THE DIRECTORY OF DIRECTORIES™

THE DIRECTORY OF DIRECTORIES™

An Annotated Guide to Business
and Industrial Directories, Professional
and Scientific Rosters, and Other Lists
and Guides of All Kinds

FIRST EDITION

James M. Ethridge
Editor

Cecilia Ann Marlow
Assistant Editor

Published by
INFORMATION ENTERPRISES™

Distributed by
GALE RESEARCH COMPANY
Book Tower   Detroit, Michigan 48226

Staff for

The Directory of Directories
and
Directory Information Service

James M. Ethridge
Editor

Cecilia Ann Marlow
Assistant Editor

Aided by

Anna Dougan, Mary C. Jablonski,
Nancy Emmert, Arlene Gant Smith,
Patricia A. Doline

The Directory of Directories
is published every two years
in even years
and is supplemented by three issues of
Directory Information Service

(Write the Gale Research Company, Book Tower,
Detroit; Michigan, 48226 for subscription information)

Computerized photocomposition by
Computer Composition Corporation
Madison Heights, Michigan

TABLE OF CONTENTS

Indexes

The indexes are the keys to successful, easy use of *The Directory of Directories*. They are printed on colored paper in the back of the book. Look in the indexes first! (See the Introduction, page viii, for comment on the indexes and subject-classified sections.)

What the Book Contains and How It Was Compiled

The Directory of Directories

Prices shown are prices reported to be current as of December 31, 1979, unless otherwise stated. Many later prices are provided, and are so indicated.

INTRODUCTION

In introducing the material in the pages which follow, it is necessary first of all to refer to the *Directory Information Service*, which preceded the present volume.

The *DIS* appeared as a paperbound periodical, with three issues in 1977 and three in 1978. It achieved considerable recognition for usefulness and uniqueness, including being selected by the Library of Congress as one of only 500 works to be included in the working library assembled for the White House Conference on Library and Information Services.

As publication of the *DIS* proceeded, the need for a cumulated edition of material already published became more and more apparent, and the decision was made to concentrate during 1979 on preparation of this cumulation, *The Directory of Directories*. It is expected that future editions of the *DOD* will be published at two-year intervals, with supplementary issues of the *DIS* being published between cumulations.

This cumulation includes about 5,200 entries, of which more than 1,400 are new. Like the entries which appeared originally in the *DIS*, the new entries have been compiled primarily from questionnaires completed by the publishers, and manuscripts of all entries have been submitted to publishers for approval.

OLD ENTRIES HAVE BEEN CAREFULLY REVISED

All entries which previously appeared in the *DIS* were submitted to publishers of the individual directories for updating. Through repeated mailings and several hundred telephone calls, updated information on the status of previously listed directories was secured for all but perhaps one or two percent of the old entries. Some proved to be defunct, and have been listed in the Title Index as "Discontinued."

A small number were deleted (but not noted as discontinued) because mail to last-known addresses was returned, and no new addresses or telephone numbers could be found. The one or two percent of entries which could not be confirmed, but for which mail was not returned and

apparently valid telephone numbers existed, have been run with the note, "Not verified."

REVISION CONTINUED INTO 1980

Revision began in the summer of 1979, and the text reflects changes known to the editors in February, 1980. Prices shown are those which were in effect for current publications at the end of December, 1979; 1980 prices have also been given in many cases, and are so identified. (Users are urged to read the "Framework and Content of a Listing" section for additional information on compilation practices.)

SCOPE OF THE DIRECTORY OF DIRECTORIES

Directory is often used for publications which would be better described as catalogs, encyclopedias, checklists, or some other type of compilation. Conversely, these alternative terms are sometimes used to describe publications which should be classed as directories. Webster considers a directory as "an alphabetical or classified list containing names and addresses." The American Library Association's *A.L.A. Glossary of Library Terms* describes a directory as a list of persons or organizations, systematically arranged, usually in alphabetical or classed order, giving addresses, affiliations, etc., for individuals, and address, officers, functions, and similar data for organizations."

A common element in these definitions is that *directories contain addresses*, and this is the principal criterion used to delimit compilations coming within the scope of the *DOD*. (The criterion is flexible; lists of leading businesses, for example, often do not include street addresses though they may include headquarters city and state. Nevertheless, addresses are usually found in publications cited in the *DOD*.)

By omission, the definitions establish another characteristic of directories — directories contain names and addresses and often other types of statistical or descriptive material, but not extensive text.

Any publication which has the characteristics discussed above is within the scope of the *DOD*, except limited-interest directories of small local clubs, etc.

Thus, the *DOD* lists a wide range of publications, including general commercial and manufacturing directories; general and specialized lists of cultural institutions; directories of individual industries, trades, and professions; rosters of professional and scientific societies. It also includes membership lists of special-interest groups of all kinds — political, recreational, cultural, etc.; state and federal government publications listing their own activities or the programs supported by them; and a wide variety of lists and guides on other subjects.

CONTENT OF
THE DIRECTORY OF DIRECTORIES

The Directory of Directories contains three sections:

1. Directory Section
2. Title Index
3. Subject index

Directory Section — Within this section, entries are divided into fifteen subject categories — Business, Industry, and Labor; Education; Health and Medicine; etc. Entries are numbered serially, and entry numbers are cited in the indexes, in addition to titles.

Within subject categories, entries are arranged alphabetically according to title.

Unlike assigning index subjects, which permits a single publication to be placed under several headings, putting directories into one of the fifteen subject areas is an either/or matter. The wide diversity of subject matter and the diversity within individual publications make the classifications into subject areas less than scientifically precise.

The major content or point of view of a publication has been the basis for assigning it to one of the major classifications. For example, several directories of arts and crafts shows and fine arts exhibits are listed. These directories are concerned primarily with events at which professional or serious semiprofessional artists offer their work for sale. These directories appear in the Arts and Entertainment category. On the other hand, there are directories of crafts and model supplies and suppliers which have hobbyists as their principal audience, and these have been assigned to the Hobbies, Travel, and Leisure category.

Similarly, directories concerned with education or training in a given subject have been assigned to the classification concerned with that subject, *not* to the Education category.

Subject Index — The subject index is the fastest way to locate *DOD* listings on specific subjects. There is no need to check through the general subject category. Commonly used, narrow, specific terms have been chosen for

subject headings wherever possible, and numerous cross-references have been provided.

The name of the directory as well as the entry number are both given in the subject index, thus permitting a speedy decision about whether it appears to fit the search requirement.

For users unfamiliar with some of the problems of subject indexing, it should be mentioned that there are numerous considerations of vocabulary, depth, comprehensiveness, etc., which individual indexers tend to handle in their own individual ways — none of which is any more "right" than another so long as the result is an index which guides a user to an answer. A capsule illustration is available in *Cross Reference Index* (R.R. Bowker, 1974) which attempts "to indicate to researchers the most appropriate subject headings in catalogs and indexes." The *CRI* compares the usage of six standard reference and cataloging publications with respect to about 2,500 common subjects; it is seldom that all six use the same subject heading and not uncommon for at least three or four of the six to use completely different terms for the same material.

Users, of course, may consult an index with an equally varying set of terms in their minds, and it is for that reason, as well as because the wide range of subjects covered presents special problems, that the *DOD* index contains an unusual number of cross-references.

The editors believe the subject index is an outstanding feature of the *DOD*, and would welcome users' comments, pro or con.

Title Index — Titles of all directories listed in the *DOD* are given in a single alphabetical sequence in the title index, along with the entry number. The title index includes:

1. Titles under which directories are listed.
2. Former titles, cross-referenced to the title used in the listing.
3. Variant titles (cover titles, for example, if significantly different from title used on title page), cross-referenced to the title used in the listing.
4. Discontinued titles, listed with the note, "Discontinued."

THANKS ARE DUE TO MANY PEOPLE

A project such as the *DOD* is made much more manageable and has a greater chance of successful completion if a competent and hard-working staff has the help and support of other people who are able to lend special support when it is needed. Many such people have helped bring the *DOD* to completion.

Foremost among them is Frederick G. Ruffner, Jr., my friend and colleague, president of the Gale Research Company. His generous counsel and support from the conception of the *Directory Information Service* through the final stages of the *Directory of Directories* have been invaluable, and have helped make both publications useful realities. One of Fred's highest compliments is to say that someone is "a directory person," which implies a special talent in conceiving useful reference directories and compiling them, and surely he deserves the title perhaps more than anyone else in publishing today.

Other Gale people who were particularly helpful were Doris D. Goulart; Theresa Lafaro; Geraldine McIntosh; Robert C. Thomas; Miranda Herbert; Barbara McNeil; Dennis La Beau; Arthur Chartow; and Nancy Yakes.

Among others who provided assistance or counsel are: George McFarlane, Office of the Superintendent of Documents, Government Printing Office; Sylvia Mechanic, Librarian, Business Library, Brooklyn Public Library (home of one of the country's finest directory collections), and staff member Kaye Shepherd; Lorna M. Daniells, Reference Librarian, Baker Library, Graduate School of Business Administration, Harvard University, and staff member Steve Wolff; David Parish, Milne Library, State University College of Arts and Science, Geneseo, New York; John Trytten, Management and Marketing Services, Inc., Royal Oak, Michigan; Richard Wiener, Richard Wiener, Inc., New York; James Hibler, Librarian, Market Opinion Research Company, Detroit; Charlotte Georgi, Chief Librarian, Graduate School of Management, University of California,

Los Angeles; Joseph Hanson, Editor and Publisher, *Folio* Magazine, New Canaan, Connecticut; Elizabeth Rumics, Reference Librarian, Upsala College, East Orange, New Jersey.

I hope that all the foregoing and the many others who helped in one way or another will feel that their efforts had a worthwhile result.

COMMENTS AND SUGGESTIONS INVITED

Users are invited to send comments and suggestions concerning the *DOD* to:

Editor
The Directory of Directories
Information Enterprises
Post Office Drawer 829
Detroit, Michigan 48231

Publishers of directories are welcome to submit their publications for listing in the DOD. They are strongly urged to send sample copies, if at all possible, in addition to fully descriptive brochures.

James M. Ethridge

FRAMEWORK AND CONTENT OF A LISTING

For convenience in scanning entries in the *Directory of Directories*, the seventeen parts of a listing are arranged in a standardized manner and the descriptive information concerning each directory is broken down into categories. Each category is preceded by a standardized bold face heading. The following notes explain the arrangement and content of a typical listing.

1. Entry Number — A sequential number precedes each entry and is used as a reference in the indexes.

2. Title of Directory — To a casual user, the titles of publications perhaps seem rather cut and dried: Titles are what appear on title pages. This is not true, however, for the purposes of a publication such as the *DOD*. Copying title pages uncritically would result in the *DOD*'s being full of titles such as "Membership Directory," "Buyer's Guide," and "List of Members" — none of them very distinctive or informative, especially in an index. Therefore, publications which have merely generic titles are cited and alphabetized according to the names of the organizations issuing them, with the generic titles following, as, "Society of Widget Designers — Membership Directory." If the "Buyer's Guide" is part of or issued by a periodical, it is listed under the name of the periodical, as, "Western Widget World — Buyer's Guide Issue." (Librarians will recognize that Rule 6 of the *Anglo-American Cataloging Rules* has been followed in establishing titles under which publications are entered, except that perhaps more forms of titles have been considered generic than the discussion of Rule 6 in *LC Information Bulletin* 33 anticipates.)

Titles present another problem, also, in that publishers often do not use titles of their publications in a consistent way. This is particularly true of association directories and special issues of periodicals. One association described the same publication under four different titles, using one title on the questionnaire, another on the publication itself, and two others on the brochure and order form. In many cases, publishers returned questionnaires on which they had filled in straightforward directory titles and on which they made no reference to companion periodicals; accompanying brochures or sample copies, however, often revealed that the directory was a 13th issue of a periodical or

that the directory material was included in a regular issue with a special subtitle. Publishers (and others) commonly cite simply as *"Directory of . . ."* a publication straightforwardly identified on the book itself as *"Jones' Directory of . . .,"* or vice versa. As a standard practice, the *DOD* assigned the longer form whenever there was a conflict, and made a cross-reference from the shorter form.

Cross-references have been provided in both the text and the title index for all significant variant forms of titles which have come to the editors' attention, and for former titles changed since 1970.

3. Publisher/Compiler — Normally, the name mentioned in the address at the beginning of each entry is the name of the organization or publishing company which both compiled and issued the directory. When the compiler and the publisher are known to be different, the name of the compiling organization appears in the address, and the name of the publisher appears in the section "Send orders to," at the end of the listing.

4. Address and Telephone — These items refer to the specific office responsible for the directory. Some publishers have directory offices in several cities which are responsible for individual publications; the *DOD* address and phone are for the office responsible for the specific directory listed. Varying telephone numbers may appear for the same office, since some editors have given direct-dial numbers.

5. Covers/Number of listings/Publication includes — One of these headings opens most annotations. ("Description" or "Background" may be used in some cases.) "Covers" is used to introduce a brief description of the scope of the work — number of entries, industry or profession covered, geographical area covered, etc.; minor features are not mentioned. "Number of listings" is used when the content of the directory is adequately described by the title. "Publication includes" precedes a description of directory features in a publication which is primarily non-directory in nature.

6. Entries include — This section describes the types of information contained in a single, typical entry in the principal directory section of the publication. If the publication contains two or more substantial directory sections and they differ markedly in detail provided, a separate description is given for each.

7. Arrangement — The description following this heading also applies to the principal directory section. Again, if there are two or more substantial directory sections and they differ markedly, a separate indication of arrangement is given for each. Terms most commonly used are: *Alphabetical* – e.g., by personal name if a membership list, or similar publication, or by company name if a business directory. *Geographical* – i.e., by major geographic units, usually states, and then by city, with listings alphabetical within cities. *Classified* – e.g., companies grouped under product headings, or professionals under their specialties.

8. Indexes — Comment on indexes has been omitted from many entries, because there has been obvious confusion on the part of some respondents as to what is an index and what is a major section of a directory. In the *DOD*, a brief citation of information which refers to a more detailed source is considered an index, not an independent section of the directory. For example, in an industrial directory with detailed entries which are arranged alphabetically by company name, a separate list arranged by city and state which included only the company name would be described as a geographical index.

9. Pages — The approximate number of pages in the publication described is reported. The number of pages is omitted if the directory section occupies only a portion of the publication.

10. Frequency — Joan K. Marshall commented in the introduction to her *Serials for Libraries* that, "The one thing that can be said with absolute certainty about the frequency of serial publications is that it changes frequently." The editors of the *DOD* thoroughly agree. Hundreds of telephone calls were made in the course of compiling the *DOD*, and it was found that sometimes even within the same office there was no agreement on frequency or expected publication date; questionnaires and revision forms often showed the same uncertainty. Obviously, many directories are special projects for which no specific staff is provided, and publication is achieved when, as, and if it is possible. Even some commercial publications show slippage in their schedules, although this is less likely in the case of a publication which carries advertising or of special issues of periodicals. The editors have attempted to be as specific as possible in describing fre-

quency, but considerable variation from stated frequencies and dates should be expected. Years of past as well as future editions have been mentioned for irregular publications to give some idea of possible frequency.

11. Editor(s) — Name and titles are always given, if reported.

12. Advertising accepted — Circulation follows this statement, if reported. Circulation is not mentioned if advertising is not accepted.

13. Former title — Changes occurring since 1970 are included, if reported.

14. Price — Price reported is the price of the publication in December, 1979, so far as the editors could determine. 1980 prices have also been given, if known, and are so identified. Prices for controlled circulation periodicals (publications ordinarily circulated free of charge to persons in the industry concerned) are sometimes indefinite; conflicting answers were sometimes given to queries, and single copy prices mentioned in *Standard Rate and Data Service Business Publication Rates and Data* have sometimes been found to be different from those supplied to the *DOD*. Controlled circulation publications and associations sometimes limit circulation of their directories, although copies can often be secured if a legitimate need can be shown. International Standard Serial Numbers (ISSN) have been included following the price, if provided. International Standard Book Numbers (ISBN), which were part of entries in the *Directory Information Service*, have been omitted from the *DOD*, because it became apparent during revision that the significance and proper use of ISBNs are often misunderstood; separate ISBNs were sometimes not provided for clothbound and paperbound editions, for example, or a price for a new edition might be given with the note that the ISBN of the new edition would be the same as for the old edition, etc.

15. Send orders to — When the address for orders is different from the editorial address used at the beginning of the listing, the ordering address is supplied under this heading.

16. Also includes — This phrase precedes comment on important non-directory information contained in the publication.

17. Other information — This phrase precedes comment on aspects of the directory or its publication which do not fit under other headings.

1

Business, Industry,

and Labor

★1★
AAA DIRECTORY OF TOLL BRIDGES, FERRIES, DOMESTIC STEAMSHIP LINES AND AUTO/PASSENGER LAND CARRIERS
American Automobile Association
8111 Gatehouse Road   Phone: (703) 222-6146
Falls Church, VA 22047
Covers: Toll facilities in the United States, Canada, and Mexico which enable automobiles and their passengers to complete toll non-highway portions of journeys; includes all toll bridges and toll ferries and scheduled free ferry facilities, and steamship, rail, and bus service which includes the transportation of automobiles and their passengers. **Entries include:** For bridges, ferries, and steamship lines - Terminal name and location, size restriction, toll, schedule, crossing time, services, and concession service. For rail and bus lines - Terminal and location, size restriction, fare, schedule, services. **Arrangement:** Bridges, ferries, and steamship lines are arranged by the body of water they cross; rail and bus lines are by terminal cities. **Indexes:** Geographical. **Pages** (approx.): 50. **Frequency:** Annual, spring. **Editor:** Curt Hildebrand, Manager, Highway Information. **Former title:** AAA Directory of Toll Bridges, Ferries, Domestic Steamship Lines, and Toll Roads (1975). **Price:** $5.00, plus 53¢ shipping, payment with order.

★2★
ABD—AVIATION BUYER'S DIRECTORY
Air Service Directory, Inc.
One Bank Street   Phone: (203) 325-2647
Stamford, CT 06901
Covers: Aircraft, parts, and equipment manufacturers and dealers, and service firms in the aviation industry. **Entries include:** Company name, address, phone. **Pages** (approx.): 300. **Frequency:** Quarterly. **Editor:** P. W. Speier, Publisher. **Advertising accepted.** Circulation 14,000. **Price:** $10.00 per year; $3.00 per copy (ISSN 0001-0502). **Other information:** Variant title, "Aviation Buyer's Directory."

★3★
ACADEMY OF INTERNATIONAL BUSINESS—MEMBERSHIP ROSTER
Academy of International Business
Florida International University
Tamiami Trail
Miami, FL
Number of listings: 900. **Entries include:** Name and address. **Arrangement:** Alphabetical. **Indexes:** Geographical, institution. **Pages** (approx.): 40. **Frequency:** Annual, fall. **Editor:** Duane A. Kujawa, Executive Secretary. **Former title:** Association for Education in International Business - Roster. **Price:** Roster available to members only; list on gummed labels $150.00 to nonmembers.

Ad Dollar Summary *See* LNA Multi-Media Report Service

★4★
ADCRAFTER—ROSTER ISSUE [Detroit]
Adcraft Club of Detroit
2630 Book Building   Phone: (313) 962-7225
Detroit, MI 48226
Covers: 1,850 executives of advertising agencies, advertising media, and advertising companies in Detroit metropolitan area. **Entries include:** Name, title, company name, office address and phone, business classification, membership code. **Arrangement:** Alphabetical by individual name, classified by line of business; identical information in both sections. **Pages** (approx.): 500. **Frequency:** Annual, third May issue. **Editor:** Lee H. Wilson. **Advertising accepted.** Circulation 2,600. **Price:** $10.00.

★5★
ADHESIVES [YEAR]
International Plastics Selector, Inc., Subsidiary
Cordura Publications, Inc.
2251 San Diego Avenue, Suite A216
San Diego, CA 92110
Covers: About 270 manufacturers of adhesives, sealants, and primers. **Entries include:** For each product - Commercial name, adhesive class, chemical base, recommended industry and uses, substrates, lap shear test results, manufacturer's name and address. **Arrangement:** By product. **Indexes:** Manufacturer name, chemical base, commercial name, application. **Pages** (approx.): 1,300. **Frequency:** Annual, June. **Editor:** Michael J. Howard. **Price:** $55.00, plus $2.00 shipping.

★6★
ADHESIVES RED BOOK
Palmerton Publishing Company, Inc.
6285 Barfield Road   Phone: (404) 256-9800
Atlanta, GA 30328
Covers: Adhesive formulators and suppliers of materials and services to the industry. **Entries include:** Company name, address, phone, names of principal plant personnel, list of products. **Arrangement:** Alphabetical. **Indexes:** Geographical, product. **Editor:** Art Sweum. **Frequency:** Annual, usually April. **Advertising accepted.** Circulation 11,000. **Price:** $27.50, postpaid.

Advertiser Red Book *See* Standard Directory of Advertisers

★7★

ADVERTISING AGE—AGENCIES RANKED BY GROSS INCOME ISSUE
Crain Communications, Inc.
740 N. Rush Street   Phone: (312) 649-5200
Chicago, IL 60611
Covers: About 625 advertising agencies which reported income, or whose incomes were ascertained through research. **Entries include:** For agencies with gross income over $3 million - Agency name, ranks for two years, billing, gross income, number of employees. For other agencies - Income for two years. **Arrangement:** Ranked by gross income in 1977 for first time; previously ranked by billings. **Frequency:** Annual, March. **Former title:** Advertising Age - Agencies Ranked by Billings Issue. **Price:** $2.50 (1980 edition).

Advertising Section of Marketing Service Organizations and Membership Roster of the Am. Marketing Assn. See American Marketing...

★8★

AERONAUTICAL INFORMATION SERVICES PROVIDED BY STATES [i.e., nations]
International Civil Aviation Organization
Box 400, Succursale
Place de l'aviation Internationale
Montreal H3A 2R2, Quebec, Canada
Publication includes: List of international airports. **Arrangement:** Geographical. **Frequency:** Semiannual. **Price:** $3.25 per issue (DOC 7383-AIS/503/48).

★9★

AEROSOL AGE—ANNUAL BUYERS GUIDE ISSUE
Industry Publications, Inc.
200 Commerce Road   Phone: (201) 239-5800
Cedar Grove, NJ 07009
Covers: Aerosol and pump spray packaging industries, worldwide. **Entries include:** Company name, address, phone, list of products or services. **Arrangement:** Separate lists for United States manufacturers, custom fillers and packagers, and companies abroad. **Indexes:** Product. **Frequency:** Annual, October. **Editor:** Margaret Hundley. **Advertising accepted.** Circulation 6,000. **Price:** $2.00.

★10★

AEROSPACE INDUSTRIES ASSOCIATION OF AMERICA—DIRECTORY OF VTOL AIRCRAFT
Aerospace Industries Association of America
1725 De Sales Street, N. W.
Washington, DC 20036
Publication includes: List of about 20 manufacturers of VTOL (vertical take off and landing) aircraft (helicopters). **Entries include:** Company name, address, and phone; aircraft designations and technical specifications are listed in a separate section. **Arrangement:** Alphabetical. **Pages** (approx.): 15. **Frequency:** Annual, February. **Price:** Free.

★11★

AFFILIATED WAREHOUSE COMPANIES DIRECTORY
Affiliated Warehouse Companies, Inc.
Box 295   Phone: (201) 739-2323
Hazlet, NJ 07730
Covers: About 70 warehouse companies in the United States and Canada served by Affiliated Warehouse Companies, Inc., a public warehouse sales agency. **Entries include:** Firm name, address, individuals in charge of new business, phone, square feet of area, insurance rates, areas served, trucking equipment, railroad facilities, and industries served. **Arrangement:** Geographical. **Indexes:** Cities served. **Pages** (approx.): 35. **Frequency:** Annual. **Price:** Free.

AGC Construction Education Directory See Collegiate Construction Education Directory

Agency Red Book See Standard Directory of Advertising Agencies

AIDS International—Membership Directory See Voice— Membership Directory

★12★

AIR CONDITIONING, HEATING & REFRIGERATION NEWS—DIRECTORY ISSUE
Business News Publishing Company
755 W. Big Beaver Road   Phone: (313) 362-3700
Troy, MI 48084
Covers: 1,700 manufacturers and their foreign affiliates; wholesalers and factory outlets; exporters specializing in the industry; associations. **Entries include:** For manufacturers - Company name, address, phone, names of key personnel, brand names, list of products. Similar information for other categories. **Arrangement:** Manufacturers are alphabetical and geographical; exporters are alphabetical; wholesalers are geographical. **Indexes:** Geographical index of manufacturers; product; trade name. **Pages** (approx.): 425. **Frequency:** Annual, December. **Editor:** Ronald K. Plaar. **Advertising accepted.** Circulation 32,000. **Price:** $10.00.

★13★

AIR DIFFUSION COUNCIL—DIRECTORY OF CERTIFIED PRODUCTS AND MEMBERSHIP ROSTER
Air Diffusion Council
435 N. Michigan Avenue   Phone: (312) 527-5494
Chicago, IL 60611
Publication includes: List of about 20 manufacturers of air control and distribution devices. **Entries include:** Company name, address. **Arrangement:** Alphabetical. **Pages** (approx.): 10. **Frequency:** Irregular; latest edition 1976; new edition expected early 1980. Periodic updates between editions. **Editor:** O. S. Hallett, Account Executive. **Price:** Free. **Other information:** Principal content of publication is list of air diffusion and distribution products tested and certified by the council; for each product manufacturer name and model number is supplied.

★14★

AIR FREIGHT DIRECTORY
Air Cargo, Inc.
1819 Bay Ridge Avenue   Phone: (301) 263-8054
Annapolis, MD 21403
Publication includes: Directory of more than 500 motor carriers contracting with Air Cargo, Inc. for delivery and pick up of freight. Air Cargo is a ground service specialist organization jointly owned by 25 major air freight carriers. **Entries include:** Airport city and code, firm name, address, phone, name of service manager, and services offered. **Arrangement:** Geographical. **Pages** (approx.): 100. **Frequency:** Bimonthly. **Editor:** Cheryle A. Crissman. **Advertising accepted.** **Price:** $5.00 per copy; $20.00 per year. **Also includes:** Principal content of publication is chart of service points and rates.

Air Freight Motor Carriers Conference—Membership Directory See Film, Air and Package Carriers Conference—Membership Directory

★15★

AIR FREIGHT MOTOR CARRIERS CONFERENCE—ROUTING GUIDE
Air Freight Motor Carriers Conference
1616 P Street, N. W.   Phone: (202) 797-5363
Washington, DC 20036
Covers: Motor carriers which make ground connections with air freight carriers. Publication consists of geographical listing of cities, references to airports serving them, and motor carriers providing service to and from airports. Information on carriers is included. **Frequency:** Frequent supplements. **Price:** $30.00 for current base volume, supplement service for one year, and binder.

★16★
AIR TAXI CHARTER & RENTAL DIRECTORY OF NORTH AMERICA
Aircraft Charter & Rental Tariff Information Service of North America,
Inc.
Box 3000
Oak Park, IL 60303   Phone: (217) 546-1491
Covers: 5,500 air taxi and scheduled commuter airline operators in
the United States, Canada, Mexico, and the Caribbean and Pacific.
Entries include: Aircraft listings section (600 operators) shows
company name, address, phone, name of chief executive, scheduled
connections, rates, and type of aircraft used. Air taxi operators
section shows company name, address, and phone. **Arrangement:**
Geographical within sections. **Pages** (approx.): 130. **Frequency:**
Irregular; previous edition 1975; latest edition October 1979. **Editor:**
Joseph Payton, President. **Advertising accepted. Price:** $15.00.

★17★
AIR TRANSPORT WORLD—ANNUAL MARKET DEVELOPMENT
   ISSUE
Penton/IPC
600 Summer Street   Phone: (203) 348-7531
Stamford, CT 06904
Publication includes: List of top 25 world airlines in various rankings -
by number of passengers, fleet size, number of employees, etc.
Frequency: Annual, May. **Advertising accepted. Send orders to:** Air
Transport World, 614 Superior Avenue West, Cleveland, OH 44113.

★18★
AIRCARGO—AIR FORWARDER ISSUE
Official Airline Guides Inc., Division
Dun & Bradstreet Company
888 Seventh Avenue   Phone: (212) 977-8314
New York, NY 10019
Covers: Air freight forwarders authorized by Civil Aeronautics Board,
International Air Transport Association cargo agents, and United
States Customs brokerage services available through air freight
companies. A list of foreign forwarders is also included. **Entries
include:** Firm name, address, type of authority held (domestic and/or
international), type of cargo carried. **Arrangement:** Geographical.
Advertising accepted. Circulation 17,600.

★19★
AIRLINE GUIDE TO STEWARDESS AND STEWARD CAREERS
Arco Publishing Company, Inc.
219 Park Avenue South   Phone: (212) 777-6300
New York, NY 10003
Covers: Airlines in the United States, Canada, and the Caribbean.
Entries include: Airline name, address, application instructions,
training, appearance and attitude requirements, working conditions,
routes, salary scales, etc. **Arrangement:** Alphabetical by airline name.
Pages (approx.): 130. **Frequency:** Annual, July. **Editor:** Alexander
Clark Morton. **Price:** $5.95.

★20★
AIRLINE HANDBOOK
Airline Handbook Publishing Company
Box 3694
Cranston, RI 02910
Covers: 1,400 commercial airline services (scheduled and chartered)
serving over 200 nations and territories worldwide. **Entries include:**
Airline name, addresses of main and branch offices, financial keys,
number of employees, routes and destinations, aircraft fleets,
passenger traffic totals, company history. **Arrangement:**
Alphabetical. **Indexes:** Geographical. **Pages** (approx.): 400.
Frequency: Annual, January. **Editor:** Paul K. Martin. **Price:** $10.00
(current and 1980 editions).

★21★
AIRLINE INDUSTRY DIRECTORY
Airline Publishing Group, Inc.
818 18th Street, N. W., Suite 420   Phone: (202) 466-6166
Washington, DC 20006
Covers: Scheduled and nonscheduled airlines, cargo carriers, aircraft
and equipment manufacturers, government agencies, embassies,
associations, airports, automobile rental agencies, and suppliers of
goods and services to the airline industry, worldwide. **Entries include:**
Company name, address, phone, names and titles of executives, list of
products or services. **Arrangement:** By activity. **Indexes:** Company
name, personal name. **Pages** (approx.): 800. **Frequency:** Semiannual,
spring and fall; first edition April 1979. **Editor:** Donald W. Dean, Editor
and Publisher. **Advertising accepted.** Circulation 6,000 per issue.
Price: $35.00 per copy.

★22★
AIRLINE PRIORITY "OVER-THE-COUNTER" ROUTING GUIDE
Air Freight Motor Carriers Conference
1616 P Street, N. W.   Phone: (202) 797-5363
Washington, DC 20036
Covers: Motor carriers which provide "over-the-counter" pick up and
delivery service to and from airports for small packages. Publication
consists of list of airports with list of conference members providing
service. **Price:** Free.

★23★
AIRPORT BOOK: THE PASSENGER'S GUIDE TO MAJOR AIRPORTS
   IN THE UNITED STATES AND CANADA
Airport Book Press
11205 Farmland Drive
Rockville, MD 20852
Covers: About 40 airports and related facilities. **Entries include:**
Airport name, location, brief general description, and detailed
descriptions of ground transportation, parking, car rental agencies,
restaurants, motels, and other services and features; listings for most
facilities and services include street address, phone, and hours.
Arrangement: Geographical. **Pages** (approx.): 210. **Frequency:**
Annual; first edition September 1979. **Editor:** Albert Diaz. **Price:**
$2.95, plus $1.00 shipping.

★24★
AIRPORT SERVICES MANAGEMENT—FBO BLUE BOOK ISSUE
   [Aircraft parts, etc.]
Lakewood Publications
731 Hennepin Avenue   Phone: (612) 333-0471
Minneapolis, MN 55403
Publication includes: List of manufacturers of aircraft parts,
accessories, equipment, and supplies for fixed base operators. **Entries
include:** Company name, address, phone; some listings include
executive name. **Indexes:** Product. **Frequency:** Annual, April. **Editor:**
Richard A. Coffey. **Advertising accepted.** Circulation 20,000. **Price:**
$2.50 (current and 1980 editions).

★25★
AIRPORT SERVICES MANAGEMENT—RED BOOK DIRECTORY OF
   AIRPORT PRODUCTS AND SERVICES ISSUE
Lakewood Publications
731 Hennepin Avenue   Phone: (612) 333-0471
Minneapolis, MN 55403
Publication includes: List of companies which supply ground support
equipment, materials, supplies, and services to airports and airlines.
Entries include: Company name, address, phone; some listings include
name of executive. **Indexes:** Product. **Frequency:** Annual, October.
Editor: Richard A. Coffey. **Advertising accepted.** Circulation
20,000. **Price:** $2.50.

Airports USA *See* AOPA's Airports USA

★26★
ALABAMA DIRECTORY OF MINING AND MANUFACTURING
Alabama Development Office
State Capitol   Phone: (205) 832-6980
Montgomery, AL 36130
Number of listings: About 5,000 (SIC 10-14 and 20-39). **Entries include:** Company name, address, phone, name and title of principal executive, name and address of parent company, number of employees, products or services, SIC numbers, year established. **Arrangement:** Alphabetical. **Indexes:** Geographical, product/SIC, parent company name, export/import firms, SIC number for materials used. **Pages** (approx.): 800. **Frequency:** Biennial, even years; latest edition October 1978. **Editor:** Richard W. McLaney, Supervisor, Industrial Research. **Former title:** Industrial Alabama (1976). **Price:** $20.00. **Other information:** Manufacturers' News catalog formerly listed this publication as ''Alabama Industrial Directory'' and ''Alabama Mining & Manufacturing Directory.''

Alabama Industrial Directory *See* Alabama Directory of Mining and Manufacturing

Alabama Mining & Manufacturing Directory *See* Alabama Directory of Mining and Manufacturing

★27★
ALABAMA STATE INDUSTRIAL DIRECTORY
State Industrial Directories Corporation
Two Penn Plaza   Phone: (212) 564-0340
New York, NY 10001
Number of listings: 5,000. **Entries include:** Company name, address, phone, names of key executives, number of employees, plant size, 4-digit SIC code, products, whether firm imports or exports, and whether firm has research facilities. **Arrangement:** Geographical. **Indexes:** Alphabetical, product (includes mailing address and phone for each firm). **Frequency:** Not established; first edition December 1978. **Advertising accepted. Price:** $50.00 (ISSN 0161-8563).

★28★
ALASKA BUSINESS LICENSE DIRECTORY
Alaska Department of Revenue
State Office Building
Pouch SA   Phone: (907) 465-2316
Juneau, AK 99811
Covers: 30,000 businesses licensed by the State of Alaska. **Entries include:** Company name, address, name of owner. **Arrangement:** Classified by type of business; geographical by Zip Code. **Indexes:** SIC. **Pages** (approx.): 1,000. **Frequency:** Annual, January. **Editor:** Peggie Ward, Cashier. **Price:** Available in 48X microfiche only; $20.00.

★29★
ALASKA CONSTRUCTION AND OIL—ALASKA TRANSPORTATION DIRECTORY ISSUE
Vernon Publications, Inc.
109 W. Mercer Street   Phone: (206) 285-2050
Seattle, WA 98119
Covers: Transportation firms of all types serving Alaska, freight forwarders, and port authorities. **Entries include:** Company name, address, phone, address and phone of branches serving Alaska, names and titles of key personnel, description of services. **Arrangement:** By type of service. **Frequency:** Annual, October. **Advertising accepted. Price:** $2.00.

★30★
ALASKA CONSTRUCTION & OIL—DIRECTORY OF EQUIPMENT MANUFACTURERS AND DISTRIBUTORS ISSUE
Vernon Publications, Inc.
109 W. Mercer Street   Phone: (206) 285-2050
Seattle, WA 98119
Covers: About 1,000 firms which distribute construction equipment and supplies in Alaska and manufacturers of construction equipment in the United States; state and federal agencies, trade organizations, and labor groups concerned with construction in Alaska are also listed. **Entries include:** For distributors, suppliers, and manufacturers - Company name, address, phone, names of key executives, and products and lines handled. **Arrangement:** Alphabetical. **Indexes:** Brand name. **Pages** (approx.): 140. **Frequency:** Annual, July. **Editor:** Christine Laing, Managing Editor. **Advertising accepted.** Circulation 8,000. **Price:** $10.00 (current edition); $15.00 (1980 edition).

★31★
ALASKA PETROLEUM & INDUSTRIAL DIRECTORY
Petroleum Information Corporation
409 W. Northern Lights Boulevard   Phone: (907) 279-2477
Anchorage, AK 99503
Covers: Petroleum industry in all aspects, utilities, construction, transportation, mining, fishing, forest products, services and supplies. Includes sections on government and native organizations. About 3,000 listings. **Entries include:** Company name, address, phone, key personnel. **Arrangement:** Classified by industry. **Indexes:** General index to all sections, including government and organizations. **Pages** (approx.): 290. **Frequency:** Annual, May. **Editor:** Kristen Nelson. **Advertising accepted.** Circulation 3,000. **Price:** $25.00. (Not verified)

★32★
ALL MONTANA CATALOG
All Montana Catalog
Box 8567
Missoula, MT 59807
Covers: Small businesses in Montana; a list of resource organizations with information on Montana and activities in the state is also included. **Price:** $5.00.

★33★
ALLIED DISTRIBUTION, INC.—MEMBERSHIP DIRECTORY
Allied Distribution, Inc.
6145 N. Milwaukee Avenue
Chicago, IL 60646
Covers: About 60 public warehouses in the United States and Canada which are members. **Entries include:** Company name, address, phone, principal executives, financial data, and list of services. **Arrangement:** Geographical. **Indexes:** Alphabetical, city. **Pages** (approx.): 60. **Frequency:** Annual. **Price:** Free.

★34★
ALLIED FINANCE ADJUSTERS CONFERENCE—DIRECTORY
Allied Finance Adjusters Conference
Box 489
Stockton, CA 95201
Covers: 200 automobile repossession agencies and skip tracers who are members. **Entries include:** Firm name, address, area served. **Arrangement:** Geographical. **Pages** (approx.): 200. **Frequency:** Annual, May. **Price:** Free.

★35★
ALMANAC OF THE CANNING, FREEZING, PRESERVING INDUSTRIES
Edward E. Judge & Sons, Inc.
Box 550   Phone: (301) 876-7150
Westminister, MD 21157
Publication includes: List of the industry's machinery, supply, and service firms. **Arrangement:** Alphabetical and classified. **Frequency:** Annual, July. **Advertising accepted.** Circulation 5,000. **Price:** $21.50. **Other information:** Principal content is statistical and legal data pertaining to food processing industry.

★36★

THE ALTERNATIVE HOUSE: A COMPLETE GUIDE TO BUILDING AND BUYING

Addison House
Morgan's Run   Phone: (603) 768-3903
Danbury, NH 03230
Publication includes: List of manufacturers and sources for solar houses, prefabricated houses, log cabins, and mobile homes. **Entries include:** Manufacturer name, address, products. **Arrangement:** Geographical. **Frequency:** First edition 1979. **Editor:** Rita Tatum. **Price:** $12.95, cloth; $6.95, paper.

★37★

AMCA DIRECTORY OF LICENSED PRODUCTS [Air movement and control products]

Air Movement and Control Association
30 W. University Drive
Arlington Heights, IL 60004
Covers: Member manufacturers of air movement and control products. **Entries include:** Name, address, products, model numbers, catalog numbers, sizes. **Arrangement:** Alphabetical. **Indexes:** Product. **Pages** (approx.): 40. **Frequency:** Annual, January. **Editor:** Prasad Bwatt. **Price:** Free.

★38★

AMERICAN AIRLINES TRAVEL GUIDE TO BLACK CONVENTIONS & CONFERENCES

Convention Merchandising Promotions, Inc.
5223 Georgia Avenue, N. W.
Washington, DC 20011
Covers: About 110 predominantly Black organizations holding conventions and conferences in the United States. **Entries include:** Organization name, location, and date of convention, president's name, and description of the organization and its activities. **Arrangement:** Alphabetical. **Pages** (approx.): 85. **Frequency:** Annual. **Other information:** Formerly published by American Airlines.

★39★

AMERICAN APPAREL MANUFACTURERS ASSOCIATION— DIRECTORY

American Apparel Manufacturers Association
1611 N. Kent Street, Suite 800
Arlington, VA 22209
Covers: 800 clothing manufacturers; suppliers of goods and services to manufacturers. **Entries include:** Firm name, address, phone, products. **Arrangement:** Alphabetical. **Indexes:** Product. **Pages** (approx.): 280. **Frequency:** Annual. **Price:** Apply.

★40★

AMERICAN ASSEMBLY OF COLLEGIATE SCHOOLS OF BUSINESS— DIRECTORY OF ACCREDITED INSTITUTIONS

American Assembly of Collegiate Schools of Business
11500 Olive Street Road, Suite 142   Phone: (314) 872-8481
St. Louis, MO 63141
Covers: About 210 institutions offering accredited programs of instruction in business administration at the college level. **Entries include:** Institution name, address; name and phone of department chairman or contact. **Arrangement:** Geographical. **Frequency:** Annual, fall. **Price:** $2.50.

★41★

AMERICAN ASSOCIATION OF PORT AUTHORITIES—HANDBOOK

American Association of Port Authorities
1612 K Street, N. W.   Phone: (202) 331-1263
Washington, DC 20006
Covers: Nearly 400 commissions and other administrative bodies which operate ports in the Western Hemisphere. **Entries include:** Member's name, address, phone, telex. **Arrangement:** Alphabetical. **Pages** (approx.): 160. **Frequency:** Annual, March. **Editor:** Marian E. Loughlin, Corporate Secretary. **Price:** Available to members only.

★42★

AMERICAN AUTOMATIC MERCHANDISER—BLUE BOOK DIRECTORY ISSUE

M-G Publications, Inc.
328 Frontage Road   Phone: (312) 441-6240
Northfield, IL 60093
Covers: Suppliers of products and equipment to the merchandise vending and office coffee service industries. **Entries include:** Company name, address, phone, names of executives, trade and brand names, and products or services offered. **Arrangement:** By type of business (equipment manufacturer, etc.). **Frequency:** Annual, July. **Editor:** Ben Ginsberg. **Advertising accepted.** Circulation 14,000. **Price:** $8.00 (current edition); $12.00 (1980 edition).

★43★

AMERICAN AUTOMATIC MERCHANDISER—DIRECTORY OF NATIONAL/REGIONAL OPERATIONS ISSUE

M-G Publications, Inc.
328 Frontage Road   Phone: (312) 441-6240
Northfield, IL 60093
Covers: Headquarters and branches of vending companies, juke box operators, and other automatic merchandisers which operate nationally or regionally. **Entries include:** For headquarters - Company name, address, names of principal executives. For branches - City and state, name operated under at that location, address, name of local manager. **Arrangement:** Alphabetical by parent company name. **Frequency:** Annual, October. **Editor:** Ben Ginsberg. **Advertising accepted.** Circulation 14,000. **Price:** $1.50.

American Automotive Leasing Association—Membership List
See The Vehicle

★44★

AMERICAN BLUE BOOK OF FUNERAL DIRECTORS

Kates-Boylston Publications, Inc.
1501 Broadway
Times Square   Phone: (212) 398-9266
New York, NY 10036
Covers: About 22,000 funeral homes in the United States and Canada primarily. Manufacturers and suppliers of supplies and equipment for funeral homes are also listed. **Entries include:** For funeral homes - Funeral home name and address. For manufacturers and suppliers - Company name, address, products. **Arrangement:** Funeral homes are geographical, manufactuers are alphabetical. **Frequency:** Biennial, summer of even years. **Advertising accepted.** Circulation 11,500. **Price:** $50.00.

★45★

AMERICAN BOAT AND YACHT COUNCIL—MEMBERSHIP LIST

American Boat and Yacht Council
Box 806   Phone: (516) 598-0550
Amityville, NY 11701
Covers: 800 marine engineers, marine underwriters, naval architects, marine surveyors, manufacturers of small boats and related equipment, and Coast Guard, Navy, and state government personnel. **Entries include:** Name, address, phone. **Arrangement:** Alphabetical. **Pages** (approx.): 30. **Frequency:** Annual, June. **Editor:** G. James Lippmann, Executive Director. **Price:** Available to members only.

★46★

AMERICAN BOTTLED WATER ASSOCIATION—MEMBERSHIP ROSTER

American Bottled Water Association
1411 W. Olympic Boulevard   Phone: (213) 384-3177
Los Angeles, CA 90015
Covers: About 200 bottled water plants and their suppliers. **Entries include:** Company name, address, phone, names of executives, list of products or services. **Arrangement:** Alphabetical. **Pages** (approx.): 20. **Frequency:** Annual, April. **Editor:** Brenda J. Jones. **Advertising accepted.** **Price:** Available to members only.

★47★

AMERICAN BUSINESS COMMUNICATION ASSOCIATION BULLETIN—MEMBERSHIP DIRECTORY ISSUE
C/o Professor Francis W. Weeks
911 S. Sixth Street
University of Illinois   Phone: (217) 333-1007
Champaign, IL 61820
Covers: About 1,500 college teachers and others interested in business communication of all types (correspondence, direct mail copy, public relations materials, etc.). **Entries include:** Name, address. **Arrangement:** By Zip code. **Frequency:** Annual, March. **Price:** Available in mailing list form only, $45.00.

★48★

AMERICAN BUSINESS DIRECTORY [In Ireland]
U.S. Chamber of Commerce in Ireland
20 College Green
Dublin 2, Ireland
Covers: 250 member American businesses interested in developing trade and investment in Ireland; other American Chambers of Commerce outside the United States are also listed. **Entries include:** Name, address. **Arrangement:** Alphabetical. **Indexes:** SIC. **Pages** (approx.): 130. **Frequency:** Annual, March. **Editor:** Robert P. Chalker, Executive Director. **Advertising accepted.** Circulation 1,150. **Price:** $8.00; add $5.00 shipping for airmail.

American Car Rental Association—Membership List *See* **The Vehicle**

★49★

AMERICAN CEMENT DIRECTORY
Bradley Pulverizer Company
123 S. Third Street   Phone: (215) 434-5191
Allentown, PA 18105
Covers: About 300 cement manufacturing companies in North, Central, and South America. **Entries include:** Company name, address, phone, names of principal executives, capacity, products. **Arrangement:** Geographical. **Indexes:** Company name. **Pages** (approx.): 250. **Frequency:** Annual, April. **Price:** $25.00, postpaid (1979 edition); $30.00, postpaid (1980 edition).

★50★

AMERICAN CHAIN OF WAREHOUSES—MEMBERSHIP DIRECTORY
American Chain of Warehouses
250 Park Avenue   Phone: (212) 986-7722
New York, NY 10017
Number of listings: 65. **Entries include:** Company name, address; names of executives; facilities, capital, types of storage, floor space, insured contents rate. **Arrangement:** Geographical. **Pages** (approx.): 40. **Frequency:** Annual. **Price:** Free.

★51★

AMERICAN CHAMBER OF COMMERCE IN AUSTRALIA— DIRECTORY
American Chamber of Commerce in Australia
50 Pitt Street, 8th Floor
Sydney, N. S. W. 2000, Australia
Covers: 1,450 Australian and American businesses interested in developing trade and investment within and between the two countries. **Frequency:** Annual.

★52★

AMERICAN CHAMBER OF COMMERCE IN BELGIUM—MEMBERSHIP DIRECTORY
American Chamber of Commerce in Belgium
Avenue des Arts, 50, Bte, 5
Brussels B-140, Belgium
Covers: 900 Belgian and American businesses interested in developing trade and investment within and between the two countries. **Entries include:** Company name, address, phone, cable address, telex, name of manager, line of business. **Arrangement:**

Alphabetical. **Indexes:** SIC code. **Pages** (approx.): 80. **Frequency:** Annual, July/August. **Editor:** Rosalyne Prevost. **Advertising accepted.** Circulation 5,000. **Price:** $25.00, plus $2.00 shipping. **Also includes:** Lists of other American chambers of commerce abroad; United States government consulates and embassies; United States trade and international marketing centers.

★53★

AMERICAN CHAMBER OF COMMERCE IN FRANCE—MEMBERSHIP DIRECTORY
American Chamber of Commerce in France
21, avenue George-V
Paris F-75008, France
Covers: 1,500 French and American businesses interested in developing trade and investment within and between the two countries. **Frequency:** Annual. **Price:** $30.00, plus $6.00 air mail shipping.

★54★

AMERICAN CHAMBER OF COMMERCE IN GERMANY—ANNUAL REPORT AND DIRECTORY
American Chamber of Commerce in Germany
Executive Office
Rossmarkt 12
Frankfurt Am Main 6, West Germany
Covers: German and American businesses interested in developing trade and investment within and between the two countries. **Frequency:** Annual.

American Chamber of Commerce in Italy—Membership Directory *See* **Italian American Business—Annual Directory Issue**

★55★

AMERICAN CHAMBER OF COMMERCE IN JAPAN—DIRECTORY OF MEMBERS
American Chamber of Commerce in Japan
701 Tosho Building, 2-2, Marunouchi 3-Chome
Chiyoda-Ku
Tokyo 100, Japan
Covers: 1,000 Japanese and American businessmen interested in developing trade and investment within and between the two countries. **Entries include:** Name, company affiliation, address, office and home phone numbers, photograph, membership category. **Arrangement:** Alphabetical. **Indexes:** Classified. **Pages** (approx.): 190. **Frequency:** Annual, March. **Editor:** Henry A. Samson. **Advertising accepted.** Circulation 2,000. **Price:** $40.00.

★56★

AMERICAN CHAMBER OF COMMERCE IN MOROCCO—DIRECTORY
American Chamber of Commerce in Morocco
53, Rue Allal-Ben-Abdallah
Casablanca, Morocco
Covers: 140 Moroccan and American businesses interested in developing trade and investment within and between the two countries. **Frequency:** Annual.

★57★

AMERICAN CHAMBER OF COMMERCE IN NEW ZEALAND— DIRECTORY OF MEMBERS
American Chamber of Commerce in New Zealand
Box 3408
Wellington, New Zealand
Covers: 250 New Zealand and American businesses interested in developing trade and investment within and between the two countries. **Entries include:** Company name, mailing and street addresses, phone, name and title of key executive, line of business. **Arrangement:** Alphabetical. **Indexes:** Product/service, trade name/New Zealand representative. **Pages** (approx.): 90. **Frequency:** Annual, June. **Price:** $5.00, plus $2.25 shipping.

★58★
AMERICAN CHAMBER OF COMMERCE IN REPUBLIC OF CHINA—
  ROSTER
American Chamber of Commerce in Republic of China
Chia Hsin 2d Building, Room N 1012
96 Chung San N Rd. Sec. 2
Box 17-277
Taipei, Taiwan, Republic of China
Covers: About 500 Taiwanese and American businesses interested in developing trade and investment within and between the two countries. **Entries include:** Company name, address, line of business, names of key personnel. **Arrangement:** Alphabetical. **Indexes:** Personal name. **Pages** (approx.): 100. **Frequency:** Every 8-10 months; latest edition April 1979. **Editor:** Deborah Cooke. **Price:** $10.00.

American Chamber of Commerce in the Netherlands—Trade
  Directory *See* Netherlands-American Trade Directory

★59★
AMERICAN CHAMBER OF COMMERCE OF MEXICO—MEMBERSHIP
  DIRECTORY
American Chamber of Commerce of Mexico
Lucerna 78, Esq. Viena
Mexico 6, D.F., Mexico
Covers: 2,300 Mexican and American businesses interested in developing trade and investment within and between the two countries. **Frequency:** Irregular.

★60★
AMERICAN CHAMBER OF COMMERCE OF THE DOMINICAN
  REPUBLIC—INVESTORS HANDBOOK
American Chamber of Commerce of the Dominican Republic
Box 95-2
Santo Domingo, Dominican Republic
Publication includes: List of 450 Dominican and American member firms interested in developing trade and investment within and between the two countries. **Entries include:** Member name, company name, address, phone. **Arrangement:** By type of membership, then alphabetical by company name. **Frequency:** Annual, December. **Advertising accepted.**

★61★
AMERICAN CONCRETE INSTITUTE—MEMBERSHIP DIRECTORY
American Concrete Institute
Box 19150   Phone: (313) 532-2600
Detroit, MI 48219
Covers: Over 15,000 engineers, architects, contractors, educators, and others interested in improving techniques of design, construction, and maintenance of concrete products and structures. **Entries include:** Name, address. **Arrangement:** Alphabetical. **Frequency:** Biennial, fall of odd years. **Price:** $25.00.

American Die Casting Institute—Membership Directory *See*
  Questions and Answers about Suppliers [Die casting industry]

★62★
AMERICAN DROP-SHIPPERS DIRECTORY
World Wide Trade Service
                                       Phone: (206) 641-8209
Medina, WA 98039
Covers: About 320 firms willing to drop ship single item orders at wholesale prices for mail order and other direct marketers. **Entries include:** Company name, address, and products. **Arrangement:** Alphabetical. **Pages** (approx.): 35. **Frequency:** Irregular; latest edition September 1978; new edition expected spring 1980. **Editor:** George F. Lucas, Owner/Publisher. **Advertising accepted.** Circulation 7,000. **Price:** $5.00 (current edition; tentative, 1980 edition).

★63★
AMERICAN ELECTRONICS ASSOCIATION—MEMBERSHIP
  DIRECTORY
American Electronics Association
2600 El Camino Real   Phone: (415) 327-9300
Palo Alto, CA 94306
Covers: Over 1,000 electronics and high-technology companies throughout the United States and 235 associates (financial institutions doing business with member companies). **Entries include:** Company name, address, phone, names of executives, number of employees, list of products or services, date founded, marketing method, and whether a public or private company. **Arrangement:** Alphabetical with geographic cross-references. **Pages** (approx.): 225. **Frequency:** Annual, spring; supplement update in fall. **Editor:** William H. Phillips, Director of Finance and Administration. **Former title:** Western Electronics Manufacturers Association - Directory; Wema Membership Directory. **Price:** $50.00.

★64★
AMERICAN FEDERATION OF LABOR-CONGRESS OF INDUSTRIAL
  ORGANIZATIONS BUILDING AND CONSTRUCTION TRADES
  DEPARTMENT—OFFICIAL DIRECTORY
American Federation of Labor-Congress of Industrial Organizations
Building and Construction Trades Department
815 16th Street, N. W.   Phone: (202) 347-1461
Washington, DC 20006
Covers: About 500 national, regional, and local AFL-CIO unions and councils. **Entries include:** Council or union name, address, phone, names of officials. **Arrangement:** Geographical. **Pages** (approx.): 125. **Frequency:** Semiannual, spring and fall. **Price:** For official use only.

★65★
AMERICAN FROZEN FOOD INSTITUTE—MEMBERSHIP DIRECTORY
American Frozen Food Institute
1700 Old Meadow Road, Suite 100   Phone: (703) 821-0770
McLean, VA 22102
Covers: 550 frozen food processors, suppliers, brokers, and distributors. **Entries include:** Company name, address, phone, names of principal executives, products, brand names, plant or distribution center locations. **Arrangement:** Alphabetical. **Indexes:** Product. **Pages** (approx.): 170. **Frequency:** Annual, fall. **Price:** $75.00.

American Hardboard Association—Membership List *See* Kitchen
  Business—Directory & Buyers Guide Issue

American Hotel and Motel Association—Allied Member
  Companies Directory *See* Lodging Magazine—Buyers Guide
  for Hotels and Motels Issue

★66★
AMERICAN IMPORTERS ASSOCIATION—MEMBERSHIP
  DIRECTORY
American Importers Association, Inc.
420 Lexington Avenue   Phone: (212) 490-2720
New York, NY 10017
Covers: 1,300 firms engaged in importing and member firms which provide legal, banking, insurance, custom brokerage, freight forwarding, and other services to importers. **Entries include:** Firm name, address, products or services. **Arrangement:** Aplhabetical. **Indexes:** Product/geographical, members providing import services. **Pages** (approx.): 135. **Frequency:** Biennial, spring of odd years. **Editor:** Norman Ober. **Advertising accepted.** Circulation 3,000. **Price:** $13.00, postpaid, payment with order.

★67★
AMERICAN INK MAKER—BUYERS' GUIDE ISSUE
MacNair-Dorland Company, Inc.
101 W. 31st Street   Phone: (212) 279-4457
New York, NY 10001
Covers: Raw materials, equipment, and services for manufacturers of

printing ink, carbon paper, pigments, varnishes, graphic chemicals, and similar products. **Entries include:** Company name and address. **Pages** (approx.): 150. **Frequency:** Annual, October. **Editor:** John C. Vollmuth. **Advertising accepted.** Circulation 4,100. **Price:** $2.00.

★68★
AMERICAN INTERNATIONAL TRADERS REGISTER
Trade Facilitation Information & Services Division
Commerce Department   Phone: (202) 377-2107
Washington, DC 20230
Background: Not a published directory, but a computer-based list of 30,000 United States manufacturers in all industries who have identified themselves as being "interested in" exporting and have requested listing; it is estimated that 75% are active exporters; list also includes export companies, contractors, architectural-engineering firms, etc. List is updated daily by Commerce Department field offices. Data base includes company name, address, name and title of contact person, 2-digit SIC code. List is available on 360 IBM computer tape, with company name, address, and contact name and title, or in printout or label form with "International Operations Officer" substituted for contact name; in either case, selection can be made by 2-digit SIC code (but selection by size is not possible). Sequence can be alphabetical or by state in zip code order. If more than one 2-digit code is selected, list is alphabetical without regard to SIC numbers. **Price:** $350.00 for entire list or any part (charge established by congressional action) payment must accompany order; 3¢ per name additional for labels.

★69★
AMERICAN LABOR SOURCEBOOK
McGraw-Hill, Inc.
1221 Avenue of the Americas   Phone: (212) 997-1221
New York, NY 10020
Publication includes: Lists of more than 200 labor unions and professional and state employee associations, and labor publications and federal and state agencies devoted to labor relations and collective bargaining. **Entries include:** Name of union, publication, agency, etc., address, phone; most listings also include names of staff members or other contacts. **Frequency:** Published 1979. **Editors:** Bernard Rifkin and Susan Rifkin. **Price:** $39.95. **Other information:** Principal content is articles and tables, many reproduced from government sources, on labor history, legislation, wages, unemployment, etc.

★70★
AMERICAN MACHINE TOOL DISTRIBUTORS ASSOCIATION—
    DIRECTORY OF MEMBERS
American Machine Tool Distributors Association
4720 Montgomery Lane
Washington, DC 20014
Number of listings: 250. **Entries include:** Company name, address, names and titles of key personnel, machine tool lines handled. **Arrangement:** Alphabetical. **Pages** (approx.): 500. **Frequency:** Annual, May. **Editor:** Al Scolnik. **Price:** $25.00, postpaid, payment with order.

★71★
AMERICAN MARKETING ASSOCIATION—MEMBERSHIP ROSTER
American Marketing Association
222 S. Riverside Plaza   Phone: (312) 648-0536
Chicago, IL 60606
Covers: 16,000 individual members and about 500 paid listings for member research and service firms. **Entries include:** For individuals - member name, position, address, home and office phone numbers. For firms - company name, address, phone, names of principal executives, description of services. **Frequency:** Biennial, spring of odd years. **Editor:** Dini Sterngold. **Advertising accepted.** Circulation 14,000. **Former title:** Directory of Marketing Services and Membership Roster. **Price:** Roster with advertising section, $25.00; advertising section only, $15.00. **Other information:** Cover and title page of roster bear title, "Advertising Section of Marketing Service

Organizations and Membership Roster of the American Marketing Association." Separate advertising section has title, "Directory of Marketing Service Organizations."

American Monument Association—Membership Directory *See* Red Book [Retail monument dealers and suppliers]

★72★
AMERICAN MOTOR CARRIER DIRECTORY—Specialized Services
    Edition
Guide Services, Inc.
6291 Barfield Road, N. E.   Phone: (404) 252-9210
Atlanta, GA 30328
Covers: All licensed specialized motor carriers and related services, including refrigerated carriers, heavy haulers, bulk haulers, riggers, and specified commodity carriers. **Entries include:** Company name, address, phone, services or commodities handled, territory served, executive names, bank references. **Arrangement:** Geographical. **Pages** (approx.): 200. **Frequency:** Annual, January. **Editor:** James Frassetto, President. **Advertising accepted.** Circulation 10,000. **Price:** $15.00.

★73★
AMERICAN MOTOR CARRIER DIRECTORY
Guide Services, Inc.
6291 Barfield Road, N. E.   Phone: (404) 252-9210
Atlanta, GA 30328
Publication includes: List of all licensed general commodity carriers, nationwide. Also includes lists of state and federal regulatory bodies governing the trucking industry, tariff publishing bureaus, freight claim councils, industry associations, etc. **Entries include:** Carrier listings include company name, address of headquarters and terminals, phones, tariffs followed, names of executives, insurance, and equipment information. **Arrangement:** Alphabetical. **Pages** (approx.): 1,300 total. **Frequency:** National edition is semiannual, January and July; regional editions are annual, as follows: Pacific States, February; Illinois-Missouri, March; Southeastern, May; Middle Atlantic, August; New England, September. **Editor:** James Frassetto, President. **Advertising accepted.** Circulation 14,000 for national edition; 7,000 each regional. **Price:** $65.00 annually for national edition; $15.00 for each regional edition. **Also includes:** Principal content of publication is listing of direct point-to-point services of general commodity carriers throughout the United States and to Canada and Mexico.

American Package Express Carriers Association—Member Directory *See* Film, Air and Package Carriers Conference—Membership Directory

★74★
AMERICAN PACKAGE EXPRESS CARRIERS ASSOCIATION—
    SERVICE DIRECTORY
American Package Express Carriers Association
1616 P Street, N. W.   Phone: (202) 797-5363
Washington, DC 20036
Covers: Motor carriers which make ground connections with air carriers transporting small packages. Publication consists of individual page for each member showing complete information on service and operating area, supplemented by map of territory. **Price:** $10.00.

★75★
AMERICAN PUBLIC GAS ASSOCIATION—DIRECTORY
American Public Gas Association
301 W. Maple Avenue, Suite G, Section 4   Phone: (703) 281-2910
Vienna, VA 22180
Covers: About 1,000 municipally owned gas systems throughout the United States. **Entries include:** Name of system, address, phone, contact person's name, number of meters, number of employees, name of supplier of natural gas, miles of transmission and distribution lines, and date it became a municipal utility. **Arrangement:** Geographical. **Frequency:** Annual, March. **Advertising accepted.** Circulation 600. **Price:** $10.00 (current and 1980 editions).

★76★

AMERICAN PUBLIC WORKS ASSOCIATION—DIRECTORY

American Public Works Association
1313 E. 60th Street   Phone: (312) 947-2520
Chicago, IL 60637
Covers: 19,500 engineers, administrators, and others active in the public works field. **Arrangement:** Alphabetical. **Indexes:** Geographical. **Pages** (approx.): 570. **Frequency:** Annual, March. **Editors:** Rodney R. Fleming and Alfred J. Kuhn. **Price:** $20.00 (current and 1980 editions).

★77★

AMERICAN RECOVERY ASSOCIATION—DIRECTORY

American Recovery Association
4040 W. 70th Street   Phone: (612) 929-9669
Minneapolis, MN 55435
Covers: 385 firms specializing in the repossession of goods, primarily automobiles, sold on credit. **Entries include:** Company name, address, phone number, name of principal executive. **Arrangement:** Geographical by location of members' offices, with cross references from other towns served. **Pages** (approx.): 425. **Frequency:** Annual, January. **Editor:** Dorothy S. Anderson, General Manager. **Advertising accepted.** Circulation 40,000. **Price:** Free.

★78★

AMERICAN REGISTER OF EXPORTERS AND IMPORTERS

American Register of Exporters and Importers Corporation
38 Park Row   Phone: (212) 227-4030
New York, NY 10038
Covers: About 30,000 United States manufacturers and distributors who engage in export/import trade, and service firms interested in foreign customers; also includes airlines, steamship lines, freight forwarders, banks and government agencies related to the industry. **Entries include:** Company name, address, products in which it deals; advertiser entries may include phone, officers, brand names, etc. **Arrangement:** By product, in about 1,300 product categories; other sections for banks active in international trade, steamship lines, etc. **Indexes:** Lists of product classifications in English, Spanish, French, German. **Pages** (approx.): 830. **Frequency:** Annual, May. **Editor:** S. John Cousins. **Advertising accepted. Price:** $50.00.

★79★

AMERICAN SHOEMAKING DIRECTORY

Shoe Trades Publishing Company
15 East Street   Phone: (617) 542-0190
Boston, MA 02111
Covers: Shoe manufacturers in the United States and Canada. **Entries include:** Company name, address, phone, names of executives, product information. **Arrangement:** Geographical. **Pages** (approx.): 170. **Frequency:** Annual, spring. **Editor:** Thomas O'Rowan. **Price:** $11.00 (current edition); $12.00 (1980 edition).

★80★

AMERICAN SOCIETY FOR INDUSTRIAL SECURITY—ANNUAL DIRECTORY OF MEMBERS AND AFFILIATES

American Society for Industrial Security
2000 K Street, N. W.   Phone: (202) 331-7887
Washington, DC 20006
Covers: 11,000 persons concerned with physical security of offices, plants, and institutions, and the security of proprietary information, computer data bases, credit card systems, works of art, etc. **Entries include:** Member name, address, and company affiliation. **Pages** (approx.): 300. **Indexes:** Geographical, affiliation. **Frequency:** Annual, June. **Editor:** Shari Mendelson, Publications Manager. **Advertising accepted. Price:** Available to members only.

American Society for Training and Development—Membership Directory *See* Who's Who in Training and Development

★81★

AMERICAN SOCIETY OF INTERNATIONAL EXECUTIVES—ROSTER

American Society of International Executives
Box 11568
Philadelphia, PA 19116
Covers: About 400 persons holding positions in international trade. **Frequency:** Annual. **Price:** Available to members only.

★82★

AMERICAN SOCIETY OF PROFESSIONAL ESTIMATORS— NATIONAL ROSTER [Construction industry]

American Society of Professional Estimators
7789 Othello Street, Suite A   Phone: (714) 565-7950
San Diego, CA 92111
Covers: 1,825 members allied to the building industry as construction estimators. **Entries include:** Name, address, phone, business address and phone, category of membership. **Arrangement:** By numbered chapter. **Indexes:** Alphabetical. **Pages** (approx.): 100. **Frequency:** Annual, March. **Editor:** Shirley Campbell, Membership Secretary. **Price:** Available to members only.

★83★

AMERICAN SOCIETY OF TRAVEL AGENTS—MEMBERSHIP ROSTER

American Society of Travel Agents
711 Fifth Avenue   Phone: (212) 486-0700
New York, NY 10022
Covers: 9,000 travel agents and wholesale tour operators in the United States and Canada, 2,000 overseas, and 5,500 allied members of the ASTA (airlines, car rental companies, cruise lines, etc.). **Entries include:** Company name, address, phone, name of principal executive and other officials, and telex/cable addresses. **Arrangement:** Geographical by category. **Indexes:** Personal name, company. **Pages** (approx.): 670. **Frequency:** Annual, spring. **Editor:** Robert C. Eichel, Director of Sales. **Advertising accepted.** Circulation 19,000. **Price:** $35.00.

★84★

AMERICAN SUBSIDIARIES OF GERMAN FIRMS

German American Chamber of Commerce
666 Fifth Avenue   Phone: (212) 582-7788
New York, NY 10019
Number of listings: 825. **Entries include:** Name, address and phone of American firm; name and address of German parent company; percentage of German participation; type of company (manufacturer, sales agent, etc.); and products. **Arrangement:** Alphabetical. **Indexes:** Parent firm, product, geographical. **Pages** (approx.): 100. **Frequency:** Annual, September. **Price:** $40.00.

★85★

AMERICAN SUPPLY ASSOCIATION—MEMBERSHIP DIRECTORY [Plumbing-heating]

American Supply Association
221 N. LaSalle Street   Phone: (312) 236-4082
Chicago, IL 60601
Covers: 2,300 wholesalers handling plumbing, heating and cooling materials and supplies. **Entries include:** Company name, address, phone, names of executives, list of products or services. **Arrangement:** Geographical. **Pages** (approx.): 130. **Frequency:** Annual, May. **Price:** $25.00.

★86★

AMERICAN TEXTILE MACHINERY ASSOCIATION—OFFICIAL DIRECTORY

American Textile Machinery Association
1730 M Street, N. W., Suite 804   Phone: (202) 296-1460
Washington, DC 20036
Covers: 100 textile machinery manufacturers worldwide who are ATMA members (SIC 3552). Text in English, French, German, and Spanish. **Entries include:** Manufacturer name, address, phone, list of products and descriptions, and photographs and illustrations of textile

machinery manufactured. **Pages** (approx.): 130. **Frequency:** Biennial, July of odd years. **Editor:** Chris R. Beverino, Staff Vice President. **Price:** $20.00.

★87★

AMERICAN WAREHOUSEMEN'S ASSOCIATION—MEMBERSHIP DIRECTORY
American Warehousemen's Association
222 W. Adams Street   Phone: (312) 726-5550
Chicago, IL 60606
Covers: About 550 warehouse firms specializing in the storage and handling of non-refrigerated items; coverage includes United States, Canada, Mexico, Costa Rica, Dominican Republic, Panama, and Venezuela. **Entries include:** Company name, address, facilities, services, contact names, square feet. **Arrangement:** Geographical. **Pages** (approx.): 20. **Frequency:** Annual, May. **Price:** Free.

American Water Works Association Yearbook *See* Journal of the American Water Works Association—Buyers' Guide Issue

★88★

AMERICAN WOOD PRESERVERS INSTITUTE—MEMBER AND PRODUCT DIRECTORY
American Wood Preservers Institute
1651 Old Meadow Road   Phone: (703) 893-4005
McLean, VA 22102
Covers: About 100 firms producing pressure-treated wood products and their suppliers. **Entries include:** Company name, address, phone, list of products. **Arrangement:** Geographical. **Indexes:** Alphabetical, product, companies classified by types of preservatives used, geographical. **Pages** (approx.): 30. **Frequency:** Annual, fall. **Editor:** Theodore J. Duke, Executive Vice President. **Advertising accepted.** Circulation 60,000. **Price:** $1.50.

★89★

AMUSEMENT RIDES AND GAMES BUYERS GUIDE
Billboard Publications, Inc.
Box 24970   Phone: (615) 748-8120
Nashville, TN 37202
Covers: Manufacturers, importers, and suppliers of amusement rides and games. **Entries include:** Company name, address, phone, name of principal executive, list of products or services. **Pages** (approx.): 40. **Frequency:** Annual, September. **Editor:** Paul Curran. **Advertising accepted. Former title:** Guide to Amusement Rides. **Price:** $3.50.

★90★

ANGLO AMERICAN TRADE DIRECTORY
American Chamber of Commerce (United Kingdom)
75 Brook Street
London W1Y 2EB, England
Covers: About 13,000 British and American businesses interested in developing trade and investment within and between the two countries. **Entries include:** Name, address, phone, cable address, name and title of key executive or contact, trading interests, name of distributor, subsidiary, agent, or other commercial link. **Arrangement:** Alphabetical. **Indexes:** Product/service. **Pages** (approx.): 435. **Frequency:** Annual. **Editor:** Robert F. Templeton. **Advertising accepted.** Circulation 3,500. **Price:** $60.00, postpaid; add $8.00 for airmail postage.

Annual Fire Protection Reference Directory *See* Fire Protection Reference Directory

★91★

AOPA'S AIRPORTS USA
Aircraft Owners and Pilots Association
7315 Wisconsin Avenue   Phone: (301) 654-0500
Washington, DC 20014
Covers: 13,500 landing facilities, including airports, heliports, and seaplane bases. **Entries include:** Airport type, city, descriptive information, hours operated, communications frequencies, fixed base

operators, and facilities and services available to pilots. **Arrangement:** Geographical. **Pages** (approx.): 530. **Frequency:** Annual, January. **Editor:** Marla L. St. Peter. **Former title:** AOPA Airport Directory (1975). **Price:** $10.00 (1980 edition).

Apartment Construction News—Directory Issue *See* Multi-Housing News—Directory Issue

★92★

APPAREL TRADES BOOK
Dun & Bradstreet, Inc.
99 Church Street   Phone: (212) 285-7383
New York, NY 10007
Covers: About 125,000 apparel retailers and wholesalers in the United States which are rated by Dun & Bradstreet and included in its national "Reference Book." A separate "Apparel Trades Book" is published for each state; Illinois and New York are also available in editions which exclude Chicago and New York City, and separate Chicago and New York City editions are available. **Entries include:** Company name, principal lines of merchandise carried in order of importance, the D-U-N-S number and composite credit appraisal. **Arrangement:** Geographical. **Frequency:** Quarterly, in February, May, August, and November. **Editor:** John I. Scotto, National Manager, Business Data Bank. **Price:** Approximately $20-$75 per quarterly issue, depending on state. Available only to subscribers to the Dun & Bradstreet Credit Service.

★93★

APPLIANCE—PURCHASING DIRECTORY ISSUE
Dana Chase Publications, Inc.
York Street and Park Avenue   Phone: (312) 834-5280
Elmhurst, IL 60126
Covers: Suppliers to manufacturers of consumer, commercial, and business appliances. **Entries include:** Company name, address, phone, list of products or services. **Pages** (approx.): 110. **Frequency:** Annual, January. **Editor:** James Stevens. **Advertising accepted.** Circulation 24,000. **Former title:** Appliance Industry - Purchasing Directory Issue. **Price:** $12.00 (current edition); $14.00 (1980 edition).

Appliance Industry—Purchasing Directory Issue *See* Appliance—Purchasing Directory Issue

★94★

APPLIANCE MANUFACTURER—ANNUAL DIRECTORY ISSUE
Cahners Publishing Company
Five S. Wabash Avenue   Phone: (312) 372-6880
Chicago, IL 60603
Covers: About 3,500 appliance manufacturers, mass merchandisers, and suppliers. **Entries include:** Company name, address, phone, list of products or services. **Arrangement:** Alphabetical. **Indexes:** Product. **Pages** (approx.): 130. **Frequency:** Annual, June. **Editor:** Arnold P. Consdorf. **Advertising accepted.** Circulation 26,000. **Price:** $10.00.

★95★

ARAB BLACKLIST UNVEILED
Landia Publishing Company
256 S. Robertson Boulevard
Beverly Hills, CA 90211
Publication includes: Appendix of 5,000 international companies included in lists judged favorable to Israel or to be doing business with Israel and therefore included in the boycott list published by the Arab Boycott Office and participating governments. Includes those formerly included and now removed. **Frequency:** Published fall 1977. **Editor:** Edward Hotaling. **Price:** $49.95. **Also includes:** Report on history of boycott and its operation, the anti-boycott movement in the United States, and the position of the United States government. (Not verified)

★96★

ARABIC DIRECTORY ON AMERICAN BUSINESS

News Circle Publishing Company

2007 Wilshire Boulevard, Suite 900   Phone: (213) 483-5111

Los Angeles, CA 90057

Covers: Manufacturers, universities, hospitals, trade organizations, and other entities in the United States of interest to the Arab World; also includes federal government agencies, diplomatic missions, chamber of commerce in the United States, etc. The directory is in Arabic, except for names and addresses. **Entries include:** Organization or company name, address. Paid listings and listings for other organizations may include phone, telex, and description of services. **Arrangement:** Manufacturers, hospitals, and others with goods and services to sell are by product. **Indexes:** Only paid listings are included in the alphabetical index. **Pages** (approx.): 320. **Frequency:** First edition expected 1980. **Advertising accepted. Price:** Not yet determined. **Other information:** Mideast Business Exchange is mentioned as publisher in some promotion.

★97★

ARCHITECTS' GUIDE TO GLASS, METAL & GLAZING

U.S. Glass Publications, Inc.

2158 Union Avenue, Suite 401   Phone: (901) 272-2956

Memphis, TN 38104

Publication includes: List of suppliers of flat glass, architectural metal and related products. **Entries include:** Company name, address, contact name, products, brand names. **Arrangement:** Alphabetical. **Frequency:** Annual, June. **Editor:** John K. Lawo, Jr., Editor and Publisher. **Advertising accepted.** Circulation 12,700. **Price:** $3.00.

★98★

ARCHITECTURAL ALUMINUM CERTIFICATION PROGRAM DIRECTORY

Architectural Aluminum Manufacturers Association

35 E. Wacker Drive   Phone: (312) 782-8256

Chicago, IL 60601

Covers: Over 200 manufacturers of aluminum prime windows, sliding glass doors, and combination storm windows and doors certified to meet association and American National Standards Institute specifications. **Entries include:** Company name, address. **Arrangement:** Alphabetical. **Indexes:** Product. **Frequency:** Annual. **Price:** Free.

★99★

AREA CODE 800

Lansford Publishing Company, Inc.

1088 Lincoln Avenue   Phone: (408) 287-3105

San Jose, CA 95155

Covers: About 1,000 firms in many lines of business which have 800-(toll-free) telephone numbers. **Entries include:** Company name, address, phone, regular and toll-free phone numbers, brief note on product or service. **Arrangement:** Classified by product or service. **Indexes:** Company. **Pages** (approx.): 75. **Frequency:** Not established; first edition late 1977; new edition planned. **Price:** $9.95, payment with order. **Other information:** Includes a smaller number of listings than some similar directories, but appears to cover a wider variety of companies.

★100★

ARGENTINE-AMERICAN BUSINESS REVIEW/DIRECTORY

Motivational Communications, Inc.

175 Fifth Avenue   Phone: (212) 260-0800

New York, NY 10010

Covers: About 900 import/export firms, manufacturers, and national agencies (United States and Argentina) concerned with commerce between the two countries. **Entries include:** Company or agency name, address, phone, and products or services. **Arrangement:** Alphabetical. **Pages** (approx.): 75. **Frequency:** Annual, January. **Editor:** Barry V. Conforte. **Advertising accepted.** Circulation 50,000. **Price:** $25.00, plus $2.50 shipping (current and 1980 editions). **Other information:** Official publication of the Argentine-American Chamber of Commerce; contains the chamber roster.

Argentine-American Chamber of Commerce—Roster *See* Argentine-American Business Review/Directory

★101★

ARIZONA BUSINESS DIRECTORY [Phoenix area only]

Arizona Business Directory, Inc.

4747 N. 16th Street, Suite D-102

Phoenix, AZ 85016

Covers: 30,000 retail, service and manufacturing businesses in the Phoenix metropolitan area only. **Entries include:** Company name, address, phone; date established; number of employees; officers, directors, and executives; annual sales; subsidiaries; SIC classifications; and products or services. **Arrangement:** Classified by principal SIC code. **Indexes:** Alphabetical index of company names. **Pages** (approx.): 900. **Frequency:** Annual; first edition to be published fall 1977. **Editor:** Dixon H. Harris. **Advertising accepted.** Circulation 3,000 (planned). **Price:** $44.60, postpaid. (Not verified)

★102★

ARIZONA BUSINESS/INDUSTRY—"WHERE TO FIND IT" DIRECTORY ISSUE

Trailbeau Publications, Inc.

7319 E. Stetson Drive, Suite 4   Phone: (602) 945-4435

Scottsdale, AZ 85251

Covers: 5,000 manufacturers, suppliers, distributors, and other commercial firms in industrial and service lines located in Arizona and western states; listings are paid. **Entries include:** Company name, address, phone, trade and brand names, products and/or services. **Arrangement:** By products and services. **Pages** (approx.): 70. **Frequency:** Annual, January. **Editor:** Dorothy La Traille, Editor and Co-publisher. **Advertising accepted.** Circulation 5,225. **Price:** $1.75 (1980 edition).

Arizona Directory of Manufacturers *See* Directory of Arizona Manufacturers

★103★

ARIZONA MEDIA GUIDE

Phoenix Chapter

Public Relations Society of America

1515 E. Osborn Road

Phoenix, AZ 85014

Covers: Wire services, newspapers, radio and television stations located in Arizona. **Entries include:** Name, address, phone. **Arrangement:** By type of media. **Frequency:** Latest edition September 1979. **Price:** $12.50, payment with order.

★104★

ARIZONA USA INTERNATIONAL TRADE DIRECTORY

Arizona Office of Economic Planning and Development

1700 W. Washington, Room 505   Phone: (602) 271-3737

Phoenix, AZ 85007

Covers: About 275 Arizona enterprises currently involved in international trade. **Entries include:** Company name, address, phone, name of principal executive, number of employees, list of products or services, SIC numbers, date established, and countries dealt with. **Arrangement:** Alphabetical. **Indexes:** SIC, geographical. **Pages** (approx.): 75. **Frequency:** Irregular; latest edition 1977, with 1978 supplement. **Former title:** Arizona Exports and Imports (1977). **Price:** Free.

Arkansas Directory of Industries *See* Directory of Manufacturers in Arkansas

Arkansas Manufacturers Directory *See* Directory of Manufacturers in Arkansas

★105★

ART AND INGENUITY OF THE WOODSTOVE: A BOOK OF HISTORY AND USE

Everest House, Publishers
1133 Avenue of the Americas   Phone: (212) 764-3400
New York, NY 10036
Publication includes: List of woodstove manufacturers and retailers of stoves and related products. **Frequency:** First edition 1979. **Editor:** Jan Adkins. **Price:** $12.95.

★106★

ASHRAE HANDBOOK & PRODUCT DIRECTORY [Heating, refrigerating, and air conditioning]

American Society of Heating, Refrigerating, and Air-Conditioning Engineers
345 E. 47th Street   Phone: (212) 644-7953
New York, NY 10017
Covers: About 4,500 manufacturers of heating, cooling, and air conditioning equipment. **Entries include:** Company name, location. **Arrangement:** Classified by product. **Frequency:** Directory consists of four volumes published in rotation. Volumes are "Systems" (due May 1980), "Equipment" (1979), "Applications" (1978), and "Fundamentals" (1977). **Advertising accepted.** **Price:** $40.00 per volume, plus $2.00 shipping, payment with order.

★107★

ASSOCIATED BUILDERS AND CONTRACTORS—MEMBERSHIP DIRECTORY AND ASSOCIATION GUIDE

Associated Builders and Contractors
444 N. Capitol Street, N. W.   Phone: (202) 637-8800
Washington, DC 20001
Covers: About 14,000 member construction contractors and suppliers. **Entries include:** Company name, address, phone, name of principal executive; supplier listings show trade and brand names handled. **Arrangement:** Geographical. **Pages** (approx.): 500. **Frequency:** Annual, December. **Editor:** Maurice Cox. **Advertising accepted.** Circulation 14,000. **Former title:** Associated Builders and Contractors - National Membership Directory (1977). **Price:** $100.00.

Associated Business Writers of America—Directory *See* **Directory of Business Writers**

Associated Equipment Distributors—Membership Directory *See* **Compilation of Nationally Averaged Rental Rates and Model Reference Data**

Associated Equipment Distributors—Membership Directory *See* **Construction Equipment Distribution—Directory Issue**

★108★

ASSOCIATED FUNERAL DIRECTORS SERVICE—BULLETIN AND ROSTER

Associated Funeral Directors Service
810 Stratford Avenue   Phone: (813) 228-9105
Tampa, FL 33603
Publication includes: 2,500 funeral homes in United States and Canada, plus some abroad. **Entries include:** Home name and phone. **Arrangement:** Geographical. **Pages** (approx.): 60. **Frequency:** Quarterly. **Editor:** Frank P. Pryor, Executive Director. **Advertising accepted.** Circulation 15,500. **Price:** Free.

★109★

ASSOCIATED GENERAL CONTRACTORS OF AMERICA—NATIONAL ASSOCIATE DIRECTORY

Associated General Contractors of America
1957 E Street, N. W.   Phone: (202) 393-2040
Washington, DC 20006
Covers: More than 1,500 associate member firms which supply equipment and materials to firms engaged in building, highway, heavy, industrial, municipal utilities, and railroad construction. **Entries**

include: Company name, address, phone, names of principal executives, and products. **Arrangement:** Geographical. **Indexes:** Alphabetical, type of service. **Pages** (approx.): 70. **Frequency:** Annual, December. **Editor:** Diane Snow. **Advertising accepted.** **Price:** $25.00.

Associated General Contractors of America Collegiate Construction Education Directory *See* Collegiate Construction Education Directory

Associated General Contractors of America MBE Directory *See* Constructor—Associated General Contractors of America MBE...

★110★

ASSOCIATED TELEPHONE ANSWERING EXCHANGES—MEMBERSHIP DIRECTORY

Associated Telephone Answering Exchanges
5203 Leesburg Pike, Suite 205   Phone: (703) 998-5702
Falls Church, VA 22041
Number of listings: 850. **Entries include:** Bureau name, address, name of contact. **Arrangement:** Geographical. **Pages** (approx.): 220. **Frequency:** Annual, spring. **Price:** Free.

★111★

ASSOCIATED WAREHOUSES, INC.—DIRECTORY OF MEMBERS

Associated Warehouses, Inc.
370 Lexington Avenue, Room 2215   Phone: (212) 685-0160
New York, NY 10017
Number of listings: 90. **Entries include:** Warehouse name, address, phone, telex, executives' names, and descriptive information (railroad siding and service data, storage area available, insurance rates, financial references, and facilities). **Arrangement:** Alphabetical by name of city. **Indexes:** Geographical and warehouse name. **Pages** (approx.): 100. **Frequency:** Annual. **Price:** Free. **Other information:** Variant title, "AWI Red Book Directory."

★112★

ASSOCIATION AND SOCIETY MANAGER—CONVENTION CENTER, AUDITORIUM, AND ARENA GUIDE ISSUE

Brentwood Publishing Corporation
825 S. Barrington Avenue   Phone: (213) 826-8388
Los Angeles, CA 90049
Entries include: Facility name, address, type, capacity, special features. **Arrangement:** Geographical. **Frequency:** Annual, December/January. **Advertising accepted.** Circulation 15,000. **Price:** $5.00.

Association for Education in International Business—Roster *See* Academy of International Business—Membership Roster

★113★

ASSOCIATION MANAGEMENT—CONVENTION HALL DIRECTORY ISSUE

American Society of Association Executives
1101 16th Street, N. W.   Phone: (202) 659-3333
Washington, DC 20036
Covers: 300 convention halls, auditoriums, and arenas in the United States and Canada. **Entries include:** Name of hall, address, manager, phone, exhibit space available, lodging facilities, storage space, parking capacity, number of meeting rooms, capacity of largest facilities for meal functions, and distance from major hotel and business district. **Arrangement:** Geographical. **Pages** (approx.): 25. **Frequency:** Annual, February. **Editor:** Elaine Jorpeland. **Advertising accepted.** Circulation 11,000. **Price:** $2.00 (current and 1980 editions).

★114★
ASSOCIATION OF CONSULTING MANAGEMENT ENGINEERS—
DIRECTORY OF MEMBER FIRMS
Association of Consulting Management Engineers
230 Park Avenue   Phone: (212) 697-9693
New York, NY 10017
Covers: About 55 management consulting firms. **Entries include:** Firm name, address, description of services offered, areas of expertise, locations of branch offices and affiliates. **Arrangement:** Alphabetical. **Pages** (approx.): 60. **Frequency:** Biennial, even years. **Price:** Free.

Association of Diesel Specialists—Directory *See* Diesel & Gas Turbine Progress—Association of Diesel Specialists Directory Issue

Association of Executive Recruiting Consultants—Roster *See* Directory of Executive Recruiters

★115★
ASSOCIATION OF GRAPHIC ARTS CONSULTANTS—DIRECTORY
Association of Graphic Arts Consultants
Printing Industries of America
1730 N. Lynn Street
Arlington, VA 22209
Covers: About 50 consultants to the printing industry. **Entries include:** Name, address, qualifications. **Arrangement:** Alphabetical. **Frequency:** Irregular; previous edition 1978; latest edition 1979. **Editor:** Edward W. Hill, Jr. **Price:** Free.

★116★
ASSOCIATION OF MANAGEMENT CONSULTANTS—DIRECTORY
OF MEMBERSHIP AND SERVICES
Association of Management Consultants
331 Madison Avenue   Phone: (212) 686-9676
New York, NY 10017
Number of listings: 110. **Entries include:** Company name, address, phone number, names and background of staff members, list of products or services. **Pages** (approx.): 100. **Frequency:** Base list published irregularly, updated in February, June, and October. **Editor:** Robert Gitelman, Executive Secretary. **Price:** Base list and year's updates, $25.00.

★117★
ASSOCIATION OF PRIVATE POSTAL SYSTEMS—MEMBERSHIP
DIRECTORY
Association of Private Postal Systems
4100 E. Iliff Avenue   Phone: (303) 758-6388
Denver, CO 80222
Covers: About 55 mail delivery services. **Entries include:** Company name, address, phone, year established, area covered, maximum quantity and rate, names and titles of key personnel, delivery date, delivery method, area selection, delivery agent, other services available. **Arrangement:** Geographical. **Pages** (approx.): 20. **Frequency:** Annual.

★118★
ASSOCIATION OF RECORDS MANAGERS AND
ADMINISTRATORS—POCKET DIRECTORY
Association of Records Managers and Administrators
4200 Somerset, Suite 215   Phone: (913) 341-3808
Prairie Village, KS 66208
Covers: About 120 officers, committee chairmen, and chapter presidents of the association. **Entries include:** For officers - Name, title, address, phone. For committee chairmen - Name, committee, address, phone. For chapter presidents - Name of chapter, name of president, address, phone. **Arrangement:** Chapter presidents are

geographical. **Pages** (approx.): 35. **Frequency:** Annual. **Price:** Available to members only.

Association of Steel Distributors—Roster *See* Metal Distribution

★119★
ATLANTA MANUFACTURING DIRECTORY [Georgia]
Atlanta Chamber of Commerce
Box 1740
Atlanta, GA 30301
Covers: About 1,500 firms in the 15-county Atlanta SMSA manufacturing products within SIC classifications 20-39. **Entries include:** Company name, address, phone, names of principal executives, number of employees, list of products or services, 4-digit SIC numbers, date established, market served. **Arrangement:** By county and by SIC number; identical information in each arrangement. **Pages** (approx.): 140. **Frequency:** Irregular, about every two years; next edition spring 1981. **Price:** $7.25. **Other information:** Consists of listings taken from "Georgia Manufacturing Directory."

★120★
ATLANTIC CITY BUILDING TRADES DIRECTORY
Glasco Associates, Inc.
33 S. Presbyterian Avenue   Phone: (609) 345-0909
Atlantic City, NJ 08404
Covers: About 5,000 companies and suppliers of products and services to the building and construction trade; developers, contractors, and subcontractors doing business in southern New Jersey. **Entries include:** Company name, address, phone, name of contact. **Arrangement:** By product or service. **Frequency:** Annual, spring. **Editor:** Gerald Mitchell, Editor-in-Chief. **Advertising accepted.** Circulation 20,000. **Price:** $20.00.

★121★
AUDARENA STADIUM GUIDE
Billboard Publications, Inc.
Box 24970   Phone: (615) 748-8120
Nashville, TN 37202
Covers: More than 5,000 arenas, auditoriums, stadiums, exhibit halls, and coliseums in the United States, Canada, and, in less depth, Europe and South America. **Entries include:** Site name, name of owning or operating company, address, phone, name of contact, description of facilities, capacity, services. **Arrangement:** Geographical. **Pages** (approx.): 300. **Frequency:** Latest edition September 1979. **Advertising accepted.** **Price:** $30.00, postpaid, payment with order.

★122★
AUDIO-VISUAL COMMUNICATIONS—AV EQUIPMENT BUYING
GUIDE AND PRODUCTION DIRECTORY
United Business Publications, Inc., Subsidiary
Media Horizons, Inc.
475 Park Avenue South   Phone: (212) 725-2300
New York, NY 10016
Covers: About 1,200 manufacturers of, or distributors with exclusive rights to, audiovisual equipment and supplies. **Entries include:** Company name, address, phone, description of products. **Arrangement:** Classified by type of equipment. **Indexes:** Manufacturer. **Pages** (approx.): 150. **Frequency:** Annual, October. **Editor:** Frances H. Lee. **Advertising accepted.** Circulation 32,000. **Price:** $5.75.

★123★
AUDIO-VISUAL COMMUNICATIONS—VIDEO PRODUCTION
SERVICES & VTR COMPATIBILITY GUIDE ISSUE
United Business Publications, Inc., Subsidiary
Media Horizons, Inc.
475 Park Avenue South   Phone: (212) 725-2300
New York, NY 10016
Covers: About 700 firms offering services in video production and

manufacturers of compatible videotape recorders-playbacks. **Entries include:** Company name, address, phone, keys indicating services. **Arrangement:** Geographical. **Pages** (approx.): 100. **Frequency:** Annual, April. **Editor:** Frances H. Lee. **Advertising accepted. Price:** $1.25 (current and 1980 issues).

★124★
AUSTRALIAN-AMERICAN BUSINESS REVIEW/DIRECTORY
Motivational Communications, Inc.
175 Fifth Avenue   Phone: (212) 260-0800
New York, NY 10010
Covers: About 900 import/export firms, manufacturers, and national agencies (United States and Australia) concerned with commerce between the two countries and recognized by the Australian Government Trade Commission. **Entries include:** Company name, address, phone, and products or services offered. **Arrangement:** Alphabetical. **Pages** (approx.): 75. **Frequency:** Irregular; latest edition September 1979. **Editor:** Barry V. Conforte. **Advertising accepted.** Circulation 50,000. **Price:** $25.00.

★125★
AUSTRIAN-AMERICAN BUSINESS REVIEW
Motivational Communications, Inc.
175 Fifth Avenue   Phone: (212) 260-0800
New York, NY 10010
Covers: Import/export firms, manufacturers, and federal agencies (United States and Austria) concerned with commerce between the two countries. **Entries include:** Company name, address, phone, and products or services. **Arrangement:** Alphabetical. **Frequency:** Annual, September. **Editor:** Anne Bauso. **Advertising accepted.** Circulation 50,000. **Price:** $25.00, plus $2.50 shipping.

★126★
AUTHOR'S GUIDE TO JOURNALS IN BUSINESS
Haworth Press
149 Fifth Avenue   Phone: (212) 228-2800
New York, NY 10010
Number of listings: About 450. **Entries include:** Publication name, address for manuscripts, publication orientation and subject interests, usual review time and delay in publication of accepted manuscripts, early publication options (if any). **Frequency:** Not established; first edition expected late spring 1980. **Price:** $16.95.

★127★
AUTO TRIM NEWS—DIRECTORY OF PRODUCT SOURCES ISSUE
National Association of Auto Trim Shops
1623 Grand Avenue   Phone: (516) 223-4334
Baldwin, NY 11510
Publication includes: Major suppliers, manufacturers, and installers of interior and exterior trim and accessory products used in customizing cars, trucks, vans, and boats. **Entries include:** Company name, address, phone, contact person. **Arrangement:** Alphabetical. **Indexes:** Product. **Pages** (approx.): 50. **Frequency:** Annual, November. **Editor:** Nat Danas. **Price:** $4.00.

★128★
AUTOMATION IN HOUSING & SYSTEMS BUILDING NEWS—BUYERS' GUIDE ISSUE
CMN Associates, Inc.
5144 W. Main Street   Phone: (312) 674-8392
Skokie, IL 60076
Publication includes: About 600 manufacturers and suppliers to the industrialized/manufactured (pre-fabricated) housing industry. **Entries include:** Company name, address, phone, name of sales executive. **Arrangement:** Alphabetical. **Indexes:** Product. **Frequency:** Annual, January. **Editor:** Don Carlson, Publisher. **Advertising accepted.** Circulation 21,000. **Price:** 5.00 (current edition); $10.00 (1980 edition).

★129★
AUTOMATION IN HOUSING & SYSTEMS BUILDING NEWS—TOP 100 SURVEY ISSUE
CMN Associates, Inc.
5144 W. Main Street   Phone: (312) 674-8392
Skokie, IL 60076
Publication includes: List of 100 leading home builders in terms of dollar volume; 25 leading builders in terms of units built. **Entries include:** Company name, chief executive, type of housing built, dollar volume, number of units built. **Arrangement:** By volume and units. **Indexes:** Alphabetical. **Frequency:** Annual, July-August issue. **Editor:** Don O. Carlson. **Advertising accepted.** Circulation 21,000. **Price:** $3.00 (current edition); $5.00 (1980 edition).

★130★
AUTOMOTIVE AFFILIATED REPRESENTATIVES—MEMBERSHIP ROSTER
Automotive Affiliated Representatives
10800 N. Military Trail, Suite 222   Phone: (305) 626-8380
Palm Beach Gardens, FL 33410
Covers: 2,000 manufacturers' agents and about 200 manufacturers serving the automotive parts and equipment aftermarket industry. **Entries include:** For agents' firms - Company name, address, name, home and business phone of owner, branch locations, name of manager (if any), services and facilities, number of salesmen employed, territory covered, list of products handled. For manufacturers - Company name, address, phone, contact. **Indexes:** Agent (salesman) name. **Pages** (approx.): 120. **Frequency:** Annual, March. **Editor:** Melvin H. Steinbrenner, Executive Vice-President. **Price:** Free.

★131★
AUTOMOTIVE AGE—BUYER'S GUIDE ISSUE
Freed-Crown Publishing Company, Inc.
6931 Van Nuys Boulevard   Phone: (213) 873-1320
Van Nuys, CA 91405
Covers: Over 1,200 companies that offer products and services for new car dealerships; also lists manufacturers of domestic and imported cars and trucks, special purpose vehicles, vehicle converters, kit cars, and specialty cars. **Entries include:** Company name, headquarters address and phone, names and titles of sales executives, cities and phone numbers of outlets. **Arrangement:** Alphabetical. **Indexes:** Product. **Frequency:** Annual, December. **Editor:** Chris Hosford. **Advertising accepted. Price:** $5.00.

★132★
AUTOMOTIVE BODY REPAIR NEWS BUYERS GUIDE
Stanley Publishing Company
300 W. Lake Street   Phone: (312) 332-0210
Chicago, IL 60606
Covers: Manufacturers and suppliers of equipment and materials for repair of automobile bodies. Also includes lists of manufacturers' representatives and warehouse distributors. **Entries include:** Company name, address, phone, products and services. **Arrangement:** Manufacturers and representatives are alphabetical, distributors are geographical. **Indexes:** Product, brand names. **Frequency:** Annual, June. **Advertising accepted.** Circulation 63,200. **Price:** $15.00.

★133★
AUTOMOTIVE BOOSTER CLUBS INTERNATIONAL—ROSTER
Automotive Booster Clubs International
605 E. Algonquin Road   Phone: (312) 593-8350
Arlington Heights, IL 60005
Covers: 500 officers and committee members of 51 local groups of ABCI, an organization of sales executives, manufacturers' agents, and direct factory salesmen in automotive aftermarket and service industries. **Entries include:** Name, address, phone, local group affiliation. **Arrangement:** According to office held. **Pages** (approx.): 25. **Frequency:** Annual, January.

★134★
AUTOMOTIVE INDUSTRIES SALES PLANNING & MARKETING DIRECTORY
Chilton Company
Chilton Way   Phone: (215) 687-8200
Radnor, PA 19089
Covers: Over 3,500 United States and Canadian automotive plants and parts suppliers with over 200 employees. **Entries include:** Company name, address, phone, number of employees, list of key personnel, types of activity, SIC number, list of products. **Arrangement:** Geographical. **Indexes:** Product. **Frequency:** Formerly annual, now irregular; latest edition 1978; no editions planned for 1979 or 1980. **Price:** $100.00.

★135★
AUTOMOTIVE MARKETING—BUYER'S GUIDE ISSUE
Chilton Company
Chilton Way   Phone: (215) 687-8200
Radnor, PA 19089
Publication includes: More than 1,000 manufacturers of products, tools, and equipment useful in the installation and repair of automotive systems. **Entries include:** Company name, address, phone. **Arrangement:** Alphabetical. **Indexes:** Product. **Frequency:** Annual, September. **Editor:** Rick Bay. **Advertising accepted. Price:** $3.00.

Automotive News—Almanac Issue *See* Automotive News—Market Data Book Issue

★136★
AUTOMOTIVE NEWS—MARKET DATA BOOK ISSUE
Crain Automotive Group, Inc.
965 E. Jefferson Avenue   Phone: (313) 567-9520
Detroit, MI 48207
Publication includes: List of automobile, truck, parts, accessories, and dealership equipment manufacturers; "Who's Who in the Auto Industry" section gives brief biographical data and photographs of executives of major firms. **Pages** (approx.): 225. **Frequency:** Annual, last Wednesday in April. **Editor:** Richard A. Wright. **Advertising accepted.** Circulation 60,000. **Former title:** Automotive News - Almanac Issue (1976). **Price:** $12.50 (current and 1980 editions). **Other information:** Also includes production, sales, financial, advertising expenditure, and other data; federal regulations; domestic and import car specifications.

★137★
AUTOMOTIVE PARTS REBUILDERS ASSOCIATION—MEMBERSHIP ROSTER & TRADE DIRECTORY
Automotive Parts Rebuilders Association
6849 Old Dominion Drive, Suite 352   Phone: (703) 790-1050
McLean, VA 22101
Covers: Over 700 production rebuilders of automotive parts; over 250 suppliers and manufacturers' representatives servicing rebuilders. **Entries include:** Company name, address, phone, names of executives, products or services. **Arrangement:** Rebuilders are geographical; others are alphabetical. **Pages** (approx.): 45. **Frequency:** Annual, April. **Editor:** Rose Marie Flanagan, Secretary - Membership Records. **Former title:** Automotive Parts Rebuilders Association Buyer's Guide (1973). **Price:** $20.00 (current edition); $30.00 (1980 edition).

★138★
AUTOMOTIVE REBUILDER—PURCHASING DIRECTORY ISSUE
Babcox Publications
11 S. Forge Street   Phone: (216) 535-6117
Akron, OH 44304
Covers: About 350 manufacturers of components and equipment for rebuilding automotive parts and about 60 companies which supply rebuildable parts to rebuilders and manufacturers. **Entries include:** Company name, address, phone; most listings also include name of president or contact. **Arrangement:** Alphabetical within manufacturer and core supplier categories. **Indexes:** Product. **Pages** (approx.): 180.

Frequency: Annual, January. **Editor:** Andrew J. Doherty. **Advertising accepted.** Circulation 18,000. **Price:** $3.00.

★139★
AUTOMOTIVE SERVICE INDUSTRY ASSOCIATION—MEMBERSHIP DIRECTORY
Automotive Service Industry Association
444 N. Michigan Avenue   Phone: (312) 836-1300
Chicago, IL 60611
Covers: Wholesalers, manufacturers, distributors, and other commercial firms supplying the automotive servicing industry. **Entries include:** Company name, address, phone, and whether a distributor, manufacturer, or wholesaler. **Arrangement:** Alphabetical. **Frequency:** Annual. **Price:** Available to members only.

★140★
AUTOMOTIVE WAREHOUSE DISTRIBUTORS ASSOCIATION—MEMBERSHIP DIRECTORY
Automotive Warehouse Distributors Association
1719 W. 91st Place   Phone: (816) 444-3500
Kansas City, MO 64114
Covers: Over 600 automotive parts distributors and 240 manufacturers. **Entries include:** Company name, address, phone, names of key personnel, products distributed or manufactured, territories served, number and location of branches. **Arrangement:** Alphabetical. **Indexes:** Geographical index of distributors and manufacturers. **Pages** (approx.): 165. **Frequency:** Annual, March. **Price:** $50.00, postpaid (current and 1980 editions).

Aviation Buyer's Directory *See* ABD—Aviation Buyer's Directory

★141★
AVIATION DIRECTORY
E. A. Brennan & Company, Inc.
9355 Chapman Avenue   Phone: (714) 539-8931
Garden Grove, CA 92641
Covers: Airports, fixed base operators and service firms, other firms serving general aviation, and aircraft owners; separate editions for Pacific and western, southwestern and Gulf, mid-continent, northeast, and mid-Atlantic and southern states. **Entries include:** For airports - Airport name, phone, name of manager, name of owner and operator, location, and runway, lighting, radio, and other data. For firms - Name only, in airport section (geographical); name, address, phone in alphabetical and product-classified sections. For owners - Name, address, phone in alphabetical section. **Frequency:** Annual. **Advertising accepted. Former title:** Pacific Coast Aviation Directory and Buyer's Yellow Pages (1979). **Price:** Free; controlled circulation.

★142★
AVIATION WEEK & SPACE TECHNOLOGY—MARKETING DIRECTORY ISSUE
McGraw-Hill, Inc.
1221 Avenue of the Americas   Phone: (212) 997-2061
New York, NY 10020
Covers: 5,000 manufacturers and service firms concerned with military, commercial, governmental, and corporate aviation and aircraft, rockets, missiles, space vehicles, avionics, etc. **Entries include:** Company name, address, phone, names of executives, and products or services. **Arrangement:** Alphabetical. **Indexes:** Product (2,000 headings). **Pages** (approx.): 370. **Frequency:** Annual, December. **Editor:** Ines Peressini, Marketing Directory Manager. **Advertising accepted.** Circulation 96,000. **Price:** $4.00.

AWI Red Book Directory *See* Associated Warehouses, Inc.—Directory of Members

Baccalaureate Programs in Hotel, Restaurant, Institutional Management in the United States *See* Senior College Programs in Hotel...

★143★

BAKERY PRODUCTION AND MARKETING—BUYERS GUIDE ISSUE
Gorman Publishing Company
5725 E. River Road   Phone: (312) 693-3200
Chicago, IL 60631
Covers: Over 1,200 manufacturers of equipment and supplies for
bakeries. **Entries include:** Company name, address, phone, and name
of contact; regional-only manufacturers include a code indicating
geographic region served. **Arrangement:** Alphabetical. **Indexes:**
Product. **Frequency:** Annual, December. **Advertising accepted.**
Circulation 31,000. **Price:** $15.00.

★144★

BAKERY PRODUCTION AND MARKETING—RED BOOK ISSUE
Gorman Publishing Company
5725 E. River Road   Phone: (312) 693-3200
Chicago, IL 60631
Covers: About 2,000 wholesale, multi-unit retail, grocery chain, and
co-op bakery companies and plants in the United States and Canada,
manufacturing bread, cakes, cookies, crackers, pretzels, snack foods,
frozen bakery products, etc. Also includes about 1,200 bakery
product distributors, dealers, jobbers, brokers, and manufacturers'
representatives. **Entries include:** For major bakeries - Name,
headquarters, address, phone, type of operation, number of plants,
stores, officers, number of employees, sales, brands. For individual
bakeries - Name, address, phone, type, products, sales, employees.
For distributors - Name, address, phone, type of service, products
offered, marketing area, sales, personnel. **Arrangement:** Bakery
company headquarters are alphabetical; individual plants are
geographical; distributors are grouped in six regions. **Indexes:**
Alphabetical index to bakeries. **Pages** (approx.): 275. **Frequency:**
Annual, June. **Editor:** Vivien Gorman. **Advertising accepted.**
Circulation 31,000. **Price:** $65.00 (current and 1980 editions).

★145★

BARGAIN HUNTING IN THE BAY AREA [California]
Wingbow Press
2940 Seventh Street   Phone: (415) 549-3030
Berkeley, CA 94710
Covers: Over 300 factory outlets; catalog stores; sample stores;
warehouses and showrooms; customs, freight, police, and storage
auctions; salvage and wrecking yards; rummage sales, and other
vendors of articles at 20% to 70% discount. **Entries include:** Outlet
name, address, specialties, discounts offered. **Arrangement:** By type
of establishment. **Pages** (approx.): 150. **Frequency:** Irregular; latest
edition July 1978. **Editor:** Sally Socolich. **Price:** $4.50, plus 75¢
shipping.

★146★

BARRON'S GUIDE TO GRADUATE BUSINESS SCHOOLS
Barron's Educational Series, Inc.
113 Crossways Park Drive   Phone: (516) 921-8750
Woodbury, NY 11797
Publication includes: About 225 colleges offering Master of Business
degree, primarily in eastern states. **Entries include:** Name of school,
location, description of the graduate program, admission
requirements, availability of financial aid. **Arrangement:** Geographical.
Pages (approx.): 350. **Frequency:** Irregular; first edition 1978; new
edition expected April 1980. **Editor:** Eugene Miller. **Price:** $4.95, plus
50¢ shipping (current and 1980 editions). **Other information:** Includes
information on applications, selection of school, tests, etc.

★147★

BARTER COMMUNIQUE QUARTERLY
Full Circle Marketing Corporation
5700 Midnight Pass Road   Phone: (813) 349-3300
Sarasota, FL 33581
Covers: Business and publications which deal in barter, i.e., which
offer accomodations, services, etc., for advertising space, or vice
versa. **Entries include:** Company name, address, phone, products/
services needed/offered. **Pages** (approx.): 50 (tabloid size).

Frequency: Quarterly. **Editor:** Robert J. Murley. **Advertising
accepted.** Circulation 40,000. **Price:** $20.00 per year.

★148★

BATTERY MAN—SLIG BUYERS' GUIDE ISSUE
Independent Battery Manufacturers Association
100 Larchwood Drive   Phone: (813) 586-1409
Largo, FL 33540
Covers: About 2,000 manufacturers and rebuilders of heavy-duty
storage batteries, primarily for motor vehicles, and their suppliers,
worldwide. Includes firms in other areas of starting, lighting, ignition,
and generating systems. **Entries include:** Firm name, address,
products. **Arrangement:** Battery manufacturers are geographical,
suppliers are by product or service. **Indexes:** Alphabetical (includes
addresses). **Pages** (approx.): 100. **Frequency:** Biennial, spring of odd
years. **Editor:** Dan A. Noe, Executive Secretary. **Advertising
accepted.** Circulation 8,500. **Price:** $5.00, payment with order.

★149★

BAY AREA EMPLOYER DIRECTORY [California]
James R. Albin
431 Bridgeway   Phone: (415) 332-6438
Sausalito, CA 94965
Covers: About 1,800 employers in the Bay Area with 100 or more
employees, including both private and governmental employers.
Entries include: Firm or agency name, address, phone, year
established, type of business or activity, number of employees, sales,
names and titles of local chief executive and personnel manager.
Arrangement: Alphabetical. **Indexes:** Occupations hired by firms
listed. **Pages** (approx.): 200. **Frequency:** Irregular; new edition
expected 1980. **Editor:** James R. Albin. **Advertising accepted.**
Price: $19.95.

★150★

**BAY AREA EMPLOYMENT AGENCY AND EXECUTIVE RECRUITER
    DIRECTORY [California]**
James R. Albin
431 Bridgeway   Phone: (415) 332-6438
Sausalito, CA 94965
Covers: Over 600 employment agencies handling temporary and/or
permanent personnel and executive recruiting firms in the 10-county
San Francisco Bay Area (Alameda, Contra Costa, Marin, Napa, San
Francisco, San Mateo, Santa Clara, Santa Cruz, Solana, and Sonoma
counties). **Entries include:** Agency name, address, phone, names of
executives, number of counselors, whether applicant or employer pays
agency fee, whether permanent and/or temporary positions are
handled. Listings do not indicate agency's occupational specialties.
Arrangement: Alphabetical. **Indexes:** Occupations handled, indicating
whether entry level or experienced applicants are served. **Pages**
(approx.): 150. **Frequency:** Annual, fall. **Editor:** James R. Albin.
Advertising accepted. **Former title:** Bay Area Employment Agency
Directory. **Price:** $9.95.

★151★

BEAUTY FASHION—BATH DIRECTORY ISSUE
Beauty Fashion, Inc.
48 E. 43rd Street   Phone: (212) 687-6190
New York, NY 10017
Covers: Manufacturers of bath products and related items for men
and women. **Entries include:** Company name, address, phone, trade
and brand names. **Arrangement:** Alphabetical. **Indexes:** Trade name.
Frequency: Annual, May. **Editor:** John G. Ledes. **Advertising
accepted.** Circulation 18,000. **Price:** This issue, $10.00;
subscription, $10.00 per year.

★152★

BEAUTY FASHION—COSMETIC DIRECTORY ISSUES
Beauty Fashion, Inc.
48 E. 43rd Street   Phone: (212) 687-6190
New York, NY 10017
Covers: Manufacturers of color cosmetics for women. **Entries**

include: Company name, address, phone. **Arrangement:** Alphabetical. **Indexes:** Brand name. **Frequency:** Annual, October (Part 1), November (Part 2). **Editor:** John G. Ledes. **Advertising accepted.** Circulation 18,000. **Price:** This issue, $10.00; subscription, $10.00 per year.

★153★

BEAUTY FASHION—CTFA CONVENTION ISSUE
Beauty Fashion, Inc.
48 E. 43rd Street   Phone: (212) 687-6190
New York, NY 10017
Covers: Suppliers of goods and services to cosmetic industry manufacturers represented at Cosmetic, Toiletry and Fragrance Association convention. **Entries include:** Company name, address, phone, name of contact, list of products or services. **Arrangement:** Classified. **Frequency:** Annual, February. **Editor:** John G. Ledes. **Advertising accepted.** Circulation 18,000. **Price:** This issue, $10.00; subscription, $10.00 per year.

★154★

BEAUTY FASHION—FRAGRANCE DIRECTORY ISSUE
Beauty Fashion, Inc.
48 E. 43rd Street   Phone: (212) 687-6190
New York, NY 10017
Covers: Manufacturers of perfumes, colognes, and other fragrances for men and women. **Entries include:** Company name, address, phone, trade and brand names. **Arrangement:** Alphabetical. **Indexes:** Trade name. **Frequency:** Annual, June. **Editor:** John G. Ledes. **Advertising accepted.** Circulation 18,000. **Price:** This issue, $10.00; subscription, $10.00 per year.

★155★

BEAUTY FASHION—MEN'S DIRECTORY ISSUE
Beauty Fashion, Inc.
48 E. 43rd Street   Phone: (212) 687-6190
New York, NY 10017
Covers: Manufacturers of men's fragrances, toiletries and related products. **Entries include:** Company name, address, phone, trade and brand names. **Arrangement:** Alphabetical. **Indexes:** Trade name. **Frequency:** Annual, April. **Editor:** John G. Ledes. **Advertising accepted.** Circulation 18,000. **Price:** This issue, $10.00; subscription, $10.00 per year.

★156★

BEAUTY FASHION—SUN PRODUCTS ISSUE
Beauty Fashion, Inc.
48 E. 43rd Street   Phone: (212) 687-6190
New York, NY 10017
Covers: Manufacturers of sun tan products and special sun products for men and women. **Entries include:** Company name, address, phone, trade and brand names. **Arrangement:** Alphabetical. **Indexes:** Trade name. **Frequency:** Annual, January. **Editor:** John G. Ledes. **Advertising accepted.** Circulation 18,000. **Price:** This issue $10.00; subscription, $10.00 per year.

★157★

BEAUTY FASHION—TREATMENTS DIRECTORY ISSUE
Beauty Fashion, Inc.
48 E. 43rd Street   Phone: (212) 687-6190
New York, NY 10017
Covers: Manufacturers of treatment (cosmetic) products. **Entries include:** Company name, address, phone, trade and brand names. **Arrangement:** Alphabetical. **Indexes:** Trade name. **Frequency:** Annual, March. **Editor:** John G. Ledes. **Price:** This issue, $10.00; subscription, $10.00 per year.

★158★

BECKER GUIDE [Chicago-area corporations]
Becker Warburg Paribas Group
Two First National Plaza   Phone: (312) 630-5554
Chicago, IL 60603
Covers: 270 major publicly held corporations and financial institutions in northern Illinois. **Entries include:** Company name, headquarters location and phone, brief description of product lines and organizational structure, list of key personnel, consolidated balance sheet in abbreviated form, consolidated income statement, number of employees, date of annual meeting, and other stockholder information. **Pages** (approx.): 330. **Frequency:** Annual, summer. **Editor:** Mary L. Merker. **Price:** $19.50.

Bedding Buyers' Guide and Composite Catalog *See* Bedding
    Magazine—Bedding Industry Yearbook and Supplies Guide
    Issue

★159★

**BEDDING MAGAZINE—BEDDING INDUSTRY YEARBOOK AND
    SUPPLIES GUIDE ISSUE**
National Association of Bedding Manufacturers
1150 17th Street, N. W.   Phone: (202) 872-0600
Washington, DC 20036
Covers: Manufacturers of components, equipment, and services used by manufacturers of mattresses and foundations. **Entries include:** Company name, address, phone, list of products or services. **Arrangement:** Alphabetical. **Indexes:** Product. **Pages** (approx.): 120. **Frequency:** Annual, December. **Editor:** Nancy H. Butler. **Advertising accepted.** Circulation 2,600. **Former title:** Bedding Buyers' Guide and Composite Catalog. **Price:** $5.00.

★160★

**BELGIAN AMERICAN CHAMBER OF COMMERCE IN THE UNITED
    STATES—TRADE DIRECTORY**
Belgian American Chamber of Commerce in the U. S.
50 Rockefeller Plaza, Suite 1003-1005
New York, NY 10020
Covers: 1,400 United States firms with plants or offices in Belgium and Luxembourg. **Entries include:** Company name, address, telex and phone numbers, names of principal executives, subsidiaries, description of products or services. **Arrangement:** Alphabetical. **Pages** (approx.): 170. **Frequency:** Irregular; previous edition 1977; latest edition July 1979. **Price:** $28.00.

★161★

BELL HELICOPTER OPERATORS DIRECTORY
Bell Helicopter Textron
Box 482   Phone: (817) 280-2011
Fort Worth, TX 76101
Covers: Over 350 United States and Canadian commercial helicopter operators. **Entries include:** Company name, address, phone, names and titles of key personnel, aircraft operated, type of operation. **Arrangement:** Alphabetical. **Frequency:** Latest edition 1979. **Price:** Free.

★162★

BEST BETS [New York City]
Quick Fox, Inc.
33 W. 60th Street   Phone: (212) 246-0325
New York, NY 10023
Description: Information on colorful, exceptional, and otherwise notable restaurants, boutiques, amusement places, etc., selected from "Best Bets" section of "New York Magazine." **Pages** (approx.): 145. **Frequency:** First published 1977. **Author:** Ellen Stock Stern. **Price:** $3.95.

★163★

BEST'S SAFETY DIRECTORY
A. M. Best Company, Inc.
Ambest Road   Phone: (201) 439-2200
Oldwick, NJ 08858
Covers: Nearly 2,000 manufacturers and distributors of safety, industrial hygiene, security, and pollution control products and services. **Arrangement:** Manufacturers are classified. **Indexes:** Distributor location. **Pages** (approx.): 1,500 in two volumes. **Frequency:** Annual, October. **Advertising accepted.** Circulation 15,000. **Price:** $30.00, postpaid, payment with order. **Also includes:** Reference material on governmental safety standards.

★164★

BEVERAGE INDUSTRY—ANNUAL MANUAL ISSUE
Magazines for Industry, Inc.
747 Third Avenue   Phone: (212) 838-7778
New York, NY 10017
Covers: Over 700 companies supplying equipment and materials to the soft drink, beer, wine, bottled water, and juice industries; industry associations; bottling and supply franchise companies. **Entries include:** For suppliers - Company name, address, phone, code to indicate products. For associations - Name, address, phone, name of president; some association listings also include meeting date and location and names of other executives. Franchise company listings include name, address, phone, names and titles of executives, number of plants, number of franchised plants, products, foreign involvement. **Arrangement:** State associations and supplier associations are geographical, other listings are alphabetical. **Indexes:** Trade and brand name, product. **Frequency:** Annual, September. **Editor:** Paul Mullins. **Advertising accepted.** Circulation 9,000. **Price:** $30.00.

★165★

BEVERAGE WORLD—BUYERS GUIDE ISSUE
Keller Publishing Corporation
150 Great Neck Road   Phone: (516) 829-9210
Great Neck, NY 11021
Covers: Suppliers to the beverage industry. **Entries include:** Company name, address. **Arrangement:** By product. **Frequency:** Annual, September. **Editor:** Barbara Spiegel. **Price:** $2.00.

★166★

BEVERAGE WORLD—SOFT DRINK FRANCHISE COMPANY DIRECTORY ISSUE
Keller Publishing Corporation
150 Great Neck Road   Phone: (516) 829-9210
Great Neck, NY 11021
Publication includes: List of about 60 soft drink companies which offer bottler franchises. **Entries include:** Company name, headquarters address, names of principal executives, brand names, phone, number of franchises operating, number of countries in which represented. **Arrangement:** Alphabetical. **Frequency:** Irregular; about every 2 years; new edition January 1980. **Editor:** Richard V. Howard. **Price:** $2.00 (1980 edition).

★167★

BIG BOOK [Building Industry Guide for New England]
Slater Publications, Inc.
679 Highland Avenue   Phone: (617) 449-3916
Needham Heights, MA 02194
Covers: Over 33,000 architects, engineers, developers, general contractors, sub-contractors, suppliers, consultants, and others in the building industry in New England (Maine, New Hampshire, Vermont, Massachusetts, Connecticut, and Rhode Island). Also includes a list of 5,000 manufacturers and agents and lists of trade associations and government agencies. **Entries include:** Company name, address, phone; and codes for years in business, annual sales volume, and maximum bonding capacity. **Arrangement:** Classified, geographical within categories. **Indexes:** Alphabetical company name index. **Pages** (approx.): 930. **Frequency:** Annual, November. **Editor:** Robert T. Slater, Publisher. **Advertising accepted.** Circulation 10,000. **Price:**

$40.00, payment with order; $41.75, billed.

★168★

BILLBOARD INTERNATIONAL RECORDING EQUIPMENT AND STUDIO DIRECTORY
Billboard Publications, Inc.
9000 Sunset Boulevard   Phone: (213) 273-7040
Los Angeles, CA 90069
Covers: Recording studios, equipment manufacturers and importers, independent record producers, and tape bulk raw and blank loaded cassette manufacturers in the United States and over 25 other countries. **Entries include:** Company name, address, phone, names of principal executives, trade or brand names and/or list of products or services. **Arrangement:** United States and Canadian recording studios are geographical; all other lists are alphabetical within categories. **Indexes:** Recording equipment and products. **Pages** (approx.): 165. **Frequency:** Annual, October. **Editors:** Earl Paige, Special Issues Editor (Los Angeles), and Bob Hudoba, Manager, Directory Services (Cincinnati). **Advertising accepted.** **Price:** $15.00. **Send orders to:** Billboard Magazine Directories, 2160 Patterson St. Cincinnati, OH 45214 (513-381-6450).

★169★

BILLBOARD TAPE/AUDIO/VIDEO MARKET SOURCEBOOK
Billboard Publications, Inc.
9000 Sunset Boulevard   Phone: (213) 273-7040
Los Angeles, CA 90069
Covers: Tape/audio/video equipment manufacturers, wholesalers, and importers; videotape libraries; pre-recorded tape, tape service and supply companies; accessories; store fixtures and merchandising aids; manufacturers and importers in the United States, Belgium, Canada, France, German Federal Republic, Italy, Mexico, Netherlands, Switzerland, and the United Kingdom. **Entries include:** Company name, address, phone, names of principal executives, trade and brand names and/or list of products or services. **Arrangement:** Classified by product or service; tape services are geographical, other sections are alphabetical. **Pages** (approx.): 60. **Frequency:** Annual, May. **Editors:** Earl Paige, Special Issues Editor (Los Angeles), and Bob Hudoba, Manager, Directory Services (Cincinnati). **Advertising accepted.** **Price:** $10.00. **Send orders to:** Billboard Magazine Directories, 2160 Patterson St., Cincinnati, OH 45214 (513-381-6450).

★170★

BILLBOARD'S INTERNATIONAL BUYER'S GUIDE
Billboard Publications, Inc.
9000 Sunset Boulevard   Phone: (213) 273-7040
Los Angeles, CA 90069
Covers: Record companies; music publishers; record and tape wholesalers; services and supplies for the music-record-tape industry; record and tape dealer accessories, fixtures, and merchandising aids; includes United States and over 65 other countries. **Entries include:** Company name, address, phone, names of principal executives, trade and brand names and/or list of products and services. **Arrangement:** Classified by product or service; record and tape wholesalers and some services and supplies are geographical, other sections are alphabetical. **Pages** (approx.): 400. **Frequency:** Annual, September. **Editors:** Earl Paige, Special Issues Editor (Los Angeles), and Bob Hudoba, Manager, Directory Services (Cincinnati). **Advertising accepted.** **Price:** $35.00. **Send orders to:** Billboard Magazine Directories, 2160 Patterson St., Cincinnati, OH 45214 (513-381-6450).

★171★

BILLBOARD'S INTERNATIONAL DISCO SOURCEBOOK
Billboard Publications, Inc.
9000 Sunset Boulevard   Phone: (213) 273-7040
Los Angeles, CA 90069
Covers: Record companies, discotheque equipment and service companies in the United States and abroad. **Entries include:** Company name, address, phone, names of principal executives, trade and brand

names and/or list of products or services. **Arrangement:** Alphabetical within major categories. **Indexes:** Equipment and services. **Pages** (approx.): 115. **Frequency:** Annual, April. **Editors:** Earl Paige, Special Issues Editor (Los Angeles), and Bob Hudoba, Manager, Directory Services (Cincinnati). **Price:** $10.00. **Send orders to:** Billboard Magazine Directories, 2160 Patterson St., Cincinnati, OH 45214 (513-381-6450).

★172★
BIRMINGHAM AREA INDUSTRIAL DIRECTORY [Alabama]
Birmingham Area Chamber of Commerce
Box 10127   Phone: (205) 323-5461
Birmingham, AL 35202
Covers: About 1,200 manufacturing establishments in Jefferson, Shelby, St. Clair, and Walker counties. **Entries include:** Company name, address, phone, name of principal executive, number of employees, products or services, SIC numbers. **Arrangement:** Alphabetical, geographical, and product-by-SIC sections contain same information. **Pages** (approx.): 225. **Frequency:** Irregular; latest edition 1979. **Price:** $13.50, plus $1.00 shipping (ISSN 0147-2097). **Other information:** Format and content identical with "Alabama Directory of Mining and Manufacturing" for listed firms; $15.00, plus $1.00 shipping.

Black Book *See* **Directory Iron and Steel Plants**

★173★
BLACK BUSINESS DIRECTORY [Baltimore, MD]
Black Economic Research Team
Box 13513   Phone: (301) 675-6600
Baltimore, MD 21203
Publication includes: Shopping guide to Black-owned/operated businesses and Black professionals in the Baltimore, MD area. **Entries include:** Name, address, phone. **Arrangement:** Alphabetical by line of business. **Pages** (approx.): 50. **Frequency:** Irregular; new edition expected March 1980. **Editor:** Talbert L. Gwynn, Editor/Vice President. **Advertising accepted.** Circulation 100,000. **Price:** $2.00 (1980 edition).

★174★
BLACK ENTERPRISE—LEADING BLACK BUSINESSES ISSUE
Earl G. Graves Publishing Company
295 Madison Avenue   Phone: (212) 889-8220
New York, NY 10017
Covers: 100 Black-owned or Black-controlled businesses with sales of $4.2 million or above, 49 banks with total assets of $2 million or more, 40 savings and loan associations with total assets of $100,000 or more, and 39 insurance companies with total assets of about $200,000 or more. **Entries include:** Company name, city and state, name of chief executive, year founded, financial data. **Arrangement:** Ranked by financial size. **Frequency:** Annual, June. **Editor:** Earl G. Graves. **Advertising accepted. Price:** $2.00 (current and 1980 editions). **Also includes:** Analyses of the lists and of the industries in which firms listed operate.

★175★
BLACKBOOK BUSINESS AND REFERENCE GUIDE [Chicago]
National Publications Sales Agency, Inc.
840 E. 87th Street, Suite 202   Phone: (312) 994-5100
Chicago, IL 60619
Covers: About 1,500 Black-owned consumer-oriented businesses in the Chicago area. Limited to advertisers. **Entries include:** Firm name, address, phone, whether Black-owned or Black-managed. **Arrangement:** Classified. **Pages** (approx.): 125. **Frequency:** Annual, March. **Editor:** Donald C. Walker. **Price:** $4.35, postpaid (1980 edition).

★176★
BLUE BOOK OF MAJOR HOMEBUILDERS
CMR Associates, Inc.
11-A Village Green   Phone: (301) 261-6363
Crofton, MD 21114
Covers: 2,000 major homebuilding firms. **Entries include:** Company name, address, phone, key executives, areas in which firm operates, construction methods, number of units constructed in each of last four years and plans for current year, nonresidential building, remodeling activity, property management, performance record, sales price and rental ranges, money requirements, land requirements, government housing activity. **Arrangement:** Geographical. **Indexes:** Alphabetical. **Pages** (approx.): 325. **Frequency:** Annual, February. **Editor:** Donald F. Spear, President. **Price:** $105.00 (current edition); $115.00 (1980 edition); regional editions (northeast, midwest, south and west), $40.00 each (current edition); $45.00 each (1980 edition). **Other information:** Variant title, "Who's Who in Residential Construction."

Blue Book of the Soap, Detergent. . .Industries *See* **Soap/Cosmetics/Chemical Specialties Blue Book**

★177★
BLUE BOOK/CONTRACTORS REGISTER [New York, New Jersey, Connecticut]
Contractors Register, Inc.
30 Undercliff Avenue   Phone: (914) 592-8200
Elmsford, NY 10523
Covers: About 18,700 contractors, subcontractors, and suppliers of construction materials located in the New York, New Jersey, and Connecticut area. **Entries include:** Company name, address, phone. **Arrangement:** By product or service, then geographical. **Pages** (approx.): 2,000. **Frequency:** Annual, February. **Editor:** Edmund J. Kiernan. **Advertising accepted.** Circulation 27,000. **Price:** Free.

★178★
BLUE-COLLAR JOBS FOR WOMEN
E. P. Dutton, Inc.
Two Park Avenue   Phone: (212) 725-1818
New York, NY 10016
Publication includes: List of apprenticeship information offices, trade unions, and other sources of information concerning opportunities for women in the skilled trades. **Entries include:** Source name, address, title of publication (if any). **Frequency:** Published 1979. **Editor:** Muriel Lederer. **Price:** $12.95, cloth; $7.95, paper. **Other information:** Principal content of publication is description of skilled trade jobs, including pay, training, apprenticeship, work conditions, amount of work available, physical requirements, and advancement opportunities.

★179★
BM/E—THE SOURCE ISSUE
Broadband Information Services, Inc.
295 Madison Avenue   Phone: (212) 685-5320
New York, NY 10017
Covers: About 900 manufacturers, manufacturers' representatives, and distributors of equipment and supplies used in the radio and television broadcasting industries. **Entries include:** For manufacturers - Company name, address, phone, branches, products. For representatives and distributors - Company name, address, phone, name of manufacturers represented (if advertisers in this issue). **Arrangement:** Manufacturers are alphabetical, others are geographical. **Indexes:** Product. **Frequency:** Annual, September. **Advertising accepted.** Circulation 32,000. **Price:** $3.00.

★180★
THE BOOK [Advertiser services, northeastern states]
The Book Ltd.
431 Post Road East   Phone: (203) 226-4207
Westport, CT 06880
Covers: Over 4,000 professionals in the artistic, photographic, writing, and communications fields in Connecticut, New York, New Jersey, Rhode Island, and Massachusetts. Also includes related

technical service suppliers and production shops, model agencies, advertising agencies, audiovisual services, etc. **Entries include:** Name, address, phone. **Arrangement:** Within 12 categories (art and photo supplies, photo processing, typesetters, etc.). **Pages (approx.):** 200. **Frequency:** Annual, early in year. **Editor:** Heloisa Centner, President. **Advertising accepted.** Circulation 8,500. **Price:** $12.00 (current edition); $16.00 (1980 edition).

★181★
BOXBOARD CONTAINERS—BOXMAKERS' BUYING GUIDE ISSUE
Maclean-Hunter Publishing Corporation
300 W. Adams Street   Phone: (312) 726-2802
Chicago, IL 60606
Covers: Manufacturers and suppliers of equipment, services, and products used in boxmaking. **Entries include:** Company name, address. For sales representatives - Name, address, phone. **Arrangement:** Manufacturers are alphabetical; representatives are alphabetical by manufacturer, then geographical. **Indexes:** Product. **Frequency:** Annual, January. **Advertising accepted.** **Price:** $1.50 (1980 edition).

★182★
BRADFORD'S DIRECTORY OF MARKETING RESEARCH AGENCIES AND MANAGEMENT CONSULTANTS IN THE UNITED STATES AND THE WORLD
Bradford's Directory of Marketing Research Agencies
Box 276
Fairfax, VA 22030
Covers: About 500 marketing research agencies and management consultants in market research; associations concerned with market research; international coverage. **Entries include:** For agencies and consultants - Individual or firm name, address, phone, region covered, how long firm has been established, number of staff, names of key personnel, description of services offered. For associations - Name, address, phone, name of director, description of purpose, activities, and publications (if any). **Arrangement:** Agencies are geographical, associations are alphabetical. **Indexes:** Service, personal name, branch office location. **Pages (approx.):** 300. **Frequency:** Irregular; latest base volume 1971; biennial updates. **Editor:** Ernest S. Bradford. **Price:** Base volume and updates, $25.50. (Not verified)

★183★
BRAZIL BUSINESS
Motivational Communications, Inc.
175 Fifth Avenue   Phone: (212) 260-0800
New York, NY 10010
Covers: About 900 import/export firms, manufacturers, and federal agencies (United States and Brazil) concerned with commerce between the two countries. **Entries include:** Company name, address, phone, and products or services. **Arrangement:** Alphabetical. **Pages (approx.):** 75. **Frequency:** Annual, winter. **Editor:** Barry V. Conforte. **Advertising accepted.** Circulation 50,000. **Price:** $25.00 (current and 1980 editions).

★184★
BRAZILIAN-AMERICAN BUSINESS REVIEW DIRECTORY
Brazilian American Chamber of Commerce
22 W. 48th Street   Phone: (212) 575-9030
New York, NY 10036
Covers: Brazilian and American businesses interested in developing trade and investment within and between the two countries. **Arrangement:** Alphabetical. **Frequency:** Annual.

★185★
BREWERS DIGEST—BUYERS GUIDE & BREWERY DIRECTORY
Siebel Publishing Company, Division
Ammark Publishing Company
4049 W. Peterson Avenue   Phone: (312) 463-3400
Chicago, IL 60646
Covers: All breweries in the Western Hemisphere. Includes list of sources of equipment and supplies. **Entries include:** For breweries -

Company name, address, principal executive and operating personnel, products, brands, capacities. For suppliers - Company name, address, products. **Arrangement:** Breweries are geographical, suppliers are alphabetical. **Indexes:** Product. **Pages (approx.):** 130. **Frequency:** Annual, January. **Editor:** Ross Heuer. **Advertising accepted.** Circulation 3,000. **Price:** $5.00 (current and 1980 editions).

★186★
BRITISH-AMERICAN CHAMBER OF COMMERCE—YEARBOOK AND CLASSIFIED DIRECTORY
British-American Chamber of Commerce
10 E. 40th Street   Phone: (212) 889-0680
New York, NY 10016
Covers: 600 British and American businesses interested in developing trade and investment within and between the two countries. **Entries include:** Company name, address. **Arrangement:** Classified by product or service. **Frequency:** Annual, December. **Advertising accepted.** **Price:** Apply.

★187★
BROADCAST ENGINEERING—BUYERS GUIDE ISSUE
Intertec Publishing Corporation
Box 12901   Phone: (913) 888-4664
Overland Park, KS 66212
Covers: 700 manufacturers of communications equipment for radio, television, and recording applications. **Entries include:** Company name, address. **Arrangement:** Alphabetical. **Indexes:** Product. **Pages (approx.):** 200. **Frequency:** Annual, September. **Editor:** Bill Rhodes, Editorial Director. **Advertising accepted.** Circulation 35,000. **Price:** $10.00.

Broadcast Management/Engineering—Source Issue *See* BM/E— The Source Issue

★188★
BROOME COUNTY CHAMBER OF COMMERCE—DIRECTORY OF INDUSTRY [New York State]
Broome County Chamber of Commerce
Box 995   Phone: (607) 772-8860
Binghamton, NY 13902
Covers: About 250 manufacturers in Broome and contiguous counties. **Entries include:** Company name, address, phone, name of principal executive, number of employees, SIC numbers, list of products or services. **Arrangement:** Alphabetical. **Indexes:** SIC. **Pages (approx.):** 60. **Frequency:** Irregular; latest edition 1979. **Editor:** David H. Treichler, Vice President, Industrial Development. **Price:** $10.50.

★189★
BUILDING SERVICES CONTRACTOR—BUYERS' GUIDE ISSUE
MacNair-Dorland Company, Inc.
101 W. 31st Street   Phone: (212) 279-4456
New York, NY 10001
Covers: Supplies, equipment, and services for firms doing cleaning under contract. **Entries include:** Company name and address. **Frequency:** Annual, December. **Editor:** Joseph A. Thorsen. **Advertising accepted.** Circulation 6,500. **Price:** $2.00.

★190★
BUILDING SUPPLY NEWS—BUYERS GUIDE ISSUE
Cahners Publishing Company
Five S. Wabash Avenue   Phone: (312) 372-6880
Chicago, IL 60603
Covers: Manufacturers of building supply materials and products in the United States. **Entries include:** Company name, address, trade and brand names, list of products. **Arrangement:** Classified. **Pages (approx.):** 230. **Frequency:** Annual, November. **Editor:** Nancy Rademacher. **Advertising accepted.** Circulation 34,000. **Price:** $25.00.

★191★
BUILDING SUPPLY NEWS—GIANTS ISSUE
Cahners Publishing Company
Five S. Wabash Avenue   Phone: (312) 272-6880
Chicago, IL 60603
Covers: Over 500 building supply retailing companies with volumes of $5 million or more and over 50 building supply wholesalers with volumes of $15 million or more. **Entries include:** Company name, headquarters, number of units, volume sales, whether publicly or privately held, brief note on company plans, activity, etc. **Arrangement:** Ranked by sales volume. **Indexes:** Company name. **Frequency:** Annual, January. **Editor:** Patricia Coleman. **Advertising accepted. Former title:** Building Supply News - Retailing Giants Issue. **Price:** $25.00 (current and 1980 editions).

Building Supply News—Retailing Giants Issue *See* Building Supply News—Giants Issue

★192★
BULK LIQUID TERMINALS DIRECTORY
Independent Liquid Terminals Association
1101 15th Street, N. W., Room 509   Phone: (202) 659-2301
Washington, DC 20005
Covers: About 50 member companies which own and operate over 165 waterside bulk liquid terminals. **Entries include:** Company name, address, terminal names and locations; for each terminal, tank capacity, products handled, dock size, water depth, barreling or other services, and vessel, truck, rail, and pipeline handling capabilities. **Arrangement:** Alphabetical. **Indexes:** Geographical. **Pages** (approx.): 100. **Frequency:** Annual, March. **Price:** $50.00 (current and 1980 editions); includes 12 monthly issues of newsletter on legislation and regulation of industry.

★193★
BUS GARAGE INDEX
Friendship Publications, Inc.
Box 1472   Phone: (509) 328-9181
Spokane, WA 99210
Covers: Over 600 garages and service centers in the United States and Canada offering services to buses on charter service and tours. **Entries include:** Company name, address, phone, name of maintenance manager, list of services. **Arrangement:** Geographical. **Pages** (approx.): 105. **Frequency:** Biennial, spring of odd years. **Editor:** William A. Luke. **Advertising accepted.** Circulation 3,000. **Price:** $5.00. **Also includes:** Maps showing bus garages.

★194★
BUS INDUSTRY DIRECTORY
Friendship Publications, Inc.
Box 1472   Phone: (509) 328-9181
Spokane, WA 99210
Covers: Over 2,800 intercity and charter bus companies and local transit authorities in the United States and Canada; about 900 suppliers to the industry; associations and consultants. **Entries include:** For bus companies - Name, address, phone, names of executives, types of service, number of buses. For suppliers - Company name, address, phone, trade or brand names, list of products or services. **Arrangement:** Main section geographical; suppliers, alphabetical. **Indexes:** Product index to supplier list. **Pages** (approx.): 220. **Frequency:** Biennial, spring of even years. **Editor:** William A. Luke. **Advertising accepted.** Circulation 2,000. **Price:** $22.50 (current edition); $25.00 (tentative, 1980 edition).

★195★
BUSINESS BOOKS AND SERIALS IN PRINT
R. R. Bowker and Company
1180 Avenue of the Americas   Phone: (212) 764-5100
New York, NY 10036
Publication includes: List of about 1,600 publishers of books and serials on business-related subjects, including economics, finance, management, etc. **Entries include:** Name, address. **Frequency:**

Irregular; latest edition 1977; supplement 1978. **Price:** $37.50, 1977 edition; $24.00, supplement; postpaid, payment with order (ISSN 0146-5953 and 0000-0582 respectively). **Send orders to:** R. R. Bowker Co., Box 1807, Ann Arbor, MI 48106 (313-761-4700). **Other information:** Principal content of publication is bibliography of books and serials in author and title sequences. There is also a subject index. Based on "Books in Print," described in separate listing.

Business Directory of San Diego County [California] *See* San Diego Chamber of Commerce—Business Directory [California]

★196★
BUSINESS EDUCATION FORUM—PROFESSIONAL LEADERSHIP ROSTER ISSUE
National Business Education Association
1906 Association Drive   Phone: (703) 860-0213
Reston, VA 22091
Covers: Key personnel in business education, primarily at secondary level, including officers of national, regional, state associations and state and local supervisory personnel in business and distributive education. **Pages** (approx.): 20. **Frequency:** Annual, December. **Editor:** O. J. Byrnside, Jr., Executive Director. **Advertising accepted.** Circulation 23,000. **Price:** $2.50.

★197★
BUSINESS FIRMS DIRECTORY OF THE DELAWARE VALLEY [Pennsylvania, New Jersey, Delaware]
Greater Philadelphia Chamber of Commerce
1617 J. F. Kennedy Boulevard, Suite 1960 Phone: (215) 568-4040
Philadelphia, PA 19103
Covers: 6,500 businesses in the 11-county Delaware Valley area of Pennsylvania, New Jersey, and Delaware. Also lists hospitals and educational institutions. **Entries include:** Company name, address, phone, names of executives, number of employees, SIC numbers, and whether the firm is a direct importer or exporter. **Arrangement:** Geographical. **Indexes:** Alphabetical, SIC. **Pages** (approx.): 335. **Frequency:** Irregular; latest edition July 1979; new edition expected July 1980. **Editor:** Robert S. Barr, Research Director. **Advertising accepted.** Circulation 2,000. **Price:** $40.00. **Other information:** Issued by PENJERDEL Corporation, regional affiliate of the Chamber's publication bureau.

★198★
BUSINESS ORGANIZATIONS AND AGENCIES DIRECTORY
Gale Research Company
Book Tower   Phone: (313) 961-2242
Detroit, MI 48226
Covers: Information sources of all kinds which are helpful in solving business problems, including state, national, and international organizations; government agencies; trade, business, commercial, and labor organizations; commodity and stock exchanges; United States and foreign diplomatic offices; regional planning and development agencies; convention, fair, and trade organizations; franchise companies; airline offices; hotel/motel systems; publishers; newspapers; information centers; data processing services; research centers; graduate schools of business; special libraries; etc. **Entries include:** Names, addresses, and contact persons. **Arrangement:** Classified by activity, service, type of entity, etc. **Indexes:** Individual sections have special indexes as required. **Pages** (approx.): 875. **Frequency:** Not established; first edition March 1980. **Editors:** Anthony T. Kruzas and Robert C. Thomas. **Price:** $65.00.

Business Publication Rates & Data *See* Standard Rate & Data Service—Business Publication Rates & Data

★199★
BUSINESS RADIO BUYER'S GUIDE
Cardiff Publishing Company
3900 S. Wadsworth Boulevard   Phone: (303) 988-4670
Denver, CO 80235
Publication includes: Lists of manufacturers, suppliers, and manufacturers' representatives of business radio and related equipment. **Entries include:** Company name, address, phone, names of key executives, and a general description of products or services. **Arrangement:** Alphabetical. **Indexes:** Product. **Pages** (approx.): 100. **Frequency:** Annual, January. **Editor:** Barbara Martin. **Advertising accepted.** Circulation 20,000. **Price:** $8.95.

★200★
BUSINESS RESOURCE DIRECTORY [New England]
Federal Reserve Bank of Boston
Urban Affairs Section
30 Pearl Street   Phone: (614) 426-7100
Boston, MA 02106
Covers: 750 resource and assistance groups (chambers of commerce, colleges and universities, community development corporations, banks having development departments) in New England offering free or low-cost technical aid to business. **Entries include:** Name of organization, address, phone number, name of chief executive, classification code, brief description of the organization's activities and services. **Arrangement:** Geographical. **Indexes:** Resources. **Pages** (approx.): 270. **Frequency:** Irregular; latest edition (1975) out of print; new edition expected 1980. **Editor:** William R. Osgood, Manager of Urban Affairs. **Price:** Free.

★201★
BUSINESS TELEPHONE & EQUIPMENT DIRECTORY OF THE INTERCONNECT INDUSTRY
North American Telephone Association
1030 15th Street, N. W., Suite 360   Phone: (202) 393-7446
Washington, DC 20005
Covers: Over 300 manufacturers of non-utility telephone terminal equipment (switchboards, key and PBX, intercoms, desk instruments, etc.) and over 1,300 firms which supply and maintain such equipment. Also lists state interconnect associations. **Entries include:** Firm name, address, phone, names of key executives, products. **Arrangement:** Geographical and alphabetical. **Indexes:** Alphabetical. **Pages** (approx.): 135. **Frequency:** Annual, fall. **Advertising accepted.** **Former title:** North American Telephone Association - Directory. **Price:** $30.00.

★202★
BUSINESS WEEK—CORPORATE SCOREBOARD ISSUE
McGraw-Hill, Inc.
1221 Avenue of the Americas   Phone: (212) 997-1221
New York, NY 10020
Publication includes: List of 1,200 major companies in all business, industrial, and financial categories, with extensive analytical text. **Entries include:** Company name, several types of sales and earnings data. **Arrangement:** Alphabetical within line of business categories. **Frequency:** Surveys on about 900 companies are published in May, August, and November issues; 1,200 company round-up appears in a March issue; December issue lists earning estimates on 900 companies for year ahead. **Editor:** Robert Mims. **Advertising accepted.** **Former title:** Business Week - Survey of Corporate Performance Issue. **Price:** $1.25.

★203★
BUSINESS/PROFESSIONAL ADVERTISING ASSOCIATION— DIRECTORY OF MEMBERS
Business/Professional Advertising Association
205 E. 42nd Street   Phone: (212) 661-0222
New York, NY 10017
Covers: About 3,100 business communications professionals in the fields of advertising, marketing communications, and marketing. **Entries include:** Name, company with which affiliated, address.

Arrangement: Alphabetical within chapter. **Pages** (approx.): 65. **Frequency:** Biennial, fall of even years. **Editor:** R. L. Coleman, Managing Director. **Price:** $10.00.

★204★
BUYERS' GUIDE AND DEALER DIRECTORY [Building supplies, northeastern states]
Lumber Co-Operator, Inc.
339 East Avenue   Phone: (716) 325-1626
Rochester, NY 14604
Covers: About 2,000 New England and New York retail lumber and building supply dealers; manufacturers and wholesalers who have advertisements in the directory; industry associations. **Entries include:** Dealer listings include company name, address, phone, names of executives. Advertising manufacturer and wholesaler listings include similar data and a list of products. **Arrangement:** Dealers are geographical, advertisers are alphabetical. **Indexes:** Product. **Pages** (approx.): 250. **Frequency:** Annual, October. **Editor:** Horace G. Pierce, Executive Vice President. **Advertising accepted.** Circulation 3,400. **Price:** $75.00.

Buyers Guide and Directory of Maine Manufacturers *See* **Maine Marketing Directory**

★205★
BUYERS GUIDE OF USED MACHINE TOOLS & METALWORKING EQUIPMENT
Machinery Dealers National Association
1110 Spring Street   Phone: (301) 585-9494
Silver Spring, MD 20910
Covers: 440 dealers in used metalworking equipment who are members of the association. **Entries include:** Company name, address, phone, names of executives, telex number. **Arrangement:** Alphabetical. **Indexes:** Personal name. **Pages** (approx.): 70. **Frequency:** Annual. **Price:** Free.

★206★
BUYER'S GUIDE TO IMPORTED GERMAN PRODUCTS
German American Chamber of Commerce
666 Fifth Avenue   Phone: (212) 582-7788
New York, NY 10019
Covers: 3,000 German manufacturers selling in the United States and 1,800 United States representatives, and subsidiaries of German manufacturers and importers of German-made products. **Entries include:** For German firms - Name and address, and name and address of United States representative for each product or product group. For United States firms - Name, address, and products handled, and names and addresses of German manufacturers represented. **Arrangement:** Alphabetical. **Indexes:** Product. **Pages** (approx.): 360. **Frequency:** Irregular; latest edition 1977; new edition expected 1980. **Advertising accepted.** Circulation 5,000. **Price:** $18.00, plus $2.00 shipping.

★207★
BUYER'S GUIDE TO MANUFACTURED HOMES
Hawthorn Books, Division
Elsevier-Dutton Publishing Co., Inc.
Two Park Avenue   Phone: (212) 725-1818
New York, NY 10016
Publication includes: List of about 125 manufacturers of mobile, modular, and panelized homes, log homes, kit homes, and geodesic dome homes. **Entries include:** Manufacturer name, address, types of homes offered, areas available. **Arrangement:** Geographical. **Pages** (approx.): 310. **Frequency:** First edition November 1979; new edition expected March 1980. **Editor:** Tom Philbin. **Price:** $22.50.

★208★

BUYER'S GUIDE TO MICROGRAPHIC EQUIPMENT, PRODUCTS, AND SERVICES

National Micrographics Association
8719 Colesville Road   Phone: (301) 587-8202
Silver Spring, MD 20910

Publication includes: 260 manufacturers, suppliers, and service companies which are members of the association. **Entries include:** Company name, address, phone. **Arrangement:** Alphabetical. **Indexes:** Product. **Frequency:** Annual, January; June supplement. **Editor:** Denise L. Harlow. **Advertising accepted.** Circulation 20,000. **Price:** Free.

★209★

BUYERS' GUIDE TO MINORITY BUSINESS [Arizona]

Arizona Minority Purchasing Council
Phoenix Business Development Corp.
4227 N. 16th Street   Phone: (602) 274-4647
Phoenix, AZ 85016

Covers: Minority firms in Arizona offering commercial and industrial products and services. **Entries include:** Company name, address, phone, contact, date established, number of employees, facilities, description of products or services, references. **Arrangement:** Classified by line of business. **Frequency:** Irregular; latest edition 1977; new edition expected January 1980; semiannual updates. **Price:** $10.00 (current and 1980 editions); updates, $5.00 each.

★210★

BUYERS' GUIDE TO MINORITY BUSINESSES [Charlotte, NC]

Carolinas Association of Regional Minority Purchasing Councils
Box 16458   Phone: (919) 275-2571
Greensboro, NC 27406

Covers: Nearly 200 firms offering professional, commercial, industrial, and consumer products and services. **Entries include:** Company name, address, phone, principal executive, number of employees, financial data, products or services, trade or brand names, production facilities, customer references, and bank references. **Arrangement:** Classified. **Indexes:** Company name. **Pages** (approx.): 180. **Frequency:** Irregular; latest edition August 1979; monthly updates. **Advertising accepted.** Circulation 500. **Price:** Base volume $20.00; updates $10.00 per year.

★211★

BUYERS GUIDE TO OUTDOOR ADVERTISING

Institute of Outdoor Advertising
485 Lexington Avenue   Phone: (212) 986-5920
New York, NY 10017

Covers: Outdoor advertising companies and their markets, rates, etc. **Entries include:** Company list shows company name, mail and shipping addresses, phone, manager's name, reference code number, population, number of illuminated and non-illuminated posters, cost. **Arrangement:** Geographical. **Pages** (approx.): 700. **Frequency:** Semiannual, January and September. **Editor:** James McGay. **Advertising accepted.** Circulation 800. **Price:** $50.00, annual subscription; $30.00 per issue. Ordering in advance of publication date advised.

★212★

BUYERS GUIDE TO PRODUCTS MANUFACTURED ON AMERICAN INDIAN RESERVATIONS

Indian Industrial Development Office
Economic Development Administration
Commerce Department   Phone: (202) 377-5321
Washington, DC 20230

Covers: About 125 companies with facilities on Indian reservations. **Entries include:** Company name, address, phone, SIC number, number of employees, list of products, asterisk for Indian-owned firms. **Arrangement:** Geographical. **Indexes:** SIC. **Frequency:** Irregular; latest edition June 1979. **Price:** Free. **Other information:** Published with the Bureau of Indian Affairs.

★213★

BUYER'S GUIDE TO THE NEW YORK MARKET [Children's wear]

Earnshaw Publications, Inc.
393 Seventh Avenue   Phone: (212) 563-2742
New York, NY 10001

Covers: New York City showrooms and offices for children's wear manufacturers and representatives. **Entries include:** Company name, address, phone, names of executives and showroom sales personnel, and products. **Arrangement:** Alphabetical. **Indexes:** By building location. **Pages** (approx.): 200. **Frequency:** Annual, April. **Editor:** Diane Specht, Editorial Director. **Advertising accepted.** Circulation 10,000. **Price:** $1.00.

Buying Offices & Accounts *See* Salesman's Guide Nationwide Directory: Buying Offices & Accounts

★214★

CABLE COMMUNICATIONS—ANNUAL DIRECTORY AND BUYER'S GUIDE ISSUE

Pryde Publications Ltd.
165 Bloor Street, E.   Phone: (416) 924-1214
Toronto, Ontario M4W 1C8, Canada

Covers: About 225 manufacturers and distributors of cable television, broadcasting and telecommunications equipment; primarily covers United States and Canada. **Entries include:** Company name, address, phone. **Arrangement:** Alphabetical. **Indexes:** Product. **Frequency:** Annual, March. **Editor:** Udo Salewsky. **Advertising accepted.** Circulation 5,250. **Former title:** Canadian Telephone and Cable Television Journal (1973). **Price:** $12.00 (current and 1980 editions).

★215★

CALIFORNIA INDUSTRIAL SERVICES REGISTER

Times Mirror Press
1115 S. Boyle Avenue   Phone: (213) 265-6767
Los Angeles, CA 90023

Covers: 10,000 firms which offer services and products to California manufacturers (including sales representative firms, distributors, and others). **Entries include:** Company name, address, names and titles of key personnel, phone, service or product, number of employees, SIC numbers, sales volume, year established. **Arrangement:** Alphabetical. **Indexes:** Geographical (with address and SIC number), SIC number, product (with address). **Pages** (approx.): 660. **Frequency:** Annual, November. **Editor:** Phyllis Newman. **Advertising accepted.** **Price:** $60.00, postpaid.

California Manufacturers Association—Directory *See* California Manufacturers Register

★216★

CALIFORNIA MANUFACTURERS REGISTER

Times Mirror Press
1115 S. Boyle Avenue   Phone: (213) 265-6767
Los Angeles, CA 90023

Covers: 19,000 manufacturing plants in California with four or more employees; includes membership of California Manufacturers Association. **Entries include:** Company name, address, phone, names of executives, number of employees, sales volume, products, SIC numbers, and date established. **Arrangement:** Alphabetical. **Indexes:** Geographical, product, importer/exporter companies, SIC. **Pages** (approx.): 850. **Frequency:** Annual, January. **Editor:** P. Newman. **Advertising accepted.** **Price:** $72.50, postpaid. **Other information:** Sponsored by the California Manufacturers Association.

★217★

CALIFORNIA MINORITY BUSINESS ENTERPRISES DIRECTORY

Source Publications, Inc.
1900 Powell Street, Suite 1145   Phone: (415) 547-6670
Emeryville, CA 94608

Covers: 2,200 firms offering professional, commercial, and industrial products and services. **Entries include:** Company name, address, phone, contact person, description of products or services. **Frequency:** Annual, March. **Price:** $35.00 (current edition); $38.00 (1980 edition). **Other information:** Variant title, "Minority Business Enterprises Directory."

California Publicity Outlets *See* Metro California Media

Canadian Investment in New York *See* International Investment in New York

Canadian Steel Service Centre—Roster *See* Metal Distribution

Canadian Telephone and Cable Television Journal—Annual Directory Issue *See* Cable Communications—Annual Directory and Buyer's Guide Issue

★218★
CANDY AND SNACK INDUSTRY BUYING GUIDE
Magazines for Industry, Inc.
777 Third Avenue   Phone: (212) 838-7778
New York, NY 10017
Publication includes: List of about 300 suppliers of ingredients, equipment, and supplies to the candy and snack industry; also includes list of federal and state offices concerned with enforcement of laws governing food quality. **Entries include:** For suppliers - Company name, address. For agencies - Agency name, address, contact name. **Arrangement:** Alphabetical. **Indexes:** Product. **Frequency:** Annual, November. **Editor:** Louis J. Lassus. **Advertising accepted.** Circulation 5,500. **Price:** $15.00.

★219★
CANDY BUYERS' DIRECTORY
Manufacturing Confectioner Publishing Company
175 Rock Road   Phone: (201) 652-2655
Glen Rock, NJ 07452
Covers: Wholesale confectionery manufacturers, candy importers, and 500 candy brokers. **Entries include:** Company name, address, phone, name of sales manager (for manufacturers and importers), and products and brand names manufactured or distributed. Broker and importer listings also show territory covered and countries imported from. **Arrangement:** Alphabetical; brokers are listed geographically. **Indexes:** Brand and trade name, product. **Pages** (approx.): 130. **Frequency:** Annual, January. **Editor:** Allen R. Allured. **Advertising accepted. Price:** $25.00, payment with order (1980 edition). **Other information:** "The Directory of Candy Brokers" is the title of a section of the "Candy Buyers' Directory;" not published separately.

★220★
CANDY MARKETER ALMANAC & BUYERS DIRECTORY
Magazines For Industry, Inc.
777 Third Avenue   Phone: (212) 838-7778
New York, NY 10017
Covers: Manufacturers and importers of candy and other confectionery products. **Entries include:** Company name, address, phone, names of sales executives, area served, warehouse locations, brand names, types of products handled. **Arrangement:** Alphabetical within separate lists for manufacturers and importers. **Indexes:** Product. **Pages** (approx.): 70. **Frequency:** Annual, December. **Editor:** Louis J. Lassus. **Advertising accepted.** Circulation 12,000. **Price:** $10.00.

★221★
CANVAS PRODUCTS ASSOCIATION INTERNATIONAL—BUYERS GUIDE
Canvas Products Association International
Endicott Building, No. 350   Phone: (612) 222-2508
St. Paul, MN 55101
Covers: 1,200 manufacturers of industrial fabrics and end products in the United States and Canada, including fibers, fabrics, films and nonwovens, and tents, inflatable structures, sails and other marine products, tarpaulins, etc.; suppliers are also listed. **Entries include:**

Company name, address, phone, financial keys. **Arrangement:** Alphabetical. **Indexes:** Product. **Pages** (approx.): 120. **Frequency:** Annual, January. **Editor:** Michael Coughlin. **Advertising accepted.** Circulation 7,000. **Price:** $5.00 (1979 edition); $7.50 (1980 edition).

★222★
CAROLINAS COMPANIES
Interstate Securities Corporation
2700 NCNB Plaza
Charlotte, NC 28280
Covers: More than 150 publicly traded companies based in North and South Carolina engaged in manufacturing, banking, insurance, and real estate. **Entries include:** Company name, address, principal executives, products or services, financial data. **Arrangement:** Classified by line of activity. **Pages** (approx.): 175. **Frequency:** Annual, June. **Former title:** North Carolina Companies. **Price:** Free.

★223★
CARPET & RUG INDUSTRY—BUYERS GUIDE ISSUE
Rodman Publishing Corporation
26 Lake Street   Phone: (201) 825-2552
Ramsey, NJ 07446
Covers: Manufacturers of mill equipment used in the manufacture of carpets and rugs. **Entries include:** Company name, address, product description. **Arrangement:** By product. **Indexes:** Company name. **Frequency:** Annual, September. **Editor:** Edward Fox. **Advertising accepted.** Circulation 5,500. **Price:** $2.00.

★224★
CARPET AND RUG INSTITUTE—DIRECTORY AND REPORT
Carpet and Rug Institute
Box 2048   Phone: (404) 278-3176
Dalton, GA 30720
Covers: About 350 manufacturers of carpets, rugs, bathmats, and bedspreads and their suppliers. **Entries include:** Company name, address, phone, names of executives, list of products. **Arrangement:** Alphabetical. **Indexes:** Product. **Pages** (approx.): 150. **Frequency:** Annual, September. **Editor:** Richard N. Hopper, Director of Consumer Affairs. **Advertising accepted.** Circulation 3,500. **Price:** $10.00.

★225★
CATALOG SHOWROOM BUSINESS—SUPPLIER DIRECTORY & BUYERS GUIDE ISSUE
Gralla Publications
1515 Broadway   Phone: (212) 869-1300
New York, NY 10036
Covers: 2,100 firms which sell to chain and independent catalog showrooms and catalog coordinating companies. Includes "Who's Who of Catalog Coordinators and Independent Publishers," and a national regional representatives guide. **Entries include:** Company name, address, phone. Entries in product section also include a code indicating types of merchandise offered in 79 categories from air conditioners to woodenware. **Arrangement:** Alphabetical; classified by product category. **Pages** (approx.): 150. **Frequency:** Annual, December. **Editor:** Deborah J. Miller. **Advertising accepted.** Circulation 7,000. **Price:** $2.00.

★226★
CATALOG SHOWROOM MERCHANDISER—CSM SUPPLIERS DIRECTORY ISSUE
CSM Marketing, Inc.
131-L Brook Avenue   Phone: (516) 242-5959
Deer Park, IL 11729
Publication includes: Directory of manufacturers of jewelry; small appliances; giftware; luggage; electronics; sporting goods; toys; lawn, garden, office, hardware, and photography equipment; and other items sold through catalog showrooms. **Entries include:** Company name, address, phone, executives, and list of products or services. **Arrangement:** Classified in major product categories. **Indexes:** Product, department, company. **Pages** (approx.): 165. **Frequency:**

Annual, December. **Editor:** Stephen Flanagan. **Advertising accepted.** Circulation 12,500. **Price:** $5.00.

★227★

CATALYST NATIONAL NETWORK OF CAREER RESOURCE CENTERS [Women's counseling and employment]

Catalyst
14 E. 60th Street   Phone: (212) 759-9700
New York, NY 10022

Covers: About 150 centers offering individual and group counseling to women in matters of employment, career development, continuing education, etc. **Entries include:** Name of center, name of sponsoring college or university, address, phone, hours, code indicating type of resources and if fee is charged. **Arrangement:** Geographical. **Frequency:** Semiannual, June and December. **Editor:** Jean Clarkson, Manager, Women's Network. **Price:** Free.

★228★

CATTARAUGUS COUNTY INDUSTRIAL AND STATISTICAL CATALOG [New York]

Cattaraugus County Industrial Development Agency
303 Court Street   Phone: (716) 938-9111
Little Valley, NY 14755

Covers: Business, industrial, and service firms located in Cattaraugus, New York. **Entries include:** For firms - Company name, address, phone, names of president and general manager, number of employees, SIC number, and description of products or services. **Arrangement:** Alphabetical. **Pages** (approx.): 150. **Frequency:** Irregular; annual updates. **Editor:** Carol J. Milks, Executive Director. **Price:** Free. **Also includes:** County statistics.

★229★

CDE STOCK OWNERSHIP DIRECTORY: TRANSPORTATION

Corporate Data Exchange, Inc.
198 Broadway, Suite 707   Phone: (212) 962-2980
New York, NY 10038

Covers: About 200 major transportation companies, including 30 railroads, 20 airlines, 43 truck and bus lines, 38 water carriers, 51 oil and gas pipelines, and 15 freight forwarders. **Entries include:** Company name, address; selected financial and operating statistics; law firms representing the company and their recent fees; principal investment bank handling the company's security offerings; product or service breakdown; comments on recent corporate events (including mergers, changes in control, questionable payments, stockholder actions, etc.); detailed breakdown of stock structure, showing for each class of stock the number of shares outstanding, names of principal individual and other stockholders, total votes of each, etc. **Frequency:** Not established; first edition August 1977. **Editors:** Stephen Abrecht, Michael Locker. **Price:** $60.00, libraries and nonprofit organizations; $250.00, corporations. **Other information:** This publication is the first in a planned series. The second study has been published (see separate listing for "CDE Stock Ownership Directory: Agribusiness"), and additional studies are planned in Banking and Finance (fall 1979), Energy (1980), Defense (1980), Mass Media, and Mining. Studies are prepared from detailed examinations of the investment portfolios of about 2,000 institutions and of the reports filed by the corporations with the Securities and Exchange Commission and four other government regulatory agencies. For background on CDE and the editors of the directories, see "New York Times" business-finance section, August 14, 1977, and "Newsday" business-finance section, May 22, 1977.

CDE Stock Ownership Directory Series *See* CDE Stock Ownership Directory: Transportation

★230★

CEE/CONTRACTORS' ELECTRICAL EQUIPMENT—PRODUCT REFERENCE ISSUE

Sutton Publishing Company, Inc.
707 Westchester Avenue   Phone: (914) 949-8500
White Plains, NY 10604

Covers: Manufacturers of products used in the electrical construction industry. **Entries include:** Company name, address, phone, name of principal executive, trade and brand names, list of products or services. **Arrangement:** By product classification. **Pages** (approx.): 400. **Frequency:** Annual, August. **Editor:** Bernadette Sabatino, Content Coordinator. **Advertising accepted.** Circulation 68,000. **Price:** $10.00.

Central Atlantic States Manufacturers Directory *See* Directory of Central Atlantic States Manufacturers

★231★

CERAMIC DATA BOOK—SUPPLIERS' CATALOG AND BUYERS' DIRECTORY

Cahners Publishing Company, Inc.
Five S. Wabash Avenue   Phone: (312) 373-6880
Chicago, IL 60603

Covers: About 3,500 manufacturers and distributors of equipment and materials for the fine ceramics and heavy clay products industries (SIC 3632, 3633). **Entries include:** Company name, address. **Arrangement:** Classified by product. **Pages** (approx.): 250. **Frequency:** Annual, October. **Editor:** J. J. Svec. **Price:** $5.00. **Also includes:** Metric conversion tables, pertinent engineering data, and supplier catalogs.

★232★

CERTIFICATED TOWING COMPANIES HOLDING AUTHORITY FROM THE INTERSTATE COMMERCE COMMISSION

Interstate Towing Association
21635 E. Nine Mile Road
St. Clair Shores, MI 48080

Number of listings: 115. **Entries include:** Company name, address, contact, phone. **Arrangement:** Geographical. **Pages** (approx.): 30. **Frequency:** Annual, January. **Editor:** Dianne Yovanovich, Staff Secretary. **Price:** Free.

★233★

CERTIFIED SAFETY PROFESSIONALS—DIRECTORY

Board of Certified Safety Professionals
501 S. Sixth Street, Suite 101   Phone: (217) 359-9263
Champaign, IL 61820

Number of listings: About 5,500 safety engineers, industrial hygienists, safety managers, fire protection engineers, and others certified by the board. **Entries include:** Name, address. **Arrangement:** Alphabetical. **Indexes:** Geographical. **Pages** (approx.): 130. **Frequency:** Biennial, fall of odd years. **Price:** Available to members only.

★234★

CHAIN STORE AGE GENERAL MERCHANDISE EDITION—TOP 100 CHAINS ISSUE

Lebhar-Friedman, Inc.
425 Park Avenue   Phone: (212) 371-9400
New York, NY 10022

Publication includes: List of 100 largest chain store operations according to dollar volume. **Entries include:** Chain name, volume, number of stores for preceding year, financial analysis. **Arrangement:** By sales volume. **Frequency:** Annual, June. **Editor:** Murray Forseter. **Former title:** Chain Store Age General Merchandise Edition - Top 200 Chains Issue. **Price:** $1.00.

★235★
CHAIN STORE AGE SUPERMARKETS EDITION—TOP 100 FOOD CHAINS ISSUE
Lebhar-Friedman, Inc.
425 Park Avenue   Phone: (212) 371-9400
New York, NY 10022
Publication includes: List of leading grocery store chains based on annual retail sales. **Entries include:** Chain name, number of stores, annual sales, and estimated annual sales per store. **Arrangement:** By sales volume. **Frequency:** Annual, July. **Price:** Included in subscription, $6.00 per year.

★236★
CHAIN STORE LIST [California]
Business Extension Bureau
1335 S. Flower Street   Phone: (213) 749-0151
Los Angeles, CA 90015
Covers: Parent companies of grocery, drug, liquor, variety, department, and discount stores and convenience markets with stores in California. **Entries include:** Company name, address, phone, names of executives, trade styles, headquarters, number of stores, buyers (and their hours), future plans. **Arrangement:** Alphabetical. **Indexes:** Trade style. **Pages** (approx.): 320. **Frequency:** Irregular; latest edition August 1979. **Editor:** Robert L. Hicks **Price:** $30.00.

Chamber of Commerce Executives *See* Directory of State Chamber of Commerce and Association of Commerce and Industry Executives

★237★
CHAMBER OF COMMERCE OF GREATER KANSAS CITY— MEMBERSHIP DIRECTORY AND BUYER'S GUIDE
Chamber of Commerce of Greater Kansas City
600 Ten Main Center   Phone: (816) 221-2424
Kansas City, MO 64105
Covers: 2,400 member businesses in the 7-county area of greater Kansas City. **Entries include:** Company name, address, phone, names of executives, and list of products or services. **Frequency:** Annual, February. **Price:** Available to members only.

★238★
CHAMBERS OF COMMERCE IN OHIO
Ohio Chamber of Commerce
17 S. High Street   Phone: (614) 228-4201
Columbus, OH 43215
Number of listings: 300. **Entries include:** Chamber name, phone, name and address of executive secretary or other contact. **Arrangement:** Geographical. **Pages** (approx.): 30. **Frequency:** Annual, December. **Editor:** Edmond Loewe, Director of Organizational Services. **Price:** $10.40.

★239★
CHARLOTTE MECKLENBERG DIRECTORY OF MANUFACTURING [North Carolina]
Greater Charlotte Chamber of Commerce
129 W. Trade Street   Phone: (704) 377-6911
Charlotte, NC 28202
Number of listings: 675. **Entries include:** Company name, address, name of principal executive, number of employees, whether firm exports or imports, SIC numbers, list of products or services. **Arrangement:** Alphabetical. **Indexes:** SIC. **Pages** (approx.): 75. **Frequency:** Annual, January. **Price:** $6.00.

★240★
CHARLOTTE MECKLENBURG MAJOR EMPLOYERS [North Carolina]
Greater Charlotte Chamber of Commerce
129 W. Trade Street   Phone: (704) 377-6911
Charlotte, NC 28202
Covers: About 290 firms which employ 100 or more and are located in Mecklenburg County. **Entries include:** Company name, address, name of key executive, phone, number of employees, year established in area, and SIC code. **Arrangement:** By SIC numbers. **Indexes:** Alphabetical, employee size. **Pages** (approx.): 40. **Frequency:** Annual, spring. **Price:** $5.00 (current edition); $6.00 (1980 edition).

★241★
CHARTER COACH GUIDE
Russell's Guides, Inc.
817 Second Avenue, S. E.
Cedar Rapids, IA 52406
Covers: About 300 companies which have motor coaches available for group charter; international coverage. **Entries include:** Company name, address, phone, names of contact persons, bases of operation, services available, languages, number of coaches available, and other descriptive information. **Arrangement:** Geographical. **Pages** (approx.): 75. **Frequency:** Annual, September. **Editor:** William A. Luke. **Advertising accepted.** Circulation 2,000. **Price:** $10.00 **Other information:** Published with and also available from: Friendship Publications, Inc., Box 1472, Spokane, WA 99210.

★242★
CHASE'S CALENDAR OF ANNUAL EVENTS: SPECIAL DAYS, WEEKS, AND MONTHS
Apple Tree Press, Inc.
Box 1012   Phone: (313) 234-5451
Flint, MI 48501
Covers: 2,300 special days and events worldwide. **Entries include:** Name, purpose, and inclusive dates of event, name and address of sponsor, and name of person from whom additional information may be obtained. **Arrangement:** Chronological. **Pages** (approx.): 130. **Frequency:** Annual, November. **Editor:** William D. Chase. **Price:** $9.95, postpaid, payment with order.

Chatauqua County Chamber of Commerce Industrial Directory [New York] *See* Jamestown Area Chamber of Commerce— Industrial Directory [New York]

★243★
CHEAP CHIC UPDATE [Stores]
Harmony Books
Crown Publishers, Inc.
One Park Avenue   Phone: (212) 532-9200
New York, NY 10016
Publication includes: Retail stores, flea markets, and mail order houses in the United States, England, and France where one can purchase "fashionable" clothes at reasonable prices. **Frequency:** Irregular; previous edition 1975; latest edition 1978. **Editors:** Caterine Milinaire and Carol Troy. **Former title:** Cheap Chic (1978). **Price:** $6.95.

★244★
CHEM SOURCES—USA
Directories Publishing Company, Inc.
Box 1372   Phone: (904) 673-1241
Ormond Beach, FL 32074
Publication includes: List of 800 United States chemical producers and distributors. **Entries include:** Company name, address, phone, location of manufacturing plants, locations of sales offices, telex number. **Arrangement:** Alphabetical. **Pages** (approx.): 900. **Frequency:** Annual, January. **Price:** $120.00 (current and 1980 editions). **Other information:** Principal content of directory is listing of about 80,000 chemical products listed alphabetically by chemical nomenclature. Publisher also issues "Chem Sources - Europe" containing similar data and covering about 500 companies; $100.00 (March 1980 edition price).

★245★
CHEMICAL & ENGINEERING NEWS—FACTS AND FIGURES ISSUE
American Chemical Society
1155 16th Street, N. W.   Phone: (202) 872-4600
Washington, DC 20036
Publication includes: List of 50 largest chemical producers in terms of total chemical sales. Frequency: Annual, first May issue. Editor: Michael Heylin. Advertising accepted. Price: $1.50. Also includes: Extensive statistical data on the chemical industry.

★246★
CHEMICAL ENGINEERING—EQUIPMENT BUYER'S GUIDE ISSUE
McGraw-Hill, Inc.
1221 Avenue of the Americas   Phone: (212) 997-2379
New York, NY 10020
Publication includes: Over 3,500 firms supplying equipment and machinery to the chemical processing industry. Entries include: Company name, address, phone, sales office locations and phones. Arrangement: Alphabetical. Indexes: Product, trade name. Pages (approx.): 750. Frequency: Annual, July. Editor: Joseph A. Callahan, Manager. Advertising accepted. Circulation 60,000. Price: $25.00, postpaid, payment with order (current and 1980 editions).

★247★
CHEMICAL EXECUTIVE DIRECTORY
Executive Directories
Box 234   Phone: (312) 256-2782
Kenilworth, IL 60043
Covers: More than 300 companies in the chemical, oil, paint, drug, plastics, paper, and allied industries, and their executives. Publication is a company rather than an executive directory, in that it is arranged by company and has no personal name index. Entries include: Company name, address, phone, names of divisions and subsidiaries, and names and titles of up to 40 or 50 executives. Indexes: Company/division/subsidiary. Pages (approx.): 100. Frequency: Not established; first edition December 1977. Editor: M. E. Baade. Price: $9.75, payment with order, $10.75 billed.

★248★
CHEMICAL NEW PRODUCT DIRECTORY
Marketing Development
402 Border Road   Phone: (617) 369-5382
Concord, MA 01742
Publication includes: List of about 180 companies whose stock is publicly traded and who introduced "significant new chemical products" during the preceding year. Entries include: Company name, address, number of new products, products by SIC categories. Arrangement: Alphabetical. Indexes: Product by SIC categories. Frequency: Annual, April. Price: $350.00. Also includes: Principal content of publication is description of new products.

★249★
CHEMICAL PURCHASING—CHEMICALS DIRECTORY ISSUE
Myers Publishing Company, Inc.
2135 Summer Street
Stamford, CT 06905
Covers: Suppliers of 7,500 chemicals and raw materials. United States manufacturers' products listed free; companies abroad and all distributors and agents receive listings in proportion to ad space. Trade name section limited to advertisers. Entries include: Name of supplier, address, principal sales office, phone. Arrangement: Supplier section alphabetical by company name, product section by product name. Pages (approx.): 560. Frequency: Annual, October. Editor: Ting Gough, Managing Editor. Advertising accepted. Circulation 14,600. Price: $12.50.

★250★
CHEMICAL WEEK—BUYERS GUIDE ISSUE
McGraw-Hill, Inc.
1221 Avenue of the Americas   Phone: (212) 997-2379
New York, NY 10020
Covers: About 2,500 manufacturers and distributors of chemical raw materials to the chemical process industries. Entries include: Company name, address, phone, and local addresses and phone numbers for up to 25 sales locations. Arrangement: Alphabetical. Indexes: Product, trademark. Pages (approx.): 760. Frequency: Annual, October. Editor: Joseph A. Callahan, Manager. Advertising accepted. Circulation 50,000. Price: $30.00, cloth; paperbound issue included in subscription, $20.00 per year. Also includes: Manufacturers' catalogs.

★251★
CHEMICAL WEEK—CHEMICAL WEEK 300 ISSUE
McGraw-Hill, Inc.
1221 Avenue of the Americas   Phone: (212) 997-6212
New York, NY 10020
Publication includes: Ranked list of leading chemical process industry firms with annual sales over $100 million. Entries include: Company name, sales, profit and profit ratios, per share data. Arrangement: By size within industry segment. Frequency: Quarterly in last issues of February, May, August, and November. Editor: Homer Starr. Advertising accepted. Price: $5.00.

Chicago: Trade Show, Convention, Meeting Guide *See* Chicago Convention & Tourism Guide

★252★
CHICAGO BUYER'S GUIDE
Chicago Association of Commerce and Industry
130 S. Michigan Avenue
Chicago, IL 60603
Covers: More than 5,500 industrial, commercial, and service firms in the Chicago area; not limited to members. Entries include: Company name, address, and phone. Arrangement: Product. Indexes: Company name. Pages (approx.): 400. Frequency: Annual. Advertising accepted. Circulation 50,000. Price: Free.

★253★
CHICAGO CONVENTION & TOURISM GUIDE
Chicago Convention and Tourism Bureau
332 S. Michigan Avenue
Chicago, IL 60604
Description: A guide to local restaurants and hotels of the usual tourist sort, but includes other features such as companies and institutions which offer facility tours, special events for women, a calendar of events for the year, etc. Pages (approx.): 100. Frequency: Annual, December. Former title: Chicago: Trade Show, Convention, Meeting Guide. Price: $3.95.

★254★
CHICAGO, COOK COUNTY AND ILLINOIS INDUSTRIAL DIRECTORY
National Publishing Corporation
2720 Des Plaines Avenue   Phone: (312) 297-5115
Des Plaines, IL 60018
Covers: Over 28,000 manufacturers, wholesalers, distributors, service firms, etc. Entries include: Company name, address, phone, names of principal executives, number of employees, capitalization, parent firm (if applicable), date established, product or service. Arrangement: Geographical except in Chicago, which is by Zip code. Indexes: Product, alphabetical. Pages (approx.): 1,275. Frequency: Annual, January. Advertising accepted. Price: $75.00 (current edition); $80.00 (1980 edition).

★255★

CHICAGO MEDIA DIRECTORY

Chicago Convention and Tourism Bureau

332 S. Michigan Avenue   Phone: (312) 922-3530

Chicago, IL 60604

Covers: Executive and editorial personnel at Chicago's major daily newspapers, downtown weeklies, and wire services, as well as radio and television station personnel. **Entries include:** For newspapers - Publication name, address, phone, names of personnel and titles or usual assignments. For radio and TV - Station name, address, phone, names of personnel, names of major programs interested in public relations materials and names of their producers. **Arrangement:** Alphabetical within type of medium or outlet. **Pages** (approx.): 30. **Frequency:** Annual, January. **Editor:** Wayne Dunham, Director of Public Relations. **Former title:** Publicity in Chicago. **Price:** Free.

Children's Wear Directory *See* Earnshaw's Infants, Girls, Boys Wear—Children's Wear Directory Issue

★256★

CHILTON'S CONTROL EQUIPMENT MASTER

Chilton Company

Chilton Way

Radnor, PA 19089

Covers: Over 5,000 manufacturers and suppliers of control and instrumentation equipment. **Entries include:** Company name, address, phone; sales offices are listed for some companies. **Arrangement:** Alphabetical. **Indexes:** Product. **Frequency:** Annual, July. **Price:** $45.00 (current edition); $55.00 (1980 edition). **Also includes:** Catalogs of products of 300 companies.

★257★

CHINA, GLASS, AND TABLEWARE—RED BOOK DIRECTORY ISSUE

Ebel-Doctorow Publications, Inc.

Box 2147   Phone: (201) 779-1600

Clifton, NJ 07015

Covers: Importers, distributors, manufacturers, and their representatives supplying china, crystal, and table top accessories to the retail industry; related associations are listed separately. **Entries include:** Company name, address, phone, names of executives, trade and brand names, and products or services offered. **Arrangement:** Alphabetical. **Indexes:** Product, backstamp, pattern name. **Pages** (approx.): 110. **Frequency:** Annual, fall. **Editor:** Susan Grisham. **Advertising accepted. Price:** Included in subscription, $12.00 per year; not available separately.

★258★

CLARK'S DIRECTORY OF SOUTHERN TEXTILE MILLS

Clark Publishing Company

106 E. Stone Avenue   Phone: (803) 242-5300

Greenville, SC 29602

Entries include: Name of mill; city located in; number of spindles, looms, etc.; mailing address; phone; list of personnel with titles; list of products. **Arrangement:** Geographical. **Pages** (approx.): 190. **Frequency:** Annual, March. **Editor:** Randolph Taylor, Publisher. **Advertising accepted.** Circulation 3,500. **Price:** $9.50, plus $1.00 shipping (current edition); $10.00, plus $2.00 shipping, payment with order (1980 edition).

★259★

CLASSIFIED BUSINESS DIRECTORY OF THE STATE OF CONNECTICUT

Connecticut Directory Company, Inc.

322 Main Street   Phone: (203) 324-1222

Stamford, CT 06901

Covers: Manufacturers, banks, schools, service companies, distributors, wholesalers, restaurants, and motels in Connecticut and surrounding states. All listings are paid. **Entries include:** Company name, address, phone. **Arrangement:** By type of business, then geographical. **Pages** (approx.): 560. **Frequency:** Annual, February. **Editor:** Marilyn Kahn, President. **Advertising accepted.** Circulation

16,000. **Price:** $29.95 (current edition); $32.95 (1980 edition). No sales in Connecticut except to libraries; available to Connecticut libraries tax free.

★260★

CLASSIFIED DIRECTORY OF WISCONSIN MANUFACTURERS

Wisconsin Manufacturers and Commerce

111 E. Wisconsin Avenue   Phone: (414) 271-9428

Milwaukee, WI 53202

Number of listings: 6,500. **Entries include:** Company name, address, phone, telex and TWX numbers, names of principal executives, number of employees, net worth, SIC numbers, products, brand names. **Arrangement:** Geographical. **Indexes:** Multistate and multinational company, product, alphabetical, Zip code, brand name, SIC (includes company name, address, and phone). **Pages** (approx.): 850. **Frequency:** Annual, November. **Editor:** Jean C. Peterson. **Advertising accepted. Price:** $50.00, payment with order. **Other information:** Manufacturers' News catalog lists this publication as, "Wisconsin Manufacturers Directory."

★261★

CLEVELAND BUSINESS LEAGUE—ROSTER AND CATALOG OF SERVICES

Cleveland Business League

10518 Superior Avenue   Phone: (216) 421-7147

Cleveland, OH 44106

Covers: About 400 members of the league, an organization of Black businesspersons. **Entries include:** Company name, address, phone, name of member. **Arrangement:** Classified. **Pages** (approx.): 90. **Frequency:** Biennial, April. **Advertising accepted.** Circulation 2,000. **Price:** Free. (Not verified)

★262★

COLLEGE PLACEMENT ANNUAL

College Placement Council

65 E. Elizabeth Avenue   Phone: (215) 868-1421

Bethlehem, PA 18018

Covers: 1,300 firms interested in hiring college graduates. **Entries include:** Company name, address, nature of business, year established, number of employees, and occupations for which they wish to hire college graduates. **Arrangement:** Alphabetical. **Indexes:** Occupational, geographical, special employment categories. **Pages** (approx.): 480. **Frequency:** Annual, September. **Editor:** Joan Bowser. **Advertising accepted.** Circulation 437,000. **Price:** $5.00, postpaid (ISSN 0069-5734).

★263★

COLLEGIATE CONSTRUCTION EDUCATION DIRECTORY

Associated General Contractors of America

1957 E Street, N. W.

Washington, DC 20006

Covers: Construction and construction-related programs at junior colleges, and universities. **Pages** (approx.): 80. **Frequency:** Irregular; latest edition August 1979. **Former title:** Construction Education Directory (1978). **Price:** $3.00.

★264★

COLORADO FOREIGN TRADE DIRECTORY

Denver Chamber of Commerce

1301 Welton Street   Phone: (303) 534-3211

Denver, CO 80204

Covers: About 335 Colorado importers and exporters, engineering and architectural consultants, and agencies, institutions, and other companies offering services of interest to Colorado firms involved in international trade. **Entries include:** For importers and exporters - Company name, address, phone, name of principal executive, number of employees, financial data, products or services, SIC, country or area with which trading. For services - Firm or agency name, address, phone, names of key executives; some listings include type of services offered. **Arrangement:** By activity. **Indexes:** Product. **Pages** (approx.): 100. **Frequency:** Irregular; latest edition 1979. **Editor:**

David A. Sondag, Economic Development. **Price:** $20.00.

★265★

COMMERCIAL CAR JOURNAL—BUYERS' GUIDE ISSUE
Chilton Company
Chilton Way   Phone: (215) 687-8200
Radnor, PA 19089
Covers: Suppliers of products and services used by operators of truck, bus, and passenger car fleets. **Entries include:** Company name, address, phone, trade names. **Arrangement:** By product; company listings repeated under various headings as necessary. **Frequency:** Annual, October. **Editor:** James D. Winsor. **Advertising accepted.** Circulation 75,000. **Price:** $5.00.

★266★

COMMERCIAL CAR JOURNAL—TOP 100 ISSUE
Chilton Company
Chilton Way   Phone: (215) 687-8200
Radnor, PA 19089
Covers: Top 100 for-hire motor carriers. **Entries include:** Company name, headquarters city, rank, gross operating revenue, number of vehicles owned, total equipment expenditures, etc. **Arrangement:** Ranked by gross operating revenue. **Frequency:** Annual, June. **Editor:** James D. Winsor. **Advertising accepted.** **Price:** $5.00 (current and 1980 editions).

★267★

COMMERCIAL DIRECTORY OF PUERTO RICO-VIRGIN ISLANDS
The Witcom Group, Inc.
El Caribe Building, 15th Floor   Phone: (809) 725-8075
San Juan, PR 00901
Covers: Over 11,000 retailers and 7,000 distributors and wholesalers of consumer products. **Entries include:** Firm name, address, phone, name of contact, number of employees, branches. **Arrangement:** Classified by type of merchandise (automotive, clothing, etc.). **Indexes:** Alphabetical. **Pages** (approx.): 650. **Frequency:** Annual, October. **Editor:** Nan S. Caso, President. **Advertising accepted.** **Price:** $60.00.

★268★

COMPILATION OF NATIONALLY AVERAGED RENTAL RATES AND MODEL REFERENCE DATA FOR CONSTRUCTION EQUIPMENT
Associated Equipment Distributors
615 W. 22nd Street   Phone: (312) 654-0650
Oak Brook, IL 60521
Publication includes: About 325 firms (members of Associated Equipment Distributors) that sell, rent, and service construction equipment. **Entries include:** Company name, location, and type of equipment available for rent. **Arrangement:** Geographical. **Frequency:** Annual, June. **Price:** $18.00. **Also includes:** Section of equipment specifications and average daily, weekly, and monthly rates on operated and maintained construction equipment of all types.

★269★

COMPJOB [Computer industry employment]
Employment Information Services
Box 3265
Chico, CA 95927
Covers: Over 100 companies with a continuing need for employees with computer programming, operation, and other computer-related skills; listings are free. **Entries include:** Company name, address; description of line of business, type of computer, language used, etc. **Arrangement:** Geographical. **Pages** (approx.): 60. **Frequency:** Triennial, spring; latest edition 1978. **Editor:** John Henry Westlund. **Price:** $6.95, postpaid.

★270★

COMPLETE BOOK OF WOODBURNING STOVES
Sterling Publishing Company, Inc.
Two Park Avenue   Phone: (212) 532-7160
New York, NY 10016
Publication includes: List of manufacturers of woodburning stoves and list of chimney sweeps. **Entries include:** For manufacturers - Company name, address, products. For chimney sweeps - Name, address. **Arrangement:** Manufacturers are alphabetical, chimney sweeps are geographical. **Frequency:** First edition June 1979. **Editor:** David Ivins. **Price:** $6.95.

Complete Guide to New England Markets and Media *See* New England Advertising Week—Complete Guide to New England Markets and Media Issue

Computer Directory & Buyers Guide *See* Computers and People—Computer Directory & Buyers Guide Issue

★271★

COMPUTER PERIPHERALS REVIEW
GML Information Service
594 Marrett Road
Lexington, MA 02173
Publication includes: Directory of computer peripheral equipment manufacturers. **Frequency:** Three issues a year. **Price:** $150.00 per year; add $25.00 for overseas postage. **Other information:** Principal content of publication is tabulated specifications of magnetic tape units, disks, printers, and other data processing peripheral equipment.

★272★

COMPUTER REVIEW
GML Information Service
594 Marrett Road
Lexington, MA 02173
Publication includes: Directory of computer main frame manufacturers. **Frequency:** Three issues a year. **Price:** $95.00 per year; add $25.00 for overseas postage. **Other information:** Principal content of publication is specification sheets covering all commercially available computers costing more than $50,000.

★273★

COMPUTERS AND PEOPLE—COMPUTER DIRECTORY AND BUYERS' GUIDE ISSUE
Berkeley Enterprises, Inc.
815 Washington Street   Phone: (617) 332-5453
Newtonville, MA 02160
Covers: Companies which offer hardware, software, and computing or data processing services; colleges and universities which use computers in administration, education, instruction, research, and/or offer commercial service. Includes list of computer user groups. **Entries include:** Company entries show name, address, phone, names of principal executives, number of employees, products or services. Institution listings show similar data. **Arrangement:** Alphabetical. **Indexes:** Geographical, product. **Pages** (approx.): 130. **Frequency:** Annual, August. **Editor:** Edmund C. Berkeley. **Price:** $24.00.

★274★

CONCRETE INDUSTRIES YEARBOOK
Pit & Quarry Publications, Inc.
105 W. Adams Street   Phone: (312) 726-7151
Chicago, IL 60603
Publication includes: List of advertisers of equipment for the production of concrete block/brick, pipe, tile, and prestressed and precast concrete units. **Entries include:** Company name, address, and phone. **Arrangement:** Alphabetical. **Frequency:** Annual, July. **Editor:** Charles P. Holmes. **Advertising accepted.** Circulation 8,200. **Price:** $35.00.

★275★
CONNECTICUT & RHODE ISLAND DIRECTORY OF MANUFACTURERS
Commerce Register, Inc.
213 First Street   Phone: (201) 445-3000
Hohokus, NJ 07423
Covers: 7,500 industrial firms with five or more employees. **Entries include:** Company name, address, phone, names of principal executives; product descriptions and SIC codes; banking affiliation, attorneys, auditors; plant size, number of employees, and sales. **Arrangement:** Geographical. **Indexes:** Company name, SIC. **Pages** (approx.): 400. **Frequency:** Annual, May; first edition May 1979. **Price:** $59.50, plus 95¢ shipping.

★276★
CONNECTICUT MEDIA DIRECTORY
New England Newsclip Agency, Inc.
Five Auburn Street   Phone: (617) 879-4460
Framingham, MA 01701
Covers: 290 newspapers, periodicals, college publications, and 95 radio and television broadcasting stations operating in Connecticut. New York City radio and television stations which reach Connecticut are also listed. **Price:** $19.00. **Other information:** Entry content, arrangement, etc., same as "New England Media Directory," described in separate listing.

★277★
CONNECTICUT MINORITY BUSINESSES
Connecticut Department of Economic Development
210 Washington Street   Phone: (203) 566-4051
Hartford, CT 06106
Covers: More than 200 minority-owned enterprises. **Entries include:** Company name, address, phone, principal executive, type of ownership, number of employees, primary products or services, related capabilities, major equipment, primary customers. **Arrangement:** Classified. **Pages** (approx.): 40. **Frequency:** Annual, fall. **Price:** Free.

★278★
CONNECTICUT STATE INDUSTRIAL DIRECTORY
State Industrial Directories Corporation
Two Penn Plaza   Phone: (212) 564-0340
New York, NY 10001
Number of listings: 6,000. **Entries include:** Company name, address, phone, names of key executives, number of employees, plant size, 4-digit SIC code, products, whether firm imports or exports, and whether firm has research facilities. **Arrangement:** Geographical. **Indexes:** Alphabetical, product (includes mailing address and phone for each firm). **Pages** (approx.): 310. **Frequency:** Annual, February. **Advertising accepted. Price:** $45.00, plus $2.75 shipping (ISSN 0096-6186).

★279★
CONNECTICUT WOMEN IN BUSINESS
Connecticut Department of Economic Development
210 Washington Street   Phone: (203) 566-4051
Hartford, CT 06106
Covers: About 125 firms owned or managed by women. **Entries include:** Company name, address, phone, names and titles of female executives, list of products or services. **Arrangement:** Classified. **Pages** (approx.): 20. **Frequency:** Annual, fall. **Price:** Free.

Conover-Mast Purchasing Directory See **U.S. Industrial Directory**

★280★
CONSTRUCTION—DIRECTORY & BUYER'S GUIDE ISSUE [Southeast]
Construction Publishing Company
2420 Wilson Boulevard   Phone: (703) 524-6611
Arlington, VA 22201
Covers: Construction equipment distributors in Maryland, District of Columbia, Virginia, and North Carolina. **Entries include:** For equipment distributors and manufacturers - Company name, address, phone, products manufactured or carried; branch offices are included for distributors. For municipal government listings (towns over 3,000) - Name, city hall address, phone, council meeting dates, key personnel. Similar information is given for other government listings. For associations (national, state, local) - Association name, address, phone, name of executive director. For aggregate, bituminous, and ready-mix suppliers - Company name, address, phone, number of plants and their locations. **Frequency:** Annual, March. **Editor:** Jack C. Lewis. **Advertising accepted.** Circulation 6,600. **Price:** $15.00.

★281★
CONSTRUCTION BULLETIN—DIRECTORY ISSUE [Upper Midwest]
Chapin Publishing Company
8441 Wayzata Boulevard, Suite 180   Phone: (612) 546-1811
Golden Valley, MN 55426
Covers: Distributors and other suppliers of materials and services to the construction industry in Minnesota, North Dakota, and South Dakota, and manufacturers with outlets in the area. Includes separate list of state highway department personnel. **Entries include:** For distributors, etc. - Company name, address, phone, names of executives, manufacturers represented. For manufacturers - Company name, address, phone, products. **Arrangement:** Manufacturers are alphabetical, distributors are geographical. **Indexes:** Product. **Pages** (approx.): 300. **Frequency:** Annual, March. **Editor:** Robert Siegel. **Advertising accepted.** Circulation 6,000. **Price:** $10.00 (current and 1980 editions).

★282★
CONSTRUCTION DIGEST—BUYER'S GUIDE AND DIRECTORY
Construction Digest, Inc.
101 E. 14th Street   Phone: (317) 634-7374
Indianapolis, IN 46206
Covers: 2,300 distributors of construction equipment and suppliers and manufacturers with distribution in the area; associations; auctioneers. Two editions: West Edition covers Illinois, eastern Missouri, and northwestern Indiana; East Edition covers Indiana, Kentucky, and Ohio. **Entries include:** Company name, address, phone, list of products or services. **Arrangement:** Manufacturers are alphabetical, distributors are geographical. **Indexes:** Product, trade name. **Pages** (approx.): 400. **Frequency:** Annual, March. **Editor:** Art Graham. **Advertising accepted.** Circulation 14,600. **Price:** $10.00.

★283★
CONSTRUCTION EMPLOYMENT DIRECTORY [California]
Construction Employment Directory
Box 255488   Phone: (916) 485-5915
Sacramento, CA 95825
Description: Not a directory. Lists without fee persons with construction-related experience, mostly in California, who are seeking employment, and provides brief description of qualifications. Employers then contact job seekers through the publisher. Subscription price to employers is $500.00 per year for monthly issues. There is no further fee to either party.

★284★
CONSTRUCTION EQUIPMENT—AMERICA'S EQUIPMENT-OWNING GIANTS
Cahners Publishing Company
Five S. Wabash Avenue   Phone: (312) 372-6880
Chicago, IL 60603
Publication includes: More than 200 of the largest equipment-owning heavy construction contractors, engaged in earthmoving, paving, building, and materials production. **Entries include:** Firm name, location, chief officer, equipment ownership rank, equipment replacement value, current equipment factor, general description of type and location of work. **Arrangement:** By equipment ownership rank. **Indexes:** Alphabetical. **Frequency:** Annual, September. **Editor:** John Rehfield. **Advertising accepted.** Circulation 74,000. **Price:** $2.00.

★285★
CONSTRUCTION EQUIPMENT BUYERS GUIDE
Cahners Publishing Company
Five S. Wabash Avenue　　　　　Phone: (313) 372-6880
Chicago, IL 60603
Covers: Over 1,500 manufacturers of construction equipment, plus their distributors; brief list of financing, bonding, and management services, and trade associations. **Entries include:** For manufacturers - Company name, address, names of executives, major types of equipment or services offered, where products can be bought, code indicating whether company sells through distributors. For distributors - Company name, address, phone, contacts, code indicating manufacturers served. **Arrangement:** Separate lists of manufacturers and distributors. **Indexes:** Trade name, product. **Frequency:** Annual, May. **Editor:** John Rehfield. **Advertising accepted.** Circulation 74,000. **Price:** $20.00.

★286★
CONSTRUCTION EQUIPMENT DISTRIBUTION—DIRECTORY ISSUE
Associated Equipment Distributors
615 W. 22nd Street　　　　　Phone: (312) 654-0650
Oak Brook, IL 60521
Covers: About 1,600 members of the association, including manufacturers and distributors of construction equipment; publishers; suppliers of parts and services; and financial institutions involved in construction equipment distribution; international coverage. **Entries include:** Company name, address, phone, name of principal executive. **Arrangement:** By type of membership. **Pages** (approx.): 190. **Frequency:** Annual, May. **Editor:** Art Faber. **Advertising accepted.** Circulation 4,300. **Price:** $10.00.

★287★
CONSTRUCTION INDUSTRY MANUFACTURERS ASSOCIATION— MEMBERSHIP AND ACTIVITIES DIRECTORY
Construction Industry Manufacturers Association
111 E. Wisconsin Avenue, Suite 1700　　　Phone: (414) 272-0943
Milwaukee, WI 53202
Covers: About 200 firms engaged in the manufacture of construction machinery and components and allied equipment. **Pages** (approx.): 80. **Frequency:** Annual. **Price:** Available to members only.

★288★
CONSTRUCTION INDUSTRY REFERENCE BOOK [Arizona]
Arizona Society of Architects
1121 N. Second Street　　　　　Phone: (602) 257-1992
Phoenix, AZ 85004
Covers: About 4,000 contractors, architects, engineers, financial institutions, and suppliers of equipment and materials to the construction industry who are members of construction industry associations active in Arizona. National associations are also listed. **Entries include:** For individuals - Name, office address, phone, title and affiliation (if appropriate). For associations - Name, address, phone. **Arrangement:** By association name. **Pages** (approx.): 300. **Frequency:** Biennial, September of even years. **Price:** $15.00, plus $1.00 shipping (current edition); $25.00 (tentative, 1980 edition).

★289★
CONSTRUCTION NEWS—DIRECTORY & BUYER'S GUIDE ISSUE [Mid-South]
Construction News, Inc.
715 W. Second Street　　　　　Phone: (501) 376-1931
Little Rock, AR 72203
Covers: Suppliers and distributors of construction machinery in Oklahoma, Arkansas, western Tennessee, Louisiana, and Mississippi, and manufacturers with representation in the area. **Entries include:** Company name, address, phone, names of executives. **Arrangement:** Geographical. **Frequency:** Annual, March. **Editor:** Lee Russell. **Advertising accepted.** Circulation 6,300. **Price:** $6.00. **Other information:** Auctioneers, lending institutions, and associations serving the construction industry.

★290★
CONSTRUCTION REVIEW—DIRECTORY OF NATIONAL TRADE ASSOCIATIONS, PROFESSIONAL SOCIETIES...OF THE CONSTRUCTION...INDUSTRIES ISSUE
Construction and Building Products Division
Commerce Department　　　　　Phone: (202) 377-3601
Washington, DC 20230
Covers: Full title is "Directory of National Trade Associations, Professional Societies, and Labor Unions of the Construction and Building Products Industries." **Entries include:** Organization name, address. **Arrangement:** By field of activity (finance, highways, etc.). **Frequency:** Latest issue containing directory was March/April 1978; revised irregularly. **Editor:** Aaron Sarghir. **Price:** $1.50 (ISSN 0010-6917).

★291★
CONSTRUCTION SPECIFICATIONS INSTITUTE—MEMBER DIRECTORY
Construction Specifications Institute
1150 17th Street, N. W., Suite 300
Washington, DC 20036
Number of listings: 13,000. **Entries include:** Name of member, address, and chapter affiliation. **Arrangement:** Geographical. **Indexes:** Alphabetical. **Frequency:** Annual, January. **Editor:** Donald Day. **Advertising accepted.** Circulation 13,000. **Price:** $25.00, plus $1.50 shipping.

★292★
CONSTRUCTIONEER—DIRECTORY ISSUE [New York, New Jersey, Pennsylvania, Delaware]
Reports Corporation
One Bond Street　　　　　Phone: (201) 635-6450
Chatham, NJ 07928
Covers: Producers of crushed stone, sand, and gravel, bituminous products, ready mix concrete, prestressed concrete, and slag for the construction and public works industries of New York, New Jersey, Pennsylvania, and Delaware. Also includes federal and state agencies, county and city officials, associations, consultants, and equipment manufacturers and distributors. **Entries include:** Company name, address, trade and brand names, list of products or services. **Pages** (approx.): 300. **Frequency:** Annual, March. **Editor:** Kenneth A. Hanan. **Advertising accepted.** Circulation 17,000. **Price:** $10.00.

★293★
CONSTRUCTOR—ASSOCIATED GENERAL CONTRACTORS OF AMERICA MBE CONTRACTOR DIRECTORY [Minority contractors]
Associated General Contractors of America
1957 E Street, N. W.
Washington, DC 20006
Covers: About 8,000 construction contractors and subcontractors believed by AGC to be minority enterprises within the meaning of government regulations requiring participation of minority business in public projects. **Entries include:** Firm name, address, phone, name of contact, description of specialties. **Arrangement:** Geographical. **Indexes:** Specialty. **Pages** (approx.): 115. **Frequency:** Not established; first edition summer 1978; second edition October 1979. **Advertising accepted.** **Former title:** Associated General Contractors of America MBE Directory. **Price:** $35.00.

★294★
CONSTRUCTOR—DIRECTORY ISSUE
Associated General Contractors of America
1957 E Street, N. W.　　　　　Phone: (202) 393-2040
Washington, DC 20006
Covers: More than 8,000 member firms engaged in building, highway, heavy, industrial, municipal utilities, and railroad construction. (SIC 1541, 1542, 1611, 1622, 1623, 1629.) Also includes listing of state and local chapter officers with titles and addresses. **Entries include:** Company name, address, phone, names of principal executives, and code indicating type of construction undertaken.

Arrangement: Geographical. Indexes: Alphabetical by company name. Pages (approx.): 330. Frequency: Annual, July. Editor: Diane Snow. Advertising accepted. Circulation 26,000. Price: $35.00 (current and 1980 editions).

★295★
CONSULTANTS AND CONSULTING ORGANIZATIONS DIRECTORY
Gale Research Company
Book Tower   Phone: (313) 961-2242
Detroit, MI 48226
Covers: Over 6,000 firms, individuals, and organizations active in the consulting field. Entries include: Individual or organization name, address, phone, specialties. Arrangement: Geographical. Indexes: Subject-location, personal name, organization name. Pages (approx.): 950. Frequency: Triennial; latest edition 1979; updated semiannually by "New Consultants." Editor: Paul Wasserman. Price: $95.00; supplement service, $85.00 per year.

★296★
CONSULTANTS DIRECTORY [Personnel management]
International Association for Personnel Women
Box 3057
Grand Central Station   Phone: (212) 734-8160
New York, NY 10017
Covers: About 120 women available for consulting assignments in personnel and human resources management. Entries include: Name, business address, phone, geographic area served, consulting skills. Arrangement: Alphabetical. Indexes: Topic, geographical. Pages (approx.): 90. Frequency: Irregular; latest edition 1978; new edition expected 1981. Editor: Connie Sternberg, Executive Director. Price: $5.00 (current and new editions).

Consulting Engineers of Idaho—Membership Roster See Manufacturing Directory of Idaho

★297★
CONSUMER ELECTRONICS MANUFACTURERS DIRECTORY
Marketing Development
402 Border Road   Phone: (617) 369-5382
Concord, MA 01742
Covers: About 1,500 manufacturers of consumer electronic products (calculators, digital watches, video products, etc.) sold in the United States. Entries include: Company name, address, phone, products, names and titles of key personnel, number of employees, and sales revenue. Arrangement: Alphabetical. Indexes: Product. Pages (approx.): 200. Frequency: First edition 1979. Price: $75.00.

★298★
CONSUMER ELECTRONICS MONTHLY—BUYER'S GUIDE ISSUE
CES Publishing Corporation
325 E. 75th Street   Phone: (212) 794-0500
New York, NY 10021
Publication includes: Lists of manufacturers and suppliers of consumer electronics devices such as video and stereo equipment, telephones, calculators and watches, video games, home and CB radios, and personal computers. Each list appears in a section devoted to a category of products. Entries include: Company name, address, phone, names of executives. Arrangement: Alphabetical. Frequency: Annual, January. Editor: Art Levis. Advertising accepted. Price: $15.00 (current edition); $10.00 (1980 edition); postpaid.

★299★
CONTAINER NEWS—ANNUAL BUYERS' GUIDE ISSUE [Freight transportation]
Communication Channels, Inc.
6285 Barfield Road   Phone: (404) 256-9800
Atlanta, GA 30328
Covers: Over 2,500 manufacturers and suppliers of equipment, services, and products to the intermodal transportation industry; international coverage. Entries include: Company name, address, phone, products or services. Arrangement: By product/service.

Pages (approx.): 50. Frequency: Annual, August. Editor: Art Sweum, Buyers' Guide Editor. Advertising accepted. Circulation 30,000. Price: $2.00.

★300★
CONTRA COSTA COUNTY DEVELOPMENT ASSOCIATION— DIRECTORY OF INDUSTRIES [California]
Contra Costa County Development Association
838 Escobar Street   Phone: (415) 228-0800
Martinez, CA 94553
Covers: 525 companies involved in manufacturing or industrial service. Entries include: Company name, address, name of principal executive, number of employees, list of products or services, SIC numbers. Arrangement: Geographical. Indexes: Alphabetical. Pages (approx.): 80. Frequency: Irregular; about every two years; latest edition October 1979. Editor: Paul F. Hughey, General Manager. Price: $5.84.

★301★
CONTRACT—DIRECTORY ISSUE
Gralla Publications
1515 Broadway   Phone: (212) 869-1300
New York, NY 10036
Covers: Manufacturers and suppliers of commercial-grade furniture, lighting, and other furnishings for offices and industrial settings; trade associations are also listed. Entries include: Company name, address, phone, name of contact, products. Arrangement: Alphabetical. Indexes: Product. Pages (approx.): 300. Frequency: Annual, January. Editor: Lenid Corlin. Advertising accepted. Circulation 27,000. Price: $3.00, payment with order (1980 edition).

Contract Carriers Conference—Membership Directory See National Directory of Contract Carriers

★302★
CONTRACTORS TRADE DIRECTORY (The Green Book)
Contractors Trade Directory, Inc.
2538 W. Peterson Avenue   Phone: (312) 583-6100
Chicago, IL 60659
Covers: Construction trade in Illinois, Indiana, Wisconsin, Michigan, and Iowa. Entries include: Company name, address, phone. Arrangement: Classified by type of business. Pages (approx.): 540. Frequency: Annual, June. Editor: Harvey Oleck, President. Advertising accepted. Circulation 15,000. Price: $50.00.

Control Equipment Master See Chilton's Control Equipment Master

★303★
CONVENIENCE STORES—ANNUAL REPORT OF THE CONVENIENCE STORE INDUSTRY ISSUE
Progressive Grocer Company
708 Third Avenue   Phone: (212) 490-1000
New York, NY 10017
Publication includes: Lists of leading publicly and nonpublicly held convenience store chains. Entries include: Company name, headquarters city, number of stores, and dollar volume. Frequency: Annual, September/October. Editor: Robert Rossner. Advertising accepted. Price: $2.75 (ISSN 0193-919X).

Copper and Brass Servicenter Association—Roster See Metal Distribution

★304★
CORPORATE BUYERS OF DESIGN SERVICES/USA
BIDS, Inc.
1301 20th Street, N. W., Suite 104   Phone: (202) 785-2133
Washington, DC 20036
Covers: 4,000 U. S. corporations. Entries include: Company name, address; name and title of executive responsible for selecting architects, engineers and related consulting services; codes indicating

preferred contact procedures, nonproprietary project plans, approximate square footage of construction, and geographic area of project(s). **Pages** (approx.): 270. **Frequency:** Annual, fall. **Editor:** Raymond L. Gaio, President. **Price:** $190.00, payment with order (ISSN 0145-3017).

★305★
CORPORATE DIAGRAMS AND ADMINISTRATIVE PERSONNEL OF THE CHEMICAL INDUSTRY
Chemical Economic Services
Box 468
Palmer Square   Phone: (609) 921-8468
Princeton, NJ 08540
Covers: 375 major and 720 medium-sized chemical processing and manufacturing firms. **Entries include:** Firm name, address, names and titles of top and middle management, products, sales; similar information for plants and subsidiaries. **Pages** (approx.): 265. **Frequency:** Every four years; latest edition 1979. **Editor:** Kenneth R. Kern. **Price:** $150.00 including looseleaf binder; $137.50 without binder; $3.00 shipping.

★306★
CORPORATE DIRECTORY [OF] STATE OF ALASKA
Corporations Division
Alaska Department of Commerce and Economic Development
State Office Building, 9th Floor
Pouch D
Juneau, AK 99801
Covers: 10,260 domestic, foreign, and nonprofit corporations in the department's active files. **Entries include:** Name of corporation, date of incorporation or of filing in Alaska, name of registered agent, address of registered office, state of domicile. **Arrangement:** Alphabetical. **Frequency:** Annual, December; June supplement. **Price:** $12.00; supplement, $1.50. (Not verified)

★307★
CORPORATE REPORT FACT BOOK
Dorn Communications
7101 York Avenue, South   Phone: (612) 835-6855
Minneapolis, MN 55435
Covers: In separate regional editions, 300 corporations in the Ninth Federal Reserve District (Minnesota, the Dakotas, Montana, upper Michigan, and western Wisconsin), and 320 corporations in the Tenth Federal Reserve District (Wyoming, Colorado, Nebraska, Kansas, Oklahoma, northern New Mexico, and northwest Missouri) whose stock is actively traded and publicly held by 200 or more shareholders. Also includes a list of privately owned companies with over 100 employees, regional federal facilities with over 100 employees, and subsidiaries. **Entries include:** Company name, address, phone, officers and directors and principal executives, profile, balance sheet and five year earnings history, number of employees, number of stockholders, general counsel, auditors. **Arrangement:** Alphabetical. **Pages** (approx.): 450 (9th district edition). **Frequency:** 9th district edition - Annual, November; midyear supplement. 10th district edition - Annual, December. **Editor:** Lynn D. Dunn. **Advertising accepted. Price:** $49.00 (9th and 10th district editions); 9th district supplement, $5.00; postpaid.

★308★
CORPUS CHRISTI ECONOMIC DEVELOPMENT CORPORATION MINORITY SMALL BUSINESS DIRECTORY [Texas]
Corpus Christi Economic Development Corporation
1801 S. Staples, Suite 202   Phone: (512) 883-3887
Corpus Christi, TX 78404
Covers: About 125 firms offering primarily consumer services and products. **Entries include:** Company name, address, phone, name of contact. **Arrangement:** Classified. **Frequency:** Irregular; latest edition summer 1977. **Price:** Free. (Not verified)

★309★
CORROSION ENGINEERING BUYER'S GUIDE
National Association of Corrosion Engineers
1440 South Creek   Phone: (713) 492-0535
Houston, TX 77084
Covers: 700 manufacturers of products used in corrosive environments. **Entries include:** Company name, address, phone, name of principal executive, trade and brand names, list of products or services. **Arrangement:** Alphabetical. **Indexes:** Trade name. **Pages** (approx.): 150. **Frequency:** Biennial, October of even years. **Editor:** Jerry R. Castleberry, Executive Editor. **Advertising accepted.** Circulation 13,500. **Former title:** Materials Performance Buyer's Guide (1976). **Price:** $10.00 (current edition); $13.00 (1980 edition).

Corset, Bra and Lingerie Directory See Intimate Fashion News Directory of Resources Issue

Cosmetic, Toiletry and Fragrance Association—Membership Directory See Who's Who in the Cosmetic Industry

Council of Fleet Specialists—Membership Directory See Heavy Duty Trucking—Council of Fleet Specialists Equipment Buyers' Guide...

★310★
COUNTRY INNS OF THE FAR WEST
101 Productions
834 Mission Street   Phone: (415) 495-6040
San Francisco, CA 94103
Covers: 75 country inns in California, Nevada, Oregon, and Washington, and British Columbia, Canada chosen by the editors for their lack of similarity to modern commercial accommodations. **Entries include:** Inn name, address, phone, number of rooms, facilities available, rates, meal service, restrictions, seasons open, whether credit cards are accepted; historical or other information of interest. **Arrangement:** Geographical area. **Indexes:** State/inn name. **Pages** (approx.): 230. **Frequency:** Irregular; previous edition 1977; latest edition 1979. **Editors:** Jacqueline Killeen, Charles C. Miller, and Rachel Bard. **Price:** $4.95, plus 75¢ shipping.

★311★
COUNTRY INNS OF THE OLD SOUTH
101 Productions
834 Mission Street   Phone: (415) 495-6040
San Francisco, CA 94103
Covers: Over 60 country inns in southern and southeastern states chosen by the author for their lack of similarity to modern commercial accommodations. **Entries include:** Inn name, address, phone, number of rooms, facilities available, rates, meal service, restrictions, seasons open, whether credit cards are accepted; historical or other information of interest. **Arrangement:** Geographical. **Indexes:** State/inn name. **Pages** (approx.): 180. **Frequency:** Irregular; first edition 1978. **Editor:** Robert W. Tolf. **Price:** $4.95, plus 75¢ shipping.

Crane and Rigging Association—Roster See Heavy-Specialized Carriers Conference Directory

★312★
CREATIVE BLACK BOOK [Advertiser services]
Friendly Publications
80 Irving Place   Phone: (212) 228-9750
New York, NY 10003
Covers: 12,000 art suppliers, photographers, printers, illustrators and designers, model and advertising agencies, color labs, and others whose products or services are used in advertising. Includes five geographical sections - the South, Midwest, Northeast, West, and International. **Entries include:** Company name, address, and phone. **Pages** (approx.): 700. **Frequency:** Annual, January. **Editors:** Stuart Waldman and Marty Goldstein, Publishers. **Advertising accepted.** Circulation 40,000. **Former title:** Sales Executives Guide. **Price:**

$20.00, plus $2.00 shipping.

★313★

CREATIVE DIRECTORY OF THE SUN BELT [Advertiser services]
Ampersand, Inc.
1103 S. Shepherd   Phone: (713) 523-0506
Houston, TX 77019
Covers: More than 5,000 artists, designers, illustrators, photographers, writers, public relations and advertising agencies, motion picture companies, graphic arts suppliers, TV film companies, musicians, talent agencies, audiovisual services, and others concerned with advertising in California, Florida, Texas, Arizona, New Mexico, Louisiana, Alabama, and other Sun Belt states. **Entries include:** Company or firm name, address. **Arrangement:** Classified by service. **Frequency:** Annual, December. **Price:** $15.00, plus $2.95 shipping.

★314★

CREATIVE DIRECTORY/CHICAGO [Advertiser services]
Creative Directory, Inc.
333 N. Michigan, Suite 311   Phone: (312) 236-7337
Chicago, IL 60601
Covers: 3,000 advertising agencies, marketing services, photographers, public relations firms, sound studios, talent agencies, audiovisual services, and others offering creative and production services. **Entries include:** For most listings - Company name, address, phone, list of officers, description of services. For freelance listings - Name, talent, address, phone. **Arrangement:** By specialty. **Pages** (approx.): 275. **Frequency:** Annual, January. **Editor:** Beaver Hansen. **Advertising accepted.** Circulation 5,000. **Price:** $20.00 (1980 edition).

★315★

CREMATION ASSOCIATION OF NORTH AMERICA—MEMBERSHIP DIRECTORY
Cremation Association of North America
15300 Ventura Boulevard, Suite 305   Phone: (213) 990-5966
Sherman Oaks, CA 91403
Covers: About 290 crematories and 20 suppliers of urns and other equipment. **Entries include:** Crematory or supplier name, address, phone, key personnel; supplier listings include list of products and services and trade and brand names. **Arrangement:** Geographical. **Pages** (approx.): 70. **Frequency:** Annual, January. **Editor:** Paul G. Bryan, Secretary. **Price:** Available to members only.

★316★

CRONER'S REFERENCE BOOK FOR WORLD TRADERS
Croner Publications, Inc.
211 Jamaica Avenue   Phone: (212) 464-0866
Queens Village, NY 11428
Covers: In Volume 1, government agencies concerned with foreign trade, other sources of information on trade subjects, and steamships, airlines, freight forwarders, and other companies providing trade services. Volumes 2 and 3 provide similar information for foreign countries, plus lists of advertising agencies, hotels, publications, etc. **Entries include:** Company or organization name, address, phone, services. **Arrangement:** By type of organization. **Pages** (approx.): 1,600, in 3 looseleaf volumes. **Frequency:** Triennial; periodic supplements. **Price:** $65.00 (includes one year's supplements), plus $4.95 shipping, payment with order.

Cultured Marble Institute—Membership List *See* Kitchen Business—Directory & Buyers Guide Issue

★317★

CURTAIN DRAPERY & BEDSPREAD BUYERS GUIDE
Columbia Communications, Inc.
370 Lexington Avenue   Phone: (212) 532-9290
New York, NY 10017
Covers: Manufacturers of curtains, draperies, bedspreads, and related products, and resident buying offices of department store and specialty chains in major cities. **Entries include:** Company name,

address, phone; buying office listings include number and types of stores represented. **Arrangement:** Manufacturers are alphabetical, buyers are geographical. **Indexes:** Product. **Frequency:** Annual, May. **Advertising accepted.** **Price:** $5.00 (current and 1980 editions).

★318★

CUSTOM ENGINEERED P/M PARTS AND PRODUCTS MANUFACTURERS DIRECTORY INTERNATIONAL
Metal Powder Industries Federation
Box 2054   Phone: (609) 799-3300
Princeton, NJ 08540
Covers: 245 firms in the international powdered metals industry. Includes members of the Powder Metallurgy Parts Association, P/M Industries Association, Refractory Metals Association. **Entries include:** Firm name, address, phone, name of contact, coded products list, branch or division addresses, phone numbers. **Arrangement:** By association, then alphabetical. **Pages** (approx.): 25. **Frequency:** Annual, May. **Price:** Free; request on company letterhead.

★319★

CUSTOM HOUSE GUIDE [United States]
North American Publishing Company
401 N. Broad Street   Phone: (215) 574-9600
Philadelphia, PA 19108
Publication includes: Principal ports in the United States which have customs facilities, with their customs officials, port authorities, chambers of commerce, and other relevant organizations and agencies; other ports of entry; shipping companies and related trades. **Entries include:** For each principal port - Name of organization or agency, address, phone, names and titles of key personnel; description and limitations of port facilities, port charges, and activities. **Indexes:** General. **Frequency:** Annual, spring. **Editor:** Edward H. Kiernan. **Advertising accepted.** **Price:** $98.00 (current edition); $125.00 (1980 edition) (ISSN 0070-2250). **Other information:** Principal content is tariff schedules, customs regulations, trade agreements, etc.

★320★

CUTTING TOOL DIRECTORY
Cutting Tool Manufacturers Association
6735 Telegraph Road, Suite 120   Phone: (313) 647-4747
Birmingham, MI 48010
Covers: Over 160 member companies which manufacture metalworking cutting tools. **Entries include:** Company name, address, phone, products, trade names. **Arrangement:** Alphabetical. **Indexes:** Product. **Pages** (approx.): 30. **Frequency:** Biennial, even years. **Editor:** Welles Jatho, Executive Secretary. **Price:** $1.00.

Cutting Tool Manufacturers Association—Membership Directory *See* Cutting Tool Directory

★321★

DAILY NEWS RECORD'S DIRECTORY OF MEN'S & BOYS' WEAR FIRMS AT...[Major New York addresses]
Fairchild Publications, Division
Capital Cities Media, Inc.
7 E. 12th Street   Phone: (212) 741-4000
New York, NY 10003
Description: Full title is, "Daily News Record's Directory of Men's & Boy's Wear Firms at 1290 Avenue of the Americas and 350 Fifth Avenue." **Entries include:** Firm name, name of chief executive, building, room and phone number. **Arrangement:** By building, then alphabetical. **Indexes:** Merchandise type, brand name, firm name. **Pages** (approx.): 100. **Frequency:** Annual, January. **Advertising accepted.** Circulation 28,000. **Price:** $5.00 (current and 1980 editions).

★322★

DALTON'S DIRECTORY OF BUSINESS AND INDUSTRY
[Philadelphia, South New Jersey, Delaware]
Dalton's Directory of Business and Industry
410 Lancaster Avenue   Phone: (215) 649-2680
Haverford, PA 19041
Covers: Over 10,000 firms in Philadelphia and Bucks, Chester, Montgomery, and Delaware counties in Pennsylvania; Camden, Gloucester, Burlington, Mercer, and Salem counties in New Jersey; New Castle county in Delaware. Includes manufacturing, service, retail, and other firms. **Entries include:** Company name, address, phone, number of employees, products or services, names of principal executives. **Arrangement:** Geographical. **Indexes:** Alphabetical, product. **Pages** (approx.): 525. **Frequency:** Annual, summer. **Price:** $55.00.

★323★

DATA COMMUNICATIONS BUYERS' GUIDE
McGraw-Hill, Inc.
1221 Avenue of the Americas   Phone: (212) 997-3139
New York, NY 10020
Covers: Manufacturers of data communications, distributed data processing, and computer network equipment and services, worldwide. **Entries include:** Company name, address, phone, number of employees, financial keys, list of products; listings may also include locations of sales offices. **Arrangement:** Geographical. **Indexes:** Product. **Pages** (approx.): 200. **Frequency:** Annual, November. **Editor:** Harry Karp. **Advertising accepted.** Circulation 25,000. **Price:** $15.00.

★324★

DATAMATION—TOP 50 U.S. COMPANIES ISSUE [Data processing]
Technical Publishing Company
35 Mason Street   Phone: (212) 489-2200
Greenwich, CT 06830
Covers: 50 leading United States manufacturers of data processing equipment. **Entries include:** Company name, rank, street address, phone, data processing equipment revenues for the previous year, net income, number of employees, total revenues for three preceding years. **Arrangement:** Ranked by data processing revenues. **Frequency:** Annual, June. **Editor:** John L. Kirkley. **Advertising accepted. Price:** $3.00.

Datapro Directory of Software *See* **Datapro Reports**

Datapro Directory of Suppliers *See* **Datapro 70**

Datapro EDP Solutions *See* **Datapro Reports**

★325★

DATAPRO REPORTS
Datapro Research Corporation
1805 Underwood Boulevard   Phone: (609) 764-0100
Delran, NJ 08075
Background: The "Datapro Reports" series includes separate reports on minicomputers, data communications, electronic data processing support systems and equipment, word processing, software, office automation systems, copiers and duplicators, retail automation equipment, and banking automation equipment. (See also "Datapro 70" listing.) **Entries include:** Each series includes descriptions of each equipment model offered by each manufacturer in the field and comparison charts and lists of suppliers, associations, etc., with addresses and phone numbers. Individual descriptions include a summary and detailed reports on technical characteristics and operation. Reports are loose-leaf, in several volumes. **Frequency:** Base volumes current to date supplied upon subscription; updates sent monthly. **Price:** Datapro Reports on Minicomputers, $430.00 per year...Data Communications, $390.00; ...EDP Solutions, $230.00; ...Word Processing, $290.00; ...Office Systems, $430.00; ...Copiers and Duplicators, $290.00; ...Retail Automation, $290.00; ...Banking

Automation, $290.00; Datapro Directory of Software, $270.00.

Datapro Reports on Banking Automation *See* **Datapro Reports**

Datapro Reports on Copiers and Duplicators *See* **Datapro Reports**

Datapro Reports on Data Communications *See* **Datapro Reports**

Datapro Reports on Minicomputers *See* **Datapro Reports**

Datapro Reports on Office Systems *See* **Datapro Reports**

Datapro Reports on Retail Automation *See* **Datapro Reports**

Datapro Reports on Word Processing *See* **Datapro Reports**

★326★

DATAPRO 70
Datapro Research Corporation
1805 Underwood Boulevard   Phone: (609) 764-0100
Delran, NJ 08075
Publication includes: List of nearly 900 companies which offer data processing products and services. **Entries include:** Company name, address, size, sales and service organization, and description of products. Directory section is offered separately as "Datapro Directory of Suppliers," $15.00. **Arrangement:** Alphabetical. **Other information:** Principal content of publication is descriptions and evaluations of data processing products and services offered by the manufacturers in the directory section. **Price:** $615.00, includes three base volumes (looseleaf format) and monthly updates.

★327★

DAVISON'S KNIT GOODS TRADE (The Red Book)
Davison Publishing Company, Inc.
175 Rock Road   Phone: (201) 455-3135
Glen Rock, NJ 07452
Covers: 10,000 company listings, including 2,200 knitting mills plus dyers, bleachers, and finishers in the United States and Canada. Includes separate lists of mill agents, wholesalers, chain stores and retailers who handle knit goods, plus a buyers' guide. **Entries include:** Company name, address, phone, principal executive, and products or services. **Arrangement:** Classified by products and functions. **Indexes:** Alphabetical index of mills. **Pages** (approx.): 600. **Frequency:** Annual, July. **Editor:** Norman L. Vought, President. **Advertising accepted.** Circulation 1,800. **Price:** $35.00. **Send orders to:** Davison Publishing Co., Inc., Box 477, Ridgewood, NJ 07451.

★328★

DAVISON'S SALESMAN'S BOOK
Davison Publishing Company, Inc.
175 Rock Road   Phone: (201) 445-3135
Glen Rock, NJ 07452
Covers: 7,000 mills, dyers, finishers, laminators, and bonders in the United States and Canada. **Entries include:** Company name, address, phone, name of executives, machinery in use, yarns and fibers used, products, and sales agents. **Arrangement:** Geographical. **Pages** (approx.): 500. **Frequency:** Annual, February. **Editor:** Norman L. Vought, President. **Price:** $20.00. **Send orders to:** Davison Publishing Co., Inc., Box 477, Ridgewood, NJ 07451.

★329★

DAVISON'S TEXTILE BLUE BOOK
Davison Publishing Company, Inc.
175 Rock Road   Phone: (201) 445-3135
Glen Rock, NJ 07452
Covers: Over 19,000 companies in the textile industry in the United States and Canada, including about 8,000 textile plants. Covers mills, manufacturers, dyers, bleachers, finishers, dealers, importers, exporters, brokers, shippers, and agents for various textiles, fibers, yarns, and cordage. **Entries include:** Listings generally include

company name, address, phone, names of executives, and a description of products or services, including trade names. Mill and other production facility listings include data on equipment and capacity. **Arrangement:** Divided by industry segment; mills and manufacturers are listed geographically and by process or product category, dyers according to process employed. **Indexes:** Alphabetical index of mills and processors. **Pages** (approx.): 700. **Frequency:** Annual, January. **Editor:** Norman L. Vought, President. **Advertising accepted.** Circulation 4,500. **Price:** $50.00. **Send orders to:** Davison Publishing Co., Inc., Box 477, Ridgewood, NJ 07451. **Also includes:** Lists of trade names, textile schools, testing and research laboratories, and trade associations.

★330★
DAVISON'S TEXTILE BUYER'S GUIDE (The Gold Book)
Davison Publishing Company, Inc.
175 Rock Road   Phone: (201) 445-3135
Glen Rock, NJ 07452
Covers: Suppliers of equipment, materials, and services for the textile industry. **Entries include:** Company name and address, list of products or services. **Arrangement:** Alphabetical. **Indexes:** Classified lists of products and services refer to supplier section. **Pages** (approx.): 300. **Frequency:** Annual, May. **Editor:** Norman L. Vought, President. **Advertising accepted.** Circulation 7,500. **Former title:** Davison's Textile Catalog and Buyer's Guide. **Price:** $25.00. **Send orders to:** Davison Publishing Co., Inc., Box 477, Ridgewood, NJ 07451.

Davison's Textile Catalog and Buyer's Guide (The Gold Book) See Davison's Textile Buyer's Guide (The Gold Book)

★331★
DAYTON AREA MINORITY BUSINESS DIRECTORY [Ohio]
Dayton Human Relations Council
40 S. Main Street, Suite 721   Phone: (513) 225-5336
Dayton, OH 45402
Covers: About 350 firms offering professional, commercial, industrial, and consumer products and services. **Entries include:** Company name, address, phone, name of contact. **Arrangement:** Classified. **Indexes:** Company. **Pages** (approx.): 50. **Frequency:** Annual, fall. **Price:** Free.

★332★
DEALERSCOPE MAGAZINE—NATIONAL BUYER'S GUIDE ISSUE
[Consumer hardgoods]
Dealerscope
115 Second Avenue   Phone: (617) 890-5124
Waltham, MA 02154
Covers: Manufacturers, distributors, and manufacturer representatives in the major appliance and consumer electronic industries (stereo equipment, calculators, etc.). **Entries include:** For manufacturers - Manufacturer name, address, phone, distributor or representative, and city and state in which distributor located. For distributors - Distributor or representative name, address, and phone. **Arrangement:** Manufacturers are alphabetical, distributors are geographical. **Frequency:** Annual, December; May update. **Editor:** James M. Barry. **Advertising accepted.** Circulation 38,500. **Former title:** Distributor Directory & Where to Buy It Guide. **Price:** $25.00.

★333★
DECOR—SOURCES ISSUE
Commerce Publishing Company
408 Olive Street
St. Louis, MO 63102
Covers: More than 500 wholesale suppliers of pictures, picture frames, interior accessories, sculpture, mirrors, etc. to art galleries, picture framers, and home accessories retailers. **Entries include:** Supplier name, address, and phone. **Arrangement:** By product. **Indexes:** Product. **Pages** (approx.): 450. **Frequency:** Annual, July. **Editor:** W. Humberg. **Advertising accepted.** Circulation 21,000. **Price:** $6.00.

★334★
DECORATING RETAILER—DIRECTORY OF THE WALLCOVERINGS
INDUSTRY ISSUE
National Decorating Products Association
9334 Dielman Industrial Drive   Phone: (314) 991-3470
St. Louis, MO 63132
Covers: About 1,000 manufacturers and distributors of wallcoverings and related products. **Entries include:** Company name, address, phone, executives; manufacturer listings include information on wallcovering lines, collection characteristics, book serial numbers and expiration dates, brand and trade names; distributor listings include brands carried. **Arrangement:** Alphabetical. **Indexes:** Collection/ trade/brand names, pattern numbers. **Pages** (approx.): 210. **Frequency:** Annual, December. **Editor:** Jack Fulwiler. **Advertising accepted.** Circulation 20,000. **Price:** $10.00, postpaid.

★335★
DE/DOMESTIC ENGINEERING—BOOK OF GIANTS ISSUE
Construction Industry Press, Inc.
110 N. York Road
Elmhurst, IL 60126
Covers: About 200 mechanical contracting firms having annual volumes of $3,000,000 or more. **Entries include:** Company name, location, gross volume, specialties. **Arrangement:** By volume. **Indexes:** Alphabetical. **Pages** (approx.): 230. **Frequency:** Annual, August. **Advertising accepted.** Circulation 40,000. **Price:** $2.00.

★336★
DEEP FOUNDATIONS INSTITUTE—MEMBERSHIP ROSTER
[Construction industry]
Deep Foundations Institute
66 Morris Avenue   Phone: (201) 379-1100
Springfield, NJ 07081
Covers: About 200 individuals concerned with piling, caissons, and other deep support for structures or deep excavation; consulting firms, foundation contractors, materials and equipment suppliers. **Entries include:** Name, address; affiliation and title given for members who are employed by corporate members, or who are trustees, officers, or committee members of the Institute. **Arrangement:** By membership category. **Pages** (approx.): 20. **Frequency:** Annual, March. **Editor:** Mrs. Fern McNerney, Executive Secretary. **Price:** Available to members only.

★337★
DEFENSE INDUSTRY ORGANIZATION SERVICE
Carroll Publishing Company
1058 Thomas Jefferson Street, N. W.   Phone: (202) 333-8620
Washington, DC 20007
Covers: In organization chart form, about 80 companies and 6,000 individuals responsible for nearly 60% of total Department of Defense contract awards. **Entries include:** Company name, address, names and titles of key personnel, phone. **Arrangement:** By company. **Frequency:** Current set of charts delivered at time of subscription; updated semiannually. **Price:** $435.00 per year.

★338★
DEFENSE LOGISTICS AGENCY—MINORITY BUSINESS DIRECTORY
Defense Logistics Agency
Defense Department
Alexandria, VA 22314
Covers: Minority business firms with capability of participating in defense contracts or working with other defense contractors. **Frequency:** Not established; first edition April 1978. **Price:** Free.

★339★
DELAWARE DIRECTORY OF COMMERCE AND INDUSTRY
Delaware State Chamber of Commerce
1102 West Street
Wilmington, DE 19801
Covers: About 5,000 manufacturers, retailers, wholesalers, and service establishments. **Entries include:** Company name, address,

phone, names of principal executives, number of employees, list of products or services, SIC numbers, number of branches, whether firm exports or imports. **Arrangement:** Alphabetical. **Indexes:** Geographical, SIC. **Pages** (approx.): 275. **Frequency:** Irregular; latest edition 1979. **Price:** $20.00, postpaid.

★340★
DELAWARE STATE INDUSTRIAL DIRECTORY
State Industrial Directories Corporation
Two Penn Plaza   Phone: (212) 564-0340
New York, NY 10001
Number of listings: 600. **Entries include:** Company name, address, phone, names of key executives, number of employees, plant size, 4-digit SIC code, products, whether firm imports or exports, and whether firm has research facilities. **Arrangement:** Geographical. **Indexes:** Alphabetical, product (includes mailing address and phone for each firm). **Frequency:** Annual, spring. **Advertising accepted. Price:** $15.00, plus $2.75 shipping (ISSN 0148-5652).

★341★
DELI NEWS—DELI PRODUCTS DIRECTORY ISSUE [California]
Delicatessen Council of Southern California
12028 Venice Boulevard, Suite 7   Phone: (213) 391-1982
Mar Vista, CA 90066
Covers: About 150 suppliers of delicatessen foods, and supplies and equipment used in a delicatessen operation; listings include brokers and distributors. Coverage limited to California. **Entries include:** Company name, address, phone, products and brand names. **Arrangement:** By broker, distributor/supplier, or service/equipment. **Indexes:** Product/brand name. **Pages** (approx.): 20. **Frequency:** Annual, January. **Editor:** John R. Cates. **Advertising accepted.** Circulation 6,000. **Price:** $1.50, payment with order. **Other information:** Title of deli product section is, "Directory of Delicatessen Products."

★342★
DEPARTMENT OF DEFENSE PRIME CONTRACTORS IN THE CHICAGO REGION
Small Business Office
Defense Contract Administration Services Region, Chicago
Defense Logistics Agency
Box 66475   Phone: (312) 694-3031
Chicago, IL 60666
Covers: About 800 firms which supply products, services, and equipment directly to the Defense Department in Illinois, Wisconsin, and Indiana. **Entries include:** Company name, address, product or size, code for number of employees, name of contact. **Arrangement:** Geographical. **Indexes:** 1980 edition to include product index. **Pages** (approx.): 85. **Frequency:** Approximately annual; latest edition May 1979. **Price:** Free.

★343★
DESIGN NEWS ELECTRICAL/ELECTRONIC DIRECTORY
Cahners Publishing Company
221 Columbus Avenue   Phone: (617) 536-7780
Boston, MA 02116
Covers: About 5,500 manufacturers and suppliers of electrical/ electronic components to the OEM (original equipment manufacturer) market in SIC groups 34-39. **Entries include:** Company name, address, phone; advertiser listings include listings for sales offices and distributors. **Arrangement:** Alphabetical. **Indexes:** Product, trade name. **Pages** (approx.): 160. **Frequency:** Annual, November. **Editor:** Steve Kern. **Advertising accepted.** Circulation 90,200. **Former title:** Design News Reference Editions. **Price:** $6.00. **Other information:** See other listings under "Design News..." for information on power transmission, fluid power, fastening, and materials editions.

★344★
DESIGN NEWS FASTENING DIRECTORY
Cahners Publishing Company
221 Columbus Avenue   Phone: (617) 536-7780
Boston, MA 02116
Covers: About 5,300 manufacturers and suppliers of fastening products to the OEM (original equipment manufacturer) market in SIC groups 34-39. **Frequency:** Annual, July. **Advertising accepted.** Circulation 92,200. **Price:** $6.00. **Other information:** Content, arrangement, etc., same as "Design News Electrical/Electronic Directory," described separately.

★345★
DESIGN NEWS FLUID POWER DIRECTORY
Cahners Publishing Company
221 Columbus Avenue   Phone: (617) 536-7780
Boston, MA 02116
Covers: About 5,300 manufacturers and suppliers of fluid power products to the OEM (original equipment manufacturer) market in SIC groups 34-39. **Frequency:** Annual, May. **Advertising accepted.** Circulation 49,700. **Price:** $6.00. **Other information:** Content, arrangement, etc., same as "Design News Electrical/Electronic Directory," described separately.

★346★
DESIGN NEWS MATERIALS DIRECTORY
Cahners Publishing Company
221 Columbus Avenue   Phone: (617) 536-7780
Boston, MA 02116
Covers: About 5,300 manufacturers and suppliers of materials (e.g., ferrous, nonferrous, and plastic bearings, gears, and chains) to the OEM (original equipment manufacturer) market in SIC groups 34-39. **Frequency:** Annual, September. **Advertising accepted.** Circulation 87,000. **Price:** $6.00. **Other information:** Content, arrangement, etc., same as "Design News Electrical/Electronic Directory," described separately.

★347★
DESIGN NEWS POWER TRANSMISSION DIRECTORY
Cahners Publishing Company
221 Columbus Avenue   Phone: (617) 536-7780
Boston, MA 02116
Covers: About 5,300 manufacturers and suppliers of power transmission products to the OEM (original equipment manufacturer) market in SIC groups 34-39. **Frequency:** Annual, March. **Advertising accepted.** Circulation 56,700. **Price:** $6.00. **Other information:** Content, arrangement, etc., same as "Design News Electrical/ Electronic Directory," described separately.

Design News Reference Editions *See* Design News Electrical/ Electronic Directory

★348★
DESIGNERS WEST RESOURCE DIRECTORY
Arts Alliance Corporation
8564 Melrose Avenue   Phone: (213) 657-8231
Los Angeles, CA 90069
Covers: About 3,600 firms supplying products to professional interior designers, architects, and contractors in western states. **Entries include:** Company name, address, phone, showroom addresses and key personnel, list of products or services. **Arrangement:** Alphabetical. **Indexes:** Product. **Pages** (approx.): 320. **Frequency:** Semiannual, spring and fall. **Editor:** Kathleen L. Schultz. **Price:** $5.00.

Dial 800 *See* Dial Free: Dial 800

★349★
DIAL FREE: DIAL 800
JMO Publishing, Inc.
Box 995
Radio City Station
New York, NY 10019
Covers: About 4,000 companies, organizations, hotels, airlines, etc., with 800- (toll-free) telephone numbers. **Arrangement:** By line of business. **Former title:** Dial 800. **Price:** $2.99, plus 50¢ shipping.

★350★
DIEMAKERS & DIECUTTERS ASSOCIATION—MEMBERSHIP
        ROSTER [Packaging]
Diemakers & Diecutters Association
3255 S. U.S. 1   Phone: (305) 465-9450
Fort Pierce, FL 33450
Covers: About 350 commercial and inplant diemakers, diecutters, and suppliers primarily for the packaging, and folding and corrugated box industry. **Entries include:** Company name, address, phone, voting and associate representatives; some listings include products. **Arrangement:** Alphabetical. **Pages** (approx.): 10. **Frequency:** Annual, May. **Editor:** Cyndi Schulman, Executive Director. **Price:** Available to members only.

★351★
DIESEL & GAS TURBINE PROGRESS—ASSOCIATION OF DIESEL
        SPECIALISTS DIRECTORY ISSUE
Diesel Engines, Inc.
11225 W. Bluemound Road   Phone: (414) 771-4562
Milwaukee, WI 53226
Publication includes: 725 service firms which are members of the Association of Diesel Specialists, including about 250 overseas members. **Entries include:** Firm name, address, phone, services. **Arrangement:** Geographical. **Frequency:** Annual, March. **Price:** $15.00.

★352★
DIESEL & GAS TURBINE PROGRESS—EGSMA MEMBERSHIP/
        PRODUCT DIRECTORY OF LEADING COMPANIES ISSUE
Diesel Engines, Inc.
11225 W. Bluemound Road   Phone: (414) 771-4562
Milwaukee, WI 53226
Covers: About 180 members of the Electrical Generating Systems Marketing Association; includes manufacturers, manufacturers' representatives, distributors, and dealers in electricity generating equipment. Trade associations, publishers, and consultants are also listed. **Entries include:** Company name, address, phone, names and titles of key personnel, line of business, type of membership and year initiated; products, services, or companies represented as appropriate. **Arrangement:** Alphabetical. **Indexes:** Product/service. **Pages** (approx.): 50. **Frequency:** Annual, February. **Editor:** Hattie Banbury, Executive Director. **Advertising accepted. Price:** $7.50, payment with order. **Send orders to:** Electrical Generating Systems Marketing Assn., 435 N. Michigan Ave., No. 1717, Chicago, IL 60611 (312-644-0828).

★353★
DIESEL DIRECTORY
Calcom Publications
Toadtown   Phone: (916) 872-1200
Magalia, CA 95954
Covers: 8,400 service stations and truck stops which offer diesel fuel. **Entries include:** Facility name, location. **Arrangement:** Geographical by regions. **Indexes:** State. **Pages** (approx.): 240. **Frequency:** Latest edition spring 1978. **Editor:** Robert Behme. **Price:** $6.95, postpaid. **Other information:** Reports on 1978 diesel cars and recreational vehicles.

★354★
DIESEL FUEL DIRECTORY
Light Oils Department
Amoco Oil Company
200 E. Randolph Drive
Chicago, IL 60601
Covers: 960 stations in 45 states and the District of Columbia which sell diesel fuel. **Entries include:** Station name, address, kind of fuels sold in each. **Arrangement:** Geographical. **Frequency:** Annual, spring. **Price:** Free.

★355★
DIESEL FUEL GUIDE
Diesel Fuel Services, Inc.
Box 256   Phone: (212) 684-3818
South Salem, NY 10590
Covers: 11,300 diesel fuel stations in United States and Canada. **Entries include:** Brand name of fuel, street address or nearest intersection. **Arrangement:** Geographical. **Pages** (approx.): 210. **Frequency:** Annual, winter. **Former title:** A Directory of Diesel Fuel Stations Coast to Coast. **Price:** $6.95.

★356★
DIESEL STOP DIRECTORY AND ROAD ATLAS
Hammond, Inc.
515 Valley Street   Phone: (201) 763-6000
Maplewood, NJ 07040
Covers: 11,000 service stations and other outlets which stock diesel fuel. **Entries include:** Station name and location. Except for stations in small communities or highly congested areas, locations are also shown on maps for individual states. **Arrangement:** Geographical. **Pages** (approx.): 100. **Frequency:** Annual, December. **Price:** $4.95 (1978 edition). **Other information:** This is the same publication mentioned in some sources as being published by Mercedes-Benz, whose dealers are listed in a special edition of this directory.

Direct Mail List Rates & Data *See* Standard Rate & Data
        Service—Direct Mail List Rates & Data

★357★
DIRECT MARKETING MARKETPLACE
Hilary House Publishers, Inc.
1033 Channel Drive
Hewlett Harbor, NY 11557
Covers: Several thousand direct marketing companies, service firms and suppliers, and creative and consulting services concerned with direct marketing (including mail, radio and television broadcasting). **Entries include:** Company name, address, phone; description of products and services, names and titles of key personnel. Some listings also include gross sales volume, advertising budget, and amounts spent in marketing media. **Arrangement:** By type of firm. **Indexes:** General company and personnel index, with full addresses and phone numbers. **Pages** (approx.): 300. **Frequency:** Not established; first edition January 1980. **Editor:** Edward L. Stern. **Price:** $25.00, plus $2.00 shipping; payment or purchase order must accompany order. **Other information:** Library orders only should be sent to R. R. Bowker Co., Box 1807, Ann Arbor, MI 48106 (313-761-4700).

★358★
DIRECT SELLING ASSOCIATION—GUIDE TO COMMITTEES AND
        DIRECTORY OF MEMBERS
Direct Selling Association
1730 M Street, N. W., Suite 610   Phone: (202) 293-5760
Washington, DC 20036
Publication includes: 160 member direct selling companies and their suppliers. Associations and firms are concerned with selling of consumer products door-to-door and through party plans. **Entries include:** For member companies - Company name, address, phone, names and titles of key personnel, products or services. **Arrangement:** Alphabetical. **Pages** (approx.): 60. **Frequency:** Annual,

summer. **Editor:** Mills Edwards, Director, Information Services. **Price:** $20.00.

★359★
DIRECT SELLING WORLD DIRECTORY
Direct Selling Association
1730 M Street, N. W., Suite 610   Phone: (202) 293-5760
Washington, DC 20036
Covers: 25 direct selling associations, associated member companies, and the World Federation of Direct Selling Associations and the European Federation of Direct Selling Associations. Associations and firms are concerned with selling of consumer products door-to-door and through party plans. **Entries include:** Organization name, address, phone. National association listings include names of association officers and their affiliations. Member company listings include products. **Arrangement:** Geographical. **Pages** (approx.): 45. **Frequency:** Annual, May. **Editor:** William L. Wight, Manager, International Affairs. **Price:** $7.50.

★360★
DIRECTORIO PROFESIONAL HISPANO [Spanish-speaking professional in Connecticut, New Jersey, and New York]
Blanca Balbi
Box 408   Phone: (212) 762-1432
Flushing, NY 11352
Covers: About 1,700 Hispanic doctors, optometrists, dentists, lawyers, architects, and accountants with offices in Connecticut, New Jersey, or New York. **Entries include:** Name, address, and phone. **Arrangement:** By profession. **Indexes:** Medical specialists. **Pages** (approx.): 45. **Frequency:** Annual, June/July. **Editor:** George E. Balbi. **Advertising accepted.** Circulation 10,000. **Price:** Free.

★361★
DIRECTORY: FASHION ACCESSORIES SALES REPRESENTATIVES
Business Journals, Inc.
22 S. Smith Street   Phone: (203) 853-6015
Norwalk, CT 06855
Covers: 470 representatives of manufacturers of handbags, gloves, belts, and other accessories; international coverage. **Entries include:** Name of representative or of firm, address, phone, states in territory. **Arrangement:** Geographical. **Pages** (approx.): 40. **Frequency:** Not established; first edition 1979. **Advertising accepted.** **Price:** $15.00, payment with order. **Other information:** Advertised under title, "Directory of Accessories Sales Representatives."

★362★
DIRECTORY—METROPOLITAN BUFFALO INDUSTRY
Buffalo Area Chamber of Commerce
107 Delaware Avenue   Phone: (716) 849-6677
Buffalo, NY 14202
Covers: 1,100 manufacturing firms located in Erie and Niagara counties of New York. **Entries include:** Company name, address, phone, name of principal executive, number of employees, products or services, SIC numbers, and square footage. **Arrangement:** Alphabetical. **Indexes:** Product. **Frequency:** Irregular; previous edition 1976; latest edition November 1979. **Former title:** Industrial Directory Metropolitan Buffalo. **Price:** $7.17 (1976 edition).

★363★
DIRECTORY IRON AND STEEL PLANTS (The Black Book)
Association of Iron and Steel Engineers
Three Gateway Center, Suite 2350   Phone: (412) 281-6324
Pittsburgh, PA 15222
Covers: More than 1,300 companies, 2,500 plants, and 15,000 technical and administrative personnel in United States and Canada engaged in blast furnace operations, steel production, coking, steel works and rolling mills and allied operations. Separate list of major suppliers. Some foreign companies included. **Entries include:** All

listings include company name, plant name, address, phone, names of principal executives and operating personnel; listings may also include data on capacity, equipment, railroad and shipping facilities, number of employees, and products. **Arrangement:** Classified by principal activity. **Indexes:** Geographical, alphabetical. **Pages** (approx.): 500. **Frequency:** Annual, February. **Price:** $25.00, payment must accompany order (current and 1980 editions). **Other information:** Not to be confused with "Directory of Iron and Steel Works of the U. S. and Canada," published by the American Iron and Steel Institute.

Directory of Accessories Sales Representatives *See* Directory: Fashion Accessories Sales Representatives

★364★
DIRECTORY OF ALTERNATIVE DELIVERY SYSTEMS
Circulation Systems, Inc.
Box 41
Agawam, MA 01001
Covers: Companies involved in the hand delivery of shopping guides, circulars, samples, magazines, etc., including hand delivery companies and brokers, hand delivered publications, circulation suppliers, and shopping guides and community newspapers offering total coverage. **Entries include:** Delivery company listings include company name, address, phone, year established, method of delivery, names of personnel, days required for delivery, whether service is audited, area served and possible circulation, major accounts, delivery rates, special services, payment terms, commissions, representatives. Publication listings include foregoing, as applicable, and deadlines, availability of color, mechanical requirements, etc. **Arrangement:** Classified by type of service. **Frequency:** Annual, first quarter of year. **Advertising accepted.** **Price:** $12.00, postpaid. (Not verified)

★365★
DIRECTORY OF AMERICAN BUSINESS IN AUSTRIA
American Chamber of Commerce in Austria
Turkenstrasse 9
Vienna, Austria A-1090
Covers: 1,400 American companies doing business in or with Austria; subsidiaries, affiliates, representatives, agents, and distributors located in Austria are listed for each company; members of the American Chamber of Commerce in Austria are also listed. **Entries include:** Company name, address. **Arrangement:** Alphabetical. **Pages** (approx.): 300. **Frequency:** Irregular; latest edition 1977; new edition expected 1979-80. **Editor:** Ursula Kreyl, Chief Editor. **Advertising accepted.** Circulation 1,500. **Price:** AS 250.

★366★
DIRECTORY OF AMERICAN FIRMS IMPORTING FROM THE PEOPLE'S REPUBLIC OF CHINA
National Council for US-China Trade
1050 17th Street, N. W., Room 350
Washington, DC 20036
Number of listings: More than 800. **Entries include:** Company name, address, products handled. **Arrangement:** Alphabetical. **Indexes:** Product. **Pages** (approx.): 30. **Frequency:** Not established; first edition fall 1977. **Price:** $35.00.

★367★
DIRECTORY OF ARIZONA MANUFACTURERS
Phoenix Metropolitan Chamber of Commerce
Chamber of Commerce Center
34 W. Monroe, Suite 900   Phone: (602) 254-5521
Phoenix, AZ 85003
Covers: More than 2,000 manufacturers or manufacturer/distributors whose activity is at least 50% manufacturing; also includes 110 industrial parks. **Entries include:** For manufacturers - Company name, address, phone, names of executives, number of employees, products, SIC numbers, type of ownership, market area. For industrial parks - Name, address, phone, acreage or square feet, name of agent. **Arrangement:** Alphabetical. **Indexes:** Product, geographical. **Pages** (approx.): 150. **Frequency:** Annual, January. **Former title:** Directory

of Manufacturers in the Metropolitan Phoenix Area (1973). **Price:** $20.00, plus $2.50 shipping. **Other information:** State Industrial Directories Corp. and Manufacturers' News catalogs list this publication as, "Arizona Directory of Manufacturers."

Directory of Arkansas Industries *See* Directory of Manufacturers in Arkansas

Directory of Black Businesses [St. Petersburg, Florida] *See* Minority Business Directory, St. Petersburg, Florida

★368★
DIRECTORY OF BLACK FASHION SPECIALISTS
Harlem Institute of Fashion
157 W. 126th Street   Phone: (212) 666-1320
New York, NY 10027
Covers: Designers, dressmakers, tailors, milliners, fashion commentators and coordinators, and others engaged in the fashion business. **Entries include:** Company name, address, phone, name of principal executive. **Arrangement:** Classified. **Indexes:** Alphabetical, company, occupation. **Frequency:** Irregular; latest edition 1970; new edition expected 1980. **Editor:** Lois K. Alexander. **Price:** Free; restricted circulation. **Other information:** Published in cooperation with the National Association of Milliners, Dressmakers, and Tailors.

★369★
DIRECTORY OF BUSINESS AND FINANCIAL SERVICES
Special Libraries Association
235 Park Avenue South   Phone: (212) 777-8136
New York, NY 10003
Covers: 1,000 publications of about 420 publishers of business and financial information services in the United States (817), Canada (81), England (63), and other countries. **Entries include:** Name and type of service, frequency, and description of coverage. **Arrangement:** Alphabetical. **Indexes:** Publisher, subject. **Pages** (approx.): 230. **Frequency:** Irregular; latest edition 1976. **Editors:** Mary McNierney Grant and Norma Cote. **Price:** $18.80. **Also includes:** An appendix of stock exchanges in many countries.

★370★
DIRECTORY OF BUSINESS AND ORGANIZATIONAL COMMUNICATORS
International Association of Business Communicators
870 Market Street, Suite 928   Phone: (415) 433-3400
San Francisco, CA 94102
Covers: About 7,000 members of the association in public, corporate, employee, and alumni relations, and in other communications fields. **Entries include:** Name, address, title, code indicating type of business or organization, phone. **Arrangement:** Alphabetical. **Indexes:** Geographical, type of business. **Pages** (approx.): 175. **Frequency:** Annual, spring. **Price:** $30.00 (current and 1980 editions).

★371★
DIRECTORY OF BUSINESS WRITERS
Associated Business Writers of America
1450 S. Havana, Suite 620   Phone: (303) 751-7844
Aurora, CO 80012
Covers: About 100 member professional business and industrial writers. **Entries include:** Name, address, phone, area covered, subject specialization. **Arrangement:** Alphabetical. **Indexes:** Geographical, classification by specialty. **Pages** (approx.): 40. **Frequency:** Annual, February; semiannual updates. **Editor:** Donald E. Bower, Director. **Advertising accepted.** Circulation 500. **Price:** $10.00.

Directory of Candy Brokers *See* Candy Buyers' Directory

★372★
DIRECTORY OF CAREER TRAINING AND DEVELOPMENT PROGRAMS
Ready Reference Press
Box 4288
Thousand Oaks, CA 91359
Covers: Management training programs, executive training programs, summer training programs, professional development programs, field sales training programs, and other training and development programs offered by business, government, and professional organizations. **Entries include:** Organization name, program title, purpose, number of persons selected, type of training, qualifications, location of training, selection process, length of training, name and address of contact. **Arrangement:** Alphabetical. **Indexes:** Subject, geographical. **Pages** (approx.): 400. **Frequency:** Not established; first edition 1979. **Price:** $37.50.

Directory of Central and South Atlantic States Manufacturers *See* Directory of Central Atlantic States Manufacturers

★373★
DIRECTORY OF CENTRAL ATLANTIC STATES MANUFACTURERS
Seaboard Publishing Company, Inc.
714 E. Pratt Street   Phone: (301) 539-5774
Baltimore, MD 21202
Covers: About 27,000 companies in Maryland, Delaware, Virginia, West Virginia, North Carolina, and South Carolina. Includes variety of nonmanufacturers such as newspapers, computer programming services, etc. **Entries include:** Company name, address, phone, name of principal executive, number of employees, list of products or services, SIC numbers. **Arrangement:** Geographical. **Indexes:** Product. **Pages** (approx.): 525. **Frequency:** Biennial, January of even years. **Editor:** David B. Baker, Jr. **Former title:** Directory of Central and South Atlantic States Manufacturers. **Price:** $60.00 (current edition); $50.00 (1980 edition). **Other information:** Variant title, "Central Atlantic States Manufacturers Directory."

★374★
DIRECTORY OF CHAMBERS OF COMMERCE IN ILLINOIS
Illinois State Chamber of Commerce
20 N. Wacker Drive   Phone: (312) 372-7373
Chicago, IL 60606
Covers: 300 local chambers of commerce. Includes list of state and national chambers and associations related to chambers of commerce. **Entries include:** Chamber name, address, phone, staff accreditation status. **Arrangement:** Geographical. **Pages** (approx.): 30. **Frequency:** Annual, January. **Editor:** Patrick Glynn, Executive Director, Center for Business Management. **Price:** $3.00 (current and 1980 editions).

★375★
DIRECTORY OF CHEMICAL PRODUCERS U.S.A.
SRI International
333 Ravenswood Avenue   Phone: (415) 326-6200
Menlo Park, CA 94025
Covers: Over 1,300 United States chemical producers, over 10,000 chemicals produced in the United States in commercial quantities at 4,200 plant locations. **Entries include:** For companies - Company name, division or subsidiary names, corporate address, phone, telex, location of each subsidiary, division, and manufacturing plant, and all products made at each plant location. For products - Producers' names and plant locations, alternate product names (if any), and plant-by-plant capacities for over 245 major chemicals. **Arrangement:** Companies alphabetical by parent company, products alphabetical and by group (dyes, pesticides, etc.), plants geographical. **Pages** (approx.): 1,100 in annual bound volume, plus cumulative supplements. **Frequency:** Bound volume annually in April; supplements in May and October. **Editor:** Elaine M. Klapproth, Manager. **Former title:** Western Chemical Producers. **Price:** $450.00 for first year subscription, lower rates for renewals. **Other information:** Subscription price includes both bound volume and supplements, plus access to the directory's staff for consultation and inquiries.

★376★
DIRECTORY OF COLLEGE RECRUITING PERSONNEL
College Placement Council
65 E. Elizabeth Avenue   Phone: (215) 868-1421
Bethlehem, PA 18018
Covers: Companies with staff assigned to maintaining relations with college placement offices and to visiting campuses to recruit new employees; about 1,400 listings. **Entries include:** Company name, nature of business, number of employees, names of recruiting personnel, their office addresses and phones; names of secondary contacts. **Arrangement:** Alphabetical. **Indexes:** Personal name. **Pages** (approx.): 240. **Frequency:** Annual, January. **Editor:** Joan Bowser. **Price:** $8.00, postpaid (current and 1980 editions).

★377★
DIRECTORY OF COLLEGES AND UNIVERSITIES WITH SPECIALIZATIONS IN DISTRIBUTIVE TEACHER EDUCATION
Council for Distributive Teacher Education
C/o Dr. Leroy M. Buckner
Florida Atlantic University   Phone: (305) 395-5100
Boca Raton, FL 33431
Number of listings: 110. **Entries include:** Institution name, address, phone, names of faculty, description of program including courses, degrees offered, etc. **Arrangement:** Alphabetical. **Indexes:** Geographical. **Pages** (approx.): 120. **Frequency:** Triennial; latest edition 1979; new edition expected July 1982. **Editor:** Dr. Leroy M. Buckner. **Price:** $10.00.

★378★
DIRECTORY OF COLORADO MANUFACTURERS
Business Research Division
College of Business
University of Colorado
Campus Box 420   Phone: (303) 492-8227
Boulder, CO 80309
Entries include: In geographical section - Company name, mailing address, plant address, phone; Standard Metropolitan Statistical Area in which located; names and titles of up to two executives; date founded; distribution area; approximate employment; list of products. In product section - Company name, address, phone; approximate employment; area of distribution, major products. In alphabetical section - Company name, city and county in which located; SIC product codes. **Pages** (approx.): 290. **Frequency:** Every 18 months; latest edition April 1979; new edition expected July 1980. **Editor:** Gerald L. Allen, Research Economist. **Price:** $25.00 (current edition); $30.00 (1980 edition).

★379★
DIRECTORY OF COMMERCE & INDUSTRY—NASSAU AND SUFFOLK COUNTIES [New York]
Long Island Association of Commerce and Industry
425 Broad Hollow Road, Suite 205   Phone: (516) 752-9600
Melville, NY 11747
Number of listings: 5,200. **Entries include:** Company name, address, phone, names of principal executives, product description, plant size and property size, number of employees, whether firm imports or exports. **Arrangement:** By product. **Indexes:** Alphabetical, geographical. **Pages** (approx.): 375. **Frequency:** Biennial; latest edition summer 1979. **Price:** $49.15, postpaid. **Other information:** Variant title, "Long Island Directory of Commerce and Industry."

★380★
DIRECTORY OF CONSTRUCTION ASSOCIATIONS
Professional Publications, Division
Metadata, Inc.
441 Lexington Avenue   Phone: (212) 687-3836
New York, NY 10017
Covers: About 3,000 local, regional, and national professional societies, technical associations, trade groups, manufacturer bureaus, government agencies, labor unions, and other construction information sources; includes Canada. **Entries include:** Organization name, address, phone, contact. **Pages** (approx.): 300. **Frequency:** Annual, summer; periodical supplements. **Price:** $17.50.

★381★
DIRECTORY OF CONSULTANTS [Utility and transportation industries]
National Association of Regulatory Utility Commissioners
Box 684
Washington, DC 20044
Covers: About 120 consultants and consulting firms active in utility and transportation industries. **Entries include:** Firm or individual name, address, and phone; names of regulatory agencies by which engaged in the past and the purpose and dates of the engagements; areas of specialization; qualifications and experience. **Arrangement:** Alphabetical. **Pages** (approx.): 95. **Frequency:** Annual, September-October. **Price:** $6.00, postpaid, payment with order.

★382★
DIRECTORY OF CONTRACT PACKAGERS AND THEIR FACILITIES
The Packaging Institute, USA
342 Madison Avenue   Phone: (212) 687-8875
New York, NY 10017
Covers: 350 contract packagers in the United States and abroad. **Entries include:** Firm name, address, type of products handled, physical properties and types of packaging forms produced. **Arrangement:** Geographical. **Pages** (approx.): 200. **Frequency:** Irregular; latest edition 1977; new edition expected 1980. **Price:** $17.50.

★383★
DIRECTORY OF CONVENTIONS
Bill Communications, Inc.
1422 Chestnut Street   Phone: (215) 563-0680
Philadelphia, PA 19102
Covers: Over 18,000 meetings of North American national, regional, and state and local organizations. **Entries include:** Name of organization; title and address of executive in charge of event; dates; site; expected attendance; scope of event - whether international, national, regional, state, or district; whether exhibits are included. **Arrangement:** Geographical by meeting location, then chronological. **Indexes:** By organization name. **Pages** (approx.): 360, annual issue; 170, supplement. **Frequency:** Annual, January; supplement, July. **Price:** $55.00, including supplement. **Send orders to:** Directory of Conventions, 633 Third Ave., New York, NY 10017 (212-986-4800).

★384★
DIRECTORY OF CORPORATE AFFILIATIONS
National Register Publishing Company, Inc., Subsidiary
Standard Rate & Data Service, Inc.
5201 Old Orchard Road   Phone: (312) 966-8500
Skokie, IL 60077
Covers: 3,750 United States parent companies and about 46,000 domestic and foreign divisions, subsidiaries, and/or affiliates. **Entries include:** For parent companies - Company name, address, phone, stock exchange symbol and exchange, state in which incorporated and date, annual sales, number of employees, principal industry in which active, and names and titles of principal officers, name and address of corporate counsel. For subsidiaries - Company name, address, phone, state in which incorporated, annual sales, number of employees, principal industry, and name of chief executive officer. **Arrangement:** Alphabetical. **Indexes:** Subsidiaries; geographical index in separate booklet. **Pages** (approx.): 1,400. **Frequency:** Annual, January; five updating bulletins. **Editor:** Bob Weicherding. **Advertising accepted.** Circulation 10,000. **Price:** $117.00, plus $6.00 shipping (current and 1980 editions).

★385★
DIRECTORY OF CUSTOM PLASTICS PROCESSORS
Organization of Plastics Processors
53 Church Street   Phone: (202) 535-3869
Stonington, CT 06378
Number of listings: 550. **Entries include:** Company name, address, and phone. **Arrangement:** Classified by processing method, then geographical. **Indexes:** Company name. **Pages** (approx.): 35. **Frequency:** First edition 1978. **Advertising accepted.** **Price:** $10.00.

Directory of Defense Electronic Products: U.S. Manufacturers
See Directory of Defense Electronic Products and Services: United...

★386★
DIRECTORY OF DEFENSE ELECTRONIC PRODUCTS AND SERVICES: UNITED STATES SUPPLIERS
Information Clearing House, Inc.
500 Fifth Avenue   Phone: (212) 354-2424
New York, NY 10036
Covers: Manufacturers of telecommunicatons, command and control, and other systems; fire control, navigation, test, airborne, and meteorological equipment and instruments; transponders; cameras; data displays, etc. **Entries include:** Company name, address, phone, trade and brand names, products and systems. **Arrangement:** Alphabetical. **Indexes:** Product. **Pages** (approx.): 180. **Frequency:** Annual, January. **Advertising accepted.** Circulation 4,000. **Former title:** Directory of Defense Electronic Products: U. S. Manufacturers. **Price:** $30.00 (current and 1980 editions). **Other information:** Published for the Electronic Industries Association.

Directory of Delicatessen Products [California] *See* Deli News— Deli Products Directory Issue [California]

Directory of Diesel Fuel Stations Coast to Coast *See* Diesel Fuel Guide

★387★
DIRECTORY OF DIRECTORS IN THE CITY OF BOSTON AND VICINITY [Massachusetts]
Bankers Service Company
14 Beacon Street   Phone: (617) 742-5786
Boston, MA 02108
Covers: Executives, directors, and trustees of corporations and institutions located in the Boston area; corporations and institutions; accountants and auditors; architects and engineers; lawyers; insurance agencies; real estate companies; banks and trust companies; and New York and Boston Stock Exchange members with offices in the Boston area. **Entries include:** For individuals - Name, address, title, and companies with which affiliated. For companies and corporations - Name, address, names and titles of president, vice presidents, and directors. **Arrangement:** By profession or type of company. **Pages** (approx.): 1,100. **Frequency:** Annual, June. **Advertising accepted.** **Price:** $160.00.

★388★
DIRECTORY OF DIRECTORS IN THE CITY OF NEW YORK
Directory of Directors Company, Inc.
Box 462   Phone: (212) 924-6705
Southport, CT 06490
Covers: About 15,000 directors, officers, trustees, and partners of about 4,000 corporations and firms located within 75 miles of New York City or which have two or more directors living in this area. **Entries include:** Individual name, address (residence address if permitted by individual), and companies with which individual is affilated. **Arrangement:** Alphabetical by individual name. **Pages** (approx.): 825. **Frequency:** Annual, spring. **Editor:** J. Joseph. **Advertising accepted.** **Price:** $100.00.

★389★
DIRECTORY OF ELECTRICAL WHOLESALE DISTRIBUTORS AND MARKET PLANNING GUIDE
McGraw-Hill, Inc.
1221 Avenue of the Americas   Phone: (212) 997-2378
New York, NY 10020
Covers: About 5,000 electrical wholesalers; separate list of manufacturers of electrical products. **Entries include:** For wholesalers - Company name, address, phone, names of key personnel, locations of branches and affiliates, number of employees, number of sales personnel, geographic area served, amount of floor space, dollar value of inventory, product lines, year established, and association memberships. For manufacturers - Company name, address, phone, products, selling practices, warehousing facilities, percentage of sales through distributors, training programs, advertising allowance, and other details. **Arrangement:** Wholesalers are geographical, manufacturers are alphabetical. **Pages** (approx.): 550. **Frequency:** Biennial, July of even years. **Editor:** George Ganzenmuller, Editor-in-Chief. **Former title:** Directory of Verified Electrical Wholesale Distributors (1976). **Price:** $210.00.

★390★
DIRECTORY OF EMPLOYEE ORGANIZATIONS IN NEW YORK STATE
Division of Research and Statistics
New York Labor Department
Two World Trade Center   Phone: (212) 488-4806
New York, NY 10047
Covers: Principal officers of 5,300 local, state, and national or international employee organizations representing workers in New York State. **Entries include:** Name of organization, principal officer, address. **Arrangement:** Separate sections for international, national, and statewide organizations; area councils and federations; and local organizations in the private sector and in the public sector; some councils and local organizations are arranged by trade. **Indexes:** Officers, local labor organizations. **Pages** (approx.): 280. **Frequency:** Irregular; about every three or four years; new edition expected 1980. **Editor:** Nicholas Neufeld. **Former title:** Directory of Labor Organizations in New York State (1971). **Price:** $5.00. **Send orders to:** Office of Public Information, NYS Department of Labor, Building 12, State Campus, Albany, NY 12240 (518-457-6330).

★391★
DIRECTORY OF EXECUTIVE RECRUITERS
Kennedy & Kennedy, Inc.
Templeton Road   Phone: (603) 585-2200
Fitzwilliam, NH 03447
Covers: More than 1,800 executive search firms and certified public accounting firms which do executive recruiting; covers North America; firms operating on a contingent fee basis are listed in separate section. **Entries include:** Firm name, address, industry-functional specialty, salary minimum; members of the Association of Executive Recruiting Consultants are identified. **Arrangement:** Alphabetical. **Indexes:** Geographical, SIC, and management function. **Pages** (approx.): 190. **Frequency:** Irregular; new edition expected December 1980. **Editor:** James H. Kennedy. **Price:** $10.00, payment with order; $11.00, billed. **Other information:** Although not stated in promotion, publisher claims in book the right to forbid commercial mailing list use of directory, and sends bills for such use.

★392★
DIRECTORY OF EXPERTS ON ORGANIZATION AND MANAGEMENT OF CONSTRUCTION
Construction Engineering Research Laboratory
United States Army
Defense Department
Box 4005
Champaign, IL 61820
Covers: About 75 persons in 20 countries selected by the Working Commission on Organization and Management of Construction, International Council for Building Research Studies Documentation. **Entries include:** Name, address, professional experience, publications,

honors, interests. **Arrangement:** Alphabetical. **Pages** (approx.): 125. **Frequency:** Irregular; latest edition summer 1979.

★393★
DIRECTORY OF EXPOSITIONS AUDITED BY EA
Exposition Audit, Division
Business Publications Audit of Circulation, Inc.
360 Park Avenue South   Phone: (212) 532-6880
New York, NY 10010
Covers: About 100 currently active expositions, trade shows, major convention exhibits, etc., audited by Exposition Audit since 1973. **Entries include:** Name, date, and location of exposition, total registered attendance, total square footage, number of exhibitors, and name and address of current show manager. **Arrangement:** Alphabetical by name of exposition. **Pages** (approx.): 10. **Frequency:** Annual, February. **Editor:** Michael J. Moonitz, Manager. **Price:** Free.

★394★
DIRECTORY OF FEE-BASED INFORMATION SERVICES
Information Alternative
Box 657   Phone: (914) 679-2549
Woodstock, NY 12498
Covers: Over 200 information brokers, free-lance librarians, independent information specialists, public and institutional libraries, and others who provide information for a fee. **Entries include:** Company library, or individual name, address, phone, hours, rates, fairly detailed description of services, specialties, etc. **Arrangement:** Geographical. **Indexes:** Name. **Pages** (approx.): 75. **Frequency:** Annual, spring; bimonthly supplements in "Journal of Fee-based Information Services." **Editor:** Kelly Warnken. **Price:** $5.00 (current and 1980 editions).

★395★
DIRECTORY OF FIRMS EMPLOYING 100 OR MORE [Greensboro, North Carolina]
Greensboro Chamber of Commerce
Box 3246   Phone: (919) 275-8675
Greensboro, NC 27402
Number of listings: 155. **Entries include:** Firm name, address, name of chief executive, year established in Greensboro, line of business, and number of employees. **Arrangement:** Alphabetical. **Frequency:** Irregular; latest edition November 1978; new edition expected 1980. **Price:** $2.50.

★396★
DIRECTORY OF FLORIDA INDUSTRIES
Florida Chamber of Commerce
Box 5497   Phone: (904) 222-2831
Tallahassee, FL 32301
Covers: About 10,000 manufacturing, mining, and processing concerns. **Entries include:** Company name, address, phone, names of principal executives, number of employees, list of products or services, SIC numbers, whether firm imports or exports. **Arrangement:** By county and by SIC number; identical information in each arrangement. **Indexes:** Alphabetical. **Pages** (approx.): 750. **Frequency:** Annual, fall. **Advertising accepted. Price:** $37.00, plus $1.50 shipping, payment with order.

★397★
DIRECTORY OF FOREIGN FIRMS OPERATING IN THE UNITED STATES
World Trade Academy Press, Inc.
50 E. 42nd Street   Phone: (212) 697-4999
New York, NY 10017
Entries include: Company name, American office address and phone, description of product or services. **Arrangement:** Alphabetical. **Pages** (approx.): 750. **Frequency:** Irregular; latest edition 1978. **Price:** $85.00.

Directory of Foreign Investment *See* Probe Directory of Foreign Direct Investment in the United States

★398★
DIRECTORY OF FOREIGN MANUFACTURERS IN THE UNITED STATES
Publishing Services Division
College of Business Administration
Georgia State University
University Plaza   Phone: (404) 658-4253
Atlanta, GA 30303
Covers: 3,400 United States companies involved with chemicals, machinery, electrical and electronic equipment, food, fabricated metals, primary metals, instruments, textiles, rubber and plastic products, printing and publishing, and transportation equipment (SIC 28, 35, 36, 20, 34, 33, 38, 22, 30, 27, 37), and the 1,800 firms abroad which own them. **Entries include:** Company name, address, list of products, SIC numbers, parent company name and address. **Arrangement:** Alphabetical by company name. **Indexes:** Parent company (alphabetically), parent company (geographically), subsidiary (geographically), products by SIC number. **Pages** (approx.): 300. **Frequency:** Irregular; latest edition 1979; new edition expected 1982-83. **Editors:** Jeffrey S. Arpan, David A. Ricks. **Price:** $29.95, postpaid, payment must accompany orders from individuals.

★399★
DIRECTORY OF FRANCHISING ORGANIZATIONS
Pilot Books
347 Fifth Avenue   Phone: (212) 685-0736
New York, NY 10016
Covers: Over 600 companies in 40 consumer and service fields which offer franchises. **Entries include:** Company name, address, investment required, product or service covered by franchise, etc. **Arrangement:** Classified by product or service. **Frequency:** Annual, January. **Editor:** Samuel Small. **Price:** $3.50 (current and 1980 editions).

★400★
DIRECTORY OF GOVERNMENT PRODUCTION PRIME CONTRACTORS
Government Data Publications
1661 McDonald Avenue   Phone: (212) 627-0819
Brooklyn, NY 11230
Covers: Organizations which received government production prime contracts during the past fiscal year. **Entries include:** Contractor's name and address. **Arrangement:** First section alphabetical by firm name; second section by Zip code. **Frequency:** Annual, November. **Editor:** Siegfried Lobel. **Price:** $15.00. **Send orders to:** Government Data Publications, 422 Washington Bldg., Washington, DC 20005.

★401★
DIRECTORY OF HELICOPTER OPERATORS IN THE UNITED STATES, CANADA, AND PUERTO RICO
Aerospace Industries Association
1725 DeSales Street, N. W.   Phone: (202) 347-2315
Washington, DC 20036
Covers: More than 3,000 operators with total of 8,000 craft; separate lists for commercial, company and executive, and governmental operators; includes list of helicopter flight schools. **Entries include:** For operators - Name, address, phone; some entries include name of one executive, number and type of helicopters operated, types of flight services provided (agriculture, construction, external load, etc.). For flight schools - Name, address, phone, name of owner. **Arrangement:** Geographical. **Pages** (approx.): 210. **Frequency:** Biennial, even years. **Price:** Free.

★402★

DIRECTORY OF HELIPORTS IN THE UNITED STATES, CANADA, AND PUERTO RICO
Aerospace Industries Association
1725 DeSales Street, N. W.   Phone: (202) 347-2315
Washington, DC 20036
Covers: More than 3,300 public, private, and hospital heliports; does not include oil production platform sites or Forest Service landing areas. **Entries include:** Name of heliport, location and/or street address, phone, size of landing area, services available, ownership, whether private or public or reserved for special use, whether ground level or roof top. **Arrangement:** Geographical. **Indexes:** Hospital heliports. **Pages** (approx.): 300. **Frequency:** Biennial, even years. **Price:** Free.

★403★

DIRECTORY OF HIGH-DISCOUNT MERCHANDISE AND PRODUCT SOURCES FOR DISTRIBUTORS AND MAIL-ORDER WEALTH BUILDERS
International Wealth Success, Inc.
24 Canterbury Road
Rockville Centre, NY 11570
Covers: Over 1,000 suppliers of high-discount merchandise such as yo-yos, stuffed toys, oils and lubricants, CB radios, belt buckles, etc. **Entries include:** Company name, address; most listings also include phone, and name of contact. **Arrangement:** By product. **Pages** (approx.): 100. **Frequency:** Semiannual, January and July. **Price:** $17.50, payment with order.

★404★

DIRECTORY OF HOTEL & MOTEL SYSTEMS
American Hotel Association Directory Corporation
888 Seventh Avenue   Phone: (212) 265-4506
New York, NY 10019
Covers: Approximately 300 hotel, motel, and resort chain organizations owning or operating three or more hotels, including some foreign chains. A list of referral organizations is also included. **Entries include:** Company name, address, phone, names of executives, properties owned and their locations and numbers of rooms. **Arrangement:** Alphabetical. **Pages** (approx.): 220. **Frequency:** Annual, July. **Editor:** Rose Vinckus. **Price:** $15.00.

★405★

DIRECTORY OF HOTEL AND RESTAURANT MANAGEMENT PROGRAMS
Holiday Inn University
1150 E. Goodman Road   Phone: (601) 895-2941
Olive Branch, MS 38654
Covers: Schools and colleges offering training courses in hotel and restaurant management; a separate list of international schools is available. **Entries include:** Name of school, address, degrees, certificates or diplomas offered, and requirements for admission. **Arrangement:** Geographical. **Pages** (approx.): 70. **Frequency:** Irregular; latest edition 1978. **Price:** $8.00 for United States edition; $10.00 for international edition.

★406★

DIRECTORY OF IMPORTERS AND EXPORTERS [St. Louis, Missouri]
St. Louis Regional Commerce and Growth Association
10 Broadway   Phone: (314) 231-5555
St. Louis, MO 63102
Number of listings: More than 400. **Entries include:** Company name, address, and merchandise or commodities imported or exported. **Arrangement:** Alphabetical. **Indexes:** Product. **Pages** (approx.): 115. **Frequency:** Annual, spring. **Price:** $7.00.

★407★

DIRECTORY OF INCENTIVE TRAVEL INTERNATIONAL
Incentive Group Marketing, Inc.
5535 Balboa Boulevard, Suite 101   Phone: (213) 990-9810
Encino, CA 91316
Covers: Hotels, resorts, cruise lines, airlines, ground tour operators, incentive travel houses, group travel operators, tour wholesalers. **Entries include:** Company name, address, phone, names of executives, list of products or services. **Arrangement:** Geographical. **Pages** (approx.): 400. **Frequency:** Semiannual, spring and fall. **Editor:** J. Robert Skalnik, Executive Editor. **Advertising accepted.** Circulation 37,200. **Price:** $7.50.

★408★

DIRECTORY OF INDIAN BUSINESS ENTERPRISES—MUSKOGEE AREA [Oklahoma]
Muskogee Area Office
Bureau of Indian Affairs
Interior Department
Muskogee, OK 74401
Covers: About 350 businesses owned by American Indians in Oklahoma which provide commercial, industrial, and consumer services and products. **Entries include:** Company name, address, phone, line of business, and name of contact. **Arrangement:** By agency. **Frequency:** Irregular; latest edition November 1978. **Former title:** Minority Business Directory. **Price:** Free.

★409★

DIRECTORY OF INDUSTRIAL DEVELOPMENT ORGANIZATIONS [ILLINOIS]
Illinois Department of Business and Economic Development
222 S. College Street   Phone: (217) 782-6861
Springfield, IL 62706
Covers: In addition to local organizations, also lists railroads, utilities, banks, regional organizations. **Entries include:** Organization or company name, address, phone, contact person. **Pages** (approx.): 50. **Frequency:** Annual, summer. **Editor:** Sandra Main, Administrative Assistant. **Price:** Free.

★410★

DIRECTORY OF INDUSTRIAL DISTRIBUTORS
Morgan-Grampian Publishing Company
Two Park Avenue   Phone: (212) 340-9700
New York, NY 10016
Number of listings: 9,000. **Entries include:** Company name, address, phone, names of principal executives, financial keys, type of products carried. **Arrangement:** Geographical. **Indexes:** Company name, product. **Pages** (approx.): 650. **Frequency:** Triennial; new edition expected 1981. **Editor:** George J. Berkwilt. **Price:** $275.00.

★411★

DIRECTORY OF INDUSTRIAL HEAT PROCESSING AND COMBUSTION EQUIPMENT
Industrial Heating Equipment Association
1901 N. Moore Street   Phone: (703) 525-2513
Arlington, VA 22209
Covers: About 100 manufacturers of industrial furnaces, industrial ovens, combustion equipment, induction and dielectric heating equipment, and other industrial heating devices. Includes advertisers only, but not limited to association members. **Entries include:** Manufacturer name, address, product picture, applications, technical specifications. **Pages** (approx.): 135. **Frequency:** Biennial, January of odd years. **Advertising accepted.** **Price:** $20.00. **Send orders to:** Book Publishing Division, Information Clearing House, Inc., 500 Fifth Avenue, New York, NY, 10036 (212-354-2424).

★412★

DIRECTORY OF INDUSTRIES—TAMPA/HILLSBOROUGH COUNTY [Florida]

Greater Tampa Chamber of Commerce
801 E. J. F. Kennedy Boulevard   Phone: (813) 228-7777
Tampa, FL 33601

Number of listings: 750. Also includes list of distributors and suppliers of building materials and industrial products. **Entries include:** For manufacturers - Company name, address, phone, name of principal executive, SIC numbers and product descriptions, number of employees, whether firm exports or imports. For distributors - Company name and address. **Arrangement:** Manufacturers arranged alphabetically and by product; identical information in each section; distributors classified by product. **Frequency:** Irregular; previous edition 1978; latest edition fall 1979. **Price:** $5.00.

Directory of Industry and Corporations [Stamford, Connecticut]
    See Directory of Manufacturing Industries and Corporations...

★413★

DIRECTORY OF IOWA MANUFACTURERS

Iowa Development Commission
250 Jewett Building   Phone: (515) 281-3925
Des Moines, IA 50309

Covers: About 3,900 Iowa manufacturers and hybrid seed corn processors. **Entries include:** Company name, address, phone, names of principal executives, number of employees, products or services, parent company (if applicable). **Arrangement:** Alphabetical, geographical, SIC number; similar information in each part. **Indexes:** Product. **Pages** (approx.): 575. **Frequency:** Biennial, June of odd years. **Price:** $12.00, postpaid, payment with order. **Other information:** Manufacturers' News catalog lists this publication as, "Iowa Manufacturers Directory" ($26.00).

★414★

DIRECTORY OF IRON AND STEEL WORKS OF THE UNITED STATES AND CANADA

American Iron and Steel Institute
1000 16th Street, N. W.   Phone: (202) 452-7100
Washington, DC 20036

Number of listings: 200. **Entries include:** Company, address, names of executives, financial keys, capacity, equipment, list of products. **Arrangement:** Alphabetical. **Pages** (approx.): 400. **Frequency:** Irregular; previous edition 1977; new edition expected 1980. **Editor:** Robert Platt, Director of Statistics. **Price:** $15.00 (both 1977 and 1980 editions). **Other information:** Not to be confused with "Directory Iron and Steel Plants" published by the Association of Iron and Steel Engineers.

★415★

DIRECTORY OF ISRAEL PRODUCTS AND SERVICES IN THE U.S.

Government of Israel Trade Center
350 Fifth Avenue   Phone: (212) 560-0660
New York, NY 10001

Covers: Over 600 firms which import from Israel, and Israeli firms such as banks, shipping companies, travel agencies, and others which have offices in the United States. **Entries include:** Company name, address, phone, and products or services. **Arrangement:** Geographical. **Indexes:** Product or trade. **Pages** (approx.): 90. **Frequency:** First edition 1978. **Price:** Free.

★416★

DIRECTORY OF JAPANESE FIRMS, OFFICES, AND SUBSIDIARIES IN NEW YORK, NEW JERSEY, AND CONNECTICUT

Japan External Trade Organization
Japan Trade Center
1221 Avenue of the Americas   Phone: (212) 997-0400
New York, NY 10020

Entries include: Name, address, phone, name of the parent company and location of the headquarters in Japan, and type of business. **Indexes:** Product. **Frequency:** Annual, summer. **Price:** Free. **Other**

information: Not to be confused with "Japanese Firms, Offices, and the Other Organizations in the United States."

★417★

DIRECTORY OF KANSAS MANUFACTURERS AND PRODUCTS

Kansas Department of Economic Development
503 Kansas Avenue, 6th Floor   Phone: (913) 296-3481
Topeka, KS 66603

Covers: About 4,400 firms, principally manufacturers but including poultry, crop preparation, crushed and broken stone and limestone, sand and gravel, radio, television, blueprinting, and motion pictures SIC classifications. **Entries include:** Company name, address, phone, name of principal executive, list of products, whether firm exports. **Arrangement:** Alphabetical, geographical, SIC number; identical information in all three sections. **Pages** (approx.): 325. **Frequency:** Annual, summer. **Editor:** Norman L. Allen. **Price:** $15.00.

★418★

DIRECTORY OF KANSAS MANUFACTURING FIRMS IN EXPORT

Kansas Department of Economic Development
503 Kansas Avenue, 6th Floor   Phone: (913) 296-3481
Topeka, KS 66603

Entries include: Company name, address, phone, name of principal executive, number of employees, list of products or services, SIC numbers. **Arrangement:** Classified by SIC group. **Pages** (approx.): 30. **Frequency:** Biennial, summer of odd years. **Editor:** Norman L. Allen. **Price:** $5.00. **Other information:** Variant title, "Kansas Manufacturers and Products in Export."

★419★

DIRECTORY OF KANSAS MINORITY BUSINESSES

Minority Business Division
Kansas Department of Economic Development
503 Kansas, 6th Floor   Phone: (913) 296-3481
Topeka, KS 66603

Covers: About 115 minority businesses and 45 organizations which assist minority enterprises in Kansas. **Entries include:** For businesses - Name, address, phone, code to indicate type of ownership, name of contact, number of employees, annual sales, whether firm is a government contractor, sales or service area, product or service, SIC number, date established. For others - Name, address, phone. **Arrangement:** Alphabetical. **Indexes:** Geographical, SIC number. **Pages** (approx.): 50. **Frequency:** Biennial, odd years. **Editor:** Enos Cooper, Director. **Price:** Free.

Directory of Labor Education *See* Directory of Workers Education

★420★

DIRECTORY OF LABOR ORGANIZATIONS [Massachusetts]

Division of Statistics
Massachusetts Department of Labor & Industries
100 Cambridge Street   Phone: (617) 727-3593
Boston, MA 02202

Covers: Over 250 national and international labor organizations; over 120 delegate labor organizations (composed of delegates from similar-trade locals or same-locality locals); and over 2,200 local unions in Massachusetts. **Entries include:** For national organizations - Name, address, name of corresponding officer, name of Massachusetts representative, if any. For delegate organizations - Name, address, names of officers, phone, meeting place and time. For local unions - Name and charter number, meeting place and time, names of two officers, address, phone. **Arrangement:** National and delegate organizations are alphabetical, local unions are geographical. **Pages** (approx.): 200. **Frequency:** Annual, July. **Price:** $1.20, plus 60¢ shipping. **Send orders to:** State Bookstore, State House, Room 116, Boston, MA 02133 (617-727-2834). **Also includes:** Number of local unions in an industry and membership statistics for current and previous two years.

Directory of Labor Organizations in New York State *See* Directory of Employee Organizations in New York State

★421★
DIRECTORY OF LABOR-MANAGEMENT COMMITTEES [Concerned with productivity]
National Center for Productivity and Quality of Working Life
C/o Productivity Information Center/NTIS
425 13th Street, N. W. Phone: (202) 724-3369
Washington, DC 20004
Covers: About 215 labor-management committees concerned with improvement in labor productivity and the quality of working life. **Entries include:** Names of management and labor groups involved in the committee; names, affiliations, addresses, and telephone numbers of individuals representing each group; date founded; number of employees affected; brief description of history and activities. **Arrangement:** Geographical. **Indexes:** Type of committee, unions, companies. **Pages** (approx.): 200. **Frequency:** Irregular; previous edition October 1976; latest edition spring 1978. **Price:** $4.00 (S/N 052-003-00522-1). **Send orders to:** Government Printing Office, Washington, DC 20402.

★422★
DIRECTORY OF LEAD CASTERS
Lead Industries Association
292 Madison Avenue Phone: (212) 578-4750
New York, NY 10017
Covers: About 60 manufacturers of cast lead products (other than battery grids). **Entries include:** Company name, address, contact, and descriptive information including type of casting method, products and auxiliary services offered. **Arrangement:** Geographical. **Pages** (approx.): 15. **Frequency:** Irregular; latest edition fall 1979. **Price:** Free.

Directory of LI Business Services *See* LI Business Review—Directory Issues

Directory of Louisiana Importers and Exporters *See* Louisiana International Trade Directory

Directory of Louisiana Manufacturers *See* Louisiana Directory of Manufacturers

★423★
DIRECTORY OF MAIL DROPS IN THE UNITED STATES AND CANADA
Loompanics Unlimited
Box 264
Mason, MI 48854
Covers: 800 services which will receive and forward mail, including about 40 abroad. **Entries include:** Service name and address. **Arrangement:** Geographical. **Pages** (approx.): 25. **Frequency:** Irregular; latest edition spring 1979. **Editor:** Michael Hoy. **Price:** $4.00.

★424★
DIRECTORY OF MAILING LIST HOUSES
B. Klein Publications, Inc.
Box 8503
Coral Springs, FL 33065
Covers: About 2,000 mailing list compilers, brokers, and managers. **Entries include:** Firm name, address, phone, year founded, name of principal executive, types of lists handled. **Arrangement:** Geographical. **Indexes:** Categories of lists handled. **Pages** (approx.): 240. **Frequency:** Irregular; latest edition December 1976. **Editor:** Bernard Klein. **Price:** $30.00.

★425★
DIRECTORY OF MANAGEMENT CONSULTANTS
Kennedy & Kennedy, Inc.
Templeton Road Phone: (603) 585-2200
Fitzwilliam, NH 03447
Covers: 550 management consulting firms. **Entries include:** Firm name, address, phone, name of principal executive, date founded, number of employees, annual volume, services offered, SIC numbers of industries served, plus brief description of firm. **Indexes:** Services, industries served, geographical. **Pages** (approx.): 250. **Frequency:** Biennial, spring of odd years. **Editor:** James H. Kennedy. **Price:** $37.50, payment with order. **Other information:** Although not stated in promotion, publisher claims in book the right to forbid commercial mailing list use of directory, and sends bills for such use.

★426★
DIRECTORY OF MANUFACTURERS AND PRODUCTS OF THE HANDWRITING AND MARKING INSTRUMENT MANUFACTURING INDUSTRY
Writing Instrument Manufacturers Association
1625 I Street, N. W. Phone: (202) 331-1429
Washington, DC 20006
Covers: About 75 member manufacturers. **Arrangement:** Alphabetical. **Frequency:** Biennial, January of odd years. **Advertising accepted.** Circulation 1,000. **Price:** $10.00.

★427★
DIRECTORY OF MANUFACTURERS, GREENSBORO, N. C.
Greensboro Chamber of Commerce
Box 3246 Phone: (919) 275-8675
Greensboro, NC 27402
Number of listings: 350. **Entries include:** Firm name, address, name of chief executive, year established, line of business, number of employees. **Arrangement:** Alphabetical. **Indexes:** Product/service. **Frequency:** Irregular; latest edition January 1978; new edition expected January 1980. **Price:** $2.50.

★428★
DIRECTORY OF MANUFACTURERS IN ARKANSAS
Arkansas Industrial Development Foundation
Box 1784 Phone: (501) 371-2302
Little Rock, AR 72203
Covers: About 2,200 firms. **Entries include:** Company name, address, phone, names of principal executives, number of employees, list of products or services, SIC numbers, whether company exports, name of parent company if firm is a subsidiary. **Arrangement:** Geographical. **Indexes:** Alphabetical, SIC. **Pages** (approx.): 275. **Frequency:** Annual, February. **Advertising accepted.** Circulation 3,500. **Former title:** Directory of Arkansas Industries. **Price:** $25.00. **Other information:** Manufacturers' News catalog formerly listed this publication as, "Arkansas Manufacturers Directory;" now cites it as, "Arkansas Directory of Industries."

Directory of Manufacturers in the Metro Phoenix Area [Arizona] *See* Directory of Arizona Manufacturers

★429★
DIRECTORY OF MANUFACTURERS OF STEEL BUILDING CONSTRUCTION PRODUCTS
American Iron and Steel Institute
1000 16th Street, N. W.
Washington, DC 20036
Covers: 400 manufacturers of steel building products in the United States and Canada. **Entries include:** Company name, address, phone. **Arrangement:** By product. **Pages** (approx.): 10. **Frequency:** Irregular; latest edition 1979. **Former title:** Manufacturers List Guide of Steel Building Construction Products. **Price:** Free.

★430★
DIRECTORY OF MANUFACTURERS, STATE OF HAWAII
Chamber of Commerce of Hawaii
735 Bishop Street   Phone: (808) 531-4111
Honolulu, HI 96813
Number of listings: 3,500. **Entries include:** Company name, address, phone, name of principal executive, number of employees, list of products or services, sales, date established. **Arrangement:** By SIC. **Indexes:** Product, geographical, brand and trade name. **Pages** (approx.): 100. **Frequency:** Biennial, October of odd years. **Price:** $15.00, plus $2.00 shipping. **Other information:** Cited in Manufacturers' News catalog as, "Hawaii Directory of Manufacturers."

★431★
**DIRECTORY OF MANUFACTURING INDUSTRIES AND
        CORPORATIONS [Stamford, Connecticut]**
Southwestern Area Commerce and Industry Association
One Landmark Square   Phone: (203) 359-3220
Stamford, CT 06901
Covers: 900 industrial firms and corporate headquarters in Stamford, Old Greenwich, Byram, Greenwich, Darien, New Canaan, Norwalk, Wilton, Weston, and Westport, Connecticut. **Entries include:** Company name, address, phone, names of key officers, nature of business. **Indexes:** Product. **Pages** (approx.): 130. **Frequency:** Biennial, fall of odd years. **Former title:** Directory of Industry and Corporations. **Price:** $10.00.

Directory of Marketing Service Organizations *See* American
    Marketing Association—Membership Roster

Directory of Marketing Services and Membership Roster *See*
    American Marketing Association—Membership Roster

★432★
DIRECTORY OF MARYLAND EXPORTERS-IMPORTERS
Business Directories Office
Maryland Department of Economic and Community Development
2525 Riva Road   Phone: (301) 269-2705
Annapolis, MD 21401
Number of listings: Over 920; includes list of service organizations. **Entries include:** Company name, address, phone number, telex and cable address, names and titles of principal executives, bank, number of employees, and products. **Arrangement:** Alphabetical. **Indexes:** Product. **Pages** (approx.): 140. **Frequency:** Triennial; latest edition September 1976. **Editor:** Fred E. Ziegenhorn. **Price:** $6.00, postpaid, payment with order.

★433★
DIRECTORY OF MARYLAND MANUFACTURERS
Business Directories Office
Maryland Department of Economic and Community Development
2525 Riva Road   Phone: (301) 269-2705
Annapolis, MD 21401
Number of listings: Over 3,100. **Entries include:** Company name, address, names of principal executives, phone, year established, whether firm exports or imports, research facilities available, products, SIC numbers, number of employees. **Arrangement:** Geographical, SIC; similar information in both sections. **Indexes:** Alphabetical, product. **Pages** (approx.): 500. **Frequency:** Biennial, odd years. **Editor:** Fred E. Ziegenhorn. **Price:** $18.00, postpaid, payment with order.

★434★
DIRECTORY OF MASSACHUSETTS MANUFACTURERS
George D. Hall Company
20 Kilby Street   Phone: (617) 523-3745
Boston, MA 02109
Entries include: Company name, address, phone, key executives, number of employees, list of products or services, SIC number, financial keys. **Arrangement:** Geographical. **Indexes:** Alphabetical,

product. **Frequency:** Annual, January. **Advertising accepted.** Circulation 3,000. **Price:** $39.00.

★435★
DIRECTORY OF MICHIGAN MANUFACTURERS
Pick Publications, Inc.
8543 Puritan Avenue   Phone: (313) 864-9388
Detroit, MI 48238
Covers: 15,000 manufacturers and 1,500 manufacturers' agents. **Entries include:** For manufacturers - Company name, address, phone, names of principal executives, number of employees, date established, branch plants, SIC numbers, product descriptions, parent company, and, for some companies, annual sales, plant square footage, whether firm imports or exports. For agents - Same information, as relevant, and products carried and area served. **Arrangement:** Geographical. **Indexes:** Alphabetical, SIC. **Pages** (approx.): 500. **Frequency:** Annual, March; biennial until 1976 edition. **Editor:** M. R. Pickell, **Advertising accepted. Price:** $80.00 (current and 1980 editions).

Directory of Mining and Manufacturing [New Mexico] *See*
    Directory of New Mexico Manufacturing and Mining

Directory of Minnesota Exporters *See* Minnesota International
    Trade Directory

★436★
**DIRECTORY OF MINORITY BUSINESS [Southeast and central
        Alabama]**
Business Development Center
Tuskegee Institute
440 Clay Street   Phone: (205) 263-0239
Montgomery, AL 36104
Covers: Minority-owned or -controlled business firms in 21 counties of central and southeast Alabama. **Entries include:** Company name, address, phone, SIC number. **Arrangement:** Geographical, line of business; same data in each list. **Pages** (approx.): 75. **Frequency:** Irregular; latest edition 1978; new edition expected March 1980. **Editor:** Gregg Jennings. **Price:** Free (current and 1980 editions).

★437★
**DIRECTORY OF MINORITY BUSINESS RESOURCES OF THE
        AMERICAN MARKETING ASSOCIATION**
Office of Minority Business Enterprise
Commerce Department   Phone: (202) 377-3024
Washington, DC 20230
Covers: American Marketing Association volunteers available to work with minority businessmen. **Entries include:** Volunteer's name, office address, career data, and areas of special competence. **Pages** (approx.): 100. **Frequency:** Irregular. **Editors:** David J. Barnaby and Gerald E. Hills (Marketing Professors). **Price:** Free.

★438★
**DIRECTORY OF MINORITY BUSINESSES IN FORSYTH AND
        GUILFORD COUNTIES, NORTH CAROLINA**
Northwest Piedmont Council of Governments
                                     Phone: (919) 722-9346
Winston-Salem, NC 27101
Covers: About 450 firms offering professional, commercial, industrial, and consumer services and products. **Entries include:** Company name, address, phone, name of contact, number of employees, annual sales range. **Arrangement:** Geographical, then by line of business. **Frequency:** Irregular; latest edition 1977.

Directory of Minority Businesses (Oregon) *See* Minority Vendors
    Directory of Oregon

Directory of Minority Businesses Serving the State of Maryland
    See Economic Opportunity in the Maryland Marketplace—
    Minority...

★439★

DIRECTORY OF MINORITY CONSTRUCTION CONTRACTORS AND SUBCONTRACTORS [Northern California]

San Francisco Redevelopment Agency
939 Ellis Street　　　　　　　　Phone: (415) 771-8800
San Francisco, CA 94109
Covers: Over 800 firms in northern California which offer products and services to the construction industry. **Entries include:** Company name, license number, address, phone, contact. **Arrangement:** Classified by product or trade. **Pages** (approx.): 90. **Frequency:** Irregular; previous edition November 1977; March 1978 supplement; latest edition December 1979. **Editor:** Benson Hattem. **Price:** $15.00.

★440★

DIRECTORY OF MINORITY CONTRACTORS WITH A MARITIME CAPABILITY

Maritime Administration
Commerce Department
Washington, DC 20230
Entries include: Name of contractor, address, phone, facilities or equipment, name of contact. **Pages** (approx.): 80. **Frequency:** Not established; first edition 1977. **Price:** Free.

★441★

DIRECTORY OF MINORITY TRUCKERS [Northern California]

San Francisco Redevelopment Agency
939 Ellis Street　　　　　　　　Phone: (415) 771-8800
San Francisco, CA 94109
Number of listings: 150. **Entries include:** Company name, address, PUC license number, phone, name of contact, list of equipment. **Arrangement:** Alphabetical. **Pages** (approx.): 20. **Frequency:** Irregular; latest edition 1977 with updates; next edition April 1980. **Editor:** Benson Hattem. **Price:** $3.00 (current and new editions).

★442★

DIRECTORY OF MINORITY-OWNED BUSINESS [Illinois]

Northern Illinois Business Corporation
Rockford, IL
Covers: About 250 firms and shops in the Rockford-Freeport area offering professional, commercial, and consumer products and services. **Entries include:** Company name, address, phone, contact. **Arrangement:** Classified. **Frequency:** Latest edition September 1977. **Price:** Free. **Send orders to:** Human Resources Dept., City of Rockford, Illinois, 425 E. State St., Rockford, IL 61104 (815-987-5781). **Other information:** Northern Illinois Business Corporation ceased operations June 30, 1979.

★443★

DIRECTORY OF MOBILE AND MODULAR HOUSING MANUFACTURERS

Hardison Publishing Company
6229 Northwest Highway　　　　Phone: (312) 774-2525
Chicago, IL 60631
Covers: About 700 mobile home and modular housing manufacturers in the United States and Canada, and about 225 distributors of aftermarket products. **Entries include:** For manufacturers - Company name, address, phone, type of unit produced, whether a branch (and name and location of parent, if so), type of unit produced, names of key personnel; home office listings show locations of other facilities. For distributors - Name, address, phone, products handled. **Arrangement:** Alphabetical within state; distributors follow manufacturers. **Pages** (approx.): 85. **Frequency:** Annual, April. **Price:** $4.00. **Other information:** A slightly abridged version of material which appears in "Manufactured Housing Dealer - Annual Directory and Buyer's Guide Issue" (see separate listing).

★444★

DIRECTORY OF MOLDER SERVICES [Plastics industry]

Society of the Plastics Industry
3150 Des Plaines Avenue　　　　Phone: (312) 297-6150
Des Plaines, IL 60018
Covers: About 340 plastic molding firms which are members of the molders division of the society. **Entries include:** Company name, address, phone, contact person, process and types of materials used, press specifications, specialty, in-house services provided, and coding to indicate whether a custom shop and whether proprietary or captive. **Arrangement:** Geographical. **Pages** (approx.): 45. **Frequency:** Irregular; latest edition 1977; 1980 edition planned. **Price:** $5.00.

★445★

DIRECTORY OF MONTANA MANUFACTURERS

Montana Department of Community Affairs
1424 Ninth Avenue　　　　　　Phone: (406) 449-2896
Helena, MT 59601
Entries include: Company name, address, phone, name of principal executive, number of employees, and products or services. **Arrangement:** Alphabetical; geographical; classified by SIC numbers. **Pages** (approx.): 70. **Frequency:** Irregular; approximately every two years; previous edition August 1977; new edition expected January 1980. **Editor:** Tom Dundas. **Price:** $10.00 (current and 1980 editions). **Other information:** State Industrial Directories Corp. catalog lists this directory as, "Montana Directory of Manufacturers;" Manufacturers' News catalog lists it as, "Montana Manufacturers Directory and Buyers Guide."

Directory of Motor Vehicle Related Associations See MVMA **Directory of Motor Vehicle Related Associations**

★446★

DIRECTORY OF MUSIC COMPANIES: United States and Foreign

Instrumentalist Company
1418 Lake Street
Evanston, IL 60204
Covers: Manufacturers and distributors of musical instruments, accessories, uniforms, and related merchandise, plus music publishers, textbook publishers, and agents. **Entries include:** Company name, address, brand names, and product information. **Arrangement:** Alphabetical. **Pages** (approx.): 60. **Editor:** J. W. Worrel. **Former title:** Directory of the Music Industry. **Price:** $4.50.

Directory of National and International Labor Unions in the United States See **Directory of National Unions and Employee Associations**

★447★

DIRECTORY OF NATIONAL UNIONS AND EMPLOYEE ASSOCIATIONS

Bureau of Labor Statistics
Labor Department
Fourth and G Streets, N. W.　　　Phone: (202) 523-1535
Washington, DC 20212
Covers: More than 200 national unions and professional and state employee associations engaging in labor representation. **Entries include:** Name, address, names of elected officials and department heads, publications, conventions, membership figures, number of locals. **Arrangement:** Separate sections for AFL-CIO, railroad unions, other federations, and individual national unions. **Indexes:** Alphabetical, personal name. **Pages** (approx.): Base publication, 150 pages. **Frequency:** Biennial in odd years, with supplements in even years; 1979 edition delayed. **Editor:** Harry P. Cohany, Chief, Division of Industrial Relations. **Former title:** Directory of National and International Labor Unions in the United States (1971). **Price:** $2.75 for base volume (1977 edition; 1975 data); $2.40 for supplement (published 1978). **Send orders to:** Government Printing Office, Washington, DC 20402. Also available from Bureau of Labor Statistics regional offices. **Also includes:** Historical and statistical data on labor movement and unions. **Other information:** Base volume,

published 1977, includes year date "1975" in title, but the list of unions is corrected to February 1977.

★448★
DIRECTORY OF NEBRASKA MANUFACTURERS AND THEIR PRODUCTS
Nebraska Department of Economic Development
Box 94666   Phone: (402) 471-3111
Lincoln, NE 68509
Number of listings: 2,000. **Entries include:** Company name, address, phone, name of principal executive, SIC numbers, list of products, code for number of employees. **Arrangement:** Geographical. **Indexes:** Alphabetical, SIC. **Pages** (approx.): 200. **Frequency:** Biennial, spring of even years. **Price:** $10.00 (current and 1980 editions). **Other information:** State Industrial Directories Corp. catalog lists this publication as, "Nebraska Manufacturers Directory."

Directory of Nevada Businesses *See* **Nevada Industrial Directory**

★449★
DIRECTORY OF NEW ENGLAND MANUFACTURERS
George D. Hall Company
20 Kilby Street   Phone: (617) 523-3745
Boston, MA 02109
Covers: About 27,000 manufacturers and banks in Connecticut, Maine, Massachusetts, New Hampshire, Rhode Island, and Vermont. **Entries include:** For manufacturers - Company name, address, phone, names of principal executives, SIC numbers, list of products or services, number of employees, whether firm exports or imports. For banks - Same types of information as applicable. **Arrangement:** Geographical; manufacturers and banks in separate sections. **Indexes:** Alphabetical, product, SIC. **Pages** (approx.): 925. **Frequency:** Annual, January. **Advertising accepted. Price:** $84.00 (1980 edition). **Other information:** Manufacturers' News catalog lists this publication as, "New England Manufacturers Directory."

Directory of New England Newspapers, College Publications, Periodicals, Radio and Television Stations *See* **New England Media Directory**

★450★
DIRECTORY OF NEW MEXICO MANUFACTURING AND MINING
Bureau of Business and Economic Research
University of New Mexico   Phone: (505) 277-2216
Albuquerque, NM 87131
Number of listings: 700. **Entries include:** Company name, address, phone, name of principal executive, number of employees, SIC numbers, list of products; manufacturer listings also show date established; mining listings also show whether underground, pit, etc., and name of mine. **Arrangement:** Manufacturers arranged geographically, alphabetically, and by SIC code; same information in all sections. **Pages** (approx.): 160. **Frequency:** Biennial in August of even years. **Former title:** Directory of Mining and Manufacturing. **Price:** $15.00. **Other information:** Cover title is, "New Mexico Directory of Manufacturing and Mining."

Directory of North American Rubber Product Manufacturers and...Suppliers *See* **Rubber & Plastics News—Rubbicana Issue [Directory issue]**

★451★
DIRECTORY OF NORTH CAROLINA MANUFACTURING FIRMS
Industrial Development Division
North Carolina Commerce Department
430 N. Salisbury St.   Phone: (919) 733-7980
Raleigh, NC 27611
Number of listings: About 6,800. **Entries include:** Company name, address, names and titles of principal executives, phone, name and address of parent company, area served, SIC numbers, list of products or services, number of employees, year established. **Arrangement:** Geographical and by SIC numbers; similar information

in each section. **Indexes:** Alphabetical. **Pages** (approx.): 600. **Frequency:** Biennial, fall of even years. **Price:** $20.00, payment must accompany order.

★452★
DIRECTORY OF NORTH DAKOTA MANUFACTURERS
North Dakota Business and Industrial Development Department
513 E. Bismarck Avenue
Bismarck, ND 58505
Number of listings: 1,100. **Entries include:** Company name, address, phone, name of principal executive (in some listings), number of employees, list of products, SIC numbers. **Arrangement:** Geographical; alphabetical, SIC; similar information in each section. **Pages** (approx.): 140. **Frequency:** Biennial, February of even years. **Price:** Free. **Other information:** Manufacturers' News catalog lists this publication as, "Directory of North Dakota Manufacturing."

Directory of North Dakota Manufacturing *See* **Directory of North Dakota Manufacturers**

Directory of Ohio Manufacturers *See* **Ohio Industrial Directory**

★453★
DIRECTORY OF OREGON MANUFACTURERS
Oregon Department of Economic Development
155 Cottage Street   Phone: (503) 373-1200
Salem, OR 97310
Number of listings: 4,600. **Entries include:** Company name, address, phone, name of principal executive, number of employees, SIC numbers, list of products, whether firm exports or imports, parent company information (if applicable). **Arrangement:** By SIC classification. **Indexes:** Alphabetical, geographical. **Pages** (approx.): 325. **Frequency:** Biennial, January of even years. **Editor:** Scott Hannigan. **Price:** $25.00 (1980 edition). **Other information:** Manufacturers' News catalog lists this publication as, "Oregon Manufacturers Directory."

Directory of Overseas Summer Jobs *See* **Overseas Summer Jobs**

★454★
DIRECTORY OF PACKAGING SUPPLIERS TO THE DRUG AND COSMETIC INDUSTRY
Focus Publishing Company, Inc.
Box 814
Amherst, MA 01002
Covers: About 1,000 companies which manufacture containers (aerosols, bottles, tubes, tablet dispensers, etc.) or do contract packaging, decorating, sealing, or assembly. **Entries include:** Company name, address, phone, name of contact, products or services, number of employees. **Arrangement:** Alphabetical. **Indexes:** Product/service. **Pages** (approx.): 125. **Frequency:** Annual, June. **Editor:** Joel Frados. **Advertising accepted.** Circulation 3,000. **Price:** $12.00.

★455★
DIRECTORY OF PARTICLEBOARD AND MEDIUM DENSITY FIBERBOARD MANUFACTURERS
National Particleboard Association
2306 Perkins Place   Phone: (301) 587-2204
Silver Spring, MD 20910
Number of listings: 20 member manufacturers. **Entries include:** Company name, address; names, titles, and phone numbers of key personnel; trade names, products, product specifications including wood type, size, thickness; size of plant, capacity, location, and number of employees. **Arrangement:** Alphabetical. **Indexes:** Product. **Frequency:** Annual. **Price:** Free.

★456★
DIRECTORY OF PLASTICS-KNOWLEDGEABLE GOVERNMENT PERSONNEL
Plastics Technical Evaluation Center
Army Armament Research and Development Command
Picatinny Arsenal   Phone: (201) 328-4222
Dover, NJ 07801
Covers: 1,500 personnel knowledgeable in plastics in government agencies and the armed forces. **Entries include:** Person's name, name of government organization where employed, working group with telephone listing, and area of specialization. **Arrangement:** Classified by agency or command. **Indexes:** Subject specialty. **Pages** (approx.): 110. **Frequency:** Irregular; latest edition February 1975. **Editors:** Richard J. Valles and John Nardone. **Price:** $20.00. **Send orders to:** National Technical Information Service, Springfield, VA 22161.

★457★
DIRECTORY OF PLUMBING RESEARCH RECOMMENDATIONS
International Association of Plumbing and Mechanical Officials
5032 Alhambra Avenue   Phone: (213) 223-1471
Los Angeles, CA 90032
Covers: About 1,500 manufacturers of approximately 10,000 plumbing products and appliances. **Entries include:** Manufacturer name, address, product name, model number, product description. **Arrangement:** Alphabetical. **Indexes:** Product. **Pages** (approx.): 300. **Frequency:** Monthly. **Editor:** Tom Higham. **Price:** $25.00 per year.

★458★
DIRECTORY OF PREMIUM, INCENTIVE & TRAVEL BUYERS
Salesman's Guide, Inc.
1140 Broadway   Phone: (212) 684-2985
New York, NY 10001
Covers: About 10,300 firms that purchase premium incentive merchandise and travel incentive programs. **Entries include:** Company name, address, phone, names of premium/incentive buyers, executives, and titles. **Arrangement:** Geographical. **Indexes:** Company name. **Pages** (approx.): 550. **Frequency:** Irregular; latest edition 1979; quarterly updates. **Advertising accepted.** **Price:** $110.00, including quarterly updates.

Directory of Private Employment Agencies *See* **National Association of Personnel Consultants—Membership Directory**

★459★
DIRECTORY OF PRODUCTIVITY AND QUALITY OF WORKING LIFE CENTERS
National Center for Productivity and Quality of Workinglife
C/o Productivity Information Center/NTIS
425 13th Street, N. W.   Phone: (202) 724-3369
Washington, DC 20004
Covers: About 30 United States centers and some centers abroad. **Entries include:** For United States centers - Center name, address, phone, names of key staff, type of organization, objectives, programs, publications, etc. For foreign centers - Center name, address, director's name. **Frequency:** Issued 1978. **Price:** $3.00 (S/N 052-003-00597-2). **Send orders to:** Government Printing Office, Washington, DC 20402.

★460★
DIRECTORY OF PUBLIC AFFAIRS OFFICERS
Public Affairs Council
1220 16th Street, N. W.
Washington, DC 20036
Covers: 200 corporation executives with public affairs/government relations/social responsibility assignments. **Arrangement:** Alphabetical, geographical. **Pages** (approx.): 200. **Frequency:** Biennial. **Price:** Available to members only.

★461★
DIRECTORY OF PUBLIC REFRIGERATED WAREHOUSES
International Association of Refrigerated Warehouses
7315 Wisconsin Avenue   Phone: (301) 652-5674
Washington, DC 20014
Covers: 650 member warehouses and 64 associate members supplying products and services to the refrigerated warehousing industry. **Entries include:** Company name, address, space, temperature ranges, type of refrigeration, truck and rail platform capacity, rail lines service, and insurance rates and service. **Arrangement:** Geographical. **Pages** (approx.): 165. **Frequency:** Annual, January. **Advertising accepted.** Circulation 4,000. **Price:** $35.00 (current and 1980 editions); free to food industry.

★462★
DIRECTORY OF RECREATIONAL VEHICLE MANUFACTURERS
Hardison Publishing Company
6229 Northwest Highway   Phone: (312) 774-2525
Chicago, IL 60631
Covers: About 800 recreational vehicle manufacturers. **Entries include:** Company name, address, names of key personnel, types of vehicles manufactured, and whether a branch (and name and location of parent, if so). **Arrangement:** Alphabetical within state. **Pages** (approx.): 85. **Frequency:** Annual, April. **Price:** $4.00. **Other information:** An abridged version of material which appears in "RV Dealer - Directory and Buyer's Guide Issue" (see separate listing).

★463★
DIRECTORY OF RESEARCH, DEVELOPMENT AND DEMONSTRATION PROJECTS [Mass transportation]
Urban Mass Transit Administration
Transportation Department
Washington, DC 20590
Covers: About 120 research projects being conducted by federal and state governmental agencies and other organizations concerned with mass transit. **Entries include:** Name of sponsoring organization, name of project, name, address, and phone of investigator; description of project. **Arrangement:** By type of transportation. **Indexes:** Subject, name of contractor, project number. **Pages** (approx.): 160. **Frequency:** Annual. **Price:** Apply.

★464★
DIRECTORY OF RESEARCH SERVICES PROVIDED BY MEMBERS OF THE MARKETING RESEARCH ASSOCIATION
Marketing Research Association
Box 1415
Grand Central Station   Phone: (212) 532-9065
New York, NY 10017
Covers: Over 400 market research companies and field interviewing services in United States and Canada who are members. **Entries include:** Company name, address, phone, names of executives, list of services, special interviewing capabilities. **Arrangement:** Geographical. **Pages** (approx.): 140. **Frequency:** Irregular; latest edition April 1979; new edition expected September 1980. **Editor:** William J. Callahan. **Advertising accepted.** Circulation over 950. **Price:** $30.00 (current edition); $35.00 (1980 edition). **Send orders to:** Callahan Research Associates, 31 E. 28th St., New York, NY 10016 (212-532-9065). **Also includes:** Separate geographical listing for firms with one-way mirror facilities, central telephone facilities, and permanent shopping mall locations. **Other information:** Cover title is, "MRA Research Service Directory."

★465★
DIRECTORY OF SAN FRANCISCO IMPORTERS AND EXPORTERS [California]
San Francisco Area World Trade Association
San Francisco Chamber of Commerce
465 California Street, 9th Floor   Phone: (415) 392-4511
San Francisco, CA 94104
Number of listings: About 70. **Entries include:** Company name, address, phone, and list of items imported and/or exported.

Arrangement: Alphabetical. **Pages** (approx.): 4. **Frequency:** Annual. **Editor:** Jayne Einhorn, Trade Information Officer. **Price:** Free.

★466★
DIRECTORY OF SEATTLE-KING COUNTY MANUFACTURERS [Washington]
Seattle Chamber of Commerce
215 Columbia Street   Phone: (206) 447-7210
Seattle, WA 98104
Number of listings: 1,600. **Entries include:** Company name, address, phone, name of principal executive, number of employees, list of products, SIC numbers, markets served, date established, annual gross sales. **Arrangement:** Alphabetical. **Indexes:** Product and SIC number. **Pages** (approx.): 80. **Frequency:** Biennial, January of odd years. **Editor:** Carole A. Aaron, Research Manager. **Advertising accepted. Price:** $12.50.

Directory of Shipowners, Shipbuilders and Marine Engineers *See* Marine Week Directory of Shipowners, Shipbuilders and Marine Engineers

★467★
DIRECTORY OF SHOP-BY-MAIL BARGAIN SOURCES
Pilot Books
347 Fifth Avenue   Phone: (212) 685-0736
New York, NY 10016
Covers: 700 mail-order houses offering goods and services at discount prices. **Entries include:** Company name, address, cost of literature (if any), and product or services offered. **Arrangement:** Alphabetical. **Pages** (approx.): 65. **Frequency:** Irregular; first edition February 1978; new edition expected 1981. **Editors:** Margaret A. Boyd and Sue Scott-Martin. **Price:** $2.95.

Directory of Solar Energy Equipment Manufacturers and Solar Energy Architects and Engineers *See* Illinois Solar Energy Directory

★468★
DIRECTORY OF SOUTH CAROLINA PORT SERVICES
South Carolina State Ports Authority
176 Concord Street   Phone: (803) 723-8651
Charleston, SC 29402
Covers: About 350 custom house brokers, transportation companies, terminals and warehouses, tugboat operators, ship repair yards, and others offering services to the shipping industry in South Carolina. **Entries include:** Name of organization, business, or individual, mailing address, location, and phone. **Arrangement:** Classified by product or service. **Pages** (approx.): 25. **Frequency:** Annual. **Editor:** David A. Harman. **Price:** Free.

Directory of South Dakota Industries *See* South Dakota Manufacturers and Processors Directory

★469★
DIRECTORY OF SPEAKERS [Personnel management]
International Association for Personnel Women
Box 3057
Grand Central Station   Phone: (212) 734-8160
New York, NY 10017
Covers: About 70 women qualified to speak on topics related to personnel management, such as affirmative action, employment, labor relations, and manpower planning. **Entries include:** Name, business address, phone, chapter with which affiliated, if any, geographic availability, and topics. **Arrangement:** Alphabetical. **Indexes:** Topic. **Pages** (approx.): 30. **Frequency:** Irregular; latest edition spring 1978; new edition expected 1980. **Editor:** Connie Sternberg, Executive Director. **Price:** $5.00 (current and 1980 editions).

★470★
DIRECTORY OF SPECIALIZED FURNITURE CARRIERS
National Furniture Traffic Conference
335 E. Broadway
Gardner, MA 01440
Covers: Firms specializing in transportation of furniture. Does not include household moving firms. **Frequency:** Latest edition September 1979. **Price:** $19.95.

★471★
DIRECTORY OF STATE CHAMBER OF COMMERCE AND ASSOCIATION OF COMMERCE AND INDUSTRY EXECUTIVES
Chamber of Commerce of the United States
1615 H Street, N. W.   Phone: (202) 659-6000
Washington, DC 20062
Covers: About 465 officers, presidents, and other chief executive officers of state chambers of commerce. **Entries include:** Name, address; chamber address. **Arrangement:** Geographical. **Pages** (approx.): 35. **Frequency:** Irregular; latest edition December 1979. **Former title:** Chamber of Commerce Executives. **Price:** $5.00.

★472★
DIRECTORY OF STEEL FOUNDRIES IN THE UNITED STATES, CANADA, AND MEXICO
Steel Founders' Society of America
20611 Center Ridge Road   Phone: (216) 333-9600
Rocky River, OH 44116
Covers: About 450 steel foundries in the United States, Canada, and Mexico. **Entries include:** Company name, address, phone, principal executives, types and sizes of castings produced, processes employed, equipment available for melting, heat treating, and quenching; use of product. **Arrangement:** Alphabetical. **Indexes:** Geographical (with size of castings produced and other specifications data). **Pages** (approx.): 275. **Frequency:** Biennial, summer of odd years. **Editor:** Cheryl M. Hallstrom, Administrative Assistant. **Price:** $15.00.

★473★
DIRECTORY OF SUPPLIERS TO THE DIRECT SELLING INDUSTRY
Direct Selling Association
1730 M Street, N. W., Suite 610   Phone: (202) 293-5760
Washington, DC 20036
Covers: Nearly 100 associate members of the association who supply products, equipment, and materials to the direct selling industry. **Entries include:** Company name, address, phone, names of key personnel, products or services. **Arrangement:** Alphabetical. **Indexes:** Product/service. **Pages** (approx.): 35. **Frequency:** Annual, spring. **Editor:** Mills C. Edwards, Director, Information Services. **Price:** $5.00.

★474★
DIRECTORY OF SYSTEMS HOUSES & MINICOMPUTER OEM'S
Sentry Computer Services, Inc.
Five Kane Industrial Drive   Phone: (617) 562-9308
Hudson, MA 01749
Covers: Over 3,000 systems houses, turnkey suppliers, dealers, and other firms which manufacture or sell equipment containing minicomputer components purchased from others. **Entries include:** Company name, address, phone, names and titles of key personnel, type of equipment handled, industries and applications, number of employees, annual sales, mini- and microcomputers used in products. **Arrangement:** Alphabetical. **Indexes:** Geographical, application, computer model used. **Pages** (approx.): 400. **Frequency:** Annual, January. **Editor:** Carol G. Grace. **Advertising accepted. Price:** $347.00.

Directory of Tennessee Industries *See* Tennessee Directory of Manufacturers

★475★

DIRECTORY OF TEXAS MANUFACTURERS

Bureau of Business Research
University of Texas at Austin
Box 7457
Austin, TX 78712

Covers: About 15,000 manufacturers in Texas and Texarkana, Arkansas; includes SIC manufacturing classifications and "Products recovered from natural gas," "Mined sulfur," and certain classes of shell products. **Entries include:** Company name, address, phone, year established, area served, form of company organization, number of employees, products, SIC numbers. **Arrangement:** Geographical and SIC with similar information in each. **Indexes:** Alphabetical. **Pages** (approx.): 1,000 (in two volumes). **Frequency:** Annual, fall. **Editor:** Ida M. Lambeth. **Price:** $60.00. **Other information:** Supplemented by "Texas Industrial Expansion," monthly; see separate listing. "Directory of Texas Manufacturers" is listed in Manufacturers' News catalog as "Texas Manufacturers Directory."

★476★

DIRECTORY OF THE AMERICAN URANIUM INDUSTRY [Cancelled]

Dames & Moore
500 Sansome Street
San Francisco, CA

Background: Widely announced in the trade press during the spring of 1978, the publication was reported cancelled when Information Enterprises requested information from the publishers.

★477★

DIRECTORY OF THE CANNING, FREEZING, PRESERVING INDUSTRIES

CFP Directory
Box 550   Phone: (301) 876-7150
Westminster, MD 21157

Covers: 1,700 North American packers of canned fruits, vegetables, juices, preserves, jams and jellies (SIC 2033); canned specialties (SIC 2032); frozen fruits and vegetables (SIC 2037); frozen specialties (SIC 2038); pickles, sauces and salad dressings (SIC 2035); canned and cured seafood (SIC 2091); fresh or frozen packaged fish (SIC 2092); canned meats (SIC 20138); and frozen meats. **Entries include:** Company name, address, phone, divisions, subsidiaries, factories, pack volume, key personnel, container sizes, association affiliation, brands, products by factory and process. **Arrangement:** Alphabetical. **Indexes:** Geographical, product, and brand name. **Pages** (approx.): 560. **Frequency:** Biennial, April of even years. **Editor:** James J. Judge. **Price:** $50.00.

Directory of the Institutional Food Market *See* **Thomas Grocery Register**

Directory of the Music Industry *See* **Directory of Music Companies: United States and Foreign**

★478★

DIRECTORY OF TOP COMPUTER EXECUTIVES

Applied Computer Research
3003 W. Northern Avenue, Suite 3   Phone: (602) 995-5929
Phoenix, AZ 85021

Covers: Executives with major data processing responsibilities in over 6,000 companies with gross annual sales of over $50 million and/or EDP budgets over $250,000. **Entries include:** Company name, address, phone, subsidiary and/or division names, major systems installed, names and titles of top executives. **Arrangement:** Classified by broad business areas. **Indexes:** Industry, Geographical. **Pages** (approx.): 270. **Frequency:** Semiannual, February and August. **Editor:** Phillip C. Howard. **Price:** $75.00 per copy; $120.00 per year.

★479★

DIRECTORY OF TRAILER RESEARCH RECOMMENDATIONS [Recreational vehicle plumbing]

International Association of Plumbing and Mechanical Officials
5032 Alhambra Avenue   Phone: (213) 223-1471
Los Angeles, CA 90032

Covers: About 200 manufacturers of plumbing products used in recreational vehicles and mobile homes. **Entries include:** Company name, address, product name, model number, product description. **Arrangement:** Alphabetical. **Indexes:** Product. **Pages** (approx.): 225. **Frequency:** Monthly. **Editor:** Tom Higham. **Price:** $25.00 per year.

★480★

DIRECTORY OF TYPOGRAPHIC SERVICES

National Composition Association
1730 N. Lynn Street
Arlington, VA 22209

Covers: 4,800 typesetting plants in the United States; includes nonmembers. **Entries include:** Company name, address, phone, key personnel, type of equipment. **Arrangement:** Geographical. **Frequency:** Not established; first edition 1979. **Price:** $10.00. **Other information:** Compiled with staff of "Typeworld."

★481★

DIRECTORY OF UNITED STATES ELECTRONIC MAIL DROPS

Tahoe Information and Business Services
Box 4031   Phone: (702) 588-3866
Stateline, NV 89449

Covers: Over 200 services in over 180 cities where facsimile equipment (telecopiers) is available on fee basis for use in transmission and receipt of documents. Coverage includes Canada, Puerto Rico, and London, England. **Entries include:** Service name, address, phone, type of equipment used, and scope of transmission and receiving services offered. **Arrangement:** Geographical. **Pages** (approx.): 40. **Frequency:** Annual, spring. **Editor:** Laurence J. Foley. **Price:** $8.85, payment with order (current and 1980 editions). **Also includes:** Table of interstate transmission line charges, airline mileage table, map showing location of facsimile services, international routing codes, rates, and direct dialing procedures to foreign cities.

★482★

DIRECTORY OF UNITED STATES IMPORTERS

Journal of Commerce
110 Wall Street   Phone: (212) 425-1616
New York, NY 10005

Covers: 30,000 importers in the United States and Canada. **Entries include:** Firm name, address, names of principal executives, products dealt in, annual volume and other statistics. **Arrangement:** Geographical. **Indexes:** Product (by Standard International Trade Classification number). **Pages** (approx.): 1,200. **Frequency:** Biennial, November of odd years. **Price:** $150.00.

★483★

DIRECTORY OF UNITED STATES TRADE SHOWS, EXPOSITIONS, AND CONVENTIONS [Of interest to businesses abroad]

U. S. Travel Service
Commerce Department   Phone: (202) 377-3715
Washington, DC 20230

Number of listings: Over 500. **Entries include:** Name of event, description, dates and locations for two coming years, name and address of contact for full information, and, where applicable, code indicating show participation in Commerce Department programs to internationalize trade shows. **Arrangement:** Classified by line of business. **Indexes:** Chronological. **Pages** (approx.): 75. **Frequency:** Annual, January. **Price:** Free.

★484★
DIRECTORY OF U.S. AND CANADIAN MARKETING SURVEYS AND SERVICES
Charles H. Kline & Company, Inc.
330 Passaic Avenue   Phone: (201) 227-6262
Fairfield, NJ 07006
Covers: 150 firms publishing a total of about 2,100 multi-client marketing reports and syndicated continuing services. **Entries include:** Company name, address, phone, and executive names, plus report or service title, issue date or frequency, and price. **Arrangement:** Alphabetical by company name. **Indexes:** Subject. **Pages** (approx.): 160. **Frequency:** Irregular; latest edition April 1979. **Price:** $125.00, with binder and mid-'79, -'80 updates.

★485★
DIRECTORY OF U.S. & INTERNATIONAL EXECUTIVE RECRUITERS
United Consultants
Box 232   Phone: (312) 256-5068
Wilmette, IL 60091
Covers: About 1,400 recruiting firms handling executive openings; international coverage. **Entries include:** Company name, address, and areas of specialization. **Arrangement:** By job classification. **Pages** (approx.): 60. **Frequency:** Six times yearly. **Editor:** J. Richards. **Price:** $10.00 (current edition); $11.00 (1980 edition).

★486★
DIRECTORY OF UTAH MANUFACTURERS
Utah Job Service
Utah Department of Employment Security
174 Social Hall Avenue   Phone: (801) 533-2296
Salt Lake City, UT 84111
Number of listings: 1,900. **Entries include:** Company name, address, number of employees, products. **Arrangement:** Geographical and SIC; similar information in each section. **Indexes:** Product, alphabetical. **Pages** (approx.): 150. **Frequency:** Biennial, March of odd years. **Price:** Free.

Directory of Utility and Transportation Consultants *See* Directory of Consultants [Utility and transportation industries]

Directory of Verified Electrical Wholesale Distributors *See* Directory of Electrical Wholesale Distributors and Market Planning Guide

★487★
DIRECTORY OF VIRGINIA MANUFACTURING
Virginia State Chamber of Commerce
611 E. Franklin Street   Phone: (804) 643-7491
Richmond, VA 23219
Covers: Over 4,000 manufacturers and mining and quarrying firms with five or more employees. **Entries include:** Company name, address, phone, names of principal executives, number of employees, SIC number, parent company (if applicable). Separate list of firms with foreign affiliations gives parent company, country, and product only. **Arrangement:** Alphabetical. **Indexes:** SIC, geographical. **Pages** (approx.): 200. **Frequency:** Biennial, early in even years. **Editor:** Richard S. Gillis, Jr. **Price:** $30.00 (current and 1980 editions). **Other information:** Manufacturers' News catalog lists this publication as, "Virginia Industrial Directory." The cover title is "Industrial Directory of Virginia."

★488★
DIRECTORY OF WASHINGTON CREATIVE SERVICES
Constance A. Miller, Publisher
1506 19th Street, N. W.   Phone: (202) 232-8572
Washington, DC 20036
Covers: Over 300 Washington-based individuals and firms supplying products and services to graphics arts, advertising, and related firms. Includes art suppliers, photographers, printers, illustrators and designers, commercial artists, talent agencies, and others. All listings are paid. **Entries include:** Firm or individual name, address, phone;

sample of representative copy or art work provided for freelancers. **Arrangement:** By type of service. **Indexes:** Alphabetical. **Pages** (approx.): 130. **Frequency:** First edition 1979; new edition expected 1980. **Editor:** Constance A. Miller. **Price:** $15.00, plus 75¢ shipping (current and 1980 editions). **Other information:** 1980 edition will include over 1,000 listings.

Directory of Washington Manufacturers *See* Washington Manufacturers Register

★489★
DIRECTORY OF WATERBED RESOURCES AND INFORMATION
Flotation Sleep Industry Magazine
1700 East Dyer Road, Suite 250   Phone: (714) 557-2961
Santa Ana, CA 92705
Publication includes: Approximately 400 manufacturers and distributors of waterbed mattresses, frames, and accessories. **Entries include:** Company name, address, phone. **Arrangement:** Classified. **Frequency:** Annual, January. **Editor:** Steve McGonigal. **Advertising accepted. Price:** $5.00 (1979 edition); $6.00 (1980 edition).

Directory of Wholesalers in the United States and Canada [Shoe repair] *See* Shoe Service Wholesalers in the United States and...

★490★
DIRECTORY OF WIRE COMPANIES OF NORTH AMERICA
Business Information Services, Inc.
10 Lookout Drive   Phone: (203) 438-4323
Ridgefield, CT 06877
Covers: About 1,000 companies manufacturing wire and wire products, with history and product profiles on 750 of these firms. **Entries include:** For profiled firms - Company name, address, phone, history, product and market information, names of principal executives. For other firms - Company name, address, phone. **Arrangement:** Alphabetical. **Indexes:** Geographical. **Pages** (approx.): 250. **Frequency:** Annual, spring. **Editor:** Richard J. Callahan. **Advertising accepted.** Circulation 3-5,000. **Price:** $35.00, plus $2.50 shipping (current edition); $40.00, plus $2.50 shipping (1980 edition).

★491★
DIRECTORY OF WOMEN BUSINESS OWNERS [Westchester, New York]
Westchester Association of Women Business Owners
Box 171   Phone: (914) 592-3188
Scarborough, NY 10510
Covers: About 100 member firms with at least 50% ownership by a woman located in Westchester, New York and surrounding area. **Entries include:** Company name, address, phone, name of owner, products or services. **Arrangement:** Same information is given by line of business and by town or city. **Pages** (approx.): 60. **Frequency:** Annual, January. **Editor:** Maloue Edelson, President. **Advertising accepted.** Circulation 1,000. **Price:** $5.00, plus 50¢ shipping.

★492★
DIRECTORY OF WOMEN IN BUSINESS AND PROFESSIONS [Knoxville, Tennessee]
Knoxville Chapter
National Association of Social Workers
Box 9097
Knoxville, TN 37920
Covers: Women business owners, self-employed professional women, and women free-lancers in the Knoxville area. **Frequency:** Irregular; first edition January 1978. **Other information:** First edition presently out of print. (Not verified)

★493★
DIRECTORY OF WOMEN-OWNED BUSINESSES: [AREA]
National Association of Women Business Owners
2000 P Street, N. W., Suite 511   Phone: (202) 338-8966
Washington, DC 20036
Covers: Washington/Baltimore edition includes 1,150 businesses offering more than 330 types of goods and services; Chicago and Boston editions have similar coverage. **Entries include:** Company name, address, phone, owners' names and titles, company's products or services, percentage of business owned by women, whether a minority business. **Arrangement:** Alphabetical. **Indexes:** Product/service. **Frequency:** Annual. **Editors:** Juanita M. Weaver, Paulette D. Waters. **Price:** $10.00 each edition.

★494★
DIRECTORY OF WORKERS EDUCATION
Workers Education Local 189
Box 818   Phone: (304) 292-0496
Morgantown, WV 26505
Covers: 300 American and foreign members who are concerned with educational issues related to labor organization and union objectives. Also includes lists of labor unions with education departments, universities with labor education programs, and resources available to workers' educators. **Entries include:** Member listings show name, address, and home and/or work phone. Other lists show similar information. **Arrangement:** Alphabetical within lists. **Pages** (approx.): 50. **Frequency:** Biennial, odd years. **Editor:** Lee Balliet, Treasurer. **Former title:** Directory of Labor Education. **Price:** $2.00.

Directory/Census of Manufactured Housing *See* Packaged
    Directory [Manufactured housing]

Disco Sourcebook *See* Billboard's International Disco Sourcebook

★495★
DISCOUNT MERCHANDISER—ANNUAL MARKETING STUDY ISSUE
Chartcom, Inc.
641 Lexington Avenue   Phone: (212) 935-2636
New York, NY 10022
Publication includes: List of discount merchandisers with $50 million or more in sales in preceding year. **Entries include:** Company name, number of stores, total volume, sales per unit. **Arrangement:** By sales volume. **Frequency:** Annual, May issue. **Editor:** Nathaniel Schwartz. **Advertising accepted.   Price:** $10.00. **Also includes:** Other statistics on the discount industry.

★496★
DISCOUNT MERCHANDISER—$100 MILLION CLUB ISSUE
Chartcom, Inc.
641 Lexington Avenue   Phone: (212) 935-2636
New York, NY 10022
Covers: Chain store discount companies with sales of $100 million or more. **Entries include:** Company name, name and photograph of president or chairman, sales for past five years; text accompanies each listing and describes company plans, etc. **Arrangement:** Ranked by sales. **Frequency:** Annual, June. **Editor:** Nathaniel Schwartz. **Advertising accepted.** Circulation 45,000. **Price:** $10.00.

★497★
DISCOUNT STORE NEWS—TOP 100 CHAINS ISSUE
Lebhar-Friedman, Inc.
425 Park Avenue   Phone: (212) 371-9400
New York, NY 10022
Entries include: Chain name, location, estimated sales for current year and sales and earnings for previous year, number of stores, total store square footage. **Arrangement:** By sales volume. **Frequency:** Annual, second September issue. **Price:** $1.00.

★498★
DISTRIBUTION WORLDWIDE—DISTRIBUTION GUIDE ISSUE
Chilton Company
Chilton Way   Phone: (215) 687-8200
Radnor, PA 19089
Covers: Rail piggyback carrier services; liquid bulk terminals; air carriers; ports; interstate motor carriers; bulk and liquid bulk transfer points; container carriers; public warehouses; and manufacturers, lessors, and suppliers of material handling and container equipment and supplies. **Entries include:** Each listing includes name of company and address; most listings include phone and name of contact; descriptive information including services and products, commodities handled, number of carriers and load capacity, routes and ports of call is given as appropriate. **Arrangement:** By activity. **Frequency:** Annual, July. **Advertising accepted. Price:** $15.00.

Distributor Directory & Where to Buy It Guide [Consumer
    Hardgoods] *See* Dealerscope Magazine—National Buyer's
    Guide Issue

★499★
DISTRIBUTORS CONFIDENTIAL BEAUTY & BARBER BUYING GUIDE
Service Publications, Inc.
100 Park Avenue   Phone: (212) 532-5588
New York, NY 10017
Covers: About 1,000 manufacturers of supplies and equipment for barbers and beauticians, 100 manufacturers' agents, 2,400 distributors, 100 barber schools, and 3,000 beauty schools. **Entries include:** For manufacturers and agents - Company name, address, phone, names of principal executives. For distributors - Company name, address, phone, name of owner of president, number of salesmen, Standard Metropolitan Statistical Area in which located. For schools - Name, address, phone, SMSA, whether private or vocational; accredited schools are coded. **Arrangement:** Manufacturers are alphabetical; agents, distributors, and schools are geographical. **Indexes:** Trade name. **Pages** (approx.): 400. **Frequency:** Annual, July. **Editor:** Florence Kaplan. **Advertising accepted.** Circulation 3,000. **Price:** $30.00.

★500★
DIXIE CONTRACTOR—DIRECTORY ISSUE
Dixie Contractor
525 Marshall Street   Phone: (404) 377-2683
Decatur, GA 30031
Covers: Construction equipment distributors and manufacturers serving Alabama, Florida, Georgia, South Carolina, and middle and east Tennessee. **Entries include:** Company name, address, phone, key personnel, trade and brand names. **Arrangement:** Geographical. **Frequency:** Semiannual, March and August. **Advertising accepted. Price:** $10.00 (current and 1980 editions).

Domestic Engineering—Book of Giants Issue *See* DE/Domestic
    Engineering—Book of Giants Issue

★501★
DOW JONES-IRWIN GUIDE TO FRANCHISES
Dow Jones-Irwin Division
Richard D. Irwin, Inc.
1818 Ridge Road   Phone: (312) 798-6000
Homewood, IL 60430
Covers: More than 500 franchises available in such fields as employment services, fast foods, restaurants, drive-ins and carry-outs, motels-hotels, printing, etc. **Entries include:** Company name, address, phone, contact person, and description of franchise with amount of capital required, type of financing available, training provided, and managerial assistance available. **Arrangement:** By type of franchise. **Indexes:** Company name. **Pages** (approx.): 300. **Frequency:** Irregular; first edition January 1979. **Editors:** Peter G. Norback and Craig T. Norback. **Price:** $14.95. **Also includes:** Descriptive information on the International Franchise Association, and franchise information and assistance available from the

Commerce Department and the Small Business Administration.

★502★

DRIVER'S GUIDE TO LOW UNDERPASSES

J. J. Keller & Associates, Inc.
145 W. Wisconsin Avenue   Phone: (414) 722-2848
Neenah, WI 54956
Covers: Over 10,000 vertical clearances 14 feet 6 inches or less on United States highways; highway scale locations are also listed. **Entries include:** Highway route number, location, and amount of clearance provided. **Arrangement:** Geographical. **Pages** (approx.): 385. **Frequency:** Irregular; latest edition 1978. **Editor:** Patricia Laux. **Advertising accepted. Price:** $6.00.

★503★

DROP SHIPPING SOURCE DIRECTORY OF MAJOR CONSUMER
PRODUCT LINES

Consolidated Marketing Services, Inc.
507 Fifth Avenue   Phone: (212) 688-8797
New York, NY 10017
Covers: Firms which will drop ship single units of their products direct to the customers of retailers, mail order firms, firms offering premiums, etc., at the wholesale price, and similar listings of firms which will drop ship wholesale quantities to retail stores. Drop shippers listed handle thousands of products. **Entries include:** Company name, address, and products handled. **Arrangement:** Divided into 25 consumer merchandise classifications (luggage, housewares, etc.). **Frequency:** Irregular; first edition 1976; monthly updates in "Drop Shipping News." **Price:** $5.00. **Other information:** Some mentions of this directory still appear with former name of publisher, Decision Computers.

★504★

DRUG & COSMETIC CATALOG

Harcourt Brace Jovanovich, Inc.
757 Third Avenue   Phone: (212) 888-2132
New York, NY 10017
Covers: About 4,000 pharmaceutical and cosmetic manufacturers, and 350 manufacturers of packaging, packaging equipment, private formulas, aerosols, and raw materials used in drug and cosmetic manufacturing. **Entries include:** Company name, address, products, trade and brand names, name of contact. **Arrangement:** By activity. **Pages** (approx.): 180. **Frequency:** Annual, August. **Editor:** Donald A. Davis. **Advertising accepted.** Circulation 5,000. **Price:** $10.00.

★505★

DUN & BRADSTREET REFERENCE BOOK

Dun & Bradstreet, Inc.
99 Church Street
New York, NY 10007
Covers: Tens of thousands of firms of all sizes in the United States and Canada in all lines of business (the most comprehensive and largest of the general business directories); lacks addresses. **Entries include:** Company name; line of business expressed in SIC code; name of parent company and relationship; and codes indicating whether firm is branch of a foreign concern, estimated financial strength and composite credit rating, and whether change in rating has occurred since previous edition. **Arrangement:** Geographical; listings for each locality begin with locality name, population, county or parish, code for Dun & Bradstreet reporting office, and names of banks, principal bank officers, and bank assets. **Frequency:** Bimonthly. **Price:** Apply; available to subscribers to Dun & Bradstreet "Business Information Reports" only. **Other information:** Each firm listed is described in a much more detailed report available to Dun & Bradstreet subscribers; data in the "Reference Book" are stored in computer readable form and are available in varied arrangements and selections.

★506★

DUN & BRADSTREET REFERENCE BOOK OF CORPORATE
MANAGEMENTS

Dun & Bradstreet, Inc.
99 Church Street
New York, NY 10007
Covers: Presidents, directors, vice presidents, and officers of corporations in the United States. Controllers and assistant officers are not listed unless the corporation requests. **Entries include:** Company name, corporate headquarters address, phone; names of executives with abbreviated titles, asterisk if a director, business and professional occupations and dates, educational data, business affiliations outside the corporation, date of birth, and marital status; includes name and business affiliation of non-officer directors. **Arrangement:** Alphabetical by company name. **Indexes:** Personal name (with abbreviated title and company affiliation). **Frequency:** Annual, fall. **Price:** $95.00 (current and 1980 editions).

★507★

DUN & BRADSTREET STATE SALES GUIDE

Dun & Bradstreet Inc.
99 Church Street
New York, NY 10007
Covers: All businesses in each state which are rated by Dun & Bradstreet and included in its national "Reference Book." A separate "State Sales Guide" is published for each state and the District of Columbia; special state break-outs also available for California, New York, and Illinois. **Entries include:** Company name, 4-digit SIC number, estimated financial strength, credit rating, code indicating date business was established. **Arrangement:** Geographical. **Frequency:** Quarterly, in January, March, July, and September. **Editor:** John I. Scotto, National Manager, Business Data Bank. **Price:** Lease basis; approximately $25-$100 per quarterly issue, depending on state. Available only to subcribers to the Dun & Bradstreet Credit Service.

★508★

DURHAM BUSINESS & PROFESSIONAL CHAIN [North Carolina]

Durham Business & Professional Chain, Inc.
116 W. Parrish Street   Phone: (919) 688-7356
Durham, NC 27702
Covers: Minority businesses and professional firms in Durham. **Entries include:** Company name, address, phone, list of products or services. **Pages** (approx.): 5. **Frequency:** Quarterly. **Editor:** Norma Wood. **Price:** Free.

★509★

EARL CLARK'S DIRECTORY OF WORLD ELECTRIC LINES

Earl W. Clark
2958 Westridge Avenue   Phone: (513) 661-0042
Cincinnati, OH 45238
Covers: 1,000 electrically operated railroads and operating museums, worldwide. Includes appendices for museums displaying non-operating equipment and for recently abandoned lines. **Entries include:** Railway name, location, type of equipment operated, number of cars, track gauge, route mileage, and descriptive annotation. **Arrangement:** Geographical. **Pages** (approx.): 40. **Frequency:** Irregular; latest edition 1976; new edition expected 1980. **Editor:** Earl W. Clark. **Advertising accepted.** Circulation 750. **Price:** $3.50 (current edition); $7.00 (1980 edition).

★510★

EARNSHAW'S INFANTS, GIRLS, BOYS WEAR REVIEW—
CHILDREN'S WEAR DIRECTORY ISSUE

Earnshaw Publications, Inc.
393 Seventh Avenue   Phone: (212) 563-2742
New York, NY 10001
Covers: 600 children's apparel and accessory firms with offices or showrooms in the United States. **Entries include:** Company name, address, phone, names of executives, products and brand names. **Arrangement:** Alphabetical. **Indexes:** Product, brand name.

Frequency: Annual, December. **Editor:** Diane Specht, Editorial Director. **Advertising accepted.** Circulation 8,000. **Price:** $5.00; available to trade only. **Also includes:** Trade associations, children's apparel buyers, and suppliers to the industry.

★511★

EASTERN AUTOMOTIVE JOURNAL—DIRECTORY AND BUYERS
    GUIDE ISSUE

Eastern Automotive Journal
Box 373   Phone: (516) 295-3680
Cedarhurst, NY 11516

Covers: Manufacturers, manufacturers' representatives, and wholesale warehouse distributors of automotive aftermarket parts and services. **Arrangement:** Separate alphabetical lists of manufacturers, representatives, and distributors. **Indexes:** Geographical indexes of representatives and distributors. **Frequency:** Annual, January. **Editor:** William Dogan. **Advertising accepted.** **Price:** $10.00 (current and 1980 editions).

Eastern Manufacturers and Industrial Directory *See* Interstate
    Manufacturers and Industrial Directory

★512★

ECONOMIC OPPORTUNITY IN THE MARYLAND MARKETPLACE—
    MINORITY BUSINESS DIRECTORY

Office of Minority Business Enterprise
Maryland Department of Economic and Community Development
1748 Forest Drive   Phone: (301) 269-2682
Annapolis, MD 21401

Covers: About 400 firms offering professional, commercial, and industrial products and services. **Entries include:** Company name, address, phone, name of contact, SIC numbers, type of business, date established, number of employees, dollar limit on usual size of projects. **Arrangement:** By county. **Indexes:** Alphabetical, SIC. **Pages** (approx.): 80. **Frequency:** Annual, fall. **Former title:** Directory of Minority Businesses Serving the State of Maryland; Maryland Minority Business Directory. **Price:** Free.

★513★

ECONOMIC WORLD DIRECTORY OF JAPANESE COMPANIES IN
    USA

Economic Salon Ltd.
60 E. 42nd Street   Phone: (212) 986-1588
New York, NY

Covers: More than 450 companies in the United States which are subsidiaries, divisions, etc., of parent Japanese firms. **Entries include:** United States company name, address, phone, branch facilities, financial data, type of business, names of executives, number of Japanese and United States employees, history, current company information, and similar but less extensive data on parent company. **Arrangement:** Alphabetical. **Frequency:** Irregular; latest edition September 1979. **Price:** $120.00.

★514★

ECOTECHNICS: INTERNATIONAL POLLUTION CONTROL
    DIRECTORY

Ecopress Ltd.
C. P. 466
1211 Geneva 1, Switzerland

Covers: 35,000 manufacturers and service organizations worldwide (about 10,000 in the United States and Canada) concerned with pollution control related to water, air, solid wastes, noise, and vibration. **Entries include:** Company name, address, phone, telex, list of products or services. **Arrangement:** By product. **Pages** (approx.): 450. **Frequency:** Biennial, fall of even years. **Advertising accepted.** **Former title:** Ecotechnics: An International Ecology Directory. **Price:** $65.00. **Send orders to:** Fairchild Books, 7 E. 12th St., New York, NY 10003 (212-741-4280).

★515★

EDUCATIONAL PROGRAMS IN PUBLIC WORKS

American Public Works Association
1313 E. 60th Street   Phone: (312) 947-2520
Chicago, IL 60637

Covers: Universities and colleges which offer interdisciplinary programs in public works. **Frequency:** Annual.

★516★

ELECTRIC COMFORT CONDITIONING NEWS—FACT BOOK ISSUE

EIP, Inc.
2132 Fordem Avenue   Phone: (608) 244-3528
Madison, WI 53701

Covers: Manufacturers of air conditioners, electrical heating systems, and other electric comfort products, and their related controls and accessories. Limited to advertisers. **Entries include:** Company name, address, phone, name of principal executive, and illustrated product descriptions. **Arrangement:** Alphabetical. **Frequency:** Annual, spring. **Editor:** Jeanne Conners. **Advertising accepted.** Circulation 17,000. **Price:** $2.00 (current and 1980 editions).

★517★

ELECTRIC VEHICLE NEWS—INTERNATIONAL DIRECTORY OF THE
    ELECTRIC VEHICLE INDUSTRY ISSUE

Porter Corporation
Box 533   Phone: (203) 226-4600
Westport, CT 06880

Covers: About 300 companies concerned with the manufacture of electric vehicles and their components; organizations concerned with the development of electric vehicles; international coverage. **Entries include:** Organization or company name, address, phone, line of business or products. **Arrangement:** Alphabetical. **Indexes:** Product. **Pages** (approx.): 20. **Frequency:** Annual, February. **Editor:** G. Rogers Porter. **Price:** $4.00 (current and 1980 editions).

★518★

ELECTRICAL APPARATUS MAGAZINE—ELECTROMECHANICAL
    BENCH REFERENCE ISSUE

Barks Publications, Inc.
400 N. Michigan Avenue   Phone: (312) 321-9440
Chicago, IL 60611

Covers: Manufacturers, rebuilders, and distributors serving the electrical apparatus industry. **Entries include:** Company name, address, phone. **Arrangement:** Manufacturers and remanufacturers are alphabetical, distributors are geographical. **Indexes:** Product. **Pages** (approx.): 75. **Frequency:** Annual, spring. **Editor:** Ann Ogden, Directory Editor. **Advertising accepted.** **Price:** $3.00 (current and 1980 editions).

★519★

ELECTRICAL BUSINESS—BUYERS' GUIDE ISSUE

Rickard Publishing Company
1807 Glenview Road   Phone: (312) 998-5810
Glenview, IL 60025

Covers: About 800 manufacturers of electrical products and their distributors. **Entries include:** Manufacturer name, distributor name, address, phone. **Arrangement:** Geographical; separate issues for east, south, midwest, and west. **Indexes:** Product. **Frequency:** Annual, January. **Advertising accepted.** Circulation 67,700.

★520★

ELECTRICAL BUSINESS—ELECTRICAL CONTRACTING'S FOUR
    HUNDRED ISSUE

Rickard Publishing Company
1807 Glenview Road   Phone: (312) 998-5810
Glenview, IL 60025

Covers: 400 largest electrical contracting firms. **Entries include:** Company name, address, phone; name of treasurer; type of business; sales for current year; number of employees. **Arrangement:** Ranked by sales. **Frequency:** Annual, September. **Advertising accepted.** Circulation 67,700. **Price:** Apply.

★521★

**ELECTRICAL CONTRACTOR—ELECTRICAL PRODUCT
LITERATURE FILE ISSUE**

National Electrical Contractors Association, Inc.
7315 Wisconsin Avenue   Phone: (301) 657-3110
Washington, DC 20014
Covers: 400 manufacturers and suppliers of products and services to the electrical contracting industry. **Entries include:** Company name, address, phone. **Arrangement:** Alphabetical. **Indexes:** Product. **Frequency:** Annual, December. **Advertising accepted.** Circulation 48,500. **Price:** Apply; controlled circulation.

Electrical Generating Systems Marketing Association—Roster
See Diesel & Gas Turbine Progress—EGSMA Membership/
Product. . .Issue

★522★

ELECTRICAL WORLD DIRECTORY OF ELECTRIC UTILITIES

McGraw-Hill, Inc.
1221 Avenue of the Americas   Phone: (212) 997-4933
New York, NY 10020
Covers: Over 3,500 investor-owned, municipal, rural cooperative, and government electric utility systems in the United States and Canada; also lists associations, commissions, power pools, and consulting engineering firms. **Entries include:** For utilities - Company name, address, phone, names of corporate and operating personnel, number of employees, statistics on capacities, sales, etc. **Arrangement:** Geographical. **Indexes:** Alphabetical. **Pages** (approx.): 1,000. **Frequency:** Annual, October. **Editor:** Eileen S. Macdonald, Manager. **Price:** $125.00.

Electrical/Electronic Directory *See* Design News Electrical/
Electronic Directory

★523★

**ELECTRO BUYERS' GUIDE TO ELECTRONIC DISTRIBUTORS and
Sales Representatives in the San Francisco Bay Area
[California]**

Jack K. Ayre, Publisher
21801 Wright Terrace   Phone: (408) 732-7518
Sunnyvale, CA 94087
Covers: Electronic products available through distributors and manufacturers' sales representatives in the San Francisco Bay area. **Entries include:** Company name, address, phone, and products. **Arrangement:** Separate alphabetical lists of manufacturers, distributors, and sales representatives. **Indexes:** Product. **Pages** (approx.): 330. **Frequency:** Annual, summer. **Editor:** Jack K. Ayre, Publisher. **Advertising accepted.** **Price:** $10.80 (tentative).

★524★

ELECTROMECHANICAL BENCH REFERENCE

Barks Publications, Inc.
400 N. Michigan Avenue   Phone: (312) 321-9440
Chicago, IL 60611
Covers: Manufacturers, distributors, and remanufacturers of electrical apparatus. **Entries include:** Company name, address, phone, products. **Arrangement:** Alphabetical within line of business. **Indexes:** Product; distributors are also indexed geographically. **Pages** (approx.): 100. **Frequency:** Annual, February. **Editor:** Ann Ogden. **Advertising accepted.** Circulation 15,250. **Price:** $5.00, plus $1.50 shipping.

★525★

ELECTRONIC BUSINESS—ELECTRONIC BUSINESS 100 ISSUE

Cahners Publishing Company
221 Columbus Avenue   Phone: (617) 536-7780
Boston, MA 02116
Covers: 100 companies with greatest revenues from sales of electronic products. **Entries include:** Company name; rank for current and prior year; electronic revenues; total revenues; total net income; productivity as measured by total sales per employee and net income per employee; R&D as percent of total sales; return on equity; return

on investment; compound growth rate in sales and net income. **Arrangement:** Ranked by electronic revenues. **Frequency:** Annual, February. **Editor:** Saul Goldweitz. **Advertising accepted.** **Price:** $1.50.

★526★

**ELECTRONIC BUSINESS—TOP 20 MILITARY CONTRACTORS
ISSUE**

Cahners Publishing Company
221 Columbus Avenue   Phone: (617) 536-7780
Boston, MA 02116
Covers: 20 largest defense contractors in all fields of industry. **Entries include:** Company name, rank, brief analysis of company's contracts and activities. **Arrangement:** Ranked by total amount of military contract awards received in preceding year. **Frequency:** Annual, September. **Editor:** Saul Goldweitz. **Advertising accepted.** **Price:** $1.50.

★527★

ELECTRONIC DESIGN MASTER DIRECTORY—THE GOLD BOOK

Hayden Publishing Company, Inc.
50 Essex Street   Phone: (201) 843-0550
Rochelle Park, NJ 07662
Covers: 9,800 electronic manufacturers and 1,400 distributors of electronic products. **Entries include:** Company name, address, phone, names of executives, number of employees, financial keys, trade and brand names, list of products or services, SIC numbers, TWX and telex numbers, Federal Supply Code for Manufacturers. **Arrangement:** Manufacturers are alphabetical, distributors are geographical. **Indexes:** Product, trade name. **Pages** (approx.): 2,000. **Frequency:** Annual, July. **Editor:** George Weingarten. **Advertising accepted.** **Price:** $35.00 (current edition); $40.00 (1980 edition). **Other information:** Principal content of publication is manufacturers' catalogs.

Electronic Distributors Master Catalog *See* Off the Shelf: The
Electronic Distributors Master Catalog

★528★

**ELECTRONIC INDUSTRIES ASSOCIATION—TRADE DIRECTORY
AND MEMBERSHIP LIST**

Electronic Industries Association
2001 I Street, N. W.   Phone: (202) 457-4900
Washington, DC 20006
Number of listings: 300. **Entries include:** Company name, address, phone, names of executives, trade and brand names, list of products or services, division assignment, registered code symbol. **Arrangement:** Alphabetical. **Pages** (approx.): 180. **Frequency:** Annual, February. **Editor:** Terry Sutter. **Price:** $10.00 (current and 1980 editions).

★529★

ELECTRONIC INDUSTRY TELEPHONE DIRECTORY

Harris Publishing Company
2057-2 Aurora Road   Phone: (216) 425-9143
Twinsburg, OH 44087
Covers: Nearly 19,000 manufacturers, manufacturers' agents, distributors, and principal aircraft and missile users of electronics. **Entries include:** Company name, address, phone. **Arrangement:** Same information given alphabetically and classified by product. **Pages** (approx.): 400. **Frequency:** Annual, June. **Editor:** Beatrice R. Harris, Vice President. **Advertising accepted.** **Price:** $21.75, postpaid, payment with order.

★530★

ELECTRONIC MARKETING DIRECTORY

National Credit Office Division
Dun & Bradstreet, Inc.
1290 Avenue of the Americas   Phone: (212) 957-2470
New York, NY 10019
Covers: About 6,600 electronic component manufacturers listed with

Dun & Bradstreet credit reporting service (but directory does not include credit information). **Entries include:** Company name, address, phone; plants and divisions; purchasing names and titles of personnel; products; volume of sales; number of employees. **Arrangement:** Same information given geographically and by product. **Indexes:** Product. **Pages** (approx.): 1,500. **Frequency:** Annual, June; bimonthly updates. **Editor:** Philip J. LoMedico, Manager. **Price:** $505.00, including updates for one year, postpaid (1980 edition).

★531★
ELECTRONIC NEWS—FINANCIAL FACT BOOK & DIRECTORY
Fairchild Books
Fairchild Publications, Inc.
7 E. 12th Street   Phone: (212) 741-4280
New York, NY 10003
Covers: 700 publicly held electronics and electronics-affiliated companies in the United States and Canada. **Entries include:** Company name; corporate address and phone; corporate officers and directors; nature of business and description of products; divisions, subsidiaries, and affiliates with locations and phone numbers; acquisitions and mergers; transfer agents with addresses; number of employees, plant size and growth, dates and earnings, and stock information for up to five years; financial data for the current and previous year, including income account, assets, and liabilities, and breakdown of revenue by line of business. **Arrangement:** Alphabetical. **Indexes:** Subsidiaries. **Pages** (approx.): 600. **Frequency:** Annual, September. **Editor:** Robin Feldman, Research Editor. **Price:** $80.00.

★532★
ELECTRONIC NEWS—LEADING FIRMS ISSUE
Fairchild Publications, Inc.
7 E. 12th Street   Phone: (212) 741-4000
New York, NY 10003
Publication includes: List of 50 leading United States electronic firms in terms of sales; similar data on leading foreign companies. **Entries include:** Company name, electronic sales, percent of sales in electronics, gross sales in all lines. **Arrangement:** By sales. **Frequency:** Annual, usually early July issue. **Editor:** James Lydon. **Advertising accepted. Price:** $1.00.

★533★
ELECTRONIC PACKAGING AND PRODUCTION MAGAZINE— PRINTED CIRCUITS DIRECTORY ISSUE
Milton S. Kiver Publications, Inc.
222 W. Adams Street   Phone: (312) 263-4866
Chicago, IL 60606
Publication includes: Over 1,700 manufacturers and suppliers of equipment and materials used in the manufacture of printed circuit boards. **Entries include:** Company name, address, phone. **Arrangement:** Alphabetical. **Indexes:** Product. **Pages** (approx.): 200. **Frequency:** Annual, December. **Editor:** Donald J. Levinthal. **Advertising accepted.** Circulation 27,550. **Price:** $20.00.

★534★
ELECTRONIC PACKAGING AND PRODUCTION MAGAZINE— VENDOR SELECTION ISSUE
Milton S. Kiver Publications, Inc.
222 W. Adams Street   Phone: (312) 263-4866
Chicago, IL 60606
Publication includes: Over 4,000 manufacturers and suppliers of equipment and materials used in the production, testing, and packaging of electronic devices and systems. **Entries include:** Company name, address, phone; some listings also include name of executive and products. **Arrangement:** Alphabetical. **Indexes:** Product. **Pages** (approx.): 330. **Frequency:** Annual, July. **Editor:** Michael Driscoll. **Advertising accepted.** Circulation 26,000. **Price:** $20.00 (current and 1980 editions).

★535★
ELECTRONIC REPRESENTATIVE DIRECTORY
Harris Publishing Company
2057-2 Aurora Road   Phone: (216) 425-9143
Twinsburg, OH 44087
Covers: 3,500 independent electronic manufacturers' representatives. **Entries include:** Company name, address, phone, sales personnel, lines handled, territory served, and facilities. **Arrangement:** Alphabetical; geographical. **Pages** (approx.): 140. **Frequency:** Annual, January. **Editor:** Jeanne Ring. **Advertising accepted.** Circulation 11,000. **Price:** $10.00, plus $1.00 shipping (current and 1980 editions). **Other information:** Reprinted from "Who's Who in Electronics."

Electronic Representatives Association—Membership Directory *See* **Electronics Industry Directory of Manufacturers' Representatives**

★536★
ELECTRONIC REPRESENTATIVES ASSOCIATION—MID-LANTIC CHAPTER MEMBERSHIP DIRECTORY
Mid-Lantic Chapter
Electronic Representatives Association
C/o George Carroll
Box 344   Phone: (215) 664-9755
Narbeth, PA 19072
Entries include: Company name, address, phone, key personnel, branch offices; lines carried and area served are given in separate list. **Arrangement:** Alphabetical. **Indexes:** Product. **Frequency:** Biennial, fall of odd years. **Price:** Free.

★537★
ELECTRONIC REPRESENTATIVES ASSOCIATION—SOUTHERN CALIFORNIA CHAPTER ROSTER
Southern California Chapter
Electronic Representatives Association
23987 Craftsman Road   Phone: (213) 888-9909
Calabasas, CA 91302
Covers: About 150 firms representing approximately 1,200 manufacturers of electronic products. **Entries include:** Company name, address, phone, TWX, branch offices, company officials, number of employees, services offered, manufacturers and products represented. **Arrangement:** Alphabetical. **Indexes:** Manufacturer, product. **Pages** (approx.): 100. **Frequency:** Annual, January/February. **Price:** Free.

Electronic Specifying and Procurement *See* **Who's Who in Electronics**

★538★
ELECTRONIC V.I.P. CLUB—MEMBERSHIP DIRECTORY
Electronic V.I.P. Club
C/o Sanford Levey
Electronic Distributors, Inc.
4900 N. Elston Avenue   Phone: (312) 283-4800
Chicago, IL 60630
Covers: About 500 individuals who have made significant contributions to the electronics industry. **Entries include:** Name, address, phone, company name, spouse's name, home phone and address. **Arrangement:** Alphabetical. **Frequency:** Annual, April. **Editor:** Sanford Levey, Executive Vice President. **Price:** Available to members only.

★539★
ELECTRONICS ASSOCIATION OF CALIFORNIA—DIRECTORY OF MEMBER FIRMS
Electronics Association of California
185 San Gabriel Drive   Phone: (408) 736-7600
Sunnyvale, CA 94086
Covers: About 300 small and medium-sized electronic firms. **Entries include:** Company name, address, phone, names and titles of key

personnel, products. **Arrangement:** Alphabetical. **Pages** (approx.): 125. **Frequency:** Annual, March. **Price:** $25.00.

★540★

ELECTRONICS BUYERS' GUIDE

McGraw-Hill, Inc.
1221 Avenue of the Americas   Phone: (212) 997-2544
New York, NY 10020
Covers: 6,000 companies worldwide manufacturing 4,000 electronic components, equipment, and allied products and materials. **Entries include:** Company name, address, phone, number of employees, financial data, products or services, trade names, name of sales contact, and local sales offices. **Arrangement:** Alphabetical. **Indexes:** Product, trade name. **Pages** (approx.): 900. **Frequency:** Annual, June. **Advertising accepted.** Circulation 30,000. **Price:** $30.00 (1980 edition).

★541★

ELECTRONICS INDUSTRY DIRECTORY OF MANUFACTURERS' REPRESENTATIVES

Electronic Representatives Association
233 E. Erie, Suite 1003   Phone: (312) 649-1333
Chicago, IL 60611
Number of listings: 1,850 member firms; international coverage. **Entries include:** Firm name, address, phone; names of owners; facilities; states in territory; association divisional memberships; number of employees; branch offices' addresses, phone numbers, telex, and names of managers. Type of product handled is shown in separate tabulation at end of each chapter section. **Arrangement:** Geographical, by chapter. **Indexes:** Personal name (of representative). **Pages** (approx.): 220. **Frequency:** Annual, June. **Editor:** Janet L. Hipp, Communications Director. **Advertising accepted. Price:** $5.00.

★542★

ELECTRONICS NEW PRODUCT DIRECTORY

Marketing Development
402 Border Road   Phone: (617) 369-5382
Concord, MA 01742
Publication includes: List of about 500 companies whose stock is publicly traded and who introduced "significant new electronic products" during the preceding year. **Entries include:** Company name, address. **Arrangement:** By product category. **Indexes:** Company name. **Frequency:** Annual, spring. **Price:** $450.00. **Also includes:** Principal content of publication is description of new products.

★543★

ELEVATOR WORLD—DIRECTORY ISSUE

Elevator World
345 Morgan Avenue   Phone: (205) 479-4514
Mobile, AL 36606
Covers: Elevator manufacturers, contractors, and suppliers who advertise during the year of publication. **Entries include:** Company name, address, phone, list of products or services. **Arrangement:** Alphabetical. **Frequency:** Annual, October. **Editor:** William C. Sturgeon. **Advertising accepted. Price:** $7.00.

★544★

EMBROIDERY DIRECTORY

Schiffli Lace and Embroidery Manufacturers Association
512 23rd Street   Phone: (201) 863-7300
Union City, NJ 07087
Covers: 70 merchandisers, 66 embroiderers, 48 allied trades (sources of equipment, yarn, design studios, etc.), 36 banking, insurance, and other agencies primarily in the northwestern New Jersey and New York City area (SIC 2397). **Entries include:** Company name, address, phone, and type of product or service. **Arrangement:** Classified into sections by trade or service type. **Pages** (approx.): 140. **Frequency:** Annual, November. **Editor:** I. Leonard Seiler. **Advertising accepted.** Circulation 2,000. **Price:** $5.00.

★545★

EMPLOYMENT MANAGEMENT ASSOCIATION—MEMBERSHIP ROSTER

Employment Management Association
20 William Street   Phone: (617) 235-8878
Wellesley, MA 02181
Covers: Employment and personnel executives in business, education, and industry. **Entries include:** Name, title, company, address. **Arrangement:** Alphabetical. **Indexes:** Company. **Pages** (approx.): 65. **Frequency:** Annual, September. **Editor:** John D. Erdlen, Executive Director. **Price:** Apply.

★546★

EMPLOYMENT OPPORTUNITIES IN THE LOUISIANA OFFSHORE MARINE INDUSTRY

Offshore Research Service
Box 2606 NSU
Thibodaux, LA 70301
Covers: Employment and training opportunities for entry level and licensed personnel for crewboats and supply vessels servicing the offshore oil exploration, production, and marine construction industry; includes list of marine companies with domestic and foreign fleets, and list of vocational schools offering marine-related courses. **Arrangement:** By topic. **Indexes:** Alphabetical index of courses and programs; geographical index of marine companies. **Pages** (approx.): 30. **Frequency:** Irregular; latest edition April 1979. **Editor:** John Rochelle. **Price:** $3.00, postpaid, payment with order.

★547★

ENCYCLOPEDIA OF BUSINESS INFORMATION SOURCES

Gale Research Company
Book Tower   Phone: (313) 961-2242
Detroit, MI 48226
Covers: Publishers of thousands of books on business-oriented topics, and live sources of information in the field, including trade associations, professional societies, etc. **Entries include:** Source name, address; some listings may contain additional information. **Arrangement:** Classified by highly specific subjects (helicopters, industrial diamonds, etc.); within each category, sources are arranged by type. **Indexes:** Detailed table of contents, with subject cross references. **Pages** (approx.): 665. **Frequency:** Irregular; latest edition 1976; new edition expected May 1980. **Editors:** Paul Wasserman, et al. **Price:** $52.00. **Other information:** See also listing for "Encyclopedia of Geographic Information Sources."

★548★

ENCYCLOPEDIA OF CONTEMPORARY TYPESETTING

Graphic Arts Technical Foundation
4615 Forbes Avenue   Phone: (412) 621-6941
Pittsburgh, PA 15213
Publication includes: List of manufacturers of phototypesetting equipment; equipment is described in detail in other sections of the book. **Entries include:** Company name, address. **Arrangement:** Alphabetical. **Pages** (approx.): 200. **Frequency:** Irregular; latest edition 1978. **Editor:** Charles Shapiro. **Price:** $36.00.

★549★

ENCYCLOPEDIA OF INFORMATION SYSTEMS AND SERVICES

Gale Research Company
Book Tower   Phone: (313) 961-2242
Detroit, MI 48226
Covers: More than 2,500 "storage and retrieval services, data base producers and publishers, online vendors, computer service companies, computerized retrieval systems, micrographic firms, libraries, government agencies, networks and consortia, information centers, data banks, clearinghouses, research centers, associations, and consultants" (subtitle) using data processing equipment and techniques in the collection, processing, storage, retrieval, dissemination, and utilization of information. Omits general purpose data management systems, conventional abstracting and indexing services, libraries with housekeeping or conventional reference

systems only, and hardware manufacturers. **Entries include:** Name of parent organization, name of system, address, phone, year founded, name of unit head, size of staff, names of any affiliated organizations, general description of system and its objectives, principal areas of interest or type of activity, sources of data for the system, type and quantity of stored information in all forms, publications, microform products and services, computer-based products and services, other services, clientele served, name of contact. **Arrangement:** Alphabetical. **Indexes:** Institution or company name, personal name, geographical, subject; additional indexes of data base producers and publishers, computer readable data bases, library and information networks, abstracting and indexing services, and several other categories. **Pages** (approx.): 1,200. **Frequency:** Formerly irregular; previous edition 1974, latest edition September 1978; biennial thereafter; supplemented by "New Information Systems and Services." **Editor:** Anthony T. Kruzas. **Price:** $110.00; supplement service, $70.00.

★550★
ENERGY SYSTEMS PRODUCT NEWS—BUYERS GUIDE & DIRECTORY ISSUE
Business Communications Inc., Subsidiary
Thomas Publishing Company
One Penn Plaza   Phone: (212) 695-0500
New York, NY 10001
Covers: Manufacturers, distributors, and other suppliers of power generating equipment, products, and related services used by public utilities and private industry. **Entries include:** Company name, address, phone, products or services. **Arrangement:** Alphabetical. **Indexes:** Product. **Pages** (approx.): 160. **Frequency:** Annual, July; first edition expected 1980. **Editor:** Michael E. Brown. **Advertising accepted.** Circulation 42,000. **Price:** $10.00.

★551★
ENGINEERING NEWS-RECORD—TOP 400 CONSTRUCTION CONTRACTORS ISSUE
McGraw-Hill, Inc.
1221 Avenue of the Americas   Phone: (212) 997-1221
New York, NY 10020
Covers: 400 United States contractors receiving largest dollar volumes of contracts in preceding calendar year. Separate list of 50 largest construction management firms. **Entries include:** For contractors - Company name, headquarters location, total value of contracts received in preceding year and of foreign contracts, construction specialties, rank. For construction managers - Same, except no specialty information. **Arrangement:** By contract value. **Frequency:** Annual, in an April issue. **Editor:** Arthur J. Fox. **Advertising accepted.** Circulation 102,000. **Price:** $3.00.

★552★
ENGINEERING NEWS-RECORD—TOP INTERNATIONAL CONTRACTORS ISSUE
McGraw-Hill, Inc.
1221 Avenue of the Americas   Phone: (212) 997-1221
New York, NY 10020
Covers: 200 contractors (including United States firms) competing outside their own national borders who received largest dollar volume of contracts in preceding calendar year. **Entries include:** Company name, headquarters location, total value of contracts received in preceding year, construction specialties, rank. **Arrangement:** By contract value. **Frequency:** Annual, issue not fixed; first list appeared in December 6, 1979 issue. **Editor:** Arthur J. Fox. **Advertising accepted.** Circulation 102,000. **Price:** $3.00.

★553★
ENGINEERING NEWS-RECORD—TOP SPECIALTY CONTRACTORS ISSUE
McGraw-Hill, Inc.
1221 Avenue of the Americas   Phone: (212) 997-1221
New York, NY 10020
Covers: Largest United States specialty subcontractors in mechanical

contracting (90 firms), electrical (90), excavation-foundation (25), steel erection (25), roofing-sheet metal (20), demolition-wrecking (20), glazing (12). **Entries include:** Company name, headquarters location, total value of contracts received in preceding year and of foreign contracts, construction specialties, rank. **Arrangement:** By contract value. **Frequency:** Annual, in an August issue. **Editor:** Arthur J. Fox. **Advertising accepted.** Circulation 102,000. **Price:** $3.00.

★554★
ENGINEERING NEWS-RECORD DIRECTORY OF CONTRACTORS
McGraw-Hill, Inc.
1221 Avenue of the Americas   Phone: (212) 997-2534
New York, NY 10020
Background: Limited to advertisers. **Entries include:** Company name, address, branch locations, subsidiaries, list of key personnel, territory served, capabilities. **Frequency:** Biennial, fall of even years. **Price:** $12.50 (1978 edition); $12.95 (tentative, 1980 edition).

ENR Directory of Contractors *See* Engineering News-Record Directory of Contractors

Environmental Wastes Control Manual & Catalog File *See* Public Works Manual

★555★
EVANSVILLE AREA MANUFACTURERS DIRECTORY [Indiana]
Metropolitan Evansville Chamber of Commerce
329 Main Street   Phone: (812) 425-8147
Evansville, IN 47708
Covers: About 425 firms in Vanderburgh, Warrick, Posey, and Gibson counties. **Entries include:** Company name, address, name of principal executive, number of employees, list of products. **Arrangement:** Geographical. **Indexes:** Product. **Pages** (approx.): 30. **Frequency:** Irregular; latest edition 1979. **Editor:** Larry E. Adams, Director of Organizational Affairs. **Former title:** Evansville Area Industrial Directory. **Price:** $5.00.

★556★
EXECUTIVE EMPLOYMENT GUIDE
American Management Associations
135 W. 50th Street   Phone: (212) 586-8100
New York, NY 10020
Covers: About 135 executive search firms personnel agencies, job registers, and job counselors. **Entries include:** Firm name, address, phone, type of firm, kinds of positions handled, minimum salary of jobs handled, and whether firm will review resumes and interview uninvited applicants. **Frequency:** Three or four cumulative revisions per year. **Price:** $2.00 per revision.

Exhibit Designers & Producers Association—Directory *See* National Trade Show Exhibitors Association—Exhibit Industry Guide

Exhibit Service Contractors Association—Directory *See* National Trade Show Exhibitors Association—Exhibit Industry Guide

★557★
EXHIBITS SCHEDULE: ANNUAL DIRECTORY OF TRADE AND INDUSTRIAL SHOWS
Bill Communications, Inc.
1422 Chestnut Street   Phone: (215) 563-0680
Philadelpha, PA 19102
Covers: Trade, industrial, and public shows, worldwide, which include exhibits. **Entries include:** Show name, name and address of contact, number of booths, dates, location, expected attendance, headquarters, show frequency. **Arrangement:** By industry and/or profession. **Indexes:** Geographical by show site, chronological. **Pages** (approx.): 200, annual; 100, supplement. **Frequency:** Annual, January; supplement, July. **Price:** $65.00, including supplement (current and 1980 editions). **Send orders to:** Exhibits Schedule, 633 Third Ave., New York, NY 10017 (212-986-4800).

★558★

EXPANDED SHALE, CLAY & SLATE INSTITUTE—ROSTER OF MEMBERS

Expanded Shale, Clay & Slate Institute
7401 Wisconsin Avenue, Suite 414   Phone: (301) 654-0140
Bethesda, MD 20014
Covers: About 30 producers of lightweight aggregate of expanded shales, clays, and slates by the rotary kiln method; international coverage. **Entries include:** Company name, address, brand names. **Arrangement:** Geographical. **Frequency:** Annual, September. **Editor:** Harry C. Robinson, Managing Director. **Price:** Free.

★559★

EXPORT—ANNUAL BUYERS GUIDE ISSUE

Johnston International Publishing Corporation
386 Park Avenue   Phone: (212) 689-0120
New York, NY 10016
Covers: 350 manufacturers and exporters of hardware, air conditioning and refrigeration equipment, tools, building materials, and consumer goods. Limited to advertisers. **Entries include:** Company name, address, phone, names of contacts. **Arrangement:** Alphabetical. **Indexes:** Product. **Frequency:** Annual, January/February issue. **Editor:** Robert Weingarten. **Advertising accepted.** **Price:** $10.00 (current and 1980 editions).

★560★

EXPORTERS & IMPORTERS, BUFFALO-NIAGARA AREA [New York]

Buffalo Area Chamber of Commerce
107 Delaware Avenue   Phone: (716) 849-6600
Buffalo, NY 14202
Number of listings: 600. **Entries include:** Company name, address, phone, and list of products. **Arrangement:** Alphabetical. **Indexes:** Product. **Pages (approx.):** 50. **Frequency:** Irregular. **Price:** $1.00.

★561★

EXPORTERS DIRECTORY/U.S. BUYING GUIDE

Journal of Commerce
110 Wall Street   Phone: (212) 425-1616
New York, NY 10005
Covers: 40,000 manufacturers with export interests, export managers, and export merchants in the United States. **Entries include:** Firm name, address, phone, names of principal executives, statistics, products, brand names. **Arrangement:** Geographical. **Indexes:** Company name, product (by Standard International Trade Classification number). **Pages (approx.):** 1,400. **Frequency:** Biennial, fall of even years. **Advertising accepted.** **Price:** $150.00.

★562★

FACTORY OUTLET SHOPPING GUIDE FOR NEW ENGLAND

Bird Associates, Inc.
449 Second Street
Oradell, NJ 07649
Covers: Factory, wholesaler's, distributor's, and importer's outlets, plus clearance centers and discount stores. **Entries include:** Company name, address, phone, hours of business, description of merchandise sold, store policies, range of discounts, and travel directions. **Arrangement:** Alphabetical. **Indexes:** Geographical, merchandise category. **Pages (approx.):** 90. **Frequency:** Annual, August. **Editor:** Jean D. Bird, Vice President. **Price:** $2.95. **Send orders to:** FOSG Publications, Box 239, Oradell, NJ 07649 (201-384-2500). **Also includes:** Glossary of manufacturers' and jobbers' terms.

★563★

FACTORY OUTLET SHOPPING GUIDE FOR NEW JERSEY AND ROCKLAND COUNTY [New York]

Bird Associates, Inc.
449 Second Street
Oradell, NJ 07649
Other information: 80 pages. Published annually in August. Content, price, etc., same as "Factory Outlet Shopping Guide for New England," described in separate listing.

★564★

FACTORY OUTLET SHOPPING GUIDE FOR NEW YORK/LONG ISLAND/WESTCHESTER

Bird Associates, Inc.
449 Second Street
Oradell, NJ 07649
Other information: 90 pages. Published annually in August. Content, price, etc., same as "Factory Outlet Shopping Guide for New England," described in separate listing.

★565★

FACTORY OUTLET SHOPPING GUIDE FOR NORTH AND SOUTH CAROLINA

Bird Associates, Inc.
449 Second Street
Oradell, NJ 07649
Other information: 40 pages. Annual, August. Content, price, etc., same as "Factory Outlet Shopping Guide for New England," described in separate listing.

★566★

FACTORY OUTLET SHOPPING GUIDE FOR PENNSYLVANIA

Bird Associates, Inc.
449 Second Street
Oradell, NJ 07649
Number of listings: 400. **Other information:** 80 pages. Published annually in August. Content, price, etc., same as "Factory Outlet Shopping Guide for New England," described in separate listing.

★567★

FACTORY OUTLET SHOPPING GUIDE FOR WASHINGTON, DC/ Maryland/Delaware/Virginia

Bird Associates, Inc.
449 Second Street
Oradell, NJ 07649
Other information: 50 pages. Published annually in August. Content, price, etc., same as "Factory Outlet Shopping Guide for New England," described in separate listing.

★568★

FACTORY STORE GUIDE TO ALL NEW ENGLAND

Globe Pequot Press, Inc.
Old Chester Road
Chester, CT 06412
Covers: About 265 factory outlet stores. **Entries include:** Store name, address, phone, hours, credit cards accepted, and description of merchandise lines carried. **Arrangement:** Geographical. **Indexes:** Type of merchandise. **Pages (approx.):** 200. **Frequency:** Irregular; latest edition June 1979. **Editors:** A. Miser and A. Pennypincher. **Price:** $4.50.

★569★

FAIRCHILD'S FINANCIAL MANUAL OF RETAIL STORES

Fairchild Books
Fairchild Publications, Inc.
7 E. 12th Street   Phone: (212) 741-4280
New York, NY 10003
Covers: 500 publicly held companies in the United States and Canada which are partly or exclusively retail. **Entries include:** Company name, corporate address and phone, corporate officers and directors, nature of business and/or description of products, subsidiaries and divisions with their locations, acquisitions and mergers, transfer agents with addresses, financial data for current and previous year including income, assets, and liabilities, plus number of stores, sales and earnings, and stock information for up to five years, breakdown of revenue by line of business. **Arrangement:** Alphabetical. **Pages (approx.):** 400. **Frequency:** Annual, October. **Editor:** Robin Feldman, Research Editor. **Price:** $45.00.

★570★

FAIRCHILD'S MARKET DIRECTORY OF WOMEN'S AND CHILDREN'S APPAREL [New York City]
Fairchild Books
Fairchild Publications, Inc.
7 E. 12th Street   Phone: (212) 741-4280
New York, NY 10003
Covers: Manufacturers of women's and children's apparel in New York City. **Entries include:** Firm name, address, phone, and room location. **Arrangement:** Classified by merchandise category and building address. **Frequency:** Irregular; latest edition September 1979. **Price:** $9.50. **Also includes:** Garment District map, Manhattan street guide, and travel information.

★571★

FAIRCHILD'S TEXTILE & APPAREL FINANCIAL DIRECTORY
Fairchild Books
Fairchild Publications, Inc.
7 E. 12th Street   Phone: (212) 741-4280
New York, NY 10003
Covers: 275 publicly owned textile and apparel corporations. **Entries include:** Company name, address, phone, names of executives, trade and brand names, financial data, list of products or services. **Arrangement:** Alphabetical. **Indexes:** Trademark. **Pages** (approx.): 285. **Frequency:** Annual, fall. **Editor:** Ms. Robin Feldman. **Price:** $40.00.

★572★

FALL RIVER AREA CHAMBER OF COMMERCE—DIRECTORY OF MANUFACTURERS [Massachusetts]
Fall River Area Chamber of Commerce
101 Rock Street   Phone: (617) 676-8226
Fall River, MA 02722
Entries include: Company name, address, phone, name of principal executive, number of employees, list of products. **Arrangement:** Alphabetical. **Frequency:** Annual. **Price:** $10.00.

★573★

FASHION ACCESSORIES MAGAZINE—BLUEBOOK DIRECTORY OF ACCESSORIES MANUFACTURERS
Business Journals, Inc.
22 S. Smith Street   Phone: (203) 853-6015
Norwalk, CT 06855
Covers: 1,600 manufacturers, importers, and sales representatives producing or handling belts, gloves, handbags, scarves, hosiery, jewelry, sunglasses, and umbrellas. **Entries include:** Company name, address, and phone. **Arrangement:** Classified by product. **Frequency:** Annual, January. **Editor:** Joanne Lombardo, Listings Editor. **Advertising accepted.** Circulation 11,000. **Former title:** Handbags, Gloves, and Accessories - Directory Issue (1973). **Price:** $7.00 (current edition); $10.00 (1980 edition); payment with order.

★574★

FASTENER FINDER: SURPLUS INVENTORY DIRECTORY
Resource Publications, Inc.
Covers: About 200 domestic and foreign manufacturers of fasteners; and importers, jobbers, and end users of fasteners with excess stocks for sale. **Entries include:** Name, address, phone, name of contact, minimum billing, specialties (for manufacturers and jobbers), and general information on fasteners available. **Arrangement:** Alphabetical. **Indexes:** Surplus fasteners by item and by vendor. **Pages** (approx.): 2,000. **Frequency:** Semiannual, spring and fall. **Editor:** Warren Neil Olsen, Jr. **Advertising accepted.** Circulation 2,000. **Price:** $155.00 per issue. (Not verified)

★575★

FDS GUIDE TO AMERICAN INLAND TOWBOAT FLEETS
Fleet Data Service
6362 Windswept, Suite 220   Phone: (713) 780-2582
Houston, TX 77057
Covers: About 1,000 inland towboat fleets serving the Mississippi

River system, the Gulf intra-coastal waterway system, and other Gulf Coast rivers. **Entries include:** Fleet name, address, phone, vessel name, year built, length, draft, continuous horsepower, engine make and model, and other specification data. **Arrangement:** In three volumes: Louisiana-based fleets; fleets serving non-Mississippi River points; and fleets serving the Mississippi River. Alphabetical by fleet name within volumes. **Indexes:** Vessel name. **Frequency:** Annual; first edition March 1979. **Price:** $125.00, for set of three volumes; $50.00 each.

★576★

FDS GUIDE TO AMERICAN OFFSHORE VESSELS
Fleet Data Service
6362 Windswept, Suite 220   Phone: (713) 780-2582
Houston, TX 77057
Covers: About 150 American offshore fleets and their 1,600 petroleum-service vessels (both United States and foreign flag), including tug and supply vessels, utility boats, crewboats, survey and service vessels over 60 feet. **Entries include:** Fleet name, address, phone, TWX/telex number, names of vessels, and flag, year built, length, continuous horsepower, engine make and model, tankage, and capacity for each vessel. **Arrangement:** Alphabetical. **Indexes:** Vessel name. **Frequency:** Annual, May. **Price:** $95.00.

★577★

FDS GUIDE TO MAJOR AMERICAN TUG FLEETS
Fleet Data Service
6362 Windswept, Suite 220   Phone: (713) 780-2582
Houston, TX 77057
Covers: About 70 tugboat fleets with over 850 tugs with petroleum-service and other offshore capabilities. **Entries include:** Fleet name, address, names of vessels, and, for each vessel, year built, length, horsepower, bow configuration, winch availability. **Arrangement:** Alphabetical. **Indexes:** Vessel name. **Frequency:** Annual, February. **Price:** $50.00.

★578★

FDS SPECIFICATIONS OF LARGE FOREIGN OFFSHORE VESSELS
Fleet Data Service
6362 Windswept, Suite 220   Phone: (713) 780-2582
Houston, TX 77057
Covers: Over 70 foreign fleets with more than 500 petroleum-service and other vessels of 165 feet or larger (including diving support, geophysical, well service vessels, and others). **Entries include:** Fleet name, address, phone, TWX/telex number, names of vessels, and year built, length, continuous horsepower, engine make and model, tankage, and capacity for each vessel. **Arrangement:** Alphabetical. **Indexes:** Vessel name. **Frequency:** Annual, summer. **Price:** $95.00.

Feature Writers, Photographers, and Syndicates Directory *See* **Working Press of the Nation**

★579★

FEDERAL SUPPLY CODE FOR MANUFACTURERS
Defense Logistics Service Center
Defense Logistics Agency
Defense Department
Battle Creek, MI 49016
Covers: About 92,000 companies, primarily manufacturers, that produce or maintain design control for products cataloged by federal government agencies. **Entries include:** Company name, address, five-digit Federal Supply Code for Manufacturers, and letter code indicating active or inactive status or other attributes; some listings include previous company name, previous location, or other information. **Arrangement:** "Name to Code" section is alphabetical by company name; "Code to Name" section is numerical by code number. **Frequency:** Six times yearly. **Price:** "Name to Code," $18.30 per year, $3.25 per issue (microfiche only; S/N 008-007-80003-5); "Code to Name," $14.45 per year, $2.50 per issue (microfiche only; S/N 008-007-80004-3).

★580★

FENCE INDUSTRY—DIRECTORY ISSUE
Communication Channels, Inc.
6285 Barfield Road   Phone: (404) 256-9800
Atlanta, GA 30328
Covers: Manufacturers of fence materials. **Entries include:** Company name, address. Entries for advertisers also show phone, list of products, foreign suppliers. **Arrangement:** Alphabetical. **Indexes:** Product, brand name. **Pages** (approx.): 160. **Frequency:** Annual, December. **Editor:** William Coker. **Advertising accepted.** Circulation 13,000. **Former title:** International Directory of Fence Materials. **Price:** $6.00.

Fiber Optics Handbook and Marketing Guide *See* International Fiber Optics and Communications—Handbook and Buyer's Guide Issue

★581★

FIBER PRODUCER—BUYERS GUIDE ISSUE
W. R. C. Smith Publishing Company
1760 Peachtree Road, N. W.   Phone: (404) 874-4462
Atlanta, GA 30357
Publication includes: Manufacturers and suppliers of equipment, supplies, and services used in the man-made fibers industry. **Entries include:** Company name, address, phone. **Frequency:** Annual, October. **Editor:** Ann W. Barrett. **Advertising accepted.** Circulation 8,100. **Price:** $10.00.

★582★

FILM, AIR AND PACKAGE CARRIERS CONFERENCE—MEMBERSHIP DIRECTORY
Film, Air and Package Carriers Conference
1616 P Street, N. W.   Phone: (202) 797-5363
Washington, DC 20036
Covers: About 225 motor carriers specializing in the transportation of films, air freight, or air express packages usually requiring expedited ground handling. Conference is composed of National Film Carriers, Air Freight Motor Carriers Conference, and American Package Express Carriers Association, and is affiliated with American Trucking Associations. **Entries include:** Firm name, address, telephone and telex numbers, names of key personnel, ICC certificate number (if any), airports served, branches, services. **Arrangement:** Geographical. **Indexes:** Firm name (with division, location, services). **Pages** (approx.): 35. **Frequency:** Annual, January. **Price:** $5.00 (current and 1980 editions).

★583★

FINANCIAL PERFORMANCE PROFILE OF PUBLIC APPAREL COMPANIES
Kurt Salmon Associates, Inc.
350 Fifth Avenue   Phone: (212) 564-3690
New York, NY 10001
Covers: About 125 publicly held apparel manufacturers. **Entries include:** Company name, address, names of principal officers, products, stock exchange on which listed, balance sheets, profit and loss statements, and analysis of key financial ratios. **Pages** (approx.): 650. **Frequency:** Annual, May. **Price:** $200.00. **Also includes:** Financial data are also provided and analyzed for the apparel industry as a whole.

★584★

FINANCIAL PERFORMANCE PROFILE OF PUBLIC TEXTILE COMPANIES
Kurt Salmon Associates, Inc.
350 Fifth Avenue   Phone: (212) 564-3690
New York, NY 10001
Covers: About 100 publicly held textile manufacturers. **Entries include:** Company name, address, names of principal officers, products, stock exchange on which listed, balance sheets, profit and loss statements, and analysis of key financial ratios. **Pages** (approx.): 650. **Frequency:** Annual, May. **Price:** $200.00. **Also includes:** Financial data are also provided and analysed for the textile industry as a whole.

Finder's Directory [Shoe repair] *See* Shoe Service Wholesalers in the United States and Canada

★585★

FINDEX: THE DIRECTORY OF MARKET RESEARCH REPORTS, STUDIES AND SURVEYS
Find/SVP
500 Fifth Avenue   Phone: (212) 354-2424
New York, NY 10036
Covers: Publishers and research firms which publish over 4,000 market research reports, subscription research reports, audits, client studies, and other consumer and industrial surveys and studies. **Entries include:** Publisher name, address. For reports - Title, date of publication, number of pages, price, description of content, publisher name. **Arrangement:** Publishers are alphabetical, reports are by subject/industry. **Indexes:** Subject. **Pages** (approx.): 360. **Frequency:** Annual, January; semiannual supplement. **Editor:** Diana Degen. **Price:** $110.00 including supplement, postpaid, payment with order.

★586★

FIRE & SECURITY DIRECTORY
Penton/IPC
614 Superior Avenue West   Phone: (216) 696-0300
Cleveland, OH 44113
Covers: Manufacturers of fire protection and security equipment. **Entries include:** Company name and address. **Arrangement:** Alphabetical; classified by product category. **Frequency:** Annual, May or June. **Editor:** Peter J. Sheridan. **Advertising accepted.** Circulation 54,000. **Price:** $2.00 (1980 edition).

★587★

FIRE PROTECTION REFERENCE DIRECTORY
National Fire Protection Association
470 Atlantic Avenue   Phone: (617) 482-8755
Boston, MA 02210
Covers: Manufacturers of fire protection products. **Entries include:** Company name, address, phone, list of products or services. **Arrangement:** By product categories. **Pages** (approx.): 190. **Frequency:** Annual, December. **Editor:** Denise L. Babcock. **Advertising accepted.** Circulation 55,000. **Price:** $5.00.

★588★

FIRMS IN THE 8(A) BUSINESS DEVELOPMENT PROGRAM
Small Business Administration
1441 L Street, N. W.   Phone: (202) 653-6407
Washington, DC 20416
Covers: About 900 minority-owned or minority-controlled businesses which are receiving assistance from the Small Business Administration. **Entries include:** Firm name, address, phone, name of owner or president, line of business, minority code. **Arrangement:** Geographical. **Frequency:** Irregular; latest edition May 1979. **Price:** Free.

★589★

500 CONTRACTORS RECEIVING THE LARGEST DOLLAR VOLUME OF MILITARY PRIME CONTRACT AWARDS FOR RDT&E
Directorate for Information Operations & Reports
Washington Headquarters Services
Defense Department
Pentagon, Room 4B 938   Phone: (202) 697-3182
Washington, DC 20301
Covers: 500 largest contractors (including business, nonprofit organizations, foreign contractors, and government agencies) for research, development, test, and evaluation projects. **Entries include:** Company name, total dollar value of awards, rank, location of individual facilities and amount of local awards; symbol indicates whether classified as a small business. **Arrangement:** By type of

organization, then by rank. **Indexes:** Alphabetical. **Pages** (approx.): 25. **Frequency:** Annual. **Price:** Free.

★590★

FLEET OWNER—SPECS AND BUYERS' DIRECTORY ISSUE
McGraw-Hill, Inc.
1221 Avenue of the Americas
New York, NY 10020
Publication includes: Lists of manufacturers and of suppliers, distributors, and manufacturers' representatives of equipment and materials used in the operation, management, and maintenance of truck and bus fleets. **Entries include:** Company name, address, phone. **Arrangement:** Manufacturers are classified by product; others are geographical. **Frequency:** Annual, October. **Advertising accepted.** Circulation 75,000. **Price:** $2.50. **Also includes:** State weight limits, state trucking associations, specifications for equipment and components, training aids and courses, OSHA and BMCS offices, and manufacturers' service managers.

★591★

FLEXIBLE PACKAGING ASSOCIATION—MEMBERSHIP DIRECTORY
Flexible Packaging Association
12025 Shaker Boulevard   Phone: (216) 229-6373
Cleveland, OH 44120
Covers: Over 175 member companies which manufacture flexible packaging (primarily bags), and supplies and equipment used in its manufacturing. **Entries include:** Company name, address, phone, names of representatives to association. **Arrangement:** By type of membership. **Indexes:** Geographical, product. **Pages** (approx.): 25. **Frequency:** Annual, September. **Price:** Available to members only.

★592★

FLIGHT INTERNATIONAL—WORLD AIRLINE DIRECTORY ISSUE
IPC Transport Press Ltd.
Dorset House
Stamford Street
London SE1 9LU, England
Covers: Over 500 scheduled airlines and charter companies operating commercial fixed and rotary wing aircraft for passenger and freight service, worldwide. **Entries include:** Airline name, address, telex number, date established, type of ownership, names of subsidiaries, services offered, number and type of aircraft in service and on order, and number, manufacturer, and type of simulators operated. **Arrangement:** Alphabetical. **Indexes:** Geographical. **Frequency:** Annual, May. **Editor:** J. M. Ramsden. **Advertising accepted. Price:** 40 pounds (1980 edition).

★593★

FLOOR COVERING WEEKLY—HANDBOOK OF CONTRACT FLOOR COVERING ISSUE
Bart Publications, Inc., Division
Cox Broadcasting Corporation
919 Third Avenue   Phone: (212) 759-8050
New York, NY 10022
Covers: Floor covering manufacturers. **Entries include:** Company name, address, phone, and name of contact. **Arrangement:** Alphabetical. **Indexes:** Product. **Frequency:** Annual, May. **Advertising accepted.** Circulation 37,500. **Price:** $10.00 (current edition); $15.00 (1980 edition); postpaid. **Also includes:** Principal content is technical specifications for over 1,000 commercial flooring products.

★594★

FLOOR COVERING WEEKLY—LOCAL PRODUCT SOURCE DIRECTORY ISSUE
Bart Publications, Inc., Division
Cox Broadcasting Corporation
919 Third Avenue   Phone: (212) 759-8050
New York, NY 10022
Covers: Manufacturers and importers of carpet, rugs, carpet cushion, and fiber, resilient tile and sheet, wood, and ceramic floor coverings. Separate listing of distributors. **Entries include:** For manufacturers -

Company name, address, phone, regional sales offices, local distributors, products, association memberships. For distributors - Company name, address, phone, manufacturers represented. **Arrangement:** Alphabetical. **Indexes:** Geographical index of distributors. **Frequency:** Annual, October. **Advertising accepted. Price:** $5.00.

★595★

FLOORING—DIRECTORY AND BUYING GUIDE ISSUE
Harcourt Brace Jovanovich, Inc.
757 Third Avenue   Phone: (212) 888-4354
New York, NY 10017
Covers: 1,000 manufacturers, 1,000 workrooms, 100 manufacturers' representatives, and 2,000 distributors of floor, wall, and other interior surfacing products and equipment in the United States and Canada. Includes lists of 10,000 brand names and 90 trade associations. **Entries include:** Company name, address, phone, key personnel, brand names, and list of products or services. **Arrangement:** Divided into sections: products and equipment; brand names (alphabetical); manufacturers (alphabetical); distributors, workrooms, and representatives sections (all geographical); trade associations (alphabetical and geographical). **Pages** (approx.): 300. **Frequency:** Annual, November. **Editor:** Michael Korsonsky. **Advertising accepted. Price:** $5.00.

★596★

FLORIDA AIRPORT DIRECTORY
Bureau of Aviation
Florida Department of Transportation
605 Suwannee Street   Phone: (904) 488-8444
Tallahassee, FL 32301
Covers: 140 public use airports; 290 private airports; heliports, and seaplane bases. **Entries include:** For public airports - Name, coordinates, major city served; name and address of owner; name and phone of manager; flight and service data. Other listings show facility name, city served, address, phone, manager name, length and type of landing surface, coordinates. **Arrangement:** By type of facility, then geographical. **Indexes:** Airport name/city served. **Pages** (approx.): 180. **Frequency:** Irregular; latest edition May 1979. **Editor:** William Stockton, Airport Licensor. **Price:** $4.00, postpaid.

★597★

FLORIDA BUILDER MAGAZINE—PRODUCT DIRECTORY ISSUE
Peninsular Publishing Company, Inc.
3300 Henderson Boulevard, Suite 105   Phone: (813) 870-2445
Tampa, FL 33609
Covers: Manufacturers of equipment and products for the building industry (residential, commercial, and roadbuilding). **Entries include:** Company name, address, trade and brand names, list of products. **Arrangement:** Alphabetical. **Indexes:** Product. **Pages** (approx.): 50. **Frequency:** Annual, February. **Editor:** Ann R. Griffin. **Advertising accepted.** Circulation 9,000. **Price:** $1.00 (1979 edition); $1.25 (1980 edition).

★598★

FLORIDA FORUM—DESKBOOK DIRECTORY ISSUE [Roofing, sheet metal, and air conditioning contracting]
Florida Roofing Sheet Metal & Air Conditioning Contractors Association
1040 S. Semoran Boulevard   Phone: (305) 671-9232
Winter Park, FL 32792
Covers: Manufacturers, distributors, and manufacturers' representatives in the air conditioning, roofing, and sheet metal industries in Florida. **Entries include:** Company name, address, phone, locations and phone numbers for branches, and products. **Arrangement:** By roofing, sheet metal, or air conditioning, then by type of firm. **Frequency:** Annual, January. **Editor:** Steve Munnell. **Advertising accepted.** Circulation 3,500. **Price:** $1.50 (current and 1980 editions).

★599★
FLORIDA GOLDEN PAGES [Advertiser services]
Florida Golden Pages
15221 N. E. 21st Avenue   Phone: (305) 233-6510
North Miami Beach, FL 33162
Covers: Art suppliers, photographers, illustrators and designers, and others whose products or services are used in motion picture, television, and audiovisual industries in Florida. **Entries include:** Company name, address, and phone. **Arrangement:** By type of service. **Pages** (approx.): 300. **Frequency:** Annual, January. **Price:** $19.95, postpaid, payment with order (1980 edition).

★600★
FLORIDA INDUSTRIES GUIDE
Industries Guides, Inc.
203 E. Park Lake Street   Phone: (305) 841-7911
Orlando, FL 32802
Number of listings: 9,000. **Entries include:** Company name, address, phone number, name of contact, list of products, SIC number. **Pages** (approx.): 200. **Frequency:** Annual, fall. **Editor:** Richard J. McHenry. **Price:** $25.00.

★601★
FLORIDA STATE INDUSTRIAL DIRECTORY
State Industrial Directories Corporation
Two Penn Plaza   Phone: (212) 564-0340
New York, NY 10001
Number of listings: 8,700. **Entries include:** Company name, address, phone, names of key executives, number of employees, plant size, 4-digit SIC code, products, whether firm imports or exports, and whether firm has research facilities. **Arrangement:** Geographical. **Indexes:** Alphabetical, product (includes mailing address and phone for each firm). **Frequency:** Annual; first edition May 1979. **Advertising accepted. Price:** $50.00 (current and 1980 editions).

★602★
FLORIDA TREND—DIRECTORY OF FLORIDA'S PUBLIC COMPANIES ISSUE
Trend Publications, Inc.
Box 2350   Phone: (813) 247-5411
Tampa, FL 33601
Covers: About 300 companies which are publicly traded and headquartered in Florida. **Entries include:** Company name, address, phone; exchange and exchange symbol; current stock price and range of current year; profits to earning ratio figure; annual dividend figure; line of business; names of subsidiaries; names of officers; five-year summary figures for sales/revenues, net income, earnings and dividends per share; financial data; number of shares outstanding. **Arrangement:** Alphabetical. **Frequency:** Annual, July. **Editor:** Walker Roberts. **Advertising accepted.** Circulation 35,000. **Price:** $2.00, postpaid, payment with order.

★603★
FLORIST—BUYERS' DIRECTORY ISSUE
Florist Transworld Delivery Association
29200 Northwestern Highway   Phone: (313) 355-9300
Southfield, MI 48076
Covers: 1,200 suppliers in floral industry; 7,000 product listings. **Entries include:** Company listings include name, address, phone, and products. Product listings include company name only. **Arrangement:** Classified by product, in alphabetical order; companies listed alphabetically. **Pages** (approx.): 230. **Frequency:** Annual, August. **Editor:** William Golden. **Advertising accepted.** Circulation 24,000. **Price:** $2.00 (current and 1980 editions).

★604★
FLUID POWER HANDBOOK & DIRECTORY
Penton/IPC
614 Superior Avenue West   Phone: (216) 696-0300
Cleveland, OH 44113
Covers: 950 manufacturers and distributors of fluid power products in the United States and Canada. **Entries include:** Entries generally give company name and address. Advertisers' section includes sales executives' names, phones, and sales outlets. **Arrangement:** Manufacturers are alphabetical, distributors geographical. **Indexes:** Product, trade names. **Pages** (approx.): 1,170. **Frequency:** Biennial, December of odd years. **Editor:** Tobi Goldoftas. **Advertising accepted.** Circulation 29,000. **Price:** $25.00, plus $2.00 shipping.

★605★
FLYING ANNUAL & BUYERS' GUIDE
Ziff-Davis Publishing Company
One Park Avenue
New York, NY 10016
Publication includes: List of manufacturers of aircraft and avionic equipment. **Entries include:** Company name, address, products. **Arrangement:** Alphabetical. **Frequency:** Annual. **Editor:** Robert Parke. **Former title:** Flying Annual and Pilots' Buying Guide. **Price:** $3.00, postpaid, payment with order.

★606★
FOCUS—METRO MARKETING DIRECTORY ISSUE [Philadelphia, Pennsylvania advertising services]
Focus
1015 Chestnut Street   Phone: (215) 925-8545
Philadelphia, PA 19107
Covers: About 500 advertising and public relations agencies, market research firms, graphic arts services, and other companies of interest to marketing managers in the Philadelphia area. **Entries include:** Company or firm name, address, name and title of principal executive, free-lance services used, year established, whether corporation or other form of organization, number of employees, amount and type of billings, names of accounts (when furnished). **Arrangement:** By type of service. **Frequency:** Annual, June. **Indexes:** Alphabetical. **Editor:** Vijay S. Kothare. **Price:** $3.00 (current edition); $5.00 (1980 edition).

Food Brokers of the United States *See* Grocery Communications—Food Broker Issue

★607★
FOOD ENGINEERING MASTER
Chilton Company
Chilton Way   Phone: (215) 687-8200
Radnor, PA 19089
Publication includes: Over 2,000 manufacturers and suppliers of equipment and products for food processing plants. **Entries include:** Company name, address, phone. **Arrangement:** Alphabetical. **Indexes:** Product. **Pages** (approx.): 1,800. **Frequency:** Annual, July. **Editor:** Pat O'Donnell. **Advertising accepted.** Circulation 20,000. **Price:** $55.00. **Also includes:** Catalogs of over 500 companies.

★608★
FOOD ENGINEERING'S DIRECTORY OF U.S. FOOD PLANTS
Chilton Company
Chilton Way   Phone: (215) 687-8200
Radnor, PA 19089
Covers: More than 11,000 food and beverage plants with 20 or more employees, food and beverage research and development facilities, and company headquarters. **Entries include:** Company name, address, number of employees, phone, SIC codes. **Arrangement:** Alphabetical. **Indexes:** SIC, geographical. **Pages** (approx.): 400. **Frequency:** Not established; first edition January 1978. **Price:** $195.00, postpaid, payment with order.

Food Equipment Distributors Association—Roster *See* Food Service Equipment Specialist—Buyer's Guide and Product Directory Issue

Food Industry Directory [Washington, Alaska] *See* Grocery Industry Directory of Washington State and Alaska

Food Processing—Catalog of Ingredients, Equipment & Supplies Issue *See* Food Processing—Guide & Directory to Ingredients, Equipment...

★609★
FOOD PROCESSING—GUIDE & DIRECTORY TO INGREDIENTS, EQUIPMENT & SUPPLIES
Putman Publishing Company
430 N. Michigan Avenue   Phone: (312) 644-2020
Chicago, IL 60611
Covers: Over 2,200 food ingredient and equipment manufacturers (SIC 201-209). **Entries include:** Company name, address, phone, **Arrangement:** Alphabetical. **Indexes:** Product. **Frequency:** Annual, July. **Editor:** Roy G. Hlavacek, Publishing Director. **Advertising accepted.** Circulation 56,000. **Former title:** Food Processing - Catalog of Ingredients, Equipment & Supplies Issue. **Price:** $25.00.

Food Processing Machinery and Supplies Association— Membership Directory *See* Food Processor's Guide

★610★
FOOD PROCESSOR'S GUIDE
Food Processing Machinery and Supplies Association
1828 L Street, N. W., Suite 700   Phone: (202) 833-5770
Washington, DC 20036
Covers: More than 425 association members who exhibit at the International Exposition for Food Processors. **Entries include:** Company name, address, phone, names of executives, products and services, length of membership in the association, and hotel and booth number when available. **Arrangement:** Alphabetical. **Pages** (approx.): 260. **Frequency:** Annual, January/February. **Advertising accepted.** Circulation 12,000. **Former title:** Food Processor's Guide to Production, Processing, and Packaging Equipment, Supplies and Services. **Price:** Free.

Food Processor's Guide to Production, Processing, and Packaging Equipment, Supplies and Services *See* Food Processor's Guide

★611★
FOOD SERVICE MARKETING—DIRECTORY OF FOOD, EQUIPMENT, SUPPLIES AND SERVICES ISSUE
EIP, Inc.
2132 Fordem Avenue   Phone: (608) 244-3528
Madison, WI 53704
Covers: About 450 food companies, equipment and supply companies, and other suppliers to the food service industry. **Entries include:** Company name, address, phone, name of contact. **Arrangement:** Alphabetical within above categories. **Indexes:** Product. **Pages** (approx.): 150. **Frequency:** Annual, May. **Editor:** Jeanette Riechers. **Advertising accepted.** Circulation 106,000. **Price:** Not sold separately; $24.00 per year.

★612★
FOOD SERVICE MARKETING—ELECTRIC FOOD SERVICE EQUIPMENT ISSUE
EIP, Inc.
2132 Fordem Avenue   Phone: (608) 244-3528
Madison, WI 53704
Number of listings: 450, paid. **Entries include:** Food equipment photograph, model number, dimensions, capacity, trade name, plus company name, address, phone, and name of executive. **Arrangement:** Alphabetical by company. **Frequency:** Annual, August. **Editor:** Jeanette Riechers. **Advertising accepted.** Circulation 106,000. **Price:** Not sold separately; $24.00 per year.

Foodservice Consultants Society International—Membership Roster *See* Foodservice Equipment Specialist—Buyer's Guide & Product Directory...

Foodservice Equipment Dealer—Buyer's Guide and Product Directory Issue *See* Foodservice Equipment Specialist— Buyer's Guide...Issue

★613★
FOODSERVICE EQUIPMENT SPECIALIST—BUYER'S GUIDE AND PRODUCT DIRECTORY ISSUE
Cahners Publishing Company, Inc.
Five S. Wabash Avenue   Phone: (312) 372-6880
Chicago, IL 60603
Publication includes: Over 1,000 manufacturers of foodservice equipment and supplies; membership rosters for Food Equipment Distributors Association, National Association of Food Equipment Manufacturers, Food Equipment Manufacturers Association, and Foodservice Consultants Society, International; list of peripheral trade associations. **Entries include:** Company or individual name, address; associations list and rosters include phone and name of contact. **Arrangement:** Alphabetical. **Indexes:** Trade and brand name (interspersed in manufacturer's directory), product. **Pages** (approx.): 140. **Frequency:** Annual, September or October. **Editor:** Russ Carpenter. **Advertising accepted.** Circulation 13,000. **Price:** $12.00.

★614★
FOODSERVICE/WEST—BRANDS/SOURCES GUIDE & DIRECTORY COVERING CALIFORNIA, ARIZONA, NEVADA
Harlequin Publications
Box 875   Phone: (213) 375-8196
Palos Verdes, CA 90274
Covers: About 3,000 brokers, distributors, manufacturers and manufacturers' representatives, service companies, and other companies providing equipment, supplies, and food to the foodservice industry in California, Arizona, and Nevada. **Entries include:** Company name, address, phone; name of parent company, if any; addresses and phone numbers of branch offices, if any. Broker and manufacturer representative listings also include products, memberships, and names of principals in broker index. **Arrangement:** Alphabetical. **Indexes:** Broker/representative firm name, equipment manufacturer/ representative company name, product, brand name. **Pages** (approx.): 120. **Frequency:** Annual, July. **Editor:** Audrey M. Dodd. **Advertising accepted.** Circulation 10,000. **Price:** $10.00, postpaid.

★615★
FOOTWEAR NEWS—DIRECTORY ISSUE
Fairchild Publications, Inc.
7 E. 12th Street   Phone: (212) 741-4320
New York, NY 10003
Covers: Manufacturers and importers of footwear in the United States; separate list of wholesalers. **Entries include:** Company name, address, phone, code for category of footwear manufactured or imported; divisions or subsidiaries, if any, and wholesale price range. **Arrangement:** By type of shoe (women's, athletic, etc.). **Indexes:** Brand name (with company name, category, and price range). **Frequency:** Latest edition July 1978. **Editor:** Kenneth Share, Publisher. **Price:** $10.00, postpaid, payment with order.

★616★
FORBES MAGAZINE—ANNUAL REPORT ON AMERICAN INDUSTRY ISSUE
Forbes, Inc.
60 Fifth Avenue   Phone: (212) 620-2200
New York, NY 10011
Publication includes: List of about 1,000 leading industrial firms. **Entries include:** Company name, sales, profits, earnings growth rate, dividends, stock price gain. **Arrangement:** Ranked by profit, earnings growth rate, and stock price gain (three lists). **Indexes:** Company by industry and profit and growth. **Frequency:** Annual, January. **Editor:** Malcolm Forbes. **Advertising accepted.** Circulation 670,000. **Price:** $2.50 (current and 1980 editions).

★617★
FORBES MAGAZINE—CHIEF EXECUTIVE COMPENSATION SURVEY ISSUE
Forbes, Inc.
60 Fifth Avenue   Phone: (212) 620-2200
New York, NY 10011
Publication includes: List of about 800 firms and compensation of their chief executive officers. **Entries include:** (In chart form) Company name, name of chief executive officer, rank, compensation in salary and bonus, total remuneration, years with company, age, business background (whether in sales, administration, etc.). **Frequency:** Annual, in a June issue. **Advertising accepted.** Circulation 670,000. **Price:** $2.50 (current and 1980 editions).

★618★
FORBES MAGAZINE—500 LARGEST CORPORATIONS ISSUE
Forbes, Inc.
60 Fifth Avenue   Phone: (212) 620-2200
New York, NY 10011
Publication includes: "The 500 Largest Corporations" ranked in mid-May issue by revenues, profits, assets, market value of stock. **Entries include:** Company name, statistics related to ranking. **Indexes:** Alphabetical (with further statistical data). **Frequency:** Annual, mid-May issue. **Editor:** Malcolm Forbes. **Advertising accepted.** Circulation 670,000. **Price:** $2.50 (current and 1980 editions).

★619★
FOREIGN TRADE MARKETPLACE
Gale Research Company
Book Tower   Phone: (313) 961-2242
Detroit, MI 48226
Publication includes: Lists of United States ports, ocean shipping and air freight lines, export managers, banks having an interest in international trade, franchisers who operate overseas, federal and state government agencies active in international trade, United States diplomatic posts abroad, organizations (including those abroad) active in international trade, schools and programs in foreign trade, trade centers (United States and other) abroad, and foreign trade zones in the United States and abroad. Also includes numerous sections on facilities, companies, etc., abroad, including private and governmental export and import organizations and trading companies, major distributors and sales agents handling United States products, and others. **Entries include:** Company, organization or agency name, address, and name of contact are usually given; phone may be given; activity, product, service, etc., is mentioned if not evident from classification. **Arrangement:** Classified by type of activity. **Indexes:** Subject/geographic. **Pages** (approx.): 650. **Frequency:** Not established; first published August 1977. **Editor:** George J. Schultz. **Price:** $52.00.

★620★
FORGING CAPABILITY CHART
Forging Industry Association
55 Public Square   Phone: (216) 781-6260
Cleveland, OH 44113
Covers: 155 producers of ferrous and nonferrous forgings who are members. **Entries include:** Company name, address, phone; relative size of company; major pieces of equipment operated; minimum/maximum weights of forgings produced, by material. **Arrangement:** By process. **Frequency:** Latest edition June 1979; new edition expected January 1981. **Price:** Free.

Forging Industry Association—Membership Directory *See* Forging Capability Chart

Formed Fabric Industry—Fabric Manufacturers Guide Issue *See* Nonwovens Industry—Fabric Manufacturers Guide Issue

★621★
FORT WORTH BUYERS GUIDE AND MEMBERSHIP DIRECTORY [Texas]
Fort Worth Chamber of Commerce
700 Throckmorton Street   Phone: (817) 336-2491
Fort Worth, TX 76102
Number of listings: 2,200; limited to chamber of commerce members. **Entries include:** Company name, address, phone, name of key executive, product or service. **Arrangement:** Alphabetical. **Indexes:** Product. **Pages** (approx.): 120. **Frequency:** Annual, September. **Editor:** Barbara Winkle. **Advertising accepted.** Circulation 10,000. **Price:** $15.00, plus $1.00 shipping.

★622★
FORTUNE DOUBLE 500 DIRECTORY
Time, Inc.
Time and Life Building   Phone: (212) 556-2581
New York, NY 10020
Covers: 500 largest United States corporations (published in a May issue each year), second 500 largest (published in a June issue), and the 50 largest commercial banks, utilities, life insurance companies, diversified-financial companies, retailers, and transportation companies (published in a July issue). **Entries include:** Company name, headquarters city, sales, net income, employees, comparative earnings per share for several years, and various other statistical and financial information. **Arrangement:** By annual sales, where appropriate; otherwise by assets. **Indexes:** Alphabetical. **Pages** (approx.): 80. **Frequency:** Annual, September. **Editor:** Evelyn Benjamin, Board of Editors. **Price:** $7.00, payment with order. **Send orders to:** Fortune Directory, Box 8001, Trenton, NJ 08607.

Fortune 500 Directory *See* Fortune Double 500 Directory

★623★
FRAGRANCE FOUNDATION REFERENCE GUIDE
Fragrance Foundation
116 E. 19th Street   Phone: (212) 673-5580
New York, NY 10003
Covers: Manufacturers of over 500 fragrances available in the United States. **Entries include:** Company name, address, phone. **Arrangement:** Alphabetical. **Indexes:** Product with date of introduction and description. **Frequency:** Latest edition September 1979. **Price:** $25.00.

★624★
FRANCHISE ANNUAL
Info Press Inc.
736 Center Street   Phone: (716) 754-4669
Lewiston, NY 14092
Covers: 1,300 franchisors, distributors, licensors, franchise consultants, and joint ventures. **Entries include:** Name, address, and phone of franchisor, line of business, length of time in franchising, year established, number of units authorized, initial investment, and approximate total investment. **Arrangement:** U.S. or Canadian, then by type of business. **Indexes:** Company name. **Pages** (approx.): 125. **Frequency:** Annual, January. **Editor:** Edward L. Dixon, Jr. **Price:** $12.95 (current edition); $14.95 (1980 edition; ISSN 0318-8752); plus 75¢ shipping. **Also includes:** Information on becoming a franchisee. **Other information:** Updated monthly by "Info Franchise Newsletter," which includes new franchisors, legislation, and litigation developments, $24.00 per year.

★625★
FRANCHISE OPPORTUNITIES HANDBOOK
Industry and Trade Administration
Commerce Department
Washington, DC 20230
Covers: Over 860 franchisors in some 40 lines of business (auto rentals, campgrounds, foods, security systems, etc.). **Entries include:** Company name, address, name of contact, description of the business operation franchised, number of franchisees, date company began,

amount of capital needed, whether financial assistance is available, and what training and managerial assistance are provided. **Arrangement:** Classified. **Pages** (approx.): 390. **Frequency:** Annual, summer. **Price:** $6.50. **Send orders to:** Government Printing Office, Washington, DC 20402. **Other information:** Also includes general information on securing franchises and operating franchised businesses. Users of the directory are cautioned that the Commerce Department has not verified statements in the listings for the various franchisors.

★626★
FREIGHT SHIPPING DIRECTORY [Port of Los Angeles]
Port of Los Angeles
Box 151   Phone: (213) 548-7962
San Pedro, CA 90733
Covers: Shipping lines operating out of the Port of Los Angeles; container terminals, passenger services, special commodities handling facilities and other services are included. **Entries include:** For shipping lines - Name of line, pier address, headquarters address and phone, other ports served from Los Angeles. **Arrangement:** Alphabetical. **Pages** (approx.): 30. **Frequency:** Annual. **Price:** Free.

★627★
FROZEN FOOD FACTBOOK AND DIRECTORY
National Frozen Food Association
One Chocolate Avenue   Phone: (717) 534-1601
Hershey, PA 17033
Covers: 1,260 companies worldwide who are members, including 350 distributors; 350 packers; 400 brokers, suppliers, retailers, and others. Also covers 3,500 industry executives, listed alphabetically with their telephone numbers. **Entries include:** Company name, address, phone, names of executives, products or services, trade and brand names. **Arrangement:** Geographical within membership category; supplier members and packers listed in product classifications. **Indexes:** Company name. **Pages** (approx.): 370. **Frequency:** Annual, fall. **Editor:** Dorothy Williamson. **Advertising accepted.** Circulation 3,500. **Price:** $50.00.

★628★
FUEL OIL NEWS—SOURCE BOOK ISSUE
Publex Corporation
Box 308   Phone: (201) 534-9023
Whitehouse, NJ 08808
Covers: Nearly 400 manufacturers and suppliers of oil handling, delivery, heating, and cooling equipment, and related products and services. **Entries include:** Company name, address, phone, name of contact, coded product list, brand names. **Arrangement:** Alphabetical. **Indexes:** Product. **Frequency:** Annual, December. **Editor:** George Schultz. **Advertising accepted.** Circulation 16,500. **Price:** $3.00.

★629★
FUR AGE WEEKLY—ANNUAL DIRECTORY ISSUE
Fur Vogue Publishing Company
127 W. 30th Street   Phone: (212) 239-4983
New York, NY 10001
Publication includes: Directory for companies and resident buyers in New York City, plus a capsule review of the past year. **Entries include:** Company name, address, and phone. **Arrangement:** Alphabetical. **Pages** (approx.): 40. **Frequency:** Annual, March. **Editor:** E. R. Harrowe. **Advertising accepted.** Circulation 5,000. **Former title:** Fur Age Weekly - Annual Review Number. **Price:** $10.00. **Other information:** Annual directory issue now includes "Building-By-Building Fur Source Directory," formerly published separately.

Fur Age Weekly—Annual Review Number *See* Fur Age Weekly— Annual Directory Issue

Fur Age Weekly—Building-By-Building Fur Source Directory Issue *See* Fur Age Weekly—Annual Directory Issue

★630★
FUR AGE WEEKLY—CLASSIFIED FUR SOURCE DIRECTORY ISSUE
Fur Vogue Publishing Company
127 W. 30th Street   Phone: (212) 239-4983
New York, NY 10001
Covers: New York City wholesale fur industry, including garment manufacturers, designers, repairers, remodelers, converters, cleaners, buyers, and brokers. **Entries include:** Company name, address, phone number, and products or services. **Arrangement:** Alphabetical; classified by product. **Pages** (approx.): 200. **Frequency:** Annual, October. **Editor:** E. R. Harrowe. **Advertising accepted.** Circulation 5,000. **Price:** $5.00.

★631★
FURNITURE METHODS & MATERIALS—ANNUAL DIRECTORY AND
    BUYER'S GUIDE
Associations Publications, Inc.
3116 Forest Hill Road   Phone: (901) 754-4890
Germantown, TN 38138
Publication includes: List of suppliers of products and services to the furniture manufacturing industry. **Entries include:** Supplier name, address, phone, and name of sales contact. **Arrangement:** Alphabetical. **Indexes:** Product. **Frequency:** Annual, November. **Editor:** James D. Powell. **Advertising accepted.** Circulation 15,000. **Price:** $10.00.

★632★
FURNITURE PRODUCTION—BLUE BOOK DIRECTORY ISSUE
Production Publishing Company
804 Church Street   Phone: (615) 255-7667
Nashville, TN 37203
Covers: Over 1,500 suppliers of products and services to the furniture industry. **Entries include:** Company name, address, phone, name and title of principal executive. **Arrangement:** By product and service categories. **Frequency:** Annual, December. **Editor:** J. H. Whaley, Jr., Publisher. **Advertising accepted.** Circulation 17,000. **Price:** $10.00.

★633★
GARDENA VALLEY, CALIFORNIA CHAMBER OF COMMERCE—
    MEMBERSHIP DIRECTORY
Gardena Valley Chamber of Commerce
1551 W. Redondo Beach Boulevard   Phone: (213) 532-9905
Gardena, CA 90247
Number of listings: 300. **Entries include:** Company name, address, phone, names of executives, number of employees, products or services offered. **Arrangement:** Alphabetical. **Pages** (approx.): 15. **Frequency:** Irregular; latest edition March 1979; new edition expected 1980. **Editor:** Anita E. Bell, Secretary/General Manager. **Price:** $5.00.

★634★
GARMENT MANUFACTURERS INDEX
Klevens Publications, Inc.
7600 Avenue V   Phone: (805) 944-4111
Little Rock, CA 93543
Covers: Manufacturers and suppliers of products and services used in the manufacture of men's, women's, and children's apparel. **Entries include:** Company name, address, phone, list of products or services, brief description of product. **Arrangement:** Classified (fabrics, trimmings, supplies and service, and equipment). **Indexes:** Supplier. **Pages** (approx.): 150. **Frequency:** Annual, November. **Editor:** Herbert Schwartz. **Advertising accepted.** Circulation 18,500. **Price:** $4.95.

★635★
GAS INDUSTRY TRAINING DIRECTORY
American Gas Association
1515 Wilson Boulevard
Arlington, VA 22209
Covers: Over 600 programs available from gas transmission and distribution companies, manufacturers of gas-fired equipment,

consultants, etc., and from gas associations. **Entries include:** Name, address, phone of source of program, name of contact, program description. **Indexes:** Subject. **Frequency:** Annual, May. **Price:** $20.00 (current and 1980 editions).

Gavel Annual International Directory *See* Meetings and
    Conventions—Gavel Annual International Directory Issue

Gebbie House Magazine Directory *See* Working Press of the
    Nation

★636★
GENERAL AVIATION AIRCRAFT
Aircraft Owners and Pilots Association
7315 Wisconsin Avenue   Phone: (301) 654-0500
Washington, DC 20014
Covers: 80 manufacturers of ten categories of aircraft: Single engine fixed gear and retractable gear, multiengine piston, turboprop, turbojet, STOL, AG planes, rotary wing, sailplanes, and balloons. **Entries include:** Manufacturer, address, specifications, performance, price data. **Arrangement:** Classified by type of aircraft. **Pages** (approx.): 20. **Frequency:** Annual, March. **Editor:** Don C. Johnson, Special Projects Editor. **Price:** $5.00.

George D. Hall's Directory of Massachusetts Manufacturers *See*
    Directory of Massachusetts Manufacturers

★637★
GEORGIA DIRECTORY OF INTERNATIONAL SERVICES
Research Committee International Council
Georgia Chamber of Commerce
Commerce Building, Room 1200
Atlanta, GA 30303
Covers: Georgia exporting and importing companies, trade organizations, financial institutions concerned with foreign investment, transportation services, and other cultural, service, and commercial organizations concerned with international trade and exchange. **Entries include:** Company or organization name, address, phone, description of service or international interests. **Arrangement:** By line of business or activity. **Pages** (approx.): 100. **Editor:** Hariette C. Hawkins. **Price:** $3.50.

★638★
GEORGIA MANUFACTURING DIRECTORY
Georgia Department of Industry and Trade
1400 N. Omni International
Atlanta, GA 30303
Covers: About 5,300 firms manufacturing products within SIC classifications 20-39. **Entries include:** Company name, address, phone, names of principal executives, number of employees, list of products or services, 4-digit SIC numbers, date established, market served. **Arrangement:** By county and by SIC number; identical information in each arrangement. **Indexes:** Alphabetical, parent company, import/export. **Pages** (approx.): 750. **Frequency:** Annual, January. **Editor:** Susan D. Barnett. **Price:** $15.00 (current and 1980 editions; ISSN 0435-5482).

★639★
GEORGIA STATE INDUSTRIAL DIRECTORY
State Industrial Directories Corporation
Two Penn Plaza   Phone: (212) 564-0340
New York, NY 10001
Number of listings: 5,600. **Entries include:** Company name, address, phone, names of key executives, number of employees, plant size, 4-digit SIC code, products, whether firm imports or exports, and whether firm has research facilities. **Arrangement:** Geographical. **Indexes:** Alphabetical, product (includes mailing address and phone for each firm). **Frequency:** Annual, December. **Advertising accepted.** **Price:** $50.00 (ISSN 0161-8571).

★640★
GEYER'S "WHO MAKES IT" DIRECTORY [Office equipment]
Geyer-McAllister Publications, Inc.
51 Madison Avenue   Phone: (212) 689-4411
New York, NY 10010
Covers: Manufacturers and wholesalers of office equipment and supplies. **Entries include:** Company name, address, phone, list of products. **Arrangement:** Alphabetical; classified by product category. **Indexes:** Advertiser. **Pages** (approx.): 220. **Frequency:** Annual, January. **Editor:** Mary Conyers, Production Manager. **Advertising accepted.** **Price:** Available only with subscription to "Geyer's Dealer Topics," $11.00 (current and 1980 editions). **Also includes:** Lists of trade associations and trade names.

★641★
GIFT AND DECORATIVE ACCESSORY BUYERS DIRECTORY
Geyer-McAllister Publications, Inc.
51 Madison Avenue   Phone: (212) 689-4411
New York, NY 10010
Covers: Manufacturers, importers, jobbers, and manufacturers' representatives for gifts, china and glass, lamps and home accessories, stationery, greeting cards, and related products. **Entries include:** Company name, address, product lines, trade and brand names; some entries also include phone. **Arrangement:** Sources are listed alphabetically and classified by merchandise category. **Indexes:** Advertiser. **Pages** (approx.): 450. **Frequency:** Annual, August. **Editor:** Phyllis Sweed, Editor/Vice President. **Advertising accepted.** Circulation 32,000. **Price:** Available only with subscription to "Gifts and Decorative Accessories" magazine, $15.00 per year. **Also includes:** Lists of trade names and brands, domestic and foreign trade associations, national and international fairs, and tenants of all permanent gift marts in the United States.

Gift & Housewares Buyers *See* Salesman's Guide Nationwide
    Directory: Gift & Housewares Buyers

★642★
GIFT AND TABLEWARE REPORTER GIFTGUIDE
Gralla Publications
1515 Broadway   Phone: (212) 869-1300
New York, NY 10036
Covers: 2,600 manufacturers, importers, distributors, and representatives in gift/tableware field, including stationery, costume jewelry, chinaware, glassware, stainless steel flatware, cooking utensils, etc.; wholesale centers; New York, Los Angeles, and Chicago resident buying firms; trade associations; foreign manufacturers (keyed to importers). **Entries include:** Manufacturer list shows address, phone, type of operation, and major showrooms. **Arrangement:** Alphabetical. **Indexes:** Product. **Pages** (approx.): 160. **Frequency:** Annual, August. **Editor:** Debbie Miller. **Advertising accepted.** **Former title:** Gift and Tableware Reporter Resources for Retailers (1977). **Price:** $10.00. **Also includes:** Trademarks, patterns, and cuttings section, with brand name, description of article, and name of firm in main section which handles it.

★643★
GIFTWARE NEWS—TABLEWARE DIRECTORY & MANAGEMENT GUIDE ISSUE
Talcott Communications Corporation
1111 E. Touhy Avenue   Phone: (312) 299-8438
Des Plaines, IL 60018
Publication includes: About 350 manufacturers, suppliers, distributors, and their representatives supplying china, glassware, linen, and tabletop accessories to the retail industry. **Entries include:** Company name, address, phone, lines or products handled. **Arrangement:** Alphabetical by company. **Indexes:** Product. **Pages** (approx.): 80. **Frequency:** Annual, January. **Advertising accepted.** Circulation 41,000. **Former title:** Giftware News - Management Guide & Tableware Directory Issue. **Price:** $1.50 (current and 1980 editions).

★644★
GLASS FACTORY DIRECTORY
National Glass Budget
Box 7138   Phone: (412) 682-5136
Pittsburgh, PA 15213
Covers: 500 glass manufacturers in United States and Canada.
Entries include: Company name, address, phone, names of
executives, list of products, capacity. **Arrangement:** Geographical.
Indexes: Alphabetical. **Pages** (approx.): 170. **Frequency:** Annual,
spring-summer. **Advertising accepted.** Circulation 1,500. **Price:**
$5.00 (current and 1980 editions).

★645★
GLASS INDUSTRY—DIRECTORY ISSUE
Magazines for Industry, Inc.
777 Third Avenue   Phone: (212) 838-7778
New York, NY 10017
Covers: Lists of primary and secondary glass manufacturers (including
foreign), suppliers to the glass industry, glass associations and unions,
independent research labs, and glass educational institutions.
Arrangement: Classified into groups mentioned above, then
alphabetical; foreign manufacturers are geographical. **Indexes:**
Product. **Pages** (approx.): 200. **Frequency:** Annual, October. **Editor:**
Lowell E. Perrine. **Advertising accepted.** Circulation 3,000. **Price:**
$12.00.

Gold Book [Electronics] *See* **Electronic Design Master Directory**

★646★
GOLF COURSE BUILDERS OF AMERICA—MEMBERSHIP
  DIRECTORY
Golf Course Builders of America
725 15th Street, N. W.   Phone: (202) 638-0555
Washington, DC 20005
Number of listings: 40. **Entries include:** Individual or company name,
address, phone, biographical information for individuals, histories of
golf courses built by the member. **Arrangement:** Alphabetical. **Pages**
(approx.): 50. **Frequency:** Annual, December. **Advertising accepted.**
Price: Free.

★647★
GOMER'S BUDGET TRAVEL DIRECTORY
Hammond Incorporated
515 Valley Street   Phone: (201) 763-6000
Maplewood, NJ 07040
Covers: About 4,500 motels, hotels, country inns, and tourist homes
offering double bed, double occupancy rooms for $20.00 per night or
less. **Entries include:** Name of facility, street address, phone, rate,
additional charge for cots, whether pets are allowed, number of units,
credit cards accepted, and whether air conditioning, pool, restaurant,
and TV are available. **Arrangement:** Geographical. **Pages** (approx.):
225. **Frequency:** Annual, spring. **Editor:** Gomer Lewis. **Price:** $5.95.
Other information: Formerly published as "Gomer's Guides from the
Mississippi to the Pacific," with similar volume for eastern states.

Gomer's Guides... *See* **Gomer's Budget Travel Directory**

★648★
GOOD PACKAGING—DIRECTORY ISSUE [Western states]
Pacific Trade Journals
1315 E. Julian Street   Phone: (408) 286-1661
San Jose, CA 95116
Covers: Over 2,100 manufacturers and suppliers of packaging
machinery, packages, packaging materials, and material handling
equipment with offices in the western United States. **Entries include:**
Manufacturer's name, name of representative company, address, and
phone. **Arrangement:** Alphabetical. **Indexes:** Product. **Frequency:**
Annual, July. **Advertising accepted.** Circulation 7,100. **Price:**
$10.00 (current and 1980 editions).

★649★
GOODALE CONTRACTORS' DIRECTORY [Florida]
Goodale Contractors' Directory
5674 Bayview Drive   Phone: (813) 391-6206
Seminole, FL 33542
Covers: Contractors and suppliers of equipment and services to
contractors of the west coast of Florida. **Entries include:** Company
name, address, phone, product or service. **Arrangement:** By city, then
type of business. **Frequency:** Annual. **Price:** $15.00.

Government Contracts Directory *See* **Government**
  Primecontracts Monthly

★650★
GOVERNMENT PRIMECONTRACTS MONTHLY
Government Data Publications
1661 McDonald Avenue   Phone: (212) 627-0819
Brooklyn, NY 11230
Covers: Firms which received prime contract for production of goods
from federal government agencies during preceding month. **Entries**
include: Name and address of awardee, agency, description of
material, quantity, contract number, and amount. **Arrangement:** By
product. **Frequency:** Monthly. **Editor:** Siegfried Lobel. **Former title:**
Government Contracts Directory, an annual. **Price:** $60.00 per year.
Send orders to: Government Data Publications, 422 Washington
Bldg., Washington, DC 20005.

★651★
GOVERNMENTAL PURCHASING
White Eagle, Inc.
2550 Kuser Road   Phone: (609) 586-2056
Trenton, NJ 08650
Covers: National suppliers to governmental agencies. **Entries include:**
Company name, address. **Arrangement:** By product. **Pages** (approx.):
50. **Frequency:** Bimonthly. **Editor:** Isabelle Selikoff, Editor.
Advertising accepted. Circulation 4,600. **Price:** $5.00 per copy.

Graduate Study in Management *See* **Guide to Graduate**
  Management Education

★652★
GRAPHIC ARTS GREEN BOOK TRADE DIRECTORY AND REGISTER
A. F. Lewis & Company, Inc.
15 Spinning Wheel Road   Phone: (312) 323-9777
Hinsdale, IL 60521
Covers: 10,000 printing plants, bookbinders, typographers,
photoengravers, paper merchants, paper manufacturers and dealers,
and others serving the graphic arts industry in Illinois, Indiana,
Wisconsin, and Michigan (SIC 2600, 2700). **Entries include:**
Company name, address, phone, names of executives, name of buyer,
number of employees, line of business. **Arrangement:** By line of
business; printers and lithographers, geographical. **Pages** (approx.):
430. **Frequency:** Annual, winter. **Editor:** Edward Schuller, Publisher.
Advertising accepted. Circulation 10,000. **Price:** $45.00, plus
$1.85 shipping. **Other information:** Same publisher's "Printing
Trades Blue Book" covers other geographic areas (see separate
listings).

★653★
GRAPHIC ARTS MARKETPLACE
Coast Publishing, Inc.
3255 S. U.S. 1   Phone: (305) 465-9450
Fort Pierce, FL 33450
Covers: Over 2,300 manufacturers and suppliers of graphic arts
equipment, electronic and computer-based systems, and services for
printers and publishers; 350 periodicals and associations. **Entries**
include: Company name, address, phone, names of principal
executives, description of products or services. **Arrangement:**
Classified. **Pages** (approx.): 265. **Frequency:** Annual. **Former title:**
Graphic Communications Marketplace. **Price:** $15.00, plus $2.50
shipping (current and 1980 editions). **Other information:** Formerly

published by Technical Information, Inc. of South Lake Tahoe, CA (through 1979).

Graphic Communications Marketplace *See* Graphic Arts Marketplace

★654★
GREAT BOOK OF CATALOGS
Pinkerton Marketing, Inc.
135 Oak Terrace   Phone: (312) 234-5533
Lake Bluff, IL 60044
Covers: Over 2,000 mail order companies which publish catalogs. **Entries include:** Company name, address, product lines, catalog cost (if any), special services. **Arrangement:** By product. **Indexes:** Company name. **Pages** (approx.): 180. **Frequency:** First edition fall 1979; new edition expected fall 1980. **Editor:** Steve Pinkerton. **Price:** $8.95, plus $1.00 shipping. **Other information:** Supplement included in initial purchase; updated monthly by ''The Best to You by Mail,'' $24.00 per year.

★655★
GREAT LAKES RED BOOK
Fourth Seacoast Publishing Company, Inc.
24145 Little Mack   Phone: (313) 779-5570
St. Clair Shores, MI 48080
Covers: Over 300 commercial Great Lakes fleets and 1,400 vessels. Includes a listing of bulk and general cargo docks, shipyards. **Entries include:** Name of vessel; dimensions; names of captain, chief engineer, owners, operators, and addresses. **Arrangement:** Classified. **Pages** (approx.): 375. **Frequency:** Annual, May. **Price:** $4.25.

★656★
GREATER BOSTON CONVENTION & MEETING PLANNERS GUIDE [Massachusetts]
Greater Boston Convention & Tourism Bureau
900 Boylston Street   Phone: (617) 536-4100
Boston, MA 02115
Covers: Convention and exhibit services, hotels and other meeting facilities, visitor attractions, radio and television stations, tour packages, and recreational facilities in Oston area. **Entries include:** Company, facility, or site name, address, phone, services or attractions. Hotels and other convention sites include number of rooms, meeting rooms, square footage, and seating capacities. **Arrangement:** By type of service, etc. **Pages** (approx.): 65. **Frequency:** Annual, March. **Former title:** Meeting Planner's Guide to Greater Boston. **Price:** Free.

★657★
GREATER CHARLOTTE CHAMBER OF COMMERCE—MEMBERSHIP DIRECTORY & BUYER'S GUIDE [North Carolina]
Greater Charlotte Chamber of Commerce
Box 32785
Charlotte, NC 28232
Entries include: Company name, address, phone, name of chief executive. **Arrangement:** Alphabetical. **Indexes:** Product/service. **Frequency:** Annual. **Price:** $5.00, plus 50¢ shipping.

★658★
GREATER CHICAGO MINORITY VENDORS DIRECTORY [Illinois]
Chicago Regional Purchasing Council
6 N. Michigan Avenue, Suite 1308   Phone: (312) 263-0105
Chicago, IL 60602
Covers: About 1,000 firms offering professional, commercial, and industrial products and services. **Entries include:** Company name, address, phone, name of contact, capability number, number of employees, gross revenue, other information on business background and capabilities. **Arrangement:** Alphabetical. **Indexes:** Product, capability number. **Pages** (approx.): 1,000. **Frequency:** Irregular; latest edition November 1978. **Price:** $10.00.

★659★
GREATER CINCINNATI CHAMBER OF COMMERCE—BUSINESS AND INDUSTRY DIRECTORY [Ohio]
Greater Cincinnati Chamber of Commerce
120 W. Fifth Street   Phone: (513) 721-3300
Cincinnati, OH 45202
Covers: 4,000 member firms and nonmember manufacturing firms in the Cincinnati SMSA (Hamilton, Clermont, and Warren counties in Ohio; Boone, Campbell, and Kenton counties in Kentucky; Dearborn county in Indiana). **Entries include:** Company name, address, phone, names of principal executives, number of employees, list of products or services, SIC numbers, date established, whether firm imports or exports, branches. **Arrangement:** By SIC classification. **Indexes:** Alphabetical, product. **Pages** (approx.): 220. **Frequency:** Annual, January. **Editor:** Ann M. Oswald. **Advertising accepted.** Circulation 9,500. **Price:** $25.00 (current edition); $27.50 (1980 edition).

★660★
GREATER CLEVELAND GROWTH ASSOCIATION—MEMBERSHIP DIRECTORY, BUYERS/SELLERS GUIDE [Ohio]
Greater Cleveland Growth Association
Union Commerce Building, Room 690   Phone: (216) 621-3300
Cleveland, OH 44115
Covers: Company name, address, phone, names of executives. **Frequency:** Annual, April. **Advertising accepted.** Circulation 10,000. **Former title:** Manufacturers Directory. **Price:** $15.00, payment with order.

★661★
GREATER HARTFORD MANUFACTURERS DIRECTORY [Connecticut]
Greater Hartford Chamber of Commerce
250 Constitution Plaza   Phone: (203) 525-4451
Hartford, CT 06103
Covers: 1,600 manufacturers in 33 towns which comprise the Greater Hartford area. **Entries include:** Firm name, address, phone, name of chief executive, number of employees, products, whether firm imports or exports, SIC. **Arrangement:** Alphabetical. **Indexes:** Geographical, product. **Pages** (approx.): 140. **Frequency:** Biennial, odd years. **Advertising accepted.** Circulation 1,500. **Price:** $20.00, plus $2.00 shipping, payment with order.

★662★
GREATER PITTSBURGH CHAMBER OF COMMERCE—BUYERS GUIDE [Pennsylvania]
Greater Pittsburgh Chamber of Commerce
411 Seventh Avenue   Phone: (412) 391-3400
Pittsburgh, PA 15219
Number of listings: 775 members of the chamber. **Entries include:** Company name, address, phone number, name of contact, line of business, SIC category (without SIC number). **Arrangement:** By SIC descriptors (without numbers), then alphabetical. **Indexes:** Chamber member name (with line of business and phone). **Pages** (approx.): 90. **Frequency:** Annual, summer. **Editor:** Kay Hofmeister. Manager of Communications Division. **Advertising accepted.** Circulation 5,000. **Former title:** Greater Pittsburgh Chamber of Commerce Membership Directory and Buyers Guide. **Price:** $3.00.

Green Book: Distributors & Manufacturers Confidential Beauty & Barber Guide *See* Distributors Confidential Beauty & Barber Buying Guide

Green Book *See* International Directory of Marketing Research Houses and Services

★663★
GREEN BOOK OF HOME IMPROVEMENT CONTRACTORS
CMR Associates, Inc.
11-A Village Green   Phone: (301) 261-6363
Crofton, MD 21114
Covers: More than 10,000 home improvement contractors in 24

major markets in California, Colorado, District of Columbia-Virginia-Maryland, Florida, Georgia, Illinois, Indiana, Kansas, Kentucky, Massachusetts, Michigan, Minnesota, Missouri, New York, Ohio, Pennsylvania, Texas, and Washington. **Entries include:** Company name, address, phone, key personnel, business operations, sales volume, business profile, number of employees, owner's comments, list of products or services. **Arrangement:** Geographical; separate reports for each market. **Frequency:** Irregular; latest edition for above July 1978, new edition expected spring 1980; additional market reports issued August 1979 for areas in above states as well as Alabama, Arizona, Connecticut, Delaware, Iowa, Louisiana, Nebraska, Nevada, New Jersey, New Mexico, the Carolinas, Oklahoma, Oregon, Rhode Island, Tennessee, Utah, and Wisconsin. **Price:** Varies by market. **Also includes:** Market studies on types of work done and volume of each, gross sales, etc.

★664★
GREENWOOD'S GUIDE TO GREAT LAKES SHIPPING
Freshwater Press, Inc.
258 The Arcade   Phone: (216) 241-0373
Cleveland, OH 44114
Covers: Companies which ship water-carried commodities on the Great Lakes-St. Lawrence Seaway system. **Entries include:** Company name, address, phone, names of executives, services. **Arrangement:** By service and equipment. **Pages** (approx.): 650. **Frequency:** Annual, April. **Editor:** John O. Greenwood, President. **Advertising accepted.** Circulation 2,500. **Price:** $30.00 (current edition); $33.00 (tentative, 1980 edition).

Greeting Card Magazine—Buyers Guide Issue *See* Greetings
    Magazine—Buyers Guide Directory Issue

★665★
GREETINGS MAGAZINE—BUYERS GUIDE DIRECTORY ISSUE
Mackay Publishing Company
95 Madison Avenue   Phone: (212) 679-6677
New York, NY 10016
Covers: Producers of greetings material (gift wrap, social stationery, novelties, greeting cards, party goods, and gifts). **Entries include:** Company name, address, brand names, and products or services. **Indexes:** Product. **Pages** (approx.): 70. **Frequency:** Annual, July. **Editor:** Milton J. Kristt. **Advertising accepted.** Circulation 6,000. **Former title:** Greeting Card Magazine - Buyers Guide Issue. **Price:** $6.00, postpaid, payment with order (current and 1980 editions).

★666★
GROCER'S SPOTLIGHT—MEGA-2 MARKET STUDY AND WHO'S
    WHO ISSUE
Shamie Publishing Company
22725 Mack Avenue   Phone: (313) 779-4940
St. Clair Shores, MI 48080
Covers: Food retailers, wholesalers, and distributors in Illinois, Indiana, Iowa, Kansas, Kentucky, Michigan, Minnesota, Missouri, Nebraska, North Dakota, Ohio, western Pennsylvania, West Virginia, and Wisconsin. **Entries include:** Company name, address, names and titles of key personnel, phone; number of stores; sales volume for previous year or estimate for current year; plans for new construction or remodeling; buying hours; key source of supply. **Arrangement:** Geographical. **Frequency:** Annual, August 15 issue. **Advertising accepted. Price:** $15.00, plus $1.00 shipping. **Other information:** Principal content of publication is market evaluation with number of stores, estimated volume, and percentage of market given for each market area, state, SMSA, and county.

★667★
GROCER'S SPOTLIGHT WEST—MARKET STUDY AND WHO'S
    WHO OF THE WEST ISSUE
Shamie Publishing Company
1800 N. Argyle Avenue   Phone: (213) 461-3627
Los Angeles, CA 90028
Covers: Food retailers, wholesalers, and distributors in Alaska,

Arizona, California, Colorado, Hawaii, Idaho, Montana, Nevada, New Mexico, Oregon, Utah, Washington, and Wyoming. **Entries include:** Company name, address, names and titles of key personnel, phone; number of stores; sales volume for previous year or estimate for current year; plans for new construction or remodeling; buying hours; key source of supply. **Arrangement:** Geographical. **Frequency:** Annual, August 15 issue. **Advertising accepted.** Circulation 65,180. **Price:** $5.00, plus $1.00 shipping. **Other information:** Principal content of publication is market evaluation, with number of stores, estimated volume, and percentage of market given for each market area, state, SMSA, and county.

★668★
GROCERY COMMUNICATIONS—FOOD BROKER ISSUE
GroCom Group, Inc.
94 County Road   Phone: (401) 245-1332
Barrington, RI 02806
Covers: 2,200 food brokers in the United States. **Entries include:** Company name, address, phone, coding to indicate lines handled. **Arrangement:** Geographical. **Pages** (approx.): 100. **Frequency:** Semiannual, March and December. **Editor:** Brad McDowell, Publisher/Editor. **Advertising accepted.** Circulation 15,000. **Price:** $2.00. **Other information:** Cover title is, "Food Brokers of the United States."

★669★
GROCERY COMMUNICATIONS—FOOD INDUSTRY DIRECTORY
    ISSUE
GroCom Group, Inc.
94 County Road   Phone: (401) 245-1332
Barrington, RI 02806
Covers: 2,500 manufacturers, wholesalers, brokers, distributors, and other suppliers of food and beverage products, general merchandise, produce and flowers, frozen foods, and other food industry-related products, equipment, and supplies. Coverage is limited to 11 western United States. **Entries include:** Company name, address, phone. **Arrangement:** Alphabetical. **Indexes:** Brand/trade name. **Pages** (approx.): 180. **Frequency:** Annual, January. **Editor:** Jayne Clark, Managing Editor. **Advertising accepted.** Circulation 15,000. **Price:** $20.00 (1980 edition).

★670★
GROCERY DISTRIBUTION MAGAZINE—DIRECTORY OF
    WAREHOUSE EQUIPMENT/FIXTURES/SERVICES ISSUE
Market Publications
39 S. LaSalle Street, Room 312   Phone: (312) 263-1057
Chicago, IL 60603
Covers: More than 200 national suppliers of products and services to food industry warehouses. **Entries include:** Company name, address, phone, and products or services. **Arrangement:** Alphabetical. **Indexes:** Product. **Pages** (approx.): 50. **Frequency:** Annual, November/December. **Editor:** Richard Mulville, Publisher. **Advertising accepted.** Circulation 15,000. **Price:** $2.00.

★671★
GROCERY INDUSTRY DIRECTORY OF WASHINGTON STATE AND
    ALASKA
Washington State Food Dealers' Association
120 Sixth Avenue, North   Phone: (206) 622-7015
Seattle, WA 98109
Covers: About 75 buying offices for groups of three or more grocery stores; and about 2,800 grocery stores, supermarkets, convenience stores, and deli stores in Washington and Alaska. A separate buyer's guide section includes advertisements by suppliers to the industry. **Entries include:** Store name, name of owner or manager, address, phone. **Arrangement:** Geographical. **Indexes:** Store name. **Pages** (approx.): 125. **Frequency:** Annual, March. **Editor:** Marge Olson, Managing Editor. **Advertising accepted.** Circulation 4,000. **Former title:** Food Industry Directory (1979). **Price:** $5.00, payment with order.

★672★
GUIDE FOR THE DEVELOPMENT AND PRE-OPENING OF A MOTEL
Hospitality Media
15912 Windy Meadow
Dallas, TX 75248
Publication includes: List of suppliers of equipment, fixtures, and services needed for new motels. **Entries include:** Company name, address, phone. **Indexes:** Product. **Frequency:** Latest edition spring 1978. **Editor:** Arlie L. Taylor. **Price:** $100.00. **Other information:** Principal content is detailed information on steps necessary to carry out a new motel project through the opening phase. (Not verified)

Guide To Amusement Rides *See* Amusement Rides and Games Buyers Guide

★673★
GUIDE TO 50 MAIL ORDER COMPANIES
Elysium Publishing Company
3010 Santa Monica Boulevard
Santa Monica, CA 90404
Entries include: Company name, address, description of types of merchandise handled, catalogs available. **Frequency:** First edition spring 1978. **Price:** $2.00, postpaid. (Not verified)

Guide to Graduate Business Schools—Eastern Edition *See* Barron's Guide to Graduate Business Schools

Guide to Graduate Business Schools *See* Barron's Guide to Graduate Business Schools

★674★
GUIDE TO GRADUATE MANAGEMENT EDUCATION
Graduate Management Admission Council
Educational Testing Service
Box 966   Phone: (609) 921-9000
Princeton, NJ 08541
Publication includes: List of about 430 graduate management schools. **Entries include:** School name, address, information on programs offered. **Arrangement:** Alphabetical by university name. **Frequency:** Annual, September. **Former title:** Programs of Graduate Study in Business; Graduate Study in Management (1979). **Price:** $3.95, postpaid.

★675★
GUIDE TO INFORMATION SOURCES FOR THE CONSTRUCTION INDUSTRY
Producers Council
1717 Massachusetts Avenue, N. W.   Phone: (202) 667-8727
Washington, DC 20036
Covers: Trade associations; publishers of trade journals, indexes, and directories; federal government agencies; trade unions; and other organizations which produce material concerning the construction industry. **Entries include:** Publication title; name, address, and phone of publisher. **Arrangement:** By type of publication or source. **Pages** (approx.): 115. **Frequency:** Published 1979. **Editors:** F. M. Garfield and C. W. Vollmer of Koppers Company, Inc. **Price:** $17.50, postpaid.

Guide to Manufactured Homes *See* NAHM's Guide to Manufactured Homes

Guide to Minority Business Directories *See* Guide to Obtaining Minority Business Directories

★676★
GUIDE TO MINORITY SUPPLIERS—METROPOLITAN WASHINGTON AREA [District of Columbia]
Metropolitan Washington Minority Purchasing Council
1705 De Sales Street, N. W.   Phone: (202) 833-8960
Washington, DC 20036
Covers: Over 500 minority-owned businesses in the metropolitan Washington, DC area. **Entries include:** Company name, address,

phone, description of services or products. **Arrangement:** By product/service. **Indexes:** Alphabetical. **Pages** (approx.): 100. **Frequency:** Annual, March. **Editor:** William H. Bass, Executive Director. **Price:** Free.

★677★
GUIDE TO OBTAINING MINORITY BUSINESS DIRECTORIES
National Minority Business Campaign
1201 12th Avenue, North   Phone: (612) 377-2402
Minneapolis, MN 55411
Covers: About 115 organizations which publish directories of minority businesses; includes local directories covering commercial, industrial, professional, and/or retail business in all lines, and directories of wider geographical scope which tend to cover single lines of business. **Entries include:** Publisher or source name, address, phone, type of publication, date of publication. **Arrangement:** City and state directories are geographical; others listed randomly in separate section. **Pages** (approx.): 15. **Frequency:** Annual, January. **Editor:** Rose Meyerhoff, Executive Director. **Former title:** Guide to Minority Business Directories. **Price:** $2.75.

★678★
GUIDE TO THE RECOMMENDED COUNTRY INNS OF NEW ENGLAND
Globe Pequot Press
Old Chester Road   Phone: (203) 767-2231
Chester, CT 06412
Covers: About 150 New England country inns chosen by the authors on the basis of quality of food, atmosphere, accomodations, and uniqueness. **Entries include:** Name, location, directions, photo or line drawing of inn, type of accomodations available, other facilities, recreational activities available, entertainment offered, type of cuisine, and further data indicating "uniqueness." **Arrangement:** Geographical. **Pages** (approx.): 300. **Frequency:** Annual, January. **Editors:** Elizabeth Squier and Suzy Chapin. **Price:** $4.95 (current edition); $5.95 (1980 edition).

★679★
GUITAR'S FRIEND MAIL ORDER GUIDE TO MUSICAL INSTRUMENTS AND SUPPLIES
The Guitar's Friend
Box 200, Route 1   Phone: (208) 263-7640
Sandpoint, ID 83864
Background: Not a directory but a catalog of stringed instruments and related items sold by the company.

Hammond Diesel Stop Directory and Road Atlas *See* Diesel Stop Directory and Road Atlas

Handbags, Gloves, and Accessories—Directory Issue *See* Fashion Accessories Magazine—Bluebook Directory

★680★
HANDBOOK OF BUILDING SECURITY PLANNING AND DESIGN
McGraw-Hill, Inc.
1221 Avenue of the Americas
New York, NY 10020
Publication includes: List of manufacturers and distributors of security products and equipment, and a list of security consultants. **Entries include:** For manufacturers and distributors - Company name, address, products. For consultants - Name, address, affiliation, area of expertise. **Arrangement:** Alphabetical. **Frequency:** Published 1979. **Price:** $34.50. **Other information:** Principal content of publication is discussion of various security devices and their value.

★681★
HANDBOOK OF INDEPENDENT ADVERTISING AND MARKETING SERVICES
Executive Communications, Inc.
400 E. 54th Street   Phone: (212) 421-3713
New York, NY 10022
Covers: 300 services for marketing and advertising. **Entries include:**

Company name, address, phone, names of executives, and description of services, including method of operation, compensation system, etc. **Arrangement:** Alphabetical within ten subject-oriented sections - sales promotion, new product workshops, etc. **Pages** (approx.): 180. **Frequency:** Annual, January. **Editor:** Susan Fulton, Marketing Editor. **Price:** $40.00 (current and 1980 editions).

★682★
HANDLING & SHIPPING MANAGEMENT—NORTH AMERICAN PORTS DIRECTORY ISSUE
Penton/IPC, Inc.
Penton Plaza   Phone: (216) 696-7000
Cleveland, OH 44114
Covers: About 80 United States and Canadian ports. **Entries include:** Name of port, address of administrative agency or authority, name and title of administrator; description of port including amount of warehouse space, container facilities, bulk facilities, other facilities available, rail service, whether foreign trade zone. **Arrangement:** Geographical. **Frequency:** Annual, September. **Advertising accepted.** Circulation 75,000. **Price:** $1.50.

★683★
HARDWARE AGE—WHO MAKES IT BUYER'S GUIDE ISSUE
Chilton Company
Chilton Way   Phone: (215) 687-8200
Radnor, PA 19089
Publication includes: About 5,000 manufacturers of automotive, electrical, lawn and garden, plumbing products, and building supplies, hardware, housewares, paint, sporting goods, tools, toys, and warehouse equipment, and wholesalers of those products. **Entries include:** Name, address, and phone; wholesaler listings show products handled. **Arrangement:** Manufacturers are alphabetical, wholesalers are geographical. **Indexes:** Product. **Pages** (approx.): 550. **Frequency:** Annual, December. **Editors:** George Headley and Arthur Slepian. **Advertising accepted.** Circulation 57,000. **Price:** $15.00.

★684★
HARDWARE AGE "WHO'S WHO" VERIFIED DIRECTORY OF HARDLINES DISTRIBUTORS
Chilton Company
Chilton Way   Phone: (215) 687-8200
Radnor, PA 19089
Covers: More than 4,200 hardware wholesalers, specialty distributors, manufacturers' representatives, and retail chains (hardware, general retail, home and auto supply, specialty stores). **Entries include:** All listings show firm name, address, phone, date established, sales volume, names of principal executives, area served, buyers and/or lines handled, special services, if any (drop shipments, warehousing, etc.); chain listings show type of outlet, other categories show number of salesmen. **Arrangement:** Geographical within separate sections for each type of operation. **Pages** (approx.): 430. **Frequency:** Biennial, summer of even years. **Editors:** George Headley and Arthur Slepian. **Price:** $125.00 (current edition); $175.00 (1980 edition).

Hardwood Plywood Manufacturers Association—Membership List *See* Kitchen Business—Directory & Buyers Guide Issue

★685★
HARRIS COUNTY SHOPPING CENTER DIRECTORY [Texas]
Houston Chamber of Commerce
1100 Milam Building, Suite 2560   Phone: (713) 651-1313
Houston, TX 77002
Number of listings: 200. **Entries include:** Name, location, census tracts, year established, number of stores, square footage, parking spaces, store names by SIC groups, and number of eating, drinking, and non-retail establishments. **Arrangement:** Geographical. **Indexes:** Alphabetical (with street, census tract location, and square footage). **Editor:** H. N. Martin, Director of Research. **Pages** (approx.): 130. **Frequency:** Irregular; latest edition 1976; new edition possible 1982. **Price:** $25.00, plus $2.50 shipping.

★686★
HARRIS MICHIGAN INDUSTRIAL DIRECTORY
Harris Publishing Company
2057-2 Aurora Road   Phone: (216) 248-8540
Twinsburg, OH 44087
Number of listings: 14,000. **Entries include:** Company name, address, phone, names of executives, year established, plant size, approximate annual sales, number of employees, major SIC number, brief description of products. **Arrangement:** Geographical. **Indexes:** Alphabetical, SIC, product. **Pages** (approx.): 500. **Frequency:** Annual, May. **Editor:** Peg Edmunds. **Former title:** Harris Michigan Manufacturers Industrial Directory. **Price:** $58.75 (current and 1980 editions).

★687★
HAT LIFE YEAR BOOK
Hat Life Year Book
551 Summit Avenue
Jersey City, NJ 07306
Covers: About 1,000 hat manufacturers, wholesalers, renovators, and importers of men's headwear, plus trade suppliers. Includes some 120 foreign manufacturers (SIC 2253, 2352, 5036). **Entries include:** Company name, address, phone, and trade and brand names. **Arrangement:** Product-classified. **Frequency:** Annual, March. **Advertising accepted.** Circulation 6,800. **Price:** $4.00 (current and 1980 editions).

★688★
HAWAII BUSINESS DIRECTORY
Hawaii Business Directory, Inc.
765 Amana Street, Suite 208   Phone: (808) 944-5123
Honolulu, HI 96814
Covers: About 25,000 manufacturers, wholesalers, retailers, service firms, and other businesses and professionals. **Entries include:** Company name, address, phone, names of owners or corporation executives and directors, industry classification, date established, number of employees, annual sales, type of firm (partnership, etc.), products or services. **Arrangement:** Alphabetical. **Indexes:** SIC. **Pages** (approx.): 600. **Frequency:** Annual, fourth quarter. **Editor:** John L. Witwer, President and Publisher. **Advertising accepted.** Circulation 12,000. **Former title:** State of Hawaii Business Directory (1974). **Price:** $64.50 (current and 1980 editions). **Also includes:** Business profile and market data.

★689★
HAWAII BUYER'S GUIDE: AN AUTHORITATIVE GUIDE TO INDUSTRIAL PRODUCTS & SERVICES IN HAWAII
Hawaii Business Publishing Corporation
825 Keeaumoku Street   Phone: (808) 946-3978
Honolulu, HI 96808
Covers: Distributors and representatives of 12,000 manufacturers who sell industrial and commercial products in Hawaii. **Entries include:** Company name, phone, trade and brand names. **Arrangement:** Alphabetical. **Indexes:** Product. **Pages** (approx.): 325. **Frequency:** Annual, spring. **Advertising accepted.** Circulation 6,000. **Price:** $15.00 (current and 1980 editions).

Hawaii Directory of Manufacturers *See* Directory of Manufacturers, State of Hawaii

Hearing Dealer Buyers Guide *See* Hearing Instruments—Annual Industry Directory Issue

★690★
HEARING INSTRUMENTS—ANNUAL INDUSTRY DIRECTORY ISSUE
Harcourt Brace Jovanovich, Inc.
One E. First Street   Phone: (218) 727-8511
Duluth, MN 55802
Publication includes: 200 manufacturers and distributors of hearing aids, ear molds, audiometric test equipment, audio meters, and noise control products, worldwide. **Entries include:** Company name,

address, phone, names of executives, trade or brand names, and list of products or services. **Arrangement:** Alphabetical. **Frequency:** Annual, May. **Editor:** Marjorie D. Skafte. **Advertising accepted.** **Price:** $5.00 (current and 1980 editions).

★691★
HEATING/COMBUSTION EQUIPMENT BUYERS GUIDE AND DATA FILE [Process energy management]
Business Communications, Inc., Subsidiary
Thomas Publishing Company
250 W. 34th Street   Phone: (212) 695-0500
New York, NY 10001
Covers: Sources of equipment, services, and engineering data for persons responsible for process heat and combustion operations in metallurgical, casting, ceramic, and petrochemical industries. **Entries include:** Company name, address, phone, and products or services. **Indexes:** Trade name. **Frequency:** Annual, October. **Editor:** Michael E. Brown, Managing Editor. **Advertising accepted.** Circulation 30,000. **Price:** $5.00.

★692★
HEATING/PIPING/AIR CONDITIONING—INFO-DEX ISSUE
Reinhold Publishing Company, Subsidiary
Penton/IPC
Two Illinois Center Building, Suite 1300   Phone: (312) 861-0880
Chicago, IL 60601
Publication includes: 3,500 manufacturers in the heating/piping/air conditioning industry, and 175 associations and government agencies concerned with standards for the industry. **Entries include:** Company name, address, phone. **Arrangement:** Alphabetical. **Indexes:** Product, trade name. **Frequency:** Annual, June. **Editor:** Robert T. Korte. **Advertising accepted.** Circulation 37,500. **Price:** $10.00 (current and 1980 editions).

★693★
HEAVY DUTY TRUCKING—COUNCIL OF FLEET SPECIALISTS EQUIPMENT BUYERS' GUIDE & SERVICES DIRECTORY
Heavy Duty Trucking Magazine
Box W   Phone: (714) 833-0512
Newport Beach, CA 92663
Covers: 400 Council of Fleet Specialists member manufacturers and wholesalers specializing in heavy duty truck parts and repairs. **Entries include:** Company name, address, phone, names of executives, parts or services manufactured or available; wholesaler listings also show area served. **Arrangement:** Wholesalers are geographical, manufacturers alphabetical. **Indexes:** Alphabetical index to wholesalers. **Pages** (approx.): 100. **Frequency:** Annual, January. **Editor:** Kent Powell. **Advertising accepted.** Circulation 110,000. **Price:** Free. **Other information:** A special section of "Heavy Duty Trucking" magazine prepared by the Council of Fleet Specialists, 8245 Nieman Rd., Suite 111, Shawnee Mission, KS (913-492-1620).

★694★
HEAVY-SPECIALIZED CARRIERS CONFERENCE DIRECTORY
Heavy-Specialized Carriers Conference
American Trucking Associations
1155 16th Street, N. W.   Phone: (202) 797-5407
Washington, DC 20036
Covers: About 650 members of the conference's transportation section and Crane and Rigging Association, specializing in handling of large and heavy loads. **Entries include:** Company name, address, and services and equipment provided. **Frequency:** Annual, January. **Price:** Free.

★695★
HELICOPTER ASSOCIATION OF AMERICA—INTERNATIONAL DIRECTORY OF MEMBERS
Helicopter Association of America
1156 15th Street, N. W., Suite 610   Phone: (202) 466-2420
Washington, DC 20005
Covers: 725 companies which own and operate helicopters for hire

and/or use helicopters for private and corporate transport, and companies which manufacture helicopters or provide service to the industry. **Entries include:** Company name, address, phone, names of executives, list of products or services, and type of equipment operated or serviced. **Arrangement:** Classified by membership category. **Indexes:** Geographical, company name. **Pages** (approx.): 80. **Frequency:** Semiannual, spring and fall. **Editor:** Robert Richardson, Executive Director. **Price:** $10.00. **Also includes:** VTOL Aircraft Designation Chart arranged by manufacturer, showing for each aircraft civil and military designations and technical information.

Heliports in the United States, Canada, and Puerto Rico *See* **Directory of Heliports in the United States, Canada, and Puerto Rico**

★696★
HEMI ELECTRONICS DIRECTORY [Northern California]
Hemi Publications
825 Opal Drive   Phone: (408) 248-2418
San Jose, CA 95117
Covers: Manufacturers and distributors in the "Silicon Valley" area of northern California who manufacture or stock electronic components, accessories, materials, etc. **Entries include:** Company name, address, phone, type of products. **Arrangement:** Alphabetical. **Indexes:** Product. **Pages** (approx.): 200. **Frequency:** Irregular; previous edition January 1977; latest edition July 1979. **Editor:** E. M. Hannon. **Advertising accepted.** **Price:** $5.00.

★697★
HFD-RETAILING HOME FURNISHINGS—DIRECTORY OF SUPPLIERS ISSUE [Telephone and equipment]
Fairchild Publications, Inc.
7 E. 12th Street   Phone: (212) 741-4000
New York, NY 10003
Covers: About 150 manufacturers and suppliers of residential telephone equipment. **Entries include:** Company name, address, phone, name of contact, products, brand names. **Arrangement:** Alphabetical. **Pages** (approx.): 20. **Frequency:** Not established; first edition September 1978. **Editor:** Manning Greenberg. **Advertising accepted. Price:** 50¢.

★698★
HIGH TECH: THE INDUSTRIAL STYLE & SOURCE BOOK FOR THE HOME
Clarkson N. Potter, Inc., Division
Crown Publishers, Inc.
One Park Avenue   Phone: (212) 532-9200
New York, NY 10016
Publication includes: List of hundreds of suppliers, manufacturers, and distributors of industrial products which are suggested for use as home furnishings. **Entries include:** Company name, address, products; some listings include prices and illustrations. **Arrangement:** Alphabetical. **Frequency:** Published November 1978. **Author:** Joan Kron and Suzanne Slesin. **Price:** $30.00, plus $1.25 shipping. **Other information:** "High-tech" is a term describing a style of interior decorating which uses industrial and commercial products such as testubes, scaffolding, lockers, small parts bins, etc., as home furnishings.

★699★
HOME AND AUTO [STORES] BUYER'S GUIDE
Harcourt Brace Jovanovich, Inc.
757 Third Avenue   Phone: (212) 888-3300
New York, NY 10017
Covers: Manufacturers and distributors of home and automotive products sold to public through automotive chains, department stores, etc., including automobile accessories, hardware, paint, sporting goods, lawn and garden merchandise; includes list of manufacturers' agents. **Entries include:** Company name, address, phone, and list of products. Manufacturers' agents listings also show terrritory traveled. **Arrangement:** Alphabetical. **Indexes:** Product. **Pages** (approx.): 75.

Frequency: Annual, July. **Editor:** Richard P. Weinberg. **Advertising accepted.** Circulation 22,000. **Price:** $5.00. **Send orders to:** Harcourt Brace Jovanovich, Inc., 1 E. First St., Duluth, MN 55802 (218-727-8511).

Hot Rod Industry News—Performance and Custom Directory Issue *See* **Hot Rod Magazine—Performance and Custom Directory Issue**

★700★

HOT ROD MAGAZINE—PERFORMANCE AND CUSTOM DIRECTORY ISSUE

Petersen Publishing Company

8490 Sunset Boulevard   Phone: (213) 657-5100

Los Angeles, CA 90069

Covers: About 3,900 manufacturers, dealers, distributors, and service companies supplying performance and custom products for racing, street, and off-road vehicle applications; international coverage. **Entries include:** Company name, address, phone, company officers, and products or services offered. **Arrangement:** Alphabetical within separate sections for manufacturers, dealers and distributors, and service companies. **Indexes:** Product, geographical. **Pages** (approx.): 200. **Frequency:** Annual, November. **Editor:** Ormel Duke. **Advertising accepted.** Circulation 35,000. **Former title:** Hot Rod Industry News - Performance and Custom Directory Issue (1978). **Price:** $5.95.

★701★

HOTEL & MOTEL MANAGEMENT—BUYERS GUIDE AND REFERENCE ISSUE

Robert Freeman Publishing Corporation

1713 Central Street   Phone: (312) 328-4111

Evanston, IL 60201

Covers: 900 companies supplying products or services to the hotel and motel industry. **Entries include:** Company name, address, phone number, principal executive, products or services, and brand names. **Arrangement:** Alphabetical. **Indexes:** Brand name, product. **Frequency:** Annual, February. **Advertising accepted.** Circulation 30,000. **Price:** $2.00 (current and 1980 editions).

★702★

HOTEL & MOTEL RED BOOK

American Hotel Association Directory Corporation

888 Seventh Avenue   Phone: (212) 265-4506

New York, NY 10019

Covers: About 8,500 hotels, motels, resort hotels, and condominiums with rental programs in the United States, Canada, Mexico, and the Caribbean; most are members of the association. **Entries include:** Property name, address, phone, toll-free or TWX number, manager's name, number of rooms, rates. Similar information for condominiums. **Arrangement:** Geographical. **Indexes:** Hotel name. **Pages** (approx.): 675. **Frequency:** Annual, May. **Editor:** Barbara Rugowski, General Manager. **Advertising accepted.** Circulation 31,000. **Price:** $25.00 (current and 1980 editions).

★703★

HOTEL & TRAVEL INDEX

Ziff-Davis Publishing Company

One Park Avenue   Phone: (212) 725-3833

New York, NY 10016

Covers: Over 30,000 hotels, motels, resorts, inns, and guest houses, worldwide; airline headquarters and branch offices; hotel and motel systems; hotel representatives and reservations services; railroad offices. **Entries include:** All entries show company name, address, phone; hotel listings show rates, manager's name, hotel representative, telex number, travel agency commission. **Arrangement:** Geographical, alphabetical. **Pages** (approx.): 1,700. **Frequency:** Quarterly, late February, May, August, November. **Editor:** Jerry Preece. **Advertising accepted.** Circulation 28,000. **Price:** $20.00 per copy; $60.00 per year. **Other information:** The first and probably the largest of the travel industry's hotel directories, "Hotel &

Travel Index" has grown from a system of hotel brochure racks first placed in California hotels in 1928 by founder Elwood Ingledue.

★704★

HOUSE BEAUTIFUL'S DIRECTORY OF MATCHING SERVICES FOR CHINA, SILVER, AND GLASS

Hearst Magazines

717 Fifth Avenue, Room 958

New York, NY 10022

Covers: Sources for securing matching pieces of fine china, quality earthenware, sterling, silver plate, stainless steel, American pressed and cut glass, and European crystal. **Frequency:** Irregular; latest edition spring 1978. **Price:** 50¢, postpaid.

★705★

HOUSEHOLD & PERSONAL PRODUCTS INDUSTRY—COSMETICS AND TOILETRIES BUYERS' GUIDE ISSUE

Rodman Publishing Corporation

26 Lake Street   Phone: (201) 825-2552

Ramsey, NJ 07446

Covers: Suppliers to manufacturers of cosmetics, toiletries, soaps, detergents, and related household and personal products. **Entries include:** Supplier names and addresses. **Arrangement:** Alphabetical. **Indexes:** Product, trade name. **Frequency:** Annual, February. **Editor:** Hamilton C. Carson. **Advertising accepted.** Circulation 14,000. **Price:** $2.00.

★706★

HOUSING—DIRECTORY OF PRODUCTS AND MANUFACTURERS ISSUE

McGraw-Hill, Inc.

1221 Avenue of the Americas   Phone: (212) 997-6908

New York, NY 10020

Covers: About 1,700 manufacturers of building supplies primarily for residential construction; about 120 manufacturers of modular, sectional, panelized, prefabricated, and precut housing; and 85 trade associations. **Entries include:** Company name, address. Phone is given for building supply manufacturers in alphabetical listing; products are given in building supply manufacturers classified listing and for housing manufacturers. **Arrangement:** Building supply manufacturers are alphabetical and classified, housing manufacturers and trade associations are alphabetical. **Pages** (approx.): 125. **Frequency:** Annual, July; first edition August 1979. **Editor:** Jenny Kahn. **Advertising accepted.** Circulation 85,000. **Price:** $3.00, postpaid.

★707★

HOUSTON—TOP 100 PUBLIC COMPANIES AND LEADING FINANCIAL INSTITUTIONS ISSUE [Texas]

Houston Chamber of Commerce

1100 Milam Building, 25th Floor   Phone: (713) 651-1313

Houston, TX 77002

Entries include: Company name, total sales or revenues for current and previous year, rank for current and previous year, and percentage of change in net income per share. **Arrangement:** Ranked by total sales or revenues for previous year. **Frequency:** Irregular; latest appeared in February 1978 issue. **Editor:** Richard Stanley. **Advertising accepted.** **Price:** $1.50.

★708★

HOUSTON PUBLIC COMPANIES [Texas]

Cordovan Corporation

5314 Bingle Road   Phone: (713) 688-8811

Houston, TX 77092

Covers: About 140 publicly owned companies in Houston which have provided information, plus about 90 others listed in an appendix for lack of full information, change in status, etc. **Entries include:** Company name, address, phone, stock's trading symbol, names of officers and directors, number of employees, SIC number, corporate history, financial keys, and other data. **Arrangement:** Alphabetical. **Pages** (approx.): 300. **Frequency:** Annual, summer. **Editor:** Mike Weingart. **Advertising accepted.** Circulation 3,000. **Price:** $9.95.

★709★
HOUSTON-GULF COAST MANUFACTURERS DIRECTORY
Houston Chamber of Commerce
1100 Milam, 25th Floor   Phone: (713) 651-1313
Houston, TX 77002
Covers: 3,340 manufacturing plants in the Houston area (including Harris, Brazoria, Chambers, Fort Bend, Galveston, Liberty, Montgomery, and Waller counties). **Entries include:** Plant name, parent company name, plant street address, plant mailing address, parent company address, phone, census tract number if in Harris County or county name, type of organization, year plant began operations in county, year plant began operations at present address, distribution area, number of employees (coded), names and titles of key personnel, products with 4-digit SIC number for each. **Arrangement:** Alphabetical. **Indexes:** SIC number. **Pages** (approx.): 270. **Frequency:** Triennial; latest edition 1978; new edition expected 1981. **Editor:** H. N. Martin, Director of Research. **Price:** $40.00, plus $4.00 shipping.

★710★
HOW TO BUY METALWORKING MACHINERY AND EQUIPMENT
Industrial Machinery News Corporation
29516 Southfield Road
Southfield, MI 48037
Publication includes: Directory of machine tool distributors and dealers. **Entries include:** Company name, address, phone, lines handled. **Arrangement:** Geographical. **Frequency:** Irregular; first edition 1977. **Price:** $39.95. **Other information:** Principal content of publication is descriptions, diagrams, etc., of metalworking equipment.

★711★
HOW TO FIND INFORMATION ABOUT COMPANIES
Washington Researchers
918 16th Street, N. W.   Phone: (202) 828-4800
Washington, DC 20006
Covers: Over 1,500 state government agencies, federal government agencies, investigative firms, libraries, local organizations, information services, computerized data bases, trade associations, labor unions, and other organizations, agencies, and firms which collect information on public and private companies. **Entries include:** Name, address; phone is included for many listings; description of services, information, etc. **Arrangement:** By type of organization. **Indexes:** Subject. **Pages** (approx.): 280. **Frequency:** Not established; first edition August 1979. **Price:** $45.00, postpaid, payment with order; $48.00, billed.

★712★
HSMA OFFICIAL HOTEL-MOTEL DIRECTORY AND FACILITIES GUIDE
Hotel Sales Management Association (International)
333 N. Gladstone Avenue   Phone: (609) 832-1979
Margate, NJ 08402
Covers: About 5,000 hotels and motels throughout the world with one or more HSMA members on their staffs. **Entries include:** Facility's name, address, phone, cable, and teletype numbers; name of principal and other executives; chain affiliation; number of rooms; description of facilities and services. **Arrangement:** Geographical. **Indexes:** Alphabetical. **Pages** (approx.): 190. **Frequency:** Annual, January. **Editor:** David C. Dorf, Director of Education. **Advertising accepted.** Circulation 25,000. **Price:** $5.00 (current and 1980 editions). **Send orders to:** Hotel Sales Management Association (International), 362 Fifth Ave., New York, NY (212-868-3466).

★713★
HVI-CERTIFIED HOME VENTILATING PRODUCTS DIRECTORY
Home Ventilating Institute
4300-L Lincoln Avenue   Phone: (312) 359-8160
Rolling Meadows, IL 60008
Covers: 30 manufacturers of home ventilating products (ventilating range hoods, exhaust fans, powered attic space ventilators, etc.). **Entries include:** Company name, address, products, ratings in air delivery and sound. **Arrangement:** By product. **Pages** (approx.): 10. **Frequency:** Annual, spring. **Editor:** D. W. Sanford, Executive Director. **Price:** Free.

★714★
IC MASTER [Integrated circuits]
United Technical Publications, Division
Cox Broadcasting Corporation
1333 Lawrence Expressway, Suite 420   Phone: (408) 248-8044
Santa Clara, CA 95051
Publication includes: List of manufacturers and distributors of integrated circuits. **Entries include:** Company name, address, phone, integrated circuits available. **Arrangement:** Alphabetical. **Indexes:** Product. **Frequency:** Annual, January; supplements in March, June, September, and November. **Editor:** John Darago. **Price:** $65.00; includes a year's supplements. **Send orders to:** United Technical Publications, 645 Stewart Avenue, Garden City, NY 11530. **Also includes:** Major portion of publication is buyer's guide to integrated circuits, their applications, and possible substitutions.

Idaho Concrete and Aggregate Producers Association—Roster
    See Pacific Builder & Engineer—Buyers Guide & Directory
    Issue

Idaho Manufacturers Directory See Manufacturing Directory of
    Idaho

Idaho Manufacturing Directory See Manufacturing Directory of
    Idaho

Idaho Mining Association—Membership Roster See
    Manufacturing Directory of Idaho

★715★
IFT WORLD DIRECTORY & GUIDE [Food industry]
Institute of Food Technologists
221 N. LaSalle Street   Phone: (312) 782-8424
Chicago, IL 60601
Covers: 18,000 members of the institute, scientific and technical personnel concerned with food processing, product development, and research. Also includes sections on suppliers, consultants, and testing laboratories. **Entries include:** For members - Name, affiliation, address. **Arrangement:** Alphabetical within membership classifications. **Indexes:** Affiliation. **Pages** (approx.): 450. **Frequency:** Annual, December. **Editor:** John B. Klis. **Advertising accepted.** Circulation 18,000. **Former title:** Directory and Guide (1979). **Price:** Available to members only.

★716★
IG ENERGY DIRECTORY [Insulation, roofing, etc.]
Guide Publications
Box 508   Phone: (515) 236-7029
Grinnell, IA 50112
Covers: 20,000 suppliers to the roofing, siding, storm window, and insulation industry. **Entries include:** Company name, address, phone, names of principal executives, products. **Arrangement:** By general product line. **Indexes:** Geographical, product. **Frequency:** Annual, October; first edition 1979. **Editor:** Jerry L. Vitera. **Advertising accepted.** **Price:** $10.00, plus $3.00 shipping.

★717★
ILLINOIS DIRECTORY OF LUMBER RETAILERS
Illinois Lumber and Material Dealers Association
400 Leland Building   Phone: (217) 544-5405
Springfield, IL 62701
Entries include: Company name, address, phone, names of executives, trade and brand names, list of products or services. **Arrangement:** Geographical. **Pages** (approx.): 90. **Frequency:** Annual, June. **Editor:** Edwin F. Sembell. **Advertising accepted.** Circulation 1,000. **Price:** $17.50.

★718★

ILLINOIS MANUFACTURERS DIRECTORY

Manufacturers' News, Inc.

Three E. Huron Street   Phone: (312) 337-1084

Chicago, IL 60611

Number of listings: 27,000. **Entries include:** Company name, address, phone, names of principal executives, number of employees, net worth, list of products or services, SIC numbers, year established. **Arrangement:** Geographical. **Indexes:** Alphabetical, product number. **Pages** (approx.): 1,200. **Frequency:** Annual, February. **Advertising accepted. Price:** $89.00.

★719★

ILLINOIS SERVICES DIRECTORY

Manufacturers' News, Inc.

Three E. Huron Street   Phone: (312) 337-1084

Chicago, IL 60611

Covers: 11,000 wholesalers, jobbers, contractors, retailers, services, etc. **Entries include:** Firm name, address, phone, names of executives, number of employees, SIC number. **Arrangement:** Zip code sequence. **Indexes:** Alphabetical, SIC. **Pages** (approx.): 960. **Frequency:** Annual, June. **Advertising accepted. Price:** $65.00.

★720★

ILLINOIS SOLAR ENERGY DIRECTORY

Illinois Institute of Natural Resources

325 W. Adams Street   Phone: (217) 785-2800

Springfield, IL 62706

Covers: Distributors and manufacturers of solar equipment and components; solar energy consultants; associations concerned with solar energy and alternative forms of energy; solar energy education programs in Illinois. **Entries include:** Organization name, address, description of activity or product. **Arrangement:** By product or activity. **Frequency:** Irregular; latest edition November 1978; new edition expected January 1980. **Editor:** Gary W. Mielke. **Former title:** Directory of Solar Energy Equipment Manufacturers and Solar Energy Architects and Engineers. **Price:** Free (ILLDOE 78/04). **Other information:** Also available from National Technical Information Service, Springfield, VA 22161; $6.50, paper; $3.00, microfiche (PB 293-063).

★721★

IMMS DIRECTORY OF CERTIFIED PROFESSIONALS [Material handling]

International Material Management Society

3310 Bardaville Drive   Phone: (517) 321-6713

Lansing, MI 48906

Covers: About 1,400 members certified by the association in materials handling, materials management, or a combination of those areas. **Entries include:** Name, address, code to indicate area of certification. **Arrangement:** Alphabetical. **Indexes:** Geographical. **Frequency:** Not established; first edition January 1979. **Price:** $25.00.

★722★

IMPLEMENT & TRACTOR—PRODUCT FILE EDITION

Intertec Publishing Corporation

Box 12901   Phone: (913) 888-4664

Overland Park, KS 66212

Publication includes: Lists of manufacturers, wholesalers, exporters/importers, distributors, and their representatives supplying products and services to the farm equipment industry. **Entries include:** Company name, address, and phone; some listings include names of sales contacts, coding to indicate type of firm, and products handled. **Arrangement:** Alphabetical. **Indexes:** Product, brand name. **Pages** (approx.): 350. **Frequency:** Annual, March. **Advertising accepted.** Circulation 28,000. **Price:** $4.00 (current edition; tentative, 1980 edition).

★723★

IMPORTED HARDWOOD PRODUCTS ASSOCIATION—DIRECTORY

Imported Hardwood Products Association

Box 1308   Phone: (703) 836-6696

Alexandria, VA 22313

Number of listings: About 250. **Entries include:** Company name, address, phone, names of executives, financial keys, list of products or services, telex and cable addresses. **Arrangement:** Classified by type of membership. **Pages** (approx.): 130. **Frequency:** Annual, fall. **Editor:** O. Keister Evans, Executive Vice President. **Advertising accepted. Price:** $25.00.

★724★

IMPORTERS AND EXPORTERS TRADE PROMOTION GUIDE

World Wide Trade Service

Medina, WA 98039

Covers: Over 300 foreign trade organizations concerned with world trade, foreign chambers of commerce and associations in the United States, American chambers of commerce in foreign countries, American chambers of commerce which have foreign trade services, and publishers of books and periodicals of assistance in world trade. **Entries include:** Name, address; publications (if any). Publisher listings include frequency, price, description of contents. **Arrangement:** By type of organization. **Pages** (approx.): 25. **Frequency:** Irregular; latest edition 1979. **Price:** $5.00, postpaid.

★725★

IMPORTERS CONFIDENTIAL DROP-SHIP DIRECTORY

World Wide Trade Service

Medina, WA 98039

Covers: About 90 foreign companies willing to make small drop shipments; foreign government trade information offices in the United States; about a dozen publications concerned with world trade. **Entries include:** For drop shippers - Company name, address, products. For publications - Title, publisher; some listings mention price or describe content. **Arrangement:** Information offices are alphabetical, suppliers are geographical. **Pages** (approx.): 15. **Frequency:** Irregular; latest edition 1977. **Advertising accepted. Price:** $3.00, postpaid.

★726★

INC.—THE INC. 100 ISSUE [Fastest growing small companies]

United Marine Publishing Company, Inc.

38 Commercial Wharf   Phone: (617) 227-4700

Boston, MA 02110

Publication includes: List of 100 fastest growing, publicly held companies in manufacturing and service industries which had revenues of less than $25 million in 1975; some companies which became publicly owned in 1976 or 1977 are included. **Entries include:** Company name, headquarters city, type of business, date incorporated, name of chief executive officer, numer of employees, 1974 and 1978 sales, and income and growth statistics. **Arrangement:** By sales growth. **Frequency:** Annual, May; first edition 1979. **Editor:** Bradford W. Ketchum, Jr., Senior Editor. **Advertising accepted.** Circulation 400,300. **Price:** $1.50.

★727★

INCENTIVE MARKETING—DIRECTORY OF INCENTIVE SOURCES ISSUE

Bill Communications, Inc.

633 Third Avenue   Phone: (212) 986-4800

New York, NY 10017

Covers: 1,000 suppliers of products (including travel) used as advertising and promotional premiums and incentives for other uses, and services needed to conduct a premium or incentive campaign. Includes trading stamp services and specialists in various forms of promotion (contests and sweepstakes, close outs, bank and financial promotion, etc.), and manufacturers' representatives. **Entries include:** Company name, address, phone, name of contact, information on product or service. **Arrangement:** Classified by product or service. **Pages** (approx.): 200. **Frequency:** Annual, January. **Editor:** Murray Elman. **Advertising accepted.** Circulation 35,000. **Price:** $2.00

(current and 1980 editions).

Independent Liquid Terminals Association—Membership Directory *See* Bulk Liquid Terminals Directory

★728★
INDIANA INDUSTRIAL DIRECTORY
Indiana State Chamber of Commerce
Board of Trade Building   Phone: (317) 634-6407
Indianapolis, IN 46204
Covers: About 12,000 manufacturers, processors, and wholesalers. **Entries include:** Company name, address, phone, name of principal executive, number of employees, list of products or services. **Arrangement:** Geographical. **Indexes:** Alphabetical, product. **Pages** (approx.): 380. **Frequency:** Biennial, fall of even years. **Editor:** Max R. Jackson. **Advertising accepted.** Circulation 7,200. **Price:** $30.00, plus $3.00 shipping.

★729★
INDIANA INTERNATIONAL TRADE DIRECTORY
Indiana Department of Commerce
336 State House   Phone: (317) 633-4538
Indianapolis, IN 46204
Covers: About 1,100 Indiana business firms interested in international trade. Includes list of export management companies. **Entries include:** Company name, address, SIC number and product description. **Arrangement:** Alphabetical and by SIC code; identical information in both sections; exporters and importers listed separately. **Pages** (approx.): 140. **Frequency:** Irregular; latest edition 1977. **Price:** Free.

★730★
INDIANA STATE INDUSTRIAL DIRECTORY
State Industrial Directories Corporation
Two Penn Plaza   Phone: (212) 564-0340
New York, NY 10001
Number of listings: 13,800. **Entries include:** Company name, address, phone, names of key executives, number of employees, plant size, 4-digit SIC code, products, whether firm imports or exports, and whether firm has research facilities. **Arrangement:** Geographical. **Indexes:** Alphabetical, product (includes mailing address and phone for each firm). **Frequency:** Annual, September. **Advertising accepted.** **Price:** $6.00.

★731★
INDIANAPOLIS BUSINESS AND INDUSTRY DIRECTORY
Indianapolis Chamber of Commerce
320 N. Meridian Street   Phone: (317) 635-4747
Indianapolis, IN 46204
Covers: 2,100 manufacturers and other business firms. **Entries include:** Company name, address, phone, name of principal executive, list of products or services, SIC numbers. **Arrangement:** Alphabetical. **Indexes:** Product/service, SIC number. **Pages** (approx.): 90. **Frequency:** Annual, June. **Editor:** Ann Overturf. **Advertising accepted.** Circulation 5,000. **Former title:** Indianapolis Chamber of Commerce - Buyer's Guide and Membership Directory. **Price:** $15.60, plus $1.50 shipping, payment with order.

Indianapolis Chamber of Commerce—Buyer's Guide and Membership Directory [Indiana] *See* Indianapolis Business and Industry Directory...

Industrial Alabama *See* Alabama Directory of Mining and Manufacturing

★732★
INDUSTRIAL DEVELOPMENT—MILLION DOLLAR PLANTS COLUMN
Conway Publications, Inc.
Peachtree Air Terminal
1954 Airport Road   Phone: (404) 458-6026
Atlanta, GA 30341
Covers: Significant new or expanding industrial facilities. **Entries include:** Company name, address, nature and dollar value of change or expansion, planned use of new facilities. **Arrangement:** Geographical. **Frequency:** In each monthly issue. **Editor:** H. M. Conway, President. **Price:** $7.00 per copy; $39.00 per year (ISSN 0097-3033).

★733★
INDUSTRIAL DEVELOPMENT IN THE TVA AREA DURING [YEAR]
Division of Power Utilization
Tennessee Valley Authority
801 Power Building
Sixth & Market Streets   Phone: (615) 755-2319
Chattanooga, TN 37401
Covers: New industrial operations established in the Tennessee Valley Authority service area during the preceding year, and existing plants which announced plans for expansion. **Entries include:** Company name, town, SIC number, product or operation, type of development and its estimated completion date, and estimated increases in kilowatt demand, investment, and employment. **Arrangement:** Geographical by county. **Pages** (approx.): 40. **Frequency:** Annual, April. **Editor:** Leila M. Dicks, Statistical Clerk. **Price:** Free. **Also includes:** Summary statistics in numeric and graphic form.

★734★
INDUSTRIAL DIRECTORY—MANUFACTURING FACILITIES IN ALLEGHENY COUNTY [Pennsylvania]
Greater Pittsburgh Chamber of Commerce
411 Seventh Avenue   Phone: (412) 391-3400
Pittsburgh, PA 15219
Covers: About 280 manufacturing plants in Allegheny County which employ 50 people or more. **Entries include:** Company name, address, phone, name of principal executive, products, SIC number, and average number of employees. **Arrangement:** Geographical. **Indexes:** Alphabetical, SIC number. **Pages** (approx.): 50. **Frequency:** Irregular; latest edition 1979. **Price:** $5.00.

★735★
INDUSTRIAL DIRECTORY [Bartholomew County, Ohio]
Columbus Chamber of Commerce
500 Franklin
Columbus, OH
Number of listings: Over 300 firms in Bartholomew County, Ohio. **Entries include:** Company name, address, phone; name of chief executive officer; number of employees; lines of business. **Arrangement:** By general industry (agriculture, communications, construction, etc.). **Frequency:** Latest edition 1978. **Price:** $3.00.

★736★
INDUSTRIAL DIRECTORY [Gardena Valley, California]
Gardena Valley Chamber of Commerce
1551 W. Redondo Beach Boulevard   Phone: (213) 532-9905
Gardena, CA 90247
Covers: About 1,200 industrial firms in the Gardena Valley, California area. Membership in the chamber is not a requirement for listing. **Entries include:** Company name, address, phone, name of chief executive, line of business, number of employees, parent company if any. **Arrangement:** By industry. **Indexes:** Product/service. **Pages** (approx.): 65. **Frequency:** Biennial, October of even years. **Editor:** Anita E. Bell, Secretary/General Manager. **Price:** $10.00.

★737★

INDUSTRIAL DIRECTORY FOR STOCKTON AND SAN JOAQUIN COUNTY, CALIFORNIA
Greater Stockton Chamber of Commerce
1105 N. El Dorado Street　　　　Phone: (209) 466-7066
Stockton, CA 95202
Covers: 450 industrial firms in Stockton and San Joaquin county. **Entries include:** Company name, address, phone, name of principal executive, and number of employees. **Arrangement:** By product. **Indexes:** Alphabetical. **Frequency:** Irregular; previous edition 1977; latest edition July 1979. **Price:** $7.50, payment with order. **Other information:** Published with San Joaquin Economic Development Association.

Industrial Directory Metropolitan Buffalo *See* **Directory— Metropolitan Buffalo Industry**

★738★

INDUSTRIAL DIRECTORY OF ROCHESTER AND MONROE COUNTY, NEW YORK
Rochester Area Chamber of Commerce
555 St. Paul Street　　　　Phone: (716) 454-2220
Rochester, NY 14604
Number of listings: 850. **Entries include:** Company name, address, phone, name of principal executive, number of employees, and products or services. **Arrangement:** Alphabetical. **Indexes:** Product. **Pages** (approx.): 80. **Frequency:** Irregular; approximately every two years; latest edition 1979. **Editor:** Michael P. Vadala, Manager, Economic Development. **Price:** $20.00.

★739★

INDUSTRIAL DIRECTORY OF SOUTH CAROLINA
South Carolina State Development Board
Box 927　　　　Phone: (803) 758-3055
Columbia, SC 29202
Number of listings: Over 2,700. **Entries include:** Company name, address, phone, parent company (if applicable), plant address, names of principal executives, whether firm exports or imports, number of employees, products, SIC numbers. **Arrangement:** By county and by SIC classification; same information in both sections except executives' names omitted in SIC. **Indexes:** Alphabetical. **Pages** (approx.): 400. **Frequency:** About every 18 months; latest edition 1978; new edition expected January 1980. **Editor:** Grace G. McKown. **Price:** $20.00 (current and 1980 editions). **Also includes:** Classified list of companies serving international trade. Entries include company name, address, phone, foreign representatives. **Other information:** Cover title, "South Carolina Industrial Directory."

★740★

INDUSTRIAL DIRECTORY OF THE COMMONWEALTH OF PENNSYLVANIA
Pennsylvania Department of Commerce
Health & Welfare Building, Room 630B　　　　Phone: (717) 787-7532
Harrisburg, PA 17120
Number of listings: 14,500. **Entries include:** Company name, address, phone, number of employees, name of principal executive. **Arrangement:** By SIC number within counties. **Indexes:** Alphabetical, SIC. **Pages** (approx.): 900. **Frequency:** Annual, spring. **Editor:** Joanne L. Young. **Price:** $15.00, postpaid, payment with order.

Industrial Directory of Virginia *See* **Directory of Virginia Manufacturing**

Industrial Directory of York and York County [Pennsylvania] *See* **York County Industrial Directory [Pennsylvania]**

★741★

INDUSTRIAL FABRIC PRODUCTS REVIEW—DIRECTORY OF AVAILABLE EQUIPMENT ISSUE
Canvas Products Association International
Endicott Building, Room 350　　　　Phone: (612) 222-2508
St. Paul, MN 55101
Publication includes: List of about 75 manufacturers and distributors of new and used equipment for handling industrial fabrics, including sewing machines, heat sealers, cutting knives, grommeting equipment, etc. **Entries include:** Company name, address, phone, products. **Arrangement:** Alphabetical. **Frequency:** Annual, December. **Editor:** Michael E. Coughlin. **Advertising accepted.** Circulation 4,200. **Price:** $5.00.

Industrial Gas—Directory of....Equipment and Systems Issue *See* **Modern Industrial Energy—Annual Directory...Issue**

Industrial Gas and Energy Utilization—Annual Directory of Energy Management and Conservation Equipment Issue *See* **Modern Industrial...**

★742★

INDUSTRIAL PARK GROWTH
Conway Publications, Inc.
Peachtree Air Terminal
1954 Airport Road　　　　Phone: (404) 458-6026
Atlanta, GA 30341
Publication includes: List of about 4,000 United States and Canadian office and industrial parks. **Entries include:** Project name, name and address of developer. **Arrangement:** Geographical. **Pages** (approx.): 400. **Frequency:** First published 1979. **Editors:** H. M. Conway, L. L. Liston, R. J. Saul. **Price:** $39.00. **Also includes:** Discussion of development of park concept, performance standards, etc.

★743★

INDUSTRIAL PARKS AND DISTRICTS IN PENNSYLVANIA
Division of Research and Planning
Pennsylvania Department of Commerce
Health and Welfare Building, Room 632　　　　Phone: (717) 787-9610
Harrisburg, PA 17120
Covers: About 500 industrial parks in Pennsylvania. **Entries include:** Name of park or district; total acreage; acreage available for sale or lease; name, address, phone of agent and/or owners; transportation and types of utilities available; industries located in facility. **Arrangement:** Geographical. **Pages** (approx.): 360; supplement, 110. **Frequency:** Main directory issued in 1973; supplement in 1976. **Editor:** Keith A. Gingrich. **Price:** Free.

★744★

INDUSTRIAL RELATIONS RESEARCH ASSOCIATION— MEMBERSHIP DIRECTORY
Industrial Relations Research Association
Social Science Building, Room 7226
University of Wisconsin　　　　Phone: (608) 262-2762
Madison, WI 53706
Covers: About 5,000 businessmen, union leaders, government officials, lawyers, arbitrators, teachers and others interested in labor relations. **Entries include:** Name, office address, career data, writings. **Arrangement:** Alphabetical. **Indexes:** Geographical, occupation. **Pages** (approx.): 400. **Frequency:** Every six years; latest edition 1979. **Editor:** David R. Zimmerman, IRRA Secretary-Treasurer. **Price:** $12.00, plus $1.25 shipping.

Industrial Research/Development—Yellow Pages of Instrumentation, Equipment, and Supplies Issue *See* **Yellow Pages of Instrumentation...**

★745★

INDUSTRY—NEW AND EXPANDING [Alabama]
Alabama Development Office
State Capitol   Phone: (205) 832-6980
Montgomery, AL 36130
Entries include: Company name, address, products, nature of expansion if appropriate. **Arrangement:** Geographical. **Indexes:** Alphabetical, SIC. **Pages** (approx.): 40. **Frequency:** Annual, January. **Editor:** Richard W. McLaney, Research Supervisor. **Price:** $1.00 (current and 1980 editions).

★746★

INDUSTRY ANALYSTS IN THE FEDERAL GOVERNMENT
Washington Researchers
918 16th Street, N. W.   Phone: (202) 828-4800
Washington, DC 20006
Covers: Over 100 industry analysts and specialists in the Department of Commerce and Bureau of Census. **Entries include:** Name, office address and phone. **Arrangement:** By department, then by industry, then by product. **Indexes:** SIC. **Pages** (approx.): 30. **Frequency:** Annual, summer. **Price:** $10.00, payment with order; $11.50, billed.

★747★

INLAND EMPIRE MANUFACTURERS GUIDE [Northwestern United States]
Spokane Area Development Council
Box 2147   Phone: (509) 624-9285
Spokane, WA 99210
Covers: 1,200 manufacturing firms in a 36-county area - eastern Washington, northern Idaho, western Montana, Umatilla County, Oregon (SIC 20-39). **Entries include:** Company name, address, phone, principal executive, principal product, market area, number of employees, secondary activity (e.g., wholesale, distributor, manufacturers representative). Alphabetical and geographical section entries list the company's name and SIC code. **Arrangement:** Classified by SIC code. **Indexes:** Alphabetical, geographical. **Pages** (approx.): 95. **Frequency:** Irregular; latest edition June 1979. **Editor:** David Walsh, Assistant Manager. **Price:** $10.00, plus $1.00 shipping.

★748★

INLAND RIVER GUIDE [Barge companies, etc.]
Waterways Journal, Inc.
319 N. Fourth Street, Suite 666   Phone: (314) 241-7354
St. Louis, MO 63102
Covers: Barge and towing companies operating on Mississippi River System, Warrior-Tombigbee System, Gulf Intracoastal Waterway; all inland and Gulf Coast shipyards; public and private terminals on waterways; contracting and dredging firms; government agencies dealing with waterways, etc. **Entries include:** Company name, address, phone, names of executives, list of products or services. **Arrangement:** By category. **Pages** (approx.): 500. **Frequency:** Annual, September. **Editor:** Dan Owen. **Advertising accepted.** Circulation 2,300. **Price:** $25.00.

★749★

INLAND RIVER RECORD [Towboats and other equipment]
Waterways Journal
319 N. Fourth Street, Suite 666   Phone: (314) 241-7354
St. Louis, MO 63102
Covers: Over 3,500 commercial towboats and tugs, U. S. Corps of Engineer vessels, and Coast Guard vessels navigating the Mississippi River and its tributaries, the Gulf Intracoastal Waterway, and the Warrior-Tombigbee System. Includes a separate list of passenger vessels and certain private craft. **Entries include:** Boat name, builder, year built, dimensions, engines and horsepower, reduction, previous owners, and present owner, with address. **Pages** (approx.): 400. **Frequency:** Annual, July. **Editor:** Dan Owen. **Advertising accepted.** Circulation 1,750. **Price:** $20.00.

★750★

INNOVATION IN PUBLIC TRANSPORTATION
Urban Mass Transportation Administration
Transportation Department
Washington, DC
Covers: 130 mass transportation projects in the areas of bus and paratransit technology and operations, rail transit technology, automated guideway transit technology and operations, socio-economic projects, safety and product qualification, etc. Includes illustrations and bibliography of project reports. **Entries include:** Project name, location, sponsor, nature of activities. **Pages** (approx.): 90. **Frequency:** Annual. **Price:** $2.30 (S/N 050-014-00014-2). **Send orders to:** Government Printing Office, Washington, DC 20402.

★751★

IN-PLANT PRINTER GOLD BOOK DIRECTORY
Innes Publishing Company
425 Huehl Road, Building 11-B   Phone: (312) 564-5940
Northbrook, IL 60062
Covers: Manufacturers of equipment for the in-plant graphic arts industry. **Entries include:** Company name, address, phone, list of products. **Arrangement:** By product categories. **Pages** (approx.): 70. **Frequency:** Annual, December. **Advertising accepted.** Circulation 22,000. **Price:** $3.00.

★752★

INSITE [Concession industry]
National Association of Concessionaires
35 E. Wacker Drive   Phone: (312) 236-3858
Chicago, IL 60601
Covers: About 400 member equipment manufacturers, suppliers, jobber/distributors, popcorn processors, theaters, amusement parks, stadiums, rinks, and other concession operators in the United States and Canada. **Entries include:** For operators - Company name, phone, name of contact. For manufacturers and suppliers - Company name, address, phone, names and titles of up to four executives, brief description of service or products. **Arrangement:** By type of concession or business activity. **Indexes:** Personal name, geographical, product. **Pages** (approx.): 125. **Frequency:** Annual, January; first edition under new title, 1980. **Editor:** Anne Davis, Communications Director. **Advertising accepted.** Circulation 3,500. **Former title:** National Association of Concessionaires - Membership Directory. **Price:** $35.00.

★753★

INSTALLATION SPECIALIST MAGAZINE—BUYERS' GUIDE ISSUE [Floor covering]
Specialist Publications, Inc.
17835 Ventura Boulevard   Phone: (213) 873-1411
Encino, CA 91316
Covers: About 6,000 manufacturers and distributors of equipment and supplies used in the installation, cleaning, and maintenance of floor coverings. **Entries include:** Comapny name, address, phone, products or services. **Arrangement:** Alphabetical. **Indexes:** Product. **Pages** (approx.): 150. **Frequency:** Annual, May. **Editor:** Howard Olansky. **Advertising accepted.** Circulation 16,000. **Price:** $5.00 (1980 edition).

Institute of Food Technologists—Directory and Guide *See* IFT World Directory & Guide

★754★

INSTITUTE OF INTERNAL AUDITORS—MEMBERSHIP DIRECTORY
Institute of Internal Auditors
249 Maitland Avenue   Phone: (305) 830-7600
Altamonte Springs, FL 32701
Covers: 20,000 auditors, controllers, and accountants in internal auditing positions in corporations, government, and institutions. **Entries include:** Name, company name and address or home address. **Arrangement:** Alphabetical. **Frequency:** Annual, fall. **Price:** Available to members only.

★755★
INSTITUTE OF MANAGEMENT CONSULTANTS—DIRECTORY OF MEMBERS
Institute of Management Consultants
19 W. 44th Street   Phone: (212) 686-7338
New York, NY 10036
Number of listings: 800 individuals who practice management consulting as individuals or members of firms. **Entries include:** Name, firm, address, phone, areas of competence. **Arrangement:** Alphabetical by member's name. **Indexes:** Geographical. **Pages** (approx.): 60. **Frequency:** Annual. **Editor:** John F. Hartshorne. **Price:** $5.00.

★756★
INSTITUTIONS/VOLUME FEEDING—ANNUAL 400 ISSUE
Cahners Publishing Company
Five S. Wabash Avenue   Phone: (312) 372-6880
Chicago, IL 60603
Publication includes: Lists of 400 largest away-from-home food service companies, 100 leading hotels and motels and other suppliers of lodging (including the military), and 500 regional and local food and lodging operations with a volume of $1 million or more. **Entries include:** For 400 list - Company name, location, rank, foodservice volume and number of units for two preceding years, brief summary of activities and prospects. For 100 list - Company name, location, rank, room sales for two preceding years, number of properties and beds. For 500 list - Company name, location, volume, type of operation, number of seats or beds, meals served (breakfast...), number of employees. **Arrangement:** 400 and 100 list ranked by sales volume, 500 list divided by regions, then alphabetically by company or institution. **Frequency:** Annual, July 15 issue. **Editor:** Jane Young Wallace. **Advertising accepted.** Circulation 105,000. **Price:** $15.00 (current edition); $20.00 (1980 edition).

★757★
INSULATION/CIRCUITS DESK MANUAL
Lake Publishing Corporation
700 Peterson Road   Phone: (312) 362-8711
Libertyville, IL 60048
Covers: Suppliers of products and services used in manufacturing electronic products. Also includes a list of distributors, manufacturers' agents, jobbers, and representatives not directly employed by manufacturers. **Entries include:** Company name and address. **Arrangement:** Suppliers alphabetical; distributors and agents geographical. **Pages** (approx.): 300. **Frequency:** Annual, June/July. **Editor:** Lincoln R. Samelson, Publisher. **Advertising accepted.** Circulation 35,000. **Former title:** Insulation/Circuits Directory Encyclopedia. **Price:** $25.00.

★758★
INSURANCE CONFERENCE PLANNER
Bayard Publications, Inc.
695 Summer Street   Phone: (203) 327-0800
Stamford, CT 06901
Publication includes: Guide to selected conference and meeting sites; there are sometimes special sections on specific areas, e.g., a section on Florida facilities. Includes list of convention and tourist bureaus. **Entries include:** Facility name, address, phone; sales director's name; data on size and services. **Arrangement:** Geographical. **Frequency:** Every two months. **Editor:** George Lowden. **Advertising accepted.** Circulation approximately 11,000. **Former title:** Insurance Magazine's Green Book of Convention Planning (1976). **Price:** $5.00 per April issue, and $2.00 for other issues; $10.00 per year.

Insurance Magazine's Green Book of Convention Planning *See* Insurance Conference Planner

★759★
INTERACTIVE COMPUTING DIRECTORY
Association of Time-Sharing Users
75 Manhattan Drive   Phone: (303) 499-1722
Boulder, CO 80303
Covers: About 250 companies offering time-sharing services, equipment, and software. **Entries include:** Company name, address, phone, description of product or service. **Arrangement:** Issued in parts, each devoted to a specific function or service - data bases, graphics programs, etc. **Indexes:** Geographic section includes all firms in other sections. **Pages** (approx.): 600. **Frequency:** Annual, with bimonthly supplements. **Editor:** Hillel Segal, President. **Price:** $70.00.

★760★
INTERAVIA ABC—WORLD DIRECTORY OF AVIATION AND ASTRONAUTICS
Interavia Publications
1633 Vista del Mar   Phone: (213) 461-4981
Hollywood, CA 90028
Covers: 50,000 aviation and aerospace manufacturers, airlines, associations, government agencies, etc., worldwide. **Entries include:** For companies - Company name, address, principal departments or divisions, names of principal executives, branch offices and factories with addresses, description of products or services. Listings for associations and agencies include similar detail. Entries are ordinarily in the language of the country. **Arrangement:** Geographical, then classified by industry or activity. **Indexes:** Personal name, company name. **Pages** (approx.): 1,300. **Frequency:** Annual, March. **Advertising accepted. Price:** $72.00.

★761★
INTERIOR DECORATORS' HANDBOOK
Columbia Communications, Inc.
370 Lexington Avenue   Phone: (212) 532-9290
New York, NY 10017
Covers: Manufacturers and distributors of furniture, accessories, floor coverings, fabrics, wallcoverings, etc., and services related to these products. **Entries include:** Manufacturer or distributor name, address, phone, brands carried. Similar information for importers, jobbers, and agents. **Arrangement:** Alphabetical. **Indexes:** Product, trade name. **Pages** (approx.): 500. **Frequency:** Semiannual, April and October. **Editor:** Laura R. Blank. **Advertising accepted.** Circulation 19,000. **Price:** $12.00 per year.

★762★
INTERIOR DESIGN—BUYERS' GUIDE ISSUE
Whitney Communications Corporation
850 Third Avenue   Phone: (212) 593-2100
New York, NY 10022
Covers: 2,000 manufacturers and suppliers of furniture and furnishings for contract and residential designers. **Entries include:** Company name, address, phone. **Arrangement:** Alphabetical. **Indexes:** Keyword, product, geographical. **Pages** (approx.): 325. **Frequency:** Annual, December. **Editor:** Loretta Wasserman, Directory Editor. **Advertising accepted.** Circulation 26,500. **Price:** $5.00.

Internal Publications Directory *See* Working Press of the Nation

★763★
INTERNATIONAL ADVERTISING ASSOCIATION—MEMBERSHIP DIRECTORY
International Advertising Association
475 Fifth Avenue   Phone: (212) 684-1583
New York, NY 10017
Covers: 2,700 advertisers, advertising agencies, media and other firms involved in advertising who are members, worldwide. **Entries include:** Company name, address, phone, name of principal executive. **Arrangement:** Contents classified geographically, then by function or service. **Pages** (approx.): 150. **Frequency:** Annual, January/February. **Editor:** John S. W. Wasley, Executive Director. **Advertising accepted.** Circulation 3,000. **Price:** $50.00 (current and 1980

editions).

International Association for Personnel Women—Consultants Directory *See* Consultants Directory [Personnel Management]

★764★
INTERNATIONAL ASSOCIATION FOR PERSONNEL WOMEN— MEMBERSHIP ROSTER
International Association for Personnel Women
Box 3057
Grand Central Station   Phone: (212) 734-8160
New York, NY 10017
Number of listings: 1,500 members-at-large and members of affiliated chapters. **Entries include:** Individual name, office address, office phone, coding to indicate duties in position and number of employees served. **Arrangement:** By type of membership. **Pages** (approx.): 90. **Frequency:** Annual, November. **Editor:** Connie Sternberg, Executive Director. **Price:** $100.00.

International Association for Personnel Women—Speaker Roster *See* Directory of Speakers [Personnel management]

★765★
INTERNATIONAL ASSOCIATION OF AMUSEMENT PARKS AND ATTRACTIONS—MANUAL AND GUIDE
International Association of Amusement Parks and Attractions
7222 W. Cermak Road, Suite 303   Phone: (312) 442-5866
North Riverside, IL 60546
Covers: Outdoor amusement industry manufacturers and suppliers, including 360 ride manufacturers; also includes membership rosters of IAAPA (850 entries) and International Association of Fairs and Expositions (350 entries) as well as a directory of 1,050 permanent outdoor amusements and attractions and 1,100 of their concessionaires. **Entries include:** For manufacturers, suppliers, and IAAPA roster - Name, address, phone number, name of executives. IAFE roster - Event or park name, address, contact. For listing of parks - Name, address, contact, names of executives, phone number, owner's name, attendance, and park features and equipment. For concessionaires - Name and type of concession, park name. **Arrangement:** Manufacturer, suppliers and IAAPA roster, alphabetical; IAFE roster, parks and concessionaires, geographical. **Indexes:** Product. **Frequency:** Annual, February. **Editor:** Grace Urban. **Advertising accepted.** Circulation 3,500. **Price:** $25.00, payment with order (current and 1980 editions).

★766★
INTERNATIONAL ASSOCIATION OF AUDITORIUM MANAGERS— MEMBERSHIP DIRECTORY
International Association of Auditorium Managers
111 E. Wacker Drive, Room 620   Phone: (312) 565-4100
Chicago, IL 60601
Covers: Over 800 auditorium, arena, stadium, exhibit hall, and coliseum managers and their facilities. **Entries include:** Member's name, name of facility, address, phone, initial year of membership. **Arrangement:** Alphabetical. **Indexes:** Geographical (with facility seating capacity, square feet of exhibit space). **Pages** (approx.): 50. **Frequency:** Annual, fall. **Price:** $60.00; controlled circulation.

International Association of Business Communicators— Membership Directory *See* Directory of Business and Organizational Communicators

★767★
INTERNATIONAL ASSOCIATION OF CONVENTION & VISITOR BUREAUS—GENERAL INFORMATION AND MEMBERSHIP DIRECTORY
International Association of Convention & Visitor Bureaus
702 Bloomington Road
Champaign, IL 61820
Covers: Over 100 member bureaus, worldwide. **Entries include:** Bureau name, address, phone, name and title of representative.

Arrangement: Geographical; United States listings by city name. **Pages** (approx.): 15. **Frequency:** Semiannual, September and March. **Price:** Free.

International Association of Refrigerated Warehouses—Roster *See* Directory of Public Refrigerated Warehouses

★768★
INTERNATIONAL CONGRESS CALENDAR
Union of International Associations
1, rue aux Laines
1000 Brussels, Belgium
Covers: 3,000 international meetings scheduled up to three or more years in the future. **Entries include:** Name and address of sponsoring body, theme, meeting place, estimated number of participants, concurrent exhibition, if any. **Arrangement:** Identical information listed geographically and chronologically. **Indexes:** Subject, sponsoring organization. **Pages** (approx.): 330. **Frequency:** Annual, March; supplemented monthly in "Transnational Associations." **Advertising accepted.** Circulation 15,000. **Price:** $38.00, calendar only; $63.50, calendar plus monthly supplements; postpaid (current and 1980 editions).

International Directory of Fence Materials *See* Fence Industry— Directory

★769★
INTERNATIONAL DIRECTORY OF MARKETING RESEARCH HOUSES AND SERVICES (The Green Book)
New York Chapter
American Marketing Association
420 Lexington Avenue   Phone: (212) 687-3280
New York, NY 10017
Covers: More than 600 marketing research consultants and suppliers (computer services, interviewing services, etc.) of marketing research needs primarily in the United States with some in Canada and abroad. Includes a list of computer programs for market research. **Entries include:** Company name, address, phone, name of principal executive, list of products and services. **Arrangement:** Alphabetical. **Indexes:** Geographical, principals, computer programs. **Pages** (approx.): 150-200. **Frequency:** Annual, February. **Editor:** William Knobler, Publications Director. **Advertising accepted.** Circulation 3,200. **Price:** $25.00, payment with order (1980 edition).

★770★
INTERNATIONAL DIRECTORY OF PUBLISHED MARKET RESEARCH
Undine Corporation
221 E. 78th Street
New York, NY 10021
Covers: Over 400 market research and consulting firms which have published over 5,000 studies covering markets worldwide. **Entries include:** Title of study, name and address of research firm, scope of report, language or languages in which available, price. **Arrangement:** By product or industry (with SIC number cross-references). **Indexes:** Research source. **Pages** (approx.): 500. **Frequency:** Annual, March. **Price:** $39.95, plus $3.20 shipping. **Other information:** Compiled by British Trade Overseas Board and Research & Finance Management (International) Ltd.

★771★
INTERNATIONAL DIRECTORY OF THE NONWOVEN FABRIC INDUSTRY
INDA, Association of the Nonwoven Fabrics Industry
10 E. 40th Street   Phone: (212) 686-9170
New York, NY 10016
Covers: About 500 manufacturers of nonwoven fabrics and suppliers of materials, equipment, and machinery to them, as well as fabric finishers and end product converters/fabricators; international coverage. **Entries include:** Name, address, contact, membership affiliation, cross-reference to product section. **Arrangement:** Contents classified into 8 main sections - Company name

(alphabetical); Material Suppliers, Machinery and Equipment Manufacturers, Nonwoven Fabric Producers/Suppliers (by types of structures and by product application); Commission Services, including Finishing and Converting (by service); Finished Product (by product); Trademarks and Brand Names (alphabetical). **Pages** (approx.): 210. **Frequency:** Biennial, summer of odd years. **Editor:** Janet Rosen. **Advertising accepted.** Circulation 3,000. **Former title:** Nonwoven Fabrics and Disposable Soft Goods Directory; Nonwoven Fabrics Industry - International Directory. **Price:** $25.00, payment with order. **Other information:** Association name was changed from "International Nonwovens and Disposables Association" (1977).

★772★
**INTERNATIONAL DOWNTOWN EXECUTIVES ASSOCIATION—
   MEMBERSHIP ROSTER**
International Downtown Executives Association
1101 17th Street, N. W., Suite 1001   Phone: (202) 296-5874
Washington, DC 20036
Covers: About 250 downtown improvement organizations, plus affiliated interests. **Entries include:** Organization name, city, name of contact, office address, office phone. **Arrangement:** Geographical. **Frequency:** Annual, January. **Price:** Available to members only.

International Federation of Forwarding Agents Associations—
   Membership Directory *See* International Federation of Freight
   Forwarders ...

★773★
**INTERNATIONAL FEDERATION OF FREIGHT FORWARDERS
   ASSOCIATIONS—MEMBERSHIP DIRECTORY**
International Federation of Freight Forwarders Associations
Box 177
CH 8026 Zurich, Switzerland 241 80 45
Covers: 60 freight forwarding associations and 1,200 international freight forwarding firms, worldwide. **Entries include:** Company name, address. **Arrangement:** Geographical. **Frequency:** Annual, January. **Editor:** W. Zeilbeck, Director General. **Price:** Free. **Other information:** Name changed from International Federation of Forwarding Agents Associations.

★774★
**INTERNATIONAL FIBER OPTICS AND COMMUNICATIONS—
   HANDBOOK AND BUYERS' GUIDE ISSUE**
Information Gatekeepers, Inc.
167 Corey Road, Suite 111   Phone: (617) 739-2022
Brookline, MA 02146
Publication includes: List of about 350 manufacturers and suppliers of fiber optics and communications products; international coverage. **Entries include:** Company name, address, products, phone, key personnel. **Arrangement:** Alphabetical within United States and foreign lists. **Indexes:** Product. **Pages** (approx.): 140. **Frequency:** Annual, September. **Former title:** Fiber Optics Handbook and Marketing Guide (1980). **Price:** $75.00. **Other information:** Principal content of publication is discussion of current uses of fiber optics worldwide. **Also includes:** Glossary of terms.

★775★
**INTERNATIONAL FILE OF MICROGRAPHICS EQUIPMENT AND
   ACCESSORIES**
Microform Review, Inc.
520 Riverside Avenue   Phone: (203) 226-6967
Westport, CT 06880
Covers: Vendors of micrographics equipment and accessories, worldwide. Consists of microfiche copies of vendor's product catalogs and a printed index of companies and products. **Frequency:** Biennial, June of odd years. **Price:** $250.00.

★776★
**INTERNATIONAL FOODSERVICE MANUFACTURERS
   ASSOCIATION—MEMBERSHIP DIRECTORY**
International Foodservice Manufacturers Association
875 N. Michigan Avenue, Suite 3460   Phone: (312) 944-3838
Chicago, IL 60611
Covers: 260 food manufacturers supplying processed foods to restaurants, hotels, clubs, hospitals, schools, institutions, etc. **Entries include:** Company name, address, phone, names of principal and other executives, and list of products or services. **Arrangement:** Alphabetical within membership category. **Frequency:** Annual, April. **Editor:** Judith German Loeb, Director of Information Services. **Advertising accepted.** **Price:** $10.00 (current edition); $25.00 (1980 edition).

★777★
**INTERNATIONAL FRANCHISE ASSOCIATION—MEMBERSHIP
   DIRECTORY**
International Franchise Association
1025 Connecticut Avenue, N. W.   Phone: (202) 659-0790
Washington, DC 20036
Covers: 275 companies which offer franchises; nearly all are American. **Entries include:** Company name, line of business, address, phone. **Arrangement:** Classified. **Pages** (approx.): 50. **Frequency:** Annual. **Advertising accepted.** **Price:** $1.50.

★778★
**INTERNATIONAL FROZEN FOOD ASSOCIATION—MEMBERSHIP
   DIRECTORY**
International Frozen Food Association
1700 Old Meadow Road   Phone: (703) 821-0770
McLean, VA 22101
Covers: About 60 processors and distributors in the international frozen food market. **Entries include:** Company name, address, phone, principal executives, plant locations, geographic distribution, and products or nature of business. **Pages** (approx.): 40. **Frequency:** Annual, January. **Price:** $15.00.

★779★
INTERNATIONAL GLASS/METAL CATALOG
Artlee Catalog, Inc.
110 E. 42nd Street   Phone: (212) 682-7681
New York, NY 10017
Covers: Manufacturers, importers, and other suppliers who furnish the products and services used by wholesalers, fabricators, distributors, retailers, and installers of flat glass, architectural metal, and related products. **Entries include:** Supplier name, address, phone, and when furnished, cable, TWX, and telex numbers. **Arrangement:** Alphabetical. **Indexes:** Product, brand name. **Pages** (approx.): 280. **Frequency:** Annual, November. **Editor:** Oscar S. Glasberg, Publisher. **Advertising accepted.** Circulation 11,000. **Price:** $25.00. **Other information:** Published in both English and French; includes catalogs of some manufacturers.

International Import Index *See* International Intertrade Index of
   New Imported Products

★780★
**INTERNATIONAL INSTRUMENTATION & CONTROLS—BUYERS
   GUIDE ISSUE**
Keller Publishing Corporation
150 Great Neck Road   Phone: (516) 829-9210
Great Neck, NY 11021
Covers: Suppliers of precision instrument products and services and biomedical equipment. **Entries include:** Firm name, address, phone, product type. **Arrangement:** Alphabetical. **Indexes:** Product. **Frequency:** Annual, October. **Editor:** Dennis Lynds. **Advertising accepted.** Circulation 57,000. **Price:** Controlled circulation.

★781★

INTERNATIONAL INTERTRADE INDEX OF NEW IMPORTED PRODUCTS
International Intertrade Index
744 Broad Street, Suite 3400   Phone: (201) 623-2864
Newark, NJ 07101
Covers: Manufacturers of new products that are announced at foreign trade fairs. **Entries include:** Company name, address, description of new products, and prices. **Arrangement:** Geographical. **Pages** (approx.): 8 per issue. **Frequency:** Monthly. **Editor:** John E. Felber. **Former title:** International Import Index. **Price:** $15.00 per year (ISSN 0020-7004).

★782★

INTERNATIONAL INVESTMENT IN NEW YORK
Buffalo Area Chamber of Commerce
107 Delaware Avenue   Phone: (716) 849-6677
Buffalo, NY 14202
Covers: Foreign-owned firms engaged in engineering, wholesale and retail trade, sales, warehousing, assembly, and manufacturing in Erie and Niagara counties of New York State. **Pages** (approx.): 15. **Frequency:** Annual, January or February. **Former title:** Canadian Investment in New York. **Price:** $5.00, plus 50¢ shipping.

★783★

INTERNATIONAL MAGNESIUM ASSOCIATION—BUYER'S GUIDE
International Magnesium Association
1406 Third National Building
Dayton, OH 45402
Covers: Companies which supply magnesium metal, specialize in magnesium work, manufacture magnesium products, or conduct research in magnesium; international coverage. **Entries include:** Company name, address, phone, telex number, and cable address. **Arrangement:** By activity. **Pages** (approx.): 15. **Frequency:** Annual, late spring. **Price:** Free.

International Material Management Society—Certified Member Directory *See* IMMS Directory of Certified Professionals...

★784★

INTERNATIONAL PERSONNEL RESOURCES
Bank Personnel Division
American Bankers Association
1120 Connecticut Avenue, N. W.   Phone: (202) 467-6322
Washington, DC 20036
Covers: Over 100 organizations and workshops concerned with administration of employees of United States corporations in assignments abroad. Also includes newsletters, checklists, books, etc. **Frequency:** Not established; first edition early 1978. **Price:** $60.00.

International Pulp & Paper Directory *See* PPI International Pulp & Paper Directory

International Recording Equipment & Studio Directory *See* Billboard International Recording Equipment...

★785★

INTERNATIONAL REGISTRY OF TRAILER, CONTAINER, AND CHASSIS EQUIPMENT
Equipment Interchange Association
1616 P Street, N. W.   Phone: (202) 797-5273
Washington, DC 20036
Covers: About 100 operators of trailer, container, and chassis equipment, primarily trucking companies. **Entries include:** Company name, address, name of contact; and, in tabular form, type of equipment, specifications, capacity, and number of units of each type owned. **Arrangement:** Alphabetical. **Pages** (approx.): 140. **Frequency:** Semiannual, September and March. **Editor:** Kenneth R. Hauck. **Price:** $10.00 per copy; $20.00 per year. **Other information:** Listings are available to all transportation companies.

★786★

INTERNATIONAL RESOURCE DIRECTORY [Training and development]
American Society for Training and Development
Box 5307   Phone: (608) 274-3440
Madison, WI 53705
Covers: Advertisers offering training and development products and services. **Entries include:** Basic paid listings include organization or company name, address, phone, name of contact; additional details may be included in larger listings. **Arrangement:** Alphabetical. **Indexes:** Product/service, geographical. **Frequency:** Latest edition 1978. **Advertising accepted. Price:** $9.95, postpaid, payment must accompany order.

★787★

INTERNATIONAL SHIPPING AND SHIPBUILDING DIRECTORY
Benn Publications Ltd.
25 New Street Square
London EC4A 4JA, England
Covers: Several thousand shipowners, managers, and lines; seaborne container companies and services; ship building and repair firms and other service firms; suppliers of ships machinery and equipment. **Entries include:** Firm name, address, phone, Telex and cable addresses; branch offices; names of principal executives; agents; parent and associated companies; and, for shipowners and lines, detailed information on ships owned, capacity, etc. **Arrangement:** Classified by type of activity. **Indexes:** Firm, product, service, ship name. **Pages** (approx.): 850. **Frequency:** Annual, fall. **Advertising accepted. Circulation** 2,800. **Price:** 35 pounds. **Send orders to:** Nichols Publishing Co., Box 96, New York, NY 10024.

★788★

INTERNATIONAL SOCIETY OF HOTEL ASSOCIATION EXECUTIVES—DIRECTORY OF MEMBERS
International Society of Hotel Association Executives
141 W. 51st Street   Phone: (212) 247-0800
New York, NY 10019
Number of listings: 55. **Entries include:** Name of association, name of executive, address, phone. **Arrangement:** Alphabetical if national, geographical if state or local; single alphabet. **Pages** (approx.): 5. **Frequency:** Annual, February or March; updated in July or August. **Price:** Available to members; others, apply.

★789★

INTERNATIONAL SUBSCRIPTION AGENTS: AN ANNOTATED DIRECTORY
Resources and Technical Services Division
American Library Association
50 E. Huron Street   Phone: (312) 944-6780
Chicago, IL 60611
Covers: 240 agents handling orders for foreign periodicals and serials. **Entries include:** Dealer name, address, countries of specialization, types of materials supplied, discounts, special services, ratings by user libraries, general acquisitions procedures. **Arrangement:** Alphabetical. **Indexes:** Countries of specialization. **Pages** (approx.): 125. **Frequency:** Irregular; latest edition 1978. **Editor:** Nancy Buckeye. **Price:** $4.00.

International Tape Association—Membership Directory *See* ITA Source Directory [Audio and video tapes]

International Trade Directory for the State of Oregon *See* Oregon International Trade Directory

★790★

INTERNATIONAL TRADE SERVICES DIRECTORY [Charlotte, North Carolina]
Greater Charlotte Chamber of Commerce
129 W. Trade Street   Phone: (704) 377-6911
Charlotte, NC 28202
Covers: International or port of entry services such as interpreters,

banking, freight forwarders, customhouse brokers; includes list of foreign firms located in Charlotte, North Carolina. **Entries include:** Name, address, phone, service provided, list of products, and geographical area served. **Arrangement:** Classified by type of service. **Pages** (approx.): 20. **Frequency:** Biennial, October of even years. **Editor:** G. Jackson Burney, Manager. **Price:** $5.00 (current edition); $6.00 (1980 edition); plus $1.00 shipping.

★791★
INTERNATIONAL WAREHOUSE AND STORAGE DIRECTORY
IPC Industrial Press Ltd.
Dorset House, Stamford Street
London SE1 9LU, England
Covers: Over 5,000 warehouse and storage companies and their branches; international coverage. **Entries include:** Company name, address, phone, telex; warehouse capacity, minimum ceiling height, and volume capacity for bulk liquids/solids in metric measures; description of facilities available (railroad sidings, security, etc.). **Arrangement:** Geographical. **Pages** (approx.): 250. **Frequency:** Annual, spring. **Editor:** Eric Straker. **Advertising accepted.** Circulation 4,000. **Price:** 15 pounds (current and 1980 editions).

★792★
INTERSTATE EXIT DIRECTORY
Adventure Publishing Company
2910 Fleetwood Avenue, S. W.   Phone: (703) 989-9300
Roanoke, VA
Description: A series of publications, each covering one interstate highway, primarily along Eastern seaboard. For each highway the numbers and names of each exit are given, the mileage between exits is given, and names and locations of motels, restaurants, service stations, hospitals, etc., at the exit are shown on maps. In a separate section of paid listings some establishments at most exits are described in detail, with information on location, hours of operation, services offered, credit cards accepted, phone. **Arrangement:** By state and exit number. **Frequency:** Irregular; first edition 1979. **Price:** Varies; about $3.50.

★793★
INTERSTATE MANUFACTURERS AND INDUSTRIAL DIRECTORY
Bell Directory Publishers, Inc.
1995 Broadway   Phone: (212) 787-5888
New York, NY 10023
Covers: Firms in 22 states, primarily in the east, south, and west. **Entries include:** Firm name, address, phone. **Arrangement:** Classified by product. **Pages** (approx.): 240. **Frequency:** Annual. **Advertising accepted.** Circulation 15,000. **Former title:** Eastern Manufacturers and Industrial Directory (1975). **Price:** $20.00 (1980 edition).

Interstate Towing Association—Membership Directory *See* **Certificated Towing Companies Holding Authority from the Interstate Commerce...**

★794★
INTIMATE FASHION NEWS—DIRECTORY OF RESOURCES ISSUE
Mackay Publishing Corporation
95 Madison Avenue   Phone: (212) 679-6677
New York, NY 10016
Covers: Foundation and lingerie manufacturers and suppliers. **Entries include:** Company name, address, phone, names of executives, trade and brand names, list of products or services. **Arrangement:** Alphabetical lists of both manufacturers and suppliers. **Indexes:** Supplies. **Frequency:** Annual, July. **Editor:** Milton Kristt. **Advertising accepted.** Circulation 6,500. **Former title:** Corset, Bra and Lingerie Directory. **Price:** $5.00.

★795★
INVENTORY OF POWERPLANTS IN THE UNITED STATES
Office of Energy Data Operations
Energy Information Administration
Energy Department
1000 Independence Avenue, N. W.   Phone: (202) 252-6401
Washington, DC 20585
Covers: Existing and projected powerplants within electric utility systems. **Entries include:** Plant name and number, company name, county of location, nameplate rate, type of unit, primary fuel consumed, alternate fuel capability, date operation began or will begin, date of verification of data, and whether unit is jointly owned. **Arrangement:** By type of unit (existing and projected electrical generation units, jointly owned units, and projected construction units), then geographical within federal regions. **Frequency:** Annual. **Price:** $6.00 (DOE/EIA-0095). **Send orders to:** Government Printing Office, Washington, DC 20402.

Iowa Exporting Companies Directory *See* **Iowa International Directory**

★796★
IOWA INTERNATIONAL DIRECTORY
Iowa Development Commission
250 Jewett Building
914 Grand Avenue
Des Moines, IA 50309
Covers: Over 900 Iowa manufacturing companies exporting products in 266 Standard Industrial Classification (SIC) categories. **Entries include:** Company name, address, phone, chief executive, list of products or services, SIC numbers. **Arrangement:** By SIC category. **Indexes:** Product, alphabetical. **Pages** (approx.): 180. **Frequency:** Biennial, August of odd years. **Former title:** Iowa Exporting Companies Directory. **Price:** Free.

Iowa Manufacturers Directory *See* **Directory of Iowa Manufacturers**

★797★
IRON AGE—METAL INDUSTRY FINANCIAL ANALYSIS ISSUE
Chilton Company
Chilton Way   Phone: (215) 687-8200
Radnor, PA 19089
Covers: About 25 nonferrous metal firms and about 35 iron and steel firms. **Entries include:** Company name, rank, net sales, operating profit, operating profit as percentage of sales, U. S. and foreign income taxes, etc. **Arrangement:** Ranked by net sales. **Frequency:** Annual, last April issue. **Advertising accepted.** **Price:** $1.00 for report reprints, payment with order.

Iron Age Census Of Metalworking *See* **Iron Age Metalworking Data Bank**

★798★
IRON AGE METALWORKING DATA BANK
Chilton Company
Chilton Way   Phone: (215) 687-8200
Radnor, PA 19089
Covers: 46,000 metalworking plants employing 20 or more people, in 2 volumes. **Entries include:** Plant name, division name, address, phone, number of employees, SIC numbers (6 digit), Dun's number, activity code. **Arrangement:** Volume 1, alphabetical; Volume 2 by SIC code. **Pages** (approx.): 500 per volume. **Frequency:** Annual, April. **Former title:** Iron Age Census of Metalworking. **Price:** $375.00 per volume; $500.00 per set (current and 1980 editions).

Iron Castings Society—Directory of Members *See* **Sources for Iron Castings: A Buyers Guide and Directory of Members**

ISSD: International Shipping and Shipbuilding Directory *See* International Shipping and Shipbuilding Directory

★799★
ITA SOURCE DIRECTORY [Audio and video tapes]
International Tape Association
10 W. 66th Street   Phone: (212) 787-0910
New York, NY 10023
Covers: More than 350 member manufacturers and suppliers of audio and video tape products and services, users of the medium, and government agencies and trade associations concerrned with audio and video tape use; international coverage. **Entries include:** Company or asssociation name, address, phone, contact person, and description of company products, services, or interests. **Arrangement:** Alphabetical. **Indexes:** Product. **Pages** (approx.): 55. **Frequency:** Annual, spring. **Advertising accepted.** **Price:** Free; controlled circulation.

★800★
ITALIAN AMERICAN BUSINESS—ANNUAL DIRECTORY ISSUE
American Chamber of Commerce in Italy
Main Office
Via Agnello 12
20121 Milan, Italy
Covers: 2,700 Italian and American businesses interested in developing trade and investment within and between the two countries. **Entries include:** For members - Company name, address, phone, cable address, telex, names and titles of key personnel, coded product/service list, names of American companies represented, name of American parent company. For American firms represented in Italy - Company name and location, products, Italian firm and address, coding to indicate relationship (subsidiary, affiliate). Nonmember listings also include phone, cable, telex, and chief executive. **Arrangement:** Alphabetical within above categories. **Indexes:** Product/service. **Pages** (approx.): 415. **Frequency:** Annual, October. **Editor:** Gabriella Gabet. **Advertising accepted.** Circulation 4,000. **Price:** $40.00 (ISSN 0021- 2873).

★801★
ITEM (Interference Technology Engineers Master)
R & B Enterprises
Box 328   Phone: (215) 823-6236
Plymouth Meeting, PA 19462
Publication includes: Sales offices of manufacturers and suppliers of products and services to the electrical interference technology field who advertise in ITEM. **Arrangement:** Contents arranged in 23 product categories (Analysis and recording equipment, Anechoic material & chambers, etc.). **Indexes:** Product and Service. **Pages** (approx.): 200. **Frequency:** Annual, January. **Editor:** Robert D. Goldblum, Publisher. **Advertising accepted.** Circulation 25,000. **Price:** $20.00 (current edition); $25.00 (1980 edition). **Other information:** Principal content of publication is paid catalog pages with product description, specifications, and illustrations.

★802★
IWP WORD PROCESSING INDUSTRY DIRECTORY
International Word Processing Association
Maryland Road   Phone: (215) 657-3220
Willow Grove, PA 19090
Covers: Manufacturers of word processing equipment; word processing consultants; word processing service bureaus; educational institutions offering word processing courses or curriculums; personnel agencies serving word processing personnel and users. **Entries include:** Name, address. **Arrangement:** Alphabetical within categories above. **Pages** (approx.): 60. **Frequency:** Annual. **Price:** $7.00.

★803★
JAMESTOWN AREA CHAMBER OF COMMERCE—INDUSTRIAL DIRECTORY OF CHATAUQUA COUNTY [New York]
Jamestown Area Chamber of Commerce
101 W. Fifth Avenue   Phone: (716) 484-1101
Jamestown, NY 14701
Number of listings: About 500. **Entries include:** Company name, address, phone, names of principal executives, short description of business and products, number of employees. **Arrangement:** Geographical. **Indexes:** Product. **Pages** (approx.): 55. **Frequency:** Irregular; previous edition 1977; latest edition fall 1979. **Advertising accepted.** **Price:** $5.50, plus $1.36 shipping. **Other information:** Publisher recently changed its name from Chatauqua County Chamber to Jamestown Area Chamber of Commerce.

★804★
JANE'S FREIGHT CONTAINERS: PORTS, OPERATORS, MANUFACTURERS
Macdonald and Jane's Publishers Ltd.
8 Shepherdess Walk
London N1 7LW, England
Covers: About 270 ports and the container operations of each; when possible inland depots of each operation or port are also included. Suppliers of equipment and services are listed in separate sections. **Entries include:** For ports and container operations - Port name, location, company names, addresses, services. For manufacturers and suppliers - Company name, address, phone, officials, products or services. **Arrangement:** Ports are geographical, manufacturers are alphabetical. **Indexes:** Named ships, general. **Pages** (approx.): 700. **Frequency:** Annual, March. **Editor:** Patrick Finlay. **Advertising accepted.** **Price:** $72.50. **Send orders to:** Franklin Watts, Inc., 730 Fifth Avenue, New York, NY 10019. (Not verified)

★805★
JANE'S WORLD RAILWAYS & RAPID TRANSIT SYSTEMS
Macdonald and Jane's Publishers Ltd.
8 Shepherdess Walk
London N1 7LW, England
Publication includes: List of manufacturers of locomotives and rolling stock and of track maintenance, signaling, control, and other equipment for railways and transit systems. **Entries include:** Company name, address, phone, officials, products. **Arrangement:** Alphabetical. **Pages** (approx.): 700. **Frequency:** Annual, June. **Editor:** Paul Goldsack. **Advertising accepted.** **Price:** $72.50. **Send orders to:** Franklin Watts, Inc., 730 Fifth Avenue, New York, NY 10019. **Also includes:** Description of railway systems in 99 countries in detail (110 in tabulated form) and rapid transit systems in 90 cities; international associations; consultants.

Japanese Firms, Offices and Subsidiaries in the United States *See* Japanese Firms, Offices and the Other Organizations...

★806★
JAPANESE FIRMS, OFFICES, AND THE OTHER ORGANIZATIONS IN THE UNITED STATES
Japan External Trade Organization
Japan Trade Center
232 N. Michigan Avenue   Phone: (312) 726-4390
Chicago, IL 60601
Covers: About 880 Japanese-owned companies operating about 1,650 offices and subsidiaries in the United States. **Entries include:** Company name, address, phone, products or services. **Arrangement:** Geographical. **Indexes:** Product, U.S. company name, parent Japanese company name. **Pages** (approx.): 150. **Frequency:** Triennial; latest edition December, 1978. **Former title:** Japanese Firms, Offices, and Subsidiaries in the United States. **Price:** $16.00. **Send orders to:** California Business Corporation, 900 Wilshire Boulevard, Suite 414, Los Angeles, CA 90017 (213-625-0808). **Other information:** Not to be confused with "Directory of Japanese Firms, Offices, and Subsidiaries in New York, New Jersey, and Connecticut."

★807★

JEWELERS' CIRCULAR-KEYSTONE—JEWELERS' DIRECTORY ISSUE

Chilton Company

Chilton Way   Phone: (215) 687-8200
Radnor, PA 19089

Covers: About 8,000 manufacturers' suppliers and retailers' suppliers, manufacturers, importers, and wholesale jewelers providing merchandise and supplies to the jewelry retailing industry. Trade associations are also listed. **Entries include:** For all companies - Company name, address, phone. For associations - Name, address, and names of officers. **Arrangement:** Manufacturers' suppliers and retailers' suppliers are listed separately and grouped by product or service. Associations, manufacturers, and importers are alphabetical. Wholesale jewelers are geographical. **Indexes:** Product. **Pages** (approx.): 830. **Frequency:** Annual, June. **Editor:** George Holmes. **Advertising accepted.** Circulation 21,000. **Price:** $7.00.

★808★

JOB HUNTER'S GUIDE TO EIGHT GREAT AMERICAN CITIES

Brattle Publications

Four Brattle Street, Suite 306   Phone: (617) 661-7467
Cambridge, MA 02138

Covers: Government agencies, employment agencies, executive recruiters, temporary help agencies, business and trade organizations, top 300 employers, and other firms of possible interest to the job hunter in Atlanta, Boston, Denver, Phoenix, Portland, San Diego, San Francisco, and Seattle. **Entries include:** Agency, organization, or firm name, address, phone, and products or services. **Arrangement:** By city, then by type of organization. **Pages** (approx.): 160. **Frequency:** Biennial, spring of even years. **Editor:** Richard D. Salmon, Editor and Publisher. **Price:** $12.50 (current edition); $13.50 (1980 edition). **Also includes:** Section for each city includes introduction discussing climate, cost of living, commuting, and other topics.

★809★

JOB HUNTER'S GUIDE TO THE ROCKY MOUNTAIN WEST

Brattle Publications

Four Brattle Street, Suite 306   Phone: (617) 661-7467
Cambridge, MA 02138

Covers: Employment opportunities and services in the Rocky Mountain region. Scope and format same as "Job Hunter's Guide to Eight Great American Cities," described in separate listing. **Frequency:** Not established; first edition expected October 1980. **Price:** $13.50.

★810★

JOB HUNTER'S GUIDE TO THE SUNBELT

Brattle Publications

Four Brattle Street, Suite 306   Phone: (617) 661-7467
Cambridge, MA 02138

Covers: Employment opportunities and services in the lower southern and southwestern states. Scope and format same as "Job Hunter's Guide to Eight Great American Cities," described in separate listing. **Frequency:** Not established; first edition expected June 1980. **Price:** $12.50.

★811★

JOBBER TOPICS—ANNUAL MARKETING DIRECTORY ISSUE [Automotive aftermarket]

Irving-Cloud Publishing Company

7300 N. Cicero Avenue   Phone: (312) 588-7300
Chicago, IL 60646

Covers: Manufacturers, remanufacturers, warehouse distributors, jobbers, manufacturers' agents, and trade associations in the automotive aftermarket field. **Entries include:** All listings include name of contact and association membership; distributor and agent listings show number of salesmen and lines handled; jobber listings show number of salesmen and branch offices; remanufacturer listings show parts handled. **Arrangement:** Remanufacturers and jobbers are geographical, others are alphabetical. **Indexes:** Geographical indexes for distributors and agents. **Frequency:** Annual, July. **Editor:** Jack

Creighton, Editorial Director. **Advertising accepted.** Circulation 33,000. **Former title:** Jobber Topics - Directory and Buyer's Guide Issue. **Price:** $10.00, postpaid.

Jobber Topics—Directory and Buyer's Guide Issue *See* Jobber Topics—Annual Marketing Directory Issue [Automotive aftermarket]

Johnson's World Wide Chamber of Commerce Directory *See* World Wide Chamber of Commerce Directory

★812★

JOURNAL [OF THE] AMERICAN WATER WORKS ASSOCIATION— BUYERS' GUIDE ISSUE

American Water Works Association

6666 W. Quincy Avenue   Phone: (303) 794-7711
Denver, CO 80235

Covers: Member suppliers and distributors of water supply products and services, contractors for water supply projects, and engineering consultants. **Entries include:** Company name, address, names of executives, trade and brand names, products and services offered. **Arrangement:** Suppliers and distributors are alphabetical; engineering consultants both alphabetical and geographical. **Indexes:** Product. **Pages** (approx.): 125. **Frequency:** Annual, November. **Editor:** Mary A. Parmelee. **Advertising accepted.** Circulation 42,000. **Price:** Included in subscription; not available separately.

★813★

JUVENILE MERCHANDISING—ANNUAL DIRECTORY & BUYERS GUIDE ISSUE

Columbia Communications, Inc.

370 Lexington Avenue   Phone: (212) 532-9290
New York, NY 10017

Covers: Manufacturers of juvenile products, including furniture, pre-school toys, infant wear, etc. **Entries include:** Company name, address, phone, name of principal executive, list of products, brand names. **Arrangement:** Alphabetical. **Indexes:** Product, brand name. **Pages** (approx.): 150. **Frequency:** Annual, August. **Editor:** Lee Clarke Neumeyer. **Advertising accepted.** Circulation 11,000. **Price:** $5.00.

Kansas Manufacturers and Products in Export *See* Directory of Kansas Manufacturing Firms in Export

Kansas Minority Industrial Directory *See* Directory of Kansas Minority Businesses

★814★

KENTUCKY AIRPORT DIRECTORY

Division of Aeronautics

Kentucky Department of Transportation

419 Ann Street   Phone: (502) 564-4480
Frankfort, KY 40601

Number of listings: About 75. **Entries include:** Location, elevation, runway information, traffic control, radio frequencies, lighting information, services available, name of manager, operator, navigation data, aerial photograph. **Arrangement:** Geographical. **Pages** (approx.): 170. **Frequency:** Annual, summer. **Price:** Free.

★815★

KENTUCKY DIRECTORY OF MANUFACTURERS

Kentucky Department of Commerce

Capital Plaza Office Tower   Phone: (502) 564-4886
Frankfort, KY 40601

Number of listings: 2,700. **Entries include:** Company name, address, phone, names of principal executives, number of employees, list of products or services, parent company, date established. **Arrangement:** Geographical. **Indexes:** Alphabetical, SIC, parent company. **Pages** (approx.): 375. **Frequency:** Annual, January. **Editor:** Dorothy D. Lea. **Price:** $15.00 (current and 1980 editions). **Other information:** Manufacturers' News catalog lists this publication as, "Kentucky Manufacturers Directory" ($28.00).

★816★
KENTUCKY DIRECTORY OF SELECTED INDUSTRIAL SERVICES
Kentucky Department of Commerce
Capitol Plaza Tower
Frankfort, KY 40601
Covers: Consulting engineering firms, coal testing laboratories, electric motor repair shops, heat treating facilities, industrial equipment suppliers, metal finishers and metal supply houses, public warehouses, and tool, die, machine, and pattern shops located in Kentucky and in nearby cities in adjacent states. **Entries include:** Company name, address, phone, names of executives, services. **Arrangement:** By service groups. **Indexes:** Alphabetical, geographical. **Frequency:** Biennial, spring of even years. **Price:** $4.00 (current edition; tentative, 1980 edition).

Kentucky Exporters Directory *See* Kentucky International Trade Directory

★817★
KENTUCKY INTERNATIONAL TRADE DIRECTORY
International Division
Kentucky Department Of Commerce
Capital Plaza Tower, 24th Floor   Phone: (502) 564-2170
Frankfort, KY 40601
Covers: 500 manufacturers in Kentucky engaged in import and export, and firms providing international trade services. **Arrangement:** Classified. **Pages** (approx.): 200. **Frequency:** Biennial in January of even years. **Editor:** Cary W. Blankenship, International Economist. **Former title:** Kentucky Exporters Directory. **Price:** $15.00 (1980 edition).

Kentucky Manufacturers Directory *See* Kentucky Directory of Manufacturers

★818★
KENTUCKY MODIFIED MINORITY PURCHASING GUIDE
Office of Minority Business Enterprise
Kentucky Department of Commerce
2329 Capital Plaza Tower   Phone: (502) 564-2064
Frankfort, KY 40601
Covers: About 170 firms offering commercial and industrial products and services. **Entries include:** Company name, address, phone, name of contact, products or services. **Arrangement:** Classified. **Frequency:** Annual, summer. **Price:** Free.

★819★
KENTUCKY STATE INDUSTRIAL DIRECTORY
State Industrial Directories Corporation
Two Penn Plaza   Phone: (212) 564-0340
New York, NY 10001
Number of listings: 2,600. **Entries include:** Company name, address, phone, names of key executives, number of employees, plant size, 4-digit SIC code, products, whether firm imports or exports, and whether firm has research facilities. **Arrangement:** Geographical. **Indexes:** Alphabetical, product (includes mailing address and phone for each firm). **Frequency:** Not established; first edition summer 1979. **Advertising accepted. Price:** $25.00 (ISSN 0190-1354).

★820★
KIDS' STUFF
Pantheon Books, Inc.
201 E. 50th Street   Phone: (212) 751-2600
New York, NY 10022
Covers: About 250 manufacturers of children's furniture, play equipment, and toys. **Entries include:** Manufacturer name, address, description and photograph of item. **Arrangement:** By type of product. **Pages** (approx.): 210. **Frequency:** Not established; first edition 1979. **Author:** Linda Foa and Geri Brin. **Price:** $17.95, cloth; $8.95, paper.

★821★
KITCHEN BOOK
Crown Publishers, Inc.
One Park Avenue
New York, NY 10016
Publication includes: Listing of manufacturers and suppliers of equipment, products, and services described in the text. **Entries include:** Company name, address. **Arrangement:** By product. **Frequency:** Published October 1977. **Author:** Terence Conran. **Price:** $30.00.

★822★
KITCHEN BUSINESS—DIRECTORY & BUYERS GUIDE ISSUE
Gralla Publications
1515 Broadway   Phone: (212) 869-1300
New York, NY 10036
Covers: About 900 manufacturers, distributors, dealers, and designers of residential built-in kitchen and bath products, such as cabinets, vanities, appliances, sinks, cast marble, plastic laminates, other materials, and tools. Trade associations are also listed, and membership lists for the following are included: American Hardboard Association, Cultured Marble Institute, Hardwood Plywood Manufacturers Association, National Association of Plastic Fabricators, National Kitchen Cabinet Association, and National Particleboard Association (SIC 2434). **Entries include:** For manufacturers, etc. and associations not fully treated - Name, address, phone. For associations fully treated - Name, address, phone, names of directors and key personnel, description of membership and types of membership, dues, services. For companies in membership lists - Company name, address; some listings also include phone. **Arrangement:** Manufacturers are both alphabetical and classified (with coded product lists). Associations are alphabetical. **Pages** (approx.): 240. **Frequency:** Annual, February. **Editor:** B. Leslie Hart. **Advertising accepted.** Circulation 22,500. **Price:** $2.00 (current edition); $3.00 (1980 edition); available to trade only. **Also includes:** Oven, range, and decorator front specifications.

★823★
KITCHEN BUSINESS—WHO'S WHO IN KITCHEN CABINETS ISSUE
Gralla Publications
1515 Broadway   Phone: (212) 869-1300
New York, NY 10036
Publication includes: Special section on 150 leading manufacturers of kitchen cabinets (SIC 2434). **Entries include:** Company name, address, phone, principal executives, region served, types of products, history of firm. **Frequency:** Annual, July. **Advertising accepted.** Circulation 25,000. **Price:** $3.00; available to the trade only.

★824★
KLINE GUIDE TO THE CHEMICAL INDUSTRY
Charles H. Kline & Company, Inc.
330 Passaic Avenue   Phone: (201) 227-6262
Fairfield, NJ 07006
Covers: 465 leading chemical companies. **Entries include:** Company name, address, phone, financial and statistical information on the individual company. **Pages** (approx.): 300. **Frequency:** Triennial; latest edition December 1977. **Former title:** Marketing Guide to the Chemical Industry. **Price:** $95.00. **Other information:** Principal content is tables, charts, and textual analysis of the economics and technology of the industry.

★825★
KLINE GUIDE TO THE PACKAGING INDUSTRY
Charles H. Kline & Company, Inc.
330 Passaic Avenue   Phone: (201) 227-6262
Fairfield, NJ 07006
Covers: 435 major manufacturers of packaging materials and finished products. **Entries include:** Company name, address, phone, financial and statistical information on the individual company. **Arrangement:** Alphabetical. **Frequency:** Triennial; latest edition 1977. **Price:** $48.00. **Other information:** Principal content is tables, charts, and

textual analysis of the economics and technology of the industry.

★826★

KLINE GUIDE TO THE PAINT INDUSTRY
Charles H. Kline & Company, Inc.
330 Passaic Avenue   Phone: (201) 227-6262
Fairfield, NJ 07006
Covers: 225 leading paint companies. **Entries include:** Company
name, address, phone, financial and statistical information on the
individual company. **Pages** (approx.): 125. **Frequency:** Triennial;
latest edition 1978. **Former title:** Marketing Guide to the Paint
Industry. **Price:** $65.00. **Other information:** Principal content is
tables, charts, and textual analysis of the economics and technology of
the industry.

★827★

KLINE GUIDE TO THE PLASTICS INDUSTRY
Charles H. Kline & Company, Inc.
330 Passaic Avenue   Phone: (201) 227-6262
Fairfield, NJ 07006
Covers: 500 leading plastics companies. **Entries include:** Company
name, address, phone, financial and statistical information on the
individual company. **Arrangement:** Alphabetical. **Pages** (approx.):
180. **Frequency:** Not established; first edition 1978. **Price:** $90.00.
Other information: Principal content is tables, charts, and textual
analysis of the economics and technology of the industry.

★828★

KNITTING TIMES—BUYERS' GUIDE DIRECTORY ISSUE
National Knitted Outerwear Association
51 Madison Avenue   Phone: (212) 683-7520
New York, NY 10010
Covers: Suppliers to the knitting and knit apparel industries. **Entries
include:** Company name, address, phone, list of products or services.
Pages (approx.): 370. **Frequency:** Annual, September. **Editor:** Eric
Hertz. **Advertising accepted.** Circulation 10,000. **Price:** $5.00.

★829★

KNOXVILLE AREA MANUFACTURERS [Tennessee]
Greater Knoxville Chamber of Commerce
301 Church Avenue, S. E.   Phone: (615) 637-4550
Knoxville, TN 37902
Covers: Manufacturing, mining, and service industries in the Knoxville-
Knox County area. **Entries include:** Name, address, phone, chief
executive, service or product manufactured, SIC number, number of
employees, and codes indicating whether a chamber member and
whether a parent company. **Arrangement:** Alphabetical. **Indexes:**
Product/service. **Pages** (approx.): 40. **Frequency:** Biennial in even
years, with supplements in odd years. **Price:** $10.75, postpaid.

★830★

L.A. WORKBOOK [Los Angeles advertising services, etc.]
Lexy Scott
6140 Lindenhurst   Phone: (213) 657-8707
Los Angeles, CA 90035
Covers: 4,000 Los Angeles advertising agencies, photographers,
printers, TV services, free-lance artists and designers, artists'
representatives, other agency services; also includes magazines,
record companies, and department stores. **Entries include:** Company
or individual name, address, phone. **Arrangement:** By service or
product. **Pages** (approx.): 200. **Frequency:** Annual, summer. **Editor:**
Lexy Scott. **Price:** $15.00.

★831★

LABOR OFFICES IN THE UNITED STATES AND CANADA
Employment Standards Administration
State Employment Standards Division
Labor Department   Phone: (202) 523-8219
Washington, DC 20210
Covers: Federal, state, and provincial offices and agencies in the
United States and Canada which have administrative responsibility for

the performance of labor or labor-related functions. Associations of
these agencies' officials and other labor administration groups are also
listed. **Entries include:** Name of department or agency, names of
officials, address, phone; lists of divisions with officals' names,
addresses, and phones. Association listings include name, address,
phone, name and title of chief executive officer, and acronym.
Arrangement: Two geographical lists of agencies; one for United
States and one for Canada. **Pages** (approx.): 150. **Frequency:**
Biennial, even years. **Editor:** Thelma B. Smith. **Price:** Free. **Send
orders to:** U. S. Department of Labor, Employment Standards
Administration, Branch of Printing and Publications, Room C-5307,
200 Constitution Avenue, N. W., Washington, DC 20210.

★832★

LABORATORY MANAGEMENT—GOLD BOOK DIRECTORY ISSUE
United Business Publications, Inc., Division
Media Horizons, Inc.
475 Park Avenue South   Phone: (212) 725-2300
New York, NY 10017
Publication includes: List of manufacturers and suppliers of clinical
laboratory supplies and equipment. **Entries include:** Company name,
address, phone. **Arrangement:** Alphabetical. **Pages** (approx.): 90.
Frequency: Annual, December. **Editor:** Bennet Zucker. **Advertising
accepted.** Circulation 30,000. **Also includes:** Classified list of
products. **Other information:** 1979 issue out of print.

★833★

**LAND IMPROVEMENT CONTRACTORS OF AMERICA—
MEMBERSHIP AND TELEPHONE DIRECTORY**
Land Improvement Contractors of America
1300 Maybrook Drive   Phone: (312) 344-0700
Maywood, IL 60153
Covers: 4,100 land improvement, conservation, and reclamation
contractors. **Entries include:** Company name, address, phone, name
of principal executive. **Arrangement:** Geographical. **Pages** (approx.):
150. **Frequency:** Annual, May. **Editor:** Paul A. Bucha, Executive Vice-
President. **Price:** Available to members only.

★834★

LARGE EMPLOYERS OF METRO ST. LOUIS [Missouri]
St. Louis Regional Commerce and Growth Association
10 Broadway   Phone: (314) 231-5555
St. Louis, MO 63102
Covers: 950 firms in all lines of business employing 100 persons or
more in City of St. Louis, four Missouri counties (Franklin, Jefferson,
St. Charles, and St. Louis), and four Illinois counties (Clinton, Madison,
Monroe, and St. Clair); includes non-members. **Entries include:**
Company name, address, phone, names of principal executives, SIC
numbers, type of business, list of products or services. **Arrangement:**
By number of employees. **Indexes:** Alphabetical, SIC. **Pages** (approx.):
40. **Frequency:** Annual, winter. **Editor:** William M. Julius, Manager,
Business Information Center. **Price:** $10.00 (current edition);
$15.00 (1980 edition).

Leading National Advertisers Reports *See* **LNA Multi-Media
Report Service**

★835★

LEAHY'S HOTEL-MOTEL GUIDE AND TRAVEL ATLAS [Suspended]
American Hotel Register Company
2775 Shermer Road   Phone: (312) 564-4000
Northbrook, IL 60062
Covers: 47,500 hotels and motels in over 8,600 cities and towns,
listed without regard to affiliation or non-affiliation with hotel industry
associations, chains, etc. Publication does not accept advertising.
Entries include: Hotel name, postal address, rates, number of rooms,
plan of operation. **Arrangement:** Geographical. **Pages** (approx.): 300.
Frequency: Usually annual, March; publication suspended for 1980.
Editor: James F. Leahy, President. **Price:** $20.00, postpaid, payment
with order.

★836★
LEATHER AND SHOES—CHAIN SHOE STORES AND LEASED SHOE DEPARTMENT OPERATORS ISSUE

Rumpf Publishing Division
Nickerson & Collins Company
1800 Oakton Street   Phone: (312) 298-6210
Des Plaines, IL 60018
Entries include: Company name, address, phone, names of executives, types and brands of shoes sold, retail price ranges, number of units operated, types of stores operated. **Arrangement:** Geographical. **Indexes:** Alphabetical, brand name. **Pages** (approx.): 40. **Frequency:** Annual, July. **Editor:** Gloria Schroeder. **Advertising accepted.** Circulation 4,000. **Price:** $2.50 (1980 edition). **Other information:** Includes separate lists in rank order of parent companies operating 100 or more units and chains operating 50 or more units.

★837★
LEATHER AND SHOES—LEATHER BUYERS GUIDE ISSUE

Rumpf Publishing Company, Division
Nickerson & Collins Company
1800 Oakton Street   Phone: (312) 298-6210
Des Plaines, IL 60018
Covers: Tanners, finishers, curriers, and related leather industry businesses. **Entries include:** Company name, address, phone; list of officers, sales managers, and superintendents; year established; plant locations; code for product types. **Arrangement:** Alphabetical. **Indexes:** Geographical, types of leather, trade names, product. **Pages** (approx.): 100. **Frequency:** Annual, January. **Editor:** Gloria Schroeder. **Advertising accepted.** Circulation 4,000. **Price:** $4.00 (1980 edition).

Leather Buyers Guide *See* Leather and Shoes—Buyers Guide Issue

★838★
LEATHER MANUFACTURER DIRECTORY

Shoe Trades Publishing Company
15 East Street   Phone: (617) 542-0190
Boston, MA 02111
Covers: Tanneries, leather finishers, and hide processors and their suppliers in the United States and Canada. **Entries include:** Company name, address, phone, names of executives, list of products or services. **Arrangement:** Geographical. **Pages** (approx.): 350. **Frequency:** Annual, spring. **Advertising accepted.** **Price:** $11.00 (1979 edition); $12.00 (1980 edition).

★839★
LI BUSINESS REVIEW—DIRECTORY ISSUES

Long Island Business Review
303 Sunnyside Boulevard   Phone: (516) 681-8000
Plainview, NY 11803
Description: Each issue includes a directory section covering one major type of business in the area, e.g., printing, real estate, insurance, etc. **Entries include:** Firm name, address, phone, name of contact, product or service. **Arrangement:** By subcategory. **Frequency:** Monthly. **Other information:** Sometimes cited as, "Directory of LI Business Services."

Linen Supply Association of America—Roster, Buyers Guide and Handbook *See* Textile Rental Services Association—Roster-Buyers Guide

★840★
LINERS FOR SANITARY LANDFILLS AND CHEMICAL AND HAZARDOUS WASTE DISPOSAL SITES [Locations of lined sites]

Municipal Environmental Research Laboratory
Office of Research and Development
Environmental Protection Agency
Cincinnati, OH 45268
Covers: About 250 sanitary landfills and chemical and hazardous waste disposal sites and holding ponds with linings expected to be impermeable, and manufacturers and suppliers of linings. **Entries include:** For sites - Name of owner and owner's address, site name and address, name of contact, type of liner, date installed, depth and type of waste, and whether liner specifications and construction plans are available. For manufacturers - Company name, address, phone, contact. **Arrangement:** By EPA region. **Pages** (approx.): 90. **Frequency:** Published May 1978. **Price:** $6.00, paper; $3.00, microfiche (PB 293-335). May also be available from the agency. **Send orders to:** National Technical Information Service, Springfield, VA 22161.

★841★
LIST OF 8(A) APPROVED CONTRACTORS [Minority firms in SBA Seattle Region]

Seattle Regional Office
Small Business Administration
710 Second Avenue, Room 555   Phone: (206) 399-5725
Seattle, WA 98104
Covers: More than 125 approved 8(a) contractors offering industrial and commercial services and products in the Region Ten districts of Anchorage, Alaska; Boise, Idaho; Portland, Oregon; and Seattle and Spokane, Washington. **Entries include:** Company name, address, phone, name of contact, line of business. **Arrangement:** By district, then classified. **Frequency:** Semiannual. **Price:** Free.

List of Industry Analysts in the Federal Government *See* Industry Analysts in the Federal Government

List of Manufacturers and Processors [Savannah, Georgia] *See* Savannah Area Manufacturers Directory [Georgia]

★842★
LIST OF SHIPOWNERS

Lloyd's Register of Shipping
17 Battery Place   Phone: (212) 425-8050
New York, NY 10004
Covers: Owners and managers of ocean-going merchant ships in the world of 100 tons gross or more (listed in "Register of Ships" described in separate listing). **Entries include:** Name, names of ships owned or managed, address, coding to indicate type of ship. **Arrangement:** Alphabetical. **Frequency:** Annual, October. **Price:** $80.00. **Also includes:** Lists of former names of ships and compound names of ships. **Other information:** Common title is, "Lloyd's List of Shipowners."

Lithographic Preparatory Services Association—Directory *See* Lithographic Preparatory Trade Shops Services Buyer's Guide

★843★
LITHOGRAPHIC PREPARATORY TRADE SHOPS SERVICES BUYER'S GUIDE

Lithographic Preparatory Services Association
C/o Printing Industries of America
1730 N. Lynn Street
Arlington, VA 22209
Covers: About 100 member firms which offer preparatory services (negatives, plates, and color separation) for lithographic printing. **Entries include:** Firm name, address, phone, names of contact persons, type of work handled, area of specialization. **Arrangement:** Geographical. **Indexes:** Firm name. **Pages** (approx.): 20. **Frequency:** Annual, fall. **Price:** Free.

Lloyd's List of Shipowners *See* List of Shipowners

Lloyd's Register of Offshore Units, Submersibles, and Diving Systems *See* Register of Offshore Units, Submersibles, and Diving...

Lloyd's Register of Ships *See* Register of Ships

★844★

LNA MULTI-MEDIA REPORT SERVICE

Leading National Advertisers, Inc.

515 Madison Avenue, Suite 2302   Phone: (212) 888-1940

New York, NY 10022

Background: LNA analyzes advertising expenditures of 1,000 companies which use magazines, newspaper supplements, network television, spot television, network radios, or outdoor media. Data are furnished by company in order of total expenditures, by brands (about 24,000), and product category. **Frequency:** Quarterly, annual cumulations. **Price:** Apply. **Other information:** ''Ad Dollar Summary'' is the principal report in the LNA Multi-Media Report Service.

★845★

LOCKSMITH LEDGER/SECURITY REGISTER SECURITY GUIDE & DIRECTORY

Nickerson & Collins Company

1800 Oakton   Phone: (312) 298-6210

Des Plaines, IL 60018

Covers: Manufacturers, and distributors of security products; trade associations are also listed. **Entries include:** For manufacturers and distributors - Company name, address, phone, name of contact, products manufactured or lines handled. For trade associations - Name, address. **Indexes:** Trademark. **Frequency:** Annual, January. **Advertising accepted.** Circulation 26,000. **Price:** $5.00 (current and 1980 editions).

★846★

LOCKWOOD'S DIRECTORY OF THE PAPER & ALLIED TRADES

Vance Publishing Corporation

133 E. 58th Street   Phone: (212) 755-5400

New York, NY 10022

Covers: United States and Canadian pulp and paper companies and their mills; paper converters; paper merchants; and industry associations. Also lists suppliers of equipment, chemicals, technical services, and raw materials to the paper industry (SIC 26). **Entries include:** All listings usually show company name, address, phone, personnel, and products and grades manufactured or handled; paper company listings also show divisions and subsidiaries, research centers, sales officer; mill listings also show equipment and daily output; merchant lists also show nature of business (whether wholesaler, importer, etc.), processing operations offered. **Arrangement:** Paper manufacturing companies, associations, wood pulp agents, and industry suppliers are alphabetical. Paper mills, converters, general paper merchants, major waste paper and rag dealers are geographical. **Indexes:** Personal name index of personnel in company and mill sections; company name index to companies, mills, converters, and merchants. Mill and converter product index. **Pages** (approx.): 1,000. **Frequency:** Annual, January. **Editor:** Harry Dyer. **Advertising accepted.** Circulation 4,500. **Price:** $55.00, postpaid, payment with order (current and 1980 editions).

★847★

LODGING MAGAZINE—BUYERS GUIDE FOR HOTELS AND MOTELS ISSUE

American Hotel and Motel Association

888 Seventh Avenue   Phone: (212) 265-4506

New York, NY 10019

Covers: About 375 allied (supplier) members of the association. **Entries include:** Company name, address, phone, name of principal executive, list of products or services. **Pages** (approx.): 100. **Frequency:** Annual, April. **Editor:** James Pearson. **Advertising accepted.** Circulation 11,200. **Former title:** Lodging Magazine - Hotel/Motel Buyers Directory Issue (1976). **Price:** $10.00 (current edition; tentative, 1980 edition).

★848★

LOG HOME GUIDE FOR BUILDERS AND BUYERS

Muir Publishing Company Ltd.

Gardenvale, Quebec H9X 1B0, Canada

Covers: About 80 pre-cut and hand-hewn log home companies in the United States and Canada. Schools for log construction are also listed. **Entries include:** Descriptions in text form give extensive information, with illustrations, about company's products, and include full company name, address, and phone. **Arrangement:** Alphabetical. **Frequency:** Annual, November. **Advertising accepted.** **Price:** $8.50, postpaid, payment with order.

Long Island Directory of Commerce and Industry [New York] *See* Directory of Commerce & Industry—Nassau and Suffolk Counties

★849★

LOOKING FOR PRE-COATED METALS?

National Coil Coaters Association

1900 Arch Street   Phone: (215) 564-3484

Philadelphia, PA 19103

Covers: 60 suppliers of pre-coated metal coil, other than metal-plated coil, in North America who are members. **Entries include:** Company name, address, phone, names of sales executives, list of coatings available. **Arrangement:** Alphabetical. **Frequency:** Irregular; latest edition October 1979. **Price:** Free.

★850★

LOS ANGELES DIRECTORY OF TV COMMERCIAL FILM PRODUCERS AND OTHER RELATED SERVICES

Charles H. Stern Agency, Inc.

9220 Sunset Boulevard, Suite 218   Phone: (213) 273-6890

Los Angeles, CA 90069

Covers: Advertising agencies, casting services, production companies, photographers, film laboratories, film editorial services, studios, and other service firms related to advertising in southern California. **Entries include:** Company or individual name, address, phone, and name of contact. **Arrangement:** By type of activity. **Pages** (approx.): 40. **Frequency:** Annual, January. **Editor:** Charles H. Stern, President. **Advertising accepted.** Circulation 8,000. **Price:** $5.00 (current and 1980 editions).

★851★

LOS ANGELES TIMES—TIMES ROSTER OF CALIFORNIA'S 100 LEADING COMPANIES

Los Angeles Times

Times Mirror Publishing Company

Times Mirror Square

Los Angeles, CA 90053

Covers: Largest publicly held companies with headquarters in California. Includes not only industrials but financial, merchandising, and other firms as well. **Entries include:** Company name, address, names of principal executives, sales, assets, employees, and other financial and statistical data, and a brief description of the firm's business and history. **Arrangement:** Ranked by sales or revenues, within industry categories. **Frequency:** Annual, in a May Sunday issue. **Former title:** ''...Roster of California's Top Industrials.'' **Price:** $2.00. **Send orders to:** Marketing Research Department, Los Angeles Times, Times Mirror Square, Los Angeles, CA 90053.

★852★

LOUISIANA CONTRACTOR—LOUISIANA CONSTRUCTION DIRECTORY ISSUE

Rhodes Publishing Company, Inc.

18271 Jefferson Highway   Phone: (504) 292-8980

Baton Rouge, LA 70816

Covers: Contractors, architects, engineers, subcontractors, and other suppliers of equipment, materials, and services for the Louisiana construction industry. **Entries include:** Company name, address, phone. **Arrangement:** Alphabetical. **Indexes:** Geographical, type of construction. **Pages** (approx.): 300. **Frequency:** Annual, December. **Editor:** Kim Rhodes. **Advertising accepted.** Circulation 5,500. **Price:** $10.00

★853★
LOUISIANA DIRECTORY OF MANUFACTURERS
Louisiana Department of Commerce
Box 44185   Phone: (504) 342-5359
Baton Rouge, LA 70804
Number of listings: Over 2,000. **Entries include:** Company name, address, phone, name of principal executive, name of purchasing agent, date established, SIC number, products, number of employees, area served. **Arrangement:** Geographical, SIC; both sections contain similar information. **Indexes:** Alphabetical, parent company, exporter/importer, product. **Pages** (approx.): 150. **Frequency:** Irregular; latest edition 1978; new edition expected January 1980. **Former title:** Directory of Louisiana Manufacturers. **Price:** $20.00 (1980 edition). **Other information:** Manufacturers' News catalog formerly listed this publication as, "Louisiana Manufacturers Directory."

★854★
LOUISIANA INTERNATIONAL TRADE DIRECTORY
International Marketing Institute
University of New Orleans
Lakefront   Phone: (504) 283-0279
New Orleans, LA 70122
Covers: 1,000 Louisiana industries, trades, and institutions directly or indirectly engaged in international trade. **Entries include:** Company name, address, phone number, list of products or services, SIC numbers. **Arrangement:** Separate sections for importers and exporters, manufacturers, international trade services. **Indexes:** SIC. **Pages** (approx.): 180. **Frequency:** Irregular; latest edition 1977. **Editor:** Dr. Richard G. Arellano, ·Director, International Marketing Institute. **Advertising accepted. Former title:** Directory of Louisiana Importers and Exporters. **Price:** $15.00.

Louisiana Manufacturers Directory *See* Louisiana Directory of Manufacturers

★855★
LOUISIANA MINORITY BUSINESS DIRECTORY
Louisiana Association of Business and Industry
Box 3988   Phone: (504) 387-5372
Baton Rouge, LA 70821
Covers: About 105 minority firms operating in Louisiana. **Entries include:** Company name, address, phone, name of owner or manager, products or services, year established, geographic area covered. **Arrangement:** Alphabetical. **Indexes:** Product/service. **Pages** (approx.): 45. **Frequency:** Not established; first edition August 1979; new edition expected June 1980. **Editor:** Richard J. Perkins, Director of Minority Business Development. **Price:** $2.50, postpaid.

★856★
LOUISIANA STATE INDUSTRIAL DIRECTORY
State Industrial Directories Corporation
Two Penn Plaza   Phone: (212) 564-0340
New York, NY 10001
Number of listings: 2,700. **Entries include:** Company name, address, phone, names of key executives, number of employees, plant size, 4-digit SIC code, products, whether firm imports or exports, and whether firm has research facilities. **Arrangement:** Geographical. **Indexes:** Alphabetical, product (includes mailing address and phone for each firm). **Frequency:** Not established; first edition October 1979. **Advertising accepted. Price:** $20.00.

★857★
LOUISVILLE AREA DIRECTORY OF MANUFACTURERS
Louisville Area Chamber of Commerce
300 W. Liberty   Phone: (502) 582-2421
Louisville, KY 40202
Covers: 1,400 manufacturers in 13-county Louisville metropolitan area (including Indiana) (SIC 2011-3999). **Entries include:** Company name, address, phone, names of executives, number of employees, list of products or services, SIC numbers. **Arrangement:** Alphabetical by company name. **Indexes:** Product; companies by Zip code. **Pages**

(approx.): 100. **Frequency:** Irregular; latest edition 1979; new edition expected fall 1981. **Price:** $11.00, postpaid.

★858★
LUGGAGE & TRAVELWARE—DIRECTORY AND MARKET GUIDE ISSUE
Business Journals, Inc.
22 S. Smith Street   Phone: (203) 853-6015
Norwalk, CT 06855
Covers: About 500 jobbers, manufacturers, importers, and representatives in the luggage and leather goods industry (SIC 3161, 3172). **Entries include:** Company name, address, phone, names of executives, branch office and showroom locations, and whether the firm is a manufacturer, jobber, importer, or representative. **Arrangement:** Alphabetical. **Indexes:** Product, trade mark and brand name. **Pages** (approx.): 130. **Frequency:** Annual, December. **Editor:** Terry Petak. **Advertising accepted.** Circulation 6,000. **Price:** $6.00.

★859★
MACARONI JOURNAL—BUYERS GUIDE ISSUE
National Macaroni Manufacturers Association
Box 336
Palatine, IL 60067
Covers: About 50 manufacturers and suppliers of services, equipment, and materials to manufacturers of macaroni and other pasta products. **Entries include:** Company name, address, phone; trade and brand names; names, addresses, and phone numbers of manufacturers' representatives and/or distributors. **Arrangement:** Classified. **Frequency:** Annual, April. **Editor:** Robert M. Green. **Advertising accepted.** Circulation 1,010. **Price:** $2.00; available to subscribers only (ISSN 0024-8894).

★860★
MACHINE AND TOOL DIRECTORY
Hitchcock Publishing Company, Subsidiary
American Broadcasting Companies, Inc.
Hitchcock Building   Phone: (312) 665-1000
Wheaton, IL 60187
Covers: Over 3,000 manufacturers of metalworking equipment; distributors are listed separately. **Entries include:** Company name, address, phone. **Arrangement:** Alphabetical. **Indexes:** Product. **Pages** (approx.): 600. **Frequency:** Annual, February. **Editor:** Raymond Spiotta. **Advertising accepted.** Circulation 49,000. **Price:** $25.00 (current and 1980 editions). **Also includes:** Engineering handbook section.

Machinery Dealers National Association—Membership Directory *See* Buyers Guide of Used Machine Tools & Metalworking Equipment

★861★
MACRAE'S BLUE BOOK
MacRae's Blue Book Company
100 Shore Drive   Phone: (312) 325-7880
Hinsdale, IL 60521
Covers: 60,000 manufacturing firms in the United States; Volume 1 is alphabetical list of companies; Volumes 2-4 are product indexes; Volume 5 is catalog pages. **Entries include:** Volume 1 - Company name, address, products, phone, and cities and phone numbers of branches and sales outlets. Volumes 2-4 - Product-classified listings of manufacturers with address and financial key. **Indexes:** Trade name (in Volume 1). **Frequency:** Annual, March. **Editor:** Charles A. Burton, Jr., President and Publisher. **Advertising accepted. Price:** $69.25. **Also includes:** Catalogs of some companies with names and titles of key personnel, and locations and phone numbers for sales representatives.

★862★

MADE IN NEW HAMPSHIRE

New Hampshire Department of Resources and Economic Development
Box 856   Phone: (603) 271-2342
Concord, NH 03301

Covers: New Hampshire manufacturers and mining companies. **Entries include:** Company name, address, phone, products, number of employees, names of principal executives, whether firm imports or exports. **Arrangement:** Alphabetical. **Indexes:** Geographical, SIC. **Pages** (approx.): 170. **Frequency:** Biennial, spring of odd years. **Editor:** Paul H. Guilderson, Industrial Director. **Price:** $10.00.

★863★

**MADERA DISTRICT CHAMBER OF COMMERCE—INDUSTRIAL
    DIRECTORY [California]**

Madera District Chamber of Commerce
131 W. Yosemite Avenue   Phone: (209) 673-3563
Madera, CA 93637

Entries include: Company name and address. **Arrangement:** Alphabetical. **Indexes:** SIC. **Frequency:** Biennial, odd years. **Price:** $5.00.

★864★

MADISON AVENUE—TOP ADVERTISING AGENCIES ISSUE

Madison Avenue Magazine Publishing Corporation
369 Lexington Avenue   Phone: (212) 682-5250
New York, NY 10017

Publication includes: List of about 65 major advertising agencies. **Entries include:** Agency name, headquarters location, estimated billings for past and current year, number of employees, accounts gained and lost in preceding year, and description of agency philosophy and services. **Arrangement:** Alphabetical. **Frequency:** Annual, January. **Price:** $3.00.

★865★

MADISON AVENUE HANDBOOK [Advertiser services]

Peter Glenn Publications
17 E. 48th Street   Phone: (212) 688-7940
New York, NY 10017

Covers: Advertising agencies and related services in New York City, Atlanta, Boston, Chicago, Los Angeles, San Francisco, Dallas, Houston, Detroit, Florida's "Gold Coast," Toronto, and Montreal. Includes TV producers; photographers; artists, models, actors, and their agents; photographers and suppliers; sources of props and rentals, fashion houses, beauty services, and similar services. **Arrangement:** Alphabetical by service (media, agencies, etc.). **Pages** (approx.): 240. **Frequency:** Annual. **Editor:** Peter Glenn. **Price:** $11.95, plus $1.00 shipping (1979 edition); $12.95 (1980 edition).

Magazine Directory See **Working Press of the Nation**

★866★

MAIL ORDER BUSINESS DIRECTORY

B. Klein Publications
Box 8503
Coral Springs, FL 33065

Covers: 5,900 firms in the United States doing business by mail order and catalogs. **Entries include:** Name, address, name of owner or contact, and products or services. **Arrangement:** Geographical. **Pages** (approx.): 500. **Frequency:** Irregular; latest edition early 1978. **Price:** $40.00.

★867★

MAIL ORDER USA

Mail Order USA
3100 Wisconsin Avenue, N. W., Apartment B-10 Phone: (202) 686-9521
Washington, DC 20016

Covers: Over 2,000 mail order catalogs in the United States and Canada; many catalogs are free. **Entries include:** Name and address of mail order house, plus brief description of offerings and price of catalog. **Arrangement:** By type of merchandise (clothes, garden, toys, etc.). **Pages** (approx.): 180. **Frequency:** Irregular; latest edition October 1979. **Editor:** Dorothy O'Callaghan, Publisher. **Price:** $6.00.

★868★

MAINE MARKETING DIRECTORY

Maine Development Office
Executive Department   Phone: (207) 289-2656
Augusta, ME 04333

Covers: Over 1,300 manufacturers and processors. **Entries include:** Company name, address, phone, name and title of principal executive, number of employees, list of products or services, SIC numbers, parent company (if applicable). **Arrangement:** Same information given geographically and by SIC number. **Indexes:** Alphabetical. **Pages** (approx.): 350. **Frequency:** Biennial, July of even years. **Editor:** Hadley P. Atlass, Director. **Former title:** Buyers Guide and Directory of Maine Manufacturers. **Price:** $7.50. **Send orders to:** Tower Publishing Co., 163 Middle St., Portland, ME 04111 (207-774-9813).

★869★

MAINE MEDIA DIRECTORY

Maine Clipping Service
Box 360   Phone: (207) 377-2977
Winthrop, ME 04364

Covers: 180 newspapers, periodicals, and college publications, and 95 radio and television broadcasting stations operating in Maine. **Price:** $15.00. **Other information:** Entry content, arrangement, etc., same as "New England Media Directory," described in separate listing.

★870★

MAINE STATE INDUSTRIAL DIRECTORY

State Industrial Directories Corporation
Two Penn Plaza   Phone: (212) 564-0340
New York, NY 10001

Number of listings: 1,700. **Entries include:** Company name, address, phone, names and titles of key executives, number of employees, plant size, 4- and 5-digit SIC number, products, whether firm imports or exports, and whether firm has research facilities. **Arrangement:** Geographical. **Indexes:** Alphabetical, product (includes mailing address and phone for each firm). **Pages** (approx.): 220. **Frequency:** Annual, August. **Advertising accepted. Price:** $20.00, plus $1.75 shipping.

★871★

**MAINE, VERMONT, NEW HAMPSHIRE DIRECTORY OF
    MANUFACTURERS**

Commerce Register, Inc.
213 First Street   Phone: (201) 445-3000
Hohokus, NJ 07423

Covers: 4,000 industrial firms with five or more employees. **Entries include:** Company name, address, phone, names of principal executives, product descriptions, SIC codes, plant size, number of employees, sales, banking affiliation, attorneys, auditors. **Arrangement:** Geographical. **Indexes:** Company name, SIC. **Pages** (approx.): 200. **Frequency:** Annual, August; first edition August 1979. **Advertising accepted.** Circulation 1,500. **Price:** $39.50, plus 75¢ shipping.

★872★

MAINTENANCE SUPPLIES—BUYER'S GUIDE ISSUE

MacNair-Dorland Company, Inc.
101 W. 31st Street   Phone: (212) 279-4456
New York, NY 10001

Covers: Maintenance chemicals, equipment, and services for distributors of sanitary supplies. **Entries include:** Company name and address. **Pages** (approx.): 200. **Frequency:** Annual, November. **Editor:** Edward Pasternack. **Advertising accepted.** Circulation 10,000. **Price:** $3.00.

★873★

MAJOR EMPLOYERS IN METROPOLITAN CHICAGO

Chicago Association of Commerce and Industry

130 S. Michigan Avenue   Phone: (312) 786-0111

Chicago, IL 60603

Covers: About 1,130 firms employing at least 250 employees in their Chicago area plants and offices; subsidiaries, affiliates, and divisions are also listed. **Entries include:** Company name, Zip code, phone; names of major officers, corporate division officers, plant managers, division directors, personnel directors, and purchasing agents; line of business for non- manufacturers and products and SIC numbers for manufacturers; total United States sales; coding to indicate number of employees and whether manufacturer or non-manufacturer. **Arrangement:** Alphabetical. **Indexes:** Product. **Frequency:** Irregular, about every two years; previous edition 1977; new edition expected mid-summer 1980. **Price:** $31.50 (current edition); $42.00 (1980 edition).

★874★

MAJOR FIRMS IN THE PITTSBURGH METRO AREA

Greater Pittsburgh Chamber of Commerce

411 Seventh Avenue   Phone: (412) 391-3400

Pittsburgh, PA 15219

Covers: About 135 firms in the Pittsburgh area which employ 500 or more people. **Entries include:** Name of Pittsburgh division, division company name, parent company name, address, phone, names of key personnel, products, and SIC numbers. Asterisk denotes companies headquartered in Pittsburgh. **Arrangement:** Alphabetical. **Pages** (approx.): 45. **Frequency:** Annual, spring. **Price:** $5.00.

Major Mass Market Merchandisers See Salesman's Guide Nationwide Directory: Major Mass Market Merchandisers

★875★

MANAGING THE LEISURE FACILITY—BUYERS GUIDE ISSUE

Billboard Publications

Box 24970   Phone: (615) 748-8120

Nashville, TN 37202

Covers: Over 2,500 manufacturers and suppliers of products and services used at mass entertainment facilities, including amusement equipment, rides, food and beverage supplies, fireworks, novelties and souvenirs. **Entries include:** Company name, address, phone. **Indexes:** Product. **Pages** (approx.): 150. **Frequency:** Annual, March. **Editor:** Paul Curran, Editorial Director. **Advertising accepted.** Circulation 19,000. **Price:** $5.00 (current edition); $7.50 (1980 edition). **Other information:** Sometimes cited as, "Mass Entertainment Industry Buyers Guide."

★876★

MANHATTAN CLOTHES SHOPPING GUIDE

Macmillan, Inc.

866 Third Avenue   Phone: (212) 935-2000

New York, NY 10022

Covers: Sources for new and used clothing in Manhattan - classic, funky, bargain basement, and haute couture; includes shops for men, women, and children. **Entries include:** Shop name, address, phone, specialties. **Arrangement:** By area. **Frequency:** First edition November 1978. **Editor:** Elaine Louie. **Price:** $9.95, cloth; $5.95, paper.

★877★

MANUFACTURED HOUSING DEALER—ANNUAL DIRECTORY AND BUYER'S GUIDE ISSUE

Hardison Publishing Company

6229 Northwest Highway   Phone: (312) 774-2525

Chicago, IL 60631

Covers: About 700 mobile home and modular housing manufacturers in the United States and Canada, plus suppliers, distributors, wholesalers, and manufacturers' representatives for the industry. **Entries include:** For manufacturers - Company name, address, phone, names and titles of key personnel, year established, models

manufactured, price range, locations of company plants. For others - Company name, address, phone, contact. **Arrangement:** By manufacturer, supplier, distributor/wholesaler, representative, or special services; then alphabetical, except special services, which is by service. **Indexes:** Supplier, product. **Pages** (approx.): 200. **Frequency:** Annual, January. **Editor:** Renald Rooney. **Advertising accepted.** Circulation 20,000. **Former title:** Mobile-Modular Housing - Annual Directory and Buyer's Guide. **Price:** $6.00 (1980 edition). **Other information:** Also published in abridged pocket format as, "Directory of Mobile and Modular Housing Manufacturers" (see separate listing).

★878★

MANUFACTURERS' AGENTS' GUIDE [To firms that sell through agents]

Manufacturers' Agent Publishing Company, Inc.

663 Fifth Avenue   Phone: (212) 682-0326

New York, NY 10022

Covers: More than 12,700 manufacturers who distribute through agents. **Entries include:** Name of manufacturer, address, principal products, credit rating, name and title of sales executive. **Arrangement:** By industry. **Pages** (approx.): 240. **Frequency:** Biennial, March of even years. **Editor:** E. K. Sharp. **Price:** $29.95, payment with order.

★879★

MANUFACTURERS' AGENTS NATIONAL ASSOCIATION— DIRECTORY OF MEMBERS

Manufacturers' Agents National Association

2021 Business Center Drive   Phone: (714) 752-5231

Irvine, CA 92713

Covers: 6,000 independent agents and firms representing manufacturers of all types in specified territories on commission basis, as well as manufacturers, consultants, and others interested in the agency/principal method of marketing. **Entries include:** Name, address, phone, principal executive, product lines carried, territory, number of travelers, date established. **Arrangement:** Geographical. **Indexes:** Alphabetical, product. **Pages** (approx.): 400. **Frequency:** Annual, June. **Editor:** James J. Gibbons, President. **Advertising accepted.** Circulation 15,000. **Price:** $35.00 (including one-year subscription to "Agency Sales Magazine;" current and 1980 editions).

Manufacturers Directory—Charleston, S. C. See Trident Area Manufacturers Directory [South Carolina]

Manufacturers Directory [Cleveland, Ohio] See Greater Cleveland Growth Association...

Manufacturers Directory of York and York County [Pennsylvania] See York County Industrial Directory [Pennsylvania]

Manufacturers List Guide of Steel Building Construction Products See Directory of Manufacturers of Steel Building Construction Products

★880★

MANUFACTURERS, PRODUCTS OF THE COMPOSITE CAN AND TUBE INDUSTRY

Composite Can and Tube Institute

1800 M Street, N. W.   Phone: (202) 223-4840

Washington, DC 20036

Covers: About 200 manufacturers of cans, tubes, spools, cones, and similar products. **Entries include:** Company name, address, phone, locations of branch plants, names and titles of key personnel, coding to indicate products and industries served, coding to indicate whether member of Composite Can and Tube Institute. **Arrangement:** By regions. **Indexes:** State by region. **Pages** (approx.): 50. **Frequency:** Annual, August. **Price:** $5.00.

★881★

MANUFACTURING CONFECTIONER—PURCHASING EXECUTIVE'S
GUIDE ISSUE
Manufacturing Confectioner Publishing Company
175 Rock Road   Phone: (201) 652-2655
Glen Rock, NJ 07452
Covers: Suppliers of machinery, equipment, raw materials, and supplies to the confectionery industry. **Arrangement:** Geographical. **Indexes:** Product. **Pages** (approx.): 180. **Frequency:** Annual, July. **Editor:** Diane Mancini. **Advertising accepted.** Circulation 2,200. **Price:** $5.00, payment with order.

★882★

MANUFACTURING DIRECTORY OF IDAHO
Center for Business Development and Research
University of Idaho   Phone: (208) 885-6611
Moscow, ID 83843
Number of listings: About 1,100. **Entries include:** Company name, address, phone, name of principal executive, number of employees, products or services, SIC numbers, whether firm exports; also includes membership rosters of Idaho Mining Association and Consulting Engineers of Idaho. **Arrangement:** Geographical. **Indexes:** Alphabetical, SIC. **Pages** (approx.): 125. **Frequency:** About every two years; latest edition January 1979; next expected January 1981. **Editor:** George M. Armstrong. **Former title:** Idaho Manufacturers Directory. **Price:** $22.50, postpaid, payment with order. **Other information:** Manufacturers' News and State Industrial Directories Corp. catalogs list this publication as, "Idaho Manufacturing Directory." Sometimes cited as, "Idaho Manufacturers Directory."

★883★

MARCONI INTERNATIONAL REGISTER
Telegraphic Cable & Radio Registrations, Inc.
Box 14   Phone: (914) 381-2334
Larchmont, NY 10538
Covers: 45,000 firms worldwide which do business internationally. **Entries include:** Company name, address, phone, telex, cable address, brief description of business, name of president and international department manager. **Arrangement:** Alphabetical. **Indexes:** Product (geographical under 2,500 product headings, with full mailing address), cable address. **Pages** (approx.): 1,400. **Frequency:** Annual, December. **Editor:** Le Sueur G. Smith, Jr., Secretary. **Advertising accepted.** Circulation 5,000. **Price:** $55.00, payment with order.

★884★

MARINE CATALOG & BUYERS GUIDE
Simmons-Boardman Publishing Corporation
350 Broadway   Phone: (212) 966-7700
New York, NY 10013
Covers: Manufacturers and suppliers of products and equipment for firms engaged in ship and boat building, construction of petroleum drill rigs, and operation and repair of these units. Also lists consulting engineers, naval architects, and marine surveyors. **Entries include:** Company name and address, phone, products or services, trade names. **Arrangement:** Classified. **Indexes:** Product, trade name. **Frequency:** Annual, October. **Editor:** Larry J. Ospa. **Advertising accepted.** Circulation 7,500. **Price:** $15.00.

Marine Digest Pacific Coast Marine Directory *See* Pacific Coast
Marine Directory

★885★

MARINE DIRECTORY
Simmons-Boardman Publishing Corporation
350 Broadway   Phone: (212) 966-7700
New York, NY 10013
Covers: 15,000 ship owners and operators, 5,000 shipyards, and ship chandlers; international coverage. Also includes United States and Canadian port authorities, naval architects, consulting engineers, and marine surveyors. **Entries include:** For owners and operators and shipbuilders - Company name, address, phone, names of principal

personnel, list of vessels and tonnage or shipyard facilities. For port authorities - Name of authority, address, phone, names of key executives. **Arrangement:** Geographical (within type of organization or activity). **Pages** (approx.): 530. **Frequency:** Annual, March. **Editor:** Larry J. Ospa. **Advertising accepted.** Ciculation 2,500. **Price:** $80.00.

★886★

MARINE WEEK DIRECTORY OF SHIPOWNERS, SHIPBUILDERS AND
MARINE ENGINEERS
IPC Industrial Press Ltd.
Dorset House, Stamford Street
London SE1, England
Covers: Shipping, ship repairing, shipbuilding, and marine engineering companies, worldwide. **Entries include:** Company name, address, phone, names of executives, services, fleets, dock facilities. **Pages** (approx.): 1,500. **Frequency:** Annual, January. **Editor:** Simon Timm. **Advertising accepted.** Circulation 4,000. **Price:** $65.00, postpaid (1980 edition). **Send orders to:** Marine Week Sundry Sales, 40 Bowling Green Lane, London, England.

Market Research Association—Membership Directory *See*
Directory of Research Services Provided by Members of the
Marketing Research Assn

Market Statistics Key Plants *See* Marketing Economics Key
Plants—Guide to Industrial Purchasing Power

★887★

MARKETING COMMUNICATIONS EXECUTIVES INTERNATIONAL—
ROSTER
Marketing Communications Executives International
1831 Chestnut Street   Phone: (215) 567-7692
Philadelphia, PA 19103
Number of listings: 1,200. **Entries include:** Name, title, address. **Arrangement:** Geographical by chapter cities. **Indexes:** Company. **Pages** (approx.): 90. **Frequency:** Annual, February. **Editor:** A. O. Dietrich, Managing Director. **Price:** $50.00 (for professional use only).

★888★

MARKETING ECONOMICS KEY PLANTS—GUIDE TO INDUSTRIAL
PURCHASING POWER
Marketing Economics Institute Ltd.
441 Lexington Avenue   Phone: (212) 687-5090
New York, NY 10017
Covers: More than 40,000 key manufacturing plants with 100 or more employees (SIC 2011-3999); there are also editions for New England, Middle Atlantic, East North Central, West North Central, South Atlantic, East South Central, West South Central, and Mountain/Pacific regions. **Entries include:** Company name, address, number of employees, SIC numbers. **Arrangement:** Geographical and by SIC number; same data in both sections. **Pages** (approx.): 600. **Frequency:** Biennial, August of odd years. **Editor:** Alfred Hong, Managing Director. **Former title:** Market Statistics Key Plants. **Price:** $90.00, national edition; $13.00, regional editions.

Marketing Guide to the Chemical Industry *See* Kline Guide to the
Chemical Industry

Marketing Guide to the Paint Industry *See* Kline Guide to the
Paint Industry

★889★

MARKETING TIMES: JOURNAL OF CONTINUING EDUCATION—
LEADERSHIP DIRECTORY
Sales and Marketing Executives International
380 Lexington Avenue   Phone: (212) 986-9300
New York, NY 10017
Covers: About 1,100 officials of local chapters of the organization; also includes national and regional officers. **Entries include:** Chapter name, name and address of executive secretary, and names, business

affiliations, titles, addresses, and phone numbers of chapter officers. **Arrangement:** Geographical. **Pages** (approx.): 50. **Frequency:** Annual, November or December. **Editor:** Roy Alexander. **Advertising accepted.** Circulation 20,000. **Price:** $5.00.

★890★
MARKING PRODUCTS & EQUIPMENT
Marking Devices Publishing Company
666 N. Lake Shore Drive, Suite 548   Phone: (312) 943-1300
Chicago, IL 60611
Covers: Manufacturers of marking and identification products. **Entries include:** Company name, address, trade and brand names, list of products. **Arrangement:** Alphabetical. **Pages** (approx.): 100. **Frequency:** Annual, March. **Editor:** A. W. Hachmeister. **Advertising accepted.** Circulation 1,850. **Price:** $3.00 (current edition); $5.00 (1980 edition).

★891★
MARYLAND MEDIA DIRECTORY
Maryland Chamber of Commerce
60 West Street   Phone: (301) 269-0642
Annapolis, MD 21401
Covers: Publications and television and radio stations located in Maryland. **Entries include:** Name of publication or station, corporate name, address, phone, names of key executives. **Arrangement:** By county and city. **Frequency:** Annual, October. **Price:** $10.00, postpaid.

Maryland Minority Business Directory *See* **Economic Opportunity in the Maryland Marketplace—Minority Business Directory**

★892★
MARYLAND STATE INDUSTRIAL DIRECTORY
State Industrial Directories Corporation
Two Penn Plaza   Phone: (212) 564-0340
New York, NY 10001
Number of listings: 3,700. **Entries include:** Company name, address, phone, names of key executives, number of employees, plant size, 4-digit SIC code, products, whether firm imports or exports, and whether firm has research facilities. **Arrangement:** Geographical. **Indexes:** Alphabetical, product (includes mailing address and phone for each firm). **Frequency:** Irregular; latest edition May 1979. **Advertising accepted.** **Price:** $35.00, plus $2.75 shipping (ISSN 0148-5660).

Mass Entertainment Industry Buyers Guide *See* **Managing the Leisure Facility—Buyers Guide Issue**

★893★
MASS TRANSIT—BUYER'S GUIDE ISSUE
Mass Transit
555 National Press Building   Phone: (202) 638-0330
Washington, DC 20045
Covers: Over 350 manufacturers and distributors serving the mass transit industry. **Entries include:** Company name, address, phone, names and titles of key personnel, products or services. **Arrangement:** Alphabetical. **Indexes:** Product. **Frequency:** Annual, January; first edition 1979. **Editor:** C. Carrol Carter, Publisher and Editor. **Advertising accepted.** Circulation 19,500. **Price:** $2.00 (current edition); $2.50 (1980 edition).

★894★
MASS TRANSIT—GUIDE TO URBAN TRANSPORTATION CONSULTANTS ISSUE
Mass Transit
555 National Press Building   Phone: (202) 638-0330
Washington, DC 20045
Publication includes: Over 150 urban transportation architects, designers, engineers, planners, and other specialists serving the urban transportation industry. **Entries include:** Company name, address, phone; name, title, and phone of person in charge of urban

transportation; services offered. **Arrangement:** Alphabetical. **Frequency:** Annual, August. **Editor:** C. Carroll Carter, Publisher and Editor. **Advertising accepted.** Circulation 19,500. **Price:** $2.50.

★895★
MASSACHUSETTS DIRECTORY OF MANUFACTURERS
Commerce Register, Inc.
213 First Street   Phone: (201) 445-3000
Hohokus, NJ 07423
Covers: 8,500 industrial firms with five or more employees. **Entries include:** Company name, address, phone, names of principal executives, product descriptions, SIC codes, plant size, number of employees, sales, banking affiliation, attorneys, auditors. **Arrangement:** Geographical. **Indexes:** Company name, SIC. **Pages** (approx.): 400. **Frequency:** Annual, June; first edition June 1979. **Advertising accepted.** Circulation 2,500. **Price:** $49.50, plus 95¢ shipping.

★896★
MASSACHUSETTS RETAIL LIQUOR LICENSEE DIRECTORY
New England Beverage Publications
Bodwell Street   Phone: (617) 471-7750
Avon, MA 02322
Covers: All retail, wholesale, importer, and broker liquor licenses in Massachusetts. **Arrangement:** Alphabetical. **Indexes:** Geographical. **Pages** (approx.): 120. **Frequency:** Annual, spring. **Editor:** Coleman A. Goldberg. **Advertising accepted.** **Price:** $70.00 (1979 edition); $95.00 (1980 edition).

★897★
MASSACHUSETTS STATE INDUSTRIAL DIRECTORY
State Industrial Directories Corporation
Two Penn Plaza   Phone: (212) 564-0340
New York, NY 10001
Number of listings: About 10,000. **Entries include:** Company name, address, phone, names of key executives, number of employees, plant size, 4-digit SIC code, products, whether firm imports or exports, and whether firms have research facilities. **Arrangement:** Geographical. **Indexes:** Alphabetical, product (includes mailing address and phone for each firm). **Pages** (approx.): 360. **Frequency:** Annual, June. **Advertising accepted.** **Price:** $40.00, plus $2.75 shipping (ISSN 0148-7558).

★898★
MATERIAL HANDLING ENGINEERING HANDBOOK & DIRECTORY
Penton/IPC
614 Superior Avenue, West   Phone: (216) 696-0300
Cleveland, OH 44113
Covers: About 1,600 manufacturers and several thousand distributors of materials handling equipment and protective packaging machinery and supplies. **Entries include:** Name of company, address, phone. Some distributor listings show products handled. **Arrangement:** Manufacturers are alphabetical, distributors are geographical. **Indexes:** Product, trade name. **Pages** (approx.): 600. **Frequency:** Biennial in December of even years. **Editor:** Bernard Knill, Executive Editor. **Advertising accepted.** Circulation 24,000. **Price:** $25.00, plus $2.00 shipping.

★899★
MATERIAL HANDLING INSTITUTE—PRODUCT DIRECTORY
Material Handling Institute
1326 Freeport Road
Pittsburgh, PA 15238
Covers: About 360 member manufacturers of material handling equipment and systems. **Entries include:** Company name, address, phone, contact person, and products. **Arrangement:** Alphabetical. **Indexes:** Product. **Pages** (approx.): 30. **Frequency:** Annual. **Price:** Free.

★900★

MATERIAL HANDLING INSTITUTE—SPEAKERS BUREAU
Material Handling Institute
1326 Freeport Road   Phone: (412) 782-1624
Pittsburgh, PA 15238
Covers: About 160 companies which are members of the Material
Handling Institute, and 60 universities and colleges, with staff
members able to speak on various aspects of materials handling.
Entries include: Company or institution name, address, name and title
of contact, advance notification required, geographic limitations, and
topic or subject; listings also note fees required. **Arrangement:** By
type of company. **Pages** (approx.): 20. **Frequency:** Irregular; new
edition expected January 1980. **Price:** Free.

★901★

MATERIALS ENGINEERING—MATERIAL SELECTORS ISSUE
Penton/IPC Inc.
1111 Chester Avenue   Phone: (216) 696-7000
Cleveland, OH 44114
Covers: 700 manufacturers of materials (steels, metals, plastics,
rubber, ceramics, glass, fibers), parts and forms, finishes, and joining
materials used in production or manufacturing plants. **Entries include:**
Company name, address, phone. **Arrangement:** By product. **Indexes:**
Product. **Pages** (approx.): 330. **Frequency:** Annual, December.
Editor: Robert Stedfeld. **Advertising accepted.** Circulation 60,500.
Price: $10.00.

Materials Performance Buyer's Guide *See* **Corrosion Engineering
     Buyers Guide**

★902★

**MECHANICAL CONTRACTORS ASSOCIATION OF AMERICA—
     MEMBERSHIP DIRECTORY**
Mechanical Contractors Association of America
5530 Wisconsin Avenue, N. W., Suite 750   Phone: (301) 654-7960
Washington, DC 20015
Covers: 1,800 contractors in the piping systems industry who install
piping and related equipment for heating and cooling systems. Also
includes list of state and local associations. **Entries include:** Company
name, address, phone, and names of principal executives.
Arrangement: Geographical. **Indexes:** Alphabetical. **Frequency:**
Annual, February. **Editor:** Thelma Mrazek, Communications
Coordinator. **Advertising accepted.** Circulation 2,500. **Price:** $3.00
(1980 edition); available to members and advertisers only.

★903★

MEDIA [YEAR] [Illinois]
Midwest Newsclip Inc.
360 N. Michigan Avenue, Suite 700   Phone: (312) 263-4065
Chicago, IL 60601
Covers: Newspapers, magazines, and radio and television stations
located in or serving Illinois. **Entries include:** For print media - Name
of publication, address, phone, names of publisher and editors,
deadlines, photo requirements, publication dates, circulation areas and
figures, advertising rates. For radio and television stations - Address,
phone, names of general manager and news director, station format,
wire services used, newscast times, interview shows offered, names
of producers and other contacts, prime time advertising rates,
broadcast areas and hours. **Arrangement:** By type of medium, then
geographical. **Frequency:** Approximately annual; new edition expected
spring 1980. **Editor:** Jeff Hill. **Price:** $25.00 (current edition);
$45.00 (1980 edition); postpaid.

★904★

MEDIA DECISIONS—DIRECTORY OF TOP 200 BRANDS ISSUE
Decisions Publications, Inc.
342 Madison Avenue   Phone: (212) 953-1888
New York, NY 10017
Covers: Companies (such as Sears), individual product lines (Jell-O
desserts), and products (Charmin bathroom tissue) which were leading
advertisers in the preceding year. Leaders spent $8.5 million per year

or more. **Entries include:** Brand, company, media categories used and
amounts spent, names of company marketing/brand management
personnel, names of company's advertising agencies and executives
handling accounts, and brief note on company or product strategy,
budget, etc. **Arrangement:** Rank order. **Indexes:** Alphabetical. **Pages**
(approx.): 60. **Frequency:** Annual, July. **Advertising accepted.**
Circulation 25,500. **Price:** $3.00.

★905★

MEDIA DIRECTORY [OF] SAN DIEGO COUNTY [California]
San Diego Chamber of Commerce
233 A Street, Suite 300   Phone: (714) 232-0124
San Diego, CA 92101
Covers: San Diego county newspapers, magazines, news bureaus,
radio and television stations. **Entries include:** For publications - Name
of publication, address, names of executives, phone. For radio and
television stations - Call letters, frequency, address, mailing address,
names of executives, phone. **Arrangement:** By type of media. **Pages**
(approx.): 20. **Frequency:** Annual, May. **Editor:** Roger L. Conlee,
Director of Communications. **Price:** $4.00 (current and 1980
editions).

★906★

MEDIA FAX [Advertising, Atlanta, Georgia]
Terminus Media, Inc.
1819 Peachtree Road, N. W.   Phone: (404) 351-8351
Atlanta, GA 30309
Covers: Direct marketing firms, outdoor advertising firms,
newspapers, periodicals, radio and television stations involved in mass
media advertising in Atlanta. Includes list of advertising agencies and
other professionals. Also lists regional markets for newspapers,
outdoor firms, and periodicals. **Entries include:** Company name,
address, phone, and other pertinent data depending on medium (rates,
circulation figures, etc.). **Arrangement:** By medium. **Indexes:**
Company. **Pages** (approx.): 150. **Frequency:** Semiannual, March and
September. **Editor:** Hal Butts, Jr. **Advertising accepted.** Circulation
500. **Price:** $35.00 per year; no single issue sales.

Meeting Planner's Guide to Greater Boston *See* **Greater Boston
     Convention & Meeting Planner's Guide**

★907★

**MEETINGS AND CONVENTIONS—GAVEL ANNUAL
     INTERNATIONAL DIRECTORY ISSUE**
Ziff-Davis Publishing Company
One Park Avenue   Phone: (212) 725-3737
New York, NY 10016
Covers: Over 3,000 convention halls, convention bureaus, and hotels,
primarily in the United States, suitable for large meetings; suppliers of
convention services; speakers; cruise lines and theme parks. **Entries
include:** Facility listings show name, address, phone, sales contact,
total number of guest rooms and meeting rooms, largest group
accomodated, etc. Speaker listings show name, address of booking
contact, subjects and types of presentation, etc. Other listings have
similar detail. **Arrangement:** Geographical. **Indexes:** Halls, hotels.
Pages (approx.): 550. **Frequency:** Annual, March. **Editor:** Judith
Sawyer, Editor, Gavel/Special Projects. **Advertising accepted.**
Circulation 73,500. **Price:** $5.00 (1979 edition); $5.00 (tentative,
1980 edition).

**Membership Directory & Buyers Guide of Members of SPI
     [Plastics industry]** *See* **Society of the Plastics Industry—
     Membership...**

★908★

MEMPHIS MINORITY PURCHASING GUIDE [Tennessee]
Memphis Regional Purchasing Council
Box 224   Phone: (901) 523-2322
Memphis, TN 38101
Covers: About 200 firms offering professional, commercial,
industrial, and consumer products and services. **Entries include:**

Company name, address, phone, name of contact, SIC number, number of employees, date established, brief description of company history and activities. **Arrangement:** Classified. **Indexes:** Company. **Pages** (approx.): 60. **Frequency:** Irregular; new edition expected January 1980. **Price:** $5.00 (1980 edition).

★909★
MENNONITE BUSINESS AND PROFESSIONAL PEOPLE'S DIRECTORY
Mennonite Industry and Business Associates
2000 S. 15th Street, Walnut Court, D4-2   Phone: (219) 533-0979
Goshen, IN 46526
Covers: 7,500 Mennonite business, professional, and management people in United States and Canada. **Entries include:** Name, address, code indicating type of business. **Arrangement:** Geographical and by vocation; identical information in each part. **Pages** (approx.): 130. **Frequency:** Biennial, summer of even years. **Editor:** J. J. Hostetler. **Price:** $12.50 (current and 1980 editions).

Men's & Boys' Wear Buyers *See* Salesman's Guide Nationwide Directory: Men's & Boys' Wear Buyers [Excluding New York City metro area]

★910★
MEN'S WEAR—APPAREL BLUE BOOK DIRECTORY OF MEN'S AND BOYS' WEAR FIRMS ISSUE
Fairchild Publications, Division
Capital Cities Media, Inc.
7 E. 12th Street   Phone: (212) 741-4400
New York, NY 10003
Covers: Manufacturers of sportswear, accessories (including toiletries and gifts), fiber and fabric, footwear, and other men's and boys' apparel and materials. **Entries include:** Company name, address, phone. **Arrangement:** By type of article (belt, neckwear, etc.). **Indexes:** Brand name. **Frequency:** Annual, December. **Advertising accepted. Price:** $4.95.

★911★
MERCEDES-BENZ DIRECTORY OF DIESEL FUEL STATIONS
Mercedes-Benz of North America
Box 350
Montvale, NJ 07645
Covers: 13,100 diesel fuel stations in the United States and Canada. **Entries include:** Station name, address or location. **Arrangement:** Geographical. **Frequency:** Irregular. **Price:** $2.00.

★912★
MERCHANT SHIPS: NEWBUILDINGS
Nichols Publishing Company
Box 96   Phone: (212) 580-8079
New York, NY 10024
Covers: 1,500 ships constructed during preceding year which are larger than 1,000 gross registered tons; worldwide. **Entries include:** Vessel name, flag, type of vessel, gross and deadweight tonnage, dimensions, horsepower, maximum draft, number of screws, machinery, service speed, owners, builder, yard number. **Indexes:** Yard productions. **Pages** (approx.): 260. **Frequency:** Latest edition October 1977 (1976 construction). **Editor:** D. T. Hornsby. **Price:** $14.50, postpaid, payment with order.

★913★
MERCHANT VESSELS OF THE UNITED STATES (INCLUDING YACHTS)
United States Coast Guard
Transportation Department
400 Seventh Street, S. W.   Phone: (202) 426-2304
Washington, DC 20590
Covers: Merchant vessels and yachts over 75 feet under United States registration. **Entries include:** Vessel name and number, official register number, description, home port, owner name, address, tonnage, length, and type of construction. **Arrangement:** By type of

vessel. **Pages** (approx.): 2,600 (two volumes). **Frequency:** Irregular; latest edition 1978. **Price:** $26.50, for base volumes only (S/N 050-012-00148-1). **Send orders to:** Government Printing Office, Washington, DC 20402.

★914★
MESSENGER/COURIER INTERCITY ROUTING GUIDE
American Package Express Carriers Association
1616 P Street, N. W.   Phone: (202) 797-5363
Washington, DC 20036
Covers: Motor carriers which provide expedited transportation of small shipments between cities. Publication consists of geographical list of firms, with addresses, phones. **Frequency:** Latest edition September 1979. **Price:** Free.

★915★
METAL DISTRIBUTION
Fairchild Publications, Division
Capital Cities Media, Inc.
7 E. 12th Street   Phone: (212) 741-4420
New York, NY 10003
Covers: Producers of commercial and industrial metals and metal products; manufacturers of metal processing and handling equipment; and member firms of the following associations: Steel Service Center Institute, Canadian Steel Service Centre, National Association of Aluminum Distributors, Copper & Brass Servicenter Association, and Association of Steel Distributors. **Entries include:** Company name, address, phone. **Arrangement:** Producers and manufacturers are alphabetical, membership lists are geographical. **Indexes:** Product. **Frequency:** Annual, January. **Editor:** Joseph Marino. **Advertising accepted.** Circulation 14,000. **Former title:** Metal/Center News - Directory of Metal Producers Issue (1978). **Price:** $10.00 (current and 1980 editions).

★916★
METAL FINISHING—GUIDEBOOK AND DIRECTORY ISSUE
Metals and Plastics Publications, Inc.
One University Plaza   Phone: (201) 487-3700
Hackensack, NJ 07601
Publication includes: List of manufacturers and suppliers serving captive and contract metal and plastic finishing shops. **Entries include:** Company name, address, phone, products. **Arrangement:** Alphabetical. **Indexes:** Product, trade name. **Frequency:** Annual, December. **Editor:** Palmer H. Langdon, President. **Advertising accepted.** Circulation 15,000. **Price:** $7.25.

★917★
METAL POWDER PRODUCERS AND SUPPLIERS DIRECTORY INTERNATIONAL
Metal Powder Industries Federation
Box 2054   Phone: (609) 799-3300
Princeton, NJ 08540
Covers: About 60 producers and suppliers of metal powders who belong to Metal Powder Producers Association or Refractory Metals Association, which are component associations of the federation. **Entries include:** Company name, address, phone, code number indicating metals processes. **Arrangement:** By member associations; overseas listing geographical. **Pages** (approx.): 10. **Frequency:** Irregular; latest edition 1979. **Editor:** V. L. Sears. **Price:** Free.

Metal Powder Producers Association—Membership Directory *See* Metal Powder Producers and Suppliers Directory International

★918★
METAL PROGRESS—HEAT TREATING BUYERS GUIDE AND DIRECTORY ISSUE
American Society for Metals
                              Phone: (216) 338-5151
Metals Park, OH
Covers: 500 manufacturers of equipment and supplies for heat

treating industry and 400 suppliers of commercial heat treating services. **Entries include:** Company name, address, phone, list of products or services. **Arrangement:** Alphabetical within "Equipment and Supplies" and "Commercial Services" sections. **Indexes:** Product (with phone and location). **Pages** (approx.): 130. **Frequency:** Annual, November. **Editor:** Darlene Hannan. **Advertising accepted.** Circulation 47,000. **Price:** $10.00.

★919★
METAL STATISTICS
Fairchild Publications, Division
Capital Cities Media, Inc.
7 E. 12th Street   Phone: (212) 741-4426
New York, NY 10003
Publication includes: Two lists ("Where to Buy" and "Where to Sell") of firms which sell precious, ferrous and nonferrous metals, ores, finished products, alloys, and equipment and services of use in metal industries, as well as firms which purchase scrap. Listings are paid. **Entries include:** Company name, address, phone, contact person, products and services appear in advertisements. **Arrangement:** Alphabetical. **Pages** (approx.): 400. **Frequency:** Annual, June. **Advertising accepted.** **Price:** $35.00, plus $1.50 shipping.

Metal/Center News—Directory of Metal Producers Issue *See* Metal Distribution

★920★
METRO ATLANTA PUBLICITY OUTLETS AND MEDIA DIRECTORY
Metro Atlanta Publicity Outlets and Media Directory
Box 54105   Phone: (404) 892-4317
Atlanta, GA 30308
Covers: 400 publicity outlets (newspapers, magazines, radio and television stations, etc.) in 15-county area of Atlanta, Georgia (SIC 2711, 2721, 4832, 4833, 7351, 7392, 7824). **Entries include:** Company name, address, phone. **Arrangement:** By type of outlet. **Pages** (approx.): 30. **Frequency:** Annual, fall. **Editor:** Elaine Perry. **Advertising accepted.** **Price:** $49.50.

★921★
METRO CALIFORNIA MEDIA
Public Relations Plus, Inc.
Box 327   Phone: (203) 868-0200
Washington Depot, CT 06794
Covers: Newspapers, radio and television stations, magazines, and other media in 19 metropolitan areas of California. **Entries include:** Medium name, address, phone, names of editors and creative staff, with titles or indication of assignments. **Frequency:** Annual. **Editor:** Harold D. Hansen. **Former title:** California Publicity Outlets (1978). **Price:** $49.50 (current and 1980 editions).

★922★
MICHIGAN CONTRACTOR & BUILDER—BUYER'S GUIDE AND DIRECTORY ISSUE
Contractor Publishing Company
1629 W. Lafayette Boulevard   Phone: (313) 962-3337
Detroit, MI 48216
Publication includes: List of manufacturers and distributors of construction equipment and products. **Entries include:** Company name, address, phone. **Arrangement:** Alphabetical. **Indexes:** Product. **Frequency:** Annual, March. **Advertising accepted.** Circulation 3,400. **Price:** $10.00.

★923★
MICHIGAN OFFICE OF MINORITY BUSINESS ENTERPRISES— DIRECTORY
Office of Economic Development
Minority Business Division
Michigan Department of Commerce
Box 30225   Phone: (517) 373-8340
Lansing, MI 48909
Covers: About 1,000 minority contractors and commercial and industrial firms. **Entries include:** Company name, address, name of contact, phone, SIC code. **Arrangement:** Geographical. **Indexes:** SIC, product, company name. **Frequency:** Biennial, summer of odd years. **Price:** Free.

★924★
MICHIGAN STATE INDUSTRIAL DIRECTORY
State Industrial Directories Corporation
Two Penn Plaza   Phone: (212) 564-0340
New York, NY 10001
Number of listings: 14,500. **Entries include:** Company name, address, phone, names of key executives, number of employees, plant size, 4-digit SIC code, products, whether firm imports or exports, and whether firm has research facilities. **Arrangement:** Geographical. **Indexes:** Alphabetical, product (includes mailing address and phone for each firm). **Frequency:** Not established; first edition October 1979. **Advertising accepted.** **Price:** $55.00.

★925★
MICROWAVE JOURNAL—MICROWAVE ENGINEER'S HANDBOOK AND BUYERS' GUIDE ISSUE
Horizon House
610 Washington Street   Phone: (617) 326-8220
Dedham, MA 02026
Publication includes: Over 150 manufacturers of microwave electronics products and equipment. **Entries include:** Company name, address, phone, and name of key executive; sales outlets or representatives, and their addresses and phone numbers are also included for advertisers only. **Arrangement:** Alphabetical. **Indexes:** Product (with phone number of manufacturer and frequency range of product). **Pages** (approx.): 150. **Frequency:** Irregular; latest edition 1976. **Price:** $10.00.

★926★
MICROWAVE PRODUCT DATA DIRECTORY
Hayden Publishing Company, Inc.
50 Essex Street   Phone: (201) 843-0550
Rochelle Park, NJ 07662
Covers: About 4,500 United States and Canadian manufacturers of microwave equipment components, including antennas and accessories, materials and accessories, passive components, semiconductors, solid-state components, systems and subsystems, test instruments and equipment, and tubes and amplifiers. **Entries include:** Company name, address, phone, names of principal executives and list of sales offices are given in advertisers' listings. **Arrangement:** Alphabetical. **Indexes:** Product. **Pages** (approx.): 930. **Frequency:** Annual, August. **Editor:** Howard Bierman, Publisher. **Advertising accepted.** Circulation 45,000. **Price:** $18.00.

★927★
MID-AMERICA COMMERCE & INDUSTRY—BUYER'S GUIDE ISSUE
MACI, Inc.
1824 Cheyenne Road   Phone: (913) 272-5280
Topeka, KS 66604
Covers: About 100 companies supplying materials, equipment, and services to industries in Missouri, Kansas, Oklahoma, Nebraska, and parts of other midwestern states. Limited to advertisers. **Entries include:** All listings include company name, address, phone; some listings give products, services, and names of personnel. **Arrangement:** By product. **Frequency:** Annual, September. **Editor:** Ray Lippe, Editor and Publisher. **Advertising accepted.** Circulation 7,000. **Price:** $5.00.

★928★

MID-AMERICA LUMBERMENS ASSOCIATION—MEMBERSHIP DIRECTORY

Mid-America Lumbermens Association

4901 Main Street   Phone: (816) 931-2102

Kansas City, MO 64112

Covers: Lumber and building material dealers in Arkansas, Kansas, Missouri, Nebraska, Oklahoma who are members. **Entries include:** Company name, address, phone, name of contact. **Arrangement:** Geographical. **Frequency:** Annual. **Price:** $15.00. (Not verified)

★929★

MID-ATLANTIC ELECTRICAL BLUE BOOK

Gleason Publishing Company, Inc.

Box 515   Phone: (617) 545-5311

Scituate, MA 02066

Covers: Electrical manufacturers, electrical utility companies, municipal inspectors, hospitals, universities and colleges, architectural and engineering firms, electrical product distributors, manufacturers' representatives, and members of local trade associations; coverage limited to eastern Maryland, New York, New Jersey, and Delaware. **Entries include:** Company name, address, phone; most listings also include name of key executive, representative, or buyer. Representatives' listings include lines handled. **Arrangement:** By type of company, then geographical. **Indexes:** Product. **Pages** (approx.): 240. **Frequency:** Annual, June. **Advertising accepted.** Circulation 19,000. **Price:** $9.50 (1980 edition).

Middle Market Directory *See* Million Dollar Directory
    [Corporations, utilities, etc.]

★930★

MIDEAST BUSINESS GUIDE

News Circle Publishing Company

2007 Wilshire Boulevard, Suite 900   Phone: (213) 483-5111

Los Angeles, CA 90057

Covers: 4,000 businesses, manufacturing firms, trade organizations, publishers, government agencies, diplomatic missions, and others located in the Middle East or in the United States and concerned with trade in the Arab countries. **Entries include:** Company or organization name, address, phone. **Arrangement:** Middle Eastern companies and organizations are listed by service or area of interest; United States organizations are listed separately. **Indexes:** Alphabetical. **Pages** (approx.): 320. **Frequency:** Irregular; latest edition 1977; new edition expected 1980. **Editor:** Joseph R. Haiek. **Advertising accepted.** Circulation 5,000. **Price:** $12.00 (current and 1980 editions). **Also includes:** Economic review of the Middle East and North Africa including procedures for conducting business and reference information on each of the countries.

★931★

MID-WEST CONTRACTOR—CONSTRUCTION EQUIPMENT DIRECTORY ISSUE

Mid-West Records, Inc.

934 Wyandotte   Phone: (816) 842-2902

Kansas City, MO 64141

Covers: Construction equipment manufacturers and distributors. **Entries include:** Company name, address, phone, names and titles of executives, trade and brand names, and products or services. **Pages** (approx.): 200. **Frequency:** Annual, March. **Editor:** Gilbert E. Mulley, Executive Director. **Advertising accepted.** Circulation 8,500. **Price:** $10.00.

Midwest Contractor's Construction Directory *See* Mid-West
    Contractor—Construction Equipment Directory Issue

★932★

MIDWEST DIRECTORY OF COMPUTER INSTALLATIONS

C. I. Publications

233 Peachtree Street, N. E., Suite 2010   Phone: (404) 586-0143

Atlanta, GA 30303

Covers: About 2,500 data processing installations in twelve Midwestern states. **Entries include:** Company name, address, phone, name and title of contact, computer equipment configuration, languages used, applications, computer time availabilities, number of employees. **Arrangement:** Geographical. **Indexes:** Industry, equipment. **Pages** (approx.): 600. **Frequency:** Annual; first edition November 1979. **Editor:** Kimberly K. Taylor. **Advertising accepted.** **Price:** $125.00.

Midwest Graphic Arts Trade Directory and Buyers Guide *See*
    Graphic Arts Green Book Trade Directory and Register

★933★

MID-WEST PIEDMONT AREA BUSINESS DEVELOPMENT ORGANIZATION—MINORITY BUSINESS DIRECTORY [North Carolina]

Mid-West Piedmont Area Business Development Organization

623 Waughtown Street   Phone: (919) 784-7970

Winston-Salem, NC 27107

Covers: More than 600 firms in Forsyth County and the surrounding 14 counties which offer professional, commercial, industrial, and consumer products and services. **Entries include:** Company name, address, phone, name of contact, product or service, number of employees. **Arrangement:** By line of business. **Pages** (approx.): 75. **Frequency:** Not established; first edition in this format, July 1978; latest edition November 1979. **Price:** Free.

★934★

MIDWEST PURCHASING—BUYERS' GUIDE ISSUE

Bashian Publishing, Inc.

1501 Euclid Avenue   Phone: (216) 621-2858

Cleveland, OH 44115

Publication includes: Lists of manufacturers of products and suppliers of services who have advertised in "Midwest Purchasing" during the preceding twelve months. **Entries include:** Company name, address, phone. **Arrangement:** Classified by product or service. **Frequency:** Annual, July. **Editor:** Lynne A. Wallace. **Advertising accepted.** Circulation 6,800. **Price:** Included in subscription, $30.00 per year. **Other information:** Sponsored by the Purchasing Management Association of Cleveland.

★935★

MIDWEST PURCHASING—ROSTER ISSUE

Bashian Publishing, Inc.

1501 Euclid Avenue   Phone: (216) 621-2858

Cleveland, OH 44115

Covers: Almost 3,000 members of individual chapters of the National Association of Purchasing Management located in Ohio, western Pennsylvania, western New York, northern West Virginia, and northern Kentucky. **Entries include:** Name, company with which affiliated, address. **Arrangement:** By chapter (primarily cities). **Pages** (approx.): 95. **Frequency:** Annual, April. **Editor:** Lynne A. Wallace, Assistant Publisher. **Advertising accepted.** Circulation 6,900. **Price:** $25.00. **Other information:** Published for the Purchasing Management Association of Cleveland.

Military Specifications and Sources *See* Qualified Products List
    and Sources

★936★

MILLION DOLLAR DIRECTORY [Corporations, utilities, etc.]

Dun & Bradstreet, Inc.

99 Church Street

New York, NY 10007

Covers: Businesses with a net worth of $1 million or more, including industrial corporations, utilities, transportation companies, banks and trust companies, stock brokers, mutual and stock insurance companies, wholesalers, retailers, and domestic subsidiaries of foreign corporations. **Entries include:** Company name, state of incorporation, address, phone, annual sales, number of employees, company ticker symbol on stock exchange, stock exchange abbreviation, division names and functions, SIC, names, titles, and functions of principal executives. **Arrangement:** Alphabetical. **Indexes:** Geographical (with address and SIC), business by SIC (with address). **Pages** (approx.): 5,000. **Frequency:** Annual, January. **Price:** $195.00 per year (lease basis; 1980 edition). **Other information:** Companion volume is "Middle Market Directory," which provides similar information on firms with a net worth of $500,000 to a million dollars. 1980 lease price is $165.00 per year.

★937★
MINICOMPUTER REVIEW
GML Corporation
594 Marrett Road   Phone: (617) 861-0515
Lexington, MA 02173
Publication includes: Directory of minicomputer manufacturers. **Entries include:** Corporate name and address, executive names and titles,· date established, number of employees, sales revenue, net earnings, office locations, hardware products, number of units sold, software support. **Arrangement:** Alphabetical. **Frequency:** Three times yearly. **Price:** $95.00 per year; add $25.00 for overseas postage. **Other information:** Principal content of publication is specification sheets on the companies' minicomputers, mostly under $50,000.

Minneapolis/St. Paul Directory of Minority Enterprises *See* Minnesota Directory of Minority Enterprises

★938★
MINNESOTA DIRECTORY OF MANUFACTURERS
Minnesota Department of Economic Development
480 Cedar Street   Phone: (612) 296-3871
St. Paul, MN 55101
Number of listings: 5,500. **Entries include:** Company name, address, name of principal executive, phone, type of organization (cooperative, partnership, etc.), area served, number of employees, date established, SIC numbers, list of products. **Arrangement:** Geographical. **Indexes:** Alphabetical, SIC. **Pages** (approx.): 425. **Frequency:** Biennial, early in odd years. **Price:** $20.00, postpaid. **Send orders to:** Documents Section, Department of Administration, 140 Centennial Office Building, St. Paul, Minnesota 55155. **Other information:** State Industrial Directories Corp. catalog lists this publication as, "Minnesota Manufacturers Directory" ($35.00).

★939★
MINNESOTA DIRECTORY OF MINORITY ENTERPRISES
Metropolitan Economic Development Association
2021 E. Hennepin Street, Suite 370   Phone: (612) 378-0361
Minneapolis, MN 55413
Covers: Over 400 industry- and consumer-serving businesses. **Entries include:** Company name, address, phone number, SIC numbers; most listings include name of owner or president and business description. Some listings also include year established, customer names, number of employees, equipment, square feet, financial keys. **Arrangement:** Two sections - industry-serving businesses and consumer-serving businesses, then alphabetical by line of business. **Indexes:** Line of business, company name. **Pages** (approx.): 30. **Frequency:** Annual, September. **Former title:** Minneapolis/St. Paul Directory of Minority Enterprises. **Price:** Free. **Other information:** Published in cooperation with Minnesota Department of Economic Development, 480 Cedar St., St. Paul, MN 55101.

★940★
MINNESOTA INTERNATIONAL TRADE DIRECTORY
International Trade Division
Minnesota Dept. of Economic Development
480 Cedar Street   Phone: (612) 296-5023
St. Paul, MN 55101
Covers: Over 650 Minnesota firms which export. **Entries include:** Company name, address, phone, name and title of chief executive, type of ownership, year established, number of employees, extent of territory, products. **Arrangement:** By SIC number. **Indexes:** Product (includes company name with address, phone, chief executive). **Pages** (approx.): 60. **Frequency:** Latest edition April 1979. **Price:** Free.

Minnesota Manufacturers Directory *See* Minnesota Directory of Manufacturers

★941★
MINORITY BUSINESS AND PROFESSIONAL SERVICES DIRECTORY [Detroit]
Community and Economic Development Department
City of Detroit
150 Michigan Avenue   Phone: (313) 224-6350
Detroit, MI 48226
Covers: 1,500 firms offering professional, commercial, industrial, and consumer products and services. **Entries include:** Company name, address, phone, contact, date established, number of employees. **Arrangement:** Classified. **Indexes:** Company. **Pages** (approx.): 100. **Frequency:** Latest edition 1977. **Price:** Free.

★942★
MINORITY BUSINESS CAPABILITIES SURVEY [Pennsylvania]
Bureau of Minority Business Development
Pennsylvania Department of Commerce
406 South Office   Phone: (717) 787-5631
Harrisburg, PA 17120
Covers: About 400 firms offering professional, commercial, and industrial products and services. **Entries include:** Company name, address, phone, name of contact, number of employees, date of information in listing, description of product or service, capability number, vendor number. **Arrangement:** Alphabetical. **Indexes:** Capability number. **Pages** (approx.): 150. **Frequency:** Irregular; latest edition April 1977; next edition planned for early 1979. (Not verified)

★943★
MINORITY BUSINESS DIRECTORY: DENVER-BOULDER METRO AREA [Colorado]
Colorado Office of Planning and Budget
State Capitol Building, Suite 124   Phone: (303) 759-1000
Denver, CO 80203
Covers: About 1,100 firms offering professional, commercial, and industrial products and services. **Entries include:** Company name, address, phone, contact, list of products or services. **Arrangement:** Classified. **Pages** (approx.): 150. **Frequency:** Irregular; latest November 1977. **Editors:** Audrey Oliver and Wes Martin. **Price:** Free. (Not verified)

Minority Business Directory—Charlotte/Mecklenburg *See* Minority Business Directory—Mecklenburg, Gaston & Union Counties [North Carolina]

★944★
MINORITY BUSINESS DIRECTORY—MECKLENBURG, GASTON & UNION COUNTIES [North Carolina]
Charlotte Business Resource Center
502 Commerce Center
129 W. Trade Street   Phone: (704) 332-8578
Charlotte, NC 28202
Covers: About 555 firms offering primarily consumer and commercial products and services. **Entries include:** Firm name, address, phone. **Arrangement:** Classified. **Pages** (approx.): 40. **Frequency:** Annual.

Former title: Minority Business Directory - Charlotte/Mecklenburg. **Price:** Free.

Minority Business Directory [American Indians, Oklahoma] *See* Directory of Indian Business Enterprises—Muskogee Area [Oklahoma]

★945★
MINORITY BUSINESS DIRECTORY [Arkansas]
Arkansas Business Development Corporation
Union Bank Building, Suite 1055   Phone: (501) 376-0703
Little Rock, AR 72203
Covers: About 1,000 firms in Arkansas offering commercial, industrial, and consumer products and services. **Entries include:** Company name, address, phone, number of employees, name of contact. **Arrangement:** By regions of state, then by line of business. **Pages** (approx.): 50. **Frequency:** Irregular; latest edition August 1979. **Price:** Free.

★946★
MINORITY BUSINESS DIRECTORY [Bergen County, NJ]
Urban League for Bergen County
106 W. Palisade Avenue   Phone: (201) 568-4988
Englewood, NJ 07631
Frequency: Annual; latest edition December 1977. **Price:** Free.

★947★
MINORITY BUSINESS DIRECTORY [New Haven, Connecticut]
Greater New Haven Business and Professional Association
226 Dixwell Avenue   Phone: (203) 776-0272
New Haven, CT 06511
Covers: 250 firms offering professional, commercial, industrial, and consumer products and services. **Entries include:** Company name, address, phone, name of owner or manager, SIC number, description of services or products. **Arrangement:** Classified. **Indexes:** Firm name, SIC number. **Pages** (approx.): 80. **Frequency:** Irregular; latest edition 1979. **Editor:** Janice Rashed. **Former title:** Minority Business Development Directory. **Price:** Free.

★948★
MINORITY BUSINESS DIRECTORY [Pittsburgh]
Pittsburgh Regional Minority Purchasing Council
One Oliver Plaza, Suite 3004
Pittsburgh, PA 15222
Covers: About 125 firms offering industrial and commercial products and services. **Entries include:** Company name, address, phone, brief history of firm. **Arrangement:** Classified. **Indexes:** Company. **Frequency:** Irregular; latest edition 1974, with updates. **Price:** Free.

★949★
MINORITY BUSINESS DIRECTORY OF CONTRACTORS, SUBCONTRACTORS AND CONSTRUCTION SUPPLIERS IN THE CHICAGO AREA [Illinois]
Builders Association of Chicago
228 N. La Salle Street   Phone: (312) 372-4480
Chicago, IL 60601
Number of listings: Over 100. **Entries include:** Company name, address, type of business, references. **Arrangement:** Alphabetical. **Indexes:** Service. **Frequency:** Published August 1978. **Price:** Free; distribution limited to Chicago area.

★950★
MINORITY BUSINESS DIRECTORY, ST. PETERSBURG, FLORIDA
St. Petersburg Area Chamber of Commerce
Box 1371   Phone: (813) 821-4069
St. Petersburg, FL 33731
Covers: Minority firms offering professional, commercial, industrial, and consumer products and services. **Arrangement:** Classified by line of business. **Frequency:** Irregular; latest edition September 1979. **Former title:** Directory of Black Businesses.

★951★
MINORITY BUSINESS ENTERPRISE DIRECTORY OF FIRMS IN NORTHERN ILLINOIS, INDIANA, AND WISCONSIN
Defense Contract Administration Services Region, Chicago
Defense Logistics Agency
Defense Department
Box 66475, O'Hare International Airport   Phone: (312) 694-3031
Chicago, IL 60666
Covers: About 300 minority-owned firms offering professional, industrial, and commercial products and services. **Entries include:** Company name, address, phone, name of contact, description of products or services, SIC number. **Arrangement:** Classified. **Indexes:** Alphabetical. **Pages** (approx.): 35. **Frequency:** Latest edition January 1978; new edition expected January 1980. **Price:** Free.

★952★
MINORITY BUSINESS ENTERPRISES [New England]
Defense Contract Administration Services Region
Defense Logistics Agency
Defense Department
666 Summer Street   Phone: (617) 542-6000
Boston, MA 02210
Covers: About 350 firms offering professional, commercial, and industrial services. **Entries include:** Company name, address, phone, contact, list of products or services. **Arrangement:** Alphabetical. **Indexes:** Product/service. **Pages** (approx.): 60. **Frequency:** Annual, fall. **Price:** Free.

Minority Business Enterprises Directory [California] *See* California Minority Business Enterprises Directory

★953★
MINORITY BUSINESS ENTERPRISES IN WASHINGTON STATE
Small Business Division
Washington State Department of Commerce
General Administration Building
Olympia, WA 98504
Covers: More than 500 firms offering professional, commercial, industrial, and consumer products and services. **Entries include:** Company name, address, phone, name of contact, date established, number of employees, list of products or services. **Arrangement:** Classified. **Pages** (approx.): 125. **Frequency:** Irregular; latest edition July 1979. **Price:** Free.

Minority Business Guide [Ohio] *See* Ohio Minority Business Guide

★954★
MINORITY CONSTRUCTION CONTRACTORS IN ARKANSAS
Arkansas Business Development Corporation, Inc.
Union National Bank Building, Suite 1055   Phone: (501) 376-0703
Little Rock, AR 72203
Covers: About 200 minority contracting firms including general contracting, plumbing, electrical, carpentry, masonry and concrete, painting and interior decorating, excavation, trucking, etc. **Entries include:** Name of owner or manager, company name, address, phone, coding to indicate bondable and licensed contractors. **Arrangement:** By area of contracting, then geographical. **Pages** (approx.): 15. **Frequency:** Latest edition January 1979. **Price:** Apply.

★955★
MINORITY CONTRACTORS AND SUPPLIERS DIRECTORY [San Diego, Calif.]
San Diego Business Development Center
3620 30th Street, Suite E   Phone: (714) 291-4631
San Diego, CA 92104
Covers: About 500 minority firms offering products and services to the construction industry. **Entries include:** Company name, address, phone, contact. **Arrangement:** Calssified. **Pages** (approx.): 100. **Frequency:** Irregular; latest edition September 1979. **Price:** $5.00, postpaid.

Minority Enterprises in North Dakota *See* North Dakota Minority
   Enterprises

★956★

MINORITY PURCHASING GUIDE FOR THE LOUISVILLE AREA
   [Kentucky]
Louisville Area Chamber of Commerce
300 W. Liberty Street   Phone: (502) 582-2421
Louisville, KY 40202
Number of listings: 80. **Frequency:** Biennial, fall of even years.
Price: $2.00.

★957★

MINORITY SUPPLIERS IN THE GREATER DETROIT AREA
Inner City Business Improvement Forum
3049 E. Grand Boulevard   Phone: (313) 875-4700
Detroit, MI 48202
Covers: 400 manufacturers and dealers in a wide variety of products,
plus service and construction firms, owned by Blacks, Spanish-
speaking persons, and other minorities. **Entries include:** Company
name, address, phone, names of chief executives, list of products or
services, trade and brand names, and business references.
Arrangement: Classified by products and services. **Indexes:**
Company. **Frequency:** Irregular; latest edition September 1979.
Editor: Linda Darnell Harris, Procurement Analyst. **Price:** Free.

★958★

MINORITY VENDORS DIRECTORY [Houston, Texas]
Houston Regional Minority Purchasing Council
4101 San Jacinto, Suite 204   Phone: (713) 523-4497
Houston, TX 77004
Covers: About 450 firms operating in construction, manufacturing,
and general services, including some out-of-town vendors. **Entries
include:** Name of company, address, phone, name of owner, number of
employees, operating space, length of time in business, business
references, list of major equipment, estimated volume.
Arrangement: By product or service. **Indexes:** Alphabetical, product.
Pages (approx.): 500. **Frequency:** Annual, spring; semiannual
updates. **Editor:** Roy Hollister. **Price:** Available to members only.

★959★

MINORITY VENDORS DIRECTORY OF OREGON
Minority Business Opportunity Committee
C/o Small Business Administration
511 N. W. Broadway, Room 647   Phone: (503) 221-2905
Portland, OR 97204
Number of listings: Over 200. **Entries include:** Company name,
address, phone, name of principal executive, date established, number
of employees, size of contracts preferred, and types of jobs
preferred. **Arrangement:** By SIC number. **Pages** (approx.): 70.
Frequency: Irregular; latest edition October 1979. **Editors:** Erma
O'Neale, Executive Director, and D. Matsuda, Chairperson. **Former
title:** Directory of Minority Business (Oregon). **Price:** Free to
procurement entities only.

★960★

MINORITY-OWNED ENTERPRISES [San Francisco]
Defense Contract Administration Services Management Area
Defense Supply Agency
Defense Department
2155 Mariners Suare Loop
Alameda, CA
Covers: About 900 firms offering professional, commercial, and
industrial products and services. **Entries include:** Company name,
address, phone, name of contact, description of product or service.
Arrangement: Alphabetical. **Indexes:** Product/service. **Pages**
(approx.): 100. **Frequency:** Irregular; latest edition November 1976.
Price: Free. (Not verified)

★961★

MISSISSIPPI INTERNATIONAL TRADE DIRECTORY
Mississippi Marketing Council
2003 Walter Sillers State Office Building   Phone: (601) 354-6707
Jackson, MS 39205
Covers: 395 firms in Mississippi desiring to export their products.
Includes list of Mississippi ports. **Entries include:** Company name,
address, phone, name of executive, list of products, and bank
references. **Arrangement:** By SIC number. **Indexes:** Firms, products.
Pages (approx.): 120. **Frequency:** Irregular; latest edition September
1976; new edition expected July 1980. **Editor:** William A. McGinnis,
Jr., Assistant Marketing Manager. **Price:** $15.00 (current edition);
$10.00 (1980 edition). **Other information:** Directory is multilingual.

★962★

MISSISSIPPI MANUFACTURERS DIRECTORY
Mississippi Research and Development Center
3825 Ridgewood Road   Phone: (601) 982-6414
Jackson, MS
Number of listings: About 2,500. **Entries include:** Company name,
address, phone, names of principal executives, number of employees,
SIC numbers, products, name and location of parent company.
Arrangement: Geographical. **Indexes:** Alphabetical, product, SIC code
with product. **Pages** (approx.): 275. **Frequency:** Annual, usually
December; 1980 edition expected in March. **Editor:** Lorraine Vallado.
Price: $20.00, postpaid, payment with order.

★963★

MISSOURI DIRECTORY OF MANUFACTURING AND MINING
IDC Informative Data Company
3546 Watson Road   Phone: (314) 353-2244
St. Louis, MO 63139
Number of listings: 6,200, covering firms in SIC classifications
1011-1499 in mining and 2011-3999 in manufacturing. **Entries
include:** Company name, address, phone, name of principal executive,
SIC numbers, list of products or services, whether firm exports,
number of employees. **Arrangement:** Geographical. **Indexes:**
Alphabetical, SIC. **Pages** (approx.): 450. **Frequency:** Annual,
February. **Advertising accepted. Price:** $40.00 (1980 edition).

★964★

MOBILE AIR CONDITIONING—INTERNATIONAL BUYERS GUIDE &
   REFERENCE ISSUE
International Mobile Air Conditioning Association
Courtland Street
Lansdale, PA 19446
Covers: Manufacturers and suppliers of air conditioning systems,
parts, and services for cars, boats, trucks, and other vehicles. **Entries
include:** Company name, address, phone, trade and brand names, and
list of products. **Arrangement:** Alphabetical. **Indexes:** Product. **Pages**
(approx.): 150. **Frequency:** Annual, November. **Editor:** S. A. Rodman.
Advertising accepted. Circulation 8,000. **Price:** $10.00.

Mobile and Modular Home Directory *See* Recreational Vehicle
   Directory

Mobile Home Merchandiser—Annual Mobile Home Producers
   Guide Issue *See* Mobile/Manufactured Home Merchandiser—
   Annual Mobile Home Producers..

★965★

MOBILE/MANUFACTURED HOME MERCHANDISER—ANNUAL
   MOBILE HOME PRODUCERS GUIDE ISSUE
RLD Group, Inc.
5225 Old Orchard Road, Suite 7   Phone: (312) 967-0430
Skokie, IL 60077
Covers: About 240 manufacturers of mobile homes, modular homes,
and other types of manufactured housing. **Entries include:** Company
name, address, phone, names of executives, products and locations of
individual plants. **Arrangement:** Alphabetical. **Indexes:** Geographical,
classified by type of home produced, and brand name. **Pages**

(approx.): 120. **Frequency:** Annual, November. **Editor:** Jim Mack. **Advertising accepted.** Circulation 20,000. **Price:** $5.00.

Mobile-Modular Housing—Annual Directory and Buyer's Guide Issue *See* Manufactured Housing Dealer—Annual Directory and Buyer's Guide Issue

★966★
MODERN BULK TRANSPORTER—TANK TRUCK BUYERS GUIDE ISSUE
Sutherland Publications, Inc.
4801 Montgomery Lane   Phone: (301) 654-8802
Washington, DC 20014
Covers: Suppliers of products or services for companies operating tank trucks. **Entries include:** Company name, address, phone, names of executives, trade and brand names. **Pages** (approx.): 100. **Frequency:** Annual, October. **Editor:** John L. Conley. **Advertising accepted.** Circulation 11,000. **Price:** $1.50.

★967★
MODERN CASTING—BUYERS GUIDE ISSUE
American Foundrymen's Society
Golf & Wolf Roads   Phone: (312) 824-0181
Des Plaines, IL 60016
Covers: About 1,700 manufacturers, suppliers, and distributors of foundry and metal casting equipment and products. **Entries include:** Company name, address, phone. **Arrangement:** Alphabetical. **Indexes:** Product. **Frequency:** Annual, November. **Editor:** Jack H. Schaum, Publisher/Editor. **Advertising accepted.** Circulation 27,000. **Price:** $15.00.

★968★
MODERN CONCRETE—BUYER'S GUIDE ISSUE
Pit & Quarry Publications, Inc.
105 W. Adams Street   Phone: (312) 726-7151
Chicago, IL 60603
Publication includes: About 700 manufacturers and suppliers of equipment and materials to the concrete production industry (manufacturers of concrete block, pipe, ready mixed concrete, etc.). **Entries include:** Company name, address, phone. **Arrangement:** Alphabetical. **Indexes:** Product. **Pages** (approx.): 35. **Frequency:** Annual, September. **Editor:** Buren C. Herod. **Advertising accepted.** Circulation 20,000. **Price:** $2.00.

★969★
MODERN GROCER INDUSTRY DIRECTORY OF METRO NEW YORK
Grocers Publishing Company, Inc.
370 Lexington Avenue   Phone: (212) 686-0727
New York, NY 10017
Covers: Grocery store chains and cooperatives and their suppliers, including wholesalers, rack jobbers, bottlers, meat packers, produce dealers, etc. **Entries include:** Company name, address, phone, names of principal executives, trade and brand names and/or indication of product or service. **Arrangement:** Classified by major product or type of business. **Pages** (approx.): 500. **Frequency:** Annual, fall; 1979 edition delayed to January 1980. **Editor:** Howard Ackerman. **Advertising accepted.** **Price:** $27.50 (current edition); $30.00 (1980 edition).

★970★
MODERN INDUSTRIAL ENERGY—ANNUAL DIRECTORY OF ENERGY MANAGEMENT AND CONSERVATION EQUIPMENT ISSUE
Publishing Dynamics, Inc.
209 Dunn Avenue   Phone: (202) 322-7676
Stamford, CT 06905
Covers: About 350 manufacturers of industrial gas-fired and energy-utilization equipment, systems, and related products. **Entries include:** Company name, address, phone, names of contacts, and products or services. **Arrangement:** Alphabetical. **Indexes:** Product. **Pages** (approx.): 50. **Frequency:** Annual, December. **Editor:** Joseph Conlin. **Advertising accepted.** Circulation 20,000. **Former title:** Industrial

Gas - Directory of Gas-Fired & Energy Utilization Equipment and Systems Issue; Industrial Gas and Energy Utilization - Annual Directory of Energy Management and Conservation Equipment Issue (1979). **Price:** $5.00.

★971★
MODERN MACHINE SHOP—NC/CAM GUIDEBOOK ISSUE
Gardner Publications, Inc.
600 Main Street   Phone: (513) 241-5924
Cincinnati, OH 45202
Covers: About 700 manufacturers offering numerical control machine tools and other computer-assisted manufacturing products and services. **Entries include:** Name, address, phone. **Arrangement:** Alphabetical. **Indexes:** Products and services. **Frequency:** Annual, January. **Editor:** Fred W. Vogel, Editor-in-Chief. **Advertising accepted.** Circulation 75,000. **Former title:** Modern Machine Shop NC Guidebook & Directory. **Price:** $5.00 (current and 1980 editions).

★972★
MODERN MATERIALS HANDLING—CASEBOOK AND DIRECTORY ISSUE
Cahners Publishing Company
221 Columbus Avenue   Phone: (617) 536-7780
Boston, MA 02116
Publication includes: Lists of about 1,500 manufacturers of equipment and supplies used in materials handling and engineers consulting in materials handling. **Entries include:** Company name, address, phone. **Arrangement:** Alphabetical. **Indexes:** Trade name, product. **Pages** (approx.): 450. **Frequency:** Annual, June. **Editor:** Miles J. Rowan. **Advertising accepted.** Circulation 95,000. **Price:** $10.00.

★973★
MODERN PACKAGING—ENCYCLOPEDIA AND BUYER'S GUIDE ISSUE
Morgan-Grampian Publishing Company
Two Park Avenue   Phone: (212) 340-9700
New York, NY 10016
Publication includes: About 3,500 manufacturers, consultants, associations, and service organizations supplying packaging products or services. **Entries include:** Company name, address, and phone. **Arrangement:** Alphabetical. **Indexes:** Product. **Frequency:** Annual, December. **Editor:** William C. Simms. **Advertising accepted.** Circulation 60,000. **Price:** $15.00.

★974★
MODERN PLASTICS—ENCYCLOPEDIA ISSUE
McGraw-Hill, Inc.
1221 Avenue of the Americas   Phone: (212) 997-6424
New York, NY 10020
Publication includes: 4,500 plastic processors and converters and suppliers of products and services to the plastics industry in the United States and Canada. **Entries include:** Company name, address, phone, list of products or services. **Arrangement:** Classified by 350 categories of products. **Indexes:** Alphabetical index of companies. **Pages** (approx.): 900. **Frequency:** Annual, October. **Editor:** Joan Agranoff. **Advertising accepted.** **Price:** $25.95. **Other information:** A special 13th issue of "Modern Plastics" magazine.

Modern Plastics Encyclopedia *See* Modern Plastics— Encyclopedia Issue

Modern Railroads—Transit Directory of Products and Supplies Issue *See* Modern Railroads Rail Transit—Suppliers Directory Issue

★975★
MODERN RAILROADS RAIL TRANSIT—SUPPLIERS DIRECTORY ISSUE
Cahners Publishing Company
Five S. Wabash Avenue   Phone: (312) 372-6880
Chicago, IL 60603
Covers: Suppliers of products and services to the rail and rail transit industry (including signaling equipment, data and communication systems, etc.). List of trade associations with committees and executives is also included. **Entries include:** Company name, address, phone, names and titles of key personnel. **Arrangement:** Alphabetical. **Indexes:** Product. **Frequency:** Annual, September. **Advertising accepted.** Circulation 9,500. **Former title:** Modern Railroads - Transit Directory of Products and Supplies Issue. **Price:** $2.00.

★976★
MODERN RECORDING'S BUYER'S GUIDE
Cowan Publishing Corporation
14 Vanderventer Avenue   Phone: (516) 883-5704
Port Washington, NY 11050
Covers: Manufacturers of recording and music equipment, including recorders, amplifiers, studio monitors, synthesizers, etc.; international coverage. **Entries include:** Manufacturer's name, address; product, model number, price, accessories, specifications. **Arrangement:** By product, then alphabetical by company name. **Pages** (approx.): 200. **Frequency:** Annual, winter. **Editor:** Hector G. LaTorre. **Advertising accepted.** Circulation 120,000. **Price:** $2.95.

★977★
MODERN TEXTILES—MANMADE FIBER DESKBOOK ISSUE
Rayon Publishing Corporation
303 Fifth Avenue   Phone: (212) 684-0455
New York, NY 10016
Covers: About 100 producers of manmade textile fibers in the United States. **Entries include:** Company name, address, phone, trade and brand names, type of fiber product. **Arrangement:** Alphabetical. **Indexes:** Trade name. **Frequency:** Annual, March. **Editor:** Miles E. Denham. **Advertising accepted.** Circulation 11,700. **Price:** $4.00. **Other information:** Includes data on manmade textile fibers, including properties, end uses, and trade names.

★978★
MODULAR DIRECTORY [Mobile home manufacturers]
Manufactured Housing Newsletter
410 S. Grove Avenue   Phone: (312) 381-4312
Barrington, IL 60010
Covers: About 450 companies manufacturing modular homes and double-wide mobile homes. **Entries include:** Name, address, phone, names of principal executives, product description, area in which marketed, building codes to which units conform; listings for branch plants include less detail. **Arrangement:** Alphabetical. **Indexes:** Geographical. **Pages** (approx.): 115. **Frequency:** Irregular; latest edition October 1978. **Editor:** Shepard Robinson. **Price:** $36.00.

Montana Directory of Manufacturers *See* Directory of Montana Manufacturers

Montana Manufacturers Directory and Buyers Guide *See* Directory of Montana Manufacturers

Montana Ready Mix and Concrete Products Association—Roster *See* Pacific Builder & Engineer—Buyers Guide & Directory Issue

★979★
MOTOR WEST—WESTERN MANUFACTURERS' AGENTS DIRECTORY ISSUE
McHenry Publishing Company
1145 W. Collins Avenue   Phone: (714) 997-0960
Orange, CA 92667
Covers: Firms marketing automotive products in the western states.

Entries include: Company name, address, phone, key personnel. **Arrangement:** Geographical. **Frequency:** Annual, September. **Advertising accepted.** Circulation 33,600.

★980★
MOTOR/AGE—TOOLS AND EQUIPMENT BUYERS GUIDE ISSUE
Chilton Company
Chilton Way   Phone: (215) 687-8200
Radnor, PA 19089
Covers: Manufacturers of tools and equipment for automobile repair. **Entries include:** Company name, address, phone, types of products made. **Arrangement:** By principal category (brake service, engine testing); manufacturers alphabetical within categories, and listings indicate more specifically the products made within the general category. **Frequency:** Annual, March. **Editor:** Stan Stephenson. **Advertising accepted.** Circulation 141,000. **Price:** $2.00 (current and 1980 editions).

MRA Research Service Directory *See* Directory of Research Services Provided by Members of the Marketing Research Association

★981★
MULTI-HOUSING NEWS—DIRECTORY ISSUE
Gralla Publications
1515 Broadway   Phone: (212) 869-1300
New York, NY 10036
Covers: 1,500 builders and developers of multi-family housing. **Entries include:** Company name and address. **Pages** (approx.): 15. **Frequency:** Annual, July. **Editor:** Wes Wise. **Advertising accepted.** Circulation 42,000. **Former title:** Apartment Construction News - Directory Issue. **Price:** $2.00.

★982★
MULTI-LINGUAL DIRECTORY OF MACHINE TOOLS & RELATED PRODUCTS
National Machine Tool Builders' Association
7901 Westpark Drive   Phone: (703) 893-2900
McLean, VA 22102
Covers: About 375 member manufacturers of power-driven, non-portable, machines used to shape or form metal. **Entries include:** Company name, address, products. **Arrangement:** By product. **Pages** (approx.): 175. **Frequency:** Annual, September. **Price:** Free.

★983★
MULTINATIONAL MARKETING AND EMPLOYMENT DIRECTORY
World Trade Academy Press, Inc.
50 E. 42nd Street
New York, NY 10017
Covers: 7,500 American corporations operating both in the United States and overseas. Includes a marketing register covering 40 groups. **Entries include:** Company name and address of headquarters; when available, names of executives, list of products or services, countries in which operations are conducted. **Arrangement:** Alphabetical. **Indexes:** Industry. **Pages** (approx.): 1260. **Frequency:** Irregular; previous edition 1976; new edition possible 1981. **Former title:** National and International Employment Handbook. **Price:** $130.00 (out of print). **Other information:** Publisher states this publication, considered the 7th edition, is a revision and is combined with two other previous publications, "Multinational Corporations Operating Overseas" and "Angel's National Directory of Personnel Managers."

★984★
MVMA DIRECTORY OF MOTOR VEHICLE RELATED ASSOCIATIONS
Motor Vehicle Manufacturers Association
300 New Center Building
Detroit, MI 48202
Covers: 175 national and important regional associations which are active in business areas related to motor vehicles. **Entries include:** Association name, address, phone, name of executive secretary or

other official, brief description of organization's interests. **Arrangement:** Alphabetical. **Pages** (approx.): 50. **Frequency:** Every 18 months; latest edition 1978. **Price:** Free.

★985★

NAHM'S GUIDE TO MANUFACTURED HOMES [And other pre-fabricated buildings]

National Association of Home Manufacturers
6521 Arlington Boulevard   Phone: (703) 533-9606
Falls Church, VA 22042
Covers: More than 100 member companies which manufacture homes, apartments, vacation homes, log homes, geodesic dome homes, churches, and commercial structures; also lists suppliers of building materials, appliances, and professional services. **Entries include:** For manufacturers - Company name, address, sales contact, and description of types of homes or other structures produced and information on and prices for catalogs and brochures. For other firms and associations - Company or association name, address, interests or services. **Pages** (approx.): 65. **Frequency:** Not established; latest edition September 1979. **Price:** $4.00, postpaid.

★986★

NAMES AND NUMBERS: A JOURNALIST'S GUIDE TO THE MOST NEEDED INFORMATION SOURCES AND CONTACTS

John Wiley & Sons, Inc.
605 Third Avenue   Phone: (212) 867-9800
New York, NY 10016
Covers: 20,000 information sources and contacts including: airports, toll-free telephone numbers, railroads, hotels and motels, prominent Americans, special interest groups, institutions, colleges and universities, government agencies and offices, sports leagues, information and research services, foreign and United States embassies, associations and societies, television and radio stations, publishers, and others. **Entries include:** Name of organization, agency, individual, etc., address, phone. **Arrangement:** In three categories: logistics (travel information); information sources and contacts; and media. **Pages** (approx.): 525. **Frequency:** Not established; first edition November 1978. **Editor:** Rod Nordland. **Price:** $24.95. **Send orders to:** John Wiley & Sons, Inc., 1 Wiley Drive, Somerset, NJ 08873 (201-469-4400).

NATA Business Telephone and Equipment Industry *See* Business Telephone & Equipment Industry

★987★

NATIONAL AIR TRANSPORTATION ASSOCIATION—OFFICIAL MEMBERSHIP DIRECTORY

National Air Transportation Association
1010 Wisconsin Avenue, N. W.   Phone: (202) 965-8880
Washington, DC 20007
Covers: About 900 regular, associate, and affiliate members; regular members include airport service organizations, air taxi/commuter operators, and commuter airlines. **Entries include:** Company name, address, phone, and services offered. **Arrangement:** Regular members are classified by service; associate and affiliate members are alphabetical in separate sections. **Indexes:** Geographical. **Pages** (approx.): 175. **Frequency:** Annual, with quarterly updates. **Price:** $20.00, including update service (current and 1980 editions).

★988★

NATIONAL AMERICAN WHOLESALE GROCERS' ASSOCIATION— DIRECTORY

National American Wholesale Grocers' Association
51 Madison Avenue   Phone: (212) 532-8899
New York, NY 10010
Covers: 300 independent food wholesalers. **Entries include:** Company name, address, phone, name of principal executive, list of products. **Arrangement:** Alphabetical. **Pages** (approx.): 60. **Frequency:** Biennial, July of even years. **Editor:** Lowell Scher, Secretary-Treasurer. **Price:** Available to members only.

National and International Employment Handbook *See* Multinational Marketing and Employment Directory

National Apparel Suppliers and Contractors Directory *See* National Contractors and Suppliers Directory [Apparel industry]

National Art Materials Trade Association—Membership Directory *See* Who's Who in Art Materials

★989★

NATIONAL ASPHALT PAVEMENT ASSOCIATION PLANT QUALITY CERTIFICATION PROGRAM DIRECTORY

National Asphalt Pavement Association
6811 Kenilworth Avenue   Phone: (301) 779-4880
Riverdale, MD 20840
Covers: About 400 hot-mix asphalt plants meeting NAPA quality control standards and operated by 150 companies and firms in 42 states and Puerto Rico. **Entries include:** Company name and address, name and address of its plants, production capacity of plant, and an indication of its certification in the areas of environmental control, safety, personnel training, and automation of equipment. **Arrangement:** Geographical. **Pages** (approx.): 35. **Frequency:** Annual, June. **Price:** Free.

National Association of Aluminum Distributors—Roster *See* Metal Distribution

★990★

NATIONAL ASSOCIATION OF BLACK MANUFACTURERS— MEMBERSHIP DIRECTORY

National Association of Black Manufacturers
1910 K Street, N. W., Suite 600
Washington, DC 20006
Covers: About 500 minority-owned manufacturing firms. **Entries include:** Company name, address, phone, names of principal executives, description of business and facilities, market area, major customers, Federal Supply Codes. **Arrangement:** Alphabetical. **Indexes:** Geographical. **Pages** (approx.): 500. **Frequency:** Annual, January. **Price:** $30.00 (current edition); $35.00 (1980 edition).

★991★

NATIONAL ASSOCIATION OF BRICK DISTRIBUTORS—DIRECTORY

National Association of Brick Distributors
1750 Old Meadow Road   Phone: (703) 734-0110
McLean, VA 22102
Covers: About 250 distributors and dealers handling bricks and other structural clay products. **Entries include:** Company name, address, phone, name of principal executive, list of products or services. **Arrangement:** Alphabetical. **Pages** (approx.): 20. **Frequency:** Annual, spring. **Price:** $5.00; restricted distribution.

★992★

NATIONAL ASSOCIATION OF CHAIN DRUG STORES— MEMBERSHIP DIRECTORY

National Association of Chain Drug Stores
1911 Jefferson Davis Highway   Phone: (703) 979-3200
Arlington, VA 22202
Covers: About 200 chain drug retailers and their 15,000 individual pharmacies; 400 supplier companies; state boards of pharmacy and pharmaceutical and retail associations; colleges of pharmacy; drug trade associations. **Entries include:** For chain drug retailers - Firm name, headquarters address and phone, number of owned and leased pharmacies, names and titles of key personnel, buying hours, warehouse address. For suppliers - Firm name, address, phone, products, names of key personnel. For individual drug stores - Name, address; parent company not identified if not included in store name. For other listings - Company or other name, address, phone, name of chief executive. **Arrangement:** Classified by activity; stores and colleges are then geographical, other listings are alphabetical. **Indexes:** Chain drug store headquarters location, supplier product; separate

alphabetical lists with full addresses of persons in chain headquarters responsible for prescription and ethical products, cosmetics and toiletries, and security. **Pages** (approx.): 210. **Frequency:** Annual, December. **Editor:** Linda M. Williams, Directory of Publications. **Price:** $60.00.

National Association of Concessionaires—Roster *See* Insite [Concession industry]

★993★
NATIONAL ASSOCIATION OF FLEET ADMINISTRATORS—
　　REFERENCE BOOK
National Association of Fleet Administrators
295 Madison Avenue　　　　　　　Phone: (212) 689-3200
New York, NY 10017
Covers: Automobile manufacturers' sales and leasing representatives throughout the country. **Entries include:** Company name, address, phone, and name of representative. **Pages** (approx.): 120. **Frequency:** Annual, spring. **Editor:** Lynne Warshavsky, Director of Publications. **Advertising accepted.** Circulation 2,500. **Price:** $2.50.

National Association of Food Equipment Manufacturers—Roster *See* Foodservice Equipment Specialist—Buyer's Guide and Product Directory...

National Association of Home Manufacturers—Membership Directory *See* NAHM's Guide to Manufactured Homes...

★994★
NATIONAL ASSOCIATION OF INSTITUTIONAL LAUNDRY
　　MANAGERS
National Association of Institutional Laundry Managers
781 Twin Oaks Avenue　　　　　　Phone: (714) 426-6651
Chula Vista, CA 92010
Covers: 1,700 managers of in-house laundries for institutions, hotels, plants, etc. **Entries include:** Name, name of employer, address; listings for associate members show company name, address, name of chief executive, and list of products or services. **Arrangement:** By type of membership. **Pages** (approx.): 60. **Frequency:** Annual. **Editor:** Robert J. Conard, Executive Secretary. **Price:** Apply.

★995★
NATIONAL ASSOCIATION OF MARINE SURVEYORS—
　　MEMBERSHIP LIST
National Association of Marine Surveyors
86 Windsor Gate Drive　　　　　　Phone: (212) 895-3677
North Hills, NY 11040
Number of listings: About 350. **Entries include:** Name, firm name, address, phone, year elected to membership. **Arrangement:** Geographical. **Indexes:** Personal name. **Pages** (approx.): 50. **Frequency:** Annual, March; addenda in June, September, December. **Editor:** Howard I. Saffer, National Secretary. **Price:** $1.50, payment with order.

★996★
NATIONAL ASSOCIATION OF PATTERN MANUFACTURERS—
　　BUYER'S GUIDE AND DIRECTORY OF MEMBERS
National Association of Pattern Manufacturers
21010 Center Ridge Road　　　　　Phone: (216) 333-7417
Cleveland, OH 44116
Covers: About 175 independent jobbing and captive pattern producers serving the metal working industry, and their suppliers. **Entries include:** Company name, address, phone, officers, type of shop, capabilities and specialties. **Arrangement:** Geographical. **Pages** (approx.): 50. **Frequency:** Irregular; latest edition August 1979. **Editor:** B. J. Imburgia. **Advertising accepted. Price:** $15.00.

★997★
NATIONAL ASSOCIATION OF PERSONNEL CONSULTANTS—
　　MEMBERSHIP DIRECTORY
National Association of Personnel Consultants
1012 14th Street, N. W.　　　　　Phone: (202) 638-1721
Washington, DC 20005
Covers: Over 2,300 private (for-profit) employment agencies. **Entries include:** Agency name, address, phone, names and titles of individual members, whether "full service." **Arrangement:** By specialty, then geographical. **Pages** (approx.): 170. **Frequency:** Annual. **Price:** $8.50. **Other information:** Also cited as, "Directory of Private Employment Agencies." Association changed name from National Employment Association.

★998★
NATIONAL ASSOCIATION OF PLASTIC FABRICATORS—
　　MEMBERSHIP DIRECTORY AND BUYER'S GUIDE
National Association of Plastics Fabricators
1701 N Street, N. W.　　　　　　Phone: (202) 223-2504
Washington, DC 20036
Number of listings: About 200. **Entries include:** Listings for all members show company name, address, phone, names of executives, products or services; listings for regular members also show production volume, processes used, geographic area served, plant size, and number of employees. **Arrangement:** Alphabetical. **Indexes:** Product, geographical. **Pages** (approx.): 80. **Frequency:** Annual, fall. **Editor:** Jill M. Wettrich, Executive Director. **Advertising accepted. Price:** $10.00.

National Association of Plastic Fabricators—Membership List *See* Kitchen Business—Directory & Buyers Guide Issue

★999★
NATIONAL ASSOCIATION OF PLASTICS DISTRIBUTORS—
　　MEMBERSHIP DIRECTORY
National Association of Plastics Distributors
Gilson Road　　　　　　　　　　Phone: (603) 532-7221
Jaffrey, NH 03452
Covers: 160 distributors of plastics materials to the industry and 65 manufacturers who sell their products through plastics distributors. **Entries include:** Company name, address, phone, name of principal executive, and list of products or services. **Arrangement:** Alphabetical within divisions of membership. **Pages** (approx.): 60. **Frequency:** Annual, April. **Editor:** Raymond W. Kruse, Executive Director. **Price:** Available to members only.

National Association of Purchasing Management (Sixth District)—Roster *See* Midwest Purchasing—Roster Issue

★1000★
NATIONAL ASSOCIATION OF QUICK PRINTERS—SUPPLIER
　　DIRECTORY
National Association of Quick Printers
3255 S. U. S. Highway 1
Fort Pierce, FL 33450
Covers: Over 150 suppliers of printing products; only members of the association are listed. **Entries include:** Company name, address, name of contact, branch office locations. **Arrangement:** Alphabetical. **Indexes:** Product. **Frequency:** Irregular; latest edition winter 1979. **Price:** Available to members only.

★1001★
NATIONAL ASSOCIATION OF SERVICE MANAGERS—
　　MEMBERSHIP DIRECTORY
National Association of Service Managers
6022 W. Touhy Avenue　　　　　　Phone: (312) 763-7350
Chicago, IL 60648
Covers: 1,100 members responsible for product service functions of manufacturing firms in consumer, commercial, and industrial lines. **Entries include:** Member's name, company name, address, phone. **Arrangement:** Alphabetical. **Indexes:** Geographical. **Pages** (approx.):

80. **Frequency:** Annual, late spring. **Editor:** Marvin Lurie, Executive Director. **Advertising accepted. Price:** $100.00.

★1002★
NATIONAL ASSOCIATION OF STORE FIXTURE MANUFACTURERS—DIRECTORY
National Association of Store Fixture Manufacturers
5975 W. Sunrise Boulevard   Phone: (305) 587-9190
Sunrise, FL 33313
Covers: About 200 manufacturers of store, bank, and office fixtures (SIC 2541 and 2542). **Entries include:** Company name, address, phone, names of principal personnel, list of products and services, size of plant, number of employees, representative jobs, and geographical areas served. **Arrangement:** Alphabetical. **Pages** (approx.): 75. **Frequency:** Annual, July. **Editor:** Robert L. Strauss, Executive Director. **Price:** Available to members and specifiers and purchasers of fixtures.

★1003★
NATIONAL ASSOCIATION OF SUGGESTION SYSTEMS— MEMBERSHIP DIRECTORY
National Association of Suggestion Systems
435 N. Michigan Avenue, Suite 2112   Phone: (312) 644-0075
Chicago, IL 60611
Covers: About 800 companies, associations, and federal, state, county, and municipal government agencies operating or contemplating employee suggestion systems. **Entries include:** Company, association, or agency name; address; suggestion system administrator. **Arrangement:** Classified by type of membership, then alphabetical. **Pages** (approx.): 40. **Frequency:** Annual, June. **Editor:** O. S. Hallett, Executive Secretary. **Advertising accepted.** Circulation 800. **Price:** Available to members only.

National Association of Truck Stop Operators—Membership Directory *See* **Truck Stop Fuel Guide**

★1004★
NATIONAL AUTO AUCTION ASSOCIATION—MEMBERSHIP DIRECTORY
National Auto Auction Association
Box 29100   Phone: (402) 464-2170
Lincoln, NE 68529
Covers: 115 automobile auction firms. **Entries include:** Company name; address; names and phones of auction personnel; pick up, delivery, and reconditioning services available. **Arrangement:** Geographical. **Pages** (approx.): 60. **Frequency:** Annual, January. **Editor:** Bernard Hart, Executive Secretary. **Price:** Free.

★1005★
NATIONAL AUTOMATIC MERCHANDISING ASSOCIATION— DIRECTORY OF MEMBERS
National Automatic Merchandising Association
7 S. Dearborn Street
Chicago, IL 60603
Covers: 2,300 vending and food service management firms, along with vending machine manufacturers and distributors and producers of other equipment and food items. **Entries include:** For vending firms - Company name, address, phone, code indicating products carried, whether coffee service is offered, and whether the firm operates a commissary. For manufacturers, distributors, and suppliers - Company name, address, phone, products or companies represented. **Arrangement:** Vending firms are geographical, others are alphabetical within line of business. **Pages** (approx.): 70. **Frequency:** Annual, summer. **Price:** $75.00.

★1006★
NATIONAL AUTOMOTIVE DIRECTORY
W. R. C. Smith Publishing Company
1760 Peachtree Road, N. W.   Phone: (404) 874-4462
Atlanta, GA 30357
Covers: Approximately 1,000 manufacturers of automotive aftermarket equipment, parts, accessories, and supplies, and manufacturers' representatives. **Entries include:** Manufacturer listings include company name, address, phone number, trade and brand names, list of products or services, names of sales representatives; representatives' listings show name, plus territory covered. **Indexes:** Trade and brand name, product. **Pages** (approx.): 200. **Frequency:** Annual, November. **Editor:** Diane D. Sullivan. **Advertising accepted.** Circulation 21,250. **Price:** $15.00.

★1007★
NATIONAL BACKHAUL GUIDE [Freight brokers and shippers]
J. J. Keller & Associates, Inc.
145 W. Wisconsin Avenue   Phone: (414) 722-2848
Neenah, WI 54956
Covers: About 2,600 carriers, truck brokers, shippers, refrigerated haulers, packers, growers, and other haulers with loads available through backhaul (return trip) or trip-lease arrangements. **Entries include:** Company name, address, phone, coding to indicate business type, type of equipment needed, and availability of trip lease contracts. **Arrangement:** Geographical. **Pages** (approx.): 325. **Frequency:** Semiannual, supplements to looseleaf base edition, February and August. **Editor:** Patricia Laux. **Price:** Base edition, $79.00; supplements, $59.00 per year; plus $6.00 shipping.

★1008★
NATIONAL BARREL & DRUM ASSOCIATION—MEMBERSHIP AND INDUSTRIAL SUPPLY DIRECTORY
National Barrel & Drum Association
910 17th Street, N. W., No. 912   Phone: (202) 296-8028
Washington, DC 20006
Covers: About 215 container reconditioners and dealers, worldwide. **Entries include:** For members - Company name, address, phone, names and phone numbers of key executives; many listings include railroad route. **Arrangement:** Geographical. **Indexes:** Alphabetical. **Pages** (approx.): 90. **Frequency:** Annual, January. **Advertising accepted. Price:** $5.00, plus 66¢ shipping (current and 1980 editions).

★1009★
NATIONAL BEVERAGE MARKETING DIRECTORY
Beverage Marketing Corporation
261 Madison Avenue   Phone: (212) 682-2025
New York, NY 10016
Covers: About 14,000 beer wholesalers, wine and spirits wholesalers, soft drink bottlers and franchisors, breweries, wineries, distilleries, alcoholic beverage importers, bottled water companies, and trade associations, government agencies, and others concerned with the beverage and bottling industries. **Entries include:** For beverage and bottling companies - Company name, address, phone, names of key executives, number of employees, brand names, and other information including number of franchisees, number of delivery trucks, sales volume. Suppliers and related companies and organizations listings include similar but less detailed information. **Arrangement:** Geographical. **Indexes:** Personal name, supplier's product, company name. **Pages** (approx.): 600. **Frequency:** Annual, September. **Editor:** Michael C. Bellas, Publicher & Editor. **Price:** $95.00, postpaid, payment with order. **Send orders to:** Beverage Marketing Corp., Box 126, Mingo Junction, OH 43938.

★1010★
NATIONAL BUILDING MATERIAL DISTRIBUTORS ASSOCIATION— MEMBERSHIP ROSTER
National Building Material Distributors Association
55 E. Monroe Street, Suite 1616   Phone: (312) 332-7127
Chicago, IL 60603
Covers: About 1,300 wholesale distributors of building materials in the United States and Canada who are members, and manufacturers in that field who are associate members. **Entries include:** Company name, address, phone, name of principal executive, and the products and services offered. **Arrangement:** Geographical. **Indexes:** Alphabetical. **Pages** (approx.): 130. **Frequency:** Annual, April. **Editor:**

Frank E. O'Dowd, Executive Vice President. **Price:** $60.00.

★1011★
NATIONAL BURGLAR AND FIRE ALARM ASSOCIATION—ROSTER OF MEMBERSHIP
National Burglar and Fire Alarm Association
1101 Connecticut Avenue, N. W., Suite 700 Phone: (202) 857-1130
Washington, DC 20036
Covers: About 450 installers and manufacturers of electrical burglar and fire alarm equipment. **Entries include:** Company name, address, phone, key personnel, list of services, branches. **Arrangement:** Alphabetical within membership categories. **Indexes:** Geographical. **Pages** (approx.): 105. **Frequency:** Annual, July. **Advertising accepted.** Circulation 1,000. **Price:** $10.00.

★1012★
NATIONAL CERTIFIED PIPE WELDING BUREAU—MEMBERSHIP DIRECTORY [Plumbing and heating]
National Certified Pipe Welding Bureau
5530 Wisconsin Avenue, Suite 750 Phone: (301) 654-7960
Washington, DC 20015
Covers: About 675 mechanical contractors in air conditioning, plumbing, and heating who employ pipe welders and whose welding is certified. **Entries include:** Firm name, address, phone, name of contact. **Arrangement:** By each chapter, then by firm name. **Pages** (approx.): 50. **Frequency:** Annual, December-January. **Editor:** Darlene Thompson. **Price:** Available to members only.

★1013★
NATIONAL CONTRACTORS AND SUPPLIERS DIRECTORY [Apparel industry]
Denyse and Company, Inc.
6226 Vineland Avenue Phone: (213) 766-5291
North Hollywood, CA 91606
Covers: About 5,000 suppliers and contractors to the apparel manufacturing industry. **Entries include:** Company name, address, phone, name of president, and products or services. **Arrangement:** Alphabetical. **Indexes:** Product. **Pages** (approx.): 230. **Frequency:** Annual, March. **Editor:** Bobbi Zane, Managing Editor. **Advertising accepted.** Circulation 15,000. **Former title:** National Apparel Suppliers and Contractors Directory. **Price:** $10.95, plus $2.00 shipping.

★1014★
NATIONAL CUSTOMS BROKERS & FORWARDERS ASSOCIATION OF AMERICA—MEMBERSHIP ROSTER
National Customs Brokers & Forwarders Association of America
One World Trade Center, Suite 1109 Phone: (212) 432-0050
New York, NY 10048
Covers: About 400 persons and firms that are customs brokers or foreign freight forwarders; international coverage. **Entries include:** Company name, address, phone, telex number, cable address, year established, FMC license number, contact, branch or affiliate cities, and line of business. **Arrangement:** By membership class, then alphabetical. **Indexes:** Geographical by city name. **Pages** (approx.): 135. **Frequency:** Annual, February or March. **Editor:** Vincent J. Bruno, Executive Vice President. **Advertising accepted.** Circulation 3,500. **Price:** $2.00, postpaid, payment with order.

★1015★
NATIONAL DIRECTORY OF ADDRESSES AND TELEPHONE NUMBERS
Bantam Books
666 Fifth Avenue Phone: (212) 765-6500
New York, NY 10019
Covers: 50,000 business firms ($10 million annual sales or over), government offices, banks, hotels, consulates and embassies, colleges and universities, newspapers, radio and television stations, race tracks, and bail bondsmen. **Entries include:** Name, address, phone. **Arrangement:** Classified, alphabetical; same material in each section. **Pages** (approx.): 620. **Frequency:** Irregular; latest edition September

1979. **Editor:** Stanley R. Greenfield. **Price:** $14.95, plus $1.00 shipping.

★1016★
NATIONAL DIRECTORY OF BUDGET MOTELS
Pilot Books
347 Fifth Avenue Phone: (212) 685-0736
New York, NY 10016
Covers: Over 1,600 budget chain motels in 48 states, plus list of headquarters for 31 motel chains with budget-priced facilities. **Entries include:** Motel name, location, cost of overnight stay, facilities. **Frequency:** Annual, April. **Editor:** Ray Carlson. **Price:** $2.95 (current edition); $3.50 (1980 edition).

★1017★
NATIONAL DIRECTORY OF COMPUTING AND CONSULTING SERVICES
Independent Computer Consultants Association
Box 27412 Phone: (314) 567-9708
St. Louis, MO 63141
Covers: Over 260 firms supplying data processing products and services including consulting firms, systems development, education and training, processing, audits and security, financing, and legal service firms. **Entries include:** Company name, address, phone, name and title of contact, code to indicate whether a member of ICCA, services, specialties, languages, achievements. **Arrangement:** By Zip code. **Indexes:** Company name, area of expertise. **Pages** (approx.): 55. **Frequency:** Annual, January. **Editor:** Steven A. Epner, President. **Advertising accepted.** Circulation (1980 edition) 2,500. **Price:** $10.00 (current edition); $25.00 (1980 edition).

★1018★
NATIONAL DIRECTORY OF CONTRACT CARRIERS
Contract Carriers Conference
1730 Rhode Island Avenue, N. W., Suite 801 Phone: (202) 331-8811
Washington, DC 20036
Covers: About 250 trucking firms which operate on a contract basis; trade associations, suppliers, and governmental agencies are also listed. **Entries include:** For trucking firms - Company name, address, phone, names of officers and traffic managers, operating authority, equipment, commodities carried, territory, terminals and shippers served. **Arrangement:** Geographical. **Indexes:** Member name. **Frequency:** Latest edition May 1979; new edition expected January 1980. **Advertising accepted. Price:** $8.00.

★1019★
NATIONAL DIRECTORY OF MANUFACTURERS' REPRESENTATIVES
McGraw-Hill, Inc.
1221 Avenue of the Americas
New York, NY 10020
Number of listings: 5,000. **Entries include:** Agency name, address, names of owners or executives, number of representatives traveled, area covered, lines or types of products handled, special services offered. **Arrangement:** Alphabetical. **Indexes:** Geographical, with SIC subdivisions. **Pages** (approx.): 800. **Frequency:** Not established; first edition January 1979. **Editor:** Herbert F. Holtje. **Price:** $54.00.

★1020★
NATIONAL DISTRIBUTION DIRECTORY
Local and Short Haul Carriers Conference
1616 P Street, N. W. Phone: (202) 797-5414
Washington, DC 20036
Covers: Local cartage, warehousing, and distribution services throughout the United States, and carriers offering consolidation. **Entries include:** Company name, address, services, name of principal executive, bank references. **Arrangement:** Geographical. **Pages** (approx.): 225. **Frequency:** Annual, July. **Advertising accepted.** Circulation 13,000. **Price:** $15.00. **Other information:** Formerly published by Guide Services, Inc.

National Electrical Contractors Association—Roster *See* New England Electrical Blue Book

National Electrical Manufacturers Representatives Association—Roster *See* New England Electrical Blue Book

★1021★

NATIONAL ELECTRONIC DISTRIBUTORS ASSOCIATION—MEMBERSHIP DIRECTORY

National Electronic Distributors Association
1480 Renaissance Drive   Phone: (312) 298-9747
Park Ridge, IL 60068
Number of listings: 500. **Entries include:** Company name, address, branch locations, phones, names of principal executives, size of firm, products handled, territory served. **Arrangement:** Geographical. **Indexes:** Alphabetical. **Pages** (approx.): 50. **Frequency:** Biennial, summer of odd years. **Price:** $25.00.

National Employment Association—Directory *See* National Association of Personnel Consultants—Membership Directory

National Film Carriers—Membership Directory *See* Film, Air and Package Carriers Conference—Membership Directory

National Flexible Packaging Association—Roster *See* Flexible Packaging Association—Membership Directory

★1022★

NATIONAL FLUID POWER ASSOCIATION—MEMBERSHIP DIRECTORY

National Fluid Power Association
3333 N. Mayfair Road, Suite 311   Phone: (414) 259-0990
Milwaukee, WI 53222
Covers: About 200 companies which manufacture components used in transmitting power by means of a fluid under pressure. **Entries include:** Company name; address; phone, TWX, cable, and telex numbers; names of executives. **Arrangement:** Alphabetical. **Indexes:** Personal name, product. **Pages** (approx.): 230. **Frequency:** Annual, September. **Editor:** James I. Morgan, President. **Price:** $40.00.

★1023★

NATIONAL FOOD BROKERS ASSOCIATION—DIRECTORY OF MEMBERS

National Food Brokers Association
1916 M Street, N. W.   Phone: (202) 331-9120
Washington, DC 20036
Covers: About 2,400 member food brokers. **Entries include:** Firm name, address, phone, name of contact, and coding to indicate product categories, clientele, and services provided. **Arrangement:** Geographical. **Frequency:** Annual, December. **Price:** Apply on company letterhead.

★1024★

NATIONAL FROZEN PIZZA INSTITUTE—MEMBERSHIP DIRECTORY

National Frozen Pizza Institute
1700 Old Meadow Road   Phone: (703) 821-0770
McLean, VA 22102
Entries include: Company name, address, phone, principal executives, products, areas served. **Pages** (approx.): 30. **Frequency:** Annual, fall. **Price:** $30.00.

★1025★

NATIONAL FUNERAL DIRECTORS ASSOCIATION—DIRECTORY OF MEMBERS

NFDA Publications, Inc.
135 W. Wells Street   Phone: (414) 276-2500
Milwaukee, WI 53203
Covers: 14,000 members of the state funeral director associations affiliated with the National Funeral Directors Association. **Entries include:** Company name, address, phone, and principal executive. **Arrangement:** Geographical. **Frequency:** Annual, November. **Editor:**

Charles J. Zahn. **Advertising accepted. Price:** $25.00.

National Industrial Cafeteria Managers Association—Membership Directory *See* Society for Foodservice Management—Membership Directory

★1026★

NATIONAL INDUSTRIAL RECREATION ASSOCIATION—MEMBERSHIP DIRECTORY

National Industrial Recreation Association
20 N. Wacker Drive   Phone: (312) 346-7575
Chicago, IL 60606
Number of listings: About 2,200 personnel managers, recreation directors, and certified administrators in employee recreation, fitness, and services. **Entries include:** Name, address, phone. **Arrangement:** Alphabetical. **Frequency:** Annual. **Price:** Available to members only.

★1027★

NATIONAL INDUSTRIAL TRAFFIC LEAGUE—MEMBERSHIP ROSTER

National Industrial Traffic League
1909 K Street, N. W., Suite 410   Phone: (202) 296-4535
Washington, DC 20006
Number of listings: 1,800. **Entries include:** Company name, address, phone, and individual's name and title. **Arrangement:** Alphabetical. **Indexes:** Personal name. **Pages** (approx.): 60. **Frequency:** Annual, spring. **Price:** Available to members only.

★1028★

NATIONAL INSTITUTE OF PACKAGING, HANDLING AND LOGISTIC ENGINEERS—MEMBERSHIP DIRECTORY

National Institute of Packaging, Handling, and Logistic Engineers
Box 2765
Arlington, VA 22202
Covers: 225 engineers, chemists, consultants and executives. **Entries include:** Name, address, phone, and company. **Pages** (approx.): 100. **Frequency:** Semiannual, spring and fall. **Advertising accepted. Price:** $20.00 per year.

★1029★

NATIONAL INSULATION CONTRACTORS ASSOCIATION—MEMBERSHIP DIRECTORY

National Insulation Contractors Association
1120 19th Street, N. W., Suite 405   Phone: (202) 223-4406
Washington, DC 20036
Covers: More than 475 contractors who install thermal insulation in commercial and industrial facilities, and manufacturers of materials and equipment (SIC 1799). **Entries include:** Company name, address, phone, key executives. **Arrangement:** Geographical. **Indexes:** Alphabetical. **Pages** (approx.): 70. **Frequency:** Annual, June. **Editor:** D. M. Humphrey. **Advertising accepted.** Circulation 4,500. **Price:** $3.00.

National Kitchen Cabinet Association—Membership List *See* Kitchen Business—Directory & Buyers Guide Issue

★1030★

NATIONAL LICENSED BEVERAGE ASSOCIATION—INDUSTRY DIRECTORY

National Licensed Beverage Association
309 N. Washington Street
Alexandria, VA 22314
Covers: Brewing companies, distillers, importers, vintners, and soft drink companies. Includes sections listing trade associations, trade publications, and state liquor administrators. **Entries include:** Company name, address, phone, and names of company executives. **Indexes:** Personal name. **Pages** (approx.): 100. **Frequency:** Annual, January. **Editor:** Gerald E. Murphy, Executive Director. **Price:** $15.00 (current and 1980 editions).

National Machine Tool Builders' Association—Membership Directory *See* Multi-Lingual Directory of Machine Tools & Related Products

★1031★
NATIONAL MAILING-LIST HOUSES
Small Business Administration
1441 L Street, N. W.   Phone: (202) 653-6365
Washington, DC 20416
Covers: A selected group of major mailing list compilers and brokers. Pages (approx.): 8. Frequency: Irregular; latest edition June 1977; no new edition planned. Editor: Richard D. Milligan. Price: Free (Small Business Bibliography No. 29). Send orders to: Small Business Administration, Box 15434, Fort Worth, TX 76119.

★1032★
NATIONAL MARINE REPRESENTATIVES ASSOCIATION— DIRECTORY
National Marine Representatives Association
401 N. Michigan Avenue   Phone: (312) 759-7251
Chicago, IL 60611
Covers: 300 independent representatives selling pleasure craft and other small boats, motors, and marine accessories. Entries include: Name, address, phone, manufacturers represented, territories covered. Arrangement: Alphabetical. Indexes: Geographical. Frequency: Annual, January. Editor: Teddee Grace, Executive Secretary. Price: $10.00 (current and 1980 editions). Send orders to: Teddee Grace, 28-P Fernwood Dr., Bolingbrook, IL 60439 (312-759-7251).

National Micrographics Association—Membership Directory *See* Buyer's Guide to Micrographic Equipment, Products, & Services

★1033★
NATIONAL MINORITY PURCHASING COUNCIL DATA BANK— MINORITY VENDOR INFORMATION SERVICE
National Minority Purchasing Council
1500 Broadway, Suite 3001   Phone: (212) 944-2430
New York, NY 10036
Background: Not a published directory but a computerized data bank with information concerning more than 10,000 minority firms nationwide. Information available on firms by geographic region or by product or service capability; data base includes a variety of basic business facts on each company. Service available to members and subscribers only, but membership is not restricted. Price: Free to dues-paid members; $300.00 per year to subscribers.

National Office Machine Dealers Association—Roster *See* NOMDA Spokesman—Who's Who Issue

★1034★
NATIONAL OFFICE PRODUCTS ASSOCIATION—MEMBERSHIP DIRECTORY AND BUYERS' GUIDE
National Office Products Association
301 N. Fairfax Street   Phone: (703) 549-9040
Alexandria, VA 22314
Covers: 7,000 manufacturers, wholesalers, retailers and sales and marketing representatives. Entries include: Company name, address, phone, principal executives, number of employees, branch stores, and products or services. Arrangement: Alphabetical; geographical; buyers' guide classified by product category. Pages (approx.): 215. Frequency: Annual, January. Editor: Simon DeGroot, Director of Communications. Advertising accepted. Circulation 7,000. Price: $100.00 (current and 1980 editions).

National Paper Trade Association—Membership Roster *See* Who's Who in Paper Distribution

National Particleboard Association—Membership Directory *See* Directory of Particleboard and Medium Density Fiberboard Manufacturers

National Particleboard Association—Membership List *See* Kitchen Business Directory & Buyers Guide Issue

★1035★
NATIONAL PASSENGER TRAFFIC ASSOCIATION—MEMBERSHIP DIRECTORY
National Passenger Traffic Association, Inc.
122 E. 42nd Street, 17th Floor   Phone: (212) 682-0470
New York, NY 10017
Covers: 400 corporate travel managers and allied members in the United States and Canada. Entries include: Individual's name, corporate name, type of membership, office address, and phone. Arrangement: Alphabetical by individual name. Indexes: Corporation. Pages (approx.): 65. Frequency: Annual, March. Editor: Josephine Brune, Chairman, Directory Committee. Arrangement: Circulation 1,500. Price: $5.00.

★1036★
NATIONAL PETROLEUM NEWS—BUYER'S GUIDE ISSUE
McGraw-Hill, Inc.
1221 Avenue of the Americas   Phone: (212) 997-2361
New York, NY 10020
Covers: Manufacturers and marketers of petroleum products and industry-related equipment. Entries include: Firm name, address, phone, names and titles of marketing and other key executives. Arrangement: Alphabetical. Indexes: Product. Frequency: Annual, March. Advertising accepted. Circulation 19,000. Price: $1.10, plus 35¢ shipping.

★1037★
NATIONAL PETROLEUM NEWS—FACT BOOK ISSUE
McGraw-Hill, Inc.
1221 Avenue of the Americas   Phone: (212) 997-2361
New York, NY 10020
Covers: Producers, transporters, refiners, and marketers of petroleum products; oil-marketing and related industry associations. Entries include: For petroleum industries - Company name, address, phone, brand name of product, coding to indicate line of business, names and titles of marketing and other key executives. For associations - Name, address, phone, number of members, names and titles of key personnel. Arrangement: Companies are alphabetical, associations are alphabetical within national and regional categories. Indexes: General. Frequency: Annual, mid-June issue. Price: $11.00.

★1038★
NATIONAL PRECAST CONCRETE ASSOCIATION—MEMBERSHIP DIRECTORY
National Precast Concrete Association
825 E. 64th Street   Phone: (317) 253-0486
Indianapolis, IN 46220
Covers: About 625 producers of precast concrete products. Entries include: Company name, address, phone, principal executive, products or services. Arrangement: Geographical. Indexes: Product. Pages (approx.): 45. Frequency: Biennial, spring of odd years; supplement issued in even years. Editor: R. W. Walton, Executive Vice-President. Price: $2.00; available to members only.

★1039★
NATIONAL PREMIUM SALES EXECUTIVES—MEMBERSHIP DIRECTORY
National Premium Sales Executives
1600 Route 22   Phone: (201) 687-3090
Union, NJ 07083
Covers: 350 sales and marketing executives of firms selling merchandise for use as premiums, sales incentives, and prizes. Entries include: Name, title, company name, address, phone, list of products, photograph of member, year elected to membership.

Arrangement: Alphabetical. Indexes: Company, product. Pages (approx.): 90. Frequency: Annual, May. Editor: Howard C. Henry, Executive Director. Price: 30¢ shipping.

★1040★
NATIONAL RAILROAD CONSTRUCTION AND MAINTENANCE
    ASSOCIATION—DIRECTORY AND BUYER'S GUIDE
National Railroad Construction and Maintenance Association
9331 Waymond Avenue   Phone: (219) 924-1709
Highland, IN 46322
Covers: 650 companies supplying construction services and supplies and equipment from ballast to wood preserving materials. Entries include: Company name, address, phone, representatives. Arrangement: Alphabetical. Indexes: Product. Frequency: Annual, December; 1979 edition delayed to March. Price: $5.00. Other information: Association's name changed from Railroad Construction and Maintenance Association.

National Restaurant Association—Membership Directory See
    Who's Who in Food Service

★1041★
NATIONAL SASH & DOOR JOBBERS ASSOCIATION—
    MEMBERSHIP DIRECTORY
National Sash & Door Jobbers Association
20 N. Wacker Drive   Phone: (312) 263-2670
Chicago, IL 60606
Covers: 350 millwork and building products wholesale distribution centers which handle sash, doors, building woodwork, and related products, and suppliers of such products. Entries include: Firm name, address, phone, products handled or manufactured. Arrangement: Geographical. Pages (approx.): 120. Frequency: Annual, spring. Price: $15.00.

★1042★
NATIONAL SCALE MEN'S ASSOCIATION—YEARBOOK
National Scale Men's Association
214 1/2 S. Washington Street   Phone: (312) 355-4788
Naperville, IL 60540
Covers: About 2,100 persons engaged in the manufacture, construction, repair, installation, design, or sale of scales, and weights and measures officials from various governmental units. Entries include: Name, address, phone, occupation, name of employer. Arrangement: Geographical. Pages (approx.): 260. Frequency: Annual, May. Editor: Mrs. S. T. Wagner, Executive Director. Advertising accepted. Circulation 3,500. Price: $25.00 (current and 1980 editions).

★1043★
NATIONAL TANK TRUCK CARRIER DIRECTORY
National Tank Truck Carriers
1616 P Street, N. W.   Phone: (202) 797-5425
Washington, DC 20036
Covers: For-hire tank truck carriers serving petroleum, chemical, and other industries in the United States, Canada, Australia, England, Europe, Japan, Mexico, and South Africa. Also lists shippers, intermodal bulk facilities, and state and related associations affiliated with the American Trucking Associations. Entries include: Company name, address, phone, names of executives, list of products or services. Arrangement: Carrier section is geographical; shippers are listed alphabetically. Indexes: Personal name, company name. Pages (approx.): 350. Frequency: Annual, January. Editor: Melinda Duncan, Publications Manager. Advertising accepted. Circulation 2,500-3,000. Price: $7.50 (1980 edition). Also includes: Names and addresses of the Department of Transportation and Interstate Commerce Commission field personnel, a listing of dangerous articles authorized by DOT for tank truck transportation, and tank specifications.

National Tire Dealers & Retreaders Association—Membership
    Directory See Who's Who Directory [Tire industry]

★1044★
NATIONAL TOOL, DIE, AND PRECISION MACHINING
    ASSOCIATION—BUYERS GUIDE
National Tool, Die, and Precision Machining Association
9300 Livingston Road   Phone: (301) 248-6200
Washington, DC 20022
Covers: Nearly 3,000 member firms. Entries include: Company name, address, phone, facilities and job capabilities. Arrangement: Geographical. Pages (approx.): 800. Frequency: Annual, summer. Price: Apply; restricted circulation.

★1045★
NATIONAL TRADE AND PROFESSIONAL ASSOCIATIONS OF THE
    U.S. AND CANADA AND LABOR UNIONS
Columbia Books, Inc.
777 14th Street, N. W., Suite 1336   Phone: (202) 737-3777
Washington, DC 20005
Number of listings: 6,000. Entries include: Name, year established, name of chief executive, address, phone, number of staff members, budget, size of membership, date and location of annual meetings, publications, historical data. Arrangement: Alphabetical. Indexes: Geographical, key word, budget, chief executive. Pages (approx.): 400. Frequency: Annual, January. Editor: Craig Colgate, Jr. Price: $30.00, postpaid (current and 1980 editions); payment with order.

★1046★
NATIONAL TRADE SHOW EXHIBITORS ASSOCIATION—EXHIBIT
    INDUSTRY GUIDE
National Trade Show Exhibitors Association
4300-L Lincoln Avenue   Phone: (312) 359-8160
Rolling Meadows, IL 60008
Covers: About 370 members of the National Trade Show Exhibitors Association, Exhibit Designers & Producers Association, and Exhibit Service Contractors Association; also lists publishers of trade show and exhibit industry magazines, major convention facilities, and convention bureaus. Entries include: For members of the associations - Name, address, phone, name of contact, products or services. For other listings - Company name, address, phone, name and title of contact. Arrangement: By line of business or association. Pages (approx.): 80. Frequency: Annual, February. Editor: Jim Kelty, Managing Director. Price: $15.00. Also includes: List of available attendance audits.

★1047★
NATIONAL TRUCK EQUIPMENT ASSOCIATION—MEMBERSHIP
    ROSTER
National Truck Equipment Association
25900 Greenfield, Suite 410   Phone: (313) 968-3680
Oak Park, MI 48237
Covers: Over 600 distributors who install truck bodies and related equipment on chassis-cabs, and 175 manufacturers and associates. Entries include: Company name, address, phone, name of contact. Manufacturer listings include products. Arrangement: Alphabetical within activity class. Indexes: Georgraphical. Pages (approx.): 85. Frequency: Annual. Editor: James D. Carney, Executive Director. Price: $25.00. Other information: Association changed name from Truck Equipment and Body Distributors Association.

★1048★
NATIONAL WHOLESALE DRUGGISTS' ASSOCIATION—
    MEMBERSHIP & EXECUTIVE DIRECTORY
National Wholesale Druggists' Association
670 White Plains Road   Phone: (914) 723-3571
Scarsdale, NY 10583
Covers: Wholesalers, manufacturers, colleges of pharmacy, advertising agencies, and national drug trade associations. Entries include: Company name, address, phone, names of principal executives. Arrangement: Classified by type of membership and then

alphabetical. **Pages** (approx.): 100. **Frequency:** Annual, February. **Editor:** Donald F. Higgins, Director of Communications & Publications. **Price:** $25.00. **Also includes:** List of pharmacy colleges with addresses.

National Woodwork Manufacturers Association—Membership Directory See Sources of Supply [Woodwork]

National Yellow Book of Funeral Directors & Suppliers See Yellow Book of Funeral Directors and Suppliers

★1049★
NEBRASKA INTERNATIONAL TRADE DIRECTORY
Nebraska Department of Economic Development
301 Centennial Mall South   Phone: (402) 471-3111
Lincoln, NE 68509
Covers: About 350 manufacturing firms located in Nebraska which export or are interested in exporting. **Entries include:** Firm name, address, phone; name of key executive, products, SIC number, code to indicate number of employees. **Arrangement:** Alphabetical. **Indexes:** Product and manufacturer by SIC. **Pages** (approx.): 65. **Frequency:** Irregular; latest edition 1976; new edition expected 1981. **Price:** Free. **Also includes:** Demographic and other general information about Nebraska.

Nebraska Manufacturers Directory See Directory of Nebraska Manufacturers and Their Products

★1050★
NETHERLANDS-AMERICAN TRADE DIRECTORY
American Chamber of Commerce in the Netherlands
Carnegieplein 5
The Hague, Netherlands
Covers: About 8,500 Netherlands and American businesses interested in developing trade and investment within and between the two countries. **Entries include:** Company name, address, phone, cable address, telex, name of chief executive, products manufactured or imported. **Arrangement:** Alphabetical. **Indexes:** Product/service, American firms, Dutch firms with American subsidiaries, member companies. **Pages** (approx.): 550. **Frequency:** Irregular; latest edition 1977; undated supplement of member firms. **Advertising accepted.** Restricted to members only. **Price:** $55.00.

Nevada Directory of Business See Nevada Industrial Directory

★1051★
NEVADA EXPORT DIRECTORY
Reno District Office
Industry and Trade Administration
Commerce Department
777 W Second Street, Room 120   Phone: (702) 784-5203
Reno, NV 89503
Covers: About 240 Nevada firms which export their products; also listed are firms with services of interest to exporters (including banks, freight and transportation firms, etc.), chambers of commerce, embassies and legations in the United States, overseas trade centers, and others. **Entries include:** For exporting firms - Company name, address, phone, name and title of contact, products, SIC number. For other listings - Name, address; some listings also include phone. **Arrangement:** By activity. **Indexes:** Exporting firm by product. **Pages** (approx.): 110. **Frequency:** Irregular; latest edition 1979; new edition expected May 1980. **Editor:** J. Jerry Jeremy. **Price:** Free. **Other information:** Published in cooperation with the Nevada Department of Economic Development, Western Industrial Nevada, Latin Chamber of Commerce, and Nevada World Trade & International Tourism Association.

★1052★
NEVADA INDUSTRIAL DIRECTORY
Nevada Department of Economic Development
Capitol Complex   Phone: (702) 885-4322
Carson City, NV 89710
Covers: Manufacturers, wholesalers, and companies providing industrial services (SIC 2000-3900, 4225, 5063, 8911). **Entries include:** Company name, address, phone, names of principal executives, number of employees, financial keys, list of products or services, SIC numbers, date established. **Pages** (approx.): 100. **Frequency:** Irregular; latest edition March 1978. **Editor:** Fred Hinners. **Former title:** Directory of Nevada Businesses (1974). **Price:** $2.00. **Other information:** State Industrial Directories Corp. catalog lists this publication as, "Nevada Directory of Business."

★1053★
NEVADA STATE INDUSTRIAL DIRECTORY
State Industrial Directories Corporation
Two Penn Plaza   Phone: (212) 564-0340
New York, NY 10001
Number of listings: 400. **Entries include:** Company name, address, phone, names of key executives, number of employees, plant size, 4-digit SIC code, products, whether firm imports or exports, and whether firm has research facilities. **Arrangement:** Geographical. **Indexes:** Alphabetical, product (includes mailing address and phone for each firm). **Frequency:** Not established; first edition expected 1980. **Advertising accepted.** **Price:** $15.00.

New Consultants See Consultants and Consulting Organizations Directory

★1054★
NEW ENGLAND ADVERTISING WEEK—COMPLETE GUIDE TO NEW ENGLAND MARKETS AND MEDIA ISSUE
Editor and Printer Publishing Company
470 Atlantic Avenue   Phone: (617) 482-0876
Boston, MA 02210
Covers: About 30 television stations, 330 radio stations, 1,140 newspapers, 300 New England periodicals, and other media available in Connecticut, Maine, Massachusetts, New Hampshire, Rhode Island, Vermont; 725 media representatives for above media as well as taxi cab, outdoor, transit, and aerial advertising are listed. **Entries include:** For media - Medium name, address, phone, circulation or audience, name of contact. For representatives - Name, address, phone. **Arrangement:** By medium. **Pages** (approx.): 75. **Frequency:** Annual, last December issue. **Editor:** Charles E. Jackson. **Advertising accepted.** **Price:** $10.00; included in annual subscription, $7.00.

★1055★
NEW ENGLAND BUSINESS—TOP 200 INDUSTRIAL/TOP 200 SERVICE ISSUES
Yankee, Inc.
120 Tremont Street, Suite 420   Phone: (617) 482-7040
Boston, MA 02108
Covers: New England's top 100 industrial firms and top 100 service firms. **Entries include:** Company name, headquarters city, rank, sales or revenues, net income, profits. **Arrangement:** Ranked by sales/revenues. **Frequency:** Annual; industrial list beginning of June, service list, mid-June. **Editor:** Theresa Engstrom. **Advertising accepted.** **Former title:** New Englander - Top 200 Issue. **Price:** $1.00 per issue.

★1056★
NEW ENGLAND ELECTRICAL BLUE BOOK
Gleason Publishing Company, Inc.
Box 515   Phone: (617) 545-5311
Scituate, MA 02066
Covers: Electrical manufacturers, electrical utility companies, municipal inspectors, hospitals, universities and colleges, architectural and engineering firms, electrical product distributors, manufacturers' representatives, and members of the National Electrical Contractors

Association (New England) and National Electrical Manufacturers Representatives Association. **Entries include:** Company name, address, phone; most listings also include name of key executive, representative, or buyer. Representatives' listings include lines handled. **Arrangement:** By type of company, then geographical. **Indexes:** Product. **Pages** (approx.): 240. **Frequency:** Annual, January. **Editor:** Charles Pyle, Publisher. **Advertising accepted.** Circulation 15,000. **Price:** $9.50 (current and 1980 editions).

New England Manufacturers Directory *See* Directory of New England Manufacturers

★1057★
NEW ENGLAND MEDIA DIRECTORY
New England Publishing Company, Inc.
Five Auburn Street   Phone: (617) 879-4460
Framingham, MA 01701
Covers: Over 1,950 newspapers, periodicals, college publications, radio and television stations operating in New England. **Entries include:** For newspapers, periodicals, and college publications - Banner or title, address, phone, circulation, date and frequency of publication; publishing company, school, or political affiliation. College publications also include characteristics of readership. Periodicals with non-specific titles include description of contents. Newspaper listings also include process used, advertising and editorial deadlines, advertising rates, page and column size, names of editor and publisher. Editors' and executives' names, titles, and papers (daily and Sunday) are also listed in an insert with publisher address and phone. For radio and television stations - Call letters for station, channel, address, phone, broadcast area and times, network affiliation, names of station personnel. Radio stations also include description of station format. **Arrangement:** Newspapers, periodicals, and college publications are arranged by banner or title; Radio and television stations are arranged by town. **Indexes:** Newspaper by county, newspaper by name, chain newspaper by group name, radio station by call letters, television stations by call letters, general. **Pages** (approx.): 300. **Frequency:** Annual, spring; fall update. **Editor:** Thomas M. Georgon. **Former title:** Directory of New England Newspapers, College Publication, Periodicals, Radio and Television Stations (1978). **Price:** $24.00 (current edition); $27.00 (1980 edition); including update and insert.

★1058★
NEW ENGLAND REGION COMPREHENSIVE MINORITY BUSINESS LISTING
Minority Business Opportunity Committee
Boston Federal Executive Board
John F. Kennedy Federal Building
Boston, MA 02203
Covers: About 1,000 firms mostly in Massachusetts, Connecticut, Maine, Rhode Island, New Hampshire, and Vermont offering commercial, industrial, and professional products and services. **Entries include:** Company name, address, phone, name of contact, product or service. **Arrangement:** Classified. **Indexes:** Alphabetical. **Pages** (approx.): 125. **Frequency:** Semiannual, January and July. **Price:** Free.

New Englander—Top 200 Issue *See* New England Business—Top 200 Issues

★1059★
NEW FIRMS LISTING SERVICE [Long Island, N. Y.]
Long Island Association of Commerce and Industry
425 Broadhollow Road   Phone: (516) 752-9600
Melville, NY
Covers: 25 to 50 new plants, expansions, relocations, and incorporations of firms in Nassau and Suffolk counties. **Entries include:** Company name, address, name of executive contact, products or services, number of employees, and square footage of plant. **Arrangement:** Geographical. **Frequency:** Monthly. **Editor:** Alice Gelbert. **Price:** $9.50 per year to members; $25.00 to nonmembers.

★1060★
NEW HAMPSHIRE MEDIA DIRECTORY
New England Newsclip Agency, Inc.
Five Auburn Street   Phone: (617) 879-4460
Framingham, MA 01701
Covers: 150 newspapers, periodicals, college publications, and 55 radio and television broadcasting stations operating in New Hampshire. **Price:** $15.00. **Other information:** Entry content, arrangement, etc., same as "New England Media Directory," described in separate listing.

★1061★
NEW HAMPSHIRE STATE INDUSTRIAL DIRECTORY
State Industrial Directories Corporation
Two Penn Plaza   Phone: (212) 564-0340
New York, NY 10001
Number of listings: 1,500. **Entries include:** Company name, address, phone, names of key executives, number of employees, plant size, 4-digit SIC code, products, whether firm imports or exports, and whether firm has research facilities. **Arrangement:** Geographical. **Indexes:** Alphabetical, product (includes mailing address and phone for each firm). **Frequency:** Biennial, fall of odd years. **Advertising accepted.** **Price:** $20.00, plus $2.75 shipping (ISSN 0098-6216).

★1062★
NEW INDUSTRIES OF THE SEVENTIES
Conway Publications, Inc.
Peachtree Terminal
1954 Airport Road   Phone: (404) 458-6026
Atlanta, GA 30341
Covers: More than 8,000 new plants and industrial expansions announced, under construction, or completed between January 1970 and December 1977. **Entries include:** Company name, address, nature and dollar value of change or expansion, planned use of new facilities. **Arrangement:** Geographical. **Pages** (approx.): 220. **Frequency:** Published 1978. **Editors:** H. M. Conway, L. L. Liston, R. J. Saul. **Price:** $65.00. **Other information:** Compendium of "Industrial Development - Million Dollar Plants" column (see separate listing).

★1063★
NEW JERSEY BLACK DIRECTORY
Urbana, Inc.
715 Park Avenue   Phone: (201) 674-1680
East Orange, NJ 07017
Covers: Over 300 firms offering commercial and consumer services in New Jersey. **Entries include:** Company name, address, phone; larger ads include additional detail. **Arrangement:** Classified. **Frequency:** Annual, January. **Editor:** George E. Hyman. **Advertising accepted.** Circulation 50,000. **Former title:** The Black Pages. **Price:** $3.00.

★1064★
NEW JERSEY BUSINESS—TOP 100 EMPLOYERS ISSUE
New Jersey Business and Industry Association
50 Park Place   Phone: (201) 623-8359
Newark, NJ 07102
Entries include: Company name, address, name of principal executive, total number of employees in New Jersey, rank by number of employees in current and preceding year. **Arrangement:** By number of employees. **Frequency:** Annual, May. **Editor:** James T. Prior. **Advertising accepted.** **Price:** $1.00 (1980 edition).

★1065★
NEW JERSEY BUSINESS CHANGE SERVICE
State Industrial Directories Corporation
Two Penn Plaza   Phone: (212) 564-0340
New York, NY 10001
Covers: New firms, personnel changes, relocations, company closings, etc. **Entries include:** Company name, address, phone, SIC number; if a relocation, includes former address; if a new company, includes available information on size, products, etc. **Arrangement:** By county **Pages** (approx.): 30. **Frequency:** Quarterly. **Editor:** Doris Grillo.

Advertising accepted. Circulation 5,000. Price: $90.00 per year, plus $1.50 shipping (ISSN 0149-824X).

★1066★

NEW JERSEY DIRECTORY OF MANUFACTURERS
Commerce Register, Inc.
213 First Street   Phone: (201) 445-3000
Hohokus, NJ 07423
Covers: 11,500 industrial firms with five or more employees. Entries include: Company name, address, phone, names of principal executives, product descriptions, SIC codes, plant size, number of employees, sales, banking affiliation, attorneys, auditors. Arrangement: Geographical. Pages (approx.): 600. Frequency: Annual, September; first edition September 1979. Advertising accepted. Circulation 3,500. Price: $59.50.

★1067★

NEW JERSEY EN SUS MANOS
New Jersey en sus Manos
311 Elizabeth Avenue   Phone: (201) 355-3550
Elizabeth, NJ 07206
Covers: Primarily Hispanic-owned businesses offering consumer and commercial services and products. (A yellow-pages-style directory limited to advertisers.) Arrangement: Classified. Frequency: Annual, March. Advertising accepted. Circulation 100,000. Price: Free.

★1068★

NEW JERSEY INTERNATIONAL TRADE DIRECTORY
Office of International Trade
Division of Economic Development
New Jersey Department of Labor and Industry
1100 Raymond Boulevard, Room 508   Phone: (201) 648-3518
Newark, NJ 07102
Covers: 4,000 New Jersey firms which engage in international trade or are interested in doing so. Entries include: Firm name, address, phone, names of key personnel, square feet occupied, number of employees, whether firm is presently in international trade, and whether it has research facilities. Arrangement: By SIC number. Indexes: Company name; also includes references to SIC classifications from related BTN (Brussels Tariff Nomenclature) and SITC (Standard International Trade Classification) codes. Frequency: Irregular; latest edition December 1978. Editor: F. Gordon Simmons. Advertising accepted. Price: $45.00.

★1069★

NEW JERSEY MEDIA DIRECTORY
New Jersey Clipping Service
99 E. Northfield Avenue   Phone: (201) 994-3333
Livingston, NJ 07039
Covers: Over 830 New Jersey periodicals, newspapers, college publications, radio and television stations. Also includes New York City and Philadelphia daily newspapers with sections specifically for New Jersey. Pages (approx.): 105. Frequency: Annual, spring; fall update. Price: $24.00 (current edition); $27.00 (1980 edition). Other information: Content, format, and arrangement similar to that of "New England Media Directory," described in separate listing, except general index is not included.

★1070★

NEW JERSEY STATE INDUSTRIAL DIRECTORY
State Industrial Directories Corporation
Two Penn Plaza   Phone: (212) 564-0340
New York, NY 10001
Covers: About 14,500 firms with six or more employees in New Jersey. Entries include: Company name, address, phone, names of key executives, number of employees, plant size, 4-digit SIC code, products, whether firm imports or exports, and whether firm has research facilities. Arrangement: Geographical. Indexes: Alphabetical, product (includes mailing address and phone for each firm). Pages (approx.): 575. Frequency: Annual, July. Advertising accepted. Price: $87.00, plus $2.75 shipping (ISSN 0098-6224).

New Mexico Directory of Manufacturing and Mining *See* Directory of New Mexico Manufacturing and Mining

★1071★

NEW MEXICO MINORITY SUPPLIERS DIRECTORY
New Mexico Minority Purchasing Council
2040 Fourth Street, N. W., Suite C   Phone: (505) 766-3480
Albuquerque, NM 87102
Covers: About 300 firms offering professional, commercial, and industrial products and services. Entries include: Company name, address, phone, name of contact, capability number and description of product, number of employees, date established. Arrangement: Classified. Indexes: Product/service. Pages (approx.): 70. Frequency: Irregular; latest edition June 1979; new edition expected July 1980. Price: Free.

★1072★

NEW YORK AND SURROUNDING TERRITORY CLASSIFIED BUSINESS DIRECTORY
New York Directory Company, Inc.
Five Tanyard Lane   Phone: (516) 549-1256
Huntington, NY 11743
Covers: 35,000 manufacturers, wholesalers, hotels, and service companies throughout New York, New Jersey, and Connecticut. Entries include: Company name, address, phone, list of products or services. Arrangement: Classified by line of business. Pages (approx.): 1,080. Frequency: Annual, April. Advertising accepted. Price: $39.95 (current and 1980 editions).

★1073★

NEW YORK BUSINESS CHANGE SERVICE
State Industrial Directories Corporation
Two Penn Plaza   Phone: (212) 564-0340
New York, NY 10001
Covers: New firms, personnel changes, relocations, company closings, etc. Entries include: Company name, address, phone, SIC number; if a relocation, includes former address; if a new company, includes available information on size, products, etc. Arrangement: By county. Pages (approx.): 40. Frequency: Quarterly. Editor: Doris Grillo. Advertising accepted. Circulation 5,000. Price: $90.00 per year, plus $1.50 shipping (ISSN 0149-8231).

★1074★

NEW YORK CITY TRADE UNION HANDBOOK
New York City Central Labor Council, AFL-CIO
386 Park Avenue South, Room 601   Phone: (212) 685-9552
New York, NY 10016
Covers: 500 local unions in the New York City area, 13 local union councils and New York City Central Labor Council; also lists 110 international unions and national AFL-CIO. Entries include: Union name, address, phone, names of executives. Arrangement: Alphabetical by union name. Pages (approx.): 170. Frequency: Irregular; latest edition December 1977. Editor: Sally Genn. Price: Free.

★1075★

NEW YORK PORT HANDBOOK
Maritime Association of New York
80 Broad Street   Phone: (212) 425-5704
New York, NY 10004
Covers: Steamship, towing, and transportation companies, ship builders and dry dock facilities, warehouses, marine sales and service companies, banks, admiralty attorneys and other firms engaged in shipping and world trade in the Port of New York-New Jersey. Entries include: Company or organization name, address, phone, products or services. Pages (approx.): 165. Price: $5.00.

★1076★
NEW YORK STATE INDUSTRIAL DIRECTORY
State Industrial Directories Corporation
Two Penn Plaza   Phone: (212) 564-0340
New York, NY 10001
Number of listings: 20,000. **Entries include:** Company name, address, phone, names of key executives, number of employees, plant size, 4-digit SIC code, products, whether firm imports or exports, and whether firm has research facilities. **Arrangement:** Geographical. **Indexes:** Alphabetical, product (includes mailing address and phone for each firm). **Pages** (approx.): 875. **Frequency:** Annual, January. **Advertising accepted. Price:** $90.00, plus $2.75 shipping (1980 edition; ISSN 0149-8231).

★1077★
NEW YORK STATE MEDIA DIRECTORY
Burrelle's Press Clipping Service
75 E. Northfield Avenue   Phone: (212) 227-5570
Livingston, NJ 07039
Covers: Over 1,600 New York state newspapers, college publications, periodicals, radio and television stations. **Pages** (approx.): 215. **Frequency:** Annual, spring; fall update. **Price:** $26.00 (current edition); $29.00 (1980 edition). **Other information:** Content, format, and arrangement similar to that of "New England Media Directory," described in separate listing, except general index is not included.

New York-New Jersey Port Scheduled Steamship Service Directory *See* Port of New York-New Jersey Scheduled Steamship Service Directory

★1078★
NEWARK AREA CHAMBER OF COMMERCE—MANUFACTURERS LIST [Licking County, Ohio]
Newark Area Chamber of Commerce
50 W. Locust Street   Phone: (614) 345-9757
Newark, OH 43055
Number of listings: Over 200. **Entries include:** Company name, address, phone, names of executives, code for number of employees, list of products or services. **Arrangement:** Alphabetical within manufacturers and industrial services categories. **Frequency:** Annual, September. **Editor:** C. Allen Milliken, Executive Vice President. **Price:** $2.50.

Newspaper Directory *See* Working Press of the Nation

★1079★
NIAGARA FALLS INDUSTRIAL DIRECTORY [New York State]
Niagara Falls Area Chamber of Commerce
468 Third Street   Phone: (716) 285-9141
Niagara Falls, NY 14301
Covers: About 75 member industrial firms and financial institutions. **Entries include:** For industrial firms - Company name, address, phone, names and titles of principal executives; code for number of employees; products or services; SIC numbers; whether firm exports; and whether tours are offered; listings for subsidiaries include parent name and address. Similar data for banks includes branches. **Arrangement:** Manufacturers and banks in separate alphabetical lists. **Indexes:** Company name. **Frequency:** Annual, January. **Editor:** John J. Reardon, Jr., Executive Vice President. **Price:** $10.00 (current and 1980 editions).

★1080★
NOISE CONTROL DIRECTORY
Fairmont Press
134 Peachtree Street, N. E., Suite 918   Phone: (404) 892-1784
Atlanta, GA 30303
Covers: Manufacturers and distributors of noise pollution control equipment; trade associations, consulting engineers, and government agencies concerned with noise control are also listed. **Entries include:** Company name, address, phone, contact. **Arrangement:** By activity.

Pages (approx.): 115. **Frequency:** Irregular; latest edition September 1979. **Editor:** Claudia Archibald. **Price:** $24.50.

★1081★
NOMDA SPOKESMAN—WHO'S WHO ISSUE
National Office Machine Dealers Association
1510 Jarvis Avenue   Phone: (312) 593-3270
Elk Grove Village, IL 60007
Covers: 4,200 retailers and 200 manufacturers of typewriters, calculators, copying machines, and other office machines; 25 office machine repair educational programs in public and proprietary schools. **Entries include:** Company name, address, phone, names of executives; dealer listings include codes showing products handled. **Arrangement:** Dealers are geographical, manufacturers alphabetical. **Indexes:** Personal name, product. **Pages** (approx.): 200. **Frequency:** Annual, June. **Editor:** Marilyn Helfers, Publications Coordinator. **Advertising accepted. Price:** $75.00.

Nonwoven Fabrics and Disposable Soft Goods Directory *See* International Directory of the Nonwoven Fabric Industry

Nonwoven Fabrics Industry—International Directory *See* International Directory of the Nonwoven Fabrics Industry

★1082★
NONWOVENS INDUSTRY—FABRIC MANUFACTURERS GUIDE ISSUE
Rodman Publishing Company
Box 555   Phone: (201) 825-2552
Ramsey, NJ 07446
Publication includes: About 100 international manufacturers of nonwoven fabrics. **Entries include:** Company name, address, sales managers' names, phone, manufacturing method, fibers used, and trade names of company's products. **Arrangement:** Alphabetical. **Frequency:** Annual, June. **Editor:** Edward H. Silk. **Advertising accepted.** Circulation 10,500. **Former title:** Formed Fabric Industry - Fabric Manufacturers Guide Issue. **Price:** $2.50.

★1083★
NONWOVENS INDUSTRY—MACHINERY/EQUIPMENT BUYER'S GUIDE ISSUE
Rodman Publishing Company
Box 555   Phone: (201) 825-2552
Ramsey, NJ 07446
Covers: About 250 manufacturers of machinery and equipment used in the production of nonwoven fabrics and disposable soft goods. **Entries include:** Company name, address, phone; name and title of chief executive; products offered. **Arrangement:** Alphabetical. **Indexes:** Product. **Pages** (approx.): 75. **Frequency:** Annual, July. **Editor:** Ed Silk. **Advertising accepted.** Circulation 9,800. **Price:** $2.50.

★1084★
NORTH AMERICAN REGISTER OF BUSINESS AND INDUSTRY
Global Marketing Services, Inc.
19562 Ventura Boulevard   Phone: (213) 996-3500
Tarzana, CA 91356
Covers: 5,000 largest companies by sales volume, plus local advertisers. **Entries include:** For largest firms - Company name, address, phone, total number of employees, SIC number, total annual sales. For advertisers - Smallest unit of space is listing similar to large firm listings; larger units in display form may include officials, product information, etc. **Arrangement:** Largest firms are by sales volume and geographical, same information in each sequence; advertisers appear in geographical sequence only. **Indexes:** None. **Pages** (approx.): 925. **Frequency:** Annual, February. **Editor:** Burton Goldman, President. **Advertising accepted.** Circulation 13,500. **Price:** $58.00.

★1085★

**NORTH AMERICAN SOCIETY FOR CORPORATE PLANNING—
    DIRECTORY OF MEMBERS**

North American Society for Corporate Planning
1406 Third National Building
Dayton, OH 45402

Covers: 1,300 corporate planners. **Entries include:** Name, title, office address and phone number. **Arrangement:** Alphabetical within area chapter; alphabetical by company name. **Pages** (approx.): 160. **Frequency:** Annual, May. **Editor:** R. P. Palomo, Secretary. **Price:** Available to members only.

North American Telephone Association—Directory *See* **Business Telephone & Equipment Industry**

North Carolina Companies *See* **Carolinas Companies**

★1086★

NORTH CAROLINA METALWORKING DIRECTORY

Industrial Extension Service
School of Engineering
North Carolina State University
Box 5506   Phone: (919) 737-2358
Raleigh, NC 27650

Covers: About 300 metalworking shops and plants in North Carolina which will accept jobbing work. **Entries include:** Contact information and description of capablilities. **Arrangement:** By county. **Indexes:** Alphabetical and by process offered. **Pages** (approx.): 210. **Frequency:** Approximately triennial; latest edition March 1978. **Editor:** R. L. Edwards, P. E., Metalworking Specialist. **Price:** $5.00, payment with order. **Send orders to:** Industrial Extension Service, North Carolina State University, Box 1125, New Bern, NC 28560. **Other information:** Variant title, "North Carolina Metalworking Facilities Directory."

North Carolina Metalworking Facilities Directory *See* **North Carolina Metalworking Directory**

★1087★

NORTH CAROLINA MINORITY BUSINESS DIRECTORY

Office of Minority Business Enterprise
North Carolina Department of Commerce
430 N. Salisbury Street   Phone: (919) 733-4962
Raleigh, NC 27611

Covers: About 600 firms offering professional, commercial, industrial, and consumer products and services. **Entries include:** Company name, address, phone. **Arrangement:** Classified. **Frequency:** Irregular; latest edition December 1977; new edition expected February 1980. **Price:** Free.

★1088★

NORTH CAROLINA STATE INDUSTRIAL DIRECTORY

State Industrial Directories Corporation
Two Penn Plaza   Phone: (212) 564-0340
New York, NY 10001

Number of listings: 6,700. **Entries include:** Company name, address, phone, names of key executives, number of employees, plant size, 4-digit code, products, whether firm imports or exports, and whether firm has research facilities. **Arrangement:** Geographical. **Indexes:** Alphabetical, product (includes mailing address and phone for each firm). **Frequency:** Irregular; latest edition December 1979. **Advertising accepted. Price:** $50.00, plus $2.75 shipping (ISSN 0161-8571).

★1089★

NORTH DAKOTA MINORITY ENTERPRISES

Small Business Administration
653 Second Avenue North
Fargo, ND 58102

Covers: About 140 firms offering primarily consumer products and services and construction services. **Entries include:** Company name,

address, phone, line of business. **Arrangement:** Alphabetical. **Indexes:** Line of business. **Frequency:** Irregular; latest edition June 1978; new edition expected summer 1980. **Price:** Free.

★1090★

**NORTH DAKOTA RURAL ELECTRIC AND TELEPHONE
    COOPERATIVES—DIRECTORY**

North Dakota Association of Rural Electric Cooperatives
Box 727   Phone: (701) 663-6501
Mandan, ND 58554

Covers: Rural electric distribution, generation, and transmission cooperatives, rural telephone cooperatives, includes cooperatives in bordering states. Also lists local, regional, and national affiliated organizations. **Entries include:** Company name, address, phone, area served, and names of principal personnel. **Arrangement:** Alphabetical within divisions of membership. **Indexes:** Advertiser. **Pages** (approx.): 170. **Frequency:** Biennial, January of even years. **Editor:** Milton T. Vedvick. **Advertising accepted.** Circulation 1,200. **Price:** $5.00 (1980 edition).

★1091★

**NORTHAMERICAN HEATING & AIRCONDITIONING WHOLESALERS
    ASSOCIATION—MEMBERSHIP DIRECTORY**

Northamerican Heating & Airconditioning Wholesalers Association
1661 W. Henderson Road   Phone: (614) 459-2100
Columbus, OH 43220

Number of listings: 1,530 wholesalers and distributors. **Entries include:** Company name, address, phone, and names of executives. **Arrangement:** Alphabetical. **Frequency:** Annual, spring. **Price:** Available to members only.

Northwest Electric Power Directory *See* **Northwest Electric Utility Directory**

★1092★

NORTHWEST ELECTRIC UTILITY DIRECTORY

Northwest Public Power Association
1310 Main Street   Phone: (206) 694-6553
Vancouver, WA 98666

Covers: All electric utilities in Washington, Oregon, Idaho, Montana, Alaska, and British Columbia, Alberta, and the Yukon. **Entries include:** Company name, address, phone, names of executives, financial keys. **Arrangement:** Geographical. **Indexes:** Type of utility (municipal, cooperative, etc.). **Pages** (approx.): 100. **Frequency:** Annual, April. **Editor:** Al Aldrich, Communications Director. **Advertising accepted.** Circulation 3,600. **Former title:** Northwest Electric Power Directory. **Price:** $5.00 (1980 edition).

★1093★

**NORTHWESTERN-IOWA DEALER REFERENCE MANUAL [Lumber
    and building materials]**

Northwestern Lumbermen, Inc.
7300 France Avenue South   Phone: (612) 830-2910
Minneapolis, MN 55435

Covers: Retail lumber and building material dealers in Minnesota, Iowa, North Dakota, and South Dakota. Also lists manufacturers, wholesalers, and distributors who pay to advertise. **Entries include:** For dealers - Company name, address, phone, name of principal executive, trade and brand names, and list of products or services. For advertisers - Company name, commodity listings, and trade names. **Pages** (approx.): 140. **Frequency:** Annual, September. **Editor:** Robert L. Pitz, Director of Publications. **Advertising accepted.** Circulation 2,500. **Price:** $35.00.

★1094★

OAG POCKET TRAVEL PLANNER

Offical Airline Guide, Inc.
2000 Clearwater Drive   Phone: (312) 654-6000
Oakbrook, IL 60521

Covers: 2,700 hotels and 2,000 restaurants in 62 major United States cities. **Entries include:** For hotels and motels - Name, Mobil

Travel Guide rating, address, phone, and room rate range. For restaurants - Name, Mobil Travel Guide rating, address, phone, and type of menu. **Arrangement:** By city. **Pages** (approx.): 200. **Frequency:** Quarterly. **Editor:** M. E. Nester, Publication Manager. **Advertising accepted. Circulation** 20,000. **Price:** $20.00 per year. **Also includes:** A directory of toll free 800 phone numbers for car rental firms, hotel systems, airport limousines, bus and rail services.

★1095★
OAG TRAVEL PLANNER & HOTEL/MOTEL GUIDE (NORTH AMERICAN EDITION)
Official Airline Guide, Inc.
2000 Clearwater Drive   Phone: (312) 654-6000
Oakbrook, IL 60521
Covers: 12,000 destination cities, military installations (U.S. only), and colleges and universities in North America and travel information related to them; 17,000 hotels and motels, and hotel and motel systems and reservations services; calendars of events; city, state or province, and national tourist offices; tour operators; car rental agencies; airport limousine services; consulates and missions of foreign countries in North America and United States; foreign service offices, worldwide; airport and other travel facilities for handicapped persons. **Entries include:** For destinations - Place name, airport name and code or note on nearest air service; larger cities include information on hotel names, addresses, phones, rates, and Mobil Travel Guide rating. Calendar of events - Date, name, and location of event, and names, addresses, and phones of state and local tourism agencies. Airport facilities for handicapped - City and, in dot chart form, data on parking, stairs, ramps, etc. Other listings include name, address, phone. **Arrangement:** Primarily geographical. **Pages** (approx.): 675. **Frequency:** Quarterly. **Advertising accepted.** Circulation 57,000. **Price:** $18.00 per issue; $40.00 per year.

★1096★
OASIS: THE COMPLETE GUIDE TO BOTTLED WATER THROUGHOUT THE WORLD
Capra Press
629 State Street   Phone: (805) 966-4590
Santa Barbara, CA 93101
Covers: 70 brands of bottled water throughout the world in detail, and additional bottlers in less detail. **Entries include:** For main entries - Brand name, bottler name and address, reproduction of label, chemical analysis, brief history of the water or brand, and discussion of any special uses. **Pages** (approx.): 190. **Frequency:** Published 1978. **Editor:** Arthur Von Wiesenberger. **Price:** $6.95.

★1097★
O'DWYER'S DIRECTORY OF CORPORATE COMMUNICATIONS
J. R. O'Dwyer Company, Inc.
271 Madison Avenue   Phone: (212) 679-2471
New York, NY 10016
Covers: Public relations departments of 2,300 major United States companies (listed on the New York Stock Exchange or in the "Fortune" list of 1,000 largest firms). Also includes similar information on 300 large trade associations. **Entries include:** Company name, address, phone, sales, type of business; names and duties of principal public relations personnel at headquarters and other major offices, plus name and title of person to whom PR head reports; name and address of outside PR counsel, if any; PR budget. **Arrangement:** Alphabetical. **Indexes:** Geographical, product. **Pages** (approx.): 250. **Frequency:** Annual, July. **Editor:** Jack O'Dwyer. **Price:** $60.00.

★1098★
O'DWYER'S DIRECTORY OF PUBLIC RELATIONS FIRMS
J. R. O'Dwyer Company, Inc.
271 Madison Avenue   Phone: (212) 679-2471
New York, NY 10016
Covers: Over 900 public relations firms in the United States. **Entries include:** Firm name, address, phone, principal executives, branch offices, billings, date founded, and clients. **Arrangement:**

Alphabetical. **Indexes:** Specialty (beauty and fashions, finance/investor, etc.), geographical, clients. **Pages** (approx.): 200. **Frequency:** Annual, spring. **Editor:** Jack O'Dwyer. **Price:** $35.00 (current edition); $40.00 (1980 edition). **Also includes:** List of top 50 PR firms.

★1099★
OFF THE SHELF: THE ELECTRONIC DISTRIBUTORS MASTER CATALOG
United Technical Publications
645 Stewart Avenue   Phone: (516) 222-2500
Garden City, NY 11530
Covers: Electronic and electromechanical products available off-the-shelf from distributors. **Entries include:** Company name, address, phone, products and brand names. **Frequency:** Annual, November. **Editor:** Frank Egan. **Advertising accepted. Price:** $10.00.

★1100★
OFFICIAL BUS GUIDE
Russell's Guides, Inc.
817 Second Avenue, S. E.   Phone: (319) 364-6138
Cedar Rapids, IA 52406
Publication includes: List of about 475 intercity bus companies in United States, Canada, and Mexico. **Entries include:** Company name, address, phone, executives' names and titles, list of terminals and stations with terminal managers' names. **Pages** (approx.): 800. **Frequency:** Monthly. **Editor:** James E. Rogers, Senior Vice President. **Advertising accepted. Circulation** 14,000. **Price:** $41.00, plus $4.80 shipping for subscription of 12 issues, beginning with issue current at time order is received (ISSN 0036-0171). **Other information:** Principal content of publication is intercity operating timetables. Variant title is, "Russell's Official National Motor Coach Guide."

★1101★
OFFICIAL CONTAINER DIRECTORY
Magazines for Industry, Inc.
777 Third Avenue   Phone: (212) 838-7778
New York, NY 10017
Covers: Manufacturers of corrugated and solid fibre containers, folding cartons, rigid boxes, fibre cans and tubes, and fibre drums. Includes a buyers guide of equipment, materials, and services for the industry and a packaging and shipping machinery guide (SIC 2640 series). **Entries include:** Company name, address, phone, equipment, names of executives, plants, and type of containers manufactured. Guide sections include similar information. **Arrangement:** Classified by type of container manufactured, then geographically. **Indexes:** Product. **Pages** (approx.): 150. **Frequency:** Semiannual, spring and fall. **Editor:** Joel J. Shulman. **Advertising accepted.** Circulation 5,000. **Price:** $20.00 per issue; $35.00 per year.

★1102★
OFFICIAL DIRECTORY OF INDUSTRIAL AND COMMERCIAL TRAFFIC EXECUTIVES
Traffic Service Corporation
815 Washington Building
1435 G Street, N. W.   Phone: (202) 783-7325
Washington, DC 20005
Covers: 12,000 United States and Canadian firms with full-time or part-time traffic departments and 22,000 traffic executives. Also includes about 2,000 other persons in associations, federal and state regulatory agencies, and consulting firms involved in transportation and distribution-related activities. **Entries include:** Company entries show company name, address, phone, names and titles of traffic department personnel, plant and branch office locations. **Arrangement:** Alphabetical by company name. **Indexes:** Company, personal name. **Pages** (approx.): 465. **Frequency:** Annual, October. **Editor:** Callie Possinger. **Advertising accepted.** Circulation 6,000. **Price:** $35.00, postpaid, payment with order.

Official Guide of the Railways & Steam Navigation Lines *See* Official Railway Guide—North American Passenger Edition

Official Guide of the Railways & Steam Navigation Lines *See* Official Railway Guide—North American Freight Service Edition

★1103★
OFFICIAL HOTEL & RESORT GUIDE
Ziff-Davis Publishing Company
One Park Avenue   Phone: (212) 725-7460
New York, NY 10016
Covers: 20,000 hotels, resorts, and motor hotels worldwide. Volume 1 covers the U. S.; Volume 2, Europe; and Volume 3, Western Hemisphere (excluding U. S.), Africa, Asia, Australia, and the Pacific. Separate lists of golf resorts and tennis resorts; health spas in the United States. **Entries include:** Hotel/motel/resort name, address, phone, name of manager, number of rooms or units, rates, brief description of facilities, codes indicating credit cards accepted and commission rates, if any. **Arrangement:** Geographical. **Frequency:** Annual. **Editor:** Dorothy H. Rubin. **Advertising accepted.** **Price:** $155.00 for set of 3 volumes in looseleaf binder, including periodic updates.

★1104★
OFFICIAL MEETING FACILITIES GUIDE
Ziff-Davis Publishing Company
One Park Avenue   Phone: (212) 725-3858
New York, NY 10016
Covers: 1,000 national and international meeting facilities, primarily hotels in the United States. **Entries include:** Name of facility, types of accommodations, dining and entertainment available, group rates, meeting room capacities, facts for exhibitors, access and transportation data, equipment and services available. **Arrangement:** Geographical. **Pages** (approx.): 1,000. **Frequency:** Semiannual, spring and fall. **Editor:** Virginia Nonneman. **Advertising accepted.** Circulation 15,000. **Price:** $30.00 (current and 1980 editions).

★1105★
OFFICIAL MOTOR CARRIER DIRECTORY
Official Motor Carrier Directory, Inc.
1130 Canal Street   Phone: (312) 939-1434
Chicago, IL 60607
Covers: 2,100 general and specialized motor carriers, and air freight carriers. **Entries include:** Company name, address, phone, names of executives, terminals, services, tariffs, insurance. **Arrangement:** Alphabetical. **Indexes:** Geographical. **Pages** (approx.): 650. **Frequency:** Semiannual, May and November. **Editor:** Nancy Westhorpe. **Advertising accepted.** Circulation 6,000. **Price:** $19.50 per year; single copies not available.

★1106★
OFFICIAL RAILWAY GUIDE—NORTH AMERICAN FREIGHT SERVICE EDITION
National Railway Publication Company
424 W. 33rd Street   Phone: (212) 563-7300
New York, NY 10001
Covers: Railways in North America offering freight service. Includes lists of railroad associations, state railroad commissions, federal regulatory agencies. **Entries include:** Railroad name, general office, address, phone, names of executives, list of services, schedules, maps, local sales offices and their phone numbers and executives. **Arrangement:** Alphabetical. **Indexes:** Index of stations and lines serving them. **Pages** (approx.): 725. **Frequency:** Bimonthly. **Editor:** Marie A. Todor. **Advertising accepted.** Circulation 5,500. **Former title:** Official Guide of the Railways & Steam Navigation Lines... (1974). **Price:** $15.50 per issue; $55.00 per year.

★1107★
OFFICIAL RAILWAY GUIDE—NORTH AMERICAN PASSENGER TRAVEL EDITION
National Railway Publication Company
424 W. 33rd Street   Phone: (212) 563-7300
New York, NY 10001
Covers: Railways in North America offering passenger service. **Entries include:** Railroad name, address, phone, name of one executive, list of services, schedules, maps. **Indexes:** Index of stations and lines serving them. **Pages** (approx.): 250. **Frequency:** Monthly, except February and August. **Editor:** Marie A. Todor. **Advertising accepted.** Circulation 10,000. **Former title:** Official Guide of the Railways & Steam Navigation Lines... (1974). **Price:** $6.00 per issue; $35.00 per year.

★1108★
OFFICIAL SOURCE GUIDE TO FLEET SAFETY TRAINING AIDS
J. J. Keller & Associates, Inc.
145 W. Wisconsin Avenue   Phone: (414) 722-2848
Neenah, WI 54956
Publication includes: List of truck driver training schools. **Entries include:** For training aids - Title, description of content, producer, address. For schools - Name, address. **Arrangement:** Training aids are by subject, schools are geographical. **Pages** (approx.): 75. **Frequency:** Irregular; latest edition 1979; new edition expected 1980. **Editor:** George McDowell. **Price:** $10.00.

★1109★
OHIO CONTRACTOR—DIRECTORY AND BUYER'S GUIDE ISSUE
Ohio Contractors Association
41 S. High Street   Phone: (614) 228-6831
Columbus, OH 43215
Covers: 900 construction firms or construction industry suppliers who are members or associates of the association. **Entries include:** For members - Company name, address, phone, names and titles of executives, whether labor relations division member. For associates - Company name, address, phone, name of contact, addresses of branches. **Arrangement:** Alphabetical in membership categories. **Indexes:** Product. **Frequency:** Annual, May. **Editor:** Wanda Kerr Dunbar, Editor. **Advertising accepted.** Circulation 7,800. **Price:** $5.00. **Send orders to:** Wanda Kerr Dunbar, Inc., 4645 Executive Dr., Columbus, OH 43220 (614-457-8570).

★1110★
OHIO INDUSTRIAL DIRECTORY
Harris Publishing Company
2057-2 Aurora Road   Phone: (216) 425-9143
Twinsburg, OH 44087
Number of listings: 16,500. **Entries include:** Company name, address, phone, key personnel, year established, plant size, annual sales, number of employees, SIC number and product description. **Arrangement:** Geographical. **Indexes:** Product, SIC number, manufacturer name. **Pages** (approx.): 950. **Frequency:** Annual, November. **Former title:** Directory of Ohio Manufacturers (1976); Ohio Manufacturers Industrial Directory (1979). **Price:** $49.50.

Ohio Manufacturers Industrial Directory *See* Ohio Industrial Directory

★1111★
OHIO MINORITY BUSINESS GUIDE
Minority Business Development Office
Ohio Department of Economic and Community Development
Box 1001   Phone: (614) 466-5700
Columbus, OH 43216
Covers: Nearly 1,000 firms offering professional, commercial, industrial, and consumer products and services. **Entries include:** Company name, address, phone, name of owner or president, number of employees, facilities and equipment, licenses, credit references, etc. **Arrangement:** Classified. **Indexes:** Geographical, company. **Frequency:** Irregular; latest edition December 1979. **Price:** One-time

charge of $10.00, updates free.

★1112★
OHIO ROSTER [Publicly traded firms]
Edward Howard & Company
1021 Euclid Avenue   Phone: (216) 781-2400
Cleveland, OH 44115
Covers: About 140 manufacturers, retailers, service companies, transportation firms, public utilities, and financial institutions with revenues of $100 million or more located in Ohio whose stock is publicly traded. **Entries include:** Firm name, location, line of business, total revenues, net income, total assets, current and prior year's earnings and dividends per share, dividend as a percent of earnings for most recent year, stock data, and stock exchange on which traded. **Arrangement:** Ranked by total revenues. **Pages** (approx.): 15. **Frequency:** Annual; first edition October 1979. **Price:** $1.00.

★1113★
OKLAHOMA DIRECTORY OF MANUFACTURERS AND PRODUCTS
Oklahoma Industrial Development Department
507 Will Rogers Memorial Office Building   Phone: (405) 521-2181
Oklahoma City, OK 73105
Number of listings: 3,500 manufacturers and mineral producers (SIC 13, 20-29). **Entries include:** Company name, address, phone, name of principal executive, number of employees, date established, area served, SIC numbers, list of products or services. **Arrangement:** Geographical. **Indexes:** SIC, alphabetical. **Pages** (approx.): 625. **Frequency:** Biennial, early in even years. **Editor:** Lee Zimmerman, Information Specialist. **Price:** $20.00 (1980 edition).

★1114★
100 COMPANIES RECEIVING THE LARGEST DOLLAR VOLUME OF MILITARY PRIME CONTRACT AWARDS
Directorate for Information Operations & Reports
Washington Headquarters Services
Defense Department
Pentagon, Room 4B 938   Phone: (202) 697-3182
Washington, DC 20301
Entries include: Company name, subsidiary names, amount of awards, percent of total United States Defense Department awards. **Arrangement:** By dollar volume. **Indexes:** Alphabetical. **Pages** (approx.): 20. **Frequency:** Annual. **Price:** Free.

★1115★
ONLINE—"DOCUMENT DELIVERY" [Column]
Online, Inc.
11 Tannery Lane   Phone: (203) 227-8466
Weston, CT 06883
Covers: About 60 vendors able to supply originals or photocopies of government documents, patents, standards and specifications, Securities and Exchange Commission reports, journal and periodical articles, etc. **Entries include:** Vendor name, address, phone, description of materials supplied, whether paper or micrographic copies, charges, special services. **Arrangement:** Classified by type of material supplied. **Frequency:** Quarterly. **Price:** $52.00 per year. **Other information:** Present column began with review in January 1978 issue of 60 suppliers active at that time; later columns provide revisions, data on additional suppliers, etc.

★1116★
OPD CHEMICAL BUYERS DIRECTORY
Schnell Publishing Company, Inc.
100 Church Street   Phone: (212) 732-9820
New York, NY 10007
Covers: 1,700 suppliers of chemical process materials and 320 companies which transport and store chemicals in the United States. **Entries include:** Company name, address, phone, list of products or services, telex numbers. **Arrangement:** Alphabetical. **Pages** (approx.): 1,000. **Frequency:** Annual, August. **Editors:** Gaetana Carideo and Toni Neville. **Advertising accepted.** Circulation 17,000. **Price:** Available only with subscription to "Chemical Marketing Reporter,"

$32.00 a year. **Other information:** Principal content of publication is an alphabetical listing of about 10,000 chemical process materials and their suppliers.

Optical Industry and Systems Directory *See* Optical Purchasing Directory, Encyclopedia & Dictionary

★1117★
OPTICAL PURCHASING DIRECTORY, ENCYCLOPEDIA & DICTIONARY
Optical Publishing Company, Inc.
Box 1146
Berkshire Common   Phone: (413) 499-0514
Pittsfield, MA 01201
Covers: Over 1,500 United States and over 300 foreign manufacturers and suppliers listed in Volume 1, the buyers' guide. (Volume 2 is an optical industry encyclopedia and dictionary.) **Entries include:** Company, name, address, phone, names of executives and technical personnel, description of products and services. **Arrangement:** Alphabetical; foreign manufacturers arranged geo-alphabetically. **Indexes:** Geographical, product. **Pages** (approx.): 1,250 (2 volumes). **Frequency:** Annual, September. **Editor:** Mrs. Teddie C. Laurin, Publisher. **Advertising accepted.** Circulation 10,000. **Former title:** Optical Industry and Systems Directory. **Price:** $38.50 per set (ISSN 0078-5474).

★1118★
ORANGE COUNTY BUSINESS AND INDUSTRIAL DIRECTORY [California]
Orange County Chamber of Commerce
One City Boulevard West   Phone: (714) 634-2900
Orange, CA 92668
Number of listings: 5,000. **Entries include:** Company name, address, phone, names and titles of key personnel, line of business, number of employees. **Frequency:** Annual. **Price:** $28.50, payment must accompany order.

Oregon Concrete and Aggregate Producers Association—Roster *See* Pacific Builder & Engineer—Buyers Guide & Directory Issue

★1119★
OREGON INTERNATIONAL TRADE DIRECTORY
International Trade Division
Oregon Department of Economic Development
921 S.W. Washington   Phone: (503) 229-5535
Portland, OR 97205
Covers: Over 600 firms engaged in international trade. **Entries include:** Company name, address, phone, name of principal executive, trade and brand names, list of products, SIC numbers. **Arrangement:** Alphabetical (current edition); by SIC (1980 edition). **Indexes:** Product, SIC, country exported to. **Frequency:** Biennial, January of even years. **Former title:** International Trade Directory for the State of Oregon. **Price:** $5.00 (current edition); $10.00 (1980 edition).

Oregon Manufacturers Directory *See* Directory of Oregon Manufacturers

★1120★
OREGON STATE INDUSTRIAL DIRECTORY
State Industrial Directories Corporation
Two Penn Plaza   Phone: (212) 564-0340
New York, NY 10001
Number of listings: 5,000. **Entries include:** Company name, address, phone, names of key executives, number of employees, plant size, 4-digit SIC code, products, whether firm imports or exports, and whether firm has research facilities. **Arrangement:** Geographical. **Indexes:** Alphabetical, product (includes mailing address and phone for each firm). **Frequency:** Not established; first edition expected January 1980. **Advertising accepted.** **Price:** $30.00.

★1121★
OUTLET STORES IN NORTH CAROLINA
Division of Economic Development
North Carolina Department of Natural and Economic Resources
Box 27687   Phone: (919) 733-5816
Raleigh, NC 27611
Covers: Factory outlet stores. **Entries include:** Name, address, phone, and products for sale. **Arrangement:** Geographical. **Pages** (approx.): 10. **Frequency:** Irregular. **Price:** Free; one per request.

★1122★
OVERSEAS SUMMER JOBS
Vacation-Work
9 Park End Street
Oxford OX1 1HJ, England
Covers: More than 50,000 jobs, worldwide. **Entries include:** Name of employer, address, length of employment, number of positions available, pay rates, how and when to apply, name of contact. **Pages** (approx.): 170. **Frequency:** Annual, December. **Editor:** Charles James. **Former title:** Directory of Overseas Summer Jobs. **Price:** $6.95. **Send orders to:** Writer's Digest Books, 9933 Alliance Road, Cincinnati, OH 45242 (513-984-0717).

★1123★
PACIFIC BUILDER & ENGINEER—BUYERS GUIDE & DIRECTORY ISSUE
Vernon Publications, Inc.
109 W. Mercer Street   Phone: (206) 285-2050
Seattle, WA 98119
Covers: Heavy construction equipment manufacturers; distributors of such equipment; suppliers of sand, gravel, and ready-mix concrete, and equipment finance companies in Oregon, Washington, Idaho, and Montana. Includes a list of government contracting agencies. Rosters are also included for the Idaho Concrete and Aggregate Producers Association, Montana Ready Mix and Concrete Products Association, Oregon Concrete and Aggregate Producers Association, and Washington Aggregates and Concrete Association. **Entries include:** For distributors, manufacturers, and suppliers - Company name, address, phone, names of executives, trade and brand names, list of products or services. **Arrangement:** By activity; distributors are then geographical, others are alphabetical. **Pages** (approx.): 100. **Frequency:** Annual, March. **Editor:** Roscoe E. Laing. **Advertising accepted.** Circulation 9,000. **Price:** $10.00 (current and 1980 editions).

Pacific Coast Aviation Directory and Buyer's Yellow Pages *See* Aviation Directory

★1124★
PACIFIC COAST INDUSTRIAL DIRECTORY
Bender Publications, Inc.
4077 W. Pico Boulevard   Phone: (213) 737-6820
Los Angeles, CA 90019
Covers: Manufacturers, dealers, distributors, and their representatives supplying machine tools, fabrication equipment, supplies, etc., to metalworking and plastic fabricating firms in California, Oregon, Washington, and Arizona. **Entries include:** Company name, address, phone. **Arrangement:** By product. **Indexes:** Trade name. **Pages** (approx.): 325. **Frequency:** Annual, July. **Advertising accepted.** **Price:** $20.00.

★1125★
PACIFIC COAST MARINE DIRECTORY
Marine Digest, Inc.
218 National Building   Phone: (206) 682-2484
Seattle, WA 98104
Covers: About 7,500 companies offering services and products to the shipping industry in Washington, Oregon, California, Hawaii, Alaska, and British Columbia. Services include shipbuilding and ship repair, tugs, freight forwarders and other shippers, etc. Ports are also listed. **Entries include:** Company name, address, phone; many listings include names and titles of key personnel. **Arrangement:** By ports. **Pages** (approx.): 385. **Frequency:** Annual, November. **Editor:** Timothy J. Dwyer. **Advertising accepted.** Circulation 2,800. **Price:** $5.00.

★1126★
PACKAGE ENGINEERING—ANNUAL BUYER'S GUIDE ISSUE
Cahners Publishing Company
Five S. Wabash Avenue   Phone: (312) 372-6880
Chicago, IL 60603
Covers: Over 2,400 manufacturers of packaging machinery, containers, materials, and supplies used in packaging foods and other products; also lists converters, contract packagers, and testing laboratories. **Entries include:** Company name, address, phone, and products and services offered. **Arrangement:** Alphabetical. **Indexes:** Product, brand or trade name. **Frequency:** Annual, October. **Advertising accepted.** **Price:** $20.00.

★1127★
PACKAGE PRINTING—DIEMAKERS AND DIECUTTERS ANNUAL DIRECTORY ISSUE
North American Publishing Company
401 N. Broad Street   Phone: (215) 574-9600
Philadelphia, PA 19108
Covers: Commercial and in-plant diemakers and diecutters for package printers, and manufacturers and distributors of diemaking and diecutting equipment and supplies; coverage includes the United States and Canada. **Entries include:** For all listings - Company name, address. For diemakers and diecutters - Code indicating whether commercial or in-plant. **Arrangement:** Diemakers and diecutters are geographical; manufacturers and suppliers are alphabetical. **Indexes:** Product. **Frequency:** Annual, June. **Editor:** Henni Marine. **Advertising accepted.** Circulation 7,000. **Price:** $2.00.

★1128★
PACKAGED DIRECTORY [Manufactured housing]
Manufactured Housing Newsletter
410 Grove Avenue   Phone: (312) 381-4312
Barrington, IL 60010
Covers: About 630 companies which produce panels and trusses for custom home builders, panelized package homes, and log, geodesic, pre-cut kit type homes and commercial buildings. Top 25 manufacturers are listed. **Entries include:** Company name, address, phone; names and titles of key personnel, coding to indicate products, areas covered, number of homes or components produced for current and prior two years. **Arrangement:** Alphabetical. **Indexes:** Geographical. **Pages** (approx.): 130. **Frequency:** Irregular; previous edition 1976; latest edition March 1979. **Editor:** Shepard Robinson. **Former title:** Directory/Census of Manufactured Housing (1979). **Price:** $36.00.

Packaging Machinery Manufacturers Institute—Directory *See* PMMI Packaging Machinery Directory

★1129★
PACKAGING MARKETPLACE
Gale Research Company
Book Tower   Phone: (313) 961-2242
Detroit, MI 48226
Covers: More than 4,000 manufacturers, distributors, wholesalers, and others providing services, materials, and equipment to the packaging industry. **Entries include:** Company name, address, phone, name of contact; specialties are mentioned if not apparent from classification. **Arrangement:** Classified by major types of products and services. **Pages** (approx.): 290. **Frequency:** Published June 1978. **Editor:** Joseph F. Hanlon. **Price:** $45.00. **Also includes:** Each section is introduced with a description of trade practices in the segment of the industry covered, and includes a basic glossary.

★1130★
PAINT RED BOOK
Palmerton Publishing Company, Division
Communication Channels, Inc.
6285 Barfield Road   Phone: (404) 256-9800
Atlanta, GA 30328
Covers: About 1,100 paint and coatings manufacturers located in the United States, Puerto Rico, and Canada; products include production, application, and aerosol equipment; testing services and consulting laboratories are also listed. **Entries include:** Company name, address, phone, and products or services offered. **Arrangement:** Alphabetical. **Indexes:** Geographical, trade and brand name. **Pages** (approx.): 300. **Frequency:** Annual, spring. **Editor:** Art Sweum. **Advertising accepted.** Circulation 5,000. **Price:** $27.50.

★1131★
PAPER COATING ADDITIVES
Technical Association of the Pulp and Paper Industry
One Dunwoody Park   Phone: (404) 393-6130
Atlanta, GA 30338
Publication includes: List of manufacturers of paper coating chemical additives. **Entries include:** Company name, address. **Arrangement:** By product. **Pages** (approx.): 60. **Frequency:** Irregular; latest edition 1978. **Price:** $14.00. **Other information:** Principal content of publication is descriptive information of the chemicals discussed.

★1132★
PAPER, FILM & FOIL CONVERTER—ANNUAL DIRECTORY &
    BUYERS GUIDE
Maclean-Hunter Publishing Corporation
300 W. Adams Street   Phone: (312) 726-2802
Chicago, IL 60606
Covers: 1,000 companies worldwide which manufacture packaging and nonpackaging products from paper, paperboard, film or foil. Includes separate list of suppliers to the converting industry. **Entries include:** Company name, address, phone, list of executives, list of products or services, and list of branch offices and subsidiaries. **Indexes:** Product. **Pages** (approx.): 325. **Frequency:** Annual, June. **Editor:** Peter A. Rigney. **Advertising accepted.** Circulation 21,000. **Price:** $3.50 (current edition); $5.00 (1980 edition).

★1133★
PAPER INDUSTRY MANAGEMENT ASSOCIATION—MEMBERSHIP
    DIRECTORY
Paper Industry Management Association
2400 E. Oakton Street   Phone: (312) 956-0250
Arlington Heights, IL 60005
Covers: 3,000 pulp, paper mill, and paper converting production executives. **Entries include:** Name, office address and phone, home address, and name of spouse. **Arrangement:** Alphabetical by member name. **Pages** (approx.): 100. **Frequency:** Annual, July. **Editor:** William D. Hall. **Advertising accepted.** Circulation 3,000. **Price:** Available to members only.

★1134★
PARK AREAS AND EMPLOYMENT OPPORTUNITIES FOR SUMMER
    [YEAR] [National parks]
National Park Service
Interior Department
Washington, DC 20242
Covers: Seasonal job openings in five job categories anticipated in the National Park Service; regional offices are listed. **Entries include:** For regional offices - Name, address. For job openings - Location code number, name of park, state, summer season dates, estimated number of positions available within job categories and grade levels. **Arrangement:** By region. **Pages** (approx.): 10. **Frequency:** Annual. **Price:** Free.

★1135★
PARK MAINTENANCE—ANNUAL BUYERS' GUIDE ISSUE
Madisen Publishing Company
Box 1936   Phone: (414) 733-2301
Appleton, WI 54913
Covers: About 1,000 manufacturers and suppliers of materials and equipment for the maintenance of parks, golf courses, campuses, pools, and other large outdoor areas. **Entries include:** Company name, address, and products. **Arrangement:** Alphabetical. **Indexes:** Product. **Pages** (approx.): 20. **Frequency:** Annual, October. **Editor:** Erik Madisen, Jr. **Advertising accepted.** Circulation 17,000. **Price:** $2.00.

★1136★
PARKS AND RECREATION—ANNUAL BUYERS' GUIDE ISSUE
National Recreation and Park Association
1601 N. Kent Street   Phone: (703) 525-0606
Arlington, VA 22209
Covers: 530 companies supplying products and services to private and governmental park and recreation agencies. **Entries include:** Company name and address. **Arrangement:** Classified by product or service. **Pages** (approx.): 20. **Frequency:** Annual, January. **Editor:** Margaret Smith. **Advertising accepted.** Circulation 22,000. **Price:** $1.50 (current and 1980 editions).

Parts/Equipment Buyers' Guide & Services Directory [Trucks]
    See Heavy Duty Trucking—Council of Fleet Specialists
    Equipment Buyers' Guide

★1137★
PENJERDEL LOCATION AND MARKET GUIDE [Pennsylvania, New
    Jersey, Delaware]
Greater Philadelphia Chamber of Commerce
1617 J. F. Kennedy Boulevard, Suite 1960   Phone: (215) 568-4040
Philadelphia, PA 19103
Covers: About 250 industrial parks, 100 shopping centers with 20 or more stores, 600 facilities which undertake research and development projects, 250 multinational companies with operations in the area, and various services such as utilities, development assistance agencies, banks, colleges, real estate firms, etc. Also includes profiles of county and township governments and school districts, with addresses and names of officials. **Entries include:** All listings include firm or agency name, address; park listings give name, address, and phone of management firm, acreage and utilities available; R&D firm listings give list of specialties. **Arrangement:** Classified by function or service. **Pages** (approx.): 325. **Frequency:** Annual, March. **Editor:** Jody Gallagher Miller. **Advertising accepted.** Circulation 13,000. **Price:** $20.00 (current and 1980 editions). **Other information:** Principal content of publication is market, tax, demographic and other information and statistics related to selection of business sites. Publication is issued by PENJERDEL Corporation, regional affiliate of the Chamber's publication bureau.

★1138★
PENNSYLVANIA BUSINESS CHANGE SERVICE
State Industrial Directories Corporation
Two Penn Plaza   Phone: (212) 564-0340
New York, NY 10001
Covers: New firms, personnel changes, relocations, company closings, etc. **Entries include:** Company name, address, phone, SIC number; if a relocation, includes former address; if a new company, includes available information on size, products, etc. **Arrangement:** By county. **Frequency:** Quarterly. **Price:** $90.00 per year, plus $1.50 shipping.

★1139★
PENNSYLVANIA DIRECTORY OF MANUFACTURERS
Commerce Register, Inc.
213 First Street   Phone: (201) 445-3000
Hohokus, NJ 07423
Number of listings: 13,500. **Pages** (approx.): 650. **Frequency:** Annual; first edition expected February 1980. **Advertising accepted.**

Price: $59.50, plus 95¢ shipping. **Other information:** Entry content, format, etc., similar to "Connecticut & Rhode Island Directory of Manufacturers," described in separate listing.

★1140★
PENNSYLVANIA EXPORTERS DIRECTORY
Bureau of Statistics, Research and Planning
Pennsylvania Department of Commerce
Health and Welfare Building, Room 630B   Phone: (717) 787-7532
Harrisburg, PA 17120
Covers: 2,500 manufacturers who export goods from Pennsylvania. **Entries include:** Company name, address, list of products exported, SIC numbers. **Arrangement:** Alphabetical. **Indexes:** Product. **Pages** (approx.): 120. **Frequency:** Biennial, spring of odd years. **Editor:** Dr. JoAnne L. Young, Director, Bureau of Statistics, Research, and Planning. **Price:** Free.

★1141★
PENNSYLVANIA STATE INDUSTRIAL DIRECTORY
State Industrial Directories Corporation
Two Penn Plaza   Phone: (212) 564-0340
New York, NY 10001
Number of listings: 15,000. **Entries include:** Company name, address, phone, names of key executives, number of employees, plant size, 4-digit SIC code, products, whether firm imports or exports, and whether firm has research facilities. **Arrangement:** Geographical. **Indexes:** Alphabetical, product (includes mailing address and phone for each firm). **Pages** (approx.): 725. **Frequency:** Annual, March. **Advertising accepted.** **Price:** $90.00, plus $2.75 shipping (ISSN 0553-6065).

★1142★
PEORIA AREA MANUFACTURERS DIRECTORY [Illinois]
Peoria Area Chamber of Commerce
230 S. W. Adams Street   Phone: (309) 676-0755
Peoria, IL 61602
Number of listings: Over 300. **Entries include:** Company name, address, phone, name of principal executive, number of employees, list of products or services, SIC numbers. **Frequency:** Annual, fall. **Editor:** Robert G. Arnett, Manager of Economic Development. **Price:** $4.00, postpaid.

Performance Warehouse Association *See* **Specialty and Custom Dealer—Performance Warehouse Association Directory Issue**

★1143★
PETROLEUM EQUIPMENT DIRECTORY
Petroleum Equipment Institute
3739 E. 31st Street   Phone: (918) 743-9941
Tulsa, OK 74135
Covers: Over 700 manufacturers and distributors of petroleum marketing equipment worldwide who are members of the institute. **Entries include:** Company name, address, phone, names of executives, list of products or services. **Arrangement:** Manufacturers listed alphabetically, distributors listed geographically. **Frequency:** Annual, January. **Editor:** Robert N. Renkes, Administrative Director. **Advertising accepted.** Circulation 2,000. **Price:** $10.00 (1980 edition).

★1144★
PHELON'S DISCOUNT STORES
Phelon, Sheldon & Marsar, Inc.
32 Union Square East   Phone: (212) 473-2590
New York, NY 10003
Covers: 1,990 large discount and self-service stores and chain store headquarters that buy hard and soft department store merchandise; also includes 8,000 jobbers, rack jobbers, and catalog show rooms. **Entries include:** Company name, address, phone, names of executives, trade and brand names. **Arrangement:** Geographical. **Pages** (approx.): 400. **Frequency:** Biennial, August of even years. **Price:** $60.00.

★1145★
PHELON'S WOMEN'S SPECIALTY STORES
Phelon, Sheldon & Marsar, Inc.
32 Union Square East   Phone: (212) 473-2590
New York, NY 10003
Covers: Approximately 18,000 women's apparel and accessory shops and chains. **Entries include:** Name, address, headquarters, number of shops, merchandise lines, buyers and representatives, store size, price ranges. **Arrangement:** Geographical. **Pages** (approx.): 350. **Frequency:** Biennial, August of odd years. **Price:** $60.00.

★1146★
PHI DELTA GAMMA—MEMBERSHIP DIRECTORY [Women graduate students]
Phi Delta Gamma
2412 Rebecca Road   Phone: (913) 537-8227
Manhattan, KS 66502
Covers: About 8,500 women pursuing graduate studies, and alumnae members of the society. **Frequency:** Annual, May. **Price:** Available to members only.

★1147★
PHI THETA PI—MEMBERSHIP DIRECTORY [Business]
Phi Theta Pi
2103 Cortez Road   Phone: (904) 641-0964
Jacksonville, FL 32216
Covers: About 23,000 male college students pursuing majors in business who have been elected to this honor society for outstanding attainment, and alumni members of the society; includes some faculty members. **Editor:** Richard B. Glover, Grand Secretary-Treasurer. **Price:** Available to members only.

★1148★
PHILADELPHIA MARITIME EXCHANGE PORT DIRECTORY
Philadelphia Maritime Exchange
620 Lafayette Building   Phone: (215) 915-1522
Philadelphia, PA 19106
Covers: Services and facilities of the Port of Philadelphia. **Entries include:** Company name, address, phone. **Arrangement:** Classified by product or service. **Pages** (approx.): 205. **Frequency:** Annual, spring. **Editor:** William A. Harrison, Jr. **Price:** $5.00.

★1149★
PHONEFICHE [Telephone directories]
Micro Photo Division
Bell & Howell
Old Mansfield Road   Phone: (216) 264-6666
Wooster, OH 44691
Background: "Phonefiche" is a microfiche collection of telephone directories covering about 90% of cities and towns in the United States with a population of 25,000 or more, including suburban directories, in many cases; both white and yellow pages are usually provided; directories of major federal government departments are also included. The "Community Cross-Reference Guide" lists thousands of communities alphabetically and shows which telephone directory serves each community. **Frequency:** Collection is updated as new telephone directories appear. **Price:** Available separately or in groups according to number and size of areas covered; e.g., Category 1 (top 10 metropolitan areas), $129.00; Category 5 (246 metropolitan areas), $780.00. Category 6 (towns over 25,000), $1,370.00.

★1150★
PHOTO WEEKLY—BUYERS HANDBOOK & PRODUCT GUIDE ISSUE
Billboard Publications, Inc.
1515 Broadway   Phone: (212) 764-7396
New York, NY 10036
Covers: 625 manufacturers and distributors of photographic supplies and equipment, worldwide; photofinishers; photographic repair technicians; manufacturers' representatives. **Entries include:** Company name, address, phone, information on products or services. **Arrangement:** Classified. **Indexes:** Product. **Frequency:** Semiannual,

January and July. **Editor:** Sophie Smoliar, Publisher. **Advertising accepted.** Circulation 10,500. **Price:** $15.00, postpaid, payment with order.

★1151★
PHOTOGRAPHIC MANUFACTURERS & DISTRIBUTORS ASSOCIATION—MEMBERSHIP DIRECTORY
Photographic Manufacturers & Distributors Association
866 United Nations Plaza, Suite 436   Phone: (212) 688-3520
New York, NY 10017
Covers: About 70 importers, distributors, and manufacturers of photographic products. **Entries include:** Company name, address, phone, names of contacts; many listings include description of company and products. **Arrangement:** Alphabetical. **Pages (approx.):** 15. **Frequency:** Annual, spring. **Price:** Free.

★1152★
PHOTOGRAPHIC TRADE NEWS—MASTER BUYING GUIDE AND DIRECTORY ISSUE
PTN Publishing Corporation
250 Fulton Avenue   Phone: (516) 489-1300
Hempstead, NY 11550
Covers: 1,500 manufacturers of photographic equipment. **Entries include:** Company name, address, phone, names of executives, trade and brand names, list of products, distributors. **Arrangement:** Alphabetical. **Indexes:** Product. **Pages (approx.):** 500. **Frequency:** Annual, January. **Editor:** Alan Carlton. **Advertising accepted.** Circulation 14,000. **Price:** $4.00. **Other information:** Similar in content to "Photographic Trade News - Professional Photographic Equipment Directory" (see separate listing), but with emphasis on retail amateur market.

★1153★
PHOTOGRAPHIC TRADE NEWS—PROFESSIONAL PHOTOGRAPHIC EQUIPMENT DIRECTORY AND BUYING GUIDE ISSUE
PTN Publishing Corporation
250 Fulton Avenue   Phone: (516) 489-1300
Hempstead, NY 11550
Covers: Manufacturers and distributors of photographic equipment and supplies; photographic equipment repair services; photofinishing services specializing in work for professional photographers. **Entries include:** For manufacturers and distributors - Company name, address, phone, names of principal executives, trade and brand names, list of products or services. Similar data for repair and finishing services. **Arrangement:** Classified by major product or service areas. **Indexes:** Brand name. **Pages (approx.):** 300. **Frequency:** Annual, August. **Advertising accepted.** Circulation 30,000. **Price:** $10.00. **Other information:** Sometimes cited as "Professional Photographic Equipment Directory and Buying Guide."

★1154★
PIMA CATALOG: PAPER AND PULP MILL CATALOG AND ENGINEERING HANDBOOK
Paper Industry Management Association
2400 E. Oakton Street   Phone: (312) 956-0250
Arlington Heights, IL 60005
Covers: Manufacturers and distributors of chemicals, equipment, supplies, and services used in the manufacture of paper. **Entries include:** Company name, address, phone, trade and brand names, products. **Arrangement:** Alphabetical. **Indexes:** Product. **Pages (approx.):** 320. **Frequency:** Annual, January. **Editor:** William D. Hall. **Advertising accepted.** Circulation 5,000. **Price:** $25.00 (current edition); $35.00 (1980 edition). **Also includes:** Substantial portion of content is engineering and statistical data.

★1155★
PIPELINE & UNDERGROUND UTILITIES CONSTRUCTION—ANNUAL CONTRACTORS ISSUE
Oildom Publishing Company
3314 Mercer   Phone: (713) 622-0676
Houston, TX 77027
Publication includes: About 9,000 individual contracting firms concerned with the construction of oil and gas pipelines, water and sewer lines, gas distribution systems, and underground cable construction; international coverage (SIC 1623). **Entries include:** Company name, address, phone, names of executives, types of construction undertaken. **Arrangement:** Geographical. **Pages (approx.):** 200. **Frequency:** Annual, June. **Editor:** Daniel Dietsch. **Advertising accepted.** Circulation 13,000. **Price:** $20.00.

★1156★
PIT & QUARRY HANDBOOK AND BUYER'S GUIDE
Pit & Quarry Publications, Inc.
105 W. Adams Street   Phone: (312) 726-7151
Chicago, IL 60603
Publication includes: About 125 paid advertisers of supplies and equipment used in the production of nonmetallic minerals and cement. **Entries include:** Advertiser's name, address, and phone. **Arrangement:** Alphabetical. **Pages (approx.):** 700. **Frequency:** Annual, October. **Editor:** Charles P. Holmes. **Advertising accepted.** Circulation 8,500. **Price:** $65.00.

★1157★
PITTSBURGH FEDERAL EXECUTIVE BOARD MINORITY BUSINESS DIRECTORY
Minority Business Opportunity Committee
Pittsburgh Federal Executive Board
Federal Building, Room 614
1000 Liberty Avenue   Phone: (412) 644-5882
Pittsburgh, PA 15222
Covers: About 200 firms offering professional, commercial, industrial, and consumer products and services. **Entries include:** Name of business, owner, address, phone, line of business, years in operation, years of owner's experience, union affiliations, upper limit per contract, and government work performed. **Arrangement:** Classified. **Indexes:** Company, subject. **Pages (approx.):** 110. **Frequency:** Irregular; latest edition October 1979. **Editor:** Faye O. Johnson, Executive Director. **Price:** Free.

★1158★
PLACES: A DIRECTORY OF PUBLIC PLACES FOR PRIVATE EVENTS & PRIVATE PLACES FOR PUBLIC FUNCTIONS [New York area]
Tenth House Enterprises
Caller Box 810
Gracie Station
New York, NY 10028
Covers: 600 public and private facilities which can be used for exhibits, promotional meetings, conferences, rehearsals, parties, sports events, etc. Includes unusual places such as antique railroad cars, piers, vineyards, etc. **Entries include:** Name of facility, address, phone, name of contact, brief description of facility, rental fee, equipment available, uses and restrictions on use. **Arrangement:** Alphabetical; includes broad categories (e.g., auditoriums) within which listings may also be alphabetical and/or geographical. **Indexes:** Name of facility. **Pages (approx.):** 140. **Frequency:** Approximately every 18 months; latest edition 1979; new edition expected April 1980. **Editors:** Hannelore Hahn and Tatiana Stoumen. **Price:** $10.95, plus $1.00 shipping.

★1159★
PLANT AND OWNERSHIP LIST [Electric generating plants]
Office of Energy Data Operations
Energy Information Administration
Energy Department
1000 Independence Avenue, N. W.   Phone: (202) 252-6401
Washington, DC 20585
Covers: Generating plants which are illustrated on a set of maps entitled, "Principal Electric Facilities;" operating and under-construction plants are listed. **Entries include:** Plant name, type of plant, designation of the Electric Reliability Council in which the plant is located, installed capacity in megawatts, and type of ownership. **Arrangement:** Geographical. **Pages** (approx.): 90. **Frequency:** Annual. **Price:** $2.75 (S/N 061-003-00001-1). **Send orders to:** Government Printing Office, Washington, DC 20402. **Other information:** "Principal Electric Facilities" is composed of 11 regional maps which show locations of the above described electric generating plants. It also includes transmission lines, distribution substations, operating and design voltage, submarine cables, underground cables, and other similar details. To obtain maps, specify states desired; $2.00 per copy.

★1160★
PLANT ENERGY MANAGEMENT—SPECIFIERS GUIDE AND
   TECHNOLOGY REVIEW ISSUE
Walker-Davis Publications, Inc.
2500 Office Center   Phone: (215) 657-3203
Willow Grove, PA 19090
Covers: About 3,000 manufacturers and suppliers of energy conservation and energy-efficient equipment, systems, products, and services for industrial and commercial applications. **Entries include:** Company name, address, distributor name, distributor location, products. **Arrangement:** By product. **Indexes:** Geographical, alphabetical. **Pages** (approx.): 220. **Frequency:** Annual, December; first edition 1979. **Editor:** Frank McGill. **Advertising accepted.** Circulation 30,000. **Price:** $20.00.

★1161★
PLANT ENGINEERING DIRECTORY & SPECIFICATIONS CATALOG
Technical Publishing Company, Inc.
1301 S. Grove Avenue   Phone: (312) 381-1840
Barrington, IL 60010
Publication includes: List of manufacturers and suppliers of equipment and materials used in manufacturing and processing plant maintenance and engineering (SIC 20-39). **Entries include:** Company name, address, products. **Indexes:** Product. **Frequency:** Annual, March. **Advertising accepted.** Circulation 35,000.

★1162★
PLASTICS DESIGN & PROCESSING—BUYERS GUIDE ISSUE
Lake Publishing Corporation
Box 159   Phone: (312) 362-8711
Libertyville, IL 60048
Covers: Manufacturers and suppliers of reinforced plastics/composites industry. **Entries include:** Company name, address, phone, name of contact. **Arrangement:** Alphabetical. **Indexes:** Product. **Frequency:** Annual, January. **Editor:** Gary Miller. **Advertising accepted.** Circulation 45,000. **Price:** $3.00.

★1163★
PLASTICS TECHNOLOGY—SPECIAL HANDBOOK AND BUYER'S
   GUIDE ISSUE
Bill Communications, Inc.
633 Third Avenue   Phone: (212) 986-4800
New York, NY 10017
Publication includes: Suppliers of machinery, materials, chemicals, and additives for the plastics processing industry. **Entries include:** Company name, address, phone, and products or services. **Arrangement:** By product groups (equipment, etc.). **Pages** (approx.): 525. **Frequency:** Annual, May. **Editor:** Malcolm W. Riley. **Advertising accepted.** Circulation 38,600. **Price:** $19.50. **Also includes:** Product

list with specifications and descriptions of machinery, chemicals and additives, and thermoplastic materials.

★1164★
PLASTICS WEST DIRECTORY
Plastics Focus Publishing
30 E. 42nd Street, Room 1717A
New York, NY 10017
Covers: 2,000 suppliers of machinery, services, supplies, materials, film and sheet, additives, and reinforcements used in the plastic processing industry in the western United States. **Entries include:** Company name, address, phone, personnel, representatives serving the western states, branch offices, and products or services. **Arrangement:** Geographical. **Indexes:** Product. **Pages** (approx.): 200. **Frequency:** Annual, late fall. **Advertising accepted.** **Price:** $15.00, payment with order; $16.50, billed.

★1165★
PLASTICS WORLD SUPPLIERS REFERENCE FILE
Cahners Publishing Company
221 Columbus Avenue   Phone: (617) 536-7780
Boston, MA 02116
Covers: About 750 manufacturers and suppliers of products and equipment used in plastics manufacturing. **Entries include:** Company name, address, phone. **Arrangement:** Alphabetical. **Indexes:** Product, trade name. **Pages** (approx.): 150. **Frequency:** Annual, October. **Editor:** Bernard S. Miller. **Advertising accepted.** Circulation 60,000. **Price:** $12.50 (ISSN 0032-1273).

★1166★
PLAYTHINGS—DIRECTORY ISSUE
Geyer-McAllister Publications, Inc.
51 Madison Avenue   Phone: (212) 689-4411
New York, NY 10010
Covers: Toy manufacturers and suppliers, designers and inventors, manufacturers' representatives, trade names, and fairs. **Entries include:** Company name, address, phone, description of products manufactured or lines carried. **Arrangement:** Manufacturers are listed alphabetically and by product category, suppliers by product category, and manufacturers' representatives geographically. **Indexes:** Advertiser. **Pages** (approx.): 240. **Frequency:** Annual, May. **Editor:** Frank Reysen. **Advertising accepted.** **Price:** $11.00 (current and 1980 editions).

P/M Industries Association—Membership List *See* Custom
   Engineered P/M Parts and Products Manufacturers Directory
   International

★1167★
PMMI PACKAGING MACHINERY DIRECTORY
Packaging Machinery Manufacturers Institute
2000 K Street, N. W.   Phone: (202) 331-8181
Washington, DC 20006
Covers: About 175 member companies which design, manufacture, sell, and service packaging machinery. **Entries include:** Company name, address, phone, names and titles of key personnel, products and services, and names, phones, addresses, and territory of sales representatives, branch offices, and distributors. **Arrangement:** Alphabetical. **Indexes:** Product/service, alphabetical (with address). **Pages** (approx.): 315. **Frequency:** Annual, fall. **Price:** $2.00 shipping.

★1168★
POCKET LIST OF RAILROAD OFFICIALS
National Railway Publication Company
424 W. 33rd Street   Phone: (212) 563-7210
New York, NY 10001
Covers: Officials and equipment of railroads, private car companies, railroad-owned truck lines, and transit systems using or planning use of steel wheel/steel rail equipment. Also covers railroad associations, boards, departments, and commissions and their personnel, and lists Class I and Short Line railroads. **Entries include:** For companies and

associations - Name, address, phone, name of chief executive. Most railroad listings include name, address, miles of track operated, number of locomotives and other equipment. **Arrangement:** Alphabetical by line or company name. **Indexes:** Product, railroads by states. **Pages** (approx.): 880. **Frequency:** Quarterly: February, May, August, November. **Editor:** F. J. Gordon, Advertising Manager. **Advertising accepted.** Circulation 12,400. **Price:** $16.00 per year; $8.00 per issue.

★1169★

POCKETGUIDE TO CHINA'S FOREIGN TRADE ORGANIZATIONS, DOMESTIC CORPORATIONS, AND MINISTRIES

National Council for US-China Trade
1050 17th Street, N. W.
Washington, DC 20036
Covers: Foreign trade organizations, China's Foreign Trade Corporations, about 30 domestic (Chinese) corporations, and Chinese government agencies. **Entries include:** Organization or agency name, address, telex number, scope of activities. **Arrangement:** By activity. **Pages** (approx.): 70. **Frequency:** First edition 1979. **Price:** $5.00, plus $1.00 shipping.

★1170★

POLLUTION ENGINEERING—ENVIRONMENTAL YEARBOOK AND PRODUCT REFERENCE GUIDE ISSUE

Technical Publishing Company
1301 S. Grove Avenue   Phone: (312) 381-1840
Barrington, IL 60010
Covers: About 2,600 manufacturers of pollution control equipment including equipment for air, water, and noise pollution control, and for solid and liquid waste disposal. **Entries include:** Company name, address, phone, products or services. **Arrangement:** By type of equipment. **Frequency:** Annual, December. **Editor:** Nancy L. Voras, Associate Editor. **Advertising accepted.** Circulation 52,000. **Price:** $2.00.

★1171★

POLLUTION EQUIPMENT NEWS—CATALOG AND BUYER'S GUIDE ISSUE

Rimbach Publishing, Inc.
8550 Babcock Boulevard   Phone: (412) 364-5366
Pittsburgh, PA 15237
Covers: Over 2,900 manufacturers of pollution control equipment and products. **Entries include:** Company name, address, phone, and products. **Arrangement:** Alphabetical. **Indexes:** Product. **Pages** (approx.): 315. **Frequency:** Annual, November. **Editor:** David C. Lavender. **Advertising accepted.** Circulation 80,000. **Price:** $10.00.

★1172★

POLYURETHANE MANUFACTURERS ASSOCIATION— MEMBERSHIP DIRECTORY

Polyurethane Manufacturers Association
180 N. Michigan Avenue   Phone: (312) 332-5657
Chicago, IL 60601
Covers: About 110 urethane processing firms and suppliers of chemicals and equipment. **Entries include:** Company name, address, names of key personnel, branch locations, processing capabilities, and components processed. **Arrangement:** Alphabetical. **Indexes:** Geographical, process capability, components processed. **Frequency:** Annual, winter. **Price:** $10.00, payment with order.

★1173★

PORT OF DETROIT WORLD HANDBOOK

Fourth Seacoast Publishing Company, Inc.
Box 145   Phone: (313) 779-5570
St. Clair Shores, MI 48080
Covers: Commercial services and facilities at the Port of Detroit. **Arrangement:** Classified. **Pages** (approx.): 75. **Frequency:** Annual, May. **Price:** $4.50.

★1174★

PORT OF NEW YORK-NEW JERSEY SCHEDULED STEAMSHIP SERVICE DIRECTORY

Port Promotion Division
Port Authority of New York & New Jersey
One World Trade Center, Room 62 West   Phone: (212) 466-8318
New York, NY 10048
Covers: 145 steamship lines offering scheduled cargo, passenger, or cruise service at the New York-New Jersey port; active piers in port, ocean carriers, terminal operators, and railroads are also listed. **Entries include:** For steamship lines - Name of line, office address, phone, and pier location. For piers, carriers, terminal operators, and railroads - Name, address, and phone. **Arrangement:** Classified. **Indexes:** Countries to which scheduled service is provided. **Frequency:** Annual, December. **Price:** Free. **Other information:** Variant titles, "Scheduled Steamship Service Directory" and "New York-New Jersey Port Scheduled Steamship Service Directory."

★1175★

PORTLAND CAREER HUNTER'S GUIDE: A SOURCEBOOK OF LOCAL RESOURCES [Oregon]

Victoria House, Publishers
2218 N. E. Eighth Avenue   Phone: (503) 284-4801
Portland, OR 97212
Covers: 50 public and private employment agencies offering vocational guidance and placement services. **Entries include:** Agency name, address, phone, contact person, cost, eligibility standards, description of organization. **Arrangement:** By nature of service (counseling, placement, etc.) **Indexes:** Agency name. **Pages** (approx.): 145. **Frequency:** Not established; first edition 1977. **Price:** $3.95, plus 50¢ shipping.

★1176★

PORTS OF THE WORLD

Benn Publications Ltd.
25 New Street Square
London EC4A 4JA, England
Covers: About 2,150 ports, worldwide. **Entries include:** Port name; operating authority, address, and officials; container, bulk cargo, tanker, and other facilities and terminals; offshore and repair facilities; working hours and other local data. **Arrangement:** Geographical by major area (North America, Europe, etc.). **Indexes:** Ports and countries. **Pages** (approx.): 1,100. **Frequency:** Annual, October. **Advertising accepted.** **Price:** 34 pounds. **Send orders to:** Nichols Publishing Co., Box 96, New York, NY 10024.

★1177★

PORTUGUESE-AMERICAN BUSINESS REVIEW

Motivational Communications, Inc.
175 Fifth Avenue   Phone: (212) 260-0800
New York, NY 10010
Covers: About 900 import/export firms, manufacturers, and federal agencies (United States and Portugal) concerned with commerce between the two countries. **Entries include:** Company name, address, phone, and products or services offered. **Arrangement:** Alphabetical. **Pages** (approx.): 75. **Frequency:** Annual, winter. **Editor:** Barry V. Conforte. **Advertising accepted.** Circulation 50,000. **Price:** $25.00 (1980 edition).

Portuguese-American Business Review/Directory *See* Portuguese-American Business Review

★1178★

POST'S PULP & PAPER DIRECTORY

Miller Freeman Publications, Inc.
500 Howard Street   Phone: (415) 397-1881
San Francisco, CA 94105
Covers: 1,200 North American pulp and paper mills; 16,000 converters; associations, schools, and research facilities; and suppliers of equipment, services, and chemicals. **Entries include:** For mills - Company name, address, phone, names of executives, list of products

or services, equipment, and capacities. For suppliers - Company name, address, products or services, trade and brand names. **Arrangement:** Geographical. **Indexes:** Personal name index of mill officials, product. **Pages** (approx.): 675. **Frequency:** Annual, October. **Editor:** James R. Ledbetter, Managing Editor. **Advertising accepted.** Circulation 3,000. **Price:** $50.00.

★1179★
POWDER METALLURGY EQUIPMENT DIRECTORY
Powder Metallurgy Equipment Association
Box 2054   Phone: (609) 799-3300
Princeton, NJ 08540
Covers: Powder metallurgy process equipment suppliers. **Entries include:** Company name, phone, list of products or services, and product catalogs. **Pages** (approx.): 100. **Frequency:** Annual. **Price:** Free.

Powder Metallurgy Parts Association—Membership List *See* Custom Engineered P/M Parts and Products Manufacturers Directory International

★1180★
POWER GUIDE: A CATALOGUE OF SMALL SCALE POWER EQUIPMENT
Intermediate Technology Publications
9 King Street
London WC2E 8HN, England
Covers: Manufacturers of power-producing equipment including solar engines, wind-electric systems, methane digesters, hydro-mechanical and pumping systems, gas turbines and rotary engines, diesel and spark ignition engines; information sources, consultants, and R&D firms concerned with the use of power-generating equipment particularly in remote areas; worldwide coverage. **Entries include:** Company name, address. **Arrangement:** By type of equipment or firm. **Indexes:** Geographical, manufacturer name. **Frequency:** Not established; first edition August 1979. **Editor:** Peter Fraenkel. **Price:** $12.50. **Send orders to:** International Scholarly Book Services, Box 555, Forest Grove, OR 97116.

★1181★
POWER TOOL INSTITUTE—ROSTER
Power Tool Institute
605 E. Algonquin Road   Phone: (312) 593-8350
Arlington Heights, IL 60005
Covers: 200 executives of 20 manufacturers of portable, handheld, and stationary lawn and garden tools, electric and battery operated. **Entries include:** Company name, address, and phone. **Arrangement:** Alphabetical. **Pages** (approx.): 20. **Frequency:** Annual, January. **Editor:** James E. Bates, Executive Manager. **Price:** For members and other approved users only.

★1182★
POWER TRANSMISSION DESIGN HANDBOOK
Penton/IPC, Inc.
614 Superior Avenue West   Phone: (216) 696-0300
Cleveland, OH 44113
Covers: Over 650 manufacturers, distributors, and suppliers of power transmission equipment and components (bearings, controls, drives, and motors). **Entries include:** Company name, address, phone, and products. **Arrangement:** Alphabetical. **Indexes:** Product, trade name. **Pages** (approx.): 800. **Frequency:** Biennial, January of odd years. **Editor:** Tom Hughes. **Advertising accepted.** **Price:** $25.00, plus $2.00 shipping, payment with order (ISSN 0146-9134).

★1183★
PPI INTERNATIONAL PULP & PAPER DIRECTORY
Miller Freeman Publications, Inc.
500 Howard Street   Phone: (415) 397-1881
San Francisco, CA 94105
Covers: Pulp and paper mills producing over 10,000 tons of paper per year. Includes 2 sections in which producers are listed geographically

under mill grades for pulp, paper, and paperboard. Also includes buyers' guide of suppliers of equipment, chemicals, and services, and a list of trade associations. **Entries include:** Name of company (headquarters); address; phone or telex number; names of executives; number of employees; products; equipment and production capacity; subsidiary names and locations. **Arrangement:** Geographical. **Indexes:** Alphabetical (includes company address); personal name (includes company affiliation and address). **Pages** (approx.): 530. **Frequency:** Biennial, July of even years. **Editor:** Leonard E. Haas. **Advertising accepted.** Circulation 2,500. **Price:** $50.00 (current edition); $60.00 (tentative, 1980 edition).

★1184★
PR BLUE BOOK INTERNATIONAL [Information note]
PR Publishing Company, Inc.
Box 600   Phone: (603) 778-0514
Exeter, NH 03833
Description: Though still cited in current bibliographies on the field, this publication (which lists about 1,000 firms) has not been issued since 1973 (1972 data). The editor of the former edition has died, and there is no tentative date of publication for a new edition as of December 1979. **Price:** $12.50.

★1185★
PRECISION METAL—DIRECTORY ISSUE
Penton/IPC
614 Superior Avenue West   Phone: (216) 696-0300
Cleveland, OH 44113
Covers: Die and investment casters, forgers, extruders, tool and die makers, roll formers, etc., and suppliers to the industry. **Entries include:** Company name, address, phone. **Arrangement:** Classified by process, etc. **Pages** (approx.): 275. **Frequency:** Annual, January. **Editor:** Randolph B. Gold. **Advertising accepted.** **Price:** $5.50 (current and 1980 editions).

Premium Incentive & Travel Buyers *See* Salesman's Guide Nationwide Directory: Premium Incentive & Travel Buyers

★1186★
PREMIUM MERCHANDISING CLUB OF NEW YORK—DIRECTORY OF MEMBERS
Premium Merchandising Club of New York
1605 Vauxhall Road   Phone: (201) 687-3090
Union, NJ 07083
Covers: About 250 marketing executives using and supplying premiums/incentives in the development of merchandising and motivation programs. **Entries include:** Name, title, company name, address, phone, products handled. **Arrangement:** Alphabetical. **Indexes:** Company. **Pages** (approx.): 35. **Frequency:** Annual, January. **Editor:** Howard C. Henry, Executive Director. **Price:** 15¢ shipping.

★1187★
PREMIUM/INCENTIVE BUSINESS—DIRECTORY OF PREMIUM SUPPLIERS AND SERVICES ISSUE
Gralla Publications
1515 Broadway   Phone: (212) 869-1300
New York, NY 10036
Covers: 3,000 suppliers of products (including travel) used as premiums and of services needed in conducting a premium/incentive offer; also includes consultants and manufacturers' representatives. **Entries include:** Company name, address, phone; consultant and representative listings include territory, number of representatives, and memberships. **Arrangement:** Suppliers are alphabetical and classified by product (name, address, and phone in each); representatives and consultants are alphabetical. **Frequency:** Annual, February. **Editor:** Susan L. Fry, Editor/Co-Publisher. **Advertising accepted.** Circulation 26,000. **Price:** $4.00 (current and 1980 editions).

★1188★
PRESSURE SENSITIVE TAPE DIRECTORY
Pressure Sensitive Tape Council
1800 Pickwick Avenue   Phone: (312) 724-7700
Glenview, IL 60025
Publication includes: List of about 15 manufacturers of cellophane, cloth, paper, plastic, and rubber pressure sensitive tape products (excluding surgical and medical tapes). **Entries include:** Company name, address, phone, list and description of uses and characteristics of individual products. **Arrangement:** Alphabetical. **Pages (approx.):** 45. **Frequency:** Annual. **Price:** $12.00.

Principal Electric Facilities *See* Plant and Ownership List [Electric generating plants]

★1189★
PRINCIPAL EMPLOYERS OF THE METROPOLITAN WASHINGTON AREA [District of Columbia]
Metropolitan Washington Board of Trade
1129 20th Street, N.W.   Phone: (202) 857-5900
Washington, DC 20036
Covers: About 750 employers; excludes federal government departments but includes quasi-governmental bodies such as Amtrak and Washington Metro Area Transit Authority. **Entries include:** Company name, address, name of principal executive. **Arrangement:** By number of employees. **Pages (approx.):** 35. **Frequency:** Irregular; latest edition 1978. **Price:** $5.00.

★1190★
PRINCIPAL INTERNATIONAL BUSINESSES: THE WORLD MARKETING DIRECTORY
Dun & Bradstreet International Ltd.
99 Church Street   Phone: (212) 285-7256
New York, NY 10007
Covers: Approximately 50,000 major businesses, all lines, in all non-satellite countries, including the United States. (Companies are not necessarily "international" in the sense of having operations in more than one country; the coverage of the directory is simply international.) **Entries include:** Company name, address, name of chief executive, number of employees, financial keys, line of business, financial keys, SIC numbers, telex addresses, whether exporter/importer. **Arrangement:** Geographical. **Indexes:** Line of business, company. **Pages (approx.):** 2,300. **Frequency:** Annual, September. **Price:** $395.00.

Print Media Production Data *See* Standard Rate & Data Service—Print Media Production Data

★1191★
PRINTING TRADES BLUE BOOK
A. F. Lewis & Company, Inc.
79 Madison Avenue   Phone: (212) 254-9015
New York, NY 10016
Covers: Printing plants, bookbinders, typographers, photoengravers, paper merchants, paper manufacturers, printing machinery manufacturers and dealers, and others serving the graphic arts industry (SIC 2600, 2700). Four editions: New York Edition (7,000 establishments) covers metropolitan New York and the state of New Jersey. Southeastern Edition (8,600 establishments) covers Kentucky, Tennessee, Alabama, Mississippi, Louisiana, Virginia (except Washington suburbs), North Carolina, South Carolina, Georgia, and Florida. Northeastern Edition (5,600 establishments) covers Connecticut, Maine, Massachusetts, New Hampshire, New York (upstate only), Rhode Island, and Vermont. Delaware Valley-Ohio Edition (8,100 establishments) covers Pennsylvania, Maryland, Delaware, District of Columbia and its Virginia suburbs, and Ohio. **Entries include:** Company name, address, phone, names and titles of executives, name of buyer, list of products or services, year established. **Arrangement:** Geographical. **Indexes:** Personal name, company name, trade name/watermark. **Pages (approx.):** 750-900. **Frequency:** New York Edition, annual, winter; Southeastern Edition

and Delaware Valley-Ohio Edition, biennial, summer of odd years; Northeastern Edition, biennial, summer of even years. **Advertising accepted.** Circulation 5,250 each volume. **Price:** $45.00, plus $1.85 shipping. **Other information:** Same publisher's "Graphic Arts Green Book" covers midwestern states (see separate listing).

★1192★
PRIVATE CAMPGROUNDS & RV PARKS—BUYING GUIDE
Campground Marketing Associates
Box 121   Phone: (213) 373-6241
Palos Verdes Estates, CA 90274
Covers: Manufacturers or companies selling recreation products and services to privately and publicly owned campgrounds and parks. **Entries include:** Company name, address, phone, names of executives. **Arrangement:** Classified in 10 major categories (Administrative & Services, RV Site Facilities, General Store, etc.). **Pages (approx.):** 90. **Frequency:** Annual, June. **Editor:** Stuart L. Patton. **Advertising accepted.** Circulation 12,500. **Price:** $3.00; controlled circulation.

★1193★
PROBE DIRECTORY OF FOREIGN DIRECT INVESTMENT IN THE UNITED STATES
Probe International, Inc.
1492 High Ridge Road   Phone: (203) 329-9595
Stamford, CT 06903
Covers: About 1,000 foreign corporations with investments in manufacturers in the United States and about 3,000 American manufacturing firms which are partly or wholly owned by foreign corporations. **Entries include:** Foreign company listings include name, address, and investments. American company listings include company name, address, phone, product, and foreign company investor. **Arrangement:** Foreign corporations are arranged by country, American corporations are arranged alphabetically. **Indexes:** Geographical. **Frequency:** Annual. **Editor:** Mona White. **Former title:** Directory of Foreign Investment. **Price:** $90.00.

★1194★
PROCESSED PREPARED FOOD—BUYERS GUIDE ISSUE
Gorman Publishing Company
5725 E. River Road   Phone: (312) 693-3200
Chicago, IL 60631
Covers: About 1,700 manufacturers and suppliers of food processing and packaging equipment and materials; includes list of trade associations. **Entries include:** Company name, address, phone, name of contact, products. **Arrangement:** Alphabetical. **Indexes:** Product. **Pages (approx.):** 270. **Frequency:** Annual, December. **Editor:** Mary L. Gorman, Directory Manager. **Advertising accepted.** Circulation 40,000. **Former title:** Canner/Packer - Buyers Guide Issue. **Price:** $10.00.

★1195★
PRODUCT DIRECTORY OF THE REFRACTORIES INDUSTRY IN THE UNITED STATES
The Refractories Institute
One Oliver Plaza, Suite 1102   Phone: (412) 281-6787
Pittsburgh, PA 15222
Covers: About 115 manufacturers of refractories, most of whom are members (SIC 3255 and 3297). **Entries include:** Company name, address, phone, telex and TWX numbers, trade and brand names, list of products, locations of plants, SIC codes. **Arrangement:** Alphabetical. **Indexes:** Geographical, brand name, product. **Pages (approx.):** 300. **Frequency:** Irregular; latest edition 1978. **Price:** $20.00.

★1196★
PRODUCTIVITY: INFORMATION RESOURCE DIRECTORY
National Center for Productivity and Quality of Working Life
Washington, DC
Covers: Institutions and organizations which perform research or compile information on productivity and worklife; also includes

citations of published sources. **Entries include:** Source name, address, description of services or resources. **Frequency:** Published 1977. **Price:** $6.00 (PB 282-745/AS). **Send orders to:** National Technical Information Service, Springfield, VA 22161. (Not verified)

★1197★
PRODUCTS FINISHING DIRECTORY
Gardner Publications, Inc.
600 Main Street　　　　　　Phone: (513) 241-5924
Cincinnati, OH 45202
Publication includes: Firms in the metal finishing industry offering electroplating, painting, polishing, buffing, cleaning, degreasing, etc. **Entries include:** Company name, address, phone, and products or services. **Arrangement:** Alphabetical. **Indexes:** Product. **Frequency:** Annual, Septmber. **Editor:** Gerard H. Poll., Jr. **Advertising accepted.** **Price:** $3.00.

★1198★
PROFESSIONAL BUILDER & APARTMENT BUSINESS—HOUSING GIANTS ISSUE
Cahners Publishing Company
Five S. Wabash Avenue　　　　Phone: (312) 372-6880
Chicago, IL 60603
Publication includes: List of the largest volume builders in housing and light construction in the United States, including conventional builders and housing/mobile home manufacturers. **Entries include:** Company name, address, name of principal executive, financial data, and list of products or services. **Arrangement:** Classified by dollar volume of business. **Indexes:** Company name. **Pages** (approx.): 60-page section in regular issue. **Frequency:** Annual, July. **Editor:** Roy Diez. **Advertising accepted.** Circulation 105,000. **Price:** $10.00 (current and 1980 editions).

★1199★
PROFESSIONAL FURNITURE MERCHANT—RESOURCE DIRECTORY ISSUE
Gralla Publications
1515 Broadway　　　　　　Phone: (212) 869-1300
New York, NY 10036
Covers: 2,000 household furniture and furnishing manufacturers; also includes a listing of furniture marts and permanent trade exhibits. **Indexes:** Product. **Frequency:** Annual, February. **Editor:** Jane Edelstein, Managing Editor. **Advertising accepted.** **Price:** $3.00 (current and 1980 editions).

Professional Photographic Equipment Directory and Buying Guide *See* **Photographic Trade News—Professional Photographic Equipment Directory**

★1200★
PROFESSIONAL STUDIO GOLD BOOK [Photography]
Media Horizons, Inc.
475 Park Avenue South　　　　Phone: (212) 725-2300
New York, NY 10016
Covers: About 200 suppliers of materials, equipment, and services to photographers such as baby and portrait studio photographers, school, and wedding and confirmation photographers. **Entries include:** Company name, trade and brand names, and list of products or services offered. **Arrangement:** Classified by product. **Pages** (approx.): 65. **Frequency:** Irregular; latest edition October 1977; no new edition planned for 1979 or 1980. **Editor:** Frances H. Lee, Directory Editor. **Advertising accepted.** Circulation 15,000. **Price:** $5.00.

★1201★
THE PROFESSIONAL TO CONSULT—DIRECTORY OF CERTIFIED KITCHEN DESIGNERS
American Institute of Kitchen Dealers
124 Main Street　　　　　　Phone: (201) 852-0033
Hackettstown, NJ 07840
Covers: Over 500 kitchen and bath designers certified by the

institute. **Entries include:** Name, company name, address. **Arrangement:** Geographical. **Pages** (approx.): 65. **Frequency:** Annual, April/May. **Price:** Free.

★1202★
PROFESSIONAL'S GUIDE TO PUBLIC RELATIONS SERVICES
Richard Weiner, Inc.
888 Seventh Avenue　　　　Phone: (212) 582-7373
New York, NY 10019
Publication includes: Descriptions and evaluations of over 1,000 products and services useful in public relations and sales promotion. **Entries include:** Supplier name, address, phone, names of principal executives, trade and brand names, and descriptions of products or services. **Arrangement:** Classified by product or service (clipping services, film companies, etc.). **Indexes:** Supplier. **Pages** (approx.): 300. **Frequency:** Irregular; latest edition 1975; new edition planned for 1980. **Editor:** Richard Weiner. **Price:** $35.00 (1980 edition).

Programs of Graduate Study in Business *See* **Guide to Graduate Management Education**

★1203★
PROGRESSIVE GROCER—ANNUAL REPORT OF THE GROCERY INDUSTRY ISSUE
Progressive Grocer Company
708 Third Avenue　　　　　Phone: (212) 490-1000
New York, NY 10017
Publication includes: Lists of leading grocery wholesalers, publicly and nonpublicly held grocery chains, and convenience chains, ranked by sales. **Entries include:** Company name, headquarters city, number of stores, and dollar volume. **Frequency:** Annual, April. **Editor:** Edgar B. Walzer. **Advertising accepted.** **Price:** $3.50 (current edition); $3.75 (tentative, 1980 edition).

★1204★
PROGRESSIVE GROCER—GUIDE TO NEW EQUIPMENT ISSUE
Progressive Grocer Company
708 Third Avenue　　　　　Phone: (212) 490-1000
New York, NY 10017
Publication includes: List of over 600 manufacturers and suppliers of grocery store equipment, office supplies, security services, decorating services, etc. **Entries include:** Company name, address, phone, products. **Arrangement:** By product category. **Frequency:** Annual, December. **Editor:** Robert Rossner. **Advertising accepted.** **Price:** $2.50.

★1205★
PROGRESSIVE GROCER'S MARKETING GUIDEBOOK
Progressive Grocer Company
708 Third Avenue　　　　　Phone: (212) 490-1000
New York, NY 10017
Covers: Major chain and independent food retailers and wholesalers, plus food brokers, rack jobbers, candy and tobacco distributors, magazine distributors, specialty food distributors, and convenience store chains. **Entries include:** For retailers and wholesalers - Chain or company name, address, phone, number of stores served, locations of stores, major grocery supplier, three-year financial summary, buying policies, private label information, list of executives, buyers, and merchandisers. For rack jobbers - Name, address, phone, list of key personnel including buyers and their buying categories, list of items handled. **Arrangement:** By 79 Nielsen market areas. **Indexes:** General. **Pages** (approx.): 775. **Frequency:** Annual, September. **Editor:** Lucy Tarzian. **Advertising accepted.** **Price:** $149.00; regional editions for New England and Middle Atlantic States, Southeast and East Central States, West Central and Southwest States, and Pacific Region and Convenience Stores, $55.00 each.

★1206★
PROPJET
AvCom, International
Box 2398
Wichita, KS 67201
Covers: Owners of 3,900 business turboprop aircraft in service; worldwide coverage. **Entries include:** Owner identification, registration number; aircraft model, series, and serial number. **Arrangement:** By country of registration. **Indexes:** Model, region. **Pages** (approx.): 130. **Frequency:** Annual, January. **Editor:** Harry Adams. **Price:** $4.75, postpaid, payment with order.

★1207★
PUBLIC POWER—DIRECTORY ISSUE
American Public Power Association
2600 Virginia Avenue, N. W., Suite 212   Phone: (202) 333-9200
Washington, DC 20037
Covers: 2,220 local publicly owned electric utilities (municipal, public power districts, public utility districts, etc.) in United States and possessions (SIC 39). **Entries include:** Company name, address, phone, name and title of chief executive, financial keys. **Arrangement:** Geographical. **Frequency:** Annual, January-February. **Editor:** Vic Reinemer. **Advertising accepted.** Circulation 15,200. **Price:** $5.00 (current and 1980 editions).

★1208★
PUBLIC RELATIONS JOURNAL—REGISTER ISSUE
Public Relations Society of America
845 Third Avenue   Phone: (212) 826-1750
New York, NY 10022
Covers: About 9,000 public relations practitioners in business, government, education, etc., who are members. **Entries include:** Name, professional affiliation and title, address, phone, membership rank. **Arrangement:** Alphabetical. **Indexes:** Geographical, organizational. **Pages** (approx.): 475. **Frequency:** Annual, July. **Editor:** Leo J. Northart. **Advertising accepted.** **Price:** $45.00. **Other information:** Sometimes cited as, "Public Relations Register."

Public Relations Register *See* Public Relations Journal—Register Issue

Public Utilities Advertising Association—Directory *See* Public Utilities Communicators Association—Directory

★1209★
PUBLIC UTILITIES COMMUNICATORS ASSOCIATION—DIRECTORY
Public Utilities Communicators Association
C/o Jack C. Mark
Minnesota Gas Company
733 Marquette Avenue   Phone: (612) 372-4780
Minneapolis, MN 55402
Covers: 365 advertising and public relations people engaged in communications for public utilities who are members. **Entries include:** Name, company name, address, title, phone number. **Pages** (approx.): 30. **Frequency:** Annual, July. **Editor:** Jack C. Mark, Secretary. **Price:** Available to members only. **Other information:** Association name changed in 1976 from "Public Utilities Advertising Association."

Public Works Journal—Street and Highway Manual and Catalog File *See* Public Works Manual

★1210★
PUBLIC WORKS MANUAL
Public Works Journal Corporation
200 S. Broad Street   Phone: (201) 445-5800
Ridgewood, NJ 07451
Covers: Manufacturers and distributors of equipment, materials, and services used in the design, construction, maintenance, and operation of streets and highways, water systems, wastewater and solid wastes processing, and recreation areas. **Pages** (approx.): 450. **Frequency:** Annual, spring. **Editors:** James Kircher and Samuel Conner.

Advertising accepted. Circulation 34,000. **Former title:** Environment Wastes Control Manual & Catalog File. **Price:** $5.00.

Public Works Manual and Catalog File *See* Public Works Manual

Publicity in Chicago *See* Chicago Media Directory

★1211★
PUERTO RICO OFFICIAL INDUSTRIAL DIRECTORY
Witcom Group, Inc.
210 Ponce de Leon Avenue   Phone: (809) 725-8075
San Juan, PR 00901
Covers: 7,000 manufacturers and related service firms; manufacturers' representatives. **Entries include:** For manufacturers and services - Company name, address, phone, names of principal executives, year established, size, SIC number, products, Fomento-promoted status and tax-exempt status. For manufacturers' representatives - Firm name, names of principals, products. **Pages** (approx.): 675. **Frequency:** Annual, May. **Editor:** Nan S. Caso. **Advertising accepted.** **Price:** $60.00. **Other information:** Sponsored by Economic Development Administration (Fomento).

★1212★
PULP & PAPER—BUYER'S GUIDE ISSUE
Miller Freeman Publications, Inc.
500 Howard Street   Phone: (415) 397-1881
San Francisco, CA 94105
Publication includes: 2,100 manufacturers and suppliers located mostly in North America supplying equipment, chemicals, and services for the pulp and papermaking industry. **Entries include:** Company name, address, and phone. **Arrangement:** Alphabetical. **Indexes:** Product, trade name. **Frequency:** Annual, November. **Editor:** Kenneth E. Lowe. **Advertising accepted.** Circulation 21,000. **Price:** $10.00.

★1213★
PULP & PAPER—NORTH AMERICA PROFILE ISSUE
Miller Freeman Publications, Inc.
500 Howard Street   Phone: (415) 397-1881
San Francisco, CA 94105
Publication includes: About 75 United States and Canadian pulp and paper companies with a total daily capacity of 1,000 tons or more. **Entries include:** Company name, city and state or province, name of chairman and photograph, net sales and net earnings for current and prior year, review of financial and production activities, and location and production capacity of each mill. **Arrangement:** Alphabetical. **Indexes:** Company ranked by sales (with amount of sales and percentage of change from prior year), company ranked by pulp capacity, and company ranked by paper/board capacity. **Frequency:** Annual, June. **Editor:** Stephanie Pollitzer, Managing Editor. **Advertising accepted.** **Price:** $10.00. 1979 edition was last publication of this material in this format. **Other information:** Principal content of publication is industry overviews, summary of trends, industry statistics, etc.

★1214★
PURCHASING PEOPLE IN MAJOR CORPORATIONS
National Minority Business Campaign
1201 12th Avenue North   Phone: (612) 377-2402
Minneapolis, MN 55411
Covers: Minority purchasing programs in the 500 largest manufacturing companies and the 250 largest non-manufacturing companies in the United States. **Entries include:** Company name, address, phone; name of minority vendor program coordinator and addresses of corporate division and purchasing locations included in most entries. **Frequency:** Annual. **Price:** Free.

★1215★

QC QUICK CALLER AIR CARGO DIRECTORIES
Fourth Seacoast Publishing Company, Inc.
24145 Little Mack   Phone: (313) 779-5570
St. Clair Shores, MI 48080
Covers: Airlines, air freight forwarding firms, air charter firms, airports, and air cargo related services in a specific region. Directories are available for the Chicago area, Detroit area, Miami area, and Boston area. **Entries include:** Company name, address, phone, office hours, names of key executives. **Arrangement:** By type of firm or service (airlines with sales offices, airlines with operations...). **Pages** (approx.): 100. **Frequency:** Annual; Detroit edition, August; Chicago and Miami, October; Boston, February. **Editor:** Roger J. Buysse. **Advertising accepted.** Circulation 20,000 (each directory). **Price:** $3.50, plus $1.50 shipping, per volume.

★1216★

QUALIFIED PRODUCTS LIST AND SOURCES
Global Engineering Documentation Services, Inc.
3301 W. MacArthur Boulevard   Phone: (714) 540-9870
Santa Ana, CA 92704
Covers: Manufacturers of electronic, mechanical fastener, and other components conforming to military specifications in Federal Supply Class code groups 16, 31, 53, 58, 59, 61, 62, 66, and 91. **Entries include:** Manufacturer name and address. **Arrangement:** Alphabetical. **Indexes:** Military Specification Number index in numerical order includes supplier names; product index in alphabetical order includes government designation or Military Specification Number. **Pages** (approx.): 250 per issue. **Frequency:** Semiannual. **Editor:** Garnet Mills Lieblich, Vice President. **Advertising accepted.** Circulation 1,000. **Former title:** Military Specifications and Sources. **Price:** $60.00 per year; $35.00 per copy.

★1217★

QUALIFIED REMODELER—PICTORIAL BUYING GUIDE
Qualified Remodeler, Inc.
75 E. Wacker Drive   Phone: (312) 263-4291
Chicago, IL 60601
Description: Not a directory; includes descriptions and photos of products used in home remodeling industry, with reader service card number. **Arrangement:** By product. **Frequency:** Annual, November. **Editor:** David M. Sauer. **Advertising accepted. Price:** $5.00.

★1218★

QUESTIONS AND ANSWERS ABOUT SUPPLIERS [Die casting industry]
American Die Casting Institute
2340 Des Plaines Avenue   Phone: (312) 298-1220
Des Plaines, IL 60018
Covers: 125 custom die casting member companies. **Entries include:** Firm name, address, phone, name of an executive, and data on equipment capabilities, alloys cast, finishing and machining services offered. **Arrangement:** Alphabetical, geographical. **Pages** (approx.): 30. **Frequency:** Irregular; new edition expected early 1980. **Price:** Free.

★1219★

QUICK FROZEN FOODS DIRECTORY OF FROZEN FOOD PROCESSORS
Harcourt Brace Jovanovich, Inc.
One E. First Street   Phone: (218) 727-8511
Duluth, MN 55802
Covers: 3,000 frozen food processors, refrigerated warehouses, and truck and rail freight lines handling frozen foods. **Entries include:** Company name, address, phone, names of executives, volume in pounds, trade and brand names, list of products or services, what per cent of business is retail or institutional, plant locations. **Arrangement:** Processors listed by product, geographically, and by brand. **Pages** (approx.): 500. **Frequency:** Annual, May. **Editor:** Sam Martin. **Advertising accepted.** Circulation 4,000. **Price:** $30.00, plus $1.50 shipping.

★1220★

QUICK FROZEN FOODS DIRECTORY OF WHOLESALE DISTRIBUTORS—INSTITUTIONAL AND RETAIL
Harcourt Brace Jovanovich, Inc.
One E. First Street   Phone: (218) 727-8511
Duluth, MN 55802
Entries include: Company name, address, phone, names of executives, brand names and list of products. **Arrangement:** Geographical. **Indexes:** Alphabetical. **Pages** (approx.): 330. **Frequency:** Biennial, October of odd years. **Editor:** Sam Martin. **Advertising accepted.** Circulation 800. **Price:** $40.00.

★1221★

RACINE AREA MANUFACTURERS DIRECTORY [Wisconsin]
Racine Area Chamber of Commerce
731 Main Street   Phone: (414) 633-2451
Racine, WI 53403
Number of listings: About 300. **Entries include:** Company name, address, phone, name of principal executive, number of employees, list of products or services. **Arrangement:** Alphabetical. **Pages** (approx.): 50. **Frequency:** Annual, January. **Editor:** Darrell E. Wright, President. **Price:** $7.00, plus $1.50 shipping.

Railroad Construction and Maintenance Association—Directory and Buyer's Guide *See* **National Railroad Construction and Maintenance Assn.**

★1222★

RAILWAY TRACK AND STRUCTURES—RAILROAD TRACK CONTRACTORS DIRECTORY ISSUE
Simmons-Boardman Publishing Corporation
29 E. Madison   Phone: (312) 641-5815
Chicago, IL 60602
Covers: About 200 companies specializing in track construction, maintenance, and/or equipment maintenance for railways in the United States and Canada. Companies offering further specialties are also listed separately. **Entries include:** Company name, address, coding to indicate services. **Arrangement:** Geographical. **Frequency:** Annual, July. **Editor:** Merwin H. Dick. **Advertising accepted.** Circulation 6,000. **Price:** $1.00.

★1223★

REACTIVE CURE SYSTEMS: UV-IR-EB [Radiation curing and processing]
Captan Associates Inc.
13-15 Orient Way
Rutherford, NJ 07070
Covers: About 600 companies which manufacture or supply equipment, components, chemicals, materials, and services used in industrial curing and processing with radiation sources. **Entries include:** Company name, address, phone, products or services. **Arrangement:** By product. **Indexes:** Company name. **Pages** (approx.): 250. **Frequency:** Not established; first edition expected January 1980. **Editor:** Clare Bluestein. **Advertising accepted. Price:** $85.00, postpaid, payment with order; $88.50, billed.

Recreation Vehicle Dealers Association—Membership Directory *See* **Who's Who of RV Dealers**

★1224★

RECREATIONAL VEHICLE DIRECTORY [Manufacturers]
Hanley Publishing Company
3412 Main Street   Phone: (312) 677-8151
Skokie, IL 60076
Publication includes: 180 manufacturers of recreational vehicles. **Entries include:** Company name, address, and code for models produced. **Arrangement:** Alphabetical. **Frequency:** Annual, March. **Editor:** Gloria C. Krolski, Vice President. **Price:** $2.95 (current and new editions). **Also includes:** Principal content is one-page or half-page descriptions of individual models of recreational vehicles, with photographs, specifications, and layout diagrams.

★1225★
RED BOOK [Retail monument dealers and suppliers]
American Monument Association
6902 N. High Street   Phone: (614) 885-2713
Worthington, OH 43085
Covers: 5,000 retail gravestone dealers and 1,800 suppliers of granite and marble; 1980 edition will include other suppliers of equipment, services, and products. **Entries include:** For dealers - Company name, address, phone, names of owner or corporate officers and their titles. For stone suppliers - Company name, address, phone, products. **Arrangement:** Dealers are geographical, suppliers are by product. **Indexes:** Alphabetical. **Frequency:** Annual, January. **Advertising accepted. Price:** $10.00 (current edition); $12.50 (1980 edition). **Other information:** Credit information formerly included in "Red Book" is now published in a separate supplement, and is available to association members only.

Red Book *See* World Coffee & Tea—Red Book Issue

★1226★
RED BOOK OF HOUSING MANUFACTURERS
CMR Associates, Inc.
11-A Village Green   Phone: (301) 261-6363
Crofton, MD 21114
Covers: Prefabricated home manufacturers, modular home manufacturers, mobile home manufacturers, and major firms which erect production homes; 500 firms have full listings, another 900 have abbreviated listings. Also includes 500 manufacturers who make building components and building systems. **Entries include:** Full home manufacturers and builder listings include, as appropriate, company name, address, phone, names of principal executives, marketing areas and methods, production volume and facilities, gross revenues, construction methods or product line. **Pages** (approx.): 200. **Frequency:** Annual, September. **Editor:** Donald F. Spear, President. **Price:** $105.00. **Other information:** Variant title, "Who's Who in Industrialized Housing."

Reference Book for World Traders *See* Croner's Reference Book
for World Traders

Refractory Metals Association—Membership Directory *See*
Metal Powder Producers and Suppliers Directory International;
Custom Engineered P/M Parts and Products Manufacturers
Directory International

★1227★
REFRIGERATED TRANSPORTER—LTL GUIDE ISSUE
Tunnell Publications, Inc.
1602 Harold Street   Phone: (713) 523-8124
Houston, TX 77006
Covers: About 120 refrigerated carriers willing to carry less than full trailer loads; cold storage firms which offer local delivery services are also listed. **Entries include:** Name, address, phone; trucks available, geographic area covered. **Arrangement:** Alphabetical. **Frequency:** Annual, December. **Editor:** Gary Macklin. **Advertising accepted.** Circulation 16,000. **Price:** $5.00.

Refuse Removal Journal—Buyer's Guide Issue *See* Solid Wastes
Management/Refuse Removal Journal—Buyer's Guide Issue

★1228★
REGISTER OF MINORITY FIRMS [New York State]
Office of Minority Business Enterprise
New York Department of Commerce
99 Washington Avenue
Albany, NY 12245
Covers: Minority-owned construction, professional, service, manufacturing, distributing, and retail firms in New York State. **Entries include:** Firm name, address, phone, products or services.

Arrangement: By SIC classification. **Frequency:** Biennial, summer of odd years. **Price:** Free.

★1229★
REGISTER OF OFFSHORE UNITS, SUBMERSIBLES, AND DIVING SYSTEMS
Lloyd's Register of Shipping
17 Battery Place   Phone: (212) 425-8050
New York, NY 10004
Covers: Mobile drilling rigs, submersibles, diving systems, and work units. **Entries include:** Name of owner, address, telex and phone. **Arrangement:** By type of equipment/ship. **Frequency:** Annual, October. **Price:** $50.00. **Other information:** Common title is, "Lloyd's Register of Offshore Units..."

★1230★
REGISTER OF PLANNED EMERGENCY PRODUCERS
Defense Logistics Agency
Defense Department
Cameron Station
Alexandria, VA 22314
Description: "Official list of privately-owned United States and Canadian industrial firms and military departments' facilities participating in the DOD Industrial Preparedness Program." **Entries include:** Company name (including name of parent company and/or subsidiary, etc.), city and state in which located, DOD plant index number, Armed Services Production Planning Officer (ASPPO) code number; listings for government-owned plants include same type of information. **Arrangement:** Three sections containing identical information: Alphabetical; Geographical; ASPPO Number. **Pages** (approx.): 300 (looseleaf). **Frequency:** Annual, April. **Price:** $6.00 (S/N 008-007-03069-8). **Send orders to:** Government Printing Office, Washington, DC 20402.

★1231★
REGISTER OF REPORTING LABOR ORGANIZATIONS
Labor Department
200 Constitution Avenue, N. W.   Phone: (202) 523-8165
Washington, DC 20210
Covers: All unions which file reports with the United States Labor Department under the Labor-Management Reporting and Disclosure Act or under Executive Order 11491; coverage includes both private industry and government agencies, but does not include the FBI, CIA, USIA, State Department, and the TVA. **Entries include:** Union name, address, unit and file number of report. **Arrangement:** Geographical. **Pages** (approx.): 325. **Frequency:** Irregular; latest edition 1977. **Price:** $4.75 (S/N 029-000-00291-6). **Send orders to:** Government Printing Office, Washington, DC 20402. **Also includes:** Mergers, dissolutions, and name changes occurring during the years covered.

★1232★
REGISTER OF SHIPS—APPENDIX
Lloyd's Register of Shipping
17 Battery Place   Phone: (212) 425-8050
New York, NY 10004
Covers: Shipbuilders, dry and wet docks, marine insurance companies, and other shipping-related service companies. **Entries include:** Company name, telegraphic address. Shipbuilders' listings include names of existing ships built by them. **Arrangement:** Alphabetical within type of service. **Frequency:** Annual, January. **Price:** $80.00. **Other information:** Common title is, "Lloyd's Register of Ships - Appendix."

★1233★
REGISTER OF SHIPS
Lloyd's Register of Shipping
17 Battery Place   Phone: (212) 425-8050
New York, NY 10004
Covers: All known ocean-going merchant ships of 100 gross tons or more. Ship-borne barges, docking facilities, gas carriers, refrigerated

cargo installations, refrigerated stores terminals, and container terminals are now listed in a separate volume, "Register of Ships (Subsidiary Sections)." **Entries include:** Ship name, name of owner, flag, tonnages, classification, and ship specifications, including type, hull, cargo facilities, and machinery. (Owner addresses included in "Register of Ships - Appendix," described in separate listing.) Listings in "Subsidiary Sections" volume include facility or company name and address. **Arrangement:** Alphabetical. **Frequency:** Annual; "Register" in August, "Subsidiary Sections" in October; cumulative monthly supplements include new ships and changes. **Price:** $350.00 (includes "Subsidiary Sections" volume and "Register of Offshore Units, Submersibles, and Diving Systems," described in separate listing). **Other information:** Common title is, "Lloyd's Register of Ships" or ". . .Shipping."

★1234★
REGISTRY OF PROFESSIONAL [SHORTHAND] REPORTERS AND ANNUAL MEMBERSHIP DIRECTORY
National Shorthand Reporters Association
118 Park Street, S. E.   Phone: (703) 281-4677
Vienna, VA 22180
Covers: 12,000 United States, Canadian, and foreign shorthand reporters. **Entries include:** Name; office address and phone; home address and phone; professional qualifications; shorthand system used. **Arrangement:** Geographical. **Indexes:** Alphabetical. **Pages** (approx.): 300. **Frequency:** Annual, October. **Editor:** Robert N. Virkus, Communications Director. **Advertising accepted.** Circulation 12,500. **Former title:** Membership Directory. **Price:** $10.00. **Also includes:** List of state shorthand association officers, publications, and editors; list of Certified Shorthand Reporter Boards.

★1235★
RENT-A-USED-CAR
American Entrepreneurs Association
631 Wilshire Boulevard
Santa Monica, CA 90401
Publication includes: List of firms such as Lease-A-Lemon, Charlotte, N. C., and Rent-A-Heap Cheap in Houston, TX, which rent old used cars at rates considerably below conventional rental agencies. **Entries include:** Firm name, address. **Frequency:** Published 1979. **Price:** $35.00. **Other information:** Principal content of book is information on how to begin a used car rental business.

★1236★
REPROGRAPHICS—ANNUAL DIRECTORY OF DESIGN-DRAFTING AND ENGINEERING REPRODUCTION PRODUCTS AND SUPPLIES
Innes Publishing Company
425 Huehl Road, Building 11-B   Phone: (312) 564-5940
Northbrook, IL 60062
Description: Not a directory; provides product description and name of manufacturer only, plus reference to reader service card.

★1237★
RESEARCH & DEVELOPMENT DIRECTORY
Government Data Publications
1661 McDonald Avenue   Phone: (212) 627-0819
Brooklyn, NY 11230
Covers: Firms which received research and development contracts from the federal government during preceding 12 months. **Entries include:** Awardee name, address, agency, description of work, dollar amount of contract, and other pertinent data. **Arrangement:** First section alphabetical by awardee; second section geographical by awarding agency; third section classified by nature of work. Identical information in each section. **Frequency:** Annual, September. **Editor:** Siegfried Lobel. **Price:** $15.00. **Send orders to:** Government Data Publications, 422 Washington Bldg., Washington, DC 20005. **Other information:** Variant title is, "Unique 3-in-1 Research and Development Directory."

★1238★
RESEARCH TRIANGLE PARK DIRECTORY [North Carolina]
North Carolina Science and Technology Research Center
North Carolina Department of Commerce
Box 12235
Research Triangle Park, NC 27709
Covers: About 80 research and commercial organizations located in Research Triangle Park, North Carolina. **Entries include:** Company name, address, phone; corporate affiliation (if any); line of business; names of principal officers; number of employees; location in park; some listings include hours. **Arrangement:** Research organizations are alphabetical, commercial organizations are by location and/or type. **Pages** (approx.): 40. **Frequency:** Annual, January. **Editor:** D. K. Schroeder. **Price:** Free.

★1239★
RESISTANCE WELDER MANUFACTURERS ASSOCIATION— MEMBERSHIP DIRECTORY
Resistance Welder Manufacturers Association
1900 Arch Street   Phone: (215) 564-3484
Philadelphia, PA 19103
Covers: About 25 manufacturers of resistance welding equipment and supplies. **Entries include:** Company name, address, products. **Arrangement:** Alphabetical by division. **Pages** (approx.): 15. **Frequency:** Annual, February. **Price:** Free.

★1240★
RESORTS & PARKS PURCHASING GUIDE
Klevens Publications, Inc.
7600 Avenue V   Phone: (805) 944-4111
Littlerock, CA 93543
Covers: Manufacturers and suppliers of products and services for summer and winter resorts, ski areas, national parks, etc., which offer food and lodging for vacationers. **Entries include:** Company name, address, name of principal executive, brief description of product. **Arrangement:** Within general categories (recreation, food, food services, souvenirs, buildings and maintenance, etc.). **Frequency:** Annual, April. **Editor:** Herbert Schwartz. **Advertising accepted.** **Price:** $3.00.

★1241★
RESOURCES COUNCIL—SOURCE DIRECTORY [Interior decoration]
Resources Council
979 Third Avenue   Phone: (212) 752-9040
New York, NY 10022
Covers: Interior furnishings manufacturers, distributors, manufacturers' representatives, and others concerned with interior decoration; tenant firms of major interior design and decoration buildings in New York; and manufacturers' representatives of lines in major buying areas. **Entries include:** For manufacturers - Company name, address, phone; advertiser listings include description of products. For office building tenants - Name, office, phone. For representatives - Name of line, firm or individual name, address, phone. **Arrangement:** Manufacturers are alphabetical; office tenants are by building; representatives are geographical. **Indexes:** Product. **Pages** (approx.): 265. **Frequency:** Annual, May. **Editor:** Bobbye Fosse, Executive Director. **Advertising accepted.** Circulation 40,000. **Price:** $2.00; restricted circulation.

★1242★
RESTAURANT HOSPITALITY—HOSPITALITY 500 ISSUE
Penton/IPC
1111 Chester Avenue   Phone: (216) 696-7000
Cleveland, OH 44114
Covers: 500 leading food service corporations and restaurant chains on basis of sales. **Entries include:** Company name, headquarters city and state, total sales, average sales per unit, percentage in food and labor costs, number of units, number company-owned and franchised, whether liquor, wine, and beer are sold. **Arrangement:** Ranked by total sales. **Indexes:** Company name, geographical. **Frequency:**

Annual, June. **Editor:** Connie Norweb. **Advertising accepted.** Circulation 80,000. **Price:** $4.00 (current and 1980 editions).

★1243★
RETAIL CHAIN STORE DIRECTORY [Northern California]
Business News, Inc.
165 Capp Street
San Francisco, CA 94110
Covers: Over 500 retail chain stores including banks, department stores, drug stores, furniture dealers, home improvement stores, motels, restaurants, variety stores, etc., located in northern California. **Entries include:** Chain name, address, phone, name of contact. **Arrangement:** By line of business. **Frequency:** Latest edition 1979. **Price:** $35.00.

★1244★
RHODE ISLAND DIRECTORY OF EXPORTERS
Rhode Island Department of Economic Development
7 Jackson Walkway   Phone: (401) 277-2601
Providence, RI 02903
Covers: About 200 Rhode Island companies which are interested in exporting or export their products. **Entries include:** Company name, address, phone, list of products, name of contact person, number of employees, name of parent company, countries exporting to. **Arrangement:** By SIC number. **Pages** (approx.): 70. **Frequency:** Not established; first edition late 1979. **Editor:** Vincent K. Harrington. **Price:** $5.00.

★1245★
RHODE ISLAND DIRECTORY OF MANUFACTURERS
Rhode Island Department of Economic Development
One Weybosset Hill   Phone: (401) 277-2601
Providence, RI 02903
Number of listings: 2,500. **Entries include:** Company name, address, phone, list of products, name of contact person, number of employees, whether firm exports or imports, parent company. **Pages** (approx.): 275. **Frequency:** Biennial, July of odd years. **Editor:** Vincent K. Harrington. **Price:** $10.00.

★1246★
RHODE ISLAND MINORITY BUSINESS ENTERPRISES
Rhode Island Department of Economic Development
7 Jackson Walkway   Phone: (401) 277-2601
Providence, RI 02903
Covers: About 120 firms offering professional, commercial, industrial, and consumer products and services. **Entries include:** Company name, address, phone, name of owner. **Arrangement:** Classified. **Frequency:** Irregular; latest edition July 1979. **Editor:** Alan N. Addison. **Former title:** Rhode Island Minority Businesses. **Price:** $10.00.

★1247★
RHODE ISLAND STATE INDUSTRIAL DIRECTORY
State Industrial Directories Corporation
Two Penn Plaza   Phone: (212) 564-0340
New York, NY 10001
Number of listings: 2,700. **Entries include:** Company name, address, phone, names of key executives, number of employees, plant size, 4-digit SIC code, products, whether firm imports or exports, and whether firm has research facilities. **Arrangement:** Geographical. **Indexes:** Alphabetical, product (includes mailing address and phone for each firm). **Frequency:** Annual, September. **Advertising accepted.** **Price:** $20.00, plus $2.75 shipping.

★1248★
RN & WPL DIRECTORY [Textiles]
Textile Publishing Corporation
Box 50079
Washington, DC 20004
Covers: 56,000 Registered Numbers and Wool Products Labeling numbers which appear on textile and apparel products to identify their

manufacturers, importers, and distributors. **Entries include:** Number, company name, address, product/service. **Arrangement:** By number. **Indexes:** Alphabetical, product/service, geographical. **Pages** (approx.): 1,000. **Frequency:** First edition spring 1979. **Price:** $50.00, plus $2.50 shipping (Eastern U.S.); $3.50 shipping (Western U.S.).

★1249★
ROCKY MOUNTAIN CONSTRUCTION—BUYER'S GUIDE AND DIRECTORY ISSUE
Mountain Publishing Company, Inc.
2201 Stout Street   Phone: (303) 571-5400
Denver, CO 80205
Covers: Construction equipment manufacturers, their distributors, and other construction industry suppliers in Arizona, Colorado, Idaho, Nevada, New Mexico, Utah, Wyoming, and the El Paso, Texas, trade area. Includes lists of awarding authorities and construction industry associations. **Entries include:** Company name, address. **Pages** (approx.): 300. **Frequency:** Annual, March. **Editor:** Hol Wagner. **Advertising accepted.** Circulation 9,500. **Price:** $12.00.

★1250★
ROLE OF TRUCKSTOPS IN CRISIS RELOCATION
Defense Civil Preparedness Agency
Washington, DC 20301
Publication includes: List of more than 3,000 truck stops. **Entries include:** Truck stop name, location, phone, brand of products handled. **Arrangement:** Geographical. **Frequency:** Published September 1978. **Other information:** Volume 3 in series, "Postattack Impacts of the Crisis Relocation Strategy on Transportation Systems."

★1251★
ROOFING, SIDING, INSULATION—ANNUAL DIRECTORY ISSUE
Harcourt Brace Jovanovich, Inc.
757 Third Avenue   Phone: (212) 888-4354
New York, NY 10017
Covers: Manufacturers, wholesalers, jobbers, and distributors of products and equipment for the roofing, siding, and insulation industries; trade associations are also included. **Entries include:** Company name, address, phone, sales contact, and products and lines manufactured or handled. **Arrangement:** Manufacturers and associations are alphabetical, distributors are geographical. **Indexes:** Product, trade name. **Pages** (approx.): 200. **Frequency:** Annual, April. **Price:** $5.00 (ISSN 0033-7129).

★1252★
RUBBER & PLASTICS NEWS—RUBBICANA ISSUE [Directory issue]
Crain Communications, Inc.
One Cascade Plaza, Suite 1202   Phone: (216) 253-2183
Akron, OH 44308
Covers: 1,000 rubber product manufacturers and 800 suppliers of equipment, services, and materials. **Entries include:** For manufacturers - Company name, address, phone, names and titles of executives, date established, type of ownership, number and type of employees, annual gross sales, products, markets, rubbers used, and equipment used for processing. **Arrangement:** Classified by line of business. **Indexes:** Product, trade name. **Pages** (approx.): 450. **Frequency:** Annual, December. **Editor:** Cynthia Burkhardt. **Advertising accepted.** Circulation 14,000. **Price:** $45.00, plus $2.00 shipping. **Also includes:** Trade associations with name, address, phone, executive staff, purpose, and meeting titles, dates and locations. **Other information:** Variant title, "Directory of North American Rubber Product Manufacturers and Rubber Industry Suppliers."

★1253★
RUBBER RED BOOK
Palmerton Publishing Company, Division
Communication Channels, Inc.
6285 Barfield Road   Phone: (404) 393-2920
Atlanta, GA 30328
Covers: Rubber manufacturers in the United States, Canada, and Puerto Rico; separate lists of suppliers of materials and services to and independent sales agents for the rubber industry. **Entries include:** For manufacturers - Company name, address, phone, names of executives and plant personnel, number of employees, trade and brand names, type of products manufactured. **Arrangement:** Manufacturers are alphabetical; sales agents are geographical. **Indexes:** Product. **Pages** (approx.): 700. **Frequency:** Annual, January. **Editor:** Art Sweum. **Advertising accepted.** Circulation 5,000. **Price:** $39.50 (current edition); $42.00 (1980 edition).

★1254★
RUBBER WORLD BLUE BOOK: MATERIALS, COMPOUNDING INGREDIENTS AND MACHINERY FOR RUBBER
Bill Communications, Inc.
77 N. Miller Road   Phone: (216) 867-4405
Akron, OH 44313
Publication includes: List of suppliers to the rubber industry. **Entries include:** Supplier name, address, phone, trade and brand names, list of products. **Arrangement:** Alphabetical. **Frequency:** Annual, spring. **Editor:** Don R. Smith. **Advertising accepted.** Circulation 3,500. **Price:** $37.50 (current edition); $41.50 (1980 edition). **Other information:** Principal content is descriptions of materials, compounding information, etc.

Rubbicana *See* **Rubber & Plastics News—Rubbicana Issue [Directory issue]**

★1255★
RURAL AND URBAN ROADS—ANNUAL BUYER'S GUIDE INDEX OF HIGHWAY AND MUNICIPAL PRODUCTS ISSUE
Scranton-Gillette Communications
380 Northwest Highway   Phone: (312) 298-6622
Des Plaines, IL 60016
Publication includes: 625 manufacturers of equipment, machinery, and materials for use in highway construction, repair, and other municipal uses. **Entries include:** Company name and address. **Arrangement:** Alphabetical. **Indexes:** Product. **Frequency:** Annual, September. **Editor:** Jerry Mallek. **Advertising accepted.** Circulation 45,000. **Former title:** Rural and Urban Roads - Annual Buyer's Guide for Highway and Municipal Products Issue. **Price:** $1.00.

Russell's Official National Motor Coach Guide *See* **Official Bus Guide**

★1256★
RV DEALER—DIRECTORY AND BUYER'S GUIDE ISSUE [Recreation vehicles]
Hardison Publishing Company
6229 Northwest Highway   Phone: (312) 774-2525
Chicago, IL 60631
Covers: About 800 recreational vehicle manufacturers plus their suppliers, distributors, wholesalers, manufacturers' representatives, and others in the industry; coverage includes Canada. **Entries include:** For manufacturers - Company name, address, phone, location of branch plants, types of vehicles made. For suppliers - Company name, address, names of key personnel. For distributors, wholesalers, and representatives - Company name, address, phone, product lines handled, and whether OEM or aftermarket. **Arrangement:** Alphabetical within above groups, except suppliers of special services which are by service. **Indexes:** Supplier, product. **Frequency:** Annual, November. **Editors:** Renald Rooney and Marian Hoglind. **Advertising accepted.** **Price:** $6.00. **Other information:** Also published in slightly abridged pocket format as, "Directory of Recreational Vehicle Manufacturers" (see separate listing).

★1257★
SAINT LOUIS COMMERCE—ROSTER ISSUE
St. Louis Regional Commerce and Growth Association
10 Broadway   Phone: (314) 231-5555
St. Louis, MO 63102
Number of listings: 3,000. **Entries include:** Company name, address, phone, names of principal executives. **Arrangement:** Alphabetical. **Pages** (approx.): 145. **Frequency:** Annual, April. **Editor:** Robert E. Hannon. **Advertising accepted.** **Price:** Not sold separately; available with annual subscription to the magazine, $10.00; (ISSN 0036-293X).

★1258★
SAINT PAUL AREA CHAMBER OF COMMERCE—MEMBERSHIP DIRECTORY [Minnesota]
Saint Paul Area Chamber of Commerce
Osborn Building, Suite 300   Phone: (612) 222-5561
St. Paul, MN 55102
Number of listings: 2,300. **Entries include:** Company name, address, phone, name of principal executive, and type of product or service. **Arrangement:** Alphabetical and by product; essentially the same information in each section. **Pages** (approx.): 140. **Frequency:** Annual. **Advertising accepted.** **Price:** $25.00.

Sales and Marketing Executives International—Roster *See* **Marketing Times: Journal of Continuing Education—Leadership Directory**

★1259★
SALES ASSOCIATION OF THE CHEMICAL INDUSTRY—ROSTER
Sales Association of the Chemical Industry
50 E. 41st Street   Phone: (212) 686-1952
New York, NY 10017
Covers: 1,000 salesmen, managers, and executive officers engaged in sales or sales promotion for American chemical manufacturers, distributors, and exporters; purchasing agents; personnel of trade publications and advertising agencies. Primarily covers New York, New Jersey, and Connecticut. **Entries include:** Name and office address. **Arrangement:** Alphabetical. **Frequency:** Biennial, fall. **Editor:** P. B. Slawter. **Price:** Available to members only.

Sales Executives Guide *See* **Creative Black Book [Advertiser Services]**

★1260★
SALES PROSPECTOR
Prospector Research Services, Inc.
751 Main Street   Phone: (617) 899-1271
Waltham, MA 02254
Covers: Industrial, commercial, and institutional expansions and relocations in new or existing buildings; reports on 50-150 firms in each newsletter. Fifteen somewhat overlapping editions: New England; New York, New Jersey, and southern Connecticut; Pennsylvania, Delaware, and southern New Jersey; Ohio and Michigan; Ohio River Valley; Illinois and Indiana; Maryland, Virginia, West Virginia, North Carolina, South Carolina, District of Columbia; California, Arizona, Nevada, and Hawaii; Georgia, Florida, Alabama, South Carolina, North Carolina; Louisiana, Mississippi, Arkansas, Oklahoma, Kentucky, Tennessee; Texas, Oklahoma, New Mexico; Missouri, Iowa, Kansas, Nebraska; Wisconsin, Minnesota, Iowa, North Dakota, South Dakota; Colorado, Idaho, Montana, Oregon, Utah, Washington, Wyoming, Alaska; Canada. **Entries include:** Information provided varies according to nature of case being reported. A report on installation of a large new metalworking press gave technical details and comment by company president on how the acquisition would benefit the company; report on a plant enlargement included information from a company officer on size of the enlargement, contractor's name, company's plans for increased production and specific increases planned in specific products. Items include name and full address of the company reported on. **Pages** (approx.): 10-15 per regional edition. **Frequency:** Monthly. **Editor:** Herbert A. Ireland. **Price:** $76.00 yearly for each

regional edition; $498.00 yearly for complete set.

★1261★

SALESMAN'S GUIDE: WOMEN'S SPECIALTY STORES [California]
Salesman's Guide, Inc.
1140 Broadway   Phone: (212) 684-2985
New York, NY 10001
Covers: About 1,800 California women's specialty stores with net worth of $10,000 to $100,000. **Entries include:** Store name, address, phone, name of owner; names of buyers; lines carried; price and size ranges handled. **Arrangement:** Geographical. **Frequency:** Biennial, December of even years. **Editor:** Edward R. Blank. **Advertising accepted.** Circulation 500. **Price:** $35.00, postpaid, payment with order; $36.75, billed.

★1262★

SALESMAN'S GUIDE DIRECTORY OF INFANTS' TO TEENS' WEAR BUYERS [New York metro area]
Salesman's Guide, Inc.
1140 Broadway   Phone: (212) 684-2985
New York, NY 10001
Covers: Resident buying offices and department, specialty, and chain stores. **Entries include:** Buying office or store name, names of buyers and merchandise managers, buyers' sample room days and hours, prices and size ranges in which interested. **Arrangement:** Geographical. **Indexes:** Alphabetical. **Frequency:** Semiannual. **Price:** $15.00 per year, postpaid, payment with order.

★1263★

SALESMAN'S GUIDE DIRECTORY OF MEN'S & BOYS' WEAR BUYERS [New York metro area]
Salesman's Guide, Inc.
1140 Broadway   Phone: (212) 684-2985
New York, NY 10001
Covers: Resident buying offices and department, specialty, and chain stores. **Entries include:** Buying office or store name, names of buyers and merchandise managers, buyers' sample room days and hours, prices and size ranges in which interested. **Arrangement:** Geographical. **Indexes:** Alphabetical. **Frequency:** Semiannual. **Price:** $15.00 per year, postpaid, payment with order.

★1264★

SALESMAN'S GUIDE DIRECTORY OF WOMEN'S ACCESSORIES BUYERS [New York metro area]
Salesman's Guide, Inc.
1140 Broadway   Phone: (212) 684-2985
New York, NY 10001
Covers: Resident buying offices and department, specialty, and chain stores. **Entries include:** Buying office or store name, names of buyers and merchandise managers, buyers' sample room days and hours, prices and size ranges in which interested. **Arrangement:** Geographical. **Indexes:** Alphabetical. **Frequency:** Annual. **Price:** $10.00, postpaid, payment with order.

★1265★

SALESMAN'S GUIDE DIRECTORY OF WOMEN'S COATS & SUITS BUYERS [New York metro area]
Salesman's Guide, Inc.
1140 Broadway   Phone: (212) 684-2985
New York, NY 10001
Covers: Resident buying offices and department, specialty, and chain stores. **Entries include:** Buying office or store name, names of buyers and merchandise managers, buyers' sample room days and hours, prices and size ranges in which interested. **Arrangement:** Geographical. **Indexes:** Alphabetical. **Frequency:** Annual. **Price:** $10.00, postpaid, payment with order.

★1266★

SALESMAN'S GUIDE DIRECTORY OF WOMEN'S DRESSES BUYERS [New York metro area]
Salesman's Guide, Inc.
1140 Broadway   Phone: (212) 684-2985
New York, NY 10001
Covers: Over 400 resident buying offices and department, specialty, and chain stores in New York metropolitan area. **Entries include:** Buying office or store name, names of buyers and merchandise managers, buyers' sample room days and hours, prices and size ranges in which interested. **Arrangement:** Alphabetical. **Indexes:** Geographical. **Frequency:** Semiannual, June and December. **Editor:** Edward R. Blank. **Advertising accepted.** **Price:** $15.00 per year, postpaid, payment with order; $16.40, billed.

★1267★

SALESMAN'S GUIDE DIRECTORY OF WOMEN'S INTIMATE APPAREL BUYERS [New York metro area]
Salesman's Guide, Inc.
1140 Broadway   Phone: (212) 684-2985
New York, NY 10001
Covers: Over 400 resident buying offices and department, specialty, and chain stores in the New York metropolitan area. **Entries include:** Buying office or store name, names of buyers and merchandise managers, buyers' sample room days and hours, prices and size ranges in which interested. **Arrangement:** Alphabetical. **Indexes:** Geographical. **Pages** (approx.): 135. **Frequency:** Semiannual, January and July. **Editor:** Edward R. Blank. **Advertising accepted.** **Price:** $15.00 per year, postpaid, payment with order; $16.40, billed.

★1268★

SALESMAN'S GUIDE DIRECTORY OF WOMEN'S SPORTSWEAR BUYERS [New York metro area]
Salesman's Guide, Inc.
1140 Broadway   Phone: (212) 684-2985
New York, NY 10001
Covers: Over 400 resident buying offices and department, specialty, and chain stores in the New York metropolitan area. **Entries include:** Buying office or store name, names of buyers and merchandise managers, buyers' sample room days and hours, prices and size ranges in which interested. **Arrangement:** Alphabetical. **Indexes:** Geographical. **Pages** (approx.): 135. **Frequency:** Semiannual, March and September. **Editor:** Edward R. Blank. **Advertising accepted.** **Price:** $15.00 per year, postpaid, payment with order; $16.40, billed.

★1269★

SALESMAN'S GUIDE NATIONWIDE DIRECTORY: BUYING OFFICES & ACCOUNTS
Salesman's Guide, Inc.
1140 Broadway   Phone: (212) 684-2985
New York, NY 10001
Covers: About 225 paid and commission resident buying offices in New York, Miami, Chicago, and Dallas, which service about 11,000 accounts. **Entries include:** Firm name, address, phone; names and addresses of accounts serviced. **Arrangement:** Alphabetical. **Pages** (approx.): 400. **Frequency:** Annual, March. **Editor:** Edward R. Blank. **Advertising accepted.** **Price:** $30.00, postpaid, payment with order; $31.75, billed.

★1270★

SALESMAN'S GUIDE NATIONWIDE DIRECTORY: GIFT & HOUSEWARES BUYERS
Salesman's Guide, Inc.
1140 Broadway   Phone: (212) 684-2985
New York, NY 10001
Covers: Nearly 4,700 catalog showrooms and coordinators; department, discount, furniture, general merchandise, hardware, home furnishings, lawn and garden, and variety stores; florists; gift, greeting card shops; trading stamp houses; supermarkets; mail order companies; drug home centers; and rack jobbers with houseware and gift department buyers. **Entries include:** Store name, address (buying

headquarters), New York City or California buying office affiliation, type of store, number of stores, sales volume for gift and housewares department, name of president, name of general merchandise manager, names of divisional managers. **Arrangement:** Geographical. **Indexes:** Store name. **Pages** (approx.): 820. **Frequency:** Annual, with 3 supplements. **Editor:** Edward R: Blank. **Advertising accepted. Price:** $90.00, including supplements, postpaid, payment with order; $92.00, billed.

★1271★
SALESMAN'S GUIDE NATIONWIDE DIRECTORY: MAJOR MASS MARKET MERCHANDISERS [Excluding New York City metro area]
Salesman's Guide, Inc.
1140 Broadway   Phone: (212) 684-2985
New York, NY 10001
Covers: About 1,600 firms responsible for purchasing women's wear, men's wear, children's wear, and accessories to be sold in about 174,000 discount, variety, drug, factory outlet, and other retail stores; coverage does not include the New York metropolitan area. State and regional editions are also available. **Entries include:** Firm name, address, phone, names of buyers, lines purchased. **Arrangement:** Geographical. **Indexes:** Alphabetical. **Pages** (approx.): 360. **Frequency:** Annual, June. **Editor:** Edward R. Blank. **Advertising accepted. Price:** $55.00, postpaid, payment with order; $56.75, billed. Apply for prices of state editions.

★1272★
SALESMAN'S GUIDE NATIONWIDE DIRECTORY: MEN'S & BOYS' WEAR BUYERS [Excluding New York City metro area]
Salesman's Guide, Inc.
1140 Broadway   Phone: (212) 684-2985
New York, NY 10001
Covers: About 5,000 retail stores selling men's and boys' clothing, sportswear, furnishings, and accessories; coverage does not include New York metropolitan area. State and regional editions are also available. **Entries include:** Store name, address, phone; sales volume in dollars, names of executives and buyers, and resident buying offices (when part of chain or on lease basis). **Arrangement:** Geographical. **Indexes:** Store name. **Pages** (approx.): 700. **Frequency:** Annual, October with 3 supplements. **Editor:** Edward R. Blank. **Advertising accepted. Circulation** 1,000. **Price:** $60.00, including supplements, postpaid, payment with order; $62.00, billed. Apply for prices of state editions.

★1273★
SALESMAN'S GUIDE NATIONWIDE DIRECTORY: PREMIUM INCENTIVE & TRAVEL BUYERS
Salesman's Guide, Inc.
1140 Broadway   Phone: (212) 684-2985
New York, NY 10001
Covers: Over 16,000 buyers of premium/incentive and travel/incentive merchandise and programs. State and regional editions are also available. **Entries include:** Company name, address, phone, names and titles of buyers and other key personnel; types of premiums used and dollar volume are included for most listings. **Arrangement:** Geographical. **Indexes:** Alphabetical (firm name). **Pages** (approx.): 700. **Frequency:** Annual, October with 3 supplements per year. **Editor:** Edward R. Blank. **Advertising accepted. Price:** $110.00, including supplements, postpaid, payment with order; $112.50, billed. Apply for prices of state editions.

★1274★
SALESMAN'S GUIDE NATIONWIDE DIRECTORY: WOMEN'S & CHILDREN'S WEAR BUYERS [Excluding New York City metro area]
Salesman's Guide, Inc.
1140 Broadway   Phone: (212) 684-2985
New York, NY 10001
Covers: About 5,000 retail stores selling women's dresses, coats, intimate apparel, and other women's wear, infants' to teens' wear and

accessories; coverage does not include New York metropolitan area. State and regional editions are also available. **Entries include:** Store name, address, phone, sales volume in dollars, names of executives and buyers, and resident buying offices (when part of chain or on lease basis). **Arrangement:** Geographical. **Indexes:** Store name. **Pages** (approx.): 1,000. **Frequency:** Annual, January with 3 supplements. **Editor:** Edward R. Blank. **Advertising accepted. Price:** $60.00, including supplements, postpaid, payment with order; $62.00, billed. Apply for prices of state editions.

★1275★
SAN DIEGO CHAMBER OF COMMERCE—BUSINESS DIRECTORY [California]
San Diego Chamber of Commerce
110 W. C Street, Suite 1600   Phone: (714) 232-0124
San Diego, CA 92101
Covers: 2,350 firms. **Entries include:** Company name, address, name of principal executive, number of employees, year established in San Diego County, and SIC number. **Arrangement:** By product. **Indexes:** SIC, Zip code. **Pages** (approx.): 200. **Frequency:** Annual, November. **Former title:** Business Directory of San Diego County. **Price:** $15.00, plus $3.00 shipping.

★1276★
SAN FRANCISCO BUSINESS—BIG 50 ISSUE
San Francisco Chamber of Commerce
465 California Street   Phone: (415) 392-4511
San Francisco, CA 94104
Covers: 50 leading Bay Area corporations and smaller numbers of leading banks, savings and loan associations, and utilities. **Entries include:** Company name, California headquarters city, line of business, current and previous year's rank in terms of sales. **Arrangement:** Ranked by sales. **Indexes:** Alphabetical (includes sales and net worth figures). **Frequency:** Annual, July. **Advertising accepted. Price:** $1.50 (ISSN 0036-410X).

★1277★
SAN LEANDRO CHAMBER OF COMMERCE—INDUSTRIAL AND DISTRIBUTION FIRMS [California]
San Leandro Chamber of Commerce
262 Davis Street   Phone: (415) 351-1481
San Leandro, CA 94577
Entries include: Company name, address, phone, name of principal executive, number of employees, list of products or services. **Arrangement:** Alphabetical. **Frequency:** Irregular; latest edition June 1977. **Editor:** E. B. Cooper, Executive Vice-President. **Price:** $10.00.

★1278★
SAN MATEO COUNTY INDUSTRIAL FIRMS [California]
Business Information Systems
181 Second Avenue, Suite 321
San Jose, CA 94401
Covers: 3,570 companies located in San Mateo County, California; industrial parks are also included. **Entries include:** Company name, address, phone, names and titles of key executives, number of employees, line of business, SIC number, whether local company or branch of larger company. **Arrangement:** Alphabetical. **Pages** (approx.): 220. **Frequency:** Annual, fall. **Editor:** A. MacBean, President. **Advertising accepted. Circulation** 3,000. **Price:** $38.00, plus $4.00 shipping. **Other information:** Compiled for San Mateo County Development Association.

★1279★
SANITARY MAINTENANCE—BUYERS' GUIDE ISSUE
Trade Press Publishing Company
407 E. Michigan Street   Phone: (414) 271-4105
Milwaukee, WI 53201
Publication includes: Manufacturers and suppliers of equipment and products for the sanitary supplies and building service contractors industry; trade associations are included. **Entries include:** Company name, address, trade and brand names, products or services.

Frequency: Annual, January. **Editor:** Don Mulligan. **Advertising** accepted. Circulation 10,000. **Price:** $3.00 (1980 edition).

★1280★
SANITATION INDUSTRY YEARBOOK
Communication Channels, Inc.
6285 Barfield Road   Phone: (404) 256-9800
Atlanta, GA 30328
Publication includes: Listings with detailed specifications, illustrations, and manufacturer information for most of the refuse handling machinery and equipment manufactured in North America. **Pages** (approx.): 350. **Frequency:** Annual, November. **Editor:** Alan Novak. **Advertising accepted.** Circulation 22,000. **Price:** $15.00.

★1281★
SANTA CLARA COUNTY INDUSTRIAL DIRECTORY [California]
Business Information Systems, Inc.
181 Second Avenue, Suite 321
San Jose, CA 94401
Covers: 4,225 manufacturing and distribution firms located in Santa Clara County, California; industrial parks are also included. **Entries include:** Company name, address, phone, name of contact, number of employees, line of business and SIC number. **Arrangement:** Alphabetical. **Indexes:** Geographical, SIC. **Pages** (approx.): 250. **Frequency:** Annual, February. **Editor:** A. MacBean, President. **Advertising accepted.** Circulation 4,000. **Price:** $38.00, plus $4.00 shipping. **Other information:** Compiled for San Jose Chamber of Commerce.

★1282★
SANTA MONICA INDUSTRIAL DIRECTORY [California]
Santa Monica Chamber of Commerce
200 Santa Monica Boulevard   Phone: (213) 393-9825
Santa Monica, CA 90401
Entries include: Company name, address, phone, name of principal executive, list of products or services. **Arrangement:** By product. **Pages** (approx.): 50. **Frequency:** Irregular; latest edition 1975; next planned for 1978. **Price:** $2.00 (1975 edition); $5.00 (1978 edition). (Not verified)

★1283★
SAVANNAH AREA MANUFACTURERS DIRECTORY [Georgia]
Savannah Port Authority
42 E. Bay Street   Phone: (912) 233-9604
Savannah, GA 31402
Covers: 170 manufacturers and processors in Savannah and Chatham county and 70 in the surrounding area (Bryan, Bullock, Effingham, Jefferson, and Liberty counties in Georgia; Beaufort, Hampton, and Jasper counties in South Carolina). **Entries include:** Company name, address, phone, names of executives, number of employees, line of business, type of ownership or management, and SIC numbers. **Arrangement:** Geographical. **Indexes:** SIC number (with product and company). **Pages** (approx.): 50. **Frequency:** Biennial, odd years. **Editor:** W. Miles Greer, Assistant Director for Industrial Development. **Former title:** List of Manufacturers and Processors. **Price:** Free.

★1284★
SAVE ON SHOPPING DIRECTORY
S.O.S. Directory
Box 10482   Phone: (904) 733-8878
Jacksonville, FL 32207
Covers: 8,000 factory outlet stores, sample shops, retail clearance centers, and surplus distribution centers in United States and Canada, selected on basis of recommendations by shoppers. **Entries include:** Store name and mailing address, credit cards accepted, directions for reaching store, description of merchandise, and estimated savings. **Arrangement:** Geographical. Separate listing with limited information on chains. **Pages** (approx.): 380. **Frequency:** Annual, August. **Editor:** Iris Ellis, President. **Price:** $6.95, plus $1.00 shipping. **Send orders to:** Caroline House Publishers, 236 Forest Park Place, Ottawa, IL 61350 (library and bookstore orders only). **Other information:**

Updated quarterly by "Bargain News," $7.75 per year.

Scheduled Steamship Service Directory [New York] *See* Port of New York-New Jersey Scheduled Steamship Directory

★1285★
SEAFARING GUIDE & DIRECTORY OF LABOR-MANAGEMENT AFFILIATIONS
Office of Maritime Manpower
Maritime Administration, Room 3067
Commerce Department   Phone: (202) 377-5653
Washington, DC 20230
Covers: 25 maritime management organizations and trade associations, 260 shipping companies, 46 unions, 37 companies which own offshore drilling rigs, and government agencies concerned with the maritime industry. **Entries include:** Company or organization name and address; company entries include union affiliations and management association memberships; union and agency entries include principal officers and phone. **Arrangement:** Alphabetical within agency, organization, or company classification. **Pages** (approx.): 50. **Frequency:** Irregular; latest edition 1975; new edition has been planned since 1978, but was uncertain as of November 1979. **Editor:** Mrs Esther Love, Deputy Director, Office of Maritime Manpower. **Former title:** Guide to Seafaring Collective Bargaining (1975). **Price:** 75¢. **Send orders to:** Government Printing Office, Washington, DC 20402.

★1286★
SEASONAL EMPLOYMENT [National Park Service]
National Park Service
Interior Department
Washington, DC 20242
Covers: Concessionaires who operate hotels, lodges, stores, and other visitor facilities in areas administered by the National Park Service and who have seasonal employees. **Entries include:** Name of park, company name, address, coding to indicate concession facilities offered (lodging, transportation, stores, etc.). **Arrangement:** Alphabetical by name of park. **Pages** (approx.): 20. **Frequency:** Irregular. **Price:** Free. **Also includes:** Job titles and descriptions pertaining to seasonal positions in the National Park Service, and a list of regional offices.

★1287★
SEATTLE CAREER HUNTER'S GUIDE
Victoria House, Publishers
2218 N. E. Eighth Avenue   Phone: (503) 284-4801
Portland, OR 97212
Covers: About 100 private and public employment services, career counseling agencies, testing services, and other facilities useful to persons seeking employment. **Entries include:** Agency name, address, phone, contact person, cost, eligibility standards, description of organization. **Arrangement:** By nature of service (counseling, placement, etc.). **Indexes:** Agency name. **Pages** (approx.): 250. **Frequency:** Not established; first edition 1978. **Editors:** Sheri Raders, Peggy Newsom. **Price:** $5.95, plus 60¢ shipping. **Also includes:** Dot chart with agency name, services provided, and target populations.

★1288★
SEATTLE'S SUPER SHOPPER: INCLUDES TACOMA (Washington)
Writing Works, Inc.
7438 S. E. 40th Street   Phone: (206) 232-2171
Mercer Island, WA 98040
Covers: About 360 factory outlets, sample shops, liquidators, thrift stores. **Entries include:** Store name, address, phone, days and hours of operation, and brief description of merchandise handled. **Arrangement:** By product. **Indexes:** Store name. **Pages** (approx.): 160. **Frequency:** Annual, January. **Editors:** Priscilla Johnston and Dinah Stotler. **Price:** $2.95 (current edition); $3.95 (tentative, 1980 edition); plus 75¢ shipping.

★1289★
SEAWAY MARITIME DIRECTORY
Fourth Seacoast Publishing Company, Inc.
24145 Little Mack   Phone: (313) 779-5570
St. Clair Shores, MI 48080
Covers: About 50 ports in the Great Lakes and St. Lawrence Seaway area. **Entries include:** Name of port, descriptive information, list of port service firms and steamship lines with addresses, phone numbers, services offered. **Arrangement:** Alphabetical. **Pages** (approx.): 365. **Frequency:** Annual, May. **Price:** $20.00.

Second Shopper's Guide to Museum Stores *See* **Shopper's Guide to Museum Stores**

★1290★
SECURITY INDUSTRY & PRODUCT NEWS—DIRECTORY & BUYING GUIDE ISSUE [Protection]
PTN Publishing Corporation
250 Fulton Avenue   Phone: (516) 489-1300
Hempstead, NY 11550
Covers: More than 500 manufacturers and 350 distributors of locks, alarms, video equipment, radio equipment, etc., for providing physical security of premises, vaults, etc. **Entries include:** For manufacturers - Company name, address, phone, names of president and sales manager, distributors. For distributors - Company name, address, phone. **Arrangement:** Alphabetical. **Indexes:** Product, trade name. **Pages** (approx.): 250. **Frequency:** Annual, January-February. **Advertising accepted. Price:** $10.00 (current and 1980 editions).

★1291★
SECURITY WORLD—PRODUCT DIRECTORY ISSUE
Security World Publishing Company, Division
Cahners Publishing Company
2639 S. La Cienega Boulevard   Phone: (213) 836-5000
Los Angeles, CA 90034
Covers: About 935 manufacturers and suppliers of security products, including alarms, non-broadcast television equipment, and other equipment. **Entries include:** Company name, address, phone, list of products. **Arrangement:** Alphabetical. **Indexes:** Product. **Frequency:** Annual, summer. **Advertising accepted.** Circulation 40,000. **Price:** $10.00 (ISSN 0037-0703).

★1292★
SECURITY/FIRE EQUIPMENT MANUFACTURERS' DIRECTORY
Marketing Development
402 Border Road   Phone: (617) 369-5382
Concord, MA 01742
Covers: About 520 manufacturers of access control systems, locks, burglar alarms, fire extinguishers, signalling equipment, door bolts, motion detectors, and other fire and security equipment (SIC 3429, 3569, 3662, 3999). **Entries include:** Company name, address, phone, names of executives, number of employees, financial data, and products or services. **Arrangement:** Alphabetical. **Indexes:** Product. **Pages** (approx.): 180. **Frequency:** Irregular; latest edition fall 1977. **Editor:** Bud Anderson, President. **Price:** $35.00.

★1293★
SEIBT EXPORT DIRECTORY OF GERMAN INDUSTRIES
Seibt-Verlag
Rosenheimer Straase 145a
D-8000 Munchen 80, Germany
Covers: German firms interested in export business. **Entries include:** Company name, address, products. **Arrangement:** Alphabetical. **Indexes:** Product. **Pages** (approx.): 1,600. **Frequency:** Annual, spring. **Advertising accepted. Price:** 72 DM (current edition); 85 DM (1980 edition). **Other information:** Separate editions in English, Spanish, and French.

★1294★
SELECTED AND ANNOTATED BUYING GUIDE [To Asian American-owned business in California Bay area]
Asian, Inc.
1610 Bush Street   Phone: (415) 928-5910
San Francisco, CA 94109
Covers: Firms offering professional, commercial, and industrial products and services. **Entries include:** Company name, address, phone, name of contact; size of facilities; dollar volume of business for previous, current, and coming years; basis for pricing; licenses; some listings include clients. **Arrangement:** Classified by product or service. **Frequency:** Irregular; latest edition January 1978; addendum May 1979. **Price:** $5.00.

★1295★
SEM 79
Solar Engineering Publishers, Inc.
8435 N. Stemmons Freeway, Suite 880   Phone: (214) 630-6963
Dallas, TX 75247
Covers: More than 550 manufacturers of solar products; solar installation and maintenance contractors, architects, and engineers; testing laboratories with solar equipment capabilities; computer services; research consultants. **Entries include:** Company name, address, phone; manufacturer listings include names and addresses of dealers and distributors. **Arrangement:** Classified. **Indexes:** Product, trade and brand name. **Frequency:** Annual. **Advertising accepted. Price:** $15.00.

SEMI Directory *See* **SEMI Membership Directory**

★1296★
SEMI MEMBERSHIP DIRECTORY
Semiconductor Equipment and Materials Institute
625 Ellis Street, Suite 212   Phone: (415) 964-5111
Mountain View, CA 94043
Covers: Manufacturers of equipment and materials for the semiconductor industry; international coverage. Includes a list of individual members with business addresses. **Entries include:** Company name, address, phone, date founded, number of employees, type of ownership, marketing method, names of executives, list of products. **Arrangement:** Alphabetical. **Indexes:** Geographical, product. **Pages** (approx.): 50. **Frequency:** Annual, August. **Price:** $25.00.

★1297★
SEMICONDUCTOR INDUSTRY ASSOCIATION—YEARBOOK

Semiconductor Industry Association
20380 Town Center Lane, Suite 155   Phone: (408) 255-3522
Cupertino, CA 95014
Covers: 200 manufacturers of semiconductors in the United States; not limited to members. **Entries include:** For members - Company name, address, names and locations of subsidiaries, names and titles of key personnel, products. For nonmembers - Company name, address, and locations of subsidiaries and parent companies. **Arrangement:** Alphabetical. **Pages** (approx.): 40. **Frequency:** Annual, September. **Price:** $35.00, postpaid, payment with order.

★1298★
SEMICONDUCTOR INTERNATIONAL—ANNUAL BUYER'S GUIDE ISSUE
Milton S. Kiver Publications, Inc.
222 W. Adams Street   Phone: (312) 263-4866
Chicago, IL 60606
Publication includes: List of about 1,000 manufacturers and suppliers of equipment and products in the assembly, packaging, and testing of solid state devices and integrated circuits. **Entries include:** Company name, address, phone, products. **Arrangement:** Alphabetical. **Indexes:** Product. **Frequency:** Annual, November. **Editor:** Donald J. Levinthal. **Advertising accepted.** Circulation 17,000. **Price:** $10.00.

★1299★
SENIOR COLLEGE PROGRAMS IN HOTEL, RESTAURANT, INSTITUTIONAL MANAGEMENT IN THE UNITED STATES
National Restaurant Association
One IBM Plaza, Suite 2600   Phone: (312) 787-2525
Chicago, IL 60611
Number of listings: 70. **Entries include:** School name, department name, address, phone, code to indicate schools primarily oriented to dietetics. **Arrangement:** Geographical. **Frequency:** Published 1977; updated 1978. **Price:** Free. **Other information:** Also cited as, "Baccalaureate Programs in Hotel, Restaurant, Institutional Management in the United States." Prepared in cooperation with the National Institute for the Foodservice Industry.

★1300★
SERVICE REPORTER—BUYERS GUIDE ISSUE [Heating, cooling]
Technical Reporting Corporation
1098 S. Milwaukee Avenue   Phone: (312) 537-6460
Wheeling, IL 60090
Covers: Manufacturers of air conditioning, heating, ventilating, and refrigerating equipment. **Entries include:** Company name, address, phone, name of contact, and list of products. **Arrangement:** Alphabetical. **Indexes:** Product. **Frequency:** Annual, December. **Editor:** Robert Mader. **Advertising accepted. Price:** $3.00.

★1301★
SERVICE WORLD INTERNATIONAL
Cahners Publishing Company
205 E. 42nd Street   Phone: (212) 949-4377
New York, NY 10017
Covers: Manufacturers of equipment and suppliers of services for the restaurant, hotel, and institutional markets, worldwide. **Entries include:** Company name, address, phone, telex, cable, parent company, products and services, trade names, and regional and local distributors. **Arrangement:** Alphabetical by company name. **Pages** (approx.): 120. **Frequency:** Annual, December. **Editor:** Julie Woodman. **Advertising accepted.** Circulation 18,000. **Price:** $5.00.

★1302★
SEYBOLD REPORT—SYSTEM INSTALLATIONS ISSUE [Graphic arts industry]
Seybold Publications, Inc.
Box 644   Phone: (215) 565-2480
Media, PA 19063
Covers: About 1,550 newspaper and commercial copy handling and typesetting systems; some foreign installations included. **Entries include:** User name and location, circulation (if a publication), date first installed, and present configuration of the system, including host hardware, terminals, peripheral equipment, output typesetters, and type of application. **Arrangement:** By manufacturer. **Pages** (approx.): 80. **Frequency:** Irregular; latest edition September 24, 1979. **Editor:** John W. Seybold. **Price:** $172.00 per year (ISSN 0364-5517).

Sheldon's Retail Directory of the United States and Canada *See* Sheldon's Retail Stores

★1303★
SHELDON'S RETAIL STORES
Phelon, Sheldon & Marsar, Inc.
32 Union Square East   Phone: (212) 473-2590
New York, NY 10003
Covers: 1,800 large independent department stores; 500 large junior department store chains; over 100 large independent and chain home furnishing stores; 750 large independent women's specialty stores; 300 large women's specialty store chains; 500 New York resident buyers and merchandise brokers. **Entries include:** For stores - Name of store or chain, address, phone, New York and other buying offices, branch store locations, names of all department buyers and lines bought by each, names of principal executives. For buying offices - Firm name, address, buyers' names and lines bought, names of stores served. **Arrangement:** Geographical. **Indexes:** Alphabetical index of

store and chain names. **Pages** (approx.): 700. **Frequency:** Annual, February. **Price:** $60.00 (current edition); $65.00 (tentative, 1980 edition).

★1304★
SHOE FACTORY BUYERS' GUIDE
Shoe Trades Publishing Company
15 East Street   Phone: (617) 542-0190
Boston, MA 02111
Covers: Over 750 suppliers and their representatives to the shoe manufacturing industries in the United States and Canada. **Entries include:** Company name, address, trade and brand names, list of products or services. **Arrangement:** By type of product and service. **Indexes:** Trade mark. **Pages** (approx.): 700. **Frequency:** Annual, spring. **Editor:** Thomas O'Rowan. **Advertising accepted.** Circulation 4,000. **Price:** $5.00 (current edition); $8.00 (1980 edition).

★1305★
SHOE SERVICE WHOLESALERS IN THE UNITED STATES AND CANADA
Shoe Service Institute of America
222 W. Adams Street   Phone: (312) 236-2283
Chicago, IL 60606
Covers: About 280 wholesalers of findings and small tools used in shoe repair and shoe care. **Entries include:** Company name, address, phone, name of principal executive; some listings also include names of buyers. **Arrangement:** Geographical. **Pages** (approx.): 50. **Frequency:** Annual. **Former title:** Finder's Directory. **Price:** $200.00 (current and 1980 editions). **Other information:** Sometimes cited as, "Directory of Wholesalers in the United States and Canada."

★1306★
SHOPPER'S GUIDE TO MUSEUM STORES
Universe Books
381 Park Avenue South   Phone: (212) 685-7400
New York, NY 10016
Covers: Museums with shops offering products created specifically by and for the museum; covers about 700 items. **Entries include:** Product description, price, museum name, address, and phone, ordering information and information on museum membership, member discounts, and mail order catalogues published by the museum. **Pages** (approx.): 195. **Frequency:** Irregular; latest edition November 1978. **Editor:** Shelley Hodupp. **Price:** $7.95. **Other information:** 1978 edition titled, "Second Shopper's Guide to Museum Stores."

★1307★
SHOPPING CENTER DIRECTORY
National Research Bureau
424 N. Third Street   Phone: (319) 752-5415
Burlington, IA 52601
Covers: 19,000 shopping centers, in four volumes. Volume 1: Eastern States - Connecticut, Delaware, District of Columbia, Maine, Maryland, Massachusetts, New Hampshire, New Jersey, New York, Pennsylvania, Rhode Island, Vermont, Virginia, and West Virginia. Volume 2: Midwestern States - Illinois, Indiana, Iowa, Kansas, Kentucky, Michigan, Minnesota, Missouri, Nebraska, North Dakota, Ohio, South Dakota, Tennessee, and Wisconsin. Volume 3: Southern States - Alabama, Arkansas, Florida, Georgia, Louisiana, Mississippi, North Carolina, South Carolina, Texas. Volume 4: Western States - Alaska, Arizona, California, Colorado, Hawaii, Idaho, Montana, Nevada, New Mexico, Oklahoma, Oregon, Utah, Washington, Wyoming. A fifth volume includes three indexes - Centers under construction or planned; centers with space available; and centers that have expanded. **Entries include:** Center name, address, mailing address, phone; names of executives, architect, merchants' association secretary; gross sales; date opened; auditorium facilities; if air conditioned (for malls); square footage; number of stores; availability of parking; type of center (regional, community, neighborhood); name and square footage for major/anchor tenants; other tenants' names. **Arrangement:** Geographical. **Indexes:** Alphabetical, metropolis name. **Pages**

(approx.): 2,600. **Frequency:** Annual, quarterly updates. **Price:** $72.00 per regional section; $168.00 for set of five. Index volume is $38.00 with a regional volume; $72.00, alone. Price includes quarterly updates.

★1308★
SHOPPING CENTER INVENTORY OF SAN DIEGO COUNTY [California]
Economic Research Bureau of San Diego
110 W. C Street, Suite 1600   Phone: (714) 232-0124
San Diego, CA 92101
Number of listings: 200, including centers proposed but not yet built. **Entries include:** Name of center, address, number of stores, square feet of retail space, major retailers, name of leasing agent; most entries include tenant names. **Arrangement:** Geographical. **Frequency:** Irregular; latest edition October 1977; new edition expected January 1980. **Editor:** Gale D. Sonora. **Price:** $7.50 (current and 1980 editions).

★1309★
S.I.C. 20 BUYERS GUIDE
S.I.C. Publishing Company
Box 6042   Phone: (609) 896-9447
Lawrenceville, NJ 08648
Covers: 3,300 suppliers of products and services to the food processing and beverage industry (SIC 20). **Entries include:** Company name and address. **Arrangement:** Alphabetical. **Indexes:** Product. **Pages** (approx.): 250. **Frequency:** Annual, May. **Editor:** P. C. Herald, Publisher. **Advertising accepted.** Circulation 17,500. **Price:** $15.00.

★1310★
SIGNS OF THE TIMES—SIGN ERECTION AND MAINTENANCE DIRECTORY SECTION
Signs of the Times
407 Gilbert   Phone: (513) 421-2050
Cincinnati, OH 45202
Covers: 800 firms that erect and/or maintain electrical signs. **Entries include:** Company name, address, phone, services. **Arrangement:** Geographical. **Pages** (approx.): 20. **Frequency:** Monthly. **Editor:** Dave Souder. **Advertising accepted.** Circulation 14,500. **Price:** $1.50.

★1311★
SILVER BOOK [Truck equipment]
Verbiest Publishing Company
950 E. Maple, Suite 205   Phone: (313) 645-2360
Birmingham, MI 48011
Covers: Suppliers of special equipment for Chevrolet trucks. **Entries include:** Company name, address, phone, list of products and trade names. **Arrangement:** Classified. **Pages** (approx.): 180. **Frequency:** Annual, January. **Advertising accepted.** **Price:** $3.50.

★1312★
SILVER REFINERS OF THE WORLD AND THEIR IDENTIFYING INGOT MARKS
Silver Institute
1001 Connecticut Avenue, N. W.,
    Suite 1138
Washington, DC 20036
Covers: 65 refiners in 17 countries. **Entries include:** Company name, address, phone, and ingot mark. **Pages** (approx.): 75. **Frequency:** Not established; first edition 1977. **Price:** $5.00.

★1313★
SKI INDUSTRIES AMERICA—TRADE SHOW DIRECTORY
Ski Industries America
1200 17th Street, N. W.
Washington, DC 20036
Covers: 260 manufacturers and importers of ski apparel, equipment, and accessories who participate. **Entries include:** Company name, address, phone, salesmen, and products (including trade or brand names). **Arrangement:** Alphabetical. **Frequency:** Annual, March.

Editor: R. A. DesRoches, Executive Vice President. **Price:** $10.00 (current and 1980 editions).

★1314★
SKILLS DIRECTORY [Bartering]
Comstock Trading Company
1926 Tice Valley Boulevard   Phone: (415) 939-9292
Walnut Creek, CA 94595
Covers: Several thousand members who have paid $100 to join the Comstock Trading Program, devoted to bartering. **Entries include:** Barterer name, address. **Arrangement:** By skill or professional service offered. **Price:** Included in membership. **Other information:** See also listing for Comstock's "Trading Post."

SLIG Buyers' Guide [Storage battery industry] *See* Battery Man—SLIG Buyers' Guide Issue

★1315★
SMALL MOTOR MANUFACTURERS ASSOCIATION— MEMBERSHIP/PRODUCT DIRECTORY
Small Motor Manufacturers Association
435 N. Michigan Avenue, Suite 1717   Phone: (312) 644-0828
Chicago, IL 60611
Covers: About 55 manufacturers, suppliers, and others concerned with sub-fractional horsepower motors. **Entries include:** Company name, address, name of contact, list of projects. **Arrangement:** Alphabetical. **Pages** (approx.): 30. **Frequency:** Annual. **Price:** $5.00, payment with order.

★1316★
SMALL WORLD DIRECTORY [Children's products]
Earnshaw Publications, Inc.
393 Seventh Avenue   Phone: (212) 563-2742
New York, NY 10001
Covers: 200 manufacturers of juvenile furniture, wheel goods, toys, and accessories. Also lists federal agencies, showrooms, wholesalers, buyers, suppliers, trade associations, and brand names. **Entries include:** Manufacturer name, address, phone, names of executives, products, and brand names. **Arrangement:** Alphabetical. **Pages** (approx.): 100. **Frequency:** Annual, December. **Editor:** Thomas Hudson. **Advertising accepted.** Circulation 10,000. **Price:** $2.00.

★1317★
SMALLER BUSINESS ASSOCIATION OF NEW ENGLAND— MEMBERSHIP DIRECTORY
Smaller Business Association of New England
69 Hickory Drive   Phone: (617) 890-9070
Waltham, MA 02154
Number of listings: 900. **Entries include:** Company name, address, phone, names of chief executives, list of products or services. **Arrangement:** Classified by type of business. **Pages** (approx.): 120. **Frequency:** Biennial, fall of even years. **Editor:** Lewis A. Shattuck, Executive Vice President. **Advertising accepted.** Circulation 7,000. **Price:** $25.00.

★1318★
SNACK FOOD—BUYERS GUIDE ISSUE
Harcourt Brace Jovanovich, Inc.
111 E. Wacker Drive   Phone: (312) 938-2327
Chicago, IL 60601
Publication includes: List of 1,000 firms providing supplies and services to the snack food manufacturing industry. **Entries include:** Company name, address, phone, and products or services. **Arrangement:** Classified by product category; alphabetical. **Frequency:** Annual, August. **Editor:** Jerry Hess. **Advertising accepted.** **Price:** $5.00. **Send orders to:** Harcourt Brace Jovanovich, Inc., 1 E. First St., Duluth, MN 55802 (218-727-8511).

★1319★
SNACK FOOD BLUE BOOK
Harcourt Brace Jovanovich, Inc.
111 E. Wacker Drive   Phone: (312) 938-2327
Chicago, IL 60601
Covers: Over 1,100 corporate group headquarters, individual plants, distributors, and trade associations, in separate sections; international coverage. **Entries include:** All entries give name, address and names of executives; most include phone. Entries for corporate headquarters list company plants; separate list of plants includes products manufactured, equipment, number of employees. Association listings include president, number of members, meetings and events, services. **Arrangement:** Corporate offices and associations are alphabetical, plants and distributors are geographical. **Indexes:** Company name (with address). **Frequency:** Irregular; previous edition 1976; latest edition October 1979. **Editor:** Jerry Hess. **Advertising accepted.** **Price:** $40.00. **Send orders to:** Harcourt Brace Jovanovich, Inc., 1 E. First St., Duluth, MN 55802 (212-727-8511).

★1320★
SOAP/COSMETICS/CHEMICAL SPECIALTIES BLUE BOOK
MacNair-Dorland Company
101 W. 31st Street   Phone: (212) 279-4455
New York, NY 10001
Covers: Sources of raw materials, equipment, and services for the soap, cosmetic, and chemical specialties industry. Includes a list of trade association officials. **Entries include:** Company name, address, trade and brand names, list of products or services. **Pages** (approx.): 200. **Frequency:** Annual, April. **Editor:** John Vollmutl. **Advertising accepted.** Circulation 13,000. **Former title:** Blue Book of the Soap, Detergent, Cosmetic, and Chemical Specialty Industries. **Price:** $3.00 (current and 1980 editions).

★1321★
SOCIETY FOR FOODSERVICE MANAGEMENT — MEMBERSHIP DIRECTORY
Society for Foodservice Management
310 W. Liberty Street   Phone: (502) 583-3783
Louisville, KY 40202
Covers: 350 companies that own, operate, or contract food services for their own employees; contracting food service firms; and suppliers to this industry. **Entries include:** Company name, address, phone, names of executives, and number of employees. **Arrangement:** Alphabetical. **Pages** (approx.): 120. **Frequency:** Annual, March. **Editor:** Phillip S. Cooke, Executive Director. **Advertising accepted.** **Price:** Available to members only. **Other information:** Society for Foodservice Management was formed by the merger of the National Industrial Cafeteria Managers Association and the Association for Food Service Management.

★1322★
SOCIETY OF RESEARCH ADMINISTRATORS — MEMBERSHIP DIRECTORY
Society of Research Administrators
1100 Glendon Avenue, Suite 2104   Phone: (213) 825-4243
Los Angeles, CA 90024
Covers: 1,200 persons interested in the management of research of all types in all fields. **Entries include:** Name, office address and phone, highest degree held, areas of occupational specialization. **Arrangement:** Alphabetical. **Indexes:** Organization. **Pages** (approx.): 140. **Frequency:** Annual, November. **Editor:** Julie Mendelson. **Advertising accepted.** Circulation 1,200. **Price:** $30.00.

★1323★
SOCIETY OF THE PLASTICS INDUSTRY — MEMBERSHIP DIRECTORY & BUYERS GUIDE
Society of the Plastics Industry
355 Lexington Avenue   Phone: (212) 573-9400
New York, NY 10017
Covers: 1,400 manufacturers and processors of all types of plastics, producers of raw materials, manufacturers of equipment and supplies, and research and testing laboratories. **Entries include:** Company name, address, phone, names of up to three principal executives, and list of products or services. **Arrangement:** Alphabetical. **Indexes:** General business classification (machinery, film and sheet plastics, etc.), product and services (knobs, laminating service, etc.), and geographical. **Pages** (approx.): 550. **Frequency:** Annual, March. **Editor:** John G. Weigly, Director of Administrative Services. **Former title:** Directory and Buyers Guide of the SPI. **Price:** $30.00 (current and 1980 editions).

Solar Age Catalog *See* Solar Age Resource Book

★1324★
SOLAR AGE RESOURCE BOOK
SolarVision, Inc.
Church Hill   Phone: (603) 827-3347
Harrisville, NH 03450
Publication includes: List of architects, engineers, and others having some expertise in the use of solar energy, and buyers' guides for solar, wind, and wood energy products. **Frequency:** First edition under this title 1979; new edition expected 1981. **Former title:** Solar Age Catalog. **Price:** $9.95.

★1325★
SOLAR COLLECTOR MANUFACTURING ACTIVITY AND APPLICATIONS IN THE RESIDENTIAL SECTOR
Office of Energy Data Operations
Energy Information Administration
Energy Department
1000 Independence Avenue, N. W.   Phone: (202) 252-6401
Washington, DC 20585
Publication includes: In appendix - List of manufacturers of solar energy collectors. **Entries include:** Company name, address, type of collector manufactured. **Arrangement:** Alphabetical. **Frequency:** Semiannual. **Price:** $1.20 (S/N 061-000-00047-0). **Send orders to:** Government Printing Office, Washington, DC 20402.

★1326★
SOLAR ENERGY DIRECTORY
Centerline Company
401 S. 36th Street   Phone: (602) 267-0014
Phoenix, AZ 85034
Covers: About 1,400 solar energy, wind energy, and manufacturers, architects, contractors, government agencies, and other related groups and firms, primarily in the United States. **Entries include:** Company name, address, area of involvement, phone. **Arrangement:** By type of firm or activity, then geographical. **Indexes:** United States company name. **Pages** (approx.): 215. **Frequency:** Irregular; latest edition 1978. **Editor:** Jerry Kingery, Manager. **Price:** $12.50, postpaid.

★1327★
SOLAR ENERGY SOURCE BOOK: FOR THE HOME OWNER, COMMERCIAL BUILDER, AND MANUFACTURER
Solar Energy Institute of North America
1110 Sixth Street, N. W.
Washington, DC 20001
Covers: Manufacturers, distributors, architects, engineers, schools, etc., concerned with solar energy and related technology and products; includes wind energy. **Entries include:** For manufacturers - Company name, address, product information. Listings in other categories give similar data. **Arrangement:** By type of collector, and by activity or service. **Pages** (approx.): 800. **Frequency:** Annual, April. **Editor:** Christopher Wells Martz. **Price:** $30.00, cloth; $15.00, paper; plus $2.00 shipping.

★1328★
SOLAR ENGINEERING—SOLAR HOT WATER PACKAGERS [Special feature]
Solar Engineering Publishers, Inc.
8435 N. Stemmons Freeway   Phone: (214) 630-6963
Dallas, TX 75247
Publication includes: Special 12-page directory in March 1978 issue of firms supplying complete systems for solar hot water heating. **Price:** $1.50.

Solar Engineering Master Catalog *See* SEM 79

★1329★
SOLAR HEATING AND COOLING—SOLAR BUYERS GUIDE ISSUE
Gordon Publications, Inc.
20 Community Place   Phone: (201) 267-6040
Morristown, NJ 07960
Covers: Over 600 manufacturers and 3,400 distributors of solar equipment and materials; and over 2,500 solar builders, engineers, architects, and installers. **Entries include:** Company or firm name, address; manufacturer listings include phone; distributor listings include lines handled; professional service listings include services. **Arrangement:** Manufacturers are alphabetical, others are geographical. **Indexes:** Product. **Frequency:** Annual, February. **Editor:** Alison Brown. **Advertising accepted.** Circulation 11,000. **Price:** $5.00.

★1330★
SOLAR PRODUCTS SPECIFICATIONS GUIDE
SolarVision, Inc.
Church Hill   Phone: (603) 827-3347
Harrisville, NH 03450
Covers: About 225 manufacturers of over 400 products for use in solar energy systems. **Entries include:** Company name, address, phone, name of executive, and description and technical specifications of one product. **Pages** (approx.): 500. **Frequency:** Looseleaf base volume published 1978; updates every two months. **Price:** $165.00, including updates for one year (1980 price).

★1331★
SOLID STATE PROCESSING AND PRODUCTION BUYERS GUIDE AND DIRECTORY
Symcon, Inc.
14 Vanderventer Avenue
Port Washington, NY 11050
Covers: 1,500 suppliers to manufacturers and processors of solid state devices and circuits. **Entries include:** Company name, address, phone, branch offices (if any), telex and TWX numbers. **Arrangement:** Alphabetical. **Indexes:** Product/service, trade name. **Pages** (approx.): 400. **Frequency:** Irregular; new edition expected February 1980. **Advertising accepted. Price:** $40.00 (1980 edition).

★1332★
SOLID WASTES MANAGEMENT/REFUSE REMOVAL JOURNAL— BUYERS GUIDE ISSUE
Communication Channels, Inc.
6285 Barfield Road   Phone: (404) 256-9800
Atlanta, GA 30328
Publication includes: Directory of manufacturers of equipment and supplies for the solid and liquid wastes management industry (including resource recovery and hazardous wastes). **Entries include:** Firm name, address, phone. **Indexes:** Brand name, product, trade name. **Pages** (approx.): 200. **Frequency:** Annual, February. **Editor:** Alan Novak. **Advertising accepted.** Circulation 22,000. **Former title:** Refuse Removal Journal. **Price:** $3.00.

★1333★
SONOMA COUNTY ECONOMIC DEVELOPMENT BOARD— DIRECTORY OF MANUFACTURERS [California]
Sonoma County Economic Development Board
2300 County Center Drive
Building A, Suite 129   Phone: (707) 527-2406
Santa Rosa, CA 95401
Number of listings: 675. **Entries include:** Company name, address, phone, name of principal executive, number of employees, products. **Arrangement:** By SIC numbers. **Indexes:** Alphabetical, product. **Pages** (approx.): 50. **Frequency:** Annual. **Editor:** Harold V. Pederson, Development Director. **Price:** $4.00, plus 60¢ shipping (1980 edition).

S.O.S. Directory *See* Save on Shopping Directory

★1334★
SOUND AND VIBRATION—BUYER'S GUIDE ISSUES
Acoustical Publications, Inc.
27101 E. Oviatt Road   Phone: (216) 835-0101
Bay Village, OH 44140
Covers: 250 manufacturers of materials, systems, and instruments for control and measurement of sound and vibration. **Arrangement:** By product category. **Pages** (approx.): 40. **Frequency:** Materials issue in July, systems issue in August, instrumentation issue in March. **Editor:** Jack Mowry. **Editor:** Circulation 20,000. **Price:** Included in subscription, $10.00 per year.

★1335★
SOURCES FOR IRON CASTINGS: A BUYERS GUIDE AND DIRECTORY OF MEMBERS
Iron Castings Society
20611 Center Ridge Road   Phone: (216) 333-9600
Rocky River, OH 44116
Covers: 240 iron foundries which are members of the society (SIC 3321, 3322). **Entries include:** Foundry name, address, phone, type of foundry, specialty types of castings and products, casting size and use, monthly production, irons and classes, facilities and services, names of executives, and SIC numbers. **Arrangement:** By SIC, then alphabetical. **Indexes:** Geographical, personal name. **Pages** (approx.): 90. **Frequency:** Biennial, early in even years. **Editor:** T. Jerry Warden, Marketing Director. **Price:** Free.

★1336★
SOURCES OF AID AND INFORMATION FOR U.S. EXPORTERS
Washington Researchers
918 16th Street, N. W.   Phone: (202) 828-4800
Washington, DC 20006
Covers: Governmental and nongovernmental sources in the United States and abroad which offer information and assistance to firms in international trade. **Entries include:** Name of department, agency, association, etc., address, phone, services or information offered to companies engaged in export. **Arrangement:** By service. **Frequency:** Annual. **Editor:** Donna Jablonsky. **Price:** $30.00, postpaid, payment with order; $33.00, billed. **Other information:** Cited in pre-publication releases as, "Sources of Information for U.S. Exporters."

Sources of Information for U.S. Exporters *See* Sources of Aid and Information for U.S. Exporters

★1337★
SOURCES OF STATE INFORMATION ON CORPORATIONS
Washington Researchers
918 16th Street, N. W.   Phone: (202) 828-4800
Washington, DC 20006
Covers: State offices where documents are kept describing companies within that state. Information available from these sources ranges from articles of incorporation to current financial data. **Entries include:** Name of office, address, phone, which official to contact for special records (where applicable), fees for transcripts. **Arrangement:** Geographical by state, then by type of record (corporate, uniform commercial code, securities). **Pages** (approx.): 40. **Frequency:**

Annual, summer. **Price:** $17.50, postpaid, payment with order; $19.00, billed.

★1338★
SOURCES OF SUPPLY [Woodwork]
National Woodwork Manufacturers Association
205 W. Touhy Avenue   Phone: (312) 623-6747
Park Ridge, IL 60068
Covers: Over 90 manufacturers of wood windows, wood doors, frames, and other wood items; suppliers to the industry are also included. **Entries include:** Company name, address, phone, name of contact, products. **Arrangement:** Alphabetical. **Pages** (approx.): 20. **Frequency:** Annual, February. **Price:** Free.

★1339★
SOURCES OF SUPPLY DIRECTORY [Luggage and leather goods industry]
Business Journals, Inc.
22 S. Smith Street   Phone: (203) 853-6015
East Norwalk, CT 06855
Number of listings: 1,000 (SIC 3161). **Entries include:** Company name, address, phone, name of principal executive, code for type of resource. **Arrangement:** Alphabetical. **Indexes:** Product, trade name. **Pages** (approx.): 150. **Frequency:** Annual, November. **Editor:** Jo-Ann Lombardo. **Advertising accepted.** Circulation 2,500. **Price:** $5.00.

★1340★
SOURCES OF SUPPLY/BUYERS GUIDE [Paper industry]
Advertisers & Publishers Service, Inc.
300 N. Prospect Avenue   Phone: (312) 823-3145
Park Ridge, IL 60068
Covers: About 1,700 mills and converters, 2,700 merchants, and 200 manufacturers' representatives in paper, films, foils, and allied lines. Includes list of trade associations. **Entries include:** For mills and converters - Firm name, address, principal personnel, products. For merchants - Firm name, address, phone, names of executives, main and branch offices. For manufacturers' representatives - Name, address, phone, lines handled. **Arrangement:** Mills are alphabetical; merchants are alphabetical and geographical; representatives are geographical. **Indexes:** Product, brand name. **Pages** (approx.): 300. **Frequency:** Annual, April. **Editor:** Louise B. Cowan. **Advertising accepted.** Circulation 1,500. **Price:** $35.00 (current edition); $40.00 (1980 edition).

South Carolina Industrial Directory *See* Industrial Directory of South Carolina

★1341★
SOUTH CAROLINA INTERNATIONAL TRADE DIRECTORY
South Carolina State Development Board
Box 927   Phone: (803) 758-2411
Columbia, SC 29202
Covers: All manufacturers in South Carolina engaged in importing and/ or exporting. **Entries include:** Company name, address, phone, names of principal and other executives, number of employees, list of products or services, SIC numbers. **Arrangement:** Alphabetical. **Indexes:** Geographical, product. **Pages** (approx.): 200. **Frequency:** Irregular. **Editor:** Renee Oswald, Research Analyst. **Price:** Out of print; new edition in different format possible in 1981.

★1342★
SOUTH CAROLINA METALWORKING DIRECTORY
South Carolina State Development Board
Box 927   Phone: (803) 758-3055
Columbia, SC 29202
Covers: About 200 custom metalworking firms and about 160 firms with metalworking-related products in South Carolina. **Entries include:** For metalworking firms - Name, address, name and title of chief executive, phone, number of employees, principal line of business, equipment and specifications of equipment available. For other firms - Name, address, names and titles of manager and purchasing agent,

phone, products. **Arrangement:** Metalworking firms are by county, others are alphabetical. **Indexes:** Metalworking firm with machine or process, firm name with county and city. **Pages** (approx.): 345. **Frequency:** Biennial, odd years. **Price:** Free.

★1343★
SOUTH CAROLINA STATE INDUSTRIAL DIRECTORY
State Industrial Directories Corporation
Two Penn Plaza   Phone: (212) 564-0340
New York, NY 10001
Number of listings: 2,500. **Entries include:** Company name, address, phone, names of key executives, number of employees, plant size, 4-digit SIC code, products, whether firm imports or exports, and whether firm has research facilities. **Arrangement:** Geographical. **Indexes:** Alphabetical, product (includes mailing address and phone for each firm). **Frequency:** Annual, spring; first edition 1979. **Advertising accepted.** **Price:** $30.00 (current and 1980 editions; ISSN 0162-0878).

★1344★
SOUTH DAKOTA MANUFACTURERS AND PROCESSORS DIRECTORY
South Dakota Industrial Development Department
620 S. Cliff Avenue   Phone: (605) 339-6779
Sioux Falls, SD 57103
Number of listings: 825. **Entries include:** Company name, address, phone, code for number of employees, products or line of business, SIC numbers. **Arrangement:** Alphabetical. **Indexes:** Geographical, SIC, product. **Pages** (approx.): 90. **Frequency:** Annual, January. **Editor:** Richard Garness. **Price:** $5.00 (current and 1980 editions).

★1345★
SOUTH MAGAZINE—TOP 200 COMPANIES ISSUE
Trend Publications, Inc.
Ybor Square
Eighth Avenue & 13th Street
Tampa, FL 33605
Covers: Top publicly held industrial and service companies in the South. Separate lists of 25 least profitable companies, 25 most profitable, and newcomers to the Top 200 list. **Entries include:** Company name, headquarters city, rank for current and previous year, sales or revenues, net income, and other financial data, stock exchange, and description of principal business, name of key executive. **Arrangement:** Ranked by total revenues or sales. **Indexes:** Industry, state. **Frequency:** Annual, July. **Editor:** Roy B. Bain. **Advertising accepted.** **Price:** $3.00.

★1346★
SOUTHEAST DIRECTORY OF COMPUTER INSTALLATIONS
C.I.I. Publications
233 Peachtree Street, N. E., Suite 2010   Phone: (404) 586-0143
Atlanta, GA 30303
Covers: About 1,300 data processing installations and vendors in eight southeastern states. **Entries include:** Company name, address, phone, name of contact; number of data processing employees; computer equipment configuration, languages used, applications, computer time availabilities. **Arrangement:** Geographical. **Frequency:** Irregular; first edition December 1977; latest edition February 1979. **Editor:** Kimberly K. Taylor. **Price:** $90.00.

★1347★
SOUTHERN ADVERTISING/MARKETS—ANNUAL FORECAST AND REVIEW ISSUE
Ernest H. Abernethy Publishing Company
73 Third Street, N. E.   Phone: (404) 881-6442
Atlanta, GA 30308
Covers: About 2,000 advertising agencies in southern and southwestern states and the District of Columbia. **Entries include:** Agency name, address, phone, names of executives, billings, accounts. **Arrangement:** Geographical. **Pages** (approx.): 120. **Frequency:** Annual, March. **Editor:** Jack Majors, General Manager.

Advertising accepted. Circulation 8,200. **Price:** $10.00 (1980 edition).

★1348★

SOUTHERN CALIFORNIA BUSINESS DIRECTORY AND BUYERS GUIDE

Civic-Data Corporation
404 S. Bixel Street   Phone: (213) 629-0703
Los Angeles, CA 90017
Covers: Over 20,000 retailers, service firms, manufacturers, and distributors in Kings, Tulare, Inyo, San Luis Obispo, Kern, Santa Barbara, Ventura, Los Angeles, San Bernadino, Orange, Riverside, San Diego, and Imperial counties. **Entries include:** Company name, address, phone, names of principal executives, list of products or services, SIC numbers, number of employees, form of ownership (corporate, proprietorship, etc.), and whether manufacturer, retailer, etc. **Arrangement:** Product. **Indexes:** Company name. **Pages** (approx.): 1,000. **Frequency:** Annual, February. **Editor:** James R. Converse. **Advertising accepted.** **Price:** $50.00, plus $3.00 shipping (current and 1980 editions). **Other information:** Sponsored by Los Angeles Area Chamber of Commerce.

★1349★

SOUTHERN CALIFORNIA CONTRACTORS ASSOCIATION— DIRECTORY

Southern California Contractors Association
4418 Beverly Boulevard   Phone: (213) 661-2141
Los Angeles, CA 90004
Covers: About 120 heavy engineering contractors who are regular members and about 70 affiliate members supplying products and services to contractors in southern California. **Entries include:** For all listings - Company name, address, and phone. **Arrangement:** Alphabetical. **Indexes:** Product or service, contractor equipment. **Pages** (approx.): 40. **Frequency:** Annual, April. **Editor:** Mike Yurechko, Editor and Executive Secretary. **Advertising accepted.** Circulation 1,000. **Price:** $2.50 (current and 1980 editions).

Southern Furniture Manufacturers Association—Membership Directory *See* Who's Who in the Furniture Industry

★1350★

SOUTHERN PAPER TRADE ASSOCIATION—MEMBERSHIP BOOK

Southern Paper Trade Association
1704 Baptiste Court   Phone: (601) 769-7145
Pascagoula, MS 39567
Covers: 120 wholesale paper distribution merchants who are members in the first part; 175 paper mill officials and representatives who are members of The Southerners, and who sell to wholesale paper merchants in Alabama, Arkansas, Florida, Georgia, Kentucky, Louisiana, Mississippi, and Tennessee in the second part. **Entries include:** Company name, address, phone, names of principal executives; plus, in the second section, list of products. **Arrangement:** Merchants are geographical; Southerners roster is alphabetical by manufacturer. **Frequency:** Annual. **Price:** $15.00.

★1351★

SOUTHERN PULP AND PAPER MANUFACTURER—ANNUAL MILL AND PERSONNEL DIRECTORY ISSUE

Ernest H. Abernethy Publishing Company
73 Third Street, N. E.   Phone: (404) 881-6442
Atlanta, GA 30308
Covers: Pulp, paper, and paperboard mills in 14 southern states. **Entries include:** Company name, address, phone, names of executives, list of products or services, equipment, and capacity. **Pages** (approx.): 200. **Frequency:** Annual, October. **Advertising accepted.** Circulation 9,500. **Price:** $10.00.

★1352★

SOUTHWEST GEORGIA DIRECTORY OF MANUFACTURERS

Southwest Georgia Planning and Development Commission
Box 346
Camilla, GA 31730
Covers: About 500 manufacturers in a 14-county area. **Entries include:** Company name, address, name of principal executive, list of products. **Arrangement:** Alphabetical. **Indexes:** Geographical, SIC. **Pages** (approx.): 90. **Frequency:** Biennial, December of even years. **Price:** $5.00. (Not verified)

★1353★

SOUTHWEST INDUSTRIAL DIRECTORY

Bender Publications, Inc.
4077 W. Pico Boulevard   Phone: (213) 737-6820
Los Angeles, CA 90019
Covers: Manufacturers, dealers, distributors, and their representatives furnishing machine tools, fabrication equipment, supplies, etc., to metalworking and plastic fabricating firms in Texas, Oklahoma, Arkansas, New Mexico, and Louisiana. **Entries include:** Company name, address, phone. **Arrangement:** By product. **Indexes:** Trade name. **Frequency:** Annual, July; first edition 1978. **Price:** $15.00.

★1354★

SOUTHWESTERN AREA COMMERCE AND INDUSTRY ASSOCIATION DIRECTORY OF MANUFACTURING, RESEARCH AND CORPORATE HEADQUARTERS [Connecticut]

Southwestern Area Commerce and Industry Association
One Landmark Square   Phone: (203) 359-3220
Stamford, CT 06901
Covers: About 950 firms. **Entries include:** Company name, address, phone, name of representative to association, products, publications. **Arrangement:** Alphabetical by labor market area. **Indexes:** Product, compny name. **Pages** (approx.): 100. **Frequency:** Biennial, odd years. **Editor:** Thais E. Morgan. **Price:** $15.00, plus 50¢ shipping.

★1355★

SOUVENIRS AND NOVELTIES MAGAZINE—BUYER'S GUIDE ISSUE

Kane Communications
401 N. Broad Street, Suite 904   Phone: (215) 925-9744
Philadelphia, PA 19108
Covers: About 1,000 manufacturers, wholesalers, and importers of merchandise considered souvenirs and novelties. **Entries include:** Company name, address, phone, products, whether firm is manufacturer, wholesaler, or importer. **Arrangement:** By product. **Indexes:** Alphabetical. **Frequency:** Annual, August. **Editor:** Stephanie Donat. **Advertising accepted.** Circulation 10,500. **Price:** $5.00.

★1356★

SPAIN-UNITED STATES CHAMBER OF COMMERCE— MEMBERSHIP DIRECTORY

Spain-United States Chamber of Commerce
500 Fifth Avenue   Phone: (212) 354-7848
New York, NY 10036
Covers: 600 businesses in Spain and the United States interested in expanding trade between the two countries. **Entries include:** Company name, address, information on products exported, imported, and manufactured. **Arrangement:** Alphabetical. **Indexes:** Product. **Pages** (approx.): 90. **Frequency:** Annual. **Editor:** Mariano Baguena. **Advertising accepted.** Circulation 2,000. **Price:** $25.00.

★1357★

SPEC-DATA SYSTEMS—SPEC-DATA INDEX ISSUE

Construction Specifications Institute
1150 17th Street   Phone: (202) 833-2160
Washington, DC 20036
Publication includes: List of 230 manufacturers of construction products and materials, who participate in Spec-Data product information service. **Entries include:** Company name, address, phone, product category. **Arrangement:** Alphabetical. **Indexes:** Product,

trade name. **Pages** (approx.): 65. **Frequency:** Annual, June. **Editor:** James Sigel, Manager. **Advertising accepted.** Circulation 16,000. **Price:** $23.00; available only with subscription for full year. **Other information:** Product specifications sheets are issued quarterly through looseleaf updating service; subscribers receive current set.

★1358★
SPECIAL EQUIPMENT CATALOG FOR DODGE TRUCKS
Ross Roy, Inc.
2751 E. Jefferson Avenue   Phone: (313) 568-6000
Detroit, MI 48207
Covers: Suppliers of special equipment which can be installed on Dodge trucks; listings are paid. **Entries include:** Company name, address, products in advertisements. **Arrangement:** Alphabetical. **Frequency:** Annual, December. **Editor:** Sherman Ellis. **Advertising accepted.** Circulation 6,000. **Price:** $3.50.

★1359★
SPECIALTY AND CUSTOM DEALER—PERFORMANCE WAREHOUSE ASSOCIATION DIRECTORY ISSUE [Automotive parts and accessories]
Babcox Automotive Publications
11 S. Forge Street   Phone: (216) 535-6117
Akron, OH 44304
Publication includes: List of about 90 members of Performance Warehouse Association, suppliers of parts and accessories for hot rod and other high performance automobiles. **Entries include:** Name of president, company name, address, phone, products, and lines. **Arrangement:** Alphabetical. **Frequency:** Annual, June. **Editor:** Gary Gardner. **Advertising accepted.** Circulation 19,500. **Price:** $3.00.

★1360★
STANDARD & POOR'S REGISTER OF CORPORATIONS, DIRECTORS AND EXECUTIVES
Standard & Poor's Corporation
345 Hudson Street   Phone: (212) 924-6400
New York, NY 10014
Covers: About 37,000 corporations in the United States, including names and titles of over 400,000 officials (Volume 1); 75,000 biographies of directors and executives (Volume 2). **Entries include:** Company entries list name, address, phone, principal executives, number of employees, financial data, SIC numbers, and products or services. Listings for directors and executives give name, home and principal office addresses, date and place of birth, fraternal organization memberships and other business affiliations. **Arrangement:** Alphabetical. **Indexes:** Volume 3 indexes companies geographically and by SIC number, and lists new executives, new companies, and obituaries. **Pages** (approx.): 4,200. **Frequency:** Annual, January; supplements in April, July, and October. **Editor:** Thomas A. Lupo. **Advertising accepted.** Circulation 13,900. **Price:** $198.00, lease basis (1980 edition).

★1361★
STANDARD CORPORATION DESCRIPTIONS
Standard & Poor's Corporation
25 Broadway   Phone: (212) 248-2525
New York, NY 10004
Description: "This service contains descriptions of various publicly held corporations, including those listed on the New York and American Stock Exchanges and the larger unlisted and regional exchange companies. Full or standard coverage treatment is accorded to corporations included herein for a fee. Other corporations will receive less than such coverage." **Entries include:** For full coverage companies - Company name, home office address, names of officers and directors, financial data, current and historical information on company activities, names of subsidiaries, number of employees, stock data, and summary of financial information for preceding 10 years. **Indexes:** Company name, subsidiary name. **Frequency:** Quarterly updates; "Daily Corporation News," issued 5 times per week comprises the seventh volume of service. **Price:** $877.00 per year, includes quarterly updates and "Daily Corporation News."

★1362★
STANDARD DIRECTORY OF ADVERTISERS
National Register Publishing Company, Inc., Subsidiary
Standard Rate & Data Service, Inc.
5201 Old Orchard Road   Phone: (312) 966-8500
Skokie, IL 60077
Covers: About 17,000 companies which place national and/or regional advertising. **Entries include:** Company name, address, phone, annual sales, number of employees, products advertised with brand name or trade name, and management, financial, advertising, and marketing executives; listings also include name and address of advertising agencies used, amounts spent on advertising, and media used. **Arrangement:** Two editions: Classified edition, with companies arranged by line of business; and geographical edition. **Indexes:** Classified edition includes alphabetical indexes; geographical index published separately. **Pages** (approx.): 1,000. **Frequency:** Classified edition published in April, geographical in August; geographical index to classified edition published in June; supplements in other months; "Ad Change" newsletter published weekly. **Editor:** Bob Weicherding. **Advertising accepted.** Classified edition circulation, 8,000; geographical edition, 2,500. **Price:** Classified edition with geographical index, or geographical edition, each $139.00; with "Ad Change," $207.00; single copy of either edition, no supplements, $99.00; single copy of geographical index, $29.00; "Ad Change" bulletins, $59.00 per year. **Other information:** Also known as, "Advertiser Red Book."

★1363★
STANDARD DIRECTORY OF ADVERTISING AGENCIES
National Register Publishing Company, Inc., Subsidiary
Standard Rate & Data Service, Inc.
5201 Old Orchard Road   Phone: (312) 966-8500
Skokie, IL 60077
Covers: 4,400 advertising agencies. **Entries include:** Agency name, address, phone, year founded, memberships, annual billing, executives including space and time buyers and account executives, and clients. **Arrangement:** Alphabetical. **Indexes:** Geographical (includes address and phone). **Pages** (approx.): 1,000. **Frequency:** February, June, and October; supplements in other months. **Editor:** Bob Weicherding. **Advertising accepted.** Circulation 8,000. **Price:** $97.00 per year, including supplements; single copy, without supplements, $42.00. **Other information:** Also known as "Agency Red Book."

★1364★
STANDARD RATE & DATA SERVICE—BUSINESS PUBLICATION RATES & DATA
Standard Rate & Data Service, Inc.
5201 Old Orchard Road   Phone: (312) 966-8500
Skokie, IL 60077
Covers: More than 3,000 business, trade, and technical publications. Also includes about 200 publications of international circulation. **Entries include:** Publication name, address, phone, principal personnel, editorial profiles, advertising rates, discounts, mechanical requirements, copy regulations, circulation, closing and publication dates. **Arrangement:** Classified by industry or line of business. **Indexes:** Title. **Frequency:** Monthly, on 24th of the month; "Weekly Change Bulletin" optional. **Advertising accepted. Price:** $85.25 per year, plus $11.75 shipping; weekly bulletin, $8.00 shipping. **Also includes:** Details on direct response card programs.

★1365★
STANDARD RATE & DATA SERVICE—DIRECT MAIL LIST RATES & DATA
Standard Rate & Data Service, Inc.
5201 Old Orchard Road   Phone: (312) 966-8500
Skokie, IL 60077
Covers: Over 50,000 mailing lists composed of business persons and firms, general consumers, and rural and farm consumers, plus cooperative mailings and package insert programs. Includes separate listings for mailing list brokers, compilers, and managers, and suppliers of products and services to the direct mail industry (e.g., lettershops,

etc.). **Entries include:** For mailing lists - Title of list; name, address, phone of owner or broker, and name of contact; description of list, and its arrangement, maintenance, quantity, etc.; specific identification of source of list; addressing selections, method, delivery schedules; mailing services offered; restrictions on use of list; price. For brokers and compilers - Firm name, address, phone, names of principal personnel, types of lists handled, fees and deposits, mailing services offered, association memberships. **Arrangement:** Lists arranged by market classification (safety, literature and book buyers, etc.), by list name within classifications; managers, compilers, and brokers are alphabetical; suppliers classified by service. **Indexes:** Subject/market classification, list title/list owner. **Pages** (approx.): 900. **Frequency:** Quarterly (Business Lists in January and July; Consumer Lists in March and September). Change Bulletins issued semimonthly. **Advertising accepted.** **Price:** $70.00 per year, plus $3.00 shipping; $45.00 per copy; no charge for bulletins.

★1366★
STANDARD RATE & DATA SERVICE—PRINT MEDIA PRODUCTION DATA
Standard Rate & Data Service, Inc.
5201 Old Orchard Road   Phone: (312) 966-8500
Skokie, IL 60077
Covers: Business periodicals, consumer and farm periodicals, daily newspapers, and their printers. **Entries include:** Publication name, address, phone; printer name, address, phone, contact; and general shipping instructions, binding method, printing process used, production specifications, insert and bleed information, special issues, issue and closing dates. **Arrangement:** By type of publication; business publications subarranged by interests; newspapers subarranged by media category, then geographically. **Frequency:** Quarterly, February, May, August, December; change bulletins issued periodically. **Advertising accepted.** **Price:** $52.50 per year, plus $2.25 shipping; business publication section, $29.50 per year, plus $1.25 shipping; magazine and newspaper section, $29.50 per year, plus $1.25 shipping; no charge for bulletins.

★1367★
STAR DIRECTORY [Truck equipment]
Verbiest Publishing Company
950 E. Maple Road, No. 205   Phone: (313) 645-2360
Birmingham, MI 48011
Covers: Suppliers of optional equipment which can be installed on International Harvester, Mack, Peterbilt, Kenworth, White, and Freightliner trucks; international coverage. **Entries include:** Manufacturer name, address. **Arrangement:** Alphabetical. **Indexes:** Equipment. **Frequency:** Annual, January. **Advertising accepted.** Circulation 3,600. **Price:** $3.50 (current and 1980 editions).

State Car and Truck Renting and Leasing Association—
   Membership List *See* The Vehicle

State of Hawaii Business Directory *See* Hawaii Business Directory

★1368★
STATEN ISLAND CHAMBER OF COMMERCE—MEMBERSHIP DIRECTORY [New York]
Staten Island Chamber of Commerce
130 Bay Street   Phone: (212) 727-1900
Staten Island, NY 10301
Number of listings: 500. **Entries include:** Firm name, address, phone, name of principal executive or partner, line of business. **Arrangement:** Alphabetical and by line of business. **Pages** (approx.): 60. **Frequency:** Annual. **Advertising accepted.** **Price:** $10.00.

Staten Island Chamber of Commerce Business/Professional
   Directory *See* Staten Island Chamber of Commerce—
   Membership Directory [New York]

★1369★
STATISTICS OF PRIVATELY OWNED ELECTRIC UTILITIES IN THE UNITED STATES
Office of Energy Data Operations
Energy Information Administration
Energy Department
1000 Independence Avenue, N. W.   Phone: (202) 252-6401
Washington, DC 20585
Publication includes: List of privately owned electric utility companies in the United States. **Entries include:** Company name, address, financial keys. **Arrangement:** Alphabetical within Class A and Class B plants. **Frequency:** Annual. **Price:** $7.75 (S/N 061-002-00002-2). **Send orders to:** Government Printing Office, Washington, DC 20402.

★1370★
STATISTICS OF PUBLICLY OWNED ELECTRIC UTILITIES IN THE UNITED STATES
Office of Energy Data Operations
Energy Information Administration
Energy Department
1000 Independence Avenue, N. W.   Phone: (202) 252-6401
Washington, DC 20585
Publication includes: List of publicly owned electric utility companies in the United States. **Entries include:** Company name, address, financial keys. **Arrangement:** Alphabetical. **Frequency:** Annual. **Price:** $6.00 (S/N 061-002-00013-8). **Send orders to:** Government Printing Office, Washington, DC 20402.

★1371★
STEAM-ELECTRIC PLANT CONSTRUCTION COST AND ANNUAL PRODUCTION EXPENSES
Office of Energy Data Operations
Energy Information Administration
Energy Department
1000 Independence Avenue, N. W.   Phone: (202) 252-6401
Washington, DC 20585
Publication includes: List of about 690 fossil-fueled and nuclear steam-electric plants in the United States with capacities of 25 megawatts or greater. **Entries include:** Plant name and location, name and location of owner, maximum generator rating in megawatts, type of fuel, plant costs and production expenses, peak demand, other technical and financial data. **Arrangement:** Geographical. **Indexes:** Plant name. **Frequency:** Annual. **Price:** $4.50 (S/N 061-003-00008-8). **Send orders to:** Government Printing Office, Washington, DC 20402.

Steel Service Center Institute—Roster *See* Metal Distribution

★1372★
STORES—TOP 100 ISSUE
National Retail Merchants Association
100 W. 31st Street   Phone: (212) 244-8780
New York, NY 10001
Covers: 100 retail department store divisions having largest estimated sales during preceding year. **Entries include:** Name of store, city, abbreviation for parent company, number of stores included, total square feet, and total sales. **Arrangement:** Ranked by sales. **Frequency:** Annual, July. **Editor:** Joan Bergmann. **Advertising accepted.** **Price:** $2.00.

★1373★
SUCCESSFUL MEETINGS—INTERNATIONAL CONVENTION FACILITIES DIRECTORY ISSUE
Bill Communications, Inc.
1422 Chestnut Street   Phone: (215) 563-0680
Philadelphia, PA 19102
Covers: About 50 hotel chain headquarters; 40 show managements; 40 associations; 50 hotel representatives; 3,000 hotels, convention centers and convention bureaus; 225 exhibit builders and show suppliers; 100 incentive and group travel suppliers (including airlines

and cruise lines); 175 audiovisual producers; 500 convention services and products. **Entries include:** Company name, address, phone, name of principal executive, list of products or services. **Arrangement:** Geographical. **Indexes:** Alphabetical. **Pages** (approx.): 500. **Frequency:** Annual, April. **Editor:** Virginia Lofft. **Advertising accepted.** Circulation 70,000. **Price:** $10.00.

★1374★
SUMMER EMPLOYMENT DIRECTORY OF THE UNITED STATES
Writer's Digest Books
9933 Alliance Road   Phone: (513) 984-0717
Cincinnnati, OH 45242
Covers: 1,000 employers, predominantly camps, who hire temporary help for summer work; listings are paid. **Entries include:** Name and address, length of employment, pay rate, duties, qualifications, application deadline and procedure. **Arrangement:** Geographical, then by type of employer (camp, restaurant, etc.). **Pages** (approx.): 210. **Frequency:** Annual, November. **Editor:** Mynene Leith. **Advertising accepted. Price:** $8.95, cloth; $5.95, paper.

★1375★
SUPERMARKET NEWS DISTRIBUTION STUDY OF GROCERY STORE SALES
Fairchild Books
Fairchild Publications, Inc.
7 E. 12th Street   Phone: (212) 741-4280
New York, NY 10003
Covers: Major food retailers in large United States and Canadian cities and their share of market; number of supermarkets in each chain, voluntary, and co-op in these cities plus names of leading independents; location and name of principal suppliers; new supermarkets; directory of food associations. **Pages** (approx.): 200. **Frequency:** Annual. **Price:** $27.50, postpaid, payment with order (1980 edition). **Also includes:** Demographic information for 50 U. S. cities.

★1376★
SUPERMARKETING—50 LEADING PUBLICLY OWNED FOOD CHAINS ISSUE
Gralla Publications
1515 Broadway   Phone: (212) 869-1300
New York, NY 10036
Entries include: Chain name, sales for two preceding years, net income, number of stores. **Arrangement:** By dollar volume. **Frequency:** Annual, October. **Editor:** Howard Rauch. **Advertising accepted. Price:** Included in annual subscription, $20.00; not sold separately.

★1377★
SUPPLIERS' DIRECTORY [Shoe repair industry]
Shoe Service Institute of America
222 W. Adams Street   Phone: (312) 236-2283
Chicago, IL 60606
Covers: Firms which supply materials to the shoe repair industry. **Entries include:** Company name, address, trade and brand names, list of products. **Arrangement:** Alphabetical. **Indexes:** Product, trade name. **Frequency:** Irregular; latest edition 1974; new edition possible January 1980. **Price:** 1974 edition out of print; 1980 edition price not determined.

★1378★
SWEDISH SUBSIDIARY COMPANIES IN THE U.S.A.
Swedish-American Chamber of Commerce
One Dag Hammarskjold Plaza   Phone: (212) 838-5530
New York, NY 10017
Covers: Nearly 150 subsidiaries of Swedish parent companies; chambers of commerce, trade offices, embassies and consulates, information offices, and tourist offices are also listed. **Entries include:** Name of parent company, address, phone, telex; name of United States subsidiary, address, phone, name and title of key executive, products. **Arrangement:** Alphabetical (by parent company

name in Swedish). **Frequency:** Annual, May. **Price:** $15.00, postpaid, payment with order.

★1379★
SWEDISH-AMERICAN CHAMBER OF COMMERCE—MEMBERSHIP DIRECTORY
Swedish-American Chamber of Commerce
One Dag Hammarskjold Plaza   Phone: (212) 838-5530
New York, NY 10017
Covers: About 280 United States and 180 Swedish members of the chamber, concerned with promoting commercial relations between the two countries. **Entries include:** Company name, address; United States listings include phone. **Arrangement:** Separate alphabetical lists by country. **Indexes:** Product. **Pages** (approx.): 135. **Frequency:** Annual, June. **Advertising accepted. Price:** $5.00.

TAPPI Directory *See* **Technical Association of the Pulp & Paper Industry—Directory**

TARA Membership Directory *See* **Truck-Frame & Axle Repair Association—Membership Directory**

★1380★
TECHNICAL ASSOCIATION OF THE PULP & PAPER INDUSTRY—DIRECTORY
Technical Association of the Pulp and Paper Industry
One Dunwoody Park   Phone: (404) 394-6130
Atlanta, GA 30338
Covers: 15,000 executives, managers, engineers, research scientists, superintendents, and technologists in the pulp, paper, and allied industries. **Entries include:** Name, title, company affiliation, address, phone. **Arrangement:** Alphabetical. **Indexes:** Geographical. **Pages** (approx.): 250. **Frequency:** Annual, June. **Editor:** M. Kouris. **Advertising accepted. Former title:** Technical Association of the Pulp and Paper Industry Yearbook. **Price:** $75.00.

★1381★
TECHNICAL SCHOOLS, COLLEGES AND UNIVERSITIES OFFERING COURSES IN GRAPHIC COMMUNICATIONS
Education Council
Graphic Arts Industry
4615 Forbes Avenue   Phone: (412) 621-6941
Pittsburgh, PA 15213
Entries include: School name, address, phone, name of contact; types of programs offered, degrees or certificates awarded. **Arrangement:** By field, then geographical. **Frequency:** Latest edition 1978; new edition expected 1980. **Price:** Free.

★1382★
TEENS & BOYS DIRECTORY [Apparel]
Boys' Outfitter Company, Inc.
71 W. 35th Street   Phone: (212) 594-0880
New York, NY 10001
Covers: Manufacturers and wholesalers of apparel and footwear for boys through high school age. Fabric manufacturers and finishers, apparel designers, resident buying firms, trade associations, and New York hotels are also listed. **Entries include:** For New York and other cities and miscellaneous listings - Company name, address, phone. For individual markets - Company name, address, phone, list of products. **Arrangement:** New York market product classified; Boston, California, Chicago, Milwaukee, Philadelphia, Texas, and Minneapolis-St. Paul markets are alphabetical by manufacturer's name; other cities are product classified and then arranged geographically. **Pages** (approx.): 440. **Frequency:** Semiannual, April and October. **Editor:** Helen Lambert. **Price:** $2.00, plus 25¢ shipping (current and 1980 editions).

★1383★
TELEFOOD MAGAZINE—BUYER'S GUIDE ISSUE
Davies Publishing Company
136 Shore Drive   Phone: (312) 325-2930
Hinsdale, IL 60521
Publication includes: Importers, distributors, manufacturers, and suppliers to the gourmet and specialty food and beverage retail industry; trade organizations are listed separately. **Entries include:** Company name, address, phone, trade and brand names, and products or services. **Arrangement:** Alphabetical. **Indexes:** Product. **Pages** (approx.): 100. **Frequency:** Annual, December. **Advertising accepted.** Circulation 11,000. **Price:** $10.00.

★1384★
TELEPHONE ENGINEER & MANAGEMENT DIRECTORY
Harcourt Brace Jovanovich, Inc.
124 S. First Street   Phone: (312) 232-1400
Geneva, IL 60134
Covers: More than 1,000 manufacturers, training firms, distributors, and suppliers to the telephone industry; government agencies; and trade associations. Also includes separate geographical lists of independent telephone companies in the United States, telephone companies operated by the Bell System, and foreign telephone companies. **Entries include:** For manufacturers - Company name, address, names of key executives, and list of products. For phone companies - Name, address, phone, key executives, number of phones in service, exchanges, plant statistics, construction budgets. **Arrangement:** Manufacturers are alphabetical, telephone companies are geographical. **Indexes:** Product. **Pages** (approx.): 550. **Frequency:** Annual, July. **Editor:** Ray H. Smith. **Advertising accepted.** Circulation 8,000. **Price:** $28.50, plus $1.50 shipping, payment with order; $30.00, plus $1.50 shipping, billed.

★1385★
TELEPHONY'S DIRECTORY OF THE TELEPHONE INDUSTRY
Telephony Publishing Corporation
55 E. Jackson Boulevard   Phone: (312) 922-2435
Chicago, IL 60604
Covers: Bell System companies, exchanges, and officers; independent telephone companies and exchanges in the United States, Canada, and Central and South America; telephone holding companies; personnel of state and federal regulatory commissions, telephone associations, and Rural Electrification Administration. **Frequency:** Annual, July. **Editor:** Getty Barrett. **Advertising accepted.** Circulation 11,000. **Price:** $35.00 (current and 1980 editions).

★1386★
TELEVISION SPONSORS DIRECTORY
Everglades Publishing Company
Drawer Q   Phone: (813) 695-4398
Everglades, FL 33929
Covers: 9,000 nationally advertised consumer products (e. g., liquor, cigarettes, records, farm and office equipment). **Entries include:** Product listings include name of product and reference to listing for the manufacturers. Manufacturer listings include product names, parent company and divisions, address and name of chairman of the board or other chief executive. **Arrangement:** Alphabetical. **Pages** (approx.): 260. **Frequency:** Semiannual, winter and summer. **Editor:** Roger C. Foss. **Price:** $9.95 per issue.

★1387★
TELEX/TWX DIRECTORY AND BUYER'S GUIDE
Western Union Directory Services
One Lake Street
Upper Saddle, NJ 07458
Covers: About 119,000 Western Union customers with telex and TWX numbers. **Entries include:** Company name, city, telex or TWX number and answerback. **Arrangement:** Geographical. **Indexes:** Product. **Pages** (approx.): 1,800. **Frequency:** Annual, April. **Editor:** Saul Lipshitz. **Advertising accepted.** Circulation 180,000. **Price:** $5.00.

★1388★
TENNESSEE DIRECTORY OF MANUFACTURERS
Tennessee Department of Economic and Community Development
1014 Andrew Jackson Building   Phone: (615) 741-1995
Nashville, TN 37219
Covers: About 5,000 mining and manufacturing firms. **Entries include:** Company name, address, phone, names of principal executives, number of employees, products, SIC numbers, area served, whether company imports or exports, year established, parent company (if applicable). **Arrangement:** Geographical. **Indexes:** Alphabetical, product. **Pages** (approx.): 510. **Frequency:** Irregular, about every two years; latest edition August 1977. **Editor:** James C. Cotham, III, Commissioner. **Former title:** Tennessee Manufacturers Directory. **Price:** $15.00. **Other information:** State Industrial Directories Corp. catalog formerly listed this publication as, ''Directory of Tennessee Industries.''

★1389★
TENNESSEE INDUSTRIES GUIDE
Industries Guides, Inc.
203 E. Park Lake Street   Phone: (305) 841-7911
Orlando, FL 32802
Number of listings: 4,500. **Entries include:** Company name, address, phone, name of principal executive, number of employees, products, SIC numbers. **Arrangement:** Geographical. **Indexes:** Alphabetical, SIC. **Pages** (approx.): 175. **Frequency:** Annual, March. **Editor:** Richard J. McHenry. **Advertising accepted. Price:** $45.00.

Tennessee Manufacturers Directory *See* **Tennessee Directory of Manufacturers**

★1390★
TENNESSEE STATE INDUSTRIAL DIRECTORY
State Industrial Directories Corporation
Two Penn Plaza   Phone: (212) 564-0340
New York, NY 10001
Number of listings: 4,900. **Entries include:** Company name, address, phone, names of key executives, number of employees, plant size, 4-digit SIC code, products, whether firm imports or exports, and whether firm has research facilities. **Arrangement:** Geographical. **Indexes:** Alphabetical, product (includes mailing address and phone for each firm). **Frequency:** Annual, spring. **Advertising accepted. Price:** $30.00.

★1391★
TENT RENTAL DIRECTORY
Canvas Products Association International
350 Endicott Building   Phone: (612) 222-2508
St. Paul, MN 55101
Covers: Firms in the United States and Canada which rent fair, party, and commercial tents. **Entries include:** Company name, address, phone, key executives, products. **Arrangement:** Geographical. **Pages** (approx.): 5. **Frequency:** Irregular; latest edition January 1979; new edition possible January 1980. **Editor:** Mary Burczyk, Director of Public Relations. **Price:** 25¢.

★1392★
TERMINUS REPORT [Business expansions, Atlanta, Georgia]
Terminus Media, Inc.
1819 Peachtree Road, N. W.   Phone: (404) 351-8351
Atlanta, GA 30309
Covers: New businesses and business changes and new construction in five-county Atlanta metropolitan area. **Entries include:** For businesses - Company name, address, phone, name of one principal or manager, type of business, date opened, number of employees, or nature of business change. For new construction - Nature and address of project, cost, estimated completion date, and name and address, and phone of owner and contractor. **Arrangement:** By Zip code. **Frequency:** Twice weekly. **Editor:** Suzette Jack. **Price:** $240.00 per year. (Not verified)

★1393★

TEST AND MEASUREMENT EQUIPMENT MANUFACTURERS'
DIRECTORY
Marketing Development
402 Border Road   Phone: (617) 369-5382
Concord, MA 01742
Covers: About 915 manufacturers of test and measurement equipment. Also includes list of top 30 manufacturers ranked by projected sales. **Entries include:** Company name, address, phone, telex, names and titles of key personnel, products, number of employees, projected sales. Leading companies' listings have more detail. **Arrangement:** Alphabetical. **Indexes:** Product. **Pages** (approx.): 190. **Frequency:** Irregular; first edition September 1978. **Price:** $75.00, plus $2.00 shipping.

★1394★

TEXAS AIRPORT DIRECTORY
Texas Aeronautics Commission
410 E. Fifth Street   Phone: (512) 475-4768
Austin, TX 78711
Covers: About 700 public airports and private airports and landing strips open to public use in Texas. Includes heliports and helistops and seaplane bases. **Entries include:** For airports - Name; location; elevation; name, address, and phone of manager; lights; hours attended; fuel availability; facilities. For heliports - Name, latitude and longitude, services, size, ownership, elevation, use restrictions. **Arrangement:** Geographical within aircraft type. **Indexes:** Airport name. **Pages** (approx.): 175. **Frequency:** Annual. **Editor:** Nona D. Gold. **Price:** Free.

★1395★

TEXAS CONTRACTOR—BUYER'S GUIDE AND DIRECTORY ISSUE
Peters Publishing Company of Texas
2828 W. Kingsley Road   Phone: (214) 271-2693
Garland, TX 75041
Publication includes: Manufacturers and distributors of supplies and equipment for the construction industry in Texas. **Entries include:** For manufacturers - Company name, address, phone, products, and local distributors. For distributors - Company name, address, phone, name of contact, lines carried. **Arrangement:** Manufacturers are alphabetical, distributors are geographical. **Indexes:** Product. **Frequency:** Annual, March. **Editor:** William B. Morrison. **Advertising accepted.** Circulation 5,700. **Price:** $10.00.

★1396★

TEXAS INDUSTRIAL EXPANSION
Bureau of Business Research
University of Texas at Austin   Phone: (512) 471-1616
Austin, TX 78712
Covers: New and expanding manufacturing facilities in Texas (SIC 1321, 1477, 2011-3999, 4911). **Entries include:** Company name, address, name of principal executive, number of employees, financial keys, list of products or services, SIC numbers. **Arrangement:** Geographical. **Pages** (approx.): 20. **Frequency:** Monthly. **Editor:** Ida M. Lambeth. **Price:** $6.00 per year (ISSN 0040-4365). **Other information:** Supplement to the "Directory of Texas Manufacturers."

Texas Manufacturers Directory *See* Directory of Texas
    Manufacturers

★1397★

TEXTILE INDUSTRIES—BUYER'S GUIDE ISSUE
W. R. C. Smith Publishing Company
1760 Peachtree Road, N. W.   Phone: (404) 874-4462
Atlanta, GA 30357
Covers: About 3,000 manufacturers and suppliers of textiles and products used in the textile industry; worldwide coverage. **Entries include:** For manufacturers - Company name, address, phone; separate list of addresses includes products. For United States agents of foreign manufacturers - Manufacturer and agent names and addresses. **Arrangement:** Primarily alphabetical by company name.

Indexes: Product (includes supplier addresses). **Pages** (approx.): 450. **Frequency:** Annual, June. **Editor:** Diane D. Sullivan. **Advertising accepted.** Circulation 31,500. **Price:** $5.00.

★1398★

TEXTILE RENTAL SERVICES ASSOCIATION—ROSTER-BUYERS
GUIDE
Textile Rental Services Association
1250 E. Hallandale Beach Boulevard   Phone: (305) 457-7555
Hallandale, FL 33309
Publication includes: List of 1,800 companies supplying linen and towels to other industries and companies furnishing textiles and other supplies to the linen supply industry. List of local, state, regional, and foreign trade associations is also included. **Entries include:** Company name, address, phone, name of contact. **Arrangement:** Member companies are geographical; associations are alphabetical. **Indexes:** Product. **Pages** (approx.): 200. **Frequency:** Annual, November. **Editor:** Donald T. Smith. **Advertising accepted.** Circulation 3,000. **Price:** Available to members only. **Other information:** The name of the association was changed from Linen Supply Association of America in 1979.

★1399★

TEXTILE WORLD—FACT FILE/BUYER'S GUIDE ISSUE
McGraw-Hill, Inc.
1175 Peachtree Street, N. E.   Phone: (404) 892-2868
Atlanta, GA 30361
Covers: Manufacturers and distributors of machinery, equipment, and supplies used by textile mills. **Entries include:** Generic name of product or service, company, and names and addresses of suppliers. **Arrangement:** Alphabetical by product name. **Pages** (approx.): 350. **Frequency:** Annual, July. **Editor:** Charlene Hazell, Buyer's Guide Editor. **Former title:** Textile World - Buyer's Guide Issue. **Advertising accepted.** Circulation 30,000. **Price:** $6.00.

★1400★

THOMAS GROCERY REGISTER
Thomas Publishing Company
One Penn Plaza   Phone: (212) 695-0500
New York, NY 10001
Covers: Volume 1 includes 1,800 supermarket chains; 4,300 brokers; and 4,200 wholesalers and distributors having separate sections for general line groceries, frozen foods, institutional foods, specialties, produce, provisions and meats, and general merchandise; rack jobbers; dry and refrigerated warehouses. Volume 2 includes a product index of 45,000 sources for 4,000 categories of food and non-food products, exporters and import equipment machinery, supplies, and services. Volume 3 lists 58,000 companies and 440 related trade associations; includes food brand names list. **Entries include:** Volume 1 entries are geographical and list company name, address, phone, executives, and financial keys; Volume 2 entries include names of sources in geographical order; Volume 3 entries are alphabetical and include company name, address, phone, and other data. **Pages** (approx.): 2,400 (3 volumes). **Frequency:** Annual, October. **Editor:** John Kovac, General Manager. **Advertising accepted.** Circulation 5,300. **Price:** $69.00 (3 volume set); $55.00 (Volume 1 or 2 and 3). **Other information:** "Directory of the Institutional Food Market," which lists several hundred government, private, and nonprofit institutions and food service companies, is a new supplement and is included in 3-volume price.

★1401★

THOMAS REGISTER OF AMERICAN MANUFACTURERS AND
THOMAS REGISTER CATALOG FILE
Thomas Publishing Company
One Penn Plaza   Phone: (212) 695-0500
New York, NY 10001
Covers: More than 100,000 manufacturing firms in the United States; Volumes 1-8 list products, Volumes 9-10 list companies, and Volumes 11-16 are comprised of bound catalogs of more than 800 manufacturers. **Entries include:** Volumes 1-8 - Product or service,

manufacturer names. Volumes 9-10 - Manufacturer name, address, phone, asset rating; some entries include names of executives, trade and brand names, and products or services offered. **Arrangement:** Volumes 1-8: classified by product, followed by manufacturers' names geographically. Volumes 9-10: alphabetical. **Indexes:** Brand name (Volume 8). **Frequency:** Annual, January. **Editor:** Ronald J.Duchaine. **Advertising accepted. Price:** $75.00 (current edition); $120.00 (1980 edition). **Other information:** Volumes 11-16 are sometimes called "Thomcat."

Thomcat *See* Thomas Register of American Manufacturers and Thomas Register Catalog File

★1402★

TILE & DECORATIVE SURFACES—DIRECTORY AND PURCHASING GUIDE ISSUE
Tile and Decorative Surfaces Company
18327 Sherman Way, Suite 104   Phone: (213) 344-4200
Reseda, CA 91335
Covers: Over 1,000 manufacturers and distributors of tile products and tile contractors. **Entries include:** For manufacturers - Company name, address, phone (for United States companies), locations of branch offices and warehouses. For distributors - Company name, address, phone, manufacturers' lines handled. **Arrangement:** Manufacturers are alphabetical, distributors are geographical. **Indexes:** Product. **Frequency:** Annual, December. **Advertising accepted.** Circulation 10,200. **Price:** $7.50, plus $1.50 shipping.

★1403★

TODAY'S TRANSPORT INTERNATIONAL/TRANSPORTE MODERNO—FLEET DIRECTORY ISSUE
Intercontinental Publications, Inc.
Box 5017   Phone: (203) 226-7463
Westport, CT 06880
Covers: United States manufacturers and exporters worldwide who export truck and automotive products to Africa, Asia, the Middle East, and Latin America. **Entries include:** Company name, address, products and brands. **Arrangement:** Alphabetical. **Indexes:** Brand name, product. **Frequency:** Annual, February/March. **Editor:** Martin Greenburgh. **Advertising accepted.** Circulation 40,000. **Price:** $3.00 (1980 edition). **Other information:** Separate English and Spanish issues.

★1404★

TOLL FREE BUSINESS
Toll Free Planning Services
Box 102   Phone: (612) 333-5511
Minneapolis, MN 55440
Covers: About 20,000 toll-free listings, primarily in the travel field. **Entries include:** Firm name, phone, location. **Arrangement:** Classified by product or service. **Frequency:** Annual, December. **Price:** $8.95.

★1405★

TOLL FREE DIGEST: A DIRECTORY OF TOLL FREE TELEPHONE NUMBERS
Toll Free Digest Company, Inc.
Box 800   Phone: (518) 828-6400
Claverack, NY 12513
Covers: 17,000 hotels, resorts, car rental agencies, airlines, etc., and non-leisure businesses with toll-free (800) numbers. **Entries include:** Company name, city in which located, states and/or cities from which toll-free calls can be made, and toll-free number applicable in each location. **Arrangement:** Classified by service or product. **Pages** (approx.): 250. **Frequency:** Annual. **Advertising accepted. Price:** $4.50, plus 50¢ shipping.

★1406★

TOP SYMBOLS AND TRADEMARKS OF THE WORLD
Marquis Who's Who, Inc.
200 E. Ohio Street   Phone: (312) 787-2008
Chicago, IL 60611
Publication includes: List of about 6,000 companies with one or more trademarks or logos which have become widely known since 1973. **Entries include:** Logo; name and agency of designer; year created; name, address, and line of business of owner. **Arrangement:** Alphabetical by company owning logo. **Indexes:** Company's country, designer name, studio name, agency name, company line of business. **Frequency:** Irregular; base set (7 volumes) 1973, supplement 1977. **Price:** Base volumes, $150.00 per set; supplement, $25.00; plus $2.50 shipping.

★1407★

TOURIST ATTRACTIONS AND PARKS—BUYER'S GUIDE ISSUE
Kane Communications
401 N. Broad Street, Suite 904   Phone: (215) 925-9744
Philadelphia, PA 19108
Covers: Manufactured articles used or sold by amusement parks, theme parks, animal lands and zoos, national and state parks, museums, and other visitor-oriented facilities. **Entries include:** Company name, address, and phone. **Arrangement:** Alphabetical. **Indexes:** Product. **Frequency:** Annual. **Editor:** Martin Dowd. **Advertising accepted.** Circulation 15,000. **Price:** $10.00.

★1408★

TOY CENTER OFFICIAL DIRECTORY
Toy Center
200 Fifth Avenue
New York, NY 10010
Covers: 700 toy manufacturers and sales representatives who maintain sales offices and showrooms at 200 Fifth Avenue (Toy Center South) and 1107 Broadway (Toy Center North) in New York City. **Entries include:** Company name, address, room number, types of toys, key personnel. **Arrangement:** By buildings, then by floors. **Indexes:** Product, company name. **Pages** (approx.): 300. **Frequency:** Annual, February. **Editor:** Herman Robben, Executive Secretary. **Price:** $3.00.

★1409★

TRADE AND PROFESSIONAL ASSOCIATIONS IN CALIFORNIA: A DIRECTORY
California Institute of Public Affairs
226 W. Foothill Boulevard   Phone: (714) 624-5212
Claremont, CA 91711
Covers: 1,000 state and regional business and professional associations, and national associations having California offices. **Entries include:** Name, address, phone. **Arrangement:** Alphabetical. **Indexes:** Keyword and subject. **Pages** (approx.): 60. **Frequency:** Not established; first edition January 1979. **Price:** $12.00, plus $1.48 shipping.

★1410★

TRADE AND PROFESSIONAL ASSOCIATIONS IN OHIO
Ohio Chamber of Commerce
17 S. High Street   Phone: (614) 228-4201
Columbus, OH 43215
Number of listings: 310. **Entries include:** Association name, executive director or key officer, address, phone. **Arrangement:** Alphabetical. **Indexes:** Business or profession. **Pages** (approx.): 20. **Frequency:** Annual, February. **Editor:** Edmond Loewe, Director of Organizational Services. **Price:** $10.40 (current and 1980 editions).

★1411★
TRADE NAMES DICTIONARY: COMPANY INDEX
Gale Research Company
Book Tower   Phone: (313) 961-2242
Detroit, MI 48226
Covers: Nearly 30,000 companies which manufacture, distribute, import, or otherwise market consumer-oriented products. **Entries include:** Company name, address; trade names with brief product descriptions are given under the company name in a separate section. **Arrangement:** Both sections are alphabetical. **Pages** (approx.): 900. **Frequency:** Not established; first edition fall 1979. **Editor:** Ellen T. Crowley. **Price:** $95.00. **Other information:** Based on the second edition of "Trade Names Dictionary," in which trade names and descriptions are arranged alphabetically, with company entries interspersed in a single alphabet. The company index brings all products of a single company together under the name of the company.

★1412★
TRADE SHOW FACT BOOK
Sanford Organization, Inc.
4300-L Lincoln Avenue   Phone: (312) 359-8160
Rolling Meadows, IL 60008
Covers: Major United States and Canadian industrial trade shows and exhibitions. **Entries include:** Show name, dates, location, number of exhibitors, products exhibited, costs, contract provisions, expected attendance, audience, name of show manager, address, name and phone of contact. **Indexes:** Chronological, industry covered. **Pages** (approx.): 1,300. **Frequency:** Annual, fall. **Editor:** Donn W. Sanford, CAE, President. **Advertising accepted.** Circulation 4,000. **Price:** $120.00.

★1413★
TRADEMARK DIRECTORY [Paints and coatings]
National Paint & Coatings Association
1500 Rhode Island Avenue, N. W.
Washington, DC 20005
Covers: Over 60,000 trademarks representing about 6,000 paint and coatings companies. **Entries include:** Products covered, owner's name, company location, date of first use; listings for registered marks include registration symbol. **Arrangement:** By type of product (chemicals or tools), then alphabetical by trade name. Separate listing for numerical trade names. **Pages** (approx.): 425, base edition; 10, supplement. **Frequency:** Every three or four years; supplements also issued. Latest edition 1976; supplement, 1978. **Price:** $20.00, base edition; $2.50, supplement. **Also includes:** A sample trademark listing form, information on trademark ownership, advice on selecting a new trademark, and the mechanics of trademark procurement.

★1414★
TRADESHOW/CONVENTION GUIDE
Budd Publications, Inc.
228 E. 45th Street   Phone: (212) 347-8724
New York, NY 10017
Covers: 14,000 conventions and trade shows, worldwide, local companies which supply services such as photography, exhibit design, etc., and halls and hotels catering to conventions and shows. **Entries include:** For shows - Name of sponsoring group, address, name of principal executive, show dates, attendance figures, number and size of booths. For suppliers - Company name, address, phone. **Arrangement:** Show entries arranged by industry or subject; supplier entries are geographical. **Indexes:** Geographical by location of event, alphabetical by event name. **Pages** (approx.): 800. **Frequency:** Annual, October. **Editor:** Kitty Huffer. **Advertising accepted.** Circulation 11,200. **Former title:** Tradeshow. **Price:** $55.00.

★1415★
TRADING POST [Bartering]
Comstock Trading Company
1926 Tice Valley Boulevard   Phone: (415) 939-9292
Walnut Creek, CA 94595
Publication includes: Lists of persons interested in bartering collectibles, exchanging homes or real estate, and bartering all other types of merchandise. **Entries include:** Barterer name, address. **Arrangement:** By merchandise offered. **Frequency:** Monthly. **Price:** Included in membership in Comstock Trading Program, $100.00 per year. **Other information:** See also listing for Comstock's "Skills Directory."

★1416★
TRAFFIC WORLD—AIR FREIGHT GUIDE ISSUE
Traffic Service Corporation
1435 G Street, N. W., Suite 815   Phone: (202) 783-7325
Washington, DC 20005
Publication includes: List of about 65 airlines which have air freight services; international coverage. **Entries include:** Company name and acronym, and name, address, and phone of contact; description of services offered, restrictions on size of freight, types of containers accepted, liability limits, aircraft types available, and special services. Listings include maps. **Arrangement:** Alphabetical. **Frequency:** Annual, November. **Advertising accepted.** **Price:** Included in subscription, $75.00 per year.

★1417★
TRAILER/BODY BUILDERS—BUYERS GUIDE ISSUE
Tunnell Publications, Inc.
1602 Harold Street   Phone: (713) 523-8124
Houston, TX 77006
Covers: 5,700 products used by original equipment manufacturers of truck trailers and truck bodies. **Entries include:** Company name, address. **Arrangement:** Product-classified. **Pages** (approx.): 310. **Frequency:** Annual, July. **Editor:** Paul Schenck, President. **Advertising accepted.** Circulation 10,000. **Price:** $7.50 (current and 1980 editions).

★1418★
TRAINING WORLD—BLUE BOOK DIRECTORY ISSUE
Vanderbilt Communications Company, Inc.
60 E. 42nd Street, Suite 1026   Phone: (212) 986-8030
New York, NY 10017
Covers: About 3,000 suppliers (manufacturers, dealers, and manufacturers' representatives) of books, films, programs, services, audio equipment, instructional equipment, furniture and meeting facilities for employee training; limited to advertisers. **Entries include:** Company name, address, phone, sales contact, products or services offered, and local dealers and sales representatives. **Arrangement:** Classified by product or service. **Frequency:** Annual, September. **Advertising accepted.** Circulation 50,000. **Price:** $10.00.

★1419★
TRAINING/HRD—TRAINING'S YELLOW PAGES OF SOFTWARE AND SERVICES ISSUE
Lakewood Publications
731 Hennepin Avenue   Phone: (612) 333-0471
Minneapolis, MN 55403
Covers: Over 400 companies which supply audiovisual materials, textbooks, multimedia programs, consulting services, production services, and other products and services used in training. **Entries include:** Company name, address. **Arrangement:** Alphabetical. **Indexes:** Subject of training material (with type of product or service). **Pages** (approx.): 35. **Frequency:** Annual, August. **Editor:** Philip G. Jones. **Advertising accepted.** Circulation 40,000. **Price:** $2.00.

★1420★

TRANSMISSION AND DISTRIBUTION—SPECIFIERS AND BUYERS GUIDE ISSUE [Electrical power]
Cleworth Publishing Company
One River Road   Phone: (203) 661-5000
Cos Cob, CT 06807
Covers: Manufacturers and distributors of equipment for electric power transmission and distribution. **Arrangement:** Two alphabetical sections, Product and Supplier. **Pages** (approx.): 60 (in special section). **Frequency:** Annual, March. **Editor:** Stuart M. Lewis. **Advertising accepted.** Circulation 32,800. **Former title:** Transmission & Distribution - Annual Purchasing Issue. **Price:** $4.00 (current and 1980 editions).

★1421★

TRANSPORTATION DIRECTORY [Charlotte, North Carolina]
Greater Charlotte Chamber of Commerce
Box 32785
Charlotte, NC 28232
Covers: About 150 motor carriers, airlines, railroads, other firms, and government agencies in the transportation industry serving the greater Charlotte, North Carolina area. **Entries include:** For companies - Company name, address, phone, name of president or manager. For agencies - Name, address, phone. **Arrangement:** Alphabetical. **Frequency:** Irregular; latest edition 1979; new edition expected 1981. **Price:** $5.00, plus 50¢ shipping.

★1422★

TRANSPORTATION LIBRARIES IN THE UNITED STATES AND CANADA
Special Libraries Association
235 Park Avenue South   Phone: (212) 777-8136
New York, NY 10003
Covers: More than 200 libraries having special collections of transportation materials. **Entries include:** Library name, address, phone, description of holdings. **Arrangement:** Alphabetical. **Indexes:** Geographical, subject, personal name. **Pages** (approx.): 220. **Frequency:** Irregular; latest edition January 1978. **Price:** $10.75; payment must accompany orders from individuals.

★1423★

TRANSPORTATION LINES ON THE ATLANTIC, GULF, AND PACIFIC COASTS
Waterborne Commerce Statistics Center
U. S. Army Engineer Lower Mississippi Valley Division
Defense Department   Phone: (504) 865-1121
New Orleans, LA 70161
Covers: Commercial vessels and operators (except ferries, floating equipment, and recreational boats) using navigable waters of United States in geographical area specified. **Entries include:** In operator section - Operating company name, address. In vessel section (arranged by operator) - Operating company name; vessel operating base; vessel name, type, construction, dimensions, capacity, draft, horsepower, year built or rebuilt. In operations section (arranged by operator) - Operator company name, area in which operator is working, place and type of shipping. **Pages** (approx.): 200. **Frequency:** Irregular (often described as an annual, however); latest edition October 1979 (data from 1978). **Price:** $2.00, payment with order. **Send orders to:** District Engineer, U. S. Army Engineer Division, Box 60267, New Orleans, LA 70160.

★1424★

TRANSPORTATION LINES ON THE GREAT LAKES SYSTEM
Waterborne Commerce Statistics Center
U. S. Army Engineer Lower Mississippi Valley Division
Defense Department   Phone: (504) 865-1121
New Orleans, LA 70161
Covers: Commercial vessels and operators (except ferries, floating equipment, and recreational boats) using navigable waters of United States in geographical areas specified. **Entries include:** In operator section - Operating company name, address. In vessel section (arranged by operator) - Operating company name; vessel operating base; vessel names, type, construction, dimensions, capacity, draft, horsepower, year built or rebuilt. In operations section (arranged by operator) - Operating company name, area in which operator is working, place and type of shipping. **Pages** (approx.): 30. **Frequency:** Irregular (often described as an annual, however); latest edition June 1979 (1978 data). **Price:** $1.00, payment with order. **Send orders to:** District Engineer, U. S. Army Engineer Division, Box 60267, New Orleans, LA 70160.

★1425★

TRANSPORTATION LINES ON THE MISSISSIPPI RIVER SYSTEM AND THE GULF INTRACOASTAL WATERWAY
Waterborne Commerce Statistics Center
U. S. Army Engineer Lower Mississippi Valley Division
Defense Department   Phone: (504) 865-1121
New Orleans, LA 70161
Covers: Commercial vessels and operators (except ferries, floating equipment, and recreational boats) using navigable waters of United States in geographical areas specified. **Entries include:** In operator section - Operating company name, address. In vessel section (arranged by operator) - Operating company name; vessel operating base; vessel name, type, construction, dimensions, capacity, draft, horsepower, year built or rebuilt. In operations section (arranged by operator) - Operating company name, area in which operator is working, place and type of shipping. **Pages** (approx.): 300. **Frequency:** Irregular (often described as an annual, however); latest edition October 1979 (1978 data). **Price:** $2.25, payment with order. **Send orders to:** District Engineer, U. S. Army Engineer Division, Box 60267, New Orleans, LA 70160.

★1426★

TRANSPORTATION TELEPHONE TICKLER
Twin Coast Newspapers, Inc.
99 Wall Street   Phone: (212) 425-1616
New York, NY 10005
Covers: 20,000 companies and agents in North American port districts which provide services to shippers ranging from air freight forwarding to warehousing. **Entries include:** Company names, headquarters and branch addresses and phones, names of key personnel. **Arrangement:** Geographical, in three volumes, including separate volume for Port of New York. **Frequency:** Annual, January. **Advertising accepted.** Circulation 21,000. **Price:** $25.00 per set, postpaid, payment with order; volumes not available separately. **Send orders to:** Transportation Telephone Tickler, 445 Marshall Street, Phillipsburg, NJ 08865.

Travel Agent Travel Industry Personnel Directory *See* Travel Industry Personnel Directory

★1427★

TRAVEL INDUSTRY PERSONNEL DIRECTORY
American Traveler, Inc.
Two W. 46th Street   Phone: (212) 575-9000
New York, NY 10036
Covers: Air and steamship lines, tour operators, bus lines, hotel representatives, foreign and domestic railroads, foreign and domestic tourist information offices, travel trade associations, etc. Includes names of personnel, but publication is not a personnel directory in the same way telephone book white pages enable direct lookup of individuals. **Entries include:** Agency or company name, address, phone, names of principal personnel. **Arrangement:** By companies or agencies within functional or service categories (airlines, information offices, etc.). **Pages** (approx.): 500. **Frequency:** Annual, February. **Editor:** Eric Freidheim, Publisher. **Advertising accepted.** Circulation 6,500. **Price:** $10.00.

★1428★
TRAVEL MASTER
United Technical Publications Division
Cox Broadcasting Corporation
645 Stewart Avenue   Phone: (516) 222-2500
Garden City, NY 11530
Covers: Hotels and their sales representatives, and principal offices of hotel chains, casinos, airlines, and travel organizations worldwide. **Entries include:** Hotel entries show name, address, phone, number of rooms, facilities and their capacities, etc. Separate "Yellow Pages" listings include name, address, phone for hotel suppliers. **Arrangement:** Hotel directory is geographical, others are classified. **Pages** (approx.): 1,000. **Frequency:** Semiannual, fall and spring. **Advertising accepted.** Circulation 22,000. **Price:** $12.50 per copy; $20.00 per year.

★1429★
TRAVEL RESEARCH ASSOCIATION MEMBERSHIP DIRECTORY
Travel Research Association
Bureau of Economics and Business Research
University of Utah
Box 8066
Foothill Station   Phone: (801) 581-6333
Salt Lake City, UT 84108
Covers: About 600 state and local tourism bureaus and other federal and provincial government agencies, airlines, steamship lines, hotels, university bureaus of business research, and other university departments, and research and consulting firms concerned with travel research, marketing, and promotion. **Entries include:** Firm or individual name, address, phone; company listings also include name of representative or alternate. **Arrangement:** Alphabetical. **Indexes:** Personal name, geographical. **Pages** (approx.): 100. **Frequency:** Annual, June. **Editor:** Mari Lou Wood, Executive Secretary. **Price:** $10.00, payment with order.

★1430★
TRAVEL TRADE—PERSONNEL SALES GUIDE ISSUES
Travel Trade Publications, Inc.
605 Fifth Avenue   Phone: (212) 752-3233
New York, NY 10017
Covers: Hotel representatives; tour operators; airline, railroad, and steamship line offices; car rental and sightseeing companies; and industry associations and foreign tourist offices. **Entries include:** For hotel representatives - Name, address, phone, hotels represented. For tour operators, airline, railroad, steamship lines, car rental and sightseeing companies - Name, address, name of contact, and description of routes or offerings. For associations and others - Name, address. **Arrangement:** By type of activity. **Frequency:** Semiannual, May and November. **Advertising accepted.** **Price:** Included with subscription, $5.00 per year (current and 1980 editions).

★1431★
TRAVEL WEEKLY'S WORLD TRAVEL DIRECTORY
Ziff-Davis Publishing Company, Inc.
One Park Avenue   Phone: (212) 725-3852
New York, NY 10016
Covers: 33,000 travel agencies and retail and wholesale travel agents; government tourist offices; 1,200 local sightseeing operations; 500 wholesale tour operators and local attractions; cruise lines; worldwide. **Entries include:** Company name, address, phone, names of executives, financial keys, list of services, DBAs, appointments, affiliations, limited data on offerings. **Pages** (approx.): 600. **Frequency:** Annual, February. **Editor:** Llynn Wurtzel, Managing Editor. **Advertising accepted.** Circulation 7,500. **Former title:** World Travel Directory. **Price:** $45.00 (current and 1980 editions).

★1432★
TRAVELER'S TOLL-FREE TELEPHONE DIRECTORY
Landmark Publishing Company
Box 3287   Phone: (802) 863-5333
Burlington, VT 05401
Covers: 10,000 hotels, motels, airlines, auto rental agencies, and other travel-related businesses, and 10,000 other businesses and government agencies. **Entries include:** Company name, toll-free phone number, location. **Arrangement:** Classified by product or service. **Pages** (approx.): 350. **Frequency:** Annual, January. **Editor:** Jerome T. Smith. **Advertising accepted.** **Price:** $10.95, plus $1.00 shipping (1980 edition).

★1433★
TRIDENT AREA MANUFACTURERS DIRECTORY [South Carolina]
Charleston Trident Chamber of Commerce
Box 975   Phone: (803) 577-2510
Charleston, SC 29402
Covers: 130 manufacturing companies located in Berkeley, Charleston, and Dorchester counties. **Entries include:** Company name, address, phone, name of principal executive, number of employees, list of products or services. **Arrangement:** Alphabetical. **Pages** (approx.): 20. **Frequency:** Irregular with updates two or three times yearly. **Editor:** Albert M. Hodge, Jr., Manager of Trade and Community Development. **Former title:** Manufacturers Directory - Charleston, South Carolina. **Price:** $3.00.

★1434★
TRIDENT AREA SHOPPING CENTER DIRECTORY [South Carolina]
Charleston Trident Chamber of Commerce
Box 975   Phone: (803) 577-2510
Charleston, SC 29402
Covers: Existing and proposed shopping centers and larger free-standing stores. **Entries include:** Center name; location; name, address and phone number of rental agency; physical characteristics (number of stores, space available, etc.); list of tenants. **Arrangement:** Alphabetical by center or store name. **Pages** (approx.): 50. **Frequency:** Annual, spring. **Editor:** Albert M. Hodge, Jr., Manager of Trade and Community Development. **Price:** $5.00.

★1435★
TRINC'S BLUE BOOK OF THE TRUCKING INDUSTRY
Trinc Transportation Consultants, Division
Dun & Bradstreet, Inc.
475 L'Enfant Plaza, S. W., Suite 4200   Phone: (202) 484-3410
Washington, DC 20024
Covers: About 3,000 Class I and II motor carriers of property. **Entries include:** Company name, address, types of cargoes carried, names and titles of principal executives, affiliated firms; iin separate section, financial and operating data for each firm. **Arrangement:** Alphabetical. **Frequency:** Annual. **Price:** $135.00 **Also includes:** Summary statistics and operating data by commodities.

★1436★
TRINC'S GREEN BOOK OF AIR FREIGHT & FREIGHT FORWARDERS
Trinc Transportation Consultants, Division
Dun & Bradstreet, Inc.
475 L'Enfant Plaza, S. W., Suite 4200   Phone: (202) 484-3410
Washington, DC 20024
Covers: More than 200 air freight forwarders and 75 freight forwarders in the United States. **Entries include:** Company name, address, names and titles of principal executives; in separate section, financial and operating data for each firm. **Arrangement:** Alphabetical. **Frequency:** Annual, with a six-month supplement. **Price:** $65.00, including supplement.

★1437★
TRINC'S RED BOOK OF THE TRUCKING INDUSTRY
Trinc Transportation Consultants, Division
Dun & Bradstreet, Inc.
475 L'Enfant Plaza, S. W., Suite 4200   Phone: (202) 484-3410
Washington, DC 20024
Publication includes: Selected revenue, income, expense, and traffic statistics data for nearly 3,000 motor carriers of property; carriers are named, but publication does not include directory features found in other Trinc publications described in separate listings. Frequency: Annual, quarterly supplements. Price: $135.00; includes year's supplement service. Other information: Based on carriers' quarterly reports to Interstate Commerce Commission.

★1438★
TRUCK BROKER DIRECTORY [Freight brokers and shippers]
J. J. Keller & Associates, Inc.
145 W. Wisconsin Avenue   Phone: (414) 722-2848
Neenah, WI 54956
Covers: About 2,600 truck brokers, refrigerated haulers, shippers, packers, growers, distributors, and other firms in the United States and Canada interested in return trip loads, through backhaul (return trip) or trip-lease arrangements. Entries include: Company name, address, phone, branch office location and phone, coding to indicate line of business, service offered; some listings indicate season of operation. Arrangement: Geographical. Pages (approx.): 330. Frequency: Annual. Editor: Patricia Laux, Editor. Advertising accepted. Price: $25.00.

Truck Equipment and Body Distributors Association—
    Membership Roster See National Truck Equipment
    Association—Membership Roster

Truck Equipment Catalog for GMC Dealers See Vocational
    Equipment Directory for GMC Dealers

Truck Renting and Leasing Association—Membership List See
    The Vehicle

★1439★
TRUCK STOP FUEL GUIDE
National Association of Truck Stop Operators
Box 1285
Alexandria, VA 22313
Covers: Almost 1,000 North American truck stops and their restaurants, all open 24 hours daily. Entries include: Truck stop name, phone, facilities available, credit cards accepted, owner's name. Arrangement: Geographical. Pages (approx.): 80. Frequency: Semiannual, summer and winter. Advertising accepted. Circulation 100,000. Former title: National Association of Truck Stop Operators - Membership Directory. Price: $1.00.

★1440★
TRUCK TRAILER MANUFACTURERS ASSOCIATION—
    MEMBERSHIP DIRECTORY
Truck Trailer Manufacturers Association
2430 Pennsylvania Avenue, N. W.   Phone: (202) 785-5833
Washington, DC 20037
Covers: About 100 truck and tank trailer manufacturers. Entries include: Company name, address, phone, name of contact person, and description of company's products. Arrangement: Alphabetical. Pages (approx.): 100. Frequency: Annual. Price: $12.00.

★1441★
TRUCK-FRAME & AXLE REPAIR ASSOCIATION—MEMBERSHIP
    DIRECTORY
Truck-Frame and Axle Repair Association
MEMA Building
222 Cedar Lane
Teaneck, NJ 07666
Covers: About 70 regular and associate members that repair heavy-duty trucking equipment or supply the industry. Entries include: Firm name, address, phone, name of president, coding to indicate specialties. Arrangement: Geographical. Pages (approx.): Leaflet. Frequency: Annual, December. Editor: Silvie Licitra, Administrator. Price: Free. Send orders to: Truck-Frame & Axle Repair Association, 915 E. 99th Street, Brooklyn, NY 11236 (212-257-6241).

★1442★
TRY US: NATIONAL MINORITY BUSINESS DIRECTORY
National Minority Business Campaign
1201 12th Avenue, N.   Phone: (612) 377-2402
Minneapolis, MN 55411
Covers: 4,300 minority-owned companies capable of supplying their goods or services on a national or regional level. Entries include: Company name, address, phone, name of principal executive, number of employees, date established, trade and brand names, financial keys, list of products or services, names of three customers. Arrangement: Geographical within product or service categories. Indexes: Company, product. Pages (approx.): 350. Frequency: Annual, January. Editor: Rose Meyerhoff, Executive Director. Price: $13.50 (current edition); $14.00 (1980 edition); plus $1.00 shipping.

★1443★
TULSA AREA MANUFACTURERS DIRECTORY [Oklahoma]
Metropolitan Tulsa Chamber of Commerce
616 S. Boston Avenue   Phone: (918) 585-1201
Tulsa, OK 74119
Covers: About 1,200 industrial firms in Creek, Mayes, Osage, Rogers, Tulsa, and Wagoner counties, Oklahoma. Entries include: Company name, address, phone, name of principal executive, number of employees, date established, area served, SIC numbers, list of products, parent company (if applicable), trade names. Arrangement: Alphabetical. Indexes: SIC, geographical, exporters. Pages (approx.): 80. Frequency: Formerly biennial; now annual, July, with semiannual supplement. Editor: Ray Vella. Price: $10.00, including supplements.

★1444★
TURBO MACHINERY INTERNATIONAL—TURBOMACHINERY
    CATALOG & WORKBOOK ISSUE
Business Journals, Inc.
22 S. Smith Street   Phone: (203) 853-6015
Norwalk, CT 06855
Covers: Suppliers of gas turbine engine components, equipment, and services for maintenance and repair; engineers, consultants, and contractors are listed separately. Entries include: For suppliers - Company name, address, phone, telex, and products or services offered. For consultants - Company name, address, phone, services offered, and name of contact. Arrangement: Alphabetical. Indexes: Product. Pages (approx.): 500. Frequency: Annual, March. Editor: Kurt Hallberg. Advertising accepted. Circulation 6,400. Price: Included in subscription, $15.00 per year.

TV and Radio Directory See Working Press of the Nation

UCN Register See University Consultants Network Register

Unique 3-in-1 Research & Development Directory See Research
    & Development Directory

★1445★
UNITED PESTICIDE FORMULATORS AND DISTRIBUTORS
    ASSOCIATION—ROSTER
United Pesticide Formulators and Distributors Association
2444 W. Point Road   Phone: (404) 762-0194
College Park, GA 30337
Covers: 65 suppliers to the pest control industry in United States, Canada, and Spain. Entries include: Company name, address, name of authorized representative to association. Arrangement: Alphabetical. Pages (approx.): 5. Frequency: Annual, summer. Editor: C. P. Stephenson, Secretary. Price: Free.

★1446★
U.S. AND INTERNATIONAL DIRECTORY OF HOTEL, RESTAURANT, AND INSTITUTIONAL SCHOOLS
Council on Hotel, Restaurant and Institutional Education
Human Development Building, Room 12   Phone: (814) 863-0586
University Park, PA 16802
Covers: About 150 secondary and technical schools, colleges, and universities; international coverage. **Entries include:** For member schools - School name, address, areas of study, degrees offered, name and title of contact. For nonmember schools - School name, city, Zip code. **Arrangement:** Geographical. **Pages** (approx.): 75. **Frequency:** Irregular; latest edition May 1979. **Editor:** Thomas F. Powers, Ph.D., Executive Vice-President. **Price:** $2.00.

★1447★
U.S. DIRECTORY OF THE SOFT DRINK INDUSTRY
Food Industries Directories
798 Kings Highway   Phone: (203) 366-4448
Fairfield, CT 06430
Covers: Over 3,900 plants engaged in the bottling and distribution of nonalcoholic beverages (SIC 2086). **Entries include:** Company name, address, phone, name of principal officer, type of business, key showing approximate sales and number of employees. **Arrangement:** Geographical. **Frequency:** Irregular; latest edition fall 1978; new edition expected April 1980. **Price:** $69.50, postpaid, payment with order.

★1448★
U.S. FIRMS IN FRANCE
American Chamber of Commerce in France
21, avenue George-V
Paris F-75008, France
Covers: 1,100 affiliates, branches, factories, and sales offices of American firms in France. **Entries include:** Company name, address, phone, telex, name of chief executive. **Frequency:** Latest edition 1979. **Price:** $37.00, plus $8.00 air mail shipping.

★1449★
U.S. FOAMED PLASTICS MARKETS AND DIRECTORY
Technomic Publishing Company, Inc.
265 Post Road West   Phone: (203) 226-7203
Westport, CT 06880
Covers: Producers of plastic foam shapes, chemicals, and other products, and sources of equipment and supplies. **Entries include:** Company name, address, phone, names of executives, and products. **Arrangement:** Classified by type of foamed plastic. **Frequency:** Annual, September. **Price:** $25.00. **Other information:** Principal content of volume is market projections and analyses.

★1450★
U.S. HEADQUARTERS IN EUROPE
American Chamber of Commerce in France
21, avenue George-V
Paris F-75008, France
Covers: Over 850 American firms with corporate offices in Europe (for their European or overseas operations). **Entries include:** Company name, address, phone, telex, key personnel. **Arrangement:** Alphabetical and geographical. **Frequency:** Latest edition 1979. **Price:** $30.00, plus $5.00 airmail shipping.

★1451★
U.S. INDUSTRIAL DIRECTORY
Cahners Publishing Company
1200 Summer Street   Phone: (203) 327-2450
Stamford, CT 06905
Description: Publication consists of four volumes, of which the "Industrial Telephone/Address Directory" provides company names, addresses, trade names, phone numbers, and addresses and phones of local sales offices and distributors. Other volumes include product listings with supplier names; product-classified list of companies offering catalogs and brochures (obtainable through reader service

cards); and new product information. **Frequency:** Annual. **Editor:** Lee Elkins. **Price:** $55.00.

★1452★
U.S. PUBLICITY DIRECTORY
John Wiley & Sons, Inc.
605 Third Avenue   Phone: (212) 867-9800
New York, NY 10016
Covers: In separate volumes: Radio and television stations; magazines (including newsletters and house organs); newspapers (dailies and weeklies); business and finance media (regardless of format or frequency); communications services (news bureaus, wire services, syndicates, and photo services). **Entries include:** Outlet name, address, phone, names of key personnel, special interests or formats. **Indexes:** Subject, geographical. **Frequency:** First edition expected March 1980; complete set of updated volumes to be published six months later. **Editor:** Craig T. Norback. **Price:** $185.00; includes set of updated volumes.

★1453★
UNITED STATES REPRESENTATIVES IN THE CHINA TRADE
National Council for US-China Trade
1050 17th Street, N. W., Room 350
Washington, DC 20036
Covers: 35 United States based companies with representatives in China willing to assist other American firms in establishing trade with China. **Entries include:** Company name, United States address, China address, product, special services. **Arrangement:** Alphabetical. **Indexes:** Product, service. **Pages** (approx.): 25. **Frequency:** Not established; first edition August 1979. **Price:** $10.00, plus $1.00 shipping.

★1454★
UNITED STATES TOBACCO JOURNAL SUPPLIER DIRECTORY
BMT Publishing Company
254 W. 31st Street   Phone: (212) 594-4120
New York, NY 10001
Covers: Approximately 500 suppliers, manufacturers, and importers of cigarettes, cigars, pipes, and tobacco, candy, sundries, health and beauty aids, and vending equipment. Also includes lists of tobacco distributors and members of buying syndicates. **Entries include:** For manufacturers and suppliers - Company name, address, phone, names of executives, trade and brand names, list of products, packaging. For distributors and others - Company name, address, phone. **Arrangement:** Manufacturers and suppliers are classified; distributors, geographical; others, alphabetical. **Indexes:** Product, brand name. **Pages** (approx.): 300. **Frequency:** Semiannual, July and December. **Editor:** Joanne Goldstein, Assistant to the Publisher. **Advertising accepted.** Circulation 4,800. **Price:** $10.00. **Also includes:** "Who's Who in Tobacco/Confectionery Distribution," a geographical listing of distribution firms with name, address, phone, names of executives and buyers, territory, and branches.

★1455★
U.S. TRADE AND TRANSPORT DIRECTORY
Trade and Transport Company
1527 W. Lewis Street   Phone: (714) 291-9300
San Diego, CA 92103
Covers: Over 20,000 companies in major ports and transport centers in the United States which provide shipping, trucking, rail, airline, cargo handling, custom house, and other services. **Entries include:** Company name, address, phone, trade names, type of business. **Arrangement:** Geographical, then by type of service. **Indexes:** Firm name. **Pages** (approx.): 700. **Frequency:** Annual, November. **Editor:** William J. Smith, Publisher. **Advertising accepted.** Circulation 10,000. **Price:** $35.00.

United States Trade Shows, Expositions, and Conventions *See* **Directory of United States Trade Shows, Expositions, and Conventions**

★1456★
UNITED STATES-ITALY TRADE DIRECTORY
Italy-America Chamber of Commerce
350 Fifth Avenue, Suite 3015   Phone: (212) 279-5522
New York, NY 10001
Covers: 3,000 firms. Lists importers of Italian commodities, Italian manufacturers represented in the United States, and United States companies with business interests in Italy. **Entries include:** Company name, address. **Arrangement:** By activity. **Indexes:** Commodity, brand name. **Pages** (approx.): 300. **Frequency:** Biennial, odd years. **Advertising accepted.** Circulation 5,000. **Price:** $30.00, plus $3.00 shipping. **Also includes:** Business rules, taxation, tariffs, etc.

★1457★
UNIVERSITY AND COLLEGE LABOR EDUCATION ASSOCIATION—
    DIRECTORY OF MEMBER INSTITUTIONS AND PROFESSIONAL
    STAFF
University and College Labor Education Association
308 Knapp Hall   Phone: (304) 293-3323
Morgantown, WV 26506
Covers: Universities with full time labor education programs. **Entries include:** Name, address, and phone of member institution and names and titles of professional staff. **Arrangement:** Geographical. **Pages** (approx.): 20. **Frequency:** Annual, July. **Editor:** Owen Tapper, Secretary-Treasurer. **Price:** $2.00.

★1458★
UNIVERSITY CONSULTANTS NETWORK REGISTER
Anderson Group, Inc.
Box 508   Phone: (201) 377-0085
Madison, NJ 07940
Covers: 500 faculty members of United States colleges and universities with specialties in business, industrial engineering, computer sciences who act as consultants in their field. **Entries include:** Name, address, affiliation, academic title, degrees, phone; address and phone for consulting inquiries; services; languages; experience; references; publications; major field of consulting activity; type of clientele preferred. **Indexes:** Geographical, language, alphabetical, university affiliation, problem area. **Pages** (approx.): Base edition, 480; expected supplement 250. **Frequency:** Biennial, October of odd years; annual, March supplement. **Editor:** Viola Anderson. **Price:** $65.00, including 1980 supplement; $20.00, supplement only; plus $1.50 shipping (ISSN 0160-1229).

★1459★
URBAN MASS TRANSIT: A GUIDE TO ORGANIZATIONS AND
    INFORMATION RESOURCES
California Institute of Public Affairs
226 W. Foothill Boulevard   Phone: (714) 624-5212
Claremont, CA 91711
Covers: Over 1,000 governmental agencies, associations, advocacy groups, transit systems, consultants, manufacturers, and publishers of materials concerned with urban mass transit and transportation problems of special groups. **Entries include:** For organizations, etc. - Name, address, phone, names and titles of key personnel, description of programs and projects, publications. **Arrangement:** Type of organization. **Indexes:** Subject, organization name, geographical. **Pages** (approx.): 150. **Frequency:** Not established; first edition November 1979. **Editor:** Thomas N. Trzyna. **Price:** $25.00.

★1460★
USED EQUIPMENT DIRECTORY
Reinhold Division
Penton/IPC
70 Sip Avenue   Phone: (201) 653-4440
Jersey City, NJ 07306
Publication includes: List of 600 dealers in used electrical, power, process, and material handling equipment, machine tools, etc. **Entries include:** Company name, address, phone, principal executive, types of equipment handled. **Arrangement:** Geographical. **Pages** (approx.): 550. **Frequency:** Monthly. **Advertising accepted.** Circulation

75,000. **Price:** $2.00 per copy; $15.00 per year. **Other information:** Principal content is approximately 27,000 listings of used equipment for sale, classified by type.

★1461★
UTAH STATE INDUSTRIAL DIRECTORY
State Industrial Directories Corporation
Two Penn Plaza   Phone: (212) 564-0340
New York, NY 10001
Number of listings: 2,100. **Entries include:** Company name, address, phone, names of key executives, number of employees, plant size, 4-digit SIC code, products, whether firm imports or exports, and whether firm has research facilities. **Arrangement:** Geographical. **Indexes:** Alphabetical, product (includes mailing address and phone for each firm). **Frequency:** Biennial, even years. **Advertising accepted.** **Price:** $15.00, plus $2.75 shipping (ISSN 0160-7405).

★1462★
THE VEHICLE
Conference of American Renting & Leasing Associations
1750 Pennsylvania Avenue, Suite 1303   Phone: (202) 347-2374
Washington, DC 20006
Covers: Firms engaged in automobile and truck renting and leasing; members of the following are also listed: American Automotive Leasing Association, American Car Rental Association, Truck Renting and Leasing Association, and State Car and Truck Renting and Leasing Association. **Entries include:** Company name, address, phone, names of principal executives, organization affiliations. **Indexes:** Geographical. **Frequency:** Annual, February. **Advertising accepted.** Circulation 3,000.

★1463★
VENDING TIMES—INTERNATIONAL BUYERS GUIDE AND
    DIRECTORY ISSUE
Vending Times, Inc.
211 E. 43rd Street   Phone: (212) 697-3868
New York, NY 10017
Covers: Manufacturers and suppliers of equipment and products used by vending machine industry operators, including product vendors, juke boxes, pinball and other games. **Arrangement:** Alphabetical within separate lists for vending machines and music and game devices. **Pages** (approx.): 160. **Frequency:** Annual, February. **Editor:** Arthur E. Yohalem. **Advertising accepted.** Circulation 14,000. **Price:** $7.50 (1980 edition). **Other information:** Includes specifications of major vending machines. Sometimes cited as "VT/VEND Buyer's Guide," reflecting purchase of "Vend" by Vending Times, Inc., in 1973.

Verified Directory of Hardlines Distributors *See* Hardware Age
    "Who's Who" Verified Directory of Hardlines Distributors

★1464★
VERIFIED DIRECTORY OF MANUFACTURERS' REPRESENTATIVES
Manufacturers' Agent Publishing Company, Inc.
663 Fifth Avenue   Phone: (212) 682-0326
New York, NY 10022
Covers: Nearly 16,000 manufacturers' domestic and export representatives serving all industries except food products; coverage includes Canada. **Entries include:** Firm name, address, territory served, and principal lines carried. **Arrangement:** Geographical. **Pages** (approx.): 240. **Frequency:** Biennial, March of odd years. **Editor:** E. K. Sharp. **Price:** $43.80, postpaid, payment with order; $45.80, billed (ISSN 0086-5692).

★1465★
VERIFIED DIRECTORY OF WOODWORKING AND SAWMILL
    MACHINERY
Vance Publishing Corporation
300 W. Adams Street   Phone: (312) 977-7200
Chicago, IL 60606
Covers: Manufacturers of woodworking and sawmill machinery and

equipment dealers and distributors. **Entries include:** Company name, address, phone, names of executives, type of machinery manufactured or handled. **Arrangement:** Manufacturers are alphabetical, dealers geographical. **Indexes:** Product. **Frequency:** Triennial; latest edition August 1978. **Editor:** Monte Nace. **Price:** $9.00.

★1466★
VERMONT DIRECTORY OF MANUFACTURERS
Vermont Agency of Development and Community Affairs
109 State Street   Phone: (802) 828-3211
Montpelier, VT 05602
Number of listings: Over 800. **Entries include:** Company name, address, phone, line of business, parent company, trade names, name of principal executive, SIC numbers, number of employees, whether plant tours are given, whether products are exported. **Arrangement:** Alphabetical. **Indexes:** Geographical, SIC. **Pages** (approx.): 65. **Frequency:** Annual, spring. **Editor:** George A. Donovan. **Price:** $4.00, including supplement (current and 1980 editions; ISSN 0362-9295).

★1467★
VERMONT MEDIA DIRECTORY
New England Newsclip Agency, Inc.
Five Auburn Street   Phone: (617) 879-4460
Framingham, MA 01701
Covers: 140 newspapers, periodicals, and college publications, and 50 radio and television broadcasting stations operating in Vermont. **Price:** $15.00. **Other information:** Entry content, arrangement, etc., same as "New England Media Directory," described in separate listing.

★1468★
VERMONT STATE INDUSTRIAL DIRECTORY
State Industrial Directories Corporation
Two Penn Plaza   Phone: (212) 564-0340
New York, NY 10001
Number of listings: Over 700. **Entries include:** Company name, address, phone, names of key executives, number of employees, plant size, 4-digit SIC code, products, whether firm imports or exports, and whether firm has research facilities. **Arrangement:** Geographical. **Indexes:** Alphabetical, product (includes mailing address and phone for each firm). **Pages** (approx.): 100. **Frequency:** Biennial, fall of odd years. **Advertising accepted.** **Price:** $20.00, plus $2.75 shipping (ISSN 0098-6208).

Video Bluebook *See* **Videolog: Programs for Business and Industry**

★1469★
VIDEOLOG: PROGRAMS FOR BUSINESS AND INDUSTRY
Esselte Video, Inc.
600 Madison Avenue   Phone: (212) 753-7530
New York, NY 10022
Covers: Over 100 producers and distributors of videotape programs on business subjects, including technical, social, and psychological areas of business. **Entries include:** Company name, address, phone, contact person. **Arrangement:** Alphabetical. **Indexes:** Subject. **Pages** (approx.): 275. **Frequency:** Irregular; first edition fall 1978; new edition expected November 1980. **Editor:** Lawrence Eidelberg, Director of Publications. **Former title:** The Video Bluebook (1978). **Price:** $35.00 (current and 1980 editions). **Send orders to:** Esselte Video Inc., Box 978, Edison, NJ 08817 (201-225-1900). **Other information:** Principal content is annotated entries describing about 3,300 videotapes.

★1470★
VIRGINIA DIRECTORY OF MINORITY BUSINESSES
Virginia State Office of Minority Business Enterprise
Virginia State College
Box 61   Phone: (804) 526-8981
Petersburg, VA 23803
Covers: Nearly 2,000 firms offering professional, commercial, industrial, and consumer products and services. **Entries include:**

Company name, address, phone, name of contact, floor space, products or services. **Arrangement:** Classified. **Indexes:** Company, geographical. **Pages** (approx.): 160. **Frequency:** Annual, August. **Editor:** Floresta D. Jones, Program/Information Officer. **Price:** Free.

Virginia Industrial Directory *See* **Directory of Virginia Manufacturing**

★1471★
VIRGINIA STATE INDUSTRIAL DIRECTORY
State Industrial Directories Corporation
Two Penn Plaza   Phone: (212) 564-0340
New York, NY 10001
Number of listings: 5,100. **Entries include:** Company name, address, phone, names of key executives, number of employees, plant size, 4-digit SIC code, products, whether firm imports or exports, and whether firm has research facilities. **Arrangement:** Geographical. **Indexes:** Alphabetical, product (includes mailing address and phone for each firm). **Frequency:** Annual, spring. **Advertising accepted.** **Price:** $50.00 (current and 1980 editions).

★1472★
VOCATIONAL EQUIPMENT DIRECTORY FOR GMC DEALERS
Verbiest Publishing Company
950 E. Maple, Suite 205   Phone: (313) 645-2360
Birmingham, MI 48011
Covers: Suppliers of special equipment for General Motors Corporation trucks to adapt them for various lines of business. **Entries include:** Company name, address, phone, list of products and trade names. **Arrangement:** Classified. **Pages** (approx.): 150. **Frequency:** Annual, January. **Advertising accepted.** Circulation 4,500. **Former title:** Truck Equipment Catalog for GMC Dealers. **Price:** $3.50.

★1473★
VOICE—MEMBERSHIP DIRECTORY ISSUE [Floor covering and drapery industries]
AIDS International
4420 N. Fairfax Drive, No. 100
Arlington, VA 22203
Covers: 600 firms offering rug, upholstery, and drapery sales, installation, and cleaning, and firms providing supplies and equipment. **Arrangement:** Geographical. **Frequency:** Annual, April. **Editor:** Robert F. Coleman, Executive Vice President. **Price:** $1.00 (current and 1980 editions).

VT/VEND Buyer's Guide *See* **Vending Times—International Buyers Guide and Directory Issue**

★1474★
WALDEN'S ABC GUIDE AND PAPER PRODUCTION YEARBOOK
Walden-Mott Corporation
466 Kinderkamack Road   Phone: (201) 261-2630
Oradell, NJ 07649
Covers: About 6,400 firms which manufacture, convert, and sell paper products. **Entries include:** Company name, address, phone, names of executives, and products and services offered. **Arrangement:** Geographical. **Indexes:** Product, alphabetical. **Pages** (approx.): 550. **Frequency:** Annual, January. **Editor:** Michael G. Balbian. **Advertising accepted.** Circulation 3,000. **Price:** $50.00 (1980 edition).

★1475★
WALKER'S MANUAL OF WESTERN CORPORATIONS
Walker's Manual, Inc.
5855 Naples Plaza, Suite 101   Phone: (213) 434-3468
Long Beach, CA 90803
Covers: Almost 1,200 publicly owned corporations headquartered in the 13 western United States and Canada. **Entries include:** Company name, address, phone, line of business, names of executives, names of directors and shareholdings of each, number of employees, brand names or product lines, and complete financial information (book

value, debentures, reserves, etc.). **Arrangement:** Alphabetical. **Indexes:** Alphabetical, geographical, industry classification. **Pages** (approx.): 1,600 (in two volumes). **Frequency:** Annual, fall; monthly supplements. **Advertising accepted.** **Former title:** Walker's Manual of Western Corporations & Securities (1975). **Price:** $158.00, without supplements; $77.00, supplements only.

★1476★
WALLCOVERINGS—DIRECTORY ISSUE
Publishing Dynamics, Inc.
Two Selleck Street   Phone: (203) 357-0028
Stamford, CT 06902
Covers: 1,000 manufacturers, importers, distributors, and suppliers in the wallcoverings industry, worldwide. **Entries include:** Company name, address, phone, names of executives, shipping methods, nature of firm's business, manufacturing methods used, collection names, branches; distributors are located via the "Collections" section. Wholesaler listings indicate lines carried. **Arrangement:** Alphabetical. **Indexes:** Product. **Pages** (approx.): 250. **Frequency:** Annual, September. **Editor:** Jody Stone. **Advertising accepted.** **Price:** $7.50.

Washington Aggregates and Concrete Association—Roster *See* Pacific Builder & Engineer—Buyers Guide & Directory Issue

Washington Food Dealer Magazine—Grocery Industry Directory *See* Grocery Industry Directory of Washington State and Alaska

★1477★
WASHINGTON MANUFACTURERS REGISTER
Times Mirror Press
1115 S. Boyle   Phone: (213) 265-6767
Los Angeles, CA 90023
Number of listings: 4,400. **Entries include:** Company name, address, phone, names of executives, number of employees, sales volume, list of products, SIC numbers, and date established. **Arrangement:** Alphabetical. **Indexes:** Geographical, product. **Pages** (approx.): 350. **Frequency:** Biennial, February of even years. **Editor:** P. Newman. **Price:** $38.50 (current edition); $42.50 (1980 edition).

★1478★
WASHINGTON PUBLIC PORTS ASSOCIATION—PORT DIRECTORY
Washington Public Ports Association
Box 1518   Phone: (206) 943-0760
Olympia, WA 98507
Covers: 57 ports and their officials who are members of the association. Includes a list of 15 nonmembers. **Entries include:** For members - Port name, address, county, phone, scan number, names and addresses of commissioners, names and titles of officials. For nonmembers - Name, address, list of commissioners. **Arrangement:** Geographical. **Pages** (approx.): 20. **Frequency:** Annual, January. **Price:** Free.

★1479★
WATERSIDE PLANT LOCATIONS AND EXPANSIONS [Shipping]
American Waterways Operators
1600 Wilson Boulevard, Suite 1101   Phone: (703) 841-9300
Arlington, VA 22209
Covers: New plants or expansions announced in year preceding publication which are to be constructed along national navigable waterways. **Entries include:** Location of new facility, company constructing it, type of facility, amount to be spent on construction, number of employees required for new facility. **Arrangement:** Classified by waterway, then by city. **Pages** (approx.): 25. **Frequency:** Annual, July. **Price:** Free.

★1480★
WATERWAY POINT DIRECTORY FOR THE GREAT LAKES, ATLANTIC, AND PACIFIC AREAS
U.S. Army Engineer Waterways Experiment Station
Hydraulics Laboratory
Corps of Engineers
Box 631
Vicksburg, MS 39180
Covers: Commercial docks, towns, landings, navigation locks, bridges, junctions and other points on navigable rivers, bays, streams, creeks and other waterways in the Great Lakes, Atlantic, and Pacific areas. **Entries include:** For each river point - Waterborne Commerce Statistics Center port and dock codes, title of point, point type code, area code, and location (state, county, Business Economic Area, Strategic Metropolitan Statistical Area, and Water Resource Area). **Arrangement:** By region, then by numeric code. **Indexes:** Name of waterway. **Frequency:** Irregular; latest edition January 1976. **Editors:** Larry L. Daggett and Robert W. McCarley.

★1481★
WEATHERIZATION MATERIALS HANDBOOK
Institute for Local Self-Reliance
1717 18th Street, N. W.
Washington, DC 20009
Covers: About 900 manufacturers of insulation, weatherstripping, storm doors and storm windows, and distributors and manufacturers of insulation blowing machines. **Entries include:** Name of manufacturer, address, phone, name of contact, minimum order, delivery time, whether sales are made to community action programs. **Arrangement:** By type of product, then geographical. **Pages** (approx.): 120. **Frequency:** Published 1979. **Price:** $6.50, paper; $3.00, microfiche (PB 297-212). May also be available from the publisher. **Send orders to:** National Technical Information Service, Springfield, VA 22161. **Other information:** Discussion of characteristics and uses of insulation, storm doors and windows, caulking and weather stripping, etc.

★1482★
WELDING & FABRICATING DATA BOOK
Penton/IPC
614 Superior Avenue West   Phone: (216) 696-0300
Cleveland, OH 44113
Covers: More than 2,000 independent welding supply distributors and manufacturers' sales outlets. **Entries include:** Company name, address, phone. **Arrangement:** Geographical. **Indexes:** Product. **Frequency:** Annual. **Advertising accepted.** **Former title:** Welding Data Book Product Selector and Source Guide. **Price:** $25.00, plus $2.00 shipping. **Also includes:** Substantial section of engineering data.

Welding Data Book Product Selector and Source Guide *See* Welding & Fabricating Data Book

★1483★
WELDING DESIGN & FABRICATION—WELDING AND FABRICATING BUYER'S GUIDE ISSUE
Penton/IPC, Inc.
Penton Plaza   Phone: (216) 696-7000
Cleveland, OH 44114
Covers: Over 600 manufacturers and suppliers of products and equipment for the welding and fabricating industry. **Entries include:** Firm name, address, phone, product type. **Arrangement:** Alphabetical. **Indexes:** Product. **Frequency:** Annual, January. **Editor:** Rosalie Brosilow. **Advertising accepted.** Circulation 43,000. **Price:** $2.00.

Wema Membership Directory *See* American Electronics Association—Membership Directory

★1484★
WENCO INTERNATIONAL TRADE DIRECTORY
Wenco Enterprises, Inc.
390 S. W. Salix Place
Aloha, OR 97005
Covers: 175,000 manufacturing and non-manufacturing companies in 150 countries. **Entries include:** Company name, address, year established, type of organization, number of employees, language of correspondence, SIC numbers, and business code. **Arrangement:** By SIC number within countries. **Frequency:** Biennial, spring of even years. **Editor:** William E. Noles, Sr., President and Publisher. **Advertising accepted.** Circulation 25,000. **Price:** $225.00 (two volumes), postpaid (1980 edition).

★1485★
WEST COAST METAL IMPORTERS ASSOCIATION—MEMBERSHIP ROSTER AND DIRECTORY
West Coast Metal Importers Association
C/o F. V. Swanson
333 S. Flower, Room 226
Los Angeles, CA 90071
Covers: 200 importers of steel and allied products on the West Coast, who are members. **Frequency:** Latest edition September 1979. **Price:** Available to members only.

★1486★
WEST VIRGINIA MANUFACTURING DIRECTORY
West Virginia Office of Economic and Community Development
Building 6, Room 512
1900 Washington Street, East   Phone: (304) 348-2234
Charleston, WV 25305
Number of listings: 1,500. **Entries include:** Company name, address, phone, name of principal executive, number of employees, products or services, SIC number. **Arrangement:** Alphabetical. **Indexes:** County, city, product, exporter, SIC. **Pages** (approx.): 280. **Frequency:** Biennial, January of even years. **Editor:** Michael Marlowe, Research Coordinator. **Price:** $10.00 (current edition); $15.00 (1980 edition).

★1487★
WEST VIRGINIA STATE INDUSTRIAL DIRECTORY
State Industrial Directories Corporation
Two Penn Plaza   Phone: (212) 564-0340
New York, NY 10001
Entries include: Company name, address, phone, names of key executives, number of employees, plant size, 4-digit SIC code, products, whether firm imports or exports, and whether firm has research facilities. **Arrangement:** Geographical. **Indexes:** Alphabetical, product (includes mailing address and phone for each firm). **Frequency:** Annual, fall. **Advertising accepted.** **Price:** $20.00, plus $2.75 shipping (ISSN 0160-7391).

★1488★
WESTERN BUILDER—DIRECTORY AND BUYER'S GUIDE ISSUE
  [Wisconsin, Michigan]
Western Builder Publishing Company
6526 River Parkway   Phone: (414) 453-7700
Milwaukee, WI 53213
Covers: Construction equipment distributors in Wisconsin and Upper Michigan; and manufacturers supplying equipment and products to the construction industry. **Entries include:** For distributors - Firm name, address, phone, names and titles of key personnel, manufacturers represented. For manufacturers - Company name, address, products. **Arrangement:** Alphabetical. **Indexes:** Product. **Frequency:** Annual, late March. **Advertising accepted.** Circulation 4,100. **Price:** $10.00 (current and 1980 editions; ISSN 0043-3535).

Western Chemical Producers *See* Directory of Chemical
  Producers U. S. A.

Western Electronics Manufacturers Association—Directory *See*
  American Electronics Association—Membership Directory

★1489★
WESTERN FOODSERVICE—ANNUAL WESTERN BUYERS DIRECTORY ISSUE
Young/Conway Publications, Inc.
347 Madison Avenue   Phone: (212) 986-4119
New York, NY 10017
Covers: About 1,500 wholesalers, manufacturers, brokers, dealers, designers, distributors, and other suppliers to the food service industry in the 13 western states. **Entries include:** Company name, code noting type of supplier (manufacturers' agent, broker, consultant, dealer, manufacturer, or wholesaler), address, phone, wholesale value of inventory, states services, names of executives, and code for products offered. **Arrangement:** Geographical. **Pages** (approx.): 60. **Frequency:** Annual, January. **Advertising accepted.** Circulation 21,000. **Price:** $2.00 (current and 1980 editions). **Send orders to:** "Western Foodservice," 5455 Wilshire Blvd., Ste. 711, Los Angeles, CA 90036.

★1490★
WESTERN MATERIAL HANDLING/PACKAGING/SHIPPING—BUYERS' GUIDE ISSUE
Baymer Publications, Inc.
606 Larchmont Boulevard   Phone: (213) 461-2761
Los Angeles, CA 90004
Covers: Over 600 manufacturers of material handling, packaging, and related equipment, materials, and supplies. **Entries include:** Company name, home office and western branch addresses, phone, products. **Arrangement:** Alphabetical. **Indexes:** Product. **Pages** (approx.): 75. **Frequency:** Annual, June. **Editor:** Jack Gibson. **Advertising accepted.** Circulation 15,000. **Price:** $6.00.

★1491★
WESTERN NEW YORK METROSCENE
Buffalo Area Chamber of Commerce
107 Delaware Avenue   Phone: (716) 849-6677
Buffalo, NY 14202
Publication includes: Lists of banks, colleges and universities, medical and other health care facilities, apartment complexes, real estate firms, restaurants, recreation facilities, newspaper publishers, radio and television broadcasting stations, and other firms and organizations of interest to the newcomer to Erie and Niagara counties, New York. **Entries include:** Listings generally include name, address, phone; higher education institutions include degrees offered, tuition; radio broadcasting stations include frequency, format; other information included in listings as appropriate. **Arrangement:** By activity. **Pages** (approx.): 85. **Frequency:** Biennial, even years. **Price:** $2.95, plus 75¢ shipping.

Western Packaging Directory *See* Good Packaging—Directory
  Issue [Western states]

★1492★
WESTERN PLASTICS—DIRECTORY/YEARBOOK ISSUE
Western Plastics News, Inc.
1625 17th Street   Phone: (213) 870-6683
Santa Monica, CA 90404
Covers: Plastics-oriented manufacturers west of the Mississippi. Includes a yearbook of activities and events. **Entries include:** Company name, address, phone, names of executives, number of employees, list of products or services, SIC numbers, branches and representatives. **Arrangement:** Alphabetical and classified. **Frequency:** Irregular. **Editor:** H. M. Hastings. **Advertising accepted.** Circulation 10,000. **Price:** $15.00.

★1493★
WESTERN RETAILERS—BRAND GUIDE & DIRECTORY [Grocery
    and food industry]
Harlequin Publications
Box 875
Palos Verdes, CA 90274
Phone: (213) 375-8196
Covers: About 3,000 brokers, distributors, food and non-food
manufacturers, and service companies concerned with the food
industry in California, Arizona, and Nevada. **Entries include:** Company
name, address, phone; name of parent company, if any; addresses and
phone numbers of branches, if any. Broker and manufacturer
representative index listings also include products, memberships.
Arrangement: Alphabetical. **Indexes:** Broker name, retail product,
service/supply, manufacturer/brand with source. **Pages** (approx.):
135. **Frequency:** Annual, March. **Editor:** Audrey M. Dodd.
Advertising accepted. Circulation 10,000. **Price:** $10.00, postpaid.

★1494★
WESTERN TRAVEL SALES GUIDE
Cabell Travel Publications
11411 Cumpston Street
North Hollywood, CA 91601
Phone: (213) 980-6260
Covers: Travel agents, wholesale tour operators, motor coach-
sightseeing companies, airlines, steamships, railroads, car rental
companies, foreign auto sales, state and foreign government tourist
offices, foreign consulates, hotel/motel chains and systems, hotel and
travel representatives, and special service companies throughout
western United States, western Canada, and Mexico. **Entries include:**
Company name, address, phone, names of executives. **Arrangement:**
By type of business, then geographical. **Indexes:** Alphabetical index of
travel agencies; classified index of wholesale tour operators by
destination areas (Orient, etc.). **Pages** (approx.): 415. **Frequency:**
Semiannual. **Editor:** James A. Cabell. **Advertising accepted.**
Circulation 3,500. **Price:** $20.00 per issue; $35.00 per year.

★1495★
WHERE SHALL I GO TO COLLEGE TO STUDY ADVERTISING?
Advertising Education Publications
3429 55th Street
Lubbock, TX 79413
Covers: 80 colleges and universities in 42 states with advertising
curriculums. **Entries include:** Institution name and location; program
identification and content, degrees offered, accreditation, number of
advertising students, graduates, and full-time faculty; scholarship
assistance available; admission requirements; fees; contact name.
Arrangement: Geographical. **Pages** (approx.): 40. **Frequency:**
Annual, December. **Editors:** Billy I. Ross and Donald G. Hileman. **Price:**
$1.00, payment with order.

★1496★
WHERE TO BUY HARDWOOD PLYWOOD AND VENEER
Hardwood Plywood Manufacturers Association
1825 Michael Faraday Drive
Reston, VA 22090
Phone: (703) 435-2900
Covers: 140 manufacturers and prefinishers of hardwood plywood
and their suppliers. **Entries include:** Company name, address, phone,
name of principal executive, list of products and services.
Arrangement: Alphabetical. **Pages** (approx.): 50. **Frequency:** Annual,
June. **Editor:** Clark E. McDonald, Managing Director. **Price:** Free.

★1497★
WHERE TO FIND BUSINESS INFORMATION
Wiley-Interscience, Division
John Wiley & Sons
605 Third Avenue
New York, NY 10016
Phone: (212) 867-9800
Publication includes: List of about 1,450 publishers of business
materials, including commercial publishers, organizations,
governmental units, etc., who issue books, periodicals, newsletters,
directories, etc. **Entries include:** Publisher name, address, phone,
titles of business publications. **Arrangement:** Alphabetical.

Frequency: Published June 1979. **Editors:** David M. Brownstone and
Gorton Carruth. **Price:** $34.95. **Also includes:** Annotated descriptions
of individual publications in a separate section. **Send orders to:** John
Wiley & Sons, 1 Wiley Dr., Somerset, NJ.

★1498★
WHERE TO FIND CERTIFIED MECHANICS FOR YOUR CAR
National Institute for Automotive Service Excellence
1825 K Street, N. W., Suite 515
Washington, DC 20006
Phone: (202) 833-9646
Covers: Repair establishments including new car dealers, independent
garages, service stations, mass merchandisers, specialty shops, and
body and paint shops who employ mechanics certified by the Institute.
(NIASE is a nonprofit testing organization governed by industry and
outside directors.) **Entries include:** Facility name, address, phone,
type of establishment (service station, specialty work only, etc.).
Arrangement: Geographical. **Frequency:** Latest edition 1978. **Price:**
$1.95.

Who Owns Whom: International Subsidiaries of U.S. Companies
    See Who Owns Whom: North America

★1499★
WHO OWNS WHOM: NORTH AMERICA
Dun & Bradstreet Ltd.
6-8 Bonhill Street
London EC2A 4BU, England
Covers: Companies with parent companies located in the United
States and Canada and subsidiaries in foreign countries, or parent
companies in foreign countries and subsidiaries in the United States
and Canada; domestic subsidiaries are not listed for United States
parent companies, but are listed for Canadian firms. **Entries include:**
Company name, address of parent company, subsidiaries' names,
associate company names, country of incorporation, and codes
indicating relationship to parent company, whether inactive or not, and
industry class. **Arrangement:** Alphabetical. **Indexes:** Subsidiary name.
Pages (approx.): 1,100. **Frequency:** Annual, May. **Editor:** Natalie
Stuart. **Advertising accepted.** Circulation 1,400. **Former title:** Who
Owns Whom: International Subsidiaries of U.S. Companies. **Price:**
$113.00 (current edition); $149.00 (1980 edition); ISSN 0308-
8502).**Other information:** Formerly published by O. W. Roskill and
Co.

★1500★
WHOLESALE-BY-MAIL CATALOG
St. Martin's Press
175 Fifth Avenue
New York, NY 10010
Phone: (212) 674-5151
Covers: Over 350 mail-order firms offering products at discount
prices. **Entries include:** Company name, address, phone, amount of
discount, brands or product lines handled, minimum order, shipping
costs and method of payment, sales tax or duty, return policy,
payment means, editor's evaluation code. **Arrangement:** By product
category. **Indexes:** Company name. **Pages** (approx.): 225.
Frequency: Not established; first edition July 1979. **Editor:** Rebecca
Martin. **Price:** $10.95, cloth; $5.95, paper.

★1501★
WHOLESALER—DIRECTORY OF MANUFACTURERS
    REPRESENTATIVES ISSUE [Plumbing, heating, etc.]
Scott Periodicals Corporation
135 Addison Street
Elmhurst, IL 60126
Phone: (312) 530-6172
Number of listings: 2,000 manufacturers' representatives handling
plumbing, heating, piping, air conditioning, and refrigeration products.
Entries include: Representative's name or firm name, address, phone,
territory, and lines carried. **Arrangement:** Geographical by territory
(Central States, North Pacific, etc.). **Pages** (approx.): 50 devoted to
directory section. **Frequency:** Annual, February. **Editor:** David Miller.
Advertising accepted. Circulation 23,000. **Price:** $12.00.

★1502★
WHOLESALER—WHOLESALING 100 ISSUE [Plumbing, heating, etc.]
Scott Periodicals Corporation
135 Addison Street   Phone: (312) 530-6172
Elmhurst, IL 60126
Covers: 100 leading wholesalers of plumbing-heating equipment and supplies; 50 leading wholesalers of air conditioning and refrigeration equipment and supplies. **Arrangement:** Geographical by size. **Pages** (approx.): 60. **Frequency:** Annual, July. **Editor:** David Miller. **Advertising accepted.** Circulation 23,000. **Former title:** The Wholesaler - Guide to the Industry Issue. **Price:** $2.50.

★1503★
WHOLESALER PRODUCT DIRECTORY [Plumbing, heating, etc.]
Scott Periodicals Corporation
135 Addison Street   Phone: (312) 530-6172
Elmhurst, IL 60126
Covers: Manufacturers of plumbing, heating, piping, air conditioning and refrigeration and related products in the United States and overseas. **Entries include:** Company name, address, phone, name of principal executive, list of products. **Arrangement:** Contents arranged in three alphabetical sections: product, trade name, and manufacturer. **Pages** (approx.): 250. **Frequency:** Annual, summer. **Editor:** Roy T. Wagner. **Advertising accepted.** Circulation 8,000. **Price:** $20.00 (current edition); $25.00 (1980 edition). **Other information:** Includes product catalogs.

★1504★
WHO'S WHO DIRECTORY [Tire industry]
National Tire Dealers & Retreaders Association
1343 L Street, N. W.   Phone: (202) 638-6650
Washington, DC 20005
Number of listings: 5,000 members of the association. **Entries include:** Name, address, phone, tire lines carried, membership classification (dealer, retreader, or supplier). **Arrangement:** Alphabetical. **Indexes:** Geographical. **Frequency:** Annual, January. **Editor:** C. D. Hylton III, Director, Editorial Services. **Advertising accepted.** Circulation 5,000. **Price:** Apply.

★1505★
WHO'S WHO IN ADVERTISING
Redfield Publishing Co., Inc.
Box 1256
Brattleboro, VT 05301
Covers: About 10,000 advertising agency executives, corporate advertising executives, media executives, and teachers of advertising. **Entries include:** Name, address, personal and career data, professional and community affiliations, education, military service, and awards and honors. **Arrangement:** Alphabetical. **Indexes:** Company. **Pages** (approx.): 900. **Frequency:** Biennial, odd years; latest edition December 1979. **Editor:** Catherine Quinn Serie. **Advertising accepted.** **Price:** $69.50, plus $3.50 shipping. **Send orders to:** Redfield Publishing Company, Inc., Box 325, Monroe, NY 10950.

★1506★
WHO'S WHO IN ART MATERIALS
National Art Materials Trade Association
178 Lakeview Avenue   Phone: (201) 546-6400
Clifton, NJ 07604
Covers: About 1,600 retailer members and manufacturers. **Entries include:** Company name, address, phone number, name of principal executive, trade and brand names, list of products or services. **Arrangement:** Members are geographical, manufacturers are alphabetical. **Pages** (approx.): 135. **Frequency:** Irregular; latest edition July 1979. **Editor:** Howard L. Landstrom, Executive Director. **Price:** $1.50.

★1507★
WHO'S WHO IN CALIFORNIA CONSTRUCTION
American Subcontractors Association of California
1600 Dove Street, Suite 329   Phone: (714) 752-0157
Newport Beach, CA 92660
Covers: About 2,500 subcontracting firms. **Entries include:** Firm name, address, phone, name of chief executive; memberships, awards, projects; equipment owned; dollar volume in previous year; number of tradesmen employed; licenses held; geographical area served; branch office locations. **Arrangement:** Alphabetical. **Indexes:** Trade. **Pages** (approx.): 150. **Frequency:** Not established; first edition expected February 1980. **Editor:** Jay McFadden. **Price:** $25.00, plus $1.50 shipping.

★1508★
WHO'S WHO IN ELECTRONICS
Harris Publishing Company
2057-2 Aurora Road   Phone: (216) 425-9143
Twinsburg, OH 44087
Covers: 7,000 manufacturers, 3,500 manufacturers' representatives, and nearly 2,500 distributors. **Entries include:** All entries give name, address, phone, principal personnel, information on facilities or plants, and products manufactured or handled. Other information listed includes, for manufacturers, year established and annual sales; for representatives, territory served, branch offices, and services; for distributors, outlets and annual sales. **Arrangement:** Alphabetical and geographical; distributors are listed geographically. **Indexes:** Product index listing manufacturer name, location, and phone. **Pages** (approx.): 750. **Frequency:** Annual, January. **Editor:** Jeanne Ring. **Former title:** Electronic Specifying and Procurement. **Price:** $52.00 (1980 edition).

★1509★
WHO'S WHO IN FLORICULTURE
Society of American Florists and Ornamental Horticulturists
901 N. Washington Street   Phone: (703) 836-8700
Alexandria, VA 22314
Covers: 5,600 retailers, 850 growers, 435 wholesale florists, suppliers, and allied tradesmen, 195 manufacturers and wholesalers of supplies and hardgoods, 170 affiliated organizations, 220 associate individuals who are members of the Society of American Florists. **Entries include:** Company name, address, phone, name of principal executive, number of employees. **Arrangement:** Contents arranged both geographically and alphabetically. **Pages** (approx.): 230. **Frequency:** Annual, January. **Editor:** Darryl D. McEwen. **Advertising accepted.** Circulation 7,400. **Price:** $75.00 (1980 edition).

★1510★
WHO'S WHO IN FOOD SERVICE
National Restaurant Association
One IBM Plaza, Suite 2600   Phone: (312) 787-2525
Chicago, IL 60611
Covers: 20,000 member restaurants, cafeterias, clubs, drive-ins, caterers, and other companies in the food service industry, primarily in the United States. **Entries include:** Company name, address, phone, and names of principal executives . **Arrangement:** Geographical. **Pages** (approx.): 350. **Frequency:** Annual, summer. **Price:** $50.00.

Who's Who in Industrialized Housing See Red Book of Housing Manufacturers

★1511★
WHO'S WHO IN PACKAGING: A DIRECTORY OF MEMBERSHIP, PEOPLE IN PACKAGING AND GUIDE TO PROFESSIONAL PACKAGING EXPERTISE
Packaging Institute, U.S.A.
342 Madison Avenue   Phone: (212) 687-8875
New York, NY 10017
Number of listings: 5,000. **Entries include:** Name, address, phone, areas of expertise and experience. **Arrangement:** Alphabetical. **Indexes:** Expertise, geographical. **Pages** (approx.): 300. **Frequency:**

Annual, April. **Editor:** Jean Corvington, Editor and Publications Coordinator. **Advertising accepted.** Circulation 5,000. **Price:** $18.00, plus $2.00 shipping.

★1512★
WHO'S WHO IN PAPER DISTRIBUTION
National Paper Trade Association
420 Lexington Avenue   Phone: (212) 682-2570
New York, NY 10017
Covers: 1,700 paper merchants who are members. **Frequency:** Latest edition 1977; new edition expected February 1980. **Price:** $20.00.

★1513★
WHO'S WHO IN PUBLIC RELATIONS (INTERNATIONAL)
PR Publishing Company, Inc.
14 Front Street
Exeter, NH 03833
Covers: About 4,700 individuals active in the field of public relations (approximately 20% from countries other than the United States) who were chosen by the editors on the basis of present position and level of responsibility or authority; theoretical and/or actual experience in the field; contributions to the profession; and professional prominence. **Entries include:** Name, birth date and location, degrees earned, institutions attended; career history, memberships, business and home addresses, awards, books in the field. **Arrangement:** Alphabetical. **Indexes:** Geographical. **Pages** (approx.): 700. **Frequency:** Irregular; latest edition 1976; new edition expected 1980. **Editors:** Robert L. Barbour, Adrian A. Paradis. **Price:** $35.00.

Who's Who in Residential Construction *See* Blue Book of Major Homebuilders

★1514★
WHO'S WHO IN SERVICE TOOLS AND EQUIPMENT
Equipment and Tool Institute
1545 Waukegan Road   Phone: (312) 729-8550
Glenview, IL 60025
Covers: About 75 manufacturers of service tools and equipment for the automotive repair industry. **Entries include:** Company name, address, names of delegate and alternate to association, members in vertical groups, corporate officers, principals, products manufactured. **Arrangement:** Alphabetical. **Indexes:** Product. **Pages** (approx.): 115. **Frequency:** Annual, January. **Editor:** Donn R. Proven, Executive Manager. **Price:** $25.00.

Who's Who in the Auto Industry *See* Automotive News—Market Data Book Issue

★1515★
WHO'S WHO IN THE COSMETIC INDUSTRY
Cosmetic, Toiletry and Fragrance Association
1133 15th Street, N. W.   Phone: (202) 331-1770
Washington, DC 20005
Covers: About 450 companies which are members of the association. **Entries include:** Company name; address; phone; telex/TWX number; chief executives and titles; products; services; parent company; affiliates and subsidiaries; designation as manufacturer, distributor, supplier, or private label manufacturer. **Arrangement:** Alphabetical. **Indexes:** Personal name. **Pages** (approx.): 90. **Frequency:** Annual, spring. **Price:** $20.00.

★1516★
WHO'S WHO IN THE FURNITURE INDUSTRY
Southern Furniture Manufacturers Association
Box 2436   Phone: (919) 885-5065
High Point, NC 27261
Covers: 200 manufacturers of wood and metal home, office, and institutional furniture. **Entries include:** Company name, address, phone, names of principal executives, list of products. **Frequency:** Annual, January. **Price:** $15.00.

Who's Who in the Lathing and Plastering Industry *See* Who's Who in the Wall and Ceiling Industry

Who's Who in the Office Machine Industry *See* NOMDA Spokesman—Who's Who Issue

★1517★
WHO'S WHO IN THE WALL AND CEILING INDUSTRY
Association of the Wall and Ceiling Industries-International
1711 Connecticut Avenue, N. W.   Phone: (202) 667-8402
Washington, DC 20009
Covers: Contractors, manufacturers, suppliers, unions, organizations, and periodicals affiliated with the industry. **Entries include:** Contractor section lists company name, address, phone, name of executives, and types of work done. Other sections list similar data. **Arrangement:** Classified. **Indexes:** Personal name. **Pages** (approx.): 120. **Frequency:** Annual, September. **Editor:** Gerald L. Wykoff. **Advertising accepted.** Circulation 1,500. **Former title:** Who's Who in the Lathing and Plastering Industry (1976). **Price:** $35.00. **Other information:** Former name of association is, "International Association of Wall and Ceiling Contractors/Gypsum Drywall Contractors International."

Who's Who in Tobacco & Confectionery Distribution *See* United States Tobacco Journal Supplier Directory

★1518★
WHO'S WHO IN TRAINING AND DEVELOPMENT
American Society for Training and Development
6414 Odana Road   Phone: (607) 274-3440
Madison, WI 53705
Covers: About 10,000 members concerned with training and development of business, industrial, and government personnel. **Arrangement:** Alphabetical. **Pages** (approx.): 250. **Frequency:** Annual, February. **Editor:** Michael H. Cook. **Advertising accepted.** Circulation 15,000. **Price:** $25.00 (current and 1980 editions); available to libraries only.

★1519★
WHO'S WHO OF RV DEALERS [Recreation vehicles]
Recreation Vehicle Dealers Association of North America
3251 Old Lee Highway, Suite 412   Phone: (703) 591-7130
Fairfax, VA 22030
Covers: 1,600 retail sales firms handling travel trailers, camping trailers, truck campers, and motor homes in the United States and Canada which are open for business twelve months of the year. **Entries include:** Company name, location, phone, and owner's or manager's name. **Arrangement:** Alphabetical. **Indexes:** Geographical, membership status. **Pages** (approx.): 60. **Frequency:** Annual, April. **Editor:** H. C. Peaster, Publications Executive Director. **Advertising accepted.** Circulation 5,000. **Former title:** Recreation Vehicle Dealers Association - Membership Directory. **Price:** $5.00.

★1520★
WICHITA AREA DIRECTORY OF MANUFACTURERS [Kansas]
Wichita Area Chamber of Commerce
350 W. Douglas
Wichita, KS 67202
Number of listings: 575. **Entries include:** Company name, address, phone, name of principal executive, list of products, SIC numbers, code for number of employees, whether firm exports. **Arrangement:** Alphabetical and by SIC classification; identical information in both sections. **Pages** (approx.): 90. **Frequency:** Biennial, summer of odd years. **Advertising accepted.** Circulation 4,000. **Price:** $5.00.

★1521★
WIND ENERGY DIRECTORY
Wind Power Digest
109 E. Lexington   Phone: (219) 294-2023
Bristol, IN 46514
Covers: Designers, manufacturers, and distributors of wind energy

systems, and organizations, consultants, publications, and other persons and groups active in the field. **Entries include:** For manufacturers - Company name, address, evaluation of equipment according to capacity, amount of wind required, special characteristics. **Arrangement:** Classified. **Pages** (approx.): 50. **Frequency:** Irregular; first edition 1978; new edition expected March 1980. **Price:** $4.95.

★1522★

WIND POWER DIGEST—WIND POWER ACCESS CATALOG ISSUE

Wind Power Digest
109 E. Lexington   Phone: (219) 294-2023
Bristol, IN 46514
Covers: Commercial wind energy equipment and systems. **Pages** (approx.): 40. **Frequency:** Irregular; latest edition winter 1979. **Price:** $2.00.

Wire Association International—Directory *See* Wire Journal—Directory/Catalog Issue

★1523★

WIRE JOURNAL—DIRECTORY/CATALOG ISSUE

Wire Journal, Inc.
Wire Association International
1570 Boston Post Road   Phone: (203) 453-2777
Guilford, CT 06437
Covers: Manufacturers and converters of steel and nonferrous bars, rods, strip, wire, and wire products, and electrical wire and cable (SIC 33). **Entries include:** Company name, address, phone, names of executives, trade and brand names, branch or distributor offices. **Arrangement:** Alphabetical. **Indexes:** Geographical. **Pages** (approx.): 380. **Frequency:** Annual, June. **Editor:** Barbara Chaffin. **Advertising accepted.** Circulation 11,000. **Price:** $10.00.

★1524★

WIRE TECHNOLOGY BUYERS' GUIDE

Wire Technology, Inc.
Box 480   Phone: (203) 325-2685
Stamford, CT 06904
Covers: About 2,000 suppliers of equipment and services, worldwide, to wire and wire products industry, including rod, bar, and wire companies and companies manufacturing products from these materials, producers of electric wire and cable, and makers of machinery, equipment, and supplies for the industry. **Entries include:** Company name, address, phone, name of principal executive, and list of products. **Arrangement:** Product classified. **Indexes:** Alphabetical, geographical. **Pages** (approx.): 500. **Frequency:** Annual, July. **Editor:** Richard J. Callahan. **Advertising accepted.** Circulation 5,000. **Price:** $10.00.

Wisconsin Manufacturers Directory *See* Classified Directory of Wisconsin Manufacturers

★1525★

WOMAN'S GUIDE TO HER OWN FRANCHISED BUSINESS

Pilot Books
347 Fifth Avenue   Phone: (212) 685-0736
New York, NY 10016
Publication includes: List of about 160 franchise opportunities in the fields of fast foods, accounting and tax services, health and beauty aids, candy stores, travel agencies, etc. **Entries include:** Company name, address, description of line of business, amount of investment required. **Arrangement:** By line of business. **Frequency:** Irregular; latest edition January 1979. **Author:** Anne Small and Robert S. Levy. **Price:** $2.50, plus 75¢ shipping.

★1526★

WOMEN & BUSINESS: A DIRECTORY OF WOMEN-OWNED BUSINESSES IN WASHINGTON, OREGON, IDAHO, AND ALASKA

General Services Administration
18th and F Streets   Phone: (202) 655-4000
Washington, DC 20405
Covers: About 1,000 firms specializing in services, transportation, manufacturing, retail and wholesale, and construction. **Entries include:** Firm name, address, product or service, name of owner or contact. **Arrangement:** Geographical. **Pages** (approx.): 65. **Frequency:** First edition 1979. **Price:** $3.50 (S/N 022-001-00078-7). **Send orders to:** Government Printing Office, Washington, DC 20402.

Women's & Children's Wear Buyers *See* Salesman's Guide Nationwide Directory: Women's & Children's Wear Buyers

Women's Specialty Stores [California] *See* Salesman's Guide: Women's Specialty Stores [California]

★1527★

WOOD & WOOD PRODUCTS—REFERENCE DATA/BUYING GUIDE ISSUE

Vance Publishing Corporation
300 W. Adams Street   Phone: (312) 346-7788
Chicago, IL 60606
Covers: 1,000 manufacturers and 190 dealers of machinery, equipment, and supplies for industrial woodworking applications; also lists forestry schools, wood industry consultants, trade associations. Includes some European listings. **Entries include:** For companies - Company name, address, phone. Other listings include school or other name, address, phone, contact; consultant listings include brief description. **Arrangement:** Manufacturers are alphabetical; dealers, schools, and consultants are geographical. **Indexes:** Product. **Frequency:** Annual, March. **Editor:** Russ Gager. **Advertising accepted.** Circulation 30,000. **Price:** $5.00 (current edition; tentative, 1980 edition).

★1528★

WOOD ENERGY

Garden Way Publishing
Charlotte, VT 05445
Covers: Manufacturers of wood stoves. **Entries include:** Manufacturer name, address; products; distributors' names and addresses; product catalog. **Pages** (approx.): 145. **Editor:** Mary Twitchell. **Price:** $7.95.

★1529★

WOODSTOVE DIRECTORY

Energy Communications Press
Box 4474   Phone: (603) 622-8206
Manchester, NH 03108
Covers: About 300 manufacturers of wood stoves, fireplaces, and wood furnaces and boilers; about 100 manufacturers of equipment and accessories for woodheat equipment; about 120 retailers of these products; and over 50 chimney sweeps. All listings are paid. **Entries include:** Company name, address, phone. Manufacturers' listings also include product specifications, price, description, and photograph. **Arrangement:** Manufacturers are alphabetical by name of product, others are geographical. **Indexes:** Advertisers (with address and phone). **Pages** (approx.): 210. **Frequency:** Annual, August. **Editor:** Clifford Martel, Jr. **Advertising accepted.** Circulation 200,000. **Price:** $2.00, plus 50¢ shipping.

★1530★

WOODWORKING & FURNITURE DIGEST—NEW PRODUCT REVIEW & BUYER'S GUIDE ISSUE

Hitchcock Publishing Company
25 W. 550 Geneva Road   Phone: (312) 665-1000
Wheaton, IL 60187
Covers: Suppliers of materials, machinery, tools, and services for

woodworking and furniture manufacturing processes (SIC 24, 25, 37, and 39). **Entries include:** Company name, address, phone, list of products or services. **Arrangement:** Alphabetical. **Indexes:** Product. **Frequency:** Biennial, August of odd years. **Editor:** Richard D. Rea, Editorial Director. **Advertising accepted.** Circulation 29,900. **Price:** $10.00.

★1531★

WOODWORKING MACHINERY DISTRIBUTORS' ASSOCIATION— MEMBERSHIP DIRECTORY AND BUYER'S GUIDE

Woodworking Machinery Distributors' Association
580 Shoemaker Road   Phone: (215) 265-6658
King of Prussia, PA 19406
Covers: About 100 firms specializing in sales of sawmill machinery, heavy-production woodworking machinery, and used woodworking machinery; also includes manufacturers of such machinery. **Entries include:** Company name, address, phone, names of principal executives, products. **Frequency:** Biennial, September of even years. **Price:** Free.

★1532★

WOODWORKING MACHINERY MANUFACTURERS OF AMERICA— BUYER'S GUIDE AND DIRECTORY

Woodworking Machinery Manufacturers of America
580 Shoemaker Road   Phone: (215) 265-6658
King of Prussia, PA 19406
Covers: More than 85 woodworking machinery and tool manufacturers making equipment to handle operations from green sawmills to furniture manufacture and finishing. **Entries include:** Company name, address, phone. **Arrangement:** Alphabetical. **Indexes:** Machine. **Pages** (approx.): 275. **Frequency:** Biennial, fall of even years. **Price:** Free. **Other information:** International Edition has listings in English, French, German, and Spanish.

Word Processing Industry Directory *See* **IWP Word Processing Industry Directory**

★1533★

WORK BOAT—BOATBUILDING ISSUE

H. L. Peace Publications
1700 N. Causeway Approach   Phone: (504) 626-3151
Mandeville, LA 70448
Publication includes: List of boatyards in the United States. **Entries include:** Company name, address, types of boats manufactured, additional services available, particular items manufactured for sale, and if dry dock facilities are available. **Arrangement:** By water bodies (Pacific Coast, etc.). **Frequency:** Annual, December. **Advertising accepted.** Circulation 12,000. **Price:** $3.00.

★1534★

WORKING PRESS OF THE NATION

National Research Bureau
424 N. Third Street   Phone: (319) 752-5415
Burlington, IA 52601
Covers: In separate volumes, over 6,100 daily and weekly newspapers; 13,600 radio and television stations; 4,800 magazines; 2,550 syndicates, feature writers, and photographers; and 3,500 internal house organs. **Entries include:** All listings include name of publication or station, address, phone, names of executives, editors, writers, talk show hosts, etc., as appropriate. Broadcasting and magazine volumes include data on kinds of material needed. Technical and mechanical requirements for publications are given. **Arrangement:** Magazines classified by audience; newspapers and broadcasting stations are geographical. **Frequency:** Annual, January. **Price:** Set, $198.00; The Newspaper Directory (Volume 1 of set), $71.00; The Magazine Directory (Volume 2), $71.00; The TV and Radio Directory (Volume 3), $71.00; Feature Writers, Photographers, and Syndicates (Volume 4), $71.00; Internal Publications Directory (Volume 5), $71.00; (1980 editions). **Other information:** "Internal Publications Directory" was formerly published separately as "Gebbie House Magazine Directory."

★1535★

WORLD AVIATION DIRECTORY

Ziff-Davis Publishing Company
1156 15th Street   Phone: (202) 293-3400
Washington, DC 20005
Covers: Aviation, aerospace, and missile manufacturers, including manufacturers of aircraft, spacecraft, piston and jet engines, and component manufacturers and major subcontractors; support services (fuel companies, repair stations, etc.); airports and heliports; airlines; government agencies and associations; airline caterers; air freight companies; international scope. **Entries include:** Company or organization name, address, phone, numerous executives' names; manufacturer and supplier listings also show products; airline listings also show number of employees and number and type of equipment. **Arrangement:** Classified by major activity (manufacturers, airlines, etc.). **Indexes:** Company and organization, personnel, product. **Pages** (approx.): 1,800. **Frequency:** Semiannual, March and September. **Editor:** Marjorie S. Fingeret. **Advertising accepted.** Circulation 12,000. **Price:** $50.00.

★1536★

WORLD CEMENT DIRECTORY

Cembureau
2, rue Saint-Charles
75740 Paris Cedex 15, France
Covers: Manufacturers of cement and cement products in 140 countries; institutes and associations concerned with information and research in the fields of cement and concrete are also included. **Entries include:** Company name, address, location of plants, type and number of kilns, fuel used, production and capacity, cement types produced, brand names, and number of employees. **Arrangement:** Geographical. **Frequency:** Annual. **Price:** 250 French Francs. **Other information:** Cembureau is the European cement industry trade association.

★1537★

WORLD COFFEE & TEA—RED BOOK ISSUE

McKeand Publications, Inc.
636 First Avenue   Phone: (203) 934-5288
West Haven, CT 06516
Covers: Manufacturers and suppliers of equipment to the office coffee service industry. **Entries include:** Company name, address, phone, sales offices, and a description of products and services. **Pages** (approx.): 100. **Frequency:** Annual, July. **Editor:** David H. McKeand, President. **Advertising accepted.** Circulation 9,100. **Price:** $5.00.

★1538★

WORLD CONVENTION DATES

Hendrickson Publishing Company, Inc.
79 Washington Street   Phone: (516) 483-6881
Hempstead, NY 11550
Covers: 13,300 meetings of international, national, regional, state, and district organizations, up to 10 years in advance of meeting dates. **Entries include:** Name of sponsoring organization; name, title, and address of person in charge of event; dates; site; expected attendance; scope of event (whether international, national, regional, state, or district); if event includes banquet or exhibits; headquarters hotel or other location. **Arrangement:** Geographical directory arranged according to location of event is published in January with a July update; directory classified according to major interest (medicine, insurance, science, etc.), the "Generic Directory," published in September; the "Event Planners Guide" (covering suppliers of products, facilities, and services to conventions), in four regional volumes, published in December. **Editor:** Jane Hendrickson Winter. **Advertising accepted.** Circulation 12,000. **Price:** January issue, $10.00; July update, $2.50; September issue, $20.00; December issue, $25.00.

★1539★
WORLD DIRECTORY OF FOOD AND DRINK MANUFACTURING COMPANIES
Eurofood
60 Kingly Street
London W 1R 5LH, England
Covers: 2,000 companies engaged in production of food and beverages, including meat processing, milling, baking, bottling, etc.; covers 78 countries. **Entries include:** Company name, address, names of principal executives, major lines of business, brands, subsidiary and associated companies, financial data, current corporate developments, and major shareholders. **Arrangement:** Geographical. **Indexes:** Company name, brand. **Pages** (approx.): 800. **Frequency:** Not established; first edition early 1979. **Price:** 50 pounds. **Also includes:** Statistical data on individual countries and the industry as a whole.

★1540★
WORLD DREDGING AND MARINE CONSTRUCTION—ANNUAL DIRECTORY OF WORLD'S DREDGES AND SUPPLIERS ISSUE
Symcon Publishing Company, Division
Symcon Marine Corporation
Box 31   Phone: (213) 432-6911
Long Beach, CA 90801
Covers: Owners of 2,600 dredges used worldwide, and of dredging industry suppliers. **Entries include:** For dredge owners - Owner name and address, name, size, horsepower and type of dredges owned, history of firm. For suppliers - Company name, address, types of products. **Arrangement:** Owners are geographical, suppliers are alphabetical. **Indexes:** Product. **Pages** (approx.): 80. **Frequency:** Annual, February. **Editor:** Judith Powers. **Advertising accepted.** Circulation 9,200. **Former title:** World Dredging and Marine Construction - The World's Dredges and Their Owners Issue. **Price:** $6.00 (current and 1980 editions).

★1541★
WORLD OF FASHION
R. R. Bowker Company
1180 Avenue of the Americas   Phone: (212) 764-5100
New York, NY 10036
Covers: Trade associations, organizations, fashion schools, museums with fashion collections and archives, fashion publishers, and leading fashion designers or firms; international coverage. **Indexes:** Subject/ personal name. **Pages** (approx.): 390. **Frequency:** Irregular; latest edition 1979. **Editor:** Eleanor Lambert. **Price:** $19.95, postpaid, payment with order. **Send orders to:** R. R. Bowker Co., Box 1807, Ann Arbor, MI 48106 (313-761-4700).

World Space Directory *See* **World Aviation Directory**

★1542★
WORLD TRADE CENTERS ASSOCIATION—DIRECTORY
World Trade Centers Association
One World Trade Center, 63W   Phone: (212) 466-8380
New York, NY 10048
Covers: 100 existing or developing centers devoted to increase of international trade, worldwide. **Entries include:** Name, address, phone number, telex, cable, executive officer. **Indexes:** Alphabetical, geographical, institutional. **Pages** (approx.): 10. **Frequency:** Semiannual, January and July. **Editor:** S. Alex Baker, Administrative Assistant. **Price:** Free.

★1543★
WORLD TRADE DIRECTORY [San Diego County, California]
San Diego Chamber of Commerce
110 C Street, Suite 1600   Phone: (714) 232-0124
San Diego, CA 92101
Covers: About 600 San Diego county companies involved in international trade. **Entries include:** Company name, address, line of business, countries with which involved. **Arrangement:** Alphabetical. **Frequency:** Irregular; previous edition 1975; latest edition fall 1978.

Price: $7.50.

World Travel Directory *See* **Travel Weekly's World Travel Directory**

★1544★
WORLD WIDE CHAMBER OF COMMERCE DIRECTORY
Johnson Publishing Company, Inc.
Eighth And Van Buren Streets   Phone: (303) 667-0652
Loveland, CO 80537
Covers: Chambers of commerce, or, in many cases, city offices or other local contacts, in about 7,750 localities in the United States and 275 localities abroad; American chambers of commerce abroad; foreign diplomatic offices in the United States and American offices abroad. **Entries include:** Chamber or other organization name, name of executive, address, phone, population. Foreign chambers' listings usually contain generic designation only, address, and population. Diplomatic office listings show address, phone, contact, national holidays. **Pages** (approx.): 250. **Frequency:** Annual, July. **Editor:** Jeane Buckley. **Price:** $12.00.

★1545★
WORLD WIDE SHIPPING GUIDE
World Wide Shipping Guide, Inc.
77 Moehring Drive   Phone: (914) 359-1934
Blauvelt, NY 10913
Covers: About 1,500 world ports and 45,000 firms servicing the import and export markets through the ports; published in two volumes, a United States edition and an international edition. **Entries include:** Company name, address, phone, telex, and services; some listings include names of executives. **Arrangement:** Geographical. **Pages** (approx.): 1,300. **Frequency:** Annual, February. **Editor:** Lee di Paci. **Advertising accepted.** **Price:** $30.00, payment with order; $35.00, billed. **Also includes:** In United States edition, a list of steamship conferences and a glossary.

★1546★
WORLDWIDE PETROCHEMICAL DIRECTORY
Petroleum Publishing Company
Box 1260   Phone: (918) 835-3161
Tulsa, OK 74101
Covers: More than 2,400 petrochemical plants; separate section on new construction; worldwide coverage. **Entries include:** Company name, address, phone, plant addresses and phones, key personnel; feedstocks, products, and capacities given in separate list; new plant listings include contractors, estimated costs, completion dates. **Arrangement:** Geographical. **Indexes:** Company, personal name. **Pages** (approx.): 275. **Frequency:** Annual, November. **Price:** $40.00.

Writing Instrument Manufacturers Association—Directory *See* **Directory of Manufacturers and Products of the Handwriting and Marking...**

★1547★
WYOMING DIRECTORY OF MANUFACTURING AND MINING
Wyoming Department of Economic Planning and Development
Barrett Building   Phone: (307) 777-7284
Cheyenne, WY 82002
Number of listings: 1,250. **Entries include:** Company name, address, phone, name of principal executive, products, SIC numbers. **Arrangement:** By SIC numbers. **Indexes:** Alphabetical, geographical, product. **Pages** (approx.): 120. **Frequency:** Annual, November. **Price:** $3.00.

★1548★
YAKIMA MANUFACTURERS' DIRECTORY [Washington State]
Greater Yakima Chamber of Commerce
410 E. Yakima Avenue   Phone: (509) 248-2021
Yakima, WA 98907
Covers: 450 manufacturing firms in the Yakima Valley. **Entries include:** Name of firm, year established, address, name of principal

executive, product, and number of employees. **Arrangement:** Classified by type of manufacturing. **Pages** (approx.): 50. **Frequency:** Irregular; latest edition September 1979. **Price:** 15.00.

★1549★
YELLOW BOOK OF FUNERAL DIRECTORS AND SERVICES
Nomis Publications, Inc.
Box 5122   Phone: (216) 757-3961
Youngstown, OH 44514
Covers: 23,000 United States and Canadian funeral homes; Veteran's Administration hospitals, cemeteries, and regional offices; major hospitals; foreign consulates and branch offices; daily papers; mortuary colleges. **Entries include:** Name of home, address, phone, code for shipping points, code for daily papers available for obituaries. **Arrangement:** By type of business, then geographical. **Pages** (approx.): 600. **Frequency:** Annual, October. **Editor:** Chester E. Simon, Owner and Publisher. **Advertising accepted.** Circulation 6,000. **Price:** $25.00. **Also includes:** State regulations concerning shipment of human remains. **Other information:** Cover title, "National Yellow Book of Funeral Directors and Services."

★1550★
**YELLOW PAGES OF INSTRUMENTATION, EQUIPMENT, AND
     SUPPLIES**
Technical Publishing Company
1301 S. Grove Avenue   Phone: (312) 381-1840
Barrington, IL 60010
Covers: About 950 manufacturers, distributors, and suppliers of products and equipment to the instrumentation industry. **Entries include:** Company name, address, and phone. **Arrangement:** By company name and product; identical data in each section. **Frequency:** Annual, January. **Advertising accepted.** Circulation 100,000. **Price:** $15.00 (1980 edition; ISSN 0160-4074). **Other information:** Published as a thirteenth issue of "Industrial Research/ Development."

★1551★
YORK COUNTY INDUSTRIAL DIRECTORY [Pennsylvania]
York Area Chamber of Commerce
13 E. Market Street   Phone: (717) 854-3814
York, PA 17405
Entries include: Company name, address, phone, name of principal executive, and number of employees. **Arrangement:** Alphabetical. **Indexes:** Product. **Pages** (approx.): 55. **Frequency:** Annual, spring. **Former title:** Manufacturer's Directory of York and York County (1975); Industrial Directory of York and York County (1979). **Price:** $3.88, postpaid.

★1552★
ZIP/AREA CODE DIRECTORY
Pilot Books
347 Fifth Avenue   Phone: (212) 685-0736
New York, NY 10016
Description: Arranges telephone area codes according to corresponding postal Zip codes. **Arrangement:** Geographical, then Zip code. **Frequency:** First edition published 1979. **Editor:** Ruthie Marks. **Price:** $2.95.

2

Banking, Finance,

Insurance and Real Estate

★1553★
ABA BANKING JOURNAL—BANKER'S GUIDE TO WASHINGTON ISSUE
Simmons-Boardman Publishing Corporation
350 Broadway   Phone: (212) 966-7700
New York, NY 10013
Covers: Federal agencies, offices, and organizations concerned with banking and located in Washington, DC. **Entries include:** Organization or agency name, address, phone; name of contact; services or interests. **Arrangement:** By type of organization. **Frequency:** Annual, January. **Advertising accepted.** Circulation 40,300. **Price:** $1.00.

★1554★
ACCOUNTING FIRMS & PRACTITIONERS
American Institute of Certified Public Accountants
1211 Avenue of the Americas   Phone: (212) 575-6200
New York, NY 10036
Covers: About 25,000 certified public accounting firms having one or more principals belonging to the institute, and individual practitioners who are members. **Entries include:** Name, address. **Arrangement:** Geographical. **Frequency:** Biennial, January of odd years. **Price:** Free; available to members, banks, and libraries only.

Active Registered Investment Companies *See* Index of Active Registered Investment Companies

★1555★
AGENT'S AND BUYER'S GUIDE [Insurance]
National Underwriter Company
420 E. Fourth Street   Phone: (513) 721-2140
Cincinnati, OH 45202
Publication includes: List of companies writing specialty line insurance policies; underwriting groups; and offices offering service on special lines of property and casualty insurance. **Entries include:** For companies - Company name, address, coverages included or handled. For underwriting groups - Firm name, address. For offices - Firm name, affiliation, address, lines handled. **Arrangement:** Alphabetical within types of activity. **Frequency:** Annual, March. **Editor:** Jean M. Freels, Chief Compiler. **Advertising accepted. Price:** $9.50.

★1556★
THE AIRPORT CITY
Conway Publications, Inc.
Peachtree Air Terminal
1954 Airport Road   Phone: (404) 458-6026
Atlanta, GA 30341
Publication includes: List of about 500 fly-in developments in the Western Hemisphere. **Entries include:** Name of development, name

of developer, address, length of runway, services offered. **Arrangement:** Geographical. **Pages** (approx.): 200. **Frequency:** Published 1977. **Author:** H. M. Conway, President. **Price:** $35.00.

★1557★
AMERICAN ASSOCIATION OF MINORITY ENTERPRISE SMALL BUSINESS INVESTMENT COMPANIES—MEMBERSHIP DIRECTORY
American Association of Minority Enterprise Small Business
    Investment Companies
915 15th Street, N. W.   Phone: (202) 347-8600
Washington, DC 20005
Covers: About 115 venture capital firms for minority small businesses. **Entries include:** Company name, address, phone, chief executive. **Arrangement:** Geographical. **Pages** (approx.): 20. **Frequency:** Annual, summer. **Editor:** Thomas M. Kirlin, Director, Public Relations. **Price:** Apply; controlled circulation.

★1558★
AMERICAN ASSOCIATION OF SPANISH-SPEAKING CERTIFIED PUBLIC ACCOUNTANTS—MEMBERSHIP DIRECTORY
American Association of Spanish-Speaking Certified Public
    Accountants
1010 S. Flower Street   Phone: (213) 385-2136
Los Angeles, CA 90015
Number of listings: 200. **Entries include:** Member name, address, phone, professional and biographical data, photo. **Arrangement:** Alphabetical. **Indexes:** Geographical. **Frequency:** Irregular; latest edition 1977; new edition expected 1981. **Price:** $25.00.

★1559★
AMERICAN BANK DIRECTORY
McFadden Business Publications
6364 Warren Drive   Phone: (404) 448-1011
Norcross, GA 30093
Covers: Over 14,800 banks and registered multi-bank holding companies, nationwide; also published in editions for individual states. **Entries include:** Bank name, address (including county, Federal Reserve District), phone, year established, transit number, officers and directors, condensed statement of condition, principal correspondents, population. **Arrangement:** Geographical. **Frequency:** Semiannual, May and November. **Editor:** Mary W. Little. **Price:** $60.00, single issue of national edition; $8.00 for single state edition; $4.00 for each additional state in same binder; prices do not include shipping.

★1560★
AMERICAN BANKER—500 LARGEST FREE WORLD BANKS
American Banker, Inc.
525 W. 42nd Street   Phone: (212) 563-1900
New York, NY 10036
Covers: 500 largest banks in non-communist world; also includes "Overseas Banks Ranked after the First 500" and "Compilation of Foreign Bank Activities in the United States." **Entries include:** Bank name, headquarters, rank, and amount of deposits for two previous years. Section on foreign bank activities in the United States lists geographically foreign banks with branches or agencies in the United States, and subsidiaries and securities companies in which they have an interest. **Arrangement:** Ranked by deposits. **Indexes:** Geographic listing of largest banks outside United States. **Frequency:** Annual, fall. **Editor:** W. C. Rappleye. **Advertising accepted.** Circulation 16,350. **Price:** $6.00. **Other information:** Reprinted from a July issue of "American Banker."

★1561★
AMERICAN BANKER—INTERNATIONAL ACTIVITIES OF U.S.
    BANKS ISSUE
American Banker, Inc.
525 W. 42nd Street   Phone: (212) 563-1900
New York, NY 10036
Covers: Over 300 United States banks active in international banking and finance services. **Entries include:** Bank name, name of parent company (if any), statement of international banking policy, correspondent banking relationships, locations of banking representation abroad. **Arrangement:** Geographical (state and city of United States office). **Indexes:** Geographical (countries in which active). **Pages** (approx.): 70. **Frequency:** Biennial, even years, in a March issue. **Editor:** W. C. Rappleye. **Advertising accepted.** Circulation 16,350.

★1562★
AMERICAN BANKER—LARGEST MUTUAL SAVINGS BANKS ISSUE
American Banker, Inc.
525 W. 42nd Street   Phone: (212) 563-1900
New York, NY 10036
Covers: 100 largest United States mutual savings banks and 300 largest worldwide. **Entries include:** Bank name, headquarters city, rank; total assets and deposits on January 1 of current and preceding year; number of accounts at beginning of current year; range of interest rates paid at beginning of current and preceding year. **Arrangement:** Ranked by deposits. **Frequency:** Annual. **Editor:** W. C. Rappleye. **Advertising accepted.** Circulation 16,350. **Price:** $3.00.

★1563★
AMERICAN BANKER—100 LARGEST CREDIT UNIONS IN THE U.S.
    ISSUE
American Banker, Inc.
525 W. 42nd Street   Phone: (212) 563-1900
New York, NY 10036
Entries include: Credit union name, headquarters location, rank; total assets for current year and 18 months prior; prior period's rank and gain in rank; total member savings; share drafts; number of regular share accounts; number of share draft accounts; dividend rate. **Arrangement:** Ranked by total assets. **Frequency:** Latest edition September 1978. **Editor:** W. C. Rappleye. **Advertising accepted.** Circulation 16,350. **Price:** $2.00.

★1564★
AMERICAN BANKER—100 LARGEST DOMESTIC BANK HOLDING
    COMPANY SYSTEMS ISSUE
American Banker, Inc.
525 W. 42nd Street   Phone: (212) 563-1900
New York, NY 10036
Entries include: Name of bank holding company, headquarters location; name of largest controlled bank in deposits, city; rank; total assets for current and prior year; prior year's rank and gain in rank; total deposits for current and prior year; number of controlled banks

and number of branches. **Arrangement:** Ranked by total current year's assets. **Frequency:** Latest edition June 1978. **Editor:** W. C. Rappleye. **Advertising accepted.** Circulation 16,350. **Price:** $3.00. **Other information:** Reprinted from June 1978 issue of "American Banker."

★1565★
AMERICAN BANKER—100 LARGEST FINANCE COMPANIES
American Banker, Inc.
525 W. 42nd Street   Phone: (212) 563-1900
New York, NY 10036
Entries include: Finance company name, headquarters, city, rank; total capital funds for two preceding years; capital and surplus, assets, receivables net, net income, deferred income, receivables acquired, and amount of bank credit at end of the preceding year. **Arrangement:** Ranked by size of capital funds. **Frequency:** Annual, summer. **Editor:** W. C. Rappleye. **Advertising accepted.** Circulation 16,350. **Price:** $2.00. **Other information:** Also includes similar listings of 100 largest independent or affiliated finance companies, 48 largest captive finance companies, and 58 finance companies below top 100. Reprinted from a June issue of "American Banker."

★1566★
AMERICAN BANKER—100 LARGEST REAL ESTATE INVESTMENT
    TRUSTS ISSUE
American Banker, Inc.
525 W. 42nd Street   Phone: (212) 563-1900
New York, NY 10036
Entries include: Trust name, headquarters location, rank; name and location of adviser; total assets for current and prior year; prior year's rank and places gained; total amount of loans and investments, loans, debt; reserve for loss; share equity; date of figures. **Arrangement:** Ranked by total assets. **Frequency:** Latest edition October 1977. **Editor:** W. C. Rappleye. **Advertising accepted.** Circulation 16,350. **Price:** $2.00. **Other information:** Reprinted from October 14, 1977 issue of "American Banker."

★1567★
AMERICAN BANKER—300 LARGEST MORTGAGE BANKING FIRMS
    AND 100 LARGEST COMMERCIAL BANKS IN SERVICING OF
    PERMANENT MORTGAGES ISSUE
American Banker, Inc.
525 W. 42nd Street   Phone: (212) 563-1900
New York, NY 10036
Entries include: For mortgage companies - Company name, headquarters city, rank; dollar value of mortgages serviced for current and prior year; prior year's rank and gain in rank; number of mortgages; number of investors. For commerical banks - Company name, headquarters city, rank; total dollar volume and number of mortgages serviced for investors; number of investors; prior year's rank and gain in rank; total dollar value of mortgages serviced; dollar value of mortgages owned by bank. **Arrangement:** Mortgage companies are ranked by total dollar value of mortgages serviced and commercial banks are ranked by total dollar value of mortgages serviced for investors. **Frequency:** Latest edition 1978. **Editor:** W. C. Rappleye. **Advertising accepted.** Circulation 16,350. **Price:** $2.50. **Other information:** Reprinted from a 1978 issue of "American Banker."

★1568★
AMERICAN BANKER—300 LARGEST SAVINGS AND LOAN
    ASSOCIATIONS ISSUE
American Banker, Inc.
525 W. 42nd Street   Phone: (212) 563-1900
New York, NY 10036
Entries include: Association name, city, rank; total assets, deposits, and number of accounts at end of two preceding six-month periods; range of interest rates for new accounts for same period. **Arrangement:** Ranked by deposits. **Frequency:** Semiannual, spring and fall. **Editor:** W. C. Rappleye. **Advertising accepted.** Circulation 16,350. **Price:** $2.00. **Other information:** Reprinted from a

February and an August issue of "American Banker."

★1569★
AMERICAN BANKER—300 LARGEST U.S. COMMERCIAL BANKS ISSUE
American Banker, Inc.
525 W. 42nd Street   Phone: (212) 563-1900
New York, NY 10036
Entries include: Bank name, headquarters, rank and amount of deposits at preceding June 30 and at end of two previous six-month periods. **Arrangement:** Ranked by deposits. **Frequency:** Annual, February. **Advertising accepted.** Circulation 16,350. **Price:** $5.00. **Other information:** Reprinted from a February issue of "American Banker."

American Banker Directory and Guide to the Largest U.S. Banks
   See American Banker Guide to the First 5,000 U.S. Banks

★1570★
AMERICAN BANKER GUIDE TO THE FIRST 5,000 U.S. BANKS
American Banker, Inc.
525 W. 42nd Street   Phone: (212) 563-1900
New York, NY 10036
Number of listings: 4,500. **Entries include:** Bank name, city, position in list and deposits in two most recent full years. **Arrangement:** Geographical, size of deposit. **Indexes:** Deposit order. **Frequency:** Annual, June. **Former title:** American Banker Directory and Guide to the Largest U.S. Banks With Deposits Over $25 Million. **Price:** $12.00. **Other information:** Reprinted from a March issue of "American Banker."

★1571★
AMERICAN BANKERS ASSOCIATION KEY TO ROUTING NUMBERS
Rand McNally & Company
8255 N. Central Park Avenue   Phone: (312) 673-9100
Skokie, IL 60076
Covers: All financial institutions in the United States and their routing numbers. **Entries include:** Institution name, location, routing number. **Arrangement:** By routing number, geographical. **Frequency:** Annual, July; supplements are issued. **Editor:** Edward C. McNally, Vice President, Bank Publications Division. **Price:** $25.00, including supplements.

★1572★
AMERICAN INDUSTRIAL PROPERTIES REPORT—OFFICE/ INDUSTRIAL SITE SEEKERS' DIRECTORY ISSUE
Indprop Publishing Company, Inc.
74 Shrewsbury Avenue   Phone: (201) 842-7433
Red Bank, NJ 07701
Covers: About 3,000 state, county, local, railroad, port, utility, and other offices concerned with influencing business and industry to locate within their areas; includes Canada. **Entries include:** Name of agency, address, phone, name and title of contact. **Arrangement:** Geographical, then by office sponsor - state, railroad, utility, etc. **Frequency:** Annual, March. **Editor:** Gary Stasse. **Advertising accepted.** Circulation 43,000 (directory issue only). **Price:** $10.00 (current and 1980 editions). **Also includes:** Lists of literature and feasibility studies available on each area, with reader service card number, but without address (or, sometimes name) of publisher.

★1573★
AMERICAN INSTITUTE OF CERTIFIED PUBLIC ACCOUNTANTS— LIST OF MEMBERS
American Institute of Certified Public Accountants
1211 Avenue of the Americas   Phone: (212) 575-6200
New York, NY 10036
Covers: About 130,000 individual certified public accountants who are members of the institute; international coverage. **Entries include:** Name, address, firm or affiliation, year of admission; asterisk indicates whether practicing public accounting as a partner, shareholder, or individual; if not in public practice, title is given.

Arrangement: Alphabetical. **Frequency:** Annual, July. **Price:** $12.50; available to members, banks, and libraries only. **Other information:** Cover title, "AICPA List of Members."

★1574★
AMERICAN INSTITUTE OF REAL ESTATE APPRAISERS— DIRECTORY OF MEMBERS
American Institute of Real Estate Appraisers
430 N. Michigan Avenue   Phone: (312) 440-8141
Chicago, IL 60611
Number of listings: 7,000. **Entries include:** Name, office address and phone, home address and phone. **Arrangement:** Geographical. **Indexes:** Alphabetical. **Pages** (approx.): 230. **Frequency:** Annual, January. **Editor:** Douglas McDonough, Director of Public Relations. **Price:** Free.

★1575★
AMERICAN SAVINGS AND LOAN LEAGUE—MEMBERSHIP ROSTER
American Savings and Loan League
1435 G Street, N. W., Suite 1019   Phone: (202) 628-5624
Washington, DC 20005
Covers: About 80 minority savings and loan associations in 24 states and the District of Columbia. **Entries include:** Association name, address, phone, name of principal executive. **Arrangement:** Geographical. **Pages** (approx.): 5. **Frequency:** Irregular; latest edition December 1977. **Editor:** French F. Stone. **Former title:** Directory of Minority Owned Savings and Loan institutions. **Price:** Free.

★1576★
AMERICAN SOCIETY OF REAL ESTATE COUNSELORS— DIRECTORY
American Society of Real Estate Counselors
430 N. Michigan Avenue   Phone: (312) 440-8093
Chicago, IL 60611
Number of listings: About 450. **Entries include:** Name, office address and phone, home address and phone, areas of counseling specialty. **Arrangement:** Geographical. **Indexes:** Alphabetical. **Pages** (approx.): 80. **Frequency:** Annual, midwinter. **Editor:** Lois Hofstetter, Executive Director. **Price:** $1.00 (current and 1980 editions).

Associate Mercantile Market—Membership List *See* Chicago
   Mercantile Exchange—Membership List

Association of Bank Holding Companies *See* Rand McNally
   International Bankers Directory

★1577★
BANK DIRECTORY OF NEW ENGLAND
Shawmut Bank of Boston, N. A.
One Federal Street   Phone: (617) 292-3767
Boston, MA 02211
Covers: Commercial and mutual savings banks in the New England states. **Entries include:** Name of bank, address, phone, officers, board of directors, correspondent banks, and financial information. **Arrangement:** Geographical. **Pages** (approx.): 600. **Frequency:** Annual, May. **Editor:** Lincoln E. Barber, Jr., Vice President. **Price:** $10.00 (current and 1980 editions).

Bank Directory of the Ninth Federal Reserve District *See* Bank
   Directory of the Upper Midwest

★1578★
BANK DIRECTORY OF THE UPPER MIDWEST
Financial Communications, Inc.
5100 Edina Industrial Boulevard   Phone: (612) 835-5853
Edina, MN 55435
Covers: Minnesota, North Dakota, South Dakota, Montana, northwestern Wisconsin and upper Michigan, and Wyoming. **Entries**

include: Name of bank, main office and branch addresses, phone, principal executives, financial data, banking hours, date founded, transit number, county. **Arrangement:** Geographical. **Pages** (approx.): 580. **Frequency:** Annual, early spring. **Advertising accepted.** Circulation 5,000. **Former title:** Commercial West Bank Directory of the Ninth Federal Reserve District. **Price:** $25.00 (current and 1980 editions). **Other information:** Variant title, "Bank Directory of the Ninth Federal Reserve District."

★1579★
BANK SYSTEMS AND EQUIPMENT—DIRECTORY ISSUE
Gralla Publications
1515 Broadway   Phone: (212) 869-1300
New York, NY 10036
Covers: More than 1,800 manufacturers, distributors, and other suppliers of equipment and materials to the banking industry. **Entries include:** Company name, address; names of executives and product descriptions are given for over 400 companies. **Arrangement:** Alphabetical. **Indexes:** Product. **Pages** (approx.): 250. **Frequency:** Annual, January. **Editor:** Joan Prevete Hyman. **Advertising accepted.** Circulation 22,000. **Price:** $3.00 (current and 1980 editions).

Banker's Handbook of Federal Aids to Financing *See* Handbook of Federal Assistance: Financing, Grants, Technical Aids

★1580★
BANKERS MONTHLY—ROSTER OF MAJOR FINANCE COMPANIES ISSUE
Bankers Monthly, Inc.
601 Skokie Boulevard   Phone: (312) 498-2580
Northbrook, IL 60062
Publication includes: List of leading finance companies in terms of total capital funds. **Entries include:** Company name, location, total capital funds for two years, various other financial data. **Arrangement:** By total capital funds. **Frequency:** Annual, May 15 issue. **Editor:** Alvin M. Youngpriest, Jr. **Advertising accepted.** **Price:** $1.50, payment with order.

★1581★
BANKERS SCHOOLS DIRECTORY
Bank Personnel Division
American Bankers Association
1120 Connecticut Ave., N. W.
Washington, DC 20036
Covers: Industry training programs only, and distribution is restricted.

★1582★
BEST'S AGENTS GUIDE TO LIFE INSURANCE COMPANIES
A. M. Best Company
Ambest Road   Phone: (201) 439-2200
Oldwick, NJ 08858
Number of listings: 1,300. **Entries include:** Company name, address, names of president and secretary, phone, states where licensed, Best's policyholders' rating, current and historical financial data. Also includes lists of state insurance commissions and life insurance companies ranked by assets and insurance in force. **Arrangement:** Alphabetical. **Pages** (approx.): 1,200. **Frequency:** Annual, July. **Editor:** C. Burton Kellogg, Vice President. **Price:** $15.00.

★1583★
BEST'S REVIEW: PROPERTY/CASUALTY INSURANCE EDITION— 100 LEADING COMPANIES ISSUE
A. M. Best Company
Ambest Road   Phone: (201) 439-2200
Oldwick, NJ 08858
Entries include: Company name, rank by total premiums in property and casualty business, and other financial data. **Arrangement:** By total property and casualty premiums. **Frequency:** Annual, June. **Editor:** John C. Burridge. **Advertising accepted.** **Price:** $2.00.

★1584★
BLACK'S GUIDE [To available office space]
Black's Guide, Inc.
Box 2090   Phone: (201) 842-6060
Red Bank, NJ 07701
Covers: Office space available in buildings and developments; separate issues for New York metro area, Philadelphia-South Jersey area, and Baltimore-Washington area. **Entries include:** Building name, address, name and phone number of rental agent, and size, approximate rental, and availability of space. Each listing keyed by number on area map. **Arrangement:** Geographical. **Pages** (approx.): 300. **Frequency:** Annual; New York edition in January, Philadelphia-South Jersey in May, and Baltimore-Washington in August. **Advertising accepted.** Circulation 15,000. **Price:** $25.00 per edition (current and 1980 editions).

Blue Book *See* Western Bank Directory

★1585★
BLUE BOOK OF ADJUSTERS [Insurance adjusters]
National Association of Independent Insurance Adjusters
175 W. Jackson Boulevard
Chicago, IL 60604
Covers: About 450 independent insurance adjuster offices in the United States. **Entries include:** Name of firm, address, phone, areas of expertise. **Arrangement:** Geographical. **Frequency:** Annual. **Price:** Apply; restricted circulation. **Also includes:** Names of officers with areas of jurisdiction, association committee personnel, members of National Advisory Council.

★1586★
BLUE BOOK OF PENSION FUNDS
Insurance Research, Inc.
515 National Press Building   Phone: (202) 638-1984
Washington, DC 20045
Covers: Companies or groups which have at least one defined benefit pension plan with 100 or more plan participants and $1,000,000 or more in total assets. If the same company or group has other plans of lesser size (including defined contribution plans), these are also listed. **Entries include:** Name of plan or fund; name of plan administrator, phone; effective date of plan; type of defined benefit plan; number of participants; number of employees; SIC code; names and addresses of bank, trustees, actuary, accountant, investment managers, and others providing service to the plan; date of last evaluation; actuarial and financial data. **Arrangement:** Geographical within seven regional volumes for New England, mid-Atlantic, southeastern, south-central, midwestern, southwestern and mountain, and western states. **Frequency:** First edition expected April, 1980; annual, spring, thereafter. **Price:** $365.00 per set; regional volumes range from $70.00 to $150.00.

Bond Buyer's Directory of Municipal Bond Dealers of the United States *See* Directory of Municipal Bond Dealers of the United States

★1587★
BRANCH DIRECTORY AND SUMMARY OF DEPOSITS [Banking]
Decision Research Sciences, Inc.
300 Axewood East   Phone: (215) 542-9550
Ambler, PA 19002
Description: In separate state editions, lists all known banks, federally insured credit unions, and savings and loan associations within the state. Editions for Alabama, Arizona, Arkansas, California, Delaware, District of Columbia, Georgia, Idaho, Indiana, Kentucky, Louisiana, Maine, Maryland, Massachusetts, Michigan, Mississippi, Nevada, New Hampshire, New Jersey, New Mexico, New York, North Carolina, Ohio, Oregon, Pennsylvania, Rhode Island, South Carolina, Tennessee, Utah, Vermont, Virginia, Washington. **Entries include:** Full institution name and address, deposit data, by branches and type (demand, etc.), and amount of change from previous period. **Arrangement:** Geographical; also an alphabetical listing of banks only with information similar to

that in geographical section. **Pages** (approx.): Varies. **Frequency:** Annual, March. **Price:** $210.00 per state volume.

★1588★
BRONX APARTMENT OWNERS DIRECTORY [New York City]
Standard Abstract Corporation
132 Nassau Street   Phone: (212) 732-0225
New York, NY 10038
Number of listings: 5,000. **Entries include:** Owner name, address of business, phone, and list of apartment properties owned or controlled by individual. **Arrangement:** By street and address, and alphabetical by owner name. **Pages** (approx.): 500. **Frequency:** Annual, spring. **Editor:** B. Scheckner, President. **Advertising accepted. Price:** $70.00 (current and 1980 editions).

★1589★
BROOKLYN APARTMENT OWNERS DIRECTORY [New York City]
Standard Abstract Corporation
132 Nassau Street   Phone: (212) 732-0225
New York, NY 10038
Number of listings: 5,000. **Entries include:** Owner name, address of office, phone, and list of properties owned or controlled by individual. **Arrangement:** By street and address, and alphabetical by owner name. **Pages** (approx.): 400. **Frequency:** Annual, March, with cumulative quarterly supplements. **Editor:** B. Scheckner, President. **Advertising accepted. Price:** $70.00 (current and 1980 editions).

★1590★
BUSINESS CAPITAL SOURCES
International Wealth Success, Inc.
24 Canterbury Road
Rockville Centre, NY 11570
Covers: Over 1,500 sources of loans of capital for business and real estate uses. **Entries include:** Lender name, address, requirements or restrictions on loan. **Arrangement:** Geographical. **Pages** (approx.): 150. **Frequency:** Semiannual, January and July. **Editor:** Tyler G. Hicks. **Price:** $15.00, payment with order.

★1591★
BUSINESS WEEK—BANK SCOREBOARD ISSUE
McGraw-Hill, Inc.
1221 Avenue of the Americas   Phone: (212) 997-1221
New York, NY 10020
Covers: 200 largest United States banks on basis of total assets. **Entries include:** (In chart form) Assets, deposits, and loans, and statistics on changes, earnings, etc. **Arrangement:** By total assets. **Frequency:** Annual, in an April issue. **Price:** $1.25.

Butler's Money Fund Directory *See* Donoghue's Money Fund Directory

★1592★
CALIFORNIA BUSINESS—INDUSTRIAL PARKS DIRECTORY ISSUE
California Business News, Inc.
Box 4360   Phone: (213) 843-2121
Burbank, CA 91503
Entries include: Park name, location, date established, size, percent occupied and number of tenants, types of businesses for which suited, utilities available, rail and air facilities on site or nearby, name of management firm, address, phone, name of contact; limited to advertisers. **Arrangement:** By county. **Frequency:** Not established; first issue July 1978. **Editor:** Martin Stone, Publisher. **Advertising accepted. Price:** $1.50.

★1593★
CALIFORNIA MOBILE HOME PARK GUIDE
Modern Housing, Inc.
4043 Irving Place   Phone: (213) 839-1162
Culver City, CA 90230
Covers: More than 5,000 mobile home parks and communities in California. **Entries include:** Name of park, address, manager's name, total spaces (and number of spaces assigned to single-, double-, or triple-wides), adult or family restrictions, pet restrictions, facilities available, occupancy levels, and resale frequency. **Arrangement:** By county. **Pages** (approx.): 85. **Frequency:** Annual, August. **Editor:** Edward Ely. **Advertising accepted.** Circulation 10,000. **Former title:** California Mobile Home Guide. **Price:** $6.00.

★1594★
CASUALTY ACTUARIAL SOCIETY—YEAR BOOK
Casualty Actuarial Society
One Penn Plaza   Phone: (212) 557-8637
New York, NY 10001
Covers: 700 actuaries working in insurance other than life insurance. **Entries include:** Name, office address, date admitted to society. **Arrangement:** Classified by membership categories, then alphabetical by name. **Frequency:** Annual, January.

★1595★
CHARLOTTE MECKLENBURG INDUSTRIAL PARKS [North Carolina]
Greater Charlotte Chamber of Commerce
129 W. Trade Street   Phone: (704) 377-6911
Charlotte, NC 28233
Covers: More than 30 industrial parks with available space. **Entries include:** Park name, location; land available, cost, whether development assistance is offered; details concerning rail, natural gas, water, and sewer service; types of tenants desired; restrictions; name and address of contact; list of present tenants. **Arrangement:** Alphabetical. **Pages** (approx.): 75. **Frequency:** Irregular; latest edition December 1979. **Price:** $6.00.

★1596★
CHICAGO BANKS DIRECTORY
Law Bulletin Publishing Company
415 N. State Street   Phone: (312) 644-7800
Chicago, IL 60610
Covers: 275 banks in Chicago and suburban Cook County, Illinois. **Entries include:** Bank name, address, phone, list of officers, bank statements for quarter prior to publication. **Pages** (approx.): 330. **Frequency:** Semiannual, March and September. **Editor:** S. L. McFall. **Advertising accepted.** Circulation 6,000. **Price:** $3.00.

★1597★
CHICAGO MERCANTILE EXCHANGE—MEMBERSHIP LIST
Chicago Mercantile Exchange
444 W. Jackson Boulevard   Phone: (312) 648-1000
Chicago, IL 60606
Covers: Members of the exchange and its divisions, the International Monetary Market and Associate Mercantile Market. **Entries include:** Name, address, phone, name of company associated with. **Arrangement:** By division, then alphabetical. **Pages** (approx.): 80. **Frequency:** Semiannual. **Price:** $5.00.

★1598★
COMMERCIAL WEST—BOND DIRECTORY ISSUE
Financial Communications, Inc.
5100 Edina Industrial Boulevard   Phone: (612) 835-5853
Edina, MN 55435
Covers: About 35 municipal and corporate bond underwriters and dealers with offices in the midwest. **Entries include:** Company name, address, phone; nature of firm; names and titles of managing officers, sales representatives, and staff members; types of securities handled; area served; underwriting and syndication calendar for prior year. **Arrangement:** Alphabetical. **Frequency:** Annual, early September. **Advertising accepted.** Circulation 4,500. **Price:** $1.00.

Commercial West Bank Directory of the Ninth Federal Reserve District *See* Bank Directory of the Upper Midwest

★1599★
COMMODITIES MAGAZINE REFERENCE GUIDE TO FUTURES MARKETS
Commodities Magazine, Inc.
219 Parkade   Phone: (319) 277-6341
Cedar Falls, IA 50613
Covers: All exchanges dealing in futures contracts, including commodities, foreign currencies, and financial instruments, worldwide. Also includes about 5,00 advisory services, brokerage firms, consultants, research firms, management services, etc., specializing in, or with special interest in, futures trading. **Entries include:** Company name, address, phone, branch offices, and names of principal executives. **Pages** (approx.): 95. **Frequency:** Annual, May. **Editor:** Darrell Jobman. **Advertising accepted.** Circulation 25,000. **Former title:** Directory of Commodity Futures Trading. **Price:** $6.00 (current and 1980 editions). **Also includes:** Trading reference data, such as lists of commodities traded by exchange, complete trading information by commodity, member firms of each exchange, available free literature, and editorial analysis of futures trading by category (grains, metals, meats, etc.).

Corporate Directory Service *See* Financial Trend's Corporate Directory Service

★1600★
CORPORATE INDEX DIRECTORY
Office of Reports and Information Services
Securities and Exchange Commission
500 N. Capitol Street   Phone: (202) 755-1152
Washington, DC 20549
Covers: Corporations preparing to make new stock offerings; derived from registration statements and exchange listing applications. **Entries include:** Corporation name, SEC file number, address, issuer, action codes, SIC number. **Arrangement:** Alphabetical. **Frequency:** Quarterly. **Price:** About 10¢ per page; prepared for SEC internal use; price quoted is copying cost.

★1601★
CORPORATE TRANSFER AGENTS ASSOCIATION—ROSTER AND BYLAWS
Corporate Transfer Agents Association
C/o Union Pacific Corporation
120 Broadway, Room 1722   Phone: (212) 233-6222
New York, NY 10005
Covers: 140 persons in responsible positions in corporations which transfer their own stock or who supervise stock transfer departments. **Arrangement:** Alphabetical. **Frequency:** Irregular; latest edition December 1975. **Price:** Available to members only.

★1602★
CREDIT UNION DIRECTORY
Angelo R. Venezian, Inc.
211 E. 43rd Street   Phone: (212) 661-9242
New York, NY 10017
Number of listings: 23,000. **Entries include:** Credit union name, address, asset code, number of members, type of charter (state or federal). **Arrangement:** Geographical. **Pages** (approx.): 220. **Frequency:** Biennial, spring of odd years. **Advertising accepted.** **Former title:** Credit Union Directory, Handbook, and Buyers Guide. **Price:** $40.00.

★1603★
CREDIT UNION DIRECTORY AND BUYER'S GUIDE
United Publishing Company
128 C Street, N. W.   Phone: (202) 638-0832
Washington, DC 20001
Covers: 23,000 state and federal credit unions; also lists credit union leagues. **Entries include:** Credit union name, address, total assets.

Arrangement: Geographical. **Pages** (approx.): 160. **Frequency:** Annual, June. **Editor:** Frank Joseph. **Advertising accepted.** Circulation 6,000. **Price:** $49.00.

CUSIP Corporate Directory *See* CUSIP Master Directory

★1604★
CUSIP MASTER DIRECTORY
Standard & Poor's Corporation
25 Broadway   Phone: (212) 248-2525
New York, NY 10004
Covers: Official numbers and descriptions assigned by the American Bankers Association Committee on Uniform Security Identification Procedures (CUSIP) to more than 1,000,000 stocks, bonds, and warrants of 65,000 issuers, including corporations, municipalities, and the United States and foreign governments. "CUSIP Corporate Directory" covers corporate securities only. **Arrangement:** Alphanumerical. **Frequency:** Annual, May; "Digest of Changes in CUSIP" issued every 10 days. **Price:** "Master Directory" with "Digest of Changes," $650.00; "Corporate Directory" with "Digest of Changes," $440.00; "Digest of Changes" alone, $84.00.

★1605★
DEFENSE CREDIT UNION DIRECTORY
Defense Credit Union Council
1730 Rhode Island Avenue, N. W.   Phone: (202) 848-4545
Washington, DC 20036
Covers: 400 credit unions with membership consisting wholly or partly of the military and civilian personnel of the United States defense establishment, worldwide. **Entries include:** Name, address, phone, name of principal executive. **Arrangement:** Geographical. **Pages** (approx.): 40. **Frequency:** Biennial, September of odd years. **Editor:** Col. George E. Myers (U. S. A. Ret.), Executive Director. **Price:** Available to members only.

★1606★
DEPOSIT HISTORY AND PROJECTIONS [Banks and savings and loan associations]
Decision Research Sciences, Inc.
300 Axewood East   Phone: (215) 542-9550
Ambler, PA 19002
Covers: In seventeen geographical volumes, lists all known banks and savings and loan associations in Connecticut, Maine, Massachusetts, New Hampshire, Rhode Island, Vermont; Pennsylvania; New York; Indiana and Michigan; Ohio and West Virginia; Delaware and New Jersey; District of Columbia, Maryland, Virginia; North Carolina and South Carolina; California and Hawaii; Alaska, Idaho, Oregon, Washington; Alabama, Arkansas, Louisiana, Mississippi; Arizona, Colorado, Nevada, New Mexico, Utah; Illinois and Wisconsin; Georgia, Florida, Puerto Rico; Kentucky, Missouri, Tennessee; Oklahoma and Texas; Iowa, Minnesota, Nebraska. **Entries include:** Institution name, addresses of branches, deposits by year for five preceding years, yearly growth rate, deviation, and projections for two coming years. **Arrangement:** Geographical, compatible with arrangement of data in same publisher's "Branch Directory and Summary of Deposits," described in separate listing. **Frequency:** Annual, January; first edition January 1980. **Price:** $240.00 per volume.

Directory List of Mortgage Directors *See* Insurance Companies' Directory List of Mortgage Directors

★1607★
DIRECTORY OF AMERICAN SAVINGS AND LOAN ASSOCIATIONS
T. K. Sanderson Organization
200 E. 25th Street   Phone: (301) 235-3383
Baltimore, MD 21218
Covers: 5,000 associations and their branches. **Entries include:** For main office - Name, address, phone, branch locations, key officials, insured affiliations, assets; For out-of-town branches - Address, phone. **Arrangement:** Geographical. **Pages** (approx.): Over 450. **Frequency:** Annual, January. **Price:** $40.00, postpaid. **Other**

information: Regional directories with abridged listings, $15.50 each.

★1608★
DIRECTORY OF BOND AGENTS
Standard & Poor's Corporation
25 Broadway   Phone: (212) 248-2525
New York, NY 10004
Publication includes: List of paying agents, registrars, co-registrars, trustees and conversion agents for approximately 20,000 corporate and municipal bonds. **Entries include:** Issuer's name, state of incorporation, full title of issue, interest payment dates, form of bond, exchange fee, coupon paying agent, registrar, trustee, conversion agent. **Arrangement:** Alphabetical. **Frequency:** Biennial, January of even years; current list provided at beginning of subscription; bimonthly supplements. **Price:** $315.00.

Directory of Commodity Futures Trading *See* Commodities Magazine Reference Guide to Futures Markets

★1609★
DIRECTORY OF COMPANIES REQUIRED TO FILE ANNUAL REPORTS WITH THE SECURITIES AND EXCHANGE COMMISSION
Securities and Exchange Commission
500 N. Capitol Street   Phone: (202) 755-4846
Washington, DC 20549
Covers: About 9,500 companies required to file annual reports under the Securities Exchange Act of 1934, including those whose securities are listed on national exchanges, are registered for over-the-counter trading, or are registered under the Securities Act of 1933. **Entries include:** Industry code indicating line of business, company name, SEC docket number identifying the company, month fiscal year ends. **Arrangement:** One section alphabetical, another section arranged by SEC Industry Code (based on the federal Enterprise Standard Industrial Classification). Identical information in both. **Pages** (approx.): 425. **Frequency:** Annual, fall. **Price:** $4.75 (1978 edition). **Send orders to:** Government Printing Office, Washington, DC 20402.

★1610★
DIRECTORY OF CREDIT INFORMATION PERSONNEL
Robert Morris Associates
1432 Philadelphia National Bank Building
Philadelphia, PA 19017
Covers: About 5,000 bank officials in over 2,000 major United States commercial banks who are concerned with exchange of credit information on commercial borrowers. **Entries include:** Bank name, address, phone, names of individuals who answer commercial credit information inquiries. **Arrangement:** Geographical. **Pages** (approx.): 135. **Frequency:** Annual, spring. **Former title:** Directory of Credit Data Personnel. **Price:** $10.00, payment with order.

★1611★
DIRECTORY OF FLOOR BROKERS [Commodities]
Commodity Futures Trading Commission
233 S. Wacker Drive, Suite 4600   Phone: (312) 353-7946
Chicago, IL 60606
Covers: About 3,500 registered commodities trading personnel and firms (including floor brokers, futures commission merchants, commodity trading advisors, and commodity pool operators). **Entries include:** Name, firm address; floor broker listings include exchanges. **Arrangement:** Alphabetical within above occupations. **Pages** (approx.): 45. **Frequency:** Monthly. **Price:** $5.00 (available in microfiche only). **Other information:** "Associated Persons" directory which lists floor brokers and others with firm name, and line of business (but no addresses) is available, $15.00 (microfiche only).

Directory of Investment Advisers Registered with the SEC *See* Directory of SEC Registered Investment Advisers

★1612★
DIRECTORY OF MANHATTAN OFFICE BUILDINGS [New York City]
McGraw-Hill, Inc.
1221 Avenue of the Americas
New York, NY 10020
Number of listings: 550. **Entries include:** Building name, address, location, fee owner and leaseholder names and addresses, renting agent name and address, and details concerning square footage, building equipment, special facilities, major tenants, etc. **Pages** (approx.): 230. **Frequency:** Not established; first edition January 1978. **Editor:** Robert F. R. Ballard. **Price:** $79.50.

Directory of Minority Owned Savings and Loan Institutions *See* American Savings and Loan League—Membership Roster

★1613★
DIRECTORY OF MUNICIPAL BOND DEALERS OF THE UNITED STATES
Bond Buyer, Inc.
One State Street Plaza   Phone: (212) 943-8200
New York, NY 10004
Covers: Municipal bond dealers, chief finance officers of municipalities which issue bonds, and attorneys specializing in or practicing in the field of municipal finance; also includes municipal finance consultants. **Entries include:** Firm, attorney, consultant, or officer name, address, phone; firm listings include telex numbers. **Arrangement:** By activity or service, then geographical. **Pages** (approx.): 440. **Frequency:** Three times yearly, spring, fall and winter. **Editor:** Denis F. McFeely. **Advertising accepted. Price:** $40.00 per copy.

Directory of Pension Funds *See* Financial Directory of Pension Funds

★1614★
DIRECTORY OF REGIONAL MALLS [Shopping centers]
Shopping Center Digest
Box 2   Phone: (914) 357-7690
Suffern, NY 10901
Covers: About 1,200 shopping centers in the United States and Canada, existing and planned, with 400,000 square feet or more of gross leasable area. **Entries include:** Shopping center name, location, and name of manager and promotion director; name, address, and phone of owner-developer and leasing agent; sales volume; proximity to major cities and competitors; tenants according to category (department stores, food, etc.). **Arrangement:** Geographical. **Indexes:** Chronological index of centers opening in each of next three years. **Pages** (approx.): 300. **Frequency:** Annual, fall. **Price:** $75.00, plus $5.00 shipping.

★1615★
DIRECTORY OF SEC REGISTERED INVESTMENT ADVISERS
Source Securities Corporation
70 Pine Street
New York, NY 10005
Covers: About 4,000 investment advisers registered with the Securities and Exchange Commission. **Entries include:** Name, address. **Frequency:** Irregular; latest edition summer 1978. **Price:** $1.00. **Other information:** Variant titles, "Directory of Investment Advisers Registered with the SEC;" "Investment Adviser Directory."

★1616★
DIRECTORY OF SECURITIES RESEARCH
W. R. Nelson & Company
551 Fifth Avenue   Phone: (212) 682-1116
New York, NY 10017
Covers: 2,700 publicly traded companies and the 470 brokerage firms which provide research coverage of those companies. **Entries include:** For companies - Headquarters location, primary financial contact, phone, names of brokerage firms which research the company's securities, names of analysts and their phone numbers. For

brokers - Firm name, address, phone, research executives and functions, names and assignments of analysts. **Arrangement:** By industry. **Indexes:** Research personnel; geographic index of brokers. **Pages** (approx.): 350. **Frequency:** Annual, January. **Editor:** Vicki J. Epstein. **Former title:** Nelson's Directory of Securities Research Information (1979). **Price:** $75.00.

★1617★

DIRECTORY OF SECURITY ANALYSTS SOCIETIES, ANALYST SPLINTER GROUPS, AND STOCKBROKER CLUBS

National Investor Relations Institute
1629 K Street, N. W.   Phone: (202) 223-4725
Washington, DC 20006
Covers: About 120 groups of security analysts, stockbrokers, and splinter groups (i. e., specialists in a single industry). **Entries include:** Group names; name, affiliation, business address and phone of president and program chairman; time, location, and length of meetings; number of members; specific interests; speaker policy; average attendance at meetings; procedure for speaking at meetings; group events; costs to guest company. **Arrangement:** Alphabetical within type of group. **Frequency:** Annual, December. **Editor:** Laurence F. Farrell, Executive Director. **Price:** $25.00.

★1618★

DIRECTORY OF STATE AND FEDERAL FUNDS FOR BUSINESS DEVELOPMENT

Pilot Books
347 Fifth Avenue   Phone: (212) 685-0736
New York, NY 10016
Covers: The development office of each state and a few federal agencies. **Entries include:** Name, address and phone number of agency, and very minimal information (50-150 words) on its financing capabilities. **Pages** (approx.): 65. **Frequency:** Irregular; previous edition 1968; latest edition 1977. **Price:** $5.00, plus 75¢ shipping.

★1619★

DIRECTORY OF THE MUTUAL SAVINGS BANKS OF THE UNITED STATES

National Association of Mutual Savings Banks
200 Park Avenue   Phone: (212) 973-5432
New York, NY 10017
Covers: About 465 mutual savings banks; state savings bank associations and other related organizations. **Entries include:** For banks - Name, address, phone, date of founding, branches, data on assets, deposits, mortgages, names and titles of key personnel, coding to indicate consumer services. For associations - Name, address, phone, names of personnel. **Arrangement:** Banks are geographical, associations are alphabetical. **Indexes:** Bank name (also shows rank by deposit size). **Pages** (approx.): 275. **Frequency:** Annual, September. **Price:** $25.00.

Directory of Trust Institutions *See* Trusts & Estates—Directory of Trust Institutions Issue

★1620★

DONOGHUE'S MONEY FUND DIRECTORY

P & S Publications, Inc.
Box C   Phone: (617) 429-5930
Medway, MA 02053
Covers: 65 money market mutual funds. (Money market funds are no-load mutual funds - i.e., they do not charge a sales fee - whose shares are immediately redeemable in cash and which invest in short-term financial instruments such as bank certificates of deposit, U. S. government securities, etc.). **Entries include:** Name, address, phone, adviser, minimum investment, financial data (assets, yields, etc.), services. **Frequency:** Has been very irregular; publisher states frequency is now semiannual, January and June. **Editor:** William E. Donoghue, Publisher. **Former title:** Butler's Money Fund Directory. **Price:** $10.00.

★1621★

E-R-C DIRECTORY OF EMPLOYEE RELOCATION SERVICES

Employee Relocation Council
1627 K Street, N. W.   Phone: (202) 857-0857
Washington, DC 20006
Covers: Brokers, appraisers, and other real estate professionals equipped to handle the relocation of employees; limited to advertisers. **Entries include:** For brokers - Firm name, address, number of offices, phone, code indicating services offered, list of corporations served, code indicating means of working with other brokers, names of executives. For appraisers - Name, firm affiliation (if any), address, phone, code indicating other activities. **Arrangement:** Appraisers and brokers are geographical, others are alphabetical. **Pages** (approx.): 750. **Frequency:** Annual, March. **Former title:** ERREAC Directory. **Price:** $8.00 (current and 1980 editions).

ERISA Benefit Funds *See* Financial Directory of Pension Funds

ERREAC Directory *See* E-R-C Directory of Employee Relocation Services

★1622★

EUROMONEY—"BITING INTO THE BIG APPLE" [Foreign banks in New York; article]

Euromoney Publications Ltd.
20 Tudor Street
London EC4Y OJS, England
Publication includes: List of foreign banks with offices or representation in New York City area. **Other information:** Appeared in June 1978 issue.

★1624★

E-Z TELEPHONE DIRECTORY OF BROKERS AND BANKS

E-Z Telephone Directory Corporation
666 Franklin Avenue   Phone: (212) 422-9492
Garden City, NY 11530
Covers: Stock and bond brokers and financial organizations in the New York area; banks and their branches in New York City, Queens, Nassau, Westchester, and Northern New Jersey; plus out-of-town brokers and banks with direct telephone connections to New York City. **Entries include:** Name, address, and phone, with symbols indicating stock exchange or trade association membership. **Arrangement:** Brokers and banks are alphabetical; out-of-town section is geographical. **Pages** (approx.): 200. **Frequency:** Semiannual, February and August. **Editor:** A. A. Gentile, President. **Advertising accepted.** Circulation 10,000. **Price:** $45.00 per year. **Send orders to:** E-Z Telephone Directory Corp., 80 Washington St., New York, NY 10006 (212-422-9492).

★1625★

FEDERAL HOME LOAN BANK BOARD—MINORITY-OWNED ASSOCIATIONS LIST

Office of Housing and Urban Affairs
Federal Home Loan Bank Board
320 First Street, S. W.
Washington, DC 20552
Number of listings: About 90 savings and loan associations. **Entries include:** Association name, address. Separate list includes date affiliated, docket number, assets for two previous years. **Arrangement:** Alphabetical. **Frequency:** Semiannual. **Price:** Free.

★1626★

FEDERAL HOME LOAN BANK OF NEW YORK—ANNUAL MEMBER DIRECTORY

Federal Home Loan Bank of New York
One World Trade Center, 103rd Floor   Phone: (212) 432-2000
New York, NY 10048
Covers: Members (saving banks and savings and loans associations in the second district (New Jersey, New York, Puerto Rico, Virgin Islands). **Entries include:** For main offices - Institution name,

address, phone, names of two senior officers, assets, FHLB number. Similar information for branches (listed under locations). **Arrangement:** Geographical. **Indexes:** Alphabetical. **Pages** (approx.): 180. **Frequency:** Annual, April. **Editor:** Barbara Sperrazza, Executive Secretary. **Price:** $10.00 (current and 1980 editions).

★1627★
FINANCE—COMMERCIAL BANKING DIRECTORY ISSUE
IFB Communications Ltd.
8 W. 40th Street   Phone: (212) 221-7900
New York, NY 10018
Covers: About 420 United States commercial banks having assets of $300 million or more in the prior year. **Entries include:** Bank name, address, phone, telex number, transit number, Federal Employer Identification Number; name of holding company (if any); number of branches and international subsidiaries and their locations; name and location of bank-related subsidiaries; names and titles of key personnel and phone for operating personnel; financial keys. **Arrangement:** Alphabetical. **Frequency:** Annual, September/October. **Price:** $20.00. **Also includes:** Ranking of banks according to equity capital and share of market compilations (latter arranged geographically).

★1628★
FINANCE—INVESTORS ISSUE
IFB Communications Ltd.
8 W. 40th Street   Phone: (212) 221-7900
New York, NY 10018
Publication includes: Top 400 securities dealers in United States. **Entries include:** Name of firm; type of ownership; headquarters address, phone, teletype and telex numbers; total number of offices and locations of branches; ranking by capital position; fails to deliver 30 days or older; debt to capital ratio; underwriting and syndication of corporate issues in previous year by number, type, and dollar volume; key personnel and number of employees. **Arrangement:** Alphabetical by company name. **Indexes:** Firms ranked by amount of total capital. **Frequency:** Annual. **Editor:** H. Lee Silberman. **Advertising accepted.** Circulation 54,000. **Price:** $10.00.

★1629★
FINANCIAL ANALYSTS FEDERATION—MEMBERSHIP DIRECTORY
Financial Analysts Federation
219 E. 42nd Street, Tower Suite   Phone: (212) 557-0055
New York, NY 10017
Covers: 14,000 security and financial analysts who are practicing investment analysts. **Entries include:** Name, firm affiliation and address, phone, specialty codes. **Arrangement:** Geographical (i.e., by constituent local or state societies). **Pages** (approx.): 380. **Frequency:** Annual, November-December. **Editor:** Peggy E. Kelly. **Price:** $50.00.

★1630★
FINANCIAL DIRECTORY OF PENSION FUNDS [State or area]
ERISA Benefit Funds
Insurance Research, Inc.
515 National Press Building   Phone: (202) 638-1984
Washington, DC 20045
Covers: 400,000 pension funds required to file reports under the Employee Retirement Income Security Act (ERISA) in 84 volumes covering individual states and major metropolitan areas. **Entries include:** Plan sponsor, name, title, and phone of fund administrator; type of plan (defined benefit, money purchase, profit-sharing, etc.); method of funding; number of participants; effective date and termination date; source(s) of contributions; etc. **Frequency:** Irregular; previous edition fall 1978; new edition expected spring 1980. **Former title:** Directory of Pension Funds. **Price:** Varies; $115.00-$299.00 (1980 edition). **Other information:** Variant title, "ERISA Benefit Funds."

★1631★
FINANCIAL EXECUTIVES INSTITUTE—MEMBER DIRECTORY
Financial Executives Institute
633 Third Avenue   Phone: (212) 953-0500
New York, NY 10017
Covers: Treasurers, controllers, finance managers, accounting managers, and other members who have primary or major financial responsibilities in their organizations. **Entries include:** Individual name, title, company with which affiliated (if any), address, type of membership, and membership number. **Arrangement:** By chapter (primarily geographical). **Indexes:** Personal name (with type of membership and chapter), company name (with member names, chapter). **Frequency:** Annual.

★1632★
FINANCIAL TREND'S CORPORATE DIRECTORY SERVICE
Equity Media, Inc.
7616 Lyndon B. Johnson Freeway   Phone: (214) 239-0161
Dallas, TX 75251
Covers: More than 500 publicly held southwestern corporations. **Entries include:** Company name, address, phone, stock exchange on which listed and symbol, names of executives, and company's annual or interim revenues and net earnings. **Arrangement:** Alphabetical. **Frequency:** Full directories in April and October, monthly updates other months. **Price:** $36.00 yearly for directories and updates.

★1633★
FINANCIAL WORLD—AMERICA'S BIGGEST MONEY-MAKERS ISSUE
Macro Communications, Inc.
919 Third Avenue   Phone: (212) 826-4360
New York, NY 10022
Covers: 500 United States firms showing greatest net earnings for the year. **Entries include:** Company name, rank, net earnings for two previous years, total assets, other financial and statistical data. **Arrangement:** Main list arranged by net earnings, other lists arranged by return on equity and other measures and by industry. **Frequency:** Annual, August 15 issue. **Editor:** Alfred Kingon. **Price:** $1.25.

★1634★
FINANCIAL WORLD—AMERICA'S TOP GROWTH COMPANIES DIRECTORY ISSUE
Macro Communications, Inc.
919 Third Avenue   Phone: (212) 826-4360
New York, NY 10022
Description: Companies are selected based on earnings per share growth rate over 10 year period ending with current year; minimum growth rate used is 5%. **Entries include:** Company name, current and prior year's ranking, earnings growth rate (over prior 10 years), number of years of increase over prior 10 years, revenues, dividends per share, earnings per share for current year and 10 years ago. **Arrangement:** Ranked by sales and earnings growth rate. **Indexes:** Companies ranked within industry. **Frequency:** Annual, August 15 issue. **Editor:** Alfred Kingon. **Price:** $1.25.

★1635★
FORBES MAGAZINE—MUTUAL FUNDS SURVEY ISSUE
Forbes, Inc.
60 Fifth Avenue   Phone: (212) 620-2200
New York, NY 10011
Publication includes: List of all mutual funds with assets over $2 million, rated according to historical performance (if time in business permits). **Entries include:** Fund name, investment results, performance ratings, total assets, other financial data. **Arrangement:** Alphabetical within several categories. **Frequency:** Annual, August. **Editor:** Malcolm S. Forbes. **Advertising accepted. Price:** $2.50.

★1636★
GOLD BOOK OF MULTI-HOUSING
Construction Marketing Research Associates, Inc.
11-A Village Green   Phone: (301) 261-6363
Crofton, MD 21114
Covers: About 2,000 major builders, developers, owners, and managers of apartments and condominiums, and managers of rental property. **Entries include:** Company name, address, phone, key personnel, gross revenues, list of services, financial keys. **Arrangement:** Geographical. **Indexes:** Company name. **Pages** (approx.): 280. **Frequency:** Annual, August; first edition August 1979. **Editor:** Donald F. Spear, President. **Price:** $105.00, plus $4.00 shipping.

★1637★
GUIDE TO PITTSBURGH'S GOLDEN TRIANGLE [Pennsylvania]
Greater Pittsburgh Chamber of Commerce
411 Seventh Avenue   Phone: (412) 391-3400
Pittsburgh, PA 15219
Covers: Office and public buildings in downtown Pittsburgh and Allegheny Center area; also includes brief listings for hotels, theaters, department stores, major apartment buildings, etc. **Entries include:** All listings include name, address, and phone; office building listings also include name, address, and phone of managing agent, year completed, height (in stories), net square feet, and number of tenants. **Arrangement:** By type of facility. **Pages** (approx.): 30. **Frequency:** Published 1978. **Price:** $3.00.

★1638★
GUIDE TO SELLING A BUSINESS
Capitol Publishing Corporation
Two Laurel Avenue   Phone: (617) 235-5405
Wellesley Hills, MA 02181
Covers: About 1,500 corporations interested in acquisitions, 100 companies seeking leveraged buy-outs, and about 500 business brokers, investment bankers, consultants, and commercial banks which have active acquisition and merger departments. **Entries include:** For corporations - Company name, address, name of contact, criteria, industry preferences, and histories. Similar information for other categories. **Arrangement:** Classified by type of firm. **Frequency:** Irregular; first edition 1977. **Price:** $49.50.

★1639★
GUIDE TO VENTURE CAPITAL SOURCES
Capital Publishing Corporation
Two Laurel Avenue   Phone: (617) 235-5405
Wellesley Hills, MA 02181
Covers: Venture capital firms, principally in the United States; Small Business Investment Corporations (SBICs); and selected consultants and "deal men." **Entries include:** Company name, address, phone, names of executives, financial keys, list of services, some details about investment requirements, etc. **Arrangement:** Geographical. **Indexes:** Personal name, line of business or industry preferences for investment. **Pages** (approx.): 340. **Frequency:** Irregular; approximately every three years; latest edition March 1977. **Editor:** Stanley E. Pratt. **Price:** $49.50. **Also includes:** Extensive subject classified bibliographies of articles and books on venture capital and SBIC operations.

★1640★
GUIDE TO WORLD COMMODITY MARKETS
Nichols Publishing Company
Box 96
New York, NY 10024
Covers: About 90 markets dealing in physical commodities and futures, worldwide. **Entries include:** Market or exchange name, address, phone, Telex number, names of principal officials, trading hours, trading unit and limits, names of trading members, and particulars of market operation. **Arrangement:** Geographical. **Indexes:** Commodity, member, general. **Pages** (approx.): 300. **Frequency:** Irregular; latest edition July 1979. **Editors:** Brian Reidy

and John Edwards. **Price:** $32.50.

★1641★
HANDBOOK OF FEDERAL ASSISTANCE: FINANCING, GRANTS...[Banking]
Warren, Gorham & Lamont
210 South Street
Boston, MA 02111
Covers: About 740 sources of financial assistance used in banking. **Entries include:** Types of assistance, objectives, eligibility, program operation and use, application procedure, range & average financial assistance, regulations, guidelines, contact information. **Arrangement:** Classified by topic. **Indexes:** Type of assistance, type of applicant. **Pages** (approx.): 700. **Frequency:** Irregular; latest edition 1979; new edition expected winter 1980. **Editor:** Robert C. Schaevitz. **Former title:** Banker's Handbook of Federal Aids to Financing. **Price:** $48.50.

★1642★
HANDBOOK OF FLORIDA BANKING
Hill-Donnelly Corporation
2907 Bay to Bay Boulevard   Phone: (813) 837-1009
Tampa, FL 33690
Covers: 750 insured national and state commercial banks in Florida. **Entries include:** Bank name, balance sheet and income statement data. Also includes section of ratio analysis of revenue, expense, and profit of individual banks. **Pages** (approx.): 560. **Frequency:** Annual, fall. **Editor:** Ronald W. Goff. **Price:** $145.00.

★1643★
HINE'S DIRECTORY OF INSURANCE ADJUSTERS
Hine's Legal Directory, Inc.
443 Duane Street   Phone: (312) 469-3983
Glen Ellyn, IL 60137
Covers: 1,200 independent insurance adjuster offices in the United States and Canada. **Entries include:** Company name, office address and phone, areas of occupational specialization, memberships. **Arrangement:** Geographical. **Pages** (approx.): 210. **Frequency:** Annual, October. **Editor:** James R. Collins. **Advertising accepted.** Circulation 7,000. **Price:** $8.75, postpaid.

★1644★
INDEPENDENT BANKERS ASSOCIATION OF AMERICA— MEMBERSHIP LIST
Independent Bankers Association of America
1168 S. Main Street   Phone: (612) 352-6546
Sauk Centre, MN 56378
Covers: 7,320 commercial banks in 45 states which are members of the Independent Bankers Association of America. **Entries include:** Bank name, city, state. **Arrangement:** Geographical. **Pages** (approx.): 80. **Frequency:** Annual, April. **Editor:** Bill McDonald. **Advertising accepted.** Circulation 8,000. **Price:** Available to members only.

★1645★
INDEX OF ACTIVE REGISTERED INVESTMENT COMPANIES UNDER THE INVESTMENT ACT OF 1940 AND RELATED INVESTMENT ADVISERS
Securities and Exchange Commission
500 N. Capitol Street   Phone: (202) 755-4846
Washington, DC 20549
Covers: 1,330 active companies registered under the Investment Company Act of 1940, including investment companies, investment advisers, principal underwriters, sponsors, and underlying companies. Separate sections for each type of registrant. **Entries include:** Investment company listings show company name, related underwriters, advisers, etc., and the 811 number for the investment company. Sections for other types of registrants show the same information in various permutations. No addresses or locations. **Arrangement:** Classified by function of registrants. **Pages** (approx.): 160. **Frequency:** Annual, fall. **Price:** Free.

★1646★

INSIDERS' CHRONICLE

Transamerica Media Corporation

1111 E. Putnam Avenue   Phone: (203) 637-5900

Riverside, CT 06878

Covers: Publicly held companies in whose restricted securities (144 Letter Stock) there has been significant trading by officers, directors, and those who hold 10% or more of its shares. **Entries include:** Company name, name/title of person involved, number of shares held, price per share, date of transaction. **Arrangement:** Alphabetical by company name. **Pages** (approx.): 20. **Frequency:** Weekly. **Editor:** Richard D. Moran. **Advertising accepted.** Circulation 4,500. **Price:** $3.00 per copy; $145.00 per year. **Also includes:** Market news, quotations, and statistics.

★1647★

INSTITUTIONAL INVESTOR—ALL-AMERICA RESEARCH TEAM ISSUE

Institutional Investor Systems, Inc.

488 Madison Avenue   Phone: (212) 832-8888

New York, NY 10022

Covers: About 300 analysts at 40-50 firms judged to have been outstanding in their recommendations concerning stock transactions. **Entries include:** Analyst name, firm, ranking, comments by colleagues and clients. **Arrangement:** By product. **Frequency:** Annual, October. **Advertising accepted. Price:** $7.25.

★1648★

INSTITUTIONAL INVESTOR—ANNUAL PENSIONS DIRECTORY ISSUE

Institutional Investor Systems, Inc.

488 Madison Avenue   Phone: (212) 832-8888

New York, NY 10022

Covers: About 350 of the largest corporate pension funds, 70 state retirement systems, and about 70 of the largest county and municipal funds; about 325 money management firms which have one or more clients among the funds listed; and about 60 consulting firms which specialize in serving pension fund sponsors. **Entries include:** For funds - Name of sponsoring company, location, name and title of executive responsible for pension fund, and institutions which manage fund assets. For management firms - Company name, location, name and title of one executive, total tax exempt assets under management, clients from among the largest funds. For consultants - Name and mailing address of firm, names of executives, type of firm and services offered, number of clients. **Frequency:** Annual, January. **Editor:** Peter Landau. **Advertising accepted.** Circulation 35,000. **Price:** $6.00.

★1649★

INSTITUTIONAL INVESTOR—FOREIGN BANKS IN AMERICA DIRECTORY ISSUE

Institutional Investor Systems, Inc.

488 Madison Avenue   Phone: (212) 832-8888

New York, NY 10022

Covers: Several hundred foreign banks with branches, agencies, or representatives in the United States. **Entries include:** Bank name, nationality, address, name of principal executive in United States, locations of offices. **Arrangement:** Geographical. **Pages** (approx.): 20. **Frequency:** Annual, September. **Editor:** Peter Landau. **Advertising accepted.** Circulation 40,000. **Price:** $7.25, payment with order. **Other information:** Sometimes cited as, "Where the Foreign Bankers Are."

★1650★

INSTITUTIONAL INVESTOR—TOP 300 MONEY MANAGERS ISSUE

Institutional Investor Systems, Inc.

488 Madison Avenue   Phone: (212) 832-8888

New York, NY 10022

Covers: 300 largest financial institutions in terms of total assets under management. **Entries include:** Institution name, headquarters city, rank for two previous years, total assets under management and

their composition, and total pension and employee benefit assets under management. **Arrangement:** By managed assets. **Frequency:** Annual, August. **Editor:** Peter Landau. **Advertising accepted. Price:** $7.25.

★1651★

INSURANCE ALMANAC

Underwriter Printing and Publishing Company

291 S. Van Brunt Street   Phone: (201) 569-8808

Englewood, NJ 07631

Covers: Over 2,000 companies which write fire, casualty, accident and health, life, and Lloyd's policies; also lists mutual and reciprocal companies. Includes national, state, and local insurance associations; state insurance officials; and agents, brokers, actuaries, and adjusters. **Entries include:** For companies - Company name, address, phone, names of officers and directors, lines written, territory covered; for larger firms, some history and financial data. For associations - Name, address, names of staff and officers, place and date of meetings. For agents, brokers, etc. - Name, address. **Arrangement:** Classified by insurance lines, type of activity, etc. **Indexes:** Company name. **Pages** (approx.): 700. **Frequency:** Annual, July. **Advertising accepted. Price:** $35.00.

★1652★

INSURANCE COMPANIES' DIRECTORY LIST OF MORTGAGE DIRECTORS

American Business Aids, Inc.

3605 Quentin Road

Brooklyn, NY 11234

Covers: 375 mortgage officers of major insurance companies which make real estate mortgages and related investments. **Entries include:** Company name, address, phone, name and title of mortgage officer. **Frequency:** Annual, November. **Price:** $39.50.

★1653★

INSURANCE FIELD STATE INSURANCE DIRECTORIES

Insurance Field Company

4325 Old Shepherdsville Road   Phone: (502) 459-7910

Louisville, KY 40218

Covers: Licensed property, liability, and life insurance companies and agencies, adjusters, and appraisers (SIC 094). Separate editions under title "[State] Insurance Directory" are published for Kentucky, Louisiana-Mississippi, New Jersey, New York, North and South Carolina, Tennessee, Texas (North and South editions), and Virginia. **Entries include:** For property and liability companies - Company name, home office address, date founded, president and secretary, addresses of state supervising offices and personnel, names and addresses of state managers, general agents, and fieldmen. For life companies - Same, except supervising offices are omitted and agency services are listed. For agencies - Agency name, address, date founded, names of principals, companies represented. **Arrangement:** Companies are alphabetical, agencies are geographical. **Pages** (approx.): 300-800. **Frequency:** Annual. **Editor:** Fred C. Crowell, Jr. **Price:** Varies; 1979 New York edition, for example, was $26.75.

International Monetary Market—Membership List *See* Chicago Mercantile Exchange—Membership List

★1654★

INVENTORY OF PRIVATE ISLANDS FOR SALE

Private Islands Unlimited

17538 Tulsa Street   Phone: (213) 360-8683

Granada Hills, CA 91344

Covers: 400 private islands and island properties for sale in all parts of the world. **Entries include:** Location, accessibility, description of vegetation and terrain, details on water frontage, government jurisdiction, distance from nearest supply source, and price. **Pages** (approx.): 30. **Frequency:** Annual, with irregular supplements. **Editor:** Donald C. Ward. **Price:** $10.00, supplements included.

Investment Adviser Directory *See* Directory of SEC Registered
Investment Advisers

★1655★
**INVESTMENT DEALERS' DIGEST—CORPORATE FINANCING
DIRECTORY ISSUE**
IDD, Inc.
150 Broadway
New York, NY 10038
Covers: Companies which offered corporate securities (bonds,
preferred and common stocks) during the preceding two quarters and
the underwriters that handled them. Also includes firms and individuals
offering specialized financial public relations and advertising services
to corporations and the securities industry. **Entries include:** For
corporations - Company name, description of offerings, underwriters.
For underwriters - Firm name, description of offerings handled, names
of issuers. For publicists - Agency or individual name, address, phone.
Arrangement: Issuers, underwriters, and publicists are alphabetical in
separate lists. **Frequency:** Semiannual, August and February. **Editor:**
Anthony V. Ricotta, Special Section Editor. **Advertising accepted.**
Price: $15.00 per special issue. **Other information:** Financial
publicists' listings were formerly carried in separate "Financial
Publicists Directory Issue" published in November.

★1656★
**INVESTMENT DEALERS' DIGEST—DIRECTORY OF PRIVATE
PLACEMENTS ISSUE**
IDD, Inc.
150 Broadway   Phone: (212) 227-1200
New York, NY 10038
Covers: Includes list of placements showing companies, amounts,
agents, and purchasers, but no directory information. **Frequency:**
Semiannual. **Price:** $7.00.

Investment Dealer's Digest—Financial Publicists Directory Issue
See Investment Dealer's Digest—Corporate Financing
Directory Issue

★1657★
IOWA BANK DIRECTORY
Northwestern Banker Company
306 15th Street
Des Moines, IA 50309
Entries include: Bank name, address, phone, branch addresses,
names of officers and directors, departments within the bank and their
officers, deposit, loan, and security holding figures, and correspondent
banks used. **Arrangement:** Geographical. **Pages** (approx.): 300.
Frequency: Annual, spring. **Price:** $10.00.

Kentucky Insurance Directory *See* Insurance Field State Insurance
Directories

★1658★
KIRSCHNER'S INSURANCE DIRECTORY [California, West]
Kirschner's Insurance Directories
586 N Street   Phone: (408) 998-2566
San Jose, CA 95112
Covers: Insurance companies, agents, brokers, surplus line brokers
located in the area represented by the directory; directories published
for northern California and Oregon, southern California, Washington/
Alaska, and Arizona/New Mexico. Associations and their members
may also be listed. **Entries include:** Company name, address, phone,
names of personnel. **Arrangement:** Alphabetical within activity
(broker, market, etc.). **Pages** (approx.): 200. **Frequency:** Semiannual;
Northern California and Oregon editions, April and October; Southern
California, Arizona/New Mexico, and Washington/Alaska editions,
January and July. **Advertising accepted.** Circulation 25,000. **Price:**
$6.95 each.

★1659★
**LIFE INSURANCE MARKETING AND RESEARCH ASSOCIATION—
MEMBER ROSTER**
Life Insurance Marketing and Research Association
170 Sigourney Street   Phone: (203) 525-0881
Hartford, CT 06105
Number of listings: 575. **Entries include:** Company name, address,
phone, key personnel. **Arrangement:** Alphabetical. **Indexes:**
Geographical. **Pages** (approx.): 200. **Frequency:** Annual, April. **Price:**
Available to members only.

★1660★
**LISTING OF LOW AND MODERATE INCOME HOUSING IN THE
BALTIMORE REGION [Maryland]**
Regional Planning Council of Baltimore
2225 N. Charles Street
Baltimore, MD 21218
Covers: About 450 housing projects and other types of low and
moderate housing in the Baltimore area. **Entries include:** Project
name, location, census tract, type of units, bedroom mix,
supplemental financial assistance. **Arrangement:** By jurisdiction, then
program. **Pages** (approx.): 40. **Frequency:** Semiannual, January and
July. **Editor:** Bob Lefenfeld. **Price:** Free.

Louisiana-Mississippi Insurance Directory *See* Insurance Field
State Insurance Directories

★1661★
**MICHIGAN INVESTOR—MICHIGAN BANK AND HOLDING
COMPANY DIRECTORY ISSUE**
Contractor Publishing Company
1629 W. Lafayette Boulevard   Phone: (313) 962-3337
Detroit, MI 48216
Covers: Over 1,500 Michigan banks, bank branches, and holding
companies. **Entries include:** Bank of company name, address, name
and title of chief officer or branch manager, names of other officers
of banks and holding companies, deposit standings of banks, and
assets of holding companies. **Frequency:** Annual, March; updated in
August. **Editor:** George A. Harding. **Advertising accepted.** Circulation
1,800. **Price:** $5.00.

★1662★
**MIDDLE MONEY MARKET DIRECTORY: THE SECOND TIER
PENSION FUNDS**
Money Market Directories, Inc.
818 E. High Street   Phone: (804) 977-1450
Charlottesville, VA 22902
Covers: 9,000 corporate pension fund and profit sharing plan
sponsors with $500,000-$2,000,000 in assets. **Entries include:**
Company name, address, phone, name and type of fund, custodian,
name of one or two executives, number of participants in fund, and
type of funding (purchased insurance, etc.). **Arrangement:**
Geographical. **Pages** (approx.): 750. **Frequency:** Annual, June. **Editor:**
Thomas H. Fitzgerald. **Advertising accepted.** **Price:** $140.00.

★1663★
**MINORITY ENTERPRISE SMALL BUSINESS INVESTMENT
COMPANIES**
Minority Business Development Agency
Commerce Department   Phone: (202) 377-3024
Washington, DC 20230
Number of listings: About 110. **Entries include:** Company name,
address, phone, names of principal executives, and codes indicating
preferred type, amount, location, and industry group for investments.
Arrangement: Geographical. **Frequency:** Irregular; latest edition May
1979. **Price:** Free.

★1664★
MINORITY-OWNED LIFE INSURANCE COMPANIES
Minority Business Development Agency
Commerce Department   Phone: (202) 377-3024
Washington, DC 20230
Number of listings: Over 40. Entries include: Company name, address, name of principal executive. Frequency: Irregular; latest edition 1976. Price: Free.

★1665★
MINORITY-OWNED SAVINGS & LOAN ASSOCIATIONS
Minority Business Development Agency
Commerce Department   Phone: (202) 377-3024
Washington, DC 20230
Number of listings: About 75. Entries include: Association name, address, name of president, phone, minority controlling the association. Arrangement: Alphabetical. Frequency: Irregular; latest edition 1978. Price: Free.

★1666★
MONEY MARKET DIRECTORY [Pension funds, foundations, etc.]
Money Market Directories, Inc.
818 E. High Street   Phone: (804) 977-1450
Charlottesville, VA 22902
Covers: About 9,700 tax-exempt funds (pension, endowment, and foundation funds) with over $2,000,000 in assets, and about 3,000 investment management services, bank trust departments, and insurance companies handling at least $3,000,000 in tax-exempt funds. Entries include: For tax-exempt funds - Name of company, institution, etc., address, phone, name of responsible executive; name of fund(s), name of bank, investment company, etc., administering the fund (internal administration is indicated), and approximate dollar amount. For investment services - Company name, address, phone, name of responsible executive, names of subsidiary or affiliated companies and names of portfolio managers, total assets managed. Arrangement: Classified by funds and services, then geographical. Indexes: Index of tax-exempt funds managed by individual services; index of investment service research department personnel by industry group. Pages (approx.): 925. Frequency: Annual, November. Editor: Thomas H. Fitzgerald. Advertising accepted. Circulation 5,100. Price: $224.00.

★1667★
MOODY'S BANK AND FINANCE MANUAL
Moody's Investors Service, Inc.
99 Church Street   Phone: (212) 553-0300
New York, NY 10007
Covers: More than 10,000 national, state, and private banks, insurance companies, mutual funds, mortgage and finance companies, real estate investment trusts, savings and loan associations, and other financial firms in the United States, and principal banks abroad. Includes "Special Features Section," listing largest banks, savings and loan associations, insurance companies, and mutual funds. Entries include: Company name, headquarters and branch offices, phones, names and titles of principal executives, directors, history, Moody's rating, and extensive financial and statistical data. Arrangement: Classified by type of business. Indexes: Company name. Pages (approx.): 3,200. Frequency: Annual, spring with twice-weekly supplements. Editor: Robert P. Hanson. Advertising accepted. (Subsidy required for what publisher designates as "Full Measure or Comprehensive Coverage.") Price: $350.00 per year, including supplements.

★1668★
MOODY'S INDUSTRIAL MANUAL
Moody's Investors Service, Inc.
99 Church Street   Phone: (212) 553-0300
New York, NY 10007
Covers: About 2,900 companies listed on the New York, American, or regional stock exchanges, and international companies. Entries include: Company name, headquarters address, phone, names and titles of executive officers, directors, history, Moody's rating, and extensive financial and statistical data. Arrangement: Alphabetical. Indexes: Geographical, industry. Pages (approx.): 3,900. Frequency: Annual, August; supplemented by "Moody's Industrial News Reports" twice weekly. Editor: Robert P. Hanson, Editor-in-Chief. Advertising accepted. (Subsidy required for what publisher designates as "Full Measure or Comprehensive Coverage.") Price: Manual (including News Reports) $390.00 (ISSN 0545-0217); News Reports, $340.00.

★1669★
MOODY'S OTC INDUSTRIAL MANUAL
Moody's Investors Service, Inc.
99 Church Street   Phone: (212) 553-0300
New York, NY 10007
Covers: Over 2,750 companies whose stock is traded over-the-counter. Entries include: Company name, headquarters, address and phone, names and titles of executive officers, directors, history, Moody's rating, and extensive financial and statistical data. Arrangement: Alphabetical. Indexes: Geographical, product/service. Pages (approx.): 1,420. Frequency: Annual, September; supplemented by "Moody's OTC Industrial News Reports" weekly. Editor: Robert P. Hanson, Editor-in-Chief. Advertising accepted. (Subsidy required for what publisher designates as "Full Measure or Comprehensive Coverage.") Price: Manual, $360.00 (includes News Reports; ISSN 0192-7167); News Reports, $310.00.

★1670★
MOODY'S PUBLIC UTILITY MANUAL
Moody's Investors Service, Inc.
99 Church Street   Phone: (212) 553-0300
New York, NY 10007
Covers: About 560 electric and gas utility companies, gas transmission companies, and telephone and water companies. Entries include: Company name, headquarters address and phone, names and titles of executive officers, directors, history, Moody's rating, and extensive financial and statistical data. Arrangement: Alphabetical. Pages (approx.): 2,540. Frequency: Annual; supplemented by "Moody's Public Utility News Reports" twice weekly. Editor: Robert P. Hanson, Editor-in-Chief. Advertising accepted. (Subsidy required for what publisher designates as "Full Measure or Comprehensive Coverage.") Price: Manual, $330.00 (includes News Reports; ISSN 0545-0241); News Reports, $280.00.

★1671★
MOODY'S TRANSPORTATION MANUAL
Moody's Investors Service, Inc.
99 Church Street   Phone: (212) 553-0300
New York, NY 10007
Covers: Over 1,000 railroads, airlines, steamship companies, electric railways, bus and truck lines, oil pipelines, bridge companies, and automobile and truck leasing companies. Entries include: Company name, headquarters address and phone, names and titles of principal executives, directors, history, Moody's rating, and extensive financial and statistical data. Arrangement: Classified by type of business. Indexes: Company name. Pages (approx.): 1,200. Frequency: Annual; supplemented by "Moody's Transportation News Reports" twice weekly. Editor: Robert P. Hanson, Editor-in-Chief. Advertising accepted. (Subsidy required for what publisher designates as "Full Measure or Comprehensive Coverage.") Price: Manual, $320.00 (ISSN 0545-025X); News Reports, $270.00.

★1672★
MORTGAGE INSURANCE COMPANIES OF AMERICA—
    MEMBERSHIP LIST
Mortgage Insurance Companies of America
1725 K Street, N. W., Suite 1402   Phone: (202) 785-0767
Washington, DC 20006
Entries include: Name of company, address, address of regional underwriting offices. Arrangement: Alphabetical. Pages (approx.): 12. Frequency: Annual, August. Editor: John C. Williamson, Executive

Vice-President. **Price:** Free.

★1673★
**MOTOR AND EQUIPMENT MANUFACTURERS ASSOCIATION—
    CREDIT AND SALES REFERENCE DIRECTORY**
Motor And Equipment Manufacturers Association
Credit Reporting Division
222 Cedar Lane   Phone: (201) 836-9500
Teaneck, NJ 07666
Covers: About 25,000 automotive industry distributors in North
America. **Entries include:** Company name, address, phone, names of
executives, number of employees, trade and brand names, financial
keys, list of products or services, data on distribution, correct trade
style, branches and subsidiaries, name of buyer(s), trade pattern,
payment habits. **Arrangement:** Geographical, then trade style. **Pages**
(approx.): 500. **Frequency:** Three times yearly, in January, May,
September. **Editor:** Kenneth W. Schauble, Manager of Credit
Reporting Division. **Price:** Service basis, approximately $500-$2,200
per year; available only to subscribers to other division services.

★1674★
MOUNTAIN STATES BANK DIRECTORY
Mountain States Publishing Company
Colorado Bankers Association
1550 First National Building   Phone: (303) 825-5359
Denver, CO 80293
Covers: About 565 commerical banks and holding companies in
Colorado, Wyoming, New Mexico, and Utah. **Entries include:** Bank
name, address, phone; names of directors and officers; most recent
financial statement, transfer and routing numbers; date establsihed.
Arrangement: Geographical. **Pages** (approx.): 280. **Frequency:**
Annual, May. **Editor:** Barbara Smith. **Advertising accepted.**
Circulation 3,400. **Price:** $13.00. **Also includes:** List of bank
holidays.

★1675★
NACIS FILE DIRECTORY [National Credit Information Service]
National Credit Information Service
Box 5300   Phone: (714) 937-2700
Orange, CA 92667
Covers: About 900,000 businesses that have made two or more
payments to suppliers as of the publication date which were reported
to NACIS; businesses are divided into four volumes - northeastern,
north central, southern, and western. **Entries include:** Company name,
city, and Zip code. **Arrangement:** Geographical. **Pages** (approx.):
2,500. **Frequency:** Semiannual, January and July. **Editor:** James H.
Holly, Vice President/General Manager. **Price:** $26.50 per set;
$10.50 for individual regional volume. **Other information:** Directory
is intended to be used in clarifying requests for NACIS file reports.

★1676★
NASD MANUAL [Securities dealers]
Commerce Clearing House, Inc.
4025 W. Peterson Avenue   Phone: (312) 583-8500
Chicago, IL 60646
Publication includes: List of about 2,900 securities dealers who are
members of the National Association of Securities Dealers. **Entries
include:** Company name, address, coding to indicate whether a
member of the National Securities Clearing Corporation, and
addresses of branch offices, if any. **Arrangement:** Alphabetical.
Frequency: Looseleaf format with annual updates of membership.
Price: $105.00 per year.

★1677★
**NATIONAL ASSOCIATION OF INDEPENDENT FEE APPRAISERS—
    NATIONAL MEMBERSHIP DIRECTORY [Real estate]**
National Association of Independent Fee Appraisers
7501 Murdoch Avenue   Phone: (314) 781-6688
St. Louis, MO 63119
Covers: 4,500 independent real estate apprasiers. **Entries include:**
Name, address, phone, level of membership. **Arrangement:**

Geographical. **Pages** (approx.): 200. **Frequency:** Annual, January.
Editor: Robert G. Kaestner, Executive Vice President. **Price:** $1.50.

National Association of Independent Insurance Adjusters—
    Directory *See* Blue Book of Adjusters [Insurance adjusters]

★1678★
**NATIONAL ASSOCIATION OF INDUSTRIAL AND OFFICE PARKS—
    ROSTER**
National Association of Industrial and Office Parks
1901 N. Fort Myer Drive, Suite 1100   Phone: (703) 525-5638
Arlington, VA 22209
Covers: About 1,125 firms involved in the development of industrial
and office parks. **Entries include:** Company name, address, phone,
name of principal executive, category of membership. **Arrangement:**
Alphabetical. **Indexes:** Geographical. **Frequency:** Annual, May. **Editor:**
Sid R. Peters, Executive Vice-President. **Advertising accepted.**
Circulation 2,000. **Price:** Restricted circulation; apply.

★1679★
**NATIONAL ASSOCIATION OF MINORITY CERTIFIED PUBLIC
    ACCOUNTING FIRMS—MEMBERSHIP DIRECTORY**
National Association of Minority Certified Public Accounting Firms
918 F Street, N. W., Suite 400   Phone: (202) 783-3141
Washington, DC 20004
Covers: About 130 certified public accounting firms and associate
members (non-practicing CPA's). **Entries include:** Company name,
address, phone, name of principal executive, list of specialties.
Arrangement: Geographical. **Indexes:** Alphabetical. **Pages** (approx.):
85. **Frequency:** Irregular; latest edition October 1978. **Editor:**
Doreen M. Odom, Communications Aide. **Price:** Free.

★1680★
**NATIONAL ASSOCIATION OF OTC COMPANIES—ANNUAL
    DATABOOK**
National Association of OTC Companies
Box 110   Phone: (215) 887-0312
Jenkintown, PA 19046
Covers: Over 200 member companies which trade in securities not
listed on stock exchanges. **Entries include:** Company name, address,
phone, name of key executive or association representative, number
of employees, financial data, services. **Arrangement:** Geographical.
Pages (approx.): 35. **Frequency:** Annual. **Editor:** Ralph P. Coleman,
Jr. **Price:** $10.00.

★1681★
NATIONAL ASSOCIATION OF REAL ESTATE EDITORS—ROSTER
National Association of Real Estate Editors
901 Lakeside Avenue   Phone: (216) 623-6721
Cleveland, OH 44114
Covers: About 250 writers and editors of real estate, building, and
home news or editorial matter in newspapers and periodicals of
general circulation. **Arrangement:** Alphabetical within active and
associate membership categories. **Pages** (approx.): 45. **Frequency:**
Annual, June. **Editor:** Robert F. Brennan, Executive Secretary. **Price:**
$20.00.

★1682★
**NATIONAL ASSOCIATION OF REAL ESTATE INVESTMENT
    TRUSTS—DIRECTORY OF MEMBERS**
National Association of Real Estate Investment Trusts
1101 17th Street, N. W.   Phone: (202) 785-8717
Washington, DC 20036
Covers: 130 trusts, 180 associated members (banks, law firms,
etc.). **Entries include:** Company name, address, phone, name of
principal executive, financial keys, and types of assets. **Arrangement:**
Alphabetical. **Pages** (approx.): 115. **Frequency:** Semiannual, June and
December. **Price:** $2.00, postpaid.

National Association of Realtors—Roster *See* National Roster of
　Realtors

National Association of Securities Dealers—Membership Roster
　See NASD Manual [Securities dealers]

★1683★
**NATIONAL ASSOCIATION OF SURETY BOND PRODUCERS—
　MEMBERSHIP DIRECTORY**
National Association of Surety Bond Producers
5225 Wisconsin Avenue, N. W.　　　　Phone: (202) 362-0101
Washington, DC 20015
Covers: Agencies and brokerages active in contract suretyship.
Entries include: Company name, address, phone, executives' names.
Arrangement: Geographical. **Pages** (approx.): 240. **Frequency:**
Annual, April. **Editor:** J. Martin Huber, Associate Director. **Price:**
$15.00.

★1684★
**NATIONAL BANKERS ASSOCIATION—ROSTER OF MEMBER
　BANKS**
National Bankers Association
499 Capitol Street, S. W., Suite 520　　Phone: (202) 488-5550
Washington, DC 20003
Covers: About 100 banks owned or controlled by minority group
persons or women. **Entries include:** Bank name, address, phone, name
of one executive. **Arrangement:** Geographical. **Frequency:** Annual.
Price: Free.

★1685★
NATIONAL CONSUMER FINANCE ASSOCIATION DIRECTORY
National Consumer Finance Association
1000 16th Street, N. W.　　　　Phone: (202) 638-1340
Washington, DC 20036
Covers: Over 20,000 installment credit offices in the United States
and Puerto Rico, including a special listing of the association's
members. Also lists state supervisory officials, exchange bureaus, and
state associations. **Arrangement:** Geographical. **Pages** (approx.):
230. **Frequency:** Biennial, early in even years. **Editor:** Colleen Kalb.
Price: $45.00 (current edition); $50.00 (1980 edition).

★1686★
**NATIONAL DIRECTORY OF PENSION FUNDS THAT INVEST IN REAL
　ESTATE INVESTMENTS**
American Business Aids, Inc.
3605 Quentin Road　　　　Phone: (212) 998-2985
Brooklyn, NY 11234
Number of listings: 1,000. **Entries include:** Fund name, manager's
name, address, phone, amount of investment. **Arrangement:**
Alphabetical. **Frequency:** Irregular; new edition expected early 1980.
Price: $75.00 (current and 1980 editions).

★1687★
NATIONAL INSURANCE ASSOCIATION—MEMBER ROSTER
National Insurance Association
2400 S. Michigan Avenue　　　　Phone: (312) 842-5125
Chicago, IL 60616
Covers: About 35 insurance companies owned or controlled by Blacks.
Entries include: Company name, address, phone, date founded,
states licensed in, officers. **Arrangement:** Alphabetical. **Frequency:**
Annual. **Price:** Free.

★1688★
NATIONAL REAL ESTATE INVESTOR—DIRECTORY ISSUE
Communication Channels, Inc.
6285 Barfield Road　　　　Phone: (404) 256-9800
Atlanta, GA 30328
Covers: 7,000 companies and individuals in 14 real estate fields,
including appraisers; builders, contractors, and developers; corporate
real estate managers; economic and industrial development
authorities; equity investors; housing and urban renewal authorities;

industrial property and parks; mortgage sources; property managers;
consultants and counselors; realtors and brokers; title insurance
companies; real estate investment trusts (REITs); and related
associations. **Entries include:** Company or agency name, address,
phone, and, in some cases, names of executives and additional
information. **Arrangement:** Classified by type of activity. **Frequency:**
Annual, June. **Editor:** Steve Lewis. **Advertising accepted.** Circulation
25,000. **Price:** $10.00 (current and 1980 editions).

★1689★
NATIONAL ROSTER OF REALTORS
Stamats Publishing Company
427 Sixth Avenue, S. E.　　　　Phone: (319) 364-6167
Cedar Rapids, IA 52406
Number of listings: 140,000. **Entries include:** Name, address.
Arrangement: By local boards. **Pages** (approx.): 740. **Frequency:**
Annual, May. **Editor:** Evelyn Oldridge. **Advertising accepted.**
Circulation 15,000. **Price:** $40.00. **Other information:** Publication is
official roster of National Association of Realtors.

★1690★
**NATIONAL SAVINGS AND LOAN LEAGUE—DIRECTORY OF
　MEMBER INSTITUTIONS**
National Savings and Loan League
1101 15th Street, N. W.
Washington, DC 20005
Covers: 300 savings and loan associations with insured savings
accounts and international savings and loan systems. **Entries include:**
Name, address, phone, names of executives, and financial
information. **Arrangement:** Geographical. **Pages** (approx.): 170.
Frequency: Annual, March. **Editor:** James A. Eberle, Vice President/
Communications. **Price:** Available to members only.

★1691★
NATIONAL SOCIETY OF PUBLIC ACCOUNTANTS—YEARBOOK
National Society of Public Accountants
1717 Pennsylvania Avenue, N. W.
Washington, DC 20006
Covers: Association members and committees; also includes lists of
affiliated state organizations and state revenue departments. **Entries
include:** Member listings include name, address, and code indicating
type of membership (student, etc.); other listings include name,
address, and phone. **Arrangement:** Geographical. **Pages** (approx.):
360. **Frequency:** Annual, fall. **Editor:** Elaine M. Ferri, Director of
Publications. **Advertising accepted.** Circulation 17,000. **Price:**
$10.00.

★1692★
NEBRASKA BANK DIRECTORY
Northwestern Banker Company
306 15th Street
Des Moines, IA 50309
Entries include: Bank name, address, phone, branch addresses,
names of officers and directors, departments within the bank and their
officers, deposit, loan, and security holding figures, and correspondent
banks used. **Arrangement:** Geographical. **Pages** (approx.): 200.
Frequency: Annual, spring. **Price:** $6.00.

Nelson's Directory of Securities Research Information *See*
　Directory of Securities Research

★1693★
NEW JERSEY DIRECTORY OF SUBSIDIZED RENTAL HOUSING
Division of Housing and Urban Renewal
New Jersey Department of Community Affairs
363 State Street
Trenton, NJ 08625
Covers: Housing projects in existence or contemplated which received
state or federal subsidies. **Entries include:** Project name, address,
phone; sponsor and financing information; name, address, and phone
of manager; typical rents, income limitations by size of family.

Arrangement: Geographical within agency categories. **Pages** (approx.): 125. **Frequency:** Annual, summer. **Editor:** Thomas A. Patten. **Price:** Free.

New Jersey Insurance Directory *See* Insurance Field State Insurance Directories

New York Credit and Financial Management Association— Membership Directory *See* Who's Who in Credit and Financial Management...

New York Insurance Directory *See* Insurance Field State Insurance Directories

★1694★
NEW YORK MERCANTILE EXCHANGE—MEMBERSHIP DIRECTORY
New York Mercantile Exchange
Four World Trade Center   Phone: (212) 938-2225
New York, NY 10048
Covers: About 800 members, member firms, and clearing house members, engaged in commodities futures trading. **Entries include:** Name, address, phone. **Arrangement:** Alphabetical. **Frequency:** Irregular; previous edition January 1978; latest edition June 1979. **Editor:** Jean LeBreton, Assistant Secretary. **Price:** $7.00; restricted circulation.

No-Load Mutual Fund Association—Investor Information Booklet and Directory *See* No-Load Mutual Fund Association— Membership Directory

★1695★
NO-LOAD MUTUAL FUND ASSOCIATION—MEMBERSHIP DIRECTORY
No-Load Mutual Fund Association
                                 Phone: (215) 783-7600
Valley Forge, PA 19481
Covers: About 145 mutual funds which do not charge sales commissions. **Entries include:** Fund name, address, phone, investment manager, assets, investment policies, purchase requirements, services, etc. **Arrangement:** Classified by type of fund. **Frequency:** Annual, January. **Editor:** Mildred C. Plenty, Executive Secretary. **Price:** Free. **Other information:** Variant titles, "Investor Information Booklet and Directory" and "Your Guide to Mutual Funds Without Sales Charges."

North and South Carolina Insurance Directory *See* Insurance Field State Insurance Directories

North Texas Insurance Directory *See* Insurance Field State Insurance Directories

★1696★
OHIO BANK DIRECTORY
Ohio Bankers Association
41 S. High Street   Phone: (614) 221-5121
Columbus, OH 43215
Covers: Ohio banking offices; also lists holding companies, state and federal elected officials, regulatory officials, and local Ohio Bankers Association groups. **Entries include:** For banking offices - City, city population, county, name of bank, phone, address, branch name, name and title of manager; main office listings also include financial keys, names and titles of key personnel including directors, holding company affiliations. For other officials and association groups - Name, address, phone. **Arrangement:** Banking offices are by city. Others are alphabetical within activity categories. **Frequency:** Semiannual, spring and fall. **Price:** $8.25.

★1697★
OPERATING BANKING OFFICES
Federal Deposit Insurance Corporation
550 17th Street, N. W.
Washington, DC 20429   Phone: (202) 389-4221
Covers: About 30,000 commercial and mutual savings banks in United States, possessions, and territories. **Entries include:** Bank name and city, plus identification of whether branch or main office, insured status, and class of bank. **Arrangement:** Geographical. **Pages** (approx.): 750. **Frequency:** Annual, June. **Editor:** Marcia K. Johnson. **Price:** Free.

★1698★
OTC DIRECTORY
Review Publishing Company
Box 110   Phone: (215) 887-6312
Jenkintown, PA 19046
Covers: Over 3,700 companies whose stock is traded over-the-counter. **Entries include:** Company name, address, phone, exchange symbol. **Arrangement:** Alphabetical. **Pages** (approx.): 50. **Frequency:** Not established; first edition August 1979. **Editor:** Ralph P. Coleman, Jr. **Price:** $10.50.

★1699★
PACIFIC NORTHWEST MOBILE HOME PARK GUIDE
Modern Housing, Inc.
4043 Irving Place   Phone: (213) 839-1162
Culver City, CA 90230
Covers: More than 1,700 mobile home parks and communities in Oregon, Washington, and Idaho. **Entries include:** Name of park, address; some entries also include total spaces (and number of spaces assigned to single-, double-, or triple-wides), adult or family restrictions, pet restrictions, facilities available, rates, occupancy levels, resale frequency. **Arrangement:** Geographical. **Pages** (approx.): 40. **Frequency:** Annual, spring. **Editor:** Edward Ely. **Advertising accepted.** Circulation 2,500. **Price:** $6.00.

★1700★
PENSION WORLD—PLAN SPONSOR'S DIRECTORY OF MASTER AND DIRECTED TRUST SERVICES ISSUE
Communication Channels, Inc.
6285 Barfield Road   Phone: (404) 256-9800
Atlanta, GA 30328
Covers: About 100 financial institutions with master and directed trust services. **Entries include:** Institution name, address, name of contact, number of clients, number of plans, number of portfolios under trusteeship, minimum size of portfolio accepted, fee structure, total asset value, and other information. **Arrangement:** Alphabetical. **Frequency:** Annual, December. **Editor:** George Adcock. **Price:** $3.00 (ISSN 0031-4862).

★1701★
PENSIONS AND INVESTMENTS—100 TOP RETIREMENT FUNDS ISSUE
Crain Communications
740 N. Rush Street   Phone: (312) 649-5280
Chicago, IL 60611
Publication includes: List of 100 largest retirement plans in terms of total assets. **Entries include:** Company name, total assets and other financial data for two years (not including year preceding "Top 100" issue), and brief summary of plan activity during year immediately preceding. **Arrangement:** Alphabetical. **Frequency:** Annual, first January issue. **Price:** $1.50.

★1702★
PITFALLS IN DEVELOPMENT
Conway Publications, Inc.
Peachtree Air Terminal
1954 Airport Road   Phone: (404) 458-6026
Atlanta, GA 30341
Publication includes: List of over 500 major development projects;

international coverage. **Entries include:** Project name, name of developer, address, name of principal executive. **Arrangement:** Geographical. **Frequency:** Published 1978. **Editor:** H. M. Conway, President. **Price:** $39.00.

★1703★
PLANT LOCATION
Simmons-Boardman Publishing Corporation
350 Broadway   Phone: (212) 966-7700
New York, NY 10013
Publication includes: Lists of industrial development organizations, public utilities, chambers of commerce, associations, and other agencies providing site location guidance. **Entries include:** Name of source, address, name of contact. **Arrangement:** Geographical, then by type of agency or service. **Pages** (approx.): 230. **Frequency:** Annual, April. **Editor:** Diana L. Tice. **Advertising accepted.** Circulation 42,500. **Price:** $25.00 (current and 1980 editions). **Other information:** Principal content of publication is data on population, climate, labor availability and wage rates, transportation and utility service, etc., for cities of 25,000 and over in the United States and Canada.

★1704★
PLANT LOCATION DIRECTORY [Michigan industrial plants]
Office of Economic Development
Michigan Department of Commerce
Box 30225
Lansing, MI 48909
Covers: About 400 industrial buildings and 80 industrial parks, and economic development organizations in Michigan. **Entries include:** Name, location, facilities, name of contact and phone. For organizations - Name, address, name of contact. **Arrangement:** Geographical. **Pages** (approx.): 65. **Frequency:** Annual, spring. **Price:** Free.

★1705★
POLK'S WORLD BANK DIRECTORY
R. L. Polk & Company
2001 Elm Hill Pike   Phone: (615) 889-3350
Nashville, TN 37202
Covers: Banks and their branches, worldwide; Federal Reserve System and other United States government and state government banking agencies; bank holding companies; leasing companies. In two editions: North American edition (including Mexico and Central America), International edition (non-United States). **Entries include:** Bank name, address, principal officers and directors, date established, phone, telex, financial data, memberships, attorney or counsel, correspondent banks, kind of charter. **Arrangement:** Geographical. **Pages** (approx.): North American edition, 5,000; International edition, 2,000. **Frequency:** North American edition is semiannual, spring and fall; International edition is annual, July. **Advertising accepted. Price:** North American edition, $81.00; International edition, $47.25. **Also includes:** Bank routing numbers in numeric sequence; maps; discontinued banks.

★1706★
PROFESSIONAL INDEPENDENT MASS-MARKETING ADMINISTRATORS—MEMBERSHIP DIRECTORY [Insurance]
Professional Independent Mass-Marketing Administrators
10 S. Riverside Plaza   Phone: (312) 930-1195
Chicago, IL 60606
Covers: Over 175 member insurance administrators, associates, companies, and allied members which market and service insurance lines for trade and professional associations, societies, and organizations. **Entries include:** Company name, address, phone, names and titles of individual members. **Arrangement:** Alphabetical. **Indexes:** Personal name, geographical. **Pages** (approx.): 80. **Frequency:** Annual. **Editor:** Carol Calozzo. **Price:** $25.00.

★1707★
QUEENS APARTMENT HOUSE OWNERS DIRECTORY [New York City]
Standard Abstract Corporation
132 Nassau Street   Phone: (212) 732-0225
New York, NY 10038
Number of listings: 4,000. **Entries include:** Owner name, address of office, phone, and list of apartment properties owned or controlled by individual. **Arrangement:** By street and address, and alphabetical by owner name. **Pages** (approx.): 400. **Frequency:** Annual, spring with cumulative quarterly supplements. **Editor:** B. Scheckner, President. **Advertising accepted. Price:** $70.00.

★1708★
RAND MCNALLY INTERNATIONAL BANKERS DIRECTORY
Rand McNally & Company
Box 7600   Phone: (312) 673-9100
Chicago, IL 60680
Covers: About 15,000 banks and 33,000 branches of United States banks, and foreign banks and branches engaged in exchange; members of the Association of Bank Holding Companies; banking associations; Federal Reserve system and other United States government and state government banking agencies; 500 largest commercial banks; bank clearing houses. **Entries include:** For domestic banks - Bank name, address, phone, routing number, memberships in Federal Reserve System and other banking organizations, principal officers with their titles, principal correspondent banks, and eight items of key financial data (deposits, etc.); directors are listed in separate section. For branches - Bank name, address, phone, routing number, manager's name. For foreign banks - Bank name, city; some listings contain detail comparable to listings for domestic banks. **Arrangement:** Geographical. **Pages** (approx.): 5,000. **Frequency:** Semiannual, spring and fall. **Editor:** Edward C. McNally, Vice President. **Advertising accepted.** Circulation 40,000. **Price:** $75.00, plus $3.75 shipping. **Also includes:** Economic data for more than 1,100 United States cities, bank routing numbers in numeric sequence, discontinued or changed bank names, maps.

★1709★
REAL ESTATE DIRECTORY OF MANHATTAN
Sanborn Map Company, Inc.
12 E. 41st Street   Phone: (212) 532-2705
New York, NY 10017
Covers: Owners and leaseholders of Manhattan properties, including condominium apartments. **Entries include:** Street address; block and lot number; owner of record; principal's name, address, and phone; date of transfer; lot size; building class; assessment. **Arrangement:** Main section, geographical; separate alphabetical lists of leaseholders, principals and their holdings, and condominium apartment holders. **Pages** (approx.): 1,480; quarterly supplements, 100 pages. **Frequency:** Annual, October, with quarterly updates. **Editor:** Dorothy A. Baker. **Advertising accepted.** (In quarterly supplements only); circulation 650. **Price:** $210.00 per year, rental basis.

★1710★
REAL ESTATE SECURITIES AND SYNDICATION INSTITUTE— ROSTER OF MEMBERS
Real Estate Securities and Syndication Institute
430 N. Michigan Avenue   Phone: (312) 440-8199
Chicago, IL 60611
Covers: About 2,500 members, who are realtors, realtor associates, educators, attorneys, accountants, and regulators involved with the industry in the United States, Canada, and some foreign areas. **Entries include:** Name, office address and phone, area of business activity, and professional affiliations. **Arrangement:** Alphabetical. **Indexes:** Geographical. **Pages** (approx.): 200. **Frequency:** Annual, January. **Price:** $25.00.

★1711★
REAL ESTATE TRANSFER DIRECTORY [Massachusetts]
RETD, Inc.
Box 885
Framingham, MA 01701
Covers: Real estate sales in Massachusetts, values over $1,000; about 130,000 transactions per year. Entries include: Name of buyer, name of seller, address of property, price, amount of mortgage, mortgagee, and date of closing. Arrangement: By town and street. Frequency: Monthly reports with semiannual summaries. Editor: David Hamilton. Price: Available in editions for single towns or entire state, $10-$950; single annual reports, $55-$875. Also includes: List of mortgages arranged by city then by bank or other maker.

★1712★
REALTORS NATIONAL MARKETING INSTITUTE—DIRECTORY OF CERTIFIED COMMERCIAL-INVESTMENT MEMBERS
Realtors National Marketing Institute
430 N. Michigan Avenue   Phone: (312) 440-8000
Chicago, IL 60611
Number of listings: 600. Entries include: Member name, firm name, address, and phone; home address; real estate board with which affiliated; specialties; member's photo. Arrangement: Alphabetical. Indexes: Geographical. Pages (approx.): 140. Frequency: Annual, fall. Editor: Helen Johnson. Price: Free. Other information: Has cover title, "Who's Who in Commercial-Investment Real Estate."

★1713★
REALTORS NATIONAL MARKETING INSTITUTE—DIRECTORY OF CERTIFIED RESIDENTIAL BROKERS
Realtors National Marketing Institute
430 N. Michigan Avenue   Phone: (312) 440-8000
Chicago, IL 60611
Number of listings: 650. Entries include: Member name, firm name, address, and phone; home address; real estate board with which affiliated; member's photo. Arrangement: Alphabetical. Indexes: Geographical. Pages (approx.): 150. Frequency: Annual, fall. Price: Free. Editor: Helen Johnson. Other information: Has cover title, "Who's Who in Residential Real Estate."

Reference Guide to Futures Markets *See* Commodities Magazine Reference Guide to Futures Markets

★1714★
RETAIL TENANT PROSPECT DIRECTORY
National Mall Monitor, Inc.
1321 U. S. Highway 19 South, Suite 500   Phone: (813) 531-5893
Clearwater, FL 33516
Covers: 2,000 retail firms and chains judged to be prospects for shopping center or mall leases. Entries include: Firm name, address, phone, name of executive responsible for locations. Arrangement: Alphabetical and by retail category; identical information in each section. Pages (approx.): 110. Frequency: Annual, fall. Price: $85.00.

★1715★
ROSTER OF MINORITY BANKS
Banking Staff, BGFD
Treasury Department
Annex No. 1, Room 204
Washington, DC 20226
Covers: About 90 commercial banks owned or controlled by minority group persons or women which participate in the Minority Bank Deposit Program. Entries include: Bank name, address, phone, name of president. Arrangement: Geographical. Frequency: Irregular. Price: Free. Other information: Same list available from Minority Business Development Agency, Commerce Department, Washington, DC 20230.

★1716★
SAVINGS AND LOAN NEWS—TOP 200 ISSUE
U. S. League of Savings Associations
111 E. Wacker Drive
Chicago, IL 60601
Publication includes: List of leading 200 savings and loan associations as ranked by assets and savings. Entries include: Association name, headquarters city, rank, assets and savings, and comparison with previous year. Frequency: Annual. Editor: Hoyt Matthews. Advertising accepted. Price: $1.50 (current and 1980 editions).

★1717★
SAVINGS BANK JOURNAL—SAVINGS BANKING'S 100 LARGEST INSTITUTIONS ISSUE
Thrift Publishers, Inc.
200 Park Avenue   Phone: (212) 973-5432
New York, NY 10017
Covers: 100 largest United States savings banks. Entries include: Bank name, headquarters city, rank, total deposits. Arrangement: By deposit size. Frequency: Semiannual, February and August. Editor: Richard Poriefke. Advertising accepted. Price: $3.00, payment with order.

★1718★
SAVINGS INSTITUTIONS MARKETING SOCIETY OF AMERICA—MEMBERSHIP DIRECTORY
Savings Institutions Marketing Society of America
111 E. Wacker Drive, Suite 2312   Phone: (312) 938-2570
Chicago, IL 60601
Covers: Over 2,100 bank and savings and loan employees, advertising agencies, and suppliers of promotional materials concerned with promoting saving and the services of savings institutions. Entries include: Name of individual and of company or institution with which affiliated, address, phone, title. Member firm listings include services. Arrangement: Geographical. Indexes: Alphabetical. Pages (approx.): 100. Frequency: Annual, March. Editor: SueAnn Spencer, Director of Publications. Price: $10.00 (current edition; tentative, 1980 edition). Circulation restricted; apply.

★1719★
SBIC DIRECTORY AND HANDBOOK OF SMALL BUSINESS FINANCE
International Wealth Success, Inc.
24 Canterbury Road   Phone: (516) 766-5850
Rockville Centre, NY 11570
Covers: Over 400 SBICs (Small Business Investment Companies) which lend money for 5 to 20 years to small businesses. Entries include: Company name, address, and amount and type of financing. Arrangement: Geographical. Pages (approx.): 150. Frequency: Annual, April. Editor: Tyler G. Hicks, Editor-in-Chief. Advertising accepted. Price: $15.00, payment with order.

Security Dealers of North America *See* Standard & Poor's Security Dealers of North America

★1720★
SHESHUNOFF 1,000 LARGEST U.S. BANKS
Sheshunoff and Company, Inc.
Box 13203
Capitol Station   Phone: (512) 444-7722
Austin, TX 78711
Description: Analyzes 1,000 United States banks having over $100 million in deposits with respect to numerous characteristics, including return on average assets, capital adequacy, expense control, etc. Includes compact balance sheet/income statement schedules. Arrangement: Most sections are arranged by deposit size. Frequency: Annual, May. Editor: Alex Sheshunoff. Price: $185.00.

★1721★

SHOPPING CENTER WORLD—ANNUAL FINANCE DIRECTORY
ISSUE

Communication Channels, Inc.
6285 Barfield Road   Phone: (404) 256-9800
Atlanta, GA 30328

Publication includes: About 500 financial institutions which finance
and/or invest in shopping centers. **Entries include:** Company name,
address, phone, principal executive's name, and financial services and
type of financing available. **Arrangement:** Geographical. **Frequency:**
Annual, October. **Editor:** Gail E. Brown. **Advertising accepted.**
Circulation 21,000. **Price:** $3.00, payment with order.

★1722★

SHOPPING CENTER WORLD—ANNUAL PRODUCT DIRECTORY
ISSUE

Communication Channels, Inc.
6285 Barfield Road   Phone: (404) 256-9800
Atlanta, GA 30328

Covers: About 1,500 suppliers of equipment, materials, and services
to shopping centers; also lists trade associations and suppliers of
promotional products and services. **Entries include:** Company or
organization name, address, phone. **Arrangement:** Alphabetical within
categories of general suppliers, promotional suppliers, and trade
organizations. **Indexes:** Product. **Frequency:** Annual, August. **Editor:**
Gail E. Brown. **Advertising accepted.** Circulation 21,000. **Price:**
$3.00, payment with order.

Site Selection Handbook—Corporate Real Estate Management
See Site Selection Handbook—Geo-Corporate Index Issue

Site Selection Handbook—Environment, Energy, and Industry
Issue *See* Site Selection Handbook—Geo-Political Index Issue

★1723★

SITE SELECTION HANDBOOK—GEO-CORPORATE INDEX ISSUE

Conway Publications, Inc.
Peachtree Air Terminal
1954 Airport Road   Phone: (404) 458-6026
Atlanta, GA 30341

Covers: About 2,300 industrial and service firms potentially
interested in expansion and/or new locations. **Entries include:**
Company name, address, name and title of executive in charge of
corporate real estate; some entries include type of business, principal
product or SIC number, area served, financial data. **Arrangement:**
Geographical. **Pages** (approx.): 110. **Frequency:** Annual, February.
Editor: Linda L. Liston. **Advertising accepted.** Circulation 29,000.
Former title: Site Selection Handbook - Corporate Real Estate
Management Issue (1978). **Price:** $15.00 (ISSN 0192-0901). **Also
includes:** Checklist of 1,500 site selection factors.

★1724★

SITE SELECTION HANDBOOK—GEO-ECONOMIC INDEX ISSUE

Conway Publications, Inc.
Peachtree Air Terminal
1954 Airport Road   Phone: (404) 458-6026
Atlanta, GA 30341

Covers: Some 7,000 area development bodies, including state
development agencies, city and county development offices, urban
renewal agencies, port and airport agencies, railroads, utilities, banks,
chambers of commerce, etc. Includes Canada. **Entries include:** Group
name, address, phone, name of contact. **Arrangement:** Geographical.
Pages (approx.): 175. **Frequency:** Annual, May. **Editor:** Linda L.
Liston. **Advertising accepted.** Circulation 29,000. **Former title:** Site
Selection Handbook - Industry's Guide to Geo-Economic Planning
Issue (1978). **Price:** $15.00 (ISSN 0192-0901).

★1725★

SITE SELECTION HANDBOOK—GEO-POLITICAL INDEX ISSUE

Conway Publications, Inc.
Peachtree Air Terminal
1954 Airport Road   Phone: (404) 458-6026
Atlanta, GA 30341

Covers: About 3,000 state, county, and local governmental agencies
which negotiate and administer inducements to industrial firms to
locate new offices, plants, warehouses, or other facilities within their
jurisdiction. **Entries include:** Agency name, address, phone, name of
principal executive, and indication of special services and incentives.
Arrangement: Geographical. **Pages** (approx.): 160. **Frequency:**
Annual, September. **Editor:** Linda L. Liston. **Advertising accepted.**
Circulation 29,000. **Former title:** Site Selection Handbook -
Environment, Energy, and Industry Issue (1978). **Price:** $15.00
(ISSN 0192-0901). **Also includes:** Dot chart tabulation of incentives,
financing plans, etc., offered by individual states.

★1726★

SITE SELECTION HANDBOOK—GEO-SITES INDEX ISSUE

Conway Publications, Inc.
Peachtree Air Terminal
1954 Airport Road   Phone: (404) 458-6026
Atlanta, GA 30341

Covers: About 4,000 developers of office and industrial parks, large-
scale planned unit developments, new towns, mini-cities, etc., and
developers of facilities such as airports and ports; includes Canada.
Entries include: Name of development; developer; address and phone
of executive in charge; year the park, or other unit was created; total
acreage; percent occupied; number of plants or tenants; amount of
land for sale or lease; price ranges; transportation access features
(roads, rail, etc.). **Arrangement:** Geographical. **Pages** (approx.): 135.
Frequency: Annual, November. **Editor:** Linda L. Liston. **Advertising
accepted.** Circulation 29,000. **Former title:** Site Selection Handbook -
Office and Industrial Parks Index (1978). **Price:** $15.00 (ISSN 0192-
0901).

Site Selection Handbook—Industry's Guide to Geo-Economic
Planning Issue *See* Site Selection Handbook—Geo-Economic
Index Issue

Site Selection Handbook—Office and Industrial Parks Issue *See*
Site Selection Handbook—Geo-Sites Index Issue

★1727★

SOCIETY OF ACTUARIES YEAR BOOK

Society of Actuaries
208 S. LaSalle Street   Phone: (312) 236-3833
Chicago, IL 60604

Covers: Actuaries who are members. **Entries include:** Name,
degrees, title, firm with which affiliated, office address, type of
membership, year enrolled. **Arrangement:** Alphabetical. **Frequency:**
Annual, January. **Price:** $50.00 (1980 edition).

★1728★

SOCIETY OF INDUSTRIAL REALTORS—DIRECTORY

Society of Industrial Realtors
925 15th Street, N. W.   Phone: (202) 637-6880
Washington, DC 20005

Covers: Approximately 1,200 specialists in industrial real estate.
Entries include: Company name, address, phone, name of individual
member. **Arrangement:** Geographical. **Indexes:** Company name-
personal name. **Pages** (approx.): 200. **Frequency:** Annual, spring.
Editor: Nelson B. Janes, Assistant Executive Vice President. **Price:**
Free.

★1729★
SOCIETY OF REAL ESTATE APPRAISERS—DIRECTORY OF
    DESIGNATED MEMBERS
Society of Real Estate Appraisers
645 N. Michigan Avenue   Phone: (312) 346-7422
Chicago. IL 60603
Covers: 6,700 professionally designated appraisers and analysts of all
types of real property in the United States and Canada; includes limited
overseas listings. Entries include: Company name, address, phone,
names of executives. Arrangement: Geographical. Pages (approx.):
270. Frequency: Annual, February. Editor: Lyn Swanson. Former
title: Directory of Professionally Designated Members. Price: Available
to members only.

★1730★
SOURCE GUIDE FOR BORROWING CAPITAL
Capital Publishing Company, Inc.
Two Laurel Avenue   Phone: (617) 235-5405
Wellesley Hills, MA 02181
Publication includes: About 400 commercial finance and leasing
companies, small business investment companies, community
development companies, and local development companies willing to
provide additional capital or to refinance existing debt for small
American businesses. Entries include: Company name, address,
phone, company size, activity, terms of loans. Arrangement:
Geographical. Pages (approx.): 440. Frequency: Irregular; latest
edition 1977. Editors: Leonard E. Smollen, Mark Rollison, and Stanley
M. Rubel. Price: $49.50.

South Texas Insurance Directory See Insurance Field State
    Insurance Directories

★1731★
STANDARD & POOR'S CORPORATION RECORDS
Standard & Poor's Corporation
25 Broadway   Phone: (212) 248-2525
New York, NY 10004
Covers: About 7,000 companies. Entries include: Corporation name,
address, detailed descriptions of background, financial structure, and
securities, for major corporations, with somewhat less detail on
smaller firms. Arrangement: Alphabetical. Frequency: Full set of
looseleaf analyses provided at beginning of subscription; updated by
"Daily News Section," cumulated monthly. Price: "Corporation
Records" and "Daily News Section," $877.00 per year; "Corporation
Records" only, $512.00 per year.

★1732★
STANDARD & POOR'S SECURITY DEALERS OF NORTH AMERICA
Standard & Poor's Corporation
345 Hudson Street   Phone: (212) 924-6400
New York, NY 10014
Covers: 8,900 security dealers, plus banks which handle municipal
bonds. Entries include: Company name, address, phone, main and
branch offices, departments, and names and titles of principal
personnel. Arrangement: Geographical. Pages (approx.): 1,400.
Frequency: Semiannual, March and September; monthly supplements.
Editor: Thomas A. Lupo. Advertising accepted. Circulation 5,000.
Price: $160.00 per year, $92.00 for single copy. Other
information: Variant title, "Security Dealers of North America."

★1733★
STANDARD & POOR'S STOCK REPORTS—AMERICAN STOCK
    EXCHANGE
Standard & Poor's Corporation
25 Broadway   Phone: (212) 248-2525
New York, NY 10004
Covers: All companies (about 1,100) whose securities are traded on
the American Stock Exchange. Entries include: Company name,
address, phone, names of officers and directors, names of transfer
agents and registrars, summary of current operations and outlook, net
sales, income and balance sheet data, other financial information,

recent developments, etc. Arrangement: Alphabetical in four
looseleaf volumes. Frequency: Full set of reports provided at
beginning of subscription; revisions issued as needed, with each
company's listing being updated about four times yearly. Hardbound
library editions published quarterly. Price: $440.00 per year, including
revisions and binders; library editions, $150.00 per year.

★1734★
STANDARD & POOR'S STOCK REPORTS—NEW YORK STOCK
    EXCHANGE
Standard & Poor's Corporation
25 Broadway   Phone: (212) 248-2525
New York, NY 10004
Covers: All companies (about 1,500) whose securities are traded on
the New York Stock Exchange. Entries include: Company name,
address, phone, names of officers and directors, names of transfer
agents and registrars, summary of current operations and outlook, net
sales, income and balance sheet data, other financial information,
recent developments, etc. Arrangement: Alphabetical in four
looseleaf volumes. Frequency: Full set of reports provided at
beginning of subscription; revisions issued as needed, with each
company's listing being updated about four times yearly. Hardbound
library editions published quarterly. Price: $520.00 per year, including
revisions and binders; library editions, $190.00 per year.

★1735★
STANDARD & POOR'S STOCK REPORTS—OVER-THE-COUNTER
    AND REGIONAL EXCHANGES
Standard & Poor's Corporation
25 Broadway   Phone: (212) 248-2525
New York, NY 10004
Covers: About 1,100 of the most active and widely held companies
whose securities are traded over-the-counter and on regional
exchanges; includes Canadian companies. Entries include: Company
name, address, phone, names of officers and directors, names of
transfer agents and registrars, summary of current operations, net
sales, income and balance sheet data, other financial information,
recent developments, etc. Arrangement: Alphabetical in four
looseleaf volumes. Frequency: Full set of reports provided at
beginning of subscription; revisions issued as needed, with each
company's listing being updated about four times yearly. Hardbound
library editions published quarterly. Price: $440.00 per year, including
revisions and binders; library editions, $140.00 per year.

★1736★
STANDARD'S MANHATTAN APARTMENT HOUSE DIRECTORY
Standard Abstract Corporation
132 Nassau Street   Phone: (212) 732-0225
New York, NY 10038
Entries include: Name of owner, address, phone, and holdings.
Arrangement: Geographical by street and number, alphabetical.
Frequency: Annual. Editor: B. Scheckner, President. Advertising
accepted. Price: $80.00.

★1737★
STANDARD'S MANHATTAN DIRECTORY OF COMMERCIAL AND
    INDUSTRIAL BUILDING OWNERS
Standard Abstract Corpporation
132 Nassau Street   Phone: (212) 732-0225
New York, NY 10038
Entries include: Name of property owner, address, phone, and realty
holdings. Arrangement: Geographical by street and house number,
and alphabetical. Frequency: Annual, summer. Editor: B. Scheckner,
President. Advertising accepted. Price: $80.00.

Stock Reports—American Stock Exchange See Standard &
    Poor's Stock Reports—American Stock Exchange

Stock Reports—New York Stock Exchange See Standard &
    Poor's Stock Reports—New York Stock Exchange

Stock Reports—Over-the-Counter and Regional Exchanges *See* Standard & Poor's Stock Reports—Over-the-Counter and Regional Exchanges

★1738★

STROUT REAL ESTATE VALUES

Strout Realty, Inc.
Plaza Towers   Phone: (417) 887-0100
Springfield, MO 65804
Covers: Several thousand farms, small town businesses, and rural properties for sale. **Entries include:** For each locality - Name, address, and phone of office handling properties in the area, with name of manager. For properties - Photo, acreage, description of land and any buildings, other features, price. **Arrangement:** Geographical. **Pages** (approx.): 275. **Frequency:** Quarterly. **Price:** Free.

★1739★

SWISS FINANCIAL YEARBOOK

Elvetica Edizioni SA
Box 694
Chiasso CH-6830, Switzerland
Description: Extensive organizational and operational information on 610 Swiss stock exchanges, banks, insurance companies, and finance companies. **Pages** (approx.): 450. **Frequency:** Annual. **Price:** $55.00, air mail postage paid.

Tennessee Insurance Directory *See* Insurance Field State Insurance Directories

★1740★

TEXAS BANKING RED BOOK

Banker's Digest, Inc.
1908 Mercantile Commerce Building   Phone: (214) 747-4522
Dallas, TX 75201
Number of listings: 1,500. **Entries include:** Bank name, address, phone, date established, names of officers and directors, statement of condition. **Arrangement:** Geographical. **Frequency:** Annual, April. **Editor:** Bonnie Jamison. **Advertising accepted.** Circulation 14,000. **Price:** $12.50.

★1741★

TEXAS BLUE BOOK OF LIFE INSURANCE STATISTICS

Record Publishing Company
Box 225770
Dallas, TX 75265
Covers: Life insurance companies licensed to operate in Texas. **Entries include:** Company name, address, phone. In separate lists - Company name, sales, and other financial statistics for three years; company name, names of officers, lines written, and territories. **Arrangement:** Address listing is geographical, others are alphabetical. **Indexes:** General. **Pages** (approx.): 145. **Frequency:** Annual, July. **Editor:** John A. Leslie. **Advertising accepted.** Circulation 800. **Price:** $12.00, plus $1.00 shipping (current edition); $15.00 (tentative, 1980 edition).

★1742★

TREASURY DEPARTMENT—ROSTER OF MINORITY BANKS

Banking Staff
Treasury Department
Annex No. 1, Room 204
Washington, DC 20226
Covers: About 100 commercial banks owned or controlled by minority group persons or women. **Entries include:** Bank name, address, phone, name of president. **Arrangement:** Geographical. **Frequency:** Irregular; latest edition November 1979. **Price:** Free.

★1743★

TRIDENT AREA GUIDE TO OFFICE SPACE [South Carolina]

Charleston Trident Chamber of Commerce
Box 975
Charleston, SC 29402
Covers: About 35 existing and proposed office buildings and office parks in the Charleston, North Charleston, and Trident, South Carolina area. **Entries include:** Building or park name, address, name, address, and phone of leasing agent, physical characteristics (number of buildings, number of stores, gross rentable space, etc.), lease agreement (minimum length, rental rate per square foot, etc.), year constructed. **Arrangement:** Geographical, then alphabetical by name of park or building. **Indexes:** Building/park name. **Frequency:** Annual, spring. **Editor:** Albert M. Hodge, Jr. **Price:** $5.00.

★1744★

TRUSTS & ESTATES—DIRECTORY OF TRUST INSTITUTIONS ISSUE

Communication Channels, Inc.
6285 Barfield Road   Phone: (404) 256-9800
Atlanta, GA 30328
Covers: About 5,000 trust departments in United States and Canadian banks. **Entries include:** Bank name, address, phone; names of trust department officers and officers of personal trust, corporate trust, investment, and other divisions; trust assets. **Arrangement:** Geographical. **Pages** (approx.): 200. **Frequency:** Annual, December. **Editor:** Art Sweum. **Advertising accepted.** Circulation 12,600. **Price:** $10.00. **Other information:** Variant title, "Directory of Trust Institutions."

★1745★

TUCSON SHOPPING CENTER GUIDE

Tucson Newspapers, Inc.
Box 26887
Tucson, AZ 85726
Number of listings: 70. **Entries include:** Name, address, number and kind of tenants, leasing agent name and address, gross square feet, number of parking spaces, average daily traffic count at major intersections, date opened, vacancies available. **Frequency:** Biennial, October of odd years. **Price:** Free.

★1746★

UNDERWRITERS' REPORT NORTHERN CALIFORNIA INSURANCE DIRECTORY

Underwriters' Report
667 Mission Street   Phone: (415) 981-3221
San Francisco, CA 94105
Covers: Insurance companies; surplus lines; agents and brokers; firms serving the insurance industry; and adjusters. Covers from Kern County to the Oregon border. **Entries include:** Company name, address, phone, names of principal executives. Entries for repair and service firms include list of products or services. **Arrangement:** Classified. **Pages** (approx.): 200. **Frequency:** Semiannual, January and July. **Editor:** Jeffrey J. Lloyd, Directory Manager. **Price:** $6.00.

★1747★

UNDERWRITERS' REPORT SOUTHERN CALIFORNIA INSURANCE DIRECTORY

Underwriters' Report
667 Mission Street   Phone: (415) 981-3221
San Francisco, CA 94105
Covers: Insurance companies; surplus lines; agents and brokers; firms serving the insurance industry; and adjusters. Covers from Kern County to the Mexican border. **Entries include:** Company name, address, phone, and names of principal executives. Entries for repair and service firms include list of products or services. **Arrangement:** Classified. **Pages** (approx.): 200. **Frequency:** Semiannual, April and October. **Editor:** Jeffrey J. Lloyd, Directory Manager. **Price:** $6.00.

★1748★
UNITED FARM AGENCY, INC. CATALOG
United Farm Agency, Inc.
612 W. 47th Street
Kansas City, MO 64112
Covers: Several thousand farms, small town businesses, and rural properties for sale. **Entries include:** For each locality - Description of community and name, address, and phone of real estate office handling listed properties in area. For properties - Photo, acreage, description of land and any buildings, other features, price. **Arrangement:** Geographical. **Indexes:** Sales offices. **Pages** (approx.): 290. **Frequency:** Quarterly. **Price:** Free.

Virginia Insurance Directory *See* Insurance Field State Insurance Directories

★1749★
WESTERN BANK DIRECTORY
Western Banker Publications, Inc.
58 Sutter Street, Suite 615   Phone: (415) 392-5452
San Francisco, CA 94104
Covers: Banks and their branch offices in Alaska, Arizona, California, Hawaii, Idaho, Montana, Nevada, New Mexico, Oregon, Utah, and Washington. **Entries include:** Bank name, address, phone, officers, statement of condition, date organized, correspondent banks. **Arrangement:** Geographical. **Frequency:** Annual, summer. **Price:** $14.00.

Where the Foreign Bankers Are: A Directory *See* Institutional Investor—Foreign Banks in America Directory Issue

★1750★
WHO AUDITS AMERICA
Data Financial Press
Box 801   Phone: (415) 321-4553
Menlo Park, CA 94025
Covers: 10,000 publicly held corporations which report to the Securities and Exchange Commission, and their accounting firms. **Entries include:** For companies - Name, location, SIC classification, number of employees, financial data, and abbreviation indicating accounting firm used. For accounting firms - Name only, with list of clients and their annual sales. **Arrangement:** Companies are alphabetical, accounting firms are geographical. There is a separate alphabetical section of accounting firms with clients having more than $50 million annual sales, with a list of those clients. **Frequency:** Usually, annual, fall; latest edition fall 1979. **Editor:** S. P. Harris, Publisher. **Price:** $33.50.

Who's Who in Commercial-Investment Real Estate *See* Realtors National Marketing Inst.—Directory of Certified Cmml.-Invest. Members

★1751★
WHO'S WHO IN CREATIVE REAL ESTATE
Who's Who in Creative Real Estate, Inc.
1000 Gesell Street   Phone: (213) 247-5813
Glendale, CA 91202
Covers: Licensed real estate salespersons and brokers who have completed 3-5 specified 2-6 day seminars in real estate subjects; persons listed have paid a $5.00 fee. **Entries include:** Name, firm name, address, phone, seminars completed, specialties. **Arrangement:** Geographical. **Frequency:** Annual, February. **Editor:** George Rosenberg. **Price:** $10.00 (1980 edition).

★1752★
WHO'S WHO IN CREDIT AND FINANCIAL MANAGEMENT [New York]
New York Credit and Financial Management Association
71 W. 23rd Street   Phone: (212) 741-4722
New York, NY 10010
Covers: About 4,000 credit and financial executives of manufacturing firms, wholesalers, and banks located in the metropolitan New York City area. **Entries include:** Name, firm with which affiliated, address, area of specialization. **Arrangement:** Alphabetical. **Frequency:** Biennial, January of odd years. **Editor:** John C. Adams, Executive Vice President. **Advertising accepted. Price:** Available to members only.

Who's Who in Residential Real Estate *See* Realtors National Marketing Institute—Directory of Certified Residential Brokers

★1753★
WOODALL'S FLORIDA & SOUTHERN STATES RETIREMENT AND RESORT COMMUNITIES
Woodall Publishing Company
500 Hyacinth Place   Phone: (312) 433-4550
Highland Park, IL 60035
Covers: About 800 housing communities (mobile home parks, mobile home subdivisions, single residence subdivisions, apartment complexes, condominiums, townhouses, and hotels) for persons seeking a retirement home or second home. Coverage limited to Florida and the southern United States and subdivided into regions, with climatic, demographic, economic, and sociological information on each region. **Entries include:** Name of community, address, type of terrain, utilities available or equipment furnished, security, community services, on-site recreation, fees, business history. **Arrangement:** Geographical. **Pages** (approx.): 200. **Frequency:** Annual, October. **Editor:** Linda Profaizer, Directory Manager. **Advertising accepted.** Circulation 46,500. **Price:** $5.95.

Woodall's Retirement and Resort Cummunities Directory *See* Woodall's Florida & Southern States Retirement and Resort Communities

Your Guide to Mutual Funds Without Sales Charges *See* No-Load Mutual Fund Association—Membership Directory

3

Agriculture, Forestry, Mining, and Fishing

★1754★
AGREVIEW—FARMANUAL ISSUE [Agricultural products and services]
AgReview Magazine
R. D. 1, Box 391
Fox Road   Phone: (203) 928-7778
Putnam, CT 06260
Covers: Manufacturers, suppliers, and distributors of products, services, and equipment to dairy, beef, and crop farmers in the northeast and middle Atlantic United States. **Entries include:** Company name, address, phone, name of key executive, products and services. **Arrangement:** Manufacturers are alphabetical; distributors and dealers are geographical, then alphabetical by manufacturer name. **Frequency:** Annual, December. **Editor:** Marietta Harkness, Associate Editor. **Advertising accepted.** Circulation 35,000. **Price:** $3.95.

★1755★
AGRICULTURAL & INDUSTRIAL MANUFACTURERS REPRESENTATIVES ASSOCIATION—MEMBERSHIP DIRECTORY [Farm equipment]
Agricultural & Industrial Manufacturers Representatives Association
Box 1311   Phone: (913) 262-4511
Mission, KS 66222
Number of listings: 280; coverage includes Canada. **Entries include:** Company name, address, phone, name of principal executive, territory covered. **Arrangement:** Geographical. **Pages** (approx.): 65. **Frequency:** Annual, October. **Editor:** Frank Bistrom. **Price:** Apply.

★1756★
AGRICULTURAL ENGINEERS YEARBOOK
American Society of Agricultural Engineers
Box 410   Phone: (616) 429-0300
St. Joseph, MI 49085
Publication includes: 8,000 members of ASAE, and manufacturers of agricultural equipment and components. **Entries include:** For members - Name, office or home address, technical interests, professional registration, year joined ASAE, membership grade. For manufacturers - Company name, address. **Arrangement:** Alphabetical. **Indexes:** Product, geographical (members). **Pages** (approx.): 750. **Frequency:** Annual, May. **Editors:** Joan F. Baxter and Russel Hahn. **Advertising accepted.** Circulation 8,000. **Price:** $19.50 (current and 1980 editions). **Also includes:** ASAE Standards, Recommendations, and Data (about 600 pages).

★1757★
AGRICULTURAL GUIDE TO WASHINGTON: WHOM TO CONTACT— AND WHERE
Elanco Products Company
Box 1750   Phone: (317) 261-2404
Indianapolis, IN 46206
Covers: Heads of congressional committees and subcommittees dealing with agricultural matters, and members of the executive branch and trade associations concerned with agribusiness. **Entries include:** Committee, department, or other unit name, individual name, address, and phone. **Pages** (approx.): 12. **Frequency:** Revised for each session of Congress. **Editor:** David L. Wothke, Director of Industry Affairs. **Price:** Free.

Agricultural Relations Council—Directory *See* Directory of Communicators in Agriculture

★1758★
AGRICULTURAL RESEARCH INDEX
Francis Hodgson Reference Publications
Longman House
Burnt Mill, Harlow
Essex CM20 2JE, England
Covers: Institutions, research centers, etc., involved in research in agriculture, fishing, forestry, horticulture, nutrition, and veterinary science; worldwide coverage. **Entries include:** Name of unit in native language and in English, address, affiliation or parent body, name of director of research, research interests. **Arrangement:** Geographical. **Pages** (approx.): 1,030. **Frequency:** Irregular. **Price:** 75 pounds. **Send orders to:** Longman Group Ltd., 43/45 Annandale Street, Edinburgh EH7 4AT, Scotland.

★1759★
AGRICULTURAL RESIDUES: WORLD DIRECTORY OF INSTITUTIONS
Food and Agriculture Organization of the United Nations
Via delle Terme di Caracalla
Rome 00100, Italy
Covers: About 1,000 institutions in 120 countries concerned with the use of residues produced in agriculture, fisheries, forestry, and related industries. **Entries include:** Institution name, address. **Arrangement:** Geographical. **Indexes:** Subject. **Pages** (approx.): 310. **Frequency:** Irregular; latest edition 1978. **Price:** $16.75. **Send orders to:** Unipub, Box 433, Murray Hill Station, New York, NY 10016.

★1760★

**AMERICAN ACADEMY OF VETERINARY NUTRITION—
   MEMBERSHIP DIRECTORY**

American Academy of Veterinary Nutrition
C/o Dr. Stanely G. Moum
Merck & Company, Inc.
Box 2000   Phone: (201) 574-4151
Rahway, NJ 07065
Number of listings: 130. **Frequency:** Annual.

American Agricultural Economics Association—Membership
   Directory *See* American Journal of Agricultural Economics—
   Handbook/Directory

American Agricultural Editors Association—Directory *See*
   Directory of Communicators in Agriculture

★1761★

**AMERICAN AGRICULTURAL EDITORS' ASSOCIATION—
   MEMBERSHIP DIRECTORY**

American Agricultural Editors' Association
5520-G Touhy Avenue   Phone: (312) 676-4060
Skokie, IL 60077
Covers: About 650 editors and editorial staff of farm publications.
Entries include: Name, address, title, affiliation, office address and
phone, editorial interests. **Arrangement:** Alphabetical. **Pages**
(approx.): 40. **Frequency:** Annual, March. **Editor:** Ted A. Priebe,
Secretary/Treasurer. **Price:** $25.00.

American Association of Agricultural Communicators of
   Tomorrow—Directory *See* Directory of Communicators in
   Agriculture

American Association of Agricultural Editors—Directory *See*
   Directory of Communicators in Agriculture

★1762★

**AMERICAN ASSOCIATION OF BOVINE PRACTITIONERS—
   DIRECTORY**

American Association of Bovine Practitioners
C/o Dr. H. E. Amstutz
Box 2319   Phone: (317) 494-8741
West Lafayette, IN 47906
Covers: 2,000 veterinarians who have a special interest in treatment
of dairy and beef cattle, and who are members. **Entries include:** Name
and office address. **Arrangement:** Geographical. **Pages** (approx.): 60.
Frequency: Annual, June. **Editor:** H. E. Amstutz, Executive Secretary.
Price: Free.

★1763★

**AMERICAN ASSOCIATION OF NURSERYMEN—MEMBER
   DIRECTORY**

American Association of Nurserymen
230 Southern Building
1425 H Street, N. W.   Phone: (202) 737-4060
Washington, DC 20005
Covers: 2,700 member firms. Also includes the membership
directories of Garden Centers of America, Horticultural Research
Institute, National Association of Plant Patent Owners, National
Landscape Association, and Wholesale Nursery Growers of America.
Entries include: AAN listings include firm name, address, phone, name
of one executive, description of type of business, and dues
classification. **Frequency:** Annual, May. **Price:** $8.00 (current and
1980 editions).

American Association of Veterinary Nutritionists—Membership
   Directory *See* American Academy of Veterinary Nutrition—
   Membership Directory

★1764★

AMERICAN BEET SUGAR COMPANIES

U. S. Beet Sugar Association
1156 15th Street   Phone: (202) 296-4820
Washington, DC 20005
Covers: 15 U. S. and Canadian companies. **Entries include:** Company
name, address, phone, names of officers and operating executives,
and names, locations, and capacities of plants. **Arrangement:**
Alphabetical. **Frequency:** Annual, spring. **Editor:** V. R. Olsen, Director
of Public Affairs. **Price:** Free.

★1765★

**AMERICAN BRAHMAN BREEDERS ASSOCIATION—MEMBERSHIP
   DIRECTORY [Cattle]**

American Brahman Breeders Association
1313 La Concha Lane   Phone: (713) 795-4444
Houston, TX 77054
Number of listings: About 2,050. **Entries include:** Name of member,
name of ranch, address (office, residence, ranch), phone, area
number, membership number, date of membership, color of cattle.
Arrangement: By the association's area numbers, then alphabetical.
Pages (approx.): 135. **Frequency:** Biennial, August of odd years.
Editor: Wendell E. Schronk, Executive Secretary. **Price:** Free.

★1766★

AMERICAN FARRIER'S ASSOCIATION—MEMBERSHIP DIRECTORY

American Farrier's Association
Box 695   Phone: (602) 265-7307
Albuquerque, NM 87103
Covers: About 600 member blacksmiths who shoe horses. **Entries
include:** Name and address, membership registration number.
Arrangement: By membership category. **Pages** (approx.): 40.
Frequency: Annual, May. **Editor:** Hazel Senn, Office Secretary. **Price:**
$1.00, plus 30¢ shipping.

★1767★

**AMERICAN FEED MANUFACTURERS ASSOCIATION—
   MEMBERSHIP DIRECTORY**

American Feed Manufacturers Association
1701 N. Ft. Myer Drive   Phone: (703) 524-0810
Arlington, VA 22209
Number of listings: 900. **Entries include:** Company name, address,
phone, names of key personnel, products, geographic areas served.
Arrangement: Geographical. **Pages** (approx.): 470. **Frequency:**
Annual, December. **Editor:** Rex A. Runyon, Director of
Communications. **Advertising accepted.** Circulation 2,300. **Price:**
$35.00.

★1768★

AMERICAN FISHERIES DIRECTORY AND REFERENCE BOOK

Journal Publications, Inc.
21 Elm Street   Phone: (207) 236-4342
Camden, ME 04843
Covers: Manufacturers, suppliers, and distributors of gear and
equipment for commercial fishing and seafood processing; boat
builders, boat yards, naval architects, marine surveyors, boat brokers,
and fisheries consultants; state and federal agencies concerned with
commercial fishing and seafood processing. **Entries include:** Company
or organization name, address, phone, products or services offered.
Arrangement: Alphabetical. **Indexes:** Product. **Pages** (approx.): 560.
Frequency: Irregular; first edition November 1978; new edition
expected 1980. **Editor:** Burton T. Coffey, Publisher-Editor.
Advertising accepted. **Price:** $52.00, cloth; $40.00, paper; plus
$1.50 shipping. **Other information:** 1980 edition will include seafood
buyers and brokers.

★1769★
AMERICAN FRUIT GROWER—BUYER'S DIRECTORY ISSUE
Meister Publishing Company
37841 Euclid Avenue   Phone: (216) 942-2000
Willoughby, OH 44094
Publication includes: List of manufacturers and distributors of equipment and supplies for the commercial fruit growing industry. Entries include: Company name, address. Arrangement: Classified. Pages (approx.): 100. Frequency: Annual, July. Editor: Richard T. Meister. Advertising accepted. Circulation 60,000. Price: $2.00 (current and 1980 editions).

★1770★
AMERICAN GOAT SOCIETY—ROSTER
American Goat Society
R. D. 2, Box 112   Phone: (817) 893-6431
DeLeon, TX 76444
Covers: 900 goat dairy farms, goat breeders, and others interested in goat husbandry. Entries include: Member name, farm name, address, codes for breeds kept, milk availability, stud service availability. Arrangement: Geographical. Pages (approx.): 30. Frequency: Annual, June. Editor: Wayne Hamrick, Secretary-Treasurer. Price: Free.

★1771★
AMERICAN INSTITUTE OF LANDSCAPE ARCHITECTS—
          DIRECTORY
American Institute of Landscape Architects
6810 N. Second Place   Phone: (602) 277-0096
Phoenix, AZ 85012
Number of listings: 450. Entries include: Name, specialization, office address, and phone. Arrangement: Geographical, subdivided by speciality. Pages (approx.): 40. Frequency: Annual, January. Editor: F. J. MacDonald. Advertising accepted. Circulation 1,200. Price: $75.00.

★1772★
AMERICAN JOURNAL OF AGRICULTURAL ECONOMICS—
          HANDBOOK/DIRECTORY
American Agricultural Economics Association
University of Kentucky   Phone: (606) 258-5688
Lexington, KY 40506
Number of listings: 4,000. Entries include: Name, office and home addresses, personal and career data, writings. Arrangement: Alphabetical. Indexes: Geographical, field of interest. Pages (approx.): 625. Frequency: Every five years; latest edition 1976; new edition expected 1981. Editor: Dr. John C. Redman. Price: $15.00.

★1773★
AMERICAN JOURNAL OF ENOLOGY AND VITICULTURE—
          DIRECTORY ISSUE
American Society of Enologists
Box 411   Phone: (916) 752-0385
Davis, CA 95616
Covers: 1,900 vineyard and winery owners, technicians, academicians interested in enology, and agricultural advisors. Entries include: Name, affiliation, address. Arrangement: Alphabetical. Pages (approx.): 25. Frequency: Annual, November. Editor: A. D. Webb. Price: Available to members only.

★1774★
AMERICAN MILKING SHORTHORN SOCIETY—MEMBERSHIP
          DIRECTORY
American Milking Shorthorn Society
1722-JJ South Glenstone   Phone: (417) 887-6525
Springfield, MO 65804
Covers: Breeders of purebred milking Shorthorn cattle producing both milk and beef. Arrangement: Geographical. Pages (approx.): 10. Frequency: Annual, April. Price: Available to members only.

★1775★
AMERICAN PLYWOOD ASSOCIATION—MEMBERSHIP DIRECTORY
American Plywood Association
119 A Street   Phone: (206) 272-2283
Tacoma, WA 98401
Covers: 150 manufacturers of plywood. Entries include: Mill name, address, products. Pages (approx.): 30. Frequency: Annual.

★1776★
AMERICAN POULTRY HISTORICAL SOCIETY—MEMBERSHIP
          LISTING
American Poultry Historical Society
C/o Robert Hogue
Poultry Science Building
Purdue University   Phone: (317) 743-2185
West Lafayette, IN 47907
Covers: About 240 individuals concerned with the collection, preservation, and storage of records, pictures, and other materials dealing with the development of the poultry industry. Entries include: Member name, address. Frequency: Annual. Price: Available to members only.

★1777★
AMERICAN RED ANGUS—BREEDERS DIRECTORY ISSUE
Red Angus Association of America
Box 776   Phone: (817) 387-3502
Denton, TX 76201
Covers: 1,100 breeders of Red Angus cattle. Entries include: Name, home address. Arrangement: Geographical. Frequency: Annual, June. Editor: Mark Herron, Director of Public Relations. Advertising accepted. Price: Free.

★1778★
AMERICAN ROMNEY BREEDERS ASSOCIATION—ACTIVE
          MEMBERSHIP LIST [Sheep]
American Romney Breeders Association
4375 N. E. Weslinn Drive
Corvallis, OR 97330
Covers: About 100 individuals, families, and farms which raise Romney breed sheep primarily as breeding stock. Entries include: Name, address. Arrangement: Geographical. Pages (approx.): Leaflet. Frequency: Irregular; latest edition September 1978. Editor: John H. Landers, Jr. Price: Single copies free.

American Society of Agricultural Engineers—Membership
          Directory See Agricultural Engineers Yearbook

★1779★
AMERICAN SOCIETY OF CONSULTING ARBORISTS—
          MEMBERSHIP DIRECTORY
American Society of Consulting Arborists
12 Lakeview Avenue
Milltown, NJ 08850
Covers: About 170 persons specializing in the growth and care of shade and ornamental trees. Entries include: Name, address, phone. Arrangement: Geographical. Indexes: Alphabetical. Pages (approx.): 30. Frequency: Annual, March. Editor: Spencer H. Davis, Jr., Executive Director. Price: Free.

American Society of Enologists—Roster See American Journal of
          Enology and Viticulture—Directory Issue

★1780★
AMERICAN SOCIETY OF FARM MANAGERS AND RURAL
          APPRAISERS—MEMBERSHIP DIRECTORY
American Society of Farm Managers and Rural Appraisers
360 S. Monroe, Suite 460   Phone: (303) 388-4858
Denver, CO 80209
Number of listings: 3,500. Entries include: Member name, office and home address, and whether available for management, appraisal, and/or agricultural consulting. Arrangement: Geographical. Indexes:

Alphabetical. **Pages** (approx.): 95. **Frequency:** Annual, spring. **Editor:** Carl O. Nonberg, Executive Vice President. **Price:** $100.00, as mailing labels only.

★1781★
AMERICAN SOCIETY OF LANDSCAPE ARCHITECTS—MEMBERS' HANDBOOK
American Society of Landscape Architects
1900 M Street, N. W., Suite 750   Phone: (202) 466-7730
Washington, DC 20036
Covers: 4,500 member landscape architects. **Entries include:** Name, address, chapter, membership category, year joined. **Arrangement:** Alphabetical within categories of private, public, or academic practice. **Indexes:** Geographical, affiliation. **Pages** (approx.): 400. **Frequency:** Annual, June. **Editor:** Richard A. Lippman, Director of Publications. **Advertising accepted.** Circulation 5,500. **Price:** $40.00 to individuals; $10.00 to libraries.

★1782★
AMERICAN SPICE TRADE ASSOCIATION—INFORMATION DIRECTORY
American Spice Trade Association
Box 1267   Phone: (201) 568-2163
Englewood Cliffs, NJ 07632
Covers: About 300 firms which import, grind, and distribute spices. **Entries include:** Company name, address, phone, names and titles of key personnel. **Arrangement:** Alphabetical. **Pages** (approx.): 50. **Frequency:** Annual, August. **Price:** Available to members only.

★1783★
AMERICAN SUFFOLK SHEEP SOCIETY—ACTIVE BREEDERS' LIST
American Suffolk Sheep Society
55 E. 100 North   Phone: (801) 753-2983
Logan, UT 84321
Covers: Over 1,500 member individuals and farms which breed Suffolk sheep. **Entries include:** Individual name, address. **Arrangement:** Geographical. **Pages** (approx.): 55. **Frequency:** Annual. **Price:** Available to members.

★1784★
AMERICAN VEGETABLE GROWER—BUYERS GUIDE ISSUE
Meister Publishing Company
37841 Euclid Avenue   Phone: (216) 942-2000
Willoughby, OH 44094
Covers: Manufacturers of equipment and supplies for the commercial vegetable growing industry. **Pages** (approx.): 110. **Frequency:** Annual, July. **Editor:** Richard T. Meister. **Advertising accepted.** Circulation 40,000. **Price:** $2.00 (current and 1980 editions).

★1785★
AQUACULTURE—BUYERS GUIDE ISSUE
Briggs Associates, Inc.
620 E. Sixth Street   Phone: (501) 376-1921
Little Rock, AR 72202
Covers: About 450 manufacturers and suppliers of equipment and materials used in fish farming, production, processing, marketing, and aquaculture in general; fish disease diagnostic services; and state extension services in fish and wildlife. **Entries include:** For manufacturers - Company name, address. For diagnostic services - Name of diagnostician, services or specializations, firm or university name, address, phone. For extension services - Name of specialist, title, university affiliation, address, phone. **Arrangement:** Manufacturers are alphabetical, others are geographical. **Indexes:** Product. **Frequency:** Annual, November. **Editor:** Dorothy Stuck. **Advertising accepted.** Circulation 5,000. **Former title:** Commercial Fish Farmer & Aquaculture News - Buyers Guide Issue. **Price:** $5.00.

★1786★
ARIZONA AGRIBUSINESS
Arizona Office of Economic Planning and Development
1700 W. Washington, Room 505
Phoenix, AZ 85007
Covers: About 550 manufacturers, distributors, trade associations and other organizations concerned with the development of the agricultural business in Arizona. **Entries include:** Company name, address, and type of business or organization. **Arrangement:** By commodity or service. **Indexes:** Product/business. **Pages** (approx.): 55. **Frequency:** Irregular; first edition May 1978. **Price:** Free. **Other information:** Compiled with the Department of Agricultural Economics, University of Arizona, Tucson, AZ 85721.

Associated Landscape Contractors of America—Membership Directory *See* Who's Who in Landscape Contracting

★1787★
BEDDING PLANTS—MEMBERSHIP DIRECTORY [Horticulture]
Bedding Plants
Box 268   Phone: (517) 349-3924
Okemos, MI 48864
Covers: About 2,700 wholesalers, retailers, growers, allied trades, and educators in the bedding plant industry. **Entries include:** Company name, address, phone, name of principal executive, financial keys, list of products or services. **Arrangement:** Geographical. **Indexes:** Alphabetical. **Pages** (approx.): 275. **Frequency:** Annual, June. **Editor:** William H. Carlson, Executive Secretary. **Price:** Available to members only.

★1788★
BEEF—BUYER'S GUIDE ISSUE
Webb Company
1999 Shepard Road
St. Paul, MN 55116
Covers: Over 1,000 companies manufacturing equipment and supplying products and services of interest to the cattle industry; also includes government associations, telephone market report sources, auction markets, commission firms, order buyers, purebred registry associations and other trade organizations. **Entries include:** Company or organization name, address, and products, services, or interests. **Arrangement:** Alphabetical. **Frequency:** Annual, December. **Price:** $1.00.

Bituminous Coal Data *See* Coal Data

Brown's Directory of North American Gas Companies *See* Brown's Directory of U.S. & International Gas Companies

★1789★
BROWN'S DIRECTORY OF U.S. & INTERNATIONAL GAS COMPANIES
Energy Publications, Inc., Division
Harcourt Brace Jovanovich Publications
800 Davis Building   Phone: (214) 748-4403
Dallas, TX 75221
Covers: Operating gas companies (utilities, including municipal systems), holding and transmission companies, and state public service commissions; includes major gas companies outside the United States. **Entries include:** For utilities - Company name, address, phone, officers and other key personnel, source of gas supplies, communities served, technical and operating data. For holding companies - Company name, address, names of officers and directors, subsidiaries, sales, employees, etc. For commissions - Body name, address, names of staff members; some listings include commissioners' names. **Arrangement:** By activity, then alphabetical. **Indexes:** Gas companies, communities with companies serving them. **Pages** (approx.): 300. **Frequency:** Annual, October. **Editor:** Dean Hale. **Advertising accepted.** Circulation 1,000. **Former title:** Brown's Directory of North American Gas Companies (1978). **Price:** $95.00.

Building Stone Institute—Membership Directory *See* Who's Who in the Stone Business

★1790★
CALIFORNIA AGRICULTURAL AIRCRAFT ASSOCIATION—MEMBERSHIP BOOK
California Agricultural Aircraft Association
1107 Ninth Street, Suite 900   Phone: (916) 442-1819
Sacramento, CA 95814
Covers: About 300 crop dusting firms, pilots, and industry suppliers. **Entries include:** For operators - Name and address of company, name and occasionally the phone of the authorized agent. For pilots - Name, address. For sustaining members - Company name, address, head of company, phone. **Arrangement:** Alphabetical. **Pages** (approx.): 100. **Frequency:** Annual, May. **Editor:** Sandi Kendall, Assistant Executive Director. **Price:** $10.00.

★1791★
CALIFORNIA AGRICULTURAL DIRECTORY [Includes Oregon and Washington]
California Service Agency
2855 Telegraph Avenue   Phone: (415) 644-7086
Berkeley, CA 94705
Covers: 1,500 farm cooperatives and organizations; 500 federal, state, and county organizations concerned with agriculture; covers California, Oregon, and Washington. **Arrangement:** By commodity. **Indexes:** Alphabetical. **Frequency:** Biennial, late in odd years. **Editor:** Milton L. Levy, Editor. **Price:** $20.00.

★1792★
CALIFORNIA CACTUS GROWERS' ASSOCIATION—DIRECTORY
California Cactus Growers' Association
Box 523   Phone: (714) 926-1151
Homeland, CA 92348
Number of listings: 70. **Entries include:** Company name, address, phone, name of principal executive, whether wholesale or retail, grower and/or shipper, and potter or bare root. **Arrangement:** Alphabetical. **Frequency:** Biennial, even years; addendum and corrections in odd years. **Other information:** Affiliate member of the Cactus and Succulent Society of America.

★1793★
CALIFORNIA WINE COUNTRY SERIES [Wineries]
Vintage Image
1335 Main Street
St. Helena, CA 94574
Covers: Active wineries in California. Three volumes: ''Napa Valley Wine Book,'' ''Sonoma-Mendocino Wine Book,'' and ''Central Coast Wine Book.'' **Entries include:** Wine name, address, phone, vineyards, winemaker, types and quantity of wines produced, descriptive text and illustrations. **Arrangement:** Geographical. **Frequency:** Annual. **Price:** $6.95, plus 70¢ shipping, payment with order.

Canner/Packer—Buyers Guide Issue *See* Processed Prepared Food—Buyers Guide Issue

★1794★
CDE STOCK OWNERSHIP DIRECTORY: AGRIBUSINESS
Corporate Data Exchange, Inc.
198 Broadway, Suite 707   Phone: (212) 962-2980
New York, NY 10038
Covers: About 220 of the leading companies and farm cooperatives in one or more of three areas: Agricultural inputs (fertilizers, farm machinery, etc.); food processing; food distribution (wholesale, retail, restaurant, and commodity trade); includes section on operations of foreign subsidiaries. **Frequency:** Irregular; first edition 1978; new edition expected 1981. **Price:** $75.00, libraries and nonprofit corporations; $250.00, corporations. **Other information:** Details of entry content, etc., are same as in ''CDE Stock Ownership Directory: Transportation'' (see separate entry, which also contains information about additional planned directories and references to news stories

concerning CDE).

Central Coast Wine Book *See* California Wine Country Series [Wineries]

Central Coast Wine Tour *See* Wine Tour Series [California]

★1795★
CEREAL FOODS WORLD—MEMBERSHIP DIRECTORY AND TECHNICAL GUIDE ISSUE
American Association of Cereal Chemists
3340 Pilot Knob Road
St. Paul, MN 55121
Covers: 2,000 scientists in the cereal processing industry (milling, baking, convenience foods, feeds, etc.). **Entries include:** Name, office address. **Arrangement:** Alphabetical. **Pages** (approx.): 150. **Frequency:** Annual, May. **Editor:** Jim Trevis. **Advertising accepted.** Former title: Cereal Science Today - Membership Directory Issue. **Price:** Available to members only; Technical Guide (without directory) available separately, $25.00.

★1796★
CHOOSE AND CUT [Christmas trees]
Maryland Department of Agriculture
Annapolis, MD 21401
Covers: About 30 growers of Christmas trees for sale on a cut-your-own basis in Maryland. **Entries include:** Grower, address, road directions, dates and hours of operations, types of trees. **Arrangement:** By county. **Frequency:** Annual. **Price:** Free. **Other information:** Published in cooperation with the Maryland Christmas Tree Association.

★1797★
COACHELLA VALLEY [CALIFORNIA] GRAPE SHIPPERS DIRECTORY
Federal-State Market News Service
395 Broadway   Phone: (714) 352-3562
El Centro, CA 92243
Number of listings: 17. **Entries include:** Company name, address, phone, trade and brand names, name of sales manager, and list of products. **Arrangement:** Alphabetical. **Frequency:** Annual. **Editor:** Jack R. Kloth, Officer-in-Charge. **Price:** Free.

★1798★
COAL AGE—BUYERS GUIDE ISSUE
McGraw-Hill, Inc.
1221 Avenue of the Americas
New York, NY 10020
Publication includes: Manufacturers, distributors, and suppliers of mining equipment and services. **Entries include:** Company name, address. **Arrangement:** Alphabetical. **Indexes:** Product. **Frequency:** Annual, September. **Advertising accepted.** Circulation 14,300. **Price:** $5.00.

★1799★
COAL DATA
National Coal Association
1130 17th Street, N. W.
Washington, DC 20036
Publication includes: Data on 50 largest bituminous coal mines. **Frequency:** Annual. **Editor:** King Lin. **Former title:** Bituminous Coal Data. **Price:** $50.00. **Other information:** Principal content of publication is statistical information on the coal industry.

★1800★
COKE PRODUCERS IN THE UNITED STATES
Office of Energy Data Operations
Energy Information Administration
Energy Department
1000 Independence Avenue, N. W.   Phone: (202) 252-6401
Washington, DC 20585
Covers: About 65 operating oven coke and beehive coke plants in the

United States. **Entries include:** Plant name, company name, location of plant, type of ownership, major uses of coke, coal chemical materials produced. Beehive coke plant listings also include type of ovens. **Arrangement:** Geographical. **Pages** (approx.): 5. **Frequency:** Annual. **Price:** Free (DOE/EIA-708). **Send orders to:** Energy Information Administration Clearinghouse, 1726 M St., N. W., Room 200, Washington, DC 20461 (202-634-5694).

★1801★
COLORADO SCHOOL OF MINES ALUMNI ASSOCIATION MINES MAGAZINE—DIRECTORY ISSUE
Colorado School of Mines Alumni Association
Guggenheim Hall   Phone: (303) 279-0300
Golden, CO 80401
Covers: All 10,300 graduates of the school (founded 1894). **Entries include:** Name, year of graduation, degree(s), company and position, title, address or note concerning death. **Arrangement:** Alphabetical. **Pages** (approx.): 170. **Frequency:** Annual, July. **Editor:** Patricia C. Petty. **Advertising accepted.** Circulation 5,800. **Price:** $12.50.

Commercial Fish Farmer & Aquaculture News—Buyers Guide Issue *See* Aquaculture—Buyers Guide Issue

Communications Officers of State Departments of Agriculture— Directory *See* Directory of Communicators in Agriculture

★1802★
CONNECTICUT AGRICULTURAL FAIRS
Marketing Division
Connecticut Dept. of Agriculture
State Office Building   Phone: (203) 566-4276
Hartford, CT 06115
Number of listings: 50. **Entries include:** Fair name, dates, locations, attractions, schedule of events, costs, secretary's name and address. **Arrangement:** Alphabetical by fair name. **Indexes:** Chronological. **Frequency:** Annual, May. **Price:** Free; send stamped, addressed envelope.

★1803★
COOPERATIVE BRANDS AND PROCESSED FOODS
Farmer Cooperative Service
Agriculture Department
550 GHI Building
Washington, DC 20250
Covers: More than 80 farm cooperatives which own their own brands used on processed foods. **Entries include:** Cooperative name, address, products, and brands. **Indexes:** Brand name. **Frequency:** Latest edition fall 1977. **Price:** Free.

Cooperative Editorial Association—Directory *See* Directory of Communicators in Agriculture

Country Carousel *See* Michigan Country Carousel [Farm product outlets]

★1804★
COUNTY AGENTS DIRECTORY
Century Communications, Inc.
5520-G Touhy Avenue   Phone: (312) 676-4060
Skokie, IL 60077
Covers: 15,000 county agents and other agricultural extension workers. **Entries include:** Name, office address, phone, areas of occupational specialization. **Arrangement:** Geographical. **Pages** (approx.): 140. **Frequency:** Annual, April. **Editor:** K. L. Orwig. **Advertising accepted.** Circulation 5,500. **Price:** $7.95. **Also includes:** Lists of national and state organizations active in agricultural extension and home demonstration, and of registry associations.

★1805★
CROW'S BUYERS AND SELLERS GUIDE OF THE FOREST PRODUCTS INDUSTRIES
C. C. Crow Publications, Inc.
834 S. W. St. Clair   Phone: (503) 222-9576
Portland, OR 97205
Covers: Over 5,000 manufacturers of lumber, plywood, and other forest products; wholesalers; commission lumber dealers; plywood jobbers; and exporters in the United States and western Canada. **Entries include:** Company name, address, phone. **Arrangement:** By line of business. **Frequency:** Annual, March. **Price:** $125.00, postpaid, payment with order.

★1806★
DAIRY INDUSTRIES CATALOG
Magazines for Industry, Inc.
777 Third Avenue   Phone: (212) 838-7778
New York, NY 10017
Covers: 800 suppliers of equipment and services for the dairy processing industry (SIC 202). Includes lists of dairy schools and Agriculture Department personnel in dairying. **Entries include:** Company name, address, and products or services. **Arrangement:** Alphabetical. **Indexes:** Product. **Pages** (approx.): 300. **Frequency:** Annual, July. **Editor:** Jerome Frank. **Advertising accepted.** Circulation 15,000. **Price:** $20.00. **Also includes:** Series of application handbooks on dairy packaging, processing, distribution, sanitation, ingredients.

★1807★
DAIRY RECORD—BUYERS GUIDE ISSUE
Gorman Publishing Company
5724 E. River Road   Phone: (312) 693-3200
Chicago, IL 60631
Covers: 700 manufacturers of products sold to dairy processors. Also includes geographical listings of associations. **Entries include:** Company name, address, phone, name of contact. **Arrangement:** Alphabetical. **Indexes:** Product. **Frequency:** Annual, December. **Advertising accepted.** Circulation 10,000. **Price:** $10.00.

★1808★
DIRECTORY OF AMERICAN HORTICULTURE
American Horticultural Society
       Phone: (703) 768-5700
Mt. Vernon, VA 22121
Covers: Professional, semiprofessional, and trade horticulture associations; conservation organizations; garden club associations; plant societies; libraries; federal agriculture programs; educational horticultural programs; botanical gardens, and arboreta. **Entries include:** Name of organization, publication, etc., address, and, in many cases, phone; where appropriate, special interests, publications, or services are indicated; garden and arboreta listings include information on size, plants featured, hours, name of superintendent. **Arrangement:** Classified. **Indexes:** General. **Pages** (approx.): 120. **Frequency:** Irregular; previous edition 1974; latest edition August 1977. **Editor:** Judy Powell, Publications Director. **Price:** $7.50.

★1809★
DIRECTORY OF ANGUS ASSOCIATIONS [Meat industry]
American Angus Association
3201 Frederick Boulevard   Phone: (816) 233-3101
St. Joseph, MO 64501
Covers: About 210 regional, state, local, and junior associations of breeders and owners of purebred Angus cattle. **Entries include:** Organization name; name, title, address, and phone for officers. **Arrangement:** Geographical. **Pages** (approx.): 40. **Frequency:** Annual, July. **Editor:** Keith E. Evans, Director, Public Relations. **Former title:** Directory of Aberdeen-Angus Associations. **Price:** $1.00.

★1810★
DIRECTORY OF AQUACULTURE IN THE SOUTHEAST
National Marine Fisheries Service
Commerce Department
Union National Plaza, Suite 1160   Phone: (501) 378-5888
Little Rock, AR 72201
Covers: Industrial, academic, state, and federal personnel engaged in aquaculture in the southeastern United States. **Entries include:** Personal name, or name of institution or agency with names of staff, address, specialties. **Arrangement:** Geographical. **Pages** (approx.): 30. **Frequency:** Irregular; latest edition January 1977. **Price:** Free.

★1811★
DIRECTORY OF COMMUNICATORS IN AGRICULTURE
Agricultural Relations Council
6501 El Lido Drive   Phone: (703) 356-8221
McLean, VA 22101
Covers: Members of the Agricultural Relations Council, American Agricultural Editors Association, American Association of Agricultural Editors, American Association of Agricultural Communicators of Tomorrow, Communications Officers of State Departments of Agriculture, Cooperative Editorial Association, National Association of Farm Broadcasters, and Newspaper Farm Editors of America. **Entries include:** Name, title, company or other affiliation, address, phone. **Arrangement:** By organization. **Pages** (approx.): 90. **Frequency:** Biennial.

★1812★
DIRECTORY OF COMPUTER PROGRAMS APPLICABLE TO U.S. MINING PRACTICES AND PROBLEMS
Bureau of Mines
Interior Department
18th and C Streets, N. W.
Washington, DC
Covers: Sources for more than 300 recent computer programs applicable to underground and surface mining, blasting, mine safety, etc., available from mining companies, equipment manufacturers, consulting firms, government agencies, etc. **Entries include:** Source name, address, description of program and its availability. **Arrangement:** Alphabetical by name of program. **Pages** (approx.): 550. **Frequency:** Published 1979. **Price:** $15.50, paper; $3.00, microfiche (PB 289-743/AS). **Send orders to:** National Technical Information Service, Springfield, VA 22161.

Directory of Electric Light & Power Companies *See* Midwest Oil Register—Industry Segment Directories

★1813★
DIRECTORY OF FARMER COOPERATIVES
National Council of Farmer Cooperatives
1800 Massachusetts Avenue, N.W.   Phone: (202) 659-1525
Washington, DC 20036
Covers: Some 500 of the largest farmer-owned cooperatives. **Entries include:** Cooperative name, address, phone, name of principal executive, list of services performed and products handled. **Arrangement:** Geographical. **Indexes:** Cooperative name. **Pages** (approx.): 65. **Frequency:** Triennial, September; latest edition November 1979. **Editor:** Donald K. Hanes, Vice President, Public Relations. **Price:** $10.00.

★1814★
DIRECTORY OF FARMERS' MARKETS IN WISCONSIN
Wisconsin Department of Agriculture, Trade, and Consumer Protection
801 W. Badger Road   Phone: (608) 266-9589
Madison, WI 53708
Covers: Markets which are communal in nature and operate at specific times and places for the sale of agricultural products. **Entries include:** Market name, location, day or days open. **Arrangement:** Geographical. **Frequency:** Annual, summer. **Price:** Free.

★1815★
DIRECTORY OF FERTILIZER PLANTS IN THE UNITED STATES
Economics and Marketing Research Section
Tennessee Valley Authority
Muscle Shoals, AL 35660
Covers: 7,200 firms which manufacture or merchandise fertilizers. Does not include basic producers of fertilizer materials or retailers. **Entries include:** Firm name, address, phone, name of principal executive, type of plant, storage capacity, and auxiliary services offered. **Arrangement:** Geographical. **Frequency:** Irregular; latest edition summer 1977; new edition expected summer 1980. **Price:** $4.00 (current edition); $5.00 (1980 edition). **Other information:** Prepared with the Association of American Plant Food Control Officials.

★1816★
DIRECTORY OF FISH CULTURISTS
New York Ocean Science Laboratory
Box 867
Montauk, NY 11954
Covers: Fish culturists and aquaculturists. **Entries include:** Name, office and home addresses and phones, highest degree held, institution granting degree, work experience, and areas of occupational specialization. **Arrangement:** Alphabetical, geographical. **Pages** (approx.): 80. **Frequency:** Irregular; latest edition 1977. **Editor:** Dr. Robert J. Valenti.

Directory of Gas Utility Companies *See* Midwest Oil Register—Industry Segment Directories

Directory of Geophysical & Oil Companies Who Use Geophysical Service *See* Midwest Oil Register—Industry Segment Directories

★1817★
DIRECTORY OF IOWA AGRICULTURAL EXPORTS
Iowa Department of Agriculture
Henry A. Wallace Building   Phone: (515) 281-5994
Des Moines, IA 50319
Covers: Over 180 Iowa agriculture firms and others in Iowa concerned with international trade (including seed growers, banks, chambers of commerce, meat packing companies). **Entries include:** Company name, address, phone, products; telex number, cable address, and international offices are listed for some entries. **Arrangement:** By product. **Indexes:** Alphabetical. **Pages** (approx.): 55. **Frequency:** Irregular; latest edition 1979. **Price:** Free.

★1818★
DIRECTORY OF MAJOR U.S. CORPORATIONS INVOLVED IN AGRIBUSINESS
Agribusiness Accountability Publications
3410 19th Street   Phone: (415) 626-1266
San Francisco, CA 94110
Number of listings: 25. **Entries include:** Name of company, address, principal lines of business and company's relative ranking in those lines, description of its areas of agribusiness. **Pages** (approx.): 50. **Frequency:** Irregular; latest edition 1977. **Editor:** A. V. Krebs, Co-Director. **Price:** Apply.

★1819★
DIRECTORY OF MINE SUPPLY HOUSES, DISTRIBUTORS, AND SALES AGENTS
McGraw-Hill, Inc.
1221 Avenue of the Americas   Phone: (212) 997-2974
New York, NY 10020
Covers: 675 minerals mining supply firms in the United States and Canada. **Entries include:** Company name, address, phone, names of principals, size of stocks maintained, territories served, products handled, branch offices, manufacturers represented, number of salesmen, year established. **Arrangement:** Geographical. **Pages** (approx.): 215. **Frequency:** Annual, summer. **Editor:** George F.

Nielsen. **Price:** $40.00, postpaid, payment with order; $42.00, billed.

★1820★

DIRECTORY OF MINING ENTERPRISES [Montana]
Montana Bureau of Mines and Geology
W. Park Street   Phone: (406) 792-8321
Butte, MT 59701
Covers: About 300 companies with metal, non-metal, and coal mining and processing operations located in Montana, and recently inactive mines. **Entries include:** Company name, address, name of contact. **Arrangement:** By commodity, then by county. **Pages** (approx.): 65. **Frequency:** Annual, summer. **Editor:** Don C. Lawson, Staff Field Agent. **Price:** Free; send 75¢ shipping.

Directory of Oil Marketing & Wholesale Distributors *See* Midwest Oil Register—Industry Segment Directories

Directory of Oil Refineries *See* Midwest Oil Register—Industry Segment Directories

Directory of Oil Well Drilling Contractors *See* Midwest Oil Register—Industry Segment Directories

Directory of Oil Well Supply Companies *See* Midwest Oil Register—Industry Segment Directories

★1821★

DIRECTORY OF SELECTED PRIVATE CIVIC-SERVICE ORGANIZATIONS FOR COOPERATIVE 4-H PROGRAMMING
Extension Service
Agriculture Department
Washington, DC 20250
Covers: About 40 national volunteer organizations in the United States which are of potential assistance in 4-H programs. **Entries include:** Organization name, address; number or description of source of members; number of local units; description of organization and its structure; description of program areas; publications. **Arrangement:** Alphabetical. **Pages** (approx.): 80. **Frequency:** Published July 1977 (1975 data). **Editor:** Joel R. Soobitsky, Program Leader. **Price:** Free.

★1822★

DIRECTORY OF STATEWIDE AGRICULTURAL ORGANIZATIONS IN VIRGINIA
Virginia Department of Agriculture and Consumer Services
203 N. Governor Street   Phone: (804) 786-2373
Richmond, VA 23209
Entries include: Association name, address, phone, name of principal executive. **Arrangement:** Alphabetical. **Frequency:** Annual, August. **Editor:** Meribeth Brewster, Information Technician. **Price:** Free.

★1823★

DIRECTORY OF THE FOREST PRODUCTS INDUSTRY
Miller Freeman Publications, Inc.
500 Howard Street   Phone: (415) 397-1881
San Francisco, CA 94105
Covers: 4,500 sawmills, plywood, board, and veneer mills in the United States; 12,000 loggers and pulpwood producers; over 4,000 wood products wholesalers, distributors and commission men and jobbers; 18,000 executives, owners, managers, and production, maintenance, and sales persons. **Entries include:** Company name, address, and phone; names of personnel; number of employees; products or type of business; amount of production; and species where applicable. **Arrangement:** Geographical. **Indexes:** Type of operation, lumber specialties, general. **Pages** (approx.): 750. **Frequency:** Annual, January. **Editor:** Herbert G. Lambert. **Price:** $75.00 (current and 1980 editions). **Also includes:** Industry statistics, directory of trade organizations, classified buyers guide to suppliers of specialized products and services for the forest industries.

Directory of the Wholesale Tobacco Trade *See* Geographical Index of Wholesale Tobacco Licensees

★1824★

DIRECTORY OF TRUCKERS AND TRUCK BROKERS [Michigan agricultural products]
Marketing Division
Michigan Department of Agriculture
Box 30017
Lansing, MI 48909
Covers: About 125 Michigan and about 25 out-of-state truckers and truck brokers interested in hauling Michigan agricultural products. **Entries include:** Firm or individual name, address, phone. **Arrangement:** Alphabetical. **Pages** (approx.): 55. **Frequency:** Irregular. **Price:** Free.

★1825★

DRILLING-DCW—INTERNATIONAL BUYER'S GUIDE ISSUE
Associated Publishers, Inc.
4703 W. Lovers Lane   Phone: (214) 358-3456
Dallas, TX 75209
Covers: United States-based companies (plus some foreign) offering supplies and services to the petroleum and gas well drilling, well completion, and well servicing industry. **Entries include:** Company name, address, phone, telex, sales offices, description of products or services. **Arrangement:** Alphabetical, with sales and services offices listed geographically within the main company entry. **Frequency:** Annual, February. **Editor:** Robert O. Frederick. **Advertising accepted.** Circulation 21,800.

★1826★

EARTHWORM BUYER'S GUIDE
Shields Publications
Box 669
Eagle River, WI 54521
Covers: About 300 earthworm growers; suppliers of equipment and materials used in earthworm agriculture and sales; covers United States and Canada. **Entries include:** For growers - Company name, address, types of worms grown and sold, whether wholesale or retail. For others - Company name, address, products. **Arrangement:** Alphabetical. **Pages** (approx.): 160. **Frequency:** Biennial, even years. **Editor:** Robert Shields, Publisher. **Advertising accepted.** Circulation 10,000. **Price:** $3.00 (current and new editions).

E/MJ—Buying Directory Issue *See* Engineering & Mining Journal—Buying Directory Issue

★1827★

E/MJ INTERNATIONAL DIRECTORY OF MINING AND MINERAL PROCESSING OPERATIONS
McGraw-Hill, Inc.
1221 Avenue of the Americas   Phone: (212) 997-4035
New York, NY 10020
Covers: 2,100 companies and 3,000 mines and plants producing metals and nonmetallic minerals, worldwide (SIC 1411-1499, 1011-1099, 333, and 334). Also includes a list of over 1,100 consultants, contractors, and other service firms, and a directory of mining associations, government mine bureaus and geological surveys. **Entries include:** For company headquarters - Company name, address, phone, names of executives, number of employees, sales and capital, general area explored, type of business, products, SIC numbers. For mines and plants - Company name, address, phone, primary function (consulting, contracting, etc.), specific activities and fields engaged in, number of employees, principals, branch offices. **Arrangement:** Companies and consultants are alphabetical; mines and plants are geographical. **Indexes:** Personnel, type of ore or mineral. **Pages** (approx.): 620. **Frequency:** Annual, June/July. **Editor:** Louis C. Bel. **Advertising accepted.** **Price:** $50.00, postpaid, payment with order; $52.00, billed. **Other information:** Includes tabulations of major open-pit, underground, and smelter-refinery operations, worldwide.

★1828★

ENERGY SOURCES [YEAR] [Western states]

Enercom

909 17th Street, Suite 601   Phone: (303) 571-0080

Denver, CO 80202

Covers: About 90 companies concerned with the development and production of oil and gas, coal, solar energy, geothermal energy, uranium, and other potential sources of energy in the Rockies and southwest United States. **Entries include:** Company name, address, phone, name of principal executive, financial data, brief description of company history, holdings, etc. **Arrangement:** By type of energy. **Pages** (approx.): 180. **Frequency:** Annual, fall. **Editor:** Rita Blome, Editor and Publisher. **Advertising accepted.** Circulation 20,000. **Price:** $10.95. **Also includes:** Articles on exploration, research, etc., related to the western states. **Other information:** Previous edition published by the Denver Securities Traders Association.

★1829★

ENGINEERING & MINING JOURNAL—BUYING DIRECTORY ISSUE

McGraw-Hill, Inc.

1221 Avenue of the Americas   Phone: (212) 997-2264

New York, NY 10020

Covers: Manufacturers and suppliers of mining equipment. **Entries include:** Company name, address, list of products or services, and adddress and phone number of local distributors, warehouses, sales offices, etc. **Arrangement:** Alphabetical. **Indexes:** Product. **Frequency:** Annual, fall. **Editor:** Stanley H. Dayton. **Advertising accepted.** Circulation 23,000. **Price:** $5.00.

Export Directory [Agriculture] *See* **Food and Agricultural Export Directory**

★1830★

FARM AND POWER EQUIPMENT—BUYERS DIRECTORY ISSUE

National Farm and Power Services, Inc.

10877 Watson Road   Phone: (314) 821-7220

St. Louis, MO 63127

Covers: Manufacturers of agricultural and light industrial machinery (SIC 5252). **Entries include:** Company name, address. **Arrangement:** Classified by product. **Indexes:** Trade name, product. **Pages** (approx.): 300. **Frequency:** Annual January. **Editor:** Sharon Degnan. **Advertising accepted.** Circulation 20,000. **Price:** $7.50. (current and 1980 editions; ISSN 0014-7843Z).

★1831★

FARM BUILDING NEWS—FARM BUILDERS BUYERS' GUIDE ISSUE

American Farm Building Services, Inc.

733 N. Van Buren   Phone: (414) 272-5410

Milwaukee, WI 53202

Covers: Materials and equipment used in construction of farm buildings, livestock feeding and handling systems, and grain storage and handling systems. **Entries include:** Company name, address, phone. **Arrangement:** Alphabetical. **Indexes:** Product. **Frequency:** Annual, October. **Editor:** Frank D. Lessiter. **Advertising accepted.** Circulation 33,000. **Price:** Included in subscription, $8.95 per year.

★1832★

FARM CHEMICALS HANDBOOK

Meister Publishing Company

37841 Euclid Avenue   Phone: (216) 942-2000

Willoughby, OH 44094

Covers: Manufacturers and suppliers of chemicals used in agribusiness. **Entries include:** Company name, address, trade and brand names.**Pages** (approx.): 650. **Frequency:** Annual. **Editor:** Gordon L. Berg. **Advertising accepted.** Circulation 15,000. **Price:** $32.00. **Also includes:** Dictionaries of plant foods and pesticides.

★1833★

FARM EQUIPMENT WHOLESALERS ASSOCIATION—MEMBERSHIP DIRECTORY

Farm Equipment Wholesalers Association

Box 1347

Iowa City, IA 52244

Number of listings: 125. **Entries include:** Company name, address, phone, names of executives, territory served, branches. **Arrangement:** Geographical. **Indexes:** Alphabetical. **Pages** (approx.): 120. **Frequency:** Annual, April. **Editor:** Thomas L. Irwin, Executive Director. **Price:** Free.

★1834★

FARM MARKETS OF OHIO—MEMBER DIRECTORY

Farm Markets of Ohio, Division

Ohio Agricultural Marketing Association

35 E. Chestnut Street

Columbus, OH 43216

Covers: Over 75 fresh produce markets. **Entries include:** Farm name, address, phone, directions, types of produce and merchandise available, hours, whether pick-your-own arrangement is available. **Arrangement:** Alphabetical. **Frequency:** Not established; first edition 1979; new edition expected 1980. **Price:** Free; send a stamped, self-addressed envelope.

★1835★

FARM STORE MERCHANDISING—BUYER'S GUIDE ISSUE

Miller Publishing Company

2501 Wayzata Boulevard   Phone: (612) 374-5200

Minneapolis, MN 55440

Covers: Manufacturers of farm supplies and light equipment who sell through retail farm stores and farm supply distributors; includes list of state and national associations serving agribusiness. **Entries include:** Company or association name, address, phone, list of key personnel. **Arrangement:** Alphabetical. **Indexes:** Product, brand name. **Frequency:** Annual, December. **Editor:** Richard W. Chamberlin. **Advertising accepted.** Circulation 32,500. **Price:** $10.00.

★1836★

FARM SUPPLIER—DIRECTORY OF FARM SUPPLIES ISSUE

Watt Publishing Company

Sandstone Building   Phone: (815) 734-4171

Mt. Morris, IL 61054

Covers: Manufacturers of supplies, services, and equipment handled by farm, feed, agricultural chemical, fertilizer, and poultry industry supply dealers. **Entries include:** Company name, address, phone, and trade and brand names. **Pages** (approx.): 130. **Frequency:** Annual, December. **Editor:** Mahlon C. Sweet. **Advertising accepted.** Circulation 22,000. **Price:** $10.00.

★1837★

FARMER-TO-CONSUMER DIRECTORY [Pennsylvania]

Bureau of Rural Affairs

Pennsylvania Department of Agriculture

2301 N. Cameron Street

Harrisburg, PA 17120

Covers: Several hundred outlets which sell direct to consumers. Outlets include produce stands, pick-your-own orchards and fields, milk juggers, Christmas tree farms, and markets for maple products and organically grown foods. **Entries include:** Outlet name, location, harvesting season, commodities sold. **Arrangement:** Geographical. **Frequency:** Annual, June. **Price:** Free.

★1838★

FEED MANAGEMENT—WHO'S WHO DIRECTORY ISSUE

Garden State Publishing Company

Garden State Building   Phone: (609) 263-4041

Sea Isle City, NJ 08243

Covers: About 200 basic manufacturers of liquid feed supplements for livestock and about 250 suppliers to these manufacturers. **Entries include:** For manufacturers - Firm name, address, date founded, brand names. **Arrangement:** Both sections alphabetical. **Frequency:** Annual, September. **Editor:** William C. Coleman. **Advertising accepted.** Circulation 13,000. **Price:** Included in subscription, $5.00 per year.

★1839★
FEEDSTUFFS—REFERENCE ISSUE
Miller Publishing Company
2501 Wayzata Boulevard   Phone: (612) 374-5200
Minneapolis, MN 55440
Publication includes: Listings of 1,800 suppliers of products and equipment for the feed, grain, and feeding industry; trade associations. **Entries include:** Company name, address, phone. **Arrangement:** Alphabetical. **Indexes:** Product. **Frequency:** Annual, late July. **Editor:** Wayne Anderson. **Advertising accepted.** Circulation 21,600. **Price:** $10.00 (current and 1980 editions).

Fir & Hemlock Door Association—Membership List *See* Western Wood Products Association—Buyers Manual

★1840★
FLORAL MARKETING DIRECTORY AND BUYER'S GUIDE
Produce Marketing Association
700 Barksdale Road   Phone: (302) 738-7100
Newark, DE 19711
Covers: Mass-marketing growers, wholesalers, equipment manufacturers, accessory suppliers, and supermarket retailers handling flowers and foliage plants and related products. **Entries include:** Company name, address, phone, names of executives, trade and brand names, list of products or services. **Arrangement:** Separate lists of growers, wholesalers, suppliers and supermarket retailers, all alphabetical. **Pages** (approx.): 30. **Frequency:** Annual, July. **Editor:** Jim Johnson, Director of Marketing Services. **Price:** $10.00.

★1841★
FLORIDA'S WOOD-USING INDUSTRY
Division of Forestry
Florida Department of Agriculture and Consumer Services
Collins Building   Phone: (904) 488-4274
Tallahassee, FL 32304
Covers: Woodbuyers, loggers, primary timber processors and secondary wood products manufacturers in Florida (SIC 2400, 2500, and 3731-32). **Entries include:** Company name, address, phone, number of employees, trade and brand names, list of products or services, raw materials and species used, size and type of operation. **Arrangement:** Geographical. **Indexes:** Company name by type of operation. **Pages** (approx.): 175. **Frequency:** Biennial, even years. **Editor:** Harlan S. Friensehner, Forest Economist. **Former title:** This publication is a combination of "Primary Wood-Using Industries in Florida" and "Secondary Wood-Using Industries in Florida." **Price:** Free.

★1842★
FOOD AND AGRICULTURAL EXPORT DIRECTORY
Export Trade Services Division
Foreign Agricultural Service
Agriculture Department
Washington, DC 20250
Covers: Federal and state agencies, trade associations, companies, and others willing to assist United States firms which wish to export food and agricultural products. Includes agricultural attaches and officers in American diplomatic offices abroad; periodicals concerned with foreign trade and their addresses. **Entries include:** Generally, agency or company name, address, phone, name of contact; association entries include names of several officers and their affiliations. **Arrangement:** Classified by level and unit of government or other activity. **Pages** (approx.): Base volume 100, supplement 50. **Frequency:** New edition or supplement published annually; latest edition November 1978. **Price:** Free. **Other information:** Cover title, "Export Directory."

★1843★
FOOD SERVICE DIRECTORY: SUPPLIERS OF FRESH PRODUCE
Produce Marketing Association
700 Barksdale Road   Phone: (302) 738-7100
Newark, DE 19711
Covers: About 275 suppliers of fresh produce to food service operations; includes separate list of commodity promotion groups. **Entries include:** Company name, address, phone, name of principal executive, trade and brand names, list of products or services, territory covered. **Pages** (approx.): 50. **Frequency:** Annual. **Editor:** David R. Riggs, Director of Educational Services. **Price:** $3.00.

★1844★
FOREST INDUSTRIES—ANNUAL LUMBER REVIEW & BUYERS' GUIDE ISSUE
Miller Freeman Publications, Inc.
500 Howard Street   Phone: (415) 397-1881
San Francisco, CA 94105
Covers: About 2,000 United States and Canadian sawmills; federal, state, and provincial agencies concerned with forestry and forest industries; and suppliers of products and services for the forest industries (SIC 83). Includes list of 100 leading mills. **Entries include:** For sawmills - Company name, address, lumber production. For agencies - Name, address. For suppliers - Company name, address, products or services. **Arrangement:** Alphabetical within categories. **Pages** (approx.): 115. **Frequency:** Annual, May. **Editor:** Herbert G. Lambert. **Advertising accepted.** Circulation 25,000. **Price:** $10.00.

★1845★
FOREST INDUSTRIES TELECOMMUNICATIONS—DIRECTORY OF LICENSEES
Forest Industries Telecommunications
Box 5446   Phone: (503) 485-8441
Eugene, OR 97405
Covers: Forest industry users of two-way radio as licensed by the Federal Communications Commission in the Forest Products Radio Service. **Entries include:** Company name, station locations, call sign, frequencies. **Arrangement:** Alphabetical. **Frequency:** Annual, July. **Price:** Apply.

★1846★
FOREST SERVICE ORGANIZATIONAL DIRECTORY
Forest Service
Agriculture Department
Box 2417   Phone: (202) 447-3760
Washington, DC 20013
Pages (approx.): 155. **Frequency:** Annual. **Price:** $2.65 (S/N 001-001-00433-2). **Send orders to:** Government Printing Office, Washington, DC 20402.

★1847★
FOREST TREE SEED DIRECTORY
Food and Agriculture Organization of the United Nations
Via delle Terme di Caracalla
Rome 00100, Italy
Covers: Sources of seeds of trees for forest production as well as some species of woody plants suitable for erosion control, ornamental uses, game and wildlife management, shelterbelts and windbreaks, and animal fodder. Includes list of national seed coordinating centers and other suppliers. **Entries include:** For trees or plants - Botanical name, supplying center country, number of seeds per kilogram, germination per cent, seed treatment recommendation, when to order. For centers and suppliers - Name, address. **Arrangement:** Tree genus and species. **Pages** (approx.): 280. **Frequency:** Irregular; latest edition 1975. **Price:** $10.00 (Stock No. PPH0410/TRI). **Send orders to:** Unipub, Box 433, Murray Hill Station, New York, NY 10016.

★1848★
FORESTRY SCHOOLS IN THE UNITED STATES
Forest Service
Agriculture Department
Washington, DC 20250
Number of listings: 50. **Entries include:** School name, address, narrative description of degrees available, major areas of concentration, special requirements; accreditation by Society of American Foresters is shown. **Arrangement:** Geographical. **Pages** (approx.): 30. **Price:** 35¢ (S/N 0101-00351). **Send orders to:** Government Printing Office, Washington, DC 20402.

★1849★
G & S MILL'S WASTE WOOD RESOURCE DIRECTORY [New England]
G & S Mill
75 Otis Street   Phone: (617) 393-9266
Northborough, MA 01532
Covers: Nearly 100 lumber mills and other manufacturers who have waste wood or wood by-products which can be used in residential wood stoves; coverage is limited to Massachusetts, Maine, New Hampshire, Rhode Island, Vermont, and North Carolina. **Entries include:** Company name, address, phone, name of contact, type of wood or wood products available, whether delivery is available. **Arrangement:** Geographical. **Pages** (approx.): 20. **Frequency:** Annual, summer. **Editor:** Paul Kalenian, President. **Price:** $3.00.

Garden Centers of America—Membership Directory *See* American Association of Nurserymen—Member Directory

★1850★
GARDEN SUPPLY RETAILER—GREEN BOOK ISSUE
Miller Publishing Company
2501 Wayzata Boulevard   Phone: (612) 374-5200
Minneapolis, MN 55440
Covers: 1,700 lawn and garden manufacturers, 360 manufacturers' representatives, 2,700 brand names, 200 garden and horticultural trade associations, 300 central parts distributors for mowers and other power equipment, and 1,200 distributors of lawn and garden supplies. Product-classified list of manufacturers. **Entries include:** Manufacturer listings show name, address, key personnel, company subsidiaries or divisions; brand name listings show manufacturer; product listings show manufacturer with phone; manufacturers' representative listings show name, phone, territory served, lines carried; distributor listings show address, territory served, lines carried. **Arrangement:** Manufacturers, brand names, and products are alphabetical; representatives and distributors are geographical; trade associations are by major interest. **Pages** (approx.): 200. **Frequency:** Annual, October. **Editor:** Richard W. Chamberlin. **Advertising accepted.** Circulation 40,000. **Former title:** Home & Garden Supply Merchandiser - Green Book Issue. **Price:** $10.00.

★1851★
GEOGRAPHICAL INDEX OF WHOLESALE TOBACCO LICENSEES
National Association of Tobacco Distributors
58 E. 79th Street   Phone: (212) 472-2700
New York, NY 10021
Covers: 4,000 distributors licensed to conduct wholesale tobacco business in various states of the United States and Canada. **Entries include:** Company name, address, phone, names of executives, number of employees, list of products, and territory covered. **Arrangement:** Geographical. **Pages** (approx.): 1,000. **Frequency:** Irregular; previous edition 1976; latest edition fall 1979. **Editor:** M. Jack Newman. **Former title:** Directory of the Wholesale Tobacco Trade. **Price:** $400.00 (2 volumes); available only to manufacturer suppliers.

★1852★
GEOPHYSICAL DIRECTORY
Geophysical Directory, Inc.
2200 Welch Avenue   Phone: (713) 259-8789
Houston, TX 77019
Covers: About 2,000 companies which provide geophysical equipment, supplies, or services, and mining and petroleum companies which use geophysical techniques. **Entries include:** Company name, address, phone, names of principal executives and operations and sales personnel; similar information for branch locations; international coverage. **Arrangement:** Classified by product or service. **Indexes:** Company name, personal name. **Pages** (approx.): 500. **Frequency:** Annual, March. **Advertising accepted.** Circulation 8,500. **Price:** $12.00.

★1853★
GRAHAM CENTER SEED DIRECTORY
Frank Porter Graham Center
Route 3, Box 95
Wadesboro, NC 28170
Covers: Small seed companies which specialize in traditional varieties of vegetable and flower seeds. **Pages** (approx.): 20. **Frequency:** Latest edition 1979. **Editor:** Cary Fowler. **Price:** $1.00, postpaid, payment with order.

★1854★
GRAIN TRUCKING DIRECTORY
Upper Great Plains Transportation Institute
North Dakota State University   Phone: (701) 237-7767
Fargo, ND
Covers: More than 600 truckers in North Dakota and Minnesota who haul grain. **Entries include:** Name, address, phone. **Arrangement:** Geographical. **Frequency:** Annual, November. **Price:** Free.

★1855★
GROUNDS MAINTENANCE—GROUNDS CARE MANUAL ISSUE
Intertec Publishing Corporation
9221 Quivira Road   Phone: (913) 888-4664
Overland Park, KS 66215
Covers: Manufacturers, growers, and suppliers of materials for landscaping design, construction, and maintenance. **Entries include:** Company name, address. **Arrangement:** Alphabetical. **Indexes:** Product. **Frequency:** Annual, December. **Editor:** Kathy Copley. **Advertising accepted.** **Price:** $3.00.

★1856★
GROWERS DIRECTORY [Illinois seed growers]
Illinois Crop Improvement Association
508 S. Broadway   Phone: (217) 367-4053
Urbana, IL 61801
Covers: About 350 member growers of corn, oats, or soybeans for seed in Illinois. **Entries include:** Grower name, address, seed variety grown, acreage certified. There is a separate alphabetical list of members showing only name, address, county, phone. **Arrangement:** By type of seed, then alphabetical by grower. **Pages** (approx.): 90. **Frequency:** Semiannual. **Editor:** George Keith, Manager. **Price:** Free. **Also includes:** Description of genetic parentage of seed, relative maturity, and disease resistance levels for oat and soybean seed varieties.

Guide to Hand-Operated and Animal-Drawn Equipment *See* Tools for Agriculture: A Buyer's Guide to Low-Cost Agricultural Implements

★1857★
GUIDE TO PUBLIC GARDENS
Garden Club of America
598 Madison Avenue   Phone: (212) 753-8287
New York, NY 10022
Covers: More than 1,000 parks, arboretums, public gardens, and historic sites with plantings in 36 states and the District of Columbia.

Entries include: Site name, address, hours open, fee, brief description. **Arrangement:** Geographical. **Pages** (approx.): 120. **Frequency:** Not established; first edition fall 1976. **Price:** $3.50.

★1858★

GULF COAST OIL DIRECTORY
Gulf Coast Directories, Inc., Division
Spearhead Publications, Inc.
3200 Marquart   Phone: (713) 961-4191
Houston, TX 77027
Covers: 7,000 companies in the Gulf Coast region engaged in petroleum exploration and production, and suppliers to the industry. **Entries include:** Company name, address, phone, principal executives. **Arrangement:** Classified by activity. **Indexes:** Company name. **Frequency:** Annual, September. **Advertising accepted. Price:** $25.00.

★1859★

HANK SEALE OIL DIRECTORIES
Hank Seale
1606 Jackson Street   Phone: (806) 474-1818
Amarillo, TX 79102
Covers: Oil producing companies, drilling contractors, geologists, landmen, major and independent marketing firms. In separate volumes, covers central United States, including Texas panhandle and west Texas; southeastern New Mexico and entire state of Texas; east Texas and Gulf Coast and southern states; eastern United States. **Entries include:** Company name, address; many listings also include phone, names of key personnel. **Arrangement:** Alphabetical in a single alphabet. **Indexes:** None. **Pages** (approx.): 300. **Frequency:** Annual. **Editor:** Hank Seale. **Price:** $25.00.

★1860★

HAWAII AGRICULTURE EXPORT DIRECTORY
Commodities Branch
Hawaii Department of Agriculture
Box 22159
Honolulu, HI 96822
Covers: Over 140 suppliers of fruits, vegetables, and flowers for export. **Entries include:** Company name, address, phone, products, name of sales contact. **Arrangement:** Alphabetical. **Indexes:** Product. **Pages** (approx.): 50. **Frequency:** Biennial, June of odd years. **Price:** Single copies free.

★1861★

HOG FARM MANAGEMENT—PORK PRODUCER'S PLANNER ISSUE
Miller Publishing Company
2501 Wayzata Boulevard   Phone: (612) 374-5200
Minneapolis, MN 55440
Covers: Companies offering products and services to the swine industry, and other agribusiness firms supplying requirements for crop farming. **Entries include:** Company name, address, names of contacts, phone. **Arrangement:** Swine industry suppliers are alphabetical, other suppliers classified. **Indexes:** Product (for swine industry suppliers). **Frequency:** Annual, December. **Editor:** John Byrnes. **Advertising accepted. Price:** $10.00.

Home & Garden Supply Merchandiser—Green Book Issue *See*
  Garden Supply Retailer—Green Book Issue

Horticultural Research Institute—Membership Directory *See*
  American Association of Nurserymen—Member Directory

Illinois Crop Improvement Association—Membership List *See*
  Growers Directory [Illinois seed growers]

★1862★

IMPERIAL VALLEY [CALIFORNIA] LETTUCE SHIPPERS DIRECTORY
Federal-State Market News Service
395 Broadway   Phone: (714) 352-3562
El Centro, CA 92243
Number of listings: 48. **Entries include:** Company name, address, phone, trade and brand names, name of sales manager, and list of products. **Arrangement:** Alphabetical. **Frequency:** Annual. **Editor:** Jack R. Kloth, Officer-in-Charge. **Price:** Free.

★1863★

IMPERIAL VALLEY [CALIFORNIA] PRODUCE BUYERS DIRECTORY
Federal-State Market News Service
395 Broadway   Phone: (714) 352-3562
El Centro, CA 92243
Number of listings: 90. **Entries include:** Company name, address, phone, trade and brand names, name of sales manager, and list of products. **Arrangement:** Alphabetical. **Frequency:** Annual. **Editor:** Jack R. Kloth, Officer-in-Charge. **Price:** Free.

★1864★

INDIANA CERTIFIED SEED DIRECTORY
Indiana Crop Improvement Association
3510 U. S. 52 South   Phone: (317) 474-3494
Lafayette, IN 47905
Covers: 145 growers of soybean, oats, wheat, popcorn, corn, and crownvetch for seed, whose seed is certified by the association. **Entries include:** Grower name, address, phone, and acres of each type of seed certified. **Arrangement:** Alphabetical. **Indexes:** By type of seed with grower name, county, and number of acres registered and/or certified. **Pages** (approx.): 75. **Frequency:** Semiannual, July and September. **Editor:** Larry Svajgr, Manager. **Advertising accepted.** Circulation 7,000. **Price:** Free. **Other information:** Type of seed included in directory varies according to growing season - summer directory included wheat and crownvetch.

★1865★

INDIANA HAY DIRECTORY
Indiana Department of Agriculture
State House, Room 333
200 W. Washington Street   Phone: (317) 633-4545
Indianapolis, IN 46204
Covers: 100 Indiana farmers with hay to sell. **Entries include:** Name, address, phone, type and quantity of hay, price. **Frequency:** Annual. **Price:** Free.

★1866★

INSTANT MARKET NEWS DIRECTORY
Regional Information Office
Agriculture Department
1100 Commerce Street, Room 5C40
Dallas, TX 75242
Covers: More than 80 sources in the Southwest for information by telephone concerning prices and market conditions for crops and livestock, local and national. **Entries include:** Source, phone, description of information offered. **Frequency:** Irregular; latest edition August 1979. **Price:** Free.

★1867★

INTERNATIONAL APPLE INSTITUTE REFERENCE BOOK
International Apple Institute
2430 Pennsylvania Avenue, N. W.   Phone: (202) 833-9150
Washington, DC 20037
Publication includes: 850 company members of the Institute, primarily growers, shippers, brokers, distributors, and packers. Also includes list of brand names for fruits and vegetables. **Entries include:** Company name, address, phone, and type of business. Brand name list includes company name and city. **Arrangement:** Geographical. **Frequency:** Annual, fall. **Editor:** Fred W. Burrows. **Advertising accepted.** Circulation 1,200. **Price:** $25.00.

★1868★
**INTERNATIONAL ASSOCIATION OF FAIRS AND EXPOSITIONS—
DIRECTORY [Agricultural fairs]**
International Association of Fairs and Expositions
Box 12044   Phone: (901) 452-0662
Memphis, TN 38112
Covers: 400 agricultural fairs in the United States and Canada which
are members and about 40 state associations of county fairs.
Includes list of associate members (suppliers, etc.). **Entries include:**
Name of fair, address, phone, name of principal executive, physical
data on fairgrounds. **Arrangement:** Geographical. **Indexes:**
Chronological. **Pages** (approx.): 100. **Frequency:** Annual, February.
Editor: T. W. Sparks, General Manager. **Advertising accepted.**
Circulation 3,000. **Price:** $50.00 (current and 1980 editions).

★1869★
INTERNATIONAL DIRECTORY OF FISH TECHNOLOGY INSTITUTES
Department of Fisheries
Food and Agriculture Organization of the United Nations
Via delle Terme di Caracalla
I-00100 Rome, Italy
Covers: Over 80 institutes in some 50 countries. **Entries include:**
Institute name, address, name of director, responsible authority,
source of financing, date founded, major fields of interest, description
of facilities, size of professional staff, description of program,
publications. **Arrangement:** Geographical. **Pages** (approx.): 125.
Frequency: Irregular; first edition 1976; new edition expected 1980.
Price: $9.00 (current and 1980 editions; FAO Fisheries Technical
Papers 152). **Send orders to:** Unipub, Box 433, Murray Hill Station,
New York, NY 10016.

International Directory of Mining and Mineral Processing
    Operations *See* E/MJ International Directory of Mining and
    Mineral...

★1870★
INTERNATIONAL LIVESTOCK TRANSPORTATION DIRECTORY
International Transportation Services Branch
Agriculture Department
Auditor's Building, Room 1405   Phone: (202) 447-2165
Washington, DC 20250
Covers: About 70 steamship lines, airlines, freight forwarders, charter
brokers, and other transportation firms which handled exported
livestock, and animal inspection facilities in the United States. **Entries
include:** For transportation companies - Company name, address,
phone, telex, name of contact; type of transportation facilities and
equipment available; services, United States and foreign bases. For
animal inspection facilities - Firm name, address, phone, name of
contact; capacity; equipment; distance to port. **Arrangement:** By line
of business. **Pages** (approx.): 40. **Frequency:** Irregular; latest edition
May 1979. **Editor:** Thomas Poerstel. **Price:** Free.

International Meat Industry Supply Association—Membership
    Directory *See* Meat Industry Supply and Equipment
    Association—Membership...

★1871★
INTERNATIONAL PETROLEUM ENCYCLOPEDIA
Petroleum Publishing Company
Box 1260   Phone: (918) 835-3161
Tulsa, OK 74101
Publication includes: Lists of multinational oil companies, petroleum
refineries, offshore drilling rigs, petroleum industry computer
installations, petrochemical plants, ports and tanker terminals, sulfur
plants; worldwide coverage. **Arrangement:** Classified. **Pages**
(approx.): 450. **Frequency:** Annual, July. **Advertising accepted.**
Circulation 10,000. **Price:** $42.50.

★1872★
**INTERSTATE OIL COMPACT COMMISSION AND STATE OIL AND
GAS AGENCIES—DIRECTORY**
Interstate Oil Compact Commission
Box 53127   Phone: (405) 525-3556
Oklahoma City, OK 73152
Covers: About 600 state representatives to the commission from 30
oil and gas producing states and six associate states, and committee
members from government and industry. **Entries include:** For each
state listing - Name of governor and representative and their
addresses. For committees - Committee name, and names and
addresses of members. **Arrangement:** Geographical. **Pages** (approx.):
60. **Frequency:** Annual, spring. **Editor:** W. Timothy Dowd, Executive
Director. **Price:** Free.

★1873★
IOWA CERTIFIED SEED DIRECTORY
Iowa Crop Improvement Association
112 Agronomy Building
Ames, IA 50011
Covers: About 270 Iowa growers raising crops for seed whose fields
have met certification standards of the association. Crops include
soybeans, wheat, barley, oats, forage crops, and hybrid corn. **Entries
include:** Grower name, address, phone, seeds grown. **Arrangement:**
Geographical. **Frequency:** Annual, November. **Price:** Free.

★1874★
IOWA HAY DIRECTORY
Iowa Department Of Agriculture
Wallace Building
Des Moines, IA 50319
Covers: Iowa hay producers. **Entries include:** Name, address, phone,
amounts and types of hay for sale. **Frequency:** Annual, December.
Price: Free.

★1875★
IOWA REPLACEMENT EWE DIRECTORY
Sheep Division
Iowa Department of Agriculture
Wallace Building
Des Moines, IA 50319
Covers: 200 stockmen in Iowa and 30 other states who have
replacement ewes for sale. **Entries include:** Personal or farm name,
address, phone, number of head, breeds. **Arrangement:** Geographical.
Frequency: Annual, spring. **Editor:** Lincoln M. Abney, Director. **Price:**
Free.

★1876★
IRRIGATION ASSOCIATION—MEMBERSHIP DIRECTORY
Irrigation Association
13975 Connecticut Avenue   Phone: (301) 871-1200
Silver Spring, MD 20906
Covers: 700 manufacturers, distributors, contractors, and research
personnel in the field of irrigation. **Entries include:** Company name,
address, phone, names of executives, financial keys, list of products
or services. **Arrangement:** Alphabetical. **Pages** (approx.): 80.
Frequency: Annual, December. **Editor:** Walter D. Anderson, Executive
Director. **Former title:** Sprinkler Irrigation Association - Membership
Directory. **Price:** $15.00 (current and 1980 editions).

★1877★
JOURNAL OF FORESTRY—MEMBERSHIP DIRECTORY ISSUE
Society of American Foresters
5400 Grosvenor Lane   Phone: (301) 897-8720
Bethesda, MD 20014
Covers: 20,000 foresters and scientists working in related fields.
Entries include: Name, professional affiliation, address.
Arrangement: Alphabetical. **Frequency:** Irregular; latest edition
1975. **Editor:** N. H. Sand, Director of Publications. **Advertising
accepted.** Circulation 22,000.

★1878★
KANSAS HAY DIRECTORY
Marketing Division
Kansas State Board of Agriculture
503 Kansas Avenue
Topeka, KS 66601
Covers: 110 Kansas hay dealers and producers. **Entries include:** Name of source, address, type and quantity of hay available. **Arrangement:** By county. **Pages** (approx.): 20. **Frequency:** Annual, August. **Price:** Free.

★1879★
KEYSTONE COAL INDUSTRY MANUAL
McGraw-Hill, Inc.
1221 Avenue of the Americas   Phone: (212) 997-1221
New York, NY 10020
Covers: Coal companies and mines, coke plants, coal cleaning plants, domestic and export sales organizations, electric utility plants using fossil fuels, cement plants, industrial plants burning coal, consultants, designers, mining contractors, laboratories; includes list of leading coal mining companies and mines. **Entries include:** Company or organization name, address, names of executives; coal mine directory includes tonnage, capacity, seam mined and facilities; consultants directory includes services offered. **Arrangement:** Mining, processing, and user lists are geographical; most other lists are alphabetical. **Indexes:** Subject, operating executive, sales and export executive, company. **Pages** (approx.): 1,300. **Frequency:** Annual, June. **Editor:** George F. Nielsen, Editor-in-Chief. **Advertising accepted.** **Price:** $110.00, plus $3.00 shipping (current and 1980 editions).

★1880★
LAND DRILLING AND OILWELL SERVICING CONTRACTORS DIRECTORY
Petroleum Publishing Company
Box 1260   Phone: (918) 835-3161
Tulsa, OK 74101
Covers: Onshore petroleum drilling and service firms, primarily in the United States and Canada. **Entries include:** Company name, address, phone, key personnel, areas of operation, rig data and depth ratings. **Pages** (approx.): 115. **Frequency:** Annual, August. **Price:** $30.00 (current and 1980 editions).

★1881★
LANDSCAPE INDUSTRY—INDUSTRY REFERENCE GUIDE ISSUE
Brantwood Publications, Inc.
Box 77   Phone: (414) 786-2900
Elm Grove, WI 53122
Covers: Firms which supply equipment, products, and plants, sod, and turf to the nursery and landscaping industry. **Entries include:** Company name, address, phone, products, contact. **Arrangement:** Alphabetical within manufacturer, supplier, distributor/wholesaler groups. **Frequency:** Annual, January. **Advertising accepted.** Circulation 14,500. **Price:** $2.00.

★1882★
LAWN AND GARDEN MARKETING—SOURCE BOOK ISSUE
Intertec Publishing Corporation
Box 12901   Phone: (913) 888-4646
Overland Park, KS 66212
Covers: Manufacturers of lawn and garden equipment, supplies, and accessories, recreational equipment, and chemicals; growers of plants and seeds; wholesalers of these products; and associations in the field. **Entries include:** Manufacturer listings include company names, addresses; wholesaler listings include company name, address, phone, type of business, number of salesmen traveled, products, area served. **Indexes:** Product. **Frequency:** Annual, September. **Editor:** Pat Blanton. **Advertising accepted.** Circulation 41,000. **Price:** $5.00.

★1883★
LIST OF ACCREDITED PROGRAMS IN LANDSCAPE ARCHITECTURE
American Society of Landscape Architects
1900 M Street, N. W., Suite 750   Phone: (202) 466-7730
Washington, DC 20036
Covers: About 40 schools of landscape architecture and other institutions offering programs in landscape architecture which are accredited by the society. **Entries include:** Institution name, address; name and phone of director, department chairman, or contact; degrees offered; years of latest and next accreditation review. **Arrangement:** Alphabetical. **Frequency:** Semiannual, spring and fall. **Price:** Single copies free.

★1884★
LIST OF FISHERY COOPERATIVES IN THE UNITED STATES
National Marine Fisheries Service
National Oceanic and Atmospheric Administration
Commerce Department   Phone: (202) 634-7451
Washington, DC 20230
Covers: 100 fishery cooperatives in 18 states and Puerto Rico. **Entries include:** Co-op name, address, phone, name of one officer or manager, number of members, total number of boats in co-op, type of co-op, major species of fish and shellfish caught. **Arrangement:** Geographical. **Pages** (approx.): 20. **Frequency:** Irregular; latest edition August 1979. **Price:** Free.

★1885★
LIST OF NATIONAL FISH HATCHERIES
Fish and Wildlife Service
Interior Department
18th and C Streets, N. W.   Phone: (202) 343-3518
Washington, DC 20240
Covers: 95 national fish hatcheries. Also includes similar lists of fish cultural development centers and fish hatchery biologists. **Entries include:** Hatchery name, manager, post office address, phone, county. **Arrangement:** Geographical. **Pages** (approx.): 20. **Frequency:** Irregular; latest edition September 1976. **Price:** Free.

Livestock Brands Recorded in Oregon *See* Oregon Livestock Brand Book

★1886★
MARKET NOTES [Produce markets]
United Fresh Fruit and Vegetable Association
727 N. Washington Street   Phone: (202) 293-9210
Alexandria, VA 22314
Covers: More than 40 produce terminal markets. **Entries include:** Market name, address, list of tenants, name and phone of market manager, hours of operation, recommended truck route to the market, gate fees, unloading charges, facilities. **Arrangement:** Geographical. **Frequency:** Irregular; updated three times yearly. **Price:** $8.75.

★1887★
MEAT AND POULTRY INSPECTION DIRECTORY
Meat and Poultry Inspection Program
Food Safety and Quality Service
Agriculture Department   Phone: (202) 447-7551
Washington, DC 20250
Covers: All meat and poultry plants which ship meat interstate and therefore come under U.S. Department of Agriculture inspection. Includes about 6,600 meat establishments and 2,500 poultry establishments; also includes establishments slaughtering or processing rabbit, buffalo, horse, and other meats, establishments certified for export or import operations, inedible fat shippers, foreign meat and poultry establishments, USDA veterinarians and others specially trained in foreign animal diseases, and inspection program officials nationwide. **Entries include:** For establishments - Name, address, USDA number, phone, applicant number, codes indicating types of operations performed. For veterinarians, etc. - Name, address, phone, title. **Arrangement:** By establishment number within type of establishment. **Indexes:** Geographical, alphabetical. **Pages**

(approx.): 525. **Frequency:** Semiannual, January and June. **Editor:** John Cook. **Price:** $4.75 per copy, $9.25 per year (S/N 001-016-80001-2). **Send orders to:** Government Printing Office, Washington, DC 20402.

★1888★

MEAT INDUSTRY SUPPLY AND EQUIPMENT ASSOCIATION—MEMBERSHIP DIRECTORY AND BUYERS GUIDE

Meat Industry Supply and Equipment Association
1900 Arch Street   Phone: (215) 564-3484
Philadelphia, PA 19103
Number of listings: 100. **Entries include:** Company name, address, phone, names and titles of executives, list of products. **Arrangement:** Alphabetical. **Pages** (approx.): 25. **Frequency:** Annual. **Price:** Free.

★1889★

MEAT MACHINERY MANUFACTURERS INSTITUTE—MEMBERSHIP DIRECTORY & BUYERS' GUIDE

Meat Machinery Manufacturers Institute
1900 Arch Street   Phone: (215) 564-3484
Philadelphia, PA 19103
Covers: About 30 manufacturers of machinery used in meat processing. **Entries include:** Company name, address, phone, names of executives, description of products. **Arrangement:** Alphabetical. **Pages** (approx.): 30. **Frequency:** Biennial, even years. **Editor:** R. Franklin Brown, Jr., Executive Secretary. **Price:** Free.

★1890★

MEAT PROCESSING—DIRECTORY OF SUPPLIERS ISSUE

Davies Publishing Company
136 Shore Drive   Phone: (312) 325-2930
Hinsdale, IL 60521
Covers: About 800 manufacturers, distributors, and other suppliers of equipment, machinery, and services for the meat packing and processing industries; additional section lists trade associations and educational and scientific organizations concerned with meat processing. **Entries include:** Company name, address, and phone. **Arrangement:** Alphabetical. **Indexes:** Product. **Pages** (approx.): 225. **Frequency:** Annual, December. **Editor:** Cal Morken, Executive Editor. **Advertising accepted.** Circulation 19,000. **Price:** $10.00.

★1891★

MICHIGAN AGRICULTURAL EXPORT DIRECTORY

Michigan Department of Agriculture
Box 30017   Phone: (517) 373-7807
Lansing, MI 48909
Covers: About 175 producers of fresh and processed fruits and vegetables, livestock, poultry, and wood and wood products. Also includes lists of air and motor freight carriers. **Entries include:** Company name, address, name of one executive, products, packaging available, brand names, whether private label products are available. **Arrangement:** Alphabetical. **Indexes:** Product. **Pages** (approx.): 40. **Frequency:** Annual, summer. **Price:** Free.

★1892★

MICHIGAN COUNTRY CAROUSEL [Farm product outlets]

Communications Office
Michigan Department of Agriculture
Box 30017   Phone: (517) 373-1104
Lansing, MI 48909
Covers: About 900 Michigan roadside markets and pick-your-own farms selling fruits and vegetables. **Entries include:** Market or farm name, address, and products sold. **Arrangement:** Geographical. **Frequency:** Annual, spring. **Price:** Free.

★1893★

MICHIGAN FLORIST—DIRECTORY AND BUYERS' GUIDE ISSUE

Michigan State Florists' Association
2420 Science Parkway   Phone: (517) 349-5754
Okemos, MI 48864
Covers: Member floral retailers and wholesalers, nurseries and garden

centers, and individual members. **Entries include:** Company name, owner's name, address, phone, type of business, and affiliation with floral delivery systems or services. **Arrangement:** Geographical. **Indexes:** Shop, owner name. **Pages** (approx.): 75. **Frequency:** Annual, July. **Editor:** Rich C. Northrup, Jr. **Advertising accepted.** **Price:** Available to members only.

Michigan State Florists' Association—Membership Directory *See* Michigan Florist—Directory and Buyers' Guide Issue

★1894★

MIDWEST OIL REGISTER—INDUSTRY SEGMENT DIRECTORIES

Midwest Oil Register, Inc.
Box 7248   Phone: (918) 742-9925
Tulsa, OK 74105
Description: Publisher issues separate directories for various segments of the petroleum and gas exploration, production, and distribution industries; see listing under "Price" for individual titles. **Entries include:** Company name, address, phone, names and titles of principal personnel; some listings may include additional information related to the specific activity of the company. **Frequency:** Annual, in fourth or first quarters. **Editor:** Ross Sloan. **Price:** Directory of Oil Marketing & Wholesale Distributors, $20.00; Directory of Geophysical & Oil Companies Who Use Geophysical Service, $18.00; Directory of Oil Well Drilling Contractors, $30.00; Directory of Oil Well Supply Companies, $25.00; Pipeline & Pipeline Contractors, $18.00; Refining, Construction, Petrochemical & Natural Gas Processing Plants of the World (also sometimes cited as, Directory of Oil Refineries), $22.00; Directory of Electric Light & Power Companies, $20.00; Directory of Gas Utility Companies, $18.00.

★1895★

MIDWEST OIL REGISTER—REGIONAL DIRECTORIES

Midwest Oil Register, Inc.
Box 7248   Phone: (918) 742-9925
Tulsa, OK 74105
Description: Publisher issues separate directories for petroleum industry firms and their suppliers in various states and geographical areas; see listings under "Price" for titles. **Entries include:** Company name, address, phone, names and titles of principal personnel; some listings may include additional information related to the specific activity of the company. **Frequency:** Annual, in fourth or first quarters. **Editor:** Ross Sloan. **Price:** Oil Directory of Alaska, $10.00; Oil Directory of California, $10.00; Oil Directory of Canada, $15.00; Oil Directory of Foreign Companies Outside the U.S.A. & Canada, $15.00; Oil Directory of Houston, Texas [including entire state], $10.00; Oil Directory of Kansas, $8.00; Oil Directory of Louisiana, Arkansas, Mississippi, Georgia, and Florida, $10.00; Oil Directory of Michigan, Illinois, Indiana, and Kentucky, $10.00; Oil Directory of Oklahoma, $12.00; Oil Directory of Rocky Mountain Region, Four Corners, and New Mexico, $10.00. (Prices are for current and 1980 editions.)

Milling & Baking News—Buyer's Guide to the Allied Trades in Grain and Milling Issue *See* Milling & Baking News—Grain...; ...Milling...

★1896★

MILLING & BAKING NEWS—GRAIN DIRECTORY/BUYER'S GUIDE ISSUE

Sosland Publishing
4800 Main Street   Phone: (816) 756-1000
Kansas City, MO 64112
Covers: Multiple grain elevator companies and companies owning terminal, port, and transfer grain elevators in the United States and Canada; suppliers and manufacturers of grain storage and moving equipment are also listed. **Entries include:** For grain elevator companies - Company name, address, storage capacity, names of executives in production and management, services. For manufacturers and suppliers - Company name, address, phone, names of executives. **Arrangement:** Alphabetical. **Indexes:** Product, grain

elevator. **Frequency:** Annual, September. **Editor:** Morton I. Sosland, Editor and Publisher. **Advertising accepted.** Circulation 5,000. **Former title:** Milling & Baking News - Buyer's Guide to the Allied Trades in Grain and Milling Issue; grain and milling now covered in separate issues. **Price:** $20.00.

★1897★
MILLING & BAKING NEWS—MILLING DIRECTORY/BUYER'S GUIDE ISSUE
Sosland Publishing
4800 Main Street   Phone: (816) 756-1000
Kansas City, MO 64112
Covers: Milling companies, mills, and manufacturers and suppliers of milling equipment and related products; United States, Canada, Central America, and the Caribbean area are included. **Entries include:** Company name, address, phone, names of executives, wholesale and retail brand names. **Arrangement:** Alphabetical. **Indexes:** Product, mill. **Frequency:** Annual, November. **Editor:** Morton I. Sosland, Editor and Publisher. **Advertising accepted.** Circulation 5,000. **Former title:** Milling & Baking News - Buyer's Guide to the Allied Trades in Grain and Milling Issue; grain and milling now covered in separate issues. **Price:** $20.00.

★1898★
MINERALS YEARBOOK
Bureau of Mines
Interior Department
Washington, DC
Publication includes: In Volume 2, a list of principal producers of iron ore, uranium, cement, lime, gypsum, clays, coal, sand and gravel, phosphate rock, and other minerals in the United States. **Entries include:** Company name, address, type of activity or mine, county. **Arrangement:** Geographical. **Frequency:** Annual; appears about 3 years after year covered by statistics in volume. **Editor:** Albert E. Schreck. **Price:** $10.75 (S/N 024-004-01938-7). **Send orders to:** Government Printing Office, Washington, DC 20402. **Other information:** Other 2 volumes include statistical and production information on the minerals industry in the United States and abroad.

Mines Register See **World Mines Register**

★1899★
MISSOURI HAY DIRECTORY
Missouri Department of Agriculture
Box 630
Jefferson City, MO 65102
Covers: Missouri hay dealers and producers. **Entries include:** Name, address, phone, types of hay available. **Frequency:** Annual. **Price:** Free.

★1900★
MORRISON PETROLEUM DIRECTORY OF KANSAS
John H. Morrison, Publisher
226 N. Emporia   Phone: (316) 263-8281
Wichita, KS 67202
Covers: Petroleum drilling contractors, producers, geologists, engineers, and oil companies operating in Kansas. **Entries include:** Company name, address, phone, names of executives. **Pages** (approx.): 400. **Frequency:** Annual, April. **Editor:** John H. Morrison. **Advertising accepted. Price:** $8.00.

Napa Valley Wine Book See **California Wine Country Series [Wineries]**

Napa Valley Wine Tour See **Wine Tour Series [California]**

★1901★
NATIONAL AGRICULTURAL AVIATION ASSOCIATION—MEMBERSHIP DIRECTORY
National Agricultural Aviation Association
National Press Building, Room 459   Phone: (202) 638-0542
Washington, DC 20045
Covers: Nearly 2,000 executives, pilots, and supplier companies engaged primarily in crop dusting. **Entries include:** For chapter and supplier company members - Name, spouse's name, company name, address, phone. **Arrangement:** By type of membership; chapter members are then geographical; supplier company members are by product. **Pages** (approx.): 135. **Frequency:** Annual, spring. **Editor:** Pauline Burns Perry. **Advertising accepted.** Circulation 4,500. **Price:** $7.50.

★1902★
NATIONAL AGRI-MARKETING ASSOCIATION—DIRECTORY OF MEMBERS
National Agri-Marketing Association
8340 Mission Road, No. 112   Phone: (913) 341-5445
Prairie Village, KS 66206
Covers: 2,200 persons active in agricultural advertising and marketing for manufacturers, advertising agencies, and media. **Entries include:** Member name and position, company name, address, phone. **Arrangement:** Geographical. **Indexes:** Alphabetical. **Pages** (approx.): 150. **Frequency:** Annual, September. **Editor:** Rex Parsons, Executive Director. **Price:** $65.00.

National Association of Farm Broadcasters See **Directory of Communicators in Agriculture**

National Association of Plant Patent Owners—Membership Directory See **American Association of Nurserymen—Member Directory**

★1903★
NATIONAL CATTLE FEEDLOT, MEAT PACKER AND GRAIN DEALERS DIRECTORY
TARA, Inc.
3521 34th Street
Lubbock, TX 79413
Covers: Cattle feedlots with capacities of over 1,000 head; interstate meat packers; and grain dealers with capacities to store 100,000 bushels or more. **Entries include:** Firm name, address, phone. **Arrangement:** Geographical within line of business categories. **Pages** (approx.): 610. **Frequency:** Biennial, odd years. **Advertising accepted. Price:** $25.00.

★1904★
NATIONAL FEED INGREDIENTS ASSOCIATION—DIRECTORY
National Feed Ingredients Association
One Corporate Plaza   Phone: (515) 225-9611
West Des Moines, IA 50265
Number of listings: About 700. **Entries include:** Company name, address, phone, principal personnel, branch offices, and person to contact. **Arrangement:** Alphabetical. **Indexes:** Personal name. **Pages** (approx.): 180. **Frequency:** Annual, fall. **Editor:** Joanne Kuster, Communications Director. **Advertising accepted. Price:** $20.00.

★1905★
NATIONAL HAY ASSOCIATION—YEARBOOK AND MEMBERSHIP DIRECTORY
National Hay Association
Box 1059   Phone: (517) 782-2688
Jackson, MI 49204
Covers: About 250 hay shippers, dealers, brokers, producers, and others interested in the hay industry. **Entries include:** Company name, address, phone, names of principal executives, trade or brand names, list of products, type of business. **Arrangement:** Geographical. **Pages** (approx.): 110. **Frequency:** Annual, December. **Editor:** Harry D. Gates, Jr., Executive Secretary. **Price:** Available to members only.

★1906★

NATIONAL HOG FARMER—PORK PRODUCER BUYING GUIDE ISSUE

Webb Publishing Company
1999 Shepard Road
St. Paul, MN 55116

Covers: 1,000 manufacturers of products for hog farmers. Also includes brand names, boar testing stations, breeders, and lists of officials of extension, state agricultural, and Farm Bureau offices as well as trade organizations. **Entries include:** Company name, address, phone, trade and brand names, list of products, or services. **Pages** (approx.): 200. **Frequency:** Annual, November. **Editor:** Neal Black. **Advertising accepted.** Circulation 122,000. **Price:** Annual subscription $10.00; Guide Issue not sold separately.

National Landscape Association—Membership Directory *See* American Association of Nurserymen—Member Directory

★1907★

NATIONAL PEANUT COUNCIL—MEMBERSHIP DIRECTORY

National Peanut Council
1000 16th Street, N. W., Suite 506   Phone: (202) 659-5656
Washington, DC 20036

Covers: About 150 growers, shellers, manufacturers, brokers, and allied businesses providing goods and services to the peanut industry. **Entries include:** Company name, address, phone, names of principal executives, products. **Arrangement:** Classified by type of company. **Pages** (approx.): 50. **Frequency:** Annual, summer. **Editor:** Katherine Martinez, Administrative Assistant. **Price:** $5.00.

★1908★

NEW JERSEY AGRICULTURAL ORGANIZATIONS

New Jersey Agriculture Department
John Fitch Plaza   Phone: (609) 292-8896
Trenton, NJ 08625

Covers: About 255 offices of federal and state agricultural agencies, county extension service, and agricultural associations. **Entries include:** Agency or organization name, address, names of officers or executives, and phone. **Arrangement:** By type of organization. **Indexes:** Personal name. **Frequency:** Irregular, latest edition 1977. **Editor:** Amy Collings, Public Information Officer. **Price:** Free.

★1909★

NEW MEXICO STOCKMAN—DIRECTORY OF NEW MEXICO AGRICULTURE ISSUE

Livestock Publications, Inc.
Box 7127   Phone: (505) 243-9515
Albuquerque, NM 87194

Covers: New Mexico Agriculture Department officials, livestock board inspectors, federal Agriculture Department officials; veterinarians; licensed livestock markets, dealers, and buyers; livestock carriers. **Entries include:** Company or agency name, address, phone; names of representatives, personnel, or contact person; products and services; breeds (if appropriate). **Arrangement:** By activity. **Frequency:** Annual, August. **Editor:** Chuck Stocks. **Advertising accepted.** Circulation 16,000. **Price:** $1.00.

Newspaper Farm Editors of America—Directory *See* Directory of Communicators in Agriculture

★1910★

NORTH AMERICAN FOREST HISTORY: A GUIDE TO ARCHIVES AND MANUSCRIPTS IN THE UNITED STATES AND CANADA

ABC-Clio Inc.
Riviera Campus
2040 A. P. S.   Phone: (805) 963-4221
Santa Barbara, CA 93103

Covers: About 350 archives, libraries, and other repositories of materials on the history of forestry and related topics in North America. **Entries include:** Repository name, address, phone, and description of holdings. **Arrangement:** Geographical. **Indexes:** Name,

subject, and geographical. **Pages** (approx.): 400. **Frequency:** First edition 1977. **Editor:** Richard C. Davis. **Price:** $82.75. **Other information:** Companion volume to "North American Forest and Conservation History: a Bibliography."

★1911★

NORTH AMERICAN WHOLESALE LUMBER ASSOCIATION— DISTRIBUTION DIRECTORY

North American Wholesale Lumber Association
Terminal Sales Building, Suite 218
Portland, OR 97205

Covers: About 585 member companies, including wholesalers, producers, and firms serving the industry. **Entries include:** Company name, address, phone, names of executives, and products and services. **Arrangement:** Classified by membership category. **Pages** (approx.): 75. **Frequency:** Annual, summer. **Price:** $5.00.

★1912★

NORTHWEST FARM EQUIPMENT JOURNAL—BUYERS MANUAL ISSUE

Northwest Farm Equipment Journal
1696 Eleanor Avenue   Phone: (612) 698-4246
St. Paul, MN

Covers: Manufacturers and their distributors who offer farm, light industrial, recreational, and lawn and garden care power equipment in Iowa, Nebraska, Minnesota, Montana, North Dakota, South Dakota, and Wisconsin. **Pages** (approx.): 100. **Frequency:** Annual, April. **Editor:** Robert L. Shannon. **Advertising accepted.** Circulation 3,400. **Price:** $3.50.

★1913★

NORTHWEST MINING ASSOCIATION—SERVICE DIRECTORY

Northwest Mining Association
Chamber of Commerce Building
1020 W. Riverside Avenue   Phone: (509) 624-1158
Spokane, WA 99201

Covers: 1,700 mining and mineral resource firms who are members, and firms which supply professional and technical services and equipment to the industry in United States and western Canada. **Arrangement:** Members are geographical; suppliers classified by product or service. **Pages** (approx.): 260. **Frequency:** Annual. **Editor:** Bonnie Brooks. **Advertising accepted.** Circulation 2,300. **Price:** Available to members only.

★1914★

OCEAN INDUSTRY—MARINE DRILLING RIGS DIRECTORY ISSUE

Gulf Publishing Company
3301 Allen Parkway   Phone: (713) 529-4301
Houston, TX 77001

Covers: About 550 mobile and self-contained drilling rigs, including submersibles, drillships and barges, semi-submersibles, and jack-ups. **Entries include:** Name of owner, name of rig, construction history, drilling equipment, towing equipment required (if any), operating data, quarters, company to which contracted, work area. **Arrangement:** By type of rig. **Frequency:** Annual, September. **Editor:** Don Taylor. **Advertising accepted.** Circulation 33,200. **Price:** $2.50.

★1915★

OFFSHORE—DIRECTORY OF MARINE BARGES ISSUE

Petroleum Publishing Company
Box 1260   Phone: (918) 835-3161
Tulsa, OK 74101

Publication includes: List of about 250 pipelay, work, construction, and combination barges, worldwide. **Entries include:** Barge owner, vessel name, specifications, special equipment, location, name of lessee. **Arrangement:** Geographical. **Frequency:** Annual, November. **Editor:** Robert G. Burke. **Advertising accepted.** Circulation 21,200. **Price:** $2.50.

★1916★

OFFSHORE CONTRACTORS AND EQUIPMENT DIRECTORY

Petroleum Publishing Company

Box 1260   Phone: (918) 835-3161

Tulsa, OK 74101

Covers: About 1,200 companies with 2,800 locations; includes drilling contractors and rig owners; construction contractors; geophysical companies; diving contractors; and transportation companies; worldwide coverage. Includes list of mobile and fixed drilling rigs, including those under construction. **Entries include:** For companies - Company name, address, phone, key personnel, brief historical sketch. For drilling rigs - Owner, name, location, specifications. **Arrangement:** Classified by equipment or service. **Indexes:** Company name. **Pages** (approx.): 400. **Frequency:** Annual, April. **Price:** $45.00 (current and 1980 editions).

★1917★

OFFSHORE DRILLING REGISTER

H. Clarkson & Company Ltd.

52 Bishopsgate

London EC2P 2AD, England

Covers: Self-contained mobile sea-going drilling rigs capable of operating in a minimum of 50 feet of water and of drilling to at least 3,000 feet; worldwide coverage. **Entries include:** Company name, address, and names, types, and capabilities of rigs. Separate list gives technical data and capacities of each rig. **Arrangement:** Alphabetical. **Indexes:** Rigs by maximum drilling depth. **Frequency:** Annual. **Price:** $80.00.

★1918★

OFFSHORE SERVICES AND EQUIPMENT DIRECTORY

Inter Sphere Group

17480 Hada Drive   Phone: (714) 291-9300

San Diego, CA 92127

Covers: About 10,000 suppliers of equipment and services to the offshore petroleum exploration and production industry, worldwide. **Entries include:** Company name, address, phone, trade and brand names, specialties. **Arrangement:** By continent, then alphabetical by company. **Indexes:** By specialty. **Pages** (approx.): 200. **Frequency:** Annual, fall. **Editor:** J. Garza. **Advertising accepted.** Circulation 10,000. **Price:** $15.00.

★1919★

OIL & GAS DIRECTORY

Geophysical Directory, Inc.

2200 Welch Avenue   Phone: (713) 529-8789

Houston, TX 77019

Covers: About 2,000 companies involved in petroleum exploration, drilling, and production, and suppliers to the industry. **Entries include:** Company name, address, phone, telex, names of principal personnel. **Arrangement:** Classified by activity. **Indexes:** Company name, personal name. **Pages** (approx.): 400. **Frequency:** Annual, October. **Editor:** Jack Weyand. **Advertising accepted.** Circulation 4,300. **Price:** $25.00, postpaid.

★1920★

OIL AND GAS PRODUCERS OF NEW MEXICO DIRECTORY AND
HANDBOOK

R. W. Byram and Company

Drawer 1867   Phone: (512) 478-2551

Austin, TX 78767

Covers: Oil and gas producers, gas purchasers, crude petroleum transporters and storers, refiners, treating plants, carbon black plants. **Entries include:** Company name, address, phone, names of executives and engineers, number of gas and/or oil wells, county located in; one month's representative production is given for producers only. **Arrangement:** Classified. **Pages** (approx.): 250. **Frequency:** Biennial, fall of odd years. **Editor:** C. M. Christensen, President. **Price:** $25.00.

Oil Directory of Alaska *See* Midwest Oil Register—Regional Directories

Oil Directory of California *See* Midwest Oil Register—Regional Directories

Oil Directory of Canada *See* Midwest Oil Register—Regional Directories

Oil Directory of Foreign Companies Outside the U.S.A. & Canada *See* Midwest Oil Register—Regional Directories

Oil Directory of Houston, Texas [Including entire state] *See* Midwest Oil Register—Regional Directories

Oil Directory of Kansas *See* Midwest Oil Register—Regional Directories

Oil Directory of Louisiana, Arkansas, Mississippi, Georgia, and Florida *See* Midwest Oil Register—Regional Directories

Oil Directory of Michigan, Illinois, Indiana, and Kentucky *See* Midwest Oil Register—Regional Directories

Oil Directory of Oklahoma *See* Midwest Oil Register—Regional Directories

Oil Directory of Rocky Mountain Region, Four Corners, and New Mexico *See* Midwest Oil Register—Regional Directories

★1921★

OIL DIRECTORY OF TEXAS

R. W. Byram and Company

Drawer 1867   Phone: (512) 478-2551

Austin, TX 78767

Covers: About 5,000 oil producing companies, 2,900 gas producing companies, 50 refineries, 20 cycling plants, 35 repressuring plants, 350 gasoline plants, 360 salt water hauling companies, 25 directional surveying companies, 25 treating plants, and 1,100 oil and gas purchasing, gathering, pipeline, and transporting companies. **Entries include:** Company name, address, phone, names of executives, partners, and engineers; one month's representative production is given for producers. **Pages** (approx.): 330. **Frequency:** Annual, April. **Editor:** C. M. Christensen, President. **Price:** $24.00 (1980 edition).

★1922★

OKLAHOMA AGRICULTURAL EXPORT DIRECTORY

Agricultural Marketing Programs

Oklahoma Department of Agriculture

Agricultural Hall, Room 505

Oklahoma State University   Phone: (405) 624-6084

Stillwater, OK 74074

Covers: About 150 manufacturers and growers of agricultural products for export and Oklahoma companies which offer services related to international trade. **Entries include:** Company name, address, phone, name and title of contact, products or services. **Arrangement:** By activity. **Indexes:** Product. **Pages** (approx.): 40. **Frequency:** Not established; first edition 1979; new edition expected fall 1980. **Price:** Free.

★1923★

OREGON ASSOCIATION OF NURSERYMEN—DIRECTORY AND
BUYER'S GUIDE

Oregon Association of Nurserymen

0224 S. W. Hamilton   Phone: (503) 221-1182

Portland, OR 97201

Covers: Growers and wholesalers of annual and perennial flowering plants, evergreens, fruit trees, etc. **Entries include:** Name of nursery; address; phone; name of owner; codes indicating type of operation, products handled, and membership status. **Arrangement:** Alphabetical. **Indexes:** Product, chapter affiliation. **Pages** (approx.):

100. **Frequency:** Annual, September. **Editor:** Dan O. Barnhart. **Advertising accepted.** Circulation 2,200. **Price:** $8.50.

★1924★
OREGON LIVESTOCK BRAND BOOK

Oregon Department of Agriculture
635 Capital Street, N. E.   Phone: (503) 378-3779
Salem, OR 97310
Covers: About 15,000 livestock brands registered to cattle, horse, and sheep owners in Oregon. **Entries include:** Owner name, address, location of brand, drawing of brand, and any earmarks or fleshmarks used on the animals. **Arrangement:** Alphabetical. **Pages** (approx.): 1,265. **Frequency:** Biennial, spring of odd years. **Former title:** Livestock Brands Recorded in Oregon. **Price:** $25.00.

★1925★
PACIFIC NORTHWEST GRAIN DEALERS ASSOCIATION—OFFICIAL DIRECTORY

Pacific Northwest Grain Dealers Association
200 S. W. Market Street, No. 205   Phone: (503) 227-0234
Portland, OR 97201
Covers: Grain, feed, milling and seed firms in Washington, Oregon, Montana, and Idaho. **Entries include:** Company name, address, phone, names of executive business activities. **Arrangement:** Geographical. **Pages** (approx.): 190. **Frequency:** Annual, summer. **Editor:** Don W. Munkers, Executive Secretary. **Advertising accepted.** Circulation 1,500. **Price:** $10.00. **Send orders to:** Pacific Northwest Grain Dealers Association, 1812 N. W. Kearney St., Portland, OR 97209 (503-226-2758).

★1926★
PACIFIC PACKERS REPORT

Journal Publications, Inc.
4215 21st Avenue, West   Phone: (206) 283-1150
Seattle, WA 98199
Covers: United States and Canadian fish and shellfish processors and brokers. **Entries include:** Name, address, phone, principal personnel, facilities, products or services, and brand names. **Arrangement:** Geographical. **Pages** (approx.): 100. **Frequency:** Annual, April. **Editor:** Bruce J. Cole, Pacific Editor. **Advertising accepted.** Circulation 12,000. **Price:** $3.50 (current and 1980 editions). **Also includes:** Data on United States and Canadian fish production, 1940-1977.

★1927★
PACIFIC SOUTHWEST DIRECTORY [Of grain and feed firms]

California Grain and Feed Association
510 Bercut Drive, Suite H   Phone: (916) 441-2272
Sacramento, CA 95814
Covers: Major firms in grain, feed, seed, and feeding industries in California, Arizona, Nevada, Utah, and Hawaii. **Entries include:** Company name, address, phone, names of executives, type of business, and rail service. **Arrangement:** Geographical. **Pages** (approx.): 190. **Frequency:** Annual, January. **Editor:** Judy Rook. **Advertising accepted.** Circulation 1,100. **Price:** $10.00 (current and 1980 editions).

Packer Red Book See Red Book [Produce industry]

★1928★
PALO VERDE VALLEY [CALIFORNIA] LETTUCE SHIPPERS DIRECTORY

Federal-State Market News Service
395 Broadway   Phone: (714) 352-3562
El Centro, CA 92243
Number of listings: 20. **Entries include:** Company name, address, phone, trade and brand names, name of sales manager, and list of products. **Arrangement:** Alphabetical. **Frequency:** Annual. **Editor:** Jack R. Kloth, Officer-in-Charge. **Price:** Free.

★1929★
PARTICIPANTS IN THE NATIONAL POULTRY IMPROVEMENT PLAN

Animal and Plant Health Inspection Service
Agriculture Department   Phone: (301) 344-2227
Washington, DC 20250
Covers: Poultry hatcheries, dealers, and independent flockowners who participate in a federal program to control certain hatchery-disseminated diseases. **Entries include:** Company name; address; size, if a hatchery; products sold (by trade and brand name); and disease classification of products. **Arrangement:** Geographical. **Pages** (approx.): 95. **Frequency:** Annual, January. **Editor:** Rennae L. Cager, Secretary, National Poultry Improvement Plan. **Price:** Free (Stock Number ARS-NE-9-4). **Send orders to:** Poultry Improvement Staff, Bldg. 265, BARC-East, Beltsville, MD 20705 (301-344-2227).

★1930★
PELICAN GUIDE TO GARDENS OF LOUISIANA

Pelican Publishing Company, Inc.
630 Burmaster Street   Phone: (504) 368-1175
Gretna, LA 70053
Covers: Louisiana's major gardens - Rosedown, Hodges, Rip Van Winkle, Live Oak, Longue Vue, and Jungle Gardens - as well as numerous other gardens, including sites in the New Orleans' French Quarter and Garden District. **Entries include:** Name of garden, location, directions, admissions policies, and floral highlights. **Pages** (approx.): 60. **Frequency:** Irregular; latest edition 1974. **Editor:** Joyce Y. LeBlanc. **Price:** $2.95.

★1931★
PESTICIDE HANDBOOK—ENTOMA

Entomological Society of America
Box AJ   Phone: (301) 864-1334
College Park, MD 20705
Publication includes: List of manufacturers of commercial pesticides. **Entries include:** Company name, address, phone, and description of products, including uses and ingredients. **Arrangement:** Alphabetical. **Frequency:** Biennial, fall of odd years. **Editor:** Robert L. Caswell. **Advertising accepted.** Circulation 6,000. **Price:** $8.95.

Petroleum Equipment Suppliers Association—Membership Directory See Service Point Directory [Petroleum production equipment]

★1932★
PETROLEUM REFINERIES IN THE UNITED STATES AND PUERTO RICO

Office of Energy Data Operations
Energy Information Administration
Energy Department
1000 Independence Avenue, N. W.   Phone: (202) 252-6401
Washington, DC 20585
Covers: Petroleum refineries, including operable, inoperable, shutdown, and under-construction plants. **Entries include:** For each plant - Name, company, location of plant, capacity. **Arrangement:** Geographical. **Pages** (approx.): 20. **Frequency:** Annual. **Price:** Free (DOE/EIA-0111). **Send orders to:** Energy Information Administration Clearinghouse, 1726 M St., N. W., Room 200, Washington, DC 20461 (202-634-5694).

★1933★
PICK-YOUR-OWN FRUITS AND VEGETABLES [Illinois]

College of Agriculture
University of Illinois
Urbana, IL 61801
Covers: Illinois farms that allow consumers to pick their own fruits and vegetables. **Entries include:** Farm name, owner address, fruit or vegetable grown. **Arrangement:** Alphabetical. **Frequency:** Annual. **Editors:** Roberta Archer and J. W. Courter. **Other information:** Compiled in cooperation with the Illinois Department of Agriculture.

★1934★

PIPELINE—ANNUAL DIRECTORY OF PIPELINES AND EQUIPMENT ISSUE

Oildom Publishing Company of Texas, Inc.
3314 Mercer   Phone: (713) 622-0676
Houston, TX 77027
Covers: Companies operating oil and gas transmission pipelines and manufacturers of pipeline equipment and supplies, gas distribution companies, and other gas and oil companies. **Entries include:** Company name, address, phone, names of key personnel, products or services. **Arrangement:** By activity. **Frequency:** Annual, October. **Editor:** Daniel Dietsch. **Advertising accepted.** Circulation 14,000. **Price:** $25.00.

★1935★

PIPELINE & GAS JOURNAL—BUYERS GUIDE ISSUE

Energy Publications, Inc., Division
Harcourt Brace Jovanovich Publications
800 Davis Building   Phone: (214) 748-4403
Dallas, TX 75221
Publication includes: List of 800 companies supplying products and services used in construction and operation of cross-country pipeline and gas distribution industries. **Entries include:** Company name, address, phone. **Arrangement:** Alphabetical. **Indexes:** Product. **Frequency:** Annual, April. **Editor:** Dean Hale. **Advertising accepted.** **Price:** $7.50.

Pipeline & Pipeline Contractors *See* Midwest Oil Register— Industry Segment Directories

★1936★

PLYWOOD & PANEL MAGAZINE—ANNUAL WORLDWIDE DIRECTORY AND BUYERS' GUIDE ISSUE

Curtis Publishing Company
1100 Waterway Boulevard   Phone: (317) 634-1100
Indianapolis, IN 46202
Covers: Manufacturers and suppliers of machinery, equipment, and supplies including veneers and panels to the woodworking industry; worldwide coverage. **Entries include:** Company name, address, phone, names of executives, products or services, and telex or cable address. **Arrangement:** By major product category (veneers, panels, all others), then alphabetical. **Pages** (approx.): 95. **Frequency:** Annual, January. **Editor:** Robert F. Dixon. **Advertising accepted.** Circulation 14,000. **Price:** $3.00. **Also includes:** List of trade associations and other sources of information on the wood products industry.

★1937★

POULTRY & EGG MARKETING—EGG MARKETING DIRECTORY ISSUE

Poultry & Egg News, Inc.
Drawer A   Phone: (609) 692-3100
Vineland, NJ 08360
Covers: Over 1,000 egg marketers in the United States. **Entries include:** Marketer's name, address, phone, names of principal executives, type of operation (packer, broker, drier, etc.), how product is handled (cartoned, liquid, etc.), weekly volume, geographic area served, other products, and branches, if any. **Arrangement:** Geographical. **Pages** (approx.): 35. **Frequency:** Annual, fall. **Editor:** Alfred N. Schwartz. **Advertising accepted.** Circulation 8,900. **Price:** $1.00. **Send orders to:** Poultry & Egg Marketing, Box 1338, Gainesville, GA 30501 (404-536-2476).

★1938★

POULTRY & EGG MARKETING—POULTRY DISTRIBUTOR DIRECTORY ISSUE

Poultry & Egg News, Inc.
Drawer A   Phone: (609) 692-3100
Vineland, NJ 08360
Covers: 860 poultry distributors, brokers, processors, and distributors. **Entries include:** Name, address, phone, names of principal executives, how products are handled (chill packed, frozen, etc.), whether company does cutting, weekly volume, other products, branches, if any, and their managers, addresses, and phones. **Arrangement:** Geographical. **Pages** (approx.): 35. **Frequency:** Annual, spring. **Editor:** Alfred N. Schwartz. **Advertising accepted.** Circulation 8,900. **Price:** $1.00 (current and 1980 editions). **Send orders to:** Poultry & Egg Marketing, Box 1338, Gainesville, GA 30501 (404-536-2476).

★1939★

POULTRY INDUSTRY DIRECTORY

Southeastern Poultry and Egg Association
1456 Church Street   Phone: (404) 377-6465
Decatur, GA 30030
Covers: About 800 egg, chicken, and turkey producers, processors, and wholesalers, and feed, pharmaceutical, and other suppliers to the industry. Also includes extensive lists of state and national poultry trade organizations and university poultry departments. Considerable coverage of areas outside southeastern states. **Entries include:** Firm name, address, name of principal executive, phone, and code indicating type of business. **Arrangement:** Geographical; egg producers and dealers and chicken and turkey producers and dealers are also listed separately. **Frequency:** Annual, December. **Advertising accepted.** **Price:** Controlled circulation.

Primary Wood-Using Industries in Florida *See* Florida's Wood-Using Industry

★1940★

PROFESSIONAL FORESTRY INSTRUCTION OFFERED IN THE U.S.

Society of American Foresters
5400 Grosvenor Lane   Phone: (301) 897-8720
Bethesda, MD 20014
Covers: About 50 forestry schools and institutions offering programs in forestry in the United States; 60 institutions offering pre-professional programs are also listed. **Entries include:** Institution name, address; degrees offered; accreditation status. **Arrangement:** Geographical. **Frequency:** Annual, January-February. **Price:** Free.

★1941★

PROFESSIONAL PEACH WORKERS IN PUBLIC INSTITUTIONS OF THE UNITED STATES: A DIRECTORY

National Peach Council
Box 1085
Martinsburg, WV 25401
Covers: About 165 state and 15 federal agriculture department researchers involved in research on peaches. **Entries include:** Name, title, affiliation, address, phone, duties or area of interest. **Arrangement:** Georgraphical. **Indexes:** Personal name. **Frequency:** Irregular; latest edition January 1979. **Editor:** Dr. Jere A. Brittain, chairman, Research and Education Committee. **Price:** $2.00.

★1942★

PROFESSIONAL WORKERS IN STATE AGRICULTURAL EXPERIMENT STATIONS AND OTHER COOPERATING STATE INSTITUTIONS

Science and Education Administration-Cooperative Research
Agriculture Department   Phone: (202) 447-2971
Washington, DC 20250
Covers: Academic and research personnel in all agricultural, forestry, aquacultural, home economics, and animal husbandry fields at experiment stations and academic institutions with agricultural programs. **Entries include:** Station or institution name, address, phone; names of personnel, their degrees and titles, and, in some cases, individual phones; classified by major scientific or administrative areas. **Arrangement:** Geographical. **Indexes:** Personnel. **Pages** (approx.): 225. **Frequency:** Annual, January. **Price:** $5.50 (Agriculture Handbook 305). **Send orders to:** Government Printing Office, Washington, DC 20402.

★1943★
THE PUBLIC GARDENS
Horticultural Society of New York
128 W. 58th Street   Phone: (212) 757-0915
New York, NY 10019
Covers: Public gardens in New York, New Jersey, and Connecticut. Entries include: Name of garden, features and highlights, list of flowers and plants, history, educational services, directions. Arrangement: Geographical. Pages (approx.): 60. Frequency: Irregular; latest edition fall 1979. Former title: Tri-State Garden Directory. Price: $2.00.

Red Angus Association of America—Membership Directory See American Red Angus—Breeders Directory Issue

★1944★
RED BOOK [Produce industry]
Vance Publishing Corporation
Fifth and State Streets   Phone: (913) 281-3073
Kansas City, KS 66101
Covers: 16,000 principal sources and outlets for fruits and vegetables. Also includes sections covering flower growers and shippers; truck brokers and haulers; chain store headquarters and branch offices; and truck stops having facilities for haulers of perishables. Entries include: Shipper, receiver, and other produce operator listings show firm name, address, phone, key personnel with home phones, type of operation, commodities handled, and keys indicating net worth, rating of business methods and trading practices, and paying practices. Listings in other sections give basic name/address/phone data; truck broker listings include trade performance ratings, area served, equipment, branches; chain store listings include personnel, number of stores served. Arrangement: All sections are geographical except chain stores, which are alphabetical (with cross-references in main section). Indexes: General alphabetical. Pages (approx.): 850. Frequency: Semiannual, April and October, with weekly change bulletins. Editor: Harold U. Hosterman, General Manager. Price: $250.00 per year, including updates.

★1945★
REDWOOD RANCHER—VINTAGE ISSUE [Wineries]
Sally Taylor and Friends
756 Kansas Street
San Francisco, CA 94107
Covers: Wineries in the coastal counties of California from Mendocino to Santa Barbara. Entries include: Winery name, address, phone, information on tours and tasting facilities, and whether and when the winery is open to the public. Each winery is coded and located on a map included in the directory section. Arrangement: Geographical. Frequency: Annual, July. Advertising accepted. Price: $2.00.

Refining, Construction, Petrochemical & Natural Gas Processing Plants of the World See Midwest Oil Register—Industry Segment Directories

Rocky Mountain Petroleum Directory See Western Oil Reporter Rocky Mountain Petroleum Directory

★1946★
SANITATION COMPLIANCE AND ENFORCEMENT RATINGS OF INTERSTATE MILK SHIPPERS
Food and Drug Administration
Public Health Service
Health, Education, and Welfare Department, HFF-415
Washington, DC 20204
Covers: Interstate milk shippers who meet federal sanitation standards, certified manufacturers of single-use products (milk cartons, etc.), and certified state milk sanitation rating officers and laboratory evaluation officers. Entries include: Shipper's company name, city, products, ratings, rating agency and date rated; manufacturers' name, assigned code, type of product, rating agency and date rating expires; sanitation or lab evaluation officer's name,

agency with which affiliated, and expiration date of officer's certification. Arrangement: Geographical. Pages (approx.): 130. Frequency: Quarterly.

Secondary Wood-Using Industries in Florida See Florida's Wood-Using Industry

★1947★
SEED WORLD—SEED TRADE BUYERS GUIDE ISSUE
Scranton Publishing Company, Inc.
380 Northwest Highway   Phone: (312) 298-6622
Des Plaines, IL 60016
Covers: Farm, flower, and vegetable seeds, foreign seed firms, equipment, services, resale items, and association officers. Entries include: Company name and address. Pages (approx.): 250. Frequency: Annual, January. Editor: Deborah Wyatt, Managing Editor. Advertising accepted. Circulation 4,500. Price: $5.00 (current and 1980 editions).

★1948★
SERVICE POINT DIRECTORY [Petroleum production equipment]
Petroleum Equipment Suppliers Association
9225 Katy Freeway, Suite 401   Phone: (713) 932-0168
Houston, TX 77024
Covers: About 220 member firms, including oil field drilling and production equipment manufacturers, oil field supply companies, and specialty service firms. Also lists about 4,000 domestic and 750 international offices, shops, and other branch service locations. Entries include: For companies - Company name, address, phone, name of executive, corporate affiliation, branch locations. For branches - Company name, address, phone. Arrangement: Companies are alphabetical, branches are geographical. Pages (approx.): 225. Frequency: Biennial, January of odd years. Price: $35.00, plus 36¢ shipping.

Sonoma-Mendocino Wine Book See California Wine Country Series [Wineries]

Sonoma-Mendocino Wine Tour See Wine Tour Series [California]

★1949★
SOURCES OF NATIVE SEEDS AND PLANTS
Soil Conservation Society of America
7515 N. E. Ankeny Road
Ankeny, IA 50021
Covers: About 165 companies and organizations which offer native seeds and plants for sale, retail, or wholesale. Offerings include flower, grass, tree, and shrub seeds and plants. Entries include: Firm or organization name, address, plants or seeds available. Arrangement: Geographical. Indexes: Company name. Pages (approx.): 20. Frequency: Not established; first edition 1979. Price: $2.00, postpaid.

★1950★
SOURCES OF PLANTS & RELATED SUPPLIES
American Association of Nurserymen
230 Southern Building
1425 H Street, N. W.   Phone: (202) 737-4060
Washington, DC 20005
Covers: Growers and suppliers of 1,600 varieties of commercially available nursery stock, and sources of related nursery supplies, retail products, and business services. Entries include: Firm name, address; nursery stock listings indicate whether the plants are available in bulk, whether packaged for retail, whether bareroot, etc.; supplier listings indicate whether the source is the manufacturer or distributor. Arrangement: Alphabetical. Indexes: Product. Frequency: Annual, July. Editor: Duane Jelink. Price: $3.00, payment with order.

★1951★

SOURCES/CONSULTANTS DIRECTORY FOR WYOMING [Minerals, petroleum]
Geological Survey of Wyoming
Box 3008
University Station   Phone: (307) 742-2054
Laramie, WY 82701
Covers: Sources of information on geological aspects of mining, petroleum, etc. available in Wyoming. Includes government agencies, commercial firms, and consultants. **Entries include:** Name, address, phone. **Arrangement:** Classified by type of agency, service, etc. **Indexes:** Specialty (for consultants). **Pages** (approx.): 40. **Frequency:** Irregular; latest edition June 1977; new edition expected early 1980.

★1952★

SOUTHERN CALIFORNIA FLORAL ASSOCIATION—DIRECTORY
Southern California Floral Association
756 Wall Street   Phone: (213) 627-1201
Los Angeles, CA 90014
Covers: About 1,000 growers, retailers, wholesalers and related firms which are members. **Entries include:** Name, office address and phone, home address and phone. **Arrangement:** Geographical. **Pages** (approx.): 140. **Frequency:** Annual, March. **Advertising accepted.** Circulation 1,500. **Price:** $7.50 (current edition); $10.00 (1980 edition).

★1953★

SOUTHERN FLORIST & NURSERYMAN—BUYERS' GUIDE ISSUE
Southern Florist Publishing Company
120 St. Louis Avenue   Phone: (817) 332-8236
Ft. Worth, TX 76104
Covers: Growers and wholesalers of cut flowers, plants, and seeds, and suppliers of floral supplies, equipment, and services. **Entries include:** Company name, address, form in which plant or flower is furnished (bareroot, in pots, etc.). Supplier lists indicate whether manufacturer, wholesaler, or importer. **Arrangement:** Separate sections for flowers and plants and for supplies, then by plant or product. **Pages** (approx.): 200. **Frequency:** Semiannual, spring and fall. **Editor:** James B. Martin. **Advertising accepted.** Circulation 8,000. **Price:** $3.00 (current and 1980 editions).

★1954★

SOUTHERN FOREST PRODUCTS ASSOCIATION—BUYER'S GUIDE
Southern Forest Products Association
Box 52468
New Orleans, LA 70152
Covers: About 160 plants and mills of member companies, all of which process southern pine lumber. **Entries include:** Company name, mill name, production capacity, railroad serving the mill, grademaking number, products, sales office address and phone. **Arrangement:** Geographical. **Pages** (approx.): 30. **Frequency:** Annual, spring. **Price:** Free.

★1955★

SOY PRODUCTS DIRECTORY
Soycrafters Association of North America
Sunrise Farm
Heath Road   Phone: (413) 624-5591
Colrain, MA 01340
Covers: About 250 shops which sell tofu, a cheese derived from soybeans, and dairies which produce soymilk. **Entries include:** Firm name, address, products. **Arrangement:** Geographical. **Frequency:** Irregular.

★1956★

SOYBEAN DIGEST—BLUE BOOK ISSUE
American Soybean Association
Box 158   Phone: (319) 988-3295
Hudson, IA 50634
Covers: Firms serving the soybean industry, including processors, refiners, manufacturers and handlers of soy foods and other soy products, and equipment suppliers. **Entries include:** Company name, address, phone, telex, brief description of service or product. Sections on refiners and processors also list personnel, process used, and capacity. **Arrangement:** Geographical within category (processor, equipment suppliers, etc.). **Indexes:** Product. **Pages** (approx.): 170. **Frequency:** Annual, June. **Editor:** Jamie Vroom. **Advertising accepted.** Circulation 7,000. **Price:** $25.00.

Sprinkler Irrigation Association—Membership Directory *See* Irrigation Association—Membership Directory

★1957★

STATE OF OREGON LOG BRANDS REGISTERED WITH THE STATE FORESTER
Log Brand Section
Oregon Forestry Department
2600 State Street   Phone: (503) 378-2512
Salem, OR 97310
Covers: Owners and illustrations of all log ownership brand marks registered in Oregon. **Entries include:** For owners - Name, address, current registration number, cross-reference to illustrations; for illustrations - reproduction of brand, registration number, owner's name. **Arrangement:** Owners listed alphabetically; illustrations first by prominent characteristic (letter, number, circle, etc.), then numerically by registration number. **Frequency:** Five year intervals, latest edition 1977; updates about every three months. **Editor:** Arlene Baughn, Log Brand Records Supervisor. **Price:** $10.00.

Sugar Mill Directory *See* Sugar y Azucar Yearbook

★1958★

SUGAR y AZUCAR YEARBOOK
Mona Palmer
25 W. 45th Street   Phone: (212) 586-4820
New York, NY 10036
Covers: 1,500 cane sugar and beet sugar refineries and their suppliers, worldwide. **Entries include:** Mill name, address, capacity, manager's name and corporation identification. **Arrangement:** Geographical. **Frequency:** Annual, November. **Advertising accepted.** **Price:** $30.00, postpaid. **Other information:** Sometimes cited as, "Sugar Mill Directory." Beet sugar refineries are not included in current edition.

★1959★

SUNFLOWER DIRECTORY
Sunflower Directory
Box 5193
Fargo, ND 58105
Covers: About 250 companies, trade associations, government agencies and over 400 persons concerned with the sunflower agriculture and products industry; coverage includes the United States and Canada. **Entries include:** Company or organization name, address, function, contact person, phone. Individuals' listings include name, organization, specialty, and phone - no address. **Arrangement:** Both organizations and individuals are alphabetical. **Indexes:** Organization function, organization location, individual by specialty. **Pages** (approx.): 100. **Frequency:** Irregular; latest edition July 1978; May 1979 supplement; new edition expected January 1980. **Editor:** David W. Cobia. **Advertising accepted.** Circulation 1,000. **Price:** $4.00 (current edition); $5.00 (tentative, 1980 edition); postpaid, payment with order. **Also includes:** List of relevant publications with title, publisher name and address, cost, and annotation.

★1960★

TENNESSEE HAY DIRECTORY
Tennessee Department of Agriculture
Box 40627
Melrose Station
Nashville, TN 37204
Covers: About 240 Tennessee hay producers. **Entries include:** Name, address, phone, types of hay for sale, number of bales, price per bale

or roll. **Arrangement:** By county. **Pages** (approx.): 30. **Frequency:** Annual, winter. **Price:** Free.

★**1961**★
TIMBER HARVESTERS OF NEW YORK STATE
Wood Utilization Service
School of Environmental Science and Forestry
State University of New York
Syracuse, NY 13210
Covers: About 1,400 loggers and pulpers operating in New York State. **Arrangement:** By county. **Frequency:** Not established; first edition 1978. **Price:** Free.

★**1962**★
TIMBER HARVESTING—WOOD & WOODLANDS DIRECTORY ISSUE
Hatton, Brown & Company
458 S. Lawrence Street   Phone: (205) 834-1170
Montgomery, AL 36103
Covers: Key personnel in the wood supply and woodlands operations of industrial timber corporations. **Entries include:** Firm name, division or subsidiary name, address, phone, names and titles of key personnel, contact information. **Arrangement:** Alphabetical by company name. **Frequency:** Annual, January.

★**1963**★
TOBACCO INTERNATIONAL—BUYERS' GUIDE/DIRECTORY ISSUE
Lockwood Trade Journal Company, Inc.
551 Fifth Avenue   Phone: (212) 661-5980
New York, NY 10017
Covers: Tobacco leaf processors and tobacco product manufacturers, worldwide. **Entries include:** Company name, address, phone, names of executives, list of products or services, telex, cable address. **Arrangement:** Processor list is geographical; manufacturers listed by product and geographically. **Pages** (approx.): 240. **Frequency:** Annual, October. **Editor:** Thomas Cogan. **Advertising accepted.** Circulation 3,500. **Price:** $15.00.

★**1964**★
TOBACCO INTERNATIONAL—DIXIE DIRECTORY ISSUE
Lockwood Trade Journal Company, Inc.
551 Fifth Avenue   Phone: (212) 661-5980
New York, NY 10017
Publication includes: Tobacco processors, manufacturers, and trade associations in the United States tobacco industry (SIC 41). **Entries include:** Company name, address, phone, names of executives and their addresses and photographs. **Frequency:** Annual, April. **Editor:** Thomas Cogan. **Advertising accepted.** Circulation 3,500. **Price:** $5.00 (current and 1980 editions).

★**1965**★
TOFU & SOYMILK PRODUCTION
New-Age Foods Study Center
Box 234
Lafayette, CA 94549
Publication includes: List of persons and institutions knowledgeable in tofu and soymilk production. **Entries include:** Name, address, special interests. **Frequency:** First edition 1979. **Editors:** William Shurtleff and Akiko Aoyagi. **Price:** $22.95, cloth; $17.95, paper; plus 85¢ shipping.

★**1966**★
TOOLS FOR AGRICULTURE: A BUYER'S GUIDE TO LOW-COST AGRICULTURAL IMPLEMENTS
Intermediate Technology Publications
9 King Street
London WC2E 8HN, England
Covers: 250 manufacturers of low-cost agricultural equipment, worldwide. Listings for about 600 items, including some equipment powered by small engines. **Entries include:** Brand or other identification, manufacturer name and address, illustration, and, in

most cases, technical information. **Arrangement:** Classified by type of farming operation (cultivation, sowing and plantings, etc.). **Pages** (approx.): 175. **Frequency:** Irregular; latest edition 1976; new edition possible 1980-81. **Editor:** John Boyd. **Former title:** Guide to Hand-Operated and Animal-Drawn Equipment (1976). **Price:** $11.95. **Send orders to:** International Scholarly Book Services, Box 555, Forest Grove, OR 97116.

★**1967**★
TOOLS FOR HOMESTEADERS, GARDENERS, AND SMALL-SCALE FARMERS
Rodale Press, Inc.
33 E. Minor Street   Phone: (215) 967-5171
Emmaus, PA 18049
Publication includes: Lists of manufacturers and distributors of about 700 hand and power-operated cultivating tools and other farm and garden implements which may be hard to locate; international coverage. **Arrangement:** By type of tool; text describes characteristics and use, and is followed by list of manufacturers. Additional manufacturers listed in appendix. **Indexes:** General. **Frequency:** First edition 1978. **Editor:** Diana S. Branch. **Price:** $12.95. **Other information:** Similar to "Tools for Agriculture: A Buyer's Guide to Low-Cost Agricultural Implements" (see separate listing), the publishers of which are also involved in compilation of this book.

Tri-State Garden Directory *See* The Public Gardens

★**1968**★
TURKEY WORLD—LEADING COMPANIES ISSUE
Watt Publishing Company
Sandstone Building   Phone: (815) 734-4171
Mt. Morris, IL 61054
Publication includes: Leading turkey firms in terms of live weight of processed birds. **Entries include:** Company name, brief note on nature of business, number of plants, pounds of live birds processed in previous year, cities in which company has processing and other plants. **Arrangement:** By total live weight. **Frequency:** Annual, January-February issue. **Editor:** William A. Haffert, Jr. **Advertising accepted. Price:** $1.50, payment with order.

★**1969**★
U.S. DIRECTORY OF MEAT PROCESSING PLANTS
Food Industries Directories
798 Kings Highway   Phone: (203) 366-4448
Fairfield, CT 06430
Covers: Over 6,000 plants engaged in curing, smoking, canning, and freezing meats, and manufacturing sausages, sausage casings, and other prepared meats and meat specialties from purchased carcasses; prepared meat plants operated as separate establishments are included (SIC 2013). Covers Canada. **Entries include:** Company name, address, phone, name of principal officer, type of business, key showing approximate sales and number of employees. **Arrangement:** Geographical. **Frequency:** Irregular; latest edition fall 1978; new edition expected early 1980. **Price:** $64.50 (current edition); $69.50 (tentative, 1980 edition); postpaid, payment with order.

★**1970**★
U.S. DIRECTORY OF MEAT SLAUGHTERING PLANTS
Food Industries Directories
798 Kings Highway   Phone: (203) 366-4448
Fairfield, CT 06430
Covers: Over 3,600 plants engaged in slaughtering cattle, hogs, sheep, lambs, and calves for meat to be sold or to be used in curing, canning, rendering, etc. (SIC 2011). Includes Canada. **Entries include:** Company name, address, phone, name of principal officer, type of business, key showing approximate sales and number of employees. **Arrangement:** Geographical. **Frequency:** Irregular; latest edition fall 1978; new edition expected early 1980. **Price:** $64.50 (current edition); $69.50 (tentative, 1980 edition); postpaid, payment with order.

★1971★

**U.S. DIRECTORY OF POULTRY SLAUGHTERING PLANTS AND
POULTRY AND EGG PROCESSING PLANTS**
Food Industries Directories
798 Kings Highway   Phone: (203) 366-4448
Fairfield, CT 06430
Covers: Over 3,200 plants engaged in slaughtering, dressing, cooking,
freezing, etc., poultry and small game, or in preparation of processed
poultry products from purchased carcasses; includes plants engaged in
freezing and breaking of eggs (SIC 2016, 2017). Includes Canada.
Entries include: Company name, address, phone, name of principal
officer, type of business, key showing approximate sales and number
of employees. **Arrangement:** Geographical. **Frequency:** Irregular;
latest edition fall 1978; new edition expected spring 1980. **Price:**
$89.50, postpaid, payment with order (current edition and tentative,
1980 edition).

★1972★

U.S. DIRECTORY OF RENDERERS AND BONERS
Food Industries Directories
798 Kings Highway   Phone: (203) 366-4448
Fairfield, CT 06430
Covers: Over 1,300 plants engaged in rendering fats and oils from
meat and poultry and reprocessing them into lard, shortening, etc.;
includes plants primarily engaged in boning of meat and poultry (SIC
2013, 2077). **Entries include:** Company name, address, phone, name
of principal officer, type of business, key showing approximate sales
and number of employees. **Arrangement:** Geographical. **Frequency:**
Irregular; latest edition fall 1978; new edition expected early 1980.
Price: $32.50, postpaid, payment with order (current edition);
$35.00 (tentative, 1980 edition).

★1973★

USA OIL INDUSTRY DIRECTORY
Petroleum Publishing Company
Box 1260   Phone: (918) 835-3161
Tulsa, OK 74101
Covers: Over 2,500 oil producers, pipeline companies, petroleum
marketing companies, and integrated oil firms; trade and professional
associations, state and federal government agencies are also included.
Entries include: For companies - Name, address, names and titles of
key personnel, phone, line of business. For major oil companies -
Name, address, names and titles of key personnel, phone, historical
description. **Arrangement:** By line of business. **Indexes:** Company,
personal name. **Frequency:** Annual, January. **Price:** $50.00 (current
and 1980 editions).

★1974★

USDA DATA BASE DIRECTORY
Office of Automated Data Systems
Agriculture Department
Washington, DC 20250
Covers: About 55 agencies in the Agriculture Department with
automated files and data bases. **Entries include:** Agency name, name
of management information systems coordinator, system name, data
base name, processing location, name of agency contact, data base
status, software used, number of records, record size, source of data,
further data base description, USDA programs supported, data
elements, other interested agencies. **Arrangement:** By agency. **Pages**
(approx.): 60. **Frequency:** Irregular; first edition May 1977; new
edition in preparation. **Editor:** Roxanne Williams, Director, Plans and
Policy Division. **Price:** Free.

★1975★

UTAH MINERAL INDUSTRY OPERATOR DIRECTORY
Utah Geological and Mineral Survey
606 Black Hawk Way
Research Park   Phone: (801) 581-6831
Salt Lake City, UT 84108
Covers: 1,000 mineral industry operators including mines, oil and gas
fields, and quarries. **Entries include:** Company name, address,

production. **Arrangement:** Geographical. **Pages** (approx.): 70.
Frequency: Biennial, May of odd years. **Editor:** Martha R. Smith.
Price: $3.00.

★1976★

VIRGINIA POULTRYMAN—DIRECTORY ISSUE
Virginia Poultry Federation
Box 1036   Phone: (703) 433-2451
Harrisonburg, VA 22801
Publication includes: Commercial poultry and poultry feed industries
in Virginia and West Virginia, including 70 poultry firms, 125 feed
industry firms, 635 poultry producers or servicemen, 40 university
personnel, 85 state department or agriculture personnel, 10
vocational agriculture offices. **Entries include:** Company name,
address. **Arrangement:** Classified. **Frequency:** Annual, December.
Editor: Jerry H. Gass. **Advertising accepted.** Circulation 2,800.
Price: $1.00.

★1977★

**WASHINGTON DEPARTMENT OF AGRICULTURE—FARM
PRODUCT OUTLET GUIDE**
Washington Department of Agriculture
General Administration Building, Room 406   Phone: (206) 753-5046
Olympia, WA 98504
Covers: Several hundred self-pick fields, roadside stands, and other
non-grocery store outlets for fresh fruit, produce, dairy products,
seafood, meat, honey, earthworms, and Christmas trees. **Entries
include:** Outlet name, location, products, phone; outlets are also
located on a map in each edition. **Arrangement:** Eleven editions for
groups of counties. **Frequency:** Annual, summer. **Price:** Free; specify
city, county, or area for which coverage is desired.

★1978★

WASHINGTON STATE AGRICULTURAL EXPORT DIRECTORY
Washington Department of Agriculture
General Administration Building, Room 406   Phone: (206) 753-5046
Olympia, WA 98504
Covers: About 500 firms engaged in processing, manufacturing,
distributing, financing and selling agricultural and related industry
products from the state of Washington. **Entries include:** Company
name, address, phone, telex, sales representative, brand names
offered, and packaging. **Arrangement:** Alphabetical by company
name. **Indexes:** Commodity. **Pages** (approx.): 110. **Frequency:**
Triennial, summer; latest edition 1978. **Editor:** Owen F. Cargol,
Agricultural Consultant. **Price:** Free.

Washington State Agricultural Trade Directory *See* Washington
    State Agricultural Export Directory

★1979★

WEED CONTROL MANUAL
Meister Publishing Company
37841 Euclid Avenue   Phone: (216) 942-2000
Willoughby, OH 44094
Publication includes: List of manufacturers of herbicides. **Entries
include:** Company name, address, phone, and list of products.
Arrangement: Alphabetical. **Indexes:** Trade or brand name. **Pages**
(approx.): 250. **Frequency:** Annual, December. **Editor:** Gordon L.
Berg. **Advertising accepted.** Circulation 20,000. **Price:** $12.00.
Also includes: Information on use of herbicides with weeds and
crops.

★1980★

WEST VIRGINIA DEPARTMENT OF MINES—DIRECTORY OF MINES
West Virginia Department of Mines
Room E-151, Capitol Building   Phone: (304) 348-2051
Charleston, WV 25305
Entries include: Company name, address, mines, number of
employees at each, accident statistics. **Arrangement:** Geographical.
Pages (approx.): 100. **Frequency:** Annual, July. **Price:** Free.

★1981★

WESTERN FARM EQUIPMENT—ANNUAL TRADE DIRECTORY
    ISSUE
Western Farm Equipment Magazine
Box 1657
Lake Oswego, OR 97034
Covers: 700 manufacturers of farm and irrigation equipment who
distribute in 13 western states and their wholesalers. Entries include:
For manufacturers - Company name and address. For wholesalers -
Company name, address, products handled; some entries include
names of principal personnel and phone. Arrangement: Manufacturers
are alphabetical, wholesalers are geographical. Indexes: Product.
Pages (approx.): 70. Frequency: Annual, March. Editor: M. A.
Johnson, Publisher. Advertising accepted. Circulation 5,000. Price:
$2.00. (Not verified)

★1982★

WESTERN GROWERS ASSOCIATION—MEMBERSHIP DIRECTORY
    [Fruits and vegetables]
Western Growers Association
1811 Quail Street   Phone: (714) 833-8384
Newport Beach, CA 92663
Covers: 1,000 growers and shippers of fruits and vegetables and
allied industries in California and Arizona, reported to grow nearly half
the fresh produce in the United States. Entries include: Company
name, address, phone, names of executives, list of produce grown and
when available. Arrangement: Alphabetical. Frequency: Annual, July.
Editor: Leslie V. Hubbard. Price: Available to members only.

★1983★

WESTERN GROWERS EXPORT DIRECTORY [Fruits and
    vegetables]
Western Growers Association
1811 Quail Street   Phone: (714) 833-8384
Newport Beach, CA 92663
Covers: Shippers of fresh produce and fruit in California and Arizona
who are members of the association and are interested in exporting to
Japan and/or Europe. (Separate editions for Japan and Europe.)
Entries include: Company name, address, phone, name and address
of responsible official, products available, seasons available.
Arrangement: Alphabetical. Indexes: Commodity (includes size and
type of shipping container and dates produce available). Pages
(approx.): 20. Frequency: Irregular; latest edition April 1978. Editor:
Leslie Hubbard. Price: Free.

★1984★

WESTERN LANDSCAPING NEWS—BUYERS' GUIDE ISSUE
Hester Communications, Inc.
Box 19531   Phone: (714) 979-4720
Irvine, CA 92713
Publication includes: Manufacturers, suppliers, distributors, and sales
offices serving professional landscaping industry in western United
States. Entries include: Company name, address, phone, and products
or services. Arrangement: Sources arranged alphabetically; classified
product guide. Frequency: Annual, March. Editor: Steve McGonigal.
Advertising accepted. Circulation 17,500. Price: $4.00 (current
edition); $5.00 (1980 edition).

★1985★

WESTERN MINING DIRECTORY
Howell Publishing Company
311 Steele Street, Suite 208   Phone: (303) 355-5202
Denver, CO 80206
Covers: Active and producing mines, suppliers, mining companies,
mining associations, state government agencies, mining consultants,
and mining contractors; covers 13 western states. Entries include:
Company or organization name, address, and phone. Arrangement:
Geographical. Frequency: Annual, June. Price: $13.00, plus $2.00
shipping.

★1986★

WESTERN OIL REPORTER ROCKY MOUNTAIN PETROLEUM
    DIRECTORY
Hart Publications, Inc.
Box 1917   Phone: (303) 892-1164
Denver, CO 80201
Covers: About 6,000 companies, associations, and agencies in the
petroleum industry in Rocky Mountain region. Entries include:
Company name, address, phone, names and titles of key personnel.
Arrangement: Classified. Pages (approx.): 900. Frequency: Annual,
March. Editor: Donald R. Hart, Editor and Publisher. Advertising
accepted. Circulation 14,000. Price: $22.00.

Western Red Cedar Lumber Association—Membership List See
    Western Wood Products Association—Buyers Manual

★1987★

WESTERN STATES MEAT PACKERS ASSOCIATION—
    MEMBERSHIP DIRECTORY
Western States Meat Packers Association
88 First Street   Phone: (415) 982-2466
San Francisco, CA 94105
Covers: About 320 meat packers, processors, and jobbers in 14
Western states. Entries include: Company name, address, phone,
principal executives, trade and brand names. Arrangement:
Geographical. Indexes: Alphabetical. Pages (approx.): 110.
Frequency: Biennial, July of odd years. Editor: C. A. Santare,
Executive Vice President & General Manager. Price: Available to
members only.

Western Wood Moulding and Millwork Producers—Directory See
    Wood Moulding and Millwork Producers—Directory

★1988★

WESTERN WOOD PRODUCTS ASSOCIATION—BUYERS MANUAL
Western Wood Products Association
Yeon Building, No. 1500   Phone: (503) 224-3930
Portland, OR 97204
Covers: Member companies in the lumber industry in twelve western
states; includes members of the Western Red Cedar Lumber
Association and Fir & Hemlock Door Association. Companies produce
rough and finished lumber, millwork, pressure treated lumber,
laminated products, etc. Entries include: Company name, plant
names, addresses, phone numbers, names of sales managers, shipping
services, facilities, capacities, species processed. Arrangement:
Alphabetical. Indexes: Geographical. Pages (approx.): 35. Frequency:
Irregular; latest edition spring 1978; new edition expected spring
1980. Price: Free.

★1989★

WHOLE WORLD OIL DIRECTORY
Tradex Publications, Inc.
4728 W. Alabama   Phone: (713) 623-0690
Houston, TX 77027
Covers: More than 20,000 companies in the petroleum industry,
including oil and gas companies, drilling contractors, equipment
suppliers, oil well services, transmission pipelines, refineries,
consulting services, etc. Entries include: Company name, address,
phone, telex and cable numbers; many entries include names of
principal personnel; some entries include listings for additional
locations. Arrangement: Classified by type of business; oil and gas
companies are then arranged geographically. Indexes: Company,
personal name. Frequency: Annual, spring. Price: $60.00, plus $5.00
shipping.

★1990★

**WHOLESALE FLORISTS AND FLORIST SUPPLIERS OF AMERICA—
    MEMBERSHIP DIRECTORY**
Wholesale Florists and Florist Suppliers of America
5313 Lee Highway   Phone: (703) 241-1100
Arlington, VA 22207
Entries include: Company name, address, phone, names of
executives, list of products or services. **Arrangement:** Geographical.
Indexes: Alphabetical. **Frequency:** Annual, June. **Editor:** Robert J.
Haffner, Staff Director - Operations. **Advertising accepted.**
Circulation 1,000. **Price:** $100.00 (current and 1980 editions).

Wholesale Nursery Growers of America—Membership Directory
    See American Association of Nurserymen—Member
    Directory

★1991★

WHO'S WHO IN LANDSCAPE CONTRACTING
Associated Landscape Contractors of America
1750 Old Meadow Road   Phone: (703) 821-8611
McLean, VA 22102
Covers: 600 landscape contractors and related suppliers who are
members. **Entries include:** Company name, address, phone, names of
principals, specialties. **Arrangement:** Alphabetical. **Indexes:**
Geographical, personal name. **Pages** (approx.): 70. **Frequency:**
Annual, spring. **Editor:** John S. Shaw, Executive Director. **Price:**
$100.00.

★1992★

WHO'S WHO IN MINING ENGINEERING
Society of Mining Engineers of AIME
Caller No. D   Phone: (303) 773-3424
Littleton, CO 80123
Number of listings: 25,755. **Entries include:** Name, member grade;
technical interests; job title; company name, division, and title.
Arrangement: Alphabetical. **Indexes:** Geographical. **Pages** (approx.):
290. **Frequency:** Annual, July; periodic updates. **Editor:** Marianne
Snedeker, Manager of Publications. **Advertising accepted.** Circulation
28,000. **Price:** $50.00.

★1993★

WHO'S WHO IN THE EGG AND POULTRY INDUSTRIES
Watt Publishing Company
Sandstone Building   Phone: (815) 734-4171
Mt. Morris, IL 61054
Covers: Processors and distributors of poultry meat and eggs, plus
manufacturers of supplies and equipment for the industry; poultry
breeders and hatcheries; public refrigerated warehouses; food chain
buyers of poultry meat and eggs. **Entries include:** Company name,
address, phone, executives, and list of products or services. **Pages**
(approx.): 340. **Frequency:** Annual, June. **Editor:** Mahlon C. Sweet.
Advertising accepted. Circulation 7,300. **Price:** $25.00.

★1994★

WHO'S WHO IN THE STONE BUSINESS
Building Stone Institute
420 Lexington Avenue   Phone: (212) 490-2530
New York, NY 10017
Covers: About 225 quarry owners, stone contractors, and dealers
who are members. **Entries include:** Company name, address, phone,
personnel, type of operation, branch offices. **Arrangement:**
Geographical. **Indexes:** Personal name. **Frequency:** Irregular; latest
edition 1978. **Price:** Available to members only.

★1995★

WINE DISTRIBUTION OPPORTUNITY DIRECTORY
National Wine Distributors Association
101 E. Ontario Street, Room 580   Phone: (312) 951-8878
Chicago, IL 60611
Covers: 150 wine suppliers, worldwide. Firms listed are seeking
additional distributors in United States markets. **Entries include:** Firm

name, address. **Arrangement:** Alphabetical. **Frequency:** Not
established; first edition 1979. **Price:** $50.00.

★1996★

WINE TOUR SERIES [California]
Vintage Image
1335 Main Street
St. Helena, CA 94574
Covers: Active wineries in California. Three volumes: "Napa Valley
Wine Tour," "Sonoma-Mendocino Wine Tour," and "Central Coast
Wine Tour." **Entries include:** Winery name, address, phone, hours,
whether a tasting room is operated, other facilities, and directions.
Arrangement: Geographical. **Price:** $2.95, plus 30¢ shipping, payment
with order.

★1997★

**WINERY TOURS IN OREGON, WASHINGTON, IDAHO, AND BRITISH
    COLUMBIA**
Writing Works, Inc.
7438 S. E. 40th Street
Mercer Island, WA 98040
Number of listings: About 40. **Entries include:** Winery name,
location, driving instructions and map, dates open, hours, whether
tasting room is operated, description of wines and winery.
Arrangement: Geographical. **Pages** (approx.): 130. **Frequency:**
Irregular; latest edition summer 1978. **Editor:** Tom Stockley. **Former
title:** Winery Trails of the Pacific Northwest. **Price:** $3.95.

Winery Trails of the Pacific Northwest *See* Winery Tours in
    Oregon, Washington, Idaho, and British Columbia

★1998★

**WINES AND VINES—ANNUAL DIRECTORY OF WINERIES AND
    VINEYARD INDUSTRY SUPPLIERS OF NORTH AMERICA**
Hiaring Company
703 Market Street   Phone: (415) 392-1146
San Francisco, CA 94103
Covers: All wineries and wine bottlers in the United States, Canada,
and Mexico; also lists industry suppliers. **Entries include:** Company
name, address, phone; names of principal executives; trade and brand
names; types of wines made; date founded; storage, fermenting, and
bottling capacity; area served; vineyard acreage; bonded premises
types and number; railroad serving winery. Supplier entries show
company name, address, phone, products, representatives' names.
Arrangement: Wineries are geographical; suppliers, alphabetical.
Indexes: Alphabetical index of wineries; product index of suppliers.
Pages (approx.): 200. **Frequency:** Annual, December. **Editor:** Claire
Hiaring. **Advertising accepted.** Circulation 4,500. **Price:** $15.00.
Also includes: Summary of state laws pertaining to wine.

★1999★

WINES AND VINES—ANNUAL STATISTICAL ISSUE
Hiaring Company
703 Market Street   Phone: (415) 392-1146
San Francisco, CA 94103
Publication includes: One hundred largest U. S. wineries ranked by
total storage capacity. **Frequency:** Annual, May. **Editor:** Philip Hiaring.
Price: $1.50. **Also includes:** Statistics for the wine industry.

★2000★

WISCONSIN DAIRY PLANT DIRECTORY
Food Division
Wisconsin Department of Agriculture, Trade, and Consumer Protection
801 W. Badger Road
Madison, WI 53713
Covers: 650 licensed dairy plants in Wisconsin. **Entries include:** Plant
name, address, license number, operations carried on at the plant,
name of licensee, and address of home office. **Arrangement:**
Geographical. **Indexes:** License number. **Frequency:** Annual. **Price:**
$1.50 (current and 1980 editions).

Wood & Woodlands Directory *See* Timber Harvesting—Wood &
   Woodlands Directory Issue

★2001★
WOOD MOULDING AND MILLWORK PRODUCERS—DIRECTORY
Wood Moulding And Millwork Producers
1730 S. W. Skyline   Phone: (503) 292-9288
Portland, OR 97225
Number of listings: 55 in Arizona, California, New Mexico, Oregon,
Texas, Utah, Washington. **Entries include:** Company name, address,
phone, names and titles of executives, list of products or services,
railroad. **Arrangement:** Alphabetical. **Pages** (approx.): 60.
Frequency: Annual. **Editor:** Gloria S. Gilbert, Office Manager. **Former
title:** Western Wood Moulding and Millwork Producers - Directory.
Price: Free.

★2002★
WOOL TRADE DIRECTORY
Donald A. Hansen
263 Summer Street   Phone: (617) 542-4231
Boston, MA 02210
Covers: Wool dealers and mills; banks, transportation companies and
others serving wool trade. **Pages** (approx.): 10. **Frequency:** Irregular;
new edition expected early 1980. **Editor:** Donald A. Hansen, Publisher.
Advertising accepted. Circulation 500. **Price:** $2.00 (1980 edition).

World Coal Directory *See* World Coal Industry Report and
   Directory

★2003★
WORLD COAL INDUSTRY REPORT AND DIRECTORY
Miller Freeman Publications, Inc.
500 Howard Street   Phone: (415) 397-1881
San Francisco, CA 94105
Covers: Major coal mining and processing operations throughout the
world. Also includes buyer's guide to equipment and supplies, export
agents, and associations, institutes, government agencies, etc.
Entries include: Company name, address, names of principal
executives, coal ranks, utilization, mining system, principal seams
mined and equipment used. **Arrangement:** Geographical. **Indexes:**
Personnel; coal ranks and utilizations; company size by tonnage. **Pages**
(approx.): 330. **Frequency:** Not established; first edition 1978.
Editor: George H. Roman. **Advertising accepted.** **Price:** $95.00,
postpaid, payment with order. **Other information:** Cited in early
promotion as, "World Coal Directory."

★2004★
WORLD DIRECTORY OF WOOD-BASED PANEL PRODUCERS
Miller Freeman Publications, Inc.
500 Howard Street   Phone: (415) 397-1881
San Francisco, CA 94105
Covers: Over 2,000 plants in over 80 countries which produce
plywood, blockboard, particleboard, fiberboard, and composite board.
Includes buyer's guide to equipment and supplies. **Entries include:**
Company name, mail/cable/TWX/telex addresses; production
capacity; species of wood used; exports; product specifications and
characteristics; names of principal management, production, and
marketing personnel at each location. **Arrangement:** Geographical;
buyer's guide by product. **Indexes:** Company. **Frequency:** Not
established; first edition December 1977. **Editor:** Hugh R. Fraser.
Advertising accepted. **Price:** $55.00.

★2005★
WORLD FOOD CRISIS: AN INTERNATIONAL DIRECTORY OF
    ORGANIZATIONS AND INFORMATION RESOURCES
California Institute of Public Affairs
226 W. Foothill Boulevard   Phone: (714) 624-5212
Claremont, CA 91711
Covers: 800 organizations and government agencies in United States
and abroad concerned with relief, technical assistance, etc. **Pages**
(approx.): 140. **Frequency:** Irregular; first edition 1977. **Editor:**

Thaddeus C. Trzyna. **Price:** $20.00.

★2006★
WORLD LIST OF FORESTRY SCHOOLS
Food and Agriculture Organization of the United Nations
Via delle Terme di Caracalla
Rome 00100, Italy
Covers: About 250 university-level and 425 non-university-level
schools of forestry, worldwide. **Entries include:** School name,
address. **Arrangement:** Geographical within above two categories.
Pages (approx.): 90. **Frequency:** Irregular; previous edition 1974;
latest edition 1977. **Price:** $5.50. **Send orders to:** Unipub, Box 433,
Murray Hill Station, New York, NY 10016.

★2007★
WORLD MARICULTURE SOCIETY—MEMBERSHIP DIRECTORY
World Mariculture Society
249 Agriculture Center
Louisiana State University
Baton Rouge, LA 70803
Covers: Individuals interested in mariculture (the culture of plants and
animals in saline waters for domestic purposes, usually food). **Entries
include:** Name, profession, address, phone, birthdate, degrees and
institutions granting them, key subjects of interest, and brief
experience/research description. **Arrangement:** Alphabetical. **Pages**
(approx.): 40. **Frequency:** Irregular; latest edition fall 1976. **Editors:**
Jennifer Achee and James W. Avault, Jr. **Price:** Available to members
only.

★2008★
WORLD MINES REGISTER
Miller Freeman Publicatons, Inc.
500 Howard Street   Phone: (415) 397-1881
San Francisco, CA 94105
Covers: About 1,600 headquarters and 1,700 active metals and
minerals mining and processing operations in 103 countries, and
approximately 11,000 mining executives. Also includes manufacturers
and distributors of mining and minerals industry equipment and
supplies (SIC 1011 - 21 - 31 - 41 - 44 - 51 - 61 - 92 - 94 - 99; 1472
- 73 - 74 - 75 - 77 - 79 - 99; 3331 - 32 - 33 - 34 - 39). **Entries
include:** For headquarters - Company name, address, key personnel,
mines operated, holdings, employment, financial data, other details.
For operations - Location and company name, materials handled and
type of operation (mining, smelting, etc.), names of local personnel.
For executives - Name, title, company, and country location.
Arrangement: Headquarters are geographical; executives are
alphabetical; equipment sources classified by product.**Indexes:**
Alphabetical index to companies and operations; operation's type of
mineral or metal handled. **Pages** (approx.): 480. **Frequency:** Biennial,
odd years. **Editor:** George O. Argall, E. M. P. Engineer. **Advertising
accepted.** Circulation 1,800. **Former title:** Mines Register (1973).
Price: $57.50, postpaid, payment with order.

★2009★
WORLD MINING—YEARBOOK, CATALOG, SURVEY & DIRECTORY
    ISSUE
Miller Freeman Publications, Inc.
500 Howard Street   Phone: (415) 397-1881
San Francisco, CA 94105
Publication includes: List of manufacturers of metal mining
equipment, refining machinery, and other equipment and supplies for
exploration, smelting, and other mining processes; international
coverage (SIC 10). **Entries include:** Company name, address, phone,
products or services. **Arrangement:** Alphabetical. **Pages** (approx.):
290. **Frequency:** Annual, June. **Editor:** George O. Argall, Jr., Senior
Editor. **Advertising accepted.** Circulation 15,700. **Price:** $10.00
(current and 1980 editions).

★2010★
WORLDWIDE DIRECTORY OF PIPELINES AND CONTRACTORS
Petroleum Publishing Company
Box 1260   Phone: (918) 835-3161
Tulsa, OK 74101
Covers: More than 300 operating pipeline companies and 600 construction, engineering, and service firms; worldwide coverage. **Entries include:** Company name, address, phone, branch offices, key personnel, operating, technical and financial data. **Pages** (approx.): 200. **Frequency:** Annual, July. **Price:** $30.00 (current and 1980 editions).

★2011★
WORLDWIDE REFINING AND GAS PROCESSING DIRECTORY
Petroleum Publishing Company
Box 1260   Phone: (918) 835-3161
Tulsa, OK 74101
Covers: Over 700 crude oil refineries, 875 gas processing plants, and engineering and construction firms which build and service these plants; worldwide coverage. **Entries include:** Company or plant name, address, key personnel; plant listings include capacities, downstream operations, product. **Arrangement:** Geographical. **Indexes:** Company, personal name. **Pages** (approx.): 350. **Frequency:** Annual, June. **Price:** $50.00 (current and 1980 editions).

★2012★
WYOMING CERTIFIED SEED DIRECTORY
Wyoming Seed Certification Service
Wyoming Department of Agriculture
Box 3354
University Station
Laramie, WY 82071
Covers: Over 80 Wyoming growers raising crops for seed whose fields met certification standards in year of issue. Also includes grain, feed, and seed dealers. **Entries include:** Grower or dealer name, address, phone. **Indexes:** Type of seed. **Arrangement:** Alphabetical. **Frequency:** Annual, December. **Editor:** Jack Cecil, Manager. **Price:** Free.

★2013★
WYOMING COAL DIRECTORY
Geological Survey of Wyoming
Box 3008
University Station   Phone: (307) 742-2054
Laramie, WY 82701
Covers: About 40 mining companies and 65 proposed and active mines in Wyoming. **Entries include:** For companies - Name, address, corporate affiliations (if any), name of president, data on state and federal coal leases and on major utility and industrial contracts held by company. For mines - Name, recent or planned production, location, technical information. **Arrangement:** Alphabetical by company name. **Pages** (approx.): 20. **Frequency:** Irregular; previous edition 1976; new edition expected January 1980. **Price:** $1.00.

4

Law and Government

(Including Military)

Advance Locator *See* Congressional Staff Directory Advance Locator

★2014★
ALABAMA DIRECTORY
Brown Printing Company
2734 Gunter Park Drive, West   Phone: (205) 277-4700
Montgomery, AL 36109
Covers: State departments and agencies, state universities, other institutions; the judiciary; county officials including commissioners, sheriffs, tax assessors, etc.; legislators. **Entries include:** Name of department or other unit, address, name of chief executive or other key personnel, county name; phone is included for probate judges and county commissions. **Arrangement:** By agency and political district. **Pages** (approx.): 40. **Frequency:** Annual, July. **Price:** $1.00. **Other information:** Directory based on information furnished by Alabama Secretary of State.

★2015★
ALABAMA GOVERNMENT MANUAL
Bureau of Public Administration
University of Alabama
Drawer I   Phone: (205) 348-5980
University, AL 35486
Covers: Over 200 state executive and regulatory agencies and staff functions, and offices in the legislative and judicial branches. **Entries include:** Name of agency or other unit, citation to legal basis of agencies, brief description of organization and function. (Addresses are not included.) **Arrangement:** By branch of government, then by function. **Pages** (approx.): 350. **Frequency:** Quadrennial; latest edition 1977. **Editor:** Coleman B. Ransone, Jr. **Price:** $7.95.

★2016★
ALABAMA LEGAL DIRECTORY
Legal Directories Publishing Company
8350 Central Expressway   Phone: (214) 692-5825
Dallas, TX 75206
Covers: All lawyers in Alabama. **Entries include:** All entries include name and address; entries for subscribers include phone, type of practice, and biographical details. **Arrangement:** Geographical by county, then by city. **Frequency:** Latest edition 1979. **Price:** $8.00. **Other information:** See separate listing, "Law Lists."

★2017★
ALABAMA OFFICIAL AND STATISTICAL REGISTER
Alabama Department of Archives and History
624 Washington Avenue   Phone: (205) 832-6510
Montgomery, AL 36130
Covers: Major state officials and United States congressmen; state offices, boards, etc.; county, city, and town officials; Alabama newspapers and periodicals. **Indexes:** Subject, agency, name. **Frequency:** Quadrennial; latest edition 1979. **Editor:** Milo B. Howard, Jr., Director of Archives and History Department. **Price:** Free.

★2018★
ALASKA BLUE BOOK
Division of State Libraries and Museums
Alaska Department of Education
Pouch G (MS 0571)   Phone: (907) 465-2910
Juneau, AK 99811
Publication includes: Biographical sketches of major state officials and legislators; lists state boards, commissions, etc., and their members; Constitutional Convention members. **Pages** (approx.): 270. **Frequency:** Biennial, summer of odd years. **Editor:** Robert M. Burnett. **Price:** $5.00, payment with order.

★2019★
ALASKA MUNICIPAL OFFICIALS DIRECTORY
Alaska Municipal League
204 N. Franklin Street   Phone: (907) 586-1325
Juneau, AK 99801
Covers: 150 units of local government, including officials and municipal statistics. **Entries include:** Name, address, and phone of municipality, incorporation date, population, municipal status, election date, sales tax, assembly meeting dates, mayor's name, officers' names and titles, and powers assumed by the borough or city (electricity, dock, etc.). **Arrangement:** Alphabetical by city. **Pages** (approx.): 120. **Frequency:** Annual, January. **Former title:** Directory of Borough and City Officials. **Price:** $4.00 (current edition); $5.00 (tentative, 1980 edition).

★2020★
AMERICAN ASSOCIATION OF MOTOR VEHICLE ADMINISTRATORS—PERSONNEL DIRECTORY OF MEMBER JURISDICTIONS
American Association of Motor Vehicle Administrators
1201 Connecticut Avenue, N. W., Suite
91   Phone: (202) 296-1955
Washington, DC 20036
Covers: About 130 state officials administering motor vehicle laws

and regulations in the United States and Canada. **Entries include:** Agency name, address, phone, name of head official, number of employees. **Arrangement:** Geographical. **Pages** (approx.): 100. **Frequency:** Biennial, July of odd years. **Editor:** Robert S. Brown, Jr., Director of Public Affairs. **Price:** $10.00.

★2021★
AMERICAN BANK ATTORNEYS
Capron Publishing Company
Box 187   Phone: (617) 235-0800
Wellesley Hills, MA 02181
Covers: Lawyers who represent one or more banks. **Entries include:** In geographical section: Firm name, address, name of bank represented. In biographical section (does not necessarily include all firms in geographical section): Firm name, address, names of individual attorneys and brief biographical data, clients. **Arrangement:** Geographical. **Frequency:** Semiannual, January and July. **Price:** Apply. **Other information:** A general law list. See separate listing, "Law Lists."

★2022★
THE AMERICAN BAR - THE CANADIAN BAR - THE INTERNATIONAL BAR
Reginald Bishop Forster & Associates
2344 Nicollet Avenue, Suite 100   Phone: (612) 871-1395
Minneapolis, MN 55404
Covers: 50,000 lawyers in the United States and over 90 countries abroad. **Entries include:** Firm name, type of practice, address, phone; names, educational data, and memberships of partners and associates. **Arrangement:** Geographical. **Indexes:** Personal name. **Pages** (approx.): 3,600. **Frequency:** Annual, March. **Editor:** Mary Reincke. **Price:** $120.00 (current and 1980 editions). **Other information:** A general law list. See separate listing, "Law Lists."

★2023★
AMERICAN BAR ASSOCIATION—DIRECTORY
American Bar Association
1155 E. 60th Street   Phone: (312) 947-4000
Chicago, IL 60637
Covers: About 5,000 lawyers active in the affairs of the association, including officers, members of board of governors and house of delegates, section officers and council members, committee chairpersons and members, and headquarters staff. **Entries include:** Section, council, or other unit name; names, addresses, and phone numbers of officers or chairpersons and members. **Frequency:** Annual, fall. **Price:** $5.00.

★2024★
AMERICAN LAWYERS QUARTERLY
The American Lawyers Company
East Ohio Building, Suite 1417   Phone: (216) 241-5521
Cleveland, OH 44114
Arrangement: Geographical. **Frequency:** Semiannual, January and July; monthly supplements. **Price:** Apply. **Other information:** A commercial law list. See separate listing, "Law Lists."

★2025★
AMERICAN SOCIETY OF CRIMINOLOGY—MEMBERSHIP DIRECTORY
American Society of Criminology
1314 Kinnear Road, Suite 212   Phone: (614) 422-9207
Columbus, OH 43212
Covers: 2,500 professional and academic criminologists, students of criminology in accredited universities, psychiatrists, psychologists, and sociologists. **Entries include:** Name, affiliation, address. **Arrangement:** Alphabetical. **Indexes:** Geographical. **Pages** (approx.): 85. **Frequency:** Annual, March. **Editor:** Charles H. McCaghy, Treasurer. **Price:** $25.00.

★2026★
ARKANSAS, LOUISIANA & MISSISSIPPI LEGAL DIRECTORY
Legal Directories Publishing Company
8350 Central Expressway   Phone: (214) 692-5825
Dallas, TX 75206
Frequency: Latest edition 1978. **Price:** $18.00. **Other information:** Content, arrangement, etc., same as "Alabama Legal Directory;" see separate listing. 1980-81 edition will separate three states into individual directories. (See also separate listing, "Law Lists.")

Arkansas Municipal Officials See **Directory of Arkansas Municipal Officials**

★2027★
ARKANSAS STATE DIRECTORY
Arkansas Secretary of State
Box 1371
Little Rock, AR 72203
Covers: Arkansas state governmental agencies. **Entries include:** Agency or department name, functions, names and titles of principal officials. **Pages** (approx.): 120. **Frequency:** Biennial, odd years. **Price:** $2.50, payment with order.

★2028★
ARSON CONTROL: HOW & WHY AND WHO WHAT WHERE
Insurance Committee for Arson Control
20 N. Wacker Drive, Suite 2140   Phone: (312) 558-3800
Chicago, IL 60606
Covers: About 500 organizations and firms (national through local levels) which are involved with arson control, including state arson task forces, government agencies, and trade and professional associations. **Entries include:** Organization or agency name, address, phone, name and title of contact; area of activity in arson control. **Arrangement:** Geographical. **Pages** (approx.): 360. **Frequency:** Latest edition November 1979; new edition expected April 1980. **Editor:** Morag E. Fullilove. **Price:** $15.00, postpaid (current and 1980 editions).

★2029★
ASSOCIATION OF FEDERAL INVESTIGATORS—DIRECTORY
Association of Federal Investigators
815 15th Street, N. W.
Washington, DC 20005
Covers: 2,500 persons now or formerly engaged in investigations, law enforcement and similar activities. **Entries include:** Name, home address. **Arrangement:** Geographical. **Pages** (approx.): 50. **Frequency:** Irregular; latest edition January 1976. **Editor:** Sidney D. Butterfield, Executive Director. **Price:** Available to members only.

★2030★
ASSOCIATION OF FORMER AGENTS OF THE U.S. SECRET SERVICE—MEMBERSHIP DIRECTORY
Association of Former Agents of the U. S. Secret Service
Box 31073   Phone: (202) 894-2115
Washington, DC 20031
Entries include: Name, home address. **Arrangement:** Alphabetical. **Frequency:** Annual, March. **Price:** Available to members only.

Association of State and Interstate Water Pollution Control Administrators—Membership Directory See **List of Water Pollution Control...**

★2031★
ATTORNEYS AND AGENTS REGISTERED TO PRACTICE BEFORE THE U.S. PATENT AND TRADEMARK OFFICE
Patent and Trademark Office
Commerce Department   Phone: (703) 557-3794
Washington, DC 20231
Number of listings: About 9,800. **Entries include:** Name, firm, address, phone, registration number; patent agents (otherwise qualified persons who are not lawyers) are designated by symbol. **Arrangement:** Geographical. **Indexes:** Alphabetical. **Pages** (approx.):

310. **Frequency:** Latest edition 1977 (S/N 003-004-00551-3). **Send orders to:** Government Printing Office, Washington, DC 20402.

★2032★
ATTORNEYS' DIRECTORY [San Diego County]
Transcript Publishing Company
861 Sixth Avenue
San Diego, CA 92101
Covers: 3,600 members of the county bench and bar. Also includes lists of courts, legal clubs and societies, bar associations, legal services, government officials. **Entries include:** Name, firm name, address, phone, photo, law school, year admitted to practice. **Arrangement:** Alphabetical. **Pages** (approx.): 160. **Frequency:** Annual, January. **Editor:** T. Rogers. **Advertising accepted.** Circulation 8,000. **Price:** $5.75.

★2033★
ATTORNEYS GENERAL OF THE STATES AND OTHER JURISDICTIONS
National Association of Attorneys General
C/o Council of State Governments
Iron Works Pike   Phone: (606) 252-2291
Lexington, KY 40578
Number of listings: 54. **Entries include:** Name, and personal and career data. **Arrangement:** Geographical. **Pages** (approx.): 60. **Frequency:** Annual, July. **Price:** $7.50.

★2034★
ATTORNEY'S REGISTER
Attorney's Register Publishing Company, Inc.
636 Equitable Building   Phone: (301) 685-2786
Baltimore, MD 21202
Arrangement: Geographical. **Frequency:** Annual. **Price:** Apply. **Other information:** A general law list. See separate listing, "Law Lists."

★2035★
AUTHOR'S GUIDE TO JOURNALS IN LAW, CRIMINAL JUSTICE, AND CRIMINOLOGY
Haworth Press
149 Fifth Avenue   Phone: (212) 228-2800
New York, NY 10010
Number of listings: About 450. **Entries include:** Publication name, address for manuscripts, publication orientation and subject interests, usual review time and delay in publication of accepted manuscripts, early publication options (if any). **Arrangement:** Alphabetical. **Indexes:** Subject/keyword. **Pages** (approx.): 250. **Frequency:** Not established; first editon 1978. **Editors:** Roy Mersky, Robert Berring, and James McCue. **Price:** $16.95.

★2036★
B. A. LAW LIST
B. A. Publishing Company, Inc.
Box 566
Edgewater   Phone: (216) 521-3188
Cleveland, OH 44107
Arrangement: Geographical. **Frequency:** Annual, January. **Price:** Apply. **Other information:** A commercial law list. See separate listing, "Law Lists."

★2037★
BAR REGISTER
Bar Register Company, Inc.
One Prospect Street   Phone: (201) 273-6060
Summit, NJ 07901
Arrangement: Geographical. **Frequency:** Annual. **Price:** Apply. **Other information:** A general law list. See separate listing, "Law Lists."

★2038★
BARRON'S GUIDE TO LAW SCHOOLS
Barron's Educational Series, Inc.
113 Crossways Park Drive   Phone: (516) 921-8750
Woodbury, NY 11797
Covers: About 165 American Bar Association approved law schools. List of top law schools ranked for prestige is also included. **Entries include:** School name, address, phone, LSAT score minimum, enrollment, accreditation, student-faculty ratio, size of library, calendar, degree programs offered, admission and degree requirements, costs, financial aid available. **Arrangement:** Alphabetical. **Indexes:** Geographical. **Pages** (approx.): 220. **Frequency:** Irregular; latest edition 1978. **Editors:** Elliott M. Epstein, Jerome Shostak, and Lawrence M. Troy. **Price:** $5.50, plus 55¢ shipping. **Also includes:** Sample "Law School Admission Test."

Barron's How to Prepare for the Law School Admission Test (LSAT) *See* Barron's New Guide to the Law School Admission Test...

★2039★
BARRON'S NEW GUIDE TO THE LAW SCHOOL ADMISSION TEST (LSAT)
Barron's Educational Series, Inc.
113 Crossways Park Drive   Phone: (516) 921-8750
Woodbury, NY 11797
Publication includes: Full descriptions of over 150 American law schools. **Entries include:** Name, address, admissions and degree requirements, costs, and degrees granted. **Frequency:** Irregular; latest edition 1979. **Author:** Jerry Bobrow and others. **Former title:** Barron's How to Prepare for the Law School Admission Test (LSAT). **Price:** $4.95. **Also includes:** Test preparation in areas of legal principles, logical reasoning, etc.

★2040★
BEST'S RECOMMENDED INSURANCE ATTORNEYS
A. M. Best Company, Inc.
Ambest Road   Phone: (201) 439-2200
Oldwick, NJ 08858
Number of listings: 3,000. **Entries include:** Firm name, address, phone, type of practice, names of firm members handling insurance trial work, names and brief data on partners and associates. **Arrangement:** Geographical. **Pages** (approx.): 2,000. **Frequency:** Annual. **Editor:** Stephen P. Cronin. **Price:** Apply. **Other information:** An insurance law list. See separate listing, "Law Lists."

★2041★
BILL TURNBOW'S ARIZONA ALMANAC
Arizona Secretary of State
Capitol West Wing, Suite 700   Phone: (602) 255-4285
Phoenix, AZ 85007
Covers: Administrators for about 140 state executive departments and agencies, elected state officials, legislators, members of the state judiciary, and members of state boards; also includes county officials. **Entries include:** Name of governmental unit, address, and names, titles, and terms of office of officials; many listings include personal addresses. **Arrangement:** By county, followed by state agencies. **Pages** (approx.): 95. **Frequency:** Biennial, April of odd years (but no 1979 edition). **Also includes:** Historic rosters, general information and statistics.

Bimonthly Directory of Key Congressional Aides *See* Congressional Yellow Book

Biographical Sketches of Members-Elect of the General Assembly [Vermont] *See* Biographical Sketches of State Officers...[Vermont]

★2042★
BIOGRAPHICAL SKETCHES OF STATE OFFICERS AND MEMBERS OF THE GENERAL ASSEMBLY [Vermont]
Vermont Secretary of State
109 State Street   Phone: (802) 828-2363
Montpelier, VT 05602
Pages (approx.): 75. **Frequency:** Biennial, January of odd years. **Former title:** Biographical Sketches of Members-Elect of the General Assembly. **Price:** Free.

Black Book *See* Manual for the Use of the General Court of New Hampshire

★2043★
BLACK ENTERPRISE—BLACK POLITICAL LEADERS [Special feature]
Earl G. Graves Publishing Company
295 Madison Avenue   Phone: (212) 889-8220
New York, NY 10017
Publication includes: List of about 65 Blacks appointed to major posts in the Carter administration (exclusive of White House staff); 16 Black political organizations operating at state or large city levels, with contacts, phones, and addresses. **Frequency:** Special feature in March, 1978 issue; new list possible in 1980. **Editor:** Earl G. Graves. **Advertising accepted. Price:** $1.25.

Blue Book [New York state government] *See* New York State Legislative Manual

Blue List *See* Diplomatic List (Blue List) [Washington, D.C.]

★2044★
BOOK OF THE STATES
Council of State Governments
Iron Works Pike   Phone: (606) 252-2291
Lexington, KY 40578
Publication includes: List of major state officials. **Arrangement:** Geographical. **Pages** (approx.): 675. **Frequency:** Biennial in even years. **Editor:** Jack Gardner. **Price:** $21.00 (current edition); $28.00 (1980 edition); postpaid, payment with order. **Also includes:** Principal content is survey articles and statistics related to governments of the various states.

★2045★
BOOK OF THE STATES, SUPPLEMENT ONE: STATE ELECTIVE OFFICIALS AND THE LEGISLATURES
Council of State Governments
Iron Works Pike   Phone: (606) 252-2291
Lexington, KY 40578
Covers: About 9,000 elected state officials, including legislators. **Entries include:** Name, title, home address. **Arrangement:** Geographical. **Pages** (approx.): 200. **Frequency:** Biennial, winter of odd years. **Editor:** Jack Gardner. **Price:** $10.00.

★2046★
BOOK OF THE STATES, SUPPLEMENT TWO: STATE ADMINISTRATIVE OFFICIALS CLASSIFIED BY FUNCTIONS
Council of State Governments
Iron Works Pike   Phone: (606) 252-2291
Lexington, KY 40578
Covers: State government elected and appointed officials, including governors, lieutenant governors, attorneys general, secretaries of state, chief justices, legislators, and administrative officials in about 100 functional categories (labor, health, highways, etc.). **Entries include:** Name, office address, title, phone. **Arrangement:** Classified by function (health, corrections, etc. **Pages** (approx.): 225. **Frequency:** Biennial, summer of odd years. **Editor:** Jack Gardner. **Price:** $10.00. **Other information:** Also known as "State Administrative Officials Classified by Functions."

★2047★
BOSTON MUNICIPAL REGISTER [Massachusetts]
Boston City Council
One City Hall Square   Phone: (617) 725-3042
Boston, MA 02201
Covers: Departments of the Boston municipal government. **Entries include:** Department name, address, phone, names of principal officials. **Arrangement:** Alphabetical by department name. **Frequency:** Biennial in fall of odd years. **Price:** $2.00.

★2048★
BRADDOCK'S FEDERAL-STATE-LOCAL GOVERNMENT DIRECTORY
Braddock Publications
1001 Connecticut Avenue, N. W.,
   Suite 21   Phone: (202) 296-3630
Washington, DC 22036
Covers: Federal and state government agencies and about 10,000 of their officials, plus principal officials of nation's counties and 100 largest cities. **Entries include:** Agency or department name, address, phone, officials with specific titles and functions. **Arrangement:** By level of government and by agency or department. **Pages** (approx.): 310. **Frequency:** Annual, summer. **Editor:** Bonnie Stern. **Price:** $12.95 (ISSN 0363-6275).

★2049★
CALIFORNIA BLUE BOOK
Legislative Bill Room
California Legislature
State Capitol   Phone: (916) 445-2323
Sacramento, CA 95814
Covers: State departments, agencies, institutions, boards, commissions, etc.; the judiciary; legislature. **Entries include:** Name of governmental unit, address, names of principal executives; listings for boards, legislature, etc., include names of members, personal addresses, and committee assignments. **Arrangement:** By principal units of government, with sub-units in random order. **Indexes:** Subject-department-personal name. **Pages** (approx.): 600. **Frequency:** Quadrennial, summer; latest edition 1975, publication suspended until after next election. **Price:** $10.00, plus 52¢ shipping.

★2050★
CALIFORNIA JOURNAL ALMANAC OF STATE GOVERNMENT & POLITICS
California Center for Research and Education in Government
1617 Tenth Street   Phone: (916) 444-2840
Sacramento, CA 95814
Covers: Executive and legislative branch members, committees, and departments, capitol reporters, multi-client lobbyists, and congressional delegates. Members of the judiciary are also included. **Entries include:** Biographical information and pictures are given for executive, legislative, and judiciary members. Addresses and phone are not included for judiciary. For agencies and others - Name, address, phone. Lobbyist listings include companies or groups represented. **Arrangement:** By activity. **Indexes:** General. **Pages** (approx.): 190. **Frequency:** Biennial, April of odd years. **Price:** $3.95. **Also includes:** Extensive information concerning the operation of the California state government, history, financial status, and demography.

★2051★
CALIFORNIA JOURNAL ROSTER AND GOVERNMENT GUIDE
California Center for Research and Education in Government
1617 10th Street   Phone: (916) 444-2840
Sacramento, CA 95814
Covers: State agencies; independent boards, commissions, and departments; congressional delegation; legislators; constitutional officers and governor's staff. **Entries include:** For agencies, boards, etc. - Name, address, phone, name of chief executive. For legislators and congressional delegation - Name, party, district, main district offices, phones. For officers and staff - Name, title, address, phone.

Frequency: Annual, February. **Price:** 75¢, postpaid (current edition); $1.00, postpaid (1980 edition).

★2052★
CALIFORNIA LEGAL DIRECTORY (INCLUDING ARIZONA)
Legal Directories Publishing Company
8350 Central Expressway   Phone: (214) 692-5825
Dallas, TX 75206
Indexes: Personal name index by county to lawyers in larger California counties only. **Frequency:** Latest edition 1979. **Price:** $12.00. **Other information:** Content, arrangement, etc., same as "Alabama Legal Directory;" see separate listing. (See also separate listing, "Law Lists.")

★2053★
CALIFORNIA LEGISLATIVE HANDBOOK
Legislative Bill Room
California Legislature
State Capitol   Phone: (916) 485-2323
Sacramento, CA 95814
Publication includes: List of California legislators. **Entries include:** Name, home and office addresses, personal and career data, committee assignments. **Frequency:** Biennial, odd years. **Price:** $4.50.

★2054★
CALIFORNIA ROSTER [Government]
California Secretary of State
1230 J Street
Sacramento, CA 95814
Covers: Elected and principal appointed officers of state, county, and municipal governments, including extensive list of state agencies and boards. **Entries include:** Name of governmental unit or agency, names of principal executives (and trustees, commissioners, etc., where applicable), address. City listings show population, council meeting dates. **Arrangement:** By level of government. **Indexes:** State agency. **Pages** (approx.): 215. **Frequency:** Biennial, summer of odd years. **Editor:** Irene E. Devejian, Roster Coordinator. **Price:** $3.73. **Send orders to:** Department of General Services, Publications, Box 1015, North Highlands, CA 95660. **Other information:** Variant title, "California State, County, City and Township Officials."

California State, County, City, and Township Officials *See* California Roster

★2055★
CAMPBELL'S LIST [Lawyers]
Campbell's List, Inc.
Campbell Building   Phone: (305) 644-8298
Maitland, FL 32751
Covers: About 2,500 law firms in general practice; includes some patent, copyright, and trademark firms. **Entries include:** Firm name, address, phone, and whether collection cases are accepted. **Arrangement:** Geographical. **Pages** (approx.): 290. **Frequency:** Annual, March; September supplement. **Price:** 3-year subscription, including supplements, $20.00. **Other information:** A general law list. See separate listing "Law Lists."

Catalog of Domestic Assistance *See* Catalog of Federal Domestic Assistance

★2056★
CATALOG OF FEDERAL DOMESTIC ASSISTANCE
Office of Management and Budget
726 Jackson Place, N. W.   Phone: (202) 395-3112
Washington, DC 20503
Covers: Federal programs and activities which provide assistance or benefits to state and local governments, Indian tribes, profit and nonprofit organizations and institutions, and individuals. **Entries include:** Extensive descriptions of each program, including requirements, application procedures, amounts available, availability of

guidelines for preparing grant requests for the specific program, address for application, reporting requirements, etc. **Arrangement:** Alphabetical by agency name, by program number thereafter. **Indexes:** Popular name of programs; subject area/function (agriculture, community development); state-aid programs, separate indexes of programs available to individuals, nonprofit organizations and institutions, local governments, state governments. **Frequency:** Annual, May; supplements September and December. **Editor:** Robert Brown, Management Analyst. **Price:** $20.00 (base edition and supplements; looseleaf format). **Send orders to:** Goverment Printing Office, Washington, DC 20402.

★2057★
CATALOG OF STATE ASSISTANCE PROGRAMS [Maryland]
Maryland Department of State Planning
301 W. Preston Street   Phone: (301) 383-2439
Baltimore, MD 21201
Covers: Programs, grants, loans, information, and services available to state and local agencies and to the general public. Includes licensing and regulatory services. **Entries include:** Program title, type of assistance available, eligibility requirements, application procedures, authorizing legislation, printed information available; name, address, and phone of contact; and name and address of administering agency. **Pages** (approx.): 150. **Frequency:** Latest edition October 1977; updated annually; new edition expected fall 1980. **Price:** Free.

Catalogue of State Programs of Assistance to New Jersey Local Governments *See* New Jersey State Aid Catalog for Local Governments

★2058★
CITIZENS' GUIDE TO THE LOUISIANA LEGISLATURE
Public Affairs Research Council of Louisiana
Box 3118   Phone: (504) 343-9204
Baton Rouge, LA 70821
Publication includes: List of legislators. **Entries include:** Name, address, party, district, biographical data, photograph. **Arrangement:** Alphabetical by chamber. **Pages** (approx.): 70. **Frequency:** Quadrennial; new edition expected 1980. **Price:** 50¢.

★2059★
CITY OF NEW YORK OFFICIAL DIRECTORY
City Record
Department of General Services
City of New York
Municipal Building, Room 2223
Centre and Chambers Streets   Phone: (212) 566-0494
New York, NY 10007
Covers: Agencies and key officials of the governments of New York City, counties within New York City, and New York State. Includes listings for federal government and all levels of courts. **Entries include:** Agency name, address, phone, description of functions, names and salaries of key personnel. **Pages** (approx.): 550. **Frequency:** Biennial, spring of even years. **Editor:** William Doyle. **Price:** $3.50, plus 50¢ shipping (current and 1980 editions).

★2060★
CIVIL GOVERNMENT, STATE OF VERMONT—FEDERAL, STATE, AND COUNTY OFFICIALS
Vermont Secretary of State
109 State Street   Phone: (802) 828-2363
Montpelier, VT 05602
Covers: State departments and agencies; judiciary; legislature; county governments. **Entries include:** Name of department or other unit, address, phone, and names, titles and city of residence of principal officials; legislators' listings show district represented. **Indexes:** Keyword. **Pages** (approx.): 100. **Frequency:** Annual, spring. **Price:** Free. **Other information:** Sometimes cited as, "Federal, State, and County Officials."

★2061★
CLEAN SLATE: A STATE-BY-STATE GUIDE TO EXPUNGING AN
   ARREST RECORD
Harmony Books
Crown Publishers, Inc.
One Park Avenue   Phone: (212) 532-9200
New York, NY 10016
Publication includes: State government agencies responsible for
arrest records, courts, and other organizations of assistance when
erasing an arrest record. Arrangement: Geographical. Pages
(approx.): 300. Frequency: First edition 1979. Editor: Tom Ballinger.
Price: $14.95, cloth; $8.95, paper.

★2062★
CLEARING HOUSE QUARTERLY [Lawyers]
Attorneys' National Clearing House Company
Box 8688   Phone: (813) 263-0840
Naples, FL 33941
Covers: Attorneys handling collection matters. Entries include: Name,
address, phone. Arrangement: Geographical in two volumes. Volume
1, attorneys handling claims against companies; Volume 2, attorneys
handling claims against individuals. Pages (approx.): 300. Frequency:
Annual, July. Editor: Joseph A. Birk, President. Price: Free. Other
information: A commercial law list. See separate listing, "Law Lists."

★2063★
CLERK'S MANUAL [Florida legislature]
Florida House of Representatives
State Capitol   Phone: (904) 488-1157
Tallahassee, FL 32304
Publication includes: Members of the Florida legislature. Entries
include: Name, office and home addresses, party, district, personal
data, career data, photograph. Pages (approx.): 290. Frequency:
Biennial, March of even years. Editor: Allen Morris, Clerk of the House.
Price: $3.00.

★2064★
CML GUIDE TO STATE ASSISTANCE FOR LOCAL GOVERNMENTS
   IN COLORADO
Colorado Municipal League
4800 Wadsworth Boulevard, Suite 204
Wheat Ridge, CO 80033
Covers: About 80 Colorado state agencies offering more than 200
financial or technical assistance programs for local governments;
some programs are available to, or of interest to, nonprofit agencies.
Entries include: Program name, objectives, eligibility requirements,
legal authority, application procedures, and agency name, address,
phone, and contact. Indexes: Agency name, subject. Frequency:
Latest edition late 1979. Former title: State Assistance for Local
Governments in Colorado. Price: $30.00.

★2065★
COLORADO DIRECTORY OF WATER ORGANIZATIONS
Colorado Water Congress
1111 S. Colorado Boulevard, No. 401   Phone: (303) 759-9805
Denver, CO 80222
Covers: About 125 organizations and agencies (from national through
local levels) which influence Colorado water administration,
management, and policy. Entries include: Organization name, address,
phone, name and title of contact, description of objectives and
activities. Arrangement: By level (national, regional, etc.). Pages
(approx.): 45. Frequency: Not established; first edition 1979; new
edition expected 1980. Editor: Fred Caruso, Executive Director.
Advertising accepted. Circulation 2,500. Price: $3.00, postpaid.

★2066★
COLORADO GENERAL ASSEMBLY—DIRECTORY
Colorado General Assembly
State Capitol   Phone: (303) 839-3006
Denver, CO 80203
Covers: Members of the general assembly and employees of the

House. Entries include: Name, spouse's name, district, counties,
party, occupation, home address and phone, capitol address and
phone. Employee listings include name, title, and address. Pages
(approx.): 40. Frequency: Annual, February. Price: Free (mailing list is
not maintained).

★2067★
COLORADO LEGISLATIVE DIRECTORY
Colorado Press Association
1336 Glenarm Place   Phone: (303) 571-5117
Denver, CO 80204
Covers: Legislators, legislative committees; Colorado newspapers.
Entries include: Legislator listings include name, office address and
phone, home address and phone, committee membership, voting
record, areas of interest, pictures. Arrangement: Geographical.
Pages (approx.): 150. Frequency: Biennial, January of odd years.
Editor: Bill Lindsey, CPA Administrator. Price: $25.00.

★2068★
COLUMBIA LIST [Lawyers]
Columbia Directory Company, Inc.
2003 Jericho Turnpike
New Hyde Park, NY 11040
Entries include: Firm name, address, phone. Arrangement:
Geographical; cross-references from towns which have no lawyer
listed to nearby towns which do. Pages (approx.): 400. Frequency:
Annual. Price: Apply. Other information: A commercial law list. See
separate listing, "Law Lists."

★2069★
COMMERCIAL BAR
Commercial Publishing Company, Inc.
402 Main Street   Phone: (203) 483-2611
Ridgefield, CT 06877
Arrangement: Geographical. Frequency: Annual, January. Price:
Apply. Other information: A commercial law list. See separate listing,
"Law Lists."

★2070★
COMMONWEALTH OF VIRGINIA TELEPHONE DIRECTORY
Telecommunications Council
Virginia Public Central Telephone System
Madison Building, Room No. 1   Phone: (804) 786-2201
Richmond, VA 23219
Covers: 125 state agencies, Virginia Commonwealth University, and
their principal personnel. Entries include: Agency section includes
agency address and names and phone numbers of departments.
Personnel section includes name, agency, and phone. Pages (approx.):
250. Frequency: Annual, December. Editor: Mrs. Cordelia S. Pride,
Supervisor. Price: $2.50, payment with order.

★2071★
CONFERENCE OF CHIEF JUSTICES—ROSTER
Conference of Chief Justices
National Center for State Courts
300 Newport Avenue   Phone: (804) 253-2000
Williamsburg, VA 23185
Covers: Chief justices of court of last resort in each state, District of
Columbia, and dependencies. Entries include: Name, office and home
address, length of terms in office and as chief justice, and given name
of spouse. Arrangement: Geographical. Frequency: Semiannual.
Price: Free.

★2072★
CONGRESS AND HEALTH
National Health Council
1740 Broadway
New York, NY 10019
Covers: Key legislators in Senate and House of Representatives
concerned with health, and members of Senate and House committees
and subcommittees on health and their staffs. Entries include: Name,

address, phone; legislators' listings include photograph. **Frequency:** Biennial, even years. **Price:** $6.00, payment with order; $7.00, billed.

★2073★
CONGRESSIONAL DIRECTORY
Office of the Congressional Directory
Joint Committee on Printing
United States Congress
United States Capitol, Room HB-30   Phone: (202) 225-2240
Washington, DC 20515
Background: The "Congressional Directory" covers in great detail the personnel and organization of the Congress, beginning with the official condensed biographies of members and continuing with lists of committees and their members and staff personnel, members' aides and secretaries, statistical and historical information on the Congress, etc. The "Directory" also includes in less detail information on the judicial branch of the federal government and its personnel, and on executive departments and agencies. (It lists executive units and their address, phone, and names and titles of personnel only, omitting any description of the units' activities. Compare with "United States Government Manual," described in a separate listing.) **Indexes:** Personal name. (The extensive table of contents serves as a subject and agency index.) **Pages** (approx.): 1,200. **Frequency:** Complete edition in January of odd years, coinciding with first session of each Congress, with supplement in January of even years for second session (but not in 1980). **Price:** $8.50, cloth; $6.50, paper; supplement, $2.00, paper. **Send orders to:** Government Printing Office, Washington, DC 20402. **Other information:** Variant title, "Official Congressional Directory for the Use of the U.S. Congress."

★2074★
CONGRESSIONAL DISTRICT ZIP CODES
Tyson, Belzer & Associates, Inc.
7735 Old Georgetown Road   Phone: (301) 652-4181
Bethesda, MD 20014
Description: A cross-reference index of the nation's 40,000 Zip codes to the 436 (plus District of Columbia) congressional districts. Through the use of this directory, associations, lobbyists, and others who wish to influence a particular member of Congress can select from their own or others' mailing lists names of persons in the member's own district and send literature urging letters to the member or encouraging some other action. **Arrangement:** Two sections: Congressional districts, representative name, and the Zip codes within them; Zip codes with the congressional district representing them. **Pages** (approx.): 100. **Frequency:** Biennial, March of odd years. **Price:** In book form, $65.00, payment with order, $67.00, billed; in computer tape form, $500.00. **Other information:** Variant title, "Directory of Congressional District ZIP Codes."

★2075★
CONGRESSIONAL HANDBOOK
Legislative Department
Chamber of Commerce of the United States
1615 H Street, N. W.   Phone: (202) 659-6140
Washington, DC 20062
Covers: Members of Congress. **Entries include:** List of Congress members by state includes member's party and home city; alphabetical list by members' names includes committee assignments, office building, room and phone number; committee rosters show members' names, states, parties. **Pages** (approx.): 80. **Frequency:** Annual, February or March. **Editor:** John L. K. Thomas, Director, Congressional Action Services. **Price:** $1.50.

★2076★
CONGRESSIONAL MONITOR DAILY
Congressional Monitor
499 National Press Building   Phone: (202) 347-7757
Washington, DC 20045
Covers: House and Senate committee hearings scheduled for up to two months from publication date. **Entries include:** Committee, hearings, locations, witness lists, other details. **Frequency:** Daily.

Price: $400.00 per year; hand delivered within Washington, DC area.

★2077★
CONGRESSIONAL PICTORIAL DIRECTORY
Joint Committee on Printing
United States Congress
United States Capitol, Room S-151   Phone: (202) 224-5241
Washington, DC 20515
Covers: Members of the House and Senate. **Entries include:** Photograph, name, residence, party, date term began. **Arrangement:** Geographical. **Indexes:** Personal name. **Pages** (approx.): 200. **Frequency:** Annual, January. **Price:** $2.00 (S/N 052-070-03895-1). **Send orders to:** Government Printing Office, Washington, DC 20402.

★2078★
CONGRESSIONAL STAFF DIRECTORY
Congressional Staff Directory
Box 62   Phone: (703) 765-3400
Mt. Vernon, VA 22121
Covers: Senators, congressmen, and their staffs, and key personnel of the Executive Branch of the federal government. Includes 2,500 brief biographies of congressional personnel, lists of committees and subcommittees with members and staffs, and lists of members showing their committee and subcommittee assignments. **Entries include:** For congressmen - Member name, party, state district (for representatives), direct dial phone, home state office addresses and phones with managers' names, and Washington staff names and titles. Separate section on state delegations gives additional information on members. For key staff members - Biographies give name, title, Washington address, career history. For Executive Branch departments - Principal addresses and phones, and names, titles, locations, and direct dial phone numbers for senior officials. **Pages** (approx.): 1,000. **Frequency:** Annual, May. **Editor:** Charles B. Brownson. **Price:** $22.00. **Also includes:** List of cities of over 1,500 population with district number, member name, and city population. **Other information:** The "Congressional Staff Directory" is the principal edition of three which are published from the same data base, updated for special purposes. Other publications are "Congressional Staff Directory Advance Locator" and "Congressional Staff Directory Election Index" (see separate listings).

★2079★
CONGRESSIONAL STAFF DIRECTORY ADVANCE LOCATOR
Congressional Staff Directory
Box 62   Phone: (703) 765-3400
Mt. Vernon, VA 22121
Covers: Members of Congrèss, their districts, and their staffs as of the beginning of each session. Includes updated delegation, staff, and Executive Department sections from "Congressional Staff Directory" (see separate listing). **Pages** (approx.): 500. **Frequency:** Annual, January. **Editor:** Charles B. Brownson, Editor-Publisher. **Price:** $8.00 (1980 edition).

★2080★
CONGRESSIONAL STAFF DIRECTORY ELECTION INDEX
Congressional Staff Directory
Box 62   Phone: (703) 765-3400
Mt. Vernon, VA 22121
Publication includes: Brief biographical sketches of all congressional candidates in each state. Also includes updated delegation, staff, and Executive Department sections from "Congressional Staff Directory" (see separate listing). **Pages** (approx.): 500. **Frequency:** Biennial, September of even years. **Editor:** Charles B. Brownson, Editor-Publisher. **Price:** $10.00 (1980 edition). **Also includes:** Election statistics by congressional district for four preceding congressional elections and list of town and cities in each district.

★2081★
CONGRESSIONAL YELLOW BOOK
Washington Monitor, Inc.
499 National Press Building   Phone: (202) 347-7757
Washington, DC 20045
Covers: 6,000 members of Congress, their committees, and their principal aides. **Entries include:** For members of Congress - Name, names, titles, and legislative responsibilities of principal aides, member's committee assignments and other responsibilities, district office address. For committees - Committee name, office address, phone, members' names and parties, description of committee jurisdiction. **Arrangement:** Alphabetical by member of Congress or committee name. **Frequency:** Quarterly updates (February, May, August, November) in looseleaf format. **Editor:** Michaela Buhler. **Former title:** Bimonthly Directory of Key Congressional Aides (1976). **Price:** $60.00 per year.

★2082★
CONNECTICUT LEGAL DIRECTORY
Legal Directories Publishing Company
8350 Central Expressway   Phone: (214) 692-5825
Dallas, TX 75206
Frequency: Latest edition 1979. **Former title:** Was included in former "New England Legal Directory." **Price:** $8.00. **Other information:** Content, arrangement, etc., same as "Alabama Legal Directory;" see separate listing. (See also separate listing, "Law Lists.")

★2083★
CONNECTICUT MUNICIPAL DIRECTORY
Connecticut Conference of Municipalities
956 Chapel Street   Phone: (203) 772-2168
New Haven, CT 06510
Entries include: Municipality name, mailing address, phone, names and titles of elected and appointed officials, meeting times, population. **Arrangement:** Geographical. **Frequency:** Annual, March. **Price:** $20.00.

Connecticut State Register and Manual *See* State of Connecticut Register and Manual

★2084★
COORDINATION DIRECTORY OF STATE AND FEDERAL AGENCY WATER AND LAND RESOURCES OFFICIALS [Missouri Basin]
Missouri River Basin Commission
10050 Regency Circle, Suite 403   Phone: (402) 397-5714
Omaha, NE 68114
Covers: More than 100 government officials with responsibilities in water and land resources in the 10-state Missouri River Basin area. **Arrangement:** By agency. **Indexes:** Personal name. **Pages** (approx.): 70. **Frequency:** Annual, fall. **Editor:** William C. Ramige, Information Officer. **Price:** Free.

★2085★
COUNCIL OF STATE COMMUNITY AFFAIRS AGENCIES—ADDRESS AND PHONE DIRECTORY
Council of State Community Affairs Agencies
Hall of the States
444 N. Capitol Street, Suite 312
Washington, DC 20001
Entries include: Agency name, address, name of director, phone. **Arrangement:** Geographical. **Frequency:** Irregular; latest edition 1977. **Price:** Free.

★2086★
COUNTRY EXPERTS IN THE FEDERAL GOVERNMENT
Washington Researchers
918 16th Street, N. W.   Phone: (202) 828-4800
Washington, DC 20006
Covers: Country specialists in the Departments of Commerce, State, Energy, and Agriculture, the Agency for International Development, and the Bureau of Mines. **Entries include:** Name, department and address, and phone of specialist. **Arrangement:** By country. **Pages** (approx.): 30. **Frequency:** Biennial, even years. **Price:** $15.00, payment with order; $16.50, billed.

★2087★
COUNTY INFORMATION SYSTEMS DIRECTORY
D. C. Heath & Company
125 Spring Street   Phone: (617) 862-6650
Lexington, MA 02115
Covers: Computing systems and equipment in county governments. **Entries include:** County name, location, demographic characteristics, government profile, data processing budget, equipment profile, data processing personnel profile, detailed listing of computer applications used by the county, etc. **Arrangement:** Geographical. **Indexes:** Applications, functions, computer manufacturer. **Pages** (approx.): 25. **Frequency:** Published 1976. **Editors:** Joseph R. Matthews, et al. **Price:** $33.95, payment with order.

★2088★
C-R-C ATTORNEY DIRECTORY
C-R-C Law List Company
401 Broadway   Phone: (212) 966-6126
New York, NY 10013
Arrangement: Geographical. **Frequency:** Annual. **Price:** Apply. **Other information:** A commercial law list. See separate listing, "Law Lists."

★2089★
CREDIT UNION ATTORNEY'S LEGAL DIRECTORY
Legal Directory, Inc.
110 S. McDonough   Phone: (205) 265-5365
Montgomery, AL 36103
Covers: Lawyers who represent credit unions or are willing to do so. **Entries include:** Lawyer name, address, phone, name of one credit union represented; some listings include additional personal and client data. **Arrangement:** Geographical. **Frequency:** Annual, May; first published 1977. **Former title:** National Directory of Credit Union Attorneys (1978). **Other information:** A general law list. See separate listing, "Law Lists."

★2090★
CRIMINAL JUSTICE AGENCIES IN [REGION AND NUMBER]
National Criminal Justice Information & Statistics Service
Law Enforcement Assistance Administration
Justice Department   Phone: (202) 376-2622
Washington, DC 20531
Covers: 57,575 state and local criminal justice agencies throughout the United States, including law enforcement agencies (i.e., police departments, sheriff's departments); criminal and civil courts; prosecuting attorneys; public defender offices and agencies; adult and juvenile correctional institutions; probation and parole agencies; and other agencies (e. g., prison industries, crime commissions, etc.). In ten volumes. Region I: Connecticut, Maine, Massachusetts, New Hampshire, Rhode Island, Vermont. II: New Jersey, New York. III: Delaware, District of Columbia, Maryland, Pennsylvania, Virginia, West Virginia. IV: Alabama, Florida, Georgia, Kentucky, Mississippi, North Carolina, South Carolina, Tennessee. V: Illinois, Indiana, Michigan, Minnesota, Ohio, Wisconsin. VI: Arkansas, Louisiana, New Mexico, Oklahoma, Texas. VII: Iowa, Kansas, Missouri, Nebraska. VIII: Colorado, Montana, North Dakota, South Dakota, Utah, Wyoming. IX: Arizona, California, Hawaii, Nevada. X: Alaska, Idaho, Oregon, Washington. **Entries include:** Agency name and address and county in which located; not published but included in magnetic tape are 1970 population of jurisdiction served and number of employees. **Arrangement:** Geographical by state; within states, separate lists for each function or agency. **Pages** (approx.): 100-350 per volume. **Frequency:** Irregular; last published late 1974 and early 1975; new publication planned since 1978, but uncertain at present. **Price:** (Current edition) Region I (GPO Stock No. 027- 000-00301-0) $1.95; II (-00302-8) $2.50; III (-00315-0) $2.70; IV (-00314-1) $4.20; V (-00308-7) $4.25; VI (00307-9) $3.45; VII (-00307-9)

$2.50; VIII (-00303-6) $2.20; IX (out of print); X (00304-4) $1.90.
Send orders to: Goverment Printing Office, Washington, DC 20402.

★2091★
CRIMINAL JUSTICE AUDIOVISUAL MATERIALS DIRECTORY
Office of Operations Support
Law Enforcement Assistance Administration
Justice Department
633 Indiana Avenue, N. W.   Phone: (202) 724-5884
Washington, DC 20531
Publication includes: 150 producers or distributors of films, filmstrips, and other audiovisual materials on criminal justice subjects. **Entries include:** Source name, address. **Arrangement:** Alphabetical. **Frequency:** Annual, fall; 1979 edition delayed. **Price:** $3.00 (S/N 027-000-00629-9). **Send orders to:** Government Printing Office, Washington, DC 20402. **Other information:** Principal content of publication is annotated listings of audiovisual materials.

★2092★
CRIMINAL JUSTICE EDUCATION DIRECTORY
International Association of Chiefs of Police
11 Firstfield Road   Phone: (301) 948-0922
Gaithersburg, MD 20760
Covers: More than 800 colleges and universities offering law enforcement and criminal justice degree programs. **Entries include:** Name of institution offering program and department responsible for it, address, name of dean or coordinator, degrees offered, names of courses offered, enrollment data. **Arrangement:** Geographical. **Pages** (approx.): 600. **Frequency:** Irregular; latest edition January 1978; new edition expected January 1981. **Editor:** Richard W. Kobetz, Assistant Director. **Former title:** Law Enforcement and Criminal Justice Education Directory. **Price:** $14.75, postpaid, payment with order.

★2093★
DECALOGUE SOCIETY OF LAWYERS—DIRECTORY OF MEMBERS
Decalogue Society of Lawyers
180 W. Washington Street   Phone: (312) 263-6493
Chicago, IL 60602
Covers: 1,600 lawyers of the Jewish faith. **Entries include:** Name, address. **Arrangement:** Alphabetical. **Advertising accepted.** Circulation 1,800. **Price:** Available to members only.

★2094★
DEFENSE DOCUMENTATION CENTER REFERRAL DATA BANK DIRECTORY
Defense Documentation Center
Defense Logistics Agency
Defense Department
Cameron Station
Alexandria, VA 22314
Covers: About 275 information analysis centers, special libraries, data banks, depositories, laboratories, testing directorates, and other research facilities of the Defense Department which "have the capability and willingness to serve the defense community in their fields of expertise." **Entries include:** Name of the facility or mission; names, addresses, and phone numbers of key personnel; detailed description of mission, subject interests, services and materials available, publications, and limitations on service or access. **Arrangement:** Alphabetical by mission or facility name. **Indexes:** Subject, director or contact name. **Pages** (approx.): 425. **Frequency:** Irregular; previous edition October 1976; latest edition June 1978. **Editor:** Alice L. Cox. **Price:** Apply; marked, "Approved for public distribution." (Publication DDC/TR-78/2.) Also available from National Technical Information Service, Springield, VA 22161; NTIS number not assigned.

★2095★
DELAWARE LEGISLATIVE ROSTER
Delaware State Chamber of Commerce
1102 West Street   Phone: (302) 655-7221
Wilmington, DE 19801
Covers: Principal state officials and members of the legislature. **Entries include:** Name, photo, term of office, party, district, occupation, home and office phones, birth date, education, memberships, former posts and affiliations, committee assignments. **Arrangement:** By district number. **Pages** (approx.): 40. **Frequency:** Biennial, spring of odd years. **Editor:** Debbie Facciolo. **Price:** $2.00.

★2096★
DELAWARE STATE MANUAL
Delaware Secretary of State
Townsend Building   Phone: (302) 678-4111
Dover, DE 19901
Covers: State departments, agencies, institutions, boards, commissions, colleges, legislators; includes officers of county governments. **Entries include:** Biographies and photographs for high executive and judicial officers and legislators; name, title, address for most others; salary is given in many cases. **Arrangement:** By department and level of government. **Indexes:** Agency. **Pages** (approx.): 100. **Frequency:** Has been biennial early in odd years, but no revision of 1975-76 edition is planned before 1981. **Price:** Free. **Also includes:** State history, information on industry and tourism.

★2097★
DEPARTMENT OF DEFENSE TELEPHONE DIRECTORY
Defense Department
Pentagon
Washington, DC 20301
Covers: Defense Department offices and key personnel in the metropolitan Washington area; also covers Army, Navy, and Air Force offices and personnel. **Entries include:** Department, bureau, or other unit name, address, names of principal personnel with titles, room numbers, and phone numbers. **Arrangement:** By department, bureau, etc. **Indexes:** Personal name (includes abbreviated identification and phone); includes names not in classified section. **Frequency:** Three times yearly. **Price:** $9.00 per year; $3.00 per copy (S/N 008-000-80002-2; ISSN 0363-6844). **Send orders to:** Government Printing Office, Washington, DC 20402.

Department of Energy Telephone Directory *See* DOE Telephone Directory

★2098★
DEPARTMENT OF HEALTH, EDUCATION, AND WELFARE TELEPHONE DIRECTORY
Health, Education, and Welfare Department
200 Independence Avenue, S. W.   Phone: (202) 655-4000
Washington, DC 20201
Covers: Health, Education, and Welfare Department offices and key personnel in the metropolitan Washington area, and selected offices elsewhere. **Entries include:** Office, institute, or other unit name, address, names of principal personnel with titles, room numbers, and phone numbers. **Arrangement:** By office, institute, etc. **Indexes:** Personal name (includes agency, room number, phone); includes names not in classified sections. **Frequency:** Latest edition spring 1979. **Price:** $4.00 (1979 out of print). **Send orders to:** Government Printing Office, Washington, DC 20402.

★2099★
DEPARTMENT OF LABOR TELEPHONE DIRECTORY
Labor Department
200 Constitution Avenue, N. W.
Washington, DC 20210
Covers: Labor Department offices and key personnel in the Washington metropolitan area, and principal regional and field offices. **Entries include:** Bureau, office, or other unit name, address, names of principal personnel with titles, room numbers, and phone numbers.

Arrangement: By agency, bureau, etc. **Indexes:** Personal name (gives abbreviated identification and phone for Washington personnel only); includes names not in classified section. **Frequency:** Annual, spring. **Price:** $3.25 (S/N 029-000-00315-7). **Send orders to:** Government Printing Office, Washington, DC 20402.

Department of State Telephone Directory *See* Telephone Directory—Department of State

Department of the Interior Telephone Directory *See* U.S. Department of the Interior Telephone Directory

Department of Transportation Telephone Directory *See* Directory—Department of Transportation

★2100★

DEPARTMENT OF TREASURY TELEPHONE DIRECTORY
Treasury Department
15th Street and Pennsylvania
  Avenue, N. W.
Washington, DC 20220
Covers: Treasury Department offices and key personnel in the Washington metropolitan area and selected offices nationwide. **Entries include:** Bureau, office or other unit name, address, names of principal personnel with titles, room numbers, and phone numbers, principal field offices. **Arrangement:** By unit. **Indexes:** Personal name (includes abbreviated identification and phone). **Pages** (approx.): 210. **Frequency:** Semiannual, spring and fall. **Editor:** Robert E. Barrett. **Former title:** Treasury Telephone Directory. **Price:** $6.10 per year; $3.25 per copy (S/N 048-000-80004-1). **Send orders to:** Government Printing Office, Washington, DC 20402.

★2101★

DIPLOMATIC LIST (Blue List) [Washington, D.C.]
State Department
2201 C Street, N. W.   Phone: (202) 655-4000
Washington, DC 20520
Covers: Personnel through the attache level assigned to Washington embassies. Embassy employees are listed in "Employees of Diplomatic Missions" (see separate listing). Consulates and their personnel are listed in "Foreign Consular Offices in the United States" (see separate listing). **Entries include:** Embassy name, chancery address, phone; names and ranks of personnel, names of spouses, home addresses and phones; listings also include the name and date of the principal national holiday. **Arrangement:** By country. **Pages** (approx.): 75. **Frequency:** Quarterly. **Price:** $8.00 per year; $2.00 per copy (S/N 044-000-80003-9; ISSN 0012-3099). **Send orders to:** Government Printing Office, Washington, DC 20402. **Other information:** Includes list of ambassadors in order of precedence.

★2102★

DIRECTORY: FEDERAL, STATE, COUNTY, AND MUNICIPAL OFFICIALS [Camden County, New Jersey]
Camden Planning Board
600 Market Street
Camden, NJ 08102
Covers: Elected and appointed officals for 37 Camden County cities, Camden County officials, and elected federal and state legislators representing Camden County. **Pages** (approx.): 50. **Frequency:** Annual, summer. **Price:** Free.

★2103★

DIRECTORY: VOLUNTEER LAW LIBRARIAN CONSULTANTS TO PRISON LAW LIBRARIES
American Association of Law Libraries
53 W. Jackson Boulevard   Phone: (312) 939-4764
Chicago, IL 60604
Covers: Over 200 law librarians who advise correctional institutions, free of charge, on the establishment and operation of law libraries. **Entries include:** Name, address. **Arrangement:** Geographical. **Frequency:** Latest edition December 1978. **Former title:** Directory

of Law Librarian Consultants to Correctional Institutions. **Price:** $3.00, plus 50¢ shipping.

★2104★

DIRECTORY—DEPARTMENT OF TRANSPORTATION
Office of the Secretary
Transportation Department
400 Seventh Street, S. W., M-482
Washington, DC 20590
Covers: Transportation Department offices and key personnel in metropolitan Washington area; also covers Coast Guard, Federal Aviation Administration, Federal Highway Administration, Federal Railroad Administration, National Highway Traffic Safety Administration, Research and Special Programs Administration, Urban Mass Transportation Administration. **Entries include:** Bureau, office, or other unit name, address, names of principal personnel with titles, room numbers, and phone numbers. **Arrangement:** By bureau, agency, etc. **Indexes:** Personal name (gives abbreviated identification and phone); includes some not in classified section. **Frequency:** Three times yearly. **Former title:** Department of Transportation Telephone Directory (1976). **Price:** $9.00 per year; $3.00 per copy (S/N 050-000-80001-6). **Send orders to:** Government Printing Office, Washington, DC 20402.

Directory and Manual of Oklahoma *See* Directory of Oklahoma

★2105★

DIRECTORY OF AREAWIDE PLANNING ORGANIZATIONS [Iowa]
Office for Planning and Programming
Iowa Division of Municipal Affairs
523 E. 12th Street   Phone: (515) 281-3711
Des Moines, IA 50319
Covers: 17 "voluntary associations of local governments established under state enabling legislation for the purpose of promoting intergovernmental cooperation and strengthening local units of government." **Entries include:** Name of organization; square mile area covered in planning; names and populations of governments included; names, office addresses, and phone numbers of key executives; description of policy structure, membership, and program areas; publications. **Arrangement:** By region. **Pages** (approx.): 115. **Frequency:** Annual, August. **Editor:** Harriet A. Cate, Community Planner. **Price:** Free (ISSN 0363-0013).

Directory of Arizona City and Town Officials *See* Local Government Directory [Arizona]

★2106★

DIRECTORY OF ARKANSAS MUNICIPAL OFFICIALS
Arkansas Municipal League
29th and Willow Streets   Phone: (501) 758-1610
North Little Rock, AR 72115
Entries include: City name, names and titles of officials and cities' mailing addresses, information about each municipality. **Arrangement:** Alphabetical. **Pages** (approx.): 65. **Frequency:** Annual, February. **Editor:** Don A. Zimmerman, Executive Director. **Price:** $10.00.

★2107★

DIRECTORY OF ATTORNEYS OF KING COUNTY [Washington]
Daily Journal of Commerce
Journal Building
83 Columbia Street   Phone: (206) 622-8272
Seattle, WA 98104
Covers: Attorneys in King County, Washington, and federal, county, and city judges, court reporters, county officers, and county legal officers for all counties in Washington. **Entries include:** Name, office address. **Arrangement:** Geographical. **Pages** (approx.): 90. **Frequency:** Annual, February. **Editor:** Scott Seifert. **Advertising accepted.** Circulation 8,000. **Price:** $4.50 (current edition); $5.00 (1980 edition).

★2108★

DIRECTORY OF AUTOMATED CRIMINAL JUSTICE INFORMATION SYSTEMS

National Criminal Justice Information and Statistcs Service
Law Enforcement Assistance Administration
Justice Dept.   Phone: (301) 492-9050
Washington, DC 20531
Covers: 455 computerized information systems serving police, courts, and correction agencies in federal, state, and local governments. **Entries include:** System name; functions; hardware and software configuration; operational status and other details; names, addresses, and phone numbers of key officials for follow-up inquiries. **Arrangement:** Geographical. **Pages** (approx.): 1,000. **Frequency:** Irregular; latest edition 1976; new edition expected 1980. **Price:** Free.

Directory of Borough and City Officials [Alaska] *See* **Alaska Municipal Officials Directory**

★2109★

DIRECTORY OF BROADCAST ACCESS TO COURTROOMS

Radio Television News Directors Association
1735 De Sales Street, N. W.   Phone: (202) 737-8657
Washington, DC 20036
Background: Not a directory in the usual sense, but gives general information on the rules pertaining to use of cameras and recording equipment in the various courts of each state; includes pertinent state legislation and other material. **Arrangement:** Geographical. **Pages** (approx.): 1,300. **Frequency:** Constant updating (copies reproduced as ordered). **Editors:** Joel Hamme and Scott Cairns. **Price:** $130.00.

★2110★

DIRECTORY OF CALIFORNIA JUSTICE AGENCIES SERVING JUVENILES AND ADULTS

California Department of the Youth Authority
4241 Williamsborough Drive   Phone: (916) 445-2046
Sacramento, CA 95823
Covers: All county probation offices; offices for state departments of Corrections, Youth Authority, Health, and Justice; U. S. probation offices; county sheriffs' departments; local police departments. **Arrangement:** Geographical by county. **Pages** (approx.): 140. **Frequency:** Biennial, July of odd years. **Editor:** George Smith. **Former title:** Directory of California Services for Juvenile and Adult Offenders; Directory of California Juvenile Law Enforcement Officials. **Price:** $1.60. **Send orders to:** State of California, Documents Section, Box 1015, North Highlands, CA 95660 (916-445-1020).

★2111★

DIRECTORY OF CITY AND TOWN OFFICIALS [Rhode Island]

Rhode Island Division of Housing and Government Services
150 Washington Street   Phone: (401) 277-2854
Providence, RI 02903
Covers: Elective and appointive officials; includes state officials. **Arrangement:** Geographical. **Frequency:** Annual, March. **Price:** $3.00 (1980 edition; 1979 sold out).

★2112★

DIRECTORY OF COMMUNITY CRIME PREVENTION PROGRAMS: NATIONAL AND STATE LEVELS

National Institute of Law Enforcement and Criminal Justice
Law Enforcement Assistance Administration
Justice Department
633 Indiana Avenue, N. W.
Washington, DC 20531
Covers: 30 national and 35 state level crime prevention programs; over 35 additional local programs which have received grants from the Law Enforcement Assistance Administration; and 20 agencies, association, and other groups with funding, technical assistance, materials, and training programs available to assist in the development of community crime prevention programs. **Entries include:** For programs - Organization name, program title, service area for state

programs, address, phone, name of sponsoring agency, objectives, services, resources, and publications. For grant recipients - Organization name, address, program title, grant number. For other organizations - Name, address, phone, description of organization, services, or assistance available. **Arrangement:** Alphabetical within above groups. **Pages** (approx.): 135. **Frequency:** Irregular; latest edition December 1978. **Editors:** James L. Locard, J. T. Skip Duncan, Robert N. Brenner. **Price:** $4.00 (S/N 027-000-00817-8). **Send orders to:** Government Printing Office, Washington, DC 20402.

Directory of Congressional ZIP Codes *See* **Congressional District ZIP Codes**

★2113★

DIRECTORY OF COUNTY OFFICERS OF KANSAS

Kansas Secretary of State
State Capitol, 2nd Floor
Topeka, KS 66612
Covers: Over 1,000 elected and appointed county officers. **Entries include:** County name, mailing address, names and titles of county commissioners, sheriffs, etc. **Pages** (approx.): 30. **Frequency:** Biennial, March of odd years. **Editor:** Jack H. Brier. **Price:** Free.

★2114★

DIRECTORY OF COUNTY OFFICIALS [Utah]

Utah Association of Counties
10 W. Broadway, Suite 311   Phone: (801) 359-3241
Salt Lake City, UT 84101
Entries include: County name, county seat, Zip code, phone, and names, addresses, and home phones of commissioners, plus names of clerks, sheriffs, and other officials. **Frequency:** Biennial, odd years. **Price:** Free. (Not verified)

★2115★

DIRECTORY OF COUNTY OFFICIALS IN WASHINGTON STATE

Washington Association of County Officials
105 E. Eighth Street, Suite 307
Olympia, WA 98501
Arrangement: By county. **Pages** (approx.): 25. **Frequency:** Annual, January/February. **Price:** $2.00.

★2116★

DIRECTORY OF CRIMINAL JUSTICE INFORMATION SOURCES

National Institute of Law Enforcement and Criminal Justice
Law Enforcement Assistance Administration
Justice Department
633 Indiana Avenue, N. W.
Washington, DC 20531
Covers: About 150 sources of information on criminal justice and include computerized literature search services, interlibrary loan programs, reference services and other resources of agencies and organizations in the criminal justice field. **Entries include:** Organization name, address, phone, year founded, name of sponsoring agency (if any), name and title of chief executive, number of staff, name of contact, area of concern, costs, user restrictions, objectives and activities, information services, information resources (library volumes, files, etc.), publications. **Arrangement:** Alphabetical. **Indexes:** Organization name, subject. **Pages** (approx.): 165. **Frequency:** Irregular; latest edition May 1979. **Editor:** Thomas Ketterman. **Price:** $4.50 (S/N 027-000-00821-6). **Send orders to:** Government Printing Office, Washington, DC 20402.

★2117★

DIRECTORY OF DATA PROCESSING IN SMALL LOCAL GOVERNMENTS

International City Management Association
1140 Connecticut Avenue, N. W.   Phone: (202) 293-2200
Washington, DC 20036
Covers: Cities, counties, and regional organizations or cooperating municipalities with in-house computer installations or which use data processing service bureaus. **Entries include:** For in-house installations

- City, county, or regional government name, population, code to indicate type of government, type of computer, amount of memory, principal applications, title, address, and phone of contact. For regional governments - Name; names of member jurisdictions, populations, and type of government; applications. For service bureaus users - Government name, population, name of service bureau, and applications. **Arrangement:** By type of government (city, county, etc.) and computer access, then geographical. **Indexes:** Computer. **Pages** (approx.): 125. **Frequency:** Not established; first edition 1978. **Editors:** O. Martin Anochie, Harlan J. Smolin. **Price:** $20.00.

★2118★
DIRECTORY OF ELECTION OFFICIALS
Clearinghouse on Election Administration
Federal Election Commission
1325 K Street, N. W.
Washington, DC 20463
Covers: State election agencies and election officials, and federal officials with election-related responsibilities. **Entries include:** Agency name, address, phone, and names and titles of officials. Agency responsibilities and operations are described in detail in separate section. **Arrangement:** Geographical. **Pages** (approx.): 155. **Frequency:** Annual, spring. **Editor:** Charlotte L. Ott. **Price:** $4.75 (S/N 052-006-000023). **Send orders to:** Government Printing Office, Washington, DC 20402.

★2119★
DIRECTORY OF FEDERAL AUDIT ORGANIZATIONS
Division of Financial and General Management Studies
General Accounting Office
441 G Street, N. W.
Washington, DC 20548
Covers: About 60 audit groups and their regional offices directly involved in the audit of federal funds. External audit organizations within regulatory agencies and investigators will be included in the 1980 edition. **Entries include:** Name of federal agency, name of audit group; name of group head, address, phone, place in organization structure; number of staff, location of staff, amount of funding; regional offices show name and title of group head, address, phone. **Arrangement:** Alphabetical. **Pages** (approx.): 80. **Frequency:** Irregular; new edition expected January 1980. **Editor:** George L. Egan, Jr., Associate Director. **Price:** Free.

★2120★
DIRECTORY OF FEDERAL GOVERNMENT PURCHASING OFFICES
Graftek Communications, Inc.
Box 2315   Phone: (305) 392-3768
Boca Raton, FL 33432
Number of listings: Over 1,500 offices, nationwide. **Entries include:** Agency and office name, address, phone, description of past purchases. **Arrangement:** By Zip code. **Pages** (approx.): 250. **Frequency:** Irregular; first edition 1978. **Editor:** Dirk Smith. **Price:** $14.95, payment with order.

★2121★
DIRECTORY OF FEDERAL OCCUPATIONAL HEALTH FACILITIES
U.S. Civil Service Commission
1900 E Street, N. W., Room 233K   Phone: (202) 254-6190
Washington, DC 20415
Covers: About 970 on-site health facilities provided for employees of the federal government in the United States. **Entries include:** Facility name, operating agency code, address, number of employees served, and coding to indicate services offered and cost (per employee annually). **Arrangement:** By zip code. **Pages** (approx.): 35. **Frequency:** Irregular; latest edition November 1977; new edition expected November 1980. **Editor:** Thomas T. Campagna, Chief, Occupational Health Division. **Price:** Free (BRI 40-33).

★2122★
DIRECTORY OF FEDERAL REGIONAL STRUCTURE
General Services Administration
General Services Building
18th and F Streets, N. W.   Phone: (202) 655-4000
Washington, DC 20405
Publication includes: List of regional offices of federal government agencies, and maps of the Standard Federal Regions and many non-standard structures. **Entries include:** Agency name, designation of regional offices, their addresses, and names and phone numbers of chief administrators of each region. **Pages** (approx.): 100. **Frequency:** Irregular; latest edition 1979. **Price:** $3.50 (S/N 022-003-0097-3). **Send orders to:** Government Printing Office, Washington, DC 20402.

★2123★
DIRECTORY OF FEDERAL, STATE, COUNTY, CITY, AND SPECIAL DISTRICT OFFICIALS IN NORTH DAKOTA
North Dakota Bureau of Governmental Affairs
University of North Dakota   Phone: (701) 777-3041
Grand Forks, ND 58201
Entries include: Department or agency name, names and titles of officials; most listings include phone numbers. **Arrangement:** By level and unit of government. **Pages** (approx.): 150. **Frequency:** Biennial, odd years. **Price:** $6.00. **Other information:** Includes tribal agency personnel for Indian reservations in North Dakota.

★2124★
DIRECTORY OF FEDERAL STATISTICS FOR LOCAL AREAS
Bureau of the Census
Commerce Department
Washington, DC 20233
Covers: Federal agencies which publish reports of statistics for local area (ranging from city blocks to metropolitan areas); unpublished statistics, microforms, data files, and other collections of census-type data are included. **Entries include:** For each title - Name of agency, address, level of detail, geographic area covered, frequency of publication and/or collection, report numbers, table numbers, and GPO catalog numbers when available. **Arrangement:** By subject. **Indexes:** Subject. **Pages** (approx.): 370. **Frequency:** Irregular; latest edition 1978 (1966-1976 data); update of urban content expected early 1980. **Editor:** Mary S. J. Gordon. **Price:** $5.50 (S/N 003-024-01553-6). **Send orders to:** Government Printing Office, Washington, DC 20402.

★2125★
DIRECTORY OF FIELD BIOLOGISTS AND LAW ENFORCEMENT OFFICERS ALONG THE UPPER MISSISSIPPI RIVER
Upper Mississippi River Conservation Committee
1830 Second Avenue   Phone: (309) 788-3991
Rock Island, IL 61201
Covers: Wildlife biologists, fishery biologists, and conservation officers responsible for activities in counties along the Mississippi River in Minnesota, Wisconsin, Iowa, Illinois, and Missouri. **Entries include:** County, navigation pool or river mile, and name, address, and phone of responsible wildlife and fishery biologists and conservation officer. **Arrangement:** By county. **Frequency:** Irregular; latest edition May 1979. **Price:** Free.

★2126★
DIRECTORY OF FLORIDA GOVERNMENT
Elections Division
Florida Secretary of State
State Capitol   Phone: (904) 488-4711
Tallahassee, FL 32301
Covers: State departments and agencies, legislators, judiciary; also includes county governments and their officials. **Entries include:** State listings include department or agency name, address, phone, names of executives; legislator listings include name, party, district, Tallahassee address, phone, legal residence. County government listings include county name, mailing address, names and titles of principal elective

and appointive officials. **Arrangement:** By unit and level of government. **Pages** (approx.): 40. **Frequency:** Annual, January. **Price:** 50¢.

★2127★
DIRECTORY OF GEORGIA MUNICIPAL OFFICIALS
Georgia Municipal Association
10 Pryor Street Building, Suite 220   Phone: (404) 688-0472
Atlanta, GA 30303
Frequency: Annual, semiannual updates. **Price:** $15.00, including update.

★2128★
DIRECTORY OF GOVERNMENT DOCUMENT COLLECTIONS AND LIBRARIANS
Government Documents Round Table
American Library Association
50 E. Huron Street   Phone: (312) 944-6780
Chicago, IL 60611
Covers: Nearly 2,300 government document collections, plus institutions, organizations, agencies, and 3,600 individuals concerned with document librarianship, publication, or related activities. Includes state document agencies, library schools and staff concerned with government documents. **Entries include:** Institution name; library name; division of library responsible for documents, and its address and phone; collection information; names and titles of staff working with documents; state document authorities; library schools and staff. **Arrangement:** Geographical. **Indexes:** Institution/library, document collection, special collection, personal name. **Pages** (approx.): 550. **Frequency:** Irregular; latest edition June 1978. **Editors:** Nancy Cline and Jaia Heymann. **Price:** $22.50, payment must accompany individuals' orders. **Send orders to:** Directory Orders, Congressional Information Service, 7101 Wisconsin Ave., Suite 900, Washington, DC 20014.

★2129★
DIRECTORY OF GOVERNMENT DOCUMENT DEALERS AND JOBBERS (Preliminary edition)
Government Documents Round Table
American Library Association
50 E. Huron Street
Chicago, IL 60611
Covers: 19 dealers handling United States and foreign publications, including municipal documents. **Entries include:** Dealer's name, address, phone number and ordering information. **Arrangement:** Alphabetical. **Pages** (approx.): 5. **Frequency:** Preliminary edition 1975, update planned for mid-1980. **Other information:** Appeared in "Documents to the People," September, 1975, pp. 40-44.

★2130★
DIRECTORY OF IDAHO CITY OFFICIALS
Association of Idaho Cities
3314 Grace Street
Boise, ID 83703
Number of listings: 200. **Entries include:** City name, population, county, address, phone, meeting day, and names of city officials with coding to indicate office and year term expires. **Arrangement:** Geographical. **Pages** (approx.): 50. **Frequency:** Irregular; latest edition 1978-79; new edition expected March 1980. **Price:** $12.50.

★2131★
DIRECTORY OF INTERSTATE COMPACTS AND AGENCIES [Government]
The Council of State Governments
Iron Works Pike   Phone: (606) 252-2291
Lexington, KY 40578
Covers: 50 interstate agencies created by compact or other interstate agreement. **Entries include:** Agency name, address, member states, public official representatives, professional staff. **Arrangement:** Alphabetical. **Pages** (approx.): 25. **Frequency:** Irregular; latest edition 1976. **Price:** $3.00.

★2132★
DIRECTORY OF IOWA MUNICIPALITIES
League of Iowa Municipalities
900 Des Moines Street, Suite 100   Phone: (515) 265-9961
Des Moines, IA 50316
Covers: 955 incorporated cities. **Entries include:** City name, city hall phone, Zip code, county, population, council meeting times, and names of all elected and appointed officials. **Arrangement:** By city. **Pages** (approx.): 80. **Frequency:** Biennial, spring of even years; supplement in odd years. **Price:** $10.00 (current edition; tentative, 1980 edition).

Directory of Juvenile and Adult Correctional Institutions... *See* Juvenile and Adult Correctional Departments, Institutions...

★2133★
DIRECTORY OF JUVENILE/FAMILY DOMESTIC RELATIONS COURT JUDGES
National Council of Juvenile and Family Court Judges
Box 8978
University Station   Phone: (702) 784-6012
Reno, NV 89507
Covers: 4,500 judges who have juvenile, family, or domestic relations jurisdiction; includes additional 700 non-judicial associate members. **Entries include:** Name, office address; many listings include title. **Arrangement:** Alphabetical and geographical; identical information in both parts. Associate members are alphabetical. **Pages** (approx.): 65. **Frequency:** Annual, September or October. **Editor:** N. Corinne Smith. **Former title:** Juvenile Court Judges Directory. **Price:** $8.00.

★2134★
DIRECTORY OF KANSAS PUBLIC OFFICIALS
League of Kansas Municipalities
112 W. Seventh Street   Phone: (913) 354-9565
Topeka, KS 66603
Covers: More than 25,000 officials at all levels of government in Kansas. **Entries include:** Governmental unit, address, names of officials, usually with individual mailing addresses; some types of listings include political party, occupation, and salary of incumbents. **Frequency:** Annual, August; updates published in "Kansas Government Journal." **Price:** $34.00.

★2135★
DIRECTORY OF LAW ENFORCEMENT AND CRIMINAL JUSTICE ASSOCIATIONS AND RESEARCH CENTERS
National Institute of Law Enforcement and Criminal Justice
Law Enforcement Assistance Administration
Justice Department
Washington, DC 20531
Number of listings: 300. **Entries include:** Name of organization, address, phone, name of one officer, year founded, numbers of members and staff, description of activities; affiliation, publications, meetings. **Arrangement:** Alphabetical. **Indexes:** Subject. **Pages** (approx.): 55. **Frequency:** Irregular; previous edition 1973; latest edition March 1978. **Price:** $5.25, paper; $3.00, microfiche (PB 279-246). **Send orders to:** National Technical Information Service, Springfield, VA 22161. **Other information:** Prepared by Law Enforcement Standards Laboratory, National Bureau of Standards (301-921-3161).

Directory of Law Librarian Consultants to Correctional Institutions *See* Directory: Volunteer Law Librarian Consultants to Prison Law...

★2136★
DIRECTORY OF LAW LIBRARIES
American Association of Law Libraries
53 W. Jackson Boulevard
Chicago, IL 60604
Covers: Institutional members of the association; law libraries employing at least one member of the association; other law libraries with collections of at least 10,000 volumes. **Entries include:** Library

name, address, phone, name of one or more staff members, number of volumes. **Arrangement:** Geographical. **Indexes:** Personal name. **Pages** (approx.): 120. **Frequency:** Biennial, fall of even years. **Former title:** Law Libraries in the United States and Canada. **Price:** $10.00.

★2137★
DIRECTORY OF LAW TEACHERS
Association of American Law Schools
One Dupont Circle, N. W., Suite 370   Phone: (202) 296-8851
Washington, DC 20036
Covers: Teachers of law in colleges and universities approved by the American Bar Association; colleges and universities are listed separately. **Entries include:** For teachers - Name, institution name, professional, educational, and career data, subjects taught. For schools - Name, address, faculty names, whether member of AALS and date of membership. **Arrangement:** Alphabetical. **Pages** (approx.): 1,000. **Frequency:** Annual, fall. **Editor:** Janet Kulick. **Price:** $30.00, payment with order. **Also includes:** Canadian associates.

★2138★
DIRECTORY OF LAW-RELATED EDUCATION PROJECTS
Special Committee on Youth Education for Citizenship
American Bar Association
1155 E. 60th Street   Phone: (312) 947-3960
Chicago, IL 60637
Covers: Over 300 law-related education programs for elementary and secondary teachers and curriculum developers. Individual teacher's law-related activities are not included. **Entries include:** Program sponsor, address, subject area taught, instructional activities used, instructional materials used, staff participants, and source of funding. **Arrangement:** Geographical. **Pages** (approx.): 105. **Frequency:** Irregular; latest edition 1978. **Editor:** Cynthia A. Kelly. **Former title:** Directory of Law-Related Educational Activities. **Price:** $2.00.

Directory of Legal Aid and Defender Services in the United States
    See NLADA Directory of Legal Aid and Defender Offices...

★2139★
DIRECTORY OF LEGISLATIVE COMMITTEES [Wisconsin]
Wisconsin Legislative Council
State Capitol, Room 147N   Phone: (608) 266-1340
Madison WI 53702
Publication includes: List of Legislative Council committees, including legislative and non-legislative members. **Arrangement:** By committee. **Pages** (approx.): 95. **Frequency:** Biennial, August of even years. **Price:** Free. **Other information:** Variant title, ''Directory of Legislative Council and Joint Legislative Committees.''

★2140★
DIRECTORY OF LOCAL GOVERNMENT OFFICIALS IN RHODE ISLAND
Bureau of Government Research
University of Rhode Island   Phone: (401) 792-2158
Kingston, RI 02881
Covers: Both elected and appointed town officials. **Entries include:** Municipality name, population, names and titles of officials. **Pages** (approx.): 25. **Frequency:** Annual, January. **Editor:** Anna G. Haggarty, Staff Assistant. **Price:** Free.

★2141★
DIRECTORY OF LOCAL PLANNING AGENCIES IN THE SOUTHEASTERN UNITED STATES
Bureau of City Planning
City of Tampa
One City Hall Plaza, A 8 East   Phone: (813) 223-8486
Tampa, FL 33602
Number of listings: 330. **Entries include:** Agency name, address, phone, description of purpose of agency. **Arrangement:** Geographical. **Pages** (approx.): 175. **Frequency:** Irregular; latest edition November 1976. **Price:** $7.50.

★2142★
DIRECTORY OF LOCAL PLANNING ORGANIZATIONS IN THE STATE OF NEVADA
Nevada Office of Planning Coordination
Capitol Building, Room 45   Phone: (702) 885-4865
Carson City, NV 89710
Number of listings: 40. **Pages** (approx.): 50. **Frequency:** Annual, summer. **Price:** Free.

★2143★
DIRECTORY OF LOCALITIES WITH COMMUNITY DEVELOPMENT BLOCK GRANT PROPERTY REHABILITATION FINANCING ACTIVITIES
Community Planning and Development
Housing and Urban Development Department
451 Seventh Street, N. W., Room B-237
Washington, DC 20410
Covers: More than 1,400 localities which budgeted Community Development Block Grant funds for housing rehabilitation in fiscal years 1975 and 1976. **Entries include:** Agency name; name, title, address, and phone of official responsible for local program. **Arrangement:** Geographical. **Pages** (approx.): 80. **Frequency:** Not established; first edition October 1977. **Price:** Free. **Send orders to:** Request copies from nearest Housing and Urban Development Department field office.

★2144★
DIRECTORY OF LOUISIANA CITIES, TOWNS AND VILLAGES
Louisiana Department of Transportation and Development
Box 44155
Baton Rouge, LA 70804
Background: Not a directory, but a gazetteer.

★2145★
DIRECTORY OF LOUISIANA MUNICIPAL OFFICIALS
Louisiana Municipal Association
5615 Corporate Boulevard
Baton Rouge, LA 70808
Entries include: Municipality name, Zip code, population, phone, names and titles of all elected officials, parish, and meeting times. **Frequency:** Biennial, January of odd years; frequent supplements. **Price:** $15.00; supplements $10.00 per year.

★2146★
DIRECTORY OF MARYLAND MUNICIPAL OFFICIALS
Maryland Municipal League
76 Maryland Avenue   Phone: (301) 268-5514
Annapolis, MD 21401
Entries include: Municipality name, mailing address, county, phone, meeting dates, names of elected and appointed officials. **Frequency:** Annual. **Price:** $3.00.

★2147★
DIRECTORY OF MARYLAND PLANNING AGENCIES
Maryland Department of State Planning
301 W. Preston Street   Phone: (301) 383-2439
Baltimore, MD 21201
Covers: State, county, local, and regional planning agencies, governmental departments concerned with planning, etc. **Entries include:** Agency name, address, names of commission members and administrative personnel, and summary of current activities. **Arrangement:** Classified by level of government. **Indexes:** County. **Pages** (approx.): 190. **Frequency:** Every three years; latest edition 1979. **Editor:** Allen Miles, Director of Operations. **Price:** Free.

★2148★

DIRECTORY OF MASSACHUSETTS LEGISLATORS AND OTHER ELECTED OFFICIALS

Associated Industries of Massachusetts
4005 Prudential Tower Phone: (617) 262-1180
Boston, MA 02199

Covers: Massachusetts legislators and other elected officials serving on the federal or state levels. **Entries include:** Official's name, photograph, political party, address, and area represented. **Arrangement:** Geographical by political unit. **Pages** (approx.): 50. **Frequency:** Biennial, February of odd years. **Price:** $2.00.

★2149★

DIRECTORY OF MAYORS [New Jersey]

New Jersey Department of Community Affairs
363 W. State Street Phone: (609) 292-6055
Trenton, NJ 08625

Covers: Mayors of towns and townships in New Jersey. **Entries include:** Municipality name, county, name of mayor, address, phone. **Arrangement:** Alphabetical by city name. **Pages** (approx.): 25. **Frequency:** Semiannual, January and July. **Editor:** Russell Marchetta, Public Information Officer. **Price:** Free. **Also includes:** Telephone directory for New Jersey Department of Community Affairs.

★2150★

DIRECTORY OF MEMBERSHIP, COMMITTEES, AND EMPLOYEES OF THE NEBRASKA LEGISLATURE

Clerk
Nebraska Legislature
State Capitol Phone: (402) 471-2271
Lincoln, NE 68509

Entries include: For legislators - Name, home and session address and phone, occupation, committees. For employees - Name, home address, phone. **Pages** (approx.): 50. **Frequency:** Annual, January. **Editor:** Patrick J. O'Donnell, Clerk of the Legislature. **Price:** Free (mailing list is not maintained).

★2151★

DIRECTORY OF MICHIGAN MUNICIPAL OFFICALS

Michigan Municipal League
Box 1487 Phone: (313) 662-3246
Ann Arbor, MI 48106

Covers: Approximately 5,300 elected and major appointed city and village officials in 525 Michigan municipalities. Also lists legislators and selected state and federal offices. **Entries include:** Name of city, address of city hall, phone, population, county location, form of government, names and titles of officials, council meeting date and time. **Arrangement:** Geographical. **Pages** (approx.): 90. **Frequency:** Semiannual, January and July. **Editor:** Helen M. Craft, Office Manager. **Price:** $14.00 per copy.

★2152★

DIRECTORY OF MICHIGAN SENATE AND HOUSE OF REPRESENTATIVES

Michigan Legislature
State Capitol
Lansing, MI 48903

Entries include: Member name, district, home address and phone, legislative address, committee assignments, length of legislative service. **Pages** (approx.): 60. **Frequency:** Usually semiannual. **Price:** Free (mailing list is not maintained). **Other information:** Includes listing of capitol press corps.

★2153★

DIRECTORY OF MILITARY PROCUREMENT PEOPLE [Audiovisual products]

National Audio-Visual Association
3150 Spring Street Phone: (703) 273-7200
Fairfax, VA 22031

Covers: About 900 persons responsible for purchasing audiovisual materials and equipment at military installations in the United States. **Entries include:** Installation name, location, and names, titles, and telephone numbers of the installation's procurement officer, small business specialist, and person in charge of audiovisual purchasing. **Arrangement:** Geographical. **Pages** (approx.): 80. **Frequency:** First edition December 1979. **Price:** $15.00, payment must accompany order.

★2154★

DIRECTORY OF MINNESOTA MUNICIPAL OFFICIALS

League of Minnesota Cities
300 Hanover Building
480 Cedar Street Phone: (612) 222-2861
St. Paul, MN 55101

Covers: Municipal officials in 855 Minnesota cities. **Entries include:** City name, Zip code, county in which located, form of government, population, city hall address, phone number of city hall or city clerk, names and titles of municipal officials, and regular council meeting day. **Arrangement:** Geographical. **Pages** (approx.): 90. **Frequency:** Annual, February. **Editor:** Louise Kuderling, Publications Manager. **Price:** $12.00 (current edition; tentative, 1980 edition).

★2155★

DIRECTORY OF MISSISSIPPI ELECTIVE OFFICIALS

Mississippi Secretary of State
Box 136 Phone: (601) 354-6541
Jackson, MS 39205

Covers: Major state officials, district and county attorneys, legislators, and county governments. **Entries include:** For state officials, attorneys, and legislators - Name, county or district, address. For county governments - County name, county seat, name and personal address of principal elective and appointive officials. **Arrangement:** State officials by office, then alphabetical; county governments alphabetical by county. **Pages** (approx.): 50. **Frequency:** Every four years; latest edition January 1976. **Price:** Free.

Directory of Mississippi Municipal Officials *See* Mississippi Municipal Directory

★2156★

DIRECTORY OF MISSISSIPPI MUNICIPALITIES

Bureau of Government Research
University of Mississippi Phone: (601) 232-7401
University, MS 38677

Covers: More than 280 incorporated municipalities. **Entries include:** Municipality name, county, population, municipal officials and their terms of office, business and hospitals, details of charter, etc. **Pages** (approx.): 175. **Frequency:** Latest edition 1977; no new edition planned. **Price:** $5.00.

★2157★

DIRECTORY OF MONTANA MUNICIPAL OFFICIALS

Montana League of Cities and Towns
1728 Ninth Avenue
Helena, MT 59601

Frequency: Biennial in odd years, with supplements semiannually. **Price:** $6.00, including supplements.

★2158★

DIRECTORY OF MUNICIPAL AND COUNTY OFFICIALS IN COLORADO

Colorado Municipal League
4800 Wadsworth Boulevard Phone: (303) 421-8630
Wheat Ridge, CO 80033

Covers: All incorporated places and counties in Colorado, plus regional planning commissions, congressional delegation, state and federal offices, and councils of governments. **Entries include:** City or county name, address and phone of municipal building and courthouse, names and titles of elected and appointed officials and commission members, populations, meeting times, business hours. **Pages** (approx.): 60. **Frequency:** Annual, August, with year-end supplement. **Advertising accepted.** Circulation 1,500. **Price:** $12.50, payment with order.

★2159★

DIRECTORY OF MUNICIPAL OFFICIALS [Alabama]
Alabama League of Municipalities
535 Adams Avenue
Montgomery, AL 36102
Covers: All incorporated municipalities. **Entries include:** Municipality name, mailing address, phone, population, names of mayor, clerk, and council or city commissioners. **Frequency:** Irregular; new edition expected 1980. **Price:** $10.00, including supplements (current and 1980 editions).

★2160★

DIRECTORY OF MUNICIPAL OFFICIALS [New Hampshire]
New Hampshire Municipal Association
193 N. Main Street   Phone: (603) 224-7447
Concord, NH 03301
Covers: Municipal officials, regional planning commissions, congressional delegations. **Frequency:** Annual, spring. **Price:** $20.00.

★2161★

DIRECTORY OF MUNICIPAL OFFICIALS [South Carolina]
Municipal Association of South Carolina
1213 Lady Street, Suite 200
Columbia, SC 29211
Entries include: Name of municipality, mailing address, population, name and titles of officials, budget, bonded debt, etc. **Frequency:** Annual, January. **Advertising accepted. Price:** $5.00.

★2162★

DIRECTORY OF MUNICIPAL OFFICIALS [South Dakota]
South Dakota Municipal League
214 E. Capitol   Phone: (605) 224-8654
Pierre, SD 57501
Entries include: Municipality name, mailing address, phone, form of government, meeting dates, etc., and names and titles of elected and major appointed officials. **Frequency:** Annual, July. **Price:** $7.00.

★2163★

DIRECTORY OF MUNICIPAL OFFICIALS OF NEW MEXICO
New Mexico Municipal League
Box 846   Phone: (505) 982-5573
Santa Fe, NM 87501
Entries include: Name of municipality, mailing address, phone, office hours, census figures, days of meetings of governing body, names of elected and chief appointed officials. **Pages** (approx.): 160. **Frequency:** Annual, May. **Editor:** William F. Fulginiti, Executive Director. **Price:** $15.00.

★2164★

DIRECTORY OF NEBRASKA MUNICIPAL OFFICIALS
League of Nebraska Municipalities
1335 L Street
Lincoln, NE 68508
Entries include: Municipality name, mailing address, elected and appointed officials, population, meeting times. **Frequency:** Annual, January. **Price:** $11.00.

★2165★

DIRECTORY OF NEW ENGLAND MAYORS
New England Municipal Center
Box L   Phone: (603) 868-5000
Durham, NH 03824
Entries include: City or town name, name of mayor. **Arrangement:** Geographical. **Frequency:** Irregular; latest edition 1979. **Price:** $3.00.

★2166★

**DIRECTORY OF NEW YORK CITY PUBLIC EMPLOYEE
      ORGANIZATIONS**
Office of Collective Bargaining
250 Broadway
New York, NY 10007
Covers: About 60 public employee organizations and unions for New York City. **Entries include:** Organization name, address, phone; name of chief executive; group represented. **Arrangement:** Alphabetical. **Pages** (approx.): 25. **Frequency:** Annual. **Editor:** John Pertusi.

★2167★

DIRECTORY OF NORTH CAROLINA MUNICIPAL OFFICIALS
North Carolina League of Municipalities
Box 3069   Phone: (919) 834-1311
Raleigh, NC 27602
Frequency: Biennial, early in even years. **Price:** $15.00, payment with order (current and 1980 editions).

★2168★

DIRECTORY OF NORTH DAKOTA CITY OFFICIALS
North Dakota League of Cities
Box 2235   Phone: (701) 223-3518
Bismarck, ND 58501
Entries include: Municipality name, mailing address, county, property valuation, names and titles of elected and appointed officials. **Pages** (approx.): 65. **Frequency:** Biennial, summer of even years. **Price:** $6.00.

Directory of Officials, Boards, Institutions [North Dakota] *See*
     Directory of State Officials, Agencies, Boards...North Dakota

★2169★

DIRECTORY OF OKLAHOMA
Oklahoma State Election Board
State Capitol, Room 535   Phone: (405) 521-2391
Oklahoma City, OK 73152
Covers: State departments, boards, commissions, institutions, etc.; legislature; judiciary; members of the state's congressional delegation; federal officials in Oklahoma; county and municipal governments. **Entries include:** Name of department, agency, board, etc., address, phone, and names and titles of officials; biographical sketches are given for some officials. **Arrangement:** By level and unit of government. **Pages** (approx.): 700. **Frequency:** Biennial, summer of odd years. **Editor:** Lee Slater. **Former title:** Directory and Manual of Oklahoma. **Price:** Free (mailing list is not maintained).

★2170★

DIRECTORY OF OKLAHOMA'S CITY AND TOWN OFFICIALS
Oklahoma Municipal League
201 N. E. 23rd Street   Phone: (405) 528-7515
Oklahoma City, OK 73105
Covers: About 560 communities. **Entries include:** Municipality name, mailing address, phone, population, names of elected and appointed officials. **Frequency:** Annual, July. **Price:** $10.00 (current and 1980 editions).

Directory of Organizations and Individuals Professionally Engaged
     in Governmental Research... *See* GRA Directory of
     Organizations...

★2171★

DIRECTORY OF PRIVATE INVESTIGATORS
Security Executive Publishing
1122 Bellwood Avenue   Phone: (312) 544-8813
Bellwood, IL 60104
Covers: About 11,000 persons, primarily private investigators. Includes a section of brief biographies; inclusion in this section required a handling fee of $10.00. **Entries include:** Individual name, address; biographical listings also include business name, address, phone, and brief mention of specialties. **Arrangement:** Geographical.

Pages (approx.): 175. **Frequency:** Annual. **Editor:** Alice Allen, Manager. **Price:** $25.00 (current and 1980 editions).

★2172★
DIRECTORY OF PUBLIC INFORMATION CONTACTS WASHINGTON, D.C.
Bendix Corporation
1911 N. Fort Myer Drive   Phone: (703) 841-1200
Arlington, VA 22209
Covers: Over 1,000 federal government personnel in the Washington, D.C. area; foreign embassies. **Entries include:** Agency name, address, phone; names, titles, room numbers, and phone numbers for key personnel in each agency. **Arrangement:** By agency. **Indexes:** Personal name. **Pages** (approx.): 70. **Editor:** Daniel H. Schurz. **Price:** Not available for public distribution.

★2173★
DIRECTORY OF RECOGNIZED LOCAL GOVERNMENTS
International City Management Association
1140 Connecticut Avenue, N. W.   Phone: (202) 828-3600
Washington, DC 20036
Covers: Local governments recognized by the association as having professional management. **Entries include:** Name of municipality, name of principal executive, population, legal basis, form, year of recognition. **Arrangement:** Geographical. **Pages** (approx.): 100. **Frequency:** Annual, March. **Former title:** Municipal Management Directory. **Price:** $25.00.

Directory of Regional Councils *See* **National Association of Regional Councils—Directory** [City, town, and county government associations]

★2174★
DIRECTORY OF SELECTED FEDERAL PROGRAM OFFICES
Association of American Colleges
1818 R Street, N. W.
Washington, DC 20009
Covers: Federal agencies of interest to university and college personnel. **Entries include:** Agency name, address, phone, name of contact, services offered or programs responsible for. **Pages** (approx.): 50. **Frequency:** Irregular; latest edition 1977. **Price:** $10.00, payment must accompany order.

★2175★
DIRECTORY OF SHERIFFS OF THE UNITED STATES
National Sheriffs' Association
1250 Connecticut Avenue   Phone: (202) 872-0422
Washington, DC 20036
Covers: 3,100 sheriffs and others in criminal justice work on federal, state, or county level, and some local chiefs of police who are members. **Entries include:** Name, title, agency or city affiliation, address. **Arrangement:** Geographical. **Indexes:** Alphabetical. **Pages** (approx.): 55. **Frequency:** Annual, April. **Editor:** Ferris E. Lucas. **Price:** $250.00 (current and 1980 editions).

★2176★
DIRECTORY OF SOUTH DAKOTA COUNTY OFFICIALS
South Dakota Association of County Commissioners
214 E. Capitol
Pierre, SD 57501
Entries include: County name, mailing address, phone, names and titles of principal officials. **Arrangement:** By county. **Pages** (approx.): 50. **Frequency:** Annual, January. **Price:** $3.00.

★2177★
DIRECTORY OF STAFF ASSISTANTS TO THE GOVERNORS
National Governors' Association
Hall of the States
444 N. Capitol Street   Phone: (202) 624-5300
Washington, DC 20001
Entries include: Name of governor; addresses and phone numbers of governor's main, district, and Washington offices; titles and names of staff assistants. **Arrangement:** Geographical. **Pages** (approx.): 35. **Frequency:** Semiannual. **Price:** $3.00 per issue (current and 1980 editions).

★2178★
DIRECTORY OF STATE AGENCIES [New York]
New York Secretary of State
162 Washington Avenue   Phone: (518) 474-6210
Albany, NY 12231
Entries include: Name of agency, phone, description of functions, names of personnel. **Frequency:** Annual. **Editor:** Charlotte Smart. **Former title:** Directory of State and County Officials (1975). **Price:** Free; distribution limited.

Directory of State, County....Officials Supplement to Guide to Government in Hawaii *See* **Guide to Government in Hawaii— Directory...**

★2179★
DIRECTORY OF STATE MERIT SYSTEMS
Office of Intergovernmental Personnel Programs
Office of Personnel Management
Washington, DC 20415
Covers: Civil service or other merit systems for employment in all states. **Entries include:** Agency name, address, phone, name of principal executive, agencies served. **Arrangement:** Geographical. **Pages** (approx.): 25. **Frequency:** Irregular; previous edition August 1978; latest edition October 1979. **Editor:** Teresa A. King. **Price:** Free.

★2180★
DIRECTORY OF STATE OFFICES—WEST VIRGINIA
West Virginia House of Delegates
State Capitol   Phone: (304) 348-2239
Charleston, WV 25305
Covers: State departments and agencies, Supreme Court of Appeals, principal legislative officers and employees. **Entries include:** Name of department, branch, etc., name of head, address, phone. **Arrangement:** Alphabetical. **Frequency:** Biennial, August of odd years. **Price:** Free (mailing list is not maintained).

★2181★
DIRECTORY OF STATE OFFICIALS [Alaska]
Alaska Legislative Affairs Agency
State Capitol
Pouch Y   Phone: (907) 465-3101
Juneau, AK 99811
Covers: Officials of state departments and agencies; the judiciary, including supreme, superior, and district courts; legislators; members of the congressional delegation. **Entries include:** Name of department, etc., address, phone, names of officials with home and mailing addresses; legislators' listings include committee assignments. **Arrangement:** By department or agency. **Pages** (approx.): 40. **Frequency:** Semiannual, January and August. **Price:** Free.

★2182★
DIRECTORY OF STATE OFFICIALS [Food and drug enforcement]
Division of Federal-State Relations
Food and Drug Administration
5600 Fishers Lane   Phone: (301) 443-6200
Rockville, MD 20857
Covers: Officials of state health and agriculture departments, boards of pharmacy, and other state departments charged with enforcement of food, drug, device, feed, and cosmetic laws. **Entries include:** Agency name; address; units within the agency; name, title, and phone of each unit's chief executive; areas of responsibility for the unit. **Arrangement:** Geographical. **Frequency:** Approximately annual. **Price:** Free; distribution limited.

★2183★

DIRECTORY OF STATE OFFICIALS, AGENCIES, BOARDS AND INSTITUTIONS OF THE STATE OF NORTH DAKOTA
North Dakota State Library
State Capitol   Phone: (701) 224-2492
Bismarck, ND 58505
Entries include: Name of department, agency, office, etc.; city; name of elected incumbent or appointed official, title, and city of residence. **Arrangement:** By level and unit of government. **Pages** (approx.): 25. **Frequency:** Biennial, odd years. **Editor:** Richard J. Wolfert. **Price:** Free.

★2184★

DIRECTORY OF STATE SERVICES [New Hampshire]
Office of Legislative Services
Speaker of the House of Representatives
New Hampshire General Court
State House, Room 318   Phone: (603) 271-3661
Concord, NH 03301
Covers: Boards, commissions, and agencies of New Hampshire. **Entries include:** Name, address, phone, description of services offered, publications. **Arrangement:** Alphabetical by three-letter acronym. **Pages** (approx.): 360. **Frequency:** Biennial, even years. **Editors:** Nina C. Gardner, Phillip M. Odom, and Laurie Sue Herman. **Price:** $10.00, plus $1.50 shipping.

★2185★

DIRECTORY OF TENNESSEE COUNTY OFFICIALS
County Technical Assistance Service
University of Tennessee
Capitol Hill Building   Phone: (615) 242-0358
Nashville, TN 37219
Covers: County officials, district attorney generals, circuit judges, county commissioners; County Technical Assistance staff and field officers; County Official's Association officers; and state and federal agencies in Tennessee. **Entries include:** For county officals - Name and office, phone; address given for county commissioner. Similar information given for other listings. **Arrangement:** County officials are by county; others are by activity. **Pages** (approx.): 125. **Frequency:** Annual, September. **Price:** $10.00.

★2186★

DIRECTORY OF TENNESSEE MUNICIPAL OFFICIALS
Municipal Technical Advisory Service
1000 White Avenue
University of Tennessee   Phone: (615) 974-5301
Knoxville, TN 37916
Covers: More than 325 incorporated cities in Tennessee; includes listings for government-related state agencies and federal agencies and development districts. **Entries include:** City name, address, phone, names of officials, population figures, name of county. **Arrangement:** Geographical. **Pages** (approx.): 110. **Frequency:** Annual, September. **Price:** $10.00.

★2187★

DIRECTORY OF TEXAS CITY OFFICIALS
Texas Municipal League
1020 Southwest Tower
Austin, TX 78701
Covers: More than 1,000 municipalities. **Entries include:** Municipality name, mailing address, phone, council meeting dates, population, and names and titles of all elected and appointed officials. **Frequency:** Annual, summer; changes reported in "Texas Town and City Magazine." **Price:** $15.00, payment with order.

★2188★

DIRECTORY OF THE FORMER MEMBERS OF CONGRESS
Former Members of Congress
121 Second Street, N. E.   Phone: (202) 543-1666
Washington, DC 20002
Covers: About 560 congressional alumni. **Entries include:** Name,

name of spouse, address, phone; political party, state represented, years served in House or Senate, number of first Congress. **Arrangement:** Alphabetical. **Indexes:** Geographical. **Pages** (approx.): 60. **Frequency:** Annual, May. **Editor:** Jed Johnson, Jr., Executive Director. **Price:** Available to members and Congress only.

★2189★

DIRECTORY OF THE STATE AND COUNTY OFFICIALS OF NORTH CAROLINA
North Carolina Secretary of State
101 Administration Building
116 W. Jones Street   Phone: (919) 733-7355
Raleigh, NC 27611
Covers: State departments, boards, commissions, institutions, etc.; legislature; judiciary; local-regional planning districts; members of the state's congressional delegation; county governments. **Entries include:** Name of department, board, etc., address, phone, and names and titles for principal officials; legislators' listings include party, district, occupation. **Arrangement:** By level and unit of government. **Pages** (approx.): 150. **Frequency:** Annual, March. **Editor:** John L. Cheney, Jr. **Price:** Free.

★2190★

DIRECTORY OF UNITED STATES PROBATION OFFICERS
Probation Division
Administrative Office of the United States Courts
United States Supreme Court Building
One First Street, N. E.   Phone: (202) 633-6226
Washington, DC 20544
Number of listings: 1,700. **Entries include:** Name, address, phone. **Arrangement:** By district. **Pages** (approx.): 65. **Frequency:** Irregular; previous edition May 1978; latest edition August 1979. **Price:** Free.

★2191★

DIRECTORY OF UTAH LOCAL OFFICIALS
Utah League of Cities and Towns
10 W. Broadway, Suite 305   Phone: (801) 328-1601
Salt Lake City, UT 84101
Entries include: Municipality name, Zip code, population, city hall phone, names and titles of elected and appointed officials. **Pages** (approx.): 75. **Frequency:** Biennial, April of even years. **Advertising accepted. Price:** $7.50.

★2192★

DIRECTORY OF VIRGINIA GOVERNMENTAL OFFICIALS
Virginia Municipal League
1011 E. Main Street   Phone: (804) 649-8471
Richmond, VA 23219
Covers: About 225 Virginia towns, cities, and counties. **Entries include:** City, town, or county name, mailing address, population, phone, names of elected and principal appointed officials. **Arrangement:** Alphabetical within separate sections for cities, towns, and counties. **Pages** (approx.): 135. **Frequency:** Biennial, November of even years. **Editor:** Richard L. DeCair, Executive Director. **Price:** $12.00 (current edition); $15.00 (1980 edition).

Directory of Washington Representatives of American
    Associations and Industry *See* Washington Representatives:
    Lobbyists, Consultants...

★2193★

DIRECTORY OF WOMEN LAW GRADUATES AND ATTORNEYS IN THE U.S.A.
Ford Associates, Inc.
824 E. Seventh Street   Phone: (219) 868-7611
Auburn, IN 46706
Number of listings: 15,000. **Entries include:** Name and home address only. **Arrangement:** Geographical. **Pages** (approx.): 500. **Frequency:** Irregular; latest edition 1977. **Editor:** Lee Ellen Ford. **Former title:** Directory of Women Attorneys in the United States. **Price:** $46.50 (five volumes).

★2194★
DISTRICT OF COLUMBIA BAR—LAWYER DIRECTORY
District of Columbia Bar
1426 H Street, N. W., Suite 840   Phone: (202) 638-4799
Washington, DC 20005
Covers: About 900 of the estimated 22,000 lawyers in the capital who serve primarily individuals and small businesses. Also includes a number of lawyers who serve the national public in highly specialized capacities, such as representing victims of major airline disasters, victims of poisonous chemicals, or universities and others who wish to secure federal research grants. Attorneys paid $10 each for listings. **Entries include:** Name, address, phone, fields of special interest or competency, fees for common legal procedures. **Arrangement:** By legal specialty. **Indexes:** Alphabetical. **Pages** (approx.): 200. **Frequency:** Annual, summer. **Price:** $2.00.

★2195★
DOE TELEPHONE DIRECTORY
Directorate of Administration
Energy Department
Washington, DC 20585
Covers: Employees in Energy Department offices in Washington; includes Federal Regulatory Energy Commission in separate section. **Entries include:** Name, phone, room number, mail station, building. **Arrangement:** Alphabetical. **Pages** (approx.): 180. **Frequency:** Annual, November. **Price:** $4.75 (S/N 061-000-00194-8). **Send orders to:** Government Printing Office, Washington, DC 20402.

Doing Business Abroad *See* **Joyner's Guide to Official Washington**

Election Directory *See* **Directory of Election Officials**

Election Index *See* **Congressional Staff Directory Election Index**

★2196★
ELECTIVE AND APPOINTIVE STATE OFFICERS [Michigan]
General Services Section
Michigan Department of Management and Budget
7461 Crowner Drive   Phone: (517) 322-1897
Lansing, MI 48913
Entries include: Department or agency name, names and titles of elective and appointive officials. **Pages** (approx.): 125. **Frequency:** Biennial, spring of odd years. **Price:** Free.

★2197★
EMERGENCY RADIO SERVICE STATION DIRECTORIES
CRB Research
Box 56   Phone: (516) 499-1200
Commack, NY 11725
Covers: Over 100,000 two-way radio services used by fire, police, emergency, and other public agencies. Separate volumes for: STATES - Florida, Illinois, Connecticut, Indiana, Maryland and the District of Columbia, Massachusetts, Michigan, Ohio, and Texas. AREAS AND REGIONS - New England (but New Hampshire, Maine, Rhode Island, and Vermont only); New York/New Jersey metropolitan area; Pennsylvania, except Philadelphia; Philadelphia and southern New Jersey and northern Delaware; Southern California; Pittsburgh/ Allegheny county; Cleveland and Cuyahoga and Lake counties; San Francisco Bay area; Milwaukee area; Minneapolis/St. Paul area; Suffolk county, New York, area; New York State except metropolitan area; Buffalo, New York, and Erie and Niagara counties. OTHER AREAS - Areas not covered in other volumes are covered in a "national" edition of three volumes, state desired to be specified in ordering. NON-EMERGENCY SERVICES - There are also separate VHF aeronautical (airport towers, etc.) and primary VHF railroad channel volumes, and a volume for federal government frequencies. **Entries include:** Licensee (user) name, location, frequency. **Frequency:** Irregular; varies for individual editions. **Editor:** Russ R. Walters. **Price:** $3.95 (except "Registry of U.S. Government Frequencies," $4.95).

★2198★
EMPIRE STATE REPORT—NEW YORK LEGISLATIVE COMMITTEES REFERENCE ISSUE
New York State Legislative Institute
17 Lexington Avenue
New York, NY 10010
Publication includes: Listing standing committee memberships for the following session. **Arrangement:** Alphabetical. **Frequency:** Biennial, January-February of odd years. **Editor:** Neil Fabricant. **Advertising accepted.** Circulation 5,000. **Former title:** Empire State Report - New York Legislature Reference Issue. **Price:** $3.00.

Empire State Report—New York Legislature Reference Issue *See* **Empire State Report—New York Legislative Committees Reference Issue**

★2199★
EMPLOYEES OF DIPLOMATIC MISSIONS (White List) [Washington, D.C.]
State Department
2201 C Street, N. W.   Phone: (202) 655-4000
Washington, DC 20520
Covers: Administrative, clerical, personal service, and other employees of diplomatic missions in the Washington area who are not listed in the Department's "Diplomatic List" (see separate listing). **Entries include:** Name, occupation or assignment, street address; nationality is indicated if not same as employing country. **Arrangement:** Alphabetical within country listings. **Pages** (approx.): 90. **Frequency:** Quarterly. **Price:** $7.00 per year; $1.80 per copy (S/N 044-000-80004-7; ISSN 0501-9664). **Send orders to:** Government Printing Office, Washington, DC 20402.

★2200★
ENCYCLOPEDIA OF SELECTED FEDERAL AND STATE AUTHORIZATIONS FOR SERVICES AND BENEFITS IN MASSACHUSETTS
Massachusetts Bureau of Systems Development
Executive Office for Administration and Finance
312 State House
Beacon Street   Phone: (617) 727-2050
Boston, MA 02133
Covers: Over 50 federal and state programs of assistance to Massachusetts, including social security, education, transportation, housing, and vocational rehabilitation. **Entries include:** Name of program; agency name, address, and name of contact; description of program eligibility requirements, services, benefits; information concerning regulations and financial status. **Arrangement:** Classified by type of program ("direct federal..."). **Pages** (approx.): 285. **Frequency:** Irregular; latest edition 1976; new edition expected late 1979. **Editor:** Jonathan P. A. Leopold, Jr. **Price:** $10.00.

★2201★
ENCYCLOPEDIA OF U.S. GOVERNMENT BENEFITS
William H. Wise and Company, Inc.
336 Mountain Road   Phone: (201) 864-5200
Union City, NJ 07087
Covers: Federal government agencies providing benefits such as scholarships, social security, veteran's benefits, and social services. **Entries include:** Agency name, address, contact, description of benefit or services and eligibility requirements. **Arrangement:** By type of benefit. **Pages** (approx.): 1,020. **Frequency:** Irregular; latest edition 1978; new edition expected April 1980. **Editors:** Roy A. Grishan and Paul D. McConaughty. **Price:** $14.95, plus $1.50 shipping.

★2202★

ENERGY CONSERVATION STANDARDS FOR BUILDINGS: STATUS
    OF STATES' REGULATORY ACTIVITIES
National Institute of Building Sciences
1730 Pennsylvania Avenue, N. W., Suite
42
Washington, DC 20006
Publication includes: List of state executive offices with
responsibilities for energy conservation and building standards
administration and enforcement. **Entries include:** Name of office,
address, phone. **Arrangement:** Geographical. **Pages** (approx.): 30.
Frequency: Irregular; latest edition February 1978. **Price:** May be
available without charge from publishing agency; also issued as NTIS
PB 279-936. **Send orders to:** National Technical Information Service,
Springfield, VA 22161.

Energy Department Telephone Directory *See* **DOE Telephone
    Directory**

★2203★

ENVIRONMENTAL PROGRAM ADMINISTRATORS
Office of Regional Intergovernmental Operations
Environmental Protection Agency
Washington, DC 20460
Covers: State officials responsible for water quality, water supply, air
quality, solid and industrial waste disposal, noise control, and pesticide
control; radiation and analytical laboratory directors at the state level;
interstate agencies with environmental program concerns; and
regional offices of the Environmental Protection Agency. **Entries
include:** Agency name, name and title of director, address, phone.
Arrangement: By federal region within area of concern or level.
Pages (approx.): 65. **Frequency:** Annual.

Facts and Issues *See* **Political Directory: Atlanta and Fulton
    County [Georgia]**

★2204★

FEDERAL ADVISORY COMMITTEES
Subcommittee on Reports, Accounting, and Management
Committee on Governmental Affairs
U.S. Senate
3308 Dirksen Senate Office Building
Washington, DC 20510
Covers: About 1,200 federal advisory committees, panels,
commissions, boards, councils and other such organizations with
membership totalling over 25,000 persons. **Entries include:** For each
committee - Name, date and authority for its creation, termination
date or date of report, functions, reports submitted, whether ad hoc
or continuing, dates of meetings, names and occupations of current
members, cost of operation. **Arrangement:** Alphabetical (by name of
committee). **Indexes:** Occupation affiliation (with member name,
committee code); personal name (with affiliation, committee code);
committee code (with member name, affiliation); and committee code
(then affiliation); all indexes also include state of residence for each
member. **Pages** (approx.): 5,000. **Frequency:** Irregular; latest edition
1977. **Price:** "Report," $24.00 (available as 2-roll set of 16mm
microfilm only; Microcopy No. A-1199-17 and A-1199-18); paper
indexes, $13.00 (GPO S/N 052-070-04756-9; December 1978
edition). **Send orders to:** For "Report" - Publication Sales Branch,
National Archives and Records Service, General Services
Administration, Washington, DC 20408. For indexes - Goverment
Printing Office, Washington, DC 20402.

★2205★

FEDERAL COMMUNICATIONS BAR ASSOCIATION DIRECTORY
Federal Communications Bar Association
Box 57109
Washington, DC 20037
Covers: About 1,000 lawyer members. **Entries include:** Name, office
address, phone. **Arrangement:** Alphabetical. **Pages** (approx.): 70.
Frequency: Annual, January. **Editor:** Carolyn C. Hill, Assistant

Secretary. **Price:** $3.50.

★2206★

FEDERAL COURT DIRECTORY
Want Publishing Company
Box 19510   Phone: (202) 783-1887
Washington, DC 20036
Covers: All federal court judges and clerks of court, and United States
attorneys and magistrates. **Entries include:** Court designation and
places where court is held; entries for judges show name, phone, place
from which appointed, and date appointed; entries for clerks show
name, phone, address. **Arrangement:** By district. **Pages** (approx.):
90. **Frequency:** Annual, March. **Price:** $6.50.

★2207★

FEDERAL EMPLOYMENT INFORMATION DIRECTORY [Criminal
    justice]
Institute of Contemporary Corrections and Behavioral Sciences
Sam Houston State University   Phone: (713) 295-6211
Huntsville, TX 77341
Covers: Federal agencies employing law enforcement personnel.
Entries include: Agency name, application address and procedures,
description of positions, pay scales, qualifications sought,
opportunities; does not include specific current openings.
Arrangement: By major government department or agency. **Pages**
(approx.): 185. **Frequency:** Irregular; previous edition May 1978;
latest edition October 1979. **Editors:** Daniel J. Miller and Charles R.
Keenan. **Price:** $5.00 (current edition; tentative, 1980 edition),
payment with order. **Other information:** Current openings in law
enforcement are described in the Institute's "National Employment
Listing Service for the Criminal Justice System" (see separate entry).

★2208★

FEDERAL ENERGY INFORMATION SOURCES AND DATA BASES
Noyes Data Corporation
Mill Road & Grand Avenue   Phone: (201) 391-8484
Park Ridge, NJ 07656
Covers: Federal departments, agencies, and commissions with
information and data bases available to the public dealing with energy.
Entries include: Agency, department, or commission name, address,
area of emphasis, services, publications. **Arrangement:** By type of
agency (cabinet, administrative, congressional). **Indexes:** Subject.
Pages (approx.): 115. **Frequency:** Latest edition December 1979.
Editor: Carolyn C. Bloch. **Price:** $24.00.

★2209★

FEDERAL EXECUTIVE TELEPHONE DIRECTORY
Carroll Publishing Company
1058 Thomas Jefferson Street, N. W.   Phone: (202) 333-8620
Washington, DC 20007
Covers: About 30,000 executive managers in federal government
offices, nationwide. **Entries include:** Alphabetical section includes
official's name, phone, and line reference to organization section.
Organization section includes agency name and address, with titles,
names, and phone numbers of incumbents. **Indexes:** Keyword.
Frequency: Bimonthly. **Price:** $96.00 per year.

★2210★

FEDERAL FAST FINDER: A KEY WORD TELEPHONE DIRECTORY TO
    THE FEDERAL GOVERNMENT
Washington Researchers
918 16th Street, N. W.   Phone: (202) 828-4800
Washington, DC 20006
Covers: About 1,000 principal departments, agencies, etc., of the
federal government, with their telephone numbers. Separate lists give
addresses for about 90 major offices and phone numbers for about
50 "hotlines" which provide recorded messages reporting daily news
in specific agencies or lines of business. **Arrangement:** By key word
(many offices are listed under more than one heading). **Pages**
(approx.): 50. **Frequency:** Annual. **Editor:** Matthew J. Lesko. **Price:**
$5.00, postpaid, payment with order; $6.50, billed.

★2211★
FEDERAL INFORMATION CENTERS
Office of the Administrator
General Services Administration
18th and F Streets   Phone: (202) 566-1937
Washington, DC 20405
Covers: The 38 centers in metropolitan areas nationwide maintained
by the General Services Administration to assist the public in securing
specific answers to questions involving federal government offices
and services; toll-free lines connect an additional 47 cities to the
nearest center. **Entries include:** Center name, address, phone.
Arrangement: Geographical. **Frequency:** Irregular; latest edition
1979. **Price:** Free. **Send orders to:** Consumer Information Center,
Pueblo, CO 81009.

★2212★
FEDERAL JOB DIRECTORY
Kent-Harbridge Publishing Inc.
1619 Traske Road
Encinitas, CA 92024
Covers: Occupations within the major civil service system career
fields (accounting, law, transportation, engineering, etc.). **Entries
include:** Description of the occupation, qualifications required, federal
agencies which use the skill and how and where to apply, information
on how to prepare the application, and additional steps to be taken
beyond completing the application. **Arrangement:** By occupation.
Frequency: Annual, spring. **Price:** $7.50. (Not verified)

★2213★
FEDERAL JOB INFORMATION CENTERS DIRECTORY
Office of Personnel Management
Box 52
Washington, DC 20044
Covers: About 70 OPM offices able to supply information concerning
federal employment. **Entries include:** Office address, phone.
Arrangement: Geographical. **Frequency:** Irregular; latest edition
September 1979. **Price:** Single copies free.

Federal Job Letter *See* Federal Jobs

★2214★
FEDERAL JOBS
Federal Systems, Inc.
Box 2280   Phone: (703) 471-1417
Reston, VA 22090
Covers: Over 2,000 specific job openings in the federal government
(and some non-federal jobs) in each issue. **Entries include:** Position
name, title, and General Schedule (GS) grade, closing date for
applications, announcement number, application address, phone, and
name of contact. **Arrangement:** By federal department or agency.
Pages (approx.): 35. **Frequency:** Every two weeks. **Editor:** Ann L.
Tedesco. **Advertising accepted. Price:** $70.00 per year; $18.00
for three months. **Other information:** Variant title, "Federal Job
Letter." Each issue includes listings of recorded job information for
the District of Columbia area available by telephone.

★2215★
FEDERAL ORGANIZATION SERVICE
Carroll Publishing Company
1058 Thomas Jefferson Street, N. W.   Phone: (202) 333-8620
Washington, DC 20007
Covers: In organization chart form, personnel in 1,600 civil and 900
military departments, bureaus, agencies. Volume 1 (135 charts) deals
with civil departments and Volume 2 (95 charts) the military. (Judicial
branch not included.) **Entries include:** Name of government agency;
names, titles, room numbers, addresses, and phone numbers for key
personnel. **Arrangement:** By department or agency. **Frequency:**
Current set of charts delivered upon subscription; updated regularly
thereafter. **Price:** Volume 1, $225.00 per year; Volume 2, $350.00
per year; both volumes, $500.00 per year.

★2216★
FEDERAL REGULATORY DIRECTORY
Congressional Quarterly, Inc.
1414 22nd Street, N. W.   Phone: (202) 296-6800
Washington, DC 20037
Covers: About 15 major federal regulatory agencies and about 65
smaller and less important ones. **Entries include:** For major agencies -
Agency name, address, description of responsibilities, list of key
contacts and phone numbers, breakdown of divisions and offices with
names of key officials and their phone numbers, organization chart,
information sources within the agency, and regional offices. For other
agencies - Same general information but less detail. **Indexes:**
Combined subject-agency. **Pages** (approx.): 800. **Frequency:** Annual,
July; first edition 1979. **Editor:** Robert E. Healy. **Price:** $25.00,
postpaid, payment with order; $26.50, billed. **Other information:**
Information provided on both major and minor agencies is
substantially more than is found in "United States Government
Manual."

★2217★
**FEDERAL RESEARCH SERVICE REPORT [Federal government job
openings]**
Federal Research Service, Inc.
Box 1059   Phone: (703) 281-0200
Vienna, VA 22180
Covers: About 3,000 current civil service vacancies in the United
States and overseas. **Entries include:** Position title, location, series
and grade, announcement number, closing date, application address.
Arrangement: Classified by federal agency. **Pages** (approx.): 55.
Frequency: Biweekly, Wednesday. **Editor:** J. A. German, President.
Price: $4.00 per copy; $21.00, 6 issues; $40.00, 12 issues;
$78.00, 26 issues.

Federal, State, and County Officials [Vermont] *See* Civil
Government, State of Vermont—Federal, State, and County
Officials

★2218★
FEDERAL YELLOW BOOK
Washington Monitor, Inc.
499 National Press Building   Phone: (202) 347-7757
Washington, DC 20045
Covers: White House, Executive Office of the President, and
departments and agencies of Executive Branch Nationwide, plus
25,000 of their personnel. **Entries include:** Department, office,
branch, etc., name and address, and names and titles of principal
personnel, with their room numbers and direct dial phone numbers.
Arrangement: By department or agency. **Pages** (approx.): 500.
Frequency: Up-to-date looseleaf edition furnished at time of
subscription; publisher promises two full update cycles yearly. **Editor:**
Teri Calabrese. **Price:** $95.00 per year.

★2219★
**FIRE MARSHALS ASSOCIATION OF NORTH AMERICA—
MEMBERSHIP YEARBOOK**
Fire Marshals Association of North America
1800 M Street, N. W., Suite 570 South   Phone: (202) 466-3650
Washington, DC 20036
Covers: About 1,200 municipal, county, state and provincial fire
marshals and fire prevention bureau officials. **Entries include:** Name,
address. **Arrangement:** Geographical. **Frequency:** Biennial, even
years. **Editor:** Robert B. Smith, Executive Secretary. **Price:** Available
to members only.

Fitzgerald's Legislative Manual *See* Manual of the Legislature of
New Jersey

★2220★
FOREIGN CONSULAR OFFICES IN THE UNITED STATES
State Department
2201 C Street, N. W.   Phone: (202) 655-4000
Washington, DC 20520
Entries include: Name of country, addresses of consulates, phone numbers, names of consuls and other personnel, jurisdictions. **Arrangement:** By country. **Pages** (approx.): 100. **Frequency:** Annual, fall. **Price:** $2.10 (S/N 044-000-01253-7; ISSN 0071-7320). **Send orders to:** Government Printing Office, Washington, DC 20402.

★2221★
FOREIGN GOVERNMENT OFFICES IN CALIFORNIA: A DIRECTORY
California Institute of Public Affairs
226 W. Foothill Boulevard   Phone: (714) 624-5212
Claremont, CA 91711
Covers: 255 offices of foreign governments (consulates, trade and tourism offices, and others) located in California. **Entries include:** Name of consulate or office; address; phone; and in many cases, descriptions of activities. **Pages** (approx.): 50. **Frequency:** Not established; first edition 1978. **Price:** $7.50.

★2222★
FOREIGN SERVICE LIST [State Department]
State Department
Washington, DC 20520
Other information: Publication discontinued in 1976; ''...the need to protect lives of Foreign Service personnel overseas was the overriding consideration in its elimination.''

★2223★
FORENSIC SERVICES DIRECTORY: THE NATIONAL REGISTER OF FORENSIC EXPERTS, LITIGATION CONSULTANTS & LEGAL SUPPORT SPECIALISTS
National Forensic Center
6 Ashburn Place   Phone: (201) 797-4343
Fair Lawn, NJ 07410
Covers: About 3,500 individuals willing to serve as expert witnesses or consultants during litigation. **Entries include:** Name, address, phone, degrees, affiliation, professional license (if any), specialties; many listings include biographical data. **Arrangement:** By consulting field or specialty (aviation, chemistry, testing laboratories). **Frequency:** First edition November 1979; new edition expected 1981. **Editor:** Betty Lipscher. **Advertising accepted. Price:** $47.50, plus $2.00 shipping. **Other information:** Cited in prepublication promotion as, ''National Directory of Forensic Experts.''

★2224★
FORWARDERS LIST OF ATTORNEYS
Forwarders List Company, Inc.
636 Equitable Building   Phone: (301) 837-4611
Baltimore, MD 21202
Arrangement: Geographical. **Frequency:** Annual. **Price:** Apply. **Other information:** A commercial law list. See separate listing, ''Law Lists.''

★2225★
GENERAL BAR
General Bar, Inc.
Bar Building
36 W. 44th Street   Phone: (212) 682-3695
New York, NY 10036
Arrangement: Geographical. **Frequency:** Annual. **Price:** Apply. **Other information:** A commercial law list. See separate listing, ''Law Lists.''

★2226★
GENERAL SERVICES ADMINISTRATION—TELEPHONE DIRECTORY
Automated Data and Telecommunications Service
General Services Administration
Washington, DC 20405
Covers: General Services Administration employees in District of Columbia and surrounding Region 3 (Delaware, Maryland,

Pennsylvania, Virginia, West Virginia), and regional offices and officials nationwide. Separate classified directory for principal officials in Washington. **Entries include:** Name, phone, building and room number, correspondence symbol. **Arrangement:** Alphabetical. **Pages** (approx.): 115. **Frequency:** Latest edition June 1979. **Price:** $4.00 (S/N 022-001-00328-2). **Send orders to:** Government Printing Office, Washington, DC 20402.

★2227★
GEORGIA LEGAL DIRECTORY
Legal Directories Publishing Company
8350 Central Expressway   Phone: (214) 692-5825
Dallas, TX 75206
Frequency: Latest edition 1978. **Price:** $9.00. **Other information:** Content, arrangement, etc., same as ''Alabama Legal Directory;'' see separate listing. (See also separate listing, ''Law Lists.'')

★2228★
GEORGIA OFFICIAL AND STATISTICAL REGISTER
Georgia Secretary of State
Archives and Records Building
330 Capitol Avenue, S.W.   Phone: (404) 656-2370
Atlanta, GA 30334
Publication includes: State departments and agencies; legislators; county governments; newspapers. **Entries include:** Department and agency listings include unit name, address, executives' names, personal and business addresses, party, position or title. Newspaper listings include name, address, name of editor. County government listings include elected or appointed officials, name of county seat, mailing address, population. **Arrangement:** By department or agency. **Indexes:** Agency-personal name. **Pages** (approx.): 2,100. **Frequency:** Biennial, summer of odd years; 1977-78 is latest edition as of December 1979. **Editor:** Marian B. Holmes. **Price:** $54.44, plus $1.91 shipping. **Also includes:** Election data, county historical background.

★2229★
GEORGIA OFFICIAL DIRECTORY OF STATE AND COUNTY OFFICERS
Georgia Secretary of State
State Capitol   Phone: (404) 656-2881
Atlanta, GA 30334
Covers: State departments and agencies; state, circuit, and county courts; county officials and boards; legislators. **Entries include:** Name of agency, department, board, etc., officials and their titles; most listings include mailing addresses. **Pages** (approx.): 75. **Frequency:** Annual, fall. **Price:** Free.

★2230★
GLOBAL AUTOVON TELEPHONE DIRECTORY (DEFENSE COMMUNICATIONS DIRECTORY)
Directory Management Office
Defense Communication Agency
Defense Department
Washington, DC 20305
Covers: Defense installations, worldwide, and some non-DOD agencies and installations. **Entries include:** Name of office or installation, phone, data transmission number. **Arrangement:** Geographical and departmental; same data in each arrangement. **Pages** (approx.): 100. **Frequency:** Three times yearly. **Price:** $2.75 per issue; $8.25 per year. **Send orders to:** Government Printing Office, Washington, DC 20402.

★2231★
GOVERNMENT OF THE CITY OF CHICAGO: A GUIDE TO ITS STRUCTURE AND FUNCTION, WITH A DIRECTORY OF OFFICERS
Chicago Municipal Reference Library
121 N. LaSalle Street, Room 1004   Phone: (312) 744-4992
Chicago, IL 60602
Covers: 68 departments and agencies. **Entries include:** Name of

office, office address, description of functions, and name and title of agency or department head. **Arrangement:** Alphabetical by name of agency or department. **Pages** (approx.): 30. **Frequency:** Irregular; latest edition 1978. **Editor:** Judith E. Purcell. **Price:** 50¢, payment with order. **Also includes:** List of currently serving aldermen, city government organization chart, ward map, and selected bibliography.

★2232★
GOVERNMENTAL GUIDE [Various states]
Governmental Guides, Inc.
Drawer 299   Phone: (615) 868-1636
Madison, TN 37115
Covers: State and city elected and appointed officials; legislators; judicial officials; political party committee members, state representatives to Congress, and federal judges, attorneys, and other federal officials in the state. Also includes newspapers, colleges, and universitites, etc. Individual editions for Alabama, Florida, Georgia, Louisiana, North Carolina, Tennessee, Texas. There is also a national edition, which covers Congress, cabinet departments, independent agencies, federal courts, with brief coverage of state officials. **Entries include:** Generally, agency name, address, name of one official, listings for major departments and cities include additional personnel. **Frequency:** Annual, summer. **Editor:** Mary Etta Tomlinson. **Price:** State and national editions each $6.85, postpaid, payment with order.

★2233★
GRA DIRECTORY OF ORGANIZATIONS AND INDIVIDUALS PROFESSIONALLY ENGAGED IN GOVERNMENTAL RESEARCH
Governmental Research Association
Box 387
Ocean Gate, NJ 08740
Covers: Agencies, institutions, organizations, and individuals interested in improving the operations of government and the efficiency of public services. Includes state and local taxpayer and tax reform associations, colleges with governmental research divisions or graduate curricula in public administration, reference libraries, etc. **Entries include:** For agencies - Founding date, address, phone, names of executive officer and professional research personnel. For individuals - Name, address, phone, occupation, and firm. **Arrangement:** State and local agencies and organizations are geographical, national associations and indiviudals are alphabetical. **Indexes:** Organization, individual. **Pages** (approx.): 70. **Frequency:** Biennial, spring of even years. **Editor:** Sandra J. Leibrich. **Price:** $20.00 (current and 1980 editions).

Graduate Programs in Public Affairs and Public Administration *See* **Programs in Public Affairs and Public Administration**

★2234★
GUIDE TO GOVERNMENT IN HAWAII—DIRECTORY OF STATE, COUNTY, AND FEDERAL OFFICIALS SUPPLEMENT
Hawaii Legislative Reference Bureau
State Capitol   Phone: (808) 548-6237
Honolulu, HI 96813
Covers: In supplement, state departments and agencies, legislators, judiciary; county governments; members of state congressional delegation. **Entries include:** Name of governmental unit, address; names and titles of officials (and terms of office, where applicable). **Arrangement:** By unit and level of government. **Indexes:** Agency. **Pages** (approx.): 100. **Frequency:** Supplement is biennial in odd years; base volume is irregular, latest edition 1977. **Editor:** Craig Fukuda. **Price:** $1.00 for supplement. **Other information:** Sometimes cited as, "Directory of State...Officials Supplement to Guide to Government in Hawaii."

Guide to Law Schools *See* **Barron's Guide to Law Schools**

★2235★
GUIDE TO MANAGEMENT IMPROVEMENT PROJECTS IN LOCAL GOVERNMENT
International City Management Association
1140 Connecticut Avenue, N. W.
Washington, DC 20036
Covers: About 400 projects per year conducted by municipal governments which have resulted in improvements in efficiency or cost reductions; projects are primarily concerned with application of new management techniques or technology. **Entries include:** Organization name, address, phone, contact, description of project. **Arrangement:** By type of activity (public works, social work, etc.). **Indexes:** Subject, geographical. **Frequency:** Five bimonthly issues a year; cumulative sixth issue also includes additional projects. **Former title:** Jurisdictional Guide to Productivity Improvement Projects (1976); Guide to Productivity Improvement Projects (1978). **Price:** $20.00 per year, including cumulation; available on calendar year basis only.

★2236★
GUIDE TO NEBRASKA STATE AGENCIES
Nebraska Library Commission
1420 P Street   Phone: (402) 471-2045
Lincoln, NE 68508
Covers: State government departments and agencies, and state colleges and universities. **Entries include:** Agency or college name, address, phone, state document classification number. **Arrangement:** By keyword in agency name. **Pages** (approx.): 40. **Frequency:** Annual, spring. **Editor:** Vern Buis. **Price:** Free (ISSN 0091-0716).

Guide to Productivity Improvement Projects *See* **Guide to Management Improvement Projects in Local Government**

★2237★
GUIDE TO TEXAS STATE AGENCIES
Lyndon B. Johnson School of Public Affairs
University of Texas at Austin
Drawer Y
University Station   Phone: (512) 471-4962
Austin, TX 78712
Number of listings: About 235. **Entries include:** State agency name, address, qualifications and method of selection of principal personnel, legal authority for agency, organization outline, function, and funding during the previous two years. **Arrangement:** By subject of jurisdiction (natural resources, agriculture, etc.). **Pages** (approx.): 330. **Frequency:** Irregular; latest edition 1978. **Editor:** Elaine Wogan. **Price:** $12.50, plus $1.00 shipping. **Other information:** An appendix lists agency heads' names, titles, addresses, and phone numbers.

Handbook of Election Officials *See* **Directory of Election Officials**

★2238★
HANDBOOK OF GOVERNMENTS IN TEXAS
Texas Advisory Commission on Intergovernmental Relations
Box 13206
Capitol Station   Phone: (512) 475-3728
Austin, TX 78711
Covers: Texas state government, including legislature, elected officials, boards and commissions, and agencies and departments; county and municipal governments; special districts and authorities; regional governments; federal government offices in Texas. **Entries include:** Department and agency listings include name, address, creating statutory authority, names of principal officials, number of employees, statement of programs and responsibilities, appropriations, etc. Other sections contain less extensive information, but sometimes list additional references. **Arrangement:** By governmental unit. **Indexes:** By keyword in name of governmental body. **Pages** (approx.): 700. **Frequency:** Biennial cycle by sections; all but federal section published in summer or fall of odd years following legislative session; federal section early in even years; sections

revised by quarterly supplements. **Price:** $25.00; annual update charge of $10.00, beginning one year from date of purchase.

★2239★
HANDBOOK OF ILLINOIS GOVERNMENT
Illinois Secretary of State
State House, Room 213   Phone: (217) 782-2201
Springfield, IL 62756
Publication includes: List of state legislators and the congressional delegation. **Entries include:** Name, address, district; delegation listings show party. **Frequency:** Biennial, early in odd years. **Price:** Free.

★2240★
HINES INSURANCE COUNSEL
Hines, Inc.
443 Duane Street   Phone: (312) 469-3983
Glen Ellyn, IL 60137
Covers: 2,500 law firms in the United States and Canada which handle defense in litigation involving insurance and transportation companies. **Entries include:** Firm name, address, phone, type of practice, names of partners and associates, clients, memberships in trial organizations. **Arrangement:** Geographical. **Pages** (approx.): 585. **Frequency:** Annual, November. **Editor:** James R. Collins. **Advertising accepted.** Circulation 10,000. **Price:** $10.00, plus $2.00 shipping. **Other information:** An insurance law list. See separate listing, "Law Lists."

★2241★
HOW AND WHERE [To check driver licenses and records]
American Trucking Associations
1616 P Street, N. W.
Washington, DC 20036
Covers: Offices responsible for maintaining driving records and offices to which truck accidents are to be reported, in all states and Puerto Rico. **Entries include:** Office name, address, phone, information to be supplied, fee, etc. **Arrangement:** Geographical. **Frequency:** Annual, January. **Price:** $2.00 (current edition); $2.50 (1980 edition); payment with order.

★2242★
IDAHO BLUE BOOK
Idaho Secretary of State
Statehouse, Room 203   Phone: (208) 384-2300
Boise, ID 83720
Publication includes: Elective state officials, legislators, and members of the state's congressional delegation. **Entries include:** Name, position, career and personal data, addresses. **Frequency:** Biennial, fall of odd years. **Editor:** Peter T. Cenarrusa, Secretary of State. **Price:** $3.25 (mailing list is not maintained). **Also includes:** Election and vital statistics, state history and chronology.

★2243★
ILLINOIS BLUE BOOK
Illinois Secretary of State
State House, Room 213   Phone: (207) 782-2201
Springfield, IL 62756
Covers: State departments and agencies, legislators, judiciary; college boards of governors; county governments; Chicago city government. **Entries include:** Each section includes description of the department, board, etc., and names of executives or members; legislator and some judicial listings include biography. **Indexes:** Agency-personal name. **Pages** (approx.): 675. **Frequency:** Biennial, fall of even years. **Price:** Free (mailing list is not maintained).

★2244★
ILLINOIS COUNTY OFFICERS
Illinois State Board of Elections
1020 S. Spring Street
Springfield, IL 62704
Entries include: County name, mailing address, and names, titles, and

political parties of about eight officials. **Arrangement:** By county. **Pages** (approx.): 40. **Frequency:** Biennial, January of odd years. **Price:** Free. **Other information:** Formerly included in "State of Illinois State and County Officers;" state officials now listed in, "Illinois State Officers," described in separate entry.

★2245★
ILLINOIS LEGAL DIRECTORY
Legal Directories Publishing Company
8350 Central Expressway   Phone: (214) 692-5825
Dallas, TX 75206
Frequency: Latest edition 1979. **Price:** $19.00. **Other information:** Content, arrangement, etc., same as "Alabama Legal Directory;" see separate listing. (See also separate listing, "Law Lists.")

★2246★
ILLINOIS LEGISLATIVE DIRECTORY
Illinois Legislative Council
107 State Office Building
Springfield, IL 62706
Covers: Members of the legislature and their assignments, staffs, etc. **Pages** (approx.): 60. **Frequency:** Annual. **Price:** Not for general distribution.

★2247★
ILLINOIS MUNICIPAL DIRECTORY
Illinois Municipal League
1220 S. Seventh Street   Phone: (217) 525-1220
Springfield, IL 62703
Entries include: Name of municipality, address, phone, names of executives. **Frequency:** Biennial, November of odd years. **Price:** $15.00, payment with order.

★2248★
ILLINOIS STATE OFFICERS
Illinois State Board of Elections
1020 S. Spring Street
Springfield, IL 62704
Covers: Principal elective state officials, legislators, judiciary, university trustees. **Entries include:** Department or other governmental unit name, names of officials, home address, political party, legislative or judicial district, length of term where applicable. **Pages** (approx.): 100. **Frequency:** Biennial, January of odd years. **Former title:** State of Illinois State and County Officers (1979). (county officers now covered in "Illinois County Officers"; see separate listing.) **Price:** Free (ISSN 0145-6199).

★2249★
INDIANA LEGAL DIRECTORY
Legal Directories Publishing Company
8350 Central Expressway   Phone: (214) 692-5825
Dallas, TX 75206
Frequency: Latest edition 1978. **Price:** $19.00. **Other information:** Content, arrangement, etc., same as "Alabama Legal Directory;" see separate listing. (See also separate listing, "Law Lists.")

★2250★
INSURANCE BAR
Bar List Publishing Company
550 Frontage Road   Phone: (312) 441-6767
Northfield, IL 60093
Covers: Law firms which handle defense in insurance litigation. **Arrangement:** Geographical. **Frequency:** Annual, summer. **Price:** Apply. **Other information:** An insurance law list. See separate listing, "Law Lists."

★2251★
**INTERNATIONAL ASSOCIATION OF ASSESSING OFFICERS—
     MEMBERSHIP DIRECTORY**
International Association of Assessing Officers
1313 E. 60th Street
Chicago, IL 60637
Covers: About 10,000 state and local officials concerned with assessment of property for tax purposes. **Entries include:** Name, position, address. **Pages** (approx.): 75. **Frequency:** Irregular; latest edition January 1979. **Price:** $15.00; available to members only.

★2252★
INTERNATIONAL ASSOCIATION OF LAW LIBRARIES—DIRECTORY
International Association of Law Libraries
Vanderbilt University Law Library   Phone: (615) 222-2726
Nashville, TN 37203
Covers: About 600 member law libraries and librarians throughout the world. **Entries include:** Institution name, address; names of individual members. **Arrangement:** Geographical. **Indexes:** Personal name/institution name. **Pages** (approx.): 150. **Frequency:** Irregular; latest edition August 1979. **Price:** $12.00.

★2253★
**INTERNATIONAL BRIDGE, TUNNEL, AND TURNPIKE
     ASSOCIATION—MEMBERS**
International Bridge, Tunnel, and Turnpike Association
1225 Connecticut Avenue, N. W., Suite
30   Phone: (202) 659-4620
Washington, DC 20036
Covers: More than 200 public agencies which operate bridges, tunnels, and highways which require the payment of tolls. **Entries include:** Agency name, address, name of contact. **Pages** (approx.): 40. **Frequency:** Annual, spring. **Price:** Available to members only.

International Businessman's Guide to Official Washington See
     Joyner's Guide to Official Washington

★2254★
**INTERNATIONAL CENTRE FOR SETTLEMENT OF INVESTMENT
     DISPUTES—ANNUAL REPORT**
International Centre for Settlement of Investment Disputes
1818 H Street, N. W.   Phone: (202) 477-4659
Washington, DC 20433
Publication includes: "List of Members of the Panels of Conciliators and Arbitrators" appointed from each country. Approximately 200 entries. **Entries include:** Name, principal occupation, position, or other indication of qualification; terminal date of appointment. **Arrangement:** Geographical. **Pages** (approx.): 30. **Frequency:** Annual, September. **Price:** Free.

★2255★
**INTERNATIONAL CITY MANAGEMENT ASSOCIATION—
     DIRECTORY OF ASSISTANTS**
International City Management Association
1140 Connecticut Avenue, N.W.   Phone: (202) 828-3600
Washington, DC 20036
Covers: About 2,300 persons who serve as assistants to professional city and county managers. **Entries include:** Municipality name, population, form of government, assistant's name, date appointed, education. **Pages** (approx.): 30. **Frequency:** Irregular; latest edition 1976-77; new edition possible late 1979. **Price:** $25.00.

★2256★
**INTERNATIONAL CITY MANAGEMENT ASSOCIATION—
     DIRECTORY OF MEMBERS**
International City Management Association
1140 Connecticut Avenue, N. W.   Phone: (202) 828-3600
Washington, DC 20036
Covers: 7,000 appointed administrators of cities, counties, and councils of governments. **Entries include:** Name, position, office address, career data, offices held in ICMA. **Arrangement:**

Alphabetical by individual name. **Pages** (approx.): 260. **Frequency:** Annual, fall. **Price:** $25.00 (current and 1980 editions).

★2257★
INTERNATIONAL COUNTERMEASURES HANDBOOK
EW Communications, Inc.
Box 50249   Phone: (415) 494-2800
Palo Alto, CA 94304
Publication includes: Lists of 3,500 Defense Department military and civilian personnel in development and operation of electronic warfare, and 110 advertisers who manufacture electronic warfare equipment and systems. **Entries include:** Personnel list shows name, rank, highly abbreviated organization identification, and Defense Department telephone system numbers. Manufacturer list shows company name, address, phone, TWX, names of principal executives, and geographical list of distributors, agents and branch offices with addresses and phone numbers. **Arrangement:** Both lists are alphabetical. **Frequency:** Annual, spring. **Editor:** Harry F. Eustace. **Advertising accepted.** Circulation 10,000. **Price:** $35.00, payment with order. **Other information:** Principal content is technical information on disciplines related to electronic warfare, from acoustics to radar and electro-optics, and advertisements of manufacturers in those fields. Includes descriptions, code names, etc., of United States, Soviet Union and Peoples Republic of China electronic equipment.

★2258★
**INTERNATIONAL INSTITUTE OF MUNICIPAL CLERKS—
     MEMBERSHIP DIRECTORY**
International Institute of Municipal Clerks
160 N. Altadena Drive   Phone: (213) 795-6153
Pasadena, CA 91107
Number of listings: 4,600. **Entries include:** City, Zip or postal code (for Canada), member's name, and a code indicating member's title. **Arrangement:** Geographical. **Pages** (approx.): 70. **Frequency:** Annual, March. **Editor:** John J. Hunnewell, Executive Director. **Price:** $6.00 (current and 1980 editions).

★2259★
INTERNATIONAL LAWYERS LAW LIST
International Lawyers Company, Inc.
432 Park Avenue South   Phone: (212) 685-6851
New York, NY 10016
Arrangement: Geographical. **Frequency:** Annual, April; cumulative supplements, July, October, and January. **Price:** Free; controlled circulation. **Other information:** A commercial law list. See separate listing, "Law Lists."

International Military Club Executives Association—Directory
     See Who's Who in Military Club Management

★2260★
**INTERNATIONAL NARCOTIC ENFORCEMENT OFFICERS
     ASSOCIATION—ANNUAL DIRECTORY**
International Narcotic Enforcement Officers Association
112 State Street   Phone: (518) 463-6232
Albany, NY 12207
Number of listings: 7,500. **Entries include:** Name, affiliation, address, phone. **Arrangement:** Alphabetical. **Pages** (approx.): 15. **Frequency:** Annual, January. **Editor:** Celeste Morga, Executive Editor. **Advertising accepted.** Circulation 10,000. **Price:** Available to members only.

★2261★
**INTERNATIONAL PERSONNEL MANAGEMENT ASSOCIATION—
     MEMBERSHIP DIRECTORY [Government personnel]**
International Personnel Management Association
1850 K Street, N. W., Suite 870   Phone: (202) 833-5860
Washington, DC 20006
Covers: Personnel management officials and agencies in state, county, and municipal governments, primarily in the United States.

Entries include: For agencies - Name of agency, name of personnel director, address, phone. For individuals - Name, title, affiliation, address. **Arrangement:** Agencies are geographical, individuals are alphabetical. **Pages** (approx.): 120. **Frequency:** Annual. **Editor:** Kenneth A. Fisher. **Price:** $25.00.

★2262★
IOWA LEGAL DIRECTORY
Legal Directories Publishing Company
8350 Central Expressway   Phone: (214) 692-5825
Dallas, TX 75206
Frequency: Latest edition 1979. **Price:** $17.00. **Other information:** Content, arrangement, etc., same as "Alabama Legal Directory;" see separate listing. (See also separate listing, "Law Lists.")

★2263★
IOWA OFFICIAL DIRECTORY OF STATE AND COUNTY OFFICERS
Iowa Secretary of State
State House   Phone: (515) 281-5864
Des Moines, IA 50319
Covers: Principal elective and appointive county officers; lists only names and titles for major state officials and members of the supreme court. **Entries include:** County name, address, and names, titles, phones of principal elective and appointive officials, with party affiliation where appropriate. **Arrangement:** By county name. **Pages** (approx.): 50. **Frequency:** Biennial, January of odd years. **Price:** Free.

★2264★
IOWA OFFICIAL REGISTER
Iowa State Printing Division
Grimes State Office Building   Phone: (515) 281-5231
Des Moines, IA 50319
Covers: Elected officials in executive, legislative, and judicial branches; state boards and institutions; county officials. **Pages** (approx.): 450. **Frequency:** Annual, summer. **Editor:** Joni Keith. **Price:** Free. **Other information:** Variant title, "The Red Book."

★2265★
JOURNAL-BULLETIN RHODE ISLAND ALMANAC
Providence Journal Company
75 Fountain Street   Phone: (401) 277-7393
Providence, RI 02902
Publication includes: Numerous lists pertaining to Rhode Island state, county, town, and city governments. **Entries include:** Generally, name of the governmental unit, address, names and titles of principal officials. **Frequency:** Annual, March. **Editor:** Joseph O. Mehr, Librarian. **Price:** $2.75 (current edition); $2.95 (1980 edition). **Also includes:** Historical and statistical data on the state.

★2266★
JOYNER'S GUIDE TO OFFICIAL WASHINGTON
Joyner & Associates, Inc.
11250 Roger Bacon Drive   Phone: (703) 437-5060
Reston, VA 22090
Covers: 2,000 officials in 40 government agencies, 800 government services, and 500 government publications, periodicals, and foreign market research reports of interest to international businessmen in importing, exporting, licensing, investment, and finance. Includes foreign embassies in Washington and United States embassies abroad. **Entries include:** Office address and phone of all officials listed. **Arrangement:** By subject. **Indexes:** Keyword. **Pages** (approx.): 400. **Frequency:** Annual. **Editor:** Nelson T. Joyner, Jr., President. **Former title:** International Businessman's Guide to Official Washington. **Price:** $95.00, plus $4.95 shipping. **Other information:** Variant title, "Doing Business Abroad."

Jurisdictional Guide to Productivity Improvement Projects *See* Guide to Management Improvement Projects in Local Government

★2267★
JUVENILE AND ADULT CORRECTIONAL DEPARTMENTS, INSTITUTIONS, AGENCIES AND PAROLING AUTHORITIES
American Correctional Association
4321 Hartwick Road, Suite L-208   Phone: (301) 864-1070
College Park, MD 20740
Covers: 2,500 juvenile and adult state and federal correctional departments, institutions, agencies, and paroling authories, military correctional facilities, and Law Enforcement Assistance Administration state planning agencies and regional offices. **Entries include:** Agency name, locations, phone, name of administrative officer (and other personnel for agencies), length of operation, average number and types of inmates. **Arrangement:** Primarily geographical within authority (federal, states, military, Justice Department, Canada, etc.). **Pages** (approx.): 335. **Frequency:** Annual, January. **Advertising accepted. Former title:** Directory of Juvenile and Adult Correctional Agencies of the U. S. and Canada. **Price:** $15.00 (current edition); $20.00 (1980 edition).

Juvenile Court Judges Directory *See* Directory of Juvenile/ family Domestic Relations Court Judges

★2268★
KANSAS DIRECTORY
Kansas Secretary of State
State House   Phone: (913) 296-2236
Topeka, KS 66612
Covers: State departments and agencies, legislators, judiciary; federal officials in the state; members of the state's congressional delegation. **Entries include:** Department or agency name, address, names of officials; many listings include home addresses (and political party, district, and date term expires where appropriate). **Indexes:** Subject/ agency. **Pages** (approx.): 250. **Frequency:** Biennial, August of odd years; supplement in even years. **Editor:** Jack H. Brier. **Price:** Free (mailing list is not maintained).

★2269★
KANSAS LEGAL DIRECTORY
Legal Directories Publishing Company
8350 Central Expressway   Phone: (214) 692-5825
Dallas, TX 75206
Frequency: Latest edition 1979. **Price:** $17.00. **Other information:** Content, arrangement, etc., same as "Alabama Legal Directory;" see separate listing. (See also separate listing, "Law Lists.")

★2270★
KANSAS LEGISLATIVE DIRECTORY
Halgo Publishing, Inc.
6305 Brookside Plaza   Phone: (816) 444-6455
Kansas City, MO 64113
Covers: Members of the Kansas legislature. **Entries include:** Name, address, committee assignments, party, district, number of terms served, photograph. **Arrangement:** Alphabetical. **Pages** (approx.): 170. **Frequency:** Biennial, odd years; supplement in even years. **Price:** $34.00, payment with order; $38.00, billed.

★2271★
KENTUCKY DIRECTORY OF BLACK ELECTED OFFICIALS
Kentucky Commission on Human Rights
701 W. Walnut Street
Louisville, KY 40203
Covers: 67 Blacks serving in elective positions in Kentucky in 1976. **Entries include:** Name, personal and career data. **Arrangement:** Geographical. **Pages** (approx.): 40. **Frequency:** Irregular; previous edition 1972; latest edition September 1976. **Price:** Free. (Not verified)

★2272★
KENTUCKY LEGAL DIRECTORY
Legal Directories Publishing Company
8350 Central Expressway   Phone: (214) 692-5825
Dallas, TX 75206
Frequency: Latest edition 1978. **Price:** $12.00. **Other information:**
Content, arrangement, etc., same as "Alabama Legal Directory;" see
separate listing. (See also separate listing, "Law Lists.")

★2273★
KEY OFFICERS OF FOREIGN SERVICE POSTS: GUIDE FOR
      BUSINESS REPRESENTATIVES
Foreign Affairs Document and Reference Center
State Department
Washington, DC 20520
Covers: About 275 embassies, missions, consulates general,
consulates, trade centers, and other diplomatic posts of the United
States Department of State, listing up to ten officers for each. **Entries
include:** City name, status of office (embassy, consulate, etc.),
address, phone, and officers' names and titles. **Arrangement:**
Geographical. **Pages** (approx.): 70. **Frequency:** Three times yearly
(March, July, November). **Price:** $1.50 per copy; $2.00 per year
(Publication 7877). **Send orders to:** Government Printing Office,
Washington, DC 20402.

★2274★
LAND USE PLANNING DIRECTORY OF THE 17 WESTERN STATES
Bureau of Reclamation
Interior Department
Box 25007   Phone: (303) 234-3251
Denver, CO 80225
Covers: Local, federal, and tribal planning agencies. **Entries include:**
Agency name, address, phone, names of personnel. **Arrangement:**
Geographical. **Pages** (approx.): 275. **Frequency:** Irregular; latest
edition 1976. **Price:** Free.

★2275★
LAW AND ORDER MAGAZINE—POLICE EQUIPMENT BUYER'S
      GUIDE ISSUE
Copp Organization, Inc.
76 N. Broadway, Suite 3001   Phone: (516) 931-2242
Hicksville, NY 11801
Covers: Manufacturers, dealers, and distributors of products, and
services for police departments. **Entries include:** Company name,
address, phone, product codes, code showing whether manufacturer
or dealer. **Arrangement:** Manufacturers listed alphabetically and by
product; distributors and dealers listed alphabetically and
geographically. **Frequency:** Annual, January. **Editor:** Frank G.
MacAloon. **Advertising accepted.** **Price:** $2.00 (current and 1980
editions).

Law Enforcement and Criminal Justice Education Directory *See*
      Criminal Justice Education Directory

★2276★
LAW ENFORCEMENT COMMUNICATIONS—BUYER'S GUIDE ISSUE
United Business Publications, Subsidiary
Media Horizons, Inc.
475 Park Avenue South   Phone: (212) 725-2300
New York, NY 10016
Covers: About 650 manufacturers and suppliers of law enforcement
equipment including alarms, apparel, audio communications,
reprographics equipment, weapons, laboratory equipment, and others.
Entries include: Company name, address, phone, name of contact,
products. **Arrangement:** Alphabetical. **Indexes:** Product. **Frequency:**
Annual, June. **Editor:** Cheryl Waixel. **Advertising accepted.**
Circulation 22,000. **Price:** $5.00.

Law Libraries in the United States and Canada *See* Directory of
      Law Libraries

★2277★
LAW LIBRARIES WHICH OFFER SERVICE TO PRISONERS
Committee on Law Library Service to Prisoners
American Association of Law Libraries
53 W. Jackson Boulevard   Phone: (312) 939-4764
Chicago, IL 60604
Covers: 200 law libraries which provide legal reference materials such
as photocopies of laws and court decisions to prisoners. **Entries
include:** Library name, address, limitations on prisoners served, cost of
photocopies, and whether reference services are provided.
Arrangement: Geographical. **Pages** (approx.): 50. **Frequency:**
Annual, June. **Editor:** Jeanette M. Fries, Librarian. **Price:** $3.00; free
to prison law libraries.

★2278★
LAW LISTS [Descriptive notes]
Background: "Law lists" refers to a group of directories which
provide varying amounts of information about lawyers, and which
were formerly certified by a committee of the American Bar
Association as being ethically appropriate sources in which lawyers
could make known their availability for consultation. As a result of the
United States Supreme Court decision in 1977 governing advertising
by lawyers and subsequent actions by the ABA, the Standing
Committee on Law Lists no longer certifies law lists, state or national,
as being in compliance with any rules or standards. (In response to
requests for guidance from some states, the committee prepared
proposed guidelines for state regulation of law lists which were
submitted to committees of the ABA and reported to the ABA House
of Delegates in August 1979). About sixty law lists were formerly
certified by the committee and described in the "Directory
Information Service." These listings, revised as needed, are continued
in this volume. The law list which has operated longest under a single
title is "Campbell's List," established in 1879. "Martindale-Hubbell
Law Directory" resulted from a merger of "Martindale's American Law
Directory," founded 1868, and "Hubbell's Legal Directory," founded
1870; it is currently the largest of the law lists and among the most
highly regarded. **Covers:** Martindale-Hubbell, a national list, and the
state and regional directories published by the Legal Directories
Publishing Company, Inc., are the only comprehensive law lists which
include every attorney nationally or in an area. There are no law lists
which attempt to include every attorney in a special field. In fact, the
essence of the appeal of law lists is exclusivity; all lists charge fees for
inclusion (usually based on the population of the area where a given
attorney practices, and ranging to $600 or more), except
comprehensive lists include a minimum listing without a fee; many lists
operate on the basis of "exclusive representation," i.e., they list only
one firm in a given locality. A few, such as the "Rand McNally List of
Bank-Recommended Attorneys," operate on the basis of
recommendations or sponsorships. Some lists use rating systems, and
firms listed are coded for ability, diligence, etc., as evaluated by peers.
Entries include: Even within a single law list, entries may run from a
brief name-and-address notation to one or two pages or more,
depending upon the size of the firm and how much it is willing to spend
for its listing. In a typical full entry, a firm name, address, and phone
will be given, along with names and backgrounds of partners and
names of typical clients; associates may also be listed. Many lists
include uniformly less data. **Arrangement:** The most frequent use of a
law list is in finding a lawyer in a location where the user has no
contacts. Therefore, nearly all law lists are geographical in
arrangement. **Indexes:** Alphabetical indexes by personal name may or
may not be provided. **Price:** Part of the service provided by law list
publishers is the free distribution of their lists to lawyers listed and to
others who can be assumed to be users of the services of lawyers
listed. There is no ethical restriction on the sale of law lists, but it was
the experience of the DOD staff in compiling law list material that
many publishers are not anxious to give laypersons information about
their publications or to promote commercial sales; whether this lack of
cooperation resulted from a desire to enhance the exclusive image of
their lists or for other reasons is not clear. "Apply" has been used in
the price section of listings if the publisher has not supplied prices;
copies will probably be sold, or furnished free of charge, to persons or

firms considered by the publisher to be potential users of listed lawyers, or possibly to libraries. **Other information:** As indicated, a good many publishers did not supply adequate information about their publications. Therefore, in some instances information was gathered from the publications themselves or from other sources; in some other instances it has not been possible to find the amount of descriptive information normally included in listings.

★2279★
LAW SCHOOLS OF THE WORLD
William S. Hein and Company, Inc.
1285 Main Street   Phone: (716) 882-2600
Buffalo, NY 14209
Number of listings: 1,300, worldwide. **Entries include:** Institution name, address, phone, names of key administrative officers, degrees offered. **Pages** (approx.): 425. **Frequency:** First edition 1977. **Author:** Henry P. Tseng. **Price:** $47.50.

★2280★
LAWMAKERS OF MONTANA
Montana State and Local Government Relations
Anaconda Company / Atlantic Richfield Company
2030 11th Avenue, Suite 22   Phone: (406) 443-5810
Helena, MT 59601
Covers: Members of Montana senate and house of representatives, governor, and lieutenant governor. **Entries include:** Biographies and photographs, districts represented, political party. **Arrangement:** By chamber, then alphabetical. **Pages** (approx.): 60. **Frequency:** Biennial, January of odd years. **Price:** Free (mailing list is maintained).

★2281★
LAWMAKERS OF WYOMING
Wyoming Trucking Association
109 Rancho Road   Phone: (307) 234-1579
Casper, WY 82602
Covers: Members of the Wyoming legislature. **Entries include:** Name, home address, party, personal and career data, photograph. **Arrangement:** Alphabetical. **Pages** (approx.): 30. **Frequency:** Biennial, January of odd years. **Editor:** Sharon D. Nichols, Administrative Assistant. **Price:** Free.

★2282★
LAWYER TO LAWYER CONSULTATION PANEL
Lawyer To Lawyer Consultation Panel, Inc.
5325 Naiman Parkway   Phone: (216) 248-0135
Solon, OH 44139
Covers: 450 lawyers who concentrate their practice in one field or a few related fields of law and who are certified as specialists by a recognized agency or have other acceptable distinctions in their field of specialization. **Entries include:** Name of lawyer and his firm, office address and phone, highest degree held, areas of specialization, and personal and career data. **Arrangement:** By specialty. **Indexes:** Geographical. **Pages** (approx.): 280. **Frequency:** Annual, July. **Editor:** Margo M. Newman. **Advertising accepted. Price:** $10.00. **Other information:** A general law list. See separate listing, "Law Lists."

★2283★
LAWYERS' LIST
Law List Publishing Company
402 Main Street   Phone: (203) 438-8435
Ridgefield, CT 06877
Entries include: Firm name, address, phone, type of practice, names of representative clients, names of partners and associates. **Arrangement:** Geographical. **Frequency:** Annual. **Price:** Apply. **Other information:** A general law list. See separate listing, "Law Lists."

★2284★
LAWYER'S REGISTER BY SPECIALTIES AND FIELDS OF LAW AND CORPORATE COUNSEL DIRECTORY
Lawyer to Lawyer Consultation Panel, Inc.
5325 Naiman Parkway   Phone: (216) 248-0135
Cleveland, OH 44139
Covers: Corporate legal staffs and independent practicing attorneys who are certified as specialists in, or concentrate their practice in, one or more fields of law. **Entries include:** In corporate section - Corporation name, address, phone, names of legal staff. In specialists sections - Name, address, phone, specialities, personal data. **Pages** (approx.): 300. **Frequency:** Irregular; latest edition June 1979. **Editor:** Vivian M. Kasunic. **Price:** $35.00. **Other information:** A general law list. See separate listing, "Law Lists."

★2285★
LEGAL DIRECTORY OF METROPOLITAN PHILADELPHIA
Philadelphia Printing Properties, Inc.
Box 277
Narberth, PA 19072
Covers: Over 11,000 practicing attorneys in Philadelphia and Bucks, Chester, Delaware, and Montgomery counties of Pennsylvania; judges, county officials, bar associations, and federal and state agencies are also listed. **Entries include:** Name, address, phone. **Arrangement:** Geographical. **Pages** (approx.): 450. **Frequency:** Annual, March. **Advertising accepted. Price:** $4.00 (current edition); $4.25 (1980 edition).

★2286★
LEGISLATIVE DIRECTORY [Illinois]
Chicago Association of Commerce and Industry
130 S. Michigan Avenue   Phone: (312) 786-0111
Chicago, IL 60603
Covers: Illinois, Cook County, and Chicago governmental departments, boards, agencies, etc., and the Illinois congressional delegation. **Entries include:** Unit name, address, phone, principal officials or board members; legislator entries include occupation. **Arrangement:** By level and unit of government. **Pages** (approx.): 90. **Frequency:** Biennial, spring of odd years. **Price:** $6.75.

★2287★
LEGISLATIVE DIRECTORY [Kansas]
Kansas Secretary of State
State Capitol, Second Floor   Phone: (913) 296-2236
Topeka, KS 66612
Covers: State officers, supreme court and court of appeals, legislators, and Kansas congressional delegation. **Entries include:** Officers', legislators' and congressional listings show name, home phone, business address and phone, party; district. Judicial listings show court, names of members, and phone numbers. **Pages** (approx.): 55. **Frequency:** Annual, January. **Editor:** Jack H. Brier. **Price:** Free (mailing list is not maintained).

★2288★
LEGISLATIVE MANUAL—STATE OF NEVADA
Nevada Legislative Counsel Bureau
401 S. Carson Street   Phone: (702) 885-5637
Carson City, NV 89710
Covers: State departments, boards, institutions, etc.; legislature; judiciary; city and county governments. **Entries include:** Name of department, board, county, etc., and names, titles, and addresses of principal officials; legislators' listings include party, district, occupation, biographical data. **Arrangement:** By level and unit of government. **Pages** (approx.): 250. **Frequency:** Biennial, January of odd years. **Editor:** Andrew P. Grose, Research Director. **Price:** $10.00.

★2289★
LEGISLATIVE MANUAL, STATE OF WASHINGTON
Washington Legislature
State Capitol   Phone: (206) 753-5000
Olympia, WA 98504
Publication includes: Lists of judiciary; legislature; members of the state's congressional delegation; county governments. **Entries include:** For legislators - Name, mailing address, birthplace, occupation, district and county, party. Other lists include name and county (and party, where appropriate). **Arrangement:** By level or unit of government. **Frequency:** Annual, spring. **Price:** Free.

★2290★
LEGISLATORS AND FUNCTIONARIES OF THE LEGISLATIVE
    ASSEMBLY OF PUERTO RICO
Secretary of the Commonwealth of Puerto Rico
Box 3271   Phone: (809) 724-3840
San Juan, PR 00904
Entries include: For legislators - Name, address, district, party, occupation. For employees - Name, address, title. **Frequency:** Irregular; latest edition January 1977. **Price:** Free (mailing list is not maintained). **Also includes:** Historical and statistical information on Puerto Rico. **Other information:** Text in Spanish.

★2291★
LEGISLATURE, SENATE, AND HOUSE REGISTERS, STATE OF
    MAINE
Clerk of the House
Maine State Legislature
State House   Phone: (207) 289-2866
Augusta, ME 04333
Covers: Principal state officials, members of the legislature, and legislative employees. **Entries include:** For state officials - Name, title, location. For legislators - Name, home and session addresses and phone numbers, occupation, district, party, committees. For employees - Name, home and session addresses and phone numbers. **Frequency:** Biennial, February of odd years. **Editor:** Edwin H. Pert, Clerk of the House. **Price:** Free.

List of Country Experts in the Federal Government *See* Country
    Experts in the Federal Government

★2292★
LIST OF LAWYERS FOR MOTORISTS
Automobile Legal Association
888 Worcester Street   Phone: (617) 237-5200
Wellesley, MA 02181
Arrangement: Geographical. **Frequency:** Annual. **Price:** Apply. **Other information:** A general law list. See separate listing, "Law Lists."

★2293★
LIST OF REGISTERED LOBBYISTS [Illinois]
Illinois Secretary of State
109 State House   Phone: (217) 782-7017
Springfield, IL 62756
Covers: Over 400 lobbyists registered with the State of Illinois. **Entries include:** Individual name, address; name and address of employer(s). **Arrangement:** Alphabetical. **Pages** (approx.): 5. **Frequency:** Six times yearly, January through June. **Price:** Free.

★2294★
LIST OF STATE OFFICERS, MEMBERS OF U.S. CONGRESS, STATE
    SENATORS AND STATE REPRESENTATIVES [Connecticut]
Connecticut Secretary of State
30 Trinity Street
Hartford, CT 06115
Covers: Principal state officials, Connecticut congressional delegation, and legislators. **Entries include:** Name, office held or district represented, party affiliation, mailing address. **Arrangement:** By office held or district. **Pages** (approx.): 10. **Frequency:** Biennial, January of odd years. **Price:** Free.

★2295★
LIST OF WATER POLLUTION CONTROL ADMINISTRATORS
Association of State and Interstate Water Pollution Control
    Administrators
Hall of the States, Suite 330
444 N. Capital Street, N. W.   Phone: (202) 624-7782
Washington, DC 20001
Number of listings: About 65 member administrators. **Entries include:** Name, title, agency, address, and phone. **Arrangement:** State administrators are geographical, regional administrators are by name of interstate commission. **Pages** (approx.): 10. **Frequency:** Irregular; latest edition June 1979. **Editor:** Robbi Savage, Executive Director. **Price:** Free.

★2296★
LOBBYIST AND EMPLOYER REGISTRATION DIRECTORY
    [California]
California Secretary of State
Box 1467   Phone: (916) 322-4880
Sacramento, CA 95807
Covers: In separate lists, lobbyists and employers of lobbyists registered with the State of California. **Entries include:** For lobbyists - Name, address, phone, groups represented, photo. For employers - Group or company name, address, phone, names of lobbyists employed. **Arrangement:** Both sections are alphabetical. **Pages** (approx.): 160. **Frequency:** Biennial, April of odd years. **Editor:** David B. Pitman, Manager, Political Reform Division. **Price:** $3.00.

★2297★
LOCAL GOVERNMENT DIRECTORY [Arizona]
League of Arizona Cities & Towns
1820 W. Washington Street   Phone: (602) 258-5786
Phoenix, AZ 85007
Covers: Elected and appointed city, town, and county officials. **Frequency:** Current looseleaf edition furnished at time of order; semiannual supplements available. **Price:** $10.00; supplements, $10.00 yearly. **Other information:** Variant title, "Directory of Arizona City and Town Officials."

★2298★
LOUISIANA ALMANAC
Pelican Publishing Company
630 Burmaster Street   Phone: (504) 368-1175
Gretna, LA 70053
Publication includes: Lists of principal state officials, legislators, principal county officials; colleges, public libraries; museums; television and radio stations and newspapers. **Entries include:** Name of person, institution, department, etc., address, phone; museum listings give directors, days open, type of museum; college listings give three officials, accreditation, control (and brief descriptions in separate section). **Frequency:** Irregular; about every two years; latest edition April 1979. **Editors:** James Calhoun and Helen Kempe. **Price:** $11.95, cloth; $7.95, paper.

★2299★
MAINE BAR DIRECTORY
Tower Publishing Company
163 Middle Street   Phone: (207) 774-9813
Portland, ME 04101
Covers: All lawyers in Maine (about 1,750). **Entries include:** Name, office address, phone. **Arrangement:** Alphabetical by personal name, firm name, and geographically by county; identical information in each section. **Pages** (approx.): 200. **Frequency:** Annual, February. **Editor:** Ann Hubbard. **Advertising accepted.** Circulation 700. **Price:** $17.00.

★2300★
MAINE REGISTER
Tower Publishing Company
163 Middle Street   Phone: (207) 774-9813
Portland, ME 04112
Covers: State, county, and municipal governments, manufacturers,

retail and service businesses, banks, newspapers, associations, radio and television stations, etc. **Entries include:** For state government - Name and address of branch or institution, officials. For municipal governments - Name and phone of principal official, names of numerous other officials and trustees, brief note on area, and classified list of businesses with name only. For businesses - Name and address, geographical under classified headings. For manufacturers - Company name, address, phone, name of principal executive, number of employees, whether firm exports or imports, description of products. **Pages** (approx.): 1,300. **Frequency:** Annual, August. **Editor:** Gilbert Lea, Jr., President. **Advertising accepted.** **Price:** $60.00, plus $1.25 shipping.

★2301★
MANUAL FOR THE USE OF THE GENERAL COURT OF NEW HAMPSHIRE (The Black Book)
New Hampshire General Court
State House, Room 317   Phone: (603) 271-2548
Concord, NH 03301
Covers: Members of the New Hampshire legislature. **Entries include:** Name, address, committee assignments, party, district. **Arrangement:** By chamber and district. **Pages** (approx.): 175. **Frequency:** Biennial, February of odd years. **Price:** Not for general distribution. **Also includes:** Legislative rules, constitution. **Other information:** Compare "New Hampshire Manual for the General Court (The Red Book)."

★2302★
MANUAL FOR THE USE OF THE LEGISLATURE OF THE STATE OF NEW YORK
New York Secretary of State
162 Washington Avenue   Phone: (518) 474-6210
Albany, NY 12231
Publication includes: Lists of state departments, boards, commissions, institutions, etc.; legislature; judiciary; members of the state's congressional delegation; federal offices in New York State; political party committees; county governments. **Entries include:** Unit name, address, names and titles of officials. **Arrangement:** By level and unit of government. **Indexes:** Personal name-institutional-subject. **Pages** (approx.): 1,600. **Frequency:** Biennial, fall of odd years. **Editor:** Eleanor Edwards. **Price:** $10.00, payment with order. **Also includes:** General, historical, and demographic information about the state.

★2303★
MANUAL OF THE CITY OF PHILADELPHIA
Division of Public Information
City of Philadelphia
City Hall
Philadelphia, PA 19107
Covers: Elected city officials and council members, boards, institutions, commissions, departments, etc., and federal and state officials in Philadelphia. **Entries include:** Name of office or individual, address, phone; listings for boards, departments, etc., include description of responsibilities. **Arrangement:** By level and unit of government. **Indexes:** Agency. **Pages** (approx.): 175. **Frequency:** Annual. **Price:** Free.

★2304★
MANUAL OF THE GENERAL ASSEMBLY [Georgia]
Georgia Secretary of State
State Capitol   Phone: (404) 656-2881
Atlanta, GA 30334
Publication includes: State departments and agencies, state judiciary, the state's congressional delegation, and boards and commissions. **Entries include:** Department or agency name, address, names and titles of principal personnel; listings for boards and commissions include names and personal addresses of board members. **Arrangement:** By department or board. **Frequency:** Annual, March. **Price:** Free.

★2305★
MANUAL OF THE LEGISLATURE OF NEW JERSEY (Fitzgerald's)
Edward J. Mullin
Box 2150
Trenton, NJ 08608
Publication includes: Lists of state departments, boards, commissions, institutions, etc.; legislature; courts; county and city governments; federal officials; congressional delegation; political organizations; newspapers; broadcasting stations; lobbyists; state officials and salaries. **Entries include:** Listings for units of state government include name of department, board, county, phone, etc., and name, title, and place of residence for principal officials, with salary, and, in many cases, biographical sketches of department and division heads; county government listings include county name, address, and name, title, party, and date term ends for county officials; municipality listings include population; lobbyist listings include name, address, and names of clients; media listings include name, address, transmission frequency or publication schedule, name of director or editor. **Arrangement:** By level and unit of government. **Indexes:** Subject-department. **Pages** (approx.): 975. **Frequency:** Annual, April. **Editor:** Edward J. Mullin. **Price:** $13.00, postpaid. **Also includes:** Extensive historical and statistical information. **Other information:** Cover title, "Fitzgerald's Legislative Manual;" spine title, "New Jersey Legislative Manual." Compiled "By authority of the Legislature."

★2306★
MANUAL OF THE SENATE AND HOUSE OF DELEGATES [Virginia]
General Assembly of Virginia
State Capitol
Richmond, VA 23219
Publication includes: List of members of the general assembly. **Entries include:** Name, home address, phone, occupation, photo, biographical data, district, party, committees. **Frequency:** Biennial, February of even years. **Price:** Free (mailing list is not maintained). **Also includes:** Principal content is legislative rules.

★2307★
MANUAL OF THE SENATE AND HOUSE OF DELEGATES [West Virginia]
West Virginia House of Delegates
State Capitol
Charleston, WV 25305
Publication includes: Lists of members of the legislature. **Entries include:** Name, place from which elected, party, district, biographical data, photograph; address and phone in separate roster. **Frequency:** Biennial, January of odd years. **Price:** Free (mailing list is not maintained).

★2308★
MARKHAM'S NEGLIGENCE COUNSEL [Lawyers]
Markham Publishing Corporation
219 Atlantic Street   Phone: (203) 324-5959
Stamford, CT 06901
Entries include: Firm name, address, phone, biographical data for partners and associates. **Arrangement:** Geographical. **Frequency:** Annual. **Editor:** K. M. McMahon. **Price:** Apply. **Other information:** A general law list. See separate listing, "Law Lists."

★2309★
MARTINDALE-HUBBELL LAW DIRECTORY
Martindale-Hubbell, Inc.
One Prospect Street   Phone: (201) 273-6060
Summit, NJ 07901
Covers: Most lawyers in the United States and its possessions, in Canada, and numerous lawyers abroad; includes a biographical section by firm, and separate lists of patent lawyers, law associations, about 175 public interest law firms, and legal aid and defender offices nationwide. **Entries include:** For non-subscribing lawyers - Name, year of birth and of first admission to bar, code indicating college and law school attended and degrees, firm name (or other affiliation, if any)

and relationship to firm, whether practicing other than as individual or in partnership. Subscriber listings also contain address, phone, type of practice, clients, etc. Entries in biographical section include same information plus additional personal details. **Arrangement:** Geographical. **Pages** (approx.): Various paging in seven volumes. **Frequency:** Annual, January. **Price:** $120.00 (current and 1980 editions). **Also includes:** Volume 7 includes digest of laws; Canadian and other foreign listings; list of American Bar Association committees and their members; law associations with addresses and officers; public interest law firms with name, address, phone; legal aid and public defender offices nationwide, with address and phone. **Other information:** A general law list. See separate listing, "Law Lists."

★2310★
MARYLAND GENERAL ASSEMBLY LEGISLATIVE DIRECTORY
Maryland Chamber of Commerce
60 West Street   Phone: (301) 269-0642
Annapolis, MD 21401
Covers: Principal state officials, the Maryland congressional delegation, and legislators. **Entries include:** For legislators - Name, address, phone, district, party. Other listings include similar information. **Frequency:** Annual, February. **Price:** 25¢, postpaid.

★2311★
MARYLAND GENERAL ASSEMBLY TELEPHONE DIRECTORY
Maryland General Assembly
Legislative Services Building   Phone: (301) 269-2745
Annapolis, MD 21401
Covers: Members of the legislature and state departments and agencies. **Entries include:** Legislator listings include name, house in which member serves, party, home and session addresses, office phone. Listings by committee include committee office and phone, names of members. Department listings include officials' names, phones. **Arrangement:** Alphabetical by district. **Pages** (approx.): 40. **Indexes:** Personal name. **Frequency:** Annual, January. **Editor:** Judith W. Brown, Administrative Assistant. **Price:** Free.

★2312★
MARYLAND MANUAL
Maryland Hall of Records Commission
Box 828   Phone: (301) 269-3917
Annapolis, MD 21404
Publication includes: Lists of state departments and agencies, professional boards, political organizations, legislators, federal agencies in the state, and the state's congressional delegation; county and municipal governments. **Entries include:** Name of department, institution, county, etc., address, phone, names of officials and their titles; legislator listings give district, party. **Arrangement:** By unit and level of government. **Indexes:** Subject, personal name. **Pages** (approx.): 780. **Frequency:** Biennial, spring of odd years. **Editor:** Edward C. Papenfuse. **Price:** $8.00, cloth; $6.00, paper.

★2313★
MASSACHUSETTS AND RHODE ISLAND LEGAL DIRECTORY
Legal Directories Publishing Company
8250 Central Expressway   Phone: (214) 692-5825
Dallas, TX 75206
Frequency: Latest edition 1979. **Former title:** Was included in former "New England Legal Directory." **Price:** $10.00. **Other information:** Content, arrangement, etc., same as "Alabama Legal Directory;" see separate listing. (See also separate listing, "Law Lists.")

★2314★
MASSACHUSETTS LEGISLATIVE DIRECTORY
Massachusetts Taxpayers Foundation
One Federal Street   Phone: (617) 357-8500
Boston, MA 02110
Covers: Massachusetts legislators and other elected state and federal officials. **Entries include:** Name, address, title, date of election.

Pages (approx.): 50. **Frequency:** Biennial, early in odd years. **Price:** Free.

★2315★
MASSACHUSETTS MANUAL FOR THE GENERAL COURT
Massachusetts General Court
State House   Phone: (617) 727-2834
Boston, MA 02133
Publication includes: Lists of state departments and agencies, professional boards, political organizations, legislators, federal agencies in the state, and the state's congressional delegation; city and county governments. **Entries include:** Name of department, institution, county, etc., address, phone, names of officials and their titles; legislator listings give district, party. **Arrangement:** By level and unit of government. **Indexes:** Agency. **Pages** (approx.): 850. **Frequency:** Biennial, December of odd years. **Editors:** Edward B. O'Neill and Wallace C. Mills. **Price:** $3.50, postpaid.

★2316★
MASSACHUSETTS MUNICIPAL DIRECTORY
Massachusetts Municipal Association
131 Tremont Street, 4th Floor   Phone: (617) 426-7272
Boston, MA 02111
Covers: Massachusetts municipalities and counties. **Entries include:** Municipality or county name, address, names and titles of elected and appointed officials. **Frequency:** Annual, September. **Price:** $15.00, payment with order.

★2317★
MAYORS OF AMERICA'S PRINCIPAL CITIES
National League of Cities
1620 I Street, N. W.   Phone: (202) 293-7356
Washington, DC 20006
Covers: Mayors of all United States cities belonging to the National League of Cities or the United States Conference of Mayors, plus all other cities with populations of 30,000 or more. **Entries include:** City name, city hall address, phone, name of mayor and date term expires. **Arrangement:** Geographical. **Frequency:** Semiannual, January and July. **Editor:** Nancy Pyle, Reference Librarian. **Price:** $8.00 per copy.

★2318★
MEMBERS OF TENNESSEE LEGISLATURE
Tennessee Legislative Council
State Capitol
Nashville, TN 37219
Entries include: Name, address, district, party. **Frequency:** Biennial, January of odd years. **Price:** Free.

★2319★
MEMBERS OF THE GENERAL ASSEMBLY OF GEORGIA
Georgia Secretary of State
State Capitol   Phone: (404) 656-2881
Atlanta, GA 30334
Entries include: Name, photo, party, legislative district, occupation, address, **Arrangement:** Alphabetical by chamber. **Pages** (approx.): 100. **Frequency:** Biennial, March of even years. **Price:** Free.

★2320★
METROPOLITAN WASHINGTON REGIONAL DIRECTORY
Metropolitan Washington Council of Governments
1225 Connecticut Avenue, N. W.,
   Suite 20   Phone: (202) 223-6800
Washington, DC 20036
Covers: More than 200 District of Columbia-area local governments, the Metro Washington Government Council, Maryland and Virginia general assemblies, and members of Congress from the Capital area. **Entries include:** Name of governmental unit, address, phone, and names and titles of officials, with personal phone numbers in some cases. **Pages** (approx.): 35. **Frequency:** Annual, spring. **Price:** Free.

★2321★

MICHIGAN BAR JOURNAL—DIRECTORY ISSUE
Michigan State Bar Journal Committee
306 Townsend Street
Lansing, MI 48933
Covers: Michigan lawyers, courts, and county officials. **Entries include:** For lawyers - Name, address, firm name, license number. For governmental units - Unit name, address, phone, names and titles of officials. **Indexes:** Geographical (lawyers only). **Frequency:** Annual, April. **Editor:** Nancy F. Brown. **Advertising accepted. Price:** Included in subscription, $12.00 per year (ISSN 0164-3576).

★2322★

MICHIGAN LEGISLATIVE DIRECTORY
Michigan Legislative Service Bureau
State Capitol   Phone: (517) 373-0170
Lansing, MI 48909
Covers: Members of the Michigan legislature and their committee assignments, staffs, etc. **Pages** (approx.): 60. **Frequency:** Biennial, summer of odd years. **Price:** Free.

★2323★

MICHIGAN MANUAL
General Services Section
Michigan Department of Management and Budget
7461 Crowner Drive   Phone: (517) 322-1897
Lansing, MI 48913
Publication includes: Lists of state departments and agencies, professional boards, political organizations, legislators, federal agencies in the state, and the state's congressional delegation; city and county governments; newspapers and broadcasting stations. **Entries include:** Name of department, board, county, etc., address, phone, names of officials and their titles; some listings include biographical data; legislator listings give district, party; media listings give frequency, circulation, etc., as appropriate. **Arrangement:** By level and unit of government. **Indexes:** General, personal name. **Pages** (approx.): 1,100. **Frequency:** Biennial, January of even years. **Price:** $6.00 (current edition; tentative, 1980 edition).

★2324★

MILITARY MARKET MAGAZINE—ALMANAC & DIRECTORY ISSUE
Army Times Publishing Company
475 School Street, S. W.   Phone: (202) 554-7180
Washington, DC 20024
Covers: Almanac section lists about 850 exchanges and commissaries and/or regional headquarters for smaller units. Directory section lists 7,000 products sold in military commissaries and exchanges, and lists their manufacturers; also covers 300 firms worldwide which are manufacturers' representatives to military stores. **Entries include:** Almanac entries list commissary name, exchange system, mailing address, annual sales. Directory entries list brand name of product, manufacturer name and address. **Arrangement:** Almanac entries are arranged by exchange, commissary system; the directory is arranged by product category. **Pages** (approx.): 170. **Frequency:** Annual, July. **Editor:** Bruce E. Covill. **Advertising accepted.** Circulation 11,000. **Price:** $2.50 (current and 1980 editions). **Other information:** Directory information also appears in the magazine's Buyers' Guide Issue (see separate listing).

★2325★

MILITARY MARKET MAGAZINE—BUYERS' GUIDE ISSUE
Army Times Publishing Company
475 School Street, S. W.   Phone: (202) 554-7180
Washington, DC 20024
Covers: 7,000 products sold in military commissaries and exchanges, and lists of their manufacturers. Also covers 300 firms worldwide who are manufacturers' representatives to military stores. **Entries include:** Company name and address. **Arrangement:** Classified according to product categories. Military representatives are listed alphabetically. **Pages** (approx.): 75. **Frequency:** Annual, January. **Editor:** Bruce E. Covill. **Advertising accepted.** Circulation 11,000.

Price: $2.50 (current and 1980 editions). **Other information:** Product and manufacturers' representative lists also appear in the magazine's Almanac & Directory Issue (see separate listing).

★2326★

MINNESOTA GUIDEBOOK TO STATE AGENCY SERVICES
Minnesota Office of the State Register
408 Saint Peter Street, Suite 415   Phone: (612) 296-4273
St. Paul, MN 55102
Entries include: Agency name, address, phone; description of services offered including nature of service, forms needed, fees charged, and usual time required to receive service. **Arrangement:** Alphabetical. **Indexes:** Subject. **Pages** (approx.): 600. **Frequency:** Biennial, July of odd years. **Editor:** Robin PanLener. **Price:** $5.95. **Also includes:** List of licenses and permits required in Minnesota.

★2327★

MINNESOTA LEGISLATIVE MANUAL
Minnesota Secretary of State
180 State Office Building   Phone: (612) 296-2805
St. Paul, MN 55155
Publication includes: Lists of state departments, selected state agencies, councils, boards, and commissions; state constitutional officers; legislators; federal agencies in the state; the state's congressional delegation; county officials; cities and post offices; legal newspapers in Minnesota. **Entries include:** Name of department, board, county, etc., legal authority, address, phone, names and titles of officials; legislators' listings include district, party, biographical data; listings for constitutional officers, principal administrators, judges, and members of the congressional delegation also include biographical data. **Arrangement:** By level and unit of government. **Indexes:** Agency, persons with biographies in manual. **Pages** (approx.): 650. **Frequency:** Biennial, fall of odd years. **Editor:** Joan Anderson Grove. **Price:** Free. **Also includes:** State primary general election returns.

★2328★

MINNESOTA, NEBRASKA, NORTH DAKOTA & SOUTH DAKOTA
          LEGAL DIRECTORY
Legal Directories Publishing Company
8350 Central Expressway   Phone: (214) 692-5825
Dallas, TX 75206
Frequency: Latest edition 1977. **Price:** $18.00. **Other information:** Content, arrangement, etc., same as ''Alabama Legal Directory;'' see separate listing. (See also separate listing, ''Law Lists.'')

★2329★

MISSISSIPPI LEGISLATURE—HANDBOOK
Mississippi Legislature
State Capitol   Phone: (601) 354-6790
Jackson, MS 39205
Publication includes: Biographical sketches of members of the legislature, including addresses. **Arrangement:** Separate alphabetical sections for senators and representatives. **Pages** (approx.): 50. **Frequency:** Annual, January. **Price:** Distribution limited to Mississippi residents.

★2330★

MISSISSIPPI MUNICIPAL DIRECTORY
Mississippi Municipal Association
230 Sun-N-Sand Building   Phone: (601) 353-5854
Jackson, MS 39202
Frequency: Every four years; latest edition 1977. **Frequency:** Directory of Mississippi Municipal Officials. **Price:** $5.00.

★2331★

MISSISSIPPI OFFICIAL AND STATISTICAL REGISTER
Mississippi Secretary of State
Box 136   Phone: (601) 354-6541
Jackson, MS 39205
Publication includes: Lists of state departments and agencies,

professional boards, judiciary, political organizations, legislators; federal agencies in the state; the state's congressional delegation; city and county governments. **Entries include:** Name of department, board, county, etc., address, phone, names and titles of officials; legislators' listings include district, party. **Arrangement:** By level and unit of government. **Indexes:** Subject-department. **Pages** (approx.): 500. **Frequency:** Quadrennial, following a leap year; new edition expected early 1981. **Price:** Free (mailing list is not maintained).

★2332★
MISSOURI LEGAL DIRECTORY
Legal Directories Publishing Company
8350 Central Expressway   Phone: (214) 692-5825
Dallas, TX 75206
Frequency: Latest edition 1978. **Price:** $19.00. **Other information:** Content, arrangement, etc., same as "Alabama Legal Directory;" see separate listing. (See also separate listing, "Law Lists.")

★2333★
MISSOURI MUNICIPAL OFFICIALS DIRECTORY
Missouri Municipal League
1913 William Street   Phone: (314) 635-9134
Jefferson City, MO 65101
Covers: Over 6,000 city officials, elected and appointed, in cities over 500. Also includes county court addresses, county clerks, and county judges. **Entries include:** Municipality name, mailing address, hours and phone for city hall, council meeting times, and names of numerous officials. **Frequency:** Annual, July. **Price:** $17.50.

★2334★
MONTANA STATE AND COUNTY ELECTED OFFICIALS
Montana Secretary of State
State Capitol   Phone: (406) 449-2034
Helena, MT 59601
Entries include: Name of department, board, court, etc., and names, titles and addresses of elective officials. **Arrangement:** By unit and level of government. **Frequency:** Biennial, early in odd years. **Price:** Free.

★2335★
MONTANA STATE GOVERNMENT TELEPHONE DIRECTORY
Communications Division
Montana Department of Administration
Sam W. Mitchell Building   Phone: (406) 449-2586
Helena, MT 59601
Covers: State offices and employees, statewide. **Pages** (approx.): 150. **Frequency:** Annual, January. **Price:** $1.00.

★2336★
MOODY'S MUNICIPAL & GOVERNMENT MANUAL
Moody's Investors Service, Inc.
99 Church Street   Phone: (212) 267-8800
New York, NY 10007
Covers: About 15,000 municipalities, counties, school districts, and other local taxing units with long-term debt of more than $1,000,000, plus state governments and institutions, federal government and agencies, and foreign governments, with Moody ratings. **Arrangement:** Geographical. **Frequency:** Annual; updated by "News Reports" twice weekly. **Price:** $575.00 per year.

★2337★
MOTOR CLUB OF AMERICA LAW LIST FOR MOTORISTS
Motor Club of America
484 Central Avenue   Phone: (201) 733-4114
Newark, NJ 07107
Number of listings: Over 1,000 in the United States and Canada. **Entries include:** Name, address, phone. **Arrangement:** Geographical. **Frequency:** Annual, December. **Price:** Free. **Other information:** A general law list. See separate listing, "Law Lists."

★2338★
MOUNTAIN STATES LEGAL DIRECTORY [Colorado, Idaho, Montana, New Mexico, Utah, Wyoming]
Legal Directories Publishing Company
8350 Central Expressway   Phone: (214) 692-5825
Dallas, TX 75206
Frequency: Latest edition 1978. **Price:** $19.00. **Other information:** Content, arrangement, etc., same as "Alabama Legal Directory;" see separate listing. (See also separate listing, "Law Lists.")

★2339★
MUNICIPAL DIRECTORY [Maine]
Maine Municipal Association
Community Drive
Augusta, ME 04330
Covers: About 500 cities, towns, and plantations. **Entries include:** Municipality name, Zip, phone, names of officials. **Frequency:** Annual, June. **Price:** $15.00.

★2340★
MUNICIPAL DIRECTORY [New York, New Jersey, and Connecticut]
Metropolitan Regional Council
One World Trade Center, Suite 2437   Phone: (212) 466-3850
New York, NY 10048
Covers: Federal, state, county and municipal officials serving Connecticut, New Jersey, and New York; regional agencies are also listed. **Entries include:** Individual name, title, office address, phone, and population of area served. **Indexes:** Municipality name. **Pages** (approx.): 135. **Frequency:** Irregular; previous edition 1976; latest edition November 1979. **Price:** $3.00.

★2341★
MUNICIPAL FINANCE OFFICERS ASSOCIATION—MEMBERSHIP DIRECTORY
Municipal Finance Officers Association
180 N. Michigan Avenue   Phone: (312) 977-9700
Chicago, IL 60601
Covers: 56,000 auditors, controllers, treasurers, and other finance and accounting officials of federal, state, provincial, and local governments in the United States and Canada; includes as associate members firms which supply products and services to municipal offices. **Entries include:** Name, position, address. **Arrangement:** Geographical. **Frequency:** Irregular; latest edition 1977; new edition expected 1980. **Price:** $25.00.

★2342★
MUNICIPAL INDEX—THE PURCHASING GUIDE FOR CITY, TOWNSHIP, COUNTY OFFICIALS AND CONSULTING ENGINEERS
Morgan-Grampian Publishing Company
Berkshire Common   Phone: (413) 499-2550
Pittsfield, MA 01201
Publication includes: Directory of municipal and county governments and their officials concerned with the purchasing of materials and equipment; separate listing of manufacturers of these products. **Entries include:** For governments - City or county name, names and titles of purchasing officials. For manufacturers - Name, address. **Arrangement:** Geographical. **Pages** (approx.): 900. **Frequency:** Annual, April. **Editor:** William Forestell, Editor-in-Chief. **Advertising accepted.** Circulation 31,000. **Price:** $30.00 (current and 1980 editions). **Other information:** Principal content of publication is advertisements for products and services of interest to city governments. **Also includes:** Population figures for about 5,000 governments.

Municipal Management Directory *See* **Directory of Recognized Local Governments**

★2343★

MUNICIPAL YEAR BOOK

International City Management Association
1140 Connecticut Avenue, N. W.   Phone: (202) 293-2200
Washington, DC 20036
Covers: All incorporated places in the United States over 2,500 population, and some places of lesser population; counties recognized by the association; all state municipal leagues and state associations of counties; councils of governments. Entries include: For municipalities - Municipality name, form of government, population, name of mayor and date term expires, and names and titles of city clerk, finance officer, other appointed officials, and municipal phone number. For counties having recognized managers - Name of administrator, year appointed, phone. For organizations - Name, executive name, address, phone, number of members. Pages (approx.): 450. Frequency: Annual. Editor: Barbara Gravby. Price: $28.50, payment with order; $29.50, billed (current edition; tentative, 1980 edition).

★2344★

MUNICIPALITIES [Illinois]

Illinois Board of Elections
1020 S. Spring Street   Phone: (217) 782-4141
Springfield, IL 62706
Covers: Presidents or mayors, clerks, treasurers, aldermen, trustees, and other elected and appointed key officials of Illinois towns, cities, and other municipalities. Entries include: Individual's name, address, phone, whether elected or appointed, date term expires. Arrangement: By county, then municipality. Pages (approx.): 400. Frequency: Biennial, fall of odd years. Price: Free.

★2345★

NATIONAL AERONAUTICS AND SPACE ADMINISTRATION—
    DIRECTORY

Headquarters
National Aeronautics and Space
    Administration   Phone: (202) 755-2320
Washington, DC 20546
Covers: Key NASA personnel in Washington. Entries include: Name, phone, mail code; classified list of principal officials also includes title and building. Arrangement: General list is alphabetical; list of officials classified by department. Pages (approx.): 45. Frequency: Quarterly. Price: $2.50 per copy; $8.00 per year.

★2346★

NATIONAL ASSOCIATION OF COUNTY INFORMATION OFFICERS—
    MEMBERSHIP ROSTER

National Association of County Information Officers
1735 New York Avenue, N. W.   Phone: (202) 785-9577
Washington, DC 20006
Number of listings: 1,100. Entries include: Name, title, county, address, phone. Arrangement: Geographical. Frequency: Irregular; latest edition fall 1977. Price: Available to members only.

★2347★

NATIONAL ASSOCIATION OF HOUSING AND REDEVELOPMENT
    OFFICIALS—NAHRO DIRECTORY

National Association of Housing & Redevelopment Officials
2600 Virginia Avenue, N. W., Suite 404   Phone: (202) 333-2020
Washington, DC 20037
Covers: 6,200 city-, county-, and state-assisted housing community development, redevelopment, and rehabilitation programs in the United States. Entries include: Agency name, address, phone, name of top executive, staff size, and information on activities. Arrangement: Geographical. Pages (approx.): 585. Frequency: Irregular; latest edition 1976. Former title: NAHRO Renewal Agency Directory. Price: Noncommercial users, $35.00; commercial users, $96.00.

★2348★

NATIONAL ASSOCIATION OF REGIONAL COUNCILS—DIRECTORY
    [City, town, and county area government associations]

National Association of Regional Councils
1700 K Street, N. W.   Phone: (202) 457-0710
Washington, DC 20006
Covers: About 670 associations of municipal, county, and other local government agencies operating in cooperation with one or more other agencies. ("Regional council" is defined in the directory as "a public organization encompassing a regional community; founded, sustained, and tied directly to local governments through local and/or state government actions.") Entries include: Name of association, address, phone, name of executive director, name of chairman; separate chart also shows founding date, area population, council budget, and programs administered (HUD 701, A-95, etc.), percentage of council board from elected local government officals. Arrangement: Geographical. Pages (approx.): 45. Frequency: Annual, September. Advertising accepted. Price: $20.00.

National Association of Schools of Public Affairs and
    Administration—Membership Directory See Programs in
    Public Affairs and...

★2349★

NATIONAL CONFERENCE OF STATE LIQUOR ADMINISTRATORS—
    OFFICIAL DIRECTORY

National Conference of State Liquor Administrators
Nebraska Liquor Commission
Box 95046
Statehouse Station   Phone: (402) 471-2571
Lincoln, NE 68509
Covers: State alcohol beverage control administrators in 54 jurisdictions in the United States, Puerto Rico, and the District of Columbia. Entries include: Name, office address and phone. Arrangement: Geographical. Pages (approx.): 15. Frequency: Annual, June. Editor: Terrance Micek, Executive Secretary-Treasurer. Price: Single copies free.

National Directory of Credit Union Attorneys See Credit Union
    Attorney's Legal Directory

National Directory of Forensic Experts See Forensic Services
    Directory: The National Register of Forensic Experts,
    Litigation...

★2350★

NATIONAL DIRECTORY OF LAW ENFORCEMENT
    ADMINISTRATORS

National Police Chiefs and Sheriffs Information Bureau
828 N. Broadway   Phone: (414) 272-3853
Milwaukee, WI 53202
Covers: 31,000 law enforcement and correctional officials, at state, county, and city levels. Entries include: Name, address, title or function. Frequency: Annual, June. Price: $22.50, postpaid.

★2351★

NATIONAL DIRECTORY OF STATE AGENCIES

Information Resources Press
2100 M Street, N. W., Suite 316   Phone: (202) 293-2605
Washington, DC 20037
Covers: 9,000 agencies of the 50 states, the District of Columbia, and United States possessions and territories. Entries include: Agency name, name and title of person in charge, address, and phone. Arrangement: Geographical and classified by 94 functional categories; identical information in each part. Pages (approx.): 680. Frequency: Biennial, November of even years. Editors: Nancy D. Wright, Jule G. McCartney, and Gene P. Allen. Price: $55.00, plus $2.00 shipping.

★2352★

NATIONAL EMPLOYMENT LISTING SERVICE FOR THE CRIMINAL JUSTICE SYSTEM

Institute of Contemporary Corrections and Behavioral Sciences
Sam Houston State University   Phone: (713) 295-6211
Huntsville, TX 77341
Covers: Job openings in police departments, sheriff's departments, courts, and other law enforcement agencies; correctional agencies; and universities and schools offering educational programs in criminal justice. **Entries include:** Name of position, qualifications sought, salary, name and address of office for contact. **Arrangement:** Geographical within field (law enforcement, education, courts, etc.). **Pages** (approx.): 75. **Frequency:** Monthly. **Editor:** Daniel J. Miller, Acting Managing Editor. **Price:** $16.00 to individuals; $30.00 to institutions; per year, payment with order.

★2353★

NATIONAL JAIL AND ADULT DETENTION DIRECTORY

American Correctional Association
4321 Hartwick Road, Suite L-208   Phone: (301) 864-1070
College Park, MD 20740
Covers: Over 3,000 county jails, large city jails, and adult detention centers. **Entries include:** Jail or center name, address, phone, name of sheriff or other administrator, capacity, population, type of offender, salary ranges for personnel, financial data, physical plant data, program. **Arrangement:** Geographical. **Pages** (approx.): 565. **Frequency:** Biennial, January of odd years; first edition 1979. **Price:** $20.00.

★2354★

NATIONAL LIST [Lawyers]

National List, Inc.
Box 401   Phone: (914) 962-5788
Yorktown Heights, NY 10598
Arrangement: Geographical. **Frequency:** Annual, January; three supplements yearly. **Price:** Apply. **Other information:** A commercial law list. See separate listing, "Law Lists."

★2355★

NATIONAL ROSTER OF BLACK ELECTED OFFICIALS

Joint Center for Political Studies
1426 H Street, N. W., Suite 926   Phone: (202) 638-4477
Washington, DC 20005
Covers: More than 4,600 Black Americans who hold elective public office in all 50 states, the District of Columbia, and the Virgin Islands. **Entries include:** Name, home address (address of chambers for judges), official title, jurisdiction in which person serves, date term ends. **Arrangement:** By state, then by level of office. **Pages** (approx.): 260. **Frequency:** Annual, fall. **Editor:** Dr. Michael Goldstein. **Price:** $19.50.

★2356★

NATION'S CITIES—ANNUAL DIRECTORY ISSUE

National League of Cities
1620 I Street, N. W.   Phone: (202) 293-7356
Washington, DC 20006
Covers: 200 private organizations and agencies concerned with municipal government. **Entries include:** Organization name and address, phone, description of activities related to municipal government, names of officials. **Arrangement:** Classified by area of interest. **Frequency:** Irregular; latest edition 1978; new edition possible 1980. **Advertising accepted.** Circulation 23,500. **Price:** Out of print.

★2357★

NEBRASKA BLUE BOOK

Nebraska Legislative Council
Box 94814
State House Station
Lincoln, NE 68509
Covers: State departments, boards, commissions, institutions, etc.;

members of state's congressional delegation; federal government offices in Nebraska; legislature; courts; county and city governments. **Entries include:** Name of department, board, etc., description of structure and activities, and names, titles, and addresses of principal officials; listings for some officials include photographs and biographical data. **Arrangement:** By unit and level of government. **Indexes:** Agency index includes some personal names. **Pages** (approx.): 875. **Frequency:** Biennial, spring of odd years. **Editor:** Lois A. Sasso. **Price:** $10.00 (mailing list is not maintained). (Not verified)

★2358★

NEBRASKA STATE GOVERNMENT DIRECTORY

Nebraska Department of Administrative Services
Division of Communications
1800 N. 33rd Street   Phone: (402) 471-2761
Lincoln, NE 68509
Description: In phone book format, covers state departments, boards, agencies, etc., located in Lincoln; separate list of legislators. **Entries include:** In department listings - Department name, address, phone, name of one or more officials. In personal listings - Name, department, phone. **Pages** (approx.): 125. **Frequency:** Annual, February/March. **Price:** $2.00, payment with order.

★2359★

NELSON'S LAW OFFICE DIRECTORY

Nelson Company
Box 309
Hopkins, MN 55343
Arrangement: Geographical. **Pages** (approx.): 190. **Frequency:** Annual, June. **Price:** $9.00. **Other information:** A general law list. See separate listing, "Law Lists."

★2360★

NEW ENGLAND DIRECTORY: STATE SENATE AND HOUSE LEADERSHIP AND COMMITTEES

New England Municipal Center
Box L   Phone: (603) 868-5000
Durham, NH 03824
Covers: Legislatures of the New England states. **Entries include:** Names of legislative officers and of committees and their members. **Frequency:** Irregular; previous edition July 1977; latest edition April 1979. **Price:** $2.00.

New England Legal Directory *See* Connecticut Legal Directory; Massachusetts & R. I. Legal Directory; Northern New England Legal Directory

New Guide to the Law School Admission Test *See* Barron's New Guide to the Law School Admission Test (LSAT)

★2361★

NEW HAMPSHIRE MANUAL FOR THE GENERAL COURT (The Red Book)

New Hampshire Secretary of State
State House, Room 204   Phone: (603) 271-3242
Concord, NH 03301
Publication includes: Lists of state departments, boards, institutions, etc.; legislature; judiciary; county governments; political organizations. **Entries include:** Name of department, board, county, etc., and names, titles, and addresses of principal officials; legislators' listings include party, district. **Arrangement:** By level and unit of government. **Pages** (approx.): 800. **Frequency:** Biennial, April of odd years. **Editor:** William M. Gardner. **Price:** $4.00, payment with order. **Also includes:** Historical and statistical data, election results, etc. **Other information:** Compare "Manual for the Use of the General Court of New Hampshire (The Black Book)."

★2362★

NEW HAMPSHIRE REGISTER
Tower Publishing Company
163 Middle Street   Phone: (207) 774-9813
Portland, ME 04112
Covers: State, county, and municipal governments, manufacturers, retail and service businesses, banks, newspapers, associations, radio and television stations, etc. **Entries include:** For state government - Name and address of branch or institution, officials. For municipal governments - Name and phone of principal official, names of numerous other officials and trustees, brief note on area, and classified list of businesses with name only. For businesses - Name and address, geographical, under classified headings. For manufacturers - Company name, address, phone, name of principal executive, number of employees, whether firm exports or imports, description of products. **Pages** (approx.): 850. **Frequency:** Annual, November. **Editor:** Gilbert Lea, Jr., President. **Advertising accepted. Price:** $60.00, plus $1.25 shipping.

★2363★

NEW JERSEY LEAGUE OF MUNICIPALITIES—DIRECTORY
New Jersey State League of Municipalities
433 Bellevue Avenue, Room D-403
Trenton, NJ 08618
Entries include: Municipality name, county, address, phone, names of mayors, municipal clerks, attorneys, others. **Frequency:** Annual, March. **Price:** $10.00 (current edition); $12.00 (1980 edition); payment with order.

New Jersey Legislative Manual *See* Manual of the Legislature of New Jersey

★2364★

NEW JERSEY STATE AID CATALOG FOR LOCAL GOVERNMENTS
New Jersey Department of Community Affairs
Box 2768   Phone: (609) 292-6055
Trenton, NJ 08625
Entries include: Title of program, department, type of aid, office and address to contact. **Pages** (approx.): 360. **Frequency:** Irregular; latest edition 1979. **Former title:** Catalogue of State Programs of Assistance to New Jersey Local Governments. **Price:** $4.00.

★2365★

NEW MEXICO BLUE BOOK
New Mexico Secretary of State
State Capitol   Phone: (505) 827-2717
Santa Fe, NM 87501
Publication includes: Lists of state departments, agencies, commissions, etc.; legislature; judiciary; state's congressional delegation; county governments; newspapers; broadcast media. **Entries include:** For government agencies - Department or agency name, address, name of principal official. For legislators - Name, district, party, city of residence. For media - Name or call letters, address, name of editor or manager. For county governments - County name, names and parties of elective officials. **Pages** (approx.): 150. **Frequency:** Biennial, even years. **Price:** Free (mailing list is not maintained). **Also includes:** Historical and statistical information.

★2366★

NEW YORK RED BOOK
Williams Press, Inc.
Patroon Station   Phone: (518) 434-1141
Albany, NY 12204
Publication includes: Lists of state departments, boards, commissions, institutions, etc.; legislature; judiciary; members of the state's congressional delegation; county governments. **Entries include:** Name of department, board, etc., address, phone, and names and titles for principal officials. Listings for legislators, congressional delegation, and senior state officials include biographical data. **Arrangement:** By level and unit of government. **Indexes:** Personal

name. **Pages** (approx.): 1,200. **Frequency:** Biennial, middle of odd years. **Editor:** Ira Freedman. **Price:** $30.00.

★2367★

NEW YORK STATE LEGISLATIVE MANUAL
New York State Department of State
162 Washington Avenue   Phone: (518) 474-6210
Albany, NY 12231
Publication includes: Lists of state departments and state agencies, professional boards, judiciary, political organizations, legislators; federal agencies in the state; the state's congressional delegation; city, county, and village governments. **Entries include:** Name of department, board, county, etc., address, names and titles of officials; legislators' listings include district, party. **Arrangement:** By level and unit of government. **Indexes:** Subject, department. **Pages** (approx.): 1,700. **Frequency:** Biennial, odd years. **Editor:** Eleanor Edwards. **Price:** $10.00. **Other information:** Variant title, "Blue Book."

★2368★

NEW YORK STATE TEMPORARY COMMISSION ON THE REGULATION OF LOBBYING—LOBBYIST INFORMATION LIST
New York State Temporary Commission on the Regulation of Lobbying
Alfred E. Smith State Office Building   Phone: (518) 474-7126
Albany, NY 12225
Covers: Lobbyists newly registered with the commission; cumulated list being planned. **Entries include:** Agent or counsel name, address, and name and address of firm or group represented. **Arrangement:** Alphabetical by name of lobbyist; no cross-reference by name of group represented. **Frequency:** Approximately monthly, with 75- 125 names in each list. **Price:** $9.00 per year. **Other information:** Issued as a computer print-out; formerly published by New York Department of State.

★2369★

NLADA DIRECTORY OF LEGAL AID AND DEFENDER OFFICES IN THE UNITED STATES
National Legal Aid and Defender Association
2100 M Street, N. W., Suite 601   Phone: (202) 452-0620
Washington, DC 20037
Covers: About 3,500 legal aid and defender organizations in the United States; includes programs for specific groups such as prisoners, senior citizens, handicapped, etc. **Entries include:** Agency name, address, phone, director's name. **Arrangement:** Geographical. **Indexes:** By type of service. **Frequency:** Annual. **Former title:** Directory of Legal Aid and Defender Services in the United States. **Price:** $6.00 (current and 1980 editions).

★2370★

NORTH CAROLINA GENERAL ASSEMBLY—HOUSE RULES- DIRECTORY
North Carolina General Assembly
Raleigh, NC 27611
Publication includes: List of members of the general assembly. **Entries include:** Name, home address, phone, party, district, committee assignments. **Arrangement:** Alphabetical. **Pages** (approx.): 95. **Frequency:** Biennial, January of odd years. **Price:** Free.

★2371★

NORTH CAROLINA LEGAL DIRECTORY
Legal Directories Publishing Company
8350 Central Expressway   Phone: (214) 692-5825
Dallas, TX 75206
Frequency: Latest edition 1978. **Price:** $12.00. **Other information:** Content, arrangement, etc., same as "Alabama Legal Directory;" see separate listing. (See also separate listing, "Law Lists.")

★2372★
NORTH CAROLINA MANUAL
North Carolina Secretary of State
101 Administration Building
116 W. Jones Street   Phone: (919) 733-7355
Raleigh, NC 27611
Publication includes: Lists of state departments and agencies and county and city governments. **Entries include:** Agency name, address, organization, names and titles of officials, description of functions. **Arrangement:** By level and unit of government. **Pages** (approx.): 950. **Frequency:** Biennial, August of odd years; 1979 edition delayed. **Editor:** John L. Cheney, Jr. **Price:** $8.00, cloth; $5.50, paper (1977 edition).

★2373★
NORTHERN NEW ENGLAND LEGAL DIRECTORY [Vermont, Maine, New Hampshire]
Legal Directories Publishing Company
8350 Central Expressway   Phone: (214) 692-5825
Dallas, TX 75206
Frequency: Latest edition 1979. **Former title:** Was included in former, "New England Legal Directory." **Price:** $8.00. **Other information:** Content, arrangement, etc., same as "Alabama Legal Directory;" see separate listing. (See also separate listing, "Law Lists.")

Official Congressional Directory for the Use of the U. S. Congress
See Congressional Directory

★2374★
OFFICIAL DIRECTORY AND RULES...OF THE LEGISLATURE OF SOUTH DAKOTA
South Dakota Legislature
State Capitol   Phone: (605) 224-3835
Pierre, SD 57501
Publication includes: Lists of legislators and employees of the legislature. **Entries include:** For legislators - Name, residence and session addresses and phone numbers, occupation, party, district. For employees - Name, address, title. **Pages** (approx.): 150. **Frequency:** Annual, January. **Price:** Free (mailing list is not maintained). **Other information:** Principal content of publication is rules of the legislature.

★2375★
OFFICIAL DIRECTORY OF THE LEGISLATURE: STATE OF IOWA
Iowa General Assembly
State House   Phone: (515) 281-5381
Des Moines, IA 50319
Covers: Legislators, their staffs, and general assembly employees; legislative committee membership. **Entries include:** For legislators - Name, occupation, political party, spouse's name, home address, phone, district and county, and session address and phone. For other personnel - Name, title, home and session addresses, phone. **Arrangement:** Alphabetical by chamber. **Pages** (approx.): 65. **Frequency:** Annual, January (dependent upon number of changes). **Editors:** Frank J. Stork, Secretary of the Senate, and David L. Wray, Chief Clerk of the House. **Price:** Free (mailing list is not maintained).

★2376★
OFFICIAL DIRECTORY OF THE MINNESOTA LEGISLATURE
Secretary of the Senate
Minnesota Legislature
231 State Capitol   Phone: (612) 296-2343
St. Paul, MN 55155
Covers: 1,250 members and employees of the legislature; state departments and agencies. **Entries include:** For legislature - Name, office address and phone, home address and phone. Member listings show district and session addresses and areas represented, and include photographs; employee listings show position. For agencies - Agency name, address, phone, names and titles of principal officials. **Arrangement:** Legislative listings alphabetical by chamber. **Pages** (approx.): 300. **Frequency:** Usually biennial, spring of odd years;

1980 edition due to party control change. **Editor:** Janine Mattson, Second Assistant Secretary of the Senate. **Also includes:** Senate and House committees and membership; legislative rules, constitutional and statutory provisions governing legislature.

★2377★
OFFICIAL MANUAL—STATE OF MISSOURI
Missouri Secretary of State
State Capitol, Room 209   Phone: (314) 751-2397
Jefferson City, MO 65101
Publication includes: Lists of state departments and agencies, professional boards, judiciary, political organizations, legislators; federal agencies in the state; the state's congressional delegation; city and county governments. **Arrangement:** By unit and level of government. **Pages** (approx.): 1,600. **Frequency:** Biennial, fall of odd years. **Editor:** James C. Kirkpatrick, Publisher. **Price:** Free; distribution generally restricted to Missouri.

★2378★
OFFICIAL MUNICIPAL ROSTER [Wyoming]
Wyoming Association of Municipalities
Box 2535   Phone: (307) 632-0398
Cheyenne, WY 82001
Covers: All 90 incorporated cities and towns in the state. **Entries include:** Municipality name, county, phone, population, mailing address, meeting dates, names of elected officials and appointed department heads. **Pages** (approx.): 30. **Frequency:** Annual, March; supplement in August. **Price:** $5.00.

★2379★
OFFICIAL ROSTER OF FEDERAL, STATE, AND COUNTY OFFICERS AND DEPARTMENTAL INFORMATION [Ohio]
Ohio Secretary of State
State Office Building
30 E. Broad Street, 14th Floor   Phone: (614) 466-2585
Columbus, OH 43216
Covers: Federal, state, and county departments and offices, including the legislature and the judiciary; also includes political party committees; state boards and commissions; state universities. **Entries include:** Name of department, agency, etc., address, phone, and names and titles of officials; county government listings include 11 elective and appointive officials. **Arrangement:** By level and unit of government. **Indexes:** Agency. **Pages** (approx.): 500. **Frequency:** Biennial, spring of even years. **Price:** Free. **Also includes:** Congressional district boundaries, historical rosters, etc.

★2380★
OFFICIAL ROSTER OF MONTANA LEGISLATORS
Montana Secretary of State
State Capitol   Phone: (406) 449-2034
Helena, MT 59601
Entries include: Name, home address, district, political party. **Arrangement:** Alphabetical by chamber. **Indexes:** County-district. **Pages** (approx.): Leaflet. **Frequency:** Biennial, November of odd years. **Price:** Free.

★2381★
OFFICIALS OF FLORIDA MUNICIPALITIES
Florida League of Cities
225 W. Jefferson Street   Phone: (904) 222-9684
Tallahassee, FL 32302
Frequency: Annual, March. **Price:** $15.60, payment with order.

★2382★
OFFICIALS OF WASHINGTON CITIES
Municipal Research and Services Center of Washington
4719 Brooklyn Avenue, N. E.   Phone: (206) 543-9050
Seattle, WA 98105
Entries include: City name, population, address, phone, names and titles of elected officials. **Frequency:** Biennial, March of even years. **Pages** (approx.): 65. **Price:** $15.00. **Other information:** Published

with Association of Washington Cities.

★2383★

OHIO GENERAL ASSEMBLY—ROSTER OF MEMBERS, OFFICERS, AND EMPLOYEES
Ohio General Assembly
State House
Columbus, OH 43215
Entries include: Name, phone, address; legislator listings show party, district. **Frequency:** Biennial, January of odd years. **Price:** Free.

★2384★

OHIO LEGAL DIRECTORY
Legal Directories Publishing Company
8350 Central Expressway   Phone: (214) 692-5825
Dallas, TX 75206
Frequency: Latest edition 1979. **Price:** $19.00. **Other information:** Content, arrangement, etc., same as "Alabama Legal Directory;" see separate listing. (See also separate listing, "Law Lists.")

★2385★

OHIO ROSTER OF MUNICIPAL AND TOWNSHIP OFFICERS AND MEMBERS OF BOARDS OF EDUCATION
Ohio Secretary of State
State Office Building
30 E. Broad Street, 14th Floor   Phone: (614) 466-2585
Columbus, OH 43216
Entries include: Name of governmental unit, address, phone, names and titles of officers. **Arrangement:** Geographical. **Pages** (approx.): 275. **Frequency:** Biennial, early in odd years. **Price:** Free.

★2386★

OKLAHOMA LEGAL DIRECTORY
Legal Directories Publishing Company
8350 Central Expressway   Phone: (214) 692-5825
Dallas, TX 75206
Frequency: Latest edition 1979. **Price:** $18.00. **Other information:** Content, arrangement, etc., same as "Alabama Legal Directory;" see separate listing. (See also separate listing, "Law Lists.")

★2387★

OKLAHOMA STATE AGENCIES...
Legislative Reference Division
Oklahoma Department of Libraries
200 N. E. 18th Street
Oklahoma City, OK 73105
Covers: Oklahoma state agencies, boards, commissions, courts, institutions, legislature, and officers. **Entries include:** Name of department, board, etc,. name of executives and their home cities. **Arrangement:** By level and unit of government. **Pages** (approx.): 110. **Frequency:** Annual, fall. **Editor:** Barbara Crouse, Head, Legislative Reference Division. **Price:** Free (mailing list is not maintained).

★2388★

OREGON & WASHINGTON LEGAL DIRECTORY (Including Alaska)
Legal Directories Publishing Company
8350 Central Expressway   Phone: (214) 692-5825
Dallas, TX 75206
Frequency: Latest edition 1978. **Price:** $12.00. **Other information:** Content, arrangement, etc., same as "Alabama Legal Directory;" see separate listing. (See also separate listing, "Law Lists.")

★2389★

OREGON BLUE BOOK
Oregon Secretary of State
State Capitol, Room 136   Phone: (503) 378-4139
Salem, OR 97310
Publication includes: Lists of state departments, agencies, etc.; county and local governments; federal offices in Oregon; newspapers

and radio and television stations. **Pages** (approx.): 380. **Frequency:** Biennial, February of odd years. **Editor:** Sonya Lindly Smith, Administrative Assistant. **Price:** $3.00, payment with order.

★2390★

OREGON VOTER DIGEST—WHO'S WHO IN OREGON STATE GOVERNMENT ISSUE
Oregon Voter Digest
108 N. W. Ninth Avenue   Phone: (503) 222-9794
Portland, OR 97209
Publication includes: Lists of about 50 state department, division, and commission heads, and some assistants and aides. **Entries include:** Name, office address and phone, home address, and personal, professional, and political history. **Frequency:** Biennial, late in odd years. **Editor:** C. R. Hillyer. **Advertising accepted.** Circulation 3,200. **Price:** $2.50 (ISSN 0030- 4859).

★2391★

ORGANIZATION OF AMERICAN STATES DIRECTORY
Organization of American States
17th & Constitution Avenue, N. W.   Phone: (202) 789-3000
Washington, DC 20006
Covers: Missions and delegations to the Organization of American States, Inter-American associations, and Permanent Observers. **Entries include:** For missions, delegations, and observers - Country name, address, phone, and office hours; ambassador's and representatives' names, addresses, and spouses' names. For associations - Association name, name, home and office address, and phone of director, and spouse's name. **Arrangement:** Alphabetical within categories of membership or type of organization. **Pages** (approx.): 45. **Frequency:** Quarterly. **Editor:** Luis Matho, Specialist. **Price:** $1.00 per copy.

★2392★

OUTSIDE COUNSEL: INSIDE DIRECTOR—DIRECTORY OF LAWYERS ON THE BOARDS OF AMERICAN INDUSTRY
Law Journal Seminars-Press
233 Broadway   Phone: (212) 964-9400
New York, NY 10007
Covers: 1,200 law firms with members serving on corporate boards in the United States. Sections indicating legal fees of $500,000 or more and corporations with more than one attorney-director are also included. **Entries include:** Law firm name, address, corporation served, legal fees paid by the corporation, firm member serving in corporate management. **Arrangement:** Same information is arranged by law firm, corporation, and city. **Pages** (approx.): 300. **Frequency:** Biennial, fall of even years. **Editor:** Wayne W. Bastedo, Esq. **Price:** $48.00.

★2393★

PENNSYLVANIA DEPARTMENTS OF TRANSPORTATION AND COMMUNITY AFFAIRS—BOROUGH OFFICIALS
Departments of Transportation and Community Affairs
State of Pennsylvania
Transportation and Safety Building,
   Room 11   Phone: (717) 787-2183
Harrisburg, PA 17120
Covers: About 6,500 officials of 1,000 boroughs, including mayors, council presidents, secretaries, solicitors, engineers, police chiefs, and appointed treasurers. **Entries include:** Name of official, mailing address, phone, position held. **Arrangement:** By county. **Pages** (approx.): 350. **Frequency:** Annual. **Price:** $5.50. **Send orders to:** Publications Sales Unit, State of Pennsylvania, Building 33, Harrisburg International Airport, Middletown, PA 17507 (717-787-1527).

★2394★
PENNSYLVANIA DEPARTMENTS OF TRANSPORTATION AND
     COMMUNITY AFFAIRS—CITY OFFICIALS
Departments of Transportation and Community Affairs
State of Pennsylvania
Transportation and Safety Building,
     Room 11   Phone: (717) 787-2183
Harrisburg, PA 17120
Covers: About 475 officials. Entries include: Name of official,
mailing address, phone, position held. Arrangement: By city. Pages
(approx.): 30. Frequency: Annual. Price: $1.50. Send orders to:
Publications Sales Unit, State of Pennsylvania, Building 33, Harrisburg
International Airport, Middletown, PA 17057 (717-787-1527).

★2395★
PENNSYLVANIA DEPARTMENTS OF TRANSPORTATION AND
     COMMUNITY AFFAIRS—COUNTY OFFICIALS
Departments of Transportation and Community Affairs
State of Pennsylvania
Transportation and Safety Building,
     Room 11   Phone: (717) 787-2183
Harrisburg, PA 17120
Covers: About 550 officials of Pennsylvania's 67 counties, including
commissioners, chief clerks, treasurers, solicitors and controllers.
Entries include: Name of official, mailing address, phone, and position
held. Arrangement: By county. Frequency: Annual. Price: $1.50.
Send orders to: Publications Sales Unit, State of Pennsylvania,
Building 33, Harrisburg International Airport, Middletown, PA 17507
(717-787-1527).

★2396★
PENNSYLVANIA DEPARTMENTS OF TRANSPORTATION AND
     COMMUNITY AFFAIRS—FIRST-CLASS TOWNSHIP OFFICIALS
Departments of Transportation and Community Affairs
State of Pennsylvania
Transportation and Safety Building,
     Room 11   Phone: (717) 787-2183
Harrisburg, PA 17120
Covers: About 600 officials of 100 first-class townships in
Pennsylvania, including mayor or president, manager, secretary,
treasurer, solicitor, engineer, and police chief. Entries include: Name
of official, mailing address, phone, position held. Arrangement: By
county. Pages (approx.): 40. Frequency: Annual. Price: $1.50. Send
orders to: Publications Sales Unit, State of Pennsylvania, Building 33,
Harrisburg International Airport, Middletown, PA 17507 (717-787-
1527).

★2397★
PENNSYLVANIA DEPARTMENTS OF TRANSPORTATION AND
     COMMUNITY AFFAIRS—SECOND-CLASS TOWNSHIP BOARDS
     OF SUPERVISORS
Departments of Transportation and Community Affairs
State of Pennsylvania
Transportation and Safety Building,
     Room 11   Phone: (717) 787-2183
Harrisburg, PA 17120
Covers: About 9,000 members of boards of supervisors, solicitors,
police chiefs, and engineers of 1,500 second-class Pennsylvania
townships. Entries include: Name of official, mailing address, phone,
and position held. Arrangement: By county. Pages (approx.): 500.
Frequency: Annual. Price: $5.50. Send orders to: Publications Sales
Unit, State of Pennsylvania, Building 33, Harrisburg International
Airport, Middletown, PA 17507 (717-787-1527).

★2398★
PENNSYLVANIA LEAGUE OF CITIES—DIRECTORY AND DATA
     BOOK
Pennsylvania League of Cities
2608 N. Third Street   Phone: (717) 236-9469
Harrisburg, PA 17110
Entries include: Municipality name, mailing address, names and titles

of elected and appointed officials, tax rates and revenues, etc.
Frequency: Annual, March. Price: $10.00 (current and 1980
editions).

★2399★
PENNSYLVANIA LEGAL DIRECTORY
Legal Directories Publishing Company
8350 Central Expressway   Phone: (214) 692-5825
Dallas, TX 75206
Frequency: Latest edition 1978. Price: $19.00. Other information:
Content, arrangement, etc., same as "Alabama Legal Directory;" see
separate listing. (See also separate listing, "Law Lists.")

★2400★
PENNSYLVANIA MUNICIPAL YEARBOOK
Pennsylvania Association of Boroughs
2941 N. Front Street   Phone: (714) 236-9526
Harrisburg, PA 17110
Covers: Officials of Pennsylvania boroughs and municipal statistics.
Arrangement: By borough name. Pages (approx.): 100. Frequency:
Annual, June. Editor: Robert C. Edwards. Advertising accepted.
Circulation 4,000. Price: $30.00. Other information: Published in
cooperation with Pennsylvania Local Governmental Secretaries
Association and Pennsylvania Borough Solicitors Association.

★2401★
PENNSYLVANIA SENATE LEGISLATIVE DIRECTORY
Secretary of the Senate
Pennsylvania Legislature
State Capitol, Room 462   Phone: (717) 787-2121
Harrisburg, PA 17120
Covers: Members of the senate; members of the state's
congressional delegation; state departments, agencies, and
commissions; judiciary; press. Entries include: For legislators - Name,
address, phone, party, district, brief biography, committee
assignments, photo. For departments, etc. - Department name,
address, phone, names of principal personnel. Arrangement: By level
or unit of government. Pages (approx.): 500. Frequency: Biennial,
summer of odd years. Price: Free (mailing list is maintained).

★2402★
THE PLUM BOOK
Bolder Books, Inc.
C/o Stonehill Publishing Company
Box 408
Planetarium Station
New York, NY 10024
Covers: Subtitled (on reprint): "The Official United States Guide to
Leading Positions in the Government, Presidential and Executive
Appointments, Salaries, Requirements, and Other Vital Statistics for
Job Seekers." Publication is a reprint of U. S. House of
Representatives, Committee on Post Office and Civil Service, "Policy
and Supporting Positions," covering positions outside the competitive
civil service, or, in other words, the "plum" political apppointrnents. It
also includes appointive non-political positions, such as scientists and
engineers in some departments, for which competitive exams are not
feasible. Entries include: Location and title of position, name of
incumbent as of September 1976, type of appointment, grade or
salary, tenure, and date of expiration, if any. Arrangement: By
department or agency. Pages (approx.): 140. Frequency: Irregular.
Price: $5.95. Also includes: Seven-page essay by Jack Anderson,
"Washington Merry- Go-Round," on the pervasive, self-perpetuating
nature of the federal bureaucracy.

★2403★
POLICE CALL RADIO DIRECTORY
Hollins Radio Data
Box 35002
Los Angeles, CA 90035
Covers: 150,000 radio stations used by public safety agencies
(police, fire departments, ambulances, etc.). Entries include: Name of

licensee (user), call letters, frequency, type of station, number of mobile radio units used by each; text includes explanation of how to listen to such radio systems. **Arrangement:** Nine geographical volumes. Contents classified within volumes by radio licensee and by frequency. **Pages** (approx.): 90 per volume. **Frequency:** Annual, November. **Editor:** Gene C. Hughes. **Price:** $5.95 per volume; specify area desired. **Send orders to:** Police Call, Lebanon, NJ 08833. **Other information:** Variant title, "Police Call, Fire, Emergency Radio Directory."

★2404★
POLICE CHIEF—DIRECTORY OF IACP MEMBERS AND BUYERS' GUIDE ISSUE
International Association of Chiefs of Police
11 Firstfield Road   Phone: (301) 948-0922
Gaithersburg, MD 20760
Covers: 11,500 persons in command and administrative positions in federal, state, and local law enforcement and related fields; includes some county police and sheriffs. Separate section of manufacturers and distributors of police equipment. **Entries include:** For officers - Name, title, name of law enforcement agency, address. For manufacturers and distributors - Company name, address, products. **Arrangement:** Geographical. **Indexes:** Product. **Pages** (approx.): 350. **Frequency:** Annual, October. **Editor:** Alice C. Pitcher. **Advertising accepted.** Circulation 23,000. **Price:** $10.00.

★2405★
POLICE EMPLOYMENT GUIDE
Institute of Contemporary Corrections and Behavioral Sciences
Sam Houston State University   Phone: (713) 295-6211
Huntsville, TX 77341
Covers: About 300 of the largest police departments in the United States. **Entries include:** Department name, application address and procedures, description of positions, pay scales, qualifications sought, opportunities; does not include specific current openings. **Arrangement:** Geographical. **Pages** (approx.): 500. **Frequency:** Irregular; latest edition September 1978; new edition expected January 1980. **Price:** $9.95 (current edition; tentative, 1980 edition), payment with order. **Other information:** Current openings in law enforcement are described in the Institute's "National Employment Listing Service for the Criminal Justice System" (see separate entry).

Policy and Supporting Positions *See* **The Plum Book**

★2406★
POLICY GRANTS DIRECTORY
Policy Studies Organizations
University of Illinois
361 Lincoln Hall
Urbana, IL 61801
Covers: About 80 governmental and private funding sources for policy studies research. **Entries include:** Name of funding source, address, names of contacts, phone, and description of grants available, eligibility requirements, procedures for application, and policy approaches or direction of research with which concerned. **Arrangement:** By type of funding source. **Pages** (approx.): 125. **Frequency:** Irregular; latest edition 1977. **Editors:** Stuart Nagel and Marian Neef. **Price:** $3.00 to individuals; $5.00 to libraries.

★2407★
POLICY RESEARCH CENTERS DIRECTORY
Policy Studies Organization
University of Illinois
361 Lincoln Hall
Urbana, IL 61801
Covers: 105 university and non-university centers, institutes, or organizations that conduct governmental policy studies research. **Arrangement:** Separate sections for university and non-university research centers. **Pages** (approx.): 175. **Frequency:** Irregular; latest edition 1978. **Editors:** Stuart Nagel and Marian Neef. **Price:** $3.00 to

individuals; $5.00 to libraries.

★2408★
POLICY STUDIES DIRECTORY
Policy Studies Organization
University of Illinois
361 Lincoln Hall
Urbana, IL 61801
Covers: About 140 policy studies programs, projects, etc., and interdisciplinary programs in American political science departments. **Arrangement:** By type of department (Ph.D., M.A., interdisciplinary programs). **Pages** (approx.): 150. **Frequency:** Irregular; latest edition 1976. **Editors:** Stuart Nagel and Marian Neef. **Price:** $3.00 for individuals; $5.00 for libraries.

★2409★
POLICY STUDIES PERSONNEL DIRECTORY
Policy Studies Organization
University of Illinois
361 Lincoln Hall
Urbana, IL 61801
Covers: Over 1,000 individuals interested in policy studies, primarily subscribers to "Policy Studies Journal," "Policy Analysis," or "Public Policy." **Entries include:** All listings include name, title, affiliation, and address; listings may also include degrees (with years received, institutions, fields of study), policy problems of interest, approaches of interest, publications, activities in the field of policy research. **Arrangement:** Alphabetical. **Indexes:** Approach, specific policy problem, disciplinary background, geographical, affiliation type. **Pages** (approx.): 260. **Frequency:** Irregular; first edition January 1979; new edition possible 1982. **Editors:** Stuart Nagel and Nancy Munshaw. **Price:** $3.00 to individuals; $5.00 to libraries.

Political Action Report *See* **Tyke's Register of Political Action Committees (Federal)**

★2410★
POLITICAL DIRECTORY: ATLANTA AND FULTON COUNTY [Georgia]
League of Women Voters of Atlanta-Fulton County
1372 Peachtree Street, N.E., Room 202   Phone: (404) 892-5836
Atlanta, GA 30309
Covers: About 350 elected and appointed officials of the city and county governments, and directors and members of boards and commissions. **Entries include:** Name, address, phone, salaries, terms of office and how chosen for the office. **Arrangement:** Classified by board, commission, or office. **Indexes:** Personal name. **Pages** (approx.): 45. **Frequency:** Annual, spring. **Editor:** Laura Kearney. **Former title:** Who's Who in Government. **Price:** $3.00 (current and 1980 editions). **Other information:** "Facts and Issues" is variant title.

★2411★
PRE-LAW HANDBOOK: ANNUAL OFFICIAL GUIDE TO ABA-APPROVED LAW SCHOOLS
Association of American Law Schools
One Dupont Circle, N. W., Suite 370   Phone: (202) 296-8851
Washington, DC 20036
Number of listings: 165. **Entries include:** School name, address, facilities, programs of study and services offered by the school, and standards for admission. **Arrangement:** Geographical. **Pages** (approx.): 400. **Frequency:** Latest edition 1978. **Price:** $5.00. **Other information:** Prepared by the Association of Law Schools, the Law School Admissions Council, and the Educational Testing Service.

Principal Legislative Staff Offices *See* **State Legislative Leadership, Committees, and Staff**

★2412★
PROBATE COUNSEL
Probate Counsel, Inc.
6402 E. Nubbell   Phone: (602) 945-4788
Scottsdale, AZ 85257
Arrangement: Geographical. **Frequency:** Annual, April. **Price:** $50.00. **Other information:** A probate law list. See separate listing, "Law Lists."

★2413★
PROFILES OF BLACK MAYORS IN AMERICA
Joint Center of Political Studies
1426 H Street, N. W., Suite 926   Phone: (202) 638-4477
Washington, DC 20005
Covers: 178 contemporary Black mayors who provided data in interviews, and 28 others for whom limited data were available. **Entries include:** Name; city and state; population, with percent of Blacks; whether or not the position is full time; method of election; date of incorporation of the municipality; length of term; personal and career data. **Arrangement:** Geographical by state, then alphabetical by name of mayor. **Indexes:** Personal name. **Pages** (approx.): 250. **Frequency:** Published 1977. **Editor:** Jeanne J. Fox, Associate Director, Research. **Price:** $10.00. **Also includes:** Historical perspective and statistical data.

★2414★
PROGRAMS IN PUBLIC AFFAIRS AND PUBLIC ADMINISTRATION
National Association of Schools of Public Affairs and Administration
1225 Connecticut Avenue, N. W.,
     Suite 30   Phone: (202) 785-3260
Washington, DC 20036
Number of listings: 215 member institutions are listed; about 175 have detailed descriptions. **Entries include:** For programs - Institution name, address, type of administrative structure, number of full-time faculty, degrees offered and requirements, length of time and number of hours required to complete program, enrollment figures, etc. For member institutions - Name, address, name of representative to association, phone. **Arrangement:** Geographical. **Pages** (approx.): 300. **Frequency:** Biennial, fall of even years. **Former title:** Graduate Programs in Public Affairs and Public Administration (1978). **Price:** $10.00, payment with order.

★2415★
RAND MCNALLY LIST OF BANK-RECOMMENDED ATTORNEYS
Bank Publications Division
Rand McNally & Company
8255 N. Central Park   Phone: (312) 267-6868
Skokie, IL 60076
Number of listings: 5,000. **Entries include:** Name and office address. **Arrangement:** Geographical; cross-references from towns without recommended attorneys to nearby towns with listings. **Pages** (approx.): 150. **Frequency:** Annual, summer. **Price:** $15.00. **Other information:** A commercial law list. See separate listing, "Law Lists."

Red Book *See* New Hampshire Manual for the General Court

Red Book (Iowa) *See* Iowa Official Register

★2416★
REGIONAL DIRECTORY MATCOG/MEMPHIS DELTA DEVELOPMENT DISTRICT [Planning]
Mississippi-Arkansas-Tennessee Council of Governments/Memphis
     Delta Development District
61 Adams Avenue   Phone: (901) 528-2770
Memphis, TN 38103
Covers: 45 member governments of a six-county area planning agency in the states of Mississippi, Arkansas, and Tennessee; also includes planning agencies, legislators and members of Congress from the area, etc. **Entries include:** For cities and counties - Name, state, Zip code, phone, elected officials, date, time and location of town meeting. Listings for legislators, planning agencies, etc., include similar

data. **Arrangement:** Geographical by county. **Pages** (approx.): 55. **Frequency:** Irregular; latest edition 1976. **Price:** Free.

★2417★
REGIONAL DIRECTORY OF LOCAL OFFICIALS [Illinois]
Southeastern Illinois Regional Planning and Development Commission
One N. Vine Street
Harrisburg, IL 62946
Number of listings: 65 governmental units. **Entries include:** Agency name, address, phone, names of officials. **Arrangement:** Geographical. **Pages** (approx.): 40. **Frequency:** Annual, after local elections. **Price:** $2.00.

★2418★
REPORT OF THE NEVADA SECRETARY OF STATE [ON STATE GOVERNMENT]
Nevada Secretary of State
Capitol Building   Phone: (702) 885-5203
Carson City, NV 89701
Covers: State departments, boards, institutions, etc.; legislature; judiciary; county governments. **Entries include:** Name of department, board, county, etc., and names, titles, and addresses of principal officials; listings for elective officials include party; listings for legislators include district, occupation. **Arrangement:** By unit and level of government. **Pages** (approx.): 50. **Frequency:** Biennial in even years. **Price:** Free.

★2419★
REPORT OF THE SECRETARY OF THE COMMONWEALTH TO THE GOVERNOR AND GENERAL ASSEMBLY OF VIRGINIA
Secretary of the Commonwealth
State of Virginia
Ninth Street Office Building   Phone: (804) 786-2441
Richmond, VA 23219
Covers: State departments, agencies, boards, etc.; state universities; legislature; judiciary; members of the state's congressional delegation. **Entries include:** Name of department or other unit, address, phone, and names, places of residence and terms of office of principal officials; legislators' listings include party, district. **Pages** (approx.): 475. **Frequency:** Annual, December. **Price:** $10.50, cloth; $9.50, paper (1978 edition).

★2420★
REPORT...ON THE ADMINISTRATION OF THE FOREIGN AGENTS REGISTRATION ACT OF 1938
Registration Unit
Internal Security Section
Criminal Division
Justice Department   Phone: (202) 724-6922
Washington, DC 20530
Covers: About 600 public relations firms, attorneys, and companies who represent foreign governments and are required to file reports on their activities. Full title of publication is, "Report of the Attorney General to the Congress of the United States on the Administration of the Foreign Agents Registration Act of 1938, As Amended." **Entries include:** Name of registrant, address, what government agency or company is represented, what types of activities are carried on for those clients. Additional detail on some agents is given in text of report. **Arrangement:** By country; some countries have several agents; total expenditure of all registered agents for each country is shown, but not amounts by agent or activity. **Indexes:** Agent name. **Pages** (approx.): 325. **Frequency:** Annual. **Price:** $9.00 (S/N 027-000-00854-2; 1980 issue). **Send orders to:** Government Printing Office, Washington, DC 20402. **Other information:** Copies of reports abridged in this publication are also available.

★2421★

RESEARCHER'S GUIDE TO WASHINGTON

Washington Researchers
918 16th Street, N. W.   Phone: (202) 828-4800
Washington, DC 20006
Description: Consists of numerous sections of text and directory material. The principal directory section is a telephone directory arranged by agency and department which lists about 20,000 divisions, offices, branches, etc.; this section also contains a subject/keyword index with phone numbers. Another section lists about 3,000 persons by name, with title, room number, and phone, who are considered to be subject experts; this section also has a subject index. Another section includes various congressional lists. **Pages** (approx.): 800. **Frequency:** Annual. **Editor:** Margaret S. Jennings. **Price:** $95.00, postpaid, payment with order; $96.50, billed.

★2422★

RHODE ISLAND MANUAL

Rhode Island Secretary of State
State House, Room 219   Phone: (401) 277-2357
Providence, RI 02903
Publication includes: Lists of state departments, agencies, etc.; judiciary; legislators. **Entries include:** Department name, address, names of elected officials and major administrators; biographical sketches for principal elected officials and legislators. **Indexes:** Subject-agency. **Pages** (approx.): 700. **Frequency:** Biennial, January of even years. **Editor:** Edward F. Walsh. **Price:** Free (mailing list is not maintained). **Also includes:** Election results, historical and statistical information, gazetteer.

★2423★

ROLL, COMMITTEES AND RULES OF THE GENERAL ASSEMBLY
    [Connecticut]

Connecticut General Assembly
State Capitol
Hartford, CT 06115
Publication includes: List of members. **Entries include:** Member name, district, party, age, birthplace, occupation, marital status, and home mailing address; separate list gives home and office phones and committee assignments. **Arrangement:** Alphabetical by chamber. **Frequency:** Biennial, January of odd years. **Editor:** Barbara Gross. **Price:** Free.

Roster: California State, County, City, and Township Officials...
    See California Roster

★2424★

ROSTER OF COMMISSIONS AND BOARDS—CITY OF LOS
    ANGELES

Los Angeles City Clerk
City Hall, Room 395
200 N. Spring Street   Phone: (213) 485-2121
Los Angeles, CA 90012
Entries include: Board or commission name, names and titles of officers and members; day, location, and time of meetings; phone. **Arrangement:** Alphabetical by name of board or commission. **Pages** (approx.): 10. **Frequency:** Annual, September. **Price:** Free.

★2425★

ROSTER OF INDIANA CITY OFFICIALS

Indiana Association of Cities and Towns
150 W. Market Street, Suite 408
Indianapolis, IN 46204
Entries include: City name, population, names and titles of elected and appointed officials. **Frequency:** Every four years; latest edition May 1976. **Price:** $5.00 (current edition); $6.00 (1980 edition).

Roster of Los Angeles City Government *See* Roster of
    Commissions and Boards—City of Los Angeles

★2426★

ROSTER OF OKLAHOMA: STATE AND COUNTY OFFICERS

Oklahoma State Election Board
State Capitol, Room 535   Phone: (405) 521-2391
Oklahoma City, OK 73105
Covers: Governor, state executive officers, and other elected officials of state and county governments. **Entries include:** Name of office, department, etc., address, phone, name of incumbent; county listings cover about 10 offices. **Arrangement:** By level and unit of government. **Pages** (approx.): 50. **Frequency:** Biennial, December of even years. **Price:** Free (mailing list is not maintained).

★2427★

ROSTER OF STATE AND LOCAL OFFICIALS OF THE STATE OF
    INDIANA

Indiana State Board of Accounts
State Office Building, Room 912
Indianapolis, IN 46204
Covers: State departments and agencies, legislators, judiciary; federal officials in the state; county, city, and township governments. **Entries include:** Name of governmental department or unit, address, names and titles of officials, political party in some cases; city listings include six principal officials only; township listings include selected administrators only. **Arrangement:** By level and unit of government. **Pages** (approx.): 135. **Frequency:** Annual, spring. **Price:** Free (mailing list is maintained).

★2428★

ROSTER OF STATE, DISTRICT, AND COUNTY OFFICERS OF THE
    STATE OF MISSOURI

Missouri Secretary of State
State Capitol, Room 209   Phone: (314) 751-2397
Jefferson City, MO 65101
Covers: State departments, boards, commissions, institutions, etc.; legislature; courts, including county judges and magistrates; county officials. **Entries include:** Name of department, board, court, etc., and names, titles, addresses, and phone numbers of principal officials; legislators' listings include occupation, political party, district; county government listings include about 15 officials with personal addresses. **Arrangement:** By unit and level of government. **Pages** (approx.): 225. **Frequency:** Biennial, April of odd years. **Price:** Free. **Also includes:** Election returns.

★2429★

ROSTER OF STATE OF NEW MEXICO—ELECTIVE STATE,
    LEGISLATIVE, DISTRICT, AND COUNTY OFFICIALS

New Mexico Secretary of State
State Capitol   Phone: (505) 827-2717
Santa Fe, NM 87501
Covers: Primarily county governments; lists principal state officials and all legislators. **Entries include:** For county governments - County name, address, and names, phones, and titles of commissioners and other elective officers. For legislators - Name, district, term, party, address. Name-title listings for state officials. **Pages** (approx.): 50. **Frequency:** Biennial, January of odd years. **Price:** Free (mailing list not maintained).

★2430★

RUSSELL LAW LIST

Russell Law List
365 Fifth Avenue South   Phone: (813) 261-8988
Naples, FL 33939
Covers: Law offices in general practice, worldwide. **Arrangement:** Geographical. **Frequency:** Annual, May. **Price:** Not for public sale. **Other information:** A general law list. See separate listing, "Law Lists."

★2431★
SOCIETY OF GOVERNMENT ECONOMISTS—MEMBERSHIP DIRECTORY
Society of Government Economists
Box 848
Ben Franklin Station   Phone: (202) 377-2011
Washington, DC 20044
Covers: About 600 economists who are employed by federal, state, regional, and local governments or international organizations. **Entries include:** Name, office and home addresses, office phone, areas of occupational specialization. **Arrangement:** Alphabetical. **Pages** (approx.): 50. **Frequency:** Biennial, March of odd years. **Editor:** John W. Rutter, Executive Secretary. **Price:** Available to members only. **Also includes:** Past officers and by-laws of the society.

★2432★
SOURCES OF INFORMATION FOR SELLING TO THE FEDERAL GOVERNMENT
Washington Researchers
918 16th Street, N. W.   Phone: (202) 828-4800
Washington, DC 20006
Covers: Several hundred federal government offices, persons, information centers, etc., able to provide information useful to firms wishing to sell products or services to the federal government. **Entries include:** Source name, address, phone; context indicates service or information available. **Arrangement:** By department, congressional office, etc. **Pages** (approx.): 65. **Frequency:** First edition 1978; new edition expected 1980. **Editor:** Donna Jablonski. **Price:** $22.50, postpaid, payment with order; $24.00, billed.

★2433★
SOUTH CAROLINA LEGAL DIRECTORY
Legal Directories Publishing Company
8350 Central Expressway   Phone: (214) 692-5825
Dallas, TX 75206
Frequency: Latest edition 1978. **Price:** $11.00. **Other information:** Content, arrangement, etc., same as "Alabama Legal Directory;" see separate listing. (See also separate listing, "Law Lists.")

★2434★
SOUTH CAROLINA LEGISLATIVE MANUAL
South Carolina House of Representatives
Box 11867   Phone: (803) 758-5240
Columbia, SC 29211
Covers: State departments, boards, commissions, institutions, etc.; legislature; judiciary; members of the state's congressional delegation; federal offices in the state; city and county governments. **Entries include:** Name of department, agency, board, etc., address, phone, and names and titles of officials; biographical sketches for legislators and some officials. **Arrangement:** By level and unit of government. **Indexes:** Agency. **Pages** (approx.): 400. **Frequency:** Annual, January/February. **Editor:** Lois T. Shealy. **Price:** $4.00, payment with order (mailing list is not maintained).

★2435★
SOUTH DAKOTA LEGISLATIVE MANUAL
South Dakota Bureau of Administration
Capitol Building Annex   Phone: (605) 773-3405
Pierre, SD 57501
Pages (approx.): 190. **Frequency:** Biennial, spring of odd years. **Price:** Free (mailing list is not maintained).

★2436★
SOUTHERN CALIFORNIA GROUP LEGAL SERVICES DIRECTORY
Los Angeles County Bar Association
606 S. Olive Street   Phone: (213) 627-2727
Los Angeles, CA 90014
Covers: Law firms which offer insured legal services plans (similar to health maintenance organization medical plans) to unions and other groups. **Entries include:** Firm name, address, list of services. **Pages** (approx.): 20. **Frequency:** Annual, August. **Price:** Free.

State Administrative Officials Classified By Functions *See* Book of the States—Supplement Two: State Administrative Officials

★2437★
STATE AND COUNTY OFFICERS [Maine]
Maine Secretary of State
State House   Phone: (207) 289-3501
Augusta, ME 04330
Covers: Principal executives of state departments, agencies and boards; members of the congressional delegation; principal elective county officials. **Entries include:** Name, title, home city; county listings show party and term of office. **Arrangement:** By level and unit of government. **Pages** (approx.): 10. **Frequency:** Biennial, February of odd years. **Price:** Free.

State Assistance for Local Governments in Colorado *See* CML Guide to State Assistance for Local Governments in Colorado

★2438★
STATE, CONGRESSIONAL, LEGISLATIVE, AND COUNTY OFFICERS OF WISCONSIN
Wisconsin State Election Board
121 S. Pinckney Street   Phone: (608) 266-8005
Madison, WI 53703
Covers: Major elective state officials and the state's congressional delegation; legislature; county governments. **Entries include:** For legislators - Name, address, district, party. For county governments - County name, county seat, names of about 10 elective and appointive officials. **Pages** (approx.): 15. **Frequency:** Biennial, December of even years. **Former title:** United States, State, Judicial, Congressional, Legislative, and County Officers of Wisconsin. **Price:** Free (mailing list is not maintained).

State Elective Officials and the Legislatures *See* Book of the States—Supplement One: State Elective Officials and the Legislatures

★2439★
STATE EXECUTIVE TELEPHONE DIRECTORY
Carroll Publishing Company
1058 Thomas Jefferson Street, N. W.   Phone: (202) 338-8620
Washington, DC 20007
Covers: About 30,000 executive branch state government offices (about 600 per state), in hierarchical arrangement within each state. **Entries include:** Name of department or office, specific address, name and title of incumbent, phone. **Arrangement:** By state. **Indexes:** Personal name, keyword. **Pages** (approx.): 300. **Frequency:** Three times yearly; first issue expected February 1980. **Editor:** Jocelyne Harding. **Price:** $100.00 per year; $65.00 per copy.

★2440★
STATE INFORMATION BOOK
Potomac Books, Inc., Publishers
Box 40604   Phone: (202) 338-5774
Washington, DC 20016
Covers: Four principal officials and about a dozen of the major state services (labor, health, highways, etc.) for each of the 50 states. Also includes federal installations and offices within the state and names of congressional delegation. **Entries include:** For officials - Name, office, political party, phone. For services and installations - Name, address, phone only. **Arrangement:** Geographical. **Pages** (approx.): 310. **Frequency:** Biennial, fall of odd years. **Editors:** Susan Lukowski and Cary T. Grayson, Jr. **Former title:** State Information and Federal Region Book (1977). **Price:** $17.50.

★2441★
STATE LEGISLATIVE LEADERSHIP, COMMITTEES, AND STAFF
Council of State Governments
Iron Works Pike   Phone: (606) 252-2291
Lexington, KY 40578
Covers: Legislative leaders, committee members and staff, personnel

of principal legislative staff offices. **Entries include:** For legislatures - Names, addresses, and phone numbers of all principal legislative staff agencies, and legislative leaders, and committees and their chairpersons and staff. For selected legislative officials by function (presidents, clerks, committee chairpersons) - Name, address, phone; committee names included in address for chairpersons. **Arrangement:** Legislatures are geographical; selected officials classified by function or committee, then alphabetical. **Pages** (approx.): 100. **Frequency:** Annual, spring. **Former title:** Principal Legislative Staff Offices (1979). **Price:** $6.00.

★2442★
STATE MUNICIPAL LEAGUE DIRECTORY
National League of Cities
1620 I Street, N. W.   Phone: (202) 293-7310
Washington, DC 20006
Covers: Organizations of towns and cities in 45 states, excluding Delaware, Hawaii, New York, Rhode Island, and Vermont. **Entries include:** Organization name, address, phone, names of officers and executive director, description of organization and staffing, finances and other operational information, programs, publications, census and demographic data. **Arrangement:** Geographical. **Pages** (approx.): 80. **Frequency:** Annual, June. **Editor:** Rose Bratton. **Price:** $12.95, plus $1.50 shipping.

★2443★
STATE OF CONNECTICUT REGISTER AND MANUAL
Connecticut Secretary of State
30 Trinity Street, Room 103   Phone: (203) 566-2508
Hartford, CT 06115
Covers: State departments, agencies, institutions, boards, commissions, colleges, legislators, judiciary; elective and appointive officials and board members of towns, cities, and boroughs; political party officials; school districts and personnel; non-state institutions and staffs; 1,000 chambers of commerce and membership organizations and their officers. **Entries include:** Biographies and photographs for high level officials; name, age, birthplace, occupation, mailing address for legislators; other listings include city, organization, etc., names, addresses, names of officials, additional information as appropriate. **Indexes:** Agency-organization. **Pages** (approx.): 900. **Frequency:** Annual, July. **Editor:** Ann L. Proctor, Publications Division Supervisor. **Price:** $5.00. **Other information:** Variant title, "Connecticut State Register and Manual." **Also includes:** Election statistics.

★2444★
STATE OF IDAHO CENTREX TELEPHONE DIRECTORY
Idaho Department of Administration
Len B. Jordan Building, Room 125   Phone: (208) 384-3694
Boise, ID 83720
Covers: State departments and employees, statewide. **Entries include:** Department listings include department name, names of executives and their assistants, address, phone. Personnel listings include name, phone, department. **Arrangement:** Separate sections for departments and personnel. **Pages** (approx.): 200. **Frequency:** Annual, January. **Price:** $2.00, plus $1.00 shipping.

State of Illinois State and County Officers *See* Illinois State Officers

★2445★
STATE OF LOUISIANA ROSTER OF OFFICIALS
Louisiana Secretary of State
Box 44125   Phone: (504) 925-4680
Baton Rouge, LA 70804
Covers: All elective state, parish, and city officials in Louisiana, and officials appointed by the governor. **Entries include:** Department, board, or municipality name, and names, addresses, and phone numbers of officials. **Arrangement:** By agency or unit. **Pages** (approx.): 350. **Frequency:** Irregular; latest edition 1978; new edition possible 1981. **Editor:** Paul J. Hardy. **Price:** $3.00, payment with

order.

★2446★
STATE OF MINNESOTA TELEPHONE DIRECTORY
Minnesota Department of Administration
Administration Building, Room G-4   Phone: (612) 296-6191
St. Paul, MN 55155
Covers: State agencies, statewide, and Capitol complex employees. **Arrangement:** Separate sections for Capitol agencies, Capitol employees, and outstate agencies. **Frequency:** Annual. **Price:** $3.50, postpaid, payment with order.

★2447★
STATE OF MISSISSIPPI OFFICIAL TELEPHONE DIRECTORY
Mississippi Secretary of State
Box 136   Phone: (601) 354-6541
Jackson, MS 39205
Covers: State offices and employees in Jackson only. **Entries include:** Personnel listings include name, department, building and room, phone. Department listings include department name, building and room, branch or section, phone. **Arrangement:** Separate alphabetical sections for personnel and departments. **Pages** (approx.): 75. **Frequency:** Generally every four years; latest edition January 1978. **Price:** Free (mailing list is not maintained).

★2448★
STATE OF NEW JERSEY OFFICIAL DIRECTORY
New Jersey Secretary of State
State House   Phone: (609) 292-3790
Trenton, NJ 08625
Covers: State departments, boards, commissions, etc.; legislature; county governments. **Entries include:** Name of department, board, etc., citation of governing legislation, address, phone, and names, titles, and residence for principal officials. County government listings include county name, address, names and titles of about 10 principal officials. **Arrangement:** By unit and level of government. **Indexes:** Agency. **Pages** (approx.): 100. **Frequency:** Latest edition April 1978; new edition expected April 1980. **Price:** Free.

★2449★
STATE OF OREGON TELEPHONE DIRECTORY
Oregon Department of General Services
1257 Ferry Street   Phone: (503) 378-4159
Salem, OR 97310
Covers: Oregon agencies and personnel, statewide. **Entries include:** Agency name, address, phone, name of principal executive, names of other executives. **Arrangement:** Alphabetical by agency. **Indexes:** Personal name. **Pages** (approx.): 140. **Frequency:** Annual, December. **Editor:** Robert C. Elgin, Administrator. **Price:** $3.00.

★2450★
THE STATE SLATE: A GUIDE TO LEGISLATIVE PROCEDURES AND LAWMAKERS
Federal-State Reports, Inc.
2201 Wilson Boulevard   Phone: (703) 522-5100
Arlington, VA 22201
Publication includes: Roster of elected state officials, including legislators, governors, lieutenant governors, secretaries of state, attorneys general, and party leaders. **Arrangement:** Geographical. **Pages** (approx.): 350; looseleaf format. **Frequency:** Annual, January; quarterly updates. **Editor:** Gloria Allender. **Price:** $75.00, including updates. **Also includes:** Committee assignments for legislators and a guide to procedures in each legislature.

★2451★
STATE-LOCAL GOVERNMENT DIRECTORY
Want Publishing Company
Box 19510   Phone: (202) 783-1887
Washington, DC 20036
Covers: State officials in executive, judicial, and legislative branches of state governments; mayors and attorneys for over 200 municipal

governments. **Entries include:** For state officials - Name, phone, title, agency or branch affiliation. For municipal officials - Name, phone. **Arrangement:** Geographical. **Pages** (approx.): 65. **Frequency:** Annual, March. **Price:** $7.50, plus 95¢ shipping (current and 1980 editions).

★2452★
STRUCTURE OF THE STATE: A COMPENDIUM OF NORTH DAKOTA AGENCIES, BOARDS, COMMISSIONS, AND INSTITUTIONS
North Dakota State Library
State Capitol   Phone: (701) 224-2492
Bismarck, ND 58505
Entries include: Name of agency, description of function and responsibilities, location, etc. **Arrangement:** By agency name. **Pages** (approx.): 150. **Frequency:** Irregular; latest edition September 1978; new edition expected 1981. **Editor:** Richard J. Wolfert. **Price:** $5.00.

★2453★
SURVEY OF EDUCATIONAL OFFERINGS IN THE FORENSIC SCIENCES
National Institute of Law Enforcement and Criminal Justice
Law Enforcement Assistance Administration
Justice Department
Washington, DC 20532
Covers: About 235 institutions or government agencies offering programs or courses in the forensic sciences. **Entries include:** Institution or agency name, location, courses or programs offered, degrees offered (if any), name of department (law, criminal justice, medicine, etc.). **Arrangement:** Geographical. **Pages** (approx.): 75. **Frequency:** Published 1977 (1974-75 data). **Editor:** Beth Lipskin, Forensic Sciences Foundation. **Price:** $1.40. **Send orders to:** Government Printing Office, Washington, DC 20402. **Other information:** Compiled by the Forensic Sciences Foundation, 11400 Rockville Pike, Suite 515, Bethesda, MD 20852 (301-770-2723), with data collected in 1974-75 as part of a grant from publisher.

★2454★
TAXPAYER'S GUIDE TO EFFECTIVE TAX REVOLT
Dale Books, Inc., Division
Multi-Media Enterprises Ltd.
380 Lexington Avenue
New York, NY 10017
Description: Includes survey of activities in 33 states with active tax reform or tax limitation movements as of fall 1978, with names of individuals, organizations, etc.; also describes activities of, and gives addresses for, seven national organizations concerned with tax reform. **Frequency:** Published fall 1978. **Editors:** Sharon D. Englemayer and Robert J. Wagman. **Price:** $1.95. **Also includes:** Chapters on organizing, publicizing, and operating a tax reform group (with sample forms, press releases, etc.), case histories of successful and unsuccessful movements, etc. (Not verified)

★2455★
TELEPHONE DIRECTORY—DEPARTMENT OF STATE
State Department
2201 C Street, N. W.   Phone: (202) 655-4000
Washington, DC 20520
Covers: State Department offices and key personnel in Washington metropolitan area; also covers Agency for International Development, Arms Control and Disarmament Agency, International Communications Agency, ACTION, and International Communications Agency. **Entries include:** Bureau, office, or other unit name, address, names of principal personnel with titles, room numbers, and phone numbers. **Arrangement:** By department or agency. **Indexes:** Personal name (gives abbreviated identification and phone); includes names not in classified section. **Frequency:** Quarterly. **Price:** $3.00 (S/N 044-000-01694-0). **Send orders to:** Government Printing Office, Washington, DC 20402.

★2456★
TENNESSEE BLUE BOOK
Tennessee Secretary of State
Capitol Hill Building, Room 580   Phone: (615) 741-2816
Nashville, TN 37219
Covers: State departments and agencies; legislature; judiciary; members of the state's congressional delegation; political party organizations; county governments. **Entries include:** Name of department, etc., address, phone, names and titles of officials; listings for legislators and congressional delegation include photographs and biographical sketches. **Arrangement:** By unit and level of government. **Indexes:** Personal name-department-subject. **Pages** (approx.): 580. **Frequency:** Biennial, January of even years. **Price:** Free.

★2457★
TENNESSEE LEGAL DIRECTORY
Legal Directories Publishing Company
8350 Central Expressway   Phone: (214) 692-5825
Dallas, TX 75206
Frequency: Latest edition 1978. **Price:** $12.00. **Other information:** Content, arrangement, etc., same as "Alabama Legal Directory;" see separate listing. (See also separate listing, "Law Lists.")

★2458★
TEXAS COUNTY DIRECTORY
Associated Publishing Company
116 W. Lee   Phone: (915) 646-0401
Brownwood, TX 76801
Covers: County judges, commissioners, clerks, tax assessors-collectors, treasurers, auditors, and engineers in all Texas counties. **Entries include:** County name, mailing address, names and titles of officials; phone numbers are given for some officials. **Arrangement:** Geographical. **Pages** (approx.): 80. **Frequency:** Biennial, January of odd years. **Advertising accepted.** Circulation 4,000. **Price:** $5.00.

★2459★
TEXAS LEGAL DIRECTORY
Legal Directories Publishing Company
8350 Central Expressway   Phone: (214) 692-5825
Dallas, TX 75206
Frequency: Latest edition 1979. **Price:** $18.00. **Other information:** Content, arrangement, etc., same as "Alabama Legal Directory;" see separate listing. (See also separate listing, "Law Lists.")

★2460★
TEXAS STATE DIRECTORY
Texas State Directory, Inc.
Box 12186
Capitol Station   Phone: (512) 282-3299
Austin, TX 78711
Covers: State departments, agencies, etc., legislature, judiciary; separate comprehensive register of state departmental personnel; city and county governments; chambers of commerce. **Entries include:** State listings show department name, address, phone, names of 5-10 officials with home addresses. City and county listings include unit name, address, names of officials. Chamber of commerce listings include organization name, address. **Pages** (approx.): 550. **Frequency:** Annual, January. **Editor:** Dorothy Wells. **Advertising accepted.** Circulation 5,000. **Price:** $15.00 (current and 1980 editions).

★2461★
EL TIO SAM Y USTED [Services and publications of U.S. government]
Cruzada Spanish Publications
Box 650909   Phone: (305) 595-5480
Miami, FL 33165
Publication includes: Descriptions in Spanish of several dozen federal government departments and agencies. **Pages** (approx.): 30. **Frequency:** Irregular; latest edition 1976; new edition in 1980. **Editor:** Andres Rivero. **Advertising accepted.** Circulation 13,000.

Price: $2.00 (current edition); $5.00 (1980 edition). **Also includes:** Bibliography of over 200 free government publications in Spanish.

★2462★
TRANSPORTATION AND PRODUCTS LEGAL DIRECTORY
Transportation and Products Legal Directory
31 E. Fifth Avenue, Room 202   Phone: (219) 883-6336
Gary, IN 46402
Arrangement: Geographical. **Frequency:** Annual. **Price:** Apply. **Other information:** A general law list. See separate listing, "Law Lists."

Treasury Telephone Directory *See* Department of Treasury Telephone Directory

★2463★
TRIAL COURT DIRECTORY OF THE UNITED STATES
National Association for Court Administration
300 Newport Avenue
Williamsburg, VA 23185
Entries include: Name, title, and address of trial court clerks and administrators. **Arrangement:** Geographical. **Pages** (approx.): 375. **Frequency:** Not established; first edition 1978. **Price:** $10.00.

★2464★
TYKE'S REGISTER OF POLITICAL ACTION COMMITTEES (FEDERAL)
Tyke Research Associates, Inc.
1629 K Street, N. W., Suite 537   Phone: (202) 296-7306
Washington, DC 20006
Covers: Over 2,000 corporate, association, labor, and other special interest committees that contribute funds, provide in-kind services, and campaign endorsements to federal candidates. **Entries include:** Organization name, committee name, address, phone, name of contact, description of activities, date established, objectives, etc. **Arrangement:** By type of organization, then alphabetical. **Indexes:** Committee name/geographical/personal name. **Pages** (approx.): 100. **Frequency:** Biennial, even years; monthly updates in "Political Action Report." **Editor:** Nathan J. Muller, Director of Research. **Advertising accepted.** Circulation 1,900. **Price:** $25.00; includes monthly updates. (Register not available without subscription to "Political Action Report.")

★2465★
UNDERWRITERS LIST OF TRIAL COUNSEL
Underwriters List Publishing Company, Inc.
C/o William Brinker, Inc.
48 Oakland Hills   Phone: (813) 697-3801
Rotunda West, FL 33946
Covers: Attorneys whose practice is primarily insurance claim defense. **Entries include:** Firm name, address, phone, kinds of practice (general insurance, fire insurance, etc.). **Arrangement:** Geographical. **Frequency:** Annual. **Price:** Apply. **Other information:** An insurance law list. See separate listing, "Law Lists."

★2466★
UNITED STATES BAR DIRECTORY
Attorneys' National Clearing House Company
Box 8688   Phone: (813) 263-0840
Naples, FL 33941
Entries include: Firm name, address, phone, preferred branches of practice, names of partners and associates. **Arrangement:** Geographical. **Pages** (approx.): 200. **Frequency:** Annual, October. **Editor:** Joseph A. Birk, President. **Price:** Free. **Other information:** A general law list. See separate listing, "Law Lists."

★2468★
U.S. DEPARTMENT OF THE INTERIOR TELEPHONE DIRECTORY
Interior Department
18th and C Streets, N. W.   Phone: (202) 343-7283
Washington, DC 20240
Covers: About 8,000 key employees, and offices, bureaus, and services. **Entries include:** For personal name listings - Name, branch or office, address, phone. Other listings include similar information. **Pages** (approx.): 100. **Frequency:** Semiannual. **Price:** $2.00. **Send orders to:** Government Printing Office, Washington, DC 20402

★2469★
U.S. ENVIRONMENTAL PROTECTION AGENCY ADVISORY COMMITTEES CHARTERS AND ROSTERS
Management and Organization Division
Environmental Protection Agency
401 M Street, S. W.   Phone: (202) 755-0866
Washington, DC 20460
Covers: Members of the federal advisory committees currently reporting to the Environmental Protection Agency. **Entries include:** For members - Name, address; rosters also include date term expires. **Arrangement:** By committee. **Indexes:** Personal name. **Pages** (approx.): 60. **Frequency:** Annual, winter. **Editor:** Mary Anne Beatty, EPA Committee Management Officer. **Price:** Free. **Also includes:** Charter for each advisory committee and copy of the Federal Advisory Committee Act.

★2470★
UNITED STATES GOVERNMENT MANUAL
National Archives and Records Service
General Services Administration
Washington, DC 20408
Background: The "Manual" is the official handbook of the United States government. It includes descriptions of agencies and other bodies in the legislative, judicial, and executive branches, and lists of their principal personnel, but the executive branch is covered in greatest depth. (The "Manual" devotes roughly 40 of 900 pages to the legislative branch and 15 to the judicial; the "Congressional Directory," described in a separate listing, devotes roughly 300 of 1,200 pages to the executive branch and 45 to the judicial.) Text of the listings is primarliy concerned with programs and activities rather than administrative structure, but general organization charts are given. The "Congressional Directory" and the "Manual" comprise the "data base" for principal federal government organizations and personnel. **Entries include:** For each cabinet department and independent agency or other unit, titles of major administrative posts and the names of incumbents are given, along with a description of the unit's responsibilities. Additional listings of subordinate offices and bureaus give same type of information. Addresses and phone numbers provided for units at all levels. **Arrangement:** By department and agency. **Indexes:** Personal name, agency name, subject. **Pages** (approx.): 900. **Frequency:** Annual, July. **Former title:** United States Government Organization Manual. **Price:** $6.75 (S/N 022-003-00982-5). **Send orders to:** Superintendent of Documents, Government Printing Office, Washington, DC 20402. **Other information:** Variant title, "United States Government Organization Manual."

United States Government Organization Manual *See* United States Government Manual

★2471★
UNITED STATES HOUSE OF REPRESENTATIVES—TELEPHONE DIRECTORY
Committee on House Administration
United States House of Representatives
U.S. Capitol, Suite H-326
Washington, DC 20515
Covers: Elected representatives and their staffs, including home district personnel. **Entries include:** For representatives - Name, state

and district, phone, room number. For staff - Name, staff or committee to which assigned, phone, room number; listings for home district personnel show out-of-town number. **Arrangement:** Alphabetical, classified by name of representative or committee; same information in each arrangement, and classified arrangement also shows title. **Pages** (approx.): 300. **Frequency:** Quarterly. **Price:** $2.50 per copy; $9.50 per year. **Send orders to:** Government Printing Office, Washington, DC 20402.

★2472★
UNITED STATES LAWYERS REFERENCE DIRECTORY
Legal Directories Publishing Company
8350 Central Expressway   Phone: (214) 692-5825
Dallas, TX 75206
Covers: Subscribing attorneys and principal personnel of county governments. **Frequency:** Biennial, even years. **Price:** $70.00. **Other information:** A law list. See separate listing, "Law Lists."

United States, State...Officers of Wisconsin *See* State, Congressional, Legislative, and County Officers of Wisconsin

★2474★
UTAH OFFICIAL ROSTER
Utah Department of Finance
State Capitol, Room 147   Phone: (801) 533-5801
Salt Lake City, UT 84114
Covers: State departments and agencies; legislature; judiciary; federal officials in Utah; members of the state's congressional delegation; colleges; county governments. **Entries include:** Name of department or other unit, address, phone, names and titles of principal officials; county government listings include county name, address, names of about ten officials for each. Some listings include party and length of term. **Pages** (approx.): 75. **Frequency:** Biennial, July of odd years. **Price:** Free.

★2475★
VERMONT LEGISLATIVE DIRECTORY AND STATE MANUAL
Vermont Secretary of State
109 State Street   Phone: (802) 828-2363
Montpelier, VT 05602
Covers: State departments and agencies; judiciary; legislature; county governments. **Entries include:** Name of department or other unit, no address or phone, and names, titles and city of residence of principal officials; listings for major executive department personnel and for legislators include biographical data. **Indexes:** General index includes significant non-recurrent items from previous directories, personal name. **Pages** (approx.): 225. **Frequency:** Biennial, December of odd years. **Editor:** Margaret E. Willey. **Price:** Free.

★2476★
VIRGINIA RECORD—DIRECTORY OF VIRGINIA OFFICIALS ISSUE
Virginia Publisher's Wing
Drawer 2-Y
Richmond, VA 23205
Publication includes: An entire issue is periodically devoted to Virginia state and local officials. **Frequency:** Irregular; approximately every two years; latest edition 1979. **Editor:** Clifford Dowdey. **Advertising accepted.** Circulation 5,500. **Price:** Included in subscription, $5.00 per year.

★2477★
VIRGINIAS, MARYLAND, DELAWARE & DISTRICT OF COLUMBIA LEGAL DIRECTORY
Legal Directories Publishing Company
8350 Central Expressway   Phone: (214) 692-5825
Dallas, TX 75206
Frequency: Latest edition 1977. **Price:** $18.00. **Other information:** Content, arrangement, etc., same as "Alabama Legal Directory;" see separate listing. (See also separate listing, "Law Lists.")

★2478★
WASHINGTON [Volume]: A comprehensive directory of the nation's capital...its people and institutions
Potomac Books, Inc.
Box 40604   Phone: (202) 338-5774
Washington, DC 20016
Covers: 6,000 federal and district government offices, businesses, associations, publications, radio and television stations, etc., in the District of Columbia area. **Entries include:** Name, address, phone, and other pertinent information. **Arrangement:** By subject or government agency. **Indexes:** Alphabetical. **Pages** (approx.): 560. **Frequency:** Biennial, odd years. **Editors:** Cary T. Grayson, Jr., and Susan Lukowski. **Price:** $27.50.

Washington Influence Directory *See* Washington Lobbyists/ Lawyers Directory

★2479★
WASHINGTON INFORMATION DIRECTORY
Congressional Quarterly, Inc.
1414 22nd Street, N. W.   Phone: (202) 296-6800
Washington, DC 20037
Covers: 5,000 governmental agencies, congressional committees, and non-governmental associations considered competent sources of specialized information. **Entries include:** Name of agency, committee, or association, address, phone, annotation concerning function or activities of the office, and name of contact. **Arrangement:** Classified by area of activity or competence (economics and business, housing and urban affairs, etc.). **Indexes:** Agency and organization, subject. **Pages** (approx.): 950. **Frequency:** Annual, May. **Price:** $22.50 (current edition); $25.00 (1980 edition).

★2480★
WASHINGTON INFORMATION WORKBOOK
Washington Researchers
918 16th Street, N. W.   Phone: (202) 828-4800
Washington, DC 20006
Covers: About 500 persons and offices in 21 federal departments and agencies able to provide information on specific aspects of their special fields. **Entries include:** Department, division, branch, etc., identification, and name and phone of individual sources. **Arrangement:** By department. **Pages** (approx.): 300. **Frequency:** Annual, spring. **Editor:** Margaret S. Jennings. **Price:** $35.00, postpaid, payment with order; $36.50, billed. **Other information:** Content is similar to "Directory of Federal Data Experts" section in same publisher's, "Researcher's Guide to Washington" (see separate entry). "Workbook" is described by publisher as "a companion piece" to the "Guide," but with less detail.

★2481★
WASHINGTON LEGISLATURE—PICTORIAL DIRECTORY
Washington Legislature
State Capitol   Phone: (206) 753-5000
Olympia, WA 98504
Covers: Elective state officials, senators, and representatives. **Entries include:** Name, portrait, home and Olympia addresses, party, district, term of office, biographical information. **Pages** (approx.): 50. **Frequency:** Biennial, odd years. **Price:** Free.

★2482★
WASHINGTON LOBBYISTS/LAWYERS DIRECTORY [District of Columbia]
Amward Publications
Box 137
Washington, DC 20044
Covers: Over 8,500 law, lobbying, public relations, and similar firms, and 2,400 political action committees (PAC's). **Entries include:** Name, address, phone, names of principals and account executives, and names of clients. **Arrangement:** Alphabetical. **Indexes:** Personal name (includes affiliations). **Pages** (approx.): 250. **Frequency:** Biennial, spring of odd years. **Editor:** Edward Zuckerman. **Former**

title: Washington Influence Directory (1977). **Price:** $25.00.

★2483★
WASHINGTON REPRESENTATIVES: LOBBYISTS, CONSULTANTS, REGISTERED FOREIGN AGENTS, LEGAL ADVISORS, PUBLIC RELATIONS AND GOVERNMENT AFFAIRS...
Columbia Books, Inc.
777 14th Street, N. W. Suite 1336   Phone: (202) 737-3777
Washington, DC 20005
Covers: Over 6,000 individuals and law or public relations firms registered as lobbyists or foreign agents who are representatives in Washington for companies, associations, labor unions, and special interest groups. Based on questionnaires to companies and associations as well as federal government records. **Entries include:** Lobbyist or agent listings show representative's name, title, address, phone, date registered as lobbyist or foreign agent, clients, and relevant background data. Organizations represented listings show name, headquarters' address and phone, names of representatives, and revelant background information. **Arrangement:** Alphabetical. **Indexes:** Organization subject of interest, foreign organization with individual representation. **Pages** (approx.): 395. **Frequency:** Annual, March. **Editors:** Arthur C. Close, Craig Colgate, Jr. **Former title:** Directory of Washington Representatives of American Associations and Industry; Washington Representatives: Who Does What for Whom. **Price:** $30.00 (current edition); $35.00 (1980 edition).

★2484★
WEST VIRGINIA BLUE BOOK
Clerk of the Senate
West Virginia Legislature
State Capitol, Room 215M   Phone: (304) 348-2272
Charleston, WV 25305
Publication includes: Lists of state departments and agencies; county and municipal governments; extensive list of associations and organizations. **Entries include:** For state government units - Unit name, address, names and titles of principal personnel; some listings include terms of office, city of residence, and/or photographs and biographical data. For county and municipal governments - County or city name, brief history and description, names and political parties of elective and appointive officials, mailing address. For associations - Organization name, address, name and address of president and secretary. **Indexes:** Personal name, keyword. **Pages** (approx.): 1,200. **Frequency:** Annual, February or March. **Editor:** J. C. Dillon, Jr. **Price:** Free. **Also includes:** Historical, statistical, and general information about the state.

White List See **Employees of Diplomatic Missions (White List) [Washington, D.C.]**

★2485★
WHO IS WHO IN THE OKLAHOMA LEGISLATURE
Legislative Reference Division
Oklahoma Department of Libraries
200 N. E. 18th Street
Oklahoma City, OK 73105
Entries include: Legislator's name, home and office addresses, personal and career data, party, district. **Pages** (approx.): 40. **Frequency:** Biennial, December, even years. **Editor:** Barbara Crouse, Head, Legislative Reference Division. **Price:** Free (mailing list is not maintained).

Who's Who in Government: Atlanta and Fulton County [Georgia] See **Political Directory: Atlanta and Fulton County [Georgia]**

★2486★
WHO'S WHO IN GOVERNMENT IN HAWAII
Chamber of Commerce of Hawaii
735 Bishop Street   Phone: (808) 531-4111
Honolulu, HI 96813
Covers: Elected state and county officials and members of Congress. **Entries include:** Official's name, office or home address, personal and

career data. **Arrangement:** Geographical. **Pages** (approx.): 25. **Frequency:** Biennial, January of odd years. **Price:** $3.00, plus 54¢ shipping.

★2487★
WHO'S WHO IN MILITARY CLUB MANAGEMENT
International Military Club Executives Association
1750 Old Meadow Road   Phone: (703) 821-3330
McLean, VA 22102
Covers: About 600 Naval, Army, Air Force, Marine, and Coast Guard personnel who manage military clubs; supplier members are also listed. **Entries include:** Name, office address and phone. For suppliers - Company name, address, product or service. **Arrangement:** Alphabetical. **Indexes:** Geographical. **Pages** (approx.): 65. **Frequency:** Annual, January. **Editor:** Richard B. Storey. **Advertising accepted.** Circulation 600. **Price:** $100.00.

★2488★
WHO'S WHO IN THE OREGON LEGISLATURE
Who's Who Publications, Inc.
108 N. W. Ninth Avenue   Phone: (503) 222-9794
Portland, OR 97209
Covers: Legislators and major elected state officers and administrative officials. **Entries include:** Name, office address and phone, home address, district, and personal, professional, and political history. **Arrangement:** Alphabetical within chamber. **Pages** (approx.): 125. **Frequency:** Biennial, December of even years. **Editor:** C. R. Hillyer. **Advertising accepted.** Circulation 3,200. **Price:** $2.50.

★2489★
WISCONSIN BLUE BOOK
Wisconsin Legislative Reference Bureau
State Capitol, Room 201N   Phone: (608) 266-0341
Madison, WI 53702
Publication includes: Lists of state departments and agencies; legislature; judiciary; state's congressional delegation; county governments. **Entries include:** Name of unit, address, phone, names and titles of principal officers, organization chart; some listings include biographical data and photographs. **Arrangement:** By level and unit of government. **Indexes:** Combined agency-institution-personal name index. **Pages** (approx.): 1,000. **Frequency:** Biennial, June of odd years. **Editors:** Dr. H. Rupert Theobald and Patricia V. Robbins. **Price:** $2.00, cloth; $1.00, paper. **Send orders to:** Document Sales and Distribution, 202 S. Thornton Avenue, Madison, WI 53702.

★2490★
WISCONSIN LEGAL DIRECTORY
Legal Directories Publishing Company
8350 Central Expressway   Phone: (214) 692-5825
Dallas, TX 75206
Frequency: Latest edition 1979. **Price:** $19.00. **Other information:** Content, arrangement, etc., same as "Alabama Legal Directory;" see separate listing. (See also separate listing, "Law Lists.")

★2491★
WISCONSIN LEGISLATIVE DIRECTORY
Wisconsin Association of Manufacturers and Commerce
111 E. Wisconsin Avenue, Suite 1600   Phone: (414) 271-9428
Milwaukee, WI 53202
Covers: State legislators and Wisconsin's congressional delegation. **Entries include:** Name, address, personal and career data. **Indexes:** Alphabetical, legislative district. **Pages** (approx.): 70. **Frequency:** Biennial, February of odd years. **Price:** $2.00.

★2492★
WISCONSIN MUNICIPAL DIRECTORY
League of Wisconsin Municipalities
122 W. Washington Avenue   Phone: (608) 266-9920
Madison, WI 53703
Covers: City and village, but not town, elected and appointed officials. **Frequency:** Revised monthly. **Price:** $20.00 each for lists of city or

village officials, payment with order.

★2493★
WOMEN ELECTED MUNICIPAL OFFICIALS [Massachusetts]
Massachusetts Municipal Associations
131 Tremont Street   Phone: (617) 426-7272
Boston, MA 02110
Covers: About 150 women selectmen, aldermen, or councillors in
Massachusetts. **Entries include:** Name, office address, education,
career data, areas of special knowledge or interest. **Arrangement:**
Geographical. **Pages** (approx.): 50. **Frequency:** Biennial, fall of even
years. **Editor:** Dorothy A. Holmes. **Price:** $5.00.

★2494★
WOMEN IN PUBLIC OFFICE
Center for the American Woman and Politics
Eagleton Institute of Politics
Rutgers University   Phone: (201) 828-2210
New Brunswick, NJ 80901
Covers: Over 17,000 women who served in 1976 and 1977 in
elective or appointive public office at local, state, or federal levels.
Entries include: Name, address, office. About 3,000 of the women
responded to requests for biographical information, and are listed in a
separate section; listings include name, address, phone, date of birth,
current occupation, present and former public offices held and dates,
current organizational memberships, education, party, etc.
Arrangement: By state; federal officeholders listed separately.
Indexes: Personal name. **Pages** (approx.): 600. **Frequency:** Irregular;
latest edition September 1978. **Editors:** Kathy Stanwick, Project
Director, and Marilyn Johnson, Statistical Research Director. **Price:**
$29.50. **Send orders to:** Scarecrow Press, Box 656, Metuchen, NJ
08840.

★2495★
WRIGHT-HOLMES LAW LIST
S & H Publishers, Inc.
485 Fifth Avenue, Room 907   Phone: (212) 986-8562
New York, NY 10017
Entries include: Firm name, address, percentage of practice devoted
to commercial law, and brief biographical data on firm members.
Arrangement: Geographical. **Frequency:** Annual, summer. **Price:**
Apply. **Other information:** A commercial law list. See separate listing,
"Law Lists."

★2496★
WYOMING OFFICIAL DIRECTORY
Wyoming Secretary of State
State Capitol   Phone: (307) 777-7378
Cheyenne, WY 82002
Covers: State departments and agencies; judiciary; legislature; county
governments. **Entries include:** Name of unit, address, names and
titles of principal officials; legislators' listings include district, party,
term of office; county listings include 12-15 elective and appointive
officials; some listings include photographs. **Arrangement:** By level
and unit of government. **Indexes:** Subject, personal name. **Pages**
(approx.): 225. **Frequency:** Annual, spring. **Editor:** Thyra Thomson.
Price: Free to Wyoming residents; $3.00 per copy to others. (Mailing
list is maintained.)

5

Science

and Engineering

★2497★
ACADEMIC COMPUTING DIRECTORY
Human Resources Research Organization
300 N. Washington Street   Phone: (703) 549-3611
Alexandria, VA 22314
Covers: About 375 educational institutions, ranging from elementary schools to universities, which are using computers for instructional purposes. **Entries include:** Name of school, address, description of program, list of computers employed. **Frequency:** Not established; first edition fall 1977. **Price:** $4.95.

★2498★
ACAROLOGISTS OF THE WORLD
Acarology Laboratory
Ohio State University
Columbus, OH 43210
Covers: About 1,400 persons concerned with the study of mites and ticks. **Entries include:** Name, address, interests. **Arrangement:** Alphabetical. **Indexes:** Geographical, subject. **Pages** (approx.): 155. **Frequency:** Irregular; latest edition January 1979 (1974-75 data). **Editor:** Donald E. Johnston. **Price:** $8.00, paper; $3.00, microfiche (PB 292-975-T). **Send orders to:** National Technical Information Service, Springfield, VA 22161.

★2499★
ACCREDITED PROGRAMS IN ARCHITECTURE
National Architectural Accrediting Board
1735 New York Avenue, N. W.   Phone: (202) 833-1180
Washington, DC 20006
Number of listings: 80. **Entries include:** Institution name, address, phone, name of dean, degrees awarded. **Arrangement:** Alphabetical. **Pages** (approx.): 5. **Frequency:** Annual, July. **Former title:** List of Accredited Programs in Architecture. **Price:** Free; small charge for bulk quantities.

ACS Laboratory Guide *See* Analytical Chemistry—Laboratory
    Guide Issue

★2500★
ADMINISTRATIVE DIRECTORY OF COLLEGE AND UNIVERSITY
    COMPUTER SCIENCE DEPARTMENTS AND COMPUTER
    CENTERS
Association for Computing Machinery
1133 Avenue of the Americas   Phone: (212) 265-6300
New York, NY 10036
Covers: Academic departments of computer science and data processing, college and university computer centers, and computer-

related associations. **Entries include:** For departments - Institution name, address, name of chairman of computer science department and degrees offered. For centers - Name of center and director, phone, equipment. For associations - Name, address, names and titles of staff. **Arrangement:** Departments, centers, and associations in separate lists. **Pages** (approx.): 175. **Indexes:** Chairman name, center director name. **Frequency:** Annual, January. **Editor:** J. M. Adams, Director of Operations. **Price:** $10.00.

★2501★
AEE DIRECTORY OF ENERGY PROFESSIONALS
Fairmont Press, Inc.
134 Peachtree Street, Suite 918M
Atlanta, GA 30303
Covers: Engineers, architects, and consultants in energy engineering and conservation who are members of the Association of Energy Engineers, and manufacturer and supplier members; Department of Energy regional offices and directors; state energy offices. **Entries include:** For members - Individual or company name, address, phone, services or products. For agencies - Name, address, phone, name of contact or chief executive. **Arrangement:** By activity. **Pages** (approx.): 280. **Frequency:** Not established; first edition November 1979. **Price:** $24.50. **Also includes:** Outline of hierarchy of federal agencies concerned with energy conservation.

Aerospace Medical Association—Directory *See* Aviation, Space,
    and Environmental Medicine—Directory Issue

Aerospace Medicine—Directory Issue *See* Aviation, Space, and
    Environmental Medicine—Directory Issue

★2502★
AEROSPACE RESEARCH INDEX
Francis Hodgson Reference Publications
Longman House
Burnt Mill, Harlow
Essex CM20 2JE, England
Covers: Over 4,000 institutions, research centers, etc., involved in aerospace research; worldwide coverage. **Entries include:** Name of unit, address, names of managers, number of research professionals, details of research activities. **Pages** (approx.): 700. **Frequency:** First edition expected 1980. **Price:** 75 pounds. **Send orders to:** Longman Group Ltd., 43/45 Annandale Street, Edinburgh EH7 4AT, Scotland.

★2503★

ALTERNATE ENERGY EQUIPMENT MANUFACTURERS
Synerjy
Box 4790
Grand Central Station
New York, NY 10017
Covers: 1,200 manufacturers of alternative energy equipment, including solar, other thermal sources (geothermal, heat recovery, wood, etc.), and wind and other small scale electrical energy sources, in three lists. **Frequency:** Revised several times yearly. **Editor:** Jeff Twine. **Price:** $3.50, solar list; $2.50 each for other two lists; $7.00 for all three.

★2504★

AMATEUR ENTOMOLOGISTS' SOCIETY—MEMBERSHIP LIST
Amateur Entomologists' Society
C/o 355 Hounslow Road Hansworth
Feltham, Middlesex TW13 5JH, England
Covers: 1,600 group and individual members worldwide who study insects. Includes the advisory panel of experts for the society. **Entries include:** Name, address, and area of interest. **Pages** (approx.): 40. **Frequency:** Irregular; latest edition 1978; annual supplements in November. **Editor:** P. W Scribb, General Editor. **Advertising accepted.** Circulation 1,600. **Price:** 1.50 pounds. **Send orders to:** L. Christie, 137 Gleneldon Rd., Streatham, London SW16, England.

★2505★

AMERICAN ACADEMY OF ENVIRONMENTAL ENGINEERS—ROSTER OF DIPLOMATES
American Academy of Environmental Engineers
Box 1278   Phone: (301) 762-7797
Rockville, MD 20850
Covers: 1,800 registered professional engineers with special interests and competence in engineering areas affecting the environment. **Arrangement:** Alphabetical. **Indexes:** Geographical. **Pages** (approx.): 120. **Frequency:** Annual, spring. **Editor:** Stanley E. Kappe, Executive Director. **Price:** $10.00; available only for scientific or educational purposes and commercial use at fee established by board of trustees.

American Academy of Sanitarians—Membership List *See* Professional Register—American Academy of Sanitarians

★2506★

AMERICAN ASSOCIATION FOR CRYSTAL GROWTH—DIRECTORY
American Association for Crystal Growth
C/o Ceres Corporation
411 Waverly Oaks Park   Phone: (617) 899-5522
Waltham, MA 02154
Covers: 500 physical scientists (chemists, physicists, ceramists, etc.) concerned with crystal growth theory and practice. **Entries include:** Name, office address, and home address. **Arrangement:** Alphabetical. **Pages** (approx.): 20. **Frequency:** Annual, February. **Editor:** J. F. Wenckus, Secretary. **Price:** Available to members only.

★2507★

AMERICAN ASSOCIATION FOR THE ADVANCEMENT OF SCIENCE HANDBOOK—OFFICERS, ORGANIZATION, ACTIVITIES
American Association for the Advancement of Science
1515 Massachusetts Avenue, N. W.   Phone: (202) 467-4400
Washington, DC 20005
Publication includes: Lists of officers, staff, committee members, affiliated organizations, Council members. **Pages** (approx.): 140. **Frequency:** Annual, spring. **Editor:** Catherine Borras, Assistant to the Executive Officer. **Price:** $2.50.

★2508★

AMERICAN ASSOCIATION FOR THE HISTORY OF MEDICINE— MEMBERSHIP DIRECTORY
American Association for the History of Medicine
C/o Robert P. Hudson, M.D., Department of the History of Medicine
Kansas University Medical Center   Phone: (913) 588-7040
Kansas City, KS 66103
Entries include: Name, address. **Arrangement:** Alphabetical. **Pages** (approx.): 30. **Frequency:** Biennial, July of even years. **Price:** $3.00 (current edition); $4.00 (1980 edition).

★2509★

AMERICAN ASSOCIATION OF COST ENGINEERS—DIRECTORY OF MEMBERS
AACE, Inc.
308 Monongahela Building   Phone: (304) 296-8444
Morgantown, WV 26505
Covers: 4,500 cost engineers and estimators, worldwide. **Entries include:** Name and preferred mailing address. **Arrangement:** Geographical. **Indexes:** Alphabetical. **Pages** (approx.): 50. **Frequency:** Annual, October. **Editor:** K. K. Humphreys, Executive Director. **Price:** $2.50; available to members only.

★2510★

AMERICAN ASSOCIATION OF PHYSICS TEACHERS—DIRECTORY OF MEMBERS
American Association of Physics Teachers
Graduate Physics Building
State University of New York   Phone: (516) 246-6840
Stony Brook, NY 11794
Number of listings: 10,000; international coverage. **Entries include:** Name, address, phone, membership code. **Arrangement:** Alphabetical. **Indexes:** Geographical. **Pages** (approx.): 80. **Frequency:** Approximately every five years; latest edition March 1976. **Editor:** A. A. Strassenburg, Executive Officer. **Price:** Free.

★2511★

AMERICAN ASSOCIATION OF SMALL RESEARCH COMPANIES— MEMBERS DIRECTORY
American Association of Small Research Companies
8794 W. Chester Pike   Phone: (215) 449-2333
Upper Darby, PA 19082
Covers: About 400 small research and development companies covering most scientific disciplines. **Entries include:** Company name, address, phone, name of principal executive, list of products or services. **Arrangement:** Alphabetical. **Indexes:** Geographical, discipline/technical field. **Pages** (approx.): 70. **Frequency:** Biennial, fall of even years. **Editor:** Joanne Martin. **Price:** $10.00.

★2512★

AMERICAN ASSOCIATION OF STRATIGRAPHIC PALYNOLOGISTS—MEMBERSHIP DIRECTORY
American Association of Stratigraphic Palynologists
C/o Amoco Production Company
Research Center
Box 591   Phone: (918) 627-3400
Tulsa, OK 74102
Covers: 600 persons engaged in or interested in research in all aspects of palynology (the branch of science dealing with pollen, spores, and other organic-walled microorganisms). **Entries include:** Name, office address and phone. **Arrangement:** Alphabetical and geographical. **Pages** (approx.): 60. **Frequency:** Annual, spring. **Editor:** Evan J. Kidson. **Price:** $3.00 (1980 edition).

★2513★
**AMERICAN BOARD OF CLINICAL CHEMISTRY—DIRECTORY OF
DIPLOMATES**
American Board of Clinical Chemistry
C/o Dr. Herbert E. Spiegel
Hoffman-LaRoche, Inc.
Building 34
Kingsland Street
Nutley, NJ 07110
Covers: About 640 chemists trained in clinical chemistry and certified
by the board. **Entries include:** Name, office address, home address.
Arrangement: Alphabetical. **Pages** (approx.): 30. **Frequency:**
Biennial, January of even years. **Editor:** Dr. Herbert E. Spiegel,
Secretary-Treasurer. **Price:** Available to members only.

★2514★
**AMERICAN BOARD OF PROFESSIONAL PSYCHOLOGY—
DIRECTORY OF DIPLOMATES**
American Board of Professional Psychology
2025 I Street, N. W., Suite 405   Phone: (202) 833-2730
Washington, DC 20006
Covers: 2,800 psychologists who have passed the board's
examination. **Entries include:** Name, office address, highest degree
held, areas of occupational specialization. **Arrangement:** Alphabetical.
Indexes: Geographical. **Pages** (approx.): 100. **Frequency:** Irregular;
latest edition 1980. **Editor:** Margaret Ives, Executive Officer. **Price:**
$10.00 (1980 edition).

American Board of Professional Psychology—Membership Roster
See American Psychological Association—Membership
Register

American Board of Psychological Hypnosis—Membership Roster
See American Psychological Association—Membership
Register

★2515★
**AMERICAN CERAMIC SOCIETY BULLETIN—CERAMIC COMPANY
DIRECTORY ISSUE**
American Ceramic Society
65 Ceramic Drive   Phone: (614) 268-8645
Columbus, OH 43214
Covers: 1,500 manufacturers, educational institutions, associations,
publications, etc., in the ceramic industry. **Entries include:** Name,
address, phone, telex number and cable address; year established;
description of product, service or activity; names and titles of
executives; number of employees. **Arrangement:** All types of groups
listed in single alphabet. **Indexes:** Product. **Pages** (approx.): 170.
Frequency: Annual, January. **Editor:** D. C. Snyder, Managing Editor.
Advertising accepted. Circulation 10,500. **Price:** $4.00 (current and
1980 editions).

★2516★
AMERICAN CERAMIC SOCIETY BULLETIN—ROSTER ISSUE
American Ceramic Society
65 Ceramic Drive   Phone: (614) 268-8645
Columbus, OH 43214
Covers: 7,500 personal and corporation members in the U. S. and 63
foreign countries. **Entries include:** Name, address, company
affiliation. **Arrangement:** Alphabetical. **Pages** (approx.): 230.
Frequency: Annual, October. **Editor:** D. C. Snyder. **Advertising
accepted.** Circulation 10,500. **Price:** $4.00. **Other information:**
Roster section titled, and sometimes cited separately as, ''Who's Who
in the World of Ceramics.''

★2517★
**AMERICAN CHEMICAL SOCIETY—RUBBER DIVISION MEMBERSHIP
DIRECTORY**
Rubber Division
American Chemical Society
1155 16th Street, N. W.   Phone: (202) 872-4600
Washington, DC 20036
Entries include: Name, company with which affiliated, company
address, and phone. **Arrangement:** By member name and company
name; company arrangement does not include phone. **Pages** (approx.):
145. **Frequency:** Annual. **Price:** Available to members only.

★2518★
AMERICAN CHEMICAL SOCIETY LIST OF APPROVED SCHOOLS
American Chemical Society
1155 16th Street, N. W.
Washington, DC 20036
Covers: About 550 institutions offering undergraduate programs in
chemistry which are approved by the association. **Entries include:**
Institution name, address. **Arrangement:** Geographical. **Pages**
(approx.): 10. **Frequency:** Annual, January. **Price:** Free.

★2519★
**AMERICAN COLLEGE OF LABORATORY ANIMAL MEDICINE—
DIRECTORY OF DIPLOMATES**
American College of Laboratory Animal Medicine
C/o Department of Animal Medicine
University of Massachusetts Medical School
55 Lake Avenue, North   Phone: (617) 856-3151
Worcester, MA 01605
Number of listings: 275. **Entries include:** Name, title affiliation,
office address, phone; year and school from which graduated; year
began membership in the association. Many listings also include
photograph. **Arrangement:** Alphabetical. **Indexes:** Geographical.
Pages (approx.): 55. **Frequency:** Annual, January. **Editor:** William S.
Webster, D.V.M., Ph.D., Secretary-Treasurer. **Price:** Available to
members only.

★2520★
AMERICAN CONSULTING ENGINEERS COUNCIL—DIRECTORY
American Consulting Engineers Council
1015 15th Street, N. W., Suite 802   Phone: (202) 296-5390
Washington, DC 20005
Covers: Member firms of state consulting engineering associations in
all states except West Virginia and Alaska (3,500 firms and 10,000
principals). **Entries include:** Company name, address, phone, names of
executives, number of employees, description of specialties and
services. **Arrangement:** Geographical. **Indexes:** Company, principals'
names. **Pages** (approx.): 350. **Frequency:** Annual, August. **Price:**
$25.00, payment must accompany order.

★2521★
**AMERICAN CONSULTING ENGINEERS COUNCIL—INTERNATIONAL
ENGINEERING DIRECTORY**
American Consulting Engineers Council
1015 15th Street, N. W., Suite 802
Washington, DC 20005
Covers: 75 member engineering consulting firms which practice
abroad. **Entries include:** Firm name, address, locations of branch
offices, names and titles of key personnel, services offered, areas of
expertise, selected typical projects. **Arrangement:** Alphabetical.
Indexes: Specialty. **Pages** (approx.): 200. **Frequency:** Biennial, even
years. **Price:** $10.00, payment must accompany order.

★2522★
**AMERICAN COUNCIL OF INDEPENDENT LABORATORIES—
DIRECTORY**
American Council of Independent Laboratories
1725 K Street, N. W.   Phone: (202) 659-3766
Washington, DC 20006
Covers: About 230 testing, research, and inspection laboratories.

Entries include: Firm name, address, phone, facilities, and professional memberships; some listings include names of executives. Arrangement: Alphabetical. Indexes: Geographical, services. Pages (approx.): 225. Frequency: Biennial, January of even years. Price: $4.00 (current edition); $5.00 (1980 edition); payment with order.

★2523★
AMERICAN ENGINEERING MODEL SOCIETY—MEMBERSHIP
   DIRECTORY
American Engineering Model Society
Box 2066
Aiken, SC 29801
Covers: About 600 individual, corporate, and student members interested in the creation of scale models for design, construction, and manufacturing purposes. Entries include: Company or individual name, address. Company listings show contact name; individual listings show name of employer, if any. Arrangement: By type of membership, then alphabetical. Pages (approx.): 10. Frequency: Annual, December. Editor: R. J. Hale, Executive Director. Price: Available to members only.

American Helicopter Society—Membership Directory See
   Vertiflite—American Helicopter Society Membership
   Directory Issue

★2524★
AMERICAN INSTITUTE FOR EXPLORATION—MEMBERSHIP &
   EXPEDITION DIRECTORY
American Institute for Exploration
1809 Nichols Raod   Phone: (616) 381-8237
Kalamazoo, MI 49007
Covers: About 400 members from a wide range of scientific disciplines. Entries include: Name, address, occupation, major expeditions, current field work, expedition interests. Arrangement: Alphabetical. Pages (approx.): 35. Frequency: Semiannual, April and November. Editor: Ted P. Bank II, Executive Director. Price: $4.00; controlled circulation. Also includes: Descriptions of expeditions sponsored by the institute within the past two years, with summaries of results.

★2525★
AMERICAN INSTITUTE OF ARCHITECTS—CALIFORNIA COUNCIL
   ANNUAL DIRECTORY
California Council
American Institute of Architects
1736 Stockton   Phone: (415) 986-0759
San Francisco, CA 94133
Covers: 6,500 California members of the institute. Entries include: Name, address, phone. Arrangement: By chapter. Pages (approx.): 140. Frequency: Irregular; latest edition January 1978. Editor: Melton Ferris. Advertising accepted. Circulation 12,500. Price: $1.00. Other information: Variant title, "Architectural Handbook."

American Institute of Architects—Firm Directory See Pro File/
   Architectural Firms/The American Institute of Architects

★2526★
AMERICAN INSTITUTE OF ARCHITECTS—MEMBERSHIP
   DIRECTORY
American Institute of Architects
1735 New York Avenue, N. W.   Phone: (202) 785-7264
Washington, DC 20006
Number of listings: 28,300. Entries include: Member name, firm or other affiliation, address, AIA chapter. Arrangement: Alphabetical. Indexes: Geographical. Frequency: Annual, May. Price: $60.00. Other information: Data on institute officers, board, and staff; scholarships for architecture students; list of accredited schools of architecture.

American Institute of Architects—Missouri Council Directory See
   Missouri Council of Architects Construction Industry
   Reference Book

★2527★
AMERICAN INSTITUTE OF CHEMISTS—MEMBERSHIP DIRECTORY
American Institute of Chemists
7315 Wisconsin Avenue   Phone: (301) 652-2447
Washington, DC 20014
Number of listings: More than 5,000. Entries include: Individual name and address, Arrangement: Same data listed alphabetically and geographically. Pages (approx.): 200. Frequency: Biennial, summer of odd years. Editor: David A. H. Roethel, Executive Director. Advertising accepted. Circulation 6,000. Price: $10.00; commercial use requires special permission.

★2528★
AMERICAN INSTITUTE OF PLANT ENGINEERS—MEMBERSHIP
   DIRECTORY
American Institute of Plant Engineers
3975 Erie Avenue   Phone: (513) 561-6000
Cincinnati, OH 45208
Covers: 8,000 plant engineers engaged in design, layout, construction, maintenance and/or control of fixed or mobile industrial facilities or manufacturing plants. Pages (approx.): 150. Frequency: Annual, August. Editor: Milton A. Tatter, Executive Director. Advertising accepted. Circulation 8,000. Price: Available to members only.

★2529★
AMERICAN INSTITUTE OF PROFESSIONAL GEOLOGISTS—
   MEMBERSHIP DIRECTORY
American Institute of Professional Geologists
Box 957   Phone: (303) 279-0026
Golden, CO 80401
Number of listings: 4,000; international coverage. Entries include: Name, address, phone, affiliation, certification number. Arrangement: Alphabetical. Indexes: Geographical (with specialty and field of practice). Pages (approx.): 225. Frequency: Annual, spring. Former title: Association of Professional Geological Scientists - Membership Directory (1979). Price: $12.00, plus $2.00 shipping.

American Laboratory Buyer's Guide See Laboratory Buyer's Guide

★2530★
AMERICAN LEATHER CHEMISTS ASSOCIATION—DIRECTORY
American Leather Chemists Association
Tanners' Council Laboratory
University of Cincinnati   Phone: (513) 475-2643
Cincinnati, OH 45221
Covers: About 900 chemists, leather technologists, and educators concerned with the tanning and leather industry. Entries include: Name, home address, company name, company address and phone. Arrangement: Alphabetical. Indexes: Company name. Pages (approx.): 190. Frequency: Annual, November. Advertising accepted. Circulation 1,000. Price: $10.00.

★2531★
AMERICAN MALACOLOGISTS: A NATIONAL REGISTER OF LIVING
   PROFESSIONAL AND AMATEUR CONCHOLOGISTS
American Malacologists
Box 2255   Phone: (305) 725-2260
Melbourne, FL 32901
Covers: Over 1,000 professional (about 40 percent) and amateur (about 60 percent) malacologists (mollusk and shellfish experts, paleoconchologists, and advanced shell collectors). Entries include: Name, office address, home address, personal data, career data, writings, club memberships, travels for shells, size of collection, research activities, honors. Arrangement: Alphabetical. Indexes: Place of residence, occupation, area of research. Pages (approx.): 610. Frequency: Irregular; first full edition published 1973, with

supplement in 1975; new edition expected 1980. **Editor:** Dr. R. Tucker Abbott. **Former title:** American Malacologist - A National Register of Professional and Amateur Malacologists and Private Shell Collectors and Biographies of Early American Mollusk Workers Born Between 1618 and 1900. **Price:** $12.50, cloth; $4.95, paper; 1975 supplement, $2.00. **Also includes:** Biographies of 500 important malacologists of the past.

American Mathematical Society *See* Combined Membership
    List...

★2532★
AMERICAN NUCLEAR SOCIETY—DIRECTORY
American Nuclear Society
555 N. Kensington Avenue   Phone: (312) 352-6611
La Grange, IL 60525
Number of listings: 11,000. **Entries include:** Name, address. **Arrangement:** Alphabetical. **Pages** (approx.): 140. **Frequency:** Irregular; latest edition 1976. **Price:** $28.00. **Other information:** Variant title, "Who's Who in Nuclear Energy."

★2533★
AMERICAN OIL CHEMISTS' SOCIETY—DIRECTORY OF
    MEMBERSHIP
American Oil Chemists' Society
508 S. Sixth Street   Phone: (217) 359-2344
Champaign, IL 61820
Covers: 3,800 chemical and engineering personnel concerned with processing and use of animal, vegetable, and marine fats and oils. **Entries include:** Name, home and business address, home and business phones, company affiliation, job title, committee service. **Arrangement:** Alphabetical. **Frequency:** Biennial, August (formerly annual). **Editor:** James Lyon, Executive Director. **Advertising accepted.** Circulation 3,800. **Price:** Available to members only.

★2534★
AMERICAN ORNITHOLOGISTS' UNION—MEMBERSHIP LIST
American Ornithologists' Union
National Museum of Natural History
Smithsonian Institution
Washington, DC 20560
Number of listings: 4,000. **Entries include:** Name, address, year of membership, year of class election, designation of class of membership. **Arrangement:** Alphabetical. **Pages** (approx.): 70. **Frequency:** Triennial; latest edition December 1979. **Price:** Apply. **Send orders to:** Dr. G. Woolfenden, Department of Biology, University of Florida, Tampa, Florida 33620. **Also includes:** Membership lists of Cooper Ornithological Society and Wilson Ornithological Society.

★2535★
AMERICAN PHYSICAL SOCIETY—"BULLETIN" MEMBERSHIP
    DIRECTORY ISSUE
American Physical Society
335 E. 45th Street   Phone: (212) 685-9422
New York, NY 10017
Covers: About 31,000 members in United States, Canada, and other countries. **Entries include:** Name, office or home address, daytime phone. **Arrangement:** Alphabetical. **Indexes:** Geographical, specialty. **Pages** (approx.): 240. **Frequency:** Irregular; approximately every two years; previous edition 1977; latest edition December 1979. **Editor:** Dr. W. W. Havens, Jr., Executive Secretary. **Price:** $10.00.

★2536★
AMERICAN PHYTOPATHOLOGICAL SOCIETY—DIRECTORY OF
    MEMBERS
American Phytopathological Society
3340 Pilot Knob Road   Phone: (612) 454-7250
St. Paul, MN 55121
Covers: 3,000 botanists and others interested in the control of plant diseases. **Entries include:** Name, address, phone, title, degree, date of degree, area of specialization. **Arrangement:** Alphabetical.

Frequency: Formerly biennial, previous edition 1974; now every five years, latest edition September 1979. **Editor:** Steven C. Nelson, Director of Publications. **Price:** Available to members only.

★2537★
AMERICAN PSYCHOLOGICAL ASSOCIATION—DIRECTORY
American Psychological Association
1200 17th Street, N. W.   Phone: (202) 833-7600
Washington, DC 20036
Covers: Over 49,000 members in the United States, Canada, and abroad. **Entries include:** Name, office or home address, office and/or home phone, date of birth, major field, areas of specialization, highest degree (year, field, and institution), present position(s) and immediate past positions, state licensure/certification as a psychologist, and membership and divisional affiliations. **Arrangement:** Alphabetical. **Indexes:** Geographical, divisional. **Pages** (approx.): 1,500. **Frequency:** Triennial; latest edition June 1978. **Editor:** Thomas J. Willette, Executive Editor. **Former title:** Biographical Directory of the American Psychological Association. **Price:** $50.00.

★2538★
AMERICAN PSYCHOLOGICAL ASSOCIATION—MEMBERSHIP
    REGISTER
American Psychological Association
1200 17th Street, N. W.   Phone: (202) 833-7600
Washington, DC 20036
Covers: Over 49,000 members in the United States, Canada, and abroad; also includes membership rosters of American Board of Professional Psychology and American Board of Psychological Hypnosis. **Entries include:** Name, office or home address, phone, membership and divisional affiliations. **Arrangement:** Alphabetical. **Indexes:** Divisional. **Pages** (approx.): 440. **Frequency:** Annual, April, in years when APA "Directory" is not published ("Directory" is triennial from 1978). **Editor:** Thomas J. Willette, Executive Editor. **Price:** $15.00 (current and 1980 editions).

★2539★
AMERICAN ROAD AND TRANSPORTATION BUILDERS
    ASSOCIATION—OFFICIALS AND ENGINEERS DIRECTORY
American Road and Transportation Builders Association
525 School Street, S. W.   Phone: (202) 488-2722
Washington, DC 20024
Covers: Over 4,000 administrative engineers and officials in federal, state, and county transportation agencies. Includes officials from state departments of transportation, highways, and aeronautics, and equivalent federal officials, plus federal officials concerned with railroads and urban mass transit. **Entries include:** Name, agency or department affiliation, address, phone. **Arrangement:** By agency or department. **Pages** (approx.): 135. **Frequency:** Annual, April. **Editor:** Richard M. Lauzier. **Former title:** Directory of Highway Officials and Engineers. **Price:** $7.00, postpaid.

★2540★
AMERICAN SOCIETY FOR MICROBIOLOGY—DIRECTORY OF
    MEMBERS
American Society for Microbiology
1913 I Street, N. W.   Phone: (202) 833-9680
Washington, DC 20006
Number of listings: 30,000. **Entries include:** Name, address, phone. **Arrangement:** Alphabetical. **Indexes:** Geographical indexes for American and foreign members. **Pages** (approx.): 320. **Frequency:** Irregular; latest edition 1979. **Price:** $15.00.

★2541★
AMERICAN SOCIETY OF CIVIL ENGINEERS—OFFICIAL REGISTER
American Society of Civil Engineers
345 E. 47th Street   Phone: (212) 644-7538
New York, NY 10017
Publication includes: List of state and local branches and state technical groups. **Entries include:** Name of section or group; geographical or technical areas covered; and names, offices held, and

addresses of officers. **Arrangement:** Geographical. **Indexes:** Alphabetical. **Pages** (approx.): 255. **Frequency:** Annual, January. **Editor:** Irving Amron. **Price:** Free. **Also includes:** Extensive description of divisions and committees of the society, with names only of officers and committee members.

★2542★
AMERICAN SOCIETY OF NAVAL ENGINEERS—DIRECTORY
American Society of Naval Engineers
1012 14th Street, N. W., Suite 807
Washington, DC 20005
Covers: 4,500 civilian and Naval engineers engaged in or interested in design, construction, operation, and maintenance of Naval and maritime craft, navigation, motive power, etc., as related to Navy needs. **Entries include:** Member name, title, activity or company, and home or business address. **Arrangement:** Alphabetical. **Indexes:** Alphabetical, personal name. **Pages** (approx.): 100. **Frequency:** Biennial, odd years. **Advertising accepted.** Circulation 4,500. **Price:** Available to members only.

★2543★
AMERICAN SOCIETY OF SWEDISH ENGINEERS—MEMBERSHIP DIRECTORY
American Society of Swedish Engineers
One Dag Hammarskjold Plaza, Suite 3800
New York, NY 10017
Number of listings: 200. **Entries include:** Member name, office and home addresses. **Arrangement:** Alphabetical. **Pages** (approx.): 30. **Frequency:** Annual, September. **Advertising accepted.** Circulation 300. **Price:** Apply.

★2544★
AMERICAN SOCIETY OF VETERINARY OPHTHALMOLOGY—DIRECTORY
American Society of Veterinary Ophthalmology
1820 August
Stillwater, OK 74074
Covers: 175 member veterinarians interested in animal ophthalmology. **Entries include:** Name, address, phone (office and home numbers), and year of graduation. **Arrangement:** Geographical. **Indexes:** Alphabetical, chronological. **Frequency:** Annual, December. **Editor:** Dr. Art J. Quinn, Secretary-Treasurer. **Price:** Available to members only.

★2545★
AMERICAN SOCIETY OF ZOOLOGISTS—MEMBERSHIP LIST
American Society of Zoologists
Box 2739
California Lutheran College   Phone: (805) 529-2475
Thousand Oaks, CA 91360
Covers: About 4,500 college and university professors and graduate students in the field of zoology. **Entries include:** Name, address, phone number, and divisional affiliation. **Arrangement:** Alphabetical by member name. **Pages** (approx.): 80. **Frequency:** Every four years; latest edition 1977.

American Statistical Association—Roster *See* **Directory of Statisticians**

★2546★
AMERICAN WATER WORKS ASSOCIATION—MEMBERSHIP ROSTER
American Water Works Association
6666 W. Quincy Avenue   Phone: (303) 794-7711
Denver, CO 80235
Covers: 27,000 water works managers, superintendents, educators, engineers, chemists, bacteriologists, and others interested in water supply; municipal and private water departments; manufacturers of water works equipment; consultants. **Arrangement:** Alphabetical. **Indexes:** Geographical. **Pages** (approx.): 320. **Frequency:** Irregular; previous edition 1973; latest edition January 1978. **Price:** $9.00;

available to members only.

★2547★
AMERICAN WATER WORKS ASSOCIATION—OFFICERS AND COMMITTEE DIRECTORY
American Water Works Association
6666 W. Quincy Avenue   Phone: (303) 794-7711
Denver, CO 80235
Number of listings: More than 2,200, primarily local officers and members of national technical committees. **Entries include:** Committee name, description of function, names and addresses of members. **Arrangement:** By committee name. **Pages** (approx.): 110. **Frequency:** Annual, fall. **Price:** $4.00.

★2548★
AMERICAN WATER WORKS ASSOCIATION, TEXAS SECTION—ANNUAL DIRECTORY ISSUE
Southwest and Texas Sections
American Water Works Association
Box 769   Phone: (817) 778-1313
Temple, TX 76501
Covers: 1,500 water works managers, superintendents, educators, engineers, chemists, bacteriologists, and others interested in water supply and treatment; municipal and private water departments; manufacturers of water works equipment; consultants. **Entries include:** Name, title, department, full address. **Arrangement:** Alphabetical. **Pages** (approx.): 90. **Frequency:** Annual, December. **Editor:** Walter T. Proctor. **Advertising accepted.** Circulation 5,800. **Price:** $1.00.

★2549★
ANALYTICAL CHEMISTRY—LABORATORY GUIDE ISSUE
American Chemical Society
1155 16th Street, N. W.   Phone: (202) 872-4600
Washington, DC 20036
Covers: About 1,800 manufacturers of scientific instruments, equipment, chemicals, and other supplies for research and control chemical laboratories; laboratory supply houses; analytical and research services. **Entries include:** Company name, address, phone. **Arrangement:** Alphabetical. **Indexes:** Product, chemical, service, trade name. **Pages** (approx.): 250. **Frequency:** Annual, August. **Editor:** Herbert A. Laitinen. **Advertising accepted.** Circulation 71,000. **Price:** $4.00. **Other information:** Published, titled, and numbered as an issue of "Analytical Chemistry," but frequently cited separately as "ACS Laboratory Guide;" also known as "LabGuide."

★2550★
ANIMAL RESOURCES—A RESEARCH RESOURCES DIRECTORY
Division of Research Resources
National Institutes of Health
Health, Education, and Welfare Department   Phone: (301) 496-5545
Bethesda, MD 20014
Covers: Major primate research centers of National Institutes of Health, and animal diagnostic laboratories, information projects, reference centers, and special colony and model study centers supported by the Division of Research Resources. **Entries include:** Resource name, address, phone, names of principal investigators, name of contact person, and details on the installation. **Arrangement:** By type of center. **Indexes:** Geographical. **Pages** (approx.): 60. **Frequency:** Irregular; latest edition 1978. **Editor:** Dr. Freeman Quimby, Project Manager. **Price:** Single copies free (DHEW NIH 79-1431). **Send orders to:** Research Resources Information Center, 1776 E. Jefferson St., Rockville, MD 20852 (301-881-4150).

Architectural Handbook *See* **American Institute of Architects—California Council Annual Directory**

★2551★

ARCHITECTURE SCHOOLS IN NORTH AMERICA

Association of Collegiate Schools of Architecture
1735 New York Avenue, N. W.   Phone: (202) 785-2324
Washington, DC 20006
Number of listings: 100. **Entries include:** School name, address; statistics on the student body; percent of applications accepted; tuition rates; scholarship information; names and specialties of faculty; descriptions of graduate, undergraduate and special programs; entrance requirements; application deadlines. **Arrangement:** Alphabetical. **Indexes:** Faculty specialty, school specialty. **Pages** (approx.): 250. **Frequency:** Biennial, fall of odd years. **Editor:** Roger Schluntz, Executive Director. **Former title:** Architectural Schools in North America. **Price:** $8.95. **Other information:** Published with and available from: Peterson's Guides, 228 Alexander Street, Princeton, NJ 08540 (609-924-5338).

★2552★

ARID-LANDS RESEARCH INSTITUTIONS: A WORLD DIRECTORY

Office of Arid Lands Studies
University of Arizona
Tucson, AZ 85721
Covers: 200 agencies in 40 countries, including commissions, university departments, government departments, foundations, scientific societies, and commercial research agencies. **Entries include:** Name of institution; date of information; type of institution; governing body; address of headquarters and field sites; area of specialization; projects, past, present and planned; staff; facilities; publications; institution history. **Arrangement:** Geographical. **Indexes:** Institution name. **Pages** (approx.): 270. **Frequency:** Irregular; previous edition 1967; latest edition 1977. **Editor:** Patricia Paylore. **Price:** $7.50. **Send orders to:** University of Arizona Press, Tucson, AZ 85721 (602-884-1441).

★2553★

ARPANET DIRECTORY

ARPANET Network Information Center
SRI International
Menlo Park, CA 94025
Covers: Users and host organizations on ARPANET, the Advance Research Programs Agency Network of the Defense Department. **Entries include:** User or host name, online and offline mail addresses, phone, and host affiliation of users. **Send orders to:** National Technical Information Service, Springfield, VA 22161.

★2554★

ARPANET RESOURCE HANDBOOK

ARPANET Network Information Center
SRI International
Menlo Park, CA 94025
Covers: Data bases and other resources available for use on ARPANET, the Advance Research Programs Agency Network of the Defense Department. **Entries include:** Name of host organization, address, data bases or other resources available, name and phone number of contacts, and enough descriptive procedure to permit a user to find and access resources. **Frequency:** Latest edition March 1979. **Send orders to:** National Technical Information Service, Springfield, VA 22161.

Association for Women in Science—Job Bulletin See AWIS Job Bulletin

★2555★

ASSOCIATION OF ACADEMIES OF SCIENCE—DIRECTORY AND PROCEEDINGS

Association of Academies of Science
C/o Ohio Academy Of Science
445 King Avenue   Phone: (614) 424-6045
Columbus, OH 43201
Covers: 44 state and local academies of science in 40 states affiliated with American Association for the Advancement of Science.

Entries include: Academy name and address, names and addresses of officers, academy activities and awards. **Arrangement:** Geographical. **Pages** (approx.): 100. **Frequency:** Annual, summer. **Editor:** Everett L. Wisman, President. **Price:** $5.00.

★2556★

ASSOCIATION OF CONSERVATION ENGINEERS—MEMBERSHIP DIRECTORY

Association of Conservation Engineers
Aaron J. Lane
Kansas Fish and Game Commission
Route 2, Box 54A   Phone: (316) 672-5911
Pratt, KS 67124
Covers: 160 persons with administrative or engineering background in conservation. **Frequency:** Annual. **Price:** Available to members only.

Association of Consulting Chemists and Chemical Engineers— Membership Directory See Consulting Services [Chemists and Chem. Engineers]

★2557★

ASSOCIATION OF CYTOGENETIC TECHNOLOGISTS— LABORATORY DIRECTORY

Association of Cytogenetic Technologists
616 S. Orchard Drive   Phone: (213) 226-4606
Burbank, CA 91506
Covers: About 200 laboratories (with at least one association member on the staff) which study heredity using genetic and cellular biology techniques. **Entries include:** Laboratory name, address, phone, areas of specialization, techniques, and names of director and cytogenetic technologists. **Arrangement:** Geographical. **Indexes:** Alphabetical. **Pages** (approx.): 40. **Frequency:** Annual, December. **Editor:** Barbara Kaplan. **Price:** Available to members only. **Send orders to:** Robby Nebergall, Membership Secretary, 929 N. St. Francis, Wichita, KS 67214.

★2558★

ASSOCIATION OF DATA PROCESSING SERVICE ORGANIZATIONS—MEMBERSHIP DIRECTORY

Association of Data Processing Service Organizations
1925 N. Lynn Street   Phone: (703) 522-5055
Arlington, VA 22209
Covers: 1,000 computer service organizations, worldwide. **Entries include:** Company name, address, phone, names of executives, number of employees, financial data, and products or services offered. **Arrangement:** Geographical. **Pages** (approx.): 145. **Frequency:** Annual, September. **Price:** $50.00, payment with order.

Association of Energy Engineers—Membership Directory See AEE Directory of Energy Professionals

★2559★

ASSOCIATION OF ENVIRONMENTAL ENGINEERING PROFESSORS—MEMBERSHIP LIST

Association of Environmental Engineering Professors
C/o Professor Charles R. O'Melia
Department of Environmental Science & Engineering
Univ. of North Carolina   Phone: (919) 966-1171
Chapel Hill, NC 27514
Number of listings: 350. **Entries include:** Name, title, school of affiliation, office address and phone. **Arrangement:** Alphabetical. **Pages** (approx.): 15. **Frequency:** Annual, winter. **Editor:** Charles R. O'Melia. **Price:** Available to members only.

Association of Professional Geological Scientists—Membership Directory See American Institute of Professional Geologists— Membership...

Association of Science-Technology Centers—Directory *See*
Exploring Science: Guide to Contemporary Museums of
Science and Technology

★2560★
ASTRONOMY DIRECTORY [Western states]
Astronomical Society of the Pacific
1290 24th Avenue   Phone: (415) 661-8660
San Francisco, CA 94122
Covers: Planetariums, observatories, amateur astronomy groups,
astronomy courses, stores specializing in astronomy equipment, and
other astronomy services. About 100-150 entries in each separate
edition for Northern California, Southern California, Pacific Northwest,
and Rocky Mountains. **Entries include:** Institution or company name,
address, phone, contact person; institutional listings give time, date,
cost and similar data for courses and events; commercial listings
indicate merchandise carried, discounts available to society members.
Arrangement: By type of institution or service. **Pages** (approx.): 20.
Frequency: Irregular; latest edition 1979; updates to be issued.
Editor: Janet Doughty, Program Coordinator.

★2561★
**AUTHOR'S GUIDE TO JOURNALS IN PSYCHOLOGY, PSYCHIATRY
    & SOCIAL WORK**
Haworth Press
149 Fifth Avenue   Phone: (212) 228-2800
New York, NY 10010
Number of listings: About 450. **Entries include:** Publication name,
address for manuscripts, publication orientation and subject interests,
usual review time and delay in publication of accepted manuscripts,
early publication options (if any), where publication is indexed or
abstracted. **Indexes:** Subject, title, keyword. **Pages** (approx.): 260.
Frequency: Not established; first edition 1977. **Editors:** Allan Markle
and Roger C. Rinn. **Price:** $16.95.

★2562★
**AUTOMATIC DATA PROCESSING EQUIPMENT INVENTORY IN THE
    UNITED STATES GOVERNMENT**
Automated Data and Telecommunications Service
General Services Administration   Phone: (202) 566-1594
Washington, DC 20405
Covers: Digital computers installed throughout the United States
government and/or operated by cost reimbursement-type
contractors, as of end of fiscal year. **Entries include:** Department or
agency using equipment; ADP unit number; office, command, or
bureau and city where located; manufacturer name and model number
of equipment; number owned and number leased at that location; and
supplier, if other than manufacturer. **Arrangement:** Identical data
presented in three arrangements: 1) by department or agency; 2) by
manufacturer; 3) by location. **Pages** (approx.): 600. **Frequency:**
Annual, October. **Former title:** Inventory of Automatic Data
Processing Equipment in the U. S. Government. **Price:** $9.75. **Send
orders to:** Government Printing Office, Washington, DC 20402.

★2563★
AUTOMOTIVE ENGINEERING—ROSTER ISSUE
Society of Automotive Engineers
400 Commonwealth Drive   Phone: (412) 776-4841
Warrendale, PA 15096
Covers: 30,000 members, worldwide. Includes list of student
chapters. **Entries include:** Member name, company name, address,
job title. **Arrangement:** Alphabetical by member name. **Indexes:**
Members by company name. **Pages** (approx.): 280. **Frequency:**
Annual, March. **Editor:** Larry Givens. **Advertising accepted.**
Circulation 33,000. **Price:** Available to members only.

★2564★
AVIATION AND SPACE MUSEUMS OF AMERICA
Arco Publishing Company, Inc.
219 Park Avenue South   Phone: (212) 777-6300
New York, NY 10003
Covers: Nearly 60 museums and collections in 22 states and 3
Canadian provinces. **Entries include:** Name of museum, description,
hours, fees. **Arrangement:** Geographical. **Pages** (approx.): 290.
Frequency: Not established; first edition 1975. **Editor:** Jon L. Allen.
Price: $6.95.

★2565★
**AVIATION, SPACE, AND ENVIRONMENTAL MEDICINE—
    DIRECTORY ISSUE**
Aerospace Medical Association
Washington National Airport   Phone: (703) 892-2240
Washington, DC 20001
Covers: 3,500 medical and scientific personnel engaged in aviation,
space research, and environmental medicine. **Entries include:** Name,
address. **Arrangement:** Alphabetical. **Pages** (approx.): 105.
Frequency: Annual, December. **Editor:** John P. Marberger, Ph.D.,
D.Sc. **Former title:** Aerospace Medicine - Directory Issue. **Price:**
$5.50, plus $1.00 shipping; available for personal use of members
only (ISSN 0095-6562).

★2566★
AVIATION/SPACE WRITERS ASSOCIATION—MANUAL
Aviation/Space Writers Association
Cliffwood Road   Phone: (201) 538-0050
Chester, NJ 07930
Publication includes: List of members, who are writers on aviation
and space subjects for media, industry, and government. **Entries
include:** Name, title, affiliation (if any), address, phone; type of
membership. **Arrangement:** Alphabetical. **Indexes:** Geographical,
affiliation. **Pages** (approx.): 100. **Frequency:** Annual, September.
Editor: William F. Kaiser. **Advertising accepted.** Circulation 6,000.
Price: $25.00.

★2567★
AWIS JOB BULLETIN
Association for Women in Science
1346 Connecticut Avenue, N. W., Suite 1122
Washington, DC 20036
Covers: Positions available in various scientific fields in the United
States. **Entries include:** Name of position, institution or firm with
opening, application deadline, duties or responsibilities, and application
information (contact person, address, etc.). **Frequency:** Every three
weeks. **Price:** $15.00 per year.

★2568★
BIO-ENERGY DIRECTORY
Bio-Energy Council
1625 I Street, N. W., Suite 825A   Phone: (202) 833-5656
Washington, DC 20006
Covers: More than 500 biomass programs being pursued in
government and industry, including solid waste resource recovery
projects; surveys sources of biomass materials and energy, microbial
and thermal conversion projects, and alcohol technology. **Entries
include:** Program name, objective, name of operating group, address,
names of personnel, sponsor name and its financial commitments,
summary of operation. **Arrangement:** Classified by type of operation.
Indexes: Organization name, geographical. **Pages** (approx.): 535.
Frequency: Annual, May. **Editor:** Paul F. Bente, Jr. **Price:** $40.00,
postpaid.

Biographical Directory of the American Psychological Association
    See American Psychological Association—Directory

★2569★

BIOMEDICAL ENGINEERING SOCIETY—DIRECTORY

Biomedical Engineering Society
Box 2399   Phone: (213) 789-3811
Culver City, CA 90230
Number of listings: About 550. **Entries include:** Member name, affiliation, institution (university, hospital, or company), office phone, home address and phone, short description of interests. **Arrangement:** Alphabetical. **Pages** (approx.): 80. **Frequency:** Annual, spring. **Editor:** Kay Lyou, Executive Assistant. **Advertising accepted.** Circulation 2,700. **Price:** Available to members only.

Biometric Society—Roster *See* Directory of Statisticians

★2570★

BIOTECHNOLOGY RESOURCES—A RESEARCH RESOURCES DIRECTORY

Division of Research Resources
National Institutes of Health
Health, Education, and Welfare Department   Phone: (301) 496-5545
Bethesda, MD 20014
Covers: Division of Research Resources grantee facilities (large scale and mini-computer systems, nuclear magnetic resonance spectrometers, electric spin resonancy spectrometers, etc.) which can be used by biomedical investigators. **Entries include:** Resource name, address, phone, names of principal investigators, name of contact person, and details on the installation. **Arrangement:** By research area. **Frequency:** Irregular; latest edition August 1978. **Editor:** Dr. Freeman Quimby, Project Manager. **Price:** Single copies free (DHEW NIH 79-1430). **Send orders to:** Research Resources Information Center, 1776 E. Jefferson St., Rockville, MD (301-881-4150).

★2571★

BLACK ENTERPRISE—BLACK ENGINEERING FIRMS [Article]

Earl G. Graves Publishing Company
295 Madison Avenue   Phone: (212) 889-8220
New York, NY 10017
Covers: 45 engineering firms owned or controlled by Blacks, nationwide. **Entries include:** Firm name, address, phone, name of president or partner, engineering specialties. **Arrangement:** Geographical. **Frequency:** Appears in May 1977 issue. **Editor:** Earl G. Graves. **Advertising accepted. Price:** $1.25.

★2572★

BOTANICAL SOCIETY OF AMERICA—DIRECTORY

Botanical Society of America
Biological Sciences
University of Kentucky   Phone: (606) 258-8770
Lexington, KY 40506
Covers: 3,200 members. **Entries include:** Name, address, research specializations. **Arrangement:** Alphabetical. **Pages** (approx.): 85. **Frequency:** Biennial, fall of odd years. **Former title:** Botanical Society of America - Yearbook. **Price:** $8.00, payment must accompany order.

★2573★

BUILDING OFFICIALS AND CODE ADMINISTRATORS INTERNATIONAL—MEMBERSHIP DIRECTORY

Building Officials and Code Administrators International
17926 S. Halsted   Phone: (312) 799-2300
Homewood, IL 60430
Covers: Approximately 5,500 construction and building code officials, architects, engineers, trade associations, and manufacturers. **Entries include:** Name, office address. **Arrangement:** Alphabetical within categories of membership. **Pages** (approx.): 200. **Frequency:** Annual, spring. **Editor:** William Even, Manager, Publications Service. **Advertising accepted.** Circulation 5,000. **Price:** $15.00.

★2574★

BUSINESS WEEK—R&D SCOREBOARD ISSUE

McGraw-Hill, Inc.
1221 Avenue of the Americas   Phone: (212) 997-1221
New York, NY 10020
Publication includes: List of more than 600 companies which report expenditures of at least one million dollars for research and development in preceding year. **Entries include:** (In chart form) Company name, sales in two preceding years, research and development expenses in preceding year and percent change from second preceding year, and several other statistical measures. **Arrangement:** Alphabetical within industry categories. **Frequency:** Annual, in a July issue. **Price:** $1.25 (current and 1980 editions).

★2575★

CATALOG OF FEDERAL METROLOGY AND CALIBRATION CAPABILITIES

National Measurement Laboratory
National Bureau of Standards
Commerce Department
Washington, DC 20234
Covers: About 200 federal laboratories involved in metrology and calibration; not represented as a complete list. **Entries include:** Laboratory name, location, name and phone of contact. Laboratory capabilities are shown separately in tabular form. **Arrangement:** By federal department, than alphabetical by name of facility. **Indexes:** Geographical (in form of map). **Pages** (approx.): 60. **Frequency:** Not established; first edition June 1979. **Editor:** Kathryn O. Leedy. **Price:** $5.25, paper; $3.00, microfiche (PB 297-151). **Send orders to:** National Technical Information Service, Springfield, VA 22161.

★2576★

CATALOG OF MODEL SERVICES AND SUPPLIES

American Engineering Model Society
Box 2066   Phone: (803) 649-6710
Aiken, SC 29801
Covers: About 75 vendors of services and supplies for the creation of accurate three-dimensional scale models for use in design, construction, and manufacturing, in United States and 29 other countries. Includes list of high schools, colleges, and technical schools with technical modeling programs. **Entries include:** Company name, address, name of principal executive. **Arrangement:** Alphabetical. **Indexes:** In-house capabilities, contract builders and specialties (highways and bridges, topographical models, litigation, etc.), vendors of components and supplies. **Pages** (approx.): 30. **Frequency:** Annual, July. **Editor:** R. J. Hale, Executive Director. **Price:** $3.00 (current and 1980 editions).

★2577★

CHEMICAL & ENGINEERING NEWS—CAREER OPPORTUNITIES ISSUE

American Chemical Society
1155 16th Street, N. W.   Phone: (202) 872-4600
Washington, DC 20036
Covers: 700 companies in the chemical process industry which are employers of professional and management personnel. **Pages** (approx.): 60. **Frequency:** Annual, October. **Editor:** Michael Heylin. **Advertising accepted.** Circulation 120,000. **Price:** $1.00.

★2578★

CHESAPEAKE BAY DIRECTORY

Chesapeake Research Consortium
1419 Forest Drive, Suite 207   Phone: (301) 263-0884
Annapolis, MD 21403
Covers: Academic researchers, institutions, agencies, and environmental organizations concerned with water quality of Chesapeake Bay. **Entries include:** Name of institution, agency, etc., address, phone; names and specialties of personnel are given in listings for research organizations, names of contacts in other listings. **Arrangement:** Type of organization. **Pages** (approx.): 130. **Frequency:** Not established; first edition 1978; new edition expected

1980. **Price:** Apply. Also available from National Technical Information Service, Springfield, VA 22161 (PB 285-610).

★2579★
CHICAGO LAKEFRONT DEMONSTRATION PROJECT ENVIRONMENTAL INFORMATION DIRECTORY
Illinois Coastal Zone Management Program
Marina City Office Building
300 N. State Street, Room 1010
Chicago, IL 60610
Covers: Sources of environmental data on the southern basin of Lake Michigan. **Entries include:** Name and address of source, name of contact, phone, profile of data available, geographic location of sampling points. **Arrangement:** By general subject area (coastal processes, air quality, etc.). **Indexes:** Author, subject, agency. **Pages** (approx.): 500. **Frequency:** First edition July 1977. **Editors:** Paul Borek, Russell Davenport, Carol Unzicker. **Price:** Apply. **Send orders to:** Paul Borek, City of Chicago Department of Planning, City and Community Development, 121 N. LaSalle St., Rm. 1000, Chicago, IL 60602.

★2580★
CHRISTIAN ASSOCIATION FOR PSYCHOLOGICAL STUDIES— MEMBERSHIP DIRECTORY
Christian Association for Psychological Studies
University Hills Christian Center
27000 Farmington Road   Phone: (313) 477-1350
Farmington, MI 48018
Covers: Christians involved in psychology, psychiatry, counseling, sociology, social work, the clergy, nursing, and students in these and related studies who are members. Christian colleges and agencies which offer counseling services are described separately. **Entries include:** Name, office address and phone number, home address, highest degree held, areas of occupational specialization, personal and career data. **Arrangement:** Geographical. **Pages** (approx.): 100. **Frequency:** Irregular; latest edition September 1979. **Editor:** Dr. J. Harold Ellens, Editor-in-Chief. **Price:** $10.00.

★2581★
CITIZEN'S ENERGY DIRECTORY—A GUIDE TO ALTERNATIVE ENERGY RESOURCES
Citizens' Energy Project
1110 Sixth Street, N. W.   Phone: (202) 783-0452
Washington, DC 20001
Covers: About 635 industries, individuals, and government and private organizations working in fields of alternative energy, energy conservation, and appropriate technology. Includes workers with solar energy, wind, wood, methane, geothermal energy, and hydroelectric energy innovations. **Entries include:** Company or organization name, address, phone, names of executives, number of employees, list of products or services, publications, activities and services, special interests. **Arrangement:** Geographical. **Indexes:** Subject, alphabetical. **Pages** (approx.): 200. **Frequency:** Annual, June. **Editor:** Ken Bossong, Coordinator, Ciizens' Energy Project. **Price:** $15.00.

★2582★
COLLEGE CHEMISTRY FACULTIES
American Chemical Society
1155 16th Street, N. W.   Phone: (202) 872-4589
Washington, DC 20036
Covers: 2,500 departments in 2- and 4-year colleges and universities in the United States, Canada, and Mexico with instruction in chemistry, biochemistry, chemical engineering and related disciplines. **Entries include:** Institution name, address, department name and phone, degrees offered, and names of faculty, with major teaching field, highest earned degree, and academic rank. **Arrangement:** Geographical. **Indexes:** Institution, personal name. **Pages** (approx.): 200. **Frequency:** Irregular, about every 4 years; latest edition 1977. **Editor:** Bonnie R. Blaser. **Price:** $15.00.

★2583★
COLLEGE CHEMISTRY SENIORS
American Chemical Society
1155 16th Street, N. W.
Washington, DC 20036
Covers: About 1,000 seniors who have studied chemistry and chemical engineering and wish to continue that study in graduate school. **Entries include:** Name, address, educational and personal data. **Arrangement:** Alphabetical. **Frequency:** Annual, fall. **Price:** $30.00.

★2584★
COLLEGES OF VETERINARY MEDICINE ACCREDITED OR APPROVED BY THE AMERICAN VETERINARY MEDICAL ASSOCIATION
American Veterinary Medical Association
930 N. Meacham Road   Phone: (312) 885-8070
Schaumburg, IL 60196
Number of listings: About 35; coverage includes Canada and Europe. **Entries include:** Institution name, address; name of dean, accreditation status, year of latest review. **Arrangement:** Geographical. **Pages** (approx.): 5. **Frequency:** Irregular, at least annual; latest edition October 1979. **Price:** $1.00; send stamped, self-addressed no. 10 envelope.

★2585★
COMBINED MEMBERSHIP LIST of the Am. Mathematical Soc., Mathematical Assn. of Am., and Soc. for Industrial and Applied Math.
Society for Industrial and Applied Mathematics
33 S. 17th Street   Phone: (215) 564-2929
Philadelphia, PA 19103
Covers: 40,000 mathematicians, educators, physicists, chemists, computer specialists, industrial managers, and institutions. **Entries include:** Name, title or position, and place of employment; mailing address; and affiliations. Phone numbers of universities and mathematics departments have been included. **Arrangement:** Alphabetical and geographical listings of individual members; geographical listings of academic and institutional members. **Frequency:** Annual, summer. **Advertising accepted.** Circulation 19,500. **Price:** $10.00.

★2586★
COMPANIES HOLDING BOILER AND PRESSURE VESSEL CERTIFICATES OF AUTHORIZATION FOR USE OF CODE SYMBOL STAMPS
American Society of Mechanical Engineers
345 E. 47th Street   Phone: (212) 644-7722
New York, NY 10017
Covers: About 2,500 manufacturers certified by the society's Boiler and Pressure Vessel Committee for production of one or more types of non-nuclear power boilers, heating boilers, and pressure vessels; international coverage. **Entries include:** Company name, address, code indicating authorized products. **Arrangement:** Same information is provided alphabetically, by code symbol stamp, and geographically. **Pages** (approx.): 200. **Frequency:** Annual, July; winter supplement. **Price:** $35.00, including supplement. **Other information:** Holders of nuclear certificates are now listed separately. See listing for "Companies Holding Nuclear Certificates of Authorization."

★2587★
COMPANIES HOLDING NUCLEAR CERTIFICATES OF AUTHORIZATION
American Society of Mechanical Engineers
345 E. 47th Street   Phone: (212) 644-8051
New York, NY 10017
Covers: About 700 manufacturers certified by the society's Boiler and Pressure Vessel Committee for production of one or more types of pressure vessels for nuclear applications. **Entries include:** Company name, address, and limitations of items which it is authorized by its certificate to produce. **Frequency:** Bimonthly (a complete,

revised list in each issue). **Price:** $45.00.

★2588★
COMPENDIUM OF METEOROLOGICAL TRAINING FACILITIES
World Meteorological Organization
41 Avenue Giuseppe-Motta, Case Postale No. 5
1211 Geneva 20, Switzerland
Covers: Meteorological training institutions in 90 countries. **Entries include:** Name and address of institution, nature of instruction, language of courses, duration, entrance qualifications, starting date and frequency of course, tuition, and condensed syllabus. **Arrangement:** Geographical. **Pages** (approx.): 365. **Frequency:** Irregular; previous edition 1972; latest edition 1977. **Price:** 25 Swiss Francs (WMO No. 240).

★2589★
COMPLIANCE STATUS OF MAJOR AIR POLLUTING FACILITIES
Division of Stationary Source Enforcement
Office of General Enforcement
Environmental Protection Agency   Phone: (202) 755-0103
Washington, DC 20460
Covers: 24,000 manufacturing plants and other air pollution sources in the United States. **Entries include:** Company and plant name, address (without Zip codes), SIC code, information on pollution compliance status. **Arrangement:** Alphabetical within EPA region, state, and SIC sequences, identical information in each list. **Pages** (approx.): 700. **Frequency:** Semiannual, January and June. **Price:** $16.25 (current and 1980 editions). **Send orders to:** National Information Service, Springfield, VA 22161.

★2590★
COMPUTER SCIENCE & TECHNOLOGY: GUIDE TO COMPUTER PROGRAM DIRECTORIES
Institute for Computer Sciences and Technology
National Bureau of Standards
Commerce Department
Washington, DC 20234
Covers: Publishers of about 60 software catalogs listing programs available from a wide variety of sources, and about 25 periodicals and similar publications which include information on availability of programs in most or all issues. **Entries include:** For catalogs - Name, address, and phone of publisher; type of publication (report, books, etc.), with any identifying number; author; frequency; date published and present status; description of content and subjects covered. For periodicals - Similar information; if publication does not consist entirely of software information, the name of the appropriate section, column, etc., is given. **Indexes:** Application (inventory, insurance industry, etc.), system (assemblers, data base management, etc.). **Pages** (approx.): 170. **Frequency:** Not established; first edition December 1977. **Editor:** Addie G. Chattie. **Price:** $3.25 (S/N 003-003-0187-8). **Send orders to:** Government Printing Office, Washington, DC 20402. **Other information:** Sometimes cited as, "Guide to Computer Program Directories."

★2591★
CONSULTING AND LABORATORY SERVICES
J. W. Lundy Enterprises
Box 543   Phone: (814) 234-4584
State College, PA 16801
Covers: Nearly 550 firms offering engineering and scientific consulting, testing, analytical, and research and development services in 20 midwestern and eastern states. **Entries include:** Firm name, address, name of chief executive, phone; number of research or consulting employees; percentage of external work performed; ownership; affiliation with other companies or laboratories. **Arrangement:** By service, then geographical. **Pages** (approx.): 170. **Frequency:** Not established; first edition 1979. **Price:** $34.75, plus $1.35 shipping. **Other information:** Variant title, "Directory of Consulting and Laboratory Services."

★2592★
CONSULTING SERVICES [Chemists and chemical engineers]
Association of Consulting Chemists and Chemical Engineers
50 E. 41st Street   Phone: (212) 684-6255
New York, NY 10017
Covers: About 125 consultants in chemistry, chemical engineering, metallurgy, etc. **Entries include:** Individual name, address, certificate number, qualifications, experience. **Indexes:** Specialty, materials/products, process/equipment. **Pages** (approx.): 100. **Frequency:** Irregular; latest edition summer 1978; new edition expected January 1980. **Price:** $20.00 (current edition); $25.00 (tentative, 1980 edition); postpaid.

Cooper Ornithological Society—Membership List *See* American Ornithologists' Union—Membership List

★2593★
CURRENT RESEARCH PROFILE FOR ALASKA
Arctic Environmental Information and Data Center
University of Alaska
707 A Street   Phone: (907) 279-4523
Anchorage, AK 99501
Covers: Over 1,600 research projects being conducted in Alaska and its offshore waters in the physical, biological, and social sciences. **Entries include:** Name and address of principal investigator, names of co-investigators, geographical data site, project title, and description of objectives and potential applications of the project. **Arrangement:** By subject area. **Indexes:** Investigator, affiliation, funding agency, subject. **Pages** (approx.): 530. **Frequency:** Annual, spring. **Editor:** Linda Perry Dwight, Supervisor of Information Services. **Price:** $10.00.

★2594★
CURRICULA IN THE ATMOSPHERIC AND OCEANOGRAPHIC SCIENCES—COLLEGES AND UNIVERSITIES IN THE U.S. AND CANADA
American Meteorological Society
45 Beacon Street   Phone: (617) 227-2425
Boston, MA 02108
Number of listings: 100. **Entries include:** Name and address of school, names and specialties of staff, degrees offered, courses, special facilities. **Arrangement:** Alphabetical. **Pages** (approx.): 300. **Frequency:** Biennial, January of even years. **Editor:** Evelyn Mazur, Assistant to the Executive Director. **Price:** $5.00, plus $1.50 shipping.

CUYB Directory of Software *See* International Directory of Software

★2595★
DATA BASE MAPPING MODEL AND SEARCH SCHEME TO FACILITATE RESOURCE SHARING...—DIRECTORY OF CHEMICAL DATA BASES
Information Retrieval Research Laboratory
Coordinated Sciences Laboratory
University of Illinois
Urbana, IL 61801
Covers: More than 150 bibliographic, numeric, and algorithmic chemical data bases. **Entries include:** Full and short names of data base; names, addresses, phone numbers, and names of contacts of data base producer, distributor, and generator; availability and charges for data base tapes; subject matter and scope of data on tape; indexing data, etc. **Arrangement:** By data base short name. **Pages** (approx.): 450. **Frequency:** Published December 1977. **Editors:** Martha E. Williams, et al. **Price:** Apply. Also available from National Technical Information Service, Springfield, VA 22161 (PB 283-893; $14.00, paper; $3.00, microfiche). **Other information:** Full title, "Data Base Mapping Model and Search Scheme to Facilitate Resource Sharing. Volume 2. Directory of Chemical Data Bases." (Final Report, Grant No. NSF SIS 74-18558.)

★2596★

DIRECTORY OF AEROSPACE EDUCATION

American Society for Aerospace Education
821 15th Street, N. W., Suite 432   Phone: (202) 347-2315
Washington, DC 20005
Publication includes: Resource centers, museums, organizations, institutions, and resource people interested in or useful in aerospace (aviation and space) education. **Pages** (approx.): 80. **Frequency:** Biennial, April of even years. **Advertising accepted.** Circulation 200,000. **Price:** $6.95 (1980 edition).

★2597★

DIRECTORY OF ANIMAL DISEASE DIAGNOSTIC LABORATORIES

National Veterinary Services Laboratories
Agriculture Department
Box 844   Phone: (515) 232-0250
Ames, IA 50010
Entries include: Laboratory name, address, description of services. **Arrangement:** Geographical. **Pages** (approx.): 175. **Frequency:** Annual. **Price:** Free.

Directory of Behavior and Design Research *See* International Directory of Behavior and Design Research

Directory of Black Architects and Engineers in the West *See* Directory of Black Design Firms in the West

★2598★

DIRECTORY OF BLACK DESIGN FIRMS IN THE WEST

San Francisco Redevelopment Agency
Box 646   Phone: (415) 771-8800
San Francisco, CA 94101
Covers: 60 architectural, engineering, planning and landscape design firms. **Entries include:** Firm name, address, phone. **Arrangement:** Alphabetical. **Frequency:** Annual, early in year. **Editor:** Benson Hattem. **Former title:** Directory of Black Architects and Engineers in the West. **Price:** Free.

★2599★

DIRECTORY OF CANCER RESEARCH INFORMATION RESOURCES

International Cancer Research Data Bank
National Cancer Institute
National Institutes of Health
Blair Building, Room 114
8300 Colesville Road   Phone: (301) 427-7150
Silver Spring, MD 20910
Covers: More than 750 cancer information sources, including libraries, organizations, cancer registries, and special information services; also includes data bases furnishing abstracts; bibliographies; etc. **Frequency:** Irregular; latest edition May 1979; new edition expected 1981. **Price:** $10.75 (PB 293-187). **Send orders to:** National Technical Information Service, Springfield, VA 22161.

★2600★

DIRECTORY OF CERTIFICATES OF COMPLIANCE FOR RADIOACTIVE MATERIALS PACKAGES

Office of Nuclear Material Safety and Safeguards
U. S. Nuclear Regulatory Commission
Washington, DC 20555
Publication includes: In Volume 2, certificates issued to users of packaging approved by the commission. **Indexes:** Certificates by model number. **Pages** (approx.): 550. **Frequency:** Annual, November. **Price:** Volume 2, $19.00, paper; $3.00, microfiche (PB 275-579). **Send orders to:** National Technical Information Service, Springfield, VA 22161.

Directory of College Geography of the United States *See* Schwendeman's Directory of College Geography of the United States

★2601★

DIRECTORY OF COMPUTER EDUCATION AND RESEARCH

Science and Technology Press, Inc.
Box 1040   Phone: (518) 374-7893
Schenectady, NY 12301
Covers: About 1,400 junior and senior colleges (in separate volumes) which offer major programs in computer sciences and/or use computers in instruction or research. **Entries include:** Institution name, address; degrees and programs offered; names of departments, schools, etc., which offer programs, names of principal administrators, and program descriptions; description of computer facilities and research activities; principal individual courses. **Arrangement:** Geographical. **Pages** (approx.): 1,800. **Frequency:** First edition June 1973; new edition possible spring 1980. **Editor:** T. C. Hsiao. **Price:** $50.00 (current edition); $90.00 (tentative, 1980 edition). **Other information:** Publisher offers as Volume three of this set a 1975 publication, "Who's Who in Computer Education and Research," which gives biographical data on about 2,000 persons actively engaged in teaching and research in computer science and related fields; $35.00. Publisher also offers an "International Edition" of the "Directory" which provides same information in same format for about 950 institutions outside the United States (about two-thirds of them in Great Britain, France, Canada, Japan, and Germany); international edition was published in June 1978; $150.00.

★2602★

DIRECTORY OF COMPUTERIZED ENVIRONMENTAL INFORMATION RESOURCES

Institute for Mining and Minerals Research
University of Kentucky
Lexington, KY
Entries include: Resource name, address; description of material available, functions, and services; subjects embraced; publications. **Pages** (approx.): 50. **Frequency:** Published October 1976; no new edition planned. **Editors:** Gilbert E. Smith, Donald A. Blome, and James E. Jones, Jr. **Price:** $4.00 (paper copy; PB 262-486-4WL). **Send orders to:** National Technical Information Service, Springfield, VA 22161.

Directory of Consulting and Laboratory Services *See* Consulting and Laboratory Services

★2603★

DIRECTORY OF CONTRACT SERVICE FIRMS [Engineering]

C. E. Publications, Inc.
Box A   Phone: (206) 485-7575
Kenmore, WA 98028
Covers: 600 contract firms which are actively engaged in the employment of engineering and technical personnel for "temporary" contract assignments throughout the world. **Entries include:** Company name, address, phone, name of contact, description of needs and work locations. **Arrangement:** Alphabetical. **Indexes:** Geographical by location of firm. **Pages** (approx.): 240. **Frequency:** Annual, July. **Editor:** Jerry A. Erikson. **Advertising accepted.** Circulation 5,000. **Price:** $5.00.

★2604★

DIRECTORY OF DEPARTMENT OF ENERGY RESEARCH AND DEVELOPMENT PROGRAMS

Government R&D Report
Box 85
M.I.T. Station   Phone: (617) 356-2424
Cambridge, MA 02139
Covers: Personnel of the new Department of Energy and its programs. Includes cross references from former Federal Energy Administration and Energy Research and Development Administration programs to presently responsible offices. Also includes department organizational charts. **Entries include:** Name, phone, areas of expertise or administrative responsibilities. **Arrangement:** Alphabetical. **Pages** (approx.): 90. **Frequency:** Not established; first edition fall 1977. **Editor:** William G. Margetts. **Price:** $18.00, postpaid.

Directory of Design Firms *See* Engineering-News Record
Directory of Design Firms

Directory of Energy Professionals *See* AEE Directory of Energy
Professionals

Directory of Engineering College Research and Graduate Study
See Engineering Education—Engineering College Research
and Graduate...

★2605★
DIRECTORY OF ENGINEERING (SCIENTIFIC AND MANAGEMENT)
DOCUMENT SOURCES
Global Engineering Documentation Services, Inc.
3301 W. MacArthur Boulevard   Phone: (714) 540-9870
Santa Ana, CA 92704
Covers: Over 3,500 issuers of engineering documents, primarily
government agencies. Entries include: Name, address, document
identification code, acronym or initialism. Arrangement: Alphabetical
by acronym or initialism. Pages (approx.): 385. Frequency: Irregular;
latest edition 1974. Editor: Dave Simonton. Price: $39.95.

★2606★
DIRECTORY OF ENGINEERING SOCIETIES AND RELATED
ORGANIZATIONS
Engineers Joint Council
345 E. 47th Street   Phone: (212) 644-7850
New York, NY 10017
Covers: Over 460 national, regional, Canadian, and international
organizations concerned with engineering and related fields. Indexes:
Geographical. Pages (approx.): 180. Frequency: Biennial, odd years.
Price: $23.00, payment with order.

★2607★
DIRECTORY OF ENGINEERS IN PRIVATE PRACTICE
National Society of Professional Engineers
2029 K Street, N. W.   Phone: (202) 331-7020
Washington, DC 20006
Covers: Persons belonging to NSPE who are also members of its
Professional Engineers in Private Practice division, including 2,000
consulting engineering firms, individual members, and firms which
practice internationally. Entries include: For companies - Name,
address, phone, name of principal executive, list of services. For
members - Name, address; most listings include phone. Arrangement:
Firms are geographical, then by specialty; individuals are alphabetical.
Pages (approx.): 260. Frequency: Biennial, January of even years.
Editor: Jack McKee, Staff Director, PEPP Division. Price: $30.00.

★2608★
DIRECTORY OF FEDERAL ENERGY GRANT AND CONTRACT
PROGRAMS
Government R&D Report
Box 85
M.I.T. Station   Phone: (617) 356-2424
Cambridge, MA 02139
Covers: Federal officials and agencies, and congressional committees,
responsible for federal energy grant and contract programs and energy
legislation. Entries include: By agency. Indexes: Energy grant and
contract program by type of energy and by technology/type of
activity. Pages (approx.): 430. Frequency: First edition October
1978. Editor: William G. Margetts, Editor/Publisher. Price: $29.00.

★2609★
DIRECTORY OF FEDERAL ENVIRONMENTAL RESEARCH AND
DEVELOPMENT PROGRAMS
Government R&D Report
Box 85
M.I.T. Station   Phone: (617) 356-2424
Cambridge, MA 02139
Covers: Federal officials and agencies, and congressional committees
responsible for environmental programs. Entries include: Agency,

committee, or individual name, office address, phone. Arrangement:
By agency. Indexes: R&D by type of pollution and by type of activity.
Pages (approx.): 300. Frequency: First edition March 1978. Editor:
William G. Margetts, Editor/Publisher. Price: $21.00.

★2610★
DIRECTORY OF FEDERAL EXPERTS IN FIRE TECHNOLOGY AND
RELATED FIELDS
Fire Administration
Commerce Department
Washington, DC 20230
Covers: About 150 persons employed throughout the federal
government in fire safety technology or related fields. Entries
include: Name, job title, agency, address, phone, Civil Service
classification, areas of expertise. Arrangement: Alphabetical by
personal name. Indexes: Agency, geographical, specialization. Pages
(approx.): 150. Frequency: Not established; first edition December
1978. Price: $13.25, paper; $3.00, microfiche (PB 291-963). May
also be available from the agency. Send orders to: National Technical
Information Service, Springfield, VA 22161.

★2611★
DIRECTORY OF FEDERAL TECHNOLOGY TRANSFER
Federal Council for Science and Technology
Washington, DC 20506
Covers: About 45 agencies involved in technology transfer activities,
which enable state and local governments and private industry to
benefit from federal research and development. Entries include:
Name of agency, programs, activities, contact persons.
Arrangement: Classified by agency. Pages (approx.): 200.
Frequency: Irregular; new edition due June 1977. Price: $4.80
(1975). Send orders to: National Technical Information Service,
Springfield, VA 22161. (Not verified)

★2612★
DIRECTORY OF FIRMS ENGAGED IN RESEARCH IN THE STATE OF
NEW MEXICO
Bureau of Business and Economic Research
University of New Mexico   Phone: (505) 277-2216
Albuquerque, NM 87131
Number of listings: 240. Entries include: Company name, address,
phone, name of principal executive, type of research performed.
Arrangement: Classified by type of research. Indexes: Alphabetical.
Frequency: Irregular; latest edition 1976. Price: $3.00.

★2613★
DIRECTORY OF GEOSCIENCE DEPARTMENTS-UNITED STATES
AND CANADA
American Geological Institute
5205 Leesburg Pike   Phone: (703) 379-2480
Falls Church, VA 22041
Covers: More than 700 departments of geology, geochemistry,
geophysics, and other geosciences, their staffs, and courses, including
field courses. Arrangement: Geographical. Indexes: Faculty,
specialty, institution name. Pages (approx.): 200. Frequency: Annual,
November. Advertising accepted. Price: $12.00.

★2614★
DIRECTORY OF GRADUATE RESEARCH [Chemistry]
American Chemical Society
1155 16th Street, N. W.   Phone: (202) 872-4589
Washington, DC 20036
Covers: About 520 institutions offering doctoral degrees in
chemistry, chemical engineering, biochemistry, and pharmaceutical or
medicinal chemistry located in the United States and Canada. Entries
include: Name of institution, address, phone, department name,
degrees offered, fields of specialization; names of faculty members,
their educational backgrounds, special research interests, personal
phone number, and recent publications; names and thesis titles of
recent Ph.D. graduates. Arrangement: Classified by discipline, then
alphabetical by keyword in institution name. Indexes: Personal name.

Pages (approx.): 1,000. **Frequency:** Biennial, October of odd years. **Price:** $30.00. **Also includes:** Statistics by department on staff size, degrees granted, etc.

Directory of Highway Officials and Engineers *See* Amer. Road & Trans. Builders Association—Officials and Engineers Directory

★2615★
DIRECTORY OF HYDRAULIC RESEARCH INSTITUTES AND LABORATORIES
International Association for Hydraulic Research
Rotterdamseweg 185
Box 177
Delft, Netherlands
Covers: About 300 laboratories, worldwide. **Entries include:** Laboratory name, address, phone, director's name, number of staff, financial data, and type of services. **Arrangement:** Geographical. **Pages** (approx.): 600 (looseleaf). **Frequency:** Partial revisions biennially; new edition expected March 1980. **Price:** Fl 60 (current and 1980 editions).

★2616★
DIRECTORY OF MARINE RESEARCH FACILITIES AND PERSONNEL IN MAINE
Research Institute of the Gulf of Maine
21 Vocational Drive
South Portland, ME 04106
Covers: Marine science facilities, personnel, and aquaculture and cooperative fishing organizations. **Entries include:** For facilities - Name, address, phone, description of courses or activities. For personnel - Name, affiliation and title, address, phone, research interests and projects. For organizations - Name, address, name of contact, principal catch. **Arrangement:** Classified. **Indexes:** Personal interests. **Pages** (approx.): 175. **Frequency:** Irregular; fourth edition 1978. **Editors:** Diane S. Brackett and Karen R. Moore. **Price:** $8.00, paper; $3.00, microfiche (PB 278-288). **Send orders to:** National Technical Information Service, Springfield, VA 22161.

★2617★
DIRECTORY OF MARINE SCIENTISTS IN THE STATE OF NORTH CAROLINA
Office of Marine Affairs
North Carolina Department of Administration
Administration Building
116 W. James Street
Raleigh, NC 27603
Entries include: Name, affiliation, degree, and research interests. **Frequency:** Published 1976. **Price:** Free.

★2618★
DIRECTORY OF MINORITY ARCHITECTURAL AND ENGINEERING FIRMS
American Consulting Engineers Council
1155 15th Street, N. W.
Washington, DC 20005
Covers: Over 300 minority architectural and engineering firms. **Entries include:** Firm name, address, phone, names of principals, firm size, and list of services. Firms which returned a notarized statement that they are Minority Business Enterprise and Architect-Engineer Services according to the U. S. Code of Federal Regulations are designated "Cert." **Arrangement:** Geographical. **Indexes:** Firm name, services. **Frequency:** Not established; first edition spring 1977. **Price:** $15.00 (ACEC Document 62). **Other information:** Published jointly with the American Institute of Architects.

★2619★
DIRECTORY OF MOSQUITO CONTROL AGENCIES
American Mosquito Control Association
5545 E. Shields Avenue   Phone: (209) 291-6676
Fresno, CA 93727
Covers: About 550 mosquito control agencies in the United States

and Canada, of which about 150 control other disease carriers as well. **Arrangement:** Geographical. **Pages** (approx.): 35. **Frequency:** Irregular, every 5-10 years; latest edition 1977. **Price:** $5.00.

★2620★
DIRECTORY OF NATIONAL AND INTERNATIONAL POLLUTION MONITORING PROGRAMS
Center for Short-Lived Phenomena
Smithsonian Institution
60 Garden Street   Phone: (617) 864-7910
Cambridge, MA 02138
Covers: Long-term monitoring activities worldwide concerned with 25 pollutants and water quality indicators. Compiled for United Nations Environment Programme. **Entries include:** Administering agency, pollutants monitored, physical medium monitored (air, drinking water, food, etc.), geographical areas covered, technical information on methods, etc. **Arrangement:** International programs listed by program name; national programs listed by country. **Indexes:** Pollutant, medium, country. **Pages** (approx.): 1,200. **Frequency:** First published 1974; see "Other Information," below. **Price:** $45.00 set, $20.00 each; Volume I, International Programs and National Programs, Argentina-Ghana; Volume II, National Programs, Greece-Swaziland; Volume III, National Programs, Sweden-Zaire. **Send orders to:** Unipub, Box 433, Murray Hill Station, New York, NY 10016. **Other information:** Data base is updated by the Smithsonian Institution under contract to United Nations Environment Programme and now contains data on more than 700 programs in 78 countries. 1,860 pages. Magnetic tape also available. Detailed information on request from Unipub.

★2621★
DIRECTORY OF NATURAL SCIENCE CENTERS
Natural Science for Youth Foundation
763 Silvermine Road   Phone: (203) 966-5643
New Canaan, CT 06840
Covers: 1,300 natural science centers, outdoor education projects, children's museums, museum education departments, and trailside museums, which feature active nature education programs for children, youth, adults, and educators in the United States and Canada. **Entries include:** Name, address, number of staff, facilities, acres of land, programs, annual budget and source of income, hours, and admission or parking fees. **Arrangement:** Geographical. **Pages** (approx.): 200. **Frequency:** Annual, fall. **Editor:** John Ripley Forbes, President. **Price:** $10.00.

★2622★
DIRECTORY OF NATURE CENTERS AND RELATED ENVIRONMENTAL EDUCATION FACILITIES
Environmental Information and Education Division
National Audubon Society
950 Third Avenue   Phone: (212) 832-3200
New York, NY 10022
Covers: Over 900 nature centers, resident outdoor schools, and outdoor laboratories in the United States and Canada. **Entries include:** Name, address, phone, organization responsible for operation and maintenance of facility, size of facility (in acres), formal program offerings, special features, guided and/or self-guided tours, seasons and hours open, fees, and code indicating if not open to public. **Arrangement:** Geographical. **Pages** (approx.): 335. **Frequency:** Irregular; previous edition 1975; latest edition summer 1979. **Price:** $6.95.

★2623★
DIRECTORY OF NAVY ELECTRO-OPTICAL PROFESSIONALS
Electro-Optical Technology Program Office
Naval Research Laboratory, Code 1409
Navy Department   Phone: (202) 767-3799
Washington, DC 20375
Covers: About 500 Navy personnel with special expertise in laser technology, holography, optics, sensor and display technology, etc. **Entries include:** Office, bureau, or laboratory name, address, and

names, phone numbers, and specialties of electro- optical personnel. **Pages** (approx.): 75. **Frequency:** Irregular; previously published in two parts (covering Navy and non-Navy experts) in 1974; 1978 edition updates Navy portion only; new edition expected late 1979. **Price:** Apply. Also available from National Technical Information Service, Springfield, VA 22161 (NTIS number not assigned).

★2624★
DIRECTORY OF NORTH AMERICAN ARID LAND RESEARCH SCIENTISTS
American Association for the Advancement of Science
1515 Massachusetts Avenue, N. W.
Washington, DC 20005
Covers: More than 1,000 scientists in Mexico, Canada, and the United States active in desertification studies. **Entries include:** Scientist's name, address, interests. **Arrangement:** Alphabetical. **Indexes:** Keyword, institutional affiliation. **Frequency:** Not established; first published early 1978. **Price:** $10.00, payment with order. **Other information:** Prepared for United Nations Conference on Desertification.

★2625★
DIRECTORY OF NORTH CAROLINA RESEARCH, DEVELOPMENT, AND TESTING LABORATORIES
Industrial Extension Service
North Carolina State University
Box 5506   Phone: (919) 737-2358
Raleigh, NC 27650
Covers: 100 North Carolina companies that provide commercial research, development, and testing. **Entries include:** Company name, address, phone, name of principal executive, list of products or services. **Arrangement:** Alphabetical. **Pages** (approx.): 130. **Frequency:** Irregular; previous edition 1967; current edition published fall 1976. **Editor:** Thomas F. Cecich, Manager of Technical Services. **Former title:** Industrial Research, Development, and Testing Guide. **Price:** $3.60.

★2626★
DIRECTORY OF NUCLEAR REACTORS
International Atomic Energy Agency
Box 100
Vienna A-1400, Austria
Covers: 80 power and research reactors throughout the world. Each volume describes in detail new reactors not previously described, and includes complete lists of power and research reactors to date. **Entries include:** For new reactors - Name, location, and owner of unit, with extensive technical data in tabular form, with some engineering drawings. For all reactors - Name, location, type, output, flux, date of criticality (and shut-down where applicable), volume of directory in which described. **Arrangement:** New reactors arranged by type, cumulative list by name. **Pages** (approx.): 400. **Frequency:** Irregular; latest volume, Volume X, published spring 1976. **Price:** $26.00. **Send orders to:** Unipub, Box 433, Murray Hill Station, New York, NY 10016.

Directory of Oceanographers in the United States *See* U.S. Directory of Marine Scientists

Directory of Organizations in Engineering Programs for Minorities *See* Minority Engineering Research Directory

★2627★
DIRECTORY OF PALAEONTOLOGISTS OF THE WORLD
International Palaeontological Association
C/o Curt Teichert
Department of Geological Sciences
University of Rochester   Phone: (716) 275-2409
Rochester, NY 14627
Number of listings: Over 6,000. **Entries include:** Name, office address, area of specialization or interest. **Arrangement:** Alphabetical. **Indexes:** Geographical, research interest. **Pages** (approx.): 305. **Frequency:** About every six years; latest edition

1976. **Editor:** Dr. E. Gerry. **Price:** $8.00. **Send orders to:** Universitetsforlaget, Box 7508, Skillebekk, Oslo, Norway.

★2628★
DIRECTORY OF PHYSICS AND ASTRONOMY STAFF MEMBERS
American Institute of Physics
335 E. 45th Street
New York, NY 10017
Covers: 2,900 college and university physics and astronomy departments and 27,000 staff members; federally funded research and development centers; federal government laboratories; industrial and not-for-profit laboratories. **Entries include:** Institution name, address, physics, physics-related, and astronomy departments, department heads, and faculty names, ranks, and telephone extensions; shows research programs of doctoral institutions and areas of concentration of master's programs. **Arrangement:** Departments are geographical; R&D centers and industrial laboratories are alphabetical; federal laboratories are by agency name. **Indexes:** Personal name, institution name. **Pages** (approx.): 380. **Frequency:** Annual, September. **Editor:** Dion W. J. Shea. **Former title:** Directory of Physics and Astronomy Faculties (1975). **Price:** $26.00, payment with order; $29.00, billed.

★2629★
DIRECTORY OF PSYCHOLOGY-RELATED STATE CIVIL SERVICE POSITIONS
Phillips Diversified Research Services, Division
H & H Communications
Box 20083
Tallahassee, FL 32304
Covers: Over 400 listings of positions at all levels requiring a background in psychological and mental health specialties available through state civil service agencies. **Entries include:** Position title, education and experience requirements, current salary; name, address, and phone of state personnel office or contact. **Arrangement:** Geographical. **Pages** (approx.): 140. **Frequency:** Annual, November. **Editor:** R. Lindsay Phillips. **Price:** $72.50, postpaid.

★2630★
DIRECTORY OF RESEARCH-ON-RESEARCH
Program of Research on the Management of Research and Development
C/o R. Sohngen
Department of Industrial Engineering and Management Sciences
Northwestern University
Evanston, IL 60201
Covers: About 380 projects concerned with the management of research and development activities (including budgeting, technology forecasting, and zero-based budgeting). **Entries include:** Name of principal investigator, associate investigators, title, institution name and address, description of project. **Arrangement:** By name of principal investigator. **Indexes:** Title, subject, researcher name, organization name (with address, researchers' names). **Pages** (approx.): 190. **Frequency:** Latest edition May 1979. **Editors:** Richard T. Barth and Albert H. Rubenstein. **Price:** $7.50, payment with order. **Other information:** Published in cooperation with the College on Research and Development of the Institute of Management Sciences.

★2631★
DIRECTORY OF SCHOOL PSYCHOLOGY TRAINING PROGRAMS IN THE UNITED STATES AND CANADA
Accreditation, Certification and Training Committee
National Association of School Psychologists
1511 K Street, Suite 927   Phone: (202) 347-3956
Washington, DC 20005
Number of listings: 205. **Entries include:** Institution name, address; degrees offered; admission requirements; ratio of graduates to enrollment; description of program; names and specialties of faculty. **Indexes:** Subject, personal name. **Pages** (approx.): 250. **Frequency:** Triennial; latest edition 1977. **Editors:** Douglas T. Brown, John P.

Lindstrom. **Price:** $6.95, plus 50¢ shipping. **Send orders to:** National Association of School Psychologists, 10 Overland Dr., Stratford, CT 06497.

★2632★
DIRECTORY OF SCIENCE COMMUNICATION COURSES AND PROGRAMS
Department of Chemistry
State University of New York at Binghamton Phone: (607) 798-2593
Binghamton, NY 13901
Covers: About 145 courses and programs concerned with teaching the communication of technical information to non-specialists. **Entries include:** Course name, description, frequency, enrollment, and name, address, and phone of faculty; program listings also include degrees offered, date founded. **Frequency:** Not established; first edition summer 1978. **Price:** $4.95, payment with order.

★2633★
DIRECTORY OF SCIENCE RESOURCES FOR MARYLAND
Business Directories Office
Maryland Department of Economic and Community Development
2525 Riva Road
Annapolis, MD 21401
Covers: 515 research and development firms and science-oriented services, 30 State of Maryland R&D firms, and 95 federal R&D firms. Resource list covers colleges, universities, vocation-technical and other programs, public libraries, professional organizations, and information sources. **Arrangement:** Classified by type of organization. **Indexes:** Alphabetical, geographical, principal activity, information sources. **Pages** (approx.): 230. **Frequency:** Biennial, even years. **Editor:** Fred Ziegenhorn. **Price:** $6.00 (1980 edition).

Directory of Science Training Programs for High Ability Secondary School Students *See* Science Training Program Directory...

★2634★
DIRECTORY OF SOLAR-TERRESTRIAL PHYSICS MONITORING STATIONS
Air Force Geophysics Laboratory
Defense Department
Hanscom Air Force Base, MA 01731
Covers: Over 1,000 ground-based observing stations, worldwide, engaged in the monitoring of the solar-terrestrial environment. These stations are part of the MONSEE (Monitoring Sun-Earth Environment) network. **Entries include:** Station latitude and longitude, alternate names of station, dates of operation, observing schedule, description of instruments used; form of reduced data, when it is available; regular distribution of data; name and address of station. **Arrangement:** By discipline (solar, interplanetary, geomagnetic, cosmic rays, etc.). **Indexes:** Station name, equivalent station name, subdiscipline. **Pages** (approx.): 450. **Frequency:** Irregular; first edition November 1977; new edition expected September 1980. **Editors:** H. E. Coffey, M. A. Shea. **Price:** Apply to World Data Center-A for Solar-Terrestrial Physics, National Geophysical amd Solar-Terrestrial Data Center, NOAA/EDS, Boulder, CO 80302.

★2635★
DIRECTORY OF STANDARDS LABORATORIES
National Conference of Standards Laboratories
Radio Building, Room 4001
Boulder, CO 80303
Covers: 175 measurement standards laboratories (both members of NCSL and nonmembers). Separate list shows capabilities in standards and calibration work. **Entries include:** Company name, address, phone, names of NCSL delegate or executive. **Arrangement:** Alphabetical by company or sponsor name. **Indexes:** NCSL delegates; labs by Zip code. **Pages** (approx.): 80. **Frequency:** Biennial, summer of odd years. **Price:** Free.

Directory of State and Local Environmental Libraries *See* State and Local Environmental Libraries

★2636★
DIRECTORY OF STATISTICIANS
American Statistical Association
806 15th Street, N. W. Phone: (202) 393-3253
Washington, DC 20005
Covers: More than 15,800 members of the American Statistical Association, the Biometric Society, and the Institute of Mathematical Statistics. **Entries include:** Name, position or title, address, phone, degrees received, areas of specialization, memberships in organizations sponsoring the directory. **Arrangement:** Alphabetical. **Indexes:** Geographical. **Pages** (approx.): 250. **Frequency:** Irregular; previous edition 1973; latest edition 1978. **Editors:** Edgar M. Bisgyer, Managing Director, and Jean Smith, Executive Assistant. **Price:** $25.00.

Directory of Suppliers, Manufacturers, Technical Consultants, Professional Engineers [Wood residue energy] *See* Wood Residue Energy ...

★2637★
DIRECTORY OF THE ASSOCIATION OF AMERICAN GEOGRAPHERS
Association of American Geographers
1710 16th Street, N. W. Phone: (202) 234-1450
Washington, DC 20009
Covers: 5,800 geographers and geography students. **Entries include:** Name, address, birth date and place; degrees, years received, granting institutions; employer's name, address, title; specialty; area of interest. **Arrangement:** Alphabetical. **Pages** (approx.): 350. **Frequency:** Irregular; latest edition 1978. **Advertising accepted.** Circulation 6,500. **Price:** $6.00.

Directory of the Solar Industry *See* Solar Energy Buyer's Guide and Directory

★2638★
DIRECTORY OF TRANSDUCER USERS
Telemetry Group
Range Commanders Council
White Sands Missile Range, NM 88002
Covers: About 50 government facilities, aerospace contractors, and universities which use transducers. **Entries include:** Organization name, address, names and phone numbers of contact persons, contact persons' functions, use of transducers, description of expertise in transducer use, facilities, and purpose or objectives of organization. **Arrangement:** By type of organization. **Pages** (approx.): 50. **Frequency:** Irregular; latest edition May 1978. **Price:** Apply (ADA 053564). **Send orders to:** Defense Logistics Agency, Defense Documentation Center, Cameron Station, Alexandria, VA 22314.

★2639★
DIRECTORY OF UNITED STATES STANDARDIZATION ACTIVITIES
National Engineering Laboratory
National Bureau of Standards
Commerce Department Phone: (301) 921-2587
Washington, DC 20234
Covers: Standardization activities of nearly 600 trade associations, technical and other professional societies representing industry and commerce, and state and federal governments. Includes non-engineering and non-industry groups. **Entries include:** Group name, address, description of activities. **Arrangement:** The standardization activities are grouped into three sections: associations, states, and agencies of the federal government. Each section is alphabetical. **Indexes:** Subject. **Pages** (approx.): 220. **Frequency:** Irregular; latest edition 1975; new edition expected 1983. **Editor:** Sophie J. Chumas, Technical Information Specialist. **Price:** $6.75 (S/N 003-003-01395). **Send orders to:** Goverment Printing Office, Washington, DC 20402.

★2640★

DIRECTORY OF U.S. DATA REPOSITORIES SUPPORTING THE
    INTERNATIONAL GEODYNAMICS PROJECT

World Data Center A for Solid Earth Geophysics
Environmental Data and Information Service
National Oceanic and Atmospheric Administration
Commerce Department
Boulder, CO 80303

Entries include: Repository name, address, phone, name of contact, description of well cores, logs, etc., available, and services available. **Arrangement:** By category (seismic surveys, geothermics, etc.). **Indexes:** Geographical; geographic data coverage. **Pages** (approx.): 50. **Frequency:** Published August 1978. **Price:** $4.50, paper; $3.00, microfiche (PB 288-495). May also be available from the agency. **Send orders to:** National Technical Information Service, Springfield, VA 22161.

★2641★

DIRECTORY OF WATER RESOURCES EXPERTISE

California Water Resources Center
University of California
475 Kerr Hall   Phone: (916) 752-1544
Davis, CA 95616

Covers: Over 250 University of California faculty and staff active in water resource research. **Entries include:** Name, title, office address and phone, research emphasis. **Arrangement:** Alphabetical. **Indexes:** Discipline, campus. **Pages** (approx.): 90. **Frequency:** Biennial, late fall of odd years. **Price:** Free (ISSN 0575-4968).

★2642★

DIRECTORY TO U.S. GEOLOGICAL SURVEY PROGRAM ACTIVITIES
    IN COASTAL AREAS

RALI Program
Geological Survey
Interior Department
Mail Stop 750   Phone: (703) 860-7288
Reston, VA 22092

Covers: About 340 programs or projects of the Geological Survey located in coastal areas or related to coastal problems. **Entries include:** Title of project, location, contact person, objectives, status of project. **Arrangement:** By scientific discipline. **Indexes:** Geographical. **Pages** (approx.): 155. **Frequency:** Irregular; latest edition 1976. **Editor:** Philip A. Marcus. **Price:** $1.75 (S/N 024-001-02851-4). **Send orders to:** Government Printing Office, Washington, DC 20402.

Discover and Learn at Science-Technology Centers See Exploring
    Science: Guide to Contemporary Musuems of Science and
    Technology

★2643★

ECOLOGICAL SOCIETY OF AMERICA BULLETIN—DIRECTORY OF
    MEMBERS ISSUE

Ecological Society of America
C/o Dr. Duncan Patten, Business Manager
Department of Botany and Microbiology
Arizona State University
Tempe, AZ 85281

Number of listings: 5,000. **Entries include:** Name, address, area of special competence. **Arrangement:** Alphabetical. **Indexes:** Geographical. **Frequency:** Triennial, fall; latest edition fall 1979. **Editor:** Dr. Duncan Patten, Business Manager. **Price:** $3.00.

★2644★

EDUCATORS GUIDE TO FREE SCIENCE MATERIALS

Educators Progress Service, Inc.
214 Center Street   Phone: (414) 326-3126
Randolph, WI 53956

Covers: Sources for about 1,700 films, filmstrips, slide sets, audiotapes, videotapes, scripts, phonograph records, and printed materials useful in the study of science. Materials are provided by industrial, governmental, and other sponsors for free use by teachers and other educators. **Entries include:** Title, brief description, date produced, length or running time, whether sound or scripts are available for silent tapes and films, whether color or black and white, booking details, source. **Arrangement:** By type of medium, then by subject. **Indexes:** Source, title, subject. **Pages** (approx.): 400. **Frequency:** Annual, fall. **Editors:** Mary H. Saterstrom and John W. Renner. **Price:** $14.00, plus $1.35 shipping.

★2645★

ELECTRO-OPTICAL SYSTEMS DESIGN—VENDOR SELECTION
    ISSUE

Milton S. Kiver Publications, Inc.
222 W. Adams Street   Phone: (312) 263-4866
Chicago, IL 60606

Covers: Over 1,200 manufacturers and suppliers of equipment and materials used in the production and testing of electro-optical systems and equipment. **Entries include:** Company name, address, phone, products or services. **Arrangement:** Alphabetical. **Indexes:** Product. **Pages** (approx.): 160. **Frequency:** Annual, November. **Editor:** Richard Cunningham. **Advertising accepted.** Circulation 27,300. **Price:** $7.50.

★2646★

ENCYCLOPEDIA OF GEOGRAPHIC INFORMATION SOURCES

Gale Research Company
Book Tower   Phone: (313) 961-2242
Detroit, MI 48226

Covers: Sources of information on nearly 400 countries, states, regions, and other geographical entities, worldwide; includes publications and their publishers, government and trade offices, etc. **Entries include:** Source name, address; some listings may contain additional information. **Arrangement:** Classified by geographic extent or area, with subcategories for larger entities. **Pages** (approx.): 165. **Frequency:** Irregular; latest edition 1978. **Editors:** Paul Wasserman, James Sanders, and Elizabeth Talbot Sanders. **Price:** $32.00. **Other information:** See also listing for "Encyclopedia of Business Information Sources."

★2647★

ENERGY DATA REPORTS

National Energy Information Center
Energy Information Administration   Phone: (202) 634-5694
Washington, DC 20461

Description: The center publishes more than 100 reports on specific energy-related topics, such as electricity, crude petroleum, etc. Each report includes names and addresses of experts or resource persons knowledgeable about the subject. List of subjects and a price list are available.

★2648★

ENGINEERING EDUCATION—ENGINEERING COLLEGE RESEARCH
    AND GRADUATE STUDY ISSUE

American Society for Engineering Education
One Dupont Circle, Suite 400   Phone: (202) 293-7080
Washington, DC 20036

Covers: 200 engineering colleges and their research programs. **Entries include:** Name of college; names of department chairman, admissions officer, and research director; graduate degree requirements; tuition information; off-campus or extension programs; faculty and enrollment figures; degrees granted; research areas of doctoral theses; appointments and stipends available; number of students and faculty doing engineering research and the sources of research support; and expenditures and number of projects (listed by area). **Arrangement:** Alphabetical. **Indexes:** Fields of study, fields of research. **Pages** (approx.): 250. **Frequency:** Annual, March. **Editor:** Patricia W. Samaras, Managing Editor. **Advertising accepted.** Circulation 13,000. **Price:** $10.00 (current and 1980 editions).

★2649★

ENGINEERING NEWS-RECORD—TOP 500 DESIGN FIRMS ISSUE

McGraw-Hill, Inc.

1221 Avenue of the Americas   Phone: (212) 997-1221

New York, NY 10020

Publication includes: 500 leading architectural, engineering, and specialty design firms selected on basis of annual sales. **Entries include:** Company name, location, code for type of firm, current and prior year rank in billings, type of services, number of "Engineering News-Record" subscribers. **Arrangement:** Ranked by billings. **Frequency:** Annual, May. **Editor:** Arthur J. Fox. **Advertising accepted.** Circulation 102,000. **Price:** $3.00, payment with order.

★2650★

ENGINEERING NEWS-RECORD—TOP INTERNATIONAL DESIGN FIRMS ISSUE

McGraw-Hill, Inc.

1221 Avenue of the Americas   Phone: (212) 997-1221

New York, NY 10020

Covers: 100 design firms (including United States firms) competing outside their own national borders who received largest dollar volume of contracts in preceding calendar year. **Entries include:** Company name, headquarters location, total value of contracts received in preceding year, design specialties, rank. **Arrangement:** By contract value. **Frequency:** Annual, issue not fixed; first list appeared in December 13, 1979 issue. **Editor:** Arthur J. Fox. **Advertising accepted.** Circulation 102,000. **Price:** $3.00.

★2651★

ENGINEERING NEWS-RECORD DIRECTORY OF DESIGN FIRMS

McGraw-Hill, Inc.

1221 Avenue of the Americas   Phone: (212) 997-2534

New York, NY 10020

Background: Limited to advertisers. **Entries include:** Company name, address, branch locations, subsidiaries, list of key personnel, territory served, capabilities. **Frequency:** Biennial, fall of even years. **Price:** $12.50.

ENR Directory of Design Firms *See* Engineering News-Record Directory of Design Firms

★2652★

EXPLORING SCIENCE: GUIDE TO CONTEMPORARY MUSEUMS OF SCIENCE AND TECHNOLOGY

Association of Science-Technology Centers

1016 16th Street, N. W.   Phone: (202) 452-0655

Washington, DC 20036

Covers: About 140 member science museums and businesses serving museums; international coverage. **Entries include:** Museum name, address, phone, name of director, hours of operation, admission fees; brief description of exhibit areas. **Arrangement:** Alphabetical within membership categories (associate, etc.). **Indexes:** Geographical. **Pages** (approx.): 75. **Frequency:** Biennial, summer of odd years. **Price:** $8.00, plus $1.00 shipping.

★2653★

FEDERAL ASSISTANCE PROGRAMS OF THE ENVIRONMENTAL PROTECTION AGENCY

Office of Planning and Management

Environmental Protection Agency

401 M Street, S. W.   Phone: (202) 755-2830

Washington, DC 20460

Covers: About 40 federal grants and funding programs for research, technical assistance, construction, demonstration, and training in environmental protection concerns. **Entries include:** Name of program, sponsoring agency, address, and name of contact; program objectives, eligibility requirements, application procedures, amount of funds or grants available. **Arrangement:** By EPA program office. **Frequency:** Irregular; latest edition 1977; new edition expected spring 1980. **Price:** Free. **Other information:** Based on "Catalog of Federal Domestic Assistance."

★2654★

FEDERAL ENVIRONMENTAL DATA: A DIRECTORY OF SELECTED SOURCES

Division of Science Information

National Science Foundation   Phone: (202) 632-5800

Washington, DC 20550

Covers: Major environmental data bases maintained by United States government agencies, primarily departments of Agriculture, Interior, and Energy, and the Environmental Protection Agency. **Entries include:** Source agency, name of data base, general description, size, update frequency, time reference, cost, turnaround time, contact name. **Pages** (approx.): 140. **Frequency:** Not established; first edition November 1977. **Editors:** Barbara E. Meyers, Elizabeth C. Fake, Robert V. Ausura. **Price:** $7.25, paper; $3.00, microfiche (PB 275-902). **Send orders to:** National Technical Information Service, Springfield, VA 22161. **Other information:** Prepared for NSF by Capital Systems Group Inc., 6110 Executive Boulevard, Suite 250, Rockville, MD 20852.

★2655★

FEDERAL STATISTICAL DIRECTORY

Office of Federal Statistical Policy and Standards

Commerce Department   Phone: (202) 673-7965

Washington, DC 20230

Covers: 3,600 key personnel engaged in statistical programs and related activities of agencies of the executive branch of the federal government. **Entries include:** Name, title, office address, and phone. **Arrangement:** By organizational units within each agency or department. **Indexes:** Personal name. **Pages** (approx.): 270. **Frequency:** Irregular, about every 2-3 years; fall 1979 edition delayed until April 1980. **Editor:** Suzann K. Evinger, Research Analyst, Editor, "Statistical Reporter." **Send orders to:** Government Printing Office, Washington, DC 20402.

Federal Technology Transfer Directory of Programs, Resources, Contact Points *See* Directory of Federal Technology Transfer

★2656★

FEDERATION OF SOCIETIES FOR COATINGS TECHNOLOGY— YEAR BOOK AND MEMBERSHIP DIRECTORY

Federation of Societies for Coatings Technology

1315 Walnut Street, Suite 830   Phone: (215) 545-1506

Philadelphia, PA 19107

Covers: About 6,700 chemists, technicians, and supervisory production personnel in the decorative and protective coatings industry who are members of the 26 constituent societies of the federation. **Entries include:** Name, company affiliation, address, phone. **Arrangement:** By society. **Indexes:** Alphabetical. **Pages** (approx.): 300. **Frequency:** Irregular; new edition expected March 1980. **Price:** $5.00 (1980 edition).

Federation of Societies for Paint Technology *See* Federation of Societies for Coatings Technology—Year Book and Membership Directory

★2657★

FEMINIST INTERNSHIP ROSTER [Psychology]

Association for Women in Psychology

C/o Cynthia Villis

Department of Psychology

Southern Illinois University   Phone: (618) 453-2374

Carbondale, IL 62991

Covers: Internships in psychology which offer women psychologists in training an opportunity to work with women clients or to receive supervision from women professionals. **Frequency:** Annual, August. **Editor:** Cynthia Villis. **Price:** Free.

★2658★
FIRE RESEARCH SPECIALISTS: A DIRECTORY
National Bureau of Standards
Commerce Department
Washington, DC 20234
Covers: Persons active in writing on, teaching, or research in fire science. **Entries include:** Name, affiliation, address, phone. **Arrangement:** Alphabetical. **Indexes:** Subject, affiliation. **Pages** (approx.): 140. **Frequency:** Irregular; previous edition 1973; latest edition September 1977. **Editor:** Nora H. Jason. **Former title:** Directory of Workers in the Fire Field. **Price:** $7.25 (PB 272-475/5WL). **Send orders to:** National Technical Information Service, Springfield, VA 22161.

★2659★
FLUID POWER SOCIETY—MEMBERSHIP DIRECTORY
Fluid Power Society
909 N. Mayfair Road   Phone: (414) 257-0434
Milwaukee, WI 53226
Number of listings: 3,000. **Entries include:** Name, office address, career data. **Arrangement:** Geographical. **Pages** (approx.): 100. **Frequency:** Annual, fall. **Editor:** Louise Johnson. **Price:** $50.00.

★2660★
GARBAGE GUIDE
Environmental Action Foundation
Dupont Circle Building, Suite 724
Washington, DC 20036
Description: Each four-page issue is devoted to a specific topic related to waste management, such as hazardous wastes, plastic bottles, or source reduction, and includes names and addresses of persons with special expertise in the problem. **Price:** $6.00 per year.

★2661★
GEOLOGICAL SOCIETY OF AMERICA—MEMBERSHIP DIRECTORY
Geological Society of America
3300 Penrose Place   Phone: (303) 447-2020
Boulder, CO 80301
Number of listings: 12,000. **Frequency:** Annual. **Former title:** Geological Society of America - Yearbook (1978). **Price:** Available to members only.

★2662★
GEOPHYSICS—BUYERS' GUIDE ISSUE
Society of Exploration Geophysicists
Box 3098   Phone: (918) 743-1365
Tulsa, OK 74101
Description: Not a directory; Buyers' Guide Issue contains a product index of advertisers in that issue only. **Frequency:** Annual, March. **Advertising accepted. Price:** $6.00.

★2663★
GEOTHERMAL REGISTRY
Geothermal Resources Council
111 G Street   Phone: (916) 758-2360
Davis, CA 95616
Covers: About 900 companies and institutions involved in one or more aspects of geothermal resource development, and approximately 1,300 individual members. **Entries include:** Company name, address and phone number, name of principal executive for geothermal matters, names of other executives, products or services, and branch offices where applicable. **Arrangement:** Companies are classified by field of business activity or service; members are alphabetical. **Indexes:** Alphabetical list of all companies, agencies, and individuals. **Pages** (approx.): 400. **Frequency:** Annual, winter. **Editor:** Beverly A. Hall. **Advertising accepted.** Circulation 1,000. **Price:** $15.00, postpaid (tentative, 1980 edition).

★2664★
GEOTHERMAL WORLD DIRECTORY
Geothermal World Corporation
18014 Sherman Way, Suite 169   Phone: (213) 342-4984
Reseda, CA 91335
Publication includes: Lists of about 9,000 manufacturers, utilities, governmental agencies, universities, exploration companies, and individuals working in research on, and exploration and development of, geothermal energy; international coverage. **Entries include:** Company, organization, or individual name, address, phone; business and government listings include name of contact. **Arrangement:** Manufacturers and individuals are alphabetical, most others are geographical. **Pages** (approx.): 600. **Frequency:** Annual, September. **Editor:** Karen Lee Darwin, Editor-in-Chief. **Advertising accepted.** Circulation 10,000. **Price:** $50.00.

★2665★
GEOTIMES—DIRECTORY OF SOCIETIES IN EARTH SCIENCE ISSUE
American Geological Institute
5205 Leesburg Pike   Phone: (703) 379-2480
Falls Church, VA 22041
Covers: About 430 organizations concerned with earth science; international coverage. **Entries include:** Organization name, address, description of interests. **Arrangement:** Alphabetical. **Frequency:** Annual, July. **Editor:** Wendell Cochran. **Advertising accepted.** Circulation 14,000. **Price:** $1.25 (ISSN 0016-8556).

★2666★
GRADUATE ASSISTANTSHIP DIRECTORY IN THE COMPUTER SCIENCES
Association for Computing Machinery
1133 Avenue of the Americas   Phone: (212) 265-6300
New York, NY 10036
Covers: Fellowships and assistantships in the computer sciences offered at United States and Canadian educational institutions. **Arrangement:** Geographical. **Frequency:** Annual, fall. **Price:** $5.00, payment with order; $7.00, billed.

★2667★
GRADUATE PROGRAMS IN PHYSICS, ASTRONOMY, AND RELATED FIELDS
American Institute of Physics
335 E. 45th Street   Phone: (212) 661-9404
New York, NY 10017
Covers: More than 270 academic departments in United States and Canada offering graduate programs in physics, astronomy, and related fields. **Entries include:** School name, address, department name, list of faculty and its research specialties, admission and graduate degree requirements, graduate student support available, and names of contacts for information on admissions, financial aid, and housing; departments offering master's programs include information on areas of concentration; departments offering doctorates include information on research programs. **Arrangement:** Geographical. **Pages** (approx.): 600. **Frequency:** Annual. **Editor:** Dion W. J. Shea. **Price:** $10.00, payment with order; $12.00, billed (1980 edition).

★2668★
GRADUATE STUDY IN PSYCHOLOGY
American Psychological Association
1200 17th Street, N. W.   Phone: (202) 833-7600
Washington, DC 20036
Covers: About 530 programs in the United States and Canada offering graduate education in psychology. **Entries include:** Institution name, address, name of department offering degree in psychology, department phone, year established, chairperson, size of faculty, APA accreditation, academic year system, programs and degrees offered, application procedure, admission requirements, student statistics for the previous year, degree requirements, tuition, financial aid available, and comments on special programs, goals, etc. **Arrangement:** Geographical. **Indexes:** Institution, program area (with degree

offered), geographical. **Pages** (approx.): 600. **Frequency:** Annual, late spring. **Price:** $6.00.

★2669★
GUIDANCE FOR APPLICATION OF REMOTE SENSING TO ENVIRONMENTAL MANAGEMENT
U.S. Army Engineer Waterways Experiment Station
Mobility and Environmental Systems Laboratory
Corps of Engineers
Box 631
Vicksburg, MS 39180
Covers: In appendix A, "Sources of Available Remote Sensor Imagery," are listed agencies and organizations (not including commercial, private, or academic organizations) which have files of remotely sensed (primarily aircraft and satellite) imagery. **Entries include:** Agency name, address, type of imagery, range of scales, coverage areas, coverage period and frequency, availability and characteristics of imagery, products available, and procedures for obtaining imagery. **Frequency:** Irregular; latest edition March 1978. **Editor:** John R. May.

Guide to Computer Program Directories *See* Computer Science and Technology: Guide to Computer Program Directories

★2670★
GUIDE TO CONTINUING EDUCATION—SHORT COURSES FOR ENGINEERS AND SCIENTISTS
Technological Advancement Centers
Box 891
East Brunswick, NJ 08816
Covers: Institutions, associations, private organizations, and other sponsors of short refresher or advanced courses in scientific and technical fields. **Entries include:** Sponsor, address, phone, contact person. Course listings give course name, sponsor, date, location, fees, etc. **Arrangement:** Sponsors are alphabetical, courses by keyword. **Frequency:** Bimonthly. **Price:** $48.00 per year; no single copies sold.

★2671★
GUIDE TO ENERGY SPECIALISTS
Center for International Environmental Information
300 E. 42nd Street
New York, NY 10017
Covers: Over 1,000 individuals from government, industry, and nonprofit organizations who specialize in energy technology and related fields (including economics, environmental concerns, and legal aspects). Individuals listed have agreed to answer questions by telephone from media and professionals (but not students). **Entries include:** Name, title, affiliation, address, phone, brief biographical data. **Arrangement:** Alphabetical. **Indexes:** Subject, specialty. **Pages** (approx.): 140. **Frequency:** Latest edition 1979. **Editor:** Porter B. Bennett. **Price:** $40.00.

★2672★
GUIDE TO EPA LIBRARIES
Information Resources and Services Branch (PM213)
Environmental Protection Agency
400 M Street, S. W.   Phone: (202) 755-0353
Washington, DC 20460
Number of listings: 31. **Entries include:** Library name, address, phone, name of librarian, description of collection and services. **Arrangement:** Geographical. **Pages** (approx.): 50. **Frequency:** Irregular; latest edition July 1977; new edition expected late 1979 or early 1980. **Price:** $4.00 (PB 269-601). **Send orders to:** National Technical Information Service, Springfield, VA 22161.

★2673★
GUIDE TO GRADUATE DEPARTMENTS OF GEOGRAPHY IN THE UNITED STATES AND CANADA
Association of American Geographers
1710 16th Street, N. W.   Phone: (202) 234-1450
Washington, DC 20009
Number of listings: 145. **Entries include:** Name of institution, requirements, programs, facilities, financial aid, faculty. **Indexes:** Staff. **Pages** (approx.): 275. **Frequency:** Annual, September. **Editor:** Teresa A. Mulloy. **Price:** $6.00.

★2674★
GUIDE TO GRADUATE STUDY IN BOTANY FOR THE UNITED STATES AND CANADA
Botanical Society of America
C/o P. K. Holmgren
New York Botanical Garden   Phone: (212) 220-8626
Bronx, NY 10458
Number of listings: About 140. **Entries include:** Institution name, address, degrees offered, number of graduate students, fields of specialization, titles of recent theses, and detailed information about individual faculty members. **Arrangement:** By university. **Frequency:** Irregular; previous edition 1974; latest edition 1977. **Price:** $4.00, payment with order.

★2675★
GUIDE TO SCIENTIFIC INSTRUMENTS
American Association for the Advancement of Science
1515 Massachusetts Avenue   Phone: (202) 467-4480
Washington, DC 20005
Publication includes: 2,000 manufacturers of instruments, apparatus, chemicals, furniture, software, etc., for use in all scientific disciplines in industrial, academic, governmental, and other laboratory facilities. **Entries include:** Company name, address, phone. **Arrangement:** Alphabetical. **Indexes:** Product (includes company addresses). **Pages** (approx.): 300. **Frequency:** Annual, fall. **Editor:** Philip H. Abelson, Ph.D. **Advertising accepted.** Circulation 160,000. **Price:** $6.00.

★2676★
GUIDE TO SOLAR ENERGY PROGRAMS
Solar Technology Division
Energy Department
600 E Street, N. W.   Phone: (202) 376-5711
Washington, DC 20545
Covers: Structure and activities of solar energy programs of the U. S. Energy Department. **Entries include:** Name of program, objectives, areas of primary interest, technology, source of detailed information. **Pages** (approx.): 70. **Frequency:** Irregular; previous edition early 1978; latest edition June 1978. **Editor:** Barry D. Brown. **Price:** $2.40 (S/N 061-000-00042-9). **Send orders to:** Government Printing Office, Washington, DC 20402.

★2677★
GUIDE TO TECHNICAL SERVICES AND INFORMATION SOURCES FOR ADP MANAGERS AND USERS [Federal government]
Institute for Computer Sciences and Technology
National Bureau of Standards
Commerce Department
Washington, DC 20234
Covers: About 50 technical services and resources available to federal data processing installations from other agencies of the government. **Entries include:** Agency name, address, phone, description of services offered, publications, etc. **Pages** (approx.): 50. **Frequency:** Published April 1979. **Editor:** Shirley M. Radack. **Price:** $5.25, paper; $3.00, microfiche (PB 294-845). May also be available from the agency. **Send orders to:** National Technical Information Service, Springfield, VA 22161.

★2678★

HANDBOOK FOR AUTHORS [Chemistry]
American Chemical Society
1155 16th Street, N. W.   Phone: (202) 872-4600
Washington, DC 20036
Publication includes: List of about 25 journals published by the society. **Entries include:** Journal title, address for manuscript submissions, brief description of content, editorial requirements, and editorial procedures. **Frequency:** Not established; first edition 1978. **Price:** $7.50, cloth; $3.75, paper.

★2679★

**HAZARDOUS MATERIALS AND WASTES COMPLIANCE BUYERS
        GUIDE**
Hazardous Materials Publishing Company
320 W. Main Street
Kutztown, PA 19530
Covers: Sources for documents, tools, regulations, tariffs, placards, labels, and safety equipment needed for legal handling of hazardous materials and wastes. **Entries include:** Supplier name, address, products. **Indexes:** Product. **Frequency:** Annual, summer. **Advertising accepted. Price:** $25.00.

★2680★

**HAZARDOUS WASTE MANAGEMENT FACILITIES IN THE UNITED
        STATES**
Office of Solid Waste Management Programs
Environmental Protection Agency
401 M Street, S. W.   Phone: (202) 755-9190
Washington, DC 20460
Covers: 120 hazardous waste management facilities, 12 mercury reprocessors, 7 active reprocessors of non-mercury batteries and wastes containing heavy metals, 95 solvent reclaiming operations, 19 petroleum re-refineries; 20 waste information and material exchanges; also includes 56 state agencies for solid waste management and 10 EPA regional offices. **Entries include:** For facilities listings - Company name, address, phone, and type of work done or materials handled at the facility. **Arrangement:** Geographical. **Pages** (approx.): 60. **Frequency:** Irregular; latest edition fall 1979. **Editor:** Jerry M. Johnson. **Price:** Free (SW-146.3). **Send orders to:** Office of Solid Waste Management Programs Publications Distribution, Environmental Protection Agency, 26 W. St. Clair, Cincinnati, OH 45268.

★2681★

**HERITAGE OF AVIATION MEDICINE: AN ANNOTATED DIRECTORY
        OF EARLY ARTIFACTS**
Aerospace Medical Association
Washington National Airport   Phone: (703) 892-2240
Washington, DC 20001
Covers: About 75 private collections, museums, and other collections of over 500 aviation medicine artifacts. **Entries include:** Collection or museum name, address, name of contact, description of collection including specific objects held. **Arrangement:** By type of artifact, then geographical. **Pages** (approx.): 125. **Frequency:** Published 1979. **Editor:** Robert J. Benford, M.D. **Price:** $3.50, plus $1.00 shipping, payment with order.

★2682★

**ICP SOFTWARE DIRECTORY—BUSINESS MANAGEMENT
        EDITIONS**
International Computer Programs, Inc.
9000 Keystone Crossing   Phone: (317) 844-7461
Indianapolis, IN 46240
Covers: In two separate editions - "Cross-Industry," which lists software products and services suitable for use by several industries with medium to large computers, and "Industry-Specific," which lists software products and services intended for use by specific industries with medium to large computers. **Entries include:** Software title, number of installations, description of purpose and features, maintenance service available, operating environment, price, and

source name, address, phone, and name and title of contact. **Arrangement:** Cross-Industry edition by application and language; Industry-Specific edition by industry, then application. **Indexes:** Vendor/product index with address and phone of vendor, software title index with dot chart tabulation of hardware manufacturer and language. **Pages** (approx.): Cross-Industry, 275; Industry-Specific, 400. **Frequency:** Semiannual; Cross-Industry, February and August; Industry-Specific, May and November. **Editor:** Dennis Hamilton, Editor-in-Chief. **Advertising accepted.** Circulation 4,700. **Former title:** International Computer Programs Quarterly. **Price:** Single edition per year, $65.00; 20% discount on multiple editions. **Other information:** See related directories under "ICP Software Directory" main heading.

★2683★

**ICP SOFTWARE DIRECTORY—DATA PROCESSING MANAGEMENT
        EDITION**
International Computer Programs, Inc.
9000 Keystone Crossing   Phone: (317) 844-7461
Indianapolis, IN 46240
Covers: Software products which are concerned with systems operation of large mainframe computers. **Entries include:** Software title, number of installations, description of purpose and features, maintenance service available, operating environment, price, and source name, address, phone, and name and title of contact. **Arrangement:** By application. **Indexes:** Vendor/product with address and phone, software title index with dot chart tabulation of hardware manufacturer and language. **Pages** (approx.): 425. **Frequency:** Semiannual, January and July. **Editor:** Dennis Hamilton, Editor-in-Chief. **Advertising accepted.** Circulation 4,700. **Former title:** International Computer Programs Quarterly. **Price:** $65.00 per year. **Other information:** See related directories under "ICP Software Directory" main heading.

★2684★

**ICP SOFTWARE DIRECTORY—INFORMATION PRODUCT &
        SERVICE SUPPLIERS EDITION**
International Computer Programs, Inc.
9000 Keystone Crossing   Phone: (317) 844-7461
Indianapolis, IN 46240
Covers: Suppliers of data processing products and services. **Entries include:** Company name, line of business, industry served, geographic area served, products and services, year founded, annual revenue, number of employees, names and titles of officers, addresses and phone numbers of headquarters, branch, and foreign offices. **Arrangement:** Alphabetical. **Indexes:** Product/service, industry served. **Frequency:** Semiannual, June and December. **Editor:** Dennis Hamilton, Editor-in-Chief. **Advertising accepted.** Circulation 4,700. **Former title:** International Computer Programs Quarterly. **Price:** $125.00. **Other information:** See related directories under "ICP Software Directory" main heading.

★2685★

**ICP SOFTWARE DIRECTORY—MINI-SMALL BUSINESS SYSTEMS
        EDITIONS**
International Computer Programs, Inc.
9000 Keystone Crossing   Phone: (317) 844-7461
Indianapolis, IN 46240
Covers: In two separate editions - "Cross-Industry," which lists software products and services suitable for use by several industries with minicomputers and small business computer systems, and "Industry-Specific," which lists software products and services intended for use by specific industries with mini- and small computers. **Entries include:** Software title, number of installations, description of purpose and features, maintenance service available, operating environment, price, and source name, address, phone, and name and title of contact. **Arrangement:** Cross-Industry edition by application and language; Industry-Specific edition by industry, then application. **Indexes:** Vendor/product index with address and phone of vendor, software title index with dot chart tabulation of hardware manufacturer and language. **Pages** (approx.): Cross-Industry, 350;

Industry-Specific, 250. **Frequency:** Semiannual; Cross-Industry, April and October; Industry-Specific, May and November. **Editor:** Dennis Hamilton, Editor-in-Chief. **Advertising accepted.** Circulation 4,700. **Former title:** International Computer Programs Quarterly. **Price:** Single edition per year, $65.00; 20% discount on multiple editions. **Other information:** See related directories under ''ICP Software Directory'' main heading.

★2686★

IFT'S REGIONAL GUIDE TO FOOD TESTING LABORATORIES AND CONSULTANTS

Institute of Food Technologists
221 N. LaSalle Street Phone: (312) 782-8424
Chicago, IL 60601
Covers: Independent laboratories with testing services for food firms, governments, or educational institutions, and consultants offering food testing services. **Entries include:** Laboratory or consultant's name, address, phone, name of principal executive, list of services and capabilities. **Arrangement:** Geographical. **Pages** (approx.): 50. **Frequency:** Annual, January. **Price:** $10.00 (current and 1980 editions).

★2687★

INDEX OF WELL SAMPLE AND CORE REPOSITORIES IN THE UNITED STATES AND CANADA

Branch of Oil and Gas Resources
Geological Survey
Interior Department Phone: (303) 234-5105
Denver, CO
Covers: Repositories which hold well samples, cores, and other data for wells drilled for water, mining, oil, gas, and waste disposal. **Entries include:** Repository name, address, phone, description of facilities including storage methods, examination facilities, policies of use, extent of coverage, method of organization. **Arrangement:** Geographical. **Pages** (approx.): 195. **Frequency:** Not established; first edition November 1977. **Price:** $29.25, paper copy; $3.50, microfiche copy; payment with order. (USGS Open File Report 77-567.)

Industrial Research, Development, and Testing Guide *See* Directory of North Carolina Commercial, Research, Development, Testing Guide

★2688★

INDUSTRIAL RESEARCH LABORATORIES OF THE UNITED STATES

Jaques Cattell Press
R. R. Bowker Company
2216 S. Industrial Park Drive Phone: (602) 967-8885
Tempe, AZ 85282
Covers: 10,000 publicly and privately owned industrial research facilities. **Entries include:** Firm or organization name, address, names and titles of key personnel, subsidiaries or divisions with R&D facilities or activities, description of research emphases, number of research staff with disciplines. **Arrangement:** Alphabetical. **Indexes:** Geographical, personal name, subject of research by industry. **Pages** (approx.): 775. **Frequency:** Biennial, fall of odd years. **Price:** $75.00, postpaid, payment with order (ISSN 0073-7623). **Send orders to:** R. R. Bowker Co., Box 1807, Ann Arbor, MI 48106 (313-761-4700).

★2689★

INFORMATION SERVICES ON RESEARCH IN PROGRESS

Smithsonian Science Information Exchange
1730 M Street, N. W.
Washington, DC 20036
Covers: About 180 planned, pilot, and operational ongoing research information systems; about 45 international and regional existing systems; and over 135 national and subnational systems. **Entries include:** System name; sponsoring organization name, address; names of key personnel; subject coverage; other details of the system. **Arrangement:** By type of system (planned, pilot, and operational;

regional, etc.). **Indexes:** Subject, organization/system name, organization/system acronym, personal name. **Pages** (approx.): 460. **Frequency:** Irregular; latest edition 1978; new edition expected fall 1980. **Price:** $14.50 (PB 282-025). **Send orders to:** National Technical Information Service, Springfield, VA 22161. **Other information:** Compiled in cooperation with UNESCO.

★2690★

INFO-SOURCES DIRECTORY [Scientific and technological research]

Mercury Communications
734 Chestnut Street Phone: (408) 425-8444
Santa Cruz, CA 95060
Covers: Sources of information (data banks, government agencies, publishers) on current scientific and technological research and developments. **Entries include:** Source name, address or location, name of contact, if any; description of information and services. **Arrangement:** By type of source. **Indexes:** Organization name, publication title, subject. **Pages** (approx.): 290. **Frequency:** Biennial, even years. **Editors:** Jill Ammon-Wexler, Catherine Carmel. **Price:** $44.50, postpaid.

Institute of Mathematical Statistics *See* Directory of Statisticians

★2691★

INSTITUTE OF TRANSPORTATION ENGINEERS—MEMBERSHIP DIRECTORY

Institute of Transportation Engineers
1815 N. Ft. Myer Drive Phone: (703) 527-5277
Arlington, VA 22209
Number of listings: 6,000. **Entries include:** Name, home and office addresses, office phone. **Arrangement:** Alphabetical. **Indexes:** Geographical. **Pages** (approx.): 260. **Frequency:** Annual, spring. **Editor:** Mrs. Bess Balchen. **Advertising accepted.** Circulation 6,000. **Former title:** Institute of Traffic Engineers - Membership Directory. **Price:** $20.00.

★2692★

INSTITUTIONS AND INDIVIDUALS ACTIVE IN ENVIRONMENTALLY-SOUND AND APPROPRIATE TECHNOLOGIES (PRELIMINARY EDITION)

International Referral System
United Nations Environment Programme
Box 30552
Nairobi, Kenya
Covers: Institutions, organizations, institutions, and commercial firms concerned with development of environmentally sound and appropriate technologies, and with related subjects and problems. **Entries include:** Organization name, address, code indicating subject interests, brief description of activities. **Arrangement:** Geographical. **Pages** (approx.): 285. **Frequency:** Published May 1978. **Price:** $11.00, paper; $3.00, microfiche (PB 299-352). **Send orders to:** National Technical Information Service, Springfield, VA 22161.

Instrument Society of America Directory of Instrumentation *See* ISA Directory of Instrumentation

★2693★

INTERAMERICAN SOCIETY OF PSYCHOLOGY—DIRECTORY OF MEMBERS

Interamerican Society of Psychology
Spanish Speaking Mental Health Research Center
University of California Phone: (213) 825-8886
Los Angeles, CA 90024
Covers: 1,100 psychologists in United States, Canada, Mexico, Central and South America. Includes list of Latin American training centers, journals, professional associations, and test editors. **Entries include:** Name, office address and phone number, home address, highest degree held, institution granting degree, areas of occupational specialization, languages spoken. **Arrangement:** Geographical. **Pages** (approx.): 130. **Frequency:** Biennial, fall of even years. **Editor:**

Gerardo Marin, Secretary General. **Advertising accepted.** Circulation 2,000.

★2694★

INTERNATIONAL ASSOCIATION OF ELECTRICAL INSPECTORS—
 MEMBERSHIP DIRECTORY

International Association of Electrical Inspectors
802 Busse Highway   Phone: (312) 696-1455
Park Ridge, IL 60068
Covers: 14,000 state, federal, industrial, utility, and insurance electrical inspectors, and, as associate members, electricians, manufacturers, engineers, architects, and wiremen. **Entries include:** Name, title, type of member, address, company employed by. **Arrangement:** Geographical, then by division and type of membership. **Indexes:** Personal name. **Pages** (approx.): 250. **Frequency:** Annual, April. **Editor:** L. E. LaFehr. **Advertising accepted.** Circulation 14,000. **Price:** $25.00 (current and 1980 editions).

★2695★

INTERNATIONAL ASSOCIATION OF INDIVIDUAL PSYCHOLOGY—
 DIRECTORY

International Association of Individual Psychology
37 W. 65th Street   Phone: (212) 874-2427
New York, NY 10023
Covers: About 20 member and 65 non-member societies, associations, and institutes for Adlerian or individual psychology. **Entries include:** For members - Name of organization; title, names, and addresses of the president, vice president, secretary, treasurer, liaison officer, and delegates; major activities. For non-members - Name and address. **Arrangement:** Geographical for both sections. **Pages** (approx.): 45. **Frequency:** Triennial; latest edition 1977; new edition expected 1980. **Editor:** Marven O. Nelson, Ed.D., Secretary General. **Price:** Free.

International Computer Programs Quarterly See **ICP Software Directory**—various editions

★2696★

INTERNATIONAL CONFERENCE OF BUILDING OFFICIALS—
 MEMBERSHIP ROSTER

International Conference of Building Officials
5360 S. Workman Mill Road   Phone: (213) 699-0541
Whittier, CA 90601
Covers: Government officials and others (primarily in the United States) responsible for preparing and publishing the Uniform Building Code of standards for materials and types of contruction. **Entries include:** Name, address, phone. **Arrangement:** Alphabetical. **Pages** (approx.): 120. **Frequency:** Annual, spring. **Editor:** Beverly Eicholtz, Manager of Publications. **Price:** $5.00.

★2697★

INTERNATIONAL COUNCIL OF PSYCHOLOGISTS—DIRECTORY

International Council of Psychologists
2772 N. Lake Avenue   Phone: (213) 794-0337
Altadena, CA 91001
Covers: About 1,000 psychologists and related mental health professionals. **Entries include:** Name, office and home address, personal data, career data, languages spoken and written, highest degree, fields of interest. **Arrangement:** Alphabetical. **Indexes:** Geographical. **Pages** (approx.): 40. **Frequency:** Biennial, spring of even years. **Editor:** Ms. Jan Holle-Paez. **Advertising accepted. Price:** Available to members only.

★2698★

INTERNATIONAL DIRECTORY OF AGRICULTURAL ENGINEERING
 INSTITUTIONS

Food and Agriculture Organization of the United Nations
Via delle Terme di Caracalla
Rome, Italy 00100
Covers: Central government services as well as international and national institutes dealing with land and water development, farm

power and machinery, rural electrification, farm buildings and farm work organization. **Entries include:** Institution name, scientific staff, training and research, recent publications, language of correspondence; entries in institution's chosen FAO correspondence language. **Arrangement:** Geographical by English name of the country. **Pages** (approx.): 530. **Frequency:** Irregular; previous edition 1968; latest edition 1974. **Editor:** H. von Hulst, Chief, Agricultural Engineering Service. **Price:** $10.00. **Send orders to:** Unipub, Box 433, Murray Hill Station, New York, NY 10016. (Not verified)

★2699★

INTERNATIONAL DIRECTORY OF BEHAVIOR AND DESIGN
 RESEARCH

Association for the Study of Man-Environment Relations
Box 57   Phone: (212) 948-2410
Orangeburg, NY 10962
Covers: 1,100 persons interested in behavior and design research. **Entries include:** Name, home and business address, field of interest, latest publication, current project, highest degree held and granting institution. **Arrangement:** Alphabetical. **Indexes:** Geographical, fields of interest, current projects keyword index. **Pages** (approx.): 100. **Frequency:** Irregular; previous edition 1974; latest edition fall 1977. **Editor:** Aristide H. Esser, President. **Price:** $16.00.

★2700★

INTERNATIONAL DIRECTORY OF BIOMEDICAL ENGINEERS

Alliance for Engineering in Medicine and Biology
4405 East-West Highway, Suite 404   Phone: (301) 657-4142
Bethesda, MD 20014
Covers: Over 1,300 biomedical engineers and others concerned with the involvement of engineering in the physical, biological, and medical sciences; international coverage. **Entries include:** Name, highest degree earned and/or certification, title and department, organizational affiliation, address, phone, principal occupation, memberships in professional associations, principal areas of interest. **Arrangement:** Alphabetical. **Indexes:** Area of interest. **Pages** (approx.): 115. **Frequency:** Biennial, September of even years. **Editor:** Patricia I. Horner, Director, AEMB. **Price:** $6.00 (ISSN 0190-9282).

★2701★

INTERNATIONAL DIRECTORY OF MARINE SCIENTISTS

Fishery Data Centre
Fisheries Department
Food and Agriculture Organization of the United Nations
Rome 00100, Italy
Covers: About 11,000 scientists involved in oceanographic work as identified by member governments. **Entries include:** Institution or other affiliation, address, names and scientific field of individual marine specialists. **Arrangement:** Geographical, then by institution. **Indexes:** Personal name. **Pages** (approx.): 335. **Frequency:** Irregular; latest edition fall 1977; new edition expected June 1980. **Price:** $13.75 (current edition); $15.00 (1980 edition). **Send orders to:** Unipub, Box 433, Murray Hill Station, New York, NY 10016. **Other information:** Taken from the Aquatic Sciences and Fisheries Information System data base.

★2702★

INTERNATIONAL DIRECTORY OF SOFTWARE

CUYB Publications Ltd.
633 Third Avenue   Phone: (212) 867-8833
New York, NY 10017
Covers: Producers of over 3,000 data processing software packages which are not restricted to a particular machine or available only with hardware; coverage includes Europe, Canada, Australia, and other foreign countries. **Entries include:** Company name, name of international supplier, product description including hardware compatibility, primary and secondary function, subject area, number of users, languages, year became operative. Supplier name, address, and phone are given in separate geographical list. **Arrangement:** Classified. **Indexes:** Single alphabet cross references for industry,

product type, supplier. **Pages** (approx.): 1,100. **Frequency:** Not established; first United States edition expected March 1980. **Editor:** Robert Grant. **Advertising accepted.** Circulation 10,000. **Former title:** CUYB Directory of Software. **Price:** $140.00.

★2703★

INTERNATIONAL FEDERATION FOR HOUSING AND PLANNING— YEARBOOK
IFHP General Secretariat
43 Wassenaarseweg
2596CG The Hague, Netherlands
Covers: 1,200 members of the IFHP and subsidiary regional organizations. Both corporate and individual members listed. **Entries include:** Name, address, phone, specialization, and membership in IFHP working groups or executive bodies. **Arrangement:** Geographical. **Frequency:** Biennial, spring of even years; first edition expected 1980. **Former title:** Yearbook. **Price:** Available to members only.

International Laboratory Buyer's Guide *See* Laboratory Buyer's Guide

★2704★

INTERNATIONAL UNION OF PHYSIOLOGICAL SCIENCES WORLD DIRECTORY OF PHYSIOLOGISTS
American Physiological Society
9650 Rockville Pike   Phone: (301) 530-7164
Bethesda, MD 20014
Covers: 12,000 United States physiologists, 225 Canadian, and 8,000 other foreign members. **Entries include:** Name, title, affiliation, address, phone, areas of interest, membership type, earned doctorate degree. **Arrangement:** By country, then society with which affiliated. **Indexes:** Alphabetical. **Pages** (approx.): 300. **Frequency:** Triennial; latest edition 1977; new edition expected July 1980. **Editor:** Orr E. Reynolds, Ph.D., Executive Secretary-Treasurer. **Price:** $15.00 (current edition; tentative, 1980 edition).

★2705★

INTERNSHIP PROGRAMS IN PROFESSIONAL PSYCHOLOGY, INCLUDING POST-DOCTORAL TRAINING PROGRAMS
Association of Psychology Internship Centers
University of Texas Health Science Center
San Antonio, TX
Covers: Institutions offering internship programs in professional psychology. **Entries include:** Institution name, name and address of contact, description of program including percentage of time spent in supervision and in seminar attendance, theoretical orientation, number of interns, stipend, admission requirements. **Arrangement:** Geographical. **Pages** (approx.): 360. **Frequency:** Biennial, odd years. **Price:** $6.00.

★2706★

THE INTERVAL—ANNUAL MEMBERSHIP DIRECTORY ISSUE
Society of Cable Television Engineers
1900 L Street, N. W.   Phone: (202) 293-7841
Washington, DC 20036
Covers: 2,600 cable television engineers, technicians, and managers; about 105 supplier companies are also included. **Entries include:** For individuals - Name, company with which affiliated, address. For companies - Name, location. **Arrangement:** By type of membership, then alphabetical. **Pages** (approx.): 180. **Frequency:** Annual, September. **Editor:** Judith Baer, Executive Vice President. **Advertising accepted.** Circulation 3,000. **Price:** $50.00.

Inventory of Automatic Data Processing Equipment in the U. S. Government *See* Automatic Data Processing Equipment Inventory in the...

★2707★

INVENTORY OF ENERGY RESEARCH AND DEVELOPMENT
Environmental Information Systems Group
Energy Research and Development Administration
Oak Ridge, TN 37380
Covers: 8,140 current energy-related research and development projects performed or sponsored in the United States, inventoried on a computerized data base. Includes summary table of expenditures. **Entries include:** Title, research institution, sponsor, principal investigators, project duration, expenditures, description of research, number of technical staff, research type (basic, applied, developmental), publications, and research location. **Arrangement:** Classified by type of research. **Indexes:** Institution; sponsor; investigator; location; keyword; permuted title. **Pages** (approx.): 5,000. **Frequency:** Irregular; third edition January 1976. **Editor:** Gloria M. Caton. **Price:** $12.00 (Y4. SC12:94-2/u). **Send orders to:** Government Printing Office, Washington, DC 20402. **Other information:** Committee Print, Serial U, Committee on Science and Technology, United States House of Representatives.

★2708★

IOTA SIGMA PI—MEMBERSHIP DIRECTORY [Women chemists]
Iota Sigma Pi
C/o Dr. Anne T. Sherren
Department of Chemistry
North Central College   Phone: (312) 420-3491
Naperville, IL 60540
Number of listings: 8,500. **Entries include:** Name, address, type of membership. **Arrangement:** Geographical (by chapter). **Indexes:** Alphabetical. **Frequency:** Irregular; new edition expected May 1981. **Editor:** Dr. Doris C. Warren. **Price:** Available to members only.

Iron and Steel Society of AIME—Roster *See* Iron and Steelmaker—Membership Directory Issue

★2709★

IRON AND STEELMAKER—MEMBERSHIP DIRECTORY ISSUE
Iron and Steel Society of AIME
345 E. 47th Street   Phone: (212) 644-8031
New York, NY 10017
Covers: 5,000 persons concerned with technical operations and processes in the production of iron and steel who are members. **Entries include:** Name, title, company affiliation, company address, member grade, divisional affiliation. **Arrangement:** Alphabetical. **Indexes:** Geographical. **Frequency:** Annual, September. **Editor:** Lawrence G. Kuhn. **Advertising accepted.** Circulation 5,300. **Price:** $50.00.

★2710★

ISA DIRECTORY OF INSTRUMENTATION
Instrument Society of America
Box 12277   Phone: (919) 549-8411
Research Triangle Park, NC 27709
Covers: About 2,000 manufacturers and 6,000 distributors, suppliers, and manufacturers' representatives of control and instrumentation equipment; coverage includes Canada. **Entries include:** Company name, address, phone, locations of sales offices or representatives. **Arrangement:** Alphabetical. **Indexes:** Product, trade name. **Pages** (approx.): 1,500. **Frequency:** Annual, June. **Editor:** J. Harvey Lucas. **Advertising accepted.** Circulation 26,500. **Price:** $30.00, plus $10.00 shipping (current edition); $65.00, postpaid (1980 edition).

★2711★

JOURNAL OF CHROMATOGRAPHIC SCIENCE—INTERNATIONAL CHROMATOGRAPHY GUIDE ISSUE
Preston Publications, Inc.
Box 48312   Phone: (312) 647-0566
Niles, IL 60648
Covers: About 350 manufacturers of chromatographs and/or chromatographic supplies, worldwide. **Entries include:** Company

name, address, phone, list of products or services. **Pages** (approx.): 125. **Frequency:** Annual, February or March. **Editors:** John Q. Walker and R. P. W. Scott. **Advertising accepted.** Circulation 7,000. **Price:** $15.00 (current and 1980 editions).

★2712★
JOURNAL OF METALS—METALLURGICAL SOCIETY DIRECTORY ISSUE
Metallurgical Society of American Institute of Mining, Metallurgical and Petroleum Engineers
Box 430   Phone: (412) 776-9028
Warrendale, PA 15086
Covers: 8,500 metallurgists, metallurgical engineers, and materials scientists, worldwide. **Entries include:** Name, office address, career data. **Frequency:** Annual, June. **Editor:** John B. Ballance. **Advertising accepted.** Circulation 13,000. **Price:** $50.00.

★2713★
JOURNAL WATER POLLUTION CONTROL FEDERATION— DIRECTORY ISSUE
Water Pollution Control Federation
2626 Pennsylvania Avenue, N. W.   Phone: (202) 337-2500
Washington, DC 20037
Covers: About 30,000 individuals, consultants, and firms concerned with water pollution control who are members. **Entries include:** Name, address. **Arrangement:** Alphabetical within membership categories. **Indexes:** Personal name, company name, geographical. **Pages** (approx.): 600. **Frequency:** Biennial, March of even years. **Editor:** Peter J. Piecuch. **Advertising accepted.** Circulation 30,000. **Price:** $11.50 (current and 1980 editions).

★2714★
LAB ANIMAL—BUYER'S GUIDE ISSUE
United Business Publications, Inc., Subsidiary
Media Horizons, Inc.
475 Park Avenue South   Phone: (212) 725-2300
New York, NY 10016
Covers: About 205 manufacturers and suppliers of equipment (cages, restrainer units, surgery and research equipment) and supplies (pharmaceuticals, veterinary products) to research laboratories using animals; includes Canada. **Entries include:** Company name, address, phone. **Arrangement:** Alphabetical. **Indexes:** Product. **Pages** (approx.): 80. **Frequency:** Annual, fall. **Editor:** Susan L. Fowler. **Advertising accepted.** Circulation 10,000. **Price:** $2.50.

LabGuide *See* **Analytical Chemistry—Laboratory Guide Issue**

★2715★
LABORATORY BUYER'S GUIDE
International Scientific Communications, Inc.
808 Kings Highway   Phone: (203) 576-0500
Fairfield, CT 06430
Covers: Over 1,200 manufacturers of scientific instruments, equipment, apparatus, and chemicals; over 3,600 companies selling laboratory products are also listed. **Entries include:** For manufacturers - Company name, address, phone. For dealers - Company name, phone, sales contact, and products handled. **Arrangement:** Manufacturers are alphabetical; dealers are geographical. **Indexes:** Product. **Pages** (approx.): 250. **Frequency:** Annual, November. **Editor:** Carol Galello, Publications Director. **Advertising accepted.** Circulation 225,000. **Price:** $3.00. **Other information:** Also published under titles, "International Laboratory Buyer's Guide" and "American Laboratory Buyer's Guide."

★2716★
LASER FOCUS—BUYERS' GUIDE ISSUE
Advanced Technology Publications, Inc.
1001 Watertown Street   Phone: (617) 244-2939
Newton, MA 02165
Covers: Nearly 600 manufacturers and suppliers in the laser, optical communication, and related industries. **Entries include:** Company

name, address, phone, principal executives, number of employees, list of products and services. **Arrangement:** Alphabetical. **Indexes:** Product. **Pages** (approx.): 375. **Frequency:** Annual, January/March. **Editor:** Bruce M. Weinberg. **Advertising accepted.** Circulation 18,000. **Price:** $18.00, payment must accompany order.

Lepidopterists' Society—Membership List *See* **News of the Lepidopterists' Society—Membership List Issue**

★2717★
LIAISON CONSERVATION DIRECTORY FOR ENDANGERED AND THREATENED SPECIES
Office of Endangered Species
Interior Department
18th and C Streets, N. W.   Phone: (202) 343-5634
Washington, DC 20240
Covers: Persons who act as liaison with federal agencies, state agencies, and conservation groups in the preservation of endangered and threatened species. Recovery Team leaders are also listed. **Arrangement:** Federal, state, conservation group, or Recovery Team, then alphabetical. **Pages** (approx.): 90. **Frequency:** Irregular; latest edition 1976. **Price:** Free.

★2718★
LIBRARY JOURNAL—ENERGY SOURCE DIRECTORY ISSUE
R. R. Bowker Company
1180 Avenue of the Americas   Phone: (212) 764-5100
New York, NY 10036
Publication includes: List of about 500 organizations, government agencies at all levels, companies, publishers, and other groups offering energy-related information and print and nonprint materials on energy. **Entries include:** Name, address, description of energy activities and interests, list of typical publications available (with prices). **Arrangement:** Alphabetical. **Frequency:** Not established; first published in January 1, 1977 issue. **Advertising accepted.** **Price:** $1.35. **Send orders to:** R. R. Bowker Co., Subscription Department, Box 67, Whitinsville, MA 01588.

List of Accredited Programs in Architecture *See* **Accredited Programs in Architecture**

★2719★
LIST OF CERTIFICATED PILOT SCHOOLS
Flight Standards Service
Federal Aviation Administration
Transportation Department
Washington, DC 20591
Covers: 2,950 FAA-certified pilot schools and about 30 schools offering FAA-approved Aircraft Dispatcher, Flight Navigator, and/or Flight Engineer training. **Entries include:** School name, address, certificate number, ratings or courses offered, and certificate-holding office, where appropriate. **Arrangement:** Geographical. **Pages** (approx.): 90. **Frequency:** Annual, summer. **Former title:** List of Certified Pilot Flight and Ground Schools. **Price:** Free.

List of Certified Pilot Flight and Ground Schools *See* **List of Certificated Pilot Schools**

★2720★
LISTING OF DATA SYSTEMS ELEMENTS AUTHORITIES
Data Systems Laboratory
George C. Marshall Space Flight Center
Marshall Space Flight Center, AL
Covers: Several hundred individuals concerned with space data storage and data handling in areas ranging from data generator elements through final processing and display who have special expertise in these areas. **Entries include:** Individual name, area of specialization, affiliation, business address, phone. **Arrangement:** Alphabetical within areas of expertise. **Frequency:** Not established; first edition July 1977.

★2721★
LOCAL ENERGY ACTION PROJECT—DIRECTORY MAILING LIST
Local Energy Action Project
Citizens' Energy Project
1110 Sixth Street, N. W., Suite 300　　　Phone: (202) 387-8998
Washington, DC 20001
Covers: 3,500 citizen groups, manufacturers, research institutes, government agencies, consultants, and equipment distributors. Entries include: Name and address. Arrangement: Zip code order. Pages (approx.): 100. Frequency: First edition summer 1977. Price: $5.00, payment with order.

★2722★
MAJOR OIL SPILL DIRECTORY
Center for Short-Lived Phenomena
Smithsonian Institution
60 Garden Street　　　Phone: (617) 864-7910
Cambridge, MA 02138
Covers: Marine oil spills occurring on ocean waters, 1967-1975. Entries include: Extensive details on each occurrence, including site and source of spill, date, substance involved, amount, cause, details of clean-up, information on vessel involved, etc. Pages (approx.): 140. Frequency: Irregular; first edition 1975. Price: $30.00. Send orders to: Unipub, Box 433, Murray Hill Station, New York, NY 10016.

Mathematical Association of America See Combined Membership List...

★2723★
MATHEMATICAL SCIENCES ADMINISTRATIVE DIRECTORY
American Mathematical Society
Box 6248　　　Phone: (401) 272-9500
Providence, RI 02940
Covers: 30 professional organizations concerned with mathematics; government agencies; academic institutions with mathematics departments; nonacademic organizations; and journals concerned with mathematics. Entries include: For professional organizations and government agencies - Name, address, names and titles of key personnel. For journals - Name, name and address of publisher, name and title of editor. For institutions - Name, address; name, title, and address of department chairman. Arrangement: Within type of organization, alphabetical, except institutions, which are geographical. Indexes: University or college name. Frequency: Irregular; latest edition 1978. Price: $6.00.

★2724★
MATNET MAILING LIST [Appropriate technology]
Citizens' Energy Project
1110 Sixth Street, N. W., Suite 300　　　Phone: (202) 387-8998
Washington, DC 20001
Covers: Over 3,000 individuals and groups active in alternative energy and appropriate technology issues. Coverage limited to New York, New Jersey, Pennsylvania, Delaware, Maryland, District of Columbia, Virginia, West Virginia, Ohio, and Kentucky. Entries include: Name, address. Arrangement: Zip code order. Pages (approx.): 90. Frequency: Not established; first edition March 1978. Price: $7.50, plus $1.15 shipping, payment with order.

Metallurgical Society of AIME—Membership List See Journal of Metals—Metallurgical Society Directory Issue

★2725★
METALLURGY/MATERIALS EDUCATION YEARBOOK
American Society for Metals
　　　Phone: (216) 338-5151
Metals Park, OH 44073
Covers: 1,050 professors of metallurgy, materials science, polymer and ceramics, primarily in the United States, Canada, and Europe. Entries include: For North American schools - Name of school,

address, name of department head, degrees offered, list of faculty members with specialties and phones, number of seniors and graduate students. Listings for foreign schools have less detail. Arrangement: Alphabetical by school name. Indexes: Personal name. Pages (approx.): 100. Frequency: Annual, March. Editor: Dr. Kali Mukherjee. Price: $20.00 (current and 1980 editions).

★2726★
MINICOMPUTER SOFTWARE DIRECTORY
Minicomputer Data Services
20 Coventry Lane　　　Phone: (203) 637-1755
Riverside, CT 06878
Covers: About 125 firms offering software and software design services for minicomputers. Entries include: Company name, address, services and programs available, number of employees, date founded, hardware specialties. Arrangement: By software subject. Indexes: Geographical, hardware required. Pages (approx.): 150. Frequency: Base looseleaf volume published March 1975; updated with supplements three times yearly. Editor: John W. Oplinger, Publisher. Price: $85.00 for base volumes, revisions to date, and two updates; $85.00 for annual renewals.

★2727★
MINICOMPUTER SOFTWARE QUARTERLY
International Management Services, Inc.
Two Frederick Street　　　Phone: (617) 879-5955
Framingham, MA 01701
Covers: About 500 firms offering software packages for minicomputers. Entries include: Company name, address, phone, and software package description, with operating requirements. Arrangement: By software subject. Indexes: Computer language, minicomputer system. Pages (approx.): 700. Frequency: Base looseleaf volume published 1975; updated with supplements quarterly. Editor: Raymond Wenig. Price: $85.00 for base volume and revisions to date, plus a year's subscription.

★2728★
MINORITY ENGINEERING RESOURCE DIRECTORY
Committee on Minorities in Engineering
National Research Council
2101 Constitution Avenue, N. W.　　　Phone: (202) 393-8100
Washington, DC 20418
Covers: About 255 organizations actively involved in increasing minority representation in engineering. Entries include: Organization name, address, name of contact person, objectives and activities of organization. Arrangement: Alphabetical. Pages (approx.): 110. Frequency: Irregular; latest edition January 1979. Former title: Directory of Organizations in Engineering Programs for Minorities (1979). Price: Free.

Missouri Council of Architects—Directory See Missouri Council of Architects Construction Industry Reference Book

★2729★
MISSOURI COUNCIL OF ARCHITECTS CONSTRUCTION INDUSTRY REFERENCE BOOK
Finan Publishing Company
8460 Watson Road　　　Phone: (314) 843-0043
St. Louis, MO 63119
Number of listings: 1,500 member architects of Missouri Council of Architects, American Institute of Architects. Entries include: Architect's name, name of firm (if any), address, phone. Arrangement: Alphabetical. Pages (approx.): 130. Frequency: Annual, January. Advertising accepted. Price: $5.00.

★2730★
NATIONAL ASSOCIATION FOR RESEARCH IN SCIENCE
TEACHING—DIRECTORY
National Association for Research in Science Teaching
C/o Paul H. Joslin
Reading-Learning Center
Drake Univ.
Des Moines, IA 50311
Number of listings: 700. **Entries include:** Name, address.
Arrangement: Alphabetical. **Frequency:** Semiannual, May and
November. **Editor:** Dr. Paul H. Joslin, Executive Secretary. **Price:**
Available to nonmembers in alphabetical mailing list form only,
$10.00.

★2731★
NATIONAL ASSOCIATION OF GEOLOGY TEACHERS—
MEMBERSHIP DIRECTORY
National Association of Geology Teachers
C/o Alan R. Geyer
Pennsylvania Bureau of Topographic
& Geologic Survey
Harrisburg, PA 17120
Covers: About 1,900 college, university, and high school teachers of
geology and the earth sciences. **Entries include:** Name and address.
Arrangement: Alphabetical. **Indexes:** Geographical. **Pages** (approx.):
60. **Frequency:** Annual, June. **Editor:** Alan R. Geyer, Secretary/
Treasurer. **Price:** Available to members only.

★2732★
NATIONAL COUNCIL OF ACOUSTICAL CONSULTANTS—
DIRECTORY
National Council of Acoustical Consultants
63 Morris Avenue
Springfield, NJ 07081
Covers: 25 acoustical consultants, primarily in the United States.
Entries include: Company name, address, phone, name of principal
executive, list of services, typical projects, area served, year
established. **Arrangement:** Alphabetical. **Pages** (approx.): 30.
Frequency: Annual, fall. **Editor:** John P. Bachner, Executive Secretary.
Price: $2.50 (1978 edition), payment must accompany order.

★2733★
NATIONAL DIRECTORY OF SAFETY CONSULTANTS
American Society of Safety Engineers
850 Busse Highway   Phone: (312) 692-4121
Park Ridge, IL 60068
Covers: 300 occupational health and safety consultants who are
members of the society's consultants division. **Entries include:** Name,
office address and phone, home address, highest degree held, areas of
occupational specialization, personal data, memberships, and
registrations. **Arrangement:** Alphabetical. **Indexes:** Geographical.
Pages (approx.): 40. **Frequency:** Annual, fall. **Editor:** Dwight B. Esau.
Price: $7.50.

★2734★
NATIONAL ENVIRONMENTAL/ENERGY WORKFORCE
ASSESSMENT [Postsecondary environmental education
programs]
Office of Research and Development
Environmental Protection Agency
401 M Street, N. W.
Washington, DC 20460
Description: A series of volumes including 12 directories of
postsecondary education programs at 2- and 4-year institutions in air,
noise, pesticides and toxicology, potable water, wastewater, radiation,
solid waste; combined programs in water/wastewater; and programs
in environmental engineering/technology, environmental science/
health, and environmental studies. **Entries include:** Name of
institution offering program, address, contact person, academic
program title, degree offered, and time required for completion of
program; some entries include descriptive comments. **Arrangement:**
By name of institution. **Indexes:** Geographical. **Frequency:** All volumes

in current series issued August 1979. **Price:** All volumes available in
microfiche at $3.00 each; paper copies priced as follows: Air, $4.50
(PB 298-580); Noise, $4.50 (PB 298-581); Pesticides and
Toxicology, $6.00 (PB 298-582); Potable Water, $4.50 (PB 298-
583); Wastewater, $4.50 (PB 298-584); Radiation, $4.50 (PB 298-
585); Solid Waste $4.00 (PB 298-586); Energy, $6.50 (PB 298-
587); Water/Wastewater, $6.50 (PB 298-588); Environmental
Engineering/Technology, $6.50 (PB 298-589); Environmental
Science/Health, $7.25 (PB 298-590); Environmental Studies, $9.25
(PB 298-591). **Send orders to:** National Technical Information
Service, Springfield, VA 22161.

★2735★
NATIONAL REGISTRY OF WOMEN IN SCIENCE AND ENGINEERING
Association for Women in Science Registry
1346 Connecticut Avenue, N. W.,
Suite 1122
Washington, DC 20036
Description: Not a directory but a computerized data base including
the names and qualifications of several thousand female scientists and
engineers. Lists of candidates fitting specific position descriptions are
provided for a fee of $50.00 per position for which suitable
candidates are found.

★2736★
NATIONAL SCIENCE FOUNDATION GUIDE TO PROGRAMS
National Science Foundation
1800 G Street, N. W.   Phone: (202) 632-5702
Washington, DC 20550
Publication includes: About 145 funding programs offered by the
National Science Foundation. **Entries include:** Program title, contact
address, eligibility requirements, application deadline, program
purpose, application procedures, type and amount of assistance
available. **Arrangement:** By subject area. **Frequency:** Annual. **Price:**
Single copies free; additional copies $3.50 (S/N 038-000-00421-
2). **Send orders to:** Government Printing Office, Washington, DC
20402.

★2737★
NATIONAL SCIENCE SUPERVISORS ASSOCIATION—DIRECTORY
National Science Supervisors Association
C/o Robert. A. Dean
Department of Education
6401 Linda Vista Road
San Diego, CA 92111
Covers: 750 department chairmen, science supervisors, coordinators,
consultants, and directors of science education in private, parochial,
and public schools. **Entries include:** Name and address.
Arrangement: Geographical. **Frequency:** Annual, July. **Editor:** Robert
A. Dean. **Advertising accepted.** Circulation 1,000. **Price:** $2.00.

★2738★
NATIONAL SOLAR ENERGY EDUCATION DIRECTORY
Solar Energy Information Data Bank
Solar Energy Research Institute
1617 Cole Boulevard   Phone: (303) 231-1205
Golden, CO 80401
Covers: Solar-related technical courses, programs, and curricula
offered at about 700 postsecondary institutions in the United States.
Entries include: Institution name, address, phone; courses, programs,
or curriculum offered; name of instructor; course and department
number; and number of credits offered. **Arrangement:** Alphabetical.
Indexes: Institution name, subject, degree offered. **Pages** (approx.):
300. **Frequency:** Annual, January. **Editor:** Richard A. Piekarski,
Production Coordinator. **Price:** $4.75 (S/N 061-000-00210-3).
Send orders to: Government Printing Office, Washington, DC 20402.
Other information: Compiled with the assistance of the Department
of Energy, the Congressional Solar Coalition, and the office of
Congressman George E. Brown, Jr.

★2739★
**NATIONAL SOLAR HEATING AND COOLING COMMERCIAL
    DEMONSTRATION PROGRAM: KEY PERSONNEL DIRECTORY**
Division of Solar Applications
Energy Department
Washington, DC 20545
Covers: About 300 federal and non-federal buildings participating in federal solar heating and cooling demonstration projects, and key personnel involved in each project. **Entries include:** Building name, address, and names, addresses, and phone numbers of owner, architect, solar designer, mechanical engineer, builders, and other key personnel; personal names are included in listings for firms. **Arrangement:** By federal and non-federal status, then geographical. **Pages** (approx.): 140. **Frequency:** Not established; first edition January 1979. **Price:** $3.25 (S/N 061-000-00253-7). **Send orders to:** Government Printing Office, Washington, DC 20402.

★2740★
**NATIONAL WATER WELL ASSOCIATION—MEMBERSHIP
    DIRECTORY**
National Water Well Association
500 W. Wilson Bridge Road   Phone: (614) 846-9355
Worthington, OH 43085
Covers: 8,000 water well drilling contractors, manufacturers and suppliers of equipment, and technical professionals, such as geologists and engineers in the United States, Canada, Mexico, and foreign countries. **Entries include:** Name, office address, and phone. **Arrangement:** Geographical. **Indexes:** Alphabetical. **Pages** (approx.): 110. **Frequency:** Annual, September. **Editor:** Jay H. Lehr, Executive Director. **Price:** $5.00.

★2741★
NATURALISTS' ALMANAC AND DIRECTORY (INTERNATIONAL)
World Natural History Publications
Box 550   Phone: (609) 654-6500
Marlton, NJ 08053
Covers: 4,000 active amateur and professional naturalists, worldwide, who will correspond. Includes separate listings of natural history periodicals, societies, museums, and sources of natural history supplies. **Entries include:** Name, address, interests, services. **Arrangement:** Geographical. **Indexes:** Personal name, specialty, institution. **Pages** (approx.): 260. **Frequency:** Biennial, fall of odd years. **Editor:** Dr. Ross H. Arnett, Jr. **Advertising accepted.** Circulation 5,000. **Former title:** The Naturalists' Directory (International). **Price:** $12.95, payment must accompany individuals' orders.

New Research Centers *See* Research Centers Directory

★2742★
**NEWS OF THE LEPIDOPTERISTS' SOCIETY—MEMBERSHIP LIST
    ISSUE**
Lepidopterists' Society
C/o Dave Winter
257 Common Street   Phone: (617) 326-6053
Dedham, MA 02026
Covers: About 1,450 members who share an interest, professional or amateur, in the study of butterflies and moths; international coverage. **Entries include:** Name, address, special interests. **Arrangement:** Geographical. **Indexes:** Alphabetical. **Pages** (approx.): 50. **Frequency:** Biennial, November-December of even years. **Editor:** Julian P. Donahue, Secretary. **Price:** $2.00, plus 50¢ shipping. **Send orders to:** Dr. Charles V. Covell, Jr., Department of Biology, University of Louisville, Louisville, KY 40208.

★2743★
NSF-RANN TRACE CONTAMINANTS PROGRAM DIRECTORY
Toxic Materials Information Center
Oak Ridge National Laboratory
Oak Ridge, TN 37830
Covers: Managers and principal investigators, co-principal investigators, and coordinators of each of the grants in the National Science Foundation's Trace Contaminants Program, Research Applied to National Needs. **Entries include:** Name, address, phone, brief description of research interest. **Arrangement:** Separate sections for managers and investigators. **Indexes:** Subject, personnel, keyword. **Pages** (approx.): 70. **Frequency:** Published October 1976; no new edition planned. **Editors:** P. A. Purnell, S. K. Smith, C. F. Wilkes. **Price:** $4.50 (ORNL/EIS-97). **Send orders to:** National Technical Information Service, Springfield, VA 22161.

★2744★
NUCLEAR EMPLOYMENT OUTLOOK
American Nuclear Society
555 N. Kensington Avenue   Phone: (312) 352-6611
La Grange Park, IL 60525
Covers: Companies in nuclear science and technology who are seeking employees. **Entries include:** Company name, address, name of personnel manager. **Arrangement:** Alphabetical by company. **Pages** (approx.): 20. **Frequency:** Irregular; latest edition 1977. **Editor:** Patricia Pollock, Assistant Marketing Manager. **Price:** $16.00.

★2745★
NUCLEAR NEWS—BUYERS GUIDE ISSUE
American Nuclear Society
555 N. Kensington Avenue   Phone: (312) 352-6611
LaGrange Park, IL 60525
Covers: About 500 nuclear-oriented manufacturers and suppliers of components, including some foreign firms. **Entries include:** Company name, address, phone, names of principal executives, list of products or services. **Arrangement:** Alphabetical. **Indexes:** Product. **Pages** (approx.): 450. **Frequency:** Annual, March. **Editor:** Jon Payne. **Advertising accepted.** Circulation 15,000. **Price:** $32.00, payment with order (ISSN 0029-5574).

★2746★
OCEANOGRAPHIC SHIP OPERATING SCHEDULES
Naval Oceanographic Command
Code N32
Bay St. Louis, MS 39529
Covers: Ships operated by United States organizations engaged in scientific research under the auspices of federal agencies and academic institutions. Directory's purpose is to encourage coordination and the accomodation of individual investigators and project teams. **Entries include:** Name, address, contact, and phone of ship operator or sponsor; ship's name, length, number of scientific personnel, cruising speed, and similar data; the year's cruise dates, area of operation, objectives; names of chief scientists; ports of call; map of general operations area. **Pages** (approx.): 110. **Frequency:** Annual, January. **Editor:** Cdr. Julian Wright, U.S.N. **Price:** Free. **Also includes:** Forms for research clearance requests and cruise prospectus. **Other information:** Compiled and published in conjunction with the University-National Oceanographic Laboratory System.

Online Directory of Terminal Sales and Service Offices *See* Online Terminal Guide and Directory

★2747★
ONLINE TERMINAL GUIDE AND DIRECTORY
Online, Inc.
11 Tannery Lane   Phone: (203) 227-8466
Weston, CT 06883
Covers: 3,000 computer terminal manufacturers' main and local offices, terminal leasing companies, terminal brokers, used terminal vendors, and service facilities; includes some offices outside United States. **Arrangement:** Geographical. **Frequency:** Irregular; latest edition 1978; new edition expected 1982. **Former title:** Online Directory of Terminal Sales and Service Offices. **Price:** $25.00.

★2748★
ORDER OF DAEDALIANS—ROSTER OF MEMBERS
Order of Daedalians
Building 1635   Phone: (512) 924-9485
Kelly Air Force Base, TX 78241
Covers: 11,000 persons interested in aviation and aerospace history and contemporary operations, and who are World War I and II pilots or their descendants or designates. **Entries include:** Name, address. **Arrangement:** Alphabetical. **Pages** (approx.): 140. **Frequency:** Annual, October. **Editor:** Col. Peter Cotellesse, Adjutant. **Price:** Available to members only.

★2749★
PERSONNEL INVOLVED IN THE DEVELOPMENT OF NUCLEAR
   STANDARDS IN THE UNITED STATES
Oak Ridge National Laboratory
Box X
Oak Ridge, TN 37831
Covers: About 8,000 persons involved in preparing nuclear standards and codes; about 900 committees, etc., concerned with such standards. **Pages** (approx.): 375. **Frequency:** First edition March 1977.

★2750★
PETERSON'S ANNUAL GUIDE TO CAREERS AND EMPLOYMENT
   FOR ENGINEERS, COMPUTER SCIENTISTS, AND PHYSICAL
   SCIENTISTS
Peterson's Guides, Inc.
228 Alexander Street   Phone: (609) 924-5338
Princeton, NJ 08540
Covers: Over 800 research, consulting, manufacturing, government, and technical services organizations which hire college and university graduates in engineering, computer science, and the physical sciences. **Entries include:** Organization name, address, name of contact, type of organization, number of employees, industry classification, and description of opportunities available including disciplines, level of education required, starting locations and salaries, level of experience accepted, benefits. **Arrangement:** Alphabetical. **Indexes:** Employer by type of organization, industry classification, number of employees, starting location, special benefits or interests; education level. **Pages** (approx.): 550. **Frequency:** Annual; first edition expected early 1980. **Editor:** Sandra Grundfest, Ed.D. **Advertising accepted.** **Price:** $12.00, plus $1.25 shipping (ISSN 0190-4213). **Send orders to:** Peterson's Guide Order Dept., Box 978, Edison, NJ 08817.

★2751★
PHYCOLOGICAL NEWSLETTER—BYLAWS AND MEMBERSHIP
   DIRECTORY ISSUE
Phycological Society of America
C/o Dr. Clinton J. Dawes, President
Department of Biology
University of South Florida   Phone: (813) 974-2060
Tampa, FL 33620
Covers: About 2,000 individuals and institutions interested in the study and utilization of algae. **Entries include:** Name and address. **Arrangement:** Both members and institutions are alphabetical. **Pages** (approx.): 25. **Frequency:** Biennial, even years. **Editor:** Dr. Larry Liddle. **Price:** $5.00. **Send orders to:** Dr. Larry Liddle, Southampton College, Southampton Long Island, NY 11968.

★2752★
POLLUTION ENGINEERING—DIRECTORY OF ENVIRONMENTAL
   CONSULTANTS AND SERVICE COMPANIES ISSUE
Technical Publishing Company
1031 S. Grove   Phone: (312) 381-1840
Barrington, IL 60010
Covers: About 2,500 companies providing independent services as consultants, contractors, or managers for pollution control and other industries concerned with the environment. **Entries include:** Company name, address, phone, and capabilities as stated by the company. **Arrangement:** Classified by type of service, then arranged by

Environmental Protection Agency Region. **Pages** (approx.): 150. **Frequency:** Annual, June. **Editors:** Richard A. Young, Nancy L. Voras. **Advertising accepted.** Circulation 51,000. **Price:** $2.50.

★2753★
POLLUTION RESEARCH INDEX
Francis Hodgson Reference Publications
Longman House
Burnt Mill, Harlow
Essex CM20 2JE, England
Covers: About 2,000 research centers in over 100 countries where environmental scientific research is carried on. **Entries include:** Name of center in native language and in English, address, affiliation or parent body, name of director of research, research interests. **Arrangement:** Geographical. **Indexes:** Center name, subject. **Pages** (approx.): 555. **Frequency:** Irregular; latest edition 1979. **Price:** 75 pounds. **Send orders to:** Longman Group Ltd., 43/45 Annandale Street, Edinburgh EH7 4AT, Scotland.

★2754★
PRO FILE/ARCHITECTURAL FIRMS/THE AMERICAN INSTITUTE OF
   ARCHITECTS
Archimedia, Incorporated
1900 Chestnut Building   Phone: (215) 561-2021
Philadelphia, PA 19103
Covers: Over 6,000 architectural firms, one or more of whose principals is a member of the American Institute of Architects. **Entries include:** Firm name, address, phone, principals and their primary responsibilities (for design, specification, etc.), branches, type of organization (proprietorship, etc.), number of staff personnel by discipline, types of work, geographical area served, awards. **Arrangement:** Geographical. **Indexes:** Firm name, personal name. **Pages** (approx.): 675. **Frequency:** Irregular; latest edition fall 1979. **Editor:** Henry W. Schirmer, AIA. **Price:** $96.00. **Send orders to:** Archimedia, Inc., Box 4403, Topeka, KS 66604. **Other information:** "Pro File" is an expanded version of, and replaces, the "Firm Directory" formerly published by the American Institute of Architects.

★2755★
PRODUCT STANDARDS INDEX
Pergamon Press, Inc.
Maxwell House
Fairview Park
Elmsford, NY 10523
Publication includes: More than 100 United States and 40 overseas industrial associations which publish technical and safety standards for products produced in their industries. **Entries include:** Association name, address. **Frequency:** Irregular; latest edition spring 1978. **Editor:** Verne L. Roberts. **Price:** $36.30. **Other information:** Principal content of book is classified lists of products keyed to associations which publish standards for them.

★2756★
PROFESSIONAL AND TECHNICAL CONSULTANTS ASSOCIATION—
   MEMBERSHIP DIRECTORY
Professional and Technical Consultants Association
681 Market Street, Suite 750   Phone: (415) 981-4849
San Francisco, CA 94105
Covers: More than 100 consultants involved in computer technology, management, marketing, manufacturing, engineering, etc. **Entries include:** Individual or firm name, address, phone, specialty. **Arrangement:** Geographical. **Frequency:** Annual, June. **Price:** $5.00.

★2757★
PROFESSIONAL REGISTER—AMERICAN ACADEMY OF
   SANITARIANS
American Academy of Sanitarians
Spruce Hall
Colorado State University
Fort Collins, CO 80523
Covers: More than 350 persons who possess at least a master's

degree in public health, environmental health sciences, or environmental management and have special interests or responsibilities in environment or health areas. **Entries include:** Individual name, office address, home address, educational data, and areas of professional specialization. **Arrangement:** Alphabetical. **Indexes:** Geographical. **Pages** (approx.): 165. **Frequency:** Irregular; latest edition 1977; new edition expected 1982. **Former title:** Register of Professional Sanitarians. **Price:** $2.00.

★2758★

PUBLIC ADVISORY COMMITTEES AND PANELS OF THE FOOD AND DRUG ADMINISTRATION

Office of Public Affairs
Food and Drug Administration
Public Health Service
Health, Education, and Welfare Department
5600 Fishers Lane
Rockville, MD 20857
Covers: 35 committees and their members who advise the Food and Drug Administration about foods, drugs, and medical devices. **Entries include:** Name of committee and secretary; its authority, structure, and function; meeting details; list of members with names and addresses of employers. **Arrangement:** Alphabetical by FDA bureau. **Indexes:** Committee, personal name. **Pages** (approx.): 150. **Price:** Free.

★2759★

QUALITY—BUYERS GUIDE FOR TEST AND MEASUREMENT EQUIPMENT ISSUE

Hitchcock Publishing Company
Hitchcock Building   Phone: (312) 665-1000
Wheaton, IL 60187
Covers: Manufacturers and distributors of quality control equipment for measurement, inspection, data analysis, evaluation, and destructive and nondestructive testing; also lists testing laboratories. **Entries include:** Company name, address; phone, list of products. **Arrangement:** Alphabetical. **Indexes:** Product. **Pages** (approx.): 300. **Frequency:** Annual, July. **Editor:** Loren Walsh. **Advertising accepted.** Circulation 73,000. **Price:** $10.00 (current and 1980 editions).

Regional Guide to Food Testing Laboratories and Consultants *See* IFT's Regional Guide to Food Testing Laboratories and Consultants

Register of Professional Sanitarians *See* Professional Register— American Academy of Sanitarians

★2760★

RESEARCH CENTERS DIRECTORY

Gale Research Company
Book Tower   Phone: (313) 961-2242
Detroit, MI 48226
Covers: About 6,300 university-related and other nonprofit research organizations which are established on a permanent basis and carry on continuing research programs in all areas of study. Includes research institutes, laboratories, experiment stations, computation centers, and other facilities and activities. **Entries include:** Unit name, name of parent institution, address, phone, name of director, year founded, sources of support, annual budget, principal fields of interest, publications, and special library facilities. **Arrangement:** Classified by broad subjects, then alphabetical by unit name. **Indexes:** Alphabetical, institution, subject. **Pages** (approx.): 1,125. **Frequency:** Biennial, summer of odd years. **Editors:** Robert C. Thomas and James A. Ruffner. **Price:** $90.00. **Other information:** Supplemented by ''New

Research Centers,'' edited by Archie   Palmer; inter-edition subscription, $80.00.

★2761★

RESEARCH IN CHEMISTRY AT PRIVATE UNDERGRADUATE COLLEGES

Council on Undergraduate Research
4570 W. 77th Street, Suite 275
Edina, MN 55435
Covers: About 95 private college chemistry departments with over 600 faculty members. Institutions contacted were selected based on success in getting outside research grants, reputation for research activity, and graduates pursuing Ph.D. degrees in chemistry. **Entries include:** College name, address; department chairman; enrollment, number of faculty, number of staff, facilities, size of library, equipment available, funding. For faculty members - Name, research interests, current publications, and grants received. **Arrangement:** Alphabetical. **Pages** (approx.): 265. **Frequency:** Not established; first edition January 1979. **Editor:** Brian Andreen. **Price:** $8.00, postpaid, payment with order; $9.00, billed.

★2762★

RESOURCE DIRECTORY OF HANDICAPPED SCIENTISTS

American Association for the Advancement of Science
1515 Massachusetts Avenue, N. W.   Phone: (202) 467-4497
Washington, DC 20005
Covers: More than 550 scientists and graduate students in the natural and social sciences, mathematics, engineering, and medicine who have handicapping conditions and are willing to share experiences and information, help organize action if needed, and assist in planning for handicapped scientists. **Entries include:** Name, address, phone, personal and professional data, educational and professional experience, expertise and consulting interests. **Arrangement:** Alphabetical. **Indexes:** Specialty in science, geographic, handicapping condition, sex. **Pages** (approx.): 70. **Frequency:** First edition October 1978; new edition expected 1981. **Editors:** Janette Alsford Owens and Martha Ross Redden. **Price:** $3.00. **Send orders to:** Project on the Handicapped in Science, Office of Opportunities in Science, AAAS, 1776 Massachusetts Avenue, N. W., Washington, DC 20036.

★2763★

ROBOTICS TODAY—CALENDAR OF EVENTS

Society of Manufacturing Engineers
One SME Drive   Phone: (313) 271-1500
Dearborn, MI 48128
Covers: Conferences, exhibits, seminars, etc., scheduled in the field of robot technology. **Entries include:** Event name, dates, location, sponsor, contact. **Frequency:** Quarterly. **Price:** $24.00 per year.

★2764★

ROSTER OF SCIENTISTS FOR THE MAJOR FOOD CROPS OF THE DEVELOPING WORLD

Office of Agriculture
Technical Assistance Bureau
Agency for International Development
Washington, DC 20523
Covers: Scientists chiefly concerned with improving food crop production in developing areas. Includes lists of international and regional agricultural research institutions and nonprofit organizations supporting agricultural assistance abroad. **Entries include:** Main listings show name, year of birth and citizenship, languages fluent in, academic degrees, specialities, experience, title, address. Geographical listings show name of scientist, profession, specialities and interests in chart form. **Arrangement:** Alphabetical. **Indexes:** Geographical (includes crops in which interested). **Pages** (approx.): 200. **Frequency:** Previous edition 1973; latest edition 1975. **Editors:** Martin T. Hutchinson and Elton G. Nelson. **Price:** Free.

★2765★
ROSTER OF WOMEN AND MINORITY ENGINEERING AND
    TECHNOLOGY STUDENTS
Engineering Manpower Commission
Engineers Joint Council
345 E. 47th Street   Phone: (212) 644-7850
New York, NY 10017
Covers: 4,700 women and minority engineering students and
technicians expected to graduate in the next two years from
recognized colleges and technical schools. Pages (approx.): 110.
Frequency: Annual, December. Price: $75.00.

★2766★
SCHWENDEMAN'S DIRECTORY OF COLLEGE GEOGRAPHY OF THE
    UNITED STATES
Southeast Association of American Geographers
C/o Geographical Studies and Research Center
Department of Geography
Eastern Kentucky University   Phone: (606) 622-2251
Richmond, KY 40475
Covers: 1,200 college and university geography departments, their
courses, requirements for enrollment, and faculties. Arrangement:
Two directory sections, both geographical - a departmental personnel
section and course and enrollment information section. Pages
(approx.): 90. Frequency: Annual, April. Editor: Dale R. Monsebroten.
Advertising accepted. Circulation 1,400. Former title: Directory of
College Geography of the United States. Price: $1.50.

★2767★
SCIENCE, ENGINEERING, RESEARCH, AND DEVELOPMENT
    DIRECTORY [Midwest]
Kansas City Regional Office
Small Business Administration
911 Walnut Street   Phone: (816) 374-3516
Kansas City, MO 64106
Covers: Companies engaged in research and development in SBA
Region VII (Missouri, Kansas, Iowa, and Nebraska). Entries include:
Company name, address, phone, name of chief executive, synopsis of
capabilities of each firm, numbers indicating DD Form 1630 capability
fields. Arrangement: Alphabetical. Indexes: Capabilities. Pages
(approx.): 20. Frequency: Annual, September. Editor: Felix J. Padilla,
Procurement Source Specialist. Price: Free.

★2768★
SCIENCE FOR THE PHYSICALLY HANDICAPPED IN HIGHER
    EDUCATION
Environmental Science Information Center
Library and Information Services Division
National Oceanic and Atmospheric Administration
Commerce Department
Rockville, MD 20852
Covers: Government agencies, professional societies, libraries and
information centers, and other sources of information dealing with
science education, career opportunities, and funding for physically
handicapped individuals. Entries include: Organization name, address,
phone, description of services. Pages (approx.): 30. Frequency: Not
established; published summer 1979. Editor: Gary H. Adams.

★2769★
SCIENCE TRAINING PROGRAMS DIRECTORY FOR HIGH ABILITY
    SECONDARY SCHOOL STUDENTS
Division of Scientific Personnel Improvement
National Science Foundation
Washington, DC 20550
Covers: 120 institutions with total of 4,400 openings for
academically outstanding secondary school students to obtain
intensive experience in science and mathematics during the summer.
Entries include: Institution name; address; title, dates, and duration
of program; number of students; restrictions; name of contact.
Arrangement: Geographical. Pages (approx.): 25. Frequency:
Annual, February. Former title: Directory of Science Training

Programs for High Ability Secondary School Students. Price: Free.

★2770★
SCIENTIFIC AND TECHNICAL BOOKS AND SERIALS IN PRINT
R. R. Bowker Company
1180 Avenue of the Americas   Phone: (212) 764-5100
New York, NY 10036
Publication includes: List of about 2,000 publishers of monographs
and serials in scientific subjects, including physical and biological
sciences, engineering, and technology. Entries include: Name,
address. Price: $55.00, payment with order. Send orders to: R. R.
Bowker Co., Box 1807, Ann Arbor, MI 48106 (313-761-4700).
Other information: Principal content of publication is listings of books
on scientific subjects in general classifications. There are author, title,
and subject indexes. Based on "Books in Print," described in separate
listing.

Sea Technology—Buyer's Guide/Directory Issue See Sea
    Technology Handbook Directory

★2771★
SEA TECHNOLOGY HANDBOOK DIRECTORY
Compass Publications, Inc.
1117 19th Street   Phone: (703) 524-3136
North Arlington, VA 22209
Covers: Manufacturing, service, research and development,
engineering, construction, drilling, and equipment lease and rental
firms and testing organizations providing goods and services to the
oceanographic, offshore, marine sciences, and undersea defense
industries. Entries include: Company name, address, phone,
executives' names, list of products or services. Arrangement:
Classified by product, service, etc. Principal section is alphabetical
listing of manufacturing and service firms, with product and service
buyers guide indexes; includes other lists of federal government
agencies active in oceanography, oceanographic research vessels in
active service, geophysical survey vessels in active service, and
educational institutions offering courses or degrees in oceanography
or related subjects, all with details appropriate to nature of the lists.
Pages (approx.): 200. Frequency: Annual, September. Editor: Larry
L. Booda. Advertising accepted. Circulation 10,000. Former title:
Undersea Technology Handbook Directory (1974). Price: $14.50.

★2772★
SMALL BUSINESS GUIDE TO FEDERAL R&D
Office of Small Business Research and Development
National Science Foundation
1800 G Street
Washington, DC 20550
Covers: Federal agencies and their major components which have
significant research and development programs. Entries include:
Agency name, outline of research components and programs,
description of fields of major interest, and several names for further
information or submission of proposals. Pages (approx.): 100.
Frequency: Published May 1978. Price: $6.50, paper; $3.00,
microfiche (PB 290-199). May also be available from the agency.
Send orders to: National Technical Information Service, Springfield,
VA 22161.

★2773★
SOCIETY FOR CLINICAL AND EXPERIMENTAL HYPNOSIS—
    DIRECTORY
Society for Clinical and Experimental Hypnosis
129-A Kings Park Drive   Phone: (315) 652-7299
Liverpool, NY 13088
Covers: 900 United States and Canadian physicians, psychologists
(licensed or certified), and dentists who use hypnosis in their
practices. Entries include: Name, office and home addresses, highest
degree held, areas of occupational specialization, whether diplomate
of American Board of Clinical Hypnosis and/or specialty boards of the
American Medical Association. Arrangement: Geographical. Indexes:
Alphabetical. Frequency: Irregular; previous edition 1976; latest

edition 1979. **Price:** $4.00.

Society for Industrial and Applied Mathematics *See* Combined Membership List...

★2774★
SOCIETY FOR INDUSTRIAL MICROBIOLOGY—DIRECTORY OF MEMBERS
Society for Industrial Microbiology
1401 Wilson Boulevard   Phone: (703) 527-6776
Arlington, VA 22209
Covers: About 1,400 mycologists, microbiologists, biologists, chemists, engineers, zoologists, and others interested in biological processes as applied to industrial materials and processes concerning microorganisms. **Entries include:** Name and office address. **Arrangement:** Alphabetical and geographical. **Pages** (approx.): 30. **Frequency:** Irregular; latest edition 1978; new edition possible late 1980. **Editor:** Ann Kulback, Business Secretary. **Price:** Free; controlled circulation.

Society of Cable Television Engineers—Membership Directory *See* The Interval—Annual Membership Directory Issue

★2775★
SOCIETY OF COSMETIC CHEMISTS—MEMBERSHIP DIRECTORY
Society of Cosmetic Chemists
1995 Broadway   Phone: (212) 874-0600
New York, NY 10023
Number of listings: 2,700. **Entries include:** Individual name, title and company with which affiliated, office address, phone. **Arrangement:** Alphabetical. **Frequency:** Biennial, July of odd years. **Price:** Available to members only.

★2776★
SOCIETY OF PETROLEUM ENGINEERS—MEMBERSHIP DIRECTORY
Society of Petroleum Engineers of AIME
6200 N. Central Expressway   Phone: (214) 361-6601
Dallas, TX 75206
Covers: 34,000 members involved in petroleum exploration, drilling, and production, worldwide. **Entries include:** Name, office address, election date, member grade. **Arrangement:** Alphabetical. **Indexes:** Geographical, company. **Pages** (approx.): 240. **Frequency:** Annual. **Editor:** Jim McInnis, Publications Manager. **Advertising accepted.** Circulation 3,000. **Price:** Available to members only.

★2777★
SOCIETY OF PHOTO-TECHNOLOGISTS—MEMBERSHIP DIRECTORY
Society of Photo-Technologists
Box 31474
Aurora, CO 80041
Covers: 900 camera repair technicians. **Entries include:** Name, office and home address. **Arrangement:** Geographical. **Pages** (approx.): 30. **Frequency:** Biennial, January of even years. **Editor:** Peggy Jones, Executive Director. **Advertising accepted.** Circulation 900. **Price:** $5.00.

★2778★
SOLAR ENERGY & RESEARCH DIRECTORY
Ann Arbor Science Publishers, Inc.
Box 1425   Phone: (313) 761-5010
Ann Arbor, Mi 48106
Covers: About 825 firms and institutions active in solar energy research and manufacturing in the United States and abroad. **Entries include:** Company or institution name, address, phone, name of principal executive and of the solar engineer, plus keys indicating activities or applications with which the organization is involved. **Arrangement:** Classified by principal activity or interest. **Indexes:** Geographical, subject. **Pages** (approx.): 390. **Frequency:** Irregular; latest edition summer 1977; no new edition planned. **Former title:** Solar Energy; was published by Environmental Action of Colorado.

Price: $24.00.

★2779★
SOLAR ENERGY BUYER'S GUIDE AND DIRECTORY
Solar Data
13 Evergreen Road   Phone: (603) 926-8082
Hampton, NH 03842
Covers: Over 3,000 companies in United States active in solar energy industry, including solar heating and cooling and solar electricity; includes firms in fields of wind, bioconversion, and ocean thermal conversion. **Entries include:** Company name, address, phone, names of executives, trade and brand names, list of products or services. **Indexes:** Product, geographical. **Pages** (approx.): 150. **Frequency:** Annual, July. **Editor:** Dick Livingstone. **Price:** $20.00, payment with order.

★2780★
SOLAR ENERGY FOR AGRICULTURAL AND INDUSTRIAL PROCESS HEAT
Assistant Secretary for Conservation and Solar Applications
Energy Department
Washington, DC 20545
Covers: About 175 experimental projects concerned with use of solar energy in agricultural and industrial processes. **Entries include:** Name of project, name and phone of project manager, location of project, amount of federal funding, and description. **Arrangement:** Classified by application. **Arrangement:** Geographical, alphabetical list of contractors. **Pages** (approx.): 125. **Frequency:** Published fall 1978. **Other information:** Map showing location of projects.

★2781★
SOLAR ENGINEERING—DESKBOOK DIRECTORY OF MANUFACTURERS ISSUE
Solar Engineering Publishers, Inc.
8435 N. Stemmons Freeway, Suite 880   Phone: (214) 630-6963
Dallas, TX 75247
Covers: Manufacturers of products for solar heating and cooling systems. **Entries include:** Company name, address, phone, description of products. **Arrangement:** Alphabetical. **Indexes:** Product (uses Construction Specifications Institute categories). **Frequency:** Annual, December. **Advertising accepted.** Circulation 14,000. **Price:** $2.50.

★2782★
SOLAR ENGINEERING DIRECTORY
American Consulting Engineers Council
1155 15th Street, N. W.
Washington, DC 20005
Covers: Consulting engineering firms with expertise in the solar energy field. **Entries include:** Company name, address, staff size, special capabilities. **Arrangement:** Geographical. **Price:** Free.

★2783★
SPEAKERS, TOURS, AND FILMS [Physics education]
Society of Physics Students
American Institute of Physics
335 E. 45th Street   Phone: (516) 681-3800
New York, NY 10017
Covers: Individuals willing to speak on physics and related fields; tours; and sources of films; about 1,000 listings. **Entries include:** For speakers - Name, address, topics, advance notice required, limitations of time and geographic area. For tours - Name, contact name and address, advance notice required, size restriction. For films - Title, source name and address, advance notice required, description. **Arrangement:** Speakers and tours are geographical, films are alphabetical. **Pages** (approx.): 130. **Frequency:** Annual, September. **Price:** $10.00, payment with order; $12.00, billed.

★2784★

STANDARDS ENGINEERS SOCIETY—MEMBERSHIP DIRECTORY
Standards Engineers Society
6700 Penn Avenue, South   Phone: (612) 861-4990
Minneapolis, MN 55423
Covers: 1,000 engineers, teachers, executives, predominantly in the United States and Canada, interested in promoting knowledge and use of standards. **Entries include:** Name, office address, home address, and current position. **Arrangement:** Alphabetical by individual and by company name. **Pages** (approx.): 80. **Frequency:** Annual, September. **Editor:** Byron H. Davies. **Advertising accepted.** Circulation 1,300. **Price:** Available to members only.

★2785★

STATE AND LOCAL ENVIRONMENTAL LIBRARIES: A DIRECTORY
Environmental Protection Agency
401 M Street, S. W.   Phone: (202) 755-0353
Washington, DC 20460
Covers: 450 libraries with known specialized environmental interests, including university and public libraries; general university libraries are omitted. **Entries include:** Library name, address, phone, name of librarian. **Arrangement:** Geographical. **Pages** (approx.): 30. **Frequency:** Irregular; latest edition November 1976; new edition expected 1980. **Former title:** Directory of State and Local Environmental Libraries. **Price:** $4.50 (PB 259-918/1WL). **Send orders to:** National Technical Information Service, Springfield, VA 22161. **Other information:** Compiled with National Oceanic and Atmospheric Administration.

★2786★

TECHNICIAN EDUCATION YEARBOOK
Prakken Publications, Inc.
416 Longshore Drive   Phone: (313) 769-1211
Ann Arbor, MI 48107
Publication includes: Lists of institutions offering technician training; also includes federal and state officials concerned with technician education, and professional organizations concerned with technician training. **Entries include:** For institutions - Name, address, name of key person in charge, enrollment figures, course offerings. **Arrangement:** Institutions, geographical. **Indexes:** Field of study. **Pages** (approx.): 370. **Frequency:** Biennial, October of odd years. **Editor:** Lawrence W. Prakken. **Advertising accepted.** **Price:** $20.00.

★2787★

TISSUE CULTURE ASSOCIATION—MEMBERSHIP ROSTER
Tissue Culture Association
One Bank Street, Suite 210   Phone: (301) 869-2900
Gaithersburg, MD 20760
Number of listings: 2,200. **Entries include:** Name, address, phone. **Arrangement:** Alphabetical. **Frequency:** Irregular; new edition possible 1980. **Advertising accepted.** **Price:** Available to members only.

Undersea Technology Handbook Directory *See* Sea Technology
   Handbook Directory

★2788★

U.S. DIRECTORY OF ENVIROMENTAL SOURCES
United States International Environmental Referral Center
Environmental Protection Agency
401 M Street, N. W., Room 2902 (PM-213) Phone: (202) 755-1836
Washington, DC 20460
Covers: More than 1,300 United States environmental organizations ("sources," for purposes of the directory) registered with USIERC, the U.S. National Focal Point of the United Nations Environmental Program's International Referral System (UNEP/INFOTERRA). Organizations include federal, state, and local government agencies; universities; industry; societies; laboratories; etc. **Entries include:** Organization name, address, phone, subject interests, and description of activities, group served, etc. **Arrangement:** Random, with

sequential numerical identifiers which are used in subject, alphabetical, and geographical indexes. **Pages** (approx.): 860. **Frequency:** Annual, fall. **Price:** $24.00 (PB 294-950/AS). **Send orders to:** National Technical Information Service, Springfield, VA 22161.

★2789★

U.S. DIRECTORY OF MARINE SCIENTISTS
National Academy of Sciences
2101 Constitution Avenue   Phone: (202) 389-6731
Washington, DC 20418
Number of listings: 3,020. **Entries include:** Name, office address, areas of occupational specialization. **Arrangement:** Geographical. **Indexes:** Personal name, special research interest. **Pages** (approx.): 330. **Frequency:** Irregular; new edition expected 1980. **Editor:** Richard C. Vetter, Executive Secretary. **Former title:** A Directory of Oceanographers in the United States. **Price:** $6.50 (1975 edition).

★2790★

U.S. OBSERVATORIES: A DIRECTORY AND TRAVEL GUIDE
Van Nostrand Reinhold Company, Division
Litton Educational Publishing, Inc.
135 W. 50th Street   Phone: (212) 265-8700
New York, NY 10020
Covers: Nearly 300 optical and radio observatories and planetariums. **Entries include:** Observatory and/or institution name, address, description of the facility and its equipment, details on public admission. Entries for 15 major observatories include history, brief survey of current research, more details on public accessibility, and information on local accomodations and points of interest. **Arrangement:** Geographical. **Pages** (approx.): 175. **Frequency:** Not established; first edition 1976. **Author:** H. T. Kirby-Smith. **Price:** $11.95. **Send orders to:** Van Nostrand Reinhold Co., 7625 Empire Dr., Florence, KY 41042.

★2791★

UPPER MISSISSIPPI RIVER CONSERVATION COMMITTEE—
   MEMBERSHIP LIST
Upper Mississippi River Conservation Committee
1830 Second Avenue   Phone: (309) 788-3991
Rock Island, IL 61201
Covers: About 115 biologists and law enforcement officials in Illinois, Iowa, Minnesota, Missouri, and Wisconsin concerned with natural resource management. **Entries include:** Name, address, phone, agency. **Arrangement:** Classified by specialization. **Pages** (approx.): 20. **Frequency:** Annual, May. **Editor:** Jerry L. Rasmussen, Coordinator. **Price:** Apply.

★2792★

USER'S GUIDE TO BIOME INFORMATION FROM THE UNITED
   STATES INTERNATIONAL BIOLOGICAL PROGRAM
Institute of Ecology
Butler University
Indianapolis, IN 46208
Covers: Researchers associated with the International Biological Program who have studied a particular biome. (A biome is an ecosystem, including both plant and animal life, such as a tundra biome, tropical biome, etc.) **Entries include:** Individual name, address, phone, biome studied, particular interests. **Arrangement:** Alphabetical. **Indexes:** Researcher by biome, by interest. **Pages** (approx.): 55. **Frequency:** Irregular; latest edition August 1977. **Editors:** A. Dexter Hinckley and Peter T. Haug. **Price:** $1.00. **Also includes:** Site list, map, and information sources concerned with biome research.

★2793★

VERTIFLITE—AMERICAN HELICOPTER SOCIETY MEMBERSHIP
   DIRECTORY ISSUE
American Helicopter Society
1325 18th Street, N. W.   Phone: (202) 659-9524
Washington, DC 20036
Covers: About 3,500 aeronautical engineers and others concerned

with vertical take off and landing aircraft. **Entries include:** Individual name, address, initial year of membership, affiliation and title. **Arrangement:** Alphabetical; new members listed separately. **Indexes:** Company/affiliation (with title and phone). **Frequency:** Annual, December. **Editor:** L. Kim Smith, Editor and Publisher. **Advertising accepted.** Circulation 4,000. **Price:** $3.00 (ISSN 0042-4455).

Water Pollution Control Federation—Membership Directory *See* Journal Water Pollution Control Federation—Directory Issue

★2794★
WATER QUALITY MANAGEMENT DIRECTORY
Water Planning Division
Environmental Protection Agency
401 M Street, S. W. (WH-554)   Phone: (202) 755-2117
Washington, DC 20009
Covers: 225 state and local government water quality management agencies. **Entries include:** Agency name, address, phone, name of principal executive, amount of grant award, and date water quality management plan due. **Arrangement:** By federal regions. **Pages** (approx.): 170. **Frequency:** Annual, spring. **Editor:** Hugh Burrows, Environmental Protection Specialist. **Price:** Free.

Who's Who in Computer Education and Research *See* Directory of Computer Education and Research

★2795★
WHO'S WHO IN DISPLAY HOLOGRAPHY
Museum of Holography Bookstore
11 Mercer Street   Phone: (212) 925-0526
New York, NY 10013
Covers: Individuals and companies in the United States, Canada, and Europe concerned with display holography. **Entries include:** Individual's name or company name, address, phone, specialties. **Arrangement:** Alphabetical. **Pages** (approx.): 130. **Frequency:** Biennial, fall of even years. **Price:** $12.50, plus $1.50 shipping.

★2796★
WHO'S WHO IN FEDERAL NOISE PROGRAMS
Office of Noise Abatement and Control
Environmental Protection Agency   Phone: (703) 557-8292
Washington, DC 20460
Covers: About 350 federal personnel involved in noise abatement and noise research. **Entries include:** Agency name, address, offices or branches, names and phone numbers of noise/acoustic personnel. **Arrangement:** By agency. **Indexes:** Personnel, geographical. **Pages** (approx.): 155. **Frequency:** Not established; first edition December 1977. **Price:** $8.00, paper; $3.00, microfiche (PB 279-520). **Send orders to:** National Technical Information Service, Springfield, VA 22161.

Who's Who in Nuclear Energy *See* American Nuclear Society—Directory

★2797★
WHO'S WHO IN SAFETY
Veterans of Safety
4721 Briarbend Drive   Phone: (713) 723-0522
Houston, TX 77035
Covers: 1,600 safety engineers with 15 or more years of professional safety experience, working and retired. **Entries include:** Name, office or home address. **Arrangement:** Alphabetical. **Indexes:** Geographical. **Pages** (approx.): 40. **Frequency:** Annual, October; latest edition 1978. **Editor:** Quincy V. Tuma, Secretary-Treasurer. **Price:** $25.00.

★2798★
WHO'S WHO IN THE INTERAGENCY ENERGY/ENVIRONMENT R&D PROGRAM
Office of Energy, Minerals, and Industry
Office of Research and Development
Environmental Protection Agency
Washington, DC 20460
Covers: Projects underway in more than a dozen federal agencies participating in the program. **Entries include:** In tabular form, the descriptive title of the project, and names of project contact, EPA coordinator, and performing agency coordinator. Names of contacts and coordinators appear in separate alphabetical list with title, address, and phone. **Arrangement:** By category of process, effect, or control. **Pages** (approx.): 50. **Frequency:** Irregular; latest edition June 1978. **Price:** Free. Also available from National Technical Information Service, Springfield, VA 22161 (PB 284-375; $4.50, paper; $3.00, microfiche).

Who's Who in the World of Ceramics *See* American Ceramic Society Bulletin—Roster Issue

Wilson Ornithological Society—Membership List *See* American Ornithologists' Union—Membership List

★2799★
WOOD RESIDUE ENERGY DIRECTORY
Forest Products Research Society
2801 Marshall Court
Madison, WI 53705
Covers: About 200 manufacturers, equipment suppliers, technical consultants, and engineers offering products or expertise in the conversion of wood residues to energy. **Entries include:** Company name, address, phone, product; consultant and engineer listings include area of expertise. **Arrangement:** Suppliers and manufacturers are alphabetical within major product category, others are geographical. **Pages** (approx.): 25. **Frequency:** Irregular; first edition November 1976; latest edition 1979. **Editor:** Pamela A. Lee. **Former title:** Directory of Suppliers, Manufacturers, Technical Consultants, Professional Engineers (1976). **Price:** $7.00, plus 70¢ shipping.

★2800★
WORLD ASSOCIATION OF DOCUMENT EXAMINERS— MEMBERSHIP DIRECTORY
World Association of Document Examiners
111 N. Canal   Phone: (312) 922-0856
Chicago, IL 60606
Covers: Handwriting experts specializing in the authentication of signatures, typewriting, ink, paper, and other problems concerning documents. **Entries include:** Name, address, phone. **Arrangement:** Geographical. **Frequency:** Annual, July. **Editor:** Lucille E. Range, Executive Secretary. **Price:** $1.00.

★2801★
WORLD CALENDAR OF FORTHCOMING MEETINGS: METALLURGICAL AND RELATED FIELDS
Metals Society
One Carlton House Terrace
London SW1Y 5DB, England
Covers: About 500 meetings and conferences concerned with metallurgy; worldwide coverage. **Entries include:** Meeting date, location, subject; names of sponsors or organizers; scope of meeting; registration information (including contact name and address); whether open to non-members; pre-conference materials available; languages; whether publication of proceedings is planned. **Arrangement:** Chronological. **Indexes:** Subject, sponsor/organizer name, location. **Pages** (approx.): 80. **Frequency:** Quarterly; cumulative. **Editor:** J. S. Bristow. **Price:** $36.00 per year.

★2802★
WORLD CENSUS OF TROPICAL ECOLOGISTS
Institute of Ecology
Ecology Building
University of Georgia   Phone: (404) 542-2968
Athens, GA 30602
Covers: About 2,000 scientists and researchers concerned with human ecology, ecology of disease, and environmental management in tropical areas; international coverage. **Entries include:** Name, address, research and interest subjects, country of research, taxonomic interest. **Arrangement:** Alphabetical. **Indexes:** Subject, country of research, taxonomic interest. **Pages** (approx.): 160. **Frequency:** Irregular; latest edition June 1977. **Editors:** Joan A. Yantko and F. B. Golley. **Price:** Free.

★2803★
WORLD DIRECTORY OF MATHEMATICIANS
International Mathematical Union
C/o Bureau of the World Directory of Mathematicians
Mathematics Department
Faculty of Sciences
Kyoto Univ.
Kyoto 606, Japan
Covers: About 20,000 mathematicians worldwide. **Entries include:** Name, address, title and affiliation. **Arrangement:** Alphabetical. **Indexes:** Geographical. **Pages** (approx.): 550. **Frequency:** Every four years; first edition August 1979. **Editor:** M. Nagata. **Price:** $20.00, payment with order; $30.00, billed.

★2804★
WORLD DIRECTORY OF PLANT PATHOLOGISTS
Fran. E. Fisher
Agricultural Research and Education Center
University of Florida   Phone: (813) 293-0927
Lake Alfred, FL 33880
Covers: Over 11,000 professional plant pathologists in 125 countries or areas. **Entries include:** Name, professional address, and special interests. **Arrangement:** By continent, sub-divided into countries/ areas. **Pages** (approx.): 140. **Frequency:** Every five years in late summer; latest edition 1979. **Editor:** Fran. E. Fisher. **Price:** $35.00.

★2805★
WORLD LIST OF COMPUTER PERIODICALS
United Trade Press Ltd.
33-35 Bowling Green Lane
London W1V 7LP, England
Publication includes: List of publishers of over 1,680 journals concerned with computers and data processing; international coverage. **Entries include:** For publishers - Name, address. For periodicals - Title, date of publication, frequency, "continuation of" and "continued as" information, other descriptive notes. **Arrangement:** Publishers are alphabetical. **Frequency:** Irregular; latest edition 1979. **Price:** 10 pounds.

★2806★
WORLDS BEYOND [Space development, futurism]
And/Or Press
Box 2246   Phone: (415) 849-2665
Berkeley, CA 94702
Publication includes: List of about 50 periodicals, organizations, lecturers, and other sources of information on space technology, UFOs, futurism, space settlement and industrialization. **Entries include:** For organizations - Name, address, description of types of memberships available, activities, publications, and cost of membership. For periodicals - Title, name of publisher, address, subscription rate, description of content. For lecturers - Name, name and address of booking firm. **Arrangement:** By topic, then by type of resource. **Frequency:** First published November 1978. **Editors:** Larry Geis and Fabrice Florin. **Price:** $6.95. **Other information:** Published under auspices of New Dimensions Foundation, 267 States Street, San Francisco, CA 94114. Principal content of the publication is

articles on space technology and futurism.

★2807★
WORLDWIDE DIRECTORY OF NATIONAL EARTH-SCIENCE
    AGENCIES
National Center
U. S. Geological Survey
Interior Department
12201 Sunrise Valley Drive   Phone: (703) 860-7444
Reston, VA 22092
Covers: Government agencies in about 160 countries concerned with earth sciences; about 70 major international organizations involved in earth science research, study, and promotion are also listed. **Entries include:** For government agencies - Name of agency, address, field of interest. For international organizations - Name, address. **Arrangement:** Agencies are by country, organizations are by field of interest. **Pages** (approx.): 80. **Frequency:** Irregular; latest edition 1978; new edition expected 1980. **Price:** Free. **Send orders to:** Branch of Distribution, U. S. Geological Survey, 1200 S. Eads Street, Arlington, VA 22202.

★2808★
ZOOS AND AQUARIUMS IN THE AMERICAS
American Association of Zoological Parks and Aquariums
Oglebay Park   Phone: (304) 242-2160
Wheeling, WV 26003
Covers: Zoos, aquariums, oceanariums and wildlife parks, members and nonmembers. **Entries include:** For institutional members of AAZPA - Name, address, phone, type of operation (public, private, governmental), names and titles of personnel, size of collection, acreage, number of visitors, educational programs, operating budgets, film titles and publications, number of employees. Separate list for nonmember institutions - Name, address, phone. For personal members - Name, address. **Pages** (approx.): 230. **Frequency:** Biennial, September of even years. **Advertising accepted.** Circulation 2,500. **Price:** $15.00 to educational facilities; $50.00 to others.

6

Education

★2809★
ACADEMIC YEAR AND SUMMER PROGRAMS ABROAD
American Institute for Foreign Study
102 Greenwich Avenue   Phone: (203) 869-9090
Greenwich, CT 06830
Entries include: School name, address, courses offered, application procedures, application deadline, tuition and fees. **Arrangement:** Geographical. **Pages** (approx.): 200. **Frequency:** Annual. **Price:** Free.

Accredited Higher Institutions *See* Directory of Postsecondary Schools with Occupational Programs

Accredited Institutions of Higher Education *See* Accredited Institut Ons of Postsecondary Education

★2810★
ACCREDITED INSTITUTIONS OF POSTSECONDARY EDUCATION
American Council on Education
One Dupont Circle, Suite 25   Phone: (202) 833-4700
Washington, DC 20036
Number of listings: 4,500; covers all accredited institutions and programs of postsecondary education in the United States. **Entries include:** Name of institution, control, type. **Pages** (approx.): 350. **Frequency:** Annual, September. **Editor:** Sherry Harris. **Former title:** Council on Postsecondary Accreditation - Membership List; Accredited Institutions of Higher Education. **Price:** $12.50, plus $1.00 shipping, payment with order. **Other information:** Variant title, "National Directory of Accredited Junior and Senior Colleges, Universities, Professional, and Specialized Schools."

Accrediting Commission for Business Schools—Directory *See* Assn. of Independent Colleges and Schools—Directory of Accredited Inst.

★2811★
ACUHO NEWS—DIRECTORY ISSUE [College housing]
Association of College and University Housing Officers
801 N. Jordan Avenue, Room 210   Phone: (812) 337-1764
Bloomington, IN 47405
Covers: About 520 member college and university housing officers. **Entries include:** Institution name, address, phone; coded description of institution including enrollment, number of rooms for single males, single females, and married/families; and names, titles, and phone numbers for individuals who are members of the association. **Arrangement:** Geographical, then by institution name. **Indexes:** Personal name, school name without state or province name in title, committee membership (with institution name). **Pages** (approx.): 80. **Frequency:** Annual, February. **Editor:** John H. Schuh. **Price:** $4.00;

restricted to advertisers in association publications. **Send orders to:** William R. Bierbaum, Director of Housing and Food Service, Washington State University, Pullman, WA 99164.

★2812★
ADVISORY LIST OF NATIONAL CONTESTS AND ACTIVITIES
National Association of Secondary School Principals
1904 Association Drive
Reston, VA 22091
Description: Evaluates contests, promotional activities, etc., directed at secondary school students and teachers as to suitability for inclusion in a school program or curriculum. **Price:** 50¢.

American Association of School Administrators—Roster *See* Who's Who in Educational Administration

★2813★
AMERICAN SCHOOL & UNIVERSITY—ANNUAL PLANT PLANNING DIRECTORY
North American Publishing Company
401 N. Broad Street   Phone: (215) 574-9600
Philadelphia, PA 19108
Covers: Companies supplying products and services for physical plants and business offices of schools, colleges, and universities. **Entries include:** Company name, address, trade and brand names, list of products or services. **Pages** (approx.): 100. **Frequency:** Annual, May. **Editor:** Rita Robison. **Advertising accepted.** Circulation 37,000. **Price:** $3.00 (current and 1980 editions).

★2814★
AMERICAN TRADE SCHOOLS DIRECTORY
Croner Publications, Inc.
211-05 Jamaica Avenue   Phone: (212) 464-0866
Queens Village, NY 11428
Covers: About 8,000 private and public trade, industrial, and vocational schools. **Entries include:** School name, address, description of courses, whether private or public, whether for men or women only, whether approved by state or Veterans Administration, whether home study courses are offered. **Arrangement:** Geographical. **Indexes:** Courses offered. **Pages** (approx.): 150. **Frequency:** Latest base volume (looseleaf format) 1976, monthly supplements. **Editor:** Ulrich H. Croner. **Advertising accepted.** **Price:** $35.00, plus $3.95 shipping for base volume and year's supplement service.

★2815★
AMERICAN UNIVERSITIES AND COLLEGES
American Council on Education
One Dupont Circle, N. W.   Phone: (202) 833-4784
Washington, DC 20036
Covers: 1,450 accredited four-year colleges and universities. Includes a list of statewide coordinating boards of higher education. **Entries include:** For schools - History, governing board, calendar, freshman characteristics, special academic programs, student life, ROTC, graduate work, degrees conferred, fees, student financial aid, departments and teaching staff, enrollment, foreign students, publications, library, finances, buildings and grounds, administration, separate descriptions of each major division within a university. For boards - Name, address, name of director. **Arrangement:** Geographical. **Pages** (approx.): 1,880. **Frequency:** Irregular; latest edition 1973. **Editor:** W. Todd Furniss, Director, Office of Academic Affairs. **Price:** $42.00.

American Vocational Journal—Annual Buyers Guide Issue *See* VocEd—Buyers Guide Issue

★2816★
ANNUAL LIST OF ACCREDITED INSTITUTIONS [Teacher education]
National Council for Accreditation of Teacher Education
1919 Pennsylvania Avenue, N. W.,
    Room 202
Washington, DC 20006
Covers: About 550 colleges and universities with teacher education programs accredited by the council. **Entries include:** Institution name, location; programs and degree levels accredited; year first accredited; date accreditation ends. **Arrangement:** Geographical. **Frequency:** Annual, December. **Price:** Single copies free.

★2817★
THE A'S & B'S OF ACADEMIC SCHOLARSHIPS
Octameron Associates
Box 3437   Phone: (703) 836-1019
Alexandria, VA 22302
Covers: About 25,000 academic/honor/merit scholarships offered on a no-need basis by government agencies, private sponsors, and about 600 colleges and universities. **Entries include:** Name and address of sponsor, name and description of program, eligibility requirements, deadlines. **Arrangement:** By type of sponsor. **Pages** (approx.): 30. **Frequency:** Annual, August. **Editor:** Robert Leider. **Price:** $2.00, plus 41¢ shipping. **Other information:** Useful primarily to the student with a B average or higher and combined Scholastic Aptitude Tests (SATS) of 1,000 or more, who is in the upper 25% of his or her class.

★2818★
ASSOCIATION FOR CONTINUING HIGHER EDUCATION— DIRECTORY
Association for Continuing Higher Education
Extension Building
Division of Continuing Education
University of Tennessee
Knoxville, TN 37916
Number of listings: 400. **Entries include:** Institution name, address, and names, titles, and phone numbers of several persons concerned with continuing education. **Arrangement:** Alphabetical by institution name. **Indexes:** Personal name. **Pages** (approx.): 90. **Frequency:** Annual, November. **Editor:** William D. Barton, Executive Vice President. **Former title:** Association of University Evening Colleges - Membership Directory. **Price:** Free.

Association for Programmed Learning and Educational Technology—Yearbook *See* International Yearbook of Educational and Instructional...

Association of College and University Housing Officers— Directory *See* ACUHO News—Directory Issue [College housing]

★2819★
ASSOCIATION OF COLLEGE UNIONS-INTERNATIONAL— DIRECTORY
Association of College Unions-International
701 Welch Road   Phone: (415) 382-8017
Palo Alto, CA 94304
Covers: About 2,000 persons responsible for operating about 950 college unions and the social, cultural, and recreational programs they provide. **Entries include:** Personal name, home and office addresses and phone numbers, responsibilities or special interests in field. **Arrangement:** Geographical. **Indexes:** Alphabetical. **Pages** (approx.): 90. **Frequency:** Annual, August. **Editor:** Carol Vartanian. **Advertising accepted.** Circulation 2,000. **Price:** $15.00.

★2820★
ASSOCIATION OF INDEPENDENT COLLEGES AND SCHOOLS— DIRECTORY OF ACCREDITED INSTITUTIONS [Business schools]
Association of Independent Colleges and Schools
1730 M Street, N. W., Suite 405   Phone: (202) 659-2460
Washington, DC 20036
Covers: 500 schools accredited by the association which offer training, primarily in business subjects and data processing, beyond the high school level. **Entries include:** Institution name, address, phone, name of chief executive, programs offered, other accreditation. **Arrangement:** Geographical. **Pages** (approx.): 20. **Frequency:** Annual, January. **Editor:** Victor K. Biebighauser, Assistant Executive Director. **Former title:** Accrediting Commission for Business Schools - Directory. **Price:** Free.

Association of Teachers of English as a Second Language— Directory *See* National Association of Foreign Student Affairs—Directory

Association of University Evening Colleges—Membership Directory *See* Association for Continuing Higher Education— Directory

★2821★
AUDIOVISUAL MARKET PLACE
R. R. Bowker Company
1180 Avenue of the Americas   Phone: (212) 764-5100
New York, NY 10036
Covers: 5,000 firms and other producers of audiovisual learning materials, including software producers and distributors, production companies, production services, public radio and TV program libraries, and manufacturers and dealers handling equipment and supplies. Also includes awards and festivals, associations, etc. **Entries include:** Name of firm or organization, address, phone, name of one or more executives, list of products, services, or interests. **Arrangement:** Classified. **Indexes:** Alphabetical, product. **Pages** (approx.): 440. **Frequency:** Annual, March. **Price:** $23.50 (current edition); $25.00 (tentative, 1980 edition; ISSN 0067-0553). **Send orders to:** R. R. Bowker Co., Box 1807, Ann Arbor, MI 48106 (313-761-4700).

★2822★
THE A-V CONNECTION
National Audio-Visual Association
3150 Spring Street
Fairfax, VA 22031
Covers: Sources of federal funds which may be used for audiovisual programs. **Pages** (approx.): 225. **Frequency:** Irregular; latest edition 1979. **Price:** $20.00.

★2823★
BAIRD'S MANUAL OF AMERICAN COLLEGE FRATERNITIES
Baird's Manual Foundation, Inc.
744 Lake Crest Drive   Phone: (414) 722-0360
Menasha, WI 54952
Covers: 1,000 universities and colleges having Greek-letter societies, 5,000 chapters of men's national social fraternities, 2,600 chapters of women's national social fraternities, and more than 14,000 chapters of professional, honor, and recognition societies. **Entries include:** School listings include list of Greek-letter societies on campus and information on fraternity housing. Fraternity listings include headquarters address, history and purpose, chapters, etc. **Pages** (approx.): 900. **Frequency:** Irregular; latest edition December 1977; new edition possible 1984. **Editor:** John Robson. **Price:** $17.50, postpaid, payment with order. **Also includes:** Review of legislation affecting fraternities.

★2824★
BARRON'S COMPACT GUIDE TO COLLEGE TRANSFER
Barron's Educational Series, Inc.
113 Crossways Park Drive   Phone: (516) 921-8750
Woodbury, NY 11797
Covers: About 300 public and private four-year colleges. **Entries include:** School name, location, phone, admission requirements, transfer quota, application and financial aid deadlines, tuition and fees, college calendar, housing, special programs, accreditation, enrollment, degrees offered. **Arrangement:** Alphabetical. **Pages** (approx.): 320. **Frequency:** Not established; first edition September 1979. **Editor:** Nicholas C. Proia. **Price:** $2.50, plus 40¢ shipping. **Other information:** Not to be confused with, "Barron's Handbook of College Transfer Information," which covers about 1,400 schools.

★2825★
BARRON'S COMPACT GUIDE TO COLLEGES
Barron's Educational Series, Inc.
113 Crossways Park Drive   Phone: (516) 921-8750
Woodbury, NY 11797
Covers: About 300 colleges and universities. **Entries include:** School name, address, phone, degrees offered, tuition, admission requirements, application deadlines, school calendar, financial aid available, housing, enrollment, and other descriptive information in coded format. **Arrangement:** Alphabetical. **Pages** (approx.): 310. **Frequency:** Irregular; latest edition 1978. **Price:** $2.50, plus 40¢ shipping.

★2826★
BARRON'S GUIDE TO PRIVATE SCHOOLS—EASTERN EDITION
Barron's Educational Series, Inc.
113 Crossways Park Drive   Phone: (516) 921-8750
Woodbury, NY 11797
Covers: Preparatory schools, military academies, and other private secondary schools in the eastern United States. **Entries include:** Name and address of school, tuition, programs offered, etc. **Frequency:** First edition expected 1980. **Editor:** Doris Kuller. **Price:** $4.95.

★2827★
BARRON'S GUIDE TO THE TWO-YEAR COLLEGES
Barron's Educational Series, Inc.
113 Crossways Park Drive   Phone: (516) 921-8750
Woodbury, NY 11797
Covers: In Volume 1, 1,350 regionally accredited junior, community, and four-year colleges which offer associate degrees. Volume 2 covers all majors offered and includes list of church-affiliated, men's and women's colleges. **Entries include:** For Volume 1: Institution name, enrollment, affiliation, calendar, environment, programs, admissions, fees. For Volume 2: majors offered, whether program is terminal, or transfer. **Arrangement:** Volume 1 - Contents classified geographically within three sections: community and commuter schools, residential, four-year colleges. Volume 2 - Geographical. **Pages** (approx.): Volume 1, 300; Volume 2, 100. **Frequency:**

Approximately biennial, summer of odd years. **Editor:** Carole Berglie. **Price:** Volume 1 - $10.25, cloth; $5.50, paper. Volume 2 - $7.95, cloth; $3.25, paper.

★2828★
BARRON'S HANDBOOK OF AMERICAN COLLEGE FINANCIAL AID
Barron's Educational Series, Inc.
113 Crossways Park Drive   Phone: (516) 921-8750
Woodbury, NY 11797
Covers: 1,500 colleges in chart form. **Entries include:** Name of institution, where and how to apply, and deadlines, for 18 categories of financial aid. **Arrangement:** Geographical. **Frequency:** Irregular; previous edition 1974; latest edition 1978. **Price:** $7.95.

★2829★
BARRON'S HANDBOOK OF COLLEGE TRANSFER INFORMATION
Barron's Educational Series, Inc.
113 Crossways Park Drive   Phone: (516) 921-8750
Woodbury, NY 11797
Covers: 1,400 colleges and universities listed in horizontal chart form. **Entries include:** School name, address and control, transfer officer, admission requirements, examinations, transfer quota, annual tuition, college calendar, financial aid, housing, and special programs. **Indexes:** Institution. **Pages** (approx.): 300. **Frequency:** Irregular; latest edition 1975; new edition expected June 1980. **Editor:** Carole Berglie. **Price:** $4.95 (current and 1980 editions).

★2830★
**BARRON'S HANDBOOK OF JUNIOR AND COMMUNITY COLLEGE
FINANCIAL AID**
Barron's Educational Series, Inc.
113 Crossways Park Drive   Phone: (516) 921-8750
Woodbury, NY 11797
Covers: Over 1,000 junior and community colleges with financial aid programs. **Entries include:** College name, address, whether public or private institution, financial aid officer's name, available grants and loans, applications required and their filing dates, and to whom aid is available. **Arrangement:** Geographical in chart form. **Indexes:** Institution. **Pages** (approx.): 450. **Frequency:** Irregular; latest edition August 1979. **Price:** $7.95.

★2831★
BARRON'S PROFILES OF AMERICAN COLLEGES
Barron's Educational Series, Inc.
113 Crossways Park Drive   Phone: (516) 921-8750
Woodbury, NY 11797
Covers: 1,475 colleges and universities. **Entries include:** Name and address of institution, application deadline, tuition, programs offered, physical facilities, comments on student life, rating of faculty, student-faculty ratio, housing, athletic programs, student organizations, etc. **Arrangement:** Volume 1 is geographical; Volume 2, "Index to Major Areas of Study," is arranged by subject. **Indexes:** "College Admissions Selector" (arranges colleges in seven groups according to estimated competition for admission). **Pages** (approx.): Volume 1 - 1,000; Volume 2 - 300. **Frequency:** About every two years; latest edition is 1978; new edition expected 1980. **Price:** Volume 1 - $21.75, cloth; $8.95, paper. Volume 2 - $15.25, cloth; $5.95, paper. Also available in four regional volumes - "The Northeast," "The South," "The Midwest," and "The West," $4.95 each, and as "Barron's Compact Guide to Colleges" (see separate listing).

★2832★
BILINGUAL EDUCATION RESOURCE GUIDE
National Education Association
Academic Building
Saw Mill Road
West Haven, CT 06516
Covers: Bilingual programs and grants in colleges and universities; civil rights activities general assistance centers; and teacher education programs for bilingual-bicultural education. **Entries include:** Institution or center name, address, description of activity or program, name and

phone of contact. **Arrangement:** By activity. **Pages** (approx.): 125. **Frequency:** Irregular; latest edition 1977. **Editors:** Carmel Sandoval and Susan Gann, Compilers. **Price:** $5.75, postpaid, payment with order; add $1.66 shipping for billed orders.

Blue Book of School Business Administration *See* School Business Affairs—Association of School Business Officials Directory Issue

★2833★
BRICKER'S (INTERNATIONAL) DIRECTORY OF UNIVERSITY-SPONSORED EXECUTIVE DEVELOPMENT PROGRAMS
Bricker Publications
Box 188   Phone: (617) 432-4595
South Chatham, MA 02659
Covers: Over 200 residential management development programs at academic institutions in the United States and abroad. **Entries include:** Name of program; sponsoring institution; location, dates, and duration of program; tuition fees; curriculum content; modes of instruction; size of classes; information on participants; living accomodations; faculty; special features; official contact. **Arrangement:** Geographical within two sections, general management programs and functional management programs. **Pages** (approx.): 545. **Frequency:** Annual, December. **Editor:** George W. Bricker, Publisher. **Price:** $65.00 (ISSN 0361-1108).

Bunting & Lyon Blue Book [Private schools] *See* Private Independent Schools

Bunting & Lyon's Guide to Private Schools *See* Private Independent Schools

Catholic Schools in America *See* Ganley's Catholic Schools in America—Elementary/Secondary

★2834★
CAUSE DIRECTORY OF ADMINISTRATIVE DATA PROCESSING [Colleges]
CAUSE
737 29th Street   Phone: (303) 492-7353
Boulder, CO 80303
Covers: About 1,000 individuals engaged in the development, use, and management of information systems in higher education who are members of CAUSE (formerly College & University Systems Exchange). **Entries include:** Name, office address and phone, title. **Arrangement:** Alphabetical. **Indexes:** Institution. **Pages** (approx.): 65. **Frequency:** Biennial, spring of odd years. **Editor:** Charles R. Thomas, Executive Director. **Price:** Available to members only.

★2835★
CHRISTIAN LIFE MAGAZINE—SCHOOL DIRECTORY ISSUE
Christian Life Publications
396 E. St. Charles Road   Phone: (312) 653-4200
Wheaton, IL 60187
Covers: 200 Christian colleges, universities, and seminaries in the United States. **Entries include:** School name, address, enrollment, size of faculty, tuition, room and board, books, other fees, accreditation, degrees offered, financial aid, denominational affiliation (if any). **Arrangement:** Contents classified into two sections: Christian Schools, Colleges and Universities; Seminaries. **Frequency:** Annual, June. **Editor:** Robert Walker. **Advertising accepted.** Circulation 102,500. **Price:** $1.00 (current and 1980 editions).

Chronicle College Charts *See* Chronicle Four-Year College Databook; Chronicle Two-Year College Databook

★2836★
CHRONICLE COLLEGE COUNSELING FOR TRANSFERS
Chronicle Guidance Publications, Inc.
                                          Phone: (315) 497-0330
Moravia, NY 13118
Covers: More than 2,300 colleges and universities in the United States. **Entries include:** Name of institution, address, Zip code, data on admissions, counseling and placement, orientation, housing, financial aid. **Arrangement:** Geographical. **Pages** (approx.): 160. **Frequency:** Biennial, September of odd years. **Price:** $6.25.

★2837★
CHRONICLE FOUR-YEAR COLLEGE DATABOOK
Chronicle Guidance Publications, Inc.
                                          Phone: (315) 497-0330
Moravia, NY 13118
Covers: Lists over 300 baccalaureate, master's, doctoral, and first professional programs offered by more than 1,850 colleges and universities in the United States and 165 colleges and universities in Canada. **Arrangement:** Alphabetical by college major. **Indexes:** College names and addresses. **Pages** (approx.): 270. **Frequency:** Annual, September. **Former title:** Chronicle Guide to Four-Year College Majors. **Price:** $12.50. **Also includes:** Information formerly in "Chronicle College Charts."

★2838★
CHRONICLE GUIDE TO EXTERNAL & CONTINUING EDUCATION
Chronicle Guidance Publications, Inc.
                                          Phone: (315) 497-0330
Moravia, NY 13118
Covers: Tabulates information on credit and noncredit continuing education, correspondence study, and external degree programs at more than 1,000 colleges and universities in the United States. **Entries include:** Name of institution, address, Zip code, general information, admissions, credit, time limits, tuition, general areas of study, further information sections. **Arrangement:** Geographical. **Pages** (approx.): 180. **Frequency:** Annual, September. **Price:** $6.25.

Chronicle Guide to Four-Year College Majors *See* Chronicle Four-Year College Databook

★2839★
CHRONICLE GUIDE TO GRADUATE & PROFESSIONAL STUDY
Chronicle Guidance Publications, Inc.
                                          Phone: (315) 497-0330
Moravia, NY 13118
Covers: 900 graduate and professional schools in the United States. **Entries include:** School name, address, degrees offered, regional and professional accreditation, calendar, enrollment, graduate faculty with doctorates, library facilities, housing, admissions, fees and expenses, financial aid. **Arrangement:** Geographical. **Indexes:** Majors by degrees granted. **Pages** (approx.): 230. **Frequency:** Biennial, September of odd years. **Price:** $10.00.

Chronicle Guide to Two-Year College Majors and Careers *See* Chronicle Two-Year College Databook

★2840★
CHRONICLE STUDENT AID ANNUAL
Chronicle Guidance Publications, Inc.
                                          Phone: (315) 497-0330
Moravia, NY 13118
Covers: Provides information on financial aid programs offered primarily by noncollegiate organizations, independent and AFL-CIO affiliated labor unions, and federal and state governments for undergraduate and graduate students. **Entries include:** Eligibility requirements, amount, application, procedure, etc. **Arrangement:** Alphabetical by organization. **Pages** (approx.): 300. **Frequency:** Annual, September. **Former title:** Student Aid Annual. **Price:** $12.00.

★2841★
CHRONICLE SUMMARY REPORT [Colleges and universities]
Chronicle Guidance Publications, Inc.
Phone: (315) 497-0330
Moravia, NY 13118
Covers: Two-year and four-year colleges and universities which consider late applications (after April 15) for fall enrollment. **Frequency:** Annual. **Price:** $2.00.

★2842★
CHRONICLE TWO-YEAR COLLEGE DATABOOK
Chronicle Guidance Publications, Inc.
Phone: (315) 497-0330
Moravia, NY 13118
Covers: Lists over 80 associate, certificate, occupational, and transfer programs offered by more than 1,850 technical institutes, two-year colleges, and universities in the United States. **Arrangement:** Alphabetical by college major. **Indexes:** College names and addresses. **Pages** (approx.): 130. **Frequency:** Annual, September. **Former title:** Chronicle Guide to Two-Year College Majors and Careers. **Price:** $9.25. **Also includes:** Information formerly in "Chronicle College Charts."

★2843★
CIC'S SCHOOL DIRECTORY
Curriculum Information Center, Inc.
Ketchum Place
Phone: (203) 226-8941
Westport, CT 06880
Covers: Public, Catholic, and selected private schools (grades K-12) in the United States, and school district offices. Includes names of over 120,000 school district administrators, and staff members in county and state education administration. **Entries include:** Name of school or district office, address, phone number, grade span, and enrollment figures. District entries also list superintendents; school board chairmen; curriculum, personnel, and guidance directors; and other district-level administrators. **Arrangement:** Geographical. **Indexes:** District name, county/district names. **Frequency:** Annual, December. **Former title:** National School Directory; School Universe Data Book. **Price:** $600.00 for set of 51 volumes (every state and District of Columbia). State editions, $20.00 to $30.00 each.

★2844★
COLLEGE ADMISSIONS DATA SERVICE HANDBOOK
Orchard House, Inc.
Balls Hill Road
Phone: (617) 369-0467
Concord, MA 01742
Covers: About 950 four-year regionally accredited undergraduate institutions offering liberal arts degree; national edition and 5 regional editions (Northeast, Mid-Atlantic, South, Mid-West, and West). Criteria for selection of institutions are not stated. **Entries include:** Institution name, phone, location, names of president and admissions officer, accreditation, number of students, admission policies, SAT-ACT board score distribution, costs, financial aid available, advance placement policy, subject majors offered, degrees offered, extracurricular activities, regulations. **Arrangement:** Alphabetical. **Indexes:** Geographical. **Pages** (approx.): 2,000 (2 volumes). **Frequency:** Annual, August; updating information appears in quarterly newsletter included in price. **Price:** $80.00 (looseleaf, national edition); $70.00 (bound, national edition); $20.00 for regional editions except Mid-West, $24.00; postpaid.

★2845★
COLLEGE & UNIVERSITY ADMINISTRATORS DIRECTORY
Gale Research Company
Book Tower
Phone: (313) 961-2242
Detroit, MI 48226
Covers: More than 35,000 officers, deans, managers, and other administrative personnel at about 3,200 American colleges and universities. **Entries include:** Individual name, title, institution name, complete mailing address. **Arrangement:** Alphabetical. **Indexes:** Function/title. **Pages** (approx.): 940. **Frequency:** Annual; first edition

January 1980. **Price:** $42.00 (ISSN 0195-3990). **Other information:** Based on the HEGIS XIII Institution Profile data base maintained by the National Center for Educational Statistics.

College & University Systems Exchange—Directory *See* CAUSE Directory of Administrative Data Processing [Colleges]

★2846★
COLLEGE COURSES IN HIGH SCHOOL
National Association of Secondary School Principals
1904 Association Drive
Reston, VA 22091
Publication includes: In appendix, secondary schools cooperating with colleges to offer college level courses to students still in high school. **Entries include:** High school name, address, courses offered, name of cooperating college and address. **Arrangement:** Geographical. **Frequency:** Published 1978. **Editors:** Franklin P. Wilbur and David W. Chapman. **Price:** $3.00, payment with order.

★2847★
COLLEGE DEGREES FOR ADULTS: A COMPREHENSIVE GUIDE TO OVER 120 PROGRAMS
Beacon Press
25 Beacon Street
Phone: (617) 742-2110
Boston, MA 02108
Covers: 120 programs "featuring options for off-campus learning, credit for learning through life experience and self-directed learning." **Entries include:** Institution name, address; admission requirements, curricula, tuition, and financial assistance available. **Indexes:** Subject. **Pages** (approx.): 160. **Frequency:** Not established; first edition May 1979. **Editors:** Wayne Blaze and John Nero. **Price:** $12.95, cloth; $5.95, paper. **Send orders to:** Harper & Row, Keystone Industrial Park, Scranton, PA 18512.

★2848★
COLLEGE FACTS CHART
National Beta Club
151 W. Lee Street
Phone: (803) 583-4553
Spartanburg, SC 29304
Covers: 3,300 institutions of higher learning in the United States, Puerto Rico, Canal Zone, Guam, and Virgin Islands. **Entries include:** Name of institution; address, name of president; phone; date founded; affiliation or support; level of study; if male, female, or co-ed enrollment; session plan; degrees offered; enrollment; number of teachers; tuition and room and board costs. **Arrangement:** Geographical. **Pages** (approx.): 60. **Frequency:** Annual, fall. **Editor:** George W. Lockamy, Executive Secretary. **Price:** $2.00.

★2849★
COLLEGE GUIDE FOR STUDENTS WITH DISABILITIES
Abt Books
55 Wheeler Street
Phone: (617) 492-7100
Cambridge, MA 02138
Covers: More than 500 two- and four-year colleges which provided accessibility surveys and/or reported on services available for handicapped students. **Arrangement:** Geographical. **Indexes:** Alphabetical. **Pages** (approx.): 545. **Frequency:** Not established; first edition 1976; new edition expected 1980. **Editor:** Ray Glazier. **Price:** $18.50, postpaid, payment with order.

★2850★
COLLEGE HANDBOOK [YEAR]
The College Board
888 Seventh Avenue
Phone: (212) 582-6210
New York, NY 10019
Covers: About 2,900 undergraduate schools (all undergraduate institutions covered in "Education Directory: Colleges and Universities," but described here in considerably more detail). **Entries include:** School name, address, and information on degrees and courses offered, special programs, admissions policies, tuition, financial aid, etc. **Arrangement:** Geographical. **Indexes:** Institution

name. (An index of majors offered by these schools is available separately in "College Handbook Index of Majors," $6.95.) **Pages** (approx.): 1,700. **Frequency:** Annual, fall. **Editor:** Maureen Matheson. **Price:** $9.95. **Send orders to:** College Board Publication Orders, Box 2815, Princeton, NJ 08415.

College Handbook Index of Majors See **College Handbook [year]**

★2851★
COLLEGE PLACEMENT AND CREDIT BY EXAMINATION
College Board
888 Seventh Avenue   Phone: (212) 582-6210
New York, NY 10019
Covers: About 2,500 colleges and universities which offer credit or advanced placement through examination. **Entries include:** Institution name, address, description of policy. **Arrangement:** Geographical. **Pages** (approx.): 440. **Frequency:** Irregular; latest edition 1978; new edition expected 1980. **Price:** $6.95.

★2852★
COLLEGE PLANNING/SEARCH BOOK
American College Testing Program
Box 168
Iowa City, IA 52243
Covers: Over 3,000 two- and four-year colleges in the United States. **Entries include:** Institution name, location, costs, admissions policies and procedures, financial aid availability, student characteristics, special programs, majors available and percentage of students studying in each major, accreditation, availability of R.O.T.C. Similar data given for two-year colleges. **Arrangement:** Four-year colleges are by region, then state; two-year colleges are by state. **Indexes:** Alphabetical; schools accredited by the American Association of Bible Colleges, Association of Independent Colleges and Schools, and National Association of Trade and Technical Schools; major; career program. **Frequency:** Latest edition September 1979. **Price:** $6.00, postpaid.

★2853★
COLLEGE 'SCOPE [College survey]
Allied Associates FPC, Inc.
108 Massachusetts Avenue   Phone: (617) 262-1240
Boston, MA 02115
Covers: Four-year colleges and universities accredited by regional accrediting agencies. **Entries include:** In tabular form, institution name, address, undergraduate enrollment, entrance tests required, number and total dollar value of undergraduate scholarships available, tuition, board and room costs, major fields of study. **Arrangement:** Geographical. **Frequency:** Annual, September. **Editor:** George R. Sulkin. **Price:** $2.00, payment with order.

★2854★
COLLEGES AND UNIVERSITITES OFFERING ACCREDITED PROGRAMS BY ACCREDITATION FIELD
National Center for Education Statistics
Education Division
Health, Education, and Welfare Department
400 Maryland Avenue, S. W.   Phone: (202) 245-8824
Washington, DC 20202
Covers: About 1,700 colleges and universities that offer programs in specific fields which are subject to accreditation by professional organizations or other specialized bodies, including pharmacy, architecture, art, etc. Includes list of 20 accrediting associations. **Pages** (approx.): 125. **Frequency:** Biennial; latest edition 1978. **Price:** $3.50 (S/N 017-080-01913-2). **Send orders to:** Government Printing Office, Washington, DC 20402.

★2855★
COLORADO PRIVATE VOCATIONAL SCHOOL DIRECTORY
Colorado Board for Community Colleges and Occupational Education
1525 Sherman Street, Room 207   Phone: (303) 839-2553
Denver, CO 80203
Covers: 70 private vocational schools approved in Colorado. **Entries include:** Name of school, address, phone, programs approved, accreditation, number of hours of instruction. **Arrangement:** Alphabetical by school name. **Pages** (approx.): 20. **Frequency:** Annual, fall. **Former title:** Colorado Proprietary School Directory. **Price:** Free.

Colorado Proprietary School Directory See **Colorado Private Vocational School Directory**

★2856★
COMMUNITY, JUNIOR, AND TECHNICAL COLLEGE DIRECTORY
American Association of Community and Junior Colleges
One Dupont Circle, Suite 410   Phone: (202) 293-7050
Washington, DC 20036
Covers: 1,250 nonprofit two-year colleges, primarily in the United States but including entries from Canada, Puerto Rico, American Samoa, the Canal Zone, Germany, and British Honduras. **Entries include:** College name and location, name of chief administrative officer, association membership, phone, type of academic year, accreditation, enrollment, fees, number of faculty and administrators. **Arrangement:** Geographical. **Pages** (approx.): 120. **Frequency:** Annual, spring. **Editor:** Fontelle Gilbert. **Former title:** Junior College Directory; Community and Junior College Directory. **Price:** $10.00 (current and 1980 editions).

Compact Guide to College Transfer See **Barron's Compact Guide to College Transfer**

Compact Guide to Colleges See **Barron's Compact Guide to Colleges**

★2857★
COMPARATIVE GUIDE TO AMERICAN COLLEGES FOR STUDENTS, PARENTS, AND COUNSELORS
Harper & Row Publishers, Inc.
10 E. 53rd Street   Phone: (212) 593-7000
New York, NY 10022
Covers: Accredited four-year, undergraduate colleges and universities in the United States. **Entries include:** Institution name, address, admission policy, type of institution, enrollment, religious orientation (if any), campus facilities and activities, tuition and other costs; also included separately, percentage of graduates attending graduate and professional schools, with schools attended. **Arrangement:** Alphabetical. **Indexes:** Geographical, selectivity, religion, baccalaureate degree by field. **Pages** (approx.): 745. **Frequency:** Biennial, September or early October of odd years. **Editors:** James Cass and Max Birnbaum. **Price:** $24.95, cloth; $9.95, paper.

★2858★
COMPARATIVE GUIDE TO TWO-YEAR COLLEGES AND CAREER PROGRAMS
Harper & Row, Publishers, Inc.
10 E. 53rd Street   Phone: (212) 593-7000
New York, NY 10022
Covers: About 1,750 community colleges, technical schools, junior colleges, and four-year colleges and professional schools which offer degree programs below the baccalaureate level. **Entries include:** Institution name, address, admission requirements, nature of training offered, fees and tuition. **Arrangement:** Geographical. **Indexes:** Fields of study or occupations; separate index of programs offered which lead to occupations designated by Department of Labor as having above-average opportunities. **Pages** (approx.): 550. **Frequency:** Not established; first edition fall 1976. **Editors:** James Cass and Max Birnbaum. **Price:** $6.95.

★2859★
CONSORTIUM DIRECTORY
Council for Interinstitutional Leadership
Box 6293   Phone: (205) 348-7770
University, AL 35486
Covers: 130 educational consortia, administered by at least one full-time professional and having two or more members. **Entries include:** Organization name, address, phone number, chief executive, names of member institutions, and description of programs. **Arrangement:** Alphabetical. **Pages** (approx.): 125. **Frequency:** Irregular; new edition expected February 1980; annual updates. **Price:** $8.00, postpaid (current and 1980 editions).

★2860★
CONTINUING EDUCATION: A GUIDE TO CAREER DEVELOPMENT PROGRAMS
Neal-Schuman Publishers, Inc.
64 University Place   Phone: (212) 472-5170
New York, NY 10003
Covers: Work-related courses and training programs offered to adults by about 2,000 universities and colleges and about 500 associations and other groups. (Commercial offerings are excluded.) Includes lists of television stations active in educational programming and reprint of National Home Study Council's "Directory of Accredited Home Study Schools." **Entries include:** For institutions - Name, office responsible for continuing education (if any), address, phone, general description of continuing education program, kinds of credits offered, areas in which courses are given, and brief description of special programs. For organizations - Name, address, very brief description of activities, areas in which courses are given. **Arrangement:** Classified by type of sponsorship, then institutions are geographical, organizations are alphabetical. **Indexes:** Course subject, institution/organization. **Pages** (approx.): 700. **Frequency:** Not established; first edition May 1977. **Price:** $39.95. **Send orders to:** Gaylord Professional Publications, Box 61, Syracuse, NY 13201 (315-457-5070).

Cooperative Education Opportunities Offered by the Federal Government *See* Federal Government & Cooperative Education

★2861★
CORRESPONDENCE EDUCATIONAL DIRECTORY
Racz Publishing Company
Box 287   Phone: (805) 483-8843
Oxnard, CA 93032
Covers: 450 accredited and unaccredited American, Canadian, and British schools, colleges, and universities which offer some level of educational opportunity by correspondence. **Entries include:** Name of institution, address, list of degrees or programs offered. **Arrangement:** Classified. **Pages** (approx.): 175. **Frequency:** Biennial in even years. **Editor:** John Harding Jones. **Price:** $10.00, plus $1.02 shipping.

★2862★
COUNCIL FOR THE ADVANCEMENT AND SUPPORT OF EDUCATION—MEMBERSHIP DIRECTORY
Council for the Advancement and Support of Education
One Dupont Circle, N. W.
Washington, DC 20036
Covers: 9,000 alumni, fund-raising, public relations, government relations, and publications officers at colleges, universities, community colleges, and independent schools. **Entries include:** Institution name, address, names of representatives to the Council and their titles. **Arrangement:** Geographical. **Indexes:** Personal name, institution. **Pages** (approx.): 165. **Frequency:** Annual, January. **Editor:** Mrs. T. W. Segadelli, Membership Director. **Price:** $50.00 (current and 1980 editions).

★2863★
COUNCIL ON POSTSECONDARY ACCREDITATION: THE BALANCE WHEEL FOR ACCREDITATION [Accrediting bodies]
Council on Postsecondary Accreditation
One Dupont Circle, N. W., Suite 760   Phone: (202) 452-1433
Washington, DC 20036
Publication includes: List of accrediting groups recognized by the council which accredit institutions as a whole or specialized departments or schools (architecture, dentistry, librarianship, etc.). **Entries include:** Association name, year of last review, year of next review (if scheduled), scope or level of accreditation activities, name of contact, address, and phone. **Arrangement:** Associations which accredit institutions are listed alphabetically, others are by discipline. **Frequency:** Annual, July. **Price:** Single copies free.

Council on Postsecondary Accreditation—Membership List *See* Accredited Institutions of Postsecondary Education

★2864★
CSP DIRECTORY OF SUPPLIERS OF FOREIGN LANGUAGE MATERIALS
Cruzada Spanish Publications
Box 650909   Phone: (305) 595-5480
Miami, FL 33165
Covers: Over 500 publishers and companies which supply all types of educational materials for foreign language teachers at any level. Includes sources for such items as comic books and diplomas. **Entries include:** Company name, address, phone, description of products or services, general data. **Arrangement:** Classified by language. **Pages** (approx.): 50. **Frequency:** Latest edition September 1978; new edition expected September 1980. **Editor:** Andres Rivero. **Advertising accepted.** Circulation 5,000. **Former title:** CSP Directory of Suppliers of Spanish Language Materials (1977). **Price:** $5.00.

CSP Directory of Suppliers of Spanish Language Materials *See* CSP Directory of Suppliers of Foreign Language Materials

★2865★
DATABASES AND CLEARINGHOUSES: INFORMATION RESOURCES FOR EDUCATION
National Center for Research on Vocational Education
Ohio State University
1960 Kenny Road   Phone: (614) 486-3655
Columbus, OH 43210
Covers: About 55 data bases and 30 clearinghouses concerned with education. **Entries include:** For data bases - Name, source and address, description of contents, format, etc. For clearinghouses - Name and address, name of contact, description of activity, services, publications, etc. **Arrangement:** Alphabetical. **Indexes:** Subject-title. **Pages** (approx.): 160. **Frequency:** Irregular; latest edition 1979; new edition expected 1981. **Editors:** Thelma J. Feaster, et al. **Former title:** Information Resources for Education (1979). **Price:** $9.75, postpaid, payment with order.

★2866★
DEGREE PROGRAMS AT UNIVERSITIES AND FOUR-YEAR COLLEGES IN ILLINOIS
Illinois Board of Higher Education
Four W. Old Capitol Square   Phone: (217) 782-2551
Springfield, IL 62701
Entries include: Institution name, address, degrees offered, majors offered. **Arrangement:** By institution name. **Indexes:** Majors by field and by Higher Education General Information Survey code. **Pages** (approx.): 110. **Frequency:** Irregular; latest edition 1977; new edition expected 1980. **Editor:** James M. Furman. **Price:** Free.

★2867★
DIRECTORY: EDUCATIONAL AND CAREER INFORMATION
   SERVICES FOR ADULTS
National Center for Educational Brokering
1211 Connecticut Avenue, N. W., Suite 400 Phone: (202) 466-5530
Washington, DC 20036
Covers: About 300 sources of brokering services advising on
education and career planning for adults and providing intermediation
and advocacy. Sources include degree-granting institutions, computer-
based or telephone information services, women's services, libraries,
and interinstitutional programs. Entries include: Name of firm or
organization, address, phone, name of contact, services offered.
Arrangement: Geographical. Pages (approx.): 85. Frequency:
Annual, January. Editor: James M. Hefferman, Associate Director.
Price: $2.00, payment with order (current and 1980 editions). Send
orders to: National Center for Educational Brokering, 405 Oak Street,
Syracuse, NY 13203 (315-425-5275). Other information: Variant
title, "Directory of Educational Brokering Services."

★2868★
DIRECTORY: EDUCATIONAL DOCUMENTATION AND
   INFORMATION SERVICES
International Bureau of Education
United Nations Educational, Scientific, and Cultural Organization
7 Place de Fontenoy
75700 Paris, France
Covers: Educational documentation services in 76 countries, and
regional and international services. Arrangement: Geographical.
Frequency: Irregular; latest edition 1977 (out of print); new edition
expected 1980. Price: New edition price not established.

★2869★
DIRECTORY OF ACCREDITED COSMETOLOGY SCHOOLS
Cosmetology Accrediting Commission
1735 K Street, N. W.   Phone: (202) 331-9550
Washington, DC 20006
Covers: 1,150 accredited cosmetology schools in the United States
and Puerto Rico. Entries include: School name, address, phone,
commission's code number. Arrangement: Geographical. Pages
(approx.): 50. Frequency: Annual, August; supplement in February.
Editor: Phillip A. Taylor, Executive Director. Price: Free. Also
includes: List of state boards of cosmetology.

★2870★
DIRECTORY OF ACCREDITED HOME STUDY SCHOOLS
National Home Study Council
1601 18th Street, N. W.   Phone: (202) 234-5100
Washington, DC 20009
Covers: About 90 correspondence schools accredited by the council.
Entries include: Name of school, address, year founded, and courses
offered. Arrangement: Alphabetical. Indexes: Subject taught.
Frequency: Annual, spring. Editor: Sally R. Welch. Former title:
Directory of Accredited Private Home Study Schools (1975). Price:
Free.

Directory of Accredited Institutions [Business schools] See
   Association of Independent Colleges and Schools—
   Directory...Accredited...

★2871★
DIRECTORY OF ACCREDITED NONCOLLEGIATE CONTINUING
   EDUCATION PROGRAMS
Council for Noncollegiate Continuing Education
6 N. Sixth Street
Richmond, VA 23219
Covers: About 90 consulting and training firms, noncollegiate
educational institutions, and organizations which offer programs in
continuing education accredited by the council. Entries include:
Organization name, address, phone, date of reexamination.
Arrangement: Alphabetical. Pages (approx.): Leaflet. Frequency:
Annual. Editor: Nathan S. Shaw. Price: Free.

Directory of Accredited Private Trade and Technical Schools See
   Handbook of Trade and Technical Careers and Training

Directory of Administrative Date Processing See CAUSE
   Directory of Administrative Data Processing [Colleges]

★2872★
DIRECTORY OF CALIFORNIA COLLEGES AND UNIVERSITIES
California Postsecondary Education Commission
1020 12th Street   Phone: (916) 445-7933
Sacramento, CA 95814
Covers: About 450 degree-granting public and independent
universities, colleges, and vocational and specialized schools. Entries
include: School name, address, phone, name of president, and general
and specialized accreditations. Arrangement: Classified by auspices
and level of study. Frequency: Annual. Price: Free. Other
information: For information on degrees and programs of these
institutions, see separate listing for "Inventory of Academic and
Occupational Programs in California Colleges and Universities," by
same publisher.

★2873★
DIRECTORY OF CAREER PLANNING AND PLACEMENT OFFICES
College Placement Council
65 E. Elizabeth Avenue   Phone: (215) 868-1421
Bethlehem, PA 18001
Covers: About 2,000 college and university offices concerned with
securing employment for graduates. Entries include: College name
and address; names, titles, and phones of career planning and
placement personnel; interview dates for undergraduates and
graduates; months of graduations; whether alumni placement is also
handled. Arrangement: Geographical. Indexes: Institutional, personal
name. Pages (approx.): 260. Frequency: Annual, July. Editor: Patricia
Kostelnick. Price: $8.00, postpaid (ISSN 0070-5284).

★2874★
DIRECTORY OF CARIBBEAN UNIVERSITIES AND RESEARCH
   INSTITUTES
Association of Caribbean Universities and Research Institutes
UNICA
Box 11532
Caparra Heights Station
San Juan, Puerto Rico 00922
Covers: About 50 Caribbean universities and institutes actively
involved in the development of the greater Caribbean area. Entries
include: Institution name, address, facilities, programs offered, staff
and student data. Arrangement: Alphabetical. Pages (approx.): 125.
Frequency: Irregular. Editor: Thomas Mathews, Program
Coordinator. Price: Apply.

★2875★
DIRECTORY OF COOPERATIVE EDUCATION
Cooperative Education Association
Indiana State University
247 Alumni Center   Phone: (812) 232-6311
Terre Haute, IN 47809
Covers: 685 member colleges which offer co-op courses (alternate
and parallel work and study) in 165 major course areas. Entries
include: Institution, address, phone, name of co-op program director,
credit offered, length of program, etc. Arrangement: Four-year or
two-year, then alphabetical. Indexes: Baccalaureate program, non-
baccalaureate program, field of study, geographical. Pages (approx.):
470. Frequency: Irregular; latest edition 1978; new edition in
preparation. Editor: E. R. Pettebone, Executive Secretary. Price:
$10.00.

★2876★
DIRECTORY OF EDUCATION ASSOCIATIONS
Office of Education
Health, Education, and Welfare Department   Phone: (202) 245-3381
Washington, DC 20202
Covers: More than 900 international, national, regional, and state associations related to education, college professional and recognition societies in education, foundations primarily concerned with education, and religious education associations. **Entries include:** Organization name, address, phone, names of principal officer and secretary, publications. **Arrangement:** Classified by type of organization; state associations are geographical, others are alphabetical. **Indexes:** Keyword. **Pages** (approx.): 110. **Frequency:** Annual, fall. **Editor:** Lois V. Lopez. **Price:** $4.00 (S/N 017-080-02019-0). **Send orders to:** Government Printing Office, Washington, DC 20402. **Other information:** Formerly designated as Part 4 of "Education Directory."

Directory of Educational Brokering Services *See* Directory: Educational and Career Information Services for Adults

★2877★
DIRECTORY OF EDUCATIONAL FACILITIES FOR THE LEARNING DISABLED
Academic Therapy Publications
20 Commercial Boulevard   Phone: (415) 883-3314
Novato, CA 94947
Covers: About 300 facilities which help children whose learning problems stem from difficulty in understanding and using spoken or written language. **Entries include:** Facility name, address, phone, name of director, number of staff, and coded information describing type of facility (educational, summer camp, etc.), age ranges accepted, whether coed, day-length of program, fee information, and related professional services provided. **Arrangement:** Geographical. **Pages** (approx.): 50. **Frequency:** Biennial, fall of odd years. **Editor:** Belva Finlay. **Advertising accepted.** Circulation over 50,000. **Price:** 35¢ (ISSN 0092-3257).

★2878★
DIRECTORY OF ERIC MICROFICHE COLLECTIONS [Education]
ERIC Processing and Reference Facility
4833 Rugby Avenue, Suite 303   Phone: (301) 656-9723
Bethesda, MD 20014
Covers: About 720 collections of Educational Resources Information Center (ERIC) microfiche. Collections cover at least two years of ERIC output, although they may be limited in subject coverage. About 75 collections are in foreign countries. **Entries include:** Institution or organization name, address, phone, name of contact, coverage of collection, equipment available, services, hours; asterisk denotes collections with computer search services. **Arrangement:** Geographical. **Pages** (approx.): 60. **Frequency:** Biennial, September of even years. **Editor:** Dorothy A. Slawsky. **Price:** Free.

★2879★
DIRECTORY OF ERIC SEARCH SERVICES [Education]
Educational Resources Information Center (ERIC)
National Institute of Education
Health, Education, and Welfare Department
Washington, DC 20208
Covers: About 340 organizations which provide computerized ERIC data base searches; other data bases available to each organization are also mentioned; includes Canada. **Entries include:** Organization name, address, phone, name of contact, population served, data bases available, method and format of inquiries, format of output, cost per search, time required for search, search system used, date of listing preparation. **Arrangement:** Geographical. **Pages** (approx.): 65. **Frequency:** Biennial, November of even years. **Editor:** Elizabeth Pugh. **Price:** Free. **Send orders to:** ERIC Facility, 4833 Rugby Ave., Bethesda, MD 20014 (301-656-9723).

★2880★
DIRECTORY OF EXPERTISE: GIFTED AND TALENTED [Children, California]
Gifted and Talented Management Team
California State Department of Education
721 Capitol Mall
Sacramento, CA 95814
Covers: Teacher specialists, workshop leaders, and teacher trainers selected as outstanding by their peers. **Frequency:** Published 1978. **Price:** Free.

★2881★
DIRECTORY OF FACULTY CONTRACTS AND BARGAINING AGENTS IN INSTITUTIONS OF HIGHER EDUCATION
National Center for the Study of Collective Bargaining in Higher Education
Baruch College
17 Lexington Avenue
New York, NY 10010
Covers: 600 campuses. **Entries include:** Institution name, whether two- or four-year school, name of current bargaining agent, year elected or recognized, size of bargaining unit, year first contract signed, expiration date of current contract. **Arrangement:** Geographical. **Frequency:** Annual, January. **Editor:** Molly Garfin. **Price:** $5.00 (current and 1980 editions).

★2882★
DIRECTORY OF FINANCIAL AIDS FOR WOMEN
Reference Service Press
9023 Alcott Street, Suite 201   Phone: (213) 271-1955
Los Angeles, CA 90035
Covers: Over 600 scholarships, fellowships, loan sources, grants, internships, etc., and women's credit unions and governmental educational assistance programs; includes list of other financial aid directories; some programs listed are also available to minority men. Sponsors include institutions, associations, business, government, etc. **Entries include:** Program name, sponsor name and address, type of assistance (scholarship, loan, etc.), to whom available, financial details, duration, restrictions, application details and deadline, number awarded, etc. Credit union listings show name, address, phone. **Arrangement:** Alphabetical by award name; credit unions are geographical. **Indexes:** Organization name, geographical, subject. **Pages** (approx.): 200. **Frequency:** Not established; first edition 1978. **Editor:** Gail Schlachter. **Price:** $16.95, plus $1.00 shipping.

★2883★
DIRECTORY OF GIFTED PROGRAMS IN THE NORTHEAST EXCHANGE CONSORTIUM STATES
Educational Improvement Center-South
New Jersey Department of Education
Box 209, RD 4   Phone: (609) 228-6000
Sewell, NJ 08080
Covers: Programs for gifted and talented children located in Connecticut, New Hampshire, New Jersey, Rhode Island, and Vermont. **Entries include:** Program name, address, phone, contact person, and description of program activities. **Arrangement:** Geographical. **Indexes:** Area of giftedness, district type, grade level, program type, program content. **Pages** (approx.): 70. **Frequency:** Irregular; latest edition March 1979. **Editor:** Dr. James J. Alvino. **Price:** $2.50.

★2884★
DIRECTORY OF HISTORICALLY BLACK COLLEGES AND UNIVERSITIES IN THE UNITED STATES
National Alliance of Business
1015 15th Street, N. W., Suite 500   Phone: (202) 457-0040
Washington, DC 20006
Covers: About 90 schools. **Entries include:** Institution name, address, phone, key personnel, degrees offered, enrollment, description of setting, memberships. **Arrangement:** Alphabetical. **Indexes:** Geographical (two- and four-year colleges listed separately).

Pages (approx.): 110. **Frequency:** Annual. **Former title:** Directory of Predominantly Black Colleges. **Price:** Free; charge expected for 1980 edition.

★2885★
DIRECTORY OF INTERNSHIPS, WORK EXPERIENCE PROGRAMS, AND ON-THE-JOB TRAINING OPPORTUNITIES
Ready Reference Press
100 E. Thousand Oaks Boulevard, Suite 224
Thousand Oaks, CA 91360
Covers: About 800 internships or short-term employment opportunities available from businesses, organizations, and governmental units; about 500 additional opportunities listed in supplement. **Entries include:** Name of sponsoring organization; program title; nature of assigment, duration, and eligibility; number of awards and financial data; application deadline and address for applications. **Arrangement:** Alphabetical by sponsor name. **Indexes:** Subject, geographic, program name. **Pages** (approx.): 600; supplement, 360. **Frequency:** First edition, 1976; supplement, 1978. **Editors:** Alvin Renetzky and Gail Schlachter. **Price:** $45.00; supplement, $37.50.

Directory of Interversitas *See* Interversitas—Membership Directory

★2886★
DIRECTORY OF MANAGEMENT EDUCATION PROGRAMS
American Management Associations
135 W. 50th Street   Phone: (212) 586-8100
New York, NY 10020
Covers: Over 2,200 scheduled, recurring, non-credit management education programs offered by over 600 consultants, associations, and other developers, and by colleges and universities if credit is not offered. **Entries include:** Name of group offering program, address, phone, name of contact, description of program aims, techniques used, intended participants, dates, etc. **Arrangement:** Separate volumes for programs from "Academic Sources" and "General Sources," classified by general subject areas within each volume. **Indexes:** Developer (includes name, address, phone, and brief information), industry, course name. **Pages** (approx.): 1,550. **Frequency:** Biennial in even years; supplement in odd years. **Editor:** Fred E. Voss. **Price:** $175.00.

★2887★
DIRECTORY OF MEMBER INSTITUTIONS, INSTITUTIONAL REPRESENTATIVES AND ASSOCIATES [Graduate schools]
Council of Graduate Schools in the United States
One Dupont Circle, N. W., Suite 310   Phone: (202) 223-3791
Washington, DC 20036
Covers: About 365 graduate schools in the United States which are members. **Entries include:** Institution name, address; name, title, disciplinary area, and phone of institution representatives. **Arrangement:** Geographical. **Pages** (approx.): 45. **Frequency:** Annual, April. **Editor:** John W. Ryan, Assistant to the President. **Price:** Available to members only.

★2888★
DIRECTORY OF NORTH AND SOUTH AMERICAN UNIVERSITIES
K. G. Saur Publishing, Inc.
175 Fifth Avenue   Phone: (212) 477-2500
New York, NY 10010
Covers: About 1,800 colleges and universities in 29 countries which offer doctoral degrees. **Entries include:** Name of institution, address, telephone and telex numbers, year founded, enrollment; names of president, chancellor, and director of library; departments and names of their faculty members. **Arrangement:** Geographical. **Indexes:** Name. **Pages** (approx.): 1,100. **Frequency:** Not established; first edition under this title 1978. **Editor:** Michael Zils. **Advertising accepted.** **Price:** $43.00. **Other information:** Although not so identified in promotion, this material is taken from Volume 2 of Saur's "World Guide to Universities" (1975).

★2889★
DIRECTORY OF OCCUPATIONAL EDUCATION PROGRAMS IN NEW YORK STATE
Office of Occupational and Continuing Education
University of the State of New York
State Education Department
Albany, NY 12230
Covers: Public and proprietary educational institutions with occupational education programs in New York State, not including public secondary high schools or adult evening courses. **Entries include:** Name of school, address, list of programs. **Arrangement:** Geographical, then by type of school (secondary, private, business, etc.). **Price:** 130. **Frequency:** Triennial; latest edition December 1979. **Price:** Free.

★2890★
DIRECTORY OF ORGANIZATIONS AND PERSONNEL IN EDUCATIONAL MANAGEMENT
ERIC Clearinghouse on Educational Management
University of Oregon   Phone: (503) 686-5043
Eugene, OR 97403
Covers: 160 organizations and 520 researchers in the field of educational management. **Entries include:** Listings for organizations show name, address, phone, name of chief executive, area served, general mission and specializations, publication topics, periodicals, services. Listings for researchers show name and title, address, subject interests, research affiliations, publications available from researcher. **Arrangement:** Alphabetical within separate sections for organizations and researchers. **Indexes:** Subject, organization by location. **Pages** (approx.): 80. **Frequency:** Irregular; latest edition August 1979. **Editors:** Philip K. Piele, Director, and Stuart C. Smith, Assistant Director. **Former title:** Directory of Organizations and Personnel in Educational Administration. **Price:** $5.95, payment with order.

★2891★
DIRECTORY OF POSTSECONDARY SCHOOLS WITH OCCUPATIONAL PROGRAMS
Office of Education
Health, Education and Welfare Department
400 Maryland Avenue, S. W.   Phone: (202) 245-8511
Washington, DC 20202
Covers: About 9,650 postsecondary public and private schools offering vocational programs; all schools are approved by either the state accrediting agency, a regional or association accrediting agency recognized by the Office of Education, or meet Veteran's Administration eligibility requirements or those for financial aid programs of the Office of Education. **Entries include:** Institution name, address, phone, county or city location, highest degree offered, agencies by which accredited, type of control, type of program offered (business, cosmetology, etc.), enrollment, financial aid eligibility, specific programs offered. **Arrangement:** Geographical. **Indexes:** Institution name, program. **Pages** (approx.): 405. **Frequency:** Biennial, summer of odd years. **Former title:** Accredited Higher Institutions. **Price:** $5.50 (S/N 017-080-01705-9). **Send orders to:** Government Printing Office, Washington, DC 20402. **Other information:** "Programs and Schools," a supplement, provides school name, address, and phone by program offered.

Directory of Predominantly Black Colleges *See* Directory of Historically Black Colleges and Universities in the United States

★2892★
DIRECTORY OF PRIVATE, TRADE, TECHNICAL AND ART SCHOOLS [New Jersey]
Vocational Education Division
New Jersey Department of Education
225 W. State Street   Phone: (609) 292-5662
Trenton, NJ 08625
Covers: About 65 schools which meet New Jersey's minimum state

rules. **Entries include:** School name, address, phone, name of director, and subjects offered; coding indicates whether school is approved for Veterans Administration programs and if accredited by the National Association of Trade and Technical Schools. **Arrangement:** By type of school, then alphabetical. **Pages** (approx.): 10. **Frequency:** Irregular; about twice a year. **Price:** Free.

Directory of Program Sources [Videotapes] *See* Educational & Industrial Television—Directory of Program Sources Issue [Videotapes]

★2893★
DIRECTORY OF PUBLIC SERVICE INTERNSHIPS
National Society for Internships and Experiential Education
1735 I Street, N. W., Suite 601   Phone: (202) 331-1516
Washington, DC 20006
Covers: 100 programs (most with multiple openings) offering public service internships and fellowships throughout the United States primarily to graduate students, post-graduates, and mid- career professionals. **Entries include:** Name, address, phone, and name of contact; name of administering agency, year program began, number of interns accepted each year, source of funds, description of program, geographical placement of interns, supervision, selection procedures, admissions requirements, and remuneration. **Pages** (approx.): 160. **Frequency:** Annual. **Editor:** Jane C. Kendall. **Price:** $7.00 (current and 1980 editions).

★2894★
DIRECTORY OF SCHOLARSHIPS AND LOAN FUNDS [For Boy Scouts]
Education Relationships Service
Boy Scouts of America
Box 61030
Dallas/Fort Worth Airport, TX 75261
Covers: About 30 organizations, colleges, and preparatory schools which offer scholarships or loans to Boy Scouts in particular. **Entries include:** Organization or institution name, assistance type and amount available, requirements, application procedure and deadline, address. **Arrangement:** By type of organization. **Pages** (approx.): 10. **Frequency:** Latest edition 1978; new edition expected June 1980. **Price:** Single copies free.

★2895★
DIRECTORY OF SCHOOLS, COLLEGES AND UNIVERSITIES OF THE UNITED METHODIST CHURCH
Board of Higher Education and Ministry
United Methodist Church
1001 19th Avenue, South   Phone: (615) 327-2700
Nashville, TN 37202
Number of listings: 135. Consists of five sections: Schools of Theology; Colleges and Universities; Two-Year Colleges; Secondary Schools; and Others. **Entries include:** Institution name, address, name of president, whether historically a school for Blacks. **Arrangement:** Classified by type of school. **Pages** (approx.): 20. **Frequency:** Irregular, approximately every two years; latest edition June 1979. **Price:** Free (Stock No. 1073-HE/M).

Directory of the Education Division of the Department of Health, Education, and Welfare *See* Federal Education Grants Directory

★2896★
DIRECTORY OF TITLE VII ESEA BILINGUAL EDUCATION PROGRAMS
Dissemination and Assessment Center for Bilingual Education
7703 N. Lamar   Phone: (512) 926-8080
Austin, TX 78752
Covers: Over 700 programs funded by the Office of Bilingual Education, U. S. Health, Education, and Welfare Department. Separate list of state program coordinators. **Entries include:** Program title, contact name, address, phone, language, number of students, and year

of funding. **Arrangement:** Geographical, alphabetical within cities by program title. **Indexes:** Personal name, projects by languages. **Pages** (approx.): 170. **Frequency:** Annual, winter. **Editor:** Carlos E. Perez, Director. **Price:** $7.50 (current and 1980 editions).

Directory of Undergraduate Internship Programs in the Public Sector *See* Directory of Undergraduate Internships

★2897★
DIRECTORY OF UNDERGRADUATE INTERNSHIPS
National Society for Internships and Experiential Education
1735 I Street, N. W., Suite 601   Phone: (201) 331-1516
Washington, DC 20006
Covers: 90 programs (most with multiple openings) offering public service internships throughout the United States to undergraduate students. **Entries include:** Name, address, phone, and organization of contact person; description of program, recuitment, selection procedures, admission requirements, length of assignment, remuneration, etc. **Frequency:** Annual, fall. **Editor:** Grace Hooper. **Former title:** Directory of Undergraduate Internship Programs in the Public Sector. **Price:** $7.00.

Directory of U.S. College and University Degrees for Part-Time Students *See* On Campus/Off Campus Degree Progs. for Part- Time Students

★2898★
DIRECTORY OF VISITING FULBRIGHT LECTURERS AND RESEARCH SCHOLARS
Council for International Exchange of Scholars
11 Dupont Circle, N. W.   Phone: (202) 833-4995
Washington, DC 20036
Covers: About 600 persons from abroad visiting the United States for university teaching and postdoctoral research under the Mutual Educational Exchange Program (Fulbright-Hays Act). **Entries include:** Individual name, home institution, host institution in the United States, duration of stay, and project during stay. **Arrangement:** By discipline. **Indexes:** Home country, host state. **Pages** (approx.): 40. **Frequency:** Annual, October; January supplement. **Price:** Free.

★2899★
DIRECTORY OF WASHINGTON INTERNSHIPS
National Society for Internships and Experiential Education
1735 I Street, N. W., Suite 601   Phone: (202) 331-1516
Washington, DC 20006
Covers: 200 programs (many with multiple openings) offering public service internships in the Washington metropolitan area. Primarily for openings available to undergraduate and graduate college students, but includes internships available to high school students and young professionals. **Entries include:** Sponsoring organization name, address, phone, name of contact, number of interns per term or year, time period, description of program, skills needed, etc. **Frequency:** Annual. **Editor:** Debra L. Mann. **Price:** $7.00 (current and 1980 editions). **Other information:** Based on material in the Center's "Directory of Public Service Internships."

★2900★
DON'T MISS OUT
Octameron Associates
Box 3437
Alexandria, VA 22302   Phone: (703) 836-1019
Covers: Organizations, government agencies, and others offering financial aid and scholarships to college-bound and college students. **Entries include:** Name and description of program, eligibility requirements, and name and address of sponsor. **Arrangement:** By type of sponsor. **Pages** (approx.): 30. **Frequency:** Annual, August. **Price:** $2.00.

★2901★

EDUCATION AND EDUCATION-RELATED SERIALS: A DIRECTORY
Libraries Unlimited, Inc.
Box 263   Phone: (303) 770-1220
Littleton, CO 80160
Covers: About 500 periodicals and newsletters in United States and Canada interested in manuscripts from contributors. Also includes name/address list of indexing and abstracting services for journals included in this directory. **Entries include:** Publication title, publisher, address, circulation, frequency, contact person, editorial intent and preferences, and details covering manuscript submission. **Arrangement:** Alphabetical by title. **Indexes:** Subject. **Pages** (approx.): 250. **Frequency:** Published 1977. **Editors:** Wayne J. Krepel and Charles R. Duvall. **Price:** $15.00.

★2902★

EDUCATION DIRECTORY: COLLEGES AND UNIVERSITIES
National Center for Educational Statistics
Education Division
Health, Education, and Welfare Department
400 Maryland Avenue, S. W.   Phone: (202) 245-8392
Washington, DC 20202
Covers: About 3,100 candidate or accredited educational institutions in the United States which offer at least a two-year program of college-level studies. Also includes statewide agencies of postsecondary education and higher education associations. **Entries include:** Institution name, address, phone, congressional district, county, date established, names and titles of about a dozen principal officers and executives, and data on enrollment size, fees, programs, accreditation, highest degree offered, etc. Association and agency lists show name, address, phone, name and title of executive officer. **Arrangement:** Geographical. **Indexes:** Institution name. **Pages** (approx.): 550. **Frequency:** Annual. **Editors:** Arthur Podolsky and Carolyn R. Smith. **Price:** $6.00 (S/N 017-080-02011-4). **Send orders to:** Government Printing Office, Washington, DC 20402. **Other information:** Formerly subtitled, "Higher Education," and designated as Part 3 of "Education Directory."

Education Directory: Education Associations *See* Directory of Education Associations

Education Directory: Higher Education *See* Education Directory: Colleges and Universities

★2903★

EDUCATION DIRECTORY: PUBLIC SCHOOL SYSTEMS
National Center for Education Statistics
Education Division
Health, Education, and Welfare Department
400 Maryland Avenue, S. W.   Phone: (202) 245-8824
Washington, DC 20202
Covers: About 16,000 operating local public school systems. **Entries include:** Name of system or unit, location of superintendent, Zip code, county, grade span, number of pupils, and total schools in system. **Arrangement:** Geographical, then alphabetical by system name. **Pages** (approx.): 260. **Frequency:** Annual. **Editors:** Jeffrey W. Williams and Sallie L. Warf. **Price:** $3.75 (S/N 017-080-01900-1). **Send orders to:** Government Printing Office, Washington, DC 20402. **Other information:** Formerly designated as Part 2 of "Education Directory."

★2904★

EDUCATION DIRECTORY: STATE EDUCATION AGENCY OFFICIALS
National Center for Educational Statistics
Education Division
Health, Education, and Welfare Department
400 Maryland Avenue, S. W.   Phone: (202) 245-8824
Washington, DC 20202
Covers: Principal officers (about 1,500) of state and territorial education agencies responsible for state-level administration of elementary/secondary and vocational/technical education. **Entries**

include: Department or agency name, address, phone, names and phone numbers of superintendent and principal staff members. **Arrangement:** Geographical. **Indexes:** Personal name. **Pages** (approx.): 100. **Frequency:** Annual. **Editor:** Joanell Porter. **Price:** $2.75 (S/N 017-080-01869-1). **Send orders to:** Government Printing Office, Washington, DC 20402. **Other information:** Formerly subtitled, "State Governments," and designated as Part 1 of "Education Directory."

Education Directory: State Governments *See* Education Directory: State Education Agency Officials

★2905★

EDUCATIONAL FINANCIAL AIDS [Primarily for women]
American Association of University Women
2401 Virginia Avenue, N. W.   Phone: (202) 785-7772
Washington, DC 20037
Covers: 20 undergraduate and 65 higher education programs offering fellowships, scholarships, and internships primarily available to women. **Entries include:** Sponsor, address, details of deadlines and requirements. **Pages** (approx.): 35. **Frequency:** Irregular; latest edition 1978. **Price:** $1.00.

★2906★

EDUCATIONAL MEDIA YEARBOOK
R. R. Bowker Company
1180 Avenue of the Americas   Phone: (212) 764-5100
New York, NY 10036
Publication includes: Lists of employment services and opportunities, associations, institutions offering graduate degrees in media areas, foundation and federal funding sources, and producers, distributors, and publishers of audiovisual materials. **Entries include:** All listings usually include institution or organization name, address, phone, and name of contact; most listings also contain brief additional detail pertinent to subject of listing. **Pages** (approx.): 500. **Frequency:** Annual, spring. **Editor:** James W. Brown. **Price:** $25.00, postpaid. **Send orders to:** R. R. Bowker Company, Box 1807, Ann Arbor, MI 48106 (313-761-4700). **Other information:** Principal content is articles reviewing current state of the field.

★2907★

EDUCATIONAL PRESS ASSOCIATION OF AMERICA— MEMBERSHIP ROSTER
Educational Press Association of America
Glassboro State College   Phone: (609) 445-7349
Glassboro, NJ 08028
Covers: About 700 publications for teachers and educators in the United States and Canada. **Entries include:** Title of publication, name of publisher, address, name of editor. **Arrangement:** By subject. **Pages** (approx.): 30. **Frequency:** Annual, January. **Editor:** Jack R. Gillespie, Executive Director. **Price:** $15.00, payment with order.

★2908★

EDUCATIONAL PROGRAMS THAT WORK: A RESOURCE OF EDUCATIONAL INNOVATIONS DEVELOPED BY LOCAL SCHOOL DISTRICTS
National Diffusion Network
Office of Education
Health, Education, and Welfare Department
Room 3616, ROB 3
17th And D Streets, S. W.   Phone: (301) 245-2243
Washington, DC 20202
Covers: About 200 programs approved by the Joint Dissemination Review Panel which demonstrate alternative methods of education for kindergarten through adult education, frequently with community and parent participation. **Entries include:** Program name, minimum financial requirements, criteria for implementation, program description (including ERIC descriptors), target population, services available, source of funding, contact name, address, and phone. **Arrangement:** By education area. **Indexes:** ERIC descriptor, subject, program title, geographical. **Pages** (approx.): 250. **Frequency:**

Annual; latest edition December 1979. **Editor:** Diane McIntyre, Far West Laboratory. **Price:** $5.50, postpaid, payment with order. **Send orders to:** Far West Laboratory for Educational Research and Development, 1855 Folsom Street, San Francisco, CA 94103. **Also includes:** Education Division regional offices, and state coordinators for the Title I, Follow Through, Right to Read, Title IV, and Migrant Program educational programs.

★2909★
EDUCATORS GUIDE TO FREE GUIDANCE MATERIALS
Educators Progress Service, Inc.
214 Center Street   Phone: (414) 326-3126
Randolph, WI 53956
Covers: Sources for about 2,300 films, filmstrips, slide sets, audiotapes, videotapes, scripts, phonograph records and printed materials useful in guidance work provided by industrial, governmental, and other sponsors for free use by teachers and other educators. **Entries include:** Title, brief description, date produced, length or running time, whether sound or scripts are available for silent tapes and films, whether color or black and white, booking details, source. **Arrangement:** By type of medium, then by subject. **Indexes:** Source, title, subject, items cleared for television. **Pages** (approx.): 450. **Frequency:** Annual, fall. **Editors:** Mary H. Saterstrom and Gail F. Farwell. **Price:** $14.25, plus $1.35 shipping.

Educators' Guide to Media Lists *See* Selecting Instructional Media

★2910★
EDUCATORS' PURCHASING GUIDE
American School and University
North American Publishing Company
401 N. Broad Street
Philadelphia, PA 19108
Covers: Publishers, producers, and manufacturers of educational materials, audiovisual supplies, and equipment. **Entries include:** Company name, address, phone, name of contact. **Arrangement:** By product. **Frequency:** Irregular; latest edition 1978. **Price:** $29.50, payment with order.

★2911★
**ELEMENTARY TEACHERS GUIDE TO FREE CURRICULUM
    MATERIALS**
Educators Progress Service, Inc.
214 Center Street   Phone: (414) 326-3126
Randolph, WI 53956
Covers: Sources for about 1,800 items of printed teaching materials, such as booklets, pictures, posters, and maps. Materials are provided by industrial, governmental, and other sponsors for free use by teachers and other educators. **Entries include:** Title, brief description, ordering information. **Arrangement:** By curriculum area. **Indexes:** Subject, title. **Frequency:** Annual, fall. **Editors:** Patricia H. Suttles and Kathleen Suttles Nehmer. **Price:** $13.75, plus $1.35 shipping.

★2912★
ELHI FUNDING SOURCES NEWSLETTER
Oryx Press
3930 E. Camelback Road   Phone: (602) 956-6233
Phoenix, AZ 85018
Covers: Government and foundation grants offered for support of projects in elementary, secondary, and special education. Lists grant programs having application deadlines within the six months following each issue. **Entries include:** Grant or program name, description of scope and purposes, restrictions and special requirements, application deadline, sponsor name, address, phone, name of contact. **Arrangement:** Chronological by deadline date. **Frequency:** Monthly. **Editor:** William K. Wilson. **Price:** $75.00, plus $9.50 shipping (ISSN 0149-3450).

★2913★
EL-HI TEXTBOOKS IN PRINT
R. R. Bowker Company
1180 Avenue of the Americas   Phone: (212) 764-5100
New York, NY 10036
Publication includes: List of about 400 publishers of elementary and secondary level textbooks and related teaching materials. **Entries include:** Name, address. **Frequency:** Annual, spring. **Price:** $32.50 (current edition); $35.00 (tentative, 1980 edition); postpaid, payment with order (ISSN 0070-9565). **Send orders to:** R. R. Bowker Co., Box 1807, Ann Arbor, MI 48106 (313-761-4700). **Other information:** Principal content of publication is listings of textbooks for elementary and secondary schools by subject classifications. Author, title, and series indexes are included. Based on "Books in Print," described in separate listing.

Exploring Teachers' Centers *See* Teachers' Centers Exchange
    Directory

External Degrees: Program and Student Characteristics *See*
    Guide to External Degree Programs in the United States

★2914★
FEDERAL EDUCATION GRANTS DIRECTORY
Capitol Publications
2430 Pennsylvania Avenue, N. W.   Phone: (202) 452-1600
Washington, DC 20037
Covers: 260 programs selected from the Catalog of Federal Domestic Assistance. Directory listings give education- related federal officials' titles, names, phone and room numbers, and addresses. **Indexes:** Administrator name, beneficiary eligibility, authorizing legislation, program name, U. S. code. **Pages** (approx.): 200. **Frequency:** Annual, fall. **Editor:** James Fauntleroy, Executive Editor for Special Projects. **Former title:** Directory of the Education Division of the Department of Health, Education, and Welfare; Federal Education Program Guide. **Price:** $16.00, payment must accompany order.

Federal Education Program Guide *See* Federal Education Grants
    Directory

★2915★
**FEDERAL FUNDING GUIDE FOR ELEMENTARY AND SECONDARY
    EDUCATION**
Education Funding Research Council
752 National Press Building   Phone: (202) 737-4700
Washington, DC 20045
Covers: About 150 federally financed programs. **Entries include:** Program name, responsible agency, and name, address, and phone of program administrator; eligibility and review criteria; financial data; other details. **Arrangement:** By general subject or concern. **Indexes:** General. **Pages** (approx.): 400. **Frequency:** Annual, fall. **Price:** $27.95, postpaid, payment with order; $30.70, billed (1980 edition; ISSN 0095-3342).

★2916★
FEDERAL GOVERNMENT & COOPERATIVE EDUCATION
Octameron Associates
Box 3437   Phone: (703) 836-1019
Alexandria, VA 22302
Covers: Over 500 colleges and universities and 50 two-year colleges participating in cooperative ("work-study") education programs with federal government agencies. **Entries include:** Institution name, address, phone, contact person, occupational fields covered in program, cooperating federal agencies. **Arrangement:** Geographical. **Frequency:** Annual, August. **Editor:** Robert Leider. **Price:** $1.18, postpaid, payment with order; $1.25, plus 41¢ shipping, billed. **Other information:** Inaccurately cited in literature as, "Cooperative Education Opportunities Offered by the Federal Government."

★2917★

FINANCIAL AIDS FOR HIGHER EDUCATION

William C. Brown Company, Publishers

2460 Kerper Boulevard   Phone: (319) 588-1451

Dubuque, IA 52001

Covers: Over 4,400 scholarship programs, loans, contests, and other financial aid programs for students. **Frequency:** Biennial; new edition expected January 1980. **Editor:** Oreon Keeslar. **Price:** $18.95, postpaid, payment with order (1980 edition).

★2918★

FINANCIAL AIDS TO ILLINOIS STUDENTS

Illinois Office of Education

100 N. First Street   Phone: (217) 782-7913

Springfield, IL 62701

Covers: Associations, veterans' organizations, and others which offer scholarships, grants, and loans to students; schools offering Veterans Administration approved-programs; Illinois colleges and universities; professional associations (which can provide information), Illinois high schools. **Entries include:** Name, address; sources of funding listings include description of assistance available. College listings include phone, whether public or private, whether coed, enrollment, tuition and fees, room and board, dormitory capacity. **Arrangement:** By type of organization or institution. **Pages** (approx.): 260. **Frequency:** Biennial; latest edition summer 1979. **Editor:** Marla Warner, Compiler. **Price:** Free.

★2919★

FREE AND INEXPENSIVE LEARNING MATERIALS

George Peabody College for Teachers

Box 164   Phone: (615) 327-8091

Nashville, TN 37203

Covers: About 800 sources for more than 3,000 pamphlets, posters, paperback books, slides and films, and other materials for classroom and student use. **Entries include:** Name and address of source, description of types of materials available from the source, price range, grade level; entries include information on specific titles; most entries include annotations. **Arrangement:** Classified by general subject area. **Indexes:** None. **Pages** (approx.): 250. **Frequency:** Biennial, January of odd years. **Editor:** Norman Moore. **Price:** $4.50, plus $1.00 shipping. **Send orders to:** Incentive Publications, Inc., Box 120189, Nashville, TN 37212.

★2920★

FREE UNIVERSITY DIRECTORY

Free University Network

1221 Thurston

Manhattan, KS 66502

Covers: Over 180 free (i.e., non-traditional) universities, learning exchanges, experimental colleges, and various other education projects. **Entries include:** Name, address, phone, university affiliation (if any), date founded, budget, fees, enrollment, offerings. **Arrangement:** Geographical. **Frequency:** Annual. **Price:** $1.00.

★2921★

FULBRIGHT AWARDS ABROAD: UNIVERSITY TEACHING/ ADVANCED RESEARCH

Council for International Exchange of Scholars

11 Dupont Circle, Suite 300   Phone: (202) 833-4950

Washington, DC 20036

Covers: Grants under the Fulbright-Hays Act for university lecturing and advanced research abroad by American citizens made by the Board of Foreign Scholarships and the International Communication Agency. **Entries include:** Periods in which grants are tenable; number of grants available for the country, language or other requirement; fields in which lectures and teaching are desired. **Arrangement:** Geographical. **Indexes:** Subject. **Pages** (approx.): 50. **Frequency:** Annual, March. **Former title:** Lecturing Appointments and Advanced Research Grants under the Fulbright-Hays act. **Price:** Free.

★2922★

GANLEY'S CATHOLIC SCHOOLS IN AMERICA—ELEMENTARY/ SECONDARY

Curriculum Information Center

C/o Bill Fisher

1726 Champa Street

Denver, CO 80202

Entries include: Name, address, phone, administrative personnel. **Frequency:** Annual, spring. **Price:** $30.00.

★2923★

GETTING THROUGH COLLEGE WITH A DISABILITY

President's Committee on Employment of the Handicapped

1111 20th Street, N. W.   Phone: (202) 653-5044

Washington, DC 20210

Description: Subtitle: "A Summary of Services Available on 500 Campuses for Students with Handicapping Conditions." **Pages** (approx.): 65. **Frequency:** Irregular; latest edition 1977, currently out of print. **Editor:** Paul Hippolites. **Price:** Free. **Other information:** This publication is a summary of information in "College Guide for Students with Disabilities" (see separate listing).

★2924★

GIFTED AND TALENTED: DEVELOPING ELEMENTARY AND SECONDARY SCHOOL PROGRAMS

Council for Exceptional Children

1920 Association Drive   Phone: (703) 620-3660

Reston, VA 22091

Publication includes: Directories of federal, regional, and state agencies, and lists of bibliographical resources and guides. **Frequency:** Published 1975. **Editor:** Bruce O. Boston. **Price:** $3.95. **Other information:** Variant title, "Resource Manual of Information on Educating the Gifted and Talented."

★2925★

GRADUATE PROGRAMS AND ADMISSIONS MANUAL

Graduate Record Examinations Board

Educational Testing Service   Phone: (609) 921-9000

Princeton, NJ 08541

Covers: 695 institutions which offer advanced degrees in education, arts, and sciences (out of about 900 such accredited institutions). Degrees not included are M.B.A., J.D., D.D.S., M.D., M.Div., and similar professional degrees. In four volumes: 1, Agriculture, Biological Sciences, Health Sciences, and Home Economics; 2, Arts and Humanities; 3, Physical Sciences, Mathematics, and Engineering; 4, Social Sciences and Education. **Entries include:** Over four separate sections, the following information is given for each school: Name, address, specific addresses for information on the school in general, applications, loans, housing, and assistantships; institution statistics, fees, calendar, etc.; statistics, requirements, etc., for individual programs. **Arrangement:** Geographical. **Frequency:** Biennial, September of odd years. **Price:** $16.00 per set; $4.00 per volume; postpaid, payment with order.

★2926★

GRADUATE PROGRAMS AND FACULTY IN READING

International Reading Association

800 Barksdale Road   Phone: (302) 731-1600

Newark, DE 19711

Covers: 300 graduate-level teacher education programs in reading and related fields in the United States and Canada. **Entries include:** Program director, degrees available, number of students in program, career interests of students, faculty members, faculty in related fields, special resources, courses offered. **Arrangement:** Geographical. **Indexes:** Personal name. **Pages** (approx.): 360. **Frequency:** Irregular; latest edition 1979. **Editor:** John T. Gutherie, Director of Research. **Price:** $9.00.

★2927★

GRADUATE PROGRAMS OF COOPERATIVE EDUCATION IN THE U.S. AND CANADA

National Commission for Cooperative Education
360 Huntington Avenue   Phone: (617) 437-3778
Boston, MA 02115
Covers: About 95 institutions offering co-op programs (alternate work and study) applicable to graduate students. **Entries include:** Name and type of institution, city, number of co-op students, curricula available under co-op program (engineering, natural sciences). **Arrangement:** Alphabetical. **Pages** (approx.): 20. **Frequency:** Annual. **Price:** Free.

★2928★

GRADUATE SCHOOL GUIDE

Catholic News Publishing Company
80 W. Broad Street   Phone: (914) 664-8100
Mt. Vernon, NY 10552
Covers: Colleges and universities offering programs leading to the master's or doctor's degree; separate volumes for New York State, New Jersey-Pennsylvania, New England, and Midwest. **Entries include:** School name, address, details of programs. **Pages** (approx.): 40. **Frequency:** Annual, September. **Editor:** Victor L. Ridder, Jr. **Advertising accepted. Price:** $5.00.

★2929★

GRANTS FOR GRADUATE STUDY ABROAD

Institute of International Education
809 United Nations Plaza   Phone: (212) 883-8265
New York, NY 10017
Covers: Mutual educational exchange (Fulbright-Hays) grants and grants offered by foreign governments, universities, and private donors in 50 countries whose programs are administered by the Institute. **Entries include:** Eligibility requirements, application and selection procedures, language requirements, fields of study, degree level. **Arrangement:** Geographical. **Pages** (approx.): 50. **Frequency:** Annual, May; includes information on grants for following academic year. **Price:** Free.

Guide to Educational Programs in Noncollegiate Organizations *See* National Guide to Credit Recommendations for Non-Collegiate Courses

★2930★

GUIDE TO FEDERAL ASSISTANCE [Education]

Wellborn Associates, Inc.
5791 Beaumont Avenue   Phone: (714) 454-1412
La Jolla, CA 92037
Covers: Over 500 federal assistance programs of interest to educators and to individuals. **Entries include:** For programs - Name, description, legislation originating program, deadline, eligibility requirements, Catalog of Federal Domestic Assistance program number, related federal programs, and names and addresses of state and regional program offices, when these are involved in application procedure. **Arrangement:** By program. **Indexes:** Deadline, topic, public law, agency federal contact (with phone). **Pages** (approx.): 1,200. **Frequency:** Monthly updates to base looseleaf volume. **Editor:** Jennifer M. Wellborn. **Former title:** Guide to Federal Assistance for Education. **Price:** $300.00.

Guide to Federal Assistance for Education *See* Guide to Federal Assistance [Education]

★2931★

GUIDE TO INDEPENDENT STUDY THROUGH CORRESPONDENCE INSTRUCTION

National University Extension Association
One Dupont Circle, Suite 360   Phone: (202) 659-3130
Washington, DC 20036
Covers: Schools which offer college and university credit, graduate credit, high school, junior high, and elementary school credit, and non-credit certificate program courses through correspondence. **Entries**

include: School name, address, programs offered. **Arrangement:** Geographical. **Indexes:** Program/level of credit offered. **Pages** (approx.): 35. **Frequency:** Biennial, odd years. **Price:** $2.00, plus $1.25 shipping.

Guide to Private Schools—Eastern Edition *See* Barron's Guide to Private Schools—Eastern Edition

★2932★

GUIDE TO PROFESSIONAL DEVELOPMENT OPPORTUNITIES FOR COLLEGE AND UNIVERSITY ADMINISTRATORS

Center for Leadership Development and Academic Administration
American Council on Education
One Dupont Circle   Phone: (202) 833-4700
Washington, DC 20036
Covers: 400 seminars, workshops, and conferences, and internships offering formal training in educational management and staff leadership development. **Entries include:** Name of activity, sponsor, date, location, eligibility, fees, room and board, application information, name and address of contact person, description of program. **Arrangement:** By subject. **Indexes:** Sponsoring organizations and associations. **Pages** (approx.): 130. **Frequency:** Irregular; latest edition September 1979. **Editors:** Charles F. Fisher and Isabel Coll-Pardo. **Advertising accepted.** Circulation 3,000. **Price:** $10.95, plus $1.00 shipping.

★2933★

GUIDE TO PUBLISHING IN EDUCATION

Foothills Educational Press
Faculty of Education
University of Calgary   Phone: (403) 284-5635
Calgary T2P 1N4 Alberta, Canada
Covers: 165 journals concerned with education, educational psychology, educational administration, and related disciplines; primarily United States and Canadian publications, with some British and Australian. **Entries include:** Journal name, address, frequency, subjects dealt with, and description of publication's needs and policies. **Frequency:** Irregular; latest edition 1977. **Editor:** Jack Cameron. **Price:** $7.00.

Guide to the Two-Year Colleges *See* Barron's Guide to the Two-Year Colleges

★2934★

GUIDE TO UNDERGRADUATE EXTERNAL DEGREE PROGRAMS IN THE UNITED STATES

Office on Education Credit
American Council on Education
One Dupont Circle
Washington, DC 20036
Covers: About 135 colleges and universities offering about 245 associate and undergraduate degree programs on a minimal residential and classroom basis. **Entries include:** Institution name, address, name of external degree program, subjects offered, authorization, education requirements, maximum credit given for prior learning, maximum credit given for prior experiential learning, minimum campus time required, grading system, job placement assistance offered to graduates, number of students enrolled in the external degree program, cumulative number of graduates, year program established. **Arrangement:** Geographical. **Indexes:** Institution name. **Pages** (approx.): 70. **Frequency:** Latest edition March 1978. **Editors:** Carol P. Sosdian, Laura M. Sharp. **Former title:** External Degrees: Program and Student Characteristics. **Price:** Free. **Send orders to:** National Institute of Education, Health, Education, and Welfare Department, Washington, DC 20208.

★2935★
GUIDES TO EDUCATIONAL MEDIA
American Library Association
50 E. Huron Street   Phone: (312) 944-6780
Chicago, IL 60611
Publication includes: Names and addresses of publishers of about 300 catalogs, indexes, and reviewing services which provide information about audiovisual instructional materials. Listings of individual publications mention title, publisher or sponsor, address, price, scope and content. Arrangement: Alphabetical. Indexes: General. Pages (approx.): 160. Frequency: Irregular; previous editions 1961, 1967, 1971; latest edition 1977. Editor: Margaret I. Rufsvold. Price: $5.00.

★2936★
HANDBOOK FOR THE LIFELONG LEARNER
Simon & Schuster
1230 Avenue of the Americas
New York, NY 10020
Publication includes: Lists of about 145 free universities, plus major sources for instructional audiotape cassettes, educational brokering services, and other organizations, and sources of information concerning nontraditional education for adults. Entries include: Most listings include name, address; university listings also include phone. Arrangement: By topic; universities are geographical. Indexes: General. Pages (approx.): 190. Frequency: Published 1977. Editor: Ronald Gross. Price: $9.95, cloth; $3.95, paper. Other information: Principal content of publication is textual discussion of alternative methods of learning, such as television college, learning exchanges, library services, etc.

Handbook of American College Financial Aid *See* Barron's Handbook of American College Financial Aid

Handbook of College Transfer Information *See* Barron's Handbook of College Transfer Information

Handbook of Junior and Community College Financial Aid *See* Barron's Handbook of Junior and Community College Financial Aid

★2937★
HANDBOOK OF PRIVATE SCHOOLS
Porter Sargent Publishers, Inc.
11 Beacon Street   Phone: (617) 523-1670
Boston, MA 02108
Covers: 1,900 elementary and secondary boarding and day schools. Entries include: School name, address, enrollment, facilities, names of administrators, fees. Arrangement: Geographical. Pages (approx.): 1,500. Frequency: Annual, summer. Advertising accepted. Price: $25.00, plus $1.50 shipping.

★2938★
HANDBOOK OF TRADE AND TECHNICAL CAREERS AND TRAINING
National Association of Trade and Technical Schools
2021 K Street, N. W.   Phone: (202) 296-8892
Washington, DC 20006
Covers: 530 trade schools accredited by the association offering 94 vocational programs ranging from acting and medical technology to truck driving and dog grooming. Entries include: School name, address, programs offered. Arrangement: Geographical. Indexes: Name of school, type of training. Pages (approx.): 50. Frequency: Annual, October. Former title: Directory of Accredited Private Trade and Technical Schools. Price: Free. Other information: Includes section giving brief description of various vocations and list of schools offering training in them.

★2939★
HANDBOOK ON INTERNATIONAL STUDY FOR U.S. NATIONALS
Institute of International Education
809 United Nations Plaza   Phone: (212) 883-8626
New York, NY 10017
Covers: Educational institutions abroad described from the point of view of United States students interested in attending them. Includes sections on exchange programs, awards, United States and foreign government regulations; and volunteer and trainee opportunities. Entries include: Principal sections are by country, and include information on admission requirements for United States students in the country's schools, cost, housing, language of instruction, degrees offered, academic year, programs of special interest to United States students. Listings for institutions include name, address, whether public or private, enrollment, degrees offered, etc. Arrangement: Geographical, in 3 volumes; Volume 1, "Study in Europe," Volume 2, "Study in the American Republics Area," Volume 3, "Study in the Mid-East." Indexes: Fields of study, institutions, organizations. Pages (approx.): 300 per volume. Frequency: Irregular; previous edition 1970; latest edition 1976. Price: $12.00 per volume, cloth; $6.65 per volume, paper; payment with order.

★2940★
HAWES COMPREHENSIVE GUIDE TO COLLEGES
New American Library, Inc.
1301 Avenue of the Americas   Phone: (212) 956-3800
New York, NY 10019
Covers: Over 1,500 four-year colleges and all regionally accredited 2-year colleges; colleges are rated by the editor for social achievement of graduates (based on analysis of graduates in "Who's Who in America"), and social status of schools (based on analysis of "The Social Register"). Entries include: College name, address, number of students, income range of students' families, majors offered, percentage of students continuing in graduate school, costs, description of facilities, admissions requirements, and student life. Arrangement: Geographical. Pages (approx.): 410. Frequency: Not established; first edition fall 1978. Editor: Gene R. Hawes. Price: $7.95, plus 75¢ shipping.

★2941★
HIGHER EDUCATION EXCHANGE
Peterson's Guides, Inc.
228 Alexander Street   Phone: (609) 924-5338
Princeton, NJ 08540
Covers: About 3,200 colleges, universities, and graduate and professional schools in the United States and Canada; government agencies, professional associations, foundations, and other organizations concerned with higher education; and about 4,000 companies supplying products and services to higher education. Entries include: For institutions and associations - Name, address, names of key purchasing executives, and list of institutionally owned or operated facilities. For businesses - Company name, address, name of contact. Arrangement: Institutions and organizations are geographical; companies are classified by product or service. Pages (approx.): 770. Frequency: Not established; first edition October 1978. Editor: Janet A. Mitchell. Price: $60.00, plus $1.25 shipping. Other information: Published jointly with J. B. Lippincott Company. Also includes: Gives, in tabular and graph format, statistics on enrollments, federal funds distribution, instructional media, etc.; 500 periodicals, and other materials concerned with higher education.

★2942★
HOW AND WHERE TO OBTAIN A COLLEGE DEGREE BY MAIL Even If You Are a Grade School Dropout
Education and Career Counseling
15512 Williams Street
Tustin, CA 92680
Covers: "Instant" colleges whose brochures indicate that "degrees" are granted without study or examination. Price: $12.50. (Not verified)

★2943★

HOW TO OBTAIN MONEY FOR COLLEGE: A COMPLETE GUIDE TO SOURCES OF FINANCIAL AID FOR EDUCATION

Arco Publishing, Inc.
219 Park Avenue South   Phone: (212) 777-6300
New York, NY 10003
Covers: Several hundred financial aid programs administered by state and federal governments, academic institutions, and veterans' organizations. **Entries include:** Organization name, location or address, name of program. Some listings include type of assistance, requirements, amounts available, or other details. **Arrangement:** By type of organization, or by offerings to special students. **Pages** (approx.): 200. **Frequency:** Irregular; latest edition 1976; new edition date not set. **Price:** $5.00, plus $1.00 shipping.

★2944★

INDEPENDENT SCHOOLS ASSOCIATION OF THE SOUTHWEST— MEMBERSHIP LIST

Independent Schools Association of the Southwest
Box 52297   Phone: (918) 749-5927
Tulsa, OK 74152
Covers: Independent elementary and secondary schools accredited by the association. **Entries include:** School name, address, phone, chief administrative officer, structure, and enrollment. **Arrangement:** Geographical. **Indexes:** Alphabetical. **Pages** (approx.): 5. **Frequency:** Annual, August. **Editor:** Richard W. Ekdahl, Executive Director. **Price:** Free.

★2945★

INDUSTRIAL TEACHER EDUCATION DIRECTORY—INSTITUTIONS AND PERSONNEL

National Association of Industrial and Technical Teacher Educators
C/o F. Milton Miller
103 Industrial Educational Building
University of Missouri   Phone: (314) 882-3082
Columbia, MO 65211
Covers: About 3,500 industrial education faculty members at universities and four-year colleges in the United States and Canada. **Entries include:** For institutions - Name, address, phone number for industrial education department, degrees granted in previous year, graduate assistantships available. For faculty members - Name, academic rank, highest degree held, and areas of specialization. **Arrangement:** Geographical. **Indexes:** Personal name. **Frequency:** Annual, December. **Editor:** Ervin A. Dennis. **Price:** $10.00 to commercial users. **Other information:** Published with American Council on Industrial Arts Teacher Education.

★2946★

INFACT COLLEGE CATALOG INFORMATION SYSTEM

Dataflow Systems, Inc.
7758 Wisconsin Avenue   Phone: (201) 654-9133
Bethesda, MD 20014
Background: Not a directory, but a compilation of microfilm reproductions of the complete undergraduate course catalogs of several hundred colleges and universities. **Indexes:** Index pages of each catalog are reproduced, but separate index is not provided as with INFACT medical school package. **Frequency:** Annual, winter; quarterly updates on microfilm. **Editor:** Betty Doundikoff. **Price:** $495.00 yearly; $750.00 biennially; $395.00 for renewals.

Information Resources for Education *See* Databases and Clearinghouses: Information Resources for Education

★2947★

INNOVATIVE GRADUATE PROGRAMS DIRECTORY

Center for Distance Learning
Two Union Avenue
Empire State College   Phone: (518) 587-2100
Saratoga Springs, NY 12866
Covers: 220 nontraditional graduate and post-graduate credit programs offered through 105 accredited colleges and universities, most of which are accredited. **Entries include:** Institution name, address, description of program, degree offered, name of contact, accreditation information. **Arrangement:** Alphabetical by institution name. **Indexes:** Subjects offered. **Pages** (approx.): 170. **Frequency:** Annual, November. **Editor:** Frank J. Rader. **Price:** $4.00 **Send orders to:** Educational Materials, Empire State College, Box 88, Saratoga Springs, NY 12866.

★2948★

INSIDERS' GUIDE TO PREP SCHOOLS

E. P. Dutton & Company
201 Park Avenue South   Phone: (212) 674-5900
New York, NY 10003
Covers: 60 preparatory schools, primarily in Connecticut and Massachusetts. Evaluative information is given by former students. **Entries include:** School name, address; evaluation of school including student attitude, living arrangements, sports programs, discipline procedures, curriculum; statistical information includes enrollment, costs, etc. **Arrangement:** Alphabetical. **Pages** (approx.): 240. **Frequency:** Not established; first edition May 1979. **Editors:** Joan Barrett and Sally F. Goldfarb. **Price:** $5.95.

★2949★

INSIDER'S GUIDE TO THE COLLEGES

Putnam Publishing Group
200 Madison Avenue   Phone: (212) 576-8900
New York, NY 10016
Covers: 230 colleges and universities in the United States. **Entries include:** Institution name, location; type of site, enrollment, annual expense, percentage of entering class receiving financial aid, library holdings, student-faculty ratio, number of transfer students admitted annually, percentage of students in fraternal societies, application deadline; description of campus and community, best departments and programs, entertainment, cultural, and recreational opportunities, housing, drug availability, and characteristics of the student body. **Arrangement:** Geographical. **Indexes:** Alphabetical. **Pages** (approx.): 405. **Frequency:** Latest edition 1978; new edition expected 1981. **Price:** $4.95.

★2950★

INSTITUTIONAL DIRECTORY OF HIGHER EDUCATION IN TENNESSEE

Tennessee Higher Education Commission
501 Union Building, Suite 300   Phone: (615) 741-3605
Nashville, TN 37219
Covers: About 90 associations, state agencies, and institutions of higher education (post-high school) located in Tennessee. **Entries include:** For associations and state agencies - Organization name, address, phone, description of organization's purpose and activities, list of officers and their office addresses. For institutions - School name, address, phone, names of executive staff and their titles. **Arrangement:** By type of organization. **Pages** (approx.): 35. **Frequency:** Annual, January. **Editor:** Joel D. Fryer, Public Information Assistant. **Price:** Free.

★2951★

INTERCHANGE [Learning networks]

The Learning Exchange
Box 920   Phone: (312) 864-4133
Evanston, IL 60204
Covers: About 20 "learning networks," services which bring together students who wish to study a subject and teachers who wish to teach it, generally subjects of a nonacademic and/or interdisciplinary nature; the "network" may be coordinated by an academic institution, no academic credit is involved, and teachers may have no formal credentials. **Entries include:** Name of network, address, phone, contact person. **Arrangement:** Geographical. **Frequency:** Bimonthly. **Price:** $12.00 per year.

★2952★

INTERNATIONAL ASSOCIATION OF COLLEGE AND UNIVERSITY SECURITY DIRECTORS—MEMBERSHIP DIRECTORY

International Association of College and University Security Directors
Box 98127
Atlanta, GA 30359
Covers: 725 colleges and universities and institutional representatives. **Entries include:** Name, office address, position, number of institutional representatives. **Arrangement:** Institutions listed alphabetically and geographically; representatives listed alphabetically. **Pages** (approx.): 60. **Frequency:** Annual, September. **Editor:** James L. McGovern, Executive Secretary. **Price:** Available to members only.

★2953★

INTERNATIONAL READING ASSOCIATION—DIRECTORY

International Reading Association
800 Barksdale Road   Phone: (302) 731-1600
Newark, DE 19711
Covers: About 150 affiliated organizations and committees concerned with issues and problems in reading education. **Entries include:** Name of local council, list of officers, address of the president, name and purpose of committees, names and addresses of committee chairperson, committee members. **Arrangement:** Geographical. **Indexes:** Personal name, alphabetical. **Frequency:** Annual, fall. **Price:** $1.50.

★2954★

INTERNATIONAL YEARBOOK OF EDUCATIONAL AND INSTRUCTIONAL TECHNOLOGY

Nichols Publishing Company
Box 96   Phone: (212) 580-8079
New York, NY 10024
Publication includes: Lists of institutes, universities, professional associations, and government agencies concerned with educational technology, and producers, distributors, and publishers of audiovisual materials and equipment. **Entries include:** All listings include institution or organization name, address; most listings also include products, services, or other pertinent detail. **Arrangement:** Geographical. **Pages** (approx.): 775. **Frequency:** Biennial, even years. **Editors:** Anne Howe and A. J. Romiszowski. **Price:** $25.00, payment with order. **Other information:** Principal content is articles reviewing current state of field worldwide.

★2955★

INTERVERSITAS—MEMBERSHIP DIRECTORY

Interversitas
C/o Northeastern Illinois University
5500 N. St. Louis Avenue   Phone: (312) 583-4050
Chicago, IL 60625
Covers: 325 persons in 32 countries involved in or interested in experimental, nontraditional learning programs at the postsecondary level. **Entries include:** Name, office address, highest degree held, areas of occupational specialization, personal data, career data, areas of interest. **Arrangement:** Alphabetical. **Indexes:** Geographical, area of interest, current projects, institutional affiliation. **Frequency:** Annual, December. **Editors:** Jill K. Bohlin and Reynold Feldman, Director, Interversitas. **Price:** $10.00.

★2956★

INVENTORY OF ACADEMIC AND OCCUPATIONAL PROGRAMS IN CALIFORNIA COLLEGES AND UNIVERSITIES

California Postsecondary Education Commission
1020 12th Street   Phone: (916) 445-7933
Sacramento, CA 95814
Covers: Institutions in California registered with the commission. **Entries include:** Institution name, degrees granted in specific subject. **Arrangement:** By major. **Pages** (approx.): 260. **Frequency:** Annual, March. **Price:** Free. **Other information:** For addresses of the above institutions, see separate listing for "Directory of California Colleges and Universities," by same publisher.

★2957★

IOTA LAMBDA SIGMA—MEMBERSHIP DIRECTORY [Vocational education]

Iota Lambda Sigma
C/o Raymond Christensen
Department of Industrial Education and Technology
Northwestern State University   Phone: (318) 357-6471
Natchitoches, LA 71457
Covers: About 8,600 men and women in industrial arts education, business education, distributive education, vocational education, and technical education who have been elected to this professional society in recognition of their interests, potential, and scholarship. **Entries include:** Name, address, affiliation. **Arrangement:** By chapter name (Greek alphabet). **Frequency:** Latest edition 1974; new edition expected, date not set. **Price:** Available to members only.

★2958★

JOHN DEWEY SOCIETY—MEMBERSHIP DIRECTORY [Education]

John Dewey Society
C/o Robert R. Sherman
Norman Hall
University of Florida   Phone: (904) 392-0724
Gainesville, FL 32611
Covers: 300 members, individual and institutional. **Entries include:** Name, address. **Arrangement:** Alphabetical. **Indexes:** Zip code. **Pages** (approx.): 20. **Frequency:** Annual, June. **Editor:** Robert R. Sherman, Secretary-Treasurer. **Price:** $5.00 (in mailing list form).

Junior College Directory *See* Community, Junior, and Technical College Directory

★2959★

LEARNING INDEPENDENTLY

Gale Research Company
Book Tower   Phone: (313) 961-2242
Detroit, MI 48226
Covers: Nearly 3,200 home-study programs and self-instruction resources currently available by mail in more than 400 subjects. **Entries include:** Program title, publisher name and address, type of material (cassette, filmstrip, programmed book, etc.), original date of publication, price. **Arrangement:** By subject. **Indexes:** Author, title/keyword, producer/distributor. **Pages** (approx.): 370. **Frequency:** Not established; first edition fall 1979. **Editors:** Paul Wasserman, James Sanders, and Elizabeth Talbot Sanders. **Price:** $55.00.

Lecturing Appointments and Advanced Research Grants *See* Fulbright Awards Abroad

★2960★

LIBRARIES FOR COLLEGE STUDENTS WITH HANDICAPS [Ohio]

State Library of Ohio
65 S. Front Street   Phone: (614) 466-3710
Columbus, OH 43215
Covers: Academic libraries in Ohio. **Entries include:** Library name, address, name of contact person, and information about features of building construction or arrangement which aid their use by handicapped persons. **Pages** (approx.): 30. **Frequency:** Not established; first edition published 1977. **Editor:** Diana Cohen, Assistant to the State Librarian. **Price:** Free.

★2961★

LOVEJOY'S CAREER AND VOCATIONAL SCHOOL GUIDE

Simon and Schuster, Inc.
1230 Avenue of the Americas   Phone: (212) 245-6400
New York, NY 10020
Covers: Over 2,000 vocational and career (degree-granting) schools. **Entries include:** School name, location, name changes, admission information, accreditation, tuition, programs offered. **Arrangement:** Classified by vocation. **Pages** (approx.): 350. **Frequency:** Quadrennial; latest edition March 1978. **Editor:** Clarence E. Lovejoy. **Price:** $9.95, cloth; $4.95, paper.

★2962★
LOVEJOY'S COLLEGE GUIDE
Simon and Schuster, Inc.
1230 Avenue of the Americas   Phone: (212) 245-6400
New York, NY 10020
Covers: 3,600 American colleges, universities, technical institutes, and religious institutions; and selected foreign colleges accredited by the U.S. Regional Accrediting Associations. **Entries include:** A full entry gives school name, location, date founded, name changes, enrollment figures, library size, faculty-student ratio, religious affiliation, admission information, tuition, housing, scholarships and loans, athletic programs, curricula and degrees offered, special programs, summer sessions. Some entries include less data. **Indexes:** Career, special program. **Pages** (approx.): 390. **Frequency:** Triennial; latest edition 1979. **Editor:** Clarence E. Lovejoy. **Price:** $12.95, cloth; $6.95, paper.

★2963★
LOVEJOY'S PREP SCHOOL GUIDE
Simon and Schuster, Inc.
1230 Avenue of the Americas   Phone: (212) 245-6400
New York, NY 10020
Covers: About 2,700 private, independent elementary and secondary schools; includes residential and day schools. **Entries include:** School name, address, phone, rating, grade levels included, whether coed, whether day or residential; most listings also include description of school's programs, admission requirements, facilities, special emphases (gifted, art, etc.), number of students, number of faculty, religious affiliation, tuition, accreditation, etc. **Arrangement:** Geographical. **Indexes:** Alphabetical, special program/curriculum, schools which use the Secondary School Admission Test, schools which offer scholarships, schools which are members of the National Association of Independent Schools. **Pages** (approx.): 225. **Frequency:** Irregular; latest edition 1974. **Editor:** Clarence E. Lovejoy. **Price:** $9.95, cloth; $5.95, paper; postpaid, payment with order. **Other information:** Updated monthly by "Lovejoy's Guidance Digest," available from the editor at 735 Broad Street, Shrewsbury, NJ 07701.

★2964★
MANAGEMENT AND PRODUCTIVITY: AN INTERNATIONAL
        DIRECTORY OF INSTITUTIONS AND INFORMATION SOURCES
International Labour Office
1211 Geneva 22, Switzerland
Publication includes: Over 1,600 institutions in the management development and productivity fields, worldwide. **Entries include:** Name of organization, address. List of institutions in individual countries also shows code indicating type of institution. **Arrangement:** International government organizations and international associations, federations, and institutes are alphabetical; regional organizations and institutions, and institutions in individual countries are geographical. **Pages** (approx.): 230. **Frequency:** Irregular; latest edition 1976; new edition expected 1980. **Editor:** Dr. Milan Kubr. **Price:** 25 Swiss Francs. **Send orders to:** International Labour Office, 1750 New York Ave., N. W., Washington, DC 20006.

★2965★
MASS MEDIA COLLEGE CATALOG
American Association of Community and Junior Colleges
One Dupont Circle, N. W., Suite 410
Washington, DC 20036
Covers: Over 100 open-learning undergraduate courses, all but three on videotape, covering subjects from adult development, the humanities and arts, career planning, consumerism, science and health, to social science; about 25 producers are represented. **Entries include:** For each course - Title, producer, producer's address and ordering information, length of program, subject, format. **Arrangement:** By broad subject categories. **Indexes:** Title. **Frequency:** Irregular; looseleaf format first appeared November 1977; updated irregularly, latest edition 1979. **Price:** $15.00, payment with order; includes supplements.

★2966★
MATCHING GIFT DETAILS [Gifts to educational institutions]
Council for Advancement and Support of Education
One Dupont Circle, N. W., Suite 530/600
Washington, DC 20036
Covers: About 800 corporations which have matching gift programs. (Gifts by employees of these corporations to their universities and colleges of graduation are matched by the corporation.) **Entries include:** Corporation name, address, name of corporate giving officer, description of program (restrictions, colleges recognized, etc.). **Arrangement:** Alphabetical. **Indexes:** Companies matching on a greater than one to one basis, geographical, subsidiary name. **Pages** (approx.): 125. **Frequency:** Annual, January. **Editor:** Robert C. Hodges. **Price:** $10.00. **Send orders to:** Case Publications, Box 298, Alexandria, VA 22314.

★2967★
MENTALLY GIFTED MINORS RESOURCE DIRECTORY [California]
Gifted and Talented Management Team
California State Department of Education
721 Capitol Mall
Sacramento, CA 95814
Covers: Print and nonprint curriculum resources, funding sources, resource persons, association, and other information sources concerned with education and development of gifted children. **Entries include:** Organization, publisher, or other name and address; some listings include phone, description of interests or services, etc. **Arrangement:** By type of resource. **Pages** (approx.): 25. **Frequency:** Published 1978. **Price:** 65¢.

★2968★
NATIONAL AFFILIATION FOR LITERACY ADVANCE DIRECTORY
National Affiliation for Literacy Advance
1320 Jamesville Avenue   Phone: (315) 422-9121
Syracuse, NY 13210
Covers: Over 400 local and regional councils and 800 certified volunteer trainers who teach tutors for older youth and adult English speakers with little or no reading ability, tutors in English skills for speakers of other languages, and tutors teaching writing of high interest simplified reading materials for new readers. Coverage includes Canada. **Entries include:** For groups - Name, chairman, address. For trainers - Name, type of certification, address. **Arrangement:** Geographical. **Pages** (approx.): 60. **Frequency:** Annual, January. **Editor:** Adelaide L. Silvia, Executive Secretary. **Price:** $1.50.

★2969★
NATIONAL ASSOCIATION FOR WOMEN DEANS,
        ADMINISTRATORS, AND COUNSELORS—MEMBER
        HANDBOOK
National Association for Women Deans, Administrators, and
        Counselors
1625 I Street, N. W., Suite 624-A
Washington, DC 20006
Covers: 2,300 American and foreign members. **Entries include:** Name, institution, office and home addresses, phone, education, position, committee membership. **Arrangement:** Geographical. **Indexes:** Alphabetical. **Frequency:** Annual, January. **Editor:** Suellen Gallamore, Membership Director. **Price:** $30.00.

★2970★
NATIONAL ASSOCIATION OF COLLEGE ADMISSIONS
        COUNSELORS—DIRECTORY
National Association of College Admissions Counselors
9933 Lawler Avenue, Suite 500   Phone: (312) 676-0500
Skokie, IL 60077
Covers: 1,800 member high schools, school districts, colleges and universities, and other professional associations. **Entries include:** For members - Name, address, phone number, principal representative's name. For associations - Name, address, principal representative's name. **Arrangement:** Geographical. **Pages** (approx.): 150.

Frequency: Biennial, odd years. **Editor:** Stephen M. Lefebvre, Coordinator of Association Services. **Price:** $20.00; not to be used for commercial purposes.

★2971★

NATIONAL ASSOCIATION OF COLLEGE AND UNIVERSITY ATTORNEYS—DIRECTORY AND HANDBOOK

National Association of College and University Attorneys
One Dupont Circle, N. W., Suite 650   Phone: (202) 296-0207
Washington, DC 20036
Covers: About 2,000 attorneys representing United States colleges and universities in legal matters. **Arrangement:** Alphabetical. **Indexes:** Institution, geographical. **Pages** (approx.): 200. **Frequency:** Annual, fall. **Editor:** Phillip M. Grier, Executive Director. **Price:** Available to members only.

★2972★

NATIONAL ASSOCIATION OF COLLEGE AND UNIVERSITY BUSINESS OFFICERS—DIRECTORY

National Association of College and University Business Officers
One Dupont Circle, Suite 510   Phone: (202) 296-2344
Washington, DC 20036
Number of listings: 1,900. **Entries include:** Name of institution, name of primary representative. **Arrangement:** Geographical. **Pages** (approx.): 50. **Frequency:** Annual, August. **Editor:** Abbott Wainwright, Director, Information and Publications. **Price:** Limited free distribution outside membership.

★2973★

NATIONAL ASSOCIATION OF FOREIGN STUDENT AFFAIRS— DIRECTORY

National Association of Foreign Student Affairs
1860 19th Street, N. W.   Phone: (202) 462-4811
Washington, DC 20009
Covers: Individual members of NAFSA and Association of Teachers of English as a Second Language, and other persons concerned with foreign students in the United States, United States students abroad, and general problems of international educational exchange. **Entries include:** For institutions - Name, number of foreign students enrolled and number of foreign scholars, phone, names and titles of staff members concerned with international education. For individual members - Name, address, title, and phone. **Arrangement:** Geographical. **Pages** (approx.): 120. **Frequency:** Has been biennial; beginning in 1980 will be annual, January. **Editor:** William P. Bray, Director for Information Services. **Price:** $10.00 (current and 1980 editions).

★2974★

NATIONAL ASSOCIATION OF PRIVATE SCHOOLS FOR EXCEPTIONAL CHILDREN—DIRECTORY OF MEMBERSHIP

National Association of Private Schools for Exceptional Children
130 E. Orange Avenue   Phone: (813) 676-2250
Lake Wales, FL 33853
Number of listings: 80. **Arrangement:** Alphabetical. **Indexes:** Geographical. **Pages** (approx.): 100. **Frequency:** Biennial, January of odd years. **Editor:** Mrs. Linda Phillips, Public Relations Chairman. **Price:** $5.00.

★2975★

NATIONAL ASSOCIATION OF STATE DIRECTORS OF TEACHER EDUCATION AND CERTIFICATION—ROSTER

National Association of State Directors of Teacher Education and Certification
C/o Orring Nearhoof, Director
Teacher Education and Certification
Iowa Department of Public Instruction   Phone: (515) 281-3245
Des Moines, IA 50319
Covers: Offices in each state responsible for teacher education and certification. **Entries include:** Agency name, address, phone, names and titles of several key personnel. **Arrangement:** Geographical. **Frequency:** Annual, fall. **Price:** Free.

★2976★

NATIONAL CAREER DIRECTORY: AN OCCUPATIONAL INFORMATION HANDBOOK

Arco Publishing, Inc.
215 Park Avenue   Phone: (212) 777-6300
New York, NY 10003
Covers: About 2,000 trade and professional associations, government agencies, and other bodies which offer free or inexpensive materials concerning career opportunities. **Entries include:** Source name and address, description of material available, price. **Arrangement:** Classified by general subject areas. **Pages** (approx.): 240. **Indexes:** Subject. **Frequency:** Not established; first edition November 1978. **Editors:** Barry Gale, Linda Gale. **Price:** $8.95, cloth; $5.95, paper. **Other information:** First advertised as, "National Career Directory for Free and Inexpensive Guidance Materials."

★2977★

NATIONAL COLLEGE DATABANK

Peterson's Guides, Inc.
228 Alexander Street   Phone: (609) 924-5338
Princeton, NJ 08540
Covers: Several hundred four-year colleges and universities. **Arrangement:** By shared characteristic (barrier-free campus for the handicapped, dress code required, unusual major), then geographical. **Pages** (approx.): 920. **Frequency:** Not established; first edition 1979. **Editor:** Karen C. Hegener. **Price:** $7.95, plus $1.25 shipping. **Send orders to:** Peterson's Guides, Inc., Box 978, Edison, NJ 08817.

National Directory of Accredited Junior and Senior Colleges...
   See Accredited Institutions of Postsecondary Education

National Directory of Alternative Schools in the United States and
   Canada *See* New Schools Exchange: Directory & Resource
   Guide

★2978★

NATIONAL DIRECTORY OF FOUR YEAR...TWO YEAR COLLEGES AND POST HIGH SCHOOL TRAINING PROGRAMS FOR YOUNG PEOPLE WITH LEARNING DISABILITIES

Partners in Publishing Company
Box 50347   Phone: (918) 587-5140
Tulsa, OK 74150
Covers: About 200 postsecondary institutions offering programs for learning-disabled students. **Entries include:** School name, address, and name of contact; description of program including type of program, admission policies, courses offered and curriculum modifications; enrollment; percentage of learning disabled students completing the program; remedial clinic available. **Arrangement:** Geographical. **Pages** (approx.): 75. **Frequency:** Irregular; latest edition 1977; new edition expected winter 1980. **Editors:** P. M. Fielding, Editor, and John R. Moss, Consultant. **Price:** $16.95, plus 50¢ shipping (1980 edition).

★2979★

NATIONAL DIRECTORY OF PUBLIC ALTERNATIVE SCHOOLS

National Alternative Schools Program
School of Education
University of Massachusetts   Phone: (413) 454-0941
Amherst, MA 01003
Covers: 1,300 elementary and secondary public schools offering nontraditional curriculums and educational alternatives. **Entries include:** School name, address, varying amounts and kinds of information about school. **Arrangement:** Geographical. **Pages** (approx.): 200. **Frequency:** Irregular; latest edition 1977; new edition expected 1980. **Editors:** Anne Flaxman and Kerry Christensen-Homstead, Assistant Directors. **Former title:** Public Alternative Schools: A National Directory. **Price:** $3.75, plus 65¢ shipping (current edition); $5.50 (tentative, 1980 edition). **Other information:** Supplemental lists will appear in the NASP publication, "Applesauce."

★2980★
NATIONAL DIRECTORY OF SUMMER INTERNSHIPS for
Undergraduate College Students
Career Planning Office
Haverford College   Phone: (215) 649-9600
Haverford, PA 19041
Covers: 200 companies, institutions, and organizations, each offering (one as many as 75) summer positions to undergraduate students which allow them to apply previous college training to non-routine practical situations. Data apply only to internships available for the following summer (note that directory is biennial), but many of the opportunities listed are available each year. **Entries include:** Name of the program and/or the sponsoring organization, address, location of internships, number of internships available, duration of the program, salary (if any), eligibility, application instructions, and a description of the program. **Arrangement:** Classified by field (arts, communications, etc.). **Indexes:** Alphabetical. **Pages** (approx.): 160. **Frequency:** Biennial, fall of odd years. **Editors:** Diane Y. Yannopoulos, Michael A. Raciti. **Price:** $8.50.

★2981★
NATIONAL FACULTY DIRECTORY
Gale Research Company
Book Tower   Phone: (313) 961-2242
Detroit, MI 48226
Covers: About 450,000 teaching faculty members at 3,200 junior colleges, colleges, and universities in the United States and those in Canada which give instruction in English. **Entries include:** Name, department name, institution, and address. **Arrangement:** Alphabetical. **Pages** (approx.): 2,500 (2 volumes). **Frequency:** Annual, fall. **Price:** $135.00. **Other information:** Includes a geographical list of schools covered.

★2982★
NATIONAL GUIDE TO CREDIT RECOMMENDATIONS FOR
NONCOLLEGIATE COURSES
American Council on Education
One Dupont Circle   Phone: (202) 833-4770
Washington, DC 20036
Covers: More than 900 courses offered by 80 government agencies, business firms, nonprofit groups, etc., which are recommended for educational credit by the council. **Entries include:** Name of sponsoring organization, name of course, length of time required, dates offered or established, description of course objective and instruction, credit recommendation. **Arrangement:** By name of sponsoring organization. **Indexes:** Course title. **Pages** (approx.): 230. **Frequency:** Annual. **Former title:** Guide to Educational Programs in Noncollegiate Organizations. **Price:** $12.00, postpaid, payment with order. **Other information:** Compiled by the American Council on Education, Consortium of the California State University and Colleges, North Carolina Joint Committee on Transfer Students, and the state government agencies concerned with higher education in Florida, Illinois, Massachusetts, Michigan, New Jersey, Pennsylvania, and Tennessee.

National School Directory See CIC's School Directory

★2983★
NATIONAL SOCIETY FOR PERFORMANCE AND INSTRUCTION—
MEMBERSHIP DIRECTORY
National Society for Performance and Instruction
1126 16th Street, N. W., Suite 315   Phone: (202) 833-4178
Washington, DC 20036
Covers: About 1,500 persons interested in developing technological solutions to human performance problems through programmed instruction, computer-assisted instruction, and other systematic forms of instruction. **Entries include:** Name, address, phone. **Arrangement:** Alphabetical. **Indexes:** Geographical. **Pages** (approx.): 50. **Frequency:** Annual, July. **Editor:** Kay Schaeffer, National Manager. **Advertising accepted.** Circulation 1,500. **Price:** $40.00; available to members only.

★2984★
NATIONALLY RECOGNIZED ACCREDITING AGENCIES AND
ASSOCIATIONS
Division of Eligibility and Agency Evaluation
Bureau of Higher and Continuing Education
Office of Education
Health, Education, and Welfare Department   Phone: (202) 245-9873
Washington, DC 20202
Publication includes: About 75 accrediting agencies and associations recognized by the Office of Education. **Entries include:** Name of accrediting committee, name of organization, address, phone, name of director; kinds of schools or programs accredited or states covered (if a regional association); year recognized by Education Office; year of last full review; year of next review by Education Office. **Arrangement:** Regional associations by name, others by academic area accredited. **Pages** (approx.): 25. **Frequency:** Irregular; latest edition November 1978; new edition expected early 1980. **Editor:** John R. Proffitt, Director. **Price:** Free. **Also includes:** Discussion of criteria and procedures for accepting accrediting agencies by the U.S. Commissioner of Education and list of organizations under consideration for recognition.

★2985★
NEED A LIFT? [Scholarship information]
The American Legion
Box 1055   Phone: (317) 635-8411
Indianapolis, IN 46206
Covers: Sources of career, scholarship, and loan information or assistance. **Entries include:** Name and address of source, description of information or assistance offered and any requirements or limitations. **Pages** (approx.): 135. **Frequency:** Annual, fall. **Editor:** K. Michael Ayers, Director of Education Program. **Price:** $1.00.

★2986★
NEW GUIDE TO STUDY ABROAD
Harper & Row Publishers, Inc.
10 E. 53rd Street   Phone: (212) 593-7225
New York, NY 10022
Publication includes: Several hundred foreign study programs at the college level sponsored by foreign universities for out-of-country students and by United States institutions which wish to give students experiences in schools abroad. Includes section on teaching opportunities abroad. **Entries include:** Name of school, address, brief description of program and course offerings, tuition and other fees. **Arrangement:** By type of sponsor and when program offered (regular year or summer), then geographical. **Pages** (approx.): 450. **Frequency:** Biennial, March of even years; beginning in 1980, September. **Editors:** John Garraty, Cyril Taylor, and Lily von Klemperer. **Price:** $12.50, cloth; $5.95, paper (current and 1980 editions).

★2987★
NEW SCHOOLS EXCHANGE: DIRECTORY & RESOURCE GUIDE
New Schools Exchange
                    Phone: (501) 677-2300
Pettigrew, AR 72752
Covers: About 2,000 primary and secondary schools which are non-traditional in curriculum content or design, emphases, or physical environment, and generally are non-tax-supported. **Entries include:** School name, address, phone. **Arrangement:** Geographical. **Pages** (approx.): 120. **Frequency:** Irregular; latest edition 1978. **Former title:** National Directory of Alternative Schools in the United States and Canada. **Price:** $5.00. **Other information:** Published since 1969, the number of listings has increased from 30 at that time. Only schools which answer questionnaires are listed.

★2988★

NORTH CENTRAL ASSOCIATION QUARTERLY—ROSTER ISSUE
[Secondary schools and colleges]
North Central Association of Colleges and Schools
1221 University Avenue
Boulder, CO 80302
Covers: Elementary schools, secondary schools, and colleges accredited by the association in a 19-state region; and members of the accrediting teams, business officers, and committees of the association. **Entries include:** For schools - School name, address; enrollment and other statistical data; name of president or chief executive. **Arrangement:** Schools are geographical; team members classified by assignment. **Pages** (approx.): 350. **Frequency:** Annual, fall. **Editor:** Kaye Bache-Snyder. **Price:** $3.25 (ISSN 0029- 2648). **Also includes:** Archaic names of colleges and universities.

★2989★

NORTH CENTRAL CONFERENCE ON SUMMER SCHOOLS—
MEMBERSHIP DIRECTORY [Colleges and universities]
North Central Conference on Summer Schools
C/o Thomas S. McLeRoy
University of Wisconsin-Whitewater　　　Phone: (414) 472-1100
Whitewater, WI 53190
Covers: About 150 university and college summer school directors in north central and nearby states. **Entries include:** College name, address, phone, name of director, year of initial membership. **Arrangement:** Alphabetical by institution. **Indexes:** Personal name. **Pages** (approx.): 30. **Frequency:** Annual, June. **Editor:** Thomas S. McLeRoy. **Price:** Available to members only.

★2990★

NORTH DAKOTA GUIDE TO POSTSECONDARY EDUCATION
North Dakota Education Information Center
State Library　　　　　　　　　　Phone: (701) 224-2395
Bismarck, ND 58505
Covers: Accredited post-secondary institutions in North Dakota. **Entries include:** Institution name, address, names of admissions and financial officers. **Pages** (approx.): 30. **Frequency:** Annual, fall. **Editor:** Cynthia Bates. **Price:** Free.

★2991★

NORTHWEST ASSOCIATION OF SCHOOLS AND COLLEGES—
DIRECTORY OF ACCREDITED AND AFFILIATED INSTITUTIONS
Northwest Association of Schools and Colleges
3700-B University Way, N. E.　　　Phone: (206) 543-0195
Seattle, WA 98105
Covers: Institutions in Alaska, Montana, Nevada, Idaho, Utah, Washington, and Oregon. **Entries include:** Institution, location, chief executive, enrollment, degrees offered or grade level and number of grades, year of first membership. **Arrangement:** Geographical. **Frequency:** Annual, April. **Editor:** James F. Bemis, Secretary-Treasurer. **Former title:** Northwest Association of Secondary and Higher Schools - Directory of Accredited and Affiliated Institutions (1975). **Price:** $1.00 (current edition); $1.50 (1980 edition).

Northwest Association of Secondary and Higher Schools—
Directory... *See* Northwest Association of Schools and
Colleges—Directory...

★2992★

ON CAMPUS/OFF CAMPUS PROGRAMS FOR PART-TIME
STUDENTS
National University Extension Association
One Dupont Circle, Suite 360　　　Phone: (202) 659-3130
Washington, DC 20036
Covers: About 3,000 programs at some 1,300 institutions in the United States; about two-thirds of the programs are for associate degrees, with remainder divided between bachelor's and master's programs. **Pages** (approx.): 120. **Frequency:** Biennial in odd years. **Editors:** Linda W. Gordon and Judy H. Schub. **Advertising accepted.** **Former title:** A Directory of U.S. College and University Degrees for

Part-Time Students. **Price:** $4.00.

★2993★

OPPORTUNITIES ABROAD FOR TEACHERS
Division of International Education
Office of Education
Health, Education and Welfare Dept.
Washington, DC 20202
Covers: Opportunities available for elementary and secondary teachers, college instructors, and assistant professors to attend seminars or to teach abroad under the Mutual Educational Exchange Act of 1961. **Pages** (approx.): 30. **Frequency:** Annual, September for following two calendar years (i.e., September 1979 for 1980-81). **Price:** $1.75 (DHEW Publication 79-19300).

★2994★

PATTERSON'S AMERICAN EDUCATION
Educational Directories Inc.
Box 199　　　　　　　　　　Phone: (312) 392-1811
Mount Prospect, IL 60056
Covers: School districts in the United States, including 19,000 high schools, 11,000 junior high schools, and 2,000 parochial high schools, and 9,000 colleges, universities, and graduate, military, trade, technical, and private preparatory schools in separate section, "Patterson's Schools Classified." **Entries include:** Secondary school listings usually show names of principals and superintendents in addition to school names and addresses. Postsecondary school listings usually show names of administrators or directors of admission in addition to school names and addresses. **Arrangement:** School systems are arranged geographically; "Patterson's Schools Classified" is arranged by subjects offered. **Indexes:** Alphabetical (postsecondary schools only). **Pages** (approx.): 780. **Frequency:** Annual, November. **Editor:** Norman F. Elliott. **Price:** $37.50. **Also includes:** 1,000 officials in federal and state departments of education, and 200 educational associations. **Other information:** "Patterson's Schools Classified" is also sold separately; see separate entry.

★2995★

PATTERSON'S SCHOOLS CLASSIFIED
Educational Directories Inc.
Box 199　　　　　　　　　　Phone: (312) 392-1811
Mount Prospect, IL 60056
Covers: 9,000 colleges, universities, and graduate, military, trade, technical, and private preparatory schools. **Entries include:** School name, address, president, department chairmen, or admissions officer. Many entries also include descriptive listings supplied by individual schools. **Arrangement:** Classified by subjects offered. **Pages** (approx.): 210. **Frequency:** Annual, April. **Editor:** Norman F. Elliott. **Price:** $4.75 (current edition); $5.00 (1980 edition). **Other information:** Updated from previous year's edition of "Patterson's American Education;" see separate listing.

★2996★

PETERSON'S ANNUAL GUIDE TO INDEPENDENT SECONDARY
SCHOOLS
Peterson's Guides, Inc.
228 Alexander Street　　　　　　Phone: (609) 924-5338
Princeton, NJ 08540
Covers: Over 1,100 accredited and state-approved private secondary schools in the United States and abroad. **Entries include:** School name, address, description of programs, student life, facilities, admission requirements, costs, graduation requirements, student body characteristics, athletic programs, financial aid availability, college placement records. **Arrangement:** Geographical. **Indexes:** Type of school, special offerings, special programs, merit-based scholarships availability. **Pages** (approx.): 705. **Frequency:** Annual; first edition expected January 1980. **Editor:** Thomas C. Southerland, Jr. **Advertising accepted.** **Price:** $8.95, plus $1.25 shipping. **Send orders to:** Peterson's Guides Order Dept., Box 978, Edison, NJ 08817.

★2997★
PETERSON'S ANNUAL GUIDE TO UNDERGRADUATE STUDY
Peterson's Guides, Inc.
228 Alexander Street   Phone: (609) 924-5338
Princeton, NJ 08540
Covers: 2,500 four-year undergraduate institutions in the United States and Canada. **Entries include:** School name, address, description of programs, student life, campuses, and facilities. **Arrangement:** Geographical. **Indexes:** Major offered, test score range, general characteristics. **Pages** (approx.): 1,925. **Frequency:** Annual, November. **Price:** $12.00, plus $1.25 shipping.

★2998★
PETERSON'S ANNUAL GUIDES TO GRADUATE STUDY
Peterson's Guides, Inc.
228 Alexander Street   Phone: (609) 924-5338
Princeton, NJ 08540
Covers: Over 1,350 graduate institutions in the United States and Canada. Published in five volumes: "Institutions Offering Graduate Work in the United States and Canada/An Overview," "Humanities and Social Sciences," "Biological, Agricultural, and Health Sciences," "Physical Sciences," and "Engineering and Applied Sciences." **Entries include:** In "Institutions.../An Overview" - Institution name, address, names of administrators, enrollment, facilities, research affiliations, degrees offered, and fields of study. In discipline guides - Institution name and description of programs, including degree requirements, faculty qualifications, etc. **Arrangement:** "Overview" volume is alphabetical; discipline guides are by field of study within disciplines. **Pages** (approx.): 4,000. **Frequency:** Annual, November. **Editor:** Karen C. Hegener. **Price:** "Institutions.../An Overview," $11.00; "Humanities and Social Sciences," $16.00; "Biological, Agricultural, and Health Sciences," $17.00; "Physical Sciences," $14.00; and "Engineering and Applied Sciences," $15.00. Add $1.25 shipping.

★2999★
PETERSON'S TRAVEL GUIDE TO COLLEGES
Peterson's Guides, Inc.
228 Alexander Street   Phone: (609) 924-5338
Princeton, NJ 08540
Covers: Four-year undergraduate institutions in the eastern United States and Canada, and accommodations on- and off-campus available at each. Intended to complement "Peterson's Annual Guide to Undergraduate Study," described in separate listing. Published in 2 regional editions - "Northeastern States" covering Connecticut, Maine, Massachusetts, New Hampshire, New York, Rhode Island, Vermont; and "Middle Atlantic States" covering Delaware, District of Columbia, Maryland, New Jersey, Pennsylvania, and Virginia. **Entries include:** School name, address, phone, name of director of admissions, type of institution, number of students and faculty, description of academic life (including calendar), admissions information, fees, instructions for arranging campus visits, accommodations, travel directions. **Arrangement:** Geographical. **Pages** (approx.): 125. **Frequency:** Irregular; latest edition 1977. **Editor:** Connie Hinckley. **Price:** $4.95, plus $1.25 shipping, payment must accompany order. **Send orders to:** Peterson's Guides, Box 978, Edison, NJ 08817. **Also includes:** State maps. **Other information:** Published in cooperation with Hammond, Inc.

★3000★
POSTSECONDARY EDUCATIONAL OPPORTUNITIES IN ARKANSAS
Postsecondary Education Planning Commission
1301 W. Seventh Street   Phone: (501) 371-1441
Little Rock, AR 72201
Covers: Community colleges, colleges, universities, and vocational training schools in Arkansas. **Entries include:** For schools - Name, address, phone, list of admissions personnel, enrollment figures, tuition and other fees, availability of housing, admission requirements, degrees offered, financial aid programs. For financial aid - Name, amount of assistance, eligibility, terms of repayment, where to apply, application deadline. **Arrangement:** By type of institution. **Indexes:** Geographical, areas of study. **Pages** (approx.): 250. **Frequency:**

Annual, January. **Editor:** Dr. Harriet C. Smith, Higher Education Administrator. **Price:** Free.

★3001★
PRIVATE INDEPENDENT SCHOOLS
Bunting & Lyon, Inc.
238 N. Main Street   Phone: (203) 269-3333
Wallingford, CT 06492
Covers: Over 1,300 independent schools in 46 states and 57 countries. **Entries include:** School name, address, phone, enrollment, tuition and other fees, scholarship information, headmaster's name and educational background, director of admissions, regional accreditation. **Arrangement:** Geographical. **Pages** (approx.): 900. **Frequency:** Annual, spring. **Editor:** Margaret M. Sprague. **Price:** $35.00 (current edition); $38.00 (tentative, 1980 edition). **Other information:** Variant title, "Bunting & Lyon Blue Book." Some listings are reprinted in paperback and distributed through bookstores under title, "Bunting & Lyon's Guide to Private Schools."

★3002★
PROFESSIONAL ASSOCIATIONS FOR TWO-YEAR COLLEGE STUDENT DEVELOPMENT STAFF
American College Personnel Association, Division
American Personnel and Guidance Association
5203 Leesburg Pike   Phone: (703) 820-4700
Falls Church, VA 22041
Covers: Over 425 national, state, and local associations which serve two-year college student development workers in the United States. **Entries include:** Organization name, address, phone, name of contact person, annual fee, and purpose of and persons served by the association. **Pages** (approx.): 80. **Frequency:** Published September 1977. **Editors:** Robert B. Young, et al. **Price:** Free.

Profiles of American Colleges *See* Barron's Profiles of American Colleges

Public Alternative Schools: A National Directory *See* National Directory of Public Alternative Schools

★3003★
RANDAX EDUCATION GUIDE: A GUIDE TO COLLEGES WHICH ARE SEEKING STUDENTS
Education Guide, Inc.
Box 421   Phone: (617) 961-2217
Randolph, MA 02368
Covers: About 200 two-year and four-year colleges, health care schools, and vocational schools who are actively recruiting students and advertise in the publication. **Entries include:** School name, address, phone; degrees and courses offered; date founded; type of control; enrollment; costs; admission requirements. **Arrangement:** Geographical. **Indexes:** Major, state, school name. **Pages** (approx.): 130. **Frequency:** Annual, January. **Editor:** Stephen E. Marshall. **Advertising accepted.** Circulation 30,000. **Price:** $5.75, postpaid, payment with order.

★3004★
RANDAX GRADUATE SCHOOL DIRECTORY
Education Guide, Inc.
10 Bayberry Lane   Phone: (617) 961-2217
Randolph, MA 02368
Covers: Over 900 graduate and professional schools in the United States and its possessions. **Entries include:** Name of school, address, phone, date of founding, whether private or state controlled, accreditation, degrees offered, major fields of study, and other descriptive information. **Arrangement:** Geographical. **Indexes:** Major, state, and school cross-referenced. **Pages** (approx.): 310. **Frequency:** Irregular; latest edition August 1976; new edition expected 1981. **Editor:** Robert A. Pastman. **Advertising accepted.** Circulation 4,000. **Price:** $21.50, postpaid, payment with order.

Resource Manual of Information on Educating the Gifted and
    Talented *See* Gifted and Talented: Developing Elementary
    and...Programs

★3005★
RESOURCES FOR CHANGE: A GUIDE TO PROJECTS (Education)
Fund for the Improvement of Postsecondary Education
Education Division
Health, Education, and Welfare Department
400 Maryland Avenue, S. W., Room 3123
Washington, DC 20202
Covers: About 175 projects supported by the Fund which have as
their objectives "genuine improvements in educational practice."
Entries include: Name of institution or other grantee, location, name
and address of project director, and 300-500 word description of the
project. Arrangement: Alphabetical by grantee name. Indexes:
Improvement approach, curricular content, institution type, population
served, region. Pages (approx.): 120. Frequency: Annual, November.
Editor: Diane Hayman. Price: Free.

★3006★
SCHOLARSHIPS, FELLOWSHIPS AND LOANS
Bellman Publishing Company
Box 164
Arlington, MA 02174
Covers: Volume 6 includes over 500 sources of financial aid for
students which are not controlled by institutions of higher education.
Includes Vocational Goals Index section which tabulates awards, area
of study, and requirements (such as residency, sex, citizenship, and
affiliation) to sponsoring organization (such as religious, veteran,
union, ethnic, or fraternal). Entries include: Name of organization,
address, description of program, qualifications, available funds, and
special fields of interest. Arrangement: Alphabetical. Indexes:
Alphabetical index of administering agencies, donors, and funds.
Pages (approx.): 520. Frequency: Irregular; Volume 6, 1977;
Volume 7 (new material), expected spring 1980; additional
information available in quarterly Scholarships, Fellowships and Loans
News Service. Price: $45.00; News Service, $24.00 per year (ISSN
0036-6366); Volume 6 plus one-year subscription, $62.10; postpaid,
payment with order.

★3007★
SCHOOL BUSINESS AFFAIRS—ASSOCIATION OF SCHOOL
    BUSINESS OFFICIALS OFFICIAL MEMBERSHIP DIRECTORY
    ISSUE
Association of School Business Officials of the U. S. and Canada
720 Garden Street   Phone: (312) 823-9320
Park Ridge, IL 60068
Publication includes: 5,500 school business administrators, chief
school district administrators, professors of education, and business
persons in the United States and Canada. Entries include: Name, title,
school or company, address, phone. Arrangement: Alphabetical.
Frequency: Annual. Editor: Charles G. Stolberg, Editor and Publisher.
Advertising accepted. Former title: Blue Book of School Business
Administration. Price: Apply.

★3008★
SCHOOL GUIDE
Catholic News Publishing Company
80 W. Broad Street   Phone: (914) 664-8100
Mt. Vernon, NY 10552
Covers: Over 1,000 colleges, vocational schools, nursing schools,
religious communities, high schools, and boarding schools in the United
States. Entries include: Profile of institution, including name, address,
phone, courses offered, degrees awarded. Indexes: Subject areas.
Pages (approx.): 290. Frequency: Annual, December. Editor: Victor
L. Ridder, Jr. Advertising accepted. Circulation 175,000. Price:
$3.00.

★3009★
SCHOOL SHOP—DIRECTORY OF FEDERAL AND STATE OFFICIALS
    ISSUE
Prakken Publications, Inc.
416 Longshore Drive
Ann Arbor, MI 48107
Covers: Federal and state officials concerned with vocational,
technical, and trade and industrial education in the United States and
Canada. Entries include: Agency name, names of key personnel and
their areas of responsibility. Arrangement: By agency. Frequency:
Annual, April. Editor: Lawrence W. Prakken. Price: $2.50.

★3010★
SCHOOL SHOP—SUPPLIERS DIRECTORY ISSUE
Prakken Publications, Inc.
416 Longshore Drive   Phone: (313) 769-1211
Ann Arbor, MI 48107
Covers: About 250 manufacturers and suppliers of shop equipment
and materials to vocational schools. Entries include: Company name,
address. Arrangement: By product. Frequency: Annual, April. Editor:
Lawrence W. Prakken. Price: $2.50.

School Universe Data Book *See* CIC's School Directory

★3011★
SELECTED LIST OF MAJOR FELLOWSHIP OPPORTUNITIES AND
    AIDS TO ADVANCED EDUCATION FOR FOREIGN NATIONALS
Commission on Human Resources
National Research Council
2101 Constitution Avenue
Washington, DC 20418
Covers: About 55 foundations, institutes, government agencies,
international organizations, and other organizations which offer
fellowships and educational assistance to foreign nationals. Entries
include: Name of organization, text describing purpose and types of
awards offered, description of organization, application procedure,
and address. Arrangement: Alphabetical. Pages (approx.): 25.
Frequency: Published spring 1976.

★3012★
SELECTED LIST OF MAJOR FELLOWSHIP OPPORTUNITIES AND
    AIDS TO ADVANCED EDUCATION FOR UNITED STATES
    CITIZENS
Commission on Human Resources
National Research Council
2101 Constitution Avenue
Washington, DC 20418
Covers: About 100 foundations, associations, state and federal
agencies, corporations, and other organizations which offer
fellowships, grants, and scholarships. About 25 publications listing
other sources of grants and awards are also listed. Entries include:
For organizations - Name of organization, text describing purpose and
types of awards offered as well as information on the organization,
application procedure, and address. For publications - Title, publisher,
address. Arrangement: By level of education (undergraduate,
graduate, postdoctoral, and general). Pages (approx.): 50.
Frequency: Published spring 1976.

★3013★
SELECTED LIST OF POSTSECONDARY EDUCATION
    OPPORTUNITIES FOR MINORITIES AND WOMEN
Office of Education
Education Division
Health, Education, and Welfare Department
Washington, DC 20202
Covers: Programs of private organizations which offer loans,
scholarships, and fellowship opportunities for women and minorities.
Entries include: Organization name and address, brief description of
program. Arrangement: By subject. Pages (approx.): 110.
Frequency: Annual, August. Editor: Carol J. Smith. Price: $3.75 (S/N
017-080-02040-8). Send orders to: Government Printing Office,

Washington, DC 20402.

Selecting Educational Media *See* Selecting Instructional Media

★3014★
SELECTING INSTRUCTIONAL MEDIA
Libraries Unlimited, Inc.
Box 263   Phone: (303) 770-1220
Littleton, CO 80160
Publication includes: Names and addresses of several hundred publishers of lists, bibliographies, catalogs, etc., describing audiovisual materials in specific subject areas (sex education, ethnic studies, science, etc.). Listings of individual publications mention about a dozen points regarding content (grade level, media and period covered, number of entries, etc.). **Arrangement:** By subject area. **Indexes:** Subject title, personal name. **Frequency:** Irregular; previous edition 1975; latest edition 1978. **Editor:** Mary Robinson Sive. **Former title:** Educators' Guide to Media Lists (1978). **Price:** $15.00. **Other information:** Has been cited erroneously as, "Selecting Educational Media."

Seminar Locator's Two-Step Catalog *See* Seminars: The
    Directory of Continuing & Professional Education Programs

★3015★
SEMINARS: THE DIRECTORY OF CONTINUING & PROFESSIONAL
    EDUCATION PROGRAMS
Seminar Locator
525 N. Lake Street   Phone: (608) 251-2421
Madison, WI 53703
Covers: About 150 organizations and firms sponsoring more than 2,000 seminars at various locations throughout the United States and Canada; in-house seminars are listed separately. **Entries include:** Sponsor name, program title, names of speakers, description of program, Continuing Education Units offered, fees, locations, and dates. **Arrangement:** Classified by subject. **Indexes:** Subject. **Pages** (approx.): 100. **Frequency:** Three times yearly - winter/spring, summer, and fall. **Editor:** Howard C. Nelson, Publisher. **Advertising accepted.** Circulation 5,000. **Former title:** Seminar Locator's Two-Step Catalog. **Price:** $40.00 per year; $15.00 per copy. **Other information:** Seminar Locator is a seminar broker; each issue of "Seminars" includes a reader service card which can be used to request information concerning the events listed. If registration is desired, it can be secured through Seminar Locator.

★3016★
SOCIAL EDUCATION—"GRADUATION COMPETENCIES: MORE
    THAN A FAD" [Article]
National Council for the Social Studies
2030 M Street, N. W.   Phone: (202) 296-0760
Washington, DC 20036
Covers: 10 competency-based high school graduation requirement programs in Oregon, Minnesota, and Alaska. **Frequency:** Published May 1978. **Editors:** Joe Nathan and Wayne Jennings.

★3017★
STOPOUT!: WORKING WAYS TO LEARN
Garrett Park Press
Garrett Park, MD 20766
Covers: About 140 internship opportunities available with association, government, church, and other projects to young persons with incomplete or no college training. (A "stopout" is defined as a student who leaves school prior to graduation, with implications of probable return.) Programs listed provide stipend, college credit, or both. **Entries include:** Name of internship sponsor, address, phone, description of work involved in the internship, requirements, pay (if any), whether college credit can be arranged, application information. **Arrangement:** By general subject areas (environment, communications, etc.). **Indexes:** Sponsor name, geographical. **Pages** (approx.): 215. **Frequency:** Not established; first edition fall 1978. **Editor:** Joyce Slaton Mitchell. **Price:** $7.95, payment with order;

$8.95, billed.

Student Aid Annual *See* Chronicle Student Aid Annual

★3018★
STUDENT CONSUMER'S GUIDE [Federal financial aid]
Bureau of Student Financial Assistance
Education Division
Health, Education, and Welfare Department
Seventh and D Streets, S. W.
Washington, DC 20202
Covers: Application procedures and sources of information for Basic Educational Opportunity Grants (BEOG's), Supplemental Educational Opportunity Grants, National Direct Student Loans, college work-study programs, guaranteed student loans, and health education assistance loans. **Entries include:** For each loan or grant program described - Name, eligibility requirements, type of assistance and amounts of awards or loans, repayment requirements, agency name and address for further information. **Arrangement:** By program title. **Pages** (approx.): 20. **Frequency:** Annual, January. **Price:** Free. **Send orders to:** Basic Grants, Box 84, Washington, DC 20044.

★3019★
STUDENT FINANCIAL AID HANDBOOK [North Dakota]
Student Financial Assistance Agency
North Dakota Board of Higher Education
Capitol Building, 10th Floor   Phone: (701) 224-2960
Bismarck, ND 58505
Covers: State and federal financial aid programs available to students in North Dakota. **Entries include:** For programs - Description, eligibility, application deadline and procedure. For institutions - Name, program director or financial aid officer, address, phone. **Pages** (approx.): 40. **Frequency:** Biennial, summer of odd years. **Price:** Free.

★3020★
STUDY ABROAD
United Nations Educational, Scientific, and Cultural Organization
7 Place de Fontenoy
Paris 75700, France
Covers: Over 200,000 scholarships, fellowships, and educational exchange programs offered for study in 107 countries. **Entries include:** Eligibility, form and amounts of financial assistance, sponsoring or administering agency name and address. **Arrangement:** Contents classified into two sections: International Organizations; National Institutions. **Indexes:** International organization, national institution, subject of study. **Pages** (approx.): 720. **Frequency:** Biennial, November/December of even years. **Price:** $10.80. **Send orders to:** Unipub, Box 433, Murray Hill Station, New York, NY 10016.

Study in Europe *See* Handbook on International Study for U.S.
    Nationals

Study in Mid-East *See* Handbook on International Study for U.S.
    Nationals

Study in the American Republics Area *See* Handbook on
    International Study for U.S. Nationals

★3021★
SUMMER STUDY ABROAD
Institute of International Education
809 United Nations Plaza   Phone: (212) 883-8279
New York, NY 10017
Covers: About 900 college-level, adult education summer courses sponsored by United States colleges and by foreign private or governmental institutions; courses run from as little as a week to three months or so. **Entries include:** Name of institution or other sponsor, course subject, inclusive dates, subjects offered, language of instruction, whether United States college credit is offered and how much, related travel opportunities, housing, tuition, scholarships, orientation programs, deadline, and address for application.

Arrangement: Geographical. **Pages** (approx.): 120. **Frequency:** Annual, winter. **Editor:** Gail A. Cohen. **Price:** $6.00, plus 75¢ shipping, payment with order (current and 1980 editions).

★3022★
TALENT ROSTER OF OUTSTANDING MINORITY COMMUNITY COLLEGE GRADUATES
College Entrance Examination Board
888 Seventh Avenue   Phone: (212) 582-6210
New York, NY 10019
Covers: 1,200 minority graduates of two-year colleges selected on the basis of grade point average by their colleges. **Entries include:** Name, address, grade point average, intended major. **Arrangement:** By state, then college presently attending. **Pages** (approx.): 40. **Frequency:** Annual, March. **Price:** Free.

★3023★
TEACHERS' CENTERS EXCHANGE DIRECTORY
Far West Laboratory for Educational Research and Development
1855 Folsom Street   Phone: (415) 565-3100
San Francisco, CA 94103
Covers: About 80 programs for in-service education, training, and support of teachers; supplement lists 55 others. A list of publications by teachers' centers and their publishers is also included. **Entries include:** Center name, address, description of the program, resources, staff, facilities, fees, credit available, affiliation with other groups and/or unions, and publications. For publications - Title, publisher, address. **Arrangement:** Centers are geographical; publications are classified. **Pages** (approx.): Base volume, 210; supplement, 110. **Frequency:** Irregular; latest edition April 1977; supplement, May 1978; new edition expected January 1980. **Editors:** Jeanne Lance, Ruth Kreitzman. **Former title:** Exploring Teachers' Centers (1977). **Price:** $6.50 for base volume; $6.00 for supplement; postpaid, payment with order.

★3024★
TEACHER'S GUIDE TO NON-TRADITIONAL GRADUATE STUDY
Femina Press
4691 E. Powell Avenue
Las Vegas, NV 89121
Covers: Colleges and universities offering non-traditional graduate programs, including correspondence study, credit by examination, and others. **Entries include:** Institution or group offering program, address, description of program, degrees offered, residency requirements, accreditation, etc. **Arrangement:** By type of program. **Indexes:** Degree title, institution name, geographical. **Pages** (approx.): 70. **Frequency:** Annual. **Editor:** Elaine G. Koscielniak. **Price:** $5.95, plus 55¢ shipping.

★3025★
TEACHERS' GUIDE TO OVERSEAS TEACHING: A COMPLETE AND COMPREHENSIVE DIRECTORY OF ENGLISH-LANGUAGE SCHOOLS AND COLLEGES OVERSEAS
Friends of World Teaching
Box 1049   Phone: (714) 276-1464
San Diego, CA 92112
Covers: Over 1,000 English-speaking schools and colleges in about 150 countries where American teachers may apply for employment. **Entries include:** School name, address, grade levels. **Arrangement:** Geographical. **Pages** (approx.): 145. **Frequency:** Irregular; latest edition January 1979. **Editor:** Louis A. Bajkai, Director. **Price:** $10.00.

★3026★
TEACHING ABROAD
Institute of International Education
809 United Nations Plaza   Phone: (212) 883-8200
New York, NY 10017
Covers: About 150 organizations or agencies offering overseas employment to United States elementary, secondary, and college-level teachers, and guidance counselors and education administrators;

worldwide coverage. **Entries include:** Name of organization or agency, name and address of contact, academic levels and subject areas preferred; number of openings; language of instruction; location and duration of assignment; requirements; benefits; application procedure. **Arrangement:** Geographical. **Pages** (approx.): 90. **Frequency:** Irregular; latest edition 1976; new edition expected fall 1980. **Editor:** Gail A. Cohen. **Price:** $6.00 (current edition); $7.50 (1980 edition); plus 75¢ shipping.

★3027★
TEACHING OPPORTUNITIES IN THE MIDDLE EAST AND NORTH AFRICA
America-Mideast Educational and Training Services
1717 Massachusetts Avenue, N. W.,
   Suite 100
Washington, DC 20036
Covers: Organizations and schools which recruit United States teachers for positions in the Middle East and North Africa. **Entries include:** Name of organization, address, brief description of organization, eligibility of teachers, etc. **Arrangement:** Geographical. **Pages** (approx.): 25. **Frequency:** Biennial; latest edition August 1979. **Editor:** Nancy Searles, Program Officer, Educational Services Department. **Price:** $3.50. **Other information:** Formerly published by American Friends of the Middle East.

★3028★
TRAINING AND DEVELOPMENT ORGANIZATIONS DIRECTORY
Gale Research Company
Book Tower   Phone: (313) 961-2242
Detroit, MI 48226
Covers: About 1,000 companies, institutes, graduate schools, consulting groups, and other organizations which conduct managerial and supervisory training courses for business and government. **Entries include:** Organization name, address, phone, date founded, staff size and names of director and principal staff, subject or functional specialties, and details concerning courses or training offered. **Arrangement:** Alphabetical. **Indexes:** Geographical, subject, personal name. **Pages** (approx.): 600. **Frequency:** Not established; first edition 1978; new edition expected fall 1980. **Editors:** Paul Wasserman and Marlene Palmer. **Price:** $64.00.

★3029★
TRAINING OPPORTUNITIES IN JOB CORPS
Employment and Training Administration
Labor Department
601 D Street, N. W.   Phone: (202) 376-6866
Washington, DC 20213
Covers: Vocational courses offered at over 100 Job Corps centers in 42 states and Puerto Rico. **Entries include:** Center name, assigned number, capacity, operator, courses offered, address, phone, and travel directions. **Arrangement:** Alphabetical by center name. **Indexes:** Geographical. **Pages** (approx.): 50. **Frequency:** Irregular; latest edition 1979. **Price:** Free. **Also includes:** List of federal Job Corps regions, states covered within each region, and regional office address and phone.

★3030★
UNDERGRADUATE PROGRAMS OF COOPERATIVE EDUCATION IN THE U.S. AND CANADA
National Commission for Cooperative Education
360 Huntington Avenue   Phone: (617) 437-3778
Boston, MA 02115
Covers: Over 1,000 institutions offering co-op programs (alternate work and study). **Entries include:** Name and type of institution, city, number of co-op students, curricula available under co-op program (agriculture, humanities, etc.), length of co-op work term, number of work terms the co-op program provides, number of years required for degree, amount of credit given for co-op work. **Arrangement:** Geographical. **Pages** (approx.): 60. **Frequency:** Annual, spring. **Price:** Free.

★3031★
U.S. COLLEGE-SPONSORED PROGRAMS ABROAD
Institute of International Education
809 United Nations Plaza   Phone: (212) 883-8279
New York, NY 10017
Covers: Over 800 study-abroad programs, both undergraduate and graduate, conducted during the academic year by U.S. colleges and universities; worldwide coverage. Courses last at least one quarter. **Entries include:** Program name, sponsoring institution, courses, credits, housing, scholarships, language of instruction, related travel, teaching methods, tuition and other costs, prerequisites, etc. **Arrangement:** Geographical. **Indexes:** Institution, field. **Pages** (approx.): 175. **Frequency:** Annual, winter. **Editor:** Gail A. Cohen. **Price:** $6.00 (current and 1980 editions), plus 75¢ shipping; payment must accompany order.

★3032★
VIDEO REGISTER
Knowledge Industry Publications, Inc.
Two Corporate Park Drive   Phone: (914) 694-8686
White Plains, NY 10604
Covers: Over 1,300 companies, hospitals, universities, and religious and cultural organizations which use private or closed-circuit television for training, etc.; about 200 manufacturers of video hardware; about 200 publishers; and about 300 production and postproduction service companies concerned with television and videotaping. **Entries include:** Company or organization name, address, phone, telex, names of president and marketing officer. **Arrangement:** Users by type of organization, others by type of business. **Indexes:** Product of manufacturer. **Pages** (approx.): 200. **Frequency:** Published winter 1979; new edition expected October 1980. **Advertising accepted.** Circulation 5,000. **Price:** $34.95, plus $1.00 shipping.

★3033★
VINCENT/CURTIS EDUCATIONAL REGISTER
Vincent/Curtis
224 Clarendon Street
Boston, MA 02116
Covers: About 400 advertising independent schools, summer study programs, and camps in the United States. **Entries include:** School or program name, address, description of program, name of contact. **Arrangement:** Geographical. **Pages** (approx.): 300. **Frequency:** Annual, April. **Advertising accepted. Price:** $1.00.

★3034★
VOCED—BUYERS GUIDE ISSUE
American Vocational Association
2020 N. 14th Street   Phone: (703) 522-6121
Arlington, VA 22201
Publication includes: About 225 manufacturers and publishers of equipment and teaching aids for vocational education. **Entries include:** Company name, address. **Arrangement:** Alphabetical. **Indexes:** Product. **Frequency:** Annual, January. **Editor:** John Young, Managing Editor. **Advertising accepted.** Circulation 57,000. **Former title:** American Vocational Journal - Annual Buyers Guide Issue. **Price:** $1.00 (current and 1980 editions).

★3035★
WEEKEND EDUCATION SOURCE BOOK
Harper & Row, Publishers, Inc.
10 E. 53rd Street   Phone: (212) 593-7000
New York, NY 10022
Covers: 320 institutions which offer short residential programs for adults, usually non-degree programs and often scheduled on weekends. **Entries include:** Institution name, address, and non-specific descriptions of the institution's offerings in residential courses (as distinct from traditional extension or correspondence courses). **Arrangement:** Geographical. **Indexes:** Institution, general. **Frequency:** Published 1976. **Editor:** Wilbur Cross. **Price:** $6.95. **Other information:** Principal content of book is discussion of history and development of the concept of short residential programs and

their present status, scope, cost, etc.

★3036★
WESTERN ASSOCIATION OF SCHOOLS AND COLLEGES—
DIRECTORY
Western Association of Schools and Colleges
1614 Rollins Road   Phone: (415) 697-7711
Burlingame, CA 94010
Covers: Colleges and universities in California and Hawaii and elementary and secondary schools in California, Hawaii, Guam, American Samoa, and East Asia. **Entries include:** Institution name and address. College listings include president, degrees offered, enrollment. **Arrangement:** Alphabetical by type of institution. **Indexes:** Secondary schools by district. **Pages** (approx.): 100. **Frequency:** Annual, September. **Editor:** Lyle E. Siverson, Secretary-Treasurer. **Price:** Free.

★3037★
WHO'S WHO IN EDUCATIONAL ADMINISTRATION
American Association of School Administrators
1801 N. Moore Street   Phone: (703) 528-0700
Arlington, VA 22209
Covers: Over 18,000 school administrators in the United States, its trust territories, and foreign countries. **Entries include:** Name, position, year position assumed, education. Address is included for retired members and those for whom no position data is given. **Arrangement:** Geographical. **Indexes:** Alphabetical. **Pages** (approx.): 270. **Frequency:** Irregular; latest edition 1976; new edition expected early 1980. **Editor:** Mary R. Moncure, Director, Membership Division. **Former title:** American Association of School Administrators - Roster of Members. **Price:** $100.00 (current and 1980 editions).

★3038★
WORK-WISE: LEARNING ABOUT THE WORLD OF WORK FROM
BOOKS...
ABC-Clio Press
Riviera Campus
2040 Alameda Padre Serra   Phone: (805) 963-4221
Santa Barbara, CA 93103
Publication includes: List of publishers, distributors, dealers, and resource centers for materials about careers and career planning (suitable for children and young adults). **Entries include:** Publisher name, address. **Arrangement:** Alphabetical. **Indexes:** Author/title. **Frequency:** Not established; first edition fall 1979. **Editor:** Diane Gersoni-Edelman. **Price:** $14.95, postpaid, payment must accompany individuals' orders. **Other information:** Published in cooperation with Neal-Schuman Publishers. Principal content of publication is annotations of materials by career subject.

★3039★
YEARBOOK OF HIGHER EDUCATION
Marquis Academic Media
Marquis Who's Who, Inc.
200 E. Ohio Street   Phone: (312) 787-2080
Chicago, IL 60611
Publication includes: List of over 3,400 colleges and universities in the United States and Canada. **Entries include:** Name of institution, address, enrollment tuition, faculty, calendar system, list of key administrators and department heads. **Arrangement:** Geographical. **Frequency:** Annual, fall. **Price:** $44.50, plus $2.50 shipping. **Other information:** Bulk of publication is devoted to list of schools, but it also includes a list of associations, educational statistics, etc.

7

Social Sciences

and Humanities

★3040★
ABA NEWSWIRE [Author personal appearances]
American Booksellers Association
122 E. 42nd Street
New York, NY 10017
Covers: Author personal appearances and other activities related to promotion of new books. **Entries include:** Author name; national television, radio, and wire service appearances or other publicity, with dates; similar events in individual cities, with dates and places; upcoming major reviews. **Arrangement:** By author name, then by national and local events. **Frequency:** 49 issues yearly. **Price:** $35.00.

★3041★
**ACADEMIC LIBRARY INSTRUCTION PROGRAMS [YEAR]: A
WISCONSIN DIRECTORY**
Wisconsin Library Association
C/o Madison Public Library
201 Mifflin Street
Madison, WI 53703
Number of listings: 75. **Frequency:** First edition 1979. **Price:** $3.00.

ACSP-ASPO Guide to Graduate Education in Urban and Regional
    Planning *See* Guide to Graduate Education...

★3042★
**AD GUIDE: AN ADVERTISER'S GUIDE TO SCHOLARLY
PERIODICALS**
American University Press Services, Inc.
One Park Avenue   Phone: (212) 889-3510
New York, NY 10016
Number of listings: 2,500. **Entries include:** Periodical title, description of editorial content, founding date, frequency of publication, book review editor's name and address, circulation data, subscription information, advertising rates and other data, mailing list availability and cost, and name, address, and phone of editorial and advertising contacts. **Arrangement:** Classified by discipline (e.g., African studies, economics, etc.). **Pages** (approx.): 500. **Frequency:** Biennial, March of even years. **Editor:** Alice Duskey. **Price:** $50.00.

Advertiser's Guide to Scholarly Periodicals *See* Ad Guide: An
    Advertiser's Guide to Scholarly Periodicals

★3043★
ALL-IN-ONE DIRECTORY
Gebbie Press, Inc.
Box 1000   Phone: (914) 255-7560
New Paltz, NY 12561
Covers: 1,800 daily newspapers, 8,450 weekly newspapers, 7,000 radio stations, 900 television stations, 200 general-consumer magazines, 430 professional business publications, 2,900 trade magazines, 360 farm publications, list of the Black press, and a list of news syndicates. **Entries include:** For periodicals - Name, address, frequency, editor, circulation. For newspapers - Name, address, circulation. For radio and television stations - Names, addresses, network affiliations. **Arrangement:** Classified. **Pages** (approx.): 510. **Frequency:** Annual, November. **Editor:** Amalia Gebbie. **Price:** $40.00, payment with order; $47.00, billed.

★3044★
AMERICAN BOOK TRADE DIRECTORY
Jaques Cattell Press
R. R. Bowker Company
2216 S. Industrial Park Drive   Phone: (602) 967-8885
Tempe, AZ 85282
Covers: More than 16,700 bookstores and other book outlets in the United States and Canada. Also includes list of 6,500 United States book publishers, 1,000 United States and Canadian book wholesalers and paperback distributors, foreign language book dealers, book and literary appraisers, and rental library chains. **Entries include:** Bookstore listings include store name, address, phone, principal personnel, sidelines, type of business; new in the coming edition are SAN number (Standard Address Number), number of volumes stocked, square footage. **Arrangement:** Bookstores and wholesalers are geographical; other lists are alphabetical. **Indexes:** Bookseller/ wholesaler. **Pages** (approx.): 675. **Frequency:** Annual, fall; updating service available. **Price:** $49.95, postpaid (ISSN 0065-759X). **Send orders to:** R. R. Bowker Co., Box 1807, Ann Arbor, MI 48106 (313-761-4700).

American Booksellers Association—Convention Roster *See*
    Who's Who at the ABA [Bookselling]

★3045★
AMERICAN COMMITTEE FOR IRISH STUDIES—MEMBERSHIP LIST
American Committee for Irish Studies
C/o Professor Johann A. Norstedt
Department of English
Virginia Polytechnic Institute & State
    University
Blacksburg, VA 24061
Covers: About 600 academics and others who teach or are interested in the field of Irish or Irish-American studies. **Entries include:** Name,

address. **Arrangement:** Alphabetical. **Frequency:** Annual, September. **Editor:** Professor Johann A. Norstedt, Secretary. **Price:** $25.00.

American Economic Association—Membership Directory *See* American Economic Review—Survey of Members Issue

★3046★
AMERICAN ECONOMIC REVIEW—SURVEY OF MEMBERS ISSUE
American Economic Association
1313 21st Avenue South   Phone: (615) 322-2595
Nashville, TN 37212
Covers: About 20,000 educators, business executives, government administrators, and others interested in economics and its application. **Entries include:** Name, office address, personal data, career data, writings. **Arrangement:** Alphabetical. **Indexes:** Institution, specialty. **Pages** (approx.): 500. **Frequency:** Irregular; previous edition 1974; latest edition December 1978. **Editor:** C. Elton Hinshaw, Secretary. **Price:** $25.00, payment must accompany order.

★3047★
AMERICAN FORENSIC ASSOCIATION NEWSLETTER—DIRECTORY ISSUE
American Forensic Association
C/o Norma Cook, Department of Speech & Theatre
University of Tennessee
Knoxville, TN 37919
Covers: 1,500 teachers of argumentation and debate. **Entries include:** Name, office and home addresses, highest degree held. **Arrangement:** Alphabetical. **Pages** (approx.): 15. **Frequency:** Annual, October. **Advertising accepted.** Circulation 1,500. **Former title:** Journal of the American Forensic Association - Directory Issue. **Price:** Included in Subscription, $5.00.

★3048★
AMERICAN HISTORICAL ASSOCIATION—MEMBERSHIP LIST
American Historical Association
400 A Street, S. E.   Phone: (202) 544-2422
Washington, DC 20003
Covers: 15,000 members and 6,000 institutions, in United States and abroad. **Entries include:** Name and mailing address. **Arrangement:** By Zip code. **Price:** Membership list not available except on labels. $35.00 per thousand names, one-time use only.

★3049★
AMERICAN INSTITUTE OF PLANNERS—ROSTER
American Institute of Planners
1776 Massachusetts Avenue, N. W.   Phone: (202) 872-0611
Washington, DC 20036
Covers: About 12,000 persons engaged in comprehensive planning in government, environment, urban and rural development, and numerous other areas. **Entries include:** Name, position or title, address. **Arrangement:** Alphabetical. (Separate geographical edition published; see note below.) **Pages** (approx.): 170. **Frequency:** Irregular; latest edition 1976; new edition expected 1979. **Price:** $3.00. **Other information:** Geographic edition is published by American Institute of Planners, 3004 University Club Tower, Tulsa, OK 74119.

★3050★
AMERICAN LIBRARY ASSOCIATION—MEMBERSHIP DIRECTORY
American Library Association
50 E. Huron Street   Phone: (312) 944-6780
Chicago, IL 60611
Number of listings: 30,000. **Entries include:** Name, professional status, abbreviated office address, code indicating ALA division affiliations, type of membership. **Arrangement:** Alphabetical. **Pages** (approx.): 250. **Frequency:** Annual, summer. **Price:** $10.00. **Other information:** Many addresses are inadequate for mailing; not intended to be used as mailing list.

★3051★
AMERICAN LIBRARY DIRECTORY
Jaques Cattell Press
R. R. Bowker Company
2216 S. Industrial Park Drive   Phone: (602) 967-8885
Tempe, AZ 85282
Covers: About 30,000 United States and 2,700 Canadian academic, public, county, provincial, and regional libraries; library systems; medical, law, and other special libraries; and libraries for the blind and physically handicapped. Separate section lists over 300 library networks and consortia and accredited and unaccredited library school programs. **Entries include:** Library name, name of supporting or affiliated institution or firm, address, phone, names of librarian and department heads, budget, collection size, special collections. System listings include name and location. Library school listings include name, address, director, type of training and degrees, faculty size. Network/consortia listings include name, address, phone, names of affiliates, name of director, function. **Arrangement:** Most sections are geographical. **Indexes:** Institution name. **Pages** (approx.): 1,700. **Frequency:** Annual, fall; supplemented by "American Library Directory Updating Service," six times yearly. **Price:** Directory, $49.95, postpaid (ISSN 0065-910X); update, $50.00 per year (ISSN 0002-9793). **Send orders to:** R. R. Bowker Company, Box 1807, Ann Arbor, MI 48106 (313-761-4700).

★3052★
AMERICAN PHILOLOGICAL ASSOCIATION—DIRECTORY
American Philological Association
Department of Classics
University of Colorado   Phone: (303) 492-7737
Boulder, CO 80302
Number of listings: 2,800. **Entries include:** Name, address. **Arrangement:** Alphabetical lists of individual members and institutional members. **Pages** (approx.): 60. **Frequency:** Biennial, odd years; 1979 edition delayed indefinitely for computerization. **Editor:** Harold G. Evjeng, Secretary-Treasurer. **Price:** $5.00.

★3053★
AMERICAN PHILOSOPHICAL ASSOCIATION—ROSTER OF DEPARTMENT CHAIRPERSONS
American Philosophical Association
31 Amstel Avenue
University of Delaware   Phone: (302) 738-1112
Newark, DE 19711
Pages (approx.): 50. **Frequency:** Annual, winter. **Price:** $1.00.

★3054★
AMERICAN POLITICAL SCIENCE ASSOCIATION—DIRECTORY OF DEPARTMENT CHAIRPERSONS
American Political Science Association
1527 New Hampshire Avenue, N. W.   Phone: (202) 483-2512
Washington, DC 20036
Entries include: Name and department phone number of chairperson, address of institution. **Arrangement:** Alphabetical by institution name. **Pages** (approx.): 30. **Frequency:** Annual, November. **Editor:** Jean Walen. **Advertising accepted.** Circulation 1,500. **Price:** $20.00.

★3055★
AMERICAN POLITICAL SCIENCE ASSOCIATION—DIRECTORY OF MEMBERS
American Political Science Association
1527 New Hampshire Avenue, N. W.   Phone: (202) 483-2512
Washington, DC 20036
Entries include: Name and address. **Arrangement:** Alphabetical. **Pages** (approx.): 140. **Frequency:** Annual, January. **Advertising accepted.** Circulation 1,500. **Price:** $5.00 (1980 edition). **Other information:** Provides current addresses of members listed in association's "Biographical Directory," and addresses of new members enrolled between editions of the "Biographical Directory."

★3056★
AMERICAN PUBLISHER'S DIRECTORY
K. G. Saur Publishing, Inc.
175 Fifth Avenue   Phone: (212) 477-2500
New York, NY 10010
Covers: 25,000 publishers, including book, newspaper, periodical, newsletter, and any other type of publishers. **Entries include:** Publisher name, address, telex and phone, ISBN prefix, and fields of specialization. **Arrangement:** Alphabetical. **Indexes:** None. **Pages** (approx.): 500. **Frequency:** Irregular; first edition 1978; new edition possible 1980. **Editor:** Michael Zils. **Advertising accepted.** **Price:** $9.80.

American Society for Information Science—Handbook and
   Directory See ASIS Handbook and Directory

American Society for Training and Development—Consultant
   Directory See Training Resources

★3057★
AMERICAN SOCIETY OF CONSULTING PLANNERS—MEMBERSHIP
   DIRECTORY
American Society of Consulting Planners
1717 N Street, N. W.   Phone: (202) 659-2908
Washington, DC 20036
Covers: 120 private firms engaged in city and regional planning and other planning work. **Entries include:** Firm name, address, phone, names of principals, types of work, date established, geographic area served. **Arrangement:** Geographical. **Indexes:** Specialty, firm name. **Pages** (approx.): 60. **Frequency:** Annual. **Price:** $5.00, payment with order (current and 1980 editions).

★3058★
AMERICAN SOCIETY OF INTERPRETERS—MEMBERSHIP LIST
American Society of Interpreters
1629 K Street, N. W., Suite 5117
Washington, DC 20006
Covers: About 50 foreign-language interpreters and translators. **Entries include:** Name, address, and language combinations. **Arrangement:** Active members are alphabetical, inactive members are by language combination. **Pages** (approx.): 15. **Frequency:** Annual, April. **Editor:** Barbara Simon, Secretary-Treasurer. **Price:** Restricted circulation; apply.

★3059★
AMERICAN SOCIOLOGICAL ASSOCIATION—DIRECTORY OF
   MEMBERS
American Sociological Association
1722 N Street, N. W.   Phone: (202) 833-3410
Washington, DC 20036
Covers: 14,000 sociologists, worldwide. **Entries include:** Member name, preferred mailing address, and section memberships. **Arrangement:** Alphabetical. **Indexes:** Geographical. **Pages** (approx.): 200. **Frequency:** Annual, January. **Price:** $10.00.

American Translators Association—Membership Directory See
   Professional Services Directory of the American Translators
   Association

★3060★
AMERICAN TRAVELERS' TREASURY: A GUIDE TO THE NATION'S
   HEIRLOOMS
William Morrow & Company, Inc.
105 Madison Avenue   Phone: (212) 889-3050
New York, NY 10016
Covers: Buildings, parks, churches, etc., important in the nation's history, and museums of historic objects. **Entries include:** Name of building, museum, etc., address, notes concerning significance, etc., and hours of operation. **Arrangement:** Geographical. **Pages** (approx.): 600. **Frequency:** First published 1977. **Editor:** Suzanne Lord. **Price:** $5.95.

★3061★
ANTIQUARIAN BOOKSELLERS' ASSOCIATION OF AMERICA—
   MEMBERSHIP LIST
Antiquarian Booksellers' Association of America
50 Rockefeller Plaza   Phone: (212) 757-9395
New York, NY 10020
Covers: About 350 rare and out-of-print book dealers. **Entries include:** Company name, address, phone, contact or owner, specialties. **Arrangement:** Alphabetical. **Indexes:** Specialty, geographical, personal name. **Pages** (approx.): 90. **Frequency:** Irregular; latest edition July 1979; new edition expected 1980. **Price:** Send self-addressed no. 10 envelope with 41¢ postage.

★3062★
ARCHAEOLOGY IN AMERICAN COLLEGES
Archaeological Institute of America
53 Park Place   Phone: (212) 732-6677
New York, NY 10007
Covers: Over 175 United States and Canadian colleges and universities offering programs in archaeology and related fields. **Entries include:** Institution name, name and address of contact for further information, name of department, names of faculty members, and degrees offered. Many listings also include excavation sites and field schools sponsored. **Arrangement:** Alphabetical. **Indexes:** Degrees granted, by institution name. **Pages** (approx.): 80. **Frequency:** Irregular; previous edition 1970; latest edition 1974. **Price:** $2.50.

★3063★
ASIS HANDBOOK AND DIRECTORY
American Society for Information Science
1010 16th Street, N. W.   Phone: (202) 659-3644
Washington, DC 20036
Covers: About 3,500 information specialists, scientists, librarians, administrators, social scientists, and others interested in the use, organization, storage, retrieval, evaluation, and dissemination of recorded specialized information. **Entries include:** For individual members - Name, office or home address, office phone, title, chapter affiliation, special interest group affiliation. For institutions - Name, address, name of individual representative, if any. **Arrangement:** Alphabetical. **Indexes:** Chapter, special interest group. **Pages** (approx.): 100. **Frequency:** Annual, spring. **Advertising accepted.** Circulation 5,000. **Price:** $50.00 (ISSN 0066-0124).

★3064★
ASSOCIATED INFORMATION MANAGERS—MEMBERSHIP
   DIRECTORY
Associated Information Managers
316 Pennsylvania Avenue, S. E., Suite 502   Phone: (202) 544-1969
Washington, DC 20003
Covers: Over 600 persons responsible for information processing in industry, universities, nonprofit organizations, and government agencies. **Entries include:** Name, title, affiliation, address, phone. **Arrangement:** Alphabetical. **Indexes:** Geographic, affiliation. **Frequency:** Annual, September. **Editor:** Helena M. Strauch, Program Coordinator. **Price:** $8.95, payment with order.

★3065★
ASSOCIATION FOR ASIAN STUDIES—MEMBERSHIP DIRECTORY
Association for Asian Studies
One Lane Hall
University of Michigan   Phone: (313) 665-2490
Ann Arbor, MI 48109
Number of listings: 6,000, including 500 supporting members. **Entries include:** Name, address, primary discipline, primary occupation, country or region of greatest interest, regional conference of greatest participatory interest. Supporting member listings show name and address only. **Arrangement:** Alphabetical. **Pages** (approx.): 160. **Frequency:** Irregular; previous edition 1973; latest edition December 1977. **Former title:** Association for Asian Studies Membership Directory and Manpower Study. **Price:** $6.00, postpaid.

★3066★
ASSOCIATION FOR COMPARATIVE ECONOMIC STUDIES—
MEMBERSHIP LIST
Association for Comparative Economic Studies
C/o Prof. Elizabeth Clayton
Department of Economics
University of Missouri
St. Louis, MO 63121
Price: $30.00; available in form of mailing labels only. **Other information:** Created by merger of Association for the Study of Soviet-Type Economies and the Association for Comparative Economics.

★3067★
ASSOCIATION FOR UNIVERSITY BUSINESS AND ECONOMIC
RESEARCH—MEMBERSHIP DIRECTORY
Association for University Business and Economic Research
C/o Office of Research Administration
College of Business Administration
University of Wisconsin   Phone: (608) 262-1550
Madison, WI 53706
Covers: Institutions in the United States and abroad with centers, bureaus, departments, etc., concerned with business and economic research. **Entries include:** Name of bureau, center, etc.; sponsoring institution name, address, phone; names and titles of director and faculty; number of non-teaching staff; publications and frequency. **Arrangement:** Geographical within categories of membership. **Indexes:** Director name, institution name. **Frequency:** Annual, January. **Price:** $10.00.

★3068★
ASSOCIATION INTERNATIONAL DES INTERPRETES DE
CONFERENCE—MEMBERSHIP DIRECTORY
Association International des Interpretes de Conference
14, rue de l'Ancien Port
1201 Geneva, Switzerland
Covers: 1,500 persons in various countries capable of providing simultaneous translations in English, German, Dutch, French, and some 30 other languages. **Frequency:** Not established; latest edition fall 1977. **Price:** Free.

★3069★
ASSOCIATION OF AMERICAN UNIVERSITY PRESSES—DIRECTORY
Association of American University Presses
One Park Avenue   Phone: (212) 889-6040
New York, NY 10016
Number of listings: 76. **Entries include:** Press name, address, phone, cable and telex addresses, titles and names of complete editorial and managerial staffs. **Arrangement:** Alphabetical. **Indexes:** Personal name. **Pages** (approx.): 50. **Frequency:** Annual, September. **Price:** $5.00.

★3070★
ASSOCIATION OF STATE LIBRARY AGENCIES REPORT ON
INTERLIBRARY COOPERATION
Association of State Library Agencies
American Library Association
50 E. Huron Street   Phone: (312) 944-6780
Chicago, IL 60611
Covers: Multi-state library networks, state units responsible for interlibrary cooperation, sources of funding for cooperative programs, and persons administering interlibrary cooperation programs. **Arrangement:** By activity. **Pages** (approx.): 450. **Frequency:** Irregular; latest edition 1978. **Price:** $12.50.

Audio-Visual Equipment Directory *See* National Audio-Visual
   Association—Membership Directory

★3071★
AUTHOR'S GUIDE TO JOURNALS IN SOCIOLOGY & RELATED
FIELDS
Haworth Press
149 Fifth Avenue   Phone: (212) 228-2800
New York, NY 10010
Number of listings: About 450. **Entries include:** Publication name, address for manuscripts, publication orientation and subject interests, usual review time and delay in publication of accepted manuscripts, early publication options (if any). **Indexes:** Subject, title, keyword. **Pages** (approx.): 215. **Frequency:** Not established; first edition 1978. **Editor:** Marvin V. Sussman. **Price:** $16.95.

★3072★
AWARDS, HONORS & PRIZES
Gale Research Company
Book Tower   Phone: (313) 961-2242
Detroit, MI 48226
Covers: Volume 1 covers more than 5,000 awards given in the United States and Canada, primarily in recognition of service and achievement, although certain major competitive prizes (the Miss America competition, football's Superbowl, etc.) are also described. A separate volume covers similar awards made abroad and internationally. **Entries include:** Name of awarding body; address; exact title or name of the award, honor, prize, medal, or distinction; purpose of the award and terms of eligibility; exact form of the award (medal, sum of money, etc.); frequency of award; date established. **Arrangement:** Alphabetical by name of sponsoring organization. **Indexes:** Award name, subject. **Pages** (approx.): United States volume, 700; international and foreign, 520. **Frequency:** Irregular; previous edition 1975; latest United States-Canada volume October 1978; new international and foreign volume in preparation for late 1980 publication. **Editors:** Paul Wasserman and Janice McLean. **Price:** $50.00 (United States-Canada volume); $48.00 (1975 international and foreign volume); $65.00 (tentative, 1980 volume).

★3073★
AWARDS LIST [For poets, fiction writers]
Poets & Writers, Inc.
201 W. 54th Street   Phone: (212) 757-1766
New York, NY 10019
Covers: About 100 sponsors of grants, fellowships, and prizes offered to poets and fiction writers in the United States. **Entries include:** Name of sponsoring institution, address, description of award, name of contact. **Arrangement:** Alphabetical. **Pages** (approx.): 25. **Frequency:** Irregular; latest edition 1978; new edition expected 1980. **Editor:** Lisa Merrill, Managing Editor. **Price:** $2.50.

Bacon's Newspaper Directory *See* Bacon's Publicity Checker

★3074★
BACON'S PUBLICITY CHECKER
Bacon's Publishing Company
14 E. Jackson Boulevard   Phone: (312) 922-8419
Chicago, IL 60604
Covers: Over 4,000 trade and consumer magazines, 1,700 daily newspapers, and 8,000 weekly newspapers in the United States and Canada. **Entries include:** For periodicals - Publication name, address, editor's name, phone, publisher, circulation, frequency and issue date, types of publicity material used, and whether publication is a newsletter, charges for cuts, or uses photos. For daily papers - Paper name, address, phone, whether morning or evening, circulation, keys for about 20 editorial departments and positions (automotive editor, financial editor, book review editor, etc.), with names of incumbents. For weekly papers - Paper name, editor's name, address, phone, circulation, day issued. **Arrangement:** Two volumes; periodical volume is classified by subject or industry, then is alphabetical; newspaper volume divided between dailies and weeklies, then is geographical. **Pages** (approx.): 1,000. **Frequency:** Annual, October , with quarterly supplements. **Editor:** Wilfrid W. Budd, Vice President. **Former title:** Newspaper volume was formerly published separately

under title, "Bacon's Newspaper Directory." **Price:** $99.00, plus $1.95 shipping, including supplements; volumes not sold separately.

★3075★
BIRTH, MARRIAGE, DIVORCE, DEATH—ON THE RECORD
Reymont Associates
29 Reymont Avenue
Rye, NY 10580
Covers: About 300 state vital statistics bureaus and other official sources of personal and family records. **Entries include:** Name and address of agency, how far back records go, fees for copying. **Arrangement:** Geographical. **Pages** (approx.): 50. **Frequency:** Irregular; first edition 1977. **Editor:** D. J. Scherer. **Price:** $2.50, postpaid, payment with order.

★3076★
BOOK PRODUCTION INDUSTRY & MAGAZINE PRODUCTION—PUBLISHING PRODUCTION ANNUAL ISSUE
Innes Publishing Company
910 Skokie Boulevard   Phone: (312) 564-5940
Northbrook, IL 60062
Covers: Manufacturers of book papers and binding materials, book printers, and book binders. **Entries include:** For paper and binding material manufacturers - Company name, address. For book manufacturers - Company name, address, description of facilities, names and phones of sales contacts. **Arrangement:** Alphabetical. **Indexes:** Product (for materials). **Frequency:** Annual, September. **Editor:** Robert Licker. **Advertising accepted. Price:** $2.00.

★3077★
BOOK PUBLISHERS DIRECTORY
Gale Research Company
Book Tower   Phone: (313) 961-2242
Detroit, MI 48226
Covers: Subtitle reads, "Guide covering new and established, private and special interest, avant-garde and alternative, organization and association, government and institution, presses." Lists about 3,400 publishers of books and magazines. **Entries include:** Firm name, address, phone, names of principal executives, description of firm and its main subject interests, selected titles, discount and returns policies, etc. **Arrangement:** Alphabetical. **Indexes:** Subject, publisher name, and geographical. **Pages** (approx.): 200. **Frequency:** Latest edition August 1979. **Editors:** Annie M. Brewer and Elizabeth A. Geiser. **Price:** $85.00.

★3078★
BOOK PUBLISHING: A WORKING GUIDE FOR AUTHORS, EDITORS, AND SMALL PUBLISHERS [Self-publishing guide]
Bookman House, Division
D. Armstrong Company, Inc., Printers
2000-B Governor's Circle   Phone: (713) 688-1441
Houston, TX
Publication includes: List of organizations, suppliers, and others helpful to a self-publishing author. **Frequency:** Published 1979. **Editor:** Donald R. Armstrong. **Price:** $10.00.

★3079★
BOOKDEALERS IN NORTH AMERICA
Sheppard Press Limited
Box 42, Russel Chambers, Covent Garden
London WCZE, England
Covers: 1,300 dealers in secondhand and antiquarian books in Canada and United States. **Entries include:** Store name, address, phone, telegraphic address, proprietor, date established, type of premises, size of stock, specialty, if catalogues issued, association memberships. **Arrangement:** Geographical. **Indexes:** Alphabetical, specialty, permanent want list. **Pages** (approx.): 320. **Frequency:** Triennial in November; latest edition 1976. **Advertising accepted.** Circulation 5,000. **Price:** $12.00.

Bookhunter's Guide to California *See* Bookhunter's Guide to the West and Southwest

★3080★
BOOKHUNTER'S GUIDE TO THE MIDWEST, SOUTH, AND CANADA
Ephemera and Books
Box 19681   Phone: (714) 469-0833
San Diego, CA 92119
Other information: First edition published July 1978. Content, price, etc., same as "Bookhunter's Guide to the Northeast;" see separate listing.

★3081★
BOOKHUNTER'S GUIDE TO THE NORTHEAST
Ephemera and Books
Box 19681   Phone: (714) 469-0833
San Diego, CA 92119
Covers: 1,700 dealers in used, old, scarce, and rare books, paper Americana, periodicals, prints, autographs, and photographica. **Entries include:** Dealer name, address, special interests, whether store or mail order, and phone. **Arrangement:** By Zip code. **Indexes:** Special interests of dealers (about 900 subjects such as art deco, individual authors, Black studies, dance, slang, etc.). **Pages** (approx.): 140. **Frequency:** Biennial, July of odd years; first edition 1977; update in July of even years priced separately. **Editor:** Ray P. Reynolds. **Price:** $6.00, plus 60¢ shipping.

★3082★
BOOKHUNTER'S GUIDE TO THE WEST AND SOUTHWEST
Ephemera and Books
Box 19681   Phone: (714) 469-0833
San Diego, CA 92119
Other information: About 140 pages. Includes Alaska and Hawaii. Published biennially; first edition 1978. Content, price, etc., same as "Bookhunter's Guide to the Northeast;" see separate listing. (Incorporates "Bookhunter's Guide to California.")

★3083★
BOOKS IN PRINT
R. R. Bowker Company
1180 Avenue of the Americas   Phone: (212) 764-5100
New York, NY 10036
Description: "Books in Print" is the basic source of information concerning books offered for sale by publishers and distributors in the United States. It includes the most extensive list of United States book publishers available in a single source (about 7,000), along with bibliographical information on more than half-a-million books. The "Books in Print" data base is used for a number of specialized volumes containing lists of publishers, which are described in separate listings (see "Children's Books in Print," "Religious Books in Print," etc.). **Entries include:** For publishers - Company name, address. For books - Author, title, price, publisher, other bibliographic information as needed. **Arrangement:** Publishers, authors, and titles are alphabetical in separate sections. **Pages** (approx.): 8,800 in 2 author volumes and 2 title volumes. **Frequency:** Annual, fall; supplement published in spring. **Price:** $99.50, per 4-volume set; supplement, $49.50; postpaid, payment with order (ISSN 0068-0214 and 0000-0310, respectively). **Send orders to:** R. R. Bowker Co., Box 1807, Ann Arbor, MI 48106 (313-761-4700). **Other information:** The material in "Books in Print" is also available in subject-classified form in "Subject Guide to Books in Print," also published in the fall; $72.50, postpaid, payment with order (ISSN 0000-0159).

★3084★
BOWKER ANNUAL OF LIBRARY AND BOOK TRADE INFORMATION
R. R. Bowker Company
1180 Avenue of the Americas   Phone: (212) 764-5100
New York, NY 10036
Publication includes: Lists of job placement services and hotlines; accredited library schools; scholarships for education in library

science; library organizations; major libraries; publishing and bookselling organizations. **Entries include:** All listings usually include institution or organization name, address, phone, name of officer or contact; scholarship listings include requirements, value of grant; organization listings include officers, considerable detail. **Indexes:** General. **Pages** (approx.): 710. **Frequency:** Annual, spring. **Editors:** Nada Beth Glick and Filomena Simora. **Price:** $24.95, postpaid (ISSN 0068-0540). **Send orders to:** R. R. Bowker Company, Box 1807, Ann Arbor, MI 48106 (313-761-4700). **Other information:** Principal content is articles and surveys on status of library education, funding, cooperation, etc. Sponsored by the Council of National Library Associations.

★3085★
BRADY & LAWLESS'S FAVORITE BOOKSTORES
Sheed, Andrews, & McNeel, Inc.
6700 Squibb Road   Phone: (913) 362-1523
Mission, KS 66202
Covers: Several hundred bookstores in the United States and Canada. **Entries include:** Store name, address, hours open, specialty collections, and ordering information (for mail-order). **Arrangement:** Geographical. **Pages** (approx.): 250. **Frequency:** Published 1978. **Editors:** Frank Brady and Joann Lawless. **Price:** $12.95.

★3086★
BUSINESS ECONOMICS—MEMBERSHIP DIRECTORY ISSUE
National Association of Business Economists
28349 Chagrin Boulevard, Suite 201   Phone: (216) 464-7986
Cleveland, OH 44122
Covers: About 2,600 members of the association, including students. **Entries include:** Name, affiliation and title, address. **Arrangement:** By type of membership, then alphabetical. **Indexes:** Company name. **Pages** (approx.): 100. **Frequency:** Annual, March. **Editor:** William J. Brown. **Price:** $4.00; available to members and subscribers only.

★3087★
BUSINESS HISTORY CONFERENCE—MEMBERSHIP DIRECTORY
Business History Conference
C/o Fred Bateman
School of Business - 254F
Indiana University   Phone: (812) 337-8006
Bloomington, IN 47401
Number of listings: 150. **Entries include:** Name, affiliation, title, address. **Arrangement:** Alphabetical. **Pages** (approx.): 10. **Frequency:** Annual, fall.

★3088★
BUY BOOKS WHERE—SELL BOOKS WHERE: A DIRECTORY OF OUT-OF-PRINT BOOKSELLERS AND THEIR SPECIALTIES
Ruth E. Robinson, Books
Route 7, Box 162A   Phone: (304) 296-5140
Morgantown, WV 26505
Covers: Over 1,200 booksellers and book collectors in the United States and Canada interested in out-of-print materials. Also available in an abridged edition. **Entries include:** Book store or collector name, address; some listings include phone. Abridged edition listings include name, address, method of doing business, subject and author wants; some listings include phone. **Arrangement:** By subject or author wanted. Abridged edition arranged geographically. **Indexes:** Geographical. **Pages** (approx.): 130; abridged edition, 55. **Frequency:** Irregular; latest edition 1979. **Editors:** Ruth E. Robinson and Daryush Farudi. **Price:** $15.00; abridged edition, $5.00; $17.50 per set; postpaid, payment with order.

★3089★
CABELL'S DIRECTORY OF PUBLISHING OPPORTUNITIES IN BUSINESS, ADMINISTRATION, AND ECONOMICS
Cabell Publishing Company
Box 10372
Lamar University Station
Beaumont, TX 77710
Covers: 230 commercial and scholarly periodicals in business, administration, and economics. **Entries include:** Publication name, address, subject interests, editorial needs and procedures, audience and circulation of the publication, and acceptance rate. **Arrangement:** By title. **Indexes:** Discipline. **Pages** (approx.): 310. **Frequency:** Not established; first edition 1978; new edition expected 1981. **Editor:** W E. David Cabell. **Advertising accepted.** **Price:** $14.95, plus $1.50 shipping.

★3090★
CALIFORNIA LIBRARY STATISTICS AND DIRECTORY
California State Library
Library and Courts Building   Phone: (916) 445-4730
Sacramento, CA 95809
Covers: Public, academic, special, state agency, and county law libraries within California. Includes listings of systems, networks, and reference centers in California. **Entries include:** Library name, financial data, positions and salaries, collections and activities. **Arrangement:** Geographical. **Indexes:** Subject index to special collections within California libraries. **Pages** (approx.): 200. **Frequency:** Annual. **Editor:** Collin Clark, Information Manager. **Price:** $8.00. **Send orders to:** California State Department of Education, Publication Sales, Box 271, Sacramento, CA 95802. **Other information:** Published as supplement to "News Notes of California Libraries."

★3091★
CATALOG OF CITY, COUNTY, AND STATE DIRECTORIES PUBLISHED IN NORTH AMERICA
Association of North American Directory Publishers
270 Orange Street   Phone: (203) 624-3118
New Haven, CT 06509
Covers: About 50 publishers of city, county, and state directories and the several hundred directories they issue. **Entries include:** Publisher name, address, phone. **Arrangement:** Alphabetical. **Pages** (approx.): 50. **Frequency:** Annual. **Price:** $1.00. **Other information:** Principal content of this publication is list of city directories, arranged geographically and indicating by codes the name of publisher and what features are included in the directory. (Directories of this type usually include a listing of a large proportion of the residents of an area, including property owners and renters, along with their addresses, phones, marital status, etc. Arrangement is usually by surname, and a second section with similar arrangement in street order is also usually included.)

★3092★
CATALOG OF DIRECTORIES PUBLISHED ... BY MEMBERS OF INTERNATIONAL ASSOCIATION OF CROSS-REFERENCE DIRECTORY PUBLISHERS
International Association of Cross-Reference Directory Publishers
C/o Walter Bresser & Sons
684 W. Baltimore   Phone: (313) 874-0570
Detroit, MI 48202
Covers: 11 publishers of cross-reference directories and the approximately 275 directories they issue. **Entries include:** Publisher name, address, phone. **Frequency:** Annual. **Price:** Free. **Other information:** Principal content of this publication is a list of cross-reference directories, arranged geographically and indicating month or season of publication, price, area covered, and publisher. (Cross-reference directories include a street address section, with address, name of resident, and phone number arranged by street, and a telephone number section which gives the same information but is arranged by phone number.)

★3093★
CATALOG OF LITERARY MAGAZINES
Coordinating Council of Literary Magazines
80 Eighth Avenue   Phone: (212) 675-8605
New York, NY 10011
Covers: 700 magazines whose principal content is fiction, poetry, experimental prose, etc., or criticism of these forms. **Entries include:** Publication name, address, phone, description of content, frequency, subscription rate, date founded, dimensions, number of pages, circulation. **Arrangement:** Alphabetical. **Indexes:** Geographical. **Pages** (approx.): 65. **Frequency:** Irregular; latest edition 1978; new edition expected 1981. **Price:** Free.

Catholic Library Association—Handbook/Membership Directory
    See Catholic Library World—Catholic Library Association—
    Handbook/Membership...

★3094★
CATHOLIC LIBRARY WORLD—CATHOLIC LIBRARY ASSOCIATION HANDBOOK/MEMBERSHIP DIRECTORY ISSUE
Catholic Library Association
461 W. Lancaster Avenue   Phone: (215) 649-5250
Haverford, PA 19041
Number of listings: 4,000. **Arrangement:** Directory sections are both alphabetical and geographical. **Pages** (approx.): 70. **Frequency:** Annual, January. **Advertising accepted.** Circulation 4,000. **Price:** $20.00 (current and 1980 editions).

★3095★
CHAPTER ONE—CALENDAR OF AUTHOR APPEARANCES SECTION
Chapter One Marketing, Inc.
141 E. 44th Street, Suite 707
New York, NY 10017
Publication includes: List of author personal appearances. **Entries include:** Author name, title of book being promoted, name of publisher, date of appearance; some listings include location; no information on nature of event. **Arrangement:** Alphabetically by city name, then by date. **Pages** (approx.): 65. **Frequency:** Bimonthly through 1979; 10 issues per year thereafter. **Editor:** Leila Mustachi. **Advertising accepted.** Circulation 200,000. **Price:** $9.00 for 12 issues. **Also includes:** First chapters ("Chapter One") of new books, author interviews, etc.

★3096★
CHILDREN'S BOOKS: AWARDS & PRIZES
Children's Book Council
67 Irving Place   Phone: (212) 254-2666
New York, NY 10003
Covers: About 85 United States and international awards. **Entries include:** Award name, sponsor, address, history of award, criteria, and recipients. **Arrangement:** Alphabetical. **Indexes:** Title, author name, illustrator name, awards by categories. **Pages** (approx.): 210. **Frequency:** Biennial, fall of odd years. **Price:** $8.95, postpaid, payment with order.

★3097★
CHILDREN'S BOOKS IN PRINT
R. R. Bowker Company
1180 Avenue of the Americas   Phone: (212) 764-5100
New York, NY 10036
Publication includes: List of 1,000 publishers of children's books (other than textbooks) for all age levels through senior high school. **Entries include:** Name, address. **Frequency:** Annual, December. **Price:** $32.50, postpaid, payment with order (ISSN 0069-3480). **Send orders to:** R. R. Bowker Co., Box 1807, Ann Arbor, MI 48106 (313-761-4700). **Other information:** Principal content of publication is listings of children's books in author and title sequences. The material in "Children's Books in Print" is also available in subject-classified form in "Subject Guide to Children's Books in Print," also published in December; $32.50, postpaid , payment with order (ISSN 0000-0167).

★3098★
CHILDREN'S LITERARY ALMANAC: A DIRECTORY OF CHILDREN'S LITERATURE
George Kurian Reference Books
Columbus Avenue   Phone: (914) 793-0375
Tuckahoe, NY 10707
Covers: About 1,000 book and magazine publishers, organizations and book clubs in the United States concerned with children's literature. **Pages** (approx.): 115. **Frequency:** Biennial, even years. **Editor:** George Kurian. **Advertising accepted.** Circulation 5,000. **Price:** $12.95 (current edition); $19.95 (1980 edition). **Also includes:** Bibliographies, all-time juvenile bestsellers, and juvenile book awards.

★3099★
CHILDREN'S MEDIA MARKET PLACE
Gaylord Brothers, Inc.
Box 4901   Phone: (315) 457-5070
Syracuse, NY 13221
Covers: Publishers, audiovisual producers, wholesalers, distributors, bookstores, book clubs, associations, and organizations (federal agencies, awards sponsors) concerned with children's media. **Entries include:** Company name, address, phone, major personnel; description of company or organization concern, products or services; and frequency (for publications, special programs). **Arrangement:** Classified by product, service, etc. **Indexes:** Publishers and audiovisual distributors are indexed by format, subject, and special interest; also includes product or service index. **Pages** (approx.): 400. **Frequency:** Biennial, even years. **Editors:** Deidre Boyle and Stephen Calvert. **Price:** $16.95 (current and 1980 editions). **Other information:** Published in association with Neal-Schuman Publishers, Inc.

★3100★
CODA: POETS & WRITERS NEWSLETTER—VANITY PRESSES ISSUE [Article]
Poets & Writers, Inc.
201 W. 54th Street   Phone: (212) 757-1766
New York, NY 10019
Covers: About a dozen firms which offer to publish the works of authors and poets under various arrangements involving payment of costs and fees by the author. Includes descriptions of operations of vanity presses, reviews experiences of authors who have used their services. **Entries include:** Firm name, address, phone, and number of books issued yearly. **Price:** $1.50. **Other information:** Included in November-December 1976 issue, pages 3-12.

★3101★
COLLECTION, USE, AND CARE OF HISTORICAL PHOTOGRAPHS
American Association for State and Local History
1400 Eighth Avenue South   Phone: (615) 242-5583
Nashville, TN 37203
Publication includes: Names and addresses of persons, firms, and institutions able to provide assistance with problems related to the collection, storage, restoration, and use of historical photographs; an additional section lists sources for ordering supplies. **Entries include:** Individual or organization name, address, and description of assistance or products offered. **Pages** (approx.): 230. **Frequency:** First edition 1977. **Editors:** Robert A. Weinstein and Larry Booth. **Price:** $16.00.

★3102★
COMPUTER AND DATA SERVICES AVAILABLE THROUGH TYMNET
TYMNET, Inc.
20665 Valley Green Drive   Phone: (408) 446-7000
Cupertino, CA 95014
Covers: About 75 firms subscribing to TYMNET which offer public interactive computer-based services; data bases available through TYMNET subscribers; and computer software facilities offered through TYMNET to the public. **Entries include:** For subscribers - Company name, acronym, address, name and phone of contact; description of line of business, services offered, available data bases and languages, and computer hardware. For data bases - Description of content, name of source or compiler, name of subscriber offering

it. **Arrangement:** Subscribers and data bases are alphabetical. **Indexes:** Major application/software facility. **Frequency:** Irregular; latest edition June 1979. **Editor:** Nell Angelo, Publications Manager. **Former title:** Tymnet Subscriber's Directory. **Price:** $5.00.

Computer Readable Bibliographic Data Bases—A Directory and Data Source Book *See* **Computer Readable Data Bases—A Directory and Data...**

★3103★
COMPUTER READABLE DATA BASES—A DIRECTORY AND DATA SOURCE BOOK
American Society for Information Science
1010 16th Street, N. W.   Phone: (202) 659-3644
Washington, DC 20036
Covers: About 530 bibliographic and bibliographic-related data bases in the United States and Europe which are machine readable, designed for information retrieval use, and publicly or commercially available. **Entries include:** Each listing may include name of data base, producer, distributor, generator, availability, size, frequency, scope, subject matter, type of material covered (reports, journal articles, etc.), data elements in data base, correspondence with hard copy publications, processing centers, search center services, and user aids. **Arrangement:** Alphabetical by data base name. **Indexes:** Subject; name/acronym/synonym; producer; processor. **Pages** (approx.): 1500. **Frequency:** Biennial, odd years. **Editor:** Martha E. Williams, Director, Information Retrieval Research Laboratory. **Former title:** Computer Readable Bibliographic Data Bases - A Directory and Data Source Book. **Price:** $95.00. **Send orders to:** Knowledge Industry Publications, Inc., Two Corporate Park Dr., White Plains, NY 10604.

★3104★
CONFERENCE GROUP ON GERMAN POLITICS—DIRECTORY OF CURRENT RESEARCH
Conference Group on German Politics
1311 Delaware Avenue, S. W.   Phone: (202) 488-3361
Washington, DC 20024
Covers: 200 scholars who have had published or unpublished research projects on German politics or social science during the last five years. **Entries include:** Information on scholar and his project. **Arrangement:** Scholars, alphabetical; projects, by subject. **Pages** (approx.): 30. **Frequency:** Biennial, summer of even years. **Editor:** David Conradt, Research Coordinator. **Price:** $3.00. **Send orders to:** David Conradt, Department of Political Science, University of Florida, Gainesville, FL 32601 (904-376-5005).

★3105★
CONTACT—A DIRECTORY OF INTERPRETING BUSINESS/ECONOMIC EDUCATION PROGRAMS
Chamber of Commerce of the United States
1615 H Street, N. W.   Phone: (202) 659-6157
Washington, DC 20062
Covers: About 160 programs developed by corporations, chambers of commerce, and other organizations with the intent of communicating business and economic information "which generates positive attitudes toward business." **Entries include:** Name of organization, address, phone, description of program, group for which intended (teachers, clergy, general public, etc.). **Arrangement:** Alphabetical within corporate, chamber, or association categories. **Pages** (approx.): 60. **Frequency:** Irregular; latest edition March 1978; new edition expected early 1980. **Editor:** John Sullivan, Director. **Price:** $25.00 (current and 1980 editions).

★3106★
CONTEMPORARY LITERARY CRITICS
St. Martin's Press, Inc.
175 Fifth Avenue
New York, NY 10010
Covers: About 300 critics determined by the editorial board to be "important and influential" and writing in the English language. **Entries include:** Biographical information, bibliography, studies of the critic by

other authors, and an essay on the critic by the author. **Arrangement:** Alphabetical. **Pages** (approx.): 550. **Frequency:** Five year intervals; first edition January 1978. **Editor:** Elmer Borklund, English Faculty, Pennsylvania State University. **Price:** $25.00.

★3107★
COOPERATIVE INFORMATION NETWORK DIRECTORY OF LIBRARIES IN COUNTIES OF SAN MATEO, SANTA CLARA, MONTEREY, SANTA CRUZ, & SAN BENITO [CA]
Cooperative Information Network
Green Library, Room 200-A
Stanford University Libraries   Phone: (415) 329-8287
Stanford, CA 94305
Covers: 300 academic, public, special, and school libraries which are members of the information network. **Entries include:** Library name, address, name of contact; name of chief librarian; number of staff; hours of operation; phone; telex (if appropriate); description of holdings and special collections; access and inter-library loan policies; and publications. Individual school listings are less detailed. **Arrangement:** Alphabetical. **Indexes:** Subject, individual school name. **Pages** (approx.): 300. **Frequency:** Irregular; latest edition spring 1978; some sections updated periodically. **Editor:** Ronny Markoe, Coordinator. **Price:** Not for sale.

Council of Planning Librarians—Directory *See* **CPL Directory of Planning and Urban Research Libraries in the United States and...**

★3108★
CPL DIRECTORY OF PLANNING AND URBAN RESEARCH LIBRARIES IN THE UNITED STATES AND CANADA
Council of Planning Librarians
1313 E. 60th Street   Phone: (312) 947-2007
Chicago, IL 60637
Covers: About 300 special libraries or divisions of larger academic libraries dealing with planning. **Entries include:** Name, address, phone, hours, staff, holdings, services, special strengths, publications. **Arrangement:** Geographical. **Indexes:** Alphabetical, personal name. **Pages** (approx.): 100. **Frequency:** Irregular; latest edition 1979; new edition possible 1980. **Editor:** Jean S. Gottlieb. **Former title:** Directory of Planning Libraries. **Price:** $15.00, postpaid, payment with order.

★3109★
CRIME AND DETECTIVE FICTION: A HANDBOOK OF DEALERS AND COLLECTORS IN BRITAIN AND AMERICA
Trigon Press
117 Kent House Road
Beckenham
Kent BR3 1JJ, England
Covers: Out-of-print booksellers who specialize in crime and detective fiction, and specialist collectors in this field. **Entries include:** Name, address, special interests. **Arrangement:** Separate sections for dealers and collectors. **Pages** (approx.): 120. **Frequency:** First edition expected early 1979. **Editors:** R. and J. Sheppard. **Price:** $9.60.

★3110★
CURRENT BIBLIOGRAPHIC DIRECTORY OF THE ARTS AND SCIENCES
Institute for Scientific Information
University City Science Center
3501 Market Street   Phone: (215) 386-0100
Philadelphia, PA 19104
Covers: About 365,000 authors publishing in the sciences, social sciences, arts, and humanities whose articles have appeared in about 6,000 journals and 1,400 books during current year; international coverage. **Entries include:** Author name, affiliation, address, abbreviated citations for each publication during the period. **Arrangement:** Alphabetical. **Indexes:** Geographical, organization. **Frequency:** Annual; first edition spring 1979. **Price:** $200.00 (ISSN 0190-6003). **Other information:** Supersedes "Who Is Publishing in

Science,'' covering writers in the sciences and social sciences only, published 1967-78.

★3111★
DIRECTORY OF ACADEMIC LIBRARY INSTRUCTION PROGRAMS IN VIRGINIA
Virginia Library Association
C/o Donald J. Kenney
Carol M. Newman Library
Virginia Polytechnic Institute and State University
Blacksburg, VA 24061
Covers: About 80 Virginia libraries with user-oriented programs of library instruction. **Entries include:** Institution name, library name, address, enrollment, degrees offered; name, title, and phone of contact. **Arrangement:** Alphabetical. **Indexes:** Program type, evaluation method, written goals and objectives. **Pages** (approx.): 40. **Frequency:** Irregular; latest edition 1977; new edition expected 1981. **Editor:** William W. Prince. **Price:** $2.25.

★3112★
DIRECTORY OF AMERICAN PHILOSOPHERS
Philosophy Documentation Center
Bowling Green State University   Phone: (419) 372-2419
Bowling Green, OH 43403
Covers: Philosophy departments in American and Canadian collges and universities; philosophical societies; philosophical centers and institutes; publishers specializing in philosophy; and organizations awarding fellowships and assistantships in philosophy. **Entries include:** For institutions - Institution name and address, and names, ranks, and teaching fields of philosophy department faculty members. For societies, centers, publishers, etc. - Name, address, activities or interests. For fellowships and assistantships - Name of awarding body, address, type of assistance, dollar amount. **Arrangement:** Institutions are geographical; other sections by activity. **Indexes:** Personal name. **Pages** (approx.): 400. **Frequency:** Biennial, winter of even years. **Editor:** Archie J. Bahm. **Price:** $27.50 (current edition); $29.75 (1980 edition).

★3113★
DIRECTORY OF ARCHIVES AND MANUSCRIPT REPOSITORIES IN THE UNITED STATES
National Archives Trust Fund Board
                                        Phone: (202) 724-1630
Washington, DC 20408
Covers: About 3,250 repositories of all kinds in the United States which contain records of historical importance; 550 of these were non-respondents. **Entries include:** All listings include name of repository, address; respondent listings also include acquisitions policies, summary statement of holdings, whether a guide to the collection is available, user fees (if any), hours of service, etc. **Arrangement:** Geographical. **Indexes:** Type of repository (college library, religious institution, etc.), subject-personal name. **Pages** (approx.): 910. **Frequency:** First edition December 1978. **Price:** $25.00. **Send orders to:** Publications Sales Branch, National Archives and Records Service, Washington, DC 20408 (202-523-3164). **Other information:** Compiled by National Historical Publications and Records Commission guide program staff. Supersedes commission's 1961 volume by Philip M. Hamer, ''Guide to Archives and Manuscripts in the United States,'' and is intended as first unit of an exhaustive data base in the field. (See ''The NHPRC and a Guide to Manuscript and Archival Materials in the United States,'' ''American Archivist,'' Volume 40, Number 2, April 1977.)

★3114★
DIRECTORY OF AREA STUDIES ON U.S. AND CANADIAN CAMPUSES
Academy for Educational Development
World Studies Data Bank
680 Fifth Avenue   Phone: (212) 265-3350
New York, NY 10019
Covers: Institutions which offer programs of study in entire cultures of specific geographical areas of the world. **Entries include:** Institution name, address; name and phone of department chairman or contact; degrees offered; areas of study. **Frequency:** Annual. **Price:** $5.00.

★3115★
A DIRECTORY OF BIBLIOGRAPHIC INSTRUCTION PROGRAMS IN NEW ENGLAND ACADEMIC LIBRARIES
New England Chapter
Association of College and University Libraries
American Library Association
50 E. Huron Street
Chicago, IL 60611
Covers: 115 New England academic libraries with library instruction programs. **Entries include:** Institution name, library name, address, phone; description of institution and library administration's format; target audience; publicity methods; subject focus; supporting materials; documentation; contact person. **Arrangement:** Alphabetical. **Indexes:** Keyword, classified. **Pages** (approx.): 185. **Frequency:** Published 1978. **Editor:** Joan Stockard. **Price:** Apply.

★3116★
DIRECTORY OF BLACK AMERICANS IN POLITICAL SCIENCE
American Political Science Association
1527 New Hampshire Avenue, N. W.   Phone: (202) 482-2512
Washington, DC 20036
Covers: Over 370 Black advanced graduate students, academics, and professionals in the field of political science. A list of about 75 predominantly Black colleges and universities with political science programs is included. **Entries include:** Name, title, affiliation, address, degree, fields of study, research interests, skills and experiences relevant to non-academic employment. For colleges - Name, address, name of program, name of program contact; many listings also include phone. **Arrangement:** Alphabetical. **Indexes:** Field of interest. **Pages** (approx.): 110. **Frequency:** Not established; first edition 1977; new edition expected 1980. **Editor:** Maurice C. Woodard. **Price:** $5.00.

★3117★
DIRECTORY OF CHINESE AMERICAN LIBRARIANS
Chinese Culture Service, Inc.
Box 444
Oak Park, IL 60303
Number of listings: 400. **Entries include:** Name, office and home addresses, personal and career data. **Arrangement:** Alphabetical. **Pages** (approx.): 40. **Frequency:** Irregular; first edition June 1977; new edition possible 1982. **Price:** $5.00.

★3118★
DIRECTORY OF CONTINUING EDUCATION OPPORTUNITIES FOR LIBRARY/INFORMATION/MEDIA PERSONNEL
Continuing Library Education Network and Exchange (CLENE)
620 Michigan Avenue, N. E.
Washington, DC 20064
Covers: About 250 courses offered at 55 institutions. **Entries include:** Institution or sponsor name and address, course title, level or audience, frequency of course, fees, credit, teacher. **Arrangement:** By subject. **Indexes:** Geographical, teacher/leader name. **Pages** (approx.): 265. **Frequency:** Irregular; previous edition spring 1977; latest edition June 1979. **Price:** $22.80. **Send orders to:** K. G. Saur Publishing, Inc., 175 Fifth Ave., New York, NY 10010.

★3119★
DIRECTORY OF COORDINATORS OF CHILDREN'S SERVICES AND OF YOUNG ADULT SERVICES IN PUBLIC LIBRARY SYSTEMS SERVING AT LEAST 100,000 PEOPLE
Association for Library Service to Children
American Library Association
50 E. Huron Street   Phone: (312) 944-6780
Chicago, IL 60611
Covers: About 500 library systems, 375 children's coordinators, and

155 young adult coordinators. **Entries include:** Library name and address; coordinator's name, title, and whether children's or young adult coordinator. **Arrangement:** Geographical. **Pages** (approx.): 40. **Frequency:** Biennial, spring of odd years. **Editor:** Mary Jane Anderson, Executive Secretary. **Price:** $4.50, payment with order.

★3120★
DIRECTORY OF COURSES ON INDEXING IN CANADA AND THE UNITED STATES
American Society of Indexers
C/o James D. Anderson
Graduate School of Library and Information Studies
Rutgers University
4 Huntington St.
New Brunswick, NJ 08903
Covers: Courses on indexing offered by 35 library schools, information science programs, government agencies, professional associations, and private organizations. **Entries include:** Institution or organization name, address, contact, course number and title, instructor (including highest degree, title, subject area of degree, granting institution, and date), course description and lists of major and minor topics covered, total hours of instruction, course length and frequency, credits granted, admission requirements, tuition and fees, and textbooks. **Arrangement:** Geographical by region and state. **Indexes:** Type of indexing studied (concept indexing, abstracting, etc.). **Pages** (approx.): 40. **Frequency:** Irregular; latest edition 1976; new edition expected 1980. **Editor:** James D. Anderson. **Price:** $3.00, payment with order (current edition); $5.00 (tentative, 1980 editition). **Also includes:** Bibliography of indexing textbooks.

★3121★
DIRECTORY OF DEPARTMENTS OF SOCIOLOGY
American Sociological Association
1722 N Street, N. W.   Phone: (202) 833-3410
Washington, DC 20036
Covers: Sociology departments in nearly 2,000 institutions; coverage includes Canada. **Entries include:** Institution name, name and address of department, name and phone of chairperson, number of faculty, number of undergraduate sociology majors, number of graduate sociology students. **Arrangement:** Alphabetical. **Pages** (approx.): 100. **Frequency:** Annual, January/February. **Price:** $10.00, payment must accompany order.

★3122★
DIRECTORY OF EAST ASIAN COLLECTIONS IN NORTH AMERICAN LIBRARIES
Committee on East Asian Libraries
Association for Asian Studies
C/o East Asian Collection
Yale University Library   Phone: (203) 436-4810
New Haven, CT 06520
Covers: About 90 library collections in the United States and Canada concerned with China, Japan, Korea, and Vietnam. **Entries include:** Collection name, institution name, address, names and titles of personnel. **Arrangement:** Alphabetical. **Indexes:** Personal name. **Pages** (approx.): 20. **Frequency:** Annual, March. **Editor:** Hideo Kaneko, Librarian. **Price:** $3.00 (current and 1980 editions).

Directory of Exhibit Opportunities [Book publishing] *See* Exhibits Directory [Book publishing]

★3123★
DIRECTORY OF FRIENDS OF LIBRARIES GROUPS IN THE UNITED STATES
Friends of Libraries Committee
Public Relations Section
Library Administration and Management Association
American Library Association
50 E. Huron Street   Phone: (312) 944-6780
Chicago, IL 60611
Number of listings: Over 2,100. **Entries include:** Name of library

having a Friends group, address; does not include specific name of the group. **Arrangement:** Geographical. **Pages** (approx.): 300. **Frequency:** Not established; first edition June 1978. **Editor:** Sandy Dolnick, Bookfellows of Milwaukee. **Price:** $6.50.

★3124★
DIRECTORY OF GRADUATE AND UNDERGRADUATE PROGRAMS AND COURSES IN MIDDLE EAST STUDIES IN THE UNITED STATES, CANADA, AND ABROAD
Middle East Studies Association
New York University
Hagop Kevorkian Center
50 Washington Square South
New York, NY 10003
Number of listings: 180 institutions. Includes separate listing of 38 library collections on the Middle East. **Entries include:** For programs - Name of school; department name, address, and phone; degrees offered; courses; names of faculty members; graduate student support available, etc. For libraries - Name of sponsoring organization; name and address of library; name, title, and phone for contact person; size and description of holdings, etc. **Arrangement:** Programs, geographical; libraries, alphabetical by name of sponsoring organization. **Pages** (approx.): 160. **Frequency:** Irregular; latest edition summer 1976; new edition expected winter 1980. **Editor:** Ellen Hermanson (1980 edition). **Price:** $4.00 (current edition; ISSN 0026-3148).

★3125★
DIRECTORY OF GROWTH POLICY RESEARCH CAPABILITIES IN SOUTHERN UNIVERSITIES
Southern Growth Policies Board
Box 12293
Research Triangle Park, NC 27709
Covers: About 25 institutions with departments and personnel interested in the development of growth policy for southern states. **Entries include:** Department and institution, address, phone, name of director, description of growth policy research studies completed or underway, and names, titles, and specific interests of research personnel. **Pages** (approx.): 115. **Frequency:** Not established; first edition January 1978. **Editor:** David R. Godschalk. **Price:** Apply. Also available from National Technical Information Service, Springfield, VA 22161 (PB 284-355; $6.50, paper; $3.00, microfiche).

★3126★
DIRECTORY OF HISTORIC PRESERVATION ORGANIZATIONS OUTSIDE THE UNITED STATES
National Trust for Historic Preservation
Preservation Press
1785 Massachusetts Avenue, N. W.   Phone: (202) 638-5200
Washington, DC 20036
Covers: About 550 foreign and international nonprofit organizations and government agencies actively involved in the preservation and conservation of historic sites, districts, buildings or monuments. **Entries include:** Organization name, translation (if necessary), address. **Arrangement:** Geographical. **Pages** (approx.): 45. **Frequency:** Not established; first edition published May 1978. **Price:** Free.

★3127★
DIRECTORY OF HISTORICAL SOCIETIES AND AGENCIES IN THE UNITED STATES AND CANADA
American Association for State and Local History
1400 Eighth Avenue South   Phone: (615) 242-5583
Nashville, TN 37203
Covers: 4,450 historical and genealogical societies. Also lists and describes the 172 historical properties maintained by the National Park Service. **Entries include:** Organization name, address, phone, founding date, name of one official, number of members and staff, publications, brief note on major programs and period of interest. **Arrangement:** Geographical. **Indexes:** Alphabetical, subject specialty. **Pages** (approx.): 430. **Frequency:** Triennial; latest edition September 1978. **Editor:** Donna McDonald. **Price:** $24.00.

Directory of Historical Societies in New Jersey *See* Historical Organizations in New Jersey: A Directory

★3128★
DIRECTORY OF LIBRARIES AND INFORMATION SOURCES IN THE PHILADELPHIA AREA

Philadelphia Chapter
Special Libraries Association
C/o Acquisitions Department
Lippincott Library
University of Pennsylvania   Phone: (215) 243-5927
Philadelphia, PA 19104

Covers: 700 libraries and information centers in Philadelphia and eastern Pennsylvania, southern New Jersey, and Delaware. **Entries include:** Library name, address, phone, and names and titles of major staff members; descriptions of holdings; information on photocopying and microform facilities, networks or cooperative groups to which the library belongs, data bases operated by the library, and automated operations within the library. **Arrangement:** Alphabetical. **Indexes:** Special collection, personnel, subject, and network/cooperative group. **Pages** (approx.): 260. **Frequency:** Irregular; latest edition 1977; new edition expected 1981. **Editor:** Barbara Ann Holley. **Price:** $10.00.

★3129★
DIRECTORY OF LIBRARIES IN THE ST. LOUIS AREA

Higher Education Council of St. Louis
4378 Lindell Boulevard   Phone: (314) 534-2700
St. Louis, MO 63108

Covers: About 200 libraries. **Entries include:** Library name, address, phone, hours, names of principal personnel, size of holdings, groups served, services, subject specialties. **Arrangement:** Alphabetical by library name. **Indexes:** Personal name, subject collection. **Pages** (approx.): 100. **Frequency:** Biennial, fall of odd years. **Editor:** Cecilia Staudt. **Price:** $2.25, payment with order.

★3130★
DIRECTORY OF LIBRARIES PROVIDING COMPUTER-BASED INFORMATION SERVICES IN THE NEW YORK METROPOLITAN AREA

New York Metropolitan Reference and Research Library Agency
33 W. 42nd Street   Phone: (212) 398-0290
New York, NY 10036

Covers: About 75 libraries with terminals and data base access; about 100 data bases used by listed libraries are described. **Entries include:** For libraries - Organization name, library name (if different), address, phone, contact person, names of data bases available to the library, types of persons or groups allowed access. **Arrangement:** Alphabetical. **Indexes:** Library by data base system used, subject. **Pages** (approx.): 75. **Frequency:** Not established; first edition June 1978. **Editors:** Karen Kinney, Robert Richardson, and Susan Vaughn. **Price:** $10.00, payment with order; $15.00, billed (ISSN 0076-7018).

★3131★
DIRECTORY OF LIBRARY ORIENTATION AND INSTRUCTION PROGRAMS IN MARYLAND

Academic and Research Libraries Division
Maryland Library Association
C/o Bruce Sajdak
Undergraduate Library
University of Maryland
College Park, MD 20742

Covers: About 20 user-oriented programs of library instruction in Maryland libraries. **Entries include:** Institution name, address, name and title of contact, phone; type of institution; number of students; number of library staff and number involved in program; description of program; materials used; evaluation techniques; future plans. **Arrangement:** Alphabetical. **Indexes:** Table summary of program and institution features. **Pages** (approx.): 40. **Frequency:** Irregular; latest edition 1976. **Price:** Free.

★3132★
DIRECTORY OF LIBRARY REPROGRAPHIC SERVICES—A WORLD GUIDE

Microform Review, Inc.
520 Riverside Avenue   Phone: (203) 226-6967
Westport, CT 06880

Covers: Reprographic services in 500 major reference libraries, worldwide. **Entries include:** Library name, address, services offered, and price schedules. **Arrangement:** Geographical. **Frequency:** Irregular; latest edition May 1978; new edition expected June 1981. **Editor:** Joseph Z. Nitecki. **Price:** $12.95.

★3133★
DIRECTORY OF LIBRARY SCIENCE LIBRARIES

Library Education Division
American Library Association
50 E. Huron Street   Phone: (312) 944-6780
Chicago IL 60611

Covers: 24 facilities in accredited library schools. **Entries include:** Hours, seating capacity, number of periodicals held, classification system used, faculty rank, etc. **Arrangement:** Alphabetical. **Pages** (approx.): 50. **Frequency:** Irregular; first edition 1976; new edition possible 1980. **Editors:** Carol S. Nielson and Kathryn Hall. **Price:** $1.00.

★3134★
DIRECTORY OF MUSIC RESEARCH LIBRARIES Including contributors to the International Inventory of Musical Sources (RISM)

International Association of Music Libraries
School of Music
University of Iowa
Iowa City, IA 52242

Covers: 1,000 music research libraries and collections. Volume I: Canada and the United States; Volume II: Benelux countries, the Germanys, Scandinavia, Great Britain, and Ireland; Volume III: Spain, France, Italy, Portugal; Volume IV: Japan, Israel, New Zealand. Volume V (in preparation): Bulgaria, Czechoslovakia, Greece, Hungary, Poland, Romania, USSR, Yugoslavia. Volume VI (in preparation): South America, Central America, Mexico, Caribbean. **Entries include:** Collection or library name, address, phone, hours, services, catalogs, facilities for photocopying and listening, plus information on publications which describe the collection. **Arrangement:** Geographical. **Indexes:** Alphabetical. **Frequency:** Irregular; Volume I 1967, revised edition in preparation; Volume II 1970; Volume III 1975; Volume IV 1979; Volumes V and VI in preparation. **Editor:** Rita Benton. **Price:** Volume I DM 12; Volume II DM 26; Volume III DM 32; Volume IV, DM 28. **Send orders to:** Barenreiter-Verlag, Heinrich Schutz-Allee 29-37, 3500 Kassel, West Germany. **Other information:** Publication of this "RISM Series C" was taken over by Barenreiter in 1975.

★3135★
DIRECTORY OF NEW JERSEY SCHOOL MEDIA SPECIALISTS

School Media Services Section
New Jersey Department of Education
185 W. State Street   Phone: (609) 984-3285
Trenton, NJ 08625

Publication includes: Names of school media, audiovisual and library media specialists of public and private schools in New Jersey school systems; county libraries, institutions, and agencies with media specialists are also included. **Entries include:** School or district name, Zip code, name of specialist and title; similar information is included for state agencies and county libraries. **Arrangement:** Alphabetical by county, then by district. **Indexes:** Personal name. **Pages** (approx.): 130. **Frequency:** Irregular; latest edition 1976. **Price:** Free. **Other information:** Variant title, "School Media Directory."

★3136★
DIRECTORY OF NORTH CAROLINA HISTORICAL ORGANIZATIONS
Federation of North Carolina Historical Societies
C/o North Carolina Division of Archives and History
109 E. Jones Street   Phone: (919) 733-7305
Raleigh, NC 27611
Covers: More than 130 societies which supplied data; appendix lists names and addresses of about 50 non-respondents. **Entries include:** Name of society, address, name of director or president, dues, meeting information, staff, facilities, activities, research or library facilities, publications, date founded. **Frequency:** Annual. **Editors:** Jo Ann Williford, and Elizabeth F. Buford. **Price:** $5.00.

Directory of On-Line Bibliographic Data Bases *See* Directory of On-Line Information Resources

★3137★
DIRECTORY OF ONLINE DATABASES
Cuadra Associates, Inc.
1523 Sixth Street, Suite 12   Phone: (213) 451-0644
Santa Monica, CA 90401
Covers: Over 400 online bibliographic and non-bibliographic data bases. Non-bibliographic data bases include referral, numeric or statistical, chemical ·or physical properties of substances, and full textual data bases. **Entries include:** For data bases - Producer name, online organization through which it is available, type and amount of information, geographical and chronological coverage, and frequency of updating. For producers and online organizations - Name, address, phone. **Arrangement:** Producers and organizations are alphabetical in separate lists. **Indexes:** Subject, data base name, producer name, online organization name. **Frequency:** Quarterly; first edition September 1979. **Editors:** Ruth N. Landau, Judith Wanger, and Mary C. Berger. **Price:** $48.00, postpaid, payment must accompany order (ISSN 0193-6840).

★3138★
DIRECTORY OF ON-LINE INFORMATION RESOURCES
CSG Press, Division
Capital Systems Group, Inc.
6110 Executive Boulevard, Suite 250   Phone: (301) 881-9400
Rockville, MD 20852
Number of listings: About 200. **Entries include:** Data base name, subject, description, coverage, file size, name of vendor. Vendors' and producers' full names, addresses, and phone numbers in separate list. **Indexes:** Subject, vendor. **Frequency:** Semiannual, March and September; first edition 1978. **Former title:** Directory of On-Line Bibliographic Data Bases. **Price:** $8.00, payment with order; $10.00, billed; $30.00, two-year subscription.

Directory of Pennsylvania Historical Associations and Museums *See* Pennsylvania Directory of Historical Organizations

Directory of Planning Libraries *See* CPL Directory of Planning and Urban Research Libraries in the United States and Canada

★3139★
DIRECTORY OF PROGRAMS IN LINGUISTICS IN THE UNITED STATES AND CANADA
Linguistic Society of America
1611 N. Kent Street
Rosslyn Plaza
Arlington, VA 22209
Covers: About 350 institutions offering programs in linguistics. **Entries include:** Institution name, address; name and phone of department chairman or contact; degrees offered; fields of study; special resources; uncommonly taught languages; faculty; linguists in other departments. **Arrangement:** Geographical. **Frequency:** Irregular; new edition possible 1980. **Price:** $6.00, plus $1.00 shipping.

Directory of Spanish-Speaking/Spanish-Surnamed Librarians in the United States *See* Quien es Quien: A Who's Who of Spanish-Heritage..

★3140★
DIRECTORY OF SPECIAL LIBRARIES AND INFORMATION CENTERS
Gale Research Company
Book Tower   Phone: (313) 961-2242
Detroit, MI 48226
Covers: Over 14,000 special libraries, information centers, documentation centers, etc. **Entries include:** Library name, address, phone; sponsoring organization; subject interests; names and titles of staff; services (copying, etc.); size of collections; publications. Consortia and networks are listed separately. **Arrangement:** Alphabetical by name of sponsoring organization or institution. **Indexes:** Subject index in base volume, Volume 1. Volume 2 is 715-page ''Geographic-Personnel Index.'' **Pages** (approx.): 1,300. **Frequency:** Biennial, summer of odd years. Supplemented by ''New Special Libraries,'' published periodically between editions of base volume. **Editors:** Margaret Labash Young, Harold Chester Young. **Price:** Volume 1, $95.00; Volume 2, $80.00; ''New Special Libraries'' (Volume 3), $90.00 for inter-edition subscription. **Other information:** Contents of Volume 1 available in 5 separate subject volumes, $200.00 per set, $48.00 per volume. Volumes are: 1 - Business and Law; 2 - Education and Information Science; 3 - Health Sciences; 4 - Social Sciences and Humanities; 5 - Science and Technology (including Energy). **Also includes:** In appendixes - 155 libraries for the blind and physically handicapped, and 30 patent depository libraries.

★3141★
DIRECTORY OF STATE AND LOCAL HISTORY PERIODICALS
American Library Association
50 E. Huron Street   Phone: (312) 944-6780
Chicago, IL 60611
Covers: Over 700 state and local history periodicals, most of which are being published currently; also includes certain major local history periodicals now defunct which were indexed in national indexes. Most titles included are not listed in ''Ulrich's International Periodicals Directory.'' **Entries include:** Title, name and address of publisher, publishing history, frequency, where indexed, subscription price. **Arrangement:** Geographical. **Indexes:** Title. **Pages** (approx.): 135. **Frequency:** Irregular; latest edition 1977. **Editors:** Milton Crouch and Hans Raum. **Price:** $5.50.

★3142★
DIRECTORY OF TEACHER TRAINING PROGRAMS IN ESOL AND BILINGUAL EDUCATION
Teachers of English to Speakers of Other Languages
455 Nevils Building
Georgetown University   Phone: (202) 337-7264
Washington, DC 20057
Covers: More than 80 programs for training teachers of English as a foreign/second language at higher institutions of learning in United States and Canada. **Entries include:** Program name, address, length and requirements of program, degrees offered, courses, full-time staff, requirements for admission, tuition, fees and aid. **Arrangement:** Alphabetical. **Pages** (approx.): 210. **Frequency:** Biennial, spring of odd years. **Editor:** Charles H. Blatchford, Associate Professor. **Former title:** TESOL Training Program Directory. **Price:** $4.50. **Also includes:** ''Guidelines for the Certification and Preparation of Teachers of English to Speakers of Other Languages in the U. S.''

★3143★
DIRECTORY OF UNITED NATIONS INFORMATION SYSTEMS AND SERVICES
United Nations Inter-Organization Board for Information Systems
Palais des Nations
1211 Geneva 10, Switzerland
Covers: Information systems and services offered or available

through United Nations organizations and agencies. **Entries include:** Name of information system, name of United Nations organization or agency, address, name of contact, data base content, description of services. **Arrangement:** By agency. **Indexes:** Geographical, subject, information system name. **Pages** (approx.): 270. **Frequency:** Irregular; latest edition 1978. **Price:** Free.

★3144★

DIRECTORY OF WESTERN BOOK PUBLISHERS AND PRODUCTION SERVICES

Southern California Bookbuilders
710 Wilshire Boulevard, Suite 106
Santa Monica, CA 90401
Covers: About 300 publishers in the western states and 700 typesetters, book printers and binders, photographers, etc., serving the book publishing industry in the area. **Entries include:** Firm name, address, phone, names of principal personnel, date founded, types of books published. **Arrangement:** Classifed by activity. **Pages** (approx.): 100. **Frequency:** Became annual, fall, with fall 1977 edition. **Price:** Free. (Not verified)

★3145★

DIRECTORY OF WOMEN IN AMERICAN STUDIES

American Studies Association
4025 Chestnut Street
University of Pennsylvania   Phone: (215) 243-5408
Philadelphia, PA 19104
Covers: About 350 women students and teachers in American studies. **Entries include:** Individual name, office address, highest degree held, area of occupational specialization, personal and career data. **Arrangement:** Alphabetical. **Pages** (approx.): 70. **Frequency:** Biennial, summer of even years. **Price:** $3.00.

★3146★

DIRECTORY OF WOMEN IN PHILOSOPHY

Philosophy Documentation Center
Bowling Green State University   Phone: (419) 372-2419
Bowling Green, OH 43403
Covers: About 300 women actively teaching, writing, or interested in philosophy in the United States. **Entries include:** Individual name, address, phone, degree earned (date and institution), title of dissertation (if appropriate), area of specialization, publications, and current employment. **Arrangement:** Alphabetical. **Indexes:** Area of specialization. **Pages** (approx.): 45. **Frequency:** Irregular; latest edition April 1979; new edition expected December 1980. **Editor:** Caroline Whitbeck, of the Society for Women in Philosophy. **Price:** $5.00 (current and tentative, 1980 edition).

★3147★

EDITOR & PUBLISHER—ANNUAL DIRECTORY OF SYNDICATED SERVICES ISSUE

Editor & Publisher Company, Inc.
575 Lexington Avenue   Phone: (212) 752-7050
New York, NY 10022
Covers: Several hundred syndicates serving newspapers in the United States and abroad with news, columns, features, comic strips, editorial cartoons, etc. **Entries include:** Syndicate name, address, phone, name of owner or editor. **Arrangement:** Alphabetical. **Indexes:** Writers and artists handled by syndicates listed, titles of syndicated features. **Frequency:** Annual, in last issue in July. **Editor:** Gertrude A. Senk. **Advertising accepted. Price:** $5.00.

Education for Publishing *See* Peterson's Guide to Book Publishing Courses/Academic and Professional Programs

★3148★

EDUCATORS GUIDE TO FREE SOCIAL STUDIES MATERIALS

Educators Progress Service, Inc.
214 Center Street   Phone: (414) 326-3126
Randolph, WI 53956
Covers: Sources for about 3,700 films, filmstrips, slide sets,

audiotapes, videotapes, scripts, phonograph records, and printed materials useful in social studies. Materials are provided by industrial, governmental, and other sponsors for free use by teachers and other educators. **Entries include:** Title, brief description, date produced, length or running time, whether sound or scripts are available for silent tapes and films, whether color or black and white, booking details, source. **Arrangement:** By type of medium, then by subject. **Indexes:** Source, title, subject. **Pages** (approx.): 575. **Frequency:** Annual, fall. **Editors:** Patricia H. Suttles, Steven A. Suttles, and Rosella Linskie. **Price:** $15.25, plus $1.35 shipping.

★3149★

ENCYCLOPEDIA OF SELF-PUBLISHING

Communication Creativity
5644 La Jolla Boulevard   Phone: (714) 459-4489
La Jolla, CA 92037
Publication includes: List of organizations, suppliers, and others helpful to a self-publishing author. **Frequency:** Published 1979. **Editors:** Marilyn Heimberg Ross and Tom Ross. **Price:** $29.95.

★3150★

ENGLISH JOURNAL—"HOW TO GET PUBLISHED: A DIRECTORY OF ENGLISH LANGUAGE ARTS JOURNALS" [Article]

National Council of Teachers of English
111 Kenyon Road
Urbana, IL 61801
Covers: About 25 English language arts journals. **Entries include:** Journal name, address and name of sponsoring organization, name of editor, description of content and editorial policy. **Arrangement:** By journal title. **Frequency:** Appeared in January 1978 issue. **Editors:** Nancy Butler Bowden and Lee Mountain. **Price:** $2.50.

★3151★

EXHIBITS DIRECTORY [Book publishing]

Association of American Publishers
One Park Avenue   Phone: (212) 689-8920
New York, NY 10016
Covers: Over 600 national, regional, and state meetings of educational, scientific, technical, and library associations as well as international book fairs and selected merchandise trade shows at which publishers can exhibit text, general, and reference books and related media. **Entries include:** Name of organization sponsoring meeting; meeting date and site; name, address, and phone number of exhibit manager; approximate size and cost of exhibit space; sales restrictions (if any); date prospectus to be mailed; advertising rates of journal or program; estimated registration; number of publisher exhibits in ratio to total exhibits; dates and site of following year's meeting. **Arrangement:** Chronological. **Indexes:** Key word. **Pages** (approx.): 80. **Frequency:** Annual, fall. **Editor:** Ellen M. Bonn. **Former title:** Directory of Exhibit Opportunities (1975). **Price:** $20.00, payment with order (ISSN 0091-3790).

★3152★

FANTASY LITERATURE: A GUIDE TO FANTASY NOVELS, ANTHOLOGIES, AND CRITICISM

R. R. Bowker Company
1180 Avenue of the Americas   Phone: (212) 764-5100
New York, NY 10036
Publication includes: Lists of fantasy societies and organizations, fantasy awards, and fantasy collections in United States and Canadian libraries. **Entries include:** Organization name, address. For awards - Recipients, titles of winning publications, name and address of sponsor. **Arrangement:** By activity. **Indexes:** Author/title. **Pages** (approx.): 320. **Frequency:** Not established; first edition 1979. **Editors:** Robert Boyer, Marshall Tymn, and Kenneth Zahorski. **Price:** $14.95, postpaid, payment with order. **Send orders to:** R. R. Bowker Co., Box 1807, Ann Arbor, MI 48106 (313-761-4700). **Other information:** Principal content of publication is evaluations of about 240 works of fantasy.

★3153★

FEDERAL ASSISTANCE FOR MARITIME PRESERVATION
U. S. Advisory Council on Historic Preservation
1522 K Street, N. W.
Washington, DC 20005
Covers: Federal agencies offering monetary aid, technical assistance, or basic information and counseling for maritime preservation activities. **Entries include:** Agency name, address, phone, services. **Arrangement:** Alphabetical by agency name. **Pages** (approx.): 50. **Frequency:** First edition 1976. **Price:** Free.

★3154★

FEDERAL PROGRAMS FOR LIBRARIES: A DIRECTORY
State and Public Library Services Branch
Office of Libraries and Learning Resources
Office of Education
Health, Education, and Welfare Department
Washington, DC 20202
Covers: Nine federal library and 72 library-related grant programs; state library agencies. **Entries include:** Program name; name, address, and phone of sponsoring agency; description of program purpose, eligibility requirements, type of grant, amount available for current and next year, range and average of current awards, application deadline, legislation and program number. For state library agencies - Name, address, phone, name of administrator. **Arrangement:** Within library and library-related categories, alphabetical by program title. State agencies are geographical. **Indexes:** Applicant eligibility, authorizing legislation, CFDA number, federal agency, subject. **Pages** (approx.): 65. **Frequency:** Irregular; second edition November 1979. **Editor:** Lawrence E. Leonard. **Price:** Free; send self-addressed mailing label. **Also includes:** Bibliographies of library funding sources of information (including some publisher addresses) and of grantsmanship materials.

Fellowships and Grants of Interest to Historians *See* **Grants and Fellowships of Interest to Historians**

★3155★

FIELDWORK OPPORTUNITIES BULLETIN [Archaeology]
Archaeological Institute of America
53 Park Place
New York, NY 10007
Covers: Archaeological excavations and programs in progress, in United States and abroad; includes projects suitable for amateur workers. **Entries include:** Name, location, and purpose of project, requirements for workers, whether volunteers are accepted and whether paid positions are available, name and address of person receiving applications, remuneration, and whether work carries college credit. **Arrangement:** Geographical. **Frequency:** Annual, January. **Price:** $3.50, postpaid.

★3156★

FIGHTERS FOR INDEPENDENCE: A GUIDE TO SOURCES OF BIOGRAPHICAL INFORMATION ON SOLDIERS AND SAILORS OF THE AMERICAN REVOLUTION
University of Chicago Press
5801 Ellis Avenue   Phone: (312) 753-3344
Chicago, IL 60637
Covers: About 875 collections of and guides to print and nonprint military records, diaries, journals, autobiographies, and biographies. **Entries include:** For collections - Name, address, contact, type of material, names included or coverage. For guides - Title, publisher name and city, names included or coverage. **Indexes:** Subject. **Pages** (approx.): 130. **Frequency:** Published 1977. **Editors:** J. Todd White and Charles H. Lesser. **Price:** $8.00.

★3157★

FINANCIAL ASSISTANCE FOR LIBRARY EDUCATION
Standing Committee on Library Education
American Library Association
50 E. Huron Street   Phone: (312) 944-6780
Chicago, IL 60611
Covers: Scholarships, grants, etc., for assistance in library education. **Entries include:** Amount of award, number of awards available, requirements. **Arrangement:** State awards are geographical, regional and national are alphabetical. **Indexes:** Assistance for special groups and degrees other than at master's level. **Pages** (approx.): 80. **Frequency:** Annual, fall. **Editor:** Margaret Myers.

★3158★

FOLKLIFE AND THE FEDERAL GOVERNMENT: A GUIDE TO ACTIVITIES, RESOURCES, FUNDS, AND SERVICES
American Folklife Center
Library of Congress   Phone: (202) 426-5000
Washington, DC 20540
Covers: 55 federal programs and federally assisted activities of possible help to persons interested in American folklife (art, anthropology, language, etc.). **Entries include:** Program name, name of sponsoring agency, address, description of program, name of contact. **Pages** (approx.): 150. **Frequency:** First published 1978. **Editor:** Linda C. Coe. **Price:** $2.75 (S/N 030-000-00091-9). **Send orders to:** Government Printing Office, Washington, DC 20402.

★3159★

FOREIGN AREA PROGRAMS AT NORTH AMERICAN UNIVERSITIES: A DIRECTORY
California Institute of Public Affairs
Box 10   Phone: (714) 624-5212
Claremont, CA 91711
Covers: Over 700 institutions in the United States and Canada offering programs of study that deal with several aspects of one geographic area. **Entries include:** Institution name, address, phone; name and title of program director; degrees offered; general areas of research interest; countries or sub-regions of special interest; publications. **Arrangement:** Geographical (by location of institution). **Indexes:** Region, country. **Pages** (approx.): 95. **Frequency:** First edition October 1979. **Price:** $22.50, plus $1.59 shipping.

Gebbie Press All-in-One Directory *See* **All-in-One Directory**

★3160★

GOVERNMENT DEPOSITORY LIBRARIES
Joint Committee on Printing
United States Congress
Room S-151
United States Capitol   Phone: (202) 224-5241
Washington, DC 20402
Covers: About 1,225 libraries designated as government depositories. **Entries include:** District number, city, library name, address, phone, and year designated. If library name is different from institution name, both are given. **Arrangement:** Geographical. **Pages** (approx.): 45. **Frequency:** Irregular; latest edition April 1979. **Send orders to:** Government Printing Office, Washington, DC 20402. **Also includes:** Present law governing depository libraries.

★3161★

GRADUATE LIBRARY SCHOOL PROGRAMS ACCREDITED BY THE AMERICAN LIBRARY ASSOCIATION
Committee on Accreditation
American Library Association
50 E. Huron Street
Chicago, IL 60611
Covers: Over 65 institutions in the United States and Canada which offer graduate programs in library science. **Entries include:** Institution name, address; name and phone of department chairman or contact; degrees offered. **Arrangement:** Geographical. **Frequency:** Semiannual, March and October. **Price:** Free; send stamped, self-

addressed no. 10 envelope.

Graduate Study in Economics *See* Guide to Graduate Study in
Economics and Agricultural Economics

★3162★

GRANTS AND AWARDS AVAILABLE TO AMERICAN WRITERS

P. E. N. American Center
47 Fifth Avenue   Phone: (212) 255-1977
New York, NY 10003
Covers: 400 domestic and foreign grants, primarily of $500.00 or
more. **Entries include:** Name of award, address, description,
stipulations, application information, and deadline. **Arrangement:**
Alphabetical. **Pages** (approx.): 65. **Frequency:** Annual. **Former title:**
List of Grants and Awards Available to American Writers. **Price:**
$2.25 to individuals ($2.95, tentative, 1980 edition); $5.50 to
libraries; plus 50¢ shipping. **Also includes:** List of State Arts Councils.

★3163★

GRANTS AND FELLOWSHIPS OF INTEREST TO HISTORIANS

American Historical Association
400 A Street, S. E.   Phone: (202) 544-2422
Washington, DC 20003
Covers: 110 sources of funding (scholarships, fellowships,
internships) in the United States and abroad for graduate students and
researchers in history. **Arrangement:** Alphabetical. **Pages** (approx.):
70. **Frequency:** Annual, fall. **Editor:** Gregory Coin. **Former title:**
Fellowships and Grants of Interest to Historians. **Price:** $4.00.

Guide to Archives and Manuscripts in the United States *See*
Directory of Archives and Manuscript Repositories in the
United States

Guide to Book Publishing Courses... *See* Peterson's Guide to Book
Publishing Courses/Academic and Professional Programs

★3164★

GUIDE TO DEPARTMENTS OF ANTHROPOLOGY

American Anthropological Association
1703 New Hampshire Avenue, N. W.   Phone: (202) 232-8800
Washington, DC 20009
Covers: About 390 departments of anthropology in academic
institutions, museums, and research associations. **Entries include:**
Institution name, address; degrees offered; number and names of
faculty and research staff; anthropologists in other departments or
programs; graduate student support available; degree requirements;
number of degrees granted; and special programs, resources, and
facilities. **Indexes:** Personal name. **Pages** (approx.): 435. **Frequency:**
Annual, fall. **Editor:** Barbara L. Ross, Production Editor. **Price:** $8.00.
Also includes: Statistical data related to study and teaching of
anthropology.

★3165★

GUIDE TO DEPARTMENTS OF HISTORY

American Historical Association
400 A Street, S. E.   Phone: (202) 544-2422
Washington, DC 20003
Covers: 260 United States and Canadian departments of history and
research institutions, and 5,000 faculty members. **Entries include:**
School name, address, names of faculty members with their areas of
specialization, tuition, enrollment, etc. **Arrangement:** Alphabetical.
Indexes: Department specialties. **Pages** (approx.): 450. **Frequency:**
Annual, fall. **Price:** $12.50.

★3166★

GUIDE TO GRADUATE DEPARTMENTS OF SOCIOLOGY

American Sociological Association
1722 N Street, N. W.   Phone: (202) 833-3410
Washington, DC 20036
Covers: Over 200 departments of sociology offering master's and/or
Ph.D. degrees in the United States. **Entries include:** Institution name,

address, name of department, degrees offered, special programs
available, tuition cost; name and rank of faculty members, highest
degree held, institution and date of degree; student enrollment figures,
dissertation titles of recent Ph.D.s, and current positions of recent
graduates. **Arrangement:** Alphabetical. **Indexes:** Personal name,
holders of doctorates, special teaching interest. **Pages** (approx.): 300.
Frequency: Annual, February. **Price:** $10.00.

★3167★

**GUIDE TO GRADUATE EDUCATION IN URBAN AND REGIONAL
PLANNING**

Association of Collegiate Schools of Planning
C/o American Planning Association
1313 E. 60th Street   Phone: (312) 947-2560
Chicago, IL 60637
Covers: About 85 master's degree programs and 20 doctoral
programs. **Entries include:** School name, program name, application
address, admission requirements, costs, curriculum, faculty,
description of program. **Indexes:** Specializations available. **Pages**
(approx.): 400. **Frequency:** Irregular; latest edition 1978. **Editor:**
Roger Hamlin. **Former title:** ACSP-ASPO Guide to Graduate Education
in Urban and Regional Planning. **Price:** $11.95.

★3168★

**GUIDE TO GRADUATE STUDY IN ECONOMICS AND AGRICULTURAL
ECONOMICS in the United States of America and Canada**

Economics Institute
University of Colorado
Boulder, CO 80309
Number of listings: 280. **Entries include:** University name, address,
description of individual department programs. **Arrangement:**
Alphabetical. **Indexes:** Geographical. **Former title:** Irregular; latest
edition 1977. **Editors:** Wyn F. Owen and George H. Antoine.
Price: $11.50. **Send orders to:** Richard D. Irwin, Inc., 1818 Ridge
Road, Homewood, IL 60430 (312-468-9200). **Other information:**
Published under the auspices of the American Economic Association
and the American Agricultural Economics Association.

★3169★

GUIDE TO GRADUATE STUDY IN POLITICAL SCIENCE

American Political Science Association
1527 New Hampshire Avenue, N. W.   Phone: (202) 483-2512
Washington, DC 20036
Covers: Academic institutions offering master's and Ph.D. programs.
Entries include: Admissions policy, costs, financial aid, names and
specializations of faculty. **Arrangement:** Alphabetical by institution.
Indexes: Personal name. **Pages** (approx.): 380. **Frequency:** Annual,
January. **Editor:** Jean Walen. **Advertising accepted.** Circulation
4,000. **Price:** $8.00 (tentative, 1980 edition).

★3170★

GUIDE TO HUMANITIES RESOURCES IN THE SOUTHWEST

Neal-Schuman Publishers, Inc.
64 University Place   Phone: (212) 473-5170
New York, NY 10003
Covers: More than 400 library and museum collections emphasizing
the humanities and located in Arizona, Arkansas, Louisiana, New
Mexico, Oklahoma, and Texas; a separate section lists about 350
humanities scholars. **Entries include:** Library or museum name,
address, phone, and collection emphasis (fine arts, music, etc.).
Arrangement: Geographical. **Indexes:** Collection and subject. **Pages**
(approx.): 240. **Frequency:** Published 1978. **Price:** $24.50. **Send
orders to:** American Bibliographical Center - Clio Press, Riviera
Campus, 2040 A.P.S., Box 4397, Santa Barbara, CA 93103. **Other
information:** Compiled by Southwestern Library Association.

★3171★

GUIDE TO MANUSCRIPT COLLECTIONS & INSTITUTIONAL RECORDS IN OHIO

Society of Ohio Archivists
191 E. Tulane Road   Phone: (614) 262-0608
Columbus, Oh 43202
Covers: Repositories of documents with vital statistics and historical information in Ohio. **Entries include:** Repository name, address, description of records including type and date. **Arrangement:** By county. **Frequency:** Irregular; latest edition 1974. **Editor:** Frank Levstik. **Price:** $4.00.

★3172★

GUIDE TO MICROFORMS IN PRINT

Microform Review, Inc.
520 Riverside Avenue   Phone: (203) 226-6967
Westport, CT 06880
Covers: Over 400 micropublishers issuing material in microfilm and microfiche formats, worldwide, who offer more than 80,000 titles. Includes commercial, association, government, and other sources. Same list is included in publisher's ''Subject Guide to Microforms in Print.'' **Entries include:** Publisher name, address, phone. **Frequency:** Both annual, March. **Former title:** Incorporates ''International Microforms in Print.'' **Price:** $49.50 each. **Other information:** Principal content of both publications is bibliographic information concerning works published in microform. Material in ''Guide'' is arranged by author or other main entry.

★3173★

GUIDE TO NORTH CAROLINA HISTORICAL HIGHWAY MARKERS

Division of Archives and History
North Carolina Department of Cultural Resources
109 E. Jones Street
Raleigh, NC 27611
Covers: Over 1,200 highway markers for historical sites in North Carolina. **Entries include:** Marker identification code or name, location, description of site's historical significance. **Arrangement:** By historical district. **Indexes:** Subject, title, county. **Pages** (approx.): 265. **Frequency:** Irregular; latest edition 1979; new edition expected 1984. **Editor:** Jerry C. Cashion. **Price:** $2.50, plus 50¢ shipping.

Guide to Programs in Linguistics in the U.S. and Canada *See* **LSA Bulletin—Directory of Programs in Linguistics...**

★3174★

GUIDE TO U.S. ARMY MUSEUMS AND HISTORIC SITES

U. S. Army Center of Military History
Army Department
1000 Independence Avenue, S. W.   Phone: (202) 693-5041
Washington, DC 20402
Covers: 300 United States Army museums and historic sites on Army property and other Defense Department and federal museums with military history orientation, as well as private, state, and municipal military museums or museums with significant military collections. **Entries include:** Name of museum, address, phone, names of chief personnel, hours, description of collection; historic sites section includes location and description only. Appendix includes guide maps to Army posts. **Arrangement:** Geographical. **Pages** (approx.): 120. **Frequency:** Irregular; latest edition 1975. **Editor:** Norman Miller Cary, Jr., Historian. **Price:** $3.00. **Send orders to:** Government Printing Office, Washington, DC 20402.

★3175★

GUIDE TO WRITING AND PUBLISHING IN THE SOCIAL AND BEHAVIORAL SCIENCES

John Wiley & Sons, Inc.
605 Third Avenue   Phone: (212) 867-9800
New York, NY 10016
Publication includes: List of about 500 journals in social and behavioral sciences. **Entries include:** Title, address for manuscripts or queries, publication orientation and subject interests, usual review time and delay in publication of accepted manuscripts, publishing or submission fees, length and style requirements. **Arrangement:** Alphabetical. **Frequency:** Not established; first edition 1977. **Author:** Carolyn J. Mullins. **Price:** $9.95.

★3176★

GUIDEBOOK TO HISTORIC WESTERN PENNSYLVANIA

University of Pittsburgh Press
                                            Phone: (412) 624-4110
Pittsburgh, PA 15260
Covers: 1,300 historical sites in 26 counties of western Pennsylvania, including homes, churches, forts, manufacturing plants, bridges, etc., both preserved sites and ruins; includes some twentieth-century sites. **Entries include:** Site name, location, address (if applicable), description and explanation of significance, other details as relevant. **Arrangement:** Geographical. **Indexes:** Site and proper name. **Pages** (approx.): 300. **Frequency:** Published 1976. **Editor:** George Swetnam. **Price:** $12.95, cloth; $5.95, paper.

★3177★

HANDBOOK OF BLACK LIBRARIANSHIP

Libraries Unlimited, Inc.
Box 263   Phone: (303) 770-1220
Littleton, CO 80160
Publication includes: Lists of academic libraries and undergraduate schools or departments of library science in predominantly Black institutions; units of public library systems serving predominantly Black communities; libraries named for Afro-Americans; Black book publishers; Black-owned bookstores. **Entries include:** For schools - School name, address, history, degrees granted, number of faculty and student enrollment. Other entries include similar relevant details. **Arrangement:** Publishers are alphabetical; other lists are geographical. **Pages** (approx.): 400. **Frequency:** First published 1977. **Editors:** E. J. Josey and Ann Allen Shockley. **Price:** $18.50.

★3178★

HERE WAS THE REVOLUTION: HISTORIC SITES OF THE WAR FOR AMERICAN INDEPENDENCE

National Park Service
Interior Department
Washington, DC 20242
Covers: Existing sites and buildings associated with the American Revolutionary War, most open to the public. **Entries include:** Name of site, address, historical importance, descriptive information, present owner, and whether open to the public. **Arrangement:** Geographical. **Pages** (approx.): 330. **Frequency:** First edition 1976. **Price:** $6.20 (S/N 024-005-00608-7). **Send orders to:** Government Printing Office, Washington, DC 20402.

★3179★

HISPANIA—DIRECTORY ISSUE

American Association of Teachers of Spanish and Portuguese
Holy Cross College   Phone: (617) 793-2200
Worcester, MA 01610
Covers: 15,000 members. **Entries include:** Name and address. **Arrangement:** Alphabetical. **Pages** (approx.): 130. **Frequency:** Annual, October. **Editor:** Richard B. Klein. **Advertising accepted.** Circulation 15,000. **Price:** $3.75; not sold for commercial purposes.

★3180★

HISTORIC AMERICAN ENGINEERING RECORD CATALOG

National Park Service
Interior Department
Washington, DC 20242
Covers: Significant historic engineering and industrial sites for which archival documentation (including drawings, photographs, reports, and motion pictures) has been deposited in the Library of Congress. **Entries include:** Site name, address, construction date, map location, descriptive information, file number, amount and type of documentation, and type of landmark designation (National Historic Civil Engineering Landmark, etc.). **Arrangement:** Geographical. **Pages**

349

(approx.): 200. **Frequency:** First edition 1977. **Price:** $3.50.

★3181★
HISTORIC PRESERVATION GRANTS-IN-AID CATALOG
Office of Archaeology and Historic Preservation
National Park Service
Interior Department
Washington, DC 20242
Covers: 840 grant-assisted projects undertaken since 1966 to acquire and preserve properties listed in the National Register of Historic Places. **Entries include:** Name of site, address, present owner, historical significance, use of grant, project number, and amount of grant; does not include application forms or advice on winning grants. **Arrangement:** Geographical. **Pages (approx.):** 245. **Frequency:** Published 1976. **Price:** $3.15. **Send orders to:** Government Printing Office, Washington, DC 20402.

★3182★
HISTORICAL MANUSCRIPT DEPOSITORIES IN PENNSYLVANIA
Pennsylvania Historical and Museum Commission
William Penn Museum Building   Phone: (717) 787-3034
Harrisburg, PA 17120
Covers: 105 historical societies, colleges, universities, churches, libraries, and other Pennsylvania institutions. **Entries include:** Name, address, name of administrator, hours, amount and type of holdings, publications describing collection, copy services. **Arrangement:** Geographical. **Indexes:** Subject/personal name. **Pages (approx.):** 75. **Frequency:** Irregular; latest edition 1965. **Editor:** Irwin Richman. **Price:** $1.50.

★3183★
HISTORICAL ORGANIZATIONS IN NEW JERSEY: A DIRECTORY
New Jersey Historical Commission
113 W. State Street   Phone: (609) 292-6062
Trenton, NJ 08625
Covers: About 290 public and private historical organizations in New Jersey. **Entries include:** Organization name, address, phone; hours open; description of holdings; publications; programs offered; number of members and meetings. **Arrangement:** By town. **Indexes:** Organization by county; general. **Pages (approx.):** 60. **Frequency:** Irregular; latest edition 1977. **Editor:** Richard Waldron. **Former title:** Directory of Historical Societies in New Jersey. **Price:** $2.50.

★3184★
HISTORY OF SCIENCE SOCIETY—DIRECTORY OF MEMBERS
History of Science Society
"Isis" Editorial Office
215 S. 34th Street D-6
University of Pennsylvania   Phone: (215) 263-5575
Philadelphia, PA 19104
Number of listings: 1,500. **Entries include:** Name, office and home address, office and home phone numbers, highest degree held, institution granting degree, areas of occupational specialization. **Arrangement:** Alphabetical. **Indexes:** Geographical, field of expertise. **Pages (approx.):** 110. **Frequency:** Irregular; latest edition fall 1976; new edition expected January 1980. **Advertising accepted.** Circulation 1,500. **Price:** $6.00 (1980 edition).

★3185★
HISTORY TEACHER—"FEDERAL AGENCIES EMPLOYING HISTORIANS IN THE DISTRICT OF COLUMBIA AREA" [Article]
Society for History Education
California State University
Long Beach CA 90840
Number of listings: 50. **Entries include:** Agency name, name of director or contact, address, phone. **Frequency:** Appeared in February 1978 issue. **Editors:** Roberta Pigangi, et al. **Price:** Not for sale.

Information Industry Association—Membership Directory *See* Information Sources: The IIA Membership Directory

★3186★
INFORMATION MARKET PLACE
R. R. Bowker Company
1180 Avenue of the Americas   Phone: (212) 764-5100
New York, NY 10036
Covers: About 5,000 firms and individuals who produce information products or supply or service the information industry, including data processing services and equipment manufacturers, training and development organizations, indexers and translators; about 400 producers of publicly available data bases and computerized indexes and 1,000 data bases and 1,200 indexes identified by name and content; networks; information brokers. International coverage. **Arrangement:** Three sections: Production, distribution, retailing. Production and Retailing are by product type, then alphabetical with subject and specific product/service indexes. **Pages (approx.):** 270. **Frequency:** Biennial, even years. **Price:** $21.50, postpaid. **Send orders to:** R. R. Bowker Co., Box 1807, Ann Arbor, MI 48106 (313-761- 4700). **Also includes:** "Names and Numbers," an index of personnel with address and phone. **Other information:** Co-published with Learned Information (Europe) Ltd.; title outside western hemisphere is "Information Trade Directory."

★3187★
INFORMATION SOURCES: THE IIA MEMBERSHIP DIRECTORY
    [Information services and publishers]
Information Industry Association
316 Pennsylvania Avenue, S. E., Suite 502   Phone: (301) 654-4150
Washington, DC 20003
Covers: Over 120 companies producing information products, data bases, microforms, online services, on-demand services, etc., and publishers in the field. Entries are prepared by companies described. **Entries include:** Company name, address, phone, names of executives, trade and brand names, and detailed product descriptions. **Arrangement:** Alphabetical. **Indexes:** Product, personal name. **Pages (approx.):** 260. **Frequency:** Annual; new edition expected April 1980. **Price:** $10.00 (current edition); $15.00 (1980 edition).

Information Trade Directory *See* Information Market Place

★3188★
INSTITUTE OF MANAGEMENT SCIENCES/OPERATIONS RESEARCH SOCIETY OF AMERICA—COMBINED MEMBERSHIP DIRECTORY
Institute of Management Sciences
146 Westminster Street   Phone: (401) 274-2525
Providence, RI 02903
Covers: Over 11,500 managers, educators, and practicing management scientists; international coverage. **Entries include:** Name, address, affiliations within organization. **Arrangement:** Alphabetical. **Indexes:** Geographical. **Pages (approx.):** 260. **Frequency:** Biennial, even years. **Advertising accepted.** Circulation 11,500. **Price:** $15.00; restricted use.

★3189★
INSTITUTIONS WHERE SLA MEMBERS ARE EMPLOYED
Special Libraries Association
235 Park Avenue South   Phone: (212) 777-8136
New York, NY 10003
Covers: About 5,900 business firms, organizations, government agencies, and other institutions in which members of the association are employed. **Pages (approx.):** 160. **Frequency:** Published 1977. **Price:** $15.50.

★3190★
INTERDISCIPLINARY STUDIES IN THE HUMANITIES
Scarecrow Press, Inc.
52 Liberty Street   Phone: (201) 548-8600
Metuchen, NJ 08840
Covers: About 800 colleges and universities which offer formal interdisciplinary academic programs in humanities. **Entries include:** Institution name, address, descriptions of degree and non-degree

courses; many entries include names of contacts. **Arrangement:** Separate sections for two-year and four-year schools. **Indexes:** Program title. **Pages** (approx.): 1,100. **Frequency:** Not established; first edition 1977. **Editor:** Elizabeth Bayerl. **Price:** $37.50.

★3191★

INTERNATIONAL ASSOCIATION OF SCHOOL LIBRARIANSHIP—
        MEMBERSHIP DIRECTORY
International Association of School Librarianship
C/o Dr. Jean E. Lowrie, Executive Secretary
School of Librarianship
Western Michigan University   Phone: (616) 383-1849
Kalamazoo, MI 49008
Covers: 530 members engaged in some form of school library service; international coverage. **Frequency:** Biennial, January of even years. **Editor:** Bernice Wiese. **Price:** $1.50 (1980 edition).

★3192★

INTERNATIONAL DIRECTORY OF ANTIQUARIAN BOOKSELLERS
International League of Antiquarian Booksellers
3 Kron-Prinsens-Gade
1114 Copenhagen K, Denmark
Covers: 1,275 dealers in out-of-print or rare books in the United States and Europe. **Entries include:** Firm name, address, phone, names of executives, specialties. **Arrangement:** Geographical. **Indexes:** Alphabetical, specialty. **Frequency:** Irregular; previous edition 1973; latest edition fall 1976. **Editors:** Hans Bagger and Heinz Pummer. **Price:** $15.00.

★3193★

INTERNATIONAL DIRECTORY OF BOOK COLLECTORS
Trigon Press
117 Kent House Road
Beckenham
Kent BR3 1JJ, England
Number of listings: Over 2,000. **Entries include:** Name, address, collecting interests, memberships. **Indexes:** Subject, author/illustrator. **Frequency:** Triennial; latest edition 1978. **Editors:** R. and J. Sheppard. **Price:** $32.50, postpaid, payment with order. **Send orders to:** R. R. Bowker Co., Box 1807, Ann Arbor, MI 48106.

★3194★

INTERNATIONAL DIRECTORY OF BOOKSELLERS
K. G. Saur Publishing, Inc.
175 Fifth Avenue   Phone: (212) 477-2500
New York, NY 10010
Covers: More than 63,000 booksellers; includes list of national booksellers' associations. **Entries include:** Firm name, address, phone, specialties. **Arrangement:** Geographical. **Indexes:** Specialty. **Pages** (approx.): 950. **Frequency:** Annual; first edition 1978. **Editor:** Michael Zils. **Advertising accepted. Price:** $108.50.

★3195★

INTERNATIONAL DIRECTORY OF CENTERS FOR ASIAN STUDIES
Asian Research Service
Box 2232
G. P. O.
Hong Kong
Entries include: Center name, address, phone, year established, area of research, name of director, number and names of staff, publications, universities or organizations with which affiliated. **Arrangement:** Geographical. **Indexes:** Alphabetical. **Frequency:** Irregular; new edition expected January 1980. **Editor:** Nelson Leung. **Price:** $15.00 (1980 edition).

★3196★

INTERNATIONAL DIRECTORY OF LITTLE MAGAZINES AND SMALL
        PRESSES
Dustbooks
Box 1056   Phone: (916) 877-6110
Paradise, CA 95969
Covers: Over 2,500 listings for small, independent magazines, presses and papers. **Entries include:** Name, address, size, circulation, frequency, price, type of material used, number of issues or books published annually, and other pertinent data. **Arrangement:** Alphabetical. **Indexes:** Subject; regional. **Pages** (approx.): 500. **Frequency:** Annual, July. **Editor:** Len Fulton. **Advertising accepted.** Circulation 10,000. **Price:** $15.95, cloth; $11.95, paper.

★3197★

INTERNATIONAL DIRECTORY OF MEDIEVALISTS
K. G. Saur Publishing, Inc.
175 Fifth Avenue   Phone: (212) 477-2500
New York, NY 10010
Covers: About 6,000 persons worldwide who have a special interst in medieval history, including anthropologists, archaeologists, cartographers, church historians, ethnologists, linguists, art historians, natural scientists, and others. **Entries include:** Name, address, birth date, education, career, special interests, bibliography. **Arrangement:** Alphabetical. **Indexes:** Specialty. **Pages** (approx.): 1,000, two volumes. **Frequency:** Irregular; latest edition May 1979. **Price:** $129.00. **Other information:** Compiled by Centre National de la Recherche Scientifique, Paris.

★3198★

INTERNATIONAL DIRECTORY OF SOCIAL SCIENCE RESEARCH
        COUNCILS AND ANALOGOUS BODIES
K. G. Saur Publishing, Inc.
175 Fifth Avenue   Phone: (212) 477-2500
New York, NY 10010
Covers: Nearly 30 national organizations and 5 regional organizations concerned with social science research; worldwide coverage. **Entries include:** Organization name, address; names, titles, and addresses of officers; organizational structure; publications; programs; and international activities. **Arrangement:** Alphabetical. **Pages** (approx.): 170. **Frequency:** First edition 1979. **Price:** $14.80. **Other information:** Compiled by the Conference of National Social Science Councils and Analogous Bodies.

★3199★

INTERNATIONAL DIRECTORY ON ARCHIVES
K. G. Saur Publishing, Inc.
175 Fifth Avenue   Phone: (212) 477-2500
New York, NY 10010
Covers: 2,500 archives open to the public and determined by the editors to have materials of value for historical research; worldwide coverage. **Entries include:** Collection name, name of institution (if different), address; accessibility; number of volumes; nature of materials; printed guides; subject coverage. **Arrangement:** Geographical. **Pages** (approx.): 480. **Frequency:** Irregular; latest edition 1975. **Price:** $52.75. **Other information:** Edited by the International Council on Archives.

★3200★

INTERNATIONAL FEDERATION OF LIBRARY ASSOCIATIONS AND
        INSTITUTIONS—DIRECTORY
International Federation of Library Associations and Institutions
Netherlands Congress Building
The Hague, Netherlands 2508 EC
Covers: Member associations, associate members. Also includes IFLA offices, officers, general statistical information on the organization, and statutes. **Entries include:** Name of association, address, phone, list of officers. **Arrangement:** Geographical. **Indexes:** Personal name, subject. **Pages** (approx.): 150. **Frequency:** Annual, January. **Price:** Nfl. 20.00.

★3201★

INTERNATIONAL MICROFILM SOURCE BOOK

Microfilm Publishing, Inc.

Box 313

Wykagyl Station   Phone: (914) 235-5246

New Rochelle, NY 10804

Covers: Manufacturers and suppliers of microfilm and computer output microfilm equipment and other products; commercial micropublishers; COM and microfilm service bureaus. **Entries include:** Company name, address, phone, and name of contact. Manufacturer/supplier listings also include branch offices, product, whether direct sales are possible. Micropublisher listings also include type of publication. Service bureau listings include coded service and specialty lists. **Arrangement:** Manufacturers and micropublishers are alphabetical; microfilm service bureaus are geographical. **Indexes:** Product, trade name. **Pages** (approx.): 350. **Frequency:** Biennial, spring or fall of even years. **Editor:** Mitchell M. Badler. **Advertising accepted.** Circulation 9,000. **Former title:** Microfilm Source Book. **Price:** $39.50 (current edition); $47.50 (tentative, spring 1980 edition).

International Microforms in Print See **Guide to Microforms in Print**

★3202★

INTERNATIONAL SCIENCE FICTION YEARBOOK

Big O Publishing Ltd.

219 Eversleigh Road

London S. W. 11 5UY, England

Covers: Numerous aspects of science fiction activity, including book publishing, magazines, organizations, fanzines, agents, translators, libraries, book clubs, booksellers, conferences and workshops, conventions, etc. **Entries include:** Name of publication, event, service, etc., address, often phone, and one or two up to eight or ten additional types of detail as pertinent to the activity. **Arrangement:** Classified. **Pages** (approx.): 400. **Frequency:** Annual, in fall, with following year date; first edition 1978. **Editor:** Colin Lester. **Price:** $7.95. **Send orders to:** Quick Fox, Inc., 33 W. 60th st., New York, NY 10023 (212-246-0325).

★3203★

INVENTORY OF PENNSYLVANIA LIBRARY COOPERATIVE ORGANIZATIONS

Bureau of Library Development

State Library of Pennsylvania

Pennsylvania Department of Education

Box 1601   Phone: (717) 787-2646

Harrisburg, PA 17126

Number of listings: 70. **Entries include:** Organization name, address; services provided; purpose; name of members in cooperative. **Arrangement:** Alphabetical. **Indexes:** Membership by name of library, member by name of organization. **Pages** (approx.): 105. **Frequency:** Irregular; previous edition 1977; latest edition 1979. **Editor:** David R. Hoffman. **Price:** Free. **Other information:** Year prior to publication date appears at beginning of title.

★3204★

IRREGULAR SERIALS AND ANNUALS: AN INTERNATIONAL DIRECTORY

R. R. Bowker Company

1180 Avenue of the Americas   Phone: (212) 764-5100

New York, NY 10036

Covers: 32,000 current serials throughout the world which are published annually, less frequently, or irregularly, such as proceedings, transactions, handbooks, and yearbooks. Also lists serials which have ceased publication in a separate section. **Entries include:** Title, frequency of publication, publisher name and address, country of publication code, and Dewey Decimal Classification number. Additional information supplied in main text entries when appropriate or available includes translated title, ISSN, editor, distributor address, services which index the publication, year first published, and availability of

microforms. **Arrangement:** Classified by subject category; ceased publications are listed alphabetically. **Indexes:** Title; publications of international organizations. **Pages** (approx.): 1,400. **Frequency:** Biennial, spring of even years. **Editor:** Gary Ink. **Price:** $55.00 (ISSN 000-0043). **Send orders to:** R. R. Bowker Co., Box 1807, Ann Arbor, MI 48106.

★3205★—ITALICA—DIRECTORY ISSUE

American Association of Teachers of Italian

Department of Italian

Columbia University   Phone: (212) 280-2309

New York, NY 10027

Covers: 2,000 members. **Entries include:** Name and address. **Arrangement:** Alphabetical. **Pages** (approx.): 30. **Frequency:** Annual, spring. **Editor:** Olga Ragusa. **Advertising accepted.** Circulation 2,000. **Price:** $5.00.

★3206★

JOURNAL OF EDUCATION FOR LIBRARIANSHIP—DIRECTORY ISSUE

Association of American Library Schools

471 Park Lane   Phone: (814) 238-0254

State College, PA 16801

Covers: 100 graduate-level library schools in the United States and Canada who are members, and 1,900 of their faculty. **Entries include:** School name, address, phone, date established, dean, list of faculty with codes indicating subject taught. **Arrangement:** Alphabetical. **Indexes:** Personal name. **Frequency:** Annual, spring. **Editor:** Janet Phillips, Executive Secretary. **Price:** $5.00, payment with order (ISSN 0022-0604).

Journal of the American Forensic Association—Directory Issue See **American Forensic Association Newsletter—Directory Issue**

★3207★

LEONARD YELLOW PAGES LIBRARY

Leonard Yellow Pages Library

207 W. Gregory Boulevard   Phone: (913) 341-6837

Kansas City, MO 64114

Background: This is not a directory, but, rather, a source of material from directories - from the classified pages of all telephone directories published by the Bell System Associated Companies, which license the Library. Leonard states that it is able to supply any number of photocopies required from any category of listings in the yellow pages for any city, state, or region. (Not verified)

★3208★

LIBRARIANS PHONE BOOK

R. R. Bowker Company

1180 Avenue of the Americas   Phone: (212) 764-5100

New York, NY 10036

Number of listings: 51,400. **Entries include:** Librarian name, library and/or institution, city and state (but no address), and phone. **Arrangement:** Alphabetical. **Pages** (approx.): 450. **Frequency:** Not established; first edition December 1979. **Price:** $17.95 (ISSN 0195-332X).

★3209★

LIBRARIES AND INFORMATION CENTERS IN THE CHICAGO METROPOLITAN AREA

Illinois Regional Library Council

425 N. Michigan Avenue, Suite 1366   Phone: (312) 828-0928

Chicago, IL 60611

Covers: 400 libraries and information centers in the six Illinois counties of the Chicago Standard Metropolitan Statistical Area. **Entries include:** Library name, address, phone, names of staff, brief description of the library, and data on holdings, subject strengths, etc. **Arrangement:** Alphabetical. **Indexes:** Subject, geographic, personal name. **Pages** (approx.): 590. **Frequency:** Irregular; second edition published December 1976. **Editors:** Joel M. Lee and Hillis L. Griffin. **Price:** $10.00. **Also includes:** Directory of professional library organizations in the area.

Library and Documentation Journals *See* Library, Documentation, and Archives Serials

★3210★

LIBRARY AND REFERENCE FACILITIES IN THE AREA OF THE DISTRICT OF COLUMBIA

Knowledge Industry Publications, Inc.
Two Corporate Park Drive
White Plains, NY 10604
Covers: Over 400 special, public, academic, and federal libraries, reading rooms, and information centers in the Washington, DC area. **Entries include:** Library name, address (mailing and location), phone, name and title of director; number of full time staff; hours; accessibility; interlibrary loan, reprographic, and data base services; description of collection. **Arrangement:** Alphabetical. **Indexes:** Personal name, subject. **Pages** (approx.): 240. **Frequency:** Irregular; latest edition March 1979. **Editor:** Margaret Jennings. **Price:** $19.50, payment with order; $20.50, billed. **Other information:** Published in cooperation with the American Society for Information Science and Joint Venture.

★3211★

LIBRARY BUILDINGS CONSULTANTS LIST

Library Administration and Management Association
American Library Association
50 E. Huron Street   Phone: (312) 944-6780
Chicago, IL 60611
Covers: Over 60 persons, primarily present or former heads of libraries, who consult on matters pertaining to library buildings. **Entries include:** Name, address, present position, and information about experience, availability, basis of fee, etc. **Arrangement:** Alphabetical. **Pages** (approx.): 15. **Frequency:** Irregular; latest edition May 1978. **Price:** Free.

★3212★

LIBRARY, DOCUMENTATION, AND ARCHIVES SERIALS

International Federation for Documentation
7 Hofweg
The Hague, Netherlands
Covers: About 1,000 current serial publications published by international or multinational organizations or national associations, and about 60 abstracting, indexing, and current awareness services. **Entries include:** Title, name and address of publishing organization, year of first publication, brief description of usual content, frequency, price. **Arrangement:** Geographical; separate section for international organization publications. **Indexes:** Title-publisher. **Pages** (approx.): 200. **Frequency:** Irregular; latest edition 1975; new edition expected 1980. **Price:** $18.00.

★3213★

LIBRARY INSTRUCTION PROGRAMS IN ILLINOIS ACADEMIC LIBRARIES: A DIRECTORY AND SURVEY REPORT

Illinois Library Association
425 N. Michigan Avenue
Chicago, IL 60611
Covers: Over 45 user-oriented programs of library instruction in Illinois academic libraries. **Entries include:** Name of library, names of departments associated with program, program description, number of students, address. **Arrangement:** Alphabetical. **Frequency:** Irregular; latest edition 1978. **Editors:** Melissa Cain and Lois Pausch. **Price:** $2.00. **Other information:** Published with Illinois Association of College and Research Libraries.

★3214★

LIBRARY INSTRUCTIONS: A GUIDE TO PROGRAMS IN MICHIGAN

Michigan Library Association
226 W. Washtenaw
Lansing, MI 48933
Covers: About 350 community and college, public, and school libraries in Michigan with library user instruction programs. **Entries include:** Institution name, address, phone, name of contact person, type of institution, audience, instructional methods and materials, and types of publicity. **Arrangement:** By type of institution. **Pages** (approx.): 240. **Frequency:** Published 1978. **Price:** $5.00.

★3215★

LIBRARY JOURNAL—ANNUAL BUYERS' GUIDE ISSUE

R. R. Bowker Company
1180 Avenue of the Americas   Phone: (212) 764-5100
New York, NY 10036
Covers: Suppliers of products and services used by libraries from accession books and sheets to wardrobe racks. **Entries include:** Company name, address, phone, list of products or services. **Arrangement:** Alphabetical. **Indexes:** Product. **Frequency:** Annual, August. **Advertising accepted.** **Price:** $1.35. **Send orders to:** R. R. Bowker Co., Subscription Department, Box 67, Whitinsville, MA.

★3216★

LIBRARY NETWORKS

Knowledge Industry Publications
Two Corporate Park Drive   Phone: (914) 694-8686
White Plains, NY 10604
Publication includes: List of 25 computer-based library networks and consortia. **Entries include:** Network name, address, status, and name of executive director, with names and locations of member libraries. **Arrangement:** Alphabetical. **Frequency:** Biennial, summer of even years. **Editor:** Susan K. Martin. **Price:** $24.50, plus $1.00 shipping (current and 1980 editions). **Other information:** Primarily devoted to reports on network management and organizational problems, and descriptions of Ohio College Library Center and several other major networks.

★3217★

LIBRARY ORIENTATION/INSTRUCTION IN FLORIDA'S ACADEMIC LIBRARIES—A DIRECTORY

L O B I Caucus
Florida Library Association
C/o June Stillman
University of Central Florida
Box 25000
Orlando, FL 32816
Covers: Over 55 user-oriented programs of library instruction in Florida academic libraries. **Entries include:** Institution and library name, address, phone, name of contact, school enrollment, type of library, number of years program in existence, number of librarians involved, name of program, level of program, skills taught, method, print and nonprint materials used, evaluation technique. **Arrangement:** Alphabetical. **Indexes:** Subject. **Pages** (approx.): 35. **Frequency:** Irregular; latest edition 1979; new edition expected 1980. **Editor:** June Stillman. **Price:** Free; limited quantities available.

★3218★

LINGUISTIC SOCIETY OF AMERICA—ROSTER ISSUE

Linguistic Society of America
1611 N. Kent Street   Phone: (703) 528-2314
Arlington, VA 22209
Covers: 4,400 educators and linguists. **Arrangement:** Alphabetical. **Pages** (approx.): 60. **Frequency:** Annual, December. **Editor:** Victoria A. Fromkin, Secretary-Treasurer. **Advertising accepted.** Circulation 7,000. **Price:** $6.00.

List of Grants and Awards Available to American Writers *See* Grants and Awards Available to American Writers

★3219★
THE LITERARY AGENT
Society of Authors' Representatives
40 E. 49th Street   Phone: (212) 548-6333
New York, NY 10017
Covers: About 50 members of the society. **Entries include:** Name of agency, address, types of materials handled. **Price:** Free; send no. 10 self-addressed, stamped envelope.

★3220★
LITERARY AGENTS
Poets & Writers, Inc.
201 W. 54th Street   Phone: (212) 757-1766
New York, NY 10019
Publication includes: List of 40 literary agents who represent fiction writers, are willing to consider unsolicited work, and do not charge a reading fee. **Entries include:** Agency name, address, names of agents, and note on types of materials handled and submission procedure preferred; most listings specify letter contact, and do not include phone numbers. **Arrangement:** Alphabetical. **Frequency:** Not established; first published fall 1978. **Price:** $2.50, postpaid, payment with order. **Also includes:** Detailed sections on what agents are, what they do, and how to select an agent; numerous interviews with both authors and agents; chart showing sales of 22 kinds of rights (movie rights, etc.) possible from a hardcover book.

★3221★
LITERARY AND LIBRARY PRIZES
R. R. Bowker Company
1180 Avenue of the Americas   Phone: (212) 764-5144
New York, NY 10036
Covers: 370 literary prizes, library awards, fellowships, and grants in the United States, Great Britain, and Canada. 1980 edition will include 455 prizes. **Entries include:** Name of award, name and address of sponsor, names of winners, titles and publishers of winning books; conditions; rules. **Arrangement:** By type of prize. **Indexes:** Personal name/award name/sponsor name. **Pages** (approx.): 550 (660, 1980 edition). **Frequency:** Irregular; latest edition 1976; new edition expected March 1980. **Editors:** Olga Weber and Stephen J. Calvert. **Price:** $19.95 (current edition); $24.95 (tentative, 1980 edition); postpaid, payment with order (ISSN 0075-9880). **Send orders to:** R. R. Bowker Co., Box 1807, Ann Arbor, MI 48106 (313-761-4700).

★3222★
LITERARY BOOKSTORES IN THE U.S.: A LIST IN PROGRESS
Poets & Writers, Inc.
201 W. 54th Street   Phone: (212) 757-1766
New York, NY 10019
Covers: 265 bookstores which stock contemporary poetry and fiction and handle special orders. **Entries include:** Store name, address, brief description. **Pages** (approx.): 20. **Frequency:** Not established; first edition 1979. **Price:** $1.50, payment with order.

★3223★
LITERARY MARKET PLACE
R. R. Bowker Company
1180 Avenue of the Americas   Phone: (212) 764-5100
New York, NY 10036
Covers: About 1,450 book publishers in the United States who issued three or more books during the preceding year, plus book printers and binders; other suppliers to the industry; selected syndicates, newspapers, periodicals and radio and TV programs which use book reviews or news; literary agents; etc. **Entries include:** For publishers - Company name, address, phone, address for orders, principal executives and managers, date founded, number of titles in previous year, type of books published, representatives, and other affiliations. For suppliers, etc. listings usually show firm name, address, phone, executives, services, etc. **Arrangement:** Alphabetical. **Indexes:** Principal index is 25,000-item combined index of publishers, publications, personnel (called "Names and Numbers Directory," formerly also published separately); several sections have geographical

and/or subject indexes. **Pages** (approx.): 900. **Frequency:** Annual, December. **Editor:** Janice M. Blaufox. **Price:** $26.95, postpaid, payment with order (ISSN 0075-9899). **Send orders to:** R. R. Bowker Co., Box 1807, Ann Arbor, MI 48106 (313-761-4700).

★3224★
LITERARY SOCIETIES FOR BOOK COLLECTORS: BOOKMEN'S SOCIETIES AND CLUBS IN ENGLAND AND AMERICA
Trigon Press
117 Kent House Road
Beckenham
Kent BR3 1JJ, England
Covers: About 100 organizations of book collectors, including both general interest groups and special interest groups such as the Alger Society and West Country Writers Association. **Entries include:** Organization name, name and address of contact, officers, number of members, publications. **Frequency:** First edition expected 1979. **Editors:** R. and J. Sheppard. **Price:** $5.00.

★3225★
LSA BULLETIN—DIRECTORY OF PROGRAMS IN LINGUISTICS IN THE U.S. AND CANADA ISSUE
Linguistics Society of America
1611 N. Kent Street   Phone: (703) 528-2314
Arlington, VA 22209
Covers: About 175 programs. **Entries include:** Program name, address, phone, degrees offered, research projects, names of staff and areas of expertise, uncommonly taught languages offered. **Arrangement:** Geographical. **Indexes:** Personal name, institution name, language. **Frequency:** Irregular; previous edition 1975; latest edition December 1978. **Editor:** Begay Atkinson, Director of Publications. **Advertising accepted.** Circulation 6,500. **Former title:** Guide to Programs in Linguistics in the U. S. and Canada (was published by Center for Applied Linguistics). **Price:** $7.00, payment with order.

★3226★
MANAGEMENT AND ECONOMICS JOURNALS
Gale Research Company
Book Tower   Phone: (313) 961-2242
Detroit, MI 48226
Number of listings: About 160, domestic and foreign. **Entries include:** Title, address, publication orientation and scope, usual review time and delay in publication of accepted manuscripts, description of special issues and/or listings of current research and doctoral dissertations, availability of reprints or microfilm. **Arrangement:** Alphabetical. **Indexes:** Special issues, journals with research or dissertation sections, subject. **Pages** (approx.): 370. **Frequency:** Not established; first edition 1977. **Editor:** Vasile G. Tega. **Price:** $24.00.

★3227★
MAP COLLECTIONS IN THE UNITED STATES AND CANADA: A DIRECTORY
Special Libraries Association
235 Park Avenue South   Phone: (212) 777-8136
New York, NY 10003
Covers: 745 major map collections in the United States and Canada. **Entries include:** Collection name, address, phone, librarian's name, staff size, collection size, subject specialization, area specialization, services, date founded, classification system used, hours of service, statistical information. **Arrangement:** Geographical. **Indexes:** Library name. **Pages** (approx.): 215. **Frequency:** Irregular; latest edition 1978. **Editors:** David K. Carrington and Richard W. Stephenson. **Price:** $19.75.

★3228★
MASS PAPERBACK PUBLISHERS BLUEBOOK
Association of American Publishers
One Park Avenue
New York, NY 10016
Covers: Key personnel including education managers, sales managers, and rights and permissions officers of 25 paperback publishers.

Entries include: For representatives - Firm or individual's name, address, publishers represented, phone. For personnel of publishing firms - Firm name, address; names, titles, and phone numbers of personnel. Arrangement: Alphabetical. Frequency: Annual, April. Price: Free.

★3229★

MEDIA GUIDE INTERNATIONAL: AIRLINE/INFLIGHT AND TRAVEL
    MAGAZINES
Directories International, Inc.
1718 Sherman Avenue   Phone: (312) 491-0019
Evanston, IL 60201
Covers: Magazines published by airlines, hotels and motels, and travel organizations for consumers, worldwide. Entries include: Magazine name, publisher, address; company name of airline, hotel, etc.; content/audience information; circulation, rates, etc. Arrangement: Geographical within type of publication. Frequency: Annual, October. Price: $25.00.

★3230★

MEDIA LIBRARIANS DIRECTORY [New York metropolitan area]
New York Metropolitan Reference and Research Library Agency
33 W. 42nd Street   Phone: (212) 398-0290
New York, NY 10036
Covers: About 60 institutions with libraries handling media; limited to New York City area. Entries include: Institution name, library name, address, phone, and names and titles of librarians concerned with media ("media specialist," "audio-visual librarian," etc.). Arrangement: Alphabetical. Indexes: Personal name, librarians by job title. Pages (approx.): 25. Frequency: First edition September 1977. Editor: Richard Allen. Price: $5.00, payment with order (ISSN 0076-7018).

★3231★

METRO DIRECTORY OF MEMBERS [New York City area libraries]
New York Metropolitan Reference and Research Library Agency
33 W. 42nd Street   Phone: (212) 398-0290
New York, NY 10036
Covers: About 90 Agency members; includes some New Jersey and Connecticut libraries. Entries include: Library name, address, hours, description of holdings, names of librarians. Pages (approx.): 135. Frequency: Biennial, even years; 1976 is latest base volume; supplement September 1977. Price: $25.00.

Microfilm Source Book See International Microfilm Source Book

★3232★

MICROFORM MARKET PLACE
Microform Review, Inc.
520 Riverside Avenue   Phone: (203) 226-6967
Westport, CT 06880
Covers: Over 400 micropublishers issuing materials in microfilm and microfiche formats, worldwide. Entries include: Company name, address, phone, names of principal executives, and description of firm's major microform programs. Arrangement: Alphabetical. Indexes: Geographical, subjects published, personal name (with phone). Frequency: Biennial, even years. Price: $16.95 (current edition); $20.95 (1980 edition). Also includes: Calendar of related meetings and conferences.

★3233★

MIDDLE EAST LIBRARIANS' ASSOCIATION—MEMBERSHIP
    DIRECTORY
Middle East Librarians' Association
Main Library, Room 032
Ohio State University
1858 Neil Avenue   Phone: (614) 422-8389
Columbus, OH 43210
Covers: 250 librarians and others interested in those aspects of librarianship which support the study of dissemination of information about the Middle East. Entries include: Name, business address,

phone. Arrangement: Alphabetical by type of membership. Pages (approx.): 10. Frequency: Annual, month of publication varies. Editor: Marsha McClintock, Secretary-Treasurer. Price: $15.00.

★3234★

MLA DIRECTORY OF PERIODICALS: A GUIDE TO JOURNALS AND
    SERIES IN LANGUAGES AND LITERATURES
Modern Language Association of America
62 Fifth Avenue   Phone: (212) 741-7863
New York, NY 10016
Covers: 2,900 journals indexed in the "Modern Language Association International Bibliography;" journals listed are concerned with language, literature, folklore, and linguistics. Entries include: Publication title, names of editors, name and address of contact, date first published, name of sponsoring organization, acronym (assigned by MLA), frequency of publication, circulation, subscription price and year price verified, scope of content, whether book reviews are included, languages accepted for publication, whether abstracts are printed, number of articles published per year, and submission requirements for manuscripts (including article length, style, number of copies required, copyright ownership, special requirements, disposition of rejected manuscripts, average time between submission and publication decision, average time between decision and publication, and number of readers of manuscript). Arrangement: Alphabetical (by title). Indexes: Personal name, sponsoring organization name, language, subject, acronym. Frequency: Biennial, June of odd years. Editor: Eileen M. Mackesy, Managing Editor. Price: $65.00.

★3235★

MODERN LANGUAGE ASSOCIATON—JOB INFORMATION LISTS
Modern Language Association
62 Fifth Avenue   Phone: (212) 741-5593
New York, NY 10011
Covers: Listings of available positions for college teachers of English and foreign languages in four-year colleges and universities; February issue includes separate section of openings in two-year institutions. Entries include: Statement of department chairman on definite or possible openings, and any other information for job seekers (change in deadline date, or job description, notice of a vacancy filled, etc.). Arrangement: First section - statements of department chairmen; second section - list of departments reporting no vacancies. Pages (approx.): 40. Frequency: Quarterly: October, December, February, and April. Editor: Roy Chustek, Coordinator - Job Information. Advertising accepted. Circulation 7,500. Price: $20.00 per year for English edition (covering openings in English and American language and literature) or Foreign Language edition; payment with order. (Both editions contain same information on comparative literature and linguistics.)

★3236★

MONTANA LIBRARY DIRECTORY WITH STATISTICS OF MONTANA
    PUBLIC LIBRARIES
Montana State Library
930 E. Lyndale   Phone: (406) 449-3004
Helena, MT 59601
Covers: Public, school, academic, special, and institutional libraries located in Montana. Entries include: Name, address, county, name of librarian, phone, hours open. Arrangement: By type of library. Pages (approx.): 60. Frequency: Annual, January. Editor: Jo Ann Fallang, Administrative Assistant. Price: Free (ISSN 0094-873X). Also includes: Statistics of public libraries.

★3237★

MULTICULTURAL RESOURCES FOR CHILDREN
Multicultural Resources
Box 2945
Stanford, CA 94305
Publication includes: List of publishers and distributors of over 4,000 items in the areas of Black, Spanish-speaking, Asian American, American Indian, and Pacific Island cultures intended for preschool through elementary school age children. Entries include: Publisher or

distributor name, address. **Arrangement:** By culture and subject. **Pages** (approx.): 225. **Frequency:** Published 1977. **Editors:** Margaret S. Nichols and Peggy O'Neill. **Price:** $5.00. **Other information:** Principal content is bibliographical data on books and media.

Names and Numbers Directory *See* Literary Market Place

★3238★
NATIONAL AMATEUR—MEMBERSHIP LIST ISSUE
National Amateur Press Association
C/o Joseph F. Bradburn
Box 73
La Plata, MD 20646
Covers: 420 members of the National Amateur Press Association, a group interested in practicing the arts of printing, writing, and publishing amateur magazines or papers. **Entries include:** Name, address, code indicating type of membership. **Arrangement:** Geographical. **Frequency:** Semiannual, June and December. **Price:** Included in subscription, $2.00 per year (four issues).

National Amateur Press Association—Membership List *See* National Amateur—Membership List Issue

National Association of Business Economists—Membership Directory *See* Business Economics—Membership Directory Issue

★3239★
NATIONAL AUDIO-VISUAL ASSOCIATION—MEMBERSHIP DIRECTORY
National Audio-Visual Association
3150 Spring Street   Phone: (703) 273-7200
Fairfax, VA 22030
Covers: 1,000 dealers, manufacturers, producers, and suppliers of audiovisual products and materials. **Entries include:** Company name, address, phone, list of products or services. **Arrangement:** Dealers, geographical; suppliers, alphabetical. **Pages** (approx.): 60. **Frequency:** Annual, February. **Editor:** Mrs. Laurie Shirley, Assistant to Executive Vice President. **Price:** Free. **Other information:** Membership directory also included in the association's "Audio-Visual Equipment Directory," which includes product data and manufacturers' names only.

★3240★
NATIONAL FEDERATION OF ABSTRACTING AND INDEXING SERVICES—MEMBERSHIP DIRECTORY
National Federation of Abstracting and Indexing Services
112 S. 16th Street   Phone: (215) 563-2406
Philadelphia, PA 19102
Covers: About 40 major abstracting and indexing service organizations. **Entries include:** Name of organization, address, phone, names of assembly representatives and individuals to contact, description of general objectives, principal products and services, subject coverage. **Arrangement:** Alphabetical. **Pages** (approx.): 65. **Frequency:** Annual, spring. **Editor:** Toni Carbo Bearman, Executive Director. **Price:** $10.00.

★3241★
NATIONAL REGISTER OF HISTORIC PLACES
Heritage Conservation and Recreation Service
Interior Department   Phone: (202) 343-6261
Washington, DC 20243
Covers: 13,500 properties (sites, buildings, districts, structures, etc.) of local, state, or national significance in American history, architecture, archaeology, or culture; includes registrations through 1977; in two volumes. **Entries include:** Name and location of property; significant dates; description and statement of significance; ownership; accessibility; and available survey information. **Arrangement:** Geographical. **Indexes:** Place name, names of significant persons. **Pages** (approx.): 960, Volume 1; 650, Volume 2. **Frequency:** First volume (9,500 listings through 1974), 1976;

second volume (4,000 new listings through 1976), 1979. **Editor:** Sarah A. Marusin. **Price:** Volume 1, $13.00 (S/N 024-005-00645-1); Volume 2, $14.00 (S/N 024-005-00747-4). **Send orders to:** Government Printing Office, Washington, DC 20402. **Also includes:** Photographs and drawings of selected properties in each state.

★3242★
NEVADA LIBRARY DIRECTORY AND STATISTICS
Nevada State Library
Capitol Complex   Phone: (702) 885-5145
Carson City, NV 89710
Covers: Public, school, academic, institutional, and special libraries. **Entries include:** Name of library, address, phone, hours, names and addresses of staff, number of holdings, and other library statistics. **Arrangement:** Classified by type of library, then geographical. **Indexes:** Personal name. **Pages** (approx.): 120. **Frequency:** Annual, January. **Editor:** Robin Barker, Consultant. **Price:** Free.

★3243★
NEW JERSEY PUBLIC LIBRARY DIRECTORY
New Jersey State Library
185 W. State Street   Phone: (609) 292-6216
Trenton, NJ 08625
Covers: Over 325 New Jersey public libraries. **Entries include:** Name of library, address, names of director, president, and names and addresses of members of the board of trustees. **Arrangement:** By city. **Pages** (approx.): 60. **Frequency:** Annual, fall. **Editor:** Vianne Connor, Consultant. **Price:** Free.

★3244★
NEWSLETTER YEARBOOK/DIRECTORY
Newsletter Clearinghouse
44 W. Market Street   Phone: (914) 876-2081
Rhinebeck, NY 12572
Covers: About 3,000 newsletters available by subscription. **Entries include:** Title, publishing company, address, phone, names of editor and publisher, frequency, subscription price, year founded, and circulation. **Arrangement:** By subject. **Indexes:** Alphabetical, geographical. **Pages** (approx.): 190. **Frequency:** Irregular; first edition June 1977; latest edition July 1979. **Editor:** Howard Penn Hudson. **Price:** $30.00.

★3245★
OLD CHILDREN'S BOOKS: THE DEALERS IN BRITAIN AND AMERICA
Trigon Press
117 Kent House Road
Beckenham
Kent BR3 1JJ, England
Covers: Out-of-print booksellers who specialize in children's books. **Entries include:** Dealer name, address, specialties. **Pages** (approx.): 100. **Frequency:** First edition expected July 1979. **Price:** $12.00.

Operations Research Society of America—Roster *See* Institute of Management Sciences...—Combined Research Directory

★3246★
ORGANIZATIONS OFFERING SERVICES TO WRITERS IN NEW YORK STATE
Center for Arts Information
152 W. 42nd Street, Room 1239   Phone: (212) 354-1675
New York, NY 10036
Covers: About 60 national organizations, local art councils in New York, and writers' workshops that offer services and funds to playwrights, writers, and poets. **Entries include:** Organization name, address, phone, contact person, and description of services and activities. **Arrangement:** By type of program or organization. **Pages** (approx.): 10. **Frequency:** Irregular; latest edition March 1977. **Editor:** Ellen Thurston, Director. **Price:** $1.50.

★3247★
PACIFIC NORTHWEST BOOK PUBLISHERS ASSOCIATION BIBLIOGRAPHY AND DIRECTORY
Pacific Northwest Book Publishers Association
Box 122
Seattle, WA 98111
Covers: About 50 publishers in Washington, Oregon, Idaho, and Montana. Fee was charged for listing general information plus one title, with additional cost for more titles. **Entries include:** Publisher's name, address, personnel, description of interests, and one title with annotation; some listings include additional titles. **Arrangement:** Geographical. **Pages** (approx.): 35. **Frequency:** Annual, summer. **Price:** $2.00, payment with order.

★3248★
PAPERBACK BOOKS FOR YOUNG PEOPLE: AN ANNOTATED GUIDE TO PUBLISHERS AND DISTRIBUTORS
American Library Association
50 E. Huron Street   Phone: (312) 944-6780
Chicago, IL 60611
Publication includes: Lists of publishers and distributors of paperback books. **Entries include:** Distributor name, address, imprints carried, services. **Arrangement:** Geographical. **Pages** (approx.): 230. **Frequency:** Irregular; previous edition 1972; latest edition 1978. **Editor:** John Gillespie. **Price:** $9.00.

★3249★
PAPERBOUND BOOKS IN PRINT
R. R. Bowker Company
1180 Avenue of the Americas   Phone: (212) 764-5100
New York, NY 10036
Publication includes: List of about 5,600 publishers of paperbound books. **Entries include:** Name, address. **Frequency:** Semiannual, spring and fall. **Price:** $70.00 per year; $39.50 per copy; postpaid, payment with order (ISSN 0031-1235). **Send orders to:** R. R. Bowker Co., Box 1807, Ann Arbor, MI 48106 (313-761-4700). **Other information:** Principal content of publication is listings of paperbound books in all fields by author, title, and subject. Based on "Books in Print," described in separate listing.

★3250★
PARLIAMENTARY DIRECTORY
American Institute of Parliamentarians
206 Liberty Building   Phone: (515) 282-7930
Des Moines, IA 50309
Covers: 1,300 regular, certified, and certified professional parliamentarians who are members. **Entries include:** Name, residence and/or business address, phone, code indicating institute status. **Arrangement:** Geographical. **Indexes:** Alphabetical. **Price:** 40. **Frequency:** Annual, January. **Editor:** Lester L. Dahms, Executive Director. **Price:** $1.00 (current and 1980 editions).

★3251★
PENNSYLVANIA DIRECTORY OF HISTORICAL ORGANIZATIONS
Pennsylvania Historical and Museum Commission
William Penn Museum Building   Phone: (717) 787-3034
Harrisburg, PA 17120
Covers: About 250 organizations. **Entries include:** Name of organization, address, phone, officers, activities, meeting details, number of members. **Arrangement:** Geographical. **Indexes:** Alphabetical. **Pages** (approx.): 90. **Frequency:** Irregular; latest edition 1976. **Editors:** Victoria D. Brow, Deborah M. Miller. **Price:** $1.25.

★3252★
PERSONNEL SERVICES NEWSLETTER [Political scientists]
American Political Science Association
1527 New Hamsphire Avenue, N. W.   Phone: (202) 483-2512
Washington, DC 20036
Covers: Academic, governmental, and other positions currently open for political scientists. **Entries include:** Employer name, address, name of contact, description of position; some listings include phone.

Frequency: Monthly. **Price:** $10.00; available to members only.

★3253★
PETERSON'S GUIDE TO BOOK PUBLISHING COURSES/ACADEMIC AND PROFESSIONAL PROGRAMS
Peterson's Guides, Inc.
228 Alexander Street   Phone: (609) 924-5338
Princeton, NJ 08540
Covers: 200 current curricula and special courses in general publishing, and in editorial, production, design, and business areas, given by colleges, universities, trade organizations, and professional associations in the United States. **Entries include:** Name of organization, address, program purpose, special features, faculty, enrollment eligibility, level, credit hours, prerequisites, dates offered, class time required, and cost. **Arrangement:** By area of publishing covered. **Pages** (approx.): 170. **Frequency:** Published 1979; updated quarterly by "Publishing Education Newsletter" (not a Peterson's publication; see "Other information"). **Former title:** Education for Publishing. **Price:** $6.95, plus $1.50 shipping, payment with order. **Send orders to:** Association of American Publishers, One Park Avenue, New York, NY 10016 (212-689-8920). **Other information:** Published in cooperation with the Association of American Publishers; "Publishing Education Newsletter" is available from the association, $10.00 per year.

★3254★
PHONETICIAN—BIENNIAL DIRECTORY ISSUE
International Society of Phonetic Sciences
IASCP, ASB-50
University of Florida   Phone: (904) 392-2046
Gainesville, FL 32611
Covers: Over 10,000 phoneticians, phonologists, linguists, engineers, communication scientists, language teachers, speech pathologists, phoniatrists, logopedists, and national phonetic sciences organizations. **Entries include:** Name, affiliation, address, professional/scientific interests. **Arrangement:** Alphabetical. **Frequency:** Biennial, spring of even years. **Editor:** Harry Hollien, Ph.D., Secretary-General. **Advertising accepted.** Circulation 6,100. **Former title:** Circular Letters - Directory Issue. **Price:** $5.00 (current edition); $10.00 (1980 edition); postpaid.

★3255★
PICTURE SOURCES 3
Special Libraries Association
235 Park Avenue South   Phone: (212) 777-8136
New York, NY 10003
Covers: More than 1,000 United States and Canadian sources of pictures with descriptions of the collections. **Entries include:** Name, address, phone, person to contact, dates covered, types of material available, subjects covered, conditions of use. **Arrangement:** By general subject. **Indexes:** Geographical, alphabetical, numerical, subject. **Pages** (approx.): 400. **Frequency:** Irregular; latest edition 1975. **Editors:** Ann Novotny and Rosemary Eakins. **Price:** $17.00. **Other information:** Project of the Picture Division, Special Libraries Association and American Society of Picture Professionals.

★3256★
PMLA—DIRECTORY ISSUE
Modern Language Association of America
62 Fifth Avenue   Phone: (212) 741-5588
New York, NY 10011
Covers: 30,000 college and university teachers of English and modern foreign languages who are members. Also includes the following sections: Chairmen and directors of Ethnic Studies Programs; chairmen of language and area programs; women's studies programs; directory of useful addresses for individuals in language and literature; necrology; and English and foreign language department chairmen in two- and four-year colleges. **Entries include:** Member entries give name, academic affiliation, rank, language, and institutional address. **Arrangement:** Alphabetical. **Pages** (approx.): 315. **Frequency:** Annual, September. **Editor:** Dr. Joel Conarroe, Executive Director.

Advertising accepted. Circulation 34,500. **Price:** $15.00.

★3257★
POLICIES OF PUBLISHERS: A HANDBOOK FOR ORDER LIBRARIANS
Scarecrow Press, Inc.
52 Liberty Street   Phone: (201) 548-8600
Metuchen, NJ 08840
Covers: About 500 book publishers. **Entries include:** Publisher name, address, phone, address for orders, prepayment requirements, discount, return, shipping, billing, and back order policy, description of standing order or approval plans. **Arrangement:** Alphabetical. **Pages** (approx.): 150. **Frequency:** Irregular; first edition 1976; second edition 1978. **Editor:** Ung Chon Kim. **Price:** $8.50, plus 75¢ shipping.

★3258★
PRESERVATION EDUCATION FLYER: EDUCATIONAL OPPORTUNITIES IN THE PRESERVATION OF LIBRARY MATERIALS
Resources and Technical Services Division
American Library Association
50 E. Huron Street
Chicago, IL 60611
Covers: Accredited library school courses in preservation of library materials, and other courses which devote some attention to this topic; degree-granting programs in preservation; preservation workshops. **Frequency:** Irregular; first published 1976; latest edition 1979. **Editors:** Susan Swartzburg and Susan White. **Price:** $1.50, postpaid, payment with order.

★3259★
THE PRESIDENTS
White House Historical Association
726 Jackson Place
Washington, DC 20506
Covers: Existing birthplaces, residences, memorials, and other sites and buildings associated with presidents through Jimmy Carter. **Entries include:** Name of site, address, historical significance, descriptive information, and present owner. **Arrangement:** Geographical. **Pages** (approx.): 625. **Frequency:** First edition 1976; revised edition covering Carter published 1977. **Price:** $8.00 (S/N 024-005-00683-4). **Send orders to:** Government Printing Office, Washington, DC 20402. **Other information:** Published in cooperation with the National Park Service and the National Geographic Society.

★3260★
PROFESSIONAL SERVICES DIRECTORY OF THE AMERICAN TRANSLATORS ASSOCIATION
American Translators Association
Box 129   Phone: (914) 271-3260
Croton-on-Hudson, NY 10520
Covers: 1,200 translators and interpreters. **Entries include:** Name, address, languages in which proficient, subject competencies. **Arrangement:** Alphabetical. **Indexes:** Language-subject competency (with state). **Frequency:** Irregular; latest edition 1976; new edition expected July 1979.

★3261★
PUBLISHERS' INTERNATIONAL DIRECTORY
K. G. Saur Publishing, Inc.
175 Fifth Avenue   Phone: (212) 477-2500
New York, NY 10010
Covers: About 101,000 active publishers of materials of all kinds, worldwide. **Entries include:** Firm name, address, phone, publishing specialties, and ISBN prefix. **Arrangement:** Geographical. **Indexes:** ISBN (in supplement volume). **Pages** (approx.): 800. **Frequency:** Irregular; latest edition 1979. **Editor:** Michael Zils. **Price:** $129.00.

★3262★
PUBLISHERS OF THE UNITED STATES
R. R. Bowker Company
1180 Avenue of the Americas   Phone: (212) 764-5100
New York, NY 10036
Covers: 8,100 publishers listed in Books in Print (described in separate listing) and 4,000 publishers without titles currently in print. **Entries include:** Publisher name, editorial and ordering addresses, ISBN prefix. **Arrangement:** Alphabetical. **Indexes:** ISBN prefix. **Pages** (approx.): 160. **Frequency:** Not established; first edition November 1979. **Price:** $7.50, postpaid, payment with order. **Send orders to:** R. R. Bowker Co., Box 1807, Ann Arbor, MI 48106 (313-761-4700).

★3263★
PUBLISHERS' TRADE LIST ANNUAL
R. R. Bowker Company
1180 Avenue of the Americas   Phone: (212) 764-5100
New York, NY 10036
Covers: About 1,500 publishers in the United States and their catalogs. **Entries include:** Publisher name, address, phone; titles available and other bibliographic data; ordering information. **Arrangement:** Alphabetical. **Indexes:** Subject. **Frequency:** Annual, September. **Price:** $54.50, postpaid, payment with order (ISSN 0079-7855). **Send orders to:** R. R. Bowker Company, Box 1807, Ann Arbor, MI 48106 (313-761-4700).

★3264★
QUIEN ES QUIEN: A WHO'S WHO OF SPANISH-HERITAGE LIBRARIANS IN THE UNITED STATES
Bureau of School Services
College of Education
University of Arizona   Phone: (602) 884-3565
Tucson, AZ 85721
Covers: 245 Spanish-heritage librarians in the United States who have a professional degree in library science. **Entries include:** Name, home and office addresses, birth date, spouse's name, university where degree was obtained, rating of fluency in Spanish, career data, indication if writing has been published, honors, biographical publications where listed, and ethnic group. **Arrangement:** Alphabetical. **Pages** (approx.): 30. **Frequency:** Irregular; first edition fall 1976; new edition expected January 1980. **Editor:** Arnulfo D. Trejo. **Former title:** Directory of Spanish-speaking/Spanish-surnamed Librarians in the United States. **Price:** $3.00 (current edition); $5.00 (1980 edition).

★3265★
RECOGNIZED PLANNING DEGREES
American Planning Association
1776 Massachusetts Avenue, N. W.   Phone: (202) 872-0611
Washington, DC 20036
Covers: Universities which offer nearly 90 graduate programs in urban and regional planning accredited by the association. **Entries include:** Institution name, address; name and phone of department chairman or contact; degrees offered; fields of study; length of programs. **Arrangement:** Geographical. **Frequency:** Annual, January. **Price:** Free.

★3266★
REGISTER OF INDEXERS
American Society of Indexers
C/o Bill Bartenbach
11 W. 40th Street,   Phone: (212) 736-6734
New York, NY 10018
Covers: 110 freelance indexers in the United States. **Entries include:** Name, office address and phone, areas of subject specialization. **Arrangement:** Alphabetical. **Pages** (approx.): 20. **Frequency:** Latest edition 1978; new edition expected 1980. **Price:** $5.00.

★3267★

RHODE ISLAND: AN INVENTORY OF HISTORIC ENGINEERING AND INDUSTRIAL SITES

Heritage Conservation and Recreation Service
Interior Department   Phone: (202) 343-2828
Washington, DC 20240

Covers: Historic textile mills, base-metal works, utilities, bridges, railroad-related structures, lighthouses, etc., including a substantial number still surviving. **Entries include:** Name of site, address or location, details of history and significance, information on present status. **Arrangement:** Geographical. **Indexes:** Site name. **Pages** (approx.): 300. **Frequency:** Published 1978. **Editors:** Gary Kulik and Julia C. Bonham. **Send orders to:** Government Printing Office, Washington, DC 20402.

★3268★

ROSTER OF CHICANOS IN POLITICAL SCIENCE

American Political Science Association
1527 New Hampshire Avenue, N. W.   Phone: (202) 483-2512
Washington, DC 20036

Entries include: Name, address; educational, career, and personal data. **Frequency:** Latest edition 1976. **Price:** $5.00.

★3269★

ROSTER OF WOMEN ECONOMISTS

Committee on the Status of Women in the Economics Profession
C/o Professor M. A. Ferber
Department of Economics
University of Illinois
Urbana, IL 61801

Number of listings: 1,600. Roster published as computer print-out for prospective employers. **Entries include:** Name, address, employment status, number of articles and books published, and whether interested in changing jobs. **Arrangement:** By discipline, then geographical. **Frequency:** Annual, December. **Price:** $35.00 to nonprofit institutions; $50.00 to businesses.

★3270★

ROSTER OF WOMEN IN POLITICAL SCIENCE

American Political Science Association
1527 New Hampshire Avenue, N. W.   Phone: (202) 483-2512
Washington, DC 20036

Covers: 850 women political scientists. **Entries include:** Name; professional affiliation and title; home address; highest degree, school granting it, and field; research interests; skills and experience relevant to non-academic employment. **Arrangement:** Alphabetical. **Indexes:** Fields of interest. **Pages** (approx.): 150. **Frequency:** Irregular; latest edition 1976; new edition expected 1980. **Price:** $5.00 (current edition); $8.00 (tentative, 1980 edition).

★3271★

RQ—"SOURCES OF STATE VITAL STATISTICS REPORTS" [Article]

Reference and Adult Services Division
American Library Association
50 E. Huron Street   Phone: (312) 944-6780
Chicago, IL 60611

Covers: Agencies responsible for compiling and publishing the annual vital statistics reports of the states and the District of Columbia. **Entries include:** Agency name, address, title of report, price (if charge is made), and latest edition available. **Arrangement:** Geographical. **Price:** $4.00, payment with order. **Other information:** Article by Kenneth D. Sell appears in "RQ," Fall, 1976, pages 45-54.

★3272★

SCHOLARS' GUIDE TO WASHINGTON, D.C. FOR LATIN AMERICAN AND CARIBBEAN STUDIES

Smithsonian Institution Press
Box 1579   Phone: (202) 381-5143
Washington, DC 20013

Covers: Several hundred libraries, archives, museums; collections of maps, film, music, and other sound recordings; associations; government agencies, embassies; academic programs, and research centers in the Washington, DC area which have information on Latin America and the Caribbean. **Entries include:** Institution name, address, description of size and quality of holdings, and a description of activities and programs. **Arrangement:** By type of institution or collection. **Indexes:** Subject, institution name. **Pages** (approx.): 350. **Frequency:** Irregular; latest edition June 1979. **Editor:** Michael Grow. **Price:** $19.95, cloth; $7.95, paper. **Other information:** Part of a series of "Scholars' Guides" based on research conducted by the Woodrow Wilson International Center for Scholars. Other areas to be covered are Russia and East Asia (described in separate listing), Eastern Europe, and Africa.

★3273★

SCHOLARS' GUIDE TO WASHINGTON, D.C. FOR RUSSIAN/SOVIET STUDIES

Smithsonian Institution Press
Box 1579   Phone: (202) 381-5021
Washington, DC 20013

Covers: 250 libraries, archives, museums, collections of maps, film, music and other sound recordings, associations, government agencies, academic programs, and research centers which have information on the Soviet Union. **Entries include:** Name of institution, address, description of size and quality of holdings, and a description of activities and programs. **Arrangement:** By type of collection. **Indexes:** Subject, institution name. **Pages** (approx.): 400. **Frequency:** Irregular; latest edition 1977. **Editor:** Steven A. Grant. **Price:** $19.95, cloth; $6.95, paper.

School Media Directory [New Jersey] *See* **Directory of New Jersey School Media Specialists**

★3274★

SCIENCE FICTION TRADERS GUIDE: THE DEALERS, PUBLISHERS, AND FANZINES

Trigon Press
117 Kent House Road
Beckenham
Kent BR3 1JJ, England

Covers: Over 1,000 overground and underground science fiction writers, buyers, dealers, publishers, and little magazines and fanzines. **Pages** (approx.): 180. **Frequency:** Not established; first edition early 1978. **Editor:** John Lander. **Price:** 8 pounds.

★3275★

SCIENCE FICTION WRITERS OF AMERICA—MEMBERSHIP DIRECTORY

Science Fiction Writers of America
2004 Erie Street, Apartment 2
Adelphi, MD 20783

Number of listings: About 500, including many editors and agents. Also includes literary agents of members. **Entries include:** For members - Name, address, phone, literary agent. For literary agents - Name, address, phone, names of members represented. **Arrangement:** Separate alphabetical lists for authors and agents. **Pages** (approx.): 30. **Frequency:** Annual, April. **Editor:** David F. Bischoff, SFWA Secretary. **Price:** $25.00. **Send orders to:** Peter D. Pautz, SFWA Executive Secretary, 68 Countryside Apartments, Hackettstown, NJ 07840 (201-852-8531).

★3276★

SELF-PUBLISHING MANUAL: HOW TO WRITE, PRINT & SELL YOUR OWN BOOK

Parachuting Publications
Box 4232   Phone: (805) 968-7277
Santa Barbara, CA 93103

Publication includes: Lists of wholesalers, reviewers, exporters, suppliers, direct mailing list sources, publishing organizations, and others of assistance in publishing. **Entries include:** Organization or company name, address. **Arrangement:** By Zip code. **Indexes:**

General subject. **Pages** (approx.): 180. **Frequency:** Annual. **Editor:** Dan Poynter. **Price:** $14.95, cloth; $9.95, paper; postpaid.

★3277★
S.E.M. NEWSLETTER—DIRECTORY OF MEMBERS AND SUBSCRIBERS ISSUE
Society for Ethnomusicology
201 S. Main Street, Room 513   Phone: (313) 761-7787
Ann Arbor, MI 48104
Covers: About 1,350 individual members and 650 institutional members. **Entries include:** Name, address. **Arrangement:** Individuals are alphabetical, institutions are geographical. **Pages** (approx.): 45. **Frequency:** Triennial; latest edition June 1978. **Price:** $5.00.

★3278★
SERIALS IN PSYCHOLOGY AND ALLIED FIELDS
Whitston Publishing Company, Inc.
Box 958   Phone: (518) 283-4363
Troy, NY 12181
Number of listings: 800. **Entries include:** Publication name, address for manuscripts, form of payment (if any), subject interests. **Arrangement:** Alphabetical. **Pages** (approx.): 475. **Frequency:** Irregular; latest edition 1976. **Editors:** Margaret Tompkins and Norma Shirley. **Price:** $22.50.

★3279★
SMALL PRESS RECORD OF BOOKS IN PRINT
Dustbooks
Box 1056
Paradise, CA 95969
Publication includes: List of over 1,000 small, independent presses throughout the world. **Entries include:** Press name, address, names of authors whose works are listed in author section of the publication. **Arrangement:** Alphabetical. **Pages** (approx.): 425. **Frequency:** Annual, July. **Editor:** Len Fulton. **Advertising accepted.** Circulation 2,500. **Former title:** Small Press Record of Books. **Price:** $11.95. **Publication includes:** Principal content is listing by author of some 5,000 books issued by publishers described above. Listings include author, title, publication date, price, etc. There are title, publisher, and subject indexes.

Society for Ethnomusicology—Roster *See* S.E.M. Newsletter— Directory of Members and Subscribers Issue

★3280★
SOCIETY FOR HISTORIANS OF AMERICAN FOREIGN RELATIONS— ROSTER AND CURRENT RESEARCH PROJECTS
Society for Historians of American Foreign Relations
Department of History
Bowling Green State University
Bowling Green, OH 43403
Covers: About 800 members and 600 research projects. **Entries include:** For members - Name, mailing address, institutional affiliations, codes indicating major research interest and where person's projects can be located in research inventory. **Arrangement:** Membership list alphabetical; research projects are classified within geographical groups or in topical categories. **Pages** (approx.): 40. **Frequency:** Biennial, fall of even years; supplement in odd years. **Editor:** Warren F. Kimball. **Price:** $40.00. **Send orders to:** History Dept., Rutgers State Univ., Newark, NJ 08873.

★3281★
SOCIETY OF AMERICAN ARCHIVISTS—MEMBERSHIP DIRECTORY
Society of American Archivists
330 S. Wells, Suite 810   Phone: (312) 996-3370
Chicago, IL 60606
Covers: 3,500 persons concerned with management and custody of current and historical records, and with archival administration. **Frequency:** Biennial, even years. **Price:** $8.00 (current edition); $10.00 (tentative, 1980 edition).

Society of Authors' Representatives—Roster *See* The Literary Agent

★3282★
SOCIETY OF FEDERAL LINGUISTS—MEMBERSHIP DIRECTORY
Society of Federal Linguists
Box 7765
Washington, DC 20044
Covers: About 110 language specialists in the federal government. **Entries include:** Name, home and office address, home and office phone, languages. **Arrangement:** Alphabetical. **Pages** (approx.): 15. **Frequency:** Irregular; previous edition 1973; latest edition 1979. **Editors:** Wanda Feeley and Everette Larson. **Price:** Available to members only.

★3283★
SOCIETY OF THE WAR OF 1812 IN THE COMMONWEALTH OF PENNSYLVANIA—ANNUAL YEARBOOK
Society of the War of 1812 in the Commonwealth of Pennsylvania
1501 Monticello Drive   Phone: (215) 642-1946
Gladwyne, PA 19035
Covers: About 250 members of the society interested in the preservation of historical records pertaining to the War of 1812 era in the United States. **Entries include:** Individual name, address. **Arrangement:** Alphabetical. **Pages** (approx.): 20. **Frequency:** Annual, March. **Editor:** Howard Stick, Secretary. **Price:** $1.00; available to members only.

★3284★
SOURCES: A GUIDE TO PRINT AND NON-PRINT MATERIALS Available from Organs., Industry, Govt. Agencies, and Specialized Publishers
Neal-Schuman Publishers, Inc.
64 University Place   Phone: (212) 473-5170
New York, NY 10003
Covers: About 2,000 sources a year for materials which the publishers feel "escape the traditional bibliographic net," including books, periodicals, filmstrips, cassettes, posters, games, etc. **Entries include:** Publisher name, address, interests and objectives, titles of current publications (arranged by format), price. **Arrangement:** Alphabetical. **Indexes:** Title, inexpensive materials. **Pages** (approx.): 175 per issue. **Frequency:** Three times yearly. **Editor:** Maureen Crowley. **Price:** $60.00 per year (ISSN 0145-2355).

★3285★
SOUTHEASTERN BIBLIOGRAPHIC INSTRUCTION DIRECTORY: ACADEMIC LIBRARIES
Southeastern Library Association
Box 987   Phone: (404) 939-5080
Tucker, GA 30084
Covers: About 350 academic libraries in the southeastern United States which offer library orientation programs or bibliographic instruction. **Entries include:** Name of institution, name of library, address, phone, name of contact; coding to indicate college enrollment size and library collection size; degrees offered; type of institution; size of professional library staff; description of programs offered; and printed materials available. **Arrangement:** Alphabetical. **Indexes:** Program element. **Pages** (approx.): 175. **Frequency:** Irregular; first edition published 1978. **Editor:** James A. Ward, Compiler. **Price:** $6.00, payment with order.

★3286★
SOUTHEASTERN BLACK LIBRARIAN
Information Exchange System for Minority Personnel
Box 91
Raleigh, NC 27602
Covers: About 600 Black librarians in Alabama, Florida, Georgia, Kentucky, Mississippi, North Carolina, South Carolina, Tennessee, and Virginia. **Entries include:** Librarian's name, present position, business address, educational institutions attended, and degrees or certifications. **Arrangement:** Alphabetical. **Indexes:** Geographical.

Pages (approx.): 60. **Frequency:** Not established; first edition 1976. **Editor:** Dorothy May Haith, President. **Advertising accepted.** Circulation 5,000. **Price:** $6.70.

★3287★
SPECIAL LIBRARIES—ANNUAL DIRECTORY ISSUE
Special Libraries Association
235 Park Avenue South   Phone: (212) 777-8136
New York, NY 10003
Covers: About 10,600 special librarians who are members of the association. **Entries include:** Name, address, membership rank, chapter and division affiliations. **Arrangement:** Alphabetical. **Indexes:** Chapter, division. **Pages** (approx.): 350. **Frequency:** Annual, October. **Editor:** Nancy M. Viggiano. **Price:** $13.00.

Special Libraries Association—Membership Directory *See*
     Special Libraries—Annual Directory Issue

★3288★
SPECIAL LIBRARIES ASSOCIATION—SOUTHERN CALIFORNIA
     CHAPTER—MEMBERSHIP DIRECTORY
Southern California Chapter
Special Libraries Association
C/o Julia Keim
Rocketdyne
6633 Canoga Avenue
Canoga Park, CA 91304
Covers: About 300 special libraries in Southern California and their staffs. **Entries include:** Organization name, library name, address, names and phone numbers of individual members. **Arrangement:** Geographical. **Indexes:** Personal name, organization name, divisional affiliation. **Pages** (approx.): 120. **Frequency:** Irregular; latest edition fall 1979. **Price:** $20.00, postpaid, payment with order.

Special Libraries Directory: Institutions Where SLA Members Are
     Employed *See* Institutions Where SLA Members Are Employed

★3289★
SPECIAL LIBRARIES DIRECTORY OF GREATER NEW YORK
Special Libraries Association
C/o Veronica Pidala
International Nickle Company
One New York Plaza   Phone: (212) 742-4061
New York, NY 10004
Covers: About 1,200 special libraries and their collections in the New York metropolitan area. **Entries include:** Library name, address, phone, librarian's name, subject indexes, hours, staff, description of collection contents, available services, equipment, and technology. **Arrangement:** By broad subject area. **Pages** (approx.): 190. **Frequency:** Irregular; latest edition 1977; new edition expected 1980. **Editor:** Louis Hall. **Advertising accepted.** Circulation 1,400. **Price:** $18.00 (current edition); $25.00 (1980 edition).

★3290★
SPONSORS LIST [Programs for poets and writers]
Poets & Writers, Inc.
201 W. 54th Street   Phone: (212) 757-1766
New York, NY 10019
Covers: Over 600 national organizations which sponsor events for poets and fiction writers, thereby offering training, exposure for works, and opportunities for readings, teaching workshops, or short-term residencies; about 30 literary newsletters are also listed. **Entries include:** For organizations - Name, address, name of contact, description of activities. For newsletters - Publisher, address. **Arrangement:** Alphabetical. **Pages** (approx.): 50. **Frequency:** Irregular; latest edition 1979. **Editor:** Lisa Merrill, Managing Editor. **Price:** 75¢ in stamps.

★3291★
STAFF DEVELOPMENT IN LIBRARIES
Library Administration and Management Association
American Library Association
50 E. Huron Street   Phone: (312) 944-6780
Chicago, IL 60611
Covers: About 15 organizations active in staff development for libraries. **Entries include:** Organization name, address, contact person, source of funding, program areas, publications, training materials available, consultants available. **Arrangement:** Alphabetical. **Pages** (approx.): 35. **Frequency:** Irregular; latest edition 1978. **Price:** $2.00. **Also includes:** Annotated bibliography of materials on staff development and management.

★3292★
STANDARD PERIODICAL DIRECTORY
Oxbridge Communications, Inc.
183 Madison Avenue, Room 1108   Phone: (212) 689-8524
New York, NY 10016
Covers: Over 68,000 periodicals and newsletters, and annual and serial publications in the United States and Canada. **Entries include:** Publication name, publisher name, address, phone; name of editor, advertising director; description of contents and types of material used; year founded, frequency; ad and subscription rates, print method, page size, number of pages. **Arrangement:** Classified by subject. **Indexes:** Subject, title. **Pages** (approx.): 1,730. **Frequency:** Biennial, December of even years. **Price:** $90.00, postpaid, payment with order; $92.50, billed.

★3293★
STATE AND NATIONAL REGISTER OF HISTORIC PLACES [New
     Jersey]
Office of Historic Preservation
Division of Parks and Forestry
New Jersey Department of Environmental Protection
109 W. State Street   Phone: (602) 292-2023
Trenton, NJ 08625
Covers: About 500 buildings and sites designated as State Historic Places, National Historic Places, or National Historic Landmarks in New Jersey. **Entries include:** Name of site or structure, location, construction date, date placed on register(s), code to indicate whether on National Register of Historic Places or whether a National Historic Landmark. **Arrangement:** By county, then city. **Pages** (approx.): 35. **Frequency:** Annual, June. **Editor:** Nanci Kostrub Batchelor. **Price:** Free.

★3294★
STATE LIBRARY AGENCIES: A SURVEY PROJECT REPORT
Association of Specialized & Cooperative Library Agencies
50 E. Huron Street   Phone: (312) 944-6780
Chicago, IL 60611
Entries include: Agency name and address, place in state government organization, powers and duties, purpose and scope of responsibility, personnel, major functional categories, major emphases in library development, notable activities underway, special services and projects, sources of funding, current budgets, organization charts. **Pages** (approx.): 415. **Frequency:** Biennial, summer of odd years. **Editor:** Donald B. Simpson. **Price:** $15.00.

★3295★
STATISTICS OF SOUTH DAKOTA LIBRARIES
South Dakota State Library
State Library Building   Phone: (605) 773-3131
Pierre, SD 57501
Covers: About 150 public, special, and academic libraries. **Entries include:** Library name, address, type of library, name of director, phone. **Arrangement:** Geographical by city. **Pages** (approx.): 65. **Frequency:** Annual, summer. **Former title:** Statistics of South Dakota Public Libraries. **Price:** Free. **Also includes:** Major portion of publication is summary of budget and service statistics.

Statistics with Directory of Nevada Libraries and Library Personnel *See* Nevada Library Directory and Statistics

★3296★

SUBJECT COLLECTIONS [Libraries and museums]

R. R. Bowker Company

1180 Avenue of the Americas   Phone: (212) 764-5100

New York, NY 10036

Covers: Over 15,000 academic, public, and special libraries, and over 1,000 museums, in the United States, Mexico, and Puerto Rico which house collections of books, recordings, manuscripts, and other types of materials devoted to specific subjects. **Entries include:** For each collection - Name of institution, name of library, address, name of curator, number of items, topic of collection, type of materials, annual budget, photocopying and interlibrary loan policies, and other information. **Arrangement:** By subject, then geographical. **Indexes:** None. **Pages** (approx.): 1,200. **Frequency:** Irregular; latest edition January 1979. **Editor:** Lee Ash. **Price:** $47.50, postpaid, payment with order (ISSN 0000-0140). **Send orders to:** R. R. Bowker Co., Box 1807, Ann Arbor, MI 48106 (313-761-4700).

Subject Directory of Special Libraries and Information Centers *See* Directory of Special Libraries and Information Centers

Subject Guide to Books in Print *See* Books in Print

Subject Guide to Children's Books in Print *See* Children's Books in Print

Subject Guide to Microforms in Print *See* Guide to Microforms In Print

★3297★

TEACHERS OF ENGLISH TO SPEAKERS OF OTHER LANGUAGES— MEMBERSHIP DIRECTORY

Teachers of English to Speakers of Other Languages

455 Nevils Building

Georgetown University   Phone: (202) 337-7264

Washington, DC 20057

Number of listings: 7,500. **Arrangement:** Alphabetical list of individual members; geographical list of subscribing institutions. **Indexes:** Individuals geographically. **Pages** (approx.): 160. **Frequency:** Annual, September. **Price:** $4.00.

★3298★

TECHNICAL SERVICES STAFF DIRECTORY FOR ACADEMIC LIBRARIES

Inter-University Library Council Technical Services Group

C/o Brian Alley

Miami University Library

Oxford, OH 45056

Covers: Over 50 academic libraries in Indiana, Kentucky, and Ohio whose collections exceed 100,000 volumes. **Entries include:** Institution or library name, address, TWX number (if any); names, titles, and phone numbers for head of technical services, acquisitions librarian, cataloging librarian, serials librarian, contact for coordinating large purchases, and other key technical services staff members. **Arrangement:** By state, then alphabetical. **Pages** (approx.): 20. **Frequency:** Irregular; first edition October 1978; new edition expected October 1980. **Editors:** Brian Alley, Jennifer Cargill. **Price:** $2.50.

TESOL Training Program Directory *See* Directory of Teacher Training Programs in ESOL and Bilingual Education

★3299★

TRAINING RESOURCES: BUYER'S GUIDE AND CONSULTANT DIRECTORY

American Society for Training and Development

Box 5307   Phone: (608) 274-3440

Madison, WI 53705

Covers: Businesses and individual consultants offering products and services for sale to persons in corporate training and human resource development. **Entries include:** Company name, address, phone, executive names, list of products or services. **Arrangement:** Alphabetical. **Indexes:** Product, geographic. **Pages** (approx.): 50. **Frequency:** Annual. **Editor:** Joel H. Bradtke. **Advertising accepted.** Circulation 16,000. **Former title:** American Society for Training and Development - Consultant Directory. **Price:** $7.95.

★3300★

TRANSLATION AND TRANSLATORS

R. R. Bowker Company

1180 Avenue of the Americas   Phone: (212) 764-5100

New York, NY 10036

Covers: About 3,000 associations, centers, conferences, congresses, and symposia; awards, fellowships, and prizes; subsidies, training, and placement organizations; governmental and international suppliers for translation- and interpretation-related activities; and translators and interpreters; worldwide coverage. **Entries include:** Organization or sponsor name, address, phone, name and title of contact, description of products, services, or facilities as appropriate. **Arrangement:** By activity. **Indexes:** Translator-interpreter source and target language; geographical; subject. **Pages** (approx.): 245. **Frequency:** Not established; first edition September 1979. **Editor:** Stefan Congrat-Butlar. **Price:** $35.00, postpaid, payment with order. **Send orders to:** R. R. Bowker Company, Box 1807, Ann Arbor, MI 48106 (313-761-4700).

TYMNET Subscriber's Directory *See* Computer and Data Services Available Through TYMNET

★3301★

U.S. BOOK PUBLISHING YEARBOOK AND DIRECTORY

Knowledge Industry Publications

Two Corporate Park Drive

White Plains, NY 10604

Publication includes: Lists of 1,200 publishers, leading publishers by sales, book trade organizations, and courses in book publishing; also includes two-year calendar of national and international book publishing and bookselling meetings and exhibits. **Entries include:** For publishers and associations - Name, address. For leading publishers - Name, statistics on sales, share of market overall and by market segment. For courses - Institution or sponsor, location, dates, description. For meetings - Name of event, auspices, location, dates. **Indexes:** Organization name. **Pages** (approx.): 200. **Frequency:** Annual; first edition summer 1979. **Editor:** Terry Mollo. **Price:** $35.00, payment with order; $36.00, billed.

★3302★

UPPER PENINSULA OF MICHIGAN: AN INVENTORY OF HISTORIC ENGINEERING AND INDUSTRIAL SITES

Heritage Conservation and Recreation Service

Interior Department   Phone: (202) 343-2828

Washington, DC 20240

Covers: Historic mining, lumbering, and other industrial sites, bridges, etc. **Entries include:** Name of site, address or location, details of history and significance, information on present status. **Arrangement:** Geographical. **Pages** (approx.): 235. **Frequency:** Published 1978. **Price:** $4.50 (S/N 024-016-00092-7). **Send orders to:** Government Printing Office, Washington, DC 20402.

★3303★
VERMONT INTERLIBRARY LOAN POLICIES DIRECTORY
Vermont Library Association
Box 803
Burlington, VT 05402
Covers: About 50 Vermont college and special libraries participating in interlibrary loan programs. **Entries include:** Library name, institution name, address, phone, telex, name of interlibrary loan personnel, description of loan policies. **Arrangement:** Alphabetical. **Pages** (approx.): 50. **Frequency:** Irregular; latest edition spring 1977. **Price:** $3.00.

★3304★
WHERE TO WRITE FOR BIRTH AND DEATH RECORDS—UNITED STATES AND OUTLYING AREAS
National Center for Health Statistics
Public Health Service
Health, Education, and Welfare Department   Phone: (301) 346-8500
Washington, DC 20201
Covers: Vital statistics offices in each state. **Entries include:** Name and address of office, cost of full copy, cost of short form, any special requirements, dates of records held. **Arrangement:** Geographical. **Pages** (approx.): 10. **Frequency:** Irregular; latest edition 1978. **Price:** Free from NCHS (PHS 78-1142). **Send orders to:** Scientific and Technical Information Branch, National Center for Health Statistics, 3700 East-West Highway, Room 1-57, Hyattsville, MD 20782.

★3305★
WHERE TO WRITE FOR DIVORCE RECORDS—UNITED STATES AND OUTLYING AREAS
National Center for Health Statistics
Public Health Service
Health, Education, and Welfare Department   Phone: (301) 346-8500
Washington, DC 20201
Covers: Appropriate offices in each state and major city. **Entries include:** Office name and address or other information concerning proper place to send inquiry, dates of records held, and fee charged. **Arrangement:** Geographical. **Pages** (approx.): 10. **Frequency:** Irregular; latest edition 1979. **Price:** Free from NCHS. **Send orders to:** Scientific and Technical Information Branch, National Center for Health Statistics, 3700 East-West Highway, Room 1-57, Hyattsville, MD 20782.

★3306★
WHERE TO WRITE FOR MARRIAGE RECORDS—UNITED STATES AND OUTLYING AREAS
National Center for Health Statistics
Public Health Service
Health, Education, and Welfare Department   Phone: (301) 346-8500
Washington, DC 20201
Covers: Vital statistics offices in each state. **Entries include:** Name and address of office, cost of copy, dates of records held, other information. **Arrangement:** Geographical. **Pages** (approx.): 10. **Frequency:** Irregular; latest edition 1979. **Price:** Free from NCHS. **Send orders to:** Scientific and Technical Information Branch, National Center for Health Statistics, 3700 East-West Highway, Room 1-57, Hyattsville, MD 20782.

Who Is Publishing in Science *See* Current Bibliographic Directory of the Arts and Sciences

★3307★
WHO'S WHO AT THE ABA [Bookselling]
Knowledge Industry Publications, Inc.
Two Corporate Park Drive
White Plains, NY 10604
Covers: About 6,000 booksellers, publishers, agents, wholesalers, and others in bookselling and publishing. **Entries include:** Name, title, business affiliation, business address and phone; hotel at convention site. **Arrangement:** Alphabetical. **Indexes:** Publishing company name.

Pages (approx.): 120. **Frequency:** Annual, spring, at time of American Booksellers Association convention. **Editor:** Frederick Sigel. **Advertising accepted.** **Price:** $16.95, payment with order; $17.95, billed.

★3308★
WINNERS: BLUE RIBBON ENCYCLOPEDIA OF AWARDS
Facts on File
119 W. 57th Street   Phone: (212) 265-2011
New York, NY 10019
Covers: 1,000 awards given to persons of outstanding achievement in all fields; international coverage. **Entries include:** Name of awarding body; address; name of the award, prize, medal, etc.; nature of the award, i. e., whether money, certificate, etc.; frequency of award; when established; list of years award has been given and names of winners. **Arrangement:** Classified by field, subdivided by keyword. **Indexes:** Combined alphabetical index of award names, names of winners, names of organizations. **Pages** (approx.): 725. **Frequency:** Not established; first edition 1978. **Editor:** Claire Walters. **Price:** $30.00.

★3309★
WOMEN HISTORIANS OF THE MIDWEST—MEMBERSHIP DIRECTORY
Women Historians of the Midwest
Box 80021
Como Station
St. Paul, MN 55108
Number of listings: About 300. **Entries include:** Name, address, affiliation, area of interest, phone. **Arrangement:** Alphabetical. **Pages** (approx.): 10. **Frequency:** Biennial, even years. **Price:** Available to members only.

★3310★
WORLD DICTIONARY OF AWARDS AND PRIZES
Europa Publications Ltd.
18 Bedford Square
London WC1B 3JN, England
Covers: More than 2,000 awards, prizes, medals, prestigious lectureships, and other recognitions given in countries throughout the world; includes prizes in all areas of artistic, scientific, and intellectual achievement. **Entries include:** Title of award, purpose, form (medal, cash prize, etc.), frequency and time of award, date established, name and address of awarding body, recent recipients, details of eligibility. **Arrangement:** Alphabetical by award name. **Indexes:** Keyword, subject, geographical. **Pages** (approx.): 380. **Frequency:** Not established; first edition July 1979. **Price:** $45.00. **Send orders to:** Gale Research Company, Book Tower, Detroit, MI 48226.

★3311★
WORLD DIRECTORY OF MAP COLLECTIONS
International Federation of Library Associations
Netherlands Congress Building
The Hague, Netherlands
Covers: About 300 chart and map collections in nearly 50 countries, with about 40% of the collections being in the United States, Canada, the United Kingdom, and Germany. **Entries include:** Collection name, address, nature, size, and type of collection and average growth, services and policies, etc. **Arrangement:** Geographical. **Pages** (approx.): 325. **Frequency:** Not established; first edition 1976. **Editor:** Walter W. Ristow. **Price:** $20.00. **Send orders to:** Unipub, Box 433, Murray Hill Station, New York, NY 10016.

★3312★
WORLD DIRECTORY OF SOCIAL SCIENCE INSTITUTIONS
United Nations Educational, Scientific, and Cultural Organization
7 Place de Fontenoy
Paris, France 75700
Entries include: Name and address of institution, date founded, name of head, staff size, geographical areas and subjects of special interest, types of activity (research, training, etc.), how financed, research

facilities, etc. **Arrangement:** Geographical. **Pages** (approx.): 260. **Frequency:** Irregular; latest edition 1977. **Former title:** World Index of Social Science Institutions. **Price:** 72 French Francs. **Other information:** Second in series, "World Social Science Information Services."

★3313★
WORLD INDEX OF ECONOMIC FORECASTS
Gower Press Ltd.
Box 5
Epping CM16 4BY, England
Publication includes: List of economic forecasting organizations worldwide. **Entries include:** Organization name, address, name of contact; particular interest or field, if any. **Frequency:** Irregular; latest edition 1978. **Editor:** George Cyriax. **Also includes:** Principal content of publication is forecasts and development plans for major countries of world.

World Index of Social Science Institutions *See* World Directory of Social Science Institutions

★3314★
WORLD LIST OF SOCIAL SCIENCE PERIODICALS
United Nations Educational, Scientific, And Cultural Organization
7 Place de Fontenoy
Paris, France 75700
Covers: 2,300 scholarly publications in the social sciences, and abstracting and reviewing serials. **Entries include:** Title, date first published and whether still being published, abbreviated title, name and address of firm or institution with editorial responsibility (and of publisher, if different), frequency, subjects covered, book reviews and other contents, indexes, etc. **Arrangement:** Geographical. **Indexes:** Alphabetical, subject. **Pages** (approx.): 380. **Frequency:** Irregular; latest edition 1976; new edition expected in 1979. Updates twice yearly in "International Social Science Journal." **Price:** 72 French Francs. **Other information:** First in the series, "World Social Science Information Services." Text in English and French.

★3315★
WRITERS DIRECTORY
St. Martin's Press, Inc.
175 Fifth Avenue   Phone: (212) 674-5151
New York, NY 10010
Covers: Over 15,000 writers whose works are published in English; necrology; and publishers in major English-speaking countries. **Entries include:** Name; pen-names, if any; nature of work; names of publishers; address; bibliography. For publishers - Name and address. **Arrangement:** Alphabetical. **Indexes:** Subject. **Pages** (approx.): 1,500. **Frequency:** Biennial, winter of even years. **Editors:** Nancy Duin and Timothy Faulkner. **Price:** $40.00.

★3316★
WRITER'S GUIDE TO CHICAGO-AREA PUBLISHERS AND OTHER FREELANCE MARKETS
Writer's Guide Publications
9329 Crawford Avenue
Evanston, IL 60203
Covers: Over 300 firms in the Chicago area that purchase books, articles, audiovisual scripts, educational materials, and other original written matter. **Entries include:** Firm name, address, name of contact, line of business, types of materials wanted, submission procedures, rate and manner of payment, rights policy, photograph needs. **Arrangement:** By type of firm (book publisher, periodical publisher, etc.). **Indexes:** Firm name. **Pages** (approx.): 320. **Frequency:** Biennial, odd years. **Editor:** Jerold L. Kellman. **Price:** $8.95, payment with order.

★3317★
WRITERS GUILD OF AMERICA, WEST—LIST OF AGENTS
Writers Guild of America, West
8955 Beverly Boulevard   Phone: (213) 550-1000
Los Angeles, CA 90048
Covers: More than 150 writers' agents who handle material for motion pictures, television, and radio. **Entries include:** Agency name, address, phone, types of material handled. **Price:** $1.00.

★3318★
WRITER'S HANDBOOK
The Writer, Inc.
8 Arlington Street   Phone: (617) 536-7420
Boston, MA 02116
Publication includes: 2,500 markets for the sale of manuscripts, plus a list of American literary agents, writers' organizations, prize offers, and awards. **Entries include:** Market entries give publisher's editorial requirements, payment rates, address, and name of editor. **Pages** (approx.): 830. **Frequency:** Annual, spring. **Editor:** Sylvia K. Burack. **Price:** $14.95. **Also includes:** About 100 chapters by various authors and editors on writing for publication.

★3319★
WRITER'S MARKET: WHERE TO SELL WHAT YOU WRITE
Writer's Digest Books
9933 Alliance Road   Phone: (513) 984-0717
Cincinnati, OH 45242
Covers: More than 4,500 buyers of novels, articles, plays, gags, verse, fillers, and other original written material. Includes book and periodical publishers, literary agents, greeting card publishers, play producers and publishers, audiovisual material producers. **Entries include:** Name and address of buyer, phone, payment rates, editorial requirements, reporting time, how to break in. **Arrangement:** By type of publication. **Pages** (approx.): 1,000. **Frequency:** Annual, October. **Editor:** William Brohaugh. **Price:** $14.95.

8

Biographical

Directories

★3320★
AFRO-AMERICAN ARTISTS: A BIO-BIBLIOGRAPHICAL DIRECTORY
Trustees of the Boston Public Library
Copley Square   Phone: (617) 536-5400
Boston, MA 02117
Covers: 2,000 Black artists, from the eighteenth century to the
present. **Entries include:** Artist's name, birthplace and date, media,
education and training, titles of known works, places of exhibition, and
a bibliography of writings by and on the artist. **Arrangement:**
Alphabetical. **Pages** (approx.): 350. **Frequency:** Published 1973.
Editor: Theresa D. Cedarholm, Fine Arts Librarian. **Price:** $10.00.

★3321★
THE AMERICAN BENCH
Reginald Bishop Forster & Associates, Inc.
2344 Nicollet, Suite 100   Phone: (800) 328-5091
Minneapolis, MN 55404
Covers: 15,000 judges above the justice of the peace level sitting in
local, state, and federal courts. **Entries include:** Name, personal and
professional data, jurisdiction, and important cases ruled on,
memberships, previous judgeships, office phone. **Arrangement:**
Alphabetical. **Pages** (approx.): 2,000. **Frequency:** Annual, November.
Price: $80.00.

★3322★
AMERICAN CATHOLIC WHO'S WHO
National Catholic News Service
1312 Massachusetts Avenue, N. W.   Phone: (202) 659-6722
Washington, DC 20005
Covers: About 6,000 prominent laypersons and clergy (including some
Canadian); includes a necrology. **Entries include:** Name, address,
personal and career data, activities within the Church, etc.
Arrangement: Alphabetical. **Indexes:** Geographical. **Frequency:**
Biennial, early in even years. **Editor:** Joy Anderson. **Price:** $24.95
(1980 edition).

American College of Physicians—Directory *See* Biographical
   Directory of the American College of Physicians

★3323★
AMERICAN INDIAN PAINTERS
Museum of the American Indian
Broadway at 155th Street   Phone: (212) 283-2420
New York, NY 10032
Covers: 1,187 persons, mostly still living. **Entries include:** Name,
vital statistics, tribal affiliations, career notes, exhibitions, collections
in which the artist is represented. **Arrangement:** Alphabetical.
Indexes: Tribal index. **Pages** (approx.): 270. **Frequency:** Published in

1968; no new editions planned. **Editor:** Jeanne O. Snodgrass. **Price:**
$7.50, plus 50¢ shipping. **Other information:** Contributions from the
Museum of the American Indian, Vol. XXI, Part 1, 1968.

★3324★
AMERICAN MEN AND WOMEN OF SCIENCE—BIOLOGY
Jaques Cattell Press
R. R. Bowker Company
2216 S. Industrial Park Drive   Phone: (602) 967-8885
Tempe, AZ 85282
Covers: 20,100 American and Canadian biological scientists in
biology, botany, and zoology and their related specialties and
disciplines. (Listings taken from data bank for "American Men and
Women of Science," 13th edition, 1976.) **Entries include:** Name,
address, discipline, personal and career data, memberships, research
interests. **Arrangement:** Alphabetical. **Indexes:** Geographical,
discipline. **Pages** (approx.): 1,150. **Frequency:** Not established; first
published under this title spring 1977. (See "Background" note in main
entry for AMWS.) **Price:** $49.95, postpaid, payment with order. **Send
orders to:** R. R. Bowker Co., Box 1807, Ann Arbor, MI 48106 (313-
761-4700).

★3325★
AMERICAN MEN AND WOMEN OF SCIENCE—CHEMISTRY
Jaques Cattell Press
R. R. Bowker Company
2216 S. Industrial Park Drive   Phone: (602) 967-8885
Tempe, AZ 85282
Covers: 29,700 American and Canadian chemists. (Listings taken
from data bank for "American Men and Women of Science," 13th
edition, 1976.) **Entries include:** Name, address, discipline, personal
and career data, memberships, research interests. **Arrangement:**
Alphabetical. **Indexes:** Geographical, discipline. **Pages** (approx.):
1,675. **Frequency:** Not established; first published under this title
spring 1977. (See "Background" note in main entry for AMWS.)
Price: $49.95, postpaid, payment with order. **Send orders to:** R. R.
Bowker Co., Ann Arbor, MI 48106 (313-761-4700).

★3326★
AMERICAN MEN AND WOMEN OF SCIENCE—CONSULTANTS
Jaques Cattell Press
R. R. Bowker Company
2216 S. Industrial Park Drive   Phone: (602) 967-8885
Tempe, AZ 85282
Covers: 15,500 scientists with consulting experience who are listed
in "American Men and Women of Science," 13th edition (1976).
Entries include: Name, address, discipline, personal and career data,
memberships, research interests. **Arrangement:** Alphabetical.
Indexes: Geographical, discipline. **Pages** (approx.): 1,100.

Frequency: Not established; first published under this title spring 1977. (See "Background" note in main entry for AMWS.) **Price:** $38.50, postpaid, payment with order. **Send orders to:** R. R. Bowker Co., Box 1807, Ann Arbor, MI 48106 (313-761-4700).

★3327★

AMERICAN MEN AND WOMEN OF SCIENCE—MEDICAL AND HEALTH SCIENCES
Jaques Cattell Press
R. R. Bowker Company
2216 S. Industrial Park Drive   Phone: (602) 967-8885
Tempe, AZ 85282
Covers: 26,600 persons working in dentistry, health sciences, medicine, neurosciences, pharmacology, psychiatry, surgery, pharmacy, and veterinary medicine. (Listings taken from data bank for "American Men and Women of Science," 13th edition, 1976, except for persons in pharmacy and veterinary medicine, who are not found in the base volumes.) **Entries include:** Name, address, discipline, personal and career data, memberships, research interests. **Arrangement:** Alphabetical. **Indexes:** Geographical, discipline. **Frequency:** Not established; first published under this title spring 1977. (See "Background" note in main entry for AMWS.) **Price:** $49.95, postpaid, payment with order. **Send orders to:** R. R. Bowker Co., Box 1807, Ann Arbor, MI 48106 (313-761-4700).

American Men and Women of Science—Physical and Biological Sciences *See* American Men and Women of Science

★3328★

AMERICAN MEN AND WOMEN OF SCIENCE—PHYSICS, ASTRONOMY, MATHEMATICS, STATISTICS, AND COMPUTER SCIENCES
Jaques Cattell Press
R. R. Bowker Company
2216 S. Industrial Park Drive   Phone: (602) 967-8885
Tempe, AZ 85282
Covers: 24,900 American and Canadian scientists. (Listings taken from data bank for "American Men and Women of Science," 13th edition, 1976.) **Entries include:** Name, address, discipline, personal and career data, memberships, research interests. **Arrangement:** Alphabetical. **Indexes:** Geographical, discipline. **Pages** (approx.): 1,300. **Frequency:** Not established; first published under this title spring 1977. (See "Background" note in main entry for AMWS.) **Price:** $45.00, postpaid, payment with order. **Send orders to:** R. R. Bowker Co., Box 1807, Ann Arbor, MI 48106 (313-761-4700).

★3329★

AMERICAN MEN AND WOMEN OF SCIENCE—SOCIAL AND BEHAVIORAL SCIENCES
Jaques Cattell Press
R. R. Bowker Company
2216 S. Industrial Park Drive   Phone: (602) 967-8885
Tempe, AZ 85282
Covers: 24,000 persons working in economics, sociology, psychology, political science, and academic, business, and industrial administration. **Entries include:** Name, address, discipline, personal and career data, memberships, research interests. **Arrangement:** Alphabetical. **Indexes:** Geographical, discipline. **Pages** (approx.): 1,500. **Frequency:** Irregular; latest edition 1978; new edition possible fall 1981. **Price:** $69.95, postpaid, payment with order. **Send orders to:** R. R. Bowker Co., Box 1807, Ann Arbor, MI 48106 (313-761-4700).

★3330★

AMERICAN MEN AND WOMEN OF SCIENCE
Jaques Cattell Press
R. R. Bowker Company
2216 S. Industrial Park Drive   Phone: (602) 967-8885
Tempe, AZ 85282
Background: Formerly, this publication devoted separate volumes to persons in the physical and biological sciences (6 volumes, in the 12th

edition, 1971), and the social and behavioral sciences (2 volumes). There were also derivative volumes for various disciplines - economics, medical sciences, etc. 13TH EDITION (Late 1976) - This edition consisted of a single set of seven volumes (six volumes of biographical sketches in a single alphabet and one volume of geographic and discipline indexes), and covered primarily persons in the physical and life sciences. Economics was to be covered in a separate volume; sociology, psychology, and political science were omitted because they were considered to be fully covered by membership directories. Later, derivative volumes in several disciplines were published (see separate entries under main title), and a social and behavioral sciences volume was announced to cover economics and the other non-technical fields previously omitted; the latter volume was published in 1978 (see separate entry under main title). An engineering volume was also announced for early 1979 publication, but it was never issued. 14TH EDITION (August, 1979) - Same format as the 13th, with one additional biographical volume (seven in all) and an index volume. Engineers and mathematicians are included in the base set. Publisher sometimes uses subtitle "Physical and Biological Sciences" for this set. A new social and behavioral sciences volume is planned for fall 1981; plans for new derivative volumes are uncertain. **Covers:** About 131,000 United States and Canadian scientists active in the physical, biological, mathematical, and engineering fields; includes references to previous edition for deceased and non-replying former listees. **Entries include:** Name, address, personal and career data, memberships, research interests. **Arrangement:** Alphabetical. **Indexes:** Separate volume of discipline and geographical indexes. **Pages** (approx.): 7,600. **Frequency:** Irregular; previous editions 1971 and 1976; latest edition 1979. **Former title:** American Men of Science (1968). **Price:** $385.00. **Send orders to:** R. R. Bowker Company, Box 1807, Ann Arbor, MI 48106 (313-761-4700).

American Men of Science *See* American Men and Women of Science

★3331★

AMERICAN POLITICAL SCIENCE ASSOCIATION—BIOGRAPHICAL DIRECTORY
Americal Political Science Association
1527 New Hampshire Avenue, N. W.   Phone: (202) 483-2512
Washington, DC 20036
Number of listings: 12,500. **Entries include:** Biographical information on 7,000 members; entries for an additional 5,500 members contain name and address only. **Arrangement:** Alphabetical. **Pages** (approx.): 680. **Frequency:** Irregular; last published 1973. **Advertising accepted.** Circulation 15,000. **Price:** $12.50, cloth; $10.00, paper. **Other information:** Updated by APSA "Directory of Members," annual.

★3332★

ARTISTS/USA: GUIDE TO CONTEMPORARY AMERICAN ART
Foundation for the Advancement of Artists
1315 Walnut Street   Phone: (215) 546-3336
Philadelphia, PA 19107
Covers: 300 living professional American artists. **Entries include:** Name, home address, personal data, career data, reproductions of artist's current works. **Arrangement:** Alphabetical. **Pages** (approx.): 200. **Frequency:** Biennial, spring of odd years. **Price:** $30.00.

★3333★

AUTHOR BIOGRAPHIES MASTER INDEX
Gale Research Company
Book Tower   Phone: (313) 961-2242
Detroit, MI 48226
Description: ABMI is a consolidated index of more than 415,000 references covering biographical sketches dealing with some 240,000 authors of all eras and nations whose listings appear in nearly 150 English-language biographical dictionaries. Both historical and contemporary works are indexed, including Allibone's "Critical Dictionary of English Literature;" Kunitz' "British Authors Before

1800," "Twentieth Century Authors," etc.; the various Oxford Companions to national literatures; and "Contemporary Authors" and "Something About the Author." Many works devoted to specialized areas of writing - poetry, women writers, etc. - are also indexed. **Entries include:** Name, date of birth (and death, where applicable), code indicating publication in which sketch appears. **Arrangement:** Alphabetical. **Pages** (approx.): 1,200. **Frequency:** First edition summer 1978; supplement expected mid-1980. **Editor:** Dennis La Beau. **Price:** $72.00 (two volume set).

Authors and Writers Who's Who *See* International Authors and Writers Who's Who

★3334★
AUTHORS OF BOOKS FOR YOUNG PEOPLE
Scarecrow Press, Inc.
52 Liberty Street   Phone: (201) 548-8600
Metuchen, NJ 08840
Covers: About 4,000 authors, both living and deceased, who have written or illustrated books for children and young adults. **Entries include:** Name, general and brief biographical details, mention of major publications, reference to present or former city of residence (but no address); some listings include references to other sources. **Arrangement:** Alphabetical, in two volumes; base volume published 1971, supplement 1979. **Pages** (approx.): Base volume, 600 pages; supplement, 300 pages. **Frequency:** Irregular. **Editors:** Martha E. Ward and Dorothy A. Marquardt. **Price:** Base volume, $19.00; supplement, $12.00.

★3335★
BAKER'S BIOGRAPHICAL DICTIONARY OF MUSICIANS
Schirmer Books
Macmillan Publishing Company, Inc.
866 Third Avenue   Phone: (212) 935-5521
New York, NY 10022
Covers: 12,000 composers, performers, musicologists, and other figures of classical and popular music. Listings include past and present musicians, worldwide. **Entries include:** Name, career data, writings, music composed, bibliography. **Arrangement:** Alphabetical. **Pages** (approx.): 2,000. **Frequency:** Irregular; previous edition 1958, with 1965 and 1971 supplements; latest edition 1978. **Editor:** Nicolas Slonimsky (formerly, Theodore Baker). **Price:** $75.00. **Send orders to:** Macmillan Publishing Company,   100-D Brown St., Riverside, NJ 08370 (609-461-6500).

★3336★
BIO-BASE: A MASTER INDEX TO BIOGRAPHIES IN 500 BIOGRAPHICAL DICTIONARIES
Gale Research Company
Book Tower   Phone: (313) 961-2242
Detroit, MI 48226
Covers: About two million citations to sketches found in some 500 biographical dictionaries and similar works. Includes all citations in Gale's "Biographical Dictionaries Master Index" (first edition) and "Author Biographies Master Index" (first edition), and most citations in "Theatre, Film, and Television Biographies Master Index" (first edition), as well as many thousands of citations not previously included in individual publications. (Publications mentioned by title are described in separate entries in the "Directory of Directories.") **Entries include:** Name, date of birth (and death, where applicable), code indicating publication in which sketch appears. **Arrangement:** Alphabetical. **Frequency:** Base collection issued spring 1979; first supplement expected January 1980; second supplement, cumulating first and containing total of about 500,000 entries, expected late 1980. **Price:** $300.00, including two supplements; available in microfiche only. **Other information:** Each set is accompanied by printed bibliography of works indexed.

Bio-bibliographical Directory of Chicano Scholars and Writers *See* Chicano Scholars and Writers: A Bio-bibliographical Directory

★3337★
BIOGRAPHIC REGISTER [State Department]
State Department
Washington, DC 20520
Covers: State Department and other federal government personnel involved in foreign affairs. **Other information:** Effective with the 1976 edition, because of security considerations distribution of the Biographic Register to the public was discontinued, and only a limited number of copies are distributed within the government.

★3338★
BIOGRAPHICAL DICTIONARIES AND RELATED WORKS
Gale Research Company
Book Tower   Phone: (313) 961-2242
Detroit, MI 48226
Description: Not a biographical directory, but surely one of the most comprehensive guides to such works which has ever been prepared. In the base volume (1967) and two supplements (1972 and spring 1978) more than 12,000 biographical reference works and publications containing substantial numbers of biographical entries are described. Scope includes who's whos; genealogical works; dictionaries of anonyms and pseudonyms; government manuals; portrait catalogs; etc. **Entries include:** Author, title, publisher, date, pages; most entries include brief annotation. **Arrangement:** Divided by types of works: general biographical reference works; works which cover specific countries or areas; and works which cover specific vocational areas, such as the arts, athletics, education, literature, philosophy, science, religion, etc. **Indexes:** Author, title, subject. **Pages** (approx.): Base volume, 1,050; first supplement, 850; second supplement, 925. **Frequency:** Irregular. **Editor:** Robert B. Slocum. **Price:** $120.00; $40.00 per volume.

★3339★
BIOGRAPHICAL DICTIONARIES MASTER INDEX
Gale Research Company
Book Tower   Phone: (313) 961-2242
Detroit, MI 48226
Description: BDMI and its supplements constitute a consolidated index which quickly indicates whether a biographical sketch being sought is contained in one or more of about 100 biographical dictionaries listing contemporary personalities. Publications indexed include "Who's Who in America," Marquis Who's Who regional publications, all volumes in the "American Men and Women of Science" series, "Who's Who in Government," and other large biographical reference works. The base set, plus the 1979 and 1980 supplements, give 1,270,000 citations. **Entries include:** Name, date of birth (and death, where applicable), code indicating publication in which sketch appears. **Arrangement:** Alphabetical. **Editor:** Dennis La Beau. **Price:** Base set (three volumes, 1975-76), $95.00; 1979-80 supplements, together, $72.00.

Biographical Directory of Americans and Canadians of Croatian Descent with Institutions, Organizations, and Periodicals

★3340★
BIOGRAPHICAL DIRECTORY OF NEGRO MINISTERS
G. K. Hall & Company
70 Lincoln Street   Phone: (617) 423-3990
Boston, MA 02111
Arrangement: Alphabetical. **Indexes:** Geographical. **Pages** (approx.): 580. **Frequency:** Irregular; latest edition November 1975. **Editor:** Ethel L. Williams. **Price:** $28.00.

★3341★
BIOGRAPHICAL DIRECTORY OF THE AMERICAN COLLEGE OF PHYSICIANS
Jaques Cattell Press
R. R. Bowker Company
2216 S. Industrial Park Drive   Phone: (602) 967-8885
Tempe, AZ 85282
Covers: Over 28,000 internists and allied specialists who are members of the American College of Physicians. **Entries include:** Name, membership status, date of joining, certification by medical specialty boards, education, honorary degrees, personal data, internship and residencies, post-graduate training, academic and professional positions, honors and awards, memberships, military service, number of publications, address, home and/or office phone. **Arrangement:** Geographical. **Indexes:** Personal name. **Pages** (approx.): 1,900. **Frequency:** Not established; first edition October 1979. **Former title:** American College of Physicians - Directory. **Price:** $52.50, postpaid, payment with order. **Send orders to:** R. R. Bowker Co., Box 1807, Ann Arbor, MI 48106 (313-761-4700).

★3342★
BIOGRAPHICAL DIRECTORY OF THE AMERICAN PSYCHIATRIC ASSOCIATION
Jaques Cattell Press
R. R. Bowker Company
2216 S. Industrial Park Drive   Phone: (602) 967-8885
Tempe, AZ 85282
Covers: Over 23,000 psychiatrists who are members. **Entries include:** Name, office address and phone, home address, personal and career data. **Arrangement:** Alphabetical. **Indexes:** Geographical. **Pages** (approx.): 1,575. **Frequency:** About every four years; last edition 1977. Alternates with "American Psychiatric Association - Membership Directory," which contains considerably less detail in its entries. **Price:** $47.50. **Send orders to:** R. R. Bowker Co., Box 1807, Ann Arbor, MI 48106 (313-761-4700).

Biographical Encyclopedia and Who's Who of the American Theatre *See* Notable Names in the American Theatre

★3343★
BLUE BOOK: LEADERS OF THE ENGLISH-SPEAKING WORLD
Gale Research Company
Book Tower   Phone: (313) 961-2242
Detroit, MI 48226
Covers: 15,000 prominent people in government, business, arts, sciences, and the professions in the United States, Canada, Britain, Ireland, Australia, and New Zealand. **Entries include:** Name, office and home addresses, personal data, career data, awards, works (for artists, authors, composers, etc.), appearances (for entertainers, musicians, etc.). **Arrangement:** Alphabetical. **Pages** (approx.): 1,650. **Frequency:** Irregular; latest edition 1976. **Price:** $65.00. **Other information:** Formerly published by St. Martin's Press.

★3344★
CHICANO SCHOLARS AND WRITERS: A BIO-BIBLIOGRAPHICAL DIRECTORY
Scarecrow Press, Inc.
52 Liberty Street   Phone: (201) 548-8600
Metuchen, NJ 08840
Covers: More than 500 Chicanos, "as well as some Anglo Chicanistas and Latin Americans," in the social sciences, humanities, and education. **Entries include:** Name, address, educational and career data, list of writings. **Arrangement:** Alphabetical. **Pages** (approx.): 590. **Frequency:** Not established; first edition fall 1979. **Editor:** Julio A. Martinez. **Former title:** Originally advertised as, "Bio-bibliographical Directory of Chicano Scholars and Writers." **Price:** $26.50.

★3345★
CHILDREN'S AUTHORS AND ILLUSTRATORS: AN INDEX TO BIOGRAPHICAL DICTIONARIES
Gale Research Company
Book Tower   Phone: (313) 961-2242
Detroit, MI 48226
Covers: About 55,000 citations to biographical sketches of some 15,000 authors for children and young people listed in nearly 150 reference sources. **Entries include:** Name, date of birth (and death, where applicable), code indicating publication in which sketch appears. **Arrangement:** Alphabetical. **Pages** (approx.): 250. **Frequency:** Irregular; previous edition 1976; latest edition 1979. **Editor:** Adele Sarkissian. **Price:** $26.00.

★3346★
COMMUNITY LEADERS AND NOTEWORTHY AMERICANS
American Biographical Institute, Division
Historical Preservations of America, Inc.
205 W. Martin Street
Raleigh, NC 27602
Description: Lists about 9,000 persons chosen by the editorial board of the publication as distinguished and outstanding; criteria not specified. **Entries include:** Individual name, career, educational and personal data, and special awards or recognition. **Arrangement:** Alphabetical. **Frequency:** Annual, fall. **Price:** $44.95, payment with order; $49.95, billed. **Other information:** Former company name is News Publishing Company.

★3347★
CONTEMPORARY ARCHITECTS
St. Martin's Press, Inc.
175 Fifth Avenue   Phone: (212) 674-5151
New York, NY 10010
Covers: About 700 architects, worldwide. **Entries include:** Biographical data, constructed works and projects, bibliography, critical essay of the architect's work, architectural firm name and address; some entries include comments by the architect and an illustration. **Arrangement:** Alphabetical. **Pages** (approx.): 1,100. **Frequency:** First edition expected April 1980. **Editor:** Muriel Emanuel. **Price:** $60.00 (tentative).

★3348★
CONTEMPORARY ARTISTS
St. Martin's Press, Inc.
175 Fifth Avenue   Phone: (212) 674-5151
New York, NY 10010
Covers: 1,350 artists, worldwide. **Entries include:** Biographical data, one-man and group shows, collections in which represented, bibliography, addresses for artist and artist's dealer, critical essay on the artist's work; some entries include comments by the artist and an illustration. **Arrangement:** Alphabetical. **Pages** (approx.): 1,000. **Frequency:** About every five years; first edition 1977; new edition possible 1982. **Price:** $50.00, plus $1.50 shipping.

★3349★
CONTEMPORARY AUTHORS
Gale Research Company
Book Tower   Phone: (313) 961-2242
Detroit, MI 48226
Description: "Contemporary Authors" is the largest and most comprehensive collection of bio-bibliographical material concerning authors now available, and probably the largest ever compiled in equal detail. First published in the fall of 1962, it now covers about 55,000 authors who are currently active or who have lived since 1960, and the series is continuing. Until Volumes 65-68 (1977), listing in CA was limited to authors of books of a non-technical nature which were published by commercial, risk publishing houses. (Self-published authors, and the authors of works issued by vanity publishing houses, are not included.) Beginning with Volumes 65-68, the scope of the series was changed to include writers in other media, and the subtitle of the work became, "A Bio-bibliographical Guide to Current Writers in

Fiction, General Nonfiction, Poetry, Journalism, Drama, Motion Pictures, Television, and Other Fields." CA is compiled by the use of questionnaires, for the most part; some sketches are written from secondary sources, but in all cases the final manuscript is submitted to the person concerned (or his survivors) for checking. The hyphenated double-numbering system for individual volumes came about as follows: The first four volumes of CA were published as quarterlies, and carried single volume numbers; at the end of the first year, the frequency became semiannual, the size of individual volumes was doubled, and volumes carried two volume numbers; about two years later, the size of volumes was again doubled, making them four times the size of the original volumes, and the present practice of using four numbers for each physical volume began. **Entries include:** Author's name, full date of birth, place of birth, parents' names and occupations; spouse's and children's names; schools attended, with dates and degrees; politics; religion; home and office addresses; career outline; memberships; full bibliography with names of publishers and dates, and principal readers, anthologies, etc., contributed to; CA includes as unique features a description of works in progress and a section entitled "Sidelights," in which the subject's interests, philosophy, influences, etc., are discussed, often in the words of the author. (CA sets off the major sections of entries in paragraph form for ease of use, and was the first biographical directory to do so.) **Arrangement:** Each volume is alphabetical; there is no duplication between volumes. **Indexes:** A fully-cumulative index is included in alternate volumes; the index also includes references to authors represented by biographical material, or whose works are criticized in "Something About the Author" (see separate listing) and "Contemporary Literary Criticism," both published by Gale. **Pages** (approx.): 625. **Frequency:** About two volumes a year; revised volumes are published about five years after original publication; latest original edition, Volumes 85-88, published December 1979. **Editors:** Christine Nasso, general editor, "Contemporary Authors" series; Frances Carol Locher, editor, original volumes; Ann Evory, editor, revised volumes. **Price:** $48.00 per volume.

★3350★
CONTEMPORARY DRAMATISTS
St. Martin's Press
175 Fifth Avenue   Phone: (212) 674-5151
New York, NY 10010
Covers: About 350 dramatists writing in English. **Entries include:** Name, home and office addresses; personal, educational, and career data; list of plays with dates of first performances, bibliography of other works, and commentaries on playwright's work by playwright and a critic. **Arrangement:** Alphabetical. **Indexes:** Play titles. **Pages** (approx.): 1,100. **Frequency:** Every five years; latest edition 1977. **Editor:** James Vinson. **Price:** $35.00.

★3351★
CONTEMPORARY NOVELISTS
St. Martin's Press, Inc.
175 Fifth Avenue   Phone: (212) 674-5151
New York, NY 10010
Covers: About 600 novelists writing in English; necrology of post-war novelists. **Entries include:** Name, home and office addresses; personal, education, and career data; bibliography; other published bibliographies; locations of manuscript collections; critical studies; critical essay; comments by the novelist. **Arrangement:** Alphabetical. **Pages** (approx.): 1,640. **Frequency:** Five year intervals; latest edition 1976; new edition expected 1981. **Price:** $40.00.

★3352★
CONTEMPORARY POETS
St. Martin's Press
175 Fifth Avenue   Phone: (212) 674-5151
New York, NY 10010
Covers: 800 poets writing in English. **Entries include:** Name, home and office addresses; personal, educational, and career data; bibliography; entries may include comments by the poet and there is a critical essay on each entrant. **Arrangement:** Geographical. **Pages**

(approx.): 1,850. **Frequency:** Irregular; latest edition 1975; new edition expected 1980. **Editor:** James Vinson. **Former title:** Contemporary Poets of the English Language. **Price:** $35.00.

★3353★
CORPORATE REPORT WHO'S WHO IN UPPER MIDWEST BUSINESS
Ninth Federal Communications, Inc.
7101 York Avenue South   Phone: (612) 835-2700
Minneapolis, MN 55435
Covers: Principal executives in companies in the Ninth Federal Reserve District (Minnesota, North and South Dakota, Montana, Michigan Upper Peninsula, and northwest Wisconsin) which employ more than 100 persons; presidents or managing executives of banks in the area with more than $15,000,000 in deposits; and other leaders. **Entries include:** Name, position, employer, address and phone; birth date and personal data; career history; activities, memberships, and awards. **Arrangement:** Alphabetical. **Frequency:** Published 1976; no new edition planned. **Price:** $5.00.

Cum Laude Society *See* What's What with Who's Who?

★3354★
CURRENT BIOGRAPHIES OF LEADING ARCHAEOLOGISTS
Chesopiean Library of Archaeology
7507 Pennington Road   Phone: (804) 588-4254
Norfolk, VA 23505
Number of listings: Over 100. **Entries include:** Name, office and home addresses, highest degree held, occupational specialties, personal and career data, writings, and sites excavated. **Pages** (approx.): 130. **Frequency:** Irregular; first edition 1976. **Editor:** Floyd Painter. **Price:** $7.95, postpaid.

★3355★
DICTIONARY OF INTERNATIONAL BIOGRAPHY
International Biographical Centre
Melrose Press Ltd.
17/21 Churchgate Street
Soham, Ely
Cambridgeshire CB7 5DS, England
Covers: "Living men and women from all walks of life;" criteria for inclusion not specified; worldwide coverage. (Number of listings varies from edition to edition; new volumes do not repeat listings from earlier editions.) **Entries include:** Name, address; personal, education, and career data. **Arrangement:** Alphabetical. **Pages** (approx.): 1,000. **Frequency:** Annual, March. **Editor:** Ernest Kay. **Price:** $67.50. **Send orders to:** Biblio Distribution Center, 81 Adams Drive, Totowa, NJ 07512. **Other information:** Publisher also sells plaques or other forms of recognition to those listed.

Directory of American Fiction Writers *See* Directory of American Poets and Fiction Writers

★3356★
DIRECTORY OF AMERICAN POETS AND FICTION WRITERS
Poets & Writers, Inc.
201 W. 54th Street   Phone: (212) 757-1766
New York, NY 10019
Covers: 4,400 professional, contemporary poets and fiction writers who publish in America. **Entries include:** Name, office and home address, office and home phone number, areas of occupational specialization, languages spoken, latest book published. **Arrangement:** Geographical. **Indexes:** Alphabetical, with sub-index of poets who are members of ethnic groups. **Pages** (approx.): 200. **Frequency:** Biennial; first edition under this title expected June 1980. **Other information:** Supersedes "Directory of American Poets" and "Directory of American Fiction Writers." **Price:** Not set.

★3357★
DIRECTORY OF AMERICAN SCHOLARS
Jaques Cattell Press
R. R. Bowker Company
2216 S. Industrial Park Drive   Phone: (602) 967-8885
Tempe, AZ 85282
Covers: 40,000 American and Canadian humanities scholars. Volume 1 - History; Volume 2 - English, speech, and drama; Volume 3 - Foreign languages, linguistics, and philology; and Volume 4 - Philosophy, religion, and law. **Entries include:** Name, address, discipline, personal and career data, memberships, research interests. **Arrangement:** Alphabetical. **Indexes:** Geographical, showing location and discipline; also, Volume 4 includes a master alphabetical index to the entire set. **Pages** (approx.): Volume 1, 825; Volume 2, 810; Volume 3, 600; Volume 4, 700. **Frequency:** Irregular; latest edition November 1978; new edition expected 1982. **Price:** $165.00 for four volume set; $45.00 for individual volume; postpaid, payment with order (ISSN 0070-5101). **Send orders to:** R. R. Bowker Company, Box 1807, Ann Arbor, MI 48106 (313-761-4700).

★3358★
DIRECTORY OF BLACKS IN THE PERFORMING ARTS
Scarecrow Press, Inc.
52 Liberty Street   Phone: (201) 548-8600
Metuchen, NJ 08840
Covers: About 850 Blacks, including many still living, who during the last two centuries have contributed to the theater, dance, films, music, radio and television, and other entertainment media in the United States. **Entries include:** Name, birth date (and death date, if applicable), education, brief career data, list of movie or stage or other credits, hobbies, and address. **Arrangement:** Alphabetical. **Indexes:** Vocational. **Pages** (approx.): 450. **Frequency:** Not established; first edition 1978. **Editor:** Edward Mapp. **Price:** $17.50, plus $1.00 shipping.

Distinguished Young Americans Foundation See **What's What with Who's Who?**

Engineers of Distinction See **Who's Who in Engineering**

★3359★
FOURTH BOOK OF JUNIOR AUTHORS AND ILLUSTRATORS
H. W. Wilson Company
950 University Avenue   Phone: (212) 588-8400
Bronx, NY 10452
Covers: Authors (and, in most recent volume, illustrators) of books for children; each volume (see "Former titles," below) includes approximately 250 biographical sketches. Some sketches are autobiographical, some written by editors. **Entries include:** Name, dates, identification of sketch as autobiographical or biographical, the listing itself (usually, 350-600 words), a bibliography of selected works, and, in some cases, a source for additional information. Most entries also include a small photograph and an autograph. **Arrangement:** Alphabetical. **Indexes:** Cumulative name index to the series. **Pages** (approx.): 370. **Frequency:** Irregular; previous editions under various titles published 1934 (revised 1951), 1963, 1972; latest edition published 1978; new edition possible 1984. **Editors:** Doris de Montreville and Elizabeth D. Crawford. **Former title:** Junior Book of Authors; More Junior Authors; Third Book of Junior Authors. **Price:** $17.00.

★3360★
INDEX OF SOUTH DAKOTA ARTISTS
South Dakota Memorial Art Center
          Phone: (605) 688-5423
Brookings, SD 57006
Covers: 400 South Dakota artists of the nineteenth and twentieth centuries, including many living artists. **Entries include:** Artist's name, home address, highest degree held, media and/or genre, personal and career data, and major awards, collections, and publications. **Arrangement:** Alphabetical. **Pages** (approx.): 415. **Frequency:**

Irregular; latest edition 1974. **Editor:** Joseph Stuart, Director. **Price:** $25.00.

★3361★
INTERCOM: THE COMPLETE HISPANIC AMERICAN WHO'S WHO NEWSLETTER—VIVA ISSUE
Institute for the Study of the Hispanic American in U.S. Life and History
C/o Domingo Nick Reyes
Box 15096   Phone: (703) 780-6783
Alexandria, VA 22309
Covers: About 6,000 Hispanic Americans living in the United States involved in the study of Hispanic American life and history. **Entries include:** Name, office and home address, personal and career data, publications, areas of interest. **Arrangement:** Geographical. **Indexes:** Personal name, institution name. **Pages** (approx.): 600. **Frequency:** Annual. **Editor:** Domingo Nick Reyes, President. **Price:** $18.00, plus $2.16 shipping.

★3362★
INTERNATIONAL AUTHORS AND WRITERS WHO'S WHO
Gale Research Company
Book Tower   Phone: (313) 961-2242
Detroit, MI 48226
Covers: 14,000 writers, primarily American and British but including writers of other nationalities of interest in the English-speaking world. Covers novelists, poets, dramatists, editors, critics, journalists, textbook authors, radio and TV writers, etc. Based on questionnaires. Includes international list of literary agents. **Entries include:** Name, pseudonyms, personal data, principal works, other reference books in which listed, literary agent. **Arrangement:** Alphabetical. **Pages** (approx.): 1,160. **Frequency:** Irregular; latest edition September 1977; new edition expected 1981. **Editor:** Ernest Kay. **Former title:** Author's and Writer's Who's Who (1975). **Price:** $58.00. **Other information:** Compiled by, and published outside the United States and Canada by, Melrose Press Ltd.

★3363★
INTERNATIONAL WHO'S WHO
Europa Publications Ltd.
18 Bedford Square
London WC1B 3JN, England
Covers: Over 15,000 prominent persons, worldwide. **Entries include:** Name, nationality, personal and career information, honors, awards, writings, address. **Arrangement:** Alphabetical. **Pages** (approx.): 1,400. **Frequency:** Annual, fall. **Price:** $84.00 (ISSN 0074-9613). **Send orders to:** Gale Research Co., Book Tower, Detroit, MI 48226 (313-961-2242).

★3364★
INTERNATIONAL WHO'S WHO IN ART AND ANTIQUES
International Biographical Centre
Melrose Press Ltd.
17/21 Churchgate Street
Soham, Ely
Cambridgeshire CB7 5DS, England
Covers: About 5,000 living artists and collectors, writers, etc.; criteria not specified; worldwide coverage. **Entries include:** Name, address, personal, education, and career data; exhibitions, awards. **Arrangement:** Alphabetical. **Pages** (approx.): 550. **Frequency:** Irregular; latest edition 1976. **Editor:** Ernest Kay. **Price:** $37.50. **Send orders to:** Biblio Distribution Center, 81 Adams Drive, Totowa, NJ 07512.

★3365★

INTERNATIONAL WHO'S WHO IN COMMUNITY SERVICE
International Biographical Centre
Melrose Press Ltd.
17/21 Churchgate Street
Soham, Ely
Cambridgeshire CB7 5DS, England
Covers: About 5,000 persons related to community service through donation, volunteer work, or as a profession; criteria not given. **Entries include:** Name, personal and family data, current community service, address; some entries include additional detail. **Arrangement:** Alphabetical. **Pages** (approx.): 500. **Frequency:** Irregular; latest edition 1979; new edition expected 1981. **Price:** $47.50. **Send orders to:** Biblio Distribution Center, 81 Adams Drive, Totowa, NJ 07512. **Other information:** Publisher also sells plaques or other forms of recognition to those listed.

★3366★

INTERNATIONAL WHO'S WHO IN EDUCATION
International Biographical Centre
Melrose Press Ltd.
17/21 Churchgate Street
Soham, Ely
Cambridgeshire CB7 5DS, England
Covers: About 10,000 persons at all levels of teaching and educational administration; selection criteria not specified; worldwide coverage, with emphasis on English-speaking countries. **Entries include:** Name, address; personal, education, and career data. **Arrangement:** Alphabetical. **Frequency:** Irregular; new edition expected 1980. **Editor:** Ernest Kay. **Former title:** Who's Who in Education. **Price:** $54.50. **Send orders to:** Biblio Distribution Center, 81 Adams Drive, Totowa, NJ 07512. **Other information:** Publisher also sells plaques or other forms of recognition to those listed.

★3367★

INTERNATIONAL WHO'S WHO IN MUSIC AND MUSICIAN'S DIRECTORY
Gale Research Company
Book Tower   Phone: (313) 961-2242
Detroit, MI 48226
Covers: 10,000 composers, critics, managers, publishers, vocalists, instrumentalists, and others in the world of music, primarily classical and semi-classical. Appendixes include lists of orchestras, concert halls and opera houses; musical organizations, music festivals, competitions, and awards; colleges and other institutions offering courses in music. **Entries include:** Name, profession or musical specialty, personal data, professional career details, principal recordings, current management, writings, full address and phone (where supplied). **Arrangement:** Alphabetical. **Pages** (approx.): 1,170. **Frequency:** Irregular; latest edition August 1977; new edition expected July 1980. **Editor:** Adrian Gaster. **Former title:** Who's Who in Music and Musician's International Directory (1975). **Price:** $65.00. **Other information:** Compiled by, and published outside the United States and Canada by, Melrose Press Ltd.

★3368★

INTERNATIONAL WHO'S WHO IN POETRY
International Biographical Centre
Melrose Press Ltd.
17/21 Churchgate Street
Soham, Ely
Cambridgeshire CB7 5DS, England
Covers: About 5,000 living poets; worldwide coverage. Also included are poetry societies, publishers of poetry, and sponsors of poetry awards. **Entries include:** For poets - Name, address; personal, educational, and career data; bibliography. For other listings - Name, address; publisher listings include type of poetry; sponsor listings include award names and amounts. **Arrangement:** Alphabetical. **Indexes:** Pseudonym. **Pages** (approx.): 715. **Frequency:** Irregular; latest edition 1977. **Editor:** Ernest Kay. **Price:** $42.50. **Send orders to:** International Biographical Centre, Biblio Distribution Centre, 81

Adams Drive, Totowa, NJ 07512 (201-256-8600). **Also includes:** In appendixes - Name of poets laureate of the United Kingdom; names of state poets for the United States; recorded poetry; and Library of Congress holdings of recorded poetry and poet conversations.

★3369★

JOURNALIST BIOGRAPHIES MASTER INDEX
Gale Research Company
Book Tower   Phone: (313) 961-2242
Detroit, MI 48226
Covers: About 90,000 citations to textual references to and biographical sketches of historical and contemporary journalists which appear in about 200 biographical directories and other sources; includes persons in magazine and broadcast media fields as well as newspapers. **Entries include:** Name, date of birth (and death, where applicable), code indicating publication in which sketch appears. **Arrangement:** Alphabetical. **Pages** (approx.): 380. **Frequency:** Not established; first edition 1979. **Editor:** Alan E. Abrams. **Price:** $40.00.

Junior Book of Authors *See* Fourth Book of Junior Authors and Illustrators

★3370★

LEADERS IN ELECTRONICS
McGraw-Hill, Inc.
1221 Avenue of the Americas   Phone: (212) 997-1221
New York, NY 10020
Covers: Over 5,000 persons employed in key positions in the electronics industry, worldwide. **Entries include:** Name, affiliation, address, phone; home address and phone; educational, personal, and career data; awards, memberships, and achievements; patents and publications. **Arrangement:** Alphabetical. **Indexes:** Affiliation. **Pages** (approx.): 675. **Frequency:** First edition published 1979; new edition expected 1982. **Price:** $39.50, postpaid, payment with order. **Send orders to:** McGraw-Hill Order Dept., Box 699, Hightstown, NJ 08520 (609-448-1700). **Other information:** Compiled by the editors of "Electronics Magazine."

★3371★

MARQUIS WHO'S WHO PUBLICATIONS/INDEX TO ALL BOOKS
Marquis Who's Who, Inc.
200 E. Ohio Street   Phone: (312) 787-2008
Chicago, IL 60611
Description: Gives 250,000 names listed in most of the Marquis Who's Who biographical reference publications in a single alphabet. Does not include the "Directory of Medical Specialists" and covers only Volume VI of "Who Was Who in America." **Entries include:** Name, volume in which listed. **Arrangement:** Alphabetical. **Pages** (approx.): 550. **Frequency:** Annual, January. **Price:** $14.50, plus $2.50 shipping (current and 1980 editions).

★3372★

MEN AND WOMEN OF DISTINCTION
International Biographical Centre
Melrose Press Ltd.
17/21 Churchgate Street
Soham, Ely
Cambridgeshire CB7 5DS, England
Covers: "Living men and women of particular achievement;" criteria not specified; worldwide coverage. **Entries include:** Name, address; personal, education, and career data. **Arrangement:** Alphabetical. **Pages** (approx.): 600. **Frequency:** First edition expected 1980; irregular thereafter. **Editor:** Ernest Kay. **Price:** $125.00. **Send orders to:** Biblio Distribution Center, 81 Adams Drive, Totowa, NJ 07512. **Other information:** Publisher also sells plaques or other forms of recognition to those listed.

★3373★
MEN OF ACHIEVEMENT
International Biographical Centre
Melrose Press Ltd.
17/21 Churchgate Street
Soham, Ely
Cambridgeshire CB7 5DS, England
Covers: "Living men of particular achievement;" criteria not specified; worldwide coverage. **Entries include:** Name, address; personal, education, and career data; majority of entries include photograph. **Arrangement:** Alphabetical. **Pages** (approx.): 700. **Frequency:** Annual, spring. **Editor:** Ernest Kay. **Price:** $65.00. **Send orders to:** Biblio Distribution Center, 81 Adams Drive, Totowa, NJ 07512. **Other information:** Publisher also sells plaques or other forms of recognition to those listed.

Merit's Who's Who among American High School Students *See* Who's Who among American High School Students

More Junior Authors *See* Fourth Book of Junior Authors and Illustrators

National Beta Club *See* What's What with Who's Who?

National High School Award for Excellence *See* What's What with Who's Who?

National Honor Society *See* What's What with Who's Who?

National Honorary Society-Order of Lambda *See* What's What with Who's Who?

National Panorama of American Youth *See* What's What with Who's Who?

National Society of Student Leaders *See* What's What with Who's Who?

★3374★
NEW YORK TIMES BIOGRAPHICAL SERVICE
Arno Press, Subsidiary
New York Times Company
Three Park Avenue
New York, NY 10016
Description: Reproduces clippings of major biographical articles from news sections of the "New York Times" as well as obituaries. **Arrangement:** Random. **Indexes:** Alphabetical name index in each issue, with annual cumulation. **Pages** (approx.): Looseleaf. **Frequency:** Monthly. **Price:** $85.00 per year (ISSN 0161-2433).

★3375★
NOTABLE AMERICANS
American Biographical Institute, Division
Historical Preservations of America, Inc.
205 W. Martin Street
Raleigh, NC 27602
Description: Lists about 8,000 persons chosen by the editorial board of the publication as distinguished or outstanding; criteria not specified. **Entries include:** Individual name, career, educational, and personal data, and special awards or recognition. **Arrangement:** Alphabetical. **Indexes:** Geographical. **Frequency:** Irregular. **Editor:** J. S. Thomson. **Price:** $39.95, payment with order; $49.95, billed. **Other information:** Former company name is News Publishing Company.

★3376★
NOTABLE NAMES IN THE AMERICAN THEATRE
James T. White Company
1700 State Highway 3   Phone: (201) 773-9300
Clifton, NJ 07013
Covers: 3,000 living or recently deceased actors, actresses,

producers, playwrights, stage and costume designers, choreographers, composers, lyricists, conductors, casting directors, teachers, critics, educators, authors, historians, etc., who have made notable contributions to the American theater. **Entries include:** Names, personal and career data, affiliations, etc. **Arrangement:** Alphabetical. **Pages** (approx.): 1,250. **Frequency:** Irregular; previous edition 1966; latest edition 1976. **Editor:** Raymond D. McGill. **Former title:** Biographical Encyclopedia and Who's Who of American Theatre. **Price:** $69.00. **Send orders to:** Publisher or Gale Research Co., Book Tower, Detroit, MI (313-961-2242). **Also includes:** List of New York performances since 1900; premieres throughout America, with production data; premieres of American plays abroad; theater awards and recipients; theater group histories; theater building biographies; necrology; bibliography.

★3377★
O'DWYER'S DIRECTORY OF PUBLIC RELATIONS EXECUTIVES
J. R. O'Dwyer Company, Inc.
271 Madison Avenue   Phone: (212) 679-2471
New York, NY 10016
Covers: More than 2,000 corporation and public relation agency executives. **Entries include:** Name, business affiliation, address, personal and career data. **Pages** (approx.): 175. **Frequency:** Not established; first edition 1979. **Price:** $50.00.

Outstanding Teenagers of America *See* What's What with Who's Who

★3378★
PERSONALITIES OF AMERICA
American Biographical Institute, Division
Historical Preservations of America, Inc.
205 W. Martin Street
Raleigh, NC 27602
Description: Lists about 7,000 persons chosen by the editorial board of the publication as distinguished or outstanding; criteria not specified. **Entries include:** Individual name, career, educational and personal data, and special awards or recognition. **Arrangement:** Alphabetical. **Indexes:** Geographical. **Frequency:** Irregular. **Editor:** J. S. Thompson. **Price:** $45.00, payment with order; $55.00, billed. **Other information:** Former company name is News Publishing Company.

★3379★
PERSONALITIES OF THE SOUTH
American Biographical Institute, Division
Historical Preservations of America, Inc.
205 W. Martin Street
Raleigh, NC 27602
Description: Lists about 10,000 persons chosen by the editorial board of the publication as distinguished or outstanding; criteria not specified. **Entries include:** Individual name, career, educational and personal data, and special awards or recognition. **Arrangement:** Alphabetical. **Indexes:** Geographical. **Frequency:** Annual. **Price:** $39.95, payment with order; $49.95, billed. **Other information:** Former company name is News Publishing Company.

★3380★
PERSONALITIES OF THE WEST AND MIDWEST
American Biographical Institute, Division
Historical Preservations of America, Inc.
205 W. Martin Street
Raleigh, NC 27602
Description: Lists about 10,000 persons chosen by the editorial board of the publication as distinguished or outstanding; criteria not specified. **Entries include:** Individual name, career, educational and personal data, and special awards or recognition. **Arrangement:** Alphabetical. **Frequency:** Biennial. **Price:** $39.95, payment with order; $49.95, billed. **Other information:** Former company name is News Publishing Company.

Prep All Americans *See* What's What with Who's Who?

★3381★
SCIENCE FICTION AND FANTASY LITERATURE
Gale Research Company
Book Tower   Phone: (313) 961-2242
Detroit, MI 48226
Publication includes: 1,450 biographical sketches on science fiction
and fantasy authors, including many still living. **Entries include:** Name,
dates, personal and career data, first professional sale, agent's or
personal address, memberships, avocations and interests, and,
frequently, a personal statement by the author. **Arrangement:**
Alphabetical. **Indexes:** Title, series, award, and Ace and Belmont
Doubles. **Pages** (approx.): 1,140 in two volumes. **Frequency:**
Irregular; first edition November 1979. **Editor:** Robert Reginald.
Price: $64.00. **Also includes:** Checklist of nearly 16,000 English-
language first editions of books of science fiction, fantasy, and
supernatural literature, and of nonfiction works on these subjects,
published between 1700 and 1974.

★3382★
SELECTED BLACK AMERICAN AUTHORS: AN ILLUSTRATED BIO-
    BIBLIOGRAPHY
G. K. Hall and Company
70 Lincoln Street   Phone: (617) 423-3990
Boston, MA 02111
Covers: 455 Black American authors from colonial times to present.
Entries include: Individual name, biographical data, and works
published. **Arrangement:** Alphabetical. **Pages** (approx.): 400.
Frequency: Irregular; first edition December 1977. **Editor:** James A.
Page. **Price:** $30.00.

Society of Distinguished American High School Students *See*
    What's What with Who's Who?

★3383★
SOMETHING ABOUT THE AUTHOR
Gale Research Company
Book Tower   Phone: (313) 961-2242
Detroit, MI 48226
Covers: In each volume, over 200 authors and illustrators of
children's books. Series includes nearly 3,000 authors now living or
who have died since 1960; beginning with Volume 15, SATA also
includes lengthy sketches of authors and illustrators who died before
1960. **Entries include:** Author name, address, birth date (and death
date, where needed), personal and career data, full bibliography
(including works illustrated), picture of author, illustration pertaining to
one of author's works; most entries include fairly lengthy personal
statement in ''Sidelights'' section. **Arrangement:** Each volume is
alphabetical; there is no duplication between volumes. **Indexes:**
Cumulative personal name index of authors and illustrators; SATA
authors are also listed in the cumulative indexes published in alternate
volumes of ''Contemporary Authors'' (see separate listing). **Pages**
(approx.): 250-275. **Frequency:** About two volumes a year; latest
volume, Volume 17, published December 1979. **Editor:** Anne
Commire. **Price:** $30.00.

★3384★
TEXTILE WORLD'S LEADERS IN THE TEXTILE INDUSTRY
McGraw-Hill, Inc.
1221 Avenue of the Americas   Phone: (212) 997-1221
New York, NY 10020
Covers: 1,500 individuals active in textile manufacturing, marketing,
design, research, and other textile-related fields. **Entries include:**
Name, title, affiliation, address; home address; personal, educational,
and career data; areas of expertise, awards, inventions, etc. **Indexes:**
Company of affiliation, geographical. **Pages** (approx.): 330.
Frequency: Not established; first edition September 1979. **Editors:**
Laurence A. Christiansen, Theodore V. Shumeyko, Richard G.
Mansfield. **Price:** $31.95.

★3385★
THEATRE, FILM AND TELEVISION BIOGRAPHIES MASTER INDEX
Gale Research Company
Book Tower   Phone: (313) 961-2242
Detroit, MI 48226
Covers: About 100,000 citations to biographical sketches in more
than 40 biographical dictionaries and directories devoted to the stage,
screen, opera, popular music, radio, and television. Includes
performers, directors, writers, composers, and others. **Entries
include:** Name, date of birth (and death, where applicable), code
indicating publication in which sketch appears. **Arrangement:**
Alphabetical. **Pages** (approx.): 475. **Frequency:** Not established; first
edition 1979. **Editor:** Dennis La Beau. **Price:** $38.00.

Third Book of Junior Authors *See* Fourth Book of Junior Authors
    and Illustrators

★3386★
TRUSTEES OF WEALTH
Taft Corporation
1000 Vermont Avenue, N. W., Suite 600   Phone: (202) 347-0788
Washington DC 20005
Covers: About 7,800 private and corporate foundation officers.
Entries include: Name, office address, foundation and other non-
business affiliations, titles, birth year, education, employment history,
publications, home city. **Arrangement:** Alphabetical. **Indexes:**
Geographical, foundation name. **Pages** (approx.): 475. **Frequency:**
Biennial in odd years. **Editor:** Jean Brodsky. **Price:** $90.00, payment
with order; $95.00, billed.

★3387★
TWENTIETH CENTURY CHILDREN'S WRITERS
St. Martin's Press
175 Fifth Avenue   Phone: (212) 674-5151
New York, NY 10010
Covers: 600 English-language authors of fiction, poetry, and drama
for children. **Entries include:** Name, home address, highest degree
held, personal data, career data, full bibliographies, entrant's
comments on his own writing, critical essay for each writer. **Pages**
(approx.): 1,700. **Frequency:** First edition September 1978;
publication every five years is planned. **Editor:** Daniel Kirkpatrick.
Price: $40.00.

★3388★
WALTER SKINNER'S WHO'S WHO IN WORLD OIL AND GAS
Financial Times Ltd.
Minster House
Arthur Street
London EC4R 9BH, England
Covers: About 4,500 senior executives, technologists, scientists,
government representatives, and consultants in the petroleum and gas
industry. **Entries include:** Name, nationality, personal and educational
data, languages used, business positions and affiliations, office
address, phone, and telex. **Arrangement:** Alphabetical. **Indexes:**
Company, geographical. **Pages** (approx.): 750. **Frequency:** Annual,
fall. **Editor:** Walter Skinner. **Price:** $55.00.

★3389★
WARD'S WHO'S WHO AMONG U.S. MOTOR VEHICLE
    MANUFACTURERS
Ward's Communications, Inc.
28 W. Adams Street   Phone: (313) 962-4433
Detroit, MI 48226
Covers: 8,000 motor vehicle industry executives, engineers, and
managers, and principal personnel from auto-related associations,
governmental agencies, unions, and the automotive press. Includes
separate ''Directory of Automotive Suppliers'' section. **Entries
include:** Name, title, business address and phone, birth date,
education, spouse's name, business or professional background,
honors, memberships. Suppliers section gives biographical information
on executives and descriptions of companies and their products.

Arrangement: Alphabetical. Indexes: Job function. Pages (approx.): 600. Frequency: First edition March 1977. Price: $29.75. Also includes: Corporate organization charts and history of automotive Big Four, and portraits of many of the persons listed.

★3390★
WHAT'S WHAT WITH WHO'S WHO?
National Association of Secondary School Principals
1904 Association Drive   Phone: (703) 860-0200
Reston, VA 22091
Background: There are now a number of publishers offering "recognition" in the form of listings, plaques, etc., to high school students. The foreword of this booklet comments that, "Many legitimate questions are being raised as to the value, if any, of this type of recognition.... Our only interest is to point out what appear to be evidences of acceptable standards in the who's who field, and prevent exploitation of students where standards are conspicuous by their absence. The text reports on the association's contacts with the following groups, not known to be defunct: Who's Who among High School Seniors; Who's Who among Catholic High School Seniors; Who's Who among Fraternities and Sororities; Society of Distinguished American High School Students; Who's Who among American Student Leaders; Who's Who in National High School Football; Who's Who in National High School Athletics; National Panorama of American Youth; National Honorary Society - Order of Lambda; Who's Who in American High Schools; Distinguished Young Americans Foundation; National Society of Student Leaders; Prep All Americans; Cum Laude Society; National Beta Club; National High School Award for Excellence; National Honor Society; Outstanding Teenagers of America; Who's Who among American High School Students. Frequency: Latest edition September 1978. Editor: Gilbert R. Weldy. Price: $2.00, payment with order.

★3391★
WHO'S WHO AMONG AMERICAN HIGH SCHOOL STUDENTS
Educational Communications, Inc.
3202 Doolittle Drive   Phone: (312) 564-2020
Northbrook, IL 60062
Covers: 320,000 juniors and seniors in United States high schools who have been recommended for inclusion by their schools or youth organizations on the basis of academic attainment or leadership in extra-curricular activities, athletics, or community service, and who have maintained at least a "B" grade point average. Entries include: Name, personal data, high school attended, achievements, honors, future plans. Does not include personal addresses. Arrangement: Alphabetical. Pages (approx.): Six regional volumes of about 800 pages each. Frequency: Annual, November. Editor: Paul C. Krouse. Former title: Merit's Who's Who among American High School Students (1971). Price: $17.95, plus $3.00 shipping for each regional volume (1979 edition). Publisher states copies are distributed without charge to participating high schools and to public and college libraries. Other information: Publisher's literature examined emphasizes that purchase of volume is not required for inclusion; other sources indicate purchase of books, plaques, and other items related to listing are strongly promoted, and that a $3.00 listing fee is charged. Publisher offers to send summary of recognition program guidelines of National Association of Secondary School Principals and statement of related "Who's Who among American High School Students" policies upon request.

Who's Who among American High School Students *See also* What's What with Who's Who?

Who's Who among American Student Leaders *See* What's What with Who's Who?

★3392★
WHO'S WHO AMONG BLACK AMERICANS
Who's Who among Black Americans, Inc.
3202 Doolittle Drive   Phone: (312) 564-2020
Northbrook, IL 60062
Covers: 13,000 Black leaders in the professions, government, sports, etc. Entries include: Name, address, education, career and family data, publications, etc. Arrangement: Alphabetical. Indexes: Geographical, occupational. Pages (approx.): 770. Frequency: February of every third year; new edition expected 1981. Price: $49.95.

Who's Who among Catholic High School Seniors *See* What's What with Who's Who?

Who's Who among Fraternities and Sororities *See* What's What with Who's Who?

Who's Who among High School Seniors *See* What's What with Who's Who?

★3393★
WHO'S WHO AMONG LATIN AMERICANS IN WASHINGTON
Gama, Inc.
4000 Saul Road   Phone: (301) 942-8288
Kensington, MD 20795
Covers: 500 living "men and women of Latin American ancestry whose civic, political, social, and professional achievements" should be remembered. Text in English and Spanish. Entries include: Name, home and office addresses, personal and career data, writings, awards, memberships. Arrangement: Alphabetical. Frequency: First edition published September, 1976; new edition expected 1980. Editor: Gabriel Mantilla. Price: $29.95 (current and 1980 editions). Other information: Publisher's promotion mentioned that nominees would be asked to make a $20 one-time contribution, and stated that no one would be omitted for failing to do so.

★3394★
WHO'S WHO AMONG PROFESSIONAL INSURANCE AGENTS
Underwriter Printing and Publishing Company
291 S. Van Brunt Street   Phone: (201) 569-8808
Englewood, NJ 07631
Entries include: Name, company, address, education, business career, memberships, agency volume and number of employees, companies represented, and specialty lines written. Frequency: Annual, September. Price: $30.00.

★3395★
WHO'S WHO AMONG STUDENTS IN AMERICAN UNIVERSITIES AND COLLEGES
Randall Publishing Company
1700 26th Avenue   Phone: (205) 349-2991
Tuscaloosa, AL 35401
Covers: Students at about 1,400 schools chosen by the editors on the basis of participation in school committees and activities and scholastic records. Entries include: Name, place and date of birth, parents' names, and scholastic achievements. Arrangement: Alphabetical by college. Indexes: Personal name. Pages (approx.): 1,600. Frequency: Annual, July. Editor: Pattus Randall II. Price: $24.95, payment with order; $27.20, billed.

★3396★
WHO'S WHO IN ALASKAN POLITICS: A BIOGRAPHICAL DICTIONARY OF ALASKAN POLITICAL PERSONALITIES, 1884-1974
Alaska Historical Commission
C/o Binfords and Mort
2536 S. E. 11th Avenue   Phone: (503) 238-9666
Portland, OR 97202
Number of listings: 1,100. Entries include: Name, occupation, dates of birth (and death, if applicable), education, religion, political

affiliation, and address. **Arrangement:** Alphabetical. **Pages** (approx.): 135. **Frequency:** Irregular; first edition 1977. **Editors:** Evangeline Atwood and Robert N. DeArmond. **Price:** $10.00.

★3397★
WHO'S WHO IN AMERICA
Marquis Who's Who, Inc.
200 E. Ohio Street   Phone: (312) 787-2008
Chicago, IL 60611
Covers: 72,000 persons, primarily in the United States, considered to be of current national reference interest because of achievement or position; includes necrology. **Entries include:** Name; personal, educational, and career data; memberships; special achievements; writings; address; "Thoughts on My Life," written by person listed, is included in some sketches. **Arrangement:** Alphabetical. **Indexes:** A "regional index" lists persons in the Marquis Who's Who regional directories who are not in "Who's Who in America." **Frequency:** Biennial, June of even years. **Price:** $79.50, plus $2.50 shipping.

★3398★
WHO'S WHO IN AMERICAN ART
Jaques Cattell Press
R. R. Bowker Company
2216 S. Industrial Park Drive   Phone: (602) 967-8885
Tempe, AZ 85282
Covers: About 10,000 persons active in visual arts, including sculptors, painters, illustrators, printmakers, collectors, curators, writers, educators, dealers, critics, patrons, and museum executives. Also includes cumulative necrology 1953-1978. **Entries include:** All listings include name, professional classification, address; artists' listings include dealer's name and address, preferred media, works in public collections, awards, publications, teaching positions, etc.; other listings may include same information as pertinent, plus statement of research interests, etc. **Arrangement:** Alphabetical. **Indexes:** Geographical, professional classification. **Pages** (approx.): 950. **Frequency:** Biennial, spring of even years. **Price:** $42.50, postpaid, payment with order (ISSN 0000-0191). **Send orders to:** R. R. Bowker Co., Box 1807, Ann Arbor, MI 48106 (313-761-4700).

Who's Who in American High Schools *See* What's What with Who's Who?

★3399★
WHO'S WHO IN AMERICAN LAW
Marquis Who's Who, Inc.
200 E. Ohio Street   Phone: (312) 787-2008
Chicago, IL 60611
Covers: 34,000 lawyers, judges, law school deans and professors, and other legal professionals. **Entries include:** Name, home and office addresses, office phone, place and date of birth, educational background, career history, civic positions, professional memberships, writings, awards, special achievements. **Arrangement:** Alphabetical. **Pages** (approx.): 1,000. **Frequency:** Biennial, fall of odd years. **Price:** $7.50, plus $2.50 shipping.

★3400★
WHO'S WHO IN AMERICAN POLITICS
Jaques Cattell Press
R. R. Bowker Company
2216 S. Industrial Park Drive   Phone: (602) 967-8885
Tempe, AZ 85282
Covers: About 21,800 persons ranging from principal local, state, and national officials to men and women active and influential behind the scenes. **Entries include:** Name; legal and mailing addresses; birthplace and date; party affiliation; present and previous political, governmental, and business positions; achievements; memberships; writings. **Arrangement:** Geographical. **Indexes:** Alphabetical. **Pages** (approx.): 1,350. **Frequency:** Biennial, fall of odd years. **Price:** $52.50, postpaid, payment with order. **Send orders to:** R. R. Bowker Co., Box 1807, Ann Arbor, MI 48106 (313-761-4700).

★3401★
WHO'S WHO IN CALIFORNIA
Who's Who Historical Society
Box 4240   Phone: (714) 498-0600
San Clemente, CA 92672
Number of listings: 2,400. **Entries include:** Name, title, home and office addresses, personal and career data, writings. **Pages** (approx.): 450. **Frequency:** Biennial, fall of odd years. **Editor:** Sarah Alice Vitale. **Price:** $50.00.

Who's Who in Education *See* International Who's Who in Education

★3402★
WHO'S WHO IN ENGINEERING
Engineers Joint Council
345 E. 47th Street   Phone: (212) 644-7840
New York, NY 10017
Covers: About 10,000 engineers who have received awards, honors, or some other form of professional recognition. **Arrangement:** Alphabetical. **Indexes:** Geographical, field of interest. **Pages** (approx.): 600. **Frequency:** Irregular; latest edition 1978; new edition expected March 1980. **Former title:** Engineers of Distinction (1978). **Price:** $50.00. **Also includes:** List of awards offered by engineering societies.

★3403★
WHO'S WHO IN FINANCE AND INDUSTRY
Marquis Who's Who, Inc.
200 E. Ohio Street   Phone: (312) 787-2008
Chicago, IL 60611
Covers: Over 18,000 men and women in all business fields. **Entries include:** Name; home and office addresses; personal, career, and family data; civic and political activities; memberships; writings; awards. **Arrangement:** Alphabetical. **Pages** (approx.): 750. **Frequency:** Biennial, fall of odd years. **Price:** $57.50, plus $2.50 shipping.

★3404★
WHO'S WHO IN GOVERNMENT
Marquis Who's Who, Inc.
200 E. Ohio Street   Phone: (312) 787-2008
Chicago, IL 60611
Covers: About 18,000 state, local, and national government officials. **Entries include:** Name; home and office addresses; personal, career, and family data; civic and political activities, including offices held; memberships, writings; awards. **Arrangement:** Alphabetical. **Indexes:** Federal office, state or county office, local or city office. **Pages** (approx.): 750. **Frequency:** Irregular; latest edition 1977. **Price:** $55.50, plus $2.50 shipping.

★3405★
WHO'S WHO IN HEALTH CARE
Aspen Systems Corporation
20010 Century Boulevard   Phone: (301) 428-0700
Germantown, MD 20767
Covers: 8,000 persons, including educators, researchers, government officials, executives in health-related industries (insurance, pharmaceuticals, instruments, etc.), and others. **Entries include:** Name, birth date, personal and career data, memberships, address. **Arrangement:** Alphabetical. **Indexes:** Geographical, affiliation, discipline. **Frequency:** Not established; first edition November 1977; new edition expected January 1981. **Price:** $60.00.

★3406★
WHO'S WHO IN INSURANCE
Underwriter Printing and Publishing Company
291 S. Van Brunt Street   Phone: (201) 569-8808
Englewood, NJ 07631
Covers: Over 5,000 insurance officials, brokers, agents, and buyers. **Entries include:** Name, title, company name, address, home address,

educational background, professional club and association memberships, personal and career data. **Arrangement:** Alphabetical. **Pages** (approx.): 860. **Frequency:** Annual, February. **Price:** $35.00 (current and 1980 editions).

★3407★
WHO'S WHO IN LABOR
Arno Press
Three Park Avenue   Phone: (212) 725-2050
New York, NY 10016
Covers: 3,800 leaders of labor and organizations that deal with labor. Includes a roster of unions and employee associations. **Entries include:** For individuals - Name; union or organization; office address and phone; extensive career and personal data; spouse's and parents' names and occupations. For unions - Name, address, names of president and secretary-treasurer, number of locals, total membership. **Arrangement:** Alphabetical. **Indexes:** Individuals by union or organization. **Frequency:** Not established; first edition spring 1976. **Editor:** Stanley R. Greenfield. **Price:** $65.00.

★3408★
WHO'S WHO IN LAW ENFORCEMENT IN AMERICA
National Association of Chiefs of Police
2000 P Street, N. W., Suite 615   Phone: (202) 989-9088
Washington, DC 20036
Covers: Persons in supervisory or command positions in law enforcement agencies. Not limited to members. Also includes directory of suppliers of police equipment. **Entries include:** Name, office address and phone, highest degree held, areas of occupational specialization, personal and career data, awards and honors; some entries include photos. **Arrangement:** Alphabetical. **Pages** (approx.): 200. **Frequency:** Irregular, about every three years; latest edition 1976; new edition expected 1980. **Editor:** Gerald S. Arenberg, Captain. **Price:** $20.00 (current edition); $35.00 (1980 edition).

Who's Who in Music *See* International Who's Who in Music and Musician's Directory

Who's Who in National High School Athletics *See* What's What with Who's Who?

Who's Who in National High School Football *See* What's What with Who's Who?

★3409★
WHO'S WHO IN OCEAN AND FRESHWATER SCIENCE
Francis Hodgson Reference Publications
Longman House
Burnt Mill
Harlow
Essex CM20 2JE, England
Covers: About 4,000 directors and heads of departments of research and scientists concerned with oceanography, marine biology, ecology, underwater technology, and related fields; worldwide coverage. **Entries include:** Individual's name, address, title, personal and educational data, membership in scientific societies, career data, subject interests. **Arrangement:** Alphabetical. **Pages** (approx.): 340. **Frequency:** Irregular; first edition 1978. **Price:** 60 pounds, plus 2 pounds shipping. **Send orders to:** Longman Group Ltd., 43/45 Annandale Street, Edinburgh EH7 4AT, Scotland.

★3410★
WHO'S WHO IN OPERA
Arno Press
Three Park Avenue   Phone: (212) 725-2050
New York, NY 10016
Covers: 2,350 singers, conductors, stage directors, producers, and administrators, and set, costume, and lighting designers involved with opera worldwide. Also includes profiles of 101 opera companies and list of international artists' agents. **Entries include:** Name, home address, personal and career data, awards and honors, videotape and

movie productions. **Arrangement:** Alphabetical. **Frequency:** Not established; first edition summer 1976. **Editor:** Maria F. Rich, Editor, "Central Opera Service Bulletin." **Price:** $65.00. **Other information:** Eligibility of artists was based on their engagements with one or more of the major companies; e.g., the minimum requirement for singers was five major roles since beginning of the 1971-72 season.

★3411★
WHO'S WHO IN RAILROADING AND RAIL TRANSIT
Simmons-Boardman Publishing Corporation
350 Broadway   Phone: (212) 966-7700
New York, NY 10013
Covers: 3,500 railroad executives, labor leaders, lawyers active in the industry, etc. **Entries include:** Name, address, personal and business biographical details. **Arrangement:** Alphabetical. **Frequency:** Irregular; previous edition 1971; latest edition fall 1977. **Former title:** Who's Who in Railroading. **Price:** $50.00.

★3412★
WHO'S WHO IN RELIGION
Marquis Who's Who, Inc.
200 E. Ohio Street   Phone: (312) 787-2008
Chicago, IL 60611
Covers: 17,500 church officials (both lay and clergy), religious educators, directors of religious charities, editors and writers for major religious publications, priests, rabbis, ministers, and other religious leaders. **Entries include:** Name, home and office addresses, career and personal data, civic and political activities, memberships, writings, and special achievements and awards. **Arrangement:** Alphabetical. **Pages** (approx.): 600. **Frequency:** Irregular; latest edition 1977. **Price:** $55.50, plus $2.50 shipping.

★3413★
WHO'S WHO IN RISK MANAGEMENT
Underwriter Printing and Publishing Company
291 S. Van Brunt Street   Phone: (201) 569-8808
Englewood, NJ 07631
Covers: Persons in charge of buying worker's compensation, corporate liability and employee health, safety and benefits insurance for large firms. **Entries include:** Name, company, office and home addresses, business career, education and personal data, memberships, etc. **Arrangement:** Alphabetical. **Indexes:** Company, geographical. **Pages** (approx.): 200. **Frequency:** Annual, August. **Editor:** Donald E. Wolff. **Price:** $30.00.

★3414★
WHO'S WHO IN ROCK MUSIC
Atomic Press
1421 N. 34th Street   Phone: (206) 632-0550
Seattle, WA 98103
Covers: Over 6,000 musicians and groups considered "rock" artists but also including blues artists. Compiled from record jackets. **Entries include:** For individual artist - Name, group (if any); instrument; discography. For groups - Name, names and instruments of members; brief history of group; discography. **Arrangement:** Alphabetical. **Pages** (approx.): 260. **Frequency:** Not established; first edition 1978; new edition expected 1980. **Author:** William York. **Price:** $6.95 (current edition); $7.95 (tentative, 1980 edition).

★3415★
WHO'S WHO IN SCIENCE FICTION
Taplinger Publishing Company, Inc.
200 Park Avenue South   Phone: (212) 533-6110
New York, NY 10003
Covers: 400 writers, editors, illustrators, and other creative persons in science fiction, primarily Americans. **Arrangement:** Alphabetical. **Pages** (approx.): 220. **Frequency:** Published December 1976. **Editor:** Brian Ash. **Price:** $10.95, cloth; $4.95, paper.

★3416★
WHO'S WHO IN TECHNOLOGY TODAY
Technology Recognition Corporation
1382 Old Freeport Road   Phone: (412) 963-6757
Pittsburgh, PA 15238
Covers: 7,500 engineers, scientists, inventors, and researchers in the fields of electrical, mechanical, chemical, civil, and biomedical engineering, and in the earth sciences, physics, and other technological fields. **Entries include:** Name, title, affiliation, address; personal, educational, and career data; publications, inventions, expert witness experience; technical field of activity; area of expertise. **Arrangement:** By major field, then by discipline. **Indexes:** Personal name, keyword, discipline. **Pages** (approx.): 1,500 (six volumes). **Frequency:** Annual, October; first edition expected October 1980. **Editors:** Donald H. Jones and Lorraine D. Ferrari. **Price:** $660.00, including one year's updates; $390.00 without updates; $65.00 per volume. Add $2.00 shipping per volume.

★3417★
WHO'S WHO IN THE EAST
Marquis Who's Who, Inc.
200 E. Ohio Street   Phone: (312) 787-2008
Chicago, IL 60611
Covers: About 18,000 persons, including some also listed in "Who's Who in America," living in Connecticut, Delaware, District of Columbia, Maine, Maryland, Massachusetts, New Hampshire, New Jersey, New York, Pennsylvania, Rhode Island, Vermont, West Virginia, plus the Canadian provinces of New Brunswick, Newfoundland, Nova Scotia, Prince Edward Island, Quebec, and the eastern half of Ontario. **Entries include:** Name; personal, educational, and career data; memberships; special achievements; writings; address. **Arrangement:** Alphabetical. **Indexes:** All persons listed in "Who's Who in America" living in above areas. **Pages** (approx.): 890. **Frequency:** Biennial, summer of odd years. **Price:** $57.50, plus $2.50 shipping.

★3418★
WHO'S WHO IN THE MIDWEST
Marquis Who's Who, Inc.
200 E. Ohio Street   Phone: (312) 787-2008
Chicago, IL 60611
Covers: About 18,000 persons, including some also listed in "Who's Who in America," living in Illinois, Indiana, Iowa, Kansas, Michigan, Minnesota, Missouri, Nebraska, North Dakota, Ohio, South Dakota, and Wisconsin, plus the Canadian provinces of Manitoba and western Ontario. **Entries include:** Name; personal, educational, and career data; memberships; special achievements; writings; address. **Arrangement:** Alphabetical. **Indexes:** All persons listed in "Who's Who in America" living in above areas. **Pages** (approx.): 825. **Frequency:** Biennial, summer of even years. **Price:** $52.50, plus $2.50 shipping.

★3419★
WHO'S WHO IN THE SECURITIES INDUSTRY
Economist Publishing Company
12 E. Grand Avenue   Phone: (312) 944-1204
Chicago, IL 60611
Covers: About 1,000 investment bankers. **Entries include:** Banker's name, and personal and career data. **Arrangement:** Alphabetical. **Pages** (approx.): 100. **Frequency:** Annual, November. **Editor:** George R. Stearns. **Advertising accepted.** Circulation 6,000. **Price:** $5.00.

★3420★
WHO'S WHO IN THE SOUTH AND SOUTHWEST
Marquis Who's Who, Inc.
200 E. Ohio Street   Phone: (312) 787-2080
Chicago, IL 60611
Covers: About 20,000 persons, including some also listed in "Who's Who in America," living in Alabama, Arkansas, District of Columbia, Florida, Georgia, Kentucky, Louisiana, Maryland, Mississippi, North Carolina, Oklahoma, South Carolina, Tennessee, Texas, Virginia, plus

Puerto Rico and the Virgin Islands. **Entries include:** Name; personal, education, and career data; memberships; special achievements; writings; address. **Arrangement:** Alphabetical. **Indexes:** All persons listed in "Who's Who in America" living in above areas. **Pages** (approx.): 900. **Frequency:** Biennial, fall of even years. **Price:** $52.50, plus $2.50 shipping.

★3421★
WHO'S WHO IN THE THEATRE
Gale Research Company
Book Tower   Phone: (313) 961-2242
Detroit, MI 48226
Covers: 2,500 actors, actresses, directors, playwrights, producers, and designers; international coverage. **Entries include:** Name (original and stage names, where applicable), date and place of birth, education and other personal data, theatrical credits (with dates), favorite parts, recreations and hobbies, club memberships, and address. **Arrangement:** Alphabetical. **Pages** (approx.): 1,400. **Frequency:** Irregular, about every five years; latest edition spring 1977; new edition expected late 1980. **Editor:** Ian Herbert. **Price:** $60.00. **Also includes:** Broadway, Off-Broadway, and London playbills, lists of long runs, necrology, etc. **Other information:** Formerly published by Pitman, London.

★3422★
WHO'S WHO IN THE WEST
Marquis Who's Who, Inc.
200 E. Ohio Street   Phone: (312) 787-2008
Chicago, IL 60611
Covers: About 18,000 persons, including some also listed in "Who's Who in America," living in Alaska, Arizona, California, Colorado, Hawaii, Idaho, Montana, Nevada, New Mexico, Oregon, Utah, Washington, and Wyoming, and Alberta, British Columbia, and Saskatchewan. **Entries include:** Name; personal, education, and career data; memberships; special achievements; writings; address. **Arrangement:** Alphabetical. **Indexes:** All persons listed in "Who's Who in America" living in above areas. **Pages** (approx.): 850. **Frequency:** Biennial, spring of even years. **Price:** $52.50, plus $2.50 shipping.

★3423★
WHO'S WHO IN THE WORLD
Marquis Who's Who, Inc.
200 E. Ohio Street   Phone: (312) 787-2008
Chicago, IL 60611
Covers: 22,000 persons considered to be of current international reference interest because of achievement or position. **Entries include:** Name; personal, education, and career data; memberships; special achievements; writings; address. **Arrangement:** Alphabetical. **Pages** (approx.): 1,030. **Frequency:** Biennial, fall of even years. **Price:** $55.50, plus $2.50 shipping.

★3424★
WHO'S WHO IN WORLD AGRICULTURE
Francis Hodgson Reference Publications
Longman House
Burnt Mill, Harlow
Essex CM20 2JE, England
Covers: Over 8,000 directors and heads of departments of research establishments and other researchers and administrators in all areas of agricultural research; worldwide coverage. **Entries include:** Name, address, qualifications, subjects of major interest, memberships, scientific and research interest, positions held during past 10 years. **Arrangement:** Alphabetical. **Pages** (approx.): 840. **Frequency:** First edition 1979. **Price:** 75 pounds. **Send orders to:** Longman Group Ltd., 43/45 Annandale Street, Edinburgh EH7 4AT, Scotland.

★3425★
WHO'S WHO IN WORLD MEDICINE
Francis Hodgson Reference Publications
Longman House
Burnt Mill, Harlow
Essex CM20 2JE, England
Covers: 13,000 research workers in medicine; worldwide coverage. **Entries include:** Name, address, qualifications, present and past positions, memberships, research interests. **Arrangement:** Alphabetical. **Pages** (approx.): 1,300. **Frequency:** First edition expected 1980. **Price:** 90 pounds. **Send orders to:** Longman Group Ltd., 43/45 Annandale Street, Edinburgh EH7 4AT, Scotland.

Who's Who in World Oil and Gas *See* Walter Skinner's Who's Who in World Oil and Gas

★3426★
WHO'S WHO OF AMERICAN COMIC BOOKS [Artists, writers, etc.]
Jerry G. Bails
21101 E. 11 Mile Road
St. Clair Shores, MI 48081
Covers: 2,500 artists, writers, and editors who have contributed to the American 4-color comics magazine industry since 1929. Includes several hundred illustrations. **Entries include:** Name, personal and career information, writings, and credits. **Arrangement:** Alphabetical. **Pages** (approx.): 360. **Frequency:** Present 4-volume edition published about one volume per year, completed 1978. **Editors:** Jerry Bails and Hames Ware. **Price:** $23.75, postpaid.

★3427★
WHO'S WHO OF AMERICAN WOMEN
Marquis Who's Who, Inc.
200 E. Ohio Street   Phone: (312) 787-2008
Chicago, IL 60611
Covers: About 21,000 women in all fields. **Entries include:** Name; personal, educational, and career data; memberships; special achievements; writings; address. **Arrangement:** Alphabetical. **Pages** (approx.): 900. **Frequency:** Biennial, spring of odd years. **Price:** $52.50, plus $2.50 shipping.

★3428★
WHO'S WHO OF CROATIANS IN THE U.S.A. AND CANADA
Research Center for Canadian Ethnic Studies
1628 W. Morse Avenue   Phone: (312) 262-6381
Chicago, IL 60626
Covers: 625 persons who are college-educated and of Croatian descent in the United States and Canada. Also includes lists of institutions and periodicals. **Entries include:** Biographical listings show name, office address, personal and career data, writings. Other listings show institution or other name, address, officers or editors, etc., as appropriate. **Arrangement:** Alphabetical within classifications. **Indexes:** Geographical, occupational. **Pages** (approx.): 200. **Frequency:** Irregular; latest edition 1978; new edition expected early 1980. **Editors:** Francis H. Eterovich and Vladimir Markotic. **Advertising accepted.** Circulation 600. **Former title:** Biographical Directory of Americans and Canadians of Croatian Descent, with Institutions, Organizations, and periodicals. **Price:** 1978 edition out of print; $20.00 (1980 edition).

★3429★
WORLD WHO'S WHO OF WOMEN
International Biographical Centre
Melrose Press Ltd.
17/21 Churchgate Street
Soham, Ely
Cambridgeshire CB7 5DS, England
Covers: About 10,000 "women of particular achievement, including well-known local, national, and international figures;" criteria not specified; worldwide coverage. **Entries include:** Name, address; personal, educational, and career data; majority of entries include a photograph. **Arrangement:** Alphabetical. **Pages** (approx.): 1,200.

Frequency: Formerly irregular; now biennial, even years. **Editor:** Ernest Kay. **Price:** $65.00. **Send orders to:** Biblio Distribution Center, 81 Adams Drive, Totowa, NJ 07512. **Other information:** Publisher also sells plaques or other forms of recognition to those listed.

★3430★
WRITERS FOR YOUNG ADULTS: BIOGRAPHIES MASTER INDEX
Gale Research Company
Book Tower   Phone: (313) 961-2242
Detroit, MI 48226
Covers: About 43,000 citations to biographical sketches of some 9,000 young adult writers (grades 7-12) listed in nearly 265 reference sources. **Entries include:** Name, date of birth (and death, where applicable), code indicating publication in which sketch appears. **Arrangement:** Alphabetical. **Pages** (approx.): 200. **Frequency:** Not established; first edition 1979. **Editor:** Adele Sarkissian. **Price:** $24.00.

9

Arts and
Entertainment

★3431★
ACA ARTS YELLOW PAGES
American Council for the Arts
570 Seventh Avenue   Phone: (212) 354-6655
New York, NY 10018
Covers: 1,200 community, state, and federal arts agencies; arts centers, arts advocacy groups, arts publications, and fundraising councils, in the United States and Canada. **Entries include:** Name of organization or publication, names of executives, address, phone. **Arrangement:** Classified by type of activity. **Pages** (approx.): 125. **Frequency:** Current (1978) edition is last edition expected. **Editor:** Ellen Stodolsky Daniels, Director of Publications. **Price:** $7.50. **Other information:** Publisher changed name in mid-1977 from Associated Council of the Arts.

★3432★
ACCESS—FILM AND VIDEO EQUIPMENT: A DIRECTORY
American Film Institute
J. F. Kennedy Center
Washington, DC 20566
Covers: Publicly available video and film production equipment and facilities. **Entries include:** Name of company or facility, address, contact, hours of operation, equipment access policy, services and resources, description of facility, equipment inventory. **Arrangement:** Geographical. **Indexes:** Company name. **Pages** (approx.): 215. **Frequency:** First edition summer 1978. **Editor:** Nancy Legge. **Price:** $2.00.

★3433★
AMATEUR CHAMBER MUSIC PLAYERS—DIRECTORY
Amateur Chamber Music Players
15 W. 67th Street   Phone: (212) 877-9561
New York, NY 10023
Covers: 6,000 member performers in the United States and 60 other countries, in North American and overseas editions. **Entries include:** Name, address, phone, instrument played, and level of accomplishment. **Arrangement:** Geographical. **Frequency:** North American directory biennial, even years; overseas directory biennial, odd years. **Editor:** Helen Rice, Honorary Secretary. **Price:** No charge; a contribution is suggested.

★3434★
AMERICAN ART DIRECTORY
Jaques Cattell Press
R. R. Bowker Company
2216 S. Industrial Park Drive   Phone: (602) 967-8885
Tempe, AZ 85282
Covers: About 2,900 museums and art organizations and 1,550 art schools; also includes lists of state school art directors and supervisors, corporations having art holdings for public viewing, newspapers which carry art notes, art scholarships and fellowships, and 190 national, regional, and state open art exhibitions. **Entries include:** All entries usually carry institution or group name, address, phone, name of director, curator, or other contact; newspaper listings include names of art critics; museum listings include budget, hours open, publications, special collections; exhibit listings include deadlines, exhibit dates; school listings include faculty names, majors, degrees offered. **Arrangement:** Geographical. **Indexes:** Collections, personal name. **Pages** (approx.): 700. **Frequency:** Biennial, even years. **Price:** $42.50, postpaid, payment with order (ISSN 0065-6968). **Send orders to:** R. R. Bowker Co., Box 1807, Ann Arbor, MI 48106 (313-761-4700).

★3435★
AMERICAN ARTIST—DIRECTORY OF ARTS SCHOOLS AND WORKSHOPS ISSUE
Billboard Publications, Inc.
1515 Broadway   Phone: (212) 764-7364
New York, NY 10036
Covers: Arts schools (including some abroad), summer schools, private art teachers, and travel art workshops. **Entries include:** School and workshop listings include name, address, art student to teacher ratio, art courses available, whether scholarships are available, type of academic year, enrollment, number of faculty, memberships and accreditation, what educational degrees are available and how many students received them during the previous year. Workshop listings include additional information on itineraries, etc. **Arrangement:** Schools are geographical, teachers and workshops are alphabetical. **Pages** (approx.): 40. **Frequency:** Annual, March. **Editor:** Robert Hudoba, Manager, Directory Services. **Advertising accepted.** Circulation 140,000. **Former title:** American Artist - Art School Directory Issue (1977). **Price:** $1.50, postpaid, payment with order (current and 1980 editions).

★3436★
AMERICAN DANCE DIRECTORY
Association of American Dance Companies
162 W. 56th Street   Phone: (212) 265-7824
New York, NY 10019
Covers: About 170 professional dance companies in the United States. **Entries include:** Company name, artistic director, manager (with address and phone), booking manager (with address and phone), founding date, number of dancers, touring availability, whether artistic director tours, residency activities, stage dimensions, taped or live music, special programs, details of home theater, length of home season, photograph, artistic statement, active touring repertory. **Arrangement:** Alphabetical. **Indexes:** Geographical, type of dance,

touring availability, companies that operate schools, American Guild of Musical Artists companies. **Pages** (approx.): 200. **Frequency:** Biennial, summer of odd years. **Editor:** Mindy N. Levine. **Price:** $10.00.

★3437★
AMERICAN FILM INSTITUTE GUIDE TO COLLEGE COURSES IN FILM AND TELEVISION
American Film Institute
Kennedy Center for the Performing Arts   Phone: (202) 833-9300
Washington, DC 20566
Covers: About 1,100 schools in the United States, and a list of foreign film schools. **Entries include:** For United States schools - School name; address of related department; person to contact; degree offered; number of film and television majors; scholarships and assistantships available, distinctive programs; names of department members; equipment and facilities. For schools abroad - Name, address. **Arrangement:** Geographical. **Indexes:** Degrees offered, courses and programs offered. **Pages** (approx.): 475. **Frequency:** Triennial since 1975; latest edition April 1978. **Editors:** Dennis Bohnenkamp and Sam L. Grogg, Jr. **Price:** $9.75, plus $1.25 shipping. **Send orders to:** Peterson's guides, Book Order Dept., Box 978, Edison, NJ 08817.

★3438★
AMERICAN GUILD OF ENGLISH HANDBELL RINGERS—ROSTER
American Guild of English Handbell Ringers
R.D. 1, Box 118   Phone: (402) 782-2243
Bennet, NE 68317
Covers: About 3,400 members, most of them being directors of handbell choirs or organizations having handbell choirs. **Entries include:** Name, address, sponsoring organization. **Arrangement:** Geographical. **Pages** (approx.): 130. **Frequency:** Annual, January. **Editor:** Mary V. Kettelhut, Registrar. **Price:** $2.00, plus 60¢ shipping.

★3439★
AMERICAN MUSICOLOGICAL SOCIETY—DIRECTORY OF MEMBERS AND SUBSCRIBERS
American Musicological Society
201 S. 34th Street   Phone: (215) 243-8698
Philadelphia, PA 19104
Covers: About 4,500 members of the association and subscribers to its "Journal." **Entries include:** Name, address. **Arrangement:** Members are alphabetical, subscribers are geographical. **Pages** (approx.): 25. **Frequency:** Annual, January. **Editor:** Alvin H. Johnson, Executive Director. **Former title:** American Musicological Society - List of Members and Subscribers (1979). **Price:** Available to members and subscribers only.

★3440★
AMERICAN RECORDER SOCIETY—DIRECTORY AND BYLAWS
American Recorder Society
13 S. 16th Street   Phone: (212) 675-9042
New York, NY 10003
Number of listings: 3,000. **Arrangement:** Geographical. **Pages** (approx.): 60. **Frequency:** Annual, March. **Editor:** Mary Ann Fleming, Administrative Assistant. **Advertising accepted.** Circulation 3,500. **Price:** Available to members only.

American Society of Artists—Directory *See* Directory of
American Professional Artists & Craftspeople

★3441★
AMERICAN SOCIETY OF BOOKPLATE COLLECTORS AND DESIGNERS—MEMBERSHIP LIST
American Society of Bookplate Collectors and Designers
1206 N. Stoneman Avenue, No. 15   Phone: (213) 283-1936
Alhambra, CA 91801
Covers: 250 (membership limited to this number). **Entries include:** Name, address. **Frequency:** Irregular; latest edition fall 1977. **Editor:** Audrey Spencer Arellanes, Director. **Price:** Available to members only.

Other information: "Year Book" of the society, published in 1973, was devoted to biographical sketches of members and included numerous illustrations of bookplates. Included in membership fee, $25.00.

★3442★
AMERICAN SOCIETY OF COMPOSERS, AUTHORS, AND PUBLISHERS—LIST OF MEMBERS
American Society of Composers, Authors, and Publishers
One Lincoln Plaza   Phone: (212) 595-3050
New York, NY 10023
Covers: About 5,000 music publishers and their divisions and affiliates and about 18,000 composers and lyricists who can be reached through the society and whose works are licensed for performance by it. **Entries include:** For publishers - Company name, symbols indicating recent membership or relationship to ASCAP. For composers, etc. - Member name, symbols indicating recent membership, and if name is a pseudonym. **Arrangement:** Alphabetical within publisher and composer groups. **Pages** (approx.): 125. **Frequency:** Annual, usually January. **Price:** Free.

American Society of Magazine Photographers—Membership
Directory *See* ASMP—Directory

★3443★
AMERICAN SQUARE DANCE—VACATION ISSUE
Burdick Enterprises
216 Williams Street   Phone: (419) 433-2188
Huron, OH 44839
Covers: Square dance clubs and other activities of interest to square dancers. **Entries include:** Club name, address, name and phone of contact. **Arrangement:** Geographical. **Pages** (approx.): 100. **Frequency:** Annual, April. **Editors:** Stan and Cathie Burdick. **Advertising accepted.** Circulation 15,000. **Price:** $1.00 (current and 1980 editions).

★3444★
AMUSEMENT BUSINESS—COUNTRY MUSIC BOOKING GUIDE ISSUE
Billboard Publications, Inc.
Box 24970   Phone: (615) 748-8120
Nashville, TN 37202
Covers: Country music performers and their booking agencies. **Entries include:** Booking agency name, address, phone, names of performers, size of group, types of facilities performers play, etc. **Indexes:** Performer name. **Frequency:** Annual, October. **Advertising accepted.** **Price:** $3.00, postpaid, payment with order. **Other information:** Sometimes cited as, "Country Music Booking Guide." Not to be confused with "Billboard's Country Music Sourcebook," published from Los Angeles.

★3445★
ANGELS [Theater and film backers]
Leo Shull Publications
134 W. 44th Street   Phone: (212) 586-6900
New York, NY 10036
Covers: Several thousand investors in theatrical and motion picture productions, nationwide. Separate volumes for backers of theatrical and film productions. **Entries include:** Name, address, amounts invested, and names of productions. **Frequency:** Annual, September. **Editor:** Leo Shull. **Price:** $35.00 for theater edition; $65.00 for film edition; postpaid, payment must accompany order; back issues $50.00 each.

★3446★
ANNOTATED DIRECTORY OF PARTS AND SERVICES FOR AUDIO-VISUAL EQUIPMENT
Association of Audio-Visual Technicians
Box 9716   Phone: (303) 733-3137
Denver, CO 80209
Covers: About 1,200 manufacturers and other sources of parts for

audiovisual equipment; some sources provide parts which are no longer manufactured or are hard to locate. **Entries include:** Manufacturer or source name, address, name of service manager, phone, trade names or equipment brands stocked, manuals available, and policies on minimum orders, back orders, etc. **Arrangement:** Alphabetical. **Indexes:** Brand name. **Pages** (approx.): 120. **Frequency:** Biennial, September of even years. **Editor:** Elsa C. Kaiser. **Price:** $20.00, payment with order; $22.00 billed. **Other information:** Published in cooperation with the EPIE Institute.

★3447★
ANTIQUES DEALER—ANTIQUES SHOW CALENDAR SECTION
Ebel-Doctorow Publications, Inc.
1115 Clifton Avenue   Phone: (201) 779-1600
Clifton, NJ 07013
Publication includes: Antiques shows in all sections of the United States, up to one year in advance; approximately 500 shows in each issue. **Entries include:** Date of show, location, name of promoter or manager. **Arrangement:** Chronological. **Frequency:** Monthly. **Editor:** Stella Hall. **Advertising accepted.** Circulation 10,000. **Price:** $8.00 per year.

★3448★
ART AND CRAFT FAIR BULLETIN
American Society of Artists
1297 Merchandise Mart Plaza   Phone: (312) 751-2500
Chicago, IL 60654
Covers: Shows accepting high quality art and craft work, nationwide. **Entries include:** Show name, where held, sponsor, name and address of contact, dates, requirements, etc. **Arrangement:** Chronological. **Frequency:** Latest edition July 1979. **Price:** Available to members only.

Art Books in Print 1950-1979 *See* Art Books 1950-1979

★3449★
ART BOOKS 1950-1979
R. R. Bowker Company
1180 Avenue of the Americas   Phone: (212) 764-5100
New York, NY 10036
Covers: Books and serials related to the visual arts published since 1950; also includes list of catalogs of permanent collections published by museums worldwide. There is no directory of book publishers, but full information for ordering museum publications is given. **Frequency:** Not established; first edition (covering 1950-1979) December 1979. **Price:** $75.00, postpaid, payment with order. **Send orders to:** R. R. Bowker Co., Box 1807, Ann Arbor, MI 48106 (313-761-4700). **Other information:** Originally promoted under title, ''Art Books in Print 1950-1979;'' museum catalog section sometimes referred to as, ''International Directory of Museum Permanent Collection Catalogs.'' Principal content of publication is listings of books and serials on art subjects in author and title sequences. There is also a subject index. Based, except for museum listings, on ''American Book Publishing Record.''

★3450★
ART DIRECTORS' INDEX TO PHOTOGRAPHERS
Camera/Graphic Press Ltd.
Box 1702
F.D.R. Station
New York, NY 10022
Covers: 4,000 commercial photographers, worldwide; 1,700 are in the United States. **Entries include:** Personal or studio name, address, name of agent, phone, telex number, specialties. **Arrangement:** Geographical. **Indexes:** Specialty. **Pages** (approx.): 425. **Frequency:** Annual. **Price:** $42.00. (Not verified)

★3451★
ART LIBRARIES SOCIETY OF NORTH AMERICA—DIRECTORY OF MEMBERS
Art Libraries Society of North America
7735 Old Georgetown Road   Phone: (301) 656-2160
Washington, DC 20014
Number of listings: About 1,000. **Entries include:** Name; office address and phone; home address and phone; special interests. **Arrangement:** Alphabetical. **Indexes:** Geographical. **Pages** (approx.): 150. **Frequency:** Annual, fall. **Editor:** Amy R. Navratil. **Advertising accepted.** Circulation 1,000. **Price:** Available to members only.

★3452★
ART LOVERS ART & CRAFT FAIR BULLETIN [Illinois]
American Society of Artists
1297 Merchandise Mart Plaza
Chicago, IL 60654
Entries include: Fair name, location, dates. **Frequency:** Quarterly. **Price:** $5.00 per year.

★3453★
ART SCENE [Arts and crafts fairs]
Jacob Martin Jo Publishing Corporation
1025 N. H Street   Phone: (305) 968-9029
Lake Worth, FL 33460
Covers: Arts and crafts fairs and exhibits during coming eight months; includes name and address list of promoters. **Entries include:** Fair name, address, location, name and address of sponsor or other contact, fees, registration procedures. **Arrangement:** Geographical. **Pages** (approx.): 12. **Frequency:** Monthly, except August-September issues combined. **Editor:** Jim Ready. **Advertising accepted.** Circulation 3,000. **Former title:** Southern Crafts and Art News. **Price:** $10.00 per year; $1.15 per copy; postpaid, payment with order.

Art Show News *See* Colorado Art Show News

★3454★
ARTISTS ASSOCIATIONS IN THE U.S.A.
Boston Visual Artists Union
14 Reservoir Road   Phone: (617) 358-4204
Wayland, MA 01778
Covers: About 1,600 professional and amateur fine arts and handicrafts associations, about 400 of which are described in annotated listings, based on questionnaires completed by the associations. **Entries include:** All listings include association name, address; annotated listings include name of an official, number of members, brief history and description of the organization. **Arrangement:** Geographical. **Pages** (approx.): 300. **Frequency:** First edition 1977. **Editor:** Helen Shlien. **Price:** $4.00.

★3455★
ARTIST'S MARKET: WHERE TO SELL YOUR ARTWORK
Writer's Digest Books
9933 Alliance Road   Phone: (513) 984-0717
Cincinnati, OH 45242
Covers: 3,000 buyers in United States and Canada for freelance art work, including ad agencies, art studios, clip art firms, audiovisual firms, television film producers, periodicals, record companies, book publishers, others. **Entries include:** Name of buyer, address, phone, payment rates, special submission requirements, reporting time, how to break in. **Arrangement:** By type of market. **Pages** (approx.): 500. **Frequency:** Annual, September. **Editors:** Cathy Bruce, Betsy Wones. **Former title:** Arts & Crafts Market; divided (1978) into this publication and ''Craftworker's Market'' (see separate listing). **Price:** $10.95.

Artist's Market [California arts and crafts shows] *See* Arts/Crafts Exhibition Directory [California]

★3456★
ARTS AND CRAFTS DIRECTORY [Indiana]
Indiana Arts Commission
155 E. Market Street, Suite 614   Phone: (317) 633-5649
Indianapolis, IN 46204
Covers: Over 1,000 historic preservation societies, arts and crafts associations, shops, fairs and festivals, art museums, galleries, publishing houses, colleges and universities, television and radio stations, bands, choral groups, dance groups, theaters, literary societies, and other organizations concerned with the arts in Indiana. **Entries include:** All listings include name of organization, festival, historic site, etc. and address; most also include phone, name of contact. Listings for associations and societies include description of activities or function. Listings for shops, galleries, fairs, and museums include hours open or date held. Listings for performing arts groups include description of group (number of musicians, music type, etc.). **Arrangement:** Classified by type of art or activity. **Pages** (approx.): 85. **Frequency:** Annual, fall. **Editor:** Jane Ford, Public Information Director. **Price:** Free. **Other information:** Co-sponsored by Indiana Department of Commerce, Tourism Development Division.

Arts & Crafts Market *See* Craftworker's Market: Where to Sell Your Crafts; Artist's Market: Where to Sell Your Artwork

★3457★
ARTS AND CRAFTS NEWSLETTER [New England]
Kemp Krafts
Whalley Road   Phone: (802) 425-2463
Charlotte, VT 05445
Covers: Forthcoming arts and crafts fairs, mainly in New England. **Entries include:** Name and dates of show, name and address of contact. **Arrangement:** Chronological. **Frequency:** Quarterly. **Editor:** Richard T. Kemp. **Price:** $2.00 per year.

★3458★
ARTS DIRECTORY [New England]
Arts Extension Service
Hasbrouck Hall
University of Massachusetts   Phone: (413) 545-2013
Amherst, MA 01003
Covers: 500 graphic artists, craftspersons, musicians, dancers, filmmakers, and others in the arts in New England, primarily Massachusetts, and related regional business services. **Entries include:** Listings are in the form of advertisements for individual artists and generally contain name, address, phone, information on product or skill offered; some include personal background and fees. **Arrangement:** Classified by type of art. **Pages** (approx.): 20 (tabloid form). **Frequency:** Irregular; approximately annually; latest edition June 1979. **Editor:** Barbara Schaffer-Bacon, Artist Resource Coordinator. **Advertising accepted.** Circulation 2,000. **Price:** $3.50 per issue.

Arts Yellow Pages *See* ACA Arts Yellow Pages

★3459★
ARTS/CRAFTS EXHIBITION DIRECTORY [California]
Artist's Market
Box 2798
Laguna Hills, CA 92653
Covers: Arts and crafts shows in California; separate list of demonstrations, classes, etc. **Entries include:** Name and type of show, location, sponsors (if any), name of contact, commission fees, etc. **Arrangement:** Chronological by month, then geographical. **Pages** (approx.): 20. **Frequency:** Bimonthly. **Editor:** Karen Kuczynzki, Publisher. **Advertising accepted.** Circulation 2,500. **Former title:** Artist's Market. **Price:** $1.50 per issue; $6.00 per year.

★3460★
ARTSOURCE [Texas]
Dallas Public Library
1954 Commerce   Phone: (214) 748-9071
Dallas, TX 75201
Covers: Over 300 clubs, groups, institutions, councils, etc., and local government agencies concerned with the arts (including dance, music, drama, literary arts, and visual arts and crafts). **Entries include:** Organization name, address, phone, name of contact, description of purpose, activities, facilities. For artists' studios - Artist name, address, phone, medium. **Arrangement:** By area of activity. **Indexes:** Organizations with workshops or auditions, organization name. **Pages** (approx.): 120. **Frequency:** Not established; first edition 1978. **Editor:** Marian Waite.

★3461★
ARTWEEK—GALLERY CALENDAR SECTION
Artweek, Inc.
1305 Franklin Street   Phone: (415) 763-0422
Oakland, CA 94612
Publication includes: Screened list of galleries in the west, mostly California, which exhibit fine arts, photography, and handicrafts; listings are paid. **Entries include:** Gallery name, address, phone, hours, and name of show, artist or genre featured, etc. **Arrangement:** Geographical. **Frequency:** 44 issues yearly. **Advertising accepted.** Circulation 13,500. **Price:** $1.00 per copy; $16.00 per year (ISSN 0004-4121). **Also includes:** Art competitions and festivals are also listed without charge in each issue in separate sections; listings include name and address of contact and other data as appropriate.

★3462★
ASCAP SYMPHONIC CATALOG
American Society of Composers, Authors, and Publishers
One Lincoln Plaza   Phone: (212) 595-3050
New York, NY 10023
Covers: Works of over 20,000 composers, arrangers, and music publishers who are ASCAP members, plus the works of many foreign composers whose compositions are performed in the United States under ASCAP licenses. Since publishers' names and addresses are provided, the catalog is in effect a directory of mailing addresses for the composers represented. **Entries include:** Composer name, title of work, opus number (if any), date of publication, instrumentation, source of text or libretto and name of librettist when a text or libretto is employed, performance time, and source of sheet music or manuscripts. **Arrangement:** By names of composers and arrangers. **Pages** (approx.): 580. **Frequency:** Irregular; latest edition spring 1977. **Price:** $25.00, postpaid, payment with order (ISSN 0145-5265). **Send orders to:** R. R. Bowker Co., Box 1807, Ann Arbor, MI 48106 (313-761-4700).

★3463★
ASMP/THE SOCIETY OF PHOTOGRAPHERS IN COMMUNICATIONS—MEMBERSHIP DIRECTORY
ASMP/The Society of Photographers in Communications
205 Lexington Avenue   Phone: (212) 889-9144
New York, NY 10016
Covers: 1,200 professional photographers. **Entries include:** Name; address; phone; and in some cases, list of specialties. **Arrangement:** By type of membership, then alphabetical. **Indexes:** Geographical. **Pages** (approx.): 110. **Frequency:** Irregular; latest edition December 1977; new edition expected early 1980. **Editor:** Barbara O'Neill. **Advertising accepted.** Circulation 5,000. **Former title:** American Society of Magazine Photographers - Membership Directory. **Price:** $3.50.

★3464★

ASSOCIATION OF COLLEGE, UNIVERSITY AND COMMUNITY ARTS
　　ADMINISTRATORS—MEMBERSHIP LIST [Performing arts]
Association of College, University and Community Arts Administrators
Box 2137　　　　　　　　　　　　　Phone: (608) 262-0004
Madison, WI 53701
Covers: About 1,000 presenters of performing arts in the United
States. **Entries include:** Organization name, address, phone, names of
executives. **Arrangement:** Geographical. **Pages** (approx.): 60.
Frequency: Three times a year. **Price:** $75.00 per copy.

★3466★

AUDIO-VISUAL COMMUNICATIONS—WHO'S WHO IN AUDIO-
　　VISUAL PRESENTATION ISSUE
United Business Publications, Inc.
475 Park Avenue South　　　　　　　Phone: (212) 725-2300
New York, NY 10016
Covers: About 1,500 firms offering audiovisual production and design
services, and motion picture laboratory services. **Entries include:**
Company name, coded description of services offered. **Arrangement:**
Geographical. **Frequency:** Annual, June. **Editor:** Frances H. Lee.
Advertising accepted. Price: $5.00.

★3467★

BACK STAGE FILM/TAPE/SYNDICATION DIRECTORY
Back Stage Publications
165 W. 46th Street　　　　　　　　Phone: (212) 581-1080
New York, NY 10036
Covers: Over 3,500 producers and service firms involved in the non-
theatrical and industrial film and videotape industries, plus ad agencies
and TV stations. **Entries include:** Company name, address, phone, and
principal executives. **Arrangement:** Classified by type of company.
Indexes: Geographical. **Pages** (approx.): 350. **Frequency:** Annual,
March. **Editor:** Allen Zwerdling. **Advertising accepted.** Circulation
6,000. **Price:** $8.00, payment with order.

★3468★

BAND MUSIC GUIDE
Instrumentalist Company
1418 Lake Street　　　　　　　　　Phone: (312) 328-6000
Evanston, IL 60204
Publication includes: 250 principal publishers of band music with
their addresses, plus additional list of smaller companies with names
and addresses of their distributors. **Pages** (approx.): 380. **Frequency:**
Irregular; previous edition 1975; current edition fall 1977. **Price:**
$14.50. **Other information:** Publication consists primarily of listings
of musical scores published for band use, listed by title in classified
groupings (concert and marching music, marching routines, etc.) with
composer index.

★3469★

BAY AREA DANCER'S GUIDE [San Francisco, California]
Caroline House
Box 738
Ottawa, IL 61350
Covers: Dance classes, companies, and dance supply sources in the
San Francisco Bay Area. **Arrangement:** By activity or service.
Frequency: First edition October 1979. **Editor:** Beth Witrogen. **Price:**
$8.95. **Send orders to:** Caroline House, Box 161, Thornwood, NY
10594.

★3470★

BIG BOOK OF HALLS OF FAME IN THE UNITED STATES AND
　　CANADA—SPORTS
Jaques Cattell Press
R. R. Bowker Company
2216 S. Industrial Park Drive　　　　Phone: (602) 967-8885
Tempe, AZ 85282
Covers: 175 halls of fame in 30 sports fields, plus nearly 10,000
biographical sketches of varying comprehensiveness treating the lives
and accomplishments of persons and animals inducted. **Entries
include:** Name, address, nature of hall and its displays, history and
major statistics on the activity represented. **Arrangement:** Classified
by subject. **Other information:** First announced under title,
"Everyone's Guide to Halls of Fame in the United States and Canada."
Pages (approx.): 1,040. **Frequency:** Published 1978. Was to have
been published as four volumes covering sports and other fields; only
this first volume has been published and the series has been
discontinued. **Price:** $29.95, postpaid, payment with order. **Send
orders to:** R. R. Bowker Co., Box 1807, Ann Arbor, MI 48106 (313-
761-4700).

★3471★

BILLBOARD—INTERNATIONAL TALENT DIRECTORY ISSUE
Billboard Publications, Inc.
9000 Sunset Boulevard　　　　　　　Phone: (213) 273-7040
Los Angeles, CA 90069
Covers: Recording artists, booking agents, personal managers; hotel,
club, theater and campus facilities; festivals; state fairs; promoters;
staging and costume services; ticket printers; sound and lighting
companies; recording companies; and other services in the United
States and major countries abroad. **Entries include:** For artists -
Name, name of booking agent, personal manager (if appropriate),
nature of performance and/or size of group, record label. For personal
managers and booking agents - Firm name, address, phone. For
campus facilities, festivals, state fairs, and theaters - Name, address,
phone; some listings include contact person, capacity, facilities,
services. **Arrangement:** Artists, booking agents, and personal
managers are alphabetical; all others are geographical, then classified
by service. **Pages** (approx.): 185. **Frequency:** Annual, fall. **Editors:**
Earl Paige, Bob Hudoba. **Advertising accepted.** Circulation 38,000.
Price: $25.00, plus $2.00 shipping. **Send orders to:** Billboard, 2160
Patterson St., Cincinnati, OH 45214. **Other information:** Also cited
as "Biillboard's International Talent Directory"; includes some
features from now-defunct publications, "Billboard Campus
Attractions" and "Billboard's On Tour."

Billboard Campus Attractions *See* Billboard—International Talent
　　Directory Issue

★3472★

BILLBOARD'S COUNTRY MUSIC SOURCEBOOK
Billboard Publications, Inc.
9000 Sunset Boulevard　　　　　　　Phone: (213) 273-7040
Los Angeles, CA 90069
Covers: Country music artists, fan clubs, booking agents, personal
managers, promoters, record labels, label promotion, radio stations,
organizations, state fairs booking country music talent. **Entries
include:** Company, organization, club, etc.; name, address, phone,
name of principal executives or contact. **Arrangement:** All sections
alphabetical, except radio stations, which are geographical. **Pages**
(approx.): 75. **Frequency:** Annual, June. **Editors:** Earl Paige, Special
Issues Editor (Los Angeles), Bob Hudoba, Manager, Directory Services
(Cincinnati). **Advertising accepted. Editors: Price:** $10.00. **Other
information:** Not to be confused with Billboard Publications' "Country
Music Booking Guide," published by its "Amusement Business"
Division, Nashville.

Billboard's International Talent Directory *See* Billboard—
International Talent Directory Issue

Billboard's "On Tour" *See* Billboard—International Talent
Directory Issue

★3473★
BILLBOARD'S TALENT IN ACTION
Billboard Publications, Inc.
9000 Sunset Boulevard   Phone: (213) 273-7040
Los Angeles, CA 90069
Covers: Top recording artists (as determined by music popularity charts) and their booking agents and personal managers. **Entries include:** Artist's name, booking agent and personal manager names, addresses, and phones. **Arrangement:** Alphabetical. **Pages** (approx.): 100. **Frequency:** Annual, December. **Editors:** Earl Paige, Special Issues Editor (Los Angeles), and Bob Hudoba, Manager, Directory Services (Cincinnati). **Advertising accepted.** **Price:** $5.00, plus $1.75 shipping. **Also includes:** Numerical rankings of the top records, artists, producers, music publishers, and talent box office attractions.

★3474★
BLACK THEATRE: A RESOURCE DIRECTORY
Black Theatre Alliance
410 W. 42nd Street   Phone: (212) 564-2266
New York, NY 10036
Covers: Black theater and dance companies, playwrights, directors, arts administrators, and technicians concerned with the production of Black theater and dance. **Entries include:** Name, address, phone; area of interest or expertise. Most listings include list of productions or works, if appropriate. **Arrangement:** By acitivity. **Frequency:** Irregular; latest edition 1973; new edition expected 1980. **Price:** $2.00.

Black Theatre Alliance—Membership List *See* BTA Touring
Brochure [Black Theatre Alliance]

★3475★
BLUEGRASS DIRECTORY [Music]
Bluegrass Directory
4005 Lara Lane
Chattanooga, TN 37416
Covers: About 200 firms and individuals able to supply instruments, repairs, music, etc., for performance and study of old-time music, particularly bluegrass. **Entries include:** Name, address, note on product or service. **Arrangement:** Alphabetical. **Indexes:** Product. **Pages** (approx.): 60. **Frequency:** One-time edition in July 1977; publication planned two or three times a year. **Editor:** Mike Bailey. **Advertising accepted.** **Price:** $2.50, plus 50¢ shipping.

★3476★
BLUEGRASS UNLIMITED—FESTIVAL GUIDE ISSUE [Music]
Bluegrass Unlimited
Box 111
Broad Run, VA 22014
Covers: About 500 bluegrass and old-time music festivals. **Entries include:** Event name, dates, location, name and address of contact. **Frequency:** Annual, April. **Price:** $1.00, postpaid.

★3477★
BLUES WHO'S WHO [Music]
Arlington House
165 Huguenot Street
New Rochelle, NY 10801
Covers: About 575 blues singers and musicians in rock, soul, jazz, and folk music styles whose work is influenced by the blues. **Entries include:** Individual name, career and personal data, discography. **Price:** $35.00.

★3478★
BROADCASTING CABLE SOURCEBOOK
Broadcasting Publications, Inc.
1735 De Sales Street, N. W.   Phone: (202) 638-1022
Washington, DC 20036
Covers: 3,700 cable television systems serving 8,000 communities in the U. S. **Entries include:** Company name, address, phone, names of executives, areas served. **Arrangement:** Geographical. **Pages** (approx.): 350. **Frequency:** Annual, October (but not in 1980). **Editor:** Sol Taishoff, Chairman. **Advertising accepted.** Circulation 6,000. **Price:** $2.00. **Other information:** Content of this publication will be included in "Broadcasting Weekly - Yearbook Issue" 1980 edition (described in separate listing).

★3479★
BROADCASTING WEEKLY—YEARBOOK ISSUE
Broadcasting Publications, Inc.
1735 De Sales Street, N. W.   Phone: (202) 638-1022
Washington, DC 20036
Covers: All TV and radio stations in the United States and Canada, networks, station representatives, film companies, advertising agencies, trade associations, schools, and suppliers. **Entries include:** Company name, address, phone, names of executives. Station listings include power, other operating details. **Arrangement:** Stations geographical, other sections alphabetical. **Indexes:** Alphabetical. **Pages** (approx.): 800. **Frequency:** Annual, March. **Editor:** Sol Taishoff. **Advertising accepted.** Circulation 30,000. **Price:** $42.50 (current edition); $55.00 (1980 edition). **Other information:** 1980 edition will incorporate cable television data from "Broadcasting Cable Sourcebook," described in separate listing.

Broadcasting Yearbook *See* Broadcasting Weekly—Yearbook
Issue

★3480★
BTA TOURING BROCHURE [Black Theatre Alliance]
Black Theatre Alliance
410 W. 42nd Street   Phone: (212) 564-2266
New York, NY 10036
Covers: Over 50 member dance and theater companies. **Entries include:** Company name, address, performance fees, workshops, member names and biographical data, types of performances. **Arrangement:** Alphabetical. **Frequency:** Irregular. **Price:** $3.00.

★3481★
BUYERS' BOOK OF AMERICAN CRAFTS
American Craft Enterprises
Box 10
New Paltz, NY 12561
Covers: 475 craftspeople who offer their works for sale. **Entries include:** Artist's name, address, photograph of piece for sale, price, career data. **Arrangement:** By medium. **Indexes:** Artist's name, geographical. **Pages** (approx.): 180. **Frequency:** Not established; first edition 1979; new edition expected 1980. **Price:** $15.00, plus $1.50 shipping.

Cable Handbook *See* Cable/Broadband Communications Book

★3482★
CABLE/BROADBAND COMMUNICATIONS BOOK
Communications Press, Inc.
1346 Connecticut Avenue, N. W.   Phone: (202) 785-0865
Washington, DC 20036
Publication includes: Bibliographical references for individual sections include numerous short lists, with addresses, of professional and nonprofessional groups and associations which are active in cable/broadband communications. **Frequency:** Biennial, late in odd years. **Former title:** Cable Handbook (1977). **Price:** $15.50, plus $1.25 shipping.

★3483★
CALENDAR OF ARTS EVENTS [New York]
Associated Art Organizations
207 Delaware Avenue   Phone: (716) 856-6530
Buffalo, NY 14202
Covers: Regional art shows held in the western New York state area.
Entries include: Name of show, name and address of sponsor, location if different, dates. Frequency: Quarterly. Price: $1.00 per year.

★3484★
CALENDAR OF SUMMER ARTS FAIRS [Iowa]
Iowa Arts Council
State Capitol   Phone: (515) 281-4451
Des Moines, IA 50319
Covers: About 75 arts and crafts fairs occurring during the summer in Iowa. Entries include: Event name, location, dates, sponsor name, contact name and address, other data. Arrangement: Chronological. Frequency: Annual. Price: Free.

Callerlab—International Association of Square Dance Callers—Directory See Direction Roster

Campus Arts to Community Program Handbook and Catalog of Cultural Events [Indiana] See Indiana Touring Handbook and Catalog...

★3485★
CANADA CRAFTS—"CRAFT CALENDAR" COLUMN
G. P. Page Publications
380 Wellington Street West   Phone: (416) 366-4608
Toronto M5V 1E3, Ontario, Canada
Covers: Crafts shows in Canada and northern United States. Entries include: Show name, location, dates, name and address of sponsor or contact. Arrangement: Chronological. Frequency: Bimonthly. Advertising accepted. Circulation 10,000. Price: $12.00 per year; $2.00 per issue.

★3486★
CARNIVAL & CIRCUS BOOKING GUIDE
Billboard Publications, Inc.
Box 24970   Phone: (615) 748-8120
Nashville, TN 37202
Number of listings: 350. Entries include: Show name, owning or operating company, description, and name, address, and phone of carnival or circus. Frequency: Annual, August. Advertising accepted. Price: $3.50, postpaid, payment with order.

★3487★
CASTING CONTACTS [Theatrical; New York City area]
Leo Shull Publications
136 W. 44th Street   Phone: (212) 586-6900
New York, NY 10036
Covers: Casting offices and agencies, theaters, showcases, modeling agencies, clubs, radio stations and networks, game shows, and chorus and group opportunities available the year around in New York City area for new talent. Entries include: Firm name, address, phone, usual type of talent needed. Pages (approx.): 75. Frequency: Annual. Editor: Leo Shull. Advertising accepted. Price: $2.50, payment with order.

★3488★
CATALOG OF MUSEUM PUBLICATIONS AND MEDIA
Gale Research Company
Book Tower   Phone: (313) 961-2242
Detroit, MI 48226
Covers: Media (books, periodicals, filmstrips, videotapes, etc.) prepared, published, or distributed by about 1,000 museums, art galleries, etc. Entries include: Name, address, and phone of institution, and title and full descriptions and prices of items issued by the institution. Arrangement: By institution name. Indexes: Title/

keyword, periodical title, subject, geographical. Pages (approx.): 1,050. Frequency: Irregular; previous edition 1974; latest edition January 1980. Editors: Paul Wasserman and Esther Herman. Former title: Museum Media (1980). Price: $92.00.

★3489★
CAVALCADE OF ACTS & ATTRACTIONS
Billboard Publications, Inc.
Box 24970   Phone: (615) 748-8120
Nashville, TN 37202
Covers: Entertainers, touring shows, fireworks display companies, rodeo companies, etc. Arrangement: Classified by type of attraction. Pages (approx.): 200. Frequency: Annual, December. Advertising accepted. Price: $18.00.

★3490★
CELEBRITY BULLETIN
Celebrity Service, Inc.
171 W. 57th Street   Phone: (212) 757-7979
New York, NY 10019
Covers: New York edition is typical of the five editions published. It indicates arrivals of celebrities in the vicinity (including dates, purpose, etc.), their upcoming activities, and contacts for them during their visits. Separate list of daily activities for celebrities already in the area. Frequency: New York edition is daily; Hollywood, London, Paris, and Rome editions are twice weekly. Editor: Douglas Kesten. Price: New York edition is $40.00 per month; other editions' prices vary. Other information: Subscribers accepted only after interview.

★3491★
CELEBRITY SERVICE INTERNATIONAL CONTACT BOOK
Celebrity Service, Inc.
171 W. 57th Street   Phone: (212) 757-7979
New York, NY 10019
Covers: Subtitle: "International Trade Directory of the Entertainment, Media, and Allied Industries," covering "Stage, motion pictures, television-radio, music, dance, sports, producers, agents, managers, publicity agents, advertising agencies, recording companies, newspapers, magazines, publishers, hotels, restaurants, night clubs, airlines, etc." Entries include: Name, address, phone. Arrangement: Geographical, then by category. Pages (approx.): 190. Frequency: Biennial, October. Editor: Barbara A. McGurn. Advertising accepted. Price: $8.00, payment with order.

★3492★
CERAMICS MONTHLY—"WHERE TO SHOW" COLUMN
Professional Publications, Inc.
Box 12448   Phone: (614) 488-8236
Columbus, OH 43212
Entries include: Show name, location, sponsor address, dates. Arrangement: Chronological. Frequency: 10 times a year. Advertising accepted. Circulation 45,000. Price: $12.00 per year.

★3493★
CHICAGO ART REVIEW
Krantz Company
3300 N. Lake Shore Drive   Phone: (312) 935-6723
Chicago, IL 60657
Covers: 60 art galleries and 10 museums with works by 750 artists; limited to Chicago and vicinity. Entries include: Gallery or museum name, address, hours, methods of acquisition, artists' collected, special and permanent exhibits. Arrangement: Alphabetical. Indexes: Artist name. Pages (approx.): 115. Frequency: Irregular; previous edition 1977; latest edition fall 1979. Editor: Leslie J. Krantz. Price: $5.95, plus $1.00 shipping.

★3494★
COLLECTING PHOTOGRAPHS: A GUIDE TO THE NEW ART BOOM
E. P. Dutton & Company, Inc.
Two Park Avenue South
New York, NY 10016
Publication includes: Lists of galleries, dealers, auction houses, conservatorial suppliers, and museum and library collections of photographs, and photograph-related suppliers; international coverage. **Entries include:** Organization or company name, address, interests or assistance available. **Arrangement:** Alphabetical. **Pages** (approx.): 175. **Frequency:** Published June 1977. **Editors:** Landt Dennis and Lisl Dennis. **Price:** $12.95, cloth; $6.95, paper.

★3495★
COLORADO ART SHOW NEWS
Colorado Art Shows, Inc.
Box 609   Phone: (303) 795-7487
Littleton, CO 80160
Publication includes: List of local and out-of-state arts shows, craft fairs, competitions, exhibitions, and show promoters. **Arrangement:** Chronological. **Pages** (approx.): 20. **Frequency:** Quarterly. **Editor:** Margaret J. Hook, Managing Editor. **Advertising accepted.** Circulation 1,000. **Price:** $10.00 per year. **Other information:** Effective January 1980 issue, publication will extend coverage to nationwide and will change title to "Art Show News."

★3496★
COMMUNITY ARTS AGENCIES: A HANDBOOK AND GUIDE
American Council for the Arts
570 Seventh Avenue   Phone: (212) 354-6655
New York, NY 10018
Publication includes: List of names and addresses of about 1,400 community arts agencies, both private and public, with additional information on budgets, activities, physical facilities, etc., on about 700 of the organizations. **Entries include:** Full descriptions contain group name, address, budget level, name of director or contact, date founded, organization structure, priorities, phone, description of activities. **Arrangement:** Geographical. **Pages** (approx.): 410. **Frequency:** Irregular; latest edition June 1978 (1976 data). **Editors:** Robert Porter and Ellen Stodolsky Daniels. **Former title:** Guide to Community Arts Agencies (1978). **Price:** $12.50, postpaid. **Other information:** Includes extensive text on organizing and operating a community arts agency.

★3497★
COMPOSIUM ANNUAL DIRECTORY OF NEW MUSIC
Crystal Record Company
2235 Willida Lane   Phone: (206) 856-4779
Sedro Woolley, WA 98284
Publication includes: Biographical sketches of composers whose works are listed, which works must have been composed and/or published within two years of the directory date and for which scores and parts must be available. **Entries include:** Name of composer, biographical data, compositions, where to obtain copies, code indicating difficulty of the music. **Arrangement:** Alphabetical by composer. **Indexes:** By instrumentation, cumulated index of composers in past and present issues. **Pages** (approx.): 100. **Frequency:** Annual, May. **Editor:** Carol Cunning. **Price:** $8.95 (current and 1980 editions); back issues available from 1972.

Concert Music Broadcasters Association Directory *See* Concert Music Broadcasting Directory

★3498★
CONCERT MUSIC BROADCASTING DIRECTORY
Radio Seaway, Inc.
WFMT-Chicago
500 N. Michigan   Phone: (312) 751-7100
Chicago, IL 60611
Covers: About 400 commercial and non-commercial radio stations which broadcast classical music, and related record companies,

program syndication sources, trade press, and national radio sales representatives. **Entries include:** For stations - Call letters, frequency, address, phone, names of executives, syndicated programs used, percentage of programming in classical music, hours on air, and antenna height/power; some listings include licensee name. Other listings usually include company name, address, phone, and name of contact. **Arrangement:** Classified by activity or service; radio stations are geographical; other lists are alphabetical. **Indexes:** Station call letters. **Pages** (approx.): 90. **Frequency:** Annual, spring. **Editor:** C.K. Patrick, President. **Advertising accepted.** Circulation 500. **Former title:** Concert Music Broadcasters Association Directory. **Price:** $1.00.

★3499★
CONTEMPORARY AMERICAN COMPOSERS: A BIOGRAPHICAL DICTIONARY
G. K. Hall and Company
70 Lincoln Street   Phone: (617) 423-3990
Boston, MA 02111
Covers: 4,000 composers born after 1870 who have lived in the United States. **Entries include:** Composer's name, present address, biographical data, and major works. **Arrangement:** Alphabetical. **Pages** (approx.): 125. **Frequency:** Irregular; latest edition 1976; new edition expected spring 1980. **Editor:** E. Ruth Anderson. **Price:** $50.00.

★3500★
CONTEMPORARY AMERICAN THEATER CRITICS
Scarecrow Press, Inc.
52 Liberty Street   Phone: (201) 548-8600
Metuchen, NJ 08840
Number of listings: Nearly 300. **Entries include:** Critic name, biographical data, address, excerpts from published work. **Arrangement:** Alphabetical. **Indexes:** Geographical, employer name, title of work. **Pages** (approx.): 1,020. **Frequency:** Not established; first edition 1977; supplements planned. **Editors:** M. E. Comtois and Lynn F. Miller. **Price:** $35.00.

★3501★
CONTEMPORARY MUSIC PERFORMANCE DIRECTORY
American Music Center
250 W. 57th Street, Suite 626   Phone: (212) 247-3121
New York, NY 10019
Covers: 550 American ensembles which perform contemporary music exclusively or include it in their programs; 600 sponsoring organizations whose interests include contemporary music; 350 performance facilities suited to smaller groups; 200 concert series and festivals which concentrate on or include contemporary music. **Entries include:** For ensembles - Group name, type of music, names of conductor and performers, permanent address, agent's name and address. For sponsors - Name, address, activities, special interests. For facilities - Facility name, address, seating capacity, equipment, rental information, concert manager. For festivals - Event name, location, dates, type of music, participants. **Arrangement:** Geographical. **Indexes:** Alphabetical index of musicians, administrators, and organizations. **Pages** (approx.): 240. **Frequency:** Published 1975; no new edition planned. **Editor:** Judith Greenberg Finell. **Price:** $12.00, cloth; $6.00, paper; plus $1.00 shipping.

Contests, Festivals & Grants *See* Gadney's Guide to 1800 International Contests, Festivals & Grants In Film & Video, Photography...

Country Music Booking Guide *See* Amusement Business— Country Music Booking Guide Issue

County Crafts Art Fair List *See* Midwest Art Fare

★3502★
CRAFTS BULLETIN [New York]
New York State Craftsmen
27 W. 53rd Street   Phone: (212) 586-0026
New York, NY 10019
Covers: New York State craft exhibitions, fairs, workshops, seminars, films, and conferences. **Frequency:** Monthly. **Price:** $20.00 per year.

★3503★
CRAFTS FAIR GUIDE
Crafts Fair Guide
Box 262
Mill Valley, CA 94941
Covers: Participant evaluations of about 500 recurring West Coast arts and crafts shows which took place during three months covered by each quarterly issue. Intent is to enable craftspersons to decide whether to attend same event in following year. Includes list of promoters. Monthly supplements are devoted to upcoming fairs. **Entries include:** Name of event, location, date, description of the fair site, estimate of attendance, name and address of promoter, comments and ratings by participants. **Arrangement:** Chronological. **Indexes:** Fairs by city. **Pages** (approx.): 90. **Frequency:** Quarterly; monthly supplements. **Editor:** Lee Spiegel. **Price:** $6.00 per issue; $16.00 per year; supplements, 50¢ each.

★3504★
CRAFTS REPORT—"FAIR SHARE" COLUMN [Art fairs]
Crafts Report
700 Orange Street
Wilmington, DE 19801
Publication includes: List of forthcoming arts and crafts shows, with contact information. **Arrangement:** Chronological. **Frequency:** Eleven issues a year. **Editor:** Michael Scott. **Advertising accepted.** Circulation 10,000. **Former title:** Working Craftsman. **Price:** $13.50 per year.

★3505★
CRAFTWORKER'S MARKET: WHERE TO SELL YOUR CRAFTS
Writer's Digest Books
9933 Alliance Road   Phone: (513) 984-0717
Cincinnati, OH 45242
Covers: 3,500 outlets in the United States and Canada where craftworkers can sell their work, including shops and galleries, shows and fairs, museums, architectural firms, show promoters, artists' agents, etc. Includes opportunities for apprenticeships and internships. **Entries include:** For outlets - Name of buyer, address, phone, payment rates, special submission requirements, reporting time, how to break in, profile of outlet. **Arrangement:** By type of outlet. **Pages** (approx.): 700. **Frequency:** Annual, October. **Editor:** Lynne Lapin. **Former title:** Arts & Crafts Market; divided (1978) into this publication and "Artist's Market" (see separate listing). **Price:** $11.95.

★3506★
CULTURAL DIRECTORY: GUIDE TO FEDERAL FUNDS AND
     SERVICES FOR CULTURAL ACTIVITIES
American Council for the Arts
570 Seventh Avenue   Phone: (212) 354-6655
New York, NY 10018
Covers: Over 300 funds and services available to cultural activities from more than 250 federal and quasi-federal government programs as well as 50 federal boards, committees and commissions concerned with the arts. **Entries include:** Name and description of the program, eligibility, examples of previous assistance, previous budget, enabling legislation by title and public law number, address for inquiries. **Arrangement:** Alphabetical by federal agency. **Frequency:** Irregular; new edition expected, date not set. **Editor:** Linda Coe. **Price:** $4.00. **Other information:** New edition to be published by the Federal Council for the Arts and Humanities.

★3507★
DANCE CATALOG
Harmony Books
Crown Publishers, Inc.
One Park Avenue   Phone: (212) 532-9200
New York, NY 10016
Covers: Suppliers of dance equipment and clothing; ballet, modern, ethnic, and mime dance companies; dance schools; colleges and universities with dance programs; grants, fellowships, and awards for the study of dance and production of dance performances. **Arrangement:** By activity. **Pages** (approx.): 260. **Frequency:** First edition published 1979. **Editor:** Nancy Reynolds. **Price:** $15.95, cloth; $8.95, paper.

★3508★
DANCE DIRECTORY—PROGRAMS OF PROFESSIONAL
     PREPARATION IN AMERICAN COLLEGES AND UNIVERSITIES
American Alliance for Health, Physical Education, and Recreation
1201 16th Street, N. W.   Phone: (202) 833-5557
Washington, DC 20036
Covers: 215 institutions with dance curriculums at undergraduate or graduate levels. **Entries include:** Institution name, address, course offerings, teaching personnel, enrollment, degrees offered. **Arrangement:** Geographical. **Pages** (approx.): 100. **Frequency:** Irregular; latest edition 1978; new edition possible 1981. **Editor:** Betty Toman. **Price:** $4.00.

★3509★
DANCE DIRECTORY FOR KING COUNTY [Washington]
Arts Resource Services
119 Blanchard Street   Phone: (206) 624-6815
Seattle, WA 98121
Covers: About 275 dance companies, performers, instructors, supporting artists, technical equipment suppliers, service organizations, and funding organizations concerned with dance. **Entries include:** Name, address, phone, and descriptive information (references, technical requirements, fees, activity or program, and scope). **Arrangement:** Classified by type of dance or service. **Indexes:** Name indexes for performers, instructors, and supporting artists. **Pages** (approx.): 250. **Frequency:** First edition 1977. **Editor:** Karen Huffman. **Price:** Free.

★3510★
DANCE HORIZONS TRAVEL GUIDE TO SIX OF THE WORLD'S
     DANCE CAPITALS
Dance Horizons
1801 E. 26th Street
Brooklyn, NY 11229
Covers: Dance schools, dance companies, festivals, shops for dance attire, current events calendars, theaters and other dance facilities, and other dance-related places and activities in New York, Washington, London, Paris, Leningrad, and Moscow. **Entries include:** Name, address, phone, description. **Arrangement:** By city, then by type of dance-related facilities or events. **Pages** (approx.): 325. **Frequency:** First edition 1978; new edition expected 1982. **Editors:** Sally and Eric Jacobson. **Price:** $7.95.

★3511★
DANCE MAGAZINE—SUMMER DANCE CALENDAR SUPPLEMENT
Danad Publishing Company, Inc.
1180 Avenue of the Americas   Phone: (212) 921-9300
New York, NY 10036
Covers: Dance workshops, special programs for students, performances, conventions and conferences, and special dance tours; international coverage. **Entries include:** All listings include name of event, location, date, and name, address, and phone of contact. Workshops and student programs also include type of dance, length of program, accompaniment, credit hours available; performance listings include name of performing company; convention listings include name of sponsoring organization, purpose of meeting; tour listings include description of itinerary. **Arrangement:** By above four categories, then

geographical and chronological. **Pages** (approx.): 35. **Frequency:** Annual, May. **Editor:** Heidi von Obenauer. **Advertising accepted.** Circulation 135,000. **Price:** Free.

★3512★
DANCE MAGAZINE ANNUAL
Danad Publishing Company
1180 Avenue of the Americas   Phone: (212) 921-9300
New York, NY 10036
Covers: Dancers, dance companies, managers and artists' representatives, dance and mime attractions, support personnel and services, funding sources, dance sponsors, booking organizations, dance education. **Entries include:** Generally, name, address, phone, and relevant details as appropriate. **Arrangement:** Classified by type of dance, activity, or service. **Pages** (approx.): 315. **Frequency:** Annual, December. **Editor:** Heidi von Obenauer. **Advertising accepted.** Circulation 8,000. **Price:** $15.00.

★3513★
DANCE MAGAZINE COLLEGE GUIDE: A DIRECTORY TO DANCE IN
NORTH AMERICA COLLEGES AND UNIVERSITIES
Danad Publishing Company
1180 Avenue of the Americas   Phone: (212) 921-9300
New York, NY 10036
Covers: Over 500 college-level dance programs offered by two- and four-year schools. **Entries include:** College name; name, address, phone, and name of contact for dance department; degrees and majors offered; degree requirements; facilities; number of faculty; special programs; admission requirements; tuition and fees; financial aid available. **Arrangement:** Alphabetical. **Indexes:** Level of program (major, non-major, non-credit), geographical. **Pages** (approx.): 135. **Frequency:** Biennial, early in even years; first edition 1978. **Editor:** Heidi von Obernauer. **Advertising accepted. Price:** $7.50, payment must accompany orders from all but schools and libraries.

Dance Magazine Directory of College and University Dance *See* Dance Magazine College Guide

★3514★
DANCE WORLD
Crown Publishers
One Park Avenue   Phone: (212) 532-9200
New York, NY 10016
Covers: About 340 dance companies located in the United States and Canada, including regional, professional, and city dance companies. **Entries include:** Dance company name (but not address), administrative and technical staff, principal artists and soloists, repertoire. **Arrangement:** Alphabetical by company. **Indexes:** Personal name and title of program. **Pages** (approx.): 240. **Frequency:** Annual, March (for preceding year). **Editor:** John Willis. **Price:** $16.95 (current edition); $19.95 for 1979 edition due March 1980. **Also includes:** Biographical data on dancers and choreographers.

★3515★
DESIGN DIRECTORY
Wefler & Associates
Box 1591
Evanston, IL 60204
Covers: Over 700 design firms in the United States, including industrial, graphic, interior, and fashion design. **Entries include:** Firm name, address, phone; year established; number of employees; locations of branches (if any); names and titles of key personnel; and areas of specialization. **Arrangement:** Geographical. **Frequency:** Annual; first edition 1979. **Editor:** W. Daniel Wefler. **Price:** $38.00, postpaid, payment with order (ISSN 0195-4326).

★3516★
DIRECTION ROSTER [Square dancing]
Callerlab-International Association of Square Dance Callers
Box 679   Phone: (717) 646-8411
Pocono Pines, PA 18350
Covers: About 1,250 members of the association. **Entries include:** Name, address, year joined, accreditation status. **Arrangement:** Alphabetical. **Frequency:** Annual, June. **Editor:** John Kaltenthaler, Executive Secretary. **Price:** Available to members only.

★3517★
DIRECTORS GUILD OF AMERICA—DIRECTORY OF MEMBERS
Directors Guild of America
7950 Sunset Boulevard   Phone: (213) 656-1220
Hollywood, CA 90046
Covers: 5,500 motion picture, television, and radio directors and their assistants in film and tape for entertainment, and in commercial, industrial, and other non-entertainment fields, worldwide. **Entries include:** Name, office address and phone; some entries give home addresses and phone; areas of occupational specialization; brief description of experience and credits for productions. **Arrangement:** Alphabetical. **Indexes:** Geographical. **Pages** (approx.): 430. **Frequency:** Annual, usually January. **Editor:** Olive Kelsay. **Advertising accepted.** Circulation 6,000. **Price:** $7.50 (current and 1980 editions).

★3518★
DIRECTORY FOR THE ARTS: SERVICES, PROGRAMS, AND FUNDS
FOR ARTS ORGANIZATIONS, LOCAL SPONSORS, AND
ARTISTS IN NEW YORK STATE
Center for Arts Information
152 W. 42nd Street, Room 1239   Phone: (212) 354-1675
New York, NY 10036
Covers: 145 organizations and government agencies; also includes New York State community arts councils; video resource centers; performing arts management services; arts periodicals. **Entries include:** Organization name, address, phone, name of principal executive, purpose of organization, geographic area served, services, membership, and publications. **Arrangement:** Alphabetical. **Indexes:** Subject, organization name, acronym. **Pages** (approx.): 110. **Frequency:** Irregular; latest edition 1978; new edition expected 1980. **Editor:** Ellen Thurston, Director. **Price:** $10.00, cloth; $6.00, paper.

★3519★
DIRECTORY OF AMERICAN FILM SCHOLARS
Gordon Press
Box 459
Bowling Green Station
New York, NY 10004
Covers: 3,000 United States and Canadian faculty members teaching film study, production, and aesthetics. **Entries include:** Faculty member's name, office and home addresses, writings, and personal and career data. **Arrangement:** Alphabetical. **Indexes:** Geographical. **Pages** (approx.): 475. **Frequency:** Biennial; latest edition July 1979. **Editors:** Leona and Jill Phillips. **Advertising accepted.** Circulation 6,900. **Price:** $99.95.

★3520★
DIRECTORY OF AMERICAN PROFESSIONAL ARTISTS &
CRAFTSPEOPLE
American Society of Artists
1297 Merchandise Mart Plaza   Phone: (312) 751-2500
Chicago, IL 60654
Number of listings: 500 society members. **Entries include:** Name, address, phone, art medium; listings may also include works available, slides or photos on file, shows in which participated. **Arrangement:** Alphabetical. **Frequency:** Approximately semiannual, December and July. **Price:** Available to members only.

★3521★
DIRECTORY OF ART & ANTIQUE RESTORATION
Directory of Art & Antique Restoration
465 California Street, Suite 815
San Francisco, CA 94104
Covers: Artisans throughout the United States who repair and restore art objects and antiques, including persons or firms who do general restoration, those who specialize in replacing missing parts or perform specific services (carousel parts, clock parts, diamond drilling, glass panel bending), or repair specific items (battle flags, clock paintings, automatic musical devices). **Entries include:** Name, address, phone. **Arrangement:** Five sections: Antique Restoration; Art Restoration; Parts; Restoration and Repair Services; Repair of Specific Items. **Indexes:** Items and services. **Pages** (approx.): 250. **Frequency:** Biennial. **Editor:** Elizabeth Taylor. **Advertising accepted.** Circulation 2,000. **Price:** $8.50. (Not verified)

★3522★
DIRECTORY OF ART LIBRARIES AND VISUAL RESOURCE COLLECTIONS IN NORTH AMERICA
Neal-Schuman Publishers, Inc.
64 University Place   Phone: (212) 473-5170
New York, NY 10003
Covers: More than 1,300 art-related book and visual resource (photographs, slides, microforms, etc.) collections in institutions of the United States and Canada. **Entries include:** Name of institution, address, phone, size of holdings, subject areas, special collections, circulation policies, services (reprographic, reference, etc.). **Arrangement:** Geographical. **Indexes:** Institutions; art libraries have subject index to special collections; visual resource collections have index to collection emphases, subscription series, and subject index to special collections. **Pages** (approx.): 300. **Frequency:** First edition September 1978; second edition expected 1981. **Editors:** Judith A. Hoffberg and Stanley W. Hess. **Price:** $39.95. **Send orders to:** American Bibliographical Center - Clio Press, Riviera Campus, 2040 A.P.S., Box 4397, Santa Barbara, CA 93103. **Other information:** Compiled for the Art Libraries Society of North America.

Directory of Art Schools and Workshops *See* American Artist— Directory of Arts Schools and Workshops Issue

★3523★
DIRECTORY OF ARTISTS AND RELIGIOUS COMMUNITIES
Center for Contemporary Celebration
410 S. Cornell Avenue   Phone: (312) 834-8352
Villa Park, IL 60181
Covers: Over 700 dancers, story tellers, folk musicians, and other performers as well as graphic artists who serve religious communities. **Entries include:** Name, address, phone number, years of experience, description of services such as consulting or traveling. **Arrangement:** Alphabetical. **Indexes:** Geographical, art speciality. **Pages** (approx.): 145. **Frequency:** Irregular; latest edition 1975. **Editor:** Sister Adelaide Ortegel, Associate Director. **Price:** $4.00.

Directory of Artists' Associations in the U.S.A. *See* Artists Associations in the U.S.A.

★3524★
DIRECTORY OF GRADUATE PROGRAMS IN THE SPEECH COMMUNICATION ARTS AND SCIENCES
Speech Communication Association
5205 Leesburg Pike   Phone: (703) 379-1888
Falls Church, VA 22041
Number of listings: 300 departments. **Entries include:** Institutional and departmental name and address, degrees offered, areas of specialization, financial aid available. **Arrangement:** Geographical, alphabetical. **Indexes:** Institutions offering doctorate degrees. **Pages** (approx.): 300. **Frequency:** Biennial, November of even years. **Editor:** Robert N. Hall, Associate Executive Secretary. **Price:** $8.00.

★3525★
DIRECTORY OF GRADUATE PROGRAMS IN THEATRE DESIGN AND TECHNOLOGY
United States Institute for Theatre Technology
1501 Broadway
New York, NY 10036
Covers: Programs at colleges and universities in the United States and abroad. **Entries include:** Institution name, address, theater design and technology programs offered, with course description and requirements. **Pages** (approx.): 450. **Frequency:** Not established; first edition fall 1978. **Editor:** Robert Lewis Smith. **Price:** $8.50.

Directory of Modeling Schools and Agencies *See* Models Mart Directory of Model Agencies, Talent Agents, and Modeling Schools

★3526★
DIRECTORY OF MUSIC FACULTIES IN COLLEGES AND UNIVERSITIES, U.S. AND CANADA
College Music Society
C/o Regent Box 44
University of Colorado   Phone: (303) 492-5049
Boulder, CO 80309
Covers: 22,000 members of music faculties at about 1,400 colleges and universities. **Entries include:** Name, institution and department, address, teaching area, highest degree in music. **Arrangement:** Alphabetical by faculty member name. **Indexes:** Geographical, teaching area, graduate music degree. **Pages** (approx.): 800. **Frequency:** Biennial, December of even years. **Editor:** Craig Short, Executive Secretary. **Former title:** Directory of Music Faculties in American Colleges and Universities. **Price:** $15.00.

★3527★
DIRECTORY OF MUSIC LIBRARIANS IN THE UNITED STATES AND CANADA
Music Library Association
2017 Walnut Street
Philadelphia, PA 19103
Covers: 600 practicing music librarians. **Entries include:** Names, office and home addresses, degrees. **Indexes:** Type of library, fields of specialization. **Pages** (approx.): 50. **Frequency:** Irregular; latest edition 1976. **Editor:** Don Phillips. **Price:** $3.00.

★3528★
DIRECTORY OF NATIONALLY CERTIFIED TEACHERS [Music]
Music Teachers National Association
413 Carew Tower   Phone: (513) 421-1420
Cincinnati, OH 45202
Number of listings: 2,700. **Entries include:** Name, address, area of teaching. **Arrangement:** Geographical, then by area of teaching. **Pages** (approx.): 20. **Frequency:** Annual, September. **Editor:** Mariann H. Clinton, Executive Director. **Price:** Free.

★3529★
DIRECTORY OF NEW ENGLAND THEATRE-PRODUCING GROUPS
New England Theatre Conference
50 Exchange Street   Phone: (617) 893-3120
Waltham, MA 02154
Covers: Regional, resident, summer, and touring theaters, plus professional theater schools, listed under the categories of Children's Theaters, College Theaters, Community Theaters, and Professional Theaters. **Entries include:** Name and address. **Arrangement:** Geographical within each section. **Pages** (approx.): 50. **Frequency:** Irregular; approximately every five years; latest edition 1972; new edition expected 1980. **Editor:** Marie L. Philips, Executive Secretary. **Price:** $10.00 (current edition); $20.00 (1980 edition).

★3530★
DIRECTORY OF PRIVATE PRESSES AND LETTERPRESS PRINTERS AND PUBLISHERS
Press of Arden Park
861 Los Molinos Way
Sacramento, CA 95825
Covers: About 500 private presses and hobbyist printers worldwide who use the letterpress process of reproduction. **Entries include:** Press name, address, phone, information on press and types, kinds of work produced, whether samples will be exchanged, brief statement on goals, printing philosophy, etc. **Arrangement:** Alphabetical. **Indexes:** Proprietor name. **Pages** (approx.): 50. **Frequency:** Annual, August. **Editor:** Budd Westreich. **Price:** $6.50.

★3531★
DIRECTORY OF PROFESSIONAL PHOTOGRAPHY
Professional Photographers of America
1090 Executive Way   Phone: (312) 299-8161
Des Plaines, IL 60018
Covers: Over 18,000 portrait, commercial, and industrial photographers who are members of PPA, and member repair technicians; also includes guide to photographic equipment and supply manufacturers and distributors. **Entries include:** For members - Name, office address; listings for members available for assignments also show phone and specialties. For suppliers - Company name, address, phone, list of products. **Arrangement:** Separate geographical sections for members available for assignment, industrial photographers (employed by businesses, etc.), and associate members. **Indexes:** Personal name. **Pages** (approx.): 225. **Frequency:** Annual, June. **Editor:** Scott Schwar, Promotion Manager. **Advertising accepted.** Circulation 16,000. **Price:** $12.50 (current and 1980 editions).

Directory of Public Telecommunications *See* People in Public Telecommunications

★3532★
DIRECTORY OF RIGHTS AND PERMISSIONS OFFICERS [Television broadcasting]
Association of Media Producers
1707 L Street, Suite 515   Phone: (202) 296-4710
Washington, DC 20036
Covers: Personnel at member television networks, distributors of programs, some Public Broadcasting System stations, and nonprofit television agencies to contact for permission to use copyrighted materials. **Entries include:** Firm name, address, phone and name of contact. **Frequency:** Not established; first edition fall 1978. **Price:** Free; send stamped and self-addressed business envelope.

★3533★
DIRECTORY OF SPEAKERS [General]
Oryx Press
3930 E. Camelback Road, Suite 206   Phone: (602) 254-6156
Phoenix, AZ 85018
Covers: Individuals available for public speaking on such topics as abortion, regional areas, consumer affairs, health and medicine, self-defense, warfare, etc. **Entries include:** Individual name, home address and phone (if permitted), name, address, and phone of booking agent; subjects; format of presentation; compensation; educational, career data; geographic region willing to travel. **Frequency:** First edition late 1979. **Editor:** Howard J. Langer. **Price:** $29.95.

★3534★
DIRECTORY OF TEACHERS OF ORAL INTERPRETATION
Speech Communication Association
5205 Leesburg Pike
Falls Church, VA 22041
Frequency: Latest edition 1977. **Editors:** Lee Hudson and Jill O'Brien. **Price:** $3.35.

★3535★
DIRECTORY OF UNIQUE MUSEUMS
Creative Communications
2552 Strathmore
Kalamazoo, MI 49009
Covers: Over 200 specialized or unique museums in the United States and Canada. Listings include museums for barbed wire, trotters, toy trains, Mummers, dentistry, country music, medical quackery, Edgar Allen Poe, and spiders. **Entries include:** Museum name, mailing address, phone, description of collection, hours open. **Arrangement:** Geographical. **Indexes:** Specialty. **Pages** (approx.): 100. **Frequency:** Not established; first edition 1979. **Editor:** Bill Truesdell. **Price:** $3.50, plus 50¢ shipping.

★3536★
EDUCATIONAL AND INDUSTRIAL TELEVISION—DIRECTORY OF PROGRAM SOURCES ISSUE
C. S. Tepfer Publishing Company, Inc.
51 Sugar Hollow Road
Danbury, CT 06810
Covers: Over 450 producers and distributors of video-format programs covering subjects such as business, entertainment, contemporary affairs, medicine, and education. **Entries include:** Company name, address, phone, name of contact. **Arrangement:** By subject. **Frequency:** Annual, November. **Editor:** Mary M. Woolf. **Price:** $2.00.

★3537★
EDUCATIONAL RESOURCES DIRECTORY OF NEW YORK CITY'S MUSEUMS, ZOOS, BOTANICAL GARDENS
Museums Collaborative
15 Gramercy Park South   Phone: (212) 674-0300
New York, NY
Covers: Educational programs, materials, and services offered by 51 museums and 25 community arts organizations in New York City. **Entries include:** Institution or organization name, address, name of contact, description of programs, materials, and services. **Frequency:** Annual. **Price:** $5.00, plus 50¢ shipping.

★3538★
EDUCATORS GUIDE TO FREE AUDIO AND VIDEO MATERIALS
Educators Progress Service, Inc.
214 Center Street   Phone: (414) 326-3126
Randolph, WI 53956
Covers: Sources for about 1,150 audiotapes, videotapes, scripts, and phonograph records in all subject areas provided by industrial, governmental, and other sponsors for free use by teachers and other educators. **Entries include:** Title, brief description, date produced, running time, speed (revolutions per minute or inches per second), booking details, source. **Arrangement:** By curriculum areas. **Indexes:** Source, title, subject. **Pages** (approx.): 200. **Frequency:** Annual, fall. **Editors:** James L. Berger and Walter A. Wittich. **Former title:** Educators Guide to Free Tapes, Scripts, and Transcriptions (1977). **Price:** $12.25, plus $1.35 shipping.

★3539★
EDUCATORS GUIDE TO FREE FILMS
Educators Progress Service, Inc.
214 Center Street   Phone: (414) 326-3126
Randolph, WI 53956
Covers: Sources for about 4,500 educational and recreational films in all subject areas provided by industrial, governmental, and other sponsors for free use by teachers and other educators. **Entries include:** Title, brief description, date produced, running time, whether silent or sound and color or black and white, booking details, source. **Arrangement:** By curriculum area. **Indexes:** Source, title, subject, films cleared for television. **Pages** (approx.): 750. **Frequency:** Annual, fall. **Editors:** John C. Diffor and Mary Foley Horkheimer. **Price:** $16.25, plus $1.35 shipping.

★3540★
EDUCATORS GUIDE TO FREE FILMSTRIPS
Educators Progress Service, Inc.
214 Center Street   Phone: (414) 326-3126
Randolph, WI 53956
Covers: Sources for about 600 filmstrips and slide sets in all subject areas provided by industrial, governmental, and other sponsors for free use by teachers and other educators. **Entries include:** Title, brief description, date produced, number of frames or slides, whether accompanying script or sound is available, whether color or black and white, booking details, source. **Arrangement:** By curriculum area. **Indexes:** Source, title, subject. **Pages** (approx.): 200. **Frequency:** Annual, fall. **Editors:** John C. Diffor and Mary Foley Horkheimer. **Price:** $11.75, plus $1.35 shipping.

Educators Guide to Free Tapes, Scripts, and Transcriptions *See* **Educators Guide to Free Audio and Video Materials**

★3541★
ENJOYING THE SUMMER THEATRES OF NEW ENGLAND
The Pequot Press
Old Chester Road
Chester, CT 06412
Covers: 40 Equity and non-Equity professional theaters in Connecticut, Rhode Island, Massachusetts, Vermont, New Hampshire, and Maine, plus 30 major music and dance festivals in the same area. **Entries include:** Theater name, address, phone, and producer's name, plus ticket prices, performance times (but not season dates), travel directions, and a 200-300 word description of the theater, its history, the quality of its productions, etc. **Arrangement:** Geographical. **Pages** (approx.): 150. **Editor:** Anne Goodrich. **Price:** $3.50.

Everyone's Guide to Halls of Fame *See* **Big Book of Halls of Fame**

★3542★
FEATURE FILMS ON 8MM, 16MM, AND VIDEOTAPE
R. R. Bowker Company
1180 Avenue of the Americas   Phone: (212) 764-5100
New York, NY 10036
Publication includes: List of film companies and distributors for 20,350 feature films and 1,500 videocassettes in the United States and Canada. **Entries include:** For film companies and distributors - Company name, address. For films and videocassettes - Title, producer, distributor, director, cast, and technical data (length, etc.). **Arrangement:** Alphabetical. **Pages** (approx.): 450. **Frequency:** Irregular; latest edition February 1979. **Editor:** James L. Limbacher. **Price:** $24.00, postpaid, payment with order (ISSN 0071-4100). **Send orders to:** R. R. Bowker Co., Box 1807, Ann Arbor, MI 48106 (313-761-4700).

★3543★
FEMALE ARTISTS PAST AND PRESENT
Women's History Research Center
2325 Oak Street   Phone: (415) 548-1770
Berkeley, CA 94708
Covers: 1,000 women in the visual arts, including practicing artists and female art teachers, museum personnel, etc. **Entries include:** Name, areas of occupational specialization, source for personal data, and home and/or office address for living subjects. **Arrangement:** Contents classified by artist's medium or role. **Indexes:** Supplement includes combined personal name index to both volumes. **Pages** (approx.): 160; supplement, 70. **Frequency:** Irregular; latest edition 1974; supplement 1975; no further editions expected. **Editor:** Vicki Lynn Hill; editor of supplement, Louisa Moe. **Price:** $7.00; supplement, $4.00; plus 50¢ shipping.

Film Buff's Bible *See* **Film Buff's Checklist of Motion Pictures**

★3544★
FILM BUFF'S CHECKLIST OF MOTION PICTURES
Hollywood Film Archive
8344 Melrose Avenue   Phone: (213) 933-3345
Hollywood, CA 90069
Publication includes: "Selected Companies Guide" section listing 200 major American and foreign film distributors. **Entries include:** Firm name, address, phone. **Arrangement:** Alphabetical. **Frequency:** Irregular; previous edition 1972; latest edition 1979. **Editor:** D. Richard Baer. **Former title:** Film Buff's Bible. **Price:** $19.95, cloth; $25.95, library binding; plus $1.75 shipping. **Other information:** Principal content of publication is an alphabetized list of 19,000 film titles (including documentaries and television movies) from 1912 through 1979. Leading actors, directors, alternate titles, release dates, running times, countries of origin, distributors or studios, and ratings are given for each film.

★3545★
FILM SERVICE PROFILES [New York state]
Center for Arts Information
152 W. 42nd Street   Phone: (212) 354-1675
New York, NY 10036
Covers: About 100 museums and 25 public library systems in New York which show and/or collect films, and about 50 film service organizations and related service organizations. **Entries include:** Organization name, address, name of key executive. For service organizations, listings also include number of members, publications, aims, services, special resources, and whether or not inquiries are invited and handled. **Arrangement:** Service organizations are alphabetical, museums and libraries are geographical. **Pages** (approx.): 150. **Frequency:** Not established; first edition November 1979. **Editor:** Kay Salz, Film Specialist. **Price:** Not determined.

★3546★
FILMMAKERS CONNECTION—INTERNATIONAL DIRECTORY
Filmmaker's Connection
Los Angeles Cinematheque
Box 2509
Los Angeles, CA 90028
Entries include: Individual name, address, phone, age, languages understood, list of completed projects, areas of interest, professional experience, goals. **Arrangement:** Geographical. **Frequency:** Annual, December. **Editor:** Tee Bosustow. **Price:** $2.00. **Other information:** Also cited as, "International Directory;" those listed have paid a $2.00 application fee.

★3547★
FINDING THE RIGHT SPEAKER
American Association of Association Executives
1101 16th Street, N. W.
Washington, DC 20036
Covers: 700 speakers previously used and recommended by one or more member association executives. **Entries include:** Name, address, phone, specialties of the speaker, and a reference able to furnish information on the person's speaking and subject competence. **Arrangement:** Alphabetical. **Indexes:** Geographical, subject. **Pages** (approx.): 200. **Frequency:** Biennial, October of odd years. **Price:** $10.00. **Editor:** Elissa Matulis Myers. **Advertising accepted.** Circulation 20,000. **Also includes:** Articles on effective use of speakers in meetings, on working with speakers bureaus, on working with government speakers, and on establishing a speakers bureau. Also includes list of 200 not-for-profit speakers bureaus.

★3548★
FINE ARTS MARKET PLACE
R. R. Bowker Company
1180 Avenue of the Americas   Phone: (212) 764-5100
New York, NY 10036
Covers: Over 8,000 art dealers, art book dealers, museum stores, publishers of art reproductions, packers and movers specializing in works of art, art restorers and framers, sources of art materials and

gallery equipment, art associations, and art exhibits. **Entries include:** Firm, institution, or association name, address, phone, and details as relevant to the classification. **Arrangement:** Classified by activity or service. **Indexes:** General. **Pages** (approx.): 410. **Frequency:** Irregular; latest edition 1977. **Editor:** Paul Cummings. **Price:** $19.95, postpaid, payment with order (ISSN 0000-0361). **Send orders to:** R. R. Bowker Co., Box 1807, Ann Arbor, MI 48106 (313-761-4700).

First New England Catalogue *See* Only in New England

500 TV-Film Producers [New York City] *See* Who's Who in N.Y. Filmmakers

★3549★
FM ATLAS AND STATION DIRECTORY
FM Atlas Publishing Company
Box 24
Adolph, MN 55701
Covers: 4,800 FM stations located in North America. **Entries include:** Call letters, city in which station is located, musical format, network with which affiliated (if any), primary and secondary coverage radii in miles, whether stereo or monaural, and other descriptive information. **Arrangement:** Geographical, then by frequency. **Pages** (approx.): 115. **Frequency:** Irregular; latest edition fall 1978; new edition expected 1980. **Editor:** Bruce Elving. **Price:** $3.95, postpaid.

★3550★
F.M. RADIO GUIDE
And/Or Press
Box 2246   Phone: (415) 526-6939
Berkeley, CA 94702
Covers: Over 2,600 FM radio stations in the United States. **Entries include:** Station call letters, location, frequency, format, broadcasting range, hours of operation. **Arrangement:** Geographical. **Pages** (approx.): 130. **Editor:** Krompotich. **Price:** $2.95, plus $1.00 shipping, payment must accompany order.

★3551★
FOLK MUSIC: MORE THAN A SONG
Lippincott & Crowell, Publishers
521 Fifth Avenue
New York, NY 10017
Covers: Primarily, traditional and contemporary folk singers and instrumentalists; includes some listings for festivals, organizations, etc. About 350 entries of all types. **Entries include:** Performers' listings include name and biographical data centered on musical activities, along with recording information; many entries include photographs. **Arrangement:** Alphabetical. **Pages** (approx.): 450. **Frequency:** Published 1976. **Editors:** Kristin Baggelaar and Donald Milton. **Price:** $14.95.

★3552★
FOLK MUSIC SOURCEBOOK
Alfred A. Knopf, Inc.
201 E. 50th Street   Phone: (212) 572-2134
New York, NY 10022
Publication includes: About 1,150 manufacturers of folk instruments, book and music publishers, record companies, and mail-order outlets; also lists organizations, archives, festivals, and centers concerned with the preservation, promotion, and development of folk music (including blues, ragtime, ethnic, and contemporary); international coverage. **Entries include:** Name of organization or company and address; organization listings include publications. **Arrangement:** Organizations are geographical; manufacturers classified by instrument; all other sections are alphabetical. **Indexes:** General. **Pages** (approx.): 275. **Frequency:** First edition 1976. **Editors:** Larry Sandberg and Dick Weissman. **Price:** $7.95. **Also includes:** Largest section of book consists of brief comments on styles, instrumentation, etc., of individual folk music artists and groups with discographies and bibliographies; numerous photographs.

★3553★
FOTO FINDER [Photography]
Photosearch International
                                      Phone: (715) 248-3800
Osceola, WI 54020
Covers: About 1,700 photographers who subscribe to the "Photoletter" and offer photos for sale. **Entries include:** Individual's name, address. **Arrangement:** Random. **Indexes:** Subjects available, photographer name. **Pages** (approx.): 160. **Frequency:** Biennial, summer of odd years. **Editor:** Rohn Engh. **Advertising accepted.** **Former title:** Specialization Directory. **Price:** $10.00. **Other information:** Variant title, "Photofinder."

★3554★
FREE STOCK PHOTOGRAPHY DIRECTORY
Infosource Business Publications
1600 Lehigh Parkway East   Phone: (215) 433-6264
Allentown, PA 18103
Covers: About 260 federal, state, and local governments and a few corporations which will provide photographs free of charge for commercial use. **Entries include:** Name of librarian, organization name, address, phone, and description of photographs available. **Arrangement:** Geographical, subject. **Frequency:** Annual, June. **Editor:** Neil Deutsch. **Price:** $10.00, postpaid.

★3555★
GADNEY'S GUIDE TO 1800 INTERNATIONAL CONTESTS FESTIVALS & GRANTS IN FILM & VIDEO, PHOTOGRAPHY, TV/ RADIO BROADCASTING, WRITING...
Festival Publications
Box 10180
Glendale, CA 91209
Covers: 1,800 of what publisher calls "events" which carry awards of cash, equipment, etc.; "events" include sources of scholarships, grants, apprenticeships and internships, and loans. Emphasis is on visual arts. **Entries include:** Contest, event or award name, address, date and deadline, entry requirements, and information about eligibility requirements and fees, awards available, and sponsors and judges. **Arrangement:** By medium, then geographical. **Indexes:** Alphabetical. **Pages** (approx.): 610. **Frequency:** Biennial, odd years. **Price:** $21.95 cloth; $15.95, paper; plus $1.50 shipping. **Other information:** Variant title, "Contests, Festivals & Grants."

★3556★
GOODFELLOW CATALOG OF WONDERFUL THINGS [Craftspersons]
Goodfellow Review of Crafts
Box 4520   Phone: (415) 845-7645
Berkeley, CA 94704
Covers: Several hundred craftspersons and their work; crafts organizations; crafts schools; crafts publications. **Entries include:** For craftspersons - Name, address; personal note on background, interests, philosophy, etc.; photos of work; instructions for ordering by mail. For organizations, schools, publications - Name or title, address, relevant details. **Indexes:** Craft types and objects. **Pages** (approx.): 435. **Frequency:** Irregular; latest edition fall 1977; new edition expected summer 1980. **Editor:** Christopher Weills. **Price:** $8.95, postpaid. **Send orders to:** Berkely Publishing Corporation, 200 Madison Avenue, New York, NY 10016.

★3557★
GOODFELLOW REVIEW OF CRAFTS—CRAFTS FAIRS CALENDAR SECTION
Goodfellow Review of Crafts
Box 4520   Phone: (415) 548-2607
Berkeley, CA 94704
Publication includes: Crafts fairs in California, in separate lists for northern and southern parts of state. Approximately 50-75 shows per issue. **Entries include:** Name, location, dates, fees, other extensive details. **Arrangement:** Geographical by area, then chronological. **Frequency:** In each bimonthly issue. **Editors:** Jon Stewart and Bill

Netzer. **Advertising accepted.** Circulation 20,000. **Former title:** Goodfellow Newsletter. **Price:** $8.00 for 12 issues (2 years); $1.00 per copy.

Grants, Aid and Prizes to Individuals in the Arts *See* National Directory of Grants, Aid and Prizes to Individuals in the Arts...

★3558★
GRANTS IN PHOTOGRAPHY—HOW TO GET THEM
Amphoto, Division
Billboard Publications, Inc.
1515 Broadway   Phone: (212) 764-7300
New York, NY 10036
Covers: About 25 agencies, organizations, and other sources of funding for photographers. **Entries include:** Agency or organization name, address, name of contact; types of projects funded, amount of awards. **Pages** (approx.): 90. **Frequency:** Published 1979. **Author:** Lida Moser. **Price:** $12.50, plus $1.00 shipping. **Send orders to:** Lida Moser, 350 W. 57th St., Ste. 15A, New York, NY 10019.

Graphic Artists Guild-Illustrators Guild—Talent Directory *See* Talent Directory

★3559★
GUEST AUTHOR: A DIRECTORY OF SPEAKERS
Hermes Press
51 Lenox Street
Brockton, MA 02401
Covers: 800 authors, illustrators, and other subject specialists who are interested in speaking before meetings and other groups. **Entries include:** Speaker's name, address, preferred type of audience, subjects, whether charge is made for appearance (but no clue as to amount), and titles of one or two books by the speaker. **Arrangement:** Geographical. **Indexes:** Personal name, subject. **Pages** (approx.): 120. **Frequency:** Annual volumes do not duplicate previous volumes; 5-year cumulations planned. **Editors:** Jane Manthorne and Rose Moorachian. **Price:** $7.45, postpaid, payment with order (ISSN 0160-6565). (Not verified)

★3560★
GUIDE TO CLASSICAL MUSIC ON AMERICAN AND CANADIAN RADIO STATIONS
Musica
Box 1266
Edison, NJ 08817
Covers: Over 1,000 stations in the 50 United States and Canada. **Entries include:** Days and hours of concert broadcasts, wavelength of station, radius in miles, whether stereo, whether program guide is published. **Arrangement:** Geographical. **Pages** (approx.): 45. **Frequency:** Irregular; latest edition 1978. **Advertising accepted.** Circulation 15,000. **Former title:** Guide to Classical Music on American Radio Stations. **Price:** $4.95, postpaid, payment with order.

Guide to Community Arts Agencies *See* Community Arts Agencies: A Handbook and Guide

★3561★
GUIDE TO DANCE IN NEW YORK
Quick Fox, Inc.
33 W. 60th Street   Phone: (212) 246-0325
New York, NY 10023
Covers: Dance theaters in New York; the top 100 dance schools, teachers, and studios; bookstores, libraries, museums, publishers, and film producers concerned with dance; and other organizations and individuals with products, services, or information related to dance in New York (from dancewear shops to physical therapists). **Entries include:** For theaters - Name, address, performances, type of dance, name of company (if any). For dance education - Name of school, name of individual instructor, address, tuition, programs offered, names of graduates. For others - Name, address, phone; appropriate details concerning services, products, etc. **Pages** (approx.): 225.

Frequency: First edition August 1979. **Editors:** Ellen Jacob and Christopher Jonas. **Price:** $5.95.

★3562★
GUIDE TO INDEPENDENT FILM AND VIDEO
Anthology Film Archives
80 Wooster Street   Phone: (212) 226-0010
New York, NY 10012
Covers: Filmmaking groups, distributors of films and videotapes, foundations willing to fund independent film and video projects, theaters and other showcases, and publications about filmmaking. **Entries include:** Organization name, address, phone; some listings include description of activities, publications. **Arrangement:** Theaters are geographical; others are alphabetical by name (or as with publications, title). **Pages** (approx.): 90. **Frequency:** Not established; first edition 1976. **Editor:** Hollis Melton. **Price:** $4.00, plus 60¢ shipping.

★3563★
GUIDE TO MUSEUMS IN THE DELAWARE VALLEY
A. S. Barnes & Company, Inc.
Forsgate Drive   Phone: (609) 655-0190
Cranbury, NJ 08512
Covers: About 100 museums in the eleven counties bordering the Delaware River in Delaware, New Jersey, and Pennsylvania. **Entries include:** Name, address, phone, hours, fees, photo, description of collection, instructions on how to reach museum. **Arrangement:** Geographical. **Pages** (approx.): 130. **Frequency:** Irregular; latest edition 1976. **Editors:** Nancy Cramer and Laurie Gearhart. **Price:** $2.95. **Other information:** Compiled by Museum Council of Philadelphia.

★3564★
GUIDE TO WOMEN'S ART ORGANIZATIONS
Midmarch Associates
Box 3304   Phone: (212) 666-6990
New York, NY 10017
Covers: Organizations, performance groups, archives, registries, festivals, funding resources, etc., with a special interest in the work of women in visual arts, architecture, design, film and video, dance, music, theater, and writing. **Entries include:** Organization name, address, phone, interests and activities or services. **Arrangement:** Classified by field. **Pages** (approx.): 85. **Frequency:** First edition 1979; new edition expected 1981. **Editor:** Cynthia Navaretta. **Price:** $5.00, postpaid, payment with order.

★3565★
GUILD OF BOOK WORKERS—MEMBERSHIP LIST
Guild of Book Workers
663 Fifth Avenue   Phone: (212) 757-6454
New York, NY 10022
Covers: About 350 amateur and professional workers in the hand book crafts of bookbinding, calligraphy, illuminating, and decorative papermaking. **Entries include:** Name, address, specialties. **Arrangement:** Alphabetical. **Indexes:** Geographical. **Pages** (approx.): 20. **Frequency:** Irregular; previous edition May 1977; latest edition December 1979. **Editor:** Jeanne F. Lewisohn, Membership Chairman. **Price:** $15.00; use must be approved before sale.

★3566★
HANDBOOK OF MUSEUM RELATED RESOURCE ORGANIZATIONS
American Association of Museums
1055 Thomas Jefferson Street, N. W.   Phone: (202) 338-5300
Washington, DC 20007
Covers: Organizations concerned with the development, maintenance, and funding of museums. **Frequency:** Irregular. **Price:** $2.00.

★3567★

HISPANIC ARTS DIRECTORY

Association of Hispanic Arts

200 W. 87th Street   Phone: (212) 369-7054

New York, NY 10028

Covers: About 60 art organizations offering assistance to Hispanic artists, or otherwise promoting the development, exhibition, and support of Hispanic arts; coverage limited to New York. Arts included are dance, music, theatre, and visual arts. **Entries include:** Organization name, address, phone, name of director or contact, description of programs, activities, services. **Arrangement:** Alphabetical. **Pages** (approx.): 20. **Frequency:** Annual. **Editor:** Elba Cabrera Mondesire. **Former title:** Yellow Pages of Hispanic Arts. **Price:** $1.00, plus 50¢ shipping.

★3568★

HOLLYWOOD FOREIGN PRESS ASSOCIATION—MEMBERSHIP
    DIRECTORY

Hollywood Foreign Press Association

8732 Sunset Boulevard, Suite 210   Phone: (213) 657-1731

Los Angeles, CA 90069

Number of listings: 95. **Entries include:** Name, address, phone and/or telex, countries in which work is published. **Arrangement:** Alphabetical. **Pages** (approx.): 20. **Frequency:** Annual, August. **Price:** Free.

★3569★

HOW TO BE A COMPLEAT CLOWN

Stein & Day Publishers

Scarborough House   Phone: (914) 762-2151

Briarcliff Manor, NY 10510

Publication includes: List of clown schools and clubs, and businesses which supply clown props, costumes, etc. **Entries include:** Organization name, address, phone; interests, activities, or services. **Frequency:** Published November 1978. **Author:** Toby Sanders. **Price:** $9.95.

★3570★

HOW TO BREAK INTO MOTION PICTURES, TELEVISION,
    COMMERCIALS & MODELING

Doubleday & Company, Inc.

245 Park Avenue   Phone: (212) 953-4561

New York, NY 10017

Publication includes: In appendixes - Craft union offices, university drama schools, acting workshops and coaches, agencies, makeup classes, modeling schools, and other training, professional, and placement groups for acting and modeling. **Entries include:** Organization or school name, address, services. **Arrangement:** Alphabetical within activity. **Pages** (approx.): 240. **Frequency:** Published 1978. **Editor:** Nina Blanchard. **Price:** $8.95, plus 50¢ shipping. **Send orders to:** Doubleday & Company, Inc., Garden City, NY 11530.

★3571★

HOW TO FIND THE A-V JOB TRAINING MARKET IN YOUR AREA

National Audio-Visual Association

3150 Spring Street   Phone: (703) 273-7200

Fairfax, VA 22031

Covers: Over 800 organizations which receive federal funds for job training programs. **Entries include:** Organization name, address, name of contact. **Arrangement:** Geographical. **Pages** (approx.): 80. **Frequency:** Published May 1978. **Price:** $15.00, payment must accompany order.

★3572★

HOW TO SELL YOUR ARTWORK

Prentice-Hall, Inc.

                              Phone: (201) 592-2000

Englewood Cliffs, NJ 07632

Publication includes: Lists of about 1,800 United States and Canadian art schools and colleges and universities offering art training;

about 45 art organizations; about 60 art periodicals; and about 150 organizations (other than colleges and universities previously listed) which offer scholarships, fellowships, and awards for art studies. **Entries include:** For schools - School name, address, and coding to indicate courses offered, whether coeducational, degrees offered, scholarships available, when classes are held, etc. For organizations - Name, address. For publications - Title, publisher, address, cost, frequency. For grants - Name and address of sponsor, amount and length of grant, qualifications, and frequency. **Arrangement:** Schools are geographical, others are alphabetical. **Frequency:** Latest edition 1978. **Editor:** Milton K. Berlye. **Former title:** Selling Your Artwork (1978). **Price:** $14.95, cloth; $7.95, paper.

★3573★

HOW YOU CAN APPEAR IN TV COMMERCIALS

Pilot Books

347 Fifth Avenue   Phone: (212) 685-0736

New York, NY 10016

Publication includes: About 350 theatrical and Screen Actors Guild agents located in Los Angeles, San Diego, San Francisco, California; New York metropolitan area; Arizona; Colorado; Florida; Chicago, Illinois; Detroit, Michigan; New Mexico; and Dallas, Texas. **Entries include:** Agent name, office address. **Arrangement:** Geographical. **Pages** (approx.): 70. **Frequency:** Irregular; latest edition 1978. **Editors:** Raymond Carlson and Ron Milkie. **Price:** $2.95.

★3574★

IFPA FILM AND VIDEO COMMUNICATORS—MEMBERSHIP
    ROSTER

Information Film Producers of America

750 E. Colorado Boulevard, Suite 6   Phone: (213) 874-2266

Pasadena, CA 91101

Number of listings: 1,000. **Entries include:** For corporations - Name, address, phone, and name of representative. For individuals - Name, office address and phone, company name, and title. **Arrangement:** Individuals are geographical; sustainers are alphabetical. **Pages** (approx.): 100. **Frequency:** Annual, February. **Editor:** Robert B. Montague, Editorial Vice President. **Advertising accepted.** Circulation 1,000. **Price:** Available to members only.

Illustrators Guild—Roster *See*
    Talent Directory

Index to Educational Audio Tapes *See* Index to Producers and
    Distributors [Audiovisual materials]

Index to Educational Overhead Transparencies *See* Index to
    Producers and Distributors [Audiovisual materials]

Index to Educational Records *See* Index to Producers and
    Distributors [Audiovisual materials]

Index to Educational Slides *See* Index to Producers and
    Distributors [Audiovisual materials]

Index to Educational Video Tapes *See* Index to Producers and
    Distributors [Audiovisual materials]

Index to 8mm Motion Cartridges *See* Index to Producers and
    Distributors [Audiovisual materials]

Index to Free Educational Materials *See* Index to Producers and
    Distributors [Audiovisual materials]

★3575★
INDEX TO PRODUCERS AND DISTRIBUTORS [Educational audiovisual materials]
National Information Center for Educational Media
University of Southern California
University Park   Phone: (213) 741-6681
Los Angeles, CA 90007
Covers: 16,000 producers and distributors of educational audiovisual materials whose products are described in these NICEM publications: Index to 16mm Educational Films; Index to 35mm Educational Films; Index to Educational Overhead Transparencies; Index to Educational Audio Tapes; Index to Educational Video Tapes; Index to Educational Records; Index to 8mm Motion Cartridges; Index to Educational Slides; Index to Free Educational Materials. **Entries include:** Producer or distributor name, address. **Arrangement:** Alphabetical. **Frequency:** Every two and a half years; latest edition 1977; new edition expected 1980. **Price:** $21.50, plus $2.50 shipping, paper; $11.00, microfiche.

Index to 16mm Educational Films *See* Index to Producers and Distributors [Audiovisual materials]

Index to 35mm Educational Films *See* Index to Producers and Distributors [Audiovisual materials]

Indiana Arts and Crafts Directory *See* Arts and Crafts Directory [Indiana]

★3576★
INDIANA TOURING HANDBOOK AND CATALOG OF CULTURAL EVENTS FOR COMMUNITIES
Indiana Arts Commission
155 E. Market Street   Phone: (317) 633-5649
Indianapolis, IN 46204
Covers: About 25 arts organizations which offer touring programs and are funded by the commission; colleges and universities with theater, dance, music, and art programs funded under the commission's Campus Arts to Community program are also listed. **Entries include:** Name of program, description of program and target audience, number of personnel included, length of program, set-up time required, equipment and facility requirements, dates available, name, address, and phone of contact. **Arrangement:** Arts organizations and colleges are by art form in separate lists. **Pages** (approx.): 55. **Frequency:** Annual, July. **Former title:** Campus Arts to Community Program Handbook and Catalog of Cultural Events (1978). **Price:** Apply.

★3577★
INDUSTRIAL DESIGNERS SOCIETY OF AMERICA—MEMBERSHIP DIRECTORY
Industrial Designers Society of America
1717 N Street, N. W.
Washington, DC 20036
Number of listings: 1,100. **Entries include:** Individual name, address, phone, membership category, and employment classification. **Arrangement:** Alphabetical. **Indexes:** Geographical. **Frequency:** Annual, September/October. **Price:** $100.00, payment with order.

★3578★
INSTRUMENTALIST—DIRECTORY OF SUMMER MUSIC CAMPS, CLINICS, AND WORKSHOPS ISSUE
Instrumentalist Company
1418 Lake Street   Phone: (312) 328-6000
Evanston, IL 60204
Publication includes: Directory of summer music camps, clinics, and workshops in the United States, plus some Canadian and foreign camps. **Entries include:** Camp name, location, director, opening and closing dates, tuition and any extra costs, and courses offered. **Arrangement:** Geographical. **Pages** (approx.): 35; supplement, 15. **Frequency:** Annual, March; supplement, April. **Editor:** Kenneth L. Neidig, Editor/Advertising Manager. **Advertising accepted.** Circulation 22,500. **Price:** $1.50 per issue.

★3579★
INTERNATIONAL ART AND ANTIQUES YEARBOOK
National Magazine Company Ltd.
Chestergate House
Vauxhall Bridge Road
London SW1V 1HF, England
Covers: About 13,000 art and antique dealers throughout the world; also lists auction houses; dates and locations of major antiques fairs; fine art packers and shippers; art periodicals; art and antiques associations. **Entries include:** For dealers - Dealer name, address; many listings include description of dealer's stock or specialty. Other listings include similar detail. **Arrangement:** Geographical. **Indexes:** Specialist index for each country; detailed town maps and street indexes show dealer locations. **Pages** (approx.): 880. **Frequency:** Annual. **Editor:** Marcelle d'Argy Smith. **Advertising accepted.** **Price:** $42.00. **Send orders to:** Gale Research Company, Book Tower, Detroit, MI 48226. **Other information:** British coverage is limited to advertisers; full British coverage is provided in the companion volume, "British Art and Antiques Yearbook," also available from Gale; $28.00.

International Association of Concert and Festival Managers—Membership List *See* International Society of Performing Arts Administrators

International Directory [Of filmmakers] *See* Filmmakers Connection—International Directory

★3580★
INTERNATIONAL DIRECTORY OF ARTS
Art Address Verlag Muller
GMBH & Co. Kg.
Frankfurt/Main, Germany
Covers: More than 110,000 art museums, art schools, art associations, art restorers, antique dealers, coin dealers, art galleries and dealers, auctioneers, publishers, periodicals, booksellers specializing in art, artists, and collectors. **Entries include:** Individual or organization name, address; names of key personnel, specialties, publications are listed as appropriate. Listings for artists include biographical data. **Arrangement:** By activity. **Pages** (approx.): 1,800 in two volumes. **Frequency:** Irregular; latest edition October 1978. **Advertising accepted.** **Price:** $70.00, plus $2.50 shipping. **Send orders to:** Marquis Who's Who, Inc., 200 E. Ohio, St., Chicago, IL 60611 (312-787-2008).

International Directory of Museum Permanent Collection Catalogs *See* Art Books 1950-1979

★3581★
INTERNATIONAL FILM GUIDE
Tantivy Press
136-148 Tooley Street
London SE1 2TT, England
Publication includes: Lists of film production companies, distributors, organizations, and government agencies concerned with film in major countries of the world. Also includes film festivals, non-theatrical film distributors in the United States, sources of films for collectors, film archives, television networks, services for the industry, and film schools. **Entries include:** All entries include company or organization name, address; listings for festivals and following categories in foregoing list include additional details. **Arrangement:** Geographical. **Pages** (approx.): 560. **Frequency:** Annual, January. **Editor:** Peter Cowie. **Advertising accepted.** **Price:** $7.95 (current and 1980 editions). **Send orders to:** A. S. Barnes & Company, Inc., Forsgate Drive, Cranbury, NJ 08512.

★3582★
INTERNATIONAL FOLK MUSIC COUNCIL—LIST OF MEMBERS
International Folk Music Council
Department of Music
Queen's University   Phone: (613) 544-6226
Kingston, Ontario, Canada
Covers: 1,000 persons and institutions interested in folk music.
Entries include: Name, address. **Arrangement:** Alphabetical.
Frequency: Irregular.

International Industrial Television Association—Membership
   Directory *See* International Television Association—
   Membership Roster

★3583★
INTERNATIONAL MIMES AND PANTOMIMISTS DIRECTORY
International Mimes and Pantomimists
C/o August Freundlich, Dean of College of Visual & Performing Arts
200 Crouse College
Syracuse University   Phone: (315) 423-2611
Syracuse, NY 13210
Covers: Over 400 mimes and pantomimists throughout the world; also
covers courses available on the subject. **Entries include:** Name, home
address and phone, area of specialization, courses taught, and
performance description. **Arrangement:** Geographical. **Indexes:**
Alphabetical. **Pages** (approx.): 130. **Frequency:** Biennial, spring of
even years. **Price:** $12.00 (current edition); $9.00 (1980 edition).

★3584★
INTERNATIONAL MOTION PICTURE ALMANAC
Quigley Publishing Company, Inc.
159 W. 53rd Street   Phone: (212) 247-3100
New York, NY 10019
Covers: Motion picture producing companies, firms serving the
industry, equipment manufacturers, casting agencies, literary
agencies, advertising and publicity representatives, motion picture
theater circuits, buying and booking organizations, drive-in theaters,
international film festivals, associations. **Entries include:** Generally,
company name, address, phone; manufacturer and service listings may
include description of products and services and name of contact;
producing company listings include additional detail; drive-in listings
show owner and capacity. **Arrangement:** Classified by service or
activity, then generally geographical. **Pages** (approx.): 700.
Frequency: Annual, January. **Editor:** Richard Gertner. **Advertising
accepted.** **Price:** $35.00, plus $2.00 shipping. **Also includes:**
"Who's Who in Motion Pictures and Television" section giving brief
biographical details and lists of motion picture, television and other
performances, and positions and achievements for about 4,000
actors, actresses, producers, playwrights, etc. List of feature films
released during preceding year, with cast and other details. List of
feature pictures released since 1955, with principal cast, producer,
date released, running time. (These sections also appear in
"International Television Almanac.")

★3585★
**INTERNATIONAL RADIO AND TELEVISION SOCIETY—ROSTER
   YEARBOOK**
International Radio and Television Society
420 Lexington Avenue   Phone: (212) 867-6650
New York, NY 10017
Covers: About 1,300 persons professionally involved in television or
radio or connected with them through teaching, publishing, or
business. **Entries include:** Name, title (where applicable), business
address and phone. **Arrangement:** Alphabetical in two sections - those
within 50-mile radius of New York City, and those elsewhere. **Indexes:**
Classified. **Pages** (approx.): 145. **Frequency:** Annual, January.
Advertising accepted. Circulation 1,500. **Price:** Available to
members only. **Also includes:** A list of companies that provide goods
and services related to the industry.

★3586★
INTERNATIONAL ROSTER OF ORGAN TEACHERS
National Association of Organ Teachers
7938 Bertram Avenue   Phone: (219) 844-3395
Hammond, IN 46324
Frequency: Irregular; approximately every five years; latest edition
1979. **Editor:** Jack C. Grieg. **Former title:** National Roster of Organ
Teachers (1979). **Price:** Available to members only. **Also includes:**
List of audition centers and chairmen.

★3587★
**INTERNATIONAL SOCIETY OF PERFORMING ARTS
   ADMINISTRATORS—MEMBERSHIP LIST**
International Society of Performing Arts Administrators
C/o Earl R. Williams
Emens Auditorium
Ball State University   Phone: (317) 285-1539
Muncie, IN 47306
Covers: 200 concert managers and other performing arts
administrators in the United States and Canada. **Entries include:**
Administrator's name, title, and office address. **Arrangement:**
Alphabetical. **Pages** (approx.): 15. **Frequency:** Annual, January.
Editor: Clinton E. Norton, Membership Chairperson. **Former title:**
International Association of Concert and Festival Managers -
Membership List. **Price:** Available to members only.

★3588★
INTERNATIONAL TELEVISION ALMANAC
Quigley Publishing Company, Inc.
159 W. 53rd Street   Phone: (212) 247-3100
New York, NY 10019
Covers: Television networks, major program producers, major group
station owners, cable television companies, distributors, firms serving
the industry, equipment manufacturers, casting agencies, literary
agencies, advertising and publicity representatives, television stations,
associations. **Entries include:** Generally, company name, address,
phone; manufacturer and service listings may include description of
products and services and name of contact; producing, distributing,
and station listings include additional detail. **Arrangement:** Classified
by service or activity, then generally geographical. **Pages** (approx.):
650. **Frequency:** Annual, January. **Editor:** Richard Gertner.
Advertising accepted. **Price:** $35.00, plus $2.00 shipping. **Also
includes:** "Who's Who in Motion Pictures and Television" section
giving brief biographical details and lists of motion pictures, television
and other performances, and positions and achievements for about
4,000 actors, actresses, producers, playwrights, etc. List of feature
films released during preceding year, with cast and other details. List
of feature pictures released since 1955, with principal cast, producer,
date released, running time. (These sections also appear in
"International Motion Picture Almanac.")

★3589★
**INTERNATIONAL TELEVISION ASSOCIATION—MEMBERSHIP
   ROSTER**
International Television Association
26 South Street   Phone: (201) 464-6747
New Providence, NJ 07974
Covers: About 3,000 persons engaged in communications needs
analysis, script writing, producing, directing, consulting and operations
management in the videotape and non-broadcast television fields in
the United states, Canada, and Europe. **Entries include:** Name,
company affiliation, office address and phone, areas of occupational
specialization. **Arrangement:** Alphabetical. **Indexes:** Company with
which affiliated. **Pages** (approx.): 40. **Frequency:** Annual, July.
Editor: Bobette Kandle, Director of Operations. **Former title:**
International Industrial Television Association - Membership Directory.
Price: Available to members only.

★3590★
JAZZ PUBLICITY II
Reese Markewich, M. D.
Bacon Hill
Pleasantville, NY 10570
Covers: Several hundred jazz critics and jazz periodicals, worldwide. **Entries include:** Names and addresses. **Pages** (approx.): 25. **Frequency:** Irregular; latest edition 1977; new edition expected 1980. **Editor:** Reese Markewich. **Price:** 1977 edition out of print; $7.00 (tentative, 1980 edition).

Jazzman's Reference Book *See* Recordings & Bookings Worldwide [Jazz]

★3591★
LISTING OF M.F.A. PROGRAMS [Master of Fine Arts programs]
College Art Association of America
16 E. 52nd Street   Phone: (212) 755-3532
New York, NY 10022
Covers: Master of Fine Arts degree programs offered at over 100 institutions. **Entries include:** Institution name, name of department, address; admission requirements, application deadline, areas of concentration, tuition, and degree requirements. **Arrangement:** Alphabetical. **Pages** (approx.): 25. **Frequency:** Irregular; latest edition 1976; new edition expected 1980 or 1981. **Price:** $1.00, postpaid.

★3592★
LOCUS [Art and photography, New York City]
Filsinger & Company Ltd.
150 Waverly Place   Phone: (212) 243-7421
New York, NY 10014
Covers: 4,000 artists and photographers (both contemporary and retrospective) and galleries in New York City which handle their work. **Entries include:** Gallery name, address, phone, name of director, hours, types of works handled, artists for whom gallery acts as representative, artists whose works are carried. **Arrangement:** Alphabetical. **Indexes:** Artist name. **Pages** (approx.): Base volume 200, update 100. **Frequency:** Irregular; base volume 1975; update May 1977; new edition expected 1980. **Editor:** Cheryl Filsinger. **Price:** Base volume, $10.00, plus 75¢ shipping; update, $10.00, plus 50¢ shipping (current edition); $25.00 (1980 edition).

★3593★
LONG WINTER CATALOGUE—A Guide to the Craftspeople of Cape Cod
Fleming/Kapp, Publishers
Marstons Mills, MA 02648
Entries include: Name of craftsperson, address, articles produced or field of specialization, where work can be seen/purchased. **Arrangement:** Geographical. **Indexes:** Name, specialty. **Frequency:** Irregular; first edition 1974. **Price:** $2.25.

★3594★
MANHATTAN DANCE SCHOOL DIRECTORY [New York]
Marcel Dekker, Inc.
270 Madison Avenue   Phone: (212) 889-9595
New York, NY 10016
Number of listings: Over 80. **Entries include:** School name, address, phone, name of instructor, size of classes, classes offered, fees. **Arrangement:** Alphabetical. **Frequency:** Not established; first edition 1978. **Editor:** Barbi Leifert O'Reilly. **Price:** $8.95.

★3595★
MARIETTA COLLEGE CRAFTS DIRECTORY USA
Marietta College Crafts Directory USA
Marietta College   Phone: (614) 373-8027
Marietta, OH 45750
Covers: Subtitle: "Includes Listings of 5,000 Amateur and Professional Artists/Craftspersons and 1,000 Crafts Organizations." Persons listed are preponderantly professional. **Entries include:** For craftspersons - Name, studio address, phone, home phone, place and

date of birth, whether amateur or professional, preferred media. For organizations - Name, address. **Arrangement:** Craftspersons are geographical, then divided by media; organizations are in Zip code order. **Indexes:** Personal name. **Pages** (approx.): 275. **Frequency:** Published 1976. **Price:** $10.25, plus 75¢ shipping.

Media News Keys *See* Radio-TV Contact Service

★3596★
MIDWEST ART FARE
Midwest Art Fare
1056 56th Street
Des Moines, IA 50311
Covers: Art fairs and shows around the upper Midwest - Iowa, Illinois, Wisconsin, and Minnesota, and mid-Plains - Nebraska, Missouri, and Kansas. **Entries include:** Name of fair, city held in, name and address of contact, fees, deadlines, entry requirements. **Arrangement:** Chronological. **Pages** (approx.): 5-10. **Frequency:** Monthly. **Editors:** Bill and Diane Jacobsen. **Former title:** County Crafts Art Fair List (1975). **Price:** $1.00 per issue; $8.00 per calendar year.

Mime Directory *See* International Mimes and Pantomimists Directory

★3597★
MODELS GUIDE [Photographers', etc.; New York City]
Leo Shull Publications
134 W. 44th Street   Phone: (212) 586-6900
New York, NY 10036
Covers: Model agencies, photographers, TV commercial producers, and other companies using models in New York City and vicinity; includes services for models, such as hair stylists, cosmetologists, etc. **Entries include:** Name, address, and area of specialization. **Arrangement:** Classified by field. **Pages** (approx.): 130. **Frequency:** Annual. **Editor:** Leo Shull. **Advertising accepted.** **Price:** $6.85, postpaid, payment with order.

★3598★
MODELS MART DIRECTORY OF MODEL AGENCIES, TALENT AGENTS, AND MODELING SCHOOLS
Peter Glenn Publications
17 E. 48th Street   Phone: (212) 688-7940
New York, NY 10017
Entries include: School or agency name, address, phone, name of director or manager, whether an agency or school. **Arrangement:** Geographical. **Pages** (approx.): 130. **Frequency:** Irregular; latest edition 1977; new edition possible 1980. **Editor:** Rose Marie Taylor. **Advertising accepted.** **Price:** $7.50 (current edition); $10.00 (1980 edition).

Motion Picture Almanac *See* International Motion Picture Almanac

★3599★
MOTION PICTURE TV AND THEATRE DIRECTORY
Motion Picture Enterprises Publications, Inc.
          Phone: (212) 245-0969
Tarrytown, NY 10591
Covers: Companies providing services and products to the motion picture and television industries. **Entries include:** Company name, address, phone. **Arrangement:** By type of product or service, then geographical. **Indexes:** Alphabetical. **Pages** (approx.): 150. **Frequency:** Semiannual, spring and fall. **Advertising accepted.** Circulation 40,000. **Price:** $3.50.

★3600★
MOTION PICTURES, TELEVISION AND RADIO: A UNION CATALOGUE OF MANUSCRIPT AND SPECIAL COLLECTIONS IN THE WESTERN UNITED STATES
G. K. Hall and Company
70 Lincoln Street　　　　　　Phone: (617) 423-3990
Boston, MA 02111
Publication includes: List of nearly 75 libraries and archives with significant collections. **Entries include:** Library name, collection name, address, name of administrator, hours of service, services, restrictions on use (if any), description of collection including dates covered, size, contents. **Arrangement:** Geographical. **Indexes:** General, occupation. **Pages** (approx.): 205. **Frequency:** Irregular; latest edition 1977. **Editor:** Linda Harris Mehr. **Price:** $27.00. **Other information:** Publication sponsored by Film and Television Study Center. Principal content of publication is bibliographical citations with location codes.

★3601★
MOVIE COLLECTOR'S CATALOG
Cummington Publishing, Inc.
Box 466
New Rochelle, NY 10801
Description: Includes sources for 8mm and 16mm prints of collectible motion pictures, with price guides; dealers in projectors and equipment; collectors' names, addresses, and interests. Similar data given for videocassettes in supplement. **Editor:** Ken Weiss. **Price:** $5.95, plus 75¢ shipping (film edition); $1.50, plus 50¢ shipping (video supplement).

★3602★
MUSEUM COMPUTER NETWORK DIRECTORY
Museum Computer Network
C/o Center for Contemporary Arts & Letters
Library E-2340
State University of New York　　　Phone: (516) 246-6077
Stony Brook, NY 11794
Covers: 90 institutions, institution representatives, and individual members concerned with the use of computers in museum work. **Entries include:** For institutional representatives and other individual members - Name, title, museum name, address, phone. For institutions - Name, membership category, name of liaison officer. **Arrangement:** Alphabetical. **Frequency:** Irregular; latest edition November 1979. **Editor:** David Vance, President. **Price:** Free.

Museum Media *See* **Catalog of Museum Publications and Media**

★3603★
MUSEUM STUDIES PROGRAMS IN THE U.S. AND ABROAD
Office of Museum Programs
Arts & Industries Building, Room 2235
Smithsonian Institution　　　　Phone: (202) 381-6551
Washington, DC 20560
Covers: About 350 museums and universities which offer museum administration and curatorship training programs. **Entries include:** Institution name, address, affiliated museum (if not offered by a museum), description of program including length required for completion, degrees offered, length and conditions of internship, etc. **Arrangement:** Geographical. **Indexes:** Alphabetical. **Pages** (approx.): 100. **Frequency:** Irregular; latest edition 1976; October 1978 addendum. **Price:** Single copies free.

★3604★
MUSEUMS IN NEW YORK
Quick Fox
33 W. 60th Street　　　　　　Phone: (212) 246-0325
New York, NY 10023
Covers: About 90 art, historical, and other types of museums located in New York City. **Entries include:** Museum name, address, restaurant and gift shop facilities, description of collections, admission fees (if any), hours and days open. **Pages** (approx.): 350. **Frequency:**

Irregular; previous edition 1973; latest edition 1978. **Editor:** Fred W. McDarrah. **Price:** $5.95. **Also includes:** List of 155 landmarks by borough.

Music Educators Journal—MENC Official Directory Issue *See* **Music Educators National Conference—Official Directory**

★3605★
MUSIC EDUCATORS NATIONAL CONFERENCE—OFFICIAL DIRECTORY
Music Educators National Conference
1902 Association Drive　　　　Phone: (703) 860-4000
Reston, VA 22091
Covers: Officers and other leadership at national, divisional, and state levels in Music Educators National Conference. **Entries include:** Names and addresses of elected officials; members of committees and commissions. **Arrangement:** Geographical. **Frequency:** Annual, September. **Editor:** John Aquino. **Price:** Free.

★3606★
MUSIC JOURNAL—FESTIVALS ISSUE
Elemo Publishing Company
149 Hampton Road　　　　　　Phone: (516) 283-2360
Southhampton, NY 11968
Covers: About 200 music festivals sponsored by music schools, colleges and universities, private agencies, tourist agencies, etc. **Entries include:** Festival name, dates, name of sponsor, address, phone; most listings mention type of music offered; some listings include other details. **Arrangement:** Geographical. **Frequency:** Annual, April. **Price:** $2.00.

★3607★
MUSIC JOURNAL—NORTH AMERICAN MUSIC SCHOOLS DIRECTORY ISSUE
Elemo Publishing Company
149 Hampton Road　　　　　　Phone: (516) 283-2360
Southampton, NY 11968
Covers: About 1,000 private music schools, music departments of colleges and universities, and conservatories. **Entries include:** Institution name, address, phone, enrollment, number of faculty, whether a member of the National Association of Schools of Music and type of membership, degrees granted, name of director, and name of manager of lecture and performing arts series. **Arrangement:** Geographical. **Pages** (approx.): 100. **Frequency:** Annual, July; updated January. **Editor:** Mary Cummings. **Advertising accepted.** Circulation 18,000. **Price:** $2.50.

★3608★
MUSIC JOURNAL ARTISTS DIRECTORY
Elemo Publishing Company
20 Hampton Road　　　　　　Phone: (516) 283-2360
Southampton, NY 11968
Covers: About 600 symphony orchestras, 150 opera companies, 130 music festivals, 650 concert series organizations, and 175 artists' representatives and managers in United States and Canada. Also lists about 3,300 performers and performing groups in separate list keyed to list of representatives and managers. **Entries include:** Listings for orchestras, opera companies, festivals, and concert series show name, address, name of conductor or manager, phone, place of performances and its capacity, number of performances annually, and budget. Artists' representatives listings show name, address, and phone, with key used to identify agent in the artist list. **Arrangement:** By type of event or organization, then geographically. **Indexes:** Alphabetical list of artists and attractions, list of artists and attractions by specialty. **Pages** (approx.): 170. **Frequency:** Annual, November. **Editor:** Hannah Hanani. **Advertising accepted.** Circulation 10,000. **Price:** $5.00 (current and 1980 editions).

★3609★

MUSIC RETAILER'S DIRECTORY OF RECORD AND TAPE RETAIL STORES

Larkin Publications, Inc.
210 Boylston Street   Phone: (617) 964-5100
Chestnut Hill, MA 02167
Covers: About 450 headquarters offices for discount, department stores, and variety chains; 40 record and tape chains; rack jobbers; and 10,700 listings for retail stores handling records and tapes. **Entries include:** Headquarters listings include chain name, address, phone. Retailer listings include store name, address, phone. **Arrangement:** Geographical. **Frequency:** Irregular; previous edition summer 1978; latest edition September 1979. **Advertising accepted. Price:** $75.00, postpaid.

★3610★

MUSIC TRADES—PURCHASERS GUIDE TO THE MUSIC INDUSTRY ISSUE

Music Trades Corporation
80 West Street   Phone: (201) 871-1965
Englewood, NJ 07670
Covers: 2,000 musical instrument manufacturers and wholesalers, publishers of sheet music, and manufacturers of musical accessories, internationally. **Entries include:** Company name, address, phone, names of executives, trade and brand names, list of products or services. **Arrangement:** Alphabetical. **Frequency:** Annual, fall. **Advertising accepted.** Circulation 8,000. **Price:** 13th issue of Music Trades Magazine; included in subscription, $10.00 per year.

★3611★

MUSICAL AMERICA INTERNATIONAL DIRECTORY OF THE PERFORMING ARTS

ABC Leisure Magazines, Inc.
The Publishing House
Great Barrington, MA 01230
Covers: Orchestras, musicians, singers, performing arts series, dance and opera companies, festivals, contests, foundations and awards, publishers of music, artist managers, booking agents, music magazines, and service and professional music organizations. Section for United States and Canada also includes listings of choral groups, music schools and departments, and newspaper music critics; international directory section also lists concert managers. **Entries include:** All entries include name of organization, institution, address, phone, and most include name of a contact - manager, conductor, etc. Schools include number of students and faculty. Orchestra entries include number of concerts and seats. Other entries show similar details as appropriate. **Arrangement:** Classified by type of presentation, etc. **Indexes:** Advertiser (includes names of all performers and groups mentioned in ads, alphabetically and by category). **Pages** (approx.): 575. **Frequency:** Annual, December. **Editor:** Shirley Fleming. **Advertising accepted.** Circulation 10,000. **Price:** $25.00.

★3612★

MUSICAL MERCHANDISE REVIEW—MUSIC INDUSTRY DIRECTORY ISSUE

Columbia Communications, Inc.
370 Lexington Avenue   Phone: (212) 532-9290
New York, NY 10017
Covers: 1,000 manufacturers plus wholesalers, jobbers, importers, exporters, teaching institutions, publishers, organizations, manufacturers representatives connected with the musical instrument and accessories industry. **Entries include:** Company name, address, phone, names of executives, trade and brand names, list of products or services. **Arrangement:** Classified. **Indexes:** Product, trade name. **Pages** (approx.): 100. **Frequency:** Annual, June. **Editor:** John Metcalfe. **Advertising accepted.** Circulation 11,000. **Price:** $2.00.

★3613★

NATIONAL ARTS GUIDE

National Arts Guide, Inc.
200 E. Ontario Street, Suite 607   Phone: (312) 642-9001
Chicago, IL 60611
Covers: About 1,400 museums, commercial galleries, and other locations with current special exhibits or exhibits planned for the near future. **Entries include:** Facility name, address, phone, name of director; descriptions of current and coming exhibits include exhibit name, names of artists involved, media shown, dates, fees, catalog (if any) title and price. **Arrangement:** By geographic region. **Indexes:** Exhibit title, artist name, traveling exhibition; catalog index is planned; there is an annual index cumulation. **Pages** (approx.): 135. **Frequency:** Six times yearly. **Editor:** Helyn D. Goldenberg, Publisher. **Advertising accepted. Price:** $50.00 per year.

National Association of Educational Broadcasters Public Telecommunications Directory *See* People in Public Telecommunications

★3614★

NATIONAL ASSOCIATION OF SCHOOLS OF ART—DIRECTORY

National Association of Schools of Art
11250 Roger Bacon Drive, No. 5   Phone: (703) 437-0700
Reston, VA 22090
Covers: 100 independent and university-affiliated schools of art which are members. **Entries include:** Institution name, address, phone, names of executives, major programs (drawing, graphic design, etc.) and duration, summer programs, degrees. **Arrangement:** Geographical. **Frequency:** Annual. **Editor:** Samuel Hope. **Price:** $2.50.

★3615★

NATIONAL ASSOCIATION OF SCHOOLS OF MUSIC—DIRECTORY

National Association of Schools of Music
11250 Roger Bacon Drive, No. 5   Phone: (703) 437-0700
Reston, VA 22090
Covers: 490 college and university departments of music, and music conservatories, accredited by the association. **Entries include:** School name, address, type of membership, description of music program, name of chief administrator, phone, degree programs offered. **Arrangement:** Geographical. **Pages** (approx.): 100. **Frequency:** Annual, January. **Editor:** Samuel Hope, Executive Director. **Price:** $2.50, plus 75¢ shipping (current and 1980 editions).

★3616★

NATIONAL CALENDAR OF INDOOR-OUTDOOR ART FAIRS

Henry and Mildred Niles
5423 New Haven Avenue
Fort Wayne, IN 46803
Covers: About 200 independent shows and an additional 150-200 shows managed by professional art show directors or companies, in Midwest and East, and some in the West. **Entries include:** Event name, date held, closing date for entries, location, entry fee, name of person in charge with address and phone, plus additional information where appropriate. **Arrangement:** Chronological. **Pages** (approx.): 40. **Frequency:** Quarterly. **Editor:** Henry Niles. **Advertising accepted.** Circulation 1,600. **Price:** $3.00 per copy; $10.00 per year.

★3617★

NATIONAL CALENDAR OF OPEN COMPETITIVE ART EXHIBITIONS

Henry and Mildred Niles
5423 New Haven Avenue
Fort Wayne, IN 46803
Covers: 25-50 juried fine art exhibitions in Midwest and East, and some in the West. **Entries include:** Event name, dates, location, entry fee and date due, date work due, awards, media accepted, name of person in charge with address and phone, commission. **Arrangement:** Chronological. **Pages** (approx.): 10. **Frequency:** Quarterly. **Editor:** Henry Niles. **Price:** $3.00 per copy; $10.00 per year.

★3618★

NATIONAL DIRECTORY FOR THE PERFORMING ARTS AND CIVIC CENTERS

John Wiley & Sons, Inc.
605 Third Avenue   Phone: (212) 867-9800
New York, NY 10016
Covers: 4,000 facilities and performing arts organizations, including theaters, concert halls, auditoriums, civic centers, etc., and dance companies, orchestras and other musical groups, theater companies, vocal groups, mime groups, and festivals. **Entries include:** For facilities - Name, address, phone, name of contact, architect and date of construction, size and type of facility, rental information, names of resident groups. For organizations - Name, address, phone, names of principal staff and officers, size of paid and volunteer staff, number of paid and volunteer artists, budget, sources of income, performance facility used, dates active. **Arrangement:** Geographical. **Pages** (approx.): 1,050. **Frequency:** Irregular; latest edition spring 1978. **Editor:** Beatrice Handel. **Price:** $50.00. **Send orders to:** John Wiley & Sons, Inc. 1 Wiley Drive, Somerset, NJ 08873.

★3619★

NATIONAL DIRECTORY FOR THE PERFORMING ARTS/ EDUCATIONAL

John Wiley & Sons, Inc.
605 Third Avenue   Phone: (212) 867-9800
New York, NY 10016
Covers: Over 2,000 private, state, county, and city two- and four-year schools offering 5,000 curriculums in dance, music, theater, visual arts, television, and film. **Entries include:** For each school - Name, address, phone, auspices, length of programs, fields in which instruction is given. For each curriculum - Name of chairman, number of faculty and students, degrees offered, courses offered, financial assistance available, and performing groups, workshops and festivals associated with the school. **Arrangement:** Geographical. **Pages** (approx.): 670. **Frequency:** Irregular; latest edition spring 1978. **Editor:** Beatrice Handel. **Price:** $45.00. **Send orders to:** John Wiley & Sons, Inc., 1 Wiley Drive, Somerset, NJ 08873.

★3620★

NATIONAL DIRECTORY OF ARTS SUPPORT BY BUSINESS CORPORATIONS

Washington International Arts Letter
325 Pennsylvania Avenue, S. E.   Phone: (202) 488-0800
Washington, DC 20003
Covers: About 700 corporations and their 2,800 affiliates, divisions, and subsidiaries which budget some assistance to the arts and humanities. **Entries include:** Corporation name, address, phone, names of officers; listings for affiliates, divisions, and subsidiaries include city and state only. **Arrangement:** Alphabetical. **Indexes:** Officer name. **Pages** (approx.): 225. **Frequency:** Irregular; first edition 1979; new edition possible 1982. **Editor:** Daniel Millsaps. **Former title:** Private Foundations and Business Corporations Active in Arts, Humanities & Education (1977). **Price:** $65.00, prepaid.

★3621★

NATIONAL DIRECTORY OF ARTS SUPPORT BY PRIVATE FOUNDATIONS

Washington International Arts Letter
325 Pennsylvania Avenue, S. E.   Phone: (202) 488-0800
Washington, DC 20003
Covers: 1,250 private foundations offering grants in the arts. **Entries include:** Name of foundation, address, names of officers (many with home addresses), typical grants, code indicating area of interest (arts administration, architecture, dance, theater, etc.). **Pages** (approx.): 260. **Frequency:** Irregular; latest edition September 1977; new edition expected 1980. **Editor:** Daniel Millsaps. **Former title:** Private Foundations and Business Corporations Active in Arts, Humanities & Education (1977). **Price:** $55.00 (current edition); $65.00 (1980 edition).

★3622★

NATIONAL DIRECTORY OF GRANTS, AID AND PRIZES TO INDIVIDUALS IN THE ARTS, INTERNATIONAL

Washington International Arts Letter
Allied Business Consultants, Inc.
Box 9005
Washington, DC 20003
Covers: 1,500 sources of grants, special aid, and monetary prizes of over $1,000.00 for students and professionals in all the arts, including music, crafts, dance, radio, film, architecture, writing, and graphics. **Entries include:** Name, address, amount of award, and any restrictions such as age or nationality. **Indexes:** Subject. **Pages** (approx.): 250. **Frequency:** Every four years; latest edition November 1979. **Editor:** Daniel Millsaps, Publisher. **Former title:** Grants, Aid and Prizes to Individuals in the Arts. **Price:** $15.95.

★3623★

NATIONAL GUILD OF COMMUNITY SCHOOLS OF THE ARTS— MEMBERSHIP DIRECTORY [Music schools]

National Guild of Community Schools of the Arts
175 Fifth Avenue, Suite 516   Phone: (212) 673-0980
New York, NY 10010
Covers: About 60 member music schools, conservatories, and departments of music, and about 50 individual members; coverage includes Canada. **Entries include:** For institutions - School name, address, phone, year established, name and title of director. For individuals - Name, title, affiliation, address, phone. **Arrangement:** Institutions are geographical, individuals are alphabetical. **Pages** (approx.): 10. **Frequency:** Semiannual, March and September. **Editor:** Marcy Horwitz, Executive Director.

★3624★

NATIONAL OPERA ASSOCIATION—MEMBERSHIP DIRECTORY

National Opera Association
C/o Marajean Marvin, Vice-President, Regions
National Opera Association
250 S. Estes Drive, No. 53
Chapel Hill, NC 27514
Covers: 750 Music and singing teachers, singers, directors, and others interested in opera; includes schools and colleges. **Entries include:** Name, address, phone, and occupation. **Arrangement:** Alphabetical within membership divisions. **Frequency:** Annual, January. **Editor:** Marajean Marvin, Vice President, Regions. **Price:** $15.00. **Send orders to:** Constance Eberhart, Hotel Wellington, Room 823, 7th Ave. at 55th St., New York, NY 10019 (212-247-3900).

★3625★

NATIONAL PLAYWRIGHTS DIRECTORY

O'Neill Theater Center
Waterford, CT 06385
Covers: 500 American playwrights. **Entries include:** Playwright's name and photo; education; career data (theatrical and non-theatrical); address; phone; agent's name, address, and phone; title, availability, and productions (if any) of all his/her plays; whom to contact for manuscripts; synopsis of at least one listed play. **Arrangement:** Alphabetical by playwright. **Indexes:** Play title. **Pages** (approx.): 370. **Frequency:** Not established; first edition November 1977; new edition expected 1981. **Editor:** Phyllis Johnson Kaye. **Price:** $24.00. **Send orders to:** Gale Research Company, Book Tower, Detroit, Michigan 48226 (313-961-2242).

★3626★

NATIONAL RADIO PUBLICITY DIRECTORY

Peter Glenn Publications Ltd.
17 E. 48th Street   Phone: (212) 688-7940
New York, NY 10017
Covers: Over 3,500 network, syndicated, and local talk shows in the nation's 200 major markets and 4,500 local and college radio stations. **Entries include:** For stations - Call letters, address, phone, AM/FM dial positions, network affiliation, watts, coverage, format,

and names of the program director, public service director, and the news, sports, and business editors. For local talk shows - Name of show, host, topics, days and times aired, sister station airtime, contact, phone, show requirements, audience size, and source of survey. **Arrangement:** Geographical. **Indexes:** Station format, talk show content. **Pages** (approx.): 420. **Frequency:** Annual, summer; semiannual update. **Editor:** Brian J. Smith. **Advertising accepted.** **Price:** $70.00, including supplement, plus $3.00 shipping.

National Roster of Organ Teachers *See* International Roster of Organ Teachers

★3627★
NATIONAL SCULPTURE SOCIETY—MEMBERSHIP DIRECTORY
National Sculpture Society
15 E. 26th Street   Phone: (212) 838-5218
New York, NY 10010
Number of listings: 350. **Entries include:** Name, address, date of election. **Arrangement:** Alphabetical within membership categories. **Pages** (approx.): 70. **Frequency:** Triennial in fall; latest edition 1979. **Editor:** Claire A. Stein, Executive Director. **Price:** Free.

★3628★
NATIONAL SQUARE DANCE DIRECTORY
National Square Dance Association
Box 54055   Phone: (601) 825-6831
Jackson, MS 39208
Covers: 7,000 square dance, round dance, clogging, and contra clubs, worldwide. **Entries include:** Club type, name, address, and phone of contact, time and location of dances, level of dancing. **Arrangement:** Geographical. **Pages** (approx.): 130. **Frequency:** Biennial, May of odd years. **Editor:** Gordon Gross. **Advertising accepted.** Circulation 20,000. **Price:** $4.00, plus $1.50 shipping.

Network Rates & Data *See* Standard Rate & Data Service—
    Network Rates & Data

★3629★
NEW ENGLAND THEATRE CONFERENCE—MEMBERSHIP
    DIRECTORY
New England Theatre Conference
50 Exchange Street   Phone: (617) 893-3120
Waltham, MA 02154
Number of listings: 325 individuals; 125 groups. **Entries include:** Individuals' listings show name, address, professional or avocational affiliations, and theatrical interest (children's, professional, etc.). Group listings also give names and addresses of four delegates. **Arrangement:** Alphabetical by membership category for individuals; geographical for group members. **Pages** (approx.): 20. **Frequency:** Annual, January. **Editor:** Marie L. Philips, Executive Secretary. **Price:** $10.00 to commercial users; $5.00 to others (1980 edition).

★3630★
NEW YORK ON STAGE
Theatre Development Fund
1501 Broadway   Phone: (212) 221-0013
New York, NY 10036
Covers: Theatrical, dance, and musical productions planned for or in performance at theaters, clubs, halls, etc., in Manhattan, in Broadway, Off-Broadway, and off Off-Broadway areas; depending on season, an issue may include more than 300 listings. **Entries include:** Name of performing company or production, location, dates, ticket prices. **Pages** (approx.): 75. **Frequency:** Monthly. **Price:** $1.25 per copy; $8.00 per year. **Other information:** Also cited as, "Off Off-Broadway Theatre Calendar" and "OOBA Guide."

★3631★
NEW YORK PUBLICITY OUTLETS
Public Relations Plus, Inc.
Box 327   Phone: (203) 868-0200
Washington Depot, CT 06794
Covers: Consumer media in metropolitan New York area, including over 100 radio and TV stations, about 200 radio and TV interview shows, and about 500 daily and weekly newspapers. Also includes consumer magazines, Black and other ethnic media, syndicates, news services, etc. **Entries include:** Outlet name, address, phone, names of executive and editorial personnel, including names of specialized editors (business, style, art, etc.). **Arrangement:** Classified by type of outlet. **Pages** (approx.): 250. **Frequency:** Annual, March; August supplement. **Editor:** Harold D. Hansen. **Price:** $47.50, including supplement (current and 1980 editions).

★3632★
NEW YORK REVIEW OF ART
Krantz Company
3300 N. Lake Shore Drive   Phone: (312) 935-6723
Chicago, IL 60657
Covers: About 120 art galleries and nearly 30 art museums holding the works of 1,750 artists. **Entries include:** Gallery or museum name, address, methods of acquisition, exhibitions, hours. **Arrangement:** Alphabetical. **Indexes:** Artist name. **Pages** (approx.): 145. **Frequency:** Biennial, even years. **Editor:** Leslie J. Krantz. **Price:** $6.95, plus $1.00 shipping.

★3633★
NORTH AMERICAN FILM AND VIDEO DIRECTORY
R. R. Bowker Company
1180 Avenue of the Americas   Phone: (212) 764-5100
New York, NY 10036
Covers: Over 2,000 college, public, special, museum, or archival libraries and media centers with collections of 25 or more 16mm films. **Entries include:** Library or center name, address, number of staff, size and subject emphasis of collection, loan or rental policies, budget, publications, income, facilities. **Arrangement:** Geographical. **Indexes:** Special collection. **Pages** (approx.): 285. **Frequency:** Irregular; latest edition 1976. **Price:** $25.00, postpaid, payment with order (ISSN 0362-7802). **Send orders to:** R. R. Bowker Co., Box 1807, Ann Arbor, MI 48106 (313-761-4700). **Also includes:** List of film cooperatives and circuits.

★3634★
NORTH AMERICAN RADIO TV STATION GUIDE
Howard W. Sams & Company, Inc.
4300 W. 62nd Street   Phone: (317) 298-5400
Indianapolis, IN 46206
Covers: About 12,500 AM, FM, and television stations currently in operation, temporarily off the air, and under construction in the United States, Canada, Cuba, Mexico, and the West Indies. **Entries include:** Station call letters, city and state of location, channel or frequency, and coded information about the station (power, antenna height, network member, etc.). **Arrangement:** Separate sections arranged by frequency or channel for AM, FM, and TV stations, and by location, with similar information in each. **Indexes:** Call letters. **Pages** (approx.): 200. **Frequency:** Irregular; latest edition 1979. **Editor:** Van A. Jones. **Price:** $6.95.

★3635★
OCULAR—THE DIRECTORY OF INFORMATION AND
    OPPORTUNITIES FOR THE VISUAL ARTS
Ocular Publishing Company
1549 Platte Street
Denver, CO 80202
Publication includes: Sections in each issue list grants and fellowships for artists and arts organizations, and art exhibits and competitions. **Entries include:** Award name, sponsor, address, amount, conditions or requirements, deadline. **Frequency:** Quarterly. **Price:** $14.00 per year.

Off Off Broadway Alliance—Member Theatres *See* OOBA Guidebook of Theatres [off Off-Broadway]

★3636★
OFFICIAL MUSEUM DIRECTORY
National Register Publishing Company, Inc., Subsidiary
Standard Rate & Data Service, Inc.
5201 Old Orchard Road   Phone: (312) 966-8500
Skokie IL 60077
Covers: 5,300 institutions of art, history, and science in the United States, including general museums, college and university museums, children's and junior museums, company museums, national park and nature center displays, highly specialized museums. **Entries include:** Museum name, address, phone, founding date, personnel, governing authority, brief description of museum and type of collections, facilities, activities, publications, hours and admission prices, membership fees. Personnel index listings show name, title, affiliation, city, state, Zip. Type of museum index listings show museum name, city, state, Zip. **Arrangement:** Geographical. **Indexes:** Personnel, museums by type. **Pages** (approx.): 900. **Frequency:** Annual, fall. **Editor:** Bob Weicherding. **Advertising accepted.** Circulation 4,000. **Price:** $48.50, plus $2.50 shipping.

★3637★
OFFICIAL TALENT & BOOKING DIRECTORY
Specialty Publications, Inc.
7033 Sunset Boulevard, Suite 222   Phone: (213) 464-8300
Los Angeles, CA 90028
Covers: Live entertainment and phonograph recording industries, including: 8,000 artists recording popular music; 4,500 personal managers; 3,300 booking agents; 1,050 phonograph record companies; 2,100 talent promoters; 650 sound companies; 350 lighting companies; 350 theatrical ticket printing companies; 500 musical instrument and recording equipment manufacturers; 4,500 hotels and clubs which use live entertainment; 800 colleges which book live entertainment; auditoriums, arenas, etc., and businesses catering to entertainment industry in 250 cities. **Entries include:** Most entries include company name, address, phone; recording artist listings include manager name, address, phone, and name of agent; college listings include enrollment, names and seating capacities of facilities, and names of program director, etc.; city directories include extensive technical, general, and box office information on principal facilities, and lists of ticket agencies, media, and services. **Arrangement:** Most lists are alphabetical; colleges and clubs are geographical. **Indexes:** Promoter, sound company sections include individual name indexes; club section includes alphabetical index of club names. **Pages** (approx.): 800. **Frequency:** Annual, fall. **Editor:** Steve Tolin. **Advertising accepted.** Circulation 10,000. **Price:** $53.25 (current edition); $64.00 (1980 edition).

Off-Off Broadway Theatre Calendar *See* New York on Stage

On Location—Motion Picture and Television Location Directory *See* On Location—The National Film and Videotape Production Directory

★3638★
ON LOCATION—THE NATIONAL FILM AND VIDEOTAPE PRODUCTION DIRECTORY
On Location Publishing, Inc.
6464 Sunset Boulevard, Suite 570
Los Angeles, CA 90028
Covers: Facilities and services useful to motion picture and television units filming on location. National section includes state film commissions; government offices; national parks; historic districts; military establishments; castles and mansions; railroads; Indian bureaus; etc. available in 113 major cities. **Entries include:** Facility or company name, address, phone. **Arrangement:** Geographical. **Pages** (approx.): 700. **Frequency:** Annual, January. **Editor:** Ray Herbeck, Jr. **Advertising accepted.** Circulation 10,000. **Former title:** On Location - Motion Picture and Television Location Directory. **Price:** $40.00 per

issue, plus $2.50 shipping (1980 edition).

★3639★
ONLY IN NEW ENGLAND
Pequot Press, Inc.
Old Chester Road   Phone: (203) 526-9571
Chester, CT 06412
Covers: Over 500 mail-order shops, individual craftspersons, organizations and other sources for craft materials, gadgets, and handmade products; also lists museums and historic places located in New England. **Entries include:** For mail-order sources - Organization or company name, description of products and services, and address; prices also included for products. For museums and historic places - Name, address, description of significance or collection, hours or seasons open. **Indexes:** Geographical. **Pages** (approx.): 160. **Frequency:** Irregular; latest edition 1977. **Editor:** J. Chandler Hill. **Former title:** First New England Catalogue. **Price:** $4.95.

OOBA Guide *See* New York on Stage

★3640★
OOBA GUIDEBOOK OF THEATRES [Off Off-Broadway]
Off Off Broadway Alliance
162 W. 56th Street, Room 206   Phone: (212) 757-4473
New York, NY 10019
Covers: 230 member theaters located off Off-Broadway in Manhattan. **Entries include:** Theater name, address, description, history. **Arrangement:** Alphabetical. **Pages** (approx.): 200. **Frequency:** Irregular; new edition expected 1980. **Editor:** Mindy Levine. **Price:** $3.00 (current edition); $4.95 (tentative, 1980 edition).

★3641★
OPPORTUNITIES FOR STUDY IN HAND BOOKBINDING AND CALLIGRAPHY
Guild of Book Workers
663 Fifth Avenue   Phone: (212) 757-6454
New York, NY 10022
Covers: About 150 professionals worldwide who are also teachers. **Entries include:** Craftsperson's name, address, special interests, source of expertise, whether apprentices are desired, and (for schools and other centers) names and addresses of instructors and courses offered. **Arrangement:** Geographical by state or nation. **Pages** (approx.): 20. **Frequency:** Latest edition May 1977, supplement in October 1978; new edition expected 1980. **Price:** $1.00, payment with order.

★3642★
ORGANIZATIONS OF INTEREST TO PHOTOGRAPHERS IN NEW YORK STATE
Center for Arts Information
152 W. 42nd Street, Room 1239   Phone: (212) 354-2068
New York, NY 10036
Covers: About 125 organizations and galleries which serve photographers. **Entries include:** Organization name, address, phone, name of contact, description of services. **Arrangement:** Alphabetical. **Pages** (approx.): 20. **Frequency:** Irregular; latest edition August 1977. **Editor:** Ellen Thurston, Director. **Advertising accepted.** Circulation 4,000. **Price:** $2.00.

★3643★
PEOPLE IN PUBLIC TELECOMMUNICATIONS
National Association of Educational Broadcasters
1346 Connecticut Avenue, N. W.   Phone: (202) 785-1100
Washington, DC 20036
Covers: 500 public television and CPB-qualified radio stations and 3,000 individuals in public (educational) broadcasting. Includes national telecommunication agencies, with staff listings. **Arrangement:** Stations are by call letters, individuals are alphabetical. **Pages** (approx.): 140. **Frequency:** Annual, July. **Editor:** Wayne Jackson. **Former title:** Telecommunications Directory, Public

Telecommunications Directory, Directory of Public Telecommunications. **Price:** $10.00.

★3644★
THE PERFORMING WOMAN [Women musicians]
Janice D. Dinneen
26910 Grand View Avenue   Phone: (415) 881-1423
Hayward, CA 94542
Covers: Women musicians (including soloists, groups featuring women, group musicians needing a group, and free-lancers). **Entries include:** Performer name, address, musical skills, experience and interests. **Arrangement:** Geographical. **Indexes:** Performer name, free-lancers by instrument. **Pages** (approx.): 40. **Frequency:** Semiannual, June and December. **Editor:** Janice D. Dinneen, Editor and Publisher. **Advertising accepted. Price:** $3.00 per copy; $6.00 per year.

Photo Artist USA *See* Sunshine Artists USA

Photofinder *See* Foto Finder [Photography]

★3645★
PHOTOGRAPHER'S MARKET: WHERE TO SELL YOUR PHOTOS
Writer's Digest Books
9933 Alliance Road   Phone: (513) 984-0717
Cincinnati, OH 45242
Covers: Over 3,000 companies and publications which purchase original photographs, including ad agencies, public relations agencies, book and periodical publishers, stock photo agencies, etc. Includes photographic clubs, galleries, and competitions. **Entries include:** Name of buyer, address, phone, payment rates, requirements, reporting time, how to break in. **Arrangement:** By type of market. **Pages** (approx.): 700. **Frequency:** Annual, October. **Editor:** Melissa Milar. **Price:** $12.95.

★3646★
PHOTOGRAPHY MARKET PLACE
R. R. Bowker Company
1180 Avenue of the Americas   Phone: (212) 764-5100
New York, NY 10036
Covers: Buyers of photographic work and suppliers of services and products used by the commercial, journalistic, or amateur photographer. Includes photographer's agents. **Entries include:** Firm, publication, or individual name, address, phone, and names of key personnel. **Arrangement:** Classified by product or service. **Indexes:** General index of firms and persons. **Pages** (approx.): 500. **Frequency:** Irregular; latest edition 1977. **Editor:** Fred W. McDarrah. **Price:** $15.50, postpaid, payment with order (ISSN 0095-439X). **Send orders to:** R. R. Bowker Co., Box 1807, Ann Arbor, MI 48106 (313-761-4700).

★3647★
PHOTOLETTER
Photosearch International
        Phone: (715) 248-3800
Star Prairie, WI 54026
Covers: Magazine and book publishers currently soliciting photographs for publication; 10-12 listings per issue. **Entries include:** Company name, name of contact, address, phone, and nature of photos sought; newsletter format. **Pages** (approx.): 5. **Frequency:** Semimonthly (except monthly in August and January). **Editor:** Rohn Engh. **Price:** $46.00 per year (22 issues).

★3648★
PIANO FOR TWO DIRECTORY
Piano for Two Directory
8417 Franklin Avenue   Phone: (213) 654-4006
Los Angeles, CA 90069
Covers: 200 piano players experienced in, or interested in, duet and two piano playing. Most listings are in California. **Entries include:** Name, address, level of skill, phone, number of pianos or other

keyborads (harpsichords, fortepianos, etc.). **Arrangement:** Geographical. **Pages** (approx.): 25. **Frequency:** Annual, April. **Editor:** Manya Schaff. **Price:** $3.00.

★3649★
PIANO TECHNICIANS JOURNAL—OFFICIAL DIRECTORY ISSUE
Piano Technicians Guild
113 Dexter Avenue North
Seattle, WA 98109
Covers: About 3,500 piano tuners and repair persons; manufacturers and suppliers of piano maintenance equipment and supplies are also listed. **Entries include:** Name, address, phone. **Arrangement:** Members are alphabetical and geographical; manufacturers and suppliers are alphabetical. **Frequency:** Annual, October. **Editor:** Don L. Santy, Executive Editor. **Advertising accepted.** Circulation 3,500. **Price:** $25.00 (ISSN 0031 9562).

★3650★
POCKET GUIDE TO THE LOCATION OF ART IN THE UNITED STATES
Emma Lila Fundabark, Publisher
Box 231   Phone: (205) 335-3171
Luverne, AL 36049
Covers: Museums, galleries, art centers, art fairs, art festivals, art councils, art associations, historical societies, chambers of commerce, and other groups or events with art collections and information in 4,300 cities and towns in the United States. **Entries include:** Name, address. **Arrangement:** Geographical. **Pages** (approx.): 320. **Frequency:** First published 1977. **Editor:** Mary Douglass Foreman. **Price:** $5.00, plus 75¢ shipping.

★3651★
PRINTS AND THE PRINT MARKET: A HANDBOOK FOR BUYERS, COLLECTORS, AND CONNOISSEURS
Lippincott & Crowell, Publishers
521 Fifth Avenue   Phone: (212) 687-3980
New York, NY 10017
Publication includes: In appendices: Print publishers in the United States and Great Britain, print dealers and galleries, and art booksellers. **Entries include:** Company name, address, phone, and specialty. **Arrangement:** Alphabetical. **Pages** (approx.): 500. **Frequency:** Published 1977. **Editor:** Theodore B. Donson. **Price:** $19.95.

Private Foundations and Business Corporations Active in Arts...
    See National Directory of Arts Support by Private...; by Business...

★3652★
PROFESSIONAL PICTURE FRAMERS ASSOCIATION— MEMBERSHIP DIRECTORY
Professional Picture Framers Association
5633 S. Laburnum Avenue   Phone: (804) 226-0430
Richmond, VA 23231
Covers: Over 4,000 galleries, picture framing firms, and suppliers located in the United States and 24 foreign countries. **Entries include:** Company name, address, phone, name of association representative, and activity in industry. **Arrangement:** Geographical. **Indexes:** Alphabetical. **Pages** (approx.): 135. **Frequency:** Annual, March. **Editor:** Dorothy Robinson, Administrative Assistant to the Executive Director. **Advertising accepted.** Circulation 4,500. **Price:** Available to members only.

★3653★
PROGRAMS ACCREDITED BY THE FOUNDATION FOR INTERIOR DESIGN EDUCATION RESEARCH
Foundation for Interior Design Education Research
730 Fifth Avenue   Phone: (212) 586-7266
New York, NY 10019
Covers: About 45 interior design programs in the United States and Canada certified to be in conformance with the accreditation

standards of the foundation. **Entries include:** Type of program, name of institution, address, name of department chairman or program head, date of next certification review, degrees offered. **Arrangement:** Alphabetical by school in three sections: baccalaureate, three-year professional, and two-year para-professional and pre-professional programs. **Pages** (approx.): 10. **Frequency:** Semiannual, April and November. **Price:** Free; send stamped, self-addressed no. 10 envelope.

★3654★

PUBLICIST'S TV NEWSFILM HANDBOOK

Cambridge Media Resources
36 Shepard Street   Phone: (617) 491-1743
Cambridge, MA 02138
Covers: Over 300 television broadcasting stations which solicit publicity newsfilms. (An additional 400 stations which were surveyed are also listed.) **Entries include:** Station call letters, channel address, name and title of contact, preferred format of newsfilm, rate of use, network affiliation, market rank, number of households in audience. For non-responding stations - Call letters, address. **Arrangement:** Geographical. **Pages** (approx.): 140. **Frequency:** Not established; first edition 1979; new edition expected 1981. **Price:** $70.00, postpaid, payment with order; $75.00, billed.

Puppeteers of America—Roster *See* Puppetry Journal—
    Puppeteers of America International Membership Directory
    Supplement

★3655★

**PUPPETRY JOURNAL—PUPPETEERS OF AMERICA
    INTERNATIONAL MEMBERSHIP DIRECTORY SUPPLEMENT**

Puppeteers of America
2015 Novem Drive   Phone: (312) 825-2526
Fenton, MO 63026
Covers: 2,750 member individuals and organizations interested in puppetry; affiliated guilds are also listed. Coverage includes Canada and other foreign countries. **Entries include:** Name, address; name of performance group, contact or affiliation given for some listings; name of president given for guilds. Consultant listings include qualifications and specialty. **Arrangement:** Consultants by specialty; guilds and foreign members, alphabetical; United States members, geographical. **Pages** (approx.): 60. **Frequency:** Annual, February. **Editor:** Don Avery. **Advertising accepted.** Circulation 2,600. **Price:** Available to members only; apply for commercial use.

Purchasers Guide to the Music Industry *See* Music Trades—
    Purchasers Guide to the Music Industry Issue

★3656★

RADIO CONTACTS

Larimi Communications Associates Ltd.
151 E. 50th Street   Phone: (212) 935-9262
New York, NY 10022
Covers: 3,000 local, syndicated, and network radio programs interested in guests or outside scripts or information. **Entries include:** Station call numbers, address, phone, power, names of staff members, format, audience figures, programs desiring material and type of material wanted. **Arrangement:** Geographical. **Pages** (approx.): 600. **Frequency:** Annual with monthly updates. **Editor:** Michael Smith. **Price:** $126.00 per year.

★3657★

RADIO PROGRAMMING PROFILE

BF/Communication Services, Inc.
7 Cathy Court   Phone: (516) 676-7070
Glen Head, NY 11545
Covers: 3,000 AM and FM radio stations in top 200 markets, with format information (type of music, news, etc.) for each. **Entries include:** Station call letters, address, phone, names of executives, hour-by-hour format information. **Arrangement:** Geographical. Volume 1 has top 70 markets, Volume 2 has next 130. **Pages**

(approx.): Volume 1, about 400; Volume 2 about 375. **Frequency:** Three times a year. **Editor:** W. M. Fromm, President. **Advertising accepted.** Circulation 1,000. **Price:** $161.00 per year, per volume; no single copies sold.

★3658★

**RADIO-TELEVISION NEWS DIRECTORS ASSOCIATION—
    DIRECTORY**

Radio-Television News Directors Association
1735 De Sales Street, N. W.   Phone: (202) 737-8657
Washington, DC 20036
Number of listings: 2,000; includes Canada and some foreign countries. **Arrangement:** Geographical. **Pages** (approx.): 80. **Frequency:** Annual, January. **Editor:** Bill Sprague, Publications Editor. **Advertising accepted.** Circulation 2,000. **Price:** Available to members only.

★3659★

RADIO-TV CONTACT SERVICE

Media News Keys
150 Fifth Avenue   Phone: (212) 924-0320
New York, NY 10011
Covers: Radio and television programs (both local and network) which use guests and originate in the New York City area. **Entries include:** Program name, station name, address, phone, name of host, types of guests desired. **Pages** (approx.): 3x5 card format. **Frequency:** Subscribers receive current card file and monthly updates. **Editor:** Jerry Leichter. **Price:** $30.00, including revisions. **Other information:** Publisher also offers a weekly update service in newsletter format, "Media News Keys," which covers changes in radio, television, newspaper, magazine, syndicate, and other personnel important to public relations activities; $70.00 per year.

★3660★

RECORDINGS & BOOKINGS WORLDWIDE [Jazz]

International Jazz Federation
1697 Broadway, Suite 1203
New York, NY 10019
Covers: Over 4,000 jazz-oriented organizations; record companies, distributors, and retail stores; discographers; record collectors; concert agencies and promoters; festivals; clubs and lounges; radio stations; critics and reviewers; publications. **Entries include:** Name of group, company, etc., address; some entries include additional information. **Arrangement:** By activity or interest. **Pages** (approx.): 150. **Frequency:** Annual, fall. **Price:** $10.00, postpaid, payment with order.

★3661★

SAN FRANCISCO BAY AREA THEATER RESOURCE DIRECTORY

Theater Communications Center of the Bay Area
1182 Market Street, Room 208
San Francisco, CA 94102
Covers: Over 70 Bay Area theater troupes, plus listings for rehearsal and performance facilities, schools, theatrical supply houses, etc. **Entries include:** Troupe name, sponsoring organization (if any), address and phone for contact, type of performance, number of performers. Similar detail for other categories. **Arrangement:** Alphabetical. **Pages** (approx.): 150. **Frequency:** Irregular; first edition April 1979; new edition expected early 1980. **Price:** $4.50 (current edition); $5.00 (tentative, 1980 edition); payment with order.

★3662★

SEE AMERICA FIRST—ON FILM

Reymont Associates
29 Reymont Avenue   Phone: (914) 967-8185
Rye, NY 10580
Covers: Sources for about 165 16mm color films on regional, state, and local travel attractions in the United States. **Entries include:** Film title, name and address of source, length of film, fees or rental costs, description of subject. **Arrangement:** Geographical. **Pages** (approx.): 30. **Frequency:** Irregular; latest edition 1979. **Editor:** D. J. Scherer.

Price: $2.25, plus 25¢ shipping.

Selling Your Artwork See How to Sell Your Artwork

★3663★
SHORTWAVE LISTENER'S GUIDE
Howard W. Sams & Company, Inc.
4300 W. 62nd Street   Phone: (317) 298-5400
Indianapolis, IN 46206
Covers: Short wave radio stations worldwide which can be received in North America. **Entries include:** Frequency, address. **Arrangement:** Geographical. **Indexes:** News broadcasts by time and country. **Pages** (approx.): 145. **Frequency:** Annual, January. **Price:** $4.95 (current edition); $5.95 (1980 edition).

★3664★
SHUTTLE, SPINDLE, AND DYEPOT—"CALENDAR" COLUMN
   [Weaving exhibits, art fairs]
Handweavers Guild of America
65 La Salle Road   Phone: (203) 233-5124
West Hartford, CT 06107
Publication includes: Weaving exhibits, arts and crafts fairs. **Entries include:** Event name, location, dates, sponsor, contact name and address. **Frequency:** Quarterly. **Editor:** Kevin Chase. **Advertising accepted. Price:** $12.50 per year.

★3665★
SIMON'S DIRECTORY OF THEATRICAL MATERIALS, SERVICES,
   AND INFORMATION—WHERE TO BUY, TO RENT, TO LEASE,
   TO FIND OUT
Package Publicity Service
1501 Broadway   Phone: (212) 354-1840
New York, NY 10036
Covers: 22,000 listings for industries in the United States and Canada of use to the theater. Some, such as scene shops, stage lighting companies, ticket companies, a major belly dancer's boutique in Walnut Valley, CA, and a source for breakaway bottles in choice of wine, beer, Scotch, or cola are exclusively theatrical; others are more general and are not used exclusively by theaters (plastics suppliers, costume accessories shops, photographers, sign painters, etc.). **Entries include:** Company name, address, phone, and products or services. **Arrangement:** Classified by 91 categories, then geographical. **Indexes:** Product. **Pages** (approx.): 390. **Frequency:** Irregular; approximately every three years; latest edition, December 1975, is out of print; new edition expected November 1980. **Editor:** Avivah Simon. **Advertising accepted.** Circulation 10,000. **Price:** $14.95, plus 75¢ shipping (1980 edition). **Also includes:** General theater information - awards, periodicals, organizations,and playwriting contests - plus New York and regional theaters, new theaters, theater architects, theater consultants, etc.

★3666★
SINGERS IN NEW YORK: A Guide to Opportunities and Services
William-Frederick Press
55 E. 86th Street   Phone: (212) 722-7272
New York, NY 10028
Pages (approx.): 120. **Frequency:** Irregular; latest edition 1977; new edition expected February 1980. **Editor:** Edward J. Dwyer. **Price:** $6.50 (1980 edition).

★3667★
SOCIETY OF ANIMAL ARTISTS NEWSLETTER—DIRECTORY ISSUE
Society of Animal Artists
151 Carroll Street
City Island   Phone: (212) 885-2181
Bronx, NY 10464
Covers: 105 wildlife artists, worldwide. Includes prospectus of coming exhibitions of animals in art. **Entries include:** Name, home address, personal and career data, published or exhibited works, information on exhibitions. **Pages** (approx.): 4. **Frequency:** Irregular; latest edition March 1979. **Editor:** Patricia Bott, Secretary. **Price:**

Available only to members, museums and art galleries.

★3668★
SOCIETY OF PHOTOGRAPHER AND ARTIST REPRESENTATIVES—
   MEMBERSHIP DIRECTORY [New York City area]
Society of Photographer and Artist Representatives
Box 845
F.D.R. Station   Phone: (212) 832-3123
New York, NY 10022
Entries include: Representative name, phone, address, names of artists and photographers represented. **Frequency:** Annual, summer. **Price:** $5.00, plus self-addressed large envelope with 24¢ postage.

★3669★
SONGWRITER'S ANNUAL DIRECTORY
Music-by-Mail
Box 6101
Broadway Station   Phone: (212) 247-4620
Long Island City, NY 11106
Covers: Markets for songwriters, including music publishers, record companies, performers, etc. **Entries include:** Publisher, record company, or artist's name, address. **Frequency:** Annual. **Editor:** Syde Berman. **Former title:** Songwriter's Review - Annual Directory Issue (1979).

★3670★
SONGWRITER'S MARKET
Writer's Digest Books
9933 Alliance Road   Phone: (513) 984-0717
Cincinnati, OH 45242
Covers: 2,000 music publishers, jingle writers, advertising agencies, audiovisual firms, radio and television stations, and other buyers of musical compositions and lyrics. **Entries include:** Buyer's name and address, phone, payment rates, submission requirements, etc. **Arrangement:** By type of outlet. **Pages** (approx.): 500. **Frequency:** Annual, October. **Editor:** William Brohaugh. **Price:** $10.95.

Songwriter's Review—Annual Directory Issue See Songwriter's
   Annual Directory

★3671★
SONNECK SOCIETY—MEMBERSHIP DIRECTORY
Sonneck Society
C/o Nicholas Tawa
69 Undine Road   Phone: (617) 787-2283
Boston, MA 02135
Covers: 400 musicologists, ethnomusicologists, conductors, performers, and others interested in American music. **Entries include:** Name, office address and phone, home address, areas of occupational specialization, career data, special interests in American music. **Arrangement:** Alphabetical. **Pages** (approx.): 20. **Frequency:** Annual, fall. **Editor:** Nicholas E. Tawa. **Price:** $5.00.

★3672★
SOURCE DIRECTORY [Native American crafts]
Indian Arts and Crafts Board
Interior Department   Phone: (202) 343-2773
Washington, DC 20240
Covers: About 150 Native American-owned and operated businesses which produce and/or sell authentic Native American hand crafted products. **Entries include:** Business name, address, general location, phone, hours, description of products. **Arrangement:** Geographical. **Frequency:** Irregular; latest edition 1978; new edition expected 1980. **Former title:** Combined (1978) two previous publications, "Source Directory 1: Indian and Eskimo Organizations Marketing Native American Arts and Crafts" and "Source Directory 2: Indian and Eskimo Individuals Marketing Native American Arts and Crafts." **Price:** Free.

★3673★
SOURCETAP: A DIRECTORY OF PROGRAM RESOURCES FOR RADIO
National Federation of Community Broadcasters
1000 11th Street, N. W., Third Floor   Phone: (202) 789-1200
Washington, DC 20001
Covers: Over 100 groups that produce radio programs for noncommercial, public radio stations. **Entries include:** Group name, address, phone, name of contact, description of group, programs available, price, ordering information. **Arrangement:** Alphabetical. **Indexes:** Subject. **Pages** (approx.): 200. **Frequency:** Annual, June. **Editor:** Theresa R. Clifford, Associate Director. **Price:** $25.00 (current edition); $35.00 (1980 edition).

Southern Crafts and Art News *See* Art Scene [Arts and crafts fairs]

★3674★
SPEAKERS AND LECTURERS: HOW TO FIND THEM
Gale Research Company
Book Tower   Phone: (313) 961-2242
Detroit, MI 48226
Covers: About 4,200 speakers on a wide range of subjects who are available through 230 commercial booking agencies, companies, organizations, universities, etc. **Entries include:** Agency, organization, etc., name, address, phone, note on types of speakers provided and other details, fees, and names and topics of speakers. **Arrangement:** Alphabetical by agency name. **Indexes:** Speaker name, lecture title/keyword, geographical, subject. **Pages** (approx.): 475. **Frequency:** Not established; first edition March 1979. **Editors:** Paul Wasserman and Jacqueline R. Bernero. **Price:** $52.00.

★3675★
SPEAKERS DIRECTORY AND MEETING PLANNERS HANDBOOK
International Speakers Network, Inc.
175 E. Delaware Place, Suite 4601   Phone: (312) 266-0260
Chicago, IL 60611
Covers: 1,200 public speakers and entertainers, primarily in the United States, selected on the basis of references furnished by persons requesting listing. **Entries include:** Name, office address and phone, personal data, career data, speaking experience, and speech title. **Arrangement:** Alphabetical by subject area (Black history, creativity, conservation, etc.). **Indexes:** Personal name. **Pages** (approx.): 280. **Frequency:** Latest edition 1976; 1977 supplement. **Editor:** Robert A. Bouque. **Advertising accepted.** Circulation 10,000. **Price:** $10.00.

Specialization Directory [Photography] *See* Foto Finder [Photography]

★3676★
SPEECH COMMUNICATION DIRECTORY
Speech Communication Association
5205 Leesburg Pike   Phone: (703) 379-1888
Falls Church, VA 22041
Covers: 6,000 secondary and postsecondary teachers in the speech field (drama, debate, rhetoric, radio-TV, etc.), including some practitioners in government, business and industry in the United States and other countries. Includes list of institutions granting graduate degrees in speech. **Entries include:** Name, office and home address, phone, highest degree held, areas of occupational specialization, career data, type of membership, membership in regional/state associations. **Arrangement:** Alphabetical. **Indexes:** Geographical. **Pages** (approx.): 250. **Frequency:** Annual, January. **Editor:** William Work, Executive Secretary. **Advertising accepted.** Circulation 2,500. **Price:** $9.50 (current and 1980 editions).

Spot Radio Rates & Data *See* Standard Rate & Data Service— Spot Radio Rates & Data

Spot Radio Small Markets Edition *See* Standard Rate & Data Service—Spot Radio Small Markets Edition

Spot Television Rates & Data *See* Standard Rate & Data Service—Spot Television Rates & Data

★3677★
SQUARE DANCING—DIRECTORY ISSUE
American Square Dance Society
462 N. Robertson Boulevard   Phone: (213) 652-7434
Los Angeles, CA 90048
Covers: About 1,400 square dance associations, callers' associations, archives centers, periodicals, and information volunteers, worldwide but primarily in the United States. **Entries include:** Association, periodical, or individual name, and address; information volunteer listings include phone. **Arrangement:** Geographical. **Frequency:** Annual, August. **Editor:** Bob Osgood. **Advertising accepted.** Circulation 28,000. **Price:** $1.00.

★3678★
SQUARE DANCING—SQUARE DANCE DATE BOOK COLUMN
American Square Dance Society
462 N. Robertson Boulevard   Phone: (213) 652-7434
Los Angeles, CA 90048
Covers: About 75 coming square dance festivals, workshops, and other events involving square dancing, usually for two months ahead. **Entries include:** Event name, location, dates. **Arrangement:** Chronological. **Frequency:** Monthly. **Editor:** Bob Osgood. **Advertising accepted.** Circulation 28,000. **Price:** $8.00 per year.

★3679★
STANDARD RATE & DATA SERVICE—NETWORK RATES & DATA
Standard Rate & Data Service, Inc.
5201 Old Orchard Road   Phone: (312) 966-8500
Skokie, IL 60077
Covers: Radio and television networks, their owned stations, and affiliated stations. **Entries include:** Network or group name, advertising representatives, basic required groups and basic optional groups of stations, discounts, production facilities and services, closing times for advertising material. **Arrangement:** By network and area. **Frequency:** Bimonthly. **Advertising accepted.** **Price:** $15.50 per year, plus 50¢ shipping.

★3680★
STANDARD RATE & DATA SERVICE—SPOT RADIO RATES & DATA
Standard Rate & Data Service, Inc.
5201 Old Orchard Road   Phone: (312) 966-8500
Skokie, IL 60077
Covers: About 4,350 AM stations and 2,100 FM stations. **Entries include:** Call letters, name of owning company, address, phone, name of firm or individual representing station for advertising, special program features, participating programs, commissions. **Arrangement:** Geographical, then by call letters. **Frequency:** Monthly, on 1st of the month; "Weekly Change Bulletin" optional. **Advertising accepted.** **Price:** $82.00 per year, plus $6.00 shipping; weekly bulletin, $8.00 shipping. **Also includes:** Market and census data, farm data, ethnic and Black programming information.

★3681★
STANDARD RATE & DATA SERVICE—SPOT RADIO SMALL MARKETS EDITION
Standard Rate & Data Service, Inc.
5201 Old Orchard Road   Phone: (312) 966-8500
Skokie, IL 60077
Covers: Radio stations in markets of 25,000 or less. **Entries include:** Call letters, owner's name, address, name of one staff member, name of firm or individual representing station for advertising, format (Top 40, all news, country-western, etc.), facilities, affiliations, rates, commissions. **Arrangement:** Geographical, then by call letters. **Frequency:** Semiannual, April and October. **Advertising accepted.**

Price: $27.25 per year, plus 75¢ shipping.

★3682★
STANDARD RATE & DATA SERVICE—SPOT TELEVISION RATES & DATA
Standard Rate & Data Service, Inc.
5201 Old Orchard Road   Phone: (312) 966-8500
Skokie, IL 60077
Covers: All television stations and regional networks and groups. Includes separate section showing video tape recording capabilities of stations. **Entries include:** Call letters, name of owning company, address, phone, name of firm or individual representing station for advertising, special features, participation programs, rates, commissions. Video recording capability section shows call letters, address, and type of recording equipment. **Arrangement:** Geographical, then by call letters. **Frequency:** Monthly, on 15th of month; "Weekly Change Bulletin" optional. **Advertising accepted. Price:** $76.25 per year, plus $3.25 shipping; weekly bulletin, $8.00 shipping. **Also includes:** Market and census data.

★3683★
STOCK PHOTO AND ASSIGNMENT SOURCE BOOK
R. R. Bowker Company
1180 Avenue of the Americas   Phone: (212) 764-5100
New York, NY 10036
Covers: 4,000 sources for stock photos, including photo agencies, commercial and industrial firms, national and international agencies, historical collections, and film libraries. Also includes photographers who work on assignment, photography researchers, dealers in historical illustrations, photographic associations, and photo publications. **Entries include:** Name of source, person, etc., address, names of key personnel, types and subject specialties of material collected or photographed. **Arrangement:** Classified by photo subjects (Accidents and Disasters, Politics and Causes, etc.). **Indexes:** Subject, personal name. **Pages** (approx.): 485. **Frequency:** Not established; first edition September 1977. **Editor:** Fred W. McDarrah. **Price:** $19.95, postpaid, payment with order (ISSN 0146-5961). **Send orders to:** R. R. Bowker Co., Box 1807, Ann Arbor, MI 48106 (313-761-4700).

★3684★
STUBS—METROPOLITAN NEW YORK EDITION [Theaters, etc.]
Stubs Publications
234 W. 44th Street   Phone: (212) 398-8370
New York, NY 10036
Covers: Seating plans for theaters, music halls, and sports stadia in metropolitan New York and Washington, D. C. **Entries include:** Facility name, seating plan, address, and box office phone. **Pages** (approx.): 100. **Frequency:** Irregular; latest edition 1979; new edition expected 1980. **Editors:** Ronald S. and Patricia Lee, Owner-Publishers. **Advertising accepted.** Circulation 30,000. **Price:** $3.95, plus $1.00 shipping (current and 1980 editions).

★3685★
SUMMER ARTS FESTIVAL CALENDAR [New York]
Associated Arts Organizations
207 Delaware Avenue   Phone: (716) 856-6530
Buffalo, NY 14202
Covers: Visual arts festivals held during the summer in western New York state. **Entries include:** Festival name, name and address of sponsor, location if different, dates. **Frequency:** Annual. **Price:** $1.00.

★3686★
SUMMER THEATRE DIRECTORY [American Theatre Association]
American Theatre Association
1000 Vermont Avenue, N. W., Suite 902   Phone: (202) 628-4634
Washington, DC 20005
Number of listings: 300. **Entries include:** Name and address of theater, contact person, length of season, type and capacity of building, types of plays produced, salaried and unsalaried positions

available, application requirements, related conditions of employment, brief description. **Arrangement:** Geographical. **Frequency:** Annual, February. **Editor:** Kevin Hoggard. **Price:** $3.50 (current and 1980 editions); orders under $10.00 must be prepaid.

★3687★
SUMMER THEATRE DIRECTORY [Leo Shull]
Leo Shull Publications
134 W. 44th Street   Phone: (212) 586-6900
New York, NY 10036
Covers: Several hundred operating summer theaters in the United States and Canada. **Entries include:** Theatrical company name, address, casting policies, contact person, production data, and acting, technical, and apprentice openings. **Arrangement:** Geographical. **Pages** (approx.): 175. **Frequency:** Annual, March. **Editor:** Leo Shull. **Advertising accepted.** Circulation 20,000. **Price:** $6.00, postpaid, payment must accompany order.

★3688★
SUNSHINE ARTISTS USA—Arts and Crafts Calendar
Sun Country Enterprises, Inc.
501 Virginia Avenue
Winter Park, FL 32789
Covers: 1,000 arts and crafts and photography shows, nationwide. Separate section includes reports on attendance, management, etc., of recent events. **Entries include:** Event name, dates, location, contact, entry details. **Arrangement:** Chronological within states. **Frequency:** Monthly. **Editor:** J. L. Wahl. **Advertising accepted.** Circulation 18,000. **Price:** $15.00 per year; no single issues sold. **Other information:** Incorporated "Photo Artist USA" in 1979.

★3689★
SURVEY OF ARTS ADMINISTRATION TRAINING IN THE U.S. AND CANADA
American Council for the Arts
570 Seventh Avenue   Phone: (212) 354-6655
New York, NY 10018
Covers: About 30 institutions offering graduate programs, seminars, internships, and other special programs that train persons to be administrators for performing arts companies, museums, and other similar organizations. **Entries include:** Institution name, name of program or department, address, phone, description of program including admission requirements, degrees offered and degree requirements; internships, seminars, and workshops offered. **Arrangement:** By type of program. **Pages** (approx.): 75. **Frequency:** Irregular; latest edition September 1979. **Price:** $6.95, postpaid, payment with order.

★3690★
SURVEY OF PH.D. PROGRAMS IN ART HISTORY
College Art Association of America
16 E. 52nd Street   Phone: (212) 755-3532
New York, NY 10022
Covers: Over 40 programs in the United States and Canada. **Entries include:** Institution name, address; description of program including admission requirements, degrees offered, degree requirements, tuition, fees. **Arrangement:** Alphabetical. **Pages** (approx.): 70. **Frequency:** Irregular; latest edition 1978. **Price:** $3.00, postpaid.

★3691★
TALENT DIRECTORY [Graphic artists]
Graphic Artists Guild
30 E. 20th Street
New York, NY 10003
Covers: Graphic artists who are members. **Entries include:** Artist name, address, phone, accounts served, experience and background, kinds of work desired, and, usually, a photo of the artist. **Arrangement:** Classified by type of work (design, fashion, textile design, etc.). **Pages** (approx.): 160. **Frequency:** Annual. **Former title:** Graphic Artists Guild-Illustrators Guild - Talent Directory. **Price:** Free.

★3692★
TALK-BACK TV: TWO-WAY CABLE TELEVISION
TAB Books
Box 40   Phone: (717) 794-2191
Blue Ridge Summit, PA 17214
Publication includes: "Two-Way TV Directory." Pages (approx.): 240. Frequency: Published October 1976. Editor: Peter L. Deksnis. Price: $9.95, cloth; $5.95, paper.

★3693★
TECHNICAL ASSISTANCE FOR ARTS FACILITIES: A SOURCEBOOK
Educational Facilities Laboratories
680 Fifth Avenue   Phone: (212) 397-0040
New York, NY 10019
Covers: Organizations offering advice concerning physical facilities required by performing and visual arts groups, such as finding quarters, remodeling, and paying for them. Entries include: Name of organization, address, services. Pages (approx.): 30. Editor: Nancy Ambler. Price: $2.00.

Telecommunications Directory See People in Public Telecommunications

Television Almanac See International Television Almanac

★3694★
TELEVISION CONTACTS
Larimi Communications Associates Ltd.
151 E. 50th Street   Phone: (212) 935-9262
New York, NY 10022
Covers: About 900 television stations, networks, and syndicates interested in guests or outside scripts, films, etc. Entries include: For stations - Call letters, affiliation, channel number, address, phone, key station personnel; also gives news and other shows, names of contacts, and types of material used. Similar information for networks and syndicates. Arrangement: By market. Indexes: Call letter, geographical. Pages (approx.): 600. Frequency: Annual, with monthly and daily update services. Editor: Lisa Merrell. Price: $117.00.

★3695★
TELEVISION FACTBOOK
Television Digest, Inc.
1836 Jefferson Place, N. W.   Phone: (202) 872-9200
Washington, DC 20036
Covers: Commercial and noncommercial television stations and networks, worldwide; North American cable television systems; television equipment manufacturers, program and service suppliers, consulting engineers, brokers, attorneys practicing before the Federal Communications Commission, station sales representatives; colleges and universities offering radio-television degrees; etc. Entries include: Station listings show call letters, licensee name and address, studio address and phone, identification of owners, sales and legal representatives, chief station personnel, rates, technical data, map of service area, and Arbitron circulation data. Manufacturer and supplier listings include company name, address, phone, contact name. Arrangement: Classified by activity or service; stations are geographical, other sections largely alphabetical. Indexes: Call letters; general subject. Pages (approx.): 2,350 (in two volumes). Frequency: Annual, March with weekly updates. Editor: Albert Warren, Publisher. Advertising accepted. Circulation 9,500. Price: $127.50, including supplements.

★3696★
TELEVISION/RADIO AGE—TEN CITY DIRECTORY
Television Editorial Corporation
1270 Avenue of the Americas   Phone: (212) 757-8400
New York, NY 10020
Covers: 4,000 commercial radio and television stations, networks, and groups and their representatives; trade organizations; trade publications; advertising agencies; program distributors; and transportation, hotels, and restaurants. Includes: New York, Chicago,

Los Angeles, San Francisco, Detroit, Atlanta, Dallas-Fort Worth, St. Louis, Philadelphia, and Minneapolis-St. Paul. Entries include: Station or company name, address, phone. Arrangement: By city, then by type of business or activity. Pages (approx.): 100. Frequency: Annual, spring. Editor: Ms. Lee Sheridan, Coordinator. Advertising accepted. Price: $5.00, payment with order. Also includes: List of top 50 national spot advertisers.

Ten City Directory [Advertising] See Television/Radio Age—Ten City Directory

★3697★
TEXAS MUSEUM DIRECTORY
Texas Historical Commission
Box 12226
Austin, TX 78711
Covers: About 410 museums in Texas. Entries include: Museum name, address, name of director, admission fee, hours, phone, publications, description of contents. Arrangement: By city. Indexes: County. Pages (approx.): 80. Frequency: Irregular, about every two to three years; latest edition 1978. Editors: Kit Fontaine and Vincent Scanio. Price: Free.

★3698★
TEXTILE COLLECTIONS OF THE WORLD
Van Nostrand Reinhold Ltd.
450 W. 33rd Street   Phone: (212) 594-8660
New York, NY 10001
Covers: Museums having textile collections. Volume 1 covers 60 museums in the United States and Canada; volume 2 covers 40 museums in England, Scotland, and Ireland. Entries include: Name of collection, detailed survey, and evaluation of the collection. Arrangement: Geographical. Indexes: General index for each volume. Pages (approx.): 320, Volume 1; 220, Volume 2. Former title: First two volumes published August 1976. Editor: Cecil Lubell. Price: $35.00, Volume 1; $30.00, Volume 2. Also includes: Photographs showing representative pieces from different periods. They are arranged chronologically and by country of origin and are included in the general index.

★3699★
THEATRE CRAFTS DIRECTORY
Rodale Press, Inc.
250 W. 57th Street, Suite 312   Phone: (212) 582-4110
New York, NY 10019
Covers: About 120 undergraduate theater programs, 80 graduate theater programs; about 55 summer theaters; and over 350 manufacturers and suppliers of products and services in the technical theater and related fields. Entries include: For colleges - Name, address; degrees and programs offered; name and title of department chairman; number of students in technical and in theater arts, number of faculty, number of courses; memberships; admission requirements; deadline for admission; degree requirements; opportunities for production activities; performance facilities; tuition, and financial aid available. For summer theaters - Name, location, name and address of contact, season, description of theater emphasis, facilities, positions available, and application procedure. For suppliers - Company name, address, phone, name and title of contact, line of business, contact, address, and phone for branch offices, distributors, and representatives. Arrangement: Suppliers are alphabetical and geographical; others are geographical. Pages (approx.): 260. Frequency: Biennial, February of odd years. Editor: Patricia MacKay. Advertising accepted. Circulation 15,000. Price: $10.00.

★3700★
THEATRE DIRECTORY [National, nonprofit]
Theatre Communications Group
355 Lexington Avenue   Phone: (212) 697-5230
New York, NY 10017
Covers: Over 170 professional, nonprofit theaters, and 30 related organizations. Entries include: Name, address, phone, directors and

managers, general performance information. **Arrangement:** Alphabetical. **Indexes:** Regional. **Pages** (approx.): 50. **Frequency:** Annual, October. **Editor:** David J. Skal. **Price:** $3.00.

★3701★
THEATRE PROFILES [National, nonprofit]: An Informational
   Handbook
Theatre Communications Group
355 Lexington Avenue   Phone: (212) 697-5230
New York, NY 10017
Covers: Over 160 resident, noncommercial theatrical companies. **Entries include:** Name, address, and names of directors, and descriptive, statistical, and fiscal information; illustrated. **Arrangement:** Alphabetical. **Indexes:** Names, play titles. **Pages** (approx.): 220. **Frequency:** Biennial, fall of odd years. **Editor:** David J. Skal. **Price:** $12.95.

★3702★
THEATRICAL CALENDAR
Celebrity Service, Inc.
171 W. 57th Street   Phone: (212) 757-7979
New York, NY 10019
Covers: Current Broadway, Off-Broadway, and off Off-Broadway productions; productions opening the current week and later; shows in preview, tryout, and rehearsal; future shows definite and indefinite. Covers New York metropolitan region, primarily, but includes national information, also. **Entries include:** For current shows - Show name; theater name; names of producer and principal staff, with phones; date opened. For other shows - Same data, plus additional information on location, cast, dates, etc., as available. **Arrangement:** Separate lists for shows in various stages. **Indexes:** Show name. **Frequency:** Weekly. **Editor:** Roslyn M. Lipps. **Price:** $3.50 per issue; $95.00 for fourteen months.

★3703★
THEATRICAL INDEX
Theatrical Index
888 Eighth Avenue
New York, NY 10019
Covers: Theatrical presentations in pre-production stage which are seeking investors; also covers producers and agents. **Entries include:** Production name, brief details, contact; agents' and producers' listings include name, address, phone. **Frequency:** Weekly. **Price:** $4.50 per copy.

★3704★
TRAVELING FM RADIO GUIDE
And/Or Press
Box 2246   Phone: (415) 849-2665
Berkeley, CA 94702
Covers: 2,600 stations. **Entries include:** Geographical listings give city name and stations located there; station listings follow listings for cities in each state, in order by call letters, and give frequency, city, power, type of programming. **Pages** (approx.): 125. **Frequency:** Published April 1977. **Advertising accepted. Price:** $2.95, postpaid.

T.U.B.A. Membership Roster *See* Tubists Universal Brotherhood
   Association—Membership Roster

★3705★
TUBISTS UNIVERSAL BROTHERHOOD ASSOCIATION—
   MEMBERSHIP ROSTER
Tubists Universal Brotherhood Association
C/o Donald C. Little
School of Music
North Texas State University   Phone: (817) 788-2791
Denton, TX 76203
Covers: About 1,500 persons who are players or teachers of the tuba or euphonium. **Entries include:** Name, address, phone, status as tuba or euphonium player, affiliation or occupation. **Arrangement:** Alphabetical. **Pages** (approx.): 30. **Frequency:** Annual, spring. **Editor:**

Donald C. Little. **Price:** $5.00; commercial use not permitted.

★3706★
TV PUBLICITY OUTLETS NATIONWIDE
Public Relations Plus, Inc.
Box 327   Phone: (203) 868-0200
Washington Depot, CT 06794
Covers: 2,000 local and network television programs which use outside scripts, film, or guests. **Entries include:** Station location and call letters; program name and time; name, address, and phone of host; whether syndicated or carried on network; description of subject matter and visual material used; rated audience size. **Arrangement:** Geographical. **Pages** (approx.): 90. **Frequency:** Quarterly. **Editor:** Harold D. Hansen. **Price:** $89.50 per year.

★3707★
UNITED STATES INSTITUTE FOR THEATRE TECHNOLOGY—
   MEMBERSHIP DIRECTORY
United States Institute for Theatre Technology
1501 Broadway, Room 1408   Phone: (212) 354-5360
New York, NY 10036
Covers: 2,700 members concerned with theater architecture, engineering, and administration. **Entries include:** Name, address. **Frequency:** Annual. **Price:** Available to members.

★3708★
VIDEO PROGRAMS INDEX [Videotape distributor directory]
National Video Clearinghouse, Inc.
Box 3   Phone: (516) 364-3686
Syosset, NY 11791
Covers: About 400 entertainment and non-entertainment video tape program distributors and retailers. **Entries include:** Company name, address, phone, subject specialty, formats available, means of acquistion (rent, loan, purchase, etc.). **Arrangement:** Entertainment and non-entertainment distributors listed separately. **Indexes:** Subject, free loan, free duplication, trade-in/used, rental/loan. **Pages** (approx.): 55. **Frequency:** Annual, November. **Editor:** Ken Winslow. **Advertising accepted.** Circulation 20,000. **Price:** $6.95.

★3709★
VIDEO SOURCE BOOK [Video products and distributors]
National Video Clearinghouse, Inc.
Box 3   Phone: (516) 364-3686
Syosset, NY 11791
Covers: Nearly 400 producers and distributors of over 15,000 pre-recorded videotapes and videodiscs. **Entries include:** Name, address, phone, titles available, subject area. **Arrangement:** By title. **Indexes:** Category, distributor name. **Pages** (approx.): 900. **Frequency:** Annual, November. **Editor:** Maxine K. Reed. **Advertising accepted.** Circulation 40,000. **Price:** $19.95, plus $1.00 shipping (current edition); $50.00 (tentative, 1980 edition). **Other information:** Principal content of publication is listing of titles available with descriptive data.

★3710★
VIDEOLOG: PROGRAMS FOR GENERAL INTEREST AND
   ENTERTAINMENT
Esselte Video, Inc.
600 Madison Avenue   Phone: (212) 753-7530
New York, NY 10022
Covers: Over 100 producers and distributors of videotape programs of general interest, including self-help, recreation, child care, and other subjects. **Entries include:** Company name, address, phone, contact person. **Arrangement:** Alphabetical. **Indexes:** Subject, titles by company name. **Pages** (approx.): 300. **Frequency:** Annual. **Editor:** R. Beardsley. **Price:** $20.00. **Send orders to:** Esselte Video, Inc., Box 978, Edison, NJ 08817 (201-225-1900). **Other information:** Primary content is annotated entries describing about 4,500 videotapes and 600 movies on videotapes.

★3711★
WAFL BOOK—A GUIDE TO FILM AND VIDEO IN THE
　　WASHINGTON, DC AREA
Washington Area Filmmakers League
Box 6475　　　　　　　　　　Phone: (202) 462-1192
Washington, DC 20009
Covers: Paid listings of about 200 freelance film editors, artists, photographers, stuntpersons, etc.; about 25 business firms offering production services; and about 75 film organizations, libraries, archives, and educational programs in filmmaking in the greater Washington, DC area. **Entries include:** For freelance artists - Name, address, phone, skills, years of experience, references (if listed with WAFL), and description of experience. For businesses - Name, address, phone, and "review" of firm (by panel of 20 filmmakers) including history of firm, equipment, services. For others - Name, address, phone, name of contact, description of activities or program. **Arrangement:** Alphabetical within activity categories. **Indexes:** Freelance artist by type of work, firm by product or service, production company name. **Pages** (approx.): 200. **Frequency:** Every 18 months; latest edition 1978; new edition expected early 1980. **Editor:** Greg Epler. **Advertising accepted.** Circulation 7,000. **Price:** $4.95, plus 50¢ shipping, payment with order (current and 1980 editions).

★3712★
WASHINGTON INTERNATIONAL ARTS LETTER—DIRECTORY OF
　　PANELISTS AND CONSULTANTS OF THE NATIONAL
　　ENDOWMENT FOR THE ARTS ISSUES
Washington International Arts Letter
Box 9005　　　　　　　　　　Phone: (202) 488-0800
Washington, DC 20003
Covers: Individuals who serve as consultants to the National Endowment of the Arts. **Entries include:** Individual name, home address, phone, area of specialization, and career data, and NEA affiliation. **Arrangement:** Classified by discipline or specialization. **Pages** (approx.): 10. **Frequency:** Irregular; last appeared in May and June 1978 issues. **Editor:** Daniel Millsaps. **Price:** $10.00.

★3713★
WASHINGTON INTERNATIONAL ARTS LETTER—"SELECTED
　　DIRECTORY OF NATIONAL ARTS SERVICE ORGANIZATIONS"
　　ISSUES
Washington International Arts Letter
325 Pennsylvania Avenue, S. E.　　Phone: (202) 488-0800
Washington, DC 20003
Covers: Organizations serving the arts - visual arts, architecture, literature, museums, theater, poetry, dance, film, television, etc. **Entries include:** Organization name, address, services (publications, meetings, etc.). **Arrangement:** Alphabetical. **Frequency:** Not established; first published in February and March 1978 issues, with supplement in November 1979. **Editor:** Daniel Millsaps. **Price:** $10.00 for these two directory issues and supplements.

★3714★
WESTART—SHOW CALENDAR SECTION
WestArt
198 Hillmont Avenue　　　　Phone: (916) 885-0969
Auburn, CA 95603
Publication includes: "Time to Show," a regular calendar covering 125-150 coming arts and crafts shows in the United States, with emphasis on the West Coast. Shows which charge admission are required to pay for listing. **Entries include:** Show location, date, deadline date for entering, description of craft types, entry restrictions and requirements, names of jurors (if available), awards or prize amounts, name and address of contact; some listings also include phone. **Arrangement:** By month of deadline, then alphabetical by city name. **Frequency:** Twice monthly. **Editor:** Jean L. Couzens. **Advertising accepted.** Circulation 7,500. **Price:** $8.00 per year, payment must accompany order (ISSN 0008-1124).

★3715★
WHERE AND HOW TO SELL YOUR PHOTOGRAPHS
Amphoto, Division
BPI
1515 Broadway
New York, NY 10036
Publication includes: About 300 book and magazine publishers and other markets for photographs. **Entries include:** Firm name, address, phone, and size and type of photograph desired. **Arrangement:** By type of market. **Pages** (approx.): 265. **Frequency:** Irregular; latest edition 1979; new edition expected 1981. **Editor:** Dena Bennet. **Former title:** Where and How to Sell Your Pictures. **Price:** $9.95.

★3716★
WHITMARK DIRECTORY—SOURCE BOOK OF TALENT, FASHION,
　　AND AUDIO-VISUAL SERVICES IN THE SOUTHWEST
Whitmark Associates
4120 Main Street　　　　　　Phone: (214) 826-9400
Dallas, TX 75226
Covers: 800 illustrated listings for adult and juvenile actors, actresses, and models in the Southwest, primarily Texas; motion picture and videotape production facilities in the Southwest. **Entries include:** Name, acting or performing specialties, and agency contact; audiovisual production services are presented in individual suppliers' ads. **Arrangement:** Classified by sex and age of performers and types of audiovisual service offered. **Indexes:** Personal name. **Pages** (approx.): 400. **Frequency:** Annual, September. **Editor:** Margaret F. Murrell. **Advertising accepted.** Circulation 2,000. **Former title:** Whitmark Talent Directory. **Price:** $37.50, plus $1.50 shipping.

★3717★
WHO'S WHERE [Theater, media]
Leo Shull Publications
134 W. 44th Street　　　　　Phone: (212) 586-6900
New York, NY 10036
Covers: 2,000 producers, directors, casting agents, trade unions, theaters, literary agents, columnists and theater reporters, press agents, TV stations and staff. **Entries include:** Name, phone, and address. **Arrangement:** Classified by activity or service. **Pages** (approx.): 100. **Frequency:** Irregular; approximately every two years; latest edition January 1979. **Editor:** Leo Shull. **Advertising accepted.** **Price:** $4.50, postpaid, payment must accompany order.

★3718★
WHO'S WHO IN HOLLYWOOD—1900-1976
Arlington House Publishers
165 Huguenot Street　　　　Phone: (914) 636-3850
New Rochelle, NY 10801
Covers: About 20,000 screen performers who appeared in films released in the United States; sections are Living Players, Late Players (1900-1974), Players Who Died in 1975 and 1976, "Lost" Players, and "Lost" Child Players ("lost" meaning whereabouts unknown). **Entries include:** Individual name, personal and career data, specialization (comedy, drama, etc.), selected films, and general area of residence. **Arrangement:** Alphabetical within section. **Pages** (approx.): 900. **Frequency:** First edition 1977. **Editor:** David Ragan. **Price:** $30.00.

★3719★
WHO'S WHO IN N.Y. FILMMAKERS
Leo Shull Publications
134 W. 44th Street　　　　　Phone: (212) 586-6900
New York, NY 10036
Entries include: Firm name, address, phone, type of films or tapes produced (commercials, shorts, features, etc.), names of executives, casting heads, and details of job application procedures. **Pages** (approx.): 50. **Frequency:** Semiannual. **Editor:** Leo Shull. **Former title:** 500 TV-Film Producers. **Price:** $3.00, payment with order.

★3720★
WOMEN ARTISTS NEWS—"ART ALMANAC" SECTION [Show directory]
Midmarch Associates
Box 3304
Grand Central Station   Phone: (212) 666-6990
New York, NY 10017
Publication includes: List of forthcoming fine arts and arts and crafts fairs and exhibits and other markets; also solo and group shows for individual artists. **Entries include:** For fairs - Show name, location, sponsor, contact, dates. Other types of listings include similar detail. **Frequency:** Monthly. **Editor:** Cynthia Navaretta. **Advertising accepted.** Circulation 4,000. **Price:** $6.00 per year.

Working Craftsman—"Fair Share" Column See Crafts Report—"Fair Share" Column

★3721★
WORLD A.V. PROGRAMME DIRECTORY [Audiovisual materials]
R. R. Bowker Company
1180 Avenue of the Americas   Phone: (212) 764-5100
New York, NY 10036
Description: Covers producers of audiovisual materials of all kinds, including films, videotapes, filmstrips, slides, etc.; coverage limited to English-speaking countries. Publication consists of microfiche reproductions of producer's catalogs; there is a printed subject index to the microfiche. Available in separate sections devoted to "Science and Technology," "Arts and Humanities," "Training and Self-Development," and "Entertainment and Leisure." **Frequency:** Annual, with at least three microfiche update supplements per year, and three revised indexes. **Price:** $360.00 per year for complete directory; $150.00 per year per subject section. **Send orders to:** R. R. Bowker Co., Box 1807, Ann Arbor, MI 48106 (313-761-4700). **Other information:** Compiled by Videofilm Centre.

★3722★
WORLD DIRECTORY OF INSTITUTIONS OFFERING COURSES IN INDUSTRIAL DESIGN
International Council of Societies of Industrial Design
United Nations Industrial Development Organization
Box 707
Z-1011 Vienna, Austria
Covers: Institutions worldwide which offer courses in industrial design. **Entries include:** Institution name, address, name of department(s) related to design, funding, size of staff and enrollment, admission requirements, length and description of courses offered, fees, financial aid. **Arrangement:** Geographical. **Indexes:** Institution name (with language requirements, range of courses). **Pages** (approx.): 80. **Frequency:** Irregular; latest edition 1976. **Price:** Free.

★3723★
WRITERS GUILD DIRECTORY [Broadcast and film media]
Writers Guild of America, West
8955 Beverly Boulevard   Phone: (213) 550-1000
Los Angeles, CA 90048
Covers: About 1,250 writers for motion pictures, television, and radio; includes a few listings for members of Writers Guild of America, East; total listings are about 20% of the combined membership of the two organizations, representing only those who requested inclusion. Name-only list of all members of both Guilds is included. **Entries include:** Name, address, phone, name of agent, recent work. **Arrangement:** Alphabetical. **Pages** (approx.): 120. **Frequency:** Biennial, March of odd years. **Price:** $10.00, payment with order.

★3724★
WTFDA TV STATION GUIDE
Worldwide TV-FM DX Association
Box 202
Whiting, IN 46394
Covers: 1,500 television stations currently operating in North and Central America. Published for persons having a special interest in long distance television reception. **Entries include:** Station name, channel, location, offset pattern, state, call letters, network, power, antenna height, TV Guide serving area. **Arrangement:** Stations listed by channel. **Pages** (approx.): 60. **Frequency:** Irregular; latest edition September 1979. **Editor:** Frank Aden, Jr. **Advertising accepted.** Circulation 500. **Price:** $5.00.

Yellow Pages of Hispanic Arts See Hispanic Arts Directory

10

Public Affairs
and Social Concerns

★3725★
**ACCESSIBILITY ASSISTANCE—A DIRECTORY OF CONSULTANTS
ON ENVIRONMENTS FOR HANDICAPPED PEOPLE**
National Center for a Barrier Free Environment
1140 Connecticut Avenue, N. W.   Phone: (202) 466-6896
Washington, DC 20036
Covers: Over 400 designers, architects, rehabilitation professionals,
groups of disabled persons and others willing to serve as consultants in
barrier free design. **Entries include:** Individual or group name,
address, phone, services, accessibility projects, name of contact,
names and addresses of references. **Arrangement:** Geographical.
Indexes: Personal name, profession. **Pages** (approx.): 200.
Frequency: Not established; first edition November 1978; new
edition expected fall 1980. **Editor:** Margaret Milner, Project Director.
Price: $3.25, postpaid, payment with order; $4.25, billed.

★3726★
**ACCREDITED JOURNALISM AND MASS COMMUNICATION
EDUCATION**
American Council on Education for Journalism
School of Journalism
University of Missouri   Phone: (314) 882-6362
Columbia, MO 65201
Covers: About 80 institutions with accredited programs in journalism.
Entries include: Institution name, address; name and phone of
department chairman or contact; fields of study; accreditation, and
date accredited. **Arrangement:** Geographical. **Frequency:** Annual,
July. **Editor:** Milton Gross. **Former title:** Accredited Programs in
Journalism.

Accredited Programs in Journalism *See* Accredited Journalism
And Mass Communication Education

★3727★
**AFFIRMATIVE ACTION: A COMPREHENSIVE RECRUITMENT
MANUAL**
Garrett Park Press
          Phone: (301) 946-2553
Garrett Park, MD 20766
Publication includes: Lists of predominantly Black four- and two-year
colleges and universities; colleges and universities with relatively large
Hispanic, Native American, and Asian American student enrollments;
predominantly Black fraternities and sororities; newspapers and
periodicals with minority group readership; radio and television
broadcasting stations with minority group audiences; minority
consulting employment firms; skill banks; state and local commissions
concerned with equal opportunity employment; organizations which
provide housing assistance to minorities; minority public accounting

firms; regional minority purchasing councils; Black-owned insurance
companies; minority-owned banks. **Entries include:** All listings include
organization name, address; Black four-year college listings also
include phone, name of placement director, enrollment, code to
indicate accreditation, and number of degrees awarded by degree and
field; other minority college listings include code for two-year colleges.
Fraternity and sorority listings include number of chapters and number
of chapters on college campuses. Newspaper and periodical listings
include frequency and circulation. **Arrangement:** Primarily by activity
then by minority group. Colleges, newspapers, radio and television
stations, and banks are then geographical; insurance companies are
ranked by size; others are alphabetical. **Frequency:** First edition April
1979. **Editor:** Robert Calvert, Jr. **Price:** $14.00, postpaid, payment
must accompany orders from individuals; $15.00, billed. **Other
information:** Principal content of publication is discussion of methods
of recruitment of minority employees, particularly college graduates.

★3728★
AFFIRMATIVE ACTION: A GUIDE FOR THE PERPLEXED
Institute for Community Development
Continuing Education Service
Michigan State University
S. Harrison Road   Phone: (517) 355-0100
East Lansing, MI 48824
Publication includes: List of about 200 federal civil rights agencies
and departments concerned with affirmative action. **Entries include:**
Organization name, address, states covered by regional offices.
Arrangement: By region within national agency listing. **Pages**
(approx.): 205. **Frequency:** Published 1977. **Author:** Gregory D.
Squires. **Price:** $4.50, payment must accompany order.

★3729★
AFFIRMATIVE ACTION REGISTER
Affirmative Action, Inc.
8356 Olive Boulevard   Phone: (314) 991-1335
St. Louis, MO 63132
Covers: In each issue, about 200 positions at a professional level
(most requiring advanced study) available to minorities and the
handicapped; listings are advertisements placed by employers with
affirmative action programs. **Entries include:** Company or
organization name, address, name of contact; description of position
including title, requirements, duties, application procedure, salary, etc.
Arrangement: By profession. **Pages** (approx.): 20. **Frequency:**
Monthly. **Advertising accepted.** Circulation 55,000. **Price:** $15.00
per year; distributed free to minority and handicapped candidate
sources (ISSN 0146-2113).

★3730★

AGENCIES AND ORGANIZATIONS REPRESENTED IN AAPOR MEMBERSHIP
American Association for Public Opinion Research
Box 17   Phone: (609) 924-8670
Princeton, NJ 08540
Covers: About 75 firms engaged in opinion research. **Entries include:** Firm name, address, phone, name of contact, services. **Arrangement:** Alphabetical. **Indexes:** Geographical. **Pages** (approx.): 40. **Frequency:** Annual. **Editor:** June R. Christ. **Price:** Free.

★3731★

ALL THE HELP YOU CAN GET [Massachusetts]
Direct Information Service
Jones Library
43 Amity Street   Phone: (413) 256-0121
Amherst, MA 01002
Covers: Nationwide, regionwide, and statewide services available in Hampshire County, Massachusetts. **Entries include:** Name of organization, address, phone, hours, eligibility, list of services, fees. **Arrangement:** By type of aid provided. **Indexes:** Topics, organization name. **Pages** (approx.): 200. **Frequency:** Has been biennial, even years; new edition expected March 1980; annual updates beginning in 1980. **Price:** $10.00 (1980 edition).

★3732★

ALL TOGETHER JOURNAL—LIFESTYLE DIRECTORY [Column]
All Together
205 W. Wacker Drive, Suite 1416   Phone: (312) 782-4398
Chicago, IL 60606
Publication includes: List of organizations and businesses which serve people pursuing alternative lifestyles including singles, gays, single parents, divorced and widowed persons, corporate families, etc. **Entries include:** Location, hours, features, lifestyle interest, special offers to members, general comments. **Frequency:** Quarterly. **Editor:** Lloyd M. Levin, President. **Price:** Included in membership, $10.00 per year.

★3733★

ALONE AND SURVIVING [Widowhood]
Walker and Company
720 Fifth Avenue   Phone: (212) 265-3632
New York, NY 10019
Publication includes: Lists (in appendixes) of counseling services for widows and for their children, financial and employment guidance services, and publications of assistance to widows. **Entries include:** Name of service or publication, address, phone, and, for services, name of contact. Most listings also include a description of the services offered or publication content. **Arrangement:** By type of service; local counseling services are then listed by state. **Frequency:** Previous edition 1977; latest edition July 1979. **Price:** $4.95, plus 75¢ shipping.

★3734★

ALPHABETIZED DIRECTORY OF AMERICAN JOURNALISTS
Alphabetized Directory of American Journalists
Box 231   Phone: (317) 452-2033
Kokomo, IN 46901
Covers: About 25,000 editorial staff of about 1,750 daily newspapers in the United States and staff of Associated Press and United Press International. **Entries include:** Journalist's name, position or assignment, and name of paper only. Street address and phone are obtained from a separate list of papers. **Arrangement:** Journalists are arranged alphabetically, newspapers geographically. **Pages** (approx.): 300. **Frequency:** Irregular; latest edition June 1979. **Price:** $11.50, postpaid.

★3735★

ALTERNATIVE AMERICA
Richard Gardner, Publisher
Box 134
Harvard Square Station
Cambridge, MA 02139
Covers: 5,000 groups concerned with alternative lifestyles, social change, consumerism, appropriate technology, cooperative living and ventures, etc. Includes associations, publishers, nonprofit and cooperative undertakings, etc. **Entries include:** Group name, address, keywords indicating major concerns; listings limited to one 120-character line of computer print. **Arrangement:** Zip code. **Indexes:** Subject, group name. **Frequency:** Not established; first edition 1976; new edition planned, date uncertain. **Editor:** Richard Gardner. **Price:** $4.00, postpaid.

★3736★

ALTERNATIVE CELEBRATIONS CATALOGUE
Alternatives
4274 Oaklawn Drive   Phone: (601) 366-8468
Jackson, MS 39206
Publication includes: About 60 people and earth groups and 20 self-help craft groups active in celebrating holidays more simply and less expensively by emphasizing non-commercial values. **Entries include:** Group or craftsperson's name, address, and activities. **Pages** (approx.): 250. **Frequency:** Irregular; latest edition 1978. **Advertising accepted.** **Former title:** The Alternate Catalogue (1974), The Alternate Celebrations Catalogue (1975). **Price:** $5.00, payment with order.

★3737★

ALTERNATIVE PRESS DIRECTORY
Alternative Press Syndicate
116 E. 27th Street   Phone: (212) 481-0140
New York, NY 10010
Covers: 220 alternative newspapers and magazines, worldwide. **Entries include:** For United States listings - Name of publication, address, phone; names of publisher, advertising director, and editor; format, pages, price, circulation, year founded, ad rates, frequency. For foreign listings - Paper name, address. **Arrangement:** Geographical. **Frequency:** Irregular; latest edition 1979; new edition expected 1980. **Editors:** Craig Silver and Dan Taylor. **Former title:** Underground Press Directory. **Advertising accepted.** Circulation 10,000. **Price:** $6.00, plus 25¢ shipping.

★3738★

ALTERNATIVE WORK SCHEDULE DIRECTORY
National Council for Alternative Work Patterns
1925 K Street, N. W.   Phone: (202) 466-4467
Washington, DC 20006
Covers: 290 public and private organizations utilizing flextime, compressed workweek, job sharing, and part-time work schedules. **Entries include:** Firm name, address, contact, and program description. **Arrangement:** Geographical. **Indexes:** Alphabetical, type of industry, type of alternative work schedule program. **Pages** (approx.): 190. **Frequency:** Not established; first edition 1978. **Editors:** Gail S. Rosenberg, Marion C. Long, and Susan W. Post. **Price:** $25.00.

★3739★

ALTERNATIVES IN PRINT
ALA/SRRT Task Force on Alternatives in Print
C/o Neal-Schuman Publishers, Inc.
64 University Place   Phone: (212) 473-5170
New York, NY 10003
Covers: 2,600 small presses, associations, and institutions which publish alternate culture, social change books, periodicals, tapes, films, etc.; includes 750 foreign publishers. **Entries include:** Publisher name, address, and titles, authors, and prices of publications. **Arrangement:** Alphabetical by publisher name. **Indexes:** Subject, geographical, author, title. **Pages** (approx.): 700. **Frequency:** Irregular; latest

edition October 1979. **Price:** $39.95, plus $1.25 shipping.

★3740★
**AMERICAN ASSOCIATION FOR MARRIAGE AND FAMILY
   THERAPY—MEMBERSHIP DIRECTORY**
American Association for Marriage and Family Therapy
924 W. Ninth   Phone: (714) 981-0888
Upland, CA 91786
Covers: 5,000 members throughout the United States and Canada,
plus national and international affiliates. **Entries include:** Name, office
address, highest degree held, and any special rank in association.
Arrangement: Alphabetical and geographical, with identical
information in each. **Pages** (approx.): 300. **Frequency:** Biennial, fall of
odd years. **Price:** $10.00.

★3741★
**AMERICAN ASSOCIATION FOR PUBLIC OPINION RESEARCH—
   DIRECTORY OF MEMBERS**
American Association for Public Opinion Research
Box 17   Phone: (609) 924-8670
Princeton, NJ 08540
Number of listings: 1,100. **Entries include:** Name, business or home
address, phone. **Arrangement:** Alphabetical. **Indexes:** Geographical.
Pages (approx.): 110. **Frequency:** Annual, fall. **Editor:** Diane
Schrayer. **Price:** Available to members only.

American Association of Marriage and Family Counselors—
   Membership Directory *See* American Association for Marriage
   and Family...

★3742★
**AMERICAN ASSOCIATION OF SUICIDOLOGY—MEMBERSHIP
   ROSTER**
American Association of Suicidology
Box 3264   Phone: (713) 644-7911
Houston, TX 77001
Covers: About 500 psychologists, psychiatrists, social workers,
nurses, health educators, physicians, directors of suicide prevention
centers, clergy and others concerned with suicide prevention. **Entries
include:** Name, address, office phone, geographical area covered.
Arrangement: Alphabetical. **Pages** (approx.): 25. **Frequency:** Annual,
June. **Price:** $10.00.

★3743★
**AMERICAN COUNCIL ON CONSUMER INTERESTS—MEMBERSHIP
   LIST**
American Council on Consumer Interests
162 Stanley Hall
University of Missouri   Phone: (314) 882-3817
Columbia, MO 65201
Number of listings: 3,000. **Other information:** Available in mailing
list form only.

★3744★
**AMERICAN GROUP PSYCHOTHERAPY ASSOCIATION—
   MEMBERSHIP DIRECTORY**
American Group Psychotherapy Association
1995 Broadway, 14th Floor   Phone: (212) 787-2618
New York, NY 10023
Covers: 3,000 physicians, psychologists, and other mental health
professionals interested in treatment of emotional problems by group
methods. **Entries include:** Name, office or home address, highest
degree held, affiliate society of which a member. **Arrangement:**
Alphabetical. **Indexes:** Geographical. **Pages** (approx.): 160.
Frequency: Biennial, odd years. **Price:** $10.00.

★3745★
AMERICAN HUMANE AGENCY DIRECTORY
American Humane Association
5351 S. Roslyn Street   Phone: (303) 779-1400
Englewood, CO 80111
Covers: Over 2,000 animal protection agencies; coverage is mostly
American, but Canadian and some other foreign countries are included.
Entries include: Agency name, address. **Arrangement:** Geographical.
Pages (approx.): 200. **Frequency:** Irregular; latest edition 1977;
semiannual updates. **Editor:** Shirley Gates, Membership Secretary.
Price: $35.00.

American Society of Association Executives—Directory *See*
   Who's Who in Association Management

★3746★
**AMERICAN SOCIETY OF JOURNALISTS AND AUTHORS—
   DIRECTORY OF PROFESSIONAL WRITERS**
American Society of Journalists and Authors
1501 Broadway, Suite 1907   Phone: (212) 997-0947
New York, NY 10036
Covers: About 550 nonfiction writers who are members. **Entries
include:** Writer's name, home and office addresses and phones,
specialties, areas of expertise; name, address, and phone of agent;
memberships; books; periodicals contributed to; awards; employment
history. **Arrangement:** Alphabetical. **Indexes:** Subject specialty,
geographical. **Pages** (approx.): 200. **Frequency:** Annual, January.
Former title: Society of Magazine Writers - Directory of Professional
Writers (1975). **Price:** $35.00 (current edition; tentative, 1980
edition).

★3747★
ANN ARBOR PEOPLE'S YELLOW PAGES
Community Switchboard
608 N. Main   Phone: (313) 663-1111
Ann Arbor, MI 48104
Covers: Co-ops, collectives, nonprofit groups, businesses which
accept work exchange as payment, public services, and individuals and
groups with services or information of general interest. **Entries
include:** Name, location, phone, hours, services offered, fee
schedules, population normally served, other pertinent data.
Arrangement: Alphabetical. **Frequency:** Irregular; previous edition
1974; new edition due May 1978. **Editors:** M. Bodine, R. Rice,
Coordinators. **Price:** 50¢ (1978 edition).

★3748★
ANNOTATED BIBLIOGRAPHY ON SELF-HELP MUTUAL AID
National Self-Help Clearinghouse
Graduate Center / City University of New York
33 W. 42nd Street
Room 1227
New York, NY 10036
Covers: Authors of articles on self-help mutual aid groups and topics
which appeared during 1975-77. **Entries include:** Article title,
periodical in which it appeared, date, annotation, author's name and
address. **Arrangement:** Alphabetical by title. **Pages** (approx.): 60.
Frequency: Irregular; latest edition 1978 (with 1975-77
information). **Editor:** H. Carson Briggs. **Price:** $3.25, postpaid;
payment or purchase order must accompany order. **Other
information:** Based on computer printout supplied by the National
Clearinghouse on Mental Health Information of the National Institute
for Mental Health.

★3749★
ANNUAL INDEX FOUNDATION REPORTS [Maryland]
Maryland Attorney General's Office
One S. Calvert Street   Phone: (301) 383-3737
Baltimore, MD 21202
Number of listings: 275. **Entries include:** Foundation name, address,
employer identification number, foundation manager, assets.
Additional information available for personal research in files.

Arrangement: Alphabetical. **Frequency:** Photocopies prepared from current records as need arises. Records include Internal Revenue Service forms 990-PF and 990-AR for preceding or second preceding year. **Price:** $5.00 photocopy fee, payment with order.

★3750★
ANNUAL REGISTER OF GRANT SUPPORT
Marquis Academic Media
Marquis Who's Who, Inc.
200 E. Ohio Street   Phone: (312) 787-2008
Chicago, IL 60611
Covers: 2,400 current grant programs offered by government agencies, private foundations, educational and professional associations, corporations, unions, church groups and other organizations; special emphasis on programs offering grants to individuals for study, travel, etc. **Entries include:** Organization name, address, and phone; major interests; program names and purposes; nature and amounts of support; eligibility requirements; application instructions; names of persons to whom inquiries are to be submitted. **Arrangement:** By grant purpose (e.g. special populations, humanities, international affairs, etc.). **Indexes:** Subject, organization and program, geographical, and personnel. **Pages** (approx.): 750. **Frequency:** Annual, fall. **Price:** $57.50, plus $2.50 shipping.

★3751★
**APPROPRIATE TECHNOLOGIES FOR THIRD WORLD
    DEVELOPMENT**
St. Martin's Press
175 Fifth Avenue   Phone: (212) 674-5151
New York, NY 10010
Publication includes: List of participants in conference held by the International Economic Association, Teheran, Iran, September 18-23, 1976. **Entries include:** Name, affiliation, address. **Pages** (approx.): 440. **Frequency:** Published 1979. **Editor:** Austin Robinson. **Price:** $32.50. **Other information:** Book is primarily devoted to proceedings of the conference.

★3752★
**APPROPRIATE TECHNOLOGY—A DIRECTORY OF ACTIVITIES AND
    PROJECTS**
National Science Foundation
1800 G Street, N. W., Room 1108   Phone: (202) 634-4333
Washington, DC 20550
Covers: 325 groups, organizations, institutions, etc., concerned with developing simple, low-cost, labor intensive, and decentralized intermediate, or appropriate, technology for use in developing countries and in alternate life styles in urbanized nations. Also lists resource groups in Washington, DC. **Entries include:** Group or project name and address, 75-100 word description of activities. **Arrangement:** Classified by principal interest. **Pages** (approx.): 70. **Frequency:** Irregular; latest edition April 1977. **Editors:** Edward Bryan, Robert Lamson. **Former title:** Directory of Appropriate Technology. **Price:** Free. **Other information:** A Project of National Science Foundation/Research Applied to National Needs.

★3753★
ARCHITECTURAL BARRIERS REMOVAL
Office for Handicapped Individuals
Health, Education, and Welfare Department
Washington, DC 20201
Covers: About 10 national organizations and agencies concerned with architectural barriers which hamper mobility of handicapped persons; also covers sources of funding for their removal, for barrier-free design research, etc. **Entries include:** Organization or agency name, address, description of publications, activities, services, etc.; listings for fund sources include eligibility information and application procedure. **Frequency:** Published May 1979. **Price:** $2.25 (S/N 017-090-00046-1). **Send orders to:** Government Printing Office, Washington, DC 20402.

★3754★
ARIS FUNDING MESSENGERS [Grant alert newspapers]
Academic Research Information System
2330 Clay Street, Suite 205   Phone: (415) 922-8890
San Francisco, CA 94115
Covers: Grant and fellowship programs of the larger foundations and government agencies. Three editions: "Creative Arts and Humanities Report," 8 issues a year, $58; "Social and Natural Sciences Report," 8 issues and 8 supplements a year, $85; "Medical Sciences Report, 8 issues and 8 supplements a year, $85. **Entries include:** Name of funding source, address, program information with particular attention to procedures and deadlines.

★3755★
ASPEN HANDBOOK ON THE MEDIA
Aspen Institute Program on Communications and Society
360 Bryant Street   Phone: (415) 327-2270
Palo Alto, CA 94301
Covers: 700 communications publications; United States, Canadian, overseas, and international organizations; universities and other organizations conducting research; organizations supporting research; media action groups; guides to United States and Canadian government policymaking bodies; communications law courses. **Entries include:** Name of organization, address, names of chief personnel, brief description of activities, services, publications, etc. **Arrangement:** By type of organization (university conducting research, media action group, etc.) and subject of publication (journalism, broadcasting, etc.). **Pages** (approx.): 450. **Frequency:** Biennial, odd years. **Editors:** William L. Rivers, Wallace Thompson, and Michael J. Nyhan. **Price:** $8.95.

★3756★
ASSOCIATED PRESS CALENDAR [Washington, D. C., events]
Associated Press
2021 K Street, N. W.   Phone: (202) 833-5300
Washington, DC 20006
Covers: Press conferences, meetings, hearings, etc., to occur during the following 24-36 hours in the Washington, D. C., area which are expected to have newsworthy aspects. **Entries include:** Place, time, names of persons or organizations involved, nature of event, etc. **Frequency:** Twice daily, via teletype to subscribers in the Washington area. **Editor:** John Wilson. (Also see separate DOD entry for United Press International Daybook.)

★3757★
**ASSOCIATION FOR WORLD EDUCATION—DIRECTORY OF
    MEMBER INSTITUTIONS**
Association for World Education
Box 589   Phone: (516) 423-9641
Huntington, NY 11743
Covers: 400 member institutions throughout the world concerned with education in areas affecting development, peace, and social justice. **Entries include:** Institution name, address, and international education programs and activities. **Arrangement:** Geographical. **Pages** (approx.): 50. **Frequency:** Irregular; latest edition 1976, 1977 supplement. **Editor:** Leah R. Karpen. **Price:** $1.50.

★3758★
ASSOCIATION HANDBOOK OF METROPOLITAN WASHINGTON
Metropolitan Washington Board of Trade
1129 20th Street, N. W., Suite 200
Washington, DC 20036
Covers: 1,800 national, regional, and local associations with headquarters in the metropolitan area. **Entries include:** Association name, address, phone, name of principal officer, year founded, scope, staff size, memberships, annual operating budget. **Arrangement:** Alphabetical. **Price:** $15.00.

★3759★

ASSOCIATION OF INTERNATIONAL COLLEGES AND UNIVERSITIES—DIRECTORY

International University Press
501 E. Armour Boulevard   Phone: (816) 231-5177
Kansas City, MO 64109
Covers: About 275 individuals, organizations, and institutions active in international education and exchange of information. **Entries include:** Name, address; organization listings include number of members. **Arrangement:** Alphabetical. **Pages** (approx.): 50. **Frequency:** Annual, December. **Editor:** Dr. John Wayne Johnston. **Advertising accepted.** Circulation 1,000. **Price:** $10.00.

★3760★

ASSOCIATIONS OF THE DELAWARE VALLEY [Pennsylvania, New Jersey, Delaware]

Greater Philadelphia Chamber of Commerce
1617 J. F. Kennedy Boulevard   Phone: (215) 568-4040
Philadelphia, PA 19103
Covers: 650 businessmen's, chamber of commerce, civic, cultural, economic development, professional, service, trade, and women's groups. **Entries include:** Organization name and its address, phone and executive director, if so organized, with names of president and secretary; for smaller organizations, officers' names and address of secretary. **Arrangement:** Classified by type of organization. **Indexes:** Alphabetical, keyword. **Frequency:** Irregular; previous edition June 1978; latest edition September 1979. **Editor:** Robert S. Barr, Research Director. **Price:** $12.19, postpaid, payment with order. **Other information:** Issued by PENJERDEL Corporation, regional affiliate of the Chamber's publication bureau.

★3761★

AYER DIRECTORY OF PUBLICATIONS

Ayer Press
210 W. Washington Square
Philadelphia, PA 19106
Covers: Over 22,000 magazines and newspapers in a single geographical arrangement; also, in separate geographical groups with abbreviated information, lists of newspaper feature editors; agricultural, college, foreign language, Jewish, Black, fraternal, religious, and trade publications; general magazines; newspapers. **Entries include:** Publication name, address, phone, names of editor, publisher, and national advertising manager, base advertising rate, page specifications, subscription rate, circulation, frequency. **Arrangement:** Geographical. **Indexes:** Title. **Pages** (approx.): 1,250. **Frequency:** Annual, March. **Editor:** William J. Luedke, Publisher. **Price:** $59.00, plus $1.50 shipping.

★3762★

AYER PUBLIC RELATIONS & PUBLICITY STYLEBOOK

Ayer Press
One Bala Avenue   Phone: (215) 664-6205
Bala Cynwyd, PA 19004
Publication includes: List of feature editors of newspapers with circulation over 100,000. **Entries include:** Editor name, paper name, address, phone, circulation. **Arrangement:** Geographical. **Frequency:** Irregular; latest edition 1979. **Price:** $11.95, plus 90¢ shipping. **Other information:** Principal content is information on public relations and journalistic style.

★3763★

BAY AREA MEN'S RESOURCE CATALOG [California]

Bay Area Men's Resource Catalog Collective
Box 6072
San Francisco, CA 94110
Covers: 200 resources in San Francisco Bay area providing low-cost and alternative services for men. **Arrangement:** By subject (Aging, Counseling and Therapy, Health, Media, Men's Movement, Military, Parenting/Children, etc.). **Pages** (approx.): 60. **Frequency:** Irregular; latest edition December 1978; new edition expected June 1980. **Editors:** C. Piller, M. Massmiller, D. Chillcott. **Advertising accepted.**

Circulation 2,500. **Price:** $1.50, plus 50¢ shipping (current and 1980 editions).

★3764★

BOSTON PEOPLE'S YELLOW PAGES

Vocations for Social Change
107 South Street   Phone: (617) 423-1621
Boston, MA 02111
Covers: 1,400 social service/social change groups in Boston. **Entries include:** Name of group, address, phone, hours, brief description. **Arrangement:** By subject (Aging, Children, Political Action, etc.). **Pages** (approx.): 200. **Frequency:** Irregular; latest edition 1976 with 1977 supplement; new edition expected spring 1980. **Price:** $2.60 (1976 edition and supplement), payment with order. **Other information:** This People's Yellow Pages was the first widely known publication of this type, and in many ways a model for those which have followed.

★3765★

BUFFALO AREA CHAMBER OF COMMERCE—SPEAKERS/MEDIA

Buffalo Area Chamber of Commerce
107 Delaware Avenue   Phone: (716) 849-6677
Buffalo, NY 14202
Covers: Speakers in the western New York area from a variety of organizations and companies; daily and weekly newspapers, shopping news, college and business newspapers and newsletters; and radio and television broadcasting stations in the western New York area. **Entries include:** For speakers - Topic, title of lecture, whether visual aids are available, fees, name of speaker, and name, address, and phone of organization or company. For daily and weekly newspapers and shopping news - Title, name, address, and phone of publisher, name of editor, geographic area included in circulation or group. For other publications - Publisher name, address, phone, name of editor, title. For broadcasting stations - Call letters, channel, address, phone, names and titles of key personnel. **Arrangement:** Speakers are by topic, others are by type of media. **Pages** (approx.): 40. **Frequency:** Annual, winter. **Price:** $5.00, plus $1.00 shipping.

Business and Civic Organizations Directory [Buffalo, New York]
See **Directory of Western New York Business and Civic Organizations**

★3766★

CALIFORNIA & NEVADA LSC LEGAL SERVICES PROGRAMS DIRECTORY

Western Center on Law and Poverty
3535 W. Sixth Street   Phone: (213) 487-7211
Los Angeles, CA 90020
Covers: Agencies offering legal counsel and representation to persons unable to afford conventional services, and to groups whose activities may cause change in institutions affecting the poor. **Entries include:** Agency name; address; phone; names and titles of staff. **Arrangement:** Geographical. **Pages** (approx.): 55. **Frequency:** Every four months. **Editor:** Dorothy A. Huff. **Price:** $6.50.

★3767★

CALIFORNIA AND THE WORLD: A DIRECTORY OF CALIFORNIA ORGANIZATIONS CONCERNED WITH INTERNATIONAL AFFAIRS

California Institute of Public Affairs
226 W. Foothill Boulevard   Phone: (714) 624-5212
Claremont, CA 91711
Covers: About 550 governmental agencies and private associations, foundations, and university programs that are concerned with international relations and are located in California. **Entries include:** Organization or agency name, address, phone; description of activities; publications; name of contact. **Arrangement:** Alphabetical. **Indexes:** Subject, geographical. **Pages** (approx.): 70. **Frequency:** Not established; first edition January 1979. **Price:** $12.00, plus $1.00 shipping.

California Environment Yearbook & Directory *See* California Environmental Directory

★3768★

CALIFORNIA ENVIRONMENTAL DIRECTORY: A GUIDE TO ORGANIZATIONS AND RESOURCES

California Institute of Public Affairs

226 W. Foothill Boulevard   Phone: (714) 624-5212
Claremont, CA 91711

Covers: 1,300 organizations in California concerned with environmental quality. **Entries include:** Name, address, phone, description of activities and structure. **Arrangement:** By type of organization (state agency, research and educational organization, etc.). **Pages** (approx.): 170. **Frequency:** Irregular; latest edition 1977; new edition possible 1980. **Former title:** California Environment Yearbook & Directory. **Price:** $16.75, plus $1.00 shipping.

★3769★

CAMPUS CO-OP DIRECTORY

North American Student Cooperative Organization

Box 7293   Phone: (313) 663-0889
Ann Arbor, MI 48107

Covers: 450 student cooperatives in the United States and Canada, except food cooperatives, which are now included in the "Food Co-op Directory" (see separate listing). Lists housing, bookstore, and miscellaneous service cooperatives, and federations of individual cooperatives. **Entries include:** Name, address, type of cooperatives (housing, etc.), restrictions on membership or service (if any), and whether school-owned and/or managed. **Arrangement:** Geographical by state/province, then by Zip code. **Pages** (approx.): 30. **Frequency:** Biennial, November of odd years. **Editor:** Margaret Lamb. **Former title:** Directory of Campus Cooperatives in North America. **Price:** $1.50.

★3770★

CATALOG: METROPOLITAN YOUTH RESOURCES [Minneapolis-St. Paul]

Enablers, Inc.

Wright Building, No. 320
2233 University   Phone: (612) 647-0711
St. Paul, MN 55114

Covers: 400 social service agencies in the seven-county Minneapolis-St. Paul area which serve youth (aged 6-25) and their families. **Entries include:** Name of agency, services provided, days and hours, ages and neighborhoods served, Board of Directors, funding sources, budget, size of staff. **Arrangement:** By 16 primary service categories (Chemical Dependency, Corrections, Counseling, etc.). **Indexes:** Alphabetical, geographical, subject. **Pages** (approx.): 200. **Frequency:** Irregular; latest edition fall 1978. **Editor:** Joan Hummel, Information Coordinator. **Price:** $8.00.

★3771★

CATALOG OF FEDERAL PROGRAMS RELATED TO COMMUNITY EDUCATION

Office of Education

Health, Education, and Welfare Department
Washington, DC 20202

Covers: Federal programs available for support of community education and related activities to enable citizens to identify their own needs and problems. **Entries include:** Program title, administering agency office address and phone, regional offices where guidelines may be obtained, purpose of grant, target populations, federal funds available, grant restrictions, and application suggestions. **Arrangement:** By agency. **Indexes:** Subject, Catalog of Domestic Assistance number and title, program number by category and by federal agency. **Pages** (approx.): 190. **Frequency:** Has been biennial, odd years; no new edition planned. **Price:** $3.75 (S/N 017-080-01774-1). **Send orders to:** Government Printing Office, Washington, DC 20402.

★3772★

CENSORED

Bayliss Corbett

Box 1526
Bonita Springs, FL 33923

Covers: 500 publishers of periodicals, booksellers, and organizations which are sources of news and background on domestic and international affairs. Mostly pro-freedom viewpoints range from religious-conservative to libertarian-rightist; many are scholarly and non-ideological. **Entries include:** Title or organization name, address, brief description of publication. **Arrangement:** By organization type or special interest/geographic area. **Pages** (approx.): 35. **Frequency:** Irregular; latest edition November 1978. **Editor:** Bayliss Corbett, Publisher. **Former title:** Some Hard-to-Locate Sources of Information on Current Affairs. **Price:** $7.00, postpaid, payment with order (ISSN 0163-2280).

★3773★

CHAMBERS OF COMMERCE & CIVIC AGENCIES, TRADE & PROFESSIONAL ORGANIZATIONS, WOMEN'S ORGANIZATIONS [Pittsburgh, Pennsylvania]

Greater Pittsburgh Chamber of Commerce

411 Seventh Avenue   Phone: (412) 391-3400
Pittsburgh, PA 15219

Number of listings: 100 chambers of commerce and civic agencies, 190 trade and professional organizations, and 30 women's organizations in the greater Pittsburgh area. **Entries include:** Organization name, address, phone; name of director; names, addresses, and phone numbers for president and secretary if there is no formal office for the association. **Arrangement:** Alphabetical within above groups. **Pages** (approx.): 100. **Frequency:** Irregular; latest edition 1978; new edition expected February 1980. **Price:** $5.00. **Other information:** 1980 title, "Organizations Directory."

★3774★

CHARITABLE FOUNDATIONS DIRECTORY OF OHIO

Charitable Foundations Section

Ohio Attorney General's Office
30 E. Broad Street, 15th Floor   Phone: (614) 466-3180
Columbus, OH 43215

Covers: 3,500 charitable organizations and trusts registered in Ohio. **Entries include:** Foundation name, address, contact person, phone number, restrictions, purpose of trust, amount of assets, trust number, and total amount of grants given. **Arrangement:** Alphabetical. **Indexes:** Geographic, purpose of grant. **Pages** (approx.): 140. **Frequency:** Irregular; latest edition 1977; new edition possible 1980. **Editor:** Susan Boone, Accountant. **Price:** $4.00 (current edition); $5.00 (tentative, 1980 edition).

★3775★

CHARITABLE TRUST DIRECTORY [Washington State]

Washington Attorney General's Office

Temple of Justice
Olympia, WA 98504

Number of listings: 460. **Arrangement:** Alphabetical. **Pages** (approx.): 100. **Frequency:** Annual; published mid-year for previous year. Based on records in the attorney general's office. **Editor:** Jeanette Dieckman, Administrative Assistant. **Price:** $3.00, payment with order.

★3776★

CHILD ABUSE AND NEGLECT

Lexington Books, Division

D. C. Heath & Company
125 Spring Street   Phone: (617) 862-6650
Lexington, MA 02173

Publication includes: List of social agencies concerned with child abuse. **Entries include:** Agency name, address. **Arrangement:** Geographical. **Frequency:** Published spring 1978. **Price:** $25.00. **Other information:** Full title of this monograph by Joseph J. Costa and Gordon K. Nelson is, "Child Abuse and Neglect: Legislation, Reporting, and Prevention."

★3777★

CHILD ABUSE AND NEGLECT PROGRAMS
National Center on Child Abuse and Neglect
Health, Education and Welfare Department
Box 1182
Washington, DC 20013
Covers: More than 2,200 private and public service-oriented child abuse and neglect programs; 10 regional editions. Entries include: Name and address of parent organization, name of child abuse program, name of contact, description of services, staffing, organization, and funding. Arrangement: By state, then alphabetical by organization name. Indexes: Director name, organization name, subject. Frequency: Irregular; previous edition March 1978; latest edition summer 1979. Price: Free.

★3778★

CHILD WELFARE LEAGUE OF AMERICA—DIRECTORY OF MEMBER
    AGENCIES AND ASSOCIATES
Child Welfare League of America
67 Irving Place   Phone: (212) 254-7410
New York, NY 10003
Covers: Provisional, accredited, and general members and associates. Includes member agencies of the Florence Crittenton Division. Entries include: Agency name, address, phone number, name of executive director, list of services, indicates if public or voluntary. Arrangement: Geographical. Frequency: Annual, January. Editor: Arlene W. Stern, Director of Publications. Price: $8.00.

Christian Movement for Peace International Work Camps See A
    Unique Encounter [Christian work camps]

★3779★

CITIZENS MEDIA DIRECTORY
National Citizens Committee for Broadcasting
1530 P Street, N. W.   Phone: (202) 462-2520
Washington, DC 20005
Covers: 400 national and local media reform groups, public access centers, community radio stations, alternative news services, film and video producers, distributors, and film and video services. Entries include: Name, address, and phone. Some sections also list contact persons, brief description of the group. Arrangement: By type of group or business. Pages (approx.): 170. Frequency: Irregular; 1979 supplement. Editor: Pamela Draves, Intern. Price: $7.50.

★3780★

CIVITAN INTERNATIONAL—CLUB DIRECTORY
Civitan International
Box 2102   Phone: (205) 591-8910
Birmingham, AL 35201
Covers: 1,000 clubs in the United States and abroad. Entries include: Club name, name and address of president and secretary, day and place of meeting. Arrangement: Geographical. Pages (approx.): 75. Frequency: Annual. Price: Available to members only.

★3781★

CLEARINGHOUSE FOR HUMANE EDUCATION MATERIALS [A
    directory]
American Humane Association
5251 S. Roslyn Street   Phone: (303) 779-1400
Englewood, CO 80111
Covers: About 90 agencies, societies, etc., which publish materials for use in public education in humane treatment of animals. Entries include: Source name, address, description of materials published. Arrangement: Geographical. Indexes: Subject, source, film. Pages (approx.): 350. Frequency: Irregular; latest edition 1978; new edition expected 1981. Editor: Jill Williams, Associate Director, Research and Education. Price: $14.50, payment with order.

★3782★

CLUBS AND ORGANIZATIONS DIRECTORY [Gardena Valley,
    California]
Gardena Valley Chamber of Commerce
1551 W. Redondo Beach Boulevard   Phone: (213) 532-9905
Gardena, CA 90247
Covers: About 200 clubs, associations, churches, schools, and parent-teacher organizations in Gardena Valley, California, area. Entries include: Organization name, address, phone, names of president and secretary, time and place of meetings. Arrangement: Alphabetical. Pages (approx.): 15. Frequency: Irregular; latest edition February 1979; new edition expected 1980. Editor: Anita E. Bell, Secretary/General Manager. Price: $3.00.

★3783★

COLLEGE WOMEN'S MARKET [Advertising]
Charles D. Oliver Company
38 Witch Lane   Phone: (203) 853-0051
Rowayton, CT 06853
Covers: Colleges with predominantly female student populations. Entries include: College name, address, and campus radio stations, youth marketing firms, and daily newspapers. Arrangement: Geographical. Pages (approx.): 40. Frequency: Annual, fall. Editor: Charles Oliver, Publisher. Price: $50.00, payment with order. (Not verified)

★3784★

COLLEGES AND UNIVERSITIES WITH ACCREDITED
    UNDERGRADUATE SOCIAL WORK PROGRAMS
Council on Social Work Education
345 E. 46th Street   Phone: (212) 697-0467
New York, NY 10017
Number of listings: 265. Entries include: Name of school, social work department name and address, name of contact, phone, year of accreditation, year of next review. Arrangement: Geographical within accreditation and candidacy categories. Pages (approx.): 20. Frequency: Annual, July. Editor: A. Stamm, Director of Accreditation. Price: Single copies free.

★3785★

COLLEGE/UNIVERSITY MEDIA SURVEY—A GUIDE TO
    ADVERTISING OPPORTUNITIES AT CAMPUS
Charles Oliver Company
38 Witch Lane   Phone: (203) 853-0051
Rowayton, CT 06853
Number of listings: 170. Entries include: College name, address, and campus radio stations, youth marketing firms, and daily newspapers. Arrangement: Geographical. Pages (approx.): 50. Frequency: Annual, summer. Editor: Charles D. Oliver. Price: $35.00, payment with order.

★3786★

COLORADO FOUNDATION DIRECTORY
Junior League of Denver
1805 S. Bellaire
Denver, CO 80222
Number of listings: About 260. Entries include: Foundation name, address, assets, total grants, fields of interest, preferred forms of contact, application information. Pages (approx.): 50. Frequency: Irregular; first edition February 1978 with 1976-77 Colorado Attorney General's office tax data; new edition expected January 1980. Editor: Chris Whitman. Price: $5.50, postpaid, payment with order.

★3787★

COMMITTEE FOR ELIMINATION OF DEATH—PUBLICATIONS/
    ORGANIZATIONS
Committee for Elimination of Death
Box 696
San Marcos, CA 92069
Covers: About 45 associations, institutes, societies, foundations,

movements, agencies that qualify as immortalist or life-extension organizations. **Entries include:** Organization name, address, phone, name of chief executive or contact; some listings include title of periodical or newsletter. **Arrangement:** Alphabetical. **Frequency:** Irregular. **Editor:** A. Stuart Otto, Chairman. **Price:** $1.00. **Also includes:** A bibliography of immortalist and life-extension literature.

★3788★
COMMUNICATION DIRECTORY
Council of Communication Societies
Box 1074   Phone: (301) 953-7100
Silver Spring, MD 20910
Covers: About 380 communication associations; about 85 communication research centers; about 570 colleges and universities offering communication specialties. **Entries include:** For associations and research centers - Name, address, staff, purposes and mission, publications, and (for associations) speaker and meeting data. For colleges and universities - Level of degree or certification. **Arrangement:** Associations and research centers are alphabetical, colleges and universities are geographical. **Indexes:** Subject, personal name. **Pages** (approx.): 185. **Frequency:** Irregular; latest edition 1974; new edition expected 1980. **Editor:** Dr. Vernon M. Root, Executive Director. **Former title:** Directory of Communication Organizations. **Price:** $4.00, payment with order; $8.00, billed (ISSN 0070-5292).

★3789★
COMMUNITIES—DIRECTORY OF INTENTIONAL COMMUNITIES ISSUE
Communities Publication Cooperative
Twin Oaks Community
Box 426   Phone: (703) 894-5126
Louisa, VA 23093
Publication includes: List of about 125 known active intentional communities or communes. **Entries include:** In chart form: Community name, address, year established, number of members, number of acres, style of organization, and details of religion, diet, form of group government, sexual relationships predominating, and whether new members are desired. Brief descriptions of each group are given in a separate section. **Arrangement:** Zip code. **Frequency:** Not established; first publication under this sponsorship January 1978. **Editors:** Chip Coffman, Mikki Wenig, and Jubal. **Advertising accepted. Price:** $2.00. **Other information:** Produced cooperatively with Green Revolution Magazine. Replaces commune directories formerly published separately by each magazine. Cover title of this issue is, "Directory of Intentional Communities."Communities Publication Cooperative issued in 1979 "A Guide to Cooperative Alternatives," which also contains a list of communes; see separate listing.

★3790★
COMMUNITY [Syracuse, New York]
Syracuse Peace Council
924 Burnet Avenue
Syracuse, NY 13203
Covers: Community resources in Onandaga County, New york. (A people's-yellow-pages type of publication.) **Entries include:** Name, address, phone, and other pertinent information. **Arrangement:** By type of resource (crafts, day care, education, etc.). **Pages** (approx.): 60. **Frequency:** Annual, fall. **Price:** $1.00.

Community Grants Resource Catalogue: A Directory of Philanthropic Foundations in...Massachusetts See **Grants Resource Manual [MA]**

★3791★
COMMUNITY JOBS
The Youth Project
1704 R Street, N. W.
Washington, DC 20009
Covers: About 1,500 organizations and agencies per year with open positions in community service projects and other social change programs. **Entries include:** Organization name, address, name of contact, phone; job or internship available and description of duties. **Arrangement:** Geographical. **Pages** (approx.): 25. **Frequency:** Monthly. **Editors:** Doyle Nieman and David Parker, Publishers. **Advertising accepted.** Circulation 2,500. **Price:** $9.00 to individuals; $12.00 to community organizations; $24.00 to institutions; per year.

Community Publication Rates & Data See **Standard Rate & Data Service—Community Publication Rates & Data**

★3792★
COMMUNITY SERVICE DIRECTORY, WICHITA AND SEDGWICK COUNTY [Kansas]
United Way of Wichita/Sedgwick County
Insurance Building   Phone: (913) 267-4327
Wichita, KS 67201
Entries include: Name of agency, address, phone, hours. **Editor:** Arthur Binford, Information and Referral Coordinator. **Former title:** Directory of Community Services; Guide to Social Service Agencies. **Price:** $10.00. **Other information:** Joint project with City of Wichita, Social Rehabilitation Services.

★3793★
COMMUNITY SERVICES MANUAL [Akron, Ohio area]
United Way of Summit County
Box 1260
Akron, OH 44309
Covers: Human service agencies in Summit County, Ohio. **Entries include:** Agency name, address, phone, services. **Price:** $7.50.

★3794★
COMSEARCH PRINTOUTS [Foundation grants]
Foundation Center
888 Seventh Avenue   Phone: (212) 975-1120
New York, NY 10019
Covers: Grants made in latest year for which complete data are available by about 400 of the largest foundations. Based on Foundation Grants Data Bank, and printed out in over 55 subject groupings - medical education, libraries, higher education, special projects, child welfare, etc. **Entries include:** Foundation name, address, amount and date of grant, name and address of recipient, and information on purpose of grant. **Arrangement:** By state, then by foundation name. **Price:** $11.00 per subject for paper copy; $3.00 for microfiche.

★3795★
CONSERVATION DIRECTORY
National Wildlife Federation
1412 16th Street, N. W.   Phone: (202) 483-1550
Washington, DC 20036
Covers: About 100 federal agencies, 300 national and international organizations, 1,030 state government agencies and citizens groups, and 70 Canadian agencies and groups concerned with conservation of natural resources and preservation of the environment; colleges and universities with environmental education programs are also listed. **Entries include:** Agency name, address, addresses of branches or subsidiary units, names of personnel (often, several names and titles are given), publications, and description of interests and activities. **Arrangement:** Classified. **Indexes:** Personal name. **Pages** (approx.): 270. **Frequency:** Annual, January. **Editor:** Jeannette Bryant. **Price:** $4.00, payment must accompany individuals' orders (current and 1980 editions). **Also includes:** List of National Wildlife Refuges, National Forests, and National Seashores.

★3796★
CONSUMER COMPLAINT GUIDE
Macmillan Information, Division
Macmillan, Inc.
866 Third Avenue   Phone: (212) 935-2000
New York, NY 10022
Covers: Over 8,000 companies. **Entries include:** Company name, address, phone, name of person responsible for consumer complaints. **Arrangement:** Alphabetical. **Pages** (approx.): 470. **Author:** Joseph Rosenbloom. **Price:** $12.50, cloth; $5.95, paper. **Also includes:** Information on guarantees and warranties, suggestions for making complaints, etc.

Consumer Magazine and Farm Publication Rates & Data *See* Standard Rate & Data Service—Consumer Magazine and Farm Publication Rates...

★3797★
CONSUMER SOURCEBOOK
Gale Research Company
Book Tower   Phone: (313) 961-2242
Detroit, MI 48226
Covers: Federal, state, and city agencies providing aid and information to the consumer in such areas as consumer finance, health, safety, environmental concerns, social welfare, law, product safety and reliability, etc.; non-governmental associations, centers, institutes, etc., active in consumer affairs; newspaper, radio, and television features concerned with consumerism; and more than 17,000 large and small companies manufacturing or distributing consumer goods. **Entries include:** Agency, association, and media listings include name, address, and, where needed, note on interests; some entries include names of contacts. Company listings include company name, address, product; company section includes brand name cross-references. **Indexes:** Organization, personnel, publications. **Pages** (approx.): 1,600 pages (two volumes). **Frequency:** Irregular; previous edition 1974; latest edition summer 1978. **Editors:** Paul Wasserman and Jean Morgan. **Price:** $58.00.

★3798★
CONSUMERS DIRECTORY
International Organization of Consumers Unions
9 Emmastraat
2595EG The Hague, Netherlands
Covers: 200 international, national and principal local consumer organizations in 55 countries. Also covers intergovernmental and national government bodies and agencies with a direct and continuing role in consumer protection. **Entries include:** Organization or agency name, address, date founded, aims, activities, publications, membership, finances, and principal officers. **Arrangement:** Geographical. **Pages** (approx.): 200. **Frequency:** Biennial; latest edition 1978; new edition expected early 1980. **Price:** Dfl. 25.00 (current edition); Dfl. 30.00 (1980 edition).

★3799★
CONSUMER'S RESOURCE HANDBOOK
Office of Consumer Affairs
Health, Education, and Welfare Department   Phone: (202) 755-8875
Washington, DC 20201
Publication includes: A complaint handling section, a guide to federal consumer services, and a directory of state and local consumer offices. **Frequency:** Not established; first edition November 1979. **Price:** Free. **Send orders to:** Consumer Information Center, Department 532G, Pueblo, CO 81009.

★3800★
CONTACTS—SOCIAL, BUSINESS, EDUCATIONAL, RECREATIONAL
  [New York metro area]
Venture Publishing Company
155 W. 72nd Street   Phone: (212) 873-7580
New York, NY 10023
Covers: Several hundred clubs, societies, and organizations in the New York metropolitan area. **Entries include:** Organization name, address, phone, description of activities. **Arrangement:** By activity (sports and recreation, arts and culture, etc.). **Indexes:** Subject, organization name. **Pages** (approx.): 125. **Frequency:** Not established; first edition September 1979. **Editor:** Howard E. Fischer. **Price:** $10.95, postpaid, payment with order.

Continental Association of Funeral and Memorial Societies—Roster *See* Manual of Death Education and Simple Burial; *also in* Funeral and Memorial Societies

★3801★
CO-OPERATIVE DIRECTORY
Co-Operative Directory Association
Box 4218   Phone: (505) 247-3278
Albuquerque, NM 87196
Covers: 4,000 food co-ops, co-op warehouses, collective nonprofit bakeries and restaurants, mills, truckers, co-op storefronts, and other cooperatives (including banks, factories, information centers, educational programs) in the United States and Canada. **Entries include:** Co-op name, address, and phone, with key indicating type of co-op facility, products. Many entries also include name of contact. **Arrangement:** Regional warehouses and groups listed separately. Local co-ops listed by Zip code within state. **Pages** (approx.): 130. **Frequency:** Annual, fall. **Advertising accepted.** Circulation 13,000. **Former title:** Food Co-Op Directory (1979). **Price:** $4.00 to individuals; $7.00 to others; payment with order. **Other information:** Non-food cooperative projects were included for the first time in the 1979 edition.

★3802★
CRISIS BULLETIN—EMERGENCY AFTER-HOURS FACILITIES [Los Angeles County]
Information and Referral Service of Los Angeles County
621 S. Virgil Avenue   Phone: (213) 736-1300
Los Angeles, CA 90005
Covers: 409 voluntary and tax-supported health and welfare services available from 5 P.M. to 8 A.M. and on weekends and holidays in Los Angeles County. Reports on sources for help with 31 different problems from "alchoholism" to "welfare." **Entries include:** Name of agency, address, after-hours phone, hours of service, and brief description of service provided. **Arrangement:** Law enforcement and medical emergency sections are geographical, others are alphabetical by agency name. **Pages** (approx.): 95. **Frequency:** Irregular; latest edition June 1979. **Editor:** Dona Clark. **Price:** $5.00, postpaid, payment with order.

★3803★
CUE MEDIA GUIDE [Oregon]
Center for Urban Education
0245 S. W. Bancroft   Phone: (503) 221-0984
Portland, OR 97201
Covers: Oregon newspapers; radio and television stations; special interest periodicals, newsletters, and little magazines; government publications; Indian publications. **Entries include:** Medium name, address, phone; for broadcast media, channel or frequency, licensee, coverage, hours, principal personnel, information on community service programming; for print media, owner, frequency, circulation, coverage, personnel. **Arrangement:** By regions of the state. **Indexes:** City. **Pages** (approx.): 65. **Frequency:** Irregular; latest edition fall 1979. **Editor:** Rhoda Epstein. **Price:** $5.00, plus 50¢ shipping. **Other information:** Update for Portland area only expected spring 1980.

★3804★

CUMULATIVE LIST OF ORGANIZATIONS... [Internal Revenue Service]
Office of Employee Plans and Exempt Organizations
Internal Revenue Service
Treasury Department
1111 Constitution Avenue, N. W.
Washington, DC 20224
Description: Complete title is, "Cumulative List of Organizations Described in Section 170 (c) of the Internal Revenue Code of 1954" (i.e., organizations to which contributions have been determined by the Internal Revenue Service to be deductible from income for federal tax purposes). About 186,000 such organizations are listed; individual religious congregations or other subordinate groups under a central organization holding an exemption letter are not listed separately. **Entries include:** Organization name, city, state; may also include a code indicating that the group listed is a central organization, a private foundation or other group with limited deductibility, etc. **Arrangement:** Alphabetical. **Pages** (approx.): 1,200. **Frequency:** Annual, with three quarterly supplements. **Price:** $14.00 per year, including supplements (current and 1980 editions; T 22.2:Or 3/980: ISSN 0499-6453). **Send orders to:** Government Printing Office, Washington, DC 20402.

★3805★

DEVELOPMENT DIRECTORY—HUMAN RESOURCE MANAGEMENT
Advanced Personnel Systems
756 Lois Avenue   Phone: (406) 736-2433
Sunnyvale, CA 94087
Covers: About 250 organizations which offer about 900 seminars and conferences relating to personnel management, labor relations, training and development, etc. **Entries include:** Seminar title, sponsor, instructor, dates, locations, subject descriptors, cost, and address and phone for additional information. **Indexes:** Subject. **Frequency:** Semiannual; bimonthly supplements. **Editor:** Richard B. Frantzreb, Editor and Publisher. **Price:** $95.00 per year.

★3806★

DIRECTORY: INNOVATIVE DEVELOPMENTS IN AGING
Project IDEA
Department of Social & Behavioral Sciences
University of California-San Francisco
3835 Mission Street   Phone: (415) 666-3236
San Francisco, CA 94110
Covers: About 800 programs for the aging throughout the United States; limited to programs which include distinctive new features; appendixes list state and local agencies and additional information resources for the aging and in gerontology. **Entries include:** Agency or organization name, address, and name of contact person; description of program, including goals, activities, advocates, geographic area and target population, funding sources, current status of program. **Arrangement:** By major subject within separate volumes for state level data and for local level data. **Indexes:** Keyword. **Pages** (approx.): 900 (in two volumes). **Frequency:** Irregular; latest state edition August 1979; first local edition February 1979. **Editor:** Tedi Dunn. **Price:** $25.00, plus $2.50 shipping per volume.

★3807★

DIRECTORY—PRIVATE FUNDING FOR RURAL PROGRAMS: FOUNDATIONS AND OTHER PRIVATE SECTOR RESOURCES
National Rural Center
1828 L Street, N. W.
Washington, DC 20036
Covers: About 55 foundations that have provided grants for rural-oriented programs. **Entries include:** Foundation name, address, phone, name of contact, primary interests, rural interests (may include actual grants made), geographic area served, financial data, assets, grants amount paid, number and value range of grants made, whether an annual report is available. **Arrangement:** Alphabetical. **Indexes:** Subject, geographic area served. **Pages** (approx.): 65. **Frequency:** Irregular; latest edition September 1978. **Editor:** Barbara Stephens

Adams. **Price:** $2.00. **Also includes:** Sources of information for additional information, including publishers of foundation directories, trade unions, church organizations, and a list of Foundation Center libraries and collections (all with addresses).

★3808★

DIRECTORY [OF] FEDERALLY FUNDED COMMUNITY MENTAL HEALTH CENTERS
Operations Liaison and Program Analysis Section
National Institute of Mental Health
Public Health Service
Health, Education, and Welfare Department   Phone: (301) 443-4673
Rockville, MD 20857
Number of listings: About 720. **Entries include:** Center name, address, name of director, phone, type of center, whether in a designated poverty area, number and types of grants. **Arrangement:** Geographical. **Pages** (approx.): 65. **Frequency:** Biennial, spring of odd years. **Editor:** Frances H. Premo, Chief. **Price:** $3.50 (S/N 017-024-00952-1). **Send orders to:** Government Printing Office, Washington, DC 20402.

★3809★

DIRECTORY FOR REACHING MINORITY AND WOMEN'S GROUPS
Employment and Training Administration
Labor Department
200 Constitution Avenue, N. W.
Washington, DC 20210
Covers: More than 5,000 federal, state, county, regional, and municipal agencies and organizations active in community action, ethnic services, civil rights, human resource utilization and development, etc., and many organizations in business and the media concerned with improving the economic, social, and education status of minorities and women. **Entries include:** Organization name, address, phone. **Arrangement:** Geographical. **Pages** (approx.): 300. **Frequency:** Irregular; previous edition 1970; latest edition 1979. **Price:** $4.50 (S/N 029-000-00357-2). **Send orders to:** Government Printing Office, Washington, DC 20402.

★3810★

DIRECTORY OF AGENCIES: U.S. VOLUNTARY, INTERNATIONAL VOLUNTARY, INTERGOVERNMENTAL [Social work]
National Association of Social Workers
1425 H Street, Suite 600   Phone: (202) 628-6800
Washington, DC 20005
Number of listings: 300; does not include national governmental agencies. **Entries include:** Agency name, address, date of founding, name of an officer, membership purpose, activities, and publications. **Arrangement:** Alphabetical. **Indexes:** Keyword and subject. **Pages** (approx.): 100. **Frequency:** Irregular; previous edition 1975; latest edition 1978. **Price:** $5.00.

Directory of Appropriate Technology See **Appropriate Technology—A Directory of Activities and Projects**

Directory of Approved Counseling Agencies See **Directory of Counseling Services**

★3811★

DIRECTORY OF BETTER BUSINESS BUREAUS
Council of Better Business Bureaus
1150 17th Street, N. W.   Phone: (202) 862-1200
Washington, DC 20036
Covers: About 150 Better Business Bureaus in the United States, Canada, Israel, and Venezuela. **Entries include:** Address, phone. **Arrangement:** Geographical. **Pages** (approx.): Leaflet. **Frequency:** Annual, January. **Price:** Single copies free; $5.00 per 100.

Directory of Campus Cooperatives in North America See **Campus Co-Op Directory**

★3812★

DIRECTORY OF CAREER RESOURCES FOR WOMEN

Ready Reference Press
Box 4288
Thousand Oaks, CA 91359
Covers: Associations, agencies, institutions and other organizations of assistance to women in career education and planning. **Entries include:** Organization name, address, phone, purpose and functions, career resources offered (publications, services, programs), special resources offered (scholarships, fellowships, funding, etc.). **Arrangement:** Alphabetical. **Indexes:** Subject, geographical. **Pages (approx.):** 400. **Frequency:** Not established; first edition 1979. **Price:** $37.50.

★3813★

DIRECTORY OF CHARITABLE FUNDS IN NEW HAMPSHIRE

Division of Charitable Trusts
New Hampshire Attorney General's Office
State House Annex
Concord, NH 03301
Number of listings: 400. **Entries include:** Foundation or trust name, address, donor, assets, purpose, date established. **Arrangement:** Alphabetical. **Indexes:** Geographical, subject. Appendix showing grants by fields by each foundation. **Pages (approx.):** 110. **Frequency:** Irregular; third edition June 1976, based on 1974-75 records in the Attorney General's office; annual June supplement. **Price:** $3.00, base edition and current supplement.

★3814★

DIRECTORY OF CHARITABLE ORGANIZATIONS [Pennsylvania]

Pennsylvania Attorney General's Office
Capitol Annex
Harrisburg, PA 17120
Number of listings: 1,200. **Arrangement:** Alphabetical and by purpose; identical information in each part. **Pages (approx.):** 150. **Frequency:** Irregular; latest edition April 1974. Based on records in Attorney General's office. **Price:** Out of print, but widely available in libraries.

★3815★

DIRECTORY OF CLUBS AND ORGANIZATIONS OF UPPER ROCK ISLAND COUNTY [Illinois]

Chamber of Commerce of Upper Rock Island County
622 19th Street   Phone: (309) 762-3661
Moline, IL 61265
Number of listings: 500. **Entries include:** Organization name, name of contact, address, and phone. **Arrangement:** Alphabetical. **Frequency:** Annual, spring/summer. **Price:** $4.00.

Directory of Communication Organizations *See* Communication Directory

★3816★

DIRECTORY OF COMMUNITY CARE FACILITIES [California]

California Department of Social Services
744 P Street   Phone: (916) 445-3284
Sacramento, CA 95814
Covers: Adoption and home finding agencies, residential care facilities for adults and children, preschool care centers, and day care centers located in California and licensed by the California Department of Social Services. Health facilities are not listed. **Entries include:** Facility name, address, phone; name of director or administrator; capacity; license limitations (age, sex, hours of care, etc.). **Arrangement:** By county. **Pages (approx.):** 550. **Frequency:** Annual, March. **Price:** Free. **Also includes:** List of district offices of social services department licensing division for community care facilities; list includes addresses, phone, and counties served.

★3817★

DIRECTORY OF COMMUNITY ORGANIZATIONS IN CHICAGO

Institute of Urban Life
14 E. Chestnut Street   Phone: (312) 787-7525
Chicago, IL 60611
Covers: About 100 organizations having an office and a staff of one or more. **Entries include:** Name of organization, address, names of key executives, phone. **Frequency:** Annual, spring. **Editor:** Mary Schlitz. **Price:** $2.00.

★3818★

DIRECTORY OF COMMUNITY RESOURCES IN KALAMAZOO COUNTY [Michigan]

Kalamazoo Public Library
315 S. Rose Street   Phone: (616) 342-9837
Kalamazoo, MI 49006
Covers: Over 300 sources of health and medical care, financial and other aid for needy people, services for special groups (handicapped, drop-outs, aged, etc.), counseling, and other community aids. **Entries include:** Source name, address, phone, office hours, name of chief staff member, goal, services, eligibility, how to contact, geographic area served, source of financial support, and by whom licensed (where applicable). **Arrangement:** Alphabetical. **Indexes:** Subject. **Pages (approx.):** 75. **Frequency:** Irregular; latest edition 1976; new edition expected 1980. **Editor:** Mabel Stenesh, Head, Reference Division. **Price:** $1.75 (1976 edition).

★3819★

DIRECTORY OF COMMUNITY SERVICES: THE BRONX, MANHATTAN, AND STATEN ISLAND

Office of Adult Services
The New York Public Library
8 E. 40th Street   Phone: (212) 790-6451
New York, NY 10016
Covers: Over 2,500 organizations and groups which offer programs and services at a neighborhood level; included are community and citizens' groups, and educational, cultural, recreational, and social service agencies. **Entries include:** Name, address, phone, description of services, hours of operation, fees, name of contact. **Arrangement:** Alphabetical. **Indexes:** Subject (English and Spanish). **Pages (approx.):** 500 per volume (English and Spanish volumes). **Frequency:** Annual, fall. **Editor:** Beth E. Waldis, Community Information Project. **Price:** $40.00, plus $2.00 shipping, payment with order.

Directory of Community Services [Wichita, Kansas] *See* Community Service Directory, Wichita and Sedgwick County [Kansas]

★3820★

DIRECTORY OF CONSERVATIVE AND LIBERTARIAN SERIALS, PUBLISHERS, AND FREELANCE MARKETS

Dennis D. Murphy
3404 N. Romero Road
Tuscon, AZ 85705
Covers: About 200 conservative or libertarian serials and publishers. Specifically excludes racist or antisemitic organizations and publications. **Entries include:** Publication name, address, frequency, price, and description. Codes indicate free lance policies. **Arrangement:** Alphabetical. **Indexes:** Subject. **Pages (approx.):** 65. **Frequency:** Not established; previous edition 1977; latest edition 1979. **Editor:** Dennis D. Murphy. **Price:** $4.95, plus 75¢ shipping, payment must accompany individuals' orders (ISSN 0149-7847).

★3821★

DIRECTORY OF CONSULTANT SERVICES FOR COMMUNITY ACTION AGENCIES

National Center for Community Action
1328 New York Avenue, N. W.   Phone: (202) 667-8970
Washington, DC 20005
Covers: About 90 consultants in varying fields who have been recommended by community action agencies nationwide to the

National Center for Community Action. **Entries include:** Firm name, address, phone, field of specialization, and name of community action agency representative making recommendation. **Arrangement:** Geographical. **Frequency:** Irregular; latest edition 1977. **Editor:** Carol Valverde. **Price:** $10.00, payment with order.

★3822★

DIRECTORY OF CONSULTANTS FOR THE DEVELOPMENT OF FACILITIES FOR THE AGING

American Association of Homes for the Aging

1050 17th Street, N. W., Suite 770   Phone: (202) 296-5960

Washington, DC 20036

Covers: About 165 housing consultants, planners, architects, and financial advisors who are available on a consulting basis to assist in the development and management of facilities for the elderly. **Entries include:** Firm name or individual name, address, phone, line of business, specialty, services, experiences relevant to the aging (project name) with name, address, and phone of contact. **Arrangement:** Geographical. **Indexes:** Firm/individual name. **Pages** (approx.): 170. **Frequency:** Irregular; latest edition 1977; new edition expected 1981. **Editor:** William D. Hughes, Director, Housing Department. **Price:** $5.00.

★3823★

DIRECTORY OF COUNSELING SERVICES

International Association of Counseling Services

Two Skyline Place, Suite 400

5203 Leesburg Pike   Phone: (703) 820-4710

Falls Church, VA 22041

Covers: 385 member counseling agencies in the United States and Canada that have been or are being evaluated and accredited by the association. **Entries include:** Name, address, phone number, memberships, fee, hours, sponsor, types of counseling, other services offered, clientele, method of applying, director's name and background, number and professions of staff. **Arrangement:** Geographical. **Frequency:** Annual, January. **Editor:** Jean P. Whittaker, Associate Administrative Officer. **Former title:** Directory of Approved Counseling Agencies. **Price:** $6.00.

★3824★

DIRECTORY OF DIOCESAN AGENCIES OF CATHOLIC CHARITIES IN THE UNITED STATES, PUERTO RICO AND CANADA

National Conference of Catholic Charities

1346 Connecticut Avenue, N. W.   Phone: (202) 785-2757

Washington, DC 20036

Covers: Over 600 member community and social service agencies affiliated with the Roman Catholic Church. Listings include Catholic schools of social work, diocesan agencies, and councils and conferences of Catholic organizations. **Entries include:** Organization name, address, name and title of director, phone. **Arrangement:** Geographical within categories of agencies, schools, and conferences. **Pages** (approx.): 75. **Frequency:** Annual, spring. **Price:** $3.50.

Directory of Direct Service Providers [Pennsylvania] *See* **Directory of Human Services in the Delaware Valley [Pennsylvania]**

★3825★

DIRECTORY OF ENVIRONMENTAL GROUPS IN NEW ENGLAND

Office of Public Affairs

Region 1

Environmental Protection Agency

John F. Kennedy Federal Building   Phone: (617) 223-7223

Boston, MA 02203

Covers: About 350 nonprofit organizations concerned with the protection of the environment; listings include health planning agencies, land conservation and acquisition associations and firms, state and federal government agencies, nature centers and clubs, zoos, etc. **Entries include:** Organization or agency name, address, phone, contact person, publications, and description of activities. **Arrangement:** Classified by type of group (government, national,

etc.); local groups are geographical. **Pages** (approx.): 60. **Frequency:** Irregular; latest edition 1979; new edition expected spring 1980. **Editor:** Chris Jendras. **Former title:** Directory of Environmental Organizations for Connecticut, Maine, Massachusetts, New Hampshire, Rhode Island, and Vermont. **Price:** Free.

Directory of Environmental Organizations for CT, ME, MA, NH, RI, and VT *See* **Directory of Environmental Groups in New England**

Directory of Environmental Organizations for Pacific Northwest *See* **Environmental Organizations Directory [Pacific Northwest]**

★3826★

DIRECTORY OF ERDA INFORMATION CENTERS [Energy R&D]

Technical Information Center

Energy Research and Development Administration

Box 62

Oak Ridge, TN 37830

Covers: 30 major information analysis centers and data centers operated by ERDA or its contractors. **Entries include:** Center name, address, phone, name of director, annotation covering scope, sponsors, services, qualified users. **Arrangement:** Alphabetical. **Pages** (approx.): 50. **Frequency:** Irregular; latest edition spring 1977. **Price:** Free (TID-4590).

★3827★

DIRECTORY OF FACULTY DEVELOPMENT PROJECTS IN ENERGY

Education Programs Division

Office of the Assistant Secretary for Intergovernmental and Institutional Re

Energy Department

Washington, DC 20585

Covers: About 75 workshops for teachers conducted by colleges under the sponsorship of the Energy Department. **Entries include:** Workshop name, address or location, cost, dates. **Arrangement:** Geographical. **Pages** (approx.): 20. **Frequency:** Annual. **Price:** Free.

★3828★

DIRECTORY OF FEDERAL CONSUMER OFFICES

Office of Consumer Affairs

Health, Education, and Welfare Department   Phone: (202) 245-6877

Washington, DC 20201

Covers: 65 federal departments and agencies with consumer programs. **Entries include:** Agency and department names, address, and toll-free phones and hot lines. **Arrangement:** Alphabetical by program. **Frequency:** Irregular; latest edition November 1977. **Former title:** Guide to Federal Consumer Services. **Price:** Free. **Send orders to:** 532G, Consumer Information Center, Pueblo, CO 81009.

★3829★

DIRECTORY OF FEDERAL, STATE AND LOCAL GOVERNMENT CONSUMER OFFICES

Office of Consumer Affairs

Health, Education, and Welfare Department   Phone: (202) 755-8875

Washington, DC 20201

Covers: 600 main and branch government consumer affairs offices at federal, state, county, and city level and lists of Federal Information Centers and state public utility commissions. **Entries include:** Name of director, address, phone. **Arrangement:** Geographical. **Pages** (approx.): 30. **Frequency:** Latest edition 1977. **Price:** $2.00 (S/N 017-000-00197- 3). **Send orders to:** Government Printing Office, Washington, DC 20402.

★3830★

DIRECTORY OF FOUNDATIONS AND CHARITABLE TRUSTS REGISTERED IN OREGON

Charitable Trust Section
Oregon Department of Justice
500 Pacific Building
520 S. W. Yamhill   Phone: (503) 229-5278
Portland, OR 97204
Covers: 330 general purpose, grant-making foundations and charitable trusts operating in Oregon. **Entries include:** Address, names of trustees or officers, purpose, and financial data, including assets and amount of grants during last reporting year. **Arrangement:** Alphabetical. **Pages** (approx.): 80. **Frequency:** Irregular; latest edition November 1973; supplement published November 1975. **Editor:** Virgil D. Mills, Administrator of Charitable Trusts. **Former title:** Directory of Charitable Corporations, Foundations, and Trusts Registered in Oregon. **Price:** $5.00.

★3831★

DIRECTORY OF FOUNDATIONS IN MASSACHUSETTS

Division of Public Charities
Massachusetts Department of the Attorney General
One Ashburton Place
Boston, MA 02108
Covers: 725 foundations, primarily those making grants totaling more than $1,000 per year. **Entries include:** Foundation name, address, phone, trustees, financial data, interests, application procedures. **Arrangement:** Divided according to whether grants are primarily to individuals or organizations. **Indexes:** Index-appendixes of grant amounts, geographic restrictions, purposes, loans, non-scholarship loans, scholarships. **Pages** (approx.): 135. **Frequency:** Not established; latest edition September 1977. Based on Internal Revenue Service forms 990-PF and 990-AR from 1975 and data from foundations. **Editor:** Carol Fubini. **Price:** $7.50, plus 50¢ shipping. **Send orders to:** Associated Foundations of Greater Boston, 294 Washington, Rm. 501, Boston, MA 02108 (617-426-2606).

★3832★

DIRECTORY OF FOUNDATIONS IN THE COMMONWEALTH OF MASSACHUSETTS

Eastern Connecticut State College Foundation
Box 431   Phone: (203) 456-3231
Willimantic, CT 06226
Number of listings: 960. Appendixes of initial returns, relocations in Massachusetts, previously existing foundations appearing for the first time, and deleted foundations which appeared in first edition. **Arrangement:** Alphabetical. **Indexes:** Geographical, largest grants. **Pages** (approx.): 160. **Frequency:** Irregular; second edition 1976. Based on Internal Revenue Service forms 990-PF and 990-AR from 1974. **Editor:** John Parker Huber. **Price:** $15.00, payment with order.

★3833★

DIRECTORY OF FOUNDATIONS IN THE STATE OF CONNECTICUT

Eastern Connecticut State College Foundation
Box 431   Phone: (203) 456-3231
Willimantic, CT 06226
Number of listings: 590. Includes lists of relocations and changes. **Arrangement:** Alphabetical. **Indexes:** Geographical, grant purposes, largest single grants. **Pages** (approx.): 170. **Frequency:** Irregular; third edition 1976. Based on Internal Revenue Service forms 990-PF and 990-AR from 1973. **Editor:** John Parker Huber. **Price:** $7.00, payment with order; $8.00, billed.

★3834★

DIRECTORY OF FOUNDATIONS IN THE STATE OF NEW HAMPSHIRE

Eastern Connecticut State College Foundation
Box 431   Phone: (203) 456-3231
Willimantic, CT 06226
Number of listings: 140. **Arrangement:** Alphabetical. **Indexes:** Geographical, interests, asset amount, grant amounts. **Frequency:**

Irregular; second edition 1975. Based on Internal Revenue Service forms 990-PF and 990-AR from 1973. **Editor:** John Parker Huber. **Price:** $5.00, payment with order.

★3835★

DIRECTORY OF FOUNDATIONS IN THE STATE OF VERMONT

Eastern Connecticut State College Foundation
Box 431   Phone: (203) 456-3231
Willimantic, CT 06226
Number of listings: 40. **Arrangement:** Alphabetical. **Indexes:** Geographical, interests, asset amount, grant amounts. **Pages** (approx.): 25. **Frequency:** Irregular; first edition 1975. Based on Internal Revenue Service forms 990-PF and 990-AR from 1972. **Editor:** John Parker Huber. **Price:** $3.00, payment with order.

Directory of Funeral and Memorial Societies *See* Manual of Death Education and Simple Burial

★3836★

DIRECTORY OF HOMOSEXUAL ORGANIZATIONS AND PUBLICATIONS

Homosexual Information Center
6715 Hollywood Boulevard, Suite 210   Phone: (213) 464-8431
Hollywood, CA 90028
Covers: 250 homosexual organizations and publications in United States, Canada, and several foreign countries. **Arrangement:** Geographical. **Indexes:** Organization type (i.e., religious, social, etc.). **Pages** (approx.): 40. **Frequency:** Irregular; latest edition July, 1979. **Editors:** Don Slater and Ursula Enters Copely. **Former title:** Homosexual National Classified Directory (1973). **Price:** $5.00.

Directory of Housing Cooperatives in the United States *See* National Directory of Housing Cooperatives

★3837★

DIRECTORY OF HUMAN SERVICE AGENCIES IN RHODE ISLAND

Council for Community Services
229 Waterman Street   Phone: (401) 361-6500
Providence, RI 02906
Covers: About 700 public and private nonprofit human service agencies and organizations. **Entries include:** Agency name, address, phone, name of contact or director; description of services; hours open; eligibility requirements; ages and geographic area served; fee for service; funding. **Arrangement:** Alphabetical. **Indexes:** Service, alphabetical, government agency. **Pages** (approx.): 350. **Frequency:** Biennial, summer of odd years. **Editor:** Nancy L. Fisher. **Price:** $10.00.

★3838★

DIRECTORY OF HUMAN SERVICES IN THE DELAWARE VALLEY [Pennsylvania]

Community Resource Information Service, Division
Community Services Planning Council of Southeastern Pennsylvania
7 Benjamin Franklin Parkway   Phone: (215) 568-3750
Philadelphia, PA 19103
Covers: About 3,000 health and social services programs providing services directly to clients in the greater Philadelphia, Pennsylvania area. Published in microfiche format with paper and microform indexes. **Entries include:** Service site name, address, purpose, area served, programs, eligibility requirements, costs, waiting times for service intake and delivery, facility accessibility, client conveniences. **Arrangement:** Random. **Indexes:** Site name, geographical, service, KWIC. **Pages** (approx.): 5,000. **Frequency:** Three times yearly, January, May, and September. **Editor:** Thomas F. Deahl, CRIS Director. **Former title:** Directory of Direct Service Providers. **Price:** $300.00 per year (current and 1980 editions).

★3839★
DIRECTORY OF IEC ASSISTANCE AND SERVICES [Family planning]
East-West Communication Institute
East-West Center
1776 East-West Road   Phone: (808) 947-8160
Honolulu, HI 96882
Covers: Organizations in United States and Europe which provide financial and technical assistance for communication activities to family planning programs in developing countries, primarily in Asia. **Entries include:** Organization name, addresses of headquarters and field offices; types of assistance provided, including training programs, financial aid, publications, consultative services, and its interests in population/family planning. **Pages** (approx.): 210. **Frequency:** Irregular; latest edition 1976. **Editor:** Elizabeth Bentzel Buck, Research Associate. **Price:** Free, if sent by surface mail.

Directory of Intentional Communities *See* Communities—
    Directory of Intentional Communities Issue

★3840★
DIRECTORY OF JEWISH FEDERATIONS, WELFARE FUNDS, AND
    COMMUNITY COUNCILS
Council of Jewish Federations
575 Lexington Avenue   Phone: (212) 751-1311
New York, NY 10022
Number of listings: 230. **Entries include:** Name, address, phone, date of founding, name of president and executive director. **Arrangement:** Geographical. **Frequency:** Annual. **Price:** $5.00.

★3841★
DIRECTORY OF KANSAS ASSOCIATIONS
Kansas Department of Economic Development
503 Kansas Avenue, 6th Floor   Phone: (913) 296-3481
Topeka, KS 66603
Number of listings: About 255. **Entries include:** Association name, composition of membership, number of members, number of paid staff members, name of chief executive, address and phone of headquarters in Kansas, whether an annual meeting is held, and whether a regular publication is available. **Arrangement:** By area of interest (agriculture, business and trade, etc.). **Indexes:** Association name. **Pages** (approx.): 45. **Frequency:** Biennial, spring of odd years. **Editor:** Norman L. Allen. **Price:** Free.

★3842★
DIRECTORY OF KANSAS FOUNDATIONS
Association of Community Arts Councils of Kansas
509-A Kansas Avenue   Phone: (913) 296-4092
Topeka, KS 66603
Number of listings: 255. **Entries include:** Foundation name, address, contact name, names of trustees, phone, assets, areas of interest, geographical area covered, arts-related contributions, range of amounts awarded. **Arrangement:** Alphabetical. **Pages** (approx.): 60. **Frequency:** Latest edition September 1979; biennial updates. **Editor:** Molly Wiseman. **Price:** $5.00, plus 80¢ shipping, payment with order.

★3843★
DIRECTORY OF NATIONAL ORGANIZATIONS CONCERNED WITH
    LAND POLLUTION CONTROL
Freed Publishing Company
Box 1144
F.D.R. Station   Phone: (212) 753-2769
New York, NY 10022
Covers: 400 companies, associations, labor unions, and federal agencies that are conducting efforts to prevent or reduce land pollution in such areas as solid waste management, strip mining, land reclamation, and litter and vandalism. **Entries include:** Organization name, key official to contact, address, phone, and major interests in the field of land pollution control. **Arrangement:** Alphabetical. **Pages** (approx.): 60. **Frequency:** Irregular; latest edition 1974; new edition expected 1980. **Editor:** Laura E. Freed. **Price:** $15.00.

★3844★
DIRECTORY OF NATIONAL TRAFFIC SAFETY ORGANIZATIONS
    with Full Time Field Staffs and Services
National Safety Council
425 N. Michigan Avenue   Phone: (312) 527-4800
Chicago, IL 60611
Covers: 12 organization headquarters and 200 field offices, regional representatives, etc. **Entries include:** Organization name, headquarters address, phone, field staff or state or regional representatives, organizational objectives, publications, and services. **Arrangement:** Geographical. **Pages** (approx.): 30. **Frequency:** Annual, September. **Editor:** Gladys M. Blodgett, Safety Organization Consultant. **Price:** Single copy free to letterhead request.

★3845★
DIRECTORY OF NEW JERSEY FOUNDATIONS
Mitchell Guides
Box 413   Phone: (609) 924-6689
Princeton, NJ 08540
Covers: About 335 foundations with grants in excess of $5,000 per year, and all businesses in New Jersey (not necessarily donors) with over 500 employees. **Entries include:** Foundation name, address, managers' names, financial and grant data. **Pages** (approx.): 90. **Frequency:** Irregular; first edition 1977; new edition expected early 1980. **Editor:** Janet A. Mitchell. **Price:** $20.00, postpaid, payment with order (1980 edition). **Other information:** Now part of series, "Mitchell Guides to Foundations, Corporations, and Their Managers."

★3846★
DIRECTORY OF NEWSPAPER LIBRARIES IN THE UNITED STATES
    AND CANADA
Special Libraries Association
235 Park Avenue, South   Phone: (212) 777-8136
New York, NY 10003
Covers: 300 newspaper libraries and their personnel. **Entries include:** Name of library, address, phone, list of personnel, circulation figures, hours, resources, special collections, and services available. **Arrangement:** Geographical. **Indexes:** Alphabetical, personal name. **Pages** (approx.): 340. **Frequency:** Irregular; latest edition 1976. **Editor:** Grace D. Parch. **Price:** $9.75.

★3847★
DIRECTORY OF NUCLEAR ACTIVISTS
Environmental Action of Colorado
Box 545
La Veta, CO 81055
Covers: 250 persons and organizations opposed to further development of nuclear power and nuclear weapons. **Entries include:** Name of person or organization, address, phone, description of major interests, activities, capabilities, and resources. **Arrangement:** Geographical. **Indexes:** Subject/resource. **Pages** (approx.): 140. **Frequency:** Irregular; latest edition November 1975. **Editor:** Ben Billings, Coordinator. **Price:** $5.00.

★3848★
DIRECTORY OF OKLAHOMA FOUNDATIONS
University of Oklahoma Press
1005 Asp Avenue
Norman, OK 73069
Number of listings: 275. **Arrangement:** Alphabetical. **Indexes:** Foundation grant activities. **Pages** (approx.): 300. **Frequency:** Irregular; latest edition 1974. Based on Internal Revenue Service forms 990-PF and 990-AR from 1971 and 1972. **Editor:** Thomas E. Broce. **Price:** $12.50, cloth; $5.95, paper.

★3849★
DIRECTORY OF ORGANIZATIONS IN BALTIMORE COUNTY
    [Maryland]
Baltimore County Public Library
320 York Road   Phone: (301) 296-8500
Towson, MD 21204
Covers: Over 2,000 organizations including 25 community councils, 290 improvement associations, 500 churches, 180 parent-teacher groups, and other social, volunteer, professional, and trade associations. **Entries include:** Name of organization; name, address, and phone of president or chairman, month of annual election, district, subject interest. **Indexes:** Councilmanic district, subject interest. **Frequency:** Annual. **Editor:** Richard Parsons. **Price:** $4.50, plus 50¢ shipping (February 1980 edition).

★3850★
DIRECTORY OF ORGANIZATIONS IN GREATER LOS ANGELES
    [California]
Institute of Industrial Relations
405 Hilgard Avenue   Phone: (213) 825-9191
Los Angeles, CA 90024
Covers: Both voluntary associations and government and private agencies and services in Los Angeles County. **Entries include:** Organization name, address, phone, names of executives, brief description of activities and services. **Arrangement:** By type of organization, then geographical. **Indexes:** Organization and association name. **Pages** (approx.): 240. **Frequency:** Irregular; previous edition 1976; latest edition September 1979. **Editor:** Paul Bullock, Research Economist. **Former title:** Directory of Organizations in South and East Los Angeles (1973). **Price:** $6.50, postpaid, payment with order.

★3851★
DIRECTORY OF PENNSYLVANIA FOUNDATIONS
Regional Foundation Center
Free Library of Philadelphia
Logan Square   Phone: (215) 686-5423
Philadelphia, PA 19103
Number of listings: About 1,100 foundations with assets over $50,000. **Entries include:** Foundation name, address, names of executives, codes indicating fields of interest, assets, grant amounts with names of recipient organizations, grant application procedures, deadline, requirements. **Arrangement:** By five regions of state. **Pages** (approx.): 305. **Frequency:** Not established; first edition 1978; new edition expected January 1981. **Editor:** S. Damon Kletzien. **Price:** $14.00, postpaid, payment with order.

★3852★
DIRECTORY OF PERSONAL IMAGE CONSULTANTS
Editorial Services Company
1140 Avenue of the Americas   Phone: (212) 354-5025
New York, NY 10036
Covers: About 100 firms which provide counseling in speech and public appearance, dress, personal public relations, and career selection. **Entries include:** Company name, address, phone, teaching methods, fees, experience or background, staff size, principal corporate clients. **Arrangement:** By specialty category. **Indexes:** Geographical. **Frequency:** Annual, winter. **Editor:** Jacqueline Thompson. **Advertising accepted.** Circulation 3,000. **Price:** $10.95, postpaid, payment with order (ISSN 0163-6537).

Directory of Professional Social Workers *See* NASW Professional
    Social Workers Directory

Directory of Professional Writers *See* American Society of
    Journalists and Authors—Directory of Professional Writers

★3853★
DIRECTORY OF PUBLISHING OPPORTUNITIES IN JOURNALS AND
    PERIODICALS
Marquis Academic Media
Marquis Who's Who, Inc.
200 E. Ohio Street   Phone: (312) 787-2008
Chicago, IL 60611
Covers: More than 3,400 scholarly and technical journals. **Entries include:** Publication name, address, phone, names of key staff, submission requirements, subjects and types of material in which interested, payment, etc. **Arrangement:** Classified by general subject area. **Indexes:** Title, subject, publisher/sponsor, personal name. **Pages** (approx.): 725. **Frequency:** Irregular; previous edition 1975; latest edition January 1979. **Editor:** C. Edward Wall. **Price:** $44.50, plus $2.50 shipping.

★3854★
DIRECTORY OF RESEARCH GRANTS
Oryx Press
3930 E. Camelback Road   Phone: (602) 956-6233
Phoenix, AZ 85018
Covers: More than 2,000 research grants available from governmental, business, foundation, and private sources. **Entries include:** Grant name, name and address of sponsor, description of purpose of grant, qualifications, amounts of money available, application deadline, etc. **Arrangement:** By subject. **Indexes:** Grant name, sponsor name, and sponsoring organization by type. **Pages** (approx.): 325. **Frequency:** Annual. **Editor:** William K. Wilson. **Price:** $37.50, plus $1.25 shipping. **Other information:** An edited cumulation of material published in the quarterly issues of "Grant Information System;" see separate entry.

★3855★
DIRECTORY OF RESOURCES FOR AFFIRMATIVE RECRUITMENT
Equal Employment Opportunity Commission
2401 E Street, N. W.
Washington, DC 20506
Covers: About 75 national organizations and commercial placement agencies, and about 100 such regional groups, which refer minority and women applicants to employers or otherwise aid in affirmative recruitment. **Entries include:** Referral organization's name and address, contact person's name, title and phone, purpose of organization, and services available to employers. **Arrangement:** National and regional sections, divided by type of referral agency. **Pages** (approx.): 90. **Frequency:** Irregular; latest edition December 1976. **Editor:** Richard Dickerson, Chief, Education Branch, Voluntary Programs. **Price:** Free.

★3856★
DIRECTORY OF RIGHTIST PUBLICATIONS THROUGHOUT THE
    WORLD
Robert Pate
Box 5203
Huntsville, AL 35805
Covers: About 60 newspapers and magazines in 12 countries that are to the right in the political spectrum, and mostly of a racial nature. **Entries include:** Name, address, languages in which published. **Arrangement:** Geographical. **Pages** (approx.): 2. **Frequency:** Irregular; previous edition August 1978; latest edition November 1979. **Editor:** Robert Pate. **Price:** $2.00.

★3857★
DIRECTORY OF RURAL ORGANIZATIONS
National Rural Center
1828 L Street, N. W.   Phone: (202) 331-0258
Washington, DC 20036
Covers: 150 national organizations involved in rural revitalization and development. **Entries include:** Organization name, address, phone, key personnel, year established, goals and activities, services rendered, rural focus, interests, publications, code indicating

activities, including whether organization lobbies. **Arrangement:** Alphabetical. **Pages** (approx.): 50. **Frequency:** Irregular; latest edition October 1977. **Editor:** Lawrence W. Newlin, Assistant Director for Community Development. **Price:** $2.00, payment with order.

★3858★
DIRECTORY OF SAN FRANCISCO CLUBS AND ORGANIZATIONS [California]
San Francisco Chamber of Commerce
465 California Street   Phone: (415) 392-4511
San Francisco, CA 94104
Number of listings: Over 700. **Entries include:** Name, address, phone, name of principal executive. **Arrangement:** By subject or interest. **Pages** (approx.): 35. **Frequency:** Annual, May. **Price:** $5.00, payment with order (current and 1980 editions).

Directory of Selected Training Facilities in Family Planning *See* Training Facilities in Population and Family Planning

★3859★
DIRECTORY OF SERTOMA CLUBS
Sertoma International
1912 E. Meyer Boulevard   Phone: (816) 333-8300
Kansas City, MO 64132
Covers: 15 regions of Sertoma International, plus over 900 Sertoma clubs. **Entries include:** International entries list the international, state, and district officers and their addresses; club entries give the president's and secretary's names and addresses. **Arrangement:** Geographical. **Pages** (approx.): 40. **Frequency:** Annual, August. **Editor:** Ginger M. Graham. **Price:** 75¢; available for non-commercial uses only.

★3860★
DIRECTORY OF SMALL MAGAZINE/PRESS EDITORS AND PUBLISHERS
Dustbooks
Box 100
Paradise, CA 95969
Covers: About 3,000 publishers and editors. **Entries include:** Individual name, title of publication, and address and phone number of publisher. **Arrangement:** Alphabetical. **Pages** (approx.): 250. **Frequency:** Annual, June. **Editor:** Len Fulton. **Price:** $8.95, plus 95¢ shipping. **Other information:** A companion directory to "International Directory of Little Magazines and Small Presses" (see separate listing).

★3861★
DIRECTORY OF SOCIAL AND HEALTH AGENCIES OF NEW YORK CITY
Columbia University Press
562 W. 113th Street   Phone: (212) 678-6794
New York, NY 10025
Covers: Over 1,000 major social and health agencies and their affiliates in New York City or with headquarters there and sponsored by government, private, or nonprofit organizations. **Entries include:** Name, address, phone, officers, description of services, eligibility requirements, year established, languages spoken, hours, fees, and subdivisions. **Arrangement:** Alphabetical. **Indexes:** Subject, personal name. **Pages** (approx.): 650. **Frequency:** Biennial, spring of odd years. **Editors:** Rowena McDade and William James Smith. **Price:** $24.00, plus $1.30 shipping, payment with order. **Send orders to:** Columbia University Press, 136 S. Broadway, Irvington-on-Hudson, NY 10533 (914-591-9111). **Also includes:** "Selected Information and Referral Services Outside New York City," a listing of major social service organizations in the United States and Canada, arranged geographically.

★3862★
DIRECTORY OF SPECIAL PROGRAMS FOR MINORITY GROUP MEMBERS: CAREER INFORMATION SERVICES, EMPLOYMENT SKILLS BANKS, FINANCIAL AID SOURCES
Garrett Park Press
Garrett Park, MD 20766   Phone: (301) 946-2553
Covers: About 2,100 private and governmental agencies offering financial aid, employment assistance, and career guidance programs for minorities. **Entries include:** Organization or agency name, address, phone, name of contact, type of organization, purpose, description of services and activities in the equal opportunity employment area. **Arrangement:** Alphabetical. **Indexes:** Alphabetical, type of program. **Pages** (approx.): 610. **Frequency:** Irregular; latest edition 1975; new edition expected January 1980. **Editor:** Willis L. Johnson. **Price:** $19.00, payment with order; $20.00, billed (1980 edition).

★3863★
DIRECTORY OF STATE AGENCIES CONCERNED WITH LAND POLLUTION
Freed Publishing Company
Box 1144
FDR Station   Phone: (212) 753-2769
New York, NY 10022
Covers: State government agencies (1-8 per state) that deal with solid wastes, soil erosion, strip mines, litter, or other ground pollutants, plus those concerned with land use and land use planning. **Entries include:** Agency name, key official to contact, address, phone, description of agency's major areas of interest and responsibility. **Arrangement:** Geographical. **Pages** (approx.): 40. **Frequency:** Irregular; latest edition 1979. **Editor:** Laura E. Freed. **Price:** $10.00.

★3864★
DIRECTORY OF STATE AND LOCAL CONSUMER ORGANIZATIONS
Consumer Federation of America
1012 14th Street, N. W., Suite 901
Washington, DC 20005
Number of listings: 300. **Entries include:** Name, address, phone, name of contact, areas of interest. **Frequency:** Published 1978. **Price:** $5.00.

★3865★
DIRECTORY OF SUICIDE PREVENTION/CRISIS INTERVENTION AGENCIES IN THE UNITED STATES
American Association of Suicidology
Box 3264   Phone: (713) 644-7911
Houston, TX 77001
Covers: About 200 suicide prevention centers. **Entries include:** Center name, sponsoring organization (if different), address, phone, emergency phone number, year established, hours of service, services available, source of funding. **Arrangement:** Geographical. **Pages** (approx.): 250. **Frequency:** Irregular; latest edition 1971; new edition expected 1980. **Price:** 1971 edition out of print; 1980 edition price not determined.

★3866★
DIRECTORY OF TEXAS FOUNDATIONS
Texas Foundations Research Center
Box 5494   Phone: (512) 474-6046
Austin, TX 78763
Covers: Over 1,100 Texas foundations having assets above $20,000 and/or distributed total grants above $1,000; separate list of about 285 foundations which do not meet these criteria. **Entries include:** Foundation name, address, activities supported, income, assets, total amount and number of grants, name of contact. **Arrangement:** Alphabetical. **Indexes:** Geographical, activities supported. **Pages** (approx.): 200. **Frequency:** Biennial, fall of even years. Based on Internal Revenue Service forms 990-PF and 990-AR from prior year. **Editor:** William T. Hooper, Jr. **Price:** $15.00, postpaid, payment with order; $16.25, billed (current edition); $18.00, postpaid, payment with order; $19.50, billed (1980 edition). **Also includes:** 300

foundations not meeting criteria listed with addresses, assets, and total grants. Research service is available.

★3867★
DIRECTORY OF THE AMERICAN LEFT
Editorial Research Service
Box 1832
Kansas City, MO 64141
Covers: Over 1,775 socialist, communist, collectivist, welfare statist, and other left-wing organizations and periodicals in the United States, Canada, and the British Commonwealth, primarily national or regional in scope. **Entries include:** Organization or publication name, address, special interests, code indicating major political or philosophical category. **Frequency:** Biennial, October of odd years; supplement in even years. **Editor:** Laird M. Wilcox. **Price:** $9.95, postpaid. **Other information:** Updated bimonthly by "The Wilcox Report," $24.00 per year (ISSN 0049-7630). Same publisher also issues "Directory of the American Right," described in separate listing.

★3868★
DIRECTORY OF THE AMERICAN RIGHT
Editorial Research Service
Box 1832
Kansas City, MO 64141
Covers: 1,800 conservative, anti-communist, libertarian, free market, racial nationalist, tax revolt, right-to-life, and other right-wing organizations and periodicals in the United States and the British Commonwealth, primarily national or regional in scope. **Entries include:** Organization or publication name, address, special interests, code indicating major political or philsophical category. **Frequency:** Irregular; latest edition October 1979. **Editor:** Laird M. Wilcox. **Price:** $9.95, postpaid, payment with order. **Other information:** Updated bimonthly by "The Wilcox Report," $24.00 per year (ISSN 0049-7630). Same publisher also issues "Directory of the American Left;" see separate entry.

★3869★
DIRECTORY OF THE COLLEGE STUDENT PRESS IN AMERICA
Oxbridge Communications, Inc.
183 Madison Avenue   Phone: (212) 689-8524
New York, NY 10016
Covers: About 6,000 student-run newspapers, magazines, and yearbooks on 2,500 college campuses. **Entries include:** For colleges - Name, address, phone, name of president, enrollment. For publications - Title, name of advisor, description of contents, advertsing and subscription rates, trim size and print method, frequency, circulation, budget and method of financing. **Arrangement:** Geographical. **Indexes:** Title. **Pages** (approx.): 650. **Frequency:** Biennial, even years. **Editor:** Dario Politella, Ph.D. **Price:** $25.00 (current edition); $35.00 (1980 edition); postpaid, payment with order.

★3870★
DIRECTORY OF THE MAJOR GREATER BOSTON FOUNDATIONS
J. F. Gray Company
Box 748
Islington Station
Westwood, MA 02090
Number of listings: 50. **Arrangement:** Alphabetical. **Pages** (approx.): 45. **Frequency:** Irregular; latest edition 1974. Based on Internal Revenue Service forms 990-PF and 990-AR from 1972. **Price:** $14.95. (Not verified)

Directory of Trade and Professional Associations in North Carolina See North Carolina Directory of Trade and Professional Assns.

★3871★
DIRECTORY OF VOLUNTEER BUREAUS AND VOLUNTARY ACTION CENTERS
Association of Volunteer Bureaus
801 N. Fairfax Street
Alexandria, VA 22314
Covers: 375 member bureaus and centers. **Entries include:** Name of bureau or center, address, name of executive director, population of community served, organization structure, affiliations. **Arrangement:** Geographical. **Frequency:** Annual, summer. **Editor:** Jean V. Varney, AVB Administrative Coordinator. **Price:** $2.00.

★3872★
DIRECTORY OF VOLUNTEER ORGANIZATIONS IN TEXAS
Convention Services
Box 475   Phone: (512) 472-7544
Austin, TX 78767
Covers: 2,000 associations, societies, clubs, and fraternal groups in Texas. **Entries include:** Name of organization, address, phone, scope of organization, annual meeting and/or size of membership, names of paid personnel and/or elected officers. **Arrangement:** Alphabetical by key word in organization name. **Indexes:** Organization name. **Pages** (approx.): 225. **Frequency:** Biennial, fall, with supplement in other year. **Editor:** Leta Faye Voss. **Price:** $42.75, plus $1.00 shipping.

★3873★
DIRECTORY OF WESTERN NEW YORK BUSINESS AND CIVIC ORGANIZATIONS
Buffalo Area Chamber of Commerce
107 Delaware Avenue   Phone: (716) 849-6677
Buffalo, NY 14202
Covers: Over 400 business organizations; luncheon and service clubs; women's organizations; and art centers; also lists newspapers, radio/TV stations, and employee organization publications; includes list of available speakers and their topics. **Entries include:** Association name, address, phone, name of president and/or secretary, purpose, meeting schedule, election month. **Arrangement:** Alphabetical. **Pages** (approx.): 75. **Frequency:** Annual, spring. **Price:** $12.00, plus 75¢ shipping.

★3874★
DIRECTORY OF WOMEN AND MINORITY MEN IN ACADEMIC JOURNALISM/COMMUNICATION
Association for Education in Journalism
431 Murphy Hall
University of Minnesota   Phone: (612) 376-7100
Minneapolis, MN 55455
Covers: Over 800 professionals, academics, or graduate students. **Entries include:** Name, office address, highest degree held, areas of occupational specialization, personal and career data, and professional, research, and teaching experience. **Arrangement:** Alphabetical. **Indexes:** Teaching/research interest. **Pages** (approx.): 100. **Frequency:** Irregular; latest edition 1977. **Price:** $7.50, payment with order.

Directory of Women's Media See Media Report to Women Index/ Directory of Women's Media

★3875★
DOLLARS & SENSE—"TAX REVOLT INDEX" COLUMN
National Taxpayers Union
325 Pennsylvania Avenue, S. E.   Phone: (202) 546-2085
Washington, DC 20003
Publication includes: Descriptions of efforts being made in 32 states to achieve tax relief similar to that under California's Proposition 13. **Entries include:** Name and address of group or groups within the state working for tax reform, name of contact person, and various amounts of detail on each state's efforts, including details of proposals, wording of proposals, goals, etc. **Frequency:** Monthly. **Editor:** Lance Lamberton. **Price:** Included in membership; $15.00 per year.

★3876★
DRUGS: A MULTIMEDIA SOURCEBOOK FOR YOUNG ADULTS
ABC-Clio Press
Riviera Campus
2040 Alameda Padre Serra   Phone: (805) 963-4221
Santa Barbara, CA 93103
Publication includes: List of publishers, distributors, dealers, resource centers, and agencies with drug information resources and publications. **Entries include:** Publisher name, address. Agency listings include description of materials available. **Indexes:** Author/title. **Frequency:** Not established; first edition fall 1979. **Editors:** Sharon Ashenbrenner Charles and Sari Feldman. **Price:** $14.95, postpaid, payment must accompany individuals' orders. **Other information:** Published in cooperation with Neal-Schuman Publishers. Principal content of publication is annotated bibliographies.

★3877★
ECONOMICS OF ELECTRIC UTILITY RATE REFORM: A DIRECTORY OF ECONOMISTS
Public Interest Economics Foundation
1714 Massachusetts Avenue, N. W.   Phone: (202) 872-0313
Washington, DC 20036
Covers: Professional economists willing to serve as consumer witnesses and experts in proceedings directed toward utility rate restructuring, on a volunteer or low-fee basis. **Arrangement:** Geographical. **Frequency:** Not established; first edition April 1977; new edition possible 1980. **Price:** $2.25.

★3878★
EDITOR & PUBLISHER INTERNATIONAL YEAR BOOK
Editor & Publisher Company, Inc.
575 Lexington Avenue   Phone: (212) 752-7050
New York, NY 10022
Covers: Daily and Sunday newspapers in the United States and Canada; weekly newspapers; foreign daily newspapers; special service newspapers; newspaper syndicates; news services; journalism schools; foreign language and Black newspapers in the United States; advertising clubs; trade associations; clipping bureaus; house organs; journalism awards; also lists manufacturers of equipment and supplies. **Entries include:** For daily papers - Publication name, address, phone, names of executives and departmental editors (business, financial, book, food, etc.), circulation and advertising data. Similar but less detailed information for other publications. **Arrangement:** Publications and schools geographical, most other lists alphabetical. **Pages** (approx.): 600. **Frequency:** Annual, March. **Editor:** Michael Olver. **Advertising accepted. Price:** $30.00 (current edition); $35.00 (1980 edition).

★3879★
EDITOR & PUBLISHER JOURNALISM AWARDS DIRECTORY
Editor & Publisher Company, Inc.
575 Lexington Avenue   Phone: (212) 752-7050
New York, NY 10022
Covers: Over 200 cash prizes, scholarships, fellowships, and grants available to journalism personnel for work on special subjects or in specific fields. **Entries include:** Award name, donor, address, deadlines, and requirements; many listings include winners for previous year. **Arrangement:** Alphabetical. **Frequency:** Annual, January. **Editor:** Robert U. Brown. **Price:** $3.00, postpaid, payment with order. **Other information:** Reprinted from last December issue of previous year.

★3880★
EM COMPLAINT DIRECTORY FOR CONSUMERS
Everybody's Money
Credit Union National Association
Box 431   Phone: (608) 241-1211
Madison, WI 53701
Covers: Federal, state, and local government agencies; senators and representatives; radio and television broadcasters; food producers, manufacturers, and others to whom to address complaints or inquiries.

Entries include: Name, address. **Arrangement:** By type of organization. **Pages** (approx.): 55. **Frequency:** Annual, January. **Editor:** Sharon Stark, Editor. **Price:** $2.00, payment must accompany order (current and 1980 editions).

★3881★
EMERGING AGING NETWORK: A DIRECTORY OF STATE AND AREA AGENCIES ON AGING
Select Committee on Aging
House of Representatives
United States Congress
Washington, DC 20515
Covers: Nearly 60 state agencies and 600 area agencies concerned with the aging. **Entries include:** Agency name, address, phone, and name of director. **Arrangement:** Geographical. **Pages** (approx.): 135. **Frequency:** First edition 1978. **Price:** $3.00 (S/N 052-070-04793-3). **Send orders to:** Government Printing Office, Washington, DC 20402.

★3882★
ENCYCLOPEDIA OF ASSOCIATIONS
Gale Research Company
Book Tower   Phone: (313) 961-2242
Detroit, MI 48226
Covers: 14,000 active organizations divided into 17 classifications: trade, business, and commercial; agricultural organizations and commodity exchanges; legal, governmental, public administration, and military; scientific, engineering, and technical; educational; cultural; social welfare; health and medical; public affairs; fraternal, foreign interest, nationality, and ethnic; religion; veteran, hereditary, and patriotic; hobby and avocational; athletic and sports; labor; chambers of commerce; Greek letter. **Entries include:** Organization name, address, phone, principal official, staff size, date founded, number of members, description of objectives, activities, committees, publications, former names, convention dates and places for three years ahead. **Arrangement:** By subject keyword within classifications above. **Indexes:** Combined keyword/organization name index in Volume 1; Volume 2 consists of complete geographical index with organization name, address, phone, and name of principal executive, and complete executive personal name index with same information. **Pages** (approx.): Volume 1, 1,550; Volume 2, 815. **Frequency:** Annual, November; periodic supplements between editions. **Editor:** Denise Akey. **Price:** Volume 1, "National Organizations of the United States," $90.00; Volume 2, "Geographic and Executive Index," $75.00; Volume 3 (supplements), "New Associations and Projects," $85.00 for inter-edition subscription. **Other information:** During 1980, direct computer access to the 14th edition of the "Encyclopedia of Associations" will be available to users through Lockheed Information Systems, an international computer search company located in Palo Alto, CA.

★3883★
ENCYCLOPEDIA OF OHIO ASSOCIATIONS
Publications Committee
Ohio State University Libraries
Main Library, Room 001
1858 Neil Avenue Mall
Columbus, OH 43210
Covers: 5,000 Ohio nonprofit associations which are state-wide in scope or interest. Includes both national and regional organizatons which have headquarters or chapters in the state as well as those which do not, and many local organizations. **Entries include:** Association name, name and address of secretary or other officer, number of Ohio members, and a description of the organization's purposes and activities. Nonrespondents are listed, but with less detail. **Arrangement:** Classified by geographic scope (national, state, local). **Indexes:** Geographical, type of association, keyword, acronym, periodical. **Pages** (approx.): 525. **Frequency:** Not established; first edition 1977. **Editors:** Martha S. Alt, Marjorie Adams Harf, and Rita Hirschman. **Price:** $13.95, plus $1.50 shipping.

★3884★
ENERGY: A GUIDE TO ORGANIZATIONS AND INFORMATION RESOURCES IN THE UNITED STATES

California Institute of Public Affairs
226 W. Foothill Boulevard   Phone: (714) 624-5212
Claremont, CA 91711
Covers: 1,500 federal, state, interstate, and local government agencies; trade, professional, and citizens' associations; research and development and information centers; and major energy utilities. **Entries include:** Name, address, phone, names and titles of principal personnel, organization structure, activities, publications. **Arrangement:** Classified by principal interest. **Indexes:** Organization name, acronym, subject of interest. **Pages** (approx.): 225. **Frequency:** Irregular; previous edition 1974; latest edition 1978. **Editor:** Thaddeus C. Trzyna. **Price:** $20.00, plus $1.66 shipping.

★3885★
ENERGY: A MULTIMEDIA GUIDE FOR CHILDREN AND YOUNG ADULTS

ABC-Clio Press
Riviera Campus
2040 Alameda Padre Serra   Phone: (805) 963-4221
Santa Barbara, CA 93103
Publication includes: List of publishers, distributors, dealers, and resource centers offering energy conservation and alternative energy materials. **Entries include:** Publisher name, address. **Arrangement:** Alphabetical. **Indexes:** Author, title. **Pages** (approx.): 195. **Frequency:** Not established; first edition 1979. **Editor:** Judith H. Higgins. **Price:** $14.95, postpaid, payment must accompany individuals' orders. **Other information:** Published in cooperation with Neal-Schuman Publishers. Principal content of publication is annotated bibliographies.

★3886★
ENERGY DIRECTORY UPDATE SERVICE

Environment Information Center, Inc.
292 Madison Avenue   Phone: (212) 949-9471
New York, NY 10017
Covers: 3,000 organizations active in the energy field, divided into these individually bound chapters: Energy Information Locator; Federal Government/Executive Branch; Federal Government/Congress; State and Regional Government; Trade, Professional, and Non-Governmental Organizations; Industry; and Cumulative Index. **Entries include:** Organization name, personnel, address, phone, programs, projects, publications, and information services. **Indexes:** Alphabetical, geographical, subject. **Pages** (approx.): 600. **Frequency:** Base edition, 1975; bimonthly updates. **Editor:** Monica Pronin, Director of Editorial Productions. **Price:** Base edition and updates for one year, $295.00; updates only, $195.00. **Other information:** Updates "The Energy Directory," published in 1975.

★3887★
ENERGY POLICY MAKING IN THE NORTHEAST: A DIRECTORY OF STATE PROGRAMS AND INSTITUTIONS

Applied Science Research Applications
National Science Foundation
Washington, DC 20550
Covers: Energy-related duties and programs of legislative and executive branches of state governments in Connecticut, Delaware, Maine, Massachusetts, New Hampshire, New Jersey, New York, Pennsylvania, Rhode Island, and Vermont. **Entries include:** Agency name, address, phone, names and titles of key personnel, energy-related programs and responsibilities. **Arrangement:** Geographical. **Pages** (approx.): 135. **Frequency:** Not established; first edition September 1977. **Price:** $7.25, paper copy; $3.00, microfiche (PB 277-503). **Send orders to:** National Technical Information Service, Springfield, VA 22161.

★3888★
ENERGY TRAILS: A GUIDEBOOK

Energy Department
Box 62
Oak Ridge, TN 37830
Covers: Volume 1, "Northeastern States," includes about 25 major energy sites, power plants, science museums, etc., open to public visits in Vermont, Massachusetts, New York, New Jersey, Pennsylvania, Maryland, and the District of Columbia. Volumes for other areas in preparation. **Entries include:** Facility name, location, map, hours, fees, contact information, phone, and information concerning the nature and history of the facility. **Arrangement:** Geographical. **Pages** (approx.): 100. **Frequency:** Not established; first edition fall 1976; publication dates of additional volumes not known at present. **Editor:** Joseph A. Angelo, Jr. **Price:** Free.

★3889★
ENVIRONMENTAL INFORMATION RESOURCES FOR STATE AND LOCAL ELECTED OFFICIALS: GENERAL REFERENCE GUIDE

Office of Regional Intergovernmental Operations
Environmental Protection Agency
Washington, DC 20460
Covers: Non-documentary sources concerned with environmental problems generally, including trade, professional, and industry associations, publication staffs, reference and referral services, etc., and primary and secondary literature sources. **Arrangement:** By type of source. **Pages** (approx.): 150. **Frequency:** Not established; first edition 1977. **Editors:** G. W. Rivkin and S. L. Brecher. **Price:** $7.25, paper copy; $3.00, microfiche (PB 278-682). **Send orders to:** National Technical Information Service, Springfield, VA 22161.

★3890★
ENVIRONMENTAL INFORMATION RESOURCES FOR STATE AND LOCAL ELECTED OFFICIALS: SURFACE MINING

Office of Regional Intergovernmental Operations
Environmental Protection Agency
Washington, DC 20460
Publication includes: List of organizations, associations and individuals with special knowledge of strip mining. **Entries include:** Organization or individual name, address, special area of interest. **Frequency:** Not established; first edition 1977. **Editors:** G. W. Rivkin and S. L. Brecher. **Price:** $6.50, paper copy; $3.00, microfiche (PB 278-684). **Send orders to:** National Technical Information Service, Springfield, VA 22161. **Also includes:** General review of impact of strip mining, pollution control and reclamation technology and costs, legislation, etc.

★3891★
ENVIRONMENTAL INFORMATION RESOURCES FOR STATE AND LOCAL ELECTED OFFICIALS: SOLID WASTE

Office of Regional Intergovernmental Operations
Environmental Protection Agency
Washington, DC 20460
Covers: Non-documentary sources especially concerned with solid waste management, such as trade, professional, and industry associations, public interest groups, referral services, and reference services; includes documentary sources such as published bibliographies, abstract journals, etc. **Arrangement:** By type of source. **Pages** (approx.): 185. **Frequency:** Not established; first edition 1977. **Editors:** G. W. Rivkin and S. L. Brecher. **Price:** $9.00, paper copy; $3.00, microfiche (PB 278-683).**Send orders to:** National Technical Information Service, Springfield, VA 22161.

★3892★
ENVIRONMENTAL ORGANIZATIONS DIRECTORY [Pacific Northwest]

Environmental Protection Agency, Region 10
1200 Sixth Avenue, Mail Stop 635   Phone: (206) 442-1203
Seattle, WA 98101
Covers: Regional voluntary organizations, EPA regional offices, and state, local, and provincial environmental and pollution control

agencies in Alaska, Idaho, Oregon, Washington, and British Columbia. **Entries include:** Organization name, address, phone, regional representative, and brief narrative on the organization's purpose, goals, committees, local chapters, and other data. **Arrangement:** By type of organization (regional, agency, etc.). **Pages** (approx.): 40. **Frequency:** Biennial, fall of even years. **Editor:** Donald R. Bliss, Jr., Director, Public Affairs. **Price:** Free. **Other information:** Variant title, "Directory of Environmental Organizations for Alaska, Idaho, Oregon, Washington, and the Province of British Columbia."

★3893★
EQUAL RIGHTS HANDBOOK
Avon Books, Division
Hearst Corporation
959 Eighth Avenue   Phone: (212) 262-5700
New York, NY 10019
Publication includes: Several hundred national, regional, and local organizations working for passage of the Equal Rights Amendment to the United States Constitution, and a list of principal organizations opposing the amendment. **Entries include:** Organization name, address; listings for some supporters include additional details; listings for opponents include a discussion of their activities and tactics. **Frequency:** Published 1978. **Editor:** Riane Tennenhaus Eisler. **Price:** $1.95.

★3894★
EVIST RESOURCE DIRECTORY—A DIRECTORY OF PROGRAMS AND COURSES IN...ETHICS AND VALUES IN SCIENCE AND TECHNOLOGY
American Association for the Advancement of Science
1776 Massachusetts Avenue, N. W.   Phone: (202) 467-4464
Washington, DC 20036
Covers: Over 1,800 courses and programs offered at over 500 colleges and universities oriented to and related to ethics and values in science and technology (EVIST). Fields of study include science and technology and human values, environmental concerns, biomedical concerns, industry and society, and public policymaking. **Entries include:** For programs oriented to EVIST - Institution name, address, program name, name of director; description of content and intent of program; program details including audience, funding, and year program began. For courses oriented to EVIST - Course title, name of instructor, name and address of institution, description. **Arrangement:** By subject. **Pages** (approx.): 215. **Frequency:** Irregular; first edition 1978. **Editor:** Joseph M. Dasbach, Program Associate. **Price:** Free.

★3895★
EXOTIC WEAPONS
Loompanics Unlimited
Box 264
Mason, MI 48854
Covers: Over 300 dealers in weapons such as blowguns, boomerangs, bolas, tear gas batons, tomahawks, sonic weapons, robots, and others. Publishers and organizations concerned with exotic weapons are also listed. **Entries include:** Dealer name, address, description of product. **Arrangement:** Alphabetical. **Pages** (approx.): 100. **Frequency:** Irregular; latest edition 1979; new edition expected 1981. **Editor:** Michael Hoy. **Price:** $6.95, plus $1.00 shipping.

Faculty Alert Bulletins [Grants] *See* **Grant Information System**

★3896★
FAMILY CIRCLE GUIDE TO SELF-HELP
Ballantine Books, Division
Random House, Inc.
201 E. 50th Street   Phone: (212) 751-2600
New York, NY 10022
Publication includes: List of names, addresses, and interests of 450 self-help groups in the United States and Canada. **Frequency:** Published 1979. **Editor:** Glen Evans. **Price:** $3.00, postpaid, payment with order. **Send orders to:** Ballantine Books, 455 Hahn Road,

Westminster, MD 21157.

★3897★
FAMILY PAGE DIRECTORY
Public Relations Plus, Inc.
Box 327   Phone: (203) 868-0200
Washington Depot, CT 06794
Covers: 550 newspapers with family-interest pages or sections. **Entries include:** Newspaper name, address, phone, and circulation, plus names of five principal special-interest editors (beauty, fashion, food, etc.). **Arrangement:** Geographical. **Pages** (approx.): 24. **Frequency:** Three times yearly. **Editor:** Harold D. Hansen. **Price:** $45.00 per year. **Also includes:** List of newspapers ranked by circulation.

Family Planning Programs—A Guide to Sources of Family Planning Program Assistance *See* **Population Reports—Family Planning Programs Issue**

★3898★
FAMILY SERVICE ASSOCIATION OF AMERICA—DIRECTORY OF MEMBER AGENCIES
Family Service Association of America
44 E. 23rd Street   Phone: (212) 674-6100
New York, NY 10010
Covers: 300 accredited and provisional member agencies in United States and Canadian cities. **Entries include:** Agency name, address, executive director, and information on areas served by each agency. **Arrangement:** Geographical. **Pages** (approx.): 100. **Frequency:** Annual, January; directory changes issued bimonthly. **Price:** $8.00, plus $1.00 shipping; directory changes $2.50 per year.

★3899★
FEDERAL ASSISTANCE FOR PROGRAMS SERVING THE HANDICAPPED
Office for Handicapped Individuals
Rehabilitation Services Administration
Health, Education, and Welfare Department
338D Hubert H. Humphrey Bldg.   Phone: (202) 245-1961
Washington, DC 20201
Covers: About 150 programs of the federal government for assistance to physically and mentally handicapped persons; includes listings for organizations and state agencies concerned with handicapping conditions. **Entries include:** Program name, extensive description, name of administering agency and address for application. **Indexes:** Subject, eligibility. **Pages** (approx.): 375. **Frequency:** Annual. **Price:** Free from issuing agency; $7.00 from Government Printing Office (S/N 017-000-00228-7).

Federally Funded Mental Health Centers *See* **Directory [of] Federally Funded Community Mental Health Centers**

Federation of Organizations for Professional Women—Directory *See* **Washington Women: A Directory of Women and Women's Organizations...**

★3900★
FEMINISM IN THE MID-1970S
Ford Foundation
320 E. 43rd Street   Phone: (212) 573-5000
New York, NY 10017
Publication includes: List of 150 associations, societies, clubs, and other organizations and about 25 non-organization publications concerned with the women's movement in the United States. **Entries include:** For organizations - Group name, address, name of publication (if any). For publications - Title, name and address of publisher, name of editor. **Pages** (approx.): 65. **Frequency:** First edition 1977. **Author:** Maren Lockwood Carden. **Price:** $3.95. **Send orders to:** Ford Foundation, Box 559, Naugatuck, CT 06770. **Other information:** Updates the author's "The New Feminist Movement" (1974).

★3901★

FINDING A JOB: A RESOURCE BOOK FOR THE MIDDLE-AGED AND RETIRED

Adelphi University Press
South Avenue   Phone: (516) 248-2020
Garden City, NY 11530

Covers: State offices concerned with the aging, nonprofit placement services for the retired and elderly, and senior community service employment programs (established under the Older Americans Act); ACTION regional offices are also listed. **Entries include:** Organization or agency name, address, name of director, services. **Arrangement:** Geographical. **Pages** (approx.): 140. **Frequency:** Not established; first edition 1978; new edition expected mid-1980. **Editors:** Norman Sprague and Hilary Fleming Knatz. **Price:** 1978 edition out of print; 1980 edition price not determined.

★3902★

FIRST MEN'S DIRECTORY FOR THE PACIFIC NORTHWEST

Metrocenter YMCA
909 Fourth Avenue   Phone: (206) 447-4551
Seattle, WA 98104

Covers: Over 100 individuals and groups which are involved in or interested in men's issues including sexuality, divorce, homosexuality, spouse abuse, single parenting, etc. in the Pacific Northwest area. **Entries include:** Name of organization or individual, address, phone. Most listings include description of interests, programs, or services; some listings also include hours. **Arrangement:** Geographical, then organizations, then individuals. **Pages** (approx.): 20. **Frequency:** Not established; first edition 1979; new edition expected spring 1980. **Advertising accepted.** Circulation 200. **Price:** 75¢ (current edition); $1.00 (tentative, 1980 edition); postpaid, payment with order.

★3903★

FOLIO MAGAZINE—FOLIO 400 ISSUE [Periodical industry]

Folio Magazine Publishing Corporation
125 Elm Street   Phone: (203) 972-0761
New Canaan, CT 06840

Publication includes: Lists of leading American magazines ranked according to circulation, advertising sales, pages of advertising, and several other characteristics. **Entries include:** Rankings by total sales revenue include 400 magazines and twelve other characteristics (advertising sales, circulation, etc.). Other groupings are smaller and give less detail. **Frequency:** Annual, January; first published January 1980. **Editor:** J. J. Hanson. **Advertising accepted. Price:** $4.00.

★3904★

FOLIO MAGAZINE—GUIDE TO MAGAZINE SUPPLIERS ISSUE

Folio Magazine Publishing Corporation
125 Elm Street   Phone: (203) 972-0761
New Canaan, CT 06840

Covers: Graphic arts, paper, fulfillment, and other companies offering products and services to the magazine publishing industry. **Entries include:** Company name, address, phone, name of contact, and description of products or services. **Arrangement:** Classified by service or product. **Frequency:** Annual, May. **Editor:** J. J. Hanson. **Advertising accepted. Price:** $10.00 (current and 1980 editions).

★3905★

FOOD CO-OP DIRECTORY [California]

California Department of Consumer Affairs
1020 N Street   Phone: (916) 322-7674
Sacramento, CA 95814

Covers: About 300 food cooperatives, buying clubs, direct charge co-ops, collectives, and warehouses. **Entries include:** Co-op name, address. **Arrangement:** By county; separate editions for northern and southern California. **Frequency:** Annual, April. **Price:** Free.

Food Co-Op Directory [National] *See* Co-Operative Directory

★3906★

FOR BETTER, FOR WORSE: A FEMINIST HANDBOOK ON MARRIAGE AND OTHER OPTIONS

Charles Scribner's Sons
597 Fifth Avenue   Phone: (212) 486-2700
New York, NY 10017

Publication includes: Lists of organizations concerned with wife abuse, lesbianism, and other aspects of the women's movement, and publishers and publications related to the movement. **Entries include:** Organization or publisher name, address; some organization listings are annotated; publication listings include date, price, annotation. **Indexes:** General. **Frequency:** Not established; first edition 1977. **Editors:** Jennifer Baker Fleming and Carolyn Kott Washburne. **Price:** $14.95, cloth; $7.95, paper.

★3907★

FOUNDATION CENTER NATIONAL DATA BOOK

Foundation Center
888 Seventh Avenue   Phone: (212) 975-1120
New York, NY 10019

Covers: More than 21,000 nonprofit organizations in the United States classified as private foundations by the Internal Revenue Service. Based on information returns to the IRS. **Entries include:** Foundation name, address, principal officer, assets, amount of grants made, and gifts received during most recent period reported. **Arrangement:** Same information is given in alphabetical order and geographically, then by annual grants amount. **Indexes:** None. **Frequency:** Annual, September. **Price:** $40.00, 2 volume set, payment with order.

★3908★

FOUNDATION CENTER SOURCE BOOK PROFILES

Foundation Center
888 Seventh Avenue   Phone: (212) 975-1120
New York, NY 10019

Covers: About 1,000 of the largest national and regional grant-making organizations, at rate of about 85 new profiles per issue. Updates and expands "Foundation Center Source Book," which is no longer published. **Entries include:** Foundation name, address, name of director, detailed statements of policies, programs, application procedures, statistical grants analysis (by subject, type of grant, and type of recipient), and listing of sample grants for latest year available. **Frequency:** Two-year cycle, with bimonthly updates. **Price:** $200.00 per year, payment with order (includes 500 new full profiles and revisions for all 1,000).

★3909★

FOUNDATION DIRECTORY

Foundation Center
888 Seventh Avenue   Phone: (212) 975-1120
New York, NY 10019

Covers: Over 3,100 of the largest foundations in the United States, all having more than $1 million in assets and awarding more than $100,000 in grants in a recent year. **Entries include:** Foundation name, address, phone, form of organization, names of major donors, purpose and activities, fields of interest, name of officers, trustees, or directors; and financial data. Includes information on grant application procedure. **Arrangement:** Geographical. **Indexes:** Foundation by city, subject interest, and names of donors, trustees, and administrators. **Pages** (approx.): 600. **Frequency:** Biennial, fall of odd years. **Editor:** Marianna O. Lewis. **Price:** $40.00, plus $1.50 shipping. **Send orders to:** Columbia University Press, 136 S. Broadway, Irvington-on-Hudson, NY 10533.

★3910★

FOUNDATION GRANTS INDEX

Foundation Center
888 Seventh Avenue   Phone: (212) 975-1120
New York, NY 10019

Covers: Grants awarded in previous year by about 400 philanthropic foundations (approximately 15,000 grants are described).

Arrangement: Geographical. **Indexes:** Recipient organization name, foundation name, subject, keyword/phrase. **Pages** (approx.): 480. **Frequency:** Annual, April. **Editor:** Lee Noe. **Price:** $21.00. **Send orders to:** Columbia University Press, 136 S. Broadway, Irvington-on-Hudson, NY 10533.

★3911★
FOUNDATION GRANTS TO INDIVIDUALS
Foundation Center
888 Seventh Avenue   Phone: (212) 975-1120
New York, NY 10019
Covers: About 1,000 foundations which made more than 40,000 individual grants totaling more than $56,000,000 "in the most recent year of record." **Entries include:** Foundation name, address, phone, contact person, asset size, total number of grants, portion of grants going to individuals, number of individuals receiving grants, application information, and description of grant program. **Arrangement:** Classified by subject areas of grants. **Indexes:** Subject, foundation name, company-sponsored foundation. **Pages** (approx.): 250. **Frequency:** Biennial, fall of odd years. **Editor:** Carol Kurzig. **Price:** $15.00; prepaid or charge card orders only.

★3912★
FOUNDATION REPORTER
Taft Corporation
1000 Vermont Avenue, N. W., Suite 600   Phone: (202) 347-0788
Washington, DC 20005
Covers: About 230 philanthropic foundations with national interests and giving patterns; an additional 300 foundations are covered in the nine regional editions. **Entries include:** Foundation name; contact name, title, address, and phone; officers and trustees including biographical data; financial data including size and type of typical grants; operating and historical information. **Indexes:** Subject, others. **Pages** (approx.): 750. **Frequency:** Annual, fall; updated monthly by "News Monitor/Taft Report." **Editor:** Jean Brodsky. **Price:** $195.00, postpaid, payment with order; $200.00, billed; includes "Foundation Reporter," 12 issues of "News Monitor," and one regional edition; additional regional editions, $30.00 each.

★3913★
FOUNDATIONS IN NEW JERSEY
Governmental Reference Office
Division of the State Library, Archives and History
New Jersey Department of Education
185 W. State Street   Phone: (609) 292-6220
Trenton, NJ 08625
Number of listings: About 800. **Entries include:** Foundation name, address, name of executor or bank. **Arrangement:** By county. **Indexes:** Foundation name (with IRS number and county). **Pages** (approx.): 45. **Frequency:** Irregular; first edition June 1978. Based on Internal Revenue Service forms 990-PF and 990-AR from 1976 and 1977. **Price:** 1978 edition out of print; available in libraries.

★3914★
FOUNDATIONS IN WISCONSIN: A DIRECTORY
Marquette University Memorial Library
1415 W. Wisconsin Avenue   Phone: (414) 224-1515
Milwaukee, WI 53233
Number of listings: 700. **Entries include:** Foundation name, address, phone, assets, total grants, grant range, median grant, number of grants, interests, and manager's name. **Arrangement:** Alphabetical. **Indexes:** Personal name, geographical, area of interest. **Pages** (approx.): 340. **Frequency:** Biennial, fall of even years. Based on Internal Revenue Service forms 990-PF and 990-AR from second preceding year. **Editor:** Margaret Marik. **Price:** $12.50, payment must accompany order. **Also includes:** Lists of top 20 Wisconsin granting foundations, inactive foundations, and recently terminated foundations.

★3915★
FOUNDATIONS THAT SEND THEIR ANNUAL REPORT
Public Service Materials Center
415 Lexington Avenue
New York, NY 10017
Covers: 475 foundations with assets over $1,000,000 or grants over $200,000 which will send their annual report on request at no charge. **Entries include:** Foundation name, address. **Arrangement:** Alphabetical. **Frequency:** Irregular; latest edition 1979. **Price:** $4.75.

★3916★
FUNDING IN AGING: PUBLIC, PRIVATE AND VOLUNTARY
Adelphi University Press
Levermore Hall 103
South Avenue   Phone: (516) 294-8700
Garden City, NY 11530
Covers: About 525 federal and state government agency programs, foundations, corporations, and voluntary organizations which provide funding or technical assistance to programs serving the elderly. **Entries include:** All listings include organization name, address, type of assistance offered. Government listings also include legislative authorization, eligibility and use requirements, application procedures, range and average amount of grant. Foundation listings also include assets, emphasis, grants given to aged, application procedure. Other listings include activities, purpose, description of assistance. **Arrangement:** Government agencies are by subject, foundations are geographical, other organizations are alphabetical. **Indexes:** Organization name/subject. **Pages** (approx.): 300. **Frequency:** Irregular; latest edition May 1979; new edition possible 1982. **Editors:** Lilly Cohen, Marie Oppedisand-Reich, and Kathleen Hamilton Gerardi. **Former title:** National Guide to Government and Foundation Funding Sources in the Field of Aging (1979). **Price:** $18.00, plus 80¢ shipping. **Other information:** Compiled with the cooperation of the Nassau County Department of Senior Citizen Affairs and Office of Housing and Intergovernmental Affairs.

★3917★
FUNERAL AND MEMORIAL SOCIETIES
Continental Association of Funeral and Memorial Societies
1828 L Street, N. W.   Phone: (202) 293-4821
Washington, DC 20036
Covers: 160 nonprofit memorial societies which assist members in obtaining simple funeral arrangements at reasonable cost. Includes members of the Memorial Society Association of Canada. **Entries include:** Name, address, phone. **Arrangement:** Geographical. **Frequency:** Semiannual. **Editors:** Elizabeth Clemmer and Ernest Morgan. **Price:** Free.

★3918★
THE FUTURE: A GUIDE TO INFORMATION SOURCES
World Future Society
4916 St. Elmo Avenue   Phone: (301) 656-8274
Washington, DC 20014
Covers: 560 futurists and/or individuals with a special interest in the future; also includes 270 organizations now engaged in futures research in North America, Europe, Asia, and elsewhere; 400 educational programs; 120 research projects. **Entries include:** For futurists - Name, office address and phone, home address, highest degree held, personal and career data, specializations, writings. For organizations, etc. - Name, address, key personnel or faculty, description of activities and objectives. **Arrangement:** Alphabetical within field of activity. **Indexes:** Geographical, subject. **Pages** (approx.): 720. **Frequency:** Latest edition 1979; new edition possible 1981. **Editor:** Edward Cornish. **Former title:** Resources Directory for America's Third Century. **Price:** $25.00, postpaid, payment with order.

★3919★
FUTURE FILE
Learning Concepts
2501 N. Lamar Street   Phone: (512) 474-6911
Austin, TX 78705
Publication includes: List of associations and groups concerned with study of the future, and manufacturers, publishers, audiovisual material producers, and others offering materials and services in this field. **Entries include:** Company, organization, or personal name, address, phone. **Arrangement:** By service or product. **Pages** (approx.): 260. **Frequency:** Irregular; previous edition 1977; latest edition 1979. **Price:** $13.95, plus $1.12 shipping. **Other information:** Formerly published by Rawson Wade Publishers.

★3920★
FUTURES DIRECTORY
Westview Press
5500 Central Avenue   Phone: (303) 444-3541
Boulder, CO 80301
Covers: About 400 organizations and 600 individuals involved in long-range planning and research on the future; worldwide coverage. **Entries include:** For organizations - Name of chief officer, type of organization, primary emphasis, methodology used, funding source, number employed, and address. For individuals - Name, address, age, sex, educational data, past work, direction of current work, and funding. **Arrangement:** Alphabetical by name of organization or last name of individual. **Indexes:** Geographical, methodology, subject. **Pages** (approx.): 400. **Frequency:** Published 1977; no other edition planned. **Editors:** John McHale and Magda Cordell McHale. **Price:** $47.25. **Other information:** Based on project of the Center for Integrative Studies, University of Houston and the United Nations Institute for Training and Research.

★3921★
GAIA'S GUIDE [Primarily lesbian orientation]
Gaia's Guide
651 Brannan Street, Suite 5
San Francisco, CA 94107
Covers: About 3,000 homosexual, primarily lesbian, organizations, publications, groups, bars, bookstores, switchboards, centers, resources, etc., in the United States and major western European cities. **Entries include:** Name of group, establishment, etc., address, phone, description of facilities or services; hours, meeting days, code indicating type of clientele included where appropriate. **Arrangement:** Geographical, then by type of activitiy. **Pages** (approx.): 300. **Frequency:** Annual, March. **Editor:** Ms. Sandy Horn, Editor/Publisher. **Advertising accepted.** Circulation 10,000. **Price:** $7.50 (current edition); $8.00 (1980 edition).

★3922★
GAY SOURCE: A CATALOG FOR MEN
Coward, McCann & Geoghegan, Inc.
200 Madison Avenue   Phone: (212) 883-5500
New York, NY 10016
Covers: Business and service establishments nationwide serving homosexual men, including bookstores, bars, clothing stores, hotlines, etc. **Arrangement:** By type of establishment or subject. **Frequency:** Not established; first edition August 1977. **Editor:** Dennis Sanders. **Price:** $6.95.

★3923★
GAYELLOW PAGES: A Classified Directory of Gay Services and Businesses in USA and Canada
Renaissance House
Box 292
Village Station   Phone: (212) 929-7720
New York, NY 10014
Covers: Gay- or lesbian-oriented business enterprises, organizations, churches, restaurants, and publications. Includes a separate listing of national firms. **Entries include:** Name, address, phone, business hours, and an annotation describing programs, products, or services.

Arrangement: Geographical; national listings are classified by subject category. **Pages** (approx.): 80. **Frequency:** Annual, fall. **Editor:** Frances Green. **Advertising accepted.** Circulation 15,000. **Price:** $5.00.

★3924★
GEORGIA FOUNDATION DIRECTORY
Foundation Collection
Atlanta Public Library
10 Pryor Street, S. W.
Atlanta, GA 30303
Number of listings: About 550. **Entries include:** Name only. **Arrangement:** Geographical, alphabetical, subject. **Frequency:** Published 1979. **Price:** Free. **Other information:** This publication is essentially an index to the more detailed "Guide to Georgia Foundations," described in separate entry.

★3925★
GIRLS CLUBS OF AMERICA—ROSTER OF MEMBER ORGANIZATIONS
Girls Clubs of America
205 Lexington Avenue   Phone: (212) 689-3700
New York, NY 10016
Number of listings: 255 local clubs. **Arrangement:** Geographical. **Frequency:** Semiannual, June and December. **Price:** Available to members only.

★3926★
GIVE BUT GIVE WISELY [Philanthropic organizations]
Philanthropic Advisory Service
Council of Better Business Bureaus
1150 17th Street, N. W.
Washington, DC 20036
Covers: About 360 nonprofit organizations separated into two lists: those which meet the Council's BBB Standards for Charitable Solicitations, and those which do not; selection for this listing based on frequency of inquiry; chosen from the file of approximately 10,000 national and international organizations maintained by the Council. **Entries include:** Organizations which meet Council's standards are listed by name only; organizations which do not meet standards are listed with keys indicating areas in which groups do not meet standards. **Frequency:** Quarterly. **Price:** $1.00, plus stamped, self-addressed business envelope.

★3927★
GLOBAL LISTING OF APPROPRIATE TECHNOLOGY ORGANIZATIONS AND SOURCES
Agency for International Development
State Department
Washington, DC 20523
Covers: About 1,200 diverse government agencies, private organizations, research institute, development groups, and commercial firms involved in some aspect of appropriate technology; about 375 are in the United States. **Entries include:** Agency or other unit name, address; some listings include name of contact. **Arrangement:** By country; United States entries are subdivided by state. **Pages** (approx.): 160. **Frequency:** Not established; first edition summer 1979. **Price:** $9.00, paper; $3.00, microfiche (PB 296-635). May also be available from the agency. **Send orders to:** National Technical Information Service, Springfield, VA 22161.

★3928★
GRADUATE AND PROFESSIONAL SCHOOL OPPORTUNITIES FOR MINORITY STUDENTS
Educational Testing Service
Carter and Rosedale Roads   Phone: (609) 921-9000
Princeton, NJ 08540
Covers: Universities which actively practice affirmative action with regard to minority groups. Includes list of sources for further information on graduate study in various fields, and sources of financial aid for minority students. **Entries include:** University name,

address, name of contact, standard tests used, application fee and dates, total number of students, number of minority students and faculty, whether minorities are actively recruited, aid offered. **Arrangement:** By field of study, then alphabetical. **Pages** (approx.): 250. **Frequency:** Irregular; latest edtion 1975-77. **Price:** $3.00, payment with order.

★3929★
GRANT INFORMATION SYSTEM
Oryx Press
3930 E. Camelback Road   Phone: (602) 956-6233
Phoenix, AZ 85018
Covers: Annually, 2,000 grant support programs available from federal and state agencies, private foundations, and business, professional, and religious organizations. **Entries include:** Grant name, name and address of sponsor, description of purpose of grant, qualifications, amounts of money available, application deadline, CFDA number, whether program requires state review, etc. Supplemented by monthly "Faculty Alert Bulletins" which contain similar information, with emphasis on deadlines, but do not include addresses. **Arrangement:** By discipline. **Frequency:** Issued in cumulative quarterly parts. **Editor:** William K. Wilson. **Price:** $375.00 per year, plus $30.00 shipping, including bulletins (ISSN 0099-0213). **Other information:** Final cumulation is also published as, "Directory of Research Grants;" see separate entry.

★3930★
GRANTS REGISTER: POSTGRADUATE AWARDS IN THE ENGLISH-SPEAKING WORLD
St. Martin's Press
175 Fifth Avenue   Phone: (212) 674-5151
New York, NY 10010
Covers: About 2,000 sources in the United Kingdom, Ireland, Australia, Canada, the United States, and other English-speaking areas which award financial aid for graduate study, research, or travel, including scholarships, fellowships, grants, awards for creative work, etc. Many are not available to United States nationals. **Entries include:** Name of awarding organization, name of award, address, subjects, purpose, number of awards offered and their value, place and duration of tenancy, eligibility requirements, application procedure. **Arrangement:** Alphabetical. **Indexes:** Subject, geographical, awards and awarding bodies. **Pages** (approx.): 775. **Frequency:** Biennial, March of odd years. **Editor:** Roland Turner. **Price:** $26.50.

★3931★
GRANTS RESOURCE MANUAL [Massachusetts]
Government Research Publications
Box 122
Newton Centre, MA 02159
Covers: 550 Massachusetts governmental agencies and philanthropic foundations offering grants and grant information. **Arrangement:** Alphabetical. **Indexes:** Subject interests. **Frequency:** Irregular; latest edition June 1979. Based on Internal Revenue Service forms 990-PF and 990-AR. **Editors:** Don Levitan and Daniel F. Donahue. **Price:** $15.00, plus 80¢ shipping. Supersedes "Community Grants Resource Catalogue: A Directory of Philanthropic Foundations in the Commonwealth of Massachusetts."

★3932★
GRANTSMANSHIP CENTER NEWS—"THE BIG SEARCH" ISSUE
Grantsmanship Center
1031 S. Grand Avenue   Phone: (213) 749-4721
Los Angeles, CA 90015
Publication includes: "How to Locate a Hidden Treasure (of Information about Foundations)," an article describing information in Internal Revenue Service forms 990-AR which all tax exempt foundations are required to file with the IRS and with the states in which they are chartered. Gives list by state of the state government office responsible for receiving 990s and making them available, name of contact, address, phone, hours, restrictions on use. Also includes

extensive bibliography of foundation directories with publisher addresses which is approximately equalled by coverage of these materials in the DOD, but which provides additional details in some cases. **Editor:** Timothy Saasta. **Advertising accepted.** **Price:** $3.50. **Other information:** Appears in October-December 1977 issue.

★3933★
GRAY PANTHER NETWORK—DIRECTORY COLUMN
Gray Panthers
3700 Chestnut Street
Philadelphia, PA 19104
Publication includes: Nationwide list of local groups in each issue. **Frequency:** Quarterly. **Price:** $3.00 per year.

Green Revolution—Community Directory Issue See
    Communities—Directory of Intentional Communities Issue

★3934★
GREEN REVOLUTION—LAND REFORM DIRECTORY ISSUE
School of Living
Box 3233   Phone: (717) 755-1561
York, PA 17402
Covers: 250 community land trusts, private land trusts, and other groups and individuals interested in reforming the system of land holding and land use in the United States. Includes apprenticeship opportunities. **Frequency:** Irregular; latest appears in March 1978 issue. **Advertising accepted.** Circulation 3,000. **Price:** $1.25.

★3935★
GUIDE TO CALIFORNIA FOUNDATIONS
Northern California Foundations Group
Box 5646   Phone: (415) 626-1650
San Francisco, CA 94101
Covers: 440 California foundations with assets exceeding $500,000, or which grant $25,000 or more annually. **Entries include:** Foundation name, address, phone, contact person, purpose, assets, total grants, grant ranges, sample grants, officers and directors, limitations or restrictions, deadlines, preferred form of contact. **Arrangement:** Alphabetical. **Indexes:** Foundation name, granting interest, geographical interest, community foundations. **Pages** (approx.): 300. **Frequency:** Biennial, even years. **Editor:** Malinda Marble. **Price:** $6.00, payment with order. **Other information:** Prepared by the San Francisco Study Center.

★3936★
GUIDE TO CHARITABLE FOUNDATIONS IN THE GREATER AKRON AREA
United Way of Summit County
Box 1260   Phone: (216) 762-7601
Akron, OH 44309
Number of listings: 50. **Entries include:** Foundation name, address, phone, name of contact, interests. **Pages** (approx.): 65. **Frequency:** Not established; first edition 1978. **Price:** $2.50.

★3937★
GUIDE TO CONSUMER SERVICES IN WESTERN PENNSYLVANIA
Pittsburgh Federal Executive Board
1000 Liberty Avenue
611 Federal Building   Phone: (412) 644-6607
Pittsburgh, PA 15222
Covers: Federal, state, and local government agencies, non-governmental consumer services, trade associations, consumer action panels, and other organizations which provide consumer protection services, consumer education and information, mediation services, and lobbying; coverage limited to western Pennsylvania. **Entries include:** Organization or agency name, purpose, functions, address, phone, fees, publications. **Arrangement:** By type of organization. **Indexes:** Organization type, subject. **Pages** (approx.): 55. **Frequency:** Irregular; previous edition July 1975; latest edition September 1979. **Price:** Free.

Guide to Convivial Tools *See* LJ Special Report Guide to Convivial Tools

★3938★
GUIDE TO COOPERATIVE ALTERNATIVES
Communities Publication Cooperative
Box 426   Phone: (703) 894-5126
Louisa, VA 23093
Covers: Several hundred groups, organizations, and individuals active in community organization and alternative life styles as they related to food, health, energy and the environment, appropriate technology, cooperatives, communes, etc.; includes a list of communes. **Entries include:** Organization or individual name, address, phone, interests or activities. **Arrangement:** By subject or type of activity. **Pages** (approx.): 190. **Frequency:** First edition 1979. **Editors:** Paul Freundlich, Chris Collins, and Mikki Wenig. **Price:** $5.95, plus 55¢ shipping.

★3939★
GUIDE TO FEDERAL BENEFITS AND PROGRAMS FOR HANDICAPPED CITIZENS AND THEIR FAMILIES
National Association for Retarded Citizens
1522 K Street, N. W., Suite 516   Phone: (202) 785-3388
Washington, DC 20005
Covers: More than 250 federal government programs concerned with physically and mentally handicapped individuals; also lists several hundred agencies, congressional committees, state government units, etc., interested in the handicapped. **Entries include:** Program descriptions, application requirements, contact addresses for additional information. **Pages** (approx.): 450. **Frequency:** Irregular; latest edition 1979. **Price:** $30.00. **Other information:** Based on "Catalog of Federal Domestic Assistance," but material has been rewritten and supplemented.

Guide to Federal Consumer Services *See* Directory of Federal Consumer Services

★3940★
GUIDE TO FEDERAL PROGRAMS: PROGRAMS AND ACTIVITIES RELATED TO HISTORIC PRESERVATION—SUPPLEMENT
National Trust for Historic Preservation
Preservation Press
1785 Massachusetts Avenue, N. W.   Phone: (202) 638-5200
Washington, DC 20036
Covers: About 40 programs of government agencies, including those in the legislative branch, with funding for which historic preservation programs are eligible. **Entries include:** Agency name, program name, general program subject, brief description of program, examples, eligibility, information contact. **Arrangement:** By type of agency (federal, quasi-governmental, private, etc.). **Pages** (approx.): 110. **Frequency:** Irregular; latest edition 1976. **Editor:** Nancy D. Schultz, Principal Consultant. **Price:** $3.00, plus 50¢ shipping. **Other information:** Base edition published in 1974, covered 200 programs from 49 agencies; now out of print.

Guide to Federal Programs for Historic Preservation *See* Guide to Federal Programs: Programs and Activities Related to Historic...

★3941★
GUIDE TO FOUNDATIONS OF THE SOUTHEAST
Davis-Taylor Associates, Inc.
Route 3, Box 289
Mt. Morgan Road
Williamsburg, KY 40769
Covers: About 2,525 foundations in eleven southern states. Volume 1: Kentucky, Tennessee, Virginia (about 675 foundations); Volume 2: North Carolina, South Carolina (about 550 foundations); Volume 3: Georgia and Florida (about 825 foundations); Volume 4: Alabama, Arkansas, Louisiana, and Mississippi (about 475 foundations). **Entries include:** Foundation name, address, officers, assets, total amount of grants made, and description of sample grants. **Arrangement:** Alphabetical within state sections. **Indexes:** Officer name. **Frequency:** Irregular; latest edition 1975, except Volume 4, 1976. Based on Internal Revenue Service forms 990-PF and 990-AR for 1973 and 1974. **Editor:** Jerry C. Davis. **Price:** Out of print, but available in many libraries.

★3942★
GUIDE TO GEORGIA FOUNDATIONS
State Economic Opportunity Unit
Office of District Programs
Department of Human Resources
618 Ponce de Leon Avenue
Atlanta, GA 30308
Covers: About 550 foundations in Georgia, only about one percent of which have more than $1,000,000 in assets. **Entries include:** Foundation name, address, name of contact, largest and smallest grants ever made. **Frequency:** Published 1979. **Price:** Free. **Other information:** A list which gives names of foundations in this publication in alphabetical, geographical, and subject order is described in separate entry for "Georgia Foundation Directory."

★3943★
GUIDE TO GLOBAL GIVING
Movement for a New Society
4722 Baltimore Avenue
Philadelphia, PA 19143
Covers: Major relief agencies and numerous smaller ones active in international aid. **Entries include:** Agency name, address, programs and goals, compostion of staff, areas served, financial data. **Pages** (approx.): 65. **Frequency:** Published 1976. **Editor:** Phyllis Taylor. **Price:** $1.75.

★3944★
GUIDE TO INDIANA FOUNDATIONS
Davis-Taylor Associates, Inc.
Route 3, Box 289
Mt. Morgan Road
Williamsburg, KY 40769
Number of listings: 335. **Arrangement:** Alphabetical. **Pages** (approx.): 110. **Frequency:** Irregular; latest edition 1975. Based on Internal Revenue Service forms 990-PF and 990-AR for 1973 and 1974. **Editor:** James H. Taylor. **Price:** Out of print, but available in many libraries.

★3945★
GUIDE TO LONG ISLAND LEADERS
Long Island/BUSINESS
303 Sunnyside Boulevard   Phone: (516) 349-8200
Plainview, NY 11557
Covers: Clubs, institutions, newspapers and other media, economic development groups, governmental bodies, and 100 major companies in Long Island, New York. **Entries include:** Association, institution, etc., name, address, phone, name of principal executive; some listings include additional information. **Arrangement:** By type of activity. **Pages** (approx.): 45. **Frequency:** Annual, summer. **Editor:** Paul B. Townsend. **Price:** $10.00. **Other information:** Published in segments during the year in "Long Island/BUSINESS."

★3946★
GUIDE TO MINNESOTA FOUNDATIONS
Minnesota Council on Foundations
Foshay Tower, Suite 413   Phone: (612) 338-1989
Minneapolis, MN 55402
Number of listings: 575. **Entries include:** Foundation name, address, name of contact, type of foundation, directors, assets, grants in year reported on, fields of interest; some entries include name, address, and estimated assets only. **Arrangement:** Divided into grant-making, operating, scholarship and educational, and recently dissolved foundations. Appendix of out-of-state grants. **Pages** (approx.): 75. **Frequency:** Not established; first edition 1977. **Price:** $10.00.

★3947★
GUIDE TO NEWSPAPER INDEXES IN NEW ENGLAND
New England Library Association
1113 Main   Phone: (617) 829-6545
Holden, MA
Covers: Locations of indexes to newspapers presently or formerly published in New England, and to newspapers published outside the region but indexed in New England. **Entries include:** Newspaper title, frequency, format, inclusive dates of its index, whether index is published or unpublished, scope of the index, and location. **Arrangement:** Geographical (state, then city), then alphabetical by title. **Indexes:** Title, libraries surveyed. **Pages** (approx.): 95. **Frequency:** Not established; first edition 1978. **Price:** $5.00.

★3948★
GUIDE TO OREGON FOUNDATIONS
Tri-County Community Council of Portland
718 W. Burnside Street   Phone: (503) 223-1030
Portland, OR 97209
Covers: About 285 foundations based in Oregon, and national foundations particularly active in Oregon; includes trusts and scholarship funds. **Entries include:** Foundation name, address, name of contact, restrictions on grants, total grants and range of size of individual grants, sample grants, funding restrictions, timetables, whether letter, interview, etc., is preferred as first contact. **Arrangement:** Geographical. **Indexes:** Alphabetical. **Pages** (approx.): 265. **Frequency:** Biennial, even years; first edition spring 1978; update fall 1979. Based on Internal Revenue Service forms 990-PF and 990-AR for second preceding year. **Price:** $7.50, plus 50¢ shipping (current edition); $10.00 (tentative, 1980 edition).

Guide to Social Service Agencies [Wichita and Sedgwick County]
See **Community Service Directory, Wichita and Sedgwick County** [Kansas]

★3949★
GUIDE TO STATE HISTORIC PRESERVATION PROGRAMS
National Trust for Historic Preservation
Preservation Press
1785 Massachusetts Avenue, N. W.   Phone: (202) 638-5200
Washington, DC 20036
Publication includes: Interior Department and state sources of grants, state arts councils; individual state editions. **Arrangement:** Geographical. **Frequency:** Irregular; latest edition 1976. **Editor:** Betts Abel. **Price:** 50¢ each, plus 50¢ shipping.

★3950★
GUIDE TO TEXAS FOUNDATIONS
Southern Resource Center
Box 5593
Dallas, TX 75222
Number of listings: 215. **Arrangement:** Four geographical categories. **Pages** (approx.): 100. **Frequency:** Irregular; latest edition 1975. Based on data from cooperating foundations or 1973-74 records in the attorney general's office. **Price:** $7.50. (Not verified)

★3951★
GUIDE TO WASHINGTON, D.C., FOUNDATIONS
Guide Publishers
Box 5849   Phone: (301) 530-1643
Washington, DC 20014
Number of listings: 280. **Entries include:** Foundation name, address, reporting period for data, net worth, total number and total value of grants made, amount and recipient of two largest grants and grants exceeding $5,000; purpose, special interest, names and titles of officials. **Arrangement:** Alphabetical. **Indexes:** Officer name. **Pages** (approx.): 60. **Frequency:** Irregular; second edition 1975. Based on Internal Revenue Service forms 990-PF and 990-AR from 1973. **Editor:** Francis de Bettencourt. **Price:** $8.00.

★3952★
GUIDE TO WOMEN'S PUBLISHING
Dustbooks
Box 100
Paradise, CA 95969
Covers: More than 100 women's journals and newspapers; agencies distributing women's publications, and women's presses with their histories and editorial policies are also listed. **Entries include:** For publications - Name, address, price, publishing frequency, content. **Arrangement:** Alphabetical. **Pages** (approx.): 300. **Frequency:** Irregular; first edition April 1978; new edition expected March 1980. **Editors:** Polly Joan and Andrea Chesman. **Price:** $9.95, cloth; $4.95, paper (current edition); $11.95, cloth; $6.95, paper (1980 edition). **Also includes:** List of directories, review media, libraries, archives, and bookstores for women.

★3953★
HANDBOOK OF CORPORATE SOCIAL RESPONSIBILITY
Human Resources Network
2010 Chancellor Street
Philadelphia, PA
Covers: Corporate giving programs of about 200 corporations with a total of 750 programs.

★3954★
HANDBOOK OF FUTURES RESEARCH
Greenwood Press, Inc.
51 Riverside Avenue   Phone: (203) 226-3571
Westport, CT 06880
Publication includes: Lists of organizations concerned with futures research, college-level research and study programs in the subject, and futures-oriented journals and periodic reports. **Frequency:** Not established; first edition spring 1978. **Editor:** Jib Fowles. **Price:** $39.95, postpaid, payment with order. **Other information:** Principal content of publication is articles concerned with individual social and environmental problems (environmental decay, food, population) and research techniques (simulation modeling and gaming, forecasting, etc.).

★3955★
HANDBOOK ON APPROPRIATE TECHNOLOGY
Canadian Hunger Foundation
323 Chapel Street   Phone: (613) 237-0180
Otta K1N 7Z2, Ontario, Canada
Publication includes: Lists of groups working in development of appropriate technology. **Entries include:** Name, address, brief note on interests and activities. **Frequency:** Volumes published irregularly; revised edition of Volume 1, May 1979; Volume 2 expected late 1979 or early 1980. **Price:** Revised Volume 1, $14.50 Canadian. **Also includes:** Information on appropriate technology and case studies. **Other information:** Available in English, French, and Spanish editions.

★3956★
HANDICAPPED FUNDING DIRECTORY
Research Grant Guides
Box 357
Oceanside, NY 11572
Covers: More than 400 foundations, associations, and government agencies which grant funds for projects related to handicapped persons. **Entries include:** Name of granting organization, address, information concerning type and size of grants, application details. **Arrangement:** Geographical. **Indexes:** Alphabetical. **Pages** (approx.): 160. **Frequency:** Biennial, spring of even years. **Editor:** Burton J. Eckstein. **Price:** $14.50 (current edition); $16.50 (1980 edition); postpaid.

★3957★
HEALTH & RESOURCE GUIDE [San Diego County, California]
County of San Diego
Administrative Center
1600 Pacific Highway   Phone: (714) 236-2722
San Diego, CA 92101
Covers: Over 300 agencies and organizations offering health and
welfare services. Crisis lines, emergency ambulance services, welfare
agencies, and women's and children's services are included. Entries
include: Agency or organization name, address, phone. Arrangement:
By type of service. Pages (approx.): 225. Frequency: Irregular; latest
edition 1979.

★3958★
HELP: THE INDISPENSABLE ALMANAC OF CONSUMER
      INFORMATION
Everest House Publishers
1133 Avenue of the Americas   Phone: (202) 737-1190
New York, NY 10036
Publication includes: Numerous short lists of sources of information
and assistance on consumer problems, related to extensive text on the
problems; reports independent ratings of philanthropic organizations.
Entries include: Name, address. Indexes: General. Pages (approx.):
425. Frequency: Annual, fall. Editor: Arthur E. Rowse. Former title:
Help: The Useful Almanac. Price: $7.95. Other information:
Formerly published by Consumer News, Inc.

Help: The Useful Almanac See Help: The Indispensable Almanac
      of Consumer Information

★3959★
THE HELP BOOK
Charles Scribner's Sons
597 Fifth Avenue
New York, NY 10017
Covers: Local, state, and national agencies and organizations able to
assist with child abuse, rape, assault, suicide prevention, education,
emergencies and disasters, legal services, transportation and travel,
and volunteerism, etc. Entries include: Organization or agency name,
address, phone, description of services. Arrangement: By subject or
concern. Pages (approx.): 420. Frequency: First edition November
1979. Editor: J. L. Barkas. Price: $19.95, cloth; $9.95, paper. Send
orders to: Charles Scribner's Sons, Vreeland Avenue, Totowa, NJ
07512.

★3960★
HELP FOR THE CITIZENS OF WAKE COUNTY [Raleigh, North
      Carolina]
Wake County Information and Referral Center
Wake County Public Libraries
104 Fayetteville Street   Phone: (919) 755-6089
Raleigh, NC 27601
Covers: 800 social service, mental health, medical, educational,
recreational, cultural, and other community agencies or organizations
which offer direct services to citizens of Wake County, North
Carolina. Entries include: Organization name, address, phone, brief
description of services and activities, other pertinent information.
Arrangement: Alphabetical. Indexes: Subject. Pages (approx.): 180.
Frequency: Irregular; latest edition July 1979. Editor: Carol H. Reilly,
Extension Librarian, Information and Referral Center. Price: $1.00,
payment with order.

Holistic Health Directory See New Age Directory [Alternative
      lifestyles and philosophies]

★3961★
HOME ECONOMICS IN INSTITUTIONS GRANTING BACHELOR'S OR
      HIGHER DEGREES
American Home Economics Association
2010 Massachusetts Avenue, N. W.   Phone: (202) 862-8300
Washington, DC 20036
Entries include: Institution name, address; name and phone of
department chairman or contact; degrees offered; fields of study;
fellowships and financial aid offered. Arrangement: Geographical.
Frequency: Annual. Price: $3.00.

Homosexual National Classified Directory See Directory of
      Homosexual Organizations and Publications

★3962★
HOTLINES [U.S. government]
Public Citizen
Box 19404
Washington, DC 20036
Covers: 18 federal government toll-free hotline services which
provide information on, and accept reports concerning, a wide variety
of consumer and citizen problems, including runaways, job safety,
flood insurance, solar heating, commodity futures trading, etc. Entries
include: Name of service, name of sponsoring department or agency,
description of service provided or information given, toll-free number.
Frequency: First edition summer 1978. Price: Free; send business-
size stamped and self-addressed envelope. Other information: Public
Citizen is a Ralph Nader group.

★3963★
HOUSING RESOURCE MANUAL [New York City]
Pratt Institute Center for Community and Environmental Development
275 Washington Avenue   Phone: (212) 622-5026
Brooklyn, NY 11205
Covers: Private and governmental organizations and individuals who
assist tenants and homeowners with housing problems in New York
City. Entries include: Name, address, phone, name of contact.
Frequency: Irregular; updated periodically. Price: $3.50 for base
edition and updates, plus $1.50 shipping.

★3964★
HUDSON'S WASHINGTON NEWS MEDIA CONTACTS DIRECTORY
Howard Penn Hudson
44 W. Market Street   Phone: (914) 876-2081
Rhinebeck, NY 12572
Covers: 2,800 editors, free lance writers, and news correspondents,
plus 2,500 United States, Canadian, and foreign newspapers, radio-TV
networks and stations, magazines, and periodicals based or
represented in Washington, DC. Entries include: For publications and
companies - Name, address, phone, and name of editor or key
personnel. For individuals - Name, assignment. Arrangement:
Classified by activity (e.g., correspondents), media type, etc.
Newspapers and radio-TV stations sections are arranged
geographically; specialized periodicals section is arranged by subject.
Pages (approx.): 260. Frequency: Annual, January; updates in April,
July, and October. Editors: Howard Penn Hudson and Mary Elizabeth
Hudson. Advertising accepted. Price: $48.00 (current edition);
$55.00 (1980 edition); per year, postpaid, payment with order. Send
orders to: Hudson's Directory, 2626 Pennsylvania Ave., N. W.,
Washington, DC 20037 (202-333-5444).

Human Rights Directory See North American Human Rights
      Directory

★3965★
HUMAN RIGHTS HANDBOOK
Facts on File
119 W. 57th Street   Phone: (212) 265-2011
New York, NY 10019
Covers: About 250 human rights organizations, worldwide. Entries
include: Organization name, address, phone, name of contact,

background, function. **Frequency:** Not established; first edition 1979. **Editor:** Marguerite Garling. **Price:** $25.00.

★3966★

HUMAN RIGHTS ORGANIZATIONS AND PERIODICALS DIRECTORY
Meiklejohn Civil Liberties Institute
1715 Francisco Street   Phone: (415) 848-0599
Berkeley, CA 94703
Covers: 500 organizations, many periodicals, concerned with social change and human rights, especially those providing information or assistance on legal questions and engaging in litigation. **Entries include:** Organization name, address, brief description of purpose, and publications (including frequency and rate). **Arrangement:** Alphabetical. **Indexes:** Subject. **Pages** (approx.): 100. **Frequency:** Biennial, odd years. **Editor:** David Christiano, Librarian. **Price:** $10.00.

★3967★

ILLINOIS DIRECTORY OF ENVIRONMENTAL INFORMATION
Illinois Institute of Natural Resources
309 W. Washington   Phone: (312) 793-3870
Chicago, IL 60606
Covers: Environmental groups, neighborhood recycling centers, markets for recyclable materials, and state agencies in Illinois. **Entries include:** For groups and centers - Name, address, phone, name of director; center listings also include hours of operation and materials recycled. Agency listings include name, address, phone. **Arrangement:** By county. **Pages** (approx.): 240. **Frequency:** Irregular; latest edition 1977; new edition expected April 1980. **Editor:** Anna L. Englehardt. **Price:** $7.25, paper copy; $3.00 microfiche (1977 edition; PB 281-070/AS). **Send orders to:** National Technical Information Service, Springfield, VA 22161. **Other information:** Single copies of 1980 edition free from publisher.

★3968★

ILLINOIS FOUNDATION DIRECTORY
Foundation Data Center
123 E. Grant Street   Phone: (612) 870-4434
Minneapolis, MN 55403
Covers: Estimated 1,900 active and inactive foundations. **Entries include:** Foundation name, address, phone, names of trustees and managers, foundation type, year established, principal contributors, territory interested in, financial data, list of gifts and grants. **Arrangement:** Alphabetical. **Pages** (approx.): 700. **Frequency:** Published 1978; annual updates. Based on Internal Revenue Service forms 990-PF and 990-AR, from second preceding year. **Editors:** Beatrice J. Capriotti and Frank J. Capriotti, III. **Price:** $425.00 (base volume); $200.00, annual update; individuals' orders must be accompanied by payment.

★3969★

ILLINOIS FOUNDATION PROFILES
Davis-Taylor Associates, Inc.
Route 3, Box 289
Mt. Morgan Road
Williamsburg, KY 40769
Covers: About 320 foundations with assets of $400,000 or which have made grants totaling $100,000. **Entries include:** Foundation name, address, officers, assets, total amount of grants made, and description of sample grants. **Arrangement:** Alphabetical. **Pages** (approx.): 100. **Frequency:** Irregular; latest edition 1976. Based on Internal Revenue Service forms 990-PF and 990-AR for 1973 and 1974. **Editor:** James H. Taylor. **Price:** Out of print, but available in many libraries.

★3970★

ILLINOIS WOMEN'S DIRECTORY
Midwest Women's Center
53 W. Jackson Street
Chicago, IL 60604
Covers: 2,000 Illinois associations and state and local branches of national organizations, 600 services for women, 190 Illinois and

national hotlines; includes surveys of resources in about 30 specific fields, such as where to find financial aid. Appropriate entries include Spanish text. **Arrangement:** By organization name, with city and subject cross-references in same alphabet. **Pages** (approx.): 170. **Frequency:** Not established; first edition December 1978. **Editor:** Kathleen Ligare. **Price:** $5.20, postpaid, payment with order. **Other information:** Published in cooperation with Swallow Press, Inc.

★3971★

INFO DIRECTORY [Social services, Los Angeles, California]
Information and Referral Service of Los Angeles County
621 S. Virgil Avenue   Phone: (213) 736-1300
Los Angeles, CA 90005
Covers: Over 3,600 sources for health, welfare, vocational, and recreational services. **Arrangement:** By type of service. **Indexes:** Alphabetical, service, geographical. **Frequency:** Irregular; previous edition 1975; latest edition November 1978. **Price:** $18.50, postpaid, payment must accompany order.

International Association of Counseling Services—Directory *See* **Directory of Counseling Services**

★3972★

INTERNATIONAL DIRECTORY OF ORGANIZATIONS CONCERNED WITH THE AGING
Department of Economic and Social Affairs
United Nations
New York, NY 10017
Covers: About 115 organizations and institutions, about one-third of which are in North America. **Entries include:** Institution name, address, name of principal executive and other personnel, description of objectives and activities, periodicals issued, languages used. **Arrangement:** Geographical. **Pages** (approx.): 60. **Frequency:** Not established; first edition summer 1977. **Price:** $4.00 (Sales No. E.77.IV.10).

★3973★

INTERNATIONAL DIRECTORY OF PRISONERS AID AGENCIES
International Prisoners Aid Association
C/o Department of Sociology
University of Louisville   Phone: (502) 588-6836
Louisville, KY 40208
Publication includes: 45 prisoners aid agencies around the world about which some details are given and 50 additional public agencies and private organizations with name and address only. **Arrangement:** Geographical. **Pages** (approx.): 45. **Frequency:** Irregular; latest edition 1975; new edition expected July 1980. **Editor:** Dr. Badr-El-Din Ali, Executive Director. **Price:** $1.00 (current edition); $2.50 (tentative, 1980 edition). **Also includes:** Survey of penal system, correctional trends, financing, and probation and after-care services in each country.

★3974★

INTERNATIONAL DIRECTORY OF SEX RESEARCH AND RELATED FIELDS
Institute for Sex Research
Indiana University   Phone: (812) 337-7686
Bloomington, IN 47405
Covers: Over 1,600 individuals in 50 countries concerned with sex behavior, sex variations, sex education, contraception, marriage, divorce, sex and media, etc. **Entries include:** Name, title, affiliation, address, degrees, phone, statement of research interests and competence, bibliography of selected publications. **Arrangement:** Alphabetical. **Indexes:** Subject, geographical. **Frequency:** Not established; first edition 1976. **Editor:** Joan Brewer, Information Service Officer. **Price:** $100.00. **Send orders to:** G. K. Hall & Co., 70 Lincoln St., Boston, MA 02111 (617-423-3990). **Other information:** Current information maintained by institute's Information Service.

★3975★
INTERNATIONAL DIRECTORY OF WOMEN'S DEVELOPMENT ORGANIZATIONS
Office of Women in Development
Agency for International Development
Washington, DC 20523
Covers: About 600 organizations which are primarily of interest to women or which may have resources available to women; local, national, and international organizations are listed with emphasis on local and national organizations of developing countries. **Entries include:** Name of organization, location and mailing address, phone; affiliation with international organizations, if any; names and addresses of principal officers, method of selection, name of executive director, if any; number of chapters, number of members; date established; publications, conferences, and meetings; language used; functions, activities, and areas of interest; achievements of organization. **Arrangement:** Geographical within categories of organization type. **Indexes:** (In tabular format) Geographic region, country, organization name, whether affiliated with another group, number of chapters, number of members, whether a federation, activity, date established, language used, whether active on an international level. **Pages** (approx.): 315. **Frequency:** Irregular; first edition 1977 (1975 data); new edition expected summer 1980. **Editor:** Franziska P. Hosken. **Price:** Free.

★3976★
INTERNATIONAL DIRECTORY OF YOUTH INTERNSHIPS
United Nations Headquarters Non-Governmental Organizations Youth Caucus
Social Development Division
United Nations, Room DC-977
New York, NY 10017
Covers: Internship opportunities with the United Nations, its specialized agencies, non-governmental organizations, and university programs related to the United Nations. Also lists United Nations Information Centers and United Nations Development Program Offices worldwide. **Entries include:** Name of intern program, name and address of sponsor, description of positions, number available, remuneration (most programs do not offer salaries or expenses), application details. **Arrangement:** Classified by type of sponsor. **Frequency:** Irregular; latest edition 1977; new edition expected 1980. **Price:** $2.00.

★3977★
INTERNATIONAL EDUCATION: A COMPENDIUM OF FEDERAL AGENCY PROGRAMS
Office on International Education Policy
American Council on Education
One Dupont Circle
Washington, DC 20036
Covers: Over 100 education grants by federal agencies for international educational research programs or international exchange programs. **Entries include:** Agency name, address, program description including objectives, eligibility requirements, name of contact, etc. **Arrangement:** Alphabetical. **Pages** (approx.): 80. **Frequency:** Irregular; latest edition 1977; new edition expected 1981. **Editor:** Becky H. Owens. **Price:** $5.00, payment with order.

★3978★
INTERNATIONAL MEALS ON WHEELS DIRECTORY
National Association of Meal Programs
C/o Capitol Hill United Methodist Church
421 Seward Square, S. E.   Phone: (202) 564-1000
Washington, DC 20003
Covers: About 1,000 programs (mostly privately financed) which provide hot meals at a nominal fee to ill or elderly persons; coverage includes United States, Canada, Guam, Puerto Rico, and the Virgin Islands. **Entries include:** Program name, address of kitchen, contact name, special dietary needs met. **Arrangement:** Geographical. **Pages** (approx.): 100. **Frequency:** Annual. **Editor:** Neil Scott. **Former title:** National Directory of Meals on Wheels Programs. **Price:** $1.50,

postpaid.

★3979★
INTERNATIONAL UNION FOR THE SCIENTIFIC STUDY OF POPULATION—DIRECTORY OF MEMBERS' SCIENTIFIC ACTIVITIES
International Union for the Scientific Study of Population
Rue Forgeur 5
B-4000 Liege, Belgium
Covers: 1,300 members in 90 countries. **Entries include:** Name, nationality, date of birth, home or office address, position, publications, areas of research - past, current, and projected. **Arrangement:** Geographical. **Pages** (approx.): 440. **Frequency:** Irregular; latest edition November 1975; new edition expected late 1980. **Price:** $18.00.

★3980★
INVENTORY OF PRIVATE AGENCY POPULATION RESEARCH
Interagency Committee on Population Research
National Institutes of Health
Public Health Service
Health, Education, and Welfare Department   Phone: (301) 496-1971
Bethesda, MD 20014
Covers: About 415 population research projects sponsored by the Ford Foundation, the Population Council, and the Rockefeller Foundation. **Entries include:** Title of project (including organism and/or anatomical site if applicable), name of principal investigator, name and location of grantee institution, name of sponsoring agency and agency subdivision, whether a grant or intramural funding, agency project number, prior year's funding amount, project period and total project funds. **Arrangement:** By focus of research, then by principal investigator name. **Indexes:** Investigator name. **Pages** (approx.): 90. **Frequency:** Annual, winter. **Editor:** Margaret R. Garner, Technical Information Specialist/Biologist. **Price:** Free (ISSN 0360-0610).

★3981★
INVEST YOURSELF [Volunteer service opportunities]
Commission on Voluntary Service and Action
475 Riverside Drive, Room 1126   Phone: (212) 870-2801
New York, NY 10027
Covers: Work camps, apprenticeships, seminars, community action projects, and other programs involving community service and personal involvement. Most service opportunities provide little or no compensation, but do include some room and board; some involve personal expenditures, especially for travel. Includes list of agencies. **Entries include:** Description of activity available, length of involvement expected, any special requirements, compensation or expense, agency handling recruitment. Agency list includes agency name, address, name of contact. **Arrangement:** Classified by type of service. **Pages** (approx.): 60. **Frequency:** Annual, December. **Editor:** Susan Angus, Editorial Coordinator. **Former title:** Invest Your Summer. **Price:** $2.00, postpaid, payment with order.

★3982★
JOURNALISM CAREER AND SCHOLARSHIP GUIDE
The Newspaper Fund
Box 300   Phone: (609) 452-2000
Princeton, NJ 08540
Covers: About 3,000 scholarships, fellowships, assistantships, and internships with a value of over $100 and available through over 200 colleges and universities. Also lists aid available through journalism associations, individual newspapers, etc. **Entries include:** School name, address, name of department responsible for journalism curriculum, name and phone of chairman, programs offered, degrees offered, average yearly school costs, and description of aid available. Similar information for non-institutional awards. **Arrangement:** Schools are geographical, others are alphabetical within type of aid. **Indexes:** Institution. **Pages** (approx.): 130. **Frequency:** Annual, December. **Former title:** Journalism Scholarship Guide. **Price:** Free. **Also includes:** Information on journalism as a career, job search procedures, employment forecast, school enrollment forecast.

★3983★

JOURNALISM EDUCATOR—DIRECTORY ISSUE

Association for Education in Journalism
431 Murphy Hall
University of Minnesota   Phone: (612) 376-7100
Minneapolis, MN 55455

Covers: Over 260 journalism schools and departments in four-year colleges and universities; journalism education associations at the college and university level; national funds, fellowships, and foundations in journalism; college and scholastic journalistic services; media and professional associations; and professional and student societies; coverage includes the United States and Canada. **Entries include:** For journalism schools and departments - School name, address, phone, names of faculty and administrators; facilities; description of educational programs. For other listings - Name, address, phone, name of contact. **Arrangement:** Schools are geographical, others are alphabetical within organization type. **Pages** (approx.): 65. **Frequency:** Annual, January. **Editor:** William Roepke, Professor. **Advertising accepted.** Circulation 2,000. **Price:** $5.00 (current and 1980 editions).

Journalism Scholarship Guide *See* Journalism Career and Scholarship Guide

★3984★

KANSAS CITY CLUBS AND ORGANIZATIONS

Chamber of Commerce of Greater Kansas City
600 Ten Main Center   Phone: (816) 221-2424
Kansas City, MO 64105

Entries include: Name, address, phone, name of officers. **Arrangement:** Classified by type of organization. **Pages** (approx.): 50. **Frequency:** Irregular; latest edition May 1976; new edition possible 1981. **Price:** 1976 edition out of print.

★3985★

KIBBUTZ VOLUNTEER

Vacation-Work
9 Park End Street
Oxford, England

Covers: More than 200 kibbutzim in Israel which desire volunteer workers. **Entries include:** Name, address, phone, work available, what is provided for volunteers without charge (food, etc.), entertainment offered, accomodations available, languages spoken, etc. **Arrangement:** Alphabetical. **Pages** (approx.): 135. **Frequency:** Biennial; new edition expected January 1980. **Editor:** John Bedford. **Price:** $6.95 (1980 edition; ISSN 0413-3881). **Send orders to:** Writer's Digest Books, 9933 Alliance Rd., Cincinnati, OH 45242 (513-984-0717).

★3986★

KIWANIS INTERNATIONAL DIRECTORY

Kiwanis International
101 E. Erie Street   Phone: (312) 943-2300
Chicago, IL 60611

Covers: About 7,500 local clubs of business and professional men. **Entries include:** Club name, president, name and address of secretary, meeting place and time. **Arrangement:** Geographical. **Pages** (approx.): 245. **Frequency:** Annual, November. **Editor:** R. P. Merridew. **Price:** Available to members only.

★3987★

LEAP YEAR PAPERS [Co-op resources]

Cascadian Regional Library
454 Willamette Street   Phone: (503) 485-0366
Eugene, OR 97401

Publication includes: Over 600 groups and individuals with information and/or experience in organizing co-ops, including food co-ops and political and citizens' organizations; primarily Oregon, Washington, and Idaho are covered. **Entries include:** Group or individual name, address, phone. **Arrangement:** Alphabetical. **Pages** (approx.): 65. **Frequency:** Published 1976. **Price:** $1.95.

★3988★

LIST OF PROFESSIONAL WOMEN'S GROUPS [National organizations]

American Association of University Women
2401 Virginia Avenue, N. W.   Phone: (202) 785-7730
Washington, DC 20037

Covers: About 85 professional associations and women's organizations committed to the advancement of women; groups listed offer one or more types of employment services, and include many organizations with both male and female members. **Entries include:** Organization name, address, name of principal official, and name and address of chairperson of women's unit (if organization includes men). **Frequency:** Annual. **Price:** 50¢.

★3989★

LISTING OF NEIGHBORHOOD ORGANIZATIONS IN SAN FRANCISCO [California]

Neighborhood Services Office
San Francisco Planning and Urban Research Association
414 Clement Street, Room 5   Phone: (415) 221-0414
San Francisco, CA 94118

Covers: About 110 neighborhood improvement associations, merchants associations, planning councils, etc. **Entries include:** Organization name, address, phone, name of president. **Arrangement:** Alphabetical. **Frequency:** Quarterly. **Price:** $3.00 per year, payment with order. **Other information:** List, on mailing labels, of 27,000 California organizations also available. Apply for price, etc.

★3990★

LJ SPECIAL REPORT GUIDE TO CONVIVIAL TOOLS

R. R. Bowker Company
1180 Avenue of the Americas   Phone: (212) 764-5100
New York, NY 10036

Covers: About 500 publishers (worldwide) of a wide variety of book and periodical materials useful in "research on radical alternatives to a commodity-intensive society" (from introduction by Ivan Illich), referred to as "radical technologies." Includes annotated entries on about 900 books and 125 periodicals. **Arrangement:** Books are by author, periodicals by title. **Indexes:** Subject/co-author/title. **Pages** (approx.): 300. **Frequency:** First edition fall 1979; proposed frequency is triennial. **Editor:** Valentina Borremans, former director, Centro Intercultural de Documentacion (CIDOC). **Price:** $5.95, payment with order; $7.00, billed (ISSN 0362-448X). **Send orders to:** R. R. Bowker Company, Box 1817, Ann Arbor, MI 48106. **Other information:** Published as no. 13 in "Library Journal Special Reports" series.

★3991★

LOS ANGELES PEOPLE'S YELLOW PAGES

Los Angeles People's Yellow Pages, Inc.
510 Pacific Avenue, No. 4   Phone: (213) 399-5736
Venice, CA 90291

Covers: About 500 community resources important in social change and daily living, with emphasis on inexpensive and reliable services. Includes resources in arts, consumerism, women's movement, child care, education, etc. **Entries include:** Resource name, address, phone, brief description. **Arrangement:** Classified by area of activity. **Indexes:** Zip code. **Pages** (approx.): 175. **Frequency:** Annual, summer. **Editor:** Ross Moster. **Price:** $2.50 donation requested. (Not verified)

★3992★

MAGAZINE INDUSTRY MARKET PLACE

R. R. Bowker Company
1180 Avenue of the Americas   Phone: (212) 764-5100
New York, NY 10036

Covers: About 3,100 periodical publishers, printers, other suppliers to the industry, direct mail services, associations and organizations, agents, etc. **Entries include:** For publishers - Company name, address, phone, address for orders, principal executives and managers, date founded, periodical titles, representatives. For suppliers and other listings - Firm name, address, phone, executives, services, etc. **Arrangement:** Alphabetical. **Indexes:** Principal index is 20,000-item combined index of publishers, publications, personnel ("Names and Numbers"). **Pages** (approx.): 610. **Frequency:** Annual; first edition December 1979. **Editor:** Janice M. Blaufox. **Advertising accepted. Price:** $24.50, postpaid, payment with order. **Send orders to:** R. R. Bowker Company, Box 1807, Ann Arbor, MI 48106 (313-761-4700). **Other information:** Originally advertised as, "Magazine Market Place Directory."

Magazine Market Place Directory *See* Magazine Industry Market Place

★3993★
MAGAZINES FOR LIBRARIES
R. R. Bowker Company
1180 Avenue of the Americas   Phone: (212) 764-5100
New York, NY 10036
Covers: About 6,500 periodicals. **Entries include:** Title, publisher name and address, year first published, frequency, price, editor, where indexed, editorial content. **Arrangement:** By subject. **Indexes:** Readership. **Pages** (approx.): 950. **Frequency:** Irregular; latest edition November 1978. **Editors:** Bill Katz and Berry G. Richards. **Price:** $37.50, postpaid, payment with order. **Send orders to:** R. R. Bowker Co., Box 1807, Ann Arbor, MI 48106 (313-761-4700).

★3994★
MAINE NATURAL RESOURCE ORGANIZATIONS DIRECTORY
Resource Planning Division
Maine State Planning Office
184 State Street
Augusta, ME 04330
Entries include: Name, address, description of activities. **Pages** (approx.): 40. **Frequency:** Not established; latest edition 1979. **Price:** Free.

★3995★
MANUAL OF DEATH EDUCATION AND SIMPLE BURIAL
Celo Press
Route 5   Phone: (704) 675-4925
Burnsville, NC 28714
Publication includes: "Directory of Funeral and Memorial Societies" covering about 175 local societies concerned with simplifying funerals through pre-planning; societies are members of the Continental Association of Funeral and Memorial Societies in the United States and the Memorial Society Association of Canada. **Entries include:** Society name, address, phone. **Arrangement:** Geographical. **Frequency:** Irregular; new edition expected January 1980. **Editor:** Ernest Morgan. **Price:** $2.50 (tentative, 1980 edition). **Other information:** Includes information to help the consumer plan a funeral without the assistance of a memorial society and on organizing a society.

★3996★
MARYLAND ASSOCIATION, BUSINESS, CHAMBER OF COMMERCE, PROFESSIONAL SOCIETY, AND TRADE ASSOCIATION DIRECTORY
Maryland Association Management Corporation
Box 67
Annapolis, MD 21401
Covers: 500 organizations with offices in Maryland. **Entries include:** Association name, address, phone, name of principal officer; number of committees; meetings; and publications. **Arrangement:** By type of organization. **Frequency:** Annual. **Advertising accepted.** Circulation 5,000. **Price:** $8.00.

★3997★
MARYLAND ENVIRONMENTAL DIRECTORY
Maryland Conservation Council
2574 Riva Road, Suite 15A
Annapolis, MD 21401
Covers: About 125 organizations, federal and state government agencies, and other groups in Maryland concerned with conservation and the environment. **Entries include:** Organization or agency name, address, phone, name of contact, description of purpose and activities, publications. **Arrangement:** By type of organization. **Indexes:** Topic, personal name, publication title. **Pages** (approx.): 100. **Frequency:** Irregular; latest edition 1978. **Editor:** William G. Wilson. **Price:** $4.00, payment with order; $4.50, billed.

★3998★
MEDIA AWARDS HANDBOOK
Milton L. Levy
621 Sheri Lane   Phone: (415) 837-6598
Danville, CA 94526
Covers: Major honor awards and contests for radio, television, newspapers, magazines, and allied fields. **Entries include:** Name of contest or award, sponsor, address, deadline, media of concern, entry categories, form of entry, rules, awards, announcement date, purpose. **Arrangement:** Alphabetical. **Pages** (approx.): 200. **Frequency:** Irregular; previous edition 1974; latest edition fall 1979. **Editor:** Milton L. Levy. **Price:** $20.00.

★3999★
MEDIA GUIDE INTERNATIONAL: NEWSPAPERS AND NEWS MAGAZINES
Directories International, Inc.
1718 Sherman Avenue   Phone: (312) 491-0019
Evanston, IL 60201
Covers: Newspapers and news magazines, international, national, and regional in scope, from 111 countries, including the United States. **Entries include:** Publication name, name and address of publisher, name of advertising manager, name of United States representative, advertising rates in U. S. dollars and local currency, circulation, mechanical data, etc. **Arrangement:** By geographic region; multicontinental publications listed separately. **Frequency:** Annual, February. **Advertising accepted.** Circulation 1,300. **Price:** $58.00.

★4000★
MEDIA GUIDE TO FREE CIRCULATION NEWSPAPERS, SHOPPING GUIDES, AND PRIVATE DISTRIBUTION SYSTEMS
National Association of Advertising Publishers
313 Price Place
Madison, WI 53705
Covers: 145 free circulation newspapers, 870 shopping guides, and 475 private distribution systems. **Entries include:** Publication or service name, publisher or company name, address, phone, rate and other information, Zip code areas covered. **Arrangement:** Geographical. **Pages** (approx.): 160. **Frequency:** Annual, July. **Editor:** Joel Bradtke. **Advertising accepted.** Circulation 2,400. **Price:** $12.50 (current edition); $13.00 (tentative, 1980 edition). **Also includes:** List of audited publications.

★4001★
MEDIA REPORT TO WOMEN INDEX/DIRECTORY OF WOMEN'S MEDIA
Women's Institute for Freedom of the Press
3306 Ross Place, N. W.   Phone: (202) 966-7783
Washington, DC 20008
Covers: 500 women's media (feminist-oriented periodicals, publishers, film makers, radio/TV groups, etc.) and 800 women who work in these and traditional media. **Entries include:** Media list includes company or publication name, address, phone, and name of contact, plus short description. Media women section includes name, office address and phone, home address, and brief comment on media work. **Arrangement:** Media sections are by Zip code, individual section is alphabetical. **Indexes:** Each geographical section has alphabetical index and media women section has Zip code index. **Pages** (approx.): 60. **Frequency:** Annual, January. **Editor:** Martha Leslie Allen. **Advertising accepted. Price:** $8.00 (current and 1980 editions). **Other information:** Associates of the institute are included in the media women list.

Memorial Society Association of Canada—Roster *See* Manual of Death Education and Simple Burial

★4002★
MEN'S AWARENESS NETWORK NEWSLETTER ("MAN")
Knoxville Men's Resource Center
Box 8060
UT Station
Knoxville, TN 37921
Covers: Men's Movement activities, organizations, periodicals and other publications, seminars and courses, etc. **Entries include:** Name of periodical, organization, etc., plus appropriate details. **Frequency:** Irregular; several times yearly. **Price:** $5.00 per year. (Not verified)

★4003★
MENTAL HEALTH ALMANAC
Garland Publishing, Inc.
136 Madison Avenue   Phone: (212) 686-7492
New York, NY 10016
Covers: Organizations concerned with mental health issues; graduate programs in mental health; and professional and service organizations. **Entries include:** For organizations - Name, address, phone, contact; target population, specific mental health issue, or profession with which concerned. For graduate programs - Institution name, address, phone, contact; description of program including degrees, field experience, tuition, length of time required. **Arrangement:** Within categories of population, concern, and profession, by subject. **Pages** (approx.): 415. **Frequency:** Published 1978. **Editor:** Robert D. Allen. **Price:** $17.50, postpaid, payment with order.

★4004★
MICHIGAN FOUNDATION DIRECTORY
Michigan League for Human Services
200 Mill Street
Lansing, MI 48933
Covers: Nearly 300 Michigan foundations having assets of $200,000 or more and/or making grants of at least $25,000 annually. Separate list of over 500 foundations with assets of $1,000 to $200,000 or grants of $5,000 to $25,000. **Entries include:** Foundation name, address, phone, year established and name of principal donor, purpose, assets, total grant amounts and highest and lowest grants, names and titles of officers and trustees, name of contact, deadline and other grant details. **Arrangement:** Alphabetical. **Indexes:** Geographical, asset size. **Pages** (approx.): 70. **Frequency:** Irregular; latest edition 1978; new edition expected 1981. Based on Internal Revenue Service forms 990-PF and 990-AR. **Price:** $7.50, payment with order. **Other information:** Prepared with Council of Michigan Foundations.

★4005★
MINDING THE CORPORATE CONSCIENCE [Public interest groups]
Council on Economic Priorities
84 Fifth Avenue   Phone: (212) 691-8550
New York, NY 10011
Covers: About 150 public interest groups (Accuracy in Media, Center for Auto Safety, etc.) with primary or incidental interest in social accountability of corporations. **Entries include:** All entries include group name and address; more than 80 include a description of activities, publications, etc. **Arrangement:** Alphabetical. **Pages** (approx.): 130. **Frequency:** Irregular; latest edition 1978. **Editor:** Steven Lydenberg. **Price:** $75.00.

★4006★
MINNESOTA FOUNDATION DIRECTORY: PROPOSAL GUIDELINES AND DEADLINES
Foundation Data Center
123 E. Grant Street   Phone: (612) 870-4434
Minneapolis, MN 55403
Covers: Over 50 Minnesota foundations, but in greater detail than "Minnesota Foundation Directory" (see separate listing). **Entries include:** Foundation name, address, phone, assets, contact, principal contributors, and discussion of foundation's background, interests, grant procedures, etc. **Arrangement:** Alphabetical. **Pages** (approx.): 105. **Frequency:** Published 1976. Based on Internal Revenue Service forms 990-PF and 990-AR from 1973, 1974, and 1975. **Editor:** Beatrice J. Capriotti and Frank J. Capriotti, III. **Price:** $50.00.

★4007★
MINNESOTA FOUNDATION DIRECTORY
Foundation Data Center
123 E. Grant Street   Phone: (612) 870-4434
Minneapolis, MD 55403
Covers: 600 Minnesota foundations, including out-of-state foundations with special Minnesota interests. Includes "Guidelines and Deadlines" section also published separately as "Minnesota Foundation Directory: Proposal Guidelines and Deadlines" (see separate listing). **Entries include:** Foundation name, address, names of trustees and managers, principal contributors, territory interested in, financial data, list of gifts and grants. **Arrangement:** Alphabetical. **Indexes:** Donor/foundation names, personal names of administrators and trustees, banks and trust companies as trustees. **Pages** (approx.): 275. **Frequency:** Not established; latest edition 1976; semiannual updates between editions; new edition possible 1979-80. Based on Internal Revenue Service forms 990-PF and 990-AR from 1973 and 1974. **Editors:** Beatrice J. Capriotti and Frank J. Capriotti, III. **Price:** $250.00; updating service, $150.00.

★4008★
MINORITY WOMEN'S ORGANIZATIONS AND RECRUITING WOMEN FOR TRADITIONALLY "MALE" CAREERS
Project on the Status and Education of Women
Association of American Colleges
1818 R Street, N. W.   Phone: (202) 387-1300
Washington, DC 20009
Publication includes: List of minority women's organizations in the United States. **Entries include:** Organization name, address, and name of contact person. **Arrangement:** By ethnic category. **Pages** (approx.): 15. **Frequency:** Published October 1977. **Price:** Free. **Also includes:** Review of special programs for recruiting women and lists of publications, research groups, and resources helpful in recruiting minority women.

★4009★
MISSOURI NEWSPAPER DIRECTORY
Missouri Press Association
Eighth & Locust Streets
Columbia, MO 65201
Covers: Over 300 newspapers which are members of the Missouri Press Association. **Entries include:** Banner; publisher name and address; open display and classified rates; mechanical requirements; names of editor, advertising manager, and circulation manager. **Arrangement:** By banner. **Indexes:** By county. **Pages** (approx.): 50. **Frequency:** Annual, February. **Editor:** Edward L. Steele. **Price:** $12.50.

Missouri Press Association—Directory *See* Missouri Newspaper Directory

Mitchell Guides to Foundations, Corporations and Their Managers *See* Directory of New Jersey Foundations

★4010★
NASW PROFESSIONAL SOCIAL WORKERS DIRECTORY
National Association of Social Workers
1425 H Street, N. W., Suite 600   Phone: (202) 628-6800
Washington, DC 20005
Covers: 77,700 social workers who are members. **Entries include:** Name, address, phone, title, affiliation, certification or licensure information, education; some listings include vocational, educational, and volunteer activities, and honors received. **Arrangement:** Alphabetical. **Pages** (approx.): 1,735. **Frequency:** Irregular; previous edition 1972; latest edition September 1978. **Editor:** Ilse Schaffer,

Administrator. **Price:** $40.00, plus $2.50 shipping. **Other information:** Variant title, "Directory of Professional Social Workers."

★4011★

NASW REGISTER OF CLINICAL SOCIAL WORKERS
National Association of Social Workers
1425 H Street, N. W., Suite 600   Phone: (202) 628-6800
Washington, DC 20005
Covers: Over 10,000 clinical social workers who applied for listing under established criteria, which include education, certification by Academy of Certified Social Workers or state licensing, and supervised and clinical experience. **Entries include:** Name; office address and phone; home address and phone; highest degree; area of specialization; personal data; career data; licensing, certification, and registration information. **Arrangement:** Alphabetical. **Indexes:** Geographical. **Pages** (approx.): 690. **Frequency:** Biennial, fall of even years. **Editor:** Ilse Schaffer, Administrator. **Price:** $30.00, plus $1.25 shipping.

National Association of Housing Cooperatives—Membership Directory *See* National Directory of Housing Cooperatives

National Association of Social Workers—Membership Directory *See* NASW Professional Social Workers Directory

★4012★

NATIONAL ASSOCIATION OF VAN POOL OPERATORS— MEMBERSHIP DIRECTORY
National Association of Van Pool Operators
Box 2197   Phone: (713) 965-2229
Houston, TX 77001
Covers: About 250 corporations or agencies operating van pools, as expansion of ride-sharing and as alternative commuting method; includes vendors dealing in van pool equipment and services, and others. **Entries include:** Company name, representative name, address, phone. **Arrangement:** Classified by membership category, then alphabetical. **Pages** (approx.): 15. **Frequency:** Annual, June. **Editor:** Toni Nelson, Managing Editor. **Price:** Available to members only. **Send orders to:** Executive Secretary, National Association of Van Pool Operators, 610 Ivystone Lane, Cinnaminson, NJ 08077.

★4013★

NATIONAL CHILDREN'S DIRECTORY
Urban Information Interpreters, Inc.
Box AH
College Park, MD 20740
Covers: About 700 organizations concerned with improving social and legal conditions for children and youth. Includes lists of government agencies concerned with children and alternative education programs. **Entries include:** Organization name, address, phone, purposes or concerns, activities, newsletters or other publications, and sources of funding. **Arrangement:** National organizations are alphabetical, others geographical. **Pages** (approx.): 300. **Frequency:** Not established; first edition spring 1977. **Editors:** Mary Lee Bundy and Rebecca Glenn Whaley. **Price:** $39.95.

★4014★

NATIONAL CIVIL RIGHTS DIRECTORY
Urban Information Interpreters, Inc.
Box AH
College Park, MD 20740
Covers: About 550 organizations (including about 350 local) that work to promote racial justice. **Entries include:** For organizations - Name, address, phone, description of activities. **Pages** (approx.): 185. **Frequency:** Not established; first edition 1979. **Editors:** Mary Lee Bundy and Irvin Gilchrist. **Price:** $19.95.

★4015★

NATIONAL COUNCIL OF MARRIAGE AND DIVORCE LAW REFORM AND JUSTICE ORGANIZATIONS—DIRECTORY
National Council of Marriage and Divorce Law Reform and Justice Organizations
C/o G. F. Doppler
Box 60   Phone: (215) 353-3462
Broomall, PA 19008
Covers: 165 organizations concerned with reform of marriage and divorce laws, father's rights, etc. **Entries include:** Organization name, address, name and phone of contact. **Frequency:** Copied for distribution as requested; continuous updating. **Price:** $1.00, plus stamped, self-addressed envelope for listings covering a single area. Request quotation for larger lists.

★4016★

NATIONAL DIRECTORY OF CHILDREN & YOUTH SERVICES
CPR Directory Services Company
1301 20th Street, N. W.   Phone: (202) 785-4061
Washington, DC 20036
Covers: Child and youth-oriented social services, health and mental health services, and juvenile court and youth advocacy services in state agencies, major cities, and 3,100 counties; also covers runaway youth centers, child abuse projects, wife abuse projects, and national organizations concerned with child health and welfare. **Entries include:** Agency listings include agency name, address, phone, names of principal executives and staff, description of services. **Arrangement:** Geographical. **Pages** (approx.): 525. **Frequency:** Annual; first edition September 1979. **Advertising accepted.** Circulation 5,000. **Price:** $39.00, postpaid, payment with order (ISSN 0190-7476).

★4017★

NATIONAL DIRECTORY OF EDUCATIONAL PROGRAMS IN GERONTOLOGY
Administration on Aging
Office of Human Development
Health, Education, and Welfare Department
Washington, DC 20201
Covers: Types of programs and specific courses offered which are concerned with some aspect of aging as offered by about 1,300 colleges and universities. **Entries include:** Name and address of institution, name and phone number of contact, and descriptions of courses, degree programs, financial aid available, research projects, etc., often with name and phone of instructor, director, etc. **Arrangement:** Geographical. **Indexes:** Institution name, subject. **Pages** (approx.): 1,600. **Frequency:** Not established; first edition 1976. **Price:** $9.35 (S/N 017-062-00105-7). **Send orders to:** Government Printing Office, Washington, DC 20402. **Other information:** Prepared by Faye McBeath Institute on Aging and Adult Life, University of Wisconsin, Madison, WI, with the cooperation of the Association for Gerontology in Higher Education.

★4018★

NATIONAL DIRECTORY OF HOUSING COOPERATIVES
National Association of Housing Cooperatives
1828 L Street, N. W., Suite 1100   Phone: (202) 872-0550
Washington, DC 20036
Number of listings: 1,300. **Entries include:** Name, address, number of units, cost to move in, and approximate monthly charges. **Arrangement:** Geographical. **Indexes:** Type of financing. **Pages** (approx.): 60. **Frequency:** Irregular; latest edition November 1977. **Editor:** Ernie Eden, Executive Director. **Advertising accepted.** Circulation 1,000. **Price:** $50.00. **Other information:** Variant title, "Directory of Housing Cooperatives in the United States."

National Directory of Meals on Wheels Programs *See* International Meals on Wheels Directory

★4019★

NATIONAL DIRECTORY OF NEWSLETTERS AND REPORTING SERVICES

Gale Research Company
Book Tower　　　　　　　　　　Phone: (313) 961-2242
Detroit, MI 48226
Covers: Periodicals of a newsletter format or nature issued on a regular basis by both commercial and noncommercial publishers. The planned four issues, each covering about 750 newsletters, will constitute the second edition of a book published previously. **Entries include:** Newsletter title, name and address of publisher or sponsoring organization, phone, name of editor, brief description of the newsletter's scope and purpose, year first published, frequency, cost of subscription, circulation (in some cases), size, etc. **Arrangement:** Alphabetical. **Indexes:** Cumulative title, subject, and publisher indexes. **Frequency:** Four issues published 1978-1980. **Editor:** Robert C. Thomas. **Price:** $42.00 for four-issue set.

★4020★

NATIONAL DIRECTORY OF PRIVATE SOCIAL AGENCIES

Croner Publications, Inc.
211-05 Jamaica Avenue　　　　　　Phone: (212) 464-0866
Queens Village, NY 11428
Number of listings: Over 14,000. **Entries include:** Agency name, address, description of services. **Arrangement:** Geographical. **Indexes:** Type of service or agency. **Frequency:** Latest base volume (looseleaf format) 1976, monthly supplements. **Price:** $35.00, plus $3.95 shipping for base volume and year's supplement service.

★4021★

NATIONAL DIRECTORY OF RUNAWAY PROGRAMS

National Youth Work Alliance
1346 Connecticut Avenue, N. W., Suite 502 Phone: (202) 785-0764
Washington, DC 20036
Covers: 215 programs serving runaway youth. **Entries include:** Sponsoring agency, address, name and phone of contact, facilities and services offered, funding sources, number of staff, number of runaways served, success and other statistics. **Arrangement:** Geographical. **Pages** (approx.): 130. **Frequency:** Irregular; latest edition 1979. **Former title:** National Directory of Runaway Centers. **Price:** $5.00, postpaid, payment with order.

★4022★

NATIONAL DIRECTORY OF SISTER CITIES IN THE UNITED STATES

Town Affiliation Association of the United States
1625 I Street, Suite 424-26　　　　Phone: (202) 293-5504
Washington, DC 20006
Covers: About 700 U.S. cities which are affiliated through this program with cities in other nations in order to encourage better international understanding in the fields of education, culture, and economic and social relationships. **Entries include:** Name of city, population, date program founded, name of foreign affiliates, and name, address, phone of mayor and of United States chairperson. **Arrangement:** Geographical. **Pages** (approx.): 40. **Frequency:** Annual, July. **Editor:** Richard Oakland, Director of Member Services. **Price:** $2.50.

★4023★

NATIONAL DIRECTORY OF WEEKLY NEWSPAPERS

National Newspaper Association
1627 K Street, N. W., Suite 400　　Phone: (202) 466-7200
Washington, DC 20006
Number of listings: 7,800. **Entries include:** Name of newspaper, address, county, type of area, circulation, day published, name of publisher, and information on advertising and production. **Arrangement:** Geographical. **Pages** (approx.): 450. **Frequency:** Annual, April. **Advertising accepted.** Circulation 2,900. **Price:** $30.00, postpaid, payment with order (1980 edition). **Also includes:** State county/city maps.

★4024★

NATIONAL DIRECTORY OF WOMEN'S EMPLOYMENT PROGRAMS

Wider Opportunities for Women
1649 K Street, N. W.　　　　　　Phone: (202) 638-4868
Washington, DC 20006
Covers: 140 women's employment programs sponsored by associations, business, and government. **Entries include:** Organization name, address, phone, description of purpose of organization, programs and services offered, target population, number of staff, type of funding, name of contact, publications. **Arrangement:** Geographical. **Pages** (approx.): 130. **Frequency:** Annual, October; first edition 1979. **Price:** $7.50, plus 50¢ shipping, payment must accompany order.

★4025★

NATIONAL EMPLOYMENT LISTING SERVICE FOR HUMAN SERVICES

Institute of Contemporary Corrections and Behavioral Sciences
Sam Houston State University　　　Phone: (713) 295-6211
Huntsville, TX 77341
Covers: Positions available in mental health and mental retardation; rehabilitation services; children, youth, and family services; community service, and academic and educational services. **Entries include:** Agency or institution name, application address and procedures, description of position, pay scale, qualifications sought. **Arrangement:** Geographical within specialty (mental health, rehabilitation, etc.). **Pages** (approx.): 75. **Frequency:** Monthly. **Editor:** Daniel J. Miller, Acting Managing Editor. **Price:** $16.50 to individuals; $31.00 to institutions; per year, payment with order.

★4026★

NATIONAL FIRE PROTECTION ASSOCIATION—YEARBOOK

National Fire Protection Association
470 Atlantic Avenue　　　　　　Phone: (617) 482-8755
Boston, MA 02210
Publication includes: 125 association committees on specific hazards and safety practices and 3,000 committee members. **Entries include:** Committee name, description of duties, and names, titles, and full addresses of committee members. **Arrangement:** Alphabetical by technical committee name. **Frequency:** Annual, January or February. **Price:** Available to members only.

National Guide to Government and Foundation Funding Sources in the Field of Aging *See* Funding in Aging: Public, Private and...

★4027★

NATIONAL JEWISH COMMUNITY RELATIONS ADVISORY COUNCIL—DIRECTORY OF CONSTITUENT ORGANIZATIONS

National Jewish Community Relations Advisory Council
55 W. 42nd Street　　　　　　　Phone: (212) 564-3450
New York, NY 10036
Covers: Over 10 national and 105 local Jewish community relations agencies. **Entries include:** Agency name, address, phone, officers, regional offices, and representatives. **Arrangement:** Alphabetical. **Pages** (approx.): 30. **Frequency:** Annual, spring. **Editor:** Lynne Ianniello, Director, Public Information. **Price:** Free; restricted to community relations agencies.

★4028★

NATIONAL PRESS PHOTOGRAPHERS ASSOCIATION—MEMBERSHIP DIRECTORY

National Press Photographers Association
Box 1146　　　　　　　　　　Phone: (919) 489-3700
Durham, NC 27702
Number of listings: 6,000. **Entries include:** Name, home address, and employer. **Arrangement:** Alphabetical. **Indexes:** Geographical. **Frequency:** Annual, December. **Advertising accepted.** **Price:** $25.00.

★4029★

NATIONAL REGISTER OF CERTIFIED SEX EDUCATORS, CERTIFIED SEX THERAPISTS

American Association of Sex Educators and Counselors
5010 Wisconsin Avenue, N. W.   Phone: (202) 686-2523
Washington, DC 20016
Number of listings: 1,300 sex educators, 1,000 sex therapists, and 65 sex counselors. **Entries include:** Name, address, highest degree. **Arrangement:** Separate geographical sections for educators, therapists, and counselors. **Pages** (approx.): 120. **Frequency:** Annual, February. **Editor:** Beatrice K. Brody. **Price:** $5.00, payment with order (current and 1980 editions). **Also includes:** Certification requirements and procedures.

★4030★

NATIONAL STUDENT VOLUNTEER PROGRAM TRAINING SCHEDULE

ACTION
Washington, DC 20525
Covers: Training seminars for coordinators of high school and college service-learning programs. **Frequency:** Annual. **Price:** Free.

★4031★

NATIONAL TRUST EDUCATION SERVICES AND OPPORTUNITIES

National Trust for Historic Preservations
1785 Massachusetts Avenue, N. W.   Phone: (202) 673-4000
Washington, DC 20036
Covers: Conferences, workshops, and other educational programs sponsored by the National Trust for current year. **Entries include:** Program name, dates, content, name and address of contact. **Frequency:** Annual. **Price:** Free.

★4032★

NEW AGE DIRECTORY [Alternative lifestyles and philosophies]

Survival Foundation, Inc.
Box 64   Phone: (203) 974-2440
Woodstock Valley, CT 06282
Covers: Over 2,500 New Age centers, publishers, periodicals, bookstores, and products; health resorts; traditional and non-traditional physicians interested in holistic approaches; natural healing centers; communes; spiritual centers and courses; and extensive listings of vegetarian, fruitarian, and other natural food resources. **Entries include:** Organization or personal name, address, description of product, service, or interest. **Arrangement:** By subject. **Indexes:** Subject, organization. **Pages** (approx.): 180. **Frequency:** Annual. **Editor:** Viktoras Kulvinskas. **Price:** $3.45. **Other information:** Variant titles, "Holistic Health Directory;" "New Age Holistic Health Directory."

New Age Holistic Health Directory *See* New Age Directory [Alternative lifestyles and philosophies]

★4033★

NEW ENGLAND RESOURCES ON THE ENVIRONMENT

New England Municipal Center
Box L   Phone: (603) 868-5000
Durham, NH 03824
Covers: About 400 federal and state agencies and citizen groups. **Entries include:** Name, address; name, title, and phone of contact; description of purpose, activities; subcommittees or divisions; year founded; publications. **Arrangement:** National, regional, or state, then by organization type. **Indexes:** Topic. **Pages** (approx.): 115. **Frequency:** Irregular; latest edition October 1976. **Price:** $3.00.

★4034★

NEW JERSEY DIRECTORY FOR SENIOR CITIZENS

New Jersey Health Products Information Committee
971 Stuyvesant Avenue   Phone: (201) 687-7272
Union, NJ 07083
Covers: Public and private agencies in New Jersey which provide legal aid, health services, financial assistance, and community and consumer services at no cost to the aged. **Entries include:** Agency name, phone number. **Arrangement:** By area of concern (legal aid, health, etc.). **Pages** (approx.): 5. **Frequency:** Published 1979; new edition expected February 1980. **Editor:** Adrienne Bechtle. **Price:** Free.

★4035★

NEW JERSEY PERIODICAL DIRECTORY

Guggenheim Memorial Library
Monmouth College   Phone: (201) 222-6600
West Long Branch, NJ 07764
Covers: 360 New Jersey periodicals regularly issued at least semiannually. Also includes lists of new titles, title changes, changes of address, titles which have ceased. **Entries include:** For currently published periodicals: Title, publisher, editor's name, address, frequency, circulation, subscription cost, year first issued. **Arrangement:** Alphabetical by title. **Indexes:** Subject (Burlington, NJ, dance, trees, etc.). **Pages** (approx.): 35. **Frequency:** Irregular; previous edition 1976; latest edtion 1979. **Editor:** Robert F. Van Benthuysen, Library Director. **Price:** $1.50, postpaid.

★4036★

NEW WEST TRAILS' PEOPLE'S YELLOW PAGES [Tucson, Arizona]

New West Trails Collective
C/o Joyce Hardin
2237 E. 18th Street   Phone: (602) 624-9644
Tucson, AZ 85719
Covers: 2,000 listings of human services, cooperatives, alternative groups in many fields, etc. **Entries include:** Name, address, phone, contact person, description of service, cost, hours, etc. **Arrangement:** Classified by activity or service. **Indexes:** Keyword, alphabetical. **Frequency:** Annual, fall. **Price:** $3.95, postpaid, payment with order. **Other information:** Some reviews have cited as, "Tucson People's Yellow Pages."

★4037★

NEW YORK FOUNDATION PROFILES

Davis-Taylor Associates, Inc.
Route 3, Box 289
Mt. Morgan Road
Williamsburg, KY 40769
Number of listings: 950. **Arrangement:** Alphabetical. **Pages** (approx.): 260. **Frequency:** Irregular; latest edition 1976. Based on Internal Revenue Service forms 990-PF and 990-AR for 1974 and 1975. **Editor:** James H. Taylor. **Price:** $29.95.

★4038★

NEW YORK SELF-HELP HANDBOOK: A STEP BY STEP GUIDE TO NEIGHBORHOOD IMPROVEMENT PROJECTS

Citizens Committee for New York City
Three W. 29th Street, 6th Floor   Phone: (212) 578-4747
New York, NY 10001
Covers: About 100 subjects of interest to New Yorkers, such as safety, graffiti, park planning, block club organziation, etc., and describes how each project or problem can be approached. Information is generally applicable to other urban communities. Each section includes names and addresses of one or more similar established projects, national organizations concerned with the problem or activity, governmental organizations active in the field, etc. **Arrangement:** Classified by type of project (safety and security, sanitation, consumer affairs, etc.). **Pages** (approx.): 145. **Frequency:** Irregular; latest edition 1978. **Editor:** Karin Carlson, Project Director. **Price:** $4.95, plus 75¢ shipping.

★4039★

NEW YORK WOMEN'S YELLOW PAGES

St. Martin's Press, Inc.
175 Fifth Avenue   Phone: (212) 674-5151
New York, NY 10010
Publication includes: Directory listings of facilities, organizations, institutions, etc., of interest or service to women in connection with

special women's problems, such as children, rape, law and discrimination, medicine and health, etc. **Entries include:** Name of source, address, phone, description of activity or service. **Arrangement:** Classified by type of service. **Pages** (approx.): 525. **Frequency:** Not established; first edition 1978. **Price:** $12.95, cloth; $5.95, paper. **Other information:** Prepared by the Boston Women's Collective.

★4040★
NEWS BUREAUS IN THE U.S.
Richard Weiner, Inc.
888 Seventh Avenue   Phone: (212) 582-7373
New York, NY 10019
Covers: 500 news bureaus operated by 200 major newspapers, magazines, business publications, wire services, and syndicates. Included are state capital, suburban, and regional bureaus, bureaus in Washington, D. C., and all bureaus nationwide of The Associated Press, United Press International, etc. **Entries include:** Bureau name, address, phones, and names of editorial personnel. **Arrangement:** Geographical. **Indexes:** Alphabetical. **Pages** (approx.): 150. **Frequency:** Biennial, odd years. **Editor:** Richard Weiner. **Price:** $20.00. **Also includes:** A discussion of publishing trends and their influence on the growth of bureau operations.

News Monitor/Taft Report *See* **Foundation Reporter**

★4041★
NEWSPAPER GUILD—ADDRESS LIST OF LOCAL OFFICERS
Newspaper Guild
1125 15th Street, N. W.   Phone: (202) 296-2990
Washington, DC 20005
Covers: 79 locals and 6 district councils of The Newspaper Guild. Also lists international and staff members. **Entries include:** Local name, number, and names of officers and staff with their addressess or the local address. **Arrangement:** Alphabetical by local name. **Pages** (approx.): 5. **Frequency:** Semiannual, November and April. **Editor:** Anita Rynning, Office Manager. **Price:** Free.

★4042★
NEWSPAPER INDEXES: A LOCATION AND SUBJECT GUIDE FOR RESEARCHERS
Scarecrow Press, Inc.
52 Liberty Street   Phone: (201) 548-8600
Metuchen, NJ 08840
Covers: Libraries, historical and genealogical societies, and individuals having indexes to newspapers of general circulation, foreign language newspapers, church publications, etc.; Volume 1 lists 300 repositories, Volume 2, 250 additional repositories. **Entries include:** For sources - Repository name, address, subjects indexed, cost of having an index searched, charges for photocopying. For newspapers - Group or area is used as heading, then individual papers are listed, with dates of index coverage and symbol referring to the geographically arranged repository list. **Pages** (approx.): Volume 1, 210; Volume 2, 205. **Frequency:** Volume 1, summer 1977; Volume 2, summer 1979. **Editor:** Anita Cheek Milner. **Price:** Volume 1, $8.50; Volume 2, $10.00.

Newspaper Rates & Data *See* **Standard Rate & Data Service—Newspaper Rates & Data**

★4043★
NIPPON CLUB—DIRECTORY [Japan]
Nippon Club
145 W. 57th Street   Phone: (212) 581-2223
New York, NY 10019
Covers: About 2,600 Japanese and other persons who have a special interest in Japan, and who wish to promote friendship and better cultural, economic, and political relations between Japan and the United States. Includes 350 affiliated companies. **Entries include:** Name, address, phone. **Arrangement:** Alphabetical. **Pages** (approx.): 275. **Frequency:** Annual, November. **Advertising accepted.**

Circulation 4,000. **Price:** Apply.

★4044★
NONSEXIST MATERIALS: A SELECTION GUIDE FOR CHILDREN AND YOUNG ADULTS
ABC-Clio Press
Riviera Campus
2040 Alameda Padre Serra   Phone: (805) 963-4221
Santa Barbara, CA 93103
Publication includes: List of publishers, distributors, dealers, and resource centers offering materials that "depict nonsexist roles, values and attitudes, relationships, activities, and lifestyle options." **Entries include:** Publisher name, address. **Arrangement:** Alphabetical. **Indexes:** Author/title. **Frequency:** Not established; first edition winter 1979. **Editor:** Donna Barkman. **Price:** $14.95, postpaid, payment must accompany individuals' orders. **Other information:** Published in cooperation with Neal-Schuman Publishers. Principal content of publication is annotated bibliographies.

★4045★
NORTH AMERICAN HUMAN RIGHTS DIRECTORY
Human Rights Internet
1502 Ogden Street, N. W.   Phone: (202) 462-4320
Washington, DC 20010
Covers: About 200 organizations based in the United States which are engaged in work in international human rights; organizations concerned with human rights only within the United States are not included. **Entries include:** Organization name, address, phone, names of principal staff members, publications, whether tax exempt or registered with United Nations, and brief description of origin, purposes, and programs. **Arrangement:** Alphabetical. **Indexes:** Subject, geographical-interest. **Pages** (approx.): 175. **Frequency:** Annual, March. **Former title:** Human Rights Directory (1980). **Price:** $5.00.

★4046★
NORTH CAROLINA DIRECTORY OF TRADE AND PROFESSIONAL ASSOCIATIONS
Center for Applied Research
School of Business and Economics
University of North Carolina at Greensboro   Phone: (919) 379-5430
Greensboro, NC 27412
Number of listings: 275. **Entries include:** Most listings include name of organization, address, phone, director's name; some also show number of members, publications, services, and purpose or intent of association. **Arrangement:** Alphabetical. **Indexes:** Subject. **Pages** (approx.): 75. **Frequency:** Biennial; new edition possible spring 1981. **Editor:** Robert D. Norton, Research Associate. **Price:** $7.00.

Northern California Food Co-Op Directory *See* **Food Co-Op Directory [California]**

★4047★
OCEAN COUNTY DIRECTORY OF CLUBS AND ORGANIZATIONS [New Jersey]
Ocean County Library
15 Hooper Avenue   Phone: (201) 349-6200
Toms River, NJ 08753
Covers: About 500 military, educational, social service, cultural, religious, and other organizations located in Ocean County, New Jersey. **Entries include:** Organization name, president's name, address, and phone. **Arrangement:** Classified by subject (civic, fraternal, and service organizations, beach and yacht clubs, etc.). **Pages** (approx.): 40. **Frequency:** Irregular; latest edition September 1978. **Editor:** Stella Kern. **Other information:** Publication may be discontinued and replaced by computerized referral service.

★4048★
OFFICIAL DIRECTORY OF OPTIMIST INTERNATIONAL [Clubs]
Optimist International
4494 Lindell Boulevard   Phone: (314) 371-6000
St. Louis, MO 63108
Covers: About 3,500 local Optimist Clubs. **Entries include:** Club name, president, address, meeting place and time. **Arrangement:** Geographical. **Frequency:** Annual, October. **Editor:** Ralph J. Gentles, Associate Executive Secretary. **Price:** Available to members only.

★4049★
OHIO FOUNDATION PROFILES
Davis-Taylor Associates, Inc.
Route 3, Box 289
Mt. Morgan Road
Williamsburg, KY 40769
Covers: About 255 foundations with assets of $400,000 or which have made grants totaling $100,000. **Entries include:** Foundation name, address, officers, assets, total amount of grants made, and description of sample grants. **Arrangement:** Alphabetical. **Pages** (approx.): 65. **Frequency:** Irregular; latest edition 1976. Based on Internal Revenue Service forms 990-PF and 990-AR for 1973 and 1974. **Editor:** James H. Taylor. **Price:** $29.95.

★4050★
OLDER AMERICANS HANDBOOK
Van Nostrand Reinhold Company
135 W. 50th Street   Phone: (212) 265-8700
New York, NY 10020
Covers: Services, agencies, programs, etc., available to older persons, including both governmental and private resources. **Entries include:** Most entries include names and addresses only. **Arrangement:** Classified by type of program or service. **Pages** (approx.): 310. **Frequency:** Published 1977. **Editors:** Craig and Peter Norback. **Price:** $8.95.

★4051★
OPEN DALLAS: A GUIDE TO SERVICES AND SPECIAL RESOURCES
Dallas Public Library
1954 Commerce   Phone: (214) 748-9071
Dallas, TX 75201
Covers: 3,000 agencies and organizations in the Dallas and North Central Texas areas that in some way serve as a community resource. **Entries include:** Name of organization; address; phone; description of activities or services; staff, hours, and director's name where applicable. **Arrangement:** By type of organization or subject, then alphabetical by name or keyword. **Indexes:** Organization name/subject. **Pages** (approx.): 340. **Frequency:** Irregular; latest edition spring 1979; new edition expected spring 1981. **Editor:** Margaret Warren, Systems Resources. **Price:** $4.50, postpaid. **Other information:** Cover title, "Open Dallas: Discover Your City."

Optimist International—Directory *See* Official Directory of Optimist International [Clubs]

★4052★
OREGON WOMAN'S RESOURCE GUIDE
Continuing Education Publications
1633 S. W. Park Avenue   Phone: (503) 229-4843
Portland, OR 97207
Covers: 660 resource places for women in Oregon. **Entries include:** Name, address, phone, type of service offered, appropriateness for certain situations. **Arrangement:** By type of resource. **Pages** (approx.): 140. **Frequency:** Irregular; latest edition 1976. **Editors:** Marilyn Schmalle-Clark and Nancy Bridgeford. **Price:** $3.00.

Organizations Directory [Pittsburgh, Pennsylvania] *See* Chambers of Commerce & Civic Agencies, Trade & Professional Organizations,...

★4053★
ORGANIZATIONS OF THE YORK AREA [Pennsylvania]
York Area Chamber of Commerce
13 E. Market Street   Phone: (717) 854-3814
York, PA 17405
Entries include: Organization name, president's and secretary's names, addresses, phones, date of election, place and time of meetings. **Arrangement:** Alphabetical. **Pages** (approx.): 35. **Frequency:** Annual. **Price:** $2.65, postpaid.

★4054★
OVER 55 IS NOT ILLEGAL: A RESOURCE BOOK FOR ACTIVE OLDER PEOPLE
Houghton Mifflin Company
Two Park Street   Phone: (617) 725-5000
Boston, MA 02107
Publication includes: Lists of resources for information on employment, volunteering, and education for the retired and elderly. **Entries include:** Organization or agency name, address, phone, contact person, type of information or assistance available. **Arrangement:** Geographical within area of concern. **Frequency:** Published April 1979. **Author:** Frances Tenenbaum. **Price:** $14.95, cloth; $7.95, paper; plus 85¢ shipping.

★4055★
OXBRIDGE DIRECTORY OF NEWSLETTERS
Oxbridge Communications, Inc.
183 Madison Avenue, Room 1108   Phone: (212) 689-8524
New York, NY 10016
Covers: About 5,000 newsletters in the United States and Canada. **Entries include:** Publication name, publisher name, address, phone; name of editor, advertising director; description of contents and types of material used; year founded; frequency; ad and subscription rates, print method, page size, number of pages. **Arrangement:** Classified by subject. **Indexes:** Subject. **Pages** (approx.): 250. **Frequency:** Biennial, odd years; first edition 1979. **Price:** $35.00, plus $2.00 shipping. **Other information:** Based on material in "Standard Periodical Directory" (see separate listing).

★4056★
PARENTS' YELLOW PAGES
Anchor Press
Doubleday & Company, Inc.
245 Park Avenue   Phone: (212) 953-4561
New York, NY 10017
Publication includes: Lists of organizations, government agencies, and other groups (including manufacturers, publishers, etc.) which have services or products or assistance to parents. **Entries include:** Organization name, address; some listings include notes as to services, products, etc. **Arrangement:** Topical. **Frequency:** Not established; first edition 1978. **Editor:** Frank Caplan, Princeton Center for Infancy. **Price:** $7.95.

★4057★
PENNSYLVANIA NEWSPAPER PUBLISHERS ASSOCIATION DIRECTORY
Pennsylvania Newspaper Publishers Association
2717 North Front Street   Phone: (717) 234-4067
Harrisburg, PA 17110
Covers: About 325 daily and weekly newspapers and 40 affiliate members (companies involved in the newspaper and printing industry); membership lists of the Pennsylvania Society of Newspaper Editors, Pennsylvania Press Photographers, and Pennsylvania Women's Press Association are also provided. **Entries include:** Paper name, address, phone, names of executives, company or owner name, mechanical data, advertising rates, and circulation. **Arrangement:** Alphabetical. **Indexes:** Geographical by county. **Pages** (approx.): 80. **Frequency:** Annual, January. **Editor:** Linda L. Miller, Managing Editor. **Advertising accepted.** Circulation 1,100. **Price:** $10.00 (current and 1980 editions).

Pennsylvania Press Photographers *See* Pennsylvania Newspaper Publishers Association Directory

Pennsylvania Society of Newspaper Editors *See* Pennsylvania Newspaper Publishers Association Directory

Pennsylvania Women's Press Association *See* Pennsylvania Newspaper Publishers Association Directory

★4058★
PEOPLE HELPING PEOPLE HELP THEMSELVES
Charles Stewart Mott Foundation
Mott Foundation Building   Phone: (313) 238-5651
Flint, MI 48502
Covers: About 95 centers in the United States which develop community education programs, lend technical assistance, train, etc., to enable community involvement in decisions concerning it. **Entries include:** Center name, director's name, address, phone; some entries include assistants' names. **Arrangement:** Geographical. **Pages** (approx.): 25. **Frequency:** Irregular; latest edition 1979. **Price:** Free. **Also includes:** State associations of community education and other resources.

★4059★
PERIODICALS OF PUBLIC INTEREST ORGANIZATIONS
Commission for the Advancement of Public Interest Organizations
1875 Connecticut Avenue, N. W., Suite 103
Washington, DC 20009
Covers: About 100 periodicals published by public interest organizations. **Entries include:** Publication name, organization name, address, phone, frequency, subscription price, brief annotation. **Pages** (approx.): 60. **Frequency:** Not established; first edition 1979. **Price:** $5.00, postpaid, payment with order.

★4060★
PERIODICALS THAT PROGRESSIVE SCIENTISTS SHOULD KNOW ABOUT
Tallahassee Science for the People
Progressive Technology Company
Box 20049   Phone: (904) 222-7080
Tallahassee, FL 32304
Covers: About 295 publications concerned with scientific and technological topics of current interest issued by United States and foreign publishers; topics range from childbirth at home and organic gardening to socialism and paranormal phenomena. **Entries include:** Publication title, publisher, address, and topic of publication. **Arrangement:** Alphabetical. **Pages** (approx.): 10. **Frequency:** First edition June 1977. (Not verified)

★4061★
PITTSBURGH AREA FOUNDATION DIRECTORY
Community Action Pittsburgh
Fulton Building
Pittsburgh, PA 15227
Number of listings: 200. **Arrangement:** Alphabetical. **Pages** (approx.): 100. **Frequency:** Irregular; latest edition 1976. Based on Internal Revenue Service forms 990-PF and 990-AR from 1971-74. New edition expected February 1980. **Price:** $10.00.

★4062★
PLANNED PARENTHOOD AFFILIATES & CHAPTERS
Planned Parenthood Federation of America
810 Seventh Avenue   Phone: (212) 541-7800
New York, NY 10019
Number of listings: 220. **Entries include:** Affiliate or chapter name, address, phone, code for whether medical, educational, or provisional member. **Arrangement:** Geographical. **Pages** (approx.): 30. **Frequency:** Annual, January. **Editor:** Gina Johnson, Director of Publications. **Former title:** Affiliate Directory. **Price:** Apply (ISSN 0192-7078).

★4063★
POPULATION: AN INTERNATIONAL DIRECTORY OF ORGANIZATIONS AND INFORMATION RESOURCES
California Institute of Public Affairs
226 W. Foothill Boulevard   Phone: (714) 624-5212
Claremont, CA 91711
Covers: Over 600 organizations worldwide concerned with population and family planning. **Entries include:** Organization name, address, phone, names of key personnel responsible for population programs, description of programs and activities, and publications issued. **Arrangement:** By type of organization (intergovernmental, international non-governmental, etc.). **Indexes:** Organization, subject, acronyms, initialisms. **Pages** (approx.): 160. **Frequency:** Irregular; latest edition 1976. **Editor:** Thaddeus C. Trzyna. **Price:** $18.75, plus $1.66 shipping.

★4064★
POPULATION REPORTS—FAMILY PLANNING PROGRAMS ISSUE
Population Information Program
George Washington University Medical Center
1343 H Street, N. W.   Phone: (202) 676-4848
Washington, DC 20005
Covers: About 60 organizations and government agencies concerned with population control and family planning; international coverage. **Entries include:** Organization name, address, phone, cable and telex codes when available. **Pages** (approx.): 25. **Frequency:** Irregular; latest edition March 1977. **Editor:** Lois E. Bradshaw, et al. **Price:** Free. **Also includes:** Text of report describes the agencies and organizations and their activities and budget figures.

★4065★
THE PORTLAND BOOK [Oregon]
Center for Urban Education
0245 S. W. Bancroft   Phone: (503) 284-9465
Portland, OR 97212
Covers: About 2,000 organizations located in the Portland, Oregon area or in the state of Oregon which are sources of information on Portland; listings include government agencies, trade and professional associations, publishers, research centers, medical and emergency services, etc. **Entries include:** Most listings include company or organization name, address, phone, services, and information provided. **Arrangement:** By type of organization. **Indexes:** General. **Pages** (approx.): 200. **Frequency:** Annual; first edition May 1979. **Editor:** Steve Johnson. **Price:** $6.95. **Other information:** Updates "The Chinook Centrex."

★4066★
PORTLAND WOMEN'S YELLOW PAGES [Oregon]
Portland Women's Yellow Pages
1912 S. E. Ankeny Street
Portland, OR 97214
Covers: Over 400 women in the Portland area with skills to share. **Entries include:** Name, address, phone, skills. **Arrangement:** Skill or topic. **Pages** (approx.): 130. **Frequency:** Irregular; latest edition summer 1979. **Price:** $2.00, plus 60¢ shipping, payment with order. **Send orders to:** Parting, Inc., 1628 S.E. Ankeny, Portland, OR 97214.

★4067★
PRIVATE ORGANIZATIONS IN THE POPULATION FIELD
Population Crisis Committee
1120 19th Street, N. W., Suite 550   Phone: (202) 659-1833
Washington, DC 20036
Covers: About 35 organizations concerned with population issues and family planning; international coverage. **Entries include:** Organization name, address, phone, names of director and president or chairpersons, description of activities and concerns. **Arrangement:** Alphabetical. **Pages** (approx.): Leaflet. **Frequency:** Irregular; previous edition 1976; latest edition August 1979. **Editor:** Sharon L. Camp, Director, Education and Public Policy. **Price:** Free.

★4068★
PRODUCTIVITY RESOURCE INFORMATION GUIDE
Productivity Institute
College of Business Administration
Arizona State University   Phone: (602) 965-7626
Tempe, AZ 85281
Covers: About 70 organizations and individuals with special knowledge of factors which influence worker productivity. **Frequency:** Not established; first edition 1978; new edition expected May 1980. **Price:** $5.00 (current edition); $25.00 (tentative, 1980 edition).

★4069★
PROFESSIONAL FREELANCE WRITERS DIRECTORY
National Writers Club
1450 S. Havana, Suite 620   Phone: (303) 751-7844
Aurora, CO 80012
Covers: About 100 member writers (out of 6,000), who have published on a free-lance basis. **Entries include:** Name, address, phone (home and business numbers), special fields of writing competence, titles of books published by royalty firms, mention of contributions to specific magazines, journals, newspapers or anthologies, recent awards received, relevant activities and skills (photography, etc.). **Arrangement:** Alphabetical. **Indexes:** Geographical and subject specialty. **Pages** (approx.): 45. **Frequency:** Annual, February. **Editor:** Donald E. Bower, Director. **Price:** $10.00.

★4070★
PUBLIC WELFARE DIRECTORY
American Public Welfare Association
1155 16th Street, N. W.
Washington, DC 20036
Covers: Federal, state, territorial, county, and major municipal public welfare agencies. **Entries include:** Agency name, address, phone, names of key personnel, type of service or clientele. **Arrangement:** Geographical. **Pages** (approx.): 400. **Frequency:** Annual, August. **Price:** $35.00, payment with order. **Other information:** Also includes general information about numerous subjects related to public welfare - child support enforcement, Medicaid eligibility and claims, probation and parole services, etc.

★4071★
PURPLE PAGES
Hawthorn Books, Inc.
260 Madison Avenue   Phone: (212) 725-7740
New York, NY 10016
Covers: About 1,700 consumer protection agencies, better business bureaus, organizations, media and action hotlines, and other sources offering assistance to consumers. **Entries include:** Name, address, phone; some entries include additional detail. **Arrangement:** By type of service or concern. **Pages** (approx.): 225. **Frequency:** First edition 1979. **Editor:** Jeffrey Feinman. **Price:** $6.95.

★4072★
RACINE: WHERE TO TURN [Community services, Wisconsin]
Community Services Department
City of Racine
800 Center Street   Phone: (414) 636-9210
Racine, WI 53403
Covers: 130 community services agencies. **Entries include:** Agency name, address, phone, and information concerning agency services. **Pages** (approx.): 90. **Frequency:** Annual, January. **Editor:** Charles R. Tyler, Director. **Price:** Free.

★4073★
RAINBOOK: RESOURCES FOR APPROPRIATE TECHNOLOGY
RAIN Magazine
2270 N. W. Irving   Phone: (503) 227-5110
Portland, OR 97210
Covers: About 1,500 publications concerned with appropriate technology, alternative culture, environmental and social concerns, etc. However, the arrangement and selection of material, and the full addresses and other information provided in each entry, put "Rainbook" in the access catalog or directory rather than the bibliography category. Principal sections are: Appropriate Technology; Place; Economics; Community Building; Communications; Transportation; Shelter; Agriculture; Health; Waste Recycling; Energy. **Indexes:** General. **Pages** (approx.): 250. **Frequency:** Not established; first edition July 1977. **Editor:** Lane deMoll. **Price:** $15.00, cloth; $7.95, paper. **Send orders to:** Schocken Books, Inc., 200 Madison Ave., New York, NY 10016 (212-685-6500). **Other information:** "Rainbook" is based on and supplemented by material in "RAIN Magazine," published from the Oregon address above 10 times a year. Subscription, Regular, $15.00 per year; "Living Lightly" rate (income less than $5,000), $7.50.

★4074★
REACT TEAM DIRECTORY [Citizen's band radio monitors]
REACT International
75 E. Wacker Drive, Suite 405   Phone: (312) 346-0978
Chicago, IL 60601
Covers: 2,000 groups of people who monitor citizen's band radio Channel 9 (for local emergencies). **Entries include:** Team name, location, identification number, call sign. **Arrangement:** Geographical. **Pages** (approx.): 20. **Frequency:** Annual, December. **Editor:** Gerald H. Reese, Managing Director. **Price:** $1.00.

★4075★
RECOVERY, INCORPORATED—DIRECTORY OF GROUP MEETING INFORMATION
Recovery, Inc.
116 S. Michigan Avenue   Phone: (312) 263-2292
Chicago, IL 60603
Covers: Approximately 1,100 weekly group meetings providing a professionally developed method of self-help aftercare to help prevent relapses in former mental patients and chronic conditions in nervous patients. **Entries include:** Group meeting location, time and date. **Arrangement:** Geographical. **Pages** (approx.): 50. **Frequency:** Annual, February. **Price:** $1.00 (members and professionals only; current and 1980 editions).

★4076★
REGISTRY OF PRIVATE FAIR HOUSING ORGANIZATIONS/GROUPS
Office of Fair Housing and Equal Opportunity
Housing and Urban Development Department
451 Seventh Street, S. W., Room 5100
Washington, DC 20410
Covers: About 375 organizations concerned with the elimination of discrimination in housing; also lists more than 1,500 organizations believed to have such interests and activities, but which did not respond to questionnaire. **Entries include:** For responding organizations - Organization name, address, phone, hours, name of contact, data on the group, percentage of activity devoted to fair housing, and specific areas of interest and fair housing services provided. For non-respondents - Name, address, and, usually, name of contact. **Arrangement:** Geographical. **Pages** (approx.): 210. **Frequency:** Published 1977. **Price:** Free. **Other information:** . Prepared for the department by National Newspaper Publishers Association.

★4077★
RELEVANCE OF A.T. DEVELOPMENTS IN THE U.S. TO THE THIRD WORLD [Appropriate technology]
TRANET
Box 567
Rangeley, ME 04970
Covers: About 30 major organizations in the United States working in appropriate technology, and about 25 individuals working in the field. **Entries include:** For organizations - Name, address, phone, names of key personnel, areas of expertise, and 400-500 words describing the organization and its objectives. For individuals - Name, address, phone, areas of expertise, and 200-300 words describing experience and interests. **Pages** (approx.): 150. **Frequency:** Published spring

1979. **Editor:** Frederick W. Smith. **Price:** $8.00, paper; $3.00, microfiche (PB 295-955). May also be available from the agency. **Send orders to:** National Technical Information Service, Springfield, VA 22161. **Other information:** Prepared for Agency for International Development, Organization of Economic Cooperation and Development, and International Bank for Reconstruction and Development.

★4078★
RESOURCE DIRECTORY FOR AFFIRMATIVE RECRUITMENT IN CONNECTICUT
Connecticut Commission on Human Rights and Opportunities
90 Washington Street   Phone: (203) 566-3350
Hartford, CT 06115
Covers: Over 150 governmental agencies, associations, and other organizations working for affirmative action in hiring of minority and handicapped persons and women. **Entries include:** Name of organization, address, name and phone number of contact, and description of organization's purpose and activities. **Arrangement:** By labor market area. **Pages** (approx.): 45. **Frequency:** Irregular; latest edition June 1979. **Editor:** Elizabeth Theiss Smith, Public Information Officer. **Price:** Free.

Resources Directory for America's Third Century *See* **The Future: A Guide to Information Sources**

Rhode Island Health, Recreation, Welfare Agencies *See* **Directory of Human Service Agencies in Rhode Island**

★4079★
ROTARY INTERNATIONAL—OFFICIAL DIRECTORY
Rotary International
1600 Ridge Avenue   Phone: (312) 328-0100
Evanston, IL 60201
Covers: More than 17,000 local Rotary clubs, a service organization of business executives and professional men. **Entries include:** Name and address of president and secretary, meeting day, time and place. Includes hotels, inns, motels, and motor courts owned or operated by Rotarians, and list of licensed suppliers of Rotary jewelry and merchandise. **Arrangement:** Geographical. **Frequency:** Annual, spring. **Advertising accepted.** **Price:** $3.00 (available to members only through local club secretaries).

★4080★
RURAL SOCIOLOGICAL SOCIETY DIRECTORY
Rural Sociological Society
325 Morgan Hall
University of Tennessee   Phone: (615) 974-7231
Knoxville, TN 37916
Covers: Educators and others employed in the field of rural sociology. **Entries include:** Name, office or home address, phone, highest degree held, present position, personal data, areas of occupational specialization. **Pages** (approx.): 65. **Frequency:** Biennial, fall of odd years. **Editor:** Frank O. Leuthold, Treasurer. **Price:** $3.00.

★4081★
SAN FRANCISCO BAY AREA PEOPLE'S YELLOW PAGES [California]
San Francisco Bay Area People's Yellow Pages
Box 31291
San Francisco, CA 94131
Covers: Organizations, shops, and agencies offering alternative goods and services. **Entries include:** Organization, name, address, phone, hours, prices, services offered, eligibility requirements. **Arrangement:** By type of service offered. **Pages** (approx.): 200. **Frequency:** Irregular; latest edition July 1975; new edition expected 1980. **Editors:** Jan Zobel and Diane Sampson. **Advertising accepted.** Circulation 20,000. **Price:** $3.50 (1975 edition); $4.65 (1980 edition); payment with order.

★4082★
SCHOOLS OF SOCIAL WORK WITH ACCREDITED MASTER'S DEGREE PROGRAMS
Council on Social Work Education
345 E. 46th Street   Phone: (212) 242-3800
New York, NY 10017
Covers: Institutions in North America with graduate programs in social work education accredited by the council. **Entries include:** Program name and address, name and phone of director or dean, year first accredited, year of next accreditation review. **Arrangement:** Geographical. **Pages** (approx.): 20. **Frequency:** Annual, July. **Price:** Free.

★4083★
SCIENCE, TECHNOLOGY, AND SOCIETY: A GUIDE TO THE FIELD
Program on Science, Technology, and Society
Cornell University
628 Clark Hall
Ithaca, NY 14853
Covers: 400 United States colleges and universities and 150 institutes, programs, etc., with a total of more than 2,300 interdisciplinary courses in science, technology, and society (STS), sometimes variously called science and technology policy, ethics and values in science and technology, technology assessment and forecasting, technology and human affairs, etc. STS-related activities of selected professional organizations, research corporations, etc., are also listed. **Entries include:** Entries in course description section show institution name and address, course number and/or name, very brief annotation, faculty member(s) involved, level, number of times offered, average number of students. Program profiles for schools and for nonacademic groups show name, address, details of STS activities. **Arrangement:** Geographic. **Indexes:** Course, government and research institution. **Pages** (approx.): 575. **Frequency:** Not established; first edition October 1976 (1975 data). **Editors:** Ezra D. Heitowit, Janet Epstein, Gerald Steinberg. **Price:** $13.50 (PB 262-487/AS). **Send orders to:** National Technical Information Service, Springfield, VA 22161. **Other information:** Sponsored by Division for Science Education Development and Research, Directorate for Science Education, National Science Foundation, Washington, DC 20550.

★4084★
SEATTLE PEOPLE'S YELLOW PAGES [Washington State]
Seattle Metrocenter YMCA
909 Fourth Avenue   Phone: (206) 447-4551
Seattle, WA 98104
Frequency: Latest edition November 1979. **Price:** $3.64 (1978 edition).

★4085★
SELF-HELP IN THE HUMAN SERVICES
Jossey-Bass, Inc. Publishers
433 California Street   Phone: (415) 433-1740
San Francisco, CA 94104
Publication includes: Appendix, "Directory of Self-Help Groups." **Number of listings:** 130. **Frequency:** Published fall 1977. **Price:** $12.95, postpaid. **Also includes:** Principal content of book, written by Alan Gartner and Frank Riessman, is a discussion and examination of self-help concepts and practices.

Service Directory of National Organizations Affiliated...with...*See* **Service Directory of National Voluntary Health & Social Welfare...**

Service Directory of National Organizations, Voluntary and Govermental *See* **Service Directory of National Voluntary Health & Social...**

★4086★
SERVICE DIRECTORY OF NATIONAL VOLUNTARY HEALTH &
    SOCIAL WELFARE ORGANIZATIONS
National Assembly of National Voluntary Health and Social Welfare
    Organizations
291 Broadway, 11th Floor   Phone: (212) 267-1700
New York, NY 10007
Covers: About 105 organizations, national in scope and services,
which are sources of aid and/or information for social welfare
concerns. (Includes YMCA, National Association for Retarded Persons,
Girl Scouts, etc.) **Entries include:** Organization name, address, phone,
name of director, purpose, services or programs. **Arrangement:**
Alphabetical. **Frequency:** Biennial, even years. **Former title:** Service
Directory of National Organizations Affiliated and Associated with the
National Social Welfare Assembly; Service Directory of National
Organizations, Voluntary and Governmental. **Price:** $5.00, payment
with order. **Other information:** The association has had two recent
name changes - originally known as the National Social Welfare
Assembly, the name changed to the National Assembly for Social
Policy and Development, and, more recently, the National Assembly of
National Voluntary Health and Social Welfare Organizations.

★4087★
SERVICES FOR FAMILIES AND YOUTH [St. Louis County, Missouri]
Office of County Youth Programs
St. Louis County Department of Human Resources
10262 Page
Overland, MO 63132
Covers: Over 80 programs available from agencies for counseling,
education, employment, health, legal assistance, and recreation in St.
Louis County, Missouri. **Entries include:** Agency name, address,
phone, office hours, description of services and programs, fees.
Arrangement: Alphabetical. **Frequency:** Irregular; latest edition
1978; new edition expected February 1980. **Price:** Free.

★4088★
SHARE: A DIRECTORY OF FEMINIST LIBRARY WORKERS
Women Library Workers
Box 9052   Phone: (415) 654-8822
Berkeley, CA 94709
Number of listings: 200 members. **Entries include:** Name, home and
business address and phone; brief note on occupation, skills, and
interests, and what the individual is willing to share, from living
accomodations to experience in specific problems. **Arrangement:**
Geographical. **Indexes:** Organization name, publication title, subject,
personal name. **Pages** (approx.): 65. **Frequency:** Formerly biennial,
even years; effective with February 1980 edition frequency will be
annual. **Former title:** SHARE: Sisters Have Resources Everywhere.
Price: $3.00, payment with order (current edition); $4.00, payment
with order; $5.00, billed (1980 edition). **Other information:**
Compiled by Carole Leita.

★4089★
SIGMA PHI GAMMA—MEMBERSHIP DIRECTORY
Sigma Phi Gamma
1814 Briarcrest Lane   Phone: (817) 277-8011
Arlington, TX 76012
Covers: About 7,700 women in business and other occupations who
conduct various projects for the promotion of friendship among, and
advancement of, women. **Frequency:** Annual. **Price:** Available to
members only.

★4090★
SOCIETY FOR INTERNATIONAL DEVELOPMENT—DIRECTORY OF
    MEMBERS
Society for International Development
Palazzo Civilta del Lavoro
00144 Rome, Italy
Number of listings: About 6,000. **Entries include:** Name, office or
home address. **Arrangement:** Geographical. **Indexes:** Alphabetical.
Pages (approx.): 60. **Frequency:** Irregular; latest edition fall 1977.

Editor: Andrew E. Rice. **Price:** $4.00, payment with order.

Society of Magazine Writers—Directory *See* American Society
    of Journalists and Authors—Directory of Professional Writers

Some Hard-to-Locate Sources of Information on Current Affairs
    See Censored

★4091★
SOURCE LIST [Single-parent adoptions]
Committee for Single Adoptive Parents
Box 4074
Washington, DC 20015
Covers: About 50 agencies and organizations which are sources of
adoptable children and have accepted unmarried applicants for
adoption; international coverage. **Entries include:** Agency or
organization name, address, name of director, types of children
available, estimated time required for adoption process, estimated
cost, and special interest information. **Arrangement:** Geographical.
Pages (approx.): 20. **Frequency:** Every 18 months; updated at 6
month intervals. **Editor:** Hope Marindin, Chairman. **Price:** $5.00;
available to unmarried members only.

★4092★
SOURCES OF SERIALS: AN INTERNATIONAL PUBLISHER AND
    CORPORATE AUTHOR DIRECTORY TO "ULRICH'S" AND
    "IRREGULAR SERIALS"
R. R. Bowker Company
1180 Avenue of the Americas   Phone: (212) 764-5100
New York, NY 10036
Covers: Over 60,000 publishers of serials and annuals, worldwide.
Entries include: Publisher name, address, and titles of firm's
publications. **Arrangement:** Geographical, then by publisher. **Pages**
(approx.): 1,600. **Frequency:** Not established; first edition 1977.
Price: $52.50, postpaid, payment with order (ISSN 0000-0523).
Send orders to: R. R. Bowker Co., Box 1807, Ann Arbor, MI 48106
(313-761-4700).

★4093★
SOUTH CAROLINA FOUNDATION DIRECTORY
Reader Services Department
South Carolina State Library
Box 11469
Columbia, SC 29211
Covers: About 200 foundations, about 90% of which have less than
$1,000,000 in assets. **Entries include:** Foundation name, address,
assets, total grant amount, fields of subject and geographic interest.
Frequency: Published 1978. **Price:** No charge, but send 70¢ in stamps.

Southern California Food Co-Op Directory *See* Food Co-Op
    Directory [California]

★4094★
SOUTHERN CALIFORNIA MEDIA DIRECTORY and PCLA
    Membership Roster
Publicity Club of Los Angeles
1533 Wilshire Boulevard   Phone: (213) 483-8077
Los Angeles, CA 90058
Covers: 1,000 newspapers, magazines, radio and TV stations, and
other media in eight-county Southern California area; also covers 210
members of Publicity Club of Los Angeles and suppliers of public
relations products and services. **Entries include:** Media entries include
publication name, address, phone, personnel (up to 30-40 editors,
columnists, producers, etc.), circulation, and dates of publication.
PCLA entries include company affiliation, address, phone, and
residence address and phone. Supplier entries include company name,
address, phone, contact name, list of products or services.
Arrangement: Alphabetical for members, geographical for media.
Pages (approx.): 200. **Frequency:** Annual. **Advertising accepted.**
Circulation 1,000. **Price:** $20.00.

★4095★
SPACES FOR LEARNING, PLAYING AND STAYING [Day care facilities in Orange County, California]
Orange County Commission on the Status of Women
810 C N. Broadway	Phone: (714) 834-6880
Santa Ana, CA 92701
Covers: About 350 child care centers in Orange County, California. **Entries include:** Center name, address, phone; size of center, hours of operation, ages of children accepted, hot meals offered, programs available. **Arrangement:** Alphabetical. **Pages** (approx.): 90. **Frequency:** Irregular; latest edition winter 1979. **Price:** $1.00, plus 50¢ shipping.

★4096★
STANDARD RATE & DATA SERVICE—COMMUNITY PUBLICATION RATES & DATA
Standard Rate & Data Service, Inc.
5201 Old Orchard Road	Phone: (312) 966-8500
Skokie, IL 60077
Covers: Weekly newspapers and shopping guides, including audited, non-audited, and free (National Association of Advertising Publishers members) publications. **Entries include:** Publication name, company name, personnel, rates, closing time, mechanical requirements, and circulation. **Arrangement:** Classified by type of area served and type of publication (metro or non-metro, etc.). **Frequency:** Semiannual, May and November. **Advertising accepted.** **Former title:** Standard Rate & Data Service - Weekly Newspaper & Shopping Guide Rates & Data. **Price:** $12.25 per year, plus $1.25 shipping.

★4097★
STANDARD RATE & DATA SERVICE—CONSUMER MAGAZINE AND FARM PUBLICATION RATES & DATA
Standard Rate & Data Service, Inc.
5201 Old Orchard Road	Phone: (312) 966-8500
Skokie, IL 60077
Covers: About 930 consumer and 200 farm periodicals. **Entries include:** Publication name, address, phone, principal personnel, editorial profiles, advertising rates, discounts, mechanical requirements, copy regulations, circulation, closing and publication dates. **Arrangement:** Classified by subject interest. **Indexes:** Frequency, shopping advertising pages. **Frequency:** Monthly, on 27th of the month; "Weekly Change Bulletin" optional. **Advertising accepted.** **Price:** $77.25 per year, plus $5.25 shipping; weekly bulletin (optional), $8.00 shipping. **Also includes:** Details on agricultural direct response card programs, and market and census data.

★4098★
STANDARD RATE & DATA SERVICE—NEWSPAPER RATES & DATA
Standard Rate & Data Service, Inc.
5201 Old Orchard Road	Phone: (312) 966-8500
Skokie, IL 60077
Covers: More than 1,600 newspapers and newspaper groups, including newspaper-distributed magazines, nationally and locally edited comics, religious newspapers, Black newspapers, specialized newspapers, and daily newspapers with preprinted inserts. **Entries include:** Publication name, address, phone, principal personnel, advertising rates, special features, contract and copy regulations, mechanical requirements, and circulation. Information on cooperative and classified advertising for each publication in separate sections. Circulation breakdown in "Newspaper Circulation Analysis," a separate volume published annually. **Arrangement:** Geographical. **Frequency:** Monthly, on 12th of the month; "Newspaper Circulation Analysis" included with August issue; "Weekly Change Bulletin" optional. **Advertising accepted.** **Price:** $80.50 per year, plus $6.00 shipping; weekly bulletin (optional), $8.00 shipping; additional copies of "Newspaper Circulation Analysis," $25.00. **Also includes:** Market and census data.

Standard Rate & Data Service—Weekly Newspaper & Shopping Guide Rates & Data *See* Standard Rate & Data Service—Community Publication Rates..

★4099★
SUBURBAN NEWSPAPERS OF AMERICA—MEMBERSHIP DIRECTORY
Suburban Newspapers of America
111 E. Wacker Drive
Chicago, IL 60601
Entries include: For newspapers - Publication name, publishing company name, address, phone, names of key personnel, mechanical specifications, principal communities served. For suppliers - Company name, address, phone, names of principal personnel, products or services. **Arrangement:** Members are geographical; associate and professional members are random. **Pages** (approx.): 50. **Frequency:** Annual, summer. **Advertising accepted.** Circulation 1,000. **Price:** $10.00.

★4100★
SURVEY OF GRANT-MAKING FOUNDATIONS
Public Service Materials Center
415 Lexington Avenue
New York, NY 10017
Covers: Over 1,000 foundations with assets of over $1,000,000 or grants totalling over $200,000. **Entries include:** Foundation name, address, phone, name of contact person; meeting schedule, geographic area with which concerned, types of grants made. **Arrangement:** Alphabetical. **Frequency:** Irregular; latest edition 1976; new edition expected January 1980. **Price:** $10.00 (1980 edition).

★4101★
SURVEY OF THE EMERGING SOLAR ENERGY INDUSTRY
Solar Energy Information Services
18 Second Avenue	Phone: (415) 347-2640
San Mateo, CA 94401
Covers: 400 companies and 165 research groups, associations, etc. **Pages** (approx.): 405. **Frequency:** Not established; first edition fall 1977; new edition expected January 1980. **Author:** Justin A. Bereny. **Price:** $69.50, cloth; $60.00, paper (current edition); $79.50, cloth; $70.00, paper (1980 edition).

★4102★
SYNDICATED COLUMNISTS
Richard Weiner, Inc.
888 Seventh Avenue	Phone: (212) 582-7373
New York, NY 10019
Publication includes: List of several hundred major syndicated newspaper columnists. **Entries include:** Columnist's name, personal or private office address, name of syndicate handling his work. **Arrangement:** Alphabetical. **Indexes:** By column type. **Pages** (approx.): 200. **Frequency:** Biennial, June of odd years. **Editor:** Richard Weiner. **Price:** $20.00, includes updates. **Also includes:** History of early columnists and syndicates, analysis of major newspapers using syndicated columns, and other material on the subject.

★4103★
SYNERJY/A DIRECTORY OF ENERGY ALTERNATIVES
Synerjy
Box 4790
Grand Central Station	Phone: (212) 865-9595
New York, NY 10017
Covers: Over 5,000 organizations, publishers, individuals, resources, articles, books, etc., interested in or dealing with alternatives to fossil fuels and atomic power. **Entries include:** For individuals, organizations, etc. - Name, address, few words on interest, specialty, etc. For articles, books, etc. - Bibliographic citations. **Arrangement:** Subject-classified. **Frequency:** Semiannual, January and July; January issue cumulated in July issue. **Editor:** Jeffrey M. Twine. **Price:**

$24.00 per year; $14.00, July issue; $12.00, January issue; plus $1.00 shipping per issue, payment must accompany individuals' orders.

★4104★
SYNTHESIS [Libertarian socialist newsletter]
League for Economic Democracy
Box 1858   Phone: (213) 833-2633
San Pedro, CA 90733
Publication includes: Directory of about 150 libertarian socialist organizations. **Entries include:** Organization name, address, activities, publications. **Frequency:** Irregular; about twice a year. **Former title:** Solidarity Newsletter. **Price:** $2.50 (five issues) to individuals; $5.00 (five issues) to institutions.

★4105★
TAFT CORPORATE FOUNDATION DIRECTORY
Taft Corporation
1000 Vermont Avenue, N. W., Suite 600   Phone: (202) 347-0788
Washington, DC 20005
Covers: About 320 company-sponsored foundations of varying size and importance which make grants. **Entries include:** Foundation name, address, names of foundation officers and board members, name of contact person, information on grants (types, average amounts, typical grants, application procedures, etc.), and information on the company supporting the foundation (products, sales, number of employees, etc.). **Arrangement:** Alphabetical. **Indexes:** Geographical, interest, personal name, company name. **Pages** (approx.): 375. **Frequency:** Biennial, odd years. **Editor:** Laura Brown. **Price:** $125.00, postpaid, payment with order.

★4106★
TEXAS TRADE AND PROFESSIONAL ASSOCIATIONS AND OTHER SELECTED ORGANIZATIONS
Bureau of Business Research
University of Texas at Austin
Box 7459
University Station   Phone: (512) 471-1616
Austin, TX 78712
Covers: 600 Texas associations or national associations with an office in Texas. **Entries include:** Association name, address, phone, executive officer, number of members, title of publication (if any). **Arrangement:** Alphabetical according to keyword. **Indexes:** Alphabetical, geographical. **Pages** (approx.): 80. **Frequency:** Annual. **Editor:** Rita J. Wright, Librarian. **Price:** $3.50.

★4107★
TORONTO WAGES FOR HOUSEWORK CAMPAIGN BULLETIN
Toronto Wages for Housework Committee
Box 38
Station E   Phone: (416) 466-7457
Toronto M6H 4E1, Ontario, Canada
Covers: Wages for Housework movement activities in Canada, United States, and Europe, with reports and addresses on about 15 local committees. **Frequency:** Latest edition June 1979. **Price:** Free.

Training Facilities in Demography, Family Planning and Physiology of Reproduction See **Training Facilities in Population and Family...**

★4108★
TRAINING FACILITIES IN POPULATION AND FAMILY PLANNING in the Western Hemisphere Region
International Planned Parenthood Federation
105 Madison Avenue   Phone: (212) 679-2230
New York, NY 10016
Number of listings: 70. **Entries include:** Institution or facility name, address, name of contact, description of program and/or courses offered, application deadline, starting date, fellowships. **Arrangement:** Classified by subject, then geographical. **Pages** (approx.): 60. **Frequency:** Latest edition October 1979. **Former title:**

Directory of Selected Training Facilities in Family Planning and Allied Subjects; Training Facilities in Demography, Family Planning and Physiology of Reproduction. **Price:** Free.

★4109★
TRANET (TRANSNATIONAL NETWORK FOR APPROPRIATE/ ALTERNATIVES TECHNOLOGIES) [Newsletter]
TRANET, Inc.
Box 567   Phone: (207) 864-2252
Rangeley, ME 04870
Publication includes: Directory of appropriate/alternative technology centers, worldwide. **Entries include:** Center name, address, director, and brief description of activities. **Arrangement:** Geographical by region (Africa, Asia and the Pacific, etc.). **Pages** (approx.): 25. **Frequency:** Quarterly, non-cumulative. **Editor:** William N. Ellis. **Price:** Available with TRANET membership: $15.00 annually for individuals, $100.00 annually for organizations. **Other information:** The directory section of the publication is devoted to one specific field each issue (bicycle transportation, self-help housing, small scale agriculture, etc.). Publication includes news items on developments in field, with names and addresses for contact.

Tucson People's Yellow Pages See **New West Trails' People's Yellow Pages**

★4110★
ULRICH'S INTERNATIONAL PERIODICALS DIRECTORY
R. R. Bowker Company
1180 Avenue of the Americas   Phone: (212) 764-5100
New York, NY 10028
Covers: 61,000 current periodicals published throughout the world. Includes a list of over 2,000 periodicals that have ceased or suspended publication. **Entries include:** Name of publication, Dewey Decimal Classification number, country code and ISSN, subtitle, language(s) of text, year first published, frequency, subscription price in country of origin and U. S. rate, sponsoring organization, publisher name and address, editor, regular features (reviews, advertising, abstracts, bibliographies, trade literature, etc.), indexes, circulation, format, availability of microforms, services which index or abstract the periodical, former title. **Arrangement:** Classified by subject. **Indexes:** Titles of new periodicals; titles of publications of international organizations; all titles, including variant and former titles. **Pages** (approx.): 2,200. **Frequency:** Biennial, fall of odd years. **Editor:** Gary Ink. **Price:** $64.50, postpaid, payment with order (ISSN 0000-0175). **Send orders to:** R. R. Bowker Co., Box 1807, Ann Arbor, MI 48106. **Other information:** Supplemented by "Ulrich's Quarterly, A Supplement to 'Ulrich's International Periodicals Directory' and 'Irregular Serials and Annuals,'" $28.00 per year (ISSN 0000-0507).

Ulrich's Quarterly See **Ulrich's International Periodicals Directory**

Underground Press Directory See **Alternative Press Directory**

★4111★
A UNIQUE ENCOUNTER [Christian work camps]
Christian Movement for Peace
121 Avenue Road   Phone: (416) 921-2360
Toronto, Ontario, M5R 2G3, Canada
Covers: About 150 summer volunteer work opportunities directed by the movement; international coverage. Includes list of associated work camp movements. **Entries include:** For camps - Work camp location, nature of work, number of participants, conditions or requirements for acceptance. For associated movements - Name, description of activities, address. **Arrangement:** Geographical. **Pages** (approx.): 30. **Frequency:** Annual, April. **Former title:** Christian Movement for Peace International Work Camps (1978). **Price:** $2.00.

★4112★

UNITED FUND OF HOUSTON AND HARRIS COUNTY—DIRECTORY OF COMMUNITY RESOURCES AND SERVICES [Texas]

United Fund of Houston and Harris County
1010 Waugh Drive   Phone: (713) 529-5913
Houston, TX 77019
Covers: 400 human care services in the Houston/Harris County and surrounding areas. **Entries include:** Agency name; address; phone; executive's name and title; list of services provided, showing name of supervisor, name of contact, eligibility, application procedure, and fee policy for each; list of each office location showing address, phone, special hours, geographical area served, 24-hour phone, and availability and level of Spanish-speaking staff for each. **Arrangement:** Alphabetical. **Indexes:** Keyword, special programs, and topics. **Pages** (approx.): 400. **Frequency:** Biennial, odd years. **Editor:** Ruben Jimenez. **Price:** $15.00.

★4113★

UNITED PRESS INTERNATIONAL DAYBOOK [Washington, D. C., events]

United Press International
315 National Press Building   Phone: (202) 628-6621
Washington, DC 20045
Covers: Press conferences, meetings, congressional hearings, etc., to occur during following 24-36 hours in the Washington, D. C., area which are expected to have newsworthy aspects. **Entries include:** Place, time, names of persons or organizations involved, nature of event, etc. **Frequency:** Twice daily, via teletype to subscribers in major cities. **Editor:** Jim Welch, Manager. (Also see separate DOD entry for Associated Press Calendar.) "UPI International Future File" covers same as above but is published each Friday for following week.

United Press International Future File [Washington, D.C. events]
See United Press International Daybook [Washington, D. C. events]

★4114★

U.S. NON-PROFIT ORGANIZATIONS IN DEVELOPMENT ASSISTANCE ABROAD

American Council of Voluntary Agencies for Foreign Service
200 Park Avenue South
New York, NY 10003
Covers: About 450 nonprofit organizations headquartered in the United States which operate or support development assistance programs in Africa, East Asia and the Pacific, Latin America, and Near East-South Asia. Includes voluntary agencies, church missions, foundations, associations, and projects of business and labor. **Entries include:** Agency name, address, staff, history, objectives, programs, countries served, financial data, publications. **Indexes:** Agency name, country served, type of assistance. **Pages** (approx.): 525. **Frequency:** Irregular; latest edition 1978. **Price:** $6.00, postpaid, payment with order.

★4115★

VOICESPONDENCE CLUB—DIRECTORY

Voicespondence Club
R.D. 2
173 Highland Estates
Kutztown, PA 19530
Covers: About 400 blind and 100 sighted persons who have access to a tape recorder and who exchange tape recordings of ideas, conversation, music, and copies of phonograph records. **Entries include:** Name, address, occupation, hobbies. **Arrangement:** Alphabetical. **Pages** (approx.): 25. **Frequency:** Annual, August. **Editor:** Howard McClelland. **Advertising accepted.** Circulation 500. **Price:** Available to members only.

★4116★

VOLUNTEER "VACATIONS" ON AMERICA'S PUBLIC LANDS

Signpost Publications
16812 36th Avenue West   Phone: (206) 743-3947
Lynnwood, WA 98036
Covers: Volunteer Conservation Corps programs sponsored by the American Hiking Society in National Forest and state park areas. **Entries include:** Program identification and location, skills needed, benefits offered (insurance, free lodging, etc.), equipment needed, length of stay expected, dates program operates. **Arrangement:** By park or forest area. **Pages** (approx.): 50. **Frequency:** Irregular; first edition summer 1978; new edition expected 1980. **Price:** $2.95, postpaid, payment with order.

★4117★

VOLUNTEERS WHO PRODUCE BOOKS: BRAILLE, TAPE, LARGE TYPE

National Library Service for the Blind and Physically Handicapped
Library of Congress   Phone: (202) 882-5500
Washington, DC 20542
Covers: Organizations and individuals who produce books for visually and physically handicapped persons. Includes proofreaders and special education specialists. **Entries include:** Organization entries include organization name, address, and phone; chairperson's name, address, phone; type of media, specialty. Individual listings include name, address. **Arrangement:** Geographical within service category. **Indexes:** Specialty. **Pages** (approx.): 70. **Frequency:** Biennial; latest edition 1978. **Price:** Free. **Other information:** Available in Braille or large type editions.

★4118★

WASHINGTON CONSUMERS' CHECKBOOK [District of Columbia]

Washington Center for the Study of Services
1518 K Street, N. W., Suite 406   Phone: (202) 347-9612
Washington, DC 20005
Covers: A specific type of consumer-oriented business or service industry in each issue; issues have been published thus far on health services and auto repair services, and issues are planned on financial services, TV repair shops, and a number of other consumer-oriented businesses. (Coverage limited to Washington metropolitan area.) **Entries include:** In the directory sections, large numbers of firms are mentioned by name and address, and details on their policies, prices, and competence derived from the firms and from customer reports are given. In general information sections, suggestions are given on diagnosing common problems (to avoid exaggeration of problems by shops), on choosing a shop, etc. **Pages** (approx.): 140. **Frequency:** Quarterly. **Editor:** Robert Krughoff, President. **Price:** $14.00 per year; $4.95 per copy. **Other information:** Persons interested in preparing publications such as the "Checkbook" for their own areas can secure a report prepared by the Center, "Guide for Starting a Local Service Evaluation Magazine," $3.00.

★4119★

WASHINGTON GUIDE FOR BATTERED WOMEN [District of Columbia]

Task Force on Abused Women
Women's Legal Defense Fund
1010 Vermont Avenue, N. W.   Phone: (202) 529-5991
Washington, DC 20005
Publication includes: List of emergency shelters, legal aid services, and other organizations of assistance to abused spouses in Washington, DC. **Entries include:** Shelter or service name, address, phone, description of services, fee charged (if any). **Frequency:** Irregular; latest edition 1979. **Price:** $1.00.

★4120★

WASHINGTON WOMEN: A DIRECTORY OF WOMEN AND WOMEN'S ORGANIZATIONS IN THE NATIONAL CAPITAL
Federation of Organizations for Professional Women
2000 P Street, N. W., Suite 403   Phone: (202) 466-3547
Washington, DC 20036
Covers: About 100 organizations, and 675 women that monitor public policy issues of concern to women in Washington; also includes female members of Congress and women with influential positions on congressional staffs or in federal offices in Washington. **Entries include:** For organizations - Name, address, phone, brief description of interests; some listings include names of women on staff or board, etc. For women in government - Name, affiliation, title, phone; some listings include addresses. For individual women (who may or may not be listed in the other sections) - Name, affiliation, title, address, phone. **Arrangement:** Classified. **Pages** (approx.): 170. **Frequency:** First edition November 1978; new edition is planned. **Price:** $8.00, postpaid, payment with order. **Also includes:** List of publications that follow women's concerns. **Other information:** Supersedes ''Federation of Organizations for Professional Women - Directory.''

Weekly Newspaper & Shopping Guide Rates & Data *See* Standard Rate & Data Service—Community Publication Rates & Data

★4121★

WHERE AMERICA'S LARGE FOUNDATIONS MAKE THEIR GRANTS
Public Service Materials Center
355 Lexington Avenue   Phone: (212) 687-0646
New York, NY 10017
Covers: More than 600 of the largest United States foundations. **Entries include:** Foundation name, address, total amount of grants for latest available year and details on all or a substantial portion of grants made during the period. Listings also include a note concerning special interests of individual foundations, best approaches, etc. **Arrangement:** Geographical. **Pages** (approx.): 250. **Frequency:** Irregular; previous edition 1977; new edition expected January 1980. **Editor:** Joseph Dermer. **Price:** $24.00 (current edition); $34.50 (1980 edition).

★4122★

WHERE THE MONEY'S AT [California foundations]
Irving R. Warner
3235 Berry Drive   Phone: (213) 654-0540
Studio City, CA 91604
Covers: 525 foundations in California which have made grants of $10,000 or more. **Entries include:** Foundation name, address, phone; contact names; assets, total gifts, typical gifts; names of directors, trustees, and administrative officers; and suggestions for grant seekers. **Arrangement:** Alphabetical. **Indexes:** Geographical, personal name. **Frequency:** Not established; first edition January 1978. **Editor:** Patricia Tobey. **Price:** $17.00, postpaid.

★4123★

WHOLE EARTH CATALOG [Note on 1980 edition]
Point
27 Gate 5 Road
Sausalito, CA 94965
Background: The original ''Whole Earth Catalog'' (1969) was the forerunner of a new type of publication, generally known as the ''access catalog.'' It was a blend of directory, bibliography, and topical survey, all focused on a specific subject - ecology, conservation, etc., in the case of the ''Catalog.'' It was followed by ''Whole Earth Epilog,'' and later by a periodical which contained the same type of material and is called, ''Co-Evolution Quarterly.'' The Winter 1979-80 issue of the ''Quarterly'' announced that a new edition of ''Whole Earth Catalog'' was being planned for probable publication late in 1980, under the editorship of Art Kleiner. No price was announced, and it was requested that no orders be placed.

★4124★

WHO'S INVOLVED WITH HUNGER: AN ORGANIZATION GUIDE
World Hunger Education Service
2000 P Street, N. W., Suite 205   Phone: (202) 223-2995
Washington, DC 20036
Covers: 200 international, federal, and private nonprofit organizations in the United States and abroad concerned with scientific and political aspects of food supply. **Entries include:** Organization name, address, phone; name of key executive; branch offices; description of purpose and activities; publications. **Pages** (approx.): 45. **Frequency:** Latest edition November 1979. **Editor:** Patricia L. Kutzner. **Price:** $2.00, plus 50¢ shipping. **Other information:** First edition published with American Freedom from Hunger Foundation (now defunct).

★4125★

WHO'S WHO IN ASSOCIATION MANAGEMENT
American Society of Association Executives
1101 16th Street, N. W.   Phone: (202) 659-3333
Washington, DC 20036
Covers: 8,000 paid executives who are members of the American Society of Association Executives. **Entries include:** Name, address, phone, associations represented, and codes indicating type of association, budget, and scope. **Arrangement:** Alphabetical. **Indexes:** Associations, geographical, keyword. **Pages** (approx.): 400. **Frequency:** Annual, January. **Advertising accepted.** Circulation 10,000. **Price:** $25.00 (current and 1980 editions).

★4126★

WHO'S WHO IN SOLAR AND WIND ENERGY [Iowa]
Citizens United for Responsible Energy
1342 30th Street   Phone: (515) 277-0253
Des Moines, IA 50311
Covers: Over 400 persons, companies, and organizations in Iowa involved with alternative energy research and the selling and demonstration of alternative systems. **Entries include:** Name, address, activity or interest. **Arrangement:** Alphabetical. **Indexes:** Geographical. **Pages** (approx.): 20. **Frequency:** Annual. **Price:** $5.00, plus $1.00 shipping.

★4127★

WIC DIRECTORY OF SPECIAL SUPPLEMENTAL FOOD PROGRAMS FOR WOMEN, INFANTS AND CHILDREN
Children's Foundation
1420 New York Avenue, N. W., Suite 800   Phone: (202) 347-3300
Washington, DC 20005
Covers: 1,430 local, state, and Agriculture Department directors of the Supplemental Food Programs for Women, Infants, and Children (WIC). **Entries include:** Director name, department or agency name, institution name (for local programs) program title, address, phone. **Arrangement:** By level of program, then geographical. **Pages** (approx.): 100. **Frequency:** Annual, spring. **Price:** $2.50. **Also includes:** County maps.

Wilcox Report *See* Directory of the American Right; Directory of the American Left

★4128★

WISE GIVING GUIDE
National Information Bureau, Inc.
419 Park Avenue South   Phone: (212) 532-8595
New York, NY 10016
Covers: 400 national organizations which solicit contributions from the public, and which have supplied, or been requested to supply, operating and financial data to the bureau. Bureau requests audit by independent auditors, detailed annual budget, etc. Evaluations are then reported in the ''Wise Giving Guide'' by listing the organization under one of five major headings, from ''Meet NIB Standards'' to ''Do Not Meet One or More NIB Standards.'' More detailed evaluations of up to three organizations per request are available without charge. **Frequency:** Monthly. **Editor:** Jane Pendergast, Assistant Director. **Price:** $20.00 per year; single copies free; discounts on quantities.

★4129★
WOMEN IN CALIFORNIA: A Guide to Organizations and Resources
California Institute of Public Affairs
226 W. Foothill Boulevard   Phone: (714) 624-5212
Claremont, CA 91711
Covers: 1,600 governmental and private organizations in California that are concerned with women's rights and problems. **Entries include:** Organization name; address; phone, and, in most cases, programs, activities, publications, and services offered. **Pages** (approx.): 150. **Arrangement:** Classified by major subject of concern of the organization (general, children, education, lifestyles, etc.). **Frequency:** Irregular; latest edition 1977. **Price:** $16.75, plus $1.66 shipping.

★4130★
WOMEN IN COMMUNICATIONS—NATIONAL MEMBERSHIP DIRECTORY
Women in Communications
Box 9561   Phone: (512) 345-8922
Austin, TX 78766
Entries include: Name; home address and phone; name of firm; business title; firm address and phone. For campus chapters - Name, title, and address of faculty adviser; name of student president. **Arrangement:** Geographical (by chapter); campus chapters are by institution name. **Indexes:** Personal name. **Pages** (approx.): 160. **Frequency:** Biennial, fall of even years. **Editor:** Karen Allen, Communications Director. **Advertising accepted.** Circulation 8,000. **Former title:** National Directory of Professional Members (1974). **Price:** $6.00.

Women Library Workers—Membership List *See* SHARE: A Directory of Feminist Library Workers

★4131★
WOMEN'S HISTORY SOURCES—A GUIDE TO ARCHIVES AND MANUSCRIPT COLLECTIONS IN THE UNITED STATES
R. R. Bowker Company
1180 Avenue of the Americas   Phone: (212) 764-5100
New York, NY 10036
Covers: About 1,600 libraries, institutions, and other organizations with about 18,000 primary source collections in women's history. **Entries include:** Organization name, collection title, address, phone, description of collection, including type of materials, inclusive dates, type of bibliographic control, accessibility, and contents. **Arrangement:** Alphabetical. **Indexes:** Subject, personal name, geographical. **Pages** (approx.): 1,900 in two volumes. **Frequency:** Published fall 1978. **Editor:** Andrea Hinding. **Price:** $175.00, postpaid, payment with order. **Send orders to:** R. R. Bowker Company, Box 1807, Ann Arbor, MI 48106 (313-761-4700). **Also includes:** Bibliography of secondary sources.

Women's Institute for Freedom of the Press—Directory of Associates *See* Media Report to Women Index/Directory of Women's Media

★4132★
WOMEN'S ORGANIZATIONS & LEADERS DIRECTORY
Today News Service, Inc.
National Press Building   Phone: (202) 628-6663
Washington, DC 20045
Covers: 25,000 national and local groups, government agencies, professional and trade associations, companies, libraries, colleges and universities, and individuals with interest or involvement in women's issues, particularly the movement for equal rights for women; international coverage. **Entries include:** For organizations - Name, address, phone, names of officers and director, affiliated groups and chapters, activities, subject interest, geographic area served, publications. For individuals - Name, affiliation, address, phone; organizational responsibility, activities and achievements in the field. **Arrangement:** Alphabetical. **Indexes:** Organization/personal name, geographical, periodical title, subject area. **Pages** (approx.): 800.

Frequency: Irregular; previous edition 1975; latest edition 1979. Expected to be published about every 18-24 months in the future. **Editor:** Lester A. Barrer, Editor and Publisher. **Advertising accepted.** **Price:** $60.00.

★4133★
WORK CAMP PROGRAMME DIRECTORY
Coordinating Committee for International Voluntary Service
United Nations Educational, Scientific, and Cultural Organization
1, rue Miollis
75015 Paris, France
Frequency: Annual. **Price:** Free.

Work Schedule Directory *See* Alternative Work Schedule Directory

★4134★
WORKING FOR CONSUMERS—A DIRECTORY OF STATE AND LOCAL ORGANIZATIONS
State and Local Organizing Project
Consumer Federation of America
1012 14th Street, N. W.   Phone: (202) 737-3732
Washington, DC 20005
Covers: About 400 consumer organizations, public interest groups, self-help groups, and similar organizations concerned with consumer protection, environment, problems of the elderly, utility reform, and other consumer concerns. **Entries include:** Organization name, address, name of director, phone, and focus of services or concerns. **Arrangement:** Geographical. **Pages** (approx.): 10. **Frequency:** Annual, September. **Editor:** Steve Brobeck, Director, State and Local Project. **Price:** $2.00 to member consumer groups; $10.00 to business firms.

★4135★
WORKING ON WIFE ABUSE
Betsy Warrior
46 Pleasant Street   Phone: (617) 492-5630
Cambridge, MA 02139
Covers: Over 2,000 shelters, hotlines, YWCA's, hospitals, mental health services, legal service agencies, schools, colleges, and other organizations and agencies which offer services to abused wives in the United States and abroad; includes listings of many individuals active in the field. **Entries include:** Name, address, phone; additional information as available. **Arrangement:** Geographical. **Pages** (approx.): 130. **Frequency:** Irregular; latest edition December 1978; new edition expected January 1980. **Editor:** Betsy Warrior. **Price:** $5.00, plus 50¢ shipping, payment with order (current and 1980 editions).

★4136★
WORLD ENVIRONMENTAL DIRECTORY
Business Publishers, Inc.
818 Roeder Road   Phone: (301) 587-6300
Silver Spring, MD 20910
Covers: About 7,500 pollution control product manufacturers and other firms with environmental interests; industry lobbyists; professional consulting, design, and research services; governmental agencies and commissions; law firms with environmental interests; universities with environmental courses; environmental libraries; periodicals; trade, professional, public interest, and international organizations with environmental interests. **Entries include:** Name, address, phone, names of executives, and, if appropriate, references to product, service, or interests. **Arrangement:** Two volumes; Volume 1, United States and Canada; Volume 2, foreign countries. Within volumes, arranged by type of activity or major product field (solid waste, etc.). **Indexes:** Company name, personal name. **Frequency:** Irregular; latest edition of Volume 1, fall 1977; Volume 2, spring 1978; cumulation expected May 1980. **Editor:** Beverly A. Gough. **Price:** Volume 1, $39.00; Volume 2, $27.00; cumulation, $57.60; payment with order. **Send orders to:** Ballinger Co., 17 Dunster, Harvard Square, Cambridge, MA 02138.

★4137★

WORLD FUTURE SOCIETY BULLETIN—LOCAL GROUPS AND COORDINATORS SECTION

World Future Society
4916 St. Elmo Avenue
Washington, DC 20014

Covers: Several hundred chapter officials and local coordinators for futurist activities in the United States, Canada, and some foreign countries. **Entries include:** Name, address, phone; some listings include chapter function. **Arrangement:** Geographical. **Frequency:** Bimonthly. **Advertising accepted. Price:** Included in comprehensive membership, $27.00 per year.

★4138★

YEARBOOK OF INTERNATIONAL ORGANIZATIONS

Union of International Associations
1, rue aux Laines
1000 Brussels, Belgium

Covers: About 8,200 organizations which are "truly international" (active in at least three countries) and organizations which are more broadly defined as international in scope, including some regional organizations (African, Scandinavian, etc.). **Entries include:** Organization name in English, French, and other appropriate languages, address, name of director, history, structure, number of members and nationality, publications, place and dates of meetings, activities, and other descriptive information. **Entries include:** Alphabetical within separate sections for the "truly international" organizations and for others. **Indexes:** Subject, English organization name, French organization name, geographical, acronym, English keyword, French keyword, continent, foreign language title, personal name, date/place of creation, foundation, institute. **Pages** (approx.): 1,000. **Frequency:** Annual. **Price:** 2,300 Belgian Francs (ISSN 0084-3814).

★4139★

YOUTH-SERVING ORGANIZATIONS DIRECTORY

Gale Research Company
Book Tower   Phone: (313) 961-2242
Detroit, MI 48226

Covers: Over 1,000 organizations concerned with young people from early years through secondary school and junior college. (Selected from "Encyclopedia of Associations.") **Entries include:** Organization name, address, chief executive, phone, group's purposes and activities, convention schedule, etc. **Arrangement:** Alphabetical. **Indexes:** Keyword. **Pages** (approx.): 475. **Frequency:** Annual, early in year. **Price:** $18.00 (current edition); $24.00 (1980 edition). **Other information:** 1980 edition will include research centers (from "Research Centers Directory") and special libraries (from "Directory of Special Libraries") as well as associations.

11

Health

and Medicine

★4140★
AACP ROSTER OF TEACHERS [Pharmacy]
American Association of Colleges of Pharmacy
4630 Montgomery Avenue, Suite 201   Phone: (301) 654-9060
Bethesda, MD 22014
Covers: Faculty members teaching in accredited schools of pharmacy in the United States and Puerto Rico; similar information is given for schools outside the United States; pharmacy school librarians in separate list. **Entries include:** Name, title, rank, institution name, address, and area of instruction. **Pages** (approx.): 150. **Frequency:** Annual, January. **Price:** $5.00, payment with order.

★4141★
ACADEMY OF AMBULATORY FOOT SURGERY—MEMBERSHIP DIRECTORY
Academy of Ambulatory Foot Surgery
1405 Locust Street   Phone: (215) 735-8943
Philadelphia, PA 19102
Covers: 1,700 podiatrists performing surgery in their offices. **Entries include:** Name, address, and phone. **Arrangement:** Alphabetical. **Pages** (approx.): 35. **Frequency:** Annual, June. **Editor:** Abraim Plon, D.P.M. **Advertising accepted.** Circulation 2,200. **Price:** Available to members only.

★4142★
ACCENT ON LIVING BUYER'S GUIDE [Products for handicapped]
Accent Special Publications
Cheever Publishing, Inc.
Gillum Road and High Drive   Phone: (309) 378-2961
Bloomington, IL 61701
Covers: Over 400 manufacturers and distributors of products for disabled persons, ranging from common items such as wheelchairs to bowling ball pushers and talking calculators. **Entries include:** Company name, address. **Arrangement:** Classified. **Pages** (approx.): 75. **Frequency:** Biennial, late in odd years. **Price:** $10.00, plus 55¢ shipping.

★4143★
ACCESS: THE GUIDE TO A BETTER LIFE FOR DISABLED AMERICANS
David Obst Books
Random House, Inc.
201 E. 50th Street   Phone: (212) 751-2600
New York, NY 10022
Publication includes: Lists of facilities, manufacturers of equipment, and suppliers of services to handicapped persons in the United States. **Entries include:** Organization or company name, address; description of products, services, or assistance available. **Arrangement:** Classified. **Pages** (approx.): 255. **Frequency:** Published May 1978. **Author:** Lilly Bruck. **Price:** $12.95, cloth; $5.95, paper; plus 75¢ shipping. **Send orders to:** Random House, Inc., Westminster, MD 21157. **Other information:** Also available as a "Talking Book" from the Division for the Blind and Physically Disabled, Library of Congress (RC 12104).

Accredited Colleges of Pharmacy *See* **Colleges of Pharmacy Accredited Degree Programs**

★4144★
ACCREDITED EDUCATIONAL PROGRAMS IN MEDICAL RECORD ADMINISTRATION
American Medical Record Association
John Hancock Center, Suite 1850
875 N. Michigan Avenue   Phone: (312) 787-2672
Chicago, IL 60611
Covers: Nearly 50 schools which offer accredited baccalaureate programs in medical record administration. **Entries include:** College or university name, location, name of school or department, name of contact, prerequisites, length of program, whether a degree is awarded, month that classes begin, and codes for availability of scholarships and other details. **Arrangement:** Geographical. **Pages** (approx.): 5. **Frequency:** Annual, July. **Price:** Single copies free.

★4145★
ACCREDITED EDUCATIONAL PROGRAMS IN MEDICAL RECORD TECHNOLOGY
American Medical Record Association
John Hancock Center, Suite 1850
875 N. Michigan Avenue   Phone: (312) 787-2672
Chicago, IL 60611
Covers: About 75 accredited associate degree programs for medical record technology. **Entries include:** School name, location, prerequisites, length of program, month classes begin, name of program director. **Arrangement:** Geographical. **Pages** (approx.): 5. **Frequency:** Annual, July. **Price:** Single copies free.

★4146★
ADMISSION REQUIREMENTS OF U.S. AND CANADIAN DENTAL SCHOOLS
American Association of Dental Schools
1625 Massachusetts Avenue, N. W.   Phone: (202) 667-9433
Washington, DC 20036
Number of listings: 69. **Entries include:** School name, dean, address, program, admission requirements, calendar, expenses, and financial aid. **Arrangement:** Geographical. **Indexes:** Alphabetical. **Pages** (approx.): 200. **Frequency:** Annual, spring. **Price:** $7.50, postpaid (current and 1980 editions).

Agency Directory and Certification Manual [Methodist Church]
See Directory of United Methodist Health and Welfare
Ministries

★4147★
ALLIED HEALTH EDUCATION DIRECTORY
American Medical Association
535 N. Dearborn Street   Phone: (312) 751-6088
Chicago, IL 60610
Covers:. 3,100 health career educational programs in about 25
technical, paramedical, and administrative fields accredited by the
American Medical Association. Entries include: Name and address of
hospital or institution sponsoring program, length of program, date
classes begin, prerequisites, tuition, class size, financial aid offered,
names of program director and educational coordinator, degree or
certificate awarded, clinical affiliates. Arrangement: By occupation,
then geographically. Indexes: Institution name (with contact, address,
phone, programs). Pages (approx.): 530. Frequency: Irregular; latest
edition November 1979. Editor: Patricia L. Dedman. Former title:
Directory of Approved Allied Medical Educational Programs; Allied
Medical Education Directory. Price: $12.00. Send orders to:
American Medical Association, Box 821, Monroe, WI 53566. Also
includes: Description of the occupation and of process by which
programs become accredited.

Allied Health Education Programs in Junior and Senior Colleges—
Guidance Edition *See* Directory of Allied Health Education
Programs...

Allied Medical Education Directory *See* Allied Health Education
Directory

★4148★
AMBULATORY PEDIATRIC ASSOCIATION—MEMBERSHIP
DIRECTORY
Ambulatory Pediatric Association
4525 E. San Francisco
Tucson, AZ 85712
Covers: About 1,100 medical personnel, social workers, and others
interested in the care of children in ambulatory care facilities. Entries
include: Name, office address and phone, highest degree held.
Arrangement: Geographical. Pages (approx.): 70. Frequency:
Biennial, summer of odd years. Price: Available to members only.

★4149★
AMERICAN ACADEMY OF ALLERGY—MEMBERSHIP DIRECTORY
American Academy of Allergy
611 E. Wells Street   Phone: (414) 272-6071
Milwaukee, WI 53202
Covers: 2,825 physicians specializing in allergies and allergic
diseases. Entries include: Name, office address and phone, birth year,
educational data. Arrangement: Alphabetical and geographical. Pages
(approx.): 320. Frequency: Biennial, odd years. Advertising
accepted. Circulation 3,000. Price: $50.00. Also includes: List of
institutions offering residencies and fellowships for allergy training,
with address, number of residencies, name of program director,
programs.

★4150★
AMERICAN ACADEMY OF CHILD PSYCHIATRY—MEMBERSHIP
DIRECTORY
American Academy of Child Psychiatry
1424 16th Street, N. W., Suite 201A   Phone: (202) 462-3754
Washington, DC 20036
Number of listings: 2,100. Entries include: Name, home and/or
office address, and membership status. Arrangement: Alphabetical.
Indexes: Geographical. Pages (approx.): 70. Frequency: Annual,
October; supplements issued after January. Editor: Jean DeJarnette,
Membership and Office Coordinator. Price: $5.00.

★4151★
AMERICAN ACADEMY OF HEALTH ADMINISTRATION—
MEMBERSHIP DIRECTORY
American Academy of Health Administration
Miller Hall
University of North Carolina   Phone: (919) 966-2249
Chapel Hill, NC 27514
Number of listings: 1,500. Entries include: Name, office or home
address, job title. Arrangement: Alphabetical. Pages (approx.): 30.
Frequency: Irregular; latest edition 1977. Editor: Dr. Bob Robinson,
Executive Director. Price: Out of print.

★4152★
AMERICAN ACADEMY OF OCCUPATIONAL MEDICINE—
MEMBERSHIP DIRECTORY
American Academy of Occupational Medicine
150 N. Wacker Drive   Phone: (312) 782-2166
Chicago, IL 60606
Covers: About 500 physicians who devote full time to occupational
medicine. Entries include: Name, title, company, address, phone.
Arrangement: Geographical. Indexes: Alphabetical. Frequency:
Annual, January. Editor: Howard N. Schulz, Executive Director. Price:
$20.00.

American Academy of Optometry—Geographical Directory *See*
American Journal of Optometry and Physiological Optics—
Geographical ...

★4153★
AMERICAN ACADEMY OF ORTHOTISTS AND PROSTHETISTS—
DIRECTORY
American Academy of Orthotists and Prosthetists
1444 N Street, N. W.   Phone: (202) 234-8400
Washington, DC 20005
Covers: 1,200 orthotists and prosthetists concerned with the design,
manufacture, and fitting of orthopedic braces, artificial limbs and
other major body parts, and cosmetic replacement of minor parts.
Entries include: Name, home address, highest degree held.
Arrangement: Alphabetical. Indexes: Geographical. Pages (approx.):
90. Frequency: Annual, March. Editor: Michael V. Hines, Director of
Membership Services.

★4154★
AMERICAN ACADEMY OF PEDIATRICS—FELLOWSHIP LIST
American Academy of Pediatrics
1801 Hinman Avenue
Evanston, IL 60204
Covers: 20,700 pediatricians in the United States, Canada, and South
America. Entries include: Name, office address and phone, and year
of graduation. Arrangement: Alphabetical and geographical.
Frequency: Annual, January. Price: $21.00.

★4155★
AMERICAN ACADEMY OF PSYCHOANALYSIS—MEMBERSHIP
ROSTER
American Academy of Psychoanalysis
30 E. 40th Street
New York, NY 10016
Covers: About 875 persons interested in developing communication
among psychoanalysts and persons in other disciplines in science and
the humanities. Entries include: Name, office address and phone;
home address and phone (if given). Arrangement: Alphabetical.
Indexes: Geographical. Pages (approx.): 60. Frequency: Biennial,
spring of even years.

American Annals of the Deaf—Directory of Programs and
Services...Issue *See* American Annals of the Deaf [Reference
issue]

★4156★
AMERICAN ANNALS OF THE DEAF [Reference issue]
Convention of American Instructors of the Deaf
Conference of Executives of American Schools for the Deaf
5034 Wisconsin Avenue, N. W.			Phone: (303) 363-1327
Washington, DC 20016
Covers: In three parts: Educational programs and services, supportive and rehabilitation programs and services, and research and information programs and services focusing on the deaf and aurally handicapped. **Entries include:** Generally, name of sponsoring organization, address, and description of programs offered. School listings include staff and enrollment data. **Arrangement:** By type of organization or service. **Pages** (approx.): 330. **Frequency:** Annual, April. **Editors:** Dr. William N. Craig and Dr. Helen B. Craig. **Advertising accepted. Former title:** American Annals of the Deaf - Directory of Programs and Services for the Deaf in the United States Issue; issue no longer has distinctive title. **Price:** $6.50 (current and 1980 editions; ISSN 0002-726X).

★4157★
AMERICAN ASSOCIATION FOR MUSIC THERAPY—MEMBERSHIP DIRECTORY
American Association for Music Therapy
777 Education Building
35 W. Fourth Street				Phone: (212) 598-3491
New York, NY 10003
Covers: 450 music therapists, worldwide. **Entries include:** Name, office address, and phone, title and affiliation, home address. **Arrangement:** Alphabetical. **Pages** (approx.): 10. **Frequency:** Annual, November. **Editor:** Annabelle Sonkin, Membership Chairperson. **Former title:** Urban Federation for Music Therapists - Membership Directory. **Price:** Available to members only.

★4158★
AMERICAN ASSOCIATION OF BIOFEEDBACK CLINICIANS—DIRECTORY
American Association of Biofeedback Clinicians
2424 Dempster
Des Plaines, IL 60016
Covers: About 500 physicians, therapists, researchers, and others who conduct biofeedback training; international coverage. **Frequency:** Biennial, even years. **Editor:** Kathleen Kilkenny, Executive Secretary. **Price:** $5.50 (tentative, 1980 edition).

★4159★
AMERICAN ASSOCIATION OF DIABETES EDUCATORS—ROSTER OF MEMBERSHIP
American Association of Diabetes Educators
North Woodbury Road				Phone: (609) 589-4831
Pitman, NJ 08071
Number of listings: About 935. **Entries include:** For individual members - Name, address; some listings include title and affiliation. For institutional members - Name, address, names and titles of representatives. **Arrangement:** By membership type, then alphabetical. **Indexes:** Geographical. **Pages** (approx.): 45. **Frequency:** Annual, January/February. **Price:** $20.00; restricted circulation.

★4160★
AMERICAN ASSOCIATION OF HOMES FOR THE AGING—MEMBERSHIP DIRECTORY
American Association of Homes for the Aging
1050 17th Street, N. W., Suite 770		Phone: (202) 296-5960
Washington, DC 20036
Covers: Over 1,600 nonprofit member homes, housing, and health facilities, and 500 supplier, individual, and attorney associate members. **Entries include:** Name of home, address, phone, names of administrative staff, sponsorship, levels of care, services. **Arrangement:** Geographical. **Indexes:** Personal name. **Pages** (approx.): 110. **Frequency:** Irregular; latest edition 1979; new edition expected June 1980. **Price:** $20.00 to libraries; $30.00 to business firms.

★4161★
AMERICAN ASSOCIATION OF HOSPITAL CONSULTANTS—ROSTER OF MEMBERS
American Association of Hospital Consultants
2341 Jefferson Davis Highway			Phone: (703) 528-2700
Arlington, VA 22202
Covers: 125 persons who offer consulting services related to planning, financing, management, and operation of health facilities. **Entries include:** Individual's name and title, firm affiliation, office address, phone. **Arrangement:** By type of membership, then alphabetical. **Pages** (approx.): 20. **Frequency:** Annual, August-September. **Price:** Free.

★4162★
AMERICAN ASSOCIATION OF NEUROPATHOLOGISTS—ROSTER
American Association of Neuropathologists
C/o Department of Pathology
University of Iowa				Phone: (319) 353-3429
Iowa City, IA 52242
Number of listings: 500. **Entries include:** Name, address, phone. **Arrangement:** Alphabetical. **Indexes:** Geographical. **Frequency:** Biennial, even years. **Price:** $50.00 (1980 edition).

★4163★
AMERICAN ASSOCIATION OF PSYCHIATRIC SERVICES FOR CHILDREN—MEMBERSHIP DIRECTORY
American Association of Psychiatric Services for Children
1725 K Street, N. W.				Phone: (202) 659-9115
Washington, DC 20009
Covers: 170 mental health clinics and 145 mental health professionals in the United States and a few in Canada. **Entries include:** Individual entries include name, office address and phone number, and academic degree. **Arrangement:** Geographical. **Pages** (approx.): 40. **Frequency:** Biennial, spring of even years. **Price:** $5.00 (tentative, 1980); 1978 edition out of print.

★4164★
AMERICAN ASSOCIATION OF PUBLIC HEALTH PHYSICIANS—MEMBERSHIP ROSTER
American Association of Public Health Physicians
Box 522						Phone: (601) 453-4563
Greenwood, MS 38930
Number of listings: 500. **Entries include:** Name, address, including professional affiliation. **Arrangement:** By states in Zip code order. **Indexes:** Zip code. **Pages** (approx.): 20. **Frequency:** Annual, fall. **Editor:** Alfio Rausa, M.D., Secretary-Treasurer. **Price:** $28.00, plus $2.00 shipping.

★4165★
AMERICAN BOARD OF ORTHODONTICS—DIRECTORY OF INFORMATION
American Board of Orthodontics
225 S. Meramec Avenue				Phone: (314) 727-6162
St. Louis, MO 63105
Publication includes: List of diplomates of the board (specialists in prevention or correction of irregularities in position of teeth). **Arrangement:** Geographical. **Pages** (approx.): 50. **Frequency:** Annual, July. **Editor:** Earl E. Shepard, Executive Director. **Price:** Free. **Other information:** Formerly, American Board of Orthodontists.

★4166★
AMERICAN BURN ASSOCIATION—MEMBERSHIP DIRECTORY
American Burn Association
C/o C. E. Hartford, M.D.
Department of Surgery
University of Iowa Hospitals			Phone: (319) 356-3622
Iowa City, IA 52242
Covers: 1,400 physicians, occupational and physical therapists, nurses, social workers, dietitians, bio-medical engineers, and others with special competence or interest in care of patients suffering from burns. **Entries include:** Name, address, titles. **Arrangement:**

Alphabetical lists of active, associate, special, and honorary members. **Frequency:** Annual, July. **Editor:** Charles E. Hartford, M.D., Secretary. **Price:** Free.

★4167★
**AMERICAN CLEFT PALATE ASSOCIATION—MEMBERSHIP &
     TEAM DIRECTORY**
American Cleft Palate Association
331 Salk Hall
University of Pittsburgh
Pittsburgh, PA 15261
Covers: 1,350 physicians, dentists, speech pathologists, audiologists, psychologists, and others worldwide actively concerned with care of individuals with cleft palates and related deformities. **Entries include:** For individuals - Name, address, education, profession, phone, year of board, and present affiliation. For teams - Hospital name, address, name of director. **Arrangement:** Individuals are alphabetical, teams are geographical. **Indexes:** Individual's location. **Pages** (approx.): 265. **Frequency:** Biennial, odd years. **Editor:** Betty Jane MacWilliams, Ph.D. **Price:** $5.00, plus $1.00 shipping.

★4168★
**AMERICAN COLLEGE OF HOSPITAL ADMINISTRATORS—
     DIRECTORY**
American College of Hospital Administrators
840 N. Lake Shore Drive   Phone: (312) 943-0544
Chicago, IL 60611
Number of listings: 10,000. **Entries include:** Name, title, health service-related affiliation, address, personal and professional data. **Arrangement:** Alphabetical. **Pages** (approx.): 850. **Frequency:** Biennial, odd years. **Price:** $30.00; 1979 price not set.

★4169★
**AMERICAN COLLEGE OF OSTEOPATHIC HOSPITAL
     ADMINISTRATORS—MEMBERSHIP DIRECTORY**
American College of Osteopathic Hospital Administrators
930 Busse Highway   Phone: (312) 692-2351
Park Ridge, IL 60068
Covers: 196 fellows, members, and nominees. **Entries include:** Name, address, hospital affiliation. **Arrangement:** Alphabetical by membership classification. **Pages** (approx.): 30. **Frequency:** Annual, March. **Editor:** Lin Fish. **Price:** $10.00.

★4170★
**AMERICAN COLLEGE OF VETERINARY PATHOLOGISTS—
     MEMBERSHIP DIRECTORY**
American College of Veterinary Pathologists
N. A. D. L.
Box 70   Phone: (515) 232-0250
Ames, IA 50010
Covers: 500 veterinary and veterinary clinical pathologists. **Entries include:** Name, office address, and phone. **Frequency:** Annual, January. **Price:** $25.00 (current and 1980 editions).

★4171★
**AMERICAN DANCE THERAPY ASSOCIATION—MEMBERSHIP
     DIRECTORY**
American Dance Therapy Association
2000 Century Plaza   Phone: (301) 997-4040
Columbia, MD 21044
Number of listings: 1,100. **Entries include:** Name, address; career information is given in alternate volumes in odd years. **Arrangement:** Alphabetical. **Indexes:** Geographical. **Pages** (approx.): 50. **Frequency:** Annual, December. **Editor:** Patricia Latteri, Office Manager. **Price:** Available to members only.

★4172★
AMERICAN DENTAL DIRECTORY
American Dental Association
211 E. Chicago Avenue
Chicago, IL 60611
Covers: 130,000 dentists. Also includes list of active and historic dental schools, dental organizations, dental consultants, and state dental examining boards. **Entries include:** Name, address, year of birth, dental school, year of graduation, character of practice, membership status. **Arrangement:** Geographical. **Indexes:** Alphabetical. **Pages** (approx.): 1,400. **Frequency:** Annual, fall. **Price:** $50.00, payment with order.

★4173★
AMERICAN DRUG INDEX
J. B. Lippincott Company
E. Washington Square   Phone: (215) 574-4200
Philadelphia, PA 19105
Publication includes: Alphabetical list of manufacturers of prescription drugs and patent medicines, and other drug store items. **Entries include:** Company name, address. **Pages** (approx.): 725. **Frequency:** Annual, February. **Editor:** Norman F. Billups, Ph.D., Professor of Pharmacy. **Price:** $16.00. **Also includes:** Listings for over 20,000 prescription and over-the-counter drug items, toiletries, etc., giving information on manufacturer, forms and strengths, packaging, trade names, etc.; for drugs, correlates generic and brand names.

★4174★
AMERICAN ELECTROLYSIS ASSOCIATION—ROSTER
American Electrolysis Association
Box 204   Phone: (203) 372-7119
Evanston, IL 60204
Covers: 1,300 electrologists (persons engaged in the removal of body hair by electrical means) worldwide. **Entries include:** Name, address, phone. **Arrangement:** Geographical. **Pages** (approx.): 130. **Frequency:** Biennial, March of odd years. **Editor:** Elizabeth Albanese, Corresponding Secretary. **Price:** Free.

★4175★
AMERICAN GROUP PRACTICE ASSOCIATION—DIRECTORY
American Group Practice Association
20 S. Quaker Lane   Phone: (703) 751-1000
Alexandria, VA 22314
Covers: About 450 private group medical practices and their professional staffs, totaling about 14,000 persons. **Entries include:** Name of group member, address, phone, names of administrator and other executives, breakdown of medical specialties of the staff. **Arrangement:** Alphabetical by member group name. **Indexes:** Geographical by member group name; alphabetical by individual professionals within member groups. **Pages** (approx.): 400. **Frequency:** Irregular; new edition expected fall 1980. **Editor:** Elizabeth M. Goodfellow. **Advertising accepted.** Circulation 4,000. **Price:** $30.00 (current edition); $25.00 (tentative, 1980 edition).

★4176★
**AMERICAN GUILD OF HYPNOTHERAPISTS—MEMBERSHIP
     DIRECTORY**
American Guild of Hypnotherapists
9559 Bolsa Avenue   Phone: (714) 531-5779
Westminster, CA 92683
Covers: About 700 licensed hypnotherapists, professional hypnotists, students in these fields, and others interested in the use of hypnotherapy and hypnotism in counseling, investigation, and the healing arts. **Entries include:** Name, address, phone, specialty. **Arrangement:** Geographical. **Frequency:** Annual, October. **Editor:** Joseph R. Ross, Ph.D. **Price:** Available to members; others, apply.

★4177★

AMERICAN HOLISTIC MEDICAL ASSOCIATION—ROSTER

American Holistic Medical Association
C/o Dr. C. Norman Shealy
Route 2, Welsh Coulee
La Crosse, WI 54601

Covers: 450 doctors of medicine who practice or are interested in holistic medicine. **Entries include:** Name, address, specialty. **Arrangement:** Alphabetical. **Indexes:** Geographical. **Pages** (approx.): 30. **Frequency:** Annual. **Price:** $2.00 per state list.

★4178★

AMERICAN HOSPITAL ASSOCIATION GUIDE TO THE HEALTH CARE
    FIELD

American Hospital Association
840 N. Lake Shore Drive   Phone: (312) 280-6000
Chicago, IL 60611

Covers: 7,000 hospitals, 29,000 personal members, and 1,000 health related organizations. Also includes manufacturers and distributors of hospital and health care products. **Entries include:** For hospitals - Facility name, address, phone, administrator's name, number of beds, other statistics. For personal members - Name, affiliation. For suppliers - Company name, address, products. **Arrangement:** Hospitals arranged geographically, members and suppliers alphabetically. **Frequency:** Annual, August. **Editor:** Carol L. Keenan, Guide Coordinator. **Advertising accepted. Former title:** Hospitals - Annual Guide Issue. **Price:** $43.75, postpaid, payment with order; $47.25, billed.

★4179★

AMERICAN INDUSTRIAL HYGIENE ASSOCIATION—DIRECTORY

American Industrial Hygiene Association
475 Wolf Ledges Parkway   Phone: (216) 762-7294
Akron, OH 44311

Covers: 4,000 members concerned with the study and control of environmental factors affecting industrial workers. **Entries include:** Name, address, affiliation. **Arrangement:** Geographical. **Frequency:** Annual.

★4180★

AMERICAN INSTITUTE OF ULTRASOUND IN MEDICINE—
    MEMBERSHIP ROSTER

American Institute of Ultrasound in Medicine
6161 N. May Avenue, Suite 278   Phone: (405) 840-3721
Oklahoma City, OK 73112

Covers: About 3,000 physicians, engineers, biologists, and others interested in the use of ultrasonic radiation clinically and in research. **Arrangement:** Alphabetical. **Indexes:** Geographical. **Frequency:** Irregular; previous edition 1977; latest edition 1979. **Price:** Apply; restricted circulation.

★4181★

AMERICAN JOURNAL OF NURSING—DIRECTORY OF NURSING
    ORGANIZATIONS ISSUES

American Journal of Nursing Company
555 W. 57th Street   Phone: (212) 582-8820
New York, NY 10019

Publication includes: Directory of nursing organizations and agencies. April issue contains federal listings; May issue contains international, national, regional, and state listings. **Entries include:** Name, address, and officers or nursing representative. **Frequency:** Annual, April and May. **Editor:** Thelma Schorr, R.N. **Advertising accepted.** Circulation 340,000. **Price:** $3.00 (current and 1980 editions).

★4182★

AMERICAN JOURNAL OF OPTOMETRY AND PHYSIOLOGICAL
    OPTICS—GEOGRAPHICAL DIRECTORY, AMERICAN ACADEMY
    OF OPTOMETRY ISSUE

American Academy of Optometry
Box 565   Phone: (507) 451-0009
Owatonna, MN 55060

Covers: 2,300 members worldwide. **Entries include:** Name, title, affiliation, and office address. **Indexes:** Alphabetical, specialty. **Pages** (approx.): 70. **Frequency:** Annual, November. **Editor:** Dr. Merton Flom, University of California, Berkeley. **Price:** $1.50. **Send orders to:** Williams & Wilkins Co., 428 E. Preston, Baltimore, MD 21202.

★4183★

AMERICAN MEDICAL DIRECTORY

PSG Publishing Company, Inc.
545 Great Road
Littleton, MA 01460

Covers: About 445,000 physicians in the United States and United States physicians in foreign countries; women physicians are included in main volumes and also listed separately in "Directory of Women Physicians," a supplemental volume. **Entries include:** Name, address, year licensed, medical school, type of practice, primary and secondary specialties, and board certifications. **Arrangement:** Geographical; federal service and United States physicians abroad in separate section. **Indexes:** Alphabetical (comprises volume 1 of set). **Frequency:** Irregular; previous edition 1973; latest edition February 1979; new edition expected 1981. **Price:** Five volume set, including "Directory of Women Physicians," $225.00, plus $4.75 shipping; publisher does not quote separate price for women physicians volume.

★4184★

AMERICAN MEDICAL WRITERS ASSOCIATION—AMWA
    FREELANCE DIRECTORY

American Medical Writers Association
5272 River Road, Suite 290   Phone: (301) 986-9119
Bethesda, MD 20016

Covers: About 85 members of the association who are primarily freelance writers on medical subjects, or are interested in such assignments. Membership includes consultants, editors, photographers, translators, and educators. **Entries include:** Name, address, phone, specialties, types of media familiar with, subjects, publications in which work has appeared, other activities, whether person will travel. **Arrangement:** Alphabetical. **Indexes:** Geographical, specialty. **Pages** (approx.): 30. **Frequency:** Irregular; latest edition April 1979; new edition expected December 1980. **Price:** Free.

★4185★

AMERICAN OCCUPATIONAL MEDICAL ASSOCIATION—
    MEMBERSHIP DIRECTORY

American Occupational Medical Association
150 N. Wacker Drive   Phone: (312) 782-2166
Chicago, IL 60606

Covers: 3,800 medical directors and plant physicians specializing in industrial medicine and surgery. **Entries include:** Name, title, affiliation, address, phone, degree; codes for membership class, medical specialty certifications, and type of practice. **Arrangement:** Geographical. **Indexes:** Alphabetical. **Pages** (approx.): 150. **Frequency:** Annual, January. **Advertising accepted.** Circulation 5,000. **Price:** $25.00 (current and 1980 editions).

★4186★

AMERICAN ORTHODONTIC SOCIETY—TECHNIQUE REFERRAL
    DIRECTORY

American Orthodontic Society
8226 Douglas Street, Suite 332   Phone: (214) 363-2980
Dallas, TX 75225

Covers: About 2,400 orthodontists; international coverage. **Entries include:** Name, address, whether a member, and orthodontic specialty. **Arrangement:** Geographical. **Indexes:** Alphabetical. **Pages** (approx.): 150. **Frequency:** Has been quadrennial with annual supplements; new edition expected 1980, thereafter will be triennial with annual supplements. **Editor:** Dr. Charles D. Yates, Executive Director. **Price:** $20.00; available to members only.

★4187★

AMERICAN OSTEOPATHIC HOSPITAL ASSOCIATION—
    DIRECTORY
American Osteopathic Hospital Association
930 Busse Highway   Phone: (312) 692-2351
Park Ridge, IL 60068
Covers: 205 osteopathic hospitals. Includes list of individual and institutional members. Also lists state osteopathic associations. **Entries include:** Name of hospital, name of chief executive officer, address, phone, number of beds and other hospital data. **Arrangement:** Geographical. **Pages** (approx.): 45. **Frequency:** New edition expected January 1980. **Editor:** Lin Fish, Director of Communications. **Advertising accepted.** Circulation 700. **Price:** $25.00 (current edition); $15.00 (1980 edition); payment must accompany order.

★4188★

AMERICAN OSTEOPATHIC MEDICAL SCHOOL CATALOGUE
Osteopathic Medical School Information Center
One E. Main Street   Phone: (516) 665-8500
Bay Shore, NY 11706
Covers: 10 colleges of osteopathic medicine; state licensure boards. **Entries include:** School name, address, phone, name of dean, admission requirements, tuition. For boards - Name, address. **Arrangement:** Geographical. **Pages** (approx.): 65. **Frequency:** Irregular; latest edition 1976. **Editors:** Esther A. and Richard P. Zaretsky. **Price:** $8.00, postpaid, payment with order. **Also includes:** List of osteopathic hospitals.

★4189★

AMERICAN PSYCHIATRIC ASSOCIATION—MEMBERSHIP
    DIRECTORY
American Psychiatric Association
1700 18th Street, N. W.   Phone: (202) 232-7878
Washington, DC 20009
Covers: 25,000 psychiatrists holding MD degrees who are members. **Entries include:** Name, preferred mailing address, status in association, and year of joining. **Arrangement:** Alphabetical. **Indexes:** Geographical. **Pages** (approx.): 200. **Frequency:** New edition expected spring 1980; has been biennial, will now alternate with "Biographical Directory of the American Psychiatric Association," published by Jaques Cattell Press of the R. R. Bowker Co. (see separate listing). **Price:** 1980 price not determined.

★4190★

AMERICAN PSYCHOANALYTIC ASSOCIATION—ROSTER
American Psychoanalytic Association
One E. 57th Street   Phone: (212) 752-0450
New York, NY 10022
Number of listings: 2,700. **Entries include:** Name, address, phone. **Arrangement:** Alphabetical. **Indexes:** Geographical. **Pages** (approx.): 100. **Frequency:** Annual, fall. **Price:** $7.00. **Also includes:** Lists of accredited training institutions and affiliate societies.

★4191★

AMERICAN SOCIETY FOR ADOLESCENT PSYCHIATRY—
    MEMBERSHIP DIRECTORY
American Society for Adolescent Psychiatry
24 Green Valley Road   Phone: (215) 566-1054
Wallingford, PA 19086
Number of listings: 1,600. **Pages** (approx.): 50. **Frequency:** Irregular; latest edition fall 1979. **Editor:** Mary D. Staples, Executive Secretary. **Price:** Availabe to members only.

★4192★

AMERICAN SOCIETY FOR HOSPITAL PUBLIC RELATIONS—
    ROSTER OF MEMBERSHIP
American Society for Hospital Public Relations
840 N. Lake Shore Drive
Chicago, IL 60611
Number of listings: 1,300. **Arrangement:** Alphabetical. **Indexes:** Geographical. **Frequency:** Annual, January. **Price:** Available to members only.

★4193★

AMERICAN SOCIETY FOR HOSPITAL PURCHASING AND
    MATERIALS MANAGEMENT—ROSTER
American Society for Hospital Purchasing and Materials Management
    of the American Hospital Association
840 N. Lake Shore Drive   Phone: (312) 280-6084
Chicago, IL 60611
Number of listings: 1,200. **Entries include:** Member name, address, hospital affiliation, and phone. **Arrangement:** Geographical. **Pages** (approx.): 45. **Frequency:** Annual, July. **Former title:** American Society for Hospital Purchasing Agents - Roster. **Price:** Available to members only.

American Society for Psychoprophylaxis in Obstetrics—Directory
    See Who's Who in Childbirth Education

★4194★

AMERICAN SOCIETY OF BARIATRIC PHYSICIANS—DIRECTORY
    [Physicians concerned with obesity]
American Society of Bariatric Physicians
5200 S. Quebec Street, No. 300   Phone: (303) 779-4833
Englewood, CO 80111
Number of listings: 550. **Entries include:** Name, address, and phone. **Frequency:** Annual, July. **Editor:** Randall B. Lee, Executive Director. **Price:** $15.00.

★4195★

AMERICAN SOCIETY OF CLINICAL HYPNOSIS—MEMBERSHIP
    DIRECTORY
American Society of Clinical Hypnosis
2400 E. Devon, Suite 218
Des Plaines, IL 60018
Covers: About 3,000 physicians, dentists, and psychologists who use hypnosis. **Entries include:** Name, office address, highest degree held, areas of specialization. **Pages** (approx.): 135. **Frequency:** Biennial, spring of odd years. **Price:** Available to members only.

★4196★

AMERICAN VETERINARY MEDICAL ASSOCIATION—DIRECTORY
American Veterinary Medical Association
930 N. Meacham Road   Phone: (312) 885-8070
Schaumburg, IL 60196
Covers: 36,700 veterinarians; not limited to AVMA members. **Entries include:** Name, spouse's name, address, and codes for area of specialization, type of employer, institution granting degree, and year received. **Arrangement:** Geographical. **Indexes:** Alphabetical. **Pages** (approx.): 480. **Frequency:** Biennial, January of even years. **Editor:** Arthur V. Tennyson, V.M.D., Director, Membership and Field Services. **Advertising accepted.** Circulation 5,500. **Price:** $30.00, payment with order. **Also includes:** Extensive list of veterinary medical and related associations.

★4197★

APHA DRUG NAMES: AN INDEX
American Pharmaceutical Association
2215 Constitution Avenue, N. W.   Phone: (202) 628-4410
Washington, DC 20037
Publication includes: List of drug manufacturers, repackagers, and distributors whose products appear under proprietary names in the text. **Entries include:** Company name, address. **Arrangement:** Alphabetical. **Frequency:** Irregular; latest 1979. **Former title:**

Proprietary Names of Official Drugs. **Price:** $16.00, payment with order. **Other information:** Principal content is alphabetical list of generic drug names with names of manufacturers who sell the product in bulk and the proprietary name and company name of manufacturers repackaging it.

★4198★
APPROPRIATE TECHNOLOGY FOR HEALTH DIRECTORY
ATH Programme
World Health Organization
Avenue Appia
1211 Geneva 27, Switzerland
Covers: 210 persons worldwide concerned with appropriate technology specifically for health applications, including about 50 in North America. **Entries include:** Name, affiliation, address, and interests. **Arrangement:** Geographical. **Indexes:** Subject. **Pages** (approx.): 45. **Frequency:** Semiannual. **Price:** $5.25, paper; $3.00, microfiche (PB 297-077). **Send orders to:** National Technical Information Service, Springfield, VA 22161.

★4199★
ASSOCIATION FOR ADVANCEMENT OF BEHAVIOR THERAPY—
MEMBERSHIP DIRECTORY
Association for Advancement of Behavior Therapy
420 Lexington Avenue   Phone: (212) 682-0065
New York, NY 10017
Covers: About 3,000 psychiatrists, psychotherapists, and others interested in behavior therapy. **Entries include:** Name, office and home addresses, certifications or licenses, and personal data. **Arrangement:** Alphabetical. **Indexes:** Geographical. **Pages** (approx.): 130. **Frequency:** Biennial, fall of odd years; 1979 edition delayed to January 1980. **Price:** Available to public as mailing labels only; $45.00 per thousand.

★4200★
ASSOCIATION FOR THE ADVANCEMENT OF MEDICAL
INSTRUMENTATION—MEMBERSHIP DIRECTORY
Association for the Advancement of Medical Instrumentation
1901 N. Fort Myer Drive, Suite 602   Phone: (703) 525-4890
Arlington, VA 22209
Covers: 4,500 physicians, clinical engineers, biomedical professionals, medical equipment manufacturers. **Entries include:** Name, title, affiliation, office address, phone, code for area of occupational specialization. **Arrangement:** Alphabetical. **Indexes:** Specialty, geographical. **Frequency:** Biennial, even years. **Advertising accepted.** Circulation 3,500. **Price:** $25.00 (current and 1980 editions).

★4201★
ASSOCIATION OF HALFWAY HOUSE ALCOHOLISM PROGRAMS OF
NORTH AMERICA—MEMBERSHIP DIRECTORY
Association of Halfway House Alcoholism Programs of North America
786 E. Seventh Street   Phone: (612) 771-0933
St. Paul, MN 55106
Number of listings: 525. **Entries include:** Organization name, address, phone, director's name, number of beds, and target population and substance abused; individuals' listings show name, address. **Arrangement:** Geographical. **Pages** (approx.): 25. **Frequency:** Annual, January. **Editor:** Diane Fontaine-Adams, Executive Director. **Price:** $1.00 (current edition); $3.00 (1980 edition).

★4202★
ASSOCIATION OF MEDICAL ILLUSTRATORS—MEMBERSHIP
DIRECTORY
Association of Medical Illustrators
6022 W. Touhy Avenue   Phone: (312) 763-7350
Chicago, IL 60058
Number of listings: Over 400. **Entries include:** Name, preferred address and phone. **Arrangement:** Alphabetical. **Indexes:**

Geographical (with code for free-lance availability). **Frequency:** Biennial, fall of odd years. **Price:** Free.

★4203★
ASSOCIATION OF REHABILITATION FACILITIES—MEMBERSHIP
DIRECTORY
Association of Rehabilitation Facilities
5530 Wisconsin Avenue, Suite 955
Washington, DC 20015
Covers: 762 facilities in the United States, Canada, and Guam which operate sheltered workshops and/or homebound programs oriented toward physical, vocational, and social rehabilitation. **Entries include:** Facility name, address, phone, name and title of facility representative to the association, services offered. **Indexes:** Personal name. **Frequency:** Annual, May.

★4204★
AUTHOR'S GUIDE TO JOURNALS IN NURSING
Haworth Press
149 Fifth Avenue   Phone: (212) 228-2800
New York, NY 10010
Number of listings: About 450. **Entries include:** Publication name, address for manuscripts, publication orientation and subject interests, usual review time and delay in publication of accepted manuscripts, early publication options (if any). **Frequency:** Not established; first edition expected late spring 1980. **Price:** $16.95.

★4205★
AUTHOR'S GUIDE TO JOURNALS IN THE HEALTH FIELD
Haworth Press
149 Fifth Avenue   Phone: (212) 228-2800
New York, NY 10010
Number of listings: About 450. **Entries include:** Publication name, address for manuscripts, publication orientation and subject interests, usual review time and delay in publication of accepted manuscripts, early publication options (if any). **Arrangement:** Alphabetical. **Indexes:** Subject/keyword. **Frequency:** Not established; first edition 1978. **Editor:** Donald Ardell. **Price:** $16.95.

★4206★
AV SOURCE DIRECTORY: A SUBJECT INDEX TO HEALTH SCIENCE
AV PRODUCER/DISTRIBUTOR CATALOGS
Midwest Health Science Library Network
Library of the Health Sciences
University of Illinois at the Medical Center
Box 7509   Phone: (312) 996-2464
Chicago, IL 60680
Covers: Over 500 producers and distributors of audiovisual materials concerned with the health sciences. **Entries include:** Company name, address, phone; formats used; distribution policy; collection size; Medical Subject Heading from the National Library of Medicine thesaurus; discipline heading. **Arrangement:** Alphabetical. **Indexes:** Subject, in three parts - Producer/distributor by health sciences general coverage, broad discipline, and specific medical subject. **Pages** (approx.): 105. **Frequency:** Not established; first edition 1977. **Editor:** Bruce Ardis. **Price:** $9.75.

★4207★
BALTIMORE-WASHINGTON HEALING RESOURCES
Healing Resources, Inc.
421 Butternut Street, N. W.   Phone: (202) 829-4201
Washington, DC 20012
Covers: Practitioners of health-oriented medicine, herbal treatment, and other nontraditional health care. **Arrangement:** Alphabetical. **Indexes:** Type of healing. **Frequency:** Not established; first edition 1977. **Price:** $5.95.

★4208★
BARRON'S GETTING INTO MEDICAL SCHOOL
Barron's Educational Series, Inc.
113 Crossways Park Drive   Phone: (516) 921-8750
Woodbury, NY 11797
Publication includes: List of medical schools approved by the American Medical Association. **Entries include:** School name, address, admission requirements, costs, special programs, and minority student information. **Arrangement:** Alphabetical. **Frequency:** Irregular; previous edition 1978; latest edition June 1979. **Author:** Dr. Sanford J. Brown. **Price:** $3.75, payment with order. **Other information:** Primary content of publication is information on medical school admission policies, requirements, testing, etc.

★4209★
BARRON'S GUIDE TO FINANCIAL AID FOR MEDICAL STUDENTS
Barron's Educational Series, Inc.
113 Crossways Park Drive   Phone: (516) 921-8750
Woodbury, NY 11797
Covers: Several hundred sources of financial aid for medical students, including governmental agencies, medical schools, associations, fraternal and veterans' organizations. **Entries include:** Organization name, address, name of program, amount of assistance available, eligibility requirements, application procedures. Medical school listings include name, address, phone. **Arrangement:** By type of assistance; most are then geographical. **Pages** (approx.): 265. **Frequency:** First edition fall 1979. **Editor:** Dr. Stephen H. Lazar. **Price:** $5.95. **Other information:** Cited in pre-publication promotion as, "Complete Medical Student's Guide to Financial Aid."

★4210★
BARRON'S GUIDE TO FOREIGN MEDICAL SCHOOLS
Barron's Educational Series, Inc.
113 Crossways Park Drive   Phone: (516) 921-8750
Woodbury, NY 11797
Covers: Foreign medical schools accepting American students. **Entries include:** Name of school, address, admission and course requirements, application procedures. **Arrangement:** Geographical. **Indexes:** Subject. **Pages** (approx.): 210. **Frequency:** Not established; first edition 1979. **Author:** Carla Fine. **Price:** $4.95, payment with order. **Other information:** Originally advertised under title, "Complete Guide to Foreign Medical Schools."

★4211★
BARRON'S GUIDE TO MEDICAL, DENTAL, AND ALLIED HEALTH SCIENCE CAREERS
Barron's Educational Series, Inc.
113 Crossways Park Drive   Phone: (516) 921-8750
Woodbury, NY 11797
Covers: Accredited educational programs in the field of health care, including dentistry, dental assistantship and hygiene, electroencephalography, hospital administration, medical librarianship, medical assistantships, medical laboratory technology, medical record specialties, medicine, nuclear medicine technology, nursing (licensed and registered nurse programs), occupational therapy, optometry, osteopathy, pharmacy, physical therapy, physician's assistant, podiatry, public health, radiation therapy technology, radiologic technology, respiratory therapy, social work, speech pathology and audiology, and veterinary medicine. **Entries include:** School name, address. Medical school listings also include admission requirements, housing, grading and promotional policies, facilities, and description of curriculum. **Arrangement:** By type of program, then geographical. **Pages** (approx.): 270. **Frequency:** Irregular; latest edition 1977; free updates available. **Editor:** Dr. Saul Wischnitzer. **Price:** $5.50, plus 55¢ shipping.

Behavior Therapy and Research Society—Roster of Clinical Fellows *See* Journal of Behavior Therapy & Experimental Psychiatry...

Best Dentists in America *See* Best Doctors in America

★4212★
BEST DOCTORS IN AMERICA
Reveal Publications
2208 Woodlawn Street
Kannapolis, NC 28081
Background: A November, 1978, issue of "American Medical News" contained the following comment: "The editor, Shelby Taylor, told AMA that he selects the best physicians by a process of 'research and sorting.' He denied that a physician would have to buy the $18 book or pay a fee in order to be listed as one of the 'best doctors.' However, he declined to say how a physician's name would be selected for inclusion. 'We do it by our own process of research,' he said, but declined to describe the process, saying that 'it is impossible to go into.' " **Other information:** Reveal Publications' solicitation brochure also mentions that the firm publishes "Best Dentists in America" and "Best Lawyers in America." The "A D A News," publication of the American Dental Association, reported in its April 2, 1979 issue on solicitations for listings and purchase of books received by dentists. It described its experience in trying to secure information about the publication from the publisher as "several weeks of cat and mouse," with no satisfactory results.

★4213★
BEST DOCTORS IN THE U.S.
Seaview Books
747 Third Avenue   Phone: (212) 593-2900
New York, NY 10017
Covers: Doctors in specialties ranging from cardiology, cancer, heart surgery, urology and gastrointestinal disorders to allergies, dermatology, obstetrics, gynecology, and plastic surgery who have been named as the "best" by physicians in interviews; also includes recommended health centers and hospitals. **Entries include:** Name, address, phone. **Frequency:** Not established; first edition August 1979. **Editor:** John Pekkanen. **Price:** $8.95. **Send orders to:** Simon & Schuster, 1230 Avenue of the Americas, New York, NY 10020. **Other information:** Not to be confused with "Best Doctors in America;" see separate listing.

Best Lawyers in America *See* Best Doctors in America

★4214★
BHM SUPPORT—DIRECTORY OF GRANTS, AWARDS, AND LOANS
[Health education federal funding]
Bureau of Health Manpower
Health Resources Administration
Health, Education, and Welfare Department
Bethesda, MD 20852
Covers: Several hundred institutions having education programs in medicine, osteopathic medicine, dentistry, optometry, pharmacy, podiatric medicine, veterinary medicine, nursing, allied health sciences, and public health funded through awards of the Bureau of Health Manpower. **Entries include:** Institution name, grant number, name of contact, program title, number of awards, total amount awarded. **Arrangement:** By DHEW region, then geographical. **Indexes:** Program title (with state, number of awards, and amount awarded). **Pages** (approx.): 915. **Frequency:** Annual, December (for prior fiscal year). **Editors:** Bella U. Berman and Samuel Rosenthal. **Price:** Free (DHEW Publication No. HRA 79-19). **Send orders to:** Bureau of Health Manpower, 3700 East-West Highway, Hyattsville, MD 20782.

★4215★
BIOGRAPHICAL DIRECTORY OF THE AMERICAN PUBLIC HEALTH ASSOCIATION
Jaques Cattell Press
R. R. Bowker Company
2216 S. Industrial Drive
Tempe, AZ 85282
Covers: About 29,000 physicians, nurses, educators, engineers, environmentalists, social workers, industrial hygienists, and consumers

interested in public health; approximately 13,000 members are covered in detail (others did not respond to survey). **Entries include:** For members fully covered - Name, address, phone; career, educational, and personal data; memberships; areas of interest. For all others - Name, address. **Arrangement:** Alphabetical. **Indexes:** Geographical. **Pages** (approx.): 1,200. **Frequency:** Not established; first edition December 1979. **Price:** $54.50, postpaid, payment with order. **Send orders to:** R. R. Bowker Co., Box 1807, Ann Arbor, MI 48106 (313-761-4700).

★4216★

BIOMEDICAL COMMUNICATIONS—MEDICAL MEDIA DIRECTORY ISSUE

United Business Publications, Inc., Division
Media Horizons, Inc.
475 Park Avenue South   Phone: (212) 725-2300
New York, NY 10016
Covers: Publishers of books, periodicals, and other instructional media for medical, paramedical, and public education. **Entries include:** Company name, address, phone, contact. **Pages** (approx.): 90. **Frequency:** Annual, April. **Editor:** Cheryl Waixel. **Advertising accepted.** Circulation 23,000. **Price:** $15.00 (current and 1980 editions).

★4217★

BIRTH PRIMER: A SOURCE BOOK OF TRADITIONAL AND ALTERNATIVE METHODS IN LABOR AND DELIVERY

Running Press
38 S. 19th Street   Phone: (212) 567-5080
Philadelphia, PA 19103
Publication includes: Lists of organizations, publishers, and other sources of information concerning alternative methods of childbirth (including midwifery, psychoprophylaxis, etc.). **Entries include:** Organization, etc. name, address, description of services, programs, publications, or other information materials. **Arrangement:** By activity. **Indexes:** Subject. **Pages** (approx.): 260. **Frequency:** Not established; first edition 1977. **Editor:** Rebecca Rowe Parfitt. **Price:** $5.95, plus 60¢ shipping.

★4218★

BLUE BOOK—INTERNATIONAL DIRECTORY OF MEDICAL/ surgical SUPPLY DEALERS

Cassak Publications, Inc.
2009 Morris Avenue   Phone: (201) 687-8282
Union, NJ 07083
Covers: About 3,500 health care supply dealers; international coverage in two volumes: Volume 1 - domestic; Volume 2 - Canadian and foreign dealers. **Entries include:** Dealership name, address, phone; names of key executives; geographic area served; number of salesmen; length of time in business; association affiliation; description of primary customers through percentage breakdown of sales; sales volume. **Arrangement:** Geographical. **Indexes:** Dealer name. **Pages** (approx.): Volume 1, 830; Volume 2, 200. **Frequency:** Irregular; latest edition spring 1978. **Editor:** Selma Levy. **Advertising accepted. Price:** Volume 1, $50.00; Volume 2, $25.00; set, $60.00.

★4219★

BLUE BOOK OF OPTOMETRISTS

Professional Press, Inc.
101 E. Ontario Street, Sixth Floor   Phone: (312) 337-7800
Chicago, IL 60611
Covers: 25,400 optometrists in the United States and Canada; separate sections list optical supply houses, manufacturers and import firms, associations, and colleges concerned with optometry and opticianry. **Entries include:** For optometrists - Name, office address, phone, personal, educational, and career data, and areas of occupational specialization. **Arrangement:** Geographical. **Pages** (approx.): 800. **Frequency:** Biennial, April of even years. **Advertising accepted. Price:** $14.75 (current edition); $18.00 (1980 edition).

Center for Educational Development—Continuing Education Calendar *See* Continuing Education Calendar for Health Professionals

★4220★

CLARK'S DIRECTORY OF SOUTHERN HOSPITALS

Clark Publishing Company
106 E. Stone Avenue   Phone: (803) 242-5300
Greenville, SC 29602
Entries include: Name of hospital, city and county located in, accreditation, mailing address, phone, number of beds, type of facility (nonprofit, general, state, etc.), list of administrative personnel and chiefs of medical services with titles. **Arrangement:** Geographical. **Pages** (approx.): 340. **Frequency:** Annual, November. **Editor:** Randolph Taylor, Publisher. **Price:** $12.00, plus $1.50 shipping, payment with order.

★4221★

CLEVELAND MEDICAL DIRECTORY

Cleveland Consumer Action
532 Terminal Tower   Phone: (216) 687-0525
Cleveland, OH 44113
Covers: Over 665 general practitioners, internists, and pediatricians practicing in Cuyahoga County; hospitals and other group providers are also listed. **Entries include:** For doctors responding to the questionnaire (about 195) - Name, address, medical school attended; hospital with which affiliated, office hours, fees, and availability for house calls. For non-responding doctors - Name, address, medical school attended. For hospitals - Name, address, facilities and services. **Arrangement:** Alphabetical within specialty. **Pages** (approx.): 230. **Frequency:** Not established; first edition May 1978. **Editor:** Laura B. Chisolm. **Advertising accepted.** Circulation 1,000. **Price:** $3.65, plus 30¢ shipping.

★4222★

CLINICAL LABORATORY REFERENCE

Medical Economics Company
680 Kinderkamack Road   Phone: (201) 262-3030
Oradell, NJ 07649
Covers: About 140 manufacturers of diagnostic reagents, tests, systems, instruments, and equipment used in a clinical laboratory, and publishers and suppliers of materials used in education and training of staff; listings are paid. **Entries include:** Company name, address, phone, and products or services. **Arrangement:** Alphabetical. **Indexes:** Brand name, product, organ and disease, and continuing education materials. **Pages** (approx.): 180. **Frequency:** Annual, May; supplement in November. **Editor:** H. Mason Fackert, Publisher. **Advertising accepted.** Circulation 57,800. **Price:** $15.00, including supplement.

★4223★

CLINICAL PROGRAMS FOR MENTALLY RETARDED CHILDREN

Bureau of Community Health Services
Health Services Administration
Health, Education, and Welfare Department
5600 Fishers Lane, Room 7A20   Phone: (202) 443-4273
Rockville, MD 20857
Covers: About 250 outpatient medical facilities providing comprehensive evaluation, treatment, or followup services primarily to children suspected of or diagnosed as being mentally retarded. **Entries include:** Facility name, address, phone, name of director, geographic area served, ages accepted, source of funding, and hours open. **Arrangement:** Geographical. **Pages** (approx.): 45. **Frequency:** Irregular; latest edition 1978; new edition possible January 1980. **Editor:** Rudolf P. Hormuth, Specialist in Services for Mentally Retarded Children. **Price:** $1.60 (S/N 017-021-00029-0). **Send orders to:** Government Printing Office, Washington, DC 20402. **Other information:** Single copies available free from the Bureau of Community Health Services (DHEW Publication No. HSA 78-5291).

★4224★

COLLEGE OF OPTOMETRISTS IN VISION DEVELOPMENT— FELLOW MEMBER ROSTER
College of Optometrists in Vision Development
Box 285   Phone: (714) 425-6191
Chula Vista, CA 92012
Number of listings: About 340. **Entries include:** Name, address, and phone. **Arrangement:** Geographical. **Pages (approx.):** 25. **Frequency:** Annual, winter. **Editor:** Robert M. Wold, O.D. **Price:** 50¢ (current and 1980 editions).

★4225★

COLLEGES OF PHARMACY ACCREDITED DEGREE PROGRAMS
American Council on Pharmaceutical Education
One E. Wacker Drive   Phone: (312) 467-6222
Chicago, IL 60601
Covers: Accredited first professional degree programs of United States and Puerto Rico colleges of pharmacy. **Entries include:** College name, address, phone, dean's name, date of most recent and of next accreditation evaluation. **Arrangement:** Geographical. **Pages (approx.):** 20. **Frequency:** Annual, July. **Former title:** List of Accredited Colleges of Pharmacy in the United States of America; Accredited Colleges of Pharmacy. **Price:** Free.

★4226★

COMPENDIUM OF TUMOR IMMUNOTHERAPY PROTOCOLS
International Cancer Research Data Bank
National Cancer Institute
National Institutes of Health
8300 Colesville Road   Phone: (301) 427-8759
Silver Spring, MD 20910
Covers: Over 350 tumor immunotherapy projects, worldwide; projects listed are conducted by participants in the International Registry of Tumor Immunotherapy. **Entries include:** Project name, name and phone of chief investigator, address; description of project including hypothesis, entry criteria, drug, dosage, other project data. **Arrangement:** By organ site and tumor type. **Indexes:** Investigator name, agent, tumor, geographical, cooperative group. **Pages (approx.):** 440. **Frequency:** Annual. **Price:** $14.00 (PB80-104672). **Send orders to:** National Technical Information Service, Springfield, VA 22161. **Other information:** 1980 edition is expected to be combined with "Compilation of Clinical Protocol Summaries," described in separate listing.

★4227★

COMPILATION OF CLINICAL PROTOCOL SUMMARIES [Cancer research]
International Cancer Research Data Bank
National Cancer Institute
National Institutes of Health
8300 Colesville Road   Phone: (301) 427-8759
Silver Spring, MD 20910
Covers: Over 1,500 cancer-related research projects. **Entries include:** Project name, name and phone of chief investigator, address; description of project including hypothesis, entry criteria, drug, dosage, other project data. **Arrangement:** By registration number. **Indexes:** Subject (body site, cancer type, drug, therapy mode), protocol organization number. **Pages (approx.):** 580. **Frequency:** Irregular; latest edition April 1979; new edition expected fall 1980. **Price:** $16.25 (PB 293-186). **Send orders to:** National Technical Information Service, Springfield, VA 22161. **Other information:** Prepared by the Current Cancer Research Project Analysis Center of the Smithsonian Science Information Exchange. 1980 edition is expected to incorporate "Compendium of Tumor Immunotherapy Protocols," described in separate listing.

Complete Guide to Foreign Medical Schools *See* Barron's Guide to Foreign Medical Schools

★4228★

COMPLETE LISTING OF NORTH CAROLINA HOSPITALS (NON-FEDERAL)
Division of Facility Services
North Carolina Department of Human Resources
1330 St. Mary's Street   Phone: (919) 733-5794
Raleigh, NC 27605
Covers: About 165 non-federal hospitals in North Carolina, both existing and under construction. **Entries include:** Hospital name, city, type of license, accreditation, whether certified for Medicare and/or Medicaid, ownership, operation, medical type (general, pulmonary diseases, etc.), bed capacity, and beds in use. Address, phone, and name of administrator provided in separate alphabetical list. **Arrangement:** By county. **Pages (approx.):** 30. **Frequency:** Annual, spring. **Editor:** Ruth Hathaway, Health Facilities Planner. **Price:** Free.

★4229★

COMPLETE LISTING OF NURSING HOMES...[North Carolina]
Division of Facility Services
North Carolina Department of Human Resources
1330 St. Mary's Street   Phone: (919) 733-5794
Raleigh, NC 27605
Covers: Full title is, "Complete Listing of Nursing Homes: Skilled/Intermediate/Combination Care"; covers about 195 homes. **Entries include:** Name, address, phone, name of administrator, whether certified for Medicare and/or Medicaid, number of beds for skilled care, etc. **Arrangement:** By county. **Pages (approx.):** 20. **Frequency:** Annual, spring. **Editor:** Ruth Hathaway, Health Facilities Planner. **Price:** Free. **Other information:** Supplemented by, "Hospitals and State Institutions with Skilled Nursing, Intermediate Care, or Intermediate Care for the Mentally Retarded Beds," which covers 25 facilities.

Complete Medical Student's Guide to Financial Aid *See* Barron's Guide to Financial Aid for Medical Students

★4230★

CONSUMER HEALTH EDUCATION: A DIRECTORY
Office of Health Resources Opportunity
Public Health Service
Health, Education and Welfare Department
3700 East-West Highway   Phone: (301) 436-7222
Hyattsville, MD 20782
Covers: Voluntary organizations concerned with health education. **Entries include:** Organization name, address, phone, subject of special interest, and description of programs. **Arrangement:** Alphabetical. **Pages (approx.):** 50. **Frequency:** Latest edition 1976, out of print; new edition planned. **Price:** Free. **Other information:** Compiled by American Public Health Association.

★4231★

CONTACT LENS MANUFACTURERS ASSOCIATION—DIRECTORY OF MEMBERS
Contact Lens Manufacturers Association
C/o Bostrom Management Corporation
435 N. Michigan Avenue, Suite 1717   Phone: (312) 644-0828
Chicago, IL 60611
Number of listings: 125. **Entries include:** Company name, address, phone, names of executives. **Arrangement:** Alphabetical within membership categories. **Indexes:** Personal name. **Pages (approx.):** 45. **Frequency:** Irregular; latest edition April 1979. **Editor:** Glenn W. Bostrom, Executive Director. **Price:** Free.

★4232★

CONTINUING EDUCATION CALENDAR FOR HEALTH PROFESSIONALS
Center for Continuing Health Education
Wichita State University   Phone: (316) 689-3628
Wichita, KS 67208
Covers: 350 continuing education events for health and helping professions. **Entries include:** Name of event, date, location, subject matter and title, contact person, number of continuing education

credit hours available, sponsor, occupations applicable toward, and fee. **Arrangement:** Chronological. **Pages** (approx.): 30. **Frequency:** Annual, August; monthly supplements. **Editor:** Ms. Lin Bertsch, Director. **Advertising accepted.** Circulation 1,500. **Former title:** Center for Educational Development - Continuing Education Calendar. **Price:** $5.00.

★4233★
COPING CATALOG [Washington, DC]
Washington Area Council on Alcoholism and Drug Abuse
1221 Massachusetts Avenue, N. W., Suite A   Phone: (202) 783-1300
Washington, DC 20005
Covers: Addiction treatment resources and hotlines in the metropolitan Washington area. **Entries include:** Facility name, address, phone, hours, fees, services, name of director. **Arrangement:** Classified by type of service. **Indexes:** Facility/program name. **Pages** (approx.): 170. **Frequency:** Irregular; latest edition September 1979. **Editor:** Eleanor R. Edelstein. **Price:** $10.00.

★4234★
COTH DIRECTORY: EDUCATIONAL PROGRAMS AND SERVICES
Council of Teaching Hospitals
Association of American Medical Colleges
One Dupont Circle, N. W.   Phone: (202) 466-5100
Washington, DC 20036
Covers: About 400 medical schools' teaching hospitals, residency and internship programs, and paramedical programs belonging to the Council of Teaching Hospitals. **Entries include:** Name of facility, address, description of program, requirements for admission. **Arrangement:** Alphabetical. **Frequency:** Annual. **Price:** $6.00.

★4235★
**COUNCIL FOR HEALTH AND WELFARE SERVICES OF THE UNITED
    CHURCH OF CHRIST—DIRECTORY**
Council for Health and Welfare Services
United Church of Christ
132 W. 31st Street   Phone: (212) 239-8700
New York, NY 10001
Covers: About 120 social welfare agencies, retirement homes, children's residential homes, hospitals, and other facilities affiliated with the United Church of Christ. **Entries include:** Agency name, type of institution and summary of services offered, name of chief administrator, mailing address, phone number, and conference assignment. **Arrangement:** Geographical. **Indexes:** Classified by type of service. **Pages** (approx.): 45. **Frequency:** Annual, fall. **Editor:** Rev. J. Robert Achtermann, Executive Secretary. **Price:** Single copies free.

★4236★
**COUNCIL OF COMMUNITY BLOOD CENTERS—MEMBERSHIP
    DIRECTORY**
Council of Community Blood Centers
Box 2068   Phone: (602) 949-5727
Scottsdale, AZ 85252
Covers: About 30 blood centers and banks throughout the United States. **Entries include:** Center name, address, phone, U.S. license number, chief executives. **Arrangement:** Alphabetical. **Pages** (approx.): 10. **Frequency:** Annual, March. **Editor:** William S. Kyler, Assistant Secretary, Executive Director. **Price:** Free.

Council of Teaching Hospitals—Roster *See* COTH Directory...

Current Cancer Research *See* Special Listings of Current Cancer
    Research

★4237★
DEATH EDUCATION—HOSPICE ISSUE
Hemisphere Publishing Corporation
1025 Vermont Avenue, N. W.   Phone: (202) 783-3958
Washington, DC 20005
Publication includes: List of about 25 hospices and hospice programs in the United States. **Entries include:** Hospice name, address,

services. **Arrangement:** Geographical. **Frequency:** Published in spring/summer 1978 issue. **Editor:** Ed Davidson. **Price:** $16.95 per single copy. **Send orders to:** Hemisphere Publishing Corporation, 19 W. 44th Street, Suite 613, New York, NY 10036.

★4238★
DENTAL LAB AGE INTERNATIONAL YELLOW PAGES
ESCO Publishing Company
1405 N. Main, Suite 222   Phone: (512) 225-4057
San Antonio, TX 78212
Covers: 700 manufacturers and suppliers to dental laboratories and dental technology facilities, and 600 dealers, including mail order supply houses. **Entries include:** Company name, address, phone, name of principal executive, area served. **Arrangement:** Manufacturers are alphabetical, dealers are geographical. **Indexes:** Product. **Pages** (approx.): 70. **Frequency:** Annual, April. **Editor:** Brenda Richardson. **Advertising accepted.** Circulation 31,000. **Price:** $5.00 (current and 1980 editions).

★4239★
DENTAL SCHOOLS OUTSIDE THE U.S.
American Dental Association
211 E. Chicago Avenue   Phone: (312) 440-2500
Chicago, IL 60611
Entries include: Institution name, address, name of director. **Arrangement:** Geographical. **Pages** (approx.): 65. **Frequency:** Irregular; latest edition 1977. **Price:** Free.

★4240★
**DIRECTORY: HEALTH SYSTEMS AGENCIES, STATE HEALTH
    PLANNING AND DEVELOPMENT AGENCIES, STATEWIDE
    HEALTH COORDINATING COUNCILS**
Bureau of Health Planning and Resources Development
Public Health Service
Health, Education, and Welfare Department   Phone: (301) 436-6733
Hyattsville, MD 20782
Covers: About 300 state health coordinating councils, state health planning and development agencies, and health systems agencies established under the National Health Planning and Resources Development Act. **Entries include:** Agency or council name, address, phone, name of director. Agency listings include annual or initial designation date, budget. Health systems agency listings include name and address of chairman, population covered, congressional districts covered, and type of organization (nonprofit, etc.). **Arrangement:** Geographical within type of agency. **Pages** (approx.): 45. **Frequency:** Irregular; latest edition December 1979. **Price:** Free (DHEW Publication No. HRA 79-14024).

★4241★
**DIRECTORY—FAMILY PLANNING SERVICE SITES—UNITED
    STATES**
National Center for Health Statistics
Public Health Service
Health, Education and Welfare Department
3700 East-West Highway
Hyattsville, MD 20782
Covers: About 4,700 medical family planning services sites which responded from the 5,600 in the National Inventory of Family Planning Services. **Entries include:** Facility name, address. **Arrangement:** By state and county. **Pages** (approx.): 175. **Frequency:** Irregular; latest edition November 1977 (1975 data). **Price:** $3.50 (S/N 017-022-00605-7). **Send orders to:** Government Printing Office, Washington, DC 20402.

★4242★
DIRECTORY FOR EXCEPTIONAL CHILDREN
Porter Sargent Publishers, Inc.
11 Beacon Street   Phone: (617) 523-1670
Boston, MA 02108
Covers: Over 3,000 public and private schools, clinics, and treatment centers for disturbed, maladjusted, and handicapped children. Includes

lists of governmental and private agencies, associations, etc., concerned with exceptional children. **Arrangement:** Geographical, then by disability treated. **Indexes:** Alphabetical. **Pages (approx.):** 1,500. **Frequency:** Biennial, even years. **Editor:** Christopher Leonesio. **Advertising accepted. Price:** $25.00.

★4243★

DIRECTORY FOR EXPANDED ROLE PROGRAMS FOR REGISTERED NURSES
Bureau of Health Manpower
Health Resources Administration
Health, Education, and Welfare Department
3700 East-West Highway
Hyattsville, MD 20782
Covers: Continuing education and graduate programs. **Entries include:** Institution name, programs offered, description. **Pages (approx.):** 60. **Frequency:** Latest edition 1979. **Price:** $1.50 (S/N 017-041-00129-7). **Send orders to:** Government Printing Office, Washington, DC 20402. **Other information:** Formerly published by the American Nurses Association under title, "Preparing Registered Nurses for Expanded Roles: A Directory of Programs."

★4244★

DIRECTORY OF ACCREDITED RESIDENCY TRAINING PROGRAMS [Medical]
American Medical Association
535 N. Dearborn Street   Phone: (312) 751-6301
Chicago, IL 60610
Covers: 5,000 residency programs accredited by the Liaison Committee on Graduate Medical Education. **Entries include:** School or institution name, name and address of director, specialties available, teaching hospitals' names, number enrolled, requirements, and length of program. **Arrangement:** By specialty, then geographical. **Pages (approx.):** 500. **Frequency:** Annual, fall. **Editor:** Anne E. Crowley, Ph.D. **Former title:** Directory of Approved Internships and Residencies. **Price:** $10.00, payment with order (current and 1980 editions). **Send orders to:** American Medical Assn. Order Dept., Box 821, Monroe, WI 53566 (312-751-6765).

★4245★

DIRECTORY OF ADULT DAY CARE CENTERS
Health Standards and Quality Bureau
Health Care Financing Administration
Health, Education, and Welfare Department
1849 Gwynn Oak Avenue
Baltimore, MD 21207
Covers: Nearly 700 programs which provide restorative, maintenance, or social programs (more extensive than senior center programs) for aged and handicapped persons; psychiatric day hospitals and primarily psychiatric day care services are excluded. **Entries include:** Center name, address, name of director, date started, sponsor, funding source, nature of program, number of participants. **Arrangement:** Geographical. **Pages (approx.):** 125. **Frequency:** Irregular; latest edition May 1978; new edition expected 1980. **Editor:** Edith G. Robins. **Price:** Free.

★4246★

DIRECTORY OF AGENCIES SERVING THE VISUALLY HANDICAPPED IN THE U.S.
American Foundation for the Blind
15 W. 16th Street   Phone: (212) 620-2000
New York, NY 10011
Covers: 470 nonprofit organizations which have a full-time director and a board of directors and/or are established through local, state, or federal legislation, and offer services to the visually handicapped; about 180 low vision clinics are also listed. **Entries include:** Agency name, address, phone, name of executive officer, services offered, accreditation, memberships. **Arrangement:** State and local agencies are geographical, specialized agencies are alphabetical within type of

organization. **Indexes:** Organization name. **Pages (approx.):** 440. **Frequency:** Biennial, July of even years; quarterly correction lists. **Editor:** Mary Ellen Mulholland. **Price:** $10.00, including corrections, postpaid, payment must accompany order.

Directory of Alcoholism Services in Texas *See* Guide to Alcoholism Resources in Texas

★4247★

DIRECTORY OF ALLIED HEALTH EDUCATION PROGRAMS IN JUNIOR AND SENIOR COLLEGES
American Society of Allied Health Professions
One Dupont Circle, Suite 300   Phone: (202) 293-3422
Washington, DC 20036
Covers: Over 7,000 active programs (1980 edition). **Arrangement:** Alphabetical by occupational area (laboratory services, etc.) and by award level (Bachelor's degree, etc.). **Indexes:** Institutions and programs (by state). . **Pages (approx.):** 585. **Frequency:** Irregular; latest edition 1975; new edition expected July 1980. **Editor:** Richard S. Nunn, Project Director, Junior/Senior College Inventories. **Former title:** Allied Health Education Programs in Junior and Senior Colleges - Guidance Edition. **Price:** Free. **Send orders to:** Information Office, Bureau of Health Manpower (HRA), 3700 East-West Highway, Hyattsville, MD 20782.

Directory of Alternative Birth Services *See* NAPSAC Directory of Alternative Birth Services and Consumer Guide

Directory of Approved Allied Medical Education Programs *See* Allied Health Education Directory

Directory of Approved Internships and Residencies [Medical] *See* Directory of Accredited Residency Training Programs [Medical]

★4248★

DIRECTORY OF ARCHITECTS FOR HEALTH FACILITIES
American Hospital Association
840 N. Lake Shore Drive
Chicago, IL 60611
Covers: Architectural firms with experience or special interest in health care facilities. **Entries include:** Firm name, address, phone, average maximum number of personnel, past five years; total dollar value of work in the design or construction stages; work in health facilities as a percent of total work; other offices. **Arrangement:** Alphabetical. **Indexes:** Geographical. **Pages (approx.):** 50. **Frequency:** Biennial, odd years. **Price:** $8.25 (Pub. No. 1327).

★4249★

DIRECTORY OF BLOOD ESTABLISHMENTS
Bureau of Biologics
Food and Drug Administration
Public Health Service
Health, Education, and Welfare Department   Phone: (301) 443-5368
Bethesda, MD 20205
Covers: Over 7,000 blood banks, hospitals, and other establishments which draw, process, or use blood and blood products and which have registered with the FDA. **Entries include:** Establishment name, address, name of responsible head, type of establishment (community blood bank, hospital, etc.), products (whole blood, platelet concentrate, etc.), and functions (recruit donors, perform transfusions, etc.). **Arrangement:** Geographical. **Pages (approx.):** 815. **Frequency:** Annual, March. **Price:** $10.00, plus $2.07 shipping (DHEW Publication No. FDA 79-9001).

★4250★
DIRECTORY OF BLUE SHIELD PLANS
National Association of Blue Shield Plans
211 E. Chicago Avenue   Phone: (312) 440-5664
Chicago, IL 60611
Entries include: Name, address, phone number, and name of chief executive. **Arrangement:** Geographical. **Pages** (approx.): 10. **Frequency:** Semiannual, January and July. **Editor:** Mike Morrison, Manager of Publications. **Price:** Free.

★4251★
DIRECTORY OF CERTIFIED PSYCHIATRISTS AND NEUROLOGISTS
Marquis Academic Media
Marquis Who's Who, Inc.
200 E. Ohio Street   Phone: (312) 787-2008
Chicago, IL 60611
Covers: Over 14,500 psychiatrists and neurologists certified by the American Board of Psychiatry and Neurology. **Entries include:** Name, office address, phone; educational, career data; memberships; teaching position. **Arrangement:** Geographical. **Indexes:** Personal name. **Pages** (approx.): 690. **Frequency:** Not established; first edition March 1979. **Price:** $19.50. **Other information:** Published under the direction of the American Board of Medical Specialties. Derived from material in "Directory of Medical Specialties," described in separate listing.

★4252★
DIRECTORY OF CHILD LIFE ACTIVITY PROGRAMS IN NORTH AMERICA [Hospital care]
Association for the Care of Children in Hospitals
3615 Wisconsin Avenue, N. W.   Phone: (202) 244-1801
Washington, DC 20016
Number of listings: 270. **Entries include:** Department name, name and address of hospital, department phone, name of contact, number of beds, number of units, pediatric age range, staff number and training level, program times, number of activity centers, source of funding, administrative structure, use of volunteers, student internship availability, initial year of program. **Arrangement:** Geographical. **Pages** (approx.): 70. **Frequency:** Irregular; previous edition 1977; latest edition 1979. **Price:** $5.00, plus $1.00 shipping. **Other information:** Variant title, "Directory of Child Life and Play Programs."

Directory of Child Life and Play Programs *See* Directory of Child Life Activity Programs in North America [Hospital care]

★4253★
DIRECTORY OF CLINICAL FELLOWSHIPS IN MEDICINE
Graduate Publications
3074 Seahorse Avenue
Ventura, CA 93003
Covers: Over 450 hospitals and other medical institutions which offer over 3,000 post-residency or subspecialty clinical fellowship programs in medical specialties (including allergy-immunology, clinical pharmacology, dermatology, genetics, medicine, neurosciences, obstetrics and gynecology, pathology, pediatrics, psychiatry, radiology, and surgery). **Entries include:** Name and address of program director, daily in-patient census, monthly out-patient census, availability of research, starting date of program, number of starting positions, program length, availability of stipend, education requirements, and participating hospitals. **Arrangement:** By specialty. **Pages** (approx.): 315. **Frequency:** Biennial, fall of even years. **Editor:** Sara E. Prichard, Managing Editor. **Price:** $12.00.

★4254★
DIRECTORY OF COLLEGES AND UNIVERSITIES OFFERING DEGREES IN LEARNING DISABILITIES
Academic Therapy Publications
20 Commercial Boulevard
Novato, CA 94947
Covers: About 190 educational institutions with credential programs in learning disabilities, 55 organizations concerned with learning

disabilities, and state education offices. **Entries include:** For educational institutions - Name, address, phone, and name of contact; in coded format, description of credential program offered, including number of years required, whether undergraduate or graduate, general courses offered, terms courses are offered, grades covered by credential, graduate programs offered, and whether lab school or facilities are available. For organizations - Name, address, phone, name of contact. For state education offices - Name of administrator, address. **Arrangement:** By type of organization, then geographical. **Pages** (approx.): 65. **Frequency:** Published November 1978. **Editor:** J. B. Preston. **Price:** $2.00 (ISSN 0161-5467).

★4255★
DIRECTORY OF COLLEGES, VOCATIONAL-TECHNICAL SCHOOLS, AND DIPLOMA SCHOOLS OF NURSING [Georgia]
Georgia Educational Improvement Council
7 Martin Luther King, Jr. Drive, S. W.,
   Room 656
Atlanta, GA 30334
Covers: About 100 accredited postsecondary educational institutions in Georgia. **Entries include:** Institution name, address, phone number, names of executives, list of programs and degrees, admission and cost information. **Arrangement:** By type of institution, then alphabetical. **Pages** (approx.): 250. **Frequency:** Biennial, fall of odd years. **Editor:** Dr. James W. Mullins, Executive Director. **Former title:** Directory of Educational Opportunities in Georgia. **Price:** Free.

★4256★
DIRECTORY OF COMMUNITY HIGH BLOOD PRESSURE CONTROL ACTIVITIES
National High Blood Pressure Education Program
Public Health Service
Health, Education, and Welfare Department
7910 Woodmont Avenue, Suite 1320   Phone: (301) 652-1370
Bethesda, MD 20014
Covers: About 2,100 community and health organizations, corporations, hospitals, medical schools, health centers, and other organizations active in high blood pressure control. **Entries include:** Name of organization, address, phone, name and title of director; description of organization including setting, groups served, funding source, cooperating organizations, budget, number of staff and type, whether data system is automated; and activities (detection, education, etc.). **Arrangement:** Geographical. **Pages** (approx.): 375. **Frequency:** Irregular; latest edition 1977. **Editor:** Graham W. Ward, Program Coordinator. **Price:** Free (DHEW Publication No. NIH 77-1243).

★4257★
DIRECTORY OF COMMUNITY SERVICES IN CALIFORNIA FOR ALCOHOL ABUSE AND ALCOHOLISM
Information Clearinghouse Unit
California Department of Alcohol and Drug Abuse
111 Capitol Mall   Phone: (916) 322-4445
Sacramento, CA 95814
Covers: Community alcohol abuse service agencies, including treatment and rehabilitation units and county coordinators. **Entries include:** Name of agency, address, phone, contact person, services provided. **Arrangement:** By county. **Frequency:** Not established; first edition expected spring 1980. **Price:** Free.

★4258★
DIRECTORY OF COMPUTER USERS IN NUCLEAR MEDICINE
Biomedical Computing Technology Information Center
Oak Ridge National Laboratory
Energy Research and Development
   Administration
Oak Ridge, TN 37830
Covers: Institutions using computers in nuclear medicine and manufacturers of nuclear medicine systems. **Entries include:** For users - Institution name, address, type, size, name of contact, description of equipment, types of studies done utilizing computers, and system information. For vendors - Company name, address, short descriptions of their equipment and systems. **Pages** (approx.): 250.

Frequency: Not established; first edition 1977. **Editors:** R. L. Henne, et al. **Price:** Free.

★4259★
DIRECTORY OF CONTRACEPTIVES
International Planned Parenthood Federation
18-20 Lower Regent Street
London SW1Y 4PW, England
Covers: About 200 countries, listing as many as 100 distinct contraceptives available in each (caps, condoms, spermicides, hormonal contraceptives, and intrauterine devices); 650 brand names and 25 manufacturers; 100 IPPF offices and member associations. **Entries include:** For member associations - Name, address. **Arrangement:** Geographical, then by type and brand name. **Pages** (approx.): 90. **Frequency:** Irregular; latest edition June 1976; new edition expected September 1980. **Editors:** Philip Kestleman, Ronald Kleinman. **Price:** $10.00 (tentative, 1980 edition).

★4260★
DIRECTORY OF DEPARTMENTS OF ANATOMY OF THE UNITED STATES AND CANADA
American Association of Anatomists
C/o Dr. John E. Pauly
University of Arkansas for Medical Sciences
4301 W. Markham Street   Phone: (501) 661-5180
Little Rock, AR 72201
Covers: 3,100 anatomy department faculty members in 190 colleges of medicine, dentistry, and osteopathic and veterinary medicine in the United States and Canada. **Entries include:** Name, office address and phone, academic rank, highest degree held and granting institution, teaching and research interests. **Arrangement:** By institution name. **Indexes:** Personal name. **Pages** (approx.): 195. **Frequency:** Usually triennial; latest edition January 1979. **Editor:** Dr. John E. Pauly, Secretary-Treasurer. **Price:** $10.00, payment with order.

Directory of District of Columbia Clinics *See* Health Care for Women: A Guide to Services in the District of Columbia

★4261★
DIRECTORY OF DRUG ABUSE AND ALCOHOLIC TREATMENT PROGRAMS
National Institute on Drug Abuse
Public Health Service
Health, Education, and Welfare Department
5600 Fishers Lane
Rockville, MD 20857
Covers: 10,000 federal, state, local, and privately funded agencies administering or providing drug abuse and alcoholism treatment services; hotlines; crisis centers; and similar programs. **Entries include:** Name of agency, address, phone, whether the agency is a drug unit, alcohol unit, or both. **Arrangement:** Geographical. **Pages** (approx.): 375. **Frequency:** Irregular; latest edition September 1979. **Price:** Free. **Other information:** Based on the National Drug and Alcoholism Abuse Treatment Utilization Survey.

Directory of Drug Abuse Treatment Programs *See* Directory of Drug Abuse and Alcoholic Treatment Programs

★4262★
DIRECTORY OF DRUG EXPERIENCE RESOURCES
Division of Drug Experience
Bureau of Drugs
Food and Drug Administration
5600 Fishers Lane
Rockville, MD 20857
Covers: Persons and groups active in drug studies and drug information, worldwide. **Entries include:** Institution or agency name, name of individual, address, nature of experience or type of drug, phone. **Arrangement:** Geographical. **Pages** (approx.): 160. **Frequency:** Not established; first edition November 1977; new edition possible 1980. **Editors:** Arthur Ruskin, M.D., and Robert F.

Clarke, Ph.D. **Price:** $8.00, paper; $3.00, microfiche (PB 275-609). **Send orders to:** National Technical Information Service, Springfield, VA 22161.

Directory of Educational Opportunities in Georgia *See* Directory of Colleges, Vocational-Technical Schools, and Diploma Schools of...

★4263★
DIRECTORY OF ENGLISH-SPEAKING PHYSICIANS [Abroad]
Intermedic, Inc.
777 Third Avenue
New York, NY 10017
Covers: 215 physicians in 93 countries interested in treating English-speaking travelers. **Entries include:** Physician name, address, home and office phone. **Arrangement:** Geographical. **Frequency:** Annual, November. **Price:** Included in membership, $6.00 for individual, $10.00 for family. **Other information:** Prepared by the Executive Health Examiners Group.

★4264★
DIRECTORY OF EVANSTON AREA PRIMARY CARE PHYSICIANS [Illinois]
Consumers' Health Group of Evanston, Illinois
828 Davis Street   Phone: (312) 475-0909
Evanston, IL 60201
Covers: About 140 local primary care physicians and hospitals. **Entries include:** Physician name, office address and phone, specialty, fees, policies, procedures. For hospitals - name, address; description of staffing and services. **Arrangement:** Alphabetical. **Pages** (approx.): 135. **Frequency:** Irregular; latest edition 1979. **Editor:** Bernice Barta. **Price:** $4.00, plus $1.00 shipping. **Also includes:** Map showing bus routes to major physician office buildings and hospitals.

Directory of Family Planning Sites *See* Directory—Family Planning Service Sites—United States

★4265★
DIRECTORY OF HEALTH CARE FACILITIES [Illinois]
Division of Development and Construction
Illinois Department of Public Health
525 W. Jefferson, 4th Floor   Phone: (217) 782-5643
Springfield, IL 62761
Covers: Hospitals, state schools, long-term health care facilities, laboratories, blood banks, home health agencies, and other licensed health agencies. **Entries include:** Facility name, address, phone, chief administrator, type of control, type of service (and bed count, for hospitals). **Arrangement:** Classified by type of facility. **Indexes:** Hospitals, long-term health care facilities. **Pages** (approx.): 190. **Frequency:** Irregular; latest edition September 1977. **Editor:** Mrs. Marge Frantzreb, Clerk. **Price:** Free.

★4266★
DIRECTORY OF HEALTH OFFICERS, REGISTRARS, STATISTICIANS, AND RESEARCH DIRECTORS IN U.S. AND CANADIAN REGISTRATION AREAS
National Center for Health Statistics
Health Resources Administration
Public Health Service
Health, Education, and Welfare Department
Washington, DC 20201
Covers: Health officers, registrars, principal statisticians, and research directors for each state health department. **Entries include:** Name, title, address, phone. **Arrangement:** Geographical. **Pages** (approx.): 30. **Frequency:** Biennial, even years. **Price:** Free (Stock No. HRA 75-1141). **Send orders to:** Scientific and Technical Information Branch, National Center for Health Statistics, 5600 Fishers Lane, Room 8-20, Rockville, MD 20852.

★4267★
DIRECTORY OF HIGH-ENERGY RADIOTHERAPY CENTRES
International Atomic Energy Agency
Karntner Ring 11
Vienna A-1011, Austria
Covers: About 1,300 radiotherapy centers in 90 countries that provide treatment with high-activity radioisotopes and super-voltage accelerators. **Entries include:** Center name, address, names of radiotherapists and physicists, equipment information, isotope or energy source data. **Arrangement:** Geographical. **Indexes:** City. **Pages** (approx.): 260. **Frequency:** Irregular; previous edition 1970; latest edition fall 1976. **Price:** $15.00. **Send orders to:** Unipub, Box 433, Murray Hill Station; New York, NY 10016.

★4268★
DIRECTORY OF HOME HEALTH AGENCIES CERTIFIED AS MEDICARE PROVIDERS
National League for Nursing, Inc.
10 Columbus Circle   Phone: (212) 582-1022
New York, NY 10019
Covers: Agencies certified by the Social Security Administration to provide such services as out-of-hospital home care by public health nurses, aides, etc. **Entries include:** Agency name, address, symbol indicating whether proprietary or nonprofit agency, and type of service offered. Agencies approved by the League are identified. **Arrangement:** Geographical. **Pages** (approx.): 90. **Frequency:** Irregular; latest edition 1976. **Price:** Out of print.

★4269★
DIRECTORY OF HOMEMAKER-HOME HEALTH AIDE SERVICES
National Council for Homemaker-Home Health Aide Services
67 Irving Place   Phone: (212) 674-4990
New York, NY 10003
Covers: 145 local agencies supplying homemaker and health aide services which are accredited/approved by the Council. **Entries include:** Agency name, address, phone. **Arrangement:** Geographical. **Frequency:** Annual, January. **Price:** $1.00 shipping.

★4270★
DIRECTORY OF HOMEMAKER-HOME HEALTH AIDE SERVICES IN THE UNITED STATES, PUERTO RICO, AND THE VIRGIN ISLANDS
National Council for Homemaker-Home Health Aide Services
67 Irving Place   Phone: (212) 674-4990
New York, NY 10003
Covers: About 4,900 agencies and service units providing homemaker-home health aide services; includes about 145 local agencies accredited or approved by the council which are also listed alone in a separate publication of similar title. **Entries include:** Unit name, address, phone. **Arrangement:** Geographical. **Pages** (approx.): 200. **Frequency:** Annual, December. **Editor:** L. L. Clark. **Price:** $10.00, postpaid, payment with order (ISSN 0027-9072).

Directory of Hospital and Surgical Supply Dealers *See* Keithwood Directory of Hospital and Surgical Supply Dealers

★4271★
DIRECTORY OF INPATIENT FACILITIES FOR THE MENTALLY RETARDED [HEW]
National Center for Health Statistics
Health Resources Administration
Public Health Service
Health, Education, and Welfare Department
Washington, DC 20201
Number of listings: 1,343. **Entries include:** Facility name, address, whether nonprofit or for profit, number of beds, sex and ages of patients accepted. **Arrangement:** Geographical. **Pages** (approx.): 114. **Frequency:** Irregular. **Price:** Free (HRA 75-1230). **Other information:** Currently out of print, but may be available from National Technical Information Service, Springfield, VA 22161 in future.

★4272★
DIRECTORY OF INPATIENT FACILITIES FOR THE MENTALLY RETARDED [Reprint edition]
U. S. Directory Service, Inc.
12 S. E. First Street   Phone: (305) 371-8881
Miami, FL 33101
Number of listings: 1,343. **Entries include:** Facility name, address, whether nonprofit or for profit, number of beds, sex and ages of patients accepted. **Arrangement:** Geographical. **Pages** (approx.): 110. **Frequency:** Irregular. **Editors:** Stanley Alperin; Melvin S. Alperin, Editorial Directors. **Price:** $14.50. **Other information:** Though not so identified in promotional literature, this is a reprint of the free Health, Education, and Welfare Department publication of same title (HRA 75-1230) mentioned above.

Directory of Intern Training Hospitals (Osteopathic) *See* Directory of Osteopathic Postdoctoral Education

★4273★
DIRECTORY OF INVESTOR-OWNED HOSPITALS AND HOSPITAL MANAGEMENT COMPANIES
Federation of American Hospitals
620 E. Sixth Street   Phone: (501) 376-6818
Little Rock, AR 72203
Covers: Over 1,000 investor-owned hospitals and 33 hospital management companies in the United States and Puerto Rico. **Entries include:** For hospitals - Name, address, phone, names of administrator and chief of staff, number of beds, and, if applicable, code for name of parent company. For management companies - Company name, address, phone, officers' names, plus names of hospitals owned, addresses, phones, names of chief administrators. **Arrangement:** Hospitals are geographical, companies are alphabetical. **Pages** (approx.): 85. **Frequency:** Annual, August/September. **Editor:** John R. Walker. **Advertising accepted.** Circulation 23,000. **Price:** $20.00, payment with order.

★4274★
DIRECTORY OF LICENSED HOSPITALS
Washington Department of Social and Health Services
Airdustrial Park, Building 12, LM-13   Phone: (206) 753-5851
Olympia, WA 98504
Covers: About 115 licensed hospitals located in Washington. **Entries include:** Hospital name, address, phone, county, license number, number of beds, type of ownership, licensee, and name of administrator. **Arrangement:** Alphabetical. **Indexes:** County. **Pages** (approx.): 30. **Frequency:** Annual, fall. **Price:** Free.

Directory of Medical Facilities *See* Medicare/Medicaid Directory of Medical Facilities...

★4275★
DIRECTORY OF MEDICAL PRODUCTS DISTRIBUTORS
McKnight Medical Communications, Inc.
550 Frontage Road   Phone: (312) 446-1622
Northfield, IL 60093
Number of listings: About 2,000. **Entries include:** Company name, address, branches, phone, name of principal executives, type of distributor (i.e., hospital supply, rental, etc.), number of salesmen, financial keys, area served, association affiliations. **Arrangement:** Geographical. **Frequency:** Irregular; latest edition 1979; new edition expected spring 1980. **Price:** $50.00.

★4276★
DIRECTORY OF MEDICAL SPECIALISTS
Marquis Who's Who, Inc.
200 E. Ohio Street   Phone: (312) 787-2008
Chicago, IL 60611
Covers: About 220,000 board-certified specialists in over 20 areas of medical practice from allergy to urology. **Entries include:** Name, home and office addresses, date and place of birth, education, career data, date certified, professional memberships, selected writings,

awards, achievements. **Arrangement:** Classified by specialty, then geographical. **Indexes:** Alphabetical. **Pages** (approx.): 4,300 (three volumes). **Frequency:** Biennial, November of odd years. **Price:** $99.50. **Other information:** Compiled with the American Board of Medical Specialties.

★4277★
DIRECTORY OF NATIONAL INFORMATION SOURCES ON HANDICAPPING CONDITIONS AND RELATED SERVICES
Rehabilitation Services Administration
Office of Human Development Services
Health, Education, and Welfare Department
200 Independence Avenue, S. W.   Phone: (202) 245-7246
Washington, DC 20201
Covers: About 270 government and private organizations with an interest in handicapped individuals. **Entries include:** Organization name, address, phone, handicapping conditions served, scope of activities, and services. **Pages** (approx.): 400. **Frequency:** Irregular; latest edition 1976.

★4278★
DIRECTORY OF ON-GOING RESEARCH IN CANCER EPIDEMIOLOGY
Clearinghouse for Ongoing Research in Cancer Epidemiology
International Agency for Research on Cancer
150 Cours Albert Thomas
F-69008 Lyon, France
Covers: 1,025 ongoing cancer epidemiology research projects in over 70 countries. **Entries include:** Name of principal investigator, address; description of project; site and term of project. **Arrangement:** Geographical. **Frequency:** Annual. **Price:** $20.00. **Send orders to:** National Technical Information Service, Springfield, VA 22161. **Other information:** Collaborative effort of the International Agency for Research on Cancer, Lyon, France; German Cancer Research Center, Heidelberg, Germany; and the International Cancer Research Data Bank, National Cancer Institute, Silver Spring, MD.

★4279★
DIRECTORY OF ON-GOING RESEARCH IN SMOKING AND HEALTH
Office on Smoking and Health
Public Health Service
Health, Education, and Welfare Department
5600 Fishers Lane   Phone: (301) 443-1690
Rockville, MD 20857
Covers: Over 970 projects investigating various aspects of smoking in over 40 countries. **Entries include:** Name and address of performing organization, project title, objective, methods, results to date, plans for future, beginning date and projected termination, sources of funding. **Arrangement:** Geographical. **Indexes:** Organization, principal investigator, sponsor, subject. **Pages** (approx.): 440. **Frequency:** Biennial, summer of even years. **Editor:** Donald R. Shopland, Technical Information Officer. **Price:** Free.

★4280★
DIRECTORY OF OSTEOPATHIC POSTDOCTORAL EDUCATION
American Osteopathic Hospital Association
930 Busse Highway   Phone: (312) 692-2351
Park Ridge, IL 60068
Covers: About 80 internship programs approved by the American Osteopathic Association. **Entries include:** Name and address of hospital, names of administrator and director of medical education, operating statistics, features of internship program, and residencies offered, if any. **Arrangement:** Geographical. **Pages** (approx.): 50. **Frequency:** Annual, September. **Editor:** Lin Fish, Director of Communications. **Advertising accepted.** Circulation 2,000. **Price:** $15.00.

★4281★
DIRECTORY OF PATHOLOGY TRAINING PROGRAMS
Intersociety Committee on Pathology Information
4733 Bethesda Avenue, Suite 735   Phone: (301) 530-6783
Bethesda, MD 20014
Covers: 225 institutions offering pathologist training programs in the United States and Canada. **Entries include:** Name and address of institution, programs offered, stipends, types and numbers of appointments, facilities, type of specialization, names of staff, and information on community. **Arrangement:** Geographical. **Indexes:** Personal name. **Pages** (approx.): 470. **Frequency:** Annual, July. **Editor:** Judy Graves. **Price:** $25.00. **Other information:** Institutions listed pay a subscription fee of about $300.00.

★4282★
DIRECTORY OF PERSONNEL RESPONSIBLE FOR RADIOLOGICAL HEALTH PROGRAMS
Bureau of Radiological Health
Food and Drug Administration
Health, Education, and Welfare Department
5600 Fishers Lane
Rockville, MD 20857
Covers: About 295 individuals who conduct radiological health program activities in federal, state, and local governmental agencies. **Entries include:** Individual name and title, name of agency, address, phone; office hours listed with state heading. **Arrangement:** By level of agency and geographical. **Indexes:** Personal name. **Pages** (approx.): 40. **Frequency:** Semiannual, March and September. **Price:** Free (FDA 79-8027).

★4283★
DIRECTORY OF POISON CONTROL CENTERS
National Clearinghouse for Poison Control Centers
Food and Drug Administration
Health, Education, and Welfare Department
5600 Fishers Lane
Rockville, MD 20875
Covers: About 500 poison control centers across the United States that are officially recognized as such by their respective state departments of health. **Entries include:** Name of center, address, phone. **Arrangement:** Geographical. **Pages** (approx.): 35. **Frequency:** Annual, August. **Editor:** William H. Peterson, Jr., Poison Information Coordinator. **Price:** Free; restricted circulation.

★4284★
DIRECTORY OF PRECEPTORSHIP PROGRAMS IN THE HEALTH PROFESSIONS
National Health Council
1740 Broadway   Phone: (212) 582-6040
New York, NY 10019
Covers: About 300 institutions offering internships in nursing, school nursing, dietetics, medicine, dentistry, pharmacy, public health, etc. **Entries include:** Institution name, contact person, address, and phone; description of preceptorship offered, locations available, length of internship, supervision given; financial assistance available; and funding source for program. **Arrangement:** Two sections - Programs available to students from other institutions and closed programs; within the sections, geographical. **Indexes:** Discipline. **Pages** (approx.): 85. **Frequency:** Latest edition fall 1977; no new edition planned. **Editor:** Pamela J. Maraldo, Research Associate. **Price:** Free.

★4285★
DIRECTORY OF PROFESSIONAL ELECTROLOGISTS
Gordon Blackwell
30 E. 40th Street, Suite 505
New York, NY 10016
Covers: 600 permanent hair removal services worldwide. **Entries include:** Name, office address and phone, modalities employed (short wave, galvanic, blended current). **Arrangement:** Geographical. **Pages** (approx.): 30. **Frequency:** Annual, May. **Editor:** Gordon Blackwell. **Price:** $1.50.

★4286★
DIRECTORY OF PROVIDERS OF FAMILY PLANNING AND ABORTION SERVICES
Alan Guttmacher Institute
515 Madison Avenue   Phone: (212) 752-2100
New York, NY 10022
Covers: About 3,100 family planning and 2,600 abortion providers. **Entries include:** Name of clinic or other facility, address, phone, description of services. **Arrangement:** Geographical. **Frequency:** Not established; first edition 1977. **Price:** $5.00, postpaid, payment with order (ISSN 0148-6322).

★4287★
DIRECTORY OF REHABILITATION DIRECTORS AND REHABILITATION COORDINATORS
Association of Medical Rehabilitation Directors and Coordinators
3830 Linklea Drive   Phone: (713) 665-4253
Houston, TX 77025
Covers: 520 members primarily from United States and Canada. **Entries include:** Name, office address and phone, home address, title, whether physician or administrator, and whether certified. **Arrangement:** Alphabetical. **Indexes:** Geographical. **Pages** (approx.): 60. **Frequency:** Annual, January. **Editor:** Paul Heft, Executive Director. **Advertising accepted.** Circulation 1,000. **Price:** $4.00 (current and 1980 editions).

Directory of Resources Available to Deaf and Hard-of-Hearing Persons in the Southern California Area *See* GLAD Directory of...

Directory of Resources for the Developmentally Disabled [Florida] *See* Guide to Services for Persons with Developmental Disabilities

★4288★
DIRECTORY OF STATE REHABILITATION AGENCIES—FOR THE BLIND
Rehabilitation Services Administration
Health, Education and Welfare Department
330 C Street, S. W.   Phone: (202) 245-3498
Washington, DC 20201
Entries include: Agency name; name, title, address, and phone of key personnel. **Arrangement:** Geographical. **Pages** (approx.): 170. **Frequency:** Annual, June. **Price:** Free.

★4289★
DIRECTORY OF STATE REHABILITATION AGENCIES—GENERAL
Rehabilitation Services Administration
Health, Education and Welfare Department
330 C Street, S. W.   Phone: (202) 245-3498
Washington, DC 20201
Entries include: Agency name; name, title, address, and phone of key personnel. **Arrangement:** Geographical. **Pages** (approx.): 70. **Frequency:** Annual, June. **Price:** Free.

★4290★
DIRECTORY OF UNITED METHODIST HEALTH AND WELFARE MINISTRIES
Board of Global Ministries
United Methodist Church
1200 Davis Street   Phone: (312) 869-9600
Evanston, IL 60201
Covers: 62 hospitals, 63 child care, and 180 long-term care agencies related to the United Methodist Church. **Entries include:** Agency name, address, phone, names of executives, list of services. **Arrangement:** Classified by type of agency, then geographically. **Pages** (approx.): 30. **Frequency:** Annual, January. **Editor:** Cathie Lyons, Executive Director. **Former title:** Certification Council Manual and Directory. **Price:** Free. **Send orders to:** The Service Center, Board of Global Ministries, United Methodist Church, 7820 Reading Road, Cincinnati, OH 45237.

★4291★
DIRECTORY OF UNITED STATES HOMEOPATHIC PHYSICIANS
National Center for Homeopathy
6231 Leesburg Pike, Suite 506   Phone: (703) 534-4363
Falls Church, VA 22044
Covers: About 150 doctors of medicine or osteopathy who include homeopathy in their practices; includes short list of homeopathic pharmacists. **Entries include:** Name, address, degree, medical specialty (if any). **Arrangement:** Geographical. **Indexes:** Alphabetical. **Frequency:** Irregular; new edition expected 1980. **Price:** $1.25, payment with order.

Directory of Women Physicians *See* American Medical Directory

★4292★
DORLAND'S MEDICAL DIRECTORY [Philadelphia, PA and Camden, NJ]
Philadelphia Printing Properties, Inc.
Box 277
Narberth, PA 19072
Covers: Nearly 7,000 practicing physicians in the Philadelphia, Pennsylvania and Camden, New Jersey areas. Hospitals and their staffs are also included. **Entries include:** For physicians - Name, office and home addresses and phone numbers, medical school attended and year graduated, medical specialty, certification, hospital affiliation. For hospitals - Name, address, names and specialties of staff. **Arrangement:** Geographical. Osteopaths are listed separately. **Indexes:** Specialty, geographical, personal name. **Pages** (approx.): 760. **Frequency:** Annual, November. **Advertising accepted. Price:** $21.95, payment with order; $23.35, billed.

★4293★
DRUG ABUSE: A DIRECTORY OF COMMUNITY SERVICES IN CALIFORNIA
Information Clearinghouse Unit
California Department of Alcohol and Drug Abuse
111 Capitol Mall   Phone: (916) 322-4445
Sacramento, CA 95814
Covers: 850 community drug abuse service agencies including treatment and rehabilitation units and county drug program coordinators. **Entries include:** Name of agency, address, phone, contact person, services provided. **Arrangement:** By county. **Pages** (approx.): 80. **Frequency:** Annual, spring. **Editor:** Jack Colbert, Chief, Integrated Drug Abuse Reporting Section. **Price:** Free (No. DADA P78-3).

★4294★
DRUG TOPICS HEALTH AND BEAUTY AIDS DIRECTORY (The Pink Book)
Medical Economics Company, Subsidiary
Litton Publications
680 Kinderkamack Road   Phone: (201) 262-3030
Oradell, NJ 07649
Publication includes: List of manufacturers of over-the-counter drug and cosmetic items. **Entries include:** Company name, address, trade and brand names. **Arrangement:** Alphabetical. **Frequency:** Irregular; latest edition 1974; new edition planned for 1977. **Editor:** Jerry Levine. **Also includes:** List of 25,000 products classified by end use, with manufacturer key. **Price:** $20.00.

★4295★
DRUG TOPICS RED BOOK
Medical Economics Company, Subsidiary
Litton Publications
680 Kinderkamack Road   Phone: (201) 262-3030
Oradell, NJ 07649
Publication includes: Alphabetical list of manufacturers of prescription drugs and patent medicines, and other drug store items. **Entries include:** Cmpany name, address, trade and brand names, list of products. **Arrangement:** Alphabetical. **Pages** (approx.): 700. **Frequency:** Annual, December; cumulative supplement, August.

Editor: Charles E. Baker, Jr., Publisher. **Advertising accepted.** Circulation 68,000. **Price:** $16.00. **Also includes:** Alphabetical list of prescription and over-the-counter drug items, etc., with brand names, sizes, prices, etc.

★4296★

EDUCATIONAL OPPORTUNITIES IN COMPARATIVE PATHOLOGY, UNITED STATES AND FOREIGN COUNTRIES
Registry of Comparative Pathology
Armed Forces Institute of Pathology   Phone: (202) 576-2452
Washington, DC 20306
Covers: About 90 institutions, mostly in the United States, offering programs in comparative pathology. **Entries include:** School name, address, name of director, and description of program including residencies or preceptorships offered, degree offered, specializations possible, and extramural affiliations. **Arrangement:** Geographical. **Pages** (approx.): 30. **Frequency:** Biennial, even years. **Editor:** George Migaki. **Price:** Free.

★4297★

EDUCATIONAL PROGRAMS IN OCCUPATIONAL THERAPY
American Occupational Therapy Association
6000 Executive Boulevard, Suite 200   Phone: (301) 770-2200
Rockville, MD 20852
Covers: About 100 accredited schools in the United States which offer undergraduate and graduate programs in occupational therapy. **Entries include:** Institution name, address; name and title of department chairman or contact; level of program; year of next evaluation; whether out-of-state students are accepted. **Arrangement:** By level of program, then geographical. **Pages** (approx.): 5. **Frequency:** Annual, fall. **Price:** Free.

★4298★

EDUCATIONAL PROGRAMS IN THE HEALTH FIELD
American Hospital Association
801 N. Lake Shore Drive   Phone: (312) 280-6000
Chicago, IL 60611
Covers: Accredited educational programs in dentistry, dental assistantship and hygiene, dietetics, electroencephalography, health services administration, medical librarianship, medical assistantships, medical illustration, medical laboratory technology, medical record specialties, medicine, nuclear medicine technology, nurse anesthesia, nursing (licensed and registered nurse programs), occupational therapy, osteopathy, pharmacy, physical therapy, podiatry, public health, radiation therapy technology, radiologic technology, respiratory therapy, social work, speech pathology and audiology, and surgical technology. **Entries include:** Institution name, location; heading for each section includes statement concerning source of certification or accreditation. **Arrangement:** By specialty, then geographical. **Pages** (approx.): 45. **Frequency:** Irregular; latest edition 1979. **Editor:** Kelly Guncheon. **Price:** $7.50, postpaid, payment with order; $8.50, billed.

★4299★

EMERGENCY MEDICAL SERVICES—BUYERS GUIDE ISSUE
Emergency Medical Services
12849 Magnolia Boulevard   Phone: (213) 980-4184
North Hollywood, CA 91607
Covers: About 880 manufacturers, suppliers, and distributors of equipment and other products used in emergency medical services. Also covers 45 emergency medical service associations, state agencies, and meetings, workshops, and other conferences of interest. **Entries include:** For companies - Company name, address, phone, name of principal executive, products or services. For associations - Name, address, phone, name of director, number of members, description of membership, publications, meeting time. **Arrangement:** Alphabetical. **Indexes:** Geographical, product. **Pages** (approx.): 210. **Frequency:** Annual, November. **Editor:** Joan Hart, Managing Editor. **Advertising accepted.** Circulation 40,000. **Price:** $4.00.

★4300★

ENCYCLOPEDIA OF ALTERNATIVE MEDICINE AND SELF-HELP
Rider & Company
178-202 Great Portland Street
London W1N 6AQ, England
Publication includes: List of practitioners of holistic and alternative medicine, centers for such treatments, and associations, journals, etc., concerned with the subject; includes self-help groups. **Arrangement:** Classified by activity. **Indexes:** Ailment. **Frequency:** Not established; first edition 1978. **Editor:** Malcolm Hulke. **Price:** $12.95, cloth; $6.95, paper. **Send orders to:** Schocken Books, Inc., 200 Madison Ave., New York, NY 10016 (212-685-6500).

★4301★

EXECUTIVE DIRECTORY OF THE U.S. PHARMACEUTICAL INDUSTRY
Chemical Economic Services
Box 468-G   Phone: (609) 921-8468
Princeton, NJ 08540
Covers: About 650 companies and 6,000 middle to top management executives employed in the pharmaceutical industry. **Entries include:** For companies - Company name, address, names of key executives, other United States divisions and subsidiaries involved in health care, and a description of how each company operates. **Arrangement:** Alphabetical. **Indexes:** Executive name (includes title). **Pages** (approx.): 185. **Frequency:** Irregular; latest edition 1976-77; new edition expected 1981. **Price:** $65.00. **Also includes:** List of businesses which have ceased operation since last edition.

★4302★

FACULTY OPENINGS IN SCHOOLS OF PHARMACY
American Association of Schools of Pharmacy
4630 Montgomery Avenue, Suite 201   Phone: (301) 654-9060
Bethesda, MD 20014
Covers: Openings in about 75 schools. **Frequency:** Quarterly. **Price:** $1.00 per issue, payment with order.

★4303★

FEDERAL ASSISTANCE FOR PROGRAMS SERVING THE VISUALLY HANDICAPPED
American Foundation for the Blind
15 W. 16th Street   Phone: (212) 620-2000
New York, NY 10011
Covers: 19 federal agencies offering 136 programs for the blind or funding other programs for the blind. **Entries include:** Agency name, address, program name, and description. **Arrangement:** By agency. **Indexes:** Subject. **Pages** (approx.): 60. **Frequency:** Annual. **Editor:** Barbara D. McGarry. **Price:** $4.00, payment with order. **Other information:** Based on "Catalog of Federal Domestic Assistance."

Federation of American Hospitals Review—Directory Issue *See* **Directory of Investor-Owned Hospitals and Hospital Management Companies**

★4304★

FOREIGN MEDICAL SCHOOL CATALOGUE
Foreign Medical School Information Center
One E. Main Street   Phone: (516) 665-8500
Bay Shore, NY 11706
Covers: Medical schools in 65 foreign countries. **Entries include:** Name and address of school, admission statistics, graduates, and performances on the Education Commission for Foreign Medical Graduate exams. Some entries include data on programs, admission, and transfer requirements. **Pages** (approx.): 170. **Frequency:** Irregular; latest edition 1978. **Editor:** Charles R. Modica. **Price:** $9.95, payment with order.

★4305★
FUND SOURCES IN HEALTH AND ALLIED FIELDS
Oryx Press
3930 E. Camelback Road   Phone: (602) 956-6233
Phoenix, AZ 85018
Covers: Government (including current National Institutes of Health medical research grant programs) and foundation grants offered for support of projects in health sciences and health care. Includes grant programs with application deadlines within the six months following each issue. **Entries include:** Grant/program name, description of scope and purposes, restrictions and special requirements, application deadline, sponsor name, address, phone, name of contact. **Arrangement:** By major research areas (alcoholism, dentistry, etc.), then by deadline date. **Frequency:** Monthly. **Editor:** William K. Wilson. **Price:** $95.00, plus $9.50 shipping (ISSN 0145-6644).

★4306★
GENERAL CLINICAL RESEARCH CENTERS
Division of Research Resources
National Institutes of Health
Health, Education, and Welfare Department   Phone: (301) 496-5545
Bethesda, MD 20014
Covers: About 80 research centers located in colleges, universities, and hospitals funded by the National Institutes of Health for conducting controlled studies of human disorders. **Entries include:** Institution name; name, title, address, and phone of program director; name and title of associate director; name, title, address, and phone of principal investigator; address of facility; description of on-site resources; description of major areas of investigation. Some listings have less detailed information. **Arrangement:** Geographical. **Pages** (approx.): 90. **Frequency:** About every two years; latest edition September 1979. **Price:** Single copies free (NIH Pub. No. 80-1433). **Send orders to:** Research Resources Information Center, 1776 E. Jefferson St., Rockville, MD 20852.

Getting into Medical School *See* Barron's Getting into Medical
    School

★4307★
**GLAD DIRECTORY OF RESOURCES AVAILABLE TO DEAF AND
    HARD-OF-HEARING PERSONS IN THE SOUTHERN CALIFORNIA
    AREA**
Greater Los Angeles Council on Deafness
616 S. Westmoreland   Phone: (213) 383-2220
Los Angeles, CA 90005
Covers: Over 750 agencies and resources serving the deaf and hearing impaired in the southern California area. **Entries include:** Generally, name, address, phone, and name of contact. Some listings also include hours, services, whether teletypewriter telephone is available. **Arrangement:** By type of agency. **Indexes:** Agency name. **Pages** (approx.): 120. **Frequency:** Irregular; latest edition February 1979. **Advertising accepted. Price:** $5.00. **Other information:** Directory is updated through "Glad News," included with directory in membership, $10.00.

★4308★
GOLDBERG'S DIET CATALOG
Collier Books
Macmillan Publishing Company, Inc.
866 Third Avenue
New York, NY 10022
Publication includes: Lists of diet groups (Weight Watchers, etc.), diet and health resorts, and obesity clinics and physicians specializing in its treatment. **Entries include:** Name, address, description of philosophy, activities, etc. **Arrangement:** Classified. **Pages** (approx.): 200. **Frequency:** Not established; first edition 1977. **Editor:** Larry Goldberg. **Price:** $7.95. **Also includes:** Considerable text on medication, exercises, cookbooks, etc.

★4309★
**GUIDANCE, COUNSELING, AND SUPPORT SERVICES FOR HIGH
    SCHOOL STUDENTS WITH PHYSICAL DISABILITIES**
Technical Education Research Centers
44 Brattle Street   Phone: (617) 547-0430
Cambridge, MA 02138
Publication includes: List of sources for materials and resources for use of high school guidance personnel in assisting physically handicapped students in personal adjustment, educational placement, career development, and other areas. A separate volume lists organizations and other resources in each state concerned with high school age physically handicapped students. **Entries include:** Listings for materials include name of publisher, producer, or organization, address, date of publication, and cost. Listings for organizations include name, address, phone, interests, services offered. **Arrangement:** Materials and resources are alphabetical by producer; organizations are geographical. **Indexes:** Subject. **Pages** (approx.): 465. **Frequency:** Published 1977. **Editor:** June C. Foster, et al. **Price:** $15.00, manual and organization directory for one state; $8.50 for 50-state organization directory.

★4310★
GUIDE TO ALCOHOLISM RESOURCES IN TEXAS
Texas Commission on Alcoholism
Sam Houston State Office Building,
    Room 809
Austin, TX 78701
Covers: About 800 alcoholism services and agencies in Texas. **Entries include:** Agency name, address, phone, contact, and similar information. **Arrangement:** By type of service or agency, then by city. **Pages** (approx.): 500. **Frequency:** Irregular; previous edition 1975; latest edition fall 1978; update expected 1980. **Editor:** Mary Kay Knief, Information Specialist. **Former title:** A Directory of Alcoholism Services in Texas. **Price:** $3.00.

★4311★
**GUIDE TO CLINICAL SERVICES IN SPEECH-LANGUAGE
    PATHOLOGY AND AUDIOLOGY**
American Speech-Language-Hearing Association
10801 Rockville Pike   Phone: (301) 897-5700
Rockville, MD 20852
Covers: Accredited and nonaccredited clinical speech and hearing programs in the United States and Canada, and ASHA members in private practice; 2,500 entries. **Entries include:** For clinics - Clinic name, address, phone, director, size and certification of staff, type of clinic, referrals, and services offered. For members - Name, address, and certification status. **Arrangement:** Geographical. **Pages** (approx.): 215. **Frequency:** Annual, January. **Editor:** Kenneth O. Johnson, Ph.D., Executive Secretary. **Price:** $8.00, payment with order (current edition; tentative, 1980 edition).

Guide to Financial Aid for Medical Students *See* Barron's Guide to
    Financial Aid for Medical Students

★4312★
**GUIDE TO GRADUATE EDUCATION IN SPEECH PATHOLOGY AND
    AUDIOLOGY**
American Speech-Language-Hearing Association
10801 Rockville Pike   Phone: (301) 897-5700
Rockville, MD 20852
Covers: 215 colleges and universities offering graduate training in speech pathology and audiology. **Entries include:** Institution name, location, size, faculty, admission requirements, tuition, length of program, and availability of financial aid. **Pages** (approx.): 115. **Frequency:** Annual, spring. **Price:** $2.00.

Guide to Medical, Dental, and Allied Health Science Careers *See*
    Barron's Guide to Medical, Dental, and Allied Health Science
    Careers

★4313★

GUIDE TO PREPAID GROUP HEALTH CARE PROGRAMS [Health maintenance organizations]

Center for Information on America

Phone: (203) 868-2602

Washington, CT 06793

Publication includes: List of about 90 health maintenance organizations. **Entries include:** Organization name, address, phone. **Pages** (approx.): 130. **Frequency:** Not established; first edition 1976. **Price:** $3.00, plus 48¢ shipping, payment with order.

★4314★

GUIDE TO RESPITE CARE PROGRAMS IN MARYLAND FOR THE DEVELOPMENTALLY DISABLED

Maryland Developmental Disabilities Council

201 W. Preston Street

Phone: (301) 383-3358

Baltimore, MD 21201

Covers: About 30 existing or planned programs which provide emergency or planned substitute care for developmentally disabled persons normally cared for by their families. **Entries include:** Program name, address, phone, name of contact, area served, eligibility requirements, services provided, cost. **Arrangement:** Geographical. **Pages** (approx.): 15. **Frequency:** Irregular; latest edition fall 1978. **Editor:** Sandra G. Broda. **Price:** Free.

★4315★

GUIDE TO SERVICES FOR PERSONS WITH DEVELOPMENTAL DISABILITIES [Florida]

Florida Developmental Disabilities Planning Council

Florida Department of Health & Rehabilitative Services

1311 Winewood Boulevard, Building 5

Phone: (904) 488-4257

Tallahassee, FL 32301

Covers: Over 300 agencies in Florida providing services for victims of retardation, cerebral palsy, epilepsy, and autism. **Entries include:** Agency name, address, phone, contact, services provided, client eligibility requirements, schedule of operation, area served, and fee schedule. **Arrangement:** By district. **Indexes:** Agency/program name. **Pages** (approx.): 200. **Frequency:** Biennial, even years. **Editor:** Debbie E. Smith, Planner. **Advertising accepted.** **Former title:** Directory of Resources for the Developmentally Disabled (1978). **Price:** Free; single copies only. **Also includes:** Related associations, advocacy services, etc.

Guide to the Health Care Field *See* **American Hospital Association Guide to the Health Care Field**

★4316★

GUILD OF PRESCRIPTION OPTICIANS OF AMERICA—REFERENCE LIST OF GUILD OPTICIANS

Guild of Prescription Opticians of America, Division

Opticians Association of America

1250 Connecticut Avenue, N. W.

Phone: (202) 659-3620

Washington, DC 20036

Covers: 7,900 dispensing opticians; 500 member firms. **Entries include:** For opticians - Name, office and branch addresses, office phone, areas of specialization. For firms - Company name, address, name of manager, services. **Arrangement:** Geographical. **Frequency:** Latest edition 1976; new edition expected January 1981. **Price:** $20.00, postpaid, payment with order.

★4317★

HANDBOOK AND DIRECTORY OF NURSING HOMES [New York metropolitan area]

Basic Books, Inc.

10 E. 53rd Street

New York, NY 10022

Publication includes: 600 long-term care facilities in New York, New Jersey, and Connecticut. **Entries include:** Name of facility, type of care offered, number and size of rooms, address, medical facilities, number of employees, kinds of diets provided, waiting period for admittance, name of contact, fees, community interaction, social

programs. **Arrangement:** Alphabetical. **Indexes:** Geographical; type of care offered. **Pages** (approx.): 450. **Frequency:** Irregular; latest edition 1975. **Editor:** Paul Neuthaler. **Price:** $7.95, paper; $17.95, cloth. **Also includes:** Several chapters on health insurance and nursing homes, how to evaluate a facility, types of facilities, etc.

★4318★

HANDBOOK SCHEDULE OF CONVENTIONS [Health care]

Health Care Exhibitors Association

90 Bagby Drive, Suite 222

Phone: (205) 870-5143

Birmingham, AL 35209

Covers: 600 health care meetings in the United States, 500 of which have an exhibit program. **Entries include:** Name of association/ meeting, name and address of contact, meeting and exhibit dates for current year, membership of the association, number of exhibit booths, average cost of booth space, attendance at previous meeting, date and site for next meeting. **Arrangement:** Alphabetical by meeting name. **Indexes:** Chronological; keyword. **Pages** (approx.): 120. **Frequency:** Semiannual, September and March. **Editor:** John W. Rousseau, Executive Director. **Advertising accepted.** Circulation 700. **Price:** $50.00 for first copy; $25.00 each for additional copies; restricted circulation.

★4319★

HANDICAPPED DRIVER'S MOBILITY GUIDE

American Automobile Association

8111 Gatehouse Road

Phone: (703) 222-6345

Falls Church, VA 22047

Covers: Over 500 manufacturers of driving aids, driving schools, publishers, government agencies, universities, and other organizations and companies offering services and products to the handicapped driver; about 15 VA-approved hand control manufacturers. **Entries include:** Organization, publisher, or manufacturer name, address, phone, code for products or services. **Arrangement:** Geographical. **Pages** (approx.): 80. **Frequency:** Irregular; latest edition 1978. **Editor:** John DeLellis, Educational Consultant. **Price:** 50¢ (AAA stock number 3772). **Send orders to:** Local AAA Club office. **Also includes:** Summary of types of driving aids recommended by Veterans Administration for various handicaps.

★4320★

HAYES DIRECTORY OF DENTAL SUPPLY HOUSES

Edward N. Hayes, Publisher

4229 Birch Street

Phone: (714) 540-8470

Newport Beach, CA 92660

Number of listings: About 600. **Entries include:** Company name, address, phone, financial strength and credit rating. **Arrangement:** Geographical. **Indexes:** Alphabetical. **Frequency:** Annual, August. **Price:** $30.00.

★4321★

HAYES DIRECTORY OF PHYSICIAN AND HOSPITAL SUPPLY HOUSES

Edward N. Hayes, Publisher

4229 Birch Street

Phone: (714) 540-8470

Newport Beach, CA 92660

Number of listings: Over 1,500. **Entries include:** Company name, address, phone, financial strength, credit rating. **Arrangement:** Geographical. **Indexes:** Alphabetical. **Frequency:** Annual, August. **Price:** $40.00.

★4322★

HAYES DRUGGIST DIRECTORY

Edward N. Hayes, Publisher

4229 Birch Street

Phone: (714) 540-8470

Newport Beach, CA 92660

Covers: About 49,000 retail drug stores and about 700 major wholesale druggists. **Entries include:** Company name, address, financial strength, and credit rating. **Arrangement:** Geographical, in separate sections. **Indexes:** Alphabetical. **Frequency:** Annual, March. **Price:** $80.00.

★4323★
HEALTH CARE DIRECTORY
Medical Economics Company, Subsidiary
Litton Publications
680 Kinderkamack Road   Phone: (201) 262-3030
Oradell, NJ 07649
Covers: Companies, associations, and federal and state agencies
concerned with planning and delivering health care or producing
equipment and supplies needed in the field. Includes adoption
agencies; ambulance services; medical and hospital equipment and
supply manufacturers, Blue Cross and Blue Shield and other health
insurance organizations; organ transplant registries and transplant
centers; abortion centers; nuclear medicine centers; prosthetic
centers; health facility architects and designers; homemaker services;
specialized centers for research on and treatment of alcoholism,
allergies, arthritis, burns, cancer, colon and rectal diseases,
dermatologic diseases, epilepsy, kidney diseases, heart diseases,
respiratory diseases, speech pathology, and spinal cord injury; medical
hypnosis facilities; medical laboratories and their suppliers; attorneys
specializing in medical and health problems; medical artists and
illustrators; medical model makers; medical and health care publishers;
medical schools; nursing schools; nurse anesthetist programs; drug
companies; medical associations; prosthetic equipment; physical
rehabilitation facilities; sex change clinics; sex education and therapy
practitioners; volunteer service opportunities in medical areas;
physician assistant programs; poison control centers; Veterans
Administration hospitals and facilities. Some sections consist of
membership lists or directories published separately by associations,
government agencies, etc. **Entries include:** Generally, name, address,
and phone only; some entries include name of contact or indication of
specialties, etc. **Arrangement:** Classified by activity, service, etc.
Pages (approx.): 1,200. **Frequency:** Not established; first edition
summer 1977. **Editors:** Craig T. and Peter G. Norback. **Price:** Out of
print.

★4324★
HEALTH CARE FOR WOMEN: A GUIDE TO SERVICES IN THE
     DISTRICT OF COLUMBIA
DC Public Interest Research Group
Box 19542   Phone: (202) 676-7388
Washington, DC 20036
Covers: About 30 clinics in the District of Columbia area which
provide gynecological services; childbirth courses are also listed.
Entries include: Clinic name, address, fees, billing procedures, waiting
time for appointment, classes offered, services. Childbirth course
listings include description of methods taught. **Arrangement:**
Alphabetical. **Pages** (approx.): 70. **Frequency:** Irregular; latest edition
September 1978. **Former title:** Directory of District of Columbia
Clinics. **Price:** $2.50, plus 50¢ shipping. **Other information:** Co-
sponsored by DC Community Research Foundation. **Also includes:**
General information on birth control, abortion, etc.

★4325★
HEALTH CARE PRODUCT NEWS—DIRECTORY ISSUE
Gralla Publications
1515 Broadway   Phone: (212) 869-1300
New York, NY 10036
Covers: 2,500 manufacturers and 700 distributors of equipment,
supplies, and services for hospitals and nursing homes. **Entries
include:** For manufacturers - Company name, address, phone. For
distributors - Company name, address, phone, names of principal
executives, branch office locations. **Arrangement:** Manufacturers are
alphabetical, distributors are geographical. **Indexes:** Product.
Frequency: Annual, November. **Editor:** Gil Numeroff. **Advertising
accepted.** Circulation 80,000. **Price:** $2.50.

★4326★
HEALTH CAREERS DIGEST
Cass Martin Research Associates
Box 1463
Secaucus, NJ 07094
Covers: In each issue, about 450 executive, administrative, and
managerial career opportunities in health care. **Entries include:**
Amount of detail varies, but usually includes title of position,
requirements, some indication of salary and benefits, name and
address of employer, and name of contact. **Frequency:** Every two
weeks. **Price:** $60.00 per year; $36.00 for 6 months.

★4327★
HEALTH DATA GUIDE [Rhode Island]
Rhode Island Department of Health
401 State Health Department Building
Davis Street   Phone: (401) 277-2550
Providence, RI 02908
Covers: Hospitals, nursing homes, health maintenance organizations,
and similar health care facilities in Rhode Island. **Entries include:**
Facility name, address, phone. **Arrangement:** By type of facility.
Pages (approx.): 235. **Frequency:** Irregular; latest edition 1977; new
edition expected 1980. **Editor:** David Casey. **Former title:** Rhode
Island Department of Health Health Planning Guide (1974). **Price:**
Free. **Also includes:** Health care statistics and trend data.

★4328★
HEALTH EDUCATION—AAHE DIRECTORY OF INSTITUTIONS ISSUE
Association for the Advancement of Health Education
1201 16th Street, N. W.   Phone: (202) 833-5535
Washington, DC 20036
Covers: About 175 institutions offering undergraduate and/or
graduate programs in school health education and/or community
health education. **Entries include:** Institution name, address, program
offered; most listings include name of contact. **Arrangement:**
Geographical. **Frequency:** Biennial, November/December of even
years. **Editor:** Linda M. Moore. **Price:** Free.

★4329★
HEALTH FOODS BUSINESS—ANNUAL PURCHASING GUIDE ISSUE
Howmark Publishing Corporation
225 W. 34th Street   Phone: (212) 279-0800
New York, NY 10001
Covers: Manufacturers, suppliers, and wholesalers of health food
products; publishers of health food related books and magazines, and
associations interested in the health foods industry. **Entries include:**
Name, address, phone, names and titles of key personnel, line of
business, products or services. **Arrangement:** By type of business or
activity. **Indexes:** Product, brand name. **Pages** (approx.): 250.
Frequency: Annual, November. **Editor:** Michael Spielman. **Advertising
accepted.** Circulation 6,000. **Price:** $18.00.

★4330★
HEALTH GROUPS IN WASHINGTON: A DIRECTORY
National Health Council
1740 Broadway
New York, NY 10019
Covers: About 120 professional, voluntary, consumer, insurance,
union, business, and academic organizations with some impact on the
development of federal health policies. **Entries include:** Name of
organization, address, phone, and names of Washington
representatives. **Frequency:** Irregular; latest edition June 1979.
Former title: Private Health Organizations' Government Relations
Directory. **Price:** $2.00, payment with order; $2.75, billed.

★4331★
HEALTH MEDIA BUYER'S GUIDE
Navillus Publishing Corporation
1074 Hope Street   Phone: (203) 322-3478
Stamford, CT 06907
Covers: 1,700 publications in health field (medical, dental, hospital,

drug, etc.), which carry advertising; in 3 parts. Part 1 contains indexes, multiple publishers, and advertising representatives; Part 2- medical and surgical publications; Part 3-allied health, veterinary, etc. **Entries include:** Publisher name, address, phone; 625 paid entries also include editorial, advertising, and circulation information. **Arrangement:** Contents classified into several major sections: Multispecialty journals, multiple publishers, and representatives are alphabetical; specialty journals classified by subject (acupuncture, aerospace medicine, etc.); regional health publications are geographical; publishers are alphabetical by journal name. **Indexes:** Publication name. **Frequency:** Part 1, Semiannual; Parts 2 and 3 updated as needed. **Editor:** John W. Sullivan. **Advertising accepted.** Circulation 1,500. **Price:** $90.00 per year; includes 3 looseleaf binders and update mailings.

★4332★

HEALTH OCCUPATIONS TRAINING PROGRAMS ADMINISTERED BY HOSPITALS

Health Resources Administration
Public Health Service
Health, Education, and Welfare Department   Phone: (301) 443-1620
Bethesda, MD 20852
Covers: 4,550 programs in nursing, clinical laboratory services, dental services, diet and nutrition, emergency services, medical instrumentation, mental health, pharmacy, vision care, etc. **Entries include:** Hospital name, location, program title, number of beds, type of control (governmental, for-profit, etc.), type of services (general, obstetrics, orthopedics, etc.), description of academic program, application and financial information, program size and numbers of graduates. **Arrangement:** By major program areas (Administration, etc.), then by subareas, then geographical. **Indexes:** Program. **Pages** (approx.): 375. **Frequency:** Not established; first edition September 1977 (1976 data). **Price:** $5.75 (S/N 017-022-00585-9). **Send orders to:** Government Printing Office, Washington, DC 20402. **Other information:** Also available from National Technical Information Service, Springfield, VA 22161; $15.00, paper; $3.00, microfiche (PB 243-109).

★4333★

HEALTH ORGANIZATIONS OF THE UNITED STATES, CANADA, AND INTERNATIONALLY

P. W. Associates
7706 Edmonston Avenue
College Park, MD 20740
Covers: Several thousand professional groups, voluntary associations, foundations, and other organizations concerned with health, medicine, and related fields; includes regional organizations. **Entries include:** Organization name, address, phone, date founded, name of principal executive, and description of activities, publications, etc. **Arrangement:** Alphabetical. **Pages** (approx.): 350. **Frequency:** Irregular; latest edition 1977. **Editors:** Paul Wasserman and Jane K. Bossart. **Price:** $29.00.

Health Sciences Video Directory *See* **Videolog: Programs for the Health Sciences**

★4334★

HEALTH SERVICES ADMINISTRATION EDUCATION

Association of University Programs in Health Administration
One Dupont Circle, Suite 420
Washington, DC 20036
Covers: Undergraduate and graduate member programs in health services administration; coverage includes Canada. **Entries include:** Program name, address, department name, name of director, phone; program history and description; curriculum description; admission procedures and requirements; financial assistance available; placement services; enrollment and student characteristics; fees. **Arrangement:** Alphabetical within undergraduate and graduate groups. **Indexes:** Geographical, faculty name (with degree, title, specialty, and institution). **Pages** (approx.): 275. **Frequency:** Annual. **Editor:** Marcia S. Lane. **Former title:** International Directory of

Graduate & Undergraduate Programs and Centers for Advanced Study in Health Administration. **Price:** $5.95, postpaid, payment with order; $6.75, billed (ISSN 0160-4961).

★4335★

HEALTH SERVICES RESEARCHERS DIRECTORY

National Center for Health Services Research
Human Resources Administration
Health, Education, and Welfare Dept.
Center Bldg., Rm. 7-44
3700 East-West Hwy.   Phone: (301) 436-8970
Hyattsville, MD 20782
Covers: Over 3,000 persons in Health, Education, and Welfare Department Regions IV, VI, VII, VIII, and X who conducted research in health services, 1972-1975. **Entries include:** Researcher's name and professional identification, location and documentation research. **Arrangement:** By HEW region and state. **Frequency:** Not established; first edition 1976. **Send orders to:** National Technical Information Service, Springfield, VA 22161 (PB 262-107.) **Other information:** Compiled by Donald Clark Associates, 560 Ashbury St., San Francisco, CA 94117.

★4336★

HEARING AID JOURNAL—WORLD BUYERS GUIDE AND DIRECTORY ISSUE

Hearing Aid Journal
Benson Building, No. 627   Phone: (712) 252-2051
Sioux City, IA 51101
Covers: Manufacturers and suppliers of hearing aids, earmolds, audiometers, testing equipment, calibrators, and accessory items; hearing aid repair laboratories. Includes separate listing for Canada and other foreign countries. **Entries include:** Company name, address, phone, names and titles of executives, whether manufacturer or distributor, trade and brand names, list of products or services. **Arrangement:** Alphabetical by company name. **Pages** (approx.): 80. **Frequency:** Annual, November. **Editor:** Donald V. Radcliffe (Box A3945, Chicago, IL 60690). **Advertising accepted.** Circulation 15,500. **Former title:** National Hearing Aid Journal - World Buyers Guide and Directory for the Hearing Instruments Industry. **Price:** $3.00.

★4337★

HELP: A WORKING GUIDE TO SELF-HELP GROUPS

New Viewpoints
730 Fifth Avenue   Phone: (212) 480-7606
New York, NY 10019
Covers: 600 self-help mutual aid groups willing to provide information about their meetings or referral to another group. **Entries include:** Group name, address, phone, name and phone number of contact person, description of focus of group, qualifications for attendance, fee. **Arrangement:** Alphabetical. **Indexes:** Geographical, problem. **Frequency:** Not established; first edition summer 1979. **Editors:** Alan Gartner and Frank Riessman. **Former title:** Originally listed as, "Self-Help Directory." **Price:** $7.95, plus 50¢ shipping, payment with order. **Other information:** Supersedes "Directory of Self-Help Groups," formerly published in "Self-Help Reporter" of National Self-Help Clearinghouse.

Holistic Dimensions in Healing *See* **Wholistic Dimensions...**

★4338★

HOSPITAL & COMMUNITY PSYCHIATRY SERVICE—LIST OF MEMBER FACILITIES

Hospital & Community Psychiatry Service
American Psychiatric Association
1700 18th Street, N. W.   Phone: (202) 797-4853
Washington, DC 20009
Covers: Institutions having psychiatric units, mental retardation units, and community health centers which are members of the Hospital & Community Psychiatry Service. **Entries include:** Name of facility, address. **Arrangement:** Geographical. **Pages** (approx.): 15.

Frequency: Annual. **Former title:** Hospital and Community Psychiatry Service - List of Member Facilities. **Price:** Free to members; others, apply.

★4339★
HOSPITAL GROUP PURCHASING DIRECTORY
McKnight Medical Communications, Inc.
550 Frontage Road   Phone: (312) 446-1622
Northfield, IL 60093
Covers: About 245 hospital materials purchasing groups. **Entries include:** Name and location of buying group, total number of beds in each group, approximate dollar expenditures, executives' and purchasing directors' names. **Arrangement:** Geographical. **Frequency:** Annual. **Price:** $22.50, payment with order.

★4340★
HOSPITAL PURCHASING GUIDE
Medical Business Services, Division
IMS America Ltd.
Butler and Maple Avenues   Phone: (215) 643-0400
Ambler, PA 19002
Publication includes: List of about 1,000 manufacturers and distributors of medical-surgical products. **Entries include:** Company name, address, phone, name of contact. **Arrangement:** Alphabetical. **Indexes:** Product, manufacturer/distributor. **Frequency:** Annual, January. **Editor:** Calvin Probst. **Advertising accepted.** Circulation 7,000. **Price:** $55.00.

Hospitals—Annual Guide Issue *See* American Hospital
    Association Guide to the Health Care Field

Hospitals and State Institutions with Skilled Nursing...for the
    Mentally Retarded Beds [North Carolina] *See* Complete
    Listing Of...

★4341★
HOW TO GET INTO MEDICAL AND DENTAL SCHOOL
Arco Publishing, Inc.
219 Park Avenue, South   Phone: (212) 777-6300
New York, NY 10003
Covers: About 130 medical schools and 70 dental schools in the United States and Canada. **Entries include:** School name, address, name of dean, course requirements. **Arrangement:** By field of study. **Pages** (approx.): 145. **Frequency:** Irregular; latest edition 1977; new edition date not set. **Price:** $4.00, plus $1.00 shipping. **Also includes:** List of dentistry scholarships for the disadvantaged.

★4342★
HRA, HSA, CDC, ADAMHA PUBLIC ADVISORY COMMITTEES:
    AUTHORITY, STRUCTURE, FUNCTIONS, MEMBERS
Public Health Service
Health, Education, and Welfare Department
Rockville, MD 20857
Covers: Public advisory committees to the four agencies of the Public Health Service most directly concerned with organization, development, and delivery of health care and related research: Health Resources Administration, Health Services Administration, Center for Disease Control, and Alcohol, Drug Abuse, and Mental Health Administration. **Entries include:** Committee name; name, title, and address of chief officer(s) and of committee members; description of committee activity, how members are selected, etc. **Arrangement:** Alphabetical by agency. **Indexes:** Committee, personal name. **Pages** (approx.): 95. **Frequency:** Annual, spring. **Price:** Free.

★4343★
INFACT MEDICAL SCHOOL INFORMATION SYSTEM
Academic Information Methods, Division
Dataflow Systems, Inc.
7758 Wisconsin Avenue   Phone: (301) 654-9133
Bethesda, MD 20014
Background: Not a directory, but a compilation of microfiche

reproductions of the complete catalogs of about 120 medical schools in the United States and Canada. **Indexes:** Printed "Index/Guide" is published yearly which is a combined index of the catalogs in the microfiche collection. **Frequency:** Annual, winter; quarterly updates on microfiche. **Editor:** Betty Doundikoff. **Price:** $149.50 yearly; $258.50 biennially.

★4344★
INFORMATION FOR APPLICANTS TO SCHOOLS AND COLLEGES OF
    OPTOMETRY
American Optometric Association
243 N. Lindbergh   Phone: (314) 991-4100
St. Louis, MO 63141
Covers: 13 optometry schools. **Entries include:** School name, address, admission requirements, description of program including courses, degree requirements, and internships. **Arrangement:** Alphabetical. **Pages** (approx.): 50. **Frequency:** Annual, April. **Price:** Free.

★4345★
INTERNATIONAL ACADEMY OF BIOLOGICAL MEDICINE—
    DIRECTORY
International Academy of Biological Medicine
Box 31313
Phoenix, AZ 85046
Covers: 300 physicians in the United States, Canada, Mexico, and Europe who emphasize nutrition and other natural holistic approaches in treatment; also lists clinics and spas endorsed by the academy. **Entries include:** Name, specialty, address, phone. **Arrangement:** Geographical. **Pages** (approx.): 15. **Frequency:** Annual. **Editor:** Dr. Paavo Airola. **Price:** Free; send business-size stamped, self-addressed envelope.

★4346★
INTERNATIONAL ACADEMY OF PREVENTIVE MEDICINE—
    MEMBERSHIP DIRECTORY
International Academy of Preventive Medicine
10409 Town and Country Way, Suite 200   Phone: (713) 468-7851
Houston, TX 77024
Covers: 875 persons having doctoral degrees in one of the health care professions (medicine, osteopathy, dentistry, etc.). **Entries include:** Name, office address, highest degree held, areas of occupational specialization. **Arrangement:** Alphabetical. **Indexes:** Geographical, specialty. **Pages** (approx.): 50. **Frequency:** Annual, summer. **Editor:** Joseph A. Nowell, Executive Director. **Price:** Free.

★4347★
INTERNATIONAL ASSOCIATION FOR ORTHODONTICS—
    MEMBERSHIP DIRECTORY
Internation Association for Orthodontics
645 N. Michigan Avenue, Suite 522   Phone: (312) 642-2602
Chicago, IL 60611
Number of listings: 850. **Entries include:** Name, office address, office phone, orthodontic specialty. **Arrangement:** Geographical. **Pages** (approx.): 30. **Frequency:** Biennial, summer of even years. **Editor:** Joanna Carey, Executive Director. **Price:** $3.00 (current and 1980 editions).

International Catalog of Aids & Appliances for Blind & Visually
    Impaired Persons *See* International Guide to Aids...

★4348★
INTERNATIONAL COLLEGE OF SURGEONS—MEMBERSHIP
    DIRECTORY
International College of Surgeons
1516 N. Lake Shore Drive   Phone: (312) 642-3555
Chicago, IL 60610
Covers: 14,000 surgeons; accredited medical schools throughout the world. **Entries include:** Name, address, hospital and teaching affiliations, medical school and date graduated, specialization, and accreditation. **Arrangement:** Alphabetical; medical schools are listed

geographically. **Indexes:** Geographical. **Pages** (approx.): 470. **Frequency:** Biennial; new edition expected February 1980. **Price:** $6.00 (current edition); $10.00 (1980 edition); available only to noncommercial organizations.

★4349★

INTERNATIONAL DIRECTORY OF GENETIC SERVICES
The National Foundation-March of Dimes
1275 Mamaroneck Avenue   Phone: (914) 428-7100
White Plains, NY 10605
Covers: 900 medical genetic units engaged in research or counseling. **Entries include:** Name of unit director, unit name, address, phone, code for services offered or special capabilities. **Arrangement:** Geographical. **Indexes:** Director name (with unit services), genetic service by geographic area. **Pages** (approx.): 60. **Frequency:** Irregular; latest edition May 1977. **Editors:** Henry T. Lynch, Hoda Guirgis, Daniel Bergsma. **Price:** Free.

International Directory of Graduate & Undergraduate...Study in Health Administration See **Health Services Administration Education**

International Directory of Medical/Surgical Supply Dealers See **Blue Book—International Directory of Medical/Surgical Supply Dealers**

★4350★

INTERNATIONAL DIRECTORY OF OCCUPATIONAL SAFETY AND HEALTH SERVICES AND INSTITUTIONS
International Labor Office
CH-1211 Geneva 22, Switzerland
Covers: Institutions working in the field of occupational safety and health. **Entries include:** Name of institution, address, status, list of departments or sections, principal functions and activities, publications. (Entries in English, French, or Spanish.) **Arrangement:** Geographical by English names of countries. **Pages** (approx.): 380. **Frequency:** Irregular; latest edition 1977. **Price:** $11.95. **Send orders to:** International Labor Office, 1750 New York Ave., N. W., Suite 330, Washington, DC 20006 (202-634-6335).

★4351★

INTERNATIONAL DIRECTORY OF SPECIALIZED CANCER RESEARCH AND TREATMENT ESTABLISHMENTS
International Union Against Cancer
3 rue du Conseil-General
1205 Geneva, Switzerland
Covers: 680 major institutions with specialized competence in the field of cancer research and/or treatment in 50 countries. **Entries include:** Institution name, address, phone; affiliations; names of directors and department heads; number of personnel; amount of annual budget; annual cancer-patient statistics; description of activities; availability of postgraduate training posts; special cancer library facilities. **Arrangement:** Geographical. **Indexes:** Institution name, director name, department head name. **Pages** (approx.): 720. **Frequency:** Biennial, summer of even years. **Editor:** David W. Reed. **Price:** 100.00 Swiss Francs.

★4352★

INTERNATIONAL GUIDE TO AIDS & APPLIANCES FOR BLIND & VISUALLY IMPAIRED PERSONS
American Foundation for the Blind
15 W. 16th Street   Phone: (212) 924-0420
New York, NY 10011
Covers: Over 270 sources worldwide for 2,500 special devices for blind and visually handicapped persons. **Entries include:** Name of device, name and address of distributor, description, price. **Arrangement:** By type of device (low vision aids, etc.). **Pages** (approx.): 300. **Frequency:** Irregular; latest edition 1976; new edition possible 1980-1981. **Editor:** Mary Ellen Mulholland, Publications Director. **Former title:** International Catalog of Aids.... **Price:** $3.00, payment must accompany individuals' orders.

★4353★

INTERNATIONAL HALFWAY HOUSE ASSOCIATION—DIRECTORY OF RESIDENTIAL TREATMENT CENTERS
International Halfway House Association
2525 Victory Parkway   Phone: (513) 221-3250
Cincinnati, OH 45206
Covers: 1,600 residential treatment centers (halfway houses) which serve offenders, alcoholics, drug abusers, youth, mentally ill/retarded. **Entries include:** Name of program, address, phone, year established, director's name, capacity, age and sex restrictions, primary function. **Arrangement:** Geographical. **Pages** (approx.): 70. **Frequency:** Annual, spring; 1979 edition delayed to January 1980. **Price:** Not determined.

★4354★

INTERNATIONAL REGISTER OF RESEARCH ON BLINDNESS AND VISUAL IMPAIRMENT
American Foundation for the Blind
15 W. 16th Street   Phone: (212) 620-2000
New York, NY 10011
Covers: Non-medical research projects on problems of the blind and visually impaired, and organizations and publishers concerned with the subject. **Entries include:** For research projects - Name of researcher, institution with which affiliated, address, description of project. For organizations - Name, address, area of interest. For publishers - Title, author or editor, publisher name and address, coverage. **Arrangement:** Research projects and organizations are geographical; publishers are by title. **Indexes:** Subject, country, investigator name. **Pages** (approx.): 140. **Frequency:** Irregular; previous edition 1978; latest edition late 1979. **Editors:** J. M. Gill and L. L. Clark. **Price:** 5 pounds. **Other information:** Published in cooperation with the Warwick Research Unit for the Blind, Coventry, England.

★4355★

INTERNATIONAL TELEPHONE DIRECTORY OF THE DEAF
Telecommunications for the Deaf
814 Thayer Avenue   Phone: (301) 588-4605
Silver Spring, MD 20910
Covers: About 10,000 deaf persons in the United States with teletypewriting equipment. **Entries include:** Name, address, phone. **Arrangement:** Geographical. **Pages** (approx.): 115. **Frequency:** Annual, December. **Editor:** Barry Strassler, Executive Director. **Advertising accepted.** Circulation 10,000. **Price:** $10.00; available to members only.

★4356★

INTERNATIONAL VEGETARIAN HEALTH FOOD HANDBOOK
Vegetarian Society
Parkdale
Dunham Road
Altrincham
Cheshire WA14 4QG, England
Covers: Resources for vegetarian food throughout the world, including stores, suppliers, restaurants, and hotels; includes vegetarian publications. **Entries include:** Name, address; listings may also include phone, hours, capacity, etc. **Pages** (approx.): 200. **Frequency:** Biennial, fall of odd years. **Advertising accepted.** Circulation 20,000. **Price:** 1.20 pounds, plus 82 pence (air mail).

★4357★

JOURNAL OF BEHAVIOR THERAPY & EXPERIMENTAL PSYCHIATRY—DIRECTORY ISSUE
Behavior Therapy and Research Society
C/o Ms. Pearl Epstein
Temple University Medical School
Eastern Pennsylvania Psychiatric Institute
Philadelphia, PA 19129
Covers: About 200 clinical and clinical research fellows with training and experience in behavior therapy (psychologists and psychiatrists) who are members of the Behavior Therapy and Research Society. **Entries include:** Name, office address, highest degree held.

Arrangement: Alphabetical. Pages (approx.): 10. Frequency: Annual, December. Editor: Joseph Wolpe, M.D. Price: Free.

★4358★
JOURNAL OF NURSING ADMINISTRATION—DIRECTORY OF
    CONSULTANTS TO NURSING ADMINISTRATION ISSUE
Journal of Nursing Administration, Inc.
12 Lakeside Park
607 North Avenue   Phone: (617) 245-8944
Wakefield, MA 01880
Covers: About 200 consultants, primarily registered nurses, specializing in nursing administration, training, patient services, etc. Entries include: Name, address, phone, highest degree held, areas of occupational specialization, agency setting, geographic area of consultation, years of consulting experience. Some listings include basic fee, services. Arrangement: Alphabetical. Indexes: Category. Pages (approx.): 65. Frequency: Annual, August. Editor: Carol Higgins. Advertising accepted. Circulation 16,500. Former title: Journal of Nursing Administration - Nursing Service Consultants Directory Issue. Price: $3.00, payment with order.

Journal of Nursing Administration—Nursing Service Consultants
    Directory Issue See Journal of Nursing Administration—
    Directory of...

★4359★
KEITHWOOD DIRECTORY OF HOSPITAL AND SURGICAL SUPPLY
    DEALERS
Keithwood Company
201 W. Church Road   Phone: (215) 337-1866
King of Prussia, PA 19406
Covers: More than 4,500 dealers in the United States and abroad. Entries include: Company name, address (including branches, divisions, etc.), phone, names of principal executives, and types of products sold, with percentage of total sales for each type. Arrangement: Geographical. Indexes: Alphabetical. Pages (approx.): 400. Frequency: Biennial, January of even years. Price: $43.50 (current edition); $45.00 (1980 edition); postpaid, payment with order.

★4360★
LANSING AREA DOCTORS DIRECTORY [Michigan]
Impression 5 Museum
1400 Keystone   Phone: (517) 882-2437
Lansing, MI 48910
Covers: 275 medical and osteopathic physicians who responded to a questionnaire; over 15 local hospitals and medical facilites are also listed. Entries include: Physician's name, address, phone, degrees, specialization, personal and career data, fees, and policies. Arrangement: By medical specialty. Pages (approx.): 100. Frequency: Annual, spring. Editor: Gerald S. Fedewa. Price: $2.50, plus 48¢ shipping. Other information: One of the first publications of its kind, this directory sold over 5,000 copies in the first month it was available. Some attempts elsewhere to publish consumer directories of physicians have been thwarted by legal and professional restrictions; a federal court ruling in favor of consumer medical directories is described in "Consumer Reports," February 1977, pages 65-66.

★4361★
LIBRARIES FOR PEOPLE WITH HANDICAPS [Ohio]
State Library of Ohio
65 S. Front Street
Columbus, OH 43215
Number of listings: 250 main libraries, plus accessible branch libraries. Entries include: Library name, address, phone, special services and materials (large-print books, etc.), accessibility to the handicapped (non-slip floors, door width, etc.), and contact person. Arrangement: Geographical. Pages (approx.): 100. Frequency: Irregular; latest edition 1977. Editor: Eunice Lovejoy, Library Development Consultant, Services to the Handicapped. Price: Free. Also includes: Ohio public libraries listed by county, and information

about talking book program in Ohio.

★4362★
LIBRARY RESOURCES FOR THE BLIND AND PHYSICALLY
    HANDICAPPED
National Library Service for the Blind and Physically Handicapped
Library of Congress
1291 Taylor Street, N. W.   Phone: (202) 882-5500
Washington, DC 20542
Covers: Regional and subregional libraries throughout the United States that provide a free library service of braille and recorded books and magazines to visually and physically handicapped persons. Agencies distributing talking book and cassette machines are also indicated. Entries include: Name of library, address, phone, TWX number (if any), In-WATS number, name of librarian, contact for machines (if any), hours, list of book collections, list of special collections, list of special services. Arrangement: Geographical. Pages (approx.): 110. Frequency: Annual. Price: Free (ISSN 0364-1236).

List of Accredited Degree Programs of Pharmacy See Colleges of
    Pharmacy Accredited Degree Programs

★4363★
LIST OF CRYO-SURGEONS [Hemorrhoid specialists]
California Health Publications
Box 963
Laguna Beach, CA 92652
Covers: Physicians specializing or with special interest in treatment of hemorrhoids by rapid freezing of tissues. Frequency: Latest list is 1979. Price: Free; send self-addressed, stamped long envelope.

★4364★
LISTING OF FDA-APPROVED METHADONE TREATMENT
    PROGRAMS FOR NARCOTIC ADDICTION
Division of Methadone Monitoring
Bureau of Drugs
Food and Drug Administration   Phone: (301) 443-3414
Rockville, MD 20852
Number of listings: 750. Entries include: Name of program, address, name and address of sponsor, phone, program identifier number. Arrangement: Geographical. Pages (approx.): 120. Frequency: Annual, fall. Price: Free. Other information: FDA cautions that this list is "extremely fluid," with constant change in status and location of clinics.

★4365★
M&D-MED INSTRUMENT HANDBOOK & BUYERS GUIDE
Measurements & Data Corporation
2994 W. Liberty Avenue   Phone: (412) 343-9666
Pittsburgh, PA 15216
Covers: Manufacturers of biomedical instruments. Entries include: Manufacturer name, address, phone, name of contact. Frequency: Six sections per year,one each two months. Former title: Medical Electronics and Data - MED Equipment Buyer's Guide. Price: $15.00 per year. Also includes: Principal content of publication is technical data on instruments and equipment.

★4366★
MEDICAL AND HEALTH INFORMATION DIRECTORY
Gale Research Company
Book Tower   Phone: (313) 961-2242
Detroit, MI 48226
Covers: 12,000 medical- and health-oriented organizations; professional standards and review organizations (PSROs); federal and state government agencies; health systems agencies; (HSAs); health maintenance organizations (HMOs); Blue Cross/Blue Shield plans; dental plans; poison control centers; pharmaceutical companies; medical and allied health schools; medical book publishers; medical periodicals, review serials, etc.; medical libraries, information centers, research centers, and information systems; Veterans Administration

and other United States government MED hospitals and medical centers. **Entries include:** All entries include institution or firm names, addresses, and phone; many include names of key personnel and, when pertinent, descriptive annotations. **Arrangement:** Classified by activity, service, etc. **Indexes:** Individual sections have special indexes as required. **Pages** (approx.): 665. **Frequency:** About every two years; latest edition 1977; new edition expected March 1980. **Editor:** Anthony T. Kruzas. **Price:** $62.00, postpaid, payment with order.

★4367★
MEDICAL AND HEALTHCARE MARKETPLACE GUIDE
International Bio-Medical Information Service, Inc.
8859 S. W. 69th Court   Phone: (305) 665-4856
Miami, FL 33156
Covers: Over 1,000 American firms and 700 subsidiaries of foreign firms operating in the United States which offer medical products and services. Covers over 2,000 separate operating units. **Entries include:** Company name, address, phone, executive officers, description of products or services, trade names, financial information, number of plants, and number of employees. **Arrangement:** Alphabetical. **Indexes:** Geographical; personal name; product; subsidiary and division. **Pages** (approx.): 560. **Frequency:** Biennial; new edition expected July 1980. **Editors:** Arthur B. and Adeline B. Hale. **Price:** $175.00 (1980 edition; ISSN 0146-8022).

★4368★
MEDICAL BOOKS AND SERIALS IN PRINT
R. R. Bowker Company
1180 Avenue of the Americas   Phone: (212) 764-5100
New York, NY 10036
Publication includes: List of publishers of monographs and serials concerned with health sciences and health care, including medicine, dentistry, psychiatry, nursing, etc. **Entries include:** Name, address. **Frequency:** Annual, spring. **Price:** $43.50, postpaid, payment with order (ISSN 0000-0574). **Send orders to:** R. R. Bowker Co., Box 1807, Ann Arbor, MI 48106 (313-761-4700). **Other information:** Principal content of publication is listings of books in health care fields by author, title, and subject. Based on ''Books in Print,'' described in separate listing.

Medical Electronics and Data—MED Equipment Buyer's Guide
   See M&D-MED Instrument Handbook & Buyers Guide

★4369★
MEDICAL GROUP MANAGEMENT ASSOCIATION—
   INTERNATIONAL DIRECTORY
Medical Group Management Association
4101 E. Louisiana Avenue   Phone: (303) 753-1111
Denver, CO 80222
Covers: 2,500 member administrators of group medical practices or clinics serving three or more physicians. **Entries include:** Group or clinic name, address, phone, size, services provided, types of specialties, statistical data, name, title and personal data of administrator. **Arrangement:** Geographical. **Indexes:** Personal name, clinic name. **Pages** (approx.): 200. **Frequency:** Irregular; latest edition 1979. **Price:** $50.00.

★4370★
MEDICAL LIBRARY ASSOCIATION—DIRECTORY
Medical Library Association
919 N. Michigan Avenue, No. 3208   Phone: (312) 266-2456
Chicago, IL 60611
Covers: 4,900 individual and institutional members. **Entries include:** For individuals - Name, address, professional certificate. For institutions - Name, address, names of representatives. **Arrangement:** Individual members, alphabetical; institutions, geographical. **Pages** (approx.): 130. **Frequency:** Annual, August. **Advertising accepted.** Circulation 4,900. **Price:** $15.00.

★4371★
MEDICAL MEETINGS ANNUAL DIRECTORY
United Business Publications, Inc.
475 Park Avenue South   Phone: (212) 725-2300
New York, NY 10017
Covers: Meetings of medical, osteopathic, medical, dental, nursing, hospital and nursing home, podiatry, optometry, veterinary, chiropractic, and allied health associations and societies, local to international in scope. **Entries include:** Name of organization; address; phone; name of chief executive officer and meeting planner; meeting theme or title, date, type, site, number of attendees, number of commercial exhibits. **Arrangement:** Classified by major health care classifications. **Indexes:** Location, date. **Pages** (approx.): 180. **Frequency:** Annual, November. **Editor:** Marty Elbaum. **Advertising accepted.** Circulation 20,000. **Price:** $12.95.

★4372★
MEDICAL RESEARCH INDEX
Francis Hodgson Reference Publications
Longman House
Burnt Mill, Harlow
Essex CM20 2JE, England
Covers: Over 5,000 institutions, research centers, etc., involved in medical research and related subjects. **Entries include:** Name of center in native language and in English, address, affiliation or parent body, name of director of research, research interests. **Arrangement:** Geographical. **Indexes:** Center name, subject. **Pages** (approx.): 1,330. **Frequency:** Irregular; latest edition 1979. **Price:** 75 pounds. **Send orders to:** Longman Group Ltd., 43/45 Annandale Street, Edinburgh EH7 4AT, Scotland.

★4373★
MEDICAL SCHOOL ADMISSION REQUIREMENTS—U.S.A. AND
   CANADA
Association of American Medical Colleges
One Dupont Circle, N. W.   Phone: (202) 466-5100
Washington, DC 20036
Covers: About 140 medical schools and colleges in the United States and Canada. **Entries include:** School name, address, admission requirements, application procedures, financial aid programs. **Arrangement:** Geographical. **Frequency:** Annual. **Price:** $5.00, payment with order.

★4374★
MEDICAL SELF-CARE—SELF-CARE CLASSES [Column]
Medical Self-Care
Box 718   Phone: (415) 663-1403
Inverness, CA 94937
Covers: Existing or forming classes in medical self-care. (In early 1980, list covered over 125 classes in 35 states.) **Entries include:** Name and address of person responsible for course. **Arrangement:** Geographical. **Frequency:** Quarterly. **Former title:** First appeared as a special feature; is now a regular column. **Price:** $2.50 per issue; $10.00 per year.

★4375★
MEDICARE/MEDICAID DIRECTORY OF MEDICAL FACILITIES...
Health Standards/Quality Bureau
Health Care Financing Administration
Health, Education, and Welfare Department
330 C Street, S. W.
Washington, DC 20201
Description: Full title is, ''Medicare/Medicaid Directory of Medical Facilities, Listings of Facilities in Alphabetical Sequence by State, City within State, and Facility Name within City (with Provider Numerical Index).'' Lists hospitals, nursing homes and other long-term care facilities with skilled nursing staffs, home health agencies, and physical therapy units in various types of facilities. **Entries include:** Facility name, address, date of first participation, provider number, and, in coded form, type of billing elected, type of facility, services available and types of cases served, and accreditation. **Arrangement:**

Geographical within ten regions. **Pages** (approx.): 1,750. **Frequency:** Irregular; latest edition November 1979. **Price:** $10.25 (S/N 017-070-00306-1; 1977 edition). **Send orders to:** For 1977 edition - Government Printing Office, Washington, DC 20402. **Other information:** The 1979 edition is not available from the GPO.

★4376★
MEDICINE'S NEW TECHNOLOGY: A CAREER GUIDE
Arco Publishing, Inc.
219 Park Avenue South   Phone: (212) 777-6300
New York, NY 10003
Publication includes: List of hospital-based training programs and schools with formal courses in technically oriented health science careers, such as biomedical engineering. **Entries include:** School name, location, code for programs offered. **Arrangement:** Geographical. **Frequency:** Not established; first edition July 1979. **Author:** Janet Zhun Nassif. **Price:** $8.95, plus $1.00 shipping.

★4377★
MENTAL HEALTH DIRECTORY
National Institute of Mental Heatlh
Public Health Service
Health, Education and Welfare Department
Bethesda, MD 20014
Covers: Hospitals, treatment centers, outpatient clinics, day/night facilities, and mental health centers offering mental health assistance; not included are substance abuse programs and programs for the developmentally disabled. **Entries include:** Name, address, phone, geographic area served, type of control (i.e., government or private), and services. **Arrangement:** Geographical. **Pages** (approx.): 635. **Frequency:** Irregular; latest edition 1977; new edition possible 1980. **Price:** $7.00. **Also includes:** Lists of regional offices of the Alcohol, Drug Abuse, and Mental Health Administration, and other voluntary, self-help, and governmental mental health organizations.

★4378★
MENTAL HEALTH SERVICES INFORMATION AND REFERRAL DIRECTORY
Ready Reference Press
Box 4288
Thousand Oaks, CA 91359
Covers: In four regional editions covering the United States - Counseling centers, psychiatric hospitals, residential treatment centers, clinics, and other private and federally-funded sources for mental health services; also listed are state mental health authorities, regional alcohol and substance abuse offices of the Health, Education, and Welfare Department, voluntary mental health associations, professional mental health associations, self-help organizations for mental health, and others. **Entries include:** For mental health services - Type of facility, name, address, phone, geographic area served, name of controlling agency or organization, services, eligibility restrictions (if any). Other listings include name, address, phone. **Arrangement:** Mental health services are geographical, others are by type of organization. **Pages** (approx.): 320 per regional edition. **Frequency:** Not established; first edition 1978. **Price:** $37.50 per regional edition. **Also includes:** Mental health statistics for each area, including cost, staffing, admissions, etc. **Other information:** Regional editions are Eastern, Central, Southern, and Western.

★4379★
MENTAL HEALTH YEARBOOK/DIRECTORY
Van Nostrand Reinhold Company, Division
Litton Educational Publishing, Inc.
135 W. 50th Street   Phone: (212) 265-8700
New York, NY 10020
Covers: Federally funded mental health facilities, apparently taken from the National Institute of Mental Health's "Mental Health Directory" (see separate listing); also includes national and state organizations concerned with specific mental health problems and conditions. **Arrangement:** By type of condition or concern; hospitals

are geographical. **Pages** (approx.): 780. **Frequency:** First edition 1979. **Editor:** Judith Norback. **Price:** $39.50.

★4380★
MOBILIZATION OF COMMUNITY RESOURCES [Mental illness]
Research Utilization Laboratory
ICD Rehabilitation and Research Center
340 E. 24th Street   Phone: (212) 679-0100
New York, NY 10010
Publication includes: About 100 community-based programs for the mentally ill in the United States. **Entries include:** Agency name, address, services, client eligibility requirements. **Arrangement:** Classified by service offered. **Pages** (approx.): 130. **Frequency:** Irregular; previous edition 1977; latest edition 1978. **Editors:** Isabel Pick Robinault and Marvin Weisinger. **Price:** $4.00, postpaid.

★4381★
MUTUAL HELP GROUPS: A GUIDE FOR MENTAL HEALTH WORKERS
National Institute of Mental Health
Public Health Service
Health, Education, and Welfare Department
5600 Fishers Lane
Rockville, MD 20857
Publication includes: About 20 groups (primarily national) composed of people sharing a common problem who provide mutual assistance in dealing with the problem. **Entries include:** Organization name, address, description of program and philosophy. **Frequency:** Published 1978. **Editor:** Phyllis R. Silverman. **Price:** Free.

★4382★
NAPSAC DIRECTORY OF ALTERNATIVE BIRTH SERVICES AND CONSUMER GUIDE
National Association of Parents & Professionals for Safe Alternatives in Childbirth
Box 267   Phone: (314) 238-2010
Marble Hill, MO 63764
Covers: 3,500 birth centers, midwifery schools, midwives, doctors doing home births, childbirth educators, and others in the field of alternative childbirth throughout the United States and Canada. **Entries include:** Name, address, phone, medically related degree, and services. **Arrangement:** By Zip code order within states. **Pages** (approx.): 150. **Frequency:** Has been irregular; latest edition May 1978. New edition expected February 1980, thereafter annual, February. **Editor:** Penny Simkin, RPT, Director of Maternity Standards. **Advertising accepted. Price:** $3.50 (current edition); $4.50 (1980 edition); plus 75¢ shipping. **Other information:** List of about 45 state and regional associations belonging to NAPSAC is available separately.

★4383★
NARCOTICS AND DRUG ABUSE—A-Z
Croner Publications, Inc.
211-03 Jamaica Avenue   Phone: (212) 464-0866
Queens Village, NY 11428
Covers: Agencies, commissions, organizations, and individuals actively opposed to the use and/or abuse of narcotics and drugs, and companies having relevant products or services. Three volumes: Volume 1, Connecticut, New York, New Jersey; Volume 2, western states; Volume 3, all others. **Entries include:** For agencies, commissions, and facilities - Name, address, name of administrator, description of services. For companies - Name, location, products or activities. **Arrangement:** Alphabetical within organization types. **Frequency:** Annual, with quarterly updates. **Price:** $40.00, plus $3.95 shipping; includes base volume, binder, and year's updating service. **Also includes:** Descriptions of drugs, including slang terms used to refer to specific drugs in English and Spanish; bibliography.

★4384★
NATIONAL ACCREDITATION COUNCIL FOR AGENCIES SERVING
    THE BLIND AND VISUALLY HANDICAPPED—LIST OF
    ACCREDITED MEMBERS
National Accreditation Council for Agencies Serving the Blind and
    Visually Handicapped
79 Madison Avenue, Suite 1406   Phone: (212) 683-8581
New York, N,Y 10016
Covers: About 80 agencies and schools accredited for service to the
blind in the United States. Entries include: Organization name, name
of chief administrator, date first accredited, date of next re-
evaluation, city and state. Arrangement: Geographical. Pages
(approx.): 5. Frequency: Semiannual, January and July. Editor: Anne
F. Barber, Staff Associate for Accreditation. Price: Free.

National Ambulance Directory See Paramedical National
    Directory

★4385★
NATIONAL ASSOCIATION FOR MUSIC THERAPY—MEMBERSHIP
    DIRECTORY
National Association for Music Therapy
901 Kentucky Street, Suite 206   Phone: (913) 842-1909
Lawrence, KS 66044
Number of listings: 2,900. Entries include: Name, home address,
occupational affiliation. Arrangement: Alphabetical. Pages (approx.):
70. Frequency: Annual, spring. Editor: Margaret S. Sears, Executive
Director. Price: $3.50.

National Association of Parents & Professionals for Safe
    Alternatives in Childbirth—Roster See NAPSAC Directory of
    Alternative...

★4386★
NATIONAL ASSOCIATION OF PRIVATE PSYCHIATRIC
    HOSPITALS—MEMBERSHIP DIRECTORY
National Association of Private Psychiatric Hospitals
1701 K Street, N. W., Suite 1205   Phone: (202) 223-6691
Washington, DC 20006
Number of listings: 170. Entries include: Name of hospital, address,
name of administrator, description of treatment program,
accreditation, number of beds, length of stay permitted.
Arrangement: Alphabetical. Frequency: Irregular; about every three
years; latest edition 1977. Price: $5.00.

★4387★
NATIONAL ASSOCIATION OF PRIVATE RESIDENTIAL FACILITIES
    FOR THE MENTALLY RETARDED—DIRECTORY OF MEMBERS
National Association of Private Residential Facilities for the Mentally
    Retarded
6269 Leesburg Pike, Suite B-5   Phone: (703) 536-3311
Falls Church, VA 22044
Number of listings: 450. Entries include: Facility name, address,
phone, name of administrator; description of residents including
number, sex, age, level of retardation, and special conditions served;
licensing and certification. Arrangement: Geographical. Pages
(approx.): 50. Frequency: Annual. Price: $12.50.

National Board for Certification in Dental Technology—Directory
    See Who's Who in the Dental Laboratory Industry

National Directory of Drug Abuse Treatment Programs See
    Directory of Drug Abuse and Alcoholic Treatment Programs

★4388★
NATIONAL DIRECTORY OF HISPANIC PROFESSIONALS IN MENTAL
    HEALTH AND HUMAN SERVICES
National Coalition of Hispanic Mental Health and Human Services
    Organizations
1725 K Street, N. W., Suite 1212   Phone: (202) 466-2260
Washington, DC 20006
Covers: 1,250 Hispanics active in programs for alcoholism,
community organization, drug abuse, legal aid, planning, etc. Includes
list of about 75 national Hispanic organizations. Entries include:
Name, affiliation or profession, address, phone. Arrangement:
Classified by occupation or program. Pages (approx.): 60. Frequency:
Not established; first edition fall 1977. Price: $3.00.

★4389★
NATIONAL DIRECTORY OF MENTAL HEALTH
Wiley-Interscience Division
John Wiley & Sons, Inc.
605 Third Avenue
New York, NY 10016
Covers: Over 4,000 adult outpatient mental health services, including
clinics, community health centers, private groups and institutions,
schools, hotlines, and referral centers. Entries include: Name of
organization, address, phone, services offered, therapeutic
orientation, client/patient access, fee structure, waiting time, and
staff qualifications. Arrangement: Geographical. Pages (approx.):
500. Frequency: Irregular; first edition winter 1978-79; new edition
expected April 1980. Editor: Ellen G. Detlefsen. Price: $38.00
(tentative, 1980 edition). Send orders to: John Wiley & Sons, Inc., 1
Wiley Dr., Somerset, NJ 08873 (201-469-4400). Other
information: A Neal-Schuman publication.

National Directory of Services and Programs for Autistic Children
    See U.S. Facilities and Programs for Children with Severe ...

★4390★
NATIONAL DRUG CODE DIRECTORY
Food and Drug Administration
Public Health Service
Health, Education, and Welfare Department
5600 Fishers Lane (HFD-315)   Phone: (301) 427-7953
Rockville, MD 20857
Publication includes: List of manufacturers of commercially
marketed human prescription drugs and over-the-counter drugs (in
Volume two). Entries include: Drug company full name, address,
labeler code. Arrangement: Alphabetical by short name of company
Indexes: Drug number, drug group, drug name. Frequency: Irregular;
latest edition 1976; new edition expected 1980. Price: $18.75 (S/N
017-012-00242-1). Send orders to: Government Printing Office,
Washington, DC 20402. Also includes: Publication is primarily a
listing of about 58,000 drug products.

★4391★
NATIONAL HEALTH COUNCIL—LISTING OF MEMBER
    ORGANIZATIONS
National Health Council
1740 Broadway   Phone: (212) 582-6040
New York, NY 10019
Number of listings: 87 national voluntary agencies, health
professional associations, government agencies, and others. Entries
include: Agency name, address of national headquarters, chief
executive. Arrangement: Alphabetical. Pages (approx.): 10.
Frequency: Irregular; latest edition March 1979. Editor: Juliette
Hand, Director, Administrative Division. Price: 25¢ shipping.

★4392★
NATIONAL HEALTH DIRECTORY
Science and Health Publications
6410 Rockledge Drive, No. 208   Phone: (301) 530-1377
Bethesda, MD 20034
Covers: About 11,500 public officials at policy-making levels

concerned with health care services and delivery. Covers federal and state agencies, including personnel of state health planning agencies and health systems agencies. **Entries include:** Agency name, address, and individual names, titles, addresses, and phones. **Arrangement:** By level of government and agency. **Indexes:** Personal name. **Pages** (approx.): 725. **Frequency:** Annual, January. **Price:** $19.50 (current edition); $29.50 (1980 edition); payment with order.

★4393★
NATIONAL HEALTH PRACTITIONER PROGRAM PROFILE
Association of Physician Assistant Programs
2341 Jefferson Davis Highway, Suite 700   Phone: (703) 920-5732
Arlington, VA 22202
Covers: Over 50 programs which train physician assistants. **Entries include:** Program name, institution name, address, phone, description of program, including curriculum, selection criteria, degrees or certificates offered. **Arrangement:** Geographical. **Pages** (approx.): 140. **Frequency:** Biennial, August of even years. **Editor:** Dr. Robert S. Bloom. **Price:** $7.50, payment must accompany order.

★4394★
NATIONAL HEARING AID SOCIETY—DIRECTORY OF MEMBERS
National Hearing Aid Society
20361 Middlebelt Road   Phone: (313) 478-2610
Livonia, MI 48152
Covers: 2,000 certified hearing aid audiologists and provisional members. **Entries include:** Name, address, phone. **Arrangement:** Geographical. **Pages** (approx.): 50. **Frequency:** Annual, April. **Editor:** Anthony DiRocco, Executive Vice-President. **Advertising accepted.** Circulation 17,000. **Price:** $1.50 (current and 1980 editions). **Also includes:** Manufacturers and suppliers of hearing aids.

★4395★
NATIONAL REGISTRY OF PSYCHOANALYSTS
National Accreditation Association and American Examining Board of Psychoanalysis
80 Eighth Avenue, Suite 1210   Phone: (212) 741-0515
New York, NY 10011
Covers: Over 1,000 certified psychoanalysts, psychoanalytic psychotherapists and students at approved training institutions; coverage includes the United States, Canada, and Europe. 20 approved training institutions are also listed. **Entries include:** Name, preferred address and phone number, name of institution granting certificate, year granted, date of certification. For institutions - Name, address, name of director, areas in which accredited (by the association), school of thought, level of degree, and date of next accreditation review. **Arrangement:** Alphabetical within above categories. **Indexes:** Geographical. **Pages** (approx.): 155. **Frequency:** Annual, spring. **Editor:** Janice Hildebrand, Administrator. **Price:** $5.00. **Also includes:** Criteria for certification, code of ethics, training curriculum, research and academic affiliates, and supporters of psychoanalysis. **Other information:** In addition to providing training, the goal of this organization is the establishment of psychoanalysis as a separate profession, independent of medical education.

★4396★
NATIONAL SAFETY NEWS—SAFETY PRODUCT DATA ISSUE
National Safety Council
444 N. Michigan Avenue   Phone: (312) 527-4800
Chicago, IL 60611
Covers: Occupational health and safety equipment, products, manufacturers and distributors, and services. **Indexes:** Product. **Frequency:** Annual, March. **Editor:** Roy Fisher. **Advertising accepted.** Circulation 60,000. **Price:** $1.56 (current edition); $2.00 (1980 edition).

★4397★
NATURAL FAMILY PLANNING PROGRAM REFERRAL LIST
Human Life and Natural Family Planning Foundation
1511 K Street, N. W., Suite 305   Phone: (202) 393-1380
Washington, DC 20005
Covers: About 175 family planning program agencies which emphasize non-artificial contraception. **Entries include:** Program name, sponsoring institution, address, phone, name of director, methods taught. **Arrangement:** Geographical. **Pages** (approx.): 60. **Frequency:** Irregular; latest edition February 1977; new edition expected January 1980. **Price:** $1.50. **Other information:** 1980 edition will include extensive changes in format and coverage.

★4398★
NATUROPATH AND THE NATURAL HEALTH WORLD—
    "PROFESSIONAL DIRECTORY OF NATUROPATHIC
    PHYSICIANS" SECTION
Mrs. John W. Noble, Publisher
1920 N. Kilpatrick Street   Phone: (206) 695-0213
Portland, OR 97217
Number of listings: 25; listings are paid. **Entries include:** Name of doctor and/or clinic, address, phone; some listings include services or specialty. **Arrangement:** Geographical. **Frequency:** Monthly. **Editor:** Edward M. Jones. **Price:** $5.00 per year.

★4399★
NO-NONSENSE GUIDE TO GET YOU INTO MEDICAL SCHOOL
Simon & Schuster, Inc.
1230 Avenue of the Americas   Phone: (212) 245-6400
New York, NY 10020
Covers: About 120 United States and foreign medical schools. **Entries include:** For United States schools - Name, address; facilities, costs, application procedures, financial aid available, other descriptive information. For foreign schools - Name, address; similar but less detailed descriptive information. **Arrangement:** Geographical. **Pages** (approx.): 200. **Frequency:** Published 1979. **Editor:** Kent Bransford. **Price:** $8.95, cloth; $3.95, paper.

★4400★
NURSING [YEAR] CAREER DIRECTORY
Intermed Communications, Inc.
132 Welsh Road   Phone: (215) 657-4600
Horsham, PA 19044
Covers: Nonprofit and investor-owned hospitals and departments of the United States government which hire nurses. Does not report specific positions available. **Entries include:** Unit name, location, areas of nursing specialization, educational requirements for nurses, licensing, facilities, benefits, etc. **Arrangement:** Geographical. **Frequency:** Annual, January. **Editor:** John E. Kelly. **Advertising accepted.** Circulation 100,000. **Price:** $10.00.

★4401★
NURSING HOMES AND HOMES FOR SPECIAL SERVICES [Florida]
Office of Licensure and Certification
Florida Department of Health and Rehabilitative Services
Box 210
Jacksonville, FL 32231
Number of listings: Over 300. **Entries include:** Home name, name of owner, address, phone, type of facility, bed capacity, type of ownership, languages spoken, number and type of employees, activities, whether certified for Medicare and/or Medicaid. **Arrangement:** Geographical. **Indexes:** Facility name (with city, county). **Pages** (approx.): 70. **Frequency:** Annual, January. **Price:** Apply.

★4402★
NURSING JOB GUIDE TO OVER 7,000 HOSPITALS
Prime National Publishing Company
470 Boston Post Road   Phone: (617) 899-2702
Weston, MA 02166
Covers: Over 7,000 medical centers, infirmaries, government

hospitals, and other hospitals in the United States; in tabular format, provides information about each facility which would be of interest to nurses considering employment there, but does not list specific openings. **Entries include:** Hospital name, address, phone, name of nurse recruiter; number of beds, number of admissions, number of patient days, type of control, whether a teaching institution; nursing specialties utilized; list of fringe benefits; whether relocation assistance is given; educational opportunities; special programs. **Arrangement:** Geographical. **Pages** (approx.): 200. **Frequency:** Annual, December. **Editor:** Ira Alterman. **Advertising accepted.** Circulation 10,000. **Price:** $15.00 (ISSN 0162-9069).

★4403★
NUTRITION-MINDED DOCTORS IN THE U.S. AND CANADA
Alacer Corporation
Box 6180
Buena Park, CA 90622
Covers: Medical doctors, osteopaths, chiropractors, and dentists who emphasize nutrition in treatment; coverage includes Canada. **Entries include:** Name, specialty, address. **Arrangement:** Geographical. **Pages** (approx.): 50. **Frequency:** Every 18 months. **Price:** 50¢ (current edition); $1.00 (tentative, 1980 edition).

★4404★
OCCUPATIONAL SAFETY AND HEALTH DIRECTORY
National Institute for Occupational Safety and Health
Public Health Service
Health, Education, and Welfare Department
5600 Fishers Lane   Phone: (301) 443-2140
Rockville, MD 20857
Covers: Federal, state, and local occupational safety agencies. **Entries include:** Name of department or division, address, phone, names and titles of key personnel. **Arrangement:** Federal by department or agency; state and local, geographical. **Pages** (approx.): 90. **Frequency:** Annual. **Price:** Free (Stock No. DHEW NIOSH 79-123). **Send orders to:** Publications, National Institute for Occupational Safety and Health, 4676 Columbia Parkway, Cincinnati, OH 45226 (513-684- 4287).

★4405★
OFF DIABETES PILLS: A DIABETIC'S GUIDE TO LONGER LIFE
Public Citizen Health Research Group
2000 P Street, N. W.   Phone: (202) 872-0320
Washington, DC 20036
Publication includes: List of about 20 diabetes treatment centers which treat diabetics through diet (without oral hypoglycemics and/or insulin). **Entries include:** Center name, address, name of contact. **Arrangement:** Geographical. **Frequency:** Published 1978. **Editors:** Rebecca Warner, Sidney M. Wolfe, and Rebecca Rich. **Price:** $3.50. **Other information:** Principal content of publication is discussion of treatment of diabetes through oral hypoglycemics.

Osteopathic Medical School Catalogue *See* **American Osteopathic Medical School Catalogue**

★4406★
PACIFIC DERMATOLOGIC ASSOCIATION—MEMBERSHIP DIRECTORY
Pacific Dermatologic Association
180 Mark Twain Avenue
Reno, NV 89509
Covers: 1,100 members in Alaska, Arizona, California, Colorado, Hawaii, Nevada, New Mexico, Idaho, Montana, Oregon, and Washington. **Entries include:** Name, home and office addresses, personal data, dermatology society memberships. **Arrangement:** Alphabetical. **Indexes:** Geographical. **Pages** (approx.): 120. **Frequency:** Biennial, spring of even years. **Editor:** Florence Beardsley, Executive Secretary. **Advertising accepted.** Circulation more than 1,000. **Price:** $5.00 (current and 1980 editions); not available for commercial use.

★4407★
PAIN CLINIC DIRECTORY
American Society of Anesthesiologists
515 Busse Highway
Park Ridge, IL 60068
Covers: Clinics specializing in the treatment of acute chronic pain, including severe headache, arthritis, backache, etc. The society has not investigated the effectiveness of the clinics and does not vouch for them. **Arrangement:** Geographical. **Frequency:** Irregular; latest edition summer 1979. **Price:** $4.00.

★4408★
PARAMEDICAL NATIONAL DIRECTORY
United Publications
380 Hudson Street   Phone: (203) 522-2552
Hartford, CT 06106
Covers: Manufacturers and suppliers of ambulance equipment and related medical equipment and supplies, and emergency medical and ambulance services in the United States. **Entries include:** For suppliers and manufacturers - Company name, address. For ambulance and emergency medical services - Service name and address. **Arrangement:** Manufacturers and suppliers are classified by product or service; ambulance services are geographical. **Pages** (approx.): 315. **Frequency:** Every five years; latest edition 1977. **Editor:** Lynn Mahan, Publisher. **Advertising accepted.** **Former title:** National Ambulance Directory. **Price:** $15.00.

★4409★
PHARMACEUTICAL DIRECTORY
American Pharmaceutical Association
2215 Constitution Avenue, N. W.   Phone: (202) 628-4410
Washington, DC 20037
Covers: State associations, national organizations, colleges, and governing agencies concerned with pharmacy and pharmaceutical products. **Entries include:** Association name, address, and phone. **Frequency:** Annual. **Price:** $1.00 (current edition); $2.00 (1980 edition).

★4410★
PHARMACEUTICAL MANUFACTURERS OF THE UNITED STATES
Noyes Data Corporation
Grand Avenue
Park Ridge, NJ 07656
Covers: About 350 pharmaceutical and health care product manufacturers in the United States. **Entries include:** Company name, address, products. **Arrangement:** Alphabetical. **Pages** (approx.): 255. **Frequency:** Irregular; latest edition 1977; new edition expected 1980. **Price:** $32.00 (current edition); $36.00 (1980 edition).

★4411★
PHARMACEUTICAL MARKETERS DIRECTORY
Fisher-Stevens, Inc.
120 Brighton Road   Phone: (201) 471-2057
Clifton, NJ 07012
Covers: Personnel of pharmaceutical companies, advertising agencies with clients in the medical field, and medical publications. Also includes alphabetical list of publishers' representatives. **Entries include:** Company name, address, list of personnel by department or section with their phone numbers. **Arrangement:** By type of business (pharmaceutical company, advertising agency, or publishing company), then alphabetical by company name. **Indexes:** Personnel, geographical/classified supplier section. **Pages** (approx.): 380. **Frequency:** Annual, April. **Editor:** John C. Banghart, Publisher. **Advertising accepted.** Circulation 2,000. **Price:** $39.95.

★4412★
PHARMACY SCHOOL ADMISSION REQUIREMENTS
American Association of Colleges of Pharmacy
4630 Montgomery Avenue, Suite 201   Phone: (301) 654-9060
Bethesda, MD 22014
Covers: About 75 colleges of pharmacy accredited by the American

Council on Pharmaceutical Education. **Entries include:** School name, address, admission requirements, contact name, timetables for application and admission for two-year period in advance. **Pages** (approx.): 140. **Frequency:** Biennial. **Price:** $5.00, payment with order.

★4413★

PHYSICIAN DIRECTORY OF LANCASTER CITY AND COUNTY MEDICAL SOCIETY [Pennsylvania]

Lancaster City and County Medical Society
139 E. Walnut Street
Lancaster, PA 17603

Covers: 300 member physicians practicing in Lancaster County, Pennsylvania. **Entries include:** Name, address, office hours, specialty, hospital affiliation, basic fees, and other information. **Arrangement:** By specialty. **Indexes:** Geographic area served. **Frequency:** Not established; first edition spring 1979. **Editor:** Dr. Henry Wentz. **Price:** Free.

Pink Book *See* Drug Topics Health and Beauty Aids Directory

Preparing Registered Nurses for Expanded Roles: A Directory of Programs *See* Directory for Expanded Role Programs for R.N.S

Private Health Organizations' Government Relations Directory *See* Health Groups in Washington: A Directory

★4414★

PROOFS—BUYERS' GUIDE AND MANUFACTURERS' DIRECTORY ISSUE

Dental Economics Division
Petroleum Publishing Company
1421 South Sheridan   Phone: (918) 835-3161
Tulsa, OK 74112

Covers: Over 400 manufacturers of dental products and equipment; coverage includes Canada. **Entries include:** Company name, address, phone, key personnel, products. **Arrangement:** Alphabetical. **Indexes:** Product. **Pages** (approx.): 35. **Frequency:** Annual, December. **Editor:** Mary Elizabeth Good. **Advertising accepted.** Circulation 8,200. **Price:** $1.00, plus 25¢ shipping.

★4415★

PROOFS—DENTAL DEALER DIRECTORY ISSUE

Dental Economics Division
Petroleum Publishing Company
Box 1260   Phone: (918) 835-3161
Tulsa, OK 74101

Covers: 580 companies which are retail outlets for dental supplies, equipment, and services, and which carry inventory and serve dentists within a specific area. **Entries include:** Company name, address, phone, names of principal executives, number of outside sales representatives. **Arrangement:** Geographical. **Indexes:** Company name. **Frequency:** Annual, April. **Advertising accepted.** Circulation 6,500. **Price:** $1.25 (current and 1980 editions).

Proprietary Names of Official Drugs *See* APhA Drug Names: An Index

★4416★

PSYCHIATRIC OUTPATIENT SERVICES BULLETIN IN LOS ANGELES COUNTY [California]

Information and Referral Service of Los Angeles County
621 S. Virgil Avenue   Phone: (213) 736-1300
Los Angeles, CA 90005

Number of listings: About 125 free or low-fee clinics, programs, etc. **Entries include:** Clinic name, address, phone; title and name of administrator, medical director and professional consultant; service area; application procedure; fees; waiting period for intake/therapy; night/weekend service; treatment modalities; staffing and coverage in hours per week; ages served. **Arrangement:** Alphabetical. **Indexes:**

Age served, language. **Pages** (approx.): 40. **Frequency:** About every two years; latest edition 1979. **Editor:** Dona Clark. **Price:** $3.50, postpaid, payment with order.

★4417★

PUBLISHER SOURCE DIRECTORY [Handicapped education]

National Center on Educational Media and Materials for the Handicapped
Ohio State University   Phone: (614) 422-7596
Columbus, OH 43210

Covers: More than 1,600 publishers and producers in the United States, Canada, and Europe of instructional materials and other educational aids for sale or rent. **Entries include:** Name, address, list of products. **Arrangement:** By product. **Pages** (approx.): 140. **Frequency:** Irregular; latest edition 1977. **Price:** $9.50 (Stock No. 77:301). **Send orders to:** Ohio State University Press, 2070 Neil Avenue, Columbus, OH 45210 (614-422-6930).

★4418★

QUALIFIED HEALTH MAINTENANCE ORGANIZATIONS

Office of Health Maintenance Organizations
Public Health Service
Health, Education, and Welfare Department
5600 Fishers Lane, Room 3-32   Phone: (301) 443-2300
Rockville, MD 20857

Covers: About 100 prepaid health plans. **Entries include:** Plan name, address, phone, name of president, date qualified, loan commitment, name of compliance officer. **Arrangement:** Random. **Frequency:** Not established; latest edition July 1979. **Price:** Free.

★4419★

RADIOLOGY/NUCLEAR MEDICINE—BUYERS GUIDE ISSUE

W. G. Holdsworth & Associates, Inc.
1000 E. Northwest Highway   Phone: (312) 394-2022
Mount Prospect, IL 60056

Covers: About 1,575 manufacturers of radiology, ultrasound, tomography, and nuclear medicine equipment and supplies; dealers and distributors are also included. **Entries include:** For manufacturers - Company name, address, phone, branch office locations, and names and titles of key personnel. For dealers and distributors - Name, address, name of contact. **Arrangement:** Manufacturers are alphabetical, dealers and distributors are both geographical and alphabetical. **Indexes:** Trade and brand name, product. **Pages** (approx.): 250. **Frequency:** Annual; first edition November 1979. **Editor:** Laura M. Dreyer, Buyers Guide Manager. **Advertising accepted.** Circulation 27,350. **Price:** $45.00, postpaid, payment with order.

Red Book *See* Drug Topics Red Book

Red Book of Eye, Ear, Nose and Throat Specialists *See* Red Book of Ophthalmology

★4420★

RED BOOK OF OPHTHALMOLOGY

Professional Press, Inc.
101 E. Ontario Street   Phone: (312) 337-7800
Chicago, IL 60611

Covers: 10,700 ophthalmologists; optical supply houses, manufacturers, and importers; residencies; eye banks; etc. **Entries include:** For ophthalmologists - Name, office address and phone, highest degree, special interests, personal and career data. **Arrangement:** Geographical. **Pages** (approx.): 410. **Frequency:** Biennial, April of odd years. **Advertising accepted.** **Price:** $17.00.

★4421★

REGION IV DIRECTORY OF SERVICES FOR PERSONS WITH DEVELOPMENTAL DISABILITIES [Minnesota]

West Central Regional Development Commission
Fergus Falls Community College   Phone: (218) 739-3356
Fergus Falls, MN 56537
Covers: About 200 developmental disability services in Becker, Clay, Douglas, Grant, Otter Tail, Pope, Stevens, Traverse, and Wilkin counties in Minnesota. **Entries include:** Facility name, address, phone, hours of operation, purpose, services offered eligibility requirements, disabilities served, fees. **Arrangement:** Geographical. **Indexes:** Service provided. **Pages** (approx.): 75. **Frequency:** Irregular; latest edition June 1979. **Price:** Free.

★4422★

REHABILITATION/WORLD—HOST DIRECTORY: AMERICAN REHABILITATION FACILITIES THAT WELCOME PROFESSIONAL VISITORS

Rehabilitation International USA
20 W. 40th Street   Phone: (212) 869-0461
New York, NY 10018
Covers: About 300 rehabilitation facilities in 45 states. **Entries include:** Facility name, address, name and phone of director or contact, disabilities handled, programs offered, type of facility, number of staff, number of clients, whether guest accommodations are available. **Arrangement:** Geographical. **Pages** (approx.): 15. **Frequency:** Annual, June. **Advertising accepted.** Circulation 11,000. **Price:** Available as a reprint, $1.50.

★4423★

RESEARCH AWARDS INDEX [Health and medicine]

National Institutes of Health
Public Health Service
Health, Education, and Welfare Department
5333 Westbrand Avenue, Room OA03   Phone: (301) 496-7543
Bethesda, MD 20014
Covers: Over 30,000 PHS-supported research grants and contracts. In three volumes: subject index (9,000 headings); project identification list; principal investigator list. **Entries include:** Subject index includes project number and title; project identification list, by project number, shows project title, principal investigator's name and address; principal investigator list includes project number. **Pages** (approx.): 3,100. **Frequency:** Latest edition 1978; new edition expected spring 1980. **Price:** $35.50. **Send orders to:** Government Printing Office, Washington, DC 20402. **Other information:** Data base is partly machine readable and may be available for public use. The list of publications resulting from individual projects which was formerly included has been dropped. Sometimes cited as "Research Awards Index."

★4424★

RESEARCH DIRECTORY OF THE REHABILITATION RESEARCH AND TRAINING CENTERS

Rehabilitation Services Administration
Office of Human Development Services
Health, Education, and Welfare Department   Phone: (202) 245-0555
Washington, DC 20201
Covers: About 260 research projects of the 19 Rehabilitation Research and Training Centers. **Entries include:** Center name, address, name of director, project descriptions including name of principal investigator. **Arrangement:** By center. **Indexes:** Keyword, investigator name. **Pages** (approx.): 440. **Frequency:** Annual. **Editor:** Joseph Fenton. **Price:** $14.00, paper; $3.00, microfiche (PB 297-303). May also be available from agency. **Send orders to:** National Technical Information Service, Springfield, VA 22161.

Research Grants Index *See* Research Awards Index [Health and medicine]

Rhode Island Department of Health Health Planning Guide *See* Health Data Guide [Rhode Island]

★4425★

ROSTER OF DOCTORAL STUDENTS IN SCHOOLS OF PHARMACY

American Association of Schools of Pharmacy
4630 Montgomery Avenue, Suite 201   Phone: (301) 654-9060
Bethesda, MD 22014
Frequency: Annual. **Price:** $3.00, payment with order.

Roster of Teaching Personnel in Colleges of Pharmacy *See* AACP Roster of Teachers [Pharmacy]

Self-Help Directory *See* Help: A Working Guide to Self-Help Groups

Self-Help Reporter—Directory of Self-Help Groups Column *See* Help: A Working Guide to Self-Help Groups

★4426★

SENSORY AIDS FOR EMPLOYMENT OF BLIND AND VISUALLY IMPAIRED PERSONS: A RESOURCE GUIDE

American Foundation for the Blind
15 W. 16th Street   Phone: (212) 620-2000
New York, NY 10011
Covers: Sources for 150 special devices for blind and visually handicapped persons to enable employment. Some devices are in development. **Entries include:** Device name, function, employment application, description of device; name, address, and phone of source; availability; cost. **Arrangement:** By function categories (electrical measurements, typing aids, etc.). **Indexes:** Employment area, manufacturer and vendor name, foreign manufacturer and vendor, research and development, device. **Pages** (approx.): 210. **Frequency:** Not established; first edition 1979. **Editor:** Yvonne Russell. **Price:** $7.50 (large print or braille editions), payment must accompany orders from individuals. **Other information:** Compiled by the Sensory Aids Foundation of Palo Alto, CA.

★4427★

SEX THERAPY TODAY

Grove Press, Inc.
196 W. Houston Street   Phone: (212) 242-4900
New York, NY 10014
Publication includes: List of about 40 sex therapists. **Arrangement:** Geographical. **Indexes: Pages** (approx.): 235. **Frequency:** First published 1977. **Editors:** Patricia Gillan and Richard Gillan. **Price:** $4.95, plus 50¢ shipping. **Send orders to:** Random House, Order Department, Hahn Road, Westminster, MD 21157 (301-848-1900).

★4428★

SOCIETY OF TEACHERS OF FAMILY MEDICINE—MEMBERSHIP DIRECTORY

Society of Teachers of Family Medicine
1740 W. 92nd Street   Phone: (816) 333-9700
Kansas City, MO 64114
Covers: About 1,700 physicians and other individuals involved in teaching or promotion of family medicine; international coverage. **Entries include:** Name, office address, office phone, highest degree held, faculty title or rank. **Arrangement:** Alphabetical. **Pages** (approx.): 100. **Frequency:** Annual, summer. **Editor:** Nancy Davis, Staff Assistant. **Price:** $15.00.

★4429★

SPECIAL LISTINGS OF CURRENT CANCER RESEARCH

International Cancer Research Data Bank
National Cancer Institute
National Institutes of Health
Blair Building, Room 114
8300 Colesville Road   Phone: (301) 427-8759
Silver Spring, MD 20910
Background: "Special Listings of Current Cancer Research" is the

series names for periodic special directories of investigators and projects each covering one selected cancer research area; e. g., a recent listing covered "Gynecologic Cancer: Etiology, Epidemiology, Clinical Aspects, and Related Studies." An entry consists of a descriptive paragraph detailing each study's objectives, approach, and progress, with names, affiliations, and addresses of the principal investigator and co-investigators. Arrangement is by subject similarity within the field covered by the issue. Approximately 50-60 directories are issued each year. **Former title:** Current Cancer Research. **Price:** Available in paper copies and microfiche from National Technical Information Service, Springfield, VA 22161; prices vary according to length.

★4430★
STATE-APPROVED SCHOOLS OF NURSING—L.P.N./L.V.N.
National League for Nursing
10 Columbus Circle   Phone: (212) 582-1022
New York, NY 10019
Covers: Licensed practical nurse and licensed vocational nurse programs in 1,250 schools. **Entries include:** Name of school, address, types of programs, admission policies, type of administrative control, sources of financial support, length of program, information on state board approval and National League for Nursing accreditation. **Arrangement:** Geographical. **Pages** (approx.): 80. **Frequency:** Annual, August/September. **Price:** $4.95, postpaid, payment with order.

★4431★
STATE-APPROVED SCHOOLS OF NURSING—R.N.
National League for Nursing
10 Columbus Circle   Phone: (212) 582-1022
New York, NY 10019
Covers: Associate degree, baccalaureate degree, and diploma programs offered in 1,350 schools, leading to licensure as registered nurses. **Entries include:** Name of school, address, names of deans and directors of programs, type of administrative control, sources of financial support, and information on National League for Nursing accreditation status. **Arrangement:** Geographical. **Pages** (approx.): 75. **Frequency:** Annual, July/August. **Price:** $4.95, postpaid, payment with order.

★4432★
STRIKE BACK AT CANCER: WHAT TO DO AND WHERE TO GO FOR THE BEST MEDICAL CARE
Prentice-Hall, Inc.
Englewood Cliffs, NJ 07632
Covers: National Cancer Institute facilities, treatment centers, rehabilitation organizations, oncologists, and research specialists; coverage of treatment centers is international. **Entries include:** For treatment centers - Name, address, number of staff, number of beds, equipment available, number of reference library volumes, treatment methods. For other listings - Name, address, services. **Arrangement:** By type of service or activity, then geographical. **Pages** (approx.): 480. **Frequency:** Published 1978. **Editor:** Stephen A. Rapaport. **Price:** $12.95.

★4433★
SUMMER PROGRAMS FOR CHILDREN IN STATE SCHOOLS, STATE HOSPITALS, STATE HOSPITAL SCHOOLS [Massachusetts]
Massachusetts Department of Education
31 St. James Avenue
Boston, MA 02116
Covers: About 110 recreational summer programs for institutionalized or multiply handicapped children. **Entries include:** Camp name, address, phone; sponsor name; contact name, address, and phone; fees; description of programs; activities; number of staff; physical setting; medical facilities and personnel available. Day camp listings have slightly less detail. **Arrangement:** Geographical. **Pages** (approx.): 325. **Frequency:** Irregular; latest edition winter 1977. **Price:** Free. **Also includes:** Chart listing camps with disabilities accepted and camper characteristics.

★4434★
SURGICAL TRADE BUYERS GUIDE
Cassak Publications, Inc.
2009 Morris Avenue   Phone: (201) 687-8282
Union, NJ 07083
Covers: 2,000 manufacturers of hospital and physician's supplies and equipment; medical laboratory, oxygen therapy, and X-ray supplies and equipment; patient aid products; and orthopedic appliances. **Entries include:** For manufacturers - Company name and address. **Arrangement:** Alphabetical. **Indexes:** Product. **Pages** (approx.): 450. **Frequency:** Annual, July. **Editor:** Laurie Cassak. **Advertising accepted.** Circulation 4,600. **Price:** $15.00.

★4435★
TAY-SACHS TEST CENTER DIRECTORY & GUIDE
National Tay-Sachs & Allied Diseases Association
122 E. 42nd Street
New York, NY 10017
Covers: Centers with programs of detection, prevention, and research into Tay-Sachs and allied degenerative lysosomal and neurological diseases occuring in infants and children. **Arrangement:** Geographical. **Frequency:** Irregular; new edition expected January 1980. **Price:** Free.

★4436★
TEL-MED OFFICE DIRECTORY
Tel-Med
22700 Cooley Drive   Phone: (714) 825-6034
Colton, CA 92324
Covers: About 200 Tel-Med offices country-wide (many with state-wide toll-free numbers) which play for callers on request any of over 300 taped discussions of common medical problems (vaginitis, measles, unsatisfactory sexual response, etc.). **Entries include:** Office name, phone. **Arrangement:** Geographical. **Price:** Free.

★4437★
TRAINING DIRECTORY OF THE REHABILITATION RESEARCH AND TRAINING CENTERS
Rehabilitation Services Administration
Office of Human Development Services
Health, Education, and Welfare Department   Phone: (202) 245-0555
Washington, DC 20201
Covers: Over 300 short- and long-term courses, workshops, conferences, etc., offered by the 19 medical, vocational, mental retardation, and deafness Rehabilitation Research and Training Centers. **Entries include:** Center name and, for each course, the course name, instructor, objectives, trainees for whom course is intended, schedule, and name and address of contact. **Arrangement:** By center. **Indexes:** Keyword. **Pages** (approx.): 175. **Frequency:** Annual. **Editor:** Joseph Fenton. **Price:** $9.25, paper; $3.00, microfiche (PB 297-719). May also be available from agency. **Send orders to:** National Technical Information Service, Springfield, VA 22161.

★4438★
200 WAYS TO PUT YOUR TALENT TO WORK IN THE HEALTH FIELD
National Health Council
1740 Broadway
New York, NY 10019
Covers: Professional associations, government agencies, institutions, and other organizations offering information or assistance concerning health career education. **Entries include:** Organization name, address. **Arrangement:** By occupation. **Frequency:** Irregular; latest edition 1979. **Former title:** Where to Get Health Career Information. **Price:** Single copies free. **Send orders to:** "200 Ways," Box 40, Radio City Station, New York, NY 10019.

★4439★
U.S. FACILITIES AND PROGRAMS FOR CHILDREN WITH SEVERE MENTAL ILLNESSES: A DIRECTORY
National Institute of Mental Health
Health, Education, and Welfare Department
5600 Fishers Lane
Rockville, MD 20852
Covers: About 500 known facilities and programs; separate list of facilities believed to provide children's services. Includes associations concerned with autistic children. **Entries include:** Facility name, address, phone, type (day, residential, etc.), year established, capacity, fees, physical description, admission criteria, parent participation, staff (number of certifications, etc.), and description of program offered. **Arrangement:** Geographical. **Indexes:** Alphabetical by facility name, in form of chart showing facilities offered. **Pages** (approx.): 450. **Frequency:** Irregular; latest edition 1977. **Price:** $5.00 (S/N 017-024-00689-1). **Send orders to:** Government Printing Office, Washington, DC 20402. **Other information:** Compiled by National Society for Autistic Children. Variant title, "National Directory of Services and Programs for Autistic Children."

★4440★
U.S. MEDICAL DIRECTORY
U. S. Directory Service
121 S. E. First Street
Miami, FL 33101
Background: The Reference and Subscription Books Committee of the American Library Association found in reviewing this publication that a substantial portion of it was reprinted from a 1975 Social Security Administration directory, that the listing of physicians was "far from complete" (12 physicians in Mobile, Alabama, for example, though the American Medical Association lists over 300), and that the publisher was uncooperative, leading the committee to "assume that, for some reason, the publishers wish to withhold certain information about the compilation of this book." (For review, see "Booklist," June 15, 1978, pages 1640-41.) **Frequency:** Irregular; latest edition 1977. **Price:** $45.00 (ISSN 0091-8393).

★4441★
U.S. PHYSICIAN REFERENCE LISTING
Fisher-Stevens, Inc.
120 Brighton Road   Phone: (201) 471-4000
Clifton, NJ 07012
Covers: 175,000 physicians; data taken from American Medical Association files. **Entries include:** Physician name, address, specialty, type of practice, board certifications, professional societies, year of birth, medical school, and year of graduation. **Arrangement:** Geographical. **Indexes:** Alphabetical (includes name, city, and state). **Pages** (approx.): Geographical portion (10 volumes), 2,500; alphabetical index (3 volumes), 700. **Frequency:** Annual, June. **Price:** Available to insurance companies only per 1977 ruling by American Medical Association.

★4442★
UNLISTED DRUGS INDEX-GUIDE
Pharmaco-Medical Documentation, Inc.
205 Main Street   Phone: (201) 635-9500
Chatham, NJ 07928
Covers: Medicinal drugs presently in use which are not listed in the United States Pharmacopeia, and their manufacturers; international coverage. **Entries include:** Company name, address. **Arrangement:** Alphabetical by company name, mnemonic code name; addresses in both sections. **Indexes:** Trade and generic name, investigational-drug code number. **Pages** (approx.): 650. **Frequency:** Irregular; latest edition 1977; new edition expected 1980. **Editor:** Boris R. Anzlowar. **Price:** $340.00.

Urban Federation for Music Therapists—Membership Directory *See* American Association for Music Therapy—Membership Directory

★4443★
VIDEOLOG: PROGRAMS FOR THE HEALTH SCIENCES
Esselte Video, Inc.
600 Madison Avenue   Phone: (212) 753-7530
New York, NY 10022
Covers: Over 1,500 producers and distributors of videotape programs in health care subjects, including patient education programs. **Entries include:** Company name, address, phone, contact person. **Arrangement:** Alphabetical. **Indexes:** Subject, titles by company name. **Pages** (approx.): 400. **Frequency:** About every 18 months; latest edition 1979; new edition expected January 1981. **Editor:** Lawrence Eidelberg. **Former title:** Health Sciences Video Directory (1979). **Price:** $35.00, plus $1.00 shipping. **Send orders to:** Esselte Video, Inc., Box 987, Edison, NJ 08817 (201-225-1900). **Other information:** Primary content is annotated entries describing about 7,000 videotapes.

★4444★
WELL BEING MAGAZINE—HERBS AND HEALING COLUMN
Well Being Productions
Box 1829   Phone: (714) 234-2211
Santa Cruz, CA 95061
Publication includes: List of natural healing schools, sources for herb plants and seeds, and herb walks. **Frequency:** Column is now irregular.

★4445★
WELLNESS: THE YES! BOOKSHOP GUIDE [Holistic healing]
Yes! Bookshop
1035 31st Street, N. W.   Phone: (202) 338-7874
Washington, DC 20007
Publication includes: List of publishers of about 1,500 books on holistic health care. **Entries include:** Publisher name, address. **Arrangement:** Publishers are alphabetical, books are by subject. **Indexes:** Author. **Frequency:** Not established; first edition October 1977; new edition expected 1981. Supplements issued semiannually. **Editor:** Cris Popenoe. **Price:** $4.95, postpaid. **Other information:** Primary content of publication is annotated bibliographical listings of available publications in fields mentioned.

Where to Get Health Career Information *See* 200 Ways to Put Your Talent to Work in the Health Field

★4446★
WHERE TO GET HELP FOR KIDS: A GUIDE TO AGENCIES...FOR ABUSED, EMOTIONALLY DISTURBED AND PHYSICALLY HANDICAPPED CHILDREN
Gaylord Brothers, Inc.
Box 4901   Phone: (315) 457-5070
Syracuse, NY 13221
Covers: Public agencies and private facilities offering services for the emotionally and physically handicapped child; services range from consultation and referral to education and treatment. **Entries include:** Name of agency or service, address, eligibility, fee scale, capacity (number of beds), and programs or services available. **Arrangement:** Geographical. **Pages** (approx.): 400. **Frequency:** Biennial, fall of odd years; first edition 1979. **Editor:** Gwendolyn T. Davis. **Price:** $29.95. **Other information:** Published in association with Neal-Schuman Publishers.

★4447★
WHOLISTIC DIMENSIONS IN HEALING: A RESOURCE GUIDE
Dolphin Books
Doubleday & Company, Inc.
245 Park Avenue   Phone: (212) 953-4587
New York, NY 10017
Publication includes: Lists of associations, groups, schools, publishers, treatment facilities, and manufacturers and suppliers concerned with holistic health; includes some resources abroad. Covers hypnosis, biofeedback, astrology, preventive nutrition; art, dance, and music therapy; and other modalities. **Entries include:** Resource name, address, phone, name of contact, description of

activities, services, products, etc. **Arrangement:** By broad general subjects. **Frequency:** First edition fall 1978. **Author:** Leslie J. Kaslof. **Price:** $7..95.

★4448★

WHO'S WHO IN CHILDBIRTH EDUCATION

American Society for Psychoprophylaxis in Obstetrics
1411 K Street, N. W., Suite 200   Phone: (202) 783-7050
Washington, DC 20005
Covers: About 2,200 certified childbirth educators and physicians; includes nonmembers; international coverage. **Entries include:** Name, office address and phone, home address and phone. **Arrangement:** Alphabetical within teacher and physician member categories. **Indexes:** Geographical. **Pages** (approx.): 130. **Frequency:** Usually annual, fall. **Editor:** Cassandra Roberts, Membership Manager. **Price:** $6.00.

★4449★

WHO'S WHO IN CHIROPRACTIC INTERNATIONAL

WWIC International Publishing Company, Inc.
3152 E. Weaver Avenue   Phone: (303) 333-1581
Littleton, CO 80121
Covers: 450 leading chiropractic doctors; publisher states they were selected by peer review. **Entries include:** Name of individual, address, and personal, educational and professional data. **Arrangement:** Alphabetical. **Pages** (approx.): 215. **Frequency:** First edition 1977; new edition expected 1980; thereafter, expected to be biennial, fall of even years. **Editor:** Fern L. Dzaman. **Price:** $49.50 (current edition); $55.00 (1980 edition). **Also includes:** List of educational institutions offering programs in chiropractic. **Other information:** 1980 edition will list 1,500 doctors in 450 pages.

Who's Who in Preventive Medicine *See* International Academy of Preventive Medicine—Membership Directory

★4450★

WHO'S WHO IN THE DENTAL LABORATORY INDUSTRY

National Association of Dental Laboratories
3801 Mt. Vernon Avenue   Phone: (703) 683-5265
Alexandria, VA 22305
Covers: About 3,300 dental laboratories, 12,000 certified dental technicians, and schools of dental technology. **Entries include:** Name, address, and, for laboratories, list of products and services. **Pages** (approx.): 150. **Frequency:** Annual, January. **Editor:** Audrey J. Calomino, Managing Editor. **Advertising accepted.** Circulation 15,000. **Former title:** National Board for Certification in Dental Technology - Directory. **Price:** $30.00 (current and 1980 editions).

World Buyers Guide and Directory for the Hearing Instruments Industry *See* Hearing Aid Journal—World Buyers Guide and Directory Issue

★4451★

WORLD DIRECTORY OF MEDICAL SCHOOLS

World Health Organization
Avenue Appia
Ch-1211 Geneva 27, Switzerland
Covers: Undergraduate medical teaching institutions in 105 countries. **Entries include:** Name of institution, address, year in which instruction began, requirements of admission, duration of program, language of instruction, degree awarded, number of students and graduates broken down by nationals and foreigners. **Arrangement:** Geographical. **Pages** (approx.): 360. **Frequency:** Irregular; latest edition 1979 (1975-76 data). **Price:** 30.00 Swiss Francs. **Send orders to:** WHO Publications Center USA, 49 Sheridan Ave., Albany, NY 12210. **Other information:** Separate editions in English and French.

★4452★

WORLD DIRECTORY OF PHARMACEUTICAL MANUFACTURERS

IMSWORLD Publications Ltd.
York House, 37 Queen Square
London WC1N 3BH, England
Covers: Over 2,000 leading drug companies in over 30 major markets which account for over 90% of the non-Communist world's drug sales. **Entries include:** Company name, address, phone, telex number, list of products or services, parent company and subsidiaries (if any), company's leading products listed by trade name and therapeutic category (including approximate total number of products marketed). **Arrangement:** By country. **Pages** (approx.): 300. **Frequency:** Biennial, even years. **Editor:** N. S. Hey, Editorial Director. **Price:** $125.00.

★4453★

WORLD DIRECTORY OF SCHOOLS FOR MEDICAL ASSISTANTS

World Health Organization
Avenue Appia
Ch-1211 Geneva 27, Switzerland
Covers: Schools for medical assistants, worldwide. **Entries include:** Name of school, address, admission requirements, length of training, language of instruction, curriculum information, and graduation requirements. **Arrangement:** Geographical. **Pages** (approx.): 115. **Frequency:** Irregular; latest edition 1976 (1973 data). **Price:** 24.00 Swiss Francs. **Send orders to:** WHO Publications Center USA, 49 Sheridan Ave., Albany, NY 12210. **Other information:** Bilingual in English and French.

★4454★

WRITING FOR NURSING PUBLICATIONS

Charles B. Slack, Inc.
6900 Grove Road   Phone: (609) 848-1000
Thorofare, NJ 08086
Publication includes: List of about 60 nursing publications. **Entries include:** Name of publication, address, information on intended audience and subject content. **Arrangement:** Alphabetical. **Frequency:** Not established; first edition 1976. **Editor:** Andrea B. O'Connor. **Price:** $6.50.

★4455★

YEARBOOK AND DIRECTORY OF OSTEOPATHIC PHYSICIANS

American Osteopathic Association
212 E. Ohio Street   Phone: (312) 944-2713
Chicago, IL 60611
Entries include: Name, office or home address, institution granting degree. **Arrangement:** Alphabetical. **Indexes:** Geographical. **Pages** (approx.): 525. **Frequency:** Annual, September. **Editor:** George W. Northup, D.O. **Advertising accepted.** Circulation 14,000. **Price:** $35.00.

12

Religious, Ethnic,
and Fraternal Affairs

Accrediting Association of Bible Colleges—Directory *See* American Association of Bible Colleges—Directory

American Arabic Speaking Almanac *See* Arab Americans Almanac

★4456★
AMERICAN ASSOCIATION OF BIBLE COLLEGES—DIRECTORY
American Association of Bible Colleges
Box 1523
Fayetteville, AR 72701
Covers: 110 schools accredited or under consideration by AABC. **Entries include:** Institution name, address, phone, year accredited, years of last and next evaluations, denominational affiliation, enrollment, programs, and administrators. **Arrangement:** Alphabetical within classes of accreditation. **Pages** (approx.): 15. **Frequency:** Annual, December. **Editor:** John Mostert, Executive Director. **Former title:** Accrediting Association of Bible Colleges - Directory (1973). **Price:** 25¢.

★4457★
AMERICAN ASSOCIATION OF PASTORAL COUNSELORS— DIRECTORY
American Association of Pastoral Counselors
3000 Connecticut Avenue, N. W., Suite 300   Phone: (202) 387-0031
Washington, DC 20008
Number of listings: 1,800. **Entries include:** Name, address, and level of membership. **Pages** (approx.): 115. **Frequency:** Annual, September. **Price:** $2.00.

★4458★
AMERICAN INDIAN CALENDAR
Bureau of Indian Affairs
Interior Department
19th and C Streets   Phone: (202) 343-7445
Washington, DC 20242
Covers: Over 300 events ranging from exhibits of native art to whaling festivals to powwows in Alaska and the lower United States. Includes Bureau field offices able to provide current information. **Entries include:** Event name, description, dates, location. **Arrangement:** Geographical, then chronological. **Pages** (approx.): 95. **Frequency:** Annual, spring. **Price:** $2.25 (S/N 024-002-00067-5). **Send orders to:** Government Printing Office, Washington, DC 20402.

★4459★
AMERICAN INDIAN REFERENCE BOOK
eARTh Art, Inc.
Box 2204   Phone: (703) 683-4925
Kalamazoo, MI 49003
Covers: 800 craft shops; 100 powwows, festivals, and dances; 250 federal reservations; 300 schools; and other organizations involved with American Indians. **Entries include:** Information suppled varies with the section, but normally includes name of shop, event, etc., address, and sometimes names of contact; may also include dates, statistics, etc., as appropriate. **Arrangement:** Classified by activity, subject, etc. **Pages** (approx.): 310. **Frequency:** Biennial, fall of even years. **Editor:** Nancy Grabiak, Co-owner. **Price:** $9.95, postpaid.

★4460★
AMERICAN JEWISH LANDMARKS
Fleet Press Corporation
160 Fifth Avenue   Phone: (212) 243-6100
New York, NY 10010
Covers: Jewish landmarks (memorials, birthplaces, synagogues, famous cemeteries, libraries), restaurants, and shops in the United States. **Entries include:** Name of landmark, address, annotation. **Arrangement:** Geographical. **Frequency:** Volume 1, "The Northeast," published 1977; Volume 2, "The South and Southwest," published 1979. Volume 3, "The Middle West and the West," due 1980-81. **Author:** Bernard Postal and Lionel Koppman. **Price:** Volume 1 - $18.50, cloth; $8.50, paper; Volume 2 - $13.95, cloth; $7.50, paper; plus $1.25 shipping per volume. **Other information:** A portion of Volume 1, "The Northeast," has been reprinted and marketed separately under the title, "Jewish Landmarks of New York;" $11.95, cloth; $5.95, paper.

★4461★
AMERICAN JEWISH ORGANIZATIONS DIRECTORY
Frenkel Mailing Service
24 Rutgers Street
New York, NY 10002
Publication includes: Jewish organizations, synagogues, and schools. **Entries include:** Name, address, phone, rabbi or key person for some listings, denomination, key indicating whether school, synagogue, or organization. **Arrangement:** Geographical. **Pages** (approx.): 180. **Frequency:** Biennial, late in even years. **Editor:** Louis Frenkel. **Advertising accepted.** Circulation 5,000. **Former title:** American Synagogue Directory (1969). **Price:** $15.00.

★4462★
AMERICAN JEWISH PRESS ASSOCIATION—ROSTER OF MEMBERS
C/o Jewish Exponent
226 S. 16th Street   Phone: (215) 893-5700
Philadlephia, PA 19102
Covers: About 70 privately owned and federation owned Jewish newspapers in the United States and Canada. **Entries include:** Title, type of membership, address, name and phone of editor; some listings also include name of assistant editor. **Arrangement:** Geographical. **Pages** (approx.): 10. **Frequency:** Annual, February. **Editor:** Frank F. Wundohl. **Price:** Available to members only.

★4463★
AMERICAN JEWISH YEARBOOK
Jewish Publication Society of America
117 S. 17th Street   Phone: (215) 564-5925
Philadelphia, PA 19103
Publication includes: 1,000 national Jewish organizations; national Jewish periodicals; Jewish federations and welfare funds. **Entries include:** Name, address, officers, and aims of organizations. **Arrangement:** Classified. **Indexes:** General. **Pages** (approx.): 650. **Frequency:** Annual, November. **Editor:** David Singer, Associate Editor. **Price:** $15.00. **Other information:** Co-published with the American Jewish Committee. Includes articles, necrology, calendar, demographic statistics.

American Synagogue Directory *See* American Jewish Organizations Directory

★4464★
AMERICA'S RELIGIOUS TREASURES
Harper & Row Publications, Inc.
10 E. 53rd Street
New York, NY 10022
Covers: Historic places of worship, early meeting houses, and memorials and shrines commemorating religious events or persons. **Entries include:** Site name, location, description of significance of the site; maps and illustrations are included for some sites. **Arrangement:** Geographical. **Pages** (approx.): 290. **Frequency:** First edition 1977. **Editors:** Marion Rawson Vuilleumier and Pierre DuPont Vuilleumier. **Price:** $9.95.

★4465★
ANGLO-JEWISH MEDIA LIST
R. K. Communications
98-15 65th Road
Rego Park, NY 11374
Covers: Over 330 Jewish news services, news weeklies, biweeklies, monthlies, national publications, house organs, and specialized journals. **Entries include:** Periodical titles; name, address, and phone of editor; name of sponsor; frequency; circulation; description of publication; whether news releases or inquiries by free-lance writers are welcomed. **Arrangement:** By type of publication (news services, Canadian press, special-interest journals, etc.). **Indexes:** Title. **Pages** (approx.): 55. **Frequency:** Latest edition 1979; new edition expected 1980. **Editor:** Ray Kesterbaum. **Advertising accepted.** **Price:** $38.00.

★4466★
ANNUAL DIRECTORY, HOUSES OF PRAYER
Clarity Publishing, Inc.
75 Champlain Street   Phone: (518) 465-4591
Albany, NY 12204
Covers: Over 130 Catholic houses of prayer and over 75 prayer/study experience centers. **Entries include:** Name of house or center, address, phone, sponsor, date founded, spirituality thrust, guest policy, fee (if any), whether brochure is available. Prayer house listings include special services, list of core members. Hermitage facilities include name of director. **Arrangement:** Both lists alphabetical.

Indexes: Geographical, type of guest served, specialty or focus. **Pages** (approx.): 150. **Frequency:** Annual, May. **Editor:** Patricia A. Crewell. **Price:** $9.95 (current edition; tentative, 1980 edition).

★4467★
ANNUAL DIRECTORY OF RELIGIOUS BROADCASTING
National Religious Broadcasters
38 Speedwell Avenue   Phone: (201) 540-8500
Morristown, NJ 07960
Covers: Over 2,200 radio stations, radio programs, television stations, program producers, advertising agencies, book publishers, recording companies, equipment manufacturers, and others concerned with religious broadcasting in all faiths. To qualify, radio and television stations must carry at least 15 hours of religious programs per week. **Entries include:** For stations - Call letters, address, phone; name of contact and/or names of key personnel. Other listings include producer, manufacturer, or company name, address, phone, name of contact; description of program or product. **Arrangement:** Stations are geographical, others are alphabetical within activity. **Indexes:** Radio call letter with location and frequency, radio program title. **Pages** (approx.): 330. **Frequency:** Annual, winter. **Editor:** Dr. Benjamin L. Armstrong, Executive Director. **Advertising accepted.** Circulation 5,000. **Price:** $15.00, plus $2.00 shipping.

★4468★
ARAB AMERICANS ALMANAC
News Circle Publishing Company
Box 74637   Phone: (213) 469-7004
Los Angeles, CA 90004
Covers: Arab American communities, organizations, churches and mosques, leaders, and newspapers and radio programs. **Entries include:** Name (of community, organization, church, newspaper, etc.), address. Who's who section includes biographical material. **Arrangement:** Five directory sections: Arab American communities in United States; cultural, political and other local and national organizations; biographical sketches of prominent Arab American personalities; churches and mosques; newspapers and radio programs. **Pages** (approx.): 320. **Frequency:** Biennial; new edition expected July 1980. **Editor:** Joseph R. Haiek. **Advertising accepted.** Circulation 5,000. **Price:** $4.95 (current edition); $12.00 (1980 edition).

★4469★
ARAB-AMERICANS AND THEIR ORGANIZATIONS
American Jewish Committee
165 E. 56th Street
New York, NY 10022
Covers: Arab American political, social, religious, and other groups in the United States. **Entries include:** Organization name, address. **Pages** (approx.): 20. **Frequency:** Not established; first edition May 1978. **Editor:** Sheba Mittelman. **Price:** 50¢.

★4470★
ARIZONA COMMISSION OF INDIAN AFFAIRS—TRIBAL DIRECTORY
Arizona Commission of Indian Affairs
1645 W. Jefferson   Phone: (602) 271-3123
Phoenix, AZ 85007
Covers: Indian tribes and associations, government agencies, and other organizations concerned with Indian affairs in Arizona. **Entries include:** Listings for tribes show name, list of officers with addresses, list of council and committee members with phone numbers, meeting and election information, office address and phone; listings for associations show name, address, phone, list of officers, meeting details. **Arrangement:** Classified into 10 categories (Reservations, Indian Associations, Education, Employment, etc.). **Pages** (approx.): 70. **Frequency:** Annual, summer. **Editor:** Diane C. Dankerl, Administrative Secretary. **Price:** Free.

★4471★
ASIAN AMERICAN REFERENCE DATA DIRECTORY [Information note]
Division of Asian American Affairs
Health, Education, and Welfare Department   Phone: (202) 245-7515
Washington, DC 20201
Description: Not a directory, but a 1976 bibliography containing full abstracts of some 480 of the ''major reference materials related to the health, education, and social welfare characteristics of Asian Americans.'' **Price:** $9.25 (S/N 017-000-00193-1). **Send orders to:** Government Printing Office, Washington, DC 20402.

★4472★
ASSOCIATED CHURCH PRESS DIRECTORY
Associated Church Press
321 James Street   Phone: (312) 232-1055
Geneva, IL 60134
Covers: About 115 periodicals issued by member religious organizations of Christian denominations and their publishing houses; some Christian independent publishers are also included. **Entries include:** Title, address, phone, and name and phone of editor; name of publisher (and sponsoring organization, if different); description of publication including type or content, price, frequency, circulation, whether adveritsing is accepted, etc. **Arrangement:** Alphabetical. **Indexes:** Geographical, personal name. **Pages** (approx.): 45. **Frequency:** Annual, fall. **Editor:** Donald F. Hetzler, Executive Secretary. **Advertising accepted. Arrangement:** Circulation 500. **Price:** $20.00 to business firms; $6.00 to libraries and individuals.

★4473★
ASSOCIATION FOR CREATIVE CHANGE WITHIN RELIGIONS AND OTHER SOCIAL SYSTEMS—ANNUAL DIRECTORY
Association for Creative Change
Box 2212   Phone: (315) 424-1802
Syracuse, NY 13210
Covers: 700 members in the United States, Canada, and abroad. **Entries include:** Name, office and home addresses and phone numbers, areas of specialization. **Arrangement:** Geographical. **Indexes:** Alphabetical, specialization. **Pages** (approx.): 80. **Frequency:** Annual, September. **Editor:** Dorothy J. Brittain, Executive Director. **Former title:** Association for Religion and Applied Behavioral Science - Annual Directory. **Price:** $5.00.

Association for Religion & Applied Behaviorial Science—Annual Directory *See* Association for Creative Change within Religions...

★4474★
ASSOCIATION FOR THE SOCIOLOGY OF RELIGION—DIRECTORY OF MEMBERS
Association for the Sociology of Religion
C/o Dr. Robert McNamara
Loyola University of Chicago
6525 N. Sheridan Road   Phone: (312) 274-3000
Chicago, IL 60626
Number of listings: 1,400. **Entries include:** Name, office address, special interests in the field. **Pages** (approx.): 80. **Frequency:** Annual, January; quarterly supplements. **Editor:** Roger D. Irle, Executive Secretary. **Price:** $5.00 (1980 edition).

★4475★
ASSOCIATION OF JEWISH LIBRARIES—MEMBERSHIP LIST
Association of Jewish Libraries
C/o National Foundation for Jewish Culture
122 E. 42nd Street, Room 1512
New York, NY 10017
Covers: 450 Judaica libraries or librarians in United States, Canada, or Mexico City. **Entries include:** For libraries - Name, address, personnel. For individuals - Name, address. **Arrangement:** Geographical. **Pages** (approx.): 20. **Frequency:** Annual, March. **Editor:** Mary G. Brand, Treasurer. **Price:** $20.00.

Association of Theological Schools—Directory *See* ATS Bulletin—Directory Issue [Theological schools]

★4476★
ATS BULLETIN—DIRECTORY ISSUE [Theological schools]
Association of Theological Schools
Box 130   Phone: (513) 898-4654
Vandalia, OH 45377
Covers: About 200 seminaries and theological colleges representing nearly 50 denominations in the United States and Canada. **Entries include:** For accredited and associate schools - Name, address, phone, president or dean, denomination, enrollment, number of faculty, library resources, degrees offered. For clusters and consortia - Name, address, phone, chairman, names of member schools. **Arrangement:** Alphabetical within membership categories. **Indexes:** Geographical and by denominational affiliation. **Pages** (approx.): 65. **Frequency:** Annual, February. **Editor:** Charlotte M. Thompson, Director of Administrative Services. **Price:** $1.50, plus 60¢ shipping.

★4477★
BAPTIST MISSIONARY ASSOCIATION OF AMERICA—DIRECTORY AND HANDBOOK
Baptist News Service
Baptist Missionary Association of America
Box 97   Phone: (214) 586-8617
Jacksonville, TX 75766
Covers: Commissions, agencies, missions, and committees of the Baptist Missionary Association of America, affiliated schools, state and regional associations of congregations, individual church congregations, missionaries, ministers, and music, education, and youth directors ordained or affiliated with the association. **Entries include:** All listings include name of agency, person, or church; address. Most listings also include phone. Church listings include name of clerk and association affiliation. Church association listings include name and address of association moderator, clerk, and treasurer; names of churches, town, date founded, name of pastor, name of church clerk, membership and financial statistics. **Arrangement:** By type of organization or person's occupation; association committees and schools are alphabetical, others are primarily geographical. **Pages** (approx.): 260. **Frequency:** Annual, fall. **Editor:** Leon Gaylor, Director. **Price:** $2.50.

★4478★
BAPTIST PUBLIC RELATIONS ASSOCIATION—DIRECTORY
Baptist Public Relations Association
460 James Robertson Parkway   Phone: (615) 244-2355
Nashville, TN 37219
Number of listings: 350. **Entries include:** Name, office address and office phone. **Arrangement:** Alphabetical. **Pages** (approx.): 30. **Frequency:** Annual, April. **Editor:** Patsy Winfrey, Secretary. **Price:** $5.00 (current and 1980 editions).

Black Newspaper in America: A Guide *See* Survey of Black Newspapers in America

★4479★
BLACK PRESS PERIODICAL DIRECTORY
Black Newspaper Clipping Bureau, Inc.
68 E. 131st Street   Phone: (212) 281-6000
New York, NY 10037
Covers: Newspapers, magazines, newsletters, radio stations, and news services in the United States and abroad which are Black owned or oriented. Includes list of American Indian news sources. **Pages** (approx.): 100. **Frequency:** Biennial, odd years; upddated quarterly; 1979 edition delayed to early 1980. **Editor:** Lawrence T. Jackson, Research Director. **Advertising accepted.** Circulation 3,000. **Price:** $40.00.

Blue Book: Directory and Buyers Guide to the Churches,
    Synagogues... [New York City] *See* Tablet Directory and
    Buyers Guide...

★4480★

BORN-AGAIN CHRISTIAN CATALOG

M. Evans and Company, Inc.
216 E. 49th Street
New York, NY 10017

Covers: Camps, schools, colleges, retirement communities, nursing homes, organizations for Jewish Christians, radio and TV broadcasting stations and other organizations, publishers, and entertainment primarily for fundamentalist, evangelical Christians. **Entries include:** For camps - Name, address, phone, name and address of director. For schools - Name, address, phone, faculty size, denomination, name of chief administrator, grade levels. For colleges - Name, location, phone, denomination, curriculum and fee data, etc. For retirement and nursing facilities - Name, address, phone, denomination, number of residents, whether certified for Medicare, costs and admissions data. For Jewish Christian organizations - Name, address, name of director, activities. For TV and radio stations - Call letters, city, frequency. Other listings include name, address, description of services or products. **Arrangement:** By type of activity or service, then usually geographical. **Indexes:** General. **Pages** (approx.): 290. **Frequency:** First edition 1979. **Editor:** William Proctor. **Price:** $6.95.

★4481★

BULLETIN UNITED BIBLE SOCIETIES—WORLD ANNUAL REPORT ISSUE

United Bible Societies
Box 755
Stuttgart, West Germany

Covers: 100 Bible societies worldwide affiliated with the United Bible Societies. **Entries include:** Society name, address; characteristics of area and population served; summary of scripture translation, production, and distribution activities. **Arrangement:** Geographical. **Pages** (approx.): 170. **Frequency:** Annual, April or May. **Price:** $1.00 (1980 edition). **Send orders to:** American Bible Society, 1865 Broadway, New York, NY 10023. **Other information:** Supersedes former separate publication, "United Bible Societies - Directory."

★4482★

CALIFORNIA DIRECTORY OF PSI SERVICES

Inner-Space Interpreters
Box 1133
Magnolia Park Station   Phone: (213) 843-0476
Burbank, CA 91507

Covers: Over 400 organizations, individuals, and services concerned with psychic faculties and phenomena, including New Age groups, extrasensory perception and related subjects, esoteric wisdom, inner-self exploration, etc. **Entries include:** Name of organization or individual, address, phone, comment on interest or activities. **Pages** (approx.): 120. **Frequency:** Irregular; latest edition 1978. **Editor:** Elizabeth M. Werner. **Price:** $3.00, plus 40¢ shipping, payment with order.

★4483★

CALIFORNIA INDIANS: PRIMARY RESOURCES; A GUIDE TO MANUSCRIPTS, DOCUMENTS, SERIALS, MUSIC, AND ILLUSTRATIONS

Ballena Press
Box 1366
Socorro, NM 87801

Covers: Archives with print and nonprint materials for research on California Indians; coverage is worldwide; local historical societies and private collections are excluded. **Entries include:** Archive or institution name, address, description of holdings. **Arrangement:** Geographical. **Indexes:** Subject. **Pages** (approx.): 230. **Frequency:** Published 1977. **Editors:** Lowell John Bean and Sylvia Brakke Vane. **Price:** Out of print, no new edition planned; available in libraries.

CARA Seminary Directory *See* U.S. Catholic Institutions for the
    Training of Candidates for the Priesthood

★4484★

CAREER DEVELOPMENT OPPORTUNITIES FOR NATIVE AMERICANS

Office of Indian Educational Programs
Bureau of Indian Affairs
Interior Department
1951 Constitution Avenue, N. W.   Phone: (202) 343-7387
Washington, DC 20245

Covers: Financial aids available to American Indian and Alaskan natives at postsecondary level. **Pages** (approx.): 60. **Frequency:** Irregular; latest edition fall 1979. **Editor:** Leroy Falling, Chief, Division of Postsecondary Education. **Former title:** Scholarships for American Indians (1975). **Price:** Free.

★4485★

CATHOLIC PRESS DIRECTORY

Catholic Press Association
119 N. Park Avenue   Phone: (516) 766-3400
Rockville Centre, NY 11570

Covers: Catholic magazines and dioscesan newspapers and directories. **Entries include:** Title of publication, publisher's name, address, phone, names and titles of executives, circulation, circulation area, advertising rates, mechanical requirements. **Arrangement:** Newspapers are geographical, magazines are alphabetical. **Indexes:** Title. **Pages** (approx.): 125. **Frequency:** Annual, fall. **Editor:** Rev. Msgr. John S. Randall. **Advertising accepted.** Circulation 2,000. **Price:** $10.00. **Other information:** List of diocesan directories (with title and address), omitted from recent editions, was restored beginning with 1977 edition.

Catholic Retreat Centers in North America *See* Directory of
    Catholic Retreat Houses in United States and Canada

★4486★

CATHOLIC TELEPHONE GUIDE [New York-New Jersey]

Catholic News Publishing Company
80 W. Broad Street   Phone: (914) 664-8100
Mt. Vernon, NY 10552

Covers: 265 religious communities, 1,525 churches, 1,400 schools, and 750 other Catholic institutions within the eight dioceses in the greater New York-New Jersey area. Also includes a list of priests, Catholic organizations, nursing homes, summer camps, and Catholic publications. **Entries include:** Institution name, address, phone, name of principal, superior, etc. **Arrangement:** Geographical. **Pages** (approx.): 340. **Frequency:** Annual. **Editor:** Victor L. Ridder. **Advertising accepted.** Circulation 8,500. **Price:** $15.00 (current and 1980 editions).

★4487★

CATHOLIC THEOLOGICAL SOCIETY OF AMERICA—DIRECTORY

Catholic Theological Society of America
C/o Br. Luke Salm, F. S. C.
Manhattan College   Phone: (212) 548-1400
Bronx, NY 10471

Covers: 1,150 Catholic theologians in the United States and Canada. **Entries include:** Name, office address, highest degree held, areas of occupational specialization, personal data, writings and publications. **Arrangement:** By type of membership, then alphabetical. **Pages** (approx.): 130. **Frequency:** Irregular; latest edition 1977. Updated annually by appendix to association's "Proceedings." **Editor:** Br. Luke Salm, F. S. C., Executive Secretary. **Price:** $5.00.

★4488★

CHRISTIAN BOOKSELLERS ASSOCIATION—SUPPLIERS DIRECTORY

Christian Booksellers Association
2620 Venetucci Boulevard   Phone: (303) 576-7880
Colorado Springs, CO 80901
Covers: Over 850 manufacturers and distributors of religious books, Bibles, Sunday school and church supplies and other products sold in religious bookstores. **Entries include:** Company name, address, phone, names of key executives, list of products or services, trade policy, volume discounts available. **Arrangement:** Alphabetical. **Indexes:** Product, toll free phone number, single title order plan, blank check order system, co-op ad policy, foreign language product. **Pages** (approx.): 650. **Frequency:** Annual, February. **Editor:** Gary Foster, Publication Director. **Advertising accepted.** Circulation 5,000. **Price:** $54.95.

★4489★

CHRISTIAN YELLOW PAGES

Walter R. Thomson, Manager
Christian Yellow Pages
802 E. Imperial Highway   Phone: (209) 869-0936
Downey, CA
Background: Publications titled ''Christian Yellow Pages'' are distributed in a number of cities nationally on the basis of franchises from the Christian Yellow Pages organization. The publications consist primarily of paid product- or service-classified listings of businesses, as in conventional yellow page telephone directories. ''Christian Yellow Pages,'' however, accepts advertising only from persons who sign statements to the effect that they are ''born again Christians.'' **Other information:** The ''New York Times'' reported in its September 7, 1977 edition (page 48) that the Christian Yellow Pages organization had been made the defendant in a suit filed by the Anti-Defamation League of B'nai B'rith, charging that restriction of advertising in the publications violated various California laws relating to religious discrimination and unfair competition. In Nashville, Tennessee, local publishers of a 1979 ''Christian Yellow Pages'' defended their publication as being no different from diocesan directories published by Catholic newspapers or the ''Jewish Yellow Pages'' or ''Black Yellow Pages.'' (Not verified)

★4490★

COLLEGE GUIDE FOR JEWISH YOUTH

B'nai B'rith Career and Counseling Services
B'nai B'rith Hillel Foundations
1640 Rhode Island Avenue, N. W.
Washington, DC 20036
Covers: About 350 colleges and universities having at least 25 Jewish students; coverage includes the United States and Canada. Institutions with facilities for the handicapped are listed separately. **Entries include:** Institution name, address, enrollment (total and Jewish), type of setting, sponsorship, Jewish facilities with addresses, and other items of interest. **Arrangement:** Geographical region, then alphabetical. Institutions with handicapped facilities are also geographical, then by handicap. **Indexes:** Institution name. **Pages** (approx.): 190. **Frequency:** Irregular; latest edition 1978. **Editors:** S. Norman Feingold, Samuel Z. Fishman, and Philip B. Aaronson. **Price:** $6.95, postpaid.

★4491★

CONFERENCE OF MAJOR SUPERIORS OF MEN OF THE USA— DIRECTORY

Conference of Major Superiors of Men of the USA
1302 18th Street, N. W., Suite 601   Phone: (202) 223-4164
Washington, DC 20036
Covers: About 265 major religious superiors of the various Roman Catholic religious orders of men. **Entries include:** Name, address, phone. **Arrangement:** Classified by religious order, then alphabetical. **Pages** (approx.): 50. **Frequency:** Annual, September. **Editor:** Donald P. Skwor, SDS, Associate Secretary. **Price:** Apply.

★4492★

D.C. DIRECTORY OF NATIVE AMERICAN FEDERAL AND PRIVATE PROGRAMS

American Indian Program
Phelps-Stokes Fund
1029 Vermont Avenue, N. W., Suite 1100   Phone: (202) 638-7066
Washington, DC 20005
Covers: Over 90 programs of interest to American Indians sponsored by federal and private groups and by Indian organizations. **Entries include:** Organization name, contact, address, phone. **Pages** (approx.): 20. **Frequency:** Approximately annual, with two updates per year and irregular supplemental material. **Price:** $25.00 per year; $5.00 per copy.

★4493★

DEVI DASI'S DIRECTORY [Psychics, etc.; Florida]

Devi Dasi's Directory
3903 Loquat Avenue   Phone: (305) 444-2630
Coconut Grove, FL 33133
Covers: Over 500 individuals, organizations, and services in Florida concerned with yoga, New Age, and other spiritual activities. **Pages** (approx.): 45. **Frequency:** Usually annual; latest edition fall 1979. **Editor:** Eleanore Micelli. **Advertising accepted.** **Price:** $2.00, payment with order.

★4494★

DIRECTORIO CHICANO: A RESOURCE LISTING OF CHICANO MEDIA

Southwest Network
1020 B Street, Suite 8
Hayward, CA 94544
Covers: 300 Chicano print and film resources. Print section lists research centers, publishers, distributors/booksellers, periodicals, and pinto newsletters (prisoners' house organs); includes inactive publications and groups. Film section lists independent Chicano producers/distributors and short list of films. **Entries include:** Print section listings give resource name and address; periodical listings give title, publisher, address, frequency, language, date founded, price, geographic scope. Film section gives name and address. **Pages** (approx.): 30. **Frequency:** Irregular; third edition May 1976; next edition 1977. **Editor:** Armando Valdez. **Price:** $1.00. (Not verified)

★4495★

DIRECTORY FOR A NEW WORLD

International Cooperation Council
9025 Wilshire Boulevard, Suite 311   Phone: (213) 998-7812
Beverly Hills, CA 90211
Covers: 250 organizations (nearly all in the United States) of primarily spiritual, psychological, or metaphysical orientation working to ''foster the emergence of a new universal person and civilization based on unity in diversity among all peoples.'' Includes supplemental list of several hundred organizations active in areas of interest to ICC. **Entries include:** Main entries include statement by each organization of its interests and objectives, with name of executive, address, and phone. **Arrangement:** Alphabetical. **Indexes:** Geographical (with address and phone). **Pages** (approx.): 345. **Frequency:** Annual, January. **Editor:** Leland P. Stewart, Executive Director. **Former title:** International Cooperation Council Directory: Planetary Guide to Cooperating Organizations Fostering a New Person and Civilization. **Price:** $7.95, plus $1.00 shipping, payment with order (current and 1980 editions).

★4496★

DIRECTORY OF AFRICAN & AFRO-AMERICAN STUDIES IN THE UNITED STATES

African Studies Association
Brandeis University
Epstein Building   Phone: (617) 899-3079
Waltham, MA 02154
Covers: About 625 institutions offering programs in African and Afro-American studies; about 300 other institutions have briefer listings. **Entries include:** For principal institutions - Name, address, courses

offered, faculty, library collections available, financial aid, and area of specialized study. For other institutions - Name, address, and courses offered. **Arrangement:** Geographical. **Indexes:** Institution name, language used in teaching. **Pages** (approx.): 320. **Frequency:** Irregular; latest edition 1979. **Editors:** Mitsue Frey and David Duffy. **Former title:** Directory of African Studies in the United States. **Price:** $30.00, payment with order.

★4497★
DIRECTORY OF ARMENIAN-AMERICAN SCHOLARS
Armenian Assembly Charitable Trust
522 21st Street, N. W.   Phone: (202) 833-1367
Washington, DC 20006
Covers: Individuals of Armenian heritage in America concerned with the study and preservation of the Armenian culture. **Entries include:** Name, address, title and affiliation; educational, personal, and career data; areas of study. **Arrangement:** Alphabetical. **Frequency:** Latest edition 1976; new edition planned. **Price:** Single copies free.

★4498★
DIRECTORY OF ASIAN AND AFRICAN LIBRARIANS IN NORTH AMERICA
Asian and African Section
Association of College and Research Libraries
American Library Association
50 E. Huron Street   Phone: (312) 944-6780
Chicago, IL 60611
Covers: About 460 librarians active in library services concerned with Asia and Africa (special language capabilities, cataloging, collection development, acquisitions, instruction, etc.) or members of the Asian and African Section of ALA. **Entries include:** Name, title, address. **Arrangement:** Alphabetical. **Pages** (approx.): 35. **Frequency:** Latest edition 1978. **Editor:** Henry Scholberg.

★4499★
DIRECTORY OF CATHOLIC COMMUNICATIONS PERSONNEL
Office of Public Affairs
U. S. Catholic Conference
1312 Massachusetts Avenue, N. W.,
  Room 510
Washington, DC 20005
Covers: About 250 communication and information directors and radio and television representatives for dioceses in the United States; also lists about 30 Catholic communications centers and other organizations and agencies, worldwide. **Entries include:** Organization name, address, phone, name and title of contact. **Arrangement: Entries include:** Geographical; centers and organizations listed separately. **Frequency:** Annual. **Price:** Free. **Send orders to:** (For 1979 edition only) Catholic Communications Foundation, 222 N. 17th Street, Suite 907, Philadelphia, PA.

★4500★
DIRECTORY OF CATHOLIC RETREAT HOUSES IN UNITED STATES AND CANADA
Retreats International
1112 Memorial Library   Phone: (219) 283-2764
Notre Dame, IN 46556
Number of listings: About 400. **Entries include:** Name, address, phone, number of rooms, kinds of programs. **Arrangement:** Geographical. **Pages** (approx.): 50. **Frequency:** Annual, January. **Editor:** Thomas W. Gedeon, SJ, Executive Director. **Price:** $10.00.

★4501★
DIRECTORY OF CHRISTIAN WORK OPPORTUNITIES
Intercristo
975 John Street   Phone: (206) 623-0715
Seattle, WA 98109
Covers: About 21,000 job openings with about 400 Christian organizations and agencies worldwide. **Arrangement:** Classified by type of job. **Indexes:** Agency, geographical, length of service. **Pages** (approx.): 925. **Frequency:** Annual, winter; supplement in the spring. **Advertising accepted. Price:** $29.50.

★4502★
DIRECTORY OF DAY SCHOOLS IN THE UNITED STATES, CANADA AND LATIN AMERICA [Jewish]
Torah Umesorah-National Society for Hebrew Day Schools
229 Park Avenue South   Phone: (212) 674-6700
New York, NY 10003
Covers: Approximately 500 elementary and secondary Hebrew day schools. **Entries include:** School name, address, phone, administrative personnel, grades, language of instruction, date of founding. **Arrangement:** Geographical. **Pages** (approx.): 40. **Frequency:** Biennial; new edition expected September 1980. **Editor:** Rabbi Yaakov Fruchter, Director of Publications. **Price:** $5.00.

★4503★
DIRECTORY OF DEPARTMENTS AND PROGRAMS OF RELIGION IN NORTH AMERICA
Council on the Study of Religion
Wilfrid Laurier University
Waterloo, Ontario N2L 3C5, Canada
Covers: Detailed listing of about 250 departments of religious studies or theology and schools of theology. Appendix listing for about 1,200 other departments, programs, and schools of religion. **Entries include:** For detailed listing - Name of institution and department, address, phone, enrollment, degrees offered and recent number of degrees, description of program, listing of faculty with information on their backgrounds. For appendix listing - Name and address. **Arrangement:** Alphabetical. **Indexes:** Geographical, personal name. **Pages** (approx.): 280. **Frequency:** Irregular; latest edition 1978; new edition expected 1981. **Editor:** Harold Remus. **Former title:** Directory of Religious Studies Programs, Departments of Religion in North America. **Price:** $4.50.

★4504★
DIRECTORY OF EPISCOPAL CHURCH SCHOOLS
National Association of Episcopal Schools
815 Second Avenue   Phone: (212) 867-8400
New York, NY 10017
Covers: About 800 Episcopal schools (nursery through grade 12) in the United States and a few overseas. **Entries include:** Name of school, address, phone, date of founding, grades encompassed, type of school, diocese, accreditation, enrollment. **Arrangement:** Geographical. **Pages** (approx.): 90. **Frequency:** Triennial; latest edition 1978. **Editor:** Susie Bennett, Executive Coordinator. **Price:** $2.50.

★4505★
DIRECTORY OF ETHNIC PUBLISHERS AND RESOURCE ORGANIZATIONS
Office for Library Service to the Disadvantaged
American Library Association
50 E. Huron Street   Phone: (312) 944-6780
Chicago, IL 60611
Covers: 280 organizations and publishers with strong or exclusive interests in ethnic and minority material. Traditional publishers whose publications are easily accessible are omitted. **Entries include:** Publisher or organization name, address, phone, major purpose and emphasis, list of publications. **Arrangement:** Alphabetical. **Indexes:** Subject, publishers who maintain archival or research centers. **Pages** (approx.): 90. **Frequency:** Irregular; latest edition 1979. **Editor:** Marjorie K. Joramo, Urban Affairs Librarian, Michigan State University. **Price:** $9.50.

★4506★
DIRECTORY OF ETHNIC STUDIES LIBRARIANS
Office for Library Service to the Disadvantaged
American Library Association
50 E. Huron Street   Phone: (312) 944-6780
Chicago, IL 60611
Covers: 250 librarians concerned with ethnic studies, ethnic collections, etc. **Entries include:** Names, addresses, employers, positions, and areas of responsibility or interest. **Arrangement:**

Alphabetical. **Indexes:** Type of library, geographical, institutional, subject. **Pages** (approx.): 100. **Frequency:** Published 1976 (now out of print); new edition date not determined. **Editor:** Beth J. Shapiro, Urban Policy and Planning Librarian, Michigan State University.

★4507★
DIRECTORY OF INFORMATION ON HEALTH CAREERS FOR AMERICAN INDIANS
National Educational Laboratory Publishers, Inc.
813 Airport Boulevard
Austin, TX 78702
Covers: About 85 associations, agencies, colleges, societies, and programs which can provide information on health careers; about 60 agencies, organizations, and other providers of financial aid for American Indians pursuing health careers; and about 15 training and education programs of the Public Health Service/Indian Health Service. **Entries include:** Organization name, address. **Arrangement:** By assistance offered. **Pages** (approx.): 30. **Frequency:** Irregular; latest edition January 1977. **Editor:** Raymond D. Apodaca. **Price:** 83¢, microfiche; $2.06, paper. **Send orders to:** ERIC Clearinghouse on Rural Education and Small Schools, New Mexico State University, University Park, NM.

★4508★
DIRECTORY OF JEWISH HEALTH AND WELFARE AGENCIES
Council of Jewish Federations
575 Lexington Avenue   Phone: (212) 751-1311
New York, NY 10022
Covers: Health and welfare services for individuals and families, children, youth, and adults; vocational services; housing and nursing homes for the elderly; and hospitals, supported partly or wholly by the council; United States and Canada are included. **Entries include:** Organization or facility name, address, phone, name of director. **Arrangement:** Geographical. **Pages** (approx.): 60. **Frequency:** Biennial, even years. **Price:** $5.00.

★4509★
DIRECTORY OF JEWISH HOMES FOR THE AGED IN THE UNITED STATES AND CANADA
National Association of Jewish Homes for the Aged
2525 Centerville Road   Phone: (214) 327-4503
Dallas, TX 75228
Covers: Nonprofit Jewish homes for the aged in the United States and Canada. **Entries include:** Facility name, address, number of beds, admission requirements and procedures, name of administrator and description of residents' characteristics. **Arrangement:** Geographical. **Pages** (approx.): 205. **Frequency:** Irregular; latest edition 1979. **Editor:** Dr. Herbert Shore. **Price:** $8.50.

★4510★
DIRECTORY OF MASONIC LIBRARIES
Masonic Service Association of the United States
8120 Fenton Street   Phone: (301) 588-4010
Silver Springs, MD 20910
Covers: About 50 libraries; unattended libraries, private collections, and lodge libraries are not included. **Entries include:** Group name, name of librarian (if any), address. **Arrangement:** Geographical. **Pages** (approx.): 5. **Frequency:** Latest edition 1979. **Price:** 50¢.

★4511★
DIRECTORY OF MINORITY MEDIA [San Francisco area]
San Francisco Redevelopment Agency
Box 646   Phone: (415) 771-8800
San Francisco, CA 94101
Covers: More than 50 radio stations, television stations, and publications oriented to Asian Americans, Blacks, Native Americans, and Spanish-speaking Americans. **Entries include:** Name of medium, name of contact, address, phone. **Arrangement:** By type of medium. **Frequency:** Not established; first issued 1979. **Price:** Free.

★4512★
DIRECTORY OF PATRISTIC SCHOLARS
North American Patristic Society
Office Tower, No. 1333
University of Kentucky   Phone: (606) 257-2886
Lexington, KY 40506
Covers: 200 scholars actively engaged in research into early history of the Christian Church. **Entries include:** Name, birthdate and birthplace, address, phone, degrees and institutions granting them, areas of research. **Arrangement:** Alphabetical. **Pages** (approx.): 60. **Frequency:** Published 1976. **Editor:** Louis Roberts. **Price:** $1.50.

★4513★
DIRECTORY OF RELIGIOUS BODIES IN THE UNITED STATES
Garland Publishing, Inc.
545 Madison Avenue   Phone: (212) 935-1571
New York, NY 10022
Number of listings: 1,200. **Entries include:** Group name, headquarters address, major publications. **Arrangement:** Alphabetical. **Pages** (approx.): 320. **Frequency:** Not established; first edition 1977. **Editor:** J. Gordon Melton. **Price:** $33.00.

★4514★
DIRECTORY OF RELIGIOUS ORGANIZATIONS IN THE UNITED STATES
McGrath Publishing Company
Box 9001   Phone: (919) 763-3757
Wilmington, NC 28401
Covers: About 1,600 associations, mission groups, learned societies, ecumenical organizations, religious publishers, and other organizations in the field of religion. **Entries include:** Organization name, address, phone, name of chief executive, membership statistics, religious affiliation, purpose, and description of activities. **Arrangement:** Classified by type of activity. **Pages** (approx.): 550. **Frequency:** Biennial, even years. **Price:** $62.50 (current and 1980 editions).

★4515★
DIRECTORY OF SIGNIFICANT 20TH CENTURY MINORITY WOMEN IN THE U.S.A.
Gaylord Professional Publications, Division
Gaylord Brothers, Inc.
Box 4901   Phone: (315) 457-5070
Syracuse, NY 13221
Covers: About 750 women belonging to American Indian, Black, Hispanic, or Asian American minority groups. **Entries include:** Specific ethnic group membership (if American Indian also gives tribe, etc.), birthplace, names of parents, spouse, and children; education and career data; membership in professional, community, or business organizations; special honors or achievements; and publications; most listings include a statement of beliefs by the subject or a person close to her. **Arrangement:** Alphabetical. **Pages** (approx.): 500. **Frequency:** Not established; first edition fall 1979. **Author:** Dr. Jessie Carney Smith. **Price:** $39.95.

★4516★
DIRECTORY OF SOUTHERN BAPTIST CONVENTION CHURCHES
Southern Baptist Convention
Baptist Sunday School Board
127 Ninth Avenue, North   Phone: (615) 251-2500
Nashville, TN 37234
Pages (approx.): 500. **Frequency:** Irregular; latest edition October 1978; new edition expected October 1981. **Price:** $10.25.

★4517★
DIRECTORY OF THE AMERICAN BAPTIST CHURCHES IN THE U.S.A.
American Baptist Churches in the U. S. A.
Valley Forge, PA 19481
Covers: Denominational boards; regional and state groups; churches and pastors; and other professional leadership. **Arrangement:** Classified into sections above. **Pages** (approx.): 310. **Frequency:**

Biennial, June of odd years. **Editor:** Robert C. Campbell, General Secretary. **Price:** $4.00 (ISSN 0091-9381).

★4518★
DIRECTORY OF THE AMERICAN OCCULT AND PARANORMAL
Editorial Research Service
Box 1832
Kansas City, MO 64141
Covers: About 650 organizations and periodicals concerned with occult and paranormal groups and movements, including astrology, psychics, biorhythm, extrasensory perception, faith healing, fortune telling, magic, metaphysics, palmistry, mysticism, numerology, parapsychology, pyramid power, reincarnation, spiritualism, unidentified flying objects, voodoo, witchcraft, etc. **Frequency:** First edition expected March 1980. **Editor:** Laird M. Wilcox. **Price:** $9.95. **Other information:** Supplemented in a section of the same publisher's ''Journal of Superstition and Magical Thinking,'' semiannual, $12.00 per year.

★4519★
**ECUMENICAL DIRECTORY OF RETREAT AND CONFERENCE
        CENTERS**
Anchor Society, Inc.
2398 Pine Street
San Francisco, CA 94115
Number of listings: Over 1,300. **Entries include:** Name of center, address, phone, name of contact person; ecumenicity or not; owner, operator; facilities available, including chapel, and whether meals, leadership, or camping facilities are provided; accomodation limits and rates. **Arrangement:** Geographical. **Indexes:** Center name. **Pages** (approx.): 270. **Frequency:** Irregular; latest edition 1975; new edition expected fall 1977. **Editor:** Philip Deemer. **Advertising accepted.** **Price:** $15.00 (1975 edition); $18.00 (1977 edition). (Not verified)

★4520★
**EDUCATION ASSISTANCE FOR AMERICAN INDIANS & ALASKA
        NATIVES**
Master of Public Health Program for American Indians
School of Public Health
Earl Warren Hall
University of California   Phone: (415) 642-3228
Berkeley, CA 94720
Publication includes: Sources of information regarding health careers, training for health careers, and financial aid available to American Indians and Alaska natives from the Bureau of Indian Affairs, institutions, tribal councils, and other sources. **Entries include:** Name of organization or publisher, address, contact person, phone, and service programs offered. **Arrangement:** Subject (occupation information, specific programs, financial aid). **Pages** (approx.): 105. **Frequency:** Irregular; latest edition September 1979. **Editor:** Holly Halsey, Scholarship Information Coordinator. **Price:** $1.50.

★4521★
**ENCYCLOPEDIC DIRECTORY OF ETHNIC NEWSPAPERS AND
        PERIODICALS IN THE UNITED STATES**
Libraries Unlimited, Inc.
Box 263   Phone: (303) 770-1220
Littleton, CO 80160
Covers: About 1,000 publications of about 65 ethnic groups. **Entries include:** Title (with English translation), date first published, editorial address, phone, editor's name, language(s) used in publication, sponsoring organization, circulation, frequency, annual subscription rate, and annotation describing scope, objectives, etc. **Arrangement:** Classified into ethnic sections, then according to whether in English or other language. **Indexes:** Title. **Pages** (approx.): 250. **Frequency:** Irregular; first edition 1972; latest edition 1976. **Editors:** Lubomyr R. Wynar and Anna T. Wynar. **Price:** $15.00.

★4522★
**ENCYCLOPEDIC DIRECTORY OF ETHNIC ORGANIZATIONS IN THE
        UNITED STATES**
Libraries Unlimited, Inc.
Box 263   Phone: (303) 770-1220
Littleton, CO 80160
Covers: 1,500 organizations representing about 75 ethnic groups. Includes cultural, religious, fraternal, political, educational, professional, and scholarly organizations. **Entries include:** Name of organization, address, phone, officers, founding date, branches, membership, purpose, publications, conventions, and other descriptive data. **Arrangement:** Classified by ethnic group; multi-ethnic and research organizations listed alphabetically. **Indexes:** Organization name. **Pages** (approx.): 440. **Frequency:** Published 1975. **Editor:** Lubomyr R. Wynar, with Lois Buttlar and Anna T. Wynar. **Price:** $19.50.

★4523★
EPISCOPAL CHURCH ANNUAL
Morehouse-Barlow Company, Inc.
78 Danbury Road   Phone: (203) 762-0721
Wilton, CT 06897
Covers: The clergy of the Episcopal Church, the Anglican Communion worldwide, biographies of recently consecrated bishops, seminaries, training schools, retreat centers, and social service agencies. **Entries include:** Name and address of clergy; personal data, position, and writings of recently consecrated bishops. **Arrangement:** Clergy list is alphabetical; diocesan list is geographical. **Pages** (approx.): 520. **Frequency:** Annual, January. **Editor:** Ronald T. C. Lau. **Advertising accepted.** Circulation 5,200. **Price:** $12.95 (current and 1980 editions). **Also includes:** Information and statistics on dioceses, the structure of the church, and its institutions.

Ethnic Directory [Detroit] *See* Ethni-City: An Ethnic Guide to
        Metropolitan Detroit

★4524★
ETHNIC DIRECTORY OF CALIFORNIA
Western Publishers
Box 30193
Station B
Calgary, Alberta, Canada
Covers: Restaurants and gift shops of several dozen ethnic and nationality groups in California; includes consulates general and occasional churches and associations. **Entries include:** Activity name, address, phone. **Arrangement:** Ethnic groups alphabetical under state/city headings. **Indexes:** Ethnic group. **Pages** (approx.): 170. **Frequency:** Published 1977. **Editors:** Vladimir Markotic and T. Petrunic. **Price:** $10.65, postpaid, payment with order. **Other information:** Will be discontinued; copies still available.

★4525★
ETHNIC DIRECTORY OF NEW JERSEY
William H. Wise & Company, Inc.
336 Mountain Road   Phone: (201) 864-5200
Union City, NJ 07087
Covers: Over 1,700 ethnic organizations, churches, schools, newspapers, political clubs, national homes, dance and choral groups, and other ethnic-related organizations in New Jersey. **Entries include:** All listings include group or organization name and address; many listings include phone and name of chief officer, date founded, number of members, objectives and activities, and publications. **Arrangement:** By nationality or ethnic group. **Indexes:** Geographical. **Pages** (approx.): 290. **Frequency:** Not established; first edition 1978; new edition expected 1980. **Editor:** Zora Kipel. **Price:** $15.00, plus $1.30 shipping.

★4526★
ETHNIC DIRECTORY OF THE NORTHWEST COAST OF U.S.A.
Western Publishers
Box 30193
Station B
Calgary, Alberta, Canada
Covers: Restaurants and gift shops of several dozen ethnic and nationality groups in Alaska, Hawaii, Oregon, and Washington; includes consulates general and occasional churches and associations. **Entries include:** Activity name, address, phone. **Arrangement:** Ethnic groups alphabetical under state/city headings. **Indexes:** Ethnic group. **Pages** (approx.): 80. **Frequency:** Published 1977. **Editors:** Vladimir Markotic and T. Petrunic. **Price:** $7.55, postpaid, payment with order. **Other information:** Will be discontinued; copies still available.

★4527★
ETHNIC LIBRARY RESOURCES DIRECTORY [New England]
Ethnic Services Task Force
New England Library Board
231 Capitol Avenue   Phone: (203) 525-2681
Hartford, CT 06115
Covers: About 165 library collections of materials in a foreign language or of interest to a particular ethnic group; limited to New England and primarily collections of over 200 items. A few film collections are also listed. **Entries include:** Library name, address, name and phone of contact person; number of items, language, description of collection, access, languages spoken by staff, programs. Film collections have less detail. **Arrangement:** By ethnic group. **Indexes:** Library name, film title by ethnic group. **Frequency:** Not established; first edition April 1979. **Price:** $2.00, postpaid, payment with order; $2.50, billed.

★4528★
ETHNI-CITY: AN ETHNIC GUIDE TO METROPOLITAN DETROIT
Michigan Ethnic Heritage Studies Center
60 Farnsworth   Phone: (313) 832-7400
Detroit, MI 48202
Covers: 50 ethnic groups and over 2,000 of their organizations, institutions, churches, clubs, facilities, media, entertainment places, and activities. **Entries include:** Name, address, hours, and other details as appropriate to the type of activity. **Arrangement:** By ethnic group. **Pages** (approx.): 125. **Frequency:** About every three years; latest edition October 1976; new edition expected spring 1980. **Editor:** James M. Anderson. **Advertising accepted.** Circulation 25,000. **Former title:** Ethnic Directory. **Price:** $2.50.

★4529★
FEDERAL AND STATE INDIAN RESERVATIONS AND INDIAN TRUST AREAS
Commerce Department
Washington, DC
Entries include: Reservation or area name, location, mailing address, legal status, and information on the tribe and its history, community facilities, local economy, etc. **Arrangement:** Geographical. **Pages** (approx.): 600. **Frequency:** Published 1974. **Price:** $5.90. **Send orders to:** Government Printing Office, Washington, DC 20402.

★4530★
GOSPEL MUSIC [Year]
Gospel Music Association
38 Music Square West   Phone: (615) 242-0303
Nashville, TN 37203
Covers: Gospel musicians, composers, and artists; recording companies, studios, and production companies; talent agencies; publishers; performing rights organizations; television and radio broadcasting stations; and book stores, Bible supply stores, and other retailers. **Entries include:** All listings include name, address; some listings include phone. Broadcasting station listings include contact, program title, format (television) or number of hours devoted to gospel music. **Arrangement:** Broadcasting stations and retailers are geographical, others are alphabetical. **Pages** (approx.): 130.

Frequency: Annual, spring. **Editor:** Don Butler, Executive Director. **Advertising accepted.** Circulation 15,000. **Former title:** Gospel Music Directory & Yearbook (1979). **Price:** $5.00.

Gospel Music Directory & Yearbook *See* Gospel Music [Year]

★4531★
GUIDE TO ETHNIC MUSEUMS, LIBRARIES, AND ARCHIVES IN THE UNITED STATES
Center for Ethnic Publications
School of Library Science
Kent State University
Room 318
Kent, OH 44242
Covers: Museums, libraries, and archives of over 70 ethnic groups and about 830 cultural institutions of assistance in ethnic research. Collections in large research libraries are not included. **Entries include:** Name of institution, type, address, phone, sponsoring organization, names and titles of key personnel, number of staff, date founded, scope of coverage, accessibility, admission fees, visitors allowed, publications, collection size, and objectives, activities, and services. **Arrangement:** By ethnic group. **Pages** (approx.): 380. **Frequency:** Not established; first edition 1978. **Editors:** Lubomyr R. Wynar and Lois Buttlar. **Price:** $9.50.

★4532★
GUIDE TO JEWISH CHICAGO
American Jewish Congress
22 W. Monroe Street, Suite 2102   Phone: (312) 332-7355
Chicago, IL 60603
Covers: Synagogues, community organizations, schools, educational organizations, book stores, camps, homes for the aged, Anglo-Jewish periodicals, kosher caterers, restaurants, and funeral chapels that cater to the Jewish community. **Entries include:** For synagogues - Name, address, doctrinal orientation, phone, name of rabbi. For organizations - Name, address, phone, name of person in charge, and brief description. Restaurant and funeral homes show name, address, and phone. **Arrangement:** Alphabetical within service categories. **Pages** (approx.): 40. **Frequency:** Biennial, January of even years. **Editor:** Manuel Silver, Director, Midwest Region. **Price:** $2.50.

★4533★
GUIDE TO JEWISH STUDENT GROUPS
North American Jewish Students Network
15 E. 26th Street, No. 1350   Phone: (212) 689-0790
New York, NY 10010
Covers: 375 Jewish student groups in North America, including student organizations, student publications, chavurot, etc. **Entries include:** Name of group, description, address, phone, campus (where applicable), name of contact person. **Arrangement:** By type of activity. **Indexes:** Alphabetical, geographical. **Pages** (approx.): 200. **Frequency:** Biennial. **Editor:** Ruth Mason.

Guide to Psi Periodicals *See* International Guide to Psi Periodicals

★4534★
GUIDE TO PSI TAPE RECORDINGS
Inner-Space Interpreters
Box 1133
Magnolia Park Station   Phone: (213) 843-0476
Burbank, CA 91507
Covers: About 90 producers and distributors of cassette tapes of lectures, classes, etc., concerned with psychic faculties and phenomena. **Entries include:** Producer name, address, subjects available, prices. **Frequency:** Not established; latest edition late 1977. **Editor:** Elizabeth M. Werner. **Price:** $3.00, plus 40¢ shipping, payment with order.

★4535★
HANDBOOK OF DENOMINATIONS IN THE UNITED STATES
Abingdon Press
201 Eighth Avenue South   Phone: (615) 749-6000
Nashville, TN 37202
Publication includes: List of headquarters addresses for about 250 religious bodies. **Entries include:** Body name and address. **Arrangement:** Classified by religious "family." **Frequency:** Every five years; latest edition 1975; new edition expected March 1980. **Editor:** Frank S. Mead. **Price:** $7.95 (current and 1980 editions). **Also includes:** Principal content of book is summaries of the bodies' histories and beliefs.

Houses of Prayer Annual Directory *See* Annual Directory, Houses of Prayer

★4536★
INNER DEVELOPMENT: THE YES! BOOKSHOP GUIDE
Yes! Bookshop
1035 31st Street, N. W.   Phone: (202) 338-7874
Washington, DC 20007
Publication includes: List of publishers of about 11,000 books on religion, philosophy, spiritualism, psychic phenomena, mythology, the occult, and similar topics. **Entries include:** Publisher name, address. **Frequency:** Irregular; latest edition January 1979; new edition expected 1982. Supplements issued quarterly. **Price:** $9.95, postpaid. **Other information:** Principal content of publication is annotated bibliographical listings of available publications in fields mentioned.

★4537★
INTERNATIONAL CEMETERY DIRECTORY
American Cemetery Association
250 E. Broad Street   Phone: (614) 221-6829
Columbus, OH 43215
Covers: More than 8,000 cemeteries. **Entries include:** Name, address. **Arrangement:** Geographical. **Frequency:** Irregular; latest edition 1974; new edition expected January 1980. **Editor:** John P. Danglade. **Advertising accepted. Price:** $30.00 (1980 edition).

International Cooperation Council Directory: Planetary Guide... *See* Directory for a New World

★4538★
INTERNATIONAL GUIDE TO PSI PERIODICALS
Inner-Space Interpreters
Box 1133
Magnolia Park Station   Phone: (213) 843-0476
Burbank, CA 91507
Covers: More than 350 regularly published magazines, newsletters, and journals concerned with psychic faculties and phenomena, including New Age movement, extrasensory perception, parapsychology, phenomena, astrology, wicca, UFOs, extraterrestrial life, etc.; international coverage. **Entries include:** Publication name; publisher name, phone, and address; editor name; frequency; price; brief review of interests and subjects. **Frequency:** Irregular; latest edition 1979; new edition expected January 1980. **Editor:** Elizabeth M. Werner. **Price:** $4.00, plus 50¢ shipping, payment with order (current and 1980 editions). **Other information:** Variant title, "Guide to Psi Periodicals."

★4539★
INTERNATIONAL PSYCHIC REGISTER
Ornion Press
Box 1816
Erie, PA 16507   Phone: (814) 459-7730
Covers: More than 1,000 psychics, healers, mediums, dowsers, tarot readers, parapsychologists, and other practitioners of the psychic arts, in the United States, Canada, and Great Britain. **Entries include:** Name, address, phone, areas of specialization, organizational affiliations, whether brochure is available, whether available for mail

consultation or as speaker. **Arrangement:** Classified. **Pages** (approx.): 90. **Frequency:** Annual, February; July supplement. **Editor:** Donald A. McQuaid, Editor and Publisher. **Price:** $4.00, including supplement, payment with order (current and 1980 editions). **Other information:** Variant title, "Psychic Register."

★4540★
JEWISH EDUCATION DIRECTORY
American Association for Jewish Education
114 Fifth Avenue
New York, NY 10011
Covers: About 2,000 schools, central agencies, teacher training schools, and individuals. **Entries include:** Name, address, ideological affiliation, level of school. **Arrangement:** Geographical within type of organization. **Pages** (approx.): 60. **Frequency:** Biennial, June of odd years. **Editor:** Dr. George Pollak, Director, Department of Community Studies. **Advertising accepted.** Circulation 4,000. **Price:** $5.00.

Jewish Landmarks of New York *See* American Jewish Landmarks

★4541★
JEWISH LOS ANGELES: A GUIDE [California]
Jewish Federation-Council of Greater Los Angeles
6505 Wilshire Boulevard   Phone: (213) 852-1234
Los Angeles, CA
Covers: Kosher delicatessens, butchers; Jewish congregations; Jewish social service agencies; places for students and elderly to meet with other Jewish people; "everything for the Jewish person in Los Angeles." **Entries include:** For most listings - Name of facility, restaurant, etc., address, phone. Service facilities also include hours open; other listings have similar information as appropriate. **Arrangement:** By type of activity. **Indexes:** Topic, organization name. **Pages** (approx.): 115. **Frequency:** Published 1976. **Editor:** Neil Reisner. **Price:** $2.50, plus 50¢ shipping.

★4542★
JEWISH STUDIES IN AMERICAN AND CANADIAN UNIVERSITIES
B'nai B'rith Hillel Foundations
1640 Rhode Island Avenue, N. W.   Phone: (202) 857-6560
Washington, DC 20036
Covers: Over 300 colleges and universities in the United States and Canada which offer courses in Jewish studies; includes Jewish institutions of higher education. **Entries include:** Institution name, location; departments having courses in Jewish studies and their titles and numbers; information about degree programs in Jewish studies and related fields. **Arrangement:** Geographical. **Indexes:** Institution name, graduate program, summer program, Israel study opportunities. **Pages** (approx.): 155. **Frequency:** Irregular; latest edition October 1979. **Editors:** Samuel Z. Fishman, Judyth R. Saypol. **Price:** $3.95, postpaid, payment must accompany order.

★4543★
JEWISH YELLOW PAGES: A DIRECTORY OF GOODS AND SERVICES
Schocken Books
200 Madison Avenue   Phone: (212) 685-6500
New York, NY 10016
Covers: Products and services of interest to Jews, with emphasis on handcrafted ritual objects and other listings for educational materials, food, toys, and various services. **Entries include:** Name, address, annotation, and illustrations for many listings. **Arrangement:** Classified. **Pages** (approx.): 210. **Frequency:** Not established; first edition 1976. **Editors:** Mae Shafter Rockland and Michael Aaron Rockland. **Price:** $15.00, cloth; $7.95, paper. **Other information:** Not to be confused with 64-page section, "The Jewish Yellow Pages," included in "The Second Jewish Catalog" published by Jewish Publication Society of America (see separate listing).

★4544★
JOURNAL OF SUPERSTITION & MAGICAL THINKING—
ORGANIZATIONS AND SERIALS COLUMN
Editorial Research Service
Box 1832
Kansas City, MO 64141
Publication includes: List of occult and paranormal organizations and publishers of related serials. **Entries include:** Organization name, address, activities, critical annotation. Publisher name, address, title of serial, critical annotation, frequency. **Arrangement:** Alphabetical. **Frequency:** Semiannual, January and June. **Editor:** Laird M. Wilcox. **Price:** $6.00 per issue (ISSN 0192-4044).

★4545★
KOSHER PRODUCTS AND SERVICES DIRECTORY
Union of Orthodox Jewish Congregations of America
116 E. 27th Street   Phone: (212) 725-3400
New York, NY 10016
Covers: Consumer products and services under the rabbinical supervision of the union. **Entries include:** Product name, name and location of manufacturer. **Arrangement:** Alphabetical by food type, then by brand name. **Pages** (approx.): 60. **Frequency:** Irregular; latest edition 1977 (now out of print); new edition expected mid-1980. **Editor:** Rabbi Berel Wein, Rabbinic Administrator. **Price:** Free. **Other information:** Publication contains no listings for Passover products, which are covered separately in the Union's "Passover Products Directory," published annually in February and also available without charge.

★4546★
LATINO MATERIALS: A MULTIMEDIA GUIDE FOR CHILDREN AND
YOUNG ADULTS
ABC-Clio Press
Riviera Campus
2040 Alameda Padre Serra   Phone: (805) 963-4221
Santa Barbara, CA 93103
Publication includes: List of publishers, distributors, dealers, and resource centers for Latino, Mexican-American, and Puerto Rican materials. **Entries include:** Publisher name, address. **Arrangement:** Alphabetical. **Indexes:** Author name, title. **Pages** (approx.): 270. **Frequency:** Not established; first edition 1979. **Editor:** Daniel Flores Duran. **Price:** $14.95, postpaid, payment must accompany individuals' orders. **Other information:** Published in cooperation with Neal-Schuman Publishers. Primary content of publication is annotations of materials by grade level.

★4547★
LEADERSHIP CONFERENCE OF WOMEN RELIGIOUS OF THE
U.S.A.—DIRECTORY
Leadership Conference of Women Religious of the U.S.A.
1302 18th Street, N. W., Suite 701   Phone: (202) 293-1483
Washington, DC 20036
Covers: About 700 superiors general or provincial superiors of religious women of Roman Catholic communities in the United States, and a selected list of organizations. **Entries include:** For members and associates - Name, address, phone, sister's administrative post within her congregation, cross- reference of order for the "Official Catholic Directory." For organizations - Name, address, phone, administrator/ officer. **Arrangement:** By geographical region. **Pages** (approx.): 60. **Frequency:** Annual, February. **Price:** $2.50; restricted circulation.

★4548★
LUTHERAN ANNUAL
Concordia Publishing House
3558 S. Jefferson Avenue   Phone: (314) 664-7000
St. Louis, MO 63118
Covers: Congregations and officers of the 40 districts of the Missouri Synod. Includes affiliated educational institutions, auxiliary organizations, health and welfare agencies, and statistical information. Also lists Lutheran Church bodies in North America. **Pages** (approx.): 530. **Frequency:** Annual, December. **Editor:** R. L. Reinke, President.

Advertising accepted. Circulation 30,000. **Price:** $3.50.

★4549★
LUTHERAN CHURCH DIRECTORY FOR THE UNITED STATES
Lutheran Council/USA
360 Park Avenue South   Phone: (212) 532-6350
New York, NY 10010
Covers: 18,000 congregations; also includes Lutheran social service agencies and periodicals. **Entries include:** Congregation name, address, county, synod with which affiliated. **Arrangement:** Alphabetical. **Indexes:** Geographical. **Pages** (approx.): 300. **Frequency:** Irregular; previous edition 1976; latest edition November 1979. **Editor:** Edward A. Rauff. **Price:** $2.00.

★4550★
MASONIC HOMES, HOSPITALS, AND CHARITY FOUNDATIONS
Masonic Service Association of the United States
8120 Fenton Street   Phone: (301) 588-4010
Silver Spring, MD 20910
Entries include: Institution name, organization, management, eligibility requirements, brief description. **Arrangement:** Alphabetical. **Frequency:** Irregular; latest edition 1979. **Editor:** Stewart M. L. Pollard, Executive Secretary. **Former title:** Masonic Homes, Orphanages, Hospitals, Infirmaries, Sanitariums, and Charity Foundations. **Price:** $1.50.

★4551★
MINORITY BIOMEDICAL SUPPORT PROGRAM: A DIRECTORY OF
THE RESEARCH PROJECTS
Division of Research Resources
National Institutes of Health
Health, Education, and Welfare Department   Phone: (301) 496-5545
Bethesda, MD 20205
Covers: Institutions granting research awards to minority faculty and students engaged in biomedical research. **Entries include:** Institution name, name of program director, address, names of individual project investigator and project. **Arrangement:** Geographical. **Indexes:** Geographical. **Pages** (approx.): 70. **Frequency:** About every two years; latest edition March 1979. **Price:** Free (NIH Pub. No. 79-1432). **Send orders to:** Research Resources Information Center, 1776 E. Jefferson St., Rockville, MD 20852.

★4552★
MINORITY GROUP MEDIA GUIDE
Directories International, Inc.
1718 Sherman Avenue   Phone: (312) 491-0019
Evanston, IL 60201
Covers: Over 800 newspapers, magazines, and 420 TV and radio stations with special appeal to specific ethnic and minority groups, including Spanish-speaking Americans, Asian Americans, the handicapped, gays, the elderly, American Indian, Polish, Irish, etc. **Arrangement:** By ethnic or minority group. **Pages** (approx.): 210. **Frequency:** Annual, November. **Advertising accepted.** **Price:** $55.00. **Also includes:** Market data on each group, including population figures, income, expenditures, etc.

★4553★
MINORITY ORGANIZATIONS: A NATIONAL DIRECTORY
Garrett Park Press
Garrett Park, MD 20766
Covers: Over 2,700 groups composed of or intended to serve members of minority groups including Alaska Natives, American Indians, Blacks, Hispanics, and Asian Americans. **Entries include:** Organization name, address, description of activities, purpose, publications, etc. **Arrangement:** By minority group. **Indexes:** Organization name, geographical, program, defunct organization. **Pages** (approx.): 380. **Frequency:** Irregular; first edition 1978. **Editor:** Katherine W. Cole. **Price:** $15.00, payment with order; $16.00, billed.

★4554★

MINORITY STUDENT OPPORTUNITIES IN UNITED STATES MEDICAL SCHOOLS

Association of American Medical Colleges
One Dupont Circle, N. W., Suite 200   Phone: (202) 828-0572
Washington, DC 20036

Covers: Programs for minority group students at 110 schools. **Entries include:** Name of school, address, phone, name of contact; descriptions of recruitment, admissions, financial aid, and academic assistance programs for the minority student; statistical table on minority admissions and enrollment. **Arrangement:** Geographical. **Indexes:** School name, geographical. **Pages** (approx.): 235. **Frequency:** Irregular; new edition expected January 1980. **Editor:** Juel L. Hodge, Research Associate. **Price:** $5.00 (1980 edition). **Also includes:** List of schools offering summer programs.

★4555★

MISSION HANDBOOK: NORTH AMERICAN PROTESTANT MINISTRIES OVERSEAS

Missions Advanced Research and Communications Center
919 W. Huntington Drive   Phone: (213) 357-1111
Monrovia, CA 91016

Covers: About 625 Protestant agencies in the United States and Canada involved in mission efforts overseas. **Entries include:** Agency name, address, executive officers, branch offices, date of founding, income, description, fields of service, type of overseas institution. **Arrangement:** Geographical and by type of organization. **Pages** (approx.): 500. **Frequency:** Latest edition 1976. **Editor:** Edward R. Dayton, Director. **Price:** $15.00.

★4556★

MISSION HANDBOOK [Catholic]

United States Catholic Mission Council
1302 18th Street, N. W., Suite 702   Phone: (202) 785-9450
Washington, DC 20036

Publication includes: List of mission institutes and seminars and missionary councils, societies, and other groups which provide assistance to missions abroad. **Entries include:** Name, address, phone. **Arrangement:** Alphabetical. **Frequency:** Annual, September. **Editor:** Mary A. Godfrey. **Price:** $1.25. **Other information:** Principal content of publication is list of about 350 mission-sending groups, showing countries served and numbers in country.

★4557★

MUSIC AND DANCE RESEARCH OF SOUTHWESTERN UNITED STATES INDIANS

Information Coordinators, Inc.
1435 Randolph Street   Phone: (313) 962-9720
Detroit, MI 48226

Publication includes: Section devoted to archives which contain recorded music of the American Indian. **Entries include:** Archive name, address, description of holdings. **Frequency:** Published fall 1977. **Editor:** Charlotte J. Frisbie. **Price:** $9.75, postpaid, payment with order. **Other information:** Principal content of publication is bibliography on the subject.

★4558★

NATIONAL ASSOCIATION OF CHURCH BUSINESS ADMINISTRATORS—MEMBERSHIP ROSTER

National Association of Church Business Administrators
7112 Grandview Drive
Kansas City, MO 64137

Number of listings: Over 750. **Entries include:** Name, address of church/institution, phone, name of spouse, type of membership. **Arrangement:** Alphabetical. **Indexes:** Institution. **Frequency:** Annual, July. **Editor:** Floy Barnes. **Price:** Available to members only.

★4559★

NATIONAL CONFERENCE OF DIOCESAN DIRECTORS OF RELIGIOUS EDUCATION/CCD—DIOCESAN DIRECTORY

U. S. Catholic Conference
Department of Education
1312 Massachusetts Avenue, N. W.   Phone: (202) 659-6868
Washington, DC 20005

Covers: 425 directors and assistant directors of religious education and Confraternity of Christian Doctrine (CCD) groups for Roman Catholic dioceses. **Entries include:** Name, office address and phone, and home phone. **Arrangement:** Alphabetical by diocese. **Pages** (approx.): 40. **Frequency:** Annual, late fall. **Editor:** Rev. David E. Beebe, Executive Secretary. **Price:** $2.00.

★4560★

NATIONAL DIRECTORY OF CHICANO FACULTY AND RESEARCH

Publications Unit
Chicano Studies Research Center
3121 Campbell Hall
UCLA
405 Hilgard Avenue   Phone: (213) 825-2642
Los Angeles, CA 90024

Covers: 1,400 Spanish-surname faculty and researchers throughout the United States, and Mexican researchers with an interest in the Chicano. **Entries include:** Name; position; department name; home address and phone; type of degree, granting institution, and date received; courses taught; teaching and research interests; areas of specialization; research projects; papers and publications. **Arrangement:** Geographical. **Indexes:** Personal name. **Pages** (approx.): 110. **Frequency:** Irregular; latest edition March 1975; new edition possible 1980. **Editors:** Renee Mares and Reynaldo Macias. **Price:** $7.00, paper; $10.00, cloth.

★4561★

NATIVE AMERICAN ARTS AND CULTURE: A RESOURCE DIRECTORY

Western States Arts Foundation
428 E. 11th Avenue   Phone: (303) 832-7979
Denver, CO 80203

Covers: Foundations, federal agencies, arts agencies, religious organizations, Native American interest groups, fund-raising workshops likely to provide funding for Native American arts. **Pages** (approx.): 90. **Frequency:** Not established; first edition 1977. **Editor:** Laurie Nogg Adler. **Price:** $3.00.

★4562★

NEW CONSCIOUSNESS CATALOGUE

G. P. Putnam's Sons
200 Madison Avenue   Phone: (212) 576-8900
New York, NY 10016

Description: Subtitle reads, "A comprehensive guide to the dimensions of psychic and spiritual development." Book includes lists, with addresses and frequent annotations, of books, organizations, audiovisual materials, periodicals, and other resources. Principal content is articles on various spiritual and related concepts. **Frequency:** Published 1979. **Editors:** Nicholas Regush and June Regush. **Price:** $6.95.

★4563★

NORTH DAKOTA INDIAN AFFAIRS COMMISSION—INDIAN RESERVATION DIRECTORIES

North Dakota Indian Affairs Commission
State Capitol   Phone: (701) 224-2428
Bismarck, ND 58505

Covers: Tribal councils, arts and crafts groups, schools and other educational programs, and other tribal, federal, state and private programs and activities on reservations. Directories issued for Standing Rock, Fort Berthold, Turtle Mountain, and Fort Totten reservations. Also a directory of off-reservation agencies in North Dakota concerned with Indian Affairs. **Entries include:** Name of school, agency, program, etc.; address; phone; name of contact person. **Pages** (approx.): 5-10 each. **Frequency:** Irregular; about every 18 months; new edition expected January 1980. **Price:** Free.

★4564★
OCCULT BOOKSTORE AND SUPPLIER DIRECTORY
Stonehenge Books
Box 6578
Chicago, IL 60680
Covers: More than 400 suppliers of occult, psychic, New Age, etc., books and materials; herbalists; schools; communities. **Entries include:** Supplier listings show name, address, phone, products; other listings have similar detail. **Frequency:** Previous edition late 1977; latest edtion fall 1979. **Editors:** Edward N. C. Griggs and Gerald M. Born. **Price:** $5.25, postpaid, payment with order.

★4565★
ORTHODOX CHURCH IN AMERICA—YEARBOOK AND CHURCH DIRECTORY
Orthodox Church in America
Route 25A, Box 675   Phone: (516) 922-0550
Syosset, NY 11791
Covers: Parish churches and clergy. **Entries include:** Church name, address, phone, names and titles of clergy. **Arrangement:** Geographical by diocese. **Indexes:** Parish by state. **Pages** (approx.): 180. **Frequency:** Annual, January. **Advertising accepted.** Circulation 1,000. **Price:** $6.00 (current and 1980 editions; ISSN 0145-7950).

★4566★
OXBRIDGE DIRECTORY OF RELIGIOUS PERIODICALS
Oxbridge Communications, Inc.
183 Madison Avenue   Phone: (212) 689-8524
New York, NY 10016
Covers: Over 3,000 religious periodicals, directories, educational materials, etc., published in the United States and Canada. **Entries include:** Title, publisher, address, phone, editor, description of content, year established, frequency, subscription price, circulation, ad rates, etc. **Frequency:** Annual. **Price:** $25.00.

Passover Products Directory *See* **Kosher Products and Services Directory**

★4567★
PILGRIM'S GUIDE TO PLANET EARTH: A NEW AGE TRAVELER'S HANDBOOK AND SPIRITUAL DIRECTORY
Spiritual Community Publications
Box 1080   Phone: (415) 457-2990
San Rafael, CA 94902
Covers: Over 15,000 spiritual centers, shrines, meditation centers, monasteries and churches, vegetarian and macrobiotic restaurants, health food stores, metaphysical bookstores, New Age schools, communes, and publishers; international coverage. **Entries include:** Name, address. **Arrangement:** Geographical. **Pages** (approx.): 320. **Frequency:** Irregular; latest edition 1974; new edition expected spring 1980. **Editor:** Parmatma Singh Khalsa. **Price:** $8.95, plus $1.00 shipping (1980 edition).

Psychic Register *See* **International Psychic Register**

★4568★
RABBINICAL ALLIANCE OF AMERICA—REGISTRY
Rabbinical Alliance of America
156 Fifth Avenue   Phone: (212) 242-6420
New York, NY 10010
Covers: 400 orthodox rabbis serving in pulpits and Jewish schools worldwide. **Entries include:** Rabbi's name, address, phone, organizational affiliation. **Arrangement:** Alphabetical. **Frequency:** Triennial. **Price:** $5.00.

★4569★
REFERENCE ENCYCLOPEDIA OF THE AMERICAN INDIAN
Todd Publications
Box 535   Phone: (203) 322-5488
Rye, NY 10580
Description: Volume 1 consists of lists of tribal bodies, government agencies, organizations, libraries, etc., concerned with Native Americans, plus a lengthy bibliography of in-print books. Volume 2 is a biographical directory of over 1,200 Indians and non-Indians active in affairs related to Native Americans. **Entries include:** Organization, agency, and other lists include name of group, address, name of officer or contact, interests. Biographical listings include name, birth date, tribal affiliation (if any), occupation, educational and career data. **Arrangement:** Associations, museums, reservations, tribal councils are geographical; periodicals are alphabetical; audiovisual aids are by type of aid; biographies are alphabetical. **Pages** (approx.): Volume 1, 565; Volume 2, 220. **Frequency:** Irregular; latest edition 1978; new edition expected 1982. **Editor:** Barry Klein. **Price:** $25.00 per volume; $47.50 for set.

★4570★
REGISTER OF GRAND LODGES ACTIVE AND EXTINCT
Masonic Service Association of the United States
8120 Fenton Street   Phone: (301) 588-4010
Silver Spring, MD 20910
Entries include: Lodge name, location, date established, brief description. **Arrangement:** Alphabetical. **Indexes:** Geographical. **Frequency:** Irregular; previous edition 1977; latest edition November 1979. **Editor:** Stewart M. L. Pollard, Executive Secretary. **Price:** $1.25.

★4571★
RELIGIOUS BOOKS AND SERIALS IN PRINT
R. R. Bowker Company
1180 Avenue of the Americas   Phone: (212) 764-5100
New York, NY 10036
Publication includes: List of publishers of books on religion and related subjects, including theology, ethics, the occult, etc. **Entries include:** Name, address. **Frequency:** Biennial, even years. **Price:** $39.50, postpaid, payment with order (ISSN 0000-0612). **Send orders to:** R. R. Bowker Co., Box 1807, Ann Arbor, MI 48106 (313-761-4700). **Other information:** Principal content of publication is listings of books on religious subjects in a classified arrangement. There are author and title indexes, and separate listings for fiction and children's fiction. Based on "Books in Print," described in separate listing.

★4572★
SCHOLARSHIPS AVAILABLE TO BLACK STUDENTS-AMERICAN INDIAN STUDENTS-SPANISH-SPEAKING STUDENTS
Pasadena Community Services Commission
500 S. Pasadena Avenue   Phone: (213) 796-4300
Pasadena, CA 91105
Covers: About 225 institutions and agencies nationwide offering educational assistance available specifically to minority students. **Entries include:** Sponsor name, address, name of contact, information concerning requirements and application. **Arrangement:** Alphabetical. **Indexes:** Geographical. **Pages** (approx.): 60. **Frequency:** Irregular; previous edition 1971; latest edition 1976. **Price:** 52¢. **Other information:** 1971 edition was published by The Free Library of Philadelphia.

Scholarships for American Indians *See* **Career Development Opportunities for Native Americans**

★4573★
SECOND JEWISH CATALOG
Jewish Publication Society of America
117 S. 17th Street   Phone: (215) 564-5925
Philadelphia, PA 19103
Publication includes: "Jewish Yellow Pages" listing Jewish

institutions, products, and services, nationwide, including synagogues, craftspersons, kosher butchers and restaurants, travel agencies and services, religious giftware, etc. **Entries include:** Institution or service name, address. **Arrangement:** Classified. **Pages** (approx.): 65-page section. **Frequency:** Irregular; latest edition 1977. **Editors:** Sharon Strassfeld and Michael Strassfeld. **Price:** $7.50. **Other information:** Not to be confused with "The Jewish Yellow Pages" published by Schocken Books, 1976 (see separate listing).

★4574★

SOCIETY FOR VALUES IN HIGHER EDUCATION—DIRECTORY OF
    FELLOWS
Society for Values in Higher Education
363 St. Ronan Street   Phone: (203) 865-8839
New Haven, CT 06511
Covers: About 2,100 persons, primarily in higher education, concerned with including moral values in liberal education. **Entries include:** Name, office address, personal data, academic field. **Arrangement:** Alphabetical. **Indexes:** Geographical, institution, academic field. **Pages** (approx.): 150. **Frequency:** Usually biennial; latest edition 1978.

★4575★

SOUTHERN BAPTIST CONVENTION ANNUAL
Southern Baptist Convention
460 James Robertson Parkway   Phone: (615) 244-4465
Nashville, TN 37215
Publication includes: List of 35,000 Baptist ministers. Also includes list of state convention officials. **Pages** (approx.): 900. **Frequency:** Annual, September. **Editor:** Martin Bradley, Recording Secretary. **Price:** $10.00.

★4576★

SPECIAL PROGRAMS FOR MINORITIES AND WOMEN IN HIGHER
    EDUCATION
Council for Financial Aid to Education
680 Fifth Avenue   Phone: (212) 541-4050
New York, NY 10019
Description: Comprehensive list of significant programs maintained by business, government, and private sources which provide general assistance and help in specific careers to Blacks, Hispanics, Indians, other minorities, and women. **Frequency:** Published fall 1978. **Price:** $4.00, postpaid, payment with order.

★4577★

SPIRITUAL COMMUNITY GUIDE: THE NEW CONSCIOUSNESS
    SOURCE BOOK
Spiritual Community Publications
Box 1080   Phone: (415) 863-4788
San Rafael, CA 94902
Covers: 3,000 yoga, health, growth, and meditation centers, ashrams, natural food stores and restaurants, spiritual bookstores, and over 400 major New Age spiritual groups, mostly in the United States and Canada. **Entries include:** Name, address, and phone of the center, store, etc., and other details including products, purpose, activities, or contact name. The major spiritual groups are described at some length. **Arrangement:** Organizations are by subject, growth centers are alphabetical, and yoga classes and similar firms (paid listings) are geographical. **Indexes:** Organization name by belief. **Pages** (approx.): 255. **Frequency:** Irregular; latest edition 1978; new edition expected September 1980. **Editor:** Parmatma Singh Khalsa. **Advertising accepted.** Circulation 80,000. **Former title:** Spiritual Community Guide for North America. **Price:** $5.95, plus $1.00 shipping (ISSN 0160-0354).

★4578★

SURVEY OF BLACK NEWSPAPERS IN AMERICA
Mercer House Press
Clover Leaf Farm   Phone: (207) 282-7116
Kennebunkport, ME 04046
Entries include: Name of paper, address, phone, circulation figures,

list of staff members, advertising rates, year of founding. **Pages** (approx.): 80. **Frequency:** Irregular; previous edition 1977; latest edition June 1979. **Editor:** Henry G. La Brie III. **Former title:** The Black Newspaper in America. **Price:** $5.00. **Also includes:** Analysis and commentary on history of Black press.

★4579★

TABLET DIRECTORY AND BUYERS GUIDE: CHURCHES,
    SYNAGOGUES AND RELIGIOUS INSTITUTIONS OF BROOKLYN,
    QUEENS, NASSAU AND SUFFOLK [New York]
Tablet Publishing Company
One Hanson Place   Phone: (212) 789-1500
Brooklyn, NY 11243
Covers: Catholic, Protestant, and Jewish churches, temples, and schools, and their clergy. **Entries include:** All listings include name of church or individual, address, phone; church and school listings include name of contact or names of key personnel. **Arrangement:** By denomination, then geographical. **Pages** (approx.): 300. **Frequency:** Annual, spring. **Editor:** Arthur L. McKenna, Sales Director. **Advertising accepted.** Circulation 10,000. **Price:** $15.00 (current and 1980 editions). **Other information:** Variant title, "Blue Book: Directory and Buyers Guide to the Churches...."

★4580★

TRAINING OPPORTUNITIES—ACCESS TO A QUALITY EDUCATION
    FOR A BRIGHTER FUTURE [Minority assistance programs]
Spanish Speaking Program Staff
Office of Education
Health, Education, and Welfare Department
400 Maryland Avenue, S. W.   Phone: (202) 245-8467
Washington, DC 20202
Covers: Over 230 scholarships, fellowships, stipends, traineeships, and other financial assistance programs offered to minority students by federal agencies, institutions, universities, and foundations; about 55 training programs for minority students are also listed. **Entries include:** Program name; name, address, and phone of contact; description of program; and eligibility requirements. **Arrangement:** By type of organization. **Pages** (approx.): 175. **Frequency:** Irregular; latest edition August 1977. **Editor:** Carmen C. Cardona, Deputy Director, Spanish Speaking Program. **Price:** Free.

★4581★

UNITARIAN UNIVERSALIST ASSOCIATION—DIRECTORY
Unitarian Universalist Association
25 Beacon Street   Phone: (617) 742-2100
Boston, MA 02108
Covers: 1,000 churches and fellowships; lists of ministers and religious educators. **Entries include:** For churches - Name, address, phone, minister's name, date established, name and address of president/chairperson, number of members, church school enrollment, financial data, code indicating district located in, name of religious educator. For ministers and religious educators - Name, address, year ordained or accredited, preparation/degrees, present and recent settlements. **Arrangement:** Geographical; minister and religious educator lists are alphabetical. **Pages** (approx.): 230. **Frequency:** Annual, fall. **Editor:** Rev. Carl Seaburg, Information Officer. **Advertising accepted.** Circulation 2,200. **Price:** $10.00.

★4582★

UNITARIAN UNIVERSALIST WOMEN'S FEDERATION—
    MEMBERSHIP DIRECTORY
Unitarian Universalist Women's Federation
25 Beacon Street   Phone: (617) 742-2100
Boston, MA 02108
Number of listings: About 300 units and 500 individual members in the United States and Canada. **Entries include:** Name, address; phone given for presidents and treasurers of local units. **Arrangement:** Geographical. **Pages** (approx.): 60. **Frequency:** Annual, fall. **Editor:** Judith Christiansen, Membership Secretary. **Price:** $2.50; available to members only.

United Bible Societies—Directory *See* Bulletin United Bible Societies—World Annual Report Issue

★4583★
U.S. CATHOLIC INSTITUTIONS FOR THE TRAINING OF CANDIDATES FOR THE PRIESTHOOD (CARA SEMINARY DIRECTORY)
Center for Applied Research in the Apostolate (CARA)
3700 Oakview Terrace, N. E.   Phone: (202) 832-2300
Washington, DC 20017
Covers: 400 Catholic seminary programs in the United States and its possessions and American seminaries abroad (Canada, Rome, Belgium). **Entries include:** Name, address and phone of institution, plus diocesan affiliation, names and titles of superiors, number of staff, degrees held by staff, accreditation, memberships, sponsorship, degree majors offered, cost of tuition and other expenses, certification for governmental student aid programs, and whether scholarships available. **Arrangement:** Geographical. **Frequency:** Annual, March. **Editor:** Rev. G. Gordon Henderson, S.J. **Price:** $15.00, billed (current and 1980 editions).

★4584★
WHERE TO BUY ISRAELI GOODS—A CHICAGOLAND DIRECTORY [Illinois]
Buy Israeli Goods Council
708 Church Street, No. 233   Phone: (312) 864-1502
Evanston, IL 60201
Covers: Retail outlets in Chicago and the surrounding suburbs for Israeli manufactured products including clothing, candies and confections, flowers, and other products. **Entries include:** Store name, address, phone; some listings also include specific items or types of items carried. **Arrangement:** By product, then by area. **Pages** (approx.): 165. **Frequency:** Irregular; latest edition October 1977. Updates mailed upon request. **Editor:** Pearl Harand, Executive Director. **Advertising accepted.** Circulation 25,000.

★4585★
WHO'S WHO IN NEW THOUGHT: BIOGRAPHICAL DICTIONARY OF NEW THOUGHT—PERSONNEL, CENTERS, AND AUTHORS' PUBLICATIONS
CSA Press
Lakemont, GA 30552
Covers: Living ministers, practitioners, and other officials in the United Church of Religious Science, Religious Science International, Unity Church, and Divine Science Church; organizations, churches, centers, schools and colleges; and historical persons who have been proponents of New Thought teachings. **Arrangement:** Individuals are alphabetical; churches and centers are geographical; schools and colleges are alphabetical. **Pages** (approx.): 320. **Frequency:** Not established; first edition 1977. **Editor:** Tom Beebe. **Price:** $6.95. **Also includes:** Bibliography of works by New Thought authors. **Other information:** New Thought is concerned with mental healing, acknowledges the existence of evil and sickness, and espouses a hopeful, positive approach to life.

★4586★
WORLD DIRECTORY OF THEOLOGICAL EDUCATION BY EXTENSION
William Carey Library
1705 N. Sierra Bonita Avenue
Pasadena, CA 91104
Covers: Extension training of Christian ministers worldwide, including workshops, centers, support agencies, associations, periodicals, and publications. **Arrangement:** Geographical. **Pages** (approx.): 420; 1976 supplement, 60. **Frequency:** Published June 1973; supplement, 1976. **Editor:** Roberta H. Winter. **Price:** $5.95, includes 1976 supplement; $1.95 for supplement only.

★4587★
WORLD LITHUANIAN ROMAN CATHOLIC DIRECTORY
Lithuanian Roman Catholic Priests' League of America
351 Highland Boulevard   Phone: (212) 647-2434
Brooklyn, NY 21007
Covers: 1,000 Lithuanian Catholic clergy, parishes, and other Catholic institutions serving Lithuanians, worldwide. **Entries include:** For clergy - Name, office and home address, office and home phone, highest degree held, areas of occupational specialty. For parishes - Address, phone, staff. **Arrangement:** Clergy are alphabetical; parishes and other institutions are geographical, then alphabetical. **Indexes:** General. **Pages** (approx.): 80. **Frequency:** Irregular; latest edition fall 1978; new edition expected fall 1980. **Editor:** Rev. Casimir Pugevicius. **Advertising accepted.** Circulation 3,000. **Former title:** Elenchus. **Price:** $5.00, plus $1.00 shipping.

★4588★
YEAR BOOK AND DIRECTORY OF THE CHRISTIAN CHURCH (DISCIPLES OF CHRIST)
General Office of the Christian Church (Disciples of Christ)
Box 1986   Phone: (317) 353-1491
Indianapolis, IN 46206
Covers: Congregations and ministers and other officials; includes officials of the General Office and other denominational bodies. **Entries include:** For congregations - Church name, address, minister, phone, congregation size, annual contributions and other budget information. For ministers, church business administrators, etc. - Name, address, title or function. **Arrangement:** Congregations, geographical; ministers, alphabetical. **Pages** (approx.): 650. **Frequency:** Annual, July. **Editor:** Shirley L. Cox. **Price:** $12.95, paper; $15.95, cloth; plus 50¢ shipping (current and 1980 editions). **Send orders to:** Christian Board of Publication, Box 179, St. Louis, MO 63166 (314-371-6900).

★4589★
YEARBOOK OF AMERICAN AND CANADIAN CHURCHES
Abingdon Press
201 Eighth Avenue South   Phone: (615) 749-6347
Nashville, TN 37202
Covers: Over 500 established religious groups in the United States and Canada. Also includes lists of local church councils, theological seminaries, church-related colleges and universities, and religious periodicals. **Entries include:** Listings for religious bodies give brief summary of history and beliefs, address, of general headquarters, and names and addresses of principal officers. Other listings include name of group, school, or periodical address, and brief details. **Arrangement:** Classified. **Indexes:** Alphabetical index to entire contents. **Pages** (approx.): 270. **Frequency:** Annual, summer. **Editor:** Constant H. Jacquet, Jr. **Price:** $12.95. **Also includes:** Statistical information on denominations, membership, finances, clergy, etc.

★4590★
YEARBOOK OF THE AMERICAN LUTHERAN CHURCH
Augsburg Publishing House
426 S. Fifth Street   Phone: (612) 330-3300
Minneapolis, MN 55415
Publication includes: Officers, boards, divisions, committees, associations, institutions, clergy, congregations, and seminary graduates of the American Lutheran Church. **Entries include:** Name, address, and phone. **Pages** (approx.): 420. **Frequency:** Annual, January. **Editor:** Arnold R. Mickelson. **Advertising accepted.** Circulation 11,500. **Price:** $3.75.

★4591★
YMCA YEARBOOK & OFFICIAL ROSTER
National Board of YMCAs
291 Broadway   Phone: (212) 374-2047
New York, NY 10007
Covers: YMCA staff in the United States; local associations in the United States; retired directors; World Alliance of YMCAs staff and addresses of National Offices. **Entries include:** Staff list includes

name, title, and location of YMCA where employed. Associations list includes address, phone, type of YMCA, number of beds (if any), staff listed by name and position, chief lay officer. Retired directors list includes address. **Arrangement:** Staff and retired directors lists are alphabetical, associations list is geographical. **Frequency:** Annual, July. **Editor:** Stan Haidl, Director, Records Management and Analysis. **Price:** $15.00 per volume, payment with order; directory material is in Volume 2. **Also includes:** Volume 1 includes statistics, reports, etc.

13

Genealogical, Veterans, and Patriotic Affairs

★4592★
ADDRESS BOOK FOR GERMANIC GENEALOGY
Thode Translations
R.R. 7, Box 306 DD
Kern Road   Phone: (614) 373-3728
Marietta, OH 45750
Covers: Over 1,200 sources useful for genealogical researchers with interest in Germany, Austria, and Switzerland; includes about 110 genealogical societies abroad, 75 central European national and regional archives, 585 foreign municipal archives, 190 foreign religious archives, and numerous libraries, genealogists, organizations, etc., in the United States. **Arrangement:** By type of resource. **Pages** (approx.): 65. **Frequency:** Irregular; latest edition 1980; new edition expected 1982. **Editor:** Ernest Thode. **Price:** $6.00, plus 66¢ shipping.

★4593★
AMERICAN & BRITISH GENEALOGY & HERALDRY
American Library Association
50 E. Huron Street   Phone: (312) 944-6780
Chicago, IL 60611
Description: Not a directory, but the principal bibliographical guide in its field to more than 5,000 selected publications of use in genealogical and heraldic research; includes numerous older books with still-useful directory content, plus a list, with addresses, of about 450 individuals and publshers whose publications are included in the volume. **Pages** (approx.): 475. **Frequency:** Second edition 1975; new edition expected 1982. **Editor:** P. William Filby. **Price:** $25.00.

★4594★
AMERICAN BATTLESHIP ASSOCIATION—MASTER ROSTER
American Battleship Association
Box 11247   Phone: (714) 271-6106
San Diego, CA 92111
Covers: 1,000 former officers and crew members of U. S. Navy battleships. **Entries include:** Name, address, dates of service. **Arrangement:** By battleship in which member served. **Pages** (approx.): 30. **Frequency:** Annual; 1980 edition expected spring. **Editor:** Margaret Graham. **Advertising accepted.** Circulation 2,000. **Price:** Available to members.

★4595★
AMERICAN GENEALOGICAL RESOURCES IN GERMAN ARCHIVES
Verlag Dokumentation
Munich, West Germany
Covers: About 285 German archives with materials of interest to American genealogists; records described are mostly from the nineteenth and twentieth centuries. Also includes German documents photocopied by the Library of Congress and now held there which were later destroyed in World War II. **Entries include:** Library or archive name, address, description of holdings. **Arrangement:** Alphabetical. **Indexes:** Geographical, name, subject. **Pages** (approx.): 335. **Frequency:** Published 1977. **Editors:** Clifford Neal Smith and Anna Piszczan-Czaja Smith. **Price:** $37.50, postpaid, payment with order. **Send orders to:** R. R. Bowker Co., Box 1807, Ann Arbor, MI 48106 (313-761-4700).

★4596★
AREA KEY PUBLICATIONS
Area Keys Genealogical Research Foundation
Highway 86 and Road 21   Phone: (303) 646-4364
Kiowa, CO 80117
Background: Compilation of "area key" publications is proceeding on a cooperative basis under the new plan of operation adopted when the former publisher became a nonprofit foundation. "New York Area Key" is the first of the new series; other publications cover Colorado, Pennsylvania, and Ohio (see separate listings); there are also County Area Keys for 67 Pennsylvania and 3 Ohio counties. **Price:** All state Area Key publications are $10.00, postpaid. **Send orders to:** Keyline Publishers, Box 98, Elizabeth, CO 80107.

★4597★
ATLANTIC BRIDGE TO GERMANY [German genealogical sources]
Everton Publishers, Inc.
Box 368   Phone: (801) 752-6022
Logan, UT 84321
Publication includes: List of archives, genealogical societies, and other information sources in Germany of possible help to American genealogists. Separate volumes deal with the states of the Federal Republic of Germany as they relate to the historical jurisdictions; five volumes published to date; write publisher for details. **Author:** Charles M. Hall.

★4598★
AUGUSTAN SOCIETY—ROSTER OF MEMBERS [Genealogy]
Augustan Society
1510 Cravens Avenue
Torrance, CA 90501
Covers: Limited to 250 persons interested in genealogy, heraldry, monarchy, and chivalry. **Pages** (approx.): 35. **Frequency:** Annual, November. **Price:** $5.00.

★4599★
BLACK GENEALOGY
Prentice-Hall, Inc.
Englewood Cliffs, NJ 07632   Phone: (201) 592-2000
Publication includes: Directory of archives and other resources

particularly useful in researching Black genealogies. **Frequency:** First edition 1977. **Editors:** Charles L. Blockson and Ron Fry. **Price:** $8.95.

★4600★

BLACK GENESIS: AN ANNOTATED BIBLIOGRAPHY FOR BLACK GENEALOGICAL RESEARCH

Gale Research Company
Book Tower   Phone: (313) 961-2242
Detroit, MI 48226

Publication includes: Descriptions, with addresses, of about 250 important archival and other sources for Black genealogy. **Pages** (approx.): 330. **Frequency:** Published fall 1978. **Editors:** James M. Rose and Alice Eicholz. **Price:** $26.00. **Also includes:** General information on types and usefulness of the various sources available to the Black genealogist and annotated bibliographical notes on general references, publications, the value of oral history, migratory patterns, etc.

★4601★

CANADIAN GENEALOGICAL HANDBOOK

Wheatfield Press
2031 Portage Avenue
Winnipeg, Manitoba R3J OK7, Canada

Covers: About 1,800 government departments, societies, etc., useful in genealogical research in Canada. **Entries include:** Source name, address; many listings include additional information. **Arrangement:** Geographical, then by type of record or repository. **Pages** (approx.): 350. **Frequency:** Irregular; latest edition 1978; new edition expected 1981-82. **Editor:** Eric Jonasson. **Price:** $11.00.

Colonial Clergy of Maryland, Delaware, and Georgia *See* Pedigrees of Descendants of Colonial Clergy

Colonial Clergy of Virginia, North Carolina, and South Carolina *See* Pedigrees of Descendants of Colonial Clergy

★4602★

COLORADO AREA KEY: A GUIDE TO THE GENEALOGICAL RECORDS OF THE STATE OF COLORADO

Area Keys Genealogical Research Foundation
Highway 86 and Road 21   Phone: (303) 646-4364
Kiowa, CO 80117

Covers: Governmental, library, association, and other sources of genealogical records in Colorado. **Entries include:** Source name, address, nature of records. **Editor:** Florence Clint. **Price:** $10.00. **Also includes:** Extensive historical and bibliographical information relating to genealogical research in Colorado.

★4603★

DIRECTORY OF AFRO-AMERICAN RESOURCES

R. R. Bowker Company
1180 Avenue of the Americas   Phone: (212) 764-5100
New York, NY 10036

Covers: About 2,100 organizations and institutions in the United States with research materials useful for Black history, genealogy, etc.; includes historical societies, significant collections of personal papers, libraries, insurance associations, and other sources. **Arrangement:** Geographical. **Pages** (approx.): 485. **Frequency:** First edition 1970. **Editor:** Walter Schatz. **Price:** $24.95, postpaid, payment with order. **Send orders to:** R. R. Bowker Co., Box 1807, Ann Arbor, MI 48106 (313-761-4700). **Other information:** Compiled for the Race Relations Information Center.

★4604★

DIRECTORY OF CENSUS INFORMATION SOURCES

Summit Publications
Box 222
Munroe Falls, OH 44262

Covers: More than 200 publishers of over 1,450 different printed, historical Federal Census Schedules and Mortality Schedules for genealogists and historians plus individuals and companies who provide census search services. **Entries include:** Vendor name, address, schedules or services offered, prices. **Arrangement:** Geographical. **Pages** (approx.): 50. **Frequency:** Biennial, summer of even years. **Editor:** John Konrad. **Price:** $4.00 (current edition); $5.00 (1980 edition); postpaid.

★4605★

DIRECTORY OF GENEALOGICAL PERIODICALS

Summit Publications
Box 222
Munroe Falls, OH 44262

Covers: Over 1,100 genealogical periodicals published worldwide including general periodicals and "one-name" family periodicals. **Entries include:** Publication name, address. **Arrangement:** Classified by type of publisher (society, individual, etc.) and whether published in United States or Europe. **Pages** (approx.): 70. **Frequency:** Biennial, summer of odd years. **Editor:** John Konrad. **Price:** $5.00.

★4606★

DIRECTORY OF GENEALOGICAL SOCIETIES IN THE U.S.A. AND CANADA

Libra Publications
297 Cove Road   Phone: (301) 255-9229
Pasadena, MD 21122

Covers: 850 genealogical societies and 100 independent genealogical periodicals. Also lists defunct societies and periodicals. **Entries include:** Name, address, number of members, annual dues, size of library, library hours, area of interest, special projects. **Arrangement:** Societies are geographical, periodicals are alphabetical by title. **Pages** (approx.): 70. **Frequency:** Biennial, summer of even years. **Editor:** Mary K. Meyer. **Advertising accepted.** Circulation 1,500. **Price:** $6.00 (current edition); $8.00 (1980 edition).

★4607★

DIRECTORY OF PROFESSIONAL GENEALOGISTS AND RELATED SERVICES

Association of Professional Genealogists
Box 11601   Phone: (801) 355-1662
Salt Lake City, UT 84147

Covers: Genealogists and related research services; listings are paid. **Entries include:** Genealogist's name or company name, address; many listings include phone. **Arrangement:** By specialty or service (countries, estate settlements, tours, lectures, etc.). **Frequency:** Annual, April. **Editor:** Wilma Adkins. **Price:** $7.75, postpaid.

★4608★

ENCYCLOPEDIA OF GERMAN-AMERICAN GENEALOGICAL RESEARCH

R. R. Bowker Company
1180 Avenue of the Americas   Phone: (212) 764-5100
New York, NY 10036

Publication includes: Chapters on both European and United States sources, such as church, occupational, military, naturalization, and other records; German Jewish records are included. **Indexes:** General. **Pages** (approx.): 275. **Frequency:** First edition 1976. **Editors:** Clifford Neal Smith and Anna Piszczan-Czaja Smith. **Price:** $37.50, postpaid, payment with order. **Send orders to:** R. R. Bowker Co., Box 1807, Ann Arbor, MI 48106 (313-761-4700).

★4609★

ENGLISH FAMILY RESEARCH [Genealogy]

Summit Publications
Box 222
Munroe Falls, OH 44262

Publication includes: Hereditary and patriotic organizations for the Colonial and Revolutionary periods, federal archives, and genealogical societies and other sources in England. **Entries include:** Name, address. **Frequency:** First edition 1979. **Editor:** John Konrad. **Price:** $4.00, postpaid.

★4610★
FAMILY SURNAME PUBLICATIONS
Rebecca L. Roth
573 Woodbridge Drive   Phone: (404) 471-2788
Riverdale, GA 30274
Covers: More than 250 family newsletters, bulletins, and quarterlies. **Entries include:** Name of publication, name of publisher or responsible individual, address, surnames of interest. **Pages** (approx.): 20. **Frequency:** Latest edition 1975. **Editor:** Betty L McCay. **Price:** $3.50, postpaid.

★4611★
FINDING OUR FATHERS: A GUIDEBOOK TO JEWISH GENEALOGY
Random House
201 E. 50th Street   Phone: (212) 751-2600
New York, NY 10022
Publication includes: Extensive list of sources for Jewish genealogy in the United States; overseas sources also included, along with basic public records in the United States needed for all research. **Pages** (approx.): 400. **Frequency:** First edition 1977. **Editor:** Dan Rottenberg. **Price:** $12.95.

★4612★
FINDING YOUR ROOTS
Ballantine Books, Inc.
Random House, Inc.
201 E. 50th Street   Phone: (212) 751-2600
New York, NY 10022
Covers: Major archives and other genealogical information sources in the United States and abroad, genealogical associations, genealogical publishers, and map publishers issuing maps of value to genealogists. Numerous references (with addresses) to sources which are not repeated in the main directory section, "State-by-State Family History Help List." **Entries include:** Source name, address. **Indexes:** General. **Pages** (approx.): 300. **Frequency:** Not established; first edition 1977. **Editor:** Jeane Eddy Westin. **Price:** $1.95, plus 50¢ shipping.

★4613★
GENEALOGICAL HANDBOOK OF GERMAN RESEARCH
Everton Publishers, Inc.
Box 368   Phone: (801) 752-6022
Logan, UT 84321
Publication includes: List of record repositories, genealogical and family organizations, and other sources in Germany of possible help to American genealogists. **Entries include:** Name of source, address, other details. **Pages** (approx.): 205. **Author:** Larry O. Jensen. **Price:** $11.50, postpaid. **Also includes:** General research guidance with respect to names, localities, correspondence, useful printed sources, etc.

★4614★
GENEALOGICAL HELPER—DIRECTORY OF GENEALOGICAL SOCIETIES AND PROFESSIONALS ISSUE
Everton Publishers, Inc.
Box 368   Phone: (801) 752-6022
Logan, UT 84321
Covers: Genealogical societies, libraries, periodicals, and professional genealogists throughout the world. **Entries include:** All entries include organization or individual name and address. Periodical listings include frequency and price. Professional genealogist listings include codes indicating specialties. **Arrangement:** Geographical. **Pages** (approx.): 50-page section in regular issue. **Frequency:** Annual, July-August issue. **Editor:** George B. Everton, Jr. **Advertising accepted.** Circulation 34,000. **Price:** $3.00.

★4615★
GENEALOGICAL HELPER—FAMILY ASSOCIATION ISSUE
Everton Publishers, Inc.
Box 368   Phone: (801) 752-6022
Logan, UT 84321
Covers: Associations devoted to genealogical study of particular families. **Entries include:** Association name, address, name of president or secretary. **Arrangement:** Alphabetical. **Frequency:** Annual, May-June issue. **Editor:** George B. Everton, Jr. **Advertising accepted.** Circulation 34,000. **Price:** $3.00.

★4616★
GENEALOGICAL HELPER—"GENEALOGY AND THE PUBLIC LIBRARY" [Article]
Everton Publishers, Inc.
Box 368   Phone: (801) 752-6022
Logan, UT 84321
Covers: More than 200 public libraries nationwide which have separate genealogical collections or a special interest in such materials. **Entries include:** Library name, address. **Arrangement:** Geographical. **Author:** Melvin L. Grotberg. **Price:** $3.00. **Other information:** Article appears in July-August 1978 issue.

★4617★
GENEALOGICAL HISTORICAL GUIDE TO LATIN AMERICA
Gale Research Company
Book Tower   Phone: (313) 961-2242
Detroit, MI 48226
Publication includes: Country-by-country listing of national, provincial, departmental, and other archives in Latin America, with a detailed listing of records of genealogical value and where they may be found. **Pages** (approx.): 275. **Frequency:** Published September 1978. **Editor:** Lyman De Platt. **Price:** $24.00. **Also includes:** Discussion of conditions which affected record keeping; abbreviations in early records; glossary; political divisions; etc.

Genealogical Register of the Society of the Descendants of
    Colonial Clergy *See* Pedigrees of Descendants of Colonial
    Clergy

★4618★
GENEALOGICAL RESEARCH: METHODS AND SOURCES
American Society of Genealogists
2255 Cedar Lane   Phone: (703) 560-4496
Vienna, VA 22180
Covers: Genealogical research sources, including public records and libraries. Volume 1 covers New England, eastern states, some southern states, and four Canadian provinces; Volume 2 covers six midwestern states, five southern states, Ontario, and North American migrations. **Frequency:** Volume 1 published 1961; Volume 2, 1970. **Editors:** Volume 1, Milton Rubbicam; Volume 2, Kenn Stryker-Rodda. **Price:** $14.00.

★4619★
GENEALOGICAL RESEARCH FOR CZECH AND SLOVAK AMERICANS
Gale Research Company
Book Tower   Phone: (313) 961-2242
Detroit, MI 48226
Covers: Location and availability of vital records, parish registers, census returns, military records, land records, and other data in Europe. **Pages** (approx.): 200. **Frequency:** Published August 1978. **Editor:** Olga Miller. **Price:** $24.00. **Also includes:** Names, abbreviations, and terms found in Czech and Slovak genealogical records; chapter bibliographies; other data.

★4620★
GENEALOGICAL RESEARCH IN MARYLAND: A GUIDE
Maryland Historical Society
201 W. Monument Street   Phone: (301) 687-3750
Baltimore, MD 21201
Publication includes: Lists of genealogical and local history societies, and archives containing historic records useful to the historian and genealogist. **Frequency:** Irregular; latest edition 1976; new edition expected 1980. **Editor:** Mary K. Meyer. **Price:** $6.00, plus $1.00 shipping, payment with order.

★4621★

GENEALOGICAL SOCIETIES AND HISTORICAL SOCIETIES (WITH GENEALOGICAL INTERESTS)
Summit Publications
Box 222
Munroe Falls, OH 44262
Covers: About 1,150 groups in the United States and 200 abroad. **Entries include:** Publication name, publisher, address. **Pages** (approx.): 55. **Frequency:** Annual. **Editor:** John Konrad. **Price:** $3.50 (current edition); $4.00 (1980 edition); postpaid.

★4622★

GENEALOGICAL SOURCE HANDBOOK
George K. Schweitzer
7914 Gleason, C-1136
Knoxville, TN 37919
Covers: 750 genealogical sources with detailed instructions for obtaining genealogical information from them. **Pages** (approx.): 120. **Frequency:** Biennial, January of even years. **Editor:** George K. Schweitzer. **Price:** $7.00.

★4623★

GENEALOGIST'S GUIDE [Wisconsin counties]
Everton Publishers, Inc.
Box 368   Phone: (801) 752-6022
Logan, UT 84321
Covers: Location of records of genealogical value in Calumet, Manitowoc, and Sheboygan counties. **Frequency:** First published 1977. **Editor:** Richard N. Cote. **Price:** $10.00 for each county edition.

★4624★

GENEALOGY: AN INTRODUCTION TO CONTINENTAL CONCEPTS
Polyanthos
Drawer 51359   Phone: (504) 566-7406
New Orleans, LA 70151
Publication includes: Lists of sources, with addresses, for genealogical research in Europe, with special emphasis on French sources. **Pages** (approx.): 150. **Frequency:** Fourth French edition 1975, English translation 1977. **Editor:** Pierre Durye, Chief Curator, French National Archives; translated by Wilson Ober Clough. **Price:** $7.50, payment must accompany order. **Also includes:** Chapters on origin of genealogy; usefulness of genealogy in biology and genetics, medicine, demography, and history.

★4625★

GENEALOGY IN MICHIGAN: WHAT, WHEN, WHERE
Alloa C. Anderson
1120 Lincoln Avenue   Phone: (313) 663-2128
Ann Arbor, MI 48104
Covers: Michigan libraries and archives with material of genealogical interest; Michigan genealogical societies; Michigan counties. **Entries include:** Organization name, address; some listings include additional details on holdings, interests, etc. **Pages** (approx.): 50. **Frequency:** Irregular; latest edition September 1978. **Former title:** Genealogy in Michigan: Its What, When, Where. **Price:** $2.50, plus 75¢ shipping. **Send orders to:** Polly Bender, 2310 Ayrshire Road, Ann Arbor, MI 48105.

★4626★

GERMAN FAMILY RESEARCH MADE SIMPLE
Summit Publications
Box 222
Munroe Falls, OH 44262
Publication includes: Lists with addresses of archives, periodicals, professional researchers, and publishers of maps likely to be helpful to genealogists; covers each state within East and West Germany. **Entries include:** Name, address. **Arrangement:** Classified by type of source. **Frequency:** Second edition 1977. **Editor:** John Konrad. **Price:** $6.00, postpaid.

★4627★

GUIDE TO FOREIGN GENEALOGICAL RESEARCH
Maralyn A. Wellauer
3239 N. 58th Street
Milwaukee, WI 53216
Publication includes: Lists of genealogical archives, libraries, associations, etc., in each European country, with addresses and some brief comments. **Arrangement:** Geographical. **Pages** (approx.): 225. **Frequency:** First edition 1976. **Author:** Maralyn A. Wellauer. **Price:** $11.00, postpaid. **Also includes:** Bibliographies for each country listing the basic works for beginning genealogical research in that country.

★4628★

HANDY BOOK FOR GENEALOGISTS
Everton Publishers, Inc.
Box 368   Phone: (801) 752-6022
Logan, UT 84321
Publication includes: Places to write or visit for genealogical information - associations, societies, libraries, archives, etc. **Pages** (approx.): 300. **Frequency:** Irregular; sixth edition 1971. **Author:** George B. Everton, Sr. **Price:** $11.75, cloth; $10.80, paper; postpaid. **Also includes:** Descriptions of records and histories of the counties and states of the United States, list of printed census records, etc.

★4629★

HANDY GUIDE TO RECORD-SEARCHING IN THE LARGER CITIES OF THE U.S. [Genealogy]
Everton Publishers, Inc.
Box 368   Phone: (801) 752-6022
Logan, UT 84321
Covers: Vital records in major United States cities embracing periods prior to establishment of state registration. **Entries include:** Source, type of record, address, fees for certificates, etc. **Arrangement:** Geographical. **Pages** (approx.): 140. **Editor:** E. Kay Kirkham. **Price:** $10.25.

★4630★

HOW AND WHERE TO RESEARCH YOUR ETHNIC-AMERICAN CULTURAL HERITAGE: [ETHNIC GROUP] - AMERICANS
Robert D. Reed
18581 McFarland Avenue
Saratoga, CA 95070
Covers: Historical societies, cultural institutes, libraries, archives, publishers, and other sources for genealogical research into German, Russian, Native American, Polish, Black, Japanese, Jewish, Irish, Mexican, Italian, Chinese, and Scandinavian backgrounds; separate volumes for each ethnic group. **Pages** (approx.): 30. **Frequency:** Most volumes first published 1979. **Editor:** Robert D. Reed. **Price:** $2.95, plus 40¢ shipping, per volume.

★4631★

HOW TO FIND YOUR FAMILY ROOTS
McGraw-Hill, Inc.
1221 Avenue of the Americas   Phone: (212) 997-1221
New York, NY 10020
Publication includes: Lists of genealogical information sources, with addresses, in all states and most countries abroad; includes sources for Black and Jewish genealogy. **Frequency:** First edition spring 1978. **Editors:** Timothy Field Beard and Denise Demong. **Price:** $24.95. **Other information:** Includes extensive text concerning various genealogical documents and problems, research to discover natural parents of adoptees, record keeping, etc.

★4632★

HUNTING YOUR ANCESTORS IN SOUTH CAROLINA
Florentine Press
Box 705   Phone: (904) 358-2736
Jacksonville, FL 32201
Publication includes: A variety of sources of information in South

Carolina of value to the genealogist. **Pages** (approx.): 50. **Frequency:** Irregular; latest edition 1974. **Editor:** Evelyn McDaniel Frazier Bryan. **Price:** $5.00, postpaid.

★4633★
IRISH FAMILY RESEARCH MADE SIMPLE
Summit Publications
Box 222
Munroe Falls, OH 44262
Publication includes: Societies, organizations, archives, etc., in the United States and Ireland useful in research into Gaelic ancestry. **Frequency:** First edition 1974. **Editor:** E. J. Collins. **Price:** $3.00, postpaid.

★4634★
IRISH RESEARCH AND SOURCES [Genealogy]
Rebecca L. Roth
573 Woodbridge Drive   Phone: (404) 471-2788
Riverdale, GA 30274
Publication includes: Lists with addresses of many sources of genealogical information in both the Irish Republic and Northern Ireland. **Frequency:** Latest edition 1972. **Editor:** Betty L. McCay. **Price:** $7.00, postpaid.

★4635★
KENTUCKY GENEALOGICAL RESEARCH SOURCES
Allstates Research Company
Box 25
West Jordan, UT 84084
Covers: Court records, archives, libraries, etc., in Kentucky of value to the genealogist; gives locations. **Frequency:** Published 1974. **Editor:** Beverly W. Hathaway. **Price:** $6.45. (Not verified)

★4636★
KNOW YOUR ANCESTORS: A GUIDE TO GENEALOGICAL RESEARCH
Charles E. Tuttle Company, Inc.
28 S. Main Street
Drawer F   Phone: (802) 773-8930
Rutland, VT 05701
Publication includes: Includes complete list of sources by state for vital records, with additional material on these and other records in separate chapters. **Pages** (approx.): 315. **Frequency:** Irregular. **Editor:** Ethel W. Williams. **Price:** $8.50.

★4637★
LEST WE FORGET: A GUIDE TO GENEALOGICAL RESEARCH IN THE NATION'S CAPITAL
Annandale Stake
Church of Jesus Christ of Latter-Day Saints
3900 Howard
Annandale, VA 22003
Covers: Facilities available for genealogical research in Washington, D.C., primarily at various units of the National Archives (including information on regional archive offices) and the Library of Congress, and the libraries of the Daughters of the American Revolution and the National Genealogical Society. **Entries include:** Facility or unit name, address, phone, hours, types of material available, and, in separate sections, detailed information on what materials are available, where and how to secure access, and notes on scope, content, limitations of the materials. **Indexes:** General subject-collection name-locality index. **Pages** (approx.): 150. **Frequency:** Irregular; previous edition 1969; latest edition 1976. **Editor:** June Andrew Babbel. **Price:** $6.00, postpaid, payment with order. **Other information:** Co-published with the Potomac Region of Virginia.

★4638★
LIST OF 140 NEWSPAPERS AND PERIODICALS WITH GENEALOGICAL QUERY COLUMNS
Summit Publications
Box 222
Munroe Falls, OH 44262
Entries include: Publication name, address. **Former title:** List of 100 Newspapers and Periodicals with Genealogical Query Columns. **Price:** $2.00, postpaid.

★4639★
LIST OF 100 HEREDITARY ORGANIZATIONS FOR WHICH MEMBERSHIP IS BASED UPON ANCESTRAL RESEARCH AND BACKGROUND
Summit Publications
Box 222
Munroe Falls, OH 44262
Entries include: Organization name, address, requirements. **Former title:** List of 75 Hereditary Organizations for which Membership Is Based upon Ancestral Research and Background. **Price:** $2.00, postpaid.

★4640★
MAJOR GENEALOGICAL SOURCES IN [Country]
Genealogical Department of The Church of Jesus Christ of Latter-day Saints
50 E. North Temple   Phone: (801) 531-2331
Salt Lake City, UT 84150
Background: The Genealogical Department (called "The Genealogical Society" prior to 1976) is one of the world's leading genealogical research organizations, with a library of over 100,000 volumes and 1,000,000 rolls of microfilm, and with over 200 branch libraries. The department formerly issued a series of research papers bearing the title, "Major Genealogical Record Sources in [Country]," which includes individual guides for dozens of countries. Each research paper concerns, in general, what types of records exist, for what periods of time, what genealogical information is contained in the records, and the availability of the records to the public. Series has been discontinued, but some reports are still available, and series is widely held in libraries. Available papers sell for about $1.00 each; a complete list of available papers and their prices is available from the department without charge; enclose a large stamped, self-addressed return envelope.

★4641★
MERRILL'S MARAUDERS ASSOCIATION—DIRECTORY
Merrill's Marauders Association
C/o Anthony C. Colombo
3814 E. Poinsettia Drive   Phone: (602) 996-3839
Phoenix, AZ 85028
Covers: About 800 known Merrill Marauders, surviving members of World War II infantry unit which served in Burma under General Frank D. Merrill. **Entries include:** Name, address. **Arrangement:** Alphabetical. **Pages** (approx.): 50. **Frequency:** Annual, fall. **Editor:** Anthony C. Colombo, Executive Secretary. **Price:** $1.00 (current and 1980 editions).

★4642★
NATIONAL DIRECTORY OF GENEALOGISTS
Hartwell Company
1617 W. 261st Street   Phone: (213) 326-8603
Harbor City, CA 90710
Covers: In two sections, persons engaged in genealogy as amateurs or professionals; listings for professionals are paid. **Entries include:** In section one - Name, address of person searching for data, and names, places of origin, birth dates, or other information about persons on whom further information is sought. In section two - Name, address, phone, and services of professional genealogists. **Arrangement:** Section one is alphabetical by name of searcher; section two is classified by specialty or service. **Frequency:** First edition expected

August 1980. **Editor:** Rodney Hartwell. **Advertising accepted.** **Price:** $10.00.

★4643★
NEW HAMPSHIRE GENEALOGICAL RESEARCH GUIDE
Prince George's County Genealogical Society
3602 Maureen Lane
Bowie, MD 20715
Covers: Records of genealogical value extant in New Hampshire. **Entries include:** Source name, location, availability to public, suggestions on use. **Arrangement:** By type of record. **Pages** (approx.): 40. **Frequency:** First edition 1973. **Editor:** Laird C. Towle. **Price:** $3.50.

★4644★
NEW YORK AREA KEY: A GUIDE TO THE GENEALOGICAL RECORDS OF THE STATE OF NEW YORK
Area Keys Genealogical Research Foundation
Highway 86 and Road 21   Phone: (303) 646-4364
Kiowa, CO 80117
Covers: Governmental, library, association, and other sources of genealogical records in New York. **Entries include:** Source name, address, nature of records. **Frequency:** First edition 1979. **Price:** $10.00. **Also includes:** Extensive historical and bibliographical information relating to genealogical research in New York.

★4645★
NEWSPAPER GENEALOGICAL COLUMN DIRECTORY
Heritage Books, Inc.
3602 Maureen Lane, Suite 326
Bowie, MD 20715
Covers: About 100 columnists appearing in over 150 newspapers and periodicals and offering genealogical researchers help in nearly 250 counties and 30 states. Includes notes on non-existent or discontinued columns. **Entries include:** Columnist name, publications carrying column, mailing address, counties covered, frequency, fees, whether columns are compiled or indexed. **Pages** (approx.): 100. **Frequency:** Irregular; latest edition 1979. **Editor:** Anita Cheek Milner. **Former title:** Newspaper Genealogy Columns: A Preliminary Checklist (1979). **Price:** $8.00.

Newspaper Genealogy Columns: A Preliminary Checklist *See* Newspaper Genealogical Column Directory

★4646★
OHIO AREA KEY: A GUIDE TO THE GENEALOGICAL RECORDS OF THE STATE OF OHIO
Area Keys Genealogical Research Foundation
Highway 86 and Road 21   Phone: (303) 646-4364
Kiowa, CO 80117
Covers: Governmental, library, association, and other sources of genealogical records in Ohio. **Entries include:** Source name, address, nature of records. **Pages** (approx.): 260. **Frequency:** Irregular; first edition out of print; new edition in preparation. **Editors:** Carol Willsey Flavell and Florence Clint. **Price:** New edition, two volumes, $10.00 per volume. **Also includes:** Extensive historical and bibliographical information relating to genealogical research in Ohio. **Other information:** County area keys are available for a few Ohio counties, and others are in preparation; $8.00 each.

★4647★
OHIO GENEALOGICAL GUIDE
Carol Willsey Flavell
4649 Yarmouth Lane
Youngstown, OH 44512   Phone: (216) 782-8841
Covers: Location, content, etc., of land, tax, census, church, military, and other records in Ohio; includes lists of libraries, periodicals, etc. Guides for individual counties are in preparation. **Arrangement:** By type of source or record. **Pages** (approx.): 160. **Frequency:** Previous edition 1978; latest edition 1979. **Editor:** Carol Willsey Flavell, C. G. **Price:** $8.00, postpaid.

★4648★
ORDER OF AMERICANS OF ARMORIAL ANCESTRY—COMPLETE REGISTER OF MEMBERS, WITH COATS OF ARMS
Order of Americans of Armorial Ancestry
C/o Charles Owen Johnson
2111 Jeff Davis Highway, Apt. 109-S
Arlington, VA 22202
Covers: Americans descended from an immigrant ancestor in colonial America whose forebears in Great Britain or continental Europe had the right to bear arms. **Entries include:** Name and address of member, name and drawing of arms of ancestor. **Arrangement:** Alphabetical by member name. **Pages** (approx.): 75. **Frequency:** Latest edition 1965. **Price:** Available to members only. **Other information:** Compiled and illustrated by Ruth T. Ravenscroft.

★4649★
PEDIGREES OF DESCENDANTS OF COLONIAL CLERGY
Society of the Descendants of Colonial Clergy
C/o Mrs. Frederick W. Johnson
255 Madison Street
Dedham, MA 02026
Covers: 1,350 members of the society. **Entries include:** Member name, names of ancestors, names of spouses, birth, death, and marriage dates, address of member. **Arrangement:** By member name. **Pages** (approx.): 700. **Frequency:** Published 1976; 1978 supplement; reissued as one volume. **Editor:** Robert Glenn Thurtle. **Price:** $25.00 for combined volume; $15.00 for 1976 edition; $12.50 for supplement. **Other information:** Regional editions are also available: "The Colonial Clergy of Maryland, Delaware, and Georgia," $7.00; and "The Colonial Clergy of Virginia, North Carolina, and South Carolina," $7.00.

★4650★
PENNSYLVANIA AREA KEY: A GUIDE TO THE GENEALOGICAL RECORDS OF THE STATE OF PENNSYLVANIA
Area Keys Genealogical Research Foundation
Highway 86 and Road 21   Phone: (303) 646-4364
Kiowa, CO 80117
Covers: Governmental, library, association, and other sources of genealogical records in Pennsylvania, and professional genealogical researchers in the state. **Entries include:** For sources - Source name, address, nature of records. For specialists - Name, address, description of genealogical specialties. **Indexes:** General. **Pages** (approx.): 150. **Frequency:** Irregular; latest edition 1977. **Editor:** Florence Clint. **Price:** $10.00. **Also includes:** Extensive historical and bibliographical information relating to genealogical research in Pennsylvania. **Other information:** County area keys are available for each of Pennsylvania's 67 counties; $8.00 each.

★4651★
POLISH FAMILY RESEARCH
Summit Publications
Box 222
Munroe Falls, OH 44262
Publication includes: Archives and other locations in Poland which contain information useful to genealogists. **Frequency:** First edition 1977. **Editor:** John Konrad. **Price:** $4.00, postpaid.

★4652★
POLISH FAMILY TREE SURNAMES
Thaddeus J. Obal
739 Hillsdale Avenue   Phone: (201) 664-7836
Hillsdale, NJ 07642
Covers: More than 300 persons doing genealogical research on surnames of Polish ancestry. **Entries include:** Surname of researchers, address, names in which interested. **Arrangement:** By researcher name. **Indexes:** Surnames researched, geographical location of researcher. **Pages** (approx.): 50. **Frequency:** Latest edition 1979; annual supplements. **Editor:** Thaddeus J. Obal. **Price:** $5.00.

★4653★
P.T. BOATS ALL HANDS ROSTER
P.T. Boats, Inc.
663 S. Cooper, Suite 4   Phone: (901) 272-9980
Memphis, TN 38101
Covers: 7,500 servicemen who served in P.T. boats during World War II. **Entries include:** Name, address, squadron, base, tender. **Arrangement:** Geographical. **Frequency:** Every five years; latest edition July 1979. **Editor:** J. M. Newberry, Director. **Advertising accepted.** Circulation 8,000. **Price:** Available to members only.

Register of Alumni: 1845-[Year] *See* United States Naval
   Academy Alumni Association—Register of Alumni

★4654★
REGISTER OF THE SOCIETY OF MAYFLOWER DESCENDANTS IN
   THE DISTRICT OF COLUMBIA
Society of Mayflower Descendants in the District of Columbia
1307 New Hampshire Avenue, N. W.
Washington, DC 20036
Covers: About 750 persons, not necessarily living in the District of Columbia, whose ancestors arrived in America on the "Mayflower." **Entries include:** Member name, birth date and place, marital and family information, education, occupation, address, genealogy. **Arrangement:** Alphabetical. **Indexes:** Personal name. **Frequency:** Irregular; latest edition 1976. **Price:** $20.00. **Send orders to:** Col. Kendrick Holle, 1600 S. Eads St., Apt. 825-S, Arlington, VA 22202.

★4655★
SCOTCH-IRISH FAMILY RESEARCH MADE SIMPLE
Summit Publications
Box 222
Munroe Falls, OH 44262
Publication includes: List of government offices, archives, etc., in Scotland and Northern Ireland which are of value to the genealogist. **Frequency:** First edition 1974. **Editor:** R. G. Campbell. **Price:** $3.00, postpaid.

★4656★
SEARCH AND RESEARCH [Genealogy]
Deseret Book Company
40 E. South Temple Street   Phone: (801) 534-1515
Salt Lake City, UT 84110
Publication includes: State-by-state summaries of important libraries and archives, sources for vital records, and information on first dates of certain legal requirements, such as marriage licenses. **Indexes:** Subject. **Frequency:** Latest edition 1977. **Editor:** Noel C. Stevenson. **Price:** $4.95.

★4657★
SEARCHING FOR YOUR ANCESTORS: THE HOW AND WHY OF
   GENEALOGY
Bantam Books, Inc.
666 Fifth Avenue   Phone: (212) 765-6500
New York, NY 10019
Covers: Numerous sources of genealogical information, with references to specific organizations, archives, etc.; one of the first instruction books to give attention to the genealogical problems of American Indians and Blacks. **Frequency:** Irregular; fourth edition University of Minnesota Press, 1973, Bantam Books, 1974. **Author:** Gilbert S. Doane. **Price:** $2.25, plus $1.00 shipping.

★4658★
SOURCES AND REPOSITORIES
Ronald A. Bremer
Box 16422   Phone: (801) 359-4192
Salt Lake City, UT 84116
Publication includes: List of about 300 national, regional, and state genealogical centers or major sources of genealogical information. **Entries include:** Source name, address. **Arrangement:** Geographical. **Frequency:** New edition expected 1980. **Editor:** Ronald A. Bremer.

Price: $5.00 (current edition); $10.00 (1980 edition). **Also includes:** Bibliography of genealogical reference works.

★4659★
SOURCES FOR GENEALOGICAL SEARCHING IN ILLINOIS
Rebecca L. Roth
573 Woodbridge Drive   Phone: (404) 471-2788
Riverdale, GA 30274
Frequency: First edition 1970. **Price:** $2.50, postpaid. **Other information:** Content, format size, etc., similar to that of "Sources for Genealogical Searching in Indiana," described in separate listing.

★4660★
SOURCES FOR GENEALOGICAL SEARCHING IN INDIANA
Rebecca L. Roth
573 Woodbridge Drive   Phone: (404) 471-2788
Riverdale, GA 30274
Publication includes: Textual references covering locations of and/ or sources for securing birth and death certificates, marriage and divorce records, census records, land and tax records, immigration records, wills, military records, church records, etc. Also includes lists of genealogical periodicals especially pertinent to research in the state, and a list of libraries and historical societies in the state. **Entries include:** For record sources - Type of record, repository office, and address; some entries include details concerning composition, completeness, etc., of the material. For periodicals - Title, publisher, address, brief annotation. For libraries and societies - Name, address, description of resources, hours. **Pages** (approx.): 20. **Frequency:** Latest edition 1973. **Editor:** Betty L. McCay. **Price:** $3.50, postpaid. **Also includes:** Brief historical data on settlement patterns, boundaries, etc.; bibliography of selected basic reference books and other materials important to research on Indiana genealogies; maps.

★4661★
SOURCES FOR GENEALOGICAL SEARCHING IN KENTUCKY
Rebecca L. Roth
573 Woodbridge Drive   Phone: (404) 471-2788
Riverdale, GA 30274
Frequency: Latest edition October 1979. **Price:** $3.00, postpaid. **Other information:** Content, format, size, etc., similar to that of "Sources for Genealogical Searching in Indiana," described in separate listing. **Also includes:** Special list of microfilmed county records.

★4662★
SOURCES FOR GENEALOGICAL SEARCHING IN MARYLAND
Rebecca L. Roth
573 Woodbridge Drive   Phone: (404) 471-2788
Riverdale, GA 30274
Frequency: Latest edition 1972. **Price:** $3.50, postpaid. **Other information:** Content, format size, etc., similar to that of "Sources for Genealogical Searching in Indiana," described in separate listing. **Also includes:** List of county records destroyed by fire or otherwise.

★4663★
SOURCES FOR GENEALOGICAL SEARCHING IN NORTH CAROLINA
Rebecca L. Roth
573 Woodbridge Drive   Phone: (404) 471-2788
Riverdale, GA 30274
Frequency: Latest edition 1969. **Price:** $2.50, postpaid. **Other information:** Content, format size, etc., similar to that of "Sources for Genealogical Searching in Indiana," described in separate listing. **Also includes:** List of county records destroyed by fire or otherwise.

★4664★
SOURCES FOR GENEALOGICAL SEARCHING IN OHIO
Rebecca L. Roth
573 Woodbridge Drive   Phone: (404) 471-2788
Riverdale, GA 30274
Frequency: Latest edition 1973. **Price:** $2.50, postpaid. **Other information:** Content, format, size, etc., similar to that of "Sources

for Genealogical Searching in Indiana,'' described in separate listing. **Also includes:** List of county records destroyed by fire or otherwise.

★4665★
SOURCES FOR GENEALOGICAL SEARCHING IN PENNSYLVANIA
Rebecca L. Roth
573 Woodbridge Drive   Phone: (404) 471-2788
Riverdale, GA 30274
Frequency: Latest edition 1973. **Editor:** Betty L. McCay. **Price:** $3.50, postpaid. **Other information:** Content, format, size, etc., similar to that of ''Sources for Genealogical Searching in Indiana,'' described in separate listing.

★4666★
SOURCES FOR GENEALOGICAL SEARCHING IN TENNESSEE
Rebecca L. Roth
573 Woodbridge Drive   Phone: (404) 471-2788
Riverdale, GA 30274
Frequency: Latest edition 1970. **Price:** $2.50, postpaid. **Other information:** Content, format, size, etc., similar to that of ''Sources for Genealogical Searching in Indiana,'' described in separate listing. **Also includes:** List of county records destroyed by fire or otherwise; material on useful school records.

★4667★
SOURCES FOR GENEALOGICAL SEARCHING IN VIRGINIA AND WEST VIRGINIA
Rebecca L. Roth
573 Woodbridge Drive   Phone: (404) 471-2788
Riverdale, GA 30274
Frequency: Latest edition 1971. **Price:** $4.00, postpaid. **Other information:** Content, format, size, etc., similar to that of ''Sources for Genealogical Searching in Indiana,'' described in separate listing. **Also includes:** List of county records destroyed by fire or otherwise.

★4668★
SURVEY OF AMERICAN CHURCH RECORDS
Everton Publishers, Inc.
Box 368   Phone: (801) 752-6022
Logan, UT 84321
Covers: Records of more than 40 denominations in 48 states. **Entries include:** ''Name of county, denomination, location by city/address, kind of record, years included and the locations of the records.'' **Arrangement:** Geographical. **Pages** (approx.): 350. **Editor:** E. Kay Kirkham. **Price:** $13.50, cloth; $12.50, paper.

★4669★
SURVEY OF AMERICAN GENEALOGICAL PERIODICALS AND PERIODICAL INDEXES
Gale Research Company
Book Tower   Phone: (313) 961-2242
Detroit, MI 48226
Publication includes: List of about 500 periodicals. **Entries include:** Publication name, address, scope (regional, ethnic, specialized, etc.), frequency, and code indicating compiler's judgment as to value in various types of libraries. **Arrangement:** Alphabetical. **Frequency:** Published fall 1978. **Editor:** Kip Sperry. **Price:** $24.00. **Other information:** Principal content is description and analysis of periodical and other indexes available for genealogical research.

★4670★
TENNESSEE GENEALOGICAL RESEARCH SOURCES
Allstates Research Company
Box 25
West Jordan, UT 84084
Covers: Court records, archives, libraries, etc., in Tennessee of value to the genealogist; gives locations **Frequency:** Published 1972. **Editor:** Beverly W. Hathaway.

★4671★
TRACING YOUR ANCESTRY
Oxmoor House
Box 2262   Phone: (205) 870-4440
Birmingham, AL 35202
Publication includes: Descriptions and addresses of libraries, archives, societies, and government offices which hold records of interest to the genealogist. **Frequency:** Published 1976. **Editor:** F. Wilbur Hembold. **Price:** $9.95, cloth; $4.95, paper. **Other information:** ''Tracing Your Ancestry: Logbook'' has been published to accompany the base volume. The ''Logbook'' is a place for a permanent record of work done by the genealogist. **Price:** $3.95.

★4672★
TRACING YOUR GERMAN ROOTS
Maralyn A. Wellauer
3239 N. 58th Street
Milwaukee, WI 53216
Publication includes: Lists of publishers of German genealogical periodicals and books, and of genealogical societies in Germany. Also includes material on American records for determining immigrant ancestor's place of origin. **Frequency:** First edition 1978. **Author:** Maralyn A. Wellauer. **Price:** $5.50, postpaid.

★4673★
TRACING YOUR NORWEGIAN ROOTS
Maralyn A. Wellauer
3239 N. 58th Street
Milwaukee, WI 53216
Publication includes: Genealogical societies, libraries, archives, and other sources in Norway and United States. **Arrangement:** By type of source. **Pages** (approx.): 75. **Frequency:** First edition 1979. **Editor:** Maralyn A. Wellauer. **Price:** $5.50. **Other information:** Includes general information on Norwegian names, surnames, maps, society, etc., useful to genealogical researcher.

★4674★
UNITED STATES GUIDE TO FAMILY RECORDS
Lin-Port House
Box 59277   Phone: (312) 274-1937
Chicago, IL 60659
Covers: Public agencies able to provide information or copies of records concerning births, marriages, divorces, and deaths, and general suggestions for obtaining such information from other sources. **Entries include:** Name and address of office, cost of copy, information on how far back records in the office go, other information. **Arrangement:** By type of record, then geographical. **Pages** (approx.): 60. **Frequency:** First edition May 1978. **Editors:** Vincent and Linda Portnov. **Price:** $3.95.

★4675★
UNITED STATES NAVAL ACADEMY ALUMNI ASSOCIATION— REGISTER OF ALUMNI
United States Naval Academy Alumni Association
Alumni House   Phone: (301) 263-4448
Annapolis, MD 21402
Covers: About 62,000 graduates and former naval cadets and midshipmen, living and deceased. **Entries include:** Name, date of birth, state appointed from, address (including duty address, if still on active duty), decorations, date of resignation or death and widow's name, where applicable. **Arrangement:** By graduating class. **Indexes:** Alphabetical, geographical. **Pages** (approx.): 800. **Frequency:** Annual, January. **Editor:** Captain Roy C. Smith III, Director of Publications. **Advertising accepted.** **Price:** $12.50 (current edition); $15.00 (1980 edition).

★4676★
VITAL RECORD COMPENDIUM
Everton Publishers, Inc.
Box 368   Phone: (801) 752-6022
Logan , UT 84321
Covers: Birth, death, and marriage records through the United States
of value to genealogical researchers compiled prior to beginning of
registration, and where the existing records are housed.
Arrangement: Geographical, to county level. **Pages** (approx.): 325.
Frequency: First edition 1979. **Editors:** John D. and E. Diane
Stemmons. **Price:** $19.95, postpaid.

★4677★
WISCONSIN GENEALOGICAL ADDRESSES
Victoria Wilson
4747 N. 30th Street   Phone: (414) 442-1387
Milwaukee, WI 53209
Covers: Genealogical societies, historical societies, museums, area
research centers, publishers and booksellers, and professional
genealogists concerned with or working in Wisconsin. **Entries include:**
Group or personal name, address. **Arrangement:** Classified by type of
resource. **Pages** (approx.): 50. **Frequency:** First edition 1978; new
edition expected spring 1980. **Editor:** Victoria Wilson. **Price:** $3.50
(current edition); $5.00 (tentative, 1980 edition).

★4678★
YELLOW PAGES [Tennessee genealogical resources]
Byron Sistler & Associates
1712 Natchez Trace   Phone: (615) 297-3085
Nashville, TN 37212
Covers: Genealogical records, libraries, organizations, etc., in
Tennessee. **Price:** $7.00, postpaid.

14

Hobbies, Travel,
and Leisure

★4679★
ACCESS DALLAS [Handicapped guide]
Committee for the Removal of Architectural Barriers
Box 36402
Dallas, TX 75235
Publication includes: Information about building features (ramps, wide doors, etc.) which help make Dallas' major stores, public buildings, recreation facilities, etc., accessible to handicapped persons, and warnings about architectural barriers which might present difficulties. **Arrangement:** Classified by type of establishment or institution. **Indexes:** Alphabetical, geographical. **Pages** (approx.): 100. **Frequency:** Irregular; latest edition 1977. **Price:** $1.25 shipping.

★4680★
ACCESS TO BOSTON [Handicapped guide]
Easter Seal Society
20 Providence   Phone: (617) 482-3370
Boston, MA 02108
Publication includes: Information about building features (ramps, wide doors, etc.) which help make Boston's major stores, public buildings, museums, restaurants, theaters, etc., accessible to handicapped persons, and warnings about architectural barriers which might present difficulties. Also includes information about many places listed, including hours, special attractions, etc. **Arrangement:** Classified by type of establishment or institution. **Pages** (approx.): 65. **Frequency:** Irregular; latest edition 1976 (now out of print); new edition planned. **Former title:** Wheeling through Boston (1976).

★4681★
ACCESS TRAVEL: AIRPORTS [Handicapped facilities]
Office of Public Affairs
Federal Aviation Administration
800 Independence Avenue, S. W.   Phone: (202) 426-1960
Washington, DC 20591
Covers: Dot chart tabulation of 220 airports in 27 countries. **Entries include:** Airport name, location, description of facilities and services of special importance to persons in wheelchairs and the blind, deaf, and aged. **Arrangement:** Geographical. **Frequency:** Irregular; latest edition fall 1979. **Price:** Free. **Other information:** Published in cooperation with Airport Operators Council International and Architectural and Transportation Barriers Compliance Board.

★4682★
ACCESS WASHINGTON: HANDICAPPED GUIDE TO DISTRICT OF COLUMBIA
Information Center for Handicapped Individuals
120 C Street, N. W.   Phone: (202) 347-4986
Washington, DC 20001
Publication includes: Information about building features (ramps, wide doors, etc.) which help make Washington's major stores, public buildings, museums, theaters, etc., accessible to handicapped persons. **Arrangement:** Classified by type of establishment or institution. **Pages** (approx.): 130. **Frequency:** Irregular; second edition 1976 with addendum. **Price:** $1.00.

★4683★
AIRLINE SERVICES UNLIMITED TRAVEL GUIDE
Airline Services Unlimited
1335 Columbus Avenue   Phone: (415) 441-7300
San Francisco, CA 94133
Covers: 3,000 airlines, tours, car rentals, camper rentals, cruises, local excursions, and special attractions which allow discounts to airline employees, worldwide. **Entries include:** Name, address, and phone of facility or service; description; regular price and type and amount of discount; credit cards accepted; validity dates; booking procedures; whether parents and retired airline employees are eligible. **Arrangement:** Geographical. **Pages** (approx.): 290. **Frequency:** Quarterly; January, April, July, and October. **Editor:** Ronald A. Folkenfilk. **Advertising accepted.** Circulation 30,000. **Price:** $7.50 per issue, payment with order; available to airline personnel only.

★4684★
AMATEUR RADIO EQUIPMENT DIRECTORY
Kengore Corporation
9 James Avenue   Phone: (201) 297-6918
Kendall Park, NJ 08824
Covers: 100 manufacturers of amateur radio equipment (citizens band not included). **Entries include:** Company name, address, phone, and products, their prices and specifications, and photographs. **Pages** (approx.): 200. **Frequency:** Annual, January. **Editor:** Kenneth A. Gordon, Publisher. **Advertising accepted.** Circulation 15,000. **Price:** $5.00, postpaid (current and 1980 editions).

★4685★
AMAZING AMERICA: A GUIDE TO OVER 600 SIGHTS
Random House, Inc.
201 E. 50th Street   Phone: (301) 233-1011
New York, NY 10022
Covers: 600 contests, festivals, monuments, museums, races, and

other "extraordinary or remarkable sights in America," including the National Eye-Gouging and Ear-Biting Contest, Uncle Sam's grave, the Museum of Broadcasting, etc. **Entries include:** Name of event, site, etc., address, description, dates and hours, admission fees. **Arrangement:** By region, then by state. **Indexes:** Alphabetical, subject. **Pages** (approx.): 450. **Frequency:** Published June 1978. **Editors:** Jane and Michael Stern. **Price:** $6.95. **Send orders to:** Random House, Inc., 400 Hahn Road, Westminster, MD 21157.

★4686★
AMERICA IN WAX
Crown Publishers, Inc.
One Park Avenue   Phone: (212) 532-9200
New York, NY 10016
Covers: 96 wax museums in the Americas, primarily the United States and Canada. Includes over 600 photographs. **Entries include:** Museum name, address, description of exhibits, etc. **Arrangement:** Geographical. **Frequency:** Published 1977; no new edition planned. **Editor:** Gene Gurney. **Price:** Out of print.

★4687★
AMERICAN CAVY BREEDERS ASSOCIATION NEWS [Guinea pigs for show]
American Cavy Breeders Association
C/o Stephen & LaGene Milhollin
3304 Lafayette
Omaha, NE 68131
Publication includes: List of open and youth shows for cavies (guinea pigs). **Entries include:** Date of show, name of sponsor, name and address of contact. **Arrangement:** Chronological. **Frequency:** Quarterly. **Advertising accepted.** **Price:** $1.00, payment with order.

★4688★
AMERICAN CRAFT MAGAZINE—TRAVEL AND STUDY ABROAD ISSUE
American Crafts Council
22 W. 55th Street   Phone: (212) 397-0600
New York, NY 10019
Publication includes: List of about 30 craft programs and 10 craft tours outside the United States. **Entries include:** Sponsor, address, crafts taught or topics, dates offered. **Arrangement:** Geographical. **Frequency:** Annual, April. **Advertising accepted.** **Former title:** Craft Horizons - Travel and Study Abroad Issue. **Price:** $3.50.

★4689★
AMERICAN FIRST DAY COVER SOCIETY—MEMBERSHIP DIRECTORY
American First Day Cover Society
14 Samoset Road
Cranford, NJ 07016
Covers: 4,000 collectors of envelopes bearing stamps cancelled on the first day of issue. **Entries include:** Name, address, member registration number, code for life, charter, or junior member. **Arrangement:** Alphabetical. **Pages** (approx.): 55. **Frequency:** Biennial, even years. **Price:** $5.00 (current edition); $10.00 (tentative, 1980 edition).

★4690★
AMERICAN POLITICAL ITEM COLLECTORS [YEAR] HANDBOOK
American Political Item Collectors
1054 Sharpsburg Drive   Phone: (205) 883-1695
Huntsville, AL 35803
Number of listings: More than 2,300. **Entries include:** Name, address, occupation; coded collecting interests, age, collection size; phone. **Arrangement:** Alphabetical. **Indexes:** Geographical. **Pages** (approx.): 200. **Frequency:** Annual, May. **Editor:** Joseph D. Hayes, Secretary-Treasurer. **Price:** Available to members only.

★4691★
AMERICAN REVENUER—YEARBOOK ISSUE [Stamps]
American Revenue Association
Box 573   Phone: (515) 756-3680
Rockford, IA 50468
Covers: 1,600 member collectors and dealers interested in United States and foreign revenue stamps. **Entries include:** Name, address, collecting interest. **Arrangement:** Alphabetical. **Pages** (approx.): 25. **Frequency:** Biennial, April of even years. **Editor:** Kenneth Trettin. **Advertising accepted.** Circulation 2,000. **Price:** Included in membership, $6.00 per year (ISSN 0163-1608). **Send orders to:** Bruce Miller, Secretary, 1016 S. Fifth Ave., Arcadia, CA 91006.

★4692★
AMERICAN RHODODENDRON SOCIETY—MEMBERSHIP LIST
American Rhododendron Society
617 Fairway Drive
Aberdeen, WA 98520
Covers: About 4,500 gardeners who have a special interest in the flowering tree and shrub of the rhododendron family, and rhododendron nurseries that serve local chapters. **Entries include:** Name, address, chapter affiliation. **Arrangement:** Membership list is alphabetical; nurseries list is geographical. **Pages** (approx.): 70. **Frequency:** Every four years; latest editon March 1978. **Editor:** Mrs. Robert Berry, Executive Secretary. **Price:** Available to members only.

★4693★
AMERICAN SILKIE BANTAM CLUB—MEMBERSHIP LIST [Poultry]
American Silkie Bantam Club
2221 Blue Ridge Boulevard   Phone: (816) 254-8389
Independence, MO 64052
Covers: About 225 individuals who raise silkie bantam breed chickens to be entered in competition. **Entries include:** Name, address. **Arrangement:** Geographical. **Pages** (approx.): 10. **Frequency:** Annual, September.

★4694★
AMERICAN SOCIETY OF DOWSERS—MEMBERSHIP LIST
American Society of Dowsers
                    Phone: (802) 654-3417
Danville, VT 05828
Covers: 1,800 persons who are amateur or professional dowsers interested in locating water, oil, mineral deposits, and various objects through use of forked sticks, pendulums, rods, etc. **Frequency:** Annual.

★4695★
AMERICAN TARANTULA SOCIETY—MEMBERSHIP DIRECTORY
American Tarantula Society
Box 2312   Phone: (206) 734-6265
Bellingham, WA 98225
Covers: Over 550 individuals interested in the tarantula spider. **Entries include:** Name, address, phone. **Arrangement:** Alphabetical. **Pages** (approx.): 10. **Frequency:** Annual, May. **Editor:** Dale Lund, Founder. **Price:** Available to members only.

★4696★
AMERICAN THEATRE ORGAN SOCIETY—NATIONAL MEMBERSHIP ROSTER
American Theatre Organ Society
Box 1002   Phone: (703) 364-2423
Middleburg, VA 22117
Number of listings: 6,000; international coverage. **Entries include:** Name, address. **Arrangement:** Geographical. **Pages** (approx.): 100. **Frequency:** Irregular; latest edition 1977. **Advertising accepted.** Circulation 3,000. **Price:** $1.00, available to members and advertisers only.

★4697★

AMERICAN TOPICAL ASSOCIATION—MEMBERSHIP DIRECTORY
[Stamps]
American Topical Association
3306 N. 50th Street   Phone: (414) 444-9109
Milwaukee, WI 53216
Covers: About 14,000 member stamp collectors who collect according to stamp subject. **Arrangement:** Alphabetical. **Indexes:** Geographical, subject. **Pages** (approx.): 200. **Frequency:** Irregular; latest edition August 1978. **Editor:** Jerome Husak. **Advertising accepted.** **Price:** $25.00. **Other information:** Use of directory as mailing list requires written permission.

★4698★

ANTIQUE HUNTING IN THE BAY AREA AND NORTHERN
    CALIFORNIA
Wingbow Press
2940 Seventh Street   Phone: (415) 549-3030
Berkeley, CA 94710
Covers: More than 600 antiques and collectibles dealers, shows, auctions, and appraisers. **Entries include:** Shop or show name, address, specialties. **Arrangement:** Geographical. **Indexes:** Repair services, specialties, store name. **Pages** (approx.): 145. **Frequency:** Not established; first edition 1978. **Editor:** Nelly Hudson. **Price:** $4.50, plus 75¢ shipping.

★4699★

ANTIQUE SHOP GUIDE
Mayhill Publications
Box 90   Phone: (317) 345-5134
Knightstown, IN 46148
Covers: 3,000 antique shops, museums, flea markets, and historic homes open to the public in Illinois, Indiana, Kentucky, Michigan, Missouri, Ohio, Tennessee, western Pennsylvania, West Virginia, and Wisconsin. **Entries include:** For antique shops - Shop name, address, map reference, year established, specialty, whether reproductions are handled, hours and seasons open, phone. Listings for other categories have similar detail. **Arrangement:** Geographical. **Indexes:** Town name. **Pages** (approx.): 165. **Frequency:** Annual, March. **Editor:** Beverly McDonald. **Advertising accepted.** **Price:** $1.50 (current edition); $1.90 (1980 edition); plus 50¢ shipping. **Other information:** Variant title, "Tri-State Trader Antique Shop Guide."

★4700★

ANTIQUE SHOPS AND DEALERS U.S.A.
Crown Publishers, Inc.
One Park Avenue   Phone: (212) 532-9200
New York, NY 10016
Number of listings: Over 10,000. **Entries include:** Shop name, address, phone, date established, name of proprietor, hours, type of stock and specialties, directions for reaching shop. **Arrangement:** Geographical. **Indexes:** Specialties. **Pages** (approx.): 450. **Frequency:** Not established; latest edition 1979. **Editors:** Bette Griffin and Michael Stewart. **Price:** $9.95. **Other information:** In the American Antiques Marketplaces Series.

★4701★

ANTIQUES DEALER—ANNUAL DIRECTORY OF WHOLESALE
    BUYING SOURCES
Ebel-Doctorow Publications, Inc.
1115 Clifton Avenue   Phone: (201) 779-1600
Clifton, NJ 07013
Covers: 300 wholesale antiques dealers, appraisers, auctioneers, show managers, and suppliers to the trade who also have ads in this issue. **Entries include:** Dealer or company name, address, type of merchandise (copperware, American furniture, etc.), or products and services (appraisals, lamp parts, etc.). **Arrangement:** Geographical. **Indexes:** Product/service, alphabetical. **Pages** (approx.): 100. **Frequency:** Annual, September. **Editor:** Stella Hall. **Advertising accepted.** Circulation 10,000. **Price:** $4.00.

Art Material Directory and Product Information Guide *See*
    International Art Material Directory

Art Material Trade News Directory of Art & Craft Materials *See*
    International Art Material Directory

★4702★

ARTS & ACTIVITIES—BUYER'S GUIDE ISSUE
Publishers Development Corporation
591 Camino de la Reina, Suite 200   Phone: (714) 297-8520
San Diego, CA 92108
Covers: About 750 suppliers of school art material and equipment. **Entries include:** Company name, address, types of products offered. **Arrangement:** Alphabetical. **Indexes:** Product. **Pages** (approx.): 70. **Frequency:** Annual, February. **Editor:** Leven C. Leatherbury, Curriculum Specialist, Art Education, San Diego City Schools. **Advertising accepted.** Circulation 38,000. **Price:** $2.00 (current and 1980 editions); state grade level served.

★4703★

ASSOCIATION OF NORTH AMERICAN RADIO CLUBS—CLUB LIST
Association of North American Radio Clubs
557 N. Madison Avenue   Phone: (213) 793-0769
Pasadena, CA 91101
Covers: About 25 North American and international member radio clubs concerned with long-distance radio listening as a hobby. **Entries include:** Name of club, address, year founded, types of broadcasts of interest to club members, publications, subscription and sample copy prices, dues. **Arrangement:** Alphabetical. **Pages** (approx.): 5. **Frequency:** Semiannual, May and November. **Editor:** Dave Browne, Executive Secretary/Editor. **Price:** 50¢, postpaid. **Other information:** Association also publishes "Directory of Club Publications and Services" giving extensive detail on these activities; 50¢.

★4704★

AT YOUR SERVICE [Handicapped guide to Boston area]
Massachusetts Rehabilitation Hospital
125 Nashua Street   Phone: (617) 523-1818
Boston, MA 02114
Publication includes: Information on leisure facilities and services (social programs, sports, theaters, etc.) available to handicapped persons in Greater Boston area, with comments on architectural features of buildings which impede or enhance their use. **Arrangement:** Arranged by type of service. **Pages** (approx.): 40. **Frequency:** Irregular; latest edition 1976. **Price:** $1.00.

★4705★

AUTO ENTHUSIAST DIRECTORY
Carl Hungness Publishing
4902 W. 15th Street   Phone: (317) 244-4792
Speedway, IN 46224
Covers: Over 1,800 sources for parts, supplies, and services necessary for restoring old automobiles; includes car clubs, car museums, specialist dealers in old cars, and sources of books, repair manuals, etc. **Entries include:** Company or individual name, address, phone, annotation describing product or service; club listings give details concerning membership and activity; museum listings indicate nature of collection, hours, fees. **Arrangement:** Classified. **Pages** (approx.): 120. **Frequency:** Annual, October. **Editor:** Carl Hungness, Publisher. **Advertising accepted.** Circulation 10,000. **Price:** $5.75, postpaid.

★4706★

AUTOMOBILE LICENSE PLATE COLLECTORS ASSOCIATION—
    MEMBERSHIP ROSTER
Automobile License Plate Collectors Association
Box 712
Weston, WV 26452
Covers: About 1,300 collectors of license plates and related memorabilia. **Entries include:** Name, address, phone. **Arrangement:** Alphabetical. **Indexes:** Geographical. **Pages** (approx.): 15. **Frequency:**

Annual, February. **Editor:** Paul M. Maginnity. **Price:** Available to members only.

★4707★
AYH HOSTEL GUIDE AND HANDBOOK
American Youth Hostels
National Campus   Phone: (703) 592-3271
Delaplane, VA 22025
Covers: About 225 hostels certified by AYH to be safe and to have per night costs of from $2.00 to not more than $6.00. **Entries include:** Hostel name, address, phone, cost per night, names of houseparents, directions, sleeping capacity, and facilities available. **Arrangement:** Geographical. **Pages** (approx.): 180. **Frequency:** Annual, January. **Editor:** William A. Nelson, Director, Hostel Department. **Advertising accepted.** Circulation 85,000. **Price:** $1.75 (current edition); $2.00 (1980 edition). **Other information:** Also published by East Woods Press as, ''Hosteling USA - The Official American Youth Hostels Handbook'' (see separate listing).

★4708★
BACK BEFORE BEDTIME [Trips for Children, New York metro area]
Quick Fox, Inc.
33 W. 60th Street   Phone: (212) 246-0325
New York, NY 10023
Covers: Zoos, amusement parks, nature centers, recreation areas, science centers and exhibit halls, historical sites and villages, theaters, and other attractions and special events for children in New York, New Jersey, and Connecticut. **Entries include:** Name of site or event, location, phone; hours, seasons, or dates scheduled; driving instructions; other sites or events in the area; description of attractions; admission fee. **Arrangement:** Events are by month, then geographical; sites are geographical. **Indexes:** Each state section of sites has a type of attraction index. **Pages** (approx.): 270. **Frequency:** Not established; first edition 1978. **Editor:** Sandy Beram. **Price:** $6.95.

★4709★
BASENJI CLUB OF AMERICA—MEMBERSHIP ROSTER AND BREEDERS DIRECTORY [Dogs]
Basenji Club of America
8800 Ridgehill Drive   Phone: (512) 345-3067
Austin, TX 78759
Covers: 600 fanciers and breeders of Basenji dogs. **Entries include:** Name, address, phone, name of kennel, local club memberships, whether puppies or dogs are offered for sale, whether stud service is offered, color of dogs. **Arrangement:** Geographical. **Pages** (approx.): 30. **Frequency:** Annual, spring. **Editor:** Loretta Kelley, Secretary. **Advertising accepted. Price:** Available to members only.

Best in Motorcoach and Air Tours *See* Official Domestic Tour
   Manual U.S.A. & Canada

★4710★
BIRDWATCHER'S GUIDE TO WILDLIFE SANCTUARIES
Arco Publishing Company
219 Park Avenue South   Phone: (212) 777-6300
New York, NY 10003
Covers: 250 major and minor wildlife sanctuaries open to the public in the United States, Canada, and the Virgin Islands. **Entries include:** Sanctuary name, address, phone, directions for reaching it, size, number and species of birds sighted (including whether the species are rare and uncommon), kinds of trails and other recreational facilities available, precautions to take, and information on checklists and other material available at the sanctuary. **Arrangement:** Geographical. **Pages** (approx.): 260. **Frequency:** published 1976; no new edition planned. **Price:** $8.95, cloth; $4.95, paper.

★4711★
BIRDWATCHERS'S GUIDE TO THE EASTERN UNITED STATES
Barron's Educational Series, Inc.
113 Crossways Park Drive   Phone: (516) 921-8750
Woodbury, NY 11797
Covers: More than 700 birdwatching sites, including national parks, forests, seashores, and sanctuaries. **Entries include:** Name, address, phone; directions; hours of operation; educational programs offered; description of terrain; common and rare species spotted; availablility of a checklist; and location of nearby camping facilities. **Arrangement:** Geographical. **Indexes:** Bird name. **Pages** (approx.): 350. **Frequency:** Irregular; latest edition November 1978; new edition expected 1980. **Editor:** Alice M. Geffen. **Price:** $15.95, cloth; $6.95, paper; payment with order.

★4712★
BLUE FLAME SPECIAL MAGAZINE [Corvette interest]
Vintage Corvette Club of America
C/o Ed Thiebaud
Star Route   Phone: (805) 238-0976
Creston, CA 93432
Publication includes: 125 sources for Corvette parts and service; also lists known Corvette collectors (persons owning six or more cars in running condition), and a roster of national car clubs. **Entries include:** Name and address of supplier, collector, or club. **Pages** (approx.): 50. **Frequency:** Quarterly. **Editor:** Ed Thiebaud, President.

★4713★
BOB DAMRON'S ADDRESS BOOK
Bob Damron Enterprises
Box 14-077   Phone: (415) 626-4692
San Francisco CA 94114
Covers: 3,800 gathering places (bars, baths, bookstores, movie theaters, discos, public parks) for homosexuals in the United States, Canada, Puerto Rico, Virgin Islands, and Guam. **Entries include:** Establishment name, address, key letters indicating type of clientele, whether food and entertainment are offered. **Arrangement:** Geographical. **Pages** (approx.): 170. **Frequency:** Annual, April. **Editor:** Bob Damron. **Advertising accepted.** Circulation 100,000. **Price:** $5.00 (current edition); $7.00 (1980 edition); plus $1.00 shipping.

★4714★
BONSAI MAGAZINE—BONSAI SOURCES SUPPLEMENT
Bonsai Clubs International
4943 Clydebank Avenue   Phone: (213) 331-4257
Covina, CA 91722
Covers: About 700 florists, nurseries, gift shops, and greenhouses which handle bonsai, bonsai stock, and pots and supplies. **Entries include:** Name, address, phone, and plants, specialty, or materials offered. **Arrangement:** Geographical. **Pages** (approx.): 40. **Frequency:** Irregular; latest edition 1978. **Editor:** Mrs. Rae Francis, Bonsai Sources Correspondent. **Price:** Included in subscription, $13.00 per year (ISSN 0162-9018).

★4715★
BRITISH NORTH AMERICA PHILATELIC SOCIETY—MEMBERSHIP HANDBOOK & DIRECTORY
British North America Philatelic Society
C/o E. J. Whiting, Secretary
25 Kings Circle
Malvern, PA 19355
Covers: About 1,500 collectors of Canadian stamps. **Entries include:** Membership number, name, mailing address. **Arrangement:** Alphabetical. **Indexes:** Geographical. **Pages** (approx.): 60. **Frequency:** Biennial, odd years. **Editor:** Edward J. Whiting, Secretary. **Price:** Available to members only.

★4716★
BUCKSKIN BULLETIN—TALLY SHEET ISSUE [Western history]
Westerners International
Box 3485
College Station
Tucson, AZ 85722
Covers: 90 local units ("Corrals") of Westerners International, an organization concerned with the history of the West. **Entries include:** Corral name, names and address of officers, publications. **Arrangement:** Geographical. **Pages** (approx.): 8. **Frequency:** Annual, January. **Advertising accepted. Price:** Included in subscription to "Buckskin Bulletin," $5.00 per year (current and 1980 editions).

★4717★
CADILLAC-LASALLE CLUB—DIRECTORY [Automobile collectors]
Cadillac-LaSalle Club
3823 Shampo Drive
Warren, MI 48092
Covers: About 2,200 Cadillac and LaSalle automobile collectors. **Entries include:** Name, address, number and model of car(s) owned. **Arrangement:** Geographical. **Pages** (approx.): 50. **Frequency:** Biennial, even years; update in odd years. **Editor:** Mrs. Edith Childs. **Price:** Apply.

★4718★
CALENDAR OF FOLK FESTIVALS AND RELATED EVENTS
National Council for the Traditional Arts
1346 Connecticut Avenue, N. W., Suite 1118
Washington, DC 20036
Covers: About 1,250 folk festivals, community celebrations, ethnic events, etc. **Entries include:** Event name, location, dates; some include contact name. **Pages** (approx.): 65. **Editor:** Nan Goland. **Advertising accepted. Price:** $3.25. **Other information:** Discontinued with 1978 edition.

★4719★
CARRIAGE ASSOCIATION OF AMERICA—MEMBERSHIP ROSTER
Carriage Association of America
R. D. Box 115   Phone: (609) 935-3826
Salem, NJ 08079
Number of listings: 2,100 collectors of horse-drawn carriages and related items. **Entries include:** Name, address, coded information on member's interest, size of vehicle collection. **Arrangement:** Geographical. **Pages** (approx.): 160. **Frequency:** Annual, March. **Editor:** T. Ryder. **Price:** Available to members only. **Send orders to:** H. K. Sowles, Jr., Box 3788, Portland, ME 04104.

★4720★
CAT FANCIERS' ASSOCIATION—ANNUAL YEARBOOK
Cat Fanciers' Association
11 Globe Court   Phone: (201) 842-2470
Red Bank, NJ 07701
Publication includes: Cat clubs, cat breeders. **Pages** (approx.): 700. **Frequency:** Annual. **Editor:** Ms. Marna Fogarty. **Advertising accepted.** Breeders only. **Price:** $16.25.

★4721★
CAT FANCIERS' ASSOCIATION BREEDER'S DIRECTORY (Little Black Book)
Cat Fanciers' Association
11 Globe Court   Phone: (201) 842-2470
Red Bank, NJ 07701
Covers: Cat breeders who are members of the association and who purchase listings. **Entries include:** Cattery name, CFA registration number, owner's name, address, phone, breeds and colors interested in. **Arrangement:** Geographical, then by breeds. **Indexes:** Alphabetical by cattery name. **Frequency:** Annual, summer. **Advertising accepted. Price:** $1.50.

★4722★
CATALOGUE OF MAGIC
Simon and Schuster, Inc.
1230 Avenue of the Americas   Phone: (212) 245-6400
New York, NY 10020
Covers: Manufacturers and designers of, and dealers in, magic effects and equipment. **Entries include:** Name of company, address, products or services, and prices. **Frequency:** First edition January 1979. **Editor:** Jeffrey Feinman. **Price:** $9.95, cloth; $4.95, paper.

★4723★
CATS MAGAZINE—DIRECTORY ANNUAL OF CAT BREEDERS ISSUE
Cats Magazine
Box 37
Port Orange, FL 32019
Covers: Over 1,300 cat breeders in the United States and Canada (only). **Entries include:** Cattery name, owner, address, phone, association memberships, breeds and colors interested in, other services available. **Arrangement:** Geographical, then by breeds. **Frequency:** Annual, April. **Editor:** Jean Laux. **Advertising accepted.** Circulation 65,000. **Price:** $1.00 (current edition); $1.25 (1980 edition; ISSN 0008-8544).

★4724★
CATS MAGAZINE—"TO SHOW AND GO" SECTION
Cats Magazine
Box 37
Port Orange, FL 32019
Publication includes: List of cat shows for three month period (beginning with month of publication). **Entries include:** Location, name of sponsoring organization, organization membership, cat breeds being shown, names of judges (if known), name and address of contact; some listings include phone; entry fee, entry deadline. **Arrangement:** Chronological. **Frequency:** Monthly. **Editor:** Jean Laux. **Advertising accepted.** Circulation 65,000. **Price:** $10.45 per year (ISSN 0008-8544).

★4725★
CAVES AND CAVERNS
National Caves Association
R.D. 9, Box 106   Phone: (615) 668-3925
McMinnville, TN 37110
Covers: About 50 member caves and caverns which are commercially operated. **Entries include:** Name of cave, address, phone. **Arrangement:** Geographical. **Pages** (approx.): Leaflet. **Frequency:** Annual, usually January. **Editor:** Barbara Munson, Secretary/ Treasurer. **Price:** Free. **Also includes:** A map showing where the caves are located.

CCA Travellers Network *See* Hospitality Guide of North America

Ceramic Hobby Industry Buyers Guide *See* Ceramic Scope— Buyers Guide Issue

★4726★
CERAMIC SCOPE—BUYERS GUIDE ISSUE
Ceramic Scope
5208 W. Pico Boulevard   Phone: (213) 935-1121
Los Angeles, CA 90019
Covers: 500 manufacturers, 700 distributors, 100 traveling teachers, and 100 associations concerned with recreational ceramics; also includes arts and crafts exhibits. **Entries include:** Firm listings show name, address, phone, year founded, number of employees, names of principal executives; manufacturer listings also show service area, catalog availability, and price. Teacher listings show name, address, phone, specialties, area served. **Arrangement:** By function or service. **Indexes:** Product. **Pages** (approx.): 150. **Frequency:** Annual, January. **Editor:** Mel Fiske. **Advertising accepted.** Circulation 15,000. **Former title:** Ceramic Hobby Industry Buyers Guide. **Price:** $4.00, plus 75¢ shipping (current and 1980 editions).

★4727★

CHARLOTTE, ISABELLE, PHYLLIS & SUSAN'S N.Y.: A Woman's Guide to Shops, Services & Restaurants
Random House, Inc.
201 E. 50th Street   Phone: (212) 751-2600
New York, NY 10022
Covers: Facilities in and near the "silk-stocking district" of Manhattan's East Side favored by the "four luxury-loving" authors able to afford them. **Entries include:** Establishment name, address, phone, tips on specialties. **Arrangement:** Classified by product or service. **Pages** (approx.): 225. **Frequency:** Not established; first published 1977. **Editors:** Charlotte Ford, Isabelle Russek Leeds, Phyllis Cerf Wagner, Susan Payson Fine. **Price:** $6.95.

Charter Flight Directory *See* How to Fly for Less

★4728★

CHARTER FLIGHT, TOUR, AND CRUISE GUIDE
Altatravel, Inc.
1526 Pontius Avenue   Phone: (213) 473-6531
Los Angeles, CA 90025
Covers: More than 5,000 cruises, tours, and charter flights, worldwide. **Entries include:** Trip name, dates, origination and destination points, costs, and tour operator, carrier, etc., as relevant. **Pages** (approx.): 50. **Frequency:** Semiannual, October and January. **Editors:** E. Barrueto and M. O'Brien. **Former title:** Cruise Guide. **Price:** $2.00.

★4729★

CIRCLES OF FRIENDS: 200 New Ways to Make Friends in Washington, DC
Mail Order USA
Box 19083   Phone: (202) 686-9521
Washington, DC 20036
Covers: 250 cultural organizations, and social and sports clubs of various kinds welcoming new members or volunteers; dining clubs; house tours; educational institutions with night or continuing education courses, etc. **Entries include:** Name, address, phone, costs, etc. **Arrangement:** Classified by type of activity. **Pages** (approx.): 65. **Frequency:** Irregular; latest edition September 1979. **Editor:** Dorothy O'Callaghan. **Price:** 4.00.

★4730★

CITROEN CAR CLUB ROSTER
Citroen Car Club
C/o Tom Harper
7926 Apperson Street   Phone: (213) 352-3781
Sunland, CA 91040
Covers: 2,000 Citroen owners, service and repair shops, part suppliers, and Citroen car clubs; international coverage. **Entries include:** Name, address; some listings also include phone, and years and models of Citroens owned. **Arrangement:** Owners and clubs are listed separately from service firms; both lists are geographical. **Pages** (approx.): 60. **Frequency:** Annual, December. **Editor:** Tom Harper. **Advertising accepted.** Circulation 2,000. **Price:** $1.00. **Send orders to:** Citroen Car Club, Box 743, Hollywood, CA 90028.

★4731★

CLASSIC CAR CLUB OF AMERICA—HANDBOOK AND DIRECTORY
Classic Car Club of America
Box 443   Phone: (201) 377-1925
Madison NJ 07940
Publication includes: 4,000 members and their classic cars. **Entries include:** Member's name; address; make, model, and year of each classic car owned. **Arrangement:** Alphabetical, geographical, and by type of car. **Frequency:** Annual, March. **Editor:** Morton Y. Bullock III, Vice-President, Publications. **Price:** $2.50 (1980 edition).

★4732★

COIN WORLD ALMANAC
Amos Press, Inc.
911 Vandemark Road   Phone: (513) 492-4141
Sidney, OH 45367
Publication includes: Producers and distributors of historical and commemorative medals, coins, and other numismatic objects, including wooden money; national collections of coins; about 200 museums with coin collections; about 250 professional numismatists (dealers); and over 350 organizations and clubs for coin collectors; worldwide coverage. **Entries include:** For commemorative medal producers - Name, address, price, sculptor, other descriptive information. For other producers and distributors - Name, address. National collections - Name, location, description of history. For museums - United States entries include organization name, address, description of holdings, hours open. Foreign museums include name, location. For organizations - Name, address, name of contact. **Arrangement:** Commemorative medal producers are by event or person commemorated. Collections and museums are geographical. Organizations are primarily alphabetical except world coin organizations, which are geographical. **Indexes:** General. **Frequency:** Irregular; previous edition 1977; latest edition 1979. **Editor:** Margo Russell. **Price:** $10.00. **Other information:** Primary content of this 1,000 page publication is information on buying, selling, evaluating, and collecting coins.

★4733★

COLLECTIBLES DIRECTORY & SOURCEBOOK
Sourcebooks
Box 14141
San Francisco, CA 94114
Covers: Over 2,500 individuals, clubs, museums, periodicals, price guides, etc., concerned with collectible objects of all kinds. **Entries include:** Name of individual, publication, etc., coded designation as to type of source or interest (dealer, collector, book, etc.); listings for dealers and collectors and some publications include address. **Arrangement:** Classified by object or interst. **Pages** (approx.): 50. **Frequency:** Annual; first edition January 1980. **Price:** $5.00.

★4734★

COMPLETE FOOD CATALOGUE
Holt, Rinehart & Winston
383 Madison Avenue   Phone: (212) 688-9100
New York, NY 10017
Covers: Mail order sellers of unusual foods, kitchen equipment, and special cookbooks, worldwide. **Entries include:** Company name, address, product descriptions, whether catalog is available, and range of prices. **Arrangement:** Classified by food. **Pages** (approx.): 260. **Frequency:** Not established; first edition fall 1977. **Editors:** Jose Wilson and Arthur Leaman. **Price:** $10.95, cloth; $6.95, paper.

★4735★

COMPUTER DATA DIRECTORY [Personal computers]
Computer Data Directory
Box 598
Cleveland, OH 44107
Covers: Several hundred manufacturers of personal computer systems, peripherals, and accessories, games, and related products. Includes newsletters, home study courses, computer stores, clubs, etc. **Arrangement:** Alphabetical within product or use classifications; computer stores and clubs are geographical. **Frequency:** Annual, March. **Editor:** Brad Lynnet. **Price:** $5.98, postpaid.

Confederate Bulletin *See* Muster Roll of the C.S.A. [Philately]

Confederate Stamp Album *See* Muster Roll of the C.S.A. [Philately]

★4736★
CONTEMPORARY CRAFTS MARKET PLACE
R. R. Bowker Company
1180 Avenue of the Americas   Phone: (212) 764-5100
New York, NY 10020
Covers: 1,000 crafts shops and galleries; several thousand suppliers of materials for clay, fiber, glass, metal, wood, and miscellaneous crafts; 300 national, regional, and local crafts organizations; 275 universities, junior colleges, and crafts schools; crafts shows and related events; crafts periodicals. **Entries include:** All include company or organization name, address, some include phone; shop listings include owner name and specialties; organization listings include president or contact, activities; education listings include courses and degrees offered; supplier listings include product, whether retail or wholesale, catalog information; show listings include dates, sponsors, contacts. **Arrangement:** Shops, organizations, education lists are geographical; suppliers are alphabetical within type of craft. **Indexes:** Alphabetical index to entire publication; separate geographical indexes to suppliers for each of the six crafts classifications. **Pages** (approx.): 340. **Frequency:** Irregular; latest edition June 1977. **Price:** $15.95, postpaid, payment with order (ISSN 0095-2710). **Send orders to:** R. R. Bowker Co., Box 1807, Ann Arbor, MI 48106 (313-761-4700). **Other information:** Compiled by American Crafts Council.

★4737★
CONTEST BOOK
Harmony Books
Crown Publishers, Inc.
One Park Avenue   Phone: (212) 532-9200
New York, NY 10016
Covers: Several hundred contests and championships in all areas of competition. **Entries include:** Contest name, sponsoring organization and address, history of contest, date and location, entry requirements, rules and regulations, first year held, prizes offered. **Pages** (approx.): 200. **Frequency:** First edition 1979. **Editors:** Susan Subtle, Ruth Reichl, and Ken Dollar. **Price:** $12.95, cloth; $6.95, paper.

★4738★
COOKS' CATALOGUE
Avon Books Division
Hearst Corporation
959 Eighth Avenue   Phone: (212) 262-5700
New York, NY 10019
Covers: 250 manufacturers and distributors of kitchenware, particularly premium-quality and unusual items. Their products are described in about 4,000 numbered entries keyed to the list of manufacturers. About 1,700 illustrations. **Entries include:** Company name and address. **Arrangement:** Main section of book arranged by type of equipment (knives, casseroles and pots, etc.); manufacturer list is alphabetical. **Pages** (approx.): 575. **Frequency:** Not established; first edition 1975; revised paperback edition spring 1977. **Editors:** James Beard, et al. **Price:** $8.95.

★4739★
COOK'S STORE
Simon and Schuster, Inc.
1230 Avenue of the Americas   Phone: (212) 245-6400
New York, NY 10020
Covers: Manufacturers, retailers, and mail-order houses which offer cooking utensils and gadgets (quiche pans, pasta machines, spaetzel makers, etc.). **Entries include:** Company name, address, products offered. **Arrangement:** Classified by product. **Frequency:** First edition October 1978. **Price:** $14.95, cloth; $7.95, paper. **Other information:** Prepared by "Consumer Guide."

Country Vacations U.S.A. *See* Farm, Ranch & Country Vacations

Craft Horizons—Travel and Study Abroad Issue *See* **American Craft Magazine—Travel and Study Abroad Issue**

★4740★
CRAFT, MODEL & HOBBY INDUSTRY—ANNUAL TRADE DIRECTORY ISSUE
Hobby Publications, Inc.
225 W. 34th Street   Phone: (212) 244-1717
New York, NY 10001
Covers: 600 manufacturers, 100 hobby book and periodical publishers, 425 manufacturers' representatives and 90 chain store buyers in the crafts, model, and hobby industry. **Entries include:** Company name, address, phone, name of principal executive, list of products or services, with trade names. Wholesaler listings also show territories. **Arrangement:** Alphabetical list of manufacturers, geographical list of wholesalers. **Indexes:** Product indexes for crafts supplies, models, home winemaking tools. **Frequency:** Annual, June. **Editor:** Nanci Fishman. **Advertising accepted.** Circulation 13,000. **Price:** $10.00.

Cruise Guide *See* Charter Flight, Tour, and Cruise Guide

★4741★
DELTIOLOGY—ROSTER ISSUE [Postcard collectors]
Deltiologists of America
3709 Gradyville Road   Phone: (215) 353-1689
Newtown Square, PA 19073
Publication includes: 1,900 picture postcard collectors and dealers concerned with items produced from 1870 to present. **Arrangement:** Geographical. **Frequency:** Annual, June. **Editor:** James L. Lowe, Director. **Advertising accepted.** Circulation 2,500. **Price:** $2.00.

Directory of Art & Craft Materials *See* International Art Material Directory

Directory of Department Store Wine Shops and Wine Stores in Major U.S. Cities *See* World Wine Almanac and Wine Atlas

Directory of Homes Available for Exchange *See* Loan-a-Home

★4742★
DIRECTORY OF MINIATURES AND DOLLS
Miniature Makers
409 S. First Street
Evansville, WI 53536
Covers: Businesses which supply miniatures, dollhouses, and dolls. Also includes museums, publications, and organizations concerned with these items. **Entries include:** Firm listings show name, address, brand names, products or services. Other listings show name or title, interests or displays, etc. **Pages** (approx.): 60. **Frequency:** Irregular; latest edition 1976. **Editor:** Patricia Diedrick. **Advertising accepted.** **Price:** $3.95. (Not verified)

★4743★
DIRECTORY OF NEW ENGLAND ASTROLOGERS
Sagittarius Rising
Box 252
Arlington, MA 02174
Covers: About 60 astrologers, plus national organizations, companies offering astrological computer services, and sources in New England for securing birth dates. **Entries include:** For astrologers - Name, address, phone, birth data, astrological and counseling specialties, teaching and writing, and educational and career data; also includes a personal essay. For other entries - Name of company or organization, address, details. **Arrangement:** Astrologers are geographical, other listings are alphabetical. **Pages** (approx.): 135. **Frequency:** Latest edition 1978; spring and fall 1978 supplements. **Editor:** Tracy Marks. **Price:** $6.00, including supplements.

★4744★

DIRECTORY OF NORTH AMERICAN FAIRS AND EXPOSITIONS
Amusement Business Division
Billboard Publications, Inc.
Box 24970   Phone: (615) 748-8120
Nashville, TN 37202
Covers: 2,500 fairs and 400 expositions in United States and Canada.
Entries include: Name of event, location, dates, admissions, attendance, contact, etc. **Pages** (approx.): 90. **Frequency:** Annual, October. **Editor:** Paul Curran. **Advertising accepted. Price:** $29.95.

★4745★

DISCOVER AMERICA NATIONAL TRAVEL NEWS DIRECTORY
Discover America Travel Organizations
1899 L Street, N. W.   Phone: (202) 293-1433
Washington, DC 20036
Covers: Public relations and management officials in all sections of the travel industry, including attractions; transportation; local, state, and regional promotion agencies and convention bureaus; and newspapers, consumer magazines, broadcast outlets, etc., which reach a majority of the population. **Entries include:** Company name, medium, or agency name, address, phone, name of one or more executives. **Arrangement:** Classified. **Pages** (approx.): 60. **Frequency:** Biennial, spring of odd years. **Editor:** James O. Hughes, Director of Communications. **Price:** $15.00.

★4746★

DISCOVERING HISTORIC IOWA
Iowa Department of Public Instruction
Grimes State Office Building   Phone: (515) 281-3038
Des Moines, IA 50319
Covers: Historical societies, museums, historic landmarks, natural areas, etc. **Entries include:** Name, address, and description of the organization or facility, dues or fees, officers, and historical significance. **Arrangement:** Geographical. **Frequency:** Irregular; latest edition 1975; no new edition planned. **Editor:** LeRoy G. Pratt. **Former title:** Guide to Historic Iowa (1975). **Price:** $3.00.

Doll House Miniatures Catalog *See* **Miniatures Catalog**

★4747★

DUDE RANCH VACATIONS
Dude Ranchers' Association
Box 43   Phone: (303) 887-3777
Granby, CO 80446
Covers: 55 member ranches, primarily working ranches in nine western states; guests may usually participate in ranch work. **Entries include:** Ranch name, address, phone, name of owner or manager, and description of facilities. **Arrangement:** Geographical. **Pages** (approx.): 20. **Frequency:** Annual, November.

Dude Ranches in Wyoming *See* **Wyoming Accommodations**

★4748★

EARLY AMERICAN INDUSTRIES ASSOCIATION—DIRECTORY
Early American Industries Association
Two Winding Lane
Scarsdale, NY 10583
Covers: 2,600 Early American tool collectors, dealers, societies, libraries, and museums who are members. **Entries include:** Name; address; types of tools collected; scope of collection. **Frequency:** Annual, June. **Editor:** John S. Kebabian. **Price:** Available to members only.

★4749★

EASTER SEAL REHABILITATION CENTER OF SOUTHWESTERN CONNECTICUT—GUIDE FOR THE HANDICAPPED
Easter Seal Rehabilitation Center of Southwestern Connecticut
26 Palmer's Hill Road   Phone: (203) 325-1544
Stamford, CT 06902
Publication includes: Information about building features (ramps, wide doors, etc.) which help make southwestern Connecticut's major stores, public buildings, museums, hotels, hospitals, theaters, etc., accessible to handicapped persons, and warnings about architectural barriers which might present difficulties. **Arrangement:** Classifed by type of establishment or institution. **Pages** (approx.): 150. **Frequency:** Irregular; latest edition May 1978. **Editor:** Elizabeth Case. **Price:** Free; $1.00 donation requested.

★4750★

EDUCATIONAL MATERIALS DIRECTORY [Sewing]
Homesewing Trade News
129 Broadway   Phone: (212) 593-2710
Lynbrook, NY 11563
Covers: Firms supplying teaching aids and programs concerned with sewing and textile trades to educational institutions. **Entries include:** Company name, address, and materials offered. **Arrangement:** Alphabetical. **Pages** (approx.): 65. **Frequency:** Annual, June. **Editors:** Senta Mead and Jane Schenck. **Advertising accepted.** Circulation 15,000. **Price:** $1.00 (current and 1980 editions). **Other information:** Compiled by American Home Sewing Association.

★4751★

EPIPHYLLUM SOCIETY OF AMERICA—MEMBERSHIP DIRECTORY [Flowers]
Epiphyllum Society of America
Box 1395   Phone: (805) 259-4637
Monrovia, CA 91016
Covers: 1,000 epiphyllum fanciers and commercial dealers. **Entries include:** Name, address. **Arrangement:** Geographical. **Frequency:** Usually annual, August; 1979 edition was supplement. **Editor:** Velma Featherstone. **Price:** $1.50.

★4752★

EXCHANGE BOOK [Home exchange]
Vacation Exchange Club, Inc.
350 Broadway   Phone: (212) 966-2576
New York, NY 10013
Covers: 2,500-5,000 houses, apartments, etc., listed by individuals which are available for vacation purposes in exchange for the homes of others, or for vacation rental. No commercial listings. Also lists persons offering and/or seeking home hospitality on exchange or paid basis. Covers United States and 40 other countries. **Entries include:** Name of person offering home, address of home, description, and other details. Some entries include photos. **Arrangement:** Geographical. **Pages** (approx.): 175 (February and April combined). **Frequency:** Main directory published in February, with supplement in April. **Editor:** David G. Ostroff. **Former title:** Pan Am Home Exchange Directory; Home Exchange Directory; Vacation Exchange Club - Directory. **Price:** $12.00 (directory and supplement); $15.00 for listing (deadlines mid-December and mid-February) plus directory and supplement (current and 1980 editions); $2.00 additional for first class mail.

★4753★

EXPLORERS LTD. GUIDE TO LOST TREASURE IN THE UNITED STATES AND CANADA
Explorers Ltd.
2107 Grant Avenue   Phone: (302) 792-1778
Wilmington, DE 19809
Covers: More than 300 sites in the United States and Canada popularly believed to be the location of lost ships, mines, buried treasure, etc. **Entries include:** Popular name of the treasure, a description and history, and approximate location. **Arrangement:** Geographical. **Indexes:** General. **Pages** (approx.): 200. **Frequency:** Published fall 1977. **Editors:** Rosemarie D. Perrin and Explorers Ltd. staff. **Also includes:** Treasure trove law and sources therefor, discussion of metal detectors, directory of state and provincial archives and historical societies.

★4754★
FABRICS FOR HISTORIC BUILDINGS
National Trust for Historic Preservation
740 Jackson Place, N. W.
Washington, DC 20006
Publication includes: Names and addresses of manufacturers of 225 commercially available reproductions of fabrics used in the United States in the eighteenth and nineteenth centuries. Listings for individual fabrics show manufacturer's catalog name, historic and reproduction data, width and length of pattern repeat. Pages (approx.): 65. Frequency: Irregular; latest edition 1977; new edition expected early 1980. Author: Jane C. Nylander. Price: $5.00 (current edition); $5.95 (tentative, 1980 edition); plus $1.00 shipping, payment with order.

★4755★
FACILITIES DIRECTORY [Handicapped Guide to Topeka, Kansas]
Division for the Disabled
Topeka-Shawnee County Human Relations Commission
City Hall, Room 54　　　Phone: (913) 295-3879
Topeka, KS 66603
Publication includes: Information about building features (ramps, wide doors, etc.) which help make the major stores, public buildings, etc., of the Topeka area accessible to handicapped persons. Arrangement: Classified by type of establishment or institution. Pages (approx.): 25. Frequency: Irregular; latest edition 1979. Price: Free; send stamped, self-addressed envelope.

★4756★
FAMILY MOTOR COACH ASSOCIATION—MEMBERSHIP DIRECTORY
Family Motor Coach Association
8291 Clough Pike　　　Phone: (513) 474-3622
Cincinnati, OH 45244
Covers: 26,000 owners of motorhome vehicles; associate members who supply products and equipment are also included. Entries include: Name, location. Supplier listings include phone, products or services. Arrangement: Motorhome owners are geographical, associate members are alphabetical. Pages (approx.): 220. Frequency: Annual, February. Editor: Dave Ginter. Price: $5.95, postpaid.

★4757★
FAMILY MOTOR COACHING—ANNUAL MEMBERSHIP DIRECTORY ISSUE
Family Motor Coach Association
8291 Clough Pike　　　Phone: (513) 474-3622
Cincinnati, OH 45244
Covers: 20,000 members; includes lists of motorhome manufacturers, dealers, sources for parts and repairs, dealers in used motorhomes, and motorhome rental agencies. Entries include: For members - Name, address, codes indicating vehicle owned and whether the member is able to offer overnight facilities to other members or emergency road service. Arrangement: Geographical, alphabetical, and by membership number; same information in each section. Pages (approx.): 370. Frequency: Annual, late fall. Editor: Pamela Gramke. Advertising accepted. Circulation 24,500. Price: Available to members only.

★4758★
FARM, RANCH & COUNTRY VACATIONS
Farm & Ranch Vacations, Inc.
36 E. 57th Street　　　Phone: (212) 355-6334
New York, NY 10022
Covers: Farms, ranches, and rural lodges and inns. Entries include: Facility name, address, rates, number and type of accomodations available, activities and recreation on the property and nearby, and activities for children with or without parental guidance. Arrangement: Geographical. Pages (approx.): 225. Frequency: Biennial, winter of odd years. Editor: Pat Dickerman, Editor and Publisher. Former title: Farm, Ranch & Countryside Guide (1976); Country Vacations U. S. A. (1979). Price: $5.95, plus $1.00 shipping.

Farm, Ranch, and Countryside Guide See Farm, Ranch & Country Vacations

★4759★
FARM STEAM SHOWS—USA AND CANADA
North Plains Press
1216 S. Main　　　Phone: (605) 225-5170
Aberdeen, SD 57401
Covers: Steam threshing jamborees. Entries include: Name of event, location, etc. Pages (approx.): 470. Frequency: Irregular; latest edition 1972; no new edition planned. Editor: Judy Kernan, Book Division Manager. Price: $15.95. Other information: Over 1,000 illustrations.

★4760★
FESTIVALS SOURCEBOOK
Gale Research Company
Book Tower　　　Phone: (313) 961-2242
Detroit, MI 48226
Covers: 3,800 fairs, festivals, and other celebrations of a recurring nature; includes Canada. Entries include: Name of event, location, dates held, frequency, duration, description of activities, year of origin, and name and address of contact. Arrangement: By broad subject areas (agriculture, ethnic events, music, etc.). Indexes: Subject (includes headings more specific than general subject areas, e.g., jazz rather than music), chronological, event name, geographical. Pages (approx.): 650. Frequency: Irregular; first edition March 1977. Editors: Paul Wasserman, Esther Herman. Price: $50.00.

★4761★
FINE ARTS PHILATELISTS—MEMBERSHIP DIRECTORY
Fine Arts Philatelists
C/o Jewell Sonderegger
Box 1606　　　Phone: (315) 631-1619
Midland, MI 48640
Covers: About 500 collectors of stamps related to the fine arts including reproductions of paintings, artist's portraits, etc.; international coverage. Entries include: Name, address. Arrangement: Alphabetical. Indexes: Geographical with coded interests list. Pages (approx.): 20. Frequency: Irregular; 1978 edition out of print; new edition expected December 1980. Editor: Jewell Sonderegger, Secretary. Price: Available to members only.

★4762★
FLEA MARKET QUARTERLY—DIRECTORY SECTION
Maverick Publications
Box 243
Bend, OR 97701
Publication includes: List of flea markets occurring in United States and Canada, for approximately three months ahead. Entries include: Market name, dates, whom to contact for reservations, admission and selling space fees, manager's phone and address, type of facilities, expected/past attendance, etc. Arrangement: Chronological. Frequency: Quarterly. Advertising accepted. Price: $2.00 per issue; $6.00 per year. (Not verified)

★4763★
FLORIDA [Events calendar]
Division of Tourism
Florida Department of Commerce
Collins Building, No. 404
107 Gaines Street　　　Phone: (904) 488-8500
Tallahassee, FL 32304
Covers: Exhibitions, festivals, sports tournaments, art exhibits, theatrical events, etc., occurring during the period. Entries include: Dates, city, location, and name of each activity. Arrangement: Classified by month, then by type of event. Pages (approx.): 30. Frequency: Quarterly. Price: Free.

★4764★

FOOD CATALOG

Stonehill Publishing Company
10 E. 40th Street
New York, NY 10016

Covers: Several hundred companies selling exotic foods and special delicacies by mail. **Entries include:** Company name, address, brief note on business and products, with prices. **Arrangement:** Geographically within food categories (cheese, fruit, seafood, etc.). **Frequency:** Not established; first edition 1977. **Editor:** Nancy Hyden Woodward. **Price:** $19.95.

★4765★

FORD'S FREIGHTER TRAVEL GUIDE

Ford's Travel Guides
22151 Clarendon Street   Phone: (213) 347-1677
Woodland Hills, CA 91367

Covers: Steamship lines which operate cargo vessels with space for passengers; travel agencies which have chosen to advertise as freighter travel specialists; foreign government tourist offices in the United States. **Entries include:** For steamship lines - Company name, address, phone; text gives ships, facilities, itineraries, etc. For travel agents - Name, address, phone. For tourist bureaus - Name, address, phone, branches. **Arrangement:** Separate sections for vessels carrying 12 passengers or less, and those carrying more. **Indexes:** Name of steamship line, port of call. **Pages** (approx.): 170. **Frequency:** Semiannual, March and September. **Editor:** Merrian E. Clark. **Advertising accepted. Price:** $4.75 per issue; $8.50 per year (current and 1980 editions; ISSN 0015-7058). **Also includes:** Section entitled, "Introduction to Freighter Travel."

★4766★

FORD'S INTERNATIONAL CRUISE GUIDE

Ford's Travel Guides
22151 Clarendon Street   Phone: (213) 347-1677
Woodland Hills, CA 91367

Covers: About 100 cruise ships, their planned cruises for one year ahead, and travel agencies which have chosen to advertise as cruise specialists. **Entries include:** For ships - Ship name, registry, date built, description, photo. For cruises - Name of cruise, fare, ship used, dates, itinerary and other details, and tour operator name, address, phone and branches. For agents - Firm name, address, phone. **Arrangement:** Cruises geographical by departure ports, agents geographical by office location. **Indexes:** Ports of call, chronological by departure date and port. **Pages** (approx.): 160. **Frequency:** Quarterly. **Editor:** Merrian E. Clark. **Advertising accepted. Price:** $5.50 per copy; $20.00 per year (ISSN 0015-7066).

★4767★

FREE STUFF FOR KIDS

Meadowbrook Press
16648 Meadowbrook Lane   Phone: (612) 933-5008
Wayzata, MN 55391

Covers: About 250 manufacturers, retailers, other businesses, and groups which offer free items of interest to children (including toy instruction booklets, rule books, posters, decals, and samples). **Entries include:** Company name, address, description of item offered gratis, handling charges, if any (maximum $1.00). **Arrangement:** By subject matter. **Indexes:** Item type. **Pages** (approx.): 120. **Frequency:** Irregular; latest edition 1979; new edition expected June 1981. **Editor:** Tom Grady. **Former title:** Rainbow Book. **Price:** $2.95, plus 50¢ shipping.

Freighter Cruise Quick Reference Guide *See* Trip Log Quick
    Reference Freighter Guide

★4768★

FUN LAND U.S.A.: THE COMPLETE GUIDEBOOK TO 100 MAJOR AMUSEMENT AND THEME PARKS

Ballantine Books, Inc., Division
Random House
201 E. 50th Street
New York, NY 10022

Entries include: Park name, location, phone; price policy, parking, hours, rides, food and accommodations, guest services; specialty, theme, and other descriptive information. **Arrangement:** Geographical. **Indexes:** Park name. **Pages** (approx.): 300. **Frequency:** Published 1978. **Editor:** Tim Onosko. **Price:** $5.95.

★4769★

FUNPARKS DIRECTORY

Amusement Business Division
Billboard Publications, Inc.
Box 24970   Phone: (615) 748-8120
Nashville, TN 37202

Covers: Over 1,500 amusement parks, zoos, kiddie lands, theme parks, caves, state and national parks, and other tourist attractions with revenue-producing activities in the United States and Canada. **Entries include:** Attraction name, name of owner or key personnel, address, phone, description of attractions and equipment. **Arrangement:** Geographical. **Indexes:** Geographical (with type and whether seasonal or year-round). **Frequency:** Annual, February. **Editor:** Paul Curran. **Advertising accepted. Price:** $18.00 (current edition); $22.50 (1980 edition); postpaid, payment must accompany order.

★4770★

GEMS AND MINERALS—ALMANAC AND DIRECTORY ISSUE

Gemac Corporation
1797 Capri Avenue   Phone: (714) 794-1173
Mentone, CA 92359

Covers: Suppliers of gems, minerals, jewelry findings, and fossils; suppliers of equipment and materials used in rockhunting and lapidary. **Entries include:** For dealers in stones - Company name, address, specialties. For suppliers of equipment, etc. - Company name, address, products and services. **Arrangement:** Dealers in stones are alphabetical; suppliers of equipment are geographical. **Frequency:** Annual, September. **Editor:** Jack R. Cox. **Advertising accepted.** Circulation 40,000. **Price:** $1.25.

★4771★

GEMS AND MINERALS—"COMING EVENTS" COLUMN [Rock and lapidary crafts shows]

Gemac Corporation
1797 Capri Avenue   Phone: (714) 794-1173
Mentone, CA 92359

Entries include: Show name, location, dates, sponsor or contact address. **Frequency:** Monthly. **Editor:** Jack R. Cox. **Advertising accepted.** Circulation 40,000. **Price:** $7.95 per year; $1.25 per copy.

★4772★

GOOD (BUT CHEAP) CHICAGO RESTAURANT BOOK: WHERE TO FIND GREAT MEALS AT LITTLE NEIGHBORHOOD RESTAURANTS FROM $1.50 TO $4.95

Swallow Press, Inc.
811 W. Junior Terrace   Phone: (312) 871-2760
Chicago, IL 60613

Number of listings: Over 300. **Entries include:** Name, address, phone, whether parking is available, whether bar is provided, hours open; and authors' evaluation of menu, price, special features. **Arrangement:** By ethnic food types. **Indexes:** Geographical, alphabetical. **Pages** (approx.): 250. **Frequency:** Irregular; latest edition 1977. **Editors:** Jill Nathanson Rhode and Ron Rhode. **Price:** $2.95, plus 55¢ shipping.

★4773★
GOOD DEALS ON LOW COST CHARTER FLIGHTS AND TOURS
Good Deals
116 Summer Street
Stamford, CT 06905
Covers: Several thousand charter flights and tours within and outside the United States. **Entries include:** Tour operator, address, phone, name of tour, dates of departure and return, services, hotels used, price, etc. **Arrangement:** By destination. **Frequency:** Bimonthly. **Price:** $6.00 a year.

★4774★
GREATER CINCINNATI GUIDEBOOK FOR THE HANDICAPPED
[Ohio]
Hamilton County Easter Seal Society
7505 Reading Road   Phone: (513) 948-1615
Cincinnati, OH 45237
Publication includes: Information about building features (ramps, wide doors, etc.) which help make Cincinnati's major stores, public buildings, museums, hotels, hospitals, theaters, etc., accessible to handicapped persons, and warnings about architectural barriers which might present difficulties. **Arrangement:** Classified by type of establishment or institution. **Indexes:** Alphabetical. **Pages** (approx.): 60. **Frequency:** Irregular; latest edition September 1977. **Price:** Free. **Other information:** Compiled by Junior League of Cincinnati.

★4775★
GREEN PAGES: THE COMPLETE INDOOR PLANT CATALOG
Ballantine Books, Inc.
Random House, Inc.
201 E. 50th Street   Phone: (212) 751-2600
New York, NY 10022
Publication includes: List of nurseries, wholesalers, and other sources for house plants. **Entries include:** Name of company or source, address. **Pages** (approx.): 225. **Frequency:** First edition 1977. **Editor:** Maggie Oster. **Price:** $7.95. **Send orders to:** Ballantine Books, Order Department, Westminster, MD 21157.

★4776★
GRIFFIN BLACK BOOK [Gambling]
Publisher
Not Known
Description: Cited in "Asian Wall Street Journal," September 20, 1979, page 14, as "a who's who of slot-machine and card cheats widely used by casinos."

★4777★
GUIDE TO ANTIQUE SHOPS [South central states]
General Imports Corporation
125 East Street   Phone: (301) 662-6200
Frederick, MD 21701
Covers: 400 antiques shops and wholesalers in Pennsylvania, Delaware, Maryland, Washington, D. C., Virginia, West Virginia, and North Carolina. **Entries include:** Company name, address, phone, names of owners or managers, specialties. **Arrangement:** Geographical. **Pages** (approx.): 220. **Frequency:** Annual, fall. **Editor:** Bert Anderson. **Advertising accepted.** Circulation 40,000. **Price:** $2.50 (current and 1980 editions).

★4778★
GUIDE TO GUEST HOUSES AND TOURIST HOMES, U.S.A.
Tourist House Associates of America
Box 355   Phone: (717) 857-0856
Greentown, PA 18426
Covers: 175 tourist homes (private residences where owners rent spare bedrooms) in places of scenic, historical, or cultural interest. **Entries include:** Name of house, address, directions, phone, name of proprietor, rates, number and type of accomodations, availability of meals, local attractions, if children or pets are welcome, when open. **Arrangement:** Geographical. **Pages** (approx.): 30. **Frequency:** Annual. **Editor:** Betty R. Rundback, Director. **Advertising accepted.**

Circulation 15,000. **Price:** $3.50. **Also includes:** Four bed and breakfast organizations which make reservations at an additional 200 tourist houses and match host and guest as to interests, age, and language.

Guide to Historic Iowa *See* Discovering Historic Iowa

★4779★
GUIDE TO NORTHERN DELAWARE FOR THE DISABLED
Easter Seal Society for Crippled Children and Adults of Del-Mar
2705 Baynard Boulevard   Phone: (302) 658-6417
Wilmington, DE 19802
Publication includes: Information about building features (ramps, wide doors, etc.) which help make the major stores, public buildings, etc., of the Wilmington area accessible to handicapped persons. **Arrangement:** Classified by type of establishment or institution. **Pages** (approx.): 25. **Frequency:** Irregular; latest edition 1976-77. **Price:** Free.

★4780★
GUIDE TO OMAHA FOR THE HANDICAPPED [Nebraska]
Nebraska Easter Seal Society
Box 14204   Phone: (402) 333-9306
Omaha, NE 68114
Covers: Buildings and businesses which are accessible to the handicapped in Omaha, Nebraska. **Entries include:** Name of building or business, address, phone, whether there is parking, entry accessibility, restrooms, multi-level access, and other features. **Arrangement:** By type of business. **Pages** (approx.): 20. **Frequency:** Irregular; latest edition May 1979. **Price:** Free. **Other information:** List is also included in Northwestern Bell Company telephone book.

★4781★
GUIDE TO PHILADELPHIA FOR THE HANDICAPPED [Pennsylvania]
Mayor's Office for the Handicapped
City Hall Annex
Room 427   Phone: (215) 686-7120
Philadelphia, PA 19107
Publication includes: Information about building features (ramps, wide doors, etc.) which help make Philadelphia's major stores, public buildings, theaters, museums, restaurants, sports facilities, etc., accessible to handicapped persons, and warnings about architectural barriers which might present difficulties. **Arrangement:** Classified by type of establishment or institution. **Pages** (approx.): 50. **Frequency:** Irregular; latest edition July 1979. **Price:** Free.

★4782★
GUIDE TO SAN FRANCISCO FOR THE DISABLED [California]
Easter Seal Society
6221 Geary Boulevard   Phone: (415) 752-4888
San Francisco, CA 94121
Publication includes: Information about building features (ramps, wide doors, etc.) which help make San Francisco's major stores, public buildings, museums, theaters, restaurants, sports facilities, etc., accessible to handicapped persons, and warnings about architectural barriers which might present difficulties. **Arrangement:** By type of institution or establishment. **Pages** (approx.): 40. **Frequency:** Irregular; latest edition 1976. **Price:** Free.

★4783★
HISTORIC MICHIGAN TRAVEL
Historical Society of Michigan
2117 Washtenaw Avenue
Ann Arbor, MI 48104
Covers: More than 160 museums and 40 historic places offering dining and lodging in upper and lower Michigan. **Entries include:** Name of establishment, address, phone, hours, fees or price range, name of contact person, and historic significance; museum listings show hours. **Arrangement:** Geographical. **Pages** (approx.): 10. **Frequency:** Latest edition August 1979. **Former title:** Visitor's Guide to the Historical Museums in Michigan. **Price:** $2.50.

★4784★
HOME COMPUTER HANDBOOK
Sterling Publishing Company, Inc.
Two Park Avenue   Phone: (212) 532-7160
New York, NY 10016
Publication includes: In appendixes - Manufacturers of home
computing hardware and peripheral equipment, periodicals, computer
clubs, and computer stores. **Entries include:** For manufacturers -
Company name, address. (Product specifications in separate
appendixes.) For computer clubs - Name, contact name and address.
For stores - Name, address. For periodicals - Title, frequency, cost,
coverage, publisher name and address. **Arrangement:** Companies are
alphabetical, stores and clubs are geographical, publishers are by
periodical title. **Frequency:** Published 1978. **Editors:** Edwin
Schlossberg, John Brockman, and Lyn Horton. **Price:** $10.95, cloth;
$9.89 library edition; plus 75¢ shipping.

Home Exchange Directory *See* Exchange Book [Home exchange]

★4785★
HOME SEWING INDUSTRY RESOURCE DIRECTORY
E-Z Maid, Inc.
330 Sunrise Highway   Phone: (516) 766-1226
Rockville Centre, NY 11570
Covers: Manufacturers and suppliers of homesewing fabrics, notions,
sewing accessories, needlecraft items, etc., primarily in New York
City. **Entries include:** Firm name, address, phone, name of executive,
code indicating products sold by end use, and map key showing
location. **Arrangement:** Alphabetical. **Indexes:** Product. **Pages**
(approx.): 125. **Frequency:** Annual, January. **Editor:** Senta Head.
Advertising accepted. Circulation 13,500. **Price:** $4.00 (current and
1980 editions). **Also includes:** Lists of fiber producers and of
wholesalers (with territories covered and product lines). **Other
information:** Listed here under title page title; often cited in trade
sources as "Resource Directory of Branded Line Merchandise in the
Homesewing Industry."

★4786★
HOME WINEMAKERS INFORMATION
American Wine Society
4218 Rosewold   Phone: (313) 549-2303
Royal Oak, MI 48073
Covers: Suppliers of juice, other supplies, equipment, and services for
home winemakers. **Entries include:** Company name, address, phone.
Arrangement: Classified. **Pages** (approx.): 4. **Frequency:** Annual;
latest edition July 1979. **Price:** 75¢.

★4787★
HOSPITALITY GUIDE OF NORTH AMERICA
Corporate Communities of America
7501 Sebago Road   Phone: (301) 229-2802
Bethesda, MD 20034
Covers: Persons seeking hospitality while traveling who are willing to
reciprocate; hospitality is "a place to sleep and/or live and company."
Entries include: Individual name, address, age, phone, kind of
hospitality available, interests, hobbies, special concerns (smoking,
food habits, etc.), type of person most welcome, and phone of
persons through whom listee can be contacted if residence changes.
Arrangement: Geographical, by state then by Zip code. **Indexes:**
Personal name. **Pages** (approx.): 45. **Frequency:** Irregular;
republished as required with additions and deletions. **Editor:** J. Daniel
Loubert, Ph.D., President. **Price:** $10.00; copies available to listees
only. **Other information:** Not to be confused with "Travelers'
Directory," a similar publication published in Philadelphia (see separate
listing). The "Hospitality Guide" is now part of the CCA Travellers
Network, an expansion of the original concept of person-to-person
hospitality on which the guide was founded. CCA now serves as an
intermediary between traveler and host.

Hosteling USA: Official American Youth Hostels Handbook *See*
   AYH Hostel Guide and Handbook

★4788★
HOSTELING U.S.A.
East Woods Press
820 East Boulevard
Charlotte, NC 28203
Publication includes: List of about 225 hostels. **Frequency:**
Published May 1979. **Price:** $8.95, cloth; $5.95, paper; plus $1.00
shipping; payment must accompany orders from individuals. **Other
information:** Includes same list of hostels as in "AYH Hostel Guide and
Handbook" published by American Youth Hostels (see separate listing).
Principal content of "Hosteling U.S.A." is information on hosteling
customs and traditions, trip planning, cycling, backpacking, etc.

★4789★
HOT SPRINGS & SPAS OF CALIFORNIA
101 Productions
834 Mission Street
San Francisco, CA 94103
Covers: About 40 spas, saunas, and baths in California. **Entries
include:** Name of spa, address, description of types of baths offered,
massage techniques, overnight accommodations available, history of
spa. **Arrangement:** Geographical. **Indexes:** **Pages** (approx.): 160.
Frequency: Published September 1978. **Editors:** Laurel Cook and
Patricia Baker. **Price:** $3.95, plus 50¢ shipping. **Other information:**
Originally advertised as, "Hot Tubbing Around California."

Hot Tubbing Around California *See* Hot Springs & Spas of
   California

Hotels and Motels in Wyoming *See* Wyoming Accommodations

★4790★
HOW TO FLY FOR LESS
Travel Information Bureau
Box 105   Phone: (516) 549-9512
Kings Park, NY 11754
Covers: 600 charter operators utilizing both unscheduled and
scheduled airlines, who offer 10,000 charter flights, both domestic
and international; includes one-way flights. **Entries include:** Type of
flight, destination, airline used, duration, minimum price, and name and
address of charter operator. **Pages** (approx.): 40. **Frequency:** Annual,
winter; irregular supplements. **Editor:** Jens Jurgen. **Price:** $3.75
(current edition); $4.00 (tentative, 1980 edition); postpaid. **Other
information:** Old title of basic list, "Charter Flight Directory," is now
used only for supplements to "How to Fly for Less."

★4791★
**HOW TO SELL YOUR COLLECTIBLES, ANTIQUES, AND CRAFTS AT
   PROFIT**
Rawson Associates Publishers, Inc.
630 Third Avenue
New York, NY 10017
Publication includes: List of about 4,000 antiques dealers and
collectors. **Entries include:** Dealer/collector name, address, code
indicating whether dealer or collector, and brief note on special
interests. **Arrangement:** Classified by major interest (specialty books,
vintage clothing, etc.), then geographical. **Indexes:** General.
Frequency: Not established; first edition October 1977. **Editor:**
Marguerite Ashworth Brunner. **Price:** $9.95.

★4792★
HUPP HERALD ROSTER [Automobile collectors]
Hupmobile Club
Box AA
Rosemead, CA 91770
Covers: About 1,600 members who own Hupmobiles. **Entries
include:** Name, state or country, year and model of Hupmobile owned.
Arrangement: Geographical. **Indexes:** Model owned, alphabetical.

Pages (approx.): 25. **Frequency:** Biennial, summer of odd years. **Editor:** Lee Wilkes, Membership Chairman. **Price:** Available to members only.

★4793★
I LOVE NEW YORK
Easter Seal Society
Two Park Avenue, Suite 1815
New York, NY 10016
Covers: Recreational and historic sites in New York State. Separate publication for New York City. **Entries include:** Site name, address, phone, note on facilities and/or historic interest, dates operational, fees, keys indicating accessibility to persons in wheelchairs or with limited mobility. **Arrangement:** Geographical. **Pages** (approx.): 65. **Frequency:** Annual, spring. **Price:** Free. **Other information:** Published by New York State Department of Commerce Travel Bureau.

Inquiline [Home exchange] *See* Worldwide Temporary Homes Exchanges and Rentals

★4794★
INSIDE THE WORLD OF MINIATURES AND DOLLHOUSES
David McKay Company, Inc.
Two Park Avenue   Phone: (212) 340-9800
New York, NY 10016
Publication includes: Lists of manufacturers and mail order sources of miniatures, dollhouses, tools, etc., and clubs, museums, and periodicals. Includes shops handling these items. **Arrangement:** Manufacturers and mail-order firms are alphabetical, shops are geographical. **Indexes:** Alphabetical. **Pages** (approx.): 240. **Frequency:** Not established; first edition 1977. **Editors:** Bernard Rosner and Jay Beckerman. **Price:** $17.95, cloth; $9.95, paper.

★4795★
INTERCHANGE DIRECTORY [Home exchange]
Interchange Vacation Rentals
56 W. 45th Street   Phone: (212) 921-8070
New York, NY
Covers: Homes available for exchange for other homes for limited periods; international coverage.

★4796★
INTERLINE HOME EXCHANGE DIRECTORY
Interline Home Exchange
Box 26000
Honolulu, HI 96825
Covers: Homes listed by individuals for exchange with other individuals for vacations or other temporary use. Includes some rental units. **Entries include:** Name, address, description of property. **Arrangement:** Geographical. **Frequency:** Annual, April. **Price:** $20.00 for directory only; $15.00 if purchaser also lists a home.

★4797★
INTERNATIONAL ART MATERIAL DIRECTORY
Syndicate Magazines, Inc.
6 E. 43rd Street   Phone: (212) 949-0800
New York, NY 10017
Covers: Manufacturers and distributors of materials for fine arts and handicrafts. **Entries include:** Company name, address, phone, line of business. **Arrangement:** Alphabetical. **Indexes:** Product, trade name. **Frequency:** Annual. **Editors:** Jo Yanow and Phyllis Borea. **Advertising accepted.** Circulation 10,000. **Former title:** Art Material Trade News - Directory of Art and Craft Materials Issue (1977); Art Material Directory and Product Information Guide (1979). Also sometimes cited as, Directory of Art & Craft Materials. **Price:** $15.00.

★4798★
INTERNATIONAL ASSOCIATION FOR MEDICAL ASSISTANCE TO TRAVELLERS
Foundation for the Support of International Medical Training
350 Fifth Avenue, Suite 5620   Phone: (212) 270-6564
New York, NY 10001
Covers: 450 association centers in 120 countries, and English-speaking physicians affiliated with the association worldwide. **Entries include:** Name of center, phone, names of contacts. **Arrangement:** Geographical. **Pages** (approx.): 60. **Frequency:** Annual, May. **Editor:** V. Marcolongo, M. D., President. **Price:** Included in membership obtained by contributing to the foundation.

★4799★
INTERNATIONAL ASSOCIATION OF PET CEMETERIES— MEMBERSHIP DIRECTORY
International Association of Pet Cemeteries
27 W. 150 North Avenue   Phone: (312) 231-1117
West Chicago, IL 60185
Number of listings: About 215. **Entries include:** Name and address of cemetery, home address and phone of owner. **Arrangement:** Alphabetical. **Pages** (approx.): 6. **Frequency:** Annual, March. **Editor:** Patricia Blosser, Executive Director. **Advertising accepted.** Circulation 500. **Price:** $150.00. **Other information:** Association changed from national to international coverage.

★4800★
INTERNATIONAL ASSOCIATION OF SPACE PHILATELISTS— MEMBERSHIP DIRECTORY
International Association of Space Philatelists
Box 302
Yonkers, NY 10710
Covers: 890 collectors of philatelic items related to space exploration, astronauts, etc. **Entries include:** Name, address, membership number. **Arrangement:** Alphabetical. **Pages** (approx.): 20. **Frequency:** Biennial, fall of odd years. **Editor:** William P. York. **Advertising accepted.** Circulation 1,100. **Price:** Available to members only.

★4801★
INTERNATIONAL AVIAN DIRECTORY
Bar-J Aviary
3865 Bowen
St. Louis, MO 63116
Covers: About 2,000 bird breeders, seed companies, and other avicultural suppliers, publications, and organizations. **Entries include:** Company or organization name, address, products or activity. **Arrangement:** Geographical. **Pages** (approx.): 80. **Frequency:** Irregular; latest edition December 1979. **Advertising accepted.** **Price:** $10.00. **Also includes:** List of bird quarantine stations.

★4802★
INTERNATIONAL BRIDGE PRESS ASSOCIATION—MEMBERSHIP LIST
International Bridge Press Association
C/o Richard L. Frey, President
235 E. 87th Street   Phone: (212) 427-0198
New York, NY 10028
Covers: 400 contract bridge writers, worldwide. **Entries include:** Name, office address. **Arrangement:** Alphabetical. **Frequency:** Annual, April or May. **Price:** $10.00.

★4803★
INTERNATIONAL COUNCIL OF FAN CLUBS—DIRECTORY
International Council of Fan Clubs
206 Ashdale Avenue   Phone: (416) 466-8332
Toronto M4L 2Y9, Ontario, Canada
Covers: About 175 clubs organized to support and promote favorite performers in television; popular, classical, and country music; sports; etc., which were associated with the ICFC during the previous year. **Entries include:** Name of performer, field in which he/she is active, name and address of club president, dues, information about club

publications, activities, and rating assigned by ICFC on basis of club performance in delivering promised publications, etc. **Frequency:** Annual, February/March. **Editor:** Mrs. Jean L. Crocker, President. **Price:** $1.00 (current and 1980 editions). **Other information:** Updating information and new clubs in the "ICFC Journal."

★4804★
INTERNATIONAL DIRECTORY OF ACCESS GUIDES
Rehabilitation International USA
20 W. 40th Street   Phone: (212) 869-9907
New York, NY 10018
Covers: 275 guides to areas throughout the world which describe architectural features of buildings, airports, terminals, etc., which impede or enhance their use. **Entries include:** Title, publisher, address, area covered, price. **Arrangement:** Geographical. **Pages** (approx.): 15. **Frequency:** Irregular; latest edition summer 1979. **Editor:** Edward A. Rust. **Price:** Available free as a reprint from "Rehabilitation/WORLD."

★4805★
INTERNATIONAL DIRECTORY OF VOLUNTARY WORK
Vacation Work
9 Park End Street
Oxford, England
Covers: Organizations which offer residential and non-residential volunteer work opportunities; worldwide coverage. **Entries include:** Organization name, address, phone; description of work available including location, number of volunteers needed, length of service, requirements, stipend; description of organization including purpose, other activities. **Arrangement:** By terms of service (residential, non-residential, long-term, short-term), then geographical. **Indexes:** Organization name. **Pages** (approx.): 175. **Frequency:** Not established; first edition 1979. **Editors:** Roger Brown and David Woodworth.

★4806★
INTERNATIONAL FAN CLUB ORGANIZATION JOURNAL—
    DIRECTORY SECTION
International Fan Club Organization
Box 177
Wild Horse, CO 80862
Covers: About 175 clubs organized to support and promote favorite country music performers. **Entries include:** Name of performer, name and address of club president, rating of the club by the IFCO with respect to providing materials promised. **Pages** (approx.): 40. **Frequency:** Journal is three times yearly; each issue includes directory. **Editors:** Loudilla, Loretta, and Kay Johnson, Co-presidents. **Advertising accepted.** Circulation approximately 500. **Price:** Included in membership, $10.00 yearly.

★4807★
INTERNATIONAL FESTIVALS ASSOCIATION—ROSTER
International Festivals Association
15 S. Fifth Street   Phone: (612) 332-7412
Minneapolis, MN 55402
Covers: 125 associations, visitor bureaus, and others concerned with promoting local festivals and similar events (Edmonton Klondike Days, Puyallup Valley Daffodil Festival, etc.). **Entries include:** Event name, sponsor, manager's name, address, phone, dates. **Arrangement:** Alphabetical by name of event. **Indexes:** Geographical by city. **Pages** (approx.): 40. **Frequency:** Annual. **Price:** $5.00.

★4808★
INTERNATIONAL HANDSPINNING DIRECTORY
Doloria Chapin
2178 Pompey-Fabius Road
R. D. 1
Fabius, NY 13063   Phone: (315) 677-3837
Publication includes: Sources of products and services used by handspinners and related craftspersons, and list of sheep breeders associations. **Arrangement:** Geographical. **Pages** (approx.): 190.

Frequency: Irregular; latest edition 1975. **Editor:** Doloria M. Chapin. **Advertising accepted.** Specialized circulation, 3,000. **Price:** $6.50, plus 50¢ shipping.

★4809★
INTERNATIONAL PHILATELIC PRESS CLUB—MEMBERSHIP LIST
    [Stamps]
Philatelic Press Club
Box 114   Phone: (212) 843-4242
Richmond Hill, NY 11419
Covers: 250 professional philatelic journalists, publishers of philately catalogs. **Entries include:** Name, address, publication affiliation, member number and category. **Arrangement:** Alphabetical. **Pages** (approx.): 10. **Frequency:** Annual, February. **Former title:** Philatelic Press Club - Membership List (1978). **Price:** Available to members; others, apply.

★4810★
INTERNATIONAL WIZARD OF OZ CLUB—MEMBERSHIP
    DIRECTORY
International Wizard of Oz Club
200 N. 11th Street
Escanaba, MI 49829
Number of listings: 975. **Entries include:** Name, address. **Arrangement:** Alphabetical. **Indexes:** Geographical. **Frequency:** Annual, spring or summer. **Editor:** Fred M. Meyer, Secretary. **Price:** Available to members only.

★4811★
INTERNATIONAL WOOD COLLECTORS SOCIETY BULLETIN—
    DIRECTORY ISSUE
International Wood Collectors Society
C/o James P. Langdon
7200 N. W. Mountlake Way   Phone: (206) 694-4984
Vancouver, WA 98665
Covers: 800 scientists, hobbyists, and craftspersons who collect exotic, colorful, and historic wood. **Entries include:** Name, address, membership number, date admitted, aspect of wood in which interested (collecting, carving, turning, furniture making, etc.). **Arrangement:** Geographical. **Indexes:** Alphabetical. **Pages** (approx.): 55. **Frequency:** Annual, March. **Editor:** James P. Langdon. **Price:** Available to members only.

Jax Fax—Official Reference Directory of Charters and Inclusive
    Tours *See* Jax Fax—The Travel Marketing Magazine
    [Charters, tours]

★4812★
JAX FAX—THE TRAVEL MARKETING MAGAZINE [Charters, tours]
Jet Airtransport Exchange, Inc.
280 Tokeneke Road   Phone: (203) 655-8746
Darien, CT 06820
Covers: Over 8,000 international and domestic charter and group tours and cruises offered by over 200 national and regional tour operators. **Entries include:** Date of tour, city of departure, price, operator identification. Address, phone, contact, escrow bank in separate list. **Arrangement:** Geographical by destination. **Indexes:** Destination. **Pages** (approx.): 340. **Frequency:** Monthly. **Editor:** Mona Moore, Associate Editor. **Advertising accepted.** Circulation 16,000. **Former title:** Jax Fax - Official Reference Directory of Charters and Inclusive Tours. **Price:** $2.00 per copy; $9.00 per year (ISSN 0148-9542).

★4813★
JOURNAL OF SPORTS PHILATELY—SPORTS PHILATELISTS
    INTERNATIONAL MEMBERSHIP ROSTER ISSUE
Sports Philatelists International
3604 S. Home Avenue
Berwyn, IL 60402
Covers: About 300. **Entries include:** Name, address. **Arrangement:** Alphabetical. **Indexes:** Geographical, collecting interests (general

sports, football, etc.). **Pages** (approx.): 40. **Frequency:** Annual, March. **Editor:** John La Porta. **Advertising accepted. Price:** $5.00, available to members only.

★4814★
JUDITH BELL'S GUIDE TO U.S. COOKING SCHOOLS
Dorn Books
7101 York Avenue, S.   Phone: (612) 835-6855
Minneapolis, MN 55435
Covers: About 200 cooking schools for amateurs, schools offering preparation for restaurant careers, and traveling cooking teachers. **Entries include:** School name, address, phone, names of instructors, name and style of director, fees. Recipes submitted by the cooking schools are given separately. **Arrangement:** Amateur schools are geographical, professional schools and traveling cooks are alphabetical. **Indexes:** School name, recipe. **Pages** (approx.): 200. **Frequency:** Not established; first edition November 1979. **Editor:** Judith Bell. **Price:** $6.95, postpaid.

Junior Philatelists of America—Roster *See* Philatelic Observer—
    Junior Philatelists of America Roster Issue

★4815★
KASTLEMUSICK DIRECTORY FOR COLLECTORS OF RECORDINGS
Kastlemusick, Inc.
170 Broadway
New York, NY 10038
Covers: Part 1: 1,375 business firms worldwide concerned with the sale, production, and distribution of recordings, and 175 publications and their publishers. Part 2: 1,750 associations, clubs, and societies, and, separately, private collectors concerned with recordings. **Entries include:** Name, address, and statement of interests or offerings. **Arrangement:** Alphabetical within each section. **Pages** (approx.): 85. **Frequency:** Annual; Part 1 in February, Part 2 in August. **Editor:** Robert A. Hill. **Advertising accepted.** Circulation 3,500. **Price:** $12.95 for two-part set. **Send orders to:** Kastlemusick, Inc., 901 Washington Street, Wilmington, DE 19801.

★4816★
KEY TO JACKSON FOR THE PHYSICALLY LIMITED [Mississippi]
Junior League of Jackson, Mississippi
Box 4805
Jackson, MS 39216
Publication includes: Information about building features (ramps, wide doors, etc.) which help make Jackson's major stores, public buildings, etc., accessible to handicapped persons, and warnings about architectural barriers which might present difficulties. **Arrangement:** Classified by type of establishment or institution. **Pages** (approx.): 70. **Frequency:** Irregular. **Price:** Free.

★4817★
LEARNING VACATIONS
Acropolis Books Ltd.
2400 17th Street, N. W.
Washington, DC 20009
Covers: About 300 institutions offering more than 400 programs including college seminars, wilderness workshops, archaeological digs, travel programs, music festivals, arts and crafts workshops, writers' conferences, and foreign study programs; programs listed are offered primarily by American schools, but programs from Canada, Mexico, and the United Kingdom are also listed. **Entries include:** Name of organization or institution offering the program; address; program title, dates, cost, and content; description of living arrangements; activities available; comments on program, locale, etc.; contact person and phone. **Arrangement:** By type of program, then geographical. **Indexes:** Subject, geographical, institution. **Pages** (approx.): 200. **Frequency:** Not established; first edition June 1978. **Editor:** Gerson G. Eisenberg. **Price:** $5.95.

★4818★
LEN BUCKWALTER'S CB CHANNEL DIRECTORY
Grosset & Dunlap
51 Madison Avenue   Phone: (212) 689-9200
New York, NY 10010
Covers: About 1,500 communities in the United States and 100 in Canada; essentially, it is a Citizens Band (CB) "telephone book." **Entries include:** Community name, names of volunteer and official groups which monitor emergency and police channels, channels monitored, and hours channel is covered; same information for service stations and truck stops in area, campgrounds, marinas and boat clubs, CB clubs, special interest groups which communicate primarily by CB, and other heavy users of CB in the area (such as large firms). Also includes channels through which information can be secured about popular local gathering places for CBers. **Arrangement:** Geographical. **Pages** (approx.): 270. **Frequency:** Irregular; latest edition 1977. **Editor:** Len Buckwalter. **Price:** $12.95, cloth; $2.99, paper.

★4819★
LINCOLN ZEPHYR OWNERS CLUB—DIRECTORY [Automobile collectors]
Lincoln Zephyr Owners Club
Box 185
Middletown, PA 17057
Covers: 850 owners of the Lincoln Zephyr automobile. **Entries include:** Name, address, model and year of car owned. **Arrangement:** Geographical. **Frequency:** Annual, January. **Editor:** Chadwick Coombs. **Price:** Available to members only.

★4820★
LINN'S WORLD STAMP ALMANAC
Amos Press, Inc.
Box 29
Sydney, OH 45365
Publication includes: Membership directories of American Stamp Dealers' Association (1,500), Canadian Stamp Dealers' Association (100), and Japan Stamp Dealers' Association (25), with names and addresses; stamp columnists in nonphilatelic press with name, address, column name, and name and address of publishing periodical; philatelic periodicals, worldwide (300), with title, publisher, address, and editor; national stamp clubs, world wide, with address and name of president or secretary; local stamp clubs in United States (1,100), with name, information on place, frequency, and time of meetings and address for further information; philatelic museums and libraries, worldwide, with addresses and holding information (100); postal administrations for each country, with addresses and details of services offered to collectors. **Indexes:** General name, place, and subject index. **Frequency:** Latest edition 1978. **Price:** $10.00, postpaid.

★4821★
LITERARY TOUR GUIDE TO THE UNITED STATES
William Morrow & Company, Inc.
105 Madison Avenue   Phone: (212) 889-3050
New York, NY 10016
Covers: Homes, museums, and other landmarks associated with American writers; separate volumes for the northeastern states, south and southwest, and west and midwest. **Entries include:** Landmark location (city and state), association with writer or writer's works, address or driving directions, and hours and policies of admission. **Arrangement:** Geographical. **Indexes:** Author/title/name. **Pages** (approx.): 225-250. **Frequency:** Northeast volume (by Emilie C. Harting) published 1977; other volumes (by Rita Stein) February 1979. **Price:** $9.95 per volume, cloth; $5.95 per volume, paper; plus 50¢ shipping.

Little Black Book *See* Cat Fanciers' Association Breeder's
    Directory

★4822★
LOAN-A-HOME
Loan-a-Home
18 Darwood Place   Phone: (914) 664-7640
Mt. Vernon, NY 10533
Covers: Over 400 houses, apartments, etc., in United States and abroad which are available for long-term and vacation purposes in exchange for the homes of others, or for rental. **Entries include:** Name of person offering home, address of home, description, and other details. **Arrangement:** Geographical. **Frequency:** Directories in June and December, supplements in September and March. **Editor:** Muriel Hurwitz. **Former title:** Directory of Homes Available for Exchange. **Price:** $12.50 for a directory and supplement; $16.00 per year. **Other information:** No charge for listing of available housing; specialty is sabbatical housing.

★4823★
MAGIC CATALOGUE
E. P. Dutton & Company
201 Park Avenue South   Phone: (212) 674-5900
New York, NY 10003
Covers: Dealers in conjuring equipment and supplies; courses, societies, and conventions in the field; museums; etc. **Entries include:** Name of dealer, event, etc., address, brief additional information as appropriate. **Arrangement:** Classified. **Pages** (approx.): 250. **Frequency:** Not established; first edition 1977. **Editor:** William Doerflinger. **Price:** $19.95, cloth; $9.95, paper. **Other information:** Principal content is discussion and demonstration of magic tricks and effects.

★4824★
MAIL ORDER FOOD GUIDE
Simon and Schuster, Inc.
1230 Avenue of the Americas
New York, NY 10020
Covers: About 400 firms which offer whole wheat grains, fresh fruits and vegetables, game, cheeses, ethnic foods, camping foods, and other unusual or exotic fare by mail. **Entries include:** Company name, address, whether catalog is available, and description of product; most firms offer several products in a given category. **Arrangement:** By type of food. **Indexes:** Company name, individual foods. **Pages** (approx.): 160. **Frequency:** Not established; first edition fall 1977. **Editors:** Anne Tilson and Carol Hersh Weiss. **Price:** $10.95, cloth; $4.95, paper. (Not verified)

★4825★
MARMON NEWS—DIRECTORY ISSUE [Automobile collectors]
Marmon Club
629 Orangewood Drive   Phone: (813) 733-4736
Dunedin, FL 33528
Covers: Persons interested in the collection, restoration, and preservation of Marmon and Roosevelt automobiles. **Entries include:** Member name, address, model owned, year of model, body style, engine number, serial number, condition of car. **Arrangement:** By year of automobile (from 1902 through 1933). **Pages** (approx.): 30. **Frequency:** Annual, January. **Editors:** Leona R. and Philip W. Belote. **Former title:** Marmon Register. **Price:** Available to members only.

★4826★
MINIATURE ROOM SETTINGS
Chilton Book Company
Chilton Way   Phone: (215) 687-8200
Radnor, PA 19089
Publication includes: List of suppliers of miniature items and supplies and tools for building such items. **Entries include:** Supplier name, address, items offered. **Frequency:** First edition spring 1978. **Editor:** Helen Ruthberg. **Price:** $12.50, cloth; $8.95, paper.

★4827★
MINIATURES CATALOG
Boynton & Associates
Clifton House   Phone: (703) 830-1000
Clifton, VA 22024
Covers: 230 manufacturers and importers of dollhouses, furniture, building components, and accessories, built to a 1'' to 1' scale. **Entries include:** Manufacturer name, address, product description, and, in many cases, an illustration. **Arrangement:** By product. **Pages** (approx.): 200. **Frequency:** Irregular; new edition expected summer 1980. **Editor:** Carol Kulenguski. **Price:** $4.75, plus 75¢ shipping (current edition); $12.00, postpaid, payment with order (1980 edition). **Other information:** Publisher also uses title, "Doll House Miniatures Catalog."

★4828★
MINING AND MINERAL OPERATIONS IN [GEOGRAPHIC REGION]: A VISITOR GUIDE
Bureau of Mines
Interior Department
2401 E Street, N. W.   Phone: (202) 634-1004
Washington, DC 20241
Covers: Active and inactive mining and mineral operations and some other mineral-related locations in the United States convenient to major highways; many may be visited as well as observed from road. Regional editions for South Atlantic, New England and Mid-Atlantic, North Central, South Central, Rocky Mountain, and Pacific states. **Entries include:** Type of operation, mineral or ore being mined, company operating the site (if active), general location, map reference, and whether open to visitors. **Arrangement:** By map reference number. **Frequency:** Irregular; latest editions 1976-77. **Price:** South Atlantic, $2.70 (S/N 024-004-01895-0); New England and Mid-Atlantic, $2.30 (S/N 024-004-01889-5); North Central, $3.25 (S/N 024-004-01897-6); South Central, $4.75 (S/N 024-004-01903-4); Rocky Mountain, $2.40 (S/N 024-004-01899-2); Pacific, $2.15 (S/N 024-004-01872-1). **Send orders to:** Government Printing Office, Washington, DC 20402.

★4829★
MORGAN CAR CLUB—ROSTER OF MEMBERS
Morgan Car Club
616 Gist Avenue   Phone: (301) 585-0121
Silver Spring, MD 20910
Covers: 350 members, organizations, suppliers, libraries, and repair shops. **Entries include:** Name, address, and automobiles owned. **Pages** (approx.): 20. **Frequency:** Annual, fall. **Editor:** Edmund J. Zielinski. **Advertising accepted.** Circulation 350. **Price:** Available to members only.

★4830★
MORT'S GUIDE TO LOW COST VACATIONS AND LODGINGS ON COLLEGE CAMPUSES—U.S.A. & CANADA
CMG Publishing Company
Box 630
Princeton, NJ 08540
Entries include: College name, address, facilities offered, cost, whether limited to students or alumni or open to general public. **Arrangement:** Geographical. **Pages** (approx.): 190. **Frequency:** Irregular; latest edition spring 1978. **Price:** $6.00.

Motorcoach Tour Mart *See* Official Domestic Tour Manual U.S.A. & Canada

★4831★
MUSEUMS AND SITES OF HISTORICAL INTEREST IN OREGON
Oregon Historical Society
1230 S.W. Park Avenue   Phone: (503) 222-1741
Portland, OR 97205
Number of listings: 400. **Entries include:** Address, hours, comment on historical interest. **Arrangement:** Geographical. **Indexes:** General. **Pages** (approx.): 40. **Frequency:** Irregular; latest edition July 1979;

new edition expected spring 1980. **Editor:** Bruce T. Hamilton, Book Editor. **Price:** $5.95.

★4832★
MUSTER ROLL OF THE C.S.A. [Philately]
Confederate Stamp Alliance
C/o Patricia A. Kaufmann, Editor
1522 K Street, N. W.
Washington, DC 20005
Number of listings: 700. **Entries include:** Name, address. **Arrangement:** Alphabetical. **Pages** (approx.): 35. **Frequency:** Biennial, even years. **Editor:** Patricia Kaufmann. **Advertising accepted. Former title:** Confederate Stamp Album, Confederate Bulletin. **Price:** Available to members only. **Send orders to:** Francis J. Crown, Jr., Box 5-585, Ft. Richardson, AK 99505.

★4833★
NASH CAR CLUB OF AMERICA—DIRECTORY
Nash Car Club of America
C/o Robert Dworschack
Route 1   Phone: (319) 242-5490
Clinton, IA 52732
Number of listings: 1,300. **Entries include:** Name, address, and automobiles owned. **Arrangement:** Geographical. **Indexes:** Name. **Pages** (approx.): 70. **Frequency:** Annual, spring. **Price:** Available to members only.

★4834★
NASO INTERNATIONAL ASTROLOGICAL DIRECTORY
National Astrological Society
127 Madison Avenue   Phone: (212) 679-5676
New York, NY 10016
Covers: Individual astrologers and organizations, publications, and services, worldwide. **Pages** (approx.): 80. **Frequency:** Biennial; latest edition fall 1979. **Editor:** Henry Weingarten. **Price:** $5.00.

★4835★
NATIONAL ANTIQUE & ART DEALERS ASSOCIATION OF AMERICA—MEMBERSHIP DIRECTORY
National Antique and Art Dealers Association of America
59 E. 57th Street   Phone: (212) 355-0636
New York, NY 10022
Entries include: Firm name, address, phone, names of one or more principal executives, cable address, specialties. **Arrangement:** Alphabetical. **Pages** (approx.): 30. **Frequency:** Annual, April. **Editor:** Edward Munves, Jr., President. **Price:** Free. **Also includes:** Lists of periods for major countries and museums in New York City.

★4836★
NATIONAL ASSOCIATION OF DEALERS IN ANTIQUES—ROSTER
National Association of Dealers in Antiques
7080 Old River Road
Rural Route 6   Phone: (815) 633-8410
Rockford, IL 61103
Covers: 750 antiques dealers and show managers. **Entries include:** Name, office address and phone, hours, area of specialization. **Arrangement:** By geographic zone. **Pages** (approx.): 50. **Frequency:** Annual, March. **Editor:** Vivian Conklin, Publications Chairman. **Price:** Free.

National Association of Pet Cemeteries—Membership Directory
    See International Association of Pet Cemeteries—
    Membership Directory

★4837★
NATIONAL DIRECTORY OF CB RADIO CHANNELS
ETC Publications
Box 1627A
Palm Springs, CA 92263
Covers: Over 12,000 channel listings for citizen's band radio. **Entries include:** Call letters, frequency, "handle." **Arrangement:**

Geographical. **Pages** (approx.): 360. **Frequency:** Not established; first edition 1979. **Price:** $7.95.

★4838★
NATIONAL DIRECTORY OF FREE TOURIST ATTRACTIONS
Pilot Books
347 Fifth Avenue   Phone: (212) 685-0736
New York, NY 10016
Covers: More than 700 gardens, museums, restored villages, ships, and archeological and scenic attractions, most authentic rather than simulated or re-created. **Entries include:** Attraction name, location, brief descriptive data, visiting days and hours, and phone number of contact. **Arrangement:** Geographical. **Frequency:** **Editor:** Raymond Carlson. **Price:** $2.95 (current edition); $3.50 (1980 edition).

★4839★
NATIONAL GUIDE TO CRAFT SUPPLIES
Van Nostrand Reinhold Company
450 W. 33rd Street   Phone: (212) 594-8660
New York, NY 10001
Covers: 600 craft suppliers, primarily in the U.S.; 109 craft societies; 95 galleries and museums; 300 places of instruction; 55 fairs; 8 bookstores; 42 periodicals. **Entries include:** Name, address, phone number, catalogs available, products and services, ordering information, and retail or wholesale distribution. **Arrangement:** Classified under 43 craft categories - beads, decoupage, woodworking, etc. **Indexes:** Alphabetical. **Pages** (approx.): 220. **Frequency:** First edition November 1975. **Price:** $14.95, cloth; $7.95, paper.

National Travel News Directory See Discover America National
    Travel News Directory

★4840★
NATIONAL TURF WRITERS ASSOCIATION—ROSTER OF MEMBERSHIP
National Turf Writers Association
6000 Executive Boulevard, Suite 317   Phone: (301) 881-2266
Rockville, MD 20852
Covers: 210 newspaper and magazine writers, sports editors, and columnists who regularly write about or publish news of thoroughbred horseracing and breeding. **Entries include:** Name, address, affiliation. **Arrangement:** Alphabetical. **Frequency:** Quarterly. **Editor:** Tony Chamblin, Secretary-Treasurer. **Price:** Available to members only.

★4841★
NEW AGE—"NATURAL FOODS RESTAURANT ROUND-UP"
[Special feature]
New Age Communications, Inc.
32 Station Street   Phone: (617) 734-3155
Brookline Village, MA 02146
Covers: About 125 vegetarian restaurants. **Entries include:** Restaurant name, address; some listings also include phone, hours, type of menu, other comments. **Arrangement:** Geographical. **Frequency:** Appears in August 1979 issue. **Price:** $1.50.

★4842★
NEW COLLECTOR'S DIRECTORY
Padre Productions
Box 1275   Phone: (805) 543-5404
San Luis Obispo, CA 93406
Covers: About 100 collectors' organizations, over 40 periodicals for collectors, nearly 100 other publications for collectors, and sources of collectibles such as auction houses and dealers. **Entries include:** For organizations - Name, date of founding, dues, number of members, scope of interest, publications, and name and address of at least one officer. For periodicals - Title, publisher's address, format, specialty, type of information given. For sources - Name, address, specialty. For

books - Title, publisher, annotation. **Arrangement:** Alphabetical within categories. **Indexes:** Type of collectible, subject. **Pages** (approx.): 160. **Frequency:** First edition 1976; new edition expected January 1980. **Author:** Robert D. Connolly. **Price:** $3.50 (current edition); $5.95 (tentative, 1980 edition); plus 70¢ shipping (ISSN 0363-3284).

★4843★
NEW ENGLAND GUEST HOUSE BOOK
East Woods Press
820 East Boulevard
Charlotte, NC 28203
Covers: More than 150 guest houses and tourist homes, with information on towns in which they are located and local attractions; includes maps showing locations of homes. **Entries include:** Name of home, address, phone, name of proprietor. **Pages** (approx.): 190. **Frequency:** First edition fall 1979. **Editor:** Corinne Madden Ross. **Price:** $9.95, cloth; $6.95, paper; plus $1.00 shipping; payment must accompany orders from individuals.

★4844★
NEW YORK'S CHINESE RESTAURANTS
Atheneum Publishers
122 E. 42nd Street   Phone: (212) 661-4500
New York, NY 10017
Number of listings: Over 80. **Entries include:** Name of restaurant, location; rating; whether liquor is available or may be brought; hours open; credit cards accepted; map reference. **Arrangement:** By regional cuisine. **Indexes:** Restaurant name. **Pages** (approx.): 220. **Frequency:** Published 1977; no new edition planned. **Editors:** Stan Miller, et al. **Price:** $4.95. **Send orders to:** Book Warehouse, Inc., Vreeland Avenue, Totowa, NJ 07512.

★4845★
NSU ENTHUSIASTS USA—MEMBERSHIP LIST [Automobiles]
NSU Enthusiasts USA
20477 Nolina Court
Johnstown, CO 80534
Covers: More than 100 members of a club interested in the NSU automobile (which takes its name from initialism for Neckarsulm, the location in Wuerttemberg, Germany, of manufacturer's plant). **Entries include:** Name, address. **Arrangement:** Alphabetical. **Frequency:** Annual, fall. **Editor:** Charles C. Marsh. **Price:** Included in membership, $4.00 for first year; $3.00 thereafter.

★4846★
OFFICIAL DOMESTIC TOUR MANUAL U.S.A. & CANADA
Grace J. Talmage and Associates
2600 Martin Road   Phone: (215) 657-2278
Willow Grove, PA 19090
Publication includes: List of 10 motorcoach tour companies offering over 250 tours with 5,000 departures throughout the United States and Canada. **Entries include:** For tour companies - Name, address, phone. For tours - Dates offered, itinerary, costs. **Arrangement:** Tour operators are alphabetical, tours are by destination area. **Indexes:** Chronological, destination. **Pages** (approx.): 165. **Frequency:** Annual, March. **Editor:** Grace J. Talmage. **Advertising accepted.** Circulation 20,000. **Former title:** Motorcoach Tour Mart (1980). **Price:** $15.00. **Other information:** Cover title formerly, "Best in Motorcoach and Air Tours."

★4847★
OLD HOUSE CATALOGUE
Main Street Press
42 Main Street
Clinton, NJ 08809
Covers: 2,500 products, services, and suppliers for restoring, decorating, and furnishing the period house from Early American to 1930s modern. **Entries include:** Name of manufacturer or supplier, address, availability of additional descriptive literature, brief descriptions or evaluations. **Arrangement:** Classified into 10 major categories (structural products, woodwork and other fittings,

hardware, etc.). **Pages** (approx.): 240. **Frequency:** Biennial, fall of even years. **Editor:** Lawrence Grow. **Price:** $14.95, cloth; $7.95, paper. **Send orders to:** Universe Books, 381 Park Avenue South, New York, NY. **Other information:** Each new edition is identified by "Second," "Third," etc. as the first word of the title.

★4848★
OLD-HOUSE JOURNAL CATALOG—BUYER'S GUIDE
Old-House Journal Corporation
69A Seventh Avenue   Phone: (212) 636-4514
Brooklyn, NY 11217
Covers: 830 companies which supply parts, services, and fixtures, used in restoring houses built before 1920. **Entries include:** Company name, address, phone, code for line of business, services and products, catalog availability. **Arrangement:** Classififed. **Indexes:** Product. **Pages** (approx.): 115. **Frequency:** Annual, fall. **Editor:** Clem Labine. **Advertising accepted.** Circulation 12,000. **Price:** $8.95, plus $1.00 shipping.

★4849★
OLDSMOBILE CLUB OF AMERICA—ROSTER
Oldsmobile Club of America, Inc.
145 Latona Road   Phone: (716) 225-8146
Rochester, NY 14626
Number of listings: 2,000. **Entries include:** Name, address, model, year of Oldsmobile owned. **Arrangement:** Geographical. **Frequency:** Irregular; latest edition 1978; new edition possible 1980. **Editor:** J. F. Waller. **Advertising accepted. Price:** $2.50.

★4850★
1,001 SOURCES FOR FREE TRAVEL INFORMATION
Travel Information Bureau
Box 105   Phone: (516) 454-0319
Kings Park, NY 11754
Publication includes: List of over 1,200 tourist information bureaus, embassies, consulates, United Nations missions, airlines, railroads, chambers of commerce, state development offices, hotel chains and other sources of travel information; covers nations of the world, but most addresses are for agencies located in the United States. **Entries include:** Company or organization name, address, branch locations. **Arrangement:** Geographical. **Indexes:** General, geographical. **Pages** (approx.): 145. **Frequency:** Published August 1978; new edition possible 1982. **Editor:** Jens Jurgen. **Price:** $3.95, plus 55¢ shipping (add 40¢ for first class mailing).

★4851★
ORGANIC TRAVELER—A Guide to Organic, Vegetarian, and Health Food Restaurants
Grasshopper Press
Box 331   Phone: (315) 479-5998
Dewitt, NY 13214
Covers: 500 vegetarian, organic, and natural food restaurants and snack bars in the United States and Canada. **Entries include:** Name, address, phone, hours, price range, and symbols indicating type of foods and service. **Arrangement:** Geographical. **Indexes:** Restaurant name. **Pages** (approx.): 175. **Frequency:** Not established; latest edition fall 1975. **Editors:** Maxine W. Davis and Gregory J. Tetrault. **Advertising accepted. Price:** $2.95.

★4852★
PACKARD CLUB—ANNUAL DIRECTORY
Packard Club
306 N. Plum   Phone: (507) 645-5496
Northfield, MN 55057
Covers: 2,600 members interested in history and restoration of Packard automobiles. **Entries include:** Name, address, phone, car(s) owned. **Arrangement:** Geographical. **Pages** (approx.): 100. **Frequency:** Irregular; previous edition March 1977; latest edition August 1979. **Price:** $3.50; available to members only.

Pan Am Home Exchange Directory *See* Exchange Book [Home exchange]

★4853★

PAPILLON CLUB OF AMERICA—MEMBERSHIP LIST [Dogs]
Papillon Club of America
5707 Hillcrest Drive
Detroit, MI 48236
Covers: About 215 owners, breeders, and exhibitors of purebred Papillon dogs. **Entries include:** Name, address, phone, kennel name. **Arrangement:** Alphabetical. **Pages** (approx.): 40. **Frequency:** Annual, June. **Price:** Available to members only.

★4854★

PEAK DOLL DIRECTORY
Dick and Polly Ford, Publishers
Box 757   Phone: (303) 392-5135
Colorado Springs, CO 80901
Covers: 500-700 ads related to the doll hobby/business. Includes ads for dealers, publications, shops, museums, supply houses, doll makers, etc. **Entries include:** Individual or shop name and address, plus type of dolls or materials handled. **Arrangement:** Alphabetical by firm or individual name. **Indexes:** Classified subject. **Pages** (approx.): 200. **Frequency:** Annual, March. **Editors:** Dick and Polly Ford. **Advertising accepted.** Circulation 2,500. **Price:** $6.00 (current and 1980 editions).

★4855★

PELICAN GUIDE TO HISTORIC HOMES AND SITES OF REVOLUTIONARY AMERICA
Pelican Publishing Company, Inc.
630 Burmaster Street   Phone: (504) 368-1175
Gretna, LA 70053
Covers: Architectural and historic attractions of colonial period; covers Maine, Vermont, New Hampshire , Rhode Island, Massachusetts, and Connecticut. **Entries include:** Name of attraction, location, photographs, hours open, significant features and history, and admission fee. **Arrangement:** Geographical. **Pages** (approx.): 130. **Frequency:** First edition 1976. **Editor:** Garret G. Stearns. **Price:** $3.25.

★4856★

PELICAN GUIDE TO OLD HOMES OF MISSISSIPPI
Pelican Publishing Company, Inc.
630 Burmaster Street   Phone: (504) 368-1175
Gretna, LA 70053
Covers: About 500 architecturally and historically significant houses of Mississippi. Volume one covers Natchez and the South; volume two features Columbus and the North. **Entries include:** Name of house, address, brief history, hours open, and admission fees. **Arrangement:** Geographical. **Pages** (approx.): Volume 1, 160; volume 2, 150. **Frequency:** Irregular; latest edition May 1977. **Editor:** Helen Kerr Kempe. **Price:** $3.95 per volume.

★4857★

PELICAN GUIDE TO PLANTATION HOMES OF LOUISIANA
Pelican Publishing Company, Inc.
630 Burmaster Street   Phone: (504) 368-1175
Gretna, LA 70053
Covers: 240 architecturally and historically significant homes, many of them dating to the early nineteenth century, including both homes open to the public and private residences. **Entries include:** Name of house, address, brief history, hours open, admission fees. **Arrangement:** Geographical. **Indexes:** By name of house. **Pages** (approx.): 130. **Frequency:** Irregular; latest edition July 1977. **Editors:** Jim and Nancy Calhoun. **Price:** $2.95.

Pen Pal Directory *See* Stamp Exchangers Directory

★4858★

PEOPLE'S ACCESSIBILITY GUIDE TO ROCHESTER, NEW YORK, FOR THE DISABLED AND ELDERLY
Handicapped Independence H.E.R.E., Inc.
55 Troup Street   Phone: (716) 546-7060
Rochester, NY 14608
Publication includes: Information about building features (ramps, wide doors, etc.) which help make major Rochester-area (Monroe County) buildings of all types accessible to handicapped persons. Includes comments about features which might present difficulties. **Arrangement:** By type of institution or establishment. **Pages** (approx.): 130. **Frequency:** Irregular; latest edition November 1978. **Editor:** Gene McGinnis, Guide Book Coordinator. **Price:** 75¢ shipping.

★4859★

PEOPLE'S FOLK DANCE DIRECTORY
John C. Steele
Box 8575   Phone: (512) 454-0175
Austin, TX 78712
Covers: International folk dance groups, publications, folk dance teachers, and retailers of folk dance costumes, equipment, etc. Groups include some outside the United States. **Entries include:** For groups - Name, meeting place and time; name, address, and phone of contact. For other listings - Company or organization name, address, product or service. **Arrangement:** Geographical. **Pages** (approx.): 70. **Frequency:** Biennial, spring of even years. **Editors:** John C. Steele and Susan Hovorka. **Price:** $1.75, plus 50¢ for first class postage.

★4860★

PERIODICAL GUIDE FOR COMPUTERISTS
E. Berg Publications
1360 S. W. 199th Court
Aloha, OR 97005
Publication includes: Nearly 30 publications which contain material relevant to personal computing. **Entries include:** Publication name, address. **Arrangement:** Alphabetical. **Indexes:** Author. **Pages** (approx.): 55. **Frequency:** Annual, January (covering articles published in previous year). **Editor:** Eldon Berg. **Price:** $5.00, postpaid (current and 1980 editions; ISSN 0147-3077). **Other information:** Principal content of publication is subject index of the periodicals' content.

★4861★

PET DEALER—ANNUAL PURCHASING GUIDE ISSUE
Howmark Publishing Corporation
225 W. 34th Street   Phone: (212) 279-0800
New York, NY 10001
Covers: Manufacturers and importers of pet supplies; distributors and wholesalers of pet supplies; wholesalers, breeders, and importers of pets (livestock); trade associations; publishers of pet books and records, educational, and training materials; and grooming schools. **Entries include:** Most listings include company or organization name, address, phone, names of executives, trade and brand names, and list of products and services. **Arrangement:** Alphabetical within above categories. **Indexes:** Manufacturers and livestock suppliers are by product; manufacturers are also indexed by brand name; and wholesalers and distributors are indexed geographically. **Frequency:** Annual, April. **Editor:** William G. Reddan. **Advertising accepted.** Circulation 9,700. **Former title:** Pet Dealer - Annual Directory. **Price:** $25.00.

★4862★

PHILATELIC DIRECTORY [Stamps]
Society of Philaticians
Box 150
Salt Point Turnpike   Phone: (914) 266-3150
Clinton Corners, NY 12514
Covers: About 200 philatelic writers, publicists, associations, libraries, museums, publications. Includes a list of world-wide postal administrations. **Entries include:** Writers list shows name, home address, publications and associations affiliated with. Other lists show name and address. **Arrangement:** Four sections - Writers list and

publications and associations list are alphabetical; postal administrations list and libraries and museums list are geographical. **Indexes:** Member names geographically. **Pages** (approx.): 50. **Frequency:** Biennial, June of even years. **Editor:** Gustav Detjen, Jr. **Advertising accepted.** Circulation 1,200. **Former title:** Membership Directory. **Price:** $12.00 (current and 1980 editions).

★4863★

PHILATELIC OBSERVER—JUNIOR PHILATELISTS OF AMERICA ROSTER ISSUE
Junior Philatelists of America
Box 116
Ashton, RI 02864
Covers: About 600 members of the Junior Philatelists of America, a stamp collecting club for persons who are usually less than 20 years old. Coverage includes Canada and other foreign countries. **Entries include:** Name, address, age, member registration number, collecting interests. **Arrangement:** Alphabetical. **Indexes:** Geographical. **Pages** (approx.): 25. **Frequency:** Annual, January-February; updated every two months in Philatelic Observer. **Editor:** Cheryl Wilkinson. **Advertising accepted. Price:** 50¢. **Also includes:** List of supporting members (generally adults) with name, member registration number, city and state; list of chapters with name, address, and name and address of chapter representative.

Philatelic Press Club—Membership List *See* International Philatelic Press Club—Membership List

★4864★

PLAYING CARD COLLECTORS' ASSOCIATION—MEMBERSHIP DIRECTORY
Playing Card Collectors' Association
813 W. Orchard Street   Phone: (414) 672-6642
Milwaukee, WI 53204
Covers: About 150 individuals who collect playing cards and card games. **Entries include:** Member name, address, registration number, collecting interests. **Arrangement:** Alphabetical. **Frequency:** Semiannual; new member lists are published in quarterly issues. **Price:** Available to members only.

★4865★

PLYMOUTH ROCK FANCIERS CLUB YEARBOOK [Poultry]
Plymouth Rock Fanciers Club
15 Fort Hill Terrace
Northampton, MA 01060
Publication includes: List of member owners of Plymouth Rock poultry. **Arrangement:** Alphabetical. **Pages** (approx.): 35. **Frequency:** Annual, spring. **Editor:** Stephen Thibault, Yearbook Editor. **Advertising accepted. Price:** Available to members; others, apply. **Also includes:** Articles about Plymouth Rocks.

★4866★

PONTIAC-OAKLAND CLUB INTERNATIONAL—ROSTER
Pontiac-Oakland Club International
Box 5108   Phone: (503) 371-1350
Salem, OR 97304
Covers: About 2,600 persons who are owners of, or interested in, vintage Pontiac and Oakland automobiles. **Entries include:** Name, address, vehicle model owned. **Pages** (approx.): 80. **Frequency:** Annual, January. **Editor:** Donald A. Bougher. **Price:** Available with membership, $12.00.

★4867★

POPULAR PHOTOGRAPHY—DIRECTORY AND BUYING GUIDE ISSUE
Ziff-Davis Publishing Company, Inc.
One Park Avenue   Phone: (212) 725-3506
New York, NY 10016
Covers: About 235 manufacturers and distributors of photographic and projection equipment, accessories, and supplies. **Entries include:** Company name, address, product description. **Arrangement:**

Alphabetical. **Indexes:** Product. **Pages** (approx.): 175. **Frequency:** Annual. **Editor:** David Steigman. **Advertising accepted. Price:** $2.25, plus 30¢ shipping.

★4868★

PORSCHE OWNERS CLUB—MEMBERSHIP ROSTER
Porsche Owners Club
Box 54910, Terminal Annex
Los Angeles, CA 90054
Number of listings: 600. **Entries include:** Name, address, automobiles owned. **Arrangement:** Alphabetical. **Pages** (approx.): 30. **Frequency:** Annual, May or June. **Advertising accepted.** Circulation, 1,500. **Price:** Available to members only.

★4869★

PROCEEDINGS OF THE RADIO CLUB OF AMERICA
Radio Club of America
Box 2112
Grand Central Station
New York, NY 10017
Publication includes: List of 800 amateur radio operators in the United States. **Entries include:** Member name, grade of membership, date of joining, dates of advancement from one grade to another, address. **Frequency:** Biennial, October of odd years. **Advertising accepted.** Circulation 830. **Price:** $2.25.

★4870★

PROFITABLE CRAFT MERCHANDISING—CRAFT SUPPLY DIRECTORY ISSUE
PJS Publications Inc.
Box 1790   Phone: (309) 682-6626
Peoria, IL 61656
Covers: About 1,750 manufacturers, manufacturers' representatives, wholesalers, publishers, consultants, and trade associations supplying or concerned with the craft industry. **Entries include:** Company name, address, phone, contact person; and, as appropriate, specialties or interests in crafts, geographical area served, and availabilty and price of catalog. **Arrangement:** Manufacturers, publishers, consultants, and trade associations are alphabetical; all others are geographical. **Indexes:** Product, trade name, book subject. **Pages** (approx.): 180. **Frequency:** Annual, June. **Editor:** Geoffrey Wheeler. **Advertising accepted. Price:** $10.00, payment with order; one year subscription rate, $9.00, including directory issue.

★4871★

QUICK GUIDE TO THE WINES OF ALL THE AMERICAS
Doubleday & Company, Inc.
245 Park Avenue   Phone: (212) 953-4561
New York, NY 10017
Publication includes: Brief description of about 75 United States wineries, with comments on the specialties of each. **Arrangement:** Geographical. **Frequency:** Not established; first edition 1977. **Editor:** Robert Jay Misch. **Price:** $4.95.

★4872★

RADIO COMMUNICATIONS GUIDE
Handler Enterprises, Inc.
Box 48
Deerfield, IL 60015
Covers: Shortwave and VHF/UHF communications stations of interest to hobby listeners operated by federal and foreign government agencies and common carriers. **Entries include:** Call letters, frequency, station type, name and address of operating agency. **Pages** (approx.): 55. **Frequency:** Not established; first edition December 1979. **Editor:** Steven Handler. **Price:** $6.95, payment with order.

★4873★
RADIO CONTROL BUYERS GUIDE
Boynton & Associates
Clifton House   Phone: (703) 830-1000
Clifton, VA 22024
Covers: Over 240 manufacturers of products and accessories used for operating model aircraft, boats, cars, etc., by radio control. **Entries include:** Manufacturer name, address, product descriptions and specifications, photos. **Arrangement:** Alphabetical. **Indexes:** Product. **Pages** (approx.): 200. **Frequency:** Annual, June. **Editor:** David M. Boynton. **Advertising accepted.** Circulation 25,000. **Price:** $7.25, plus 75¢ shipping.

★4874★
RAILROADIANA COLLECTORS ASSOCIATION—DIRECTORY
Railroadiana Collectors Association
405 Byron Avenue   Phone: (205) 342-6517
Mobile, AL 36609
Covers: About 750 individuals and commercial organizations interested in railroadiana collecting and railroad history. **Entries include:** Name, address, phone, collecting interests, membership registration number (includes year). **Arrangement:** Alphabetical. **Indexes:** Geographical, collecting interest. **Pages** (approx.): 40. **Frequency:** Annual. **Editor:** Dan Moss, Secretary. **Advertising accepted.** Circulation 750. **Price:** Available to members only.

Rainbow Book *See* Free Stuff for Kids

Rehabilitation/WORLD—International Directory of Access Guides Issue *See* International Directory of Access Guides

★4875★
RENT A FURNISHED VACATION DWELLING
N. J. Arnold
Box 234
Torrance, CA 90501
Covers: Homes, villas, chalets, boats, recreational vehicles, and other "dwellings" available for rent through private owners or agents. **Entries include:** Individual or firm name, address, phone, brief description of accomodations, cost, and period of availability. **Arrangement:** By type of facility. **Pages** (approx.): 100. **Frequency:** Annual, January. **Editor:** N. J. Arnold. **Advertising accepted.** Listings are $15.00 each, including copy of publication. **Price:** $5.95, postpaid (1980 edition).

Resource Directory of Branded Line Merchandise in the Homesewing Industry *See* Home Sewing Industry Resource Directory

★4876★
ROADFOOD [Regional restaurants]
Random House, Inc.
201 E. 50th Street   Phone: (212) 572-2168
New York, NY 10022
Covers: Subtitle: "The Coast-to-Coast Guide to over 400 of America's Great Inexpensive Regional Restaurants - All within 10 Miles of a Major Highway." Includes list of fairs and festivals featuring regional food. **Entries include:** For restaurants - Restaurant name, address, rating (on a system of 4 stars), phone, hours open, and description of food, ambience, etc. For fairs - Event name, location, dates, description of food features. **Arrangement:** By region, then by state. **Pages** (approx.): 450. **Frequency:** Not established; first edition June 1978; new edition expected fall 1980. **Editors:** Jane and Michael Stern. **Price:** $5.95. **Send orders to:** Random House, Inc., 400 Hahn Road, Westminster, MD 21157.

★4877★
RQ—"ROAD MAPS AND TOURIST INFORMATION: A LIST OF CORRECT ADDRESSES" [Article]
Reference and Adult Services Division
American Library Association
50 E. Huron Street   Phone: (312) 944-6780
Chicago, IL 60611
Publication includes: List of state tourist information agencies and highway commissions or other agencies responsible for providing road maps, general tourist and state park information, and hunting, fishing, and camping information. **Entries include:** Agency name, address, key indicating type of information provided. **Arrangement:** Geographical. **Author:** James Rettig. **Price:** $4.00. **Other information:** In Winter 1977 issue, pages 129-135.

★4878★
RUBBER STAMP ALBUM
Workman Publishing Company, Inc.
One W. 39th Street   Phone: (212) 398-9160
New York, NY 10018
Publication includes: List of companies which sell rubber stamps by mail order, and ordering tips. **Entries include:** Company name, address. **Frequency:** First edition October 1978. **Pages** (approx.): 220. **Editors:** Joni Miller and Lowry Thompson. **Price:** $12.50, cloth; $6.95, paper. **Other information:** Emphasis of book is on use of rubber stamps in handicrafts.

★4879★
RV SERVICE AND REPAIR DIRECTORY [Recreation vehicles]
Recreation Vehicle Dealers Association of North America
C/o Doe's Travel Trailers
Illinois 137 and U. S. 45
Libertyville, IL 60048
Covers: 1,000 retail service and repair shops in the United States and Canada which can service all or some part of a recreation vehicle, and who have pledged their willingness to assist out-of-town vacationers and users. **Entries include:** Shop name, address, day and night phones, services available. **Arrangement:** Geographical. **Pages** (approx.): 300. **Frequency:** Annual. **Editor:** H. C. Peaster, Publications Executive Director. **Price:** $6.95.

Second Old House Catalog *See* Old House Catalog

★4880★
SEW BUSINESS—NATIONAL DIRECTORY ISSUE
Sylvan Publishing Inc.
666 Fifth Avenue, 14th Floor   Phone: (212) 586-2806
New York, NY 10019
Covers: Manufacturers and distributors of fabrics, sewing accessories, and needlework items; associations and trade groups concerned with sewing accessory retailing; and publishers of sewing and craft books and magazines. **Arrangement:** By type of activity (distributor, producer, etc.). **Indexes:** Product, brand name and trademark. **Pages** (approx.): 170. **Frequency:** Annual, July. **Editor:** Christina Holmes. **Advertising accepted.** **Price:** $4.00.

★4881★
SHOPPING FOR CRAFTS IN NEW YORK CITY
American Crafts Council
22 W. 55th Street   Phone: (212) 977-8989
New York, NY 10019
Covers: Retail outlets for crafts in Manhattan; 90 are outlets for American crafts, 26 are for imported crafts. **Entries include:** Name of shop, address, phone, hours, products. **Arrangement:** By American or imported, then alphabetical. **Pages** (approx.): 15. **Frequency:** Irregular; latest edition January 1979. **Price:** $1.50, payment with order.

★4882★

SNOW GOER TRADE—GUIDE TO SUPPLIERS ISSUE
Webb Company
1999 Shepard Road   Phone: (612) 647-7382
St. Paul, MN 55116
Covers: About 250 manufacturers of products related to the snowmobile industry, and about 150 independent distributors. **Entries include:** Company name, address, names of one or two executives, phone; some listings include similar information for company's distributors or branch offices. **Arrangement:** Separate alphabetical lists of manufacturers and distributors. **Indexes:** Product (includes both manufacturers and distributors). **Frequency:** Annual, August/September. **Editor:** Jerry Bassett. **Advertising accepted.** Circulation 12,000. **Price:** Controlled circulation.

★4883★

**SOCIETY FOR THE PRESERVATION OF POULTRY ANTIQUITIES—
    BREEDERS DIRECTORY**
Society for the Preservation of Poultry Antiquities
Route 3
Greenwood, WI 54437
Covers: About 450 member breeders of rare or unusual varieties of poultry and waterfowl. **Entries include:** Name, address. **Arrangement:** Alphabetical. **Indexes:** Geographical with breeder name, address, and varieties handled; only members who responded to a questionnaire are included. **Pages** (approx.): 120. **Frequency:** Biennial, winter of odd years. **Advertising accepted.** Circulation 1,200. **Price:** $5.00.

★4884★

**SOCIETY OF AMERICAN TRAVEL WRITERS—ROSTER OF
    MEMBERS**
Society of American Travel Writers
1120 Connecticut Avenue, N. W., Suite 940 Phone: (202) 785-5567
Washington, DC 20036
Covers: 300 newspaper and magazine travel editors and writers, syndicated travel columnists, free-lance writers, photo journalists, and radio and television broadcasters in the United States and Canada. Also covers separately 300 executives in public relations who handle tourist attractions, domestic and foreign tourist offices, carriers, hotels, and executives of public relations agencies which handle travel accounts. **Entries include:** Name, business address, phone, year joined, and spouse's given name. **Arrangement:** Alphabetical within the two major divisions of membership. **Indexes:** Geographical, company. **Pages** (approx.): 130. **Frequency:** Annual, February. **Editor:** Ken Fischer, Administrative Coordinator. **Price:** $25.00 (current edition); $40.00 (1980 edition).

★4885★

**SOCIETY OF PAPER MONEY COLLECTORS—MEMBERSHIP
    DIRECTORY**
Society of Paper Money Collectors
Box 3666
Cranston, RI 02910
Covers: About 2,500 collectors of paper money, including United States currency of various types, foreign currency, obsolete paper money, military currency, fractional currency, checks, and stock certificates. **Entries include:** Name, registration number, address, collecting specialty. **Arrangement:** Alphabetical. **Frequency:** Annual, November; updated bimonthly in "Paper Money." **Price:** Included in membership, $10.00 per year.

Society of Philatelic Americans—Membership Directory *See*
    **S.P.A. Journal—Society of Philatelic Americans Membership
    Directory Issue**

Society of Philaticians—Membership Directory *See* **Philatelic
    Directory**

Society of Wireless Pioneers—Membership List *See* Wireless
    Pioneer Almanac, Call Book/Directory

★4886★

SOHO: A GUIDE
Neal-Schuman Publishers, Inc.
64 University Place
New York, NY 10003
Covers: Galleries, performing arts theaters, shops, and restaurants located in the SoHo section of New York City. **Entries include:** Establishment name, address, attraction. **Arrangement:** By type of establishment. **Pages** (approx.): 275. **Frequency:** Published January 1979. **Author:** Helene Zucker Seeman and Alanna Siegfried. **Price:** $6.95, plus 75¢ shipping.

★4887★

**S.P.A. JOURNAL—SOCIETY OF PHILATELIC AMERICANS
    MEMBERSHIP DIRECTORY ISSUE**
Society of Philatelic Americans
58 W. Salisbury Drive   Phone: (302) 764-6649
Wilmington, DE 19809
Covers: 8,500 stamp collectors; also lists local branches. **Entries include:** Name, address, membership number. For branches - Name, number, meeting place and time, name and address of reporter. **Arrangement:** Collectors are alphabetical. **Pages** (approx.): 165. **Frequency:** Irregular; latest edition March 1979. **Editor:** Robert B. Brandeberry, Executive Secretary. **Advertising accepted.** Circulation 2,000. **Price:** $3.00; available to members only (ISSN 0036-181X).

★4888★

SPARK GAP TIMES—ROSTER ISSUE
Old Old Timers Club
Box AA   Phone: (213) 282-0014
Mamaroneck, NY 10543
Covers: 2,200 men and women active in amateur radio communication 40 or more years ago. **Entries include:** Name, home address, call, member number. **Frequency:** Annual, May-June. **Editor:** A. J. Gironda. **Advertising accepted.** Circulation 1,100. **Former title:** Blabber Mouth. **Price:** Included in subscription, $6.00 per year.

★4889★

STAMP EXCHANGERS DIRECTORY
Levine Publications
Box 175
Irvington, NJ 07011
Covers: Over 500 people worldwide who are interested in exchanging stamps and coins with Americans. **Entries include:** Name and address. **Pages** (approx.): 16. **Frequency:** Irregular; latest edition 1979; new edition expected 1980. **Editor:** L. J. Olssen, Executive Editor. **Advertising accepted.** Circulation 4,500. **Former title:** "Pen-Pal Directory" and "Stamp Exchangers Annual Directory," which merged to form the present publication. **Price:** $2.00 (current and 1980 editions).

★4890★

STATE REVENUE SOCIETY—YEARBOOK [Stamps]
State Revenue Society
1515 S. Highland
Arlington Heights, IL 60005
Covers: About 250 collectors of revenue stamps issued by federal, state, local, and foreign governments. **Entries include:** Member name, address, collecting interests, registration number. **Arrangement:** Alphabetical. **Frequency:** Biennial, fall of odd years; updated 6 times per year by "State Revenue Newsletter." **Editor:** David Drury. **Advertising accepted.** Circulation 250. **Price:** Included in subscription to "State Revenue Newsletter," $4.00 per year. **Send orders to:** Harold A. Effner, Secretary, 210 Eastern Way, Rutherford, NJ 07070 (201-939-6199).

★4891★
STEAM AND GAS SHOW DIRECTORY [Antique farm equipment]
Stemgas Publishing Company
Box 328
Lancaster, PA 17604
Covers: Nearly 400 gatherings and shows in 40 states and Canada at which antique farm tractors and other steam-driven equipment is displayed; museums are also listed. **Entries include:** Show name, location, name and phone of contact, nature of event, dates. **Arrangement:** Geographical. **Pages** (approx.): 70. **Frequency:** Annual, spring. **Editor:** Gerald S. Lestz, Editor-Publisher. **Price:** $2.50, postpaid, payment with order (current and 1980 editions).

★4892★
STEAM PASSENGER DIRECTORY
Empire State Railway Museum
Box 666
Middletown, NY 10940
Covers: About 140 rail lines, and museums which operate steam and electric trains. **Entries include:** Line or museum name, location, length of ride, schedule, fare, locomotives operating or on display, other displays, illustrations. **Pages** (approx.): 170. **Frequency:** Annual. **Price:** $4.00.

★4893★
A STEP IN TIME: SAN DIEGO FOR THE HANDICAPPED [California]
Community Service Center for the Disabled
4601 Park Boulevard   Phone: (714) 293-3500
San Diego, CA 92116
Publication includes: Information about building features (ramps, wide doors, etc.) which help make San Diego's major stores, public buildings, museums, restaurants, theaters, etc., accessible to handicapped persons, and warnings about architectural barriers which might present difficulties. Also includes information about places listed, including hours, special attractions, fees, etc. **Arrangement:** By area of the city. **Pages** (approx.): 55. **Frequency:** Irregular; latest edition 1977. **Price:** Free; send stamped, self-addressed 6" x 9" envelope. **Other information:** Prepared by the Junior League of San Diego.

★4894★
STEREO REVIEW'S STEREO DIRECTORY AND BUYING GUIDE
Ziff-Davis Publishing Company, Inc.
One Park Avenue   Phone: (212) 725-3500
New York, NY 10016
Covers: 2,000 manufacturers of stereo and high-fidelity components. **Entries include:** Company name, address, product description, specifications, price. **Arrangement:** Alphabetical. **Pages** (approx.): 250. **Frequency:** Annual, fall. **Editor:** Arthur P. Salsberg. **Advertising accepted. Former title:** Stereo Review's Stereo/Hi-Fi Directory. **Price:** $2.95.

★4895★
TOURING WITH TOWSER
Gaines Dog Research Center
250 North Street   Phone: (914) 683-4646
White Plains, NY 10625
Covers: 2,000 independent hotels and motels and about ten chains with over 4,000 units that welcome guests with pets. Includes Canada. **Entries include:** Name, address, phone, and code for restrictions. **Arrangement:** Geographical. **Pages** (approx.): 60. **Frequency:** Biennial, January of odd years. **Editor:** Tom O'Shea, Associate Director. **Price:** $1.00. **Send orders to:** Gaines TWT, Box 1007, Kankakee, IL 60901.

Toys—Directory Issue *See* Toys, Hobbies, & Crafts—Directory Issue

★4896★
TOYS, HOBBIES, & CRAFTS—DIRECTORY ISSUE
Harcourt Brace Jovanovich Publications
757 Third Avenue   Phone: (212) 888-4390
New York, NY 10017
Covers: About 3,000 manufacturers, manufacturer representatives, suppliers, character licensing organizations, and trade associations in the toy, hobby, and craft industry. **Entries include:** For manufacturers - Company name, address, phone, sales office locations, and representatives. For manufacturer representatives - Company name, address, year business was established, number of salesmen employed, and description of display rooms and warehouse facilities. For trade associations - Name, address, phone, and officers. **Arrangement:** Manufacturers are alphabetical; manufacturer representatives are geographical; character licensing companies are alphabetical by property. **Indexes:** Product, trade name. **Pages** (approx.): 300. **Frequency:** Annual, June. **Editor:** Ian Gittlitz. **Advertising accepted.** Circulation 14,000. **Former title:** Toys - Directory Issue (1977). **Price:** $5.00.

★4897★
TRAVEL 800
Cabell Travel Publications
11411 Cumpston Street   Phone: (213) 980-6260
North Hollywood, CA 91601
Covers: 15,000 locations for hotels, cruise lines, railroads, car rental agencies, and other travel-related firms which have 800 (toll-free) numbers for use of customers. **Entries include:** Company name, city in which located, states and/or cities from which toll-free calls can be made, and toll-free number applicable in each location. **Arrangement:** Classified by product or service. **Pages** (approx.): 225. **Frequency:** Quarterly. **Advertising accepted.** Circulation 18,000. **Price:** $8.00 per copy; $25.00 per year.

★4898★
TRAVELABILITY: A GUIDE FOR PHYSICALLY DISABLED TRAVELERS IN THE UNITED STATES
Macmillan, Inc.
866 Third Avenue
New York, NY 10022
Covers: About 2,000 travel agencies, airports, cruise lines, hotels and motels, train stations, bus stations, car rental companies and other travel-related organizations and firms offering information, assistance, and barrier-free facilities or equipment for the handicapped traveler in the United States, Mexico, and the Caribbean. Accessibility guides to cities are also listed. **Entries include:** Organization name, address, services. **Arrangement:** By mode of transportation; organizations devoted specifically to handicapped travel are listed geographically in an appendix. **Indexes:** General. **Pages** (approx.): 300. **Frequency:** Not established; first edition December 1978. **Editor:** Lois Reamy. **Price:** $9.95, plus $1.50 shipping.

★4899★
TRAVELERS' DIRECTORY
Tom Linn
6224 Baynton Street
Philadelphia, PA 19144
Covers: About 800 persons willing to provide short-term hospitality for travelers in return for the same; worldwide. **Entries include:** Name of host, address, age, phone, kind of hospitality available, occupation and interests, brief personal background. **Arrangement:** Geographical. **Pages** (approx.): 125. **Frequency:** Annual, with quarterly updates. **Editor:** Tom Linn. **Price:** $12.00, including updates; available only to persons listed. **Other information:** Not to be confused with "Hospitality Guide of North America," a similar publication published in Bethesda, MD (see separate listing).

★4900★
TRAVELER'S DIRECTORY OF FAST-FOOD RESTAURANTS—
    EASTERN EDITION
Pilot Books
347 Fifth Avenue   Phone: (212) 685-0736
New York, NY 10016
Covers: Over 3,800 locations of fast-food restaurants (including
McDonald's, A & W, Red Lobster Inn, etc.) in Connecticut, Delaware,
District of Columbia, Maryland, Massachusetts, New Hampshire, New
Jersey, New York, Pennsylvania, Rhode Island, and Vermont. **Entries
include:** Restaurant name, address. **Arrangement:** Geographical.
Pages (approx.): 75. **Frequency:** First edition 1979. **Editors:**
Kathleen M. Gruber. **Price:** $3.50, plus 75¢ shipping.

★4901★
TRIP LOG QUICK REFERENCE FREIGHTER GUIDE
Air & Marine Travel Service
501 Madison Avenue   Phone: (212) 371-1300
New York, NY 10022
Covers: Selected passenger freighters booked by the publisher
scheduled to depart from United States ports during the coming
(winter or summer) cruise season. **Entries include:** Cruise name,
destination, departure dates, length of cruise, expected stops, cost,
age limits, etc. **Pages** (approx.): 5. **Frequency:** Semiannual. **Price:**
$2.00 per issue. **Other information:** Variant title, "Freighter Cruise
Quick Reference Guide."

Tri-State Trader Antique Shop Guide *See* **Antique Shop Guide**

★4902★
TUCKER AUTOMOBILE CLUB OF AMERICA—ROSTER OF
    MEMBERS
Tucker Automobile Club of America
C/o Richard E. Jones
315 Arora Boulevard   Phone: (904) 264-5169
Orange Park, NJ 32073
Number of listings: 100. **Entries include:** Name, address,
membership serial number. **Arrangement:** Numerical. **Pages**
(approx.): 3. **Frequency:** Annual, March. **Editor:** Richard E. Jones,
Secretary. **Price:** Available to members only.

★4903★
UNDERGROUND BUYING GUIDE FOR HAMS, CBERS,
    EXPERIMENTERS, AND COMPUTER HOBBYISTS
PMS/King Publishing Company
12625 Lido Way
Saratoga, CA 95070
Covers: About 600 firms which offer, mostly through mail-order,
parts and equipment useful in amateur radio, personal computing,
citizens band radio, and electronic experimentation. **Entries include:**
Company name, address, phone, description of types of products with
references to specific products and their prices, and whether literature
or catalog is available. **Arrangement:** Alphabetical. **Indexes:** Product.
Pages (approx.): 185. **Frequency:** Not established; first edition
1977. **Editor:** Dennis A. King. **Price:** $5.95.

★4904★
U.S. CANCELLATION CLUB NEWS—DIRECTORY ISSUE
U. S. Cancellation Club
Box 83   Phone: (312) 446-0904
Winnetka, IL 60093
Covers: 450 philatelists collecting postal markings and cancellations.
Entries include: Name and address. **Arrangement:** Alphabetical.
Indexes: Geographical. **Pages** (approx.): 20. **Frequency:** Annual,
November. **Editor:** C. Hall Enger. **Advertising accepted.** Circulation
500. **Price:** $6.00.

★4905★
UNITED STATES 1869 PICTORIAL RESEARCH ASSOCIATES—
    REGISTER
United States 1869 Pictorial Research Associates
9469 Galecrest Drive   Phone: (513) 729-3995
Cincinnati, OH 45231
Publication includes: List of 350 member philatelists interested in
the United States 1869 postage stamp issue and related items such as
essays, proofs, special printings and covers. **Entries include:** Name,
city and state. **Arrangement:** Classified by length of membership.
Frequency: Biennial, June of odd years. **Editor:** Benjamin E. Chapman,
Editor-in-Chief. **Advertising accepted.** Circulation 500. **Price:**
$15.00 (ISSN 0360-6534). **Send orders to:** John A. Ginn, 100 W.
57th St., Apt. 5C, New York, NY 10019. **Other information:**
Principal content of publication is editorial material and research
papers.

★4906★
USA PLANT VISITS
United States Travel Service
Commerce Department
Washington, DC 20230
Covers: About 1,800 United States firms and installations ranging
from nuclear power plants to bottling plants and local fire stations
which offer guided tours through their facilities. Publication prepared
for visitors from abroad, but most of the tours listed would also be
available to residents. **Entries include:** Company or installation name,
address, phone, name of contact, hours, restrictions (group size, age,
etc.), amount of notice required. **Arrangement:** Geographical.
Indexes: Industry. **Pages** (approx.): 150. **Frequency:** Irregular, about
every two years; latest edition spring 1977. **Former title:** Plant Visits
(1977). **Price:** $2.80 (S/N 003-012-00041-7). **Send orders to:**
Government Printing Office, Washington, DC 20402.

Vacation Exchange Club—Directory [Home exchange] *See*
    Exchange Book [Home exchange]

★4907★
VINTAGE AUTO ALMANAC
Hemmings Motor News
Box 256   Phone: (802) 442-3101
Bennington, VT 05201
Covers: About 150 makes of vintage and classic automobiles with
listings on their clubs, specialized parts dealers, services, etc.; also,
list of service shops, parts dealers, etc., which specialize in restoration
and maintenance for vintage cars generally. Includes automobile
museums, salvage yards, and dealers in vintage cars. **Entries include:**
Club listings include name, address; many listings include annotation on
ages and types of cars accepted, club activities, etc., dues, and
phone. Parts and service listings include firm name, address, phone,
and usually a statement by the firm as to products, services, parts,
etc., available. Museum listings include descriptions of displays, hours,
and fees. **Arrangement:** Classified by make, service, etc. **Indexes:**
General. **Pages** (approx.): 300. **Frequency:** Irregular; previous edition
1977; latest edition October 1979. **Price:** $4.95 (ISSN 0363-4639).

★4908★
VINTAGE CORVETTE CLUB OF AMERICA—ROSTER
Vintage Corvette Club of America
C/o Ed Thiebaud
Star Route   Phone: (805) 238-0976
Creston, CA 93432
Covers: 750 members (owners of 1953-55 models) and associate
members (owners of later models). **Entries include:** Name, address,
number of cars owned, with years and serial numbers. **Pages**
(approx.): 45. **Frequency:** Quarterly. **Editor:** Ed Thiebaud, President.

Visitor's Guide to the Historical Museums of Michigan *See*
    Historic Michigan Travel

★4909★
WEEKEND CONNOISSEUR: THE ANTIQUE COLLECTOR'S GUIDE TO THE BEST IN ANTIQUING, DINING, REGIONAL MUSEUMS...
Dolphin Editions
Doubleday & Company, Inc.
245 Park Avenue   Phone: (212) 953-4561
New York, NY 10017
Covers: Antique shops, restaurants, regional museums, and other sites and facilities of interest to antique collectors. **Entries include:** Name of establishment, address, description of goods, services, or points of interest. **Arrangement:** Geographical. **Pages** (approx.): 300. **Frequency:** Published June 1979. **Editor:** Joan Bragin. **Price:** $5.95.

★4910★
WEST VIRGINIA TRAVEL GUIDE FOR THE HANDICAPPED
Structural Barriers Program
West Virginia Rehabilitation Association
1427 Lee Street East
Charleston, WV 25301
Publication includes: Information about recreational facilities (restaurants, parks, etc.) available in West Virginia for the handicapped. **Arrangement:** Geographical. **Pages** (approx.): 45. **Frequency:** Irregular; latest edition 1974; new edition expected spring 1980. **Price:** Free.

★4911★
THE WHEELCHAIR TRAVELER
The Wheelchair Traveler
Ball Hill Road
Milford, NH 03055
Covers: Over 6,000 hotels, motels, restaurants, and sight-seeing attractions judged especially convenient for the use of handicapped travelers. **Entries include:** Facility name, address, phone, specific information such as number of steps or width of door openings, and a key indicating overall usability. Some hotel entries also include information on rates, restaurants, swimming pools, etc. **Arrangement:** Geographical. **Frequency:** Annual, October. **Editor:** Douglass R. Annand (a paraplegic who travels extensively). **Advertising accepted.** Circulation 5,000. **Price:** $7.95, postpaid, payment with order.

★4912★
WHEELCHAIR VACATIONING IN SOUTH DAKOTA
Division of Tourism
State of South Dakota
Joe Foss Building
Pierre, SD 57501
Publication includes: Information about vacation facilities (parks, museums, motels, restaurants, etc.) available in South Dakota for the handicapped. **Arrangement:** Geographical. **Pages** (approx.): 35. **Frequency:** Irregular; latest edition 1979. **Price:** Free.

Wheeling through Boston [Handicapped guide] *See* Access to Boston

★4913★
WHERE TO BUY, BOARD, OR TRAIN A DOG
Gaines Dog Research Center
250 North Street
White Plains, NY 10625
Covers: About 3,500 kennels in the United States which breed, board, or train dogs; breed and obedience clubs are also listed. **Entries include:** Kennel name, address, coding to indicate breeds and services offered. For clubs - Name, name and address of contact. **Arrangement:** Geographical. **Pages** (approx.): 100. **Frequency:** Irregular; latest edition December 1979. **Price:** $1.00. **Send orders to:** Gaines Kennel Directory, Box 1007, Kankakee, IL 60901.

★4914★
WHERE TO STAY USA (FROM 50¢ TO $14 A NIGHT)
Council on International Educational Exchange
205 E. 42nd Street   Phone: (212) 661-1414
New York, NY 10017
Covers: About 1,500 places to stay and eat; also includes help lines, tourist information sources, etc. **Arrangement:** Geographical. **Frequency:** Irregular; latest edition 1978; new edition expected 1981. **Price:** $3.95.

★4915★
WHERE-TO-SELL-IT DIRECTORY
Pilot Books
347 Fifth Avenue   Phone: (212) 685-0736
New York, NY 10016
Covers: Dealers and collectors who will purchase items by mail; primarily antiques and collectibles. **Entries include:** Company, store, or individual's name, address, items desired, purchase procedures. **Arrangement:** By item desired. **Pages** (approx.): 80. **Frequency:** First edition 1979. **Editors:** Margaret A. Boyd and Sue Scott-Martin. **Price:** $3.50, plus 75¢ shipping.

★4916★
WHOLE WORLD HANDBOOK
Council on International Educational Exchange
205 E. 42nd Street   Phone: (212) 661-1414
New York, NY 10017
Covers: Work, travel, and study opportunities abroad, selected and described from the viewpoint of the United States student. **Arrangement:** Geographical. **Pages** (approx.): 300. **Frequency:** Irregular; latest edition 1978; new edition expected 1981. **Editor:** Margaret E. Sherman, Publications Editor. **Price:** $3.95.

★4917★
WHOLE-WORLD WINE CATALOG: THE EASY REFERENCE GUIDE TO THE WORLD OF WINES, WINE LABELS, AND TASTINGS
Penguin Books
625 Madison Avenue   Phone: (212) 755-4330
New York, NY 10022
Covers: Producers of domestic and foreign wines. **Entries include:** Producer, wine classification, grape variety, district, city or village, description of wine, price range symbol, and label photo. **Arrangement:** Geographical. **Pages** (approx.): 225. **Frequency:** Irregular; first edition August 1978; new edition expected February 1980. **Editor:** William I. Kaufman. **Price:** $5.95 (current edition); $4.95 (1980 edition). **Also includes:** Glossary.

★4918★
WHO'S WHO IN INDIAN RELICS
Parks-Thompson Company
1757 W. Adams   Phone: (314) 822-2409
St. Louis, MO 63122
Covers: About 130-140 persons per volume who have outstanding collections of American Indian relics. Volume 4, published 1976, also includes roster of 1,650 collectors with their addresses. **Entries include:** Biography and portrait of collector, description of collection, photographs of selected items. **Pages** (approx.): 400. **Frequency:** Irregular; about every four years; Volume 5 planned for 1981. **Editors:** Cameron W. Parks and Ben W. Thompson. **Price:** Volumes 3 and 4, $20.00 each, plus $1.00 shipping (other volumes out of print).

★4919★
WINE COUNTRY USA/CANADA
Reymont Associates
29 Reymont Avenue   Phone: (914) 967-8185
Rye, NY 10580
Covers: 200 wineries and vineyards in 22 states and several Canadian provinces. **Entries include:** Vineyard name, address, driving directions, phone, visiting days and hours, plus data on tour programs and retail sales. **Arrangement:** Geographical. **Pages** (approx.): 30. **Frequency:** Irregular; latest edition 1977. **Editor:** D. J. Scherer.

Price: $2.00, postpaid, payment with order.

★4920★
WINNEBAGO INTERNATIONAL TRAVELERS DIRECTORY
Visual Adventures, Inc.
Box 100   Phone: (602) 754-3761
Bullhead City, AZ 86430
Covers: About 25,000 owners of Winnebago recreational vehicles.
Entries include: For members - Name, spouse's name, address, unit
number. For clubs - Name, address of contact. Arrangement: Clubs
are geographical; members are alphabetical. Pages (approx.): 190.
Frequency: Annual, April. Editor: Frank J. Berberich, Director of Public
Relations. Price: Available to members only.

★4921★
WIRELESS PIONEER ALMANAC, CALL BOOK/DIRECTORY
Society of Wireless Pioneers
C/o William A. Breniman
Box 530   Phone: (707) 542-0898
Santa Rosa, CA 95402
Covers: 3,600 wireless telegraphers and others interested in the
history and contributions of this form of communication. Entries
include: Name, office address, amateur call (if any) used by member,
beginning date in field. Arrangement: Four sections - Alphabetical,
geographical, numerical by membership serial, amateur call. Pages
(approx.): 140. Frequency: Biennial, even years. Editor: William A.
Breniman. Price: $15.00, plus $1.25 shipping for those in industry;
free to qualifying public institutions. Other information: Beginning
with January 1980 edition, title will be "Wireless Register" and will no
longer include the "Almanac."

Wireless Pioneer Directory & Call Book *See* Wireless Pioneer
   Almanac, Call Book/Directory

Wireless Register *See* Wireless Pioneer Almanac, Call Book/
   directory

★4922★
WORLD ASTROLOGICAL DIRECTORY
Iao Publications
Box 5265
Station A
Toronto, Ontario, Canada M5W 1N5
Covers: Astrologers, teachers, students, organizations, research
groups. publishers of books and periodicals, manufacturers and
suppliers of products and services concerned with astrology. Entries
include: Name, address, phone. Additional data given in paid listings.
Pages (approx.): 120. Frequency: Irregular; latest edition 1977.
Editor: Robin Armstrong. Price: $10.00.

★4923★
WORLD ENCYCLOPEDIA OF COMICS
Chelsea House Publishers
70 W. 40th Street   Phone: (212) 563-3600
New York, NY 10018
Covers: 1,200 comic artists, writers and editors, living and dead,
worldwide; includes directories of comic book publishers and
newspaper syndicates which handle cartoons. Book also includes
material on history, graphic development, aesthetics, etc., of comics,
and several hundred illustrations. Entries include: Biographical entries
include personal information and data on comic books and comic strips
produced; directories include publisher or syndicate names and
addresses. Indexes: Proper name, title, media. Pages (approx.): 900,
in two volumes. Frequency: Published 1976. Editor: Maurice Horn.
Price: $42.50, postpaid, payment with order. Send orders to: R. R.
Bowker Co., Box 1807, Ann Arbor, MI 48106 (313-761-4700).

★4924★
WORLD WINE ALMANAC AND WINE ATLAS
International Wine Society
304 E. 45th Street
New York, NY 10017
Covers: 18,000 shops in Volume 2 of the two-volume set, separately
titled, "Directory of Department Store Wine Shops and Wine Stores."
Entries include: Store name, address, phone. Arrangement:
Geographical. Pages (approx.): 150 (Volume 2). Frequency: Not
established; first edition 1976. Editor: Grace Treber. Price: $30.00.
Other information: Volume 1 is titled "The World Wine Almanac and
Wine Atlas - Complete Wine Buying Guide and Catalogue of Wine
Labels," with comments on some 4,000 wines and photographs of
their labels.

★4925★
WORLD'S FAIR COLLECTOR'S SOCIETY—DIRECTORY
World's Fair Collector's Society
148 Poplar Street   Phone: (516) 741-4884
Garden City, NY 11530
Covers: 300 collectors of memorabilia of world's fairs. Entries
include: Name, address, membership number, collecting specialties.
Arrangement: Alphabetical. Pages (approx.): 16. Frequency:
Biennial, fall of even years. Editor: Michael R. Pender. Advertising
accepted. Circulation 300. Price: Available to members only.

★4926★
WORLDWIDE TAPETALK DIRECTORY OF TAPE STATIONS
Worldwide Tapetalk
35 The Gardens
West Harrow, Middlesex, England HA1 4HE
Covers: About 500-800 tape recorder owners (cassette and reel- to-
reel) interested in exchange of verbal communication, music, radio
dubbings, etc. Entries include: Name, personal data; tape recorder
equipment used; contact location preference; hobbies, sports, and
other interests. Arrangement: Geographical. Frequency: January,
May, September. Editor: Charles L. Towers. Price: Available to
members only.

★4927★
WORLDWIDE TEMPORARY HOMES EXCHANGES AND RENTALS
Inquiline, Inc.
35 Adams Street   Phone: (914) 241-0102
Bedford Hills, NY 10507
Covers: About 600 homes per year of executive and professional
owners which are offered for exchange or rental, worldwide. Entries
include: Location, description of home and personal information about
listed subscriber, mailing address. Arrangement: Geographical. Pages
(approx.): 40. Frequency: Annual, November. Editor: Benjamin T.
Kernan. Price: $30.00. Other information: Included in subscription
is "Europe Rental Program," listing rental properties available through
Inquiline.

★4928★
WYOMING ACCOMMODATIONS
Wyoming Travel Commission
Frank Norris, Jr. Travel Center
Cheyenne, WY 82002   Phone: (307) 777-7777
Covers: About 325 private campgrounds, state parks, and national
parks and national forests with camping facilities; about 550 hotels
and motels; and about 125 dude ranches and resorts. Entries include:
Facility name, address, location, number of rooms or camping sites,
season, fees and rates, attractions and facilities available.
Arrangement: By type of facility, then geographical. Pages (approx.):
25. Frequency: Biennial, odd years. Former title: "Wyoming
Campgrounds and Facilities;" "Hotels and Motels in Wyoming;" and
"Dude Ranches in Wyoming" combined into one publication. Price:
Free.

Wyoming Campgrounds and Facilities *See* Wyoming
  Accommodations

★4929★
YOUR KEY TO NEW BRITAIN [Connecticut]
New Britain Chamber of Commerce
127 Main Street   Phone: (203) 229-1665
New Britain, CT
Publication includes: Information about building features (ramps,
wide doors, etc.) which help make New Britain's major stores, public
buildings, museums, theaters, etc., accessible to handicapped
persons, and warnings about architectural barriers which might present
difficulties. **Arrangement:** Classified by type of establishment or
institution. **Frequency:** Irregular; latest edition November 1977.
Price: Free. **Other information:** Compiled by Junior League of New
Britain.

15

Sports and

Outdoor Recreation

★4930★
ACCESS NATIONAL PARKS—A GUIDE FOR HANDICAPPED VISITORS
National Park Service
Interior Department   Phone: (202) 343-7394
Washington, DC 20240
Covers: About 300 national parks, monuments, historic sites, seashore parks, recreation areas, living history areas, and living farms. **Entries include:** Name, address, phone, description, and summary of facilities and obstacles at each site, services, programs. **Arrangement:** Geographical. **Indexes:** Alphabetical by site name. **Pages** (approx.): 200. **Frequency:** Irregular; previous edition 1971; latest edition March 1978. **Editor:** A. N. Wilson. **Former title:** National Park Guide for the Handicapped (1978). **Price:** $3.50 (S/N 024-005-00691-5). **Send orders to:** Access, Consumer Information Center, Pueblo, CO 81009.

★4931★
ADVENTURE TRAVEL
Adventure Guides, Inc.
36 E. 57th Street   Phone: (212) 355-6334
New York, NY 10022
Covers: 1,000 outfitters and services for booking excursions on foot, by horse, on wheels, by boat, on water or snow, or in the air; one chapter on trips for teenagers; covers North America. **Entries include:** Company name, address, types of excursions (backpacking, mountaineering, pack trips, river running, etc.), areas and itineraries, costs, etc. **Pages** (approx.): 240. **Frequency:** Biennial, February of even years. **Author:** Pat Dickerman. **Former title:** Adventure Travel U.S.A. (1976); Adventure Travel in North America (1980). **Price:** $5.95 (current edition); $7.95 (1980 edition); plus $1.00 shipping.

Adventure Travel in North America *See* Adventure Travel

Adventure Travel U.S.A. *See* Adventure Travel

★4932★
AMATEUR ATHLETIC UNION OF THE UNITED STATES— DIRECTORY
Amateur Athletic Union of the United States
3400 W. 86th Street   Phone: (317) 297-2900
Indianapolis, IN 46107
Covers: Officers, staff, committee chairpersons, international and regional representatives, governing and voting bodies, administrators, and officials. **Entries include:** Name, affiliation, address. **Arrangement:** Classified by organization or body. **Indexes:** Personal name. **Pages** (approx.): 130. **Frequency:** Annual, January. **Price:** $4.00 (current and 1980 editions).

American Academy of Podiatric Sports Medicine—Roster *See* Jogger—Listing of Exercise-Oriented Podiatrists Issue

★4933★
AMERICAN ASSOCIATION OF OWNERS AND BREEDERS OF PERUVIAN PASO HORSES—LIST OF OWNERS AND BREEDERS
American Association of Owners and Breeders of Peruvian Paso
    Horses
Box 2035   Phone: (415) 531-5082
California City, CA 93505
Covers: About 215 members in the United States, Canada, Europe, and Central America. **Entries include:** Name, address, phone; some listings include ranch name. **Arrangement:** Geographical. **Pages** (approx.): 20. **Frequency:** Annual, spring. **Price:** Free. **Also includes:** Calendar of association- approved horse shows with dates, show name, location, and name of judge.

★4934★
AMERICAN CONNEMARA PONY SOCIETY—DIRECTORY OF BREEDERS
American Connemara Pony Society
HoshieKon Farm
R. D. 1   Phone: (203) 491-3521
Goshen, CT 06756
Entries include: Farm name, address, facilities for boarding and foaling, availability of ponies for sale, visiting arrangements, stallions standing at public stud, and scope of operation. **Arrangement:** Geographical. **Pages** (approx.): 50. **Frequency:** Irregular; previous edition 1977; latest edition 1979. **Editor:** Mrs. John E. O'Brien, Secretary, A. C. P. S. **Price:** $1.00.

★4935★
AMERICAN HORSE SHOWS ASSOCIATION RULE BOOK
American Horse Shows Association
598 Madison Avenue   Phone: (212) 759-3070
New York, NY 10022
Publication includes: List of about 1,200 horse shows held throughout the year in the United States and Canada. **Entries include:** Name and address of sponsoring organization, location of show (city and state), details of interest to prospective exhibitors. **Frequency:** Annual, late March; updated in special column in "Horse Show Magazine," monthly. **Price:** Included in membership fee, $25.00 per year.

★4936★
AMERICAN HUNTER—HUNTER'S DIRECTORY ISSUE
National Rifle Association
1600 Rhode Island Avenue, N. W.
Washington, DC 20036
Covers: State agencies providing information on hunting and fishing, guides and outfitters, and photographic guides. **Entries include:** For each state or province - Name of agency, address; seasons; regulations; permit costs. For guides and outfitters - Name, address. **Frequency:** Annual, August. **Price:** $2.50.

★4937★
AMERICAN SUNBATHING ASSOCIATION NUDIST PARK GUIDE
American Sunbathing Association
810 N. Mills Avenue   Phone: (305) 896-8141
Orlando, FL 32803
Covers: Nudist clubs in the United States and Canada. **Entries include:** For clubs affiliated with the association, entries show club name, camp name, address, and description of accomodations and facilities; for non-affiliated clubs, entries show name and address. **Arrangement:** Affiliated clubs are listed in five regional groups; non-affiliated clubs are listed along with affiliated clubs alphabetically by club name, and geographically. **Pages** (approx.): 140. **Frequency:** Irregular; latest edition 1978; new edition expected 1981. **Editor:** Roland R. Senecal. **Advertising accepted.** Circulation 10,000. **Former title:** Bare With Us Nudist Park Guide. **Price:** $4.95. **Also includes:** Information on how to join a club and answers to common questions.

★4938★
ARMWRESTLING
Marc Sheldon Publishing
777 Loren Street   Phone: (213) 969-1868
Azusa, CA 91702
Publication includes: List of associations concerned with armwrestling and names of promoters of armwrestling competitions. **Entries include:** Name, address, information on activities. **Frequency:** Published 1977. **Author:** Ernie Jeffrey. **Price:** $8.95.

★4939★
ASSOCIATION FOR EXPERIENTIAL EDUCATION—MEMBERSHIP DIRECTORY
Association for Experiential Education
Box 4625   Phone: (303) 837-8633
Denver, CO 80204
Covers: About 800 member institutions and individuals concerned with the use of experiences as learning tools; emphasis is on outdoor experiences. **Entries include:** Name, address. **Arrangement:** Alphabetical. **Pages** (approx.): 20. **Frequency:** Annual, spring. **Price:** Available to members only.

★4940★
ASSOCIATION FOR INTERCOLLEGIATE ATHLETICS FOR WOMEN—DIRECTORY
Association for Intercollegiate Athletics for Women
1201 16th Street, N. W.   Phone: (202) 833-5485
Washington, DC 20036
Covers: Athletic programs for women at two- and four-year collegiate institutions which are members; includes information on scholarships available to female athletes. **Entries include:** Institution listings include name, address, names of representatives to AIAW, phone. Program/financial aid listings show which of 25 sports are included in intercollegiate programs, and for which ones scholarship aid is available. **Arrangement:** Institution list is alphabetical; program/aid list is alphabetical by sport and state. **Frequency:** Annual, spring. **Price:** $6.00.

★4941★
ASSOCIATION OF INDEPENDENT CAMPS—BUYERS GUIDE AND CAMP DIRECTORY
Association of Independent Camps
55 W. 42nd Street   Phone: (212) 736-6595
New York, NY 10036
Covers: About 80 manufacturers and suppliers of services to private camps; listings for about 630 private camps located in the eastern United States form the major part of the directory; camps not belonging to the association are included. **Entries include:** For suppliers - Company name, address, phone, products or services. For camps - Name of camp, location, sex of campers, and name, address, and phone of director. **Arrangement:** Buyer's guide classified by product or service; camp directory alphabetical by camp name. **Pages** (approx.): 135. **Frequency:** Annual. **Advertising accepted.** **Price:** $5.00, plus 54¢ shipping (current edition); $5.40 (1980 edition).

Association of Private Camps—Buyer's Guide and Camp Directory *See* Association of Independent Camps—Buyers Guide and Camp Directory

Backpacking & Outdoor Guide *See* Rand McNally Backpacking & Outdoor Guide

★4942★
BACKPACKING AND OUTDOOR GUIDE
Rand McNally & Company
Box 7600   Phone: (312) 267-6868
Chicago, IL 60680
Publication includes: List of locations in United States where one can practice camping, hiking, rock-hounding, orienteering, wilderness survival, boating, and other outdoor activities. **Entries include:** Name of site, description of terrain or special features, suggested outdoor activities, map. **Arrangement:** By geographic region, then by state. **Pages** (approx.): 190. **Frequency:** Irregular; latest edition 1977; new edition expected February 1980. **Author:** Richard Dunlop. **Former title:** Outdoor Recreation Guide (1974). **Price:** $5.95 (current edition); $6.95 (1980 edition).

Backpacking, Hiking, & Mountaineering Clubs of USA *See* Hiking/Mountaineering Clubs of North America

★4943★
BALLOON FEDERATION OF AMERICA—PILOT MEMBERSHIP ROSTER
Balloon Federation of America
Box 346
Indianola, IA 50125
Covers: About 1,500 balloon pilots in the United States and in foreign countries; balloon manufacturers and repair companies are also listed. **Entries include:** For members - Name, address, type of license held. For companies - Name, address, contact; some listings include type of ownership, phone. **Arrangement:** Geographical (within above categories). **Pages** (approx.): 25. **Frequency:** Annual, April. **Editor:** Laurie Jones, Membership Chairman. **Price:** $1.00. **Send orders to:** Balloon Federation of America, National Aeronautic Association, 821 15th street, N. W., Suite 430, Washington, DC 20005.

★4944★
BALLOONING: A PICTORIAL GUIDE AND WORLD DIRECTORY
Thrasher Balloons
Box 1111   Phone: (305) 247-8412
Homestead, FL 33030
Covers: Over 500 licensed hot air and gas balloonists and a dozen balloon manufacturers, worldwide. **Entries include:** For balloonists - name, address. For manufacturers - Name, address, phone, photo of one of manufacturer's balloons. **Arrangement:** Balloonists are geographical, manufacturers are alphabetical. **Pages** (approx.): 160. **Frequency:** Irregular; first edition 1978; new edition expected 1980. **Author:** W. E. Thrasher. **Price:** $15.00, plus 66¢ postage (current and 1980 editions); individuals please send payment with order. **Other**

information: A 33 1/3 rpm phonograph record of network interview with author is included; book contains numerous illustrations and explanatory text.

★4945★
BALLOONING SERVICES DIRECTORY
Balloon Federation of America
Box 346
Indianola, IA 50125
Covers: Federal Aviation Administration flight examiners, safety counselors, repair stations, balloon manufacturers, balloon schools, and balloon clubs in the United States. **Entries include:** For flight examiners and safety counselors - Name, address, phone, FAA number. For repair stations - Station name, address, phone, brands repaired, type of repairs done. For manufacturers - Name of company, address, phone. For balloon schools - Name of school, address, phone, school director. **Arrangement:** Classified by service. **Pages (approx.):** 20. **Frequency:** Annual, April. **Editor:** Ruth Salzberg, Public Relations. **Price:** $1.00. **Send orders to:** Balloon Federation of America, National Aeronautic Association, 821 15th Street, N. W., Suite 430, Washington, DC 20005.

★4946★
BANTAM GREAT OUTDOOR GUIDE TO THE UNITED STATES AND CANADA: THE COMPLETE TRAVEL ENCYCLOPEDIA AND WILDERNESS GUIDE
Bantam Books, Inc.
666 Fifth Avenue   Phone: (212) 765-6500
New York, NY 10019
Covers: Outfitters, guides, lodges, camps, schools, and other groups and facilities serving major recreational areas in the United States and Canada; publishers of regional guidebooks and maps are also listed. **Arrangement:** Geographical. **Pages (approx.):** 860. **Frequency:** Published 1979. **Editor:** Val Landi. **Price:** $12.95.

Bare with Us Nudist Park Guide *See* American Sunbathing Association Nudist Park Guide

Bicycle Bibliography: Professional Supplement *See* Bicycle Resource Guide

★4947★
BICYCLE DEALER SHOWCASE—BUYER'S GUIDE ISSUE
William/Lawrence Corporation
1700 E. Dyer Road, Suite 250   Phone: (714) 540-1933
Santa Ana, CA 92705
Covers: About 2,000 manufacturers, wholesalers, and distributors of bicycles and mopeds. **Entries include:** Name of company, address, phone, sales contact. **Arrangement:** Alphabetical and geographical. **Indexes:** Brand and trade name, product. **Pages (approx.):** 90. **Frequency:** Annual, December. **Editor:** Steve Ready. **Advertising accepted.** Circulation 15,000. **Price:** $5.00. **Send orders to:** Norrma Samuels, Box 19531, Irvine, CA 91711.

★4948★
BICYCLE RESOURCE GUIDE
David J. Luebbers
78 S. Jackson
Denver, CO 80209
Covers: English and foreign language publishers and organizations related to bicycles and bicycling. Over 1,000 entries, including tour guides, repair manuals, bike histories, magazines, 175 government and local documents pertaining to bicycle transportation planning and over 100 mail order catalogs. **Entries include:** Publication name, publisher, address, description, and price. **Indexes:** Author, subject, geographic. **Pages (approx.):** 160. **Frequency:** Annual, February. **Editor:** David J. Luebbers. **Former title:** Bicycle Bibliography: Professional Supplement. **Price:** $5.00 (ISSN 0098-1230).

★4949★
BICYCLING THE MIDWEST
Contemporary Books
180 N. Michigan Avenue
Chicago, IL 60601
Covers: Bicycle routes, tours, and paths in Illinois, Indiana, Iowa, Michigan, Minnesota, and Wisconsin. **Entries include:** Route description, directions, name and address for further information. **Arrangement:** Geographical. **Pages (approx.):** 250. **Frequency:** Not established; first edition summer 1979. **Editor:** Diana Milesko-Pytel. **Price:** $6.95.

★4950★
BOAT & MOTOR DEALER—MARKET MANUAL & BUYERS GUIDE ISSUE
Dietmeier-Van Zevern Publishing Company
340 Linden Avenue   Phone: (312) 251-8301
Wilmette, IL 60091
Covers: Manufacturers, wholesalers, and sales representatives handling pleasure boats and marine products. **Entries include:** Company name, address, phone, name of principal executive. Sales representative listings also include territory covered, market. **Arrangement:** By line of business. **Indexes:** Product. **Pages (approx.):** 120. **Frequency:** Annual, December. **Editor:** George Van Zevern. **Advertising accepted.** Circulation 26,500. **Price:** $5.00.

★4951★
BOAT OWNERS BUYERS GUIDE
Ziff-Davis Publishing Company, Inc.
One Park Avenue   Phone: (212) 725-3500
New York, NY 10016
Covers: Over 8,000 manufacturers in the pleasure boating field; includes lists of naval architects and charter firms. **Arrangement:** Classified by categories of marine products and services. **Pages (approx.):** 320. **Frequency:** Annual, October. **Editor:** Martha Lostrom. **Advertising accepted.** Circulation 100,000. **Price:** $3.00, postpaid, payment with order.

★4952★
BOATING INDUSTRY—MARINE BUYERS' GUIDE
Whitney Communications Corporation
850 Third Avenue
New York, NY 10022
Covers: 3,600 manufacturers of pleasure boats and marine products and suppliers of related services. Also includes trade name directory. Not limited to advertisers. **Entries include:** Company name, address, phone, name of contact, and description of general product or service category. **Arrangement:** Alphabetical. **Indexes:** Product (not including boats), stock boats, services. **Frequency:** Annual, December. **Editor:** Charles Jones. **Advertising accepted.** Circulation 26,000. **Price:** $10.00; controlled circulation.

★4953★
BOMBARDIER'S SNOWMOBILE VACATION GUIDE
Bombardier Corporation
Box 6106
Duluth, MN 55806
Covers: Over 35 winter recreation areas that have snowmobile trails or allow snowmobiling; area hotels, motels, restaurants, entertainment facilities, and other sporting facilities are included. **Entries include:** For hotels, etc. - Name, address, brief description. **Arrangement:** Geographical. **Frequency:** Not established; first edition 1979. **Price:** $2.95.

★4954★
BOWLING AND BILLIARD BUYERS GUIDE
National Bowlers Journal, Inc.
875 N. Michigan Avenue, Suite 3734   Phone: (312) 266-7171
Chicago, IL 60611
Covers: About 500 manufacturers and suppliers of bowling equipment and their distributors; also includes chain bowling alleys. **Indexes:**

Product. **Pages** (approx.): 75. **Frequency:** Annual, January. **Editor:** Jim Dressel. **Price:** $8.00 (1980 edition). **Other information:** Published with, but separate from, "National Bowlers Journal and Billiard Review."

★4955★

BUC BOOK—THE STATISTICALLY AUTHENTICATED USED BOAT PRICE GUIDE

BUC International Corporation
1881 N. E. 26th Street, Suite 95   Phone: (305) 565-6715
Ft. Lauderdale, FL 33305

Covers: 1,200 present and former manufacturers of motorboats, sailboats, powerboats, houseboats, custom boats, and outdrives plus 21 manufacturers of outboard motors and a boat trailer section. **Entries include:** Listings for manufacturers still in business include company name, address, and Coast Guard identification code; defunct manufacturer listings show city in which last operated. All listings show model number and name, length, other data, and estimated used retail values. **Arrangement:** Alphabetical by manufacturer name. **Indexes:** Company, trade name. **Pages** (approx.): 800. **Frequency:** Semiannual, April and October. **Editor:** Walter J. Sullivan III, President. **Price:** $44.00 per copy.

★4956★

BUC'S NEW BOAT DIRECTORY

BUC International Corporation
1881 N. E. 26th Street, Suite 95   Phone: (305) 565-6715
Ft. Lauderdale, FL 33305

Covers: About 500 manufacturers of new boats of all types ranging from canoes and kayaks to motor yachts, and about 40 engine manufacturers. **Entries include:** Company name, address, Coast Guard identification code, boat model number and name, length, other data, and list price. **Arrangement:** Alphabetical. **Indexes:** Company, trade name. **Pages** (approx.): 230. **Frequency:** Annual, spring. **Editor:** Walter J. Sullivan III, President. **Former title:** BUC Boat Buyer's Annual. **Price:** $10.00.

★4957★

CAMP DIRECTORS PURCHASING GUIDE

Klevens Publications, Inc.
7600 Avenue V   Phone: (805) 944-4111
Littlerock, CA 93543

Covers: Suppliers of products and services used in the operation of children's summer camps. **Entries include:** Company name, address, name of principal executive. **Arrangement:** Product. **Pages** (approx.): 160. **Frequency:** Annual, March. **Editor:** Herbert Schwartz. **Advertising accepted.** Circulation 14,700. **Price:** $3.00.

★4958★

CAMP GUIDE [Catholic orientation]

Catholic News Publishing Company
80 W. Broad Street   Phone: (914) 664-8100
Mt. Vernon, NY 10552

Covers: 120 boarding camps for boys and girls in the East and day camps in the New York City area. **Entries include:** Camp name; address; rates; name, address, and phone number of director. **Arrangement:** Alphabetical. **Pages** (approx.): 20. **Frequency:** Annual. **Editor:** Victor L. Ridder. **Advertising accepted.** Circulation 20,000. **Former title:** Catholic Camp Guide. **Price:** 25¢ (current and 1980 editions).

★4959★

CAMPER'S PARK GUIDE

EPM Publications
Box 490
McLean, VA 22101

Covers: Nearly 1,000 recreation areas with camping facilities located in the Atlantic states and Tennessee, Kentucky, and West Virginia. **Entries include:** Park name, address, phone, directions, description of facilities, activities possible, handicapped facilities available. Each state section includes map. **Arrangement:** Geographical. **Indexes:** Activity or interest. **Pages** (approx.): 710. **Frequency:** Latest edition 1978. **Author:** Robert Shosteck. **Price:** $9.95, plus $1.25 shipping.

Campground & Trailer Park Guide *See* Rand McNally Campground & Trailer Park Guide

★4961★

CAMPGROUND MERCHANDISING MAGAZINE—BUYER'S GUIDE ISSUE

Kane Communications, Inc.
401 N. Broad Street, Suite 904   Phone: (215) 925-9744
Philadelphia, PA 19108

Publication includes: Firms supplying merchandise for resale to campers or equipment of use to campground owners. **Entries include:** Company name, address, phone, and products or services. **Arrangement:** Alphabetical. **Frequency:** Annual, March. **Editor:** Deborah Roth. **Advertising accepted.** Circulation 11,500. **Price:** $5.00 (current and 1980 editions).

★4962★

CAMPING AND BACKPACKING: A GUIDE TO INFORMATION SOURCES

Gale Research Company
Book Tower   Phone: (313) 961-2242
Detroit, MI 48226

Publication includes: Lists of about 400 manufacturers, governmental agencies, and private organizations providing information or products related to camping and backpacking. **Entries include:** Name, address; many listings include short annotation. **Arrangement:** Classified. **Frequency:** Published 1979. **Editors:** Cecil and Mary Clotfelder. **Price:** $24.00.

★4963★

CAMPING IN THE NATIONAL PARK SYSTEM

National Park Service
Interior Department
Washington, DC 20242

Covers: About 100 National Park Service camping areas. **Entries include:** Park/campground name, location, mailing address, dates open, type of area, fee, limit of stay, sanitary facilities, recreation, etc. Each entry is keyed to a map showing the area's location. **Arrangement:** Alphabetical. **Pages** (approx.): 30. **Frequency:** Latest edition 1979; new edition expected March 1980. **Price:** 85¢ (S/N 024-005-00753-9). **Send orders to:** Government Printing Office, Washington, DC 20402.

★4964★

CAMPING MAGAZINE—BUYER'S GUIDE ISSUE

American Camping Association
Bradford Woods   Phone: (317) 342-8456
Martinsville, IN 46151

Covers: 150 firms providing sporting equipment, food, infirmary supplies, etc., to children's and other organized camps. **Entries include:** Company name, address, list of products or services. **Arrangement:** Alphabetical. **Indexes:** Product. **Pages** (approx.): 5. **Frequency:** Annual, March. **Editor:** Glenn Job. **Advertising accepted.** Circulation 9,000. **Price:** $1.25 (current and 1980 editions).

★4965★

CANOE—CANOE, KAYAK & CAMPING ACCESSORIES GUIDE ISSUE

Voyager Publications, Inc.
131 E. Murray Street   Phone: (219) 456-3420
Fort Wayne, IN 46803
Entries include: Manufacturer name, address, products. **Frequency:** Annual, February. **Editor:** John Viehman. **Advertising accepted.** Circulation 80,000. **Price:** $7.50 per year.

★4966★

CANOE—CANOE/KAYAK EXPEDITIONS AND BUYER'S GUIDE DIRECTORY

Voyager Publications, Inc.
131 E. Murray Street   Phone: (219) 456-3420
Fort Wayne, IN 46803
Publication includes: Lists of all known canoe, kayak, and river raft manufacturers in the United States and Canada, with addresses and vessel specifications, and list of canoe expeditions. **Frequency:** Annual, October. **Editor:** John Viehman. **Advertising accepted.** Circulation 80,000. **Price:** $7.50 per year.

★4967★

CANOEING AND RAFTING: THE COMPLETE WHERE-TO-GO GUIDE FOR AMERICA'S BEST TAME AND WILD WATERS

William Morrow & Company, Inc.
105 Madison Avenue   Phone: (212) 889-3050
New York, NY 10016
Covers: Lakes, streams, and rivers which are navigable by canoe; canoe rental liveries and outfitters, other sources of information. **Entries include:** For each river, lake, etc. - Name, description of flow, hazards; camping sites available; level of difficulty; season; fishing, including level of chemical contamination; route; name and address for further information. For liveries - Name, address, phone, services, river supplied. **Arrangement:** Geographical; rivers are then alphabetical, suppliers are by city. **Indexes:** River name. **Pages** (approx.): 365. **Frequency:** Not established; first edition February 1979. **Editor:** Sara Pyle. **Price:** $5.95. **Send orders to:** William Morrow & Co., 6 Henderson Drive, West Caldwell, NJ 07006 (201-575-8383).

★4968★

CANOES AND KAYAKS: A COMPLETE BUYER'S GUIDE

Contemporary Books, Inc.
180 N. Michigan Avenue   Phone: (312) 782-9181
Chicago, IL 60601
Covers: Manufacturers of canoes and kayaks in the United States and Canada. **Entries include:** Company name, brand name of product, address, construction specifications, method, prices. **Arrangement:** Alphabetical. **Pages** (approx.): 125. **Frequency:** Published 1979. **Editors:** Jack Brosius and Dave LeRoy. **Price:** $9.95, cloth; $5.95, paper.

Catholic Camp Guide *See* Camp Guide [Catholic orientation]

★4969★

CHRISTIAN LIFE MAGAZINE—DIRECTORY OF CHRISTIAN COLLEGES WITH INTERCOLLEGIATE SPORTS PROGRAMS ISSUE

Christian Life Publications
396 E. St. Charles Road   Phone: (312) 653-4200
Wheaton, IL 60187
Frequency: Annual, September. **Editor:** Robert Walker. **Advertising accepted.** Circulation 87,500. **Price:** $1.00.

Colorado Campground Directory & Road Map *See* Colorado Maps, Camping & Fun Things to Do Directory

★4970★

COLORADO MAPS, CAMPING & FUN THINGS TO DO DIRECTORY

HCP Associates
5101 Pennsylvania Avenue
Boulder, CO 80303
Covers: About 125 private campgrounds which are members of the Colorado Campground Association, and Colorado tourist attractions. **Entries include:** For campgrounds - Campground name, address, phone; number of on-site trailers or tents for rent; number of cabins for rent; downhill ski areas and location; other sports facilities and activities; guide and outfitter services nearby; CB channel monitored (if any); and foreign languages spoken (if any). **Arrangement:** Geographical. **Pages** (approx.): 35. **Frequency:** Annual, January. **Editor:** Hilton C. Fitt-Peaster. **Advertising accepted.** Circulation 250,000. **Former title:** Colorado Campground Directory & Road Map. **Price:** $1.00, postpaid, payment with order.

★4971★

COMPLETE GUIDE TO SKIING IN THE MIDWEST

Contemporary Books, Inc.
180 N. Michigan Avenue   Phone: (312) 782-9181
Chicago, IL 60601
Covers: About 175 ski slopes in Indiana, Iowa, Michigan, Missouri, Illinois, Minnesota, and Wisconsin. Ski organizations for the handicapped are also listed. **Entries include:** Ski area name, location, phone; season, ski equipment availability, lodging and food facilities, special packages or services, transportatiion, local events and points of interest. For organizations - Name, address. **Arrangement:** Geographical. **Indexes:** Ski area by distance from major city. **Pages** (approx.): 290. **Frequency:** Published 1978. **Editor:** Patricia Skalka. **Price:** $9.95, cloth; $6.95, paper. **Also includes:** Phone numbers for weather reports in four states.

★4972★

COMPLETE OUTFITTING & SOURCE BOOK FOR BIRD WATCHING

Holt, Rinehart & Winston
383 Madison Avenue   Phone: (212) 688-9100
New York, NY 10017
Covers: Manufacturers and suppliers of binoculars, cameras, portable tape recorders, and other bird watching equipment; bird watching clubs; publications concerned with bird watching; birding sites; and bird watching tours in the United States and abroad. **Pages** (approx.): 200. **Frequency:** First edition 1978. **Editor:** Michael Scofield. **Price:** $12.95, cloth ; $6.95, paper. **Other information:** Compiled by the Great Outdoors Trading Company.

★4973★

CONNEMARA STUD BOOK

American Connemara Pony Society
HosheiKon Farm
R. D. 1   Phone: (203) 491-3521
Goshen, CT 06756
Covers: Connemara ponies registered or transferred to new owners during the previous year (about 300 entries). **Entries include:** Pony's name, age, height, color, markings, names of its sire and dam, and names and addresses of its owner and breeder. **Indexes:** Personal name. **Pages** (approx.): 90. **Frequency:** Annual, winter. **Editor:** Mrs. John E. O'Brien, Secretary. **Price:** $7.50.

★4974★

CROSS-COUNTRY SKI TRAILS IN THE ROCKIES

Contemporary Books
180 N. Michigan Avenue
Chicago, IL 60601
Covers: Camping facilities and resorts for cross-country skiing in the Rocky Mountains. **Entries include:** Name, address, facilities. **Frequency:** Published October 1978. **Price:** $11.95, cloth; $5.95, paper. **Also includes:** Information on equipment, techniques, and safety and survival when cross-country skiing.

★4975★

CURTIS CASEWIT'S GUIDE TO SKI AREAS AND RESORTS
Pilot Books
347 Fifth Avenue   Phone: (212) 685-0736
New York, NY 10016
Covers: 115 ski areas and resorts in over 30 states. **Entries include:** Area or resort name, location, address, phone, rates, description of runs, number of lifts, lodging availability, comments. **Arrangement:** Geographical. **Pages** (approx.): 30. **Frequency:** Not established; first edition fall 1978. **Editor:** Curtis Casewit. **Price:** $2.50.

★4976★

CURTIS CASEWIT'S GUIDE TO TENNIS RESORTS
Pilot Books
347 Fifth Avenue   Phone: (212) 685-0736
New York, NY 10016
Covers: 250 tennis resorts located in over 35 of the United States, in Puerto Rico, and in Canada; costs range from $35.00 to $50.00 and up daily per person, with meals, for a three-day stay. **Entries include:** Resort name, address, phone, rates, number of courts, comments. **Arrangement:** Geographical. **Pages** (approx.): 30. **Frequency:** Irregular; first edition 1978. **Editor:** Curtis Casewit. **Price:** $2.50.

★4977★

DIRECTORY OF ARCHITECTS AND ENGINEERS [Boating facilities]
Outboard Boating Club of America
401 N. Michigan Avenue
Chicago, IL 60611
Covers: 150 offices of architects and engineers in the fields of design, planning, supervision, and construction of recreational boating facilities. **Entries include:** Name, address, phone, and work experience. **Arrangement:** Geographical. **Pages** (approx.): 50. **Frequency:** Irregular; latest edition March 1977; new edition expected early 1980. **Price:** Free.

Directory of Dressage Instructors *See* **USDF Dressage Directory**

★4978★

DIRECTORY OF GOLF COURSE ARCHITECTS
National Golf Foundation
200 Castlewood Drive   Phone: (305) 844-2500
North Palm Beach, FL 33408
Covers: 75 golf course and clubhouse architects. **Entries include:** Company name, address, and principal executive. **Arrangement:** Alphabetical. **Frequency:** Annual, or more frequently. **Price:** 25¢.

★4979★

DIRECTORY OF GRADUATE PHYSICAL EDUCATION PROGRAMS
National Association for Sport and Physical Education
American Alliance for Health, Physical Education and Recreation
1201 16th Street, N. W.   Phone: (202) 833-5536
Washington, DC 20036
Covers: About 65 universities which offer graduate degree programs in physical education. **Entries include:** School name, department chairman or contact, address; description of school, including administrative organization, university history, enrollment, tuition fees, admission requirements; description of program, including degrees offered, areas of study, research facilities, faculty, and financial aid available. **Arrangement:** Alphabetical. **Pages** (approx.): 80. **Frequency:** Not established; first edition 1979; new edition expected 1982. **Price:** $6.75, postpaid, payment with order. **Send orders to:** AAHPERD Publications, Box 704, Waldorf, MD 20601.

★4980★

DIRECTORY OF INFORMATION RESOURCES IN HEALTH, PHYSICAL EDUCATION, AND RECREATION
ERIC Clearinghouse on Teacher Education
One Dupont Circle, Suite 616
Washington, DC 20036
Covers: Information centers in the United States and Canada concerned with health, physical education, and recreation, and the International Association for Sport Information. **Entries include:** Organization name, address, phone, name of contact; description of organization and information facilities; services and costs. **Arrangement:** Geographical. **Pages** (approx.): 30. **Frequency:** Irregular; latest edition February 1977. **Editor:** Gordon D. Jeppson. **Price:** $3.32, plus $1.14 shipping. **Send orders to:** ERIC Document Reproduction Service, Box 190, Arlington, VA 22210.

★4981★

DIRECTORY OF JEWISH RESIDENT SUMMER CAMPS
National Jewish Welfare Board
15 E. 26th Street   Phone: (212) 532-4949
New York, NY 10010
Covers: 270 camps operated under the auspices of Jewish communal organizations. **Entries include:** Name, location, program, ages served, rates, and registration requirements, dietary practice. **Arrangement:** Geographical. **Indexes:** Alphabetical. **Pages** (approx.): 100. **Frequency:** Biennial, spring of odd years. **Editor:** Sherwood Epstein. **Price:** $5.00, payment with order.

★4982★

DIRECTORY OF OUTDOOR EDUCATION DEGREE PROGRAMS IN HIGHER EDUCATION
National Educational Laboratory Publishers, Inc.
813 Airport Boulevard   Phone: (512) 385-7084
Austin, TX 78702
Covers: About 60 colleges and universities in the United States with degree programs or majors in outdoor education, environmental education, conservation education, or environmental interpretation. **Entries include:** Institution name; name, address, and phone of contact person; degree programs offered; number and qualifications of faculty; founding date of department and degree program; description of program including course titles, descriptions, credit hour requirements; number of students enrolled in or graduated from program; description of field campus or center used by institution. **Arrangement:** Alphabetical. **Indexes:** Geographical. **Pages** (approx.): 340. **Frequency:** Published June 1977. **Editor:** Russel E. Bachert, Jr. **Price:** $12.00.

★4983★

DIRECTORY OF PROFESSIONAL PREPARATION PROGRAMS IN RECREATION, PARKS, AND RELATED AREAS
American Alliance for Health, Physical Education, and Recreation
1201 16th Street, N. W.   Phone: (202) 833-4395
Washington, DC 20036
Covers: 350 colleges offering programs in recreation, parks, and related areas. **Entries include:** Name of school, brief description of program, degrees offered, enrollment, specialty areas, and other options. **Arrangement:** Geographical. **Indexes:** Degrees offered, subject. **Pages** (approx.): 110. **Frequency:** Irregular; latest edition 1973; new edition planned. **Price:** $2.75.

★4984★

DIRECTORY OF THE UNITED STATES SKI ASSOCIATION
United States Ski Association
1726 Champa Street, Suite 300   Phone: (303) 825-9183
Denver, CO 80202
Covers: About 1,500 persons, companies, organizations, etc., active in national and international sanctioned skiing activities; also includes principal ski associations and list of sanctioned events and competitions. **Entries include:** In general list - Personal, company, or organization name, affiliation (if any), address, phone. For associations - Organization name, address, phone, names of officers and staff; similar information for major committees. For events - Event name, date, location, USSA division, events. **Arrangement:** Main list and associations are alphabetical; events are geographical. **Frequency:** Annual, August. **Editor:** Evelyn Masbruch, Executive Manager. **Advertising accepted. Price:** $6.00.

★4985★

DIRECTORY OF UNDERGRADUATE PHYSICAL EDUCATION PROGRAMS

National Association for Sport and Physical Education
American Alliance for Health, Physical Education and Recreation
1201 16th Street, N. W.   Phone: (202) 833-5536
Washington, DC 20036
Covers: About 85 colleges and universities which offer undergraduate degree programs in physical education. **Entries include:** School name, department chairman or contact, address; description of school, including administrative organization, school history, enrollment, tuition fees, admission requirements, and student housing; description of program, including title, degrees offered, faculty, areas of study, curriculum requirements, program options, degree requirements, financial aid available, and accreditation. **Arrangement:** Alphabetical. **Pages** (approx.): 110. **Frequency:** Not established; first edition 1979; new edition expected 1982. **Price:** $7.75, postpaid, payment with order. **Send orders to:** AAHPERD Publications, Box 704, Waldorf, MD 20601.

★4986★

EASTER SEAL DIRECTORY OF RESIDENT CAMPS FOR PERSONS WITH SPECIAL HEALTH NEEDS

National Easter Seal Society for Crippled Children and Adults
2023 W. Ogden Avenue   Phone: (312) 243-8400
Chicago, IL 60612
Covers: Over 225 camps; camps affiliated with the National Easter Seal Society or accredited by the American Camping Association are so identified. **Arrangement:** Geographical. **Indexes:** Alphabetical; type of disability. **Pages** (approx.): 70. **Frequency:** Biennial, fall of odd years. **Price:** $2.00, payment with order.

★4987★

EASTERN COLLEGE ATHLETIC CONFERENCE—DIRECTORY AND RECORD BOOK

Eastern College Athletic Conference
Box 3   Phone: (617) 771-5060
Centerville, MA 02632
Covers: 215 athletic administrators for institutions in the Middle Atlantic and New England states. **Entries include:** Name, address, and office phone. **Arrangement:** Alphabetical by institution. **Pages** (approx.): 50. **Frequency:** Annual, September. **Editor:** Richard J. Hussey, Assistant to the Commissioner. **Price:** $2.50.

★4988★

EASTERN RUGBY UNION CLUB DIRECTORY

Eastern Rugby Union
Massachusetts Institute of Technology,
     Room 54-720
Cambridge, MA 02139
Covers: About 1,000 clubs and officers in the Eastern Rugby Union, with subsidiary information. **Entries include:** Club name, names and addresses of officers; union name, and names and addresses of officers. **Arrangement:** Geographical. **Indexes:** Club name. **Pages** (approx.): 45. **Frequency:** Annual, spring. **Editor:** J. B. Walsh, Honorary Secretary. **Advertising accepted.** Circulation 2,000. **Price:** $2.00. **Send orders to:** Matt Godek, Box 565, Merrifield, VA 22116.

★4989★

EDUCATORS GUIDE TO FREE HEALTH, PHYSICAL EDUCATION AND RECREATION MATERIALS

Educators Progress Service, Inc.
214 Center Street   Phone: (414) 326-3126
Randolph, WI 53956
Covers: Sources for about 2,400 films, filmstrips/audiotapes, videotapes, scripts, phonograph records, and printed materials useful in study of health, physical education, and recreation. Materials are provided by industrial, governmental, and other sponsors for free use by teachers and other educators. **Entries include:** Title, brief description, date produced, length or running time, whether sound or silent tapes and films, whether color or black and white, source. **Arrangement:** By type of medium, then by subject.

Indexes: Source, title, subject, items cleared for television. **Pages** (approx.): 500. **Frequency:** Annual, fall. **Price:** $15.00, plus $1.35 shipping.

★4990★

EXPLORERS LTD. SOURCE BOOK

Explorers Ltd.
2107 Grant Avenue   Phone: (302) 792-1778
Wilmington, DE 19809
Covers: Equipment, supply, and information sources for all types of wilderness recreation and exploration. **Entries include:** In each subsection (on river touring, falconry, caving, etc.) - Essay on subject, plus sources of information (associations, state and federal government departments, etc.); sources of books and periodicals and references to specific titles; sources and descriptions of typical equipment; schools or other sources of formal instruction; all with names and addresses. **Arrangement:** Seven major sections (wilderness - land, sea, air, etc.), with about 30 subsections. **Indexes:** General. **Pages** (approx.): 400. **Frequency:** Irregular; previous edition 1974; latest edition 1977. **Editor:** Alwyn T. Perrin. **Price:** $12.95, cloth; $7.95, paper.

Family River Rafting Guide *See* **River Rafting Guide**

Football Writers Association of America—Telephone Directory
     See **Telephone Service Directory [Football writers]**

★4991★

FREE BEACHES [Nude bathing]

Free Beaches
Box 132
Oshkosh, WI 54901
Covers: Several hundred beaches, lakes, and hot springs throughout the world, including many in the United States, which allow nude bathing. **Arrangement:** Geographical. **Frequency:** Annual. **Price:** $3.50, postpaid, payment with order. **Other information:** Publisher is a national organization promoting the clothes-optional beach movement and National Nude Beach Day to "Uphold the Right to Bare Arms."

★4992★

FRISBEE PLAYERS' HANDBOOK

Parachuting Publications
Box 4232   Phone: (805) 968-7277
Santa Barbara, CA 93103
Publication includes: About 250 Frisbee game clubs, competitions, and other organizations concerned with Frisbee throwing, worldwide. **Entries include:** Organization name, address, contact. **Arrangement:** By Zip code. **Frequency:** Irregular; about every one to two years. **Editor:** Dan Poynter. **Price:** $6.95, postpaid.

★4993★

GO BOATING—BLUE PAGES ISSUE [Miami]

Graphic Publications, Inc.
261 S. W. Sixth Street, Suite 200   Phone: (305) 856-3517
Miami, FL 33130
Covers: Boat leasing and rental firms, marine sales and service firms, pumping stations, boat launch ramps, and other marine-related firms and services in the Miami, Florida area. **Arrangement:** By line of business. **Frequency:** Annual. **Advertising accepted.** Circulation 55,000. **Price:** $2.00.

Golf & Country Club Guest Policy Directory *See* **Private Country Club Guest Policy Directory [Golfing and tennis]**

★4994★
GOLF BUSINESS—BUYERS GUIDE ISSUE
Harvest Publishing Company, Subsidiary
Harcourt Brace Jovanovich, Inc.
9800 Detroit Avenue   Phone: (216) 651-5500
Cleveland, OH 44102
Covers: Manufacturers and suppliers of golf course maintenance products; equipment for players; and foodstuffs, liquor, etc., needed for clubhouse operation. **Entries include:** Company name, address, and sales contact. **Arrangement:** Alphabetical. **Indexes:** Maintenance, pro shop, and clubhouse product indexes. **Frequency:** Annual, September. **Advertising accepted. Price:** $1.50.

★4995★
GOLF COLLECTORS' SOCIETY—MEMBERSHIP DIRECTORY
Golf Collectors' Society
235 E. Helena Street   Phone: (513) 224-0358
Dayton, OH 45404
Covers: About 700 golf enthusiasts who collect the artifacts of the game. **Entries include:** Name, address, phone, spouse's name, particular collecting interest. **Arrangement:** Alphabetical. **Indexes:** Geographical. **Pages** (approx.): 85. **Frequency:** Annual, March. **Editor:** Joseph S. F. Murdoch. **Price:** $10.00; available to members only.

★4996★
GOLF COURSE SUPERINTENDENTS ASSOCIATION OF AMERICA—
      MEMBERSHIP DIRECTORY
Golf Course Superintendents Association of America
1617 St. Andrews Drive   Phone: (913) 841-2240
Lawrence, KS 66044
Number of listings: 4,400. Includes separate list of member companies. **Arrangement:** Members listed alphabetically and geographically. **Pages** (approx.): 80. **Frequency:** Annual, December. **Editor:** John M. Schilling, Director of Communications. **Price:** $25.00.

★4997★
GOLF DIGEST—PLACES TO MEET GUIDE ISSUE
Golf Digest, Inc.
495 Westport Avenue   Phone: (203) 847-5811
Norwalk, CT 06856
Publication includes: Over 200 resorts and hotels that coordinate golfing facilities with accommodations for sales meetings and conventions. **Entries include:** Resort name, number of meeting and guest rooms, capacity of largest meeting room, length of golf courses. **Arrangement:** Geographical. **Pages** (approx.): 30. **Frequency:** Annual, October. **Editor:** Nick Seitz. **Advertising accepted.** Circulation 860,000. **Price:** $1.25.

★4998★
GOLF DIGEST—PLACES TO PLAY ISSUE
Golf Digest, Inc.
495 Westport Avenue   Phone: (203) 847-5811
Norwalk, CT 06856
Covers: About 1,000 golf clubs and courses in the United States. **Entries include:** Club or course name, city, par, yardage, brief description of course, whether open to the public. **Arrangement:** Geographical. **Frequency:** Annual, February. **Editor:** Rich Seitz. **Advertising accepted. Price:** Reprint of club section, 50¢, payment with order.

★4999★
GOLF INDUSTRY—DIRECTORY OF GOLF SALES
      REPRESENTATIVES ISSUE
Industry Publishers, Inc.
915 N. E. 125th Street, Suite 2C   Phone: (305) 893-8771
North Miami, FL 33161
Number of listings: 1,500. **Entries include:** Representative or company name, address, phone, states in territory, manufacturers represented and, for companies, names of personnel. **Arrangement:** Alphabetical. **Indexes:** Product (with product codes, representative or

company name, and states traveled), geographical (states traveled with representative name or company name and manufacturer represented). **Frequency:** Annual, October/November. **Editor:** Joan Whaley. **Advertising accepted.** Circulation 17,000. **Price:** $2.00.

★5000★
GOOD SAMPARK DIRECTORY/RV HOST
Trailer Life Publishing Company, Inc.
29901 Agoura Road   Phone: (213) 991-4980
Agoura, CA 91301
Covers: About 275 recreational vehicle parks and campgrounds associated with Good Sampark Association. **Entries include:** Park name, address, location, directions, local map, phone, facilities, recreation, nearby attractions. **Arrangement:** Geographical. **Pages** (approx.): 100. **Frequency:** Annual, fall. **Editor:** Alice Robison. **Advertising accepted.** Circulation 400,000. **Price:** $1.00.

★5001★
GUIDE TO BACKPACKING IN THE UNITED STATES
Macmillan, Inc.
866 Third Avenue   Phone: (212) 935-2000
New York, NY 10022
Publication includes: Names and addresses of state tourist offices, principal stations in national parks and forests, and suppliers of backpacking equipment. **Pages** (approx.): 290. **Frequency:** Latest edition 1979. **Editor:** Eric Meves. **Price:** $5.95. **Other information:** Principal content is description of backpacking areas.

★5002★
GUIDE TO CROSS COUNTRY SKIING
Times Mirror Magazines, Inc.
380 Madison Avenue   Phone: (212) 687-3000
New York, NY 10017
Publication includes: 450 cross-country ski areas in the United States and Canada, including both commercial ski centers and parks. **Arrangement:** Geographical. **Frequency:** Annual, fall. **Editors:** Michael Brady and Bob Woodward. **Advertising accepted.** Circulation 235,000. **Price:** $2.50. **Other information:** Cover title, "Ski Magazine's Guide to Cross Country Skiing."

Guide to Fish & Wildlife Management Areas *See* Guide to Wildlife
      Management Areas [New Jersey]

★5003★
GUIDE TO NORTH AMERICAN BIRD CLUBS
Avian Publications, Inc.
Box 310   Phone: (502) 769-1377
Elizabethtown, KY 42701
Covers: Many hundreds of bird clubs in the United States, Mexico, Central America, Puerto Rico, Virgin Islands, West Indies, and Bermuda; there is an extensive section of nearly 100 pages on Canada. **Entries include:** Club name; name, phone, and address of an officer or contact; phone number for recorded information, if offered; information on meeting schedules, publications, major field trips, etc. **Arrangement:** Geographical. **Pages** (approx.): 575. **Frequency:** Not established; first edition September 1978. **Editor:** Jon E. Rickert, Sr. **Price:** $15.00, postpaid, payment must accompany order.

★5004★
GUIDE TO SUMMER CAMPS AND SUMMER SCHOOLS
Porter Sargent Publishers, Inc.
11 Beacon Street   Phone: (617) 523-1670
Boston, MA 02108
Covers: Over 1,100 summer camping, recreational, pioneering, and academic programs in the U. S. and Canada, as well as travel programs in the U. S., Canada, Mexico, and abroad. Includes special programs for the handicapped, maladjusted, and those with learning disabilities. **Entries include:** Name, address, enrollment, director's winter address, fees, length of camping period, type of housing, whether camp has counselor-in-training program. **Arrangement:** Geographical. **Pages** (approx.): 450. **Frequency:** Biennial, August of odd years. **Editor:** Ann

A. Himebaugh. **Advertising accepted.** Circulation 4,000. **Price:** $12.00, cloth; $9.00, paper; plus $1.50 shipping, payment with order.

★5005★
GUIDE TO WILDLIFE MANAGEMENT AREAS [New Jersey]
Division of Fish, Game, and Shellfisheries
New Jersey Department of Environmental Protection
363 Pennington Avenue   Phone: (609) 292-9450
Trenton, NJ 08625
Covers: About 60 wildlife management areas in New Jersey open for fishing, hunting, and/or recreation sports. **Entries include:** Name of area, number of acres, location, description of type of land (marsh, etc.); game and wildlife stocked or available, suggested recreational activities; map. **Arrangement:** Alphabetical. **Pages** (approx.): 120. **Frequency:** Irregular; previous edition 1978; latest edition September 1979. **Editor:** Steve Perrone. **Former title:** Guide to Fish & Wildlife Management Areas (1978). **Price:** $3.00.

★5006★
HANG GLIDER DIRECTORY
Hang Glider Newsweekly Magazine
1554 Fifth Street   Phone: (213) 396-4241
Santa Monica, CA 90406
Covers: 30 manufacturers, 150 dealers, 30 schools, 25 clubs, 10 sites, 100 instructors, and 20 publications relating to the sport of hang gliding, the flying of pilot-carriable soaring sailplanes or powered hang gliders (so called because pilot usually hangs beneath the wing). **Entries include:** Name, address, phone, trade name, and pictorial or descriptive information. Entry format is an advertisement of uniform size. **Arrangement:** Geographical. **Pages** (approx.): 25. **Frequency:** Formerly, annual, January; 1979 edition delayed indefinitely; updated information in Hang Glider Newsweekly Magazine. **Editor:** Joseph Faust. **Advertising accepted.** Circulation 3,000. **Price:** Latest edition out of print; new edition date not determined.

★5007★
HANG GLIDING, THE BASIC HANDBOOK OF SKYSURFING
Parachuting Publications
Box 4232   Phone: (805) 968-7277
Santa Barbara, CA 93103
Covers: About 150 manufacturers and distributors of hang gliders and kites. Also includes films, periodicals, and books. **Entries include:** Manufacturer name, address, contact name, model of glider, performance specifications, product features, product photograph. **Arrangement:** By Zip code. **Pages** (approx.): 180. **Frequency:** Irregular; latest edition June 1979. **Editor:** Dan Poynter. **Price:** $11.95, cloth; $6.95, paper; postpaid.

Hardy Plant Finder *See* **House Plant Finder**

★5008★
HERE COMES THE SUN: DIRECTORY OF SUMMER PROGRAMS FOR HANDICAPPING CONDITIONS
Information Center for Handicapped Individuals
1413 K Street, N. W., Suite 1200   Phone: (202) 347-4986
Washington, DC 20005
Covers: Facilities serving the Washington, D. C., metropolitan area. **Entries include:** Facility name, address, phone, name of chief executive, financial data, and type of programs offered. **Pages** (approx.): 45. **Frequency:** Annual, summer. **Editor:** Mrs. Yetta W. Galiber, Executive Director. **Price:** Free to agencies serving the handicapped.

★5009★
HIKING/MOUNTAINEERING CLUBS OF NORTH AMERICA
Frank Ashley
Box 291   Phone: (213) 633-7821
Culver City, CA
Pages (approx.): 10. **Frequency:** Annual, April. **Editor:** Frank Ashley. **Former title:** Backpacking, Hiking & Mountaineering Clubs of USA.

Price: $3.00, payment with order (current and 1980 editions).

★5010★
HOCKEY & ARENA BIZ—BUYERS GUIDE ISSUE
Community Performance Publications, Inc.
2038 Pennsylvania Avenue, Suite 12   Phone: (608) 249-0186
Madison, WI 53704
Covers: Manufacturers of hockey and ice skating equipment, and refrigeration systems and other products and services used in construction and operation of arenas and ice rinks. **Entries include:** Company name, address. **Arrangement:** Alphabetical. **Indexes:** Product. **Frequency:** Annual, March. **Editor:** Fenton Kelsey, Jr., Publisher & Editor. **Advertising accepted.** Circulation 24,000. **Price:** $1.00.

★5011★
HORSE INDUSTRY DIRECTORY
American Horse Council
1700 K Street, N. W.   Phone: (202) 296-4031
Washington, DC 20006
Covers: 70 horse breed registries, 150 horse industry organizations, 30 state horse councils, 220 horse periodicals, 50 state extension specialists. **Entries include:** Name, address, phone. Periodical listings also show editor, closing dates for ads, circulation. **Arrangement:** Alphabetical. **Pages** (approx.): 40. **Frequency:** Annual, May. **Editor:** George Winslett. **Price:** $4.00.

★5012★
HORSEMAN'S CATALOG
McGraw-Hill, Inc.
1221 Avenue of the Americas   Phone: (212) 997-1221
New York, NY 10020
Publication includes: Lists of equine veterinarians, veterinary colleges, racetracks, museums, riding schools, breed associations, publishers, and other service firms, manufacturers, and organizations which have information and assistance for horse owners, breeders, and ranches. **Entries include:** Usually, name and address; some listings may include additional details. **Arrangement:** By subject. **Pages** (approx.): 520. **Frequency:** Not established; first edition 1979. **Editors:** Craig Norback and Peter Norback. **Price:** $24.95.

★5013★
HOST STABLE DIRECTORY
United States Dressage Federation
1212 O Street   Phone: (402) 477-1251
Lincoln, NE 68501
Covers: Stables willing to board horses on a short-term basis and/or to have horse fanciers as visitors. **Arrangement:** Geographical. **Price:** $2.50, postpaid, payment with order.

★5014★
HOUSE PLANT FINDER
HHH Horticultural
68 Brooktree Road   Phone: (609) 448-9345
Hightstown, NJ 08520
Covers: Nurseries, plant societies, gardeners, and other sources for plants not commonly available nationally; separate booklets for tender and hardy plants. **Entries include:** Source name, address, phone, species grown. **Arrangement:** Classified by plant genus. **Pages** (approx.): 15. **Frequency:** Annual. **Editor:** Carol J. McNamara. **Former title:** Tender Plant Finder. **Price:** $1.00 per set.

★5015★
ICE SKATING INSTITUTE OF AMERICA—BUILDERS AND SUPPLIERS DIRECTORY
Ice Skating Institute of America
1000 Skokie Boulevard   Phone: (312) 256-5060
Wilmette, IL 60091
Covers: Over 50 builders and suppliers to the ice rink construction and operation industry (including ice skating equipment). **Entries include:** Company name, address, phone, people to contact, description of

products and services. **Arrangement:** Classified by product or service. **Indexes:** Alphabetical, product. **Pages** (approx.): 20. **Frequency:** Annual, May. **Editor:** Thomas E. Hall, Executive Director. **Price:** Free.

★5016★
INDEX OF THE NATIONAL PARK SYSTEM AND RELATED AREAS
National Park Service
Interior Department
18th and C Streets, N. W.   Phone: (301) 343-7394
Washington, DC 20240
Covers: About 320 areas administered by the National Park Service, including parks, wild and scenic rivers, and trails, and about 20 affiliated areas. **Entries include:** Name, location, address, acreage (federal, non-federal, and gross), and outstanding characteristics. **Arrangement:** Geographical. **Indexes:** Alphabetical by area name. **Pages** (approx.): 80. **Frequency:** Irregular; latest edition September 1979. **Former title:** Index of the National Park System and Affiliated Areas (1979). **Price:** $3.25 (S/N 024-005-00763- 6). **Send orders to:** Government Printing Office, Washington, DC 20402.

★5017★
INTERNATIONAL ADVENTURE TRAVELGUIDE
American Adventurers Association
444 Ravenna Boulevard, Suite 301
Seattle, WA 98115
Covers: 2,000 outdoor adventure trips and the related outfitters, sponsors, guides, etc. **Arrangement:** Classified into land, sea, air, and underwater trips. **Indexes:** Geographical, type (backpacking, rafting, etc.). **Pages** (approx.): 500. **Frequency:** Not established; first edition late 1977. **Price:** $9.95. **Send orders to:** Random House, Inc., 201 E. 50th St., New York, NY 10022.

★5018★
INTERNATIONAL BOAT SHOWS CALENDAR
Marex
666 Third Avenue   Phone: (212) 697-1100
New York, NY 10017
Covers: About 130 boat shows held in the United States and abroad. **Entries include:** Show name and location, dates, name of sponsoring organization and address, phone (for United States shows only), name of contact. **Arrangement:** Geographical. **Pages** (approx.): 15. **Frequency:** Annual. **Price:** $2.00.

★5019★
INTERNATIONAL DIVERS GUIDE
Underwater Society of America
732 50th Street   Phone: (305) 844-1124
West Palm Beach, FL 33407
Covers: About 1,800 diving equipment shops and diving locations; worldwide coverage. **Entries include:** For shops - Name, address. For diving spots - Location, depth, visibility, level of experience suggested, description of features. **Arrangement:** Geographical. **Pages** (approx.): 300. **Frequency:** Irregular; latest edition about 1976. **Editor:** Charles Slade. **Former title:** Underwater Society International Divers Guide. **Price:** $3.98.

★5020★
INTERNATIONAL GOLF GUIDE
Pagurian Press Limited
335 Bay Street, Suite 1106
Toronto M5H 2R3, Ontario, Canada
Covers: Golf courses worldwide. **Entries include:** Course name, address, par, yardage, fees, playing season; some listings include hotels near course. **Arrangement:** Geographical. **Pages** (approx.): 190. **Frequency:** First edition 1976. **Editor:** Nicholas Van Daalen. **Price:** $4.95. **Send orders to:** Macmillan Publishing Company, 70 Bond Street, Toronto, M5B 1X3, Canada.

★5021★
INTERNATIONAL MOTORCYCLE/MOPED/BICYCLE TRADE DIRECTORY
Freed-Crown Publishing Corporation
6931 Van Nuys Boulevard   Phone: (213) 873-1320
Van Nuys, CA 91405
Covers: Firms, worldwide, which manufacture or provide products and services related to the two-wheel vehicle industry, and associations, publications, and other aspects of the industry. Headings, introductions, etc., in English, French, German, and Italian. **Indexes:** Product, trade and brand name. **Frequency:** Annual; first edition June 1979; new edition expected October 1980. **Advertising accepted.** **Price:** $50.00, postpaid.

★5022★
IOWA QUARTER HORSE NEWS—DIRECTORY ISSUE
Iowa Quarter Horse Association
Route 2, Box 5
Humboldt, IA 50548
Publication includes: Members, winners of association-sponsored events, and recipients of awards. **Entries include:** Name of members, address. **Arrangement:** Alphabetical. **Frequency:** Annual, February. **Advertising accepted.** Circulation 68,000. **Price:** Free.

★5023★
JOGGER—LISTING OF EXERCISE-ORIENTED PODIATRISTS ISSUE
National Jogging Association
919 18th Street, N. W., Suite 830   Phone: (202) 785-8050
Washington, DC 20006
Covers: About 630 podiatrists, primarily members of the American Academy of Podiatric Sports Medicine. **Entries include:** Name, location of practice, membership status in the academy. **Arrangement:** Geographical. **Frequency:** Annual, April. **Editor:** Liz Elliott, Editor-in-Chief. **Advertising accepted.** Circulation 35,000. **Price:** $1.00 (ISSN 0164-694X).

★5024★
JOGGER—SURVEY OF TREADMILLS ISSUE
National Jogging Association
919 18th Street, N. W., Suite 830   Phone: (202) 785-8050
Washington, DC 20006
Covers: About 200 facilities offering stress testing or exercise electrocardiograms to determine cardiovascular fitness. Includes clinics, health institutes and centers, universities and medical schools, private practice doctors, and YMCA facilities. **Entries include:** Name or title of facility, name of director or physician, address, phone. 1980 edition will include services offered and cost range. **Arrangement:** Geographical. **Frequency:** Annual, February. **Editor:** Liz Elliott, Editor-in-Chief. **Advertising accepted.** Circulation 35,000. **Price:** $1.00 (ISSN 0164-694X).

★5025★
KOA HANDBOOK AND DIRECTORY FOR CAMPERS
Webb Company
1999 Shepard Road   Phone: (612) 647-7403
St. Paul, MN 55116
Covers: 900 Kampgrounds of America facilities. **Entries include:** Camp name, address, phone, rates, facilities, services, and local sights. **Arrangement:** Geographical. **Pages** (approx.): 130. **Frequency:** Annual, February. **Editor:** Don Picard. **Advertising accepted.** Circulation 1,700,000. **Price:** $1.00. **Send orders to:** KOA Handbook, Box 30558, Billings, MT 59114.

★5026★
LAKESIDE RECREATION AREAS
Stackpole Books
Cameron and Kelker Streets   Phone: (717) 234-5091
Harrisburg, PA 17105
Covers: About 200 waterfront areas built by the U.S. Army Corps of Engineers in 40 states (not including sites in Michigan, Maine, New York, Florida, and six others); maps included. **Entries include:** Site

name, address, directions to site, accommodations in area, activities, and additional sites of interest in area. **Arrangement:** Geographical. **Pages** (approx.): 175. **Frequency:** First edition 1977. **Editors:** Bill Thomas, Phyllis Thomas. **Price:** $6.95.

★5027★
LAND MANAGER DIRECTORY
Signpost
16812 36th Avenue West   Phone: (206) 743-3947
Lynnwood, WA 98036
Covers: About 150 offices responsible for management of state and federal lands in Oregon and Washington, and other sources of information for trail travelers. **Entries include:** Office and agency name, address, phone; most listings include office hours. **Frequency:** Annual, spring. **Price:** 50¢, plus addressed, stamped envelope.

★5028★
LEAGUE OF AMERICAN WHEELMEN—MEMBERSHIP DIRECTORY
   [Bicycling]
League of American Wheelmen
Box 988   Phone: (301) 727-2022
Baltimore, MD 21203
Covers: Over 400 cycling clubs; includes list of bicycle shops. **Entries include:** For clubs - Club name, address, name of information director and/or legislative representative. For shops - Name and address. **Arrangement:** Geographical. **Pages** (approx.): 100. **Frequency:** Annual, spring. **Editor:** Walter K. Ezell. **Advertising accepted.** Circulation 17,000. **Price:** Available to members only.

Lloyd's Register of American Yachts *See* North American Yacht Register

MAC Book *See* Marina Architects, Consultants, Designers, & Engineers

★5029★
MANNED KITING—THE BASIC HANDBOOK OF TOW LAUNCHED
   HANG GLIDING
Parachuting Publications
Box 4232   Phone: (805) 968-7277
Santa Barbara, CA 93103
Covers: About 150 manufacturers of tow launched kites and hang gliders. Also includes periodicals, publications, clubs, and schools. **Entries include:** Company name, address, contact name, model, performance specifications, product features, product photograph. **Arrangement:** By Zip code. **Pages** (approx.): 100. **Frequency:** Latest edition 1975; new edition expected 1981. **Editor:** Dan Poynter. **Price:** $3.95, postpaid.

Mariah Magazine—Wilderness Sports and Expeditions Column *See* Outside Magazine—Wilderness Sports and Expeditions Column

★5030★
MARINA ARCHITECTS, CONSULTANTS, DESIGNERS, & ENGINEERS
National Association of Engine and Boat Manufacturers
Box 5555
Grand Central Station
New York, NY 10017   Phone: (212) 697-1100
Covers: 200 firms specializing in marina design and construction, worldwide. **Entries include:** Company name, address, phone, areas of specialization, typical projects, branch offices, code to indicate whether architect, consultant, contractor, designer, engineer, planner, or surveyor. **Arrangement:** Alphabetical. **Indexes:** Geographical. **Pages** (approx.): 25. **Frequency:** Irregular; latest edition February 1978. **Price:** $5.00. **Other information:** Also known as, ''The MAC Book.''

★5031★
MARINE RESOURCE DIRECTORY/STATE OF NEW HAMPSHIRE
Marine Advisory Program
University of New Hampshire   Phone: (603) 862-1889
Durham, NH 03824
Covers: Businesses, organizations, and individuals in New Hampshire who are involved with the ocean, such as harbormasters and marine contractors, marinas and public landings, and boat dealers and fishing equipment dealers (but also including aquarium suppliers, campgrounds, seafood restaurants, etc.). **Entries include:** Name, address, phone. **Arrangement:** Classified by business or service and alphabetical. **Pages** (approx.): 120. **Frequency:** Irregular; latest edition July 1979. **Editor:** Debby S. Truitt. **Price:** $1.50.

★5032★
MEDIA GUIDE [To professional soccer teams]
North American Soccer League
1133 Avenue of the Americas, Suite 3500   Phone: (212) 575-0066
New York, NY 10036
Number of listings: About 10. **Arrangement:** Alphabetical by team name. **Frequency:** Annual, spring. **Advertising accepted.** **Price:** $5.75.

Membership Directory for Christian Camping International, U.S.A. Division *See* Who's Who in Christian Camping

★5033★
MICHIGAN CHARTER BOAT & INLAND GUIDES DIRECTORY
Travel Bureau
Michigan Department of Commerce
Box 30226   Phone: (517) 373-1195
Lansing, MI 48909
Covers: About 230 fishing boat charter firms on the Great Lakes (except Ontario) and inland guide services in Michigan. **Entries include:** For charter boats - Lake served (and specific area if appropriate); name of port and season; name of captain; boat name, length, and passenger capacity; contact name, address, land phone, marine phone, and harbor phone; and rates. For inland guides - Name, address, phone; services; river, lake, or area covered; counties covered; availability; maximum in party; equipment furnished; and airports. **Arrangement:** Boats are by Great Lake, inland services are alphabetical by name of guide. **Pages** (approx.): 55. **Frequency:** Annual, June. **Editor:** Stanley Lievenses, Manager, Marketing & Promotion. **Former title:** Michigan Charter Boat Directory. **Price:** Free.

Midwest Auto Racing Guide *See* National Speedway Directory

★5034★
MOTORBOAT & EQUIPMENT DIRECTORY
United Marine Publishing
38 Commercial Wharf   Phone: (617) 227-0888
Boston, MA 02110
Publication includes: Over 1,000 manufacturers of motorboats and motorboat equipment. **Entries include:** Company name, address, and phone; many entries have description or photo. **Arrangement:** Manufacturers are by product and by length of boat. **Indexes:** Manufacturer, product. **Pages** (approx.): 300. **Frequency:** Annual, winter. **Editors:** Marty Luray and Eliza Harrison. **Advertising accepted. Price:** $2.95, plus 55¢ shipping (ISSN 0148-8740). **Send orders to:** ''Motorboat & Equipment Directory,'' 126 Blaine Avenue, Marion, OH 43302.

★5035★
MOTORCYCLE DEALER NEWS—BUYERS GUIDE ISSUE
Hester Communications, Inc.
1700 E. Dyer Road, Suite 250   Phone: (714) 549-4834
Santa Ana, CA 92705
Covers: Manufacturers and distributors of motorcycle parts and accessories, motorcycles, mopeds, and shop equipment and supplies; suppliers of services (insurance, financing, publications) are also listed.

Entries include: Company name, address, phone, name of one executive. Vehicle manufacturer listings include additional information. Arrangement: Separate alphabetical lists for manufacturers and distributors, vehicle manufacturers, supplies and services. Indexes: Geographical, trade name, product. Frequency: Annual, November. Editor: Steve Matchett. Advertising accepted. Circulation 7,800. Price: $7.00.

Motorcycle Product News—Suppliers Guide and Mid-Year Directory Update Issue See Motorcycle Product News—Trade Directory Issue

★5036★
MOTORCYCLE PRODUCT NEWS—TRADE DIRECTORY ISSUE
Freed-Crown Publishing Company
6931 Van Nuys Boulevard   Phone: (213) 873-1320
Van Nuys, CA 91405
Covers: About 1,700 manufacturers, distributors, importers, and manufacturers' representatives offering products and services to the motorcycle industry. Entries include: Company name, address, phone, code for line of business; alphabetical listing includes name and title of contact. Arrangement: Alphabetical and geographical; similar information in each section. Indexes: Product, trade name. Pages (approx.): 320. Frequency: Annual, January. Editor: Allen Crown. Advertising accepted. Circulation 18,000. Price: $6.00 (current and 1980 editions). Other information: Mid-year update appears in July issue, $2.50.

★5037★
NATIONAL ASSOCIATION OF CANOE LIVERIES AND OUTFITTERS—OFFICIAL RENTAL DIRECTORY OF ACCREDITED CANOE LIVERIES AND OUTFITTERS
National Association of Canoe Liveries and Outfitters
Box 515   Phone: (616) 796-3907
Big Rapids, MI 49307
Covers: About 300 members. Entries include: Livery name, address, phone, rivers served. Arrangement: Geographical. Pages (approx.): 35. Frequency: Annual, March. Editor: P. Roy Couch, Executive Director. Price: Free.

★5038★
NATIONAL ASSOCIATION OF INTERCOLLEGIATE ATHLETICS—MEMBERSHIP AND DISTRICT DIRECTORY
National Association of Intercollegiate Athletics
1221 Baltimore Street   Phone: (816) 842-5050
Kansas City, MO 64105
Covers: 515 small and middle-sized four-year colleges with developing athletic programs. Entries include: School name, location, athletic director, sports sponsored. Arrangement: Geographical by NAIA district, then by conference. Pages (approx.): 20. Frequency: Annual, December. Editor: Harry Fritz, Executive Director. Price: $2.00. Also includes: For each district a calendar of district championship events with locations.

★5039★
NATIONAL ASSOCIATION OF SPORTING GOODS WHOLESALERS—MEMBERSHIP DIRECTORY
National Association of Sporting Goods Wholesalers
Box 11344   Phone: (312) 565-0233
Chicago, IL 60611
Number of listings: 120; includes manufacturers. Entries include: For wholesalers - Name of firm, address, phone, name of key executive, territory covered, square feet of warehouse, number of retail accounts and salesmen, whether or not a catalog is issued, sales volume, and merchandise inventories. For manufacturers - Name of firm, address, phone, names of key executives, products. Arrangement: Alphabetical. Frequency: Annual, May or June. Editor: Rebecca A. Maddy, Executive Director. Price: $10.00, postpaid.

National Bowlers Journal and Billiard Review—Buyers Guide Issue See Bowling and Billiard Buyers Guide

★5040★
NATIONAL COLLEGIATE ATHLETIC ASSOCIATION—DIRECTORY
National Collegiate Athletic Association
Box 1906   Phone: (913) 384-3220
Shawnee Mission, KS 66222
Covers: About 860 member institutions. Entries include: Name of institution, address, phone, and names of president, faculty representative for athletics, and director of athletics. Arrangement: Geographical. Pages (approx.): 100. Frequency: Annual, October. Editor: Bruce L. Howard, Publications Editor. Price: $4.00.

National Directory of Accredited Camps See Parents' Guide to Accredited Camps

★5041★
NATIONAL DIRECTORY OF COLLEGE ATHLETICS [Men's edition]
Ray Franks Publishing Ranch
Box 7068   Phone: (806) 355-6417
Amarillo, TX 79109
Covers: Men's athletic departments of 2,100 senior and junior colleges in the United States and Canada. Entries include: School name, address, enrollment, colors, team nicknames, stadium and/or gym capacity; names of president, men's athletic director and physical education director and coaches for each sport; athletic department phone number; and association affiliations. Arrangement: Alphabetical. Pages (approx.): 440. Frequency: Annual, August. Editor: Ray Franks. Advertising accepted. Circulation 10,000. Price: $11.00.

★5042★
NATIONAL DIRECTORY OF COLLEGE ATHLETICS [Women's edition]
Ray Franks Publishing Ranch
Box 7068   Phone: (806) 355-6417
Amarillo, TX 79109
Covers: Women's athletic departments at 1,600 senior and junior colleges. Entries include: School name, address; enrollment, colors, stadium and/or gym capacity, team nicknames; names of president, women's athletic director and physical education director, and coaches for each sport; athletic department phone number; and association affiliations. Arrangement: Alphabetical. Pages (approx.): 210. Frequency: Annual, September. Editor: Ray Franks. Advertising accepted. Circulation 6,000. Former title: National Directory of Women's Athletics (1976). Price: $7.00.

★5043★
NATIONAL DIRECTORY OF HIGH SCHOOL COACHES
Athletic Publishing Company
Box 931   Phone: (205) 263-4436
Montgomery, AL 36102
Covers: More than 152,000 high school coaches in about 20,000 high schools. Entries include: School name, address, phone, names of coaches and codes for sports coached. Arrangement: Geographical. Pages (approx.): 520. Frequency: Annual, September. Editor: Juanita McCalman. Advertising accepted. Circulation 10,000. Price: $24.95.

National Directory of Women's Athletics See National Directory of College Athletics [Women's edition]

National Forest Guide See Rand McNally National Forest Guide

★5044★
NATIONAL HORSEMAN—"WHEN THEY COME" [Coming shows calendar section]
National Horseman
834 E. Broadway   Phone: (502) 585-4341
Louisville, KY 40204
Publication includes: Coming horse shows, including some to be held up to a year or more in the future. **Entries include:** Name of show, sponsors, breeds shown, dates, contact. **Frequency:** Regular feature of monthly issues. **Editor:** Raymond E. Sheffield. **Advertising accepted.** Circulation 5,000. **Price:** $1.50 per issue; $15.00 per year.

★5045★
NATIONAL INTERCOLLEGIATE WOMEN'S FENCING ASSOCIATION—DIRECTORY
National Intercollegiate Women's Fencing Association
18 Pleasant Place
Kearny, NJ 07032
Covers: 70 colleges and universities with women's varsity fencing teams. **Entries include:** Name of institution, address, phone; name, address, and phone of the team coach. **Arrangement:** Geographical. **Indexes:** Alphabetical. **Pages** (approx.): 15. **Frequency:** Annual, winter. **Editor:** Catherine Taylor, Executive Secretary. **Price:** Available to members only.

★5046★
NATIONAL INTRAMURAL-RECREATIONAL SPORT DIRECTORY
National Intramural Recreational Sports Association
DeWare Field House
Texas A&m University   Phone: (713) 845-7826
College Station, TX 77843
Covers: Intramural recreational sports programs in about 850 senior colleges and universities, about 350 junior colleges, and over 80 military installations; college coverage includes Canada. **Entries include:** School name, address; names of president, intramural sports director, and union director, with individual phone numbers; enrollment; names of student assistants; some listings also include sports in which clubs have formed, degrees offered in physical education, and whether graduate assistantships are available. Military listings include slightly less detail. **Arrangement:** Alphabetical within senior college, junior college, Canadian categories. **Indexes:** Alphabetical, director name. **Pages** (approx.): 200. **Frequency:** Annual, December. **Editor:** Dennis Corrington. **Advertising accepted.** Circulation 2,000. **Price:** $6.50.

★5047★
NATIONAL OUTDOOR LIVING DIRECTORY
Live Free, Inc.
Box 743   Phone: (312) 468-8805
Harvey, IL 60426
Covers: Over 1,000 organizations concerned with skiing, mountaineering and rock climbing, homesteading, fishing, hiking, scuba diving, gun collecting and shooting sports, conservation, etc. Includes some suppliers. **Entries include:** Organization name, address, and brief comment on interests or activities. **Arrangement:** Alphabetical. **Indexes:** Type of activity. **Pages** (approx.): 80. **Frequency:** Irregular; second edition late 1975; new edition expected 1980. **Editor:** James C. Jones. **Advertising accepted.** **Price:** $2.50 (current edition); $6.00 (1980 edition).

★5048★
NATIONAL OUTDOOR WRITERS DIRECTORY
Outdoor Writers Association of America
4141 W. Bradley Road   Phone: (414) 354-9690
Milwaukee, WI 53209
Number of listings: 1,600. **Entries include:** Name, home and/or business address, phone, media written for, titles of books published, honors received, name of spouse. **Arrangement:** Geographical. **Indexes:** Media. **Pages** (approx.): 100. **Frequency:** Annual, June. **Editor:** Edwin W. Hanson. **Price:** $12.00.

National Park Guide *See* Rand McNally National Park Guide

National Park Guide for the Handicapped *See* Access National Parks—A Guide for Handicapped Visitors

★5049★
NATIONAL RIFLE ASSOCIATION COLLEGIATE SHOOTING SPORTS DIRECTORY
National Rifle Association
1600 Rhode Island Avenue, N. W.   Phone: (202) 783-6505
Washington, DC 20036
Covers: About 155 shooting programs in United States colleges and universities. **Entries include:** Institution name, address, name of contact; description of program including type, whether competitive, educational, or recreational; instruction offered; eligibility requirements; facilities; conference or league memberships; coaching staff available; financial assistance available. **Arrangement:** Geographical. **Pages** (approx.): 155. **Frequency:** Irregular; latest edition 1978; new edition expected 1980. **Editor:** John Grubar, Assistant Director. **Price:** $2.00.

★5050★
NATIONAL SPEEDWAY DIRECTORY
Dray Publishing Company
666 Westway, N. W.   Phone: (616) 453-9125
Grand Rapids, MI 49504
Covers: Nearly 1,000 North American auto racing facilities, including oval tracks and road courses. **Entries include:** Track name, mailing addresses, phone, directions to the track, size, surface, and days or nights of operation, along with names of promoters and track officials and sanctioning information. **Arrangement:** Geographical. **Pages** (approx.): 450. **Frequency:** Irregular; previous edition 1977; new edition expected mid-1980. **Editors:** Larry L. Yard and Allan E. Brown. **Advertising accepted.** **Former title:** Midwest Auto Racing Guide. **Price:** $3.95, plus 55¢ shipping (current edition); $5.00, plus $1.00 shipping (1980 edition).

★5051★
NATIONAL SPORTING GOODS ASSOCIATION BUYING GUIDE
National Sporting Goods Association
717 N. Michigan Avenue   Phone: (312) 944-0205
Chicago, IL 60611
Covers: 3,700 manufacturers, their representatives, and other suppliers of sporting goods for the retailing industry, and 200 trade associations concerned with sporting goods. **Entries include:** Company name, address, phone, sales contact, and products or services offered. **Arrangement:** Alphabetical. **Indexes:** Trade or brand name, product. **Pages** (approx.): 400. **Frequency:** Annual, October. **Price:** $7.50.

★5052★
NATIONAL WHEELCHAIR BASKETBALL ASSOCIATION— DIRECTORY
National Wheelchair Basketball Association
110 Seaton Building
University of Kentucky   Phone: (606) 257-1623
Lexington, KY 40506
Covers: 315 officers, team representatives, and game officials for each conference in the National Wheelchair Basketball Association. **Entries include:** Name, address, and team name. Entries for team representatives include phone. **Arrangement:** Listed by name of conference. **Frequency:** Annual, November. **Editor:** Stan Labanowich, Commissioner. **Price:** $1.50.

★5053★
NEW AMERICAN GUIDE TO ATHLETICS, SPORTS, & RECREATION
New American Library, Inc.
1633 Broadway   Phone: (212) 397-8000
New York, NY 10019
Publication includes: Lists of organizations, professional sports leagues and teams, publications, etc. **Entries include:** Organization or

publication name, address, phone; some listings include additional information. **Arrangement:** By sport. **Pages** (approx.): 675. **Frequency:** First edition 1979. **Editors:** Craig and Peter Norback. **Price:** $19.95, cloth; $9.95, paper. **Send orders to:** New American Library Order Dept., Box 120, Bergenfield, NJ 07621.

★5054★
NEW ENGLAND BEACH BOOK
Walker & Co.
720 Fifth Avenue　　　　　　　　Phone: (212) 265-3632
New York, NY 10019
Covers: About 175 beaches, primarily state- or community-owned, in Connecticut, Rhode Island, Massachusetts, New Hampshire, and Maine. **Entries include:** Ownership; location; admission and parking fees (if any); water, surf, and beach conditions; whether alcohol and pets are permitted; hours; nearest support area and its facilities and ambiance. Listings for each locality are introduced by a description of the character of the area. **Arrangement:** Geographical. **Pages** (approx.): 170. **Frequency:** Published 1975. **Editor:** Dedria Bryfonski. **Price:** $3.95, paper; $6.95, cloth.

★5055★
NORTH AMERICAN YACHT REGISTER
Livingston Marine Services, Inc.
17 Battery Place　　　　　　　　Phone: (212) 248-1839
New York, NY 10004
Covers: About 8,000 yacht and flag owners in North America who have paid for a listing; yachts are defined as 30 feet or more in length and include charters, historical vessels, and private vessels. Includes list of yacht clubs and yacht surveyors. **Entries include:** Yacht name, former name of yacht, owner, descriptive information about the yacht including designer and builder, home port, and port of registration. **Arrangement:** Alphabetical by yacht name. **Indexes:** Flag, call letter, former name of yacht, charter service, surveyor, historical vessel, flag and yacht owner name, and yacht club. **Pages** (approx.): 1,100. **Frequency:** Annual, spring. **Editor:** Frederick F. Livingston, Publisher. **Advertising accepted.** Circulation 3,500. **Former title:** Lloyd's Register of American Yachts (1977). **Price:** $40.00 (current edition); $45.00 (1980 edition).

★5056★
OHIO DIRECTORY OF CAMPS FOR THE HANDICAPPED
Ohio Easter Seal Society
Box 27129
Columbus, OH 43227
Covers: Camps throughout Ohio which offer residential and day care programs for persons with orthopedic or neurologic handicaps. **Entries include:** Camp name, address, phone, registration information, eligibility, fees and financial aid available, dates, and sponsoring organizations. **Arrangement:** Alphabetical. **Frequency:** Annual, April. **Price:** $1.00.

Outdoor Recreation Guide *See* Backpacking and Outdoor Guide

★5057★
OUTDOORSMAN'S GUIDE TO GOVERNMENT SURPLUS
Contemporary Books, Inc.
180 N. Michigan Avenue　　　　　Phone: (312) 782-9181
Chicago, IL 60601
Publication includes: Lists of military and civilian government agencies and large commercial firms which offer government surplus supplies and equipment useful in outdoor recreation; the materials offered range from trucks to personal items, and many items would have general usefulness; many sources offer other types of surplus and sell by mail. Also includes list of sporting facilities (camp sites, etc.) created by the Army Corps of Engineers or the Interior Department's Bureau of Reclamation. **Frequency:** Not established; first edition 1978. **Editor:** David LeRoy. **Price:** $9.95, cloth; $5.95, paper.

★5058★
OUTSIDE MAGAZINE—WILDERNESS SPORTS AND EXPEDITIONS COLUMN
Mariah Publications
3401 W. Division　　　　　　　　Phone: (312) 342-7777
Chicago, IL 60651
Covers: About 100 wilderness trip guides and licensed outfitters in each issue. **Entries include:** Personal or company name, address, phone, description of specialities or services. **Arrangement:** Geographical and alphabetical. **Frequency:** Six times a year. **Editor:** Lawrence J. Burke, Publisher. **Advertising accepted.** Circulation 200,000. **Price:** $2.50. **Other information:** "Outside Magazine" was formerly "Mariah Magazine."

★5059★
PACIFIC BOATING ALMANAC
Western Marine Enterprises, Inc.
Box Q　　　　　　　　　　　　Phone: (805) 644-6043
Ventura, CA 93001
Covers: 3,000 marine facilities serving recreational boating in California, Oregon, Washington, Nevada, Arizona, British Columbia, Alaska, and Mexico's Baja area. **Entries include:** Name of facility, address, phone, name of owner, list of services. **Arrangement:** Geographical in three volumes. Volume 1, Southern California, Arizona, and Baja; Volume 2, Northern California and Nevada; Volume 3, Pacific Northwest and Alaska. **Pages** (approx.): 425 per volume. **Frequency:** Annual, January. **Editor:** Capt. William Berssen. **Advertising accepted.** Circulation 10,000 (each edition). **Former title:** Sea Boating Almanac (1977). **Price:** $5.95 per volume (current edition); $6.95 (1980 edition); plus $1.00 shipping.

★5060★
PARACHUTING—THE SKYDIVER'S HANDBOOK
Parachuting Publications
Box 4232　　　　　　　　　　　Phone: (805) 968-7277
Santa Barbara, CA 93103
Publication includes: List of parachuting drop zones, worldwide; parachute manufacturers and dealers, publishers of books and periodicals, films, etc. **Entries include:** Site name, address. For others - Name, address, product or title. **Arrangement:** By Zip code. **Frequency:** Latest edition 1978; new edition expected 1980. **Editor:** Dan Poynter. **Price:** $11.95, cloth; $5.95, paper; postpaid.

★5061★
PARENTS' GUIDE TO ACCREDITED CAMPS
American Camping Association
Bradford Woods　　　　　　　　Phone: (317) 342-8456
Martinsville, IN 46151
Covers: About 3,000 summer camps, in northeastern, midwestern, southern, and western regional volumes. **Entries include:** Name of camp, address, phone, name and permanent address of owner or director, age and sex of children accepted, programs, etc. **Arrangement:** Geographical. **Frequency:** Annual, January; first published in regional format in 1977. **Advertising accepted. Former title:** National Directory of Accredited Camps (1977). **Price:** $1.95 per volume.

★5062★
PERUVIAN HORSE WORLD—STALLION DIRECTORY ISSUE
American Association of Owners and Breeders of Peruvian Paso Horses
Box 2035　　　　　　　　　　　Phone: (415) 531-5082
California City, CA 93505
Publication includes: Section of paid advertisements of owners of stallions offered for stud. **Entries include:** Most include horse name, name of ranch, address, phone, lineage, and awards; some also include fees and other information. **Arrangement:** Random. **Indexes:** Stallion name-parentage. **Frequency:** Annual, winter. **Editors:** Angie DeLozier and Constancia Leshin. **Advertising accepted.** Circulation 3,000. **Price:** Included in subscription, $5.00 per year.

★5063★
POOL & SPA NEWS—DIRECTORY ISSUE
Leisure Publications
3923 W. Sixth Street   Phone: (213) 385-3926
Los Angeles, CA 90020
Covers: Manufacturers and distributors of pool equipment and supplies. **Entries include:** Company name, address, phone, name of principal executive, number of employees, year firm was established, trade and brand names. **Indexes:** Product, brand name. **Pages** (approx.): 350. **Frequency:** Annual, January. **Editor:** Fay Coupe. **Advertising accepted. Price:** $14.50. **Other information:** Variant title, ''Pool News - Directory Issue.''

Pool News—Directory Issue *See* Pool & Spa News—Directory
    Issue

★5064★
POPULAR SCIENCE—''MOPEDS'' [Article]
Times Mirror Magazines, Inc.
380 Madison Avenue   Phone: (212) 687-3000
New York, NY 10017
Publication includes: ''Mopeds: 100-plus MPG, but how safe - or legal?'' (pages 66-69, ff), with a brand name, company name, and address listing of about 20 United States manufacturers of these hybrids of bicycles and motorcycles. Also includes specification chart and tabulation of state laws. **Price:** $1.50. **Other information:** In July 1977 issue.

★5065★
PRIVATE COUNTRY CLUB GUEST POLICY DIRECTORY [Golfing and
    tennis]
Pazdur Publishing Company
2171 Campus Drive, Suite 320   Phone: (714) 752-6474
Irvine, CA 92715
Covers: About 1,600 private country clubs with golfing and tennis facilities which have reciprocal guest policies; major hotel and resort golf complexes are also included. **Entries include:** Club name, number of holes, whether a private club or a resort-hotel, names of club pro and manager, phone, description of golf course, season, number and type of tennis courts, other facilities available, fees, guest policy. **Arrangement:** Geographical. **Indexes:** Club name. **Frequency:** Annual, March. **Editor:** Edward F. Pazdur, Editor & Publisher. **Advertising accepted.** Circulation 450,000. **Former title:** Golf & Country Club Guest Policy Directory (1978). **Price:** $5.00 (current and 1980 editions).

★5066★
PROFESSIONAL PREPARATION DIRECTORY FOR ELEMENTARY
    SCHOOL PHYSICAL EDUCATION
American Alliance for Health, Physical Education & Recreation
1201 16th Street, N. W.
Washington, DC 20036
Covers: Colleges and universities offering a degree program in elementary physical education in the United States. **Entries include:** Institution name, address; program name, description of program including whether or not certification is available, program options and specializations, course offerings; enrollment; summer program availability; and names of teaching personnel. **Arrangement:** Geographical. **Pages** (approx.): 60. **Frequency:** Not established; first edition 1978. **Price:** $3.00.

★5067★
PRORODEO SPORTS NEWS—COMING SHOWS CALENDAR
Professional Rodeo Cowboys Association Properties, Inc.
101 Prorodeo Drive   Phone: (303) 593-8840
Colorado Springs, CO 80919
Covers: Up to about 250 rodeos (depending on season) scheduled up to four months ahead. **Entries include:** City, dates, rodeo name, events, prizes. (Compiled for prospective participants, and thus does

not include times, ticket prices, etc.). **Arrangement:** Chronological. **Frequency:** In each biweekly issue. **Editor:** Bill Crawford. **Advertising accepted.** Circulation 29,500. **Price:** $10.00 per year; 75¢ per issue.

★5069★
RAND MCNALLY CAMPGROUND & TRAILER PARK GUIDE
Rand McNally & Company
8255 Central Park Avenue
Skokie, IL 60076
Covers: About 20,000 public and private campgrounds and trailer parks in the United States, Canada, and Mexico; about 150 sources for renting recreation vehicles. **Entries include:** In chart form, park name, address, phone, directions, CB channel monitored, number of sites, dates open, fees, and keys indicating type of environment, facilities, etc. For rental sources - Source name, address, phone. **Arrangement:** Geographical. **Pages** (approx.): 630. **Frequency:** Annual, January. **Price:** $7.95 (current edition); $8.95 (1980 edition; ISSN 0079-9610).

★5070★
RAND MCNALLY NATIONAL FOREST GUIDE
Rand McNally & Company
8255 Central Park Avenue
Skokie, IL 60076
Covers: 151 national forests. **Entries include:** Name, location, capacity, facilities, etc. **Arrangement:** Geographical. **Pages** (approx.): 225. **Frequency:** Irregular; latest edition 1979. **Editor:** Len Hilts. **Price:** $6.95.

★5071★
RAND MCNALLY NATIONAL PARK GUIDE
Rand McNally & Company
8255 Central Park Avenue
Skokie, IL 60076
Covers: All national parks, plus about 200 other areas in the National Park Service system. **Entries include:** Name, location, capacity, fees, etc. **Arrangement:** Geographical. **Pages** (approx.): 225. **Frequency:** Annual, March. **Editor:** Michael Frome. **Price:** $6.95.

★5072★
RESOURCE GUIDE TO OUTDOOR EDUCATION IN NEW ENGLAND
Massachusetts Environmental Education Society
Box 241
Westwood, MA 02090
Covers: Over 240 environmental education organizations in New England. **Entries include:** Name, address, phone, contact person; type of programs offered, to whom, facilities (if any). **Arrangement:** Alphabetical. **Indexes:** By type of program or activity. **Pages** (approx.): 80. **Frequency:** Published 1977. **Editors:** Elaine Barber and Will Phillips. **Price:** $5.00.

★5073★
RIVER RAFTING GUIDE
Caroline House Publishers
Box 738
Ottawa, IL 61350
Covers: Over 200 companies in 22 states and Canada which organize and guide expeditions on whitewater rivers. **Entries include:** Company name, address, phone, rivers run, seasons, equipment needed, dates of expeditions, etc. **Arrangement:** Geographical. **Pages** (approx.): 320. **Frequency:** Not established; first edition 1979. **Editor:** Alvin Fixler. **Price:** $7.95, payment must accompany order. **Send orders**

to: Caroline House, Box 161, Thornwood, NY 10594. **Other information:** Cited in prepublication promotion as, "River Running Directory;" variant title is, "Family River Rafting Guide."

River Running Directory *See* **River Rafting Guide**

Rodeo Sports News—Coming Shows Calendar *See* **Prorodeo Sports News—Coming Shows Calendar**

★5074★
ROLEX INTERNATIONAL GUIDE TO TENNIS RESORTS
Rolex Watch U.S.A., Inc.
Rolex Building
665 Fifth Avenue   Phone: (212) 758-7700
New York, NY 10022
Covers: About 400 tennis resorts and clubs, and hotels with access to tennis facilities, worldwide. **Entries include:** Resort name, address, phone, type and number of courts, description of services, and facilities available. **Arrangement:** Geographical. **Pages** (approx.): 150. **Frequency:** Irregular; first edition 1977. **Price:** $1.00, postpaid.

★5075★
ROXY'S SKI GUIDE TO NEW ENGLAND
East Woods Press
820 East Boulevard   Phone: (204) 334-0897
Charlotte, NC 28203
Covers: Ski resorts and ski schools. **Entries include:** Resort or school name, address, description of facilities, rating. **Pages** (approx.): 190. **Frequency:** Irregular, about every two years; latest edition November 1978. **Former title:** Roxy's Guide to New England Skiing (1978). **Price:** $5.95.

★5076★
RUNNER'S GUIDE TO THE U.S.A.
Simon and Schuster, Inc.
1230 Avenue of the Americas   Phone: (212) 245-6400
New York, NY 10020
Covers: More than 200 races nationwide from 4-milers to marathons. **Entries include:** Name of race, terrain, address and other informaton needed for entering, landmarks for gauging distance, weather, altitude, clothing, and accomodations information. **Arrangement:** Geographical. **Frequency:** First edition October 1978. **Editor:** Martina D'Alton. **Price:** $11.95, cloth; $5.95, paper. **Also includes:** Places to run in 30 major American cities with maps and path descriptions.

★5077★
RUNNING THE RIVERS OF NORTH AMERICA
Barre Publishing Company, Inc.
Valley Road
Barre, MA 01005
Covers: About 50 rivers in the United States and Canada which are suitable for white water rafting, canoeing, kayaking, and other forms of boating. **Entries include:** For each river - Name, location (25 rivers have maps), degree of difficulty, type of boat needed, permit requirements, rental concessions and addresses, name and address of contact for further information. **Arrangement:** Geographical. **Pages** (approx.): 300. **Frequency:** Published 1978. **Editor:** Peter Wood. **Price:** $12.95, cloth; $5.95, paper. **Send orders to:** Crown Publishers Inc., One Park Avenue, New York, NY 10016.

★5078★
RUNNING TIMES YEARBOOK
Running Times
12808 Occoquan Road
Woodbridge, VA 22192
Publication includes: Two biblio-directories, "1,000 Great Places to Run" and a less selective and less detailed "3,000 Places to Run," both geographical. Also includes a geographical list of sources of medical help for problems and injuries related to running. **Frequency:** Annual. **Price:** $1.95.

★5079★
SAILBOAT AND EQUIPMENT DIRECTORY
United Marine Publishing
38 Commercial Wharf   Phone: (617) 227-0888
Boston, MA 02110
Publication includes: Over 2,000 sailboat and equipment manufacturers. **Entries include:** Firm name, address, phone; many entries have description or photo. **Arrangement:** Equipment listed by product; boats listed by lenngth. **Indexes:** Boat. **Pages** (approx.): 460. **Frequency:** Annual, fall. **Editor:** Bob Payne. **Advertising accepted.** Circulation 100,000. **Price:** $3.95, plus 55¢ shipping, payment with order. **Send orders to:** Sailboat and Equipment Directory, 126 Blaine Ave., Marion, OH 43302.

★5080★
SALESMAN'S GUIDE NATIONWIDE DIRECTORY: SPORTING GOODS BUYERS
Salesman's Guide, Inc.
1140 Broadway   Phone: (212) 684-2985
New York, NY 10001
Covers: About 4,200 retail stores selling athletic and recreational equipment (footwear, apparel, baseballs, tents, guns, etc.). State and regional editions are also available. **Entries include:** Store name, address, phone, sales volume in dollars, names of executives and buyers, and resident buying offices (when part of chain or on lease basis). **Arrangement:** Geographical. **Indexes:** Store name. **Pages** (approx.): 725. **Frequency:** Annual, spring with three supplements. **Price:** $75.00, including supplements, postpaid, payment with order. Apply for prices of state editions.

Sea Boating Almanac *See* **Pacific Boating Almanac**

★5081★
SEED SAVERS EXCHANGE YEARBOOK
Kent Whealy
Rural Route 2   Phone: (816) 748-3091
Princeton, MO 64673
Publication includes: About 300 gardeners who, as members of Seed Savers Exchange, swap unusual, old, or hard-to-locate vegetable seeds; includes commercial seed sources; international coverage. **Entries include:** Individual name, address, and types of seeds available and desired. **Arrangement:** Geographical. **Pages** (approx.): 40. **Frequency:** Annual, February. **Editor:** Kent Whealy. **Former title:** True Seed Exchange (1979). **Price:** $2.00 (current and 1980 editions).

★5082★
SHOOTING INDUSTRY—BUYERS GUIDE ISSUE
Publishers Development Corporation
591 Camino de la Reina, Suite 200   Phone: (714) 297-5350
San Diego, CA 92108
Covers: Manufacturers of guns and related equipment and supplies. **Entries include:** Company name, address. **Arrangement:** Alphabetical. **Indexes:** Product, trade and brand name. **Pages** (approx.): 60. **Frequency:** Annual, July. **Editor:** Jerome Rakusan, Editorial Director. **Advertising accepted.** Circulation 25,000. **Price:** $3.00; available to dealers and retailers only.

Ski Magazine's Guide to Cross Country Skiing *See* **Guide to Cross Country Skiing**

★5083★
SKIING THE BEST
Vintage Books
Random House, Inc.
201 E. 50th Street
New York, NY 10022   Phone: (212) 751-2600
Covers: About 50 ski areas in North America. **Entries include:** Resort name, address, phone; description of slopes with difficulty rating; description of accommodations and facilities available; costs; suitability for children. **Arrangement:** Alphabetical. **Pages** (approx.):

300. **Frequency:** Published November 1978. **Author:** Miles Jaffe and Dennis Krieger. **Price:** $5.95.

★5084★
SKIING USA
William Morrow and Company, Inc.
105 Madison Avenue   Phone: (212) 889-3050
New York, NY 10016
Publication includes: List of about 700 downhill ski resorts. **Entries include:** Resort name, address, phone, directions; base elevation, rental equipment, ski lifts, instruction available; rates; other recreation facilities; lodging and restaurants available; nursery services. **Arrangement:** Geographical. **Pages (approx.):** 215. **Frequency:** First edition 1977. **Author:** Lucy M. Fehr. **Price:** $4.95.

★5085★
SOCIETY FOR AMERICAN BASEBALL RESEARCH—MEMBERSHIP DIRECTORY
Society for American Baseball Research
Box 323
Cooperstown, NY 13326
Covers: About 800 people with a special interest in baseball research, statistics, and history. **Entries include:** Name, address, phone, occupation, baseball interests. **Arrangement:** Alphabetical. **Frequency:** Annual, summer. **Editor:** L. Robert Davids, Chairman, Editorial Committee. **Price:** Available to members only.

★5086★
SPECIAL OLYMPICS—LIST OF CHAPTER SPECIAL OLYMPICS PROGRAMS
Special Olympics
1701 K Street, N. W., Suite 203   Phone: (202) 331-1346
Washington DC 20006
Covers: Programs promoting physical education and athletics for the retarded. **Entries include:** Name of chapter, plus name, address, and phone number of chapter director. **Pages (approx.):** 2. **Frequency:** Annual, September. **Editor:** Robert M. Montague, Executive Director. **Price:** Free.

Sporting Goods Buyers *See* Salesman's Guide Nationwide Directory: Sporting Goods Buyers

★5087★
SPORTING GOODS DEALER'S DIRECTORY
Sporting Goods Publishing Company
1212 N. Lindbergh   Phone: (314) 997-7111
St. Louis, MO 63166
Covers: 4,500 manufacturers, 250 wholesalers, and 850 manufacturers' agents serving the sporting goods industry. **Entries include:** For manufacturers - Company name, address, phone, products. For wholesalers and agents - Company name, address, phone. **Indexes:** Product. **Pages (approx.):** 450. **Frequency:** Annual, December or January. **Advertising accepted.** Circulation 7,200. **Price:** $5.00 (current and next editions).

★5088★
SPORTING GOODS DEALER'S REGISTER
Sporting Goods Publishing Company
1212 N. Lindbergh   Phone: (314) 997-7111
St. Louis, MO 63166
Covers: More than 300 sporting goods wholesalers, 100 importers, 800 manufacturers' representatives. **Entries include:** For wholesalers - Company name, address, phone, buyer's name, goods jobbed, territory served, number of men travelled, whether company publishes a catalog. For importers - Company name, address, description of sporting goods imported. For manufacturers' representatives - Company name, address, phone, territory, and firms represented. **Frequency:** Annual, January or February. **Editor:** Rudy Weber. **Advertising accepted. Price:** $20.00.

★5089★
SPORTS: A MULTIMEDIA GUIDE FOR CHILDREN AND YOUNG ADULTS
ABC-Clio Press
Riviera Campus
2040 Alameda Padre Serra   Phone: (805) 963-4221
Santa Barbara, CA 93103
Publication includes: List of publishers, distributors, dealers, and resource centers for materials concerned with sports. **Entries include:** Publisher name, address. **Arrangement:** Alphabetical. **Frequency:** Not established; first edition fall 1979. **Editors:** Calvin Blickle and Frances Corcoran. **Price:** $14.95, postpaid; payment must accompany individuals' orders. **Other information:** Published in cooperation with Neal-Schuman Publishers. Principal content of publication is annotated bibliographies.

★5090★
SPORTS ADMINISTRATION GUIDE AND DIRECTORY
National Sports Marketing Bureau
360 Lexington Avenue
New York, NY 10017
Covers: Non-playing job opportunities in sports with major professional teams, minor league teams, college conferences, and major sports arenas. **Entries include:** Name of organization or team, address, phone, name of contact person. **Arrangement:** Classified. **Frequency:** Irregular; latest edition 1977. **Price:** $5.00. (Not verified)

★5091★
SPORTSGUIDE FOR INDIVIDUAL SPORTS
SportsGuide
211 E. 43rd Street   Phone: (212) 697-5237
New York, NY 10017
Covers: Manufacturers, organizations, broadcasting networks and syndicators, publications, trade shows, marketing services, and other groups concerned with the business and promotional aspects of alpine and cross-country skiing, badminton, bowling, fencing, golf, paddleball, paddle tennis, platform tennis, racquetball, running and jogging, squash, table tennis, tennis; includes section on multi-sport firms and services. Also lists significant tournaments, meets, and similar events. **Entries include:** Name of company, organization, etc., address, phone, names of key personnel, and description of product, services, etc.; entries for events give information on television coverage (if any). **Arrangement:** By sport. **Indexes:** General alphabetical, manufacturer (includes company name, address, phone, executives, products, advertising agency and account executive), executive (includes company or organization name and phone). **Pages (approx.):** 325. **Frequency:** First edition January 1980. **Editor:** Richard A. Lipsey. **Advertising accepted. Price:** $40.00. **Other information:** Library orders only to Gale Research Company, Book Tower, Detroit, MI 48226 (313-961-2242).

★5092★
SPORTSGUIDE FOR TEAM SPORTS
SportsGuide
211 E. 43rd Street   Phone: (212) 697-5237
New York, NY 10017
Covers: Manufacturers, organizations, broadcasting networks and syndicators, publications, trade shows, marketing services, and other groups concerned with the business and promotional aspects of baseball, basketball, boxing, curling, field hockey, football, gymnastics, ice hockey, lacrosse, rowing and crew, rugby, soccer, softball, speed and figure skating, track and field, volleyball, and wrestling; includes section on multi-sport firms and services. Also lists significant tournaments, meets, and similar events. **Entries include:** Name of company, organization, etc., address, phone, names of key personnel, and description of product, services, etc.; entries for events give information on television coverage, if any. **Arrangement:** By sport. **Indexes:** General alphabetical, manufacturer (includes company name, address, phone, executives, products, advertising agency and account executive), executive (includes company or organization name and

phone). **Pages** (approx.): 325. **Frequency:** First edition expected April 1980. **Editor:** Richard A. Lipsey. **Advertising accepted. Price:** $40.00. **Other information:** Library orders only to Gale Research Company, Book Tower, Detroit, MI 48226 (313-961-2242).

★5093★
SPYGLASS SAILBOAT RIGGING GUIDE AND EQUIPMENT MANUAL
Spyglass
2415 Mariner Square Drive   Phone: (415) 769-8410
Alameda, CA 94501
Publication includes: Lists of manufacturers of sailboats and hardware; publishers of yachting books and magazines. **Entries include:** Name of manufacturer or publisher, address, description of product, specifications, prices. **Pages** (approx.): 400. **Frequency:** Annual, January. **Editor:** Dick Moore, Managing Editor. **Advertising accepted.** Circulation 25,000. **Price:** $4.95 (current edition); $5.95 (1980 edition); plus $1.05 shipping.

Sunset Western Campground Directory *See* **Western Campsite Directory**

★5094★
SURFER'S ALMANAC: AN INTERNATIONAL SURFING GUIDE
E. P. Dutton
Two Park Avenue   Phone: (212) 725-1818
New York, NY 10016
Covers: Beaches suitable for surfing in California, Hawaii, and other locations throughout the world; includes surfing clubs, organizations, etc. **Entries include:** Locations, detailed descriptions. **Arrangement:** Geographical. **Frequency:** Published 1977. **Editors:** Gary Fairmont and R. Filosa II. **Price:** $12.95, cloth; $6.95, paper.

★5095★
TACK 'N TOGS MERCHANDISING—TACK 'N TOGS BOOK ISSUE
 [Horse and rider products]
Miller Publishing Company
2501 Wayzata Boulevard   Phone: (612) 374-5200
Minneapolis, MN 55440
Covers: Manufacturers, wholesalers, and importers of all types of products for the horse and rider industry. Includes manufacturers representatives, wholesalers and jobbers, associations. **Entries include:** For manufacturers - Company name, address, phone, names of executives, products or services, and brand names. **Indexes:** Product, brand name. **Pages** (approx.): 350. **Frequency:** Annual, May. **Editor:** Doug Dahl. **Advertising accepted.** Circulation 16,000. **Price:** $10.00 (current and 1980 editions).

★5096★
TELEPHONE SERVICE DIRECTORY [Football writers]
Football Writers Association of America
Box 1022   Phone: (405) 341-4731
Edmond, OK 73034
Covers: About 500 newspaper and magazine sportswriters covering college and professional football. **Entries include:** Name, address, home and office phone number. **Arrangement:** Geographical. **Frequency:** Annual, September. **Editor:** Volney Meece, Secretary-Treasurer. **Price:** Available to those listed only.

Tender Plant Finder *See* **House Plant Finder**

★5097★
TENNIS—PLACES TO PLAY ISSUE
Tennis Features, Inc.
495 Westport Avenue   Phone: (203) 847-5811
Norwalk, CT 06856
Covers: About 100 tennis resorts, located in the United States. **Entries include:** Resort name, address, phone, number of courts, type of court surface. **Arrangement:** Geographical. **Frequency:** Annual, February. **Editor:** Shepherd Campbell. **Advertising accepted.** Circulation 440,000. **Price:** $1.25.

★5098★
TENNIS CATALOG
Macmillan, Inc.
866 Third Avenue   Phone: (212) 935-2000
New York, NY 10022
Publication includes: Lists of resorts which emphasize tennis, tennis camps, and mail order firms which offer equipment, each with relevant detail. **Frequency:** Not established; first edition 1978. **Editor:** Moira Duggan. **Price:** $7.95.

★5099★
TENNIS DIRECTORY
Ski Earth Publications, Inc.
38 Commercial Wharf
Boston, MA 02110
Covers: Manufacturers of tennis equipment, court lighting equipment, tennis apparel, ball machines, and stringing machines; tennis resorts are also listed. **Entries include:** For manufacturers - Company name, address, product descriptions. For resorts - Name, address, number and type of courts, court fees, instruction available and costs, tennis clinics offered, name of tennis pro, phone, credit cards accepted, package plans and costs, other facilities, directions, description. **Arrangement:** Manufacturers are classified by product, resorts are geographical. **Pages** (approx.): 210. **Frequency:** Semiannual, June and December. **Editor:** Neil R. Goldhirsh. **Advertising accepted.** **Price:** $2.95, plus $1.50 shipping.

★5100★
TENNIS INDUSTRY—DIRECTORY OF TENNIS SALES
 REPRESENTATIVES ISSUE
Industry Publishers, Inc.
1545 N. E. 123rd Street   Phone: (305) 893-8771
North Miami, FL 33161
Covers: 5,000 sales representatives handling tennis products. **Entries include:** Representative or firm name, address, phone, names of sales personnel, states traveled, manufacturers represented. **Arrangement:** Alphabetical. **Indexes:** Manufacturer, representatives by states and countries traveled. **Frequency:** Annual, November. **Editor:** Joan Whaley. **Advertising accepted.** Circulation 19,800. **Price:** $2.00.

Tennis Resorts *See* **Curtis Casewit's Guide to Tennis Resorts**

★5101★
THRILL SPORTS CATALOG
E. P. Dutton
Two Park Avenue   Phone: (212) 725-1818
New York, NY 10016
Covers: Sources of information on about 25 high-risk sports, such as hang gliding and rafting. Includes associations, book publishers, periodicals. **Entries include:** Source name, address, type of information available. **Arrangement:** Classified by sport. **Frequency:** First edition 1977. **Price:** $1.98. **Send orders to:** Book Thrift, One W. 39th Street, New York, NY; no longer available from publisher.

★5102★
THROUGHBRED RACING ASSOCIATIONS OF NORTH AMERICA—
 DIRECTORY & RECORD BOOK
Thoroughbred Racing Associations of North America
3000 Marcus Avenue, Suite 2W4   Phone: (516) 328-2660
Lake Success, NY 11042
Covers: About 60 member thoroughbred race tracks in the United States and Canada, and about 60 non-member tracks. **Entries include:** For member tracks - Corporate name, track name, address, phone, names of officers and staff, track data, equipment data, capacity, prices, and brief history of the track. Listings for non-member tracks do not include descriptive data or history. **Arrangement:** Alphabetical by track name. **Pages** (approx.): 150. **Frequency:** Annual, March. **Editor:** Bill Christine, Director, Service Bureau. **Price:** $3.00. **Also includes:** Racing dates for coming season and racing statistics.

★5103★

TRAILER LIFE RV CAMPGROUND & SERVICES DIRECTORY

Trailer Life Publishing Company, Inc.

23945 Craftsman Road   Phone: (213) 888-6000

Calabasas, CA 91302

Covers: Over 20,000 campgrounds, resorts, recreational vehicle parks and service centers, recreational vehicle dealers, disposal stations, LP gas stations, tourist attractions, and truck stops with heavy duty service for recreational vehicles. **Entries include:** For campgrounds and parks - Park name, location, directions, phone, CB channels monitored by the park, facilities, recreation rating. Listings for other facilities give similar details. **Arrangement:** Geographical. **Pages** (approx.): 1,370. **Frequency:** Annual, December. **Editor:** Alice Robison. **Advertising accepted.** Circulation 350,000. **Price:** $7.95, plus $1.50 shipping.

★5104★

TRAVELING AND CAMPING IN THE NATIONAL PARK AREAS

Globe Pequot Press

Old Chester Road   Phone: (203) 526-9571

Chester, CT 06412

Covers: National parks, seashores, historic sites, monuments, and historical parks administered by the National Park Service; separate volumes for western and eastern states and mid-America. **Entries include:** Area name, address, size, historical background, activities, facilities, camping and fishing opportunities. **Arrangement:** Geographical. **Pages** (approx.): 180 per volume. **Frequency:** Western states published 1978; others expected January 1980. **Editors:** David L. Scott and Kay Woelfel Scott. **Price:** $5.95 per volume.

True Seed Exchange *See* **Seed Savers Exchange Yearbook**

★5105★

TURF-GRASS TIMES—INDUSTRY REFERENCE GUIDE ISSUE [Golf course maintenance]

Brantwood Publications, Inc.

Box 77   Phone: (414) 786-2900

Elm Grove, IL 53122

Covers: Manufacturers, suppliers, distributors, and wholesalers of machinery, equipment, chemicals, sod and turfgrass, and other materials used in golf course maintenance; trade associations and organizations are also included. **Entries include:** Company or organization name, address. **Arrangement:** By type of activity (manufacturers and suppliers, associations, etc.). **Indexes:** Product. **Frequency:** Annual, July/August. **Advertising accepted.** Circulation 16,000. **Price:** $10.00.

★5106★

UNDERWATER HOLIDAYS

Grosset & Dunlap

51 Madison Avenue   Phone: (212) 689-9200

New York, NY 10010

Publication includes: List of locations to snorkel and scuba dive in North America and the Pacific. **Entries include:** Site name; accomodations available; dive facility; costs; address (and phone, if available); description of site, including distance from shore, reef type, depth, sealife, diving season, whether surf or calm. **Arrangement:** Geographical. **Pages** (approx.): 260. **Frequency:** First edition 1978. **Editors:** Janet Viertel and Jack Viertel. **Price:** Out of print.

Underwater Society International Divers Guide *See* **International Divers Guide**

★5107★

UNITED STATES DRESSAGE FEDERATION CALENDAR OF COMPETITIONS

United States Dressage Federation

1212 O Street   Phone: (402) 477-1251

Lincoln, NE 68501

Covers: Over 150 dressage competitions recognized by the United States Dressage Federation and the American Horse Shows Association. **Entries include:** Competition name, date, location, levels of training included in competition, names of judges (if available), and name, address, and phone of contact. **Arrangement:** By geographical region. **Indexes:** Chronological. **Pages** (approx.): 70. **Frequency:** Semiannual, April and December. **Editor:** Barbara Petersen. **Advertising accepted.** Circulation 10,000. **Price:** $2.00, plus 50¢ shipping.

★5108★

UNITED STATES PARACHUTE ASSOCIATION—DIRECTORY AND REFERENCE SOURCE

United States Parachute Association

806 15th Street, N. W.   Phone: (202) 347-5773

Washington, DC 20005

Covers: 700 parachute drop zones in United States and Canada. **Entries include:** Zone identification, location, address, phone, facilities. **Arrangement:** Geographical. **Pages** (approx.): 70. **Frequency:** Semiannual, spring and fall. **Editor:** Paul C. Proctor, Editor, Parachutist Magazine. **Advertising accepted.** Circulation 20,000. **Price:** $1.50.

★5109★

UNITED STATES POLO ASSOCIATION—YEAR BOOK

United States Polo Association

1301 W. 22nd Street, Suite 706   Phone: (312) 654-1631

Oak Brook, IL 60521

Covers: 1,300 polo players, 100 independent polo clubs, and 20 school and college polo clubs. **Entries include:** For players - Name, club, address, and handicaps. For clubs - Club name, circuit, colors, and name and address of delegate to the association. **Arrangement:** Alphabetical. **Indexes:** Club by circuit. **Pages** (approx.): 210. **Frequency:** Annual. **Price:** Available to members only. **Also includes:** Extensive information on rules, standings, etc.

★5110★

UNITED STATES PROFESSIONAL TENNIS ASSOCIATION DIRECTORY

United States Professional Tennis Association

Box 1659   Phone: (813) 388-3939

Sarasota, FL 33578

Covers: About 3,000 professional and amateur tennis players, coaches, and others active in the sport. **Entries include:** Name, address, phone. **Arrangement:** Alphabetical. **Indexes:** Division. **Pages** (approx.): 300. **Frequency:** Annual, March. **Editor:** Barbara Richards, Director of Communications. **Advertising accepted.** Circulation 3,000. **Price:** Available to members only. **Also includes:** A calendar of events, USPTA by-laws, and USPTA rankings and sanctioned tournaments.

★5111★

UNITED STATES SKI ASSOCIATION—EASTERN—DIRECTORY

Eastern Ski Association

22 High Street   Phone: (802) 254-6077

Brattleboro, VT 05301

Covers: Association committee members, division members, about 500 individual members, state associations, affiliated associations, and regional ski councils. **Entries include:** For committees, divisions, associations, and councils - Organization name, name of chairperson, address, phone; additional details as appropriate. For individuals - Name, address, phone. **Arrangement:** Organizations and committees are primarily alphabetical by organization name; individuals are alphabetical. **Pages** (approx.): 75. **Frequency:** Annual, November. **Price:** $2.00, plus 50¢ shipping. **Also includes:** Calendar of events, including competitions.

★5112★
UNITED STATES SKI WRITERS ASSOCIATION—MEMBERSHIP DIRECTORY
United States Ski Writers Association
7 Kensington Road   Phone: (518) 793-1201
Glens Falls, NY 12801
Covers: 310 writers, photographers, TV and radio personnel who develop ski news and visuals. **Entries include:** Name, business and home phone numbers, affiliation or occupation. **Arrangement:** Geographical according to following regions: Eastern, Mid-America, Midwest, Rocky Mountain, Pacific Northwest, Northern California-Nevada, Southern California. **Pages** (approx.): 40. **Frequency:** Annual, November. **Editor:** Don A. Metivier, President. **Price:** Free. **Send orders to:** John Hoefling, 2039 S. E. 103rd Dr., Portland, OR 97216 (503-253-8524).

★5113★
USDF DRESSAGE DIRECTORY: INSTRUCTORS, CLINICIANS, OFFICALS
United States Dressage Federation
1212 O Street   Phone: (402) 477-1251
Lincoln, NE 68501
Covers: About 500 dressage instructors and clinicians at all levels, American Horse Shows Association licensed dressage judges, and technical delegates. **Entries include:** Name, office and home address, office and home phone, area of occupational specialization. **Arrangement:** Geographical. **Indexes:** Personal name, occupation. **Pages** (approx.): 55. **Frequency:** Annual, September. **Editor:** Barbara Petersen, Director of Information. **Advertising accepted.** Circulation 5,000. **Former title:** Directory of Dressage Instructors (1979). **Price:** $3.00, plus 50¢ shipping.

★5114★
WATERWAY GUIDE—THE YACHTMAN'S BIBLE
Waterway Guide, Inc.
238 West Street   Phone: (301) 268-9546
Annapolis, MD 21404
Covers: Inland and coastal waterways in northern, eastern, and southern United States. Three editions. Northern edition covers: Lake Ontario to Sorel, Quebec; the Hudson River; the Erie Canal; and coastal waterways from Canada to Sandy Hook, NJ. Middle Atlantic edition covers: Sandy Hook, NJ, to Florida-Georgia line. Southern edition covers: Intracoastal waterways and Gulf Coast from the Florida-Georgia line to the Texas-Mexico border; also covers the Bahamas. Includes navigation information, communications, courses, locations of marine facilities, points of interest, restaurants, etc. **Arrangement:** Geographical. **Pages** (approx.): 400. **Frequency:** Annual. **Advertising accepted.** Circulation 15,000 each edition. **Price:** $10.00 each edition (current and 1980 editions).

★5115★
WEST COAST BEACHES
E. P. Dutton
Two Park Avenue   Phone: (212) 725-1818
New York, NY 10016
Entries include: Name of beach, location, activities and facilities available (boat launch, swimming, camping, nude bathing, etc.). **Arrangement:** Geographical. **Frequency:** Published 1979. **Editors:** Sarah Dixon and Peter Dixon. **Price:** $8.95.

★5116★
WESTERN CAMPSITE DIRECTORY
Lane Publishing Company
Willow and Middlefield Roads   Phone: (415) 321-3600
Menlo Park, CA 94025
Covers: Over 8,000 campgrounds and trailer stops in Alaska, Arizona, California, Idaho, Montana, New Mexico, Colorado, Nevada, Oregon, Utah, Washington, Wyoming, Yukon Territory, Baja Mexico, Alberta, and British Columbia; maps are included. **Entries include:** Camp name, address, phone, directions, fees, reservation requirements, season, terrain and elevation, number of campsites, facilities, and nearby attractions and recreation activities available. **Arrangement:** Geographical. **Pages** (approx.): 400. **Frequency:** Annual, February. **Editor:** Kristine Valencia. **Advertising accepted.** Circulation 80,000. **Price:** $4.95 (current and 1980 editions).

★5117★
WESTERN STATES FLY-IN CAMPGROUND DIRECTORY—PILOT'S CAMPING GUIDE
Fly'N Camp Enterprises
4838 Bluebell Avenue   Phone: (213) 985-7041
North Hollywood, CA 91607
Covers: 110 airports, airstrips, landing fields, and other locations to which a light plane can fly for planeside camping or camping nearby. **Entries include:** Landing facility name, location, coordinates and other data, name and description of nearby campground, comments on the area. **Arrangement:** Geographical. **Pages** (approx.): 170. **Frequency:** Irregular; latest edition 1978; new edition expected 1981. **Editor:** George O. Deshler. **Price:** $5.95, payment with order. **Send orders to:** Fly'N Camp Enterprises, Box 6055, Burbank, CA 91510.

★5118★
WESTERN TRAVEL ADVENTURES
Lane Publishing Company
Willow & Middlefield Roads   Phone: (415) 321-3600
Menlo Park, CA 94025
Covers: More than 1,000 attractions, vacations, resorts, and trips in the western United States, Canada, and Mexico, including selected festivals, theme parks, historic hotels, dude ranches, river running and horseback expeditions, houseboat rental agencies, recreational railroads, mountaineering schools, tennis clinics, ballooning activities, bicycling tours, and other activities. **Entries include:** Site name, address, phone; additional descriptive information varies with type of attraction but may include accommodations available, hours and season open, facilities, length of tours, fees and costs. **Arrangement:** By type of attraction or activity (theme parks, bike trips, country inns, etc.). **Pages** (approx.): 200. **Frequency:** Annual, February. **Editor:** Don Bice. **Advertising accepted.** Circulation 80,000. **Price:** $2.95, plus $1.00 shipping. **Other information:** Publication will be discontinued after 1980 edition.

★5119★
WHEELERS RECREATIONAL VEHICLE RESORT AND CAMPGROUND GUIDE
Print Media Services, Ltd.
222 S. Prospect Avenue   Phone: (312) 825-1145
Park Ridge, IL 60068
Covers: Publicly and commercially operated resorts and campgrounds for tent, camper, or motor home travelers. North American edition covers about 18,000 locations; Easterner Edition covers about 10,400 locations in the south, east, midwest, and Canada's eastern provinces; Westerner Edition covers about 7,600 locations in the western states, the western provinces of Canada, and Mexico. **Entries include:** Camp name, management authority, directions for reaching site, capacity, facilities, recreation, restrictions, dates operated, CB call numbers, mailing address, code indicating if camp is commercial. **Arrangement:** Geographical. **Pages** (approx.): North American edition, 800; regional editions 300-500. **Frequency:** Annual, January. **Editor:** Gloria S. Telander, Publisher. **Advertising accepted.** Circulation of North American edition is about 20,000; regional editions about 90,000 each. **Former title:** Wheelers Trailer Resort and Campground Guide (1975). **Price:** North American edition $6.95; Westerner, $3.95; Easterner, $4.95 (current and 1980 editions). **Send orders to:** Viking Press, 625 Madison Avenue, New York, NY 10022.

Wheelers Trailer Resort and Campground Guide *See* **Wheelers Recreational Vehicle Resort and Campground Guide**

★5120★
WHITE BOOK OF SKI AREAS—U.S. AND CANADA
Inter-Ski Services, Inc.
Box 3635
Georgetown Station   Phone: (202) 342-0886
Washington, DC 20007
Covers: 1,000 lift-equipped ski area/resorts in the United States and Canada. Includes section on helicopter skiing companies and their operations. **Entries include:** Name of ski area, location, phone; ski statistics (elevation, lift capacity, etc.); season and rates; equipment and schooling available; lodging, restaurants, apres-ski, and other recreational facilities in vicinity; shops, medical services, etc.; travel instructions. **Arrangement:** Geographical within four regions - West, North Central, South, and Northwest. **Indexes:** Geographical. **Pages** (approx.): 420. **Frequency:** Annual, winter. **Editor:** Robert G. Enzel. **Advertising accepted.** Circulation 20,000. **Former title:** White Book of U.S. Ski Areas. **Price:** $7.95, plus $1.25 shipping.

★5121★
WHOLE HORSE CATALOG
Simon & Schuster, Inc.
1230 Avenue of the Americas   Phone: (212) 245-6400
New York, NY 10020
Covers: Manufacturers and suppliers of products and services useful to persons who ride, work with, or own horses. Includes discussions of equipment in general as well as specific sources, and information about organizations, etc. **Entries include:** Listings for sources include name, address, whether catalogs are available. **Arrangement:** Classified by subject ("Apparel," etc.). **Pages** (approx.): 250. **Frequency:** Published 1977. **Editor:** Steven D. Price. **Price:** $6.95.

★5122★
WHO'S WHO IN CHRISTIAN CAMPING
Christian Camping International
Box 400   Phone: (815) 786-8453
Somonauk, IL 60552
Covers: About 1,000 member camps, businesses, churches, and schools having an evangelical Christian orientation; approximately 4,000 individuals who are members are also listed. **Entries include:** For camps - Camp name, address, phone, names of key personnel, number of occupants possible. For schools, churches, and businesses - Name, address, names and addresses of two key staff members who are also members of the association. **Arrangement:** Camps are geographical, other group listings by type of establishment then alphabetical. **Indexes:** Personal name. **Pages** (approx.): 75. **Frequency:** Biennial, even years. **Editor:** Nancy Kerstetter, Communications Services Associate. **Advertising accepted.** Circulation 4,500. **Former title:** Membership Directory for Christian Camping International, U.S.A. Division. **Price:** $3.60 (current edition); $7.50 (tentative, 1980 edition).

★5123★
WHO'S WHO IN NATIONAL ATHLETICS—HIGH SCHOOL FOOTBALL
Who's Who in National Athletics
Box 5335
Torrance, CA 90503
Covers: 15,000 high school football players picked by their coaches as eligible for high school All American selection. Includes listing of National Advisory Board, college and professional coaches, and high school All American selections for the year. **Entries include:** Name, school, personal data, career statistics, college plans, other interests. **Arrangement:** Geographical. **Pages** (approx.): 500. **Frequency:** Annual, winter. **Editor:** Franco Giannetto. **Advertising accepted.** Circulation 30,000. **Price:** $14.95. (Not verified)

★5124★
WOMEN IN THE WILDERNESS
Women in the Wilderness
13 Columbus Avenue
San Francisco, CA 94111
Publication includes: A section in each issue of this newsletter includes notices of organizations, wilderness trips and other expeditions run and led by women; most are in North America. **Frequency:** Quarterly. **Price:** $10.00 per year.

★5125★
WOODALL'S CAMPGROUND DIRECTORY
Clark and Woodall Publishing Company
500 Hyacinth Place   Phone: (312) 433-4550
Highland Park, IL 60035
Covers: Commercial and public campgrounds in the United States, Canada, and Mexico. Separate listing of about 1,000 service locations for recreational vehicles. Three major editions: North America; eastern United States and Canada; and western United States, Canada, and Mexico. Also editions for Arizona and Mexico; California and Mexico; Florida; Idaho, Oregon, and Washington; Illinois and Indiana; Iowa and Missouri; Michigan; New England; New Jersey and New York; Ohio and Pennsylvania; Texas and Mexico; Virginia; Wisconsin; and the Province of Ontario. **Entries include:** Name of campground, location, directions from major highways, camping rates per night, ratings of facilities and of recreation. **Arrangement:** Geographical. **Pages** (approx.): North American edition, 1,500; eastern, 960; western, 530; states average 150. **Frequency:** All editions annual, November/December. **Editor:** Linda L. Profaizer, Associate Publisher. **Advertising accepted.** North American edition circulation 450,000; regional editions, 55,000 each. **Former title:** Woodall's Trailering Parks and Campgrounds Directory. **Price:** North American edition, $8.95; regional editions, $5.95 each; state editions, $1.95 each. **Also includes:** Sightseeing information, special events, etc.

Woodall's Trailering Park and Campgrounds Directory See **Woodall's Campground Directory**

★5126★
YACHTING YEARBOOK OF NORTHERN CALIFORNIA
Pacific Inter-Club Yacht Association
68 Post Street, Room 417   Phone: (415) 392-7076
San Francisco, CA 94104
Covers: Over 9,000 members of 65 yacht clubs and 70 one-design boat clubs in Monterey Bay, San Francisco Bay, Stockton, and Sacramento areas. **Entries include:** Name and address of yacht club; name, address, and phone of directors and officers; name of boat; name and address of owner. One-design clubs include boat specifications. **Arrangement:** Yacht clubs are alphabetical, others are call numbers, mailing address, code indicating if camp is commercial. **Arrangement:** Geographical. **Pages** (approx.): North American edition, 800; regional editions 300-500. **Frequency:** Annual, January. **Editor:** Gloria S. Telander, Publisher. **Advertising accepted.** Circulation of North American edition is about 20,000; regional editions about 90,000 each. **Former title:** Wheelers Trailer Resort and Campground Guide (1975). **Price:** North American edition $6.95; Westerner, $3.95; Easterner, $4.95 (current and 1980 editions). **Send orders to:** Viking Press, 625 Madison Avenue, New York, NY 10022.

Title Index

A

B

C

D

TITLE INDEX

E

F

G

H

I

J

K

L

M

N

O

P

Pacific Boating Almanac 5059
Pacific Builder & Engineer—Buyers Guide & Directory Issue 1123
Pacific Coast Aviation Directory and Buyer's Yellow Pages *See* Aviation Directory
Pacific Coast Industrial Directory 1124
Pacific Coast Marine Directory 1125
Pacific Dermatologic Association—Membership Directory 4406
Pacific Northwest Book Publishers Association Bibliography and Directory 3247
Pacific Northwest Grain Dealers Association—Official Directory 1925
Pacific Northwest Mobile Home Park Guide 1699
Pacific Packers Report 1926
Pacific Southwest Directory [Of grain and feed firms] 1927
Package Engineering—Annual Buyer's Guide Issue 1126
Package Printing—Diemakers and Diecutters Annual Directory Issue 1127
Packaged Directory [Manufactured housing] 1128
Packaging Machinery Manufacturers Institute—Directory *See* PMMI Packaging Machinery Directory
Packaging Marketplace 1129
Packard Club—Annual Directory 4852
Packer Red Book *See* Red Book [Produce industry]
Pain Clinic Directory 4407
Paint Red Book 1130
Palo Verde Valley [California] Lettuce Shippers Directory 1928
Pan Am Home Exchange Directory *See* Exchange Book [Home exchange]
Paper Coating Additives 1131
Paper, Film & Foil Converter—Annual Directory & Buyers Guide 1132
Paper Industry Management Association—Membership Directory 1133
Paperback Books for Young People: An Annotated Guide to Publishers and Distributors 3248
Paperbound Books in Print 3249
Papillon Club of America—Membership List [Dogs] 4853
Parachuting—The Skydiver's Handbook 5060
Paramedical National Directory 4408
Parents' Guide to Accredited Camps 5061
Parents' Yellow Pages 4056
Park Areas and Employment Opportunities for Summer [Year] [National Parks] 1134
Park Maintenance—Annual Buyers' Guide Issue 1135
Parks and Recreation—Annual Buyers' Guide Issue 1136
Parliamentary Directory 3250
Participants in the National Poultry Improvement Plan 1929
Parts/Equipment Buyers' Guide & Services Directory [Trucks] *See* Heavy Duty Trucking—Council of Fleet Specialists Equipment Buyers' Guide
Passages Gazette *(Discontinued)*
Passover Products Directory *See* Kosher Products and Services Directory
Patterson's American Education 2994
Patterson's Schools Classified 2995
Patterson's Source Guide for Educational Materials and Equipment *(Discontinued)*
Peak Doll Directory 4854
Pedigrees of Descendants of Colonial Clergy 4649
Pelican Guide to Gardens of Louisiana 1930
Pelican Guide to Historic Homes and Sites of Revolutionary America 4855
Pelican Guide to Old Homes of Mississippi 4856
Pelican Guide to Plantation Homes of Louisiana 4857
Pen Pal Directory *See* Stamp Exchangers Directory
PENJERDEL Location and Market Guide [Pennsylvania, New Jersey, Delaware] 1137
Pennsylvania Area Key: A Guide to the Genealogical Records of the State of Pennsylvania 4650
Pennsylvania Business Change Service 1138
Pennsylvania Departments of Transportation and Community Affairs—Borough Officials 2393
Pennsylvania Departments of Transportation and Community Affairs—City Officials 2394
Pennsylvania Departments of Transportation and Community Affairs—County Officials 2395
Pennsylvania Departments of Transportation and Community Affairs—First-Class Township Officials 2396
Pennsylvania Departments of Transportation and Community Affairs—Second-Class Township Boards of Supervisors 2397
Pennsylvania Directory of Historical Organizations 3251

Pennsylvania Directory of Manufacturers 1139
Pennsylvania Exporters Directory 1140
Pennsylvania League of Cities—Directory and Data Book 2398
Pennsylvania Legal Directory 2399
Pennsylvania Municipal Yearbook 2400
Pennsylvania Newspaper Publishers Association Directory 4057
Pennsylvania Press Photographers *See* Pennsylvania Newspaper Publishers Association Directory
Pennsylvania Senate Legislative Directory 2401
Pennsylvania Society of Newspaper Editors *See* Pennsylvania Newspaper Publishers Association Directory
Pennsylvania State Industrial Directory 1141
Pennsylvania Women's Press Association *See* Pennsylvania Newspaper Publishers Association Directory
Pension World—Plan Sponsor's Directory of Master and Directed Trust Services Issue 1700
Pensions and Investments—100 Top Retirement Funds Issue 1701
People Helping People Help Themselves 4058
People in Careers *(Discontinued)*
People in Public Telecommunications 3643
People's Accessibility Guide to Rochester, New York, for the Disabled and Elderly 4858
People's Energy: Community Resource Directory [Oakland, California] *(Discontinued)*
People's Folk Dance Directory 4859
People's Yellow Pages [Kansas City, MO] *(Discontinued)*
Peoria Area Manufacturers Directory [Illinois] 1142
Performance Warehouse Association *See* Specialty and Custom Dealer—Performance Warehouse Association Directory Issue
The Performing Woman [Women musicians] 3644
Periodical Guide for Computerists 4860
Periodicals of Public Interest Organizations 4059
Periodicals That Progressive Scientists Should Know About 4060
Personalities of America 3378
Personalities of the South 3379
Personalities of the West and Midwest 3380
Personnel Involved in the Development of Nuclear Standards in the United States 2749
Personnel Resources Directory for the Education of Vietnamese (Indochinese) Refugees *(Discontinued)*
Personnel Services Newsletter [Political scientists] 3252
Peruvian Horse World—Stallion Directory Issue 5062
Pesticide Handbook—Entoma 1931
Pet Dealer—Annual Purchasing Guide Issue 4861
Peterson's Annual Guide to Careers and Employment for Engineers, Computer Scientists, and Physical Scientists 2750
Peterson's Annual Guide to Independent Secondary Schools 2996
Peterson's Annual Guide to Undergraduate Study 2997
Peterson's Annual Guides to Graduate Study 2998
Peterson's Guide to Book Publishing Courses/Academic and Professional Programs 3253
Peterson's Travel Guide to Colleges 2999
Petroleum Equipment Directory 1143
Petroleum Equipment Suppliers Association—Membership Directory *See* Service Point Directory [Petroleum production equipment]
Petroleum Refineries in the United States and Puerto Rico 1932
Pharmaceutical Directory 4409
Pharmaceutical Manufacturers of the United States 4410
Pharmaceutical Marketers Directory 4411
Pharmacy School Admission Requirements 4412
Phelon's Discount Stores 1144
Phelon's Women's Specialty Stores 1145
Phi Delta Gamma—Membership Directory [Women graduate students] 1146
Phi Theta Pi—Membership Directory [Business] 1147
Philadelphia Maritime Exchange Port Directory 1148
Philatelic Directory [Stamps] 4862
Philatelic Observer—Junior Philatelists of America Roster Issue 4863
Philatelic Press Club—Membership List *See* International Philatelic Press Club—Membership List
Phonefiche [Telephone directories] 1149
Phonetician—Biennial Directory Issue 3254
Photo Artist USA *See* Sunshine Artists USA
Photo Weekly—Buyers Handbook & Product Guide Issue 1150
Photofinder *See* Foto Finder [Photography]
Photographer's Market: Where to Sell Your Photos 3645
Photographic Manufacturers & Distributors Association—Membership Directory 1151
Photographic Trade News—Master Buying Guide and Directory Issue 1152
Photographic Trade News—Professional Photographic Equipment Directory and Buying Guide Issue 1153
Photography: Source and Resource *(Discontinued)*

Q

R

Rubbicana *See* Rubber & Plastics News—Rubbicana Issue [Directory issue]

Runner's Guide to the U.S.A. 5076

Running the Rivers of North America 5077

Running Times Yearbook 5078

Rural and Urban Roads—Annual Buyer's Guide Index of Highway and Municipal Products Issue 1255

Rural Sociological Society Directory 4080

Russell Law List 2430

Russell's Official National Motor Coach Guide *See* Official Bus Guide

RV Dealer—Directory and Buyer's Guide Issue [Recreation vehicles] 1256

RV Service and Repair Directory [Recreation vehicles] 4879

S

Sailboat and Equipment Directory 5079

Saint Louis Commerce—Roster Issue 1257

Saint Paul Area Chamber of Commerce—Membership Directory [Minnesota] 1258

Sales and Marketing Executives International—Roster *See* Marketing Times: Journal of Continuing Education—Leadership Directory

Sales Association of the Chemical Industry—Roster 1259

Sales Executives Guide *See* Creative Black Book [Advertiser services]

Sales Management—Directory of Plants *(Discontinued)*

Sales Prospector 1260

Salesman's Guide: Women's Specialty Stores [California] 1261

Salesman's Guide Directory of Infants' to Teens' Wear Buyers [New York metro area] 1262

Salesman's Guide Directory of Men's & Boys' Wear Buyers [New York metro area] 1263

Salesman's Guide Directory of Women's Accessories Buyers [New York metro area] 1264

Salesman's Guide Directory of Women's Coats & Suits Buyers [New York metro area] 1265

Salesman's Guide Directory of Women's Dresses Buyers [New York metro area] 1266

Salesman's Guide Directory of Women's Intimate Apparel Buyers [New York metro area] 1267

Salesman's Guide Directory of Women's Sportswear Buyers [New York metro area] 1268

Salesman's Guide Nationwide Directory: Buying Offices & Accounts 1269

Salesman's Guide Nationwide Directory: Gift & Housewares Buyers 1270

Salesman's Guide Nationwide Directory: Major Mass Market Merchandisers [Excluding New York City metro area] 1271

Salesman's Guide Nationwide Directory: Men's & Boys' Wear Buyers [Excluding New York City metro area] 1272

Salesman's Guide Nationwide Directory: Premium Incentive & Travel Buyers 1273

Salesman's Guide Nationwide Directory: Sporting Goods Buyers 5080

Salesman's Guide Nationwide Directory: Women's & Children's Wear Buyers [Excluding New York City metro area] 1274

San Diego Chamber of Commerce—Business Directory [California] 1275

San Francisco: An Unusual Guide to Unusual Shopping *(Discontinued)*

San Francisco Bay Area People's Yellow Pages [California] 4081

San Francisco Bay Area Theater Resource Directory 3661

San Francisco Business—Big 50 Issue 1276

San Francisco Women's Business Directory *(Discontinued)*

San Leandro Chamber of Commerce—Industrial and Distribution Firms [California] 1277

San Mateo County Industrial Directory—Firms Employing Over 100 Persons [California] *(Discontinued)*

San Mateo County Industrial Firms [California] 1278

Sanitary Maintenance—Buyers' Guide Issue 1279

Sanitation Compliance and Enforcement Ratings of Interstate Milk Shippers 1946

Sanitation Industry Yearbook 1280

Santa Clara County Industrial Directory [California] 1281

Santa Monica Industrial Directory [California] 1282

Savannah Area Manufacturers Directory [Georgia] 1283

Save on Shopping Directory 1284

Savings and Loan News—Top 200 Issue 1716

Savings Bank Journal—Savings Banking's 100 Largest Institutions Issue 1717

Savings Institutions Marketing Society of America—Membership Directory 1718

SBIC Directory and Handbook of Small Business Finance 1719

Scheduled Steamship Service Directory [New York] *See* Port of New York-New Jersey Scheduled Steamship Directory

Scholars' Guide to Washington, D.C. for Latin American and Caribbean Studies 3272

Scholars' Guide to Washington, D.C. for Russian/Soviet Studies 3273

Scholarships Available to Black Students-American Indian Students-Spanish-Speaking Students 4572

Scholarships, Fellowships and Loans 3006

Scholarships for American Indians *See* Career Development Opportunities for Native Americans

School Business Affairs—Association of School Business Officials Official Membership Directory Issue 3007

School Guide 3008

School Library Supervisors Directory *(Discontinued)*

School Media Directory [New Jersey] *See* Directory of New Jersey School Media Specialists

School Shop—Directory of Federal and State Officials Issue 3009

School Shop—Suppliers Directory Issue 3010

School Universe Data Book *See* CIC's School Directory

Schools of Social Work with Accredited Master's Degree Programs 4082

Schwendeman's Directory of College Geography of the United States 2766

Science, Engineering, Research, and Development Directory [Midwest] 2767

Science Fiction and Fantasy Literature 3381

Science Fiction Traders Guide: The Dealers, Publishers, and Fanzines 3274

Science Fiction Writers of America—Membership Directory 3275

Science for the Physically Handicapped in Higher Education 2768

Science, Technology, and Society: A Guide to the Field 4083

Science Training Programs Directory for High Ability Secondary School Students 2769

Scientific and Technical Books and Serials in Print 2770

Scientific Meetings *(Discontinued)*

Scotch-Irish Family Research Made Simple 4655

Sea Boating Almanac *See* Pacific Boating Almanac

Sea Technology—Buyer's Guide/Directory Issue *See* Sea Technology Handbook Directory

Sea Technology Handbook Directory 2771

Seafaring Guide & Directory of Labor-Management Affiliations 1285

Search and Research [Genealogy] 4656

Searching for Your Ancestors: The How and Why of Genealogy 4657

Seasonal Employment [National Park Service] 1286

Seattle Career Hunter's Guide 1287

Seattle People's Yellow Pages [Washington State] 4084

Seattle's Super Shopper: Includes Tacoma (Washington) 1288

Seaway Maritime Directory 1289

Second Jewish Catalog 4573

Second Old House Catalog *See* Old House Catalog

Second Shopper's Guide to Museum Stores *See* Shopper's Guide to Museum Stores

Secondary Wood-Using Industries in Florida *See* Florida's Wood-Using Industry

Security Dealers of North America *See* Standard & Poor's Security Dealers of North America

Security Industry & Product News—Directory & Buying Guide Issue [Protection] 1290

Security World—Product Directory Issue 1291

Security/Fire Equipment Manufacturers' Directory 1292

See America First—On Film 3662

Seed Savers Exchange Yearbook 5081

Seed World—Seed Trade Buyers Guide Issue 1947

Seibt Export Directory of German Industries 1293

Selected and Annotated Buying Guide [To Asian American-owned business in California Bay area] 1294

Selected Black American Authors: An Illustrated Bio-Bibliography 3382

Selected List of Major Fellowship Opportunities and Aids to Advanced Education for Foreign Nationals 3011

Selected List of Major Fellowship Opportunities and Aids to Advanced Education for United States Citizens 3012

Selected List of Postsecondary Education Opportunities for Minorities and Women 3013

Selected Training Programs for Physician Support Personnel *(Discontinued)*

Selecting Educational Media *See* Selecting Instructional Media

Selecting Instructional Media 3014

Self-Help Directory *See* Help: A Working Guide to Self-Help Groups

Self-Help in the Human Services 4085

Self-Help Reporter—Directory of Self-Help Groups Column *See* Help: A Working Guide to Self-Help Groups

Self-Publishing Manual: How to Write, Print & Sell Your Own Book 3276

Selling Your Artwork *See* How to Sell Your Artwork

S.E.M. Newsletter—Directory of Members and Subscribers Issue 3277

SEM 79 1295

SEMI Directory *See* SEMI Membership Directory

T

Travel Agent Travel Industry Personnel Directory *See* Travel Industry Personnel Directory
Travel 800 4897
Travel Industry Personnel Directory 1427
Travel Master 1428
Travel Research Association Membership Directory 1429
Travel Trade—Personnel Sales Guide Issues 1430
Travel Weekly's World Travel Directory 1431
Travelability: A Guide for Physically Disabled Travelers in the United States 4898
Travelers' Directory 4899
Traveler's Directory of Fast-Food Restaurants—Eastern Edition 4900
Traveler's Guide to Information Sources *(Discontinued)*
Traveler's Toll-Free Telephone Directory 1432
Traveling and Camping in the National Park Areas 5104
Traveling FM Radio Guide 3704
Treasury Department—Roster of Minority Banks 1742
Treasury of Free Cookbooks *(Discontinued)*
Treasury Telephone Directory *See* Department of Treasury Telephone Directory
Trial Court Directory of the United States 2463
Trident Area Guide to Office Space [South Carolina] 1743
Trident Area Manufacturers Directory [South Carolina] 1433
Trident Area Shopping Center Directory [South Carolina] 1434
Trinc's Blue Book of the Trucking Industry 1435
Trinc's Green Book of Air Freight & Freight Forwarders 1436
Trinc's Red Book of the Trucking Industry 1437
Trip Log Quick Reference Freighter Guide 4901
Tri-State Garden Directory *See* The Public Gardens
Tri-State Trader Antique Shop Guide *See* Antique Shop Guide
Truck Broker Directory [Freight brokers and shippers] 1438
Truck Equipment and Body Distributors Association—Membership Roster *See* National Truck Equipment Association—Membership Roster
Truck Equipment Catalog for GMC Dealers *See* Vocational Equipment Directory for GMC Dealers
Truck Renting and Leasing Association—Membership List *See* The Vehicle
Truck Stop Fuel Guide 1439
Truck Trailer Manufacturers Association—Membership Directory 1440
Truck-Frame & Axle Repair Association—Membership Directory 1441
Trucks 26 Plus—Buyers Guide Issue *(Discontinued)*
True Seed Exchange *See* Seed Savers Exchange Yearbook
Trustees of Wealth 3386
Trusts & Estates—Directory of Trust Institutions Issue 1744
Try Us: National Minority Business Directory 1442
T.U.B.A. Membership Roster *See* Tubists Universal Brotherhood Association—Membership Roster
Tubists Universal Brotherhood Association—Membership Roster 3705
Tucker Automobile Club of America—Roster of Members 4902
Tucson People's Yellow Pages *See* New West Trails' People's Yellow Pages
Tucson Shopping Center Guide 1745
Tulsa Area Manufacturers Directory [Oklahoma] 1443
Turbo Machinery International—Turbomachinery Catalog & Workbook Issue 1444
Turf-Grass Times—Industry Reference Guide Issue [Golf course maintenance] 5105
Turkey World—Leading Companies Issue 1968
TV and Radio Directory *See* Working Press of the Nation
TV Publicity Outlets Nationwide 3706
Twentieth Century Children's Writers 3387
200 Ways to Put Your Talent to Work in the Health Field 4438
Tyke's Register of Political Action Committees (Federal) 2464
TYMNET Subscriber's Directory *See* Computer and Data Services Available Through TYMNET

U

UCN Register *See* University Consultants Network Register
Ulrich's International Periodicals Directory 4110
Ulrich's Quarterly *See* Ulrich's International Periodicals Directory
Undergraduate Programs of Cooperative Education in the U.S. and Canada 3030
Underground Buying Guide for Hams, CBers, Experimenters, and Computer Hobbyists 4903
Underground Press Directory *See* Alternative Press Directory
Undersea Technology Handbook Directory *See* Sea Technology Handbook Directory

Underwater Holidays 5106
Underwater Society International Divers Guide *See* International Divers Guide
Underwriters List of Trial Counsel 2465
Underwriters' Report Northern California Insurance Directory 1746
Underwriters' Report Southern California Insurance Directory 1747
A Unique Encounter [Christian work camps] 4111
Unique 3-in-1 Research & Development Directory *See* Research & Development Directory
Unitarian Universalist Association—Directory 4581
Unitarian Universalist Women's Federation—Membership Directory 4582
United Bible Societies—Directory *See* Bulletin United Bible Societies—World Annual Report Issue
United Farm Agency, Inc. Catalog 1748
United Fund of Houston and Harris County—Directory of Community Resources and Services [Texas] 4112
United Pesticide Formulators and Distributors Association—Roster 1445
United Press International Daybook [Washington, D. C., events] 4113
United Press International Future File [Washington, D.C. events] *See* United Press International Daybook [Washington, D. C. events]
U.S. and International Directory of Hotel, Restaurant, and Institutional Schools 1446
United States Bar Directory 2466
U.S. Book Publishing Yearbook and Directory 3301
U.S. Cancellation Club News—Directory Issue 4904
U.S. Catholic Institutions for the Training of Candidates for the Priesthood (CARA Seminary Directory) 4583
U.S. College-Sponsored Programs Abroad 3031
U.S. Department of the Interior Telephone Directory 2468
U.S. Directory of Enviromental Sources 2788
U.S. Directory of Marine Scientists 2789
U.S. Directory of Meat Processing Plants 1969
U.S. Directory of Meat Slaughtering Plants 1970
U.S. Directory of Poultry Slaughtering Plants and Poultry and Egg Processing Plants 1971
U.S. Directory of Renderers and Boners 1972
U.S. Directory of the Soft Drink Industry 1447
United States Dressage Federation Calendar of Competitions 5107
United States 1869 Pictorial Research Associates—Register 4905
U.S. Environmental Protection Agency Advisory Committees Charters and Rosters 2469
U.S. Facilities and Programs for Children with Severe Mental Illnesses: A Directory 4439
U.S. Firms in France 1448
U.S. Foamed Plastics Markets and Directory 1449
United States Government Manual 2470
United States Government Organization Manual *See* United States Government Manual
United States Guide to Family Records 4674
U.S. Guide to Nursing Homes *(Discontinued)*
U.S. Headquarters in Europe 1450
United States House of Representatives—Telephone Directory 2471
U.S. Industrial Directory 1451
United States Institute for Theatre Technology—Membership Directory 3707
United States Lawyers Reference Directory 2472
U.S. Medical Directory 4440
United States Naval Academy Alumni Association—Register of Alumni 4675
U.S. Non-Profit Organizations in Development Assistance Abroad 4114
U.S. Observatories: A Directory and Travel Guide 2790
United States Parachute Association—Directory and Reference Source 5108
U.S. Physician Reference Listing 4441
U.S. Plastics in Building and Construction—Marketing Guide and Company Directory *(Discontinued)*
United States Polo Association—Year Book 5109
United States Professional Tennis Association Directory 5110
U.S. Publicity Directory 1452
United States Representatives in the China Trade 1453
U.S. Sandwich Panel Manufacturing Marketing Guide *(Discontinued)*
United States Ski Association—Eastern—Directory 5111
United States Ski Writers Association—Membership Directory 5112
United States, State...Officers of Wisconsin *See* State, Congressional, Legislative, and County Officers of Wisconsin
U.S. Synthetic Organic Chemicals Industry Marketing Guide *(Discontinued)*
United States Tobacco Journal Supplier Directory 1454
U.S. Trade and Transport Directory 1455
United States Trade Shows, Expositions, and Conventions *See* Directory of United States Trade Shows, Expositions, and Conventions

Y

Z

Subject Index

A

SUBJECT INDEX

SUBJECT INDEX

B

C

D

D.C. Directory of Native American Federal and Private Programs   4492
Energy Trails: A Guidebook   3888
Guide to Antique Shops [South Central States]   4777
Guide to Washington, D.C., Foundations   3951
Here Comes the Sun: Directory of Summer Programs for Handicapping
    Conditions   5008
Lest We Forget: A Guide to Genealogical Research in the Nation's
    Capital   4637
Register of the Society of Mayflower Descendants in the District of
    Columbia   4654
United Press International Daybook [Washington, D. C., events]   4113
Washington [Volume]: A Comprehensive Directory of the Nation's
    Capital...Its People and Institutions   2478
Washington Guide for Battered Women [District of Columbia]   4119
Washington Information Directory   2479
Washington Women: A Directory of Women and Women's Organizations in
    the National Capital   4120
Who's Who Among Latin Americans in Washington   3393
Woodall's Campground Directory   5125

Diving. See **Skin and scuba diving**

Diving (commercial) (See also Offshore marine operations and services)
Offshore Contractors and Equipment Directory   1916
Register of Offshore Units, Submersibles, and Diving Systems   1229

Divorce law reform. See **Marriage and divorce law reform**

Divorce records. See **Vital statistics**

Docks, repair. See **Shipbuilding and repair industry**

Documentation services. See **Information services**

Dogs—Clubs, breeders, etc.
Basenji Club of America—Membership Roster and Breeders Directory
    [Dogs]   4709
Papillon Club of America—Membership List [Dogs]   4853
Where to Buy, Board, or Train a Dog   4913

Dolls and dollhouses
Directory of Miniatures and Dolls   4742
Inside the World of Miniatures and Dollhouses   4794
Miniatures Catalog   4827
Peak Doll Directory   4854

Dominican Republic—Import-export trade
American Chamber of Commerce of the Dominican Republic—Investors
    Handbook   60

Door-to-door selling. See **Direct selling industry**

Dowsers
American Society of Dowsers—Membership List   4694
International Psychic Register   4539

Drama therapy
Wholistic Dimensions in Healing: A Resource Guide   4447

Dramatists
Author Biographies Master Index   3333
Contemporary Authors   3349
Contemporary Dramatists   3350
National Playwrights Directory   3625
Theatre, Film and Television Biographies Master Index   3385

Dredging (See also Offshore marine operations and services)
Inland River Guide [Barge companies, etc.]   748
World Dredging and Marine Construction—Annual Directory of World's
    Dredges and Suppliers Issue   1540

Drilling rigs. See **Offshore marine operations and services**

Drive-in theaters
International Motion Picture Almanac   3584

Driver education
Handicapped Driver's Mobility Guide   4319
Official Source Guide to Fleet Safety Training Aids   1108

Driving records
How and Where [To check driver licenses and records]   2241

Drop shipping
American Drop-Shippers Directory   62
Drop Shipping Source Directory of Major Consumer Product Lines   503
Importers Confidential Drop-Ship Directory   725

Drug abuse. See **Substance abuse**

Drug industry. See **Pharmaceutical industry**

Drug trade
Hayes Druggist Directory   4322
National Association of Chain Drug Stores—Membership Directory   992
National Wholesale Druggists' Association—Membership & Executive
    Directory   1048

Dry cleaning industry. See **Laundry and dry cleaning industry**

Dude ranches
Dude Ranch Vacations   4747
Farm, Ranch & Country Vacations   4758
Western Travel Adventures   5118

E

Earth sciences (See also Geo... headings)
Worldwide Directory of National Earth-Science Agencies   2807

Earthworm growers
Earthworm Buyer's Guide   1826

Eastern orthodox denominations
Orthodox Church in America—Yearbook and Church Directory   4565

Ecology
Ecological Society of America Bulletin—Directory of Members
    Issue   2643
User's Guide to Biome Information from the United States International
    Biological Program   2792
World Census of Tropical Ecologists   2802

Economics
Contact—A Directory of Interpreting Business/Economic Education
    Programs   3105
Guide to Graduate Study in Economics and Agricultural Economics in the
    United States of America and Canada   3168
World Index of Economic Forecasts   3313

Economics periodicals—Content requirements
Cabell's Directory of Publishing Opportunities in Business, Administration,
    and Economics   3089
Management and Economics Journals   3226

Economists
American Economic Review—Survey of Members Issue   3046
American Men and Women of Science—Social and Behavioral
    Sciences   3329
Association for Comparative Economic Studies—Membership List   3066
Association for University Business and Economic Research—Membership
    Directory   3067
Business Economics—Membership Directory Issue   3086
Economics of Electric Utility Rate Reform: A Directory of
    Economists   3877
Roster of Women Economists   3269
Society of Government Economists—Membership Directory   2431

Education (See also specific levels, subjects, and places)
International Who's Who in Education   3366
John Dewey Society—Membership Directory [Education]   2958

Education—Employment services and opportunities. See
Teaching—Employment services and opportunities

Education—Publishers and publications
Databases and Clearinghouses: Information Resources for
    Education   2865
Education and Education-Related Serials: A Directory   2901
Educational Press Association of America—Membership Roster   2907
Educators Guide to Free Guidance Materials   2909
Educators' Purchasing Guide   2910
Elementary Teachers Guide to Free Curriculum Materials   2911
El-Hi Textbooks in Print   2913
Free and Inexpensive Learning Materials   2919
Guides to Educational Media   2935
Selecting Instructional Media   3014

Education—Scholarships, grants, prizes, etc.
Directory of Selected Federal Program Offices   2174
ELHI Funding Sources Newsletter   2912
Guide to Federal Assistance [Education]   2930

Education—Study and teaching
Annual List of Accredited Institutions [Teacher education]   2816

Education associations
Directory: Educational Documentation and Information Services   2868
Directory of Education Associations   2876
Education Directory: Colleges and Universities   2902
Higher Education Exchange   2941
Yearbook of Higher Education   3039

Education libraries and librarians
Directory of ERIC Microfiche Collections [Education]   2878

Electrotyping industry. *See* Graphic arts industry

Elementary education
CIC's School Directory   2843
Directory of Day Schools in the United States, Canada and Latin America [Jewish]   4502
Directory of Gifted Programs in the Northeast Exchange Consortium States   2883
Directory of School Psychology Training Programs in the United States and Canada   2631
Education Directory: Public School Systems   2903
Education Directory: State Education Agency Officials   2904
Educational Programs That Work: A Resource of Educational Innovations Developed by Local School Districts   2908
Educators Guide to Free Guidance Materials   2909
Elementary Teachers Guide to Free Curriculum Materials   2911
Federal Funding Guide for Elementary and Secondary Education   2915
Ganley's Catholic Schools in America—Elementary/Secondary   2922
Guides to Educational Media   2935
Handbook of Private Schools   2937
Independent Schools Association of the Southwest—Membership List   2944
National Directory of Public Alternative Schools   2979
New Schools Exchange: Directory & Resource Guide   2987
North Central Association Quarterly—Roster Issue [Secondary schools and colleges]   2988
Private Independent Schools   3001
School Business Affairs—Association of School Business Officials Official Membership Directory Issue   3007
Selecting Instructional Media   3014
Who's Who in Educational Administration   3037

Elevator industry
Elevator World—Directory Issue   543

Embroidery industry
Embroidery Directory   544

Emergency medical services (*See also* Hospitals and clinics)
Emergency Medical Services—Buyers Guide Issue   4299
Health Care Directory   4323
Paramedical National Directory   4408

Emergency services
Emergency Radio Service Station Directories   2197
Len Buckwalter's CB Channel Directory   4818
Police Call Radio Directory   2403
REACT Team Directory [Citizen's band radio monitors]   4074

Employee training and development. *See* Training and development

Employee-management relations. *See* Labor relations

Employment agencies. *See* Employment services and opportunities

Employment services and opportunities (*See also* Women; Minorities; Apprenticeships; specific fields)
Bay Area Employment Agency and Executive Recruiter Directory [California]   150
College Placement Annual   262
Directory of Career Planning and Placement Offices   2873
Directory of Christian Work Opportunities   4501
Directory of College Recruiting Personnel   376
Directory of State Merit Systems   2179
Directory of U.S. & International Executive Recruiters   485
Executive Employment Guide   556
Federal Job Directory   2212
Federal Job Information Centers Directory   2213
Federal Jobs   2214
Federal Research Service Report [Federal government job openings]   2217
Finding a Job: A Resource Book for the Middle-Aged and Retired   3901
Job Hunter's Guide to Eight Great American Cities   808
Job Hunter's Guide to the Rocky Mountain West   809
Job Hunter's Guide to the Sunbelt   810
Multinational Marketing and Employment Directory   983
National Association of Personnel Consultants—Membership Directory   997
Overseas Summer Jobs   1122
Seasonal Employment [National Park Service]   1286
Seattle Career Hunter's Guide   1287
Summer Employment Directory of the United States   1374
Whole World Handbook   4916

Endangered and threatened species
Liaison Conservation Directory for Endangered and Threatened Species   2717

Energy consultants
Guide to Energy Specialists   2671

Energy libraries and librarians
Directory of ERDA Information Centers [Energy R&D]   3826

Energy research and development (all sources) (*See also* Environmental concerns and conservation)
AEE Directory of Energy Professionals   2501
Directory of Department of Energy Research and Development Programs   2604
Directory of Federal Energy Grant and Contract Programs   2608
Ecotechnics: International Pollution Control Directory   514
Energy: A Guide to Organizations and Information Resources in the United States   3884
Energy Data Reports   2647
Energy Directory Update Service   3886
Energy Policy Making in the Northeast: A Directory of State Programs and Institutions   3887
Energy Sources [Year] [Western states]   1828
Energy Trails: A Guidebook   3888
Inventory of Energy Research and Development   2707
Library Journal—Energy Source Directory Issue   2718
Local Energy Action Project—Directory Mailing List   2721
National Environmental/Energy Workforce Assessment [Postsecondary environmental education programs]   2734
Who's Who in the Interagency Energy/Environment R&D Program   2798

Energy research and development (alternative sources) (*See also* Environmental concerns and conservation)
Alternate Energy Equipment Manufacturers   2503
The Alternative House: A Complete Guide to Building and Buying   36
Bio-Energy Directory   2568
Citizen's Energy Directory—A Guide to Alternative Energy Resources   2581
Directory of Faculty Development Projects in Energy   3827
Energy: A Multimedia Guide for Children and Young Adults   3885
Energy Conservation Standards for Buildings: Status of States' Regulatory Activities   2202
Federal Energy Information Sources and Data Bases   2208
Geothermal Registry   2663
Geothermal World Directory   2664
Guide to Solar Energy Programs   2676
Illinois Solar Energy Directory   720
MATNET Mailing List [Appropriate technology]   2724
National Solar Energy Education Directory   2738
National Solar Heating and Cooling Commercial Demonstration Program: Key Personnel Directory   2739
SEM 79   1295
Solar Age Resource Book   1324
Solar Collector Manufacturing Activity and Applications in the Residential Sector   1325
Solar Energy & Research Directory   2778
Solar Energy Buyer's Guide and Directory   2779
Solar Energy Directory   1326
Solar Energy for Agricultural and Industrial Process Heat   2780
Solar Energy Source Book: For the Home Owner, Commercial Builder, and Manufacturer   1327
Solar Engineering—Deskbook Directory of Manufacturers Issue   2781
Solar Engineering—Solar Hot Water Packagers [Special feature]   1328
Solar Engineering Directory   2782
Solar Heating and Cooling—Solar Buyers Guide Issue   1329
Solar Products Specifications Guide   1330
Survey of the Emerging Solar Energy Industry   4101
Synerjy/A Directory of Energy Alternatives   4103
Who's Who in Solar and Wind Energy [Iowa]   4126
Wind Energy Directory   1521
Wind Power Digest—Wind Power Access Catalog Issue   1522
Wood Residue Energy Directory   2799

Engineering. *See* specialized branches and subjects

Engineering—Employment services and opportunities
Directory of Contract Service Firms [Engineering]   2603
Peterson's Annual Guide to Careers and Employment for Engineers, Computer Scientists, and Physical Scientists   2750

Engineering—Services
American Engineering Model Society—Membership Directory   2523
Catalog of Model Services and Supplies   2576

Engineering—Study and teaching
Engineering Education—Engineering College Research and Graduate Study Issue   2648
Guide to Continuing Education—Short Courses for Engineers and Scientists   2670
Minority Engineering Resource Directory   2728

F

G

H

SUBJECT INDEX

SUBJECT INDEX

J

K

SUBJECT INDEX

L

SUBJECT INDEX

O

SUBJECT INDEX

SUBJECT INDEX

Washington Public Ports Association—Port Directory   1478
Waterway Guide—The Yachtman's Bible   5114
Waterway Point Directory for the Great Lakes, Atlantic, and Pacific
    Areas   1480
World Wide Shipping Guide   1545

Portugal—Import-export trade
Portuguese-American Business Review   1177

Portuguese language—Study and teaching
Hispania—Directory Issue   3179

Post card collectors and collections
Deltiology—Roster Issue [Postcard Collectors]   4741

Post exchanges. *See* **Military commissaries**

Postsecondary education—Nontraditional and prebaccalaureate (*See also*
Continuing education)
Chronicle Guide to External & Continuing Education   2838
Chronicle Two-Year College Databook   2842
College Courses in High School   2846
College Degrees for Adults: A Comprehensive Guide to Over 120
    Programs   2847
College Placement and Credit by Examination   2851
Comparative Guide to Two-Year Colleges and Career Programs   2858
Correspondence Educational Directory   2861
Education Directory: Colleges and Universities   2902
Education Directory: State Education Agency Officials   2904
Educational Programs That Work: A Resource of Educational Innovations
    Developed by Local School Districts   2908
Guide to Undergraduate External Degree Programs in the United
    States   2934
Interchange [Learning networks]   2951
Interversitas—Membership Directory   2955
Learning Vacations   4817
Mass Media College Catalog   2965
National Guide to Credit Recommendations for Noncollegiate
    Courses   2982
Resources for Change: A Guide to Projects (Education)   3005
Stopout!: Working Ways to Learn   3017
Teacher's Guide to Non-Traditional Graduate Study   3024

Poultry fanciers and breeders
American Silkie Bantam Club—Membership List [Poultry]   4693
Plymouth Rock Fanciers Club Yearbook [Poultry]   4865
Society for the Preservation of Poultry Antiquities—Breeders
    Directory   4883

Poultry industry
American Poultry Historical Society—Membership Listing   1776
Farm Supplier—Directory of Farm Supplies Issue   1836
Meat and Poultry Inspection Directory   1887
Participants in the National Poultry Improvement Plan   1929
Poultry & Egg Marketing—Poultry Distributor Directory Issue   1938
Poultry Industry Directory   1939
Turkey World—Leading Companies Issue   1968
U.S. Directory of Poultry Slaughtering Plants and Poultry and Egg Processing
    Plants   1971
U.S. Directory of Renderers and Boners   1972
Virginia Poultryman—Directory Issue   1976
Who's Who in the Egg and Poultry Industries   1993

Powder metallurgy industry
Custom Engineered P/M Parts and Products Manufacturers Directory
    International   318

Powder metallurgy industry—Equipment and supplies
Metal Powder Producers and Suppliers Directory International   917
Powder Metallurgy Equipment Directory   1179

Power generation
Energy Systems Product News—Buyers Guide & Directory Issue   550

Power systems (*See also* Fluid power)
Design News Power Transmission Directory   347
Power Transmission Design Handbook   1182

Precious metals industry
Metal Statistics   919
Silver Refiners of the World and Their Identifying Ingot Marks   1312

Prefabricated buildings industry. *See* **Housing industry; Construction
industry**

Premiums industry. *See* **Incentive merchandising**

Preparatory schools. *See* **Secondary education**

Preventive medicine
Directory of Medical Specialists   4276
International Academy of Preventive Medicine—Membership
    Directory   4346

Printing industry. *See* **Graphic arts industry**

Prints. *See* **Graphic arts**

Prison industries
Criminal Justice Agencies in [Region and Number]   2090

Prisoner aid
Directorio Chicano: A Resource Listing of Chicano Media   4494
International Directory of Prisoners Aid Agencies   3973
Law Libraries Which Offer Service to Prisoners   2277
NLADA Directory of Legal Aid and Defender Offices in the United
    States   2369

Prisons. *See* **Correctional headings**

Private investigators. *See* **Investigation agencies**

Private postal systems. *See* **Distribution and delivery services**

Private presses
Directory of Private Presses and Letterpress Printers and Publishers   3530

Private schools. *See* **Elementary education; Secondary education**

Proctologists
List of Cryo-Surgeons [Hemorrhoid specialists]   4363

Produce industry. *See* **Fruit and vegetable industry**

Product liability lawyers
Markham's Negligence Counsel [Lawyers]   2308
Transportation and Products Legal Directory   2462

Product service. *See* **Repair service**

Product standards. *See* **Standards (technical)**

Productivity and the quality of working life
Directory of Labor-Management Committees [Concerned with
    productivity]   421
Directory of Productivity and Quality of Working Life Centers   459
Guide to Management Improvement Projects in Local Government   2235
Productivity: Information Resource Directory   1196
Productivity Resource Information Guide   4068

Programmed instruction. *See* **Educational technology**

Prominent persons (*See also* specific professions, etc.)
Big Book of Halls of Fame in the United States and Canada—Sports   3470
Biographical Dictionaries and Related Works   3338
Biographical Dictionaries Master Index   3339
Blue Book: Leaders of the English-Speaking World   3343
Celebrity Bulletin   3490
Community Leaders and Noteworthy Americans   3346
Dictionary of International Biography   3355
International Who's Who   3363
Marquis Who's Who Publications/Index to All Books   3371
Men and Women of Distinction   3372
Men of Achievement   3373
Names and Numbers: A Journalist's Guide to the Most Needed Information
    Sources and Contacts   986
New York Times Biographical Service   3374
Notable Americans   3375
Personalities of America   3378
Personalities of the South   3379
Personalities of the West and Midwest   3380
Trustees of Wealth   3386
Who's Who in America   3397
Who's Who in American Politics   3400
Who's Who in California   3401
Who's Who in the East   3417
Who's Who in the Midwest   3418
Who's Who in the South and Southwest   3420
Who's Who in the West   3422
Who's Who in the World   3423
Who's Who of American Women   3427
World Who's Who of Women   3429

Promoters
Billboard—International Talent Directory Issue   3471
Official Talent & Booking Directory   3637
Recordings & Bookings Worldwide [Jazz]   3660

Promotion services
Incentive Marketing—Directory of Incentive Sources Issue   727
Premium/Incentive Business—Directory of Premium Suppliers and
    Services Issue   1187

Proposition 13 organizations. *See* **Tax reform**

Prostheses. *See* **Orthopedic appliances**

Psychiatrists and psychoanalysts
American Academy of Child Psychiatry—Membership Directory   4150
American Academy of Psychoanalysis—Membership Roster   4155

SUBJECT INDEX

SUBJECT INDEX

U

SUBJECT INDEX

V

Y

Z

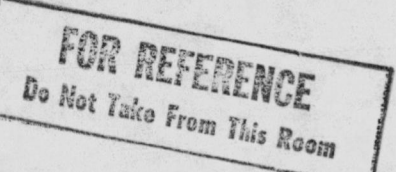